The Hockey News

D0858971

HOCKEY
ALMANAC
2000
THE COMPLETE GUIDE

ABOUT THE AUTHORS

ZANDER HOLLANDER

Zander Hollander is a veteran author who has written, co-written and edited more than 200 books, including six sports encyclopedias. A sportswriter with the *New York World Telegram* for more than 20 years, Hollander is head of Associated Features, Inc., specialists in sports and recreational publishing.

BOB McKENZIE

Bob McKenzie is the Associate Editor of *The Hockey News,* the bible of hockey fans everywhere.

GEORGE VECSEY

George Vescey is an award-winning sportswriter for *The New York Times.*

The Hockey News

HOCKEY ALMANAC 2000

THE COMPLETE GUIDE

Edited by Zander Hollander
An Associated Features Book

"Wayne's World" by Bob McKenzie, The Hockey News
Gretzky Appreciation by George Vecsey, The New York Times

Detroit • London

The Hockey News Hockey Almanac 2000
The Complete Guide

Published by Visible Ink Press®
27500 Drake Rd.
Farmington Hills, MI 48331-3535

Visible Ink Press is a trademark of Gale Group, Inc.

Most Visible Ink Press books are available at special quantity discounts when purchased in bulk by corporations, organizations, or groups. Customized printings, special imprints, messages, and excerpts can be produced to meet your needs. For more information, contact Special Markets Manager, Gale Group, Inc., 27500 Drake Rd., Farmington Hills, MI 48331-3535.

Cover Designer: Michelle DiMercurio
Page Designer: Michelle DiMercurio
Typesetting: Marco Di Vita, Graphix Group

Cover photo courtesy of *The Hockey News.*
Back cover photo used with permission of AP/WideWorld.

ISBN 1-57859-084-1
ISSN: 1524-8003
Printed in the United States of America
All rights reserved

10 9 8 7 6 5 4 3 2

CONTENTS

WAYNE'S WORLD

It was while watching the NHL awards dinner in Toronto on June 24, 1999, that it occurred to me. I'm not going to miss Wayne Gretzky. Come again? I'm not going to miss Wayne Gretzky. And the reason I'm not going to miss Wayne Gretzky is obvious—because he's not going anywhere.

Let's be honest. The Great One has been so deeply ingrained in our consciousness for so long that one could no more consider the game of hockey without No. 99 than contemplate starting a season without perusing the pages of *The Hockey News Hockey Almanac*.

For most hockey fans, Gretzky is hockey. His passion for the game—even more than his extraordinary talent, skill, and wisdom—is the very essence of what our sport is all about.

And though Gretzky will never again put on his skates to play a game in the NHL, he isn't really retiring from the sport, only from active duty. And there's a big difference.

That was highlighted on the night of the NHL awards dinner in Toronto on June 24, when Gretzky concluded his Lady Byng Trophy accep-

tance speech with this line: "For what it's worth, I thought it was a goal."

The remark was in reference to Brett Hull's Stanley Cup–winning goal for the Dallas Stars, the controversial triple-overtime score that, depending on your perspective, was either a legal goal or a crease violation.

Some have speculated that Gretzky, by endorsing the goal, was trying to do the league a favor, put a positive spin on a negative note that ended the season. Maybe. But if you know Gretzky even a little, you know the remark was typical Gretzky.

Aside from being the greatest player ever, he's always been aware of what's going on around the league and he's one of the most notorious gossips in the game. He just loves to talk hockey, and that's not about to change any time soon.

"I don't think I've ever enjoyed watching the Stanley Cup playoffs as much," said Gretzky, who kept turning up at games in a playoff city (Edmonton and Toronto, among others).

Indeed, in the hours that followed his formal retirement announcement on April 16, Gretzky

obliquely suggested he'll continue to be a significant presence, one way or another. "Everything I have in my life, and I mean everything, I owe to hockey and playing in the NHL," Gretzky said.

"I feel good about this decision because I know it's time. I can guarantee you that I won't play again. But you never know where I may turn up."

Well, that's not quite true. It seems a given that one day Gretzky will turn up in a position of prominence, likely as an owner, front and center.

"I know Wayne wants to take some time off with his family and he wants to get out golfing, too," Gretzky's agent and close friend Mike Barnett said. "But I'm sure it won't be long before he gets the itch to do something in the game.

"In the last five years, Wayne has had some serious offers to be involved in the ownership and operation of NHL franchises," Barnett continued. But we never even looked at them as long as he was playing. Now that he's retired, we'll definitely look at everything.

"I think it would be great if Mario Lemieux had ownership of the Pittsburgh Penguins and Wayne ended up with another team and they could compete against each other as owners."

There's no doubt in my mind that, sooner or later, it will happen.

Until then, I'll be satisfied with memories of Gretzky. No problem here. Look through this book, or the NHL Guide and Record Book. Gretzky is everywhere. No player has had an impact on the game like Gretzky.

He holds more than 60 NHL records to prove it, including many that will never be broken. When it's time, as it is now, to trot out the treasure trove of memories, the nonbreakables are obvious:

His 215 points in one season. His 92 goals. Fifty goals in 39 games. Points in 51 consecutive games. Four Stanley Cups. Three Canada Cups. Nine MVPs. It goes on and on.

Like many in the game, I grew up in the NHL with Gretzky. But since I also grew up in the same southern Ontario environs as the phenom from Brantford, my recollections are more personal.

I remember a 10-year-old Gretzky being discovered by the mainstream media, the subject of John Iaboni's 1971 story in the Toronto Telegram. I remember watching the World Junior Championship on Christmas Day of 1977 and being wowed by a kid who seemed so much smaller and was so much younger than the other players.

I remember taking my first newspaper job at The Sault Star in the summer of 1978, at precisely the same time that Gretzky was leaving the junior Greyhounds to sign with Indianapolis of the WHA. And I remember joking that Gretzky had to leave because Sault St. Marie wasn't big enough for both of us.

I remember going to the Gretzky home on Varadi Avenue in Brantford to do a story on Wayne's brother, Keith, and eating a pork chop dinner with Walter, his dad, and Phyllis, his mother, in their modest, middle-class home that was not so different from my own.

And I remember going there again immediately after Gretzky's retirement announcement and noting that even though the house had been expanded and the backyard is now a backyard pool, nothing much, certainly not Wayne's parents, had changed a bit.

I remember Walter's near-death experience from a brain aneurysm and Gretzky's near-and-dear friend Charlie Henry surviving heart problems, and how well they recovered. They've become walking advertisements for how precious each day really is.

I remember all the championships and honors Gretzky won, but I especially remember and appreciate how utterly gracious he was in defeat after the 1996 World Cup and 1998 Winter Olympics.

I remember writing a column criticizing Gretzky's play during the 1993 Los Angeles-

Toronto Western Conference final. I wrote that he was skating like he "had a piano on his back." Gretzky responded in Game 7 with a performance he called the best of his career, the likes of which I'll never see again.

I remember how angry he was in the immediate aftermath and how he never brought it up again. I remember being at countless press conferences where the publicity people would say, "One more question for Wayne," and he would say, "No, it's okay. I'll take as many questions are there are."

The thing is, I remember so much, so many things, big and small. Which is why, now that he's retired, I'm not going to miss Wayne Gretzky.

Even if he spent the rest of his days on Mars—and there's not much of a chance of that unless a golf course opens there—I've got enough memories and recollections to make it seems as though he's still on ice, dashing off to Jari Kurri for the one-timer or waiting for Paul Coffey on the delay.

And besides, I believe Wayne Gretzky is going to be a big player in this game for a long time.

—Bob McKenzie, Associate Editor
The Hockey News

THE LEGEND OF THE GREAT GRETZKY

He would have been the Great Jones or the Great Napier or the Great Swenson. His name just happened to be Gretzky.

He was the greatest player in the history of his sport, perhaps the single most innovative North American athlete since Babe Ruth. He changed his game.

Wayne Gretzky displayed graceful creativity amidst the macho muggers of professional hockey. He validated intuition and touch. He found openings in defenses that nobody had ever found before.

Even the goons of his business tended not to punish him, the same way American Football League defensive tackles once protected Joe Namath as their meal ticket.

He was a skinny kid with big ears from Ontario. Because of him, more than any other factor, the league could beam the Canadian sport into virgin territory in Dallas and Miami and the lunar rubble landscape of Phoenix, for goodness' sake.

He could see things behind him. He played catch with himself, flicking the puck off the net, hypnotizing defenders. He carried the puck be-

hind the net, setting up there and making the rink even larger for him. He whacked the puck off the sideboards, slipping into holes nobody could imagine. He faked Russians right out of their skates in Canada Cup matches.

He played 21 years, one in a renegade league (WHA), the rest in the National Hockey League.

It was at a momentous press conference in New York on June 24, 1999, that Gretzky announced he was retiring.

"In my heart, I know I've made the right decision," he said. "This is the right time. I'm at peace of mind."

His voice cracked a few times, but Gretzky maintained his composure, smiling often and telling a large audience of reporters: "This is a party. This is a celebration."

When nearby television monitors showed highlights of his career, his wife, the actress Janet Jones, wiped away a tear with a white handkerchief.

Gretzky leaves behind a league that will expand from 27 to 30 teams by 2001 while still

The Great One waves goodbye for a final time at Madison Square Garden on April 18, 1999.

struggling to be more than a weak fourth among top sports businesses for American audiences.

Still, the NHL features many stars, including Jaromir Jagr of Pittsburgh, Paul Kariya of Anaheim, Eric Lindros of Philadelphia, Brett Hull of Dallas, and Peter Forsberg of Colorado. But none have the charisma of Gretzky, the only hockey player some people have ever heard of, a man who acted as a missionary for the game while staying free of the legal problems and personality conflicts that have damaged the public images of some stars.

When people reminisce about the Gretzky era, as they surely will for decades, they will recall a playing style that was unlike any other. Howe, who began his career shortly after World War II, was hockey's Paul Bunyan, a mythic man, large for his era, tough for any age, a force through several decades. Orr was a comet from the late 1960s into the early 1970s who played hockey the way Jimi Hendrix played guitar, with élan that could not be copied.

Gretzky was different and appropriate for his era. As the league began importing more and more players from Europe, he played what is now recognized as a European style. Although not particularly speedy, he was a nimble skater who could stop, collect a moving puck on his stick blade, look around and pass it to an open teammate, seemingly in one motion.

At other times, Gretzky would carry the puck, stop suddenly, and delay the play a half-beat while letting others thunder by. Then he would pass or shoot through openings that only he seemed to see.

Despite his considerable wealth, Gretzky often said that he did not play hockey just for money but for the love of the game. He remains a bit of what hockey people call a "rink rat," a player who enjoys the banter of the buses, airplanes, and locker rooms.

The special moments, he said, were when you walked in for practice and teammates began to tease you about your new haircut or your new suit.

He holds 61 league scoring records, and they came from something more than endurance or power or mulish persistence. He smiles at a tape of his career highlights, the way he pranced around the ice after Stanley Cup goals, milestone goals. He is studiously modest, but not so modest that he could not enjoy the sight of himself celebrating.

He earned his goals. He was willowy when he started, at 6 feet tall and 185 pounds, and now he is almost frail-looking in comparison to the agile brutes who play this game.

As an athlete, in terms of touch and feel, he was most comparable to John McEnroe. However, McEnroe never had to take a hip check from the defense (not that it wouldn't have been a bad idea), whereas Gretzky played a sport in which strapping western Canadians were instructed to beat the stuffing out of hipper-dipper French-Canadians and later the Europeans. The kid from Ontario avoided the posse, and the sport thrived.

The funny thing was, Gretzky did not measure up to a superstar on the computer printouts. His first team—and let's get serious, he should go into the Hall of Fame in an Edmonton uniform—was in the vanguard of physical tests. Among the young Oilers of 1981, Gretzky finished dead last in just about every measurable category—weights, speed, eyesight, reflexes. His teammates ragged on him, and he set a record of 164 points that year, and he would surpass that total in seven different seasons.

"I remember him abusing the Flyers," said Mike Richter, the Rangers' goalie, who comes from Philadelphia. "What impressed me most was how often he played at the top of the game, his resiliency. His tongue would be hanging out, but he'd be tugging at the coach's elbow.

"He had a few more gears than the average player," Richter said. "He could hold the puck longer than anybody I ever saw. He had ridiculous endurance."

He was also the Great Gretzky because he recognized his role. He never bleated—as athletes do—that nobody understands the terrible pressure he was under. He would come into town, his normal pasty complexion appearing downright anemic, his minimal shoulders slumped like Willie Loman's after a bad road trip, but he would be available to the media and the fans.

In his best years, with Edmonton, Gretzky dominated the sport and led the Oilers to the four straight titles in his nine seasons with them. He had less success with the Los Angeles Kings, the St. Louis Blues, and the New York Rangers.

In his biggest goal-scoring season, 1981–82, Gretzky had an astounding 92. That combined with 120 assists for 212 points, all records. In his best season for assists, 1985–86, he collected 163, a record, of course.

Gretzky appeared in 18 All-Star Games. He won five Lady Byng trophies for sportsmanship. In NHL regular-season games, he scored a record 894 goals; Howe is second with 801. In regular-season assists, Gretzky is tops with 1,963; Paul Coffey is second with 1,102. In total points in regular-season play, Gretzky leads with 2,857; Howe is second with 1,850.

In the NHL and WHA combined, Gretzky has scored 1,072 goals, one more than Howe scored in both leagues during both regular-season and playoff games.

Howe was Gretzky's idol when Gretzky grew up in Brantford, Ontario. Gretzky joined Howe in the Hockey Hall of Fame in June 1999 when he was elected unanimously without the usual waiting period.

He realized it was time to get out, while he was still in the Kareem Abdul-Jabbar range, diminished but regal, before he became Willie Mays, an aging genius stumbling over second base.

There is no guidebook for the proper way for the great ones to bow out. Babe Ruth virtually invented the home run with his lusty swings, but finished up as a befuddled Boston Brave.

Michael Jordan was the greatest basketball player, but his mission was made easier by peers named Erving, Abdul-Jabbar, Bird, and Johnson. Gretzky said that he regretted Jordan's retirement—because his kids loved watching Jordan play.

Jim Brown had the best football retirement. Nine seasons. Led the league in rushing. And out. Chris Evert quit tennis because she loathed becoming a quarterfinalist.

Gretzky doesn't need the money. What's the sense in having a beautiful wife and three kids if your neck is in a cast?

In life as in hockey, Wayne Gretzky could see the entire rink. It was time to retire while he was still the Great One—not because of alliteration, but because of excellence.

—*George Vecsey, The New York Times*
Copyright © 1999 *The New York Times.*
Reproduced with permission.

INTRODUCTION

For us the puck flies back to 1970, when the predecessor of *The Hockey News Hockey Almanac* was born. Originally called *The Complete Encyclopedia of Hockey,* it marked the birth of the first hockey encyclopedia.

Now, nearly 30 years and eight editions later, it continues as an annual source for all that the sport has become.

This newest edition salutes the incomparable Wayne Gretzky, newly retired as the greatest player of all time.

The goal was, and is, to include not only the vital facts and figures but the drama, the history, and the heroics that have made the game so special to fans around the world. Ever since 1893, when Lord Stanley of Preston, the Earl of Derby and Governor-General of Canada, invested 10 pounds (about $49 at the time) in a squat, punch bowl–shaped trophy to symbolize amateur hockey supremacy, men have spent fortunes and lifetimes pursuing that elusive piece of silverware.

The Stanley Cup's more than 100-year history is nearly as legendary and exciting as the game of hockey itself. Lord Stanley's Cup has been tossed into a graveyard, drop-kicked into a canal, dumped out of an automobile, and Cup-napped from its showcase. Each time, however, the sacred Cup has been recovered.

For the National Hockey League, it has served as the Holy Grail since the league's beginnings in 1917 and through the decades, as hockey grew from a simple game on the frozen lakes and ponds of Canada to one played on artificial ice in huge indoor arenas across the whole of North America and in other sectors of the world. Today NHL teams perform before sellout crowds in the stadiums and millions more watching on television.

This new edition traces the sport from its earliest days and covers every NHL season, including the climactic Stanley Cup playoffs. It profiles the outstanding players of all time, including Jaromir Jagr, Ray Bourque, Paul Coffey, and Mark Messier among the actives, along with such immortals as Mario Lemieux, Gordie Howe, Bobby Hull, Bobby Orr, and, naturally, Wayne Gretzky.

A changing of the guard in recent years has been marked by Dallas's capture of its first Stan-

ley Cup in 1999, Detroit's championships in 1997 and 1998, and the emergence of first-time champions in Calgary, Pittsburgh, New Jersey, and Colorado. The birth of new franchises continues unabated as Atlanta joins the league for the 1999–2000 season, following other recent additions to the league in Anaheim, Tampa Bay, San Jose, Ottawa, Miami, and Nashville. On the way are new franchises in Columbus and Minneapolis-St. Paul, set to play in 2000–2001.

Since there is more to the complete story of hockey than the NHL, included are the departed World Hockey Association, the Olympic Games, world and collegiate championships, Canadian junior hockey and the Memorial Cup, and the IHL and AHL.

New features are numerous in this edition. The chapter formerly called "Another Part of the Ice," which covered hockey beyond the NHL, has been replaced by four separate chapters that provide expanded coverage of Canadian junior hockey, minor league hockey, U.S. college hockey, and Olympic and international competitions. A new

chapter called "Young Guns: Top Draft Picks" provides a closer look at the top 50 selections in this year's NHL Entry Draft, letting you learn more about the league's next wave of young talent.

Several existing chapters have been improved also. In the first seven chapters of the book, which provide a year-by-year overview of the NHL since its birth in 1917, playoff results and statistics have been added for each season. Chapter 8 has been expanded and rearranged. It now includes the top 100 players of all time as ranked by the *The Hockey News*. Finally, the All-Time NHL Player Register now includes plus/minus ratings for all forwards and defensemen.

Even with these additions, we're always looking for new ways to make the book even better. Please e-mail any suggestions you have to *thnhockey@galegroup.com*.

We hope that having this book by your side throughout the season and beyond will enrich your enjoyment and passion for the game.

—Zander Hollander, Associated Features

ACKNOWLEDGMENTS

They don't play hockey, but they cover it. You've seen their bylines in newspapers and magazines and books. And you've caught them on radio and television. They're the talented, dedicated writers and editors responsible for the eighth edition of what has become *The Hockey News Hockey Almanac.*

Heading the cast once more as contributing editor was Eric Compton, whose herculean task included updating and expanding the All-Time NHL Player Register. His support team included hockey maven Brad Morgan of Visible Ink Press.

Others who have lent a helping hand over the years include Lee Stowbridge, master statistician, who has figured in four editions; Benny Ercolani, the NHL's chief statistician; Bryan Lewis, the NHL's director of officiating; John Halligan, long-time N.Y. Rangers' and NHL executive; Bill Chadwick, ex-referee and member of the Hockey Hall of Fame; Frank Polnaszek of the late Hartford Whalers; Philip Pritchard of the Hockey Hall of Fame; Phyllis Hollander of Associated Features; and Judy Galens, Larry Baker, and Marty Connors of the Gale Group and Visible Ink Press. Thanks are also due to Christa Brelin for keeping

the ship afloat at all times; Matt Nowinski for keying and general support; Michelle DiMercurio for her wonderful cover and page design; Pam Reed and Mike Logusz for pulling off miracles with the photos; Carol Schwartz, Michelle Banks, Christine Tomassini, and others on the VIP staff for last-minute assistance; and Marco Di Vita of the Graphix Group for remaining patient while typesetting the book under tight deadline pressure.

We're also grateful to such previous contributors as Tim Moriarty, who played a major role in the second, third, and fourth editions; Rich Chere of the *Newark (N.J.) Star-Ledger;* Hal Bock and Ben Olan of the Associated Press; Reyn Davis of the *Winnipeg Free Press;* Doug Gould, Pat Calabria, Larry Fox, Art Friedman, Jeff Shermack, Stu Hackel, and Jim Poris.

For filling in some of the holes, we thank the NHL's Arthur Pincus, Gary Meagher, Susan Aglietti, Greg Inglis, Andrew McGowan, Alice Hanson-Leff, and Adam Schwartz, as well as the NHL team publicity directors.

Others who were there in the beginning the beginning include Maurice (Lefty) Reid, former

curator and secretary of the Hockey Hall of Fame, Red Fisher, Don Andrews, Frank Kelly, Bill Himmelman, David Rosen, Richard Sherwin, and Brian Compton.

A work as complete and vast as this one depends in part on what has been written before in newspapers, magazines, and books. Among the books that have proved helpful: *The Trail of the Stanley Cup* by Henry Roxborough; *The Hockey Encyclopedia* by Stan Fischler and Shirley Walton Fischler; *The NHL Official Guide & Record Book;* and the team media guides.

THE NHL FAMILY TREE

| '16 | '18 | '20 | '22 | '24 | '26 | '28 | '30 | '32 | '34 | '36 | '38 | '40 | '42 | '44 | '46 | '48 | '50 | '52 | '54 | '56 | '58 |

Montreal Canadiens (1917-Present)

Montreal Wanderers (1917-1918)

Ottawa Senators (1917-31) (1932-34) — St. Louis Eagles (1934-35)

Toronto Arenas (1917-19) • Toronto St. Pat's (1919-26) • Toronto Maple Leafs (1926-Present)

Quebec Bulldogs (1919-20) Hamilton Tigers (1920-25) — New York Americans (1925-41) — Brooklyn Americans (1941-42)

Boston Bruins (1924-Present)

Montreal Maroons (1924-38)

Pittsburgh Pirates (1925-30) — Philadelphia Quakers (1930-31)

New York Rangers (1926-Present)

Detroit Cougars (1926-30) — Detroit Falcons (1930-32) • Detroit Red Wings (1932-Present)

Chicago Black Hawks (1926-Present)

| '60 | '62 | '64 | '66 | '68 | '70 | '72 | '74 | '76 | '78 | '80 | '82 | '84 | '86 | '88 | '90 | '92 | '94 | '96 | '98 | '00 | '02 |

Los Angeles Kings (1967-Present)

Minnesota North Stars (1967-93) • Dallas Stars (1993-Present)

Philadelphia Flyers (1967-Present)

Pittsburgh Penguins (1967-Present)

St. Louis Blues (1967-Present)

Oakland Seals (1967-70) | California Golden Seals (1970-76) | Cleveland Barons (1976-78)

Buffalo Sabres (1970-Present)

Vancouver Canucks (1970-Present)

New York Islanders (1972-Present)

Atlanta Flames (1972-80) | Calgary Flames (1980-Present)

Kansas City Scouts (1974-76) | Colorado Rockies (1976-82) | New Jersey Devils (1982-Present)

Washington Capitals (1974-Present)

Edmonton Oilers (1979-Present)

Hartford Whalers (1979-97) • Carolina Hurricanes (1997-Present)

Quebec Nordiques (1979-95) • Colorado Avalanche (1995-Present)

Winnipeg Jets (1979-96) • Phoenix Coyotes (1996-Present)

San Jose Sharks (1991-Present)

Ottawa Senators (1992-Present)

Tampa Bay Lightning (1992-Present)

Mighty Ducks of Anaheim (1993-Present)

Florida Panthers (1993-Present)

Nashville Predators (1998-Present)

Atlanta Thrashers (1999-Present)

1

HOW IT ALL BEGAN
1917-1924

The family tree of the National Hockey League has its roots in the years around the turn of the century with branches spreading from the eastern provinces of Quebec and Ontario clear across the vast prairie land of Canada to the west and British Columbia.

It is rich with legendary hockey names—Frank and Lester Patrick, Edouard (Newsy) Lalonde, Fred (Cyclone) Taylor, Frank Nighbor, Joe Malone—men who built the game from pastime to profession and nurtured it from the frozen ponds in small mining towns to packed big-city arenas.

Hockey began as a seven-man game with upright posts embedded in the ice for goals. There were no nets, no blue lines, no red lines, and no faceoff circles on the ice. But by the time the pioneers got through with it, the game closely resembled the sport we know today.

The Amateur Hockey Association of Canada and the Ontario Hockey Association were among the first organized hockey leagues in Canada. Players and teams freely shifted from league to league in those early years.

Finally, in 1910, there were two major leagues operating in competition with each other. The Canadian Hockey Association listed Ottawa, Quebec, and three Montreal teams—the Shamrocks, the Nationals and All-Montreal. The National Hockey Association had teams in Cobalt, Haileybury, and Renfrew and two in Montreal—the Wanderers and the Canadiens.

The bidding war for players was spirited. The Patrick brothers signed with Renfrew for $3,000 each and the same club lured Cyclone Taylor away from Ottawa and offered an Edmonton player $1,000 to come east for a single game.

Aware that the war would ruin them, the two leagues came to an understanding and merged into the single National Hockey Association, a seven-team league composed of Ren-

frew, Cobalt, Haileybury, Ottawa, and three Montreal teams—the Shamrocks, the Wanderers and the Canadiens.

The Patrick brothers went west that year and organized their own league—the Pacific Coast Hockey Association, with franchises in Vancouver, Victoria, and New Westminster. The Patricks were veterans of the teamhopping in the East and started player raids of their own to lure established stars to their new league. Many, including Taylor, Lalonde, and Nighbor, went west.

With top talent migrating to it, the Pacific Coast Hockey Association gained stature and eventually a series was started, pitting the PCHA and NHA champions against each other in a playoff for the Stanley Cup.

In 1912, the NHA introduced six-man hockey and added numbers to players' jerseys. A year before, hockey's traditional two 30-minute periods had been switched to three periods of 20 minutes each. Slowly but surely, the sport was changing.

In 1913, the PCHA introduced blue lines, dividing the ice into three sections. It was the same year that, for the first time, assists as well as goals were credited to a player's scoring totals.

A year later, the NHA followed suit, crediting assists as well as goals. The Eastern circuit also allowed referees to start dropping the puck on faceoffs instead of placing it between the two sticks, thus saving a lot of bruised knuckles.

And in the West, a referee named Mickey Ion, destined to become one of the greatest officials in the history of the game, began picking an All-Star team—a custom which added considerable interest to the game.

In 1914, Canada went to war and with the conflict came problems for hockey. Many players were called up to serve in the Army and some were given deferments conditional upon their not playing hockey.

Train schedules were disrupted, causing cancellation of some games. The NHA clubs turned over the entire proceeds of their exhibition games to patriotic causes and a portion of the regular-season income to the Red Cross.

By 1917, the NHA had evolved into a six-team circuit composed of the Montreal Wanderers, Montreal Canadiens, Ottawa, Toronto, Quebec, and the Northern Fusiliers—an Army team representing the 228th Battalion of the Canadian Army.

When the 228th was ordered overseas, it was forced to withdraw from the league, leaving five teams and an unbalanced schedule. After considerable bickering, it was decided that Eddie Livingstone's Toronto team would also be dropped and its players redistributed.

There is some evidence that Livingstone was not the most popular man among his fellow owners and it was their desire to rid themselves of him that led to the creation of the new league—the National Hockey League.

Tired of intra-league squabbling, much of which had centered around the Toronto franchise and its combative owner, Eddie Livingstone, NHA owners met in Montreal's Windsor Hotel on November 22, 1917, to settle their problems once and for all.

Their solution was a simple one. They simply created their own league and left Livingstone in the NHA all by himself. The new circuit would be called the National Hockey League, with franchises going to Ottawa, the Montreal Wanderers, Montreal Canadiens, and Toronto, provided Livingstone was not included in that team's operation. Quebec was also granted a franchise, but chose not to play that first year and its players were divided among the other four teams in what turned out to be the NHL's first intra-league draft.

Major Frank Robinson, president of the NHA, bowed out and Frank Calder, secretary-treasurer of the NHA, was elected president of the new league. A 22-game schedule, running from December 19 through March 10, was adopted.

Joe Malone, Quebec's best player, wound up with the Canadiens and on opening night he scored five goals as Montreal whipped Ottawa, 7–4. Malone, playing in only 20 games, won the first NHL scoring crown with 44 goals—a pace that has never been matched.

The Wanderers opened at home with a 10–9 victory over Toronto in a game that attracted only 700 fans. That was the only victory the Wanderers ever managed in the NHL. They dropped five straight games and then, on January 2, 1918, a $150,000 fire burned Westmount Arena to the ground, leaving them without a home rink.

The Canadiens, who had shared the Arena with the Wanderers, moved into the 3,250-seat Jubilee rink for the remainder of the season but the Wanderers dropped out of the league with owner Sam Lichtenhein apparently happy to be out of what had been a losing venture.

A major rule change was adopted during the NHL's first season that was to affect the art of

Frank Calder was appointed president of the newly formed National Hockey League in 1917.

goaltending forever. Until then, goalies had been forced to stand up to defend their nets and in 1914 a rule was added by the NHA imposing $2 fines on goalies who sprawled on the ice to make a save. Now the rule was changed and goalies were permitted to assume any position they wished.

Vancouver's Fred (Cyclone) Taylor was the Pacific Coast Hockey League's scoring champion in 1917–18.

If the rule helped, the statistics don't show it. The legendary Georges Vezina of the Canadiens led the league with 84 goals allowed in 21 games—a 4.0 average that is not very good by today's standards. In addition to Malone, the top shooters were Ottawa's Cy Denneny with 36 goals in 22 games, Reg Noble of Toronto with 28 in 20 games, and Newsy Lalonde of the Canadiens, who had 23 goals in 14 games.

The Canadiens, first-half champions, and Toronto, winners of the second half, played off for the NHL title with Toronto taking the two-game, total-goals playoff, 10–7.

In the West, the PCHA, cut back to three teams by the departure of Spokane, had a tight race almost all season. But Seattle finally finished two games in front of Vancouver and four up on Portland.

Vancouver's Cyclone Taylor led the league with 32 goals, including one game-winner against Seattle scored with his back to the goal. It was a routine play for Taylor, who boasted that he once scored a goal in the NHA by skating backwards through the whole Ottawa team.

In the two-game total-goals playoff between the top two teams, Vancouver defeated Seattle, 3–2. The Millionaires traveled east to face Toronto for the Stanley Cup and split the first four games. Then the Arenas captured the deciding fifth game and the Cup, 2–1, as Corbett Denneny scored the winning goal.

1917–18

FINAL STANDINGS

First Half

	W	L	T	PTS	GF	GA
Montreal C	10	4	0	20	81	47
Toronto	8	6	0	16	71	75
Ottawa	5	9	0	10	67	79
Montreal W.	1	5	0	2	17	35

Montreal Wanderers were forced to withdraw from league after home rink burned down on January 2, 1918.

Second Half

	W	L	T	PTS	GF	GA
Toronto	5	3	0	10	37	34
Ottawa	4	4	0	8	35	35
Montreal C.	3	5	0	6	34	37

Toronto defeated Montreal Canadiens in playoffs and won regular-season championship.

LEADING SCORERS

	G
Malone, Montreal C.	44
Denneny, Ottawa	36
Noble, Toronto	28
Lalonde, Montreal C.	23
Denneny, Toronto	20
Pitre, Montreal C.	17
Cameron, Toronto	17
Darragh, Ottawa	14
Hyland, Montreal W-Ottawa	14
Gerard, Ottawa	13
Skinner, Toronto	13

No records of assists were compiled.

PLAYOFF RESULTS

Finals

Toronto d. Vancouver (PCHL), 3–2

LEADING SCORERS

	G	A	PTS
Skinner, Toronto	8	3	11
MacKay, Vancouver	5	4	9
Taylor, Vancouver	9	0	9

LEADING GOALIES

	W	SO	GAA
Lehman, Vancouver	2	0	2.86
Holmes, Toronto	3	0	4.00

1918–19

The demise of the Wanderers the year before had left the NHL with just three teams—the Montreal Canadiens, Toronto Arenas, and Ottawa Senators. There was, though, a possibility that Quebec, which had not operated in 1917–18, might join the league for its second season.

President Frank Calder, reelected for a five-year term, drew up two schedules for the new season—one for a three-team league, one for a four-team league.

When Quebec's ownership failed to meet an NHL deadline for declaring its intentions, the league suspended the franchise and went with the three-team schedule. With the end of World War I, it was expected that many players would be returning from the Army. But few were discharged in time and when the season started, the teams had much the same personnel as the year before.

The NHL adopted several important rule changes, including the adoption of the PCHA's blue-line idea. This divided the ice surface into three zones with forward passing permitted in the 40-foot-wide center area. Kicking the puck was also allowed and assists were added to regular-

The Canadiens' Joe Malone was the first NHL scoring champion, with 44 goals in 20 games in 1917–18.

season statistics. Penalty rules were reshuffled. A minor penalty would leave a team shorthanded for three minutes, a major penalty would cost five minutes and for a match penalty, no substitute would be allowed for the penalized player.

The 18-game regular season started on December 21 with Ottawa beating Montreal, 5–2. The

Joe Hall starred on defense for the Canadiens before dying of influenza in the spring of 1919.

Canadiens bounced back to lose only two more games and capture the first-half championship. Ottawa, a so-so 5–5 in the first half, won seven of eight games and took the second-half title.

Toronto, heavily favored after winning the Stanley Cup the year before, started in reverse, dropping six of its first seven games. The Arenas never righted themselves and finished in last place in both halves.

Newsy Lalonde, the Canadiens' fiery player-manager, won the scoring title with 21 goals and Ottawa's Clint Benedict was the top goalie with two shutouts and a 3.0 average in 18 games.

In the playoff between the Canadiens and Ottawa, Montreal dominated. Lalonde's team won the first three games, dropped the fourth and then wrapped up the series in the fifth game. The format had been changed from total goals in two games to a best-of-seven series.

In the PCHA, Portland's franchise was transferred to Victoria with Lester Patrick set as the team's player-manager. Lester's younger brother, Frank, was serving his sixth term as president of the league.

Seattle beat Vancouver in the opening game and held onto the league lead for six weeks before the defending champion Vancouver Millionaires took over. Vancouver won the regular-season title by one game and Cyclone Taylor again was the scoring champ with 23 goals—one more than Seattle's Bernie Morris.

There was a celebrated fight between Cully Wilson of Seattle and Vancouver's mild-mannered Mickey MacKay in which Wilson's cross-check broke MacKay's jaw. The incident cost Wilson a $50 fine, match penalty, and eventual suspension from the league.

In the two-game, total-goals playoff, Seattle defeated Vancouver, 7–5, scoring six goals in the first game. That set up the Stanley Cup series against Montreal.

The NHL champion Canadiens dropped two of the first three games, played a scoreless tie in the fourth and then tied the series by winning the fifth. But the deciding sixth game was never played. The Canadiens' ranks had been shredded by the great influenza epidemic which covered the continent. Bad Joe Hall, a defenseman, was hospitalized, and four others, including Lalonde, were confined to their hotel by the disease. The series was ended with no Cup winner—the only time in history that has happened. Hall never recovered. He died in a Seattle hospital.

1918–19

FINAL STANDINGS

First Half

	W	L	T	PTS	GF	GA
Montreal	7	3	0	14	57	50
Ottawa	5	5	0	10	39	40
Toronto	3	7	0	6	43	49

Second Half

	W	L	T	PTS	GF	GA
Ottawa	7	1	0	14	32	14
Montreal	3	5	0	6	31	28
Toronto	2	6	0	4	22	43

Montreal defeated Ottawa in playoffs and won regular-season championship.

LEADING SCORERS

	G	A	PTS
Lalonde, Montreal C.	23	9	32
Cleghorn, Montreal C.	23	6	29
Nighbor, Ottawa	18	4	22
Denneny, Ottawa	18	4	22
Pitre, Montreal C.	14	4	18
Skinner, Toronto	12	3	15
Noble, Toronto	11	3	14
Cameron, Toronto-Ottawa	11	3	14
Darragh, Ottawa	12	1	13
Randall, Ottawa	7	6	13

PLAYOFF RESULTS

Finals

No decision between Montreal Canadiens and Seattle (PCHL) (Series called off after five games due to an epidemic)

LEADING SCORERS

	G	A	PTS
Lalonde, Montreal	17	1	18
Foyston, Seattle	12	1	13

LEADING GOALIES

	W	SO	GAA
Holmes, Seattle	3	2	1.97
Lehman, Vancouver	1	0	3.50

1919–20

The player shuttle created between East and West when the Patrick brothers organized the Pacific Coast Hockey Association was in full swing.

Seattle's Frank Foyston won the PCHA scoring title in 1919–20.

Moving west from the NHL was a youngster used sparingly the year before by Toronto. But Jack Adams would one day be back and make his mark as a player, coach and executive in the NHL.

Alf Skinner and Rusty Crawford also jumped to the PCHA while Cully Wilson, a rough, tough right wing, who was banned from the coast league for his overly aggressive play, showed up in the NHL with Toronto. His style stayed the same and he was the most penalized player in the league that season, spending 79 minutes sitting out infractions.

Toronto's management, disturbed over the team's disappointing performance the year before, undertook a rebuilding job. The first step was to change the club's nickname from the Arenas to the St. Patricks, perhaps in an attempt to attract the luck of the Irish.

The Quebec Bulldogs operated their franchise and reclaimed players who had been assigned to other teams for the NHL's first two seasons. The most dominant was Joe Malone, who had won the scoring title in the league's first year of operation and now returned to Quebec from the Montreal Canadiens.

Malone was the standout on what was a dismal Quebec team. On January 31, he went on a tear of seven goals in a single game against Toronto, setting an NHL record that still stands. He almost matched that performance a little more than one month later when he scored six times against Ottawa in the final game of the season.

Malone finished the season with 39 goals and nine assists for 48 points and his second scoring title in three years. But despite his brilliance, Quebec won only four games all year and finished last. Newsy Lalonde of the Canadiens gave Malone a run for the scoring title with 37 goals and six assists for 43 points.

Ottawa's Clint Benedict was the top goalie, posting a 2.7 goals-against average and five shutouts for the 24-game season. No other netminder in the league recorded a single shutout that year.

With World War I over, Canadians began paying more attention to hockey and crowds began growing in size. On February 21, Ottawa's game at Toronto attracted 8,500—a record.

Ottawa won both halves of the NHL's split schedule, eliminating the need for the playoffs. The Senators would represent the NHL in the battle for the Stanley Cup against either Seattle, the PCHA champion, or second-place Vancouver. Frank Foyston of Seattle had won the PCHA scoring crown and he led a 6–0 romp in the second game that gave Seattle the two-game, total-goals playoff over the Millionaires, 7–3.

Seattle traveled east to play Ottawa for the Cup but when the team arrived, there was a problem. Seattle's red, white, and green uniforms closely resembled Ottawa's red, white, and black. The conflict was resolved when the Senators agreed to change to white sweaters.

Ottawa took the Cup in five games—the last two played on Toronto's artificial ice after hot weather turned Ottawa's natural surface to slush.

1919–20

FINAL STANDINGS

First Half

	W	L	T	PTS	GF	GA
Ottawa	9	3	0	18	59	23
Montreal	8	4	0	16	62	51
Toronto	5	7	0	10	52	62
Quebec	2	10	0	4	44	81

Second Half

	W	L	T	PTS	GF	GA
Ottawa	10	2	0	20	62	41
Toronto	7	5	0	14	67	44
Montreal	5	7	0	10	67	62
Quebec	2	10	0	4	47	96

LEADING SCORERS

	G	A	PTS
Malone, Quebec	39	9	48
Lalonde, Montreal C.	36	6	42
Denneny, Toronto	23	12	35
Nighbor, Ottawa	26	7	33
Noble, Toronto	24	7	31
Darragh, Ottawa	22	5	27
Arbour, Montreal C.	22	4	26
Wilson, Toronto	21	5	26
Broadbent, Ottawa	19	4	23
Cleghorn, Montreal C.	19	3	22
Pitre, Montreal C.	15	7	22

PLAYOFF RESULTS

Finals

Ottawa d. Seattle (PCHL), 3–2

LEADING SCORERS

	G	A	PTS
Foyston, Seattle	9	2	11
Nighbor, Ottawa	6	1	7

LEADING GOALIES

	W	SO	GAA
Benedict, Ottawa	3	1	2.30
Holmes, Seattle	3	1	2.57

1920–21

Quebec's dismal showing the season before left the team's owners disenchanted and the Bulldogs faded from the NHL picture for the second and final time.

Percy Thompson of Hamilton, Ontario, purchased the franchise for $5,000, moved the club to Hamilton and changed the nickname to the Tigers. It was obvious that the same players who had failed in Quebec would not do much better in Hamilton and an SOS was sent out to the other teams in the league, asking for player help.

The last time that had happened was in 1917, the NHL's first season, when the undermanned Montreal Wanderers appealed for help. The other clubs refused then and the result was Montreal's eventual dropout from the league. It was perhaps with this in mind that the NHL responded favorably to Hamilton's plight.

Toronto contributed George (Goldie) Prodgers, Joe Matte, and Cecil (Babe) Dye, Montreal ticketed Bill Couture to the Tigers and Joe Malone led the leftovers from Quebec which included Eddie Carpenter, George Carey, and Tom McCarthy.

The makeshift team stung the Canadiens with a 5–0 shutout in its home opener on December 22. Dye scored two goals and Toronto promptly reclaimed him from Hamilton and shipped Mickey Roach to take his place with the Tigers.

The move turned out to be a smart one because Dye scored more goals than anyone in the league, finishing with 35. He had 37 total points, four less than Newsy Lalonde of the Canadiens, whose 33 goals and eight assists for 41 points led

the league. It was Lalonde's second scoring title and both times he won because his assists gave him more total points than the leading goal-scorer.

After the opening victory, Hamilton slipped badly and finished in the cellar for both halves of the season, managing only six victories in 24 games. Ottawa won the first-half title with an 8–2 record, three games better than Toronto's 5–5. But the Senators, saddled by a seven-game losing streak, slipped to third in the second half, behind both Toronto and the Canadiens.

Despite the second-half slump, Ottawa's Clint Benedict finished as the top goalie with a 3.1 goals-against average and two shutouts. In the NHL playoffs against second-half champ Toronto, Benedict and the Senators regained their touch. Ottawa shut out the St. Pats, 5–0, in the opener and came back with a 2–0 whitewashing to sweep the series.

Vancouver won the PCHA title by one-half game over Seattle—the difference being a 4–4 tie which Seattle played at Victoria on March 4, Moose Johnson Night. Johnson, a veteran defenseman, was honored before the game and then the teams played through three overtimes before agreeing to let the game end as a tie.

In the two-game playoff, Vancouver romped, outscoring Seattle, 13–2. The Millionaires then met Ottawa for the Stanley Cup. The opening game attracted a record 11,000 fans. The teams split the first four games and then Ottawa won the fifth, 2–1, for the Cup.

1920–21

FINAL STANDINGS

First Half

	W	L	T	PTS	GF	GA
Ottawa	8	2	0	16	49	23
Toronto	5	5	0	10	39	47
Montreal	4	6	0	8	37	51
Hamilton	3	7	0	6	34	38

Second Half

	W	L	T	PTS	GF	GA
Toronto	10	4	0	20	66	53
Montreal	9	5	0	18	75	48
Ottawa	6	8	0	12	48	52
Hamilton	3	11	0	6	58	94

Ottawa defeated Toronto in playoffs and won regular-season championship.

LEADING SCORERS

	G	A	PTS
Lalonde, Montreal C.	33	8	41
Denneny, Ottawa	34	5	39
Dye, Toronto	35	2	37
Malone, Hamilton	30	4	34
Cameron, Toronto	18	9	27
Noble, Toronto	20	6	26
Prodgers, Hamilton	18	8	26
Denneny, Toronto	17	6	23
Nighbor, Ottawa	18	3	21
Berlinquette, Montreal C.	12	9	21

PLAYOFF RESULTS

Finals

Ottawa d. Vancouver (PCHL), 3–2

LEADING SCORERS

	G	A	PTS
Skinner, Vancouver	7	1	8
Denneny, Ottawa	4	2	6
Darragh, Ottawa	5	0	5

LEADING GOALIES

	W	SO	GAA
Benedict, Ottawa	5	2	1.71
Lehman, Vancouver	4	1	2.00

1921–22

This was a year of major changes for hockey in both the East and the West. The NHL dropped the split schedule and its first- and second-half champions, substituting instead a single schedule with playoffs between the top two teams. The PCHA introduced the penalty shot which was awarded to a player who was interfered with after breaking in alone on the goalie. There was a new league in the West and some new owners in the East.

George Kennedy, one of the founders of the NHL and owner of the Montreal club, died in 1921 and his widow sold the club to Joe Cattarinich and Leo Dandurand for $11,000. Cattarinich and Dandurand were anxious to get Sprague Cleghorn, a defenseman who had starred for the Wanderers, back to Montreal and they accomplished this in a roundabout fashion.

The NHL, still trying to help the Hamilton club, devised the plan which eventually brought Cleghorn to the Canadiens. Players with the Wanderers when the club dissolved in 1918, said the NHL, became the property of the league. Cleghorn was one of these players and the NHL simply claimed him from Ottawa and assigned him to Hamilton. Provided with this windfall, the

Tigers promptly offered Cleghorn to the Canadiens, who, they knew, were anxious to get him.

A neat package was arranged with Billy Couture and Cleghorn going to Montreal in exchange for Harry Mummery, Amos Arbour and Cully Wilson. It was the first major, multiple-player trade in the NHL.

The trade reunited Sprague Cleghorn with his brother, Odie, and the two ran wild one week in January. Each scored four goals on January 14 against Hamilton and they combined for six goals against Ottawa a few days later. Interestingly, this spree came shortly after Newsy Lalonde walked out on the team, claiming he couldn't get along with his new bosses. Frank Calder, president of the league, mediated the dispute and, after missing four games, Lalonde returned. But his days in Montreal were numbered.

On February 1, Sprague Cleghorn almost wiped out the Ottawa team singlehandedly. He cut Eddie Gerard and Cy Denneny and charged Frank Nighbor. All three Ottawa players missed two games because of injuries and Cleghorn drew a match foul plus a $15 fine. Ottawa police tried to arrest him for assault in the wake of his one-man war.

Despite Cleghorn's rambunctious play, Montreal finished third behind Ottawa and Toronto. Harry (Punch) Broadbent of Ottawa established a record with at least one goal in 16 consecutive games and a total of 25 during the streak. He finished as the leading scorer with 32 goals and 46 points.

Victoria's Ernie (Moose) Johnson was known as the man with the longest reach in hockey.

Odie Cleghorn was a star forward on the Canadiens.

Toronto defeated Ottawa, 5–4, in the first game of the total-goals playoff and then battled the Senators to a scoreless tie in the second to clinch the Stanley Cup berth.

In the West, Jack Adams, playing center for Vancouver, led the PCHA in scoring with 25 goals. But Seattle, with Frank Foyston and Jim Riley scoring 16 goals each, finished in first place.

In Victoria, a combative goalie named Norm Fowler was thrown out of two games within 10 days for fighting and the team's manager, Lester Patrick, made his debut as a goalie.

Vancouver won the playoff with goalie Hugh Lehman turning in a pair of 1–0 shutouts over Seattle.

A new league, the Western Canada Hockey League, with clubs in Calgary, Edmonton, Saskatoon, and Regina, had been formed and its players included Red Dutton, Bill Cook, and Dick Irvin. Regina finished second but knocked off pennant winner Edmonton in the playoff and challenged Vancouver for the right to represent the West in the Stanley Cup series against Toronto. Regina took the first game, 2–1, but Vancouver recovered with a 4–0 victory in the second game to clinch the playoff.

In the Stanley Cup series, Vancouver and Toronto split the first four games and then Babe Dye fired four goals, pacing a 5–1 St. Pats' victory that clinched the series and the Cup in the fifth contest.

1921–22

FINAL STANDINGS

	W	L	T	PTS	GF	GA
Ottawa	14	8	2	30	106	84
Toronto	13	10	1	27	98	97
Montreal	12	11	1	25	88	94
Hamilton	7	17	0	14	88	105

Toronto defeated Ottawa in playoffs and won regular-season championship.

LEADING SCORERS

	G	A	PTS
Broadbent, Ottawa	32	14	46
Denneny, Ottawa	27	12	39
Dye, Toronto	30	7	37
Malone, Hamilton	25	7	32
Cameron, Toronto	19	8	27

	G	A	PTS
Denneny, Toronto	19	7	26
Noble, Toronto	17	8	25
S. Cleghorn, Montreal C.	21	3	24
O. Cleghorn, Montreal C.	17	7	24
Reise, Hamilton	9	14	23

PLAYOFF RESULTS

Finals

Toronto d. Vancouver (PCHL), 3–2

LEADING SCORERS

	G	A	PTS
Dye, Toronto	11	1	12
Adams, Vancouver	7	0	7

LEADING GOALIES

	W	SO	GAA
Roach, Toronto	4	2	1.84
Lehman, Vancouver	5	4	1.98

1922–23

The split between Newsy Lalonde and Leo Dandurand could not be mended and eventually Montreal dealt its great star to Saskatoon of the new Western League. In return, the Canadiens received the rights to an amateur named Aurel Joliat, a slightly built left wing who belonged to Saskatoon but was playing with Iroquois Falls.

Joliat weighed about 140 pounds and was hardly an imposing athlete. The thought that Montreal had traded one of hockey's early greats for this little guy placed an extra burden on Joliat. But he was equal to it and was to develop into an outstanding NHL player.

In another trade, Montreal sent Bert Corbeau and Edmond Bouchard to Hamilton for Joe Malone, then in the twilight of his career. Vancouver swapped Jack Adams to Toronto for Corbett Denneny.

Joliat scored two goals in his first game for Montreal but Babe Dye had five for Toronto and the St. Pats beat the Canadiens, 7–2. It was the start of a fine season for Dye, who was to win the scoring title with 26 goals and 11 assists for 37 points.

Ottawa won the regular-season title, edging Montreal with Toronto finishing third. Clint Benedict again led the goalies with a 2.3 goals-against average and four shutouts in 24 games. It was the fifth straight year that he was the top goaltender.

Perhaps the most significant event of the season took place in Toronto's Mutual Street Arena in March 1923. That was when a young man named Foster Hewitt, sitting in an airless glass booth erected in three seat spaces and talking into an upright telephone, broadcast radio's first hockey game.

It was the start of a new era for the sport.

In the playoffs, Ottawa blanked the Canadiens, 2–0, in the first game and won the Cup berth on the basis of total goals although it lost the second game, 2–1. Billy Couture and Sprague Cleghorn played viciously in the opener, injuring several Ottawa players with their sticks and elbows. Owner Leo Dandurand was so disturbed at the display that he suspended both of them for the second game, without waiting for the league to act.

Lalonde flourished in the dual role of player-manager with Saskatoon and led the Western League in scoring with 29 goals in 26 games. But his team finished last, with Edmonton taking the regular-season title as well as the two-game, total-goals playoff over Regina.

The PCHA eliminated the position of rover and adopted six-man hockey which had been played in the East for some time. Victoria's Frank Fredrickson led the scorers with 41 goals in 30 games but Vancouver finished first and beat Victoria in the playoffs.

Ottawa, its ranks thinned by injuries, went west for the Stanley Cup playoffs and eliminated Vancouver in four games and then took Edmonton in two straight to clinch it. After watching the gritty show put on by the undermanned Senators, Frank Patrick, president of the PCHA, called them the greatest team he had ever seen.

1922–23

FINAL STANDINGS

	W	L	T	PTS	GF	GA
Ottawa	14	9	1	29	77	54
Montreal C.	13	9	2	28	73	61
Toronto	13	10	1	27	82	88
Hamilton	6	18	0	12	81	110

Ottawa defeated Montreal Canadiens in playoffs and won regular-season championship.

LEADING SCORERS

	G	A	PTS
Dye, Toronto	26	11	37
Denneny, Ottawa	21	10	31
Adams, Toronto	19	9	28
B. Boucher, Montreal C.	23	4	27
O. Cleghorn, Montreal C.	19	7	26
Roach, Hamilton	17	8	25
B. Boucher, Ottawa	15	9	24
Joliat, Montreal C.	13	9	22
Noble, Toronto	12	10	22
Wilson, Hamilton	16	3	19

PLAYOFF RESULTS

Semifinals

Ottawa d. Vancouver (PCHL), 3–1

Finals

Ottawa d. Edmonton (WCHL), 2–zero

LEADING SCORERS

	G	A	PTS
Broadbent, Ottawa	6	1	7
Denneny, Ottawa	3	1	4

LEADING GOALIES

	W	SO	GAA
Benedict, Ottawa	6	3	1.25

1923–24

Until this year, hockey players had no individual trophy for which to compete. There was the scoring championship, of course, and the satisfaction of playing for the Stanley Cup winner for some, but no single award that a player could go after and call his own.

This all changed in 1924 when Dr. David Hart, father of Cecil Hart, a manager-coach of the Montreal Canadiens, contributed a trophy to the league. The Hart Trophy was to be awarded to the Most Valuable Player in the league and the first one went to Frank Nighbor, Ottawa's smooth-skating center.

Nighbor, whose pokecheck repeatedly relieved opponents of the puck, won the award by a single vote over Sprague Cleghorn, the Canadiens' boisterous defenseman.

It was ironic that Nighbor and Cleghorn were the top contestants for the first Hart Trophy. Their styles were a study in contrasts. Nighbor was a gentlemanly sort who rarely was involved in trouble on the ice while Cleghorn seemed to cause a ruckus wherever he went.

In fact, Cleghorn's rough play caused an NHL meeting at midseason to consider his suspension. The Ottawa club claimed Cleghorn was trying to injure opponents deliberately, citing a spearing incident against Cy Denneny. The charges were rejected by the league and in Montreal's next game against Ottawa, Cleghorn charged Lionel Hitchman into the boards and received a one-game suspension.

Ottawa's Denneny won the scoring crown with 22 goals despite a bizarre experience near the end of the season. The Ottawa club was on its way to Montreal for a game when the team train became snowbound. The Senators were stuck all night and Denneny, scrounging about for some food, somehow fell down a well. Luckily he emerged without injury. The game, of course, had to be postponed.

Georges Vezina of Montreal led the goalies with a 2.0 goals-against average and three shutouts, barely edging Clint Benedict. Ottawa took the regular-season title but Montreal beat the Senators in the total-goals playoff, 5–2, with a newcomer, Howie Morenz, starring.

In the PCHA, Seattle dropped eight straight games but came out of the slump and managed to win the regular-season crown. Mickey MacKay of Vancouver led the scorers with 23 goals and teammate Hugh Lehman was the top goalie with a 2.7 goals-against average for the 30-game season.

Calgary took the Western title and Bill Cook of Saskatoon was the scoring champ with 26 goals. Regina's Red McCusker had a 2.2 goals-against average, best among the goaltenders.

Vancouver eliminated Seattle in the PCHA playoff and Calgary ousted Regina in the Western series. Then Calgary earned a bye into the Stanley Cup finals by beating Vancouver in the three-game series before both teams came east to face Montreal.

The Canadiens whipped Vancouver, 3–2 and 2–1, in the semifinals and then defeated Calgary for the Cup, winning 6–1 and 3–0.

1923–24

FINAL STANDINGS

	W	L	T	PTS	GF	GA
Ottawa	16	8	0	32	74	54
Montreal C.	13	11	0	26	59	48
Toronto	10	14	0	20	59	85
Hamilton	9	15	0	18	63	68

Montreal defeated Ottawa in playoffs and won regular-season championship.

LEADING SCORERS

	G	A	PTS
Denney, Ottawa	22	1	23
B. Boucher, Montreal C.	16	6	22
Joliat, Montreal C.	15	5	20
Dye, Toronto	17	2	19
G. Boucher, Ottawa	14	5	19
Burch, Hamilton	16	2	18
Clancy, Ottawa	9	8	17
Morenz, Montreal C.	13	3	16
Adams, Toronto	13	3	16
Noble, Toronto	12	3	15

PLAYOFF RESULTS

Semifinals

Montreal d. Vancouver (PCHL), 2–0

Finals

Montreal d. Calgary (WCHL), 2–0

LEADING SCORERS

	G	A	PTS
Morenz, Montreal	7	2	9
Joliat, Montreal	4	4	8

LEADING GOALIES

	W	SO	GAA
Vezina, Montreal	6	2	1.00

Reg Noble had to trade in his Toronto St. Pats' jersey for a Montreal Maroons' model in 1924.

2

THE YANKS ARE COMING

1924–1929

By 1924, the four-team National Hockey League had taken hold and fans were attracted to games in ever larger numbers. Hockey's popularity had grown to the point where NHL brass was seriously considering expansion into the United States. The Pacific Coast Hockey Association had been successfully operating American franchises at Seattle and Portland and there was reason to believe that a team in the eastern U.S. would enjoy similar success.

There was no problem in finding a market for expanding the prospering league. Bids for franchises came from New York, Boston, Philadelphia, and Pittsburgh. And Montreal interests were seeking a second team for that city. The league decided to move slowly on expansion, a policy that would continue for many years.

The groundwork for adding new teams was laid in 1924 when Thomas J. Duggan was granted options to operate two United States franchises. Duggan interested Boston sportsman Charles Adams and on October 12, 1924, final plans were made at Montreal's Windsor Hotel.

Adams would operate the Boston team with Art Ross, an NHL referee, chosen to manage the club. Donat Raymond and Thomas Strachan were granted a second Montreal franchise and New York would get a team for the 1926 season. The price for a new franchise was $15,000.

The league was clearly moving forward and the best proof of that was to look at the stars. Men like Newsy Lalonde and Joe Malone, who had come to the NHL as established players, were gone and in their place was a new breed featuring Aurel Joliat and Howie Morenz, who started their professional careers in the NHL and established themselves as first-line players in that league.

But with expansion came problems for the National Hockey League and its struggle to survive was to undergo a severe test in its very first year of international operation.

1924–25

With the addition of the new Boston team, called the Bruins, and the Montreal Maroons, the NHL also expanded its schedule, upping the total from 24 to 30 games. This change was to cause a minor rebellion and a player strike late in the season.

Hamilton's Red Green, one of the three players who scored five goals in a single game this season, was at the center of the squabble. The Tigers had won the regular-season race and under a new playoff plan, the first-place finishers were to meet the winners of a series between the second- and third-place teams.

But Green, acting as a spokesman for the Hamilton players, pointed out that he had signed a two-year contract the season before which called for a 24-game schedule and that now he had already played 30 and was being asked to play even more for the same salary. Green and his teammates wanted $200 each to play against the winner of the semifinal series between Toronto and the Montreal Canadiens. The Hamilton players went on strike.

Frank Calder, the NHL president, refused to yield and declared that the semifinal winner would represent the league in the Stanley Cup playoffs. On April 17, the NHL suspended the Hamilton players and fined them $200 each for their action.

The Maroons and Bruins had assembled teams composed mostly of the amateurs and old pros. Montreal came up with Clint Benedict and Harry Broadbent from Ottawa, Louis Berlinquette from Saskatoon, and Reg Noble from Toronto, among others. Alf Skinner, Bernie Morris, and Norm Fowler, all lured from the West, turned up with Boston.

The Bruins opened at home with a victory over the Maroons but then dropped 11 straight games. The Maroons inaugurated their new home, the Montreal Forum, by losing to their crosstown rivals, the Canadiens.

Toronto's Babe Dye won the scoring title with 38 goals and 44 points and Georges Vezina of the Canadiens was the top goalie with a 1.9 goals-against average and five shutouts. Billy Burch of Hamilton won the Hart Trophy as the league's MVP, and a new award donated by Lady Byng, the wife of Canada's governor general, went to Frank Nighbor, the Hart winner the year before. The Lady Byng Trophy was awarded the player who best combined sportsmanship with effective play.

The Canadiens beat Toronto, 3–2 and 2–0, in the playoffs and because of Hamilton's stand, Montreal advanced to the Stanley Cup finals against Victoria, which had joined the WCHL with Vancouver when Seattle bowed out of the PCHA, leaving that league with just two teams.

Victoria finished third behind Saskatoon and Calgary and knocked both clubs off in the WCHL playoffs, with Jack Walker starring. Victoria defeated Montreal in the first two playoff games as Walker scored four goals. The Canadiens won the third game and then Walker set up two goals by Frank Fredrickson that gave the Westerners the fourth game and the Cup.

1924–25

FINAL STANDINGS

	W	L	T	PTS	GF	GA
Hamilton	19	10	1	39	90	60
Toronto	19	11	0	38	90	84
Montreal C.	17	11	2	36	93	56
Ottawa	17	12	1	35	83	66
Montreal M.	9	19	2	20	45	65
Boston	6	24	0	12	49	119

Montreal Canadiens defeated Toronto and Hamilton in playoffs and won the regular-season title.

LEADING SCORERS

	G	A	PTS
Dye, Toronto	38	6	44
Denneny, Ottawa	27	15	42
Joliat, Montreal C.	29	11	40
Morenz, Montreal C.	27	7	34
B. Boucher, Montreal C.	18	13	31
Adams, Toronto	21	8	29
Burch, Hamilton	20	4	24
R. Green, Hamilton	19	4	23
Day, Toronto	10	12	22
Herberts, Boston	17	5	22

PLAYOFF RESULTS

Finals

Victoria (WCHL) d. Montreal Canadiens, 3–2

1925–26

The Hamilton club was sold to a New York group which paid $75,000 for the franchise. The team was renamed the Americans and rented a new sports palace, Madison Square Garden, for its home ice.

The Amerks drew 17,000 fans on opening night in the Garden and big-league hockey became an instant success in New York.

A seventh team was added to the circuit with Odie Cleghorn, the longtime Canadiens' star, named to the NHL Board of Governors to represent the new team, the Pittsburgh Pirates.

Cleghorn would also serve as playing-manager of the Pirates. The team, made up essentially of players from the United States Amateur League, fared remarkably well, with Cleghorn's rapid line changes always keeping fresh legs on the ice.

Pittsburgh spoiled the home opener of the Canadiens with a 1–0 victory and Montreal lost more than just a hockey game in that one. Midway through the game, the Canadiens' great goalie, Georges Vezina, collapsed on the ice from a high fever. Vezina, who had never missed a game in 15 years with the Canadiens, was suffering from tuberculosis and died four months later.

There were new stars around the league. Ottawa's Alex Connell had an amazing 15 shutouts and 1.2 goals-against average in 36 games and the Maroons introduced Nels Stewart, who played both center and defense, and won the scoring title with 34 goals in his rookie season. Stewart also captured the Hart Trophy and Frank Nighbor took the Lady Byng Trophy for the second consecutive year.

Canadiens' Albert (Battleship) Leduc scored vs. the N.Y. Americans in the 1925 inaugural of a new Madison Square Garden.

Ottawa won the regular-season title with two of the league's newest teams, the Maroons and the Pirates, finishing second and third. Boston was fourth and the New York Americans fifth, leaving the bottom two spots to Toronto and the Canadiens.

The Maroons eliminated Pittsburgh in the two-game, total-goals playoff, 6–4, and then whipped champion Ottawa as Clint Benedict shut out his former teammates, 1–0, in the final game.

In the West, the troubles of the old PCHA seemed to spread to the WCHL. Regina's franchise was shifted to Portland and the name Canada was dropped from the league's title, making it the Western Hockey League.

Bill Cook of Saskatoon and Dick Irvin of Portland tied for the scoring lead with 31 goals apiece and a youngster named Eddie Shore was a formidable force on defense with Edmonton, which edged Saskatoon for the regular-season title. Third-place Victoria eliminated Saskatoon and Edmonton in the playoffs and advanced to the Stanley Cup finals against the Montreal Maroons.

Nels Stewart and Clint Benedict dominated the final series as the Maroons captured the Cup. Stewart scored six goals in four games and Benedict shut out the Westerners three times.

The 1926 series was to mark the last time any league other than the NHL competed for the Stanley Cup. The floundering WHL folded its tent. Its players drifted east to the still-expanding National League, which was getting ready to add three more American teams.

1925–26

FINAL STANDINGS

	W	L	T	PTS	GF	GA
Ottawa	24	8	4	52	77	42
Montreal M.	20	11	5	45	91	73
Pittsburgh	19	16	1	39	82	70
Boston	17	15	4	38	92	85
New York A.	12	20	4	28	68	89
Toronto	12	21	3	27	92	114
Montreal C.	11	24	1	23	79	108

LEADING SCORERS

	G	A	PTS
Stewart, Montreal M.	34	8	42
Denneny, Ottawa	24	12	36

Herberts, Boston	26	5	31
Cooper, Boston	28	3	31
Morenz, Montreal C.	23	3	26
Joliat, Montreal C.	17	9	26
Adams, Toronto	21	5	26
Burch, New York A.	22	3	25
Smith, Ottawa	16	9	25
Nighbor, Ottawa	12	13	25

PLAYOFF RESULTS

Finals

Montreal Maroons d. Victoria (WHL), 3–2

LEADING SCORERS

	G	A	PTS
Stewart, Montreal M.	6	3	9

LEADING GOALIES

	W	SO	GAA
Benedict, Montreal M..	5	4	1.00
Holmes, Victoria	2	1	1.45

1926–27

Writers called this era the Golden Age of Sports, and the NHL was about to make itself a solid part of the scene that included baseball's Babe Ruth, tennis' Bill Tilden, football's Red Grange, boxing's Jack Dempsey, and golf's Bobby Jones.

The success of the New York Americans at Madison Square Garden inspired the Garden owners to seek a franchise of their own, and they were awarded one. The team, called the Rangers, was one of three new clubs added to the NHL, the others being the Detroit Cougars and the Chicago Black Hawks. With the Western and Pacific Coast Leagues now defunct, there were plenty of players available.

The 10-team league was split into two divisions, the American and the Canadian. The four Canadian teams—Ottawa, Toronto, the Montreal Maroons and Montreal Canadiens—and New York's Americans comprised the Canadian Division. The American Division listed the three new teams—the Rangers, Detroit and Chicago—along with Pittsburgh and Boston.

The players came from professional as well as amateur ranks. A package deal was arranged with the Western loop in which whole rosters of players became available for a total of $25,000 per club.

Bill Cook and his brother Bun both wound up in New York, where Conn Smythe was assem-

bling the Rangers. Eddie Shore went to Boston, where he would become perhaps the greatest defenseman in NHL history. Detroit came up with Frank Foyston and Frank Fredrickson while Dick Irvin and Mickey MacKay landed in Chicago.

Smythe had a falling-out with the Garden management and was dismissed before the Rangers ever played a game. Lester Patrick was brought in from the West to run the New York team. Smythe went home to his native Toronto, determined to get even with the New York brass. The last-place St. Pats were in trouble and up for sale and Smythe raised $160,000 and made the deal. The club's name was changed to the Maple Leafs and flourished under Smythe's shrewd control.

In Montreal, the owners of the Canadiens donated a trophy to the league in the memory of Georges Vezina to be awarded annually to the goaltender on the team which was the least-scored-upon in the league. George Hainsworth, Vezina's successor with the Canadiens, won the first one.

Howie Morenz took the Canadian Division scoring title with 32 points, including 25 goals. Bill Cook of the Rangers scored 33 goals and won the American Division scoring race with 37 points. Herb Gardiner of the Canadiens was named the MVP and Hart Trophy winner, while Billy Burch of the New York Americans got the Lady Byng.

Ottawa won the Canadian Division and the Rangers took the American Division regular-season titles. Six teams qualified for the Stanley Cup playoffs with Ottawa and Boston reaching the finals and the Senators winning in four games.

Duncan (Mickey) MacKay, a star forward from the Vancouver Millionaires, joined the Chicago Blackhawks in 1926–27.

1926–27

FINAL STANDINGS

Canadian Division

	W	L	T	PTS	GF	GA
Ottawa	30	10	4	64	86	69
Montreal C.	28	14	2	58	99	67
Montreal M.	20	20	4	44	71	68
New York A.	17	25	2	36	82	91
Toronto	15	24	5	35	79	94

	W	L	T	PTS	GF	GA
New York R.	25	13	6	56	95	72
Boston	21	20	3	45	97	89
Chicago	19	22	3	41	115	116
Pittsburgh	15	26	3	33	79	108
Detroit	12	28	4	28	76	105

LEADING SCORERS

	G	A	PTS
Bill Cook, New York R.	33	4	37
Irvin, Chicago	18	18	36
Morenz, Montreal C.	25	7	32
Frederickson, Detroit-Boston	18	13	31
Dye, Chicago	25	5	30
Bailey, Toronto	15	13	28
Boucher, New York R.	13	15	28
Burch, New York A.	19	8	27
Oliver, Boston	18	6	24
Keats, Boston-Detroit	16	8	24

PLAYOFF RESULTS

Quarterfinals

Montreal C. d. Montreal M., 2–1
Boston d. Chicago, 10 goals to 5

Semifinals

Ottawa d. Montreal C., 5 goals to 1
Boston d. New York R., 3 goals to 1

Finals

Ottawa d. Boston, 2–0 (2 ties)

LEADING SCORERS

	G	A	PTS
Oliver, Boston	4	2	6
Galbraith, Boston	3	3	6
Frederickson, Detroit	2	4	6
Denneny, Ottawa	5	0	5

LEADING GOALIES

	W	SO	GAA
Connell, Ottawa	3	0	0.60
Benedict, Montreal M..	0	0	0.91
Hainsworth, Montreal C.	1	1	1.43
Winkler, Boston	2	2	1.50
Chabot, New York R.	0	1	1.50

1927–28

There have been many hexes in sports history but none so mysterious as the eerie Curse of Muldoon which shackled the Chicago Black Hawks for 40 years. It was in 1927 that Pete Muldoon administered it.

The great Ranger line: (from left) Bill Cook, Frank Boucher, and Bun Cook.

Muldoon had been brought in to coach the new Chicago team when the NHL added three franchises in 1926. The team had done moderately well, winning 19 games in a 44-game season and finishing third to qualify for the playoffs. They were the highest-scoring team in the league with 115 goals but also allowed more goals than anyone else, 116.

So Muldoon was understandably distressed when Hawks' owner Fred McLaughlin dismissed him at the start of the 1927–28 season. In fact, Muldoon was said to be so distressed, he placed his curse on McLaughlin and the Hawks. As comeuppance for his unjust dismissal, Muldoon told McLaughlin, Chicago would never win an NHL title.

Sour grapes, one might say, but it's a fact that for 40 years the Hawks never did win the regular-season championship and only when they finally did make it was the curse wiped out.

Muldoon's successors didn't do nearly as well with the Hawks as he had done in their first season. Barney Stanley and Hugh Lehman split the job and Chicago managed only seven victories all season, finishing a dismal last in the American Division race won by Boston. The Canadiens finished first in the Canadian Division.

The individual stars were Hart Trophy winner Howie Morenz, the scoring champ with 33 goals and 51 total points, and Frank Boucher of the Rangers, who led the American Division with 35 points and won the Lady Byng Trophy.

George Hainsworth again won the goalie's Vezina Trophy but the most outstanding goaltending job was turned in by Alex Connell of Ottawa, who set a record with six straight shutouts and 446 minutes, nine seconds of scoreless hockey. Connell became the center of contention the night Lester Patrick went in to play goal.

The Rangers had advanced to the Stanley Cup final by eliminating Pittsburgh and Boston while the Montreal Maroons knocked off Ottawa and the Canadiens. The Maroons won the first game of the finals, 2–0.

Ottawa's Alex Connell set an NHL record by registering six consecutive shutouts in 1927–28.

Early in the second period of the next game, Nels Stewart fired a shot that caught Ranger goalie Lorne Chabot in the eye. Chabot could not continue and Patrick asked Eddie Gerard, manager of the Maroons, for permission to use Ottawa's Connell, who was in the stands watching the game, as a replacement.

Gerard refused and when Patrick asked permission to use a minor leaguer who was also in the stands, Gerard again refused. Patrick, seething, returned to the Ranger dressing room to tell his club what had happened.

"What do we do now?" he asked.

"How about you playing goal?" suggested Frank Boucher, half-kidding, half-serious.

Patrick, 44, had retired as a player several years earlier. But he mulled over Boucher's suggestion and said, "Okay, I'll do it."

The Rangers protected Lester like a piece of fine china. Patrick made 18 saves, allowed one goal and New York won the game in overtime.

After losing the next game, New York came back to win the final two games and the Stanley Cup.

1927-28

FINAL STANDINGS

Canadian Division

	W	L	T	PTS	GF	GA
Montreal C.	26	11	7	59	116	48
Montreal M.	24	14	6	54	96	77
Ottawa	20	14	10	50	78	57
Toronto	18	18	8	44	89	88
New York A.	11	27	6	28	63	128

American Division

	W	L	T	PTS	GF	GA
Boston	20	13	11	51	77	70
New York R.	19	16	9	47	97	79
Pittsburgh	19	17	8	46	67	76
Detroit	19	19	6	44	88	79
Chicago	7	34	3	17	68	134

LEADING SCORERS

	G	A	PTS
Morenz, Montreal C.	33	18	51
Joliat, Montreal C.	28	11	39
Boucher, New York R.	23	12	35
Hay, Detroit	22	13	35
Stewart, Montreal M.	27	7	34
Gagne, Montreal C.	20	10	30
Bun Cook, New York R.	14	14	28
Carson, Toronto	20	6	26
Finnigan, Ottawa	20	5	25
Bill Cook, New York R.	18	6	24
Keats, Chicago-Detroit	14	10	24

PLAYOFF RESULTS

Quarterfinals

Montreal M. d. Ottawa, 3 goals to 1
New York R. d. Pittsburgh, 6 goals to 4

Semifinals

Montreal M. d. Montreal C., 3 goals to 2
New York R. d. Boston, 5 goals to 2

Finals

New York R. d. Montreal M., 3–2

LEADING SCORERS

	G	A	PTS
Boucher, New York R.	7	1	8
Cook, Bill, New York R.	2	3	5

LEADING GOALIES

	W	SO	GAA
Benedict, Montreal M.	9	4	0.86

1928-29

A rule designed to hype hockey offenses was introduced in 1928, but instead it became the year of the goalie around the NHL. The new rule allowed forward passing in all three zones on the ice-that is, the defensive zone, the area between the blue lines, and the offensive zone. There was still no red line in the game and the ice was divided by only the two blue lines.

Previously, forward passing was allowed only in a team's defensive zone or center ice, but never in the offensive area. Eventually, the rule change would affect the game and open play up, but not this season.

In Montreal, little George Hainsworth almost obliterated the memory of the great Georges Vezina. In 44 games, goaltender Hainsworth recorded an incredible 22 shutouts.

Hainsworth allowed 43 goals all year-an average of less than one per game. The highest-scoring team in the league was Boston, winner of the American Division race. The Bruins scored a total of 89 goals—a shade over two per game.

One of Hainsworth's shutouts came against Ottawa on December 22, 1928, a special date for Montreal and for hockey. It marked the first NHL broadcast of a Montreal game and started an era that brought hockey into the home regularly. Arthur Dupont, founder of radio station CJAD, handled the French broadcast and columnist Elmer Ferguson did the English.

"The hockey people looked upon radio with a great deal of suspicion," noted Dupont. "They feared that if stories of the games came into the home without cost, it would ruin the attendance. So we were

Ace Bailey of Toronto took scoring honors in 1928–29.

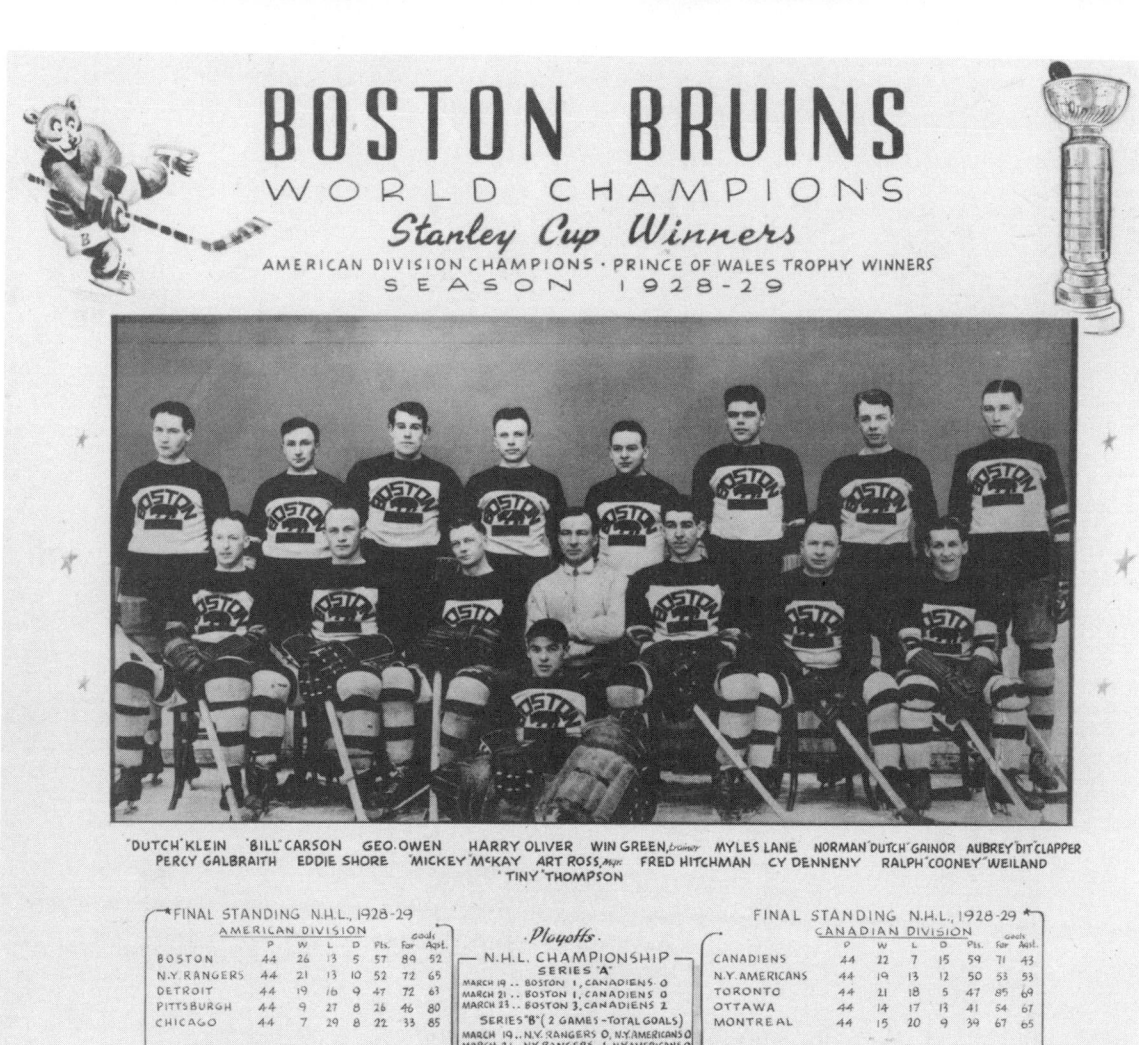

BOSTON BRUINS
WORLD CHAMPIONS
Stanley Cup Winners
AMERICAN DIVISION CHAMPIONS · PRINCE OF WALES TROPHY WINNERS
SEASON 1928-29

'DUTCH' KLEIN   'BILL' CARSON   GEO. OWEN   HARRY OLIVER   WIN GREEN, trainer   MYLES LANE   NORMAN 'DUTCH' GAINOR   AUBREY 'DIT' CLAPPER
PERCY GALBRAITH   EDDIE SHORE   'MICKEY' McKAY   ART ROSS, mgr.   FRED HITCHMAN   CY DENNENY   RALPH 'COONEY' WEILAND
'TINY' THOMPSON

FINAL STANDING N.H.L., 1928-29
AMERICAN DIVISION

	P	W	L	D	Pts.	goals for	Agst.
BOSTON	44	26	13	5	57	89	52
N.Y. RANGERS	44	21	13	10	52	72	65
DETROIT	44	19	16	9	47	72	63
PITTSBURGH	44	9	27	8	26	46	80
CHICAGO	44	7	29	8	22	33	85

Playofts
N.H.L. CHAMPIONSHIP
SERIES "A"
MARCH 19 .. BOSTON 1, CANADIENS 0
MARCH 21 .. BOSTON 1, CANADIENS 0
MARCH 23 .. BOSTON 3, CANADIENS 2
SERIES "B" (2 GAMES - TOTAL GOALS)
MARCH 19.. N.Y. RANGERS 0, N.Y. AMERICANS 0
MARCH 21.. N.Y. RANGERS 1, N.Y. AMERICANS 0
SERIES "C" (2 GAMES - TOTAL GOALS)
MARCH 19.. TORONTO 3, DETROIT 1
MARCH 21 .. TORONTO 4, DETROIT 1
SERIES "D" (2 OUT OF 3 GAMES)
MARCH 24 .. N.Y. RANGERS 1, TORONTO 0
MARCH 26.. N.Y. RANGERS 2, TORONTO 1
STANLEY CUP (FINAL - 2 OUT OF 3 GAMES)
SERIES "E"
MARCH 28.. BOSTON 2, N.Y. RANGERS 0
MARCH 29.. BOSTON 2, N.Y. RANGERS 1

FINAL STANDING N.H.L., 1928-29
CANADIAN DIVISION

	P	W	L	D	Pts.	goals for	Agst.
CANADIENS	44	22	7	15	59	71	43
N.Y. AMERICANS	44	19	13	12	50	53	53
TORONTO	44	21	18	5	47	85	69
OTTAWA	44	14	17	13	41	54	67
MONTREAL	44	15	20	9	39	67	65

Charles F. Adams, PRESIDENT

Arthur H. Ross, VICE PRES. & GEN. MGR.

Ralph F. Burkard, TREASURER

Frank Ryan, PUBLICITY DIRECTOR

The Boston Bruins took home the Cup in 1929.

limited to a brief description of the third period and afterwards a summary of the entire game."

As it developed, of course, broadcasts increased hockey interest and now the radio-television industry plays a major role in the sport.

With the goalies dominating play, Toronto's

Ace Bailey captured the scoring crown with 32 points—22 of them on goals. Carson Cooper of Detroit was the top scorer in the American Division with 18 goals and 27 points.

Hainsworth easily won the Vezina Trophy, but another goalie, Roy Worters of the New York

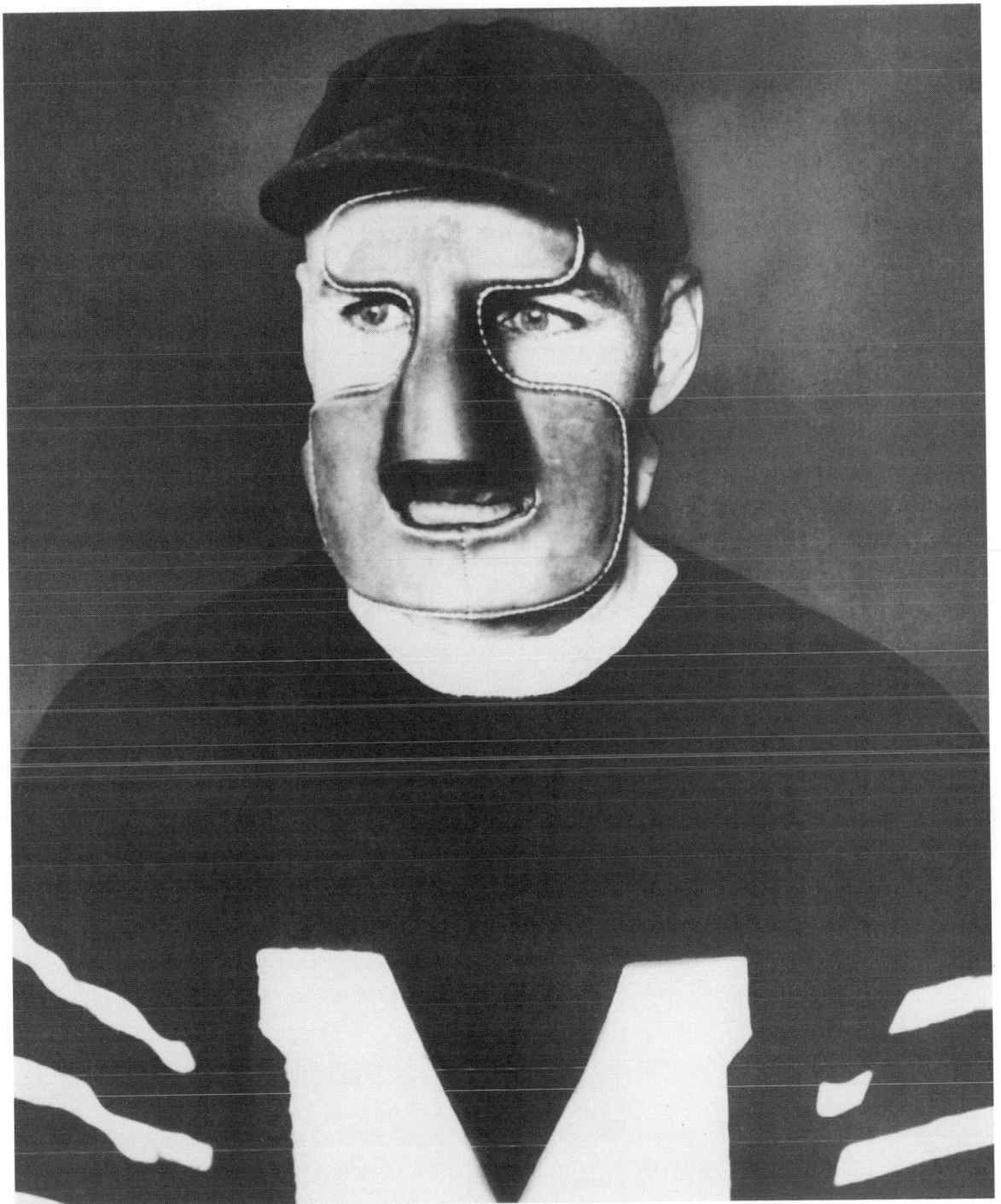

The Montreal Maroons' Clint Benedict: Hockey's first masked goalie.

Americans, took the Hart as MVP. The Rangers' Frank Boucher won the Lady Byng.

A new playoff arrangement matched the first-place, second-place and third-place teams in each division against each other. The winners of the series between second-place teams and the series between the third-place finishers clashed in the semifinal with that winner advancing to the Stanley Cup finals against the winner of the series between the two first-place clubs.

Toronto eliminated Detroit in two straight games and the Rangers knocked off the Americans in two straight. Then New York beat Toronto to advance to the finals against Boston, which had eliminated the Canadiens. The Bruins won the Cup in two games as rookie goalie Tiny Thompson turned in his third playoff shutout in five games. Thompson allowed three goals in the five games, a playoff goals-against average of 0.60.

1928–29

FINAL STANDINGS

Canadian Division

	W	L	T	PTS	GF	GA
Montreal C.	22	7	15	59	71	43
New York	19	13	12	50	53	53
Toronto	21	18	5	47	85	69
Ottawa	14	17	13	41	54	67
Montreal M	15	20	9	39	67	65

American Division

	W	L	T	PTS	GF	GA
Boston	26	13	5	57	89	52
New York R.	21	13	10	52	72	65
Detroit	19	16	9	47	72	63
Pittsburgh	9	27	8	26	46	80
Chicago	7	29	8	22	33	85

LEADING SCORERS

	G	A	PTS
Bailey, Toronto	22	10	32
Stewart, Montreal M.	21	8	29
Cooper, Detroit	18	9	27
Morenz, Montreal C.	17	10	27
Blair, Toronto	12	15	27
Boucher, New York R.	10	16	26
Oliver, Boston	17	6	23
Bill Cook, New York R.	15	8	23
Ward, Montreal M.	14	8	22
Finnigan, Ottawa	15	4	19

PLAYOFF RESULTS

Quarterfinals

New York R. d. New York A., 1 goal to 0
Toronto d. Detroit, 7 goals to 2

Semifinals

Boston d. Montreal C., 3–0
New York R. d. Toronto, 2–0

Finals

Boston d. New York R., 2–0

LEADING SCORERS

	G	A	PTS
Keeling, New York R.	3	0	3
Blair, Toronto	3	0	3
Bailey, Toronto	1	2	3

LEADING GOALIES

	W	SO	GAA
Thompson, Boston	5	3	0.60
Roach, New York R.	3	3	0.77

3

A NEW WORLD OF OFFENSE
1929–1942

The NHL had taken a firm hold in the 1920s, expanding from four teams to 10 and emerging as the sport's universally recognized major league. But in the '30s, problems would arise. There was the American Depression and the shock waves traveled right through the Canadian sport which had franchises in five United States cities. And there was the complaint that hockey was too defensive a game . . . that the offenses were stymied.

Lester Patrick, boss of the New York Rangers, agreed with the detractors to some extent.

"I believe in keeping the game wide open," said Patrick at the height of the debate over whether to remove all restrictions on forward passing. "Our followers are entitled to action . . . not for a few brief moments, but for three full 20-minute periods of a game.

"The open style of play calls for better stickhandling and speedier skating. What better system could the coaches and managers adopt to preserve and further popularize the fastest game in the world."

The NHL eventually went along with Patrick's ideas and, predictably, the game opened up considerably. The economic problems, however, caused several club shifts and a couple of franchise casualties.

But stickhandling and speed, the two qualities Patrick talked about, combined to give hockey a loyal core of fans that grew and grew, despite the Depression. The sport had its rough moments, it is true, but the game's brass, from NHL president Frank Calder on down, pulled it through the periods of crisis.

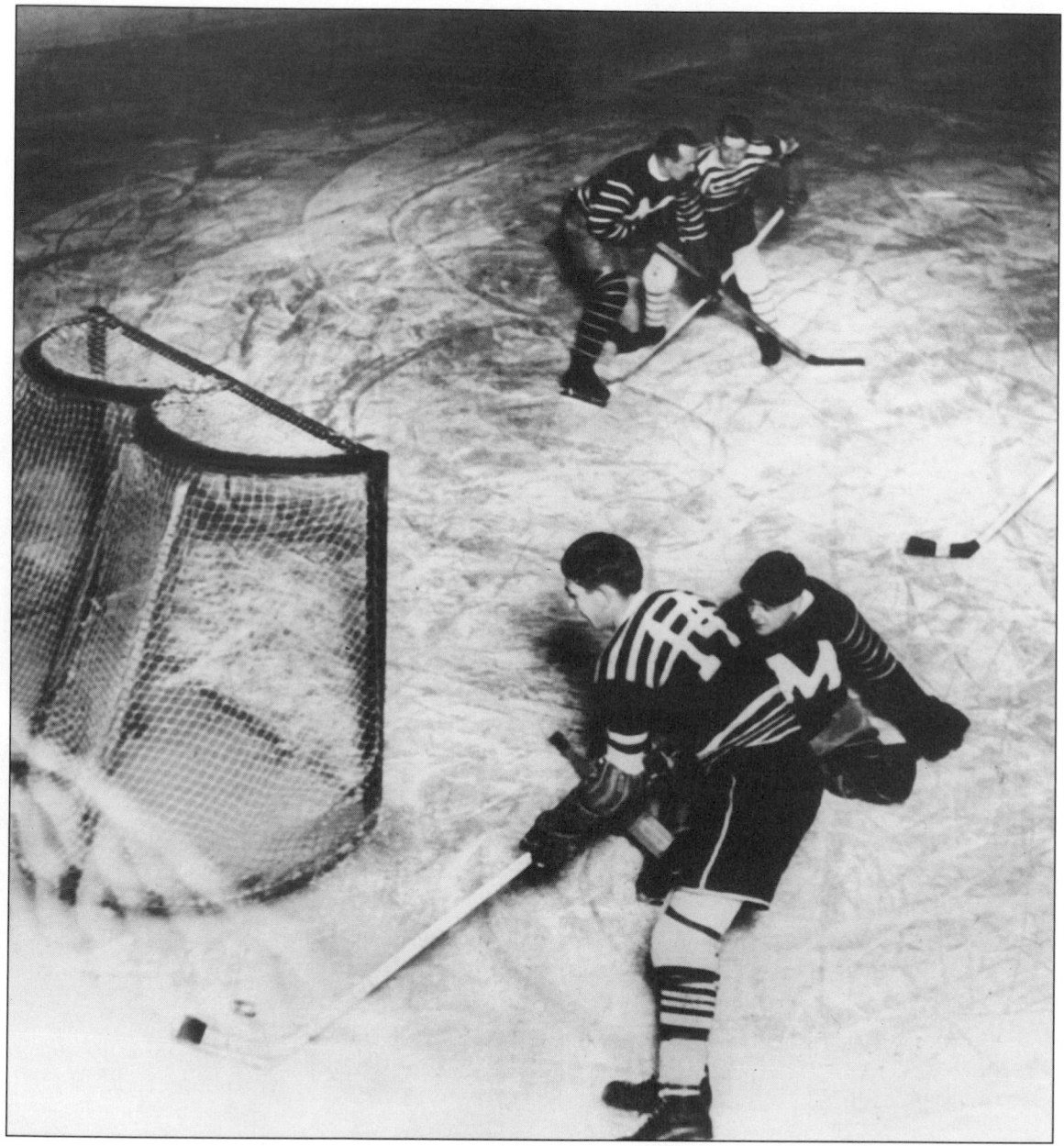

Chicago's Johnny Gottselig chases the puck in a 1929 match against the Montreal Maroons.

1929–30

It would take more than a Depression to stop Conn Smythe, who was determined to build the Toronto Maple Leafs into an NHL power, if for no other reason than to prove to Madison Square Garden's owners just how valuable a man they had lost when they fired him three years before.

Smythe needed a bigger arena for his club, but raising the money to build one was a problem.

So Smythe solved the financial question by turning to the trade unions and builders for help. As partial payment of wages, the workmen would receive stock in Maple Leaf Gardens.

The solution worked out beautifully for all parties. Smythe got his new arena and his shareholders had a part in what would become a highly successful sports and entertainment center.

But the Maple Leafs spent their next-to-last season in the old Arena Gardens and it was less than a success. They finished fourth in the Canadian Division even though they introduced a good-looking rookie named Charlie Conacher, who was destined for NHL stardom.

The new rules allowing passing in all three zones added scoring punch throughout the league and Boston's Cooney Weiland was the leading pointmaker with 73, including 43 goals. The Bruins, with Weiland setting the pace, were the highest-scoring team in the league and their goalie, Tiny Thompson, allowed the fewest goals. The combination gave Boston a fantastic 38 victories in 44 games, including one record stretch of 14 straight victories. Naturally, the Bruins won the American Division title.

Hec Kilrea of Ottawa was the leading scorer in the Canadian Division with 58 points, three more than Nels Stewart of the Montreal Maroons, who won the Hart Trophy as MVP. Tiny Thompson broke George Hainsworth's three-year hold on the Vezina Trophy and Frank Boucher took the Lady Byng again.

Roy Worters of the New York Americans was the 1930–31 Vezina Trophy winner.

The 1929–30 scoring title went to Ralph (Cooney) Weiland of Boston.

While the Bruins won their division crown by 30 points, Ottawa and the two Montreal teams staged a three-way battle for Canadian Division honors. The Maroons and Canadiens both finished with 51 points and Ottawa had 50. The Maroons were recognized as the first-place team because they had more victories (23) than the Canadiens (21).

That was a break for the Canadiens because it meant the Maroons would have to face Boston's powerhouse in the opening Stanley Cup series. Sure enough, the Bruins eliminated the Maroons in four games while the Canadiens got past Chicago in the two-game, total-goals play-off. The Rangers eliminated Ottawa but then the Canadiens took the Rangers and stunned the Bruins, winning the Cup finale in two straight games.

Clint Benedict, the Maroons' great goalie, made hockey history by using the first face mask ever that season. It happened after Howie Morenz of the Canadiens had broken Benedict's nose with a shot. Benedict didn't stay with the protection, however, and it would be almost three decades before a goalie would try a mask again.

1929–30

FINAL STANDINGS

Canadian Division

	W	L	T	PTS	GF	GA
Montreal M.	23	16	5	51	141	114
Montreal C.	21	14	9	51	142	114
Ottawa	21	15	8	50	138	118
Toronto	17	21	6	40	116	124
New York A.	14	25	5	33	113	161

American Division

	W	L	T	PTS	GF	GA
Boston	38	5	1	77	179	98
Chicago	21	18	5	47	117	111
New York R.	17	17	10	44	136	143
Detroit	14	24	6	34	117	133
Pittsburgh	5	36	3	13	102	185

LEADING SCORERS

	G	A	PTS
Weiland, Boston	43	30	73
Boucher, New York R.	26	36	62
Clapper, Boston	41	20	61
Bill Cook, New York R.	29	30	59
Kilrea, Ottawa	36	22	58
Stewart, Montreal M.	39	16	55
Morenz, Montreal C.	40	10	50
Himes, New York A.	28	22	50
Lamb, Ottawa	29	20	49
Gainor, Boston	18	31	49

LEADING SCORERS

	G	A	PTS
Weiland, Boston	1	5	6
Barry, Boston	3	3	6

LEADING GOALIES

	W	SO	GAA
Hainsworth, Montreal	5	3	1.00
Thompson, Boston	3	0	1.67

1930–31

The saga of how he financed Maple Leaf Gardens proved how determined Conn Smythe could be. In 1930, he decided that one of the things his Maple Leafs needed for improvement was a player of King Clancy's ability.

Smythe asked how much it would take to get Clancy away from Ottawa. A couple of players and cash . . . say about $35,000 . . . he was told.

Smythe had the players. The cash was another story. He had most of his assets tied up in the construction of the Leafs' new home. But if $35,000 was what he needed to get Clancy, Smythe decided he'd come up with it.

He raised some capital from friends, giving himself a little room to maneuver. Then he bet the bundle on a longshot horse—his own Rare Jewel. Naturally, the horse won and Smythe had the price for Clancy.

Smythe's wheeling and dealing was typical of the problems of Depression-burdened owners. The Pittsburgh club was forced to move to Philadelphia because of poor attendance. The Pirates changed their name to the Quakers but were doomed anyway. They lasted just that season in Philadelphia.

In Detroit, the club changed its nickname from the Cougars to the Falcons in an effort to lift sagging interest. But with money in short supply,

The Detroit Falcons' Ebbie Goodfellow led the American Division with 48 points in 1930–31.

Herb Drury was a center for the Quakers, who lasted for one season, 1930–31, in Philadelphia.

especially in the automobile capital, there was little left over to spend on watching hockey games.

Another step to inject interest around the league was the introduction of an All-Star team. The first squad selected was a study in immortals. The forward line included Howie Morenz of the Canadiens at center, his linemate Aurel Joliat at left wing and Bill Cook of the New York Rangers at right wing. The defensemen were Boston's Eddie Shore and King Clancy of Toronto. Charlie Gardiner of Chicago was picked as the goalie.

Morenz led the league in scoring with 28 goals and 51 points and won the Hart Trophy as the MVP. Frank Boucher took his fourth straight Lady Byng and Roy Worters of the New York Americans edged out Gardiner for the Vezina Trophy. Detroit's Ebbie Goodfellow led the American Division scorers with 48 points.

In the playoffs, division champs Boston and the Montreal Canadiens went five games before the Canadiens won. Three of the games went into overtime. Chicago eliminated Toronto and then whipped the Rangers, who had knocked off the Maroons.

In the final round, the Canadiens won their second straight Cup, coming from behind to beat the Black Hawks in the five-game playoffs.

Just as the Pittsburgh-Philadelphia franchise was in trouble in the American Division, the Canadian Division's Ottawa team had fallen on lean days. The Senators won just 10 games, finished in last place, and requested (and were granted) a one-year leave of absence from the league.

1930–31

FINAL STANDINGS

Canadian Division

	W	L	T	PTS	GF	GA
Montreal	26	10	8	60	129	89
Toronto	22	13	9	53	118	99
Montreal M.	20	18	6	46	105	106
New York A.	18	16	10	46	76	74
Ottawa	10	30	4	24	91	142

American Division

	W	L	T	PTS	GF	GA
Boston	28	10	6	62	143	90
Chicago	24	17	3	51	108	78
New York R.	19	16	9	46	106	87
Detroit	16	21	7	39	102	105
Philadelphia	4	36	4	12	76	184

	G	A	PTS
Morenz, Montreal C.	28	23	51
Goodfellow, Detroit	25	23	48
Conacher, Toronto	31	12	43
Bill Cook, New York R.	30	12	42
Bailey, Toronto	23	19	42
Primeau, Toronto	9	32	41
Stewart, Montreal M.	25	14	39
Boucher, New York R.	12	27	39
Weiland, Boston	25	13	38
Bun Cook, New York R.	18	17	35
Joliat, Montreal C.	13	22	35

PLAYOFF RESULTS

Quarterfinals

Chicago d. Toronto, 4 goals to 3
New York R. d. Montreal M.., 8 goals to 1

Semifinals

Montreal C. d. Boston, 3 goals to 2
Chicago d. New York R., 3 goals to 2

Finals

Montreal C. d. Chicago, 3–2

LEADING SCORERS

	G	A	PTS
Weiland, Boston	6	3	9
Gagnon, Montreal	6	2	8
Clapper, Boston	2	4	6

LEADING GOALIES

	W	SO	GAA
Roach, New York R.	2	1	1.00
Gardiner, Chicago	5	2	1.32
Hainsworth, Montreal	6	2	1.75

1931–32

The departure of Ottawa and Philadelphia left the NHL with eight clubs, four in each division. The schedule was increased to 48 games per club in an effort to increase team income during the dreary Depression days.

It was a gala night in Toronto on November 12 when Conn Smythe proudly unveiled his new Maple Leaf Gardens. A crowd of 13,542 packed the arena for the game between Toronto and Chicago. But the Black Hawks, who had never won a game in Toronto before, spoiled the party by upsetting the Leafs, 3–1.

The anger that burned within Smythe against New York and the Ranger organization could not be extinguished until he built the Leafs into a powerhouse. This was to be the year for him to get even, although it didn't start out that way. Toronto slumped into last place after one month and Smythe hired Dick Irvin to replace Art Duncan as coach. Irvin had been fired by Chicago the

year before but when he took over the Leafs, they acted like a brand-new club.

Toronto soared from last to first place with Charlie Conacher, Harvey Jackson and Joe Primeau providing the fire-power. Jackson won the Canadian Division scoring title with 53 points, three more than Primeau. Conacher finished fourth with 48 and only Howie Morenz managed to squeeze his way between the Toronto trio with 49 points.

Morenz won his second straight Hart Trophy as the MVP while Primeau ended Frank Boucher's four-year domination of the Lady Byng award. Charlie Gardiner of Chicago won the Vezina again and was named the All-Star goalie for the second time.

Jackson, a left wing, and Morenz, a center, both made the All-Star team along with right wing Bill Cook of the New York Rangers, whose 34 goals and 48 points led American Division scorers. The defensemen selected were Boston's Eddie Shore and bald-headed Ching Johnson of the Rangers, who delighted in breaking up the rushes of Montreal's Aurel Joliat by sweeping the little guy's cap off his head.

Toronto finished second behind the Canadiens in the Canadian Division while the Rangers won the American Division crown. Now, if only the playoffs worked out properly, Smythe thought, he'd finally have a chance at his revenge.

After Chicago's Charlie Gardiner shut out Toronto in the first game, the Leafs exploded for a 6–1 victory to eliminate the Black Hawks on total goals. The Maroons beat Detroit in the other quarterfinal while, happily for Smythe, the Rangers advanced to the finals by eliminating the Canadiens.

Toronto got past the Maroons in the two-game, total-goals semifinal and now it was the Leafs and the Rangers for the Stanley Cup. Conacher, Primeau, Hap Day and the other Leafs ran wild, beating the Rangers in three straight games and scoring six goals in each of them. The Stanley Cup was the ultimate ornament to adorn Smythe's new Maple Leaf Gardens. Conn's revenge was served!

A former Canadiens' star, Newsy Lalonde returned to coach his old team in 1932–33.

1931–32

FINAL STANDINGS

Canadian Division

	W	L	T	PTS	GF	GA
Montreal C.	25	16	7	57	128	111
Toronto	23	18	7	53	155	127
Montreal	19	22	7	45	142	139
New York A.	16	24	8	40	95	142

American Division

	W	L	T	PTS	GF	GA
New York R.	23	17	8	54	134	112
Chicago	18	19	11	47	86	101
Detroit	18	20	10	46	95	108
Boston	15	21	12	42	122	117

LEADING SCORERS

	G	A	PTS
Jackson, Toronto	28	25	53
Primeau, Toronto	13	37	50
Morenz, Montreal C.	24	25	49
Bill Cook, New York R.	34	14	48
Conacher, Toronto	34	14	48
Trottier, Montreal M.	26	18	44
Smith, Montreal M.	11	33	44
Siebert, Montreal M.	21	18	39
Clapper, Boston	17	22	39
Joliat, Montreal C.	15	24	39

PLAYOFF RESULTS

Quarterfinals

Toronto d. Chicago, 6 goals to 2
Montreal M. d. Detroit, 3 goals to 1

Semifinals

N. Y. Rangers d. Montreal C., 3–0

Finals

Toronto d. N.Y. Rangers, 3–0

LEADING SCORERS

	G	A	PTS
Boucher, N.Y. Rangers	3	6	9
Bun Cook, N.Y. Rangers	6	2	8
Conacher, Toronto	6	2	8
Jackson, Toronto	5	2	7

LEADING GOALIES

	W	SO	GAA
Chabot, Toronto	5	0	2.05

1932–33

In an effort to tighten belts during the height of the Depression, NHL owners decided to put a ceiling of $70,000 on club payrolls with no single player to be paid more than $7,500. That represented a 10 percent slice for most teams and the players staged a small revolution over the move.

There were big-name holdouts all over the league, including Frank Boucher of the Rangers, Reg Noble and Hap Emms of Detroit, the Canadiens' Aurel Joliat, Lorne Chabot of Toronto and Hooley Smith of the Montreal Maroons. President Frank Calder was given permission to suspend the dissidents but eventually all of the holdouts fell into line.

Seat prices were slashed, too. The top price was $3 and fans could get into most arenas for as little as 50 cents.

Ottawa returned to the league after a one-year hiatus with Cy Denneny as its coach. Other great former players also turned up as coaches: Newsy Lalonde with the Canadiens and Jack Adams in Detroit, where the team was about to adopt its third name, the Red Wings. In New York, Colonel John Hammond, who was instrumental in bringing hockey to Madison Square Garden, first with the Americans and then with the Rangers, resigned. As a result, coach Lester Patrick took on the added titles of general manager and vice president of the Rangers.

Before the season started, the Rangers sold goalie John Ross Roach to Detroit for $11,000. It was a worthwhile investment for the Cougars-Falcons-Red Wings. Roach was named the All-Star goalie on a team that included Bill Cook and Frank Boucher of the Rangers, and Baldy Northcott of the Montreal Maroons up front, and a defense of Boston's Eddie Shore and the Rangers' Ching Johnson.

Cook took the scoring title with 50 points, 28 of them goals, Boucher reclaimed the Lady Byng and Shore became the first fulltime defenseman to win the Hart Trophy. Boston's Tiny Thompson took the Vezina.

The Bruins and Detroit ended with identical records of 25–15–8 in the American Division with Boston recognized as the champion because the Bruins had scored more goals (124) than the Red Wings (111). Toronto won the Canadian Division race.

In the playoffs, the Maple Leafs eliminated the Bruins in five games. It was one of the most memorable playoff series as four of the games went into overtime and the final one lasted six extra periods.

Detroit eliminated the Montreal Maroons and the Rangers ousted the Canadiens in the quarterfinals. Then New York finished Detroit off and went up against the bone-weary Leafs in the final series.

With Toronto softened up by the prolonged series against Boston, the Rangers had an easy time, winning in four games. The heroes were the Cook brothers, Bill and Bun, and their center, Frank Boucher, all of whom had been signed for New York by Toronto's boss, Conn Smythe.

1932–33

FINAL STANDINGS

Canadian Division

	W	L	T	PTS	GF	GA
Toronto	24	18	6	54	119	111
Montreal M.	22	20	6	50	135	119
Montreal C.	18	25	5	41	92	115
New York A.	15	22	11	41	91	118
Ottawa	11	27	10	32	88	131

American Division

	W	L	T	PTS	GF	GA
Boston	25	15	8	58	124	88
Detroit	25	15	8	58	111	93
New York R.	23	17	8	54	135	107
Chicago	16	20	12	44	88	101

LEADING SCORERS

	G	A	PTS
Bill Cook, New York R.	28	22	50
Jackson, Toronto	27	17	44
Northcott, Montreal M.	22	21	43
Smith, Montreal M.	20	21	41
Haynes, Montreal M.	16	25	41
Joliat, Montreal C.	18	21	39
Barry, Boston	24	13	37
Bun Cook, New York R.	22	15	37
Stewart, Boston	18	18	36
Morenz, Montreal C.	14	21	35

PLAYOFF RESULTS

Quarterfinals

Detroit d. Montreal M. , 5 goals to 2
N.Y. Rangers d. Montreal C., 8 goals to 5

Semifinals

Toronto d. Boston, 3–2
N.Y. Rangers d. Detroit, 6 goals to 3

Finals

N.Y. Rangers d. Toronto, 3–1

LEADING SCORERS

	G	A	PTS
Dillon, N.Y. Rangers	8	2	10
Murdock, N.Y. Rangers	3	4	7

LEADING GOALIES

	W	SO	GAA
Aikenhead, N.Y. Rangers	6	2	1.60
Chabot, Toronto	4	2	1.57

1933–34

Eddie Shore was the epitome of a hockey bad man. He was a no-nonsense guy who was the scourge of the Bruins' blue line—the most feared defenseman in hockey. And in December 1933, Shore was part of one of the most dramatic incidents in the game's history.

The Bruins were at home against Toronto, with the Maple Leafs leading, 1–0, when a pair of quick penalties left Toronto two men short. Dick Irvin sent defensemen King Clancy and Red Horner and forward Ace Bailey out to kill the time.

Bailey, a former scoring champ, was an excellent puckcarrier and stickhandler—just what the Leafs needed with the Bruins enjoying a two-man edge. He won a faceoff and dodged Boston skaters, protecting the puck for a full minute before another faceoff was called because Ace was not advancing the puck.

Bailey won the second faceoff as well, again stickhandled for awhile and finally shot the puck into the Bruins' end, forcing Boston to retreat. Shore picked the rubber up and started up ice. Clancy met him and dumped him, regaining the puck for Toronto. As Shore slowly got up, he saw Bailey, still winded from his earlier one-man show, in front of him.

Eddie set sail for the Leaf star, caught him from behind and flipped him with his shoulder. Bailey hit the ice with a dull thud and lay motionless, seriously injured. When Shore grinned at Horner, skating to Bailey's aid, Red decked the Bruin defenseman with an uppercut.

Bailey hovered between life and death for several days with a severe head injury. He finally pulled through but never played hockey again. In February, Maple Leaf Gardens hosted a benefit game for Bailey between Toronto and a team of NHL All-Stars. The meeting at center ice between Bailey and Shore was shrouded in silence until the two embraced. That hug brought a thun-

Toronto fans stepped out to honor their King Clancy.

derous roar from the crowd and eased the tension that had been building before the meeting.

"I know it was an accident," said Bailey, exonerating Shore.

Toronto's Kid Line—Harvey (Busher) Jackson, Joe Primeau, and Charlie Conacher—was challenging the Cooks and Frank Boucher of the Rangers as the top scoring line in the league. The Toronto unit finished 1–2–3 in scoring in the Canadian Division with Conacher leading the league with 52 points including 32 goals, Primeau scoring 46 points and Jackson 38. Boucher's 44 points led American Division scorers.

Conacher, Primeau, and Boucher were named to the NHL All-Star team along with defensemen Clancy of Toronto and Lionel Conacher, Charlie's brother, of Chicago, and Black Hawk goalie Charlie Gardiner. Aurel Joliat of the Canadiens was the MVP and Boucher, as usual, won the Lady Byng. The Vezina went to Chicago's Gardiner, who starred in the playoffs and led the Hawks to the Stanley Cup.

Toronto finished first in the Canadian Division but lost in the playoffs to Detroit, the American Division pennant winners. Chicago eliminated the Canadiens and then the Montreal Maroons, who had finished off the Rangers.

Chicago took the Stanley Cup from Detroit in four games. Two of them went into double overtime with Gardiner shutting out the Red Wings in the last one.

In the celebration that followed the victory, Chicago's Roger Jenkins wheeled Gardiner through the city's Loop section in a wheelbarrow, never dreaming his buddy would be dead from a brain hemorrhage a scant eight weeks later.

1933–34

FINAL STANDINGS

Canadian Division

	W	L	T	PTS	GF	GA
Toronto	26	13	9	61	174	119
Montreal C.	22	20	6	50	99	101
Montreal M.	19	18	11	49	117	122
New York A.	15	23	10	40	104	132
Ottawa	13	29	6	32	115	143

American Division

Detroit	24	14	10	58	113	98
Chicago	20	17	11	51	88	83
New York R.	21	19	8	50	120	113
Boston	18	25	5	41	111	130

LEADING SCORERS

	G	A	PTS
Conacher, Toronto	32	20	52
Primeau, Toronto	14	32	46
Boucher, New York R.	14	30	44
Barry, Boston	21	17	38
Dillon, New York R	13	26	39
Stewart, Boston	21	17	38
Jackson, Toronto	20	18	38
Joliat, Montreal C.	22	15	37
Smith, Montreal M.	18	19	37
Thompson, Chicago	20	16	36

PLAYOFF RESULTS

Quarterfinals

Chicago d. Montreal C., 4 goals to 3
Montreal M. d. N.Y. Rangers, 2 goals to 1

Semifinals

Detroit d. Toronto, 3–2
Chicago d. Montreal M., 6 goals to 2

Finals

Chicago d. Detroit, 3–1

LEADING SCORERS

	G	A	PTS
Aurie, Detroit	3	7	10
Romnes, Chicago	2	7	9
Goodfellow, Detroit	4	3	7
Lewis, Detroit	5	2	7
Thompson, Chicago	4	3	7
Gottselig, Chicago	4	3	7

LEADING GOALIES

	W	SO	GAA
Gardiner, Chicago	6	2	1.33
Cude, Detroit	4	1	2.12

1934–35

The Ottawa franchise, still floundering after two more last-place finishes, was shifted to St. Louis, where the team was christened the Eagles. In a shift almost as momentous, the legendary Howie Morenz was dealt to Chicago.

Morenz and Montreal had been synonymous and the great center never acclimated himself to his new team. He finished the season with a mere eight goals, far down in the American Division scoring list. Syd Howe, who split the season between Detroit and St. Louis, led the American Division scorers with 47 points while Charlie Conacher of Toronto and his linemate, Busher Jackson, were 1–2 in Canadian Division scoring. Conacher won the title with 57 points and Jackson finished second with 44.

Toronto's Charlie Conacher won the scoring crown and led the Maple Leafs to the top of the Canadian Division in 1934–35.

The penalty shot, long a popular feature of Western League hockey, was introduced in the NHL, which now had several Western figures in its coaching ranks. There was Lester Patrick in New York, Dick Irvin in Toronto, Jack Adams in Detroit and Lester's brother, Frank Patrick, in Boston.

Scotty Bowman, purchased by Detroit along with Howe for $50,000 from St. Louis in midseason, was the first player ever to score on a penalty shot in the NHL. It came against Alex Connell, the Montreal Maroons' great goalie.

A couple of new names made their first appearances on the All-Star team. They were goalie Lorne Chabot, acquired by Chicago from Toronto to replace the deceased Gardiner, and defenseman Earl Seibert of the New York Rangers. Also chosen were Boston's Eddie Shore on defense and a forward line of Charlie Conacher and Busher Jackson from Toronto and Frank Boucher of the Rangers.

Chabot won the Vezina Trophy and Shore took the Hart Trophy. Frank Boucher won the Lady Byng for the seventh time in eight years and was awarded permanent possession of the trophy, which would be replaced by a new one.

Toronto, with the Conacher-Jackson-Joe Primeau "Kid Line" dominating the league, easily won the Canadian Division title while Boston squeezed past Chicago by one point to take the American Division.

In the playoffs, the Maple Leafs dropped the opener to Boston and then beat the Bruins three straight to advance to the Stanley Cup finals. Meanwhile, the Montreal Maroons eliminated Chicago on consecutive shutouts by Alex Connell and then knocked off the Rangers, who had topped the Canadiens.

In the final round, it was a matchup of two hot goalies—Connell of the Maroons and George Hainsworth of Toronto, who had allowed Boston just two goals in four games in the opening round. Connell proved to be hotter, giving up only four goals as the Maroons captured the Stanley Cup with three straight victories.

1934–35

FINAL STANDINGS

Canadian Division

	W	L	T	PTS	GF	GA
Toronto	30	14	4	64	157	111
Montreal M.	24	19	5	53	123	92
Montreal C.	19	23	6	44	110	145
New York A.	12	27	9	33	100	142
St. Louis	11	31	6	28	86	144

American Division

	W	L	T	PTS	GF	GA
Boston	26	16	6	58	129	112
Chicago	26	17	5	57	118	88
New York R.	22	20	6	50	137	139
Detroit	19	22	7	45	127	114

LEADING SCORERS

	G	A	PTS
Conacher, Toronto	36	21	57
Howe, Detroit-St. Louis	22	25	47
Aurie, Detroit	17	29	46
Boucher, New York R.	13	32	45
Jackson, Toronto	22	22	44
Lewis, Detroit	16	27	43
Chapman, New York A.	9	34	43
Barry, Boston	20	20	40
Schriner, New York A.	18	22	40
Stewart, Boston	21	18	39
Thompson, Chicago	16	23	39

PLAYOFF RESULTS

Quarterfinals

Montreal M. d. Chicago, 1 goal to 0
N.Y. Rangers d. Montreal C., 6 goals to 5

Semifinals

Toronto d. Boston, 3–1
Montreal M. d. N.Y. Rangers, 5 goals to 4

Finals

Montreal M. d. Toronto, 3–0

LEADING SCORERS

	G	A	PTS
Wentworth, Montreal M.	3	2	5
Jackson, Toronto	3	2	5
Conacher, Toronto	1	4	5
Northcott, Montreal M.	4	1	5

LEADING GOALIES

	W	SO	GAA
Connell, Montreal C.	5	2	1.12
Hainsworth, Toronto	3	2	1.57

1935–36

The St. Louis franchise was dissolved only one year after being moved from Ottawa. This reduced the NHL to eight teams, four in each division. The Eagles' players were distributed to other clubs around the league and there were some good ones available. Boston probably came up with the best in Bill Cowley, who developed into a star.

Carl Voss, who had started in the league with the New York Rangers three seasons earlier, continued to move from club to club. Voss had al-

Defenseman Eddie Shore of the Bruins was MVP in 1935–36.

ready played with the New York Rangers, Detroit, Ottawa, and St. Louis and that season moved on to the New York Americans after the Eagles folded. He would also play for the Montreal Maroons and Chicago Black Hawks before ending his career after six years in the NHL.

The Americans boasted the league's top scorer, second-year man Dave (Sweeney) Schriner, a left wing, who had 45 points, including 19 goals. The leading scorer in the American Division was Detroit's Marty Barry, with 21 goals and a total of 40 points.

Schriner was named to the All-Star team along with Toronto's Charlie Conacher and Hooley Smith of the Montreal Maroons, Boston defensemen Eddie Shore and Babe Siebert and Tiny Thompson, the Bruins' goalie.

Thompson also won the Vezina Trophy and wrote his name in the record book as the first goalie to assist on a scoring play. It happened on a goal by defenseman Siebert, who scored after taking a pass from the goalie.

Eddie Shore won the Hart Trophy, his third MVP award in four years, while Chicago's Doc Romnes took the Lady Byng. The Black Hawks also had the league's hottest rookie, an American-born goalie named Mike Karakas, who stepped in when Lorne Chabot was injured and played so well that the Hawks sold Chabot to the Maroons. Chicago also dealt Howie Morenz to the Rangers, a move that still left the great center homesick for Montreal.

The Montreal Maroons won the Canadian Division race by two points over Toronto while

Boston's Tiny Thompson recorded an historic goalie assist in 1935–36.

Detroit had an easier time, taking the American Division by six points over Boston. The opening game of the Stanley Cup playoffs between the Maroons and Red Wings was a memorable one.

The goalies, Detroit's Norm Smith and Lorne Chabot of the Maroons, played shutout hockey through the 60-minute regulation game and the scoreless tie lasted through five periods of overtime. Finally, with 3½ minutes remaining in the sixth extra period, Modere (Mud) Bruneteau put a shot past Chabot. The Arena clock read 2:25 a.m. and the goal ended 176 minutes, 30 seconds of play. It remains the longest game ever played.

The Red Wings went on to win the next two games, eliminating the Maroons. Toronto ousted Boston and then downed the Americans, who had beaten Chicago. Then Detroit took the Maple Leafs in the four-game finale to capture the Stanley Cup.

1935–36

FINAL STANDINGS

Canadian Division

	W	L	T	PTS	GF	GA
Montreal M	22	16	10	54	114	106
Toronto	23	19	6	52	126	106
New York A.	16	25	7	39	109	122
Montreal C.	11	26	11	33	82	123

American Division

	W	L	T	PTS	GF	GA
Detroit	24	16	8	56	124	103
Boston	22	20	6	50	92	83
Chicago	21	19	8	50	93	92
New York R.	19	17	12	50	91	96

LEADING SCORERS

	G	A	PTS
Schriner, New York A.	19	26	45
Barry, Detroit	21	19	40
Thompson, Chicago	17	23	40
Thoms, Toronto	23	15	38
Conacher, Toronto	23	15	38
Smith, Montreal M.	19	19	38
Romnes, Chicago	13	25	38
Chapman, New York A.	10	28	38
Lewis, Detroit	14	23	37
Northcott, Montreal M.	15	21	36

PLAYOFF RESULTS

Quarterfinals

Toronto d. Boston, 8 goals to 6
N.Y. Americans d. Chicago, 7 goals to 5

Semifinals

Detroit d. Montreal M., 3–0
Toronto d. N.Y. Americans, 2–1

Finals

Detroit d. Toronto, 3–1

LEADING SCORERS

	G	A	PTS
Bell, Toronto	7	3	10
Thoms, Toronto	3	5	8
Primeau, Toronto	3	4	7
Sorrell, Detroit	3	4	7

LEADING GOALIES

	W	SO	GAA
Smith, Detroit	6	2	1.34

1936–37

It was a year for the great lines. Two immortal ones broke up and another one was reunited, but with a tragic outcome.

In New York, the famous Bill Cook-Frank Boucher-Bun Cook unit was finished when the Rangers sold Bun Cook to Boston. The trio had scored more than 1,000 points playing together for the Rangers ever since the team came into the league a decade earlier. In Toronto, Joe Primeau announced his retirement, breaking up the Kid Line he had comprised along with Charlie Conacher and Busher Jackson.

In Montreal, the Canadiens brought Howie Morenz back from his two years of exile in Chicago and New York and no one was happier about the move than the veteran center.

Reunited with his old linemates, Aurel Joliat and Johnny Gagnon, Morenz played inspired hockey. He had scored 20 points at midseason when tragedy struck. Going into a corner after the puck, Morenz got his skates caught in a rut in the ice and snapped a bone in his leg.

The accident and his ability to overcome it weighed heavily on Morenz's mind as he lay in a Montreal hospital. Two months later, on March 8, his heart gave out and he died.

The funeral services were held at center ice in the Montreal Forum and 25,000 fans, many of them in tears, filed past his bier to pay their last respects to one of hockey's truly great stars.

The New York Americans, with owner Bill Dwyer in deep financial trouble, had their franchise taken over by the league. NHL president Frank Calder was to act as advisor to the club.

Toronto's Syl Apps, a former Olympic pole vaulter, was the 1936–37 Rookie of the Year.

Calder also introduced a trophy to be awarded annually to the league's top rookie. The first one went to Toronto's Syl Apps, a pole vaulter at the 1936 Berlin Olympics who turned pro with the Leafs after returning from the Games. Apps finished second in the Canadian Division scoring race with 45 points, one less than Sweeney Schriner of the New York Americans, who captured his second straight scoring crown. Detroit's Marty Barry led American Division scorers with 44 points.

The Red Wings dominated the All-Star team, gaining four of the six spots. Detroit's Larry Aurie was named at right wing, Marty Barry at center, Ebbie Goodfellow at one defense post and Norm Smith at goal. Toronto's Busher Jackson at left wing and defenseman Babe Siebert of the Montreal Canadiens were the only non-Red Wings named. Siebert won the Hart Trophy, Barry the Lady Byng and Smith the Vezina.

The Canadiens edged the Montreal Maroons for the Canadian Division title while Detroit won the American Division race. In the playoffs, the Red Wings beat the Canadiens in the first two games, then dropped two straight before winning the decisive fifth game.

The New York Rangers first eliminated Toronto and then the Maroons, who had beaten Boston. In the Stanley Cup finals, Marty Barry and substitute goalie Earl Robertson helped the Red Wings come from behind with two straight victories to capture the five-game series.

1936–37

FINAL STANDINGS

Canadian Division

	W	L	T	PTS	GF	GA
Montreal C.	24	18	6	54	115	111
Montreal M.	22	17	9	53	126	110
Toronto	22	21	5	49	119	115
New York A.	15	29	4	34	122	161

American Division

	W	L	T	PTS	GF	GA
Detroit	25	14	9	59	128	102
Boston	23	18	7	53	120	110
New York R.	19	20	9	47	117	106
Chicago	14	27	7	35	99	131

LEADING SCORERS

	G	A	PTS
Schriner, New York A.	21	25	46
Apps, Toronto	16	29	45

Barry, Detroit	17	27	44
Aurie, Detroit	23	20	43
Jackson, Toronto	21	19	40
Gagnon, Montreal C.	20	16	36
Gracie, Montreal M.	11	25	36
Stewart, Boston-New York A.	23	12	35
Thompson, Chicago	17	18	35
Cowley, Boston	13	22	35

PLAYOFF RESULTS

Quarterfinals

Montreal M. d. Boston, 2–1
N.Y. Rangers d. Toronto, 2–0

Semifinals

Detroit d. Montreal C., 3–2
N.Y. Rangers d. Montreal M., 2–0

Finals

Detroit d. N.Y. Rangers, 3–2

LEADING SCORERS

	G	A	PTS
Barry, Detroit	4	7	11
Lewis, Detroit	4	3	7
Howe, Detroit	2	5	7

LEADING GOALIES

	W	SO	GAA
Kerr, N.Y. Rangers	6	4	1.08
Smith, Detroit	3	1	1.28
Robertson, Detroit	3	2	1.41

1937–38

Clem Loughlin had set a longevity record by lasting three seasons in the revolving door for coaches operated by Chicago's boss, Major Fred McLaughlin. In 10 years, McLaughlin had employed an even dozen coaches—11 of them over the first seven seasons. When Loughlin was shown to the exit door in 1937, he was replaced by a baseball umpire and hockey referee named Bill Stewart, who would pilot Chicago to its first Stanley Cup.

A baseball umpire? Well, McLaughlin was like that, often depending for advice in running his hockey club with distinctly un-hockey types. Stewart, at least, did have some refereeing in his background.

In Boston, the Bruins assembled a new line destined for a long run of glory. Milt Schmidt was the center and his wingmen were Bobby Bauer and Woody Dumart—The Kraut Line.

Lester Patrick, coach of the New York Rangers, brought up his son, Muzz, to join his brother, Lynn, and give the Rangers three Patricks. New York also added a rookie named

Bryan Hextall who was to star during the war years and later see both his sons play in the NHL.

Toronto's Gordie Drillon won the scoring title with 52 points, 26 of them goals. Drillon was part of considerable confusion caused by the similarity in name with another fine right wing, Cecil Dillon of the Rangers. In fact, both were selected to the All-Star team—the only time in history that two players were chosen for the same position on the first team.

The other All-Stars were left wing Paul Thompson of Chicago, who led American Division scorers with 44 points, Boston's Bill Cowley at center, defensemen Eddie Shore of the Bruins and Babe Siebert of the Montreal Canadiens and Boston's Tiny Thompson, Paul's brother, in goal.

Shore recaptured the MVP Hart Trophy, his fourth in six years, Drillon was the Lady Byng winner and Tiny Thompson took the Vezina for the fourth time. Chicago's Cully Dahlstrom won the Calder Trophy as the top rookie.

Toronto and Boston won the division championships and the Maple Leafs whipped the Bruins in three straight games to advance to the final round of the Stanley Cup playoffs. Meanwhile, in an intra-city showdown, the New York Americans eliminated the Rangers and reached the semifinals against Chicago, which had come from behind to beat the Montreal Canadiens. The Black Hawks ousted the Americans and found themselves up against Toronto's powerhouse for the Stanley Cup.

Against Toronto, the Hawks were simply in over their heads. They had won just 14 of 48 games during the regular season and made the playoffs by only two points. Toronto, on the other hand, had won or tied 33 of their 48 games and had easily won the Canadian Division.

What was worse, Mike Karakas, Chicago's goalie, came up with an injured toe before the opening game. Coach Bill Stewart was not about to repeat Lester Patrick's feat of playing goal. Instead, he asked permission of the Leafs to use Dave Kerr, the Rangers' goalie. Conn Smythe re-

The Rangers' Cecil Dillon shared an All-Star berth with Toronto's Gordie Drillon in 1937–38.

fused and the Hawks wound up with Alfie Moore, a minor leaguer, in the nets, but not before Stewart and Smythe engaged in a brief jostling match outside the dressing room.

The Hawks won the opener, 3–1, and Moore thumbed his nose at the Leafs' bench. In the second game, with Moore ruled ineligible by NHL president Frank Calder, the Hawks came up with Paul Goodman, another minor leaguer who was fished out of a movie theater just two hours before the game began. He was beaten by the Leafs, 5–1, to even the series.

In the third game, Karakas returned and the Hawks won, 2–1, on Doc Romnes' goal with 4:05 left in the game. The Leafs argued that the shot had hit the post but were overruled by referee Clarence Campbell, a man who one day would become president of the NHL.

The Hawks won the fourth game and the Cup, making Stewart the toast of Chicago—for about nine months.

1937–38

FINAL STANDINGS

Canadian Division

	W	L	T	PTS	GF	GA
Toronto	24	15	9	57	151	127
New York A.	19	18	11	49	110	111
Montreal C.	18	17	13	49	123	128
Montreal M.	12	30	6	30	101	149

American Division

	W	L	T	PTS	GF	GA
Boston	30	11	7	67	142	89
New York R.	27	15	6	60	149	96
Chicago	14	25	9	37	97	139
Detroit	12	25	11	35	99	133

LEADING SCORERS

	G	A	PTS
Drillon, Toronto	26	26	52
Apps, Toronto	21	29	50
Thompson, Chicago	22	22	44
Mantha, Montreal C.	23	19	42
Dillon, New York R.	21	18	39
Schriner, New York A.	21	17	38
Thoms, Toronto	14	24	38
Smith, New York R.	14	23	37
Stewart, New York A.	19	17	36
N. Colville, New York R.	17	19	36

PLAYOFF RESULTS

Quarterfinals

N.Y. Americans d. N.Y. Rangers, 2–1
Chicago d. Montreal C., 2–1

Semifinals

Toronto d. Boston, 3–0
Chicago d. N.Y. Americans, 2–1

Finals

Chicago d. Toronto, 3–1

LEADING SCORERS

	G	A	PTS
Drillon, Toronto	7	1	8
Gottselig, Chicago	5	3	8
Seibert, Chicago	5	2	7
Thompson, Chicago	4	3	7

LEADING GOALIES

	W	SO	GAA
Karakas, Chicago	6	2	1.71
Broda, Toronto	4	1	1.85

1938–39

For years the Maroons were fighting a losing battle attracting fan support while the Canadiens enjoyed far more popularity in Montreal. Finally, the Maroons asked permission to shift to St. Louis. The league refused but did grant the franchise a one-year leave of absence to regroup its forces. But when they sold most of their players to other clubs, it became apparent that the Maroons were through for good.

The demise of the Maroons left seven teams still operating and they were grouped in a single division with six clubs qualifying for the rather crowded playoffs. Only Chicago, whose Bill Stewart was dismissed in midseason and replaced by Paul Thompson, missed.

In Boston, manager Art Ross took a dramatic step. He sold goalie Tiny Thompson, a Bruins' favorite for a decade, to Detroit. The reason was Ross' conviction that a youngster from Eveleth, Minn., was ready for the NHL. And Frank Brimsek really was ready.

Brimsek had played the Bruins' first two games while Thompson recovered from an eye ailment. Then Tiny returned and Brimsek was farmed out to Providence. But Thompson was 33 and Ross was anxious to create a spot for the promising rookie who had succeeded Chicago's Mike Karakas at Eveleth High School. On November 28, the deal was made, with the Bruins receiving $15,000 from the Red Wings. Brimsek returned two days later.

Lorne Carr of the New York Americans gets congratulations from coach Red Dutton after a winning goal against Chicago in the 1938 playoffs.

The Canadiens beat him, 2–0, in his first game and then Brimsek produced three straight shutouts. His shutout streak extended to 231 minutes, 54 seconds, breaking Thompson's modern mark of 224:47.

After Brimsek's sensational streak was broken, he started another one. Three more shutouts—one against Thompson and the Red Wings—gave him six in seven games and another unbelievable streak of 220 minutes, 24 seconds of scoreless hockey.

The Boston fans, never easy to please, were unhappy to lose Thompson, but Brimsek's fantastic debut made him an instant hero. He turned in 10 shutouts in 41 games, earning the Vezina Trophy as top goalie, the Calder Trophy as top rookie, a spot on the All-Star team and the nickname "Mr. Zero."

The other All-Stars were defensemen Eddie Shore and Dit Clapper of Boston, Toronto's center, Syl Apps, right wing Gordie Drillon of the Maple Leafs and left wing Hector (Toe) Blake of the Montreal Canadiens. Blake was the scoring champion with 47 points, including 24 goals, and captured the Hart Trophy while Clint Smith of the New York Rangers won the Lady Byng.

The Bruins won the regular-season title by 16 points over the Rangers and then the two clubs staged one of the most memorable playoff battles in history. Boston took the first three games—two of them on overtime goals by Mel Hill, an obscure 10-goal scorer during the regular season. Then the Rangers roared back to win three straight and tie the series. In the seventh game, Hill struck again, beating the Rangers eight minutes into the third overtime period and earning forever the nickname of "Sudden Death" Hill.

Toronto ripped through the New York Americans and Detroit, which had eliminated the Canadiens. In the finals, the Bruins whipped the Leafs in five games to claim their first Stanley Cup in a decade.

1938–39

FINAL STANDINGS

	W	L	T	PTS	GF	GA
Boston	36	10	2	74	156	76
New York R.	26	16	6	58	149	105
Toronto	19	20	9	47	114	107
New York A.	17	21	10	44	119	157
Detroit	18	24	6	42	107	128
Montreal	15	24	9	39	115	146
Chicago	12	28	8	32	91	132

LEADING SCORERS

	G	A	PTS
Blake, Montreal	24	23	47
Schriner, New York A.	13	31	44
Cowley, Boston	8	34	42
Smith, New York R.	21	20	41
Barry, Detroit	13	28	41
Apps, Toronto	15	25	40
Anderson, New York A.	13	27	40

Gottselig, Chicago	16	23	39
Haynes, Montreal	5	33	38
Conacher, Boston	26	11	37
Carr, New York A.	19	18	37
N. Colville, New York R.	18	19	37
Watson, New York R.	15	22	37

PLAYOFF RESULTS

Quarterfinals

Toronto d. N.Y. Americans, 2–0
Detroit d. Montreal, 2–1

Semifinals

Boston d. N.Y. Rangers, 4–3
Toronto d. Detroit, 2–1

Finals

Boston d. Toronto, 4–1

LEADING SCORERS

	G	A	PTS
Cowley, Boston	3	11	14
Drillon, Toronto	7	6	13
Conacher, Boston	6	4	10
Hill, Boston	6	3	9
Aps, Toronto	2	6	8

LEADING GOALIES

	W	SO	GAA
Brimsek, Boston	8	1	1.25
Broda, Toronto	5	2	1.94

1939–40

The guns of Europe began firing before the 1939 hockey season got underway, and before long the NHL would feel the manpower squeeze of world conflict. But, for the time being at least, the league's operations were not affected by the events overseas.

Ironically, the hottest line in the league was Boston's Milt Schmidt, Woody Dumart and Bobby Bauer, tabbed the "Kraut Line" because of their Germanic extractions. But the name proved a bit unpopular at this sensitive time so the "Kraut Line" was re-christened the "Kitchener Kids" because the trio all hailed from the Kitchener, Ontario, area.

Schmidt, the center, led the league in scoring with 52 points, 22 of them on goals. Dumart and Bauer tied for second with 43 points apiece.

The All-Star team had Schmidt at center, Bryan Hextall of the Rangers at right wing and Montreal's Toe Blake at left wing. The defensemen were Aubrey (Dit) Clapper of the Bruins and Detroit's Ebbie Goodfellow. Davey Kerr of the Rangers was the goalie.

The Bruins were at the top of the heap in 1939.

Goodfellow won the Hart Trophy and Bobby Bauer the Lady Byng. Kerr won the Vezina and a 28-year-old Ranger rookie, Kilby MacDonald, took the Calder.

For the first time since they came into the league, the Bruins had to get along without the great Eddie Shore patrolling their blue line. Shore had become owner and manager of the minor league Springfield Indians and was available only for Boston's home games. The Bruins quickly tired of this arrangement and sold Eddie to the New York Americans. Shore finished the season with the Amerks and then retired to build the Springfield club into a rewarding financial operation.

Even without Shore, the Bruins finished first in the regular-season race, again beating out the Rangers. But New York got revenge for the heartbreaking playoff loss of the year before by eliminating Boston in the Stanley Cup series, four games to two.

Toronto got by Chicago and Detroit eliminated the New York Americans in other playoff matchups. When the Maple Leafs and Red Wings met in the semifinals it turned into a little war. A 15-minute brawl marred the final game with every player on the ice and 17 who left the opposing benches joining in.

"The Wings are a bunch of hoodlums," declared the Toronto management. To which Jack Adams, manager of the Red Wings, replied, "We're just sorry we can't play the Leafs seven nights in a row."

In the Stanley Cup finale, the Rangers beat Toronto in six games, three of the New York victories coming in overtime. That wiped out the bad overtime memories Boston's "Sudden Death" Hill had left the year before.

1939–40

FINAL STANDINGS

	W	L	T	PTS	GF	GA
Boston	31	12	5	67	170	98
New York R.	27	11	10	64	136	77
Toronto	25	17	6	56	134	110
Chicago	23	19	6	52	112	120
Detroit	16	26	6	38	90	126
New York A.	15	29	4	34	106	140
Montreal	10	33	5	25	90	167

LEADING SCORERS

	G	A	PTS
Schmidt, Boston	22	30	52
Dumart, Boston	22	21	43
Bauer, Boston	17	26	43
Drillon, Toronto	21	19	40
Cowley, Boston	13	27	40
Hextall, New York R.	24	15	39
N. Colville, New York R.	19	19	38
Howe, Detroit	14	23	37
Blake, Montreal	17	19	36
Armstrong, New York A.	16	20	36

PLAYOFF RESULTS

Quarterfinals

Toronto d. Chicago, 2–0
Detroit d. N.Y. Americans, 2–1

Semifinals

N.Y. Rangers d. Boston, 4–2
Toronto d. Detroit, 2–0

Finals

N.Y. Rangers d. Toronto, 4–2

LEADING SCORERS

	G	A	PTS
Colville, N.Y. Rangers	7	2	9
Watson, N.Y. Rangers	6	3	9
Hextall, N.Y. Rangers	4	3	7

LEADING GOALIES

	W	SO	GAA
Kerr, N.Y. Rangers	8	3	1.56
Broda, Toronto	6	1	1.74

1940–41

Dick Irvin left Toronto and moved into the coaching job at Montreal, hoping to rebuild the Canadiens, who had fallen on lean times.

Before the season started, Irvin predicted a fourth-place finish for Montreal—three notches higher than they had finished the year before. Asked his thoughts about the league's top rookie, he placed the name of his own Johnny Quilty in a sealed envelope.

Quilty made it but the Canadiens didn't. Montreal finished sixth but Quilty captured the Calder Trophy as the league's best rookie. Boston's Bill Cowley won the scoring title with 62 points—only 17 of them goals. Cowley also was the MVP and Bobby Bauer of the Bruins won his second straight Lady Byng. Turk Broda of Toronto won the Vezina, edging out Detroit's Johnny Mowers on the final night of the season.

Davey Kerr of the Rangers won the Vezina Trophy and led the Stanley Cup champions in 1939–40.

It marked the first time a Maple Leaf had been the NHL's top goaltender.

The All-Star team had Broda in goal, Boston's Dit Clapper and Toronto's Wally Stanowski on defense, Cowley at center, Bryan Hextall of the Rangers and Sweeney Schriner, now with Toronto, on the wings.

The Bruins were the class of the league again and captured their fourth straight regular-season title. They set two records, going 15 games without a loss on the road over one stretch and 23 without a setback over another.

Boston finished five points in front of Toronto and knocked off the Maple Leafs in the opening round of the Stanley Cup playoffs. Detroit eliminated the Rangers and then Chicago, which had disposed of Montreal in the opening round.

In the Cup finals, the Bruins swept past the Red Wings in four straight games with Milt Schmidt and Eddie Wiseman, the player they had obtained from the Americans in the Eddie Shore deal the year before, starring.

War clouds had convinced players and executives around the league that it would not be long before the events in Europe and the Pacific would affect the NHL. Conn Smythe, owner of the Maple Leafs, advised all of his players to volunteer for military training and most of the club joined the Toronto Scottish Reserve. Other players around the league followed suit and soon many of them were trading shoulder pads and hockey sticks for field packs and rifles.

The Rangers celebrate their Stanley Cup triumph in 1940.

1940–41

FINAL STANDINGS

	W	L	T	PTS	GF	GA	
Boston	27	8	13	67	168	102	
Toronto	28	14	6	62	145	99	
Detroit	21	16	11	53	112	102	
New York R.	21	19	8	50	143	125	
Chicago	16	25	7	39	112	139	
Montreal	16	26	6	38	121	147	
New York A.	8	29	11	27	99	186	

LEADING SCORERS

	G	A	PTS
Cowley, Boston	17	45	62
Hextall, New York R.	26	18	44
Drillon, Toronto	23	21	44
Apps, Toronto	20	24	44
L. Patrick, New York R.	20	24	44
Howe, Detroit	20	24	44
N. Colville, New York R.	14	28	42
Wiseman, Boston	16	24	40
Bauer, Boston	17	22	39
Schriner, Toronto	24	14	38
R. Conacher, Boston	24	14	38
Schmidt, Boston	13	25	38

PLAYOFF RESULTS

Quarterfinals

Chicago d. Montreal C., 2–1
Detroit d. N.Y. Rangers, 2–1

Semifinals

Boston d. Toronto, 4–3
Detroit d. Chicago, 2–0

Finals

Boston d. Detroit, 4–0

LEADING SCORERS

	G	A	PTS
Schmidt, Boston	5	6	11
Wiseman, Boston	5	3	8
Howe, Detroit	1	7	8
Liscombe, Detroit	4	3	7

LEADING GOALIES

	W	SO	GAA
Kerr, N.Y. Rangers	1	0	1.88
Brimsek, Boston	0	1	2.04

1941–42

The National Hockey League season was less than one month old in December 1941, when suddenly hockey didn't seem very important anymore. It was on the morning of December 7 that Japanese bombs poured down on United States ships anchored in Pearl Harbor and plunged the U.S. into World War II.

On the night of December 7, the New York Rangers defeated Boston, 5–4, Chicago nipped the Americans, who had changed the designation of their franchise from New York to Brooklyn, 5–4, and Detroit edged Montreal, 3–2. But nobody cared about the results that night.

The next morning, many of the same fans who had packed hockey arenas the night before lined up for recruiting stations as America went to war. Hockey players, too, did their part.

Of the 14 players listed in the Ranger lineup the night of December 7, 10 eventually wound up in uniform. It was the same throughout the league as the service rolls swelled with top NHL talent. The names included Muzz and Lynn Patrick, Sid Abel, Boston's "Kraut Line" of Milt Schmidt, Woody Dumart and Bobby Bauer, Terry and Ken Reardon, Howie Meeker, Black Jack Stewart, goalies Jim Henry and Chuck Rayner and scores of others.

But, as it had 25 years before when confronted by another world conflict, the NHL continued through World War II without a single interruption in its schedule.

On the day that Japan attacked Pearl Harbor, Bryan Hextall of the Rangers and Toronto's Gordie Drillon shared the NHL scoring lead. Hextall went on to capture the championship with 56 points, two points more than his teammate Lynn Patrick. Both Rangers made the All-Star team along with Toronto center Syl Apps, defensemen Tommy Anderson of the Brooklyn Americans and Earl Seibert of Chicago and goalie Frankie Brimsek of Boston.

Anderson won the Hart Trophy as MVP, Apps took the Lady Byng, Brimsek captured the Vezina Trophy and Grant Warwick of the Rangers was the Calder Trophy winner.

Red Dutton's troubled Americans weathered one of the longest holdouts in hockey history when Busher Jackson could not reach terms with the club. Finally, in desperation, Dutton shipped Jackson to Boston for $7,500 in January. Dutton also traded Lorne Carr to Toronto for four players. But nothing worked right for the Amerks. When they finished last and their cross-town rivals, the Rangers, won the regular-season title, it

Ranger Bryan Hextall skated off with the scoring title in 1941–42.

marked the end of the Americans. They dropped out of the league at the conclusion of the season.

Toronto eliminated the first-place Rangers in the opening round of the playoffs while Detroit eliminated the Canadiens and then the Bruins, who had knocked out Chicago. That set up a final-round meeting between the Red Wings and Maple Leafs—one of the most amazing series in Stanley Cup history.

Detroit stunned the favored Leafs by winning the first three games—two of them at Toronto. Billy Taylor of the Leafs kidded newsmen before the next game, saying, "Don't worry about us, we'll beat them four straight."

Few observers, except perhaps Taylor, were prepared for what followed. The Leafs shook up their lineup and with seldom-used Don Metz and Ernie Dickens supplying the spark, won the next four games and the Stanley Cup. It was Taylor who set up Sweeney Schriner's second goal of the game and the final one of the series in Toronto's 3–1 victory in the seventh game.

1941–42

FINAL STANDINGS

	W	L	T	PTS	GF	GA
New York	29	17	2	60	177	143
Toronto	27	18	3	57	158	136
Boston	25	17	6	56	160	118
Chicago	22	23	3	47	145	155
Detroit	19	25	4	42	140	147
Montreal	18	27	3	39	134	173
Brooklyn	16	29	3	35	133	175

LEADING SCORERS

	G	A	PTS
Hextall, New York	24	32	56
L. Patrick, New York	32	22	54
Grosso, Detroit	23	30	53
Watson, New York	15	37	52
Abel, Detroit	18	31	49
Blake, Montreal	17	28	45
Thoms, Chicago	15	30	45
Drillon, Toronto	23	18	41
Apps, Toronto	18	23	41
Anderson, Brooklyn	12	29	41

PLAYOFF RESULTS

Quarterfinals

Boston d. Chicago, 2–1
Detroit d. Montreal C., 2–1

Semifinals

Toronto d. N.Y. Rangers, 4–2
Detroit d. Boston, 2–0

Finals

Toronto d. Detroit, 4–3

LEADING SCORERS

	G	A	PTS
Grosso, Detroit	8	6	14
Apps, Toronto	5	9	14
Lipscombe, Detroit	6	7	13
Stanowski, Toronto	2	8	10
Taylor, Toronto	2	8	10

LEADING GOALIES

	W	SO	GAA
LoPresti, Chicago	1	1	1.60
Henry, N.Y. Rangers	2	1	2.17
Broda, Toronto	8	1	2.38
Mowers, Detroit	7	0	3.17

4

A SOLID SIX
1942–1967

With the exit of the Americans, the NHL was down to six teams—Detroit, Chicago, Montreal, New York Rangers, Boston, and Toronto. This solid foundation would remain intact until the ambitious expansion program of the NHL's second half-century.

The war years would bring important changes to the NHL. Before the conflict was over, Frank Boucher, the creative center of the Rangers, who now coached the New York club, was to suggest the adoption of a red line at center ice to speed up the game. Overtime periods would be done away with in the interest of maintaining tight wartime travel schedules.

And Montreal's Maurice Richard emerged as the game's first superscorer. The Rocket, as Richard became known, was to be the key man on one of the most devastating teams in hockey history—the Canadiens of the mid–1950s. They were so proficient that they forced a rule change to keep them from utterly dominating the sport.

In Detroit, a young man named Gordie Howe arrived on the scene with little advance notice and established himself as hockey's greatest scorer and its longevity king. It was Howe and Richard who ruled the game in the fifties along with the Canadiens and the Red Wings.

And then came the 1960s and Bobby Hull, the dynamic blond bomber of the Chicago Blackhawks, who epitomized hockey's next era of bigger, stronger, faster players.

The period would see the shifting of the league's administration from president Frank Calder, who had been head man since the NHL's inception in 1917, to Red Dutton and then to Clarence Campbell, the ex-referee, who would be at the helm when big-league hockey swung into its most successful era.

Bloodied Jimmy Orlando of Detroit looks for support from referee King Clancy after a fight with Toronto's Gaye Stewart in 1943.

1942–43

Numerous NHL players and executives were in the service by the time the 1942 season began and early in the season a major rule change was enacted. Because of the tight train schedules during the war, NHL teams had to be precise about the length of games. Thus, they eliminated overtime.

Until then, when a game was tied at the end of three regulation periods, the teams played a 10-minute overtime period in an attempt to break the deadlock. Unlike Stanley Cup overtimes, the extra periods were not sudden death but lasted a full 10 minutes. Therefore, it was possible to have goals scored during overtime but for the game to still end in a tie.

Referee Bill Chadwick, a leading NHL official of the 1940s, felt the elimination of the extra period was a good thing for hockey. "Overtimes benefitted the stronger teams," he said. "It gave them 10 more minutes to wear down weaker competition. If a weak club held a stronger one to a tie for 60 minutes, it ought to be worth something."

With the Americans out of the league, the schedule was increased from 48 to 50 games. Red Dutton, the Amerks' head man, was disconsolate at the demise of his club but he was to be back in hockey much faster than he expected.

On his way to a meeting of the league's Board of Governors in Toronto in January, president Frank Calder suffered a heart attack. Two weeks later, he was dead. The Governors chose Dutton as president pro tem with the understanding that Clarence Campbell, the man Calder had chosen as his successor, would eventually take over.

Chicago's Bentley brothers, Doug and Max, battled Bill Cowley of Boston for the scoring title. Doug Bentley finally won the crown with 73 points, including 33 goals. Cowley had 72 points and Max Bentley 70.

Cowley and Doug Bentley made the All-Star team along with Toronto's Lorne Carr, Black Jack Stewart of Detroit and Earl Seibert of Chicago on

The Maple Leafs' Gaye Stewart was Rookie of the Year in 1942–43.

defense, and Johnny Mowers of Detroit in goal. Cowley also won the Hart Trophy while Mowers took the Vezina. The Lady Byng went to Max Bentley and Gaye Stewart of Toronto won the Calder.

In Montreal, the Canadiens introduced Maurice Richard, a young right winger, who scored five goals in 16 games before a broken ankle put him out of action.

Detroit won the regular-season title by four points over Boston while Toronto finished third and the Canadiens made it to fourth place—their highest finish in five seasons—and the final playoff spot in the six-team league. The Red Wings eliminated the Maple Leafs and Boston dropped the Canadiens in the Stanley Cup semifinals. Then, with Carl Liscombe and Sid Abel starring, Detroit flashed past the Bruins in four straight games to capture the Cup.

1942–43

FINAL STANDINGS

	W	L	T	PTS	GF	GA
Detroit	25	14	11	61	169	124
Boston	24	17	9	57	195	176
Toronto	22	19	9	53	198	159
Montreal	19	19	12	50	181	191
Chicago	17	18	15	49	179	180
New York	11	31	8	30	161	253

LEADING SCORERS

	G	A	PTS
D. Bentley, Chicago	33	40	73
Cowley, Boston	27	45	72
M. Bentley, Chicago	26	44	70
L. Patrick, New York	22	39	61
Carr, Toronto	27	33	60
Taylor, Toronto	18	42	60
Hextall, New York	27	32	59
Blake, Montreal	23	36	59
Lach, Montreal	18	40	58
O'Connor, Montreal	15	43	58

PLAYOFF RESULTS

Semifinals

Detroit d. Toronto, 4–2
Boston d. Montreal C., 4–1

Finals

Detroit d. Boston, 4–0

LEADING SCORERS

	G	A	PTS
Liscombe, Detroit	14	8	14
Abel, Detroit	5	8	13
Hollett, Boston	0	9	9
Jackson, Boston	6	3	9

LEADING GOALIES

	W	SO	GAA
Mowers, Detroit	8	2	1.94
Broda, Toronto	2	0	2.73
Brimsek, Boston	4	0	3.54

1943–44

The war had ravaged NHL rosters, leaving only youngsters, service rejects or over-age veterans. The situation was so desperate that in New York, coach Frank Boucher of the Rangers attempted a comeback at the age of 42. Boucher's return at center ice lasted 15 games and he averaged almost a point per game for hapless New York.

It was Boucher and Art Ross, Boston's manager, who pushed for, and eventually got, legislation calling for the center red line. The mid-ice divider was introduced at the start of the 1943 season in an effort to speed up the game. Boucher explained the reasoning behind it.

"My thought was that hockey had become a see-saw affair," said Boucher. "Defending teams were jammed in their own end for minutes because they couldn't pass their way out against the new five-man attack."

Before the red line was introduced, players could not pass the puck out of their defensive zone but had to carry it out themselves. This was difficult with five opposing skaters to weave through and Boucher suggested a solution.

"Why not allow teams to pass their way out of trouble, say up to mid-ice," he reasoned. "Use a red line to divide the ice. It would open the dam for the defending team and restore end-to-end play."

The idea had precisely the sought-after effect.

Boston's Herbie Cain won the scoring race with 36 goals and 82 points but missed the first All-Star team. Chicago's Doug Bentley, Lorne Carr of Toronto and Bill Cowley of Boston were named to the All-Star forward line, with Toronto's Babe Pratt and Earl Seibert of Chicago on defense and Montreal's Bill Durnan in goal. Pratt was the Hart Trophy winner, Clint Smith of Chicago took the Lady Byng, Durnan won the Vezina and Toronto's Gus Bodnar captured the Calder.

And in Montreal, coach Dick Irvin assembled a new line. He used Elmer Lach, who spoke only English, at center; Toe Blake, fluent in French and English, on left wing, and young Maurice Richard, the darling of the French-Canadian fans, on the right side. The unit was tagged the "Punch Line" and produced 82 goals—32 of them by the fiery Richard.

With Durnan doing an outstanding job in goal and the "Punch Line" racing through the league, Montreal dropped just five games and won the regular-season championship by 15 points over Detroit. It was the start of a dynasty.

There were two notable goal-scoring feats. Detroit's Syd Howe blasted six goals in a 12–2 romp over the Rangers, setting a modern mark for most goals in a single game. And Toronto's Gus Bodnar, a rookie, set a record for the fastest goal by a first-year man when he scored just 15 sec-

onds after hitting the ice in his debut, also against the Rangers.

In the Stanley Cup playoffs, Richard really took off. The Rocket scored all five goals in the Canadiens' second-game victory and Montreal finished off Toronto in the opening round before sweeping past Chicago in four straight games for the Cup. Richard set a Cup record with 12 goals in the nine playoff games.

1943–44

FINAL STANDINGS

	W	L	T	PTS	GF	GA
Montreal	38	5	7	83	234	109
Detroit	26	18	6	58	214	177
Toronto	23	23	4	50	214	174
Chicago	22	23	5	49	178	187
Boston	19	26	5	43	223	268
New York	6	39	5	17	162	310

LEADING SCORERS

	G	A	PTS
Cain, Boston	36	46	82
D. Bentley, Chicago	38	39	77
Carr, Toronto	36	38	74
Liscombe, Detroit	36	37	73
Lach, Montreal	24	48	72
Smith, Chicago	23	49	72
Cowley, Boston	30	41	71
Mosienko, Chicago	32	38	70
Jackson, Boston	28	41	69
Bodnar, Toronto	22	40	62

LEADING GOALIES

	G	GA	SO	GAA
Durnan, Montreal	50	109	2	2.18
Bibeault, Toronto	29	87	5	3.00
Karakas, Chicago	26	79	3	3.04
Dion, Detroit	26	80	1	3.08
Gardiner, Boston	41	212	1	5.17

PLAYOFF RESULTS

Semifinals

Montreal d. Toronto, 4–1
Chicago d. Detroit, 4–1

Finals

Montreal d. Chicago, 4–0

Detroit's Syd Howe scored six goals against the Rangers on February 3, 1944.

"Terrible Ted" Lindsay broke in with the Red Wings in 1944–45.

LEADING SCORERS

	G	A	PTS
Blake, Montreal	7	11	18
Richard, Montreal	12	5	17
Lach, Montreal	2	11	13

LEADING GOALIES

	W	SO	GAA
Durnan, Montreal	8	1	1.53
Karikas, Chicago	4	1	2.62

1944–45

Maurice Richard's playoff explosion the year before set the stage for the Montreal star's greatest season. The Rocket zoomed through the NHL's 50-game schedule at an incredible goal-per-game pace, scoring a record 50 times. He had 15 goals in one nine-game stretch, including five goals in one game. Ten times during the season he scored two or more goals in a single game.

Richard was the first to score 50 goals in a season and the only one ever to do it in a 50-game season. His accomplishment is often compared to the record he erased—Joe Malone's 44 goals in a 22-game season in 1917–18, the NHL's first year of operation. Malone's record was established in the era before forward passing; Richard's came in the modern era. Critics often pointed out that Richard's feat came against watered-down teams weakened by the war, but the fact remains that the Rocket was the first to hit the magic 50.

Richard's linemates also flourished from his record spree and the "Punch Line" finished 1-2-3 in scoring. Center Elmer Lach led all scorers with 80 points, Richard finished second with 73 points and left wing Toe Blake was third with 67.

The Canadiens dominated the league, winning the regular-season title again, this time by 13 points. Five Montreal players—Richard, Lach, Blake, defenseman Butch Bouchard and goalie Bill Durnan made the All-Star team with only Detroit defenseman Flash Hollett breaking the Canadiens' monopoly. Lach was the MVP, Chicago's Bill Mosienko won the Lady Byng Trophy, Durnan took the Vezina and Toronto's Frank McCool captured the Calder.

The Canadiens had lost only eight regular-season games in 1944–45 and a total of just 14 games (one in the playoffs) in two seasons while winning two straight league titles and the Stanley Cup. They were, quite naturally, favored to take the Cup again.

But Toronto stung Montreal with two quick victories in the opening round of the playoffs and eliminated the Canadiens in six games. Detroit wiped out a two-game Boston edge and whipped the Bruins in their semifinal series. That set up a final round between the Maple Leafs and Red Wings.

Detroit almost erased the memory of the embarassing Cup loss to the Leafs three years earlier, when they had blown a three-game lead. This time, it was Toronto which won the first three games—all of them shutouts by rookie goalie Frank McCool.

Suddenly the Red Wings bounced back, just as the Leafs had done in 1942. Detroit, featuring rookie Ted Lindsay, won three straight games and it looked like history was about to repeat. But Toronto finally halted the storybook comeback by winning the seventh game on defenseman Babe Pratt's goal.

1944–45

FINAL STANDINGS

	W	L	T	PTS	GF	GA
Montreal	38	8	4	80	228	121
Detroit	31	14	5	67	218	161
Toronto	24	22	4	52	183	161
Boston	16	30	4	36	179	219
Chicago	13	30	7	33	141	194
New York	11	29	10	32	154	247

LEADING SCORERS

	G	A	PTS
Lach, Montreal	26	54	80
Richard, Montreal	50	23	73
Blake, Montreal	29	38	67
Cowley, Boston	25	40	65
Kennedy, Toronto	29	25	54
Mosienko, Chicago	28	26	54
Carveth, Detroit	26	28	54
DeMarco, New York	24	30	54
Smith, Chicago	23	31	54
S. Howe, Detroit	17	36	53

LEADING GOALIES

	G	GA	SO	GAA
Durnan, Montreal	50	121	1	2.42
McCool, Toronto	50	161	4	3.22
Lumley, Detroit	37	119	1	3.22
Karakas, Chicago	48	187	4	3.90
Bibeault, Boston	26	116	0	4.46

PLAYOFF RESULTS

Semifinals

Toronto d. Montreal, 4–2
Detroit d. Boston, 4–3

Finals

Toronto d. Detroit, 4–3

LEADING SCORERS

	G	A	PTS
Carveth, Detroit	5	6	11
Kennedy, Toronto	7	2	9
Richard, Montreal	6	2	8
Lach, Montreal	4	4	8

LEADING GOALIES

	W	SO	GAA
Lumley, Detroit	7	4	2.14
McCool, Toronto	8	4	2.23

1945–46

With World War II drawing to a close, hockey players began returning to the sport. Players came back throughout the season, causing a constant shuffle of rosters throughout the NHL.

Many had lost the best hockey years of their lives while in service and found it difficult to make moves that once were second nature to them. Four years of war had robbed many of that vital extra measure of speed that separated the average players from the stars.

Some clubs, the Rangers among them, felt a sense of responsibility to the returnees and stuck with them until it became all too apparent that they just weren't able to keep up with the NHL pace anymore.

Chicago's Max Bentley got back in time to start the season with the Blackhawks and proved that his service years had not affected his hockey ability.

Bentley won the scoring title with 31 goals and 61 points and earned the Hart Trophy as the league's MVP.

Bentley was picked as the All-Star center on a team that included Montreal's Maurice Richard at right wing, Gaye Stewart of Toronto at left wing, Montreal's Butch Bouchard and Boston's Jack Crawford on defense and Montreal goalie

Bill Durnan, who won his third straight Vezina Trophy. The Lady Byng went to Montreal's Toe Blake and Edgar Laprade of the Rangers won the Calder Trophy as the NHL's best rookie.

Richard did not come close to the record goal-scoring pace he had maintained the year before and finished with 27—less than three other players, including his linemate, Toe Blake.

Despite the Rocket's reduced output, the Canadiens won their third straight regular-season title, this time by five points over Boston. But they at least looked mortal, losing 17 games—just one less than they had dropped in combined regular-season and Stanley Cup play for the previous two years.

The NHL had a new look for the service returnees. In addition to the powerful Canadiens, who had been little more than also-rans when the war started, there was the red line and a new system of three officials—two linesmen as well as a referee—for every game. Goal lights were made mandatory.

In the playoffs, the "Punch Line" carried the Canadiens to their second Stanley Cup in three years. Blake and Richard had seven goals each and Elmer Lach added five and 12 assists as Montreal shredded Chicago in four games and Boston in five to clinch the Cup.

1945–46
FINAL STANDINGS

	W	L	T	PTS	GF	GA
Montreal	28	17	5	61	172	134

"Kraut Liners" Milt Schmidt (left) and Woody Dumart (14) backcheck against the Rangers in 1945–46.

Boston	24	18	8	56	167	156
Chicago	23	20	7	53	200	178
Detroit	20	20	10	50	146	159
Toronto	19	24	7	45	174	185
New York	13	28	9	35	144	191

LEADING SCORERS

	G	A	PTS
M. Bentley, Chicago	31	30	61
Stewart, Toronto	37	15	52
Blake, Montreal	29	21	50
Smith, Chicago	26	24	50
Richard, Montreal	27	21	48
Mosienko, Chicago	18	30	48
DeMarco, New York	20	27	47
Lach, Montreal	13	34	47
Kaleta, Chicago	19	27	46
Taylor, Toronto	23	18	41
Horeck, Chicago	20	21	41

LEADING GOALIES

	G	GA	SO	GAA
Durnan, Montreal	40	104	4	2.60
Lumley, Detroit	50	159	2	3.18
Brimsek, Boston	34	111	2	3.26
Karakas, Chicago	48	166	1	3.46
Rayner, New York	40	149	1	3.72

PLAYOFF RESULTS

Semifinals

Montreal d. Chicago, 4–0
Boston d. Detroit, 4–1

Finals

Montreal d. Boston, 4–1

LEADING SCORERS

	G	A	PTS
Lach, Montreal	5	12	17
Blake, Montreal	7	6	13
Richard, Montreal	7	4	11

LEADING GOALIES

	W	SO	GAA
Durnan, Montreal	6	0	2.07
Brimsek, Boston	5	0	2.68

Boston's All-Star backliner John Crawford wore the helmet to protect his bald head.

1946–47

Red Dutton had successfully steered the NHL through the war years and before the 1946–47 season he announced his retirement. The new NHL president was Clarence Campbell, a former referee, a Rhodes scholar, a lieutenant colonel in the Canadian Army, and a member of the legal staff at the Nuremberg Trials. All this was experience that would serve Campbell well at one time or another in the ensuing years.

In Montreal, Tommy Gorman announced his retirement as general manager of the Canadiens and his replacement was Frank Selke, who for many years had played a key role in Conn Smythe's Toronto operation. Selke's move to Montreal reunited him with another ex-Smythe employee, Canadiens' coach Dick Irvin.

Detroit introduced a slope-shouldered, raw-boned right wing who would one day become hockey's top star. But Gordie Howe was just another rookie and his seven-goal season hardly portended greatness.

The league increased its schedule from 50 to 60 games and introduced a system of bonuses for All-Star selection and individual trophy winners. From then on, in addition to the honor of being selected, each player would get a $1,000 bonus from the league. In addition, the NHL boosted to $127,000 the regular-season and Stanley Cup playoff pools, making it more profitable than ever before for individuals and teams to do well.

Montreal's power-laden Canadiens reaped most of the benefits from the NHL's new afflu-

Former referee Clarence S. Campbell took over the NHL presidency in the fall of 1946.

when he scored five goals less than his record 50. The year he scored 50, the Rocket's linemate, Elmer Lach, was the MVP.

The Canadiens breezed past Boston in the five-game opening series of the Stanley Cup playoffs and then faced Toronto, which had knocked off Detroit in five games. The Canadiens won the opener of the final series, 6–0, prompting goalie Bull Durnan to scoff at the Leafs. "How did these guys get in the playoffs anyway?" needled Durnan. He soon found out.

Toronto bounced back with three straight victories that left Montreal on the brink of elimination. The Canadiens won the fifth game but the Leafs took game No. 6 and the Stanley Cup. It was in the midst of the final series that a high-sticking episode cost Richard a $250 fine and a one-game suspension by Campbell—the first of several scrapes involving the fiery Canadiens' star and the placid president of the league.

ence. They won their fourth straight regular-season title and gained four of the six first-team All-Star berths. Goalie Bill Durnan, defensemen Butch Bouchard and Kenny Reardon and right winger Maurice Richard were the Canadiens' selections. Milt Schmidt of Boston at center and Doug Bentley of Chicago at left wing completed the team.

Durnan won his fourth Vezina Trophy in a row—the first goalie to turn that trick. Richard took the Hart Trophy and Boston's Bobby Bauer was the Lady Byng winner. The Calder Trophy went to Toronto's Howie Meeker, who had been so badly wounded during the war that he was told he would never be able to play hockey again.

Chicago's Max Bentley won his second straight scoring title with 72 points—one more than Richard, who fired 45 goals. Interestingly, Richard earned the MVP designation in a season

1946–47

FINAL STANDINGS

	W	L	T	PTS	GF	GA
Montreal	34	16	10	78	189	138
Toronto	31	19	10	72	209	172
Boston	26	23	11	63	190	175
Detroit	22	27	11	55	190	193
New York	22	32	6	50	167	186
Chicago	19	37	4	42	193	274

LEADING SCORERS

	G	A	PTS
M. Bentley, Chicago	29	43	72
Richard, Montreal	45	26	71
Taylor, Detroit	17	46	63
Schmidt, Boston	27	35	62
Kennedy, Toronto	28	32	60
D. Bentley, Chicago	21	34	55
Bauer, Boston	30	24	54
R. Conacher, Detroit	30	24	54
Mosienko, Chicago	25	27	52
Dumart, Boston	24	28	52

LEADING GOALIES

	G	GA	SO	GAA
Durnan, Montreal	60	138	4	2.30
Broda, Toronto	60	172	4	2.86
Brimsek, Boston	60	175	3	2.91
Lumley, Detroit	52	159	3	3.05
Rayner, New York	58	177	5	3.05

PLAYOFF RESULTS

Semifinals

Montreal d. Boston, 4–1
Toronto d. Detroit, 4–1

Finals

Toronto d. Montreal, 4–2

1947–48

The NHL pension plan was born in 1947, with contributions by both the players and the league. In an effort to build pension revenue, an annual All-Star Game was initiated, pitting the previous season's All-Star squad against the winners of the Stanley Cup. The game was to be played just before the beginning of the regular season.

Toronto's Maple Leaf Gardens hosted the first All-Star affair and a crowd of 14,169 paid $25,865 to watch the All-Stars defeat Toronto, 4–3. Financially, the game was off to a good start. But the opening classic was marred when Bill Mosienko of Chicago fractured his left ankle.

The Maple Leafs were anxious to retain the Stanley Cup they had won the previous spring and Conn Smythe decided the best way to achieve that was to get Max Bentley into a Toronto uniform. That would not be easy since Bentley had won two straight scoring championships and, along with his brother Doug, provided Chicago with a significant gate attraction.

But the Blackhawks' farm system had not produced much in the way of NHL talent and

The Toronto Maple Leafs: Stanley Cup champions in 1946–47.

Defenseman Ken Reardon of Montreal was voted to the All-Star team in 1946–47.

Chicago was short of bodies. That gave Smythe the opening he needed. The Maple Leaf boss assembled an attractive package of Gus Bodnar, Gaye Stewart, Bob Goldham, Bud Poile, and Ernie Dickens which the Hawks could not turn down. Bentley and Cy Thomas went to the Leafs in the seven-player swap.

Smythe's bold move paid off. The Leafs soared to the top of the league and won the regular-season title as Bentley contributed 54 points, including 26 goals. The scoring title, however, went to Montreal's Elmer Lach, who had 31 goals and 61 points. The season marked the breakup of the Canadiens' potent Punch Line, on which Lach was the center. Toe Blake, the left wing, suffered a broken ankle in January that ended his playing career.

A combination of circumstances, not the least of them injuries to Blake and others, dropped the Canadiens to fifth place and out of the playoffs.

Buddy O'Connor, traded by Montreal to New York before the season, won both the Hart and Lady Byng trophies—the first player to capture both in the same season. Toronto's Turk Broda took the Vezina and Detroit's Jimmy McFadden was the Calder winner.

In Detroit, the Red Wings assembled a line of Sid Abel at center, Ted Lindsay on left wing and Gordie Howe on the right side and dubbed it the "Production Line". And it produced handsomely with 63 goals—33 of them by Lindsay.

The league was rocked late in the season by a gambling scandal which led to lifetime suspensions of two players—Billy Taylor of the Rangers and Don Gallinger of Boston. President Clarence Campbell emphasized that no games had been fixed and that Gallinger and Taylor were punished for betting on games. A similar charge had resulted in a midseason suspension for Babe Pratt two seasons earlier but Pratt was reinstated after missing nine games.

Detroit dominated the All-Star team with Ted Lindsay at left wing and Bill Quackenbush and

Toronto's Turk Broda (right) won the Vezina Trophy in 1947–48, breaking a string of four straight Vezinas by Montreal's Bill Durnan.

Jack Stewart on defense. The other choices were Broda and linemates Elmer Lach and Maurice Richard of Montreal.

While the Wings led in All-Star picks, it was the Maple Leafs who dominated the Stanley Cup playoffs. Toronto whipped Boston in five games and then clinched its second straight Cup by beating Detroit in four straight. In the final series, the Leafs held the Red Wings' vaunted Production Line to a single goal.

1947–48

FINAL STANDINGS

	W	L	T	PTS	GF	GA
Toronto	32	15	13	77	182	143
Detroit	30	18	12	72	187	148
Boston	23	24	13	59	167	168
New York	21	26	13	55	176	201
Montreal	20	29	11	51	147	169
Chicago	20	34	6	46	195	225

LEADING SCORERS

	G	A	PTS
Lach, Montreal	30	31	61
O'Connor, New York	24	36	60
D. Bentley, Chicago	20	37	57
Stewart, Toronto-Chicago	27	29	56
M. Bentley, Chicago-Toronto	26	28	54
Poile, Toronto-Chicago	25	29	54
Richard, Montreal	28	25	53
Apps, Toronto	26	27	53
Lindsay, Detroit	33	19	52
R. Conacher, Chicago	22	27	49

LEADING GOALIES

	G	GA	SO	GAA
Broda, Toronto	60	143	5	2.38
Lumley, Detroit	60	147	7	2.46
Durnan, Montreal	59	162	5	2.77
Brimsek, Boston	60	168	3	2.80
Henry, New York	48	153	2	3.19

PLAYOFF RESULTS

Semifinals

Toronto d. Boston, 4–1

Detroit d. N.Y. Rangers, 4–2

Finals

Toronto d. Detroit, 4–2

LEADING SCORERS

	G	A	PTS
Kennedy, Toronto	8	6	14
Bentley, Toronto	4	7	11
Horeck, Detroit	3	7	10

LEADING GOALIES

	W	SO	GAA
Broda, Toronto	8	1	2.15
Rayner, N.Y. Rangers	2	0	2.83
Lumley, Detroit	4	0	3.00

1948–49

When he first saw Sid Abel, Ted Lindsay, and Gordie Howe on a line together, Jack Adams knew the Detroit trio would be something special. And he was right. Starting in 1948, the Production Line led the Red Wings to one of the most successful eras in NHL history—seven straight regular-season titles.

Abel, Lindsay, and Howe meshed together like precision gears and Adams, the genial Detroit general manager, marveled at the trio's uncanny anticipation. "They could score goals in their sleep," Adams once remarked. "They always seem to know where the play will develop."

Abel, the center, was the playmaker. Lindsay, at left wing, was a fierce checker and competitor who was deadly in the corners. And right winger Howe had a marvelous shot and could control the puck for what seemed like minutes on end.

Howe, only 21, was Adams' pet. The Detroit boss had almost lost the shy youngster in his first training camp when someone forgot to furnish him with a Red Wing jacket which Adams had promised. When made aware of the problem, Adams produced the jacket in record time and Howe stayed with the Wings.

Injuries limited Howe to 40 games in 1948–49 and he scored just 12 goals. But Abel and Lindsay kept the Production Line output healthy with 54 goals between them. Goalie Harry Lumley had a 2.42 goals-against average and six shutouts as the Red Wings won the regular-season title by nine points over Boston. But

the best goaltending job was turned in by Montreal's Bill Durnan, who won his fifth Vezina Trophy in six years with a 2.10 goals-against average and 10 shutouts. Durnan had four shutouts in a row over one stretch and established a modern record by not allowing a goal for 309 minutes, 21 seconds.

Roy Conacher of Chicago and teammate Doug Bentley staged an exciting battle for the scoring title, with Conacher finally winning it. He finished with 68 points, two more than Bentley.

Conacher was chosen as the left wing on the All-Star team with Maurice Richard of Montreal at right wing and Sid Abel of Detroit at center. Two Detroit defensemen, Jack Stewart and Bill Quackenbush, and Montreal's goalie, Durnan, completed the team. Despite his limited output, Gordie Howe made the second All-Star squad.

Abel won the Hart Trophy and Quackenbush became the first defenseman to take the Lady Byng. Penti Lund of the Rangers won the Calder Trophy.

In the playoffs, the Production Line riddled Montreal, scoring 12 of Detroit's 17 goals, eight of them by Howe. That put the Red Wings in the Stanley Cup finals against Toronto, which had beaten Boston in five games.

Turk Broda, the Leafs' great goalie, was more than a match for the Production Line. Broda allowed just five goals in four games and Sid Smith's hat trick in the second game set the tone as Toronto won the Cup in four straight.

The victory, marking the Leafs' second four-game sweep in two seasons, made them the first NHL team to take three straight Stanley Cups.

1948–49

FINAL STANDINGS

	W	L	T	PTS	GF	GA
Detroit	34	19	7	75	195	145
Boston	29	23	8	66	178	163
Montreal	28	23	9	65	152	126
Toronto	22	25	13	57	147	161
Chicago	21	31	8	50	173	211
New York	18	31	11	47	133	172

LEADING SCORERS

	G	A	PTS
R. Conacher, Chicago	26	42	68
D. Bentley, Chicago	23	43	66
Abel, Detroit	28	26	54
Lindsay, Detroit	26	28	54
J. Conacher, Detroit-Chicago	26	23	49
Ronty, Boston	20	29	49
Watson, Toronto	26	19	45
Reay, Montreal	22	23	45
Bodnar, Chicago	19	26	45
Peirson, Boston	22	21	43

LEADING GOALIES

	G	GA	SO	GAA
Durnan, Montreal	60	126	10	2.10
Lumley, Detroit	60	145	6	2.42
Broda, Toronto	60	161	5	2.68
Brimsek, Boston	54	147	1	2.72
Rayner, New York	58	168	7	2.90

PLAYOFF RESULTS

Semifinals

Detroit d. Montreal, 4–3
Toronto d. Boston, 4–1

Finals

Toronto d. Detroit, 4–0

LEADING SCORERS

	G	A	PTS
Howe, Detroit	8	3	11
Kennedy, Toronto	2	6	8
Lindsay, Detroit	2	6	8
Smith, Toronto	5	2	7
Plamondon, Montreal	5	1	6

LEADING GOALIES

	W	SO	GAA
Broda, Toronto	8	1	1.57
Lumley, Detroit	4	0	2.15
Durnan, Montreal	3	0	2.18

1949–50

Detroit's Production Line, with a healthy Gordie Howe rejoining Sid Abel and Ted Lindsay, tore through the league and finished 1-2-3 in the scoring race, matching the feat which Boston's Kraut Line, Montreal's Punch Line and Toronto's Kid Line had previously achieved.

Lindsay won the scoring title with 78 points, Abel finished with 69 and Howe had 68. The trio combined for an amazing 215 points, including 92 goals—35 of them by Howe.

Despite Howe's brilliant season, he had to settle for a second-team All-Star berth. For the second straight year the right wing spot on the first team went to Montreal's Maurice Richard, who scored 43 goals, the most in the league. The intense rivalry would continue through the early 1950s with the two men occupying the two All-Star berths eight times over a nine-year period.

Throughout the league, fans argued the relative merits of the two right wingers and the extended debate created quite a feud between the Canadiens and Red Wings. Once, in a ruckus on the ice, Howe knocked Richard down. When the Rocket got up, Abel rubbed salt in the wound with a taunt. Richard wheeled and teed off on Abel, breaking his nose with a punch.

The other All-Stars in 1950 were Lindsay and Abel, defensemen Kenny Reardon of Montreal and Gus Mortson of Toronto and goaltender Bill Durnan of Montreal.

It was Durnan's sixth All-Star selection in seven seasons and he also captured his sixth Vezina Trophy. They were also his last, for he stunned Montreal by quitting in the midst of the Stanley Cup playoffs, saying that the pressure of big-league goaltending had simply become too much.

Two other goalies won individual awards that season. Chuck Rayner of the Rangers was the Hart winner and Jack Gelineau, a rookie who beat Frank Brimsek out of the Boston netminding job, took the Calder Trophy. The Lady Byng winner was Edgar Laprade of the Rangers.

Detroit finished first in the regular-season race and met Toronto in one Stanley Cup semifinal while the Rangers tangled with the Canadiens in the other. Going into the series, the Red Wings had dropped 11 straight playoff games to the Leafs and been eliminated three straight years by Toronto.

In the opening game of the series, a devastating injury almost cost Gordie Howe his life. Ted Kennedy sidestepped a Howe check and Gordie plunged face-first into the boards. He suffered a concussion, a broken nose, a fractured right cheekbone and a scratched eyeball.

The Wings, beaten 5–0 in that opener and deprived of their top scorer, gallantly bounced back and defeated the Maple Leafs in seven games. The Rangers hung three straight defeats on the Canadiens and then Bill Durnan went to Dick

Irvin before the fourth game and asked that the Montreal coach use rookie Gerry McNeil in his place. McNeil won the fourth game but New York finished Montreal off in the fifth.

In the Stanley Cup finals, the Rangers led three games to two and were leading, 4–3, in the third period of the sixth game. But goals by Ted Lindsay and Sid Abel gave the Red Wings the game and tied the series. In the seventh game, Pete Babando's overtime goal sank New York and delivered the Stanley Cup to Detroit.

1949–50

FINAL STANDINGS

	W	L	T	PTS	GF	GA
Detroit	37	19	14	88	229	164
Montreal	29	22	19	77	172	150
Toronto	31	27	12	74	176	173
New York	28	31	11	67	170	189
Boston	22	32	16	60	198	228
Chicago	22	38	10	54	203	244

LEADING SCORERS

	G	A	PTS
Lindsay, Detroit	23	55	78
Abel, Detroit	34	35	69
Howe, Detroit	35	33	68
M. Richard, Montreal	43	22	65
Ronty, Boston	23	36	59
R. Conacher, Chicago	25	31	56
D. Bentley, Chicago	20	33	53
Peirson, Boston	27	25	52
Prystai, Chicago	29	22	51
Guidolin, Chicago	17	34	51

LEADING GOALIES

	G	GA	SO	GAA
Durnan, Montreal	64	141	8	2.20
Lumley, Detroit	63	148	7	2.35
Broda, Toronto	68	167	9	2.45
Rayner, New York	69	181	6	2.62
Gelineau, Boston	67	220	3	3.28

PLAYOFF RESULTS

Semifinals

Detroit d. Toronto, 4–3
N.Y. Rangers d. Montreal, 4–1

Finals

Detroit d. N.Y. Rangers, 4–3

LEADING SCORERS

	G	A	PTS
Lund, N.Y. Rangers	6	5	11
Couture, Detroit	5	4	9
Raleigh, N.Y. Rangers	4	5	9
Gee, Detroit	3	6	9

LEADING GOALIES

	W	SO	GAA
Broda, Toronto	3	3	1.33
Lumley, Detroit	8	3	1.85
Rayner, N.Y. Rangers	7	1	2.25

1950–51

Jack Adams was never a stand-pat general manager and although Detroit had won two straight titles, the Red Wings' boss shook them up before the 1950–51 season. He engineered a mammoth nine-player trade with Chicago—the biggest deal in NHL history.

Shuttled off to Chicago were forwards Al Dewsbury, Don Morrison, and Pete Babando; defenseman Jack Stewart and goalie Harry Lumley. Babando's overtime goal had won the Stanley Cup for the Wings the season before, Stewart had made the first All-Star team three times and Lumley had turned in a 2.35 goals-against average the season before.

In return, Adams got defenseman Bob Goldham, forwards Gaye Stewart and Metro Prystai and goalie Jim Henry. Perhaps the main reason for making the trade was to give Terry Sawchuk a clear shot at the Red Wings' goalie job.

Sawchuk was not yet 21 when he became the Red Wings' regular goalie. The youngster did a spectacular job in his rookie season, with a 1.98 goals-against average and a league-leading 11 shutouts. He was the easy winner of the Calder Trophy and was named to the first All-Star team.

The other All-Stars included Detroit's Gordie Howe, who won the scoring championship with 88 points and scored 43 goals—one more than his right wing rival, Montreal's Maurice Richard. The other forwards were Howe's linemate, Ted Lindsay on left wing, and Boston's Milt Schmidt at center. Red Kelly of Detroit and Bill Quackenbush of Boston were picked as the defensemen.

Schmidt won the Hart Trophy and Kelly took the Lady Byng, becoming the second Red Wing defenseman in three years to win the trophy for gentlemanly play. In spite of Sawchuk's incredible first-year statistics, he was not the Vezina Trophy winner. That honor went to Al Rollins, who split Toronto's netminding with veteran Turk Broda. Rollins played 40 games compared to Sawchuk's 70 and had a 1.75 goals-against average.

The Red Wings finished first with 44 victories and 13 ties, accumulating a record 101 points. But they were only six points up on Toronto, which won 41 games. It was a busy season for president Clarence Campbell. He slapped three-game suspensions and $300 fines each on Ted Lindsay of Detroit and Bill Ezinicki of Boston for a midseason brawl. Gus Mortson of Toronto used his stick on Chicago's Adam Brown in March and it cost him a two-game suspension and $200 fine. Maurice Richard, still steaming over a game misconduct penalty he had drawn from referee Hugh McLean the night before, grabbed McLean in New York's Picadilly Hotel and as a result of the confrontation, Campbell fined the Rocket $500.

In the Stanley Cup opening round, the Canadiens were decided underdogs to the Red Wings. But Montreal won the first two games—both of them on overtime goals by Richard. Detroit squared the series by taking the next two but Montreal came right back and eliminated the Red Wings by winning the fifth and sixth games.

Toronto took Boston in five games and advanced to the finals against Montreal. The Maple Leafs and Canadiens set a record of sorts as all five games of their series went into overtime.

In the fifth game, Toronto was trailing, 2–1, in the final period when coach Joe Primeau yanked goalie Turk Broda to make room for an extra attacker. The maneuver paid off with Tod

Maple Leafs (from left) Sid Smith, Max Bentley, and Bill Barilko celebrate playoff victory over the Bruins en route to the 1950–51 Stanley Cup championship.

Sloan's game-tying goal with just 32 seconds remaining.

Less than three minutes into overtime, defenseman Bill Barilko won the game and the Cup for the Leafs with a goal. It was the last one he ever scored. Two months later, he was killed in a plane crash.

1950–51

FINAL STANDINGS

	W	L	T	PTS	GF	GA
Detroit	44	13	13	101	236	139
Toronto	41	16	13	95	212	138
Montreal	25	30	15	65	173	184
Boston	22	30	18	62	178	197
New York	20	29	21	61	169	201
Chicago	13	47	10	36	171	280

LEADING SCORERS

	G	A	PTS
Howe, Detroit	43	43	86
M. Richard, Montreal	42	24	66
M. Bentley, Toronto	21	41	62
Abel, Detroit	23	38	61
Schmidt, Boston	22	39	61
Kennedy, Toronto	18	43	61
Lindsay, Detroit	24	35	59
Sloan, Toronto	31	25	56
Kelly, Detroit	17	37	54
Smith, Toronto	30	21	51
Gardner, Toronto	23	28	51

LEADING GOALIES

	G	GA	SO	GAA
Rollins, Toronto	40	70	5	1.75
Sawchuk, Detroit	70	139	11	1.98
McNeil, Montreal	70	184	6	2.63
Gelineau, Boston	70	197	4	2.81
Rayner, New York	66	187	2	2.83

PLAYOFF RESULTS

Semifinals

Montreal d. Detroit, 4–2
Toronto d. Boston, 4–1 (1 tie)

Finals

Toronto d. Montreal, 4–1

LEADING SCORERS

	G	A	PTS
Richard, Montreal	9	4	13
Bentley, Toronto	11	2	13
Smith, Toronto	7	3	10

LEADING GOALIES

	W	SO	GAA
Broda, Toronto	5	2	1.10
Gelineau, Boston	1	1	1.62
Rollins, Toronto	3	0	1.71
McNeil, Montreal	5	1	1.91

1951–52

Detroit won its fourth straight regular-season championship, but the most exciting moments of the season came on March 23 in a meaningless game between New York and Chicago. That was the night Bill Mosienko made hockey history.

The Rangers and Blackhawks were out of the race for a playoff berth when they met at Madison Square Garden. New York was fifth and Chicago last. The Rangers, who had used Chuck Rayner and Emile Francis in goal during most of the season, went with Lorne Anderson in this game.

Mosienko, one of Chicago's top scorers, was playing on a line with Gus Bodnar and George Gee. At 6:09 of the third period, Bodnar fed the puck to Mosienko and the right wing fired a goal. The puck was brought back for a faceoff and at 6:20 the combination clicked again. Then another faceoff and at 6:30 another goal by Mosienko. Three goals in 21 seconds earned him a spot in the record book for the quickest hat trick in NHL history.

In Detroit, the Red Wings were dreaming about the Stanley Cup. And it was no idle dream, either. The Wings had ripped through the regular season, rolling up 100 points—just one point under the record they had established the season before. They finished 22 points ahead of second-place Montreal.

Gordie Howe won his second straight scoring title with 86 points, the same number he had posted the year before. He scored 47 goals, making a serious run at Maurice Richard's record of 50. Howe was chosen MVP and named to the right wing spot on the All-Star team. The other All-Stars were Detroit's Ted Lindsay at left wing, Montreal's Elmer Lach at center, Red Kelly of Detroit and Doug Harvey of Montreal on defense and Detroit's Terry Sawchuk in goal.

Sawchuk took the Vezina Trophy with a 1.94 goals-against average and a league-leading 12 shutouts. Toronto's Sid Smith won the Lady Byng and Montreal's Bernie Geoffrion, nicknamed Boom Boom for his jet-powered slap shots, took the Calder Trophy as the top rookie.

Montreal battled through seven games before eliminating Boston in the Stanley Cup semifinals. The Canadiens took the deciding game when Maurice Richard skated through four Bruins and

then fought off Bill Quackenbush, the last defender, before beating Jim Henry for the tie-breaking goal with four minutes to play. The significant thing about the goal is that Richard remembers very little about it. He had spent the second period of the game in the clinic at the Montreal Forum having six stitches put in his head after being pelted by Leo Labine.

"I was dizzy and a few times when I got the puck I didn't know whether I was skating toward our goal or their goal," Richard said.

Richard's heroics got the Canadiens into the final round but the Rocket couldn't help against the Red Wing juggernaut. Howe and Ted Lindsay scored five goals between them and Sawchuk turned in his third and fourth shutouts of the playoffs as Detroit swept to the Stanley Cup in four straight games. In eight playoff games, Sawchuk allowed only five goals—an incredible 0.62 goals-against average.

1951–52

FINAL STANDINGS

	W	L	T	PTS	GF	GA
Detroit	44	14	12	100	215	133
Montreal	34	26	10	78	195	164
Toronto	29	25	16	74	168	157
Boston	25	29	16	66	162	176
New York	23	34	13	59	192	219
Chicago	17	44	9	43	158	241

LEADING SCORERS

	G	A	PTS
Howe, Detroit	47	39	86
Lindsay, Detroit	30	39	69
Lach, Montreal	15	50	65
Raleigh, New York	19	42	61
Smith, Toronto	27	30	57
Geoffrion, Montreal	30	24	54
Mosienko, Chicago	31	22	53
Abel, Detroit	17	36	53

Detroit goalie Terry Sawchuk gets help from teammate Marcel Pronovost in holding off Boston's Milt Schmidt in 1952–53.

	G	A	PTS	
Kennedy, Toronto	19	33	52	
Schmidt, Boston	21	29	50	
Peirson, Boston	20	30	50	

LEADING GOALIES

	G	GA	SO	GAA
Sawchuk, Detroit	70	133	12	1.94
Rollins, Toronto	70	154	5	2.20
McNeil, Montreal	70	164	5	2.34
Henry, Boston	70	176	7	2.51
Rayner, New York	53	159	2	3.00

PLAYOFF RESULTS

Semifinals

Detroit d. Toronto, 4–0
Montreal d. Boston, 4–3

Finals

Detroit d. Montreal, 4–0

LEADING SCORERS

	G	A	PTS
Lindsay, Detroit	5	2	7
Curry, Montreal	4	3	7
Prystal, Detroit	5	2	7
Howe, Detroit	2	5	7

LEADING GOALIES

	W	SO	GAA
Sawchuk, Detroit	8	4	0.63
McNeil, Montreal	4	1	2.01
Henry, Boston	3	1	2.41

1952–53

Detroit's Production Line was broken up before the 1952–53 season when Sid Abel asked to be traded to Chicago. The Blackhawks wanted Abel as coach and Jack Adams, the Detroit general manager, did not stand in the way of his veteran center.

Abel's replacement was Alex Delvecchio, who flourished playing between Gordie Howe and Ted Lindsay. He scored 59 points, including 43 assists. The switch in centers made little difference to right winger Howe and left winger Lindsay. They finished 1–2 in scoring for the second straight year with Gordie accumulating 95 points and making his most serious run at Maurice Richard's 50-goal record, finishing with 49. Lindsay had 71 points, including 32 goals.

The departure of Abel didn't seem to hurt the Red Wings, who won their fifth straight regular-season title, but it had a major effect on Chicago, the club Abel took over. Doubling as a player-coach, Abel piloted the Blackhawks to a third-place tie with Boston for Chicago's first playoff berth in seven years.

The scoring crown was Howe's third straight and he became the first man in NHL history to put three together. Similarly, the Red Wings made NHL history with their fifth straight league title. Boston twice and Montreal once had strung four regular-season titles together, but no team had ever managed five.

Howe and Lindsay were named right wing and left wing on the first All-Star team for the third straight year. The other All-Stars were Boston center Fleming Mackell, defensemen Red Kelly of Detroit and Doug Harvey of Montreal and goalie Terry Sawchuk of Detroit.

Howe won his second consecutive Hart Trophy as MVP, Kelly was the Lady Byng winner and Sawchuk, with a 1.90 average, won the Vezina. The Calder Trophy went to New York goalie Lorne (Gump) Worsley—the third goalie in four years to be honored as the NHL's top rookie.

Early in the season, Maurice Richard scored his 324th career goal, tying the NHL record held by another Montreal great, Nels Stewart. On November 8, he scored No. 325 to set the new standard. On the same night, Richard's center, Elmer Lach, scored the 200th goal of his career.

In the playoffs, the powerful Red Wings, who had breezed to the Stanley Cup in eight straight games the year before, ruled as heavy favorites. They battered Boston, 7–0, in the opening game and looked like a sure thing to repeat as champions. But some clutch scoring by Ed Sandford and heroic goaltending by Sugar Jim Henry gave the Bruins a six-game first-round victory over Detroit.

Chicago held a three-to-two edge in games against Montreal in the other semifinal when Gerry McNeil went to coach Dick Irvin of the Canadiens and suggested that he use Jacques Plante, a rookie, in goal. It was a repeat of Bill Durnan's action during the playoffs in 1950 when he had gone to Irvin and asked to be replaced by McNeil. Plante allowed the Blackhawks one goal in two games and the Canadiens advanced to the final round against Boston.

With Plante and McNeil dividing the netminding, Montreal whipped the Bruins in five games to capture the Stanley Cup.

Boston's Jim Henry congratulates Montreal's Maurice Richard after the Canadiens eliminated the Bruins in the 1952 semifinals.

Boston	28	29	13	69	152	172
Chicago	27	28	15	69	169	175
Toronto	27	30	13	67	156	167
New York	17	37	16	50	152	211

1952–53

FINAL STANDINGS

	W	L	T	PTS	GF	GA
Detroit	36	16	18	90	222	133
Montreal	28	23	19	75	155	148

LEADING SCORERS

	G	A	PTS
Howe, Detroit	49	46	95

Lindsay, Detroit	32	39	71
M. Richard, Montreal	28	33	61
Hergesheimer, New York	30	29	59
Delvecchio, Detroit	16	43	59
Ronty, New York	16	38	54
Prystai, Detroit	16	34	50
Kelly, Detroit	19	27	46
Olmstead, Montreal	17	28	45
Mackell, Boston	27	17	44
McFadden, Chicago	23	21	44

LEADING GOALIES

	G	GA	SO	GAA
Sawchuk, Detroit	63	120	9	1.90
McNeil, Montreal	66	140	10	2.12
Lumley, Toronto	70	167	10	2.38
Henry, Boston	70	172	7	2.46
Rollins, Chicago	70	175	6	2.50

PLAYOFF RESULTS

Semifinals

Boston d. Detroit, 4–2
Montreal d. Chicago, 4–3

Finals

Montreal d. Boston, 4–1

LEADING SCORERS

	G	A	PTS
Sandford, Boston	8	3	11
Geoffrion, Montreal	6	4	10

LEADING GOALIES

	W	SO	GAA
Plante, Montreal	3	1	1.75
McNeil, Montreal	5	2	1.98
Rollins, Chicago	3	0	2.54

1953–54

The Chicago Blackhawks slipped back into the NHL's cellar after their one-season move into the playoffs and established a record for futility in 1953–54. They managed only 12 victories and lost 51 times.

Ironically, the Blackhawks did achieve one important honor. Goalie Al Rollins was named the Most Valuable Player in the league. The award might very well have been for heroism in the face of a season-long barrage of enemy shots. Four of the 12 Chicago victories were shutouts by Rollins and the 242 goals allowed by the Blackhawks were the most in the league.

Even more ironic is the fact that Harry Lumley, whom Chicago had traded to Toronto for Rollins and three other players the year before, won the Vezina Trophy, a spot on the All-Star team and a line in the NHL record book with 13 shutouts. But the MVP was Rollins.

Gordie Howe and the Detroit Red Wings again ruled the league. Howe won an unprecedented fourth straight scoring title with 81 points and the Red Wings captured a record sixth consecutive regular-season championship.

Howe and his Detroit linemate, Ted Lindsay, made the first All-Star team for the fourth straight year. Montreal center Ken Mosdell, defensemen Doug Harvey of Montreal and Red Kelly of Detroit and Lumley, Toronto's goalie, completed the team. It was the third straight All-Star berth for Kelly and Harvey.

Kelly also won his third Lady Byng Trophy in four years and captured a new award, the James Norris Trophy, as the league's top defenseman. The trophy was presented by the four children of the late former owner-president of the Detroit Red Wings. Camille Henry of New York took the Calder Trophy.

Detroit needed just five games to eliminate Toronto, and Montreal took Boston in four straight in the opening rounds of the Stanley Cup playoffs.

Then the Canadiens and Red Wings went at each other in the final round in a memorable series that stretched over seven games. The Red Wings, with Howe, Lindsay and Alex Delvecchio starring, won three of the first four contests. Then Canadiens' coach Dick Irvin changed goalies, recalling 31-year-old Gerry McNeil from the minors to replace Jacques Plante.

McNeil shut out the Red Wings in the fifth game, which Montreal won on an overtime goal by Ken Mosdell. Then he beat them, 4–1, to even the series at three games apiece.

The seventh game went into overtime tied at 1–1. With $4\frac{1}{2}$ minutes gone in the extra period, Detroit's Tony Leswick lofted a shot toward McNeil. Doug Harvey, the Canadiens' superlative defenseman, lifted his glove to flick the puck away. Instead, it glanced off Harvey's glove, over McNeil's shoulder, and into the Montreal net, giving Detroit the Stanley Cup.

The Canadiens stormed off the ice instead of congratulating the Red Wings as custom dictated. "If I had shaken hands," stormed coach Dick Irvin, "I wouldn't have meant it. I refuse to be a hypocrite."

1953–54

FINAL STANDINGS

	W	L	T	PTS	GF	GA
Detroit	37	19	14	88	191	132
Montreal	35	24	11	81	195	141
Toronto	32	24	14	78	152	131
Boston	32	28	10	74	177	181
New York	29	31	10	68	161	182
Chicago	12	51	7	31	133	242

LEADING SCORERS

	G	A	PTS
Howe, Detroit	33	48	81
M. Richard, Montreal	37	30	67
Lindsay, Detroit	26	36	62
Geoffrion, Montreal	29	25	54
Olmstead, Montreal	15	37	52
Kelly, Detroit	16	33	49
Reibel, Detroit	15	33	48
Sanford, Boston	16	31	47
Mackell, Boston	15	32	47
Mosdell, Montreal	22	24	46
Ronty, New York	13	33	46

LEADING GOALIES

	G	GA	SO	GAA
Lumley, Toronto	69	128	13	1.85
Sawchuk, Detroit	67	129	12	1.92
McNeil, Montreal	53	114	6	2.15
Henry, Boston	70	181	8	2.58
Bower, New York	70	182	5	2.60

PLAYOFF RESULTS

Semifinals

Detroit d. Toronto, 4–1
Montreal d. Boston, 4–0

Finals

Detroit d. Montreal, 4–3

LEADING SCORERS

	G	A	PTS
Moore, Montreal	5	8	13
Geoffrion, Montreal	6	5	11
Beliveau, Montreal	2	8	10

Toronto's Harry Lumley blanked 13 opponents and won the Vezina Trophy in 1953–54.

General manager Jack Adams guided Detroit to its
seventh Stanley Cup in 1954–55.

LEADING GOALIES

	W	SO	GAA
McNeil, Montreal	2	1	0.95
Sawchuk, Detroit	5	2	1.60
Plante, Montreal	5	2	1.88

1954–55

Montreal was piecing together a powerful
young team to make a run at Detroit's domination
of the NHL. There was tall Jean Beliveau, the
slick center from Quebec whom the Canadiens
wanted so badly they purchased the rights to an
entire amateur league to get him. There was flamboyant Boom Boom Geoffrion, a hard-shooting
right winger. There was cool Doug Harvey, perhaps the finest defenseman in the league since
Eddie Shore. There was colorful Jacques Plante in
goal. And there was the Rocket-Maurice Richard.

He was always No. 1 with the Canadiens'
fans. He was the heart of the club. The fiery
Frenchman with the Gallic glare was long on talent and short on temper. It was the latter that got
him in trouble, costing him the scoring title and
leading to the riot of Ste. Catherine Street which
rocked the hockey world in March 1955.

Richard, Geoffrion, and Beliveau were racing for the scoring title when the Rocket's temper
sabotaged him. It was March 13 in Boston when
Richard lost his poise, attacked Hal Laycoe of the
Bruins with his stick and took a punch at linesman Cliff Thompson.

Clarence Campbell, the league president, was
outraged by Richard's behavior and suspended the
star for the final three games of the regular season
as well as the entire playoffs. Campbell showed
up at the Montreal Forum on March 17 to watch
the Canadiens play Detroit in a battle for first
place. When the president took his seat, he was
greeted with some hooting as well as a shower of
peanuts and programs. Then a tear gas bomb was
thrown on the ice at about the same moment that a
fan approached Campbell's box with hand extended as if to shake, and then whacked the president.

Outside the building, more trouble was brew-
ing. As fans poured out of the besieged Forum,
they turned into a mob, rumbling down Ste.
Catherine Street, Montreal's main avenue, and
looting stores.

The next day, Richard went on the radio to
plead in French for calm. "I will take my punish-
ment," he said, "and come back next year to help
the club and the younger players to win the Stanley Cup."

The suspension left Richard with 74 points
and Geoffrion edged past him with 75 to win the
scoring crown. Beliveau finished third with 73.
Richard was named to the All-Star team along
with Beliveau at center and Sid Smith of Toronto
at left wing. The defensemen, again, were Doug
Harvey of Montreal and Red Kelly of Detroit
with Toronto's Harry Lumley in goal.

Smith won the Lady Byng Trophy while
Terry Sawchuk of Detroit took the Vezina with a
league-leading 12 shutouts and a 1.94 average. It

was the fifth straight season in which his goals-against average was less than two per game. The Norris Trophy went to Harvey, the Hart Trophy to Toronto's Ted Kennedy and the Calder to Ed Litzenberger of Chicago.

Detroit edged Montreal for the regular-season title, winning its seventh straight crown by just two points. In the Stanley Cup semifinals, the Red Wings whipped Toronto in four straight and the Canadiens needed five games to eliminate Boston.

In an effort to beat the Red Wings, Montreal coach Dick Irvin alternated his goalies, Jacques Plante and Charlie Hodge. But the Wings, winning all their games at home and none in Montreal, took the series and the Cup, four games to three, as Alex Delvecchio scored twice in the seventh game.

1954–55

FINAL STANDINGS

	W	L	T	PTS	GF	GA
Detroit	42	17	11	95	204	134
Montreal	41	18	11	93	228	157
Toronto	24	24	22	70	147	135
Boston	23	26	21	67	169	188
New York	17	35	18	52	150	210
Chicago	13	40	17	43	161	235

LEADING SCORERS

	G	A	PTS
Geoffrion, Montreal	38	37	75
M. Richard, Montreal	38	36	74
Beliveau, Montreal	37	36	73
Reibel, Detroit	25	41	66
Howe, Detroit	29	33	62
Sullivan, Chicago	19	42	61
Olmstead, Montreal	10	48	58
Smith, Toronto	33	21	54
Mosdell, Montreal	22	32	54
Lewicki, New York	29	24	53

LEADING GOALIES

	G	GA	SO	GAA
Sawchuk, Detroit	68	132	12	1.94
Lumley, Toronto	69	134	8	1.94
Plante, Montreal	52	110	5	2.11
Henderson, Boston	44	109	5	2.40
Worsley, New York	65	197	4	3.03

PLAYOFF RESULTS

Semifinals

Detroit d. Toronto, 4–0
Montreal d. Boston, 4–1

Finals

Detroit d. Montreal, 4–3

LEADING SCORERS

	G	A	PTS
Howe, Detroit	9	11	20
Lindsay, Detroit	7	12	19
Delvecchio, Detroit	7	8	15

LEADING GOALIES

	W	SO	GAA
Sawchuk, Detroit	8	1	2.36
Plante, Montreal	6	0	2.81

1955–56

There were important personnel changes around the league in 1955–56—both on the players' benches and behind them. After 14 seasons as coach of the Canadiens, Dick Irvin left Montreal and moved on to Chicago, where the challenge of rebuilding the Blackhawks seemed enormous. Irvin's replacement was Toe Blake, left wing on the old Punch Line. In New York, Phil Watson, always a firebrand, took over as coach, replacing Muzz Patrick, who in turn took over from Frank Boucher as the Rangers' general manager.

Detroit shook up its Stanley Cup champions and a series of trades left the Red Wings with only nine players from the squad that had captured the Cup the previous spring. In the biggest trade, Jack Adams swapped four players, including goalie Terry Sawchuk, to Boston for five Bruins. The Sawchuk deal was made because the Red Wing management felt that Terry's nerves were getting the best of him and also because Adams had a ready-made replacement in young Glenn Hall.

Adams also consummated an eight-player trade with Chicago as the Blackhawks feverishly tried to move out of the league's lower echelon. They didn't make it, but the Rangers did. New scoring punch from a group of recently graduated junior players including Andy Bathgate, Dean Prentice and Ron Murphy, as well as a stiffened defense supplied by Bill Gadsby, Harry Howell and the fans' favorite, Louie Fontinato, vaulted New York to third place—its highest finish in 14 years.

Fontinato, a rookie, accumulated 202 minutes in penalties—spending the equivalent of more than 10 periods sitting out infractions. The New York fans loved his brawling and nicknamed him Louie the Leaper.

In Montreal, Blake added three rookies—Henri Richard, the younger brother of Maurice, defenseman Jean Guy Talbot and forward

Claude Provost. The Canadiens were clearly the class of the league and finished with 100 points, losing only 15 of their 70 games. Three of the top four scorers were Canadiens, including the champion, Jean Beliveau, who had 47 goals among his 88 points.

Beliveau was named to the All-Star team along with teammates Maurice Richard, Doug Harvey and Jacques Plante. Beliveau and Richard were joined on the forward line by Detroit's Ted Lindsay while Bill Gadsby of New York won the other defense spot alongside Harvey and in front of goaltender Plante.

Plante won the Vezina Trophy with a 1.86 goals-against average, Harvey took the Norris Trophy and Beliveau was named MVP. Detroit's Earl (Dutch) Reibel won the Lady Byng while Glenn Hall, Sawchuk's replacement at Detroit, was the Calder Trophy winner.

Montreal finished off New York in five games and Detroit eliminated Toronto, also in five, in the opening rounds of the Stanley Cup playoffs. Then, with Beliveau, Bernie Geoffrion, Richard and Bert Olmstead supplying the firepower, Montreal beat Detroit in five games to win its third Stanley Cup in a decade.

1955–56

FINAL STANDINGS

	W	L	T	PTS	GF	GA
Montreal	45	15	10	100	222	131
Detroit	30	24	16	76	183	148
New York	32	28	10	74	204	203
Toronto	24	33	13	61	153	181
Boston	23	34	13	59	147	185
Chicago	19	39	12	50	155	216

LEADING SCORERS

	G	A	PTS
Beliveau, Montreal	47	41	88
Howe, Detroit	38	41	79
M. Richard, Montreal	38	33	71
Olmstead, Montreal	14	56	70
Sloan, Toronto	37	29	66
Bathgate, New York	19	47	66
Geoffrion, Montreal	29	33	62
Reibel, Detroit	17	39	56
Delvecchio, Detroit	25	26	51
Creighton, New York	20	31	51
Gadsby, New York	9	42	51

LEADING GOALIES

	G	GA	SO	GAA
Plante, Montreal	64	119	7	1.86
Hall, Detroit	70	148	12	2.11

Sawchuk, Boston	68	181	9	2.66
Lumley, Toronto	59	159	3	2.69
Worsley, New York	70	203	4	2.90

PLAYOFF RESULTS

Semifinals

Montreal d. N.Y. Rangers, 4–1
Detroit d. Toronto, 4–1

Finals

Montreal d. Detroit, 4–1

LEADING SCORERS

	G	A	PTS
Beliveau, Montreal	12	7	19
Geoffrion, Montreal	5	9	14
Richard, Montreal	5	9	14
Olmstead, Montreal	4	10	14

LEADING GOALIES

	W	SO	GAA
Plante, Montreal	8	2	1.80
Lumley, Toronto	1	1	2.76
Hall, Detroit	5	0	2.78

1956–57

Montreal's powerhouse Canadiens became the scourge of the league with a collection of the finest shooters ever to occupy a single team's roster at the same time. Maurice Richard, Jean Beliveau, Boom Boom Geoffrion, Bert Olmstead, Dickie Moore and the others were all expert marksmen. And when coach Toe Blake assembled a power play to take advantage of an enemy penalty, the Canadiens' shooters could turn a game around.

Blake used Geoffrion and Doug Harvey at the points on power plays because of their hard, accurate shots. Up front he would employ Richard at right wing, Beliveau at center and Moore or Olmstead at left wing. The effect was devastating. The Canadiens often would score two or three goals on a single penalty because at the time the rules required a penalized player to spend his full two minutes in the penalty box, regardless of how often the team with the manpower edge scored.

But the Canadiens made a travesty of the rule and eventually it had to be changed, specifically because of Montreal's proficiency. Starting in 1956–57, as soon as the team with the manpower edge scored, the penalized player was allowed to return to the ice and restore his team to full strength.

Montreal goalie Jacques Plante hurdles a fallen Maple Leaf in 1955–56, the year Plante's 1.86 goals-against average netted him the Vezina Trophy.

Detroit's assessment of Terry Sawchuk's nerves proved accurate when the ex-Red Wing goalie walked out on the Bruins in midseason, saying he was ill. The Bruins put in a hurry-up call to Springfield of the American League and came up with Don Simmons to replace Sawchuk. Ironically, on the day he left Boston, Sawchuk was named to the All-Star team for the first half of the season. With Terry sitting out the second half, Glenn Hall, his replacement at Detroit, captured the final All-Star designation.

The other All-Stars were Detroit's Red Kelly and Montreal's Doug Harvey on defense, Jean Beliveau of Montreal at center and Detroit's Ted Lindsay and Gordie Howe on the wings.

Howe won his fifth scoring championship with 89 points, including 44 goals, and also captured the Hart Trophy as MVP. The Lady Byng went to New York's Andy Hebenton, while Montreal's Jacques Plante took the Vezina, Larry Regan of Boston won the Calder and Harvey captured the Norris.

Detroit won its eighth regular-season crown in nine years, beating out the Canadiens by six points. But the Red Wings were upset by Boston's determined Bruins in the Stanley Cup semifinal series. Detroit bowed when Boston rallied for three goals in the third period to win the deciding seventh contest.

Montreal eliminated New York in five games with Geoffrion exploding for three goals in the third engagement. The Canadiens faced the Bruins for the Stanley Cup and Richard set the tone by exploding for four goals in the 5–1 opening-game victory. The Rocket scored three times in the second period and Simmons, the victim of the assault, said simply, "It was humiliating." It took the Canadiens just five games to clinch the Cup.

1956–57

FINAL STANDINGS

	W	L	T	PTS	GF	GA
Detroit	38	20	12	88	198	157
Montreal	35	23	12	82	210	155
Boston	34	24	12	80	195	174
New York	26	30	14	66	184	227
Toronto	21	34	15	57	174	192
Chicago	16	39	15	47	169	225

LEADING SCORERS

	G	A	PTS
Howe, Detroit	44	45	89
Lindsay, Detroit	30	55	85
Beliveau, Montreal	33	51	84
Bathgate, New York	27	50	77
Litzenberger, Chicago	32	32	64
M. Richard, Montreal	33	29	62
McKenney, Boston	21	39	60
Moore, Montreal	29	29	58
H. Richard, Montreal	18	36	54
Ullman, Detroit	16	36	52

LEADING GOALIES

	G	GA	SO	GAA
Plante, Montreal	61	123	9	2.02
Hall, Detroit	70	157	4	2.24
Sawchuk, Boston	34	81	2	2.38
Chadwick, Toronto	70	192	5	2.74
Rollins, Chicago	70	225	3	3.21

PLAYOFF RESULTS

Semifinals

Boston d. Detroit, 4–1
Montreal d. N.Y. Rangers, 4–1

Finals

Montreal d. Boston, 4–1

LEADING SCORERS

	G	A	PTS
Geoffrion, Montreal	11	7	18
Beliveau, Montreal	6	6	12
Richard, Montreal	8	3	11

LEADING GOALIES

	W	SO	GAA
Plante, Montreal	8	1	1.75
Simmons, Boston	5	2	2.90

1957–58

Two marvelously talented rookie left wings broke into the NHL in 1957–58. Toronto's Frank Mahovlich won the Calder Trophy as the top rookie, but it was Chicago's Bobby Hull who was to emerge as one of the game's most dynamic stars.

In Detroit, Jolly Jack Adams was again active in the player market. He took Terry Sawchuk back from the Bruins in exchange for Johnny Bucyk and made room for his returning goaltender by swapping Glenn Hall and Ted Lindsay to Chicago for four players. It was rumored that part of the reason Adams unloaded Lindsay was the veteran left wing's active participation in the formation of an NHL Players' Association.

It was the best of times and it was the worst of times for Montreal's Maurice Richard. On October 19, he scored his 500th regular-season goal,

The Canadiens' Henri Richard splits Ranger defensemen Lou Fontinato (on ice) and Harry Howell in 1956–57.

The Blackhawks unveiled dynamic Bobby Hull in 1957–58.

scoring championship with 84 points as well as an All-Star berth.

Despite the Rocket's injury, there was a Richard on the All-Star team. Brother Henri, the Pocket Rocket, who finished second to Moore in scoring with 80 points, was picked as the center. Gordie Howe of Detroit was on right wing, with Bill Gadsby of New York and Doug Harvey of Montreal as the defensemen and Chicago's Glenn Hall in goal.

Howe won Most Valuable Player honors and Harvey took the Norris Trophy as the top defenseman for the fourth straight year. Camille Henry of the Rangers won the Lady Byng, Montreal's Jacques Plante, who had started using a mask in practice, was the Vezina winner, and Toronto's Frank Mahovlich took the Calder. Mahovlich had 20 goals and 16 assists compared to Bobby Hull's 13 goals and 34 assists.

Maurice Richard, who had missed 42 regular-season games after his injury and had scored only 15 goals all year, was the spark that drove the Canadiens to their third straight Stanley Cup. Montreal swept Detroit in four games with Richard's hat trick in the final contest leading a last-period comeback that erased a two-goal deficit and gave the Canadiens a 4–3 victory.

Boston, which had eliminated New York in six games, was tied at two games apiece with Montreal when the Rocket's overtime goal in the fifth game put the Canadiens in the driver's seat. Montreal finished off Boston in the sixth game as Richard completed the 10 playoff games with 11 goals.

but less than one month later he collided with Toronto's Marc Reaume and his Achilles tendon was almost completely severed. For a time, it was feared that the 36-year-old Rocket's career might be over.

In February, the Canadiens again were jolted by an injury. This time it was Boom Boom Geoffrion, leading the league in goals at the time. The Boomer ran into teammate Andre Pronovost during a workout and ruptured a bowel. He was given the last rites of the Roman Catholic Church before major stomach surgery saved his life.

Despite the injuries, the Canadiens carried on and finished first, 19 points ahead of the surprising Rangers, who had uncovered a new scoring star in Andy Bathgate. Part of the reason for the Canadiens' success was left winger Dickie Moore, who played the last five weeks of the season with a cast on his right wrist but still won the

1957–58

FINAL STANDINGS

	W	L	T	PTS	GF	GA
Montreal	43	17	10	96	250	158
New York	32	25	13	77	195	188
Detroit	29	29	12	70	176	207
Boston	27	28	15	69	199	194
Chicago	24	39	7	55	163	202
Toronto	21	38	11	53	192	226

LEADING SCORERS

	G	A	PTS
Moore, Montreal	36	48	84
H. Richard, Montreal	28	52	80

Bathgate, New York	30	48	78
Howe, Detroit	33	44	77
Horvath, Boston	30	36	66
Litzenberger, Chicago	32	30	62
Mackell, Boston	20	40	60
Beliveau, Montreal	27	32	59
Delvecchio, Detroit	21	38	59
McKenney, Boston	28	30	58

LEADING GOALIES

	G	GA	SO	GAA
Plante, Montreal	57	119	9	2.09
Worsley, New York	37	86	4	2.32
Simmons, Boston	38	93	5	2.45
Hall, Chicago	70	202	7	2.88
Sawchuk, Detroit	70	207	3	2.96

PLAYOFF RESULTS

Semifinals

Montreal d. Detroit, 4–0
Boston d. N.Y. Rangers, 4–2

Finals

Montreal d. Boston, 4–2

LEADING SCORERS

	G	A	PTS
Mackell, Boston	5	14	19
McKenney, Boston	9	8	17
Richard, Montreal	11	4	15

LEADING GOALIES

	W	SO	GAA
Plante, Montreal	8	1	1.75
Simmons, Boston	6	1	2.41

1958–59

Conn Smythe never was a very good loser and when his Toronto Maple Leafs slipped into the NHL cellar, he decided it was time for action. Smythe sought out George (Punch) Imlach, director of player personnel for Boston, and offered him a front-office spot with the Leafs. Imlach accepted, provided that the position was that of general manager. The Leafs had no one doing that particular job, so Smythe agreed.

A week after he was named to the post, Imlach decided that Billy Reay, Toronto's coach, wasn't doing a good enough job. Imlach went on a talent hunt and lured the best man available—Punch Imlach.

The Maple Leafs had several new faces besides Imlach's. They had swapped Jim Morrison to Boston for defenseman Allan Stanley and signed another new defenseman in 21-year-old Carl Brewer. Bert Olmstead was acquired from Montreal and Imlach picked up a 33-year-old journeyman goalie, Johnny Bower, from Cleveland of the American League.

They all played a role in Toronto's helter-skelter stretch run to a playoff spot. With 20 games left to play, the Maple Leafs were in the cellar. On the final night of the regular season they won their fifth straight game while New York was losing its sixth in the last seven. As a result, Toronto sneaked into the fourth and final playoff spot, one point ahead of the embarrassed Rangers, who had to refund thousands of dollars worth of useless playoff tickets.

Montreal easily captured the regular-season title, beating Boston by 18 points. Detroit, meanwhile, had fallen on lean times and dipped all the way into the league basement despite a 32-goal season by Gordie Howe.

Dickie Moore of Montreal won his second straight scoring title with a record 96 points and earned the left wing spot on the All-Star team. Three other Canadiens also made the All-Stars, with Jacques Plante in goal, Jean Beliveau at center and Tom Johnson on defense. Johnson beat out teammate Doug Harvey, who missed the first team after seven straight selections. Right winger Andy Bathgate and defenseman Bill Gadsby of the Rangers completed the squad.

Bathgate won the Hart Trophy, Plante took his fourth straight Vezina and Johnson ended Harvey's four-year monopoly of the Norris Trophy. Montreal's Ralph Backstrom captured the Calder Trophy and Alex Delvecchio of Detroit was the Lady Byng winner.

Maurice Richard of Montreal missed 28 games with a fractured ankle and was virtually useless to the Canadiens in the playoffs. But his loss made little difference to the Montreal powerhouse. The Canadiens eliminated Chicago in six games and ousted Toronto, which had eliminated Boston, in five games for an unprecedented fourth consecutive Stanley Cup.

1958–59

FINAL STANDINGS

	W	L	T	PTS	GF	GA
Montreal	39	18	13	91	258	158
Boston	32	29	9	73	205	215

Chicago	28	29	13	69	197	208
Toronto	27	32	11	65	189	201
New York	26	32	12	64	201	217
Detroit	25	37	8	58	167	218

LEADING SCORERS

	G	A	PTS
Moore, Montreal	41	55	96
Beliveau, Montreal	45	46	91
Bathgate, New York	40	48	88
Howe, Detroit	32	46	78
Litzenberger, Chicago	33	44	77
Geoffrion, Montreal	22	44	66
Sullivan, New York	21	42	63
Hebenton, New York	33	29	62
McKenney, Boston	32	30	62
Sloan, Chicago	27	35	62

LEADING GOALIES

	G	GA	SO	GAA
Plante, Montreal	67	144	9	2.15
Bower, Toronto	39	107	3	2.74
Hall, Chicago	70	208	1	2.97
Worsley, New York	67	205	2	3.06
Sawchuk, Detroit	67	209	5	3.12

PLAYOFF RESULTS

Semifinals

Montreal d. Chicago, 4–2
Toronto d. Boston, 4–3

Finals

Montreal d. Toronto, 4–1

LEADING SCORERS

	G	A	PTS
Moore, Montreal	5	12	17
Bonin, Montreal	10	5	15
Ehman, Toronto	6	7	13
Richard, Montreal	5	8	13

LEADING GOALIES

	W	SO	GAA
Plante, Montreal	8	0	2.51
Lumley, Boston	3	0	2.85
Bower, Toronto	5	0	3.14

1959–60

The pressures of modern hockey had taken their toll on goaltenders. There was Montreal's Bill Durnan, who retired prematurely because of nerves; Montreal's Gerry McNeil, another early retiree, and Terry Sawchuk, who left Boston in midseason when he began seeing too much rub-

Montreal's Jean Beliveau (4) makes one of his league-leading 45 goals against Toronto's Johnny Bower in 1958–59.

ber. Montreal's Jacques Plante was determined not to let that happen to him.

Plante had been using a mask in practice for two years after fracturing first one and then the other cheekbone during workouts. Jacques had approached coach Toe Blake about wearing the mask during a game but Blake would not allow it.

Then, on November 1, 1959, a shot by New York's Andy Bathgate crunched into Plante's profile, inflicting a gash that took seven stitches.

When Plante subsequently emerged from the dressing room carrying a mask, he looked like a creature from outer space. How could he follow the puck through the mask's tiny eye slits? The answer was that Plante somehow saw it. That night, he beat the Rangers, 3–1, for Montreal's eighth straight game without a loss. The Canadiens tacked 10 more on to that streak as fans around the league flocked to see the masked marvel at work.

Plante captured his fifth consecutive Vezina Trophy, but the All-Star goalie berth went to Chicago's Glenn Hall. Chicago's Bobby Hull won the scoring race in an exciting battle with Boston's Bronco Horvath. Hull finished with 39 goals and 81 points—one point more than Horvath—and was the left wing on the All-Star team.

Gordie Howe of Detroit was the All-Star right wing with Montreal's Jean Beliveau at center. The defensemen were Marcel Pronovost of Detroit and Doug Harvey of Montreal. Howe won the Hart Trophy as MVP, Don McKenney of Boston was the Lady Byng winner, Harvey took

The Rocket, Montreal's Maurice Richard, battles Chicago's Elmer (Moose) Vasko in 1959–60.

the Norris and Chicago's Bill Hay, who centered for Hull, won the Calder.

The Canadiens won their third straight regular-season title, beating Toronto by 13 points. Then Montreal eliminated Chicago in four games in the opening round of the playoffs, with Plante turning in shutouts in the last two.

The Maple Leafs, perhaps inspired by a pile of 1,250 dollar bills that coach Punch Imlach placed in the middle of the dressing room floor as a reminder of the difference between winning and losing, eliminated Detroit in six games.

But Montreal swept past Toronto in the finals in four straight games to win the Stanley Cup in the minimum of eight games.

1959–60

FINAL STANDINGS

	W	L	T	PTS	GF	GA
Montreal	40	18	12	92	255	178
Toronto	35	26	9	79	199	195
Chicago	28	29	13	69	191	180
Detroit	26	29	15	67	186	197
Boston	28	34	8	64	220	241
New York	17	38	15	49	187	247

LEADING SCORERS

	G	A	PTS
Hull, Chicago	39	42	81
Horvath, Boston	39	41	80
Beliveau, Montreal	34	40	74
Bathgate, New York	26	48	74
H. Richard, Montreal	30	43	73
Howe, Detroit	28	45	73
Geoffrion, Montreal	30	41	71
McKenney, Boston	20	49	69
Stasiuk, Boston	29	39	68
Prentice, New York	32	34	66

LEADING GOALIES

	G	GA	SO	GAA
Plante, Montreal	69	175	3	2.54
Hall, Chicago	70	180	6	2.57
Sawchuk, Detroit	58	156	5	2.69
Bower, Toronto	66	180	5	2.73
Lumley, Boston	42	147	2	3.50

PLAYOFF RESULTS

Semifinals

Montreal d. Chicago, 4–0
Toronto d. Detroit, 4–2

Finals

Montreal d. Toronto, 4–0

LEADING SCORERS

	G	A	PTS
Richard, Montreal	3	9	12
Geoffrion, Montreal	2	10	12
Kelly, Detroit	3	8	11

LEADING GOALIES

	W	SO	GAA
Plante, Montreal	8	3	1.35
Bower, Toronto	4	0	2.88
Sawchuk, Detroit	2	0	2.96

1960–61

An era came to an end in 1960 when Montreal's Maurice Richard retired. After 18 professional seasons and 544 goals, the Rocket was off the ice. But that didn't keep his name out of the hockey headlines.

That was because for the first time since 1953, when Gordie Howe scored 49 times, there was a genuine threat to Richard's record of 50 goals in a season. It would be more correct to say there were two threats, but Frank Mahovlich's early-season pace obscured Bernie Geoffrion's run at Richard's mark.

By midseason, Mahovlich, Toronto's hard-skating left wing, had 37 goals and seemed a cinch to top 50. Geoffrion, on the other hand, missed six games with injuries and had only 29 goals going into the final six weeks of the season. And 14 of those had come over one 11-game stretch.

The defenses keyed on Mahovlich over those final weeks and Toronto's Big M finished with 48 goals. Geoffrion, a streaky player, hit another hot spell, exploding for 18 goals in 13 games and scoring his 50th of the season in the Canadiens' 68th game—ironically against Mahovlich's team, the Maple Leafs.

Geoffrion did not score in either of the last two games of the regular season, but won the scoring title with his 50 goals and 45 assists for 95 points. He was the All-Star right wing with Mahovlich at left wing and Jean Beliveau of Montreal at center. The defensemen were Doug Harvey of Montreal and Marcel Pronovost of Detroit, with Toronto's Johnny Bower in goal.

Bower ended Jacques Plante's five-year hold on the Vezina Trophy while Geoffrion earned the Hart Trophy and Harvey won the Norris for the sixth time. Dave Keon of Toronto was the Calder

Toronto's Ron Stewart attempts to bunt the puck past Chicago's Glenn Hall.

winner and Red Kelly, switched from defense to center after being traded to Toronto, won his fourth Lady Byng.

The Canadiens captured their fourth straight regular-season championship, beating out Toron-to by two points. And Montreal was favored to continue its string of five consecutive Stanley Cups when it opened the playoffs against third-place Chicago.

But the Blackhawks intimidated the Canadi-

ens with some tough body work and got consecutive shutouts from goalie Glenn Hall in the fifth and sixth games to beat Montreal, four games to two. The turning point may have come in the third game, won in triple overtime by Chicago on Murray Balfour's goal. Montreal coach Toe Blake was so incensed at the officiating of Dalton McArthur that he rushed on the ice and took a swing at the referee. That sortie cost Toe $2,000.

Detroit knocked out Toronto in five games, setting up the final for the Stanley Cup between the third-place Blackhawks and fourth-place Red Wings. Unflattering remarks about the officiating cost coach Rudy Pilous and general manager Tommy Ivan of the Blackhawks $500 between them but the fines didn't hurt too much because Chicago took the Cup in six games.

1960–61

FINAL STANDINGS

	W	L	T	PTS	GF	GA
Montreal	41	19	10	92	254	188
Toronto	39	19	12	90	234	176
Chicago	29	24	17	75	198	180
Detroit	25	29	16	66	195	215
New York	22	38	10	54	204	248
Boston	15	42	13	43	176	254

LEADING SCORERS

	G	A	PTS
Geoffrion, Montreal	50	45	95
Beliveau, Montreal	32	58	90
Mahovlich, Toronto	48	36	84
Bathgate, New York	29	48	77
Howe, Detroit	23	49	72
Ullman, Detroit	28	42	70
Kelly, Toronto	20	50	70
Moore, Montreal	35	34	69
H. Richard, Montreal	24	44	68
Delvecchio, Detroit	27	35	62

LEADING GOALIES

	G	GA	SO	GAA
Bower, Toronto	58	145	2	2.50
Hall, Chicago	70	180	6	2.57
Plante, Montreal	40	112	2	2.80
Bassen, Detroit	35	102	0	2.97
Sawchuk, Detroit	36	113	2	3.17

PLAYOFF RESULTS

Semifinals

Chicago d. Montreal, 4–2
Detroit d. Toronto, 4–1

Finals

Chicago d. Detroit, 4–2

LEADING SCORERS

	G	A	PTS
Howe, Detroit	4	11	15
Pilote, Chicago	3	12	15
Hull, Chicago	4	10	14

LEADING GOALIES

	W	SO	GAA
Hall, Chicago	8	2	2.10
Sawchuk, Detroit	5	1	2.32
Bassen, Detroit	1	0	2.45

1961–62

In August, the Hockey Hall of Fame erected on the Canadian National Exhibition grounds at Toronto, was officially opened. Built at a cost of $500,000, the hockey shrine honored 89 players, executives and referees from hockey's past.

But it was a player very much of the present who created the excitement: Chicago's blond bombshell, Bobby Hull. A scoring champion two years earlier at the age of 21, Hull boasted a slap shot clocked at better than 100 miles per hour.

Hull started his record run slowly and had only 16 goals after 40 games. But then, like Geoffrion had done the year before, when he tied Maurice Richard's record of 50 goals, Bobby went on a tear. Fourteen goals in nine games, including four in one night, left him 20 goals away from the record with 20 games to play. He needed an average of one goal per game and he got them. He was blanked in only four of the Hawks' final 20 games but made up for those scoreless nights with four two-goal games. He scored his 50th on the final night of the season in New York.

His 84 points gave Hull a tie for the scoring championship with New York's Andy Bathgate. Both received $1,000 from the league but Hull took the Art Ross Trophy emblematic of the scoring title because he had 22 more goals.

New York, led by Bathgate and player-coach Doug Harvey, acquired from Montreal in a trade for defensemen Lou Fontinato, made it to the playoffs for the first time in four seasons, barely beating out Detroit. A goal on a penalty shot by Bathgate against the Red Wings in New York virtually clinched the spot for New York. In the same game, Gordie Howe, killing a Detroit penalty, scored the 500th regular-season goal of his NHL career.

Bathgate was chosen at right wing on the All-Star team and Hull at left wing. The center was slender Stan Mikita of Chicago, who finished the season with 77 points, tied for third with Howe behind Hull and Bathgate. Jean Guy Talbot of Montreal and Harvey were picked on defense and Montreal's Jacques Plante in goal. It was the 10th time in 11 years that Harvey had been selected as a first-team All-Star defensemen. In the other year he made the second team.

Harvey took his seventh Norris Trophy while Plante captured the Hart Trophy as well as his sixth Vezina. The Calder Trophy went to Montreal's Bobby Rousseau and Toronto's Dave Keon took the Lady Byng.

Montreal captured its fifth straight regular-season title, but again the Canadiens went up against the rambunctious Blackhawks in the playoffs. Montreal, playing at home, won the first two games, but Chicago rebounded to take four straight games with Mikita and Hull the key men.

Toronto eliminated New York in six games, winning the pivotal fifth one in double overtime on Red Kelly's goal despite a superb performance by New York goalie Gump Worsley, who stopped 56 shots.

The Leafs went on to win the Stanley Cup in six games against Chicago, the series turning on an 8–4 romp in the fifth game in which Toronto's Bob Pulford scored three goals.

Montreal's Jacques Plante, turning away a shot by Detroit's Parker MacDonald, wound up the 1961–62 season with his sixth Vezina Trophy.

1961–62

FINAL STANDINGS

	W	L	T	PTS	GF	GA
Montreal	42	14	14	98	259	166
Toronto	37	22	11	85	232	180
Chicago	31	26	13	75	217	186
New York	26	32	12	64	195	207
Detroit	23	33	14	60	184	219
Boston	15	47	8	38	177	306

LEADING SCORERS

	G	A	PTS
Hull, Chicago	50	34	84
Bathgate, New York	28	56	84
Howe, Detroit	33	44	77
Mikita, Chicago	25	52	77
Mahovlich, Toronto	33	38	71
Delvecchio, Detroit	26	43	69
Backstrom, Montreal	27	38	65
Ullman, Detroit	26	38	64
Hay, Chicago	11	52	63
Provost, Montreal	33	29	62

LEADING GOALIES

	G	GA	SO	GAA
Plante, Montreal	70	166	4	2.37
Bower, Toronto	59	152	2	2.58
Hall, Chicago	70	186	9	2.65
Worsley, New York	60	174	2	2.90
Sawchuk, Detroit	43	143	5	3.32

PLAYOFF RESULTS

Semifinals

Toronto d. N.Y. Rangers, 4–2
Chicago d. Montreal, 4–2

Finals

Toronto d. Chicago, 4–2

LEADING SCORERS

	G	A	PTS
Mikita, Chicago	6	15	21
Horton, Toronto	3	13	16
Hull, Chicago	8	6	14

LEADING GOALIES

	W	SO	GAA
Bower, Toronto	6	0	2.28
Hall, Chicago	6	2	2.58
Simmons, Toronto	2	0	2.91

1962–63

Punch Imlach, coach of the Toronto Maple Leafs, was tired of playing bridesmaid to Montreal's bride. For three straight seasons Imlach had finished second behind the Canadiens. It wasn't Imlach's idea of success.

Punch realized he had to strengthen his defense and he decided the man who could do it was a youngster named Kent Douglas, who was playing at Springfield in the American League. Owner Eddie Shore, himself a former defenseman of considerable repute, demanded a high price. It cost Imlach five players to get Douglas in a Leaf uniform but the move paid off. Douglas became the first defenseman to win the Calder Trophy as the outstanding rookie. And the Maple Leafs put on a late surge to catch Chicago and win the regular-season title. Toronto finished one point ahead of the Blackhawks in the NHL's closest race in years. Only five points separated the Leafs in first place and Detroit in fourth.

Gordie Howe of Detroit won his sixth scoring championship with 38 goals and 86 points. Howe was also the MVP and right wing on the All-Star team. The other All-Stars were Toronto's Frank Mahovlich on left wing, Chicago's Stan Mikita at center, Pierre Pilote of Chicago and Carl Brewer of Toronto on defense and Glenn Hall of Chicago in goal.

Hall won the Vezina Trophy but had his iron-man streak of consecutive regular-season games ended at 502 when a back ailment forced him out of a game in early November. It was the first game Hall had missed since coming into the league in 1954.

In Detroit, Jack Adams ended 35 years of association with the Red Wings to become president of the Central Hockey League, where the NHL clubs had some of their most promising players developing.

But Adams' absence didn't bother Detroit fans. They were too fascinated by Howe's scoring heroics and the antics of defenseman Howie Young, who accumulated an unbelievable record 273 minutes in penalties—the equivalent of more than 4½ games.

The Red Wings kept their rooters happy in the opening round of the playoffs, eliminating Chicago in six games. Even the individual heroics of Bobby Hull, who scored eight goals despite a lame shoulder, a broken nose and a 10-stitch cut on his face, couldn't save the Blackhawks.

Montreal, weakened by late-season injuries to defensemen Lou Fontinato and Tom Johnson, bowed to Toronto in five games. Then the Maple

Leafs took Detroit in five to win the Stanley Cup for the second straight year.

1962–63

FINAL STANDINGS

	W	L	T	PTS	GF	GA
Toronto	35	23	12	82	221	180
Chicago	32	21	17	81	194	178
Montreal	28	19	23	79	225	183
Detroit	32	25	13	77	200	194
New York	22	36	12	56	211	233
Boston	14	39	17	45	198	281

LEADING SCORERS

	G	A	PTS
Howe, Detroit	38	48	86
Bathgate, New York	35	46	81
Mikita, Chicago	31	45	76
Mahovlich, Toronto	36	37	73
Richard, Montreal	23	50	73
Beliveau, Montreal	18	49	67
Bucyk, Boston	27	39	66
Delvecchio, Detroit	20	44	64
B. Hull, Chicago	31	31	62
Oliver, Boston	22	40	62

LEADING GOALIES

	G	GA	SO	GAA
Plante, Montreal	56	138	5	2.46
Sawchuk, Detroit	48	119	3	2.48
Hall, Chicago	66	166	5	2.51
Bower, Toronto	42	110	1	2.62
Worsley, New York	67	219	2	3.27

PLAYOFF RESULTS

Semifinals

Toronto d. Montreal, 4–1
Detroit d. Chicago, 4–2

Finals

Toronto d. Detroit, 4–1

LEADING SCORERS

	G	A	PTS
Howe, Detroit	7	9	16
Ullman, Detroit	4	12	16
Keon, Toronto	7	5	12

LEADING GOALIES

	W	SO	GAA
Bower, Toronto	8	2	1.60
Plante, Montreal	1	0	2.80
Sawchuk, Detroit	5	0	3.27

1963–64

Detroit's Gordie Howe entered his 19th NHL season with 540 goals—just four away from the career record held by his great rival, Montreal's Maurice Richard. Howe and the other Red Wings were affected by the record as his teammates continually sought to set him up, often ignoring their own scoring chances.

On October 27, playing in Detroit's Olympia Stadium against Richard's old team, the Canadiens, Howe tied the record at 544. The goal came despite tenacious checking by Montreal's Gilles Tremblay, who held Howe to two shots on goal all night. Defenseman Bill Gadsby earned his 400th NHL assist on Howe's historic goal.

Now, with his 544th in the books, Howe went for the record-breaker. Again the tension gripped both him and his teammates every time he took the ice. Finally, after two weeks of frustration, the break came. On November 10 at Detroit, Howe was killing a penalty against Montreal when he and Bill McNeill broke into Canadiens' ice. Gadsby flashed up the left side to make it a three-man rush and Howe fired the record-breaker.

"I knew he would get it," conceded Richard after Howe had shattered his record. "He's a great player. How about that, scoring both goals [his 544th and 545th] against my old team!"

Like his record of 50 goals in 50 games, however, Richard could point out that it took him 978 games to reach 544, while Howe needed 1,132 games to achieve 545.

Chicago teammates Bobby Hull and Stan Mikita staged an exciting battle in the scoring race. Hull's booming shot produced a league-leading 43 goals, four more than Mikita. But Mikita had 50 assists and 89 points to win the scoring championship.

For the second straight year the Blackhawks finished one point away from first place, this time behind Montreal. Many Chicago observers thought back to 1927 and the curse Pete Muldoon was alleged to have put on Chicago when he was fired as coach.

The Hawks dominated the All-Star balloting with Mikita, Hull and Ken Wharram named up front along with teammates Pierre Pilote on defense and Glenn Hall in goal. It was only the second time in history that one team had placed five men on the first All-Star squad. The only non-

Concentration is the key for Montreal's Jean Beliveau as he faces off against the Rangers' Lou Angotti in 1963–64.

Blackhawk chosen was defenseman Tim Horton of Toronto.

Montreal's Jean Beliveau won the Hart Trophy, Wharram of Chicago took the Lady Byng, Pilote won the Norris, Jacques Laperriere of Montreal captured the Calder and Charlie Hodge of Montreal, who took over when Jacques Plante was traded to New York, won the Vezina.

In February, Punch Imlach pulled off another major trade, dealing five players to New York for Andy Bathgate and Don McKenney. Eventually, the trade worked out in the Rangers' favor but its immediate effect was to help the Maple Leafs to their third straight Stanley Cup.

Bathgate and McKenney combined for nine goals and 12 assists between them as the Leafs eliminated Montreal in seven games and won the Cup in seven against Detroit.

1963–64

FINAL STANDINGS

	W	L	T	PTS	GF	GA
Montreal	36	21	13	85	209	167
Chicago	36	22	12	84	218	169
Toronto	33	25	12	78	192	172
Detroit	30	29	11	71	191	204
New York	22	38	10	54	186	242
Boston	18	40	12	48	170	212

LEADING SCORERS

	G	A	PTS
Mikita, Chicago	39	50	89
B. Hull, Chicago	43	44	87
Beliveau, Montreal	28	50	78
Bathgate, New York-Toronto	19	58	77
Howe, Detroit	26	47	73
Wharram, Chicago	39	32	71
Oliver, Boston	24	44	68
Goyette, New York	24	41	65
Gilbert, New York	24	40	64
Keon, Toronto	23	37	60

LEADING GOALIES

	G	GA	SO	GAA
Bower, Toronto	50	106	5	2.12
Hodge, Montreal	62	140	8	2.26
Hall, Chicago	65	148	7	2.30
Sawchuk, Detroit	53	138	5	2.70
Johnston, Boston	70	211	6	3.01

PLAYOFF RESULTS

Semifinals

Toronto d. Detroit, 4–3
Detroit d. Chicago, 4–3

Finals

Toronto d. Detroit, 4–3

LEADING SCORERS

	G	A	PTS
Howe, Detroit	9	10	19
Ullman, Detroit	7	10	17
Mahovlich, Toronto	4	11	15

LEADING GOALIES

	W	SO	GAA
Bower, Toronto	8	2	2.12
Hodge, Montreal	3	1	2.29
Sawchuk, Detroit	6	1	2.75

1964–65

NHL teams made two important front-office changes in 1964–65. First, in Montreal, Frank Selke retired as managing director of the Canadiens and was succeeded by Sammy Pollock, an organization man who had worked his way up through the Canadiens' vast network of farm teams. And in New York, Emile Francis succeeded Muzz Patrick as general manager of the Rangers. Francis, a journeyman goaltender in his playing days, had spent five years tutoring the top Ranger junior prospects at the club's Guelph, Ontario, farm. Included among his students were Rod Gilbert and Jean Ratelle, two developing Ranger stars.

Detroit, fed up with the penalty-drawing antics of Howie Young, had traded the defenseman to Chicago for a minor-league goalie named Roger Crozier. The Red Wings, anxious to protect the young prospect, exposed veteran Terry Sawchuk to the draft, thinking his age, 34, would deter any claim. But Punch Imlach, who had remarkable success with elderly players at Toronto, most notably goalie Johnny Bower, claimed Sawchuk. That made Crozier the Red Wings' regular goalie and he didn't disappoint.

A shrimp at 5-foot-8 and 160 pounds, Crozier displayed remarkable reflexes. He sprung at shots as though his life depended on them. It may have been a carryover from his childhood. He was one of 14 children and that can cause plenty of scrambling.

Crozier's 2.42 goals-against average earned him the Calder Trophy and a berth on the All-Star team. And, combined with the goal-scoring of Norm Ullman, Alex Delvecchio and Gordie Howe, Crozier's performance led Detroit to its first regular-season title since 1957. Ullman scored 42 goals and

finished second in the scoring race behind Chicago's Stan Mikita, who had 87 points. Howe had 29 goals and 76 points—third in the scoring race—and Delvecchio posted 25 goals and 67 points.

Ullman was the All-Star center, beating out Mikita. Chicago's Bobby Hull was picked at left wing and Claude Provost of Montreal at right wing. The defensemen were Pierre Pilote of Chicago and Jacques Laperriere of Montreal, with Crozier in goal.

Toronto's goaltending was split down the middle with Bower playing 34 games and Sawchuk 36. When the Maple Leafs finished with the fewest goals scored against them, the goalies refused to accept the Vezina Trophy unless both their names were inscribed on it and unless both received an equal cash award. The league agreed

and the two-goalie system became a permanent part of the Vezina award.

Chicago's Hull won both the Lady Byng and the Hart Trophy—the first man to take the two awards in the same year since the Rangers' Buddy O'Connor in 1947–48. Pierre Pilote was the Norris winner for the third straight season.

Hull, who had 37 goals in his first 35 games, fell victim to injuries and the worst slump of his career and finished with 39 goals for the season. But Bobby exploded during the playoffs, scoring eight goals in the seven-game semifinal victory over Detroit. The Hawks won the sixth and seventh games to take the series.

But the Canadiens, who had survived a brutal warlike series to eliminate Toronto in the semifi-

Ted Lindsay of Detroit scores the final goal of his career, No. 379, against Boston's Jack Norris, in the spring of 1965.

nals, silenced Hull in the finals. Hull scored only two goals as Montreal whipped Chicago in seven games to win the Stanley Cup. Gump Worsley's seventh-game shutout clinched it.

A new award, the Conn Smythe Trophy, honoring the outstanding player of the playoffs, went to Montreal captain Jean Beliveau, who scored eight goals in 13 playoff games.

1964–65

FINAL STANDINGS

	W	L	T	PTS	GF	GA
Detroit	40	23	7	87	224	175
Montreal	36	23	11	83	211	185
Chicago	34	28	8	76	224	176
Toronto	30	26	14	74	204	173
New York	20	38	12	52	179	246
Boston	21	43	6	48	166	253

LEADING SCORERS

	G	A	PTS
Mikita, Chicago	28	59	87
Ullman, Detroit	42	41	83
Howe, Detroit	29	47	76
B. Hull, Chicago	39	32	71
Delvecchio, Detroit	25	42	67
Provost, Montreal	27	37	64
Gilbert, New York	25	36	61
Pilote, Chicago	14	45	59
Bucyk, Boston	26	29	55
Backstrom, Montreal	25	30	55
Esposito, Chicago	23	32	55

LEADING GOALIES

	G	GA	SO	GAA
Crozier, Detroit	70	168	6	2.42
Hall, Chicago	41	99	4	2.43
Sawchuk, Detroit	36	92	1	2.56
Hodge, Montreal	52	135	3	2.60
Johnston, Boston	47	163	3	3.47

PLAYOFF RESULTS

Semifinals

Chicago d. Detroit, 4–3
Montreal d. Toronto, 4–2

Finals

Montreal d. Chicago, 4–3

LEADING SCORERS

	G	A	PTS
Hull, Chicago	10	7	17
Beliveau, Montreal	8	8	16
Rousseau, Montreal	5	8	13

LEADING GOALIES

	W	SO	GAA
Worsley, Montreal	5	2	1.68
Hodge, Montreal	3	1	2.00
Hall, Chicago	7	1	2.21

1965–66

In response to considerable pressure to expand the size of the league, the NHL decided in October 1965 to add six new teams by 1967. Four months later, franchises were awarded to Los Angeles, Oakland, Minneapolis-St. Paul, Pittsburgh, and Philadelphia. A sixth franchise was granted to St. Louis in April. The cost of joining the league would be $2 million per team.

On the ice, Bobby Hull of the Blackhawks made the big noise again. For years Hull had threatened the 50-goal mark he shared with Maurice Richard and Bernie Geoffrion. But something always stalled his drive. This time, nothing could stop him.

Hull opened the season with two hat tricks in the first week and had 15 goals in 11 games. A pair of four-goal games and three straight two-goal nights kept him on target. Hull had 44 goals in 45 games—a fantastic goal-per-game average. He hit the magic 50 mark in Chicago's 57th game. Then, he and the Hawks, feeling the record pressure, went scoreless for three games. Finally, on March 12 in Chicago, Hull scored No. 51 against New York goalie Cesare Maniago, setting off a 7½ minute demonstration by ecstatic Chicago fans. Ironically, Maniago, then playing for Toronto, had been the victim of Bernie Geoffrion's record—tying 50th goal in 1961.

Hull finished with 54 goals and a record 97 points, winning the Hart Trophy and the left wing spot on the All-Star team for the fifth time. Detroit's Gordie Howe was picked at right wing for the ninth time and Chicago's Stan Mikita made it at center for the fourth time. Jacques Laperriere of Montreal and Pierre Pilote of Chicago were the defensemen, Pilote for the fourth straight year. Chicago's "Mr. Goalie," Glenn Hall, made the team for the sixth time.

Detroit's Alex Delvecchio won the Lady Byng Trophy, Brit Selby of Toronto took the Calder and Laperriere broke Pilote's three-year grip on the Norris. The Vezina went to Montreal goalies Gump Worsley and Charlie Hodge.

The Blackhawks, led by Hull, made another run at the top but again fell short, finishing eight points behind Montreal. Toronto was third and

Chicago's Bobby Hull strikes back at one of his defensive shadows, Boston's Ed Westfall.

Detroit, pennant winners the year before, slipped to fourth.

Montreal and Toronto seemed to declare war on each other in the opening round of the playoffs. Twenty-six penalties were doled out in the second game and that was topped by record totals of 35 penalties and 154 minutes in the next game. The fights were a standoff but the Canadiens won the hockey games, sweeping four straight.

Detroit eliminated the Blackhawks, four games to two, and when the Red Wings stung the Canadiens by winning the first two games of the final series in Montreal, it appeared that Red Wing defenseman Bill Gadsby, playing in his 20th and final season, might finally drink champagne from the Stanley Cup. But it was not to be. The Canadiens roared back with four straight victories to win their second consecutive Cup. However, Roger Crozier, Detroit's heroic goalie, was awarded the Conn Smythe Trophy as the outstanding player of the playoffs.

1965–66

FINAL STANDINGS

	W	L	T	PTS	GF	GA
Montreal	41	21	8	90	239	173
Chicago	37	25	8	82	240	187
Toronto	34	25	11	79	208	187
Detroit	31	27	12	74	221	194
Boston	21	43	6	48	174	275
New York	18	41	11	47	195	261

LEADING SCORERS

	G	A	PTS
B. Hull, Chicago	54	43	97
Mikita, Chicago	30	48	78
Rousseau, Montreal	30	48	78
Beliveau, Montreal	29	48	77
Howe, Detroit	29	46	75
Ullman, Detroit	31	41	72
Delvecchio, Detroit	31	38	69
Nevin, New York	29	33	62
Richard, Montreal	22	39	61
Oliver, Boston	18	42	60

LEADING GOALIES

	G	GA	SO	GAA
Bower, Toronto	35	75	3	2.25
Worsley, Montreal	51	114	2	2.36
Hall, Chicago	64	164	4	2.63
Crozier, Detroit	64	173	7	2.78
Giacomin, New York	36	128	0	3.66

PLAYOFF RESULTS

Semifinals

Montreal d. Toronto, 4–0
Detroit d. Chicago, 4–2

Finals

Montreal d. Detroit, 4–2

LEADING SCORERS

	G	A	PTS
Ullman, Detroit	6	9	15
Tremblay, Montreal	2	9	11
Delvecchio, Detroit	0	11	11

LEADING GOALIES

	W	SO	GAA
Worsley, Montreal	8	1	1.99
Crozier, Detroit	6	1	2.34
Sawchuk, Toronto	0	0	3.00

1966–67

The NHL celebrated its 50th anniversary season by signing a $3.5-million television contract with the Columbia Broadcasting System providing for Game-of-the-Week coverage.

After laboring for 40 years under the Curse of Muldoon, which had been cast by their first coach after he felt he was unjustly fired, the Chicago Blackhawks finally broke the spell and won their first NHL regular-season title.

The Hawks won convincingly, beating Montreal by 17 points. Bobby Hull reached the 50-goal plateau for the third time in his fabulous career, finishing with 52. But the scoring crown went to teammate Stan Mikita, who set a record with 62 assists and tied Hull's mark of 97 points in a season.

The surprise team of the year was the Rangers, who flirted with first place and could have finished as high as second going into the final weekend of the season. The key men were Rod Gilbert, Phil Goyette, goalie Ed Giacomin, who had been acquired from the minors for four players two seasons earlier, and Bernie Geoffrion, lured out of retirement by general manager-coach Emile Francis. Gilbert had 28 goals, Goyette's 49 assists were second only to Mikita, Giacomin was the All-Star goalie and Geoffrion contributed 17 goals on the ice and a winning spirit in the dressing room.

Joining Giacomin on the All-Star team were New York defenseman Harry Howell, a 15-year veteran enjoying his finest season, Chicago defenseman Pierre Pilote, picked for the fifth

Boston's Bobby Orr was the obvious choice as Rookie of the Year in 1966–67.

straight year, and three Blackhawk forwards—Hull, Mikita and Ken Wharram.

Mikita, the scoring champion, also won the Hart Trophy and the Lady Byng, becoming the first triple-crown winner in NHL history. Chicago goalies Glenn Hall and Denis DeJordy shared the Vezina Trophy while Howell won the Norris and 18-year-old Bobby Orr of Boston took the Calder.

The expansion teams were busily assembling front-office staffs to scout the established teams and their farm systems for the upcoming stocking draft. Philadelphia hired Bud Poile as general manager and Keith Allen as coach. Pittsburgh came up with Jack Riley as general manager and Red Sullivan as coach. Minnesota gave both jobs to Wren Blair and St. Louis did the same with Lynn Patrick. Oakland would give both posts to Bert Olmstead and Los Angeles would name Larry Regan as general manager and Red Kelly as coach.

In the playoffs, Montreal staged a five-goal third-period rally to wipe out a Ranger lead in the first game and then burst by the demoralized New Yorkers in four straight games. Terry Sawchuk, who had achieved a landmark with his 100th career shutout during the season, led Toronto past Chicago in six games and the Maple Leafs faced the Canadiens for the Cup.

Again, it was Sawchuk's sparkling goaltending and some opportunistic scoring by Jim Pappin, Pete Stemkowski, Bob Pulford and Dave Keon that pulled the Maple Leafs through. Toronto won its 11th Stanley Cup in six games with the Smythe Trophy going to Keon.

1966–67

FINAL STANDINGS

	W	L	T	PTS	GF	GA
Chicago	41	17	12	94	264	170
Montreal	32	25	13	77	202	188
Toronto	32	27	11	75	204	211
New York	30	28	12	72	188	189
Detroit	27	39	4	58	212	241
Boston	17	43	10	44	182	253

LEADING SCORERS

	G	A	PTS
Mikita, Chicago	35	62	97
B. Hull, Chicago	52	28	80
Ullman, Detroit	26	44	70
Wharram, Chicago	31	34	65
Howe, Detroit	25	40	65
Rousseau, Montreal	19	44	63
Esposito, Chicago	21	40	61
Goyette, New York	12	49	61
Mohns, Chicago	25	35	60
Richard, Montreal	21	34	55
Delvecchio, Detroit	17	38	55

LEADING GOALIES

	G	GA	SO	GAA
DeJordy, Chicago	44	104	4	2.46
Hodge, Montreal	37	88	3	2.57
Giacomin, New York	68	173	9	2.61
Sawchuk, Toronto	28	66	2	2.81
Crozier, Detroit	58	182	4	3.35

PLAYOFF RESULTS

Semifinals

Toronto d. Chicago, 4–2
Montreal d. N.Y. Rangers, 4–0

Finals

Toronto d. Montreal, 4–2

LEADING SCORERS

	G	A	PTS
Pappin, Toronto	7	8	15
Stemkowski, Toronto	5	8	13
Beliveau, Montreal	6	5	11
Pulford, Toronto	1	10	11

LEADING GOALIES

	W	SO	GAA
Worsley, Montreal	0	0	1.50
Bower, Toronto	2	1	1.64
Vachon, Montreal	6	0	2.38

5

COAST-TO-COAST

1967–1979

It was the most ambitious undertaking ever attempted by a major sport, and many predicted it wouldn't work. But the National Hockey League went ahead with its expansion program anyway, and in a span of 11 years grew from six to 17 teams.

The biggest increase came at the start of the 1967–68 season, when the league doubled in size to 12 franchises. For the first time, hockey became a coast-to-coast sport, as teams were placed in Los Angeles and Oakland. The four other new teams were also in the U.S.—Minnesota, Philadelphia, Pittsburgh, and St. Louis.

The Montreal Canadiens continued their championship tradition in the first two seasons of expansion play, but then a young defenseman named Bobby Orr and a sharpshooting center named Phil Esposito brought the Boston Bruins into the limelight, winning the Stanley Cup in two out of the next three seasons.

Teams were added in 1970 (Buffalo and Vancouver), 1972 (New York Islanders and Atlanta), and 1974 (Kansas City and Washington), bringing the league total to 18 teams.

The Philadelphia Flyers made league history when they became the first expansion team to win the Cup in 1973–74, but after another year at the top, the Flyers gave way to a restoration of the Canadiens' dynasty as Montreal, led by super-scorer Guy Lafleur and goalie Ken Dryden, won the Cup four years in a row.

Along the way, competition from the rival World Hockey Association sent players' salaries soaring; Clarence Campbell stepped down as NHL president after serving for 31 years, replaced in 1977 by John A. Ziegler Jr., and the league was pared to 17 teams when the franchises in Cleveland and Minnesota merged in 1978.

Terry Sawchuk of Los Angeles halts scoring attempt by the New York Rangers' Orland Kurtenbach in 1967–68.

1967–68

On June 6, 1967, the most ambitious expansion program in sports history became a reality. The league doubled in size with six new teams stocked with 20 players each drafted from the established teams, and added as the NHL's West Division. The six older clubs became the East Division and a 74-game schedule was adopted.

Some good names were available and chosen by the six new clubs. Goalie Glenn Hall went to the St. Louis Blues and goalie Terry Sawchuk to the Los Angeles Kings. The Pittsburgh Penguins came up with high-scoring Andy Bathgate. The first player drafted was forward Dave Balon, picked by the Minnesota North Stars. Defensemen Bob Baun and Kent Douglas both were selected by the San Francisco-Oakland entry, called the California Seals. The Philadelphia Flyers drafted goaltenders Doug Favell and Bernie Parent.

The first meeting between an established team and an expansion team came on opening night when the Montreal Canadiens nipped the Pittsburgh Penguins, 2–1, as Jean Beliveau scored the 400th goal of his career.

For the season, expansion clubs won 40 games, lost 86 and tied 18 against the established teams. Los Angeles, coached by Red Kelly, was 10–12–2 for the best West record against the East. Of the established teams, Toronto had the most trouble with the new division. The Maple Leafs were under .500 with a 10–11–3 record and that figured importantly in their tumble to fifth place—their first season out of the playoffs in a decade. New York enjoyed the best record against the West, 17–4–3, and this helped the Rangers to a second-place finish.

In midseason the California entry decided to shed its San Francisco image and was renamed the Oakland Seals. Of the six new teams, the Seals had the toughest time at the gate and there was repeated talk about a possible shift of the

Boston's Bobby Orr breaks his stick as he knocks the puck away from New York's Phil Goyette, 1967–68.

franchise to Vancouver, British Columbia. But the Seals remained in Oakland.

Both divisions produced exciting races. Montreal finished four points ahead of the charging Rangers. New York's attack was led by Rod Gilbert and Jean Ratelle, who had played hockey together since their childhood days in Montreal. Gilbert scored 29 goals and Ratelle 32. Gilbert had four goals one night at Montreal and set an NHL record with 16 shots on net in that game. Philadelphia edged Los Angeles by one point for the West crown but the big scorer in the division was Minnesota's Wayne Connelly, who had 35 goals.

Chicago's Stan Mikita captured his fourth scoring title in five seasons with 40 goals and 87 points and repeated as a triple trophy winner,

adding the Hart and Lady Byng to his scoring championship. Gump Worsley and Rogatien Vachon of Montreal shared the Vezina Trophy while Boston's Bobby Orr took the Norris and teammate Derek Sanderson won the Calder.

Worsley was the All-Star goalie with Orr and Toronto's Tim Horton on defense and Stan Mikita and Bobby Hull of Chicago and Detroit's Gordie Howe up front. Howe celebrated his 40th birthday on the final night of the season and finished with 39 goals, his highest total in 12 seasons. Hull had 44, his lowest total in three seasons.

The new Stanley Cup playoff format provided for intra-division playoffs involved the first four teams and then a Cup final between the survivors. In the East, Montreal breezed through

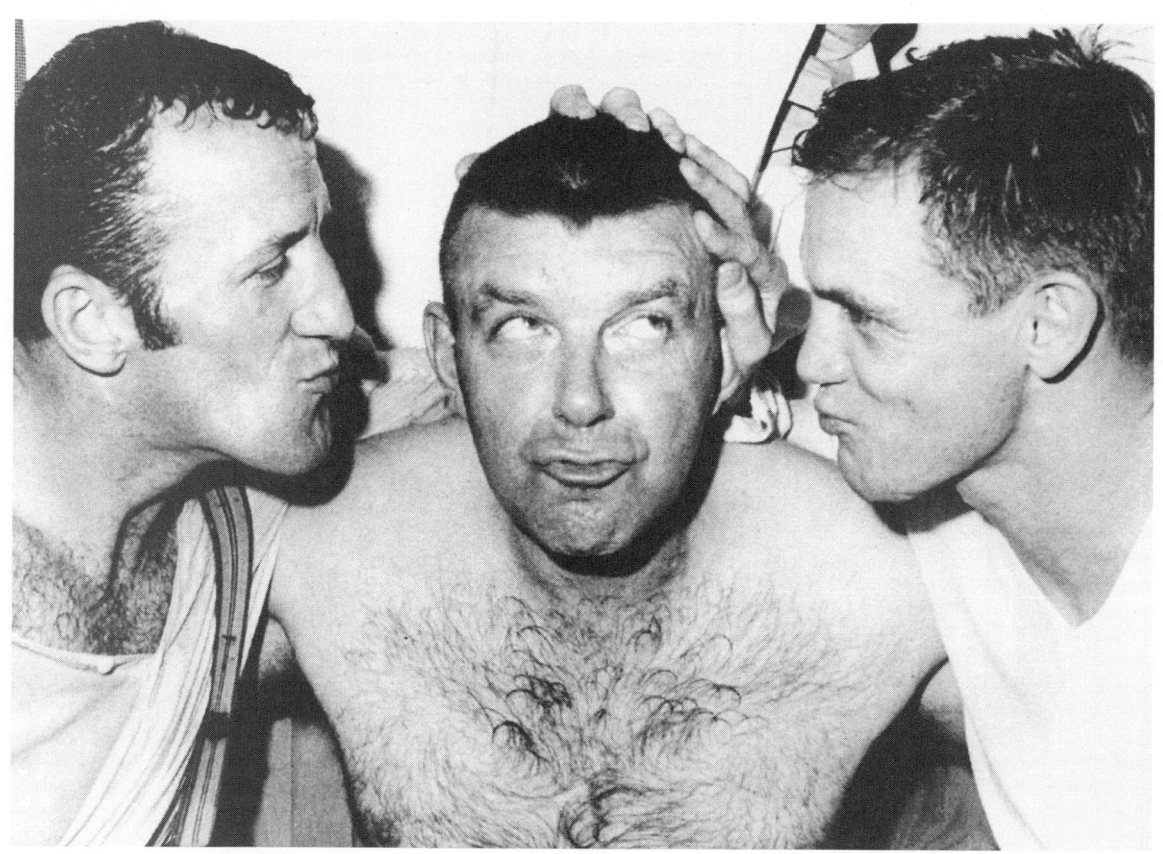

Gump Worsley is embraced by Lorne Pronovost (left) and Ralph Backstrom after the Canadiens swept the Bruins in the 1968 Stanley Cup playoffs en route to the championship.

Boston in four straight and then took Chicago in five after the Blackhawks had rallied from a two-game deficit to eliminate the Rangers. In the West, Minnesota and St. Louis emerged victorious in a pair of exciting seven-game series against Los Angeles and Philadelphia. Then the Blues struggled through seven games to beat off the North Stars.

In the finals, Montreal swept four straight games, winning the Cup. Twice the expansion Blues forced the Canadiens into overtime and each of the four games was decided by one goal. Glenn Hall, the St. Louis goalie, won the Smythe Trophy for his playoff performance.

"The expansion," NHL president Clarence Campbell said, "was successful beyond our fondest hopes."

It was a year of triumph and tragedy. The triumph was successfully doubling the size of the league. The tragedy was the death in January of Bill Masterton, a Minnesota forward, who struck his head on the ice after a collision and never regained consciousness. It was the first game-related fatality in NHL history.

1967–68
FINAL STANDINGS

East Division

	W	L	T	PTS	GF	GA
Montreal	42	22	10	94	236	167
New York	39	23	12	90	226	183
Boston	37	27	10	84	259	216
Chicago	32	26	16	80	212	222
Toronto	33	31	10	76	209	176
Detroit	27	35	12	66	245	257

Red Berenson of St. Louis scores the first of his six goals against the Philadelphia Flyers on November 7, 1968.

West Division

	W	L	T	PTS	GF	GA
Philadelphia	31	32	11	73	173	179
Los Angeles	31	33	10	72	200	224
St. Louis	27	31	16	70	177	191
Minnesota	27	32	15	69	191	226
Pittsburgh	27	34	13	67	195	216
Oakland	15	42	17	47	153	219

LEADING SCORERS

	G	A	PTS
Mikita, Chicago	40	47	87
Esposito, Boston	35	49	84
Howe, Detroit	39	43	82
Ratelle, New York	32	46	78
Gilbert, New York	29	48	77
B. Hull, Chicago	44	31	75
Ullman, Detroit-Toronto	35	37	72
Delvecchio, Detroit	22	48	70
Bucyk, Boston	30	39	69
Wharram, Chicago	27	42	69

LEADING GOALIES

	G	GA	SO	GAA
Worsley, Montreal	40	73	6	1.98
Bower, Toronto	43	84	4	2.25
Favell, Philadelphia	37	83	4	2.27
Giacomin, New York	66	160	8	2.44
Hall, St. Louis	49	118	5	2.48

PLAYOFF RESULTS

Quarterfinals

Montreal d. Boston, 4–0
Chicago d. N.Y. Rangers, 4–2
St. Louis d. Philadelphia, 4–3
Minnesota d. Los Angeles, 4–3

Semifinals

Montreal d. Chicago, 4–1
St. Louis d. Minnesota, 4–3

Finals

Montreal d. St. Louis, 4–0

LEADING SCORERS

	G	A	PTS
Goldsworthy, Minnesota	8	7	15
Marcetta, Minnesota	7	7	14
Moore, St. Louis	7	7	14
Cournoyer, Montreal	6	8	14

LEADING GOALIES

	W	SO	GAA
Parent, Philadelphia	2	0	1.35
Worsley, Montreal	11	1	1.88
Hall, St. Louis	8	1	2.43

1968–69

In his 23rd NHL season at the age of 40, Gordie Howe scored more points than he ever had before. Detroit's wonder man finished the season with an incredible 103 points, eight more than his previous high.

It was good enough for third place in the scoring race. That's because 1968–69 went down in NHL history as the year of the scorer, with records falling all around the league.

Chicago's Bobby Hull shattered the 50-goal plateau for the fourth time and pushed his own single season mark to an almost unbelievable 58 goals. He finished with 107 scoring points for second place in the scoring race.

The man of the year was Phil Esposito, a power-packing center, who set Boston and the NHL on its collective ear. Esposito, who had centered for Hull when Bobby scored 54 goals, shattered all scoring records with an amazing 126 points, including 49 goals.

Esposito, Hull, and Howe all soared past the 100-point mark, easily smashing the NHL single-season point record of 97 shared by Hull and teammate Stan Mikita. In fact, Mikita scored 97 points this year and was considered a disappointment to the Blackhawks.

The record-making wasn't confined to the established East Division teams either. In November, Red Berenson, a castoff, scored six goals for St. Louis, tying the single-game record set a quarter of a century earlier by Syd Howe of Detroit.

The St. Louis club, led by Berenson, raced to the West Division championship, winning it by a whopping 19 points. Jacques Plante, drafted from New York and lured out of retirement by the Blues, joined Glenn Hall in goal and the two veterans shared the Vezina Trophy for fewest goals allowed.

In the East, Montreal and Boston battled down to the final weekend before the Canadiens clinched first place for rookie coach Claude Ruel, who took over when Toe Blake retired.

The Canadiens and Bruins swept past New York and Toronto in four straight games as the Stanley Cup playoffs got underway. Then Montreal beat Boston in six games—three of the victories coming on overtime goals—to qualify for the Cup finals.

St. Louis shattered Philadelphia in four games and repeated the sweep against Los Angeles, which had ousted Oakland in seven. But in

the finals, the Blues were no match for Montreal. The powerful Canadiens swept to their 16th Stanley Cup in the minimum of four games, repeating their 1967–68 sweep of St. Louis.

Esposito, who led all playoff scorers with 18 points, won the Hart Trophy as MVP and was named center on the All-Star team. The other All-Stars were Hull and Howe, Boston's Bobby Orr, who broke all scoring records for defensemen with 21 goals, Toronto's Tim Horton, and St. Louis goalie Glenn Hall.

Orr won the Norris Trophy as the outstanding defenseman while Detroit's Alex Delvecchio took the Lady Byng and Danny Grant of the Minnesota North Stars won the Calder as Rookie of the Year.

1968–69

FINAL STANDINGS

East Division

	W	L	T	PTS	GF	GA
Montreal	46	19	11	103	271	202
Boston	42	18	16	100	303	221
New York	41	26	9	91	231	196
Toronto	35	26	15	85	234	217
Detroit	33	31	12	78	239	221
Chicago	34	33	9	77	280	246

West Division

	W	L	T	PTS	GF	GA
St. Louis	37	25	14	88	204	157
Oakland	29	36	11	69	219	251
Philadelphia	20	35	21	61	174	225
Los Angeles	24	42	10	58	185	260
Pittsburgh	20	45	11	51	189	252
Minnesota	18	43	15	51	189	270

LEADING SCORERS

	G	A	PTS
Esposito, Boston	49	77	126
B. Hull, Chicago	58	49	107
Howe, Detroit	44	59	103
Mikita, Chicago	30	67	97

The Esposito brothers go head-to-head: Boston's Phil against Chicago's Tony in 1969–70.

Hodge, Boston	45	45	90
Cournoyer, Montreal	43	44	87
Delvecchio, Detroit	25	58	83
Berenson, St. Louis	35	47	82
Beliveau, Montreal	33	49	82
Mahovlich, Detroit	49	29	78

LEADING GOALIES

	G	GA	SO	GAA
Hall, St. Louis	41	85	8	2.17
Edwards, Detroit	40	89	4	2.54
Giacomin, New York	70	175	7	2.56
Cheevers, Boston	52	145	3	2.80
Gamble, Toronto	61	161	3	2.80

PLAYOFF RESULTS

Quarterfinals

Montreal d. N.Y. Rangers, 4–0
Boston d. Toronto, 4–0
St. Louis d. Philadelphia, 4–0
Los Angeles d. California, 4–3

Semifinals

Montreal d. Boston, 4–2
St. Louis d. Los Angeles, 4–0

Finals

Montreal d. St. Louis, 4–0

LEADING SCORERS

	G	A	PTS
Esposito, Boston	8	10	18
Beliveau, Montreal	5	10	15
Duff, Montreal	8	6	14

LEADING GOALIES

	W	SO	GAA
Vachon, Montreal	7	1	1.42
Plante, St. Louis	8	3	1.43
Cheevers, Boston	6	3	1.68

1969–70

It had been 29 long, frustrating years between champagne sips out of the Stanley Cup for the Boston Bruins. But with a super player like Bobby Orr in the lineup, it was only a matter of time before the Bruins returned to the top. This was the year.

Orr shattered all scoring records for defensemen, exploding for 33 goals, 87 assists, and 120 points. He became the first defenseman in history to win the scoring title, only the fourth player ever to go over 100 points, and fell just six short of the record of 126 established by his teammate, Phil Esposito, the year before.

Esposito finished with 99 points for second place in the scoring race. But the family pride was protected by Phil's younger brother, Chicago's Tony, who won the Calder Trophy as Rookie of the Year and the Vezina as the Blackhawks al-

lowed fewer goals than any other team in the league.

Tony Esposito was drafted by Chicago from Montreal and took the league by storm. He turned in a record-breaking 15 shutouts and led the Hawks from a last-place finish in 1969 to first place in 1970. The East Division race was not decided until the final night of the season and then with some bizarre developments.

New York had led the East for 3½ months but wilted under an avalanche of injuries, dropping from the lead March 1. Boston and Chicago took over, battling head-to-head for the top spot. Meanwhile, New York, Detroit, and Montreal battled it out for the other three playoff berths.

In the West, St. Louis clinched its second consecutive title early and watched with interest as Philadelphia tied its way out of the playoffs. The Flyers set a record with 24 deadlocks and, although tied with Oakland in points, lost the final playoff spot in the West because the Seals had more victories.

The same thing happened in the East, where Boston and Chicago tied in points but the Blackhawks had more victories and were awarded first place. The Rangers beat out the Canadiens for fourth on the basis of more goals scored. The two teams finished with identical won-lost-tied marks and only a nine-goal binge on the final day allowed New York to make it.

Montreal's elimination ended a 22-year string of playoff appearances and marked the first time in history that no Canadian team was in the playoffs.

Boston captured the Cup, beating New York, Chicago, and St. Louis and winning the last 10 games in a row. St. Louis eliminated Minnesota and Pittsburgh before being swept out in the finals for the third straight year.

Orr became the first man in history to win four individual trophies in a single season, taking the Ross as scoring champ, the Norris as best defenseman, the Hart as regular-season MVP, and the Smythe as playoff MVP. Tony Esposito cap-

tured the Calder and Vezina and Phil Goyette of St. Louis won the Lady Byng.

The Esposito brothers made the All-Star team along with Gordie Howe of Detroit, Bobby Hull of Chicago, defensemen Brad Park of New York, and the incredible Orr.

1969–70

FINAL STANDINGS

East Division

	W	L	T	PTS	GF	GA
Chicago	45	22	9	99	250	170
Boston	40	17	19	99	277	216
Detroit	40	21	15	95	246	199
New York	38	22	16	92	246	189
Montreal	38	22	16	92	244	201
Toronto	29	34	13	71	222	242

West Division

	W	L	T	PTS	GF	GA
St. Louis	37	27	12	86	224	179
Pittsburgh	26	38	12	64	182	238
Minnesota	19	35	22	60	224	257
Oakland	22	40	14	58	169	243
Philadelphia	17	35	24	58	197	225
Los Angeles	14	52	10	38	168	290

LEADING SCORERS

	G	A	PTS
Orr, Boston	33	87	120
Esposito, Boston	43	56	99
Mikita, Chicago	39	47	86
Goyette, St. Louis	29	49	78
Tkaczuk, New York	27	50	77
Ratelle, New York	32	42	74
Berenson, St. Louis	33	39	72
Parise, Minnesota	24	48	72
Howe, Detroit	31	40	71
Mahovlich, Detroit	38	32	70
Balon, New York	33	37	70
McKenzie, Boston	29	41	70

LEADING GOALIES

	G	GA	SO	GAA
Esposito, Chicago	63	136	15	2.17
Giacomin, New York	70	163	6	2.36
Edwards, Detroit	47	116	2	2.59
Vachon, Montreal	64	162	4	2.63
Cheevers, Boston	41	108	4	2.72

PLAYOFF RESULTS

Quarterfinals

Chicago d. Detroit, 4–0
Boston d. N.Y. Rangers, 4–2
Pittsburgh d. Oakland, 4–0
St. Louis d. Minnesota, 4–2

Semifinals

Boston d. Chicago, 4–0
St. Louis d. Pittsburgh, 4–2

Finals

Boston d. St. Louis, 4–0

LEADING SCORERS

	G	A	PTS
Esposito, Boston	13	14	27
Orr, Boston	9	11	20
Bucyk, Boston	11	8	19

LEADING GOALIES

	W	SO	GAA
Plante, St. Louis	4	1	1.48
Binkley, Pittsburgh	5	0	2.10
Cheevers, Boston	12	0	2.23

1970–71

Goaltending has always been a tough way to earn a living but it never was tougher than during the 1970–71 season when the Boston Bruins assembled what may have been the greatest scoring machine in the history of hockey.

The cast was headed by Phil Esposito, the bull of a center who had set a single-season scoring record two years earlier when he totaled 126 points. Espo attacked his record with a vengeance and shattered it with an avalanche of goals and assists. He finished with 152 points, an all-time record that was split exactly down the middle with 76 goals and 76 assists. The 76 goals, a truly remarkable achievement, shattered Bobby Hull's old single-season record by 18.

Esposito thus became the fourth man in NHL history to soar past the 50-goal mark. Not long after he made it, teammate Johnny Bucyk also shot past 50, making the Bruins the first team ever to have two 50-goal scorers in the same season. Bucyk finished with 51 goals and 116 points but that total was only third in the NHL scoring race. Squeezed between scoring champion Esposito and Bucyk was Boston's fantastic defenseman, Bobby Orr, who totaled 139 points, 19 more than he had the year before when he won the scoring crown.

Fourth place in the scoring race belonged to another Bruin, Esposito's linemate, Ken Hodge, who also went over 100 points. Two more Boston players, Wayne Cashman and Johnny McKenzie, finished seventh and eighth, completing a remarkable Bruin domination of the league's top scorers.

Boston finished with a record 399 goals for the season, an average of better than five goals per game. With that kind of attack, it was no surprise that the Bruins zoomed to the East Division championship, losing only 14 games all season.

The West crown went to the Chicago Black-hawks, shifted to the expansion division in a re-alignment of teams when two new teams, Buffalo and Vancouver, were added to the East.

In the playoffs, defending champion Boston and its awesome scoring machine ranked as heavy favorites. But the Bruins ran into a hot goalie, Montreal rookie Ken Dryden, and the Canadiens eliminated Boston in seven games—a stunning first-round upset. Montreal then knocked off Minnesota to advance to the final round. Chicago eased its way past Philadelphia and then struggled in seven games, three of them stretching into overtime, before eliminating New York. That sent the Canadiens against the Black-hawks for the Cup and Montreal won it in a pul-sating seven-game showdown.

Dryden, who had played only six regular-sea-son games before the playoffs, emerged as the Canadiens' hero and won the Smythe Trophy as the Cup's MVP. The regular-season MVP was Orr, who also won his fourth straight Norris Tro-phy as the best defenseman. The Calder Trophy for Rookie of the Year went to Buffalo center Gilbert Perreault and the Lady Byng for clean play was awarded to Boston's Bucyk. Goalies Ed Giacomin and Gilles Villemure of the defensive-minded Rangers shared the Vezina Trophy as New York allowed fewer goals than any other team.

Esposito, Hodge, Bucyk, and Orr made the All-Star team along with Montreal defenseman J. C. Tremblay and Ranger goalie Giacomin.

The year was otherwise notable in that it was presumed to be the valedictory for two of the

Goaltender Ken Dryden had appeared in only six regular-season games before he led Montreal to the Stanley Cup in 1971.

NHL's greatest stars, Detroit's Gordie Howe and Montreal's Jean Beliveau. Howe scored 23 goals for a 25-year career total of 786. Beliveau scored 25, finishing his 18-year career with 507.

1970-71

FINAL STANDINGS

East Division

	W	L	T	PTS	GF	GA
Boston	57	14	7	121	399	207
New York	49	18	11	109	259	177
Montreal	42	23	13	97	291	216
Toronto	37	33	8	82	248	211
Buffalo	24	39	15	63	217	291
Vancouver	24	46	8	56	229	296
Detroit	22	45	11	55	209	308

West Division

	W	L	T	PTS	GF	GA
Chicago	49	20	9	107	277	184
St. Louis	34	25	19	87	223	208
Philadelphia	28	33	17	73	207	225
Minnesota	28	34	16	72	191	223
Los Angeles	25	40	13	63	239	303
Pittsburgh	21	37	20	62	221	240
California	20	53	5	45	199	320

LEADING SCORERS

	G	A	PTS
Esposito, Boston	76	76	152
Orr, Boston	37	102	139
Bucyk, Boston	51	65	116
Hodge, Boston	43	62	105
B. Hull, Chicago	44	52	96
Ullman, Toronto	34	51	85
Cashman, Boston	21	58	79
McKenzie, Boston	31	47	77
Keon, Toronto	38	38	76
Beliveau, Montreal	25	51	76
Stanfield, Boston	24	52	76

LEADING GOALIES

	G	GA	SO	GAA
Plante, Toronto	40	73	4	1.88
Giacomin, New York	45	95	8	2.15
Esposito, Chicago	57	126	6	2.27
Vachon, Montreal	47	118	2	2.64
Favell, Philadelphia	44	108	2	2.66

PLAYOFF RESULTS

Quarterfinals

Montreal d. Boston, 4–3
N.Y. Rangers d. Toronto, 4–2
Chicago d. Philadelphia, 4–0
Minnesota d. St. Louis, 4–2

Seminfinals

Montreal d. Minnesota, 4–2
Chicago d. N.Y. Rangers, 4–3

Finals

Montreal d. Chicago, 4–3

LEADING SCORERS

	G	A	PTS
Mahovlich, Montreal	14	13	27
Hull, Chicago	11	14	25
Cournoyer, Montreal	10	12	22
Beliveau, Montreal	6	16	22

LEADING GOALIES

	W	SO	GAA
Esposito, Chicago	11	2	2.19
Giacomin, N.Y. Rangers	7	0	2.21
Parent, Philadelphia	2	0	2.30

1971-72

There has always been considerable debate over whether there is more prestige for a team to win an NHL regular-season title or to capture the postseason Stanley Cup playoffs instead. Coming out on top of the six-month, 78-game regular-season grind is a test of staying power, but the tension and excitement of the playoffs for Lord Stanley's battered old mug have a way of stealing the thunder. People tend to remember the Stanley Cup champions longer.

The Boston Bruins solved this all very simply in 1971–72. They just won everything. Led by the scoring tandem of center Phil Esposito and defenseman Bobby Orr, the Bruins zoomed to a first-place finish in the East Division, finishing 10 points ahead of the New York Rangers and losing just 13 games, a record for the 78-game season. It was the second straight regular-season crown for the boisterous Bruins. But the season before, they had been submarined in the first round of the playoffs by Montreal. This time there was no Stanley Cup slip. Boston zipped to the Cup, losing only three of 15 postseason games.

Esposito and Orr finished 1–2 in the scoring race for the third straight season. Esposito won the title with 133 points, including 66 goals. Orr finished second with 117 points, including 37 goals, matching his total of the year before. Both made the All-Star team along with Ranger defenseman Brad Park, right wing Rod Gilbert of the Rangers, left wing Bobby Hull of Chicago, and Chicago goalie Tony Esposito.

The scoring title was the third in four years for Esposito, but he couldn't break the stranglehold Orr was establishing on the Hart Trophy as Most Valuable Player. Bobby won the MVP award for the third straight year and also took his fifth consecutive Norris Trophy as the league's finest defenseman. The Lady Byng Trophy for

clean and effective play went to Jean Ratelle of the New York Rangers, and Montreal's Ken Dryden, playoff hero a year earlier, took the Calder Trophy as Rookie of the Year. Dryden, despite his previous season's playoff heroics, was still eligible for the rookie award based on his limited regular-season duty the year before. Chicago's Tony Esposito and Gary Smith shared the Vezina Trophy as the Blackhawks achieved the league's best defensive record.

There was considerable talk around the hockey world about the establishment of another league to challenge the NHL. Most NHL officials shrugged off the talk as just that. But there was some scurrying around by the league's expansion committee and a quite sudden decision was made to add two new franchises for 1972–73. One would go to Long Island and the other to Atlanta. The development of the World Hockey Association and the establishment of those two new NHL franchises were linked. The key was a handsome new building on Long Island, the Nassau Veterans Memorial Coliseum. The WHA was eyeing the arena to house its New York team. But the NHL moved faster and placed a franchise in the building first. It was the first of many skirmishes between the two leagues.

1971-72

FINAL STANDINGS

East Division

	W	L	T	PTS	GF	GA
Boston	54	13	11	119	330	204
New York	48	17	13	109	317	192
Montreal	46	16	16	108	307	205
Toronto	33	31	14	80	209	208
Detroit	33	35	10	76	261	262
Buffalo	16	43	19	51	203	289
Vancouver	20	50	8	48	203	297

West Division

	W	L	T	PTS	GF	GA
Chicago	46	17	15	107	256	166
Minnesota	37	29	12	86	212	191
St. Louis	28	39	11	67	208	247
Pittsburgh	26	38	14	66	220	258
Philadelphia	26	38	14	66	200	236
California	21	39	18	60	216	288
Los Angeles	20	49	9	49	206	305

LEADING SCORERS

	G	A	PTS
Esposito, Boston	66	67	133
Orr, Boston	37	80	117
Ratelle, New York	46	63	109
Hadfield, New York	50	56	106
Gilbert, New York	43	54	97
F. Mahovlich, Montreal	43	53	96
B. Hull, Chicago	50	43	93
Cournoyer, Montreal	47	36	83
Bucyk, Boston	32	51	83
Clarke, Philadelphia	35	46	81
Lemaire, Montreal	32	49	81

LEADING GOALIES

	G	GA	SO	GAA
Esposito, Chicago	48	82	9	1.76
Dryden, Montreal	64	142	8	2.24
Cheevers, Boston	41	101	2	2.50
Parent, Toronto	47	116	3	2.56
Maniago, Minnesota	43	112	3	2.64

PLAYOFF RESULTS

Quarterfinals

Boston d. Toronto, 4–1
N.Y. Rangers d. Montreal, 4–2
Chicago d. Pittsburgh, 4–0.
St. Louis d. Minnesota, 4–3

Semifinals

N.Y. Rangers d. Chicago, 4–0
Boston d. St. Louis, 4–0

Finals

Boston d. N.Y. Rangers, 4–2

LEADING SCORERS

	G	A	PTS
Esposito, Boston	9	15	24
Orr, Boston	5	19	24
Bucyk, Boston	9	11	20

LEADING GOALIES

	W	SO	GAA
Smith, Chicago	1	1	1.50
Johnston, Boston	6	1	1.86
Worsley, Minnesota	2	1	2.16
Cheever, Boston	6	2	2.61

1972-73

The summer before the National Hockey League's 1972–73 season was unlike any the league had ever experienced. The offseason had always offered a serene time of recuperation for players and executives. But this summer, there was frenzied activity at all levels.

First, there was the matter of the World Hockey Association. The new league asserted itself with 12 franchises and stocked rosters by signing players whose NHL contracts were expiring. The lure of large bonuses and new challenges drew about 70 former NHL performers. The most important was Chicago star Bobby Hull, who signed a 10-year contract for $2.75 million with the new Winnipeg Jets. Hull received $1 million up front, an unprecedented bonus put together by all the franchises in the league. They knew how

Defensive play of young Brad Park, alongside Chicago's Dennis Hull here, helped the Rangers reach the Stanley Cup finals in 1972.

important an established star like Bobby would be to the new league.

Stung by the defections, the NHL went to court and sued. The legal steps prevented Hull and some others from playing early in the season but injunctions later permitted them to perform in the WHA.

While the WHA was sniping at the NHL on one front, the older league took on an internation-

Philadelphia center Bobby Clarke became the first player from the West Division to be named MVP in 1972–73.

al series against Russia's world champions, a long-awaited test of the best professionals against the best of the so-called amateurs. Many confident observers predicted an NHL sweep of the eight-game series as Team Canada (composed only of NHL players) began training in August. The first four games were to be played in early September in Canada starting in Montreal and then moving on to Toronto, Winnipeg, and Vancouver. The last four would be played in Moscow later in the month.

The Russians stunned the Canadians, winning two and tying another of the four games in Canada. When the series moved to Moscow, Team Canada finally pulled itself together and managed to win three times, taking the World Series of hockey by the barest of margins. Paul Henderson's goal in the final minute of the final game produced the deciding victory.

WHA defections hurt many NHL teams. The newly franchised New York Islanders, for example, lost seven of their 20 expansion draft choices to the new league and wound up setting an all-time futility record with 60 losses in their first season.

Montreal and Chicago won their division races and the Canadiens again captured the Stanley Cup, finishing off Chicago in six games. Boston's Phil Esposito captured his third straight scoring title and fourth in five years, leading the scorers with 130 points, including 55 goals.

Bobby Orr won the Norris Trophy as the NHL's best defenseman for a record sixth straight year. The Hart Trophy as Most Valuable Player went to Philadelphia's Bobby Clarke, a remarkable young center who became the first West Division player to take that award. Gil Perreault of Buffalo won the Lady Byng Trophy for clean and effective play, and the Calder Trophy as Rookie of the Year went to Steve Vickers of the New York Rangers.

Three Canadiens, goalie Ken Dryden, defenseman Guy Lapointe, and left winger Frank Mahovlich, made the All-Star team along with Orr on defense, Esposito at center, and Mickey Redmond of Detroit at right wing.

1972–73

FINAL STANDINGS

East Division

	W	L	T	PTS	GF	GA
Montreal	52	10	16	120	329	184
Boston	51	22	5	107	330	235
New York R.	47	23	8	102	297	208
Buffalo	37	27	14	88	257	219
Detroit	37	29	12	86	265	243
Toronto	27	41	10	64	247	279
Vancouver	22	47	9	53	233	339
New York I.	12	60	6	30	170	347

West Division

	W	L	T	PTS	GF	GA
Chicago	42	27	9	93	284	225
Philadelphia	37	30	11	85	296	256
Minnesota	37	30	11	85	254	230
St. Louis	32	34	12	76	233	251
Pittsburgh	32	37	9	73	257	265
Los Angeles	31	36	11	73	232	245
Atlanta	25	38	15	65	191	239
California	16	46	16	48	213	323

LEADING SCORERS

	G	A	PTS
Esposito, Boston	55	75	130
Clarke, Philadelphia	37	67	104
Orr, Boston	39	72	101
MacLeish, Philadelphia	50	50	100
Lemaire, Montreal	44	51	95
Ratelle, New York	41	53	94
Redmond, Detroit	52	41	93
Bucyk, Boston	40	53	93
F. Mahovlich, Montreal	38	55	93
Pappin, Chicago	41	51	92

LEADING GOALIES

	G	GA	SO	GAA
Dryden, Montreal	54	119	6	2.26
Esposito, Chicago	56	140	4	2.51
Edwards, Detroit	52	132	6	2.63
Crozier, Buffalo	49	121	3	2.76
Favell, Philadelphia	44	114	3	2.83

PLAYOFF RESULTS

Quarterfinals

Montreal d. Buffalo, 4–2
N.Y. Rangers d. Boston, 4–1
Chicago d. St. Louis, 4–1
Philadelphia d. Minnesota, 4–2

Semifinals

Montreal d. Philadelphia, 4–1
Chicago d. N.Y. Rangers, 4–1

Finals

Montreal d. Chicago, 4–2

LEADING SCORERS

	G	A	PTS
Cournoyer, Montreal	15	10	25
Hull, Chicago	9	15	24
Mahovlich, Montreal	9	14	23

LEADING GOALIES

	W	SO	GAA
Maniago, Minnesota	2	2	1.75
Giacomin, N.Y. Rangers	5	1	2.56
Dryden, Montreal	12	1	2.89
Esposito, Chicago	10	1	3.08

Ever since 1967, when the NHL orchestrated its most ambitious expansion program by doubling in size from six to 12 teams, the magic word had been parity. The lords of the NHL lived for the day when the expansion infants could compete on an even keel with the established teams. They longed to be able to say that on any given night, any team could beat any other team.

For a long time, that just wasn't so. The expansion teams always seemed a stride or two behind the established clubs. And on those rare occasions when a new club rose up to kayo one of its big brothers, the loss was considered a total disaster. The expansion teams were whipping boys. Parity was a dream for the distant future.

Then, in 1973–74, along came the Broad Street Bullies, alias Philadelphia Flyers. The team of tough guys was led by Bobby Clarke, a diabetic center with a choir-boy expression, and goalie Bernie Parent, who was the first NHL player to jump to the World Hockey Association, and also one of the first to jump back.

The Flyers lived by the coaching creed of scholarly looking Fred Shero, who often said, "If you can't beat 'em in the alley, you can't beat 'em on the ice." First Philadelphia would win the alley fight, then repeat on the ice. "We take the most direct route to the puck," philosophized Clarke, captain of the Bullies, "and we arrive in ill humor."

Most of the Flyers were acquired by general manager Keith Allen through clever trades. In one of his deals, Allen swapped goalie Parent to Toron-

The Penguins' Al Smith catches a face full of ice after making a save in the Stanley Cup playoffs against the Blues in 1970.

to to bring a forward named Rick MacLeish to Philadelphia. Parent studied for two seasons under his goaltending idol, Jacques Plante, then fled to the WHA. MacLeish, meanwhile, developed into a 50-goal scorer for the talented young Flyers.

When Parent grew disenchanted with the WHA, he let it be known that he wanted to return to the older league. Allen immediately swung a deal for his rights with Toronto and then signed the goalie to a multi-year contract with Philadelphia.

Back with the Flyers, Parent found some old friends in veteran defensemen Joe Watson and Ed Van Impe, both leftovers from the original Philadelphia expansion team, and some new friends in tough Andre Dupont and Barry Ashbee, acquired through trades, and youngsters Jim Watson and Tom Bladon, draft choices. Together, the

defensemen and Parent gave the Flyers the stingiest defense in the NHL. The goalie played in a backbreaking 73 games and compiled a sparkling 1.89 average with 12 shutouts—by far the best individual netminding numbers in the NHL.

The Flyers won the West Division crown by a comfortable seven points over Chicago—the first time the established Blackhawks had missed winning the crown in four seasons in the expansionist West Division. In the East, Boston, led by scoring champion Phil Esposito, finished a fat 14 points ahead of runnerup Montreal. Esposito won his fourth straight scoring title and fifth in the last six years with 145 points.

En route to their division crown, the Flyers led the NHL with a staggering 1,750 penalty minutes, 600 minutes more than the next-most-penalized

Bobby Clarke sipped from the Cup after the Flyers became the first expansion team to win the championship in 1974.

team. Of the total, a record 348 minutes belonged to the club's No. 1 hatchetman, Dave Schultz.

In the opening round of the playoffs, Philadelphia wiped out the surprising Atlanta Flames in four straight games and Boston did the same to Toronto. Chicago went five to eliminate Los Angeles while the New York Rangers knocked off the defending Stanley Cup champion Montreal Canadiens in six games.

The semifinals were a struggle. The Bruins eliminated Chicago in six games and Philadelphia had to go seven to beat New York. That was a landmark victory. It marked the first time an expansion team had eliminated an established club in the playoffs. Parity, it seemed, was on its way. Two weeks later, it arrived.

Paced by Parent, the Flyers defeated the Bruins in the six-game championship round and brought the Stanley Cup to Philadelphia. The clincher was a 1–0 shutout spun by Parent with the only goal scored, ironically, by MacLeish, the man for whom the goalie once was traded.

Parent, whose airtight goaltending earned him the Conn Smythe Trophy as the Most Valuable Player of the playoffs, and Chicago's Tony Esposito were co-winners of the Vezina Trophy as the netminders with the lowest goals-against average during the regular season.

Boston's Phil Esposito won the Hart Trophy as the league's MVP, while teammate Bobby Orr was the winner of the Norris Trophy as the NHL's top defenseman for a record seventh consecutive season.

New York Islander defenseman Denis Potvin won the Calder as Rookie of the Year. Boston's John Bucyk got the Lady Byng for sportsmanship and ability.

1973–74
FINAL STANDINGS

East Division

	W	L	T	PTS	GF	GA
Boston	52	17	9	113	349	221
Montreal	45	24	9	99	293	240
New York R.	40	24	14	94	300	251
Toronto	35	27	16	86	274	230
Buffalo	32	34	12	76	242	250
Detroit	20	39	10	68	255	319
Vancouver	24	43	11	59	224	296
New York I.	19	41	18	56	182	247

West Division

	W	L	T	PTS	GF	GA
Philadelphia	50	16	12	112	273	164
Chicago	41	14	23	105	272	164
Los Angeles	33	33	12	78	233	231
Atlanta	30	34	14	74	214	238
Pittsburgh	28	41	9	65	242	273
St. Louis	26	40	12	64	206	248
Minnesota	23	38	17	63	235	275
California	13	55	10	36	195	342

LEADING SCORERS

	G	A	PTS
Esposito, Boston	68	77	145
Orr, Boston	32	90	122
Hodge, Boston	30	59	89
Cashman, Boston	30	59	89
Clarke, Philadelphia	35	52	87
Martin, Buffalo	52	34	86
Apps, Pittsburgh	24	61	85
Sittler, Toronto	38	46	84
L. MacDonald, Pittsburgh	43	39	82
Park, New York R.	25	57	82
D. Hextall, Minnesota	20	62	82

LEADING GOALIES

	G	GA	SO	GAA
Parent, Philadelphia	73	136	12	1.89
Esposito, Chicago	70	141	10	2.04
Thomas, Montreal	42	111	1	2.76
Bouchard, Atlanta	46	123	5	2.77
Vachon, Los Angeles	65	175	5	2.80

PLAYOFF RESULTS

Quarterfinals
Boston d. Toronto, 4–0
N.Y. Rangers d. Montreal, 4–2
Chicago d. Los Angeles, 4–1
Philadelphia d. Atlanta, 4–0

Semifinals
Boston d. Chicago, 4–2
Philadelphia d. N.Y. Rangers, 4–3

Finals
Philadelphia d. Boston, 4–2

LEADING SCORERS

	G	A	PTS
MacLeish, N.Y. Rangers	13	9	22
Sheppard, Boston	11	8	19
Bucyk, Boston	8	10	18
Orr, Boston	4	14	18

LEADING GOALIES

	W	SO	GAA
Parent, Philadelphia	12	2	2.02
Gilbert, Boston	10	1	2.64
Giacomin, N.Y. Rangers	7	0	2.82
Esposito, Chicago	6	2	2.88

1974–75

The addition of two new franchises and realignment of the 18 teams into four divisions set the stage for a season in which the Philadelphia

Bernie Parent's net play helped the Flyers knock off Buffalo in the Cup finals in 1975.

Flyers would be seeking a repeat of their stunning Stanley Cup success.

The new entries were the Kansas City Scouts and the Washington Capitals, and the divisions, named for hockey notables, were the James Norris and Jack Adams in the Prince of Wales Conference and the Lester Patrick and Conn Smythe in the Clarence Campbell Conference.

If the newest members of the league quickly became discouraged en route to last-place finishes in their divisions, at least they could take heart in the gallant strides made by the New York Islanders. An expansion team just three years earlier, the Islanders climbed into a second-place tie with the rival New York Rangers behind the Flyers in the Patrick Division and then found themselves matched against the Rangers in the best-of-three first-round playoff series.

The teams split the first two games and in an electrifying finish the Islanders won out when J. P. Parise scored a goal in just 11 seconds of overtime—a league record.

The Islanders lost the first three games of the quarterfinal round against Pittsburgh, but rallied to win the last four, becoming the first team in 33 years to win a series after losing the first three games. In the semifinal against the Flyers, the Islanders lost the decisive seventh game after again tying a series with three straight triumphs.

Philadelphia went on to defeat the Buffalo Sabres in six games in the finals, becoming the first team to win the Stanley Cup two years in a row since Montreal won in 1968 and 1969.

Influenced by the success of the Flyers' roughhouse tactics, more players began to fight as violence in the game increased. Two players were charged with assault for their involvement in fighting incidents. Dave Forbes of the Boston Bruins was put on trial for punching Henry Boucha of the Minnesota North Stars, but the trial ended in a hung jury and the charges were dropped. And Detroit's Dan Maloney was charged with assaulting Brian Glennie of Toron-

to. But there were still victories scored by the most graceful players of the generation.

Boston defenseman Bobby Orr won his second scoring title with 135 points, ending the four-year stranglehold on the award by teammate Phil Esposito. It was the sixth straight season in which either Orr or Esposito had won the scoring championship.

Philadelphia's Bobby Clarke, the feisty center, won the Hart Trophy as Most Valuable Player for the second time in three years while Orr won the Norris as best defenseman for the seventh straight time. The Lady Byng for gentlemanly play went to Los Angeles center Marcel Dionne. Atlanta Flames left wing Eric Vail won the Calder as Rookie of the Year and goalie Bernie Parent of the Flyers won the Vezina.

Parent also won the Conn Smythe as playoff MVP and was named to the All-Star team with teammate Clarke. Others on the team were defensemen Orr and Islander Denis Potvin and wingers Guy Lafleur of Montreal and Richard Martin of Buffalo.

1974–75

FINAL STANDINGS

Prince of Wales Conference: Norris Division

	W	L	T	PTS	GF	GA
Montreal	47	14	19	113	374	225
Los Angeles	42	17	21	105	269	185
Pittsburgh	37	28	15	89	326	289
Detroit	23	45	12	58	259	335
Washington	8	67	5	21	181	446

Prince of Wales Conference: Adams Division

	W	L	T	PTS	GF	GA
Buffalo	49	16	15	113	354	240
Boston	40	26	14	94	345	245
Toronto	31	33	16	78	280	309
California	19	48	13	51	212	316

Clarence Campbell Conference: Patrick Division

	W	L	T	PTS	GF	GA
Philadelphia	51	18	11	113	293	181
New York R.	37	29	14	88	319	276
New York I.	33	25	22	88	264	221
Atlanta	34	31	15	83	243	233

Clarence Campbell Conference: Smythe Division

	W	L	T	PTS	GF	GA
Vancouver	38	32	10	86	271	254
St. Louis	35	31	14	84	269	267
Chicago	37	35	8	82	268	241
Minnesota	23	50	7	53	221	341
Kansas City	15	54	11	41	184	328

Toronto's Darryl Sittler (27) posted 100 points in 1975–76, including a 10-point night against the Bruins on February 7, 1976.

LEADING SCORERS

	G	A	PTS
Orr, Boston	46	89	135
Esposito, Boston	61	66	127
Dionne, Detroit	47	74	121
Lafleur, Montreal	53	66	119
P. Mahovlich, Montreal	35	82	117
Clarke, Philadelphia	27	89	116
Robert, Buffalo	40	60	100
Gilbert, New York	36	61	97
Perreault, Buffalo	39	57	96
Martin, Buffalo	52	43	95

LEADING GOALIES

	G	GA	SO	GAA
Parent, Philadelphia	68	137	12	2.03
Vachon, Los Angeles	54	121	6	2.24
Dryden, Montreal	56	149	4	2.69
Esposito, Chicago	71	193	6	2.74
Bouchard, Atlanta	40	111	3	2.77

Preliminary Round

Toronto d. Los Angeles, 2–1
Chicago d. Boston, 2–1
Pittsburgh d. St. Louis, 2–0
N.Y. Islanders d. N.Y. Rangers, 2–1

Quarterfinals

Philadelphia d. Toronto, 4–0
Buffalo d. Chicago, 4–1
Montreal d. Vancouver, 4–1
N.Y. Islanders d. Pittsburgh, 4–3

Semifinals

Philadelphia d. N.Y. Islanders, 4–3
Buffalo d. Montreal, 4–2

Finals

Philadelphia d. Buffalo, 4–2

LEADING SCORERS

	G	A	PTS
MacLeish, Philadelphia	11	9	20
Lafleur, Montreal	12	7	19
Drouin, N.Y. Islanders	6	12	18

LEADING GOALIES

	W	SO	GAA
Parent, Philadelphia	10	4	1.89
Stephenson, Philadelphia	2	1	1.95
Vachon, Los Angeles	1	0	2.11

1975–76

For years, the argument had reigned: could swifter, more inventive players challenge the dominance of the stronger, more aggressive teams and the style that had been popularized by the Philadelphia Flyers? The answer, it seemed, was an emphatic yes.

The Flyers' string of successes was ended not by a more violent team, but by a faster one. The Montreal Canadiens did not have anyone as powerful as Dave Schultz, the Flyer who perennially led the league in penalty minutes. But Montreal did have Guy Lafleur, a slender, graceful right wing whose name translated from French was, appropriately enough, "The Flower."

Lafleur led Montreal back into the championship ranks. After being dethroned by Philadelphia, the two-time winner, Montreal won the Stanley Cup for the 19th time. Like Lafleur, the Canadiens were simply overwhelming. They finished the season with 58 victories and 127 points—both records. They had only 11 defeats, just one more than the record they held for fewest losses in one season. They led the league in virtu-

ally every offensive and defensive category and they did it with one of the lowest penalty-minute totals of any team—an average of 12.2 a game, half of what the Flyers averaged.

In the playoffs, they won 12 of 13 games, sweeping Philadelphia in four games in the finals. In all but three of those games, the Canadiens held their opponent to three goals or fewer. Lafleur, who won the scoring title with 125 points, had 17 points in the playoffs.

This was a season marked by the trade that brought Bruin Phil Esposito to the Rangers and Brad Park to Boston. It was also a year in which Boston's Bobby Orr, operated on again because of his ailing left knee, played only 10 games. And Toronto's Darryl Sittler set a mark for most points in a game when he recorded six goals and four assists against Boston.

Philadelphia tied a league record by going unbeaten in 23 straight games (17–0–6) and the Kansas City Scouts, in their second season, set a record for futility by going 27 games without a victory (0–21–6).

Although Philadelphia was toppled as Stanley Cup champion, the Flyers did have Bobby Clarke, the winner of the Hart Trophy as Most Valuable Player. It was the third time in four years Clarke had won the award and he became only the second center, along with the legendary Howie Morenz, to win it a third time.

New York Islander center Bryan Trottier was the winner of the Calder as Rookie of the Year; Montreal goalie Ken Dryden won the Vezina and Jean Ratelle won the Lady Byng for gentlemanly play. Philadelphia's Reggie Leach, despite his team's defeat in the finals, was the Conn Smythe Trophy winner as playoff MVP after scoring a playoff record 19 goals.

Lafleur, Dryden, Clarke, and Park made the All-Star team along with defenseman Denis Potvin of the New York Islanders, who won the Norris Trophy, and left wing Bill Barber of Philadelphia.

The Flower, Guy Lafleur, led the Canadiens to their 19th Stanley Cup in 1976.

1975–76

FINAL STANDINGS

Prince of Wales Conference: Norris Division

	W	L	T	PTS	GF	GA
Montreal	58	11	11	127	337	174
Los Angeles	38	33	9	85	263	265
Pittsburgh	35	33	12	82	339	303
Detroit	26	44	10	62	226	300
Washington	11	59	10	32	224	394

Prince of Wales Conference: Adams Division

	W	L	T	PTS	GF	GA
Boston	48	15	17	113	313	237
Buffalo	46	21	13	105	339	240
Toronto	34	31	15	83	294	276
California	27	42	11	65	250	278

Clarence Campbell Conference: Patrick Division

	W	L	T	PTS	GF	GA
Philadelphia	51	13	16	118	348	209
New York I.	42	21	17	101	297	190
Atlanta	35	33	12	82	262	237
New York R.	29	42	9	67	262	333

Clarence Campbell Conference: Smythe Division

	W	L	T	PTS	GF	GA
Chicago	32	30	18	82	254	261
Vancouver	33	32	15	81	271	272
St. Louis	29	37	14	72	249	290
Minnesota	20	53	7	47	195	303
Kansas City	12	56	12	36	190	351

LEADING SCORERS

	G	A	PTS
Lafleur, Montreal	56	69	125
Clarke, Philadelphia	30	89	119
Perreault, Buffalo	44	69	113
Barber, Philadelphia	50	62	112
Larouche, Pittsburgh	53	58	111
Ratelle, New York R.-Boston	36	69	105
P. Mahovlich, Montreal	34	71	105
Pronovost, Pittsburgh	52	52	104
Sittler, Toronto	41	59	100
Apps, Pittsburgh	32	67	99

LEADING GOALIES

	G	GA	SO	GAA
Dryden, Montreal	62	121	8	2.03
Resch, New York I.	44	88	7	2.07
Bouchard, Atlanta	47	113	2	2.54
Stephenson, Philadelphia	66	164	1	2.58
Gilbert, Boston	55	151	3	2.90

PLAYOFF RESULTS

Preliminary Round

Buffalo d. St. Louis, 2–1
Toronto d. Pittsburgh, 2–1
N.Y. Islanders d. Vancouver, 2–0

Quarterfinals

Los Angeles d. Atlanta, 2–0
Phildelphia d. Toronto, 4–3
Boston d. Los Angeles, 4–3
Montreal d. Chicago, 4–0
N.Y. Islanders d. Buffalo, 4–2

Semifinals

Montreal d. N.Y. Islanders, 4–1
Philadelphia d. Boston, 4–1

Finals

Montreal d. Philadelphia, 4–0

LEADING SCORERS

	G	A	PTS
Leach, Philadelphia	19	5	24
Potvin, N.Y. Islanders	5	14	19
Lafleur, Montclair	7	10	17

LEADING GOALIES

	W	SO	GAA
Bouchard, Atlanta	0	0	1.50
Dryden, Montreal	12	0	1.92
Stanlowski, St. Louis	1	0	2.04
Gilbert, Boston	3	2	3.17
Thomas, Toronto	5	1	3.48

1976–77

If there was any doubt that the Montreal Canadiens had been restored to the National Hockey League's most privileged class, it was quickly dispelled in the 1976–77 season. Coming off their Stanley Cup success of the season before, it seemed there was little the Canadiens could do to improve upon their resounding record.

Guy Lafleur, who already had begun to establish himself as the most recognizable—and the most coveted—player of his generation was soon surrounded by invaluable helpmates. The Canadiens, in fact, were so rich in talent that they all but saved the All-Star selections for themselves.

In one of the most lopsided voting totals ever, the Canadiens placed four of their members on the first team—right wing Lafleur, defenseman Larry Robinson, goalie Ken Dryden, and Lafleur's linemate, left wing Steve Shutt. The only players to interrupt the Montreal domination were Los Angeles center Marcel Dionne and Toronto defenseman Borje Salming. Not only that, but one more Canadien, defenseman Guy Lapointe, was named to the second team.

Who could argue with the choices? The Canadiens won a record 60 games, lost a mere eight, and set another record with the total of 132 points. The Philadelphia Flyers, the team with the second-best overall record, had 20 fewer points. And the Los Angeles Kings, second to Montreal in the Norris Division, were 49 points behind. Not since the league broke into four divisions had one team so dominated a season.

In their own palace, the Montreal Forum, the Canadiens lost only once in 40 games, tying the

modern NHL record for fewest losses at home. But while the Canadiens were obviously delighted to be in their home, two other teams found new homes to start the season when the league approved a pair of franchise shifts.

The Kansas City Scouts, struggling both on the ice and in the accounting department, were sold to Denver oilman Jack Vickers, who moved the team to his home city and renamed the club the Colorado Rockies. Alas, the changes were merely cosmetic. The Rockies won only 20 games and finished with just 54 points, the second-worst total in the league.

The Cleveland Barons did not fare much better. Transplanted from Oakland, where they were known as the Seals in the NHL's six-team expansion of 1967, the Barons played in suburban Richfield in a cavernous arena that was located next to a sprawling farm. Encouraged by only a few fans willing to make the journey there, the Barons won only 25 games.

Montreal charged through the playoffs, losing only two games—both to the New York Islanders in a semifinal series—and swept the Boston Bruins in the finals when Jacques Lemaire scored an overtime goal at 4:32 in the fourth game. Montreal was once more led by Lafleur, who had finished the regular season with a league-leading 136 points, 56 of them goals.

Not surprisingly, the Canadiens swept most of the NHL postseason awards. Lafleur, besides being the Art Ross winner as scoring champion, won the Hart Trophy as Most Valuable Player and the Conn Smythe as the playoff MVP. Robinson won the Norris as best defenseman, while Willi Plett of Atlanta won the Calder as Rookie of the Year. Dionne won the Lady Byng for good conduct for the second time in three years.

The 1976–77 Lady Byng Trophy went to Marcel Dionne of Los Angeles.

1976–77

FINAL STANDINGS

Prince of Wales Conference: Norris Division

	W	L	T	PTS	GF	GA
Montreal	60	8	12	132	387	171
Los Angeles	34	31	15	83	271	241
Pittsburgh	34	33	13	81	240	252
Washington	24	42	14	62	221	307
Detroit	16	55	9	41	183	309

Prince of Wales Conference: Adams Division

	W	L	T	PTS	GF	GA
Boston	49	23	8	106	312	240
Buffalo	48	24	8	104	301	220
Toronto	33	32	15	81	301	285
Cleveland	25	42	13	63	240	292

Clarence Campbell Conference: Patrick Division

	W	L	T	PTS	GF	GA
Philadelphia	48	16	16	112	323	213
New York I.	47	21	12	106	288	193
Atlanta	34	34	12	80	264	265
New York R.	29	37	14	72	272	310

Clarence Campbell Conference: Smythe Division

	W	L	T	PTS	GF	GA
St. Louis	32	39	9	73	239	276
Minnesota	23	39	18	64	240	310
Chicago	26	43	11	63	240	298
Vancouver	25	42	13	63	235	294
Colorado	20	46	14	54	226	307

LEADING SCORERS

	G	A	PTS
Lafleur, Montreal	56	80	136
Dionne, Los Angeles	53	69	122
Shutt, Montreal	60	45	105
MacLeish, Philadelphia	49	48	97
Perreault, Buffalo	39	56	95
Young, Minnesota	29	66	95

John A. Ziegler Jr. became the fourth president of the NHL in 1977, succeeding Clarence Campbell, who had served 31 years.

Ratelle, Boston	33	61	94
McDonald, Toronto	46	44	90
Sittler, Toronto	38	52	90
Clarke, Philadelphia	27	63	90

LEADING GOALIES

	G	GA	SO	GAA
Dryden, Montreal	56	117	10	2.14
Resch, New York I.	46	103	4	2.28
Desjardins, Buffalo	49	126	3	2.63
Parent, Philadelphia	61	159	5	2.71
Vachon, Los Angeles	68	184	8	2.72

PLAYOFF RESULTS

Preliminary Round

N.Y. Islanders d. Chicago, 2–0
Buffalo d. Minnesota, 2–0
Toronto d. Pittsburgh, 2–1
Los Angeles d. Atlanta, 2–1

Quarterfinals

Philadelphia d. Toronto, 4–2
Boston d. Los Angeles, 4–2
Montreal d. St. Louis, 4–0
N.Y. Islanders d. Buffalo, 4–0

Semifinals

Montreal d. N.Y. Islanders, 4–2
Boston d. Philadelphia, 4–0

Finals

Montreal d. Boston, 4–0

LEADING SCORERS

	G	A	PTS
Lafleur, Montreal	9	17	26
Sittler, Toronto	5	16	21
Lemaire, Montreal	7	12	19

LEADING GOALIES

	W	SO	GAA
Dryden, Montreal	12	4	1.55
Resch, N.Y. Islanders	1	0	2.08
Stephenson, Philadelphia	4	1	2.59

1977–78

While the Montreal Canadiens again were the dominant force in 1977–78, at least one team served notice that it was on its way to the top. In fact, the team, the New York Islanders, turned out to be the only one that had been able to win a playoff game from the Canadiens the previous two years—and it won three of them.

The rise of the Islanders really was no surprise. It had been coming for some time. The Islanders had been known for their defense, but finally were able to add a gifted scorer, Mike Bossy, to give them the goal-getting punch they needed. It happened that the young man was born and raised in Montreal and had played outstanding junior hockey on the city's outskirts in Laval.

Yet, for some reason, Bossy had gone untouched in the first round of the amateur draft until the Islanders made him the 15th player chosen. Six other right wings already had been taken, but Bossy was confident he could help the Islanders. And when contract negotiations with his new club temporarily collapsed, Bossy boldly told general manager Bill Torrey: "I'll score 50 goals for you."

Torrey laughed. No Islander had ever scored that many goals. No rookie had ever scored that many goals. But Bossy had the last laugh. By the time he ended his rookie year, he had 53 goals and was sixth in the scoring race with 91 points, the most ever by a first-year right wing. The Islanders, with center Bryan Trottier and defenseman Denis Potvin, had three of the top six scorers in the league.

The Islanders won their first Patrick Division title, dethroning Philadelphia, and clearly were one of the most imposing threats to end Montre-

The Canadiens' Larry Robinson, checking Buffalo's Gil Perreault, was the NHL's best defenseman in 1976–77.

al's Stanley Cup reign. But the Islanders were not the only team to make a vast improvement during the season. Detroit vaulted from the league's worst record to a second-place finish behind Montreal in the Norris Division.

Still, the Canadiens again led the league during the season with 129 points, and with 59 victories failed by one to equal their own league record of 60 set the year before. The Boston Bruins, the other threat to the Canadi-

ens, had 113 points, two more than the Islanders.

But in a stunning playoff upset, the Islanders were eliminated by the Toronto Maple Leafs when Lanny McDonald scored at 4:13 of overtime in the seventh game.

After sweeping the upstart Toronto team in the semifinals, the Canadiens faced the Bruins for the second year in a row in the final round. Boston had failed to win even a single game in the championship series the year before. This time they managed to win two as the Canadiens captured the Cup for the third consecutive year. While Montreal still had the dependable scoring of Guy Lafleur, who during the season won his third straight scoring title with 132 points, it also had a mighty defense. The Canadiens allowed only 12 goals in the final series against Boston.

A major factor was the play of goaltender Ken Dryden, who shared the Vezina Trophy as the league's outstanding goalie with Michel Larocque. Others figuring in the Canadiens' success were defenseman Larry Robinson, MVP of the playoffs, and left wing Bob Gainey, who received the Frank J. Selke Trophy (awarded for the first time) as "the forward who best excels in the defensive aspects of the game."

But while Dryden was named to the All-Star team, Robinson was supplanted by Denis Potvin of the Islanders and Brad Park of the Bruins. Trottier, the Islander center, teammate Clark Gillies, a left wing, and Lafleur were the other selections. Bossy won the Calder Trophy as Rookie

Mike Bossy of the New York Islanders broke in with a bang in 1977–78 when he scored a rookie-record 53 goals.

of the Year, Lafleur won the Hart as MVP for the second straight season, Potvin regained the Norris as best defenseman, and Los Angeles' Butch Goring won the Lady Byng for gentlemanly play.

Off the ice, John A. Ziegler Jr. became the fourth president in the 61-year history of the NHL, succeeding Clarence Campbell, who had been president since 1946. A Michigan-born lawyer, Ziegler played amateur hockey and was a quarterback in football and a shortstop in baseball as a Detroit schoolboy. His bachelor and law degrees were achieved at the University of Michigan.

1977-78

FINAL STANDINGS

Prince of Wales Conference: Norris Division

	W	L	T	PTS	GF	GA
Montreal	59	10	11	129	359	183
Detroit	32	34	14	78	252	266
Los Angeles	31	34	15	77	243	245
Pittsburgh	25	37	18	68	254	321
Washington	17	49	14	48	195	321

Prince of Wales Conference: Adams Division

	W	L	T	PTS	GF	GA
Boston	51	18	11	113	333	218
Buffalo	44	19	17	105	288	215
Toronto	41	29	10	92	271	237
Cleveland	22	45	13	57	230	325

Clarence Campbell Conference: Patrick Division

	W	L	T	PTS	GF	GA
New York I.	48	17	15	111	334	210
Philadelphia	45	20	15	105	296	200
Atlanta	34	27	19	87	274	252
New York R.	30	37	13	73	279	280

Clarence Campbell Conference: Smythe Division

	W	L	T	PTS	GF	GA
Chicago	32	29	19	83	230	220
Colorado	19	40	21	59	257	305
Vancouver	20	43	17	57	239	320
St. Louis	20	47	13	53	195	304
Minnesota	18	53	9	45	218	325

LEADING SCORERS

	G	A	PTS
Lafleur, Montreal	60	72	132
Trottier, New York I.	46	77	123
Sittler, Toronto	45	72	117
Lemaire, Montreal	36	61	97
D. Potvin, New York I.	30	64	94
Bossy, New York I.	53	38	91
O'Reilly, Boston	29	61	90
Perreault, Buffalo	41	48	89
Clarke, Philadelphia	21	68	89
McDonald, Toronto	47	40	87
Paiement, Colorado	31	56	87

LEADING GOALIES

	G	GA	SO	GAA
Dryden, Montreal	52	105	5	2.05
Parent, Philadelphia	49	108	7	2.22
Resch, New York I.	45	112	3	2.55
Esposito, Chicago	64	168	5	2.63
Edwards, Buffalo	72	185	5	2.64

PLAYOFF RESULTS

Preliminary Round

Philadelphia d. Colorado, 2–0
Detroit d. Atlanta, 2–0
Toronto d. Los Angeles, 2–0
Buffalo d. N.Y. Rangers, 2–1

Quarterfinals

Boston d. Chicago, 4–0
Philadelphia d. Buffalo, 4–1
Montreal d. Detroit, 4–1
Toronto d. N.Y. Islanders, 4–3

Semifinals

Montreal d. Toronto, 4–0
Boston d. Philadelphia, 4–1

Finals

Montreal d. Boston, 4–2

LEADING SCORERS

	G	A	PTS
Lafleur, Montreal	10	11	21
Robinson, Montreal	4	17	21
Park, Boston	9	11	20

LEADING GOALIES

	W	SO	GAA
Dryden, Montreal	12	2	1.89
Grahame, Boston	2	0	2.08
Resch, N.Y. Islanders	3	0	2.32
Cheevers, Boston	8	1	2.87

1978-79

New York is a city of extremes and its fans are no different. They can be fiercely loyal and terribly impatient. They can jeer with witless vengeance and cheer with boundless passion. And for the honor of doing any of those, they will pay handsomely for their tickets.

Some even paid as much as $500 a ticket when the Rangers galvanized the city in a glorious march to the Stanley Cup finals, a march orchestrated by coach Fred Shero in his first year at the helm. "Freddie the Fog" had been hired away from the Philadelphia Flyers and almost immediately transformed the downtrodden Rangers into a success.

With the help of Swedish stars Ulf Nilsson and Anders Hedberg, who signed contracts for $300,000 a year apiece after defecting from the World Hockey Association, Shero confirmed his reputation as a genius. Although the Rangers finished in third place in the Patrick Division, they finished only four points behind second-place Philadelphia.

Not only did the Rangers then knock off Shero's old team in the quarterfinals, but they faced

the rival New York Islanders in the semifinals, an electrifying series that was a scalper's delight.

The Islanders had become the first expansion team ever to lead the league in points. They had Bryan Trottier, who led the league in scoring with 134 points, and Mike Bossy, who scored 69 goals, the second-highest total ever, including goals in 10 straight games to equal the modern NHL record. The Rangers had spirit.

Seeking their first Stanley Cup since 1940, the Rangers upset the Islanders in six games and went on to meet the defending champion Montreal Canadiens. Finally, the magic vanished. After winning the opening game, the Rangers failed to win another and Montreal won its fourth straight title.

The Rangers had to console themselves while the stunned Islanders could take heart only in a spate of postseason awards. Trottier won the Hart Trophy as Most Valuable Player and teammate Denis Potvin was given the Norris as best defenseman. Minnesota center Bobby Smith won the Calder as Rookie of the Year, Atlanta's Bob MacMillan won the Lady Byng as the most gentlemanly player and Montreal left wing Bob Gainey was named winner of both the Conn Smythe as playoff MVP and the Selke Trophy as the best defensive forward.

Three Islanders—Trottier, Potvin, and left wing Clark Gillies—were named to the All-Star team, along with right wing Guy Lafleur of Montreal and teammates Ken Dryden, goalie, and Larry Robinson, defenseman.

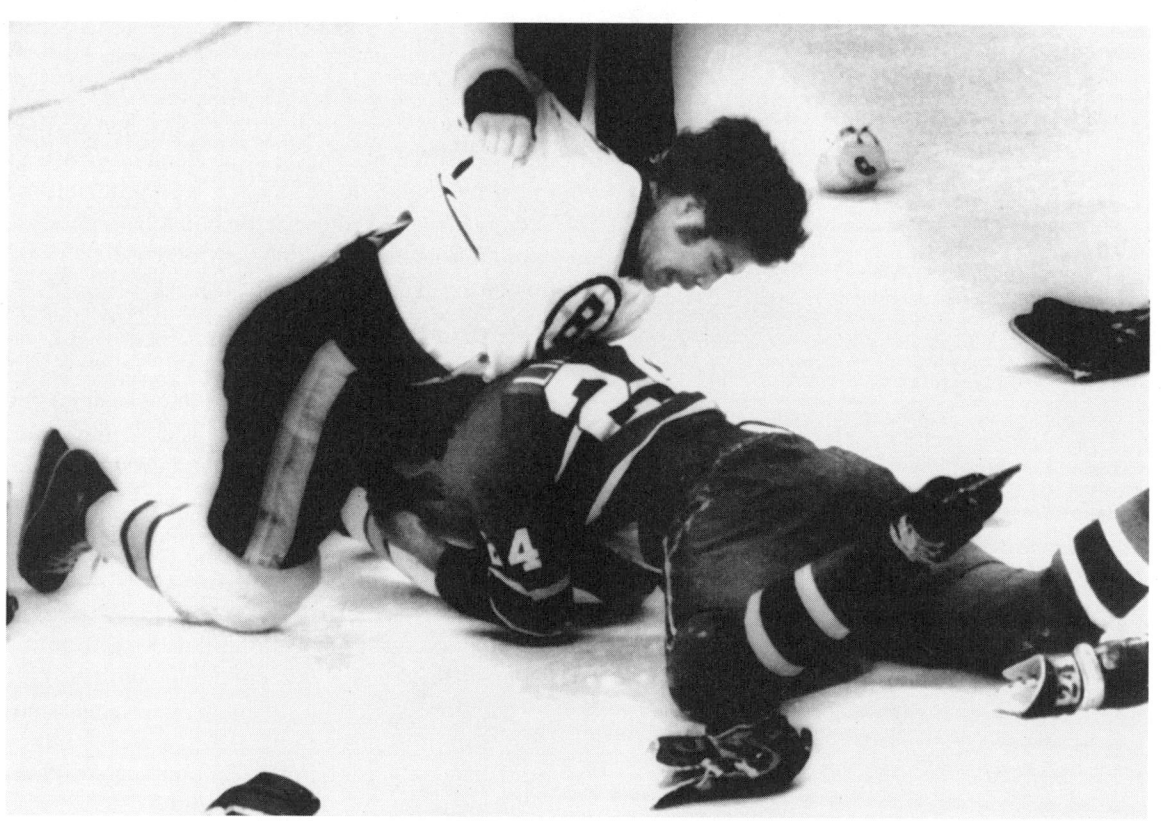

The Bruins' John Wensink won this battle, but his teammates lost the war when they were eliminated by Montreal in the 1978 finals.

1978–79

FINAL STANDINGS

Prince of Wales Conference: Norris Division

	W	L	T	PTS	GF	GA
Montreal	52	17	11	115	337	204
Pittsburgh	36	31	13	85	281	279
Los Angeles	34	34	12	80	292	286
Washington	24	41	15	63	273	338
Detroit	23	41	16	62	252	295

Prince of Wales Conference: Adams Division

	W	L	T	PTS	GF	GA
Boston	43	23	14	100	316	270
Buffalo	36	28	16	88	280	263
Toronto	34	33	13	81	267	252
Minnesota	28	40	12	68	257	289

Clarence Campbell Conference: Patrick Division

	W	L	T	PTS	GF	GA
New York I.	51	15	14	116	358	214
Philadelphia	40	25	15	95	281	248
New York R.	40	29	11	91	316	292
Atlanta	41	31	8	90	327	280

Clarence Campbell Conference: Smythe Division

	W	L	T	PTS	GF	GA
Chicago	29	36	15	73	244	277
Vancouver	25	42	13	63	217	291
St. Louis	18	50	12	48	249	348
Colorado	15	53	12	42	210	331

LEADING SCORERS

	G	A	PTS
Trottier, New York I.	47	87	134
Dionne, Los Angeles	59	71	130
Lafleur, Montreal	52	77	129
Bossy, New York I.	69	57	126
MacMillan, Atlanta	37	71	108
Chouinard, Atlanta	50	57	107
D. Potvin, New York I.	31	70	101
Federko, St. Louis	31	64	95
Taylor, Los Angeles	43	48	91
Gillies, New York I.	35	56	91

LEADING GOALIES

	G	GA	SO	GAA
Dryden, Montreal	47	108	5	2.30
Resch, New York I.	43	106	2	2.50
Palmateer, Toronto	58	167	4	2.95
Edwards, Buffalo	54	159	2	3.02
Lessard, Los Angeles	49	148	4	3.10

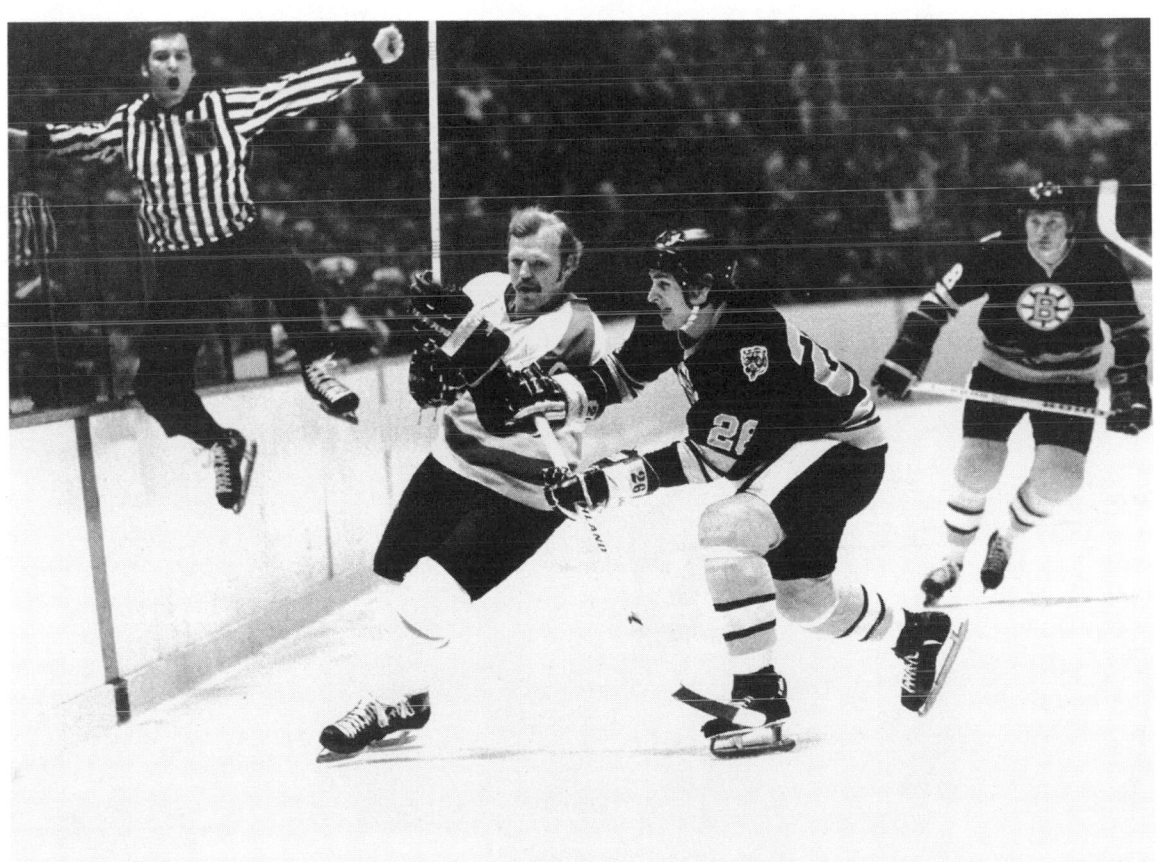

Linesman Gerard Gauthier goes aloft as the Flyers' Bob Kelly and Bruins' Mike Milbury battle for the puck in 1978.

The merger with the WHA brought superstar Wayne Gretzky to the NHL in 1979.

PLAYOFF RESULTS

Preliminary Round

Philadelphia d. Vancouver, 2–1
Toronto d. Atlanta, 2–0
Pittsburgh d. Buffalo, 2–1
N.Y. Rangers d. Los Angeles, 2–0

Quarterfinals

Montreal d. Toronto, 4–0
Boston d. Pittsburgh, 4–0
N.Y. Islanders d. Chicago, 4–0
N.Y. Rangers d. Philadelphia, 4–1

Semifinals

N.Y. Rangers d. N.Y. Islanders, 4–2
Montreal d. Boston, 4–3

Finals

Montreal d. N.Y. Rangers, 4–1

LEADING SCORERS

	G	A	PTS
Lemaire, Montreal	11	12	23
Lafleur, Montreal	10	13	23
Esposito, N.Y. Rangers	8	12	20
Maloney, N.Y. Rangers	7	13	20

LEADING GOALIES

	W	SO	GAA
Smith, N.Y. Islanders	4	1	1.90
Resch, N.Y. Islanders	2	1	2.20
Davidson, N.Y. Rangers	11	1	2.28
Dryden, Montreal	12	5	2.30

6

MERGER AND THE GRETZKY EXPLOSION

1979–1988

The costly war with the World Hockey Association finally came to an end in 1979, when the two professional leagues reached agreement on a merger. The NHL jumped from 17 to 21 franchises with the addition of four WHA clubs—the Quebec Nordiques, Edmonton Oilers, Winnipeg Jets, and Hartford Whalers. The merger, along with the signings of several European stars, changed the game dramatically.

The days of the Philadelphia Flyers' overly physical style were dwindling as the games became free-skating and wide-open. As a result, scoring totals skyrocketed. Leading the surge was Edmonton's Wayne Gretzky, who set every scoring record imaginable and became the sport's No. 1 attraction.

The Montreal Canadiens' domination was terminated in the first year of the merger as parity enabled the expansion teams of the 1970s to rise to the top. In the forefront were the New York Islanders, who ruled the game in the early 1980s. Paced by all-around center Bryan Trottier and sniper Mike Bossy, the Islanders could play either style—physical or finesse— with equal ability.

The Islanders would be succeeded by The Great Gretzky's Oilers, who made it into the winners' circle in a span that saw them win the Stanley Cup four times in five years.

More and more teams scouted Europe in search of talent. The Nordiques signed three Czechoslovakian brothers—Anton, Marian, and Peter Stastny—all of whom became stars, and other Europeans defected soon after. The league, once almost exclusively made up of Canadians, took on an international flavor.

Clearly, the 1979–80 season was an historic one for the NHL. Armistice with the World Hockey Association was achieved when the NHL agreed to absorb four of the WHA teams and in return the WHA agreed to pay off its other teams and cease operation.

With the addition of the surviving Quebec Nordiques, Winnipeg Jets, Edmonton Oilers, and Hartford Whalers, the 21-team league moved to a balanced 80-game schedule. Each team would play every other team four times, with the top 16 point-getters earning playoff spots.

Two of the new teams—Edmonton and Hartford—made the playoffs, but both were near the bottom of the league and it was obvious that by and large the talent was spread thin among the old WHA squads; indeed, the NHL had stripped the incoming teams of many of their best players in a reentry draft, with each of the four WHA teams permitted to protect only two goalies and two skaters.

One notable exception was that of a thin, pimpled 19-year-old named Wayne Gretzky, the Edmonton Oiler who was the most exciting and productive player in all of hockey. Before the merger, the Oilers struck an agreement that called for Gretzky remaining their property. It was, to say the least, a wise move.

In his first NHL season, although he technically did not qualify as a rookie because of his WHA service, Gretzky scored 51 goals and tied for the league lead in points with 137 along with Los Angeles' Marcel Dionne. But Gretzky only

Islander goalie Billy Smith chugs champagne from the Cup after conquest of the Flyers in 1980.

managed to help the Oilers claim the 16th and final playoff spot.

The biggest success of the season was that of the New York Islanders. Upset in the playoffs a year earlier and having struggled through the 1979–80 season, finally finishing fifth in points, the Islanders became only the second expansion team, along with the Philadelphia Flyers, to win a Stanley Cup. It came eight years after the team's birth in the 1972 expansion draft.

To do it, the Islanders made one of the most pivotal trades in history, landing center Butch Goring from Los Angeles right at the March trading deadline. With Goring in the lineup, the Islanders finished the season unbeaten in their last 12 games. They went on to defeat Goring's old team in the first round, Boston in the quarterfinals, and Buffalo in the semifinals.

That earned the Islanders their first berth ever in the finals against divisional rival Philadelphia. And the Islanders managed to win the opening game when Denis Potvin scored a rare power-play goal in overtime. The Islanders went on to win the series in six games on Bobby Nystrom's overtime goal.

Gretzky was the Hart Trophy winner as Most Valuable Player and winner of the Lady Byng for gentlemanly play. Montreal's Larry Robinson won the Norris as best defenseman, Boston defenseman Ray Bourque won the Calder as Rookie of the Year, Islander center Bryan Trottier won the Smythe as playoff MVP, and Montreal's Bob Gainey took the Selke Trophy as the best defensive forward for the third straight time.

Robinson, Bourque, and Dionne were named to the All-Star team, along with Montreal right wing Guy Lafleur and Los Angeles left wing Charlie Simmer.

1979–80

FINAL STANDINGS

Prince of Wales Conference: Norris Division

	W	L	T	PTS	GF	GA
Montreal	47	20	13	107	328	240
Los Angeles	30	36	14	74	290	313
Pittsburgh	30	37	13	73	251	303
Hartford	27	34	19	73	303	312
Detroit	26	43	11	63	268	306

Prince of Wales Conference: Adams Division

	W	L	T	PTS	GF	GA
Buffalo	47	17	16	110	318	201
Boston	46	21	13	105	310	234
Minnesota	36	28	16	88	311	253
Toronto	35	40	5	75	304	327
Quebec	25	44	11	61	248	313

Clarence Campbell Conference: Patrick Division

	W	L	T	PTS	GF	GA
Philadelphia	48	12	20	116	327	254
New York I.	39	28	13	91	281	247
New York R.	38	32	10	86	308	284
Atlanta	35	32	13	83	282	269
Washington	27	40	13	67	261	293

Clarence Campbell Conference: Smythe Division

	W	L	T	PTS	GF	GA
Chicago	34	27	19	87	241	251
St. Louis	34	34	12	80	266	278
Vancouver	27	37	16	70	256	281
Edmonton	28	39	13	69	301	322
Winnipeg	20	49	11	51	214	314
Colorado	19	48	13	51	234	308

LEADING SCORERS

	G	A	PTS
Dionne, Los Angeles	53	84	137
Gretzky, Edmonton	51	86	137
Lafleur, Montreal	50	75	125
Perreault, Buffalo	40	66	106
Rogers, Hartford	44	61	105
Trottier, New York I.	42	62	104
Simmer, Los Angeles	56	45	101
Stoughton, Hartford	56	44	100
Sittler, Toronto	40	57	97
MacDonald, Edmonton	46	48	94
Federko, St. Louis	38	56	94

LEADING GOALIES

	G	GA	SO	GAA
Edwards, Buffalo	49	125	2	2.57
Peeters, Philadelphia	40	108	1	2.73
Cheevers, Boston	42	116	4	2.81
Esposito, Chicago	69	205	6	2.97
Resch, New York I.	45	132	3	3.04

PLAYOFF RESULTS

Preliminary Round

Philadelphia d. Edmonton, 3–0
Minnesota d. Toronto, 3–0
Chicago d. St. Louis, 3–0
Boston d. Pittsburgh, 3–2

Quarterfinals

Buffalo d. Chicago, 4–0
Minnesota d. Montreal, 4–3
N.Y. Islanders d. Boston, 4–1
Philadelphia d. N.Y. Rangers, 4–1

Semifinals

Philadelphia d. Minnesota, 4–1
N.Y. Islanders d. Buffalo, 4–2

Finals

N.Y. Islanders d. Philadelphia, 4–2

LEADING SCORERS

	G	A	P
Trottier, N.Y. Islanders	12	17	29
Bossy, N.Y. Islanders	10	13	23
Linseman, Philadelphia	4	18	22

	W	SO	GAA
Sauve, Buffalo	6	2	2.04
Larocque, Montreal	4	1	2.20
Esposito, Chicago	3	0	2.25
Peeters, Philadelphia	8	1	2.78
Smith, N.Y. Islanders	15	1	2.80

1980–81

The New York Islanders began the 1980–81 season as Stanley Cup defenders, but there were skeptics who felt the championship was a fluke and their reign would be short-lived.

How wrong they were! Not even Edmonton's Wayne Gretzky could steal the Islanders' thunder, although he tried mightily. Gretzky, proving his share of the scoring championship the season before in his first NHL campaign was no mistake,

broke Phil Esposito's scoring record by recording an astonishing 164 points—29 more than his nearest rival—including 109 assists to break a record held by none other than Bobby Orr.

But the swift center could only lead his Edmonton team to a 15th-place finish overall in the regular-season standings. The Oilers did upset Montreal in the first round of the playoffs, but then fell in the quarterfinals to the Islanders, the team that would go on to win it all again.

There seemed to be nothing the Islanders lacked. While Gretzky piled up points, Islander Mike Bossy stockpiled goals. He scored 68 of them, one below his career high and the third-highest total in history. But Bossy's first 50 goals came in his first 50 games, tying the record set by

Pittsburgh's Randy Carlyle won the Norris Trophy as the league's top defenseman in 1980–81.

Maurice (Rocket) Richard 38 years before and unequaled since.

Even the way Bossy, a sharp-shooting right wing, grabbed a piece of the record was dramatic. He had 48 in 49 games and appeared to be falling short when the final minutes in the 50th game against the Quebec Nordiques began to tick away. But Bossy scored twice in the last four minutes, the second time with under two minutes remaining, to earn another line in the record book.

Bossy still wasn't finished. He scored a playoff record 35 points and helped the Islanders sweep the rival New York Rangers in four games in the semifinals and dispatch the Minnesota North Stars in just five games in the finals, a convincing show that finally earned the Islanders respect. But the Conn Smythe Trophy as playoff MVP went to Butch Goring, who scored five goals in the finals, including three in one game.

For his record performance, Gretzky won the Hart Trophy as Most Valuable Player for the second straight season. Pittsburgh's Randy Carlyle won the Norris as best defenseman and teammate Rick Kehoe won the Lady Byng for sportsmanship. Peter Stastny, a native of Czechoslovakia and a member of the Quebec Nordiques, won the Calder as Rookie of the Year and Montreal's Bob Gainey took the Selke Trophy as the leading defensive forward for the fourth consecutive year.

Bossy, Gretzky, and Carlyle were named to the All-Star team along with Los Angeles left wing Charlie Simmer, St. Louis goalie Mike Liut, and defenseman Denis Potvin of the Islanders.

Of any losers during the season, the Winnipeg Jets would have had to rate at the top—or the bottom. They went a record 30 games without winning a game. Overall, they were 9–57–14.

1980–81

FINAL STANDINGS

Prince of Wales Conference: Norris Division

	W	L	T	PTS	GF	GA
Montreal	45	22	13	103	332	232
Los Angeles	43	24	13	99	337	290
Pittsburgh	30	37	13	73	302	345

Butch Goring sparked the Islanders to a second Cup and was named playoff MVP in 1981.

| Hartford | 21 | 41 | 18 | 60 | 292 | 372 |
| Detroit | 19 | 43 | 18 | 56 | 252 | 339 |

Prince of Wales Conference: Adams Division

	W	L	T	PTS	GF	GA
Buffalo	39	20	21	99	327	250
Boston	37	30	13	87	316	272
Minnesota	35	28	17	87	291	263
Quebec	30	32	18	78	314	318
Toronto	28	37	15	71	322	367

Clarence Campbell Conference: Patrick Division

	W	L	T	PTS	GF	GA
New York I.	48	18	14	110	355	260
Philadelphia	41	24	15	97	313	249
Calgary	39	27	14	92	329	298
New York R.	30	36	14	74	312	317
Washington	26	36	18	70	286	317

Clarence Campbell Conference: Smythe Division

	W	L	T	PTS	GF	GA
St. Louis	45	18	17	107	352	281
Chicago	31	33	16	78	304	315
Vancouver	28	32	20	76	289	301
Edmonton	29	35	16	74	328	327
Colorado	22	45	13	57	258	344
Winnipeg	9	57	14	32	246	400

LEADING SCORERS

	G	A	PTS
Gretzky, Edmonton	55	109	164
Dionne, Los Angeles	58	77	135
K. Nilsson, Calgary	49	82	131
Bossy, New York I.	68	51	119
Taylor, Los Angeles	47	65	112
P. Stastny, Quebec	39	70	109
Simmer, Los Angeles	56	49	105
Rogers, Hartford	40	65	105
Federko, St. Louis	31	73	104
Richard, Quebec	52	51	103
Middleton, Boston	44	59	103
Trottier, New York I.	31	72	103

LEADING GOALIES

	G	GA	SO	GAA
Edwards, Buffalo	45	133	3	2.96
Peeters, Philadelphia	40	115	2	2.96
Beaupre, Minnesota	44	138	0	3.20
Lessard, Los Angeles	64	203	2	3.25
Smith, New York I.	41	129	3	3.28

PLAYOFF RESULTS

Preliminary Round

St. Louis d. Pittsburgh, 3–2
Philadelphia d. Quebec, 3–2
Buffalo d. Vancouver, 3–0
Calgary d. Chicago, 3–0
Minnesota d. Boston, 3–0
Edmonton d. Montreal, 3–0
N.Y. Islanders d. Toronto, 3–0
N.Y. Rangers d. Los Angeles, 3–1

Quarterfinals

Minnesota d. Buffalo, 4–1
Calgary d. Philadelphia, 4–3
N.Y. Islanders d. Edmonton, 4–2
N.Y. Rangers d. St. Louis, 4–2

Semifinals

N.Y. Islanders d. N.Y. Rangers, 4–0
Minnesota d. Calgary, 4–1

Finals

N.Y. Islanders d. Minnesota, 4–1

LEADING SCORERS

	G	A	P
Bossy, N.Y. Islanders	17	18	35
Payne, Minnesota	17	12	29
Trottier, N.Y. Islanders	11	18	29

| Potvin, N.Y. Islanders | 8 | 17 | 25 |
| Smith, Minnesota | 8 | 17 | 25 |

LEADING GOALIES

	W	SO	GAA
Smith, N.Y. Islanders	14	0	2.54
St. Croix, Philadelphia	4	1	2.99
Edwards, Buffalo	4	0	3.34
Meloche, Minnesota	8	0	3.52
Baker, N.Y. Rangers	7	0	4.00

1981–82

He stood a lean and bony 165 pounds, barely reached 5–11 on his tiptoes and with his thin, innocent face looked more like a schoolboy than the greatest player of his generation—maybe the greatest of any generation. Edmonton's Wayne Gretzky was 21 years old and no one had ever done what he did in 1981–82.

Having already shattered the scoring record a year earlier, Gretzky went on to destroy it, amassing 212 points, an incredible 65 more than anyone else and 107 more than his closest teammate. Included in Gretzky's total was a record 92 goals, which broke Phil Esposito's record by 16, and a record 120 assists.

The New York Islanders won their third straight Stanley Cup and won a record 15 consecutive games in the process, but it was clearly the season of No. 99, known to his Edmonton fans as "The Kid."

Gretzky became the National Hockey League's first million-dollar-a-year performer, negotiating the record pact shortly after scoring 50 goals in his first 39 games, breaking the record set by Maurice (Rocket) Richard 39 years earlier and equaled by New York Islander Mike Bossy the year before.

Taking a cue from their slender center, the Oilers vaulted from 15th place in 1980–81 to a second-place finish overall in the point standings, behind only the champion Islanders. But the Oilers were upset in the first round of the playoffs by Los Angeles, the team with the worst record of any of the 16 playoff entrants.

Edmonton's ouster only served to make the Islanders' march to their third straight title that

much easier. They became only the third franchise, joining Toronto and Montreal, to win as many as three consecutive Stanley Cups.

Bossy, the quick right wing, led the Islanders in the playoffs, earning the Conn Smythe Trophy as playoff MVP after scoring 17 goals, seven of them in a four-game finals sweep of Vancouver, tying a 26-year-old record set by Jean Beliveau.

Bossy and Gretzky were named to the All-Star team with Edmonton left wing Mark Messier, Islander goalie Bill Smith, and defensemen Ray Bourque of Boston and Doug Wilson of Chicago.

To no one's surprise, Gretzky was the first unanimous choice as Hart Trophy winner as the Most Valuable Player, joining Bobby Orr as the only player to win the award three straight seasons.

Wilson won the Norris as best defenseman, Boston center Steve Kasper took the Selke Trophy as the best defensive forward, Boston right wing Rick Middleton won the Lady Byng for sportsmanship, and Winnipeg center Dale Hawerchuk got the Calder as Rookie of the Year.

1981–82

FINAL STANDINGS

Prince of Wales Conference: Patrick Division

	W	L	T	PTS	GF	GA
New York I.	54	16	10	118	385	250
New York R.	39	27	14	92	316	306
Philadelphia	38	31	11	87	325	313
Pittsburgh	31	36	13	75	310	337
Washington	26	41	13	65	319	338

Prince of Wales Conference: Adams Division

	W	L	T	PTS	GF	GA
Montreal	46	17	17	109	360	223
Boston	43	27	10	96	323	285
Buffalo	39	26	15	93	307	273
Quebec	33	31	16	82	356	345
Hartford	21	41	18	60	264	351

Clarence Campbell Conference: Norris Division

	W	L	T	PTS	GF	GA
Minnesota	37	23	20	94	346	288
Winnipeg	33	33	14	80	319	332
St. Louis	32	40	8	72	315	349
Chicago	30	38	12	72	332	363
Toronto	20	44	16	56	298	380
Detroit	21	47	12	54	270	351

Clarence Campbell Conference: Smythe Division

	W	L	T	PTS	GF	GA
Edmonton	48	17	15	111	417	295
Vancouver	30	33	17	77	290	286
Calgary	29	34	17	75	334	345
Los Angeles	24	41	15	63	314	369
Colorado	18	49	13	49	241	362

LEADING SCORERS

	G	A	PTS
Gretzky, Edmonton	92	120	212
Bossy, New York I.	64	83	147
P. Stastny, Quebec	46	93	139
Maruk, Washington	60	76	136
Trottier, New York I.	50	79	129
D. Savard, Chicago	32	87	119
Dionne, Los Angeles	50	67	117
Smith, Minnesota	43	71	114
Ciccarelli, Minnesota	55	52	107
Taylor, Los Angeles	39	67	106

LEADING GOALIES

	G	GA	SO	GAA
Smith, New York I.	44	123	0	2.88
Fuhr, Edmonton	46	153	0	3.37
Baron, Boston	43	141	1	3.38
Meloche, Minnesota	49	164	1	3.39
Brodeur, Vancouver	50	164	1	3.40

PLAYOFF RESULTS

Division Semifinals

Boston d. Buffalo, 3–1
Quebec d. Montreal, 3–2
Chicago d. Minnesota, 3–1
St. Louis d. Winnipeg, 3–1
N.Y. Islanders d. Pittsburgh, 3–2
N.Y. Rangers d. Philadelphia, 3–1
Los Angeles d. Edmonton, 3–2
Vancouver d. Calgary, 3–0

Division Finals

Quebec d. Boston, 4–3
Chicago d. St. Louis, 4–2
N.Y. Islanders d. N.Y. Rangers, 4–2
Vancouver d. Los Angeles, 4–1

Conference Finals

N.Y. Islanders d. Quebec, 4–0
Vancouver d. Chicago, 4–1

Finals

N.Y. Islanders d. Vancouver, 4–0

LEADING SCORERS

	G	A	P
Trottier, N.Y. Islanders	6	23	29
Bossy, N.Y. Islanders	17	10	27
Potvin, N.Y. Islanders	5	16	21

LEADING GOALIES

	W	SO	GAA
Wamsley, Montreal	2	0	2.20
Smith, N.Y. Islanders	15	1	2.52
Esposito, Chicago	3	1	2.52
Brodeur, Vancouver	11	0	2.70

1982–83

As the teams went deeper into the 1982–83 season, the question seemed to be not whether the New York Islanders could win another Stanley Cup championship, but rather which team would succeed them. The Islanders slumped and suffered during the season, but when the playoffs ended, the Islanders possessed their fourth

straight title, earning themselves a slice of immortality.

They became only the second franchise to win that many consecutive championships, joining the five-time winners from Montreal (1956–60) and the Canadiens' four-time winners (1976–79). While there were record-setting performances by individuals on other teams, they seemed to pale in comparison to the Islanders' fourth championship in just their 11th season of existence.

Not even Wayne Gretzky, who again led the league in scoring with 196 points, could stop the Islanders' charge to the Cup. Gretzky was held without a goal and with just four assists as the Islanders swept the Edmonton Oilers in four games in the final series. The Islanders were led by goalie Billy Smith, who won the Conn Smythe Trophy as playoff MVP, and Mike Bossy, who set an NHL playoff record with five game-winning goals in one season.

Bossy also tied Guy Lafleur's regular-season record of six straight 50-goal seasons and became the first player to score 60 goals three straight years. Marcel Dionne of Los Angeles became the first player to score 100 points in seven consecutive seasons, breaking the mark held by Lafleur and Bobby Orr. Boston goalie Pete Peeters went 31 games without a loss, one shy of the record held by his coach, Gerry Cheevers, and the Oilers set a record by scoring 424 goals.

Still, the biggest accomplishment belonged to the Islanders. They finished a disappointing

The Great Gretzky meets Goldie Hawn and Burt Reynolds after his record-setting goal.

Peter Stastny and brothers Anton (left) and Marian (middle) led Quebec into the semifinals in the 1982 playoffs.

sixth in points during the season, the worst finish ever for a Cup winner, but defeated Washington in the preliminary round of the playoffs and the New York Rangers in the Patrick Division finals. After disposing of the Rangers, the Islanders met Boston, the team that led the league during the season with 110 points.

Following a six-game elimination of the Bruins in the Prince of Wales Conference final, the Islanders finished off the Oilers for their second straight finals sweep, adding it to the one the previous year against Vancouver. Smith was the hero. He shut out the Oilers in the opening game, 2–0, the first goalie to blank them since he did it two years earlier. He held the high-scoring Oilers to just six goals in the series while running his career playoff record to 73–24.

That represented vindication for both Smith and the Islanders. Smith failed to win a game for two months during the regular season and the Islanders went through a stretch when they could not assemble back-to-back victories for two months. The four Stanley Cups put the Islanders fifth among all NHL teams and with his 97th career playoff victory, Islander coach Al Arbour moved right behind Scotty Bowman (111) and Dick Irvin (100), who led the all-time list.

But not all the records set were glowing ones. Islander Billy Carroll, a center, set an all-time record for forwards by playing in 69 straight games without scoring a goal. And the Canadiens suffered their third straight preliminary-round elimination, which hadn't happened in the long and regal history of the franchise.

In his first season as a Bruin in 1982–83, goalie Pete Peeters posted a streak of 31 games without a defeat and won the Vezina Trophy.

Besides winning the Ross Trophy for leading the league in scoring, Gretzky also was awarded his fourth straight MVP award, the most times anyone has ever won the trophy consecutively. Peeters got the Vezina Trophy for best regular-season goaltender, Washington's Rod Langway captured the Norris Trophy for top defenseman, and Bossy took the Lady Byng Trophy for sportsmanship and high standard of playing ability. Philadelphia's Bobby Clarke won the Selke Trophy as best defensive forward and Chicago's Steve Larmer was Rookie of the Year.

The Oilers placed two players, Gretzky and Mark Messier, on the All-Star team. Joining them were Bossy, Peeters, Langway, and Philadelphia's Mark Howe.

1982–83
FINAL STANDINGS

Prince of Wales Conference: Adams Division

	W	L	T	PTS	GF	GA
Boston	50	20	10	110	327	228
Montreal	42	24	14	98	350	286
Buffalo	38	29	13	89	318	285
Quebec	34	34	12	80	343	336
Hartford	19	54	7	45	261	403

Prince of Wales Conference: Patrick Division

	W	L	T	PTS	GF	GA
Philadelphia	49	23	8	106	326	240
New York I.	42	26	12	96	302	226
Washington	39	25	16	94	306	283
New York R.	35	35	10	80	306	287
New Jersey	17	49	14	48	230	338
Pittsburgh	18	53	9	45	257	394

Clarence Campbell Conference: Norris Division

	W	L	T	PTS	GF	GA
Chicago	47	23	10	104	338	268
Minnesota	40	24	16	96	321	290

Islander goalie Billy Smith, MVP of the 1983 Stanley Cup playoffs, frustrated Wayne Gretzky (99) and his Edmonton teammates.

	W	L	T	PTS	GF	GA
Toronto	28	40	12	68	293	330
St. Louis	25	40	15	65	285	316
Detroit	21	44	15	57	263	344

Clarence Campbell Conference: Smythe Division

	W	L	T	PTS	GF	GA
Edmonton	47	21	12	106	424	315
Calgary	32	34	14	78	321	317
Vancouver	30	35	15	75	303	309
Winnipeg	33	39	8	74	311	333
Los Angeles	27	41	12	66	308	365

LEADING SCORERS

	G	A	PTS
Gretzky, Edmonton	71	125	196
P. Stastny, Quebec	47	77	124
Savard, Chicago	35	85	120
Bossy, New York I.	60	58	118
Dionne, Los Angeles	56	51	107
Pederson, Boston	46	61	107
Messier, Edmonton	48	58	106
Goulet, Quebec	57	48	105
Anderson, Edmonton	48	56	104
Nilsson, Calgary	46	58	104
Kurri, Edmonton	45	59	104

LEADING GOALIES

	G	GA	SO	GAA
Peeters, Boston	62	142	8	2.36
Melanson, New York I.	44	109	1	2.66
Smith, New York I.	41	112	1	2.87
Lindbergh, Philadelphia	40	116	3	2.98
Bannerman, Chicago	41	127	4	3.10

PLAYOFF RESULTS

Division Semifinals

Chicago d. St. Louis, 3–1
Minnesota d. Toronto, 3–1
Edmonton d. Winnipeg, 3–0
Calgary d. Vancouver, 3–1
Boston d. Quebec, 3–1
Buffalo d. Montreal, 3–0
N.Y. Islanders d. Washington, 3–1
N.Y. Rangers d. Philadelphia, 3–0

Division Finals

Chicago d. Minnesota, 4–1
Edmonton d. Calgary, 4–1
Boston d. Buffalo, 4–3
N.Y. Islanders d. N.Y. Rangers, 4–2

Conference Finals

N.Y. Islanders d. Boston, 4–2
Edmonton d. Chicago, 4–0

Finals

N.Y. Islanders d. Edmonton, 4–0

LEADING SCORERS

	G	A	P
Gretzky, Edmonton	12	26	38
Middleton, Boston	11	22	33
Pederson, Boston	14	18	32

LEADING GOALIES

	W	SO	GAA
Melanson, N.Y. Islanders	2	0	2.52
Smith, N.Y. Islanders	13	2	2.68
Bouchard, Quebec	1	0	2.73

1983–84

In his first four years in the NHL, Edmonton's Wayne Gretzky lived an everyday hockey existence that to all other players was fantasy. Yet

he still had not realized his dream—taking a victory lap with the Stanley Cup hoisted above his shoulders.

Indeed, a season earlier in the Cup finals, he had been reduced to a mere mortal for the first time in his career, held to just four assists in the Islanders' sweep of his Oilers.

From the outset of the 1983–84 season, it became apparent Gretzky would do everything possible to help earn the Oilers another shot. He scored a point in the Oilers' opener and in every game his club played in October, November, and into December. On December 18, he scored a pair of goals and assists against Winnipeg to reach the 100-point mark in only his 34th game, breaking his own league mark.

The streak continued until January 27, 1984, when Kings' goaltender Markus Mattson held the Oilers to a couple of goals in a 4–2 decision, snapping Gretzky's string at an incredible 51 games during which he amassed 153 points, including 61 goals.

His final totals of 87–118–205 left him 79 points ahead of his nearest challenger—teammate Paul Coffey—in the scoring race. The pair helped Edmonton to a 57–18–5 record and 119 points. The Oilers also established an all-time mark with 446 goals, a record 36 of them shorthanded, and set another record with three 50-plus goal scorers (Gretzky, Glenn Anderson with 54, and Jari Kurri with 52).

Gretzky and the Oilers were not the only ones to create headlines or set records. Buffalo rookie goaltender Tom Barrasso, an 18-year-old who was drafted out of high school the previous June, collected both the Vezina Trophy as top netminder and the Calder for rookie honors and earned a spot on the first All-Star team. He finished the season with a 26–12–3 record and a league-leading 2.84 goals-against average.

An unusual record was set October 30 in Philadelphia when four brothers appeared in the same game. Duane and Brent Sutter of the Islanders relived their "Hayloft Hockey" days with

twin brothers Ron and Rich, who were rookies with the Flyers. That brought to six the number of Sutters in the league, with Brian playing for St. Louis and Darryl with Chicago.

The Olympic Saddledome opened in Calgary, Quebec's Michel Goulet scored more points (121) than any left wing in one season, and on November 25 an NHL-record crowd of 21,019 jammed Joe Louis Arena in Detroit to watch the Red Wings defeat the Penguins, 7–4.

Fans in every arena got a little more for their money when, for the first time since November 21, 1942, overtime was reinstated. The five-minute, sudden-death format made its debut on October 5 when the Jets and Red Wings tied at 6–6. The first overtime goal came three nights later in the Capital Centre when the Islanders' Bob Bourne scored at 2:01 to beat Washington, 8–7. It was the first regular-season overtime goal since November 10, 1942, when the Rangers' Lynn Patrick tallied his team's fifth goal at 7:11 in a 5–3 victory. In those days, the extra session ran a full 10 minutes, no matter how many goals were scored.

While most of the early attention in the playoffs was focused on whether Al Arbour's Islanders could win their fifth straight Cup or if Edmonton could finally fulfill its promise, St. Louis and Minnesota kept everyone entertained in their Norris Division final, the North Stars winning the seventh game after six minutes of overtime on a goal by Steve Payne.

The Islanders' "Drive for Five," as they tried to match the Canadiens' feat of winning five straight titles (the Habs accomplished it in the old six-team league when it required only two post-season series victories per year), got off to a rocky start. They trailed, 2–1, in a best-of-five Patrick Division semifinal series with the Rangers, but eventually survived when Ken Morrow scored at 8:56 of overtime to win the fifth and deciding game. They got by the Capitals in five games and overcame a 2–0 deficit to oust the Canadiens in six games, winning their NHL-

Held scoreless in the Islanders' sweep to their fourth consecutive Stanley Cup, a dejected Wayne Gretzky accepts the reality of defeat in the third period of the final game, 1983.

record 19th straight playoff series to make the finals for a fifth straight year.

The Oilers, who needed just 12 games to make it to the championship round, took a page from the Islanders' style book in the opening game at Nassau Coliseum, giving a superior defensive performance in front of Grant Fuhr to beat the Islanders and Bill Smith, 1–0.

The Isles, physically battered in their previous series, rebounded with a 6–1 victory, but after that, it was Edmonton in a rout. With Gretzky and Mark Messier leading the attack, the Oilers reeled off three consecutive triumphs (7–2, 7–2, 5–2) to wrap up their first Stanley Cup. Gretzky's 35 points topped playoff scorers and Messier, with 26 points and sensational pivotal goals in

Games 3 and 4, wound up with the Conn Smythe Trophy as playoff MVP.

Washington's Rod Langway (the Norris Trophy winner), Boston's Ray Bourque, Gretzky, Goulet, and the Islanders' Mike Bossy joined Barrasso on the All-Star team, and Washington's Doug Jarvis won the Selke Trophy as best defensive forward.

Philadelphia center Bobby Clarke announced his retirement on May 15 after 15 years as a distinguished Flyer.

The biggest winners among the losers appeared to be the Penguins, who finished with 38 points, three fewer than the Devils, giving them the chance to select junior phenom Mario Lemieux in the 1984 June entry draft.

1983–84

FINAL STANDINGS

Prince of Wales Conference: Adams Division

	W	L	T	PTS	GF	GA
Boston	49	25	6	104	336	261
Buffalo	48	25	7	103	315	257
Quebec	42	28	10	94	360	278
Montreal	35	40	5	75	286	295
Hartford	28	42	10	66	288	320

Prince of Wales Conference: Patrick Division

	W	L	T	PTS	GF	GA
New York I.	50	26	4	104	357	269
Washington	48	27	5	101	308	226
Philadelphia	44	26	10	98	350	290
New York R.	42	29	9	93	314	304
New Jersey	17	56	7	41	231	350
Pittsburgh	16	58	6	38	254	390

Clarence Campbell Conference: Norris Division

	W	L	T	PTS	GF	GA
Minnesota	39	31	10	88	345	344
St. Louis	32	41	7	71	293	316
Detroit	31	42	7	69	298	323
Chicago	30	42	8	68	277	311
Toronto	26	45	9	61	303	387

Charlie Huddy, left; Paul Coffey, center; and Jari Kurri celebrate Edmonton's Cup repeat in 1985.

Clarence Campbell Conference: Smythe Division

	W	L	T	PTS	GF	GA
Edmonton	57	18	5	119	446	314
Calgary	34	32	14	82	311	314
Vancouver	32	39	9	73	306	328
Winnipeg	31	38	11	73	340	374
Los Angeles	23	44	13	59	309	376

LEADING SCORERS

	G	A	PTS
Gretzky, Edmonton	87	118	205
Coffey, Edmonton	40	86	126
Goulet, Quebec	56	65	121
P. Stastny, Quebec	46	73	119
Bossy, New York I.	51	67	118
Pederson, Boston	39	77	116
Kurri, Edmonton	52	61	113
Trottier, New York I.	40	71	111
Federko, St. Louis	41	66	107
Middleton, Boston	47	58	105

LEADING GOALIES

	G	GA	SO	GAA
Riggin, Washington	41	102	4	2.66
Barrasso, Buffalo	42	117	2	2.84
Froese, Philadelphia	48	150	2	3.14
Peeters, Boston	50	151	0	3.16
Bouchard, Quebec	57	180	1	3.20

PLAYOFF RESULTS

Division Semifinals

Montreal d. Boston, 3–0
Quebec d. Buffalo, 3–0
N.Y. Islanders d. N.Y. Rangers, 3–2
Washington d. Philadelphia, 3–0
Minnesota d. Chicago, 3–2
St. Louis d. Detroit, 3–1
Edmonton d. Winnipeg, 3–0
Calgary d. Vancouver, 3–1

Division Finals

Montreal d. Quebec, 4–2
N.Y. Islanders d. Washington, 4–1
Minnesota d. St. Louis, 4–3
Edmonton d. Calgary, 4–3

Conference Finals

N.Y. Islanders d. Montreal, 4–1
Edmonton d. Minnesota, 4–0

Finals

Edmonton d. N.Y. Islanders, 4–1

LEADING SCORERS

	G	A	P
Gretzky, Edmonton	13	22	35
Kurri, Edmonton	14	14	28
Gillies, N.Y. Islanders	12	7	19

LEADING GOALIES

	W	SO	GAA
Penny, Montreal	9	3	2.20
Liut, St. Louis	6	1	2.44

1984–85

The spotlight that had been glowing solely on Wayne Gretzky finally broke into a prism with the emergence of teammate Jari Kurri as a superstar and with the much-hyped arrival in Pittsburgh of Mario Lemieux, the youngster who had broken all of Guy Lafleur's Quebec Major Junior

All-Star Rod Langway of Washington was voted the league's leading defenseman in 1983–84.

Hockey League scoring records in 1983–84 with 133 goals and 282 points with the Laval Voisins.

Gretzky was in a race for the goal-scoring crown all season with Kurri, his sharpshooting right wing who became only the third player in history (after Phil Esposito and Gretzky) to reach the 70-goal plateau. Kurri finished with 71 goals, two behind Gretzky, who ran away with the Art Ross Trophy, scoring 208 points, 73 more than runnerup Kurri. The pair helped the Oilers go a record 15 games from the start of the season without a loss (12–0–3).

Of course, another season in the NHL meant another milestone for Gretzky. It came on December 19, when he picked up an assist for his 1,000th career point in only his 424th game, demolishing Guy Lafleur's 720-game record of being the fastest player to reach that total.

Edmonton's Mark Messier (11) was the playoff MVP as the Oilers won their first Stanley Cup in 1984, ending the Islanders' "Drive for Five."

Lemieux got off to a slow start, but began to make his presence felt as the season progressed. Lemieux got little help from teammates on a club that managed only 53 points, the next-to-worst record in the league. By the time April arrived, Lemieux had become only the third rookie (Peter Stastny and Dave Hawerchuk were the others) ever to reach the 100-point plateau. He finished with 43 goals and 57 assists and won the Calder Trophy as the league's top rookie.

Washington's Bobby Carpenter also was finally fulfilling expectations, as his 53 goals made him the first U.S.-born player ever to score 50 in a season.

The same night that Gretzky was scoring his 1,000th point, Buffalo coach Scotty Bowman was rewriting the record book, recording his 691st victory behind the bench in a career with the Canadiens and Sabres. That eclipsed former Montreal-Chicago-Toronto coach Dick Irvin. In the meantime, the Rangers were playing musical chairs with coaches, dismissing 1980 U.S. Olympic coach Herb Brooks, with general manager Craig Patrick taking over and later selecting Ted Sator.

The Islanders gave indication that a sixth consecutive appearance in the Cup finals was not likely when they finished the season in third place in the Patrick Division with 86 points, their poorest showing in 11 years.

The league's best record belonged to the resurgent Philadelphia Flyers, whose 53–20–7 mark for 113 points was four better than the defending Cup champion Oilers, whom they would meet in the finals. Philadelphia was led by goaltender Pelle Lindbergh, who led the league with 40 victories (40–17–7), and on offense by Tim Kerr, who contributed 54 goals.

The playoffs were full of memorable moments and records. One mark was set in the opening second of the postseason when Detroit's Brad Park stepped on the ice, making it the 17th consecutive year in which he participated in the playoffs.

After dropping the first two games in overtime in their opening series against Washington,

Pittsburgh's Mario Lemieux responded to his pre-NHL fanfare with a 100-point performance on the way to Rookie of the Year honors in 1984-85.

the Islanders rebounded with a 2–1 victory, then scored four times in the third period to win, 6–4, in Game 4. Bill Smith's goaltending and Brent Sutter's game-winning goal were the keys to a 2–1 victory in Game 5 as the Isles became the first team in history to win a five-game series after losing the first two.

There were no more miracles in the following round, however, when they ran up against the Flyers, who had swept the Rangers in an opening round that featured Kerr's record four goals in the second period of Game 3. The Flyers promptly defeated the Islanders in five games and then dispatched Quebec in six.

But Philadelphia didn't have enough weapons to stay with Edmonton. After losing the opener, 4–1, the Oilers ran off four straight wins to earn their second consecutive Cup.

Gretzky captured one of the few awards that had eluded him to that point—the Conn Smythe Trophy as playoff MVP, completing the postseason with a record for assists (30) and points (47). Kurri's 19 goals equaled the NHL mark.

Left wing John Ogrodnick became the first Red Wing in 12 years to be named to the first All-Star team, joining Lindbergh (Vezina), Edmonton's Paul Coffey (Norris), Boston's Ray Bourque, Gretzky, and Kurri (Lady Byng). Buffalo's Craig Ramsey won the Selke Trophy as best defensive forward.

1984–85

FINAL STANDINGS

Prince of Wales Conference: Adams Division

	W	L	T	PTS	GF	GA
Montreal	41	27	12	94	309	262
Quebec	41	30	9	91	323	275
Buffalo	38	28	14	90	290	237
Boston	36	34	10	82	303	287
Hartford	30	41	9	69	268	318

Prince of Wales Conference: Patrick Division

	W	L	T	PTS	GF	GA
Philadelphia	53	20	7	113	348	241
Washington	46	25	9	101	322	240
New York I.	40	34	6	86	345	312
New York R.	26	44	10	62	295	345
New Jersey	22	48	10	54	264	346
Pittsburgh	24	51	5	53	276	385

Clarence Campbell Conference: Norris Division

	W	L	T	PTS	GF	GA
St. Louis	37	31	12	86	299	288
Chicago	38	35	7	83	309	299
Detroit	27	41	12	66	313	357
Minnesota	25	43	12	62	268	321
Toronto	20	52	8	48	253	358

Clarence Campbell Conference: Smythe Division

	W	L	T	PTS	GF	GA
Edmonton	49	20	11	109	401	298
Winnipeg	43	27	10	96	358	332
Calgary	41	27	12	94	363	302
Los Angeles	34	32	14	82	339	326
Vancouver	25	46	9	59	284	401

LEADING SCORERS

	G	A	PTS
Gretzky, Edmonton	73	135	208
Kurri, Edmonton	71	64	135
Hawerchuk, Winnipeg	53	77	130
Dionne, Los Angeles	46	80	126
Coffey, Edmonton	37	84	121
Bossy, New York I.	58	59	117
Ogrodnick, Detroit	55	50	105
Savard, Chicago	38	67	105
Federko, St. Louis	30	73	103
Gartner, Washington	50	52	102
B. Sutter, New York I.	42	60	102

LEADING GOALIES

	G	GA	SO	GAA
Barrasso, Buffalo	54	144	5	2.66
Riggin, Washington	57	168	2	2.98
Lindbergh, Philadelphia	65	194	2	3.02
Penney, Montreal	54	167	1	3.08
Wamsley, St. Louis	40	126	0	3.26

PLAYOFF RESULTS

Division Semifinals

Montreal d. Boston, 3–2
Quebec d. Buffalo, 3–2
Philadelphia d. N.Y. Rangers, 3–0
N.Y. Islanders d. Washington, 3–2
Minnesota d. St. Louis, 3–0
Chicago d. Detroit, 3–0
Edmonton d. Los Angeles, 3–0
Winnipeg d. Calgary, 3–0

Division Finals

Philadelphia d. N.Y. Islanders, 4–1
Quebec d. Montreal, 4–3
Chicago d. Minnesota, 4–2
Edmonton d. Winnipeg, 4–0

Conference Finals

Philadelphia d. Quebec, 4–2
Edmonton d. Chicago, 4–2

Finals

Edmonton d. Philadelphia, 4–1

LEADING SCORERS

	G	A	P
Gretzky, Edmonton	17	30	47
Coffey, Edmonton	12	25	37
Kurri, Edmonton	19	12	31
Savard, Chicago	9	20	29

LEADING GOALIES

	W	SO	GAA
Lindbergh, Philadelphia	12	3	2.50
Gosselin, Quebec	9	0	3.06
Fuhr, Edmonton	15	0	3.10

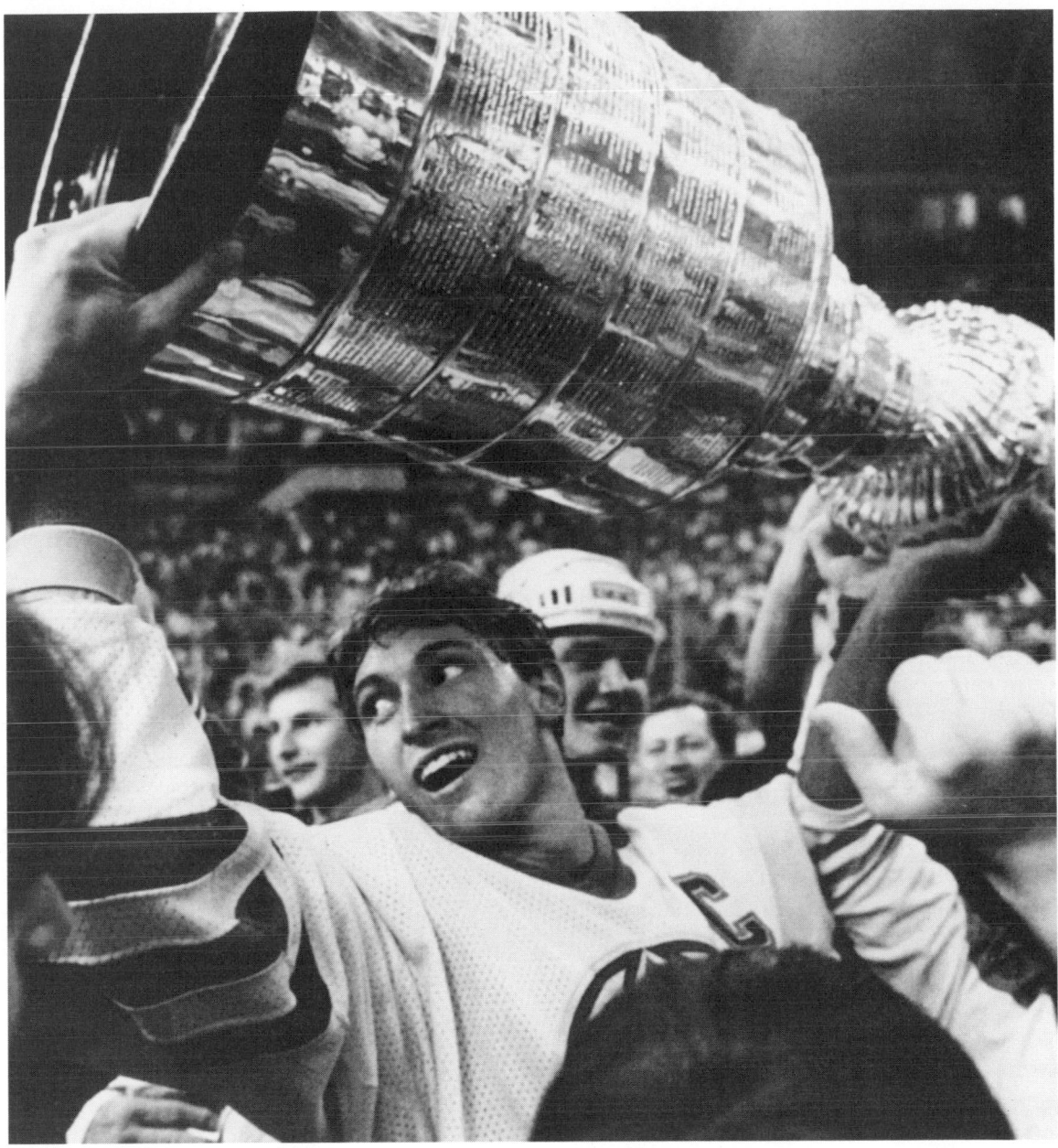

Wayne Gretzky celebrates two Cups in a row for Edmonton in 1985.

1985–86

Bobby Orr had been out of hockey for seven years, but fans kept being reminded of his greatness throughout the 1985–86 season as several of his single-season and career records for defensemen were eclipsed.

The first Orr mark to fall came on December 20 when the Islanders' Denis Potvin, in his

Oiler defenseman Paul Coffey shone in a record-breaking 1985–86 campaign that landed his second consecutive Norris Trophy.

There was change, triumph, and tragedy during the regular season. The NHL announced that fans would vote for the starting teams in the All-Star Game. In addition, the league created a new award—the Presidents' Trophy—presented to the team with the NHL's overall best record, along with a check for $100,000 to be split among the players.

The Oilers gobbled up the cash, finishing with 119 points, matching their previous club record. The Flyers placed second with 110 points and overcame the grief and shock of losing their All-Star goaltender Pelle Lindbergh, who was killed when he drove his Porsche at high speed into a wall in November.

Of course, it was Wayne Gretzky who played a major role in keeping the Oilers at the top in the regular season. He ended the season with NHL records of 215 points and 163 assists. Gretzky took the Art Ross Trophy for a sixth straight year, finishing 74 points ahead of Pittsburgh's Mario Lemieux.

Gretzky's figures dwarfed other notable accomplishments by the Flyers' Tim Kerr, who set a one-season mark with 34 power-play goals; by Minnesota center Neal Broten, who became the first U.S.-born player to record 100 or more points (105), and by Buffalo's Gilbert Perreault, who scored his 500th career goal in March.

The experts predicted that the playoffs would be another futile exercise for everyone except the Oilers. It didn't work out that way. In fact, the Oilers never got out of the Smythe Division. After dispatching the Canucks in three straight, the Oilers faced arch-rival Calgary, which had been bolstered three months earlier when it received Joey Mullen, Terry Johnson, and Rik Wilson from St. Louis for Eddy Beers, Gino Cavallini, and Charlie Bourgeois in a blockbuster trade.

The Flames, relying on rookie goaltender Mike Vernon, won the opener, 4–1, and the teams alternated victories from that point, forcing a seventh game at Northlands Coliseum. The

13th season, earned his 915th career point, surpassing Orr's total, which was accumulated in 12 seasons with the Bruins and Blackhawks. Just 39 days later, Potvin again replaced Orr at the top of a scoring list when he netted his 271st career goal.

Oiler backliner Paul Coffey tallied his 46th and 47th goals on April 2, snapping Orr's once untouchable record. Coffey finished the season at 48–90–138, one point shy of Orr's standard for defensemen.

Eight of Coffey's points came on March 14 when he tied the NHL mark for defensemen established by Philadelphia's Tom Bladon and also equaled a backliner's record for assists in one game with six. Coffey added one more record for defensemen by collecting points in 28 consecutive games.

contest was tied at two with 5:14 gone in the third period when one of the strangest plays in postseason history occurred. Rookie Oiler defenseman Steve Smith, pressured near his own net, tried to backpass to defensive partner Don Jackson. Instead, the puck ticked off goalie Grant Fuhr's left skate and slid into the net. Calgary center Perry Berezan got credit for the goal. The stunned Oilers never got the equalizer and their two-year reign as Stanley Cup champions ended in bizarre fashion.

There were other early-round surprises. The Islanders were swept for the first time in their history, ousted in three games by Washington, and Adams Division winner Quebec was bounced in the same number by fourth-place Hartford.

All but the Rangers-Capitals division final went seven games, the most thrilling between the Whalers and Canadiens when Montreal's Claude Lemieux scored at 5:55 of overtime of the seventh game.

The Blues forced the Flames to a seventh game in the Campbell Conference finals, losing 2–1, while the Canadiens ousted the Rangers in five games to set up the first all-Canadian final since Montreal and Toronto met in 1967. Calgary won the Cup final opener at home and went into overtime in Game 2. But Brian Skrudland's goal at nine seconds (the fastest overtime goal in playoff history) evened the series.

Montreal won the next three games to cop the Stanley Cup, the club's 23rd championship. Rookie goaltender Patrick Roy became the youngest Conn Smythe Trophy winner at age 20 after compiling a 15–5 record and 1.92 goals-against average.

Coffey copped the Norris Trophy for the second straight season while Ranger goaltender John Vanbiesbrouck won the Vezina, Calgary defenseman Gary Suter the Calder, Chicago center Troy Murray the Selke, and the Islanders' Mike Bossy the Lady Byng for the third time. Gretzky, Vanbiesbrouck, Bossy, Coffey, Philadelphia's Mark

Philadelphia's Tim Kerr set a single-season record with 34 power-play goals in 1985–86.

Howe, and Quebec's Michel Goulet were first-team All-Stars.

1985–86

FINAL STANDINGS

Prince of Wales Conference: Adams Division

	W	L	T	PTS	GF	GA
Quebec	43	31	6	92	330	289
Montreal	40	33	7	87	330	280
Boston	37	31	12	86	311	288
Hartford	40	36	4	84	332	302
Buffalo	37	37	6	80	296	291

Prince of Wales Conference: Patrick Division

	W	L	T	PTS	GF	GA
Philadelphia	53	23	4	110	335	241
Washington	50	23	7	107	315	272
New York I.	39	29	12	90	327	284
New York R.	36	38	6	78	280	276
Pittsburgh	34	38	8	76	313	305
New Jersey	28	49	3	59	300	374

Clarence Campbell Conference: Norris Division

	W	L	T	PTS	GF	GA
Chicago	39	33	8	86	351	349
Minnesota	38	33	9	85	327	305

A 20-year-old rookie goaltender, Montreal's Patrick Roy achieved MVP honors in the playoffs as Montreal captured the Stanley Cup in 1986.

St. Louis	37	34	9	83	302	291
Toronto	25	48	7	57	311	386
Detroit	17	57	6	40	266	415

Clarence Campbell Conference: Smythe Division

	W	L	T	PTS	GF	GA
Edmonton	56	17	7	119	426	310
Calgary	40	31	9	89	354	315
Winnipeg	26	47	7	59	295	372
Vancouver	23	44	13	59	282	333
Los Angeles	23	49	8	54	284	389

LEADING SCORERS

	G	A	PTS
Gretzky, Edmonton	52	163	215
Lemieux, Pittsburgh	48	93	141
Coffey, Edmonton	48	90	138
Kurri, Edmonton	68	63	131
Bossy, New York I.	61	62	123
P. Stastny, Quebec	41	81	122
Savard, Chicago	47	69	116
Naslund, Montreal	43	67	110
Hawerchuk, Winnipeg	46	59	105
N. Broten, Minnesota	29	76	105

LEADING GOALIES

	G	GA	SO	GAA
Froese, Philadelphia	51	116	5	2.55
Jensen, Washington	44	129	2	3.18
Malarchuk, Quebec	46	142	4	3.21
Hrudey, New York I.	45	137	1	3.21
Vanbiesbrouck, New York R.	61	184	3	3.32

PLAYOFF RESULTS

Division Semifinals

Hartford d. Quebec, 3–0
Montreal d. Boston, 3–0
N.Y. Rangers d. Philadelphia, 3–2
Washington d. N.Y. Islanders, 3–0
Toronto d. Chicago, 3–0
St. Louis d. Minnesota, 3–2
Edmonton d. Vancouver, 3–0
Calgary d. Winnipeg, 3–0

Division Finals

Montreal d. Hartford, 4–3
N.Y. Rangers d. Washington, 4–2
St. Louis d. Toronto, 4–3
Calgary d. Edmonton, 4–3

Conference Finals

Montreal d. N.Y. Rangers, 4–1
Calgary d. St. Louis, 4–1

Finals

Montreal d. Calgary, 4–1

LEADING SCORERS

	G	A	P
Gretzky, Edmonton	8	11	19
Mullen, Calgary	12	7	19
McDonald, Calgary	11	7	18
Paslawski, St. Louis	10	7	17
Lemieux, Montreal	10	5	15

LEADING GOALIES

	W	SO	GAA
Roy, Montreal	15	1	1.92
Vernon, Calgary	12	0	2.93
Millen, St. Louis	6	0	2.97

1986–87

From the moment the six-team league ballooned to 12 in 1967, there appeared to be a noticeable talent imbalance in the NHL. There always were powerhouse teams, clubs capable of competing against each other, but there also were too many teams each season that had absolutely no chance of winning the Cup or even able to keep games close on the majority of nights.

But in 1986–87, the league finally appeared to have achieved parity, with all but three of the 21 teams finishing with 70 or more points. Just two teams, league-leading Edmonton (106) and Washington (100) reached the century mark.

None of the teams in the Norris Division managed to reach the .500 level but they staged an exciting race for first place, with St. Louis finishing on top with a 32–33–15 record for 79 points, just nine more than last-place Minnesota. The Blues trailed Detroit by one point going into the season's final game, but defenseman Rob Ramage scored with 71 seconds remaining in overtime to enable St. Louis to leapfrog over Detroit into first place.

A milestone occurred during the season's opening week when, on October 9, the Kings' Marcel Dionne picked up an assist in a 4–3 loss to St. Louis, giving him 1,600 career points, the second player in league history (behind Gordie Howe) to attain that plateau.

Exactly one week later, the Islanders' Denis Potvin earned his 684th career assist, breaking Brad Park's record for defensemen. It happened 13 years to the day after Potvin had been credited with his first NHL assist and point.

A record set by Hartford's Doug Jarvis took almost as long to realize. The day after Christmas, the former Montreal and Washington center played in his 915th consecutive game, breaking Garry Unger's ironman mark. Jarvis, playing in his first full season with the Whalers, helped his team edge the Canadiens by one point to win its first Adams Division title.

New Year's Day brought more than hangovers. The Capitals sent Bobby Carpenter and a 1989 second-round draft pick to the Rangers for Kelly Miller, Mike Ridley and Bob Crawford. Just 68 days later, Carpenter was packing again, this time headed to Los Angeles for Dionne, Jeff Crossman and a future draft choice.

When the regular season ended, Wayne Gretzky had run away with the Hart Trophy for an eighth straight year with 183 points, pacing the league in both goals (62) and assists (121) and finishing 75 points ahead of teammate and runnerup Jari Kurri.

The closely contested campaign gave promise of a wide-open battle for the Stanley Cup. It also promised to be the longest road ever for the eventual champion because the best-of-five opening round was expanded to best-of-seven. That set the stage for one of the most remarkable playoff series in history—between the Islanders and Capitals. After splitting the first two games, the Caps beat the Islanders twice to open a 3–1 lead. But the Isles took the next two, forcing a seventh game.

A goal by Bryan Trottier with 5:23 remaining in regulation enabled the Isles to tie the game at

The Flyers' Ron Hextall stood tall, winning the Vezina Trophy and the Smythe Trophy, the latter despite playing for the losers in the 1987 Cup final won by Edmonton.

Left wing Luc Robitaille gave the Kings cause for cheer as he earned Rookie of the Year honors in 1986–87.

2–2. Both the Isles' Kelly Hrudey and Caps' rookie goaltender Bob Mason kicked out everything from that point as the game went into overtime after overtime. Finally, six hours and 15 minutes of agony for both teams ended in ecstasy for the Islanders when Pat LaFontaine rang a shot off the right post and into the cords at 8:15 of the fourth extra session, ending the longest game in 44 years and the fifth-longest game in NHL history.

Almost lost in the euphoria over winning the marathon at 1:55 a.m. on Easter Sunday was the fact that the Islanders had become only the third team in history to win a series after trailing 3–1. The 1942 Maple Leafs and 1975 Islanders each rebounded from 3–0 deficits.

A week later, the Isles found themselves again trailing 3–1 in a series, this time the Patrick Division final against the Flyers. Again they rallied to tie the series, but the Flyers dominated,

5–1, in Game 7. Meanwhile, Detroit rebounded from a 3–1 deficit to oust Toronto, with Glen Hanlon limiting the Leafs to just two goals in the final three games.

Edmonton avoided that kind of drama, cruising past the Kings (including a postseason record 13 goals in a 13–3 victory), Jets, and Red Wings in 15 games to earn a spot in the Cup finals. The Flyers defeated the Canadiens in six games in the Wales Conference finals, winning all three games in Montreal but needlessly expending some energy in extra-curricular activities in the process.

The league had passed an instigator rule before the season began, allowing officials to assess an additional minor penalty to a player who starts an altercation. But before the opening faceoff for the Wales Conference finale, without any officials on ice, Montreal's Claude Lemieux tried to take his customary warmup-ending shot into the opponent's net. Philadelphia's Ed Hospodar jumped Lemieux and a fight began. Players in various stages of undress came out of the locker rooms and the brawl continued for 11 minutes before the referee and linesmen were alerted and able to restore order.

With the exception of goaltender Ron Hextall's vicious slash of Edmonton's Kent Nilsson, the Flyers stuck to hockey in the finals and earned the begrudging respect of even their harshest critics when they kept coming back. After losing the first two games and trailing, 3–0, halfway through Game 3, the Flyers exploded for a 5–3 victory. Although they fell in Game 4, they survived, 4–3, in Game 5 and then scored twice in a 1:24 span to erase a 2–1 deficit in Game 6. But the Oilers took the final, 3–1, to prevail in the first seven-game final since Montreal and Chicago met in 1971.

Gretzky scored just five goals in the Oilers' 21-game postseason journey, but had a playoff-high 34 points. However, the losers' Hextall was awarded the Conn Smythe Trophy, joining Detroit goaltender Roger Crozier (1966) and the Flyers' Reggie Leach (1976) as the only MVPs from losing teams.

Hextall, who won a league-leading 37 games, copped the Vezina, Boston's Ray Bourque the Norris, Philadelphia's Dave Poulin the Selke, and Luc Robitaille of the Kings the Calder. Bourque, Hextall, Gretzky, and Kurri joined Quebec's Michel Goulet and Philadelphia's Mark Howe as first-team All-Stars.

1986–87

FINAL STANDINGS

Prince of Wales Conference: Adams Division

	W	L	T	PTS	GF	GA
Hartford	43	30	7	93	287	270
Montreal	41	29	10	92	277	241
Boston	39	34	7	85	301	276
Quebec	31	39	10	72	267	276
Buffalo	28	44	8	66	280	308

Prince of Wales Conference: Patrick Division

	W	L	T	PTS	GF	GA
Philadelphia	46	26	8	100	310	245
Washington	38	32	10	86	285	278
New York I.	35	33	12	82	279	281
New York R.	34	38	8	76	307	323
Pittsburgh	30	38	12	72	297	290
New Jersey	29	45	6	64	293	368

Clarence Campbell Conference: Norris Division

	W	L	T	PTS	GF	GA
St. Louis	32	33	15	79	281	293
Detroit	34	36	10	78	260	274
Chicago	29	37	14	72	290	310
Toronto	32	42	6	70	286	319
Minnesota	30	40	10	70	296	314

Clarence Campbell Conference: Smythe Division

	W	L	T	PTS	GF	GA
Edmonton	50	24	6	106	372	284
Calgary	46	31	3	95	318	289
Winnipeg	40	32	8	88	279	271
Los Angeles	31	41	8	70	318	341
Vancouver	29	43	8	66	282	314

LEADING SCORERS

	G	A	PTS
Gretzky, Edmonton	62	121	183
Kurri, Edmonton	54	54	108
Lemieux, Pittsburgh	54	53	107
Messier, Edmonton	37	70	107
Gilmour, St. Louis	42	63	105
Ciccarelli, Minnesota	52	51	103
Hawerchuk, Winnipeg	47	53	100
Goulet, Quebec	49	47	96
Kerr, Philadelphia	58	37	95
Bourque, Boston	23	72	95

LEADING GOALIES

	G	GA	SO	GAA
Roy, Montreal	46	131	1	2.93
Hextall, Philadelphia	66	190	1	3.00
Liut, Hartford	59	187	4	3.23
Reddick, Winnipeg	48	149	0	3.24
Mason, Washington	45	137	0	3.24

PLAYOFF RESULTS

Division Semifinals

Quebec d. Hartford, 4–2
Montreal d. Boston, 4–0
Philadelphia d. N.Y. Rangers, 4–2

Quebec left wing Michel Goulet made the first All-Star team for the third time in 1986–87.

N.Y. Islanders d. Washington, 4–3
Toronto d. St. Louis, 4–2
Detroit d. Chicago, 4–0
Edmonton d. Los Angeles, 4–1
Winnipeg d. Calgary, 4–2

Division Finals

Montreal d. Quebec, 4–3
Philadelphia d. N.Y. Islanders, 4–3
Detroit d. Toronto, 4–3
Edmonton d. Winnipeg, 4–0

Conference Finals

Philadelphia d. Montreal, 4–2
Edmonton d. Detroit, 4–1

Finals

Edmonton d. Philadelphia, 4–3

LEADING SCORERS

	G	A	P
Messier, Edmonton	12	16	28
Propp, Philadelphia	12	16	28
Anderson, Edmonton	14	13	27
Kurri, Edmonton	15	10	25

LEADING GOALIES

	W	SO	GAA
Wregget, Toronto	7	1	2.29
Fuhr, Edmonton	14	0	2.46
Hrudey, N.Y. Islanders	7	0	2.71

Indicating the time had come, Pittsburgh's Mario Lemieux broke Wayne Gretzky's stranglehold on MVP and scoring honors in 1987–88.

1987–88

The man who engraved the Hart and Art Ross Trophies through the 1980s had one of the easiest jobs in the world. Every June, all he would have to do is pull out a stencil with the name Gretzky on it and etch away. But someone new had to be lettered in after the 1987–88 season.

For the first time since entering the NHL in 1979, Wayne Gretzky was not the league MVP. For the first time since his second season, the Oiler center was not the league's scoring champion. Both honors went to Pittsburgh's Mario Lemieux, who finished his fourth season with 70 goals and 168 points, 30 goals and 19 points ahead of Gretzky, who missed 16 games because of injury. Lemieux's wins broke a string of eight straight MVP awards and seven consecutive scoring titles for Gretzky.

Lemieux's scoring prowess still was not enough to get the Penguins into the playoffs. In a remarkable finish, all six teams in the Patrick Division finished with records of better than .500. The Islanders won the division with 88 points and the Penguins finished last with 81. Calgary edged Montreal by two points for the league's best record at 48–23–9.

Individuals making headlines included Marcel Dionne, who was now wearing a Rangers' uniform. Dionne collected his 700th career goal on Halloween night to join Gordie Howe (801) and Phil Esposito (717) as the only players ever to reach that milestone. One week later, Dionne notched his 1,000th career assist, joining Gretzky and Howe in that exclusive club.

Actually, Gretzky had joined the club only three days earlier when he picked up the milestone assist in Montreal. Then, on March 1, 1988, Gretzky got the big one against Los Angeles, garnering his 1,050th assist to pass Howe and move into first place on the all-time list.

Gretzky didn't combine with Paul Coffey on any of his points in 1987–88. The All-Star defenseman held out in a contract dispute and was traded to Pittsburgh on November 24, 1987, in a seven-player deal.

Philadelphia's Ron Hextall made history on December 8 when he became the first goaltender in NHL history to actually shoot a puck into a net. Bill Smith of the Islanders had been the first goaltender to be credited with scoring a goal (November 28, 1979, in Denver), but he was simply the last Islander to touch the puck before Colorado's Rob Ramage put it into his own net.

Another goaltender, Edmonton's Grant Fuhr, set a record by playing in 75 games, two more than Bernie Parent played for the Flyers in 1973–74.

There were other significant milestones in the season. On December 19, Boston's Ken Linseman and St. Louis center Doug Gilmour made history when they scored goals two seconds apart. On January 14, the Islanders' Denis Potvin became the first defenseman ever to score 300 goals when he tallied in an 8–5 victory over Que-

bec. Calgary's Hakan Loob became the first Swedish 50-goal scorer in the NHL and teammate Joe Nieuwendyk, the Calder Trophy winner, challenged Mike Bossy's rookie goal-scoring record of 53, falling two short.

Amid all the celebrations came a note of sadness. Just three days before the February 9 All-Star Game in St. Louis was to honor him, former Blues player and coach Barclay Plager passed away from cancer.

Meanwhile, there were hurrahs in arenas where fans had been quiet for some time. In Detroit, the Red Wings finished on top of the Norris Division, the first time they had finished first since the 1964–65 season, and their 41–28–11 record (93 points) was their best in 18 years. Jacques Demers won the Jack Adams Award as Coach of the Year for an unprecedented second straight season.

And in New Jersey, the Devils produced a miracle finish to make the playoffs for the first time since moving from Colorado in 1982. They needed a victory on the final night in Chicago to jump over both the Penguins and Rangers into fourth place in the Patrick Division and got it with John MacLean scoring in Chicago with seconds left in regulation time and then again late in the five-minute overtime. The Devils' entry into the postseason set up one of the most bizarre playoff adventures in league annals.

It started in their first-round series with the Islanders. The Devils were shocked at home when Brent Sutter became the first player to score a shorthanded goal in overtime since Harvey (Busher) Jackson did it for the Bruins against the Canadiens in 1943. But the Devils rebounded to oust the Islanders in six games and face the Caps in the Patrick Division finals. Washington made it that far via Dale Hunter's fourth overtime playoff goal, coming in 5:57 of the extra session in Game 7 against the Flyers.

The Capitals went seven again against the Devils, but this time the magic belonged to New Jersey. In Game 3, the Devils' Patrik Sundstrom exploded for a playoff-record eight points

Joe Nieuwendyk of Calgary nailed down the Calder Trophy as 1987-88 Rookie of the Year with prolific goal-scoring.

(3–5–8), breaking Gretzky's mark of seven points, set on three occasions.

It was in the Wales Conference finals against the Bruins that the Devils really rocked the NHL. Their coach, the volatile Jim Schoenfeld, angered over the officiating in Game 3, confronted referee Don Koharski as the official left the ice. When others tried to keep the two apart in the corridor leading from the ice to the locker rooms, Koharski was bumped and fell.

The NHL immediately suspended Schoenfeld, but the Devils got a court injunction to get the coach behind the bench for Game 4. Game officials then refused to work the game and off-ice officials were quickly rounded up. Amid threats of lawsuits and countersuits, the Bruins went on to win the series in seven games and earn a berth in the Cup finals for the first time in 10 years.

There they faced the defending champion Oilers, who won the first three games and hoped to wrap up the series at Boston Garden. With the game tied at 3–3 at 16:37 of the second period, the lights went out. The power failure continued, the game was suspended and the series shifted back to Edmonton, where it ended as the Oilers won, 6–3, for their fourth Stanley Cup in five seasons.

Gretzky's record 31 assists in one playoff year highlighted his winning of his second Conn Smythe Trophy. The Selke Trophy went to Montreal's Guy Carbonneau and the Lady Byng to Montreal's Mats Naslund. Boston's Ray Bourque, the Norris Trophy winner, was named a first-team All-Star for the sixth time, but everyone else on the 1987–88 team was making his All-Star debut. Lemieux replaced Gretzky, joining newcomers Loob, Fuhr, Los Angeles' Luc Robitaille, and Washington defenseman Scott Stevens.

1987–88

FINAL STANDINGS

Prince of Wales Conference: Adams Division

	W	L	T	PTS	GF	GA
Montreal	45	22	13	103	298	238
Boston	44	30	6	94	300	251
Buffalo	37	32	11	85	283	305
Hartford	35	38	7	77	249	267
Quebec	32	43	5	69	271	306

Prince of Wales Conference: Patrick Division

	W	L	T	PTS	GF	GA
New York I.	39	31	10	88	308	267
Washington	38	33	9	85	281	249
Philadelphia	38	33	9	85	292	292
New Jersey	38	36	6	82	295	296
New York R.	36	34	10	82	300	283
Pittsburgh	36	35	9	81	319	316

Clarence Campbell Conference: Norris Division

	W	L	T	PTS	GF	GA
Detroit	41	28	11	93	322	269
St. Louis	34	38	8	76	278	294
Chicago	30	41	9	69	284	328
Toronto	21	49	10	52	273	345
Minnesota	19	48	13	51	242	349

Clarence Campbell Conference: Smythe Division

	W	L	T	PTS	GF	GA
Calgary	48	23	9	105	397	305
Edmonton	44	25	11	99	363	288
Winnipeg	33	36	11	77	292	310
Los Angeles	30	42	8	68	318	359
Vancouver	25	46	9	59	272	320

LEADING SCORERS

	G	A	PTS
Lemieux, Pittsburgh	70	98	168
Gretzky, Edmonton	40	109	149
Savard, Chicago	44	87	131
Hawerchuk, Winnipeg	44	77	121
Robitaille, Los Angeles	53	58	111
P. Stastny, Quebec	46	65	111
Messier, Edmonton	37	74	111
Carson, Los Angeles	55	52	107
Loob, Calgary	50	56	106
Goulet, Quebec	48	58	106

LEADING GOALIES

	G	GA	SO	GAA
Roy, Montreal	45	125	3	2.90
Lemelin, Boston	49	138	3	2.93
Malarchuk, Washington	54	154	4	3.16
Liut, Hartford	60	187	2	3.18
Hanlon, Detroit	47	141	4	3.23

PLAYOFF RESULTS

Division Semifinals

Montreal d. Hartford, 4–2
Boston d. Buffalo, 4–2
New Jersey d. N.Y. Islanders, 4–2
Washington d. Philadelphia, 4–3
Detroit d. Toronto, 4–2
St. Louis d. Chicago, 4–1
Calgary d. Los Angeles, 4–1
Edmonton d. Winnipeg, 4–1

Division Finals

Boston d. Montreal, 4–1
New Jersey d. Washington, 4–3
Detroit d. St. Louis, 4–1
Edmonton d. Calgary, 4–1

Conference Finals

Boston d. New Jersey, 4–3
Edmonton d. Detroit, 4–1

Finals

Edmonton d. Boston, 4–0

LEADING SCORERS

	G	A	P
Gretzky, Edmonton	12	31	43
Kurri, Edmonton	14	17	31
Simpson, Edmonton	13	6	19

LEADING GOALIES

	W	SO	GAA
Lemelin, Boston	6	1	2.63
Fuhr, Edmonton	16	0	2.90
Peeters, Philadelphia	7	0	3.12

7

CROWNING NEW CHAMPIONS

1988-1999

An era dawned in which fans in many NHL cities dared to dream that this would be the year their heroes would drink from the Stanley Cup. For now, no single club dominated the league. The Islanders had faded, the Canadiens moved back into the pack, the Flyers changed direction, and a surprising dismemberment of the Oilers' star-studded roster was about to begin with one of the most shocking trades in sports history.

It was an era in which Calgary, Pittsburgh, and New Jersey would win their first championships, when the Rangers would capture the division crown for the first time in more than half a century, and when the NHL would welcome the San Jose Sharks, Tampa Bay Lightning, Ottawa Senators, Florida Panthers, and Mighty Ducks of Anaheim.

It would also feature Wayne Gretzky's eclipsing the hallowed marks of Gordie Howe, the coming of a new commissioner, Gary Bettman, and a lockout that would last for 3½ months.

1988-89

Hockey was thrust onto the front pages across North America on August 9, 1988, with one of the biggest trades in the history of professional sports.

Edmonton Oilers' owner Peter Pocklington, reportedly in need of money, traded the greatest asset in hockey, Wayne Gretzky, to the Los Angeles Kings. Mike Krushelnyski and Marty McSor-ley joined Gretzky in Los Angeles in exchange for Jimmy Carson, Martin Gelinas, three first-round draft picks (1989, '91, and '93) and an estimated $15–20 million.

Another immortal had a change of address—after almost four years out of hockey. Guy Lafleur, who left the Canadiens in November 1984, signed as a free agent with the New York Rangers. Lafleur, who had only recently been inducted into the Hall of Fame, had 18 goals and 45

Introducing . . . the new king of Kings . . . Wayne Gretzky.

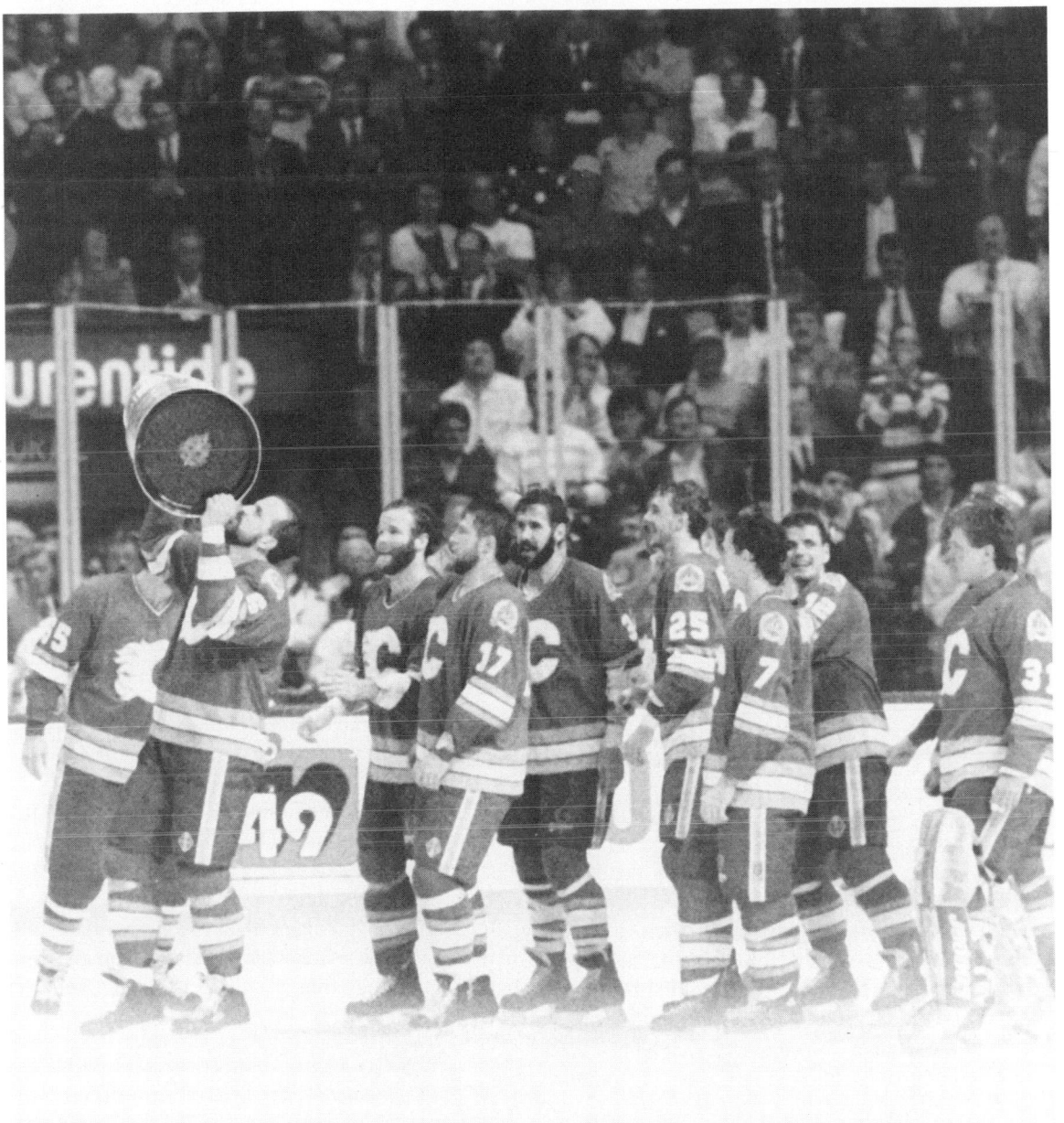

Calgary celebrated its first Stanley Cup championship in 1989.

points in 67 games and scored a goal in an emotional return to Montreal.

Playing shorthanded didn't seem as much a disadvantage as usual during the season. On Oc-tober 17, the Calgary Flames scored two short-handed goals in four seconds, setting a record and tying the record for the fastest two goals by one team in any situation. Doug Gilmour and Paul Ranheim had the goals as the Flames tied the

Nordiques, 8-8, in Quebec. Less than a month later, the Oilers' Esa Tikkanen scored two short-handed goals in 12 seconds, breaking the league record set by former Oiler Pat Hughes.

Calgary's Joe Nieuwendyk tied the NHL mark for most goals in one period (four) on January 11, 1989, scoring the four in the second period of an 8-3 win over Winnipeg. Nieuwendyk finished with his second straight 51-goal season, joining Gretzky and Mike Bossy as the only players to score 50 goals in each of their first two seasons.

Perhaps the most amazing individual feat came on New Year's Eve when Pittsburgh's Mario Lemieux, on his way to a second straight scoring title (85-114-199), tallied goals in every possible fashion in an 8-6 victory over New Jersey. Lemieux scored at even strength, on a power play, while the Penguins were shorthanded, on a penalty shot, and, finally, into an empty net.

An average of more than 19,700 fans per game at Joe Louis Arena watched Detroit win in the Norris Division behind center Steve Yzerman, who set club records in goals (65), assists (90), and points (155). Yzerman finished third in scoring behind Lemieux and Gretzky (54-114-168).

Gretzky combined with Bernie Nicholls (70 goals) to lead the Kings to a second-place finish in the Smythe, with Gretzky winning the Hart Trophy as MVP for the ninth time in 10 years. Calder Trophy winner Brian Leetch of the Rangers set the NHL mark for rookie defensemen with 23 goals and Montreal goaltender Patrick Roy, the Vezina Trophy winner, was unbeatable on Forum ice with a 25-0-3 mark. That helped the Canadiens finish second overall, their 115 points two behind the Flames.

Fittingly, the Oilers faced the Kings in the opening round of the playoffs. Edmonton, in a quest for a third straight Cup and fifth in six years, took a 3-1 lead in the series. But the Kings stormed back to win three straight games as Kelly Hrudey helped hold the Oilers to six goals.

Calgary had its own problems in its first-round matchup with Vancouver, which, despite finishing the season 43 points behind the Flames, took the series to overtime of a seventh game. Joel Otto rescued Calgary with a goal at 19:21 of the first overtime period. The Flames went on to sweep the Kings and then oust Chicago in five in the Campbell Conference finals to advance to their second Cup final in four seasons.

In the Wales Conference, Philadelphia's Ron Hextall, who a year earlier became the first goaltender to actually score a goal, became the first goalie to score in the playoffs as he hit an empty net in an 8-5 victory over Washington. The Capitals, who had just won their first Patrick Division title, were eliminated in six games.

The Flyers' next opponent was the Penguins, whose sweep of the Rangers in the opening round was their first postseason series victory since 1979. Lemieux tied Patrik Sundstrom's playoff record of eight points in a game with a five-goal, three-assist outburst in Game 5. This included four goals in the first period of a 10-7 victory, but the Flyers took the final two games to prevail. In the Wales final, Montreal bounced Philadelphia in six games to set up its second Cup matchup with Calgary in four seasons.

The Canadiens took a 2-1 edge by winning Game 3 on Ryan Walter's goal in the second overtime, but goaltender Mike Vernon and the Flames' defense held Montreal to just six goals in the next three games. Calgary won the finale, 4-2, the franchise's first championship and the first time in history that a visiting team had won the Cup in Montreal.

Calgary's Al MacInnis, whose 31 points led all playoff scorers, became the fourth defenseman to win the Conn Smythe Trophy, while Vernon tied Grant Fuhr's record with 16 playoff victories.

Other trophy winners included Montreal's Chris Chelios (Norris), Montreal's Guy Carbonneau (Selke), the Rangers' Brian Leetch (Calder), and Calgary's Joe Mullen (Lady Byng). Named as first-team All-Stars were Roy, defensemen Chelios and Pittsburgh's Paul Coffey, and for-

wards Mullen, Lemieux, and Luc Robitaille of Los Angeles.

1988–89

FINAL STANDINGS

Prince of Wales Conference: Adams Division

	W	L	T	PTS	GF	GA
Montreal	53	18	9	115	315	218
Boston	37	29	14	88	289	256
Buffalo	38	35	7	83	291	299
Hartford	37	38	5	79	299	290
Quebec	27	46	7	61	269	342

Prince of Wales Conference: Patrick Division

	W	L	T	PTS	GF	GA
Washington	41	29	10	92	305	259
Pittsburgh	40	33	7	87	347	349
New York R.	37	35	8	82	310	307
Philadelphia	36	36	8	80	307	285
New Jersey	27	41	12	66	281	325
New York I.	28	47	5	61	265	325

Clarence Campbell Conference: Norris Division

	W	L	T	PTS	GF	GA
Detroit	34	34	12	80	313	316
St. Louis	33	35	12	78	275	285
Minnesota	27	37	16	70	258	278
Chicago	27	41	12	66	297	335
Toronto	28	46	6	62	259	342

Clarence Campbell Conference: Smythe Division

	W	L	T	PTS	GF	GA
Calgary	54	17	9	117	354	226
Los Angeles	42	31	7	91	376	335
Edmonton	38	34	8	84	325	306
Vancouver	33	39	8	74	251	253
Winnipeg	26	42	12	64	300	355

LEADING SCORERS

	G	A	PTS
Lemieux, Pittsburgh	85	114	199
Gretzky, Los Angeles	54	114	168
Yzerman, Detroit	65	90	155
Nicholls, Los Angeles	70	80	150
Brown, Pittsburgh	49	66	115
Coffey, Pittsburgh	30	83	113
J. Mullen, Calgary	51	59	110
Kurri, Edmonton	44	58	102
Carson, Edmonton	49	51	100
Robitaille, Los Angeles	46	52	98

LEADING GOALIES

	G	GA	SO	GAA
Roy, Montreal	48	113	4	2.47
Vernon, Calgary	52	130	0	2.65
Lemelin, Boston	40	120	0	3.01
Sidorkiewicz, Hartford	44	133	4	3.03
Casey, Minnesota	55	151	1	3.06

PLAYOFF RESULTS

Division Semifinals

Montreal d. Hartford, 4–0
Boston d. Buffalo, 4–1
Philadelphia d. Washington, 4–2
Pittsburgh d. N.Y. Rangers, 4–0
Chicago d. Detroit, 4–2
St. Louis d. Minnesota, 4–1
Calgary d. Vancouver, 4–3
Los Angeles d. Edmonton, 4–3

Division Finals

Montreal d. Boston, 4–1
Philadelphia d. Pittsburgh, 4–3
Chicago d. St. Louis, 4–1
Calgary d. Los Angeles, 4–0

Conference Finals

Montreal d. Philadelphia, 4–2
Calgary d. Chicago, 4–1

Finals

Calgary d. Montreal, 4–2

LEADING SCORERS

	G	A	P
MacInnis, Calgary	7	24	31
Kerr, Philadelphia	14	11	25
Mullen, Calgary	16	8	24

LEADING GOALIES

	W	SO	GAA
Roy, Montreal	13	2	2.09
Vernon, Calgary	16	3	2.26
Chevrier, Chicago	9	0	2.61

1989–90

The man now called Hollywood home, so, naturally, it was with a flair for the dramatic that Los Angeles King Wayne Gretzky handled his pursuit of Hall-of-Famer Gordie Howe's NHL career scoring mark of 1,850 points.

The big moment came on October 15, 1989, in a most fitting venue, Edmonton, where the former Oiler came into the game trailing Howe's record by one point and quickly tied it by earning an assist on Bernie Nicholls' first-period goal. But, as the game progressed, it appeared the historic point would not come on this night. Just 53 seconds remained in regulation time when, with the Oilers holding a 5-4 lead, Gretzky swooped in and beat Edmonton goaltender Bill Ranford, setting the NHL's new career scoring record. Gretzky took it one step further by scoring the game-winner in overtime to end a remarkable evening.

Two more records were set in an Oilers-Kings game later in the season. On February 28 in Los Angeles, the clubs were whistled for an unprecedented 86 penalties. The Oilers had a record 45, which included 27 minors, seven majors, six misconducts, four game misconducts, and one match penalty.

Gretzky went on to regain the scoring crown he had lost to Mario Lemieux for two years, compiling 40-102-142 totals in 73 games. As for Lemieux, he missed 31 games with a back problem but still managed 45 goals (a record 13 shorthanded) and 123 points. The Pittsburgh center finished fourth in scoring, behind Gretzky, the Oilers' Mark Messier, and Detroit's Steve Yzerman.

In Toronto, former Devils' coach Doug Carpenter took over behind the bench, the Leafs' ninth head coach of the decade, matching the number of changes in Los Angeles, where Tom Webster assumed a similar position. Nothing could help Quebec, which managed just 31 points, the fewest since Washington had 21 in 1974–75, its first season. The Nordiques finished 51 points behind fourth-place Hartford in the Adams Division.

It was a different story in New York, where a well-traveled Roger Neilson guided the Rangers to first place in the Patrick, the first time since 1941–42 that the club had finished on top of any division. But that was as far as the team got. The Rangers were bounced in the second round by Washington, ending their quest for the Stanley Cup they last won a half-century ago.

A new star was emerging in St. Louis, where Brett Hull, the son of Hall of Famer Bobby Hull, set a right-wing record with a league-leading 72 goals, breaking Jari Kurri's mark by one.

Because no one team dominated the league during the regular season (Boston led with just

The pucks say it all for Wayne Gretzky and Gordie Howe in 1989.

The Oilers featured 1989–90 regular-season MVP Mark Messier (left) and they prevailed over the Bruins (Dave Poulin, 19) for the Stanley Cup.

101 points), it promised to be one of the most wide-open battles for the Cup in years.

There were knowing nods in Edmonton when the Gretzky-less Oilers fell behind, 3-1, in their Smythe Division opening-round matchup with Winnipeg. But the Oilers won a pair of one-goal games and emerged with a 4-1 victory in Game 7 to advance against the Kings. They swept that series, with Joe Murphy scoring the series winner in overtime.

Soviet import Sergei Makarov of Calgary was Rookie of the Year in 1989–90.

Meanwhile, the Oilers' Campbell Conference finals opponent, Chicago, needed 14 games to get by Minnesota and St. Louis. The Oilers eliminated the Blackhawks in six games.

In the battle for the Cup, the Oilers went up against the Bruins for the second time in three years. The Bruins had overcome a pesky Hartford club in seven games, needed five to knock off Montreal, and then swept Washington in the Capitals' first-ever conference final appearance.

In the finals, the Bruins were facing an old teammate in goaltender Bill Ranford, who had played for Boston until traded on March 8, 1988, for Andy Moog. He became the Oilers' No. 1 goaltender when shoulder surgery sidelined Grant Fuhr early in the season.

Ranford was magnificent in the playoffs, at one point going a span of 154:24 without surrendering a goal. And he was brilliant in Game 1 of the finals when he and Moog battled into a third overtime of a 2-2 thriller. Then, after 55:13 of overtime play, the Oilers' Petr Klima, acquired earlier in the season from Detroit, ended the game and, most likely, the Bruins' chances. Boston was outscored, 17-5, the rest of the way, managing only a 2-1 victory in Game 3. The Oilers earned their fifth Cup in seven years, tying them with the Bruins for the fourth-most titles in league history, but still far behind Montreal's 22.

Ranford was the clear choice for the Conn Smythe Trophy as playoff MVP. Gretzky regained the Ross Trophy and his old teammate, Messier, won the Hart as regular-season MVP. The Vezina went to Montreal's Patrick Roy, the Norris to Boston's Ray Bourque, the Selke to St. Louis' Rick Meagher, the Lady Byng to Hull, and the Calder to the Flames' Sergei Makarov.

Roy, Bourque, and Messier joined Hull, Calgary's Al MacInnis, and the Kings' Luc Robitaille as first-team All-Stars.

1989–90

FINAL STANDINGS

Prince of Wales Conference: Adams Division

	W	L	T	PTS	GF	GA
Boston	46	25	9	101	289	232
Buffalo	45	27	8	98	286	248
Montreal	41	28	11	93	288	234
Hartford	38	33	9	85	275	268
Quebec	12	61	7	31	240	407

Prince of Wales Conference: Patrick Division

	W	L	T	PTS	GF	GA
New York R.	36	31	13	85	279	267
New Jersey	37	34	9	83	295	288
Washington	36	38	6	78	284	275
New York I.	31	38	11	73	281	288
Pittsburgh	32	40	8	72	318	359
Philadelphia	30	39	11	71	290	297

Clarence Campbell Conference: Norris Division

	W	L	T	PTS	GF	GA
Chicago	41	33	6	88	316	294
St. Louis	37	34	9	83	295	279
Toronto	38	38	4	80	337	358
Minnesota	36	40	4	76	284	291
Detroit	28	38	14	70	288	323

Clarence Campbell Conference: Smythe Division

	W	L	T	PTS	GF	GA
Calgary	42	23	15	99	348	265
Edmonton	38	28	14	90	315	283
Winnipeg	37	32	11	85	298	290
Los Angeles	34	39	7	75	338	337
Vancouver	25	41	14	64	245	306

LEADING SCORERS

	G	A	PTS
Gretzky, Los Angeles	40	102	142
Messier, Edmonton	45	84	129
Yzerman, Detroit	62	65	127
Lemieux, Pittsburgh	45	78	123
Hull, St. Louis	72	41	113
Nicholls, L.A.-N.Y.R.	39	73	112
P. Turgeon, Buffalo	40	66	106
LaFontaine, New York I.	54	51	105
Coffey, Pittsburgh	29	74	103
Sakic, Quebec	39	63	102
Oates, St. Louis	23	79	102

LEADING GOALIES

	G	GA	SO	GAA
Roy, Montreal	54	134	3	2.53
Lemelin, Boston	43	108	2	2.81
Moog, Buffalo	46	122	3	2.89
Puppa, Buffalo	56	156	1	2.89
Cloutier, Chicago	43	112	2	3.09

PLAYOFF RESULTS

Division Semifinals

Boston d. Hartford, 4–3
Montreal d. Buffalo, 4–2
N.Y. Rangers d. N.Y. Islanders, 4–1
Washington d. New Jersey, 4–2
Chicago d. Minnesota, 4–3
Los Angeles d. Calgary, 4–2
Edmonton d. Winnipeg, 4–3
St. Louis d. Toronto, 4–1
Boston d. Montreal, 4–1
Washington d. N.Y. Rangers, 4–1

Division Finals

Boston d. Montreal, 4–1
Washington d. N.Y. Rangers, 4–1
Chicago d. St. Louis, 4–3
Edmonton d. Los Angeles, 4–0

Conference Finals

Boston d. Washington, 4–0
Edmonton d. Chicago, 4–2

Finals

Edmonton d. Boston, 4–1

LEADING SCORERS

	G	A	P
Simpson, Edmonton	16	15	31
Messier, Edmonton	9	22	31
Neely, Boston	12	16	28

LEADING GOALIES

	W	SO	GAA
Moog, Boston	13	2	2.21
Roy, Montreal	5	1	2.43
Ranford, Edmonton	16	1	2.53

1990–91

It was an ominous beginning for the Pittsburgh Penguins when Mario Lemieux, one of the NHL's marquee players, underwent surgery for a herniated disc in July. Without their superstar, the Penguins' outlook was at best viewed as bleak.

There would be other stars, of course, who would make the headlines, and the one who stood out over all was Brett Hull of the St. Louis Blues, who exploded for 86 goals, the third-highest total in history behind Wayne Gretzky's 92 (1981–82) and 87 (1983–84). Hull's performance, plus that of defenseman Scott Stevens, the million-dollar free-agent signee who came from the Washington Capitals, helped lead the Blues to a 105-point season, the second-best mark in the league, one point behind Chicago.

The player who put the Blackhawks on top for the first time in 24 years was rookie goaltender Ed Belfour, who had a dream season. Belfour not only won the Calder Trophy as Rookie of the Year, he also captured the Vezina Trophy with a league-leading 43 victories (43-19-7), the top goals-against average (2.47) and the leading save percentage (.910). Belfour also came within one game of Grant Fuhr's record of appearing in 75 games as the Blackhawks finished 49-23-8.

Calgary was a rude host at the Saddledome, winning 17 and tying one in a span from December 29, 1990, to March 14, 1991. Chris Nilan was rude in his own right to the visiting Whalers on March 31 when he set an NHL record with 10 penalties. As one might imagine, Nilan was not around for the final buzzer after accumulating six minors, a pair of majors, a 10-minute misconduct, and a game misconduct.

Minnesota was fighting, too—fighting for its life early in the season. The North Stars got off to a terrible start under new general manager Bobby Clarke and first-year coach Bob Gainey. The question seemed not whether the team could make the playoffs, but if it could avoid finishing with the league's worst record.

But the North Stars began to come together before midseason and finished comfortably ahead of Toronto with a 27-39-14 record. Still, their 68 points were far behind 14 other playoff qualifiers and 38 points less than Chicago, their first-round opponent.

But Cinderella came to the ball dressed in the green, white, gold and black colors of the North Stars, and the most unlikely postseason ad-

High-scoring Brett Hull of the St. Louis Blues won the Hart Trophy in his fourth season.

The Oilers had struggled through the first two rounds. It took an overtime goal by Esa Tikkanen to give the Oilers a 5-4 victory in Game 7 of their Smythe Division semifinal against the Flames. They followed that with a memorable series against the Kings, who had gotten by Vancouver in six games.

Luc Robitaille's overtime goal gave the Kings a 4-3 decision over the Oilers in the opener, but Edmonton came back on Petr Klima's overtime goal for a 4-3 victory in the second game. Game 3 went into a second overtime before Tikkanen gave the Oilers a 4-3 win. Edmonton won the fourth game, 4-2, in regulation and the Kings avoided elimination in Game 5, winning, 5-2. But the Oilers wrapped it up—appropriately once more in overtime—when Craig MacTavish scored for a 4-3 verdict.

But there would be no sixth Stanley Cup for Edmonton. The North Stars eliminated the Oilers in six games to make it back to the finals 10 years after their only appearance, when they had lost in five games to the Islanders.

Minnesota's opponent? Pittsburgh, the team that had been counted out when Lemieux had his surgery. Indeed, the Penguins, making their first-ever trip to the finals, had weathered the absence of Lemieux, who did not return until late in the season and played in only 26 games. Mark Recchi (113 points) had picked up the scoring slack during the regular season and helped the Penguins win the division title.

Lemieux's comeback, combined with the play of Recchi, Kevin Stevens, and Tom Barrasso, sparked the Penguins in the playoffs. Losing at least the first game of every series they played, Pittsburgh made it to the finals the hard way. New Jersey was the first victim in a seven-game series. The Penguins took four straight from Washington after their Game 1 loss and they came back from two defeats to oust Boston in six behind the superb goaltending of Barrasso, who had been injured.

Of course, the Penguins lost the first game, 5-4, to Minnesota in the finals. They won the

venture since the 1975 Islanders' odyssey was about to unfold.

Minnesota began in Chicago with Brian Propp's overtime goal for a 4-3 victory before dropping the next two games. But the Blackhawks didn't come close the rest of the series, scoring just two goals over the next three games. Suddenly, the NHL regular-season champions were gone.

Next up was equally fearsome St. Louis with Hull, Stevens, and 20 more victories than the Stars. The Blues had beaten Detroit in the opening round, including a two-team playoff-record 298 penalty minutes in Game 5, a 6-1 St. Louis victory. Perhaps worn out by the rough stuff, the Blues were stunned by Minnesota in six games. Now all the Stars had to do to reach the finals was knock off defending and five-time champion Edmonton.

Mario Lemieux's comeback enabled Pittsburgh to win its first Stanley Cup in 1991.

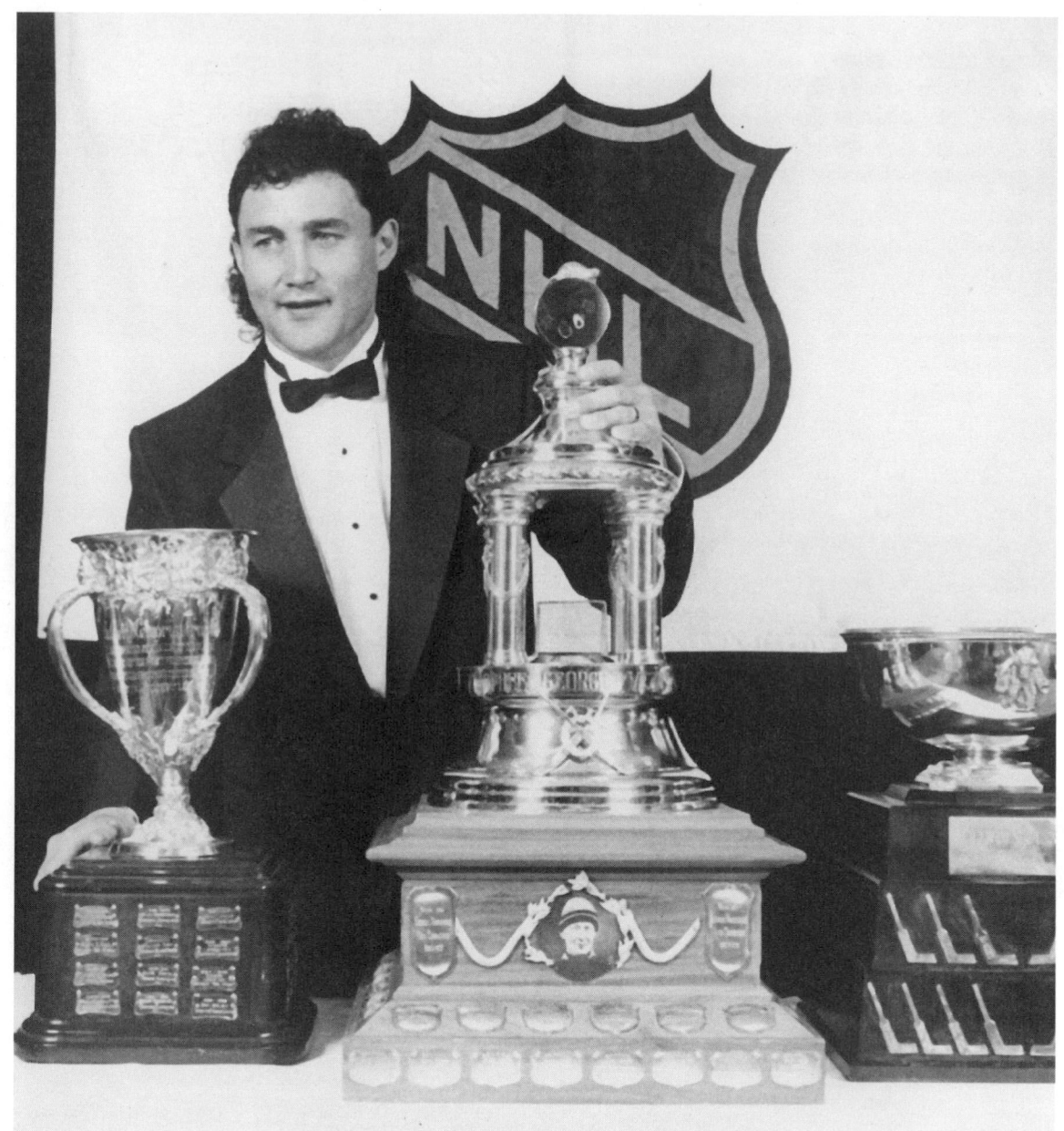

Chicago's Ed Belfour was Rookie of the Year and winner of the Vezina Trophy in 1990–91.

next, 4-1, but dropped Game 3, 3-1. Then they won three in a row, 5-3, 6-4, and 8-0—demolishing the North Stars in the finale with the largest final-round margin of victory in this century.

The Conn Smythe Trophy went to Lemieux, who had a 16-goal, 44-point playoff, the second-highest total in league annals, while Hull received the Hart Trophy.

Ray Bourque won the Norris for the fourth time and Gretzky the Ross for the ninth time with a 41-122-163 mark, 32 points better than Hull. Gretzky also was the recipient of the Lady Byng for a second time after being runnerup five times. Chicago's Dirk Graham won the Selke.

The All-Star team was made up of Belfour, Bourque, Gretzky, Hull, Robitaille, and Calgary's Al MacInnis.

1990-91

FINAL STANDINGS

Prince of Wales Conference: Adams Division

	W	L	T	PTS	GF	GA
Boston	44	24	12	100	299	264
Montreal	39	30	11	89	273	249
Buffalo	31	30	19	81	292	278
Hartford	31	38	11	73	238	276
Quebec	16	50	14	46	236	354

Prince of Wales Conference: Patrick Division

	W	L	T	PTS	GF	GA
Pittsburgh	41	33	6	88	342	305
New York R.	36	31	13	85	297	265
Washington	37	36	7	81	258	258
New Jersey	32	33	15	79	272	264
Philadelphia	33	37	10	76	252	267
New York I.	25	45	10	60	223	290

Clarence Campbell Conference: Norris Division

	W	L	T	PTS	GF	GA
Chicago	49	23	8	106	284	211
St. Louis	47	22	11	105	310	250
Detroit	34	38	8	76	273	298
Minnesota	27	39	14	68	256	266
Toronto	23	46	11	57	241	318

Clarence Campbell Conference: Smythe Division

	W	L	T	PTS	GF	GA
Los Angeles	46	24	10	102	340	254
Calgary	46	26	8	100	344	263
Edmonton	37	37	6	80	272	272
Vancouver	28	43	9	65	243	315
Winnipeg	26	43	11	63	260	288

LEADING SCORERS

	G	A	PTS
Gretzky, Los Angeles	41	122	163
Hull, St. Louis	86	45	131
Oates, St. Louis	25	90	115
Recchi, Pittsburgh	40	73	113
Cullen, Pitt.-Hart.	39	71	110
Sakic, Quebec	48	61	109
Yzerman, Detroit	51	57	108
Fleury, Calgary	51	53	104
MacInnis, Calgary	28	75	103
Larmer, Chicago	44	57	101

LEADING GOALIES

	G	GA	SO	GAA
Belfour, Chicago	74	170	4	2.47
Beaupre, Washington	45	113	5	2.64
Roy, Montreal	48	128	1	2.71

| Moog, Boston | 51 | 136 | 4 | 2.87 |
| Hrudey, Los Angeles | 47 | 132 | 3 | 2.90 |

PLAYOFF RESULTS

Division Semifinals

Boston d. Hartford, 4–2
Montreal d. Buffalo, 4–2
Pittsburgh d. New Jersey, 4–3
Washington d. N.Y. Rangers, 4–2
Minnesota d. Chicago, 4–2
St. Louis d. Detroit, 4–3
Edmonton d. Calgary, 4–3

Division Finals

Boston d. Montreal, 4–3
Pittsburgh d. Washington, 4–1
Minnesota d. St. Louis, 4–2
Edmonton d. Los Angeles, 4–2

Conference Finals

Pittsburgh d. Boston, 4–2
Minnesota d. Edmonton, 4–1

Finals

Pittsburgh d. Minnesota, 4–2

LEADING SCORERS

	G	A	P
Lemieux, Pittsburgh	16	28	44
Recchi, Pittsburgh	10	24	34
Stevens, Pittsburgh	17	16	33

LEADING GOALIES

	W	SO	GAA
Barrasso, Pittsburgh	12	1	2.60
Hrudey, Los Angeles	6	0	2.78
Beaupre, Washington	5	1	2.79

1991-92

It was the most tumultuous season in the 75-year history of the NHL, marked by the tragic death of a coach, a future superstar's refusal to sign, an expansion team, a strike, a back-to-back Stanley Cup triumph, and the ouster of the league president.

In early August, it was learned that Pittsburgh Penguins' coach Bob Johnson, who had led the team to its first Stanley Cup championship just three months earlier, was suffering from incurable brain cancer. Johnson, one of hockey's greatest good-will ambassadors, passed away on November 26.

Scotty Bowman, who had guided Montreal to five Cup titles in the 1970s, took over as the Penguins' head coach.

There would be no sign of Eric Lindros, the 19-year-old center with the potential impact of Wayne Gretzky and Mario Lemieux. The No. 1

draft pick in 1991, Lindros rejected a contract with the Quebec Nordiques and decided to sit out the NHL season. He got his ice time playing junior hockey and on the Canadian team that captured a silver medal in the 1992 Olympic Games.

The league had a new look for the first time since four teams from the WHA were absorbed in 1979 as the San Jose Sharks began operations at San Francisco's Cow Palace. Midway through the season, the expansion Tampa Bay Lightning and Ottawa Senators met their final payment obligations and were granted permanent membership in the NHL, with the teams to begin play in the 1992–93 season.

The Sharks' merchandising program proved more successful than the club's on-ice exploits, as fans across the continent sported clothing and ar-

tifacts bearing the logo of a team that finished with a 17-58-5 record, just 3-35-2 on the road.

Losses for the Sharks obviously meant victories for the rest of the league. By season's end, 18 of the 22 teams finished with at least 70 points, another indication of relative parity.

At the top of the list were the New York Rangers, who acquired Mark Messier for Bernie Nicholls and two minor leaguers on October 4 as the dismantling of the Edmonton Oiler Stanley Cup dynasty continued. Messier, who contributed 107 points and invaluable leadership on the way to winning the MVP award, spurred the Rangers to a 50-25-5 mark for 105 points and the Presidents' Trophy as the league's regular-season champion, the first time in 50 years the club had attained that status.

Down but not permanently out, Pittsburgh's Mario Lemieux suffered a broken hand in the Patrick Division final series against the Rangers, but came back to lead the Penguins to their second straight Stanley Cup championship.

There also was a resurrection in Vancouver as the Canucks established a franchise record with a 46-26-12 mark and first place in the Smythe Division. Detroit captured the Norris Division crown while Montreal, employing an air-tight defense, built an insurmountable lead in the first half of the season and coasted to a first-place finish in the Adams Division.

Eight coaching changes would come before the end of June 1992 as vacancies occurred in Buffalo, Montreal, Toronto, New Jersey, Los Angeles, Boston, St. Louis, and Hartford.

Players moved, too. Calgary's Doug Gilmour was the principal name in a 10-player deal between the Flames and Maple Leafs in early January. The Penguins, struggling through much of the regular season, were part of a three-team deal on the eve of the March trading deadline with defenseman Paul Coffey going to Los Angeles and high-scoring Mark Recchi to Philadelphia. In return, the Penguins obtained forward Rick Tocchet and defenseman Kjell Samuelsson.

It appeared all the maneuvering was in vain when, on April 1, after long and fruitless months of negotiation, the NHL Players Association went on strike. The major issues included licensing and endorsements, free agency, salary arbitration, and pension contributions.

The walkout, which threatened to bring a cancellation of the playoffs, was settled after 10 days with NHL president John Ziegler and NHLPA executive director Bob Goodenow, guided by moderates in both camps, forging a new collective bargaining agreement. Among the results were an increase to an 84-game season to generate additional revenue beginning in 1992–93, a less restrictive free-agency system, and an almost three-fold increase in the playoff bonus pool to $9 million in 1993.

The regular season resumed with teams completing the final week. That enabled the Islanders' Al Arbour to pass Dick Irvin as the leader in NHL games coached at 1,438, the record coming on April 15 in the Islanders' final game, a 7-0 victory over the Devils.

Despite missing 16 games because of injuries, the Penguins' Lemieux captured the scoring crown for a third time, finishing with 44-87-131, eight points more than teammate Kevin Stevens (54-69-123). The Kings' Gretzky, the defending scoring champion, ranked third with 31-90-121 while St. Louis' Brett Hull again ran away with the goal-scoring race with 70, 16 more than runner-up Stevens. Ranger defenseman Brian Leetch led all backliners with 22-80-102 while teammate Tony Amonte paced rookies with 35 goals and 69 points.

Montreal's Patrick Roy boasted the league's best goals-against average at 2.36 while Vancouver's Kirk McLean (38-17-9) and Detroit's Tim Cheveldae (38-23-9) paced the league in goal-tending victories.

The playoffs began with six of the eight first-round series going the full seven games, including all four in the Wales Conference. Pittsburgh came back from a 3-1 deficit to beat Washington. Vancouver did the same against Winnipeg, and Detroit survived the same deficit against Minnesota.

Game 6 of the Red Wings–North Stars series was one of the most memorable with the teams staging the first playoff scoreless tie after regulation play since the Islanders beat Chicago, 1-0, on a Mike Bossy goal in April 1979. But Sergei Fedorov's game-winning goal 18 minutes into the first overtime also proved historic because it was confirmed only after a video review by league official Wally Harris, the first time the video-replay procedure directly determined the outcome of a game.

The Penguins lost Lemieux when his left hand was broken by an Adam Graves slash five minutes into Game 2 of their Patrick Division final series with the Rangers. Joe Mullen also was lost with a leg injury, but Pittsburgh still managed to advance in six games while the Bruins were ousting the Canadiens in four games, their first sweep of the Habs in 64 years.

Chicago was rolling, establishing a one-year playoff record with 11 consecutive victories by winning the last three games against the Blues in

six games and sweeping the Wings and Oilers. Pittsburgh, sparked by the stick-handling and scoring prowess of Czechoslovakian second-year star Jaromir Jagr, beat the Bruins in four straight to earn the other berth in the finals.

That's where Chicago's streak ended. The Penguins, with Lemieux returning and goaltender Tom Barrasso making the key saves, swept the Blackhawks to equal Chicago's record 11-game playoff winning streak. Lemieux finished with 16 goals and 34 points in 15 postseason games to earn his second straight MVP award as Pittsburgh won its second straight Stanley Cup.

Trophy winners included Roy (Vezina and Jennings), Messier (Hart, as regular-season MVP, and Pearson), Lemieux (Ross and Smythe), Montreal's Guy Carbonneau (Selke), Leetch (Norris), Vancouver rookie Pavel Bure (Calder), Gretzky (Lady Byng), Boston's Ray Bourque (Clancy), the New York Islanders' Mark Fitzpatrick (Masterton), and Vancouver's Pat Quinn (Adams). Roy, Leetch, Bourque, Messier, Hull, and Kevin Stevens made the All-Star team.

In a major development in June, president Ziegler, under growing criticism from a vocal group of owners, announced his resignation, ending his 15-year tenure.

On the player front, the charismatic Lindros, a 6-foot-5, 225-pound center, landed with Philadelphia, following a tug-of-war between the Flyers and the Rangers, both teams having claimed a deal with Quebec. An arbitrator upheld the trade that provided the Nordiques with five players, a first-round draft pick and $15 million. Lindros wound up signing a six-year contract estimated at $15–20 million.

1991–92

FINAL STANDINGS

Clarence Campbell Conference: Norris Division

	W	L	T	PTS	GF	GA
Detroit	43	25	12	98	320	256
Chicago	36	29	15	87	257	236
St. Louis	36	33	11	83	279	266
Minnesota	32	42	6	70	246	278
Toronto	30	43	7	67	234	294

Clarence Campbell Conference: Smythe Division

	W	L	T	PTS	GF	GA
Vancouver	42	26	12	96	285	250
Los Angeles	35	31	14	84	287	296
Edmonton	36	34	10	82	295	297
Winnipeg	33	32	15	81	251	244
Calgary	31	37	12	74	296	305
San Jose	17	58	5	39	219	359

Prince of Wales Conference: Adams Division

	W	L	T	PTS	GF	GA
Montreal	41	28	11	93	267	207
Boston	36	32	12	84	270	275
Buffalo	31	37	12	74	289	299
Hartford	26	41	13	65	247	283
Quebec	20	48	12	52	255	318

Prince of Wales Conference: Patrick Division

	W	L	T	PTS	GF	GA
New York R.	50	25	5	105	321	246
Washington	45	27	8	98	330	275
Pittsburgh	39	32	9	87	343	308
New Jersey	38	31	11	87	289	259
New York I.	34	35	11	79	291	299
Philadelphia	32	37	11	75	252	273

LEADING SCORERS

	G	A	PTS
Lemieux, Pittsburgh	44	87	131
Stevens, Pittsburgh	54	69	123
Gretzky, Los Angeles	31	90	121
Hull, St. Louis	70	39	109
Robitaille, Los Angeles	44	63	107
Messier, New York R.	35	72	107
Roenick, Chicago	53	50	103
Yzerman, Detroit	45	58	103
Leetch, New York R.	22	80	102
Oates, St. Louis and Boston	20	79	99

LEADING GOALIES

	G	GA	SO	GAA
Roy, Montreal	67	155	5	2.36
Belfour, Chicago	52	132	5	2.70
McLean, Vancouver	65	176	5	2.74
Vanbiesbrouck, New York R.	45	120	2	2.85
Essensa, Winnipeg	47	126	5	2.88

PLAYOFF RESULTS

Division Semifinals

Montreal d. Hartford, 4–3
Boston d. Buffalo, 4–3
N.Y. Rangers d. New Jersey, 4–3
Pittsburgh d. Washington, 4–3
Detroit d. Minnesota, 4–3
Chicago d. St. Louis, 4–2
Vancouver d. Winnipeg, 4–3
Edmonton d. Los Angeles, 4–2

Division Finals

Boston d. Montreal, 4–0
Pittsburgh d. N.Y. Rangers, 4–2
Chicago d. Detroit, 4–0
Edmonton d. Vancouver, 4–2

Conference Finals

Pittsburgh d. Boston, 4–0
Chicago d. Edmonton, 4–0

Finals

Pittsburgh d. Chicago, 4–0

LEADING SCORERS

	G	A	P
Lemieux, Pittsburgh	16	18	34
Stevens, Pittsburgh	13	15	28
Francis, Pittsburgh	8	19	27

LEADING GOALIES

	W	SO	GAA
Belvour, Chicago	12	1	2.47
Cheveldae, Detroit	3	2	2.51
McLean, Vancouver	6	2	2.52

1992–93

It was a season that would be remembered as the start of the Gary Bettman Era, the end of the Penguins' dynasty and the 100th anniversary Stanley Cup winding up in Montreal for the 24th time. The season opened with Bettman taking over for John Ziegler as NHL commissioner. With the labor strife of the past season haunting him, Ziegler resigned during the off-season after 15 years in the post. The league turned its reins over to Bettman, who had been senior vice president and general counsel for the National Basketball Association.

Bettman's first task was to see that the league would continue to grow, both literally and figuratively. The addition of the Ottawa Senators and Tampa Bay Lightning gave the NHL 24 teams (four six-team divisions), with the Lightning temporarily joining the Norris Division and the Senators thrust into the tough Adams Division, where three teams would crack the 100-point barrier. Neither expansion team threatened to make the playoffs, but Tampa Bay proved to be anything but a pushover, winning a respectable total of 23 games and finishing 29 points ahead of the second-year San Jose Sharks. The Senators, meanwhile, were well-received both at home and on the road. They drew sellout crowds to the Ottawa Civic Centre and were warmly welcomed in opponents' buildings, thanks mainly to their inability to play well away from home. The Senators were so bad, in fact, that they set an NHL record with 38 straight road losses.

It wasn't until April 10, 1993, that Ottawa was able to get a point on the road, winning a 5-3 decision in New York against the Islanders. The Senators went on to lose their final two road games and finish with a 1-41 record (including a neutral-site loss) away from the Civic Centre.

The new commissioner: Gary Bettman.

At the other end of the spectrum, the two-time champion Pittsburgh Penguins showed signs that they were favorites to three-peat. Mario Lemieux was limited to 60 games due to treatment for Hodgkin's disease, but the Penguins rolled on, posting a league-high 119 points. In the process Pittsburgh smashed a league record by winning 17 straight games late in the season. From March 9, 1993, when they defeated Boston, 3-2, until April 14, when New Jersey tied them, 6-6, the Penguins were perfect, breaking the record of 15 consecutive victories set by the New York Islanders in 1981–82.

Also breaking a record was Winnipeg Jets rookie sensation Teemu Selanne, whose 76 goals were by far the most ever by a first-year player. Selanne surpassed the old mark of 53, set by the Islanders' Mike Bossy in 1977–78. Selanne's 132 points also was a rookie record, 23 more than the previous record-holder, Quebec's Peter Stastny, scored 12 years earlier.

With playoff MVP Patrick Roy in the vanguard, the Canadiens added another Stanley Cup championship to their record total in 1992–93.

The surprises started early in the first round of the playoffs. The Penguins rolled past New Jersey in five games, but the second-place team in the Patrick Division, the Washington Capitals, were not so fortunate. The Caps lost back-to-back overtime games to the Islanders and were eventually ousted in six games. The Islanders' final goal of the series was the one that rocked the NHL. It was scored by Pierre Turgeon midway through the third period, giving the Islanders an insurmountable lead and prompting Dale Hunter to charge Turgeon from behind several seconds after the goal. Turgeon suffered a separated shoulder and Hunter received a 21-game suspension to be served at the outset of the following season.

Without Turgeon, the Islanders had little hope against the powerful Penguins, but with Ray Ferraro providing the offensive punch and rookie Darius Kasparaitis distracting Lemieux and Co. with his devastating hip checks, the Islanders stunned Pittsburgh. David Volek scored in overtime of Game 7, ending the Penguins' quest for a third straight title.

In the Adams Division, Montreal appeared doomed when it dropped the first two games of its first-round series against Quebec, but Patrick Roy limited the high-powered Nordiques to nine goals over the next four games and the Canadiens went on to win the series in six games. Roy stayed hot in the conference semifinals, too, as Montreal defeated Buffalo four straight times by the score of 4-3. The Sabres, fourth in the regular season, had advanced with a stunning sweep of first-place Boston in the opening round.

In the Clarence Campbell Conference, Norris Division champion Chicago had nothing left for postseason play and was promptly eliminated in four straight games by St. Louis, which had finished 21 points behind the Blackhawks. Second-place Detroit, another 100-point-plus team, also saw its season end early when Toronto won Game 7 at Joe Louis Arena. The Maple Leafs continued their playoff magic in the next round, riding the standout goaltending of Felix Potvin to a seven-game triumph over St. Louis.

Winnipeg's Teemu Selanne set rookie scoring marks in 1992–93.

In the Smythe Division, Vancouver, which had finished first, eliminated Winnipeg in six games, while the Los Angeles Kings, continuing the run of playoff surprises, upset Calgary in six. The Kings had trailed in the series 2 games to 1 before bombarding the Flames for 21 goals in winning the next three. With the Kings' Big Three of Wayne Gretzky, Luc Robitaille, and Tomas Sandstrom leading the way, L.A. advanced to the conference finals with a six-game elimination of the Canucks.

Once the semifinals started, overtime became the Canadiens' time to shine. The outmanned Islanders gave them a tussle in the Wales final despite limited appearances by Turgeon, who tried to play with only one good shoulder. Montreal won the opener easily, 4-1, but needed a double-overtime goal from Stephan Lebeau to take Game 2.

Game 3 also went into overtime, and this time the Canadiens' Guy Carbonneau won it with a blast from the slot past Glenn Healy. Video replay showed that Montreal had seven skaters on the ice at the time, but the goal was allowed to stand, virtually ending the series. The Islanders won Game 4, but the Canadiens buried them early with a 5-2 victory in Game 5 back at Montreal.

In the Campbell final, the Maple Leafs and Kings split their first four games before the teams were forced to work overtime. Glenn Anderson scored at 19:40 of OT to give Toronto Game 5 before Gretzky rescued the Kings with an overtime goal two nights later, sending the series to a decisive Game 7. But while Toronto took advantage of home-ice in the seventh game against St. Louis, it could not do it again and the Kings rode the goaltending of Kelly Hrudey to a 5-4 triumph that propelled them into their first Stanley Cup finals.

The pressure of the finals did not affect Los Angeles. In fact, the Kings thoroughly outplayed the favored Canadiens in the first two games at the Forum. They won Game 1, 4-1, and carried a 2-1 lead into the final minutes of the second game.

But then Marty McSorley was penalized for using an illegal stick, giving the Canadiens one last chance. They tied it on the power play and then Eric Desjardins beat Hrudey 51 seconds into overtime, evening the series. The Kings would never recover. John LeClair tortured them with a pair of overtime goals in Games 3 and 4, and Roy stifled them in a 4-1 victory in Game 5 back at the Forum.

Roy was awarded the Conn Smythe Trophy as playoff MVP after going 16-4 and holding opponents to a 2.13 goals-against average. Lemieux, despite playing only 60 games, won the Ross Trophy with 69 goals and 91 assists for 160 points and was selected as league MVP for the second time. Chicago's Ed Belfour, who won 41 games, received the Vezina Trophy for the second time while teammate Chris Chelios was awarded his second Norris Trophy. The Lady Byng Trophy went to the Islanders' Turgeon, Toronto's Doug Gilmour won the Selke, and Selanne took the Calder.

Belfour, Chelios, Boston's Ray Bourque, Lemieux, Selanne, and Robitaille made the All-Star team.

1992–93

FINAL STANDINGS

Clarence Campbell Conference: Norris Division

	W	L	T	PTS	GF	GA
Chicago	47	25	12	106	279	230
Detroit	47	28	9	103	369	280
Toronto	44	29	11	99	288	241
St. Louis	37	36	11	85	282	278
Minnesota	36	38	10	82	272	293
Tampa Bay	23	54	7	53	245	332

Clarence Campbell Conference: Smythe Division

	W	L	T	PTS	GF	GA
Vancouver	46	29	9	101	346	278
Calgary	43	30	11	97	322	282
Los Angeles	39	35	10	88	338	340
Winnipeg	40	37	7	87	322	320
Edmonton	26	50	8	60	242	337
San Jose	11	71	2	24	218	414

Prince of Wales Conference: Adams Division

	W	L	T	PTS	GF	GA
Boston	51	26	7	109	332	268
Quebec	47	27	10	104	351	300
Montreal	48	30	6	102	326	280
Buffalo	38	36	10	86	335	297
Hartford	26	52	6	58	284	369
Ottawa	10	70	4	24	202	395

The Kings got as far as the Cup finals, thanks in part to Luc Robitaille, an All-Star first-team selection, for the fifth time in 1992–93.

	W	L	T	PTS	GF	GA
Pittsburgh	56	21	7	119	367	268
Washington	43	34	7	93	325	286
New York I.	40	37	7	87	335	297
New Jersey	40	37	7	87	308	299
Philadelphia	36	37	11	83	319	319
New York R.	34	39	11	79	304	308

LEADING SCORERS

	G	A	PTS
Lemieux, Pittsburgh	69	91	160
LaFontaine, Buffalo	53	95	148
Oates, Boston	45	97	142
Yzerman, Detroit	58	79	137
Selanne, Winnipeg	76	56	132
Turgeon, New York I	58	74	132
Mogilny, Buffalo	76	51	127
Gilmour, Toronto	32	95	127
Robitaille, Los Angeles	63	62	125
Recchi, Philadelphia	53	70	123

LEADING GOALIES

	G	GA	SO	GAA
Potvin, Toronto	48	116	2	2.50
Belfour, Chicago	71	177	7	2.59
Barrasso, Pittsburgh	63	186	4	3.01
Joseph, St. Louis	68	196	1	3.02
Moog, Boston	55	168	3	3.16

PLAYOFF RESULTS

Division Semifinals

Buffalo d. Boston, 4–0
Montreal d. Quebec, 4–2
Pittsburgh d. New Jersey, 4–1
N.Y. Islanders d. Washington, 4–2
St. Louis d. Chicago, 4–0
Toronto d. Detroit, 4–3
Vancouver d. Winnipeg, 4–2
Los Angeles d. Calgary, 4–2

Division Finals

Montreal d. Buffalo, 4–0
N.Y. Islanders d. Pittsburgh, 4–3
Toronto d. St. Louis, 4–3
Los Angeles d. Vancouver, 4–2

Conference Finals

Montreal d. N.Y. Islanders, 4–1
Los Angeles d. Toronto, 4–3

Finals

Montreal d. Los Angeles, 4–1

LEADING SCORERS

	G	A	P
Gretzky, Los Angeles	15	25	40
Gilmour, Toronto	10	25	35
Sandstrom, Los Angeles	8	17	25

LEADING GOALIES

	W	SO	GAA
Roy, Montreal	16	0	2.13
Joseph, St. Louis	7	2	2.27
Potvin, Toronto	11	1	2.84

1993–94

Expansion came to the league again, with the additions of the Florida Panthers and the Mighty Ducks of Anaheim, but the main stories of this season were written by Wayne Gretzky (no surprise) and the New York Rangers (quite a surprise).

The Panthers started play in Miami after being built by president Bill Torrey, who was largely responsible for the New York Islanders' dynasty in the early 1980s. The Mighty Ducks, meanwhile, became the first team to takes its name from a movie, as owner Michael Eisner of the Disney Company decided to use its hit film *The Mighty Ducks* as the inspiration for the team's logo and nickname. The expansion teams performed well in their inaugural seasons, each winning a first-season-record 33 games.

Gretzky provided the defining moment of the regular season, though, when he beat Vancouver goaltender Kirk McLean with a shot on March 23, 1994. The goal was the 802nd of Gretzky's NHL career, breaking Gordie Howe's long-standing record of 801. The Great One went on to win his 10th scoring title, recording 38 goals and 130 points in 81 games.

Others to make headlines during the season included Buffalo Sabres goaltender Dominik Hasek, who became the first netminder in 20 years to post a goals-against average of under 2.00. Hasek's 1.95 was the lowest in the league since Bernie Parent of the Flyers registered a 1.89 mark in 1973–74. Washington's Peter Bondra also left his mark in the record book when he scored four goals in a span of 4:12 against Tampa Bay's Daren Puppa at USAir Arena February 5.

On a team level, the biggest surprise of the regular season was the performance of the San Jose Sharks. In only their third season, the Sharks recorded the largest improvement of any team in NHL history, going from 24 to 82 points, earning their first playoff berth, and then shocking the heavily favored Red Wings in the first round of the playoffs.

The rise of the Rangers was not as shocking but equally dramatic. The team that won the Presidents' Trophy in 1991–92 had finished dead last in the Patrick Division last season. But this season management turned the coaching reins over to Mike Keenan, who had taken teams in Philadelphia and Chicago to the Stanley Cup finals.

The Rangers finally captured another Stanley Cup and ex-Oiler Mark Messier leads the celebration in 1994.

Dominik Hasek's sparkling 1.95 GAA with the Sabres won the Vezina Trophy in 1993–94.

Keenan told the team from the first day of training camp that they should settle for nothing less than the Stanley Cup and that by winning the Cup they could erase "The Curse of 1940"—a reference to the last time the Rangers were champions.

Whatever the motivation, the Rangers rebounded to their form of two years previous. Mark Messier, happy again under Keenan after some turbulent times with Roger Neilson, had an 84-point season and helped linemate.Adam

Detroit's Sergei Fedorov was the MVP as well as winner of the Selke Trophy in 1993–94.

Graves shatter the franchise record for goals in a season with 52. Young defensemen Sergei Zubov (89 points) and Brian Leetch (79) led the potent power play and were efficient enough in their own zone so that Mike Richter finished with a fine 42-12-6 record and 2.57 goals-against average. Still, as the playoffs approached, the old question came up again: Would the Rangers be able to maintain their pace in the playoffs?

To give the team a better chance, Keenan and general manager Neil Smith went out at the trading deadline and brought in veterans Craig MacTavish, Stephane Matteau, Glenn Anderson, and Brian Noonan, adding size, toughness, and playoff savvy to a team that already had everything else.

Once the playoffs started, the Rangers looked unbeatable. They humiliated the Islanders in a four-game sweep, then coasted past outmanned Washington in five games to reach the Eastern finals. There they would meet the resurgent New Jersey Devils, who in their first season under coach Jacques Lemaire had improved by 19 points to 106 and had cut their goals-against total from 299 to 220. The Devils advanced to the conference finals by defeating Buffalo in seven games (a classic goaltending battle between the Sabres' Dominik Hasek and the Devils' Martin Brodeur) and Boston in six.

The Western playoffs were not nearly as predictable. The Sharks were given no chance of upsetting the 100-point Red Wings, but a 5-4 victory in Game 1 set the tone for the series. Detroit came back to win Games 2 and 3, but the Sharks battled back from a 3-1 deficit to cap the fourth game and then took advantage of some erratic Red Wing goaltending to win Game 5 and take a 3-2 lead back to Detroit for the final two games.

When Detroit soared to a 7-1 triumph in Game 6, most observers felt the Sharks' magic had run out. But goals by Johan Garpenlov and Sergei Makarov gave them a 2-0 lead in the first 14 minutes of Game 7 and goalie Arturs Irbe was sensational in holding off the high-powered Red Wings. Detroit rallied on goals by Kris Draper and Vyacheslav Kozlov to tie it at 2-2, but Irbe kept his team in the game until Jamie Baker score an unassisted goal with 6:35 to go for the game-winner as nearly 20,000 Red Wings fans sat in stunned silence.

The Sharks nearly pulled off another miracle in the second round against Toronto, but Felix Potvin's goaltending helped the Leafs rally from a 3-games-to-2 deficit and win Games 6 and 7 in Toronto. That gave the Leafs a berth in the conference finals against Vancouver, which rode a dramatic road there. The Canucks were trailing 3

games to 1 against Calgary in the opening round and then incredibly won three overtime decisions.

Geoff Courtnall won Game 5 at 7:15 of extra play, and then Trevor Linden duplicated the feat two nights later with a goal at 16:13. Finally, in the decisive Game 7, the teams carried a 3-3 tie into overtime before Pavel Bure scored at 2:20 of a second overtime, propelling the Canucks into the next round. There they had far less trouble, eliminating the Dallas Stars (who had swept St. Louis in the first round) in five games.

The Western Conference finals were easy for the Canucks. After dropping a 3-2 overtime decision in Game 1 in Toronto, Vancouver came back with four straight victories, wrapping up the series on Greg Adams' goal at 0:14 of the second overtime in Game 5.

Overtime played an equally large role in the Devils-Rangers Eastern final. Stephane Richer's sudden-death goal gave New Jersey the early advantage in the series, but Richter posted a 4-0 shutout to even things up. Matteau scored in double overtime to win Game 3, but Brodeur's goaltending limited the Rangers to two goals as the Devils took Games 4 and 5.

With elimination facing them, the Rangers needed someone to step up and take them to the next level, and that turned out to be Messier. The day before Game 6, Messier calmly told the media that he "guaranteed" that the Rangers would win and force a seventh game back at Madison Square Garden.

Messier's guarantee looked flawed when the Devils jumped into a 2-0 lead at Meadowlands Arena, but New Jersey's failure to convert three two-on-one breaks in the second period proved fatal. Alexei Kovalev (on an assist from Messier) scored before the period ended, and then Messier took it from there, scoring three times in the third period to lift his team to a dramatic 4-2 victory.

That set the stage for Game 7 at the Garden. The Rangers carried a 1-0 lead into the final minute, but the Devils pulled Brodeur for an extra attacker and the move paid off when Valeri

Zelepukin scored with 7.7 seconds left, sending the game into yet another overtime. Finally, Matteau gathered a loose puck behind the net and stuffed a shot through Brodeur's pads at 4:24 of the second overtime for the 2-1 victory that put the Rangers in the finals.

Adams gave the Canucks a 1-0 lead in the series with an overtime goal, but the Rangers captured the next three games and appeared to have all the momentum heading back to New York for Game 5. Momentum is no match for the power of a 53-year curse, though. The Canucks blew a 3-0 lead before Dave Babych's goal with 10:29 left opened the doors for a 6-3 triumph that sent the series back to Vancouver, where Jeff Brown and Courtnall would score twice each in a 4-1 Canuck triumph.

Again the Rangers were facing the pressure of a must-win game. Goals by Brian Leetch and Graves gave them a 2-0 lead and when Trevor Linden scored early in the second period, Messier answered with a power-play goal, giving the Rangers a 3-1 lead entering the final period.

With a frenzied crowd roaring on every play, the Rangers managed to hold on. Linden scored again with 15:10 to go and Nathan LaFayette nearly knotted it with a shot that hit the post with six minutes left, but the Rangers never lost their cool. Finally, when Craig MacTavish won a last faceoff with 1.7 seconds left, the Rangers ended decades of frustration. Leetch, who excelled at both ends in the finals, was awarded the Conn Smythe Trophy as playoffs MVP, but it could have just as easily gone to Messier or Richter.

Detroit's Sergei Fedorov, who finished second to Gretzky for the Ross Trophy, won the Hart Trophy as league MVP and the Selke as top defensive forward, while Ray Bourque of Boston captured his fifth Norris Trophy. Hasek was an easy winner of the Vezina Trophy, while Brodeur took the Calder Trophy as the league's top rookie. Gretzky won the Lady Byng for the fourth time.

Hasek was the goalie on the All-Star team. He was joined by Bourque, the Devils' Scott Stevens, Fedorov, Bure, and the Blues' Brendan Shanahan.

1993–94

FINAL STANDINGS

Eastern Conference: Northeast Division

	W	L	T	PTS	GF	GA
Pittsburgh	44	27	13	101	299	285
Boston	42	29	13	97	289	252
Montreal	41	29	14	96	283	248
Buffalo	43	32	9	95	282	218
Quebec	34	42	8	76	277	292
Hartford	27	48	9	63	227	288
Ottawa	14	61	9	37	201	397

Eastern Conference: Atlantic Division

	W	L	T	PTS	GF	GA
New York R.	52	24	8	112	299	231
New Jersey	47	25	12	106	306	220
Washington	39	35	10	88	277	263
New York I.	36	36	12	84	282	264
Florida	33	34	17	83	233	233
Philadelphia	35	39	10	80	294	314
Tampa Bay	30	43	11	71	224	251

Western Conference: Central Division

	W	L	T	PTS	GF	GA
Detroit	46	30	8	100	356	275
Toronto	43	29	12	98	280	243
Dallas	42	29	13	97	286	265
St. Louis	40	33	11	91	270	283
Chicago	39	36	9	87	254	240
Winnipeg	24	51	9	57	245	344

Western Conference: Pacific Division7

	W	L	T	PTS	GF	GA
Calgary	42	29	13	97	302	256
Vancouver	41	40	3	85	279	276
San Jose	33	35	16	82	252	265
Anaheim	33	46	5	71	229	251
Los Angeles	27	45	12	66	294	322
Edmonton	25	45	14	64	261	305

LEADING SCORERS

	G	A	PTS
Gretzky, Los Angeles	38	92	130
Fedorov, Detroit	56	64	120
Oates, Boston	32	80	112
Gilmour, Toronto	27	84	111
Bure, Vancouver	60	47	107
Roenick, Chicago	46	61	107
Recchi, Philadelphia	40	67	107
Shanahan, St. Louis	52	50	102
Andreychuk, Toronto	53	46	99
Jagr, Pittsburgh	32	67	99

LEADING GOALIES

	G	GA	SO	GAA
Hasek, Buffalo	58	109	7	1.95
Brodeur, New Jersey	47	105	3	2.40
Roy, Montreal	68	161	7	2.50
Vanbiesbrouck, Florida	57	145	1	2.53
Belfour, Chicago	70	178	7	2.67

PLAYOFF RESULTS

Conference Quarterfinals

N.Y. Rangers d. N.Y. Islanders, 4–0
Washington d. Pittsburgh, 4–2
New Jersey d. Buffalo, 4–3
Boston d. Montreal, 4–3
San Jose d. Detroit, 4–3
Vancouver d. Calgary, 4–3
Toronto d. Chicago, 4–2
Dallas d. St. Louis, 4–0

Claude Lemieux won the Conn Smythe Trophy for his role propelling the New Jersey Devils to their first Stanley Cup in 1995.

LEADING SCORERS

	G	A	P
Leetch, N.Y. Rangers	11	23	34
Bure, Vancouver	16	15	31
Messier, N.Y. Rangers	12	18	30

LEADING GOALIES

	W	SO	GAA
Brodeur, New Jersey	8	1	1.95
Richter, N.Y. Rangers	16	4	2.07
McLean, Vancouver	15	4	2.29

1994–95

The 1994–95 season was supposed to start on October 1, 1994. It started on January 20, 1995.

Hockey almost became the first major professional sport to lose an entire season because of a labor conflict, but the NHL owners and NHL Players' Association finally settled their dispute and the games began.

Terms of the deal included: free agency for players beginning at age 32 for the first three years of the agreement and 31 for the last three years; a salary cap on entry-level players that begins at $850,000 and increases to $1,075,000 by the year 2000; and raising of the draft age to 19 (but 18-year-olds can volunteer their eligibility).

The teams would play a 48-game schedule this season (as opposed to the usual 84) and the playoffs would extend into June.

The "Game On" slogan brought hockey-starved fans back to the arenas and what they saw was a return to the defensive-style play of the 1960s. The result was a drastic dropoff in goals per game.

Even the Detroit Red Wings, known more for their offensive accent, adopted a defensive posture. They cut their defensive average from 16th to second in the league and finished with the best record (33-11-4) in the league.

Also improving dramatically—after five straight years of missing the playoffs—were the Philadelphia Flyers. Led by young superstar Eric Lindros and his Legion-of-Doom line, they rolled to the Atlantic Division title. The Quebec Nordiques' rise was swift as well. After not making the playoffs in 1993–94, they finished 30-13-5 to win the Northeast Division title.

Individual highlights of the season were provided by a pair of veterans, Pittsburgh's Joe Mullen and the Rangers' Steve Larmer, and a rookie, Washington's Jim Carey. Mullen became the first American-born player to crack the 1,000-point barrier when he scored twice in a 7-3 triumph over Florida on February 7. One month later, Larmer also reached the 1,000-point plateau when he netted a goal and three assists in a 6-4 win over New Jersey.

Carey single-handedly turned around a miserable start for the Capitals. With the team floundering with a 3-10-5 record at the end of February, the call went to Carey, who was playing with Portland in the American Hockey League. The 20-year-old goaltender proceded to go 6-0-1 and finished 18-6-3 with a 2.13 goals-against average that led the Caps into the playoffs.

But Carey and the rest of the NHL found out early in postseason play that beating the Devils would be nearly impossible. Jacques Lemaire's club, which had extended the Rangers to double-overtime of Game 7 in the Eastern Conference series the year before, shut out Boston, 5-0 and 2-0, at Boston Garden in the first two games of the conference quarterfinals. Earning the shutouts was Martin Brodeur, the young goalie. The Devils lost Game 3 at home, but then Brodeur's third shutout of the series and an overtime goal by Randy McKay restored New Jersey's two-game advantage. Back to Boston two days later, the Devils wrapped up the series with a 3-2 victory.

New Jersey went on to eliminate Pittsburgh, which had battled back from a 3-games-to-1

Philadelphia's Eric Lindros took the Hart Trophy as MVP in 1994–95.

deficit against Washington. Luc Robitaille's overtime goal rescued the Penguins in Game 5 and then Ken Wregget limited the Capitals to one goal in winning Games 6 and 7. In the other Eastern Conference bracket, the Flyers eliminated the Sabres in five games, while the Rangers surprised the Nordiques.

The turning point in the latter series came in Game 4 at Madison Square Garden when Quebec, down 2-1 in games, opened a 2-0 lead in the first period. The Nordiques broke out of their defensive zone on a 3-on-2 as Alexei Kovalev of the Rangers fell to the ice, apparently as the result of a slash. Referee Andy Van Hellemond signaled no penalty on the play and when Joe Sakic completed the rush by putting a shot past Glenn Healy, it appeared Quebec had opened a 3-0 lead. But Van Hellemond ruled that he had blown his whistle before the shot, thinking that Kovalev had been injured.

Kovalev, in fact, had faked the injury to try to draw a penalty, which was never called. The Nordiques' goal was waved off, and the Rangers rebounded to win the game, 3-2, and eventually take the series in six games.

In a postscript to the Kovalev incident, the NHL determined that Van Hellemond had erred and he was fined and removed from officiating duties for the final rounds of the playoffs.

In the next series, the bigger, younger, tougher Flyers won Games 1 and 2 in overtime and then wrapped up a sweep with two victories in New York. The Devils, meanwhile, rolled on. After stumbling in a Game 1 loss in Pittsburgh, Brodeur regained his form and limited the Penguins to five goals over the next four games, all of them Devils victories.

In the Western Conference playoffs, San Jose and Vancouver provided first-round surprises before being eliminated. The Sharks showed playoff magic for the second year in a row when Ray Whitney's goal at 1:54 of double overtime gave them a Game 7 win in Calgary. The Canucks also advanced the hard way, with Pavel Bure's two goals (his sixth and seventh of the series) providing the difference in a 5-3 Game 7 victory at St. Louis. That was quite a different playoff ending for Blues coach Mike Keenan, who the year before had led the Rangers to the Stanley Cup before leaving in a contract dispute.

Neither the Sharks nor Canucks would win another game after their first-round surprises. The Sharks were no match for the Red Wings in a four-game sweep while the Canucks managed only six goals against Chicago's Ed Belfour in a four-game elimination.

Belfour was equally hot against the Red Wings in the conference finals, but he received little help. Nicklas Lidstrom and Vladimir Konstantinov scored overtime goals to win Games 1 and 3 as the Wings broke to a 3-0 lead and went on to take the series in five games.

Back East, the Devils took the first two games in Philadelphia but the Flyers won Game 3 on an overtime goal by Lindros. When Philadelphia chased Brodeur from the net with four goals on 17 shots in a Game 4 victory, it was anybody's series. That anybody turned out to be Claude Lemieux, who fired a slap shot through Ron Hextall's pads with 45 seconds left in Game 5 to give the Devils a 3-2 triumph. They got another goal from Lemieux in a 4-2 decision that advanced them to their first Stanley Cup finals.

The year before, the Devils were eliminated by the Rangers, who had not won the Cup since 1940. Now they were going against a thirsty Red Wing team that hadn't sipped champagne since 1955.

Lemieux's goal early in the third period gave the Devils a 2-1 victory in Game 1 and then Jim Dowd's tally snapped a 2-2 tie with 1:24 remaining in Game 2. The Red Wings managed only 35 shots in the two losses.

Four different Devils scored against Mike Vernon in the first 28:20 of Game 3 as New Jersey prevailed, 5-2. Two nights later, on June 24, the latest date ever for a Stanley Cup game, Neal Broten had a pair of goals and Bill Guerin added three assists as the Devils celebrated their first Cup with a 5-2 win that capped the four-game sweep.

Lemieux won the Conn Smythe as playoffs MVP, a reward for his 13-goals-in-20-games effort. Jaromir Jagr of the Penguins became the first European to win the Art Ross Trophy as scoring champion, while Lindros was given the Hart as league MVP. Detroit's Paul Coffey won his third Norris Trophy and Sabres goalie Dominik Hasek captured the Vezina for the second year in a row. Pittsburgh's Ron Francis completed a rare double by winning the Selke and the Lady Byng, while Quebec's Peter Forsberg won the Calder as the league's top rookie.

The All-Star team was made up of Hasek, Coffey, Chicago's Chris Chelios, Lindros, Jagr, and the Flyers' John LeClair.

1994–95

FINAL STANDINGS

Eastern Conference: Northeast Division

	W	L	T	PTS	GF	GA
Quebec	30	13	5	65	185	134
Pittsburgh	29	16	3	61	181	158
Boston	27	18	3	57	150	127
Buffalo	22	19	7	51	130	119
Hartford	19	24	5	43	127	141
Montreal	18	23	7	43	125	148
Ottawa	9	34	5	23	117	174

Eastern Conference: Atlantic Division

	W	L	T	PTS	GF	GA
Philadelphia	28	16	4	60	150	132
New Jersey	22	18	8	52	136	121
Washington	22	18	8	52	136	120
New York R.	22	23	3	47	139	134
Florida	20	22	6	46	115	127
Tampa Bay	17	28	3	37	120	144
New York I.	15	28	5	35	126	158

Western Conference: Central Division

	W	L	T	PTS	GF	GA
Detroit	33	11	4	70	180	117
St. Louis	28	15	5	61	178	135
Chicago	24	19	5	53	156	115
Toronto	21	19	8	50	135	146
Dallas	17	23	8	42	136	135
Winnipeg	16	25	7	39	157	177

Western Conference: Pacific Division

	W	L	T	PTS	GF	GA
Calgary	24	17	7	55	163	135
Vancouver	18	18	12	48	153	148
San Jose	19	25	4	42	129	161
Los Angeles	16	23	9	41	142	174
Edmonton	17	27	4	38	136	183
Anaheim	16	27	5	37	125	164

LEADING SCORERS

	G	A	PTS
Jagr, Pittsburgh	32	38	70
E. Lindros, Philadelphia	29	41	70
Zhamnov, Winnipeg	30	35	65
Sakic, Quebec	19	43	62
Francis, Pittsburgh	11	48	59
Fleury, Calgary	29	29	58
Coffey, Detroit	14	44	58
Renberg, Philadelphia	26	31	57
LeClair, Mtl.-Phi.	26	28	54
Messier, New York R.	14	39	53
Oates, Boston	12	41	53

LEADING GOALIES

	G	GA	SO	GAA
Hasek, Buffalo	41	85	5	2.11
Carey, Washington	28	57	4	2.13
Belfour, Chicago	42	93	5	2.28
Lacher, Boston	35	79	4	2.41
Moog, Dallas	31	72	2	2.44

PLAYOFF RESULTS

Conference Quarterfinals

N.Y. Rnagers d. Quebec, 4–2
Philadelphia d. Buffalo, 4–1
Pittsburgh d. Washington, 4–3
New Jersey d. Boston, 4–1
Detroit d. Dallas, 4–1
San Jose d. Calgary, 4–3
Vancouver d. St. Louis, 4–3
Chicago d. Toronto, 4–3

Conference Semifinals

Philadelphia d. N.Y. Rangers, 4–0
New Jersey d. Pittsburgh, 4–1
Detroit d. San Jose, 4–0
Chicago d. Vancouver, 4–0

Conference Finals

New Jersey d. Philadelphia, 4–2
Detroit d. Chicago, 4–1

Finals

New Jersey d. Detroit, 4–0

LEADING SCORERS

	G	A	P
Fedorov, Detroit	7	17	24
Richer, New Jersey	6	15	21
Francis, Pittsburgh	6	13	19
Broton, New Jersey	7	12	19

LEADING GOALIES

	W	SO	GAA
Brodeur, New Jersey	16	3	1.67
Belfour, Chicago	9	1	2.19
Vernon, Detroit	12	1	2.31

1995–96

After its year of labor unrest, "The Coolest Game on Earth" (as it was called by one national sponsor) returned for a full slate of games. And again the sport's biggest names—Mario Lemieux, Wayne Gretzky, Patrick Roy, Paul Coffey—stole much of the spotlight. But from the glare emerged unfamiliar names—like Panthers and Avalanche.

Before the season started, the league received some good news when Lemieux, who sat

out the previous year due to back problems and Hodgkin's disease, announced he would return to the Penguins, albeit on a limited basis. Lemieux planned on playing 50 to 60 games, skipping the second nights of back-to-back contests and not making some road trips. That was the original plan, but it didn't work out that way.

The Penguin superstar wound up playing 70 games—and at the same lofty level he had reached in the early 1990s. He finished the regular season leading the NHL in goals (69), assists (92), and points (161), and was the key man on a power play that connected on a league-high 26 percent of its chances. Lemieux's amazing return and the spectacular one-on-one moves of Jaromir Jagr (149 points) helped the Penguins win the Northeast Division title.

Gretzky and Roy, two of the NHL's elite stars, also made headlines during the season, but not for their on-ice play.

Roy, the Canadiens' three-time Vezina Trophy winner, felt coach Mario Tremblay embarrassed him by leaving him in net for nine goals in an 11-1 loss to the Red Wings in Montreal on December 2. When Tremblay finally pulled Roy, the goalie skated over to team president Ronald Corey's box and told him he would never again play for the Canadiens. Four days later, Montreal traded Roy to the Colorado Avalanche for three players. The deal was to have a major effect on the rest of the league come playoff time.

Gretzky, meanwhile, was unhappy in Los Angeles as the Kings got off to a slow start and never contended for the top spot in the Pacific Di-

In midseason of 1995–96, Wayne Gretzky turned Blue, winding up in St. Louis after seven years as a King.

vision. With Gretzky approaching unrestricted free agency at the end of the season, the Kings decided to try to trade The Great One rather than possibly lose him at the end of the year and not get anything in return. So on February 27 Los Angeles sent their franchise player to the St. Louis Blues for three prospects.

Gretzky's former teammate, Coffey, now with Detroit, continued to rewrite the NHL record book for defensemen. In a December 13 win over Chicago, Coffey set up Igor Larionov's first-period goal and became the first blueliner in history to record 1,000 assists. Coffey would finish the season with 60 assists, giving him 1,038 in a re-markable 16-season career.

The rest of Coffey's teammates had a pretty good year, too. Scotty Bowman, the NHL's all-time leader in games coached and won, guided Detroit to a record-setting 62 wins, breaking the mark of 60 set by the Canadiens in 1976–77 when the league played an 80-game (instead of the current 82-game) schedule. The Red Wings finished the season with 131 points, one short of the record set by those same 1976–77 Canadiens, and won the Central Division by an astounding 37 points.

Montreal, meanwhile, never approached the lofty standards set by its predecessors but still had a memorable season when it shut the doors on the venerable Montreal Forum and ushered in a new era at the Molson Centre. The Canadiens played their last game at the Forum on March 11, beating Dallas, 4-1, then dropped the puck in their new arena five days later. Fittingly, they gave the Centre a proper baptism with a 4-2 victory over the Rangers.

Joe Sakic's scoring and playmaking brought him the Conn Smythe Trophy and the Avalanche the Stanley Cup.

When the playoffs started, it appeared that the Red Wings were a lock to break their 41-year run without a Stanley Cup. Bowman's Wings had the league's best defense, anchored by Coffey and goalies Chris Osgood and Mike Vernon, and a potent offense led by Sergei Fedorov (107 points, plus-49) and Steve Yzerman (95 points, plus-29). The other division winners, Pittsburgh, Philadelphia, and Colorado, seemed to pale in comparison to the mighty Wings. The Avalanche were overlooked by many observers simply because of their lack of name recognition. After all, the team had been known as the Quebec Nordiques since entering the league from the World Hockey Association in 1979–80, and it took awhile for people to realize that the NHL had indeed returned to Denver.

The Eastern Conference playoffs had a different look from years past as the two Florida teams, the Panthers and Tampa Bay Lightning, each made their first postseason appearance. While the Lightning's playoff stay was short, a six-game elimination by the Flyers, the Panthers' was not.

The third-year team won seven of its first 10 games in the regular season and never wavered in its bid for a playoff spot. Fans flocked to Miami Arena and supported the team with a passion that made the Panthers very tough to beat at home. Early in the season the Panthers' Scott Mellanby killed a rat that had wandered into the locker room, then he went out and scored twice. When the story made the papers, fans started bringing plastic and rubber rats to Panther games and

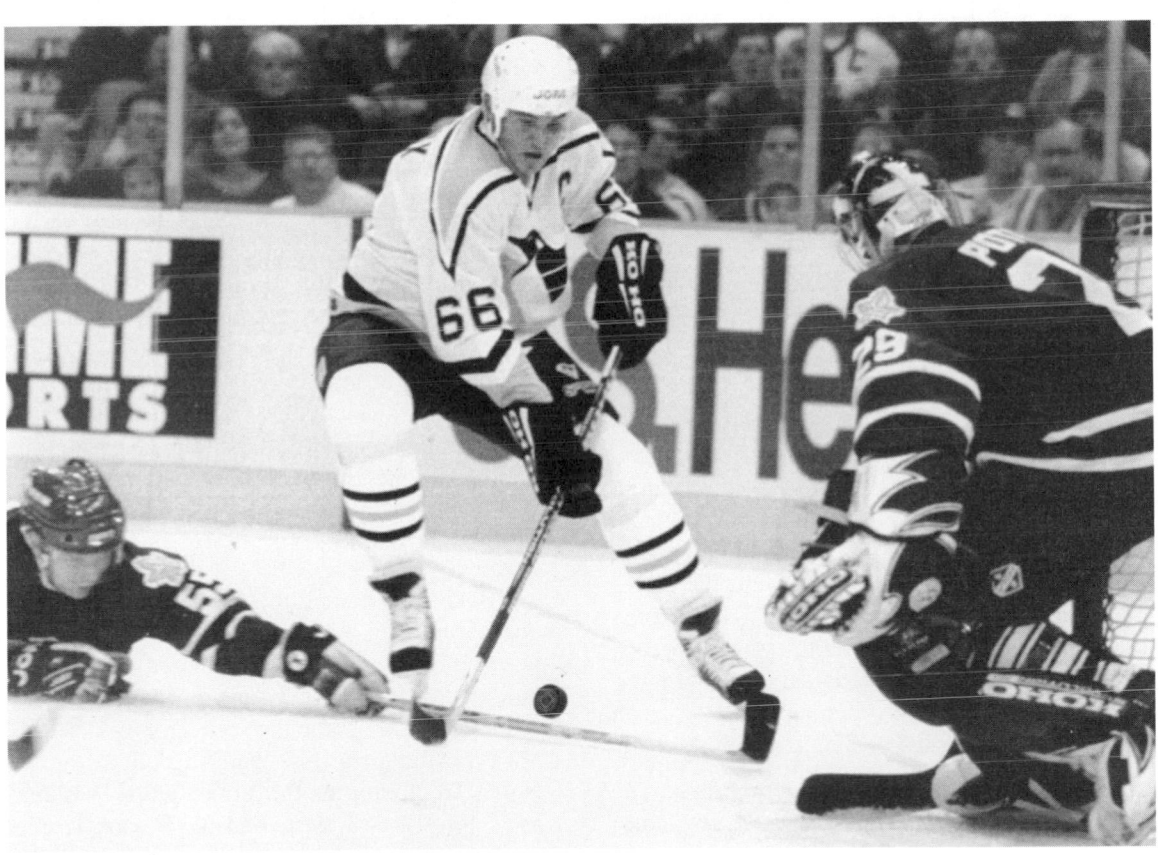

The Penguins' Mario Lemieux made a remarkable comeback in 1995–96 as he topped the NHL in scoring and captured the Hart Trophy as MVP.

throwing them onto the ice when the home team scored. The fans would have plenty of chances to throw before the playoffs were over.

The Panthers ousted the Boston Bruins in five games in the first round but were given little chance against the top-seeded Philadelphia Flyers in the conference semifinals. John Vanbiesbrouck set the tone for the series with a 2-0 shutout in Game 1 at the Spectrum as the Panthers limited the explosive Flyers to 18 shots. Philadelphia rebounded to take the next two games, but then the Panthers took over. Dave Lowry's overtime goal evened the series and Mike Hough scored in double overtime three days later to give Florida a 3-2 lead. The rats came out in Game 6 as Vanbiesbrouck stopped 34 shots in a 4-1 victory that ended the series.

Next for the Panthers were the Penguins, who had ousted the Washington Capitals and New York Rangers in the first two rounds. Again the Panthers were huge underdogs, and again they pulled off a huge upset. They played the Penguins even through six games and found themselves tied at 1-1 early in the third period of Game 7. Then, with 13:42 left, Tom Fitzgerald's 60-foot slap shot found its way past Tom Barrasso. Johan Garpenlov's goal with 2:37 remaining ensured a 3-1 triumph that sent the surprising Panthers into the Cup finals.

Waiting for them there were not the dominant Red Wings, but the Avalanche. Colorado had breezed past Vancouver in six games in the first round before running into a tough Chicago team. The Blackhawks won two of the first three games and seemed poised to take control of the series before Joe Sakic came to the rescue. Sakic scored at 4:33 of the third overtime to even the series, and the Avalanche never looked back, winning Game 5 at home before wrapping up the series on a double-overtime goal by Sandis Ozolinsh.

Detroit, meanwhile, was struggling. The Wings eliminated the Winnipeg Jets in six games but were taken to overtime of a seventh game by the Blues before Steve Yzerman's goal on a long slap shot boosted them into the conference finals.

It was there that the Red Wings' quest for their first Cup since 1955 died.

Mike Keane's overtime goal gave Colorado a Game 1 victory and then Roy stopped 35 shots in a 3-0 shutout that gave the Avalanche a two-game lead. The Red Wings climbed back into the series by splitting two games in Colorado and winning Game 5 back at Joe Louis Arena. But there was no holding off the younger, stronger Avalanche. Sakic netted his fifth game-winner of the playoffs as Colorado ended Detroit's season with a convincing 4-1 victory in the sixth game.

The finals were almost anticlimactic. Fitzgerald gave the Panthers the early lead in Game 1 with a first-period goal, but the Avalanche dominated after that. Colorado scored three times in the second period and held on for a 3-1 win, then got a first-period hat trick from Peter Forsberg in an 8-1 thrashing in Game 2. When Keane and Sakic scored less than two minutes apart to give the Avalanche a 3-2 victory in Game 3, the only question left was whether Colorado could complete a sweep of the series.

The sweep was achieved, but it didn't come easily. Roy and Vanbiesbrouck matched brilliant saves and the teams ended regulation time in a 0-0 tie. The first overtime was scoreless, as was the second. Finally, at 4:31 of the third extra period, defenseman Uwe Krupp's blast from the right point zipped past Vanbiesbrouck, giving the Avalanche the Cup. Colorado thus became the first team to win a championship in its first season after relocating.

Sakic was named the Conn Smythe winner after producing 18 goals and 16 assists in 22 postseason games. Lemieux, in addition to winning the Art Ross Trophy as the league's leading scorer, also took home the Hart Trophy as league MVP for the third time. Chris Chelios won the Norris Trophy for the third time, while Washington's Jim Carey was named the Vezina Trophy winner. Detroit's Sergei Fedorov won the Selke, Ottawa's Daniel Alfredsson captured the Calder, and Anaheim's Paul Kariya took the Lady Byng.

Lemieux, Jagr, Kariya, Chelios, Boston's Ray Bourque, and Carey were named to the All-Star team.

1995–96

FINAL STANDINGS

Eastern Conference: Northeast Division

	W	L	T	PTS	GF	GA
Pittsburgh	49	29	4	102	362	284
Boston	40	31	11	91	282	269
Montreal	40	32	10	90	265	248
Hartford	34	39	9	77	237	259
Buffalo	33	42	7	73	247	262
Ottawa	18	59	5	41	191	291

Eastern Conference: Atlantic Division

	W	L	T	PTS	GF	GA
Philadelphia	45	24	13	103	282	208
New York R.	41	27	14	96	272	237
Florida	41	31	10	92	254	234
Washington	39	32	11	89	234	204
Tampa Bay	38	32	12	88	238	248
New Jersey	37	33	12	86	215	202
New York I.	22	50	10	54	229	315

Western Conference: Central Division

	W	L	T	PTS	GF	GA
Detroit	62	13	7	131	325	181
Chicago	40	28	14	94	273	220
Toronto	34	36	12	80	247	252
St. Louis	32	34	16	80	219	248
Winnipeg	36	40	6	78	275	291
Dallas	26	42	14	66	227	280

Western Conference: Pacific Division

	W	L	T	PTS	GF	GA
Colorado	47	25	10	104	326	240
Calgary	34	37	11	79	241	240
Vancouver	32	35	15	79	278	278
Anaheim	35	39	8	78	234	247
Edmonton	30	44	8	68	240	304
Los Angeles	24	40	18	66	256	302
San Jose	20	55	7	47	252	357

LEADING SCORERS

	G	A	PTS
Lemieux, Pittsburgh	69	92	161
Jagr, Pittsburgh	62	87	149

The battered limousine was a tragic postscript for Red Wings Vladimir Konstantinov and Slava Fetisov and team masseur Sergei Mnatsakanov.

	G	A	P
Sakic, Colorado	51	69	120
Francis, Pittsburgh	27	92	119
Forsberg, Colorado	30	86	116
Lindros, Philadelphia	47	68	115
Kariya, Anaheim	50	58	108
Selanne, Winn.-Anaheim	40	68	108
Mogilny, Vancouver	55	52	107
Fedorov, Detroit	39	68	107

LEADING GOALIES

	G	GA	SO	GAA
Hextall, Philadelphia	53	112	4	2.17
Osgood, Detroit	50	106	5	2.17
Carey, Washington	71	153	9	2.26
Brodeur, New Jersey	77	173	6	2.34
Puppa, Tampa Bay	57	131	5	2.46

PLAYOFF RESULTS

Conference Quarterfinals

Philadelphia d. Tampa Bay, 4–2
Pittsburgh d. Washington, 4–2
N.Y. Rangers d. Montreal, 4–2
Florida d. Boston, 4–1
Detroit d. Winnipeg, 4–2
Colorado d. Vancouver, 4–2
Chicago d. Calgary, 4–0
St. Louis d. Toronto, 4–2

Conference Semifinals

Florida d. Philadelphia, 4–2
Pittsburgh d. N.Y. Rangers, 4–1
Detroit d. St. Louis, 4–3
Colorado d. Chicago, 4–2

Conference Finals

Florida d. Pittsburgh, 4–3
Colorado d. Detroit, 4–2

Finals

Colorado d. Florida, 4–0

LEADING SCORERS

	G	A	P
Sakic, Colorado	18	16	34
Lemieux, Pittsburgh	11	16	27
Jagr, Pittsburgh	11	12	23

LEADING GOALIES

	W	SO	GAA
Roy, Colorado	16	3	2.10
Osgood, Detroit	8	2	2.12
Hextall, Philadelphia	6	0	2.13

1996–97

The year began with Wayne Gretzky in New York, Mario Lemieux starting his farewell tour, and the Colorado Avalanche favorites to successfully defend their championship. It ended with a wild parade in Detroit as the Red Wings and their fans celebrated the team's first Stanley Cup in 42 years.

Gretzky made the biggest preseason news when he left the St. Louis Blues as a free agent and signed a two-year deal to rejoin old friend Mark Messier on the Rangers. The critics who said Gretzky was too old (36) or too fragile to withstand the rigors of the more physical Eastern Conference were proved wrong as the Great One was among the league's scoring leaders all season long. He finished the regular season with 97 points, just three shy of what would have been his 16th 100-point campaign.

Meanwhile, in Pittsburgh, Lemieux made no formal announcement until April that this would be his final season, but it was generally accepted early on that this was the case. Super Mario made his farewell campaign memorable by capturing his sixth scoring title. He netted 50 goals and added 72 assists to finish with 122 points, 13 more than runnerup Teemu Selanne of Anaheim.

While Gretzky and Lemieux were again making headlines, Colorado, led by goalie Patrick Roy, forwards Peter Forsberg and Joe Sakic, and defenseman Sandis Ozolinsh, breezed to the Presidents' Trophy with 107 points, three more than New Jersey and Dallas.

But once the playoffs started, it was the Red Wings who stole the Avalanche's thunder. After a rather disappointing regular season in which their 94 points left them 10 points behind Dallas in the Central Division, the Red Wings caught fire. They received an early scare when the St. Louis Blues went into Detroit and won, 2-0, in the opener of their first-round series, but they recovered and went on to defeat the Blues in six games.

Next came the Anaheim Mighty Ducks, and the Wings prevailed in a four-game sweep that was much tougher than it sounds. The first two games in Detroit went into overtime, with the Wings taking Game 1, 2-1, on Martin Lapointe's goal 59 seconds into sudden death and then second game, 3-2, on Slava Kozlov's score 1:31 into a third overtime period. Kozlov played the hero again as the series moved to Anaheim, scoring twice in the Red Wings' 5-3 Game 3 victory. Still, the Ducks would not quit. They took the Wings into double overtime in Game 4 before Brendan Shanahan's goal ended the series.

That set up a conference final matchup with the Avalanche, which had dispatched the Chicago Blackhawks and Edmonton Oilers in the first two

rounds. Colorado was outplayed in the first game but managed to hold on for a 2-1 victory as Roy made 34 saves.

Game 2 followed the same pattern as the Avalanche took a 2-1 lead into the third period despite being outshot, 30-11. But Roy could not perform his magic forever and the Red Wings beat him three times in the final period to win, 4-2, and even the series. The Avalanche played better when the series went to Detroit for Game 3, but Kozlov's goal with 11:40 remaining gave the Wings a 2-1 victory.

Igor Larionov and Kirk Maltby each scored twice as the Wings won, 6-0, in the fourth game but Colorado stayed alive with a 6-0 blowout in Game 5. The Avalanche's hopes of retaining the Cup ended, however, when the Red Wings went home and dominated, 3-1, in a game in which they had a 42-16 advantage in shots.

So now the Red Wings were in the Finals, where they would meet the Philadelphia Flyers. The Flyers had a relatively easy trip to the championship round as Eric Lindros and John LeClair led them past the Penguins in five games (Lemieux's last series), the Sabres in five, and the Rangers in five. But through it all there were questions about Philadelphia's goaltending. Garth Snow was adequate in the first two series. When he struggled against the Rangers, coach Terry Murray called on veteran Ron Hextall to win the final three games.

But the Red Wings were better than the Flyers in every area of the ice and coasted to a four-game sweep that was never in doubt. Detroit was in such control of the series that the Flyers held the lead for just two minutes. That lead came in the early stages of Game 3 after the Wings had posted back-to-back 4-2 victories in Philadelphia. After Hextall was beaten in the opener, Murray went to Snow for Game 2, but the young goaltender was not the answer.

LeClair scored early in Game 3 to give the Flyers the lead and some hope, but the Red Wings answered quickly. Sergei Fedorov and Martin Lapointe each scored twice as the Wings breezed to a dominating 6-1 victory that gave them a stranglehold 3-0 lead.

Murray accused his team of "choking" after the loss and the Flyers responded with an inspired effort in the first period of Game 4. But their goaltending betrayed them late in the period when Hextall allowed Nicklas Lidstrom's 55-foot shot to beat him between the pads, and the Flyers knew they were a beaten team.

Darren McCarty added a second-period goal with a sensational individual effort and the Wings held on from there, not allowing the Flyers anything until Lindros scored his only goal of the series with 14.8 seconds left. It was too little, too late.

As the clock wound down, Joe Louis Arena became awash in celebration. The Red Wings had finally done it, winning their first Stanley Cup in 42 years. Vernon was awarded the Conn Smythe Trophy as playoffs MVP, though in truth the award could have gone to any one of a number of Wings.

But the euphoria of the Detroit celebration was short-lived. Six days after winning the Cup, tragedy struck when a limousine carrying several Red Wings went off the road and struck a tree. Defenseman Vladimir Konstantinov suffered a head injury that left him in a coma, defenseman Slava Fetisov had chest lacerations and a bruised lung, and team masseur Sergei Mnatsakanov received severe head injuries.

The limo driver, Richard Gnida, was reported to have been driving with an expired license.

Buffalo's Dominik Hasek led the way in individual awards, capturing the Hart Trophy as regular-season MVP, the first goalie to do so since 1962, and the Vezina Trophy as leading goaltender. Lemieux captured his sixth Art Ross Trophy for most points in a season.

Other award winners included Buffalo's Michael Peca, Selke Trophy as top defensive forward; Buffalo's Ted Nolan, the Jack Adams Award as Coach of the Year; the Rangers' Bryan Leetch, the James Norris Trophy as No. 1 defenseman; and the Islanders' Bryan Berard, the Calder Trophy as leading rookie.

The Devils' Martin Brodeur and Michael Dunham took the William M. Jennings Trophy for goalies on the team with fewest goals against; Vancouver's Trevor Linden, the King Clancy Trophy for leadership on and off the ice; San Jose's Tony Granato, the Bill Masterton Trophy for perseverance, sportsmanship, and dedication; and the Mighty Ducks of Anaheim's Paul Kariya, the Lady Byng Trophy for sportsmanship.

1996–97

FINAL STANDINGS

Eastern Conference: Northeast Division

	W	L	T	PTS	GF	GA
Buffalo	40	30	12	92	237	208
Pittsburgh	38	36	8	84	285	280
Ottawa	31	36	15	77	226	254
Montreal	31	36	15	77	249	276
Hartford	32	39	11	75	226	256

Boston	26	47	9	61	234	300

Eastern Conference: Atlantic Division

	W	L	T	PTS	GF	GA
New Jersey	45	23	14	104	231	182
Philadelphia	45	24	13	103	274	217
Florida	35	28	19	89	221	201
New York R.	38	34	10	86	258	231
Washington	33	40	9	75	214	231
Tampa Bay	32	40	10	74	217	247
New York I.	29	41	12	70	240	250

Western Conference: Central Division

	W	L	T	PTS	GF	GA
Dallas	48	26	8	104	252	198
Detroit	38	26	18	94	253	197
Phoenix	38	37	7	83	240	243
St. Louis	36	35	11	83	236	239
Chicago	34	35	13	81	223	210
Toronto	30	44	8	68	230	273

Western Conference: Pacific Division

	W	L	T	PTS	GF	GA
Colorado	49	24	9	107	277	205
Anaheim	36	33	13	85	245	233
Edmonton	36	37	9	81	252	247
Vancouver	35	40	7	77	257	273
Calgary	32	41	9	73	214	239

Buffalo goalie Dominik Hasek won the Hart and Vezina trophies as the league's MVP and leading goalie in 1996–97.

Steve Yzerman celebrates Detroit's second straight Stanley Cup, as well as his own personal triumph after winning the Conn Smythe Trophy as Most Valuable Player of the 1997–98 Stanley Cup playoffs.

Los Angeles	28	43	11	67	214	268
San Jose	27	47	8	62	211	278

LEADING SCORERS

	G	A	PTS
Lemieux, Pittsburgh	50	72	122
Selanne, Anaheim	51	58	109
Kariya, Anaheim	44	55	99
LeClair, Philadelphia	50	47	97
Gretzky, New York R.	25	72	97
Jagr, Pittsburgh	47	48	95
Sundin, Toronto	41	53	94
Palffy, New York I.	48	42	90
Francis, Pittsburgh	27	63	90
Shanahan, Hart.-Det.	47	41	88

LEADING GOALIES

	G	GA	SO	GAA
Brodeur, New Jersey	67	120	10	1.88
Moog, Dallas	48	98	3	2.15
Hackett, Chicago	41	89	2	2.16
Hasek, Buffalo	67	153	5	2.27
Vanbiesbrouck, Florida	57	128	2	2.29

PLAYOFF RESULTS

Conference Quarterfinals

Colorado d. Chicago, 4–2
Edmonton d. Dallas, 4–3
Detroit d. St. Louis, 4–2
Anaheim d. Phoenix, 4–3
New Jersey d. Montreal, 4–1
Buffalo d. Ottawa, 4–3
Philadelphia d. Pittsburgh, 4–1
N.Y. Rangers d. Florida, 4–1

Conference Semifinals

N.Y. Rangers d. New Jersey, 4–1
Philadelphia d. Buffalo, 4–1
Colorado d. Edmonton, 4–1
Detroit d. Anaheim, 4–0

Conference Finals

Philadelphia d. N.Y. Rangers, 4–1
Detroit d. Colorado, 4–2

Finals

Detroit d. Philadelphia, 4–0

LEADING SCORERS

	G	A	PTS
Lindros, Philadelphia	12	14	26

Pittsburgh's Jaromir Jagr scores his 101st point against Boston's Byron Dafoe in the 1997–98 season finale to claim the Art Ross Trophy as the league's top scorer.

	G	A	PTS
Sakic, Colorado	8	17	25
Lemieux, Pittsburgh	13	10	23

LEADING GOALIES

	G	A	PTS
Brodeur, New Jersey	5	2	1.73
Vernon, Detroit	16	1	1.76
Richter, N.Y. Rangers	9	3	2.11

1997-98

Few expected Detroit to repeat as champs when the season dawned. Their toughest defenseman, Vladimir Konstantinov, had been seriously injured in an auto accident; their playoff MVP goalie, Mike Vernon, was traded to San Jose; and their young star center, Sergei Fedorov, was holding out for a better contract.

The NHL promised a unique season . . . and it was. The Hartford franchise moved to Raleigh, North Carolina, becoming the Hurricanes, but was forced to set up shop in Greensboro, 100 miles away. Their games were poorly attended.

Questions on the viability of Canadian franchises surfaced regularly. Edmonton was seemingly headed for Texas until community financing saved the franchise. At season's end, Vancouver, which fired both President/GM Pat Quinn and coach Tom Renny early in the year and missed the playoffs, announced it had lost $30 million.

Salaries exploded as Mark Messier's $18 million free-agent signing brought him to Vancouver, and Joe Sakic got $19 million when Colorado matched the Rangers' restricted free-agent offer sheet. In addition to Fedorov, other young stars, such as Edmonton's Bill Guerin and Anaheim's Paul Karyia, missed the season's opening weeks in search of better contracts. Fedorov held out until the Olympic break, when he signed a Carolina offer sheet that paid a $12 million lump sum bonus if the team made the semifinals. Detroit matched and he returned to their lineup. But Pittsburgh's Petr Nedved never signed and missed the entire season. Philadelphia's Eric Lindros, New Jersey's Scott Stevens, and Buffalo's Dominick Hasek all got lucrative new deals without holding out.

The three-week Olympic break stretched the season while compressing the schedule. Injuries plagued the NHL, including a troubling concussion epidemic, resulting in 238 man-games lost, more than double the previous season.

Sophisticated team defenses depressed the goals-per-game average to 5.28, the lowest since 1955–56. One hundred sixty shutouts were recorded, breaking the mark of 127 set in 1996–97. Hasek's 13 shutouts were the most since 1970. Dallas' Ed Belfour's 1.88 average was the lowest since 1972. Only Pittsburgh's Jaromir Jagr broke the 100-point barrier, the first time that happened since 1970. His scoring title was won with the lowest total since 1968.

The league instructed that all questionable goals be checked with the off-ice video replay, judge and reviewed goals became a common occurrence until the league modified its directive before midseason. Following the Olympic break, officials were urged to tighten their rulings on obstruction fouls away from the puck to aid scoring. It led to more power plays but scoring actually dropped.

Chicago missed the playoffs, its first miss in 29 seasons, as did the Rangers, who had an NHL-top $44 million payroll. But the Rangers' Wayne Gretzky recorded career assist No. 1,815, giving him more assists than anyone else had total points.

The Eastern Conference playoffs provided some big first-round upsets, none more startling than Ottawa's ousting of the Devils. Sparked by goalie Damien Rhodes, who stopped 173 of 184 New Jersey shots, the Senators won their first playoff series ever. Devils Coach Jacques Lemaire, regarded as one of hockey's best, resigned following the series.

With a balanced attack and tenacious defense, Montreal surprised the Penguins. The Habs employed defenseman Zarley Zalapsky as a checking forward against Jagr and got goals from 11 different players to eliminate Pittsburgh in six games.

The Flyers, who replaced coach Wayne Cashman with Roger Neilson late in the season,

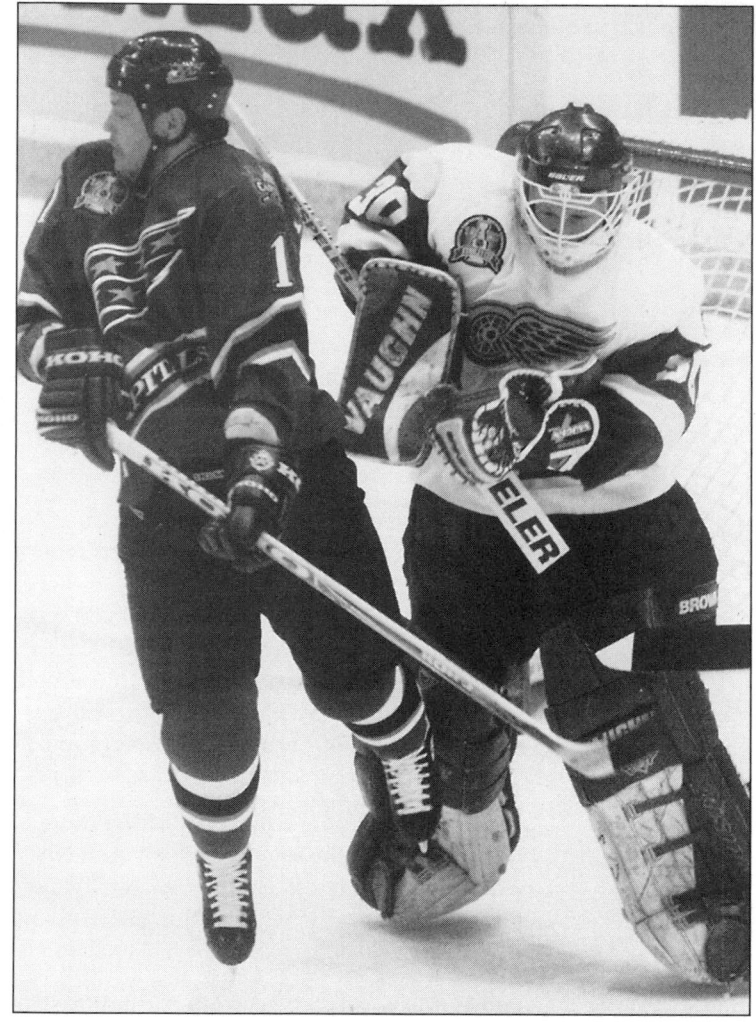

Detroit's Chris Osgood makes the save after the Capitals' Esa Tikkanen tried to deflect the puck into the net in Game 2 of the 1998 Stanley Cup finals.

skate in the crease, canceling the goal. The Caps eventually won on Brian Bellows' goal, taking the series in six games as Olaf Kolzig stopped 95 percent of Boston's shots.

Edmonton supplied the upset shocker out west, coming back from a 3–1 deficit to down Colorado in seven games. Geurin notched six goals and goalie Curtis Joseph stoned an Avalanche team that seemed to lack depth. Coach Mark Crawford was replaced by Bob Hartley following the playoffs.

Although Stars' top scorer Joe Nieuwendyk was injured early in the Dallas–San Jose series, Dallas proved too strong, winning in six games. Nieuwendyk was lost for the remainder of the playoffs.

Phoenix extended Detroit to six games before bowing, and questions arose about the play of Wings goalie Chris Osgood, who allowed soft goals early in the series.

The Kings, who sagged in late season, remained ineffective in the first round. St. Louis bombed them, 8–2, in the opener, and L.A. never recovered, being swept in its first playoff action since 1993.

seemed disorganized and dispirited in their first-round loss to Buffalo. Even in winning Game 2, the Flyers needed a questionable late-game power play to take the game. The angry Sabres outscored Philly, 10–2, over the next two games and finished them off with Michael Grosek's overtime goal in Game 5.

The Boston-Washington matchup turned on controversy. The Bruins' P. J. Axelsson scored the apparent Game 3 OT winner, but teammate Tim Taylor was detected by video review with his

In the battle of nation's capitals Kolzig's strong play in the second round halted the Senator's Cinderella ride in five games. He blanked Ottawa for the final 149 minutes of the series, posting two straight shutouts as Washington advanced to the third round for only the second time.

A surprising Game 2 hat trick made tough guy Mathew Barnaby the scoring hero for counter-attacking Buffalo, which swept Montreal

on the strength of two OT victories and Hasek's netminding.

In Joe Nieuwendyk's absence, Dallas' Belfour played his best postseason hockey since carrying Chicago to the 1992 finals, allowing the Oilers only five goals in the five-game series as Dallas headed for a showdown with Detroit.

Osgood again raised eyebrows when he allowed a long Al MacInnis goal to tie Game 3, but the Wings won in OT and took St. Louis in six games, largely on the play of Steve Yzerman, who notched nine points, and Fedorov, who got his bonus.

The third round featured a great Kolzig-Hasek goaltending matchup in the East. Even President Bill Clinton joined the Game 2 crowd at the MCI

Center arena to embrace Washington's team. He didn't stick around for the Caps' victory, one of their three overtime wins. Joe Juneau's Game 6 OT goal won the round in six games as Kolzig stopped 170 of 181 Sabre shots and the Caps were finals-bound for the first time in the team's 24-year history.

Osgood's Game 1 shutout, Yzerman's continued scoring and leadership, and the injured Konstantinov's presence in Joe Louis Arena for Game 4 sparked Detroit to a 3–1 series lead over Dallas. But with 1:25 remaining in regulation of the potential clinching Game 5, a desperate Guy Carbonneau tied the score. Then a long Jamie Langenbrunner shot eluded Osgood 46 seconds into OT to force a sixth game. But Osgood shut out Dallas and sent Detroit to its third final in four years.

A meeting of legends—and friends. Former Edmonton and New York teammates Wayne Gretzky (left) and Mark Messier face off.

Looking to become the first Cup repeaters since 1992, Detroit capitalized on Washington turnovers for first-period goals by Joe Kocur and Niklas Lidstrom just 2:14 apart in Game 1. Andrei Nikolishin got one back for Washington but Osgood held the fort and Detroit took the opener, 2–1.

Two nights later, the Wings again jumped on top, 1–0, and seemed in control when Caps defenseman Jeff Brown shot the puck the length of the ice in the second period. It barely deflected off Nikolishin's stick, which went undetected by the Wings, who eased up, believing icing was about to be called. The officials made no call and Peter Bondra took advantage of the lapse to tie the score. This upset Detroit, which surrendered two more goals for a 3–1 Caps lead at intermission.

Yzerman's second goal pulled Detroit closer but Joe Juneau answered almost immediately for a 4–2 Washington edge. Detroit stormed back with a goal by Martin LaPointe. Then came the series' critical moment: the Caps' Esa Tikkanen had Osgood trapped out of the net, but shot it through the unguarded crease, missing a chance to restore a two-goal lead. Instead, Doug Brown worked his way out of the corner to tie the score at 4–4 with less than five minutes remaining.

The game moved to overtime and LaPointe's pass out of the corner to an unguarded Kris Draper at 15:24 resulted in a Detroit victory and a 2–0 series lead.

In the first Stanley Cup finals ever held in Washington, the Wings got an early edge when Yzerman crashed the net and Tomas Holmstrom cashed in the rebound. Detroit held the lead until a third-period rebound shot by Brian Bellows tied the score at 1–1. But Federov fired a shot past Kolzig with just 4:51 remaining to give the Wings a 2–1 victory and a 3–0 series lead.

Detroit again jumped ahead in Game 4 on Brown's goal, and LaPointe made it 2–0 in the second period. Bellows got one back, but Larry Murphy's long shot restored the margin at 3–1. Brown's second goal early in the third period wrapped up a 4–1 triumph that gave Detroit its second consecutive Cup.

Yzerman, the playoffs' top scorer with 24 points in 22 games, won the Conn Smythe Trophy. Detroit's Scotty Bowman, who coached the last repeat champions in Pittsburgh in 1992, won his eighth Stanley Cup. He tied his mentor, Toe Blake, for most championships.

And the injured Vladimir Konstantinov was there to join in the celebration.

As he did in 1996–97, Hasek made off with awards galore. He again took the Hart Trophy as regular-season MVP and the Vezina Trophy as best goaltender. And he added the Pearson Award as the NHL's outstanding player.

Jagr captured the Art Ross Trophy for most points in a season, Dallas' Jere Lehtinen won the Selke Trophy as top defensive forward, and Los Angeles' Rob Blake captured the Norris Trophy as best defenseman.

Other trophy winners included Boston's Pat Burns, the Jack Adams Award as Coach of the Year; Boston's Sergei Samsonov, the Calder Trophy as Rookie of the Year; and New Jersey's Martin Brodeur and Michael Dunham, the Jennings Trophy for the second consecutive year as goalies with fewest goals against.

1997–98

FINAL STANDINGS

Eastern Conference: Northeast Division

	W	L	T	PTS	GF	GA
Pittsburgh	40	24	18	98	228	188
Boston	39	30	13	91	221	194
Buffalo	36	29	17	89	211	187
Montreal	37	32	13	87	235	208
Ottawa	34	33	15	83	193	200
Carolina	33	41	8	74	200	219

Eastern Conference: Atlantic Division

	W	L	T	PTS	GF	GA
New Jersey	48	23	11	107	225	166
Philadelphia	42	29	11	95	242	193
Washington	40	30	12	92	219	202
N.Y. Islanders	30	41	11	71	212	225
N.Y. Rangers	25	39	18	68	197	231
Florida	24	43	15	63	203	256
Tampa Bay	17	55	10	44	151	269

Western Conference: Central Division

	W	L	T	PTS	GF	GA
Dallas	49	22	11	109	242	167
Detroit	44	23	15	103	250	196
St. Louis	45	29	8	98	256	204
Phoenix	35	35	12	82	224	227
Chicago	30	39	13	73	192	199
Toronto	30	43	9	69	194	237

Western Conference: Pacific Division

	W	L	T	PTS	GF	GA
Colorado	39	26	17	95	231	205
Los Angeles	38	33	11	87	227	225
Edmonton	35	37	10	80	215	224
San Jose	34	38	10	78	210	216
Calgary	26	41	15	67	217	252
Anaheim	26	43	13	65	205	261
Vancouver	25	43	14	64	224	273

LEADING SCORERS:

	G	A	PTS
Jagr, Pittsburgh	35	67	102
Forsberg, Colorado	25	66	91
P. Bure, Vancouver	51	39	90
Gretzky, New York R.	23	67	90
LeClair Philadelphia	51	37	89
Francis, Pittsburgh	25	62	87
Selanne, Anaheim	52	34	86
Palffy, New York I.	45	41	86
Allison, Boston	33	50	83
Bondra, Washington	52	26	78
Fluery, Calgary	27	51	78
Stumpel, Los Angeles	21	57	78

LEADING GOALIES

	G	GA	SO	GAA
Belfour, Dallas	61	112	9	1.88
Brodeur, New Jersey	70	130	10	1.89
Barrasso, Pittsburgh	63	122	7	2.07
Hasek, Buffalo	72	147	13	2.09
Kidd, Carolina	47	97	3	2.17
Hextall, Philadelphia	46	97	4	2.17

PLAYOFF RESULTS

Conference Quarterfinals

Ottawa d. New Jersey, 4–2
Montreal d. Pittsburgh, 4–2
Buffalo d. Philadelphia, 4–1
Washington d. Boston, 4–2
Dallas d. San Jose, 4–2
Edmonton d. Colorado, 4–3
Detroit d. Phoenix, 4–2
St. Louis d. Los Angeles, 4–0

Conference Semifinals

Washington d. Ottawa, 4–1
Buffalo d. Montreal, 4–0
Dallas d. Edmonton, 4–1
Detroit d. St. Louis, 4–2

Conference Finals

Washington d. Buffalo, 4–2
Detroit d. Dallas, 4–2

Finals

Detroit d. Washington, 4–0

LEADING SCORERS

	G	A	P
Yzerman, Detroit	6	18	24
Federov, Detroit	10	10	20
Holmstrom, Detroit	7	12	19
Lidstrom, Detroit	6	13	19

LEADING GOALIES

	W	SO	GAA
Belfour, Dallas	10	1	1.79
Brodeur, New Jersey	2	0	1.97
Barrasso, Pittsburgh	2	0	2.71

1998–99

The last season to be played in the 20th century also became the last season with "99".

As he had so many times in his career, Wayne Gretzky took the spotlight as he announced his retirement on April 16, 1999, ending the career of the greatest player ever to don skates.

Though no longer the force he had been in the glory days with the Edmonton Oilers, Gretzky still showed flashes of brilliance and had provided one of the season's most memorable moments on March 29 against the N.Y. Islanders at Madison Square Garden.

They were in overtime when suddenly the puck landed in the front of the net. Before Islander goalie Wade Flaherty could react, Gretzky tipped the puck in to give the Rangers the victory and The Great One another record. The goal was No. 1,072 of his professional career, one more than legendary Gordie Howe had netted. It put Gretzky alone at the top of every scoring category.

With nothing left to accomplish on the ice and a nagging back injury, Gretzky decided he'd had enough. There was no formal announcement on April 15 in Ottawa before his final game on Canadian ice as the Rangers met the Senators.

As the seconds ticked down, the crowd at the Corel Centre stood as one and applauded. After the final buzzer, the prolonged standing ovation prompted Gretzky to take a few laps around the ice, with tears flowing down his face as he saluted his legion of fans.

That farewell was nothing compared to what occurred in New York three days later when Gretzky played his final NHL game against Pittsburgh. After the Rangers gave him presents in a pregame ceremony, he went out in style, setting up a Ranger goal with a pass that led to a score by Brian Leetch.

The Penguins' Jaromir Jagr rallied in overtime to hand the Rangers a 2-1 loss, but it mattered little to New York's celebrants. For more than 20 minutes the Garden crowd cheered and wept unabashedly as a teary Gretzky circled the

ice for the final time. Then, with one last wave, he was gone, taking with him an era of greatness and the number 99, which the NHL announced would never be worn by another player.

Meanwhile, a team from Texas was making its share of headlines. The Dallas Stars, after years of playoff failure, signed free agent Brett Hull in the hope he would be the missing piece to the Stanley Cup puzzle. Through the regular season Dallas breezed to the Presidents' Trophy as the team with the best overall record.

The goaltending of Eddie Belfour, combined with the scoring of Hull, Joe Nieuwendyk, and Mike Modano and a defense spearheaded by Sergei Zubov and Derien Hatcher made the Stars the favorites as the playoffs began.

The Stars swept Edmonton in the first round while their main Western Conference rivals, Detroit and Colorado, also advanced. The two-time champion Red Wings were hoping for three Cups in a row as they began by sweeping Anaheim and taking the first two games on the road against Colorado.

But the Red Wings' defense and goaltending fell apart as the Avalanche bounced back with 5-3 and 6-2 victories at Joe Louis Arena. Colorado gained the series lead behind Patrick Roy's 36 saves in a 3-0 Game 5 victory. And the Avalanche fulfilled its mission with a 5-2 triumph in the sixth game.

That set up a classic Western final between the Avalanche and Dallas, who had outlasted St. Louis in six games, three of which went into overtime. Peter Forsberg had a goal and an assist

Dominik Hasek goes low to stop Dallas's Mike Modano in the Stanley Cup finals.

Wayne Gretzky turns to teammate Adam Graves to celebrate scoring the 1,072nd goal of his career, which is a new record.

as Colorado quickly stole home-ice advantage with a 2-1 victory in Game 1, but Dallas rebounded behind a goal and assist from Modano to tie the series. The teams split the two games in Denver before Valeri Kamensky gave the Avalanche temporary control with two goals and an assist in a 7-5 triumph in Game 5. But Belfour's steady goaltending paved the way for consecutive 4-1 victories that sent Dallas into its first-ever Stanley Cup finals.

Awaiting the Stars were the surprising Buffalo Sabres, who emerged from the Eastern pack after a series of stunning early-round upsets. The top three seeds—the Devils, Senators, and Hurricanes—were all eliminated in the first round, leaving the field wide open. The Devils' loss to the Penguins was especially frustrating in New Jersey because it marked the second year in a row that the team had entered the playoffs as the No. 1 seed in the East only to lose in the first round.

The Sabres, with the umatched Dominik Hasek in goal, were never seriously threatened on the way to the finals. They swept Ottawa in the first round, skated past Boston in six games in the quarterfinals, and ousted Toronto in five games to earn their first trip to the finals since the French Connection team of 1975 lost to the Bernie Parent–led Flyers.

The Sabres had only one 40-goal scorer (Miroslav Satan), but an aggressive defense led by Jason Woolley and Alexei Zhitnik and the acrobatic goaltending of Hasek made them dangerous. In the opener Woolley scored at 15:30 of overtime to give Buffalo a rousing 3-2 triumph.

Hull got Dallas back on track in Game 2, snapping a 2-2 tie with 2:50 left, and Nieuwendyk was the hero two nights later, scoring twice in a 2-1 win that gave the Stars the lead. But in Game 4, after the teams traded goals, Buffalo's Dixon Ward scored at 7:37 of the second period and Hasek stopped all 13 shots in the third period to preserve a 2-1 victory that evened the series.

Belfour stole Hasek's thunder in the pivotal fifth game, kicking out 23 shots in a 2-0 triumph that moved the Stars to within one win of the Cup. Back in Buffalo for Game 6, Jere Lehtinen scored in the first period to give the Stars the lead, but Stu Barnes knotted it in the second period.

There was no score in the third period and the game went into overtime—one OT, another, and a third. Finally, at 14:51 of the third overtime, Modano fired a shot that Hasek stopped but couldn't control. Hull collected the rebound and shoveled it past Hasek for the Cup-winning goal.

The goal led to controversy, however, as video replay showed that Hull had his skate in the crease before firing in the rebound. The NHL ruled that the goal was good because Hull had never lost possession of the puck while it was in the crease. But at the subsequent NHL meetings, the league did away with the crease rule for the 1999–2000 season.

Nieuwendyk, who had 11 goals and 10 assists in 23 playoff games, was named the Conn Smythe Trophy winner as postseason MVP. Gretzky took one final award, his fifth Lady Byng, into retirement. Pittsburgh's Jagr bagged the Hart Trophy as league MVP, while Hasek won the Vezina, his fifth, as goalie MVP and Lehtinen got the Selke as top defensive forward.

St. Louis' Al MacInnis captured the Norris Trophy; Colorado's Chris Drury nailed the Calder as Rookie of the Year; Belfour and Roman Turek claimed the Jennings as the goalies on the team that allowed the fewest goals. Ottawa's Jacques Martin won the Adams as the top coach and Tampa Bay's John Cullen earned the Masterton for dedication to hockey.

Hasek, Jagr, Forsbeg, MacInnis, Nicklas Lidstrom of Detroit, and Paul Kariya of Anaheim made the All-Star team.

1998-99

FINAL STANDINGS

Eastern Conference: Northeast Division

	W	L	T	PTS	GF	GA
Ottawa	44	23	15	103	239	179
Toronto	45	30	7	97	268	231
Boston	39	30	13	91	214	181
Buffalo	37	28	17	91	207	175
Montreal	32	39	11	75	184	209

Eastern Conference: Atlantic Division

	W	L	T	PTS	GF	GA
New Jersey	42	24	11	105	248	196
Philadelphia	37	26	19	93	231	196
Pittsburgh	38	30	14	90	242	225
N.Y. Rangers	33	38	11	77	217	227
N.Y. Islanders	14	48	10	58	184	244

Eastern Conference: Southeast Division

	W	L	T	PTS	GF	GA
Carolina	34	30	18	86	210	202
Florida	30	34	18	78	210	228
Washington	31	45	6	68	200	218
Tampa Bay	19	54	9	47	179	292

Western Conference: Central Division

	W	L	T	PTS	GF	GA
Detroit	43	32	7	93	245	202
St. Louis	37	32	13	87	237	209
Chicago	29	41	12	70	202	248
Nashville	28	47	7	63	190	161

Western Conference: Pacific Division

	W	L	T	PTS	GF	GA
Dallas	51	19	12	114	236	168
Phoenix	39	31	12	90	205	197
Anaheim	35	34	13	83	215	206
San Jose	31	33	18	80	196	191
Los Angeles	32	45	5	69	189	222

Western Conference: Northwest Division

	W	L	T	PTS	GF	GA
Colorado	44	28	10	98	239	205
Edmonton	33	37	12	78	230	226
Calgary	30	40	12	72	211	234
Vancouver	23	47	12	58	192	258

LEADING SCORERS

	G	A	PTS
Jagr, Philadelphia	44	83	127
Selanne, Anaheim	47	60	107
Kariya, Anaheim	39	62	101
Forsberg, Colorado	30	67	97
Sakic, Colorado	41	55	96
Yashin, Ottawa	44	50	94
Lindros, Philadelphia	40	53	93
Flory, Cal.-Col.	40	53	93
LeClair, Philadelphia	43	47	90

LEADING GOALIES

	G	GA	SO	GAA
Tugnutt, Ottawa	43	75	3	1.79
Hasek, Buffalo	64	119	9	1.87
Dafoe, Boston	68	133	10	1.99
Belfour, Dallas	61	117	5	1.99

PLAYOFF RESULTS

Conference Quarterfinals

Pittsburgh d. New Jersey, 4–3
Buffalo d. Ottawa, 4–0
Boston d. Carolina, 4–2
Toronto d. Philadelphia, 4–2
Dallas d. Edmonton, 4–0
Colorado d. San Jose, 4–2
Detroit d. Anaheim, 4–0
St. Louis d. Phoenix, 4–3

Conference Semifinals

Toronto d. Pittsburgh, 4–2
Buffalo d. Boston, 4–2

Dominik Hasek stopped Brett Hull on this shot, but Hull would later score the Cup-clinching goal in triple overtime of Game 6 for Dallas.

Dallas d. St. Louis, 4–2
Colorado d. Detroit, 4–2

Conference Finals

Buffalo d. Toronto, 4–1
Dallas d. Colorado, 4–3

Finals

Dallas d. Buffalo, 4–2

LEADING SCORERS

	G	A	P
Forsberg, Colorado	8	16	24
Modano, Dallas	5	18	23
Nieuwendyk, Dallas	11	10	21
Sakic, Colorado	6	13	19
Langenbrunner, Dallas	10	7	17
Fleury, Colorado	5	12	17

LEADING GOALIES

	W	SO	GAA
Belfour, Dallas	16	3	1.67
Hasek, Buffalo	13	2	1.77
Dafoe, Boston	6	2	2.03
Fuhr, St. Louis	6	1	2.35
Joseph, Toronto	9	1	2.43
Roy, Colorado	11	1	2.66
Barrasso, Pittsburgh	6	1	2.66

8

THE TOP 100 PLAYERS IN NHL HISTORY

Selection of hockey's all-time greatest players is a pursuit that inspires lively debate among followers of the game. Older fans cling to their memories and their heroes of yore; younger rooters who never got to see the stars of the past, understandably make a case for the moderns.

The Hockey News polled 50 experts—writers, broadcasters, coaches, referees, and NHL officials—to produce its list of the 100 greatest, regardless of position.

To nobody's surprise, No. 1 in the voting was Wayne Gretzky. "If he were a mountain range he would not only be as high as the Himalayas, he would be as long as the Rockies," noted writer Jack Falla in his accompanying essay in *The Hockey News*.

Gretzky's closest competition came from Bobby Orr and Gordie Howe, No. 2 and No. 3 in the balloting, followed by Mario Lemieux and Maurice Richard.

Following are biographies on all 100 of the greatest players, arranged in numerical order, from 1 to 100.

The biographies that follow are the combined work of several veteran writers, including Tim Moriarty, Rich Chere, and Stu Hackel.

1. WAYNE GRETZKY

Wayne Gretzky and New York. The Great One and the media capital of the world. It was a celebrated marriage and nearly meant another Stanley Cup for the Rangers.

During the summer of 1996, Gretzky, the greatest scorer in the history of hockey, had become a free agent, with the opportunity to choose where he wanted to finish his career. But with the chance to reunite with old friend Mark Messier, there really was no choice to make. Gretzky accepted the Rangers' offer of a two-year deal to bring his game to the Big Apple.

Critics said Gretzky was too old (he would turn 36 in midseason) and too frail to withstand the rigors of the physical Eastern Conference. But the critics were left speechless when Gretzky not only survived but thrived. He finished the season with a team-high 97 points, narrowly missing his 16th 100-point campaign, and was even better in the playoffs, netting two hat tricks to carry the Rangers into the Eastern Conference finals, where they were worn down by the Philadelphia Flyers. Afterwards, both teams marvelled at what Gretzky had done for the Rangers.

He began his legendary career in his hometown of Brantford, Ontario, where as a 10-year-old he scored 378 goals in 85 games!

The marriage ended amicably. New York and Wayne Gretzky is over. And so is the celebrated career of the Great One.

After 21 years as a professional, the last three as a New York Ranger, Gretzky said farewell at a Madison Square Garden press conference. "It's time and, of course, I'm sad," he announced on April 17, 1999. "I've played hockey for 35 years, since I was three years old. I'm going to miss it."

And hockey will miss Wayne Gretzky.

Gretzky was only 17 when he signed his first pro contract with the Indianapolis Racers of the old World Hockey Association. When the Racers ran out of money eight games into the 1978–79 season, Wayne was sold to the Edmonton Oilers.

Wayne totaled 46 goals and 110 points in his first professional season, after which the WHA folded and the Oilers were granted an NHL franchise. Gretzky recalled his NHL baptism with a wry smile. "Everywhere I went they thought I would get killed because of my size [5-foot-11, 170 pounds]," he said. "I heard a lot of talk then that I'd never get 110 points like I did in the WHA." In fact, he did better than that, totaling 137 points on 51 goals and 86 assists.

"Wayne is a natural goal-scorer, just like I was," said Hall-of-Famer Rocket Richard. "He's moving all the time and it seems the players trying to check him can't catch him."

They couldn't catch him on the scoreboard, either. During the next nine seasons (1980–88) Gretzky led the league in scoring seven times, won eight Hart Trophies as league MVP, and captained the Oilers to four Stanley Cups. Then came the day of infamy for Oilers fans: August 9, 1988, when Gretzky was traded to the Los Angeles Kings for $15 million, three players and three first-round draft picks. In return, the Kings received Gretzky and three other players.

It was the most spectacular trade in the history of hockey—maybe of all sports.

Gretzky's assault on the record book didn't stop when he changed uniforms. The slender center became the NHL's all-time leading scorer on October 15, 1989, when he surpassed Gordie Howe's total of 1,850 points. Ironically, Wayne broke the record in Edmonton's Northlands Coliseum—his home for 10 seasons. He passed Howe with a goal with 53 seconds left in regulation, tying the game. To make the night perfect, he added another goal in overtime, giving the Kings a 4–3 victory over the Oilers.

Early in the 1990–91 season, Gretzky scored his 2,000th career point. He was then closing in on his 30th birthday. Asked if he thought he could

eventually reach 3,000 points, Gretzky said: "That might be tough. Barring injury and staying healthy, I can probably average 150 points a year, which means seven more years. I don't know if I'll play seven more years."

Gretzky was showing no signs of slowing down when he led the league in scoring for the ninth time in 1990–91 and increased his career goal total to 718. He added 31 goals in 1991–92 and finished third in scoring with 121 points (Mario Lemieux led with 131, followed by his Penguin teammate Kevin Stevens with 123).

Injuries limited Gretzky to 45 games in 1992–93, but the next season he netted his 10th scoring title with 38 goals and 92 assists for 120 points. In the process he snapped the legendary Howe's NHL record with his 802nd career goal.

Gretzky kept building on his record. He averaged a point per game in the lockout-shortened 1994–95 season, then scored 102 points in 1995–96. Late that season he was traded to the St. Louis Blues, but his stay there was brief. His contract expired after the Blues were eliminated from the playoffs, and soon after that he was on his way to New York.

As a Ranger in 1996–97 he became the first player in history to reach 1,800 assists and also the first to accumulate 3,000 points (including playoffs).

In his valedictory season, 1998–99, Gretzky added to the more than 60 NHL records that carry

Wayne Gretzky

Bobby Orr

his name, including the all-time goal, assist, and point marks.

Many of them will be forever matchless.

2. BOBBY ORR

He was always looked upon as the boy next door, the one with the winning smile and the gra-

cious manner. Square-jawed and thick-necked, there was never an ounce of fat on his 5-foot-11 frame. And he was looked upon in many quarters as the best defenseman in hockey history.

Bobby Orr was something special. "All Bobby did was change the face of hockey all by himself," said a former teammate, Phil Esposito.

Orr revolutionized the role of the defenseman with his slick passing and playmaking and end-to-end dashes. He also was responsible in part for elevating the salary structure of NHL players.

Orr signed a record bonus contract with the Boston Bruins at the age of 18 in 1966 and four years later he became the first defenseman in NHL history to win the scoring title when he led the Bruins to the Stanley Cup championship.

Appropriately enough, it was Orr's overtime goal that won the fourth and final game of the playoffs for the Bruins and brought them their first Stanley Cup in 29 years. It was his ninth goal and 20th point of the playoffs, both records for defensemen. During the regular season, Bobby had made history with record-cracking totals of 33 goals, 87 assists, and 120 points to win the scoring title.

The Bruins discovered Orr in 1962 playing midget hockey in his hometown of Parry Sound, Ontario. He was only 14 but he had everything even then. Boston moved him into junior hockey at Oshawa and in three years playing defense there, he averaged 33 goals per season, an amazing output at the time.

It cost Boston $75,000 for a two-year agreement to get young Bobby's name on an NHL contract, the best investment the team ever made.

Orr won the Calder Trophy as Rookie of the Year in 1967. "Bobby was a star from the moment they played the National Anthem in his first NHL game," said Harry Sinden, Orr's first coach in Boston.

Howell's prediction was fulfilled. Orr won the Norris Trophy as best defenseman for eight

straight years and in 1970 he became the first man in history to nail down four individual trophies in a single season. He took the Norris, the Art Ross Trophy for scoring, the Hart Trophy as the Most Valuable Player in the regular season, and the Conn Smythe Trophy as MVP in the playoffs.

Orr repeated as playoff MVP in 1972 when he led the Bruins to the Stanley Cup championship again. He also won his third consecutive Hart Trophy as regular-season MVP, becoming the first man in NHL history to win it more than two straight times.

Orr scored a career-high 46 goals and won his second scoring title with 135 points in 1974–75. He also was named to the All-Star first team for the eighth consecutive year. However, constant knee problems were slowing him down. He ended his 10-year association with the Bruins in 1976, became a free agent, and signed a $3-million, five-year contract with the Chicago Blackhawks.

He sat out the 1977–78 season after undergoing his sixth knee operation, and attempted a comeback the following year but was forced to quit after appearing in six games. "My knees can't handle playing anymore," he said. He was 30 years old.

Orr held or shared 12 individual records at the time of his retirement. He totaled 270 goals and 915 points in 657 games—remarkable figures for a defenseman. He was voted into the Hockey Hall of Fame in 1979.

Orr received his greatest accolade, though, when the *Boston Globe* conducted a poll to determine the greatest athlete in the city's history. It was not Ted Williams, Carl Yastrzemski, Bob Cousy, or Bill Russell. The winner was Bobby Orr.

3. GORDIE HOWE

Gordie Howe, looking a little uncomfortable in a tuxedo, was grinning as he approached the speaker's rostrum in the Canadian Room of the Royal York Hotel in Toronto. The occasion was the 1982 Hockey Hall of Fame dinner, and Howe

was there to receive the initial presentation of the Milestone Award, instituted by the NHL to honor players and coaches who have achieved milestones during their careers.

Howe glanced about the room, packed with almost 900 diners, and was still grinning as he began his acceptance speech. He recalled how he had dreamed during his youth of playing in the NHL. "I would have been happy to play just one season," he said. Now the audience was laughing—not at Howe but with him.

Gordie Howe was the most durable player in the history of pro hockey. He played not one season but 32—26 in the NHL and 6 in the World Hockey Association.

The 6-foot, 205-pound right wing from the wheat fields of Saskatchewan started his career with the Detroit Red Wings at the age of 18 in 1946. He finished it with the Hartford Whalers at the age of 52 in 1980.

Howe's statistics are astounding. Including playoff games, he totaled 2,421 games, 1,071 goals, 1,518 assists, 2,589 points, and 2,418 penalty minutes.

He was hailed throughout the hockey world as a seemingly indestructible man of steel. Howe's career—and his life—were almost snuffed out in his third season with the Red Wings. He collided with Toronto's Ted Kennedy during a 1950 Stanley Cup playoff game, crashed head-on into the sideboards, and suffered a severe brain injury. He hovered between life and death while surgeons operated to relieve pressure on his brain.

The injury left him with a slight facial tic; there are times when his dark eyes blink uncontrollably. His teammates called him "Blinky," and it was a mark of Howe's class that he never resented the nickname. He frequently startled newsmen with remarks like "Old Blinky was flying tonight," or "Did you see old Blinky miss that goal in the second period?"

Even in the twilight of his career, Howe remained an amazing athlete—the complete hockey player. He was big and tough and sometimes a lit-

Gordie Howe

tle rough. He could still shoot with the best NHL marksmen; he could set up plays; he acted as the triggerman on power plays; he killed penalties.

Jean Beliveau of the Montreal Canadiens claimed "Gordie Howe is the best hockey player I have ever seen."

Blessed with a powerful body, Howe would have made an ideal heavyweight boxer. He had the sloping shoulders of a fighter, his neck thick and his muscular arms dangling loosely like the limbs of an oak tree. He had his share of fights on the ice, the most memorable taking place in 1959 when he tangled with Lou Fontinato of the New York Rangers. Fontinato's nose was broken, and his whole face needed considerable repairs.

Howe, though, was no troublemaker. He just kept rolling along, content to score goals and accumulate records and honors. He was named to the NHL's All-Star team 21 times. He won the league's scoring title six times and was a six-time winner of the Hart Trophy as the league's MVP.

He ended his 25-year career with the Red Wings in 1971, sat out two years, then made an historic return in 1973 in order to play with sons Marty and Mark in the WHA.

Gordie Howe was with the Hartford Whalers when they joined three other WHA teams in the NHL in 1979. He played in all 80 games in the Whalers' first season in the NHL, then retired for the second time.

4. MARIO LEMIEUX

Mario Lemieux had heard the whispers almost from the time he broke into the NHL with the Pittsburgh Penguins in 1984. He was accused of being a floater, a player who didn't go all out every night, a man with no leadership qualities.

All those whispers were finally put to rest on a balmy May night in 1991 when Lemieux hoisted the Stanley Cup over his head and skated it around the perimeter of the Met Center in Bloomington, Minnesota.

The Penguins had wiped out the Minnesota North Stars in a six-game final series to claim their first Stanley Cup championship. And the man who contributed the most to Pittsburgh's march to victory was their captain, Mario Lemieux.

The 6-foot-4, 210-pound center totaled 12 points in five games against the North Stars and finished the playoffs with 44 points, three shy of the playoff record set by Wayne Gretzky in 1985. And he skated off with the Conn Smythe Trophy as MVP of the playoffs.

Lemieux had shown courage and determination in the way he came back from back surgery in July 1990, followed by an infection in September. He spent two months flat on his back in a hospital bed, fighting off deep-seated fears that he would never play again.

In 1991–92, he was challenged anew. Injuries caused him to miss 16 games, but he won his third scoring championship. In the playoffs, he suffered a broken left hand when slashed by the Rangers' Adam Graves in Game 2 of the Patrick Division finals. He missed the rest of that series, but came back against Chicago to bring the Penguins their second consecutive Cup. In the process, he again was playoff MVP.

Lemieux won another scoring title with 160 points (in only 60 games) in 1992–93 but the Penguins' bid for a third straight Cup was derailed by the upstart New York Islanders in the Patrick Division finals. The following season it appeared that Lemieux's career was over when he was diagnosed as having Hodgkin's disease. The treatments further weakened his back and he was forced to sit out the lockout-shortened 1994–95 season.

Lemieux was unsure whether he would ever play again, but after a year off, he decided to return for the 1995–96 season. And what a return it was! He scored nine goals in the Penguins' first eight games and became the 20th player in NHL history to record at least 500 goals. He finished the year with 161 points, winning his fifth Art Ross Trophy and third Hart Trophy.

He said before the 1996–97 season that it would likely be his last, and Lemieux went out in a blaze. He won his sixth scoring title, notching 122 points in 76 games. But the Penguins lost in the first round of the playoffs and it was all over for Super Mario. He retired with 1,494 points, sixth on the all-time list.

Lemieux, a native of Montreal, was selected first overall in the 1984 amateur draft. The Penguins finished with the worst record in the NHL and won the right to draft Lemieux.

The Penguins opened the 1984–85 season in Boston. On his first shift, Lemieux stripped the puck from All-Star defenseman Ray Bourque, skated in alone on goalie Pete Peeters and beat him to score his first NHL goal on his first shot.

By season's end Lemieux had become the third rookie in NHL history to score at least 100 points (43 goals and 57 assists). He propelled the Penguins' season point total from 38 in 1983–84 to 51 and he was picked as NHL Rookie of the Year.

A major event for Lemieux was the 1985 NHL All-Star Game at Calgary. The rookie teenager dazzled teammates, opponents, experts, and fans with two goals and an assist in sparking the Wales Conference team to a 6–4 victory. He skated away with the keys to a new car, his prize for being named the MVP of the game.

Skating and passing? Few, if any, did it better than Lemieux. He was extremely quick and mobile for a man his size (6-foot-4, 220 pounds). He had the ability to thread perfect passes through

Mario Lemieux

tangles of legs and skates, and he was big enough to reach around a forechecker to make his play.

Anticipation was another Lemieux talent. "Before I get the puck, I look where the players are and try to determine where they will be after," he said. "I try to get a crowd to go after me, then pass to who's open. It's easy."

Just as it's easy to say that Lemieux will go down as one of the greatest centers in NHL history.

5. MAURICE (ROCKET) RICHARD

Long after Maurice Richard retired in 1960, there were NHL goalies who would sit around in locker rooms, coffee shops, and taprooms and recall what it was like to face the old Rocket from Montreal.

Glenn Hall, who was an All-Star netminder with Detroit and Chicago before winding up with the St. Louis Blues, had a rather unique memory of Richard. "What I remember most about the Rocket were his eyes," Hall says. "When he came flying toward you with the puck on his stick, his eyes were all lit up, flashing and gleaming like a pinball machine. It was terrifying."

Richard terrified goalies like Hall for 18 seasons, all with the Montreal Canadiens. He totaled 544 regular-season goals, a record until Gordie Howe wiped it out in 1963. He was the first to score 50 goals in one season (1944–45), and he is the only one to have reached that figure in a 50-game schedule.

There was nothing quite so dramatic as a Richard goal. He would run, not glide, down the ice, cut in from right wing as he neared the cage and then use either a forehand or backhand shot to fool rival goalies. That was another of Richard's great, unmatched talents. He was ambidextrous, a right wing with an unorthodox left-hand shot.

"The Rocket did everything by instinct and with brute strength," said Frank Selke Sr., who was the Canadiens' general manager during Richard's record-breaking years. "He was the greatest opportunist the game has ever known."

Richard learned the rudiments of the game as a teenager in Montreal's Lafontaine Park in the years preceding World War II. He was a prolific scorer in the city's Park League, but appeared too injury-prone to become a real star. He broke an ankle while playing amateur hockey, then fractured a wrist. He was finally promoted to the Canadiens in 1942, but was sidelined early by another broken ankle. "It looks as if we have a brittle-boned player on our hands," sighed Tommy Gorman, then the Canadiens' general manager.

Gorman even considered releasing Richard, but the Rocket became stronger as he reached manhood, shook off his injuries and developed into a small bull on skates. He stood a shade under six feet and weighed 190 pounds at the height of his career. Many teams used two players to "shadow" the Rocket. He considered it a compliment. And when they got in his way, he would simply bowl them over and then glare at them with those dark, menacing eyes.

He had a mean temper that got him into frequent scrapes with players and officials. His suspension by NHL president Clarence Campbell in 1955 for carving up a Boston player with his stick and punching a linesman precipitated a riot in the Montreal Forum.

All of Richard's transgressions, though, were forgotten when he was rushed into the Hockey Hall of Fame in 1961. This honor normally wasn't bestowed on a player until at least the third year of his retirement. Maurice Richard had only been retired for nine months!

6. DOUG HARVEY

Most hockey players are content to master only a few facets of the game. Doug Harvey literally controlled every part of it during his great years as a defenseman for the Montreal Canadiens.

Pacemaking is what set him apart from his contemporaries. He could slow down or speed up

Maurice Richard

the tempo of most games with his extraordinary talents.

If the Canadiens wanted to kill time, Harvey would bring the puck up ice slowly, maneuvering his way past forechecking forwards until he reached the blue line. Then he would weave back and forth along the line, sliding soft passes to teammates and never becoming rattled.

If the Canadiens were trailing and attempting to beat the clock, it was Harvey who invariably led their fast-break up ice. And once the puck was in the enemy zone, he would station himself at the left point, waiting for a return pass and protecting against a possible breakaway by a rival player.

Harvey performed all these functions in a calm, almost lackadaisical fashion. He never seemed to fully extend himself, yet he was the unchallenged leader of the powerful Canadiens when they swept to an unprecedented five straight Stanley Cup championships from 1956 through 1960.

A native of Montreal, Harvey turned to hockey only after rejecting tempting offers from pro football and baseball scouts. It was the right choice—for him and for the Canadiens. During 13 seasons with Montreal he was named to the first All-Star team nine times and once to the second team. He earned the Norris Trophy as the league's outstanding defenseman six times.

The only fault most experts found with Harvey was a minor one: he didn't shoot enough. (The most goals he scored in a season was nine.) He claimed he would rather finesse his way to within shooting range and set up a goal for a teammate than try one of his own slapshots. "I didn't have a bonus for goals," he once said, "so why not set up the guys who needed them?"

A hero to every youngster in Montreal, Harvey encountered trouble with the Canadiens' front office when he became involved with the organization of the NHL Players' Association. In 1961 he was traded to the New York Rangers and became their player-coach, leading the league's one-time patsies into the Stanley Cup playoffs for the

Doug Harvey

first time in four years. During that same 1961–62 season he won his seventh Norris Trophy and once again was named to the All-Star team.

Harvey surrendered the coaching position after one season—he disliked the responsibility—but remained with the Rangers as a player for another 18 months. "When I was a coach, I couldn't

be one of the boys," he said. "This way if I want a beer with them, I get a beer."

He then drifted to the minors, playing in Baltimore, St. Paul, Quebec City, Pittsburgh, and Kansas City. He returned to the NHL with the St. Louis Blues during the 1968 Stanley Cup playoffs and, ironically, wound up playing against his old Montreal club in the final round.

Although he was then 45 years old, Harvey remained with St. Louis for the 1968–69 season as a defenseman and assistant coach. The next year he became defensive coach for Los Angeles before retiring.

7. JEAN BELIVEAU

The Montreal Canadiens purchased an entire hockey league in order to make Jean Beliveau a member of their team. It happened in 1953 while Beliveau was completing his third season for the Quebec Aces of the Quebec Senior League. The league was classified as "amateur," although its players received modest salaries. Modest, that is, except for Jean Beliveau. His annual salary was $20,000.

Beliveau, like many amateur tennis players in those days, claimed he couldn't afford to turn professional. It got to be extremely embarrassing for the Canadiens, who owned the negotiating rights to the young star from Trois Rivieres, Quebec. The fans were clamoring for big Jean in Montreal, but he wouldn't budge from Quebec City.

Then, in the most unusual measure ever taken to obtain a player, the Canadiens purchased the entire Quebec Senior League and the pro rights to all its players. The new owners turned the league professional, leaving Beliveau with no choice but to join Montreal. He received a $20,000 bonus for signing and a five-year, $105,000 contract, a fantastic salary for a 23-year-old rookie.

Jean Beliveau, though, was worth every Canadian penny the Montreal club paid him. He was the highest-scoring center in NHL history with 1,219 points when he retired. He finished with 507 goals in 1971 after 18 NHL seasons. That year, Beliveau had led the Canadiens to their 10th Stanley Cup since he joined the team.

To watch Beliveau in action was to marvel at the deceptive grace of this big bear on skates. A Gulliver in the icy world of comparative Lilliputians, he was 6-foot-3 and weighed 210 pounds. He didn't appear to skate quickly, but few could keep up with him. He had all the right instincts and all the right shots.

Rival players were awed by Beliveau's size and strength when he broke into the NHL. Bill Ezinicki, a vicious bodychecker in his glory days with Toronto and Boston, remembers the first time he lined up Beliveau for one of his patented hip checks. "It was like running into the side of a big oak tree," Ezinicki recalled. "I bounced right off the guy and landed on the seat of my pants."

In those days, Beliveau had only one flaw in his makeup. His disposition was better suited to the priesthood than the savage atmosphere of the hockey rink. He was crosschecked, hooked, and belted in every NHL rink. He didn't hit back because, he said, "I want to play hockey." He maintained that attitude until his third season with the Canadiens when he decided to retaliate. He wound up among the league's penalty leaders, a fact he wasn't proud of, but he also won the league's scoring title.

No longer did rival ruffians pick on Jean Beliveau. He had arrived—as a player and as a man—in the NHL. Other honors followed. In his 18 years with the Canadiens he was named to the All-Star team 10 times and twice won the Hart Trophy as the league's Most Valuable Player.

Toe Blake, Beliveau's coach for 13 years, summed up big Jean's value to the Canadiens this way: "In all the time he's been in hockey I've never heard anybody say a bad word against him. As a hockey player and a gentleman, Jean Beliveau is pretty hard to beat."

8. BOBBY HULL

It started from the instant he cradled the puck on the curved blade of his stick. One . . . two

Jean Beliveau

Bobby Hull

arrival in the NHL in 1957. In the 23 years that followed, nobody scored nearly as many goals or caused nearly as much excitement as this ruggedly handsome, blond-haired muscleman from the little Ontario town of Point Anne.

Hull was only 18 years old when he quit the junior ranks to turn pro with the Chicago Blackhawks. His great magnetism and goal-scoring ability turned a franchise that was losing money into the richest in the NHL. And as the Hawks grew in wealth, so did Bobby Hull. He became the league's first $100,000-a-year player when he signed a four-year, $400,000 contract at the start of the 1968–69 season. Other income from endorsements, several purebred cattle farms he owned, and league awards and playoff money swelled his earnings that season to approximately $200,000.

In 1972, he accepted a $1,000,000 offer from the World Hockey Association to play for the Winnipeg Jets. Despite missing 15 games because of court suits initiated by the NHL aimed at blocking his move to the new league, Hull reached the 50-goal plateau for the sixth time in his career.

strides . . . and he was in full flight, skating and slamming his way across the neutral zone and into enemy territory. By this time a chorus of sound enveloped the rink, rising into a long, drawn-out OOOHH! as this whirlwind on skates fired one of his patented slap shots.

The puck, traveling at more than 100 miles per hour, wound up high in the net and Bobby Hull had scored another goal.

This scene was enacted and reenacted an average of 40 times a season from the time of Hull's

Hull enjoyed his greatest season in 1974–75 when he scored a record 77 goals in 78 games and totaled 142 points for Winnipeg. He was playing then on a line with two Swedish imports, center Ulf Nilsson and right wing Anders Hedberg. "They make the game fun for me," Hull said. "They're also my legs."

Hull's strong legs started to weaken in 1979, the year the Jets were admitted into the NHL. He

also was experiencing shoulder problems. He ended his eight-year stay in Winnipeg late in the 1979–80 season when the Jets traded him to the Hartford Whalers. Gordie Howe also was winding up his career with the Whalers, and the two greats played on the same line in a handful of games.

Hull was the highest-scoring left wing in hockey history with 1,018 goals and 2,017 points when he retired in 1980. He was 41. He joined the New York Rangers at their training camp in 1981, attempting a comeback. But he was released before the start of the regular season and he returned to his farm in Ontario.

What made Bobby Hull so great? He was the fastest skater in hockey (28.3 miles per hour with the puck, 29.7 m.p.h. without it). He had the fastest shot: his slapshot was clocked at 118.3 m.p.h., nearly 35 m.p.h. above the league average. And then there were the Hull muscles. He didn't have an ounce of excess baggage on his 5-foot-10, 195-pound frame.

Hull totaled only 31 goals in his first two seasons with the Blackhawks, then developed the slapshot that was the bane of all goalies. He scored 50 goals in the 1961–62 season to equal a league record and progressively increased the mark to 58 in 1968–69. In his first 15 NHL seasons, he totaled 604 goals, won the league scoring championship three times and played left wing on the NHL All-Star team 12 times.

The supreme compliment came from Stan Mikita, the former Blackhawks' center. "To say that Bobby was a great hockey player is to labor the point," Mikita said. "He was all of that, of course. But the thing I admired about him was the way he handled people. He always enjoyed signing autographs for fans and was a genuine nice guy."

9. TERRY SAWCHUK

Terry Sawchuk used to quote that old nursery rhyme which insisted "Sticks and stones may break my bones, but names will never harm me." Only in Sawchuk's case it was sticks and pucks which broke his bones. And the names that people called him did hurt.

In more than two decades of professional hockey, Sawchuk overcame the following injuries and ailments to earn his place among hockey's top goalies: a broken right arm that didn't heal properly and wound up inches shorter than his left arm, severed hand tendons, a fractured instep, infectious mononucleosis, punctured lungs, ruptured discs, bone chips in his elbows that required three operations, a ruptured appendix, and innumerable cuts on his face and body, one of which almost cost him the sight in his right eye.

But the injury that hurt the most involved his pride. It happened in 1956 when he left the Boston Bruins in midseason after his bout with mononucleosis. "Those Boston reporters called me everything in the book, including a quitter," he said. "It was so bad I threatened to sue four newspapers for libel. I didn't go through with it, though. I guess those guys have to make a living, too."

He experienced his first pains of anguish when he was 10 years old back home in Winnipeg, Manitoba. His older brother, Mike, a goalie, developed a heart murmur and died. Terry inherited Mike's goalie pads and seven years later (1947) he broke into professional hockey as a fuzzy-cheeked netminder with Omaha of the United States Hockey League. He won the league's rookie award that season, spent the next two years in the American Hockey League, and then joined Detroit in 1950.

Sawchuk's unorthodox, gorilla-like crouch in the nets immediately captured the imagination of Detroit fans. It also helped him capture many awards. He won the Vezina Trophy, awarded to the NHL's most proficient goaltender, three times and shared a fourth. His goals-against average was less than two per game in each of his first five seasons with Detroit.

The Red Wings traded Sawchuk to the Bruins in 1955, reacquired him two years later, and then lost him to Toronto in the draft in 1964. He was picked up by Los Angeles in the 1967 expansion

draft and a year later returned to Detroit, then went to the New York Rangers for the 1969–70 season.

Hailed as the only NHL goalie to record more than 100 career shutouts, Sawchuk credited most of his success to his crouching style. "When I'm crouching low, I can keep better track of the puck through the players' legs on screen shots," he explained.

Ironically, this doughty figure who had survived many injuries on the ice died as a result of an off-the-ice incident in May 1970. He was elected to the Hockey Hall of Fame in 1971.

10. EDDIE SHORE

All the hockey greats—past and present—were gathered in a midtown New York restaurant for the annual Lester Patrick awards dinner in the spring of 1970. At a table near the rear of the room, the Patrick winner with the scarred features of a retired boxer was discussing hockey and how it had changed in recent years.

"The accent is on speed now," Eddie Shore said. "I guess it's better for the fans, but I liked it better in the old days. Then it was pretty much a 50-50 proposition. You socked the other guy and the other guy socked you."

Indeed, Shore had socked a lot of guys and caught a few socks in return during a brilliant 14-year career as the meanest defenseman in the NHL.

Shore came out of Edmonton, Alberta, in 1926 to join the Boston Bruins. He infused them with a

Terry Sawchuk

spirit and color which promptly lifted them from last place to second place in the NHL's American Division. Previously ignored by Bostonians, the Bruins also developed a loyal following—all because of Shore. He was a drawing card wherever he went because of his free-swinging style, his cold and brutal attacks on rival players, and his brilliance on defense. He was the most applauded player of his time—and received the most boos, too.

Hammy Moore, who was the Boston trainer during Shore's heyday, once described Eddie's style of attack. "He was the only player I ever saw who had the whole arena standing every time he rushed down the ice," Moore said. "When Shore carried the puck you were always sure something would happen. He would either end up bashing somebody, get into a fight, or score a goal."

Shore totaled 108 NHL goals, a respectable number for a defenseman, before retiring in 1940. He was named the league's Most Valuable Player four times and was voted to the All-Star team seven times.

But there are even more impressive statistics. He accumulated the astounding total of 978 stitches on his rugged body. He had his nose broken 14 times, his jaw shattered five times and he lost most of his teeth.

Shore's most celebrated fight occurred on December 12, 1933, in Toronto and it was one he always regretted. Red Horner of the Maple Leafs started it by slamming Shore into the boards. Shore picked himself up and went after Horner. He flew down the ice and, mistaking Ace Bailey for Horner, flattened Bailey with a vicious check.

Bailey's head struck the ice and he was taken to a hospital with a fractured skull. His life was saved by delicate brain surgery, but he was never able to play hockey again.

The memory of that near-tragedy haunted Shore for many years. But he continued to play great defense for the Bruins and then the New York Americans before finally hanging up his skates and becoming full-time owner of the Springfield Indians of the American Hockey League.

Eddie Shore

As a club owner, Shore remained a fighter. He fought with his players at contract time and with other owners in the committee rooms. Eddie Shore won most of those fights, too.

He was elected to the Hockey Hall of Fame in 1947.

Guy Lafleur

11. GUY LAFLEUR

La fleur means the flower, and no figure of his era—or perhaps any era—represented the romance of hockey better than Guy Lafleur. To see him move the puck up ice—fast and graceful, with definite purpose, his long blond hair flowing behind him, his arms upraised in triumph after yet another goal—was to see purity and love for the game. He collected scoring titles and Stanley Cups, scoring memorable goals for 14 years with the Montreal Canadiens.

"Hockey is my life," he said frequently, and he was quoted as placing it above his family. His dedication was evident as a child, when he would sleep wearing his equipment so he could awaken ready to go to the rink the next morning. It was again evident in his pre-game NHL ritual, as he regularly arrived for a game hours before the opening faceoff and be in full uniform long before his teammates came through the door.

He first drew national attention as an 11-year-old from Thurso, Quebec, at the 1962 International Pee-Wee Tournament, which he led in scoring despite playing against kids two and three years older. In the Quebec Major Junior League, he broke scoring records playing for the Quebec Remparts, becoming a local hero and wearing number 4 like his idol, Jean Beliveau, who had played at the other end of Highway 40 for the Montreal Canadiens.

He was drafted first by Montreal in 1971, the day after Beliveau announced his retirement. The pressures on Lefleur to replace Beliveau—in the lineup and in the hearts of Montreal's fans—were immense. He had been tabbed as a "sure thing." But he was a disappointment initially. He couldn't hit the 30-goal plateau and in fact, his totals declined in each of his first three seasons

In 1974–75, however, The Flower bloomed. He signaled the change by discarding his helmet in training camp, and the legend grew from there. Placed on right wing alongside Pete Mahovlich and Steve Shutt, he finished the season fourth in NHL scoring, becoming the Canadiens' first 50-goal man in 14 years and first 100-point scorer ever. Lafleur would reach both those plateaus for six consecutive years.

For those six seasons, he was hockey's top performer and attraction. He was named a First Team All-Star annually from 1975 though 1980, and became the youngest player ever to score 400 goals and 1,000 points. He'd arouse fans by racing up the ice and winding up for a shot after crossing the blue line, and everyone—including the opposition goaltender—knew what he was going to do. But it didn't matter. The red light almost invariably went on. He passed as well as he could shoot.

In 1975–76, Lafleur won the first of three straight Art Ross trophies as top NHL scorer and the great Montreal dynasty captured the first of four straight Stanley Cup championships. In the '76 playoffs, however, Lafleur struggled, and afterward the public discovered he had been living under the threat of a kidnapping. The following

year, he captured the Hart Trophy as the season's MVP and went on to earn playoff MVP honors as well.

For an encore in 1977–78, Lafleur again won the Hart, hitting for 60 goals as Jacques Lemaire replaced Mahovlich at center. He led all playoff scorers, as he would do again in 1978–79. But Lafleur's defining moment may have come in the '79 semifinal series against Boston, when he led a Game 7 Montreal comeback, climaxed by a dynamic tying goal in the third period's dying moments, rocking the Montreal Forum. He became toast of the town, his lifestyle and opinions a constant topic of newspaper and magazine articles.

Lafleur's instinctive style was so spontaneous and freewheeling that he was often compared to a river hockey player. "He's all over the ice and he doesn't have any idea what he's going to do," said Shutt. "So how can I know?"

An injured knee in 1979–80 marked the start of his decline. When Jacques Lemaire became coach in 1983, he cut Lafleur's ice time and Lafleur decided he no longer had a place on the team. He announced his retirement in 1984 after playing in 19 games.

But after his 1988 Hall of Fame induction, Lafleur surprised everyone by returning with the New York Rangers. He enjoyed some big nights, including a smashing return to Montreal, where he scored twice, including the game-winner. Then Lafleur skated a two-year curtain call in his old haunt, Quebec City, for the Nordiques, before retiring for good after the 1990–91 season.

12. MARK MESSIER

He has all the attributes of a hockey superstar: swift skater, strong, heavy shot, tenacious forechecker, rugged backchecker. And then there's Mark Messier's eyes!

"When he gets mad, it's like he's in another world," said former Ranger defenseman Barry Beck. "He'll look at you with those big eyes and they'll be going around in circles."

It's a look that, combined with a well-practiced elbow, has dismantled many a rival.

Messier had that look in the 1994 playoffs, and it helped the Rangers win their first Stanley Cup in 54 seasons. The Rangers had coasted through the first two rounds of the playoffs but then found themselves trailing the New Jersey Devils 3 games to 2.

Then he went out and personally delivered the victory, scoring a third-period hat trick that rallied the Rangers to a 4–2 triumph. Two nights later, the Rangers outlasted the Devils in a double-overtime Game 7 and then went from there to defeat the Vancouver Canucks for the Cup. It was just another example of Messier's leadership abilities.

In 1987, Messier was a member of the NHL squad that played the Soviets in the Rendez-Vous All-Star series. "We're sitting in the locker room before the first game," said Dave Poulin of the Boston Bruins, "and Mark stood up and outlined what we were going to do in the warmup. He said, 'Anybody have any problems with that?'

"I glanced around the room and I saw Rod Langway, Wayne Gretzky, all those people who were leaders. We looked at each other like, 'Nope, no problems at all.' Mark just took over."

It was these qualities, buttressed by his all-around play, that inspired the Rangers to acquire Messier from the Edmonton Oilers at the start of the 1991–92 season. In one of hockey's most stunning trades, the Rangers shipped three players—Bernie Nicholls, Steven Rice, and Louie DeBrusk—to Edmonton for Messier.

The 6-foot-1, 210-pound center arrived in New York with five Stanley Cup rings, one regular-season MVP award, one playoff MVP award, and three first-team All-Star selections—all of which had accumulated during 12 seasons with the Oilers.

The 30-year-old Messier had demanded a trade and was delighted to be in New York. "I'm looking forward to a new challenge," he said. "I'm starting a new career."

Mark Messier

He went on to become the Rangers' leader as they won the Patrick Division with a 105-point total, tops in the league. He wound up with his second MVP award. But the repeat-bound Penguins ended it all for Messier and the Rangers in the division final.

Messier is a native of Edmonton who grew up in Portland, Oregon, where his father was a defenseman for the Portland Buckaroos of the Western Hockey League. "My father was one tough hockey player," he said.

Messier was only 17 when he turned pro with Indianapolis of the World Hockey Association in 1978. He had played only five games when the team folded. Messier finished his first pro season with Cincinnati of the WHA and was hardly a sensation. He scored only one goal the entire season and that on a flip shot from center ice.

Glen Sather, the general manager-coach of the Oilers, picked Messier in the second round of the 1979 draft, bringing the 18-year-old hometown lad directly into the NHL. "He was no sure thing, but he could skate and he worked hard," said Sather.

After scoring 33 points in his first season and 63 the next year, Messier blossomed into a 50-goal scorer as the Oilers exploded as an NHL power in 1981–82.

He played in Wayne Gretzky's shadow during those early years in Edmonton. But one can argue that the Oilers didn't get to the top until Messier was ready to put them there. He had a bad shoulder when the Oilers reached the Cup Finals for the first time in 1983. They went down in four straight to the Islanders.

But the next year he was healthy and helped the Oilers end the Islanders' four-year reign as champions. The teams split the first two games of the Cup finals. The Oilers were trailing, 2–1, in Game 3 when Messier went the length of the ice to blow a goal past Billy Smith. It was a spectacular shot and the Oilers went on to win their first Cup in a five-game series. Messier won the Conn Smythe Trophy as playoff MVP.

After Gretzky was traded to Los Angeles in 1988, Messier was named Oiler captain. He enjoyed his most productive season in 1989–90 (129 points), helping the Oilers win their fifth Cup in seven years and winning the Hart Trophy as MVP.

After six seasons with the Rangers, he became a free agent in 1997 and signed with Vancouver. He misses Wayne Gretzky.

13. JACQUES PLANTE

From a 50-cents-per-game goaltender with a factory team in Quebec to a $35,000-a-year All-Star in the National Hockey League was the road Jacques Plante traveled during a playing career that spanned more than two decades.

It all started back in Plante's hometown of Shawinigan Falls, Quebec, when he was 15 years old. "I was playing goal for a factory team," he recalled. "We didn't get paid, so one day my father suggested that I ask the coach for some money. The coach agreed to give me 50 cents a game if I didn't tell any of the other players about it."

"Even 50 cents meant a lot to me in those days. I was the oldest of 11 children. We couldn't afford a radio. . .or luxuries of any kind. The only time we had soft drinks was at Christmas."

Plante went on from there to earn $85 a week as a netminder for Quebec City in a junior amateur league and turned pro with the Montreal Royals in the old Quebec Senior League at the age of 22 in 1951. He made his NHL debut the following season with the Montreal Canadiens in a Stanley Cup playoff game at Chicago.

That first game with the Canadiens is still stamped in Plante's memory. "I was so nervous I couldn't tie my skates," he said. But he shut out the Blackhawks, 3–0. Jacques Plante was on his way to becoming one of the highest-salaried goalies in pro hockey.

He spent 10 glorious years with the Canadiens, helping them to five straight Stanley Cup championships (1956 through 1960). He won the Vezina Trophy as the league's top netminder a record-tying six times (five in a row) and was a member of the NHL All-Star team six times. In 1962, he became only the fourth goaltender in NHL history to win the Hart (Most Valuable Player) Trophy.

Plante's flair for the dramatic and his inventiveness also marked his career at Montreal. He became a roving goalie early in his career ("One of the amateur teams I played for was so bad I

Jacques Plante

Plante was traded to New York in 1963, spent a year and a half with the Rangers, and then retired to become a salesman with a Canadian brewery. In 1968, the St. Louis Blues offered him $35,000 to make a comeback. The lanky French-Canadian, approaching his 40th birthday, couldn't resist the offer. He packed his pads and his mask and moved to St. Louis, where he shared the goaltending with 37-year-old Glenn Hall. Together, they won the Vezina Trophy and led the Blues to two consecutive West titles.

Then he was sold to Toronto in 1970 and spent three seasons with the Maple Leafs. In March 1973, Boston, looking for playoff help, purchased the 44-year-old goalie from the Leafs. He ended his career with Edmonton in the WHA in 1974–75.

14. RAY BOURQUE

Harry Sinden, president and general manager of the Boston Bruins, remembers the first time he saw Ray Bourque play hockey. "It was an All-Star junior tournament in Canada, and Ray was easily the best player on the ice," Sinden said. "He impressed me as being the perfect size for a hockey player."

"Some people look at racehorses and know just by looking which ones will be great, and I'm supposed to know that about hockey players. I looked at Ray Bourque and I said, 'We've got us a champion here.' I was right, too."

Ever since the Montreal native reached puberty, expectations have been high. In 1979, when he broke into the National Hockey League

had to always chase the puck behind the cage"), and he perfected this art with the Canadiens.

He also will be remembered as the man who popularized the goalie mask in the NHL. It happened in a game against the New York Rangers on November 1, 1959. Struck in the face by an Andy Bathgate shot, he went to the dressing room, had the wound stitched, and then returned to the ice wearing a cream-colored plastic face mask. Before long, most pro goalies adopted the mask as part of their equipment.

as an enormously talented 18-year-old rookie, the Bruins needed a star. Bourque was it.

He then was being hailed as "the best thing to come along since Bobby Orr." The comparison quickly became odious—Bourque's game is as cautious as Orr's was flashy—but Bourque ignored the hype and responded by winning the Calder Trophy as the league's best rookie. On the way, he was also selected for the All-Star first team, the only non-goalie ever to receive both honors.

That was just the beginning of Bourque's extraordinary career. He was selected to the first or second All-Star units in each of his first 17 seasons in the league and won the Norris Trophy as the league's best defenseman five times. In the 1996–97 season he became the second blueliner in history to record 1,000 assists.

Entering the 1998–99 season, he had amassed 1,411 points, second only to Paul Coffey's 1,473 in scoring by a defenseman.

Indefatigable is the word that best describes Bourque. He frequently logs between 35 and 40 minutes a game.

Bourque was born in the proletarian community of St. Laurent, Quebec, in 1960. He began playing hockey five years later. His formal education ended at 15 when he dropped out of high school to devote all his time to his junior team, the Verdun Blackhawks.

Bourque was the eighth player taken in the 1979 NHL draft, having scored 22 goals and 93 points in his final season with Verdun.

After signing his first pro contract with the Bruins, Bourque bought his father, Raymond Sr., a new car. His dad had been clocking 30,000 miles a year on a 10-year-old Buick following his son through the hockey provinces.

Bourque's debut with the Bruins was spectacular. He had a goal and two assists in his first NHL game. There would be bigger goals later. Bourque enjoyed his greatest season in 1983–84 when he totaled 31 goals and 65 assists for 96 points.

Ray Bourque

Bourque, who is 5-foot-11 and 210 pounds, is very difficult to move off the puck once he gets going. He is so stable on the ice that he seems to carve a wake behind him.

Terry O'Reilly, Bourque's former teammate and coach, said: "Ray combines speed and maneuverability and puckhandling ability. He's a terrific stickhandler and he can stop on a dime. And with that stocky, powerful body, I've seldom seen him knocked off his feet."

Bourque is the Bruins' captain in every way, which is amazing for someone who was introverted and spoke far more French than English when he first joined the team. Now he is the elder statesman who leads by both example and discourse.

Bourque is known to sportswriters as one of the most accessible and patient of athletes. He seems incapable of talking down to someone. And among the young fans who sometimes haunt practice sessions, he is known as a player who not only signs autographs but also has some friendly remark to offer.

15. HOWIE MORENZ

Babe Ruth and Bobby Jones, Bill Tilden and Jack Dempsey—these were the men who dominated America's Golden Age of Sport in the Roaring Twenties. During that same period of bathtub gin, flappers, and ragtime jazz, Canada had its own hero. He was Howie Morenz of the Montreal Canadiens, the greatest hockey player of his generation.

To the French-speaking fans of the Province of Quebec, Howie Morenz was l'homme-eclair. In English he was the same thing: the top man.

Morenz was a center for the Canadiens for 12 years and near the end of his career played with the Chicago Blackhawks and the New York Rangers. Once, in a 44-game season, he scored 40 goals—a remarkable achievement. He totaled 270 goals during his NHL career and was among the first group of players admitted to the Hockey Hall of Fame in 1945.

Howie Morenz

A happy-go-lucky man with large, smiling eyes, a receding hairline, and a heavy beard, Morenz was a typical sports hero of the 1920s. He was colorful and glamorous, hockey's fastest man on skates and a fiery competitor. Toe Blake, the most successful coach in the history of the Canadiens, was a rookie player with Montreal when Morenz was approaching the end of the line. He remembers Morenz: "He was an inspiration for all of us . . . a man with remarkable skills who laughed hard and played hard."

Dazzling speed and guile were Morenz's trademarks. A contemporary of his, Ott Heller of the Rangers, once remarked: "When Howie skates full speed, everyone else on the ice seems to be skating backward." Morenz's shot was equally impressive. Once he broke a goalie's nose with one of his bullet-like drives. Another time his shot caught a netminder square in the forehead, flipping him over on his back.

Although he never played at more than 165 pounds, Morenz bodychecked with the ferocity of a giant. He was so swift, so skillful, and so fearless that the wildly nationalistic French Canadians of Montreal were undisturbed when they discovered he was of German ancestry.

He was born in the Ontario village of Mitchell in 1902, moving with his family to Stratford, Ontario, at the age of 14. He attracted the attention of the Canadiens when he scored nine goals in an amateur game in Montreal in 1922. The following year he turned pro with the Canadiens for a $1,000 bonus and quickly earned the nickname of "The Stratford Streak."

Off the ice, Morenz's pace was just as fast. He sang and played the ukulele. He was a clothes horse; he changed his suits twice and sometimes three times a day. He wore spats. He was a charming and cosmopolitan young man living swiftly in the charming, cosmopolitan city of Montreal.

Then, suddenly, he was no longer quite so young. After 11 seasons with the Canadiens he was traded, first to Chicago in 1934 and then to the New York Rangers the following year. In 1936, he was repurchased by the Canadiens. On the night of January 28, 1937, in the midst of a fine comeback, Morenz broke four bones in his left leg and ankle in a game against Chicago. Five weeks later, the bones were knitting well when he fell to the cold floor of a Montreal hospital. An embolism had stopped his heart.

Howie Morenz was dead at the age of 34. The funeral service was held at center ice in the Montreal Forum, where thousands of fans wept openly for "Le Grand Morenz."

16. GLENN HALL

Glenn Hall once offered a terse explanation of what it is like to be a major-league goaltender. "Playing goal is a winter of torture for me," he said. "I often look at those guys who can whistle and laugh before a game and shake my head. You'd think they didn't have a care in the world. Me? I'm plain miserable before every game."

Hall's main problem was a nervous stomach. Early in his career he used to become physically ill just sitting in the locker room waiting for a game to start. The attacks became less frequent as he grew older, but the butterflies were always there.

Despite these pregame seizures of anxiety, Hall once played 502 consecutive games in the National Hockey League. He launched the streak in his first full season in the league in 1955–56 when he played all 70 games with the Detroit Red Wings. He didn't miss a game with Detroit the following season, then moved on to Chicago, where he put in five additional 70-game campaigns before the string was finally snapped in November 1962.

Hall was born and raised in Humboldt, Saskatchewan, a railway center, where he learned to tend goal on outdoor rinks. He turned pro with the old Indianapolis team in the American Hockey League in 1951, then put in three seasons with Edmonton of the Western League before moving up to the Red Wings. He was an immediate suc-

cess with Detroit, winning the Calder Trophy as the NHL's top rookie in 1956.

After two seasons with the Red Wings, he was sent to the Blackhawks in the same celebrated six-player trade that put Hall of Famer Ted Lindsay in a Chicago uniform. During 10 years with the Blackhawks, Hall won the Vezina Trophy as the league's outstanding goalie three times and was named to the All-Star first team five times.

He reached his peak in the spring of 1961 when the Blackhawks won the Stanley Cup championship for the first time in 23 years. In the semifinals against Montreal he was at his acrobatic best, holding the Canadiens scoreless for 135 minutes and 26 seconds at one stage of the series. And that Montreal team boasted such feared sharpshooters as Jean Beliveau, Bernie Geoffrion, Dickie Moore, and Henri Richard.

At the end of each season, Hall would advise the Blackhawks that he was considering retiring, but the lure of a fatter contract would always prompt him to change his mind. Then, once the season had started, he would have further doubts. "Plenty of times I'm tempted to climb into my car and head for home," he confessed.

When the St. Louis Blues plucked Hall from Chicago in hockey's first expansion draft in 1967, he was ready to quit again and become a gentleman farmer in Edmonton, Alberta. He was then 36 years old. However, the promise of the largest salary ever paid a goaltender at that time—an estimated $45,000—encouraged him to leave his 160-acre farm for St. Louis.

Glenn Hall

Hall's great goaltending led the expansion club into the finals of the 1968 Stanley Cup play-offs against Montreal. The Blues were defeated in four straight games, all of which were decided by one goal. But Hall won the Conn Smythe Trophy as the outstanding performer in the playoffs.

Then, in 1968–69 he teamed with Jacques Plante to win his third Vezina Trophy and earned his 11th All-Star team berth in 14 NHL seasons. He hung up his skates at the end of the 1970–71 season and was elected to the Hockey Hall of Fame in 1975.

17. STAN MIKITA

In a sense, there were two Stan Mikitas. For the first eight years of his NHL career, Mikita was known for his chippy, belligerent antagonism. Then, seemingly overnight, Mikita became a paragon of clean, hard play.

Mikita had the distinction of playing his entire NHL career at center with one club, the Chicago Blackhawks. He is the Blackhawks' all-time leading scorer (1,467 points) and still holds club records for most seasons (22), most games played (1,394), and most career assists (926).

He also accomplished a truly remarkable feat: In 1963–64, he led the NHL in both scoring and penalty minutes in the same season, and then—just three seasons later—he again led the NHL in scoring but amassed only 14 penalty minutes and was awarded the Lady Byng Trophy as the NHL's Most Gentlemanly Player. He also added the Hart Trophy as MVP that year, becoming the first player to win three major trophies in one season. As if that wasn't enough, he repeated the trophy hat trick a season later.

Mikita's snarly on-ice demeanor started when he was young. Born Stanislav Gvoth in 1940, he became an eight-year-old refugee from Sokolov, Czechoslovakia, and was raised by relatives in Ontario. Eventually he took their last name, but at first he didn't understand the language. When he finally learned English, he found

Stan Mikita

he was often the target of barbs from his peers. It made him a tough kid.

"I was basically hostile and so I was rough and often, downright mean," he said. "It helped in one way because I always believed that, being a so-called DP (displaced person)—somebody people picked on and looked down on—I could only

succeed by being better than everybody else. As a hockey player, I always tried that much harder."

One of the skills he perfected was playmaking, and he would become the best in the business. In 1958–59, his final season of junior hockey, he was named the Ontario Hockey Association MVP. Mikita was only 5-foot-9 and less than 170 pounds and he had to battle larger players. "That's where it all started, the chippiness, the fighting," Mikita said. "When I got to the NHL, it continued. They weren't going to push me around. It was something I believe in."

Rudy Pilous, his junior coach, became the Blackhawks' coach and summoned him to the NHL, where he became a regular from the start. In 1960–61 he was integral to the Hawks' first Stanley Cup since 1938. One of his big contributions, besides 11 playoff points, was goading Detroit hot-head Howie Young into dumb penalties during the Finals.

Hall of Fame defenseman Bill Gadsby told author Charles Wilkens the young Mikita was "a miserable little pain in the butt. He'd cross-check you, he'd spear you in the belly. You'd be going around the back of the net and he'd spear you in the calf and you'd go down. I nailed him dozens of times, but I've got to give him credit, he always got back up. I remember hitting him hard during the playoffs one year and telling him, 'Boy, one of these times you're not going to get up.' And he said, 'Get lost, you old man, that was no bodycheck at all.' I'd hit him some nights and he'd have to crawl back to the bench. But he'd always be back for his next shift. He had a lot of guts."

The season following Chicago's Cup triumph, Mikita was named First Team All-Star center, the first of six such selections. He made the second team twice.

After averaging nearly 100 penalty minutes during his first seven NHL seasons, the amazing turnaround in his play took place thanks, he says, to his young daughter. "I came home from a game one night and my daughter Meg was still up, after watching it on television. She asked me

why I spent almost the whole game sitting down while the other players were out on the ice skating around. Right then, I woke up to reality. If a two-year-old could see there was something wrong, why couldn't a supposedly intelligent 26-year old figure it out?"

He cut nearly 100 minutes off his career high total of 154 the next season and then reduced it to 12 in 1966–67. "I thought I'd try to beat the other guy with my skills instead of knocking his head off," he said.

His Chicago coach of 12 seasons, Billy Reay, may have summed up Mikita's career best when he said, "I have to say that I have never seen a better center. Maybe some could do one thing better than Stan, like skating faster or shooting harder. But none of them could do all the things that a center has to do as well as Stan does. He's the brightest hockey player I've ever seen. And one of his biggest assets is he's got a lot of pride."

18. PHIL ESPOSITO

On the night of January 9, 1981, Phil Esposito faced one of the toughest assignments of his life—his farewell address as a player. He was about to play his final game for the New York Rangers against the Buffalo Sabres at Madison Square Garden. A center-ice ceremony before the game was meant to be brief, but the crowd of 17,501 gave Esposito a lengthy standing ovation and chanted "ESPO! ESPO!"

As the applause rumbled down from the mezzanine, Esposito nodded and smiled, then raised his hands. "Please," he said. "I've been preparing for this for 10 years." The crowd roared and Esposito continued. "My world seemed to shatter when I was traded here from Boston. But after the initial shock, which took a long time, I fell in love with New York."

That was it. After 1,282 games covering 18 National Hockey League seasons, Phil Esposito was retiring as the second-highest scorer in history. He failed to score a goal that night, but he did

pick up an assist. It raised his career total to 1,590 points on 717 goals and 873 assists. At the time, only Gordie Howe had more goals (801) and more points (1,850).

Howe was at the Garden that night as the keynote speaker and presented Esposito with a number "77" sweater.

Esposito was a month shy of his 39th birthday at the time of his retirement. "I couldn't handle the pressure any more," he told friends. "It really affected me. . . . For my whole life as a hockey player, I told myself if I wasn't satisfied, I should do something else. This year I wasn't satisfied. . . .I gave it all I had, but I had nothing left to give."

Born in Sault Ste. Marie, Ontario, Esposito grew up shooting pucks at his kid brother, Tony. "He was younger," explained Phil, "so he had to be the goalie." They would play the same roles years later in the NHL.

The Blackhawks sponsored the minor hockey program in Sault Ste. Marie, and in those days that was enough for an NHL club to gain the rights to local hockey talent. That's how Phil filtered into the Chicago system. He spent two years in the minors before being called up to Chicago midway through the 1963–64 season.

Three goals in 27 NHL games gave no clue to the kind of scoring that Esposito would one day produce. A bit clumsy on his skates, Phil's major asset was his strength, and the Hawks used him to center superstar Bobby Hull. In the next three seasons, he scored 71 goals, many of them on rebounds of Hull bombs.

In 1967, the Hawks went shopping for a tough defenseman and asked Boston about Gilles Marotte. The talks expanded and finally on May 15, the deal was completed. Marotte, center Pit Martin, and minor-league goalie Jack Norris went to Chicago, with Esposito and two other forwards, Ken Hodge and Fred Stanfield, moving to the Bruins.

In 8 1/2 seasons with Boston, Espo won five scoring championships and finished second

Phil Esposito

twice. He was the first man to go over 100 points in a single season and he passed the 50-goal plateau five times. He enjoyed his greatest season in 1970–71 when he established records for most goals (76) and most points (152). Both records later were erased by Wayne Gretzky.

It is no coincidence that the Bruins ended a 29-year wait and won two Stanley Cups following the arrival of Esposito. The first Cup came in 1970 and, en route to it, Boston eliminated Chicago in four games. The scoring star for Boston was Esposito and it was accomplished at the expense of his goaltending brother, Tony, who had wound up with the Hawks after graduating from Michigan Tech.

Fans in Boston and New York were shocked when the Bruins traded Esposito to the Rangers in a five-player deal early in the 1975–76 season. The 6-foot-1, 212-pound center was shocked, too. He displayed only flashes of his old form with the Rangers—notably in the 1979 Stanley Cup playoffs when he sparked New York into the finals against the Montreal Canadiens. The Canadiens won the series in five games.

Following his retirement, Esposito became an analyst on telecasts of Ranger games. He served as general manager of the Rangers for three years (1986–89) and during that time had two brief flings as interim coach. He spearheaded a group that was granted an NHL franchise in Tampa, Fla., in 1990 and was named president of the expansion team.

Esposito re-signed as general manager in 1993 when the team was acquired by Takashi Okubo, a Japanese financier. He continued with the team, under further new ownership, through the 1997–98 season.

19. DENIS POTVIN

It was in early September 1973 when a 19-year-old rookie with a friendly smile arrived at the New York Islanders' training camp in Peterborough, Ontario. He hit speeds of more than 100-miles-an-hour in traveling from his Ottawa home in the new Mercedes Benz convertible purchased after he signed his first pro contract two months earlier.

Denis Potvin obviously was a young man in a hurry. While playing amateur hockey for Ottawa on the Ontario Hockey League, he had smashed all of Bobby Orr's league records for a defenseman. It was only natural that observers were comparing Potvin to Orr, then a Boston Bruins superstar.

"I'm not Bobby Orr and I know it," Potvin said. "You can't compare us because our styles are different. I can't skate as well as Orr, but I feel there are a couple of things I might do better, like hitting. That's a big part of my game. . . .I just hope I can accomplish some of the things Orr has done, but in my own way."

Potvin's feats during his 15 seasons in the National Hockey League are well chronicled: three-time winner of the Norris Trophy as the NHL's best defenseman, five times a first-team All-Star, and captain of four Stanley Cup championship teams with the Islanders.

Along the way, Potvin broke two of Orr's career records for a defenseman: most goals and most points. When he retired in 1988, he owned all the NHL's major scoring records for a defenseman: most goals (310), most assists (742), and most points (1,052).

So much for the numbers.

Off the ice? Intelligent, articulate, insightful, urbane—adjectives that fit Potvin like a tight pair of skates. Yet he found it difficult at times to win the respect of fans and foes.

"I don't think people looked at me as a hero-type—like a Wayne Gretzky. I was an opponent people didn't like. That's the way I'll be remembered," Potvin said.

There were times when he didn't get along with his own teammates. He acknowledges that. "I suppose," he once said, "I'm subject to a lot of prejudice and jealousy because of what I accom-

Denis Potvin

plished. I'm arrogant at times. But I think that's because I'm honest with people. I tell them what I think and they don't always like that. I have a great deal of confidence in myself."

Potvin never lacked confidence—not even as a 14-year-old growing up in Ottawa. At that tender age he joined the Ottawa team of the OHL and was pitted against players five or six years older.

He had completed five seasons of junior hockey when the Islanders made him the No. 1 pick in the 1973 amateur draft. Some of the Islanders' veterans greeted Potvin's arrival with skepticism, but they soon realized that he had the makings of a superstar.

"Denis kind of strutted into camp," said Al Arbour, the coach who took it upon himself to humble the player without diminishing his ego. "I had to blend a very strong-willed individual into a team concept, but it's no secret that we built our team around Denis."

Potvin took years to accept the method behind Arbour's manipulations. "I lived pretty much on the edge back then," Potvin said. "My emotions were on a tightrope and Al saw that and capitalized. He made me perform like a madman."

With Arbour wielding the whip, Potvin totaled 17 goals and 54 points in his first season with the Isles and won the Calder Trophy as the NHL's Rookie of the Year. He kept improving with each season and had his finest year in 1978–79 when he scored 31 goals and 101 points.

Potvin, who carried 205 pounds on a six-foot frame, was a devastating bodychecker. In 1986, he bore down on Washington's Bengt Gustaffson, breaking the Swede's leg with a clean, crunching check. And fans won't forget Potvin's career-ending check on the New York Rangers' Ulf Nilsson in 1979.

Nagging injuries started to catch up with him, beginning in 1979–80 season when he missed 49 games after surgery to correct stretched ligaments in a thumb. He later missed three months with a broken toe, then was sidelined for two months with a pulled groin muscle.

After 15 years of unconditional hard labor— all with the Islanders—Potvin retired in 1988. He was only 34. "I feel I have nothing else to prove," he said.

He was elected to the Hockey Hall of Fame in 1991, with the induction ceremonies held in Ottawa, his hometown.

20. MIKE BOSSY

The scenario rarely changed. Mike Bossy would carry the puck into the right faceoff circle or into the slot or into No-Man's Land in front of the net. Then he would shoot, quicker than a wink. Poof! The puck was in the net.

That was how Bossy scored many of the 573 goals he accumulated during his 10-year career with the New York Islanders.

Bossy was only 31 when he was forced to retire because of a chronic back problem. It is ironic that a man who endured battles with the likes of Tiger Williams was put out of commission by the same kind of injury that could be suffered by a couch potato reaching for a TV remote control.

The beginning of the end came at training camp in 1986. Bossy had finished a skating drill and bent over to catch his breath. When he stood up, there was a stabbing pain in his lower back. Rest, heat, ice, and every imaginable treatment nursed Bossy through a season he never should have played in 1986–87. With the pain and physical limitations, the thin-faced right winger registered the only sub-50-goal season of his career.

Why did Bossy push himself over the pain threshold time and again? "The pride, the feeling that I didn't want to wimp out," he said. "I went through my junior and professional career being thought of as a wimp because I wouldn't fight. I had to prove that I wasn't a wimp."

Bossy sat out the entire 1987–88 season, hoping that he would be able to resume his career. But he finally announced his retirement— through misty eyes—on October 21, 1988. "My back won the battle," he said.

Mike Bossy

The legacy Bossy left behind is awesome. He scored 50 goals or more in nine consecutive seasons—over 60 in five of those. The 53 goals he scored in his first season, 1977–78, was a rookie record. He was selected to the All-Star team eight times, earned one Conn Smythe Trophy as playoff MVP (1982), won the Lady Byng for sportsmanship three times, and helped the Islanders win four consecutive Stanley Cup championships.

It seems inconceivable that 14 NHL teams passed up the chance to pick Bossy in the first round of the 1977 amateur draft, allowing general manager Bill Torrey to make the Montreal-born youngster an Islander.

At the time, he was considered a one-dimensional sharpshooter. He later developed into an exquisite passer and playmaker. And nobody, not even Wayne Gretzky, could match Bossy's quick release when he took aim at rival goalies. Most players wait until the puck has settled on their stick before they shoot. Not Bossy.

"I felt the quicker I got the shot away, the better chance I had to score," he said. "I tried to pick a spot, high or low, but other than that I didn't think about it. I just shot."

Bossy had been shooting that way since he tied on his first pair of skates as a five-year-old. He was a pure shooter who once scored 21 goals in a single game while playing youth hockey in the Montreal suburb of Laval.

He was a homesick 20-year-old when he joined the Islanders in 1977. He had married his teenage sweetheart, Lucie, that summer and had to leave home without her. She eventually joined him and Bossy went on to his rookie-record season.

When hockey violence became an issue, Bossy always took a stand. "I didn't fight because I thought fighting was senseless," he said. "I was tougher than a lot of tough guys in the league. I didn't drop my gloves and I probably took as much abuse as anybody. But this was my way of saying that I was as tough as they were."

Bossy did get into one high-sticking duel with Dean Hopkins of the Los Angeles Kings in 1981. "I was teed off because Hopkins cross-checked me from behind," Bossy explained.

The notorious Tiger Williams shadowed Bossy during the final round of the 1982 Stanley Cup playoffs against the Vancouver Canucks, and attempted to provoke Bossy. It didn't work.

Following his retirement, Bossy returned to his home in a Montreal suburb and became involved in public relations. He was elected to the Hockey Hall of Fame in 1991.

21. TED LINDSAY

No man on skates was ever too big or too tough for Ted Lindsay to challenge. He was small (5-foot-8 and 160 pounds), but he always carried a big stick. And he used that stick—and his fists—to cut down some of the biggest, meanest men in the NHL.

His tormentors called him "Scarface" or "Terrible Ted." Lindsay didn't mind. The scar tissue on his thin but rugged face represented his badge of courage. He stopped counting the stitches when they reached 400. And the nickname "Terrible" only applied to his reputation for getting into trouble, because as a player he was magnificent.

Lindsay, a native of Renfrew, Ontario, broke into the NHL in 1944, making the big jump from the junior ranks to the Detroit Red Wings at the age of 19. Playing left wing on Detroit's memorable Production Line with Gordie Howe and Sid Abel, Lindsay helped the Red Wings win eight regular-season league titles (including seven in a row) and four Stanley Cup championships in the late 1940s and early '50s.

A member of nine All-Star teams and the league's leading scorer in 1949–50, Lindsay retired in 1960 after 16 years of service, 13 with the Red Wings and the last three with the Chicago Blackhawks. He totaled 365 goals and 458 assists, a league high for left wings until Bobby Hull passed the goals figure in 1968.

Lindsay had established a partnership with another former Detroit player, Marty Pavelich, in

Ted Lindsay

a plastics firm late in his playing career. Now he was able to devote all his time to this prosperous business. But he missed the excitement of the brawling world of hockey.

After four years of retirement, he returned to the Red Wings as a player. He was 39 years old. Asked why he would risk possible injury by attempting a comeback at that age, Lindsay said,

"It's certainly not the money. I'm well off. I just had this desire to wind up my career with the Red Wings."

The Red Wings—and their fans—welcomed Lindsay back with open arms. He launched his comeback against the Toronto Maple Leafs in Detroit's opening game of the 1964–65 season. A crowd of 14,323, the largest ever to see a Detroit home opener, greeted the old battler and he responded by dealing out several vicious body-checks to assorted Maple Leafs. Ted Lindsay was back, and soon the whole league knew it.

In a game at Montreal he drew a $25 fine for spearing Ted Harris, a rugged defenseman who towered seven inches over Lindsay and out-weighed him by 40 pounds. Claude Larose, a Montreal youngster with a reputation for being reasonably talented with his fists, tried to even matters. Lindsay gripped his stick with both hands and slashed Larose across the legs. Larose, 17 years Lindsay's junior, hobbled away in pain.

Lindsay's comeback lasted only one season, but it was a season in which the Red Wings led the league for the first time in eight years. They wouldn't have done it without old man Lindsay, who scored 14 goals and, coincidentally, was among the league leaders in penalties. Clarence Campbell, the president of the National Hockey League who had earlier scoffed at Lindsay's return, called it one of the most amazing comebacks in professional sports.

A year later, Ted Lindsay was inducted into the Hockey Hall of Fame.

22. LEONARD PATRICK (RED) KELLY

The key lyrics in that old song, "Has Anybody Here Seen Kelly?" have always served to remind fans of the most versatile All-Star in the history of the NHL. He is Leonard Patrick Kelly. And if he wasn't the Kelly mentioned in the song, he should have been, for "his hair is red and his eyes are blue and he is Irish through and through."

NHL fans first saw Red Kelly in 1947 when he joined the Detroit Red Wings as a pink-cheeked youth of 19, fresh from the junior ranks. A native of Toronto, he was ignored by the Maple Leafs when one of their scouts predicted he wasn't good enough to last 20 games in the NHL. It was a poor prediction. Kelly lasted 20 years.

Kelly spent the first 12 1/2 years of his NHL career with Detroit. During that time the Red Wings won eight regular-season championships and four Stanley Cup titles. Kelly was a defenseman then, the best rushing defenseman in the league. He was the first winner of the Norris Trophy, awarded annually to the league's outstanding defenseman, in 1954. He was named to the All-Star team six times and was a three-time winner of the Lady Byng (good sportsmanship) Trophy.

All these honors came Kelly's way while he was playing at Detroit. Then, late in the 1959–60 season, he returned home. The Maple Leafs, convinced that they had made a mistake in letting him get away the first time, talked the Red Wings into a trade after Kelly had balked at being peddled to the New York Rangers.

Kelly will never forget his first game in a Toronto uniform. "I was finally where I'd always wanted to be," he recalled. "When the people stood up and clapped and cheered me, I felt so tight I nearly burst."

The Maple Leafs, aware of Kelly's great playmaking ability, converted him into a center. He turned out to be just as valuable at his new position. In his first full season with Toronto, he propelled the previously disorganized Maple Leafs into the Stanley Cup finals, where they were finally stopped by the Chicago Blackhawks.

Toronto coach Punch Imlach called Kelly "my ace in the hole." The flaming redhead's greatest contribution to the Maple Leafs was the remarkable change he brought about in Frank Mahovlich, a brooding young man with great talent who increased his goal output from 18 to 48 the first season he played on a line with Kelly.

Red Kelly

Kelly's style was so economical he almost appeared lazy. He was a worker, though. He served two terms in the Canadian Parliament while playing for Toronto, but the extra duties as a legislator didn't hamper his play. He scored 119 goals in 7 1/2 seasons with the Maple Leafs, giving him a career total of 281, and he sipped champagne from the Stanley Cup four more times.

Following retirement as a player in 1967, Kelly became coach of the Los Angeles Kings. The Kings were picked by everybody to finish last, but Kelly—then the only pilot in the NHL without previous coaching experience—led his team to second place in the West. He moved to Pittsburgh for 1969–70 and the Penguins finished second.

Red stayed as coach of the Penguins for the next 2 1/2 seasons, piloting them to one more playoff berth before moving on to Toronto for a four-year stay.

23. BOBBY CLARKE

He is justly called The Greatest Philadelphia Flyer of all. He set standards for hard work by which Flyers have been measured ever since. No hockey player ever achieved more through raw determination than Bobby Clarke. He never took a game off, played each shift as if it were his last, and competed with a fierceness that inspired the same in teammates.

A natural leader with a choir boy visage, Clarke's appearance masked an anything-to-win attitude that was backed up by great puck skills and more than a few well-placed slashes. To long-suffering Flyer fans, he was the sainted, beloved hero of a city whose sports teams were chronic losers. Elsewhere, he was the hated, sneaky assassin who captained the Broad Street Bullies. But no matter how one emotionally reacted to Clarke, one thing is certain: His winning presence, culminating in two Stanley Cup titles, permanently turned a basketball town on to hockey.

"Between the peak years of Bobby Orr and Guy Lafleur," wrote Jay Greenberg in his defini-

tive history of the Flyers, "Clarke, the Hart Trophy winner in 1973, 1975, and 1976, was unquestionably the best player in the game."

The man who Scotty Bowman once called "the dirtiest player in hockey," was a modest, shy, soft-spoken curly blonde born in 1949 in Flin Flon, Manitoba. He played junior hockey for the Flin Flon Bombers, and his skills were such that the team retired his number 11, just as the Flyers would retire his number 16 fifteen years later.

But although he was rated a top prospect in the 1969 draft, he was picked 17th. A diabetic since 14, teams were reluctant to select him—including Philadelphia, which passed on him with the sixth pick and didn't choose him until the second round.

"I don't care if Clarke's got one arm," insisted Flyers scout Gerry Melnyk at the team's draft table. "If he can play hockey that way, take him."

Clarke had always been reluctant to talk about the illness because, "if I had a bad game, I didn't want people to say it was because I had diabetes. After the doctor told me, it made me even more determined to play hockey and prove I'm as good as everyone else. Even if a doctor told me to quit, I'd probably sneak out and play pickup games."

His point totals rose steadily in his first three NHL seasons. He was awarded the 1972 Bill Masterton Trophy for dedication and perseverance and the next season, at the age of 23, became the Flyers' captain.

Clarke also played in the '72 Summit Series, the first encounter between NHL and Soviet players. On a team stocked with talented players, Clarke tirelessly checked and scored. His most noteworthy act, however, may have been slashing Soviet star Valery Kharalmov, forcing him out of the last two games.

"I realized that somebody had to do something about him," Clarke reflected. "It's not something I'm really proud of, but I honestly can't say I was ashamed to do it."

Clarke's '73 Hart Trophy signaled the first time an expansion team player won MVP honors. He also became the first expansion player to record a 100-point season that year, a plateau he would reach three times in four seasons.

In May 1974, Clarke led Philadelphia to the Stanley Cup, upending the favored Bobby Orr and his Bruins in six games. A seven-year-old expansion team had defeated a proud Original Six team and Clarke's Game 2 performance—smashing every Bruin in sight before his OT winner knotted the series—showed his teammates they had what it took to win.

In 1974–75, the Flyers enjoyed their second straight first overall finish and second straight Cup win. With the help of linemates Bill Barber and Reg Leach, Clarke led the league in assists and a six-game victory over Buffalo. He would repeat as assist leader in 1975–76 and lead Philadelphia back to the Finals before losing to Montreal.

He returned to the Finals in 1980 and his 20 postseason points ranked among the league leaders. In 1982–83, though his offensive skills dimmed, his defensive play remained formidable and he was awarded the Selke Trophy as top defensive forward.

Mr. Flyer's retirement in 1984 was followed shortly by his appointment as general manager. With the same leadership Clarke showed on the ice, he rebuilt a Cup contender.

"He made a big impact on the game," remarked his Flyer coach Fred Shero. "I don't think there has ever been another player to have such an influence on a team. Other superstars whose teams have won were inspirational, no doubt. But they never had the same conditions as Bobby. Here's a guy who lifted an expansion team to a championship for the first time."

Clarke became the Flyer President in 1994.

24. LARRY ROBINSON

Larry Robinson, who developed into a king among defensemen in the NHL, did not have a

Bobby Clarke

regal background. He was a farm kid from eastern Ontario who remembers getting up at dawn and stumbling into the hen house to pick up eggs.

He was born in 1951 in the hamlet of Winchester, about 30 miles from Ottawa, but the family home was in Marvelville, a town of about 2,000.

"Marvelville's population is about. . . . " Robinson liked to say with a pause. "Well, if a dog dies, everybody knows about it."

From those beginnings, Robinson became an All-Star with the Montreal Canadiens. He was considered the prototype defenseman of modern hockey. Big (6-foot-3 and 212 pounds), strong, tough, mobile. He skated and handled the puck well enough to be a forward, a spot he occasionally played.

Robinson enjoyed his greatest season in 1976–77 when he totaled 19 goals and 66 assists and won the Norris Trophy as the league's outstanding defenseman. The following year, he won the Smythe Trophy as the MVP of the Stanley Cup playoffs. He sipped champagne from the Stanley Cup for the fourth straight year in 1979 and was named to the All-Star team for the third time in 1980.

Success did not spoil Larry Robinson. "When I think back to when I was a kid, I never dreamed of anything like this, like the things I have now," he admitted. "When I watched the NHL players on TV, I never thought of a hockey player as a person making a lot of money. You know what I got when I turned pro? Well, it was $7,100 a year."

He went on from there to earn $600,000 a year. However, there were times when it appeared

he would never make it to the NHL. Most pro prospects are placed on a Junior A team when they are 15 or 16, but not Robinson. He spent two years playing Tier Two in Brockville, Ontario, before moving up to the Kitchener Rangers of the Ontario Hockey Association.

Those were rough times for Robinson, then 19 years old. "I got $60 a week for playing hockey," he told Toronto reporter Al Strachan. "But I was married and that wasn't enough to feed a family. I had a job during the day working for a beverage company. I'd get up at seven and deliver soda pop all day. I'd finish about four and we'd practice at 5:30. That job paid me $80 a week.

"Then there were the games at night. It was pretty hectic. We really scraped and scraped. In the summer, I worked on road construction. I was

Larry Robinson

worried. I didn't want to live like that all my life, but what would happen if I didn't make it in hockey? What was I going to do?"

Robinson's worries eased slightly when the Canadiens made him their fourth pick (20th overall) in the 1971 amateur draft. He spent his first two seasons as a pro with Nova Scotia of the American League. Midway though his third season at Nova Scotia, he was called up to Montreal as a replacement for the injured Pierre Bouchard. He never returned to the minors.

Robinson concluded 17 seasons with the Canadiens in 1989 and signed as a free agent with the Los Angeles Kings. He was then 38 years old. "This is too tough a game and too tough a league to play in if there isn't a little fun in it," he said. "Well, it still is fun for me."

Robinson played 56 games with the Kings in 1991–92, bringing his total to 1,384 games in 20 seasons. He retired after the season, served as assistant coach with the Stanley Cup champion New Jersey Devils in 1994–95, then became head coach of the Kings in 1995–96. He was elected to the Hockey Hall of Fame in 1995.

25. KEN DRYDEN

During a timeout, he would stand in front of the net, leaning forward slightly, and using his large goalie stick as a support post. He grasped the top of the stick with his catching glove and folded his blocker over it. When he was tired, he would lower his head so that his chin rested on his forearms.

That was Ken Dryden's at-ease stance. Once play resumed and the action moved into the Montreal Canadiens' end of the rink, Dryden was a crouched panther, waiting to repulse the next enemy attack. And because he was a big man at 6-foot-4 and 205 pounds, he covered a lot of net. "He's a bleeping octopus," is the way Phil Esposito once described Dryden.

Ken Dryden also was a rarity among goalies—an articulate scholar-athlete. A native of Hamilton, Ontario, he worked his way through Cornell University on a partial hockey scholarship, then worked his way through law school with his earnings as an All-Star goalie with the Canadiens. He took a sabbatical from the Canadiens during the 1973–74 season to fulfill his law school requirements, working with a Toronto law firm which paid him $137 a week.

Some members of the hockey establishment were surprised when Dryden retired in 1979 at the age of 31. He was then at the peak of his career and earning $200,000 a year. Why retire? "This was a decision I had to make some time in my life," Dryden said. "I'm certain that I would have enjoyed playing a couple of more years. But this seems the most appropriate time to move on to new challenges."

It was expected Dryden would enter law practice or politics following his retirement. Instead, he took his wife Lynda and two children to England, settled down in a brownstone house in Cambridge, and wrote a book on his hockey experiences. He had much to write about. Consider some of his accomplishments.

He made his debut with the Canadiens at the tail end of the 1970–71 season, allowed only nine goals in six games, then sparked the Canadiens to the Stanley Cup championship and won the Smythe Trophy as the MVP of the playoffs.

• He won the Calder (Rookie of the Year) Trophy in 1971–72.

• In seven-plus seasons with the Canadiens, he totaled 46 shutouts and had a 2.24 goals-against average. His average for 112 playoff games was 2.40.

• He played in every playoff game, helping the Canadiens win six Stanley Cups, four in succession.

• He was named to the NHL All-Star team five times, led the league in shutouts four times and won or shared the Vezina Trophy five times.

Scotty Bowman, who was Dryden's coach at Montreal, always used one word to describe Dryden—consistent. "Ken would lose one game, but

Ken Dryden

he rarely lost two in a row," Bowman said. "Oh, he was so consistent."

It was Dryden's intellect, though, that set him apart from his teammates and rivals. His postgame analyses were masterpieces of logic, language and, often, self-deprecating humor.

Once, while being interviewed by Frank Orr of the *Toronto Star*, he commented on his love af-

fair with hockey. "It's a beautiful thing with its rhythms and patterns, its esthetics, although I never felt I contributed much in that way. I never liked to watch myself in game films. Before I saw myself on TV, I always figured I was Nureyev on skates, dipping and darting across the goal crease. Then I saw myself on TV and realized I was a dump truck. I was an elephant on wheels."

Dump truck? Elephant? Hardly.

Ken Dryden was what Phil Esposito labelled him—a bleeping octopus.

In May 1997 Dryden came back to hockey as President of the Toronto Maple Leafs.

26. FRANK MAHOVLICH

He was known as "The Big M," but he might have been called "The Big E" for enigma. At 6 feet and 205 pounds, Frank Mahovlich was a big man in the Original Six era and he had a big shot. He also was fine stickhandler. And in October 1962, Chicago Blackhawk owner Jim Norris agreed to a million-dollar payment to the Toronto Maple Leafs for Mahovlich. The story made headlines, but then the Leafs backed out after the news ignited a near revolt in Toronto, where kids paraded with "Don't Let the Big M Go" placards outside of Maple Leaf Gardens.

Born January 10, 1938, in the northern Ontario hockey hotbed of Timmons, young Frank assumed the responsibility for making the neighborhood's frozen pond into a rink before he was old enough to go to school. His miner father, Peter, recalled Frank regularly coming home so exhausted following an afternoon of hockey that "he would fall asleep on the sofa waiting for supper."

Teenaged Frank took the same path to the NHL that many from his region had done before him—moving to Toronto to play for St. Michael's College junior team. The Leafs had rights to all St. Mike's players and when they called Frank up for a three-game tryout in 1957, a nifty goal impressed them. He won a spot at Leaf training

Frank Mahovlich

camp that fall. A 20-goal season—then the stamp of achievement—followed and he captured the Calder Trophy as top rookie, beating out Bobby Hull, who for years would compete with the Big M for best left winger honors.

Mahovlich was part of the young corps who would mature into the Leaf dynasty that would grab four Stanley Cup titles between 1962 and 1967. But his stardom pre-dated the team's success. In the 1960–61 season, he exploded with 43 goals in his first 56 games and seemed certain to hit the exalted 50-goal mark. But, wilting under the attention and pressure, he scored only five goals in the final 14 games. Upon meeting Roger Maris, after the Yankee slugger had strained to top Babe Ruth's 60 home runs in 1961, Mahovlich told him, "I'm one fellow who is able to appreciate the ordeal you went through."

Mahovlich would never approach that mark again for Toronto. But, while he remained the Leafs' top offensive weapon, the promise of his early success was a constant source of irritation to coach Punch Imlach. "Hockey is a street car named desire," Imalch would say publicly, "and Mahovlich doesn't always catch it."

Leaf fans, too, became restless when he didn't live up to their expectations. They thought of him as slow and lazy. Fans in other NHL towns couldn't understand how anyone could boo this large guy, with his swooping, crease-crashing style and his fondness for ripping slapshots a few feet away from the goal. In one game alone, his shots knocked both Bobby Orr and Ted Green from the Boston lineup.

"He put terrible pressure on himself," said teammate Billy Harris. "He couldn't understand why they'd boo him for two periods and give him a standing ovation in the third."

An inevitable trade sent Mahovlich to Detroit in March 1968, where he partnered with Gordie Howe and Alex Delvecchio on a fearsome line. Free of Imlach and the Leaf fans, the Big M was relatively happy. He notched his 400th goal while a Wing. And he hit with 49 goals in 1968–69.

Another trade, this time to Montreal in January 1971, brightened Mahovlich even more. Montreal's management showed a concern for his emotional well-being and his hockey skills. He joined young brother Pete on the Canadiens and they contributed greatly to the Cup victory that spring. Frank led all playoff scorers with 14 goals and 27 points. In 1971–72, Mahovlich again topped the 40-goal plateau, and another Stanley Cup followed in 1972–73, with Frank again a leading playoff performer. He also was voted to the All-Star Team, an honor he had achieved in both Toronto and Detroit.

"Somehow, I'm back to the hockey feeling I haven't experienced since I was a junior," he said. After another strong season in Montreal, Ma-

hovlich returned as a long-lost hero to Toronto with the WHA Toros and played—happily—until 1978.

27. MILT SCHMIDT

He would glide behind the Boston net to pick up the puck and then start up ice. As he reached center ice he was under a full head of steam, his cowlick flying, his neck outthrust, his prominent nose sticking out like the prow of a ship. And he never had to look down at the puck, which he was shifting back and forth, left to right, right to left, on the end of his stick.

When he crossed the blue line and entered enemy territory he would skate around or barge through rival defensemen until he was close enough to the net to release his famed wrist shot. Then, bingo! The puck was in the cage and all Boston went wild.

This was Milt Schmidt in action, the kid from Kitchener, the center of the much-feared Kraut Line, who in 16 years as a player for the Bruins scored 229 goals and ranked among the most fiery competitors in the history of the NHL.

One of his greatest admirers was Art Ross, who coached and managed the Bruins during Schmidt's big years. "Schmidt was the fastest playmaker of all time," Ross said. "By that I mean no player ever skated at full tilt the way he did and was still able to make the play."

It was Ross who scouted Schmidt and signed him to a Bruins' contract in 1935. Milt played one season of minor-league hockey at Providence, then moved up to the Bruins and was reunited with two of his old school pals, Bobby Bauer and Woody Dumart. That was the beginning of the Kraut Line, so named because all three came from the Kitchener-Waterloo area of Ontario, which was predominantly German in origin.

With Schmidt as their center and leader, the Krauts led the Bruins to four straight regular-season NHL championships beginning in 1938.

Boston also won two Stanley Cup titles during that same period.

Injuries frequently slowed Schmidt but never stopped him from playing. "That's the only trouble with Milt," Ross once said. "If he would not put so much of his heart and soul into his play, he wouldn't be injured so much."

In one Stanley Cup playoff series against Toronto, when both his knees were so banged up from repeated injuries that he couldn't bend them, he had his legs taped from the ankle to the thigh and then had himself lifted off the table and onto his skates.

Referees, normally impartial, were amazed at Schmidt's courage. "Milt had more guts than any player I ever saw," said Bill Chadwick. Red Storey, another retired referee, said, "I'd take five Milt Schmidts, put my grandmother in the nets and we'd beat any team."

Schmidt was named to the NHL All-Star team four times and won the league's Most Valuable Player award in 1951 at the age of 33. He served as the Bruins' coach following his retirement as a player in 1955, then became the club's general manager.

He claimed he received his greatest thrill in 1952 when he scored the 250th goal of his career. It was Milt Schmidt Night at Boston Garden, and Bauer came out of retirement for that one game to play alongside his old Kraut linemates. "That was a great night," Schmidt said. "The goal and the ovation we got from the fans . . . I'll never forget it."

Milt Schmidt

Hockey fans—in Boston and everywhere—will never forget Milt Schmidt either.

28. PAUL COFFEY

Paul Coffey has never really gotten all the recognition he has deserved. Yes, he was selected to the first or second All-Star teams eight times in a 16-season span from 1980 through 1996. And, yes, he did win the Norris Trophy three times as the league's top defenseman during that stretch. But Coffey has always been overshadowed.

When he joined the Edmonton Oilers as a 19-year-old rookie in 1980, he came to a team that already had superstars Wayne Gretzky and Mark Messier. A trade to Pittsburgh in 1987 put him on a team that featured Mario Lemieux. Then he went to Los Angeles in 1992, reuniting with Gretzky and Jari Kurri, one of the highest-scoring right wings in NHL history. Finally, there was a trade to Detroit, where Steve Yzerman and Sergei Fedorov were superstars.

While all those stars were doing their thing, Coffey was in the background, quietly becoming the league's most prolific scoring defenseman. Entering the 1998–99 season, Coffey had amassed an incredible 1,473 points, seventh most in history. His 1,090 assists ranked a distant second to Wayne Gretzky's 1,910.

How did Coffey go where no defenseman had gone before? By using his blazing speed to join defensive rushes better than any blueliner.

"Paul plays the big offensive game because of his speed," Detroit Red Wings coach Scotty Bowman said. "His big asset is going through the neutral zone, bringing the puck up the ice.

Coffey, who was born in Weston, Ontario, played his junior hockey at Sault Ste. Marie and Kitchener in Ontario, scoring 191 points in two seasons. The Oilers took him with the sixth pick in the 1980 draft, the fourth defenseman chosen. It took Coffey awhile to acclimate himself to the NHL game, the result being a mediocre (for him) rookie season of nine goals and 23 assists in 74 games.

But Sather's philosophy of letting his defensemen join the rushes started paying off the next season. The 1981–82 Oilers led the NHL by averaging more than five goals per game, and Coffey was a huge part of their success, netting 29 goals and adding 60 assists for 89 points. He improved to 96 points in 1982–83 and helped the Oilers advance to the Stanley Cup finals for the first time.

Coffey and the Oilers fell short that time, but there was no stopping them the next two seasons. The speedy defenseman had back-to-back seasons of 126 and 121 points and the Oilers won the first of their five Stanley Cups. They ended the Islanders' quest for a fifth straight Cup with a five-game finals triumph in 1984, then easily eliminated Philadelphia in another five-game series the following year. Coffey did not win the Conn Smythe Trophy as playoffs MVP in 1985, but he might have. In only 18 playoff games, Coffey set a record for defensemen with 37 points on 12 goals and 25 assists.

Coffey stayed in Edmonton for another Cup in 1987, then was dealt to Pittsburgh in a seven-player trade. He went to Los Angeles in 1992, then to Detroit in 1993. He showed in 1995 he hadn't lost any of his scoring touch. In the strike-shortened 48-game campaign, he had 14 goals and 44 assists for 58 points, earning his third Norris Trophy. Then he contributed 18 points in as many playoff games, helping the Red Wings advance to the Stanley Cup finals before they were defeated by the New Jersey Devils.

Coffey played part of the 1996–97 season with Hartford, then with Philadelphia through 1997–98 and Carolina in 1998–99.

29. HENRI RICHARD

While most hockey fans still think of Henri Richard as the younger brother of the great Maurice (The Rocket) Richard—earning him the nick-

Paul Coffey

name "The Pocket Rocket"—one only need look in the record book to learn that Henri played on more Stanley Cup–winning teams than his older brother. In fact, no other player in NHL history has had as many—11 during a 20-year career.

"Henri is a better all-around player than I ever was," said Maurice. "He stickhandles better, controls the puck more, and skates faster. He's better in every way except goal-scoring." Which was not to say that Henri couldn't put the puck in the net, because he did it 358 times in regular-season play and another 49 times in Stanley Cup action. Plus his assist totals nearly doubled his goals in a time when assists were awarded far more strictly than today.

Fifteen years separated the brothers. Henri, born in 1936, said, "Maurice was more like an uncle to me." There was also a size difference, with Henri decidedly smaller. He weighed only 120 pounds when he starred for the Junior Canadiens, but that didn't stop him from breaking the 50-goal and 100-point plateaus in 1953–54. By the time he got the call to the NHL, Henri had filled out. But he was still a small man—5-foot-7, 165 pounds in his prime—by NHL standards. So he used his guile, tenacity, endurance, and speed to become a star.

"What made Henri Richard a great player was his desire," said teammate Jean-Guy Talbot. "When you are small you have to have more desire than anyone else to survive."

He began attending Montreal training camps at 16 and would outplay some veterans. "He just took the puck and nobody could take it away

Henri Richard

from him," noted coach Toe Blake. In 1955–56, at 19, he broke into the NHL and ultimately found himself at center on a line with Maurice and left winger Dickie Moore.

Henri was far quieter than his brother. A reporter asked Blake if Henri spoke English. "I don't even know if he speaks French," came the reply.

From the outset, Henri let his playing do the talking and his presence in the lineup coincided with the five consecutive championships Montreal won between 1956 and 1960.

Henri led the NHL in assists in 1957–58, centering for Dickie Moore, who won the scoring title despite a broken wrist. He wasn't the only Canadien Henri assisted. "Henri kept me in the league a year or two longer than I normally would have stayed," said Maurice. "The way he skated, the way he worked, he made my job easy, much easier than I would have found it otherwise." Henri even helped put the seal on Maurice's career by assisting on big brother's final goal in 1960.

Life without Maurice was a big adjustment for the Canadiens, but Henri wanted to prove he could make it on his own. Almost always over the 20-goal mark, he contributed big assists, checked top opponents, killed penalties and, when needed, fought larger men.

"You can take (Jean) Beliveau and all the others," said Ken Reardon, former Montreal defensemen and later a club executive. "Give me Henri. That little bugger could skate for five minutes without getting tired."

When the Cup returned to Montreal, Henri played a major role, scoring seven goals in the 1965 playoffs, and tallying the Cup-winner in 1966 against Detroit. The controversial goal was pure Richard determination. Driving hard to the net, he was tripped up and the puck lodged under his elbow. Henri sailed toward the net and lifted his elbow to avoid hitting the post. Goalie Roger Crozier moved to avoid collision and the puck slid across the line with Richard following.

More Cup heroics followed. In the memorable 1971 playoffs, Richard was installed on right wing with Jacques Lemaire at center in order to check Boston's Bobby Orr. "I guess it worked," Richard told author Dick Irvin, "because he didn't do as much as he usually did and we won the series."

In Game 5 of the Final against Chicago, Montreal coach Al MacNeil benched Richard, prompting Henri to tell newsmen MacNeil was "incompetent." But in Game 7, Montreal rallied from a 2–0 deficit with Richard netting the tying and Cup-winning goals.

30. BRYAN TROTTIER

Hall of Fame referee Bill Chadwick once described Bryan Trottier as the greatest hockey player he has ever seen. Other observers of the sport claim that Trottier, in his prime, was as great as Wayne (The Great One) Gretzky.

No less an authority than Gordie Howe has always favored Trottier in any Gretzky vs. Trottier debate. "I feel Bryan does more things for his team," Howe said in a 1984 interview. "He could play with any man and on any team in any era."

Trottier has always scoffed at any comparison with Gretzky. "I just wish I had some of Wayne's tools," he says with typical modesty.

A storied performer who broke into the NHL with the Islanders in 1975, Trottier won the Calder Trophy as the league's top rookie in 1976. Three years later, the gifted center captured the Art Ross Trophy as the leading scorer and the Hart Trophy as Most Valuable Player.

Trottier won six Stanley Cup rings, four with the Islanders. When the team released Trottier after 15 years of service in 1990, Islanders' general manager Bill Torrey called it "a painful decision" and had to choke back tears.

But it was not the end of the ice for Trottier, whose playing had been reduced to such a point that he was benched for the Isles' final game against the New York Rangers in their 1990 play-

Bryan Trottier

off series. A glorious era had ended for Trottier, but he signed as a free agent with the Pittsburgh Penguins and helped them win back-to-back Stanley Cups in 1991 and 1992.

He retired as a player after the 1993–94 season, finishing with career totals of 1,279 games, 524 goals, 901 assists, and 1,425 points.

Trottier was born and raised in Val Marie, Saskatchewan, a small farming and cattle-raising community close to the Montana border. He was 17 when the Islanders made him their second pick (behind Clark Gillies) in the 1974 amateur draft. Torrey shipped Trottier back to junior hockey for a season.

He was deemed ready for the Islanders after totaling 144 points for Lethbridge of the Western League in 1974–75. His coach at Lethbridge was Earl Ingarfield, a former center with the New York Rangers, who refined Trottier's talents as a center.

In his second NHL game, Trottier scored three goals and equaled a club single-game record with five points. He went on to set two league records for a rookie—most assists (63) and most points (95).

With Trottier, the Islanders finally had a center who could neutralize the other team's big guns. He was a scorer who could play defense and could win critical faceoffs. A 5-foot-11, 195-pounder, he proved a fierce and relentless checker. Once he slammed Rangers' defenseman Barry Beck, a much bigger man, into the boards with such force, a reporter at Madison Square Garden quipped, "I think the building just moved two feet."

When Mike Bossy, with his sniper's rifle, joined the Islanders in 1977, he and Trottier soon became a lethal scoring combination.

"Right off the bat, Trots knew what I was going to do and there was that chemistry . . . like we'd played together all our lives," Bossy said.

"It was eerie at times," Trottier said. "I would start a sentence and Mike would finish it. We always knew what the other was thinking."

Bossy was elected to the Hockey Hall of Fame in 1991. His longtime linemate and buddy joined him in 1998.

31. DICKIE MOORE

The Montreal Canadiens of the late 1950s won five consecutive Stanley Cups! In the process they influenced the way the game was played, the rules of the game, and the spread of hockey to Europe. The Canadiens were so star-laden that someone like Dickie Moore is often overlooked.

A Montreal native, Moore was a great sharp-shooter with an attitude. In his autobiography, the Canadiens' Jean Beliveau wrote, "Of all the stars on the 1950s Canadiens—13 of whom have been inducted into the NHL Hall of Fame—the most ferocious competitor was Richard Winston Moore." As junior hockey rivals in the Quebec League, Beliveau and Moore battled often, although Moore was five inches shorter and 30 pounds lighter.

Throughout their playoff series in 1951, when Toronto beat Montreal in five games, Beliveau recalled, "Dickie and I were running at each other all the time. The high sticking, crosschecking, elbowing, and roughing went on relentlessly, and I'm not ashamed to admit that on certain occasions, Dickie wore me down. He got as good as he gave. He was a wild man. But you could never find a better teammate, as I would discover in a few years."

Moore's Montreal junior teams won the Memorial Cup twice and, though not a big scorer in junior hockey, he was a big reason why.

An injury to Rocket Richard brought Moore into the NHL in December 1951, and Dickie responded with 18 goals and 15 assists in the remaining 33 games. Knee and shoulder injuries slowed his progress in the two seasons that followed, but when he regained his health for the 1954 playoffs, he led the Canadiens with 13 points in 11 games.

In his nine full seasons with Montreal, Moore averaged 26 goals, and despite his rugged character, he never totaled more than 68 penalty minutes in a season. Assorted injuries slowed him during his career. "Dickie's knees were arguably worse than Bobby Orr's," said Beliveau.

The most arresting tale of Moore's toughness was his drive to win the NHL scoring title in 1957–58 while playing for three months with a broken left wrist. After injuring it, he played a number of games before discovering it was broken. Given the choice of an operation or a shot at playing with a cast, Moore chose the latter.

Coach Toe Blake let Moore play, but Moore was concerned his injury might slow the production of his center, Henri Richard, neck and neck with Moore in the scoring race. Blake called a meeting and Moore explained the situation to Richard.

"I had told Pocket I thought it was unfair if I was hampering him by staying on his line but he said it was okay," said Moore. "He told me not to worry and to keep playing."

Blake switched Moore to right wing on the power play. "I could play with the one hand and catch the puck and then bring it over and shoot it or deflect it," Moore explained. He ended with 36 goals and 48 assists, beating out Richard by four points.

"They dominated," said Frank Mahovlich, who faced the Habs in two straight Cup Finals series for Toronto. "When we would get a penalty and they'd put out Geoffrion, Beliveau, Maurice Richard, Doug Harvey, and Dickie Moore on the left side, why, that was a lineup that made them change the rules. It was the best team I've ever seen to control the puck."

Until then, penalized players served a full two minutes, but when Moore and his mates began pumping in multiple goals on a single penalty, the NHL changed the rule to allow a player to exit the box following a goal.

In 1958–59 Moore captured the scoring title again. His 41 goals and 55 assists set a record of

Dickie Moore

96, breaking Gordie Howe's mark of 95. Moore's record stood until Bobby Hull totaled 97 seven years later.

He was chosen a First Team All-Star the years he won the scoring title and he garnered a Second Team selection in 1960–61, when he tallied 35 goals and 34 assists in just 57 games.

Moore retired from the Canadiens after the 1962–63 season, but he made a surprise return with the Toronto Maple Leafs for 38 games in 1964–65 after sitting out a season.

Even more surprising was his appearance in the 1968 St. Louis Blues lineup. In 18 stretch-run games and through the playoffs, the 37-year-old Moore provided a competitive spark and timely scoring as St. Louis became the first expansion team to reach the Stanley Cup Finals.

32. NEWSY LALONDE

He was the original Flying Frenchman, the greatest and most colorful player of his era. Edouard (Newsy) Lalonde scored 441 goals in a playing career that lasted 365 games over 20 years.

This was hockey in Lalonde's day: In December 1912, Lalonde's Montreal Canadiens played an exhibition game against their crosstown rivals, the Montreal Wanderers. Around the game's midway point, Lalonde smashed Odie Cleghorn of the Wanderers into the boards with such force that Odie's brother, Sprague, charged across the rink and smashed Lalonde's forehead with his stick. It just missed Newsy's eye but the laceration required a dozen stitches. Sprague received but a one-game suspension.

On another occasion, when Sprague played for Toronto, he blitzed Lalonde and was charged with assault. A bandaged Lalonde pleaded on behalf of Cleghorn to have the charges dismissed, and Sprague escaped with a $200 fine.

Those were hockey's wild, young days and if you could pass and score, as Lalonde most certainly could, you expected plenty of rough treatment. He could both take it and dish it out. "We were a different breed then, because life was a lot tougher than it is today," Lalonde told author Stan Fischler shortly before he died in 1971.

Lalonde was born in 1887 to a poor Cornwall, Ontario, family. His father ran a small shoe store and young Edouard didn't get his first pair of skates until he was 13. But having been an outstanding lacrosse player—he would be selected Canada's top lacrosse player for the first half of the 20th Century—he picked up hockey quickly.

Nicknamed "Newsie" because he had worked in a newspaper plant as a youngster, he began playing for prominent Cornwall teams in 1905, at 17. At the dawn of the pro game, he was offered $35 a week by Sault Ste. Marie in the International League. After the long train ride west, Lalonde was told by the coach that he wouldn't be used unless someone was hurt. "In those days everybody played a 60-minute game," he said. "Anyhow, I got lucky. One of the guys on our team got hurt early and I was sent out as a replacement. I scored two goals and we won the game, 3–1."

When the Ontario Professional League began in 1908, he returned East to join the Toronto franchise and led the league in scoring, the first of five scoring titles he would win.

When the NHA, the NHL's forerunner, formed in 1910, Lalonde joined the Canadiens. Though traded to Renfrew midway though the season, he still led the league in scoring, with 38 goals in 11 games.

He jumped to the Pacific Coast League in 1912, led that league in scoring and then returned to the Canadiens, where he played for the next ten seasons. In 1916, after leading the NHA in scoring, he played for the Stanley Cup, centering for Didier Petrie and Jack Laviolette, in the best-of-five Finals against Portland.

Lalonde was ill during Game 1 and missed Game 2 entirely. But he made his presence felt in Game 3, scoring a goal and getting ejected with a match penalty. He scored twice in Game 4 and

Newsy Lalonde

his Canadiens won the Cup in Game 5, his lone Cup championship.

His battles with Bad Joe Hall of Quebec were even more legendary than those against the Cleghorns. In consecutive games, Hall nearly crushed Lalonde's windpipe and carved his neck for 18 stitches. When he got back on the ice, Lalonde broke Hall's collarbone. "But there was nothing personal," said Lalonde. "When Hall later joined the Canadiens, we became friends."

He captained the Canadiens in 1916–17 and, playing a bruising style, led them to the NHA title, but lost the Cup Final to Seattle.

Lalonde became the Canadiens' playing manager when the NHL debuted in 1917–18 and, the following season, led the NHL in scoring and the Canadiens to the Finals again. He scored 17 goals in 10 playoff games and was sensational in the return engagement with Seattle, scoring all four of Montreal's goals in Game 2. But a flu epidemic which struck the team forced the series' cancellation after four games, eventually taking the life of Joe Hall.

In 1923, the Canadiens traded Lalonde to Saskatoon of the Pacific Coast League, where he was again the leading scorer. He made an NHL curtain call with a brief stint for the New York Americans in 1926–27, and was elected to the Hockey Hall of Fame in 1950.

33. SYL APPS

As great an athlete as Syl Apps was—the only man elected to the Hockey Hall of Fame, the Canadian Sports Hall of Fame, and the Canadian Amateur Athletics Hall of Fame—he was celebrated most as a human being. Selfless, devout, clean-living, and honest, Apps was "the epitome of the kind of player I wanted," said Toronto Maple Leaf owner Conn Smythe.

Apps's 10 years with the Leafs coincided with the explosive popularity of the team's radio broadcasts throughout English Canada, making him hockey's first electronic media star. Yet, he was so principled, he offered to return a portion of his salary one season because he missed half the campaign with a broken leg. He was so clean a player, he played all of 1941–42 without sitting in the penalty box.

How good a player was he? *Sport Magazine* tributed him as "A Rembrandt on ice, a Nijinksy at the goalmouth. He plays with such grace and precision, you get the impression that every move is the execution of a mental image conceived long before he goes through the motions."

Apps was a natural athlete who excelled at virtually any sport he tried. At 14, he became the youngest player in the Ontario Hockey Association. He was also a southwestern Ontario tennis champion and, gifted at track and field, he was a gold-medal pole vaulter at the 1934 British Empire Games and represented Canada at the 1936 Berlin Olympics. He was also a serious student, a

high school valedictorian, and he studied at Mc-Master University. The thought of a professional hockey career didn't actually appeal to him.

"Hockey was generally played by poorly educated, rough men," author Mike Ulmer wrote, "and gambling was an accepted part of the spectacle.... Educated men rarely considered careers as hockey players because most professions paid as much or more and promised a much longer working life."

Apps starred in football at McMaster while playing senior hockey on the side. When Conn Smythe saw him on the gridiron, "I didn't know how good a hockey player Apps was, but he was showing me that he was a great athlete." Smythe began a two-year pursuit to get Apps into a Maple Leaf uniform in the depths of the Depression. Jobs were scarce and Apps eventually signed with Toronto after the Olympics.

Apps was placed on a line between Gord Drillon and Harvey Jackson and scored 16 goals. He added an NHL-best 29 assists, losing the scoring title by a point to the New York Americans' Sweeny Schriner, but earned the Calder Trophy as Rookie of the Year.

Apps duplicated his assist lead in 1937–38, and netted 21 goals, but again was runnerup in the scoring race—to linemate Drillon. "He got as much a kick out of making sure his linemates led the league as if he had led the league himself. A real Maple Leaf type," said Smythe.

Almost always among the top scorers, he was a marvelous playmaker and his superb skating led to thrilling end-to-end dashes. His competitive spirit also sparked him to charge the net, resulting in some serious injuries. A natural leader, he became Leaf captain in 1940.

His penalty-free 1941–42 brought the Lady Byng Trophy, and that spring he sparked Toronto to the Stanley Cup championship—his first of three—in the historic comeback against Detroit when the Leafs won four straight games after losing the first three. Facing the end in Game 4, Apps scored the tying goal and set up the third-

Syl Apps

period winner. In Game 5, he had two goals and three assists. He led all playoff scorers in assists and tied for the lead in points.

After serving in World War II, he returned to the Leafs in 1945–46 and captained two more Cup teams in 1947 and 1948 before retiring to a life of civic duty and political activity. Named Canadian Father of the Year in 1949, he donated the $1,000 prize to charity.

A five-time NHL All-Star, he was inducted into the Hockey Hall of Fame in 1961. Detroit manager Jack Adams called him "the greatest center I have ever seen."

34. BILL DURNAN

Bill Durnan's career as an NHL goaltender was short in terms of service and sweet in terms of personal satisfaction.

He broke into the NHL in 1943 as a 29-year-old rookie with the Montreal Canadiens and, after seven brilliant seasons, was forced to quit the club in the middle of the 1950 Stanley Cup play-offs because of frayed nerves. But in that comparatively short time he established records which still stand.

During the 1948–49 season, Durnan set the league's modern record for the longest shutout sequence when he held the opposition scoreless for 309 minutes and 21 seconds. He was the first goalie to win the Vezina Trophy four consecutive years (1944 through 1947). Turk Broda of Toronto interrupted his string in 1948, but Durnan won the trophy for the next two years, giving him a record six in seven years.

Durnan's appearances on the league's All-Star first team matched his Vezina Trophy accomplishments. He made the squad as a rookie in 1944 and repeated each year except for 1948 when Broda again prevented him from fashioning a seven-year sweep.

Looking back on his career, Durnan once attributed his great success to the fact that he was ambidextrous.

"It was a tremendous asset and I owe that gift to Steve Faulkner, one of my coaches in a church league in Toronto when I was just a youngster," he said. "Steve showed me how to switch the stick from one hand to the other. It wasn't easy at first because I was so young and the stick seemed so heavy. But Steve kept after me and gradually the stick became lighter and I could switch it automatically."

This ability to use either hand to catch flying pucks or to bat them away with his stick was perfected by Durnan during a long career in the amateur ranks. By the time he finally turned pro with the Canadiens he was an accomplished netminder who rarely permitted a rebound in front of his cage.

In his rookie year with Montreal, Durnan gave up only 109 goals in 50 games. Sparked by Durnan's netminding and Maurice Richard's 32 goals, the Canadiens lost only five of 50 games in winning the NHL regular-season title and then skated off with the Stanley Cup.

A big, friendly man who packed 200 pounds on his 6-foot-2 frame, Durnan soon found that the pressures that eventually engulf every major-league goalie were ruining his health. "It got so bad that I couldn't sleep on the night before a game," he said. "I couldn't keep my meals down. I felt that nothing was worth that kind of agony."

Injuries—another occupational hazard of goalies—also bothered Durnan. Late in the 1949–50 season, he suffered a severely gashed head from an opponent's skate. He recovered in time for the playoffs, but midway through a semifinal series against the New York Rangers he asked to be replaced in the nets.

Bill Durnan had played his last game. In a short span of seven years in the NHL he had accomplished great feats and won many awards. His most cherished came in 1964 when he was named to the Hockey Hall of Fame.

35. PATRICK ROY

In a tense overtime at Madison Square Garden, the legend of Patrick Roy was born. It was

the 1986 Conference Championships, Montreal against New York in Game 3. The visitors led, 2–0, in games. No one had expected the Canadiens to get this far, but their eccentric 20-year-old rookie goaltender, who spoke to his goalposts and twitched his head back and forth during stoppages of play, had steered them past Boston and Hartford.

But now the desperate Rangers threw everything they had at Roy. A dozen shots, each more dangerous than the last, came his way but he turned them away. The rowdy New York fans, mangling the French pronunciation of his name, derisively chanted "Roooo-ahhhh! Roooo-ahhh!" as they attempted to unnerve him. All to no avail. The Canadiens won the game, 4–3, and proceeded to take the series in five games.

It was considered by many the finest display of overtime goaltending in memory, but the surprises didn't end there. He went on to lead the Canadiens, the league's seventh-ranked regular-season team, to the Stanley Cup. By then, no one was surprised when he was named playoff MVP. He was indisputedly Rookie of the Year as well.

For those who had followed his career, it was no surprise. He had had poor statistics playing junior hockey in Granby, but the team in front of him was awful. It afforded him the chance to face many more shots than he would have on a good club and it sharpened his game. Roy began showing his worth in the 1984–85 AHL playoffs when he backstopped the Sherbrooke Canadiens, who had finished the season under .500, to the Calder Cup title.

Bill Durnan

"I really discovered how good he was during those AHL playoffs," said Jean Perron, Roy's Montreal coach in 1986. "He was incredible on the road. He always succeeded in the most difficult circumstances—which he seemed to like very much. You could see he was cold-blooded."

A native of Quebec, he had parents who were fine athletes, and taught him confidence. With the Canadiens, he would display that confidence repeatedly over the next decade. The glories piled up: An All-Rookie Team selection, four Jennings Trophies for best-goals-against average, three Vezina Trophies for best netminder, twice the best save percentage, five postseason All-Star Team selections, nearly annual participation in the All-Star Game.

He saved his best for the playoffs, backstopping Montreal to the Finals again in 1989. In one memorable series against Boston in 1994, he suffered from appendicitis and played in great pain, even coming back immediately following surgery to try to spark a victory. In a city known for its passionate embrace of its hockey stars, no one was more beloved than Roy.

His greatest triumph came in 1993 when he led an average Montreal team to the Cup by winning a record 10 consecutive overtime games, earning a second playoff MVP. The signature moment of the Finals came in Game Four, when he stopped Los Angeles forward Tomas Sandstrom's scoring attempt. TV closeups caught Roy smiling and winking at his conquered foe.

"I knew Sandstrom was taking lots of shots, but not getting anything," Roy said. "And I knew he wasn't going to beat me."

Patrick Roy

Cocky? Perhaps, but he also was as technically sound as any goaltender in hockey. Master of the butterfly style, he was criticized early in his career for dropping to the ice too frequently to stop shots. The critics never affected him. He just perfected his craft and influenced an entire generation of goaltenders to copy his style. But none could match his success.

No matter what the hockey fortunes were in Montreal, Roy was typically in the center of things. When the team fell on hard times in 1995, Roy's feud with coach Mario Tremblay prompted a "him or me" ultimatum. The Canadiens' ownership took the view that they had never favored a player over the team, so Roy was traded to Colorado, a team managed by his good friend and former agent, Pierre Lacroix.

It was a new start for Roy. Seven months later, he backstopped the Avalanche to the 1996 Stanley Cup and won over the fans of yet another city.

Charlie Conacher

36. CHARLIE CONACHER

When the Toronto Maple Leafs first rose to prominence during the Depression, they were sparked by an infusion of youth. Among them was Charlie (The Bomber) Conacher, "the most feared forward in the game," according to premier announcer Foster Hewitt.

In his 12 seasons, Conacher either led or tied for the lead in goals five times. He was scoring champion twice and an All-Star selection five consecutive times. But mere statistics do not de-

scribe Conacher, a rollicking personality whose spirited, determined play helped build hockey's popularity.

Born into near poverty in Toronto, he would be part of Canada's most famous athletic family. Older brother Lionel was chosen as Canada's top athlete for the first half of the 20th Century. But pro hockey did not seem part of young Charlie's future. A poor skater, he was relegated to goaltender as a schoolboy. He did love shooting the puck. Leaf owner Conn Smythe would say years

later, "I believe that Charlie likes that whang of the puck against the backboards better than he does the soft sigh when the puck sags into the net."

Physically imposing even then (he'd grow to 6-foot-1, 200 pounds), he attracted attention on Toronto's frozen ponds. When Lionel made the NHL with Pittsburgh in 1925, it only fueled Charlie's determination. He became a junior star with the Toronto Marlboros and teamed with line-mate Harvey (Busher) Jackson to lead the Marlies to the 1929 Memorial Cup.

The parent Leafs called in the fall of 1929 and Conacher clicked immediately on a line with center Joe Primeau. When left winger Jackson joined them midway through the year, The Kid Line was born. It rivalled the great line of the day, New York Rangers' Bill Cook, Bun Cook, and Frank Boucher. The Kids were power personified. "When I see those big bruisers rushing in on our goal, my heart stops," said Ranger owner John Reed Kilpatrick. Conacher finished with 20 rookie goals.

In their first full year together, Conacher topped the league in goals with 31 and was third in scoring, while Primeau was first in assists. The Leafs— under 500 the year before—finished 22–13–9.

In 1931–32, Conacher again led the goal parade, including five in one game against the New York Americans. Primeau was first in assists and Jackson topped all scorers. That spring, the Leafs battled the Rangers in the Stanley Cup Finals and, in the head-to-head battle between them, the Kid Line tallied eight goals in three games to the Ranger trio's seven. Conacher had one in the first game, two in the second and two assists in the third as the Leafs swept the Rangers.

Always the joker with his teammates, Conacher was also a man about town and, during the bleak '30s, his line's exploits brought promise in the midst of woe. "If three young men could come off the pond, the open-air rinks and the frozen creeks to command international attention, there was hope for the man whose modest ambition was to find a job," wrote Toronto columnist Milt Dunnell.

For three straight years, beginning with 1933–34, Conacher led the league in goals and twice in points. While his Leafs only won that one Cup, they finished first three consecutive times, four times in six years, reaching the Finals seven times in nine seasons. For seven season in a row, at least one of the Kid Liners would be included in the league's top five scorers.

For Conacher, success had its price. His hard-charging style resulted in numerous injuries and, even during some of his best years, he played with broken bones in his hands. Toward the end of his Leaf days, hockey's hardest shooter was limited to 15 games in 1936–37 and 19 the following year. "Only a fighting heart kept him coming back," said broadcaster Hewitt.

Conacher was dealt to Detroit in 1938 and the New York Americans the following year, when he was moved back to defense for two season before retiring at age 31. He finished his career with 225 goals.

37. JAROMIR JAGR

During the Penguins' championship seasons of 1990–91 and 1991–92, the Pittsburgh Civic Arena scoreboard had a neat little gimmick. After Jaromir Jagr dazzled everyone with one of his amazing scoring plays, often created in tandem with Mario Lemieux, the scoreboard flashed the name "Jaromir," then jumbled the letters to reveal a creative anagram—"Mario Jr."

But Jagr must be considered far more than a youthful imitation. He is Lemieux's equal as a stickhandler and pinpoint shooter, and swoops to the net with the same abandon. Perhaps even more rugged than Mario, Jagr also is a superb skater. His passion for the sport seems inexhaustible—evident 90 minutes before a game when he frequently can be seen stickhandling in solitude on the ice, wearing sneakers, shorts, and an undershirt.

"If you have fun," he says, "I think you play a lot better than if you take the game too seriously."

Jagr must be having fun. In his nine NHL seasons, he's been a major contributor in two Stanley Cup championships and has earned five postseason All-Star selections—four as First Team right wing.

He has been the NHL's top scorer three times. The first was in the lockout-shortened 1994–95 season. To prove it was no fluke, he captured it again in 1997–98 when he also played for the gold-medal Czech team in Nagano, Japan. There he tied for the team lead in scoring as well.

Born in Kladno, Czechoslovakia, in 1972, he began organized hockey as a six-year-old, playing against older boys. When he became a teenager, he had three aims: "My first goal was to play for the local team in my city. My second goal was to play for the national team of Czecho- slovakia. But, my third goal was to play in the NHL."

He achieved his first goal at age 16, debuting for Poldi Kladno. In his sophomore season, he led the team in scoring. He realized his second goal by playing on both the junior and senior national teams. In June 1990, he was drafted by Pittsburgh, and realized dream three when he took the ice as a Penguin in October.

Jagr made an immediate impact, becoming a key force on a rapidly rising team. An instant teen idol in Pittsburgh because of his flowing locks and obvious enthusiasm, he had 27 goals and 57 points and made the All-Rookie Team. Just a few months past his 19th birthday, he was drinking from the Stanley Cup, having notched 13 points in 24 playoff games.

Jaromir Jagr

In the 1992 playoffs, he grabbed the reins after Lemieux had broken a hand against the Rangers. Jagr scored a penalty-shot goal in Game 4, a brilliant game-winner in pivotal Game 5, and the series clincher the next game.

Ousting Boston in the next round, Pittsburgh again reached the Finals and Jagr was in full flight. His game-tying goal in Game One against Chicago featured a zigzagging lateral sprint with the puck from the sideboards to the slot in which he eluded four players before faking goalie Ed Belfour and shooting the puck behind him. In typical fashion, Jagr removed a glove after the goal to blow kisses to the crowd. The Penguins wound up sweeping the Blackhawks for the Stanley Cup.

Jagr's point totals continued climbing—94 points in 1992–93, 99 points in 1993–94. In 1994–95, his top-scorer status was all the more impressive since Lemieux missed the season rehabilitating his injured back.

When Lemiuex returned the following year, the two waged a friendly battle for the scoring title. Lemieux won with 69 goals and 161 points to Jagr's 62 goals and 149 points. Jagr established a new mark for most points by a European-born player.

After Lemieux retired, following the 1996–97 season, Jagr racked up his second Art Ross Trophy with a league-best 67 assists and 102 points. No other player broke the century barrier in a year of reduced scoring. At age 27, Jagr's future is unlimited.

38. MARCEL DIONNE

The cover of the NHL Goal magazine in 1986 featured Marcel Dionne as "Hockey's Unknown Superstar."

If there was ever an underrated player in any sport, Dionne was he. Even today, it's a wonder that Dionne ranks relatively low among the all-time greats. He was overlooked in his day for he skated in the shadows of Guy Lafleur and Wayne Gretzky. He was long marooned in hockey's then-isolated Los Angeles Kings' outpost, piling up points night after night in a half-filled L.A. Forum, where his teams never played deep into the playoffs.

But what impressive achievements! In 18 seasons, Dionne totaled 731 goals and 1,040 assists. He topped the 100-point mark eight times. He scored at least 30 goals 14 times, 40 goals or better 10 times, and had six 50-goal seasons—five in a row. He was incredibly durable for a small man—only 5-foot-7 and 190 pounds—playing the full schedule in 11 seasons and missing more than 10 games only three times. Considered a defensive liability in his early years, he worked hard to correct that shortcoming.

"He's become an all-around star," said Montreal coach Scotty Bowman during Dionne's prime. "He has to rank right up there with the best small men who ever played the game—Henri Richard, Dave Keon, Stan Mikita. He can play for me, for anyone, any time, any place."

His first place of note was for St. Catharines in the Ontario Hockey Association, where the Drummondville, Quebec, native won two successive junior scoring titles. Born in 1951, Dionne was drafted by Detroit second overall in 1971, right after his long-time rival Lafleur. His scoring prowess was immediately evident. He followed a good rookie season with 40 sophomore goals. After a down year, he rebounded with 47 goals and 121 points in 1974–75, third in the league. Parlaying excellence with clean play, he was awarded the Lady Byng Trophy.

Although he became the Wings' 13th all-time leading scorer after just four seasons, Detroit was hardly the happy Hockeytown it is today. Constant coaching and front-office friction meant poor results, sending Dionne searching for a new home. Hockey's first modern-day superstar free agent, Dionne signed with Los Angeles in 1975, a rising team which hoped it could build a winner around him.

The move west got Dionne his first playoff action in 1975–76 and for the six seasons that followed. But the Kings only advanced to the sec-

Marcel Dionne

ond round three times, never further. Often he was accused of being the reason why, of not being able to overcome tight playoff checking. But L.A. had habitually traded top draft picks and consequently never had enough depth.

His second Kings' season saw Dionne finish behind only Lafleur in scoring, earning a First Team All-Star selection and a second Byng Trophy. But, as in Detroit, front office turmoil soured the scene.

Joe Malone

He was runner-up to Gretzky in 1980–81 as the Triple Crown Line enjoyed its best season with an accumulated 161 goals and 352 points. The Kings returned to the NHL elite that season, but Simmer's badly broken leg forced him, and ultimately the Kings, from the playoffs.

When Pat Quinn arrived to coach the Kings in 1984, he quickly dispelled the myth that Dionne was concerned only with his point totals. "Marcel is very much a team player," Quinn said. "His priority isn't personal success."

When his production finally tailed off and he was having contract problems with the Kings, Dionne was traded to the Rangers in March 1987. He rebounded in 1987–88, scoring 31 goals on a weak, non-playoff Ranger team.

When he retired at 37, Dionne was the third all-time leading scorer in the game's history. But he never came close to a Stanley Cup.

39. JOE MALONE

For students of hockey history, Joe Malone's name will always be linked to two great feats. He scored 44 goals in 22 games in 1917–18, the league's first season, and scored the most goals in one game—seven in 1920.

"Phantom Joe" played for various pro teams in five different leagues between 1908 and 1924, and he is credited with 379 goals. Oldtime observers in the pre-Gretzky era regarded Malone as the greatest all-around scorer ever. "He might have been the most prolific scorer of all time if they had played more games in those days," said Frank Selke, who saw them all in 35 years of hockey management.

Born in Sillery, Quebec, in 1890, he spent most of his career in the province. He began with the Quebec Bulldogs, then of the East Coast Hockey Association in 1909, scoring eight goals in the 12-game schedule. When Quebec was initially excluded from the formation of the National Hockey Association the next season, he jumped to Waterloo in the Ontario Pro League for

Still, Dionne produced. Centering for Dave Taylor and Charlie Simmer, the Triple Crown Line became the NHL's most feared unit. In 1978–79, Dionne finished second in scoring again. The following year, he tied young Gretzky as top scorer and was awarded the Art Ross Trophy for most goals. He was again a First Team All-Star.

a year, then returned to the Bulldogs. He captained the Bulldogs' Stanley Cup–winning teams of 1912 and 1913, scoring nine goals in one game of the 1913 Finals. He had also won the scoring title that season with 43 goals in 20 games. He'd win it again in the league's last season, 1916–17, with 41 goals in 19 games.

"Quite often," he recalled to author Stan Fischler, "I played 50 or 55 minutes a game. They didn't bother too much about changing lines, only individuals. I used to stickhandle in close and beat the goalie with the wrist shot. There was no forward passing allowed in the offensive zone."

With the formation of the NHL in 1917, Quebec dropped out and Malone jumped to the Canadiens, a shocking move at the time. Malone's line, with Newsy Lalonde and Didier Pitre, scored 84 of the team's 115 goals. With three five-goal games and a 14-game scoring streak that year, he won the first NHL scoring title. His 44 goals stood as the high mark for 27 years, until Rocket Richard's 50-goal season in 1944–45.

When the Bulldogs reformed in 1920, Malone returned for a season and again won the scoring title with 39 goals in 24 games. His seven-goal game in January 1921 against Toronto included three within two minutes. It may have been his NHL high point, but he had once scored eight in an NHA game.

"There was no great fuss made about the seven goals at the time," said Malone. "It was only a night's work as far as I was concerned. The only thing I remember about it was that it was very cold outside."

The Quebec franchise moved to Hamilton for the 1920–21 season and Malone continued to be among the league's top scorers. He returned to the Canadiens for 1922–23, but his best days were behind him. Although the Canadiens won the Cup in 1924, he played less than half the regular schedule and no playoff games. Still, when Malone retired, he did so as the NHL's all-time leading scorer, with 146 goals and 167 points in 125 games.

40. CHRIS CHELIOS

It takes a warrior's heart to excel in pro hockey and there's no better warrior than Chris Chelios. The former Chicago Blackhawks' captain has been a rock-solid performer whose all-around play on defense is rivaled among contemporaries only by Ray Bourque and Paul Coffey.

At the forefront of the great wave of Americans entering the NHL in the mid-'80s, Chelios won the Norris Trophy as top defenseman three times, the most by a U.S.-born (Chicago) blueliner. "Chelly" is also a rarity—one of the few Americans to try his skills in Canadian junior hockey. A finesse player, he shifted from forward to defense and fought regularly for the Moose Jaw Canucks in Tier II, where he was spied by the Montreal Canadiens.

"It's just fortunate that I was in the right place at the right time," he said. "I've been lucky to be on good enough teams, and some winning teams where everybody got a little bit more successful."

Montreal drafted him 40th overall in 1981, but a University of Wisconsin scholarship kept his pro career on hold. Under legendary coach Bob Johnson, Chelios developed into a Western Collegiate Hockey Association All-Star and landed a spot on the NCAA All-Tournament Team in 1983.

He played for the U.S. in the 1984 Olympics at Sarajevo. Lou Vairo, his Olympic coach, called him "one of the most competitive players I've ever coached. He'll do whatever he can to win."

Chelios jumped straight into the Canadiens' lineup after the Olympics, providing them with a key missing ingredient—a rushing defenseman. When the playoffs began, Chelios showed his worth, with a goal and ten assists in 15 postseason games.

"I had great teachers," said Chelios of his Montreal years playing alongside veterans Larry Robinson and Rick Green and for assistant coach Jacques Laperriere. "Maybe they didn't know they were teaching me. The most important thing

Chris Chelios

when I got to Montreal was that I listened and learned."

In his first full season, he tallied 55 assists, second highest total by a rookie defenseman ever. He also played in the All-Star Game and was named to the All-Rookie Team.

A knee injury forced Chelios to miss half of the 1985–86 season, but he returned as a dynamic force in the Canadiens' Stanley Cup march. Time and again, his fearless play in traffic halted the opposition, moved the puck out of danger and launched counter attacks. His toughness intimidated opposing forwards.

In some circles he was regarded as a cheap-shot artist. Partisan newspapermen in Boston, whose Bruins were Montreal's arch-rivals, sarcastically called him "Courageous Chris Chelios." But Montreal newsman Red Fisher probably described Chelios best as "a mean, aggressive, dedicated, unflinching SOB who lives and loves the game, who plays with pain and who is hated by anyone who has ever faced him."

He led Montreal back to the '89 Finals, KO-ing Flyer Brian Propp en route with a smash against the boards which reinforced his image. He also dominated games and won his first Norris Trophy. But injuries and questionable off-ice behavior forced the Canadiens to swap him to the Hawks in exchange for Denis Savard in June 1990.

The deal shocked Montreal, but it was a chance go home. A Second Team All-Star selection resulted from his first Windy City season. In perhaps Chelios' best season, he led the Hawks to the 1992 Finals and was clearly the best defenseman in the playoffs, leading all players with a plus-19 rating and all bluishliners with 21 points in 18 games.

In his prime, like Bourque and Coffey, Chelios logged an incredible amount of ice time for one so physical, but he never seemed to wear down. His grabbed a second Norris Trophy in 1993 and All-Star selections in three of the next four seasons.

He began to focus more on his defensive responsibilities by his third Norris Trophy season in

1995–96. His play did seem to tail off in 1996–97, the first time his team had ever missed the playoffs.

Chelios was sent to Detroit on March 23, 1999, the day of the trading deadline. He was traded for defenseman Anders Eriksson and first-round picks in the 1999 and 2001 entry drafts.

41. DIT CLAPPER

When young Aubrey (Dit) Clapper joined the Boston Bruins in 1927, he wore, according to a Boston newspaper, "a fancy checked cap, high boots, and a jazzbo tie." When young Gordie Howe was asked his goal as a player, he replied he wanted to last 20 years, "just like Clapper."

The NHL's first 20-year player, Dit Clapper didn't last because of any spectacular skill; rather, according to teammate Bobby Bauer, "he was so good in so many ways. But he stood out for one thing. He made so few mistakes."

Clapper was a hulking, rawboned skater, a power forward long before the term's invention. Born in Newmarket, Ontario, he was big for his day at 6-foot-2 and 195 pounds. Teammate George Owen said Clapper was considered "a tremendous physical specimen, even among the players, who were all well-built themselves. At the time, the Canadian heavyweight champion was Lionel Conacher, who also played hockey. We felt that Dit could have beat Conacher in a boxing ring."

His career began modestly, taking off in the 1929 Stanley Cup Finals. His series-opening goal, a rebound of his own shot past the Rangers' John Ross Roach, triggered a wild Boston Garden celebration and sent the Bruins winging toward their first Cup.

Clapper hit his stride the next year, playing on The Dynamite Line with tiny center Cooney Weiland and big left winger Dutch Gainor. In 44 games, Clapper popped 41 goals, second only to Weiland's 43, and added 20 assists to finish third in league scoring. In 1930–31, the trio combined

Dit Clapper

for 102 goals and 81 assists and Clapper was named a Second Team All-Star, his first of six All-Star selections. He was a Second Team pick again in 1935, when he tallied 21 goals.

Early in his career, an Ottawa Senator charged Clapper with fists cocked. Dit sent him sprawling with one right-handed chop. Another rushed him and swung. Clapper ducked, flashed his right again and dropped the second player. When a third came at him, Clapper felled him with a right to the jaw. "Three punches, three men down," recounted teammate Owen, "and not one of those punches traveled more than six inches. He could have been a great fighter, except I don't think he was mean enough."

Unappreciative of the over-aggressive tactics of the Montreal Maroon's Dave Trottier in the 1937 playoffs, Clapper punched him and continued after Trottier was down. In trying to break them up, referee Clarence Campbell swore at Clapper. Dit proceeded to punch Campbell as well. A suspension seemed in order but when Campbell admitted he had incited Clapper, the Bruin winger escaped with a fine.

The next game, Bruins manager Art Ross moved Clapper to defense, where he proved to be the star of the game with a goal and solid play. Clapper remained on defense thereafter.

Paired with Eddie Shore, Clapper became an All-Star blueliner, with First Team honors in 1938–39. The Bruins won the Cup that year, led by the Kraut Line of Bauer, Milt Schmidt, and Woody Dumart. "A lot of us were little guys," said Schmidt, "but none of us were afraid to get into scraps. We were all very brave — all because we had Dit Clapper on our side."

After Shore retired, Clapper paired with Flash Hollett and was a First Team All-Star in 1940, playing a long stretch with a broken cheekbone. In 1941, the year he scored his 200th career goal and the B's won their third Cup, Clapper partnered with Des Smith and was again a First Team selection.

Two seasons of injuries, including a severed Achilles tendon, threatened Clapper's career.

Healthy again in 1943–44, his 17th season, Clapper had an All-Star year.

But injuries in the next two seasons again limited his playing time. He became a player-assistant coach, schooling young Bruins before retiring after his 19th year. However, an injury to defenseman Jack Crawford brought Clapper out of retirement for a few games in his 20th season. He quit for good in February 1947.

The Bruins held Dit Clapper Night and his No. 5 was retired. Other teams feted him, too, and he became the first living player inducted into the Hockey Hall of Fame.

42. BERNARD GEOF-FRION

Strong and spirited, tortured and temperamental, Bernie (Boom Boom) Geoffrion was probably the most colorful of the great 1950s Montreal Canadiens. Few played with such passion and his slapshot revolutionized hockey. He retired as hockey's fifth all-time goal scorer and he was the second player to score 50 goals in a season. Maurice Richard did it in 1944–45.

Bernie Geoffrion

Geoffrion's ebullient personality always pushed teammates to bigger accomplishments. He was quick with a joke—and with his stick or fists if an opponent angered him. But his intensity gave him ulcers and often resulted in injuries. He'd usually force himself back in the lineup sooner than expected.

Born in 1931, the Montreal native didn't invent the slapper. But he popularized its use. Geof-frion began practicing the shot when he was about 11 "just as a joke," he told author Dick Irvin. "I saw that thing go pretty hard."

He began using it in junior hockey for the Montreal Nationals. "One day I was practicing at the Forum and shooting the puck hard against the boards and it was making a pretty big noise," he recalled. "A newspaper guy, Charlie Borie, asked me if it would be okay if he started calling me 'Boom Boom.' Since that day, the name stayed."

He became a young Canadiens cornerstone after playing 18 games for them in 1950–51, scoring eight goals and 14 points. He remained eligible for top rookie honors the next season, which he captured with a 30-goal campaign. By 1953, Geoffrion was one of Montreal's stars, with six goals and 10 points in a dozen playoff games for his first Stanley Cup squad.

Despite limitations in his skating, the Boomer became a consistent scorer. The only season he failed to reach the 20-goal plateau with Montreal was in 1956–57 when an elbow injury limited him to 41 games. He still managed 19 that year. But playing right wing in the era of Maurice Richard and Gordie Howe, Geoffrion was often bypassed for postseason awards.

One of Boomer's revolutionary roles was to play the point on the power play, a rarity among forwards. As his big shot flew goalward, teammates either screened the goalie or jumped on the rebound.

Boomer liked to sing after a game to all who would listen—unless he wasn't scoring. "When goals don't come," he said, "there is no song. That is a mistake, I know, but how can I sing when I'm not happy?"

He had no problems scoring in 1954–55. His 38 goals led the league. But when his idol and teammate Rocket Richard was suspended and Geoffrion's point totals surpassed Richard's, the Montreal fans booed the 24-year-old. "It really hurt me," he said. "It wasn't my fault that the Rocket got suspended."

The Habs began their unmatched Cup streak in 1956. "I have to say that was the best team ever to play hockey," he said. "Five in a row! Man, what a team!"

In 1956–57 the year his bad elbow had depressed his regular-season totals, he bagged 11 goals, one shy of Rocket's record for most goals in a postseason. His 18 points led all scorers.

The magic 50-goal mark had eluded everyone since Richard's 1944–45 campaign. But two players took aim at it in 1960–61. Toronto's

Frank Mahovlich was well ahead of the field but ran out of gas and finished with 48. The Boomer went on a tear in the last six weeks, scoring No. 50 in Montreal. "The Forum crowd rose as one and gave me the ovation of my life," he recalled. "I thought to myself that this makes up for 1955 when they booed me." He won the scoring title and the Hart Trophy as NHL MVP.

Geoffrion's production declined from that point. Following three more 20-goal seasons, he retired in 1964 to coach Montreal's Quebec farm team. He hoped to coach Montreal but, believing he would not be considered, he came out of retirement in 1966 with the Rangers.

Passions re-ignited, he scored 17 goals as a 35-year-old, excelling in games against Montreal. His championship experience provided New York with the leadership needed to make the playoffs after a four-year draught. Asked to pinpoint one thing that turned around the Rangers, teammate Donnie Marshall replied, "It was Boom Boom Geoffrion." But his ever-present ulcers flared during a second, less productive Ranger season, forcing Geoffrion to finally call it a career.

43. TIM HORTON

Today, the Canadian donut chain that bears his name is probably better known than Tim Horton ever was as a hockey player. But that speaks more to commercialism and growth of mass media than to Horton's prowess as an All-Star defenseman for the Toronto Maple Leafs.

For 22 seasons, Miles Gilbert (Tim) Horton brought his immense strength and fine athletic skills to the rink and became one of the most consistent players of the Original Six Era. "Game in and game out," said Norm Ullman, who played both with and against him, "Tim Horton has been the best defenseman in hockey over the past 15 years."

In an era when defenders were rarely involved in the game's offense, Horton had a big shot from the point and could rush the puck up

ice with speed and abandon. His excellent skating also combined with his strength to great advantage when the opposition advanced toward him. "You see the way he turns those forwards against the boards?" asked Philadelphia Flyers GM Keith Allen. "He just pins them there. They're in a trap and they know it. Nobody coming down his side wants anything to do with him."

From the hockey hotbeds of northern Ontario, where he was born in 1930, Horton followed the path many had traveled to the pros—through St. Michael's College junior hockey program in Toronto. Leaf owner Conn Smythe called him "the best defense prospect in Canada," and after a few years of seasoning in the minors, Horton came to the Leafs full time in 1952. In two years, his play was All-Star caliber, with a Second Team selection in 1954.

But the Leafs were in decline in the middle 1950s and his exciting rink-length dashes often went for naught. He also suffered serious injuries, including a badly broken leg. Still, the tales of his muscular play grew to Bunyanesque proportions. Nearsighted on the ice and bespectacled off, his teammates called him "Clark Kent."

But he rarely used his super power for evil, employing intelligence before applying muscle. Not a fighter, he needed only to wrap his arms around opponents in the "Horton Hug" or fling them to the ice in order to subdue them. He did inflict damage upon various hotel rooms in spirited highjinx during Leaf road trips, loosening door frames, unbalancing beds, and wobbling floor boards for recreation.

He only topped the 100 penalty minutes mark twice in his career. "You can't call him a really tough player because he's not mean the way Gordie Howe is," said coach Punch Imlach, who would guide Toronto and Horton to greatness in the '60s. "Tim has to be riled up. But when he is, he's the best."

Imlach's tutelage brought out the best in the entire Leaf team. In 1962, when Toronto captured their first of four Stanley Cups in the decade,

Tim Horton

Horton's 16 points in 13 playoff games set a record for defensemen.

As his skating began to slow down, he concentrated more on his defensive responsibilities and was named a First or Second Team All-Star five times in six seasons, beginning in 1963.

Bill Cook

Sabre season, his life tragically ended one night when his car turned over on the drive back to Buffalo following a game in Toronto.

"Playing with him was a wonderful experience," said his longtime Leaf defense partner Allen Stanley. "He was the finest man I ever knew, on or off the ice, a great leader without a mean streak in him."

44. BILL COOK

During the Roaring '20s, Madison Square Garden's glamorous hockey team, the New York Rangers, was the toast of the town, attracting a fur and dinner-jacket crowd. They saw a powerhouse club, coached by Lester Patrick, which would advance to the Stanley Cup Finals four times in six seasons and win the Stanley Cup twice between 1928 and 1933. The original Rangers' top player was Bill Cook, whose bullet shot and creative mind made him perhaps the best right wing of his day.

Born in 1896 in Brantford, Ontario—Wayne Gretzky's birthplace 65 years later—Cook was a star before coming to the Great White Way. He had been the top scorer in the Western Hockey League. Learning his craft from his Saskatoon Sheiks coach, the great Newsy Lalonde, the 29-year-old Cook cracked the 30-goal barrier in the league's final season playing on a line with his brother Bun.

When Conn Smythe began recruiting players for the Rangers, the Cook's Saskatchewan farm was an early destination. There, Bill told Smythe about a WHL center from Vancouver who might

Twice, he was runnerup for the Norris Trophy as best NHL defenseman.

Durable despite his physical character, he played the full schedule 13 times in his career, including nine times in 11 seasons and six in a row, coinciding with Toronto's best years.

After 18 Leaf seasons, Horton played a year each for the Rangers and Pittsburgh before being reunited with Imlach, who had become GM in Buffalo. In February 1974, during his second

fit well between the Cook Brothers, Frank Boucher. From the Rangers' opening in October 1926, this threesome, called the A Line, set the standard for NHL forward units.

Bill Cook was just reaching his peak when he joined the NHL and in that first Ranger season led the league with 33 goals and 37 points in 44 games. "We worked hard developing patterns of play," Boucher recalled. "We never put diagrams on paper. Somehow, just in describing our ideas, we'd all grasp it.

"Bill would do most of the talking. He'd say, 'Now look, Bunny (and I knew he damned well meant me, too), when I want the puck, I'll yell for it, and you get that damn puck to me.' On the ice, Bill's cry was the most amazing half-grunt, half-yell, half-groan I'd ever heard. 'When I yell, I want the puck then; don't look up to see where I am, just put it there and I'll be there.'

"So I'd be carrying the puck and I'd hear that goddam crazy noise from Bill, and I'd be sure to get the puck at that angle, in advance of the sound, sort of leading him because I knew he'd be cutting in on goal. A lot of times, I'd be lying on my back knocked down by a defenseman after I released the puck and although I didn't see anything, I'd hear the roar of the crowd and I'd know he'd banged it past the goaltender."

Cook would bang the puck past the goaltender 321 times in his professional career, second only to Nels Stewart among his contemporaries; 229 of those goals came in the NHL.

The Rangers and their A Line made the Stanley Cup playoffs nine consecutive seasons, and Bill tallied two of the most important goals in club history—their first Cup Finals goal, the historic 1928 Game 1 against the Montreal Maroons in which the 44-year-old Patrick stepped in as an emergency goaltender; and the 1933 Cup-winning goal in Game 4 against Toronto.

The unquestioned leader, Cook captained the club his entire Ranger career. They were a hard-living, night life bunch, but Boucher recalled that when the team would slump, Bill would enter the dressing room, slam his stick on the floor and declare, "Okay, boys. Everybody on the wagon!"

When the NHL began selecting postseason All-Star teams in 1931, Cook was chosen to the First Team three consecutive years and the Second Team in the fourth.

Patrick broke up the A Line as it started to fade in 1936 and moved Bill back to defense. Cook retired after the 1936–37 season but his pregame intensity was long remembered by his coach.

"He'd be a bundle of nerves," said Patrick, "just aching to get at it and break the tension. The placid player can be depended on for a safe, steady game, but for the kind of inspired hockey needed to win championships, I need the Bill Cooks. When it comes down to the crunch, the other players will follow the Bill Cooks."

45. JOHNNY BUCYK

When Johnny Bucyk would get "up" for big games, his teammates couldn't wait to hear him cough. "I get awfully nervous," he said. "which means I'm getting worked up and a little excited. I cough and gag and choke. Then one of the guys will come over and ask how I'm feeling. 'Lousy,' I'll say. 'Good,' they'll say. 'That means you're going to have a good game.' And they go away laughing."

Bucyk usually had the last laugh. The rugged, durable left winger coughed and choked his way to 556 goals and 813 assists. His 1,369 points ranked fourth all-time in NHL scoring, trailing only Gordie Howe, Phil Esposito, and Stan Mikita. He did it with characteristic Boston Bruin grit and determination, yet so expertly that penalties were rarely a part of his game.

An Edmonton native, Bucyk came from impoverished beginnings, meaning skates were not a priority. He played street hockey instead, using a broom instead of a stick until he was 10 and got hand-me-down skates. As a consequence, his skating was slow to develop.

Johnny Bucyk

Promoted to the minor pro Edmonton Flyers in 1954–55, he partnered with right wing Vic Stasiuk and center Bronco Horvath. The three were called the Uke Line, because of their supposedly shared Ukranian heritage, although Horvath was Yugoslavian. They became a sensation, with Bucyk setting rookie scoring records.

Detroit came calling on his 20th birthday and—in "complete awe of Gordie Howe and Ted Lindsay"—John spent two seasons there with mixed results. In 1957, Bucyk was sent to Boston in exchange for Terry Sawchuk. Thinking he had failed in Detroit, he was encouraged by Bruin coach Milt Schmidt to just play his grinding game, that Boston Garden's small ice surface would be perfect for his 6-foot-1, 215-pound frame.

Fortunately, the Bruins also had Horvath and Stasiuk and the Ukes were reborn. They carried the B's to the Stanley Cup Finals in 1958. The following year, with Bucyk digging in the corners for him, Horvath—who had nicknamed Bucyk "Chief"—made a serious run at the scoring title. But after injuries forced Bucyk from the lineup, Bobby Hull passed Horvath on the season's last day.

The Ukes were soon dismantled and the Bruins struggled for years. But Bucyk had gained confidence to become a consistent scorer. Frustrated Bruin fans sometimes turned on him, but he never seemed disturbed. "I was always proud to play in the NHL," he said. "There was no shame wearing a Bruin sweater. Even when we were last, we were last in the best."

Bobby Orr's arrival in 1966 changed everything. When Bucyk rifled a goal past Ranger goalie Ed Giacomin in December 1967, to take over Schmidt's spot as the Bruins all-time scorer, the same fans chanted "Chief! Chief! Chief!" for minutes after play resumed. "First you think you're dreaming, then it hits you. They're cheering for you. It's wonderful," Bucyk said. He finished with his first 30-goal season and was selected a Second Team All-Star. At 33, his best still lay ahead.

Boston began acquiring other key performers and, finally, team captain Bucyk had stars around

Sheer love for the game kept him on ponds for hours. Progressing through the local youth leagues, Bucyk was spotted by a scout for the junior Edmonton Oil Kings, who saw promise in the plodding kid with the awkward style. The scout offered him $1,500 and a job. In no position financially to turn it down, Bucyk became an Oil King.

him. He played left wing on the 1969–70 record-breaking power-play unit that included Orr, Phil Esposito, Ken Hodge, John MacKenzie, and Fred Stanfield.

The memorable 1970 play-offs allowed him to finally hoist the Cup. For an encore in 1970–71, the 35-year-old Bucyk connected for 51 goals and 116 points, was named a First Team All-Star and received the Lady Byng Trophy. But while he was gentlemanly, he was not gentle. "I never knew anyone who could hit harder, especially with a hip check," said Orr.

Bucyk's nine goals and 11 assists in the 1972 playoffs helped bring Boston a second Cup and, though the Bruins couldn't defend their title, the Chief kept rolling with a 40-goal, 93-point season in 1972–73. A second Lady Byng campaign followed that one, and then came two seasons in which he topped the 80-point plateau as he hit the age of 40.

Injuries caught Bucyk in his final two years and he hung 'em up in 1978 after 23 NHL seasons. "I didn't want to leave even then," he said.

George Hainsworth

46. GEORGE HAINSWORTH

When the legendary Montreal Canadiens goalie Georges Vezina was forced to retire with pneumonia in 1925, the team struggled to find a replacement. A tip from former Canadiens star Newsy Lalonde provided the man. George Hainsworth had starred for Lalonde in Saskatoon of the Western Hockey League and, with that league near extinction, Hainsworth was available.

Following Vezina's death, the Canadiens created the Vezina Trophy for the NHL's top goalie. The recipient in each of the first three years? George Hainsworth.

Hainsworth had been an electrician by trade and a championship amateur athlete in both baseball and hockey around Kingston, Ontario. Only 5-foot-5, he decided to give pro hockey a try with Saskatoon in 1923 and helped to drastically improve the Sheiks' fortunes. Cellar dwellers for two years, Saskatoon became a league power with Hainsworth in goal.

Arriving in Montreal in the fall of 1926, the 31-year-old rookie had a rough start. The fans remained loyal to Vezina's memory and when Hainsworth lost his first three games, he was branded "a lowly substitute" by one writer. Slowly, he began performing the same magic he had for the Sheiks. The Canadiens had finished last the previous year, but Hainsworth's play helped turn them into a second-place club.

Hainsworth only got better in each of the next two years, backstopping his team to first-place finishes. He allowed only 48 goals in 44 games in 1927–28, and his incredible performance in 1928–29, in which he recorded 22 shutouts, has never been equalled. He surrendered only 43 goals in 44 games that year. But the team could not advance past the Stanley Cup semifinals.

He won the Forum fans over for good that season, especially one January night when a pregame warmup shot broke his nose. A bloody mess, he insisted on playing. The visiting Maple Leafs stormed the goal, but George, his face swollen and feverish, seemed to laugh with each successive save. He allowed only one goal and an observer called it "his night of nights."

A master of goaltending technique, Hainsworth was "almost mechanical in his perfection," according to Montreal hockey writer Elmer Ferguson. "He did his duties with the absolute minimum of movement and utter apparent lack of effort."

To increase scoring, the NHL altered the rules for 1929–30, allowing forward passes in the offensive zone, which inflated goaltending averages. But, despite a brief illness, Hainsworth remained steady, guiding the Habs into the playoffs. They knocked off Chicago after nearly 52 minutes of overtime in Game 2 and swept the Rangers. That meant facing the mighty defending champion Bruins, who had not lost two consecutive games all season. But with a shutout in Game 1, Hainsworth led the Habs to a two-game sweep, allowing only six goals in six Cup games with three shutouts.

Now flying high, the Canadiens repeated as champs the following year, with Hainsworth

shutting out the Blackhawks and Gardiner in the deciding game. With another first-place finish in 1931–32, Hainsworth and the Canadiens appeared to be in line for the first three-peat in NHL history. But the Rangers upset them in the opening round.

Hainsworth and his team faltered thereafter. In one 1933 game, he allowed 10 goals, seven in the third period. Another subpar playoff against the Rangers sealed his fate and he was traded to Toronto. The little goalie enjoyed three more good years as the high-scoring Leafs finished first twice and a close second in 1935–36. But he could not lead Toronto past his old team in the Finals.

Hainsworth would play a total of seven games in 1936–37 with Toronto and his original team, Montreal, before conceding it was time to say goodbye.

He retired at the age of 41 with 1.91 regular-season average, 1.93 in the playoffs. He was the alltime shutout leader with 94, a mark that would stand until Terry Sawchuk surpassed it in 1964.

47. GILBERT PERREAULT

When Buffalo fans think of Gil Perreault, specific memories come to mind—the 1978 play when he went around the entire Los Angeles Kings team to score a one-handed goal, and his smart dump-in that Rene Robert converted for the OT winner through the fog against Philadelphia in the 1975 Stanley Cup Finals. But fans weren't the only ones thrilled by his marvelous skating, stickhandling, and passing.

"He'd do things on the ice and you'd look at opposing players and their jaws would drop," said teammate Larry Playfair. "Hell, we saw him all the time and we'd be catching each other with our mouths open."

Perreault's 17 NHL seasons, all with Buffalo, commenced with the first Sabre game ever in 1970, and while Pat LaFontaine and Dominick Hasek have made enormous impacts, Buffalo has never had a player to rival him. Perreault holds

Gilbert Perreault

every team career offensive record and served as captain longer than any other Sabre.

His skills were evident long before NHL stardom. He came out of Victoriaville, Quebec, to lead the Montreal Junior Canadiens to consecutive Memorial Cup titles in 1969 and 1970. He was a First Team Ontario Hockey Association All-Star both seasons and league MVP in 1970.

A spin of a wheel for the first overall draft pick in June 1970 made him a Sabre. Between two expansion teams, Buffalo held all numbers over 7, Vancouver the rest, and the wheel stopped on 11. That become Perreault's sweater number and he was "the franchise" from the outset.

The most exciting player to enter the NHL since Bobby Orr, Perreault led the Sabres in scoring (which he would do 11 times), set a new rookie record with 38 goals, and was awarded the Calder Trophy in 1970–71.

Rookie winger Richard Martin joined next season and, benefiting from Perreault's passes, popped 44 goals in 1971–72 to break that mark. Late in the season, the Sabres traded for Rene Robert, put him on the other wing, and The French Connection Line was born.

"It didn't take us too long to click," Perreault recalled. But Martin admitted his biggest problem was watching Perreault's rushes instead of complementing him. "He'd have the puck for 30 or 40 seconds at a time. It's amazing to think five guys can't take the puck away from one guy."

Their first full season together produced 105 goals as the Sabres improved by 37 points and made the playoffs for the first time. Perreault had 26 goals and 60 assists and, with only 10 penalty minutes, captured the Lady Byng Trophy. He had 10 points in the playoffs.

A broken leg accounted for his subpar 1973–74 season, but the line scored 131 goals in 1974–75 as the Sabres tied for the best record in the league. Perreault had 96 points. The Sabres advanced to the Finals against the defending champion Flyers, but were ousted in six games.

In the six seasons between 1974–75 and 1979–80, Perreault averaged 97 points a year. His best season ever, 113 points in 1975–76, also brought the first of two straight Second Team All-Star selections.

But the Sabres began struggling and Perreault asked for a trade, a request that was denied. The French Connection Line was broken up occasionally and disconnected permanently when

Robert was traded in 1979. Martin was traded in 1981, and injuries slowed Perreault in the early '80s. When healthy, he could lead the team to great heights, as in 1983–84 when his 90 points helped Buffalo finish a point behind Boston for the best Wales Conference record. Still, the lack of playoff success continued to disturb him.

"He had such high standards that anything less than perfection was not good enough for him," said teammate Bill Haijt.

What Perreault meant to the Sabres and their fans was best expressed in March 1986 when he became the 12th NHL player to score 500 goals. After beating Hartford goalie Alain Chevrier, his teammates charged off the bench. "We put him on our shoulders and carried him around as if he were a champion," said teammate Mike Foligno.

Perreault retired that spring, then returned for a final 20 games in the fall of '86. His number was later retired. In November 1995, Perreault was joined by Martin and Robert at center ice in Buffalo's Memorial Auditorium to have their numbers retired as well. The French Connection was reunited for all time.

48. MAX BENTLEY

He was called the "Dipsy Doodle Dandy from Delisle." Author Jack Batten described Max Bentley as "Fred Astaire on skates. Like Astaire, he was slim, quick, and graceful. Swift of foot, he was a dancer on ice, master of the stutter step, the feint, and the shift." But while Astaire's routines were rehearsed and practiced, Bentley may have been hockey's greatest improviser.

A virtuoso stickhandler in an age when stickhandling was crucial to offensive success, Bentley was hockey's most exciting player immediately following World War II. He was the key to the Toronto Maple Leafs becoming the first NHL team to win three consecutive Stanley Cup championships.

Born in Delisle, Saskachewan, one of 13 children in an exceptional athletic family, Bentley

was so frail-looking that he flunked tryouts with Boston and Montreal. Doctors in Montreal said he had a heart problem and suggested he stop playing. He returned to Delisle briefly, then went back to hockey. He got a tryout with Chicago on the recommendation of his older brother Doug, a Blackhawk winger.

With the Hawks, Max centered for Doug. Neither was a big man. Max was 5-foot-7 and 158 pounds. The third linemate was swift Mush March, who was even smaller than the Bentleys. But when bigger Bill Thoms joined the Bentleys in 1942–43, the line took off. In January, Max equaled the NHL record of four goals in a period. He finished three points behind Doug for the scoring title and, with only one minor penalty, captured the Lady Byng Trophy.

After two years of military service in World War II, Max returned for 1945–46. Bill Mosienko, among the fastest skaters in the game, replaced Thoms and The Pony Line was born. "To all appearances, these three players were plugged into one central nervous system," wrote Jack Batten. "They moved themselves and the puck in ways that seemed uncanny and instinctive."

"We used to talk about all kinds of ideas," said Max. "I knew we'd be all right because Doug and Mosie were the best and fastest I ever saw."

Max was better than all right, winning the scoring title in 1946, a First Team All-Star berth and, with Chicago jumping 20 points in the standings, the Hart Trophy. Then, despite the Pony Line's excellence, the Hawks descended to the basement, unable to sustain the momentum, though Max repeated as scoring champ in 1947 and was a Second Team All-Star. Things got no better the following season, when Mosienko broke his ankle in the preseason All-Star Game.

Desperately, the Hawks pulled off a shocking trade. The Hawks needed players, Toronto needed insurance against Syl Apps retiring. The Hawks got players, five of them—a complete forward line and two defensemen—and Max became a Leaf in November 1947.

Max Bentley

Brad Park

Despite missing his brother on and off the ice, Bentley became a consistent 20-goal scorer over his six Leaf seasons. But he suffered a serious back injury in the 1952–53 season and his scoring dropped off.

When the Leafs left him unprotected and the Rangers drafted him for the 1953–54 season, Max coaxed Doug out of retirement and the pair were reunited for one season, their last in the NHL.

"Max was one of the very few players who could make a fantastic play while still going at full speed," said Boston's Milt Schmidt. "We'd say before a game, 'Let's get a hold of Bentley and we'll win.' But we never could catch him."

49. BRAD PARK

Misfortune and heartbreak walked hand in hand with Brad Park during most of his career. Yet he overcame all to become a standout defenseman in the NHL. He played on knees that had no cartilage and on ankles weakened by fractures, and became a hero to fans in two cities.

His heart was broken on a November day in 1975 when the New York Rangers traded him and Jean Ratelle to the Boston Bruins for Phil Esposito and Carol Vadnais. Park, who had been the Rangers' captain and the darling of the gallery gods at Madison Square Garden, quickly shook off the shock of that trade and eventually became a favorite at Boston Garden.

Misfortune seized Park early in life. A native of Toronto, he was only 17 when he suffered torn cartilage in his left knee while playing in a Junior

With Apps and Ted Kennedy already on board, the Leafs now had three Hall of Fame centers. Playing with wingers unfamiliar with his moves, Bentley baffled his new linemates. But in a strategic move that would have lasting repercussions, coach Hap Day moved him to the point on the power play. Bentley's slick playmaking made him the first power play "quarterback," giving the Leafs the NHL's best power play and helping guide them to three Stanley Cups between 1947 and 1949.

A game. The following season he required surgery for ligament damage in his right knee. He fractured his right ankle in his second season with the Rangers in 1969.

Park's knee problems followed him to Boston. In his first season with the Bruins, he caught his left skate in a hole on the ice against the Islanders in Nassau Coliseum and required surgery to remove torn cartilage. Park's fourth and last cartilage surgery (two in each knee) occurred during the 1978–79 season, but his right-knee problems persisted.

He considered retiring in 1980, changed his mind and enjoyed an injury-free season in 1980–81. "Brad had a sensational season," said Harry Sinden, the Bruins' general manager. "There wasn't a better defenseman in the NHL."

On December 11, 1980, but Park became only the second defenseman in NHL history to collect 500 assists. The first was Bobby Orr, who was Park's teammate for a brief period during the 1975–76 season. When they skated onto the ice for a Boston power play, taking up positions on opposite points, rivals shuddered.

Park always was a dangerous point man. During the 1981–82 and 1982–83 seasons, he scored 13 of his 24 goals on power plays and he completed 1982–83 with 600 career assists, fifth-highest among active playmakers in the NHL.

Park grew up in the Toronto Maple Leafs' junior system and was drafted by the Rangers in 1966 when the Leafs, through an oversight, left him unprotected in the amateur draft. King Clancy, a Toronto vice president, used to moan over that mistake. "I don't know how we ever let that boy get away," he said.

Park was barely 20 years old when he showed up at the Rangers' training camp in 1968. He was the last player cut before the season started and was sent to the American League for more seasoning. But his minor-league career lasted just 17 games. The Rangers lost Harry Howell with an injury and Park was called up as his replacement. Park never saw the minors again.

Early in his rookie season, Park cracked the NHL record book when he assisted on four goals in a game against Pittsburgh. Later in the season, he scored his first NHL goal—the final one in a 9–0 romp over the Bruins. Delighted by the goal, he leaped high in the air and landed ingloriously on his backside. When he picked himself up and brushed himself off, Park grinned and said, "I'm okay. That first goal was worth it."

Park was named to the All-Star first team five times and twice to the second team. He appeared in the Stanley Cup playoffs for 17 consecutive years from 1969 through 1985. He was signed as a free agent by the Detroit Red Wings in 1983, played two more seasons and had a brief fling as coach of the Red Wings in 1986. He was elected to the Hockey Hall of Fame in 1988.

50. JARI KURRI

Would Wayne Gretzky have recorded such astronomical scoring stats without his right wing Jari Kurri?

An unusual question, because most people think it's Kurri who owes his career to Gretzky. Even one-time Edmonton coach Glen Sather once said, "A fire hydrant could get 40 goals playing next to Gretzky."

"Jari could never escape the stigma that he's made it because he's been Wayne's right winger." said Oilers defenseman Kevin Lowe.

Gretzky himself said, "Without Jari, I still would have been a good player, sure, but there's no way I would have accomplished what I did. He and I just clicked on the ice like we were twins."

As Gretzky's Oiler teammate for 600 games, Kurri scored 397 goals and 451 assists. He became the first European player to record a 50-goal NHL season and the first to reach 70. "Somebody once calculated that Jari had a hand in 630 of my 1,669 points in Edmonton," Gretzky said.

Kurri didn't argue the point. "Wayne helped me a lot, but I think I helped him, too," he said.

Jari Kurri

When Kurri concluded his NHL career in 1998, he retired as the all-time leading scorer among European-born players and played more games and on more Stanley Cup teams than any other European.

A native of Helsinki, he played three seasons for the Finnish club Jokerit and was spotted by

Oiler management in 1980 when the club conducted training camp in Finland. Kurri's play in exhibition games against the Oilers led them to scout him closely, which Kevin Lowe called "a major major move in the ascendancy of our franchise."

In 1980, Finnish players were still something of an NHL rarity, so 68 players were drafted before Kurri, who turned out to be a fourth-round steal. He immediately stepped into the Oiler lineup and scored at a point-per-game clip in that inaugural season.

It wasn't long before Gretzky learned he and Kurri "were almost telepathic." By his third season in 1992–93, Kurri had broken the 100-point barrier. He scored three of the Oilers' six goals in the Stanley Cup Finals won by the New York Islanders. Kurri was runnerup that season to Philadelphia's Bobby Clarke for the Selke Trophy for defensive play.

He proved a master at shooting the puck off the pass without stopping it. Kurri also was employed to kill penalties and, with Gretzky, set new records for shorthanded goals. "I tell my players, when you see those two coming down on a two-on-one, just race back to the center ice faceoff circle, because that's where you'll see the puck next," joked Vancouver coach Harry Neale in 1983–84.

Kurri, Gretzky, and Glenn Anderson all topped the 50-goal plateau in 1983–84 as the Oilers became the first NHL team with three 50-goal scorers in one season. Kurri also was named a Second Team All-Star, the first of five All-Star selections. In the playoffs, his 14 goals led the pack as the Oilers won their first Stanley Cup.

With 71 goals the following year, the most by a right wing in a season, and a career high in points, Kurri finished second only to Gretzky for the scoring title. He became a First Team All-Star and won the Lady Byng Trophy. In the 1985 Cup triumph, his four playoff hat tricks, including three in one series, were both records as he tied the mark for most goals with 19. His 67 goals led the NHL in 1988–86 and when the Oilers won the Cup in 1987 and 1988, Kurri led all playoff goal scorers both years.

Many wondered whether his numbers would dip when Gretzky was traded to Los Angeles in 1988, but playing with a few different centers, Kurri was again an All-Star, scoring 44 goals and 102 points in 1988–89.

In 1990 Kurri's seventh playoff hat trick, which tied the NHL record, helped the Oilers capture their fifth title in seven seasons. After playing a year in Italy, he returned to the NHL for the 1991–92 season, reunited with Gretzky in Los Angeles, and enjoyed some success there, playing a major role in the Kings' trip to the 1993 Finals. His strong skating kept him in the NHL as his offensive skills faded and he continued as a defensive specialist with the Rangers, Anaheim and, in 1997–98, Colorado.

He stands eighth in goals and 11th in points alltime, and in Stanley Cup play, second in goals, third in assists, and third in points.

"If Jari Kurri doesn't make the Hall of Fame," said Gretzky, "they ought to board the thing up."

Nels Stewart

51. NELS STEWART

Few players have had so meteoric a rookie season as did 23-year-old Nels Stewart in 1925–26. Playing for the Montreal Maroons in his hometown, Stewart led the league in scoring and topped the playoff scorers as the Maroons captured the Stanley Cup.

The 6-foot-1, 195-pound center made off with the Hart Trophy as Most Valuable Player. He was built like a defenseman, but was kept on the forward line because of his knack for being in position for a shot on goal.

Stewart's skating style was deceptive. He appeared slow next to more nimble forwards. But he had a deadly shot that enabled him to twice lead the league in scoring.

He scored 324 regular-season goals during a 15-year career that took him to Boston in 1933, after seven years in Montreal, and then to New York. Stewart wound up his 15-year career with the N.Y. Americans in 1940.

He was nicknamed "Old Poison" for good reason. He left the game as the most penalized player in league history with 953 minutes. Stewart was elected to the Hockey Hall of Fame in 1962.

52. FRANK (KING) CLANCY

He was only 5-foot-9, one of the smallest defenseman in NHL annals. Despite his size, he stood up to the biggest and toughest players. Which is not to say he didn't often end up on the short end of many a confrontation.

Frank Clancy inherited the nickname "King" from his football-playing father, but young Clancy took a while before becoming "King" in his own right. The Ottawa native embarked on his 16-year

Frank "King" Clancy

Bill Cowley

career in 1922, reaching his first peak in the 1926–27 season when he played a major role in the Senators winning the Stanley Cup.

Traded to Toronto in 1930—for an estimated $35,000 and two players—Clancy led the Maple Leafs to their first Stanley Cup in 1931–32. Clancy played the rest of this career with Toronto and although he never drank from another Cup, he continued as an indomitable force. For four consecutive years he made the first or second All-Star team and landed in the Hockey Hall of Fame in 1958.

Clancy coached the Montreal Maroons in 1937–38 and after a long gap returned to Toronto to lead the Maple Leafs in 1953–54, 1954–55, and 1955–56, then for short stints again in 1966–67 and 1971–72.

Along the way he became a referee for 11 seasons, and assistant GM with Toronto and a hockey goodwill ambassador for the rest of his life.

53. BILL COWLEY

A master stickhandler who became a legend in Boston, Bill Cowley centered the Bruins to the Stanley Cup in 1939 and 1941. Twice winner of the Hart Trophy, this native of Bristol, Quebec, made the NHL All-Star Team four times. Cowley was the NHL scoring champion in 1941 and paced the league in assists three times. Injuries—a broken jaw for one—cost him half a season in 1943–44. At the time he had totaled 71 points in 36 games.

Cowley also proved a solid contributor in the playoffs, highlighted by 14 points in 1939 when the Bruins won the Cup after a nine-year drought.

54. ERIC LINDROS

His 6-foot-4 inch frame alone makes him a formidable force on the ice for the Philadelphia

Eric Lindros

Harvey Jackson

Flyers. Team that physical presence with skills and skating ability and you have one of the most compelling figures in the game.

At the age of 26, Eric Lindros is a natural as captain of the Flyers. In 1994–95 he won the Hart Trophy as Most Valuable Player and the Pearson Award as outstanding player chosen by the NHL Players' Association. And made the All-Star first team.

A native of London, Ontario, Lindros was an Ontario Hockey League All-Star and Canadian Hockey League Player of the Year in 1990–91. He captained Team Canada in the 1996 World Cup and in the 1998 Olympic Games.

Lindros was acquired from Quebec in the summer of 1992 in a nine-player deal that had a profound affect on the Flyers' outlook. Among other milestones, he posted a team record six as-

sists against Ottawa in 1997. His future is unlimited.

55. HARVEY JACKSON

He was known as a party boy who frequently was at odds with his coaches, first in Toronto (10 years starting in 1930), then with the N.Y. Americans and Boston. In all, Harvey Jackson played for 15 years.

It was a career marked by his scoring skills, initially on Toronto's Kid Line with Charlie Conacher and Joe Primeau. Jackson led the league in points in 1932. He made the first or second All-Star team five times.

Sold to the N.Y. Americans with three other players for Sweeney Schriner in 1939, Jackson's production declined and he was sold after two seasons to Boston. He was at his best playing

Peter Stastny

Ted Kennedy

there with his brother Art and Bill Cowley. In the 1942–43 playoffs Jackson scored the winning goal in overtime to eliminate Montreal. But the Bruins lost to Detroit in the finals.

Jackson finished his career the following season. He had more ups than downs and a highlight was his election to the Hall of Fame in 1961.

56. PETER STASTNY

His dramatic escape from Czechoslovakia is for the movies or television: How Peter Stastny—and his brother Anton—made it to Quebec and a new life in the National Hockey League.

The Stastnys, along with older brother Marian, were one of the most productive forward lines in Europe in the 1970s. But they sought a fresh challenge in North America's National Hockey League.

First they had to plot a route to Canada. Eluding border guards in Czechoslovakia, they got to the safety of the Canadian embassy in Austria. Then, capping their cloak-and-dagger adventure, they caught a plane to Montreal.

The final destination was Quebec City and the Nordiques. For both Stastnys, but especially for Peter, success in the NHL was immediate. In that first season, 1980–81, the 6-foot-1, 200-pound center was sixth in points with 109 and captured the Calder Cup as Rookie of the Year.

Stastny became the Nordiques' mainstay, seven times going over the 100-point mark in 10 seasons before being traded to New Jersey at the end of the 1989–90 campaign. After three years with the Devils, Stastny played briefly for St. Louis in 1993–94 and 1994–95 before retiring. He was named to the Hockey Hall of Fame in 1999.

Andy Bathgate

Pierre Pilote

Walter Broda

57. TED KENNEDY

The chant of "Come o-n-n-n-n Teeder" rang out for Ted Kennedy for 14 years in Toronto, starting in 1942. The face-off specialist would lead the Maple Leafs to five Stanley Cups and he would win the Hart Trophy as Most Valuable Player in 1954–55 despite only five goals.

The 5-foot-11, 180-pound center starred in the 1945 playoffs when he paced the Maple Leafs to an upset of Montreal and a Stanley Cup triumph over Detroit. He was elected to the Hockey Hall of Fame in 1966.

58. ANDY BATHGATE

In a 17-year NHL career (the first 12 with the N.Y. Rangers), Andy Bathgate won the Hart Trophy as Most Valuable Player in 1958–59. Known for his shooting and puckhandling, he twice topped the NHL in assists and tied Bobby Hull for the scoring title in 1962.

The Rangers never won a Stanley Cup in Bathgate's years, but, as a Maple Leaf, Andy finally figured in one in 1964. He played at Toronto for two years, then with Pittsburgh for two more before briefly appearing with Vancouver in the World Hockey Association in 1974–75.

As a Ranger he made a significant shot into the face of Montreal goalie Jacques Plante in 1959. It resulted in Plante's donning a face mask that changed the face of hockey's netminders forever.

Bathgate twice made the All-NHL first team and twice the second team. He was picked for the Hockey Hall of Fame in 1978.

59. PIERRE PILOTE

A rugged defenseman who regularly landed on the All-Star team, Pierre Pilote spent all but one of his 14 NHL seasons with Chicago. He was chosen first or second All-Star for eight consecutive years, starting in 1960. Pilote was captain of the Blackhawks when they won the Stanley Cup in 1961. He captured the Norris Trophy in three consecutive years, 1963, 1964, 1965, and twice was runner-up.

For five years, starting in 1956–57, he didn't miss a game. What was further significant about Pilote was the fact that he didn't play in a regular game until he was 16. He made the Hall of Fame in 1975.

60. WALTER (TURK) BRODA

Professional hockey can thank an anonymous school principal for launching the career of one of the outstanding clutch goaltenders of all time.

It all began for Walter (Turk) Broda when he was a chubby youngster in Brandon, Manitoba, where he was born on May 15, 1914. One day the principal at his public school announced he was organizing a hockey team. Young Broda, called "Turkey Egg" because of the freckles on his face, tried out for a defense position. It was a bad choice.

"I'm sorry," his principal said, "we have all the defenseman we need." Broda started to leave the ice. "Wait a minute," the principal said. "We need a goaltender, Walter. Get into the goal."

Turk Broda was a goaltender from that day. He started his pro career in the Detroit organization and landed with Toronto through sheer luck. Conn Smythe, the Toronto club owner, was seeking a replacement for Hall of Famer George Hainsworth in 1936 when he scouted a minor-league playoff game between the Detroit Olympias and the Windsor (Ontario) Bulldogs.

Smythe had received glowing reports on the Windsor goalie, Earl Robertson. "I like the fellow tending goal for the other team," Smythe said. The other goalie was Broda. Smythe wasted no time

Frank Boucher

purchasing Broda from Detroit for $8,000. Early in the 1936–37 season, Turk replaced Hainsworth as the Maple Leafs' regular goalie. He held the job for 14 seasons, during which he helped Toronto win five Stanley Cup championships. He twice won the Vezina Trophy as the NHL's top netminder and earned berths on three All-Star teams.

Broda was always at his best when the pressure was greatest, especially in playoff games. He allowed only 211 goals (a 2.08 average) in 101 playoff games. In the 1949 championship playoffs he gave up only four goals as the Maple Leafs swept Detroit in four straight games. In the 1951 playoffs he was again brilliant, allowing only nine goals in eight games.

A happy-go-lucky man of Polish extraction, Broda was inclined to be overweight, a condition which frequently aroused the ire of Smythe. Early

Cy Denneny

Bernie Parent

in the 1949–50 season, when the Leafs failed to win in six games, Smythe called the chubby Broda into his office. "I'm not running a fat man's team," the owner said. "I'm taking you out of the nets and you're not coming back until you get down to 190 pounds." At the time Broda scaled almost 200.

The goalie knew Smythe wasn't kidding. He launched a crash diet. He turned his back on desserts. He went to a gym and was steamed, boiled, and pounded. It was a Herculean effort for Broda, who regained his job after missing only one game.

61. FRANK BOUCHER

Frank Boucher was born in Ottawa in 1901 and he went on to become a symbol of the N.Y. Rangers as a distinguished center and then the New Yorkers' coach and general manager.

He played for the Ottawa Senators for one year, 1921–22, and the Rangers for 13 years, starting in 1926. Assigned to the pivot spot between Bun and Bill Cook, Boucher starred for Stanley Cup winners in 1928 and 1933. He was outstanding in 1928 when he scored seven goals as the Rangers won their first Cup.

Known for his sportsmanship and clean play, he won the Lady Byng Trophy seven times. Boucher retired after the 1937–38 season, but came back briefly (15 games) to fill a need in 1944 when he was the Ranger coach. Boucher made it to the Hall of Fame in 1958.

62. CY DENNENY

A pioneer performer in 1917–18, the first year of the NHL, Cy Denneny was a leading scorer for 11 seasons as left wing for the Ottawa

Senators. Using his curved stick, he averaged more than a goal a game for four seasons and was always among the top pointmakers. He won the scoring crown with 22 goals in 1923–24.

Denneny led the way to the Stanley Cup four times with Ottawa and once more as a player-coach with Boston in 1928–29. He returned as coach to Ottawa for the 1932–33 season.

63. BERNIE PARENT

He stopped shots with his glove, his stick, his cheek, his arms, his skates. He stopped them from up close and from far away. He stopped the ones that came hurtling at him straight on and he stopped the ones that caromed off sticks and skates and darted in new directions.

"This is what the game is all about," said Bernie Parent as champagne spritzed around him following Philadelphia's Stanley Cup wrap up of Buffalo in 1975. It was the second consecutive year that Parent had achieved a shutout in the final game, marking a four games to two series.

Parent had won the Conn Smythe Trophy again, the first time anyone had two in a row as MVP of the playoffs. He'd also captured the Vezina Trophy he'd shared in 1974 with Chicago's Tony Esposito for fewest goals yielded during the regular season.

These were the highlights of Parent's 14 years in the NHL that began with Boston in 1965–66 and continued in Philadelphia and Toronto (and a year with the Philadelphia Blazers in the World Hockey Association) before a six-year return to the Flyers.

64. BRETT HULL

Talk about growing up in the shadow of a famous father. When Brett Hull was growing up in Belleville, Ontario, his father was dominating hockey as the sport's best left wing. In the 1990s, Brett had reached the same level, but as a right wing with the St. Louis Blues.

Brett Hull

Brett and his father share the same build, not especially tall (5-foot-10) but stocky in the upper body (203 pounds). Each has (or had) a blazing slap shot. But the similarities end there. For while Bobby threw himself into the action with reckless abandon, Brett relies more on a passive approach, waiting for the right moment to uncoil a blazing slapper that is often in the net before the goaltender can react.

"My whole game is based on deception," Brett said. "I'm there, and then I'm not. I don't do a lot because I don't want to be noticed. I barely raise my arms when I score. I don't want people mad at me for making them look stupid."

Opponents have had a number of reasons to be upset since Brett broke in to the NHL with the Calgary Flames in the 1986 playoffs. The Flames had drafted him in the sixth round of the 1984 draft after he had scored an amazing 105 goals in

Aurel Joliat

Toe Blake

56 games with Penticton in a juniors league. After two productive years at Minnesota—Duluth (84 goals in 90 college games), he joined the Flames for the '86 playoffs and went scoreless in two games. It was an omen of what his stay in Calgary would be.

He spent much of the following season with Moncton of the American Hockey League before joining Calgary for good at the start of the 1987–88 season. Though he scored 26 goals in 52 games with the Flames, the team was unhappy with what they thought was his lackadaisical attitude. People wanted Brett to show the same fire as his father, and that wasn't part of the younger Hull's game.

"I've got a reputation as a lazy, mostly un-skilled player, without the great competitive edge—and it looks like it'll never leave me," Hull said at the time.

It wasn't until Hull was traded to St. Louis late in the 1987–88 season that his innate ability broke through. Two years later, he set an NHL record for right wings with 72 goals. The following season he was even better, scoring 86 goals in only 78 games. He led the league again with 70 goals in 1991–92, then followed up with seasons of 54 and 57 goals.

Still, Hull felt unfulfilled because of the Blues' failure to succeed in the playoffs. Not even the arrival of Coach Mike Keenan in 1994, immediately after he had led the Rangers to their first Stanley Cup in 54 years, could bring the Blues a title. "People can say you're a superstar or whatever they want to call you, but you never really feel like one until you become a part of the Stanley Cup," Hull once said. In 1999 he got the chance to feel like one when he scored the Cup-clinching goal for his latest team, the Dallas Stars.

65. AUREL JOLIAT

Picture a fullback in football weighing 136 pounds at 5-foot-6. That was Aurel Joliat with the Ottawa Rough Riders before he broke his leg and turned to hockey, of all sports. He became a combative left winger with Montreal in 1922.

From then on there was no stopping him. Joliat played for 15 years, all with the Canadiens, and proved an elusive figure teamed with the great Howie Morenz. The opposition often brushed off his black cap to tantalize him. It simply inspired Joliat to a career marked by a Hart Memorial Trophy in 1933–34 and first or second-team All-Star selection four times. In the process, Montreal won the Stanley Cup three times.

66. TOE BLAKE

Toe Blake found a home with the Montreal Canadiens in 1935–36 after originally signing with the Montreal Maroons. He would come to be known as "Lamplighter" because of his scoring skills.

The rugged left winger won the Hart Memorial Trophy as MVP and the Art Ross Trophy with 48 points in 1938–39. And captured the Lady Byng Trophy for sportsmanship in 1945–46. Blake teamed with Maurice Richard and Elmer Lach to form the "Punch Line" and he scored the winning goals that brought Montreal the Stanley Cup in 1944 and 1946.

Three times he made the first All-Star team and twice the second team. After retiring follow-

Frank Brimsek

Elmer Lach

Grant Fuhr

ing the 1947–48 season, Blake came back in 1955 to coach the Canadiens to the Stanley Cup eight times—five of them came in a row, from 1956 through 1960.

67. FRANK BRIMSEK

It was his rookie season in the NHL and no wonder they soon nicknamed him "Mr. Zero." Frank Brimsek recorded 10 shutouts in 1938–39. That was the year the American-born Bruin led his team to the Stanley Cup with a 1.25 goals against average (it was a mere 1.56 during the regular season). Brimsek captured the Calder Memorial Trophy as outstanding rookie and the Vezina Trophy awarded to the goalie who gives up the fewest goals during the regular season.

Boston would win another Cup and Brimsek a second Vezina two years later. His career was in-

terrupted for two years in the U.S. Coast Guard when he served in the South Pacific during World War II. He never returned to his prewar level and retired after the 1949–50 season with Chicago.

All but one season were with the Bruins, with whom he made the All-Star first team twice and the second team six times.

68. ELMER LACH

When teammate Maurice Richard surpassed him in 1953–54, Montreal's Elmer Lach had reigned for two years as the NHL's all-time assists leader. A matchless passer and stickhandler, Lach played center on the Canadiens' vaunted Punch Line.

His entire career, starting in 1940 and winding up in 1954, was with Montreal and he collected the Hart Memorial Trophy as MVP once and

Dave Keon

the Art Ross Trophy twice. And he played for three Stanley Cup winners. Lach made the first All-Star team three times and the second team twice in the course of enduring a fractured jaw, cheek, and leg.

69. DAVE KEON

He played for 23 years, 15 with Toronto on four Stanley Cup champions, and captured the Conn Smythe Trophy as MVP in 1967 and Calder

Memorial Trophy as Rookie of the Year in 1960–61.

As a two-way center, Dave Keon scored 986 points (396 goals) and was heralded for the way he repelled opposing centers. He twice won the Lady Byng Trophy for clean play. Keon's career included four years in the WHA before he returned for a three-year stretch in the NHL with Hartford that ended his career in 1981–82.

70. GRANT FUHR

Veteran goalie Grant Fuhr of the St. Louis Blues moved into fourth place in all-time wins (413 in 18 years) in 1998–99. Terry Sawchuk has the record with 447, followed by Jacques Plante, 434, and Tony Esposito, 423.

Fuhr was outstanding from the beginning of his career with Edmonton in 1980–81 when he was runner-up to the N.Y. Islanders' Billy Smith for Rookie of the Year. In a decade with the Oilers, Fuhr proved a cool, gifted performer vital to the team's five-time harvest of the Stanley Cup. In 1987–88 he won the Vezina Trophy awarded to the goalie whose team gives up the fewest goals during the regular season.

Traded to Toronto in 1991, Fuhr moved on to Buffalo in 1992–93, was traded to Los Angeles during 1994–95, and signed as a free agent with St. Louis in 1995, where he played in an NHL record 79 games, 76 in a row, in 1995–96.

Brain Leetch

Earl Seibert

Doug Bentley

Borje Salming

71. BRIAN LEETCH

Known for its oil and its Cowboys, the state of Texas can also boast of a hockey defenseman who captures headlines for the N.Y. Rangers.

He is Brian Leetch, born in Corpus Christie and born to be a hockey star. His father, Jack, played hockey at Boston College and Brian followed in his skates. Leetch was the Rangers' first-round pick (ninth overall) in the 1986 Entry Draft. In 1988–89, his first full season, he scored 23 goals and 71 points, winning the Calder Trophy as Rookie of the Year.

His achievements and awards have continued to grow, highlighted by the Rangers' Stanley Cup championship and Leetch's earning the Conn Smythe Trophy as playoff MVP in 1994. He was the first American-born player to win the Smythe. He also added the James Norris Memorial Trophy as the league's best defenseman in 1996–97.

72. EARL SEIBERT

A superb rushing defenseman, Earl Seibert made the first or second All-Star team for 10 consecutive years with the N.Y. Rangers and Chicago from 1934–35 through 1943–44.

Seibert drew his share of penalties for his aggressive play, and he would regret the night in 1937 in Montreal when he checked the celebrated Howie Morenz into the boards. Morenz broke bones in his left leg and ankle. He was recovering but within weeks an embolism killed him.

In 1944–45, when Seibert was winding down with Detroit, he scored two goals in 36 seconds to win a game against Boston. It was an appropriate feat to mark the end of Seibert's career.

Georges Vezina

Chuck Gardiner

73. DOUG BENTLEY

There were great expectations for 23-year-old Doug Bentley when he reported to the Chicago Blackhawks in 1939. But it took three years before the left wing from Saskatoon began to make headlines. Playing with his brother Max, the center, Bentley broke loose in 1942–43 when he became the NHL's leading scorer with 73 points. The next season he was up to 77, but that was only good enough for runner-up to Boston's Herbie Cain at 83.

Doug was outstanding in the 1949 playoffs on a line with Clint Smith and Bill Mosienko. But Chicago was eliminated in the finals by the Canadiens. His achievements were formally recognized in 1950 when Bentley was chosen as the Hawks' "Best Player of the Half-Century."

74. BORJE SALMING

He never experienced the thrill of a Stanley Cup celebration, but Swedish-born Borje Salming was saluted for his all-around play in 17 NHL seasons. All but one year, his last, was spent with Toronto, starting in 1973.

Twice Salming was runner-up for the James Norris Memorial Trophy as best defenseman and he stands third on the Maple Leafs' all-time scoring list.

As a pioneering European in the NHL, Salming had to gain acceptance from the North American players. It helped that he had a hard shot that enabled him to top the 70-point mark four times. He was a first-team All-Star selection once and second team five times.

Clint Benedict

Steve Yzerman

75. GEORGES VEZINA

Goaltending, as Georges Vezina knew it in the first quarter of the century, was a different art than it is today. He played when a netminder was not permitted to sprawl on the ice to block shots. So Vezina stood straight and tall in front of the net during a brilliant 15-year career with the Montreal Canadiens from 1910 to 1925.

A product of northern Quebec, he came to the attention of the Canadiens when they played an exhibition game against Chicoutimi, an amateur team. The pros were startled by the gangling, six-foot goalie who shut them out. Montreal immediately signed up Vezina.

He went on to lead the Canadiens to two National Hockey Association championships and the Stanley Cup twice. The coolest of performers, Vezina became known as the "Chicoutimi Cucumber."

It was on November 28, 1925, that Vezina and the Canadiens faced Pittsburgh at the old Mt. Royal Arena. Vezina left the ice, bleeding from the mouth, after a scoreless first period. He returned for the start of the second period, but collapsed again. He had tuberculosis. Four months later, at the age of 39, he passed away. A trophy bearing his name is awarded each year to the NHL's outstanding goaltender.

76. CHUCK GARDINER

His career was short-lived, as was his life, but Charlie (Chuck) Gardiner proved a mighty presence in goal during his seven years with Chicago.

Originally from Scotland, Gardiner moved to Winnipeg as a youngster and found a home on the ice from 1927 through 1934. In his brief career, he posted 42 shutouts, twice won the Vezina Trophy

as the goalie yielding the fewest regular-season goals, and was a three-time first-team All-Star.

His career goals against average was 2.02 (1.73 in 1933–34) and he and his many fans had great expectations before a brain tumor felled him in 1934. He was only 29.

77. CLINT BENEDICT

The first goalie mask and Clint Benedict are synonymous. As a Montreal Maroon in the 1929–30 season, he donned a mask after a shot by the Montreal Canadiens' Howie Morenz broke his nose.

The protective shield not only limited his vision on low shots, it didn't prevent Benedict from suffering another broken nose later in the same season. Result: He and the mask retired at the end of the season.

Not until November 1, 1959, after the Canadiens' Jacques Plante was drilled in the face by a shot from the N.Y. Rangers' Andy Bathgate, did the mask emerge again. Plante donned one in that same game and it would soon become vital equipment for all goalies.

Benedict played for seven years with Ottawa, starting in the NHL's inaugural season, 1917–1918, and a year later began a string of five consecutive seasons with the league's lowest goals against average. He would achieve a 1.51 GAA with the Montreal Maroons in 1926–27. He won three Stanley Cup rings with Ottawa and one with the Maroons.

78. STEVE YZERMAN

All-around master of the Red Wings, Steve Yzerman has twice led the team to the Stanley Cup crown (1997, 1998). The longest-serving captain in the NHL (starting in 1986–87), he made the All-Rookie team in 1983–84 when he scored 87 points.

Yzerman has since won the Conn Smythe Trophy as playoff MVP, his 24 points leading all play-

Tony Esposito

ers, and the popular center is only one of four players to top 150 points in a season. The others? Wayne Gretzky, Mario Lemieux, and Phil Esposito.

He played for Team Canada in the inaugural World Cup in 1996 and was assistant captain in the 1998 Winter Olympics. Born in British Columbia, Yzerman grew up in the Ottawa suburb of Napeon, where there is now a Steve Yzerman Arena.

Yzerman has never been a first or second-team All-Star, thanks largely to the presence of Gretzky, Lemieux, and Mark Messier. No complaint from Yzerman. He can stand on his record.

79. TONY ESPOSITO

Tony Esposito becomes rueful when he recalls what it was like growing up in Sault Ste. Marie, Ontario, with his brother Phil. "It was al-

Billy Smith

Serge Savard

Alex Delvecchio

ways 'Phil did this' and 'Phil did that' and it used to make me feel awful inferior," the younger Esposito said.

That was back in the late 1950s when the Espositos were teenagers. Everybody was predicting hockey stardom for Phil Esposito, while Tony's future was slightly blurred. He even quit hockey for one year and concentrated on high school football.

Tony shrugged off that inferior feeling once he reached the NHL. For while Phil was setting scoring records with the Boston Bruins, his brother developed into an All-Star goalie with the Chicago Blackhawks.

Unlike Phil, Tony went to college—Michigan Tech on a hockey scholarship—and led the team to the NCAA title in 1965, was chosen an All-American, and was drafted by the Montreal Canadiens.

It was during his one year with Montreal (1968–69) that the Esposito brothers opposed each other for the first time since their street-hockey days in Sault Ste. Marie. Phil, the Boston center, scored two goals, but the game ended in a 2–2 tie.

In the summer of 1969 the Blackhawks plucked Tony off Montreal's unprotected list and he responded with a brilliant first season. He won the Vezina Trophy with a 2.17 goal against average, recorded 15 shutouts, made the All-Star team, and won the Calder (Rookie of the Year) Trophy.

He went on to earn a share of the Vezina on two other occasions, helped Chicago win four straight division titles, and earned a reputation as a workhorse, averaging more than 60 games a season.

Babe Dye

Lorne Chabot

80. BILLY SMITH

The President was Ronald Reagan, who will always be known as "The Gipper" for the football role he played in *Knute Rockne, All-American*. But in the White House in 1983 he was on the receiving end of a goalie's stick inscribed "The Puck Stops Here."

It was appropriately presented by Billy Smith, the impenetrable goaltender who had enabled the N.Y. Islanders to sweep Edmonton in 1983 for their fourth straight Stanley Cup. Smith had won the Conn Smythe Trophy as MVP of the playoffs.

A year earlier, Smith had taken the Vezina Trophy given the goalie yielding the fewest goals during the regular season. These were the glory days for the Islanders and the veteran from Ontario who played for 17 Islander seasons.

He retired in 1989 with 88 playoff wins, a record since surpassed by Patrick Roy with Montreal and Colorado.

81. SERGE SAVARD

Known for his defensive feats when Montreal captured the Stanley Cup eight times during his 15-year Canadiens' playing career, Serge Savard would later show his talent as GM with Montreal. He won the Conn Smythe Trophy as Stanley Cup MVP in 1969, only his second season, and in 1970–71 and 1971–72 Savard suffered leg fractures.

But little else could slow him down. The Winnipeg Jets picked him up on waivers—for a $2,500 fee—in 1981 and he played for the Jets for two seasons before retiring. But that wasn't the end for Savard. He came back to the Canadiens as

Sid Abel

Bob Gainey

GM in 1983 and Montreal won the Cup three more times before he retired for good in 1995.

82. ALEX DELVECCHIO

Longevity instantly suggests Gordie Howe. Nobody played more seasons—26—than Gordie. But who's next? Alex Delvecchio and Tim Horton. Each endured 24 seasons and each made The Top 100.

Delvecchio had a never-miss-a-game approach and, indeed, the Detroit iron man only sat out 43 games, 22 of them due to an ankle injury. And he was so clean a player that he won the Lady Byng Trophy three times.

A Red Wing center, starting in 1951, Delvecchio joined the team three years after Howe's arrival and played through 1973–74, three years after Howe left the NHL on the way to Houston

in the WHA. He played on three Stanley Cup champion teams, had a cheery attitude, and never minded hearing someone say, "Oh, you're on Gordie Howe's team."

83. BABE DYE

Slick with the stick and boasting a bullet shot, Babe Dye was deemed a cocky rookie when he reported to the Toronto St. Pats in 1919. But his teammates soon discovered that he was a power packed little guy who could score. In his first 169 games, the 5-foot-7 right wing racked up 174 goals.

He was third in the NHL in scoring in 1920–21 when he led the league with 44 points on 38 goals and six assists. He played seven years with Toronto, leading the St. Pats to the Stanley Cup in 1922.

Johnny Bower

Sprague Cleghorn

A broken leg, suffered in the Chicago Black-hawks' training camp in 1927, cut short his promising career. Dye quit the game in 1931 after a season with the N.Y. Americans and then a six-game attempt with his original Toronto team. Dye did return as a referee for six years.

84. LORNE CHABOT

To historians, Lorne Chabot is best known as the N.Y. Ranger goalie responsible for a rare moment in NHL history. It happened on April 7, 1928, when a shot by the Montreal Maroons' Nels Stewart drilled into Chabot's left eye.

Unconscious, Chabot was carried off the ice and replaced by 44-year-old Lester Patrick, the Rangers' manager and coach. Patrick not only survived in that one-game appearance, but New York went on to win the Stanley Cup.

Chabot would figure in other notable happenings in a distinguished 11-season career that took him to Toronto, the Canadiens, Chicago, Montreal Maroons, and the N.Y. Americans for six games in his finale in 1935–36. He was the Maroons' goalie when they lost, 1–0, to Detroit in a record sixth overtime in 1936. It was the longest game in history: 176 minutes, 30 seconds.

Chabot won the Vezina Trophy with Chicago in 1934–35 as the goalie yielding the fewest goals. That was the year he was a first-team All-Star selection. He also made history of sorts when he punched a goal judge in 1932. Result: a one-game suspension.

85. SID ABEL

As a player, coach and general manger, Sid Able stands as a revered figure in Detroit history.

Mike Gartner

Norm Ullman

Prior to and during the early years of World War II, the astute center from Saskatoon established himself as the heart of the Red Wings.

He led Detroit to the Stanley Cup in 1943 and, after the war, he and Ted Lindsay were joined by a promising recruit named Gordie Howe. They became known as the Production Line.

With Abel as the playmaker, they won seven consecutive regular-season titles.

Abel won the Hart Trophy as MVP in 1948–49 and he was a first or second-team All-Star four times. The Production Line was broken up when Abel became player-coach of the Chicago Blackhawks.

During the 1957–58 season, Abel came home to coach Detroit, where he remained on the bench, except for 1968–69, until the end of the 1969–70 season. He also served as GM from 1963–64 until midway in 1970–71.

86. BOB GAINEY

"Le Capitaine." Bob Gainey was one of the best checking forwards and penalty-killers during his 16 years with the Canadiens. He won the Conn Smythe Trophy as MVP in the Stanley Cup playoffs in 1979.

Gainey was a four-time winner of the Frank Selke Trophy awarded to the forward "excelling in the defensive aspects of the game." He played 1,160 games and figured prominently in his team's winning the Stanley Cup five times. He captained Montreal for seven seasons.

The Montreal Star captured Gainey with this description: "He starts from the moment he gathers the puck in the graceful curve of his stick.

Sweeney Schriner

Joe Primeau

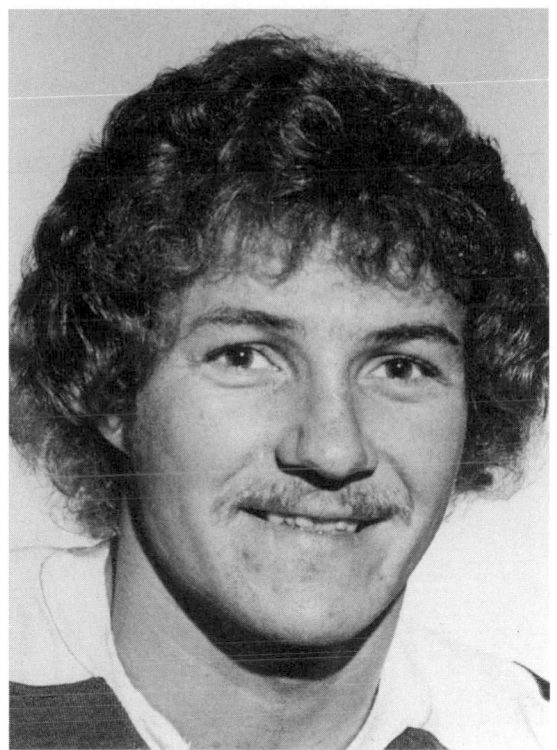

Darryl Sittler

Head up, eyes blazing like hot coals, he gets beyond one man, then another, and by now there is
no longer a crowd in the Montreal Forum, but a
noise engulfing it. This is Bob Gainey."

87. JOHNNY BOWER

He began life in the NHL as a N.Y. Ranger in
1953 when he was 29 years old. But after a rookie season with a 2.60 GAA, playing in all 70
games, Johnny Bower didn't become a force in
the game until he landed with Toronto in 1958.

Bower played for 12 years as a Maple Leaf,
capped by four Stanley Cups, a Vezina Trophy
for yielding fewest goals in 1960–61, and another one he shared with Terry Sawchuk in
1964–65. His career ended after he played in
just one game in 1969–70. As a 45-year-old,
Bower was entitled.

88. SPRAGUE CLEGHORN

There were two Cleghorns—brothers Odie
and Sprague—who played in the NHL and before
that, starting in 1911, with the National Hockey
Association.

Sprague, younger than Odie by a year, makes
the Top 100 because of his scoring feats as a defenseman with the NHA's Wanderers and in the
NHL. Sprague was known for his sensational
end-to-end dashes and for scoring five goals in an
NHA game. He even appeared in one game as a
goaltender. In his 10 years in the NHL, Sprague
played with Ottawa, the Toronto St. Pats, Montreal, and Boston. Brother Odie, a right wing and
center, was with the Canadiens and Pittsburgh Pirates in the NHL.

Joe Sakic

Dominik Hasek

89. MIKE GARTNER

Dangerous from anywhere inside the blue line, Mike Gartner was a sniper with a cannon shot that peppered goalies for 20 years. The relentless right wing retired in 1998 after a career that started with the Cincinnati Stingers in the WHA in 1978–79 when he was runner-up to Edmonton's Wayne Gretzky for Rookie of the Year.

Gartner played for a decade with Washington, followed by Minnesota, New York, Toronto, and Phoenix. His 708 goals made him the fifth-leading scorer in NHL history behind Gretzky, Gordie Howe, Marcel Dionne, and Phil Esposito.

He never won a major trophy and his teams never bagged a title, but Gartner left the game as one of its most treasured performers.

90. NORM ULLMAN

One day, perhaps, someone will break Norm Ullman's record: two goals in five seconds, registered against Chicago in the 1965 playoffs. Outstanding at center, Ullman set the mark with Detroit, where he played from 1961 until 1968 when he was traded to Toronto in a multiplayer deal for four players, including Frank Mahovlich.

Ullman was also known for his forechecking during a 17-year career that wound up with two seasons at Edmonton in the WHA. He was 41 when he retired.

91. SWEENEY SCHRINER

There are a few firsts that mark left winger Dave ("Sweeney") Schriner's 11-year career. First, he was the first Russian-born player to appear in the NHL. He was first in the Rookie of

Babe Pratt

Yvan Cournoyer

the Year (Calder Memorial Trophy) voting in 1934–35 and first in points scored (Art Ross Trophy) in 1935–36 and 1936–37.

The trophies came when Schriner was with the N.Y. Americans, where he played for five years before being traded to Toronto for Ralph ("Busher") Jackson and three others in 1939.

As a Maple Leaf, he twice led his team to the Stanley Cup. Toronto won it in 1942 when he scored two goals in the seventh game against Detroit. The second Cup came in 1945 when Toronto won the seventh game, again against Detroit, on a goal by Babe Pratt.

Schriner played another year before retiring from the NHL. But that didn't keep him from coming back in 1948 for a season with Regina in the Western Canada Senior League.

92. JOE PRIMEAU

He was the quiet center on Toronto's "Kid Line" in the early to mid-'30s. With Busher Jackson and Charlie Conacher, Joe Primeau had the passing touch that enabled the Maple Leafs to capture the Stanley Cup over the N.Y. Rangers in 1932.

Primeau, who broke in full-time with Toronto in the 1929–30 season, was twice runner-up in NHL scoring—once to Jackson and once to Conacher. He surprised everyone when he abruptly retired at the age of 30 after only seven full seasons and went into the concrete business. But he did come back—as coach of Toronto's Stanley Cup winner in 1951.

93. DARRYL SITTLER

It is safe to say that Darryl Sittler had a unique season in 1975–76. In one game the

Jack Stewart

Bill Gadsby

Frank Nighbor

Toronto center collected 10 points against Boston and in another, in the playoffs, he scored five goals against Philadelphia.

Those are highlights of a 15-year career over 11 seasons with the Maple Leafs, the balance with Philadelphia and Detroit. Sittler posted highs of 117 points in 1977–78 and 100 in 1975–76, and owns all sorts of Toronto records. But his team never won Lord Stanley's Cup.

94. JOE SAKIC

Four times he had been over the 100-point mark and he set an NHL record for most game-winning goals (6) in the 1996 playoffs. Center Joe Sakic drove the Colorado Avalanche to the Stanley Cup in 1996, the year he won the Conn Smythe Trophy as playoffs MVP.

Sakic has been an annual All-Star Game selection since 1990 when the team played in Quebec as the Nordiques. His 120 points in the championship season are his high mark in 11 seasons. He understandably has a fan following in Barnaby, British Columbia, where he was born.

95. DOMINIK HASEK

Despite all of his awards, Buffalo goaltender Dominik Hasek hasn't been able to drink from the most treasured of all, the Stanley Cup. He and his teammates lost their chance when the Dallas Stars won it in 1998–99, so Hasek will have to live on his many laurels.

They include the Hart Memorial Trophy (2) as overall MVP and the Vezina Trophy (4) as goalie MVP. He was the first goalie to win the Hart since Montreal's Jacques Plante in 1962.

That says nothing of Hasek's many other achievements, including the Czech Republic's gold-medal victory in the 1998 Winter Olympics. Hasek was Goalie of the Year five times and Player of the Year three times in Czechoslovakia before coming to play in America.

He didn't make it in Chicago, which traded him to the Sabres before the 1992–93 season, but since then he has found a home, if not a championship, in Buffalo.

96. BABE PRATT

Big and brawny, Babe Pratt came out of Stony Mountain, Manitoba, to launch a rewarding 12-year NHL career in 1936, first with the N.Y. Rangers and then with Toronto.

He was a vital Ranger when the team won the Stanley Cup in 1940. With Toronto he couldn't have been more valuable, winning the Hart Memorial Trophy in 1944 and playing a key role in the Maple Leafs' Stanley Cup triumph in 1945. It was Pratt's goal that beat Detroit, 2–1, in the seventh game of the 1945 playoffs.

"If he'd looked after himself, he could have played until he was 50," wrote Conn Smythe in his memoir, *If You Can't Beat 'Em in the Alley.* "But he was as big a drinker and a playboy as he was a hockey player."

97. JACK STEWART

He was fearless and feared, and it was King Clancy who noted, "He wasn't dirty but he was the roughest sonofagun you'd ever want to meet."

Black Jack Stewart wasn't that big (5-foot-11, 185) but he was, as Milt Dunnell of the *Toronto Star* recalled, "Tougher than a pine knot. Dour, dedicated, and full of pride. He was fast for a defenseman."

Stewart figured in two Stanley Cup championships, 1943 and 1950. He played for the Red Wings from 1938–39 through 1949–50. He finished his career with two seasons in Chicago. They

didn't give awards to defenseman in those days. If they had, Black Jack would have been a winner.

98. YVAN COURNOYER

One of the most explosive players in history, Yvan Cournoyer had a dashing skating style that featured his 16 seasons in the NHL, all with Montreal. The 5-foot-7, 168-pound right wing figured in 10 Stanley Cup triumphs, copping the Conn Smythe Trophy as MVP in 1973. It was Cournoyer's goal against Chicago in the sixth game that clinched the Cup and set an NHL playoff mark of 15 goals.

As a little man he took a pounding but he never surrendered. To build strength he did muscle-building exercises to enable him to bounce off checks. Cournoyer was nicknamed the "Roadrunner" for his quickness and speed. It all came to an end in 1979 when he was felled by a back injury.

99. BILL GADSBY

He survived the rigors of hockey for 20 years, but Bill Gadsby had been a survivor long before he took the ice with the Chicago Blackhawks in 1946.

As a 12-year-old, Gadsby, accompanied by his mother, was on the *Athenia* when it was torpedoed by Germany on the day World War II began in 1939. On their way home from London to Calgary, the Gadsbys were rescued after five hours in the Atlantic.

Seven years later, in 1946, Gadsby was in a Blackhawk uniform for the start of a 20-year career as a rushing defenseman and playmaker. He played for Chicago for six years before being traded to New York, where he made the All-Star first team three times.

It was with the Rangers in 1958–59 that he registered an NHL mark for assists by a defenseman—46. He finished his career with five seasons as a Detroit Red Wing.

100. FRANK NIGHBOR

"Skating backward and waving his stick in wand-like fashion, Frank Nighbor was ready to deliver his devastating poke check," wrote Charles Coleman in *The Trail of the Stanley Cup*.

That was the picture of Nighbor in action with the Ottawa Senators during an NHL career (after the NHA) in which he was saluted for his all-around skills. Nighbor was a center and left wing who could play offense and defense.

Nicknamed "Dutch," he was the first winner in 1923–24 of the Hart Memorial Trophy as Most Valuable Player. He led Ottawa to the Stanley Cup four times. Twice in the NHL he registered five-goal games and he had six-goal games in the NHA and the PCHA.

9

THE
STANLEY CUP

Lord Stanley, the Canadian Governor-General who donated the Stanley Cup in 1893, ironically never saw a Cup game.

One of his aides, Lord Kilcoursie, had more than a passing role in Lord Stanley's decision to initiate the Cup. Lord Kilcoursie played hockey with Lord Stanley's sons and his deep interest in the sport had spread to his boss.

Lord Stanley's guidelines for presenting the Cup were simple enough. It was to go to the leading hockey club in Canada.

In 1893, the first Cup went to the Montreal Amateur Athletic Association team, champion of the Amateur Hockey Association of Canada. There was no playoff; Montreal AAA had simply won the most games in the regular season.

In 1894, Montreal AAA defeated the Montreal Victorias, 3-2, and then the Ottawa Generals, 3-1, in a one-game final of the first-ever playoffs to capture the Cup. But Lord Stanley was gone. He had returned to his native England.

He designated two Ottawa sportsmen—Sheriff Sweetland and P.D. Ross—as trustees of the Cup, and they sifted through the various challenges from leagues all over Canada that wanted their chance to play for the trophy.

In those early days, hockey was an amateur sport played by seven-man teams on outdoor rinks built for curling. Two portable poles, embedded in the ice with no net between them, constituted the goals, and goal judges stood behind these makeshift targets with no padding to protect them. Conditions were truly primitive and it was an appropriate setting for the most fantastic Cup challenge in history—that of Dawson City in 1905.

The Ottawa Silver Seven were the Cup holders from 1903 through 1906, successfully defending it against nine challenges from all parts of Canada. But none of the challengers could match the 1905 Yukon team's effort.

Colonel Joe Boyle, a wealthy Dawson City prospector, bankrolled the team's 23-day journey to Ottawa. The happy-go-lucky gold diggers traveled by dog sled, boat and train to cover the 4,400 miles. They made 46 miles by dogs the first day and 41 the second. Some of the players were forced to remove their boots because of blistered feet on the third day, with the temperature dropping to 20 below zero.

They missed a boat connection at Skagway by two hours and had to wait five days at the docks before catching another boat from Seattle to Vancouver. Then they took a train on to Ottawa. They arrived in Ottawa, January 12, 1905, a day before the best-of-three series against the Silver Seven was to begin.

It was all for naught. The team that traveled the farthest to try for the Cup suffered the most lopsided elimination. The Klondikers lost the first game, 9-2, and the second and final game, 23-3. Frank McGee of Ottawa scored an unbelievable 14 goals in the second-game rout—eight of them in a span of eight minutes, twenty seconds. What makes it truly unbelievable is that McGee was blind in one eye.

The year before the Klondike challenge, Ottawa had beaten off the Brandon Wheat Kings

and the only notable thing about that challenge was the fact that Brandon goalie Doug Morrison incurred a penalty and was replaced in the nets by a teammate, Lester Patrick. A quarter of a century later, Patrick, then 44 and coach of the New York Rangers, would duplicate the feat and take over in goal during another Stanley Cup game.

The prestige of fielding a winning hockey team—possibly a Stanley Cup winner—was quite tantalizing to Canadian communities and the better players found themselves being offered fat contracts. Hockey's amateur posture was disappearing, and soon the Stanley Cup's would, too.

By 1907 the Eastern Canadian Amateur Hockey Association had deleted the "Amateur" from its name. And in 1910 when the National Hockey Association—forerunner of the National Hockey

The Montreal Shamrocks won their first Stanley Cup in 1899.

League—came into existence, the Stanley Cup became the goal of professional hockey teams.

When Lester Patrick and his brother Frank moved westward to organize the Pacific Coast Hockey League in 1913, a Stanley Cup series matching East and West was inaugurated. After the PCHL went out of business in 1927, the trophy became exclusively an NHL award.

Although there were no American teams in the NHL until 1924, it was seven years earlier that a U.S. team first captured the cherished Cup. In 1917, the Seattle Metropolitans, coached by Pete Muldoon, beat the Montreal Canadiens in the Cup series and transported the Cup below the border for the first time.

Through the years, the Cup has had varied adventures. It has been the most sought and at the same time most neglected trophy in sport.

Shortly after the turn of the century, following one of the Ottawa Silver Seven's several successful defenses, some members of the team were lugging the trophy back from a victory banquet. For kicks no doubt, it was suggested by one of the players that he could successfully boot the mug into Rideau Canal. And just to prove his point, he did.

The next day, when they realized what they had done, the Ottawa players rushed back to Rideau. Luckily the canal had been frozen over, and there, slightly the worse for wear but still intact, sat the Stanley Cup.

Shortly after that, the Cup did a brief turn as a flower pot. That happened when the Montreal team gathered around the silver mug for a picture in a local photographer's studio. When the posing was over, the players left the studio, and the Cup as well.

The photographer's mother found the deserted silverware and, not knowing its significance, filled it with earth and planted geraniums. Eventually, the photographer discovered it and rescued Lord Stanley's Cup.

Ottawa right wing Jack Darragh played on four Stanley Cup championship teams, the first in 1911.

Goalie Paddy Moran helped the Quebec Bulldogs win back-to-back Cups in 1912 and 1913.

In 1924, the Montreal Canadiens were celebrating their Cup victory at a downtown hotel when it was suggested that the celebration be moved to owner Leo Dandurand's home. A group of players, the Cup in tow, started out driving for Dandurand's home when a tire blew out. In the course of changing the tire, the Cup somehow was removed from the car and placed on the sidewalk. When the repairs were completed, the celebrants took off for Dandurand's again.

It wasn't until the Canadiens reached their destination that they missed the Cup. They scurried back to the spot and, sure enough, sitting there undisturbed, waiting for them, was the Cup.

Another time, an official of the Kenora Thistles stormed out of a meeting of hockey executives with the Cup under his arm. Angered over the refusal of his colleagues to authorize the use of two borrowed players during a Cup series, he was prepared to act drastically.

"Where are you going with the Cup?" he was asked. He replied quite simply: "I'm going to throw it in the Lake of Woods."

There are those who swear he would have, too, had compromise not been reached on the use of the two disputed players.

Once, during the Ottawa Silver Seven's Cup reign, one member of the team decided to cap off a celebration by taking the mug home with him to show to his mother. The idea wasn't terribly popular with his teammates and in the ensuing scuffle, the Cup was tossed over a cemetery fence.

In 1962, the Cup was on display in the lobby of the Chicago Stadium while the Blackhawks and Montreal Canadiens battled for it on the ice inside the arena. When Chicago took a commanding edge in the game, a Montreal fan left his seat. He went to the lobby, broke into the showcase, lifted out the Cup and was on his way out the door before he was stopped. He, too, had a simple explanation.

"I was taking it back to Montreal, where it belongs," he said.

Stanley Cup play is hockey's World Series. Through the years it has been packed with indi-

vidual and team heroics that live on and even tend to expand as the years go by. The stories include some of hockey's most cherished lore.

• **1919**—The only time no decision was reached. The Montreal Canadiens had traveled west to play Seattle for the Cup and the teams split the first five games (one tie). But the great flu epidemic had riddled the ranks of the Montreal team, leaving five players bedridden. The series was halted because of the wave of illness and no Cup champion was declared. Joe Hall, one of the Canadiens' stars, never recovered and died in a Seattle hospital.

• **1922**—When Lester Patrick, boss of the Vancouver team, allowed crippled Toronto to use defenseman Eddie Gerard as an emergency replacement. Gerard starred in two straight Toronto victories that cost Vancouver the Cup. Six years later, Patrick, the New York Ranger coach, went to Gerard, then general manager of the Montreal Maroons, and asked permission to use a borrowed goaltender when regular Lorne Chabot was injured. Gerard refused and Patrick, at age 44, went in to play goal, won the game and the inspired Rangers went on to take the Cup.

• **1936**—When the longest game in hockey history was played. Modere Bruneteau, a rookie who had scored only two goals during the regular season for Detroit, broke the scoreless tie against the Montreal Maroons with the only goal of the night at 16:30 of the sixth overtime period, ending 176 minutes, 30 seconds of scoreless hockey.

• **1939**—When Mel (Sudden Death) Hill of Boston personally slew the Rangers. Hill, a Ranger reject, scored the winning overtime goal in three of the Bruins' four victories over New York that year.

• **1942**—When the Detroit Red Wings beat Toronto in the first three games and with their mouths watering for a taste of Stanley Cup champagne, went into an incredible collapse, losing four straight, the series and the Cup.

• **1951**—When Toronto beat Montreal in five games, all of them going into overtime. The win-

Russell (Barney) Stanley wears a Calgary Tigers' uniform here, but in 1915 he played for the Cup-winning Vancouver Millionaires.

ning goal in the final game was scored by defenseman Bill Barilko, who was in midair when his shot went in. It was the last goal he ever scored. A few months later, Barilko died in a plane wreck.

• **1952**—When Detroit swept through to the Stanley Cup in eight straight games and goalie Terry Sawchuk allowed a total of just five goals for an astounding 0.62 Stanley Cup average. Sawchuk's feat overshadowed Montreal's Maurice Richard, who emerged from a first-aid room with six stitches holding his forehead together to score the Canadiens' winning goal against Boston in the semifinals.

• **1964**—When Toronto defenseman Bob Baun was carried off the ice on a stretcher during the sixth game against Detroit when his right leg crumpled under him. Baun demanded that the doctors pump some pain-killer into the leg and he skated out to score the winning, sudden-death goal. Only after the Leafs took game No. 7 and the Cup, did the defenseman consent to have X-rays taken. That's when they found a broken bone in his ankle.

• **1980**—When the Islanders' Bob Nystrom scored in overtime of the sixth game to defeat Philadelphia and bring the New York area its first Stanley Cup in four decades. The Islanders won six of seven overtime games in the march to their first Cup.

• **1981**—When Butch Goring, who scored five goals in the finals, three in one game, to become playoff MVP, and record-setting Mike

The strong defense of Red Kelly (left) enabled Detroit to defeat Montreal for the Cup in 1954.

Gump Worsley in goal and Jacques Laperriere on defense were major factors as Montreal swept Boston in a preliminary round of the playoffs in 1968. Phil Esposito (7) and Ted Green (right) are the Bruins.

Bossy wrapped up the Islanders' second straight Cup in a five-game series against Minnesota.

• **1982**—When Mike Bossy scored 17 goals in the playoffs, seven in a four-game finals wipe-

out of Vancouver, to make it three Cups in a row for the Islanders.

• **1983**—When Islander goalie Billy Smith, who hadn't won a game for two months in the reg-

Henri Richard grasps hockey's Holy Grail after Montreal downed Chicago in the 1973 finals.

ular season, caught fire in the playoffs. He limited the Oilers to six goals in the finals as the Islanders swept the series for their fourth straight Cup.

• **1984**—When Edmonton, led by Wayne Gretzky and Mark Messier, and in only its fifth NHL season, captured the Cup for the first time, breaking the Islanders' string of four.

• **1985**—When Wayne Gretzky won his first Conn Smythe Trophy as playoff MVP as Edmonton downed Philadelphia for its second straight Stanley Cup.

• **1986**—When Montreal won its first Cup since 1979, defeating Calgary in five games. Mats Naslund topped the Canadiens in playoff scoring and 20-year-old goaltender Patrick Roy, became the youngest winner of the Conn Smythe Trophy as playoff MVP.

• **1987**—When the Islanders' Pat LaFontaine scored the game-winning goal in the fourth overtime of Game 7 of the Patrick Division semifinal against Washington. But it was Edmonton that emerged as the Cup-holder over Philadelphia in seven games.

• **1988**—When the lights went out in Boston Garden and Game 4 against Edmonton had to be suspended with the score 3-3. The lights shone brightly for the Oilers when the series went back to Edmonton, where Wayne Gretzky led the way to a sweep of the Bruins.

• **1989**—When Calgary, paced by goaltender Mike Vernon and defenseman Al MacInnis, captured its first Cup, vanquishing Montreal in six games.

• **1990**—When ex-Bruin goaltender Bill Ranford got his chance with Edmonton in the playoffs and wound up as the MVP after stopping his old Boston team in the finals.

• **1991**—When Mario Lemieux capped a spectacular comeback from injury by leading Pittsburgh to its first Cup. Vanquishing Minnesota in the finals, the Penguins did it all after losing the first game of every playoff series.

• **1992**—When the Penguins, with Mario Lemieux, who came back after breaking his hand in the Patrick Division finals, and Jaromir Jagr leading the way, swept the Blackhawks to win their second Cup in a row.

• **1993**—When the Montreal Canadiens overcame a 2-games-to-0 deficit against Quebec in the first round, then won 16 of 20 games to capture their 24th Cup, 23rd as a member of the NHL. Patrick Roy won his second Conn Smythe Trophy after holding foes to 2.13 goals per game in the playoffs.

• **1994**—When the New York Rangers ended 54 years of frustration by beating the Vancouver Canucks in Game 7 of the Cup finals. Brian Leetch and Mark Messier provided the firepower and Mike Richter was solid in goal as the Rangers outlasted the Canucks for their first Cup since 1940.

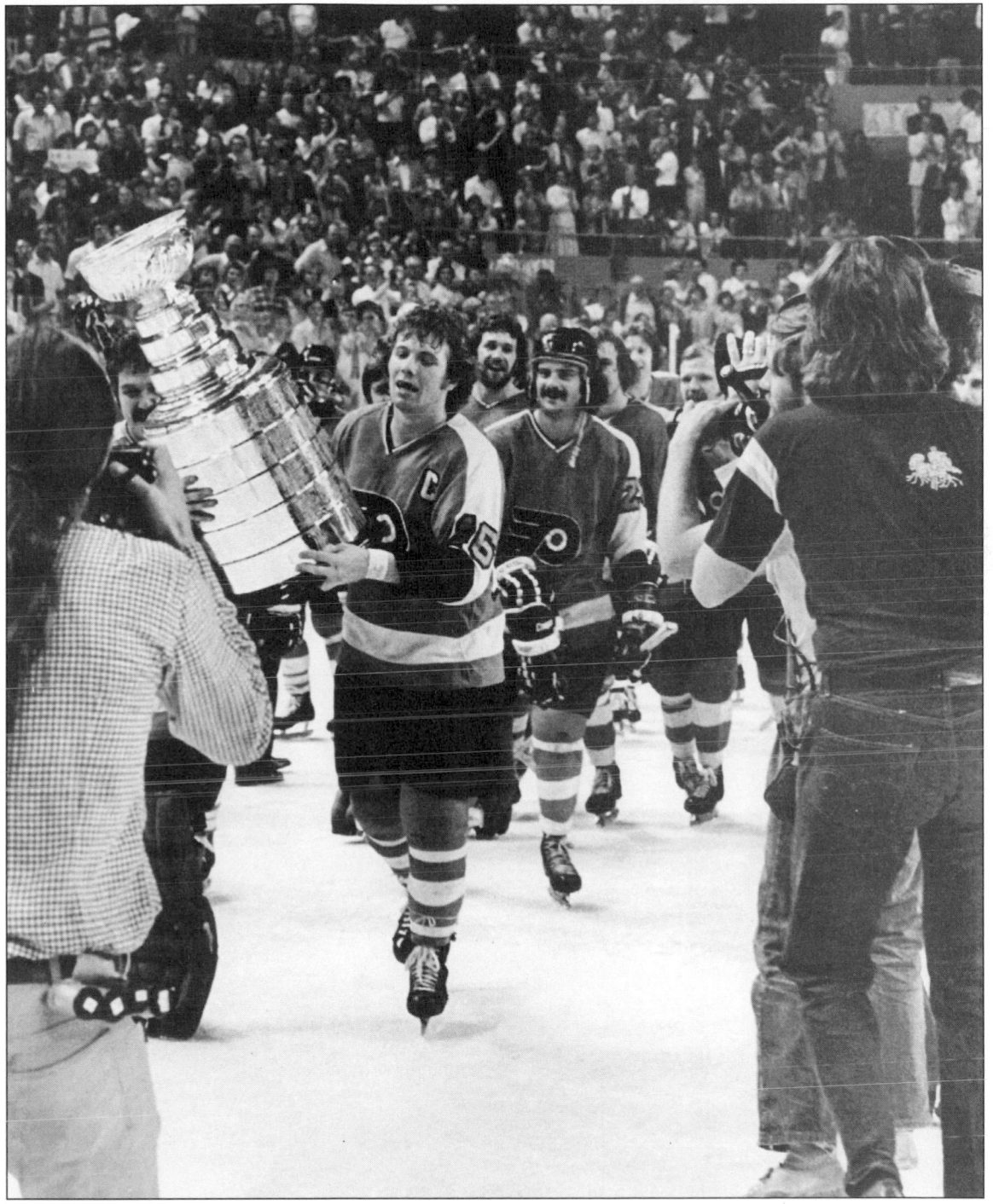

Captain Bobby Clarke leads triumphant Flyers after Philadelphia ousted Buffalo for the Cup in 1975.

• **1995**—When the New Jersey Devils, led by playoff MVP Claude Lemieux and a stifling defense, swept the Detroit Red Wings in four games to win their first Cup.

• **1996**—When the Colorado Avalanche, playing their first season in Denver, swept the Florida Panthers to win their first Cup.

• **1997**—When the Detroit Red Wings, captained by 14-year veteran Steve Yzerman, celebrated their first championship since 1955, sweeping the Philadelphia Flyers in four games, capped by a 2-1 finale.

• **1998**—When Scotty Bowman won a record-tying eighth championship as a coach as the Detroit Red Wings swept the Washington Capitals in four games. Steve Yzerman took the Smythe Trophy as MVP of the playoffs.

• **1999**—When the Dallas Stars defeated the Buffalo Sabres for their first Stanley Cup on a controversial goal by Brett Hull (replays show a possible crease violation) at 14:51 of the third overtime period in the sixth game.

STANLEY CUP PLAYOFF RECORDS

Team

Most Stanley Cup championships—24, Montreal Canadiens.

It's all over: Bobby Nystrom has just beaten Philadelphia goalie Pete Peeters with the overtime goal that brought the New York Islanders their first Stanley Cup in 1980.

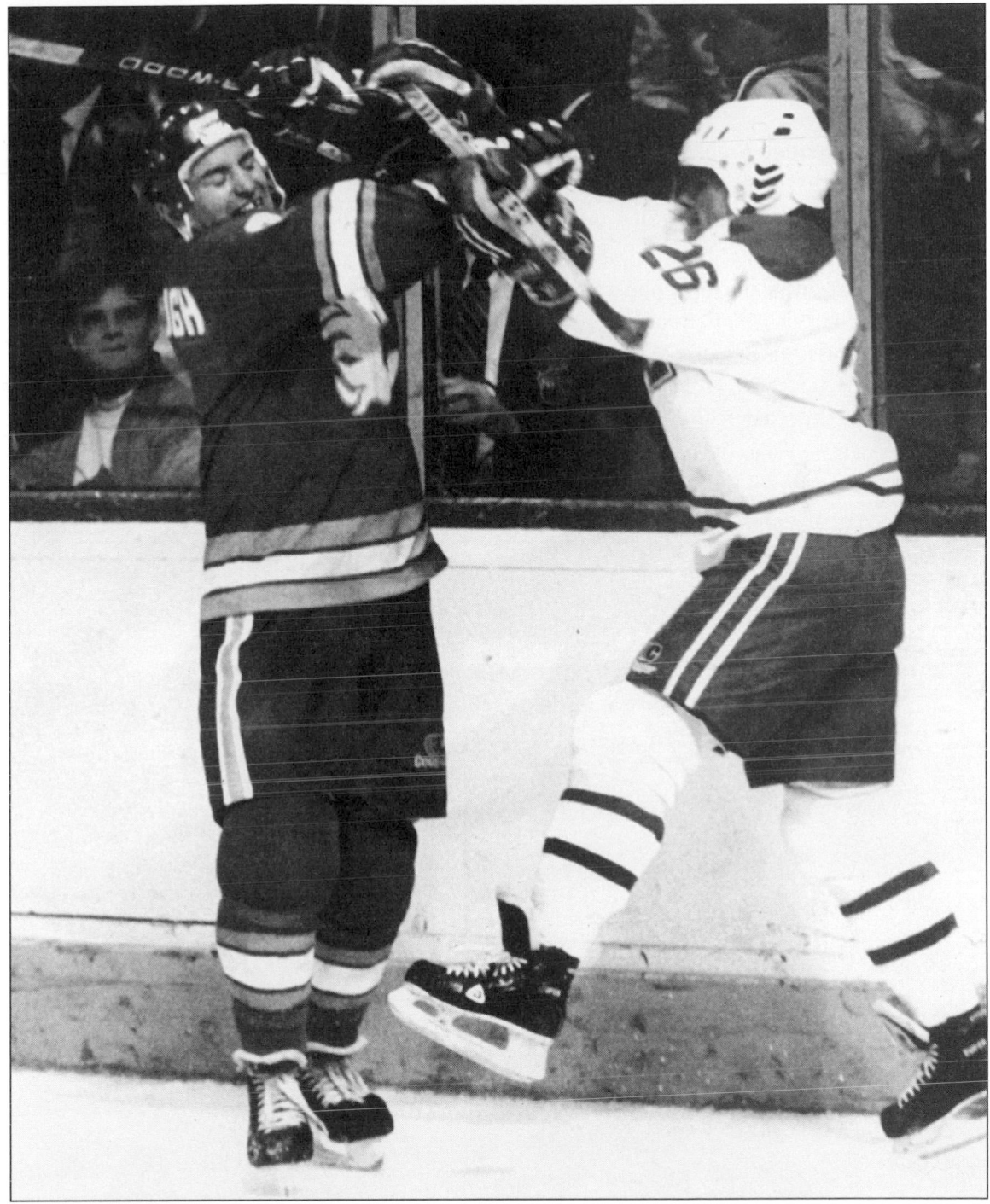

It's no-holds-barred for Calgary's Doug Risebrough (left) and Montreal's Mats Naslund in the 1986 finals. The Canadiens settled things by winning four in a row after losing the first game.

Most final series appearances—34, Montreal Canadiens.

Most years in playoffs—71, Montreal Canadiens.

Most consecutive Stanley Cup championships—5, Montreal Canadiens (1956-60).

Most consecutive final series appearances—10, Montreal (1951-60).

Most consecutive playoff appearances—29, Boston (1968-96).

Most goals, both teams, one series—69, Edmonton 44, Chicago 25, six games, 1985 conference finals.

Most goals, one team, one series—44, Edmonton, vs. Chicago, 1985.

Most goals, both teams, four-game series—36, three times, most recently Edmonton 25, Chicago 11, conference final, 1983.

Most goals, one team, four-game series—28, Boston, vs. St. Louis, semifinal, 1972.

Most goals, both teams, five-game series—52, Edmonton 32, Los Angeles 20, 1987 division semifinal.

Most goals, one team, five-game series—35, Edmonton, vs. Calgary, 1983 division final.

Most goals, both teams, six-game series—69, Edmonton 44, Chicago 25, 1985 conference final.

Most goals, one team, six-game series—44, Edmonton, vs. Chicago, 1985 conference final.

Bill Ranford's saves earned him MVP honors as Edmonton vanquished Boston for the Cup in 1990.

Most goals, both teams, seven-game series—61, Calgary 35, San Jose 26, 1995 conference quarterfinal.

Most goals, one team, seven-game series—35, Calgary, vs. San Jose, 1995 conference quarterfinal.

Fewest goals, both teams, four-game series—9, Toronto 7, Boston 2, 1935 semifinal.

Fewest goals, one team, four-game series—2, Boston, vs. Toronto, 1935 semifinal; Montreal, vs. Detroit, 1952 final.

Fewest goals, both teams, five-game series—11, Montreal Maroons 6, New York Rangers 5, 1928 final.

Fewest goals, one team, five-game series—5, New York Rangers, vs. Montreal Maroons, 1928 final; Edmonton Oilers, vs. Dallas Stars, 1998 conference semifinals.

Fewest goals, both teams, six-game series—22, Toronto 17, Boston 5, 1951 semifinal; Dallas 13, Buffalo 9, 1999 final.

Fewest goals, one team, six-game series—5, Boston, vs. Toronto, 1951 semifinal.

Fewest goals, both teams, seven-game series—18, Toronto 9, Detroit 9, 1945 final.

Fewest goals, one team, seven-game series—9, Toronto, vs. Detroit, 1945 final; Detroit, vs. Toronto, 1945 Stanley Cup final.

The Ranger faithful celebrated a long-sought return of the Cup in 1994.

Captain Scott Stevens and his teammates had a Devil of a finish in bringing the Cup to New Jersey for the first time in 1995.

Most goals, both teams, one game—18, Los Angeles 10, Edmonton 8, 1982 division semifinal.

Most goals, one team, one game—13, Edmonton, vs. Los Angeles (3), April 9, 1987.

Most goals, both teams, one period—9, New York Rangers 6, Philadelphia 3, third period, April 24, 1979; Los Angeles 5, Calgary 4, second period, April 10, 1990.

Most goals, one team, one period—7, Montreal Canadiens, vs. Toronto, third period, March 30, 1944, in 11-0 win.

Longest overtime—116 minutes, 30 seconds, Detroit vs. Montreal Maroons at Montreal, March 24-25, 1936. Mud Bruneteau scored at 16:30 of sixth overtime period.

Shortest overtime—9 seconds, Montreal at Calgary, May 18, 1986. Montreal's Brian Skrudland scored to give Canadiens 3-2 win.

Most overtime games, one season—28, 1993 (85 games played).

Fewest overtime games, one season—0, 1963 (16 games played).

Most overtime-game wins, one team, one playoff season—10, Montreal Canadiens, 1993.

Most overtime games, final series—5, Toronto vs. Montreal, 1951.

Most overtime games, semifinal series—4, three times, most recently, St. Louis vs. Minnesota, 1968.

Most consecutive playoff game wins—14, Pittsburgh (May 9, 1992 to April 25, 1993).

Most consecutive wins, one playoff year—11, Chicago and Pittsburgh, 1992; Montreal, 1993.

Longest playoff losing streak—16 games, Chicago, 1975-80.

Most shutouts, one playoff year, all teams—16, 1994.

Fewest shutouts, one playoff year, all teams—0, 1959 (18 games played).

Most shutouts, both teams, one series—5, Toronto 3, Detroit 2, 1945 final; Toronto 3, Detroit 2, 1950 semifinal.

Most penalties, both teams, one series—219, New Jersey 119 vs. Washington 110, 1988 division final, seven games.

Most penalty minutes, both teams, one series—656, New Jersey 351 vs. Washington 305, 1988 division final, seven games.

Most penalties, one team, one series—119, New Jersey, vs. Washington, 1988 division final.

Most penalty minutes, one team, one series—351, New Jersey, vs. Washington, 1988 division final.

Most penalty minutes, both teams, one game—298, Detroit 152, St. Louis 146, at St. Louis, April 12, 1991.

Most penalties, both teams, one game—66, Detroit 33, St. Louis 33, at St. Louis, April 12, 1991.

Most penalties, one team, one game—33, Detroit and St. Louis, at St. Louis, April 12, 1991.

Most penalty minutes, one team, one game—152, Detroit, at St. Louis, April 12, 1991.

Most penalties, both teams, one period—43, New York Rangers 24, Los Angeles 19, at Los Angeles, first period, April 9, 1981.

Most penalty minutes, both teams, one period—248, New York Islanders 124, Boston 124, at Boston, first period, April 17, 1980.

Most penalties and most penalty minutes, one team, one period—24 penalties, 125 minutes, New York Rangers, at Los Angeles, first period, April 9, 1981.

Most power-play goals, one team, one playoff year—35, Minnesota, 1991.

Most power-play goals, both teams, one playoff series—21, four times, most recently Minnesota 15, Chicago 6, 1991 division semifinal.

Most power-play goals, one team, one series—15, New York Islanders, vs. Philadelphia, 1980 final; Minnesota, vs. Chicago, 1991 division semifinal.

Most power-play goals, one team, one game—6, Boston, vs. Toronto, in 10-0 win April 2, 1969.

Most power-play goals, both teams, one game—8, Minnesota 4, St. Louis 4, at Minnesota, April 24, 1991.

Fastest two goals, both teams—5 seconds, Pittsburgh at Buffalo, first period, April 14, 1979. Gil Perreault scored for Buffalo at 12:59 and Jim Hamilton for Pittsburgh at 13:04.

The goaltending of Colorado's Patrick Roy enabled the Avalanche to achieve the cherished Cup in 1996.

Fastest two goals, one team—5 seconds, Detroit, vs. Chicago, second period, April 11, 1965. Norm Ullman scored at 17:35 and 17:40.

Fastest three goals, both teams—21 seconds, Chicago at Edmonton, third period, May 7, 1985. Chicago's Behn Wilson scored at 19:22, Edmonton's Jari Kurri scored at 19:36 and Edmonton's Glenn Anderson scored at 19:43.

Fastest three goals, one team—23 seconds, Toronto, vs. Atlanta, first period, April 12, 1979. Darryl Sittler scored at 4:04 and again at 4:16 and then Ron Ellis scored at 4:27.

Fastest four goals, one team—2 minutes, 35 seconds, Montreal, vs. Toronto, third period, March 30, 1944. Toe Blake scored at 7:58 and 8:37, Maurice Richard at 9:17 and Ray Getliffe at 10:33 in 11-0 win.

Detroit captain Steve Yzerman holds the Cup high in 1997 after the Red Wings swept the Flyers to end a 41-year dry spell.

Fastest five goals, one team—3 minutes, 36 seconds, Montreal, vs. Toronto, third period, March 30, 1944. Toe Blake scored at 7:58 and 8:37, Maurice Richard at 9:17, Ray Getliffe at 10:33 and Buddy O'Connor at 11:34 in 11-0 win.

Most shorthanded goals, one team, one playoff year—10, Edmonton, 1983 (16 games).

Most shorthanded goals, one team, one series—6, Calgary, vs. San Jose, 1995 conference quarterfinal; Vancouver, vs. St. Louis, 1995 conference quarterfinal.

Most shorthanded goals, one team, one game—3, Boston, at Minnesota, April 11, 1981; New York Islanders, at New York Rangers, April 17, 1983; Toronto, at San Jose, May 8, 1994.

Most shorthanded goals, one team, one period—2, 22 times, most recently Vancouver, at St. Louis, second period, May 15, 1995.

Individual

Most years in playoffs—20, Gordie Howe, Detroit and Hartford; Larry Robinson, Montreal and Los Angeles.

Most consecutive years in playoffs—20, Larry Robinson, Montreal and Los Angeles, 1973-92.

Most playoff games—236, Mark Messier, Edmonton and New York Rangers.

Most points in playoffs—382, Wayne Gretzky, Edmonton, Los Angeles, St. Louis and New York Rangers.

Most goals in playoffs—122, Wayne Gretzky, Edmonton, Los Angeles, St. Louis and New York Rangers.

Most assists in playoffs—260, Wayne Gretzky, Edmonton, Los Angeles, St. Louis and New York Rangers.

Most overtime goals in playoffs—6, Maurice Richard, Montreal.

Most penalty minutes in playoffs—699, Dale Hunter, Quebec, Washington, and Colorado.

Most shorthanded goals in playoffs—14, Mark Messier, Edmonton and New York Rangers.

Most power-play goals in playoffs—35, Mike Bossy, New York Islanders.

Most shutouts in playoffs—15, Clint Benedict, Ottawa and Montreal Maroons.

Most playoff games, goaltender—179, Patrick Roy, Montreal and Colorado.

Most points, one playoff year—47, Wayne Gretzky, Edmonton, 1985.

Most goals, one playoff year—19, Reggie Leach, Philadelphia, 1976; Jari Kurri, Edmonton, 1985.

Most assists, one playoff year—31, Wayne Gretzky, Edmonton, 1988.

Most points by a defenseman, one playoff year—37, Paul Coffey, Edmonton, 1985.

Most points by a rookie, one playoff year—21, Dino Ciccarelli, Minnesota, 1981.

Most goals by a defenseman, one playoff year—12, Paul Coffey, Edmonton, 1985.

Most goals by a rookie, one playoff year—14, Dino Ciccarelli, Minnesota, 1981.

Most power-play goals, one playoff year—9, Mike Bossy, New York Islanders, 1981; Cam Neely, Boston, 1991.

Most shorthanded goals, one playoff year—3, five times, most recently Wayne Presley, Chicago, 1989.

Most assists by a defenseman, one playoff year—25, Paul Coffey, Edmonton, 1985.

Most wins by a goaltender, one playoff year—16, Grant Fuhr, Edmonton, 1988; Mike Vernon, Calgary, 1989; Bill Ranford, Edmonton, 1990; Tom Barrasso, Pittsburgh, 1992; Patrick Roy, Montreal, 1993; Mike Richter, New York Rangers, 1994; Martin Brodeur, New Jersey, 1995; Patrick Roy, Colorado, 1996; Mike Vernon, Detroit, 1997; Chris Osgood, Detroit, 1998; Ed Belfour, Dallas, 1999.

Most shutouts, one playoff year—4, nine times, most recently, Mike Richter, New York Rangers and Kirk McLean, Vancouver, 1994.

Most consecutive shutouts—3, Clint Benedict, Montreal Maroons, 1926; John Roach, New York Rangers, 1929; Frank McCool, Toronto, 1945.

Most points in final series—13, Wayne Gretzky, Edmonton, vs. Boston, 1988.

Most goals in final series—9, Babe Dye, Toronto, vs. Vancouver, 1922.

Most assists in final series—10, Wayne Gretzky, Edmonton, vs. Boston, 1988.

Most points, one game—8, Patrik Sundstrom, New Jersey, vs. Washington, April 22, 1988 (three goals, five assists); Mario Lemieux, Pittsburgh vs. Philadelphia, April 25, 1989 (five goals, three assists).

Most goals, one game—5, Newsy Lalonde, Montreal, vs. Ottawa, March 1, 1919; Maurice Richard, Montreal, vs. Toronto, March 23, 1944; Darryl Sittler, Toronto, vs. Philadelphia, April 22, 1976; Reggie Leach, Philadelphia, vs. Boston, May 6, 1976; Mario Lemieux, Pittsburgh, vs. Philadelphia, April 25, 1989.

Most assists, one game—6, Mikko Leinonen, New York Rangers, vs. Philadelphia, April 8, 1982; Wayne Gretzky, Edmonton, vs. Los Angeles, April 9, 1987.

Most points by a defenseman, one game—6, Paul Coffey, Edmonton, vs. Chicago, May 14, 1985 (one goal, five assists).

Most penalty minutes, one game—42, Dave Schultz, Philadelphia, at Toronto, April 22, 1976.

Most points, one period—4, 11 times, most recently, Mario Lemieux, Pittsburgh vs. Washington, second period, April 23, 1992.

Most goals, one period—4, Tim Kerr, Philadelphia, at New York Rangers, second period, April 13, 1985; Mario Lemieux, Pittsburgh, vs. Philadelphia, first period, April 25, 1989.

Most assists, one period—3, 62 times, most recently, Vyacheslav Kozlov, Detroit, vs. San Jose, third period, May 21, 1995.

Fastest two goals—5 seconds, Norm Ullman, Detroit, vs. Chicago, April 11, 1965.

Fastest goal from start of game—6 seconds, Don Kozak, Los Angeles, vs. Boston, April 17, 1977.

Fastest goal from start of period—6 seconds, Don Kozak, Los Angeles, vs. Boston, April 17, 1977; Pelle Eklund, Philadelphia, at Pittsburgh, April 25, 1989.

Most three-goal-or-more games—10, Wayne Gretzky, Edmonton, Los Angeles, St. Louis and New York Rangers.

Most three-goal-or-more games, one play-off year—4, Jari Kurri, Edmonton, 1985.

Most three-goal-or-more games, one play-off series—3, Jari Kurri, Edmonton, vs. Chicago, 1985 conference final.

STANLEY CUP WINNERS

YEAR	TEAM	MANAGER	COACH
1892–93	Montreal A.A.A.	—	—
1894–95	Montreal Victorias	—	Mike Grant*
1895–96	Winnipeg Victorias	—	—
1896–97	Montreal Victorias	—	Mike Grant*
1897–98	Montreal Victorias	—	F. Richardson
1898–99	Montreal Shamrocks	—	H. J. Trihey*
1899–1900	Montreal Shamrocks	—	H. J. Trihey*
1900–01	Winnipeg Victorias	—	—
1901–02	Montreal A.A.A.	—	R. R. Boon*
1902–03	Ottawa Silver Seven	—	A. T. Smith
1903–04	Ottawa Silver Seven	—	A. T. Smith
1904–05	Ottawa Silver Seven	—	A. T. Smith
1905–06	Montreal Wanderers	—	—
1906–07	Kenora Thistles (January)	F. A. Hudson	Tommy Phillips*
1906–07	Montreal Wanderers (March)	R. R. Boon	Cecil Blachford
1907–08	Montreal Wanderers	R. R. Boon	Cecil Blachford
1908–09	Ottawa Senators	—	Bruce Stuart*
1909–10	Montreal Wanderers	R. R. Boon	Pud Glass*
1910–11	Ottawa Senators	—	Bruce Stuart*
1911–12	Quebec Bulldogs	M. J. Quinn	C. Nolan
**1912–13	Quebec Bulldogs	M. J. Quinn	Joe Marlowe*
1913–14	Toronto Blue Shirts	Jack Marshall	Scotty Davidson*
1914–15	Vancouver Millionaires	Frank Patrick	Frank Patrick
1915–16	Montreal Canadiens	George Kennedy	George Kennedy
1916–17	Seattle Metropolitans	Pete Muldoon	Pete Muldoon
1917–18	Toronto Arenas	Charlie Querrie	Dick Carroll
***1918–19	No champion		
1919–20	Ottawa Senators	Tommy Gorman	Pete Green
1920–21	Ottawa Senators	Tommy Gorman	Pete Green
1921–22	Toronto St. Pats	Charlie Querrie	Eddie Powers
1922–23	Ottawa Senators	Tommy Gorman	Pete Green
1923–24	Montreal Canadiens	Leo Dandurand	Leo Dandurand
1924–25	Victoria Cougars	Lester Patrick	Lester Patrick
1925–26	Montreal Maroons	Eddie Gerard	Eddie Gerard
1926–27	Ottawa Senators	Dave Gill	Dave Gill
1927–28	New York Rangers	Lester Patrick	Lester Patrick
1928–29	Boston Bruins	Art Ross	Cy Denneny
1929–30	Montreal Canadiens	Cecil Hart	Cecil Hart
1930–31	Montreal Canadiens	Cecil Hart	Cecil Hart
1931–32	Toronto Maple Leafs	Conn Smythe	Dick Irvin
1932–33	New York Rangers	Lester Patrick	Lester Patrick
1933–34	Chicago Black Hawks	Tommy Gorman	Tommy Gorman
1934–35	Montreal Maroons	Tommy Gorman	Tommy Gorman
1935–36	Detroit Red Wings	Jack Adams	Jack Adams
1936–37	Detroit Red Wings	Jack Adams	Jack Adams
1937–38	Chicago Black Hawks	Bill Stewart	Bill Stewart
1938–39	Boston Bruins	Art Ross	Art Ross
1939–40	New York Rangers	Lester Patrick	Frank Boucher
1940–41	Boston Bruins	Art Ross	Cooney Weiland
1941–42	Toronto Maple Leafs	Conn Smythe	Hap Day
1942–43	Detroit Red Wings	Jack Adams	Jack Adams
1943–44	Montreal Canadiens	Tommy Gorman	Dick Irvin
1944–45	Toronto Maple Leafs	Conn Smythe	Hap Day
1945–46	Montreal Canadiens	Tommy Gorman	Dick Irvin
1946–47	Toronto Maple Leafs	Conn Smythe	Hap Day
1947–78	Toronto Maple Leafs	Conn Smythe	Hap Day
1948–49	Toronto Maple Leafs	Conn Smythe	Hap Day
1949–50	Detroit Red Wings	Jack Adams	Tommy Ivan
1950–51	Toronto Maple Leafs	Conn Smythe	Joe Primeau
1951–52	Detroit Red Wings	Jack Adams	Tommy Ivan
1952–53	Montreal Canadiens	Frank Selke	Dick Irvin
1953–54	Detroit Red Wings	Jack Adams	Tommy Ivan
1954–55	Detroit Red Wings	Jack Adams	Jimmy Skinner
1955–56	Montreal Canadiens	Frank Selke	Toe Blake
1956–57	Montreal Canadiens	Frank Selke	Toe Blake
1957–58	Montreal Canadiens	Frank Selke	Toe Blake
1958–59	Montreal Canadiens	Frank Selke	Toe Blake
1959–60	Montreal Canadiens	Frank Selke	Toe Blake
1960–61	Chicago Black Hawks	Tommy Ivan	Rudy Pilous
1961–62	Toronto Maple Leafs	Punch Imlach	Punch Imlach
1962–63	Toronto Maple Leafs	Punch Imlach	Punch Imlach
1963–64	Toronto Maple Leafs	Punch Imlach	Punch Imlach
1964–65	Montreal Canadiens	Sam Pollock	Toe Blake
1965–66	Montreal Canadiens	Sam Pollock	Toe Blake
1966–67	Toronto Maple Leafs	Punch Imlach	Punch Imlach
1967–68	Montreal Canadiens	Sam Pollock	Toe Blake
1968–69	Montreal Canadiens	Sam Pollock	Claude Ruel
1969–70	Boston Bruins	Milt Schmidt	Harry Sinden
1970–71	Montreal Canadiens	Sam Pollock	Al MacNeil
1971–72	Boston Bruins	Milt Schmidt	Tom Johnson
1972–73	Montreal Canadiens	Sam Pollock	Scotty Bowman
1973–74	Philadelphia Flyers	Keith Allen	Fred Shero
1974–75	Philadelphia Flyers	Keith Allen	Fred Shero
1975–76	Montreal Canadiens	Sam Pollock	Scotty Bowman
1976–77	Montreal Canadiens	Sam Pollock	Scotty Bowman
1977–78	Montreal Canadiens	Sam Pollock	Scotty Bowman
1978–79	Montreal Canadiens	Irving Grundman	Scotty Bowman
1979–80	New York Islanders	Bill Torrey	Al Arbour
1980–81	New York Islanders	Bill Torrey	Al Arbour
1981–82	New York Islanders	Bill Torrey	Al Arbour
1982–83	New York Islanders	Bill Torrey	Al Arbour
1983–84	Edmonton Oilers	Glen Sather	Glen Sather
1984–85	Edmonton Oilers	Glen Sather	Glen Sather
1985–86	Montreal Canadiens	Serge Savard	Jean Perron
1986–87	Edmonton Oilers	Glen Sather	Glen Sather
1987–88	Edmonton Oilers	Glen Sather	Glen Sather
1988–89	Calgary Flames	Cliff Fletcher	Terry Crisp
1989–90	Edmonton Oilers	Glen Sather	John Muckler
1990–91	Pittsburgh Penguins	Craig Patrick	Bob Johnson
1991–92	Pittsburgh Penguins	Craig Patrick	Scotty Bowman
1992–93	Montreal Canadiens	Serge Savard	Jacques Demers
1993–94	New York Rangers	Neil Smith	Mike Keenan
1994–95	New Jersey Devils	Lou Lamoriello	Jacques Lemaire
1995–96	Colorado Avalanche	Pierre Lacroix	Marc Crawford
1996–97	Detroit Red Wings	Scotty Bowman	Scotty Bowman
1997–98	Detroit Red Wings	Ken Holland	Scotty Bowmam
1998–99	Dallas Stars	Bob Gainey	Ken Hitchcock

* Indicates captain. In the early years the teams were frequently run by the captain.

** Victoria defeated Quebec in challenge series. No official recognition.

*** In the spring of 1919 the Montreal Canadiens traveled to Seattle to meet Seattle, PCHL champions. After five games had been played-teams were tied at two wins each and one tie-the series was called off by the local Department of Health because of the influenza epidemic that hospitalized a number of Montreal players, including Joe Hall, who died from it.

\# Split season

10

HOCKEY'S
MEMORABLE MOMENTS

In the history of the National Hockey League, there have been many memorable moments—individual feats, team performances and rare games. The editor has chosen these unforgettable happenings on ice.

APRIL 7, 1928

MAROONS VS. RANGERS

The New York Rangers entered the finals of the 1928 Stanley Cup playoffs at a distinct disadvantage. Because of previous commitments, their own arena, Madison Square Garden, was unavailable and the entire series had to be played on the home ice of the Montreal Maroons. Montreal took advantage of the situation and won the first game of the best-of-five series, 2-0.

After a scoreless first period in the second game, the outlook appeared even more grim for the orphaned New Yorkers. A few minutes into the second session, Nels Stewart, the big Maroon center who was the greatest scorer of his time, skated in slowly on the New York goal and let loose a blistering shot that hit the goalie, Lorne Chabot, in the left eye.

Chabot fell unconscious, with blood dripping down his cheek. The crowd of 12,000 in Montreal's Forum sat silently as he was carried off on a stretcher.

There was no such thing as a substitute goalie in those days. Lester Patrick, a once-great defenseman who served as manager and coach of the Rangers, had only 10 minutes to find a replacement.

Alex Connell, a big-league goalie for Ottawa, was in the stands, but Eddie Gerard, the Maroons' manager, refused to let him play. "If I let you take Connell, it could cost me. Suckers were born yesterday and you're talking to the wrong man. I can't hear you," Gerard laughed.

So Patrick returned to his players and told them they would have to finish the game with a goalie from their own squad. It took Frank Boucher, the irrepressible center, to break the gloom. "How about you playing goal?" he asked.

Patrick, 44 years old and long since retired as a player, demurred. "I'm too old," he protested.

At age 44, Lester Patrick donned the goalie's pads in a memorable Stanley Cup game.

But he and his players knew that he had had at least some goaltending experience. Back in hockey's dark ages, goaltenders when penalized had to serve time in the penalty box like any other player. And one of the other members of the team had to take over goal. On the rare occasions when this was necessary, Patrick drew the assignment. Surveying the desperate situation this night of April 7, 1928, Patrick knew he would have to do it again.

Patrick was actually trembling as his players helped him into more elaborate goalie equipment than he had ever worn before, and, on shaky legs, he skated onto the ice to kick out a few of the easy test shots his players made sure he couldn't miss.

Then he announced he was ready and the Rangers went out to play the most inspired game of their lives. They flattened every Montreal player who dared skate near the nets guarded by their white-haired leader and, 30 seconds into the third period, took a 1-0 lead on a goal by Bill Cook. However, with six minutes to play, Montreal tied the game on a shot by Stewart and it went into overtime.

Frustrated at being stymied by an old man and with the crowd cheering the visitors, the enraged Maroons mounted attack after attack on the Ranger goal. But, after 7:05 of overtime, the clever Boucher stole the puck, broke in alone and scored the winner.

Patrick, in tears, was half-dragged and half-carried off the ice by his players to a tremendous ovation from the crowd.

He didn't attempt an encore. A rookie, Joe Miller, was in goal when the Rangers won two of the next three games to capture the Stanley Cup—the perfect ending for the series in which the gallant Lester Patrick had provided their finest hour.

MARCH 24–25, 1936

RED WINGS VS. MAROONS

The clock in Montreal's Forum the night of March 24, 1936, showed 8:34 P.M. when the ref-

eree dropped the puck to start the first-round Stanley Cup playoff series between the Montreal Maroons, champion of the National Hockey League's Canadian Division, and the Detroit Red Wings, titlist in the American Division.

Playoffs games, especially in the early going, usually are played close to the vest and nobody was surprised when the first period was scoreless and marked only by three minor penalties.

The second period was more of the same, the only excitement being a mild scuffle that drew two-minute penalties for Marty Barry of the Wings and Jimmy Ward of the Maroons. The third period also was scoreless and the fans were getting restless.

After a brief intermission, the teams went into a 20-minute sudden-death overtime session. No score. Then a second overtime period. No score. And a third. And a fourth. Near the end of the fifth overtime, Barry, the Detroit center, set up left winger Herb Lewis with a perfect pass. Lewis appeared to have Maroon goalie Lorne Chabot beaten, but his shot hit the post and bounced out.

That flurry finished the action in the fifth overtime, which amounted to the eighth 20-minute period. After 4:46 of the sixth overtime, the Red Wings and Maroons owned the record for the longest Cup playoff game. They broke the mark of 144 minutes, 46 seconds set in 1933 when Toronto defeated Boston, 1-0.

In that game, after about 100 minutes of overtime, league president Frank Calder had refused a request that the game be resumed the following night. Calder, however, was willing to toss a coin to decide the winner, but his plan was vetoed by the Maple Leafs.

The Red Wings and Maroons knew they had to play to a decision. The break didn't come until 16:30 had elapsed in the sixth overtime, or just short of three regulation games. Detroit goalie Norm Smith repulsed a Maroon rush with his 90th save and Hec Kilrea headed up ice in a two-man dash with rookie Mud Bruneteau. Bruneteau, who had scored only two goals all

season, managed to skate past the weary Maroon defense. As Lionel Conacher lost his footing on the rough ice, Mud took a pass from Kilrea, faked Chabot, who had stopped 66 shots, out of position and poked home the winner into an open net.

At 2:25 A.M. on March 25, five hours and 51 minutes after play had begun, hockey's longest game ended. The defeat seemed to take something out of the Maroons, who lost the next two games and were eliminated from the playoffs while the Red Wings went on to win the Stanley Cup.

MARCH 23, 1944

CANADIENS VS. MAPLE LEAFS

Stanley Cup playoff games usually emphasize defense. The checking is tight and rough. In the short series with a lot at stake, errors can be fatal. The Montreal Canadiens had run away with the regular-season championship of 1943–44. They lost only five games out of 50 on the schedule (with seven ties) and finished 25 points ahead of second-place Detroit.

The Stanley Cup series opened in Montreal with the Canadiens playing third-place Toronto. In a close-checking game, the Maple Leafs won the opener, 3-1. The two teams met again two nights later, March 23, 1944, in Montreal's Forum as the fans wondered how long the Leafs could hold off the powerful Canadiens, namely Maurice (Rocket) Richard.

Bob Davidson, a big, close-checking forward for the Leafs, always drew the assignment of guarding Richard. The Rocket, a 23-year-old French-Canadian, was only in his second season in the NHL but already merited special attention. Davidson and the Leafs were successful through a scoreless first period. But in the second period the home team broke loose.

Taking passes from Toe Blake and defensemen Mike McMahon, Richard wheeled in and beat Leaf goalie Paul Bibeault for the first goal of the game at 1:48. Seventeen seconds later Richard scored again on assists from his famous linemates, Blake and Elmer Lach.

Now that Montreal had a two-goal lead, Toronto had to abandon its conservative checking game. The Leafs needed goals. They got one from Reg Hamilton after 8:50 of the second period, but Richard matched that with his third goal of the night on assists from Lach and Blake at 16:46. The fiery-tempered Richard achieved his hat trick in a single period even though he twice had been set down for two-minute penalties.

The crowd gave its idol an ovation as he left the ice after the second period, but there was more to come. The Canadiens were determined not to sit on their two-goal lead. The fabulous Flying Frenchmen came out flying for the final period. After only a minute of play, Richard again was set up by Lach and Blake on the famous Punch Line, and he scored his fourth goal. And, at 8:34 he scored a fifth. The final score of the game was Richard 5, Toronto 1.

After NHL games at the Forum, the three top stars of the contest are honored. This time the crowd of 12,500 was able to give a continuous ovation. Star No. 3, Star No. 2 and Star No. 1—all Maurice Richard! Richard's five goals—tying Newsy Lalonde's Stanley Cup record that would not be equaled until 32 years later by Darryl Sittler and Reggie Leach—demoralized the Leafs, who lost the next three games as well, the final by an 11-0 score.

"I didn't know until after the game that the five goals set a record," Richard recalled. "I only had six or seven shots on net all game and each goal was scored in a different way. The funny thing is that when we beat the Leafs 11-0, I only scored two goals.

"The Leafs always were a close-checking club and they used to put Bob Davidson out to check me every game. Sometimes he stayed so close to me that I got angry and that night, I guess, I took it out on him—and the puck."

APRIL 21, 1951

MAPLE LEAFS VS. CANADIENS

Bill Barilko never really seemed destined for fame. Curly-haired and good-looking, he was a 190-pound defenseman for the Toronto Maple Leafs. Only 19 when the Leafs called him up from the minors at the end of the 1946–47 season, Barilko quickly established himself as a defensive defenseman, the kind who doesn't score goals, doesn't make All-Star teams, and doesn't get his picture in the papers very often.

Only among rival players, whom he delighted in belting into the boards, did Barilko gain any real measure of fame and respect. He never scored more than seven goals in a season in the

NHL and his most outstanding statistic was the 147 minutes in penalties he amassed in 1947–48, his first full year in the NHL. That penalty total led the league and for most of his short career he was up among the penalty leaders.

But, while he wasn't a star, Barilko was no slouch, either, and in each of his first three seasons he played an important role as the Maple Leafs won the Stanley Cup. The Leafs lost in the first round of the 1950 playoffs to Detroit, the eventual winner, and in 1951 Toronto found itself back in the finals against the Montreal Canadiens.

The Maple Leafs won the Cup, four games to one, but the series was not as one-sided as it appeared. Every game was decided in sudden-death overtime.

Toronto's Bill Barilko (5) scored the winning goal to clinch the Stanley Cup in 1951. It was his last goal.

Barilko was a key figure in the first game. Near the end of regulation time, Maurice Richard fired what seemed a sure goal at an open Toronto net, only to see Barilko dive full-length to block the shot and preserve the 2-2 tie. Sid Smith then scored the winner for Toronto after 5:51 of overtime. The second game went to Montreal, 3-2, after 2:55 of overtime on a goal by Maurice Richard.

The series moved to Montreal for the next two games and Toronto took both. Ted Kennedy won the first game, 2-1, after 4:47 of overtime and Harry Watson the second, 3-2, after 5:15.

The Leafs returned home to a joyous greeting at Maple Leaf Gardens as they prepared to clinch the Cup in the fifth game on April 21, 1951. For once it didn't look as if the game would go into overtime. With a minute to go, Montreal held a 2-1 lead. But Toronto coach Joe Primeau pulled his goalie and, with an extra skater on the ice, the Leafs got a goal from Tod Sloan with 32 seconds left to force the game into overtime.

After only 2:53, it was sudden death for the Canadiens. Barilko, who hadn't recorded a goal or an assist in the series, took a pass from Howie Meeker at mid-ice and in blind desperation fired a shot at the goal as he crossed the blue line. He actually flung himself in the air with the force of his effort and the puck skipped past Montreal goalie Gerry McNeil. The Stanley Cup returned to Toronto.

After the season, Barilko went home to Timmons, a mining town in northern Ontario. For the first time he was a national hero. He didn't get to enjoy it for long. That August, he and a friend,

Three goals in 21 seconds put Chicago's Bill Mosienko into ecstasy and the record book in 1952.

Dr. Henry Hudson, flew into northern Canada on a fishing trip in the doctor's private plane. They were never heard from again.

Some 15 years later, what was believed to be the wreckage of their plane was discovered, reviving briefly memories of the low-scoring but hard-hitting defenseman who once won a Stanley Cup for Toronto.

MARCH 23, 1952

BLACKHAWKS VS. RANGERS

Bill Mosienko, a 30-year-old right winger for the Chicago Blackhawks, and Lorne Anderson, a 20-year-old goalie for the amateur New York Rovers, each had a hope as the 1952 hockey season went into its final days before the Stanley Cup playoffs. Mosienko, looking at the NHL record book with some friends, remarked, "Gee, it would be nice to have my name in there with some of the hockey greats." Anderson's wish was more simple: to play in the NHL.

The dream came true for both, but for Anderson it was more like a nightmare.

The Rangers faced their final three games of the season already eliminated from the playoffs, Cincinnati, a minor-league team, had owned the rights to Ranger goalie Emile (Cat) Francis, so the NHL regular was shipped down to help that American Hockey League team in its playoff quest. As a result, the Rangers called up Anderson to finish the season.

The New Yorkers won Anderson's first game, 6-4, over Boston, but lost the second, 6-3, to Detroit. The final game of the 1952 season was played on March 23 with the Rangers and Blackhawks performing before a mere 3,254 fans in Madison Square Garden.

This was what is called a "brother-in-law" game. The final placings had long since been decided and nobody wanted to get hurt. With virtually no checking, referee George Gravel did not call a single penalty in the entire 60-minute game.

However, that's not to say there wasn't plenty of action. The Blackhawks' Gus Bodnar scored first with Mosienko getting an assist. Then the Rangers scored three times before the visitors tallied again—and it was still only the first period! The Rangers scored twice more for a 5-2 lead after two periods and expanded this margin to 6-2 in the opening minutes of the third as Ed Slowinski completed the three-goal hat trick.

But then, in a shocking explosion, Mosienko, the speedy 5-foot-6 right winger, made hockey history.

In almost leisurely but precise fashion, the Hawks formed for the attack. Bodnar, the center, passed off to Mosienko and his little winger beat the defenseman to rap home a goal from in front of the net. The time was 6:09 of the third period.

After the goal, there was a faceoff at center ice. Bodnar won the draw and hit the streaking Mosienko just as Bill was crossing the blue line. Mosienko took the pass, shot and scored. The time was 6:20 of the third period. Only 11 seconds had elapsed.

Again there was a faceoff, again Bodnar controlled the puck, but this time he passed off to George Gee on the left wing. Gee carried over the Ranger blue line, spotted Mosienko breaking toward the net and laid a perfect pass on the right winger's stick. Mosienko fired it past Anderson and, as the red light flashed again, the clock showed 6:30 had elapsed. Mosienko had scored three goals in 21 seconds. No player—or team—had ever scored three times in such a short period of time. Mosienko's dream had come true. He landed in the record book, breaking the old mark by 43 seconds as the Hawks scored twice more to win, 7-6.

Mosienko went on to play three more full seasons for the Blackhawks and retired at age 32 after the 1954–55 campaign with a career total of 258 goals.

As for the unfortunate Anderson, who had surrendered 17 goals in his brief trial, he never played in another NHL game.

NOVEMBER 1, 1959

CANADIENS VS. RANGERS

By 1959, Jacques Plante's reputation as one of the greatest hockey goaltenders of all time was firmly established. He had already won four Vezina Trophies, the award that annually goes to the top goalie in the NHL. And his success as a roving goalie for the Montreal Canadiens had revolutionized the techniques of playing his position.

But, as he skated out on the ice against the Rangers in New York on November 1, 1959, he also had some other souvenirs of his dangerous profession: the scars of 200 stitches in his face, a nose broken four times, a fractured skull, and two broken cheekbones.

The fractured cheekbones had come in each of Plante's first two NHL seasons. Both times he was hurt in practice from a shot by a teammate. After the second injury he had a plastic mask designed and he wore it in workouts.

The mask was a bit awkward, but during the 1958–59 season, Plante learned that a mask had been developed that would fit snugly against his face. It was just what he wanted, for now the blind spots of the old mask were eliminated. Before the season, Plante asked coach Toe Blake if he could wear the mask during games.

It was not unprecedented; Clint Benedict of the Montreal Maroons had worn one briefly in 1929, but discarded it. Goalies were traditionally barefaced after that and Blake was a traditionalist. He turned down Plante.

However, in less than two months, tradition was broken. It happened in this game against the Rangers, scoreless for eight minutes until Andy Bathgate, the New Yorkers' hardest shooter, let loose a 25-foot backhander from the left of the net.

Plante, screened by the mass of players, never saw the puck until it smashed into his face, ripping open his cheek and nose. He fell to the ice, blood staining his uniform and the Garden ice. But he recovered with a towel held against his face. It took seven stitches to close the wound.

At that time, NHL teams did not carry a spare goalie. It was up to the home club to have someone on hand who could fill in during an emergency. Some teams called on their assistant trainer; others, in Canada especially, would have available the teenage goalie from their junior team in the same city. The Rangers used a fortyish and pudgy weekend amateur named Joe Schaefer. When Schaefer had to play, it really was an emergency.

That was the situation as Plante sat up on the first-aid table. Twenty minutes had elapsed. The game had to resume. Plante looked at Blake, "I won't go back on unless I can wear the mask," he said grimly. Blake, who had fought the new device so stubbornly, had to agree. And hockey history was made.

Fortunately, Plante played well with the mask. The Canadiens beat the Rangers, 3-1, with the losers' only goal coming in the final period. Montreal had arrived at the Garden with an unbeaten streak of seven. They made it eight against the Rangers and finally extended it to 18 before losing to Toronto, 1-0. In the last 11 games of the streak, or all the time he wore the mask, Plante gave up only 13 goals.

The Montreal management reluctantly went along with Plante. "I had to show good results to keep the mask," he later commented, and he did, winning three more Vezina Trophies. And masks for goalies eventually became commonplace.

NOVEMBER 10, 1963

RED WINGS VS. CANADIENS

It was like Babe Ruth's 714 home runs. When Maurice Richard retired from the NHL in 1960 with 544 goals in regular-season play, nobody was even close. And nobody, Rocket's French-Canadian fans insisted, would ever approach his scoring record.

But when the 1963–64 campaign began, Gordie Howe, Detroit's durable right winger, was close. He started the season with 540 and

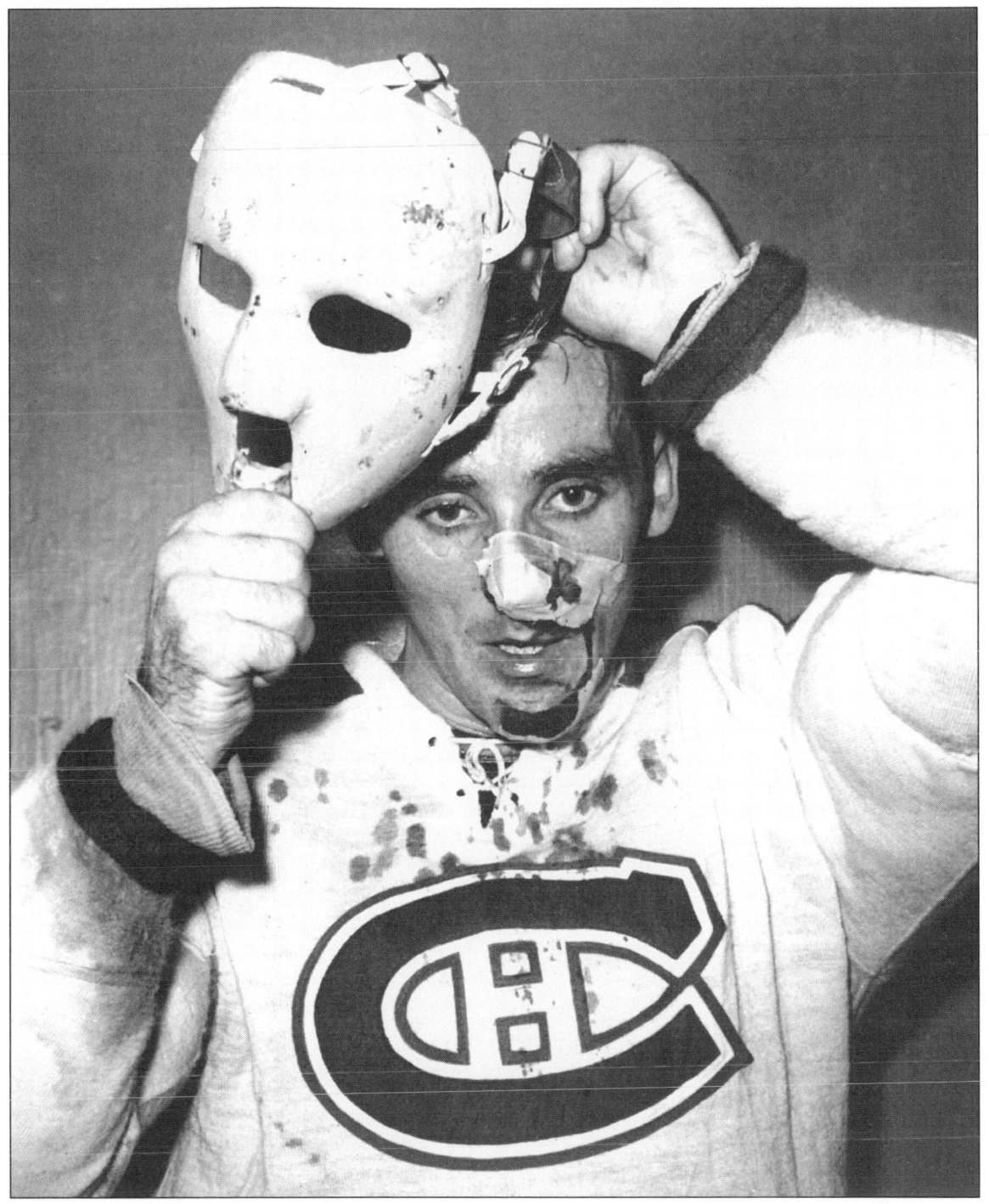

Montreal's bloodied Jacques Plante dons a mask for the first time in 1959 against the Rangers.

it seemed only a matter of time until he passed the Rocket. Only an injury could stop the husky, slope-shouldered Howe from overtaking Richard.

On October 27, 1963, Howe and the Red Wings were playing host to the Canadiens. Gordie had 543 goals and the proud Habitants were determined that Howe would not join the Rocket in the record book at their expense. Toe Blake, coach of the Canadiens, made sure that a line centered by Richard's brother, Henri, was always on ice against Howe's line. It was more than a psychological ploy. When Henri was on the ice, he controlled the puck. And Howe couldn't score without it.

Then Blake assigned Gilles Tremblay, a Montreal winger, to forget about scoring himself and to concentrate on shadowing Howe.

The strategy almost worked. Howe was limited to only two shots all game. But the second was a goal. At 11:04 of the third period, Howe got a step on Tremblay and deflected Bruce Mac-Gregor's goal-mouth pass past Montreal netminder Gump Worsley. It wasn't a picture goal, but it counted and Jean Beliveau, captain of the Canadiens, gravely skated over to shake Howe's hand.

However, the battle was only half over for Howe, then 34 and in his 18th pro season. Now he had to break the record and, game after game, the pressure mounted. Detroit had lost to Montreal, 6-4, the night Howe tied Richard after failing to score in 10 previous games, and the whole team suffered as the Red Wings tried to help their captain register No. 545.

But there was nothing coach Sid Abel could do. The Wings lost three of their next five games. Howe's nervous twitch became more pronounced, and newsmen and photographers ran out of clean shirts as they followed Howe from city to city in hope of recording the monumental goal.

Two weeks later, they found themselves back in Detroit's glistening Olympia Stadium. Another sellout crowd of more than 15,000 jammed the building—and again Montreal provided the opposition. The only major change was that instead of Gump Worsley, the Canadiens had little Charlie Hodge in goal.

Again the Canadiens were determined to protect the Rocket's record and again they concentrated solely on stopping Howe. The first period was scoreless but Detroit scored twice in 47 seconds to take a 2-0 lead after 5½ minutes of the second period. At the 13:57 mark, Alex Faulkner of the Wings was penalized five minutes for high-sticking and the redoubtable Howe came along with Billy McNeill to help kill the penalty.

The Canadiens mounted one of their fierce power assaults when McNeill dug out the puck from against the boards deep in the Detroit zone. Howe moved behind him and yelled, "Get along!" The little winger took off down the right wing and swung to the middle of the ice as he crossed into Montreal territory with Howe behind him to the right and defenseman Bill Gadsby on the left wing. As they approached the Canadiens' goal, McNeill slid the puck to Howe, who, with one motion, swiped a 15-foot shot just off the ice past Hodge and into the cage.

As the red light flashed with 15:06 gone in the period, Hodge slammed his stick against the top of the cage and skated to the sidelines. He knew there would be a prolonged ovation after what McNeill called a "perfect goal."

It was also perfect as Howe passed the Rocket by scoring when his team was short a man. And, unlike the night he tied the record, it came when his team was winning, not losing. To Howe, that was as important as any record.

MARCH 12, 1966

BLACKHAWKS VS. RANGERS

Maurice (Rocket) Richard of the Montreal Canadiens became the first player in NHL history to score 50 goals during the 1944–45 season. Then, in 1960–61, Bernie (Boom-Boom) Geoffrion of the same team did it, too. And the following year

Bobby Hull of the Chicago Blackhawks also turned the trick in the final game of the season.

Now it was the end of the 1965–66 campaign. Hull, the Golden Jet, had missed five games because of torn knee ligaments but he already had his 50 after 57 games of the 70-game schedule.

The sky seemed the limit for Hull, then 27 years old and a handsome, husky, muscular athlete. But game 58 passed, and Hull didn't score; then game 59 and game 60 and still the powerful left winger appeared anchored at 50 goals.

On the night of March 12, Hull skated out on the ice of massive Chicago Stadium as 21,000 fans—4,000 more than listed capacity—watched to see if he could make his 51st goal against the fifth-place New York Rangers.

The first period was scoreless and then the Rangers scored twice in the second 20 minutes to take a 2-0 lead as the rest of the Blackhawks seemed to be standing around waiting for Hull to get his record.

As the third period opened, Hull assisted on a goal by teammate Chico Maki and then, with 4:05 gone, Harry Howell of the Rangers was sent off with a two-minute penalty for slashing.

Back on the ice went Hull as perhaps hockey's most explosive point man on the power play. Howell had been in the penalty box almost a minute and a half when the Hawks gathered to start another rush against the undermanned Rangers. Bill Hay and Lou Angotti fed the puck up to Hull and then watched, almost as spectators, as the Golden Jet moved slowly to his left, stopped, crossed the New York blue line and then, as his teammates swooped toward the net, fired a deceptively swift wrist shot at Ranger goalie Cesare Maniago.

Eric Nesterenko, another Blackhawks forward, was near the goal-mouth at the time and he tipped Maniago's stick as the Ranger goalie, who had also given up Geoffrion's 50th goal, tried vainly to make a split save.

Chicago's Bobby Hull netted his record-setting 51st goal against the Rangers in 1966.

As the puck zipped past Maniago and the red light flashed to signify a score, the crowd erupted into what was to be a 7½ minute ovation. But Hull, for a moment, stood still, nerves tingling. If Nesterenko had tipped the puck on its way past Maniago, he, not Hull, would get the goal.

But the official scorer settled all doubts. Hull had his 51st goal after 5:34 of the third period. He skated over to the section where his wife was sitting and whispered to her through the protective glass, "Well, I did it." Then, as he skated around the ice to acknowledge the applause, Hull reached down and put on one of the dozens of hats that frenzied fans had skimmed onto the ice.

It was a glorious moment for Hull. A couple of weeks earlier, the normally placid star had exploded into a fistfight with a close-checking rival. He had considered quitting because of the pres-

sure of the 51-goal quest. But now the tensions were past. The Hawks went on to win the game, 4-2, and Bobby proceeded to score three more goals during the rest of the season to put the record at 54. But, as Hull could testify, the 51st was the hardest.

MARCH 2, 1969

BRUINS VS. PENGUINS

The NHL was founded in 1917 and for more than 50 years no player had ever scored 100 points in a single season.

For awhile, the scoring mark belonged to Dickie Moore, a shifty left wing who totaled 96 points for Montreal in 1958–59. Then, in 1965–66, Chicago's Bobby Hull boosted the mark to 97 and a year later, another Blackhawk, Stan Mikita, also reached 97.

Mikita's 97 points came in the last year that the NHL operated with just six teams. The next year, six new clubs were added and even though scoring predictably increased, it was spread around more. Mikita repeated as scoring champion, but his total fell to 87 points, 10 below the standard he shared with Hull.

That same year, Chicago swapped a center named Phil Esposito to Boston. Espo had been Hull's center in Bobby's 97-point season and was considered a caddy for the great left wing. But he proved to more than that. Much more.

Esposito gave Mikita a battle for the scoring crown that year, finishing with 84 points, only three less than the Chicago pivot. The next year, Espo exploded, scoring points at a record-setting pace. It became apparent in February that the NHL's 100-point plateau was going to be broken by the sad-eyed center who set up shop in front of goalies and refused to be moved out of there.

With linemates Ken Hodge on the right and Ron Murphy on the left, Esposito flourished. As the season turned into March, its final month, he had 97 points. On March 1, in a game against the

New York Rangers, Esposito cracked the mark with point No. 98. He had been stopped on 10 shots in the first two periods by goalie Ed Giacomin before finally slipping a shorthanded goal past the New York netminder. Later, he assisted on a goal by Bobby Orr for his 99th point.

That set the stage for Pittsburgh's visit to Boston Garden the next night. The Penguins were determined to keep Espo off the scoreboard. He was going to get point No. 100 some place, but Pittsburgh didn't want to be the victim.

"Joe Daley was the Pittsburgh goaltender and he did a good job over the first two periods," Esposito would recount. "I had two shots and no goals."

As the Bruins returned to the ice for the game's final 20 minutes, a young fan shouted to Esposito. "Please get that one-hundredth point, Phil. I want to be able to say I saw it."

Esposito obliged. With only 17 seconds gone in the period, passes from Ted Green and Hodge sprung Espo, cutting in from the left side. "Daley moved to his right," recalled Esposito, "and hit the ice. I spilled it underneath him."

The fans showered Espo with all kinds of debris, including a football helmet, saluting the historic 100th point. Espo added 26 more points that year for the first of five scoring championships in six seasons. In each of those years, he scored more than 100 points and in 1970–71 he reached his high with 152 points, including 76 goals.

Both records would stand for a decade—until a young man named Wayne Gretzky surfaced as an unprecedented scoring machine.

FEBRUARY 7, 1976

MAPLE LEAFS VS. BRUINS

It did not figure to be an exciting game. In fact, it shaped up as a mismatch. The Boston Bruins came into Maple Leaf Gardens on the night of February 7, 1976, as the hottest team in the NHL. They were unbeaten in seven games and had lost

only one of the previous 17 outings. And now they were about to face the Maple Leafs, who had won but one of their last seven games.

A day earlier, Harold Ballard, the Leafs' bombastic owner, claimed he was "determined to find a sensational center" to play between the team's top wingers, Lanny McDonald and Errol Thompson. "We'd set off a time bomb if we had a helluva center in there," Ballard said.

Coach Red Kelly had inserted Darryl Sittler into the spot earlier in the week—mainly because Sittler also had been in a slump with only five goals in his previous 17 games. It turned out to be a dynamite move.

Sittler, performing before a sellout crowd of 16,485, rewrote the NHL record book that night, scoring six goals (on 10 shots) and adding four assists in the Leafs' 11-4 thumping of the Bruins and a rookie goalie named Dave Reece.

Sittler's 10 points smashed the one-game NHL standard of eight, set by Maurice (Rocket) Richard of the Montreal Canadiens in 1944 (five goals, three assists), and equaled by teammate Bert Olmstead (four goals, four assists) 10 years later. Sittler's six goals tied the "modern era" record set by Syd Howe of Detroit in 1944 and matched by Red Berenson of St. Louis in 1968.

Joe Malone set the all-time one-game goal mark with seven while playing for the Quebec

Boston's Phil Esposito snapped Stan Mikita's one-season scoring mark with his 98th point on March 1, 1969. The next night, he became the first player to crack the 100-point barrier.

Bulldogs in 1920. However, an unofficial split exists in NHL history, created by the 1943 introduction of the center red line, which loosely divides the early and modern eras.

Sittler, 25 years old at the time of his epic performance, was numbed by it all. "It was a night when every time I had the puck something seemed to happen," he said. "Sure, I got some bounces, and I don't think it was one of their goalie's greatest nights."

Oddly, Sittler did not score a goal in the opening period, but he did pick up two assists. In the second period, he had three goals and two assists. He completed his big night with three more goals in the final period. It was the first time an NHL player scored hat tricks in consecutive periods.

Dave Reece, the sad rookie who served as Sittler's sleeve, was never to be permitted to forget that memorable night. He appeared in 13 other games for the Bruins that season, then drifted back to the minor leagues.

FEBRUARY 24, 1982

SABRES VS. OILERS

Phil Esposito was shadowing Wayne Gretzky. Everywhere that Gretzky went, Esposito was sure to follow. The trail began in Edmonton, then it was on to Detroit and, finally, it was time to shuffle off to Buffalo.

The date was February 24, 1982, and the Edmonton Oilers, led by the Great Gretzky, were playing the Buffalo Sabres in Memorial Auditorium. Esposito was the most interested spectator in the capacity crowd of 16,433 that night. Eleven years earlier, he had scored a record 76 goals in 78 games while playing for the Boston Bruins.

Gretzky had equaled Espo's record against the Red Wings in Detroit at the start of the Oilers' road trip. Now it was three nights later and Esposito squirmed in his seat as the Oilers and the Sabres carried a 3-3 tie into the final 10 minutes. Gretzky had taken seven shots at Buffalo goalie

Toronto's Darryl Sittler exploded for 10 points against Boston in 1976.

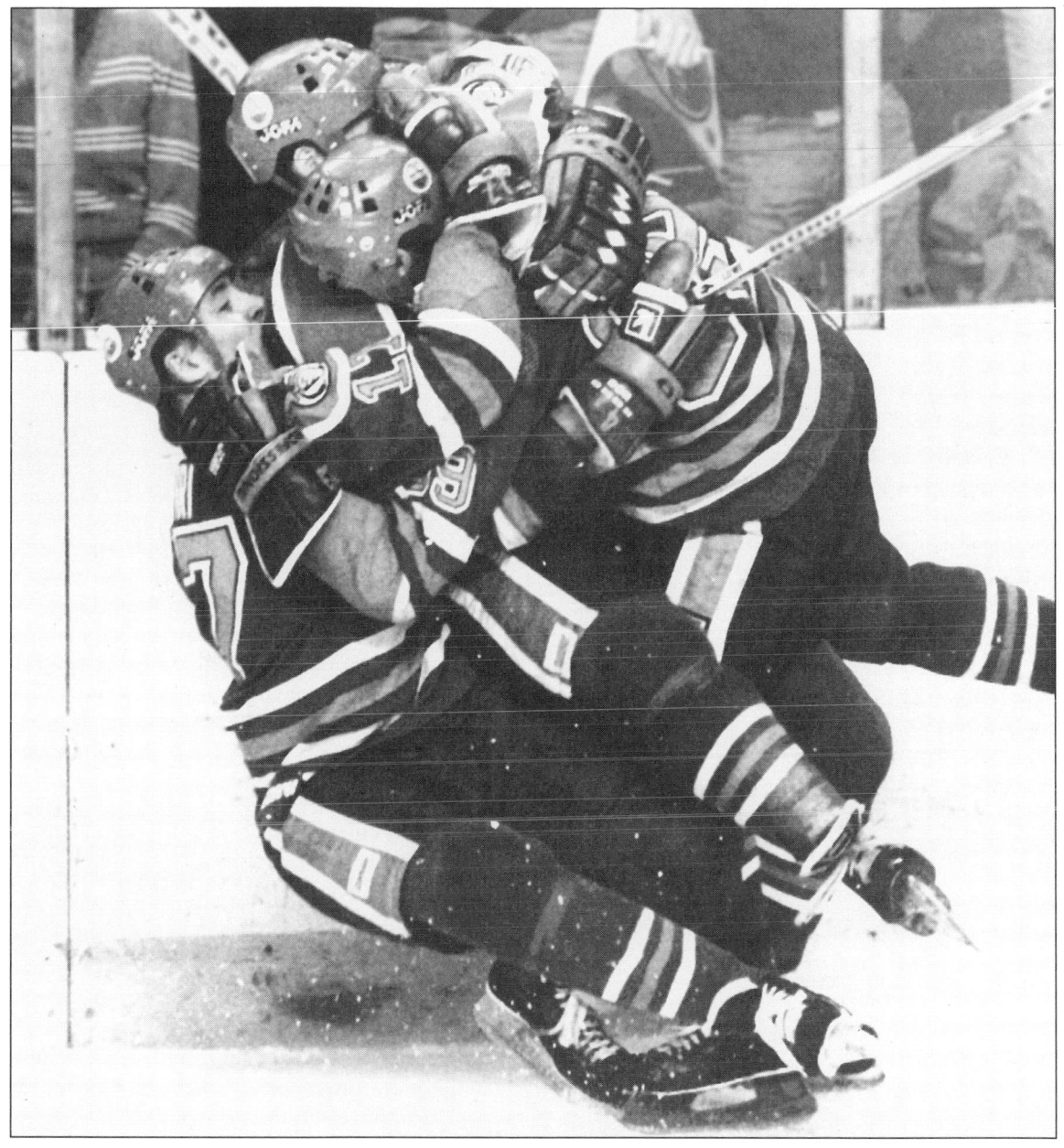

His Edmonton teammates mob Wayne Gretzky after he broke Phil Esposito's goal-scoring record.

Don Edwards without scoring. Would Wayne have to wait another night for the record-breaker?

Then, with less than seven minutes left to play, Gretzky stole the puck from Buffalo's Steve Patrick just inside the Sabres' blue line. As Gretzky skated into the slot, Buffalo defenseman Richie Dunn attempted to slow him down by hooking his stick across Gretzky's arms. Gretzky brushed the stick away and shot the puck low,

from about 12 feet. It went between Edwards' legs, and the record was broken.

Esposito came onto the ice to congratulate the 21-year-old center. "Attaway, Wayne," Esposito said. "Now I can get back to New York."

A year earlier, Esposito had retired as a player and became a television commentator for Ranger games. He knew from the moment Gretzky arrived on the NHL scene that his record was in jeopardy. So did Patsy Esposito, Phil's father. The elder Esposito had seen Gretzky play amateur hockey in Sault Ste. Marie, Ontario, where Phil was born and raised, and predicted then that Gretzky would be a record-breaker.

Gretzky did not stop at goal No. 77 against the Sabres. He added two more in the final two minutes, giving him 79 in 64 games. He completed the season with an astounding 92 goals, 120 assists and 212 points.

Gretzky received a telegram of congratulations from Ronald Reagan, President of the United States. That impressed him. He was also impressed by the fact that Don Edwards, the man who surrendered the record goal, skated the length of the ice to shake his hand.

Gretzky predicted his record also would be broken eventually. "Maybe I'll break it," he said with a grin.

MAY 17, 1983

OILERS VS. ISLANDERS

For the 65 years before the spring oif 1983, there was only one true dynasty in the NHL and that was the Montreal Canadiens. They had won 22 Cups, including four straight Cups (1976–1979).

The New York Islanders—with a star-studded corps led by Denis Potvin, Mike Bossy, Bryan Trottier, and Billy Smith—had won three consecutive Cups starting in 1980 under the leadership of general manager Bill Torrey and head coach Al Arbour. Only the Toronto Maple Leafs, Detroit Red Wings, and the Islanders, apart from the Canadiens, had ever won three in a row.

But the Islanders' opponent in the '83 Cup finals was the Edmonton Oilers—not Montreal, not Toronto, not Detroit. These Oilers were led by Wayne Gretzky and they were determined to snap the Islander streak.

"We've had young players who grew up together," Torrey said. "All of them being together all this time has been important. They got knocked off together in the playoffs by Toronto in 1978 and then by the Rangers in 1979, but ever since they've won together."

In the opening game, goalie Billy Smith posted a 2-0 shutout in Edmonton and incurred the wrath of Oiler fans when he slashed Glenn Anderson. Oilers' coach Glen Sather demanded that Smith be suspended and on the day of Game 2 an Edmonton newspaper ran a full-page color photo of a human eye with the headline: "Evil Eye on Smith."

Jeered by the Edmonton crowd which held up hundreds of Evil Eyes, Smith was again sharp as the Islanders skated to a 6-3 victory that sent them back home with a 2-0 advantage in the best-of-seven series.

The Islanders romped in Game 3, 5-1, and their fans were ready to celebrate when Game 4 began on May 17. Trottier, John Tonelli and Bossy scored goals in the first period as the Isles took a 3-0 lead. But Edmonton's Jari Kurri scored on a Gretzky setup just 35 seconds into the second period and Mark Messier tallied with 21 seconds remaining to cut the Isles' lead to 3-2.

Smith, the Islander goalie, and his Edmonton counterpart, Andy Moog, didn't yield a goal for nearly 19 minutes of the third period. The Oilers removed Moog for an extra skater and Islander defenseman Ken Morrow found the open net at 18:51 to give his team a 4-2 victory and its fourth consecutive Cup.

Smith had turned aside 24 of 26 shots in the clincher and he finished with a 13-3 record and 2.68 goals-against average in the playoffs. He was an overwhelming choice for MVP.

The home crowd of 15,317 thrilled to the song, "We Are the Champions," and the knowledge that the Islanders had a dynasty of their own.

APRIL 25, 1989

FLYERS VS. PENGUINS

In the 48 hours leading up to the evening of April 25, 1989, the Pittsburgh Penguins wondered if captain Mario Lemieux's strained neck would permit him to play against the Philadelphia Flyers in Game 5 of the Patrick Division finals.

Lemieux had been knocked out of action in Game 4 after butting heads with teammate Randy Cunneyworth. Lemieux was in considerable pain the next morning. Although his condition improved in the hours prior to the fifth game, there was the question of risking further injury by rushing Lemieux back into the lineup.

He did not participate in the morning skate and only tested his neck during the pregame skate. A crowd of 16,025 at Pittsburgh's Civic Arena and his concerned teammates awaited the decision.

The news was good. Lemieux said he would play and the Flyers soon discovered he couldn't be stopped. Just 2:15 into the opening period, Lemieux skated in on a breakaway and tucked a backhander past Philadelphia goaltender Ron Hextall. At 3:45, Lemieux deflected a pass across the crease and into the net for a 2-0 lead. Before the game was seven minutes old, he completed a hat trick by picking up a loose puck and firing a snap shot through Hextall's pads.

"Once I got the first goal, I thought we could have a big night," Lemieux said later. "There was not a lot of pain and I had my range of motion back."

It was the Flyers who had the pain. In the second period, Lemieux stole the puck from Hextall and scored his fourth goal, lifting up the goalie's stick to take the puck and flipping it inside the far post.

Lemieux set up all three Pittsburgh goals in the second period as the Penguins opened up a 9-3 lead after 40 minutes of play. Topping off the lopsided game, Lemieux made the record book when he added an empty-net goal, his fifth of the game, for a 10-3 Penguin rout.

"Considering that he was hurt, we definitely didn't expect it from him," said Hextall, the vanquished goalie.

Lemieux's feat enabled him to tie Patrik Sundstrom's record for most points (eight) in a Stanley Cup playoff game. Sundstrom had set the mark with the New Jersey Devils in a 10-4 victory over the Washington Capitals on April 22, 1988. Sundstrom had three goals and five assists in that contest.

Lemieux's five goals equaled the NHL record for goals in a playoff game held by Reggie Leach (Philadelphia), Darryl Sittler (Toronto), Maurice Richard (Montreal Canadiens), and Newsy Lalonde (Montreal Canadiens).

MAY 25, 1989

FLAMES VS. CANADIENS

For 16 years, ever since the birth of the Flames' franchise in Atlanta, general manager Cliff Fletcher had been saying, "Wait till next year." He'd reiterated it in Atlanta and then in Calgary when the team moved there in May 1980.

They'd never won the Stanley Cup and, as with every player, coach, general manager, and fan, this was the ultimate goal. Fletcher, a native of the Montreal suburb of Ville St. Laurent, had spent 10 years working part-time for the Montreal Canadiens before moving on to the St. Louis Blues and the Flames.

And now the Cup was within grasp as Calgary and Montreal met in the finals in 1989. The teams split the first two games and the Canadiens appeared to be on the way to yet another Cup when Ryan Walter's goal gave Montreal a 4-3 victory in the second overtime in Game 3.

Calgary veteran Lanny McDonald earned the right to hold the Cup aloft in 1989.

However, Al MacInnis' third-period game-winner (4-2) again evened the series in Game 4. A crowd of 20,002 at the Olympic Saddledome watched the Flames score a 3-2 victory in Game 5, sending the teams back to Montreal. If Montre-

al lost, it would be the first Canadiens' team ever to lose the Cup on home ice.

After sitting out three games, 16-year veteran Lanny McDonald returned to the Flames' lineup

on May 25 for Game 6. "Lanny was rested," coach Terry Crisp explained. "When you put Lanny Mc-Donald in your lineup and the 'C' back on his chest, you could feel the dressing room start to go. We felt he would give us an emotional lift."

It went beyond that. After the Flames' Colin Patterson and Montreal's Claude Lemieux exchanged goals, McDonald put the Flames ahead, 2-1, in the second period. Doug Gilmour's power-play goal at 11:02 of the third period made it 3-1.

Then Rick Green's goal at 11:53 brought the Canadiens within a goal. But it was Gilmour who ended Montreal's hopes when he scored an empty-net goal at 18:57 for a 4-2 victory and the first Cup in Calgary history.

MacInnis, who scored at least one point in 17 consecutive playoff games for Calgary, won the Conn Smythe Trophy as MVP of the playoffs.

Two days later, the Flames were cheered at a victory parade in the rain. "Next year" had finally arrived for Cliff Fletcher and Calgary.

OCTOBER 15, 1989

KINGS VS. OILERS

It was as inevitable as the cold winds of an Alberta winter, yet Wayne Gretzky somehow managed to make it as thrilling as the first gush from an Edmonton oil well.

For more than a decade, Gretzky had pursued Gordie Howe's record as the NHL's all-time leading scorer. Now, Howe's standard of 1,850 career points was about to fall.

Fittingly, The Great One saved his feat for Edmonton's Northlands Coliseum, where he had played for 10 seasons before the August 9, 1988, trade to the Los Angeles Kings. A sellout crowd of 17,503 cheered wildly as Gretzky returned to the scene of so many triumphs.

At the 4:32 mark of the opening period, Gretzky tied Howe's record with an assist on a goal by Bernie Nicholls. From the right wing boards, No. 99 passed the puck to defenseman Tom Laidlaw between the faceoff circles. Laidlaw found Nicholls just outside the goal crease for a shot that beat goaltender Bill Ranford.

The drama began to build. The Oilers, who would go on to win the Stanley Cup that season, shut Gretzky down at that point and it appeared the crowd might go home disappointed. With 3:29 remaining in the third period, Gretzky fed the puck to teammate Luc Robitaille, who gave it to Nicholls for a shot on goal. Nicholls' wrist shot had Ranford beaten, but the puck glanced off the post. So close.

Now time was running out. The Kings had removed goalie Mario Gosselin for an extra skater, but Mark Messier won the draw with Nichols. He got the puck back to defenseman Kevin Lowe, who was unable to clear the zone.

Steve Duchesne kept the puck in the offensive zone, driving it in deep. The disc hopped over Lowe's stick and bounced off King forward Dave Taylor's knee to Gretzky in front. The crowd gasped as Gretzky struck for the record-breaking goal. There were 53 seconds left in the game.

The crowd exploded as "1851" flashed on the scoreboard and the game was stopped while a red carpet was rolled onto the ice for a fitting ceremony. Gretzky was hugged by his father, Walter, before receiving gifts from Messier representing the Oilers, Robitaille and Taylor representing the Kings, and NHL president John Ziegler.

"This is the greatest feeling in the world," Gretzky said. "It will be the highlight of my life."

When the game, now tied at 4-4, resumed, Gretzky added to the magic of the evening. There was no score in the time that remained, but after 3:24 of sudden-death overtime, Gretzky beat Ranford for No. 1,852 and a 5-4 Kings' victory.

Howe, who had remained close to the events for eight days as Gretzky pursued his record, was gracious when it was finally broken.

"I am so proud of the fact that we have gotten along over the years," Howe said. "He calls me his friend and that's one of the greatest things

Badger Bob Johnson led Lemieux & Co. to the summit in the spring of 1991. The Penguins' coach didn't have a chance to repeat. Johnson died of brain cancer in the fall of 1991.

in my life. I feel more gain than loss. I lost a record, but I have gained a lot of friends."

"Wayne finished it and he finished it with style," said Nicholls.

MAY 25, 1991

PENGUINS VS. NORTH STARS

In Pittsburgh, May had traditionally been the month when sports fans debated how well the Steelers had done in the NFL draft and how far the Pirates might go in baseball's National League Central. The Penguins had always packed up in April because they rarely made the playoffs.

But on the night of May 25, 1991, a city known for its Super Bowl champions (four) and

World Series winners (five) sat glued to television and radio to find out if the Penguins could bring their very first Stanley Cup championship home from Minnesota.

After getting past the New Jersey Devils, Washington Capitals and Boston Bruins, the Penguins faced a North Stars' team with as much of a Cinderella story as their own. The Penguins lost the first game of the Cup finals on their home ice and went to Minnesota after a split.

A loss at the Met Center in Bloomington, Minn., in Game 3 appeared to suggest the end of Pittsburgh. Mario Lemieux did not play because of back spasms and it was uncertain if he would be able to return in the series. The Penguins had endured most of the 1990–91 season without their captain, but the playoffs became a different story.

To the delight of his teammates, Lemieux was healthy enough to play in Game 4 and he was magnificent. He scored one goal and set up another as the Pens evened the finals with a 5-3 triumph.

Returning to Pittsburgh's Civic Arena for the fifth game, Mark Recchi ended a four-game scoring slump with two goals as the Pens skated to a 6-4 victory. They were now just one victory away from what had once seemed impossible.

Penguins' forward Troy Loney recalled the feeling in the visitors' dressing room before Game 6. "The guys were so nervous, so ready, so keyed up that it was scary," Loney said. "I could see we were going to win it, that we were going to win the Cup. You could feel it."

No one felt it more than Lemieux. He was unstoppable. Ulf Samuelsson broke the ice with a wrist shot from the left point that gave Pittsburgh a 1-0 lead at 2:00 of the first period and Lemieux took a Larry Murphy pass off the boards, broke in alone and scored a shorthanded goal at 12:19 for a 2-0 lead. Joey Mullen scored 55 seconds later and it was 3-0.

Bob Errey scored on a Jaromir Jagr rebound midway through the second period, followed by goals from Ron Francis and Mullen again. Jim

Paek and Murphy added third-period goals for an 8-0 rout and Pittsburgh finally had its first Stanley Cup. It was the largest margin of victory for a final-series game in this century.

Goalie Tom Barrasso played the final game with a bad groin injury, but finished the playoffs with a 12-7 record and 2.60 goals-against average. Lemieux wound up with an aching back and the Conn Smythe Trophy as the Most Valuable Player of the playoffs. He led all scorers with 16 goals and 28 assists for 44 points in 23 games.

When the final seconds had ticked off the Met Center clock, the Penguins swarmed onto the ice to celebrate with head coach Bob Johnson and general manager Craig Patrick.

Even Recchi, who had been carried off the ice one hour prior after being knocked unconscious by a Jim Johnson check, was able to join the party.

"It can't get any better than this," he said. "It's an unbelievable thrill that so many players never get to experience."

"Boy, I'm so proud right now for the city of Pittsburgh," Loney said. "It's been a 20-year struggle for our fans, but they stuck with us. This is the reward. For all of us."

Although the clincher was played in Minnesota, Pittsburgh fans had their own celebration, clogging downtown streets and, at 3:30 A.M., greeting the champions at Greater Pittsburgh International Airport.

Two days later, they cheered as Lemieux raised the Cup at Point State Park. Before the celebration was over, the Cup would sit in the grass on Barrasso's front lawn and be dunked in the swimming pool at Lemieux's home.

MARCH 23, 1994

KINGS VS. CANUCKS

Wayne Gretzky had been known as The Great One since he burst onto the NHL scene in

Wayne Gretzky will forever cherish the puck that sent a hallowed mark into the shavings.

1979. On this night, however, Gretzky became The Greatest One.

Three days earlier, the Los Angeles Kings' Gretzky had scored a pair of goals against the San Jose Sharks, tying Gordie Howe's career record of 801 NHL goals. Those goals had been a long time in coming, since a case of the flu had limited Gretzky to just one goal in seven games over a three-week span. He finally caught up with Howe in the game against the Sharks, tying the game and the record when he scored in the final minute of what wound up a 6-6 deadlock. That set up the media crush for the Kings' next game, at home against Vancouver.

A sellout crowd of 16,005, including Gretzky's parents and NHL commissioner Gary Bettman, was on hand hoping to witness the milestone. They were disappointed in the first pe-

riod, which ended scoreless, and in the second period when the Canucks opened a 2-1 lead.

Then, when Vancouver's Jiri Slegr was penalized for holding the stick at 13:16 of the period, Gretzky and the Los Angeles power play went to work. Luc Robitaille carried the puck into the offensive zone and dropped the puck to Gretzky, who sent a lateral pass to Marty McSorley. McSorley returned the pass to Gretzky in the left circle and No. 99 fired the puck past an out-of-position Kirk McLean. "When I got the puck back, I saw the whole net," Gretzky said. "I can't believe I saw it."

The game was stopped as Gretzky's teammates poured onto the ice and highlights of his career were shown on the scoreboard. Gretzky's family joined him on the ice, as did Bettman.

"I want to congratulate you," the commissioner said. "It's an honor and a pleasure to see you break your idol's record. You've always been The Great One. Tonight, you became the greatest."

When asked afterwards if No. 802 meant the most of his many records, Gretzky said, "Yes, by far. There is no comparison. I don't think I've ever had a moment when I felt like this."

But he went on to warn that his record was in no way untouchable. "The records that are the best are the hardest ones to break," he said. "Somebody is going to have to play 16 years at 50 goals a year. That may happen. People like (Teemu) Selanne, (Sergei) Fedorov and (Eric) Lindros, if he stays healthy, those three guys have a strong chance."

In a way, it was fitting that Gretzky had set his mark against the Canucks. After all, it was Vancouver's Glen Hanlon who had surrendered The Great One's first NHL goal, way back on October 14, 1979.

JUNE 14, 1994
RANGERS VS. CANUCKS

"1940. 1940."

The chant had rung in the ears of the Rangers and their fans for some time now, a reminder that the team had gone quite awhile since winning its last Stanley Cup. Tonight, everyone connected with the team hoped, would be the night when the chant died.

The Rangers and Vancouver Canucks would be playing Game 7 of the Stanley Cup finals at Madison Square Garden. The Rangers had a chance to wrap up the series when they carried a 3-games-to-1 lead into Game 5 at the Garden, but the Canucks had staved off elimination with a 6-3 win that night and then a 4-1 victory back in Vancouver two nights later.

Now it was down to one game for the championship. A win, and the Rangers would never again have to hear about 1940. A loss, and the chant would be back, probably with more intensity, the following year. Ranger fans were hoping for the best, but fearing the worst. Before the game, scalpers were getting as much as $2,500 per ticket and those fans who couldn't get into the Garden waited outside in the street, hoping they would have something to celebrate at the end of the night.

After the clubs got over their early jitters, Brian Leetch gave the Rangers a 1-0 lead when he beat Canuck goalie Kirk McLean with a shot from the left circle at 11:02 of the first period. And it looked like the Rangers would have an easy time of it when Adam Graves added a power-play goal less than four minutes later. But Ranger fans knew not to start partying too early, for their team had a habit of giving up late goals to opponents.

Vancouver defenseman Jeff Brown was called for interference early in the second period, giving the Rangers a chance to break the game open. But the Canucks' Trevor Linden beat Mike Richter for a shorthanded goal that made it 2-1 and created a near-panic in the Garden. Mark Messier temporarily eased the tension with a power-play goal at 13:29 of the period, and now all the Rangers had to do was protect a two-goal lead down the stretch.

It wasn't easy. Linden scored again, this time on a power play, with 15:10 left, slicing the Rangers' lead to the slimmest of margins. Richter and McLean were both strong in net, keeping the

score at 3-2 as the minutes ticked away. Then, with about six minutes left, Vancouver pressed for the equalizer. But Nathan LaFayette's shot from close range clanged off the crossbar behind Richter, causing an audible sigh of relief from the partisan crowd.

Given that reprieve, the Ranger defense did its job in the final minutes, clearing rebounds and forcing the Canucks to shoot from bad angles. Three minutes. Then two. Finally, the clock went inside a minute. The Rangers were called for icing three times but the Canucks could not take advantage of the faceoffs in the offensive zone. Then, with 1.7 seconds left and the Garden crowd roaring, Craig MacTavish leaned over for the faceoff that would spell the end of 54 years of frustration. MacTavish won the draw, sending the puck into the corner, and the Rangers owned the Cup.

And "1940" would be heard no more.

APRIL 26, 1997
PENGUINS VS. FLYERS

It has been written that Philadelphia fans would boo Santa Claus. Philadelphia Flyers fans in particular are known to be the most passionate, vociferous fans in all of sports, showing their disapproval of not only the opponents but also the Flyers when things are not going well. But on this night—April 26, 1997—the CoreStates Center capacity crowd came not to boo the opponent but to salute him. The opponent's name was Mario Lemieux.

Lemieux had entered the league in 1984–85 and had battled Hodgkin's disease and a series of back injuries to become one of the greatest centers ever to play the game. But his love for the game began to wane in 1995–96 (even though he was the league's leading scorer). Lemieux let it be known early in 1996–97 that it would likely be his last campaign.

As the regular season ended, Mario made it official: Once the Penguins were out of the playoffs, his career would be over. Decimated by injuries late in the season, the Penguins had little chance against the powerful Flyers in the first round of playoffs. They dropped the first three games in mundane fashion before rebounding to take Game 4 in Pittsburgh. But with the series returning to Philadelphia for the fifth game, no one gave the Penguins a chance to win on the road and extend the series. So as the teams took to the ice that night, everyone in the arena knew that this would likely be Lemieux's last game.

As it turned out, the game itself was secondary to the event. Lemieux gave the Penguins brief hope when he beat Garth Snow at 15:54 of the first period, giving Pittsburgh a 2-1 lead, but the bigger, stronger Flyers gradually took over. Rod Brind'Amour scored twice before the period ended to give the Flyers a 3-2 lead, and though Ron Francis tied it early in the second period, Philadelphia proved to be too much. Goals by John LeClair and Trent Klatt made it 5-3 entering the third period, and then rookie Vaclav Prospal added an empty-netter in the final minute.

What happened then provided one of the more touching moments in NHL history. With the win insured, the crowd rose as one and started cheering—not for the Flyers, but for Lemieux. As the horn sounded and the teams lined up to shake hands, the salute to Lemieux became louder and louder. Several of the Flyers leaned over to whisper words of encouragement into Lemieux's ear, but it's doubtful he could have heard them. Finally, the handshakes completed, Lemieux raised his arms to the crowd to acknowledge the cheers. That only made the roar louder. The spectators were saying goodbye to a legend. After averaging better than two points a game over 745 regular-season contests and battling back from injuries, Lemieux was saying farewell. Mario accommodated his well-wishers, staying behind his teammates for a lap around the ice as the ovation continued. Then, after about five minutes of sustained applause, he left the ice for the final time.

When asked in the locker room if there was any chance he would reconsider and play again, Lemieux said simply, "Never. I played for 12 years and I feel pretty comfortable having won two cups, two Conn Smythes, and whatever else I've accomplished throughout my career."

JUNE 16, 1998

RED WINGS VS. CAPITALS

Detroit led, 2–1, when Red Wings trainer John Wharton leaned over to ask right wing Darren McCarty, "Do you see Vladdie?"

McCarty answered, "Where?"

"Behind the 'Believe' sign."

McCarty looked away from the action to find his former teammate in the stands. "No way!"

But there he was, Vladimir Konstantinov, once among the game's top defensemen, one of the two men for whom the Red Wings had dedicated the season. Arriving at the MCI Center in Washington in the second period of Game 4 of the 1998 Stanley Cup Finals, Konstantinov proved an inspirational force. The victim of a limo crash six days after winning the 1997 Cup, he could barely walk or talk, but that was progress. And here he was.

Minutes later, Larry Murphy would make it 3–1, then Doug Brown's second goal wrapped it up at 4–1.

"Believe" had become the team's slogan following the accident that severely injured Konstantinov and team masseur Sergei Mnastakanov, and slightly injured defenseman Slava Fetisov. The Wings had entered the new season with a pledge to win for Vladdie and Sergei.

Detroit faced additional adversity. Mike Vernon, the 1997 playoff MVP goalie, had been dealt to San Jose. Star center Sergei Fedorov held out most of the season with contract squabbles. Still they believed—in themselves and the ultimate rehabilitation of their fallen comrades.

They had a good season under Scotty Bowman, the winningest coach in the game's history, whose hardened methods had alienated some earlier in his career. But Bowman was a winner, the Wings knew it and paid heed to his instructions—no matter how puzzling they may have seemed. "He's in charge of this team," said captain Steve Yzerman. "The players have grown extremely fond of him. He's the guy who drives the team, and he puts fire into the team. He doesn't allow the players to get big egos or get overconfident or get too comfortable."

In the playoffs, Detroit always seemed to make things difficult for themselves, allowing Phoenix, St. Louis, and Dallas to extend them to six games in the earlier rounds. But they always found a way to win, a different player the hero each night. Even in the Finals against Washington, a club that had never played for the Cup before, each of the previous three games had been one-goal Detroit victories. In each, Washington had a chance to win. In each, Detroit would not be beaten.

On the bench, the legendary Bowman had a tear rolling down his cheek.

It would be a memorable night for many Wings. Fedorov had to regain conditioning and win back the fans. Goalie Chris Osgood played in Vernon's MVP shadow and overcame lingering questions about his performance. Yzerman, a veteran superstar who somehow escaped recognition, would be named this year's playoff MVP. Bowman would pilot his eighth Cup team, tying the record held by Montreal's Toe Blake. Everyone connected with Detroit would find a special reason to celebrate.

But no one attracted more sentiment than Konstantinov. At the final buzzer, the Wings deliriously mobbed each other, and then their inspiration was wheeled on to the ice, wearing his old number 16 sweater, joining his teammates in celebration, smiling, waving, holding a victory cigar. When Yzerman was presented with the Cup, the first person he passed it to was Vladdie. In a scene unlike any in Stanley Cup history, the traditional parade around the ice was led by a man in a wheelchair holding the trophy as thousands cheered.

"That was one of the greatest moments I've ever had" said right wing Brerdan Shanahan. "Not too often does a moment in hockey transcend sports, but that was one of them. That's a greater victory than winning the Stanley Cup."

Vladimir Konstantinov brought tears to the eyes of many hockey fans when he joined his teammates on the ice at the MCI Center to celebrate the Red Wings' second Stanley Cup.

11

THE
ALL-STAR GAME

I t's the showcase event on fans' calendars—when they have a chance to watch the league's best players display their artistry. It's the NHL's All-Star Game, which dates back to 1947.

The original format of the game pitted the Stanley Cup champions from the preceding season playing a team composed of All-Stars from the five other teams. These players were selected in a vote of hockey writers and broadcasters.

The Stanley Cup champion vs. All-Star team format remained until 1951, when it was changed to a true All-Star Game in which the First Team All-Stars from the previous season would play the Second Team All-Stars. That system was used for only two seasons, though, and in 1953 the league reverted to its Stanley Cup winners vs. All-Stars formula.

The game was played just before the start of the regular season and it would remain that way until expansion brought a change in 1967. The NHL's addition of six teams had resulted in two six-team divisions, called the East and West, and the All-Star Game, the first to be played in midseason, pitted the champion Montreal Canadiens against stars from the other 11 teams. The following season, the All-Star Game became a contest between the East All-Stars and West All-Stars, with the Eastern players representing the six original NHL franchises and the Western stars the six expansion franchises.

The addition of the Atlanta Flames and New York Islanders in 1972 did not affect the All-Star Game, but the expansion to Vancouver and Buffalo did two years later. That was when the NHL split into four divisions, with two divisions in the newly formed Wales Conference and two in the Campbell Conference. It was Wales vs. Campbell until 1994, and then Eastern Conference vs. Western Conference after the two conferences were renamed. The only exceptions were 1979, when a group of NHL All-Stars played a Soviet Union All-Star squad in a three-game Challenge Cup series, and in 1987, when the NHL stars and Soviet stars met in Rendez-Vous '87, a two-game series that replaced the All-Star Game.

In 1998, the format of the game was switched again. To spark interest, the game featured North American stars against stars from around the world.

Since 1985, the starting six players on the two teams have been selected in a poll of fans, while the remainder of each squad is chosen by the two All-Star coaches. One requirement is that each of the NHL teams has at least one representative.

There's no Stanley Cup at stake, but nobody likes to lose and there is an additional incentive for winning: $250,000, to be split among the players, coaches and trainers. The losers? Zero.

Players who compete in the skills competition that is part of the All-Star weekend do have a chance, however, to reap cash awards.

FIRST GAME
October 13, 1947 at Toronto
All-Stars 4, Toronto 3

Left wing Doug Bentley of the Chicago Blackhawks broke a 3-3 tie by drilling a shot past goalie Turk Broda in the second minute of the third period to give the All-Stars a 4-3 victory over the Maple Leafs.

Maurice Richard of Montreal and Syl Apps of the Leafs also starred. Richard assisted on the game-winning goal and scored once himself while Apps collected a goal and an assist.

Bill Mosienko, Chicago right wing, suffered a fractured left ankle when he was checked into the boards early in the second period.

All-Stars: Goal—Durnan (Montreal), Brimsek (Boston). Defense—Bouchard (Montreal), Reardon (Montreal), Stewart (Detroit), Quackenbush (Detroit). Forwards—M. Bentley (Chicago), D. Bentley (Chicago), Mosienko (Chicago), Warwick (New York), M. Richard (Montreal), Laprade (New York), Lindsay (Detroit), Dumart (Boston), Schmidt (Boston), Bauer (Boston), Leswick (New York), Coach—Dick Irvin (Montreal).

Toronto: Goal—Broda. Defense—Goldham, Stanowski, Mortson, Thomson, Barilko. Forwards—Watson, N. Metz, Poile, Kennedy, Apps, Ezinicki, Lynn, Meeker, Stewart, Klukay, Mackell. Coach—Hap Day.

Referee—King Clancy. Linesmen—Ed Mepham, Jim Primeau.

First Period: 1. Toronto, Watson (Ezinicki) 12:29. Penalties—Mortson, Leswick, Ezinicki 2, Reardon.

Second Period: 2. Toronto Ezinicki (Apps, Watson) 1:03. 3. All-Stars, M. Bentley (Reardon) 4:39. 4. Toronto, Apps (Watson, Mortson) 5:01. 5. All-Stars, Warwick (Laprade, Reardon) 17:35. Penalties—Lynn, Reardon 2.

Third Period: 6. All-Stars, M. Richard (unassisted) 0:28. 7. All-Stars, D. Bentley (Schmidt, M. Richard) 1:26. Penalties—Mortson 2, Bouchard, Ezinicki, Schmidt.

Attendance—14,138.

SECOND GAME
November 3, 1948 at Chicago
All-Stars 3, Toronto 1

Goals by Gaye Stewart, Ted Lindsay and Woody Dumart enabled the All-Stars to defeat the Maple Leafs, 3-1. Dumart accounted for the most spectacular tally when he skated the length of the ice and put the puck past goalie Turk Broda at 3:06 of the second period.

Dumart's goal gave the All-Stars a 2-0 lead. Max Bentley scored for Toronto two minutes later. Stewart, however, added an insurance goal for the visitors with only 28 seconds remaining in the second period. Only eight penalties were handed out by referee Bill Chadwick.

All-Stars: Goal—Brimsek (Boston), Durnan (Montreal). Defense—Stewart (Detroit), Quackenbush (Detroit), N. Colville (New York), Reardon (Montreal), Bouchard (Montreal). Forwards—Lindsay (Detroit), D. Bentley (Chicago), M. Richard (Montreal), Laprade (New York), Howe (Detroit), Stewart (Chicago), Dumart (Boston), Schmidt (Boston), Lach (Montreal),

Leswick (New York), Poile (Chicago). Coach—Tommy Ivan (Detroit).

Toronto: Goal—Broda. Defense—Thomson, Mortson, Boesch, Barilko, Mathers, Juzda. Forwards—H. Watson, M. Bentley, Klukay, Kennedy, Meeker, Ezinicki, Lynn, Costello, Mackell, Gardner. Coach—Hap Day.

Referee—Bill Chadwick. Linesman—Sam Babcock, Mush March.

First Period: No scoring. Penalties—Ezinicki, Reardon.

Second Period: 1. All-Stars, Lindsay (M. Richard, Lach) 1:35. 2. All-Stars, Dumart (unassisted) 3:06. 3. Toronto, M. Bentley (Costello) 5:13. 4. All-Stars, Stewart (D. Bentley) 19:32. Penalties—Mortson, Howe (major), Stewart, Bouchard, Juzda.

Third Period: No scoring. Penalty—Bouchard.

Attendance—12,794.

THIRD GAME
October 10, 1949 at Toronto
All-Stars 3, Toronto 1

Bob Goldham, a Chicago defenseman, registered the tying goal and assisted on the winner by Paul Ronty as the All-Stars defeated the Maple Leafs, 3-1, for their third straight victory over the Stanley Cup champions.

In the 15th minute of the second period, Goldham, after a rink-long dash, passed neatly to Boston's Ronty, who put the All-Stars ahead, 2-1. Goldham had tied the score with two minutes left in the opening period after Bill Barilko had found the nets for the Leafs three minutes earlier.

All-Stars: Goal—Durnan (Montreal), Rayner (New York). Defense—Stewart (Detroit), Goldham (Chicago), Egan (New York), Quackenbush (Boston), Harmon (Montreal), Reardon (Montreal). Forwards—O'Connor (New York), R. Conacher (Chicago), D. Bentley (Chicago), Mosienko (Chicago), M. Richard (Montreal),

Laprade (New York), Abel (Detroit), Howe (Detroit), Lindsay (Detroit), Leswick (New York) Ronty (Boston). Coach—Tommy Ivan (Detroit).

Toronto: Goal—Broda. Defense—Thomson, Boesch, Juzda, Barilko. Forwards—Watson, M. Bentley, Klukay, Meeker, Lynn, Mackell, Kennedy, Gardner, Timgren, Dawes, Smith. Coach—Hap Day.

Referee—Bill Chadwick. Linesman—Ed Mepham, Jim Primeau.

First Period: 1. Toronto, Barilko (Watson, Gardner) 15:22. 2. All-Stars, Goldham (Laprade) 18:03. Penalties—M. Richard, Meeker, Thomson, Howe.

Second Period: 3. All-Stars, Ronty (Goldham) 14:42. Penalties—Harmon, Thomson, Boesch, Egan, Smith.

Third Period: 4. All-Stars, D. Bentley (Quackenbush) 2:38. Penalties—None.

Attendance—13,541.

FOURTH GAME
October 8, 1950 at Detroit
Detroit 7, All-Stars 1

Left wing Ted Lindsay scored three goals in leading the Red Wings to a 7-1 triumph over the All-Stars, snapping the Stars' three-year winning streak.

Lindsay beat goalie Chuck Rayner of the Rangers only 19 seconds after the opening face-off. He scored again with three minutes remaining in the first period and registered No. 3 with five minutes left in the game.

Terry Sawchuk, a rookie, also was a standout for the Red Wings. He made 25 saves in goal, several of them spectacular stops.

All-Stars: Goal—Rayner (New York), Broda (Toronto). Defense—Stewart (Chicago), Mortson (Toronto), Thomson (Toronto), Harmon (Montreal), Quackenbush (Boston), Bouchard (Montreal). Forwards—D. Bentley (Chicago), Mosienko

(Chicago), M. Richard (Montreal), Laprade (New York), Kennedy (Toronto), Leswick (New York), Ronty (Boston), Smith (Toronto), Peirson (Boston). Coach—Lynn Patrick (Boston).

Detroit: Goal—Sawchuk. Defense—Goldham, Kelly, Reise, Fogolin, Pronovost. Forwards—Lindsay, Gee, Howe, Peters, Stewart, Abel, McFadden, Prystai, Pavelich, Carveth, Black, Couture. Coach—Tommy Ivan.

Referee—George Gravel. Linesmen—George Hayes, Doug Young.

First Period: 1. Detroit, Lindsay (Howe) 0:19. 2. Detroit, Lindsay (Abel) 17:12. Penalties—M. Richard, Leswick 2, Abel, Pronovost, D. Bentley.

Second Period: 3. Detroit, Howe (Lindsay, Kelly) 11:12. 4. Detroit, Peters (Prystai, Kelly) 18:36. 5. Detroit, Pavelich (Prystai, Peters) 19:44. Penalty—Couture.

Third Period: 6. Detroit, Prystai (Pavelich) 7:36. 7. Detroit, Lindsay (unassisted) 14:28. 8. All-Stars, Smith (Peirson) 18:27. Penalties—Peters, Stewart.

Attendance—9,166.

FIFTH GAME

October 9, 1951 at Toronto

First Team All-Stars 2, Second Team All-Stars 2

Ken Mosdell's goal midway through the third period and two fistfights highlighted a 2-2 tie between the First and Second All-Star teams.

Mosdell, a Montreal forward, forged the deadlock for the Second Team when he converted passes from Tod Sloan and Gus Mortson at 9:25 of the final session.

The fisticuffs involved Detroit's Gordie Howe and Montreal's Maurice Richard in one match and Detroit's Ted Lindsay and Toronto's Ted Kennedy in the other.

First Team: Goal—Sawchuk (Detroit), Lumley (Chicago). Defense—Kelly (Detroit), Quackenbush (Boston), Eddolls (New York), Fogolin (Chicago), Dewsbury (Chicago). Forwards—Schmidt (Boston), Howe (Detroit), Lindsay (Detroit), Raleigh (New York), Peirson (Boston), Sandford (Boston), Sinclair (New York), D. Bentley (Chicago), Stewart (New York), Bodnar (Chicago). Coach—Joe Primeau (Toronto).

Second Team: Goal—Rayner (New York), McNeil (Montreal). Defense—Thomson (Toronto), Reise (Detroit), Bouchard (Montreal), Harvey (Montreal), Mortson (Toronto). Forwards—Kennedy (Toronto), Abel (Detroit), M. Richard (Montreal), Smith (Toronto), M. Bentley (Toronto), Sloan (Toronto), Watson (Toronto), Mosdell (Montreal), Meger (Montreal), Curry (Montreal). Coach—Dick Irvin (Montreal).

Referee—Bill Chadwick. Linesmen—Sam Babcock, Bill Morrison.

First Period: 1. First Team, Howe (Lindsay, Schmidt) 7:59. Penalties—Curry, Eddolls, Sloan.

Second Period: 2. Second Team, Sloan (Watson, M. Bentley) 2:26. 3. First Team, Peirson (Stewart, Raleigh) 16:49. Penalties—Raleigh, Lindsay.

Third Period: 4. Second Team, Mosdell (Sloan, Mortson) 9:25. Penalties—Lindsay, Howe.

Attendance—11,469.

SIXTH GAME

October 5, 1952 at Detroit

First Team All-Stars 1, Second Team All-Stars 1

Maurice (Rocket) Richard, taking a pass from defenseman Hy Buller, scored at 1:36 of the third period to give the Second Team All-Stars a 1-1 tie with the First Team.

Marty Pavelich of Detroit had put the First Team in front at 9:57 of the second period after taking passes from Bill Mosienko of Chicago and Dave Creighton of Boston.

After Richard, Montreal's great right wing, tied the score, each team had several scoring opportunities but no success against goalies Terry Sawchuk of Detroit and Gerry McNeil of Montreal.

First Team: Goal—Sawchuk (Detroit). Defense—Kelly (Detroit), Harvey (Montreal), Mortson (Chicago), Quackenbush (Boston), Reise (New York), Goldham (Detroit). Forwards—Lach (Montreal), Howe (Detroit), Lindsay (Detroit), Creighton (Boston), Sandford (Boston), Pavelich (Detroit), Mosienko (Chicago), Leswick (Detroit), Sinclair (Detroit). Coach—Tommy Ivan (Detroit).

Second Team: Goal—Henry (Boston), McNeil (Montreal). Defense—Thomson (Toronto), Buller (New York), Johnson (Montreal), Flaman (Toronto), Bouchard (Montreal). Forwards—Schmidt (Boston), M. Richard (Montreal), Smith (Toronto), Watson (Toronto), Geoffrion (Montreal), Sloan (Toronto), Curry (Montreal), Reay (Montreal), Mosdell (Montreal), Megar (Montreal). Coach—Dick Irvin (Montreal).

Referee—Bill Chadwick. Linesmen—Doug Young, George Hayes.

First Period: No scoring. Penalties—Buller, Thomson, M. Richard.

Second Period: 1. First Team, Pavelich (Mosienko, Creighton) 9:57. Penalties—Bouchard, Thomson 2.

Third Period: 2. Second Team, M. Richard (Buller) 1:36. Penalty—Lach.

Attendance—10,680.

SEVENTH GAME

October 3, 1953 at Montreal
All-Stars 3, Montreal 1

Wally Hergesheimer of the New York Rangers scored two power-play goals in the opening period and paced the All-Stars to a 3-1 victory over the Canadiens.

Both of Hergesheimer's tallies came on plays originated by Detroit defenseman Red Kelly. Maurice Richard put Montreal on the scoreboard in the fifth minute of the third period. However, Detroit's Alex Delvecchio put the game out of reach with a goal into an empty net with 33 seconds left to play.

Kelly and Montreal's Bert Olmstead received major penalties for fighting in the third period.

All-Stars: Goal—Sawchuk (Detroit). Defense—Kelly (Detroit), Quackenbush (Boston), Gadsby (Chicago), Thomson (Toronto), Reise (New York), Mortson (Chicago). Forwards—Howe (Detroit), Lindsay (Detroit), Delvecchio (Detroit), Sandford (Boston), Smith (Toronto), Prystai (Detroit), Hergesheimer (New York), Mosienko (Chicago), Ronty (New York), Watson (Toronto). Coach—Lynn Patrick (Boston).

Montreal: Goal—McNeil. Defense—Harvey, St. Laurent, Bouchard, Johnson, MacPherson. Forwards—Moore, Curry, Olmstead, Beliveau, Geoffrion, Gamble, M. Richard, MacKay, Lach, McCormack, Mosdell, Meger, Davis, Mazur. Coach—Dick Irvin.

Referee—Red Storey. Linesmen—Sam Babcock, Doug Davies.

First Period: 1. All-Stars, Hergesheimer (Ronty, Kelly) 4:06. 2. All-Stars, Hergesheimer (Kelly) 5:25. Penalties—MacPherson, Lindsay.

Second Period: No scoring. Penalties—Mortson, St. Laurent, Howe, Richard.

Third Period: 3. Montreal, M. Richard (Harvey, Beliveau) 4:30. 4. All-Stars, Delvecchio (un-assisted) 19:27. Penalties—Kelly, Olmstead, Smith.

Attendance—14,153.

EIGHTH GAME

October 2, 1954 at Detroit

Detroit 2, All-Stars 2

Toronto's Gus Mortson and Boston's Doug Mohns fired second-period goals that enabled the All-Stars to gain a 2-2 deadlock with the Red Wings.

The game was highlighted by the stellar goaltending of Terry Sawchuk, who played all 60 minutes for the Wings, and Toronto's Harry Lumley and Chicago's Al Rollins, who split the netminding chores for the Stars.

Alex Delvecchio and Gordie Howe collected Detroit's goals, Delvecchio midway in the opening period and Howe 10 minutes later.

All-Stars: Goal—Lumley (Toronto), Rollins (Chicago). Defense—Harvey (Montreal), Mortson (Chicago), Horton (Toronto), Gadsby (Chicago), Howell (New York), Quackenbush (Boston). Forwards—Geoffrion ((Montreal), Mackell (Boston), Smith (Toronto), M. Richard (Montreal), Kennedy (Toronto), Beliveau (Montreal), Sandford (Boston), Raleigh (New York), Mosdell (Montreal), Ronty (New York), Mohns (Boston). Coach—King Clancy (Toronto).

Detroit: Goal—Sawchuk. Defense—Goldham, Pronovost, Kelly, Woit, Allen. Forwards—Lindsay, Leswick, Howe, Prystai, Skov, Reibel, Delvecchio, Wilson, Dineen, Poile, Bonin. Coach—Jim Skinner.

Referee—Bill Chadwick. Linesmen—George Hayes, Bill Morrison.

First Period: 1. Detroit, Delvecchio (Lindsay, Reibel) 9:50. 2. Detroit, Howe (Reibel, Kelly) 19:55. Penalties—Mortson, Bonin 2, Mackell, Howell.

Second Period: 3. All-Stars, Mortson (Gadsby, Kennedy) 4:19. 4. All-Stars, Mohns (Beliveau) 13:10. Penalties—Dineen, Bonin, Howell, Sandford, Mohns.

Third Period: No scoring. Penalties—Lindsay, Mortson, Woit.

Attendance—10,689.

NINTH GAME

October 2, 1955 at Detroit

Detroit 3, All-Stars 1

Earl (Dutch) Reibel scored twice as the Red Wings extended their unbeaten streak on home ice to 26 games by downing the All-Stars, 3-1.

The Wings, who finished the 1954–55 season with 19 victories and six ties at the Olympia, took the lead 57 seconds into the second period when Gordie Howe beat Toronto's Harry Lumley. Reibel made it 2-0 five minutes later. Doug Harvey of Montreal scored the Stars' only goal at 16:38 of the third period.

With a minute left in the game, All-Star coach Dick Irvin replaced goalie Terry Sawchuk with an extra forward and Reibel slid a long shot into the empty cage.

All-Stars: Goal—Lumley (Toronto), Sawchuk (Boston). Defense—Harvey (Montreal), Flaman (Boston), Morrison (Toronto), Stanley (Chicago), Martin (Chicago). Forwards—Beliveau (Montreal), M. Richard (Montreal), Smith (Toronto), Mosdell (Montreal), Geoffrion (Montreal), Lewicki (New York), Sullivan (Chicago), Litzenberger (Chicago), Stewart (Toronto), Labine (Boston), Watson (Chicago). Coach—Dick Irvin (Chicago).

Detroit: Goal—Hall. Defense—Goldham, Pronovost, Kelly, Godfrey, Hillman, Hollingworth. Forwards—Lindsay, Reibel, Howe, Delvecchio, Pavelich, Sandford, Chevrefils, Dineen, Toppazzini, Bucyk, Corcoran. Coach—Jim Skinner.

First Period: No scoring. Penalties—Flaman, Corcoran, Geoffrion, Stewart, Bucyk, Stanley, Morrison.

Second Period: 1. Detroit, Howe (Reibel, Delvecchio) 0:57. 2. Detroit, Reibel (Howe, Lindsay) 5:43. Penalties—Corcoran, Hollingworth.

Third Period: 3. All-Stars, Harvey (Beliveau, Smith) 16:38. 4. Detroit, Reibel (Goldham, Lindsay) 19:33. Penalties—Hollingworth, Harvey.

Attendance—10,111.

TENTH GAME

October 9, 1956 at Montreal

Montreal 1, All-Stars 1

The Canadiens and All-Stars played to a 1-1 tie in a game that marked the introduction of the new power-play regulation.

Maurice Richard clicked on a power play for Montreal only 33 seconds after the Rangers' Red Sullivan had been penalized for holding in the 15th minute of the second period.

Sullivan came out of the penalty box immediately after Richard's tally. Before the rule change, a player serving a minor penalty had to spend the full two minutes in the penalty box even if his team was scored against while shorthanded.

Detroit's Ted Lindsay evened the score four minutes after Richard's tally.

All-Stars: Goal—Hall (Detroit), Sawchuk (Boston). Defense—Gadsby (New York), Kelly (Detroit), Flaman (Boston), Mortson (Chicago), Morrison (Toronto), Bolton (Toronto). Forwards—Lindsay (Detroit), Sloan (Toronto), Howe (Detroit), Delvecchio (Detroit), Labine (Boston), Duff (Toronto), Armstrong (Toronto), Mickoski (Chicago), Wilson (Chicago), Hergesheimer (Chicago), Creighton (New York), Sullivan (New York). Coach—Jim Skinner (Detroit).

Montreal: Goal—Plante. Defense—Harvey, St. Laurent, Johnson, Turner, Talbot. Forwards—Beliveau, Geoffrion, Olmstead, Curry, Leclair, M. Richard, Moore, H. Richard, Marshall, Provost. Coach—Toe Blake.

Referee—Red Storey. Linesmen—Doug Davies, Bill Roberts.

First Period: No scoring. Penalties—Flaman, Beliveau 2.

Second Period: 1. Montreal, M. Richard (Olmstead, Harvey) 14:58. 2. All-Stars, Lindsay (Mortson) 18:48. Penalties—Mortson, Sullivan.

Third Period: No scoring. Penalties—Labine, Mortson.

Attendance—13,095.

ELEVENTH GAME

October 5, 1957 at Montreal

All-Stars 5, Montreal 3

Gordie Howe of the Detroit Red Wings and Dean Prentice of the New York Rangers each scored in the third period to give the All-Stars a 5-3 triumph over the Canadiens.

Howe broke a 3-3 tie at 8:11 and Prentice registered an insurance marker with 3:10 left in the game.

The Canadiens had taken a 3-2 lead in the second period on goals by Bert Olmstead and Stan Smrke, but the Rangers' Andy Bathgate tied it for the Stars at 18:14 of the second period on assists from Prentice and Chicago's Ed Litzenberger.

All-Stars: Goal—Hall (Chicago). Defense—Kelly (Detroit), Flaman (Boston), Gadsby (New York), Morrison (Toronto), M. Pronovost (Detroit), Stanley (Boston). Forwards—Howe (Detroit), Lindsay (Chicago), Litzenberger (Chicago), Chevrefils (Boston), Bathgate (New York), Duff (Toronto), Delvecchio (Detroit), Prentice (New York), Migay (Toronto), Armstrong (Toronto), McKenney (Boston). Coach—Milt Schmidt (Boston).

Montreal: Goal—Plante. Defense—Harvey, St. Laurent, Johnson, Turner, Talbot. Forwards—Beliveau, M. Richard, Curry, Olmstead, Smrke, Moore, Provost, H. Richard, Bonin, Goyette, A. Pronovost, Marshall. Coach—Toe Blake.

Referee—Red Storey. Linesmen—Doug Davis, Bill Morrison.

First Period: 1. All-Stars, Kelly (unassisted) 1:06. 2. Montreal, M. Richard (H. Richard, Moore) 10:53. 3. All-Stars, Stanley (Prentice, Migay) 19:55. Penalties—Migay, Talbot, Howe 2, Harvey.

Second Period: 4. Montreal, Olmstead (Johnson) 0:33. 5. Montreal, Smrke (Bonin) 9:13. 6. All-Stars, Bathgate (Prentice, Litzenberger) 18:14. Penalties—Talbot, Chevrefils, Johnson.

Third Period: 7. All-Stars, Howe (Chevrefils, Morrison) 8:11. 8. All-Stars, Prentice (Bathgate, Litzenberger) 16:50. Penalties—Flaman 2, Olmstead.

Attendance—13,003.

TWELFTH GAME
October 4, 1958 at Montreal
Montreal 6, All-Stars 3

Maurice Richard scored Montreal's first and final goals as the Canadiens defeated the All-Stars, 6-3, and ended a three-year non-winning streak for the Stanley Cup champions.

Referee Eddie Powers handed out six minor penalties and four led to goals. Andy Bathgate of the Rangers scored twice for the All-Stars while Bob Pulford of Toronto notched the visitors' other goal.

The Canadiens' Bernie (Boom Boom) Geoffrion suffered pulled neck and chest muscles from a bodycheck by Detroit's Red Kelly.

All-Stars: Goal—Hall (Chicago). Defense—Gadsby (New York), Flaman (Boston), M. Pronovost (Detroit), Mohns (Boston), Kelly (Detroit), St. Laurent (Chicago). Forwards—Howe (Detroit), Bathgate (New York), Henry (New York), Sullivan (New York), Delvecchio (Detroit), Toppazzini (Boston), Harris (Toronto), Duff (Toronto), Litzenberger (Chicago), McKenney (Boston), Pulford (Toronto). Coach—Milt Schmidt (Boston).

Montreal: Goal—Plante. Defense—Harvey, Johnson, Turner, Talbot, Cushenan. Forwards—Beliveau, Geoffrion, Backstrom, M. Richard, Moore, Provost, McDonald, H. Richard, Bonin, Goyette, Marshall, A. Pronovost. Coach—Toe Blake.

Referee—Eddie Powers. Linesmen—George Hayes, Bill Morrison.

First Period: 1. Montreal, M. Richard (Harvey, Moore) 9:19. 2. Montreal, Geoffrion (H. Richard) 16:20. Penalties—Henry, Harvey.

Second Period: 3. Montreal, Marshall (Provost) 2:33. 4. Montreal, H. Richard (Talbot, Moore) 5:08. 5. All-Stars, Pulford (Toppazzini, Harris) 11:39. Penalty—Turner.

Third Period: 6. All-Stars, Bathgate (Litzenberger, Henry) 3:55. 7. Montreal, McDonald (Provost, Marshall) 7:43. 8. All-Stars, Bathgate (Pulford, Sullivan) 13:54. 9. Montreal, M. Richard (Moore, H. Richard) 16:04. Penalties—Mohns, Duff, Provost.

Attendance—13,989.

THIRTEENTH GAME
October 3, 1959 at Montreal
Montreal 6, All-Stars 1

Big Jean Beliveau scored twice and defenseman Doug Harvey collected three assists as the Canadiens trounced the All-Stars, 6-1.

The Stars were considerably weakened by the absence of holdouts Bobby Hull, Tod Sloan and Pierre Pilote of Chicago and Bob Pulford, Dick Duff and Tim Horton of Toronto. They had not signed contracts for the season and therefore were ineligible to play.

Leading by 2-1 going into the third period, Montreal buried the Stars under a four-goal avalanche in the final 20 minutes. The marksmen were Beliveau, Dickie Moore, Henri Richard and Andrew Pronovost.

All-Stars: Goal—Sawchuk (Detroit). Defense—M. Pronovost (Detroit), Gadsby (New York), Flaman (Boston), Brewer (Toronto), Mohns (Boston). Forwards—Bathgate (New York), Howe (Detroit), Delvecchio (Detroit), Sullivan (New York), Toppazzini (Boston), Mahovlich (Toronto), Olmstead (Toronto), Litzenberger (Chicago), McKenney (Boston), Armstrong (Toronto). Coach—Punch Imlach (Toronto).

Montreal: Goal—Plante. Defense—Johnson, Harvey, Turner, Langlois, J.C. Tremblay. Forwards—Beliveau, Moore, H. Richard, Geoffrion, Backstrom, Hicke, M. Richard, Provost, McDonald, Bonin, Goyette, Marshall, A. Pronovost. Coach—Toe Blake.

Referee—Frank Udvari. Linemen—George Hayes, Bob Frampton.

First Period: No scoring. Penalties—None.

Second Period: 1. Montreal, Beliveau (Hicke, Harvey) 4:25. 2. Montreal, McDonald (Backstrom, Geoffrion) 13:43. 3. All-Stars, McKenney (Litzenberger) 18:30. Penalties— None.

Third Period: 4. Montreal, Moore (H. Richard, Johnson) 7:44. 5. Montreal, H. Richard (Moore, Harvey) 9:31. 6. Montreal, Beliveau (Hicke, Bonin) 11:54. 7. Montreal, Pronovost (Harvey) 15:51. Penalties—Tremblay, Bathgate, Turner.

Attendance—13,818.

FOURTEENTH GAME

October 1, 1960 at Montreal

All-Stars 2, Montreal 1

Andy Hebenton took a pass from his New York Ranger teammate, Red Sullivan, and beat goalie Jacques Plante at 15:51 of the second period to give the All-Stars a 2-1 victory over the Canadiens.

Frank Mahovlich of Toronto got the other Stars' goal in the opening minutes of the second period and Claude Provost tied the score for the Canadiens 11 minutes later.

This was the first All-Star game in which Maurice Richard, the Canadiens' brilliant right wing, did not participate. He had announced his retirement as a player the previous month.

All-Stars: Goal—Hall (Chicago). Defense— M. Pronovost (Detroit), Stanley (Toronto), Pilote (Chicago), Gadsby (New York), Kelly (Toronto), Armstrong (Boston). Forwards—Howe (Detroit), Hull (Chicago), Horvath (Boston), Stasiuk (Boston), Ullman (Detroit), Bathgate (New York), Hay (Chicago), Hebenton (New York), Sullivan (New York), McKenney (Boston), Mahovlich (Toronto), Pulford (Toronto). Coach—Punch Imlach (Toronto).

Montreal: Goal—Plante. Defense—Harvey, Langlois, Johnson, Turner, Talbot. Forwards— Beliveau, Geoffrion, Bonin, Backstrom, Hicke,

Moore, Provost, H. Richard, Marshall, A. Pronovost. Coach—Toe Blake.

Referee—Eddie Powers. Linesmen—George Hayes, Neil Armstrong.

First Period: No scoring. Penalty—Talbot.

Second Period: 1. All-Stars, Mahovlich (Pilote, Kelly) 0:40. 2. Montreal, Provost (Backstrom, A. Pronovost) 11:40. 3. All-Stars, Hebenton (Sullivan) 15:51. Penalties—Sullivan, Hull, Johnson.

Third Period: No scoring. Penalties— Hicke, Gadsby, Pilote, Harvey.

Attendance—13,949.

FIFTEENTH GAME

October 7, 1961 at Chicago

All-Stars 3, Chicago 1

Teammates Gordie Howe and Alex Delvecchio of the Detroit Red Wings each scored one goal and assisted on another to lead the All-Stars to a 3-1 triumph over the Blackhawks.

Delvecchio opened the scoring in the 12th minute of the opening period and Howe closed it in the 12th minute of the second session. Norm Ullman, another Red Wing, assisted on both tallies.

Eric Nesterenko beat Toronto goalie Johnny Bower for Chicago's only tally at 6:26 of the second period.

All-Stars: Goal—Bower (Toronto), Worsley (New York). Defense—Harvey (New York), Pronovost (Detroit), Boivin (Boston), Stanley (Toronto), Brewer (Toronto), Mohns (Boston). Forwards—Richard (Montreal), McKenney (Boston), Ullman (Detroit), Bathgate (New York), Geoffrion (Montreal), Howe (Detroit), Provost (Montreal), Mahovlich (Toronto), Moore (Montreal), Delvecchio (Detroit), Goyette (Montreal). Coach—Sid Abel (Detroit).

Chicago: Goal—Hall. Defense—Turner, Pilote, Vasko, Evans, Fleming, St. Laurent. Forwards—Hall, Balfour, Horvath, Murphy, Hay,

Melnyk, McDonald, Nesterenko, Hull, Wharram, Maki, Mikita. Coach—Rudy Pilous.

Referee—Frank Udvari. Linesmen—George Hayes, Neil Armstrong.

First Period: 1. All-Stars, Delvecchio (Ullman, Howe) 11:37. Penalties—Mahovlich, Hay, Vasko.

Second Period: 2. All-Stars, McKenney (Pronovost, Bathgate) 2:37. 3. Chicago, Nesterenko (Pilote, Hull) 6:26. 4. All-Stars, Howe (Delvecchio, Ullman) 11:38. Penalties—Goyette, Nesterenko 3, McKenney, Mahovlich 2.

Third Period: No scoring. Penalties—Pilote, Richard, Hull.

Attendance—14,534.

SIXTEENTH GAME
October 6, 1962 at Toronto
Toronto 4, All-Stars 1

The Maple Leafs erupted for all their goals in the opening period against Montreal goalie Jacques Plante and went on to defeat the All-Stars, 4-1, for their first victory in the annual classic.

Dick Duff, Bob Pulford, Frank Mahovlich and Eddie Shack beat Plante, who had captured the Vezina Trophy the previous season.

Detroit's Gordie Howe scored the only goal for the Stars. It was his seventh in the competition and enabled him to tie the record held by the retired Maurice Richard.

All-Stars: Goal—Plante (Montreal), Hall (Chicago), Worsley (New York). Defense—Harvey (New York), Talbot (Montreal), Pilote (Chicago), Mohns (Boston), Boivin (Boston). Forwards—McKenney (Boston), Howe (Detroit), Hull (Chicago), Geoffrion (Montreal), Bathgate (New York), Ullman (Detroit), Delvecchio (Detroit), Backstrom (Montreal), Prentice (New York). Coach—Rudy Pilous (Chicago).

Toronto: Goal—Bower. Defense—Brewer, Horton, Douglas, Baun, Hillman, Stanley. For-

wards—Kelly, Mahovlich, Nevin, Duff, Armstrong, Stewart, Keon, Harris, Pulford, Shack, MacMillan, Litzenberger. Coach—Punch Imlach.

Referee—Eddie Powers. Linesmen—Matt Pavelich, Ron Wicks.

First Period: 1. Toronto, Duff (Armstrong, Douglas) 5:22. 2. All-Stars, Howe (Delvecchio, Pilote) 7:26. 3. Toronto, Pulford (Stewart) 10:45. 4. Toronto, Mahovlich (Stanley) 13:03. 5. Toronto, Shack (Keon) 19:32. Penalties—Mohns, Nevin, McKenney, Brewer, Shack, Howe.

Second Period: No scoring. Penalties—Kelly, Howe, Brewer.

Third Period: No scoring. Penalties—Baun, Boivin, Shack.

Attendance—14,197.

SEVENTEENTH GAME
October 5, 1963 at Toronto
Toronto 3, All-Stars 3

Frank Mahovlich, Toronto's big left wing, scored two goals and collected an assist as the Leafs played a 3-3 tie with the All-Stars.

The Leafs held the lead three times, but each time the Stars rallied for a deadlock. Mahovlich scored his team's first two goals and Ed Litzenberger's tally put Toronto in front, 3-2, at 2:56 of the third period. Just 27 seconds later, Detroit defenseman Marcel Pronovost drilled the puck home from the point.

All-Stars: Goal—Hall (Chicago), Sawchuk (Detroit). Defense—Pilote (Chicago), Vasko (Chicago), Howell (New York), Johnson (Boston), Pronovost (Detroit). Forwards—Howe (Detroit), Richard (Montreal), Bathgate (New York), Hull (Chicago), Delvecchio (Detroit), Ullman (Detroit), Prentice (Boston), Oliver (Boston), Henry (New York), Bucyk (Boston), Geoffrion (Montreal), Provost (Montreal), Beliveau (Montreal). Coach—Sid Abel (Detroit).

Toronto: Goal—Bower, Simmons. Defense—Baun, Horton, Hillman, Douglas, Stanley. Forwards—Mahovlich, Shack, Kelly, Harris, Pulford, Nevin, Keon, Litzenberger, MacMillan, Stewart, Duff, Armstrong. Coach—Punch Imlach.

Referee—Frank Udvari. Linesmen—Matt Pavelich, Neil Armstrong.

First Period: 1. Toronto, Mahovlich (Armstrong, Baun) 2:22. 2. All-Stars, Richard (Henry, Howe) 4:08. 3. Toronto, Mahovlich (Keon, Litzenberger) 12:11. 4. All-Stars, Hull (Geoffrion) 19:27. Penalties—Stanley, Howell, Duff.

Second Period: No scoring. Penalties—Pronovost, Horton 2, Baun, Hull.

Third Period: 5. Toronto, Litzenberger (Mahovlich, Kelly) 2:56. 6. All-Stars, Pronovost (Bucyk, Oliver) 3:23. Penalty—Stanley.

Attendance—14,003.

EIGHTEENTH GAME

October 10, 1964 at Toronto

All-Stars 3, Leafs 2

Montreal's Jean Beliveau scored the tie-breaking goal with six minutes remaining in the second period and led the All-Stars to a 3-2 victory over the Maple Leafs.

Beliveau's goal snapped a 1-1 deadlock. Gordie Howe of Detroit and Bobby Hull of Chicago assisted on the play.

Murray Oliver of Boston put the Stars in front, 3-1, in the seventh minute of the third period, offsetting a Leafs' goal by Jim Pappin later in the session.

All-Stars: Goal—Hall (Chicago), Hodge (Montreal). Defense—Vasko (Chicago), Pilote (Chicago), Laperriere (Montreal), Howell (New York), Boivin (Boston). Forwards—Beliveau (Montreal), Howe (Detroit), B. Hull (Chicago), Delvecchio (Detroit), Gilbert (New York), Oliver (Boston), Henry (New York), Mikita (Chicago),

Bucyk (Boston), Provost (Montreal). Coach—Sid Abel (Detroit).

Toronto: Goal—Bower, Sawchuk. Defense—Horton, Douglas, Baun, Brewer, Hillman. Forwards—Pulford, Stewart, Shack, Keon, McKenney, Armstrong, Harris, Ehman, Pappin, Ellis, Bathgate, Mahovlich. Coach—Punch Imlach.

Referee—Frank Udvari. Linesmen—Ron Wicks, Neil Armstrong.

First Period: No scoring. Penalties—Bathgate, Howell, Baun, Douglas, Oliver.

Second Period: 1. All-Stars, Boivin (Laperriere, Oliver) 10:47. 2. Toronto, Douglas (Bathgate, Mahovlich) 11:45. 3. All-Stars, Beliveau (Hull, Howe) 13:51. Penalties—Laperriere, Mikita, Baun, Howell, Hodge (served by Gilbert).

Third Period: 4. All-Stars, Oliver (Bucyk, Howell) 6:11. 5. Toronto, Pappin (Ehman) 13:35. Penalties—Stewart, Pilote, Douglas, Provost.

Attendance—14,200.

NINETEENTH GAME

October 20, 1965 at Montreal

All-Stars 5, Montreal 2

Gordie Howe of Detroit shattered the career All-Star game record for goals by scoring his eighth and ninth while leading the All-Stars to a 5-2 victory over the Canadiens.

The veteran right winger, who also assisted on two other scores, broke the mark of seven goals he shared with the Canadiens' Maurice Richard. Howe broke another All-Star record by lifting his career-point total to 16. He played on a line with Norm Ullman, also of Detroit, and Chicago's Bobby Hull.

All-Stars: Goal—Hall (Chicago), Crozier (Detroit), Johnston (Boston). Defense—Gadsby (Detroit), Pilote (Chicago), Howell (New York), Pronovost (Toronto), Green (Boston), Baun (Toronto). Forwards—Ullman (Detroit), Howe (Detroit), Hull (Chicago), Ellis (Toronto), Hadfield (New York), Gilbert (New York), Oliver

(Boston), Bucyk (Boston), Mahovlich (Toronto), Nesterenko (Chicago), Delvecchio (Detroit), Mohns (Chicago). Coach—Billy Reay (Chicago).

Montreal: Goal—Hodge, Worsley. Defense—J. C. Tremblay, Harris, Laperriere, Talbot, Harper. Forwards—Beliveau, Rousseau, Duff, Backstrom, Larose, Provost, Richard, Balon, G. Tremblay, Ferguson, Berenson. Coach—Toe Blake.

Referee—Art Skov. Linesman—Matt Pavelich, Neil Armstrong.

First Period: No scoring. Penalties—Harris 2, Gadsby, Beliveau, Larose, Pronovost.

Second Period: 1. Montreal, Beliveau (Duff, Rousseau) 6:48. 2. Montreal, Laperriere (Backstrom, Larose) 11:00. 3. All-Stars, Ullman (Hull, Howe) 12:40. 4. All-Stars, Hull (Howe, Oliver) 16:35. 5. All-Stars, Howe (Ullman, Baun) 19:19. Penalty—Balon.

Third Period: 6. All-Stars, Bucyk (Gadsby, Oliver) 10:01. 7. All-Stars, Howe (unassisted) 18:39. Penalties—Ellis, Ferguson, Howell 2.

Attendance—13,351.

TWENTIETH GAME
January 18, 1967 at Montreal
Montreal 3, All-Stars 0

John Ferguson, Montreal's aggressive left wing, scored twice as the Canadiens blanked the All-Stars, 3-0, in a dull, listless contest, the first annual All-Star Game played in midseason.

Speedy Henri Richard put the Canadiens in front at 14:03 of the opening period when he converted passes from Bobby Rousseau and Terry Harper to beat Chicago's Glenn Hall, who was in the Stars' nets.

Ferguson scored less than two minutes later and again with only eight seconds remaining in the game.

All-Stars: Goal—Hall (Chicago), Giacomin (New York). Defense—Stanley (Toronto), Howell (New York), Stapleton (Chicago), Neilson (New York), Pilote (Chicago). Forwards—Ullman (Detroit), Mikita (Chicago), Keon (Toronto), Oliver

(Boston), Howe (Detroit), Gilbert (New York), Nevin (New York), B. Hull (Chicago), Mahovlich (Toronto), Bucyk (Boston), Delvecchio (Detroit). Coach—Sid Abel (Detroit).

Montreal: Goal—Hodge, Bauman. Defense—Laperriere, Talbot, Harper, J. C. Tremblay, Harris, Roberts. Forwards—Richard, Beliveau, Backstrom, Balon, Provost, Larose, Cournoyer, Rousseau, Rochefort, Duff, G. Tremblay, Ferguson. Coach—Toe Blake.

Referee—Vern Buffey. Linesmen—Matt Pavelich, Neil Armstrong.

First Period: 1. Montreal, Richard (Rousseau, Harper) 14:03. 2. Montreal, Ferguson (Larose) 15:59. Penalties—None.

Second Period: No scoring. Penalties—Howell, Richard, Ferguson.

Third Period: 3. Montreal, Ferguson (Richard, Rousseau) 19:52. Penalties—None.

Attendance—14,284.

TWENTY-FIRST GAME
January 16, 1968 at Toronto
Toronto 4, All-Stars 3

The Maple Leafs came from behind on second-period goals by Allan Stanley and Pete Stemkowski to defeat the All-Stars, 4-3, before a record All-Star crowd of 15,740.

The Stars took a 2-1 lead on Ken Wharram's goal in the opening minute of the second period. But Stanley, on passes from Stemkowski and Wayne Carleton, tied the score seven minutes later and Stemkowski put the Leafs in front to stay at 16:36.

A moment of silence was observed before the start of the game in tribute to Bill Masterton, the Minnesota forward who died the previous day from a head injury received in a game three days earlier.

All-Stars: Goal—Giacomin (New York), Hall (St. Louis). Defense—Pilote (Chicago), Howell (New York), Orr (Boston), Laperriere (Montreal), Baun (Oakland), J. C. Tremblay

(Montreal). Forwards—Mikita (Chicago), B. Hull (Chicago), Beliveau (Montreal), Ullman (Detroit), Howe (Detroit), Bucyk (Boston), Schinkel (Pittsburgh), Rochefort (Philadelphia), Balon (Minnesota), Marshall (New York). Coach—Toe Blake (Montreal).

Toronto: Goal—Gamble, A. Smith. Defense—Rupp, Horton, L. Hillman, Pronovost, Stanley. Forwards—Keon, Mahovlich, Ellis, Armstrong, Oliver, Stemkowski, Walton, Pappin, Pulford, Conacher, Carleton. Coach—Punch Imlach.

Referee—Bill Friday. Linesmen—Brent Castleman and Pat Shetler.

First Period: 1. Toronto, Oliver (Mahovlich, L. Hillman) 5:56. 2. All-Stars, Mikita (Hull, J. C. Tremblay) 19:53. Penalty—Stemkowski.

Second Period: 3. All-Stars, Wharram (Mikita) 0:35. 4. Toronto, Stanley (Stemkowski, Carleton) 7:56. 5. Toronto, Stemkowski (Carleton, Rupp) 16:36. Penalty—Howe.

Third Period: 6. Toronto, Ellis (Mahovlich, L. Hillman) 3:31. 7. All-Stars, Ullman (Howe, Orr) 8:23. Penalties—Howe, Walton.

Attendance—15,740.

TWENTY-SECOND GAME
January 21, 1969 at Montreal
East 3, West 3

For the first time, the All-Star Game pitted a squad from the new NHL West Division against one from the established East Division.

Claude Larose of Minnesota scored a goal with less than three minutes to play to give the underdog West a 3-3 standoff against the powerful East.

East All-Stars: Goal—Giacomin (New York), Cheevers (Boston). Defense—Orr (Boston), J. C. Tremblay (Montreal), Harris (Montreal), Green (Boston), Horton (Toronto), Stapleton (Chicago). Forwards—Beliveau (Montreal), Nevin (New York), Howe (Detroit), D.

Hull (Chicago), Esposito (Boston), Ullman (Toronto), Rousseau (Montreal), B. Hull (Chicago), Gilbert (New York), Mikita (Chicago), Mahovlich (Detroit). Coach—Toe Blake (Montreal).

West All-Stars: Goal—Hall (St. Louis), Parent (Philadelphia), Plante (St. Louis). Defense—Van Impe (Philadelphia), Arbour (St. Louis), Harvey (St. Louis), Vasko (Minnesota), Picard (St. Louis), Vadnais (Oakland), White (Los Angeles). Forwards—Berenson (St. Louis), O'Shea (Minnesota), Hicke (Oakland), Hampson (Oakland), Schinkel (Pittsburgh), Roberts (St. Louis), Larose (Minnesota), McDonald (St. Louis), Grant (Minnesota). Coach—Scotty Bowman (St. Louis).

Referee—John Ashley. Linesmen—Neil Armstrong, Matt Pavelich.

First Period: 1. West, Berenson (Harvey, Picard) 4:43. 2. East, Mahovlich (Rousseau, Stapleton) 17:32. Penalty—Vadnais.

Second Period: 3. West, Roberts (Berenson, Picard) 1:53. Penalties—Horton, White.

Third Period: 4. East, Mahovlich (Harris, Gilbert) 3:11. 5. East, Nevin (Ullman) 7:20. 6. West, Larose (Grant, O'Shea) 17:07. Penalties—White, Harvey.

Attendance—16,256.

TWENTY-THIRD GAME
January 20, 1970 at St. Louis
East 4, West 1

Chicago's Bobby Hull scored one goal and set up another by Gordie Howe of Detroit as the East All-Stars completely dominated the play and whipped the West, 4-1.

The East set a record with 44 shots on goal, including 20 in the last period, all of which were stopped by Jacques Plante of St. Louis. All of the East goals came in the first 30 minutes against Philadelphia's Bernie Parent. The West had just 17 shots, a record low.

Each team scored in the first 37 seconds with Jacques Laperriere hitting for the East and Pitts-

burgh's Dean Prentice for the West. The two goals were the fastest in All-Star history.

East All-Stars: Goal—Giacomin (New York), T. Esposito (Chicago). Defense—Orr (Boston), Laperriere (Montreal), Neilson (New York), Park (New York), Savard (Montreal), Brewer (Detroit). Forwards—P. Esposito (Boston), Bucyk (Boston), Howe (Detroit), Ratelle (New York), Tkaczuk (New York), Ellis (Toronto), Keon (Toronto), Lemaire (Montreal), B. Hull (Chicago), Gilbert (New York), McKenzie (Boston), Mahovlich (Detroit). Coach—Claude Ruel (Montreal).

West All-Stars: Goal—Hall (St. Louis), Parent (Philadelphia), Plante (St. Louis). Defense—Arbour (St. Louis), White (Los Angeles), Woytowich (Pittsburgh), Howell (Oakland), B. Plager (St. Louis), Vadnais (Oakland). Forwards—Berenson (St. Louis), St. Marseille (St. Louis), Clarke (Philadelphia), Goyette (St. Louis), Parise (Minnesota), Prentice (Pittsburgh), Roberts (St. Louis), O'Shea (Minnesota), Larose (Minnesota), McDonald (St. Louis), Goldsworthy (Minnesota), Grant (Minnesota), Sabourin (St. Louis). Coach—Scotty Bowman (St. Louis).

Referee—Art Skov. Linesmen—Matt Pavelich, Claude Bechard.

First Period: 1. East, Laperriere (unassisted) 0:20. 2. West, Prentice (Berenson, Woytowich) 0:37. 3. East, Howe (B. Hull, Lemaire) 7:20. Penalties—Park, St. Marseille.

All-Star alumni (from left) Phil Esposito, Bobby Orr, Gordie Howe and Bobby Hull share a laugh at the 1970 All-Star Game banquet in St. Louis.

Second Period: 4. East, B. Hull (Brewer) 3:26. 5. East, Tkaczuk (McKenzie, Bucyk) 9:37. Penalties—Woytowich.

Third Period: No scoring. Penalties—Woytowich.

Attendance—16,587.

TWENTY-FOURTH GAME

January 19, 1971 at Boston

West 2, East 1

The Chicago Blackhawks had moved from the East to the West Division at the start of the 1970–71 season and the expansion division reaped an immediate benefit in the All-Star game.

Blackhawk teammates Bobby Hull and Chico Maki scored goals in the first 4½ minutes and that was enough for a 2-1 West victory over the East. Montreal's Yvan Cournoyer got one goal for the East at 6:19 of the first period but the game was scoreless after that.

A crowd of 14,790 paid a record $79,000 to watch the defense-dominated game.

East All-Stars: Goal—Giacomin (New York), Villemure (New York). Defense—Park (New York), Tremblay (Montreal), Orr (Boston), Tallon (Vancouver), Neilson (New York), Smith (Boston). Forwards-Bucyk (Boston), P. Esposito (Boston), Hodge (Boston), Howe (Detroit), Westfall (Boston), Perreault (Buffalo), Cournoyer (Montreal), Keon (Toronto), Balon (New York), Ratelle (New York), P. Mahovlich (Montreal), F. Mahovlich (Montreal). Coach—Harry Sinden (Boston).

West All-Stars: Goal—Wakely (St. Louis), T. Esposito (Chicago). Defense—White (Chicago), Magnuson (Chicago), Harris (Minnesota), Roberts (St. Louis), B. Plager (St. Louis), Stapleton (Chicago). Forwards—Martin (Chicago), Berenson (St. Louis), B. Hull (Chicago), D. Hull (Chicago), Sabourin (St. Louis), Ecclestone (St. Louis), Clarke (Philadelphia), C. Maki (Chicago), Flett (Los Angeles), Grant (Minnesota), Mikita

(Chicago), Polis (Pittsburgh). Coach—Scotty Bowman (St. Louis).

Referee—Bill Friday. Linesmen—Neil Armstrong, John D'Amico.

First period: 1. West, C. Maki (unassisted) 0:36. 2. West, R. Hull (Flett) 4:38. 3. East, Cournoyer (D. Smith, Balon) 6:19. Penalties—Harris, F. Mahovlich, R. Hull.

Second period: No scoring. Penalties—Bucyk.

Third period: No scoring. Penalties—Stapleton, Magnuson.

Attendance—14,790.

TWENTY-FIFTH GAME

January 25, 1972 at Minnesota

East 3, West 2

Behind 2-0 on West goals by Chicago's Bobby Hull and Philadelphia's Simon Nolet, the East Division All-Stars roared back to tie the score on second-period goals by the Rangers' Jean Ratelle and Boston's Johnny McKenzie. Then Bruin Phil Esposito's third-period score gave the East the victory in the silver anniversary game.

A crowd of 15,423 braved sub-zero Minnesota temperatures to watch the clash of the two divisions. Esposito scored the winning goal against Gump Worsley, goaltender for the host Minnesota North Stars.

East All-Stars: Goal—Dryden (Montreal), Villemure (New York). Defense—Park (New York), Tremblay (Montreal), Orr (Boston), Seiling (New York), Smith (Boston). Forwards—Berenson (Detroit), R. Martin (Buffalo), P. Esposito (Boston), Gilbert (New York), Tallon (Vancouver), Perreault (Buffalo), Hadfield (New York), Cournoyer (Montreal), Henderson (Toronto), McKenzie (Boston), Ratelle (New York), F. Mahovlich (Montreal). Coach—Al MacNeil (Montreal).

West All-Stars: Goal—Worsley (Minnesota), T. Esposito (Chicago). Defense—White (Chicago), Magnuson (Chicago), Harris (Minnesota), Vadnais (California), Mohns (Minnesota), Stapleton (Chicago), Forwards—Unger (St. Louis), Goldsworthy (Minnesota), B. Hull (Chicago), D. Hull (Chicago), Lonsberry (Los Angeles), P. Martin (Chicago), Clarke (Philadelphia), C. Maki (Chicago), Nolet (Philadelphia), Mikita (Chicago), Polis (Pittsburgh). Coach—Billy Reay (Chicago).

Referee—Bruce Hood. Linesmen—Matt Pavelich, Claude Bechard.

First period: 1. West, B. Hull (P. Martin, C. Maki) 17:01. Penalty—Hadfield.

Second period: 2. West, Nolet (D. Hull) 1:11. 3. East, Ratelle (Tremblay, Gilbert) 3:48. 4. East, McKenzie (Park, Seiling) 18:45. Penalty—White.

Third period: 5. East, P. Esposito (Smith, Orr) 1:09. Penalties—White, P. Esposito, Tremblay, Mohns.

Attendance—15,423.

TWENTY-SIXTH GAME
January 30, 1973 at New York
East 5, West 4

Greg Polis, who arrived only hours before gametime following the birth of his first child in Pittsburgh, emerged as the star of the game, the first ever at New York's Madison Square Garden.

The Penguins' Polis scored two goals for the West and drove off with the car awarded to the game's Most Valuable Player. The East, however, drove off with the victory with Vancouver's Bobby Schmautz scoring the decisive goal with only six minutes left to play.

A record All-Star crowd of 17,500 watched the game.

East All-Stars: Goal—Giacomin (New York R.), Villemure (New York R.). Defense—Savard (Montreal), Park (New York R.), G. Bergman (Detroit), Orr (Boston), Lapointe (Montreal), Smith (Boston). Forwards—R. Martin (Buffalo), P. Esposito (Boston), Hodge (Boston), Schmautz (Vancouver), Cournoyer (Montreal), Keon (Toronto), Robert (Buffalo), Westfall (New York I.), Ratelle (New York R.), Henderson (Toronto), Lemaire (Montreal), F. Mahovlich (Montreal). Coach—Tom Johnson (Boston).

West All-Stars: Goal—T. Esposito (Chicago), Vachon (Los Angeles). Defense—White (Chicago), Harper (Los Angeles), Marotte (Los Angeles), Gibbs (Minnesota), B. Plager (St. Louis), Manery (Atlanta). Forwards—P. Martin (Chicago), Pappin (Chicago), Unger (St. Louis), D. Hull (Chicago), Parise (Minnesota), Dornhoefer (Philadelphia), Clarke (Philadelphia), Berry (Los Angeles), Mikita (Chicago), Polis (Pittsburgh), J. Johnston (California), MacDonald (Pittsburgh). Coach—Billy Reay (Chicago).

Referee—Lloyd Gilmour. Linesmen—Neil Armstrong, John D'Amico.

First period: No scoring. Penalties—Orr, Bergman.

Second period: 1. West, Polis (Clarke, MacDonald) 0:55. 2. East, Robert (Park) 3:56. 3. East, F. Mahovlich (unassisted) 16:27. 4. East, Henderson (P. Esposito, Hodge) 19:12. 5. West, P. Martin (D. Hull, Pappin) 19:29. Penalty—Hodge.

Third period: 6. East, Lemaire (F. Mahovlich) 3:19. 7. West, Polis (unassisted) 4:27. 8. West, Harper (Mikita) 9:27. 9. East, Schmautz (Savard) 13:59. Penalty—White.

Attendance—17,500.

TWENTY-SEVENTH GAME
January 29, 1974 at Chicago
West 6, East 4

Chicago's Stan Mikita, with a goal and two assists, and St. Louis' Garry Unger, with a goal and assist, led the expansionist West to a come-from-behind 6-4 triumph over the East.

The East jumped to a 2-0 lead in the first period but the West roared back to score three unanswered goals in the second. Unger, voted the game's Most Valuable Player, scored what proved to be the winning goal at 7:54 of the final period. The 10 goals were the most scored in an All-Star contest.

A capacity crowd of 16,426 attended the game at Chicago Stadium.

West All-Stars: Goal—Parent (Philadelphia), Esposito (Chicago). Defense—White (Chicago), Van Impe (Philadelphia), Burrows (Pittsburgh), Plager (St. Louis), Watson (Philadelphia), Awrey (St. Louis). Forwards—Berry (Los Angeles), Unger (St. Louis), P. Martin (Chicago), Hull (Chicago), Goldsworthy (Minnesota), McDonough (Atlanta), Pappin (Chicago), Clarke (Philadelphia), Johnston (California), Mikita (Chicago), MacDonald (Pittsburgh), Hextall (Minnesota). Coach—Billy Reay (Chicago).

East All-Stars: Goal—Gilbert (Boston), Dryden (Buffalo). Defense—Park (New York R.), Potvin (New York I.), Guevremont (Vancouver), Robinson (Montreal), McKenny (Toronto), Smith (Boston). Forwards—R. Martin (Buffalo), Esposito (Boston), Hodge (Boston), Ullman (Toronto), Schmautz (Vancouver), Berenson (Detroit), Cournoyer (Montreal), Cashman (Boston), Richard (Montreal), Westfall (New York I.), Redmond (Detroit), F. Mahovlich (Montreal). Coach—Scotty Bowman (Montreal).

Referee—Art Skov. Linesmen—Matt Pavelich, Willard Norris.

First period: 1. East, Mahovlich (Cournoyer, Ullman) 3:33. 2. East, Cournoyer (Ullman) 16:20. Penalty—Martin.

Second period: 3. West, Berry (Mikita) 5:59. 4. West, McDonough (Clarke, MacDonald) 13:55.. 5. West, MacDonald (Plager, Awrey) 19:07. Penalties—Hextall, Berenson.

Third period: 6. West, Mikita (Unger, White) 2:25. 7. West, Unger (White, Mikita) 7:54. 8. East, Potvin 9:55. 9. East, Redmond (Berenson) 14:55. 10. West, P. Martin (Pappin) 19:13. Penalty—Plager.

Attendance—16,426.

TWENTY-EIGHTH GAME

January 21, 1975 at Montreal
Wales Conference 7, Campbell Conference 1

NHL expansion turned the All-Star game into a battle of conferences: the Prince of Wales Conference against the Clarence Campbell Conference. In this first such pairing, Wales won easily, 7-1, at the Montreal Forum before a capacity crowd of 16,080.

Pittsburgh's Syl Apps Jr., son of a former NHL great, scored twice for Wales and was voted the game's MVP. Apps was the first son of an NHL All-Star to appear in an All-Star game.

Campbell All-Stars: Goal—Parent (Philadelphia), Smith (Vancouver). Defense—Park (New York R.), Van Impe (Philadelphia), Jarrett (Chicago), D. Potvin (New York I.), Pratt (Vancouver), Watson (Philadelphia). Forwards—Barber (Philadelphia), Unger (St. Louis), Pappin (Chicago), Vickers (New York R.), Gilbert (New York R.), Bennett (Atlanta), Lysiak (Atlanta), Clarke (Philadelphia), Nolet (Kansas City), Westfall (New York I.), Mikita (Chicago), Hextall (Minnesota). Coach—Fred Shero (Philadelphia).

Wales All-Stars: Goal—Vachon (Los Angeles), Dryden (Montreal). Defense—Harper (Los Angeles), Murdoch (Los Angeles), Orr (Boston), Korab (Buffalo), Lapointe (Montreal), Vadnais (Boston). Forwards—Luce (Buffalo), Esposito (Boston), Martin (Buffalo), Dionne (Detroit), Robert (Buffalo), Dupere (Washington), Pronovost (Pittsburgh), Lafleur (Montreal), Johnston (California), O'Reilly (Boston), Apps (Pittsburgh), Sittler (Toronto). Coach—Bep Guidolin (Boston-Kansas City).

Referee—Wally Harris. Linesmen—Leon Stickle, Claude Bechard.

First period: 1. Wales, Apps (Johnston, Vadnais) 9:38. 2. Wales, Luce (O'Reilly, Dupere) 12:02. 3. Wales, Sittler (Lafleur) 14:22. 4. Campbell, Potvin (Unger) 19:41. Penalties—None.

Second period: 5. Wales, Esposito (Lafleur, Murdoch) 19:16. Penalties—Vickers, Luce, Harper, Korab.

Third period: 6. Wales, Apps (Robert, Martin) 3:25. 7. Wales, O'Reilly (unassisted) 5:43. 8. Wales, Orr (Lafleur, Sittler) 7:19. Penalties—Watson, Clarke.

Attendance—16,080.

TWENTY-NINTH GAME

January 20, 1976 at Philadelphia
Wales Conference 7, Campbell Conference 5

Montreal's Pete Mahovlich collected a goal and three assists to pace Wales to a 7-5 victory over Campbell in the highest-scoring All-Star Game ever played.

It was a close game until midway of the second period, when Campbell coach Fred Shero inserted Philadelphia's Wayne Stephenson in goal. Wales scored on its first three shots against Stephenson to open a 6-1 lead. Wales coasted the rest of the way before a crowd of 16,436 at the Philadelphia Spectrum. Mahovlich was voted MVP.

Campbell All-Stars: Goal—Resch (New York I.), Stephenson (Philadelphia). Defense—Vadnais (New York R.), Russell (Chicago), D. Potvin (New York I.), Dupont (Philadelphia), Marks (Chicago), Watson (Philadelphia). Forwards—Unger (St. Louis), Vickers (New York R.), Paiement (Kansas City), Ververgaert (Vancouver), Barber (Philadelphia), Goldsworthy (Minnesota), Harris (New York I.), Bennett (Atlanta), Lysiak (Atlanta), Trottier (New York I.), MacLeish (Philadelphia), Leach (Philadelphia). Coach—Fred Shero (Philadelphia).

Wales All-Stars: Goal—Thomas (Toronto), Dryden (Montreal). Defense—Park (Boston), Robinson (Montreal), Burrows (Pittsburgh), Lapointe (Montreal), Korab (Buffalo), Salming (Toronto). Forwards—Larouche (Pittsburgh), Clement (Washington), Martin (Buffalo), Pronovost (Pittsburgh), Lafleur (Montreal), Ramsay (Buffalo), MacAdam (California), Sheppard (Boston), Dionne (Los Angeles), Shutt (Montreal), Mahovlich (Montreal), Maloney (Detroit). Coach—Floyd Smith (Buffalo).

Referee—Lloyd Gilmour. Linesmen—John D'Amico, Neil Armstrong.

First period: 1. Wales, Martin (Mahovlich, Lafleur) 6:01. 2. Campbell, Bennett (Dupont) 16:59. 3. Wales, Mahovlich (Lapointe, Lafleur) 18:31. 4. Wales, Park (Mahovlich, Martin) 19:00. Penalties—None.

Second period: 5. Wales, MacAdam (Maloney) 9:34. 6. Wales, Lafleur (Mahovlich, Martin) 11:54. 7. Wales, Dionne (unassisted) 13:51. 8. Wales, Maloney (Larouche, MacAdam) 16:59. Penalty—Barber.

Third period: 9. Campbell, Ververgaert (Trottier, Harris) 4:33. 10. Campbell, Ververgaert (Trottier, Harris) 4:43. 11. Campbell, D. Potvin (unassisted) 14:17. 12. Campbell, Vickers (Unger, D. Potvin) 14:46. Penalty—Marks.

Attendance—16,436.

THIRTIETH GAME

January 25, 1977 at Vancouver
Wales Conference 4, Campbell Conference 3

Rick Martin of Buffalo scored two third-period goals, including the game-winner with under two minutes to play, as Wales won their third straight over Campbell, 4-3, at the Pacific Coliseum in Vancouver.

Martin, voted MVP, scored at the four-minute mark to give the Wales a 3-2 lead. After the Rangers' Phil Esposito tied it with a goal at 12:23, Martin beat the Islanders' Chico Resch from in close with 1:56 remaining for the winning score before a crowd of 15,613.

Campbell All-Stars: Goal—Parent (Philadelphia), Resch (New York I.). Defense—Snepsts (Vancouver), Bladon (Philadelphia), Russell (Chicago), D. Potvin (New York I.), Joe Watson (Philadelphia), Jim Watson (Philadelphia). Forwards—Gilbert (New York R.), Unger (St. Louis), Paiement (Colorado), Lysiak (Atlanta), Dornhoefer (Philadelphia), Murdoch (New York R.), Clarke (Philadelphia), Young (Minnesota), MacLeish (Philadelphia), Nystrom (New York I.), Vail (Atlanta), Esposito (New York R.). Coach—Fred Shero (Philadelphia).

Wales All-Stars: Goal—Dryden (Montreal), Desjardins (Buffalo). Defense—Turnbull (Toronto), Lapointe (Montreal), Schoenfeld (Buffalo), Savard (Montreal), Robinson (Montreal), Salming (Toronto), Park (Boston). Forwards—Martin (Buffalo), McNab (Boston), McDonald (Toronto), Lafleur (Montreal), Perreault (Buffalo), Pronovost (Pittsburgh), Libett (Detroit), Charron (Washington), MacAdam (Cleveland), Gainey (Montreal), Dionne (Los Angeles). Coach—Scotty Bowman (Montreal).

Referee—Ron Wicks. Linesmen—Matt Pavelich, Ron Finn.

First period: 1. Campbell, Vail (Potvin) 2:54. 2. Wales, McDonald (Gainey, McNab) 6:22. Penalties—Campbell bench, Dornhoefer, Lapointe.

Second period: 3. Campbell, MacLeish (Nystrom, Potvin) 11:56. 4. Wales, McDonald (Perreault, Robinson) 19:27. Penalties—Potvin, Lapointe, Paiement, Joe Watson.

Third period: 5. Wales, Martin (Dionne, Robinson) 4:00. 6. Campbell, Esposito (Gilbert, Dornhoefer) 12:23. 7. Wales, Martin (Dionne, Lafleur) 18:04. Penalties—Russell, Salming.

Attendance—15,607.

THIRTY-FIRST GAME
January 24, 1978 at Buffalo
Wales Conference 3, Campbell Conference 2

Wales continued its domination of the All-Star classic, defeating Campbell, 3-2, for the fourth straight year.

Buffalo's Gil Perreault scored at 3:55 of sudden-death overtime for the winning score, but the MVP award went to New York Islander goalie Billy Smith, who stopped 16 shots in the first 30 minutes of action. A crowd of 16,433 attended the game at the Buffalo Auditorium.

Campbell All-Stars: Goal—Smith (New York I.), Stephenson (Philadelphia). Defense—Dailey (Philadelphia), Bladon (Philadelphia), Vadnais (New York R.), D. Potvin (New York I.), Watson (Philadelphia), Beck (Colorado). Forwards—Barber (Philadelphia), Bossy (New York I.), Paiement (Colorado), Gillies (New York I.), Clement (Atlanta), Ververgaert (Vancouver), Unger (St. Louis), Boldirev (Chicago), Clarke (Philadelphia), Trottier (New York I.), Esposito (New York R.), Eriksson (Minnesota). Coach—Fred Shero (Philadelphia).

Wales All-Stars: Goal—Dryden (Montreal), Vachon (Los Angeles). Defense—Savard (Montreal), Robinson (Montreal), Salming (Toronto), Park (Boston), Larson (Detroit). Forwards—Pronovost (Pittsburgh), Shutt (Montreal), Martin (Buffalo), McDonald (Toronto), Lafleur (Montreal), Perreault (Buffalo), Sirois (Washington), Cournoyer (Montreal), Dionne (Los Angeles), Maruk (Cleveland), O'Reilly (Boston), Gainey (Montreal), Sittler (Toronto). Coach—Scotty Bowman (Montreal).

Referee—Bruce Hood. Linesmen—John D'Amico, Leon Stickle.

First period: 1. Campbell, Barber (unassisted) 1:25. 2. Campbell, Potvin (Clarke) 12:12. Penalties—Salming, Gillies.

Second period: 3. Wales, Sittler (Robinson, Park) 19:32. Penalties—Dailey, Smith, McDonald, Vadnais.

Third period: 4. Wales, Martin (Dionne, O'Reilly) 18:21. Penalties—None.

Overtime: 5. Wales, Perreault (Shutt, Salming) 3:55. Penalties—None.

Attendance—16,433.

THIRTY-SECOND GAME
February 5, 1980 at Detroit
Wales Conference 6, Campbell Conference 3

After a year's absence due to the Challenge Cup series against the Soviet Union, the All-Star Game was returned to its regular format. And, as usual, Wales won, this time by a 6-3 count before 21,002 fans at Joe Louis Arena in Detroit. It was the fifth straight triumph for Wales.

Philadelphia's Reggie Leach, who scored a goal and assist for Campbell, was voted MVP, but it was 51-year-old Gordie Howe who stole the show. Hartford's Howe, playing in his final All-Star game, had an assist on the Wales' final goal and earned a long ovation from the largest crowd ever to attend an NHL game.

Campbell All-Stars: Goal—Peeters (Philadelphia), Esposito (Chicago). Defense—Lindgren (Vancouver), McEwen (Colorado), Picard (Washington), Greschner (New York R.), Watson (Philadelphia), Barnes (Philadelphia). Forwards—Barber (Philadelphia), Lukowich (Winnipeg), McDonald (Edmonton), Nilsson (Atlanta), MacLeish (Philadelphia), Bossy (New York I.), Trottier (New York I.), Federko (St. Louis), Propp (Philadelphia), Leach (Philadelphia), Esposito (New York R.), Gretzky (Edmonton). Coach—Al Arbour (New York I.).

Wales All-Stars: Goal—Edwards (Buffalo), Meloche (Minnesota). Defense—Stackhouse (Pittsburgh), Hartsburg (Minnesota), Schoenfeld (Buffalo), Robinson (Montreal), Burrows (Toronto), Larson (Detroit). Forwards—Ratelle (Boston), Cloutier (Quebec), Howe (Hartford), Lafleur (Montreal), Perreault (Buffalo), Murphy (Los Angeles), Goring (Los Angeles), Dionne (Los Angeles), Gainey (Montreal), Gare (Buffa-

lo), Payne (Minnesota), Sittler (Toronto). Coach—Scotty Bowman (Montreal).

Referee—Dave Newell. Linesmen—John D'Amico, Ray Scapinello.

First period: 1. Wales, Robinson (unassisted) 3:58. 2. Wales, Payne (Murphy, Goring) 4:19. 3. Campbell, Leach (McEwen) 7:15. Penalty—Hartsburg.

Second period: 4. Campbell, Nilsson (Federko, MacLeish) 6:03. Penalties—None.

Third period: 5. Campbell, Propp (P. Esposito, Leach) 4:14. 6. Wales, Stackhouse (Sittler, Lafleur) 11:40. 7. Wales, Hartsburg (Cloutier, Ratelle) 12:40. 8. Wales, Larson (Payne, Perreault) 13:12. 9. Wales, Cloutier (Howe) 16:06. Penalties—None.

Attendance—21,002.

THIRTY-THIRD GAME
February 10, 1981 at Los Angeles
Campbell Conference 4, Wales Conference 1

Campbell finally got into the win column as it posted a 4-1 victory over Wales. The triumph snapped the Wales' five-game victory streak.

Although outshot, 43-25, Campbell got outstanding goaltending from St. Louis' Mike Liut and Philadelphia's Pete Peeters. Liut, voted MVP, stopped 18 shots in the first period and seven more in the middle period before Peeters relieved him.

A crowd of 16,005 watched the game played at the Los Angeles Forum.

Campbell All-Stars: Goal—Liut (St. Louis), Peeters (Philadelphia). Defense—Dailey (Philadelphia), Wilson (Philadelphia), Ramage (Colorado), Potvin (New York I.), Murray (Chicago), McCarthy (Vancouver). Forwards—Barber (Philadelphia), Babych (St. Louis), Gartner (Washington), Bourne (New York I.), Lukowich (Winnipeg), Nilsson (Calgary), Holmgren (Philadelphia), Johnstone (New York R.), Williams (Vancouver), Bossy (New York I.), Fed-

erko (St. Louis), Gretzky (Edmonton). Coach—Pat Quinn (Philadelphia).

Wales All-Stars: Goal—Lessard (Los Angeles), Beaupre (Minnesota). Defense—Langway (Montreal), Picard (Toronto), Howe (Hartford), Bourque (Boston), Carlyle (Pittsburgh), Larson (Detroit). Forwards—Simmer (Los Angeles), Middleton (Boston), Kehoe (Pittsburgh), Smith (Minnesota), Dionne (Los Angeles), Rogers (Hartford), Taylor (Los Angeles), Ogrodnick (Detroit), Gare (Buffalo), Shutt (Montreal), Gainey (Montreal), P. Stastny (Quebec). Coach—Scotty Bowman (Buffalo).

Referee—Bryan Lewis. Linesmen—Jim Christison, Gerard Gauthier.

First period: 1. Campbell, Nilsson (Barber, Holmgren) :45. 2. Campbell, Barber (Johnstone) 8:02. Penalties—Bourne, Williams.

Second period: 3. Campbell, Babych (Johnstone, Federko) 16:12. Penalties—None.

Third period: 4. Wales, Ogrodnick (Howe, Kehoe) 6:13. 5. Campbell, Wilson (Bossy, Gretzky) 10:18. Penalties—None.

Attendance—16,005.

THIRTY-FOURTH GAME

February 9, 1982 at Landover, MD

Wales Conference 4, Campbell Conference 2

New York Islander Mike Bossy scored late in the second period to snap a 2-2 tie and then added an insurance goal early in the third period to send Wales to a 4-2 decision over the Campbell Conference Stars at Landover, Maryland.

While MVP Bossy was providing the offense, goaltenders Michel Dion of Pittsburgh and Don Edwards of Buffalo combined to stop 29 shots and help Wales win for the sixth time in seven games. A capacity crowd of 18,130 was on hand.

Campbell All-Stars: Goal—Fuhr (Edmonton), Meloche (Minnesota). Defense—Hartsburg (Minnesota), Coffey (Edmonton), Wilson (Chica-go), Manno (Toronto), Rautakallio (Calgary), Snepsts (Vancouver). Forwards—Gretzky (Edmonton), Savard (Chicago), Smith (Minnesota), Taylor (Los Angeles), Hawerchuk (Winnipeg), Ciccarelli (Minnesota), Lever (Colorado), Vaive (Toronto), Messier (Edmonton), Secord (Chicago), Sutter (St. Louis), Ogrodnick (Detroit). Coach—Glen Sonmor (Minnesota).

Wales All-Stars: Goal—Dion (Pittsburgh), Edwards (Buffalo). Defense—Ramsey (Buffalo), Bourque (Boston), Robinson (Montreal), Carlyle (Pittsburgh), Beck (New York R.), Langway (Montreal). Forwards—Trottier (New York I.), P. Stastny (Quebec), Acton (Montreal), Maruk (Washington), Stoughton (Hartford), Bossy (New York I.), Propp (Philadelphia), Middleton (Boston), Duguay (New York R.), Barber (Philadelphia), Tardif (Quebec), Tonelli (New York I.). Coach—Al Arbour (New York I.).

Referee—Wally Harris. Linesmen—Ron Finn, Swede Knox.

First period: 1. Campbell, Vaive (Sutter) 2:32. 2. Wales, Bourque (Maruk, Carlyle) 12:03. 3. Wales, Tardif (Middleton, Stastny) 13:27. Penalties—Tardif, Hartsburg.

Second period: 4. Campbell, Gretzky (Coffey, Ciccarelli) 0:26. 5. Wales, Bossy (Beck, Tonelli) 17:10. Penalties—Hawerchuk, Tardif.

Third period: 6. Wales, Bossy (Robinson) 1:19. Penalty—Stoughton.

Attendance—18,130.

THIRTY-FIFTH GAME

February 8, 1983 at Uniondale, N.Y.

Campbell Conference 9, Wales Conference 3

Edmonton's Wayne Gretzky scored four goals in the final period, shattering four All-Star Game records and helping the Campbell Conference post a 9-3 victory over the Wales Conference at Nassau Coliseum.

Gretzky's outburst helped the Campbell turn a close 3-2 game into a rout and hand the Wales

only their second loss in eight games. A capacity crowd of 15,230 witnessed Gretzky's feat, which won him MVP honors.

Campbell All-Stars: Goal—Bannerman (Chicago), Garrett (Vancouver). Defense—Huber (Detroit), Hartsburg (Minnesota), Murray (Chicago), Coffey (Edmonton), Wilson (Chicago), Babych (Winnipeg). Forwards—Broten (Minnesota), McDonald (Calgary), B. Sutter (St. Louis), Kurri (Edmonton), Messier (Edmonton), McCarthy (Minnesota), Vaive (Toronto), Dionne (Los Angeles), Savard (Chicago), Ciccarelli (Minnesota), Secord (Chicago), Gretzky (Edmonton). Coach—Roger Neilson (Vancouver).

Wales All-Stars: Goal—Peeters (Boston), Lindbergh (Philadelphia). Defense—Potvin (New York I.), Bourque (Boston), Howe (Philadelphia), Langevin (New York I.), Ramsey (Buffalo), Langway (Washington). Forwards—Francis (Hartford), Pederson (Boston), Walter (Montreal), Maloney (New York R.), Goulet (Quebec), Kehoe (Pittsburgh), Trottier (New York I.), Bossy (New York I.), M. Stastny (Quebec), P. Stastny (Quebec), Marini (New Jersey), Sittler (Philadelphia). Coach—Al Arbour (New York I.).

Referee—Bob Myers. Linesmen—Ryan Bozak, Leon Stickle.

First period: 1. Wales, Goulet (P. Stastny) 3:41. 2. Campbell, Babych (McDonald, Sutter) 11:37. 3. Wales, Bourque (unassisted) 19:01. Penalties—Sutter, Langevin.

Second period: 4. Campbell, Ciccarelli (Broten, Secord) 3:01. 5. Campbell, McCarthy (Ciccarelli, Murray) 14:51. Penalties—None.

A super sombrero is fitting for Wayne Gretzky after he scores four goals in the 1983 All-Star Game.

Third period: 6. Campbell, Gretzky (Kurri, Coffey) 6:20. 7. Campbell, McDonald (Sutter, Dionne) 7:29. 8. Campbell, Gretzky (Messier, Kurri) 10:31. 9. Wales, Maloney (Marini) 14:04. 10. Campbell, Gretzky (Wilson, Messier) 15:32. 11. Campbell, Vaive (unassisted) 17:15. 12. Campbell, Gretzky (Messier) 19:18. Penalties—Ramsey.

Attendance—15,230.

THIRTY-SIXTH GAME
January 31, 1984 at East Rutherford, N.J.
Wales Conference 7, Campbell Conference 6

Don Maloney of the New York Rangers tied an All-Star record with three assists and also had a goal as the Wales Conference outlasted the Campbell Conference, 7-6, at Meadowlands Arena in the highest-scoring All-Star Game ever.

Maloney won a $14,000 sports car as the game's MVP. The Wales' Mark Johnson of Hartford and the Campbell's Rick Vaive of Toronto also tied the All-Star Game record with three assists before a capacity crowd of 18,939.

Campbell All-Stars: Goal—Bannerman (Chicago), Fuhr (Edmonton). Defense—Babych (Winnipeg), Coffey (Edmonton), Lowe (Edmonton), Maxwell (Minnesota), Ramage (St. Louis), Wilson (Chicago). Forwards—Anderson (Edmonton), Bellows (Minnesota), Gretzky (Edmonton), McDonald (Calgary), Messier (Edmonton), Nicholls (Los Angeles), Ogrodnick (Detroit), Yzerman (Detroit), Rota (Vancouver), Savard (Chicago), Simmer (Los Angeles), Vaive (Toronto). Coach—Glen Sather (Edmonton).

Wales All-Stars: Goal—Peeters (Boston), Resch (New Jersey). Defense—Bourque (Boston), Cirella (New Jersey), Housley (Buffalo), Langway (Washington), O'Connell (Boston), Potvin (New York I.). Forwards—Kerr (Philadelphia), Bullard (Pittsburgh), Goulet (Quebec), Johnson (Hartford), Larouche (New York R.), Maloney (New York R.), Middleton (Boston), Naslund (Montreal), Pederson (Boston), Perreault (Buffalo), Propp (Philadelphia), P. Stastny (Quebec). Coach—Al Arbour (New York I.)

Referee—Bruce Hood. Linesmen—Ray Scapinello, John D'Amico.

First period: 1. Wales, Cirella (P. Stastny) 8:51. 2. Wales, Potvin (Kerr, Goulet) 9:30. 3. Wales, Middleton (Pederson, Housley) 14:49. 4. Wales, Naslund (Maloney, Potvin) 16:40. 5. Wales, Larouche (Johnson, Maloney) 17:14. Penalties—Housley.

Second period: 6. Campbell, Savard (Vaive, Rota) 1:23. 7. Campbell, Rota (Vaive, Savard) 5:51. 8. Campbell, Ogrodnick (Yzerman) 6:42. 9. Wales, Larouche (Maloney, Johnson) 17:34. Penalties—None.

Third period: 10. Wales, Maloney (Johnson, Cirella) 7:24. 11. Campbell, Babych (Ogrodnick) 8:11. 12. Campbell, Gretzky (Vaive, Simmer) 11:23. 13. Campbell, Bellows (Wilson) 17:37. Penalties—Maxwell, Resch.

Attendance—18,939.

THIRTY-SEVENTH GAME
February 12, 1985 at Calgary
Wales Conference 6, Campbell Conference 4

Penguin rookie Mario Lemieux had three points—including a game-clinching score in the third period—as the Wales Conference defeated the Campbell Conference, 6-4, before a crowd of 16,683 at Calgary's Olympic Saddledome.

Ray Bourque of the Wales stars set an All-Star Game record with four assists and tied a record with four points, but the 19-year-old Lemieux was voted the game's Most Valuable Player. It was his goal that gave the Wales a 5-3 lead that they protected down the stretch.

Campbell All-Stars: Goal—Fuhr (Edmonton), Moog (Edmonton). Defense—Carlyle (Winnipeg), Coffey (Edmonton), Lowe (Edmonton), MacInnis (Calgary), Reinhart (Calgary), Wilson (Chicago). Forwards—Anderson (Edmonton), Dionne (Los Angeles), Frycer (Toronto), Krushelnyski (Edmonton), Gradin (Vancouver), Gretzky (Edmonton), Hawerchuk (Winnipeg),

Kurri (Edmonton), MacLean (Winnipeg), Payne (Minnesota), Brian Sutter (St. Louis), Ogrodnick (Detroit). Coach—Glen Sather (Edmonton).

Wales All-Stars: Goal—Barrasso (Buffalo), Lindbergh (Philadelphia). Defense—Bourque (Boston), Chelios (Montreal), Langway (Washington), Ramsey (Buffalo), Russell (New Jersey), Stevens (Washington). Forwards—Bossy (New York I.), Carpenter (Washington), Francis (Hartford), Kerr (Philadelphia), Gartner (Washington), Goulet (Quebec), Hedberg (New York R.), Lemieux (Pittsburgh), Muller (New Jersey), Brent Sutter (New York I.), Tonelli (New York I.), Trottier (New York I.). Coach—Al Arbour (New York I.).

Referee—Andy van Hellemond. Linesmen—Gerard Gauthier, Bob Hodges.

First period: 1. Wales, Francis (Kerr) 1:40. 2. Wales, Kerr (Goulet, Bourque) 5:31. 3. Campbell, Dionne (Ogrodnick, MacInnis) 6:33. 4. Campbell, Frycer (Krushelnyski, Carlyle) 16:35. Penalties—Muller.

Second period: 5. Wales, Hedberg (Lemieux, Langway) 13:46. 6. Wales, Lemieux (Muller, Bourque) 17:47. Penalties—None.

Third period: 7. Campbell, Gretzky (Krushelnyski) 10:09. 8. Wales, Lemieux (Bourque) 11:09. 9. Campbell, Carlyle (Krushelnyski) 17:09. 10. Wales, Gartner (Bourque) 19:51. Penalties—Russell, Dionne.

Attendance—16,683.

The Rangers' Don Maloney won a car and a plaque as MVP of the 1984 All-Star Game.

THIRTY-EIGHTH GAME

February 4, 1986 at Hartford

Wales Conference 4, Campbell Conference 3

New York Islander teammates Mike Bossy and Bryan Trottier combined on a two-on-one in overtime to give the Wales Conference a 4-3 win over the Campbell Conference before a sellout crowd of 15,100 at the Civic Arena in Hartford.

Trottier took a pass from Bossy and beat goaltender Andy Moog of Edmonton from in close to give the Wales Conference the victory in only the second overtime All-Star Game in history. The MVP award went to Campbell goalie Grant Fuhr of Edmonton, who stopped all 15 shots he faced.

Campbell All-Stars: Goal—Fuhr (Edmonton), Moog (Edmonton). Defense—Lowe (Edmonton), Fogolin (Edmonton), Ramage (St. Louis), Coffey (Edmonton), Suter (Calgary), Wilson (Chicago). Forwards—Anderson (Edmonton), Hawerchuk (Winnipeg), Messier (Edmonton), Broten (Minnesota), Tanti (Vancouver), Clark (Toronto), Kurri (Edmonton), Taylor (Los Angeles), Savard (Chicago), M. Hunter (St. Louis), Ogrodnick (Detroit), Gretzky (Edmonton). Coach—Glen Sather (Edmonton).

Wales All-Stars: Goal—Gosselin (Quebec), Froese (Philadelphia). Defense—Mark Howe (Philadelphia), Langway (Washington), Ramsey (Buffalo), Bourque (Boston), Robinson (Montreal), Routsalainen (New York R.). Forwards—Lemieux (Pittsburgh), Muller (New Jersey), Gartner (Washington), Kerr (Philadelphia), Turgeon (Hartford), Bossy (New York I.), Trottier (New York I.), Goulet (Quebec), P. Stastny (Quebec), Poulin (Philadelphia), Propp (Philadelphia), Naslund (Montreal). Coach—Mike Keenan (Philadelphia).

Referee—Ron Wicks. Linesmen—John D'Amico, Gord Broseker.

First period: No scoring. Penalties—Suter, Gartner.

Second period: 1. Campbell, Tanti (unassisted) 7:56. 2. Wales, Propp (Naslund, Bourque) 17:56. Penalties—None.

Third period: 3. Wales, Stastny (Robinson, Turgeon) 4:45. 4. Campbell, Gretzky (Coffey, Savard) 17:09. 5. Wales, Propp (Robinson) 17:38. 6. Campbell, Hawerchuk (Savard, Coffey) 19:17. Penalties—Lowe, Turgeon, Messier, Gartner.

Overtime: 7. Wales, Trottier (Bossy) 3:05. Penalties—None.

Attendance—15,100.

THIRTY-NINTH GAME

February 9, 1988 at St. Louis

Wales Conference 6, Campbell Conference 5

Mario Lemieux's third goal of the game, an overtime tally at 1:08 of sudden death, lifted the Wales Conference All-Stars to a 6-5 victory over the Campbell Conference All-Star at The Arena in St. Louis. It was the fourth victory in a row for the Wales squad in the midseason classic.

Pittsburgh's Lemieux, the game's MVP, also added three assists to set an All-Star Game record with six points, two more than any player had ever scored. Wales teammate Mats Naslund of Montreal also broke the record with five points, all assists, in the game.

Campbell All-Stars: Goal—Fuhr (Edmonton), Vernon (Calgary). Defense—MacInnis (Calgary), McCrimmon (Calgary), Lowe (Edmonton), Ramage (St. Louis), Iafrate (Toronto), Suter (Calgary). Forwards—Adams (Vancouver), Gretzky (Edmonton), Anderson (Edmonton), Kurri (Edmonton), Savard (Chicago), Yzerman (Detroit), Bellows (Minnesota), Probert (Detroit), Nieuwendyk (Calgary), Messier (Edmonton), Hawerchuk (Winnipeg), Robitaille (Los Angeles). Coach—Glen Sather (Edmonton).

Wales All-Stars: Goal—Hextall (Philadelphia), Roy (Montreal). Defense—Howe (Philadelphia), Potvin (New York I.), Coffey (Philadelphia), K. Samuelsson (Philadelphia),

Bourque (Boston), Robinson (Montreal). Forwards—Neely (Boston), Muller (New Jersey), Dineen (Hartford), Gartner (Washington), LaFontaine (New York I.), Goulet (Quebec), Poulin (Philadelphia), Ruuttu (Buffalo), Naslund (Montreal), Stastny (Quebec), Sandstrom (New York R.), Lemieux (Pittsburgh). Coach—Mike Keenan (Philadelphia).

Referee—Denis Morel. Linesmen—Kevin Collins, Randy Mitton.

First period: 1. Campbell, Hawerchuk (Nieuwendyk, Bellows) 3:25. 2. Wales, Sandstrom (Lemieux, Naslund) 14:45. 3. Campbell, Gretzky (Probert) 18:46. Penalties—Potvin.

Second period: 4. Wales, Gartner (Lemieux) 4:28. 5. Wales, Stastny (Lemieux, Naslund) 10:08. 6. Wales, Lemieux (Naslund) 11:34. 7. Campbell, Robitaille (Savard, Lowe) 15:09. Penalties—LaFontaine, McCrimmon.

Third period: 8. Campbell, Savard (Robitaille, Anderson) 5:19. 9. Wales, Lemieux (Naslund, Dineen) 8:07. 10. Campbell, Robitaille (Anderson, Savard) 16:28. Penalties—Bellows.

Overtime: 1. Wales, Lemieux (Naslund, Dineen) 1:08. Penalties—None.

Attendance—17,878.

FORTIETH GAME

February 7, 1989 at Edmonton
Campbell Conference 9, Wales Conference 5

Los Angeles' Luc Robitaille and Edmonton's Jimmy Carson and Mark Messier scored goals in the final eight minutes as the Campbell Conference broke a four-game All-Star losing streak with a 9-5 victory over the Wales Conference at the Northlands Coliseum in Edmonton.

Wayne Gretzky, who had been traded from Edmonton to Los Angeles before the start of the season, celebrated his return by getting a goal and two assists and winning Most Valuable Player honors.

Campbell All-Stars: Goal—Fuhr (Edmonton), Vernon (Calgary). Defense—Ellett (Winnipeg), Manson (Chicago), Lowe (Edmonton), Suter (Calgary), Reinhart (Calgary), Duchesne (Los Angeles). Forwards—Gretzky (Los Angeles), J. Mullen (Calgary), Nicholls (Los Angeles), Leeman (Toronto), Messier (Edmonton), Carson (Edmonton), Ciccarelli (Minnesota), Hull (St. Louis), Kurri (Edmonton), Yzerman (Detroit), Robitaille (Los Angeles), Nieuwendyk (Calgary). Coach—Glen Sather (Edmonton).

Wales All-Stars: Goal—Lemelin (Boston), Burke (New Jersey). Defense—Stevens (Washington), Bourque (Boston), Coffey (Pittsburgh), Housley (Buffalo), Wesley (Boston), Robinson (Montreal). Forwards—Lemieux (Pittsburgh), LaFontaine (New York I.), Dineen (Hartford), Neely (Boston), MacLean (New Jersey), Smith (Montreal), Poddubny (Quebec), Brown (Pittsburgh), Tocchet (Philadelphia), B. Mullen (New York R.), Ridley (Washington), McPhee (Montreal). Coach—Terry O'Reilly (Boston).

Referee—Ron Hoggarth. Linesmen—Ron Asselstine, Wayne Bonney.

First period: 1. Campbell, Kurri (Gretzky, Robitaille) 1:07. 2. Campbell, Gretzky (Duchesne) 4:33. 3. Wales, Neely (Lemieux, Stevens) 9:47. 4. Wales, Poddubny (Ridley, Robinson) 10:38. Penalties—Messier.

Second period: 5. Wales, Wesley (LaFontaine, B. Mullen) 3:16. 6. Campbell, J. Mullen (Messier, Nieuwendyk) 7:57. 7. Campbell, Yzerman (Duchesne, Ciccarelli) 17:21. 8. Campbell, Leeman (Carson) 17:35. Penalties—Bourque.

Third period: 9. Wales, Poddubny (Tocchet, Robinson) 4:40. 10. Campbell, J. Mullen (Manson) 6:53. 11. Wales, Ridley (Bourque, Tocchet) 9:35. 12. Campbell, Robitaille (Kurri, Gretzky) 12:18. 13. Campbell, Carson (Leeman, Hull) 14:35. 14. Campbell, Messier (Nieuwendyk, J. Mullen) 17:14. Penalties—None.

Attendance—17,503.

FORTY-FIRST GAME

January 21, 1990 at Pittsburgh

Wales Conference 12, Campbell Conference 7

Playing in front of his hometown fans in Pittsburgh, Mario Lemieux scored four goals and skated off with his third Most Valuable Player award as the Wales Conference won a 12-7 shootout that was by far the highest-scoring All-Star Game in history.

Lemieux scored his first goal just 21 seconds into the game and had a hat trick before the first period was over. He tied Wayne Gretzky's record for goals in an All-Star Game with his fourth early in the third period.

Campbell All-Stars: Goal—McLean (Vancouver), Vernon (Calgary). Defense—MacInnis (Calgary), Lowe (Edmonton), Duchesne (Los Angeles), Iafrate (Toronto), Wilson (Chicago), Cavallini (St. Louis). Forwards—Gretzky (Los Angeles), Nieuwendyk (Calgary), Robitaille (Los Angeles) Mullen (Calgary), Nicholls (Los Angeles), Smail (Winnipeg), Messier (Edmonton), Gartner (Minnesota), Hull (St. Louis), Kurri (Edmonton), Yzerman (Detroit), Larmer (Chicago). Coach—Terry Crisp (Calgary).

Wales All-Stars: Goal—Puppa (Buffalo), Roy (Montreal). Defense—Leetch (New York R.), Hatcher (Washington), Housley (Buffalo), Coffey (Pittsburgh), Chelios (Montreal), Bourque (Boston). Forwards—Neely (Boston), Muller (New Jersey), Francis (Hartford), LaFontaine (New York I.), Sakic (Quebec), Turgeon (Buffalo), Andreychuk (Buffalo), Tocchet (Philadelphia), Propp (Philadelphia), Corson (Montreal), Lemieux (Pittsburgh), Richer (Montreal). Coach—Pat Burns (Montreal).

Referee—Kerry Fraser. Linesmen—Bob Hodges, Dan McCourt.

First period: 1. Wales, Lemieux (Propp, Neely) :21. 2. Wales, Andreychuk (unassisted) 5:13. 3. Wales, Turgeon (Francis) 9:22. 4. Campbell, Messier (Hull, Smail) 11:01. 5. Wales, Lemieux (Housley) 13:00. 6. Campbell, Yzerman (unassisted) 14:31. 7. Wales, Tocchet (Bourque, Muller) 16:55. 8. Wales, Lemieux (Coffey) 17:37. 9. Wales, Turgeon (Francis, Andreychuk) 18:52. Penalties—None.

Second period: 10. Wales, Muller (Coffey, Sakic) 8:47. 11. Campbell, MacInnis (Lowe) 9:03. 12. Campbell, Mullen (Nicholls) 13:00. 13. Wales, Corson (LaFontaine) 16:43. Penalties—Roy, Iafrate.

Third period: 14. Wales, Lemieux (Neely) 1:07. 15. Wales, Neely (Sakic, Hatcher) 11:20. 16. Campbell, Robitaille (Yzerman, Hull) 15:09. 17. Campbell, Robitaille (Hull, Yzerman) 16:11. 18. Wales, Muller (Tocchet) 17:50. 19. Campbell, Smail (Mullen, Nieuwendyk) 19:35. Penalties—Neely, Smail.

Attendance—16,236.

FORTY-SECOND GAME

January 19, 1991 at Chicago

Campbell Conference 11, Wales Conference 5

Vincent Damphousse, playing in his first All-Star Game, tied a record with four goals, three coming in the third period, as the Campbell Conference stars routed the Wales stars, 11-5, at Chicago Stadium.

Damphousse, the only Toronto Maple Leafs' representative, scored midway through the first period to give Campbell a 2-1 lead. He then took over in the final 11:06, beating Wales' goaltender Andy Moog of Boston to tie Wayne Gretzky and Mario Lemieux for most goals in an All-Star Game and win Most Valuable Player honors.

Campbell All-Stars: Goal—Vernon (Calgary), Ranford (Edmonton). Defense—MacInnis (Calgary), S. Stevens (St. Louis), Chelios (Chicago), Housley (Winnipeg), Suter (Calgary), S. Smith (Edmonton). Forwards—Oates (St. Louis), Fleury (Calgary), Damphousse (Toronto), Robitaille (Los Angeles), Messier (Edmonton), Gagner (Minnesota), B. Smith (Minnesota), Yzerman (Detroit), Roenick (Chicago), Larmer (Chicago), Gretzky (Los Angeles), Sandstrom (Los Ange-

les), Linden (Vancouver). Coach—John Muckler (Edmonton).

Wales All-Stars: Goal—Roy (Montreal), Moog (Boston). Defense—Leetch (New York R.), Hatcher (Washington), Coffey (Pittsburgh), Krupp (Buffalo), Galley (Boston), Bourque (Boston). Forwards—LaFontaine (New York I.), Turcotte (New York R.), Neely (Boston), Sakic (Quebec), Recchi (Pittsburgh), Tocchet (Philadelphia), Cullen (Pittsburgh), Verbeek (Hartford), K. Stevens (Pittsburgh), Christian (Boston), Savard (Montreal), Lafleur (Quebec), MacLean (New Jersey). Coach—Mike Milbury (Boston).

Referee—Terry Gregson. Linesmen—Jerry Pateman, Dan Schachte.

First period: 1. Campbell, Gagner (Larmer, Roenick) 6:17. 2. Wales, LaFontaine (Turcotte) 9:17. 3. Campbell, Damphousse (Oates) 11:36. Penalties—None.

Second period: 4. Wales, LaFontaine (Hatcher) 1:33. 5. Campbell, Suter (unassisted) 5:23. 6. Campbell, Gretzky (Sandstrom) 9:10. 7. Campbell, Oates (Yzerman) 9:48. 8. Campbell, Fleury (Messier, Chelios) 14:40. 9. Wales, Tocchet (Verbeek, Sakic) 15:36. 10. Campbell, Roenick (S. Smith, Oates) 17:07. Penalties—None.

Third period: 11. Wales, MacLean (Cullen, Bourque) 2:29. 12. Campbell, Chelios (Larmer, Roenick) 5:23. 13. Campbell, Damphousse (Oates, Housley) 8:54. 14. Campbell, Damphousse (Housley, Oates) 11:40. 15. Wales, K. Stevens (Tocchet) 13:56. 16. Campbell, Damphousse (unassisted) 17:14. Penalties—Housley 2.

Attendance—18,472.

FORTY-THIRD GAME
January 18, 1992 at Philadelphia
Campbell Conference 10, Wales Conference 6

St. Louis' Brett Hull scored twice and assisted on another to power the Campbell Conference to a 10-6 swamping of Wales. Playing on a line with Los Angeles' Wayne Gretzky, who had a goal and two assists, Hull posted his two goals in a six-goal second period that scorched Wales' goaltender Don Beaupre of Washington.

Hull won a car as MVP of the game, played before a crowd of 17,380 at the Spectrum in Philadelphia. For 40-year-old Los Angeles defenseman Larry Robinson, playing for Campbell, it marked his 10th All-Star appearance.

Campbell All-Stars: Goal—Belfour (Chicago), Cheveldae (Detroit), McLean (Vancouver). Defense—Chelios (Chicago), Ellett (Toronto), Housley (Winnipeg), MacInnis (Calgary), Robinson (Los Angeles), Tinordi (Minnesota), Wilson (San Jose). Forwards—Bellows (Minnesota), Damphousse (Edmonton), Fleury (Calgary), Hull (St. Louis), Linden (Vancouver), Gretzky (Los Angeles), Fedorov (Detroit), Oates (St. Louis), Roberts (Calgary), Robitaille (Los Angeles), Roenick (Chicago), Yzerman (Detroit). Coach—Bob Gainey (Minnesota).

Wales All-Stars: Goal—Beaupre (Washington), Richter (New York R.), Roy (Montreal). Defense—Bourque (Boston), Coffey (Pittsburgh), Desjardins (Montreal), Hatcher (Washington), Leetch (New York R.), S. Stevens (New Jersey). Forwards—Brind'Amour (Philadelphia), Burridge (Washington), Cullen (Hartford), Ferraro (New York I.), Jagr (Pittsburgh), Lemieux (Pittsburgh), Messier (New York R.), Mogilny (Buffalo), Muller (Montreal), Nolan (Quebec), Sakic (Quebec), K. Stevens (Pittsburgh), Trottier (Pittsburgh). Coach—Scotty Bowman (Pittsburgh).

Referee—Don Koharski. Linesmen—Mark Vines, Mark Pare.

First period: 1. Campbell, Linden (Roenick, Tinordi) 7:53. 2. Wales, K. Stevens (Lemieux, Jagr) 11:20. 3. Campbell, Gretzky (Hull, Robitaille) 14:56. Penalties—None.

Second period: 4. Campbell, Hull (Gretzky, Robitaille) :42. 5. Wales, S. Stevens (Mogilny, Messier) 5:37. 6. Campbell, Bellows (Fedorov, MacInnis) 7:40. 7. Campbell, Roenick (Ellett) 8:13. 8. Campbell, Fleury (Robinson) 11:06. 9. Campbell, Hull (Gretzky, Robitaille) 11:59. 10.

MVP honors went to Brett Hull of the St. Louis Blues in the 1992 All-Star Game.

Campbell, Fleury (Damphousse, Oates) 17:33. 11. Wales, Nolan (Sakic, Bourque) 19:30. Penalties—None.

Third period: 12. Wales, Trottier (Hatcher) 4:03. 13. Campbell, Bellows (Fedorov) 4:50. 14. Wales, Mogilny (Desjardins) 5:28. 15. Campbell, Roberts (Linden) 18:42. 16. Wales, Burridge (Sakic, Nolan) 19:13. Penalties—None.

Attendance—17,380.

FORTY-FOURTH GAME
February 6, 1993 at Montreal
Wales Conference 16, Campbell Conference 6

The Rangers' Mike Gartner tied an All-Star Game record with four goals, three coming in the first period, as the Wales Conference routed the Campbell Conference in the highest-scoring All-Star Game in history. Gartner scored at 3:15 and 3:37 of the opening period, then added a third at 18:02 to give the Wales a 6-0 lead. Gartner's fourth, at 3:33 of the second period, made it 8-0.

The Islanders' Pierre Turgeon had three goals and two assists for the Wales but lost out in the MVP balloting to Gartner. A crowd of 17,137 watched the game at the Montreal Forum.

Campbell All-Stars: Goal—Belfour (Chicago), Vernon (Calgary), Casey (Minnesota). Defense—Chiasson (Detroit), Chelios (Chicago), Coffey (Detroit), Butcher (St. Louis), Housley (Winnipeg), Carlyle (Winnipeg), Manson (Edmonton). Forwards—Gretzky (Los Angeles), Bure (Vancouver), Gilmour (Toronto), Modano (Minnesota), Robitaille (Los Angeles), Kisio (San Jose), Bradley (Tampa Bay), Roberts (Calgary), Yzerman (Detroit), Hull (St. Louis), Kurri (Los Angeles), Selanne (Winnipeg), Roenick (Chicago).

Wales All-Stars: Goal—Roy (Montreal), Billington (New Jersey), Sidorkiewicz (Ottawa). Defense—Lowe (New York R.), Bourque (Boston), Zalapski (Hartford), S. Stevens (New Jersey), Duchesne (Quebec), Iafrate (Washington), Marsh (Ottawa). Forwards—Gartner (New York R.), Oates (Boston), Mogilny (Buffalo), LaFontaine (Buffalo), K. Stevens (Pittsburgh), Turgeon (New York I.), Muller (Montreal), Sakic (Quebec), Recchi (Philadelphia), Bondra (Washington), Tocchet (Pittsburgh), Jagr (Pittsburgh).

Referee—Dan Marouelli. Linesmen—Kevin Collins, Ryan Bozak.

First period: 1. Wales, Gartner (Oates, Lowe) 3:15; 2. Wales, Gartner (Oates) 3:37; 3. Wales, Bondra (Oates, Gartner) 4:24; 4. Wales, Mogilny (Bourque) 11:40; 5. Wales, Turgeon (Recchi) 13:05; 6. Wales, Gartner (Oates, Bondra) 18:02. Penalties—Manson.

Second period: 7. Wales, Tocchet (K. Stevens, Recchi) :19; 8. Wales, Gartner (Turgeon) 3:33; 9. Wales, Tocchet (S. Stevens) 4:57; 10. Campbell, Roenick (Selanne) 5:52; 11. Wales, Recchi (Marsh) 9:25; 12. Campbell, Kisio (Roenick, Modano) 10:15; 13. Wales, K. Stevens (Recchi) 14:50; 14. Wales, Turgeon (Sakic, Jagr) 17:56. Penalties—None.

Third period: 15. Wales, LaFontaine (Muller, Mogilny) 8:07; 16. Wales, Jagr (Sakic, Turgeon) 9:08; 17. Wales, Marsh (K. Stevens, Recchi) 12:52; 18. Campbell, Gilmour (Coffey) 13:51; 19. Wales, Turgeon (Sakic, S. Stevens) 15:51; 20. Campbell, Selanne (Manson, Kurri) 17:03; 21. Campbell, Bure (Kisio) 18:44; 22. Campbell, Bure (unassisted) 19:31. Penalties—None.

Attendance—17,137.

FORTY-FIFTH GAME
January 22, 1994 at New York
Eastern Conference 9, Western Conference 8

Ottawa's Alexei Yashin scored with 3:42 remaining in the third period to give the Eastern Conference a come-from-behind 9-8 victory over the Western Conference before a sellout crowd of 18,200 at New York's Madison Square Garden. The East trailed 8-6 with less than 10 minutes remaining, but goals by Quebec's Joe Sakic and Florida's Bob Kudelski rallied them into a tie. Then Yashin, who had scored a goal in the first period, beat Western goalie Curtis Joseph of St. Louis for the game-winner.

Eastern Conference goaltender Mike Richter of the Rangers, who stopped 17 of 19 shots in the second period, was named MVP.

Eastern All-Stars: Goal—Roy (Montreal), Richter (New York R.), Vanbiesbrouck (Florida). Defense—Leetch (New York R.), Bourque (Boston), Galley (Philadelphia), Stevens (New Jersey), Murphy (Pittsburgh), Iafrate (Washington). Forwards—Messier (New York R.), Lindros (Philadelphia), Mogilny (Buffalo), Mullen (Pittsburgh), Recchi (Philadelphia), Graves (New York R.), Sanderson (Hartford), Oates (Boston), Turgeon (New York I.), Sakic (Quebec), Bradley (Tampa Bay), Yashin (Ottawa), Kudelski (Florida). Coach—Jacques Demers (Montreal).

Western All-Stars: Goal—Potvin (Toronto), Joseph (St. Louis), Irbe (San Jose). Defense—Chelios (Chicago), Coffey (Detroit), MacInnis (Calgary), Blake (Los Angeles), Ozolinsh (San Jose), Kasatanov (Anaheim). Forwards—Gretzky (Los Angeles), Hull (St. Louis), Bure (Vancouver), Andreychuk (Toronto), Corson (Edmonton), Selanne (Winnipeg), Taylor (Los Angeles), Shanahan (St. Louis), Nieuwendyk (Calgary), R. Courtnall (Dallas), Roenick (Chicago), Fedorov (Detroit), Gilmour (Toronto). Coach—Barry Melrose (Los Angeles).

Referee—Bill McCreary. Linesmen—Gord Broseker, Pat Dapuzzo.

First period: 1. West, Roenick (Nieuwendyk, Blake) 7:31; 2. East, Kudelski (Turgeon, Bourque) 9:46; 3. West, Fedorov (Bure, Ozolinsh) 10:20; 4. East, Lindros (unassisted) 11:00; 5. West, Shanahan (Gretzky, Hull) 13:21; 6. East, Yashin (Sakic, Turgeon) 14:29; 7. West, Andreychuk (MacInnis, Fedorov) 15:10. Penalties—None.

Second period: 8. East, Stevens (Oates, Sanderson) 10:37; 9. West, Coffey (Andreychuk, Gilmour) 12:36; 10. West, Ozolinsh (Taylor, Roenick) 14:39; 11. East, Messier (Mullen, Graves) 15:05. Penalties—None.

Third period: 12. West, Ozolinsh (Bure) :55; 13. East, Mullen (Graves, Messier) 1:28; 14.

West, Shanahan (Gretzky, Chelios) 7:40; 15. East, Sakic (Turgeon, Stevens) 10:41; 16. East, Kudelski (Messier) 13:59; 17. East, Yashin (Sakic, Turgeon) 16:18. Penalties—None.

Attendance—18,200.

(Editor's note: There was no All-Star Game in 1995 due to the lockout.)

FORTY-SIXTH GAME
January 20, 1996 at Boston
Eastern Conference 5, Western Conference 4

It was fitting that a Boston favorite, Ray Bourque, scored the goal, with 15 seconds left, that lifted the Eastern Conference to a 5-4 victory over the Western Conference at Boston's new FleetCenter. Playing before a sellout crowd of 17,565, Bourque flipped the rebound of Ranger Pat Verbeek's shot over the shoulder of Western goaltender Felix Potvin of Toronto and wound up as the game's MVP. Pittsburgh's Mario Lemieux, continuing a remarkable comeback season from Hodgkin's disease, had two assists for the East, while Detroit's Paul Coffey paced the West with a goal and assist.

Eastern All-Stars: Goal—Brodeur (New Jersey), Vanbiesbrouck (Florida), Hasek (Buffalo). Defense—Bourque (Boston), Stevens (New Jersey), Leetch (New York R.), Desjardins (Philadelphia), Schneider (New York I.), Hamrlik (Tampa Bay). Forwards—Lemieux (Pittsburgh), Shanahan (Hartford), Jagr (Pittsburgh), Turgeon (Montreal), Neely (Boston), Francis (Pittsburgh), Messier (New York R.), Bondra (Washington), MacTavish (Philadelphia), Verbeek (New York R.), LeClair (Philadelphia), Lindros (Philadelphia), Mellanby (Florida). Coach—Doug MacLean (Florida).

Western All-Stars: Goal—Belfour (Chicago), Osgood (Detroit), Potvin (Toronto). Defense—Coffey (Detroit), Chelios (Chicago), MacInnis (St. Louis), Hatcher (Dallas), Lidstrom (Detroit), Murphy (Toronto). Forwards—Gretzky (Los Angeles), Hull (St. Louis), Kariya (Anaheim), Selanne (Winnipeg), Nolan (San Jose),

Sundin (Toronto), Fleury (Calgary), Savard (Chicago), Sakic (Colorado), Forsberg (Colorado), Gartner (Toronto), Weight (Edmonton), Fedorov (Detroit), Mogilny (Vancouver). Coach—Scotty Bowman (Detroit).

Referee—Mark Faucette. Linesmen—Ron Asselstine, Brad Lazarowich.

First period: 1. Eastern, Lindros (Leetch, LeClair) 11:05; 2. Eastern, Verbeek (Lemieux, Schneider) 13:49. Penalties—Western bench (too many men).

Second period: 3. Eastern, Jagr (Lemieux, Francis) 2:07. 4. Western, Hull (Kariya, Coffey) 5:33. 5. Eastern, Shanahan (Turgeon, Neely) 8:51. 6. Western, Coffey (Fedorov, Mogilny) 11:42. 7. Western, Kariya (Sundin) 17:47. Penalties—Eastern bench (too many men).

Third period: 8. Western, Selanne (unassisted) 16:31. 9. Eastern, Bourque (Messier, Verbeek) 19:22. Penalties—None.

Attendance—17,565.

FORTY-SEVENTH GAME
January 18, 1997 at San Jose
Eastern Conference 11, Western Conference 7

Montreal's Mark Recchi scored three goals for MVP honors as he paced the Eastern Conference to an 11-7 whipping of the Western Conference at San Jose. Pittsburgh's Mario Lemieux's two goals and one assist enabled him to equal Ranger Wayne Gretzky's 20 points as the all-time All-Star Game scoring leaders. A sellout crowd of 17,442 saw San Jose's Owen Nolan make two goals just eight seconds apart in the second period, for an All-Star Game record.

Eastern All-Stars: Goal—Brodeur (New Jersey), Vanbiesbrouck (Florida), Hasek (Buffalo). Defense—Leetch (New York R.), Stevens (New Jersey), Coffey (Philadelphia), Svehla (Florida), K. Hatcher (Pittsburgh), Bourque (Boston). Forwards—Recchi (Montreal), Al-fredsson (Ottawa), LeClair (Philadelphia), Messier (New York R.), Bondra (Washington), Hawerchuk (Philadelphia), Palffy (New York I.), Sanderson (Hartford), Ciccarelli (Tampa Bay), Hunter (Washington), Lemieux (Pittsburgh), Jagr (Pittsburgh), Lindros (Philadelphia), Gretzky (New York R.). Coach—Doug MacLean (Florida).

Western All-Stars: Goal—Osgood (Detroit), Roy (Colorado), Moog (Dallas). Defense—MacInnis (St. Louis), Fetisov (Detroit), Hatcher (Dallas), Chelios (Chicago), Ozolinsh (Colorado), Tverdovsky (Phoenix). Forwards—Selanne (Anaheim), Kariya (Anaheim), Amonte (Chicago), Nolan (San Jose), Sundin (Toronto), Fleury (Calgary), Shanahan (Detroit), Hull (St. Louis), Yzerman (Detroit), Granato (San Jose), Arnott (Edmonton), Modano (Dallas), Bure (Vancouver). Coach—Ken Hitchcock (Dallas).

Referee—Bob Shick. Linesmen—Ron Asselstine, Bob Hodges, Leo Stickle.

First period: 1. East, LeClair (Bondra, Stevens) 8:52; 2. East, Lemieux (Gretzky) 9:49; 3. East, Recchi (Messier, Alfredsson) 15:32; 4. East, Hawerchuk (Lindros, Coffey) 16:19; 5. West, Bure (Sundin, Amonte) 17:36; 6. West, Kariya (Bure, Ozolinsh) 18:36. Penalties—None.

Second period: 7. East, Recchi (Svehla, Messier) 1:56; 8. East, Sanderson (Lindros) 3:21; 9. West, Bure (Selanne, Fetisov) 4:40; 10. East, Lemieux (Svehla, Ciccarelli) 6:09; 11. East, Messier (K. Hatcher, Alfredsson) 8:45; 12. East, Recchi (Oates, Lemieux) 10:57; 13. West, Shanahan (Hull, Ozolinsh) 16:38 (pp); 14. East, Hawerchuk (LeClair, Stevens) 17:28; 15. West, Nolan (Fleury, Ozolinsh) 18:54; 16. West, Nolan (Amonte) 19:02. Penalties—Coffey.

Third period: 17. East, LeClair (Bondra, Oates) 8:50; 18. West, Nolan 17:57. Penalties—K. Hatcher.

Attendance—17,442.

FORTY-EIGHTH GAME
January 18, 1998 at Vancouver
North America 8, World 7

The NHL changed its All-Star format to underscore the league's participation in the 1998 Winter Olympics. One team would represent North America; the other would comprise European-born players.

Anaheim's Teemu Selanne became the first European-born (Helsinki) player to record a hat trick in All-Star play and was the MVP. But North America prevailed, 8–7.

Two of Selanne's goals came in the first four minutes of the game as the World jumped into a 2–0 lead. It became 3–0 before the North Americans tied it up by the end of the first period. They went ahead for good near the end of the second period.

With his assist in the first period, Wayne Gretzky recaptured the all-time All-Star scoring lead from the retired Mario Lemieux. Gretzky has 22 points in 17 games, Lemieux 20 points in 8 games.

World: Goal—Hasek (Buffalo), Khabibulin (Phoenix), Kolzig (Washington). Defense—Ozolinsh (Colorado), Fetisov (Detroit), Kravchuk (Ottawa), Lidstrom (Detroit), D. Mironov (Anaheim), Zubov (Dallas). Forwards—Forsberg (Colorado), Koivu (Montreal), Sundin (Toronto), Holik (New Jersey), Larionov (Detroit), Jagr (Pittsburgh), Selanne (Anaheim), Alfredsson (Ottawa), Bondra (Washington), P. Bure (Vancouver), Kamensky (Colorado), Palffy (New York I.), Lehtinen (Dallas), Kurri (Colorado). Coach—Ken Hitchcock (Dallas).

North America: Goal—Roy (Colorado), Belfour (Dallas), Brodeur (New Jersey). Defense—Bourque (Boston), Leetch (New York R.), Chelios (Chicago), S. Niedermayer (New Jersey), S. Stevens (New Jersey), Sydor (Dallas), MacInnis (St. Louis). Forwards— Lindros (Philadelphia), Gretzky (New York R.), Modano (Dallas), Sakic (Colorado), Weight (Edmonton), Messier (Vancouver), LeClair (Philadelphia), Shanahan (Detroit),

Amonte (Chicago), Corson (Montreal), Fleury (Calgary), Recchi (Montreal), Tkachuk (Phoenix). Coach—Jacques Lemaire (New Jersey).

Referee—Paul Stewart. Linesmen—Mike Civik, Shane Heyer.

First period: 1. World, Selanne (Koivu) 0:53; 2. World, Jagr (Bondra, Mironov) 2:15; 3. World, Selanne (Lehtinen, Fetisov) 4:00; 4. North America, LeClair (Gretzky, Chelios) 4:13; 5. North America, Tkachuk (Fleury, Chelios) 10:50 (pp); 6. North America, Niedermayer (Sakic, Recchi) 18:25. Penalties—Fetisov.

Second period: 7. North America, Fleury (Modano, Tkachuk) 1:53; 8. World, Selanne (Lehtinen, Koivu) 7:11; 9. World, Kurri (Koivu, Lehtinen) 12:36; 10. North America, Lindros (Chelios, Messier) 14:46; 11. North America, Amonte (Sakic, Bourque) 16:19. Penalties—Fleury.

Third period: 12. North America, Tkachuk (Modano, Fleury) 1:36; 13. North America, Messier (Gretzky) 4:00; 14. World, Kravchuk (Sundin, Forsberg) 7:03; 15. World, Larionov (Bure) 9:41. Penalties—Weight.

Attendance —18,422.

FORTY-NINTH GAME
January 24, 1999 at Tampa Bay
North America 8, World 6

It was a fitting finale for the retiring Wayne Gretzky as he won his third All-Star Game MVP award in leading North America to an 8–6 victory over the World in Tampa Bay.

Playing in a record 18th consecutive All-Star Game, Gretzky recorded a goal and two assists. Ray Bourque's goal for the winners 17 seconds into the second period set an All-Star mark for fastest goal from the start of a period.

North America led all the way, but the World rallied to cut North America's margin to 7–5 on goals by Teemu Selanne, Pavol Demitra, Mattias Ohlund, and Mats Sundin in the third period.

But the day belonged to Gretzky.

North America: Goal—Martin Brodeur (New Jersey), Ed Belfour (Dallas), Ron Tugnutt (Ottawa). Defense—Ray Bourque (Boston), Al MacInnis (St. Louis), Rob Blake (Los Angeles), Chris Pronger (St. Louis), Larry Murphy (Detroit). Wing—Paul Kariya (Anaheim), Brendan Shanahan (Detroit), Keith Tkachuk (Phoenix), Mark Recchi (Montreal), John LeClaire (Philadelphia), Tony Amonte (Chicago), Wendell Clark (Tampa Bay), Luc Robitaille (Los Angeles), Theoren Fleury (Calgary). Center—Eric Lindros (Philadelphia), Jeremy Roenick (Phoenix), Wayne Gretzky (N.Y. Rangers).

World: Goal—Dominik Hasek (Buffalo), Nikolai Khabublin (Phoenix), Arturs Irbe (Carolina). Defense—Nicklas Lidstrom (Detroit), Teppo Numminen (Phoenix), Mattias Norstrom (Los Angeles), Matias Ohlund (Vancouver), Alexei Zhitnik (Buffalo), Sergei Zubov (Dallas). Wing—Teemu Selanne (Anaheim), Jaromir Jagr (Pittsburgh), Marcus Naslund (Vancouver), Peter Bondra (Washington), Sergei Krivokrasov (Nashville), Pavol Demitra (St. Louis), Dmitri Khristich (Boston). Center—Peter Forsberg (Colorado), Mats Sundin (Toronto), Bobby Holik (New Jersey), Alexie Yashin (Ottawa), Marco Sturm (San Jose), Martin Straka (Pittsburgh).

Referee—Paul Devorski. Linesmen—Pierre Champoux, Brian Murphy.

First period: 1. North America, Modano (Robitaille, Pronger) 4:09; 2. World, Sturm (Forsberg, Sundin) 9:42; 3. North America, Robitaille (Roenick, Clark) 10:06; 4. North America, Kariya (Amonte, Modano) 16:45; 5. North America, Recchi (Gretzky, Fleury) 17:18. Penalties—None.

Second period: 6. North America, Bourque (Modano) 0:17; 7. North America, Gretzky (Fleury, Pronger) 1:14; 8. World, Selanne (Yashin, Irbe) 2:02; 9. World, Demitra (Zhnitik, Sundin) 8:59; 10. North America, Blake (Gretzky, Recchi) 14:23; 11. World, Ohlund (Naslund, Sundin) 15:08. Penalties—None.

Third period: 12. World, Sundin (Ohlund, Jagr) 2:57; 13. North America, Sydor (Modano, Amonte) 4:02; 14. World, Zubov-Khristich, Holik) 14;20. Penalties—MacInnis.

Attendance—19,758.

ALL-STAR GAME RECORDS
Team

Most goals, both teams, one game—22, Wales 16, Campbell 6, 1993.

Fewest goals, both teams, one game—2, All-Stars 1, Montreal 1, 1956; First Team All-Stars 1, Second Team All-Stars 1, 1952.

Most goals, one team, one game—16, Wales, 1993.

Fewest goals, one team, one game—0, All-Stars vs. Montreal, 1967.

Most shots, both teams, one game—102, East 56, West 46, 1994.

Fewest shots, both teams, one game—52, Wales 40, Campbell 12, 1978.

Most shots, one team, one game—56, East, 1994.

Fewest shots, one team, one game—12, Campbell, 1978.

Most power-play goals, both teams, one game—3, three times, most recently Montreal 2, All-Stars 1, 1958.

Fewest power-play goals, both teams, one game—0, 16 times, most recently 1996.

Fastest two goals, both teams, from start of game—37 seconds, 1970.

Fastest two goals, both teams—8 seconds, Owen Nolan, West, 1997.

Fastest three goals, both teams—1:08, 1993.

Fastest four goals, both teams—3:29, 1994.

Fastest two goals, one team, from start of game—2:15, World, 1998.

Fastest two goals, one team—8 seconds, West, 1997.

Fastest three goals, one team—1:08, Wales, 1993.

Fastest four goals, one team—4:19, Campbell, 1992.

Most goals, both teams, one period—10, East 6, West 4, second period, 1997.

Most goals, one team, one period—7, Wales, first period, 1990.

Most shots, both teams, one period—39, West 21, East 18, second period, 1994.

Most shots, one team, one period—22, Campbell, third period, 1990; Wales, third period, 1991; Wales, first period, 1993.

Fewest shots, both teams, one period—9, West 7, East 2, third period, 1971; Wales 5, Campbell 4, second period, 1980.

Fewest shots, one team, one period—2, East, third period, 1971; Campbell, second period, 1978.

Individual

Most games played—23, Gordie Howe, Detroit and Hartford.

Most goals, career—13, Wayne Gretzky, Edmonton, Los Angeles, St. Louis and New York R.

Most goals, one game—4, Wayne Gretzky, Campbell, 1983; Mario Lemieux, Wales, 1990; Vincent Damphousse, Campbell, 1991; Mike Gartner, Wales, 1993.

Most goals, one period—4, Wayne Gretzky, Campbell, third period, 1983.

Most assists, career—12, Ray Bourque, Boston; Adam Oates, Washington Capitals; Joe Sakic, Colorado Avalanche; Mark Messier, Van-

couver Canucks; Wayne Gretzky, New York Rangers.

Most assists, one game—5, Mats Naslund, Wales Conference, 1988.

Most assists, one period—4, Adam Oates, Wales Conference, first period, 1993.

Most points, career—25, Wayne Gretzky, Edmonton, Los Angeles, New York R.

Most points, one game—6, Mario Lemieux, Wales Conference, 1988.

Most points, one period—4, Wayne Gretzky, Campbell Conference, third period, 1983; Mike Gartner, Wales Conference, first period, 1993; Adam Oates, Wales Conference, first period, 1993.

Most power-play goals, career—6, Gordie Howe.

Fastest goal from start of game—19 seconds, Ted Lindsay, Detroit, 1950.

Fastest goal from start of period—17 seconds, Ray Bourque, Boston, 1999.

Fastest two goals (one player) from start of game—3:37, Mike Gartner, Wales, 1993, at 3:15 and 3:37.

Fastest two goals (one player)—8 seconds, Owen Nolan, West, 1997.

Most penalty minutes—27, Gordie Howe.

Goaltenders

Most games played—13, Glenn Hall.

Most minutes played—467, Terry Sawchuk.

Most goals against—24, Patrick Roy.

Best goals-against average (minimum two games—0.68, Gilles Villemure.

12

NHL ON TV

From games broadcast with two cameras to multimillion-dollar productions with glowing pucks, television has played a huge role in the development of the National Hockey League.

The tradition that is *Hockey Night in Canada* actually began on radio in 1935 when Foster Hewitt, generally regarded as the first great hockey announcer, broadcast games from Toronto's Maple Leaf Gardens, generally on Saturday nights. With the advent of television, the Canadian Broadcasting Company began doing Maple Leaf's games in the 1950s and added the Montreal Canadiens to the scheduling rotation.

For years, either the Canadiens or Maple Leafs (or both) would play home games on Saturday night, and CBC would broadcast these games all over Canada. When the two Canadian teams met in the 1959 Stanley Cup finals, the TV ratings set an all-time high across the country.

Meanwhile, in the United States, the four American teams each had contracts with local affiliates to show their games, but the three major networks, after brief attempts, rejected plans to show the sport on a national level, claiming that the lack of interest on the West Coast would not justify paying for the air time and production costs.

When the league expanded to California in 1967, the networks began to rethink their policy, but still hockey for the most part was thought of as a regional sport. CBS, followed by NBC, became pro hockey's network outlet in the early years of NHL expansion. But in each case, low national ratings and disgruntled affiliates doomed the deal. By the late 1970s, the NHL could not find a home on U.S. broadcast network TV, and was forced to syndicate a Game of the Week and playoff coverage on independent TV stations. The league's expansion into the American southeast certainly has much to do with the game's growth as a television presence in the U.S.

Through all this time, *Hockey Night in Canada* continued to thrive, making household names out of Hewitt, Danny Gallivan, Howie Meeker, Dick Irvin, and, of course, Don Cherry, the outspoken former Boston Bruins coach whose opinionated, colorful analysis has made him one of the most popular men on Canadian television for the past 20 years.

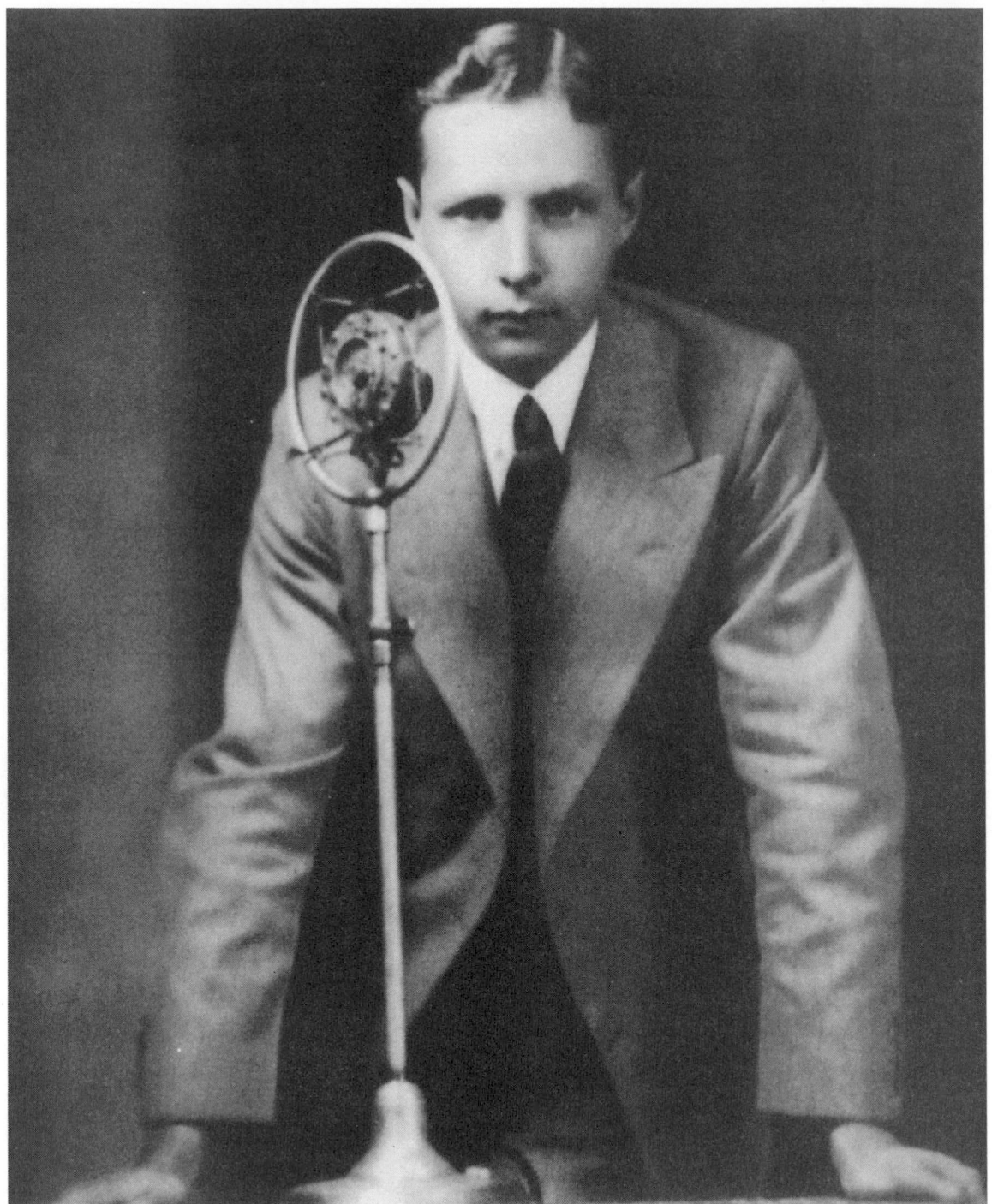

Former announcer Foster Hewitt launched a Hall of Fame career when he became the celebrated voice of Hockey Night in Canada in 1935.

But it all began with the legendary Hewitt. As *The Hockey News* noted, "When Hewitt spoke, Canada listened. His 'He shoots, he scores,' became one of the most famous phrases in hockey."

Even after his retirement from radio play-by-play in 1978, he commanded immense respect, which made his scathing criticism of the modern game sting like alcohol in a wound.

"When I tune into a game, I'll often watch for a while, then switch off the TV in disgust," Hewitt said in the Dec. 18, 1981 issue of *The Hockey News*. "And when I go to the odd game, I find I can't stomach it. It just won't go down. There's just too much attack and no defense. It's pathetic."

Hewitt was one of the many critics who felt the talent in what had become a 21-team league in 1979 had become diluted.

Terrible Ted Lindsay, the former Detroit Red Wing great, and one-time color commentator on NBC's NHL telecasts, echoed Hewitt's comments. "There's not much wrong with a lot of these players," he said, "except that they don't know how to skate, they don't know how to shoot, they don't know how to check, they don't know how to make or take a pass and they don't know how to play defense or goal."

That is an era long gone.

The sport was re-energized by the thrilling play of the Montreal, New York Islanders and Edmonton dynasties beginning in the late '70s. By the

Bill Clement, left, and Gary Thorne call the shots for U.S. viewers via ESPN.

Nobody is more colorful than Don Cherry, the ex-Bruin coach who has been a longtime favorite on CBC.

mid-1980s, the Molson's Brewery/CBC dominance of Canadian TV through *Hockey Night in Canada* in English and *La Soiree du Hockey* in French was challenged when Carling-O'Keefe Breweries started rival NHL telecasts over CTV and *Quatre Saisons*. This brought additional TV revenue to the NHL. Eventually, the competing coverage ended when Carling-O'Keefe was acquired by Molson's. But Canadian fans were still able to watch an increased number of games on the CBC's regionalized network coverage.

To combat the loss of TV revenue and exposure in the U.S., the league developed a strategy that capitalized on the growth of cable TV in the early 1980s, forging a succession of national cable deals with the USA Network, ESPN, SportsChannel America, and back to ESPN in 1994. In addition, the rise of regional sports cable networks enabled individual teams to strike their own deals, some lucrative, for local coverage of games.

By 1997, ESPN and its second network, ESPN2, had grown to the point where they were televising games nightly during the playoffs, 63 in all, called by various announcer teams, including the lead team of Gary Thorne and Bill Clement.

In Canada too, the NHL was able to augment its coverage on cable by selling rights in the 1980s to all-sports networks TSN: The Sports Network and Reseau Des Sports (RDS). Each telecast a game each week, which grew over time.

In 1990, the NHL returned to U.S. broadcast network TV when NBC telecast the All-Star Game, a deal that continued for four years. In the '93 playoffs, ABC began regionalized coverage of the playoffs on a weekly basis. The rise of the Fox Network gave the NHL a broadcast outlet hungry for attention and sports programming, and the two formed a partnership beginning with the 1994–95 season.

Fox introduced numerous innovative techniques to hockey coverage in an effort to broaden the game's viewership. Posting the score and time in a "Fox Box" throughout the game became a standard for every network and local hockey telecast. Fox also made greater use of audio from coaches and on-ice officials. But the most controversial enhancement was the 1996 unveiling of "Fox Trax," a computerized system in which micro-chips embedded in pucks resulted in the puck appearing to glow on the TV screen and be trailed by a comet-like tail when passed or shot over a certain speed. The thinking behind the Fox Trax was that viewers found the puck hard to follow on TV.

Fox Trax was a technological marvel, but reaction to the glowing puck was mixed, with some new viewers finding it helpful while longtime viewers saw it as intrusive. Fox tinkered with the system and by 1998 had eliminated the glowing aspect of it almost entirely, with only the tail remaining. A more serious concern arose when players and coaches objected to the Fox puck, saying it did not behave on the ice like a normal puck, although the NHL responded that it tested within specifications.

An era came to an end in 1998 when the NHL announced that it would award its Canadian national network contract to Labatt's Brewery, although Molson's retained local broadcasting rights to all the Canadian teams. TSN also lost its national cable contract when it was awarded to the new CTV SportsNet. TSN however, obtained regional rights for Montreal's English-language cablecasts, while CTV SportsNet acquired other teams' regional cable rights. The sale of regional cable rights was a new development in Canada and significant because it provided Canadian teams with new revenue previously only available to U.S. teams.

All these maneuverings came about amidst the backdrop of declining TV ratings on both sides of the border. For the 1997–98 regular season, CBC, TSN, Fox, and ESPN all announced slides in viewership ranging from five to 25 percent. Hockey and TV officials were at a loss to explain the drop, calling it an "aberration."

Despite the slumping ratings, Disney Corp. stepped in in late August of 1998 and signed a five-year, $600,000,000 deal with the NHL to broadcast games exclusively on ABC, ESPN, and ESPN2.

Referee Frank Udvari held on for dear life as Gordie Howe crashed an opponent into the boards in the mid-1950s.

13

THE OFFICIALS

When constabulary duty's to be done
A Policeman's lot is not a happy one.

—*Pirates of Penzance,* Act. II

It is safe to assume that Sir William Gilbert of the operatic composing team of Gilbert and Sullivan never met an ice hockey referee. He was born in Victorian London in 1838 and died in 1911, long before hockey was introduced to his country. If he were living today, he presumably would show the same compassion for referees that he did for policemen.

The lot of the hockey referee isn't a happy one either. His constabulary duties consist of bringing discipline and control to 60 minutes of speed and confusion on ice. Players skim along the frozen surface at 20 to 30 miles an hour; there are violent collisions at great speed; sticks are swung like clubs; and pucks whiz over the ice and through the air at upwards of 100 mph.

This is the referee's work day:

He skates between 15 and 20 miles in an average game. He must match the fastest player stride for stride and be on top of every play. The players' bench disgorges fresh skaters as though they were traveling through a revolving door, but the harried referee gets no rest, except between periods.

And then there are the hazards of the job. While he is trying to control the game and the players, the referee may be tripped, jammed into the corners of the rink, boarded, draped over the protective glass, slashed by a skate, hit by a flying puck or pelted with programs, fruit, vegetables, eggs, overshoes—or squid.

Squid? "You better believe it," said Bill Chadwick, the only American-born referee to be named to the Hockey Hall of Fame. "I was working a Stanley Cup playoff game in Detroit in 1952 when a fan tossed something at me which missed and landed on the ice. I went over to pick it up, but after one look I spun around and skated

off in a hurry. I thought at first it was a baby octopus. I found out later it was a squid. But octopus or squid, it sure scared the hell out of me."

Bryan Lewis, the NHL's director of officiating, was a referee for 18 years. He recalls being hit with every conceivable object. "Referees don't wear much protective equipment, so no matter where you get hit, it hurts," he said. "I got hit in the back by a thrown egg once and it swelled up the exact size of an egg. I also had plenty of cuts from pucks bouncing off me."

Referees also have been victims of assaults by players. Lewis was once punched by Barry Ashbee of the Philadelphia Flyers during a game in Pittsburgh. "Did it hurt?" said Lewis. "You bet. But Ashbee got hit, too, with an eight-game suspension."

Andy van Hellemond, who has refereed more games than any man in the history of the NHL, remembers the 1981–82 season for two reasons: he was twice assaulted by players. He was punched in the chest by Paul Holmgren of the Philadelphia Flyers during a regular-season game and was swatted in the head by Terry O'Reilly of the Boston Bruins at the conclusion of a Boston-Quebec playoff game.

Van Hellemond recalls the O'Reilly assault more vividly because it occurred in the playoffs. "As the game ended, O'Reilly started a fight with Dale Hunter [of the Nordiques]," van Hellemond said. "O'Reilly was real hot. 'I'm going to cut your eyes out,' he told Hunter.

"I tried to intercede, and O'Reilly said, 'Get out of my way or I'll go right through you.' Then

Mickey Ion (left) and Cooper Smeaton, both members of the Hockey Hall of Fame, spell out who's in charge.

Referee Bill Chadwick, calling a penalty on the Canadiens' Murph Chamberlain, blew his whistle for 16 years in the NHL.

he swung but it was more like a swat than a punch and he caught me on the side of my head."

Holmgren drew a five-game suspension for his assault and O'Reilly was suspended for 10 games. The rules dealing with abuse of officials have been tightened in recent years and can carry lengthier suspensions.

Fear grips most referees—as it does the policeman on the beat. Referees of yore like Chadwick, Red Storey, Cooper Smeaton, Mickey Ion,

Mike Rodden worked 1,187 NHL games.

Red Storey refereed from 1951 through 1959.

King Clancy and Mike Rodden were threatened with physical violence while serving in the NHL.

They learned to live with this fear and eventually wound up in the Hockey Hall of Fame because they had courage—courage to render a decision and make it stick in the face of taunts from players, coaches and hostile fans.

Van Hellemond, who retired after the 1995–96 season, showed courage in the 1995 playoffs and it cost him dearly. In Game 4 of the New York Rangers–Quebec Nordiques first-round series, van Hellemond disallowed a goal by Quebec's Joe Sakic because he thought the Rangers' Alexei Kovalev was seriously injured. Kovalev had been slashed in the back (out of van Hellemond's sight) and dropped to the ice, seemingly unable to move. The play moved to the other end of the ice, where Sakic scored to give Quebec a 3-0 lead.

After conferring with linesmen Wayne Bonney and Jay Sharrers, van Hellemond disallowed the goal, claiming he had blown his whistle before Sakic's shot. The NHL subsequently ruled van Hellemond had made a mistake, fined him and took him out of the officiating rotation for the final rounds of the playoffs. But it was small consolation to the Nordiques, who wound up losing the game to the Rangers, 3-2.

Clancy earned his berth in the Hall of Fame as a fighting defenseman. But he is also remembered as a fighting referee, a 150-pound bantam rooster of a man who never allowed himself to be intimidated by a player or coach, a club owner or a fan.

In Clancy's mind, Mickey Ion was hockey's most outstanding referee. "When Mickey refereed a game, he was in complete charge," said Clancy in an interview conducted before his death in 1986. "There's never been anyone to equal him. One night in Boston, Mickey was knocked over the boards and landed in a fan's lap. Boston scored while he was scrambling back over the boards, but Mickey didn't allow the goal. He wasn't on the ice and he said nobody was allowed to score unless he was there to see it."

Nearly two decades as a referee prepared Bryan Lewis for his current position as the NHL's director of officiating.

Clancy, who served as a referee for 11 years following his retirement as a player in 1936, never forgot the instructions Ion gave him and Rabbit McVeigh before they worked their first Stanley Cup playoff game in 1938.

"Mickey came into the officials' room and started lecturing us," Clancy said. "He said, 'Crack down on those players right from the start. And remember this: There are 15,000 idiots out there, including the players. You two guys are the only sane ones in the building.' And, you know, there were times when I think Mickey was right."

Van Hellemond refereed his first NHL game in 1972 and broke Bill Chadwick's longevity record (1,200 regular-season games) early in the 1991–92 season. The best advice van Hellemond received came from retired referee Frank Udvari.

"Frank told me to be consistent and not try to be someone else," van Hellemond said. "He also told me that acceptance was important and to guard against antagonizing people. It was good advice."

Terry Gregson, an NHL referee since 1981, admits that "a man's personality is extremely important" in his job. "You have to show quiet confidence but not arrogance," he said.

In the early days of pro hockey, referees were picked haphazardly. Retired and active players assisted in the officiating and were not paid. The first referees of the Stanley Cup playoffs were chosen from among the executives of the competing leagues.

Ion and Smeaton got their starts as referees before the first World War. They were paid—sometimes. "We got paid by the game," Smeaton recalled. "But if one of the bosses didn't like your work just once, you didn't come back. And you didn't get paid either."

The starting salary for an NHL referee in 1995–96 was $75,000 a year. Those with 21 years or more of service earn up to $200,000. In addition, referees can earn up to $29,000 more for their work in the postseason.

Salaries of linesmen range from $49,000 for rookies to $110,000 for those with 24 years or more of service—plus up to $24,000 more for postseason. They are all paid extra for preseason games.

Referee Art Skov wants no part of complaining Canadien Jean Beliveau.

The referee was the sole official in Smeaton's day. "There were no linesmen to help out," he said. "I had to call the offsides, the penalties, break up the fights and do the arguing."

Modern-day referees share the work load with two linesmen. And beginning with the 1991–92 season, referees were able to rely on video replays—but only on disputed goals.

"I'm all for it," van Hellemond said when the replays were introduced. "I know I don't feel good when I wave off a goal that is questionable. Now we have help and that should make it a better game."

Bill Chadwick recalled other problems he encountered early in his whistle-blowing career.

"When I first started refereeing [in 1941], you were more or less at the mercy of the club owners," he said. "You'd have a waiting line outside your door after every period. The owners would be there and the coaches, too. You couldn't keep 'em out. They'd walk in, give you hell and walk out.

"The referee had nobody to turn to for support. There was no referee-in-chief. All we had was the league president and he was only an intermediary. Then Clarence Campbell took over as president [in 1947] and he backed us up because he knew our problems. He had been a referee."

It was during Red Dutton's reign as NHL president that Chadwick endured his most trying experience with mob violence. He was working a

Scotty Morrison, who was referee-in-chief for more than two decades and is now chairman of the Hockey Hall of Fame, had to go by the book when the referees and linesmen went on strike before the 1969 season.

playoff game between the Canadiens and the Blackhawks in Chicago Stadium in 1943. One of his calls infuriated the Chicago fans, who went on a wild rampage, littering the ice with debris while crying for Chadwick's scalp.

The harassed referee ducked for cover, then dispatched a courier to Dutton in his front row box, asking what he should do. Dutton's answer was starkly brief: "You got yourself into this, now get yourself out."

"I needed a police escort to get out of the building that night," Chadwick said. "The next game I worked there, I was picked up at my hotel by detectives, who escorted me to the Stadium and back to the hotel after the game. Those Chicago fans really gave me a hard time."

Why so much abuse? "In no other sport are referees charged so much with the responsibility of who wins and loses," said Udvari, who was an NHL referee for 16 years. "That's why we're such a focal point for criticism."

The NHL even encourages referee identification. Although it has long been said that the best officiated games are the ones in which the referees go unnoticed, the NHL in 1977 began putting the names of officials on the back of their jerseys. Officials in other sports are usually identified by numbers.

So hockey fans are more conscious of the whistle-blowers and their respective reputations. Indeed, "Who's the ref?" is one of the first questions asked at any NHL game.

Nobody officiated more playoff games than Matt Pavelich, the first linesman elected to the Hockey Hall of Fame.

Many referees, past and present, readily admit the job has one other serious drawback. It deals with nonfraternizing. The loneliness of the long-distance runner is minor compared to the life of a referee, who is prohibited from mingling with players, club officials or fans.

Referees are not allowed to register at the same hotel as players and are advised not to frequent the same restaurants.

"It takes a certain type of person to accept that nonfraternization," Gregson said. "If you're gregarious . . . well, refereeing is not an ideal position for you."

Chadwick claimed it was even tougher when he was officiating. "The referees now have some companionship," he said. "They travel with the linesmen or arrange to meet them in various cities. In my day, the referee traveled alone and lived alone.

"You couldn't associate with the players, but I always talked to them. I figured if they talked to me off the ice, I had a better chance of dealing with them in tight situations on the ice. The big thing is to get the respect of the players."

There is no way referees can stop players from talking to them. Ron Hoggarth, who turned to refereeing while he was "a starving student" at McMaster University in Hamilton, Ontario, and who served in the NHL for more than 20 years, recalled an incident that occurred in the finals of the Stanley Cup playoffs in 1983.

Andy van Hellemond is regarded as one of the NHL's best modern referees.

Terry Gregson is in his third decade as a referee.

game and then loosen up or vice versa. A good referee has to be consistent."

Scotty Morrison, chairman of the Hockey Hall of Fame, who served as the NHL's referee-in-chief for 21 years, points out that referees have shorter careers than officials of other sports. "In hockey, the demands are so strenuous that referees are retiring at the age of 45 or 46," he said. "Beyond that, they just can't keep up with the play."

"The Islanders were playing the Oilers at Nassau Coliseum and the crowd went wild when I called three penalties in a row against the Islanders," Hoggarth said. "After I called the third one, Denis Potvin [the Islanders' captain] skated up to me and said, 'Hey, Hoggarth, how can you sleep through this noise?'"

NHL referees are under constant scrutiny by supervisors—most of whom are retired officials. The referees are rated at midseason and at the end of the regular season. The ratings are then used to determine playoff assignments.

The retired Chadwick later became an announcer and, of course, he critiqued the work of the referees.

"The only problem I've noticed among the current referees is a tendency to fluctuate," he said. "Some call every infraction at the start of a

14

HOCKEY HALL OF FAME

Winning the Stanley Cup is the ultimate team honor in hockey. Making the Hall of Fame represents the supreme individual achievement.

It is the Hall of Fame that since 1945 has perpetuated the memories of the greatest players, the sport's founders, club executives, referees, and linesmen. It also honors the writers and broadcasters.

It wasn't until August 26, 1961, that the Hall of Fame had a home. That was the day John F. Diefenbaker, Prime Minister of Canada, stood before a new structure on the grounds of the Canadian National Exhibition in Toronto and announced, "I now officially proclaim the opening of the Hockey Hall of Fame building."

Here have been housed the artifacts, photographs, and other treasures of the game. After more than 30 years, the Hall of Fame outgrew itself and moved into another venue in the spring of 1993—the historic Bank of Montreal's Upper Canadian headquarters at the center of Front and Yonge Streets in the heart of Toronto.

The Hall of Fame and Museum features state-of-the-art technical exhibits and, among other attractions, an invitation to visitors to electronically challenge the greatest hockey players of all time, two theaters for screening hockey films, a library, and an Honored Members Wall with glass plaques of the enshrinees.

Originally it took five years after retirement for a player or a referee to be eligible for membership. However, in exceptional cases the period could be shortened. Under present rules the waiting period is three years.

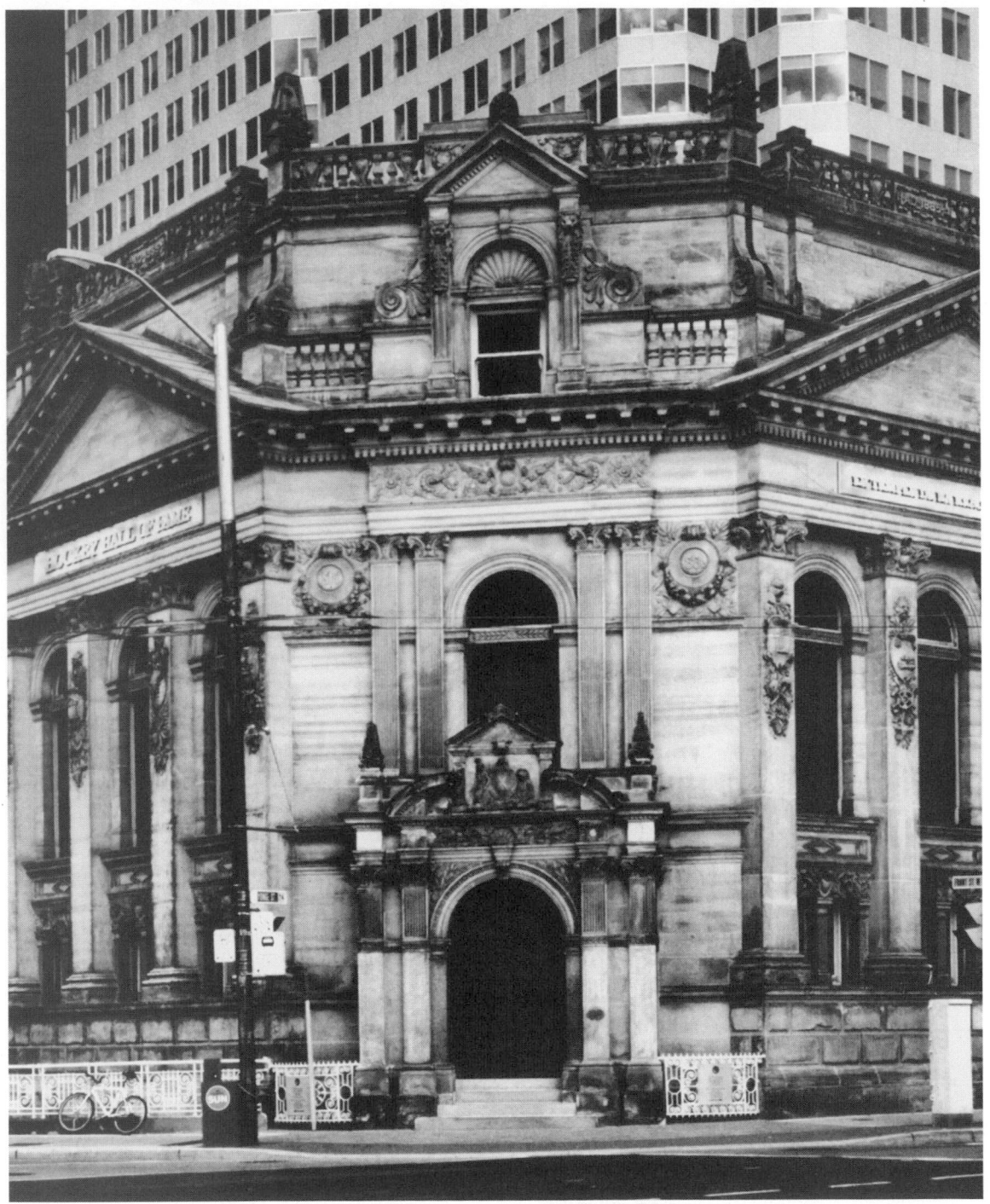

The historic Bank of Montreal was retained as the anchor of the new Hockey Hall of Fame in 1993.

Players and referees are elected by a Selection Committee headed by Dan Gallivan and made up of former players, writers, and officials. Builders are elected by a committee led by Ian P. (Scotty) Morrison, Chairman of the Hall of Fame Board of Directors.

A committee from the Professional Hockey Writers' Association selects the writers, winners of the Elmer Ferguson Memorial Award, and a committee from the NHL Broadcasters' Association selects the broadcasters, winners of the Foster Hewitt Memorial Award.

PLAYERS

Sidney Gerald (Sid) Abel: Starred on Red Wings' Production Line (with Gordie Howe and Ted Lindsay) in the 1940s. Later coached Wings to seven playoff berths in 10 seasons behind the bench. *Elected 1964.*

John James (Jack) Adams: Star forward for the Toronto Arenas, Toronto St. Pats, and Ottawa Senators. Later coached and served as general manager of the Detroit Red Wings. *Elected 1959.*

Sylvanus (Syl) Apps: A center who was the first winner of the Calder Trophy as the Rookie of the Year for 1936–37. Played entire NHL career with Toronto Maple Leafs. *Elected 1961.*

George Armstrong: One of the greatest clutch players in Toronto history. When the Leafs won four Stanley Cups in the 1960s, George had 20 goals and 20 assists in the 45 playoff games the team played. *Elected 1975.*

Irwin W. (Ace) Bailey: Right wing played only 7½ years in NHL due to fractured skull that ended career. Led league with 22 goals in 44 games in 1928–29 and was one of league's top penalty-killers. *Elected 1975.*

Dan Bain: Never played professional hockey. Was a standout center for the Winnipeg Victorias, an amateur team, in the late 1890s and early 1900s. *Elected 1945.*

Hobart (Hobey) Baker: An all-around legend at Princeton University before the First World War, he was known as a one-man hockey team. Also starred in football. Later played for the St. Nicholas amateur hockey team. *Elected 1945.*

William (Bill) Barber: Left wing tallied 420 goals and 883 points for Philadelphia from 1973 to 1984. Scored goal that sent 1976 Canada Cup final game into overtime. *Elected 1991.*

Martin A. (Marty) Barry: A center on the productive Detroit Red Wing line of the mid-1930s which included Larry Aurie and Herbie Lewis. Also played for New York Americans and Boston Bruins. *Elected 1965.*

Andrew James (Andy) Bathgate: Averaged nearly a point a game in 17-year career despite playing with a badly damaged knee. Starred for the New York Rangers in 1950s and 1960s. Was league MVP in 1958–59, when he had 88 points. *Elected 1978.*

Robert Theodore (Bobby) Bauer: A right wing on Boston's famed "Kraut Line" with Milt Schmidt and Woody Dumart, he had seven full seasons in the NHL, all with Boston, and helped the Bruins win Stanley Cups in 1939 and 1941. He tallied 123 goals and 137 assists in 327 games. *Elected 1997.*

Jean Beliveau: Scored 507 goals in 18 seasons with the Montreal Canadiens as one of the most respected players in history. Played on 10 Stanley Cup championship teams. *Elected 1972.*

Clint Benedict: A goalie on five winning Stanley Cup teams, four with Ottawa and one with the Montreal Maroons. Allowed only three goals in a four-game Cup series while with the Maroons in 1926–27. *Elected 1965.*

Douglas Wagner (Doug) Bentley: Left wing on the crack Chicago Blackhawk line with brother Max Bentley and Bill Mosienko. Played for the Hawks from 1939 to 1951. *Elected 1964.*

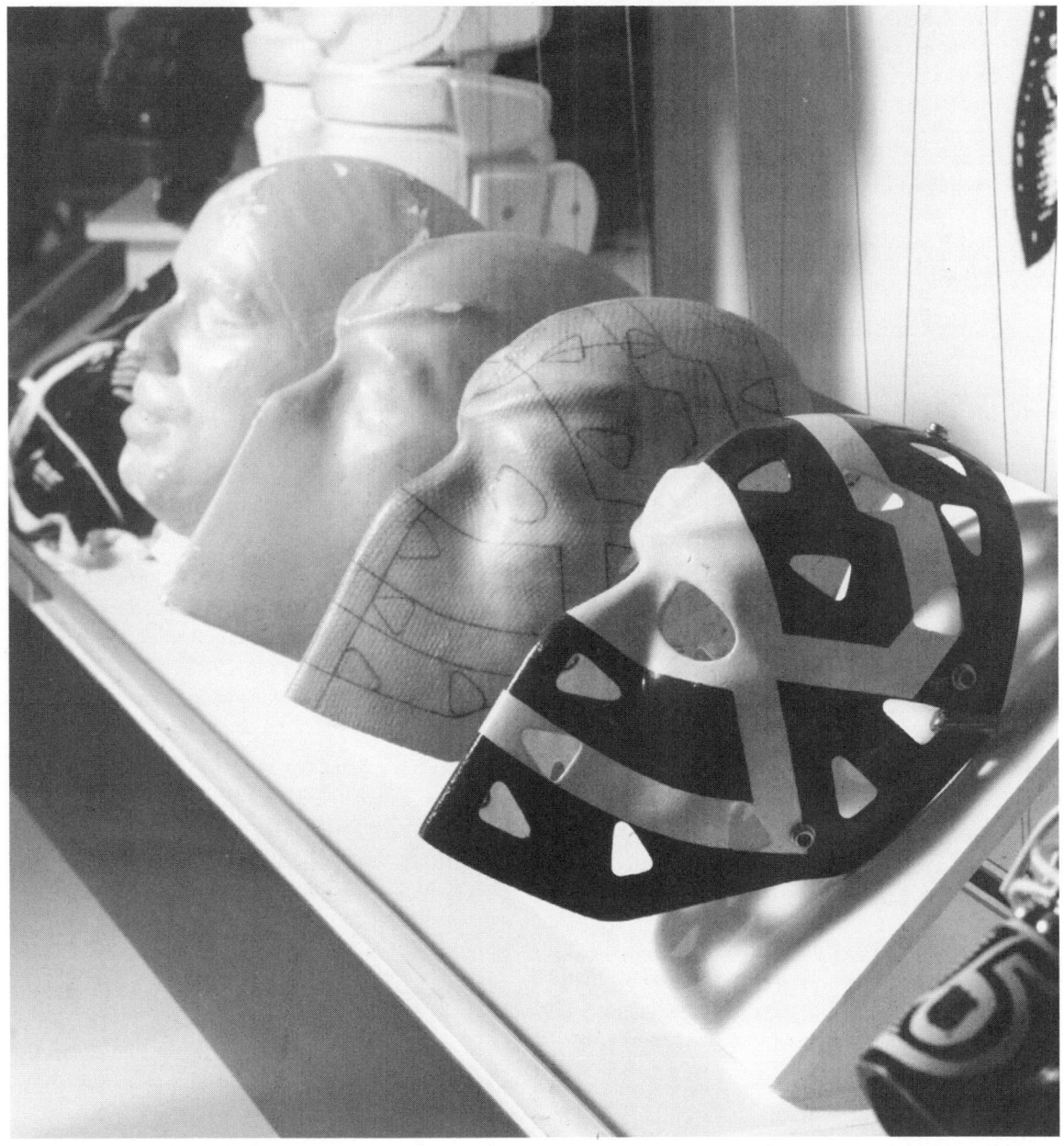

The making of a mask, a goalie's best friend.

Maxwell (Max) Bentley: A clever center and a fine stickhandler for the Chicago Blackhawks and Toronto Maple Leafs. Was voted the NHL's Most Valuable Player in 1945–46. *Elected 1966.*

Hector (Toe) Blake: A left wing for the Montreal Maroons and Montreal Canadiens. Was member of great Canadiens' line that included Maurice Richard and Elmer Lach. Later coached Canadiens to eight Stanley Cup crowns. *Elected 1966.*

Leo Joseph Boivin: Although just a 5-foot-7 defenseman, he set standard for bone-jarring checks. Played 1,150 games over 19 seasons, including 10 seasons with Boston from 1955–65. *Elected 1986.*

Richard (Dickie) Boon: Played for amateur teams in the Montreal area in the late 1890s and for the Montreal Wanderers in 1904 and 1905. *Elected 1952.*

Michael Dean (Mike) Bossy: Scored 50 or more goals in each of first nine seasons, totaling 573 goals and 1,126 points in 10 years with Islanders. Right wing set NHL rookie mark, since broken, with 53 goals in 1977–78. Conn Smythe winner in 1982. *Elected 1991.*

Emile (Butch) Bouchard: A Montreal Canadiens' defenseman for 14 years, starting in 1941–42. Named to NHL's first All-Star team three times. *Elected 1966.*

Frank Boucher: A center on the famous New York Ranger line that also included the Cook brothers, Bill and Bun. Winner of record seven Lady Byng Trophies. Also was a Ranger coach and general manager. *Elected 1958.*

George (Buck) Boucher: An older brother of Frank Boucher, he was a leading defenseman for the Ottawa Senators and Montreal Maroons from 1917 to 1929. *Elected 1960.*

John W. Bower: Didn't make his mark on a full-time basis until he was 34, when he became the workhorse goalie as Maple Leafs won four Stanley Cups in the 1960s. Had 37 career shutouts. *Elected 1976.*

Russell (Dubbie) Bowie: Was a rover for the Montreal Victorias for 10 years in the early 1900s. Had career total of 234 goals. *Elected 1945.*

Frank Brimsek: A native of Eveleth, Minn., he was nicknamed "Mr. Zero" because he twice had three consecutive shutouts as a goalie for the Boston Bruins. Starred in the late 1930s and early 1940s. *Elected 1966.*

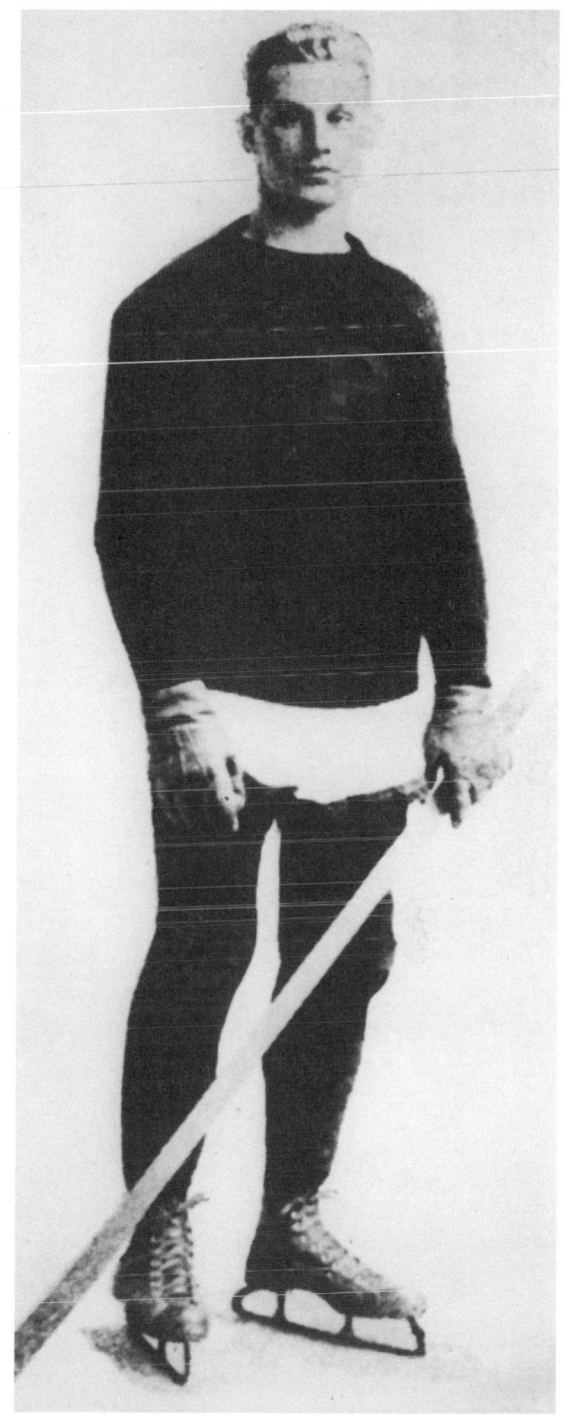

Hobey Baker never played pro hockey, but he made the Hall of Fame following a brilliant career at Princeton.

Andy Bathgate starred for 17 years in the NHL and averaged nearly a point a game.

Harry L. (Punch) Broadbent: As a forward he played for four Stanley Cup–winning teams, three as a member of the Ottawa Senators and one with the Montreal Maroons. *Elected 1962.*

Walter (Turk) Broda: Played goal 16 seasons for the Toronto Maple Leafs. Had reputation for excellence in important games. *Elected 1967.*

Turk Broda was a champ in the nets and at the dinner table.

John P. Bucyk: Played for 23 years in NHL, 21 of them with the Boston Bruins. Left wing scored 556 goals and helped Bruins win two Stanley Cups (1970, 1972). Two-time Lady Byng winner. *Elected 1981.*

William (Billy) Burch: Born in Yonkers, N.Y., in 1900, he became star center of the New York Americans in the 1920s. Led his team in scoring five times. *Elected 1974.*

Harold (Hugh) Harry Cameron: Was famous for rushes up ice while playing defense for the Toronto Arenas, Ottawa Senators, Toronto St. Pats, and Montreal Canadiens. *Elected 1962.*

Gerald Michael (Gerry) Cheevers: In Boston goal for Cup titles in 1970 and 1972. Compiled 230-94-74 record with 2.89 GAA. Coached Bruins to 204-126-46 record from 1980–84. *Elected 1985.*

Francis (King) Clancy: Was outstanding scoring defenseman for the Ottawa Senators and Toronto Maple Leafs. Also was an NHL referee and a coach for the Leafs and Montreal Maroons. *Elected 1958.*

Aubry (Dit) Clapper: Played right wing and right defense for the Boston Bruins. Spent 20 years as a player in the NHL and also coached the Bruins. *Elected 1947.*

Robert Earle (Bobby) Clarke: Feisty center overcame diabetes to amass 1,210 points in 1,144 games in 15 seasons with Philadelphia. Won Hart Trophy three times. First expansion-team player to record 100-point season. *Elected 1987.*

Sprague Cleghorn: A defenseman, he played 18 years for Ottawa, Toronto, the Montreal Canadiens, and Boston Bruins before retiring in 1928. *Elected 1958.*

Neil Colville: Center on New York Rangers' standout line of late 1930s and 1940s that included brother Mac Colville and Alex Shibicky. Later played as a defenseman for the Rangers. *Elected 1967.*

Johnny Bucyk played 21 years with the Boston Bruins and helped them win two Stanley Cups.

Charlie (Chuck) Conacher: A husky, hard-shooting right wing, he played for 10 years for the Toronto Maple Leafs. Was a member of standout line of Conacher-Joe Primeau-Harvey Jackson. Also played for Detroit and New York Americans. *Elected 1961.*

Lionel P. Conacher: One of the NHL's first great defensemen. Helped the Chicago Blackhawks and Montreal Maroons win Stanley Cups in the 1930s. *Elected 1994.*

Roy Conacher: Had 11-year career with Boston, Detroit, and Chicago that began with the Bruins in 1938. With the Blackhawks in 1948–49, he won the Art Ross Trophy for most regular-season points with 68. *Elected 1999.*

Alex Connell: As a goalie for the Ottawa Senators, he once posted a record 446 minutes, six seconds without being scored on. The streak included six consecutive shutouts. *Elected 1958.*

Frederick J. (Bun) Cook: Left wing registered 302 points in 11-year NHL career that featured Stanley Cup triumphs with the New York Rangers in 1928 and 1933. After retirement, he turned to coaching and led teams to seven American Hockey League titles. *Elected 1995.*

William (Bill) Cook: A big, strong sharpshooter from the right wing position, he played for 12 years with the New York Rangers. One of original Rangers, who came into NHL in 1926. *Elected 1962.*

Gerry Cheevers figured in two of Boston's Stanley Cup championships and later coached the Bruins.

Toronto's Happy Day coached the Leafs to five Stanley Cups after his playing days were over.

Art Coulter: Prototype defensive defenseman with Blackhawks and Rangers in the 1930s. Scored only 30 goals in 11 NHL seasons but was on three Cup winners. *Elected 1974.*

Yvan Cournoyer: Blazing speed gave him nickname "The Roadrunner" during 15-year career with the Canadiens. Played on 10 Stanley Cup winners and scored 25 or more goals 12 straight seasons. *Elected 1982.*

Bill Cowley: A clever center, he starred for the Boston Bruins in the late 1930s and early 1940s. Scored 195 goals in 13 NHL seasons. *Elected 1968.*

Samuel Russell (Rusty) Crawford: A fast-skating forward, he played amateur and professional hockey from 1906 through 1929. The Ottawa Senators and Toronto Arenas were among his teams. *Elected 1962.*

John Proctor (Jack) Darragh: A clever stickhandler and a speedy skater from the right-wing position, he was also noted for an effective backhand shot. Played mostly for the Ottawa Senators. *Elected 1962.*

Allan (Scotty) Davidson: A rugged, powerful defenseman, he starred for Kingston and Toronto before the formation of the NHL. Was shifted to forward toward the end of his career. *Elected 1950.*

Clarence (Happy) Day: A sound, steady defenseman for 10 years with the Toronto Maple Leafs and later with the New York Americans. Was also an NHL referee, coach, and general manager of the Maple Leafs. *Elected 1961.*

Alex Delvecchio: Red Wings' iron-man center who missed just 43 games in 22 seasons with club. Scored 456 goals in 1,549 games and won Lady Byng Trophy for clean play three times. *Elected 1977.*

Cyril (Cy) Denneny: A relatively slow-skating left wing, but he possessed one of the most accurate shots among players of his era. Played 11 years with Ottawa, starting in 1917, and had one season at Boston. *Elected 1959.*

Marcel Dionne: Was a leading center for 19 years (Detroit, Los Angeles, New York Rangers), winning the scoring title in 1979–80 with the Kings and the Lady Byng Trophy twice. Made the All-Star team four times. Retired with 1,771 points in third place on the all-time scoring list. *Elected 1992.*

Gordon Drillon: Averaged 22 goals a season when 20-goal scorers were rare. Played six years with Maple Leafs in the 1930s and led team in scoring three straight seasons. *Elected 1975.*

Charles Graham Drinkwater: Starred as an amateur player late in the 19th century. Played on championship teams at McGill University in Montreal and for the Montreal Victorias. *Elected 1950.*

Ken Dryden: Backbone of six Stanley Cup champions with Montreal in the 1970s. Won Smythe, Calder, and Vezina Trophies and recorded miniscule 2.24 goals-against average in 397 NHL games. *Elected 1983.*

Woody Dumart: A tenacious two-way left wing with the Boston Bruins from 1935–36 through 1953–54, he teamed with Milt Schmidt and Bobby Bauer on the Bruins' famed "Kraut Line" (later the "Kitchener Line"). Was a key figure in the Bruins' Stanley Cup crowns in 1939 and 1941. *Elected 1992.*

Thomas Dunderdale: First Australian-born player to achieve Hall of Fame status. Played 12 years in the PCHA and scored more goals than any player in the league. *Elected 1974.*

William Ronald (Bill) Durnan: Captured the Vezina Trophy six times, including four in succession, while playing for the Montreal Canadiens. Named five times as NHL's first team All-Star goalie. *Elected 1964.*

Mervyn (Red) Dutton: Starred as defenseman for Calgary of the Western Canadian League, then for the Montreal Maroons and New York Americans of NHL. Was also coach of Americans and served as league president from 1943 to 1945. *Elected 1958.*

Cecil (Babe) Dye: Greatest goal scorer of the 1920s. Playing for the Toronto St. Pats, he scored 163 goals in 149 games over six seasons. Finished career with 200 goals in 255 games. *Elected 1970.*

Phil Esposito: First player to break 100-point barrier (1968–69). Unmovable center won five scoring titles, finishing 18-year career with Chicago, Boston, and New York Rangers with 717 goals and 1,590 points. *Elected 1984.*

Tony Esposito: Five-time All-Star with Chicago played 873 games over 15 seasons. Won or shared Vezina Trophy three times, including rookie year. *Elected 1988.*

Arthur Farrell: A team-oriented forward, he was a key figure when the Montreal Shamrocks won the Stanley Cup twice in a row (1899, 1900). *Elected 1965.*

Ferdinand Charles (Fernie) Flaman: Standout 17-year defenseman for the Bruins and Leafs. Played on 1951 Toronto Stanley Cup winner. Coached AHL, WHL, and CHL teams to titles. U.S. College Coach of Year at Northeastern in 1982. *Elected 1990.*

Frank Foyston: Standout center in Western Canadian League from 1916 to 1926 while with Seattle and Victoria, compiling 186 goals. He later played two years for the Detroit Cougars. *Elected 1958.*

Frank Fredrickson: An outstanding amateur player and a star in the Pacific Coast, Western Canadian, and National Hockey Leagues. As a center, he played in the NHL for Detroit, Boston, and Pittsburgh, also coaching and managing Pittsburgh in 1930–31. *Elected 1958.*

Bill Gadsby: Overcame polio to become one of NHL's best defensemen for 20 seasons. Played for the Blackhawks, Rangers and Red Wings and was named first-team All-Star three times. *Elected 1970.*

Bob Gainey: A checking left winger during a 16-year career, all with the Montreal Canadiens,

Bernie (Boom Boom) Geoffrion got his nickname because of his crushing slapshots.

he played on five Stanley Cup championship teams. Won the Selke Trophy four times as the league's top defensive forward. *Elected 1992.*

Charles (Chuck) Gardiner: A brilliant goalie for the Chicago Blackhawks for seven consecutive seasons, starting in 1928. Twice winner

of the Vezina Trophy. Also first-team All-Star twice. *Elected 1945.*

Herbert Martin (Herb) Gardiner: Turned pro at 31 years of age with Calgary of the Western Canadian League. Defenseman joined the Montreal Canadiens four years later and was named the league's Most Valuable Player. *Elected 1958.*

James Henry (Jimmy) Gardner: Left wing played for the Montreal Shamrocks, Montreal Wanderers, and Montreal Canadiens. Also coached the Hamilton, Ont., team of the NHL in 1924–25. *Elected 1962.*

Bernie Geoffrion: Nicknamed "Boom Boom" for the sound his slapshot made as it crashed against the boards. Produced 393 goals in 16 seasons with the New York Rangers and Montreal. Coached Rangers for half a season, later coached Atlanta and did short stint at Montreal. *Elected 1972.*

Eddie Gerard: As a defenseman and captain, he led the Ottawa Senators to three Stanley Cup titles. Coached the Montreal Maroons in 1926 and was manager of the New York Americans in 1931. *Elected 1945.*

Eddie Giacomin: A 10-year goaltender with the New York Rangers, he topped the NHL in victories for three straight seasons, starting in 1966–67. Wound up career in Detroit with overall 289-206-97 record and 2.82 GAA. *Elected 1987.*

Rod Gilbert: Right wing set or equaled 20 team scoring records during brilliant 16-year career with the New York Rangers. Totaled 1,021 points in 1,065 games despite playing with a bad back. *Elected 1982.*

Hamilton Livingstone (Billy) Gilmour: Played for the Ottawa Silver Seven, winners of three straight Stanley Cup crowns, starting in 1902–03. *Elected 1962.*

Frank (Moose) Goheen: A defenseman born in White Bear, Minn., he played for St. Paul in the U.S. Amateur Association and was a member of the 1920 American Olympic team. *Elected 1952.*

Ebenezer R. (Ebbie) Goodfellow: Started out as a center, but was moved to defense by the Detroit Red Wings. Was named the NHL's Most Valuable Player in 1939–40. *Elected 1963.*

Michel Goulet: In a 16-year career, he starred as a forward with Quebec for more than a decade starting in 1979–80, followed by four seasons with Chicago. Totalled 548 goals and 604 assists. Debuted with Birmingham in the WHA in 1978–79. *Elected 1999.*

Michael (Mike) Grant: Joined the Montreal Victorias in 1894 when they won the Stanley Cup. Later organized exhibition games in the United States. *Elected 1950.*

Wilfred (Shorty) Green: Right wing played in senior league in northern Ontario until he turned pro with the Hamilton Tigers of the NHL in 1923. Later played for the New York Americans. *Elected 1962.*

Wayne Gretzky: The Great Gretzky. Unquestionably the greatest player in hockey history. Retired as a New York Ranger in 1999 after 22-year career that started in 1978–79 with Indianapolis and Edmonton in the WHA, then with Edmonton, Los Angeles, St. Louis, and the Rangers. Finished with 61 records, including nine MVP awards (unmatched in professional sports). Clearly no argument when he entered the Hall of Fame without waiting the usual three years. *Elected 1999.*

Silas (Si) Griffis: A defenseman known for his speed, he turned pro with the Kenora Thistles in 1907 when they defeated the Montreal Wan-

The Rangers' record book is dominated by Rod Gilbert.

Dick Irvin played for Chicago before becoming a successful coach in the NHL.

derers for the Stanley Cup. He captained the Vancouver Millionaires, who won the Stanley Cup in 1915. *Elected 1950.*

George Hainsworth: Recorded 22 shutouts during 44-game NHL schedule while with the Montreal Canadiens in 1928–29. Won Vezina Trophy three straight years and later was traded to Toronto. *Elected 1961.*

Glenn Hall: An All-Star goalie for 11 of his 18 years with Detroit, Chicago, and St. Louis. Set record for most consecutive games by a goaltender (502) and ended career with 2.51 goals-against average. *Elected 1975.*

Joseph Henry (Joe) Hall: Noted as a slam-bang defenseman. Played for Kenora Thistles, Montreal Shamrocks, Quebec Bulldogs, and Montreal Canadiens, through 1918–19. *Elected 1961.*

Doug Harvey: Seven-time winner of the James Norris Trophy as NHL's leading defenseman. Named to All-Star team 11 times in 17 seasons. Played the point on Montreal's awesome power play during the 1950s. *Elected 1973.*

George Hay: Was forward in western Canada with Winnipeg, Regina, and Portland until he joined the Chicago Blackhawks in 1926. Later played for Detroit Cougars and Red Wings. *Elected 1958.*

William Milton (Riley) Hern: Mostly a goalie, but played some as a forward. Starred for the Montreal Wanderers when they won the Stanley Cup in 1907, 1908, and 1910. *Elected 1962.*

Bryan Hextall: Scored 20 or more goals in seven of 12 seasons with the Rangers in the 1930s and 1940s. Three-time All-Star right wing who led NHL in scoring in 1941–42 with 56 points. *Elected 1969.*

Harry (Hap) Holmes: Starred in five professional leagues over a 15-year goaltending career. Played on four Stanley Cup champions. Memory is perpetuated by trophy carrying his name awarded to leading goalie in American Hockey League each season. *Elected 1972.*

Charles Thomas (Tom) Hooper: Played as forward for Kenora Thistles, starting in 1901. Was on the Kenora team that won Stanley Cup by defeating the Montreal Wanderers in 1907. *Elected 1962.*

G. Reginald (Red) Horner: A rough defenseman, he accumulated 1,254 penalty minutes during 12 years with the Toronto Maple Leafs, starting in 1928. *Elected 1965.*

Miles Gilbert (Tim) Horton: Inspirational leader of great Maple Leaf teams of the 1960s. Strong defenseman who played 18 years before tragic auto accident claimed his life in 1974. *Elected 1977.*

Gordie Howe: Record-setting right wing. Played for 25 years with Detroit Red Wings and was named to the All-Star team in 21 of those years. Six-time scoring champion and six-time winner of the Hart Trophy as MVP. Made remarkable comeback, playing six more seasons in the WHA, then one more in the NHL before he retired at the age of 52. *Elected 1972.*

Sydney Harris (Syd) Howe: A forward, he shares the modern record of six goals in a game made with the Detroit Red Wings in 1944. Spent 16 seasons in the NHL. *Elected 1965.*

Harry Howell: Appeared in 1,581 games, second-most among defenseman in the history of major-league hockey. Had 24-year career in NHL and WHA and was Norris Trophy winner in 1966–67 while with Rangers. *Elected 1979.*

Robert Marvin (Bobby) Hull: Left wing who scored over 900 goals in brilliant 23-year career in NHL and WHA. Most dominant scorer of the 1960s, cracking 50-goal barrier five times with Chicago. Career total of 610 NHL goals is fifth on all-time list. *Elected 1983.*

John Bower (Bouse) Hutton: Goalie for the Ottawa Silver Seven Cup champions of 1903 and 1904. Also was star goalie in lacrosse. *Elected 1962.*

Harry Hyland: A right winger, he turned pro with the Montreal Shamrocks in 1908–09.

Joined the Montreal Wanderers the next year and remained with them until 1918 when he became member of Ottawa Senators. *Elected 1962.*

James Dickenson (Dick) Irvin: Played for Regina and Portland of Western Canadian League and for Chicago Blackhawks of NHL as a forward. Also coached Blackhawks, Toronto, and Montreal Canadiens, winning four Stanley Cup titles. *Elected 1958.*

Harvey (Busher) Jackson: Gained fame on Toronto's "Kid Line" with Charlie Conacher and Joe Primeau in 1930s. Led Leafs to three NHL titles. Named to five All-Star teams and won scoring title in 1932–33. Finished career with New York Americans and Boston Bruins. *Elected 1961.*

Ernie (Moose) Johnson: Played for Montreal Wanderers until 1910 when moved to New Westminster of Pacific Coast League. Was defenseman throughout most of career, but also played forward. *Elected 1952.*

Ivan (Ching) Johnson: Was one of the original New York Rangers in 1926–27. A defenseman who relished delivering hard bodychecks, he played in the NHL for 12 years, the last with the New York Americans. *Elected 1958.*

Thomas Christian Johnson: Played on six Stanley Cup winners during 15-year career as defenseman for Montreal and Boston in the 1950s and 1960s. Norris Trophy winner in 1958–59. *Elected 1970.*

Aurel Joliat: A 140-pound left wing, he played on a line with the great Howie Morenz for the Montreal Canadiens. Was exceptionally fast and clever. Started 16-year career with Canadiens in 1922. *Elected 1947.*

Gordon (Duke) Keats: A forward, he was a long-time star in the Western Canadian League, mostly with Edmonton. Later played for Boston, Detroit, and Chicago of NHL. *Elected 1958.*

Leonard (Red) Kelly: Broke into NHL in 1947 and played 20 seasons as top defenseman for Detroit and center for Toronto. Won Lady

Byng Trophy four times and played on eight Stanley Cup winners. *Elected 1969.*

Theodore (Ted) Kennedy: As a center, he sparked the Toronto Maple Leafs to five Stanley Cup championships. Was team captain from 1948 until retirement in 1955. *Elected 1966.*

David Michael Keon: Checking center played 22 pro seasons. Won Calder Trophy with Toronto in 1960–61 and Conn Smythe in 1967. Picked up just 151 penalty minutes in 1,725 games. *Elected 1986.*

Elmer James Lach: Was center on line with Maurice Richard in 1944–45 when the Rocket scored a record 50 goals in 50 games. Played for Montreal Canadiens for 14 years,

three times being voted a first-team All-Star. *Elected 1966.*

Guy Damien Lafleur: Dazzling Montreal center was three-time scoring champion, MVP twice, and six-time All-Star. Helped Habs to four straight Cups from 1976 to 1979. Played for Rangers and Quebec after four-year retirement. *Elected 1988.*

Edouard (Newsy) Lalonde: Started pro career with Cornwall in 1905 and was one of finest scorers and roughest players of his era. Played with Montreal Canadiens of NHL and with other teams in the National Hockey Association and Pacific Coast Hockey Association. *Elected 1950.*

Jacques Laperriere: Strong and mobile backliner anchored defense on Montreal teams

Scoring champ Guy Lafleur was a point machine on four out of five championship Canadien teams.

that won six Cups during his 12-year career. Won Calder Trophy in 1962–63. *Elected 1987.*

Guy Lapointe: Solid defenseman was backbone of six Stanley Cup–winning teams in Montreal in the 1970s. Scored 622 points in 884 regular-season games and was a two-time first-team All-Star. *Elected 1993.*

Edgar L. Laprade: All-around center starred for New York Rangers from 1945 to 1955, scoring 280 points. Won Calder Trophy as Rookie of the Year in 1945–46 and four years later captured Lady Byng Trophy. *Elected 1993.*

Jean Baptiste (Jack) Laviolette: Played both as a forward and a defenseman for the Montreal Canadiens from 1909 to 1918. He had outstanding speed. Played on a line with Newsy Lalonde. *Elected 1962.*

Hughie Lehman: A professional goalie for 19 years. Standout in Pacific Coast Hockey Association for New Westminster and Vancouver. Played for Chicago Blackhawks in 1926–27, their first season in NHL. *Elected 1958.*

Jacques Gerard Lemaire: Montreal center took Stanley Cup victory lap eight times in 11 years with 139 points in 145 playoff games. Scored 366 goals and 835 points in 853 regular-season games. *Elected 1984.*

Mario Lemieux: The Hall of Fame eliminated the three-year waiting period to elect the Pittsburgh center after his retirement following the 1996–97 season. Lemieux amassed 613 goals and 1,494 points in 12 seasons with Pittsburgh, leading the Penguins to Stanley Cup triumphs in 1991 and 1992. He won the Hart Trophy as league MVP three times and the Art Ross Trophy as top scorer six times, among many awards. *Elected 1997.*

Percy LeSueur: Goalie for the Ottawa Senators from 1906 to 1913. Played for Toronto in 1914 and later coached Hamilton team of the NHL. *Elected 1961.*

Herbert Lewis: Known as "The Duke of Duluth" for his great years with Duluth in the American Hockey League, flashy, high-speed left

Guy Lapointe starred on six Stanley Cup winners with Montreal.

wing played 11 years with the Detroit Cougars, Falcons, and Red Wings. Was on two Stanley Cup championship teams and started in the first All-Star Game in 1934. *Elected 1989.*

Theodore (Ted) Lindsay: Aggressive, combative, productive left wing for Detroit Red

Montreal's Jacques Lemaire was on a Cup winner eight times.

shutouts in regular season and seven more in playoffs. *Elected 1980.*

Duncan (Mickey) MacKay: Played forward for the Vancouver Millionaires from 1914 to 1926. He joined the Chicago Blackhawks in 1926–27 and later played for Pittsburgh and Boston. *Elected 1952.*

Frank Mahovlich: A star from first season in 1957–58, when he was Rookie of Year. Left wing played on six Stanley Cup winners with Toronto and Montreal and finished career with 533 goals and 1,103 points. *Elected 1981.*

Joe Malone: Scored 44 goals during 22-game schedule in 1917–18, his first NHL season with the Montreal Canadiens. Holds NHL record of seven goals in a Stanley Cup game. *Elected 1950.*

Sylvio Mantha: Played defense for the Montreal Canadiens for 13 years, starting in 1923–24. Team finished in first place nine times during that period. Was player-coach for Boston Bruins in 1936. *Elected 1960.*

Jack Marshall: Played center for the Montreal Wanderers when they won the Stanley Cup in 1906, 1908, and 1910. Was captain of Toronto team which won Cup in 1914. *Elected 1965.*

Fred G. (Steamer) Maxwell: A star amateur who never became a professional, his position was that of rover when each team consisted of seven players. Played senior hockey in Winnipeg, starting in 1909. Later became a coach of amateur and professional teams. *Elected 1962.*

Lanny McDonald: Had a 16-year NHL career that began in Toronto in 1973 and was capped when he captained the Calgary Flames to their first Stanley Cup championship in 1989. Right wing made four All-Star Game appearances and represented Team NHL at the 1979 Challenge Cup. *Elected 1992.*

Frank McGee: A center for the Ottawa Silver Seven. In a Stanley Cup game against Dawson City in 1905, he scored 14 goals, including eight in succession during a span of eight minutes and 20 seconds. *Elected 1945.*

Wings. One of the highest career scorers at his position. Emerged from four-year retirement as player in 1964–65 to help Wings win regular-season title. *Elected 1966.*

Harry Lumley: Signed by Detroit when he was only 16, he became one of NHL's greatest goaltenders in 16-year career. Recorded 71

William George (Billy) McGimsie: Was a center for 10 years for the Kenora Thistles. Played in several Stanley Cup series against the Montreal Wanderers and Ottawa Silver Seven, the first in 1903. *Elected 1962.*

George McNamara: Helped the Toronto team win the Stanley Cup in 1914 while playing defense. Before that he was with the Montreal Wanderers and with Waterloo of the Trolley League. *Elected 1958.*

Stanley (Stan) Mikita: One of the greatest play-making centers in NHL history, he chalked up 926 assists in 22 years with the Chicago Blackhawks. Led league in scoring four times and twice won Hart and Lady Byng Trophies. *Elected 1983.*

Richard (Dickie) Moore: Twice led NHL in scoring despite assortment of serious injuries. Left wing helped Canadiens win six Stanley Cups in his 12 years there, starting in 1951. Scored 608 points in 719 NHL games. *Elected 1974.*

Patrick Joseph (Paddy) Moran: A standup goalie who used his stick to good advantage, he turned pro with the Quebec Bulldogs in 1902. Played for Haileybury in 1911, but returned to Quebec and helped the Bulldogs win the Stanley Cup in 1912 and 1913. *Elected 1958.*

Howie Morenz: A flashy, dynamic center, he starred for 14 years in the NHL, mostly with the Montreal Canadiens. Montreal traded him to Chicago in 1934 and he moved to the New York Rangers in 1935 before returning to the Canadiens for the 1936–37 campaign. *Elected 1945.*

William (Bill) Mosienko: Best remembered for scoring three goals in a record 21 seconds while playing for Chicago against the New York Rangers on March 23, 1952. Was right wing on line with Bentley brothers, Max and Doug. *Elected 1965.*

Frank Nighbor: A center, he played pro hockey in leagues in eastern and western Canada from 1915 to 1929. Starred for Vancouver Millionaires and Ottawa Senators. Scored 41 goals in 20 games in 1916–17. *Elected 1947.*

Reginald (Reg) Noble: Primarily a left wing, but played some defense for Toronto Arenas, Toronto St. Pats, Montreal Maroons, and Detroit Cougars. Helped Maroons win Stanley Cup in 1925–26. *Elected 1962.*

Herbert William (Buddy) O'Connor: Center had just 34 penalty minutes in 10-year career with Montreal and New York Rangers. Scored 60 points in 60 games for Rangers to win MVP and Lady Byng honors in 1947–48. *Elected 1988.*

Harold (Harry) Oliver: Played as a forward for 11 NHL seasons for the Boston Bruins and New York Americans. Weighed only 155 pounds and rarely was penalized. Helped Bruins win two Stanley Cup crowns. *Elected 1967.*

Murray Bert Olmstead: Tough left wing played on four Stanley Cup winners at Montreal in the 1950s before helping Toronto take the title in 1962. Amassed 421 points and 884 penalty minutes in 848 games. *Elected 1985.*

Bobby Orr: Six knee operations cut brilliant NHL career to nine years with Boston and Chicago. The only defenseman ever to win a scoring championship (he did it twice), Orr scored 915 points in 657 games. Won Norris Trophy as best defenseman eight consecutive years through 1974–75 season. *Elected 1979.*

Bernard Marcel (Bernie) Parent: Backstopped Flyers to consecutive Stanley Cup titles in 1974 and 1975, winning Conn Smythe both years. In 608 regular-season games, posted 55 shutouts and 2.55 GAA. *Elected 1984.*

Douglas Bradford (Brad) Park: High-scoring defenseman was seven-time All-Star for the Rangers, Bruins, and Red Wings in 17-year career. Scored 213 goals and 896 points in 1,113 games. Played in 161 postseason games. *Elected 1988.*

Lester Patrick: Patriarch of famous hockey family, he was an outstanding player for the Montreal Wanderers and Renfrew Millionaires. He helped form the Pacific Coast Hockey Association and, in 1926, came east to coach and manage the New York Rangers in their first NHL season. Remained with Rangers until 1946. *Elected 1947.*

Marcel Pronovost patrolled NHL blue lines for 20 years and played on five Cup winners.

Lynn Patrick: Fearing charges of nepotism, his father, Lester, wouldn't put Lynn on the New York Rangers until another club threatened to claim him. In his decade with the team, Lynn led Rangers in scoring twice and scored 335 points in 455 games. *Elected 1980.*

Gilbert Perreault: Superb skater and puck-handler scored 512 goals and 1,326 points in 1,191 games over 17 years with Buffalo. Calder Trophy winner in 1971 and Lady Byng recipient in 1972. *Elected 1990.*

Tommy Phillips: Was a hard-shooting, slick, stickhandling forward for the Kenora Thistles. In 1906, he scored seven goals in a two-game Stanley Cup series against the Montreal Wanderers. *Elected 1945.*

Pierre Pilote: Defenseman broke in with Chicago in 1956 and did not miss a game his first

five seasons. Three-time Norris Trophy winner had 498 points in 890 regular-season games. *Elected 1975.*

Didier (Pit) Pitre: Joined the Montreal Canadiens in 1909 and was noted for his blistering shot. A 200-pound forward, he played for the Canadiens until 1923, when he retired. *Elected 1962.*

Jacques Plante: The first goalie to popularize the mask, Plante had an outstanding 2.34 goals-against average in 837 games and recorded 82 shutouts. Played on six of Montreal's Stanley Cup champions. *Elected 1978.*

Denis Charles Potvin: Seven-time All-Star set NHL career records for goals, assists, and points for defensemen during 15 seasons with Islanders. Won Norris Trophy three times, Calder in 1974. Captained four Cup winners. *Elected 1991.*

Walter (Babe) Pratt: A defenseman, he began pro career with New York Rangers in January 1936 and was traded to Toronto in November 1942. A standout offensive player for a rearguard. *Elected 1966.*

A. Joseph (Joe) Primeau: Center for famous "Kid Line" that included Charlie Conacher and Harvey Jackson. A clever stickhandler and playmaker and an excellent penalty-killer for the Toronto Maple Leafs. *Elected 1963.*

Marcel Pronovost: Twenty-year veteran of NHL play who played integral role on five Stanley Cup winners. Broke in with Detroit in 1950 and played there 15 years before trade to Toronto. Solid defender scored 345 points in 1,206 games. *Elected 1978.*

Bob Pulford: Resolute left wing played on four Cup winners in Toronto. Played 16 seasons, final two with Kings, scoring 281 goals and 643 points in 1,079 games. *Elected 1991.*

Harvey Pulford: Played defense for the Ottawa Silver Seven from 1893 to 1908. Was one of the most effective bodycheckers of his era and had reputation for being a clean player. *Elected 1945.*

Bill Quackenbush: The cleanest defenseman in NHL history, he collected only 95 min-

Jean Ratelle had a 21-season career with the Rangers and Bruins.

utes of penalties in 13 seasons. A five-time All-Star with Detroit and Boston, he was Lady Byng winner in 1949. *Elected 1976.*

Frank Rankin: Played rover position when each team played with seven men. Starred for teams in Stratford, Ont., and Toronto, beginning in 1906–07. *Elected 1961.*

Jean Ratelle: Smooth-skating center scored 491 goals and 1,267 points in 1,281 games with Rangers and Bruins from 1960 to 1981. Won Lady Byng twice, spending just 276 minutes in penalty box. *Elected 1985.*

Claude Earl (Chuck) Rayner: Played 10 seasons in the NHL, all of them in New York. Had 25 career shutouts and was named to the All-Star team three times. Named winner of the Hart Trophy as Most Valuable Player in 1949–50, the second goalie to win that award. *Elected 1973.*

Kenneth (Ken) Reardon: A rugged, fearless defenseman for the Montreal Canadiens, starting in 1940–41. Voted to the NHL All-Star team four times. Later, was a front-office executive for the Canadiens. *Elected 1966.*

Henri Richard: Younger brother of Rocket Richard played on 11 All-Star champions in Montreal. Center twice led the league in assists and finished with 1,046 points in 1,256 games. *Elected 1979.*

Maurice (Rocket) Richard: Famed Montreal Canadiens' right wing had record 544 career

Henri Richard of the Canadiens (left) and Alex Delvecchio of the Red Wings were rewarded for their brilliant play with election to the Hall of Fame.

Serge Savard's defense led to seven Cups for Montreal.

goals until Detroit's Gordie Howe surpassed it. Played 18 NHL seasons before retiring after the 1959–60 campaign and was voted into the Hall of Fame nine months later. *Elected 1960.*

George Richardson: Never a professional, but an outstanding amateur from Kingston, Ont. Was with Queen's University team, which won the Allan Cup in 1909. *Elected 1950.*

Steve Shutt was a shooting star for five Cup-winning teams at Montreal.

Gordon Roberts: Played for Montreal Wanderers while attending McGill University and studying medicine. When he graduated, he moved west to practice medicinebut continued playing hockey. Set an all-time scoring record in Pacific Coast Hockey Association with 43 goals in 23 games. *Elected 1971.*

Larry Robinson: Steady defenseman helped Canadiens win six Stanley Cups in brilliant 20-season career. Played in 10 All-Star Games and set record for most playoff games (227). Scored 958 points in 1,384 games. *Elected 1995.*

Arthur Howey (Art) Ross: Turned pro with the Kenora Thistles in 1906. Also played for Haileybury and the Montreal Wanderers. Later was coach and general manager of the Boston Bruins. *Elected 1945.*

Blair Russell: A left-wing amateur star for the Montreal Victorias in the early 1900s. On February 23, 1905, he scored six goals in one game. *Elected 1965.*

Ernie Russell: Top scorer for the Montreal Wanderers, for whom he scored 32 goals during a 12-game regular-season schedule in 1910. *Elected 1965.*

J. D. (Jack) Ruttan: A leading amateur player starting in 1905–06 with the Armstrong's Point team of Winnipeg. Also played in the Manitoba University League and the Winnipeg Senior League. *Elected 1962.*

Borje Salming: A two-way defenseman from Sweden who played 17 seasons with Toronto and Detroit. He paved the way for other European players in the NHL. When he retired in 1990, he had 150 goals, 637 assists, and 787 points. *Elected 1997.*

Serge Aubrey Savard: Was key defensive stalwart on seven Montreal Cup winners over 14 seasons. Joined Winnipeg in 1981–82, helping Jets to biggest single-season improvement in NHL history. *Elected 1986.*

Terry Sawchuk: Considered one of greatest goalies in history. Played more seasons, more games, and had more shutouts than any other netminder. Appeared in 1,077 games overall, mostly with Detroit. Finished career with 103 shutouts, only goalie ever to reach the century mark. *Elected 1971.*

Fred Scanlan: A forward for the Montreal Shamrocks, winners of the Stanley Cup in 1898–99 and 1899–1900. Known for his clever play and accurate shot. *Elected 1965.*

Milton Conrad (Milt) Schmidt: A strong skater, smart stickhandler and prolific scorer, he centered Boston's famous "Kraut Line" that also included Bobby Bauer and Woody Dumart. *Elected 1961.*

David (Sweeney) Schriner: A left winger, he starred for the New York Americans and Toronto Maple Leafs. Twice won the NHL's scoring title, in 1935–36 and 1936–37. *Elected 1962.*

Earl Walter Seibert: Was noted for his ability as a rushing defenseman for the New York Rangers, Chicago Blackhawks, and Detroit Red Wings. Voted to circuit's All-Star first-team four times. *Elected 1963.*

Oliver Levi Seibert: Earl Siebert's father. Was member of the Berlin Rangers, winners of the Western Ontario Association title from 1900 to 1906. Was a forward during most of his career. *Elected 1961.*

Edward (Eddie) Shore: Generally regarded as the greatest defenseman of all time. Played for the Boston Bruins for 13½ years, then was traded to the New York Americans, for whom he played a half season. *Elected 1947.*

Steve Shutt: An uncanny shooter who set NHL record for goals by a left wing (since broken) with 60 in 1976–77. Scored 817 points in 930 games and was a member of five Canadien Stanley Cup champions in 14-year career. *Elected 1993.*

Albert (Babe) Siebert: Was outstanding left wing for Montreal Maroons. Switched to defense in the mid-1930s and continued to star with the New York Rangers, Boston Bruins, and Montreal Canadiens. *Elected 1964.*

Harold (Bullet Joe) Simpson: A fast-skating defenseman, he played for teams in Winnipeg and Edmonton before joining the New York Americans in 1925. Was general manager of the Americans from 1932 to 1935. *Elected 1962.*

Darryl Glen Sittler: Prolific center amassed 1,121 career points in 15 seasons, including record

Bullet Joe Simpson was a New York Americans' defenseman after pre-NHL career with Winnipeg and Edmonton.

10 points (six goals, four assists) in one game for Leafs in February 1976. Scored goal in overtime that won 1976 Canada Cup. *Elected 1989.*

Alfred E. (Alf) Smith: Was captain of the Ottawa Silver Seven in 1903, 1904, and 1905.

Billy Smith was the goalie who paced the Islanders to four straight Stanley Cups.

Also captained the Pittsburgh Athletic Club in 1909, his final year as a player. *Elected 1962.*

Clinton James (Snuffy) Smith: Two-time Lady Byng winner committed just 12 minor penalties in 10-year career centering for the New York Rangers and Chicago. Set then-NHL mark with 49 assists in 50-game season for the Hawks in 1943–44. *Elected 1991.*

Reginald (Hooley) Smith: Combined with Nels Stewart and Babe Siebert to form the Mon-

treal Maroons' great "S" line in the 1930s. Scored 200 goals in 17 seasons as right wing and part-time defenseman. *Elected 1972.*

Thomas Smith: An early star, he played center for three Stanley Cup championship teams before formation of the NHL. Won three scoring titles and twice scored nine goals in a single game. Also had an eight-goal game, a six-goal game, and five times scored five goals in a game. *Elected 1973.*

William (Billy) Smith: One of the greatest clutch goalies in NHL history, he led the New York Islanders to four straight Stanley Cup titles from 1980–83. Registered 305 regular-season wins and an 88-36 record in playoffs. Won Conn Smythe Trophy as playoff MVP in 1983. *Elected 1993.*

Allan Stanley: Durable defenseman played in 1,244 games over 21-year NHL career. Helped Toronto win four Stanley Cups in early 1960s and played in eight All-Star games. *Elected 1981.*

Russell (Barney) Stanley: A forward for the Stanley Cup–winning Vancouver Millionaires in the 1914–15 season. Was named general manager –coach of the Chicago Blackhawks in 1927. *Elected 1962.*

Peter Stastny: A 15-year forward with Quebec (10 years), New Jersey, and St. Louis, he posted 450 goals (1,239 points) in a career marked by a division title in 1986 and conference final berths in 1982 and 1985 with the Nordiques. Was Rookie of the Year in 1980–81. *Elected in 1999.*

John (Black Jack) Stewart: A defensive star for the Detroit Red Wings for 10 years, starting in 1938–39. Named to the league's All-Star first-team three times. *Elected 1964.*

Nelson (Nels) Stewart: A forward, he held the career scoring record of 324 goals until it was broken by Maurice Richard. Starred for the Montreal Maroons, Boston Bruins, and New York Americans. *Elected 1962.*

Bruce Stuart: A center, he played for the Portage Lakes team of Houghton, Mich., in the early 1900s. Later played for the Montreal Wanderers and the Ottawa Silver Seven. *Elected 1961.*

William (Hod) Stuart: A brother of Bruce Stuart, this defenseman played in Houghton, Mich., and for the Montreal Wanderers. *Elected 1945.*

Fred (Cyclone) Taylor: A high-scoring forward for teams in Houghton, Mich., Ottawa, Renfrew, and Vancouver. He was a whirlwind on the ice and is reported to have scored a goal once while skating backwards. *Elected 1947.*

Cecil (Tiny) Thompson: Was a goalie in the NHL for 12 seasons, 10 for the Boston Bruins and two for the Detroit Red Wings. Twice was voted to the league's All-Star first-team. *Elected 1959.*

Vladislav Tretiak: Goaltender led Soviets to 10 world titles and three Olympic gold medals from 1970–85. Registered 1.78 GAA in 98 World Championship games. First Soviet player in Hall of Fame. *Elected 1989.*

Harry Trihey: Was a rover who starred for McGill University and as captain of the Montreal Shamrocks when they won two Stanley Cup titles. *Elected 1950.*

Bryan Trottier: Elite center during 18-year career in which he posted 524 goals and 1,425 points. Was a key member of four Stanley Cup championships with the New York Islanders and two with the Pittsburgh Penguins. He retired following the 1993–94 season. *Elected 1997.*

Norm Ullman: Scored 20 or more goals in 16 of his 20 seasons in NHL. Centering for Detroit and Toronto, he scored a total of 1,229 points. He led the NHL with 42 goals in 1964–65. *Elected 1982.*

Georges Vezina: Turned pro as a goalie with the Montreal Canadiens in 1910 and played with them until November 1925. Died of tuberculosis the following year. Trophy for the goalies is awarded annually in his memory. *Elected 1945.*

John Phillip (Jack) Walker: Credited with having originated the hook check. Starred mostly on the West Coast for teams in Seattle and Victoria. Also played for Detroit in 1926–27 and 1927–28. *Elected 1960.*

Martin (Marty) Walsh: Played for Ottawa in the Eastern Canada Amateur Association, starting in 1908. Was leading scorer of the National Hockey Association for three seasons. *Elected 1962.*

Harry Watson: Played all three forward positions on crack amateur teams, including the Toronto Granites. Was with the Granites in 1924 when they represented Canada and won the Olympic title. *Elected 1962.*

Harry P. Watson: Sturdy defensive-minded left wing helped Maple Leafs win four Stanley Cups in five-year span from 1947 through 1951. Scored 443 points in 809 regular-season games and was one of cleanest players in history, with only 150 minutes of penalties in 14-year career. *Elected 1994.*

Ralph (Cooney) Weiland: Center played 11 seasons in NHL. Twice a member of Stanley Cup champions (1928–29, 1938–39), he coached Boston to the Cup in 1940–41. Also played for Ottawa and Detroit. After leaving pros, he launched a successful coaching career at Harvard University. *Elected 1971.*

Harry Westwick: Was a rover for the Ottawa Silver Seven when they won three consecutive Stanley Cup titles in the early 1900s. *Elected 1962.*

Fred Whitcroft: A prolific scorer, he played for the Kenora Thistles and Peterborough Colts. Later played for Edmonton, where he scored 49 goals in 1908. *Elected 1962.*

Gordon Allan (Phat) Wilson: Ranked among the all-time great amateur players. Was one of the stars of teams in Port Arthur, Ont., from 1918 to 1933. *Elected 1962.*

Lorne (Gump) Worsley: A two-time Vezina Trophy winner and member of four Stanley Cup winners, Worsley had 43 shutouts and a 2.93 goals-against average in 24 seasons. Played for three NHL teams and had greatest success at Montreal in the late 1960s. *Elected 1980.*

Roy Worters: Only 5-foot-3 and 135 pounds, he starred in the NHL for 12 seasons, mostly with the New York Americans. Compiled 2.36 goals-against average in 488 games and won both the Hart and Vezina Trophies. *Elected 1969.*

REFEREES, LINESMEN

Neil P. Armstrong: Began as a part-time linesman in NHL in 1957–58. Four seasons later, became a referee, never missing an assignment in 16 seasons. Officiated 1,733 regular-season games, 208 playoff games, and 10 All-Star Games. *Elected 1991.*

John Ashley: Worked 605 games over 12 NHL seasons and was regarded as league's best when he retired in 1972. *Elected 1981.*

William L. (Bill) Chadwick: A native New Yorker, he officiated NHL games for 16 years. Introduced hand signals to explain penalties such as holding and tripping. *Elected 1964.*

John D'Amico: Considered one of the finest linesmen ever, he worked over 1,700 games in a career than spanned from 1967 through 1988. Officiated in over 20 Stanley Cup finals and seven All-Star Games. *Elected 1993.*

Chaucer Elliott: Started refereeing in 1903 and worked in the Ontario Hockey Association for 10 seasons. *Elected 1961.*

George Hayes: Became first official to work in more than 1,000 games, ending 19-season career as a linesman in 1965 with 1,544 regular-season games. Officiated in 149 post-season contests and 11 All-Star games. *Elected 1988.*

Robert W. (Bobby) Hewitson: An NHL referee for almost 10 years until 1934. Later he became secretary and curator of the Hockey Hall of Fame. *Elected 1963.*

Fred J. (Mickey) Ion: Was a leading official in amateur leagues and in the Pacific Coast League and NHL until 1943. *Elected 1961.*

Matt Pavelich: First linesman to be inducted into the Hall of Fame. Colorful, steady, and respected, he set a mark for officiating most playoff games. Worked 1,727 regular-season games through April 1979. *Elected 1987.*

Michael J. (Mike) Rodden: Refereed 1,187 NHL games and was also known as a successful football coach in Canada. *Elected 1962.*

J. Cooper Smeaton: Was referee-in-chief of the NHL until 1937. Also officiated in amateur leagues and in the National Hockey Association. *Elected 1961.*

Roy A. (Red) Storey: An NHL referee from 1951 until he resigned on April 11, 1959. Worked more than 2,000 games in various circuits. *Elected 1967.*

Frank Udvari: Missed only two games in a 15-year NHL career that began in 1951. Later served as supervisor of officials. Previously refereed in the American Hockey League, where he served as referee-in-chief. *Elected 1973.*

BUILDERS

Charles F. Adams: Organizer of the Boston Bruins in 1924, first American team in the NHL. Also negotiated for the erection of the Boston Garden. *Elected 1960.*

Weston W. Adams, Sr.: Longtime president and chairman of the board of both the Boston Bruins and Boston Garden. Was a goalie at Harvard when his father, Charles F. Adams, was awarded Boston franchise, first NHL franchise in United States. *Elected 1972.*

Frank Ahearn: A director, president, and owner of the Ottawa Senators. Became president in 1922 and held that position until 1934, when the franchise was transferred to St. Louis. *Elected 1962.*

J. F. (Bunny) Ahearne: Served as president of the International Ice Hockey Federation from 1957 through 1975, organizing European, Olympic, and other international hockey events. *Elected 1977.*

Sir Montagu Allan: A Montreal financier and sportsman, he presented the Allan Cup for competition in 1908. The trophy is emblematic of the Senior Amateur Championship of Canada. *Elected 1945.*

Keith Allen: Made his contribution over a quarter of a century as coach and executive with the Philadelphia Flyers. Molded an expansion team that twice won the Stanley Cup (under coach Fred Shero) and was unbeaten for 35 games in 1979–80. *Elected 1992.*

Al Arbour: One of the winningest coaches in history, he was the driving force behind the Islanders' bench for 19 years. He was the architect behind four consecutive Stanley Cups from 1980–83. Played defense for Stanley Cup winners in Detroit, Chicago, and Toronto. His involvement in 2,227 games as a player and coach is a record. *Elected 1997.*

Harold E. Ballard: Spent much of his life building amateur and professional hockey in his native Toronto. Was principal owner of the Maple Leafs and a major force in the NHL. *Elected 1977.*

Father David Bauer, C.S.B.: Ordained Basilian priest whose hockey background included playing left wing on the Oshawa Generals' 1944 Memorial Cup winner. Conceived, developed, and coached first Canadian National Hockey Team. *Elected 1989.*

J. P. Bickell: First president, and then chairman of the board, of Maple Leaf Gardens. Award named after him is given to outstanding Toronto player each season. *Elected 1968.*

Scott Bowman: Winningest coach in NHL regular-season history. Guided Montreal to five Stanley Cup titles and expansion St. Louis to three final-round appearances, then moved to Pittsburgh, where he wan the Cup once, and De-

troit, where he won two more to tie Toe Blake at eight. Coached Team Canada to 1976 Canada Cup victory. *Elected 1991.*

George V. Brown: A pioneer of hockey in the United States. Organized the Boston Athletic Association hockey team and was the manager of the Boston Arena and Boston Garden. *Elected 1961.*

Walter A. Brown: Was president of the Boston Bruins and general manager of Boston Garden. Also coached the Boston Olympics to five U.S. national titles between 1930 and 1940. *Elected 1962.*

Frank Buckland: Coached and organized junior hockey around Toronto for 40 years and served the Ontario Hockey Association as both president and treasurer. *Elected 1985.*

J. A. (Jack) Butterfield: Largely credited with keeping minor-league hockey alive when the NHL expanded in 1967. Served as president of the American Hockey League, starting in 1966. *Elected 1980.*

Frank Calder: First president of the NHL. Served from 1917 until his death in February 1943. Trophy in his memory is awarded annually to the outstanding rookie player. *Elected 1947.*

Angus Daniel Campbell: Played an important part in the development of amateur hockey in Cobalt, Ont., area. Was the first president of the Northern Ontario Association, which was formed in 1919. *Elected 1964.*

Clarence S. Campbell: President of the NHL from September 1946 through 1976–77. Earlier was an NHL referee. *Elected 1966.*

Joseph Cattarinich: One of the original owners of the Canadiens in 1921, he was partly responsible for Montreal's proud NHL heritage. *Elected 1977.*

Joseph (Leo) Dandurand: Was among three persons who purchased the Montreal Canadiens in November 1921. He later coached the Canadiens. Was a delegate to the organizing meeting in 1914 of the Canadian Amateur Hockey Association. *Elected 1963.*

Frank Dilio: A president and secretary of the Junior Amateur Hockey Association. Later served as registrar and secretary of the Quebec Amateur Hockey Association until 1962. *Elected 1964.*

George Dudley: Was president of the Canadian Amateur Hockey Association, the Ontario Hockey Association, and the International Ice Hockey Federation. Headed the hockey section of the 1960 Olympic Games. *Elected 1968.*

Jimmie Dunn: A leading administrator and executive of junior teams and leagues in western Canada. *Elected 1968.*

Robert Alan Eagleson: Was Executive Director of the NHL Players' Association, which helped bring hockey salaries in line with other pro sports. Led negotiations to create Canada Cup series. *Elected 1989.*

Emile (The Cat) Francis: A staunch supporter of amateur hockey in the United States and former NHL goalie who became a coach and then executive with the New York Rangers, St. Louis Blues, and Hartford Whalers. *Elected 1982.*

J. L. (Jack) Gibson: Organizer of the first hockey league in the world—the International League—in 1904–05. *Elected 1976.*

Thomas Patrick Gorman: Among the founders of the NHL. Coached or managed seven Stanley Cup–winning teams while with the Montreal Canadiens and Maroons, Ottawa Senators, and Chicago Blackhawks. *Elected 1963.*

Frank A. Griffiths: Founded the company that purchased the Vancouver Canucks in 1974. Became a member of NHL Audit Committee five years later, assisting franchises in solidifying their finances, and served on NHL Board of Governors for more than 20 years. *Elected 1993.*

William (Bill) Hanley: Known as "Mr. OHA." Former timekeeper at Leafs' games, he became secretary-manager of the Ontario Hockey Association for 27 years until his retirement in 1974. *Elected 1986.*

Charles Hay: Oil-company executive coordinated negotiations for the 1972 series between Canada and Soviet Union. Organized Team Canada, which participated in historic eight-game series. *Elected 1974.*

Jim Hendy: President of the United States League and later general manager of the Cleveland Barons of the American League. Published the *Hockey Guide,* a leading statistical compendium, in the early 1930s. *Elected 1968.*

Foster William Hewitt: A hockey broadcaster for 50 years. Renowned for his exciting descriptions of games involving the Toronto Maple Leafs. *Elected 1965.*

William Abraham Hewitt: A secretary of the Ontario Hockey Association and a secretary and registrar for the Canadian Amateur Association. Was a sports editor of the *Toronto Star. Elected 1947.*

Fred J. Hume: A leading amateur hockey executive in western Canada. Later, helped develop the New Westminister professional team and the Western Hockey League. *Elected 1962.*

George (Punch) Imlach: Legendary Toronto coach and GM from 1958 through 1968–69. Guided Leafs to 10 playoff berths and four Stanley Cup titles. Became Buffalo coach and GM in 1970, rejoining Leafs in 1979 for three seasons. *Elected 1984.*

Tommy Ivan: Coached Red Wings to three Stanley Cup crowns in the early 1950s and then moved on to rebuild a struggling Chicago franchise. One of the game's greatest coaches and executives. *Elected 1974.*

W. M. (Bill) Jennings: One of the principal architects of NHL expansion in 1967. Served as president of the New York Rangers and a governor of the league for nearly 20 years. *Elected 1975.*

Bob Johnson: A Minneapolis-born star at the University of Minnesota, he went on to become a legendary coach at the University of Wisconsin before becoming coach of the Calgary Flames. After serving as executive director of USA Hockey, he coached the Pittsburgh Penguins to the Stanley Cup championship in 1990–91. He died of cancer on November 19, 1991. *Elected 1992.*

Gordon Juckes: Served the Canadian Amateur Hockey Association in executive positions from 1960 through 1978. *Elected 1979.*

General John Reed Kilpatrick: President of the New York Rangers and Madison Square Garden for 22 years. Also served on the Board of Governors of the NHL. *Elected 1960.*

Seymour H. Knox III: Brought NHL hockey to Buffalo in 1970 and made the Sabres one of the more successful expansion teams. Named *Hockey News* Executive of the Year in 1975, when the Sabres made it to the Stanley Cup finals in their fifth year of existence. *Elected 1993.*

G. A. (Al) Leader: President of the Western Hockey League for 25 years until his retirement in 1969. *Elected 1969.*

Robert LeBel: Former president of three amateur hockey groups and a life member of both the Quebec and Canadian Amateur Hockey Associations. *Elected 1970.*

Thomas F. Lockhart: Organizer and president of the Amateur Hockey Association of the United States and the Eastern Hockey League. Was also a business manager of the New York Rangers. *Elected 1965.*

Paul Lolcq: A native of Belgium, he was a president of the International Ice Hockey Federation. Credited with having helped influence the Winter Olympic Games Committee to include hockey on the program. *Elected 1961.*

John Mariucci: Developed American high school hockey programs in Minnesota. Former Blackhawk defenseman coached U.S. team to Olympic silver medal in 1956. North Stars' executive won the Lester Patrick Award in 1976–77. *Elected 1985.*

Frank Mathers: A product of Winnipeg, he became a top defenseman in the American Hock-

ey League, subsequently coaching the Hershey Bears and later becoming their president and general manager. Known as the AHL's top ambassador, he retired following the 1990–91 season and was fittingly honored by the Bears with a "Frank Mathers Night." *Elected 1992.*

Major Frederic McLaughlin: Pioneered professional hockey in Chicago. Was an owner and the first president of the Blackhawks and nicknamed the team in honor of the Blackhawk division he commanded during World War I. *Elected 1963.*

John Calverley (Jake) Milford: Discerning judge of talent coached 14 seasons in Ranger system before assuming GM positions in Los Angeles and Vancouver. Built Vancouver Canucks' club that made the 1982 Stanley Cup finals. *Elected 1984.*

Sen. Harland de Montarville Molson: Former owner of the Montreal Canadiens. *Elected 1973.*

Monsignor Atoll (Pere) Murray: Legendary creator of Notre Dame college hockey program in Wilcox, Saskatchewan. More than 100 alumni of his program have been selected in various NHL Entry Drafts. *Elected 1999.*

Francis Nelson: A vice-president of the Ontario Hockey Association and an OHA Governor to the Amateur Athletic Union of Canada. *Elected 1947.*

Bruce A. Norris: Became one of the youngest owners in pro sport in 1955 when he took over the Detroit Red Wings at age 31. Ran the Detroit franchise until 1982. *Elected 1969.*

James Norris: He purchased Detroit's NHL franchise in 1933 and changed the name of the team from the Falcons to the Red Wings. He was also an owner of the Detroit Olympia and Chicago Stadium. *Elected 1958.*

James D. Norris: Became a co-owner of the Chicago Blackhawks in 1946 after helping his father, James Norris, with the administrative duties of the Detroit Red Wings. *Elected 1962.*

William M. Northey: President of the Montreal Amateur Athletic Association and a managing director of the Montreal Forum. Was the first trustee of the Allan Cup when it was presented for amateur competition. *Elected 1947.*

John Ambrose O'Brien: Helped with the formation of the National Hockey Association in December 1909, a five-team league which included the Montreal Canadiens and the Montreal Wanderers. *Elected 1962.*

Brian F. O'Neill: Joined the NHL as Director of Administration in 1966 and served in a variety of roles until stepping down as executive vice-president in 1992. Supervised amateur and expansion drafts and scheduling, and handled all disciplinary action as part of his functions. *Elected 1994.*

Frederick Page: Served the game of hockey as player, coach, on-ice official, and administrator for more than 50 years. Member of Directorate for five World Championships and three Olympic Games. *Elected 1993.*

Frank Patrick: With his brother, Lester Patrick, he played for the famed Renfrew Millionaires. The two later organized the Pacific Coast Hockey Association. Frank also coached the Boston Bruins and was a general manager of the Montreal Canadiens. *Elected 1958.*

Allan W. Pickard: An executive for several teams and leagues in western Canada. He was a president of the Saskatchewan Amateur Association and the Canadian Amateur Association. *Elected 1958.*

Rudy Pilous: At age 28 in 1942, he established the junior club in St. Catharines, making the playoffs the next three seasons. Coached Chicago's 1961 Stanley Cup winner, Denver's WHL champs in 1964, and managed Winnipeg to two WHA titles. *Elected 1985.*

Norman Robert (Bud) Poile: Served hockey for a half century as an All-Star NHL center, minor-league coach, GM at Philadelphia and Vancouver, WHA vice president, and long-term commissioner of the CHL and IHL. *Elected 1990.*

Sam Pollock: Director of personnel for the Canadiens from 1964 through 1978, during which time the team won nine Stanley Cup titles. Assembled Team Canada '76, winners of the Canada Cup. *Elected 1978.*

Senator Donat Raymond: A president of the Montreal Maroons and the Montreal Canadiens, he headed the Canadian Arena Company which financed the construction of the Montreal Forum in 1924. *Elected 1958.*

John Ross Robertson: A member of the Canadian Parliament, he donated trophies to the winners of the senior, intermediate, and junior divisions of the Ontario Hockey Association. *Elected 1947.*

Claude C. Robinson: Was the first secretary of the Canadian Amateur Association and managed the Canadian team in the 1932 Olympic Games. *Elected 1947.*

Philip D. Ross: Named by Lord Stanley one of the trustees of the Stanley Cup in 1893 and served in that role for 56 years. *Elected 1976.*

Dr. Gunther Sabetzki: Helped popularize hockey in numerous countries around the world. Founding member of German Hockey Association in 1963 and was involved in 1972 Canada-Russia Summit Series and the foundation of the Canada Cup tournament. *Elected 1995.*

Glen Sather: As coach and general manager of the Edmonton Oilers, he was the architect of the team that won five Stanley Cups between 1984 and 1990. Played left wing from 1967 through 1975–76 with Boston, Pittsburgh, New York Rangers, St. Louis, Montreal, and Minnesota. Finished with Edmonton in the WHA in 1976–77. *Elected 1997.*

Frank J. Selke: Worked as coach, manager, and front-office executive for almost 60 years. Was with the Toronto Maple Leafs in various capacities before becoming managing director of the Montreal Canadiens in 1946. Remained director until 1964, during which time they won six Stanley Cup titles. *Elected 1960.*

Harry Sinden: Never played in the NHL, but made his mark as coach and general manager of the Boston Bruins. Coached team to first championship in 29 years in 1970 and was GM of the Bruins' Cup-winning team two years later. *Elected 1983.*

Frank D. Smith: A founder in 1911 and later secretary-treasurer of the Beaches Hockey League, which became the Toronto Hockey League. *Elected 1962.*

Conn Smythe: Longtime, fiery president of the Toronto Maple Leafs. Was instrumental in the building of Maple Leaf Gardens, which opened in November 1931. *Elected 1958.*

Ed Snider: Lobbied to bring NHL hockey to Philadelphia in the 1967 expansion. Part of group that arranged construction of The Spectrum as home for Flyers. Built organization that won the Stanley Cup in its seventh year. *Elected 1988.*

Lord Stanley of Preston: As Governor General of Canada in 1893, he donated the Stanley Cup to the championship hockey club of the Dominion. *Elected 1945.*

Captain James T. Sutherland: An organizer of teams and leagues in the Kingston, Ont., area, he coached the Kingston Junior team and served as president of the Ontario Hockey Association and the Canadian Amateur Hockey Association. *Elected 1947.*

Anatoli V. Tarasov: Generally regarded as the architect of hockey in the Soviet Union. Coached Soviets to nine amateur titles and three Olympic gold metals before retiring in 1972. *Elected 1974.*

Bill Torrey: Architect of the New York Islanders, who went from expansion team to four-time Stanley Cup champions in only 11 years. Moved to the Florida Panthers in 1993 and made that club the most successful first-year team in NHL history. *Elected 1995.*

Lloyd Turner: Helped organize the Western Canadian League in 1918. Coached and managed

the Fort William, Ont., team and was a founder of teams and leagues in Calgary, Alta. *Elected 1958.*

W. Thayer Tutt: Instrumental in the progress of amateur hockey in the United States. Helped start NCAA tournament and later served as International Ice Hockey Federation president. *Elected 1978.*

Carl P. Voss: Named first referee-in-chief of NHL in 1950 and made enormous contributions in the scouting of referees and linesmen. *Elected 1974.*

Fred Waghorne: A native of England, he was among the founders of the Toronto Hockey League. As a referee, he was responsible for introducing a whistle for stopping play during a game. A bell had been used previously. *Elected 1961.*

Arthur M. Wirtz: Got into the hockey business in 1931 when, in partnership with James Norris, he bought the Detroit Red Wings. Switched holdings to native Chicago in 1954, where he rebuilt Blackhawks into one of NHL's most prosperous franchises. *Elected 1971.*

William Wirtz: Joined Chicago Blackhawks in 1952 and served two terms as chairman of the NHL Board of Governors. Helped formulate expansion plans and was largely responsible for their success. *Elected 1976.*

John A. Ziegler: Became the fourth NHL president and CEO since 1917 in September 1977. Negotiated settlement with the WHA in 1979, ending costly talent war. During tenure, oversaw other expansions in 1991 and 1992. *Elected 1987.*

ELMER FERGUSON MEMORIAL AWARD WINNERS

In recognition of members of the newspaper profession whose words have brought honor to journalism and hockey.

Barton, Charlie, *Buffalo Courier Express*
Beauchamp, Jacques, *Montreal Matin/Journal de Montreal*
Brennan, Red, *Toronto Star*
Burchard, Jim, *New York World-Telegram*
Burnett, Red, *Toronto Star*
Carroll, Dink, *Montreal Gazette*
Coleman, Jim, *Southam Newspapers*
Darnata, Ted, *Chicago Daily News*
Delano, Hugh, *New York Post*
Desjardins, Marcel, *Montreal La Presse*
Dulmage, Jack, *Windsor Star*
Dunnell, Milt, *Toronto Star*
Ferguson, Elmer, *Montreal Newspapers*
Fisher, Red, *Montreal Star/Gazette*
Fitzgerald, Tom, *Boston Globe*
Frayne, Trent, *Toronto Telegram/Globe and Mail/Sun*
Gross, George, *Toronto Telegram*
Johnston, Dick, *Buffalo News*
Laney, Al, *New York Herald-Tribune*
Larochelle, Claude, *Le Soleil*
L'Esperance, Zotique, *le Journal de Montreal*
Mayer, Charles, *le Journal de Montreal*
MacLeod, Rex, *Toronto Globe and Mail*
Monahan, Leo, *Boston Herald*
Moriarty, Tim, *UPI/Newsday*
Nichols, Joe, *The New York Times*
O'Brien, Andy, *Weekend Magazine*
Orr, Frank, *Toronto Star*
Olan, Ben, *Associated Press (N.Y.)*
O'Meara, Basil, *Montreal Star*
Proudfoot, Jim, *Toronto Star*
Pedneault, Yvon, *TV Analyst*
Raymond, Bertrand, *le Journal de Montreal*
Rosa, Fran, *Boston Globe*
Strachan, Al, *Montreal Gazette/Toronto Globe and Mail*
Vipond, Jim, *Toronto Globe and Mail*
Lewis, Walter, *Detroit Times*
Young, Scott, *Toronto Globe and Mail/Telegram*

FOSTER HEWITT MEMORIAL AWARD WINNERS

In recognition of broadcasters who made outstanding contributions to their profession and hockey.

Cole, Bob, *Toronto*
Cusick, Fred, *Boston*
Darling, Ted, *Buffalo*

Gallivan, Danny, *Montreal*
Hewitt, Foster, *Toronto*
Irvin, Dick, *Montreal*
Kelly, Dan, *St. Louis*
Lecavelier, Rene, *Montreal*
Lynch, Budd, *Detroit*
Martyn, Bruce, *Detroit*
McDonald, Jiggs, *New York Islanders*
McKnight, Wes, *Toronto*
Meeker, Howie, *TV Analyst*
Petit, Lloyd, *Chicago*
Shaver, Al, *Minnesota*
Smith, Doug, *Montreal*
Wilson, Bob, *Boston*

UNITED STATES HOCKEY HALL OF FAME

The United States Hockey Hall of Fame is located in Eveleth, Minn., which bills itself as "The Hockey Capital of the U.S.A." This midwestern mining community has sent more than a dozen players to the NHL, including goalie Frank (Mr. Zero) Brimsek, a legendary performer with the Boston Bruins. One of its natives, Mark Pavelich, starred on the 1980 U.S. gold-medal Olympic hockey team.

Opened in 1973, the Hall of Fame honors notable American players and their feats, and it tributes the game's innovators. Its "Evolution of Hockey Time Tunnel" traces the course of the sport on every level—youth, college, international, professional.

Enshrinees, in addition to players, include coaches, administrators, and a referee, Bill Chadwick, who is among a number of others in Toronto's Hall of Fame as well. Enshrinees are selected annually.

Players

Abel, Clarence (Taffy)
Baker, Hobart (Hobey)
Bartholome, Earl
Bessone, Peter
Blake, Robert
Boucha, Henry
Brimsek, Frank

Cavanagh, Joel
Chaisson, Ray
Chase, John
Christian, Roger
Christian, William
Cleary, Robert
Cleary, William
Conroy, Anthony
Dahlstrom, Carl (Cully)
DesJardins, Victor
Desmond, Richard
Dill, Robert
Everett, Doug
Ftorek, Robbie
Garrison, John
Garrity, Jack
Goheen, Frank (Moose)
Grant, Wally
Harding, Austin
Iglehart, Stewart
Johnson, Virgil
Karakas, Mike
Kirrane, Jack
Lane, Myles
Langevin, David
Larson, Reed
Linder, Joseph
LoPresti, Sam
Mariucci, John
Matchefts, John
Mayasich, John
McCartan, Jack
Moe, William
Morrow, Ken
Moseley, Fred
Murray, Hugh (Muzz)
Nelson, Hubert (Hub)
Olson, Eddie
Owen, George
Palmer, Winthrop (Ding)
Paradise, Robert
Purpur, Clifford (Fido)
Riley, William
Romnes, Elwin (Doc)
Rondeau, Richard
Sheehy, Timothy
Williams, Tommy
Winters, Frank (Coddy)
Yackel, Ken

Coaches

Almquist, Oscar
Bessone, Amo
Brooks, Herb
Ceglarski, Len
Gordon, Malcolm
Fullerton, James
Harkness, Ned
Heyliger, Victor
Holt, Charles
Ikola, Willard
Jeremiah, Edward
Johnson, Bob
Kelley, John (Snooks)
Kelly, John H.
Pleban, John (Connie)
Riley, Jack
Ross, Larry
Thompson, Clifford
Stewart, William
Winsor, Alfred (Ralph)

Administrators

Brown, George
Brown, Walter
Bush, Walter
Clark, Donald
Claypool, James
Gibson, J.C. (Doc)
Jennings, William
Kahler, Nick
Lockhart, Thomas
Marvin, Cal
Ridder, Robert
Schulz, Charles M. (Peanuts)
Trumble, Harold
Tutt, William
Wirtz, William
Wright, Lyle

Referee

Chadwick, Bill

15

NHL RECORDS

INDIVIDUAL

Most seasons played—26, Gordie Howe, Detroit, 1946–47 through 1970–71; Hartford, 1979–80.

Most games played—1,767, Gordie Howe, Detroit and Hartford.

Most goals—894, Wayne Gretzky, Edmonton, Los Angeles, St. Louis and New York Rangers.

Most assists—1,963, Wayne Gretzky, Edmonton, Los Angeles, St. Louis and New York Rangers.

Most points—2,857, Wayne Gretzky, Edmonton, Los Angeles, St. Louis and New York Rangers.

Most goals by a center, career—894, Wayne Gretzky, Edmonton, Los Angeles, St. Louis and New York Rangers.

Most assists by a center, career—1,963, Wayne Gretzky, Edmonton, Los Angeles, St. Louis and New York Rangers.

Most points by a center, career—2,857, Wayne Gretzky, Edmonton, Los Angeles, St. Louis and New York Rangers.

Most goals by a left wing, career—610, Bobby Hull, Chicago, Winnipeg and Hartford.

Most assists by a left wing, career—813, John Bucyk, Detroit and Boston.

Most points by a left wing, career—1,369, John Bucyk, Detroit and Boston.

Most goals by a right wing, career—801, Gordie Howe, Detroit and Hartford.

Most assists by a right wing, career—1,049, Gordie Howe, Detroit and Hartford.

Most points by a right wing, career—1,850, Gordie Howe, Detroit and Hartford.

Most goals by a defenseman, career—385, Paul Coffey, Edmonton, Pittsburgh, Los Angeles, Detroit, Hartford, Philadelphia, and Carolina.

Most assists by a defenseman, career—1,102, Paul Coffey, Edmonton, Pittsburgh, Los Angeles, Detroit, Hartford, Philadelphia, and Carolina.

Most points by a defenseman, career—1,487, Paul Coffey, Edmonton, Pittsburgh, Los Angeles, Detroit, Hartford, Philadelphia, Carolina.

Most penalty minutes, career—3,966, Dave Williams, Toronto, Vancouver, Detroit, Los Angeles and Hartford, 1974–75 through 1987–88.

Quebec's Peter Stastny set a record with 109 points in his rookie season (1980–81).

Most consecutive games—964, Doug Jarvis, Montreal, Washington and Hartford, from Oct. 8, 1975 to Oct. 10, 1987.

Most games appeared in by a goaltender, career—971, Terry Sawchuk, Detroit, Boston, Toronto, Los Angeles and New York Rangers, 1949–50 through 1969–70.

Most consecutive complete games by a goaltender—502, Glenn Hall, Detroit and Chicago, 1955–56 to 1962–63.

Most shutouts by a goaltender, career—103, Terry Sawchuk, Detroit, Boston, Toronto, Los Angeles and New York Rangers, 1949–50 through 1969–70.

Most times scoring three or more goals, game—49, Wayne Gretzky, Edmonton, Los Angeles, St. Louis and New York Rangers.

Most 40-or-more-goal seasons—12, Wayne Gretzky, Edmonton, Los Angeles, St. Louis and New York Rangers.

Most 50-or-more goal seasons—9, Mike Bossy, New York Islanders; Wayne Gretzky, Edmonton, Los Angeles, St. Louis and New York Rangers.

Most 60-or-more goals seasons—5, Mike Bossy, New York Islanders; Wayne Gretzky, Edmonton, Los Angeles, St. Louis and New York Rangers.

Most 100-or-more point seasons—14, Wayne Gretzky, Edmonton, Los Angeles, St. Louis and New York Rangers.

Most goals, season—92, Wayne Gretzky, Edmonton, 1981–82.

Most assists, season—163, Wayne Gretzky, Edmonton, 1985–86.

Most points, season—215, Wayne Gretzky, Edmonton, 1985–86.

Most goals, one season, including playoffs—100, Wayne Gretzky, Edmonton, 1983–84.

Most assists, one season, including playoffs—174, Wayne Gretzky, Edmonton, 1985–86.

Most points, one season, including playoffs—255, Wayne Gretzky, Edmonton, 1984–85.

Most goals, season, by a defenseman—48, Paul Coffey, Edmonton, 1985–86.

Most assists, season, by a defenseman—102, Bobby Orr, Boston, 1970–71.

Most points, season, by a defenseman—139, Bobby Orr, Boston, 1970–71.

Most goals, season, by a rookie—76, Teemu Selanne, Winnipeg, 1992–93.

Most assists, season, by a rookie—70, Peter Stastny, Quebec, 1980–81; Joe Juneau, Boston, 1992–93.

Most points, season, by a rookie—132, Teemu Selanne, Winnipeg, 1992–93.

Most power-play goals, one season—34, Tim Kerr, Philadelphia, 1985–86.

Most shorthanded goals, season—13, Mario Lemieux, Pittsburgh, 1988–89.

Most penalty minutes, season—472, Dave Schultz, Philadelphia, 1974–75.

Most shutouts by a goalie, season—22, George Hainsworth, Montreal, 1928–29; modern record: 15, Tony Esposito, Chicago, 1969–70.

Longest undefeated streak, goaltender—32, Gerry Cheevers, Boston, 1971–72 (24 wins, 8 ties).

Most games, goalie, season—76, Grant Fuhr, St. Louis, 1995–96.

Most wins, goalie, season—47, Bernie Parent, Philadelphia, 1973–74.

Longest consecutive point-scoring streak—51 games, Wayne Gretzky, Edmonton, 1983–84.

Longest consecutive point-scoring streak, defenseman—28 games, Paul Coffey, Edmonton, 1985–86.

Longest consecutive goal-scoring streak—16 games, Punch Broadbent, Ottawa, 1921–22; modern record, 13 games, Charlie Simmer, Los Angeles, 1979–80.

Longest consecutive assist-scoring streak—23 games, Wayne Gretzky, Los Angeles, 1990–91.

Longest consecutive shutout streak, goalie—461 minutes, 29 seconds, Alex Connell, Ottawa, 1927–28; modern record: 309 minutes, 21 seconds, Bill Durnan, Montreal, 1948–49.

Most goals, season, by a center—92, Wayne Gretzky, Edmonton, 1981–82.

Most goals, season, by a right wing—86, Brett Hull, St. Louis, 1990–91.

Most goals, season, by a left wing—63, Luc Robitaille, Los Angeles, 1992–93.

Most assists, season, by a center—163, Wayne Gretzky, Edmonton, 1985–86.

Most assists, season, by a right wing—83, Mike Bossy, New York Islanders, 1981–82.

Most assists, season, by a left wing—70, Joe Juneau, Boston, 1992–93.

Most goals, season, by a rookie defenseman—23, Brian Leetch, New York Rangers, 1988–89.

Most assists, season, by a rookie defenseman—60, Larry Murphy, Los Angeles, 1980–81.

Most points, season, by a center—215, Wayne Gretzky, Edmonton, 1985–86.

Most points, season, by a right wing—147, Mike Bossy, New York Islanders, 1981–82.

Most points, season, by a left wing—125, Luc Robitaille, Los Angeles, 1992–93.

Most points, season, by a rookie defenseman—76, Larry Murphy, Los Angeles, 1980–81.

Most points, season, by a goaltender—14, Grant Fuhr, Edmonton, 1983–84.

Most goals, one game—7, Joe Malone, Quebec, vs. Toronto, Jan. 31, 1920.

Most assists, one game—7, Billy Taylor, Detroit, at Chicago, March 16, 1947; Wayne Gretzky, Edmonton, vs. Washington, Feb. 15, 1980; Wayne Gretzky, Edmonton, at Chicago, Dec. 11, 1985; Wayne Gretzky, Edmonton, vs. Quebec, Feb. 14, 1986.

Most points, one game—10, Darryl Sittler, Toronto, vs. Boston, Feb. 7, 1976 (6 goals, 4 assists).

Most goals, one game, by a defenseman—5, Ian Turnbull, Toronto, vs. Detroit, Feb. 2, 1977.

Most assists, one game, by a defenseman—6, Babe Pratt, Toronto, vs. Boston, Jan. 8, 1944; Pat Stapleton, Chicago, vs. Detroit, Mar. 30, 1969; Bobby Orr, Boston, at Vancouver, Jan. 1, 1973; Ron Stackhouse, Pittsburgh, vs. Philadelphia, Mar. 8, 1975; Paul Coffey, Edmonton, vs. Detroit, Mar. 14, 1986; Gary Suter, Calgary, vs. Edmonton, Apr. 4, 1986.

Most points, one game, by a defenseman—8, Tom Bladon, Philadelphia, vs. Cleveland, Dec. 11, 1977; Paul Coffey, Edmonton, vs. Detroit, Mar. 14, 1986.

Most penalties, one game—10, Chris Nilan, Boston, vs. Hartford, Mar. 31, 1991.

Most penalty minutes, one game—67, Randy Holt, Los Angeles, at Philadelphia, Mar. 11, 1979.

Most goals, one period—4, Busher Jackson, Toronto, at St. Louis, Nov. 20, 1934; Max Bentley, Chicago, vs. New York Rangers, Jan. 28, 1943; Clint Smith, Chicago, vs. Montreal, Mar. 4, 1945; Red Berenson, St. Louis, at Philadelphia, Nov. 7, 1968; Wayne Gretzky, Edmonton, vs. St. Louis, Feb. 18, 1981; Grant Mulvey, Chicago, vs. St. Louis, Feb. 3, 1982; Bryan Trottier, New York Islanders, vs. Philadelphia, Feb. 13, 1982; Al Secord, Chicago, vs. Toronto, Jan. 7, 1987; Joe Nieuwendyk, Calgary, vs. Winnipeg, Jan. 11, 1989; Peter Bondra, Washington, vs. Tampa Bay, Feb. 5, 1994.

Most assists, one period—5, Dale Hawerchuk, Winnipeg, at Los Angeles, Mar. 6, 1984.

Most points, one period—6, Bryan Trottier, New York Islanders, vs. New York Rangers, Dec. 23, 1978.

Fastest goal from start of game—5 seconds, Doug Smail, Winnipeg, vs. St. Louis, Dec. 20, 1981; Bryan Trottier, New York Islanders, at

Boston, Mar. 22, 1984; Alexander Mogilny, Buffalo, at Toronto, Dec. 21, 1991.

Fastest goal from start of period—4 seconds, Claude Provost, Montreal, vs. Boston, Nov. 9, 1957; Denis Savard, Chicago, vs. Hartford, Jan. 12, 1986.

Fastest two goals—4 seconds, Nels Stewart, Montreal Maroons, vs. Boston, Jan. 3, 1931.

Fastest three goals—21 seconds, Bill Mosienko, Chicago, at New York Rangers, Mar. 23, 1952.

TEAM

Most points, season—132, Montreal Canadiens, 1976–77.

Fewest points, season—8, Quebec Bulldogs, 1919–20; modern: 21, Washington Capitals, 1974–75.

Most victories, season—62, Detroit Red Wings, 1995–96.

Fewest victories, season—4, Quebec Bulldogs, 1919–20, and Philadelphia Quakers, 1930–31; modern: 8, Washington Capitals, 1974–75.

Most losses, season—71, San Jose Sharks, 1992–93.

Fewest losses, season—5, Ottawa Senators, 1919–20, Boston Bruins, 1929–30, and Montreal Canadiens, 1943–44; modern: 8, Montreal Canadiens, 1976–77.

Most ties, season—24, Philadelphia Flyers, 1969–70.

Most home victories, season—36, Philadelphia Flyers, 1975–76.

Most road victories, season—27, Montreal Canadiens, 1976–77 and 1977–78.

Most home losses, season—32, San Jose Sharks, 1992–93.

Most road losses, season—40, Ottawa Senators, 1992–93.

Fewest home victories, season—2, Chicago Blackhawks, 1927–28; modern: 6, Chicago Blackhawks, 1954–55 and Washington Capitals, 1975–76.

Fewest road victories, season—0, Toronto Arenas, 1918–19, Quebec Bulldogs, 1919–20, Pittsburgh Pirates, 1929–30; modern: 1, Washington Capitals, 1974–75, Ottawa Senators, 1992–93.

Fewest home losses, season—0, Ottawa Senators, 1922–23, Montreal Canadiens, 1943–44; modern: 1, Montreal Canadiens, 1976–77.

Fewest road losses, season—3, Montreal Canadiens, 1928–29; modern: 6, Montreal Canadiens, 1972–73, 1974–75 and 1977–78.

Longest winning streak—17 games, Pittsburgh Penguins, Mar. 9, 1993 through Apr. 10, 1993.

Longest undefeated streak—35 games, Philadelphia Flyers, Oct. 14, 1979 through Jan. 6, 1980 (25 wins, 10 ties).

Longest home undefeated streak—34 games, Montreal Canadiens, Nov. 1, 1976 through Apr. 2, 1977 (28 wins, 6 ties).

Longest winning streak, home—20 games, Boston Bruins, Dec. 3, 1929 through Mar. 18, 1930; Philadelphia Flyers, Jan. 4, 1976 through Apr. 3, 1976.

Longest winning streak, road—10, Buffalo Sabres, Dec. 10, 1983 through Jan. 23, 1984.

Longest undefeated streak, road—23 games, Montreal Canadiens, Nov. 27, 1974 through Mar. 12, 1975.

Longest losing streak—17 games, Washington Capitals, Feb. 18, 1975 through Mar. 26, 1975; San Jose Sharks, Jan. 4, 1993 through Feb. 12, 1993.

Longest losing streak from start of season—11 games, New York Rangers, 1943–44.

Longest home losing streak—11 games, Boston Bruins, Dec. 8, 1924 through Feb. 17, 1925; Washington Capitals, Feb. 18, 1975 through Mar.

30, 1975; Ottawa Senators, Oct. 27, 1993 through Dec. 8, 1993.

Longest road losing streak—38 games, Ottawa Senators, Oct. 10, 1992 through Apr. 3, 1993.

Longest winless streak—30 games, Winnipeg Jets, Oct. 19, 1980 through Dec. 20, 1980 (23 losses, 7 ties).

Longest winless streak from start of season—15 games, New York Rangers, 1943–44 (14 losses, 1 tie).

Longest home winless streak—15 games, Chicago Blackhawks, Dec. 16, 1928 through Feb. 28, 1929; Montreal Canadiens, Dec. 16, 1939 through Mar. 7, 1940.

Longest road winless streak—38 games, Ottawa Senators, Oct. 10, 1992 through Apr. 3, 1993.

Longest non-shutout streak—264 games, Calgary Flames, Nov. 12, 1981 through Jan. 9, 1985.

Most consecutive shutout losses—8, Chicago Blackhawks, 1928–29.

Most shutouts, season—22, Montreal Canadiens, 1928–29; modern: 15, Chicago Blackhawks, 1969–70.

Most goals, season—446, Edmonton Oilers, 1983–84.

Fewest goals, season—33, Chicago Blackhawks, 1928–29; modern: 133, Chicago Blackhawks, 1953–54.

Most goals allowed, season—446, Washington Capitals, 1974–75.

Fewest goals allowed, season—42, Ottawa Senators, 1925–26; modern: 131, Toronto Maple Leafs, 1953–54 and Montreal Canadiens, 1955–56.

Most power-play goals, season—119, Pittsburgh Penguins, 1988–89.

Most power-play goals allowed, season—122, Chicago Blackhawks, 1988–89.

Most shorthanded goals, season—36, Edmonton Oilers, 1983–84.

Most shorthanded goals allowed, season—22, Pittsburgh Penguins, 1984–85; Minnesota North Stars, 1991–92.

Most penalty minutes, season—2,713, Buffalo Sabres, 1991–92.

Most goals, one team, game—16, Montreal Canadiens, at Quebec, Mar. 3, 1920.

Most goals, both teams, game—21, Montreal Canadiens (14) vs. Toronto St. Patricks (7), at Montreal, Jan. 10, 1920; Edmonton Oilers (12) at Chicago Blackhawks (9), Dec. 11, 1985.

Most consecutive goals, one team, game—15, Detroit Red Wings, vs. New York Rangers, Jan. 23, 1944.

Most points, one team, game—40, Buffalo Sabres, vs. Washington Capitals, Dec. 21, 1975 (14 goals, 26 assists).

Most points, both teams, game—62, Edmonton Oilers (12 goals, 24 assists) at Chicago Blackhawks (9 goals, 17 assists), Dec. 11, 1985.

Most shots, one team, game—83, Boston Bruins, vs. Chicago, Mar. 4, 1941.

Most shots, both teams, game—141, New York Americans (73) vs. Pittsburgh Pirates (68), Dec. 26, 1925.

Most penalties, one team, game—44, Edmonton Oilers, at Los Angeles, Feb. 28, 1990.

Most penalties, both teams, game—85, Edmonton Oilers (44) at Los Angeles Kings (41), Feb. 28, 1990.

Most penalty minutes, one team, game—211, Minnesota North Stars, at Boston, Feb. 26, 1981.

Most penalty minutes, both teams, game—406, Minnesota North Stars (211) at Boston Bruins (195), Feb. 26, 1981.

Most goals, one team, period—9, Buffalo Sabres, vs. Toronto, Mar. 19, 1981.

Most goals, both teams, one period—12, Buffalo Sabres (9) vs. Toronto Maple Leafs (3), Mar. 19, 1981; Edmonton Oilers (6) at Chicago Blackhawks (6), Dec. 11, 1985.

Most points, one team, one period—23, New York Rangers, vs. California, Nov. 21, 1971; Buffalo Sabres, vs. Washington, Dec. 21, 1975; Buffalo Sabres, vs. Toronto, Mar. 19, 1981.

Most shots, one team, one period—33, Boston Bruins, vs. Chicago, Mar. 4, 1941.

Most penalties, both teams, one period—67, Minnesota North Stars (34) at Boston Bruins (33), Feb. 26, 1981.

Most penalty minutes, both teams, one period—372, Philadelphia Flyers (188) vs. Los Angeles Kings (184), Mar. 11, 1979.

Most penalty minutes, one team, one period—188, Philadelphia Flyers, vs. Los Angeles, Mar. 11, 1979.

Fastest six goals, both teams—3 minutes, 15 seconds, Montreal (4) vs. Chicago (2), Jan. 4, 1944.

Fastest five goals, both teams—1 minute, 24 seconds, Chicago (3) at Toronto (2), Oct. 15, 1983.

Fastest five goals, one team—2 minutes, 7 seconds, Pittsburgh Penguins, vs. St. Louis, Nov. 22, 1972.

Fastest four goals, both teams—53 seconds, Chicago (3) at Toronto (1), Oct. 15, 1983.

Fastest four goals, one team—1 minute, 20 seconds, Boston Bruins, vs. New York Rangers, Jan. 21, 1945.

Fastest three goals, both teams—15 seconds, New York Rangers (2) at Minnesota North Stars (1), Feb. 10, 1983.

Fastest three goals, one team—20 seconds, Boston Bruins, vs. Vancouver, Feb. 25, 1971.

Fastest two goals, both teams—2 seconds, St. Louis Blues (1) at Boston Bruins (1), Dec. 19, 1987.

Fastest two goals, one team—4 seconds, Montreal Maroons, vs. Boston, Jan. 3, 1931; Buffalo Sabres, vs. California, Oct. 17, 1974; Toronto Maple Leafs, at Quebec, Dec. 29, 1988; Calgary Flames, at Quebec, Oct, 17, 1989.

Fastest two goals from start of period, both teams—14 seconds, New York Rangers (1) at Quebec Nordiques (1), Nov. 5, 1983.

Fastest two goals from start of game, one team—24 seconds, Edmonton Oilers, at Los Angeles, Mar. 28, 1982.

Fastest two goals from start of period, one team—21 seconds, Chicago Blackhawks, at Minnesota, Nov. 5, 1983.

ALL-TIME CAREER LEADERS: REGULAR SEASON

GAMES

1.	Gordie Howe	1,767
2.	Alex Delvecchio	1,549
3.	John Bucyk	1,540
4.	Tim Horton	1,446
5.	Harry Howell	1,411
6.	Norm Ullman	1,410
7.	Stan Mikita	1,394
8.	Doug Mohns	1,390
9.	Larry Robinson	1,384
10.	Dean Prentice	1,378

GOALS

1.	Wayne Gretzky	894
2.	Gordie Howe	801
3.	Marcel Dionne	731
4.	Mike Gartner	723
5.	Phil Esposito	717
6.	Mario Lemieux	613
7.	Bobby Hull	610
	Mark Messier	610
9.	Dino Ciccarelli	608
10.	Jari Kurri	596

ASSISTS

1.	Wayne Gretzky	1,963
2.	Paul Coffey	1,102
3.	Gordie Howe	1,049
4.	Ray Bourque	1,083
5.	Mark Messier	1,045
6.	Marcel Dionne	1,040
7.	Ron Francis	1,037
8.	Stan Mikita	926
9.	Bryan Trottier	901
10.	Dale Hawerchuk	891

POINTS

1.	Wayne Gretzky	2,857
2.	Gordie Howe	1,850
3.	Marcel Dionne	1,771
4.	Mark Messier	1,660
5.	Phil Esposito	1,590
6.	Mario Lemieux	1,494
7.	Paul Coffey	1,473
8.	Stan Mikita	1,467
9.	Bryan Trottier	1,425
10.	Dale Hawerchuk	1,409

PENALTY MINUTES

1.	Dave Williams	3,966
2.	Dale Hunter	3,446
3.	Marty McSorley	3,218
4.	Chris Nilan	3,043
5.	Tim Hunter	3,011
6.	Bob Probert	2,701
7.	Rick Tocchet	2,626
8.	Will Plett	2,572
9.	Basil McRae	2,445
10.	Scott Stevens	2,440

GOALTENDERS

WINS

1.	Terry Sawchuk	447
2.	Jacques Plante	434
3.	Tony Esposito	423
4.	Patrick Roy	412
5.	Glenn Hall	407
6.	Grant Fuhr	398
7.	Roger Vachon	378
8.	Andy Moog	372
9.	Gump Worsley	335
10.	Harry Lumley	333

SHUTOUTS

1.	Terry Sawchuk	103
2.	George Hainsworth	94
3.	Glenn Hall	84
4.	Jacques Plante	82
5.	Tiny Thompson	81
6.	Alex Connell	81
7.	Tony Esposito	76
8.	Lorne Chabot	73
9.	Harry Lumley	71
10.	Roy Worters	66

ALL-TIME CAREER LEADERS: PLAYOFFS

GAMES

1.	Mark Messier	236
2.	Larry Robinson	227
3.	Glenn Anderson	225
4.	Bryan Trottier	221
5.	Kevin Lowe	214
6.	Wayne Gretzky	208
7.	Jari Kurri	196
8.	Paul Coffey	189
9.	Denis Potvin	185
10.	Bobby Smith	184

GOALS

1.	Wayne Gretzky	122
2.	Mark Messier	109
3.	Jari Kurri	106
4.	Glenn Anderson	93
5.	Mike Bossy	85
6.	Maurice Richard	82
7.	Jean Beliveau	79
8.	Dino Ciccarelli	73
9.	Bryan Trottier	71
10.	Mario Lemieux	70
	Claude Lemieux	70

ASSISTS

1.	Wayne Gretzky	260
2.	Mark Messier	186
3.	Paul Coffey	136
4.	Jari Kurri	127
5.	Ray Bourque	125
6.	Glenn Anderson	121
7.	Doug Gilmour	117
8.	Larry Robinson	116

9.	Bryan Trottier	113
10.	Denis Potvin	108

POINTS

1.	Wayne Gretzky	382
2.	Mark Messier	295
3.	Jari Kurri	233
4.	Glenn Anderson	214
5.	Paul Coffey	195
6.	Bryan Trottier	184
7.	Jean Beliveau	176
8.	Doug Gilmour	171
9.	Denis Savard	170
10.	Denis Potvin	164

GOALTENDERS

GAMES

1.	Patrick Roy	179
2.	Grant Fuhr	150
3.	Billy Smith	132
	Andy Moog	132
5.	Mike Vernon	131
6.	Glenn Hall	115
7.	Ken Dryden	112
	Jacques Plante	112
9.	Turk Broda	101
10.	Tony Esposito	99

WINS

1.	Patrick Roy	110
2.	Grant Fuhr	92
3.	Billy Smith	88
4.	Ken Dryden	80
5.	Mike Vernon	77
6.	Jacques Plante	71
7.	Andy Moog	68
8.	Turk Broda	58
9.	Terry Sawchuk	54
10.	Tom Barrasso	51

ALL-TIME SINGLE SEASON LEADERS

GOALS

1.	Wayne Gretzky, Edmonton, 1981–82	92
2.	Wayne Gretzky, Edmonton, 1983–84	87
3.	Brett Hull, St. Louis, 1990–91	86
4.	Mario Lemieux, Pittsburgh, 1988–89	85
5.	Phil Esposito, Boston, 1970–71	76
	Alexander Mogilny, Buffalo, 1982–83	76
	Teemu Selanne, Winnipeg, 1992–93	76
8.	Wayne Gretzky, Edmonton, 1984–85	73
9.	Brett Hull, St. Louis, 1989–90	72
10.	Wayne Gretzky, Edmonton, 1982–83	71
	Jari Kurri, Edmonton, 1984–85	71

ASSISTS

1.	Wayne Gretzky, Edmonton, 1985–86	163
2.	Wayne Gretzky, Edmonton, 1984–85	135
3.	Wayne Gretzky, Edmonton, 1982–83	125
4.	Wayne Gretzky, Los Angeles, 1990–91	122
5.	Wayne Gretzky, Edmonton, 1986–87	121
6.	Wayne Gretzky, Edmonton, 1981–82	120
7.	Wayne Gretzky, Edmonton, 1983–84	118
8.	Wayne Gretzky, Los Angeles, 1988–89	114
	Mario Lemieux, Pittsburgh, 1988–89	114
10.	Wayne Gretzky, Edmonton, 1980–81	109
	Wayne Gretzky, Edmonton, 1987–88	109

POINTS

1.	Wayne Gretzky, Edmonton, 1985–86	215
2.	Wayne Gretzky, Edmonton, 1981–82	212
3.	Wayne Gretzky, Edmonton, 1984–85	208
4.	Wayne Gretzky, Edmonton, 1983–84	205
5.	Mario Lemieux, Pittsburgh, 1988–89	199

6.	Wayne Gretzky, Edmonton, 1982–83	196
7.	Wayne Gretzky, Edmonton, 1986–87	183
8.	Mario Lemieux, Pittsburgh, 1987–88	168
	Wayne Gretzky, Los Angeles, 1988–89	168
10.	Wayne Gretzky, Edmonton, 1980–81	164

PENALTY MINUTES

1.	Dave Schultz, Philadelphia, 1974–75	472
2.	Paul Baxter, Pittsburgh, 1981–82	409
3.	Mike Peluso, Chicago, 1991–92	408
4.	Dave Schultz, L.A.–Pitt., 1977–78	405
5.	Marty McSorley, Los Angeles, 1992–93	399
6.	Bob Probert, Detroit, 1987–88	398
7.	Joe Kocur, Detroit, 1985–86	377
8.	Tim Hunter, Calgary, 1988–89	375
9.	Steve Durbano, Pitt.–K.C., 1975–76	370
10.	Tim Hunter, Calgary, 1986–87	361

GOALTENDERS

WINS

1.	Bernie Parent, Philadelphia, 1973–74	47
2.	Bernie Parent, Philadelphia, 1974–75	44
	Terry Sawchuk, Detroit, 1950–51	44
	Terry Sawchuk, Detroit, 1951–52	44
5.	Tom Barrasso, Pittsburgh, 1992–93	43
	Ed Belfour, Chicago, 1990–91	43
	Martin Brodeur, New Jersey, 1997–98	43
8.	Jacques Plante, Montreal, 1955–56	42
	Jacques Plante, Montreal, 1961–62	42
	Ken Dryden, Montreal, 1975–76	42

SHUTOUTS

1.	George Hainsworth, Montreal, 1928–29	22
2.	Alex Connell, Ottawa, 1925–26	15
	Alex Connell, Ottawa, 1927–28	15
	Hal Winkler, Boston, 1927–28	15
	Tony Esposito, Chicago, 1969–70	15
6.	George Hainsworth, Montreal, 1926–27	14
7.	Clint Benedict, Montreal Maroons, 1926–27	13
	Alex Connell, Ottawa, 1926–27	13
	George Hainsworth, Montreal, 1927–28	13
	Dominik Hasek, Buffalo, 1997–98	13
	John Roach, New York Rangers, 1928–29	13
	Roy Worters, New York Americans, 1928–29	13
	Harry Lumley, Toronto, 1953–54	13

THE TROPHIES

Hart Memorial Trophy

Awarded to the player "most valuable to his team." Selected in a vote of hockey writers and broadcasters. The award was presented by the National Hockey League in 1960 after the original Hart Trophy was retired to the Hockey Hall of Fame. The original Hart Trophy was donated in 1923 by Dr. David A. Hart, father of Cecil Hart, former manager-coach of the Montreal Canadiens.

1923–24	Frank Nighbor, Ottawa
1924–25	Billy Burch, Hamilton
1925–26	Nels Stewart, Montreal M.
1926–27	Herb Gardiner, Montreal C.
1927–28	Howie Morenz, Montreal C.
1928–29	Roy Worters, New York A.
1929–30	Nels Stewart, Montreal M.
1930–31	Howie Morenz, Montreal C.
1931–32	Howie Morenz, Montreal C.
1932–33	Eddie Shore, Boston

Hart Trophy

1933–34	Aurel Joliat, Montreal C.
1934–35	Eddie Shore, Boston
1935–36	Eddie Shore, Boston
1936–37	Babe Siebert, Montreal C.
1937–38	Eddie Shore, Boston
1938–39	Toe Blake, Montreal C.
1939–40	Ebbie Goodfellow, Detroit
1940–41	Bill Cowley, Boston
1941–42	Tommy Anderson, New York A.
1942–43	Bill Cowley, Boston
1943–44	Babe Pratt, Toronto
1944–45	Elmer Lach, Montreal C.
1945–46	Max Bentley, Chicago
1946–47	Maurice Richard, Montreal
1947–48	Buddy O'Connor, New York
1948–49	Sid Abel, Detroit
1949–50	Charlie Rayner, New York
1950–51	Milt Schmidt, Boston
1951–52	Gordie Howe, Detroit
1952–53	Gordie Howe, Detroit
1953–54	Al Rollins, Chicago
1954–55	Ted Kennedy, Toronto
1955–56	Jean Beliveau, Montreal
1956–57	Gordie Howe, Detroit
1957–58	Gordie Howe, Detroit
1958–59	Andy Bathgate, New York
1959–60	Gordie Howe, Detroit
1960–61	Bernie Geoffrion, Montreal
1961–62	Jacques Plante, Montreal
1962–63	Gordie Howe, Detroit
1963–64	Jean Beliveau, Montreal
1964–65	Bobby Hull, Chicago
1965–66	Bobby Hull, Chicago
1966–67	Stan Mikita, Chicago
1967–68	Stan Mikita, Chicago
1968–69	Phil Esposito, Boston
1969–70	Bobby Orr, Boston

1970–71	Bobby Orr, Boston
1971–72	Bobby Orr, Boston
1972–73	Bobby Clarke, Philadelphia
1973–74	Phil Esposito, Boston
1974–75	Bobby Clarke, Philadelphia
1975–76	Bobby Clarke, Philadelphia
1976–77	Guy Lafleur, Montreal
1977–78	Guy Lafleur, Montreal
1978–79	Bryan Trottier, New York I.
1979–80	Wayne Gretzky, Edmonton
1980–81	Wayne Gretzky, Edmonton
1981–82	Wayne Gretzky, Edmonton
1982–83	Wayne Gretzky, Edmonton
1983–84	Wayne Gretzky, Edmonton
1984–85	Wayne Gretzky, Edmonton
1985–86	Wayne Gretzky, Edmonton
1986–87	Wayne Gretzky, Edmonton
1987–88	Mario Lemieux, Pittsburgh
1988–89	Wayne Gretsky, Edmonton
1989–90	Mark Messier, Edmonton
1990–91	Brett Hull, St. Louis
1991–92	Mark Messier, New York R.
1992–93	Mario Lemieux, Pittsburgh
1993–94	Sergei Fedorov, Detroit
1994–95	Eric Lindros, Philadelphia
1995–96	Mario Lemieux, Pittsburgh
1996–97	Dominik Hasek, Buffalo
1997–98	Dominik Hasek, Buffalo
1998–99	Jaromir Jagr, Pittsburgh

Art Ross Trophy

Awarded to the player who compiles the highest number of scoring points during the regular season.

If players are tied for the lead, the trophy is awarded to the one with the most goals. If still tied, it is given to the player with the fewer number of games played. If these do not break the deadlock, the trophy is presented to the player who scored his first goal of the season at the earliest date.

The trophy was presented by Art Ross, the former manager-coach of the Boston Bruins, to the NHL in 1947.

Art Ross Trophy

SEASON	PLAYER, CLUB	GAMES PLAYED	GOALS	ASSTS	PNTS
1917–18	Joe Malone, Mont. C	20	44	—	44
1918–19	Newsy Lalonde, Mont. C	17	23	9	32
1919–20	Joe Malone, Quebec	24	39	9	48
1920–21	Newsy Lalonde, Mont. C	24	33	8	41
1921–22	Punch Broadbent, Ottawa	24	32	14	46
1922–23	Babe Dye, Toronto	22	26	11	37
1923–24	Cy Denneny, Ottawa	21	22	1	23
1924–25	Babe Dye, Toronto	29	38	6	44
1925–26	Nels Stewart, Montreal	36	34	8	42
1926–27	Bill Cook, N.Y. Rangers	44	33	4	37
1927–28	Howie Morenz, Mont. C	43	33	18	51
1928–29	Ace Bailey, Toronto	44	22	10	32
1929–30	Cooney Weiland, Boston	44	43	30	73
1930–31	Howie Morenz, Mont. C	39	28	23	51
1931–32	Harvey Jackson, Toronto	48	28	25	53
1932–33	Bill Cook, N.Y. Rangers	48	28	22	50
1933–34	Charlie Conacher, Toronto	42	32	20	52
1934–35	Charlie Conacher, Toronto	48	36	21	57
1935–36	Dave Schriner, NYA	48	19	26	45
1936–37	Dave Schriner, NYA	48	21	25	46
1937–38	Gordie Drillon, Toronto	48	26	26	52
1938–39	Toe Blake, Mont. C	48	24	23	47
1939–40	Milt Schmidt, Boston	48	22	30	52
1940–41	Bill Cowley, Boston	46	17	45	62
1941–42	Bryan Hextall, New York R	48	24	32	56
1942–43	Doug Bentley, Chicago	50	33	40	73
1943–44	Herbie Cain, Boston	48	36	46	82
1944–45	Elmer Lach, Montreal	50	26	54	80
1945–46	Max Bentley, Chicago	47	31	30	61
1946–47	Max Bentley, Chicago	60	29	43	72
1947–48	Elmer Lach, Montreal	60	30	31	61
1948–49	Roy Conacher, Chicago	60	26	42	68
1949–50	Ted Lindsay, Detroit	69	23	55	78
1950–51	Gordie Howe, Detroit	70	43	43	86
1951–52	Gordie Howe, Detroit	70	47	39	86
1952–53	Gordie Howe, Detroit	70	49	46	95
1953–54	Gordie Howe, Detroit	70	33	48	81
1954–55	Bernie Geoffrion, Montreal	70	38	37	75
1955–56	Jean Beliveau, Montreal	70	47	41	88
1956–57	Gordie Howe, Detroit	70	44	45	89
1957–58	Dickie Moore, Montreal	70	36	48	84
1958–59	Dickie Moore, Montreal	70	41	55	96
1959–60	Bobby Hull, Chicago	70	39	42	81
1960–61	Bernie Geoffrion, Montreal	64	50	45	95
1961–62	Bobby Hull, Chicago	70	50	34	84
1962–63	Gordie Howe, Detroit	70	38	48	86
1963–64	Stan Mikita, Chicago	70	39	50	89
1964–65	Stan Mikita, Chicago	70	28	59	87
1965–66	Bobby Hull, Chicago	65	54	43	97
1966–67	Stan Mikita, Chicago	70	35	62	97
1967–68	Stan Mikita, Chicago	72	40	47	87

1968–69	Phil Esposito, Boston	74	49	77	126
1969–70	Bobby Orr, Boston	76	33	87	120
1970–71	Phil Esposito, Boston	78	76	76	152
1971–72	Phil Esposito, Boston	76	66	67	133
1972–73	Phil Esposito, Boston	78	55	75	130
1973–74	Phil Esposito, Boston	78	68	77	145
1974–75	Bobby Orr, Boston	80	46	89	135
1975–76	Guy Lafleur, Montreal	80	56	69	125
1976–77	Guy Lafleur, Montreal	80	56	80	136
1977–78	Guy Lafleur, Montreal	78	60	72	132
1978–79	Bryan Trottier, New York I.	76	47	87	134
1979–80	Marcel Dionne, L.A.	80	53	84	137
1980–81	Wayne Gretzky, Edmonton	80	55	109	164
1981–82	Wayne Gretzky, Edmonton	80	92	120	212
1982–83	Wayne Gretzky, Edmonton	80	71	125	196
1983–84	Wayne Gretzky, Edmonton	74	87	118	205
1984–85	Wayne Gretzky, Edmonton	80	73	135	208
1985–86	Wayne Gretzky, Edmonton	80	52	163	215
1986–87	Wayne Gretzky, Edmonton	79	62	121	183
1987–88	Mario Lemieux, Pittsburgh	77	70	98	168
1988–89	Mario Lemieux, Pittsburgh	76	85	114	199
1989–90	Wayne Gretzky, L.A.	73	40	102	142
1990–91	Wayne Gretzky, L.A.	78	41	122	163
1991–92	Mario Lemieux, Pittsburgh	64	44	87	131
1992–93	Mario Lemieux, Pittsburgh	60	69	91	160
1993–94	Wayne Gretzky, L.A.	81	38	92	130
1994–95	Jaromir Jagr, Pittsburgh	48	32	38	70
1995–96	Mario Lemieux, Pittsburgh	70	69	92	161
1996–97	Mario Lemieux, Pittsburgh	76	50	72	122
1997–98	Jaromir Jagr, Pittsburgh	77	35	67	102
1998–99	Jaromir Jagr, Pittsburgh	81	44	83	127

Maurice Richard Trophy

Awarded for the first time in 1999, the trophy is given to the player who scores the most goals in a season. It is named for Hall of Famer Maurice Richard, known throughout the hockey world as "The Rocket."

SEASON	PLAYER, CLUB	GOALS
1998–99	Teemu Selanne, Anaheim	47

Vezina Trophy

Awarded to the goalie voted most valuable by the hockey writers and broadcasters. Up until the 1981–82 season, the trophy was awarded to the goalie or goalies for the team which gave up the fewest goals during the regular season.

The trophy was presented to the NHL in 1926–27 by the owners of the Montreal Canadiens in memory of Georges Vezina, former Canadien goalie.

Vezina Trophy

1926–27	George Hainsworth, Montreal C.
1927–28	George Hainsworth, Montreal C.
1928–29	George Hainsworth, Montreal C.
1929–30	Tiny Thompson, Boston
1930–31	Roy Worters, New York A.
1931–32	Charlie Gardiner, Chicago
1932–33	Tiny Thompson, Boston
1933–34	Charlie Gardiner, Chicago
1934–35	Lorne Chabot, Chicago
1935–36	Tiny Thompson, Boston

1936–37	Normie Smith, Detroit
1937–38	Tiny Thompson, Boston
1938–39	Frank Brimsek, Boston
1939–40	Davey Kerr, New York
1940–41	Turk Broda, Toronto
1941–42	Frank Brimsek, Boston
1942–43	Johnny Mowers, Detroit
1943–44	Bill Durnan, Montreal
1944–45	Bill Durnan, Montreal
1945–46	Bill Durnan, Montreal
1946–47	Bill Durnan, Montreal
1947–48	Turk Broda, Toronto
1948–49	Bill Durnan, Montreal
1949–50	Bill Durnan, Montreal
1950–51	Al Rollins, Toronto
1951–52	Terry Sawchuk, Detroit
1952–53	Terry Sawchuk, Detroit
1953–54	Harry Lumley, Toronto
1954–55	Terry Sawchuk, Detroit
1955–56	Jacques Plante, Montreal
1956–57	Jacques Plante, Montreal
1957–58	Jacques Plante, Montreal
1958–59	Jacques Plante, Montreal
1959–60	Jacques Plante, Montreal
1960–61	Johnny Bower, Toronto
1961–62	Jacques Plante, Montreal
1962–63	Glenn Hall, Chicago
1963–64	Charlie Hodge, Montreal
1964–65	Terry Sawchuk, Toronto
	Johnny Bower, Toronto
1965–66	Lorne Worsley, Montreal
	Charlie Hodge, Montreal
1966–67	Glenn Hall, Chicago
	Denis DeJordy, Chicago
1967–68	Lorne Worsley, Montreal
	Rogatien Vachon, Montreal
1968–69	Glenn Hall, St. Louis

Frank J. Selke Trophy

James Norris Memorial Trophy

	Jacques Plante, St. Louis
1969–70	Tony Esposito, Chicago
1970–71	Ed Giacomin, New York
	Gilles Villemure, New York
1971–72	Tony Esposito, Chicago
	Gary Smith, Chicago
1972–73	Ken Dryden, Montreal
1973–74	Bernie Parent, Philadelphia
	Tony Esposito, Chicago
1974–75	Bernie Parent, Philadelphia
1975–76	Ken Dryden, Montreal
1976–77	Ken Dryden, Montreal
	Michel Larocque, Montreal
1977–78	Ken Dryden, Montreal
	Michel Larocque, Montreal
1978–79	Ken Dryden, Montreal
	Michel Larocque, Montreal
1979–80	Bob Sauve, Buffalo
	Don Edwards, Buffalo
1980–81	Richard Sevigny, Montreal
	Denis Herron, Montreal
	Michel Larocque, Montreal
1981–82	Bill Smith, New York I.
1982–83	Pete Peeters, Boston
1983–84	Tom Barrasso, Buffalo
1984–85	Pelle Lindbergh, Philadelphia
1985–86	John Vanbiesbrouck, New York R.
1986–87	Ron Hextall, Philadelphia
1987–88	Grant Fuhr, Edmonton
1988–89	Patrick Roy, Montreal
1989–90	Patrick Roy, Montreal
1990–91	Ed Belfour, Chicago
1991–92	Patrick Roy, Montreal
1992–93	Ed Belfour, Chicago
1993–94	Dominik Hasek, Buffalo
1994–95	Dominik Hasek, Buffalo
1995–96	Jim Carey, Washington

1996–97	Dominik Hasek, Buffalo
1997–98	Dominik Hasek, Buffalo
1998–99	Dominik Hasek, Buffalo

Frank J. Selke Trophy

Awarded to the forward "who best excels in the defensive aspects of the game." Selection is by the hockey writers and broadcasters.

The trophy was presented to the NHL in 1977 in honor of Frank J. Selke, who spent more than 60 years in the game as coach, manager and front-office executive.

1977–78	Bob Gainey, Montreal
1978–79	Bob Gainey, Montreal
1979–80	Bob Gainey, Montreal
1980–81	Bob Gainey, Montreal
1981–82	Steve Kasper, Boston
1982–83	Bobby Clarke, Philadelphia
1983–84	Doug Jarvis, Washington
1984–85	Craig Ramsay, Buffalo
1985–86	Troy Murray, Chicago
1986–87	Dave Poulin, Philadelphia
1987–88	Guy Carbonneau, Montreal
1988–89	Guy Carbonneau, Montreal
1989–90	Rick Meagher, St. Louis
1990–91	Dirk Graham, Chicago
1991–92	Guy Carbonneau, Montreal

1992–93	Doug Gilmour, Toronto
1993–94	Sergei Fedorov, Detroit
1994–95	Ron Francis, Pittsburgh
1995–96	Sergei Fedorov, Detroit
1996–97	Mike Peca, Buffalo
1997–98	Jere Lehtinen, Dallas
1998–99	Jere Lehtinen, Dallas

James Norris Memorial Trophy

Awarded to the league's best defenseman. Selected by a vote of hockey writers and broadcasters.

It was presented in 1953 by the four children of the late James Norris Sr., in memory of the former owner-president of the Detroit Red Wings.

1953–54	Red Kelly, Detroit
1954–55	Doug Harvey, Montreal
1955–56	Doug Harvey, Montreal
1956–57	Doug Harvey, Montreal
1957–58	Doug Harvey, Montreal
1958–59	Tom Johnson, Montreal
1959–60	Doug Harvey, Montreal
1960–61	Doug Harvey, Montreal
1961–62	Doug Harvey, New York
1962–63	Pierre Pilote, Chicago
1963–64	Pierre Pilote, Chicago
1964–65	Pierre Pilote, Chicago
1965–66	Jacques Laperriere, Montreal
1966–67	Harry Howell, New York R.
1967–68	Bobby Orr, Boston
1968–69	Bobby Orr, Boston
1969–70	Bobby Orr, Boston
1970–71	Bobby Orr, Boston
1971–72	Bobby Orr, Boston
1972–73	Bobby Orr, Boston
1973–74	Bobby Orr, Boston
1974–75	Bobby Orr, Boston
1975–76	Denis Potvin, New York I.
1976–77	Larry Robinson, Montreal
1977–78	Denis Potvin, New York I.
1978–79	Denis Potvin, New York I.
1979–80	Larry Robinson, Montreal
1980–81	Randy Carlyle, Pittsburgh
1981–82	Doug Wilson, Chicago
1982–83	Rod Langway, Washington
1983–84	Rod Langway, Washington
1984–85	Paul Coffey, Edmonton
1985–86	Paul Coffey, Edmonton
1986–87	Ray Bourque, Boston
1987–88	Ray Bourque, Boston
1988–89	Chris Chelios, Montreal
1989–90	Ray Bourque, Boston
1990–91	Ray Bourque, Boston
1991–92	Brian Leetch, New York R.
1992–93	Chris Chelios, Chicago
1993–94	Ray Bourque, Boston
1994–95	Paul Coffey, Detroit
1995–96	Chris Chelios, Chicago
1996–97	Brian Leetch, New York R.
1997–98	Rob Blake, Los Angeles
1998–99	Al MacInnis, St. Louis

Calder Memorial Trophy

Awarded to the league's outstanding rookie. Selected by a vote of hockey writers and broadcasters. It was originated in 1937 by Frank Calder, first president of the NHL. After his death in 1943, the league presented the Calder Memorial Trophy in his memory.

Calder Memorial Trophy

To be eligible to receive the trophy, a player cannot have participated in more than 20 games in any preceding season or in six or more games in each of any two preceding seasons.

From 1932–33 to 1936–37 the top rookies were named but no trophy was presented.

1932–33	Carl Voss, Detroit
1933–34	Russ Blinco, Montreal M.
1934–35	Dave Schriner, New York A.
1935–36	Mike Karakas, Chicago
1936–37	Syl Apps, Toronto
1937–38	Cully Dahlstrom, Chicago
1938–39	Frank Brimsek, Boston
1939–40	Kilby MacDonald, New York R.
1940–41	Johnny Quilty, Montreal C.
1941–42	Grant Warwick, New York R.
1942–43	Gaye Stewart, Toronto
1943–44	Gus Bodnar, Toronto
1944–45	Frank McCool, Toronto
1945–46	Edgar Laprade, New York R.
1946–47	Howie Meeker, Toronto
1947–48	Jim McFadden, Detroit
1948–49	Pentti Lund, New York R.
1949–50	Jack Gelineau, Boston
1950–51	Terry Sawchuk, Detroit
1951–52	Bernie Geoffrion, Montreal
1952–53	Lorne Worsley, Montreal
1953–54	Camille Henry, New York R.
1954–55	Ed Litzenberger, Chicago

Conn Smythe Trophy

Lady Byng Trophy

1955–56	Glenn Hall, Detroit
1956–57	Larry Regan, Boston
1957–58	Frank Mahovlich, Toronto
1958–59	Ralph Backstrom, Montreal
1959–60	Bill Hay, Chicago
1960–61	Dave Keon, Toronto
1961–62	Bobby Rousseau, Montreal
1962–63	Kent Douglas, Toronto
1963–64	Jacques Laperriere, Montreal
1964–65	Roger Crozier, Detroit
1965–66	Brit Selby, Toronto
1966–67	Bobby Orr, Boston
1967–68	Derek Sanderson, Boston
1968–69	Danny Grant, Minnesota
1969–70	Tony Esposito, Chicago
1970–71	Gil Perreault, Buffalo
1971–72	Ken Dryden, Montreal
1972–73	Steve Vickers, New York R.
1973–74	Denis Potvin, New York I.
1974–75	Eric Vail, Atlanta
1975–76	Bryan Trottier, New York I.
1976–77	Willi Plett, Atlanta
1977–78	Mike Bossy, New York I.
1978–79	Bobby Smith, Minnesota
1979–80	Ray Bourque, Boston
1980–81	Peter Stastny, Quebec
1981–82	Dale Hawerchuk, Winnipeg
1982–83	Steve Larmer, Chicago
1983–84	Tom Barrasso, Buffalo
1984–85	Mario Lemieux, Pittsburgh
1985–86	Gary Suter, Calgary
1986–87	Luc Robitaille, Los Angeles
1987–88	Joe Nieuwendyk, Calgary
1988–89	Brian Leetch, New York R.
1989–90	Sergei Makarov, Calgary
1990–91	Ed Belfour, Chicago
1991–92	Pavel Bure, Vancouver

1992–93	Teemu Selanne, Winnipeg
1993–94	Martin Brodeur, New Jersey
1994–95	Peter Forsberg, Quebec
1995–96	Daniel Alfredsson, Ottawa
1996–97	Bryan Berard, New York I.
1997–98	Sergei Samsonov, Boston
1998–99	Chris Drury, Colorado

Conn Smythe Trophy

Awarded to the Most Valuable Player in the Stanley Cup playoffs. Selected in a vote of the NHL Governors.

The trophy was presented by Maple Leaf Gardens Ltd. in 1964 to honor the former coach, manager, president and owner of the Toronto Maple Leafs.

1964–65	Jean Beliveau, Montreal
1965–66	Roger Crozier, Detroit
1966–67	Dave Keon, Toronto
1967–68	Glenn Hall, St. Louis
1968–69	Serge Savard, Montreal
1969–70	Bobby Orr, Boston
1970–71	Ken Dryden, Montreal
1971–72	Bobby Orr, Boston
1972–73	Yvan Cournoyer, Montreal
1973–74	Bernie Parent, Philadelphia
1974–75	Bernie Parent, Philadelphia

William M. Jennings Trophy

The trophy was presented to the NHL in 1982 in memory of William M. Jennings, an architect of the league's expansion from six teams to the present 21.

1981–82	Denis Herron, Montreal
	Rick Wamsley, Montreal
1982–83	Billy Smith, New York I.
	Roland Melanson, New York I.
1983–84	Al Jensen, Washington
	Pat Riggin, Washington
1984–85	Tom Barrasso, Buffalo
	Bob Sauve, Buffalo
1985–86	Bob Froese, Philadelphia
	Darren Jensen, Philadelphia
1986–87	Patrick Roy, Montreal
	Brian Hayward, Montreal
1987–88	Patrick Roy, Montreal
	Brian Hayward, Montreal
1988–89	Patrick Roy, Montreal
	Brian Hayward, Montreal
1989–90	Andy Moog, Boston
	Rejean Lemelin, Boston
1990–91	Ed Belfour, Chicago
1991–92	Patrick Roy, Montreal
1992–93	Ed Belfour, Chicago
1993–94	Dominik Hasek, Buffalo
	Grant Fuhr, Buffalo
1994–95	Ed Belfour, Chicago
1995–96	Chris Osgood, Detroit
	Mike Vernon, Detroit
1996–97	Martin Brodeur, New Jersey
	Mike Dunham, New Jersey
1997–1998	Martin Brodeur, New Jersey
	Mike Dunham, New Jersey
1998–99	Ed Belfour, Dallas
	Roman Turek, Dallas

Lady Byng Trophy

Awarded to the player combining the highest type of sportsmanship and gentlemanly conduct plus a high standard of playing ability. Selected by a vote of hockey writers and broadcasters.

Lady Byng, the wife of the Governor-General of Canada in 1925, presented the trophy to the NHL during that year.

1924–25	Frank Nighbor, Ottawa
1925–26	Frank Nighbor, Ottawa
1926–27	Billy Burch, New York A.
1927–28	Frank Boucher, New York R.
1928–29	Frank Boucher, New York R.
1929–30	Frank Boucher, New York R.
1930–31	Frank Boucher, New York R.
1931–32	Joe Primeau, Toronto
1932–33	Frank Boucher, New York R.
1933–34	Frank Boucher, New York R.
1934–35	Frank Boucher, New York R.
1935–36	Doc Romnes, Chicago
1936–37	Marty Barry, Detroit
1937–38	Gordie Drillon, Toronto
1938–39	Clint Smith, New York R.
1939–40	Bobby Bauer, Boston
1940–41	Bobby Bauer, Boston
1941–42	Syl Apps, Toronto
1942–43	Max Bentley, Chicago
1943–44	Clint Smith, Chicago
1944–45	Bill Mosienko, Chicago
1945–46	Toe Blake, Montreal
1946–47	Bobby Bauer, Boston
1947–48	Buddy O'Connor, New York R.
1948–49	Bill Quackenbush, Detroit
1949–50	Edgar Laprade, New York R.

1975–76	Reggie Leach, Philadelphia
1976–77	Guy Lafleur, Montreal
1977–78	Larry Robinson, Montreal
1978–79	Bob Gainey, Montreal
1979–80	Bryan Trottier, New York I.
1980–81	Butch Goring, New York I.
1981–82	Mike Bossy, New York I.
1982–83	Billy Smith, New York I.
1983–84	Mark Messier, Edmonton
1984–85	Wayne Gretzky, Edmonton
1985–86	Patrick Roy, Montreal
1986–87	Ron Hextall, Philadelphia
1987–88	Wayne Gretzky, Edmonton
1988–89	Al MacInnis, Calgary
1989–90	Bill Ranford, Edmonton
1990–91	Mario Lemieux, Pittsburgh
1991–92	Mario Lemieux, Pittsburgh
1992–93	Patrick Roy, Montreal
1993–94	Brian Leetch, New York R.
1994–95	Claude Lemieux, New Jersey
1995–96	Joe Sakic, Colorado
1996–97	Mike Vernon, Detroit
1997–98	Steve Yzerman, Detroit
1998–99	Joe Nieuwendyk, Dallas

William M. Jennings Award

Awarded to the goalie or goalies on the team that gives up the fewest goals during the regular season. To be eligible, a goalie must play at least 25 games.

Bill Masterton Trophy

Jack Adams Award

1950–51	Red Kelly, Detroit
1951–52	Sid Smith, Toronto
1952–53	Red Kelly, Detroit
1953–54	Red Kelly, Detroit
1954–55	Sid Smith, Toronto
1955–56	Earl Reibel, Detroit
1956–57	Andy Hebenton, New York R.
1957–58	Camille Henry, New York R.
1958–59	Alex Delvecchio, Detroit
1959–60	Don McKenney, Boston
1960–61	Red Kelly, Toronto
1961–62	Dave Keon, Toronto
1962–63	Dave Keon, Toronto
1963–64	Ken Wharram, Chicago
1964–65	Bobby Hull, Chicago
1965–66	Alex Delvecchio, Detroit
1966–67	Stan Mikita, Chicago
1967–68	Stan Mikita, Chicago
1968–69	Alex Delvecchio, Detroit
1969–70	Phil Goyette, St. Louis
1970–71	Johnny Bucyk, Boston
1971–72	Jean Ratelle, New York R.
1972–73	Gil Perreault, Buffalo
1973–74	John Bucyk, Boston
1974–75	Marcel Dionne, Detroit
1975–76	Jean Ratelle, NYR-Boston
1976–77	Marcel Dionne, Los Angeles
1977–78	Butch Goring, Los Angeles
1978–79	Bob MacMillan, Atlanta
1979–80	Wayne Gretzky, Edmonton
1980–81	Rick Kehoe, Pittsburgh
1981–82	Rick Middleton, Boston
1982–83	Mike Bossy, New York I.
1983–84	Mike Bossy, New York I.
1984–85	Jari Kurri, Edmonton
1985–86	Mike Bossy, New York I.
1986–87	Joe Mullen, Calgary
1987–88	Mats Naslund, Montreal

1988–89	Joe Mullen, Calgary
1989–90	Brett Hull, St. Louis
1990–91	Wayne Gretzky, Los Angeles
1991–92	Wayne Gretzky, Los Angeles
1992–93	Pierre Turgeon, New York I.
1993–94	Wayne Gretzky, Los Angeles
1994–95	Ron Francis, Pittsburgh
1995–96	Paul Kariya, Anaheim
1996–97	Paul Kariya, Anaheim
1997–98	Ron Francis, Pittsburgh
1998–99	Wayne Gretzky, New York R.

Bill Masterton Trophy

Awarded by the Professional Hockey Writers' Association to "the NHL player who exemplifies the qualities of perseverance, sportsmanship and dedication to hockey." Named for the late Minnesota North Star player.

1967–68	Claude Provost, Montreal
1968–69	Ted Hampson, Oakland
1969–70	Pit Martin, Chicago
1970–71	Jean Ratelle, New York R.
1971–72	Bobby Clarke, Philadelphia
1972–73	Lowell MacDonald, Pittsburgh
1973–74	Henri Richard, Montreal
1974–75	Don Luce, Buffalo
1975–76	Rod Gilbert, New York R.
1976–77	Ed Westfall, New York I.
1977–78	Butch Goring, Los Angeles
1978–79	Serge Savard, Montreal
1979–80	Al MacAdam, Minnesota

King Clancy Memorial Trophy

Lester Patrick Trophy

1980–81	Blake Dunlop, St. Louis
1981–82	Glenn Resch, Colorado
1982–83	Lanny McDonald, Calgary
1983–84	Brad Park, Detroit
1984–85	Anders Hedberg, New York R.
1985–86	Charlie Simmer, Boston
1986–87	Doug Jarvis, Hartford
1987–88	Bob Bourne, Los Angeles
1988–89	Tim Kerr, Philadelphia
1989–90	Gord Kluzak, Boston
1990–91	Dave Taylor, Los Angeles
1991–92	Mark Fitzpatrick, New York I.
1992–93	Mario Lemieux, Pittsburgh
1993–94	Cam Neely, Boston
1994–95	Pat LaFontaine, Buffalo
1995–96	Gary Roberts, Calgary
1996–97	Tony Granato, San Jose
1997–98	Jamie McLennon, St. Louis
1998–99	John Cullen, Tampa Bay

Jack Adams Award

Awarded by the National Hockey League Broadcasters' Association to the "NHL coach adjudged to have contributed the most to his team's success." It is presented in memory of the late Jack Adams, longtime coach and general manager of the Detroit Red Wings.

1973–74	Fred Shero, Philadelphia
1974–75	Bob Pulford, Los Angeles
1975–76	Don Cherry, Boston

1976–77	Scotty Bowman, Montreal
1977–78	Bobby Kromm, Detroit
1978–79	Al Arbour, New York I.
1979–80	Pat Quinn, Philadelphia
1980–81	Red Berenson, St. Louis
1981–82	Tom Watt, Winnipeg
1982–83	Orval Tessier, Chicago
1983–84	Bryan Murray, Washington
1984–85	Mike Keenan, Philadelphia
1985–86	Glen Sather, Edmonton
1986–87	Jacques Demers, Detroit
1987–88	Jacques Demers, Detroit
1988–89	Pat Burns, Montreal
1989–90	Bob Murdoch, Winnipeg
1990–91	Brian Sutter, St. Louis
1991–92	Pat Quinn, Vancouver
1992–93	Pat Burns, Toronto
1993–94	Jacques Lemaire, New Jersey
1994–95	Marc Crawford, Quebec
1995–96	Scotty Bowman, Detroit
1996–97	Ted Nolan, Buffalo
1997–98	Pat Burns, Boston
1998–99	Jacques Martin, Ottawa

King Clancy Memorial Trophy

Awarded the player who best exemplifies leadership qualities on and off the ice and has made a noteworthy humanitarian contribution to his community. The award is in honor of the Hall of Fame defenseman.

1987–88	Lanny McDonald, Calgary

Lester B. Pearson Award

Presidents' Trophy

1988–89	Bryan Trottier, New York I.
1989–90	Kevin Lowe, Edmonton
1990–91	Dave Taylor, Los Angeles
1991–92	Ray Bourque, Boston
1992–93	Dave Poulin, Boston
1993–94	Adam Graves, New York R.
1994–95	Joe Nieuwendyk, Calgary
1995–96	Kris King, Winnipeg
1996–97	Trevor Linden, Vancouver
1997–98	Kelly Chase, St. Louis
1998–99	Rob Ray, Buffalo

Lester Patrick Trophy

Awarded for outstanding service to hockey in the United States. Eligible recipients are players, officials, coaches, executives and referees.

Selected by a six-man committee consisting of the President of the NHL, an NHL Governor, a hockey writer for a U.S. national news service, a nationally syndicated sports columnist, an ex-player in the Hockey Hall of Fame and a sports director of a U.S. national radio-television network.

Presented by the New York Rangers in 1966 to honor the memory of the long-time general manager and coach of the New York Rangers.

1965–66	Jack Adams
1966–67	Gordie Howe
	Charles Adams
	James Norris, Sr.
1967–68	Tom Lockhart
	Walter Brown
	John R. Kilpatrick
1968–69	Bobby Hull
	Edward Jeremiah
1969–70	Eddie Shore
	Jim Hendy
1970–71	Bill Jennings
	John Sollenberger
	Terry Sawchuk
1971–72	Clarence Campbell
	John Kelly
	Cooney Weiland
	James D. Norris
1972–73	Walter Bush, Jr.
1973–74	Alex Delvecchio
	Murray Murdoch
1974–75	Donald Clark
	Bill Chadwick
	Tommy Ivan
1975–76	Stan Mikita
	George Leader
	Bruce Norris
1976–77	John Bucyk
	Murray Armstrong
	John Mariucci

1977–78	Phil Esposito
	Tom Fitzgerald
	Bill Tutt
	William Wirtz
1978–79	Bobby Orr
1979–80	Robert Clarke
	Edward Snider
	Fred Shero
	U.S. Olympic hockey team
1980–81	Charles Schulz
1981–82	Emile Francis
1982–83	Bill Torrey
1983–84	John A. Ziegler, Jr.
	Arthur Howie Ross
1984–85	Jack Butterfield
	Arthur M. Wirtz
1985–86	John MacInnes
	Jack Riley
1986–87	Hobey Baker
	Frank Mathers
1987–88	Keith Allen
	Fred Cusick
	Bob Johnson
1988–89	Dan Kelly
	Lou Nanne
	Lynn Patrick
	Bud Poile
1989–90	Len Ceglarski
1990–91	Rod Gilberg
	Mike Illitch
1991–92	Al Arbour
	Lou Lamoriello
	Art Berglund
1992–93	Frank Boucher
	Red Dutton
	Bruce McNall
	Gil Stein
1993–94	Wayne Gretzky
	Robert Ridder
1994–95	Brian Mullen
	Joe Mullen
	Bob Fleming
1995–96	George Gund
	Ken Morrow
	Milt Schmidt
1996–97	Seymour H. Knox
	Bill Cleary
	Pat LaFontaine
1997–98	Neil Broten
	John Margasick
	Max McNab
	Peter Karmanos
1998–99	Harry Sinden
	U.S. Women's Olympic Hockey Team

Lester B. Pearson Award

Presented to the NHL's outstanding player as selected by members of the NHL Players' Association. Lester B. Pearson was Prime Minister of Canada.

1970–71	Phil Esposito, Boston
1971–72	Jean Ratelle, New York R.
1972–73	Bobby Clarke, Philadelphia
1973–74	Phil Esposito, Boston
1974–75	Bobby Orr, Boston
1975–76	Guy Lafleur, Montreal
1976–77	Guy Lafleur, Montreal
1977–78	Guy Lafleur, Montreal
1978–79	Marcel Dionne, Los Angeles
1979–80	Marcel Dionne, Los Angeles
1980–81	Mike Liut, St. Louis
1981–82	Wayne Gretzky, Edmonton
1982–83	Wayne Gretzky, Edmonton
1983–84	Wayne Gretzky, Edmonton
1984–85	Wayne Gretzky, Edmonton
1985–86	Mario Lemieux, Pittsburgh
1986–87	Wayne Gretzky, Edmonton
1987–88	Mario Lemieux, Pittsburgh
1988–89	Steve Yzerman, Detroit

Prince of Wales Trophy

1989–90	Mark Messier, Edmonton
1990–91	Brett Hull, St. Louis
1991–92	Mark Messier, New York R.
1992–93	Mario Lemieux, Pittsburgh
1993–94	Sergei Fedorov, Detroit
1994–95	Eric Lindros, Philadelphia
1995–96	Mario Lemieux, Pittsburgh
1996–97	Dominik Hasek, Buffalo
1997–98	Dominik Hasek, Buffalo
1998–99	Jaromir Jagr, Pittsburgh

Presidents' Trophy

Awarded the club finishing the regular season with the best overall record. The winner receives $200,000, half to the club and the other half to be split among the players.

1985–86	Edmonton 56–17–7
1986–87	Edmonton 50–24–6
1987–88	Calgary 48–23–9
1988–89	Calgary 54–17–9
1989–90	Boston 46–25–9
1990–91	Chicago 49–23–8
1991–92	New York R. 50–25–5
1992–93	Pittsburgh 56–21–7
1993–94	New York R. 52–24–8
1994–95	Detroit 33–11–4
1995–96	Detroit 62–13–7
1996–97	Colorado 49–24–9
1997–98	Dallas 49–22–11
1998–99	Dallas 51–19–12

Clarence S. Campbell Bowl

Prince of Wales Trophy

The Prince of Wales donated the trophy to the NHL in 1924. From 1927–28 to 1937–38, it was presented to the team finishing first in the American Division of the NHL. From 1938–39 through 1966–67, it was given to the first-place team in the one-division league. It was subsequently awarded to the first-place finisher in the East Division. Beginning with 1981–82, the trophy has gone to the team advancing to the Stanley Cup finals as the winner of the Wales Conference.

1924–25	Montreal C.
1925–26	Montreal M.
1926–27	Ottawa
1927–28	Boston
1928–29	Boston
1929–30	Boston
1930–31	Boston
1931–32	New York R.
1932–33	Boston
1933–34	Detroit
1934–35	Boston
1935–36	Detroit
1936–37	Detroit

1937–38	Boston
1938–39	Boston
1939–40	Boston
1940–41	Boston
1941–42	New York R.
1942–43	Detroit
1943–44	Montreal
1944–45	Montreal
1945–46	Montreal
1946–47	Montreal
1947–48	Toronto
1948–49	Detroit
1949–50	Detroit
1950–51	Detroit
1951–52	Detroit
1952–53	Detroit
1953–54	Detroit
1954–55	Detroit
1955–56	Montreal
1956–57	Detroit
1957–58	Montreal
1958–59	Montreal
1959–60	Montreal
1960–61	Montreal
1961–62	Montreal
1962–63	Montreal
1963–64	Montreal
1964–65	Detroit
1965–66	Montreal
1966–67	Chicago
1967–68	Montreal
1968–69	Montreal
1969–70	Chicago
1970–71	Boston
1971–72	Boston
1972–73	Montreal
1973–74	Boston
1974–75	Buffalo
1975–76	Montreal
1976–77	Montreal
1977–78	Montreal
1978–79	Montreal
1979–80	Buffalo
1980–81	Montreal
1981–82	New York I.
1982–83	New York I.
1983–84	New York I.
1984–85	Philadelphia
1985–86	Montreal
1986–87	Philadelphia
1987–88	Boston
1988–89	Montreal
1989–90	Boston
1990–91	Pittsburgh
1991–92	Pittsburgh
1992–93	Montreal
1993–94	New York R.
1994–95	New Jersey
1995–96	Florida
1996–97	Philadelphia
1997–98	Washington
1998–99	Buffalo

Clarence S. Campbell Bowl

Named for the former president of the NHL, the award originally was given to the champions of the West Division. Since 1981–82, it has gone to the team advancing to the Stanley Cup finals as the winner of the Campbell Conference.

1967–68	Philadelphia
1968–69	St. Louis
1969–70	St. Louis
1970–71	Chicago
1971–72	Chicago
1972–73	Chicago
1973–74	Philadelphia
1974–75	Philadelphia

1975–76	Philadelphia
1976–77	Philadelphia
1977–78	New York I.
1978–79	New York I.
1979–80	Philadelphia
1980–81	New York I.
1981–82	Vancouver
1982–83	Edmonton
1983–84	Edmonton
1984–85	Edmonton
1985–86	Calgary
1986–87	Edmonton
1987–88	Edmonton
1988–89	Calgary
1989–90	Edmonton
1990–91	Minnesota
1991–92	Chicago
1992–93	Los Angeles
1993–94	Vancouver
1994–95	Detroit
1995–96	Colorado
1996–97	Detroit
1997–98	Detroit
1998–99	Dallas

THE ALL-STAR TEAMS

Selected by a vote of hockey writers and broadcasters in each NHL city at the end of the season. The balloting originated with the 1930–31 campaign.

1930–31

FIRST		SECOND
Gardiner, Chicago	Goal	Thompson, Boston
Shore, Boston	Defense	Mantha, Montreal C.
Clancy, Toronto	Defense	Johnson, New York R.
Morenz, Montreal C.	Center	Boucher, New York R.
Bill Cook, New York R.	Right Wing	Clapper, Boston
Joliat, Montreal C.	Left Wing	Bun Cook, New York R.

1931–32

Gardiner, Chicago	Goal	Worters, New York A.
Shore, Boston	Defense	Mantha, Montreal C.
Johnson, New York R.	Defense	Clancy, Toronto
Morenz, Montreal C.	Center	Smith, Mont. M
Bill Cook, New York R.	Right Wing	C. Conacher, Toronto
Jackson, Toronto	Left Wing	Joliat, Montreal C.

1932–33

Roach, Detroit	Goal	Gardiner, Chicago
Shore, Boston	Defense	Clancy, Toronto
Johnson, New York R.	Defense	L. Conacher, Mont. M
Boucher, New York R.	Center	Morenz, Montreal C.
Bill Cook, New York R.	Right Wing	C. Conacher, Toronto
Northcott, Mont. M	Left Wing	Jackson, Toronto

1933–34

Gardiner, Chicago	Goal	Worters, New York A.
Clancy, Toronto	Defense	Shore, Boston
L. Conacher, Chicago	Defense	Johnson, New York R.
Boucher, New York R.	Center	Primeau, Toronto
C. Conacher, Toronto	Right Wing	Bill Cook, New York R.
Jackson, Toronto	Left Wing	Joliat, Montreal C.

1934–35

Chabot, Chicago	Goal	Thompson, Boston
Shore, Boston	Defense	Wentworth, Mont. M
Seibert, New York R.	Defense	Coulter, Chicago
Boucher, New York R.	Center	Weiland, Detroit
C. Conacher, Toronto	Right Wing	Clapper, Boston
Jackson, Toronto	Left Wing	Joliat, Montreal C.

1935–36

Thompson, Boston	Goal	Cude, Montreal C.
Shore, Boston	Defense	Siebert, Chicago
Seibert, Boston R.	Defense	Goodfellow, Detroit
Smith, Mont. M	Center	Thoms, Toronto
C. Conacher, Toronto	Right Wing	Dillon, New York R.
Schriner, New York A.	Left Wing	Thompson, Chicago

1936–37

Smith, Detroit	Goal	Cude, Montreal C.
Seibert, Montreal C.	Defense	Seibert, Chicago
Goodfellow, Detroit	Defense	C. Conacher, Mont. M
Barry, Detroit	Center	Chapman, New York A.
Aurie, Detroit	Right Wing	Dillon, New York R.
Jackson, Toronto	Left Wing	Schriner, New York A.

1937–38

Thompson, Boston	Goal	Kerr, New York R.
Shore, Boston	Defense	Coulter, New York R.
Siebert, Montreal C.	Defense	Seibert, Chicago
Cowley, Boston	Center	Apps, Toronto
*Dillon, New York R.	Right Wing	*Drillon, Toronto
Thompson, Chicago	Left Wing	Blake, Montreal C.

* Dillon and Drillon tied for first place in the voting and shared positions on the first and second teams.

1938–39

Brimsek, Boston	Goal	Robertson, New York A.
Shore, Boston	Defense	Seibert, Chicago
Clapper, Boston	Defense	Coulter, New York R.
Apps, Toronto	Center	N. Colville, New York R.
Drillon, Toronto	Right Wing	Bauer, Boston
Blake, Montreal C.	Left Wing	Gottselig, Chicago

1939–40

Kerr, New York R.	Goal	Brimsek, Boston
Clapper, Boston	Defense	Coulter, New York R.
Goodfellow, Detroit	Defense	Seibert, Chicago
Schmidt, Boston	Center	N. Colville, New York R.
Hextall, New York R.	Right Wing	Bauer, Boston
Blake, Montreal C.	Left Wing	Dumart, Boston

1940–41

Broda, Toronto	Goal	Brimsek, Boston
Clapper, Boston	Defense	Seibert, Chicago
Stanowski, Toronto	Defense	Heller, New York R.
Cowley, Boston	Center	Apps, Toronto
Hextall, New York R.	Right Wing	Bauer, Boston
Schriner, Toronto	Left Wing	Dumart, Boston

1941–42

Brimsek, Boston	Goal	Broda, Toronto
Seibert, Chicago	Defense	Egan, New York A.
Anderson, New York A.	Defense	McDonald, Toronto
Apps, Toronto	Center	Watson, New York R.
Hextall, New York R.	Right Wing	Drillon, Toronto
L. Patrick, New York R.	Left Wing	Abel, Detroit

1942–43

Mowers, Detroit	Goal	Brimsek, Boston
Seibert, Chicago	Defense	Crawford, Boston
Stewart, Detroit	Defense	Hollett, Boston
Cowley, Boston	Center	Apps, Toronto
Carr, Toronto	Right Wing	Hextall, New York R.
D. Bentley, Chicago	Left Wing	L. Patrick, New York R.

1943–44

Durnan, Montreal	Goal	Bibeault, Toronto
Seibert, Chicago	Defense	Bouchard, Montreal
Pratt, Toronto	Defense	Clapper, Boston
Cowley, Boston	Center	Lach, Montreal
Carr, Toronto	Right Wing	Richard, Montreal
D. Bentley, Chicago	Left Wing	Cain, Boston

1944–45

Durnan, Montreal	Goal	Karakas, Chicago
Bouchard, Montreal	Defense	Harmon, Montreal
Hollett, Detroit	Defense	Pratt, Toronto

Lach, Montreal	Center	Cowley, Boston
Richard, Montreal	Right Wing	Mosienko, Chicago
Blake, Montreal	Left Wing	S. Howe, Detroit

1945–46

Durnan, Montreal	Goal	Brimsek, Boston
Crawford, Boston	Defense	Reardon, Montreal
Bouchard, Montreal	Defense	Stewart, Detroit
M. Bentley, Chicago	Center	Lach, Montreal
Richard, Montreal	Right Wing	Mosienko, Chicago
Stewart, Toronto	Left Wing	Blake, Montreal

1946–47

Durnan, Montreal	Goal	Brimsek, Boston
Reardon, Montreal	Defense	Stewart, Detroit
Bouchard, Montreal	Defense	Quackenbush, Detroit
Schmidt, Boston	Center	M. Bentley, Chicago
Richard, Montreal	Right Wing	Bauer, Boston
D. Bentley, Chicago	Left Wing	Dumart, Boston

1947–48

Broda, Toronto	Goal	Brimsek, Boston
Quackenbush, Detroit	Defense	Reardon, Montreal
Stewart, Detroit	Defense	N. Colville, New York
Lach, Montreal	Center	O'Connor, New York
Richard, Montreal	Right Wing	Poile, Chicago
Lindsay, Detroit	Left Wing	Stewart, Chicago

1948–49

Durnan, Montreal	Goal	Rayner, New York
Quackenbush, Detroit	Defense	Harmon, Montreal
Stewart, Detroit	Defense	Reardon, Montreal
Abel, Detroit	Center	D. Bentley, Chicago
Richard, Montreal	Right Wing	Howe, Detroit
Conacher, Chicago	Left Wing	Lindsay, Detroit

1949–50

Durnan, Montreal	Goal	Rayner, New York
Mortson, Toronto	Defense	Reise, Detroit
Reardon, Montreal	Defense	Kelly, Detroit
Abel, Detroit	Center	Kennedy, Toronto
Richard, Montreal	Right Wing	Howe, Detroit
Lindsay, Detroit	Left Wing	Leswick, New York

1950–51

Sawchuk, Detroit	Goal	Rayner, New York
Kelly, Detroit	Defense	Thomson, Toronto
Quackenbush, Boston	Defense	Reise, Detroit
Schmidt, Boston	Center	Abel, Detroit
Kennedy, Toronto		Howe, Detroit
	Right Wing	Richard, Montreal
Lindsay, Detroit	Left Wing	Smith, Toronto

1951–52

Sawchuk, Detroit	Goal	Henry, Boston
Kelly, Detroit	Defense	Buller, New York
Harvey, Montreal	Defense	Thomson, Toronto
Lach, Montreal	Center	Schmidt, Boston
Howe, Detroit	Right Wing	Richard, Montreal
Lindsay, Detroit	Left Wing	Smith, Toronto

1952–53

Sawchuk, Detroit	Goal	McNeil, Montreal
Kelly, Detroit	Defense	Quackenbush, Boston
Harvey, Montreal	Defense	Gadsby, Chicago
Mackell, Boston	Center	Delvecchio, Detroit
Howe, Detroit	Right Wing	Richard, Montreal
Lindsay, Detroit	Left Wing	Olmstead, Montreal

1953–54

Lumley, Toronto	Goal	Sawchuk, Detroit
Kelly, Detroit	Defense	Gadsby, Chicago
Harvey, Montreal	Defense	Horton, Toronto
Mosdell, Montreal	Center	Kennedy, Toronto
Howe, Detroit	Right Wing	Richard, Montreal
Lindsay, Detroit	Left Wing	Sandford, Boston

1954–55

Lumley, Toronto	Goal	Sawchuk, Detroit
Harvey, Montreal	Defense	Goldham, Detroit
Kelly, Detroit	Defense	Flaman, Boston
Beliveau, Montreal	Center	Mosdell, Montreal
Richard, Montreal	Right Wing	Geoffrion, Montreal
Smith, Toronto	Left Wing	Lewicki, New York

1955–56

Plante, Montreal	Goal	Hall, Detroit
Harvey, Montreal	Defense	Kelly, Detroit
Gadsby, New York	Defense	Johnson, Montreal
Beliveau, Montreal	Center	Sloan, Toronto
M. Richard, Montreal	Right Wing	Howe, Detroit
Lindsay, Detroit	Left Wing	Olmstead, Montreal

1956–57

Hall, Detroit	Goal	Plante, Montreal
Harvey, Montreal	Defense	Flaman, Boston
Kelly, Detroit	Defense	Gadsby, New York
Beliveau, Montreal	Center	Litzenberger, Chicago
Howe, Detroit	Right Wing	M. Richard, Montreal
Lindsay, Detroit	Left Wing	Chevrefils, Boston

1957–58

Hall, Chicago	Goal	Plante, Montreal
Harvey, Montreal	Defense	Flaman, Boston
Gadsby, New York	Defense	Pronovost, Detroit
H. Richard, Montreal	Center	Beliveau, Montreal
Howe, Detroit	Right Wing	Bathgate, New York
Moore, Montreal	Left Wing	Henry, New York

1958–59

Plante, Montreal	Goal	Sawchuk, Detroit
Johnson, Montreal	Defense	Pronovost, Detroit
Gadsby, New York	Defense	Harvey, Montreal
Beliveau, Montreal	Center	H. Richard, Montreal
Bathgate, New York	Right Wing	Howe, Detroit
Moore, Montreal	Left Wing	Delvecchio, Detroit

1959–60

Hall, Chicago	Goal	Plante, Montreal
Harvey, Montreal	Defense	Stanley, Toronto
Pronovost, Detroit	Defense	Pilote, Chicago
Beliveau, Montreal	Center	Horvath, Boston
Howe, Detroit	Right Wing	Geoffrion, Montreal
Hull, Chicago	Left Wing	Prentice, New York

1960–61

Bower, Toronto	Goal	Hall, Chicago
Harvey, Montreal	Defense	Stanley, Toronto
Pronovost, Detroit	Defense	Pilote, Chicago
Beliveau, Montreal	Center	H. Richard, Montreal
Geoffrion, Montreal	Right Wing	Howe, Detroit
Mahovlich, Toronto	Left Wing	Moore, Montreal

1961–62

Plante, Montreal	Goal	Hall, Chicago
Harvey, New York	Defense	Brewer, Toronto
Talbot, Montreal	Defense	Pilote, Chicago
Mikita, Chicago	Center	Keon, Toronto
Bathgate, New York	Right Wing	Howe, Detroit
Hull, Chicago	Left Wing	Mahovlich, Toronto

1962–63

Hall, Chicago	Goal	Sawchuk, Detroit
Pilote, Chicago	Defense	Horton, Toronto
Brewer, Toronto	Defense	Vasko, Chicago
Mikita, Chicago	Center	Richard, Montreal
Howe, Detroit	Right Wing	Bathgate, New York
Mahovlich, Toronto	Left Wing	Hull, Chicago

1963–64

Hall, Chicago	Goal	Hodge, Montreal
Pilote, Chicago	Defense	Vasko, Chicago
Horton, Toronto	Defense	Laperriere, Montreal
Mikita, Chicago	Center	Beliveau, Montreal
Wharram, Chicago	Right Wing	Howe, Detroit
Hull, Chicago	Left Wing	Mahovlich, Toronto

1964–65

Crozier, Detroit	Goal	Hodge, Montreal	
Pilote, Chicago	Defense	Gadsby, Detroit	
Laperriere, Montreal	Defense	Brewer, Toronto	
Ullman, Detroit	Center	Mikita, Chicago	
Provost, Montreal	Right Wing	Howe, Detroit	
B. Hull, Chicago	Left Wing	Mahovlich, Toronto	

1965–66

Hall, Chicago	Goal	Worsley, Montreal	
Laperriere, Montreal	Defense	Stanley, Toronto	
Pilote, Chicago	Defense	Stapleton, Chicago	
Mikita, Chicago	Center	Beliveau, Montreal	
Howe, Detroit	Right Wing	Rousseau, Montreal	
B. Hull, Chicago	Left Wing	Mahovlich, Toronto	

1966–67

Giacomin, New York	Goal	Hall, Chicago	
Pilote, Chicago	Defense	Horton, Toronto	
Howell, New York	Defense	Orr, Boston	
Mikita, Chicago	Center	Ullman, Detroit	
Wharram, Chicago	Right Wing	Howe, Detroit	
B. Hull, Chicago	Left Wing	Marshall, New York	

1967–68

Worsley, Montreal	Goal	Giacomin, New York	
Orr, Boston	Defense	J. C. Tremblay, Mont.	
Horton, Toronto	Defense	Neilson, New York	
Mikita, Chicago	Center	Esposito, Boston	
Howe, Detroit	Right Wing	Gilbert, New York	
B. Hull, Chicago	Left Wing	Bucyk, Boston	

1968–69

Hall, St. Louis	Goal	Giacomin, New York	
Orr, Boston	Defense	Green, Boston	
Horton, Toronto	Defense	Harris, Montreal	
Esposito, Boston	Center	Beliveau, Montreal	
Howe, Detroit	Right Wing	Cournoyer, Montreal	
B. Hull, Chicago	Left Wing	F. Mahovlich, Detroit	

1969–70

Esposito, Chicago	Goal	Giacomin, New York	
Orr, Boston	Defense	Brewer, Detroit	
Park, New York	Defense	Laperriere, Montreal	
Esposito, Boston	Center	Mikita, Chicago	
Howe, Detroit	Right Wing	McKenzie, Boston	
B. Hull, Chicago	Left Wing	F. Mahovlich, Detroit	

1970–71

Giacomin, New York	Goal	Plante, Toronto	
Orr, Boston	Defense	Park, New York	
Tremblay, Montreal	Defense	Stapleton, Chicago	
Esposito, Boston	Center	Keon, Toronto	
Hodge, Boston	Right Wing	Cournoyer, Montreal	
Bucyk, Boston	Left Wing	B. Hull, Chicago	

1971–72

Esposito, Chicago	Goal	Dryden, Montreal	
Orr, Boston	Defense	White, Chicago	
Park, New York	Defense	Stapleton, Chicago	
Esposito, Boston	Center	Ratelle, New York	
Gilbert, New York	Right Wing	Cournoyer, Montreal	
B. Hull, Chicago	Left Wing	Hadfield, New York	

1972–73

Dryden, Montreal	Goal	Esposito, Chicago	
Orr, Boston	Defense	Park, New York R.	
Lapointe, Montreal	Defense	White, Chicago	
Esposito, Boston	Center	Clarke, Philadelphia	
Redmond, Detroit	Right Wing	Cournoyer, Montreal	
F. Mahovlich, Montreal	Left Wing	D. Hull, Chicago	

1973–74

Parent, Philadelphia	Goal	Esposito, Chicago	
Orr, Boston	Defense	White, Chicago	
Park, New York R.	Defense	Ashbee, Philadelphia	
Esposito, Boston	Center	Clarke, Philadelphia	
Hodge, Boston	Right Wing	Redmond, Detroit	
Martin, Buffalo	Left Wing	Cashman, Boston	

1974–75

Parent, Philadelphia	Goal	Vachon, Los Angeles	
Orr, Boston	Defense	Lapointe, Montreal	
D. Potvin, New York I.	Defense	Salming, Toronto	
Clarke, Philadelphia	Center	Esposito, Boston	
Lafleur, Montreal	Right Wing	Robert, Buffalo	
Martin, Buffalo	Left Wing	Vickers, New York R.	

1975–76

Dryden, Montreal	Goal	Resch, New York I.	
D. Potvin, New York I.	Defense	Salming, Toronto	
Park, Boston	Defense	Lapointe, Montreal	
Clarke, Philadelphia	Center	Perreault, Buffalo	
Lafleur, Montreal	Right Wing	Leach, Philadelphia	
Barber, Philadelphia	Left Wing	Martin, Buffalo	

1976–77

Dryden, Montreal	Goal	Vachon, Los Angeles	
Robinson, Montreal	Defense	D. Potvin, New York I.	
Salming, Toronto	Defense	Lapointe, Montreal	
Dionne, Los Angeles	Center	Perreault, Buffalo	
Lafleur, Montreal	Right Wing	McDonald, Toronto	
Shutt, Montreal	Left Wing	Martin, Buffalo	

1977–78

Dryden, Montreal	Goal	Edwards, Buffalo	
D. Potvin, New York I.	Defense	Robinson, Montreal	
Park, Boston	Defense	Salming, Toronto	
Trottier, New York I.	Center	Sittler, Toronto	
Lafleur, Montreal	Right Wing	Bossy, New York I.	
Gillies, New York I.	Left Wing	Shutt, Montreal	

1978–79

Dryden, Montreal	Goal	Resch, New York I.	
D. Potvin, New York I.	Defense	Salming, Toronto	
Robinson, Montreal	Defense	Savard, Montreal	
Trottier, New York I.	Center	Dionne, Los Angeles	
Lafleur, Montreal	Right Wing	Bossy, New York I.	
Gillies, New York I.	Left Wing	Barber, Philadelphia	

1979–80

Esposito, Chicago	Goal	Edwards, Buffalo	
Robinson, Montreal	Defense	Salming, Toronto	
Bourque, Boston	Defense	Schoenfeld, Buffalo	
Dionne, Los Angeles	Center	Gretzky, Edmonton	
Lafleur, Montreal	Right Wing	Gare, Buffalo	
Simmer, Los Angeles	Left Wing	Shutt, Montreal	

1980–81

Liut, St. Louis	Goal	Lessard, Los Angeles	
Potvin, New York I.	Defense	Robinson, Montreal	
Carlyle, Pittsburgh	Defense	Bourque, Boston	
Gretzky, Edmonton	Center	Dionne, Los Angeles	
Bossy, New York I.	Right Wing	Taylor, Los Angeles	
Simmer, Los Angeles	Left Wing	Barber, Philadelphia	

1981–82

Smith, New York I.	Goal	Fuhr, Edmonton	
Wilson, Chicago	Defense	Coffey, Edmonton	
Bourque, Boston	Defense	Engblom, Montreal	
Gretzky, Edmonton	Center	Trottier, New York I.	
Bossy, New York I.	Right Wing	Middleton, Boston	
Messier, Edmonton	Left Wing	Tonelli, New York I.	

1982–83

Peeters, Boston	Goal	Melanson, New York I.	
Howe, Philadelphia	Defense	Bourque, Boston	
Langway, Washington	Defense	Coffey, Edmonton	
Gretzky, Edmonton	Center	Savard, Chicago	
Bossy, New York I.	Right Wing	McDonald, Calgary	
Messier, Edmonton	Left Wing	Goulet, Quebec	

1983–84

Barrasso, Buffalo	Goal	Riggin, Washington	
Langway, Washington	Defense	Coffey, Edmonton	
Bourque, Boston	Defense	Potvin, New York I.	
Gretzky, Edmonton	Center	Trottier, New York I.	
Bossy, New York I.	Right Wing	Kurri, Edmonton	
Goulet, Quebec	Left Wing	Messier, Edmonton	

1984–85

Lindbergh, Philadelphia	Goal	Barrasso, Buffalo
Coffey, Edmonton	Defense	Langway, Washington
Bourque, Boston	Defense	Wilson, Chicago
Gretzky, Edmonton	Center	Hawerchuk, Winnipeg
Kurri, Edmonton	Right Wing	Bossy, New York I.
Ogrodnick, Detroit	Left Wing	Tonelli, New York I.

1985–86

Vanbiesbrouck, NYR	Goal	Froese, Philadelphia
Coffey, Edmonton	Defense	Robinson, Montreal
Howe, Philadelphia	Defense	Bourque, Boston
Gretzky, Edmonton	Center	Lemieux, Pittsburgh
Bossy, New York I.	Right Wing	Kurri, Edmonton
Goulet, Quebec	Left Wing	Naslund, Montreal

1986–87

Hextall, Philadelphia	Goal	Liut, Hartford
Bourque, Boston	Defense	Murphy, Washington
Howe, Philadelphia	Defense	MacInnis, Calgary
Gretzky, Edmonton	Center	Lemieux, Pittsburgh
Kurri, Edmonton	Right Wing	Kerr, Philadelphia
Goulet, Quebec	Left Wing	Robitaille, Los Angeles

1987–88

Fuhr, Edmonton	Goal	Roy, Montreal
Bourque, Boston	Defense	Suter, Calgary
Stevens, Washington	Defense	McCrimmon, Calgary
Lemieux, Pittsburgh	Center	Gretzky, Edmonton
Loob, Calgary	Right Wing	Neely, Boston
Robitaille, Los Angeles	Left Wing	Goulet, Quebec

1988–89

Roy, Montreal	Goal	Vernon, Calgary
Chelios, Montreal	Defense	MacInnis, Calgary
Coffey, Pittsburgh	Defense	Bourque, Boston
Lemieux, Pittsburgh	Center	Gretzky, Los Angeles
J. Mullen, Calgary	Right Wing	Kurri, Edmonton
Robitaille, Los Angeles	Left Wing	Gallant, Detroit

1989–90

Roy, Montreal	Goal	Puppa, Buffalo
Bourque, Boston	Defense	Coffey, Pittsburgh
MacInnis, Calgary	Defense	Wilson, Chicago
Messier, Edmonton	Center	Gretzky, Los Angeles
Hull, St. Louis	Right Wing	Neely, Boston
Robitaille, Los Angeles	Left Wing	Bellows, Minnesota

1990–91

Belfour, Chicago	Goal	Roy, Montreal
Bourque, Boston	Defense	Chelios, Chicago
MacInnis, Calgary	Defense	Leetch, New York R.
Gretzky, Los Angeles	Center	Oates, St. Louis
Hull, St. Louis	Right Wing	Neely, Boston
Robitaille, Los Angeles	Left Wing	K. Stevens, Pittsburgh

1991–92

Roy, Montreal	Goal	McLean, Vancouver
Leetch, New York R.	Defense	Housley, Winnipeg
Bourque, Boston	Defense	S. Stevens, New Jersey
Messier, New York R.	Center	Lemeiux, Pittsburgh
Hull, St. Louis	Right Wing	Recchi, Philadelphia
K. Stevens, Pittsburgh	Left Wing	Robitaille, Los Angeles

1992–93

Belfour, Chicago	Goal	Barrasso, Pittsburgh
Chelios, Chicago	Defense	Murphy, Pittsburgh
Bourque, Boston	Defense	Iafrate, Washington
Lemieux, Pittsburgh	Center	LaFontaine, Buffalo
Selanne, Winnipeg	Right Wing	Mogilny, Buffalo
Robitaille, Los Angeles	Left Wing	K. Stevens, Pittsburgh

1993–94

Hasek, Buffalo	Goal	Vanbiesbrouck, Florida
Bourque, Boston	Defense	MacInnis, Calgary
S. Stevens, New Jersey	Defense	Leetch, New York R.
Fedorov, Detroit	Center	Gretzky, Los Angeles
Bure, Vancouver	Right Wing	Neely, Boston
Shanahan, St. Louis	Left Wing	Graves, New York R.

1994–95

Hasek, Buffalo	Goal	Belfour, Chicago
Coffey, Detroit	Defense	Bourque, Boston
Chelios, Chicago	Defense	Murphy, Pittsburgh
E. Lindros, Philadelphia	Center	Zhamnov, Winnipeg
Jagr, Pittsburgh	Right Wing	Fleury, Calgary
LeClair, Mont.–Phil.	Left Wing	Tkaczuk, Winnipeg

1995–96

Carey, Washington	Goal	Osgood, Detroit
Chelios, Chicago	Defense	Konstantinov, Detroit
Bourque, Boston	Defense	Leetch, New York R.
Lemieux, Pittsburgh	Center	Lindros, Philadelphia
Jagr, Pittsburgh	Right Wing	Mogilny, Vancouver
Kariya, Anaheim	Left Wing	LeClair, Philadelphia

1996–97

Hasek, Buffalo	Goal	Brodeur, New Jersey
Leetch, New York R.	Defense	Chelios, Chicago
Ozolinsh, Colorado	Defense	Stevens, New Jersey
M. Lemieux, Pittsburgh	Center	Gretzky, New York R.
Selanne, Anaheim	Right Wing	Jagr, Pittsburgh
Kariya, Anaheim	Left Wing	LeClair, Philadelphia

1997–98

Hasek, Buffalo	Goal	Brodeur, New Jersey
Blake, Los Angeles	Defense	Salanne, Anaheim
Lidstrom, Detroit	Defense	Tkachuk, Phoenix
Forsberg, Colorado	Center	Gretzky, New York R.
Jagr, Pittsburgh	Right Wing	Pronger, St. Louis
LeClair, Philadelphia	Left Wing	Niedermayer, New Jersey

1998–99

Hasek, Buffalo	Goal	Dafoe, Boston
MacInnis, St. Louis	Defense	Bourque, Boston
Lidstrom, Detroit	Defense	Desjardins, Philadelphia
Forsberg, Colorado	Center	Yashin, Ottawa
Jagr, Pittsburgh	Right Wing	Selanne, Anaheim
Kariya, Anaheim	Left Wing	LeClair, Philadelphia

NHL ENTRY DRAFT

1969

First Round

1. Montreal—Rejean Houle, Montreal Jr. Canadiens; 2. Montreal—Marc Tardif, Montreal Jr. Canadiens; 3. Boston—Don Tannahill, Niagara Falls; 4. Boston—Frank Spring, Edmonton Oil Kings; 5. Minnesota—Dick Redmond, St. Catharines; 6. Philadelphia—Bob Currier, Cornwall; 7. Oakland—Tony Featherstone, Peterborough; 8. New York R.—Andre Dupont, Montreal Jr. Canadiens; 9. Toronto—Ernie Moser, Estevan; 10. Detroit—Jim Rutherford, Hamilton; 11. Boston—Ivan Boldirev, Oshawa; 12. New York R.—Pierre Jarry, Ottawa; 13. Chicago—J.P. Bordileau, Montreal Jr. Canadiens; 14. Minnesota—Dennis O'Brien, St. Catharines.

Second Round

15. Pittsburgh—Rick Kessell, Oshawa; 16. Los Angeles—Dale Hoganson, Estevan; 17.

Philadelphia—Bobby Clarke, Flin Flon; 18. Oakland—Ron Stackhouse, Peterborough; 19. St. Louis—Mike Lowe, Loyola College; 20. Toronto—Doug Brindley, Niagara Falls; 21. Detroit—Ron Garwasiuk, Regina; 22. Boston—Art Quoquochi, Montreal Jr. Canadiens; 23. New York R.—Bert Wilson, London; 24. Chicago—Larry Romanchych, Flin Flon; 25. Minnesota—Gilles Gilbert, London; 26. Pittsburgh—Michel Briere, Shawinigan Falls; 27. Los Angeles—Greg Boddy, Edmonton Oil Kings; 28. Philadelphia—Bill Brossart, Estevan.

1970

First Round

1. Buffalo—Gilbert Perreault, Montreal Jr. Canadiens; 2. Vancouver—Dale Tallon, Toronto Marlboros; 3. Boston—Reg Leach, Flin Flon; 4. Boston—Rick MacLeish, Peterborough; 5. Montreal—Ray Martiniuk, Flin Flon; 6. Montreal—Chuck Lefley, Canadian Nationals; 7. Pittsburgh—Greg Polis, Estevan; 8. Toronto—Darryl Sittler, London; 9. Boston—Ron Plumb, Peterborough; 10. Oakland—Chris Oddleifson, Winnipeg Jets; 11. New York R.—Norm Gratton, Montreal Jr. Canadiens; 12. Detroit—Serge Lajeunesse, Montreal Jr. Canadiens; 13. Boston—Bob Stewart, Oshawa; 14. Chicago—Dan Maloney, London.

Second Round

15. Buffalo—Butch Deadmarsh, Brandon; 16. Vancouver—Jim Hargreaves, Winnipeg Jets; 17. . Minnesota—Fred Harvey, Hamilton; 18. Philadelphia—Bill Clement, Ottawa; 19. Oakland—Pete Laframboise, Ottawa; 20. Minnesota—Fred Barrett, Toronto Marlboros; 21. Pittsburgh—John Stewart, Flin Flon; 22. Toronto—Errol Thompson, Charlottetown; 23. St. Louis—Murray Keogan, U. of Minnesota; 24. Los Angeles—Al McDonough, St. Catharines; 25. New York R.—Mike Murphy, Toronto Marlboros; 26. Detroit—Bobby Guindon, Montreal Jr. Canadiens; 27. Boston—Dan Bouchard, London; 28. Chicago—Mike Archambault, Drummondville.

1971

First Round

1. Montreal—Guy Lafleur, Quebec Remparts; 2. Detroit—Marcel Dionne, St. Catharines; 3. Vancouver—Jocelyn Guevremont, Montreal Jr. Canadiens; 4. St. Louis—Gene Carr, Flin Flon; 5. Buffalo—Rick Martin, Montreal Jr. Canadiens; 6. Boston—Ron Jones, Edmonton Oil Kings; 7. Montreal—Chuck Arnason, Flin Flon; 8. Philadelphia—Larry Wright, Regina; 9. Philadelphia—Pierre Plante, Drummondville; 10. New York R.—Steve Vickers, Toronto Marlboros; 11. Montreal—Murray Wilson, Ottawa; 12. Chicago—Dan Spring, Edmonton Oil Kings; 13. New York R.—Steve Durbano, Toronto Marlboros; 14. Boston—Terry O'Reilly, Oshawa.

Second Round

15. California—Ken Baird, Flin Flon; 16. Detroit—Henry Boucha, U.S. Nationals; 17. Vancouver—Bobby Lalonde, Montreal Jr. Canadiens; 18. Pittsburgh—Brian MaKenzie, St. Catherines; 19. Buffalo—Craig Ramsay, Peterborough; 20. Montreal—Larry Robinson, Kitchener; 21. Minnesota—Rod Norrish, Regina; 22. Toronto—Rick Kehoe, Hamilton; 23. Toronto—Dave Fortier, St. Catherines; 24. Montreal—Michel Deguise, Sorel; 25. Montreal—Terry French, Ottawa; 26. Chicago—Dave Kryskow, Edmonton Oil Kings; 27. New York R.—Tom Williams, Hamilton; 28. Boston—Curt Ridley, Portage.

1972

First Round

1. New York I.—Billy Harris, Toronto Marlboros; 2. Atlanta—Jacques Richard, Quebec Remparts; 3. Vancouver—Don Lever, Niagara Falls; 4. Montreal—Steve Shutt, Toronto Marlboros; 5. Buffalo—Jim Schoenfeld, Niagara Falls; 6. Montreal—Michel Larocque, Ottawa; 7. Philadelphia—Bill Barber, Kitchener; 8. Montreal—Dave Gardner, Toronto Marlboros; 9. St. Louis—Wayne Merrick, Ottawa; 10. New York—Albert Blanchard, Kitchener; 11. Toronto—George Ferguson, Toronto Marlboros; 12. Minnesota—Jerry Byers,

Kitchener; 13. Chicago—Phil Russell, Edmonton Oil Kings; 14. Montreal—John Van Boxmeer, Edmonton Oil Kings; 15. New York R.—Bobby MacMillan, St. Catharines; 16. Boston—Mike Bloom, St. Catharines.

Second Round

17. New York I.—Lorne Henning, New Westminster; 18. Atlanta—Dwight Bialowas, Regina; 19. Vancouver—Brian McSheffrey, Ottawa; 20. Los Angeles—Don Kozak, Edmonton Oil Kings; 21. New York R.—Larry Sacharuk, Saskatoon; 22. California—Tom Cassidy, Kitchener; 23. Philadelphia—Tom Bladon, Edmonton Oil Kings; 24. Pittsburgh—Jack Lynch, Oshawa; 25. Buffalo—Larry Carriere, Loyola College; 26. Detroit—Pierre Guite, St. Catharines; 27. Toronto—Randy Osburn, London; 28. California—Stan Weir, Medicine Hat; 29. Pittsburgh—Bernie Lukowich, New Westminster; 30. New York R.—Rene Villemure, Shawinigan; 31. Boston—Wayne Elder, London.

1973

First Round

1. New York I.—Denis Potvin, Ottawa; 2. Atlanta—Tom Lysiak, Medicine Hat; 3. Vancouver—Dennis Ververgaert, London; 4. Toronto—Lanny McDonald, Medicine Hat; 5. St. Louis—John Davidson, Calgary Centennials; 6. Boston—Andre Savard, Quebec Remparts; 7. Pittsburgh—Blaine Stoughton, Flin Flon; 8. Montreal—Bob Gainey, Peterborough; 9. Vancouver—Bob Dailey, Toronto Marlboros; 10. Toronto—Bob Neeley, Peterborough; 11. Detroit—Terry Richardson, New Westminster; 12. Buffalo—Morris Titanic, Sudbury; 13. Chicago—Darcy Rota, Edmonton Oil Kings; 14. New York R.—Rick Middleton, Oshawa; 15. Toronto—Ian Turnbull, Ottawa; 16. Atlanta—Vic Mercredi, New Westminster.

Second Round

17. Montreal—Glen Goldup, Toronto Marlboros; 18. Minnesota—Blake Dunlop, Ottawa; 19. Vancouver—Paulin Bordeleau, Toronto Marlboros; 20. Philadelphia—Larry Goodenough, London; 21. Atlanta—Eric Vail, Sudbury; 22. Montreal—Peter

Marrin, Toronto Marlboros; 23. Pittsburgh—Wayne Bianchin, Flin Flon; 24. St. Louis—George Pesut, Saskatoon; 25. Minnesota—John Rogers, Edmonton Oil Kings; 26. Philadelphia—Brent Levins, Swift Current; 27. Pittsburgh—Colin Campbell, Peterborough; 28. Buffalo—Jean Landry, Quebec Remparts; 29. Chicago—Reg Thomas, London; 30. New York R.—Pat Hickey, Hamilton; 31. Boston—Jim Jones, Peterborough; 32. Montreal—Ron Andruff, Flin Flon.

1974

First Round

1. Washington—Greg Joly, Regina; 2. Kansas City—Wilf Paiement, St. Catharines; 3. California—Rick Hampton, St. Catharines; 4. New York I.—Clark Gillies, Regina; 5. Montreal—Cam Connor, Flin Flon; 6. Minnesota—Doug Hicks, Flin Flon; 7. Montreal—Doug Risebrough, Kitchener; 8. Pittsburgh—Pierre Larouche, Sorel; 9. Detroit—Bill Lochead, Oshawa; 10. Montreal—Rick Chartraw, Kitchener; 11. Buffalo—Lee Fogolin, Oshawa; 12. Montreal—Mario Tremblay, Montreal Jrs.; 13. Toronto—Jack Valiquette, Sault; 14. New York R.—Dave Maloney, Kitchener; 15. Montreal—Gord McTavish, Sudbury; 16. Chicago—Grant Mulvey, Calgary Centennials; 17. California—Ron Chipperfield, Brandon; 18. Boston—Dan Larway, Swift Current.

Second Round

19. Washington—Mike Marson, Sudbury; 20. Kansas City—Glen Burdon, Regina; 21. California—Bruce Affleck, U. of Denver; 22. New York I.—Bryan Trottier, Swift Current; 23. Vancouver—Ron Sedlbauer, Kitchener; 24. Minnesota—Rick Nantais, Quebec Remparts; 25. Boston—Mark Howe, Toronto Marlboros; 26. St. Louis—Bob Hess, New Westminster; 27. Pittsburgh—Jacques Cossette, Sorel; 28. Atlanta—Guy Chouinard, Quebec Remparts; 29. Buffalo—Danny Gare, Calgary Centennials; 30. Montreal—Gary McGregor, Cornwall; 31. Toronto—Dave Williams, Swift Current; 32. New York R.—Ron Greschner, Swift Current; 33. Montreal—Gilles Lupien, Montreal Jrs.; 34. Chicago—Alain Daigle,

Trois Rivieres; 35. Philadelphia—Don McLean, Sudbury; 36. Boston—Peter Sturgeon, Kitchener.

1975

First Round

1. Philadelphia—Mel Bridgman, Victoria; 2. Kansas City—Barry Dean, Medicine Hat; 3. California—Ralph Klassen, Saskatoon; 4. Minnesota—Bryan Maxwell, Medicine Hat; 5. Detroit—Rick Lapointe, Victoria; 6. Toronto—Don Ashby, Calgary Centennials; 7. Chicago—Greg Vaydik, Medicine Hat; 8. Atlanta—Richard Mulhern, Sherbrooke; 9. Montreal—Robin Sadler, Edmonton Oil Kings; 10. Vancouver—Rick Blight, Brandon; 11. New York I.—Pat Price, Brandon; 12. New York R.—Wayne Dillon, Toronto Marlboros; 13. Pittsburgh—Gord Laxton, New Westminster; 14. Boston—Doug Halward, Peterborough; 15. Montreal—Pierre Mondou, Montreal Jrs.; 16. Los Angeles—Tim Young, Ottawa; 17. Buffalo—Bob Sauve, Laval; 18. Washington—Alex Forsyth, Kingston.

Second Round

19. Washington—Peter Scamurra, Peterborough; 20. Kansas City—Don Cairns, Victoria; 21. California—Dennis Maruk, London; 22. Montreal—Brian Engblom, U. of Wisconsin; 23. Detroit—Jerry Rollins, Winnipeg Jr. Jets; 24. Toronto—Doug Jarvis, Peterborough; 25. Chicago—Daniel Arndt, Saskatoon; 26. Atlanta—Rick Bowness, Montreal Jrs.; 27. St. Louis—Ed Staniowski, Regina; 28. Vancouver—Brad Gassoff, Kamloops; 29. New York I.—David Salvian, St. Catharines; 30. New York R.—Doug Soetaert, Edmonton Oil Kings; 31. Pittsburgh—Russ Anderson, U. of Minnesota; 32. Boston—Barry Smith, New Westminster; 33. Los Angeles—Terry Bucyk, Lethbridge; 34. Montreal—Kelvin Greenbank, Winnipeg Jr. Jets; 35. Buffalo—Ken Breitenbach, St. Catharines; 36. St. Louis—Jamie Masters, Ottawa.

1976

First Round

1. Washington—Rick Green, London; 2. Pittsburgh—Blair Chapman, Saskatoon; 3. Minnesota—Glen Sharpley, Hull; 4. Detroit—Fred Williams, Saskatoon; 5. California—Bjorn Johansson, Sweden; 6. New York R.—Don Murdoch, Medicine Hat; 7. St. Louis—Bernie Federko, Saskatoon; 8. Atlanta—Dave Shand, Peterborough; 9. Chicago—Real Cloutier, Quebec Remparts; 10. Atlanta—Harold Phillipoff, New Westminster; 11. Kansas City—Paul Gardner, Oshawa; 12. Montreal—Peter Lee, Ottawa; 13. Montreal—Rod Schutt, Sudbury; 14. New York I.—Alex McKendry, Sudbury; 15. Washington—Greg Carroll, Medicine Hat; 16. Boston—Clayton Pachal, New Westminster; 17. Philadelphia—Mark Suzor, Kingston; 18. Montreal—Bruce Baker, Ottawa.

Second Round

19. Pittsburgh—Greg Malone, Oshawa; 20. St. Louis—Brian Sutter, Lethbridge; 21. Los Angeles—Steve Clippingdale, New Westminster; 22. Detroit—Reed Larson, U. of Minnesota; 23. California—Vern Stenlund, London; 24. New York R.—Dave Farrish, Sudbury; 25. St. Louis—John Smrke, Toronto Marlboros; 26. Vancouver—Bob Manno, St. Catharines; 27. Chicago—Jeff McDill, Victoria; 28. Atlanta—Bobby Simpson, Sherbrooke; 29. Pittsburgh—Peter Marsh, Sherbrooke; 30. Toronto—Randy Carlyle, Sudbury; 31. Minnesota—Jim Roberts, Ottawa; 32. New York I.—Mike Kaszycki, Sault; 33. Buffalo—Joe Kowal, Hamilton; 34. Boston—Larry Gloeckner, Victoria; 35. Philadelphia—Drew Callander, Regina; 36. Montreal—Barry Melrose, Kamloops.

1977

First Round

1. Detroit—Dale McCourt, St. Catharines; 2. Colorado—Barry Beck, New Westminster; 3. Washington—Robert Picard, Montreal Jrs.; 4. Vancouver—Jere Gillis, Sherbrooke; 5. Cleveland—Mike Crombeen, Kingston; 6. Chicago—Doug Wilson, Ottawa; 7. Minnesota—Brad Maxwell, New Westminster; 8. New York R.—Lucien DeBlois, Sorel; 9. St. Louis—Scott Campbell, London; 10. Montreal —Mark Napier, Toronto Marlboros; 11. Toronto—John Anderson, Toronto Marlboros; 12. Toronto—Trevor Johan-

son, Toronto Marlboros; 13. New York R.—Ron Duguay, Sudbury; 14. Buffalo—Ric Seiling, St. Catharines; 15. New York I.—Mike Bossy, Laval; 16. Boston—Dwight Foster, Kitchener; 17. Philadelphia—Kevin McCarthy, Winnipeg Monarchs; 18. Montreal—Norm Dupont, Montreal Jrs.

Second Round

19. Chicago—Jean Savard, Quebec Remparts; 20. Atlanta—Miles Zaharko, New Westminster; 21. Washington—Mark Lofthouse, New Westminster; 22. Vancouver—Jeff Bandura, Portland; 23. Cleveland—Daniel Chicoine, Sherbrooke; 24. Toronto—Bob Gladney, Oshawa; 25. Minnesota—Dave Semenko, Brandon; 26. New York R.—Mike Keating, St. Catharines; 27. St. Louis—Neil Labatte, Toronto Marlboros; 28. Atlanta—Don Laurence, Kitchener; 29. Toronto—Rocky Saganiuk, Lethbridge; 30. Pittsburgh—Jim Hamilton, London; 31. Atlanta—Brian Hill, Medicine Hat; 32. Buffalo—Ron Areshenkoff, Medicine Hat; 33. New York I.—John Tonelli, Toronto Marlboros; 34. Boston—Dave Parro, Saskatoon; 35. Philadelphia—Tom Gorence, U. of Minnesota; 36. Montreal—Rod Langway, U. of New Hampshire.

1978
First Round

1. Minnesota—Bobby Smith, Ottawa; 2. Washington—Ryan Walter, Seattle; 3. St. Louis—Wayne Babych, Portland; 4. Vancouver—Bill Derlago, Brandon; 5. Colorado—Mike Gillis, Kingston; 6. Philadelphia—Behn Wilson, Kingston; 7. Philadelphia—Ken Linseman, Kingston; 8. Montreal—Danny Geoffrion, Cornwall; 9. Detroit—Willie Huber, Hamilton; 10. Chicago—Tim Higgins, Ottawa; 11. Atlanta—Brad Marsh, London; 12. Detroit—Brent Peterson, Portland; 13. Buffalo—Larry Playfair, Portland; 14. Philadelphia—Danny Lucas, Sault; 15. New York I.—Steve Tambellini, Lethbridge; 16. Boston—Al Secord, Hamilton; 17. Montreal—Dave Hunter, Sudbury; 18. Washington—Tim Coulis, Hamilton.

19. Minnesota—Steve Payne, Ottawa; 20. Washington—Paul Mulvey, Portland; 21. Toronto—Joel Quenneville, Windsor; 22. Vancouver—Curt Fraser, Victoria; 23. Washington—Paul MacKinnon, Peterborough; 24. Minnesota—Steve Christoff, U. of Minnesota; 25. Pittsburgh—Mike Meeker, Peterborough; 26. New York R.—Don Maloney, Kitchener; 27. Colorado—Merlin Malinowski, Medicine Hat; 28. Detroit—Glenn Hicks, Flin Flon; 29. Chicago—Doug Lecuyer, Portland; 30. Montreal—Dale Yakiwchuk, Portland; 31. Detroit—Al Jensen, Hamilton; 32. Buffalo—Tony McKegney, Kingston; 33. Philadelphia—Mike Simurda, Kingston; 34. New York I.—Randy Johnston, Peterborough; 35. Boston—Graeme Nicolson, Cornwall; 36. Montreal—Ron Carter, Sherbrooke.

1979
First Round

1. Colorado—Rob Ramage, London; 2. St. Louis—Perry Turnbull, Portland; 3. Detroit—Mike Foligno, Sudbury; 4. Washington—Mike Gartner, Niagara Falls; 5. Vancouver—Rick Vaive, Sherbrooke; 6. Minnesota—Craig Hartsburg, Sault; 7. Chicago—Keith Brown, Portland; 8. Boston—Ray Bourque, Verdun; 9. Toronto—Laurie Boschman, Brandon; 10. Minnesota—Tom McCarthy, Oshawa; 11. Buffalo—Mike Ramsey, U. of Minnesota; 12. Atlanta—Paul Reinhart, Kitchener; 13. New York R.—Doug Sulliman, Kitchener; 14. Philadelphia—Brian Propp, Brandon; 15. Boston—Brad McCrimmon, Brandon; 16. Los Angeles—Jay Wells, Kingston; 17. New York I.—Duane Sutter, Lethbridge; 18. Hartford—Ray Allison, Brandon; 19. Winnipeg—Jimmy Mann, Sherbrooke; 20. Quebec—Michel Goulet, Quebec Remparts; 21. Edmonton—Kevin Lowe, Quebec Remparts.

Second Round

22. Philadelphia—Blake Wesley, Portland; 23. Atlanta—Mike Perovich, Brandon; 24. Washington—Errol Rausse, Seattle; 25. New York I.—

Tomas Jonsson, Sweden; 26. Vancouver—Brent Ashton, Saskatoon; 27. Montreal—Gaston Gingras, Hamilton; 28. Chicago—Tim Trimper, Peterborough; 29. Los Angeles—Dean Hopkins, London; 30. Los Angeles—Mark Hardy, Montreal Jrs.; 31. Pittsburgh—Paul Marshall, Brantford; 32. Buffalo—Lindy Ruff, Lethbridge; 33. Atlanta—Pat Riggin, London; 34. New York R.—Ed Hospodar, Ottawa; 35. Philadelphia—Pelle Lindbergh, Sweden; 36. Boston—Doug Morrison, Lethbridge; 37. Montreal—Mats Naslund, Sweden; 38. New York I.—Billy Carroll, London; 39. Hartford—Stuart Smith, Peterborough; 40. Winnipeg—Dave Christian, U. of North Dakota; 41. Quebec—Dale Hunter, Sudbury; 42. Minnesota—Neal Broten, U. of Minnesota.

1980

First Round

1. Montreal—Doug Wickenheiser, Regina; 2. Winnipeg—Dave Babych, Portland; 3. Chicago—Denis Savard, Montreal Jrs.; 4. Los Angeles—Larry Murphy, Peterborough; 5. Washington—Darren Veitch, Regina; 6. Edmonton—Paul Coffey, Kitchener; 7. Vancouver—Rick Lanz, Oshawa; 8. Hartford—Fred Arthur, Cornwall; 9. Pittsburgh—Mike Bullard, Brantford; 10. Los Angeles—Jimmy Fox, Ottawa; 11. Detroit—Mike Blaisdell, Regina; 12. St. Louis—Rik Wilson, Kingston; 13. Calgary—Denis Cyr, Montreal Jrs.; 14. New York R.—Jim Malone, Toronto Marlboros; 15. Chicago—Jerome Dupont, Toronto Marlboros; 16. Minnesota—Brad Palmer, Victoria; 17. New York I.—Brent Sutter, Red Deer; 18. Boston—Barry Pederson, Victoria; 19. Colorado—Paul Gagne, Windsor; 20. Buffalo—Steve Patrick, Brandon; 21. Philadelphia—Mike Stothers, Kingston.

Second Round

22. Colorado—Joe Ward, Seattle; 23. Winnipeg—Moe Mantha, Toronto Marlboros; 24. Quebec—Normand Rochefort, Quebec Remparts; 25. Toronto—Craig Muni, Kingston; 26. Toronto—Bob McGill, Victoria; 27. Montreal—Ric Nattress, Brantford; 28. Chicago—Steve

Ludzik, Niagara Falls; 29. Hartford—Michel Galarneau, Hull; 30. Chicago—Ken Solheim, Medicine Hat; 31. Calgary—Tony Curtale; Brantford; 32. Calgary—Kevin LaVallee, Brantford; 33. Los Angeles—Greg Terrion, Brantford; 34. Los Angeles—Dave Morrison, Peterborough; 35. New York R.—Mike Allison, Sudbury; 36. Chicago—Len Dawes, Victoria; 37. Minnesota—Don Beaupre, Sudbury; 38. New York I.—Kelly Hrudey, Medicine Hat; 39. Calgary—Steve Konroyd, Oshawa; 40. Montreal—John Chabot, Hull; 41. Buffalo—Mike Moller, Lethbridge; 42. Philadelphia—Jay Fraser, Ottawa.

1981

First Round

1. Winnipeg—Dale Hawerchuk, Cornwall; 2. Los Angeles—Doug Smith, Ottawa; 3. Washington—Bobby Carpenter, St. John's H.S.; 4. Hartford—Ron Francis, Sault; 5. Colorado—Joe Cirella, Oshawa; 6. Toronto—Jim Benning, Portland; 7. Montreal—Mark Hunter, Brantford; 8. Edmonton—Grant Fuhr, Victoria; 9. New York R.—James Patrick, U. of North Dakota; 10. Vancouver—Garth Butcher, Regina; 11. Quebec—Randy Moller, Lethbridge; 12. Chicago—Tony Tanti, Oshawa; 13. Minnesota—Ron Meighan, Niagara Falls; 14. Boston—Normand Leveille, Chicoutimi; 15. Calgary—Al MacInnis, Kitchener; 16. Philadelphia—Steve Smith, Sault; 17. Buffalo—Jiri Dudacek, Kladno; 18. Montreal—Gilbert Delorme, Chicoutimi; 19. Montreal—Jan Ingman, Sweden; 20. St. Louis—Marty Ruff, Lethbridge; 21. New York I.—Paul Boutilier, Sherbrooke.

Second Round

22. Winnipeg—Scott Arniel, Cornwall; 23. Detroit—Claude Loiselle, Windsor; 24. Toronto—Gary Yaremchuk, Portland; 25. Chicago—Kevin Griffin, Portland; 26. Colorado—Rick Chernomaz, Victoria; 27. Minnesota—Dave Donnelly, St. Albert; 28. Pittsburgh—Steve Gatzos, Sault; 29. Edmonton—Todd Strueby, Regina; 30. New York R.—Jan Erixon, Skelleftea; 31. Minnesota—Mike Sands, Sudbury; 32. Montreal—

Lars Eriksson, Brynas; 33. Minnesota—Tom Hirsch, Patrick Henry H.S.; 34. Minnesota—Dave Preuss, St. Thomas Academy; 35. Boston—Luc Dufour, Chicoutimi; 36. St. Louis—Hakan Nordin, Sweden; 37. Philadelphia—Rich Costello, Natick H.S.; 38. Buffalo—Hannu Virta, TPS Finland; 39. Los Angeles—Dean Kennedy, Brandon; 40. Montreal—Chris Chelios, Moose Jaw; 41. Minnesota—Jali Wahlsten, TPS Finland; 42. New York I.—Gord Dineen, Sault Ste. Marie.

1982

First Round

1. Boston—Gord Kluzak, Nanaimo; 2. Minnesota—Brian Bellows, Kitchener; 3. Toronto—Gary Nylund, Portland; 4. Philadelphia—Ron Sutter, Lethbridge; 5. Washington—Scott Stevens, Kitchener; 6. Buffalo—Phil Housley, South St. Paul H.S.; 7. Chicago—Ken Yaremchuk, Portland; 8. New Jersey—Rocky Trottier, Nanaimo; 9. Buffalo—Paul Cyr, Victoria; 10. Pittsburgh—Rich Sutter, Lethbridge; 11. Vancouver—Michel Petit, Sherbrooke; 12. Winnipeg—Jim Kyte, Cornwall; 13. Quebec—David Shaw, Kitchener; 14. Hartford—Paul Lawless, Windsor; 15. New York R.—Chris Kontos, Toronto Marlboros; 16. Buffalo—Dave Andreychuk, Oshawa; 17. Detroit—Murray Craven, Medicine Hat; 18. New Jersey—Ken Daneyko, Seattle; 19. Montreal—Alain Heroux, Chicoutimi; 20. Edmonton—Jim Playfair, Portland; 21. New York I.—Patrick Flatley, U. of Wisconsin.

Second Round

22. Boston—Brian Curran, Portland; 23. Detroit—Yves Courteau, Laval; 24. Toronto—Gary Leeman, Regina; 25. Toronto—Peter Ihnacak, Czech. National Team; 26. Buffalo—Mike Anderson, N. St. Paul H.S.; 27. Los Angeles—Mike Heidt, Calgary Wranglers; 28. Chicago—Rene Badeau, Quebec Remparts; 29. Calgary—Dave Reierson, Prince Albert; 30. Buffalo—Jens Johansson, Sweden; 31. Montreal—Jocelyn Gauvreau, Granby; 32. Montreal—Kent Carlson, St. Lawrence U.; 33. Montreal—David Maley, Edina H.S.; 34. Quebec—Paul Gillis, Niagara Falls; 35. Hartford—Mark Paterson, Ottawa; 36. New York

R.—Tomas Sandstrom, Sweden; 37. Calgary—Richard Kromm, Portland; 38. Pittsburgh—Tim Hrynewich, Sudbury; 39. Boston—Lyndon Byers, Regina; 40. Montreal—Scott Sandelin, Hibbing H.S.; 41. Edmonton—Steve Graves, Sault; 42. New York I.—Vern Smith, Lethbridge.

1983

First Round

1. Minnesota—Brian Lawton, Mt. St. Charles H.S.; 2. Hartford—Sylvain Turgeon, Hull; 3. New York I.—Pat LaFontaine, Verdun; 4. Detroit—Steve Yzerman, Peterborough; 5. Buffalo—Tom Barrasso, Acton—Boxboro H.S.; 6. New Jersey—John MacLean, Oshawa; 7. Toronto—Russ Courtnall, Victoria; 8. Winnipeg—Andrew McBain, North Bay; 9. Vancouver—Cam Neely, Portland; 10. Buffalo— Normand Lacombe, U. of New Hampshire; 11. Buffalo—Adam Creighton, Ottawa; 12. New York R.—Dave Gagner, Brantford; 13. Calgary—Dan Quinn, Belleville; 14. Winnipeg—Bobby Dollas, Laval; 15. Pittsburgh—Bob Errey, Peterborough; 16. New York I.—Gerald Diduck, Lethbridge; 17. Montreal—Alfie Turcotte, Porland; 18. Chicago—Bruce Cassidy, Ottawa; 19. Edmonton—Jeff Beukeboom, Sault; 20. Hartford—David Jensen, Lawrence Academy; 21. Boston—Nevin Markwart, Regina.

Second Round

22. Pittsburgh—Todd Charlesworth, Oshawa; 23. Hartford—Ville Siren, Ilves (Finland); 24. New Jersey—Shawn Evans, Peterborough; 25. Detroit—Lane Lambert, Saskatoon; 26. Montreal—Claude Lemieux, Trois Rivieres; 27. Montreal—Sergio Momesso, Shawinigan; 28. Toronto—Jeff Jackson, Brantford; 29. Winnipeg—Brad Berry, St. Albert; 30. Vancouver—David Bruce, Kitchener; 31. Buffalo—John Tucker, Kitchener; 32. Quebec—Yves Heroux, Chicoutimi; 33. New York R.—Randy Heath, Portland; 34. Buffalo—Richard Hajdu, Kamloops; 35. Montreal—Todd Francis, Brantford; 36. Minnesota—Malcolm Parks, St. Albert; 37. New York I.—Grant McKechney, Kitchener; 38. Minnesota—Frantisek

Musil, Czech. National Team; 39. Chicago—Wayne Presley, Kitchener; 40. Edmonton—Mike Golden, Reading H.S.; 41. Philadelphia—Peter Zezel, Toronto Marlboros; 42. Boston—Greg Johnston, Toronto Marlboros.

1984

First Round

1. Pittsburgh—Mario Lemieux, Laval; 2. New Jersey—Kirk Muller, Guelph; 3. Chicago—Ed Olczyk, Team USA; 4. Toronto—Al Iafrate, Belleville; 5. Montreal—Petr Svoboda, Czech. Jrs.; 6. Los Angeles—Craig Redmond, Team Canada; 7. Detroit—Shawn Burr, Kitchener; 8. Montreal—Shayne Corson, Brantford; 9. Pittsburgh—Doug Bodger, Kamloops; 10. Vancouver—J.J. Daigneault, Longueuil; 11. Hartford—Sylvain Cote, Quebec Remparts; 12. Calgary—Gary Roberts, Ottawa; 13. Minnesota—David Quinn, Kent H.S.; 14. New York R.—Terry Carkner, Peterborough; 15. Quebec—Trevor Stienburg, Guelph; 16. Pittsburgh—Roger Belanger, Kingston; 17. Washington—Kevin Hatcher, North Bay; 18. Buffalo—Bo Mikael Andersson, Sweden; 19. Boston—Dave Pasin, Prince Albert; 20. New York I.—Duncan MacPherson, Saskatoon; 21. Edmonton—Selmar Odelein, Regina.

Second Round

22. Philadelphia—Greg Smyth, London; 23. New Jersey—Craig Billington, Belleville; 24. Los Angeles—Brian Wilks, Kitchener; 25. Toronto—Todd Gill, Windsor; 26. St. Louis—Brian Benning, Portland; 27. Philadelphia—Scott Mellanby, Henry Carr; 28. Detroit—Doug Houda, Calgary Wranglers; 29. Montreal—Stephane Richer, Granby; 30. Winnipeg—Peter Douris, U. of New Hampshire; 31. Vancouver—Jeff Rohlicek, Portland; 32. St. Louis—Anthony Hrkac, Orillia; 33. Calgary—Ken Sabourin, Sault; 34. Washington—Stephen Leach, Matignon H.S.; 35. New York R.—Raimo Helminen, Ilves (Finland); 36. Quebec—Jeff Brown, Sudbury; 37. Philadelphia—Jeff Chychrun, Kingston; 38. Calgary—Paul Ranheim, Edina

H.S.; 39. Buffalo—Doug Trapp, Regina; 40. Boston—Ray Podloski, Portland; 41. New York I.—Bruce Melanson, Oshawa; 42. Edmonton—Daryl Reaugh, Kamloops.

1985

First Round

1. Toronto—Wendel Clark, Saskatoon; 2. Pittsburgh—Craig Simpson, Michigan State; 3. New Jersey—Craig Wolanin, Kitchener; 4. Vancouver—Jim Sandlak, London; 5. Hartford—Dana Murzyn, Calgary Wranglers; 6. New York I.—Brad Dalgarno, Hamilton; 7. New York R.—Ulf Dahlen, Ostersund; 8. Detroit—Brent Fedyk, Regina; 9. Los Angeles—Craig Duncanson, Sudbury; 10. Los Angeles—Dan Gratton, Oshawa; 11. Chicago—David Manson, Prince Albert; 12. Montreal—Jose Charbonneau, Drummondville; 13. New York I.—Derek King, Sault; 14. Buffalo—Carl Johansson, Sweden; 15. Quebec—Dave Latta, Kitchener; 16. Montreal—Tom Chorske, Minneapolis H.S.; 17. Calgary—Chris Biotti, Belmont Hill H.S.; 18. Winnipeg—Ryan Stewart, Kamloops; 19. Washington—Yvon Corriveau, Toronto Marlboros; 20. Edmonton—Scott Metcalfe, Kingston; 21. Philadelphia—Glen Seabrooke, Peterborough.

Second Round

22. Toronto—Ken Soangler, Calgary Wranglers; 23. Pittsburgh—Lee Giffin, Oshawa; 24. New Jersey—Sean Burke, Toronto Marlboros; 25. Vancouver—Troy Gamble, Medicine Hat; 26. Hartford—Kay Whitmore, Peterborough; 27. Calgary—Joe Nieuwendyk, Cornell; 28. New York R.—Mike Richter, Northwood Prep; 29. Detroit—Jeff Sharples, Kelowna; 30. Los Angeles—Par Edlund, Sweden; 31. Boston—Alain Cote, Quebec Remparts; 32. New Jersey—Eric Weinrich, North Yarmouth; 33. Montreal—Todd Richard, Armstrong H.S.; 34. New York I.—Brad Lauer, Regina; 35. Buffalo—Benoit Hogue, St. Jean; 36. Quebec—Jason Lafreniere, Hamilton; 37. St. Louis—Herb Raglan, Kingston; 38. Calgary—Jeff Wenaas, Medicine Hat; 39. Winnipeg—Roger Ohman, Sweden; 40. Washington—John Druce, Peterborough; 41.

Edmonton—Todd Carnelly, Kamloops; 42. Philadelphia—Bruce Rendall, Chatham.

1986

First Round

1. Detroit—Joe Murphy, Michigan State; 2. Los Angeles—Jimmy Carson, Verdun; 3. New Jersey—Neil Brady, Medicine Hat; 4. Pittsburgh—Zarley Zalapski, Team Canada; 5. Buffalo—Shawn Anderson, Team Canada; 6. Toronto—Vincent Damphousse, Laval; 7. Vancouver—Dan Woodley, Portland; 8. Winnipeg—Pat Elynuik, Prince Albert; 9. New York R.—Brian Leetch, Avon Old Farms H.S.; 10. St. Louis—Jocelyn Lemieux, Laval; 11. Hartford—Scott Young, Boston U.; 12. Minnesota—Warren Babe, Lethbridge; 13. Boston—Craig Janney, Boston College; 14. Chicago—Everett Sanipass, Verdun; 15. Montreal—Mark Pederson, Medicine Hat; 16. Calgary—George Pelawa, Bemidji H.S.; 17. New York I.—Tom Fitzgerald, Austin Prep; 18. Quebec—Tom McRae, Sudbury; 19. Washington—Jeff Greenlaw, Team Canada; 20. Philadelphia—Kerry Huffman, Guelph; 21. Edmonton—Kim Issel, Prince Albert.

Second Round

22. Detroit—Adam Graves, Windsor; 23. Philadelphia—Jukka Seppo, Finland; 24. New Jersey—Todd Copeland, Belmont Hill H.S.; 25. Pittsburgh—Dave Capuano, Mt. St. Charles H.S.; 26. Buffalo—Greg Brown, St. Mark's; 27. Montreal—Benoit Brunet, Hull; 28. Philadelphia—Kent Hawley, Ottawa; 29. Winnipeg—Teppo Numminen, Tappara (Finland); 30. Minnesota—Neil Wilkinson, Selkirk; 31. St. Louis—Mike Posma, Buffalo Jrs.; 32. Hartford—Marc LaForge, Kingston; 33. Minnesota—Dean Kolstad, Prince Albert; 34. Boston—Pekka Tirkkonen, Sapko (Finland); 35. Chicago—Mark Kurzawski, Windsor; 36. Toronto—Darryl Shannon, Windsor; 37. Calgary—Brian Glynn, Saskatoon; 38. New York I.—Dennis Vaske, Armstrong H.S.; 39. Quebec—Jean M. Routhier, Hull; 40. Washington—Steve Seftel, Kingston; 41. Quebec—

Stephane Guerard, Shawinigan; 42. Edmonton—Jamie Nichols, Portland.

1987

First Round

1. Buffalo—Pierre Turgeon, Granby; 2. New Jersey—Brendan Shanahan, London; 3. Boston—Glen Wesley, Portland; 4. Los Angeles—Wayne McBean, Medicine Hat; 5. Pittsburgh—Chris Joseph, Seattle; 6. Minnesota—David Archibald, Portland; 7. Toronto—Luke Richardson, Peterborough; 8. Chicago—Jimmy Waite, Chicoutimi; 9. Quebec—Bryan Fogarty, Kingston; 10. New York R.—Jayson More, New Westminster; 11. Detroit—Yves Racine, Longueuil; 12. St. Louis—Keith Osborne, North Bay; 13. New York I.—Dean Chynoweth, Medicine Hat; 14. Boston—Stephane Quintal, Granby; 15. Quebec—Joe Sakic, Swift Current; 16. Winnipeg—Bryan Marchment, Belleville; 17. Montreal—Andrew Cassels, Ottawa; 18. Hartford—Jody Hull, Peterborough; 19. Calgary—Bryan Deasley, U. of Michigan; 20. Philadelphia—Darren Rumble, Kitchener; 21. Edmonton—Peter Soberlak, Swift Current.

Second Round

22. Buffalo—Brad Miller, Regina; 23. New Jersey—Rickard Persson, Ostersund; 24. Vancouver—Rob Murphy, Laval; 25. Calgary—Stephane Matteau, Hull; 26. Pittsburgh—Richard Tabaracci, Cornwall; 27. Los Angeles—Mark Fitzpatrick, Medicine Hat; 28. Toronto—Daniel Marois, Chicoutimi; 29. Chicago—Ryan McGill, Swift Current; 30. Philadelphia—Jeff Harding, St. Michael's; 31. New York R.—Daniel Lacroix, Granby; 32. Detroit—Gordon Kruppke, Prince Albert; 33. Montreal—John Leclair, Bellows Academy; 34. New York I.—Jeff Hackett, Oshawa; 35. Minnesota—Scott McCrady, Medicine Hat; 36. Washington—Jeff Ballantyne, Ottawa; 37. Winnipeg—Patrik Eriksson, Brynas; 38. Montreal—Eric Desjardins, Granby; 39. Hartford—Adam Burt, North Bay; 40. Calgary—Kevin Grant, Kitchener; 41. Detroit—Bob

Wilkie, Swift Current; 42. Edmonton—Brad Werenka, Northern Michigan.

1988

First Round

1. Minnesota—Mike Modano, Prince Albert; 2. Vancouver—Trevor Linden, Medicine Hat; 3. Quebec—Curtis Leschyshyn, Saskatoon; 4. Pittsburgh—Darrin Shannon, Windsor; 5. Quebec—Daniel Dore, Drummondville; 6. Toronto—Scott Pearson, Kingston; 7. Los Angeles—Martin Gelinas, Hull; 8. Chicago—Jeremy Roenick, Thayer Academy; 9. St. Louis—Rod Brind'Amour, Notre Dame; 10. Winnipeg—Teemu Selanne, Jokerit (Finland); 11. Hartford—Chris Govedaris, Toronto Marlboros; 12. New Jersey—Corey Foster, Peterborough; 13. Buffalo—Joel Savage, Victoria; 14. Philadelphia—Claude Boivin, Drummondville; 15. Washington—Reginald Savage, Victoriaville; 16. New York I.—Kevin Cheveldayoff, Brandon; 17. Detroit—Kory Kocur, Saskatoon; 18. Boston—Robert Cimetta, Toronto Marlboros; 19. Edmonton—Francois Leroux, St. Jean; 20. Montreal—Eric Charron, Trois—Rivieres; 21. Calgary—Jason Muzzatti, Michigan State.

Second Round

22. New York R.—Troy Mallette, Sault; 23. New Jersey—Jeff Christian, London; 24. Quebec—Stephane Fiset, Victoriaville; 25. Pittsburgh—Mark Major, North Bay; 26. New York R.—Murray Duval, Spokane; 27. Toronto—Tie Domi, Peterborough; 28. Los Angeles—Paul Holden, London; 29. New York I.—Wayne Doucet, Hamilton; 30. St. Louis—Adrien Plavsic, U. of New Hampshire; 31. Winnipeg—Russ Romaniuk, St. Boniface; 32. Hartford—Barry Richter, Culver Academy; 33. Vancouver—Leif Rohlin, VIK (Sweden); 34. Montreal—Martin St. Amour, Verdun; 35. Philadelphia—Pat Murray, Michigan State; 36. Washington—Tim Taylor, London; 37. New York I.—Sean LeBrun, New Westminster; 38. Detroit—Serge Anglehart, Drummondville; 39. Edmonton—Petro Koivunen, K—Espoo (Finland); 40. Minnesota—Link Gaetz, Spokane; 41. Washington—Wade

Bartley, Dauphin; 42. Calgary—Todd Harkins, Miami of Ohio.

1989

First Round

1. Quebec—Mats Sundin, Nacka (Sweden); 2. New York I.—Dave Chyzowski, Kamloops; 3. Toronto—Scott Thornton, Belleville; 4. Winnipeg—Stu Barnes, Tri—Cities; 5. New Jersey—Bill Guerin, Springfield; 6. Chicago—Adam Bennett, Sudbury; 7. Minnesota—Doug Zmolek, John Marshall; 8. Vancouver—Jason Herter, U. of North Dakota; 9. St. Louis—Jason Marshall, Vernon; 10. Hartford—Bobby Holik, Jihlava (Czech.); 11. Detroit—Mike Sillinger, Regina; 12. Toronto—Rob Pearson, Belleville; 13. Montreal—Lindsay Vallis, Seattle; 14. Buffalo—Kevin Haller, Regina; 15. Edmonton—Jason Soules, Niagara Falls; 16. Pittsburgh—Jamie Heward, Regina; 17. Boston—Shayne Stevenson, Kitchener; 18. New Jersey—Jason Miller, Medicine Hat; 19. Washington—Olaf Kolzig, Tri—Cities; 20. New York R.—Steven Rice, Kitchener; 21. Toronto—Steve Bancroft, Belleville.

Second Round

22. Quebec—Adam Foote, Sault St. Marie; 23. New York I.—Travis Green, Spokane; 24. Calgary—Kent Manderville, Notre Dame; 25. Winnipeg—Dan Ratushny, Cornell; 26. New Jersey—Jarrod Skalde, Oshawa; 27. Chicago—Michael Speer, Guelph; 28. Minnesota—Mike Craig, Oshawa; 29. Vancouver—Robert Woodward, Deerfield; 30. Montreal—Patrice Brisebois, Laval; 31. St. Louis—Rick Corriveau, London; 32. Detroit—Bob Boughner, Sault; 33. Philadelphia—Greg Johnson, Thunder Bay; 34. Philadelphia—Patrik Juhlin, Sweden; 35. Washington—Byron Dafoe, Portland; 36. Edmonton—Richard Borgo, Kitchener; 37. Pittsburgh—Paul Laus, Niagara Falls; 38. Boston—Mike Parson, Guelph; 39. Los Angeles—Brent Thompson, Medicine Hat; 40. New York R.—Jason Prosofsky, Medicine Hat; 41. Montreal—Steve Larouche, Trois—Rivieres; 42. Calgary—Ted Drury, Fairfield Prep.

1990

First Round

1. Quebec—Owen Nolan, Cornwall; 2. Vancouver—Petr Nedved, Seattle; 3. Detroit—Keith Primeau, Niagara Falls; 4. Philadelphia—Mike Ricci, Peterborough; 5. Pittsburgh—Jaromir Jagr, Kladno (Cezch.); 6. New York I.—Scott Scissons, Saskatoon; 7. Los Angeles—Darryl Sydor, Kamloops; 8. Minnesota—Derian Hatcher, North Bay; 9. Washington—John Slaney, Cornwall; 10. Toronto—Drake Berehowsky, Kingston; 11. Calgary—Trevor Kidd, Brandon; 12. Montreal—Turner Stevenson, Seattle; 13. New York R.—Michael Stewart, Michigan State; 14. Buffalo—Brad May, Niagara Falls; 15. Hartford—Mark Greig, Lethbridge; 16. Chicago—Karl Dykhuis, Hull; 17. Edmonton—Scott Allison, Prince Albert; 18. Vancouver—Shawn Antoski, North Bay; 19. Winnipeg—Keith Tkachuk, Malden Catholic; 20. New Jersey—Martin Brodeur, St. Hyacinthe; 21. Boston—Bryan Smolinski, Michigan State.

Second Round

22. Quebec—Ryan Hughes, Cornell; 23. Vancouver—Jiri Slegr, CHZ Litvinov (Czech.); 24. New Jersey—David Harlock, Michigan; 25. Philadelphia—Chris Simon, Ottawa; 26. Calgary—Nicolas Perreault, Hawkesbury; 27. New York I.—Chris Taylor, London; 28. Los Angeles—Brendy Semchuk, Canadian National; 29. New Jersey—Chris Gotziaman, Roseau; 30. Washington—Rod Pasma, Cornwall; 31. Toronto—Felix Potvin, Chicoutimi; 32. Calgary—Vesa Vitakoski, SaiPa; 33. St. Louis—Craig Johnson, Hill—Murray H.S.; 34. New York R.—Doug Weight, Lake Superior; 35. Winnipeg—Mike Muller, Wayzata; 36. Hartford—Geoff Sanderson, Swift Current; 37. Chicago—Ivan Droppa, Partizan (Czech.); 38. Edmonton—Alexandre Legault, Boston U.; 39. Montreal—Ryan Kuwabara, Ottawa; 40. Philadelphia—Mikael Renberg, Pitea (Sweden); 41. Calgary—Etienne Belzile, Cornell; 42. Philadelphia—Terran Sandwith, Tri—Cities.

1991

First Round

1. Quebec—Eric Lindros, Oshawa; 2. San Jose—Pat Falloon, Spokane; 3. New Jersey—Scott Niedermayer, Kamloops; 4. New York I.—Scott Lachance, Boston U.; 5. Winnipeg—Aaron Ward, Michigan; 6. Philadelphia—Peter Forsberg, MoDo (Sweden); 7. Vancouver—Alex Stojanov, Hamilton; 8. Minnesota—Richard Matvichuk, Saskatoon; 9. Hartford—Patrick Poulin, St. Hyacinthe; 10. Detroit—Martin Lapointe, Laval; 11. New Jersey—Brian Rolston, Detroit Comp.; 12. Edmonton—Tyler Wright, Swift Current; 13. Buffalo—Phillippe Boucher, Granby; 14. Washington—Pat Peake, Detroit; 15. New York R.—Alexei Kovalev, Dynamo Moscow; 16. Pittsburgh—Markus Naslund, MoDo (Sweden); 17. Montreal—Brent Bilodeau, Seattle; 18. Boston—Glen Murray, Sudbury; 19. Calgary—Niklas Sundblad, AIK (Sweden); 20. Edmonton—Martin Rucinsky, CHZ Litvinov (Czech.); 21. Washington—Trevor Halverson, North Bay; 22. Chicago—Dean McAmmond, Prince Albert.

Second Round

23. San Jose—Ray Whitney, Spokane; 24. Quebec—Rene Corbet, Drummondville; 25. Washington—Eric Lavigne, Hull; 26. New York I.—Zigmund Palffy, AC Nitra (Czech.); 27. St. Louis—Steve Staios, Niagara Falls; 28. Montreal—Jim Campbell, Northwood Prep; 29. Vancouver—Jassen Cullimore, Peterborough; 30. San Jose—Sandis Ozolinsh, Dyanamo Riga; 31. Hartford—Martin Hamrlik, TJ Zlin (Czech.); 32. Detroit—Jamie Pushor, Lethbridge; 33. New Jersey—Donevan Hextall, Prince Albert; 34. Edmonton—Andrew Verner, Peterborough; 35. Buffalo—Jason Dawe, Peterborough; 36. Washington—Jeff Nelson, Prince Albert; 37. New York R.—Darcy Werenka, Lethbridge; 38. Pittsburgh—Rusty Fitzgerald, Duluth East H.S.; 39. Chicago—Michael Pomichter, Springfield Jr. B; 40. Boston—Jozef Stumpel, AC Nitra (Czech.); 41. Calgary—Francois Groleau, Shawinigan; 42. Los Angeles—Guy Leveque, Cornwall; 43. Mon-

treal—Craig Darby, Albany Academy; 44. Chicago—Jamie Matthews, Sudbury.

1992

First Round

1. Tampa Bay—Roman Hamrlik, ZLIN; 2. Alexei Yashin, Ottawa, Dynamo Moscow; 3. San Jose—Mike Rathje, Medicine Hat; 4. Quebec—Todd Warriner, Windsor; 5. New York I.—Darius Kasparaitis, Dynamo Moscow; 6. Calgary—Cory Stillman, Windsor; 7. Philadelphia—Ryan Sittler, Nichols; 8. Toronto—Brandon Covery; 9. Hartford—Robert Petrovicky, Dukla Trencin; 10. San Jose—Andrei Nazarov, Dynamo Moscow; 11. Buffalo—David Cooper, Medicine Hat; 12. Chicago—Sergei Krivokrasov, CSKA; 13. Edmonton—Joe Hulbig, St. Sebastian's; 14. Washington—Sergei Gonchar, Chelybinsk; 15. Philadelphia—Jason Bowen, Tri—City; 16. Boston—Dmitri Kvartalnov, San Diego; 17. Winnipeg—Sergei Bautin, Dynamo Moscow; 18. New Jersey—Jason Smith, Regina; 19. Pittsburgh—Martin Straka, Plzen; 20. Montreal—David Wilkie, Kamloops; 21. Vancouver—Libor Polasek, Vitkovice; 22. Detroit—Curtis Bowen, Ottawa; 23. Toronto—Grant Marshall, Ottawa; 24. New York R.—Peter Ferraro, Waterloo Jr. A.

Second Round

25. Ottawa—Chad Penney, North Bay; 26. Tampa Bay—Drew Bannister, Sault Ste. Marie; 27. Winnipeg—Boris Mironev, CSKA; 28. Quebec—Paul Brousseau, Hull; 29. Quebec—Tuomas Gronman, Tacoma; 30. Calgary—Chris O'Sullivan, Catholic Memorial; 31. Philadelphia—Denis Metlyuk, Lada Togliatti; 32. Washington—Jim Carey, Catholic Memorial; 33. Montreal—Valeri Buri, Spokane; 34. Minnesota—Jarkko Varvio, HPK; 35. Buffalo—Josef Cierny, Zvolen; 36. Chicago—Jeff Shantz, Regina; 37.an Edmonton—Martin Reichel, Freiburg; 38. St. Louis—Igor Korolev, Dynamo Moscow; 39. Los Angeles—Justin Hocking, Spokane; 40. Vancouver—Mike Peca, Ottawa; 41. Chicago—Sergei Klimovich, Dynamo Moscow; 42. New Jersey, Sergei Brylin, CSKA; 43. Pittsburgh—Marc Hussey, Moose Jaw; 44.

Montreal—Keli Corpse, Kingston; 45. Vancouver—Mike Fountain, Oshawa; 46. Detroit—Darren McCarty, Belleville; 47. Hartford—Andrei Nikolishin, Dynamo Moscow; 48. New York R.—Mattias Norstrom, AIK.

1993

First Round

1. Ottawa—Alexandre Daigle, Victoriaville; 2. Hartford—Chris Pronger, Peterborough; 3. Tampa Bay—Chris Gratton, Kingston; 4. Anaheim—Paul Kariya, U. Of Maine; 5. Florida—Rob Neidermayer, Medicine Hat; 6. San Jose—Viktor Kozlov, Dynamo Moscow; 7. Edmonton—Jason Arnott, Oshawa; 8. New York R.—Niklas Sundstrom, MoDo; 9. Dallas—Todd Harvey, Detroit; 10. Quebec—Jocelyn Thibault, Sherbrooke; 11. Washington—Brendan Witt, Seattle; 12. Toronto—Kenny Jonsson, Rogle Angelholm; 13. New Jersey—Denis Pederson, Prince Albert; 14. Quebec—Adam Deadmarsh, Portland; 15. Winnipeg—Mats Lindgren, Skelleftea; 16. Edmonton—Nick Stajduhar, London; 17. Washington—Jason Allison, London; 18. Calgary—Jesper Mattsson, Malmo; 19. Toronto—Landon Wilson, Dubuque; 20. Vancouver—Mike Wilson, Sudbury; 21. Montreal—Saku Koivu, TPS Turku; 22. Detroit—Anders Eriksson, MoDo; 23. New York I.—Todd Bertuzzi, Guelph; 24. Chicago—Eric Lecompte, Hull; 25. Boston—Kevyn Adams, Miami (Ohio); 26. Pittsburgh—Stefan Bergqvist, Leksand.

Second Round

27. Ottawa—Radim Bicanek, Dukla Jihlava; 28. San Jose—Shean Donovan, Ottawa; 29. Tampa Bay—Tyler Moss, Kingston; 30. Anaheim—Nikolai Tsulygin, Salavat Yulalev Ufa; 31. Winnipeg—Scott Langkow, Portland; 32. New Jersey—Jay Pandolfo, Boston U.; 33. Edmonton—David Vyborny, Sparta Praha; 34. New York R.—Lee Sorochan, Lethbridge; 35. Dallas—Jamie Langenbrunner, Cloquet; 36. Philadelphia—Janne Ninimaa, Karpat Oulu; 37. St. Louis—Maxim Bets, Spokane; 38. Buffalo—Denis Tsygurov, Lada Togliatti; 39. New Jer-

sey—Brendan Morrison, Penticton; 40. New York I.—Bryan McCabe, Spokane; 41. Florida—Kevin Weekes, Owen Sound; 42. Los Angeles—Shayne Toporowski, Prince Albert; 43. Winnipeg—Alexei Budayev, Kristall Elektrostal; 44. Calgary—Jamie Allison, Detroit; 45. San Jose—Vlastimil Kroupa, Chemopetrol Litvinov; 46. Vancouver—Rick Girard, Swift Current; 47. Montreal—Rory Fitzpatrick, Sudbury; 48. Detroit—Jonathan Coleman, Andover Academy; 49. Quebec—Ashley Buckberger, Swift Current; 50. Chicago—Eric Manlow, Kitchener; 51. Boston—Matt Alvey, Springfield; 52. Pittsburgh—Domenic Pittis, Lethbridge.

1994

First Round

1. Florida—Ed Jovanovski, Windsor; 2. Anaheim—Oleg Tverdovsky, Soviet Wings; 3. Ottawa—Radek Bonk, Las Vegas; 4. Edmonton—Jason Bonsignore, Niagara Falls; 5. Hartford—Jeff O'Neill, Guelph; 6. Edmonton—Ryan Smyth, Moose Jaw; 7. Los Angeles—Jamie Storr, Owen Sound; 8. Tampa Bay—Jason Wiemer, Portland; 9. New York I.—Brett Lindros, Kingston; 10. Washington—Nolan Baumgartner, Kamloops; 11. San Jose—Jeff Friesen, Regina; 12. Quebec—Wade Belak, Saskatoon; 13. Vancouver—Mattias Ohlund, Pitea; 14. Chicago—Ethan Moreau, Niagara Falls; 15. Washington—Alexander Kharlamov, CSKA Moscow; 16. Toronto—Eric Fichaud, Chicoutimi; 17. Buffalo—Wayne Primeau, Owen Sound; 18. Montreal—Brad Brown, North Bay; 19. Calgary—Chris Dingman, Brandon; 20. Dallas—Jason Boptteril, Michigan; 21. Boston—Evgeni Ryabchikov, Molot Perm; 22. Quebec—Jeffrey Kealty, Catholic Memorial; 23. Detroit—Yan Golubovsky, CSKA Moscow; 24. Pittsburgh—Chris Wells, Seattle; 25. New Jersey—Vadim Sharifijanov, Salavat Yulayev Ufa; 26. New York R.—Dan Cloutier, Sault Ste. Marie.

Second Round

27. Florida—Rhett Warrener, Saskatoon; 28. Anaheim—Johan Davidsson, HV 71; 29. Ottawa—Stanislav Neckar, Ceske Budejovice; 30. Winnipeg—Deron Quint, Seattle; 31. Florida—Jason Podollan, Spokane; 32. Edmonton—Mike Watt, Stratford; 33. Los Angeles—Matt Johnson, Peterborough; 34. Tampa Bay—Colin Cloutier, Brandon; 35. Quebec—Josef Marha, Dukla Jihlava; 36. Florida—Ryan Johnson, Thunder Bay; 37. San Jose—Angel Nikolov, Litvinov; 38. New York I.—Jason Holland, Kamloops; 39. Vancouver—Robb Gordon, Powell River; 40. Chicago—Jean—Yves Leroux, Beauport; 41. Washington—Scott Cherrey, North Bay; 42. Vancouver—Dave Scatchard, Portland; 43. Buffalo—Curtis Brown, Moose Jaw; 44. Montreal—Jose Theodore, St.—Jean; 45. Calgary—Dmitri Ryabykin, Dynamo—2; 46. Dallas—Lee Jinman, North Bay; 47. Boston—Daniel Goneau, Laval; 48. Toronto—Sean Haggerty, Detroit; 49. Detroit—Mathieu Dandenault, Sherbrooke; 50. Pittsburgh—Richard Park, Belleville; 51. New Jersey—Patrik Elias, Kladno; 52. New York R.—Rudolf Vercik, Slovan Bratislava.

1995

First Round

1. Ottawa—Bryan Berard, Detroit; 2. New York I.—Wade Redden, Brandon; 3. Los Angeles—Aki—Petteri Berg, Kiekko—67 Turku; 4. Anaheim—Chad Kilger, Kingston; 5. Tampa Bay—Daymond Langkow, Tri—City; 6. Edmonton—Steve Kelly, Prince Albert; 7. Winnipeg—Shane Doan, Kamloops; 8. Montreal—Terry Ryhan, Tri—City; 9. Boston—Kyle McLaren, Tacoma; 10. Florida—Radek Dvorak, HC Ceske Budejovice; 11. Dallas—Jarome Iginla, Kamloops; 12. San Jose—Teemu Rihijarvi, Kiekko—Espoo; 13. Hartford—Jean—Sebastien Giguere, Halifax; 14. Buffalo—Martin Biron, Beauport; 17. Washington—Brad Church, Prince Albert; 18. New Jersey—Petr Sykora, Detroit; 19. Chicago—Dmitri Nabokov, Soviet Wings; 20. Calgary—Denis Gauthier, Drummondville; 21. Boston—Sean Brown, Belleville; 22. Philadelphia—Brian Boucher, Tri—City; 23. Washington—Miikka Elomo, Kiekko—67 Turku; 24. Alexei Morozov, Soviet Wings; 25. Colorado—

Marc Denis, Chicoutimi; 26, Detroit—Maxim Kuznetsov, Dynamo Moscow.

Second Round

27. Ottawa—Marc Moro, Kingston; 28. New York I.—Jan Hlavac, Sparta Praha; 29. Anaheim—Brian Wesenberg, Guelph; 30. Tampa Bay—Mike McBain, Red Deer; 31. Edmonton—Georges Laraque, St.—Jean; 32. Winnipeg—Marc Chouinard, Beauport; 33. Los Angeles—Donald MacLean, Beauport; 34. Winnipeg—Jason Doig, Laval; 35. Hartford—Sergei Fedotov, Dynamo Moscow; 36. Florida—Aaron MacDonald, Swift Current; 37. Dallas—Patrick Cote, Beauport; 38. San Jose—Peter Roed, White Bear Lake; 39. New York R.—Christian Dube, Sherbrooke; 40. Vancouver—Chris McAllister, Saskatoon; 41. New York I.—Denis Smith, Windsor; 42. Buffalo—Mark Dutiaume, Brandon; 43. Washington—Dwayne Hay, Guelph; 44. New Jersey—Nathan Perrott, Oshawa; 45. Chicago—Christian Laflamme, Beauport; 46. Calgary—Pavel Smirnov, Molot Perm; 47. Boston—Paxton Schafer, Medicine Hat; 48. Philadelphia—Shane Kenny, Owen Sound; 49. St. Louis—Jochen Hecht, Mannheim; 50. Los Angeles—Pavel Rosa, Chemopetrol Litninov; 51. Colorado—Nic Beaudoin, Detroit; 52. Detroit—Philippe Audet, Granby.

1996

First Round

1. Ottawa—Chris Phillips, Prince Albert; 2. San Jose—Andrei Syuzin, Salavat Yulayev UFA; 3. New York I.—Juan—Pierre Dumont, Val d'Or; 4. Washington—Alexander Volchkov, Barrie; 5. Dallas—Richard Jackman, Sault Ste. Marie; 6. Edmonton—Boyd Devereaux, Kitchener; 7. Buffalo—Erik Rasmussen, U. of Minnesota; 8. Boston—Jonathan Aitken, Medicine Hat; 9. Anaheim—Ruslan Salei, Las Vegas; 10. New Jersey—Lance Ward, Red Deer; 11. Phoenix—Dan Focht, Tri—City; 12. Vancouver—Josh Holden, Regina; 13. Calgary—Derek Morris, Regina; 14. St. Louis—Marty Reasoner, Boston College; 15. Philadelphia—Danius Zubrus, Pembroke; 16. Tampa Bay—Mario Larocque, Hull; 17. Washington—Jaroslav Svejkovsky, Tri—City; 18. Montre-al—Matt Higgins, Moose Jaw; 19. Edmonton—Matthieu Descoteau, Shawingan; 20. Florida—Marcus Nilson, Djurgarden Stockholm; 21. San Jose—Marco Sturm, Landshut; 22. New York R.—Jeff Brown, Sarnia; 23. Pittsburgh—Craig Hillier, Ottawa; 24. Phoenix—Daniel Briere, Drummondville; 25. Colorado—Peter Ratchuk, Shattuck St. Mary's; 26. Detroit—Jesse Wallin, Red Deer.

Second Round

27. Buffalo—Cory Sarich, Saskatoon; 28. Pittsburgh—Pavel Skrbek, HC Kladno; 29. New York I.—Dan Lacouture, Jr. Whalers; 30. Los Angeles—Josh Green, Medicine Hat; 31. Chicago—Remi Royer, St. Hyacinthe; 32. Edmonton—Chris Hajt, Guelph; 33. Buffalo—Darren Van Oene, Brandon; 34. Hartford—Trevor Wasyluk, Medicine Hat; 35. Anaheim—Matt Cullen, St. Cloud State; 36. Toronto—Marek Posmyk, Dukla Jihlava; 37. Los Angeles—Marian Cisar, Slovan Bratislava; 38. New Jersey—Wesley Mason, Sarnia; 39. Calgary— Travis Bigley, Lethbridge; 40. Calgary—Steve Begin, Val d'Or; 41. New Jersey—Joshua DeWolf, Twin Cities; 42. Chicago—Jeff Paul, Niagra Falls; 43. Washington—Jan Bulis, Barrie; 44. Montreal—Mathieu Garon, Victoriaville; 45. Boston—Henry Kuster, Medicine Hat; 46. Chicago—Geoff Peters, Niagara Falls; 47. New Jersey—Pierre Dagenais, Moncton; 48. New York R.—Daniel Goneau, Granby; 49. New Jersey—Colin White, Hull; 50. Toronto—Francis Larivee, Laval; 51. Colorado—Yuri Babenko, Krylja Sovetov; 52. Detroit—Aren Miller, Spokane.

1997

First Round

1. Boston—Joe Thornton, Sault Ste. Marie; 2. San Jose—Patrick Marleau, Seattle; 3. Los Angeles—Olli Jokinen, IFK Helsinki (Finland); 4. New York I.—Roberto Luongo, Val d'Or; 5. New York I.—Eric Brewer, Prince George; 6. Calgary—Daniel Tkaczuk, Barrie; 7. Tampa Bay—Paul Mara, Sudbury; 8. Boston—Sergei Samsanov, Detroit; 9. Washington—Nicholas Boynton, Ottawa; 10. Vancouver—Brad Ference, Spokane; 11. Montreal—Jason Ward, Erie; 12. Ottawa—Mari-

an Hossa, Dukla Trencin; 13. Chicago—Daniel Cleary, Belleville; 14. Edmonton—Michel Riesen, HC Biel (Switz.); 15. Los Angeles—Matt Zultek, Ottawa; 16. Chicago—Ty Jones, Spokane; 17. Pittsburgh—Robert Dome, Las Vegas; 18. Anaheim—Mikael Holmqvist, Djurgarden (Sweden); 19. New York R.—Stefan Cherneski, Brandon; 20. Florida—Mike Brown, Red Deer; 21. Buffalo—Mike Noronen, Tappara (Finland); 22. Carolina—Nikos Tselios, Belleville; 23. San Jose—Scott Hannan, Kelowna; 24. New Jersey—Jean—Francois Damphousse, Moncton; 25. Dallas—Brenden Morrow, Portland; 26. Colorado—Kevin Grimes, Kingston.

Second Round

27. Boston—Ben Clymer, U. of Minnesota; 28. Carolina—Brad DeFauw, North Dakota; 29. Los Angeles—Scott Barney, Peterborough; 30. Philadelphia—Jean—Marc Pelletier, Cornell; 31. New York I.—Jeff Zehr, Windsor; 32. Calgary—Evan Lindsay, Prince Albert; 33. Tampa Bay—Kyle Kos, Red Deer; 34. Vancouver—Ryan Bonni, Saskatoon; 35. Washington—J. F. Fortin, Sherbrooke; 36. Vancouver—Harold Druken, Detroit; 37. Montreal—Gregor Baumgartner, Laval; 38. New Jersey—Stanislav Grow, Slovan Bratislava; 39. Chicago—Jeremy Reich, Seattle; 40. St. Louis—Tyler Rennette, North Bay; 41. Edmonton—Patrick Dovigi, Erie; 42. Calgary—John Tripp, Oshawa; 43. Phoenix—Juha Gustafsson, Espoo (Sweden); 44. Pittsburgh—Brian Gaffaney, North Iowa; 45. Anaheim—Maxim Balmochnykh, Lada Togliatti; 46. New York R.—Wes Jarvis, Kitchener; 47. Florida—Kristian Huselius, Farjestad Karlstad; 48. Buffalo—Henrik Tallinder, AIK (Sweden); 49. Detroit—Yuri Butsayev, Lada Togliatti; 50. Philadelphia—Pat Kavanagh, Peterborough; 51. Calgary—Dimitri Kokorev, Dynamo Jr.; 52. Dallas—Roman Lyashenko, Yaroslavl; 53. Colorado—Graham Belak, Edmonton.

1998

First Round

1. Tampa Bay—Vincent Lecavalier, Romouski; 2. Nashville—David Legwand, Plymouth; 3. San Jose—Brad Stewart, Regina; 4. Vancouver—Bryan Allen, Oshawa; 5. Anaheim—Vitaly Vishnevsky, Yaroslav; 6. Calgary—Rico Fata, London; 7. N.Y. Rangers—Manny Malhotra, Guelph; 8. Chicago—Mark Bell, Ottawa; 9. N.Y. Islanders—Michael Rupp, Erie; 10. Toronto—Nikolai Antropov, UST—Kamenog; 11. Carolina—Jeff Heerema, Sarnia; 12. Colorado—Alex Tanguay, Halifax; 13. Edmonton—Michael Henrich, Barrie; 14. Phoenix—Patrick DesRochers, Sarnia; 15. Ottawa—Mathieu Chouinard, Shawnigan; 16. Montreal—Eric Chouinard, Quebec; 17. Colorado—Martin Skoula, Barrie; 18. Buffalo—Domitri Kalinin, Chelyabinsk; 19. Colorado—Robyn Regehr, Kamloops; 20. Colorado—Scott Parker, Kelowna; 21. Los Angeles—Mathieu Biron, Shawinigan; 22. Philadelphia—Simon Gagne; 23. Pittsburgh—Milan Craft, Pizen (Cze); 24. St. Louis—Christian Backman, Frolunda Swe); 25. Detroit—Jim Fischer, Hull; 26. New Jersey—Mike Van Ryn, U. of Michigan; 27. New Jersey—Scott Gomez, Tri City.

Second Round

28. Colorado—Ramzi Abid, Chicoutimi; 29. San Jose—Jonathon Cheecho, Belleville; 30. San Jose—Kyle Rossiter, Spokane; 31. Vancouver—Artem Chubarov, Dynamo (Russian); 32. Anaheim—Stephen Peat, Red Deer; 33. Calgary—Blair Betts, Prince George; 34. Buffalo—Andrew Peters, Oshawa; 35. Toronto—Petr Svoboda, Havi (Czech); 36. N.Y. Islanders—Chris Nielsen, Calgary; 37. New Jersey—Christian Berglund, Forlestad (Sweden); 38. Colorado—Philippe Sauve, Rimouski; 39. Dallas—John Erskine, London; 40. N.Y. Rangers—Randy Copley, Cape Breton; 41. St. Louis—Maxim Linnik, St. Thomas; 42. Philadelphia—Jason Beckett, Seattle; 43. Phoenix—Ossi Vaananen, Jokerit (Finland); 44. Ottawa—Mike Fisher, Sudbury; 45, Montreal—Mike Ribeiro, Rouyn—Norando; 46. Los Angeles—Justin Papineau, Belleville; 47. Buffalo—Norman Milley; 48. Boston—Jonathan Girard, Laval; 49. Washington—Jomar Cruz, Brandon; 50. Buffalo—Jaroslav Kristek, Zlin

(Czech.); 51. Philadelphia—Ian Forbes, Guelph; 52. Boston—Bobby Allen, Boston College; 53. Colorado—Steve Moore, Harvard; 54. Pittsburgh—Alexander Zevakhin, CSKA Russia; 55. Detroit—Ryan Barnes, Sudbury; 56. Detroit—Tomek Valtonen, Ilves (Finland); 57. Dallas—Tyler Bouck, Prince George. 58. Ottawa—Chris Bala, Harvard.

Third Round

59. Washington—Todd Hornung, Portland; 60. Nashville—Denis Arhipov, Russia; 61. Florida—Joe DiPenta, Boston University; 62. Calgary—Paul Manning, Colorado College; 63. Florida—Lance Ward, Red Deer; 64. Tampa Bay—Brad Richards, Rimouski; 65. San Jose—Eric LaPlante, Halifax; 66. N.Y. Rangers—Jason Labarbera, Portland; 67. Edmonton—Alex Henry, London; 68. Vancouver—Jarkko Ruutu, HIFK (Helsinki); 69. Toronto—Jamie Hodson, Brandon. 70. Carolina—Kevin Holdridge, Plymouth; 71. Carolina—Erik Cole, Clarkson College; 72. Tampa Bay—Dimitry Afanasenkov, Yarasloval (Russia); 73. Phoenix—Pat O'Leary, Armstrong H.S. (Minn.); 74. Ottawa—Julian Vauclair, Lugano (Switzerland); 75. Montreal—Francois Bauchemin, Laval; 76. Los Angeles—Alexey Volkov, Krylia (Russia); 77. Mike Pandolfo, St. Sebastian's H.S. (Massachusetts). 78. Boston, Peter Nordstrom, Farjestad (Sweden); 79. Colorado—Evgeny Lazarev, Ukraine; 80. Pittsburgh—David Cameron, Prince Albert; 81. Vancouver—Justin Morrison, Colorado College; 82. New Jersey—Brian Gionta, Boston College; 83. St. Louis—Matt Walker, Portland; 84. Detroit—Jake McCracken, Sault St. Marie; 85. Nashville—Geoff Koch, U. of Michigan; 86. Dallas—Gabriel Karlsson, Sweden.

1999

First Round

1. Atlanta—Patrik Stefan, Long Beach; 2. Vancouver—Daniel Sedin, MoDo; 3. Vancouver—Henrik Sedin, MoDo; 4. N.Y. Rangers—Pavel Brendl, Calgary; 5. N.Y. Islanders—Tim Connolly, Erie; 6. Nashville—Brian Finley, Bar-

rie; 7. Washington—Kris Beech, Calgary; 8. N.Y. Islanders—Taylor Pyatt, Sudbury; 9. N.Y. Rangers—Jamie Lundmark, Moose Jaw; 10. N.Y. Islanders—Branislav Mezei, Belleville; 11. Calgary—Oleg Saprykin, Seattle; 12. Florida—Denis Shvidki, Barrie; 13. Edmonton—Jani Rita, Jokerit; 14. San Jose—Jeff Jillson, Michigan; 15. Phoenix—Scott Kelman, Seattle; 16. Carolina—David Tanabe, Wisconsin; 17. St. Louis—Barret Jackman, Regina; 18. Pittsburgh—Konstantin Kaltsov, Cherepovec; 19. Phoenix—Kiril Safranov, SKA; 20. Buffalo—Barrett Heisten, Maine; 21. Boston—Nick Boynton, Ottawa; 22. Philadelphia—Maxime Ouellett, Quebec; 23. Chicago—Steve McCarthy, Kootenay; 24. Toronto—Luca Cereda, Ambri; 25. Colorado—Mikhail Kuleshov, Cherepovec; 26. Ottawa—Martin Havlat, Trinec; 27. New Jersey—Ari Ahonen, JYP; 28. N.Y. Islanders—Kristian Kudroc, Michalovce.

Second Round

29. Washington—Michal Sivek, Czech Senior League; 30. Atlanta—Luke Sellars, Ottawa; 31. Washington—Charlie Stephens, Guelph; 32. Dallas—Michael Ryan, Boston College H.S.; 33. Nashville—Jonas Andersson, Sweden Juniors; 34. Washington—Ross Lupaschuk, Prince Albert; 35. Buffalo—Milan Bartovic, Slovakia; 36. Edmonton—Alexei Semenov, Sudbury; 37. Washington—Nolan Yonkman, Kelowna; 38. Calgary—Dan Cavanaugh, Boston University; 39. Montreal—Alexander Buturlin, Russian Seniors; 40. Florida—Alexander Auld, North Bay; 41. Edmonton—Tony Salmelainen, Finland Juniors; 42. New Jersey—Mike Commodore, North Dakota; 43. Los Angeles—Andrei Shefer, Russia; 44. Anaheim—Jordan Leopold, Minnesota; 45. Colorado—Martin Grenier, Quebec; 46. Chicago—Dimitri Levinski, Russia; 47. Tampa Bay—Sheldon Keefe, Barrie; 48. Ottawa—Simon Lajeunesse, Moncton; 49. Carolina—Brett Lysak, Regina; 50. New Jersey—Brent Clouthier, Kingston; 51. Pittsburgh—Matt Murley, RPI; 52. Nashville—Adam Hall, Michigan State; 53. Phoenix—Brad Ralph, Oshawa; 54. Nashville—Andrew Hutchinson, Michigan State; 55. Buffa-

lo—Doug Janik, Maine; 56. Boston—Matt Zultec, Ottawa; 57. Pittsburgh—Jeremy Van Hoof, Ottawa; 58. Montreal—Matt Carkner, Peterborough; 59. N.Y. Rangers—David Inman, Notre Dame; 60. Toronto—Peter Reynolds, London; 61. Nashville—Ed Hill, Barrie; 62. Ottawa—Teemu Sainomaa, Jakarit; 63. Chicago—Stepan Mokhov, Russia; 64. Buffalo—Michael Zigomanis, Kingston; 65. Nashville—Jan Lasak, Slovakia; 66. Dallas—Dan Jancevski, London.

Third Round

67. Tampa Bay—Evgeny Konstantinov, Ak Bars; 68. Atlanta—Zdenek Blatny, Seattle; 69. Vancouver—Rene Vydareny, Slovakia; 70. Florida—Niklas Hagman, Finland; 71. Phoenix—Jason Jaspers, Sudbury; 72. Nashville—Brett Angel, North Bay; 73. Buffalo—Tim Preston, Seattle; 74. Los Angeles—Jason Crain, Ohio State; 75. Tampa Bay—Brett Scheffelmaier, Medicine Hat; 76. Los Angeles—Frantisek Kaberle, Sweden; 77. Calgary—Craig Anderson, Guelph; 78. N.Y. Islanders—Mattias Weinhandl, Sweden; 79. N.Y. Rangers—Johan Asplund, Sweden; 80. Florida—Jean-Francois Laniel, Shawnigan; 81. Edmonton—Adam Hauser, Minnesota; 82. San Jose—Mark Concannon, Winchendon H.S.; 83. Anaheim—Niklas Havelid, Malma; 84. Carolina—Brad Fast, Prince George; 85. St. Louis—Peter Smrek, Des Moines; 86. Pittsburgh—Sebastien Caron, Rimouski; 87. N.Y. Islanders—Brian Collins, St. John's H.S.; 88. Tampa Bay—Jimmie Olvestad, Sweden; 89. Boston—Kyle Wanvig, Kootenay; 90. N.Y. Rangers—Patrick Aufiero, Boston University; 91. Edmonton—Mike Comrie, Michigan; 92. Los Angeles—Cory Campbell, Belleville; 93. Nashville—Branko Radivojevic, Belleville; 94. Ottawa—Chris Kelly, London; 95. New Jersey—Andre Lakos, Barrie; 96. Dallas—Mathias Tjarnqvist, Sweden.

16

WORLD
HOCKEY ASSOCIATION

The World Hockey Association was an enigma. Loved by some but hated by others, the WHA led a turbulent seven years (1972–79) of existence that rocked hockey institutions.

Many would say the WHA was nothing more than a carpet-bagging league, constantly on the prowl for gullible owners in new cities populated by naive fans.

But others would argue long into the night, extolling the merits of the league, not the least of which was bargaining power for players and the emergence of major-league hockey in areas that would have been forever overlooked by the National Hockey League.

At one time or another, the league embraced 32 teams in 24 cities, 20 of which were eventually abandoned.

Reliable estimates say the owners of those 32 teams lost $50 million while the 803 players who performed in the WHA earned $120 million. The agents—virtually unheard of until the new league came along—collected 10 percent of their bounty.

Almost every player in professional hockey benefited in some way from the WHA. Owners of NHL teams scrambled to keep their organizations intact, even if it meant doubling or tripling the salaries of minor leaguers.

Born of enterprising Californians, buoyed by the creation of the American Basketball Association, their original brainchild, the WHA was founded by Gary Davidson and Dennis Murphy.

Not steeped in hockey, both would be gone before the league would reach its third anniversary.

Two players, each a legend in his time, made the WHA go. Bobby Hull, a personable, 33-year-old superstar with the Chicago Blackhawks, left the NHL and its followers aghast when he signed a $2.75-million contract to coach and play for the Winnipeg Jets.

Possessed of a pioneer spirit and the notion that he was improving the lot of all players, Hull joined the league on June 27, 1972. Enticing him, too, was $1 million up front.

Other established players followed him to the new league. Among them were Gerry Cheevers, Dave Keon, Johnny McKenzie, Frank Mahovlich and J. C. Tremblay.

But no signing had the impact Gordie Howe's did. In a historic event, the 46-year-old NHL immortal and his teenage sons, Mark and Marty, joined the Houston Aeros in June 1973.

It was more than a publicity stunt. Not only did he play 419 games, collecting 508 points, but he was a two-time All-Star on right wing and won MVP honors once.

Fittingly, the league championship trophy was sponsored by a finance company, Avco.

The Avco Cup was won by Winnipeg on three occasions as the Jets blended Europeans and Canadians into a championship team. Perhaps the finest line in professional hockey at the time was the combination of Hull and two young Swedes, Ulf Nilsson and Anders Hedberg.

Houston, led by the Howes, won the Avco Cup twice while the Quebec Nordiques and New England Whalers were champions once.

Although the league died in June 1979, it left a legacy. Four of its original teams—the Edmonton Oilers, Hartford (New England) Whalers, Quebec Nordiques and Winnipeg Jets—were admitted to the NHL. They had proven themselves.

1972-73

The WHA thought big. Twelve teams drafted 1,081 persons, not all of them players. One would-be general manager, Scotty Munro of the Calgary Broncos, picked Soviet Premier Alexei Kosygin.

Unable to post $100,000 performance bonds, two franchises—Miami and Calgary—pulled out before the season began. Cleveland and Chicago took their places.

The first player signed was left winger Steve Sutherland, swiped off the Port Huron Wings International League roster by the Los Angeles Sharks.

By August, most than 300 players were under contract. Among them was a center, Derek Sanderson, who signed a 10-year pact with the Philadelphia Blazers for a reported $2.325 million. He played only eight games and was bought out for $1 million.

An Alberta right winger, Ron Anderson, scored the WHA's first goal on October 11 in Ottawa. The Oilers won, 7-4.

The New England Whalers did the best job of recruiting and reaped their just reward—winning the first WHA championship.

Based in Boston, where they divided their time between the Arena and the Garden, the Whalers were led by a stout defense manned by such stalwarts as Rick Ley and Brad Selwood, plucked off the roster of the Toronto Maple Leafs, Jim Dorey, from the New York Rangers, and Ted Green, the former Bruin who would show he could bounce back from a serious head injury. Their coach was Jack Kelley, a respected tactician from Boston University.

New England (46-30-2) won the Eastern Division while the Western was won by Winnipeg (43-31-4). They met in a best-of-seven league final, with the Whalers winning in five games.

Center Andre Lacroix of Philadelphia won the first scoring championship with 50 goals and 74 assists.

1972–73
FINAL STANDINGS

Eastern Division

	W	L	T	PTS	GF	GA
New England	46	30	2	94	318	263
Cleveland	43	32	3	89	287	239
Philadelphia	38	40	0	76	288	305
Ottawa	35	39	4	74	279	301
Quebec	33	40	5	71	276	313
New York	33	43	2	68	303	334

Western Division

	W	L	T	PTS	GF	GA
Winnipeg	43	31	4	90	285	249
Houston	39	35	4	82	284	269
Los Angeles	37	35	6	80	259	250
Alberta	38	37	3	79	269	256
Minnesota	38	37	3	79	250	269
Chicago	26	50	2	54	245	295

LEADING SCORERS

	G	A	PTS
Lacroix, Philadelphia	50	74	124
Ward, New York	51	67	118
Lawson, Philadelphia	61	45	106
Webster, New England	53	50	103
Hull, Winnipeg	51	52	103
Beaudin, Winnipeg	38	65	103
Bordeleau, Winnipeg	47	54	101
Caffery, New England	39	61	100
Labossiere, Houston	36	60	93
Carleton, Ottawa	42	49	91

LEADING GOALIES

	G	GA	SO	GAA
Cheevers, Cleveland	52	149	5	2.83
Gillow, Los Angeles	38	96	2	2.88
Rutledge, Houston	37	110	0	2.96
Norris, Alberta	64	189	1	3.06
Curran, Minnesota	44	131	4	3.09
Smith, New England	51	162	3	3.17

Derek Sanderson played only eight games in the WHA (with the Philadelphia Blazers) before bolting back to Boston and the NHL in 1972–73.

1973-74

The Houston Aeros were older than most teams. Many of their players had been stars in the old Western Hockey League.

However, their coach, Bill Dineen, had his eye on two youngsters. Mark and Marty Howe were showing signs of becoming excellent hockey players with a junior team, the Toronto Marlies.

Bill Dineen knew he couldn't sign any Canadian youngsters before their 19th birthday. But the Howe boys were Americans.

Not one to take advantage of his friend, Dineen thought he should call Gordie to seek his permission. Howe, idle and disgruntled in his self-described role as vice-president in charge of paper clips for the Detroit Red Wings, asked Dineen if he would like to make it a threesome— Gordie to return to active play, joined by his sons.

The caper was pulled off and the Aeros finished in first place (48-25-5) in the Western Division, then roared through the playoffs, sweeping the Chicago Cougars in four straight games for the championship.

It was a season in which the Ottawa Nationals became the Toronto Toros, Philadelphia moved to Vancouver and the New York Raiders became the Golden Blades and then the Jersey Knights when bill collectors chased them out of New York to Cherry Hill, New Jersey, a suburb of Philadelphia.

The Howe family—father Gordie and sons Marty (center) and Mark—take the ice for their first WHA game together on September 25, 1973.

Mike (Shakey) Walton of the Minnesota Fighting Saints won the league scoring championship with 57 goals and 60 assists. But the league's Most Valuable Player was none other than Gordie Howe, a 47-year-old phenomenon.

1973–74

FINAL STANDINGS

Eastern Division

	W	L	T	PTS	GF	GA
New England	43	31	4	90	291	260
Toronto	41	33	4	86	304	272
Cleveland	37	32	9	83	266	264
Chicago	38	35	5	81	271	273
Quebec	38	36	4	80	306	280
New Jersey	32	42	4	68	268	313

Western Division

	W	L	T	PTS	GF	GA
Houston	48	25	5	101	318	219
Minnesota	44	32	2	90	332	275
Edmonton	38	37	3	79	268	269
Winnipeg	34	39	5	73	264	296
Vancouver	27	50	1	55	278	345
Los Angeles	25	53	0	50	239	339

LEADING SCORERS

	G	A	PTS
Walton, Minnesota	57	60	117
Lacroix, New Jersey	31	80	111
G. Howe, Houston	31	69	100
Hull, Winnipeg	53	42	95
Connelly, Minnesota	42	53	95
Carleton, Toronto	37	55	92
Lawson, Vancouver	50	38	88
Campbell, Vancouver	27	61	88
Bernier, Quebec	37	49	86
Lund, Houston	33	53	86

LEADING GOALIES

	G	GA	SO	GAA
McLeod, Houston	49	127	3	2.56
Cheevers, Cleveland	59	180	4	3.03
Smith, New England	55	164	2	3.08
Newton, Chicago	45	143	1	3.14
Curran, Minnesota	40	130	2	3.27
Wakely, Winnipeg	37	123	3	3.27

1974–75

Interest in the WHA was at an all-time high. An All-Star team represented Canada in an eight-game series with the Soviet National team. Although it was able to win only one game, the WHA did receive considerable publicity for itself and its players.

The Indianapolis Racers and Phoenix Roadrunners were accepted as expansion franchises. The New Jersey Knights finally found a home,

moving to San Diego, where they became the Mariners, and the New England Whalers, lured by a new convention center, left Boston for Hartford, Conn.

The Los Angeles Sharks were on the move, too. They headed for Detroit and became the Michigan Stags, then the Baltimore Blades. Slowly, they were going down the tubes.

The 14-team league was divided into three divisions—the Canadian, Western and Eastern. The head office was moved from Newport Beach, Cal., to Toronto. And the league bank was located in Winnipeg, where Ben Hatskin sat as chairman of the Board.

League attendance jumped from 2.7 million to 4.1 with the Howes and Houston leading the way.

Bobby Hull was creating a stir, too, frolicking beside his new Swedish linemates, Anders Hedberg and Ulf Nilsson, in Winnipeg.

Hull scored 77 goals in 78 games. But the scoring championship went to Andre Lacroix of San Diego with 41 goals and 106 assists on a line with Wayne Rivers and Rick Sentes. Rivers had 54 goals.

Sparked by Ron Grahame's three shutouts and Mark Howe's 22 points, Houston breezed through the playoffs, suffering only one loss. The Quebec Nordiques were no match for the Aeros in the final as Houston won in four straight games.

1974–75

FINAL STANDINGS

Canadian Division

	W	L	T	PTS	GF	GA
Quebec	46	32	0	92	331	299
Toronto	43	33	2	88	349	304
Winnipeg	38	35	5	81	322	293
Vancouver	37	39	2	76	256	270
Edmonton	36	38	4	76	279	279

Eastern Division

	W	L	T	PTS	GF	GA
New England	43	30	5	91	274	279
Cleveland	35	40	3	73	236	258
Chicago	30	47	1	61	261	312
Indianapolis	18	57	3	39	216	338

Western Division

	W	L	T	PTS	GF	GA
Houston	53	25	0	106	369	247
San Diego	43	31	4	90	326	268
Minnesota	42	33	3	87	308	279
Phoenix	39	31	8	86	300	265
Baltimore	21	53	4	46	205	341

LEADING SCORERS

	G	A	PTS
Lacroix, San Diego	41	106	147
Hull, Winnipeg	77	65	142
Bernier, Quebec	54	68	122
Nilsson, Winnipeg	26	94	120
Lund, Houston	33	75	108
Rivers, San Diego	54	53	107
Hedberg, Winnipeg	53	47	100
G. Howe, Houston	34	65	99
Dillon, Toronto	29	66	95
Walton, Minnesota	48	45	93

LEADING GOALIES

	G	GA	SO	GAA
Grahame, Houston	43	131	4	3.03
Rutledge, Houston	35	113	2	3.24
Wakely, San Diego	41	131	3	3.25
Cheevers, Cleveland	52	167	4	3.26
Norris, Phoenix	33	107	1	3.27
Garrett, Minnesota	58	180	2	3.28

1975–76

The Winnipeg Jets were a unique hockey club. They were owned by no one. More than 5,000 citizens had put up amounts ranging from $25 to $25,000 to keep the team viable. Shares were non-redeemable.

Some donors actually put their shares in the name of their pets. But the Jets weren't going to the dogs.

Their lineup included nine Europeans—two Finns and seven Swedes. They trained in Finland and Sweden and even stopped off in Prague, Czechoslovakia, for two exhibition games against the National team.

Returning the favor, the Czechs flew the Jets home to Canada free of charge.

Then, at Christmas, the Jets traveled to Moscow for the Izvestia Cup. They became a better hockey club, perfecting a whirling style of play that frustrated their opponents.

Fourteen teams started the season but only 12 finished. The Minnesota Fighting Saints and Denver Spurs went by the wayside. The Spurs, a new entry owned by Ivan Mullenix of St. Louis, lasted only 41 games, then moved to Ottawa. The Vancouver Blazers moved to Calgary, where they became the Cowboys. The Cincinnati Stingers joined up and the Chicago Cougars dropped out.

The Indianapolis Racers (35-39-6), Houston Aeros (53-27-0) and Winnipeg (52-27-2) won divisional titles, and the Jets emerged as league champions. They swept the defending champions from Houston in the Avco Cup final.

The Quebec Nordiques gained some consolation when left winger Marc Tardif won the scoring championship with 71 goals and 77 assists for 148 points, a league record.

1975–76

FINAL STANDINGS

Canadian Division

	W	L	T	PTS	GF	GA
Winnipeg	52	27	2	106	345	254
Quebec	50	27	4	104	371	316
Calgary	41	35	4	86	307	282
Edmonton	27	49	5	59	268	345
Toronto	24	52	5	53	335	398

Eastern Division

	W	L	T	PTS	GF	GA
Indianapolis	35	39	6	76	245	247
Cleveland	35	40	5	75	273	279
New England	33	40	7	73	255	290
Cincinnati	35	44	1	71	285	340

Western Division

	W	L	T	PTS	GF	GA
Houston	53	27	0	106	341	263
Phoenix	39	35	6	84	302	287
San Diego	36	38	6	78	303	290
Minnesota	30	25	4	64	211	212
Ottawa	14	26	1	29	134	172

LEADING SCORERS

	G	A	PTS
Tardif, Quebec	71	77	148
Hull, Winnipeg	53	70	123
Cloutier, Quebec	60	54	114
Nilsson, Winnipeg	38	76	114
Ftorek, Phoenix	41	72	113
Bordeleau, Quebec	37	72	109
Hedberg, Winnipeg	50	55	105
Houle, Quebec	51	52	103
Bernier, Quebec	34	68	102
G. Howe, Houston	32	70	102

LEADING GOALIES

	G	GA	SO	GAA
Dion, Indianapolis	31	85	0	2.74
Daley, Winnipeg	61	170	5	2.84
Norris, Phoenix	41	128	1	3.18
Wakely, San Diego	67	208	3	3.26
Grahame, Houston	57	182	3	3.27
Garrett, Minn.-Tor.	61	210	3	3.38

1976-77

The WHA, upon completing its fourth season, had survived longer than anyone had thought. Its teams had gradually grown stronger, and challenges were sought.

Even the warlords of the NHL had begun to mellow. Passively, they agreed to a 14-game exhibition series in September. The benefits would be twofold. The games would not only serve as preseason conditioners, but the competition between leagues would serve as a built-in rivalry.

When the series was over, the NHL teams had won 9 games, tied one and lost four.

"Game in and game out, our teams can play with their teams," insisted Howard Baldwin, the WHA president.

Political points, to be sure.

Internally, the new league continued to lose teams and gain cities. A second edition of the Minnesota Fighting Saints lasted only 42 games. The Toronto Toros moved to Birmingham, Ala., and became the Bulls.

But the big newsmakers were the Quebec Nordiques, Robbie Ftorek, the Howes and Anders Hedberg, the Swedish Express of the Winnipeg Jets.

Suffering from a case of "Bolinitis"—a malady named after the difficult Houston Aero owner, George Bolin—the Howes left Texas for New England. Ftorek, a small but dynamic center with the lowly Phoenix Roadrunners, became the first American-born athlete to win MVP honors in major professional hockey.

Hedberg, a 25-year-old right winger, broke one of hockey's most prestigious records, scoring 51 goals in 49 games, breaking the "50 in 50" mark previously set in the NHL by Maurice (The Rocket) Richard.

The Nordiques won their first Avco Cup by beating Winnipeg in a final series that went the full seven games. Veteran center Serge Bernier was a terror in the playoffs, collecting 14 goals and 22 assists in 17 games. The scoring champion was his teammate, Real (Buddy) Cloutier, with 66 goals, 75 assists for 141 points.

1976-77

FINAL STANDINGS

Eastern Division

	W	L	T	PTS	GF	GA
Quebec	47	31	3	97	353	295
Cincinnati	39	37	5	83	354	303
Indianapolis	36	37	8	80	276	305
New England	35	40	6	76	275	290
Birmingham	31	46	4	66	289	309
Minnesota	19	18	5	43	136	129

Western Division

	W	L	T	PTS	GF	GA
Houston	50	24	6	106	320	241
Winnipeg	46	32	2	94	366	291
San Diego	40	37	4	84	284	283
Edmonton	34	43	4	72	243	304
Calgary	31	43	7	69	252	296
Phoenix	28	48	4	60	281	383

LEADING SCORERS

	G	A	PTS
Cloutier, Quebec	66	75	141
Hedberg, Winnipeg	70	61	131
Nilsson, Winnipeg	39	85	124
Ftorek, Phoenix	46	71	117
Lacroix, San Diego	32	82	114
Tardif, Quebec	49	60	109
Leduc, Cincinnati	52	55	107
Bordeleau, Quebec	32	75	107
Stoughton, Cincinnati	52	52	104
Napier, Birmingham	60	36	96
Sobchuk, Cincinnati	44	52	96
Bernier, Quebec	43	53	96

LEADING GOALIES

	G	GA	SO	GAA
Grahame, Houston	39	107	4	2.74
Caron, Cincinnati	24	61	3	2.83
Wakely, San Diego	46	129	2	3.09
Raeder, New England	26	69	2	3.12
Rutledge, Houston	42	132	2	3.15
Landon, New England	23	59	1	3.17

1977-78

Howard Baldwin was in tears as he stood in the lobby of the Auberge des Gouverneurs in Quebec City the morning after the WHA's sixth All-Star Game. His bags were packed and he was on his way home to Hartford to inspect the damage. At 4 A.M., he had received a call informing him that the roof of the Hartford Civic Center had collapsed under the weight of snow.

Baldwin, the Whalers' trustee and president of the WHA, could barely speak. The hopes and dreams of his franchise hinged on the building that injected new life into downtown Hartford. However, nearby Springfield, in Massachusetts, came to the rescue by making the arena available to the Whalers.

Mike Walton soared, but the Minnesota Fighting Saints fell by the wayside in 1975–76.

It was the second piece of bad news the WHA had received. The other haymaker landed earlier in the boardrooms where men representing the Winnipeg Jets announced details of an offer two of their top players had received from the New York Rangers. Anders Hedberg and Ulf Nilsson would eventually go for $2.4 million.

Now, the National Hockey League was raiding the WHA.

Only eight teams surfaced for the sixth season. Ray Kroc (McDonald's hamburger king) decided he had wasted enough money on the San Diego Mariners. The Phoenix Roadrunners lost their backers, too, and so did the Calgary Cowboys.

The survivors were lumped into one division. As a novelty, All-Star teams from the Soviet Union and Czechoslovakia played eight-game schedules in the WHA.

Scoring champ and MVP was Marc Tardif, the Quebec left winger who shattered his own record with 65 goals and 89 assists for 154 points.

The Birmingham Bulls, coached by Glen Sonmor, were the rogues of the league. Before each game a Baptist minister would read the invocation. Then the brawling would start. After the games, Sonmor would lead the fans in song at The Bar Across The Street.

The Jets, however, were the class of the league. Reeling off 50 wins in the regular season, they gathered momentum in the playoffs to eliminate Birmingham in five and New England in four to win their second Avco Cup.

Anders Hedberg and Ulf Nilsson enabled Winnipeg to win the Avco Cup in 1978, then skated off to the NHL.

1977–78

FINAL STANDINGS

	W	L	T	PTS	GF	GA
Winnipeg	50	28	2	102	381	270
New England	44	31	5	93	335	269
Houston	42	34	4	88	296	302
Quebec	40	37	3	83	349	347
Edmonton	38	39	3	79	309	307
Birmingham	36	41	3	75	287	314
Cincinnati	35	42	3	73	298	332
Indianapolis	24	51	5	53	267	353
Soviet All-Stars	3	4	1	7	27	36
Czechoslovakia	1	6	1	3	21	40

LEADING SCORERS

	G	A	PTS
Tardif, Quebec	65	89	154
Cloutier, Quebec	56	73	129
U. Nilsson, Winnipeg	37	89	126
Hedberg, Winnipeg	63	59	122
Hull, Winnipeg	46	71	117
Lacroix, Houston	36	77	113
Ftorek, Cincinnati	59	50	109
K. Nilsson, Winnipeg	42	65	107
G. Howe, New England	34	62	96
M. Howe, New England	30	61	91

LEADING GOALIES

	G	GA	SO	GAA
Smith, New England	55	174	2	3.22
Daley, Winnipeg	37	114	1	3.30
Bromley, Winnipeg	39	124	1	3.30
Wakely, Cin.-Hou.	57	192	2	3.41
Dryden, Edmonton	48	150	2	3.49
Dion, Cincinnati	45	140	4	3.57

1978–79

No one really believed the WHA's seventh season would be its last. Hopes had been built up before. As early as April 1973, the WHA and NHL had met to discuss a possible merger.

Gradually, the number of teams was dwindling. What had once been a 14-team league was now reduced to six. The league was running out of cities. But there was a movement afoot to incorporate a division in Europe.

Wayne Gretzky made sure he'd be an Edmonton Oiler for a while when he signed a 20-year contract in 1979.

The WHA was alive and kicking as evidenced by two shrewd moves. Nelson Skalbania, the flamboyant Vancouver businessman, had robbed the cradle of Canadian hockey. Acting on behalf of his team, the Indianapolis Racers, Skalbania signed Wayne Gretzky, a 17-year-old sensation, to a personal services contract.

Indianapolis fans, who had never heard of him before, showed only a casual interest in the skinny, blond kid. With only a few season tickets sold, Skalbania started looking for a buyer. He found two prospects in Winnipeg's Michael Gobuty and Edmonton's Peter Pocklington.

Boarding a plane in Indianapolis, Gretzky didn't know where it would land. Pocklington sweetened his offer. The pilot was instructed to proceed to Edmonton. Days later, the Racers folded.

The Jets had already spent a bundle, buying 12 contracts from the folding Houston Aeros.

Real (Buddy) Cloutier of Quebec won his second scoring championship with 75 goals, 54 assists for a total of 129 points.

Edmonton, led by Gretzky's 110 points, finished on top with a 48-30-2 record. But the Oilers couldn't capture their first and the last Avco Cup.

Sparked by the Houston acquisitions, most notably Terry Ruskowski, Rich Preston and Morris Lukowich, the Jets whipped Edmonton in five games in the league final.

The last Avco Cup was theirs. And still is.

1978–79
FINAL STANDINGS

	W	L	T	PTS	GF	GA
Edmonton	48	30	2	98	340	266
Quebec	41	34	5	87	288	271
Winnipeg	39	35	6	84	307	306
New England	37	34	9	83	298	287
Cincinnati	33	41	6	72	274	284
Birmingham	32	42	6	70	286	311

LEADING SCORERS

	G	A	PTS
Cloutier, Quebec	75	54	129
Ftorek, Cincinnati	39	77	116
Gretzky, Edmonton	46	64	110
M. Howe, New England	42	65	107
K. Nilsson, Winnipeg	39	68	107
Lukowich, Winnipeg	65	34	99
Tardif, Quebec	41	55	96
Lacroix, New England	32	56	88
Sullivan, Winnipeg	46	40	86
Ruskowski, Winnipeg	20	66	86

LEADING GOALIES

	G	GA	SO	GAA
Dryden, Edmonton	63	170	3	2.89
Brodeur, Quebec	42	126	3	3.11
Corsi, Quebec	40	126	3	3.30
Smith, New England	40	132	1	3.31
Dion, Cincinnati	39	93	0	3.32
Liut, Cincinnati	54	184	3	3.47

17

WHA PLAYER REGISTER

I n its stormy seven years of existence, the World Hockey Association was home to some of the biggest names to ever play the game of hockey—Wayne Gretzky, Bobby Hull, Gordie and Mark Howe, Gerry Cheevers, and Frank Mahovlich, to name a few—but it was also home to a large group of players who found their niche in the WHA, not the NHL.

These players toiled away in the upstart league, some hoping for a shot at the NHL, others content to play in a league that put an emphasis on the players. For every Wayne Gretzky there was a John Gray, who served in the WHA for five years with Phoenix, Houston, and Winnipeg, scoring more than 30 goals four times.

The following sections (the first covering forwards and defensemen; the second, goalies) include the record of every player who played in the WHA but never played a game in the NHL. Those who did make it to the NHL are listed, with WHA statistics, in Chapter 25, the All–Time NHL Player Register.

Where information is missing, it was unavailable.

Players listed by name only, with no statistics, are listed in Chapter 25

The following are the abbreviations for the various teams, Canadian provinces and column headings.

Alb	Alberta Oilers
Balt	Baltimore Blades
Birm	Birmingham Bulls
Calg	Calgary Cowboys
Chi	Chicago Cougars
Cinn	Cincinnati Stingers
Clev	Cleveland Crusaders
Den	Denver Spurs
Edm	Edmonton Oilers
Hart	Hartford Whalers
Hous	Houston Aeros
Ind	Indianapolis Racers
LA	Los Angeles Sharks
Mich	Michigan Stags
Minn	Minnesota Fighting Saints
NE	New England Whalers
NJ	New Jersey Knights
NY	New York Golden Blades, Raiders
Ott	Ottawa Nationals
Phil	Philadelphia Blazers
Phoe	Phoenix Roadrunners
Que	Quebec Nordiques
SD	San Diego Mariners
Tor	Toronto Toros
Van	Vancouver Blazers
Winn	Winnipeg Jets

CANADIAN PROVINCES

Alta.	Alberta
B.C.	British Columbia
Man.	Manitoba
N.B.	New Brunswick
Nfld.	Newfoundland
N.S.	Nova Scotia
Ont.	Ontario
P.E.I.	Prince Edward Island
Que.	Quebec
Sask.	Saskatchewan
Yuk.	The Yukon
N.W.T.	Northwest Territories

COLUMN HEADINGS

A	Assists
AVG.	Goals against average
G	Goals
GP	Games Played
L	Losses
MIN	Minutes
PIM	Penalty Minutes
PTS	Points
SO	Shutouts
T	Ties
W	Wins

FORWARDS AND DEFENSEMEN

SEASON	TEAM	GP	G	A	PTS	PIM

ABBEY, Bruce *6–1 185 D*
B. Aug. 15, 1951

75–76	Chi	17	1	0	1	12

ABGRALL, Dennis

ABRAHAMSSON, Thommy

ADAIR, Jim *5–11 180 C*
B. Brockville, Ont., Sept. 28, 1948

73–74	Van	70	12	17	29	10

ADDUONO, Ray *5–9 175 C*
B. Fort William, Ont., Jan. 21, 1947

73–74	Clev.	2	0	0	0	0
74–75	SD	78	15	59	74	23
75–76	SD	80	23	67	90	22
76–77	Minn–SD	53	6	24	30	22
77–78	Ind	8	1	2	3	0
Totals		221	45	152	197	67

Playoffs

74–75	SD	10	5	9	14	13
75–76	SD	11	4	7	11	6
76–77	SD	7	3	2	5	19
Totals		28	12	18	30	38

ADDUONO, Rick

AHEARN, Kevin *5–10 160 LW*
B. Milton, Mass., June 20, 1948

72–73	NE	78	20	22	42	18

Playoffs

72–73	NE	14	1	2	3	9

ALEXANDER, Claire

ALLEN, Jeffrey

ALLEY, Steve

AMODEO, Michael

ANDERSON, Ron *6–0 190 D*
B. Dryden, Ont., Nov. 15, 1948

72–73	Chi	74	3	26	29	34
73–74	Chi	2	0	0	0	0
74–75	Clev	39	0	9	9	10
Totals		115	3	35	38	44

ANDERSON, Ronald

ANDRASCIK, Steve

ANDREA, Paul

ANTONOVICH, Mike

ARBOUR, Jack

ARCHAMBAULT, Michel

ARNDT, Danny *5–10 170 LW*
B. Saskatoon, Sask., Mar. 26, 1955

75–76	NE	69	8	8	16	10
76–77	NE–Edm	47	8	14	22	11
77–78	Birm	4	0	1	1	0
Totals		120	16	23	39	21

Playoffs

75–76	NE	8	0	0	0	0

ASH, Bob *5–9 170 D*
B. Broadview, Sask., Sept. 29, 1943

72–73	Winn	73	3	14	17	39
73–74	Winn	60	2	18	20	30
74–75	Ind	64	1	14	15	19
Totals		199	6	46	52	88

Playoffs

72–73	Winn	13	1	3	4	4
73–74	Winn	4	0	1	1	2
Totals		17	1	4	5	6

SEASON	TEAM	GP	G	A	PTS	PIM

ASHTON, Ron *6–2 210 LW*
B. Regina, Sask., May 11, 1954

74–75	Winn	36	1	3	4	66

ASMUNDSON, Duke *6–2 195 D*
B. Vita, Man., Aug. 17, 1943

72–73	Winn	76	2	14	16	54
73–74	Winn	72	5	14	19	85
74–75	Winn	38	4	15	19	53
75–76	Winn	72	5	11	16	19
Totals		258	16	54	70	211

Playoffs

72–73	Winn	12	1	2	3	8
73–74	Winn	4	0	1	1	2
75–76	Winn	13	3	2	5	11
Totals		29	4	5	9	21

ATKINSON, Steven

BACKSTROM, Ralph

BAILEY, Ace

BAIRD, Kenneth

BALL, Terry

BALON, Dave

BALTIMORE, Byron

BARBER, Butch *5–10 172 D*
B. Fairview, Alta., Aug. 31, 1943

72–73	Chi	75	4	19	23	39
73–74	NJ	3	0	0	0	2
Totals		78	4	19	23	41

BARLOW, Robert

BARRIE, Douglas

BATEMAN, Jamie *6–1 185 D*
B. Thetford Mines, Que., Sept. 16, 1954

74–75	SD	24	0	3	3	96
75–76	SD	17	1	0	1	4
Totals		41	1	3	4	100

BATHGATE, Andy

BAXTER, Paul

BEATON, Frank

BEAUDIN, Norman

BEAUDOIN, Serge

BEAULE, Alain *6–0 195 D*
B. St. Romain, Que., Apr. 7, 1948

73–74	Que	78	4	36	40	93
74–75	Que–Winn	76	4	21	25	43
Totals		154	8	57	65	136

BENNETT, John *6–1 175 LW*
B. Cranston, R.I., Jan. 19, 1950

72–73	Phil	34	4	6	10	18

BENNETT, Wendall *6–2 185 RW*
B. Loon Lake, Sask., Mar. 24, 1950

74–75	Phoe	36	4	15	19	92

Playoffs

74–75	Phoe	5	1	2	3	6

BENZELOCK, Jim *5–11 187 RW*
B. Winnipeg, Man., June 21, 1947

72–73	Alb–Chi	69	10	13	23	33
73–74	Chi	53	6	7	13	19
74–75	Chi	10	0	2	2	14
75–76	Que	31	2	5	7	6
Totals		166	18	27	45	72

Playoffs

73–74	Chi	18	2	2	4	36
75–76	Que	3	0	0	0	0
Totals		21	2	2	4	36

SEASON	TEAM	GP	G	A	PTS	PIM

BERGERON, Yves

BERGMAN, Thommie

BERNIER, Jean *5–10 170 D*
B. St. Hyacinthe, Que., July 21, 1954

74–75	Que	34	1	13	14	13
75–76	Que	81	4	26	30	10
76–77	Que	72	2	13	15	23
77–78	Que	74	10	32	42	4
Totals		261	17	84	101	50

Playoffs

74–75	Que	9	0	1	1	2
75–76	Que	4	0	1	1	0
76–77	Que	9	0	2	2	0
77–78	Que	10	3	4	7	2
Totals		32	3	8	11	4

BERNIER, Serge

BERRY, Douglas

BIGNELL, Larry

BILODEAU, Gilles

BILODEAU, Yvon *6–3 210 D*
B. Vimy, Alta., Jan. 18, 1951

75–76	Calg	4	0	0	0	2

BLACK, Milt *6–0 190 RW*
B. Winnipeg, Man., June 20, 1949

72–73	Winn	77	18	16	34	31
73–74	Winn	47	6	9	15	14
74–75	Winn	65	4	6	10	10
Totals		189	28	31	59	55

Playoffs

72–73	Winn	14	1	3	4	2

BLACKBURN, Don

BLAIN, Jacques *5–11 180 C*
B. Gatineau, Que., July 19, 1947

72–73	Que	69	1	10	11	78

BLANCHETTE, Bernie *6–0 165 RW*
B. N. Battleford, Sask., July 11, 1947

72–73	Alb–Chi	47	7	7	14	10

BLOCK, Kenneth

BLOOM, Michael

BODDY, Gregg

BOLAND, Michael

BOLDUC, Daniel

BOND, Kerry *6–0 190 LW*
B. Sudbury, Ont., July 18, 1945

74–75	Ind	71	22	15	37	23
75–76	Ind	15	2	0	2	9
Totals		86	24	15	39	32

Playoffs

75–76	Ind	7	1	0	1	11

BORDELEAU, Christian

BORDELEAU, Paul

BORGESON, Don *5–11 175 LW*
B. N. Battlefield, Sask., May 20, 1945

74–75	Phoe	74	29	28	57	38
75–76	Ott–NE	71	30	24	54	30
Totals		145	59	52	111	68

Playoffs

74–75	Phoe	5	0	1	1	2
75–76	NE	3	1	1	2	0
Totals		8	1	2	3	2

BOUCHA, Henry

SEASON	TEAM	GP	G	A	PTS	PIM
BOUDREAU, Michel						
72–73	Phil	33	7	7	14	4
73–74	Van	3	1	0	1	0
Totals		36	8	7	15	4

BOUDRIAS, Andre

BOWLES, Brian *5–11 185 D*
B. Drummondville, Que., Feb. 18, 1952

75–76	Clev	3	0	0	0	0

BOWMAN, Robert

BOYD, Bob *6–0 190 D*
B. Toronto, Ont., Nov. 27, 1951

73–74	Minn	41	1	14	15	14
74–75	Minn	13	0	0	0	21
Totals		54	1	14	15	35

Playoffs

73–74	Minn	7	0	0	0	4

BOYD, Jim *5–9 180 C*
B. Calgary, Alta., June 4, 1949

74–75	Phoe	76	26	44	70	18
75–76	Phoe	80	23	34	57	44
76–77	Calg	13	0	2	2	6
Totals		169	49	80	129	68

Playoffs

74–75	Phoe	5	1	1	2	2
75–76	Phoe	5	3	2	5	2
Totals		10	4	3	7	4

BOYER, Walter

BOYLAN, Dean *6–0 185 D*
B. Boston, Mass., Jan. 28, 1951

76–74	NY–NJ	61	1	5	6	112
74–75	SD	3	0	0	0	10
Totals		64	1	5	6	122

BRACKENBURY, Curt

BRADLEY, Brian *5–10 185 LW*
B. Sudbury, Ont., Dec. 14, 1944

72–73	NY	78	22	33	55	20
73–74	NY–NJ	78	15	23	38	12
74–75	SD	24	4	5	9	6
Totals		180	41	61	102	38

Playoffs

74–75	SD	6	0	1	1	2

BRAY, Duane *6–2 195 D*
B. Flin Flon, Man., Sept. 24, 1954

76–77	Phoe	46	2	6	8	62

BREDIN, Gary *6–0 185 RW*
B. Edmonton, Alta., May 25, 1948

74–75	Ind–Balt	77	18	23	41	37
75–76	Ott–SD	66	8	8	16	12
Totals		143	26	31	57	49

BREWER, Carl

BRINDLEY, Douglas

BROWN, Arnie

BROWN, Bob *6–1 195 D*
B. Toronto, Ont., Dec. 18, 1950

72–73	Phil–NY	21	0	4	4	8
73–74	NY–NJ	59	7	13	20	38
Totals		80	7	17	24	46

BRUBAKER, Jeffrey

BUCHANAN, Ronald

BUETOW, Brad *6–3 196 LW*
B. St. Paul, Minn., Oct. 28, 1950

73–74	Clev	25	0	0	0	4

SEASON	TEAM	GP	G	A	PTS	PIM
BURGESS, Don *6–0 170 LW*						
B. Fort Edward, Ont., June 8, 1946						
72–73	Phil	74	20	22	42	15
73–74	Van	78	30	36	66	8
74–75	Van	62	11	18	29	19
75–76	SD	73	14	11	25	35
76–77	SD	77	20	22	42	8
77–78	Ind	79	11	12	23	2
78–79	Ind	3	1	1	2	0
Totals		446	107	122	229	87

Playoffs

72–73	Phil	4	1	0	1	0
75–76	SD	11	1	7	8	4
76–77	SD	7	2	2	4	0
Totals		22	4	9	13	4

BUSNIUK, Ronald

BUTTERS, William

BYE, Brian *5–10 180 C*
B. Brantford, Ont., June 27, 1954

75–76	SD	1	0	0	0	0

BYERS, Michael

CADLE, Brian *6–1 170 LW*
B. Vancouver, B.C., Sept. 13, 1948

72–73	Winn	56	4	4	8	39

CAFFREY, Terrance

CALLIGHEN, Brett

CAMPBELL, Bryan

CAMPBELL, Colin

CAMPBELL, Scott

CAMPEAU, Dick *6–0 165 RW*
B. Montreal, Que., Apr. 9, 1952

72–73	Phil	75	1	18	19	72
73–74	Van	7	0	0	0	2
Totals		82	1	18	19	74

Playoffs

72–73	Phil	4	1	0	1	17

CARDIFF, Jim *5–9 165 D*
B. Dauphin, Man., Aug. 29, 1944

72–73	Phil	78	3	24	27	185
73–74	Van	78	1	21	22	188
74–75	Van	44	0	2	2	25
Totals		200	4	47	51	398

CARDWELL, Stephen

CARLETON, Kenneth

CARLIN, Brian

CARLSON, Jack

CARLSON, Jeff *6–3 210 RW*
B. Virginia, Minn., July 20, 1953

75–76	Minn	7	0	1	1	14

CARLSON, Steven

CARLYLE, Steve *5–10 180 D*
B. Lacombe, Alta., Mar. 10, 1950

72–73	Alb	67	7	10	17	35
73–74	Edm	50	2	13	15	18
74–75	Edm	73	4	25	29	46
75–76	Edm	28	0	11	11	10
Totals		218	13	59	72	109

Playoffs

73–74	Edm	5	0	1	1	4

CARON, Alain

CARROLL, Gregory

SEASON	TEAM	GP	G	A	PTS	PIM
CARTIER, Jean *5–9 180 D*						
B. Verdun, Que.						
72–73	Que	15	0	3	3	8

CASSOLATO, Anthony

CHARLEBIOS, Chuck

CHARTER, Claude *6–0 180 C*
B. Grande–Riviere, Que., Dec. 21, 1949

72–73	NY	12	2	3	5	0
73–74	NY–NJ	5	0	0	0	0
74–75	Balt	1	0	0	0	0
Totals		18	2	3	5	0

CHERNOFF, Michael

CHIPCHASE, Jack *5–11 205 D*
B. Seaforth, Ont., Apr. 5, 1945

72–73	Phil	4	0	0	0	2

CHIPPERFIELD, Ronald

CHRISTIANSEN, Keith *5–6 155 C*
B. Fort Frances, Ont., Apr. 8, 1947

72–73	Minn	64	12	30	42	24
73–74	Minn	74	11	25	36	36
Totals		138	23	55	78	60

Playoffs

72–73	Minn	5	1	0	1	0
73–74	Minn	10	0	1	1	2
Totals		15	1	1	2	2

CLACKSON, Kim

CLARK, Gordie

CLARKE, Jim *6–3 215 D*
B. Toronto, Ont., Aug. 11, 1954

75–76	Phoe	59	1	9	10	57

Playoffs

75–76	Phoe	1	0	0	0	0

CLEARWATER, Ray *5–11 175 D*
B. Winnipeg, Man., Nov. 10, 1942

72–73	Clev	78	11	36	47	41
73–74	Clev	68	12	23	35	47
74–75	Clev	66	4	18	22	51
75–76	Minn	2	0	0	0	2
Totals		214	27	77	104	141

Playoffs

72–73	Clev	9	1	2	3	8
73–74	Clev	5	0	0	0	2
74–75	Clev	4	1	1	2	0
Totals		18	2	3	5	10

CLIMIE, Ron *5–11 180 LW*
B. Hamilton, Ont., Mar. 5, 1950

72–73	Ott	31	12	19	31	2
73–74	Edm	76	38	36	74	22
74–75	Edm–NE	74	23	31	54	27
75–76	NE	65	25	20	45	17
76–77	NE	3	0	0	0	0
Totals		249	98	106	204	68

Playoffs

72–73	Ott	4	1	0	1	2
73–74	Edm	5	0	0	0	0
74–75	NE	6	3	0	3	0
Totals		15	4	0	4	2

CLOUTIER, Real

COATES, Brian *6–0 196 LW*
B. Carmen, Man., Sept. 22, 1952

73–74	Chi	50	10	3	13	14
74–75	Chi	35	12	9	21	26
75–76	Ind	59	11	16	27	24
76–77	Ind	16	1	5	6	4
77–78	Cinn	42	8	10	18	18
Totals		202	42	43	85	86

Playoffs

SEASON	TEAM	GP	G	A	PTS	PIM
	Chi	17	0	3	3	35
	Ind	4	0	0	0	6
Totals		21	0	3	3	41

COLBORNE, Hal F
| 73–74 | Edm | 2 | 0 | 0 | 0 | 0 |

COLE, Jim F
| 76–77 | Winn | 2 | 0 | 1 | 1 | 0 |

CONACHER, Brian

CONNELLY, Gary 6–0 186 RW
B. Rovyn, Que., Dec. 22, 1950
| 73–74 | Chi | 4 | 0 | 1 | 1 | 2 |

CONNELLY, Wayne

CONNOR, Cam

CONROY, Mike 6–0 180 LW
B. North Bay, Ont., Aug. 28, 1951
| 75–76 | Clev | 4 | 0 | 1 | 1 | 2 |

CONSTANTIN, Charlie 6–1 192 LW
B. Montreal, Que., Apr. 17, 1954
74–75	Que	20	2	4	6	9
75–76	Que	41	8	7	15	77
76–77	Ind	77	14	19	33	93
77–78	Ind	54	4	5	9	50
Totals		192	28	35	63	229

Playoffs
| 75–76 | Que | 5 | 0 | 1 | 1 | 4 |
| 76–77 | Que | 15 | 0 | 1 | 1 | 15 |

CORMIER, Michel 5–9 170 LW
B. Trois Rivieres, Que., Dec. 22, 1945
74–75	Phoe	78	36	38	74	26
75–76	Phoe	46	21	15	36	4
76–77	Phoe	58	13	16	29	22
Totals		182	70	69	139	52

Playoffs
| 74–75 | Phoe | 5 | 1 | 0 | 1 | 2 |

COTE, Alain

COTE, Roger 5–9 184 D
B. Belleterre, Que., Dec. 22, 1939
72–73	Alb	61	3	5	8	46
73–74	Edm	59	0	3	3	34
74–75	Ind	36	0	6	6	24
Totals		156	3	14	17	104

Playoffs
| 73–74 | Edm | 2 | 0 | 0 | 0 | 0 |

COURNOYER, Norm 5–10 170 C
B. Drummondville, Que., Mar. 17, 1951
73–74	Clev	13	3	5	8	6
76–77	SD	19	1	2	3	8
Totals		32	4	7	11	14

CRASHLEY, Bart

CRITCH, Glen D
| 75–76 | Ind | 3 | 0 | 0 | 0 | 0 |

CROSS, Jim D
| 77–78 | Edm | 2 | 0 | 0 | 0 | 0 |

CROWDER, Keith

CROWLEY, Paul 5–9 182 RW
| 75–76 | Tor | 4 | 0 | 0 | 0 | 0 |

CUDDIE, Steve 5–10 190 D
B. Toronto, Ont., June 18, 1950
72–73	Winn	77	7	13	20	121
73–74	Tor	74	5	18	23	65
74–75	Tor	70	5	16	21	49
Totals		221	17	47	64	235

Playoffs

SEASON	TEAM	GP	G	A	PTS	PIM
72–73	Winn	12	0	1	1	10
73–74	Tor	8	1	4	5	14
74–75	Tor	6	0	4	4	8
Totals		23	1	9	10	32

CUNNIFF, John 5–9 175 LW
B. South Boston, Mass., July 9, 1944
72–73	NE	33	3	5	8	16
73–74	NE	30	7	5	12	14
75–76	Que	2	0	0	0	5
Totals		65	10	10	20	35

Playoffs
72–73	NE	13	1	1	2	2
73–74	NE	5	1	1	2	0
Totals		18	2	2	4	2

CUNNINGHAM, Gary 6–0 184 D
B. Welland, Ont., Aug. 28, 1950
| 73–74 | Edm | 2 | 0 | 0 | 0 | 0 |

CUNNINGHAM, Rick 5–10 190 D
B. Toronto, Ont., Mar. 3, 1951
72–73	Ott	78	9	32	41	121
73–74	Tor	75	2	19	21	88
74–75	Tor	71	7	18	25	117
75–76	Tor	36	5	14	19	57
Totals		260	23	83	106	383

Playoffs
73–74	Tor	11	0	4	4	31
74–75	Tor	5	0	1	1	0
Totals		16	0	5	5	31

CUNNINGHAM, Robert

CURTIS, Paul

D'ALVISE, Bob 5–11 185 C
B. Etobicoke, Ont., Dec. 23, 1952
| 75–76 | Tor | 59 | 5 | 8 | 13 | 10 |

DANBY, John 5–10 165 C
B. Toronto, Ont., July 20, 1948
72–73	NE	77	14	23	37	10
73–74	NE	72	2	2	4	6
75–76	NE	1	0	0	0	0
Totals		150	16	25	41	16

Playoffs
73–74	NE	7	1	0	1	0
74–75	NE	4	0	1	1	0
Totals		11	1	1	2	0

DAVID, Richard

DAVIDSON, Blair 5–10 185 D
B. Cartwright, Man., Oct. 4, 1955
| 76–77 | Phoe | 2 | 0 | 0 | 0 | 2 |

DAVIS, Bill 6–1 195 D
B. Lindsay, Ont., Aug. 22, 1954
77–78	Winn	12	0	0	0	2
78–79	Winn	5	1	2	3	0
Totals		17	1	2	3	2

DAVIS, Kelly 6–0 175 D
B. Grande Prairie, Alta., Sept. 23, 1958
| 78–79 | Cinn | 18 | 0 | 1 | 1 | 20 |

DEADMARSH, Ernest

DEAN, Barry

DEBOL, David

DELORME, Ronald

DEMARCO, Ab

DERKSON, Brian 5–10 190 D
B. Borden, Sask., Nov. 29, 1951
| 73–74 | LA | 1 | 0 | 0 | 0 | 2 |

SEASON	TEAM	GP	G	A	PTS	PIM

DESCOTEAUX, Norm 5–9 170 D
B. Montreal, Que., Jan. 3, 1948
72–73	Que	2	0	1	1	0
73–74	Que	35	1	6	7	6
Totals		37	1	7	8	6

DESJARDINE, Ken 6–0 180 D
B. Toronto, Ont., Aug. 23, 1947
72–73	Que	38	2	6	8	36
73–74	Que	70	2	10	12	44
74–75	Ind	46	0	8	8	68
75–76	Calg	1	0	0	0	0
Totals		155	4	24	28	148

DEVLIN, Pete D

Playoffs
| 75–76 | NE | 1 | 0 | 0 | 0 | 0 |

DI LORENZI, Ray 5–10 185 RW
74–75	Van	3	0	0	0	0
75–76	Calg	39	8	12	20	4
Totals		42	8	12	20	4

DILLABOUGH, Robert

DILLON, Wayne

DOBEK, Bob 6–0 175 C
B. Detroit, Mich., Oct. 4, 1952
75–76	SD	14	3	1	4	2
76–77	SD	58	7	17	24	17
Totals		72	10	18	28	19

Playoffs
75–76	SD	11	1	2	3	0
76–77	SD	5	0	0	0	4
Totals		16	1	2	3	4

DONALDSON, Gary

DONNELLY, John 6–0 190 D
B. Sept. 28, 1948
| 72–73 | Ott | 15 | 1 | 1 | 2 | 44 |

DONNELLY, Pat 5–10 170 C
B. Feb. 24, 1953
| 75–76 | Cinn | 23 | 5 | 7 | 12 | 4 |

DONNELLY, Peter 5–8 155
B. Detroit, Mich., June 14, 1948
| 73–74 | Van | 52 | 0 | 1 | 1 | 9 |

DOREY, Jim

DORNSEIF, Dave 6–3 205 D
B. Edina, Minn., Aug. 12, 1956
77–78	Ind	3	0	1	1	0
78–79	Cinn	1	0	0	0	0
Totals		4	0	1	1	0

DOUGLAS, Jordy

DOUGLAS, Kent

DRISCOLL, Peter

DUBE, Normand

DUDLEY, Rick

DUBOIS, Mike 5–11 181 D
B. Montreal, Que., Nov. 7, 1954
75–76	Ind–Que	55	2	5	7	127
76–77	Que	4	0	0	0	0
Totals		59	2	5	7	127

Playoffs
75–76	Que	1	0	0	0	0
76–77	Que	2	0	1	1	0
Totals		3	0	1	1	0

DUFOUR, Guy 5–11 185 RW
B. LaTuque, Que., Feb. 9, 1946
| 72–73 | Que | 9 | 3 | 2 | 5 | 2 |

SEASON TEAM	GP	G	A	PTS	PIM
73–74 Que	74	27	23	50	30
Totals	83	30	25	55	32

DUNN, David

DUPRAS, Rich *6–0 185 C*
B. Montreal, Que., Jan. 1, 1950

73–74 Tor	2	0	0	0	0

DURBANO, Steve

EARL, Tom *6–0 180 RW*
B. Niagara Falls, Ont., Sept. 24, 1947

72–73 NE	77	10	13	23	4
73–74 NE	78	10	10	20	29
74–75 NE	72	3	8	11	20
75–76 NE	66	8	11	19	26
76–77 NE	54	9	14	23	37
Totals	347	40	56	96	116

Playoffs

72–73 NE	15	2	3	5	10
73–74 NE	7	0	2	2	2
74–75 NE	6	1	1	2	12
75–76 NE	17	0	5	5	4
76–77 NE	1	0	0	0	0
Totals	46	3	11	14	28

EOUR, Thomas

ERICKSON, Grant

ERIKSSON, Rolie

EVANS, Christopher

EVO, Bill *6–2 187 RW*
B. Royal Oak, Mich., Feb. 21, 1954

74–75 Balt	49	13	9	22	32
75–76 Edm–Clev	48	1	9	10	32
Totals	97	14	18	35	64

FALKENBERG, Robert

FALKMAN, Craig *5–11 190 RW*
B. St. Paul, Minn., Aug. 1, 1943

72–73 Minn	45	1	5	6	12

FARDA, Dick *5–9 175 C*
B. Brno, Czech., Nov. 8, 1945

74–75 Tor	66	6	25	31	2
75–76 Tor	63	19	35	54	8
76–77 Birm	48	9	26	35	2
Totals	177	34	86	120	12

FEATHERSTONE, Tony

FEDERKO, Mike *F*

76–77 Hous	4	0	0	0	0

FERGUSON, Norman

FISHER, John *D*

72–73 Alb	40	0	5	5	0

FITCHNER, Robert

FLEMING, Reggie

FLETT, William

FOLCO, Peter

FOLEY, Rick

FONTAINE, Leonard

FONTEYNE, Val

FORBES, David

FORD, Mike *6–1 185 D*
B. Ottawa, Ont., July 26, 1952

74–75 Winn	73	12	22	34	68
75–76 Winn	81	13	43	56	70
76–77 Calg	76	8	34	42	34
77–78 Winn	3	0	0	0	0

SEASON TEAM	GP	G	A	PTS	PIM
Totals	233	33	99	132	172

Playoffs

75–76 Winn	12	1	12	13	8
76–77 Winn	20	3	13	16	12
77–78 Winn	2	1	0	1	0
Totals	34	5	15	20	20

FORTIER, David

FORTIER, Florent *D*

75–76 Que	4	1	1	2	0

Playoffs

75–76 Que	1	0	0	0	0

FORTUNATO, Joe *5–10 170 LW*
B. Bari, Italy, Jan. 1, 1955

76–77 Edm	1	0	0	0	0

FOTIU, Nicholas

FRASER, Rick *5–10 177 D*
B. Sarnia, Ont., Oct. 7, 1954

74–75 Ind	4	0	0	0	2

FRENCH, John *5–11 175 LW*
B. Orillia, Ont., Aug. 25, 1950

72–73 NE	74	24	35	59	43
73–74 NE	77	24	48	72	31
74–75 NE	75	12	41	53	28
75–76 SD	76	25	39	64	16
76–77 SD	44	14	21	35	6
77–78 Ind	74	9	8	17	6
Totals	420	108	192	300	130

Playoffs

72–73 NE	15	3	11	14	2
73–74 NE	7	4	2	6	2
74–75 NE	4	1	2	3	0
75–76 SD	11	4	7	11	0
76–77 SD	7	2	3	5	2
Totals	44	14	25	39	6

FTOREK, Robert

GAMBUCCI, Gary

GALLANT, Gordon *5–11 175 LW*
B. Shedlac, B.C., Oct. 27, 1950

73–74 Minn	72	7	15	22	223
74–75 Minn	66	10	13	23	203
75–76 Que	64	4	15	19	297
76–77 Minn	71	10	16	26	126
Totals	273	31	59	90	849

Playoffs

73–74 Minn	11	1	2	3	67
74–75 Minn	1	1	0	1	0
75–76 Que	2	0	0	0	31
Totals	14	2	2	4	98

GARNEAU, J.C. *5–9 165 LW*
B. Quebec City, Que., Oct. 19, 1943

74–75 Que	17	0	5	5	27

GARTNER, Michael

GARWASIUK, Ron *5–8 160 LW*
B. St. Paul, Alta., Feb. 17, 1949

73–74 LA	51	6	13	19	100

GATEMAN, Marty *6–0 185 D*
B. Southampton, Ont., Dec. 7 1952

75–76 NE	12	0	1	1	6

GAUDETTE, Andre *5–7 165 C*
B. Sherbrooke, Que., Dec. 16, 1947

72–73 Que	78	27	44	71	12
73–74 Que	78	24	44	68	16
74–75 Que	67	10	17	27	6
Totals	223	61	105	166	34

Playoffs

74–75 Que	9	0	1	1	0

SEASON TEAM	GP	G	A	PTS	PIM

GAUTHIER, Jean

GELLARD, Sam *6–0 190 LW*
B. Port of Spain, Trinidad, Mar. 14, 1950

72–73 Phil	5	0	0	0	0
73–74 Van	23	7	4	11	15
Totals	28	7	4	11	15

GENDRON, Jean

GEOFFRION, Daniel

GEORGE, Wes *6–2 220 LW*
B. Young, Sask., Sept. 26, 1958

78–79 Ind–Edm	12	4	2	6	34

GIBBONS, Brian *6–3 190 D*
B. St. John's, Nfld., July 7, 1947

72–73 Ott	73	7	35	42	62
73–74 Tor	78	4	31	35	84
74–75 Tor	73	4	22	26	105
75–76 Ott	2	0	0	0	0
Totals	226	15	88	103	251

Playoffs

72–73 Ott	5	1	2	3	12
73–74 Tor	12	2	5	7	10
Totals	17	3	7	10	22

GIBBONS, Gerry *6–1 185 D*
B. St. John's, Nfld., Jan. 17, 1953

73–74 Tor	26	1	4	5	23
75–76 Tor	5	1	0	1	7
Totals	31	2	4	6	30

Playoffs

73–74 Tor	1	0	0	0	0

GIBSON, Jack *6–0 185 LW*
B. Picton, Ont., Aug. 18, 1948

72–73 Ott	59	22	13	35	48
73–74 Tor	61	16	9	25	60
75–76 Tor	2	0	0	0	0
Totals	122	38	22	60	108

Playoffs

72–73 Ott	1	1	0	1	5
73–74 Tor	12	1	3	4	11
Total 13	2	3	5	16	

GIBSON, John

GILBERT, Edward

GILBERT, Jean

GILLIGAN, Bill *5–11 175 C*
B. Beverly, Mass., Aug. 5, 1954

77–78 Cinn	54	10	14	24	59
78–79 Cinn	74	17	26	43	54
Totals	128	27	40	67	

Playoffs

78–79 Cinn	3	1	0	1	0

GILMORE, Tom *5–11 190 LW*
B. Flin Flon, Man., May 14, 1948

72–73 LA	71	17	18	35	191
73–74 Edm	57	19	23	42	164
74–75 Edm	74	12	19	31	84
Totals	202	48	60	108	439

Playoffs

72–73 LA	5	1	3	4	2
73–74 Edm	5	1	4	5	15
Totals	10	2	7	9	17

GILMOUR, Dave *5–9 165 LW*
B. Kingston, Ont.

75–76 Calg	1	0	0	0	0

GINGRAS, Gaston

GIROUX, Rejean *5–11 160 RW*
B. Quebec City, Que., Sept. 13, 1952

SEASON	TEAM	GP	G	A	PTS	PIM
72–73	Que	59	10	12	22	41
73–74	Que	12	5	6	11	14
Totals		71	15	18	33	55

GIVENS, Dan

SEASON	TEAM	GP	G	A	PTS	PIM
74–75	Van	1	0	0	0	0

GLENWRIGHT, Brian *6–3 206 LW*
B. Windsor, Ont., Oct. 8, 1949

SEASON	TEAM	GP	G	A	PTS	PIM
72–73	Chi	50	2	5	7	0
73–74	LA	15	3	2	5	0
Totals		65	5	7	12	0

GLOBENSKY, Allan *6–14 190 D*
B. Montreal, Que., Apr. 17, 1951

SEASON	TEAM	GP	G	A	PTS	PIM
72–73	Que	3	0	0	0	0
74–75	Que	5	0	0	0	5
75–76	Que	34	1	2	3	13
Totals		42	1	2	3	18

Playoffs

SEASON	TEAM	GP	G	A	PTS	PIM
74–75	Que	2	1	0	1	0

GOLDSWORTHY, William

GOLDTHORPE, Bill *5–11 173 LW*
B. Thunder Bay, Ont., June 20, 1953

SEASON	TEAM	GP	G	A	PTS	PIM
74–75	Balt	7	0	0	0	26
75–76	SD–Ott	26	1	0	1	61
Totals		33	1	0	1	87

Playoffs

SEASON	TEAM	GP	G	A	PTS	PIM
73–74	Minn	3	0	0	0	25

GOLEMBROSKY, Frank *6–0 190 RW*
B. Calgary, Alta., May 3, 1945

SEASON	TEAM	GP	G	A	PTS	PIM
72–73	Phil–Que	60	8	12	20	44

GORDON, Don *5–11 184 RW*
B. Timmins, Ont., Apr. 17, 1948

SEASON	TEAM	GP	G	A	PTS	PIM
73–74	LA–Chi	52	13	10	23	33
74–75	Chi	42	4	5	9	10
Totals		94	17	15	32	43

Playoffs

SEASON	TEAM	GP	G	A	PTS	PIM
73–74	Chi	18	4	8	12	4

GORMAN, David

GOSSELIN, Rich *C*

SEASON	TEAM	GP	G	A	PTS	PIM
78–79	Winn	3	0	0	0	0

GOULET, Michel

GRATTON, Bill *6–3 200 LW*
B. Brantford, Ont.

SEASON	TEAM	GP	G	A	PTS	PIM
75–76	Calg	6	0	1	1	2

GRATTON, Jean *5–9 169 RW*
B. St. Ann De Plaines, Que., Mar. 8, 1947

SEASON	TEAM	GP	G	A	PTS	PIM
72–73	Winn	71	15	12	27	37
73–74	Winn	68	12	21	33	13
74–75	Winn	49	4	8	12	2
Totals		188	31	41	72	52

Playoffs

SEASON	TEAM	GP	G	A	PTS	PIM
72–73	Winn	12	1	1	2	4
73–74	Winn	2	0	0	0	0
Totals		14	1	1	2	4

GRAVEL, John *D*
B. Montreal, Que., Ont. 27, 1943

SEASON	TEAM	GP	G	A	PTS	PIM
72–73	Phil	8	1	3	4	0

GRAY, John *5–10 185 LW*
B. Little Current, Ont., Aug. 13, 1949

SEASON	TEAM	GP	G	A	PTS	PIM
74–75	Phoe	75	35	33	68	107
75–76	Phoe	79	35	45	80	136
76–77	Phoe–Hous	75	31	30	61	84
77–78	Hous	77	35	23	58	80
78–79	Winn	57	10	15	25	51
Totals		363	146	146	292	458

Playoffs

SEASON	TEAM	GP	G	A	PTS	PIM
74–75	Phoe	5	2	3	5	12
75–76	Phoe	5	1	1	2	7
76–77	Hous	6	0	1	1	8
77–78	Hous	6	0	3	3	10
78–79	Winn	1	0	0	0	0
Totals		23	3	8	11	37

GREEN, Ted

GREIG, Bruce

GRENIER, Richard

GRESDAL, Gary *6–0 195 LW*
B. Kingston, Ont.

SEASON	TEAM	GP	G	A	PTS	PIM
75–76	Que	2	0	1	1	5

GRETZKY, Wayne

GRIERSON, Don *6–0 185 RW*
B. North Bay, Ont., June 18, 1947

SEASON	TEAM	GP	G	A	PTS	PIM
72–73	Hous	78	22	22	44	83
73–74	Hous	65	11	18	29	45
Totals		143	33	40	73	128

Playoffs

SEASON	TEAM	GP	G	A	PTS	PIM
73–74	Hous	14	1	5	6	23

GRIGG, Chris *6–1 174*
B. Ottawa, Ont., Feb. 2, 1953

SEASON	TEAM	GP	G	A	PTS	PIM
75–76	Ott	2	0	0	0	0

GRUEN, Patrick

GUITE, Pierre *6–2 190 LW*
B. Montreal, Que., Apr. 17, 1952

SEASON	TEAM	GP	G	A	PTS	PIM
72–73	Que	65	10	8	18	136
73–74	Que	72	14	20	34	106
74–75	Balt	35	19	12	31	70
75–76	Cinn	52	20	24	44	80
76–77	Cinn–Que	62	12	14	26	99
77–78	Que–Edm	78	16	26	42	86
78–79	Edm	12	1	1	2	8
Totals		376	92	105	197	585

Playoffs

SEASON	TEAM	GP	G	A	PTS	PIM
76–77	Que	17	5	0	5	9
77–78	Edm	5	1	1	2	20
Totals		22	6	1	7	29

GULKA, Bud *F*

SEASON	TEAM	GP	G	A	PTS	PIM
74–75	Van	5	1	0	1	10

GUINDON, Robert

GUSTAFSSON, Bengt

HAAS, Derek *6–0 170 LW*
B. Trail, B.C., May 1, 1955

SEASON	TEAM	GP	G	A	PTS	PIM
75–76	Calg	30	5	9	14	6

Playoffs

SEASON	TEAM	GP	G	A	PTS	PIM
75–76	Calg	1	0	0	0	0

HAGMAN, Matti

HALE, Larry

HALL, Del

HALL, Murray

HAMILTON

HAMPSON, Edward

HANDRAHAN, Alf *5–9 185 RW*
B. Alberton, P.E.I., Dec. 27, 1949

SEASON	TEAM	GP	G	A	PTS	PIM
77–78	Cinn	14	1	3	4	42

HANEY, Merv *F*

SEASON	TEAM	GP	G	A	PTS	PIM
72–73	Ott	7	0	1	1	4

HANGSLEBEN, Alan

HANMER, Craig *6–2 210 D*

SEASON	TEAM	GP	G	A	PTS	PIM
B. St. Paul, Minn., Jan. 6, 1956						
74–75	Ind	37	1	0	1	15

HANNA, John

HANSIS, Ron *6–2 195 RW*
B. Brownsville, Tex., Nov. 12, 1952

SEASON	TEAM	GP	G	A	PTS	PIM
76–77	Hous	11	4	3	7	6
77–78	Hous	78	13	9	22	51
Totals		100	17	12	29	57

Playoffs

SEASON	TEAM	GP	G	A	PTS	PIM
76–77	Hous	8	1	1	2	4
77–78	Hous	6	1	1	2	4
Totals		14	2	2	4	8

HANSON, David

HARBARUK, Nick

HARDY, Jocelyn

HARGREAVES, James

HARGREAVES, Ted *5–11 175 LW*
B. Weyburn, Sask.

SEASON	TEAM	GP	G	A	PTS	PIM
73–74	Winn	74	7	12	19	15

Playoffs

SEASON	TEAM	GP	G	A	PTS	PIM
73–74	Winn	4	0	1	1	10

HARKER, Derek *6–0 185 D*
B. Edmonton, Alta., Jan. 7, 1951

SEASON	TEAM	GP	G	A	PTS	PIM
72–73	Alb–Phil	29	0	5	5	46

HARRIS, George

HARRIS, Hugh

HARRISON, James

HART, Dick *6–0 195 D*
B. Boston, Mass., Oct. 5, 1952

SEASON	TEAM	GP	G	A	PTS	PIM
76–77	Birm	4	0	0	0	0

HARVEY, Mike *5–10 182 C*
B. Alma, Que., Jan. 31, 1938

SEASON	TEAM	GP	G	A	PTS	PIM
72–73	Que	40	6	13	19	14

HATOUM, Edward

HEATLEY, Murray *5–8 180 RW*
B. Calgary, Alta., Nov. 7, 1948

SEASON	TEAM	GP	G	A	PTS	PIM
73–74	Minn	71	26	32	58	23
74–75	Minn–Ind	51	20	17	37	56
75–76	Ind	34	2	5	7	7
Totals		156	48	54	102	86

Playoffs

SEASON	TEAM	GP	G	A	PTS	PIM
73–74	Minn	10	1	0	1	2

HEAVER, Paul *6–3 195 D*
B. Paddington, England

SEASON	TEAM	GP	G	A	PTS	PIM
75–76	Tor	66	2	12	14	83
76–77	Birm	5	0	0	0	0
Totals		71	2	12	14	83

HEDBERG, Anders

HEGGEDAL, Howie *RW*
B. Sept. 15, 1949

SEASON	TEAM	GP	G	A	PTS	PIM
72–73	LA	8	2	1	3	0

Playoffs

SEASON	TEAM	GP	G	A	PTS	PIM
72–73	LA	1	0	0	0	0

HEINDL, William

HEISKALA, Earl

HENDERSON, Paul

HENRY, Pierre *5–10 180 LW*
B. Montreal, Que., Mar. 10, 1952

SEASON	TEAM	GP	G	A	PTS	PIM
72–73	Phil	19	2	3	5	13

HERRIMAN, Don 5-10 165 LW
B. Sault Ste. Marie, Ont., Jan. 2, 1948

SEASON	TEAM	GP	G	A	PTS	PIM
72-73	Phil	78	24	48	72	63
73-74	NY-NJ	44	11	21	32	59
74-75	Edm	33	1	2	3	21
Totals		155	36	71	107	143

Playoffs

72-73	Phil	4	1	0	1	14

HICKEY, Patrick

HICKS, Glenn

HILLMAN, Larry

HILLMAN, Wayne

HINSE, Andre

HISLOP, Jamie

HOBIN, Mike 5-11 180 C
B. Sarnia, Ont.

75-76	Phoe	9	1	1	2	2
76-77	Phoe	68	17	18	35	14
Totals		77	18	19	37	16

Playoffs

75-76	Phoe	1	0	0	0	0

HODGSON, Edward

HOEKSTRA, Edward

HOGANSON, Dale

HOLBROOK, Terry

HOLLAND, Jerry

HOLMGREN, Paul

HORNUNG, Lawrence

HOULE, Rejean

HOWE, Gordie

HOWE, Mark

HOWE, Marty

HOWELL, Harry

HUCK, Anthony

HUGHES, Brent

HUGHES, Frank

HUGHES, John

HULL, Robert

HULL, Steve 5-10 180 LW
B. Ottawa, Ont., Aug. 29, 1952

75-76	Calg	58	11	15	26	6
76-77	Calg	2	0	2	2	0
Totals		60	11	17	28	6

HUNTER, David

HURLEY, Paul

HUSTON, Ronald

HUTCHISON, David

HYNDMAN, Mike 6-1 205 RW
B. Quebec City, Que., Dec. 8, 1945

73-74	LA	8	0	1	1	0

Playoffs

72-73	LA	6	0	3	3	17

HYNES, David

INGLIS, Lee 5-10 190 LW
B. Latchford, Ont., Aug. 31, 1947

73-74	NY-NJ	5	0	0	0	0
74-75	SD	5	0	2	2	0
Totals		10	0	2	2	0

INKPEN, Dave 6-0 185 D
B. Edmonton, Alta., Sept. 4, 1954

75-76	Cinn	80	4	24	28	95
76-77	Cinn-Ind	80	7	26	33	81
77-78	Edm-Que-Ind	67	1	11	12	60
78-79	Ind-NE	66	1	15	16	37
Totals		293	13	76	89	273

Playoffs

76-77	Ind	9	0	2	2	8
78-79	NE	5	0	1	1	4
Totals		14	0	3	3	12

IRWIN, Glen 5-11 195 D
B. Edmonton, Alta., Mar. 1, 1951

74-75	Hous	70	2	11	13	153
75-76	Hous	72	3	8	11	116
76-77	Hous	44	2	4	6	168
77-78	Hous-Ind	23	0	0	0	72
78-79	Ind	24	0	1	1	124
Totals		233	7	24	31	623

Playoffs

74-75	Hous	13	0	2	2	8
75-76	Hous	5	0	0	0	9
Totals		18	0	2	2	17

ISRAELSON, Larry 6-1 180 LW
B. Wetaskiwin, Sask.

74-75	Van	46	12	9	21	10
75-76	Calg	57	10	22	32	26
76-77	Calg	2	0	0	0	0
Totals		105	22	31	53	36

Playoffs

75-76	Calg	3	0	0	0	0

JACKWITH, Gary 6-0 200 D
B. Lynn, Mass., May 30, 1948

75-76	SD	2	0	0	0	0

JACQUES, Jeff 5-11 180 C
B. Preston, Ont., Apr. 4, 1953

74-75	Tor	39	12	8	20	26
75-76	Tor	81	17	33	50	113
76-77	Birm	79	21	27	48	92
Totals		199	50	68	118	231

Playoffs

74-75	Tor	6	0	4	4	2

JAKUBO, Mike 6-0 190 C
B. Sudbury, Ont., July 7, 1947

72-73	LA	7	0	0	0	0

JARRETT, Gary

JARRY, Pierre

JODZIO, Richard

JOHNSON, Daniel

JOHNSON, Jim

JOHNSTON, Lawrence

JOHNSTONE, Edward

JONES, James H.

JONES, James W.

JONES, Robert

JORDAN, Ric 6-3 200 D
B. Toronto, Ont., Mar. 31, 1950

72-73	NE	34	1	5	6	12
73-74	NE	34	0	3	3	14
74-75	Que	56	6	8	14	75
75-76	Que	54	4	7	11	75
76-77	Calg	5	0	0	0	4
Totals			11	23	34	180

Playoffs

73-74	NE	7	0	0	0	6

JOYAL, Edward

JUSTIN, Dan 6-1 201 D
B. Palo Alto, Cal., Jan. 12, 1955

75-76	Cinn	17	0	0	0	2
76-77	Cinn	6	0	2	2	4
Totals		23	0	2	2	6

KANNEGIESSER, Gordan

KARLANDER, Allan

KASSIAN, Dennis 5-11 170 LW
B. Vegreville, Alta., July 14, 1941

72-73	Alb	50	6	7	13	14

KEELER, Mike 5-10 185 D
B. Toronto, Ont., May 21, 1950

73-74	NE	1	0	0	0	0

Playoffs

73-74	NE	1	0	0	0	0

KENNEDY, Jamie 5-8 175 RW
B. Dorchester, N.B., Sept. 7, 1946

72-73	NY	54	4	6	10	11

KENNETT, Murray 5-10 175 D
B. Kamloops, B.C., June 28, 1952

74-75	Ind-Edm	78	5	17	22	25
75-76	Edm	28	3	4	7	14
Totals		106	8	21	29	39

KEOGAN, Murray 5-10 175 C
B. Biggar, Sask., Jan. 14, 1950

74-75	Phoe	78	35	29	64	68
75-76	Phoe-Calg	46	7	13	20	23
Totals		124	42	42	84	91

Playoffs

74-75	Phoe	5	0	1	1	0

KEON, David

KERSLAKE, Doug 5-11 200 RW
B. Saskatoon, Sask., Mar. 23, 1950

74-75	Edm	10	4	0	4	10
75-76	Edm	13	1	1	2	4
Totals		23	5	1	6	14

KETOLA, Veli

KETTER, Kerry

KING, Steve 5-10 185 RW
B. Toronto, Ont., Sept. 8, 1948

72-73	Ott	69	18	34	52	28
73-74	Tor	67	14	22	36	26
Totals		136	32	56	88	54

Playoffs

72-73	Ott	5	0	1	1	7
73-74	Tor	12	0	3	3	11
Totals		17	0	4	4	18

KIRK, Gavin 5-10 165 C
B. London, England, Dec. 6, 1951

72-73	Ott	78	28	40	68	54
73-74	Tor	78	20	48	68	44
74-75	Tor	78	15	58	73	69
75-76	Tor-Calg	77	36	46	82	46
76-77	Birm-Edm	81	17	46	63	50
78-79	Birm	30	1	5	6	16
Totals		422	117	243	360	279

Playoffs

72-73	Ott	5	2	3	5	12

73–74	Tor	12	2	4	6	4
74–75	Tor	6	5	6	11	2
75–76	Calg	10	4	6	10	19
76–77	Edm	5	1	0	1	4
Totals		38	14	19	33	41

KLATT, Bill *5–11 185 RW*
B. St. Paul, Minn., Oct. 16, 1947

72–73	Minn	78	36	22	58	22
73–74	Minn	65	14	6	20	12
Totals		143	50	28	78	34

Playoffs

72–73	Minn	5	1	3	4	5
73–74	Minn	11	3	2	5	18
Totals		16	4	5	9	23

KNIBBS, Darrel *6–1 185 RW*
B. Medicine Hat, Alta., Sept. 21, 1949

| 72–73 | Chi | 41 | 3 | 8 | 11 | 0 |

KOKKOLA, Keith *6–3 204 D*
B. Windsor, Ont., May 4, 1949

74–75	Chi	33	0	2	2	69
75–76	Ott	16	0	3	3	40
76–77	Birm	5	0	0	0	21
Totals		54	0	5	5	130

KONIK, George

KRAKE, Philip

KREZANSKI, Reggie *5–10 200 D*
B. New Westminster, B.C., Jan. 1, 1948

| 74–75 | SD | 2 | 0 | 0 | 0 | 2 |

KRUPICKA, Pat *5–9 160 RW*
B. Brno, Czech., Mar. 15, 1946

| 72–73 | LA–NY | 36 | 2 | 2 | 4 | 6 |

KRYSKOW, David

KUZMICZ, George *6–1 200 D*
B. Montreal, Que., May 24, 1952

74–75	Tor	34	0	12	12	22
75–76	Tor	1	0	0	0	0
Totals		35	0	12	12	22

LABOSSIERE, Gordan

LABRAATEN, Daniel

LACH, Milt   *F*

Playoffs

| 73–74 | Winn | 4 | 1 | 1 | 2 | 8 |

LACOMBE, Francois

LACROIX, Andre

LAFRAMBOISE, Peter

LAGACE, Pierre *6–2 210 LW*
B. Montreal, Que., Oct. 27, 1957

76–77	Birm	78	2	25	27	110
77–78	Que	17	2	4	6	2
78–79	Que	21	0	1	1	12
Totals		116	4	30	34	124

Playoffs

77–78	Que	1	0	0	0	0
78–79	Que	3	0	1	1	2
Totals		4	0	1	1	2

LAHACHE, Floyd *5–10 185 D*
B. Caughnawaga, Que., Sept. 17, 1957

| 77–78 | Cinn | 11 | 0 | 3 | 3 | 13 |

LAING, Bill *6–2 190 C*
B. Harris, Sask., Mar. 24, 1953

74–75	Edm	43	2	4	6	32
75–76	Edm	54	8	12	20	67
Totals		97	10	16	26	99

LALONDE, Rick *6–0 202 D*
B. Ottawa, Ont., Feb. 19, 1955

| 75–76 | SD | 2 | 0 | 0 | 0 | 0 |

LANGEVIN, David

LANGWAY, Rod

LAPIERRE, Camille *5–10 160 C*
B. Chicoutimi, Que., Feb. 8, 1951

72–73	Phil	24	5	9	14	2
73–74	Van	9	0	3	3	0
Totals		33	5	12	17	2

Playoffs

| 72–73 | Phil | 4 | 0 | 2 | 2 | 0 |

LARIVIERE, Garry

LAROSE, Claude

LAROSE, Ray *D*
B. Quebec City, Que., Nov. 20, 1941

72–73	Hous	67	1	10	11	25
73–74	NY–NJ	18	0	1	1	20
Totals		85	1	11	12	45

LARWAY, Don *6–1 192 RW*
B. Oar Lake, Minn., Feb. 2, 1954

74–75	Hous	76	21	13	34	59
75–76	Hous	79	30	20	50	56
76–77	Hous	75	11	13	24	112
77–78	Hous	69	24	35	59	52
78–79	Ind	25	8	10	18	39
Totals		324	94	91	185	318

Playoffs

74–75	Hous	13	3	1	4	8
75–76	Hous	16	7	5	12	21
76–77	Hous	3	1	0	1	0
77–78	Hous	6	1	2	3	4
Totals		38	12	8	20	33

LAUGHTON, Michael

LAVENDER, Brian

LAWSON, Daniel

LeBLANC, J.P.

LECLERC, Rene

LEDUC, Bob *5–10 185 LW*
B. Sudbury, Ont., May 24, 1944

72–73	Ott	77	22	33	55	71
73–74	Tor	61	22	29	51	29
74–75	Tor	19	3	4	7	9
Totals		157	47	66	113	109

Playoffs

72–73	Ott	5	0	2	2	4
73–74	Tor	12	4	6	10	42
Totals		17	4	8	12	46

LeDUC, Richard

LEGGE, Barry

LEGGE, Randy

LEITER, Robert

LEMIEUX, Richard

LEROUX, Gerry *5–7 160 LW*
B. St. Bernadin, Que., June 9, 1958

| 78–79 | Ind | 10 | 0 | 3 | 3 | 2 |

LESUK, William

LEY, Rick

LIDDINGTON, Robert

LILYHOLM, Len *5–8 163 LW*
B. Minneapolis, Minn., Apr. 1, 1941

| 72–73 | Minn | 77 | 8 | 13 | 21 | 37 |

Playoffs

| 72–73 | Minn | 5 | 1 | 0 | 1 | 0 |

LINDH, Mats *6–1 180 D*
B. Sept. 12, 1947

75–76	Winn	65	19	15	34	12
76–77	Winn	73	14	17	31	2
Totals		138	33	32	65	14

Playoffs

75–76	Winn	13	2	2	4	4
76–77	Winn	20	2	7	9	2
Totals		33	4	9	13	6

LINDSKOG, Doug *6–1 186 LW*
B. Red Deer, Alta., Aug. 12, 1955

| 76–77 | Calg | 2 | 0 | 0 | 0 | 2 |

LINSEMAN, Ken

LLOYD, Owen *5–11 164 D*
B. Vancouver, B.C., Apr. 30, 1957

| 77–78 | Edm | 3 | 0 | 1 | 1 | 4 |

LOCAS, Jacques *5–8 170 C*
B. St. Jerome, Que., Jan. 7, 1954

74–75	Balt–Ind	23	1	5	6	6
75–76	Cinn	80	27	46	73	70
76–77	Cinn–Calg	67	21	17	38	29
77–78	Cinn	17	0	2	2	6
Totals		187	49	70	119	111

LOMENDA, Mark *6–0 186 RW*
B. Esterhary, Sask., Apr. 14, 1954

74–75	Chi	69	16	33	49	21
75–76	Ott–Ind	39	6	16	22	11
76–77	Ind	56	9	12	21	14
Totals		164	31	61	92	46

Playoffs

| 76–77 | Ind | 9 | 3 | 1 | 4 | 17 |

LONG, Barry

LONG, Ted *6–1 185 D*
B. Woodstock, Ont., Jan. 26, 1955

| 76–77 | Cinn | 1 | 0 | 0 | 0 | 0 |

LUKOWICH, Bernard

LUKOWICH, Morris

LUKSA, Charles

LUND, Larry *6–0 190 C*
B. Penticton, B.C., Sept. 9, 1940

72–73	Hous	77	21	45	66	120
73–74	Hous	75	33	53	86	109
74–75	Hous	78	33	75	108	68
75–76	Hous	73	24	49	73	50
76–77	Hous	80	29	38	67	36
77–78	Hous	76	9	17	26	36
Totals		459	149	277	426	419

Playoffs

72–73	Hous	10	3	7	10	24
73–74	Hous	14	9	14	23	56
74–75	Hous	13	5	13	18	13
75–76	Hous	5	1	1	2	4
76–77	Hous	11	2	8	10	17
77–78	Hous	6	0	2	2	2
Totals		59	20	45	65	116

LUNDE, Leonard

LYLE, George

MacDONALD, Blair

MacGREGOR, Bruce

MacGREGOR, Gary *5–11 176 C*

SEASON	TEAM	GP	G	A	PTS	PIM

B. Kingston, Ont., Sept. 21, 1954

SEASON	TEAM	GP	G	A	PTS	PIM
74–75	Chi	78	44	34	78	26
75–76	Ott–Clev	73	21	17	38	24
76–77	NE–Ind	46	8	13	21	8
77–78	Edm	37	11	2	13	29
78–79	Ind	17	8	4	14	0
Totals		251	92	70	162	87

Playoffs

75–76	Clev	3	0	0	0	4

MacKENZIE, Al *5–10 165 D*
B. Windsor, Ont., Feb. 2, 1952

73–74	Chi	2	0	0	0	0

MacKINNON, Paul

MacMILLAN, Robert

MacNEIL, Bernie

MacSWEYN, Donald

MAGGS, Darryl

MAHOVLICH, Frank

MARA, Pete *5–7 167 C*
B. Point Edward, Ont., July 5, 1947

74–75	Chi	57	17	21	38	16
75–76	Ott	40	3	7	10	8
Totals		97	20	28	48	24

MAROTTE, Gilles

MARRIN, Peter *5–10 160 C*
B. Toronto, Ont., Aug. 3, 1953

73–74	Tor	31	1	4	5	4
74–75	Tor	4	3	1	4	0
75–76	Tor	64	22	16	38	16
76–77	Birm	79	23	37	60	36
77–78	Birm	80	28	43	71	53
78–79	Birm	20	4	11	15	18
Totals		278	81	112	193	127

Playoffs

73–74	Tor	3	0	1	1	0
74–75	Tor	6	0	4	4	2
75–76	Birm	5	0	3	3	2
Totals		14	0	8	8	4

MARSH, Jim *6–0 180 D*
B. Quesnel, B.C., July 9, 1951

76–77	Birm	1	0	0	0	0

MARSH, Peter

MARTIN, Thomas

MAVETY, Larry *5–11 196 D*
B. Woodstock, Ont., May 29, 1942

72–73	LA–Phil–Chi	73	10	40	50	89
73–74	Chi	77	15	36	51	157
74–75	Chi–Tor	74	10	31	41	150
75–76	Ott	14	0	4	4	14
76–77	Ind	10	2	2	4	8
Totals		248	37	113	150	418

Playoffs

73–74	Chi	18	4	8	12	46
74–75	Tor	6	0	3	3	6
Totals		24	4	11	15	52

MAXWELL, Bryan

MAYER, James

MAZUR, John

77–78	Hous	1	0	0	0	0

McANEELEY, Bob *5–9 180 C*
B. Cranbrook, B.C., Nov. 7, 1950

72–73	Alb	51	5	7	12	24
73–74	Edm	52	12	11	23	49
74–75	Edm	71	12	16	28	60
Totals		174	29	34	63	133

Playoffs

73–74	Edm	4	1	0	1	0
74–75	Edm	3	1	0	1	0
Totals		7	2	0	2	0

McANEELEY, Edward

McCALLUM, Duncan

McCASKILL, Edward

McCRIMMON, Jim

McCULLOUGH, Don *6–2 190 D*
B. Little Current, Sask., Mar. 23, 1951

74–75	Van	51	1	9	10	42

McDONALD, Alvin

McDONALD, Brian

McDONOUGH, Al

McGLYNN, Dick *6–2 185 D*
B. Medford, Mass., July 19, 1948

72–73	Chi	30	0	0	0	12

McKAY, Raymond

McKENZIE, Brian

McKENZIE, John

McLEOD, Allan

McLEOD, Don *6–0 190 D*
B. Trail, B.C., Aug. 24, 1946

75–76	Calg	63	0	13	13	4

McMAHON, Michael

McMANAMA, Robert

McMASTERS, Jim *5–10 195 D*
B. High River, Alta., Sept. 20, 1952

72–73	Clev	74	1	7	8	34
73–74	Clev	9	0	0	0	4
Totals		83	1	7	8	38

Playoffs

72–73	Clev	9	0	1	1	6

McMULLEN, Dale *LW*

77–78	Edm	1	0	0	0	0

McNAMARA, Mike *F*
B. Mar. 28, 1949

72–73	Que	19	0	0	0	5

McNAMEE, Pete *5–11 198 D*
B. Jamaica, W.I., Sept. 11, 1950

73–74	Van	3	0	0	0	0
74–75	Van–Phoe	66	11	20	31	92
75–76	Phoe–SD	65	2	5	7	59
76–77	SD	41	3	6	9	38
Totals		175	16	31	47	189

Playoffs

74–75	Phoe	5	1	0	1	2
75–76	SD	11	0	1	1	28
76–77	SD	2	0	0	0	2
Totals		18	1	1	2	32

MEEHAN, Gerald

MELOCHE, Denis *5–9 175 C*
B. Montreal, Que., June 19, 1952

72–73	Phil	4	1	1	2	0
73–74	Van	41	6	13	19	18
Totals		45	7	14	21	18

MELOFF, Chris *5–11 180 D*
B. Toronto, Ont., May 7, 1952

72–73	Ott	21	1	6	7	40

MELROSE, Barry

MERCREDI, Victor

MERRELL, Barry *D*

76–77	Edm	10	1	3	4	0

MESSIER, Mark

METHE, Gerry *5–10 170 LW*
B. Willowdale, Ont., Dec. 12, 1951

74–75	NE	5	0	1	1	4

MICHELLETTI, Joseph

MIGNEAULT, John *5–11 180 LW*
B. Thompkins, Sask., Feb. 14, 1949

72–73	Phil	54	10	8	18	38
73–74	Van	74	21	26	47	27
74–75	Van–Phoe	61	10	15	25	28
75–76	Phoe	68	8	12	20	14
Totals		257	49	61	110	107

Playoffs

75–76	Phoe	3	0	0	0	0

MILANI, Tom *5–6 170 RW*
B. Thunder Bay, Ont., Apr. 13, 1952

76–77	Minn	2	0	0	0	0

MILLER, Perry

MILLER, Warren

MISZUK, John

MOFFAT, Lyle

MONONEN, Larry *6–0 185 RW*
B. Joensuv, Finland, Mar. 22, 1950

75–76	Phoe	75	15	21	36	19
76–77	Phoe	67	21	29	50	0
Totals		142	36	50	86	19

Playoffs

75–76	Phoe	5	1	3	4	2

MORENZ, Brian *5–10 185 C*
B. Brampton, Ont., May 11, 1949

72–73	NY	30	7	1	8	23
73–74	NY–NJ	75	20	30	50	44
74–75	SD	78	20	19	39	76
75–76	SD	40	6	7	13	22
Totals		223	53	57	110	165

Playoffs

74–75	SD	10	0	3	3	6
75–76	SD	11	2	1	3	11
Totals		21	2	4	6	17

MORETTO, Anthony

MORGAN, Ron *5–11 190 LW*
B. Toronto, Ont.

73–74	Clev	4	0	1	1	7

Playoffs

73–74	Clev	2	1	0	1	0

MORIN, Wayne *5–10 185 D*
B. Progress, B.C., May 13, 1955

76–77	Calg	13	2	0	2	25

MORRIS, Billy *6–0 185 LW*
B. Toronto, Ont., June 26, 1949

74–75	Edm	36	4	8	12	6

MORRIS, Pete *5–8 165 LW*
B. Edmonton, Alta., June 29, 1955

75–76	Edm	75	7	13	20	34
76–77	Edm	3	0	0	0	2
Totals		78	7	13	20	36

Playoffs

75–76	Edm	3	0	1	1	7

SEASON	TEAM	GP	G	A	PTS	PIM

MORRIS, Rick *5–11 176 LW*
B. Hamilton, Ont., July 5, 1946

72–73	Chi	76	31	17	48	84
73–74	Chi	76	17	16	33	140
74–75	Chi	78	15	13	28	110
75–76	Ott–Edm	73	20	31	51	110
76–77	Edm	79	18	17	35	76
77–78	Edm–Que	30	1	6	7	47
Totals		412	102	100	202	567

Playoffs

73–74	Chi	18	4	3	7	42
76–77	Edm	5	0	1	1	4
Totals		23	4	4	8	46

MORRISON, George

MORRISON, Kevin

MORROW, Dave *6–0 190 C*
B. Edmonton, Alta., Apr. 21, 1957

78–79	Ind	10	2	10	12	29

MORTSON, Keke *5–9 170 RW*
B. Arnfield, Que., Mar. 29, 1934

72–73	Hous	67	13	16	29	95
77–78	Hous	6	0	1	1	7
Totals		73	13	17	30	102

Playoffs

72–73	Hous	10	0	3	3	16
77–78	Hous	2	0	1	1	0
Totals		12	0	4	4	16

MOSDELL, Wayne *6–3 185 D*
B. Montreal, Que., Dec. 3, 1944

72–73	Phil	8	0	1	1	12

MOTT, Darwin *5–9 165 LW*
B. Creelman, Sask., Aug. 19, 1950

72–73	Phil	1	0	0	0	0

MOTT, Morris

MOWAT, Bob *5–9 170 RW*
B. Kamloops, B.C., Oct. 5, 1949

74–75	Phoe	53	9	10	19	34

MULION, John

MYERS, Murray *6–0 185 RW*
B. Yellow Grass, Sask., Feb. 9, 1952

72–73	Phil	7	0	0	0	0
73–74	Van	61	22	20	42	28
74–75	Van	24	1	1	2	4
75–76	Cinn	56	14	15	29	12
Totals		148	37	36	73	44

NAPIER, Mark

NEALE, Robert *6–0 185 C*
B. Brandon, Man., Apr. 17, 1953

73–74	Clev	43	8	9	17	30
74–75	Clev–Winn	16	1	5	6	8
Totals		59	9	14	23	38

Playoffs

73–74	Clev	5	0	0	0	4

NEDOMANSKY, Vaclav

NEELD, Greg *6–0 192 D*
B. Vancouver, B.C., Feb. 25, 1955

75–76	Tor	17	0	1	1	18

NEVIN, Robert

NEWELL, Rick

NIEKAMP, James

NILSSON, Kent

NISTICO, Louis

NORIS, Joseph

NORWICH, Craig

NUGENT, Kevin *6–5 210 RW*
B. Little Falls, Minn., June 7, 1955

78–79	Ind	25	2	8	10	20

O'CONNELL, Tim *5–11 170 RW*
B. Chicago, Ill., Oct. 26, 1963

76–77	SD	16	0	3	3	4

O'DONNELL, Fred

O'DONOGHUE, Donald

ODROWSKI, Gerry

OLDS, Wally *6–2 200 D*
B. Warroad, Minn., Aug. 17, 1949

72–73	NY	61	5	7	12	4
75–76	Calg	28	0	5	5	6
Totals		89	5	12	17	10

Playoffs

75–76	Calg	9	0	2	2	4

O'NEIL, Paul

ORR, Bill *5–10 185 D*
B. South Porcupine, Ont., June 12, 1948

73–74	Tor	46	3	9	12	16

Playoffs

73–74	Tor	12	1	0	1	6

O'SHEA, Daniel

O'SHEA, Kevin

OUIMET, Francois *5–10 175 D*
B. Montreal, Que., Oct. 14, 1951

75–76	Minn	9	0	2	2	2
76–77	Cinn	16	1	8	9	10
Totals		25	1	10	11	12

PAIEMENT, Joseph

PAIEMENT, Pierre *D*

72–73	Phil	8	1	0	1	18

PARADISE, Dick *5–11 194 D*
B. St. Paul, Minn., Apr. 21, 1945

72–73	Minn	77	3	15	18	189
73–74	Minn	67	2	7	6	71
Totals		144	5	22	27	260

Playoffs

72–73	Minn	5	0	1	1	2
73–74	Minn	7	0	0	0	6
Totals		12	0	1	1	8

PARIZEAU, Mike

PATENAUDE, Rusty *5–9 175 RW*
B. Williams Lake, B.C., Oct. 17, 1949

72–73	Alb	77	29	27	56	59
73–74	Edm	71	20	23	43	55
74–75	Edm	56	20	16	36	38
75–76	Edm	77	42	30	72	88
76–77	Edm	73	25	16	41	57
77–78	Ind	76	23	19	42	71
Totals		430	159	131	290	368

Playoffs

73–74	Edm	4	0	2	2	2
75–76	Edm	4	1	4	5	12
76–77	Edm	2	0	0	0	8
Totals		10	1	6	7	22

PATRICK, Craig

PATRICK, Glenn

PATTERSON, Dennis

PATRY, Denis *5–8 165 RW*
B. Asbestos, Que., Dec. 3, 1953

74–75	Que	3	1	2	3	2

PAYETTE, Jean *6–0 170 C*
B. Cornwall, Ont., Mar. 29, 1946

72–73	Que	71	15	29	44	46
73–74	Que	41	4	11	15	6
Totals		112	19	40	59	52

PEACOSH, Gene *5–11 190 LW*
B. Sherridan, Man., Sept. 28, 1948

72–73	NY	67	37	34	71	25
73–74	NY–NJ	68	21	32	53	17
74–75	SD	78	43	36	79	22
75–76	SD	79	37	33	70	35
76–77	Edm–Ind	75	27	30	57	35
Totals		367	165	165	330	134

Playoffs

74–75	SD	10	7	5	12	4
75–76	SD	11	2	1	3	21
76–77	Ind	9	3	3	6	2
Totals		30	12	9	21	27

PEARSON, Mel

PELOFFY, Andre

PELYK, Michael

PENTLAND, Dwayne *5–10 180 D*
B. Vancouver, B.C., Feb. 8, 1953

76–77	Hous	29	1	2	3	6

Playoffs

76–77	Hous	2	0	0	0	0

PERKINS, Ross *5–10 176 C*
B. Tisdale, Sask., Nov. 4, 1946

72–73	Alb	71	21	37	58	19
73–74	Edm	78	16	40	56	43
74–75	Edm	76	7	16	23	33
Totals		225	44	93	137	95

Playoffs

73–74	Edm	5	1	3	4	2

PERRY, Brian

PESUT, George

PETERS, Garry

PHANEUF, Jean–Luc *5–8 165 C*
B. Montreal, Que., Oct. 26, 1955

75–76	Tor	48	8	8	16	4
76–77	Birm	30	2	7	9	2
Totals		78	10	15	25	6

PINDER, Garry

PIZUNSKI, Ed *5–10 185 D*
B. Toronto, Ont., Oct. 8, 1954

75–76	Ott	1	0	0	0	0

PLANTE, Michel *5–10 170 LW*
B. Drummondsville, Que., Jan. 19, 1952

72–73	Phil	70	13	12	25	35
73–74	Van	22	3	2	5	2
Totals		92	16	14	30	37

PLEAU, Lawrence

PLUMB, Ronald

POLANO, Nick *6–0 187 D*
B. Sudbury, Ont., Mar. 25, 1941

72–73	Phil	17	0	3	3	24

POPIEL, Jan *5–9 183 LW*
B. Virum, Denmark, Oct. 9, 1947

72–73	Chi	76	31	34	65	77
73–74	Chi	63	22	17	39	36
74–75	Chi	60	18	22	40	74
75–76	Ott–Hous	68	4	7	11	59
76–77	Phoe	28	3	2	5	8
Totals		295	78	82	160	254

SEASON	TEAM	GP	G	A	PTS	PIM

Playoffs

Season	Team	GP	G	A	PTS	PIM
73–74	Chi	18	8	5	13	12
75–76	Hous	8	1	1	2	4
Totals		26	9	6	15	16

POPEIL, Paul

POWIS, Trevor

PRENTICE, Bill *6–1 196 D*
B. Oshawa, Ont., Aug. 3, 1950

Season	Team	GP	G	A	PTS	PIM
72–73	Hous	3	0	1	1	0
73–74	Hous	55	1	2	3	35
74–75	Hous	17	0	3	3	19
75–76	Ind–Que	.59	6	7	13	181
76–77	Edm	3	0	0	0	2
77–78	Ind	21	1	1	2	28
Totals		158	8	14	22	265

Playoffs

Season	Team	GP	G	A	PTS	PIM
73–74	Hous	10	0	0	0	5
75–76	Que	5	0	0	0	17
Totals		15	0	0	0	22

PRESTON, Richard

PRIMEAU, Kevin

PRITCHARD, Jim *5–9 175 D*
B. Winnipeg, Man., Feb. 14, 1948

Season	Team	GP	G	A	PTS	PIM
74–75	Chi	2	0	0	0	0

PROCEVIAT, Dick *6–0 179 D*
B. Whitemouth, Man., June 25, 1946

Season	Team	GP	G	A	PTS	PIM
72–73	Chi	53	4	14	18	33
73–74	Chi	77	2	20	22	55
74–75	Chi–Ind	63	1	31	32	62
75–76	Ind	73	7	13	20	31
76–77	Ind	55	2	12	14	33
Totals		321	16	90	106	214

Playoffs

Season	Team	GP	G	A	PTS	PIM
73–74	Chi	13	0	4	4	10
75–76	Ind	7	0	0	0	2
Totals		20	0	4	4	12

PUMPLE, Rich *6–3 200 LW*
B. Kirkland Lake, Ont., Feb. 11, 1948

Season	Team	GP	G	A	PTS	PIM
72–73	Clev	77	21	20	41	45
73–74	Clev	17	2	2	4	16
74–75	Ind	34	4	8	12	29
Totals		128	27	30	57	90

Playoffs

Season	Team	GP	G	A	PTS	PIM
72–73	Clev	9	3	5	8	11

RAUTAKALLIO, Pekka

REED, Bill *5–11 190 D*
B. Toronto, Ont., May 25, 1954

Season	Team	GP	G	A	PTS	PIM
74–75	Balt	11	0	0	0	12
75–76	Calg	29	0	5	5	14
Totals		40	0	5	5	26

REICHMUTH, Craig *5–11 185 LW*
B. Russell, Mass., Sept. 22, 1947

Season	Team	GP	G	A	PTS	PIM
72–73	NY	73	13	14	27	127
73–74	NY–NJ	72	10	8	18	114
74–75	SD–Balt	44	2	3	5	81
Totals		189	25	25	50	322

REPO, Seppio *5–10 180 C*
B. Turku, Finland, Sept. 21, 1947

Season	Team	GP	G	A	PTS	PIM
76–77	Phoe	80	29	31	60	10

RHINESS, Brad *5–9 165 C*
B. Huntsville, Ont., Nov. 6, 1956

Season	Team	GP	G	A	PTS	PIM
76–77	SD	58	9	14	23	14
77–78	Ind	12	3	3	6	2
Totals		70	12	17	29	16

Playoffs

Season	Team	GP	G	A	PTS	PIM
76–77	SD	1	0	1	1	0

RICHARDSON, Steve *6–1 185 C*
B. Olds, Alta., May 4, 1949

Season	Team	GP	G	A	PTS	PIM
74–75	Ind–Balt	66	9	22	31	74
75–76	NE	6	0	0	0	0
Totals		72	9	22	31	74

RIIHIRANTA, Hiekki *5–11 190 LW*
B. Helsinki, Finland, Oct. 4, 1948

Season	Team	GP	G	A	PTS	PIM
74–75	Winn	64	8	14	22	30
75–76	Winn	70	1	8	9	26
76–77	Winn	53	1	16	17	28
Totals		187	10	38	48	84

Playoffs

Season	Team	GP	G	A	PTS	PIM
75–76	Winn	4	0	4	4	6

RILEY, Ron *F*
B. July 20, 1948

Season	Team	GP	G	A	PTS	PIM
72–73	Ott	22	0	5	5	2

RIVERS, John

RIZZUTO, Garth

ROBERTO, Phillip

ROBERTS, Douglas

ROBERTS, Gordan

ROBERTSON, Joe *5–11 180 C*
B. Windsor, N.S., Mar. 10, 1948

Season	Team	GP	G	A	PTS	PIM
74–75	Ind–Minn	29	5	8	13	27

ROCHON, Frank *5–11 181 LW*
B. Montreal, Que., Apr. 18, 1953

Season	Team	GP	G	A	PTS	PIM
73–74	Chi	71	12	11	23	27
74–75	Chi	69	27	29	56	19
75–76	Ott–Ind	60	17	12	29	41
76–77	Ind	57	15	8	23	8
Totals		257	71	60	131	95

Playoffs

Season	Team	GP	G	A	PTS	PIM
73–74	Chi	9	2	1	3	0
76–77	Ind	5	0	1	1	0
Totals		14	2	2	4	0

ROGERS, Alfred

ROGERS, Michael

ROLLINS, Jerry *6–3 195 D*
B. New Westminster, B.C., Mar. 22, 1955

Season	Team	GP	G	A	PTS	PIM
75–76	Tor	52	5	7	12	185
76–77	Birm–Phoe	71	4	10	14	186
78–79	Ind	7	0	1	1	7
Totals		130	9	18	27	378

ROMBROUGH, Lorne *5–11 190 LW*
B. Apr. 2, 1948

Season	Team	GP	G	A	PTS	PIM
73–74	LA	3	1	2	3	0

ROSELLE, Bob *6–2 185 LW*
B. Montreal, Que., Oct. 17, 1950

Season	Team	GP	G	A	PTS	PIM
75–76	Ind	1	0	0	0	0

ROTA, Randy

ROULEAU, Mike *5–10 176 C*
B. Hull, Que., Sept. 28, 1944

Season	Team	GP	G	A	PTS	PIM
72–73	Phil–Que	58	7	15	22	157
73–74	Que	4	0	4	4	2
74–75	Que–Balt–SD	53	6	16	22	130
Totals		115	13	35	48	289

ROUSSEAU, Dunc *6–0 195 LW*
B. Bissett, Man., Feb. 10, 1945

Season	Team	GP	G	A	PTS	PIM
72–73	Winn	74	16	17	33	75
73–74	Winn	60	10	8	18	39
Totals		134	26	25	51	114

Playoffs

Season	Team	GP	G	A	PTS	PIM
72–73	Winn	14	3	2	5	2
73–74	Winn	4	0	0	0	0
Totals		18	3	2	5	2

ROY, Pierre *6–0 175 D*
B. Amos, Que., Mar. 12, 1952

Season	Team	GP	G	A	PTS	PIM
72–73	Que	64	7	12	19	169
73–74	Que	44	2	7	9	137
74–75	Que	61	1	18	19	118
75–76	Que	78	6	30	36	258
76–77	Que–Cinn	68	6	17	23	176
78–79	NE	1	0	0	0	2
Totals		316	22	84	106	860

Playoffs

Season	Team	GP	G	A	PTS	PIM
74–75	Que	15	0	9	9	40
75–76	Que	5	1	2	3	29
76–77	Cinn	3	0	1	1	7
Totals		23	1	12	13	76

RUHNKE, Kent

RUPP, Duane

RUSKOWSKI, Terry

RUSSELL, Bob *5–9 167 C*
B. Toronto, Ont., Feb. 5, 1955

Season	Team	GP	G	A	PTS	PIM
75–76	Edm	58	13	18	31	19
76–77	Edm	57	7	6	13	41
Totals		115	20	24	44	60

Playoffs

Season	Team	GP	G	A	PTS	PIM
75–76	Edm	4	1	0	1	0
76–77	Edm	1	0	0	0	0
Totals		5	1	0	1	0

RYAN, Terry *5–10 178 C*
B. Grand Falls, Nfld., Sept. 10, 1952

Season	Team	GP	G	A	PTS	PIM
72–73	Minn	76	13	6	19	13

Playoffs

Season	Team	GP	G	A	PTS	PIM
72–73	Minn	5	0	2	2	0

RYCROFT, Allen *5–9 170 RW*
B. Beaver Lodge, Alta., Jan. 9, 1950

Season	Team	GP	G	A	PTS	PIM
72–73	Clev	7	0	2	2	0

RYDMAN, Blaine *6–2 195 F*
B. Weyburn, Sask., Dec. 16, 1949

Season	Team	GP	G	A	PTS	PIM
72–73	NY–Minn	31	0	1	1	69
73–74	Minn	8	0	0	0	21
Totals		39	0	1	1	90

SACHARUK, Lawrence

ST. SAUVEUR, Claude

SANDBECK, Cal *6–1 218 D*
B. International Falls, Minn., Jan. 28, 1956

Season	Team	GP	G	A	PTS	PIM
77–78	Edm	11	1	2	3	39
78–79	Edm	6	0	0	0	2
Totals		17	1	2	3	41

Playoffs

Season	Team	GP	G	A	PTS	PIM
77–78	Edm	5	0	0	0	10

SANDERS, Frank *6–3 230 D*
B. North St. Paul, Minn., Mar. 8, 1949

Season	Team	GP	G	A	PTS	PIM
72–73	Minn	77	8	8	16	94

Playoffs

Season	Team	GP	G	A	PTS	PIM
72–73	Minn	4	0	1	1	0

SANDERSON, Derek

SANZA, Nick *5–11 178 D*
B. Feb. 6, 1955

Season	Team	GP	G	A	PTS	PIM
75–76	Ott	1	0	0	0	0

SARNIER, Craig

SARRAZIN, Richard

SATHER, Glen

SCHARF, Ted *5–11 185 RW*
B. Penticton, Ont., Dec. 3, 1948

Season	Team	GP	G	A	PTS	PIM
72–73	NY	29	2	2	4	72
73–74	NY–NJ	63	4	2	6	107

SEASON TEAM	GP	G	A	PTS	PIM
74–75 SD	67	3	1	4	94
75–76 Ind	74	7	14	21	56
76–77 Edm	5	0	2	2	14
Totals	238	16	21	37	343

Playoffs

75–76 Ind	7	0	0	0	5

SCHELLA, John

SCHNEIDER, Buzz *5–11 175 LW*
B. Babbitt, Minn., Sept. 14, 1954

76–77 Birm	4	0	0	0	2

SCHRAEFEL, Jim *6–1 180 D*
B. Dauphin, Man., Aug. 23, 1948

73–74 Edm	34	1	1	2	0

Playoffs

73–74 Edm	5	0	3	3	0

SELBY, Brit

SELWOOD, Bradley

SEMENKO, David

SENTES, Dick *5–11 180 RW*
B. Regina, Sask., Jan. 10, 1947

72–73 Ott	73	22	19	41	78
73–74 Tor	64	26	34	60	46
74–75 SD	74	44	41	85	52
75–76 Calg	72	25	24	49	33
76–77 Calg–SD	53	20	25	45	24
Totals	336	137	143	280	233

Playoffs

72–73 Ott	5	3	1	4	2
73–74 Tor	12	7	4	11	19
74–75 SD	10	0	2	2	0
75–76 Calg	8	0	1	1	8
76–77 SD	5	0	4	4	12
Totals	40	10	12	22	41

SERAFINI, Ronald

SERVISS, Tom *5–10 185 RW*
B. Moose Jaw, Sask., May 25, 1948

72–73 LA	73	11	26	37	32
73–74 LA	74	6	15	21	37
74–75 Balt	61	12	17	29	18
75–76 Que	71	7	19	26	12
76–77 Calg	8	2	1	3	2
Totals	287	38	78	116	101

Playoffs

75–76 Que	5	0	0	0	0

SHANAHAN, Sean

SHEEHAN, Robert

SHEEHY, Timothy

SHERIDAN, John *6–1 190 C*
B. Minneapolis, Minn., Sept. 18, 1954

74–75 Ind	58	17	11	28	20
75–76 Ind	11	1	2	3	0
Totals	69	18	13	31	20

SHERRIT, Jim *5–7 170 C*
B. Glasgow, Scotland, Sept. 29, 1948

73–74 Hous	76	30	28	58	18
74–75 Hous	77	22	25	47	25
75–76 Ott	40	11	19	30	16
Totals	193	63	72	135	59

Playoffs

73–74 Hous	14	5	7	12	2
74–75 Hous	13	3	3	6	6
Totals	27	8	10	18	8

SHIRTON, Glen *D*

73–74 Clev	4	0	0	0	0

SHMYR, Johnny *D*
B. Cudworth, Sask., Jan. 2, 1945

72–73 Winn	7	0	0	0	2
73–74 LA	43	1	3	4	13
74–75 Van	39	1	5	6	43
Totals	89	2	8	10	58

Playoffs

72–73 Van	3	0	1	1	2

SHMYR, Paul

SHUTT, Byron *6–1 195 LW*
B. Toronto, Ont., Oct. 26, 1955

78–79 Cinn	65	10	7	17	115

SICINSKI, Bob *5–9 175 C*
B. Toronto, Ont., Nov. 13, 1946

72–73 Chi	77	25	63	88	18
73–74 Chi	69	11	29	40	8
74–75 Ind	77	19	34	53	12
75–76 Ind	70	9	34	43	4
76–77 Ind	60	12	24	36	14
Totals	353	76	184	260	56

Playoffs

73–74 Chi	18	6	8	14	0
75–76 Ind	7	0	0	0	2
76–77 Ind	9	0	3	3	4
Totals	34	6	11	17	6

SILTANEN, Risto

SIMPSON, Tom *5–9 190 RW*
B. Bowmanville, Ont., Aug. 15, 1952

72–73 Ott	57	10	7	17	44
73–74 Tor	74	33	20	53	27
74–75 Tor	70	52	28	80	48
75–76 Tor	73	20	21	41	15
76–77 Birm–Edm	40	10	8	18	26
Totals	314	125	84	209	160

Playoffs

72–73 Ott	5	1	0	1	0
73–74 Tor	12	4	1	5	5
74–75 Tor	5	1	1	2	0
Totals	22	6	2	8	5

SITTLER, Gary *6–1 187 D*
B. Kitchener, Ont.

74–75 Mich–Balt	5	1	1	2	14

SJOBERG, Lars-Erik

SLATER, Pete *5–9 170 RW*
B. Renfrew, Ont., Jan. 31, 1948

72–73 LA	73	12	12	24	87
73–74 LA	19	1	1	2	2
Totals	92	13	13	26	89

SLEEP, Mike *D*

75–76 Phoe	9	2	0	2	0
76–77 Phoe	13	2	2	4	6
Totals	22	4	2	6	6

Playoffs

75–76 Phoe	3	0	0	0	0

SLEIGHER, Louis

SMEDSMO, Dale

SMITH, Brian *F*

72–73 Hous	48	7	6	13	19

Playoffs

72–73 Hous	10	0	2	2	0

SMITH, Guy *6–1 188 RW*
B. Ottawa, Ont., Jan. 2, 1950

72–73 NE	23	3	3	6	6
73–74 NE	16	1	5	6	25
Totals	39	4	8	12	31

Playoffs

72–73 NE	11	2	0	2	4

SMITH, Richard

SMITH, Ross *6–0 184 RW*
B. Fawcett, Alta., Nov. 20, 1953

74–75 Ind	15	1	6	7	19

SNELL, Ronald

SOBCHUK, Dennis

SOBCHUK, Eugene

SPECK, Frederick

SPEER, William

SPENCER, Irvin

SPRING, Dan *6–0 180 C*
B. Rossland, B.C., Oct. 31, 1951

73–74 Winn	66	8	16	24	8
74–75 Winn	60	19	24	43	22
75–76 Edm	75	12	11	23	8
Totals	201	39	51	90	38

Playoffs

73–74 Winn	4	0	1	1	0
75–76 Edm	2	1	1	2	0
Totals	6	1	2	3	0

SPRING, Franklin

STANFIELD, Jack

STAPLETON, Pat

STEELE, Billy *5–7 F*
B. Edinburgh, Scotland, Nov. 13, 1952

75–76 Cinn	3	2	0	2	0
76–77 Cinn	81	9	22	31	21
Totals	84	11	22	33	21

Playoffs

76–77 Cinn	2	0	0	0	0

STEPHENSON, Ken *F*

72–73 Ott	77	3	16	19	93
73–74 Winn	29	0	7	7	24
Totals	106	3	23	26	117

Playoffs

72–73 Ott	5	1	1	2	8
73–74 Winn	3	0	2	2	10
Totals	8	1	3	4	18

STEPHENSON, Robert

STEVENS, Mike *5–11 188 D*
B. Winnipeg, Man., Oct. 13, 1950

74–75 Phoe	70	2	16	18	69
75–76 Hous	6	0	0	0	2
Totals	76	2	16	18	71

Playoffs

74–75 Phoe	5	0	1	1	0

STEWART, John *5–11 170 C*
B. Toronto, Ont., Jan. 2, 1954

74–75 Clev	59	4	7	11	8
75–76 Clev	42	2	9	11	15
76–77 Birm	52	17	24	41	33
Totals	153	23	40	63	56

Playoffs

74–75 Clev	1	0	0	0	0
77–78 Birm	5	1	1	2	6
Totals	6	1	1	2	6

STEWART, John A.

STEWART, Paul

STOESZ, Andy *D*

Playoffs

		GP	G	A	PTS	PIM
75–76	Winn	1	0	0	0	0

STOUGHTON, Blaine

SULLIVAN, Peter

SUTHERLAND, Steve *5–11 172 LW*
B. Noranda, Que., Sept. 1, 1946

		GP	G	A	PTS	PIM
72–73	LA	44	11	6	17	98
73–74	LA	72	20	12	32	182
74–75	Balt–Que	78	15	20	35	151
75–76	Que	74	22	19	41	197
76–77	Que	36	6	9	15	34
77–78	Que	75	23	10	33	143
Totals		379	97	76	173	805

Playoffs

72–73	LA	6	0	2	2	8
74–75	Que	13	0	3	3	34
75–76	Que	4	2	1	3	17
76–77	Que	17	5	0	5	16
77–78	Que	11	2	0	2	37
Totals		51	9	6	15	112

SUTHERLAND, William

SWAIN, Garry

SWENSON, Cal *5–8 176 C*
B. Naicam, Sask., Apr. 16, 1948

		GP	G	A	PTS	PIM
72–73	Winn	76	7	21	28	19
73–74	Winn	25	5	4	9	2
Totals		101	12	25	37	21

Playoffs

72–73	Winn	14	1	5	6	7
73–74	Winn	1	0	0	0	0
Totals		15	1	5	6	7

SYVRET, Dave *6–0 190 D*
B. Hamilton, Ont., Oct. 28, 1954

75–76	Tor	50	1	11	12	14
76–77	Birm	8	0	0	0	0
Totals		58	1	11	12	14

SZURA, Joseph

TAJCNAR, Rudy *5–11 225 F*
B. Bratislava, Czech.

78–79	Edm	2	0	0	0	0

TAMMINEN, Juha *5–11 185 RW*
B. Turku, Finland, May 26, 1950

75–76	Clev	65	7	14	21	0
76–77	Phoe	65	10	29	39	22
Totals		130	17	43	60	22

Playoffs

75–76	Clev	1	0	0	0	0

TANNAHILL, Donald

TARDIF, Marc

TAYLOR, Ted

TEBBUTT, Gregory

TERBENCHE, Paul

TETREAULT, Jean *D*

75–76	Minn	3	0	0	0	0

THOMAS, Reginald

TIDEY, Alexander

TITCOMB, Gord *5–11 186 F*
B. Dalhousie, N.B., Sept. 3, 1953

74–75	Tor	2	0	1	1	0

TONELLI, John

TOPOLINSKI, Craig *D*

		GP	G	A	PTS	PIM
77–78	Edm	1	0	2	2	4

TREMBLAY, J.C.

TREVELYN, Tom *5–10 185 C*
B. Toronto, Ont., Apr. 8, 1949

74–75	SD	20	0	2	2	4

TROGNITZ, Willie *6–0 205 LW*
B. Thunder Bay, Ont., June 11, 1953

77–78	Cinn	29	2	1	3	94

TROOLEN, Jerry *D*

72–73	Chi	2	0	0	0	0

TROTTIER, Guy

TROY, Jim *6–2 200 RW*
B. Boston, Mass., Jan. 21, 1953

75–76	NE	14	0	0	0	0
76–77	NE	7	0	0	0	7
77–78	Edm	47	2	0	2	124
Totals		38	2	0	2	131

Playoffs

75–76	NE	2	0	0	0	29
77–78	Edm	2	0	0	0	0
Totals		4	0	0	0	29

TURKIEWICZ, Jim *5–10 185 D*
B. Peterborough, Ont., Apr. 13, 1955

74–75	Tor	78	3	27	30	28
75–76	Tor	77	9	29	38	55
76–77	Birm	80	6	25	31	54
77–78	Birm	78	3	21	24	45
78–79	Birm	79	3	17	20	52
Totals		392	24	119	143	234

Playoffs

74–75	Tor	6	0	2	2	0
77–78	Birm	5	1	1	2	0
Totals		11	1	3	4	0

TURNBULL, Frank *5–8 155*
B. Trenton, Ont., Jan. 13, 1953

75–76	Edm	3	0	0	0	0

ULLMAN, Norm

VAN HORLICK, John *6–0 195 D*
B. Vancouver, B.C., Feb. 19, 1949

75–76	Tor	2	0	0	0	12

VENERUZZO, Gary

VIAU, Pierre *6–2 187 D*
B. Montreal, Que., Jan. 29, 1952

72–73	Chi	4	0	0	0	0

VOLMAR, Douglas

WALKER, Russell

WALL, Robert

WALSH, Brian *5–8 172 C*
B. Cambridge, Mass., Nov. 6, 1954

76–77	Calg	5	0	2	2	12

WALTER, Dave *6–0 181 C*
B. Niagara Falls, Ont., May 6, 1952

73–74	Chi	4	0	1	1	0
74–75	Chi	6	1	0	1	2
75–76	SD	16	1	2	3	6
Totals		26	2	3	5	8

WALTERS, Ron *6–0 175 RW*
B. Castor, Alta., Mar. 9, 1948

72–73	Alb	78	28	26	54	37
73–74	LA	71	14	14	28	28
74–75	Ind	17	2	1	3	9
Totals		166	44	41	85	74

WALTON, Michael

WALTON, Rob *5–9 165 C*
B. Toronto, Ont., Sept. 3, 1949

		GP	G	A	PTS	PIM
73–74	Minn–Van	73	16	38	54	26
74–75	Van	75	24	33	57	28
75–76	Calg	2	0	0	0	0
Totals		150	40	71	111	54

WARD, Ronald

WARNER, James

WARR, Steve *5–11 185 D*
B. Peterborough, Ont., Jan. 5, 1951

72–73	Ott	71	3	8	11	79

Playoffs

73–74	Tor	2	0	0	0	0

WATSON, Bryan

WATSON, James

WEBSTER, Thomas

WEIR, Stan

WEIR, Wally

WEST, Steve *5–8 150 C*
B. Peterborough, Ont., Mar. 20, 1952

74–75	Mich	50	15	18	33	4
76–77	Hous	3	0	0	0	2
77–78	Hous	71	11	21	32	23
78–79	Winn	18	3	11	14	6
Totals		142	29	50	79	35

Playoffs

75–76	Hous	7	0	1	1	0
76–77	Hous	6	0	0	0	0
77–78	Hous	6	1	0	1	0
78–79	Winn	6	2	3	5	2
Totals		25	3	4	7	2

WESTRUM, Pat *5–10 185 D*
B. Minneapolis, Minn., Mar. 3, 1948

74–75	Minn	23	0	3	3	48
75–76	Minn–Calg	63	3	12	15	121
76–77	Minn–Birm	74	2	20	22	90
77–78	Birm	77	2	10	12	97
Totals		237	7	45	52	356

Playoffs

75–76	Calg	6	0	1	1	19
77–78	Birm	3	0	1	1	0
Totals		9	0	2	2	19

WHITE, Alton *5–8 175 RW*
B. Amherst, N.S., May 31, 1945

72–73	NY–LA	70	21	21	42	24
73–74	LA	48	8	13	21	13
74–75	Mich	27	9	12	21	8
Totals		145	38	46	84	45

WHITE, Anthony

WHITLOCK, Robert

WIDING, Juha

WILKINS, Barry

WILLIAMS, Thomas

WILLIAMS, Warren

WILLIAMSON, Gary *5–10 175 LW*
B. Montreal, Que., May 25, 1950

73–74	Hous	9	2	6	8	0

Playoffs

73–74	Hous	12	0	0	0	0

WILLIS, Hal *6–2 215 D*
B. Liverpool, N.S., June 8, 1946

72–73	NY	74	3	21	24	159
73–74	LA	18	1	2	3	24
Totals		92	4	23	27	183

SEASON	TEAM	GP	G	A	PTS	PIM
WINOGRAD, Bob D						
B. Winnipeg, Man., June 6, 1946						
72–73	NY	52	0	12	12	23
73–74	NY–NJ	7	1	0	1	0
76–77	SD	1	0	0	0	0
Totals		60	1	12	13	23

WISTE, James

WOYTOWICH, Robert

WYROZUB, Randy

YAKIWCHUK, Dale *6–4 205 C*
B. Calgary, Alta., Oct. 17, 1958

78–79	Winn	4	0	0	0	0

SEASON	TEAM	GP	G	A	PTS	PIM
YOUNG, Bill *6–2 195 LW*						
B. St. Catharines, Ont., July 5, 1947						
72–73	LA–Minn	73	19	18	37	66
73–74	Clev–LA	69	9	12	21	74
Totals		142	28	30	58	140
Playoffs						
72–73	Minn	5	1	1	2	4

YOUNG, Howard

ZAINE, Rodney

ZANUSSI, Joseph

SEASON	TEAM	GP	G	A	PTS	PIM
ZRYMIAK, Jerry *6–1 195 D*						
B. Regina, Sask., Oct. 19, 1948						
72–73	LA	1	0	0	0	0
73–74	LA	27	2	8	10	8
74–75	Balt	49	3	9	12	53
75–76	Minn–Tor	39	0	13	13	27
76–77	Minn	40	2	10	12	14
Totals		156	7	40	47	102
Playoffs						
72–73	LA	2	1	0	1	2

ZUK, Wayne *C*

73–74	Edm	2	0	0	0	0

ZUKE, Michael

GOALIES

SSN	TEAM	GP	MIN	W	L	T	GA	SO	AVG

ABRAHAMSSON, Christer *6–2 180*
B. Leksand, Sweden, Apr. 12, 1947

SSN	TEAM	GP	MIN	W	L	T	GA	SO	AVG
74–75	NE	15	870	8	6	1	47	1	3.24
75–76	NE	41	2385	18	18	2	136	2	3.42
76–77	NE	45	2484	15	22	4	159	0	3.84
Totals		101	5739	41	46	7	342	3	3.58

Playoffs

75–76	NE	1	1	0	0	0	0	0	0.00
76–77	NE	2	90	0	1	0	5	0	3.33
Totals		3	91	0	1	0	5	0	3.30

ARCHAMBAULT, Yves *6–0 170*
B. June 22, 1952

72–73	Phil	6	260	1	3	0	17	0	3.92
73–74	Van	5	263	1	4	0	27	0	6.16
Totals		11	523	2	7	0	44	0	5.05

Playoffs

72–73	Phil	3	153	0	2	0	11	0	4.31

AUBRY, Serge *5–9 160*
B. Jan. 2, 1942

72–73	Que	52	3036	25	22	2	182	2	3.60
73–74	Que	26	1395	11	11	2	90	1	3.87
74–75	Que	31	1762	17	11	0	109	0	3.71
75–76	Cinn	12	549	6	4	0	38	1	4.15
76–77	Que	21	769	6	5	0	51	1	3.98
Totals		142	7511	65	53	4	470	5	3.75

Playoffs

76–77	Que	3	18	0	0	0	1	0	3.33

BERGLUND, Bill *6–1 187*
B. Everett, Mass., Sept. 24, 1948

73–74	NE	3	180	2	1	0	10	1	3.33
74–75	NE	2	36	0	0	0	3	0	5.00
Totals		5	216	2	1	0	13	0	3.61

BINKLEY, Les

BLANCHET, Bob *5–8 175*
B. Authier–Nord, Que., Feb. 24, 1954

74–75	SD	3	179	2	1	0	7	1	2.35
75–76	SD	1	32	0	1	0	4	0	7.50
Totals		4	211	2	2	0	11	1	3.13

BLUM, Frank *6–0 180*
B. June 29, 1952

72–73	Ott	2	28	0	0	0	3	0	6.43
73–74	Tor	5	130	1	0	0	5	0	2.31
Totals		7	158	1	0	0	8	0	3.04

Playoffs

73–74	Winn	2	120	0	2	0	15	0	7.50

BRODERICK, Kenneth

BRODEUR, Richard

BROMLEY, Gary

BROWN, Andrew

BROWN, Kenneth

BURCHELL, Randy *6–1 175*
B. Montreal, Que., July 2, 1955

75–76	Ind	5	136	1	0	0	8	0	3.53

CARON, Jacques

CHEEVERS, Gerry

COOLEY, Gaye *5–10 185*
B. North Bay, Ont., Feb. 8, 1945

Playoffs

75–76	NE	1	1	0	0	0	0	0	0.00

CORSI, James

COTTRINGER, Tom *5–8 162*
B. Quebec City, Que., Feb. 18, 1920

SSN	TEAM	GP	MIN	W	L	T	GA	SO	AVG
72–73	Phil	2	122	1	1	0	8	0	3.93

COUTU, Rick

73–74	Chi	20	1207	9	10	1	75	0	3.73
74–75	Chi	1	60	0	1	0	5	0	5.00
75–76	Cinn	3	149	9	13	1	97	0	4.11

CURRAN, Mike *5–9 175*
B. International Falls, Minn., Apr. 14, 1945

72–73	Minn	43	2540	23	17	2	131	4	3.09
73–74	Minn	40	2382	23	14	2	130	2	3.27
74–75	Minn	26	1367	11	10	1	90	0	3.95
75–76	Minn	5	240	2	2	0	22	1	5.50
76–77	Minn	16	848	4	7	3	50	0	3.54
Totals		130	7377	63	50	8	423	7	3.44

Playoffs

72–73	Minn	2	90	0	2	0	9	0	6.00
73–74	Minn	5	289	2	3	0	14	0	2.91
Totals		7	379	2	5	0	23	0	3.64

DALEY, Joe

DEGUISE, Michel *5–8 150*
B. June 11, 1951

73–74	Que	32	1750	12	13	1	96	1	3.29
75–76	Que	18	835	6	5	2	60	0	4.35
Totals		50	2585	18	18	3	156	1	3.62

DESJARDINS, Gerard

DION, Michel

DONNELLY, Peter *5–8 155*
B. Detroit, Mich., June 14, 1948

72–73	NY	47	2606	22	19	2	155	2	3.57
73–74	Van	49	2824	22	24	0	179	3	3.80
74–75	Que	4	129	0	1	0	10	0	4.65
Totals		100	5559	44	44	2	344	5	3.71

DOYLE, Gary

73–74	Edm	1	60	1	0	0	4	0	4.00

DUMAS, Richard

74–75	Chi	1	1	0	0	0	0	0	0.00

DRYDEN, David

DYCK, Edwin

GARDNER, Bud

GARRETT, John

GILL, Andre

GILLOW, Russ *5–10 165*
B. Hespeler, Ont., Sept. 2, 1940

72–73	LA	38	1982	17	13	2	96	2	2.91
73–74	LA	18	1041	4	13	0	69	1	3.98
74–75	SD	30	1653	15	11	2	94	1	3.41
75–76	SD	23	1037	1	10	2	74	0	4.28
Totals		109	5713	37	47	6	333	4	3.50

Playoffs

72–73	LA	5	247	1	2	0	12	0	2.91
74–75	SD	3	79	0	0	0	5	0	3.80
75–76	Calg	1	20	0	0	0	0	0	0.00
Totals		9	346	1	2	0	17	0	2.95

GRAHAME, Ron

GRATTON, Gilles

GRIGG, Chris *6–1 174*
B. Ottawa, Ont., Feb. 2, 1953

75–76	Denv–Ott	2	80	0	0	0	13	0	9.75

HOGANSON, Paul

HOLDEN, Bill

SSN	TEAM	GP	MIN	W	L	T	GA	SO	AVG
73–74	Tor	1	10	0	0	0	0	0	0.00

HOLMQUIST, Leif *5–11 175*
B. Gayle, Sweden, Sept. 22, 1942

| 75–76 | Ind | 19 | 1079 | 6 | 9 | 3 | 54 | 0 | 3.00 |

HUGHES, Bill
B. Kirkland Lake, Ont., Nov. 7, 1947

| 72–73 | Hous | 3 | 170 | 0 | 1 | 1 | 11 | 0 | 3.88 |

INNESS, Gary

JOHNSON, Robert

JUNKIN, Joseph

KAMPURRI, Hannu

| 78–79 | Edm | 2 | 90 | 0 | 1 | 0 | 10 | 0 | 6.67 |

KIELY, John *6–3 190*
B. Aug. 3, 1952

| 75–76 | Cinn | 22 | 1087 | 6 | 8 | 1 | 78 | 0 | 4.31 |

KURT, Gary

LANDON, Bruce *5–10 180*
B. Kingston, Ont., Oct. 5, 1949

72–73	NE	30	1671	15	11	1	100	1	3.59
73–74	NE	24	1386	11	9	2	82	0	3.55
74–75	NE	7	339	2	3	0	19	0	3.36
75–76	NE	38	2181	14	19	5	126	0	3.47
76–77	NE	23	1118	8	8	1	59	1	3.17
Totals		122	6695	50	50	9	386	2	3.46

Playoffs

73–74	NE	1	40	0	0	0	3	0	4.50
75–76	NE	4	197	3	0	0	7	0	2.13
76–77	NE	3	152	1	2	0	11	0	4.34
Totals		8	389	4	2	0	21	0	3.24

LAPOINTE, Norm *6–1 180*
B. Laval, Que., Aug. 13, 1955

75–76	Cinn	12	641	4	6	0	55	0	5.15
76–77	Cinn	52	2817	21	25	2	175	2	3.73
77–78	Cinn	13	647	5	6	1	50	0	4.64
Totals		77	4105	30	37	3	280	2	4.09

Playoffs

| 76–77 | Cinn | 4 | 273 | 0 | 3 | 0 | 16 | 0 | 3.52 |

LARSSON, Curt *5–11 171*
B. Dec. 11, 1944

74–75	Winn	26	1514	12	11	1	100	1	3.96
75–76	Winn	23	1287	11	10	1	83	0	3.87
76–77	Winn	19	1019	7	9	0	82	0	4.83
Totals		68	3820	30	30	2	265	1	4.16

Playoffs

75–76	Winn	2	110	2	0	0	6	0	3.27
76–77	Winn	1	20	0	0	0	1	0	3.00
Totals		3	130	2	0	0	7	0	3.23

LEVASSEUR, Jean-Louis

LIUT, Michael

LOCKETT, Kenneth

MATTSSON, Markus

McCARTAN, Jack

McDUFFE, Peter

McLEOD, Donald

McLEOD, James

MIO, Edward

NEWTON, Cameron

NORRIS, Jack

OUIMET, Ted

PAILLE, Marcel

PARENT, Bernie

PARK, Jim *6–1 190*
B. Toronto, Ont., June 22, 1952

75–76	Ind	11	572	6	4	0	23	0	2.41
76–77	Ind	31	1727	14	12	4	114	1	3.96
77–78	Ind	12	584	3	7	0	41	0	4.21
Totals		54	2883	23	23	4	178	1	3.70

Playoffs

| 75–76 | Ind | 6 | 294 | 3 | 2 | 0 | 12 | 0 | 2.45 |

PERREAULT, Robert

PLANTE, Jacques

READER, Cap *5–11 170*
B. Needham, Mass., Oct. 8, 1953

75–76	NE	3	100	0	1	0	8	0	4.80
76–77	NE	26	1328	12	10	1	69	2	3.12
Totals		29	1428	12	11	1	77	2	3.24

Playoffs

75–76	NE	14	819	7	7	0	31	2	2.27
76–77	NE	1	60	0	1	0	7	0	7.00
Totals		15	879	7	8	0	38	2	2.59

RIGGIN, Patrick

RUTLEDGE, Wayne

SANZA, Nick *5–11 178*
B. Feb. 6, 1955

| 75–76 | Denv–Ott | 1 | 20 | 0 | 1 | 0 | 5 | 0 | 15.00 |

SHAW, Jim *6–1 185*
B. Saskatoon, Sask., Oct. 18, 1945

74–75	Tor	21	1055	7	9	1	70	0	3.98
75–76	Tor	16	777	4	7	1	63	0	4.86
Totals		37	1832	11	16	2	133	0	4.36

Playoffs

| 74–75 | Tor | 5 | 262 | 2 | 2 | 0 | 18 | 0 | 4.12 |

SMITH, Allan

SMITH, Gary

SULLIVAN, Danny

72–73	Phil	1	60	1	0	0	3	0	3.00
73–74	Van	1	60	0	1	0	7	0	7.00
Totals		2	120	1	1	0	10	0	5.00

TATARYN, David

TUMILSON, Gordie
B. Winnipeg, Man., July 17, 1951

| 72–73 | Winn | 3 | 106 | 0 | 2 | 0 | 10 | 0 | 5.66 |

TURNBULL, Frank *5–8 155*
B. Trenton, Ont., Jan. 13, 1953

75–76	Edm	3	106	0	1	0	9	0	5.06
77–78	Edm	1	60	0	1	0	6	0	6.00
Totals		4	166	0	2	0	15	0	5.42

VIEN, Mario *5–7 166*
B. Aug. 7, 1955

| 75–76 | Tor | 26 | 1228 | 4 | 14 | 3 | 105 | 0 | 5.13 |

WAKELY, Ernie

WALSH, Ed *5–10 180*
B. Arlington, Mass., Aug. 18, 1951

| 78–79 | Edm | 3 | 144 | 0 | 2 | 0 | 9 | 0 | 3.75 |

SSN	TEAM	GP	MIN	W	L	T	GA	SO	AVG

WETZEL, Carl

WHIDDEN, Bob *5–10 180*
B. Sudbury, Ont., July 27, 1946

SSN	TEAM	GP	MIN	W	L	T	GA	SO	AVG
72–73	Clev	26	1609	11	12	3	88	0	3.28
73–74	Clev	22	1232	7	12	3	80	0	3.90
74–75	Clev	29	1654	9	16	1	89	1	3.23
75–76	Clev	21	1230	7	11	2	70	1	3.41
Totals		98	5725	34	51	9	327	2	3.43

WILKIE, Ian *5–9 175*
B. Edmonton, Alta., July 20, 1949

SSN	TEAM	GP	MIN	W	L	T	GA	SO	AVG
72–73	NY	5	253	1	3	0	27	0	6.40
73–74	LA–Edm	28	1513	14	10	0	91	1	3.61
Totals		33	1766	15	13	0	118	1	4.01

WOOD, Wayne
B. Toronto, Ont., June 5, 1951

SSN	TEAM	GP	MIN	W	L	T	GA	SO	AVG
74–75	Van	11	512	4	4	0	30	0	3.52

SSN	TEAM	GP	MIN	W	L	T	GA	SO	AVG
75–76	Calg–Tor	32	1661	15	10	1	107	1	3.87
76–77	Birm	23	1132	7	12	0	78	0	4.13
77–78	Birm	32	1551	12	10	2	99	1	3.83
78–79	Birm	6	311	1	3	0	21	0	4.05
Totals		104	5167	39	39	3	335	2	3.89
Playoffs									
77–78	Birm	1	29	0	0	0	3	0	6.21

WORTHY, Chris

ZIMMERMAN, Lynn *5–7 155*
B. Fort Erie, Ont., July 13, 1942

SSN	TEAM	GP	MIN	W	L	T	GA	SO	AVG
75–76	Denv–Ott	8	495	2	5	1	31	0	3.76
77–78	Hous	20	1166	10	9	0	84	0	4.32
Totals		28	1661	12	14	1	115	0	4.15
Playoffs									
77–78	Hous	4	239	1	2	0	21	0	5.27

18

THE WOMEN'S GAME

Women have played competitive hockey for 100 years, but true recognition didn't come until Feb. 17, 1998, in Nagano, Japan.

That was the historic day when the United States defeated Canada, 3–1, to win gold in the first women's Olympic hockey tournament. The red, white, and blue captured all six of its games, including a 7–4 come-from-behind triumph over Canada in the preliminary round.

Gretchen Ulion of the United States scored the first goal of the game in the second period, and teammate Shelly Looney made it 2–0 in the third period before Danielle Goyette put Canada on the scoreboard. Sandra Whyte added an empty-net goal with eight seconds remaining to wrap up the U.S. triumph.

Cammi Granato, the U.S. captain and sister of San Jose Sharks right wing Tony Granato, credited goaltender Sarah Tueting with "saving the game for us." She had 21 saves, the same number as Canada's Manon Rheaume.

Finland took the bronze medal for third place.

The Olympics were a victory as well for women's hockey in general. The sport features strong skating and passing, plus an emphasis on positional play. Unlike men's hockey, North American and International rules prohibit intentional body contact, so that players of different ages and sizes may play together. But anyone watching the U.S. and Canada compete in their pre-Olympic and Olympic Games recognized that there was no shortage of collisions or intensity.

The women's talent pool is still quite small compared to that of men's hockey, so it is uncertain if the Nagano spotlight can quickly translate into a professional league. But a byproduct of Olympic participation is increased participation in women's play at all levels of competition.

The Olympics have also provided the impetus for revealing and examining the forgotten history of women's hockey, through the publication of such books as *Too Many Men on the Ice,* by Joanna Avery and Julie Stevens. They trace the origins of the women's game to none other than Frederick Arthur, Lord Stanley of Preston, Canada's sixth governor-general.

Canada's Danielle Goyette holds her neck after falling to the ice in a preliminary-round game against the United States at the 1998 Olympics. Behind Goyette is Victoria Movsessian of the U.S. team.

Stanley's great passion for the game in the late 19th century led him to donate the Stanley Cup as a prize to Canada's best team. He also played the game himself and encouraged his family (a wife, eight sons, and two daughters) to join him on Ottawa's Rideau Canal. His daughter Isobel was one of the first female players in Canada and a member of the Government House women's team, which played against the Rideau Ladies around 1890 in perhaps the first organized women's game.

Newspaper photos of Isobel and her friends inspired women throughout Canada to emulate them. While women in eastern Canada often formed their own teams—often in the face of discouragement from men—out west they often played side-by-side with men during the game's infancy. The first all-women's league was organized in Quebec in 1900, and similar leagues would sprout over the next three decades. In Red Deer, Alberta, a prominent women's team formed in 1908 as an outgrowth of an organization providing assistance for the local hospital, so their games became charitable events to raise money. Tournaments also proved to be popular, with the first Ontario championship played in 1914. The growth of women's teams, leagues, and tournaments accelerated in Canada after World War I, when the sponsors were schools or businesses.

It was unheard of for women of the day to wear pants, so they played in long woolen skirts to keep them warm. Some goaltenders got the idea of putting buckshot pellets in the hem, providing additional weight to keep the skirt at ice level. The first competition between Canadian

Canada's Vicky Sunohara (right) tries to elude Colleen Coyne of the U.S. in the gold-medal game.

women and U.S. women dates back to this era, at a 1916 tournament in Cleveland.

Throughout Canada, women's games grew more competitive and some players, such as Bobbie Rosenthal of the Patterson Pats of Toronto, were so accomplished that newspapers of the '20s noted that they could earn places on the top men's junior teams. As the game moved indoors, dress and equipment was modified to compare with men's and admission was charged for games. A game between the Pats, the Ladies Ontario Hockey Association champs, and Quebec champions Verdun Electric drew 12,000 to the Montreal Forum in 1929.

While Clint Benedict became the first goaltender to wear a mask in NHL action in 1930, Queen's University's Elizabeth Graham preceded him by three years when she used a wire fencing mask for intercollegiate games.

Games between U.S.- and Canadian-based teams continued in the '30s, but the Depression claimed some aspects of women's hockey. The Canadian Intercollegiate Women's Ice Hockey League, formed in 1922, disbanded in 1933. But one women's team that survived enjoyed immense popularity and success during the 1930s. The Preston Rivulettes "almost single-handedly brought credibility, respect, and admiration to women's hockey," wrote Avery and Stevens. Led by forwards Hilda Ranscombe and Marm Schmuck and goalie Nellie Ranscombe, they posted 350 victories, three ties, and two losses in a 10-year period, and were annually the Ontario women's champions.

Cammi Granato (left) and Karen Bye let their gold medals say it all for the U.S. women in Nagano, Japan in 1998.

The first recipients of the Lady Bessborough Trophy in 1933, presented for winning the national title in the Dominion Women's Hockey Championships, they won each successive Dominion title until World War II forced the team to disband in 1941. The Rivulettes as a team were inducted into the Canadian Hockey Hall of Fame in 1963.

The Red Deer team, later called the Amazons, became a western version of the Rivulettes, popular and dominant in the provincial play of the '30s.

Progress was much slower and more isolated in the U.S., where the culture frowned on women's athletics in general at the beginning of the 20th century. Teams at various colleges and universities began forming as early as 1910, the largest contingent in Minnesota, where teams were based in industrial settings. Ivy League colleges in New England also had teams, but the Depression prevented the sport from spreading.

Following World War II, there were only a few organized leagues and teams. There were also instances of female players on male teams. One of the most celebrated was eight-year-old Abigail Hoffman, who registered as "Ab," cut her hair, and starred on defense in the Toronto Hockey League in 1955. When her gender was discovered by league officials, she made national news. She was not prohibited from playing but, despite

Canada's Therese Brisson takes a tumble as Jennifer Schmidgall (left), Gretchen Ullion (center), and Shelly Looney of the U.S. race for the puck in the gold-medal game won, 3–1, by the United States.

her abilities, pressure from coaches and other players forced her to quit and find women's teams to play with.

Over the next three decades, the issue of girls in boys' hockey raged in Canada. In some locales, it was because no comparable girls teams existed; in others, they did, but players sought to compete with the boys. The controversy ended in 1987, when a Canadian Supreme Court ruling affirmed the right of girls to play with boys.

Community hockey, through tournaments and house leagues, helped to keep women's hockey alive where it was played during the postwar dark ages, and the game received a boost when collegiate hockey reawakened in the 1960s.

Toronto's Queen's University revived its women's team, providing the impetus for other schools to follow.

In 1964, Brown University iced the first postwar U.S. women's collegiate team and, by 1967, began competing against Canadian teams. Cornell would join them over the next five years. Title IX legislation, which in 1972 mandated U.S. women collegiate athletes to receive equal opportunity in all collegiate sports, had little immediate impact. By 1977, however, the Ivy League was able to stage an annual women's hockey championship.

The first U.S. hockey boom in the 1970s, sparked by the fever around Bobby Orr and the Boston Bruins' Stanley Cup team, brought about

There was no joy for Stacy Wilson (left), Therese Brisson (center), and Danielle Goyette after Canada lost the gold medal to the United States.

a rise in community hockey, like the Massport/ American Girls Hockey Association in East Boston, which grew into a successful program. It inspired other communities to start similar programs, which developed women players for collegiate teams. One of their early stated goals was to see women's hockey made an Olympic sport. The Amateur Hockey Association of the United States (now USA Hockey) first petitioned the International Olympic Committee to include women's hockey in 1975.

European and Asian women began playing hockey with greater sophistication in the 1970s, and a team from Ontario toured Finland in 1979. In 1984, the Finnish National Women's Team, which would become the best outside North America, played six games in Ontario. The European championship tournament was inaugurated in 1989.

Canada's first women's national senior championship was contested in 1982. The U.S. senior women had a similar championship a year earlier, having conducted the first girls' championship in 1980. In both countries, championships at different age levels have periodically been added. Eventually the effects of Title IX kicked in for hockey, although the U.S. continued to lag behind Canada in the women's game: there were about 10 women's teams in Canada for every one in the U.S. in 1985.

National teams from Canada and the U.S. met for the first time in tournament competition at the inaugural Women's Invitational Tournament, played in 1987 in Ontario. It would grow into the Women's World Championship, the most significant international tournament prior to the Olympics. Established in 1990 and sanctioned by the International Ice Hockey Federation, the first tourney was played in Ottawa.

Canada won the first four biannual competitions, led by Angela James, who was considered the top women's player in the world. In 20 championship games, Canada outscored opponents 146 to 24. In 1997, the U.S. and Canada were tied after regulation time in the title game, before an overtime goal by Nancy Droulet enabled Canada to retain its crown. The gap between the top two nations has narrowed at the elite level.

Canada defeated the U.S. 3–1 in the gold medal game of the 1999 Women's World Championship at Espoo, Finland. The teams were tied 1–1 after two periods before Canada's Danielle Goyette and Geraldine Heaney tallied to produce the victory.

Canada's goalie, Sami Joe Small, made the All-Star team along with teammates Jayna Hefford and Hayley Wickenheiser. They were joined by Sue Merz and Jenny Schmidgall of the United States and Finland's Kirsi Hanninen.

Until the Olympics, probably the biggest story ever to involve a female player was when Canada's national team goalie, Manon Rheaume, was invited to the 1993 Tampa Bay Lightning training camp. She played briefly in a preseason game against NHL competition. She subsequently played in Tampa's minor pro organization. While she did perform well in spots, it was clear that she needed more practice time against her male counterparts.

Other women appeared in men's minor pro hockey, including U.S. National Team goalie Kelly Dyer, who played a handful of games in the Sunshine Hockey League.

19

JUNIOR HOCKEY: CANADA'S BEST

The Canadian Hockey League is to junior hockey what the NHL is to professional hockey—the best of the best. The league is the largest hockey league in the world, with 53 teams competing in three smaller leagues for the chance to win the Memorial Cup, the CHL's version of the Stanley Cup. The league features the best young talent from around the world. Recent statistics compiled by the CHL show that 65 percent of the players who played in the NHL in the 1997–98 season had spent time playing in the CHL, and fully 70 percent of the NHL's coaches and general managers got their start in the CHL, either as a player, coach, or manager.

While it might follow that those percentages would have fallen in recent years due to the increasing European presence in the NHL, that is not the case. In the 1999 NHL Entry Draft held in June, 112 CHL players were selected, including seven of the first 10 picks. Seven other CHL stars were drafted later in the first round.

The list of NHL stars who launched their careers in the CHL is a long and storied one. It starts, of course, with the Great One himself, Wayne Gretzky, and it also includes Mario Lemieux, Mike Bossy, Guy Lafleur, Theo Fleury, Denis Savard, Pat LaFontaine, Bobby Orr, Al MacInnis, Paul Coffey, Felix Potvin, and countless others.

With the parade of stars who marched through the CHL, it's no surprise that several future NHL stars made CHL history when they scored the goal that clinched the Memorial Cup for their teams. Among the members of this exclusive club are Andy Bathgate (Guelph, 1951), Pete Stemkowski (Toronto, 1964), Mark Howe (Toronto, 1973), Doug Gilmour (Cornwall, 1981), and Cam Neely (Portland, 1983).

The CHL has been a springboard to the NHL for coaches as well. Tom Kenney led the Kamloops Blazers to the league championship in 1992, then went on to coach the Vancouver Canucks. Ted Nolan, who led Sault Ste. Marie to the title in 1993, guided the Buffalo Sabres to a

division title in 1996–97. And Don Hay, one of only five men to coach consecutive Memorial Cup winners (Kamloops, 1994, 1995), moved up to coach the Phoenix Coyotes in 1996.

The CHL is divided into three separate leagues: the Ontario Hockey League, the Quebec Major Junior Hockey League, and the Western Hockey League. Teams from all three leagues compete for the most sought-after trophy in junior hockey, the Memorial Cup, which is awarded each May. Since 1972, the champions of each league have met in a round-robin series, with the top two teams playing in a sudden-death game for the Cup. Since the round-robin format was introduced, the Western League has produced 13 champions, the Ontario League has won 10 times, and the QMJHL, five times.

The trophy was originally named the OHA Memorial Cup. It was donated by the Ontario Hockey Association in 1919 in remembrance of the many soldiers who gave their lives for Canada in World War I.

MEMORIAL CUP WINNERS

SEASON	TEAM	COACH
1919	U. of Toronto Schools	Frank Carroll
1920	Toronto Canoe Club Paddlers	Ron Carroll
1921	Winnipeg Falcons	Connie Neal
1922	Fort William War Veterans	Stan Bliss
1923	U. of Manitoba Bisons	Hal Moulden
1924	Owen Sound Grays	Jim Jamieson
1925	Regina Patricias	Al Ritchie
1926	Calgary Canadians	Eddie Poulin
1927	Owen Sound Grays	Bill Hancock/Fr. J. Spratt
1928	Regina Monarchs	Howie Milne
1929	Toronto Marlboros	Frank Seike
1930	Regina Pats	Al Ritchie
1931	Elmwood Millionaires	Jack Hughes
1932	Sudbury Cub Wolves	Sam Rothschild
1933	Newmarket Redmen	Bill Hancock
1934	Toronto St. Michael's Majors	Jerry LaFlamme
1935	Winnipeg Monarchs	Harry Neil
1936	West Toronto Nationals	Clarence Day
1937	Winnipeg Monarchs	Harry Neil
1938	St. Boniface Seals	Mike Kryschuk
1939	Oshawa Generals	Tracy Shaw
1940	Oshawa Generals	Tracy Shaw
1941	Winnipeg Rangers	Lawrence Northcut
1942	Portage la Prairie Terriers	Addie Bell
1943	Winnipeg Rangers	Bob Kinnear
1944	Oshawa Generals	Charlie Conacher
1945	Toronto St. Michael's Majors	Joe Primeau
1946	Winnipeg Monarchs	Walter Monson
1947	Toronto St. Michael's Majors	Joe Primeau
1948	Port Arthur West End Bruins	Ed Lauzon
1949	Montreal Royals	Tag Millar
1950	Montreal Jr. Canadiens	Sam Pollock/Bill Reay
1951	Barrie Flyers	Leighton Emms
1952	Guelph Biltmore Mad Hatters	Alf Pike
1953	Barrie Flyers	Leighton Emms
1954	St. Catharines Tee Pees	Rudy Pilous
1955	Toronto Marlboros	Walter Broda
1956	Toronto Marlboros	Walter Broda
1957	Flin Flon Bombers	Bobby Kirk
1958	Ottawa-Hull Canadiens	Scotty Bowman
1959	Winnipeg Braves	Bill Allum
1960	St. Catharines Tee Pees	Max Kaminsky
1961	Toronto St. Michael's Majors	Fr. David Bauer
1962	Hamilton Red Wings	Eddie Bush
1963	Edmonton Oil Kings	Buster Brayshaw
1964	Toronto Marlboros	Jim Gregory
1965	Niagara Falls Flyers	Bill Long
1966	Edmonton Oil Kings	Ray Kinasewich
1967	Toronto Marlboros	Gus Bodnar
1968	Niagara Falls Flyers	Paul Emms
1969	Montreal Jr. Canadiens	Roger Bedard
1970	Montreal Jr. Canadiens	Roger Bedard
1971	Quebec Ramparts	Maurice Filion
1972	Cornwall Royals	Orval Tessier
1973	Toronto Marlboros	George Armstrong
1974	Regina Pats	Bob Turner
1975	Toronto Marlboros	George Armstrong
1976	Hamilton Fincups	Bert Templeton
1977	New Westminster Bruins	Ernie McLean
1978	New Westminster Bruins	Ernie McLean
1979	Peterborough Petes	Gary Green
1980	Cornwall Royals	Doug Carpenter
1981	Cornwall Royals	Bob Kilger
1982	Kitchener Rangers	Joe Crozier
1983	Portland Winter Hawks	Ken Hodge
1984	Ottawa 67's	Brian Kilrea
1985	Prince Albert Raiders	Terry Simpson
1986	Guelph Platers	Jacques Martin
1987	Medicine Hat Tigers	Bryan Maxwell
1988	Medicine Hat Tigers	Barry Melrose
1989	Swift Current Broncos	Graham James
1990	Oshawa Generals	Rick Comacchia
1991	Spokane Chiefs	Bryan Maxwell
1992	Kamloops Blazers	Tom Renney
1993	Sault Ste. Marie Greyhounds	Ted Nolan
1994	Kamloops Blazers	Don Hay
1995	Kamloops Blazers	Don Hay
1996	Granby Predateurs	Michel Therrien
1997	Hull Olympiques	Claude Julien
1998	Portland Winter Hawks	Brent Peterson
1999	Ottawa '67s	Brian Kilrea

ONTARIO HOCKEY LEAGUE

OHL CHAMPIONS

SEASON	TEAM	COACH
1933–34	St. Michael's College	—
1934–35	Kitchener (By default of Oshawa)	—
1935–36	West Toronto	—
1936–37	St. Michael's College	—
1937–38	Oshawa	—
1938–39	Oshawa	T. Shaw
1939–40	Oshawa	T. Shaw
1940–41	Oshawa	T. Shaw
1941–42	Oshawa	C. Conacher
1942–43	Oshawa	C. Conacher
1943–44	Oshawa	C. Conacher
1944–45	St. Michael's	J. Primeau
1945–46	St. Michael's	J. Primeau
1946–47	St. Michael's	J. Primeau
1947–48	Barrie	Hap Emms
1948–49	Barrie	Hap Emms
1949–50	Guelph	Alf Pike
1950–51	Barrie	Hap Emms
1951–52	Guelph	Alf Pike
1952–53	Barrie	Hap Emms
1953–54	St. Catharines	Rudy Pilous
1954–55	Toronto	Turk Broda
1955–56	Toronto	Turk Broda
1956–57	Guelph	Ed Bush
1957–58	Toronto	Turk Broda
1958–59	Peterborough	Scotty Bowman
1959–60	St. Catharines	Max Kaminsky
1960–61	St. Michael's	Rev. David Bauer
1961–62	Hamilton	Ed Bush
1962–63	Niagara Falls	Hap Emms
1963–64	Toronto	Jim Gregory

1964–65	Niagara Falls	Bill Long
1965–66	Oshawa	Armand "Bep" Guidolin
1966–67	Toronto	Angus Bodnar
1967–68	Niagara Falls	Paul Emms
1968–69	Montreal	Roger Bedard
1969–70	Montreal	Roger Bedard
1970–71	St. Catharines	Frank Milne
1971–72	Peterborough	Roger Neilson
1972–73	Toronto	George Armstrong
1973–74	St. Catharines	Paul Emms
1974–75	Toronto	George Armstrong
1975–76	Hamilton	Bert Templeton
1976–77	Ottawa	Brian Kilrea
1977–78	Peterborough	Gary Green
1978–79	Peterborough	Gary Green
1979–80	Peterborough	Mike Keenan
1980–81	Kitchener	Orval Tessier
1981–82	Kitchener	Joe Crozier
1982–83	Oshawa	Paul Theriault
1983–84	Ottawa	Brian Kilrea
1984–85	Sault Ste. Marie	Terry Crisp
1985–86	Guelph	Jacques Martin
1986–87	Oshawa	Paul Theriault
1987–88	Windsor	Tom Webster
1988–89	Peterborough	Dick Todd
1989–90	Oshawa	Rick Comacchia
1990–91	Sault Ste. Marie	Ted Nolan
1991–92	Sault Ste. Marie	Ted Nolan
1992–93	Peterborough	Dick Todd
1993–94	North Bay	Bert Templeton
1994–95	Detroit	Paul Maurice
1995–96	Peterborough	Dave MacQueen
1996–97	Oshawa	Bill Stewart
1997–98	Guelph	George Burnett
1998–99	Belleville	Louis Crawford

RED TILSON TROPHY— MOST VALUABLE PLAYER

YEAR	PLAYER	TEAM
1944–45	Doug McCurdy	St. Catharines
1945–46	Tod Sloan	St. Michael's
1946–47	Ed Sandford	St. Michael's
1947–48	George Armstrong	Stratford
1948–49	Gil Mayer	Barrie
1949–50	George Armstrong	Toronto
1950–51	Glenn Hall	Windsor
1951–52	Bill Harrington	Kitchener
1952–53	Bob Attersley	Oshawa
1953–54	Brian Cullen	St. Catharines
1954–55	Hank Ciesla	St. Catharines
1955–56	Ron Howell	Guelph
1956–57	Frank Mahovlich	St. Michael's
1957–58	Murray Oliver	Hamilton
1958–59	Stan Mikita	St. Catharines
1959–60	Wayne Connelly	Peterborough
1960–61	Rod Gilbert	Guelph
1961–62	Pit Martin	Hamilton
1962–63	Wayne Maxner	Niagara Falls
1963–64	Yvan Cournoyer	Montreal
1964–65	Andre Lacroix	Peterborough
1965–66	Andre Lacroix	Peterborough
1966–67	Mickey Redmond	Peterborough
1967–68	Walt Tkaczuk	Kitchener
1968–69	Rejean Houle	Montreal
1969–70	Gilbert Perreault	Montreal
1970–71	Dave Gardner	Toronto
1971–72	Don Lever	Niagara Falls
1972–73	Rick Middleton	Oshawa
1973–74	Jack Valiquette	Sault Ste. Marie
1974–75	Dennis Maruk	London
1975–76	Peter Lee	Ottawa
1976–77	Dale McCourt	St. Catharines
1977–78	Bob Smith	Ottawa
1978–79	Mike Foligno	Sudbury
1979–80	Jim Fox	Ottawa
1980–81	Ernie Godden	Windsor
1981–82	Dave Simpson	London
1982–83	Doug Gilmour	Cornwall
1983–84	John Tucker	Kitchener
1984–85	Wayne Groulx	Sault Ste. Marie
1985–86	Ray Sheppard	Cornwall
1986–87	Scott McCrory	Oshawa
1987–88	Andrew Cassels	Ottawa
1988–89	Bryan Fogarty	Niagara Falls
1989–90	Mike Ricci	Peterborough
1990–91	Eric Lindros	Oshawa
1991–92	Todd Simon	Niagara Falls
1992–93	Pat Peake	Detroit
1993–94	Jason Allison	London
1994–95	David Ling	Kingston
1995–96	Alyn McCauley	Ottawa
1996–97	Alyn McCauley	Ottawa
1997–98	David Legwand	Plymouth
1998–99	Brian Campbell	Ottawa

EDDIE POWERS MEMORIAL TROPHY— TOP SCORER

YEAR	PLAYER	TEAM
1933–34	J. Graboski	Oshawa
1934–35	J. Good	Toronto Lions
1935–36	John O'Flaherty	West Toronto
1936–37	Billy Taylor	Oshawa
1937–38	Hank Goldup	Toronto
1938–39	Billy Taylor	Oshawa
1939–40	Jud McAtee	Oshawa
1940–41	Gaye Stewart	Toronto
1941–42	Bob Wiest	Brantford
1942–43	Norman "Red" Tilson	Oshawa
1943–44	Ken Smith	Oshawa
1944–45	Leo Gravelle	St. Michael's
1945–46	Tod Sloan	St. Michael's
1946–47	Fleming Mackell	St. Michael's
1947–48	George Armstrong	Stratford
1948–49	Bert Giesebrecht	Windsor
1949–50	Earl Reibel	Windsor
1950–51	Lou Jankowski	Oshawa
1951–52	Ken Laufman	Guelph
1952–53	Jim McBurney	Galt
1953–54	Brian Cullen	St. Catharines
1954–55	Hank Ciesla	St. Catharines
1955–56	Stan Baliuk	Kitchener
1956–57	Bill Sweeney	Guelph
1957–58	John McKenzie	St. Catharines
1958–59	Stan Mikita	St. Catharines
1959–60	Chico Maki	St. Catharines
1960–61	Rod Gilbert	Guelph
1961–62	Andre Boudrias	Montreal
1962–63	Wayne Maxner	Niagara Falls
1963–64	Andre Boudrias	Montreal
1964–65	Ken Hodge	St. Catharines
1965–66	Andre Lacroix	Peterborough
1966–67	Derek Sanderson	Niagara Falls
1967–68	Tom Webster	Niagara Falls
1968–69	Rejean Houle	Montreal
1969–70	Marcel Dionne	St. Catharines
1970–71	Marcel Dionne	St. Catharines
1971–72	Bill Harris	Toronto
	Dave Gardner	Toronto
1972–73	Blake Dunlop	Ottawa
1973–74	Jack Valiquette	Sault Ste. Marie
	Rick Adduono	St. Catharines
1974–75	Bruce Boudreau	Toronto
1975–76	Mike Kaszycki	Sault Ste. Marie
1976–77	Dwight Foster	Kitchener
1977–78	Bob Smith	Ottawa
1978–79	Mike Foligno	Sudbury
1979–80	Jim Fox	Ottawa
1980–81	John Goodwin	Sault Ste. Marie
1981–82	Dave Simpson	London
1982–83	Doug Gilmour	Cornwall
1983–84	Tim Salmon	Kingston
1984–85	Dave MacLean	Belleville
1985–86	Ray Sheppard	Cornwall
1986–87	Scott McCrory	Oshawa
1987–88	Andrew Cassels	Ottawa
1988–89	Bryan Fogarty	Niagara Falls
1989–90	Keith Primeau	Niagara Falls
1990–91	Eric Lindros	Oshawa
1991–92	Todd Simon	Niagara Falls
1992–93	Andrew Brunette	Owen Sound
1993–94	Jason Allison	London
1994–95	Marc Savard	Oshawa
1995–96	Aaron Brand	Sarnia
1996–97	Marc Sarvard	Oshawa

1997–98	Peter Sarno	Windsor
1998–99	Peter Sarno	Sarnia

MAX KAMINSKY TROPHY— TOP DEFENSEMAN

YEAR	PLAYER	TEAM
1969–70	Ron Plumb	Peterborough
1970–71	Jocelyn Guevremont	Montreal
1971–72	Denis Potvin	Ottawa
1972–73	Denis Potvin	Ottawa
1973–74	Jim Turkiewicz	Peterborough
1974–75	Mike O'Connell	Kingston
1975–76	Rick Green	London
1976–77	Craig Hartsburg	Sault Ste. Marie
1977–78	Brad Marsh	London
	Rob Ramage	London
1978–79	Greg Theberge	Peterborough
1979–80	Larry Murphy	Peterborough
1980–81	Randy Boyd	Ottawa
1981–82	Ron Meighan	Niagara Falls
1982–83	Allan Macinnis	Kitchener
1983–84	Brad Shaw	Ottawa
1984–85	Bob Halkidis	London
1985–86	Jeff Brown	Sudbury
	Terry Carkner	Peterborough
1986–87	Kerry Huffman	Guelph
1987–88	Darryl Shannon	Windsor
1988–89	Bryan Fogarty	Niagara Falls
1989–90	John Slaney	Cornwall
1990–91	Chris Snell	Ottawa
1991–92	Drake Berehowsky	North Bay
1992–93	Chris Pronger	Peterborough
1993–94	Jamie Rivers	Sudbury
1994–95	Bryan Berard	Detroit
1995–96	Bryan Berard	Detroit
1996–97	Sean Blanchard	Ottawa
1997–98	Chris Allen	Kingston
1998–99	Brian Campbell	Ottawa

DAVE PINKNEY TROPHY— FEWEST GOALS AGAINST, GOALTENDERS

YEAR	PLAYERS	TEAM
1948–49	Gil Mayer	Barrie
1949–50	Don Lockhart	Toronto
1950–51	Don Lockhart	Toronto
	Lorne Howes	Barrie (tie)
1951–52	Don Head	Torontos
1952–53	John Henderson	Toronto
1953–54	Dennis Riggin	Hamilton
1954–55	John Albani	Toronto
1955–56	Jim Crockett	Toronto
1956–57	Len Broderick	Toronto
1957–58	Len Broderick	Toronto
1958–59	Jacques Caron	Peterborough
1959–60	Gerry Cheevers	St. Michael's
1960–61	Bud Blom	Hamilton
1961–62	George Holmes	Montreal
1962–63	Chuck Goddard	Peterborough
1963–64	Bernie Parent	Niagara Falls
1964–65	Bernie Parent	Niagara Falls
1965–66	Ted Ouimet	Montreal
1966–67	Peter McDuffe	St. Catharines
1967–68	Jim Rutherford	Hamilton
	Gerry Gray	Hamilton
1968–69	Wayne Wood	Montreal
	Ted Tucker	Montreal
1969–70	John Garrett	Peterborough
1970–71	John Garrett	Peterborough
1971–72	Michel Larocque	Ottawa
1972–73	Mike Palmateer	Toronto
1973–74	Don Edwards	Kitchener
1974–75	Greg Millen	Peterborough
1975–76	Jim Bedard	Sudbury
1976–77	Pat Riggin	London
1977–78	Al Jensen	Hamilton
1978–79	Nick Ricci	Niagara Falls
	Glen Ernst	Niagara Falls
1979–80	Rick LaFerriere	Peterborough

	Terry Wright	Peterborough
1980–81	Jim Ralph	Ottawa
1981–82	Marc D'Amour	Sault Ste. Marie
	John Vanbiesbrouck	S.S. Marie
1982–83	Peter Sidorkiewicz	Oshawa
	Jeff Hogg	Oshawa
1983–84	Darren Pang	Ottawa
	Greg Coram	Ottawa
1984–85	Scott Mosey	Sault Ste. Marie
	Marty Abrams	Sault Ste. Marie
1985–86	Kay Whitmore	Peterborough
	Ron Tugnutt	Peterborough
1986–87	Jeff Hackett	Oshawa
	Sean Evoy	Oshawa
1987–88	Todd Bojcun	Peterborough
	John Tanner	Peterborough
1988–89	John Tanner	Peterborough
	Todd Bojcun	Peterborough
1989–90	Jeff Wilson	Kingston
	Sean Gauthier	Kingston
1990–91	Mike Lenarduzzi	Sault Ste. Marie
	Kevin Hodson	Sault Ste. Marie
1991–92	Kevin Hodson	Sault Ste. Marie
1992–93	Chad Lang	Peterborough
	Ryan Douglas	Peterborough
1993–94	Sandy Allan	North Bay
	Scott Roche	North Bay
1994–95	Mark McArthur	Guelph
	Andy Adams	Guelph
1995–96	Dan Cloutier	Guelph
	Brett Thompson	Guelph
1996–97	Craig Hillier	Ottawa
	Tim Keyes	Ottawa
1997–98	Craig Hillier	Ottawa
	Seamus Kotyk	Ottawa
1998–99	Robert Holsinger	Plymouth

F. W. "DINTY" MOORE TROPHY— ROOKIE GOALTENDER WITH LOWEST G.A.A.

YEAR	PLAYER	TEAM
1975–76	Mark Locken	Hamilton
1976–77	Barry Heard	London
1977–78	Ken Ellacott	Peterborough
1978–79	Nick Ricci	Niagara Falls
1979–80	Mike Vezina	Ottawa
1980–81	John Vanbiesbrouck	S.S. Marie
1981–82	Shawn Kilroy	Peterborough
1982–83	Dan Burrows	Belleville
1983–84	Gerry Iuliano	Sault Ste. Marie
1984–85	Ron Tugnutt	Peterborough
1985–86	Paul Henriques	Belleville
1986–87	Jeff Hackett	Oshawa
1987–88	Todd Bojcun	Peterborough
1988–89	Jeff Wilson	Kingston
1989–90	Sean Basilio	London
1990–91	Kevin Hodson	Sault Ste. Marie
1991–92	Sandy Allan	North Bay
1992–93	Ken Shepard	Oshawa
1993–94	Scott Roche	North Bay
1994–95	David MacDonald	Sudbury
1995–96	Brett Thompson	Guelph
1996–97	Shawn DeGagne	Kitchener
1997–98	Seamus Kotyk	Ottawa
1998–99	Lavente Szuper	Ottawa

EMMS FAMILY AWARD—TOP ROOKIE

YEAR	PLAYER	TEAM
1972–73	Dennis Maruk	London
1973–74	Jack Valiquette	Sault Ste. Marie
1974–75	Danny Shearer	Hamilton
1975–76	John Tavella	Sault Ste. Marie
1976–77	Mike Gartner	Niagara Falls
1977–78	Wayne Gretzky	Sault Ste. Marie
1978–79	John Goodwin	Sault Ste. Marie
1979–80	Bruce Dowie	Toronto
1980–81	Tony Tanti	Oshawa
1981–82	Pat Verbeek	Sudbury
1982–83	Bruce Cassidy	Ottawa
1983–84	Shawn Burr	Kitchener

1984–85	Derek King	Sault Ste. Marie
1985–86	Lonnie Loach	Guelph
1986–87	Andrew Cassels	Ottawa
1987–88	Rick Corriveau	London
1988–89	Owen Nolan	Cornwall
1989–90	Chris Longo	Peterborough
1990–91	Cory Stillman	Windsor
1991–92	Chris Gratton	Kingston
1992–93	Jeff O'Neill	Guelph
1993–94	Vitali Yachmenev	North Bay
1994–95	Bryan Berard	Detroit
1995–96	Joe Thornton	Sault Ste. Marie
1996–97	Peter Sarno	Windsor
1997–98	David Legwand	Plymouth
1998–99	Sheldon Keefe	Barrie

MATT LEYDEN TROPHY—
COACH OF THE YEAR

YEAR	COACH	TEAM
1971–72	Gus Bodnar	Oshawa
1972–73	George Armstrong	Toronto
1973–74	Jack Bownass	Kingston
1974–75	Bert Templeton	Hamilton
1975–76	Jerry Toppazzini	Sudbury
1976–77	Bill Long	London
1977–78	Bill White	Oshawa
1978–79	Gary Green	Peterborough
1979–80	Dave Chambers	Toronto
1980–81	Brian Kilrea	Ottawa
1981–82	Brian Kilrea	Ottawa
1982–83	Terry Crisp	Sault Ste. Marie
1983–84	Tom Barrett	Kitchener
1984–85	Terry Crisp	Sault Ste. Marie
1985–86	Jacques Martin	Guelph
1986–87	Paul Theriault	Oshawa
1987–88	Dick Todd	Peterborough
1988–89	Joe McDonnell	Kitchener
1989–90	Larry Mavety	Kingston
1990–91	George Burnett	Niagara Falls
1991–92	George Burnett	Niagara Falls
1992–93	Gary Agnew	London
1993–94	Bert Templeton	North Bay
1994–95	Craig Hartsburg	Guelph
1995–96	Brian Kilrea	Ottawa
1996–97	Brian Kilrea	Ottawa
1997–98	Gary Agnew	London
1998–99	Peter DeBoer	Plymouth

WILLIAM HANLEY TROPHY—
MOST GENTLEMANLY PLAYER

YEAR	PLAYER	TEAM
1960–61	Bruce Draper	St. Michael's
1961–62	Lowell MacDonald	Hamilton
1962–63	Paul Henderson	Hamilton
1963–64	Fred Stanfield	St. Catharines
1964–65	Jimmy Peters	Hamilton
1965–66	Andre Lacroix	Peterborough
1966–67	Mickey Redmond	Peterborough
1967–68	Tom Webster	Niagara Falls
1968–69	Rejean Houle	Montreal
1969–74	No award presented	
1974–75	Doug Jarvis	Peterborough
1975–76	Dale McCourt	Hamilton
1976–77	Dale McCourt	St. Catharines
1977–78	Wayne Gretzky	Sault Ste. Marie
1978–79	Sean Simpson	Ottawa
1979–80	Sean Simpson	Ottawa
1980–81	John Goodwin	Sault Ste. Marie
1981–82	Dave Simpson	London
1982–83	Kirk Muller	Guelph
1983–84	Kevin Conway	Kingston
1984–85	Scott Tottle	Peterborough
1985–86	Jason Lafreniere	Belleville
1986–87	Scott McCrory	Oshawa
	Keith Gretzky	Hamilton
1987–88	Andrew Cassels	Ottawa
1988–89	Kevin Miehm	Oshawa
1989–90	Mike Ricci	Peterborough

1990–91	Dale Craigwell	Oshawa
1991–92	John Spoltore	North Bay
1992–93	Pat Peake	Detroit
1993–94	Jason Allison	London
1994–95	Vitali Yachmenev	North Bay
1995–96	Jeff Williams	Guelph
1996–97	Alyn McCauley	Ottawa
1997–98	Matt Bradley	Kingston
1998–99	Brian Campbell	Ottawa

WESTERN HOCKEY LEAGUE

WHL CHAMPIONS

YEAR	TEAM	COACH
1966–67	Moose Jaw Canucks	Brian Shaw
1967–68	Estevan Bruins	Ernie McLean
1968–69	Flin Flon Bombers	Pat Ginnell
1969–70	Flin Flon Bombers	Pat Ginnell
1970–71	Edmonton Oil Kings	Bill Hunter
1971–72	Edmonton Oil Kings	Brian Shaw
1972–73	Medicine Hat Tigers	Jack Shupe
1973–74	Regina Pats	Bob Turner
1974–75	New Westminster Bruins	Ernie McLean
1975–76	New Westminster Bruins	Ernie McLean
1976–77	New Westminster Bruins	Ernie McLean
1977–78	New Westminster Bruins	Ernie McLean
1978–79	Brandon Wheat Kings	Dunc McCallum
1979–80	Regina Pats	Bryan Murray
1980–81	Victoria Cougars	Jack Shupe
1981–82	Portland Winter Hawks	Ken Hodge
1982–83	Lethbridge Broncos	John Chapman
1983–84	Kamloops Junior Oilers	Bill LaForge
1984–85	Prince Albert Raiders	Terry Simpson
1985–86	Kamloops Blazers	Ken Hitchcock
1986–87	Medicine Hat Tigers	Bryan Maxwell
1987–88	Medicine Hat Tigers	Bryan Melrose
1988–89	Swift Current Broncos	Graham James
1989–90	Kamloops Blazers	Ken Hitchcock
1990–91	Spokane Chiefs	Bryan Maxwell
1991–92	Kamloops Blazers	Tom Renney
1992–93	Swift Current Broncos	Graham James
1993–94	Kamloops Blazers	Don Hay
1994–95	Kamloops Blazers	Don Hay
1995–96	Brandon Wheat Kings	Bob Lowes
1996–97	Lethbridge Hurricanes	Parry Shockey
1997–98	Portland Winter Hawks	Brent Peterson
1998–99	Calgary Hitmen	Dean Clark

FOUR BRONCOS MEMORIAL TROPHY—
MOST VALUABLE PLAYER

YEAR	PLAYER	TEAM
1966–67	Gerry Pinder	Saskatoon
1967–68	Jim Harrison	Estevan
1968–69	Bobby Clarke	Flin Flon
1969–70	Reg Leach	Flin Flon
1970–71	Ed Dyck	Calgary
1971–72	John Davidson	Calgary
1973–74	Ron Chipperfield	Brandon
1974–75	Brian Trottier	Lethbridge
1975–76	Bernie Federko	Saskatoon
1976–77	Barry Beck	New Westminster
1977–78	Ryan Walter	Seattle
1978–79	Perry Turnbull	Portland
1979–80	Doug Wickenheiser	Regina
1980–81	Steve Tsujiura	Medicine Hat
1981–82	Mike Vernon	Calgary
1982–83	Dennis Sobchuk	Regina
1982–83	Mike Vernon	Calgary
1983–84	Ray Ferraro	Brandon
1984–85	Cliff Ronning	New Westminster
1985–86	Rob Brown	Kamloops
	Emanuel Viveiros	Prince Albert
1986–87	Rob Brown	Kamloops
	Joe Sakic	Swift Current
1987–88	Joe Sakic	Swift Current

YEAR	PLAYER	TEAM
1988–89	Stu Barnes	Tri–City
1989–90	Glen Goodall	Seattle
1990–91	Ray Whitney	Spokane
1991–92	Steve Konowalchuk	Portland
1992–93	Jason Krywulak	Swift Current
1993–94	Sonny Mignacca	Medicine Hat
1994–95	Marty Murray	Brandon
1995–96	Jarome Iginla	Kamloops
1996–97	Peter Schaefer	Brandon
1998–99	Cody Rudkowsky	Seattle

YEAR	PLAYER	TEAM
1989–90	Petr Nedved	Seattle
1990–91	Donevan Hextall	Prince Albert
1991–92	Ashley Buckberger	Swift Current
1992–93	Jeff Friesen	Regina
1993–94	Wade Redden	Brandon
1994–95	Todd Robinson	Portland
1995–96	Chris Phillips	Prince Albert
1996–97	Donovan Nunweiler	Moose Jaw
1997–98	Marian Hossa	Portland
1998–99	Pavel Brendl	Calgary

BOB CLARKE TROPHY—TOP SCORER

YEAR	PLAYER	TEAM
1966–67	Gerry Pinder	Saskatoon
1967–68	Bobby Clarke	Flin Flon
1968–69	Bobby Clarke	Flin Flon
1969–70	Reg Leach	Flin Flon
1970–71	Chuck Amason	Flin Flon
1971–72	Tom Lysiak	Medicine Hat
1972–73	Tom Lysiak	Medicine Hat
1973–74	Ron Chipperfield	Brandon
1974–75	Mel Bridgman	Victoria
1975–76	Bernie Federko	Saskatoon
1976–77	Bill Derlago	Brandon
1977–78	Brian Propp	Brandon
1978–79	Brian Propp	Brandon
1979–80	Doug Wickenheiser	Regina
1980–81	Brian Varga	Regina
1981–82	Jock Callander	Regina
1982–83	Dale Derkatch	Regina
1983–84	Ray Ferraro	Brandon
1984–85	Cliff Ronning	New Westminster
1985–86	Rob Brown	Kamloops
1986–87	Rob Brown	Kamloops
	Craig Endean	Regina
1987–88	Theoren Fleury	Moose Jaw
	Joe Sakic	Swift Current
1988–89	Dennis Holland	Portland
1989–90	Len Barrie	Kamloops
1990–91	Ray Whitney	Spokane
1991–92	Kevin St. Jacques	Lethbridge
1992–93	Jason Krywulak	Swift Current
1993–94	Lonny Bohonos	Portland
1994–95	Daymond Langkow	Tri–Cities
1995–96	Mark Deyell	Saskatoon
1996–97	Todd Robinson	Portland
1997–98	Sergei Varlamov	Swift Current
1998–99	Pavel Brendl	Calgary

BILL HUNTER TROPHY—TOP DEFENSEMAN

YEAR	PLAYER	TEAM
1966–67	Barry Gibbs	Estevan
1967–68	Gerry Hart	Flin Flon
1968–69	Dale Hoganson	Estevan
1969–70	Jim Hargreaves	Winnipeg
1970–71	Ron Jones	Edmonton
1971–72	Jim Watson	Calgary
1972–73	George Pesut	Saskatoon
1973–74	Pat Price	Saskatoon
1974–75	Rick Lapointe	Victoria
1975–76	Kevin McCarthy	Winnipeg
1976–77	Barry Beck	New Westminster
1977–78	Brad McCrimmon	Brandon
1978–79	Keith Brown	Portland
1979–80	Dave Babych	Portland
1980–81	Jim Benning	Portland
1981–82	Gary Nylund	Portland
1982–83	Gary Leeman	Regina
1983–84	Bob Rouse	Lethbridge
1984–85	Wendel Clark	Saskatoon
1985–86	Emanuel Viveiros	Prince Albert
	Glen Wesley	Portland
1986–87	Wayne McBean	Medicine Hat
	Glen Wesley	Portland
1987–88	Greg Hawgood	Kamloops
1988–89	Dan Lambert	Swift Current
1989–90	Kevin Haller	Regina
1990–91	Darryl Sydor	Kamloops
1991–92	Richard Matvichuk	Saskatoon
1992–93	Jason Smith	Regina
1993–94	Brendan Witt	Seattle
1994–95	Nolan Baumgartner	Kamloops
1995–96	Nolan Baumgartner	Kamloops
1996–97	Chris Phillips	Lethbridge
1997–98	Michal Rozsival	Swift Current
1998–99	Brad Stuart	Calgary

JIM PIGGOT MEMORIAL TROPHY— ROOKIE OF THE YEAR

YEAR	PLAYER	TEAM
1966–67	Ron Garwasiuk	Regina
1967–68	Ron Fairbrother	Saskatoon
1968–69	Ron Williams	Edmonton
1969–70	Gene Carr	Flin Flon
1970–71	Stan Weir	Medicine Hat
1971–72	Dennis Sobchuk	Regina
1972–73	Rick Blight	Brandon
1973–74	Cam Connor	Flin Flon
1974–75	Don Murdoch	Medicine Hat
1975–76	Steve Tambellini	Lethbridge
1976–77	Brian Propp	Brandon
1977–78	Keith Brown	Portland
	John Ogrodnick	New West.
1978–79	Kelly Kisio	Calgary
1979–80	Grant Fuhr	Victoria
1980–81	Dave Michayluk	Regina
1981–82	Dale Derkatch	Regina
1982–83	Dan Hodgson	Prince Albert
1983–84	Cliff Ronning	New Westminster
1984–85	Mark Mackay	Moose Jaw
1985–86	Ron Shudra	Kamloops
	Dave Waldie	Portland
	Neil Brady	Medicine Hat
1986–87	Dennis Holland	Portland
	Joe Sakic	Swift Current
1987–88	Stu Barnes	New Westminster
1988–89	Wes Walz	Lethbridge

DEL WILSON TROPHY—TOP GOALTENDER

YEAR	PLAYER	TEAM
1966–67	Ken Brown	Moose Jaw
1967–68	Chris Worthy	Flin Flon
1968–69	Ray Martyniuk	Flin Flon
1969–70	Ray Martyniuk	Flin Flon
1970–71	Ed Dyck	Calgary
1971–72	John Davidson	Calgary
1972–73	Ed Humphreys	Saskatoon
1973–74	Garth Malarchuk	Calgary
1974–75	Bill Oleschuk	Saskatoon
1975–76	Carey Walker	New Westminster
1976–77	Glen Hanlon	Brandon
1977–78	Bart Hunter	Portland
1978–79	Rick Knickle	Brandon
1979–80	Kevin Eastman	Victoria
1980–81	Grant Fuhr	Victoria
1981–82	Mike Vernon	Calgary
1982–83	Mike Vernon	Calgary
1983–84	Ken Wregget	Lethbridge
1984–85	Troy Gamble	Medicine Hat
1985–86	Mark Fitzpatrick	Medicine Hat
1986–87	Kenton Rein	Prince Albert
	Dean Cook	Kamloops
1987–88	Troy Gamble	Spokane
1988–89	Danny Lorenz	Seattle
1989–90	Trevor Kidd	Brandon
1990–91	Jamie McLennan	Lethbridge
1991–92	Corey Hirsch	Kamloops
1992–93	Trevor Robins	Brandon
1993–94	Norm Maracle	Saskatoon

1994–95	Paxton Schafer	Medicine Hat
1995–96	David Lemanowicz	Spokane
1996–97	Brian Boucher	Tri-City
1997–98	Brent Belecki	Portland
1998–99	Cory Rudkowski	Seattle

DUNC MCCALLUM MEMORIAL TROPHY—COACH OF THE YEAR

YEAR	COACH	TEAM
1968–69	Scotty Munro	Calgary
1969–70	Pat Ginnell	Flin Flon
1970–71	Pat Ginnell	Flin Flon
1971–72	Earl Ingarfield	Regina
1972–73	Pat Ginnell	Flin Flon
1973–74	Stan Dunn	Swift Current
1974–75	Pat Ginnell	Victoria
1975–76	Ernie McLean	New Westminster
1976–77	Dunc McCallum	Brandon
1977–78	Dave King	Billings
	Jack Shipe	Victoria
1978–79	Dunc McCallum	Brandon
1979–80	Doug Sauter	Calgary
1980–81	Ken Hodge	Portland
1981–82	Jack Sangster	Seattle
1982–83	Darryl Lubiniecki	Saskatoon
1983–84	Terry Simpson	Prince Albert
1984–85	Doug Sauter	Medicine Hat
1985–86	Terry Simpson	Prince Albert
1986–87	Graham James	Swift Current
	Ken Hitchcock	Kamloops
1987–88	Marcel Comeau	Saskatoon
1988–89	Ron Kennedy	Medicine Hat
1989–90	Ken Hitchcock	Kamloops
1990–91	Tom Renney	Kamloops
1991–92	Bryan Maxwell	Spokane
1992–93	Daryl Lubiniecki	Saskatoon
1993–94	Bob Brown	Kamloops
1994–95	Kelly McCrimmon	Brandon
1995–96	Tim Speltz	Spokane
1996–97	Todd McLellan	Swift Current
1997–98	Ken Hodge	Portland
1998–99	Don Hay	Tri-City

BRAD HORNUNG TROPHY—MOST SPORTSMANLIKE

YEAR	PLAYER	TEAM
1966–67	Moris Stefaniw	Estevan
1967–68	Bernie Blanchette	Saskatoon
1968–69	Bob Liddington	Calgary
1969–70	Randy Rota	Calgary
1970–71	Lorne Henning	Estevan
1971–72	Ron Chipperfield	Brandon
1972–73	Ron Chipperfield	Brandon
1973–74	Mike Rogers	Calgary
1974–75	Danny Arndt	Saskatoon
1975–76	Blair Chapman	Saskatoon
1976–77	Steve Tambellini	Lethbridge
1977–78	Steve Tambellini	Lethbridge
1978–79	Errol Rausse	Seattle
1979–80	Steve Tsujiura	Medicine Hat
1980–81	Steve Tsujiura	Medicine Hat
1981–82	Mike Moller	Lethbridge
1982–83	Darren Boyko	Winnipeg
1983–84	Mark Lamb	Medicine Hat
1984–85	Cliff Ronning	New Westminster
1985–86	Randy Smith	Saskatoon
	Ken Morrison	Kamloops
1986–87	Len Nielsen	Regina
	Dave Archibald	Portland
1987–88	Craig Endean	Regina
1988–89	Blair Atcheynum	Moose Jaw
1989–90	Bryan Bosch	Lethbridge
1990–91	Pat Falloon	Spokane
1991–92	Steve Junker	Spokane
1992–93	Rick Girard	Swift Current
1993–94	Lonny Bohonos	Portland
1994–95	Darren Ritchie	Brandon
1995–96	Hnat Domenichelli	Kamloops
1996–97	Kelly Smart	Brandon

| 1997–98 | Cory Cyrenne | Brandon |
| 1998–99 | Matt Kinch | Calgary |

DARRYL (DOC) SEAMAN TROPHY—SCHOLASTIC PLAYER OF THE YEAR

YEAR	PLAYER	TEAM
1983–84	Ken Baumgartner	Prince Albert
1984–85	Mark Janssens	Regina
1985–86	Mark Janssens	Regina
1986–87	Casey McMillan	Lethbridge
1987–88	Kevin Cheveldayoff	Brandon
1988–89	Jeff Nelson	Prince Albert
1989–90	Jeff Nelson	Prince Albert
1990–91	Scott Niedermayer	Kamloops
1991–92	Ashley Buckberger	Swift Current
1992–93	David Trofimenkoff	Lethbridge
1993–94	Byron Penstock	Brandon
1994–95	Perry Johnson	Regina
1995–96	Bryce Salvador	Lethbridge
1996–97	Stefan Chernski	Brandon
1997–98	Kyle Rossiter	Spokane
1998–99	Chris Nielson	Calgary

QUEBEC MAJOR JUNIOR HOCKEY LEAGUE

QMJHL CHAMPIONS

YEAR	TEAM	COACH
1969–70	Quebec Remparts	Maurice Filion
1970–71	Quebec Remparts	Maurice Filion
1971–72	Cornwall Royals	Orval Tessier
1972–73	Quebec Remparts	Orval Tessier
1973–74	Quebec Remparts	Marc Picard
1974–75	Sherbooke Castors	Ghislain Delage
1975–76	Quebec Remparts	Ronald Racetti
1976–77	Sherbrook Castors	Ghislain Delage
1977–78	Trois-Rivieres Draveurs	Michel Bergeron
1979–80	Cornwall Royals	Doug Carpenter
1980–81	Cornwall Royals	Bob Kilger
1981–82	Sherbrook Castors	Andre Boisvert
1982–83	Verdun Junior	Pierre Cramer
1983–84	Laval Boisons	Jean Begin
1984–85	Verdun Canadien Junior	Jean Begin
1985–86	Hull Olympiques	Pat Burns
1986–87	Longueuil Chevaliers	Guy Chouinard
1987–88	Hull Olympiques	Alain Vigneault
1988–89	Laval Titan	Paulin Bordeleau
1989–90	Laval Titan	Pierre Cramer
1990–91	Chicoutimi Saqueerens	Jos Canale
1991–92	Verdun College Francais	Claude Therien
1992–93	Laval Titan	Robert Hartley
1993–94	Chicoutimi Sagueerens	Gasten Drapeau
1994–95	Hull Olympiques	Robert Mongrain
1995–96	Granby Predateurs	Michel Therrien
1996–97	Hull Olympiques	Claude Julien
1997–98	Val-d'Or Foreurs	Michel Georges
1998–99	Acadie-Bathurst	Roger Dejoie

JEAN BELIVEAU TROPHY—SCORING CHAMPION

YEAR	PLAYER	TEAM
1969–70	Luc Simard	Trois-Rivieres
1970–71	Guy Lafleur	Quebec
1971–72	Jacques Richard	Quebec
1972–73	Andre Savard	Quebec
1973–74	Pierre Larouche	Sorel
1974–75	Normand Dupont	Montreal
1975–76	Sylvain Locas	Chicoutimi
	Richard Dalpe	Trois-Rivieres
1976–77	Jean Savard	Quebec
1977–78	Ron Carter	Sherbrooke
1978–79	Jean-Francois Sauve	Trois-Rivieres

1979–80	Jean–Francois Sauve	Trois-Rivieres
1980–81	Dale Hawerchuk	Cornwall
1981–82	Claude Verret	Trois-Rivieres
1982–83	Pat LaFontaine	Verdun
1983–84	Mario Lemieux	Laval
1984–85	Guy Rouleau	Longueuil
1985–86	Guy Rouleau	Hull
1986–87	Marc Fortier	Chicoutimi
1987–88	Patrice Lefebvre	Shawinigan
1988–89	Stephane Morin	Chicoutimi
1989–90	Patrick Lebeau	Victoriaville
1990–91	Yanic Perreault	Trois-Rivieres
1991–92	Patrick Poulin	St–Hyacinthe
1992–93	Rene Corbet	Drummondville
1993–94	Yanick Dube	Laval
1994–95	Patrick Carignan	Shawinigan
1995–96	Daniel Briere	Drummondville
1996–97	Pavel Rosa	Hull
1997–98	Ramzi Abid	Chicoutimi
1998–99	Mike Ribeiro	Quebec

MICHEL BRIERE MEMORIAL TROPHY— MOST VALUABLE PLAYER

YEAR	PLAYER	TEAM
1972–73	Andre Savard	Quebec
1973–74	Gary MacGregor	Cornwall
1974–75	Mario Viens	Cornwall
1975–76	Peter Marsh	Sherbrooke
1976–77	Lucien Deblois	Sorel
1977–78	Kevin Reeves	Montreal
1978–79	Pierre Lacroix	Trois-Rivieres
1979–80	Denis Savard	Montreal
1980–81	Dale Hawerchuk	Cornwall
1981–82	John Chabot	Sherbrooke
1982–83	Pat LaFontaine	Verdun
1983–84	Mario Lemieux	Laval
1984–85	Daniel Berthiaume	Chicoutimi
1985–86	Guy Rouleau	Hull
1986–87	Robert Desjardins	Longueuil
1987–88	Marc Saumier	Hull
1988–89	Stephane Morin	Chicoutimi
1989–90	Andrew McKim	Hull
1990–91	Yanic Perreault	Trois-Rivieres
1991–92	Charles Poulin	St–Hyacinthe
1992–93	Jocelyn Thibault	Sherbrooke
1993–94	Emmanuel Fernandez	Laval
1994–95	Frederic Chartier	Laval
1995–96	Christian Dube	Sherbrooke
1996–97	Daniel Corso	Victoriaville
1997–98	Ramzi Abid	Chicoutimi
1998–99	Mathieu Chouinard	Shawinigar

EMILE BOUCHARD TROPHY— DEFENSEMAN-OF-THE-YEAR

YEAR	PLAYER	TEAM
1975–76	Jean Gagnon	Quebec
1976–77	Robert Picard	Montreal
1977–78	Mark Hardy	Montreal
1978–79	Raymond Bourque	Verdun eperviers
1979–80	Gaston Therrien	Quebec
1980–81	Fred Boimistruck	Cornwall
1981–82	Paul–Andre Boutilier	Sherbrooke
1982–83	Jean–Jacques Daigneault	Longueuil
1983–84	Billy Campbell	Verdun
1984–85	Yves Beaudoin	Shawinigan
1985–86	Sylvain Cote	Hull
1986–87	Jean–Marc Richard	Chicoutimi
1987–88	Eric Desjardins	Granby
1988–89	Yves Racine	Victoriaville
1989–90	Claude Barthe	Victoriaville
1990–91	Patrice Brisebois	Drummondville
1991–92	Francois Groleau	Shawinigan
1992–93	Benoit Larose	Laval
1993–94	Steve Gosselin	Chicoutimi
1994–95	Stephane Julien	Sherbrooke
1995–96	Denis Gauthier Jr.,	Drummondville
1996–97	Stephane Robidas	Shawinigan
1997–98	Derrick Walser	Rimouski
1998–99	Jiri Fischer	Hull

JACQUES PLANTE MEMORIAL TROPHY— GOALTENDER WITH LOWEST GAA

YEAR	PLAYER	TEAM
1969–70	Michel Deguise	Sorel
1970–71	Raynald Fortier	Quebec
1971–72	Richard Brodeur	Cornwall
1972–73	Pierre Perusse	Quebec
1973–74	Claude Legris	Sorel
1974–75	Nick Sanza	Sherbrooke
1975–76	Tim Bernhardt	Cornwall
1976–77	Tim Bernhardt	Cornwall
1977–78	Tim Bernhardt	Cornwall
1978–79	Jacques Cloutier	Trois-Rivieres
1979–80	Micalef Corrado	Sherbrooke
1980–81	Michel Dufour	Sorel
1981–82	Jeff Barratt	Montreal
1982–83	Tony Haladuick	Laval
1983–84	Tony Haladuick	Laval
1984–85	Daniel Berthiaume	Chicoutimi
1985–86	Robert Desjardins	Hull
1986–87	Robert Desjardins	Longueuil
1987–88	Stephane Beauregard	St–Jean
1988–89	Stephane Fiset	Victoriaville
1989–90	Pierre Gagnon	Victoriaville
1990–91	Felix Potvin	Chicoutimi
1991–92	Jean–Francois Labbe	Trois-Rivieres
1992–93	Jocelyn Thibault	Sherbrooke
1993–94	Philippe DeRouville	Verdun
1994–95	Martin Biron	Beauport
1995–96	Frederic Deschenes	Granby
1996–97	Marc Denis	Shawinigan
1997–98	Mathieu Garon	Victoriaville
1998–99	Maxime Ouellet	Quebec

MICHEL BERGERON TROPHY—ROOKIE OF THE YEAR, 1969–70 TO 1979–80, OFFENSIVE ROOKIE, SINCE 1980–81

YEAR	PLAYER	TEAM
1969–70	Serge Martel	Verdun
1970–71	Bob Murphy	Cornwall
1971–72	Bob Murphy	Cornwall
1972–73	Pierre Larouche	Sorel
1973–74	Michael Bossy	Laval
1974–75	Denis Pomerleau	Hull
1975–76	Jean–Marc Bonamie	Shawinigan
1976–77	Rick Vaive	Sherbrooke
1977–78	Normand Rochefort	Trois-Rivieres
1978–79	Alain Grenier	Laval
	Denis Savard	Montreal
1979–80	Dale Hawerchuk	Cornwall
1980–81	Claude Verret	Trois-Rivieres
1981–82	Sylvain Turgeon	Hull
1982–83	Pat LaFontaine	Verdun
1983–84	Stephane Richer	Granby
1984–85	James C. Carson	Verdun
1985–86	Pierre Turgeon	Granby
1986–87	Rob Murphy	Laval
1987–88	Martin Gelinas	Hull
1988–89	Yanic Perreault	Trois-Rivieres
1989–90	Martin Lapointe	Laval
1990–91	Rene Corbet	Drummondville
1991–92	Alexandre Daigle	Victoriaville
1992–93	Steve Brule	St–Jean
1993–94	Christian Dube	Sherbrooke
1994–95	Daniel Briere	Drummondville
1995–96	Pavel Rosa	Hull
1996–97	Vincent Lecavalier	Rimouski
1997–98	Mike Ribeiro	Rouyn–Noranda
1998–99	Ladislav Nagy	Moosehead

ROOKIE OF THE YEAR AWARD

YEAR	PLAYER	TEAM
1992–93	Steve Brule	St–Jean
1993–94	Alexei Lojkin	Chicoutimi
1994–95	Martin Biron	Beauport
1995–96	Pavel Rosa	Hull

1996–97	Vincent Lecavalier	Rimouski
1997–98	Mike Ribeiro	Rouyn–Noranda
1998–99	Ladislav Nagy	Moosehead

GUY LAFLEUR TROPHY—MOST VALUABLE PLAYOFFS PLAYER

YEAR	PLAYER	TEAM
1977–78	Richard David	Trois-Rivieres
1978–79	Jean–Francois Sauve	Trois-Rivieres
1979–80	Dale Hawerchuk	Cornwall
1980–81	Alain Lemieux	Trois-Rivieres
1981–82	Michel Morissette	Sherbrooke
1982–83	Pat LaFontaine	Verden
1983–84	Mario Lemieux	Laval
1984–85	Claude Lemieux	Verden
1985–86	Sylvain Cote	Hull
	Luc Robitaille	Hull
1986–87	Marc Saumier	Longueuil
1987–88	Marc Saumier	Hull
1988–89	Donald Audette	Laval
1989–90	Denis Chalifoux	Laval
1990–91	Felix Potvin	Chicoutimi
1991–92	Robert Guillet	Verden
1992–93	Emmanuel Fernandez	Laval
1993–94	Eric Fichaud	Chicoutimi
1994–95	Jose Theodore	Hull
1995–96	Jason Doig	Granby
1996–97	Christian Bronsard	Hull
1997–98	Jean–Pierre Dumont	Val D'Or
1998–99	Mathieu Benoit	Acadie-Bathurst

RON LAPOINTE TROPHY— COACH OF THE YEAR

YEAR	COACH	TEAM
1992–93	Guy Chouinard	Sherbrooke
1993–94	Richard Martel	St–Hyacinthe

1994–95	Michel Therrien	Laval
1995–96	Jean Provonost	Shawinigan
1996–97	Clement Jodoin	Halifax
1997–98	Guy Chouinard	Quebec
1998–99	Guy Chouinard	Quebec

FRANK J. SELKE MEMORIAL TROPHY— MOST GENTLEMANLY PLAYER

YEAR	PLAYER	TEAM
1970–71	Normand Dube	Sherbrooke
1971–72	Gerry Teeple	Cornwall
1972–73	Claude Larose	Drummondville
1973–74	Gary MacGregor	Cornwall
1974–75	Jean–Luc Phaneuf	Montreal
1975–76	Normand Dupont	Montreal
1976–77	Michael Bossy	Laval
1977–78	Kevin Reeves	Montreal
1978–79	Jean–Francois Sauve	Trois-Rivieres
	Raymond Bourque	Verdun eperviers
1979–80	Jean–Francois Sauve	Trois-Rivieres
1980–81	Claude Verret	Trois-Rivieres
1981–82	Claude Verret	Trois-Rivieres
1982–83	Pat LaFontaine	Verdun
1983–84	Jerome Carrier	Verdun
1984–85	Patrick emond	Chicoutimi
1985–86	James C. Carson	Verdun
1986–87	Luc Beausoleil	Laval
1987–88	Stephan Lebeau	Shawinigan
1988–89	Steve Cadieux	Shawinigan
1989–90	Andrew McKim	Hull
1990–91	Yanic Perreault	Trois-Rivieres
1991–92	Martin Gendron	St–Hyacinthe
1992–93	Martin Gendron	St–Hyacinthe
1993–94	Yanick Dube	Laval
1994–95	Eric Daze	Beauport
1995–96	Christian Dube	Sherbrooke
1996–97	Daniel Briere	Drummondville
1997–98	David Thibeaut	Victoriaville
1998–99	Eric Chouinard	Quebec

20

MINOR LEAGUE HOCKEY: STEPPING-STONE TO THE NHL

AMERICAN HOCKEY LEAGUE

The American Hockey League was founded in 1936 in eight eastern cities as a developmental league for the training of professional players. In the past 61 years, the league has worked hand in hand with the National Hockey League, supplying the latter with players who have honed their skills in a highly competitive setting.

How effective has the AHL been in supplying talent to the NHL? Well, in the 1995–96 season two-thirds of all NHL players had played in the AHL at some point in their careers, and the scoring leaders of six teams were graduates of the AHL. In addition, of the 92 shutouts recorded by NHL goalies in 1995–96, 71 of them were by AHL alumni. In all, 90 former AHL players have been elected to the Hockey Hall of Fame.

The charter franchises in 1936 were located in Providence, Rhode Island; New Haven, Connecticut; Philadelphia; and Springfield, Massachusetts (East Division); and Syracuse, New York; Buffalo; Pittsburgh; and Cleveland (West Division). The Buffalo franchise had to suspend operations six weeks into play when a fire gutted its arena, forcing the league to finish the season with seven teams. The Syracuse Stars took the inaugural championship, defeating the Philadelphia Ramblers three games to one in the final series.

The Hershey Bears joined the AHL in 1938, making it an eight-team league again; the Bears have remain in the league to this day. Through all the years and changes in the past six decades, the one constant in the AHL is the team playing at venerable Hershey Park Arena. The Bears have served as the top farm team for six NHL clubs and have won six Calder Cups as AHL champions.

The outbreak of World War II forced the league to cut back operations, which caused membership to drop from 10 teams in 1941–42 to six teams just two years later. But by 1948–49 the AHL was stronger than ever, with 11 franchises and a rash of new stars back from the war. One of the brightest stars was goaltender Terry Sawchuk, who began his road to the Hockey Hall of Fame by leading the Indianapolis Capitols to the Calder Cup in 1950.

Another AHL goalie who found his way into the Hall of Fame was Johnny Bower, one of the

league's best goaltenders from 1947 to 1953. The following year, he moved up to the NHL, where he helped the Toronto Maple Leafs win four Stanley Cups.

The league fluctuated between six and 12 teams through the 1950s, '60s, and '70s, and crossed the border into Canada, with Quebec joining in time for the 1959–60 season. Franchises in New Brunswick and Nova Scotia followed in the late 1970s and early 1980s.

Numerous future NHL stars over the years apprenticed in the AHL. The list includes Hall of Famers Tim Horton, Gump Worsley, Gerry Cheevers, Ed Giacomin, Doug Harvey, Leo Boivin, Andy Bathgate, Pierre Pilote, Jean Ratelle, Allen Stanley, Marcel Pronovost, Jacques Plante, Larry Robinson, Guy Lapointe, Ken Dryden, and Bill Barber.

In the last two decades, the AHL has positioned itself primarily as a development league for the NHL. Young players who graduated to the big leagues include such stars as Ron Hextall, Steve Larmer, Mike Vernon, Guy Carbonneau, Jozef Stumpel, Martin Brodeur, Jason Allison, Chris Osgood, Nikolai Khabibulin, Donald Audette, Olaf Kolzig, and Adam Oates.

The AHL set a league record by drawing over four million fans in the 1997–98 season, the first time in the league's 62-year history. The Philadelphia Flyers' farm club, the Philadelphia Phantoms (which plays in the old Philadelphia Spectrum next door to the Flyers' home arena, the CoreStates Center), won the league championship in 1997–98. They also set an AHL record with an average attendance of 11,809, breaking the old mark of 11,208, set in 1971–72 by the Boston Braves.

YEAR	TEAM	
1943–44	Buffalo Bisons	Art Chapman
1944–45	Cleveland Barons	Bun Cook
1945–46	Buffalo Bisons	Frank Beisler
1946–47	Hershey Bears	Don Penniston
1947–48	Cleveland Barons	Bun Cook
1948–49	Providence Reds	Terry Reardon
1949–50	Indianapolis Capitols	Ott Heller
1950–51	Cleveland Barons	Bun Cook
1951–52	Pittsburgh Hornets	King Clancy
1952–53	Cleveland Barons	Bun Cook
1953–54	Cleveland Barons	Bun Cook
1954–55	Pittsburgh Hornets	Howie Meeker
1955–56	Providence Reds	John Crawford
1956–57	Cleveland Barons	Jack Gordon
1957–58	Hershey Bears	Frank Mathers
1958–59	Hershey Bears	Frank Mathers
1959–60	Springfield Indians	Pat Egan
1960–61	Springfield Indians	Pat Egan
1961–62	Springfield Indians	Pat Egan
1962–63	Buffalo Bisons	Billy Reay
1963–64	Cleveland Barons	Fred Glover
1964–65	Rochester Americans	Joe Crozier
1965–66	Rochester Americans	Joe Crozier
1966–67	Pittsburgh Hornets	Baz Bastien
1967–68	Rochester Americans	Joe Crozier
1968–69	Hershey Bears	Frank Mathers
1969–70	Buffalo Bisons	Fred Shero
1970–71	Springfield Kings	John Wilson
1971–72	Nova Scotia Voyageurs	Al MacNeil
1972–73	Cincinnati Swords	Floyd Smith
1973–74	Hershey Bears	Chuck Hamilton
1974–75	Springfield Kings	Ron Stewart
1975–76	Nova Scotia Voyageurs	Al MacNeil
1976–77	Nova Scotia Voyageurs	Al MacNeil
1977–78	Maine Mariners	Bob MacCammon
1978–79	Maine Mariners	Bob MacCammon
1979–80	Hershey Bears	Doug Gibson
1980–81	Adirondack Red Wings	Tom Webster/J.P. LeBlanc
1981–82	New Brunswick Hawks	Orval Tessier
1982–83	Rochester Americans	Mike Keenan
1983–84	Maine Mariners	Tom McVie/John Paddock
1984–85	Sherbrooke Canadiens	Pierre Creamer
1985–86	Adirondack Red Wings	Bill Dineen
1986–87	Rochester Americans	John Van Boxmeer
1987–88	Hershey Bears	John Paddock
1988–89	Adirondack Red Wings	Bill Dineen
1989–90	Springfield Indians	Jim Roberts
1990–91	Springfield Indians	Jim Roberts
1991–92	Adirondack Red Wings	Barry Melrose
1992–93	Cape Breton Oilers	George Burnett
1993–94	Portland Pirates	Barry Trotz
1994–95	Albany River Rats	Robbie Ftorek
1995–96	Rochester Americans	John Tortorella
1996–97	Hershey Bears	Robert Hartley
1997–98	Philadelphia Phantoms	Bill Barber
1998–99	Providence Bruins	Peter Laviolette

Les Cunningham Award

Awarded to the player deemed "Most Valuable" in the league during the season by AHL media and players. It is named for the player who averaged more than a point a game in 10 seasons with the Cleveland Barons. Les Cunningham played in the NHL for the New York Americans and Chicago Black Hawks in the late 1930s.

YEAR	PLAYER	TEAM
1947–48	Carl Liscombe	Providence
1948–49	Carl Liscombe	Providence
1949–50	Les Douglas	Cleveland
1950–51	Ab DeMarco	Buffalo
1951–52	Ray Powell	Providence
1952–53	Eddie Olson	Cleveland
1953–54	George Sullivan	Hershey
1954–55	Ross Lowe	Springfield
1955–56	Johnny Bower	Providence
1956–57	Johnny Bower	Providence
1957–58	Johnny Bower	Cleveland

AHL CHAMPIONS—CALDER CUP

YEAR	TEAM	COACH
1936–37	Syracuse Stars	Eddie Powers
1937–38	Providence Reds	Bun Cook
1938–39	Cleveland Barons	Bill Cook
1939–40	Providence Reds	Bun Cook
1940–41	Cleveland Barons	Bill Cook
1941–42	Indianapolis Capitols	Herb Lewis
1942–43	Buffalo Bisons	Art Chapman

YEAR	PLAYER	TEAM
1958–59	Billy Hicke	Rochester
	Rudy Migay	Rochester
1959–60	Fred Glover	Cleveland
1960–61	Phil Maloney	Buffalo
1961–62	Fred Glover	Cleveland
1962–63	Denis DeJordy	Buffalo
1963–64	Fred Glover	Cleveland
1964–65	Art Stratton	Buffalo
1965–66	Dick Gamble	Rochester
1966–67	Mike Nykoluk	Hershey
1967–68	Dave Creighton	Providence
1968–69	Gilles Villemure	Buffalo
1969–70	Gilles Villemure	Buffalo
1970–71	Fred Speck	Baltimore
1971–72	Garry Peters	Boston
1972–73	Billy Inglis	Cincinnati
1973–74	Art Stratton	Rochester
1974–75	Doug Gibson	Rochester
1975–76	Ron Andruff	Nova Scotia
1976–77	Doug Gibson	Rochester
1977–78	Blake Dunlop	Maine
1978–79	Rocky Saganiuk	New Brunswick
1979–80	Norm Dube	Nova Scotia
1980–81	Pelle Lindbergh	Maine
1981–82	Mike Kaszycki	New Brunswick
1982–83	Ross Yates	Binghamton
1983–84	Garry Lariviere	St. Catharines
	Mal Davis	Rochester
1984–85	Paul Gardner	Binghamton
1985–86	Paul Gardner	Rochester
1986–87	Tim Tookey	Hershey
1987–88	Jody Gage	Rochester
1988–89	Stephan Lebeau	Sherbrooke
1989–90	Paul Ysebaert	Utica
1990–91	Kevin Todd	Utica
1991–92	John Anderson	New Haven
1992–93	Don Biggs	Binghamton
1993–94	Rich Chernomaz	St. John's
1994–95	Steve Larouche	P.E.I. Senators
1995–96	Brad Smyth	Carolina
1996–97	Jean–Francois Labbe	Hershey
1997–98	Steve Guolla	Kentucky
1998–99	Randy Robitaille	Providence

Jack A. Butterfield Trophy

Awarded to the MVP of the playoffs. The trophy is named in honor of the former league president (28 years). It is voted by the coaches.

YEAR	PLAYER	TEAM
1983–84	Bud Stefanski	Maine
1984–85	Brian Skrudland	Sherbrooke
1985–86	Tim Tookey	Hershey
1986–87	Dave Fenyves	Rochester
1987–88	Wendell Young	Hershey
1988–89	Sam St. Laurent	Adirondack
1989–90	Jeff Hackett	Springfield
1990–91	Kay Whitmore	Springfield
1991–92	Allan Bester	Adirondack
1992–93	Bill McDougall	Cape Breton
1993–94	Olaf Kolzig	Portland
1994–95	Corey Schwab	Albany
	Mike Dunham	
1995–96	Dixon Ward	Rochester
1996–97	Mike McHugh	Hershey
1997–98	Mike Maneluk	Philadelphia
1998–99	Peter Ferraro	Providence

John B. Sollenberger Trophy

Was awarded to the player who has scored the most points during the regular season. It is named after John Sollenberger, who was manager and president of the Hershey Bears and former Chairman of the Board of Governors of the AHL.

YEAR	PLAYER	TEAM
1947–48	Carl Liscombe	Providence
1948–49	Sid Smith	Pittsburgh
1949–50	Les Douglas	Cleveland
1950–51	Ab DeMarco	Buffalo
1951–52	Ray Powell	Providence
1952–53	Eddie Olson	Cleveland
1953–54	George Sullivan	Hershey
1954–55	Eddie Olson	Cleveland
1955–56	Zellio Toppazzini	Providence
1956–57	Fred Glover	Cleveland
1957–58	Willie Marshall	Hershey
1958–59	Billy Hicke	Rochester
1959–60	Fred Glover	Cleveland
1960–61	Bill Sweeney	Springfield
1961–62	Bill Sweeney	Springfield
1962–63	Bill Sweeney	Springfield
1963–64	Gerry Ehman	Rochester
1964–65	Art Stratton	Buffalo
1965–66	Dick Gamble	Rochester
1966–67	Gordon Labossiere	Quebec
1967–68	Simon Nolet	Quebec
1968–69	Jeannot Gilbert	Hershey
1969–70	Jude Drouin	Montreal
1970–71	Fred Speck	Baltimore
1971–72	Don Blackburn	Providence
1972–73	Yvon Lambert	Nova Scotia
1973–74	Steve West	New Haven
1974–75	Doug Gibson	Rochester
1975–76	Jean–Guy Gratton	Hershey
1976–77	Andre Peloffy	Springfield
1977–78	Gordie Brooks	Philadelphia
	Rick Adduono	Rochester
1978–79	Bernie Johnson	Maine
1979–80	Norm Dube	Nova Scotia
1980–81	Mark Lofthouse	Hershey
1981–82	Mike Kaszycki	New Brunswick

Eddie Shore Award

Awarded to the player chosen by the media and players as the best defenseman in the league. Eddie Shore, a member of the Hockey Hall of Fame, rates as one of the sport's all-time defensemen. He played for 13 seasons with the Boston Bruins and later became a part-owner and manager of the AHL's Springfield Indians.

YEAR	PLAYER	TEAM
1958–59	Steve Kraftcheck	Rochester
1959–60	Larry Hillman	Providence
1960–61	Bob McCord	Springfield
1961–62	Kent Douglas	Springfield
1962–63	Marc Reaume	Hershey
1963–64	Ted Harris	Cleveland
1964–65	Al Arbour	Rochester
1965–66	Jim Morrison	Quebec
1966–67	Bob McCord	Pittsburgh
1967–68	Bill Needham	Cleveland
1968–69	Bob Blackburn	Buffalo
1969–70	Noel Price	Springfield
1970–71	Marshall Johnston	Cleveland
1971–72	Noel Price	Springfield/Nova Scotia
1972–73	Ray McKay	Cincinnati
1973–74	Gordie Smith	Springfield
1974–75	Joe Zanussi	Providence
1975–76	Noel Price	Nova Scotia
1976–77	Brian Engblom	Nova Scotia
1977–78	Terry Murray	Maine
1978–79	Terry Murray	Maine
1979–80	Rick Vasko	Adirondack
1980–81	Craig Levie	Nova Scotia
1981–82	Dave Farrish	New Brunswick
1982–83	Greg Tebbutt	Baltimore
1983–84	Garry Lariviere	St. Catharines
1984–85	Richie Dunn	Binghamton
1985–86	Jim Wiemer	New Haven

1986–87	Brad Shaw	Binghamton
1987–88	Dave Fenyves	Hershey
1988–89	Dave Fenyves	Hershey
1989–90	Eric Weinrich	Utica
1990–91	Norm Maciver	Cape Breton
1991–92	Greg Hawgood	Cape Breton
1992–93	Bobby Dollas	Adirondack
1993–94	Chris Snell	St. John's
1994–95	Jeff Serowik	Providence
1995–96	Barry Richter	Binghamton
1996–97	Darren Rumble	Philadelphia
1997–98	Jamie Heward	Philadelphia
1998–99	Ken Sutton	Albany

Happy (Hap) Holmes Memorial Award

Awarded to the league's outstanding goaltender. From 1948 to 1971 it was given to the goaltender with the lowest goals against average who appeared in at least 50 percent of his team's regular season games. Since 1972, the award been awarded to the goaltender or goaltenders with the lowest goals against average—each has to appear in a minimum of 25 games. Hap Holmes had two stints in the NHL—18 games with Toronto in 1917–18 and 1918–19, followed by 43 games with Detroit in 1926–27 and 44 in 1927–28.

YEAR	PLAYER	TEAM
1947–48	Baz Bastien	Pittsburgh
1948–49	Baz Bastien	Pittsburgh
1949–50	Connie Dion	Buffalo
1950–51	Gil Mayer	Pittsburgh
1951–52	Johnny Bower	Cleveland
1952–53	Gil Mayer	Pittsburgh
1953–54	Gil Mayer	Pittsburgh
1954–55	Gil Mayer	Pittsburgh
1955–56	Gil Mayer	Pittsburgh
1956–57	Johnny Bower	Providence
1957–58	Johnny Bower	Cleveland
1958–59	Bobby Perreault	Hershey
1959–60	Ed Chadwick	Rochester
1960–61	Marcel Paille	Springfield
1961–62	Marcel Paille	Springfield
1962–63	Dennis DeJordy	Buffalo
1963–64	Roger Crozier	Pittsburgh
1964–65	Gerry Cheevers	Rochester
1965–66	Les Binkley	Cleveland
1966–67	Andre Gill	Hershey
1967–68	Bobby Perreault	Rochester
1968–69	Gilles Villemure	Buffalo
1969–70	Gilles Villemure	Buffalo
1970–71	Gary Kurt	Cleveland
1971–72	Dan Bouchard Ross Brooks	Boston
1972–73	Michel Larocque Michel Deguise	Nova Scotia
1973–74	Jim Shaw and Dave Elenbaas	Nova Scotia
1974–75	Ed Walsh and Dave Elenbaas	Nova Scotia
1975–76	Ed Walsh and Dave Elenbaas	Nova Scotia
1976–77	Ed Walsh and Dave Elenbaas	Nova Scotia
1977–78	Bob Holland and Maurice Barrett	Nova Scotia
1978–79	Robbie Moore and Pete Peeters	Maine
1979–80	Robbie Moore and Rick St. Croix	Maine
1980–81	Robbie Moore and Pelle Lindbergh	Maine
1981–82	Bob Janecyk and Warren Skorodenski	New Brunswick
1982–83	Brian Ford and Clint Malarchuk	Fredericton
1983–84	Brian Ford	Fredericton
1984–85	Jon Casey	Baltimore

1985–86	Sam St. Laurent and Karl Friesen	Maine
1986–87	Vincent Riendeau	Sherbrooke
1987–88	Vincent Riendeau and Jocelyn Perreault	Sherbrooke
1988–89	Randy Exelby and Francois Gravel	Sherbrooke
1989–90	Jean–Claude Bergeron and Andre Racicot	Sherbrooke
1990–91	David Littman and Darcy Wakaluk	Rochester
1991–92	David Littman	Rochester
1992–93	Corey Hirsch and Boris Rousson	Binghamton
1993–94	Byron Dafoe and Olaf Kolzig	Portland
1994–95	Mike Dunham and Corey Schwab	Albany
1995–96	Manny Legace and Scott Langkow	Springfield
1996–97	Jean–Francois Labbe	Hershey
1997–98	Tyler Moss and Jean–Sebastien Giguere	Saint John
1998–99	Martin Biron Tom Draper	Rochester

Aldege (Baz) Bastien Memorial Trophy

Awarded to the goaltender considered the best at his position by the broadcasters and writers. Baz Bastien had a long history with the AHL—as a player he was the league's top goaltender with Pittsburgh in 1947–48 and 1948–49. He appeared in five games with Toronto in the NHL in 1945–46. At his death in 1983, he was GM of the NHL's Pittsburgh Penguins.

YEAR	PLAYER	TEAM
1983–84	Brian Ford	Fredericton
1984–85	Jon Casey	Baltimore
1985–86	Sam St. Laurent	Maine
1986–87	Mark Laforest	Adirondack
1987–88	Wendell Young	Hershey
1988–89	Randy Exelby	Sherbrooke
1989–90	Jean–Claude Bergeron	Sherbrooke
1990–91	Mark Laforest	Binghamton
1991–92	Felix Potvin	St. John's
1992–93	Corey Hirsch	Binghamton
1993–94	Frederic Chabot	Hershey
1994–95	Jim Carey	Portland
1995–96	Manny Legace	Springfield
1996–97	Jean–Francois Labbe	Hershey
1997–98	Scott Langkow	Springfield
1998–99	Martin Biron	Rochester

Dudley (Red) Garrett Memorial Award

Awarded to the Rookie of the Year as voted by the media and players. Red Garrett died during World War II while serving in the Canadian Navy.

YEAR	PLAYER	TEAM
1947–48	Bob Solinger	Cleveland
1948–49	Terry Sawchuck	Indianapolis
1949–50	Paul Meger	Buffalo
1950–51	Wally Hergesheimer	Cleveland
1951–52	Earl Reibel	Indianapolis
1952–53	Guyle Fielder	St. Louis
1953–54	Don Marshall	Buffalo
1954–55	Jimmy Anderson	Springfield
1955–56	Bruce Cline	Providence
1956–57	Bo Elik	Cleveland
1957–58	Bill Sweeney	Providence
1958–59	Bill Hicke	Rochester

1959–60	Stan Baluik	Providence
1960–61	Chico Maki	Buffalo
1961–62	Les Binkley	Cleveland
1962–63	Doug Robinson	Buffalo
1963–64	Roger Crozier	Pittsburgh
1964–65	Ray Cullen	Buffalo
1965–66	Mike Walton	Rochester
1966–67	Bob Rivard	Quebec
1967–68	Jerry Des Jardin	Cleveland
1968–69	Ron Ward	Rochester
1969–70	Jude Drouin	Montreal
1970–71	Fred Speck	Baltimore
1971–72	Terry Caffery	Cleveland
1972–73	Ron Anderson	Boston
1973–74	Rick Middleton	Providence
1974–75	Jerry Holland	Providence
1975–76	Greg Holst	Providence
	Pierre Mondou	Nova Scotia
1976–77	Rod Schutt	Nova Scotia
1977–78	Norm Dupont	Nova Scotia
1978–79	Mike Meeker	Binghamton
1979–80	Darryl Sutter	New Brunswick
1980–81	Pelle Lindbergh	Maine
1981–82	Bob Sullivan	Binghamton
1982–83	Mitch Lamoureux	Baltimore
1983–84	Claude Verret	Rochester
1984–85	Steve Thomas	St. Catharines
1985–86	Ron Hextall	Hershey
1986–87	Brett Hull	Moncton
1987–88	Mike Richard	Binghamton
1988–89	Stephan Lebeau	Sherbrooke
1989–90	Donald Audette	Rochester
1990–91	Patrick Lebeau	Fredericton
1991–92	Felix Potvin	St. John's
1992–93	Corey Hirsch	Binghamton
1993–94	Rene Corbet	Cornwall
1994–95	Jim Carey	Portland
1995–96	Darcy Tucker	Fredericton
1996–97	Jaroslav Svejkovsky	Portland
1997–98	Daniel Briere	Springfield
1998–99	Shane Willis	New Haven

Louis A. R. Pieri Memorial Award

Awarded the outstanding coach in the AHL, it is voted by the broadcasters and writers. Pieri was a longtime force in the league as owner of the Providence Reds.

YEAR	PLAYER	TEAM
1967–68	Vic Stasiuk	Quebec
1968–69	Frank Mathers	Hershey
1969–70	Fred Shero	Buffalo
1970–71	Terry Reardon	Baltimore
1971–72	Al MacNeil	Nova Scotia
1972–73	Floyd Smith	Cincinnati
1973–74	Don Cherry	Rochester
1974–75	John Muckler	Providence
1975–76	Chuck Hamilton	Hershey
1976–77	Al MacNeil	Nova Scotia
1977–78	Bob McCammon	Maine
1978–79	Parker MacDonald	New Hampshire
1979–80	Doug Gibson	Hershey
1980–81	Bob McCammon	Maine
1981–82	Larry Kish	Binghamton
1982–83	Jacques Demers	Fredericton
1983–84	Gene Ubriaco	Baltimore
1984–85	Bill Dineen	Adirondack
1985–86	Bill Dineen	Adirondack
1986–87	Larry Pleau	Binghamton
1987–88	John Paddock	Hershey
	Mike Milbury	Maine
1988–89	Tom McVie	Utica
1989–90	Jim Roberts	Springfield
1990–91	Don Lever	Rochester
1991–92	Doug Carpenter	New Haver
1992–93	Marc Crawford	St. John's
1993–94	Barry Trotz	Portland
1994–95	Robbie Ftorek	Albany
1995–96	Robbie Ftorek	Albany
1996–97	Greg Gilbert	Worcester

1997–98	Bill Stewart	Saint John
1998–99	Peter Laviolette	Providence

Fred Hunt Memorial Award

Awarded by broadcasters and writers to the player who best exemplifies sportsmanship, determination, and dedication. Fred Hunt was a player and GM for the Buffalo Bisons.

YEAR	PLAYER	TEAM
1977–78	Blake Dunlop	Maine
1978–79	Bernie Johnston	Maine
1979–80	Norm Dube	Nova Scotia
1980–81	Tony Cassolato	Hershey
1981–82	Mike Kaszycki	New Brunswick
1982–83	Ross Yates	Binghamton
1983–84	Claude Larose	Sherbrooke
1984–85	Paul Gardner	Binghamton
1985–86	Steve Tsujiura	Maine
1986–87	Glenn Merkosky	Adirondack
1987–88	Bruce Boudreau	Springfield
1988–89	Murray Eaves	Adirondack
1989–90	Murray Eaves	Adirondack
1990–91	Glenn Merkosky	Adirondack
1991–92	John Anderson	New Haven
1992–93	Tim Tookey	Hershey
1993–94	Jim Nesich	Cape Breton
1994–95	Steve Larouche	PEI Senators
1995–96	Ken Gernander	Binghamton
1996–97	Steve Passmore	Hamilton
1997–98	Craig Charron	Rochester
1998–99	Mitch Lamoureux	Hershey

INTERNATIONAL HOCKEY LEAGUE

The International Hockey League began in 1945 with four teams, all based in the Detroit and Windsor, Ontario, area. Fifty-two years later, the league encompassed 19 teams from as far north as Quebec, as far south as San Antonio, as far east as Orlando, and as far west as Long Beach, California.

The original intent of the league was to create playing opportunities for men returning to the Detroit area following World War II. Two teams from Detroit, the Goodyears and the Detroit Auto Club, and two from Windsor, the Spitfires and Godfredsons, competed that first season, playing a 15-game schedule. The Auto Club defeated the Goodyears 2–1 in the final series to capture the first Turner Cup, emblematic of the league championship.

The league expanded to Toledo in 1947 and five years later had grown to nine teams, though all four of the original teams had disbanded. One of the new teams, the Cincinnati Mohawks, dominated the league in the mid-1950s, winning five consecutive titles. The Mohawks were helped greatly by their affiliation with the Montreal

Canadiens, who would send them young players for seasoning.

In the 1960s the league varied between six and eight teams, with all franchises located in the United States. The star of the decade was Fort Wayne Komets forward Len Thomson, who won seven Most Valuable Player awards in a 10-year period.

Teams in Kalamazoo and Milwaukee were added in the 1970s, and Toledo and Indianapolis joined the league early in the following decade. When Salt Lake City was awarded a franchise in 1984–85, the league truly began to break away from its regional thinking. The next year the IHL revolutionized hockey thinking by adopting a shootout to settle tie games.

During the 1990s, the league continued to grow. In one sense, it returned to its roots by placing a franchise in the Detroit area, with the Vipers playing at the Palace of Auburn Hills. This was part of a brief IHL movement probing the NHL's market. A team was also placed in Chicago, and both of these clubs promoted themselves as an inexpensive alternative to the NHL.

The IHL also ventured into former NHL cities, including Quebec, Kansas City, Cleveland, and briefly, Minnesota, which then moved to Manitoba following the departure of the Winnipeg Jets. The IHL also put a team in Houston, which had been identified by the NHL as a potential expansion market.

That movement lost steam when some of the smaller IHL markets had trouble competing fiscally with the newer, larger ones, and some NHL teams ended their farm team affiliation agreements with IHL clubs.

Through all its changes, the IHL has never been afraid to be different. Many traditionalists ridiculed the idea of using a shootout to determine games, but the idea is immensely popular. In 1992 the IHL became home to Manon Rheaume, the first woman to play in a regular season professional hockey game. In her first ap-pearance for the Atlanta Knights, she stopped five of six shots in one period of action.

Another IHL event that generated publicity was the Detroit Vipers' signing of Gordie Howe to play one shift of the opening game of the 1997–98 season. The 69-year-old Hall of Famer got in shape at the Vipers' training camp and became the only player to appear professionally in six decades.

Entering the 1999–2000 season, the league remains on fairly strong footing. While the older American Hockey League may send more of its players on to the NHL than the IHL does, the upstart league has its share of budding NHL stars. Sergei Samsonov of the Boston Bruins played for the Vipers the year before he won the Calder Trophy as NHL Rookie of the Year in 1998. And, in 1999, Patrik Stefan of the Long Beach Ice Dogs made headlines when he was selected first overall by the Atlanta Thrashers in the annual NHL Entry Draft.

In addition to players making the jump to the NHL, coaches have recently used the IHL as a springboard. At the end of the 1998–99 season, Steve Ludzik, head coach of the Vipers, was named head coach of the NHL's Tampa Bay Lightning. Just a week before Ludzik received his big break, Don Fraser of the Orlando Solar Bears was tabbed to take over the top spot of the expansion Atlanta Thrashers.

TURNER CUP WINNERS

YEAR	TEAM	COACH
1945–46	Detroit Auto Club	Jack Ward
1946–47	Windsor Spitfires	Ebbie Goodfellow
1947–48	Toledo Mercurys	Andy Mulligan
1948–49	Windsor Hettche Spitfires	Jimmy Skinner
1949–50	Chatham Maroons	Bob Stoddart
1950–51	Toledo Mercurys	Alex Wood
1951–52	Toledo Mercurys	Alex Wood
1952–53	Cincinnati Mohawks	Buddy O'Conner
1953–54	Cincinnati Mohawks	Roly McLenahan
1954–55	Cincinnati Mohawks	Roly McLenahan
1955–56	Cincinnati Mohawks	Roly McLenahan
1956–57	Cincinnati Mohawks	Roly McLenahan
1957–58	Indianapolis Chiefs	Leo Lamoureux
1958–59	Louisville Rebels	Leo Gasparini
1959–60	St. Paul Saints	Fred Shero
1960–61	St. Paul Saints	Fred Shero
1961–62	Muskegon Zephyrs	Moose Lallo
1962–63	Fort Wayne Komets	Ken Ullyot
1963–64	Toledo Blades	Moe Benoit
1964–65	Fort Wayne Komets	Eddie Long

1965–66	Port Huron Flags	Lloyd Maxfield
1966–67	Toledo Blades	Terry Slater
1967–68	Muskegon Mohawks	Moose Lallo
1968–69	Dayton Gems	Larry Wilson
1969–70	Dayton Gems	Larry Wilson
1970–71	Port Huron Flags	Ted Garvin
1971–72	Port Huron Wings	Ted Garvin
1972–73	Fort Wayne Komets	Marc Boileau
1973–74	Des Moines Capitols	Dan Belisle
1974–75	Toledo Goaldiggers	Ted Garvin
1975–76	Dayton Gems	Ivan Prediger
1976–77	Saginaw Gears	Don Perry
1977–78	Toledo Goaldiggers	Ted Garvin
1978–79	Kalamazoo Wings	Bill Purcell
1979–80	Kalamazoo Wings	Doug McKay
1980–81	Saginaw Gears	Don Perry
1981–82	Toledo Goaldiggers	Bill Inglis
1982–83	Toledo Goaldiggers	Bill Inglis
1983–84	Flint Generals	Dennis Desrosiers
1984–85	Peoria Rivermen	Pat Kelly
1985–86	Muskegon Lumberjacks	Rick Ley
1986–87	Salt Lake Golden Eagles	Wayne Thomas
1987–88	Salt Lake Golden Eagles	Paul Baxter
1988–89	Muskegon Lumberjacks	Blair MacDonald
1989–90	Indianapolis Ice	Darryl Sutter
1990–91	Peoria Rivermen	Bob Plager
1991–92	Kansas City Blades	Kevin Constantine
1992–93	Fort Wayne Komets	Al Sims
1993–94	Atlanta Knights	John Paris, Jr.
1994–95	Denver Grizzlies	Butch Goring
1995–96	Utah Grizzlies	Butch Goring
1996–97	Detroit Vipers	Steve Ludzik
1997–98	Chicago Wolves	John Anderson
1998–99	Houston Aeros	Dave Tippett

1984–85	Peoria Rivermen	Pat Kelly
1985–86	Fort Wayne Komets	Rob Laird
1986–87	Fort Wayne Komets	Rob Laird
1987–88	Muskegon Lumberjacks	Rick Ley
1988–89	Muskegon Lumberjacks	Blair MacDonald
1989–90	Muskegon Lumberjacks	Blair MacDonald
1990–91	Peoria Rivermen	Bob Plager
1991–92	Kansas City Blades	Kevin Constantine
1992–93	San Diego Gulls	Rick Dudley
1993–94	Las Vegas Thunder	Butch Goring
1994–95	Denver Grizzlies	Butch Goring
1995–96	Las Vegas Thunder	Chris McSorley
1996–97	Detroit Vipers	Steve Ludzik
1997–98	Long Beach Ice Dogs	John Von Boxmeer
1998–99	Houston Aeros	Dave Tippett

James Gatschene Memorial Trophy

The Gatschene Trophy is awarded to the player judged to be the league's most valuable player during the regular season.

YEAR	PLAYER	TEAM
1946–47	Herb Jones	Detroit Auto Club
1947–48	Lyle Dowell	Detroit Bright's Goodyears
1948–49	Bob McFadden	Detroit Jerry Lynch
1949–50	Dick Kowcinak	Sarnia Sailors
1950–51	John McGrath	Toledo Mercurys
1951–52	Ernie Dick	Chatham Maroons
1952–53	Donnie Marshall	Cincinnati Mohawks
1953–54	Award not in competition	
1954–55	Phil Goyette	Cincinnati Mohawks
1955–56	George Hayes	Grand Rapids Rockets
1956–57	Pierre Brillant	Indianapolis Chiefs
1957–58	Pierre Brillant	Indianapolis Chiefs
1958–59	Len Thornson	Fort Wayne Komets
1959–60	Billy Reichart	Minneapolis Millers
1960–61	Len Thornson	Fort Wayne Komets
1961–62	Len Thornson	Fort Wayne Komets
1962–63	Len Thornson	Fort Wayne Komets
	Eddie Long	Fort Wayne Komets
1963–64	Len Thornson	Fort Wayne Komets
1964–65	Chick Chalmers	Toledo Blades
1965–66	Gary Schall	Muskegon Mohawks
1966–67	Len Thornson	Fort Wayne Komets
1967–68	Len Thornson	Fort Wayne Komets
	Don Westbrooke	Dayton Gems
1968–69	Don Westbrooke	Dayton Gems
1969–70	Cliff Pennington	Des Moines Oak Leafs
1970–71	Lyle Carter	Muskegon Mohawks
1971–72	Len Fontaine	Port Huron Flags
1972–73	Gary Ford	Muskegon Mohawks
1973–74	Pete Mara	Des Moines Capitals
1974–75	Gary Ford	Muskegon Mohawks
1975–76	Len Fontaine	Port Huron Flags
1976–77	Tom Mellor	Toledo Goaldiggers
1977–78	Dan Bonar	Fort Wayne Komets
1978–79	Terry McDougall	Fort Wayne Komets
1979–80	Al Dumba	Fort Wayne Komets
1980–81	Marcel Comeau	Saginaw Gears
1981–82	Brent Jarrett	Kalamazoo Wings
1982–83	Claude Noel	Toledo Goaldiggers
1983–84	Darren Jensen	Fort Wayne Komets
1984–85	Scott Gruhl	Muskegon Lumberjacks
1985–86	Darrell May	Peoria Rivermen
1986–87	Jock Callander	Muskegon Lumberjacks
	Jeff Pyle	Saginaw Generals
1987–88	John Cullen	Flint Spirits
1988–89	Dave Michayluk	Muskegon Lumberjacks
1989–90	Michel Mongeau	Peoria Rivermen
1990–91	David Bruce	Peoria Rivermen
1991–92	Dmitri Kvartalnov	San Diego Gulls
1992–93	Tony Hrkac	Indianapolis Ice
1993–94	Rob Brown	Kalamazoo Wings
1994–95	Tommy Salo	Denver Grizzlies
1995–96	Stephane Beauregard	San Francisco Spiders
1996–97	Frederic Chabot	Houston Aeros
1997–98	Patrice Lefebvre	Las Vegas Thunder
1998–99	Brian Wiseman	Houston Aeros

Fred A. Huber Jr. Memorial Trophy

The Huber Trophy is awarded to the league's regular season points leader. Between 1947 and 1954, the award was called the J. P. McGuire Trophy.

YEAR	TEAM	COACH
1946–47	Windsor Staffords	Jack Ward
1947–48	Windsor Spitfires	Jack Dent & Ebbie Goodfellow
1948–49	Toledo Mercurys	Andy Mulligan
1949–50	Sarnia Sailors	Dick Kowcinak
1950–51	Grand Rapids Rockets	Lou Trudell
1951–52	Grand Rapids Rockets	Lou Trudell
1952–53	Cincinnati Mohawks	Buddy O'Conner
1953–54	Cincinnati Mohawks	Roly McLenahan
1954–55	Cincinnati Mohawks	Roly McLenahan
1955–56	Cincinnati Mohawks	Roly McLenahan
1956–57	Cincinnati Mohawks	Roly McLenahan
1957–58	Cincinnati Mohawks	Bill Goold
1958–59	Louisville Rebels	Leo Gasparini
1959–60	Fort Wayne Komets	Ken Ullyot
1960–61	Minneapolis Millers	Ken Yackel
1961–62	Muskegon Zephyrs	Moose Lallo
1962–63	Fort Wayne Komets	Ken Ullyot
1963–64	Toledo Blades	Moe Benoit
1964–65	Port Huron Flags	Lloyd Maxfield
1965–66	Muskegon Mohawks	Moose Lallo
1966–67	Dayton Gems	Warren Back
1967–68	Muskegon Mohawks	Moose Lallo
1968–69	Dayton Gems	Larry Wilson
1969–70	Muskegon Mohawks	Moose Lallo
1970–71	Muskegon Mohawks	Moose Lallo
1971–72	Muskegon Mohawks	Moose Lallo
1972–73	Fort Wayne Komets	Marc Boileau
1973–74	Des Moines Capitols	Dan Belisle
1974–75	Muskegon Mohawks	Moose Lallo
1975–76	Dayton Gems	Ivan Prediger
1976–77	Saginaw Gears	Don Perry
1977–78	Fort Wayne Komets	Gregg Pilling
1978–79	Grand Rapids Owls	Moe Bartoli
1979–80	Kalamazoo Wings	Doug McKay
1980–81	Kalamazoo Wings	Doug McKay
1981–82	Toledo Goaldiggers	Bill Inglis
1982–83	Toledo Goaldiggers	Bill Inglis
1983–84	Fort Wayne Komets	Ron Ullyot

Leo P. Lamoureux Memorial Trophy

The Lamoureux Trophy is awarded to the league's regular season scoring champion. The trophy was originally known as the George H. Wilkinson Trophy from 1947 (the first year it was awarded) until 1960, when the name was changed.

YEAR	PLAYER	TEAM
1946–47	Harry Marchand	Windsor Spitfires
1947–48	Dick Kowcinak	Detroit Auto Club
1948–49	Leo Richard	Toledo Mercurys
1949–50	Dick Kowcinak	Sarnia Sailors
1950–51	Herve Parent	Grand Rapids Rockets
1951–52	George Parker	Grand Rapids Rockets
1952–53	Alex Irving	Milwaukee Chiefs
1953–54	Don Hall	Johnstown Jets
1954–55	Phil Goyette	Cincinnati Mohawks
1955–56	Max Mekilok	Cincinnati Mohawks
1956–57	Pierre Brillant	Indianapolis Chiefs
1957–58	Warren Hynes	Cincinnati Mohawks
1958–59	George Ranieri	Louisville Rebels
1959–60	Chick Chalmers	Louisville Rebels
1960–61	Ken Yackel	Minneapolis Millers
1961–62	Len Thornson	Fort Wayne Komets
1962–63	Moe Bartoli	Minneapolis Millers
1963–64	Len Thornson	Fort Wayne Komets
1964–65	Lloyd Maxfield	Port Huron Flags
1965–66	Bob Rivard	Fort Wayne Komets
1966–67	Len Thornson	Fort Wayne Komets
1967–68	Gary Ford	Muskegon Mohawks
1968–69	Don Westbrooke	Dayton Gems
1969–70	Don Westbrooke	Dayton Gems
1970–71	Darrel Knibbs	Muskegon Mohawks
1971–72	Gary Ford	Muskegon Mohawks
1972–73	Gary Ford	Muskegon Mohawks
1973–74	Pete Mara	Des Moines Capitols
1974–75	Rick Bragnalo	Dayton Gems
1975–76	Len Fontaine	Port Huron Flags
1976–77	Jim Koleff	Flint Generals
1977–78	Jim Johnston	Flint Generals
1978–79	Terry McDougall	Fort Wayne Komets
1979–80	Al Dumba	Fort Wayne Komets
1980–81	Marcel Comeau	Saginaw Gears
1981–82	Brent Jarrett	Kalamazoo Wings
1982–83	Dale Yakiwchuk	Milwaukee Admirals
1983–84	Wally Schreiber	Fort Wayne Komets
1984–85	Scott MacLeod	Salt Lake Golden Eagles
1985–86	Scott MacLeod	Salt Lake Golden Eagles
1986–87	Jock Callander	Muskegon Lumberjacks
	Jeff Pyle	Saginaw Generals
1987–88	John Cullen	Flint Spirits
1988–89	Dave Michayluk	Muskegon Lumberjacks
1989–90	Michel Mongeau	Peoria Rivermen
1990–91	Lonnie Loach	Fort Wayne Komets
1991–92	Dmitri Kvartalnov	San Diego Gulls
1992–93	Tony Hrkac	Indianapolis Ice
1993–94	Rob Brown	Kalamazoo Wings
1994–95	Stephane Morin	Minnesota Moose
1995–96	Rob Brown	Chicago Wolves
1996–97	Rob Brown	Chicago Wolves
1997–98	Patrice Lefebvre	Las Vegas Thunder
1998–99	Brian Wiseman	Houston Aeros

Governors' Trophy

The Governors' Trophy is awarded to the league's outstanding defenseman.

YEAR	PLAYER	TEAM
1964–65	Lionel Repka	Fort Wayne Komets
1965–66	Bob Lemieux	Muskegon Mohawks
1966–67	Larry Mavety	Port Huron Flags
1967–68	Carl Brewer	Muskegon Mohawks
1968–69	Al Beaule	Dayton Gems
	Moe Benoit	Dayton Gems
1969–70	John Gravel	Toledo Blades

YEAR	PLAYER	TEAM
1970–71	Bob LePage	Des Moines Oak Leafs
1971–72	Rick Pagnutti	Fort Wayne Komets
1972–73	Bob McCammon	Port Huron Flags
1973–74	Dave Simpson	Dayton Gems
1974–75	Murray Flegel	Muskegon Mohawks
1975–76	Murray Flegel	Muskegon Mohawks
1976–77	Tom Mellor	Toledo Goaldiggers
1977–78	Michel LaChance	Milwaukee Admirals
1978–79	Guido Tenesi	Grand Rapids Owls
1979–80	John Gibson	Saginaw Gears
1980–81	Larry Goodenough	Saginaw Gears
1981–82	Don Waddell	Saginaw Gears
1982–83	Jim Burton	Fort Wayne Komets
	Kevin Willison	Milwaukee Admirals
1983–84	Kevin Willison	Milwaukee Admirals
1984–85	Lee Norwood	Peoria Rivermen
1985–86	Jim Burton	Fort Wayne Komets
1986–87	Jim Burton	Fort Wayne Komets
1987–88	Phil Bourque	Muskegon Lumberjacks
1988–89	Randy Boyd	Milwaukee Admirals
1989–90	Brian Glynn	Salt Lake Golden Eagles
1990–91	Brian McKee	Fort Wayne Komets
1991–92	Jean–Marc Richard	Fort Wayne Komets
1992–93	Bill Houlder	San Diego Gulls
1993–94	Darren Veitch	Peoria Rivermen
1994–95	Todd Richards	Las Vegas Thunder
1995–96	Greg Hawgood	Las Vegas Thunder
1996–97	Brad Werenka	Indianapolis Ice
1997–98	Dan Lambert	Long Beach Ice Dogs
1998–99	Greg Hawgood	Houston Aeros

James Norris Memorial Trophy

The Norris Trophy is awarded to the league's outstanding goaltender.

YEAR	PLAYER	TEAM
1955–56	Bill Tibbs	Troy Bruins
1956–57	Glenn Ramsay	Cincinnati Mohawks
1957–58	Glenn Ramsay	Cincinnati Mohawks
1958–59	Don Rigazio	Louisville Rebels
1959–60	Rene Zanier	Fort Wayne Komets
1960–61	Ray Mikulan	Minneapolis Millers
1961–62	Glenn Ramsay	Omaha Knights
1962–63	Glenn Ramsay	Omaha Knights
1963–64	Glenn Ramsay	Toledo Blades
1964–65	Chuck Adamson	Fort Wayne Komets
1965–66	Bob Sneddon	Port Huron Flags
1966–67	Glenn Ramsay	Toledo Blades
1967–68	Tim Tabor, Bob Perani	Muskegon Mohawks
1968–69	Pat Rupp, John Adams	Dayton Gems
1969–70	Gaye Cooley	Des Moines Oak Leafs
	Bob Perreault	
1970–71	Lyle Carter	Muskegon Mohawks
1971–72	Glenn Resch	Muskegon Mohawks
1972–73	Robbie Irons	Fort Wayne Komets
	Don Atchison	
1973–74	Bill Hughes	Muskegon Mohawks
1974–75	Bob Volpe	Flint Generals
	Merlin Jenner	
1975–76	Don Cutts	Muskegon Mohawks
1976–77	Terry Richardson	Kalamazoo Wings
1977–78	Lorne Molleken	Saginaw Gears
	Pierre Chagnon	
1978–79	Gord Laxton	Grand Rapids Owls
1979–80	Larry Lozinski	Kalamazoo Wings
1980–81	Claude Legris	Kalamazoo Wings
	Georges Gagnon	
1981–82	Lorne Molleken	Toledo Goaldiggers
	Dave Tardich	
1982–83	Lorne Molleken	Toledo Goaldiggers
1983–84	Darren Jensen	Fort Wayne Komets
1984–85	Rick Heinz	Peoria Rivermen
1985–86	Rick St. Croix	Fort Wayne Komets
	Eldon "Pokey" Reddick	
1986–87	Alain Raymond	Fort Wayne Komets
	Michel Dufour	
1987–88	Steve Guenette	Muskegon Lumberjacks
1988–89	Rick Knickle	Fort Wayne Komets
1989–90	Jimmy Waite	Indianapolis Ice
1990–91	Guy Hebert	Peoria Rivermen
	Pat Jablonski	

YEAR	PLAYER	TEAM
1991–92	Arturs Irbe	Kansas City Blades
	Wade Flaherty	
1992–93	Rick Knickle	San Diego Gulls
	Clint Malarchuk	
1993–94	J.C. Bergeron	Atlanta Knights
	Mike Greenlay	
1994–95	Tommy Salo	Denver Grizzlies
1995–96	Tommy Salo	Utah Grizzlies
	Mark McArthur	
1996–97	Rich Parent, Jeff Reese	Detroit Vipers
1997–98	Mike Buzak	Long Beach Ice Dogs
	Kay Whitmore	
1998–99	Kevin Weekes	Detroit Vipers
	Andrei Trafilov	

Garry F. Longman Memorial Trophy

The Longman Trophy is awarded to the league's top rookie player.

YEAR	PLAYER	TEAM
1961–62	Dave Richardson	Fort Wayne Komets
1962–63	John Gravel	Omaha Knights
1963–64	Don Westbrooke	Toledo Blades
1964–65	Bob Thomas	Toledo Blades
1965–66	Frank Golembrosky	Port Huron Flags
1966–67	Kerry Bond	Columbus Checkers
1967–68	Gary Ford	Muskegon Mohawks
1968–69	Doug Volmar	Columbus Checkers
1969–70	Wayne Zuk	Toledo Blades
1970–71	Corky Agar	Flint Generals
	Herb Howdle	Dayton Gems
1971–72	Glenn Resch	Muskegon Mohawks
1972–73	Danny Gloor	Des Moines Capitols
1973–74	Frank DeMarco	Des Moines Capitols
1974–75	Rick Bragnalo	Dayton Gems
1975–76	Sid Veysey	Fort Wayne Komets
1976–77	Ron Zanussi	Fort Wayne Komets
	Garth MacGuigan	Muskegon Mohawks
1977–78	Dan Bonar	Fort Wayne Komets
1978–79	Wes Jarvis	Port Huron Flags
1979–80	Doug Robb	Milwaukee Admirals
1980–81	Scott Vanderburgh	Kalamazoo Wings
1981–82	Scott Howson	Toledo Goaldiggers
1982–83	Tony Fiore	Flint Generals
1983–84	Darren Jensen	Fort Wayne Komets
1984–85	Gilles Thibaudeau	Flint Generals
1985–86	Guy Benoit	Muskegon Lumberjacks
1986–87	Michel Mongeau	Saginaw Generals
1987–88	John Cullen	Flint Spirits
	Ed Belfour	Saginaw Hawks
1988–89	Paul Ranheim	Salt Lake Golden Eagles
1989–90	Rob Murphy	Milwaukee Admirals
1990–91	Nelson Emerson	Peoria Rivermen
1991–92	Dmitri Kvartalnov	San Diego Gulls
1992–93	Mikhail Shtalenkov	Milwaukee Admirals
1993–94	Radek Bonk	Las Vegas Thunder
1994–95	Tommy Salo	Denver Grizzlies
1995–96	Konstantin Shafranov	Fort Wayne Komets
1996–97	Sergei Samsonov	Detroit Vipers
1997–98	Todd White	Indianapolis Ice
1998–99	Marty Turco	Michigan K-Wings

Ken McKenzie Trophy

The McKenzie Trophy is awarded to the top American-born rookie to play in the league that season.

YEAR	PLAYER	TEAM
1977–78	Mike Eruzione	Toledo Goaldiggers
1978–79	Jon Fontas	Saginaw Gears
1979–80	Bob Janecyk	Fort Wayne Komets
1980–81	Mike Labianca	Toledo Goaldiggers
	Steve Janaszak	Fort Wayne Komets
1981–82	Steve Salvucci	Saginaw Gears
1982–83	Paul Fenton	Peoria Prancers
1983–84	Mike Krensing	Muskegon Mohawks
1984–85	Bill Schafhauser	Kalamazoo Wings
1985–86	Brian Noonan	Saginaw Generals
1986–87	Ray LeBlanc	Flint Spirits
1987–88	Dan Woodley	Flint Spirits
1988–89	Paul Ranheim	Salt Lake Golden Eagles
1989–90	Tim Sweeney	Salt Lake Golden Eagles
1990–91	C.J. Young	Salt Lake Golden Eagles
1991–92	Kevin Wortman	Salt Lake Golden Eagles
1992–93	Mark Beaufait	Kansas City Blades
1993–94	Chris Rogles	Indianapolis Ice
1994–95	Chris Marinucci	Denver Grizzlies
1995–96	Brett Lievers	Utah Grizzlies
1996–97	Brian Felsner	Orlando Solar Bears
1997–98	Eric Nickulas	Orlando Solar Bears
1998–99	Mark Moweis	Milwaukee Admirals

N. R. "Bud" Poile Trophy

The Poile Trophy is awarded to the player who is judged to be the most valuable player of the playoffs.

YEAR	PLAYER	TEAM
1988–89	Dave Michayluk	Muskegon Lumberjacks
1989–90	Mike McNeill	Indianapolis Ice
1990–91	Michel Mongeau	Peoria Rivermen
1991–92	Ron Handy	Kansas City Blades
1992–93	Eldon "Pokey" Reddick	Fort Wayne Komets
1993–94	Stan Drulia	Atlanta Knights
1994–95	Kip Miller	Denver Grizzlies
1995–96	Tommy Salo	Utah Grizzlies
1996–97	Peter Ciavaglia	Detroit Vipers
1997–98	Alexander Semak	Chicago Wolves
1998–99	Mark Freer	Houston Aeros

Commissioner's Trophy

The Commissioner's Trophy is awarded to the league's coach of the year.

YEAR	PLAYER	TEAM
1984–85	Rick Ley	Muskegon Lumberjacks
	Pat Kelly	Peoria Rivermen
1985–86	Robbie Laird	Fort Wayne Komets
1986–87	Wayne Thomas	Salt Lake Golden Eagles
1987–88	Rick Dudley	Flint Spirits
1988–89	Blair "B.J." MacDonald	Muskegon Lumberjacks
	Phil Russell	Muskegon Lumberjacks
1989–90	Darryl Sutter	Indianapolis Ice
1990–91	Bob Plager	Peoria Rivermen
1991–92	Kevin Constantine	Kansas City Blades
1992–93	Al Sims	Fort Wayne Komets
1993–94	Bruce Boudreau	Fort Wayne Komets
1994–95	Butch Goring	Denver Grizzlies
1995–96	Butch Goring	Utah Grizzlies
1996–97	John Van Boxmeer	Long Beach Ice Dogs
1997–98	John Torchetti	Fort Wayne Komets
1998–99	Dave Tippett	Houston Aeros

21

U.S. COLLEGE HOCKEY: ON THE RISE

From somewhat modest beginnings, collegiate hockey in the United States has grown tremendously since the National Collegiate Athletic Association started its annual championship hockey tournament in 1948.

The collegians started with one division. Now there are three, with the highest level of competition in Division I. Each NCAA division has its own playoffs, leading to respective champions.

A long-ago player at Princeton, Hobart (Hobey) Baker, never appeared in the NHL or its predecessor leagues, but he's listed in the players' section of the Hockey Hall of Fame. Synonymous with amateur hockey in the U.S., he was notable as a pre–World War I performer. The Hobey Baker Trophy is awarded annually to the outstanding collegian.

Colleges in the U.S. recruit players from Canada as well as the U.S. and the program has become almost as extensive as the one the schools follow in tracking down talented football players. Most collegiate rosters are stacked with Canadian imports, but in recent years more and more American-born youths are playing hockey in college.

The U.S. triumph in the 1980 Olympic Games provided incentive for home-grown talent to pursue their sport. The number of those moving into the professional ranks is increasing as more youngsters recognize the value of a college education before trying pro hockey.

DIVISION I

NATIONAL CHAMPIONSHIP

YEAR	SCHOOL	COACH
1948	Michigan	Vic Heyliger
1949	Boston College	John "Snooks" Kelley
1950	Colorado College	Cheddy Thompson
1951	Michigan	Vic Heyliger
1952	Michigan	Vic Heyliger
1953	Michigan	Vic Heyliger
1954	Rensselaer	Ned Harkness
1955	Michigan	Vic Heyliger
1956	Michigan	Vic Heyliger
1957	Colorado College	Thomas Bedecki
1958	Denver	Murray Armstrong
1959	North Dakota	Bob May
1960	Denver	Murray Armstrong
1961	Denver	Murray Armstrong
1962	Michigan Tech	John MacInnes
1963	North Dakota	Barry Thorndycraft
1964	Michigan	Allen Renfrew
1965	Michigan Tech	John MacInnes
1966	Michigan State	Amo Bessone
1967	Cornell	Ned Harkness
1968	Denver	Murray Armstrong
1969	Denver	Murray Armstrong
1970	Cornell	Ned Harkness
1971	Boston U.	Jack Kelley

1972	Boston U.	Jack Kelley
1973	Wisconsin	Bob Johnson
1974	Minnesota	Herb Brooks
1975	Michigan Tech	John MacInnes
1976	Minnesota	Herb Brooks
1977	Wisconsin	Bob Johnson
1978	Boston U.	Jack Parker
1979	Minnesota	Herb Brooks
1980	North Dakota	John "Gino" Gasparini
1981	Wisconsin	Bob Johnson
1982	North Dakota	John "Gino" Gasparini
1983	Wisconsin (33-10-4)	Jeff Sauer
1984	Bowling Green (34-8-2)	Jerry York
1985	Rensselaer (35-2-1)	Mike Addesa
1986	Michigan State	Ron Mason
1987	North Dakota	John "Gino" Gasparini
1988	Lake Superior State	Frank Anzalone
1989	Harvard	Bill Cleary
1990	Wisconsin	Jeff Sauer
1991	Northern Michigan	Rick Comley
1992	Lake Superior State	Jeff Jackson
1993	Maine	Shawn Walsh
1994	Lake Superior State	Jeff Jackson
1995	Boston U.	Jack Parker
1996	Michigan	Gordon "Red" Berenson
1997	North Dakota	Dean Blais
1998	Michigan	Gordon "Red" Berenson
1999	Maine	Shawn Walsh

1994	Sean Tallaire	Lake Superior St.
1995	Chris O'Sullivan	Boston U.
1996	Brendan Morrison	Michigan

HOBEY BAKER MEMORIAL AWARD

Awarded to the top college hockey player as voted on by an 18-member panel of coaches, scouts, and media members. Named after former Princeton hockey star Hobey Baker, who died during World War I.

YEAR	PLAYER	SCHOOL
1999	Jason Krog	New Hampshire
1998	Chris Drury	Boston University
1997	Brendan Morrison	Michigan
1996	Brian Bonin	Minnesota
1995	Brian Holzinger	Bowling Green
1994	Chris Marinucci	Minnesota-Duluth
1993	Paul Kariya	Maine
1992	Scott Pellerin	Maine
1991	David Emma	Boston College
1990	Kip Miller	Michigan State
1989	Lane McDonald	Harvard
1988	Robb Stauber	Minnesota
1987	Tony Hrkac	North Dakota
1986	Scott Fusco	Harvard
1985	Bill Watson	Minnesota-Duluth
1984	Tom Kurvers	Minnesota-Duluth
1983	Mark Fusco	Harvard
1982	George McPhee	Bowling Green
1981	Neal Broten	Minnesota

MOST OUTSTANDING PLAYER AWARD

YEAR	PLAYER	COACH
1948	Joe Riley	Dartmouth
1949	Dick Desmond	Dartmouth
1950	Ralph Bevins	Boston U.
1951	Ed Whiston	Brown
1952	Kenneth Kinsley	Colorado Col.
1953	John Matchefts	Michigan
1954	Abbie Moore	Rensselaer
1955	Philip Hilton	Colorado Col.
1956	Lorne Howes	Michigan
1957	Bob McCusker	Colorado Col.
1958	Murray Massier	Denver
1959	Reg Morelli	North Dak.
1960	Bob Marquis	Boston U.
	Barry Urbanski	Boston U.
	Louis Angotti	Michigan Tech
1961	Bill Masterton	Denver
1962	Louis Angotti	Michigan Tech
1963	Al McLean	North Dak.
1964	Bob Gray	Michigan
1965	Gary Milroy	Michigan Tech
1966	Gaye Cooley	Michigan St.
1967	Walt Stanowski	Cornell
1968	Gerry Powers	Denver
1969	Keith Magnuson	Denver
1970	Daniel Lodboa	Cornell
1971	Dan Brady	Boston U.
1972	Tim Regan	Boston U.
1973	Dean Talafous	Wisconsin
1974	Brad Shelstad	Minnesota
1975	Jim Warden	Michigan Tech
1976	Tom Vanelli	Minnesota
1977	Julian Baretta	Wisconsin
1978	Jack O'Callahan	Boston U.
1979	Steve Janaszak	Minnesota
1980	Doug Smail	North Dak.
1981	Marc Behrend	Wisconsin
1982	Phil Sykes	North Dak.
1983	Marc Behrend	Wisconsin
1984	Gary Kruzich	Bowling Green
1985	Chris Terreri	Providence
1986	Mike Donnelly	Michigan St.
1987	Tony Hrkac	North Dak.
1988	Bruce Hoffort	Lake Superior St.
1989	Ted Donato	Harvard
1990	Chris Tancill	Wisconsin
1991	Scott Beattie	Northern Mich.
1992	Paul Constantin	Lake Superior St.
1993	Jim Montgomery	Maine

LEADING SCORER, PLAYOFFS

YEAR	PLAYER	COACH
1948	Wally Gacek	Michigan
1949	Gil Burford	Michigan
1950	Chris Ray	Colorado Col.
	Tony Frasca	Colorado Col.
1951	Omer Brandt	Colorado Col.
1952	George Chin	Michigan
	Doug Philpott	Michigan
1953	George Chin	Michigan
	Doug Philpott	Michigan
1954	Dick Dougherty	Minnesota
	John Mayasich	Minnesota
	Bill McFarland	Michigan
1955	Bill Cleary	Harvard
	Bill McFarland	Michigan
1956	Neil MacDonald	Michigan
1957	Bob McCusker	Colorado Col.
1958	Grant Childerhose	Clarkson
	Bob Van Lammers	Clarkson
1959	Reg Morelli	North Dakota
1960	Paul Coppo	Michigan Tech.
1961	Bill Masterton	Denver
1962	John Ivanitz	Michigan Tech.
1963	Al McLean	North Dakota
	Bob Hamill	Denver
1964	Tom Polonik	Michigan
	Gordon Wilkie	Michigan
1965	Gary Milroy	Michigan Tech.
1966	John McLennan	Clarkson
1967	Walt Stanowski	Cornell
	Sandy McAndrew	Michigan
	Tom Mikkola	Michigan St.
1968	Brian Cornell	Cornell
	John Hughes	Cornell
1969	Keith Magnuson	Denver
1970	Bob Poffenroth	Wisconsin
1971	Dean Blais	Minnesota
1972	Ron Anderson	Boston U.
	Ric Jordan	Boston U.

	David Westner	Cornell
	Gary Winchester	Wisconsin
1973	Vacated	
1974	Jim McMahon	Harvard
1975	Bob D'Alvise	Michigan Tech.
	Terry Meagher	Boston U.
	Bill Robbins	Boston U.
1976	Tom Vanelli	Minnesota
1977	Rick Meagher	Boston U.
	David Silk	Boston U.
1978	Jack O'Callahan	Boston U.
	David Silk	Boston U.
1979	Mark Taylor	North Dakota
1980	Phil Sykes	North Dakota
1981	Aaron Broten	Minnesota
1982	Phil Sykes	North Dak.
1983	Pat Flatley	Wisconsin
1984	Lyle Phair	Michigan St.
1985	Bill Watson	Minn.-Duluth
1986	Lane MacDonald	Harvard
	Mitch Messier	Michigan St.
1987	Tony Hrkac	North Dakota
1988	Pete Lappin	St. Lawrence
1989	Rob Gaudreau	Providence
1990	Tony Amonte	Boston U.
1991	Dave Trombley	Clarkson
1992	Brian Rolston	Lake Superior
1993	Jim Montgomery	Maine
1994	Gerald Tallaire	Lake Superior
1995	Nick Checco	Minnesota
	Kaj Linna	Boston U.
	Steve Thomton	Boston U.
1996	Brendan Concannon	Mass.-Lowe
	Brendan Morrison	Michigan
	Bill Muckalt	Michigan
1997	Casey Hankinson	Minnesota
	Matt Henderson	North Dakota
1998	Matt Herr	Michigan
	Mark Kosick	Michigan

DIVISION II

NATIONAL CHAMPIONSHIP

YEAR	SCHOOL	COACH
1978	Merrimack	Thom Lawler
1979	Mass.-Lowell	Bill Riley
1980	Mankato St.	Don Brose
1981	Mass.-Lowell	Bill Riley
1982	Mass.-Lowell	Bill Riley
1983	Rochester Inst.	Brian Mason
1984	Bemidji St.	Bob Peters
1993	Bemidji St.	Bob Peters
1994	Bemidji St.	Bob Peters
1995	Bemidji St.	Bob Peters
1996	Ala.-Huntsville	Doug Ross
1997	Bemidji St.	Bob Peters
1998	Ala.-Huntsville	Doug Ross
1999	St.Michael's	

MOST OUTSTANDING PLAYER AWARD

YEAR	PLAYER	COACH
1978	Jim Toomey	Merrimack
1979	Craig MacTavish	Mass.-Lowell
1980	Steve Carroll	Mankato St.
1981	Tom Mulligan	Mass.-Lowell
1982	Paul Lohnes	Mass.-Lowell
1983	Dave Burkholder	Rochester Inst.
1984	Joel Otto	Bemidji St.

LEADING SCORERS, PLAYOFFS

YEAR	PLAYER	COACH
1978	Jim Toomey	Merrimack

1979	Craig MacTavish	Mass.-Lowell
1980	Mike Carr	Mass.-Lowell
1981	Tom Mulligan	Mass.-Lowell
1982	Scott Swanson	Gust. Adolphus
1983	Mike Carr	Mass.-Lowell
1984	Drey Bradley	Bemidji St.
1993	Jamie Erb	Bemidji St.
1994	Bernie Adlys	Bemidji St.
1995	Eric Fulton	Bemidji St.
	Jude Boulianne	Bemidji St.
1996	Tony Guzzo	Ala.-Huntsville
1997	Marc Lafleur	Bemidji St.
1998	Mike Hamlin	Ala.-Huntsville
	John McCabe	Ala.-Huntsville
	Colin Schmidt	Ala.-Huntsville
	Shane Stewart	Ala.-Huntsville

DIVISION III

NATIONAL CHAMPIONSHIP

YEAR	PLAYER	COACH
1984	Babson	Rob Riley
1985	Rochester Inst.	Bruce Delventhal
1986	Bemidji St.	R. H. Peters
1987	Plattsburgh St.	Steve Hoar
1988	Wis.-River Falls	Rick Kozuback
1989	Wis.-Stevens Point	Mark Mazzoleni
1990	Wis.-Stevens Point	Mark Mazzoleni
1991	Wis.-Stevens Point	Mark Mazzoleni
1992	Plattsburgh St.	Bob Emery
1993	Wis.-Stevens Point	Joe Baldarotta
1994	Wis.-River Falls	Dean Talafous
1995	Middlebury	Bill Beaney
1996	Middlebury	Bill Beaney
1997	Middlebury	Bill Beaney
1998	Middlebury	Bill Beaney
1999	Middlebury	Bill Beaney

MOST OUTSTANDING PLAYER AWARD

YEAR	PLAYER	COACH
1984	Paul Donato	Babson
1985	Chet Hallice	Rochester Inst.
1986	Mike Alexander	Bemidji St.
1987	Chris Panek	Plattsburgh St.
1988	Not awarded	
1989	Shawn Wheeler	Wis.-Stevens Point
1990	Paul Caufield	Wis.-Stevens Point
(Award not presented since 1990)		

LEADING SCORER PLAYOFFS

YEAR	PLAYER	COACH
1984	Maurice Montambault Inst.	Rochester
1985	Dave Piromalli	Plattsburgh St.
	Peter DeArmas	Plattsburgh St.
1986	Ritchie Herbert	Rochester Inst.
1987	Chris Panek	Plattsburgh St.
1988	Arron Scott	Wis.-River Falls
1989	Paul Caufield	Wis.-Stevens Point
1990	Ralph Barahona Point	Wis.-Stevens Point
	Jim Duran	Plattsburgh St.
1991	Paul Caufield	Wis.-Stevens Point
1992	Dan Bates	Salem St.
	Chris Campbell	Wis.-Superior
1993	Steve Moore	Plattsburgh St.
1994	Jeff Lupu	Fredonia St.
1995	Russ Johnson	Wis.-River Falls
1996	Steve Toll	Rochester Inst.
1997	Mike Anatasio	Middlebury
	Mark Spence	Middlebury
1998	Eric Seidel	Plattsburgh St.

22

THE OLYMPIC GAMES AND INTERNATIONAL COMPETITIONS

OLYMPIC GAMES

The world of hockey is by no means limited to the National Hockey League, and when the NHL agreed to send its players to the 1998 Winter Olympics, it marked a new stage in the sport's competitive development and marketing. For the first time, the world's best players would represent their countries on the world's biggest stage.

As with all Olympic competition, the Olympic hockey tournament originally featured amateur players exclusively. From the 1950s though 1984, the hockey teams from capitalist nations continued to be composed of amateur players, but while the socialist countries insisted their players were amateurs as well, the rest of the world considered them professionals. Beginning in 1988, the best available players, regardless of whether they were amateur or professional, were allowed to represent their homeland in the Olympics, but those who played in the NHL could not compete because they were participating in their regular season.

The NHL's initiative in suspending its 1997-98 season to allow for 1998 Olympics participation in Nagano, Japan, had many sides to it, besides raising the tournament's competitive level. It would provide unprecedented exposure for NHL players, regardless of their homeland, and would hopefully create new stars and personalities to market. And because the Olympics enjoy high TV viewership, the U.S. network telecasts had the potential to break new ground in the sport.

The success of the U.S. at the World Cup in 1996 backed the belief that the U.S. would be a major factor. Most of the same players were selected for the Olympic team, including Mike Richter, Brian Leetch, Chris Chelios, John LeClair, Brett Hull, and Jeremy Roenick.

Similarly, the Canadians, who had finished second to the U.S. at the World Cup, had high hopes for the Olympics with a roster featuring such NHL stars as Patrick Roy, Eric Lindros, and Wayne Gretzky.

In order to keep the NHL from a lengthier moratorium, the Olympic format was redesigned to accommodate the countries with the highest number of NHL players.

The U.S. Olympic team that won the "Miracle on Ice" sings the national anthem as it accepts its gold medals at the 1980 Olympics in Lake Placid.

In a preliminary qualifying round, Italy, Austria, Slovakia, Germany, Japan, and France were eliminated, and Kazakhstan and Belarus advanced.

The teams were then placed into two divisions for a three-game round-robin schedule. Group A consisted of Canada, Sweden, the U.S., and Belarus; Group B included Russia, the Czech Republic, Finland, and Kazakhstan. Canada and Russia went undefeated in group play, while the U.S. lost two of its three. All the teams were then re-seeded for a quarterfinal single-elimination phase, leading to the medal games.

In the quarterfinals, Dominik Hasek, who had allowed only four goals in Group B play, shut down the U.S., eliminating them. Following the game, members of the U.S. team engaged in some horseplay in the Olympic Village that resulted in damage to the athletes' dormitories and disrupted the sleep of other athletes. Despite threats from Olympic and NHL officials, the offending team members were never publicly identified, as the entire team remained silent. The unfortunate incident was probably the most highly publicized chapter of the Nagano Olympics, and embarrassed the NHL.

Canada became Hasek's next victim. The Czech goalie blanked Canada for nearly 59 minutes, until a late deflection by Trevor Linden sent the game into overtime. But a 1-1 tie forced a shootout. Hasek then stopped all five shots taken by Canada.

Patrick Roy stopped four Czech shots, but Robert Reichel scored to send the Czechs into the gold-medal game. Mark Crawford, the Canadian coach, was criticized afterward for not selecting Gretzky as one of his shooters. Canada subsequently lost to Finland, 3-2, in its quest for third place and a bronze medal.

The Russians beat Sweden and Finland to advance to the Finals against Czechoslovakia, but with the gold on the line, Hasek proved unbeatable, stopping all 21 shots for a 1-0 victory. He allowed only six goals in six games, stopping 96 percent of the shots he faced and recording two shutouts to solidify his reputation as the top goaltender in the world.

The Winter Olympics go back to 1924. The sport was added to the Olympic program in 1920, when there was a single competition instead of separate winter and summer Olympics.

Canada dominated at first, winning the championship in each of the first four Olympic competitions. The Canadians won two more titles following World War II before the Soviet Union started a domination which led to eight championships in the next ten Olympics through 1992. The two times the Russians missed during that period were in 1960 and 1980, and in both cases it was the United States that pulled major upsets.

The Americans were given little chance to win in 1960, but were determined to score an upset. We knew with a couple of breaks we could upset the odds,' recalled goaltender Jack McCartan. The U.S. team had one thing going for them: the Games were held at Squaw Valley, California.

After winning four games in the preliminaries, the Americans passed a big test by edging Canada, 2-1, as McCartan made 39 saves. The U.S. squad then rallied to stun the Russians, 3-2, setting up the championship game against Czechoslovakia. Again the Americans rallied, scoring six times in the final period to win, 9-4, and take the gold.

Twenty years later, another group of young Americans gave their country an even bigger thrill as they came from nowhere to skate off with the Olympic gold.

The 1980 Games were again held in the United States-at Lake Placid, New York-and once more the U.S. team was a heavy underdog. Just a few days before the Games began, the Americans lost, 11-3, to the Russians in an exhibition game. U.S. coach Herb Brooks was hoping his team could get a silver or bronze medal.

They didn't; they came home with the gold. After tying Sweden with a last-minute goal in their opening game, the Americans raced to four

straight wins to advance to the semifinals. Awaiting them there were the vaunted Soviets. Before the game, Brooks told his players, You were born to be hockey players. You were meant to be here. This moment is yours.'

And the game was theirs, too, as Mike Eruzione snapped a tie with 10 minutes left and the U.S. held on for a stunning 4-3 victory. That sent the Americans into the finals against Finland in a game that would settle it all.

The U.S. squad, which averaged just 20 years of age, spotted the Finns a 2-1 lead going into the last period but then roared back for three goals. When the game ended, thousands of fans started singing God Bless America' and waving American flags. The Soviet streak of four consecutive

Olympic gold medals had been stopped. The U.S. had its gold and the Russians had to settle for silver.

There would be no repeat performance in the 1984 Olympics at Sarajevo, Yugoslavia. The U.S. featured what was described as a Diaper Line' consisting of three high-school players (Pat La-Fontaine, David A. Jensen, and Ed Olczyk) and they had some big moments, including a 3-3 tie with Norway and a 7-3 rout of Austria. But the team wound up seventh in the final standings.

The Soviet Union won all seven of its games to take the gold medal ahead of Czechoslovakia, Sweden and Canada.

In 1988, the Americans unleashed a high-scoring team that scored goals by the half-dozen, but they also yielded them by the half-dozen. No-

Goalie Dominik Hasek (bottom left) is surrounded by jubilant teammates after the Czech Republic won the gold medal at the 1998 Winter Olympics in Nagano, Japan with a 1–0 win over Russia.

body had beaten the Soviet Union since the U.S. did it in 1980 and the Americans came within a ricocheted slapshot of tying the Russians after being behind by four goals. The Soviet Union won the game, 7-5, and went on to capture the title.

The Soviets no longer carried CCCP on their jerseys at the 1992 Olympics. Reflecting the new independence of nations in the Soviet sphere, they were called the Unified Team in the hockey competition at Meribel, France. But nothing changed in the superior quality of their game as the Unified Team took the gold again, defeating Canada, 3-1, in the final.

Both the silver-winning Canada and the United States made bold challenges, with the Canadians featuring Eric Lindros, the celebrated NHL holdout, high-scoring Joe Juneau and goalie Sean Burke.

The U.S. squad, with minor leaguer Ray LeBlanc starring in goal, raised hopes of another Miracle on Ice' when it went unbeaten going into the final round. But losses to the Unified Team (5-2) and bronze-winning Czechoslovakia (6-1) resulted in a fourth-place finish and no medal for the U.S.

In 1994, the Unified Team was ousted, 4-3, in the semifinals by Sweden, which won the gold, 3-2, in a sudden-death shootout with Canada.

The U.S. (1-4-3) was eighth in the standings.

An increasing number of players have graduated from the collegiate and Olympic ranks into the NHL. They date back to Red Berenson, the super center of the NHL's expansion West Division in the late 1960s who led all collegiate scorers when he

Action at the 1932 Winter Olympics in Lake Placid, as Germany (black uniforms) opposes Canada.

was at Michigan in 1961-62, and Tony Esposito, an All-American goalie at Michigan Tech.

Forward Tommy Williams, who played for eight years with the Boston Bruins in the 1960s, was a member of the U.S. championship Olympic team in 1960. The 1980 gold-medal U.S. squad was the NHL springboard for such others as Ken Morrow, Mike Ramsey, Neil Broten and Dave Christian. Pat LaFontaine, Chris Chelios, Al Iafrate and Ed Olczyk are among the graduates of the 1984 U.S. Olympic team and the 1988 contingent produced Brain Leetch, Craig Janney and Kevin Stevens.

The list of Olympic medal winners follows:

Men

1920

1. Canada
2. USA
3. Czechoslovakia

1924

1. Canada
2. USA
3. Great Britain

1928

1. Canada
2. Sweden
3. Switzerland

1932

1. Canada
2. USA
3. Germany

1936

1. Great Britain
2. Canada
3. USA

1940 AND 1944

No Olympics held.

1948

1. Canada
1. Czechoslovakia
3. Switzerland

1952

1. Canada
2. USA
3. Sweden

1956

1. Soviet Union
2. USA
3. Canada

1960

1. USA
2. Canada
3. Soviet Union

1964

1. Soviet Union
2. Sweden
3. Czechoslovakia

1968

1. Soviet Union
2. Czechoslovakia
3. Canada

1972

1. Soviet Union
2. USA
3. Czechoslovakia

1976

1. Soviet Union
2. Czechoslovakia
3. West Germany

1980

1. USA
2. Soviet Union
3. Sweden

1984

1. Soviet Union
2. Czechoslovakia
3. Sweden

1988

1. Soviet Union
2. Finland
3. Sweden

1992

1. Unified Team
2. Canada
3. Czechoslovakia

1994

1. Sweden
2. Canada
3. Finland

1998

1. Czech Republic
2. Russia
3. Finland

Women

Another historic Olympic hockey chapter was written in Nagano by the women hockey players of the world. For the first time, women's hockey became an Olympic sport. The U.S. women's team fared better than the men's, winning the gold medal in the six-team tournament with a 3-1 win in the final game against Canada. For more information on the women, see chapter 19.

1998

1. USA
2. Canada
3. Finland

INTERNATIONAL COMPETITIONS

WORLD CHAMPIONSHIPS

Except for the Olympic years of 1984 and 1988-and time out for World War II-hockey has staged World Championships annually since 1924. The Soviet Union monopolized the competition, winning the crown nine straight years from 1963 through 1971 and in 23 years overall.

The Russians were generally acknowledged as the best amateur' players in the world, especially remarkable when one considers that they didn't even take up hockey until the late 1940s. The Soviet Union played as a unit virtually year-round and it showed in world competition, when they frequently played teams that get together for a relatively short period before the competition.

But the breakup of the Soviet Union in recent years has changed the picture; the Russians last won in 1993. Canada has won twice since then-1994 and 1997. Finland took the title in 1995 and the Czech Republic prevailed in 1996.

The tournament introduced a new format in 1998, making the semifinals each a two-game, total-goals affair. Sweden captured the 1998 title, defeating Finland 1-0 in Game 1, and holding the Finns to a 0-0 tie in Game 2.

For Sweden's Kent Forsberg, one of the world's top coaches and father of Peter Forsberg of the Colorado Avalanche, it was his farewell.

He announced his retirement. Appropriately, his son played on the gold-medal team.

The list of World Championship results follows:

1924
1. Canada
2. USA
3. Great Britain

1928
1. Canada
2. Sweden
3. Switzerland

1930
1. Canada
2. Germany
3. Switzerland

1931
1. Canada
2. USA
3. Austria

1932
1. Canada
2. USA
3. Germany

1933
1. USA
2. Canada
3. Czechoslovakia

1934
1. Canada
2. USA
3. Germany

1935
1. Canada
2. Switzerland
3. Great Britain

1936
1. Great Britain
2. Canada
3. USA

1937
1. Canada
2. Great Britain
3. Switzerland

1938
1. Canada
2. Great Britain
3. Czechoslovakia

1939
1. Canada
2. USA
3. Switzerland

1947
1. Czechoslovakia
2. Sweden
3. Austria

1948
1. Canada
2. Czechoslovakia
3. Switzerland

1949
1. Czechoslovakia
2. Canada
3. USA

1950
1. Canada
2. USA
3. Switzerland

1951
1. Canada
2. Sweden
3. Switzerland

1952
1. Canada
2. USA
3. Sweden

1953
1. Sweden
2. German Federal Republic
3. Switzerland

1954
1. Soviet Union
2. Canada
3. Sweden

1955
1. Canada
2. Soviet Union
3. Czechoslovakia

1956
1. Soviet Union
2. USA
3. Canada

1957
1. Sweden
2. Soviet Union
3. Czechoslovakia

1958
1. Canada
2. Soviet Union
3. Sweden

1959
1. Canada
2. Soviet Union
3. Czechoslovakia

1960
1. USA
2. Canada
3. Soviet Union

1961
1. Canada
2. Czechoslovakia
3. Soviet Union

1962
1. Sweden
2. Canada
3. USA

1963
1. Soviet Union
2. Sweden
3. Czechoslovakia

1964
1. Soviet Union
2. Sweden
3. Czechoslovakia

1965
1. Soviet Union
2. Czechoslovakia
3. Sweden

1966
1. Soviet Union
2. Czechoslovakia
3. Canada

1967
1. Soviet Union
2. Sweden
3. Canada

1968
1. Soviet Union
2. Czechoslovakia
3. Canada

1969
1. Soviet Union
2. Sweden
3. Czechoslovakia

1970
1. Soviet Union
2. Sweden
3. Czechoslovakia

1971
1. Soviet Union
2. Czechoslovakia
3. Sweden

1972
1. Czechoslovakia
2. Soviet Union
3. Sweden

1973
1. Soviet Union
2. Sweden
3. Czechoslovakia

1974
1. Soviet Union
2. Czechoslovakia
3. Sweden

1975
1. Soviet Union
2. Czechoslovakia
3. Sweden

1976
1. Czechoslovakia
2. Soviet Union
3. Sweden

1977
1. Czechoslovakia
2. Sweden
3. Soviet Union

1978
1. Soviet Union
2. Czechoslovakia
3. Canada

1979
1. Soviet Union
2. Czechoslovakia
3. Sweden

1980
1. USA
2. Soviet Union
3. Sweden

1981
1. Soviet Union
2. Sweden
3. Czechoslovakia

1982
1. Soviet Union
2. Czechoslovakia
3. Canada

1983
1. Soviet Union
2. Czechoslovakia
3. Canada

1985
1. Czechoslovakia
2. Canada
3. Soviet Union

1986
1. Soviet Union
2. Sweden
3. Canada

1987
1. Sweden
2. Soviet Union
3. Czechoslovakia

1989
1. Soviet Union
2. Canada
3. Czechoslovakia

1990
1. Soviet Union
2. Sweden
3. Czechoslovakia

1991
1. Sweden
2. Canada
3. Soviet Union

1992
1. Sweden
2. Finland
3. Czechoslovakia

1993

1. Russia
2. Sweden
3. Czechoslovakia

1994

1. Canada
2. Finland
3. Sweden

1995

1. Finland
2. Sweden
3. Canada

1996

1. Czech Republic
2. Canada
3. Russia

1997

1. Canada
2. Sweden
3. Czech Republic

1998

1. Sweden
2. Finland
3. Czech Republic

INTERNATIONAL CHALLENGES

The Soviet Union's dominance of the Olympics and other world competitions led to the inevitable argument over who was better: the Russians or the National Hockey League professionals. One way to settle it was head-to-head on ice.

The first confrontation came in 1972, when the NHL All-Stars played the Russians in an eight-game series. The NHL team won, but just barely, when Paul Henderson scored in the last minute of the final game, to give his squad a 4-3-1 edge in games.

In 1976, the NHL stars of Team Canada defeated Czechoslovakia on an overtime goal by Darryl Sittler that enabled Canada to capture the Canada Cup tournament.

The NHL All-Stars met the Soviets in a three-game Challenge Cup series at New York's Madison Square Garden in February 1979 and the Russians rallied after dropping the first game to take the set, two games to one. The USSR continued its winning ways in the 1981 Canada Cup. The Soviets walloped the Canadians, 8-1, in the final game to take home the Cup.

Over the years since then, Soviet teams have played various Canadian and U.S. units-NHL All-Stars, Team Canada, Team USA and a range of NHL clubs. From 1972 through 1991, the last time the competition was held, the Russians won 83 of 140 games.

For the NHL, its greatest success came in a tour of Leningrad, Moscow, Kiev and Riga in September 1989. Playing against Dynamo Moscow, Dynamo Riga, the Red Army and the Soviet Wings, the Washington Capitals and Calgary Flames each won three games and lost one in the eight-game series.

A new eight-nation tournament, the World Cup, the successor of the Canada Cup, was organized in 1996 as a joint venture of the NHL and the NHL Players' Association. The countries involved were the U.S., Canada, Russia, Sweden, Finland, the Czech Republic, Germany and Slovakia. The games were played in North America and Europe.

Many NHL players took part in the tournament, giving up the latter part of their summer to attend training camp in various parts of the world. Once play began, it became clear that the two best teams in the tournament were the United States and Canada. The U.S. was led by Tony Amonte of the Blackhawks, Phoenix's Keith Tkachuk, the Devils' Bill Guerin, Colorado's Adam Deadmarsh, and Ranger stars Brian Leetch and Mike Richter, while Canada's stars included Mark Messier and Wayne Gretzky of the Rangers, Eric Lindros of the Flyers and Oilers goalie Curtis Joseph.

Both teams breezed through the round-robin play and reached the best-of-three final series. The U.S. lost the opener in overtime but came back to win Game 2, setting up a winner-take-all third game, to be played in Montreal's Molson Centre. With a wildly cheering crowd behind them, the Canadians took a lead into the final periods but could not break the game open due to the fabulous goaltending of Richter. Finally, the inspired U.S. team broke through the Canadians' defense, scoring three times in the final minutes to post a stunning 5-2 triumph and the first-ever World Cup championship.

23

YOUNG GUNS:
TOP DRAFT PICKS

I n recent NHL Entry Drafts, European players have played an increasingly larger role. Past entry drafts have produced such European-born NHL superstars as Pittsburgh's Jaromir Jagr, Buffalo's Dominik Hasek, and Colorado's Peter Forsberg. After reviewing the results of the 1999 draft, it appears that another group of talented players from across the pond will soon be joining the ranks of the NHL.

Leading the way is Czechoslovakia's Patrik Stefan, the No. 1 pick of the newborn Atlanta Thrashers; the Swedish brothers Daniel and Henrik Sedin, debuting with the Vancouver Canucks; and Czechoslovakia's Pavel Brendl, the N.Y. Rangers' choice to help make them a playoff contender. The champion Dallas Stars' first pick, in the second round, was Michael Ryan, an 18-year-old Boston schoolboy who is expected to play at Northeastern University in 1999–2000.

While the first four picks may have garnered most of the media and fan attention in the days following the draft, there were plenty of great players picked later in the draft. Here is a brief run-down of the top 50 players selected in the draft:

1. **Patrik Stefan.** A season-ending head injury in 1999 didn't keep Atlanta from opting for the 6-foot-1, 205 pound center who starred in 1997–98 and 1998–99 for the IHL's Long Beach Ice Dogs. Stefan's size, strength, and scoring skills make him a sure bet for stardom in the NHL—assuming he doesn't fall victim to injuries of the sort that caused him to miss half of the regular season and all of the 1999 playoffs.

2. **Daniel Sedin.** The goal-scoring 19-year-old left wing from Sweden excelled against men in the Swedish Elite League. Daniel is proficient without the puck and is a wily forechecker who angles well. A consistent point producer at every level he's played at, Sedin figures to do the same with Vancouver in the NHL, especially with the presence of twin brother Henrik.

3. **Henrik Sedin.** The other twin at Vancouver. He and brother Daniel were named to Sweden's 1998 and 1999 World Junior Championship squads. They were on the 1999 Swedish World Championship team that earned a bronze medal in Norway. "Henrik is a worker on both ends of the ice and a team player," noted Per Beckman, his coach at MoDo.

4. **Pavel Brendl.** He lit up the WHL with his goal-scoring fireworks in 1998–99 when he led the league in scoring with 134 points and helped the Calgary Hitmen advance to the Memorial Cup. Brendl produced 21 goals and 46 points in 20 playoff games after scoring a league-leading 73 goals during the regular season. He was noted for game-breaking performances that were likened to those of the NHL's superstars. He'll have a chance to show it all with the N.Y. Rangers.

5. **Tim Connolly.** The top-rated American from Baldwinsville, NY, Connolly is a gifted center regarded as the leading American in the 1999 draft. He led the Erie Otters for two years in the OHL. The league's Rookie of the Year in 1997–98, he suffered a broken leg that ended his season in 1999. The N.Y. Islanders need him.

6. **Brian Finley.** The top goaltending prospect, Finley has the credentials to become a dominant NHL figure. At 6-foot-2, 180 pounds, Finley has, in the words of one scout, the "size, positioning, and quickness" to make it in the NHL. He played for Barrie in the OHL in 1997–98 and 1998–99. He was backup for Roberto Luongo in the 1999 WJC. Nashville awaits him.

7. **Kris Beech.** Drafted by Washington, Beech centered the Memorial Cup-bound Calgary Hitmen. Known as a playmaker who would rather pass than shoot, he scored 67 points on 26 goals and 41 assists in the WHL in 1998–99.

8. **Taylor Pyatt.** The son of former NHL center Nelson Pyatt, Taylor is an imposing 6-foot-3, 220-pound left wing. He had the speed to win the fastest skater competition in the CHL's

Prospects' Game in 1999. He played two seasons with the Sudbury Wolves.

9. **Jamie Lundmark.** He'll make the jump from Moose Jaw to New York without a hitch. That's how the Rangers view the Warriors' center, who made 40 goals and 51 assists in the WHL in 1998–99. Lundmark is known for operating at a high tempo.

10. **Branislav Mezei.** Selected by the Islanders. Few come bigger that the 6-foot-4, 221-pound Slovakian defenseman. A two-year mainstay for Belleville in the OHL, Mezei was on the bronze-medal Slovak team at the 1999 World Junior Championships.

11. **Olag Saprykin.** It was a new experience for Saprykin, playing for the first time in America, in the WHL. The pesky center/left wing from Russia brought his aggressive fame to Seattle in 1998-99 and proved an imposing and productive force. He scored 47 goals and 97 points in 66 games. The Calgary Flames like his style.

12. **Denis Shvidki.** To some, Denis Shvidki's first season with Barrie in the OHL was something of a disappointment despite the fact that the Ukranian right wing recorded 94 points on 35 goals and 59 assists. In the 1999 WJC he played for the gold-medal winning Russian entry. Selected by Florida.

13. **Jani Rita.** Finland's pride and joy made an impression in the 1999 WJC with a blast under the crossbar that U.S. goalie Chris Madden couldn't stop. The 200-pound right wing from Helsinki gets his chance in the NHL with Edmonton.

14. **Jeff Jillson.** A 6-foot-3, 219-pound defenseman from North Smithfield, Rhode Island, Jillson starred as a U. of Michigan freshman noted for his strength and competitiveness. The San Jose Sharks look for big things from this big guy who prepped at Mt. St. Charles.

15. **Scott Kelman.** The Phoenix Coyotes disregarded Kelman's minimal goal-scoring in two seasons centering Seattle in the WHL. They liked his playmaking and competitive drive enough to make him their No. 1 pick in the draft.

16. David Tanabe. His skating skills as a freshman at the U. of Wisconsin inspired the Carolina Hurricanes to go for the defenseman out of White Bear Lake, Minnesota. Tanabe played for the U.S. in the 1999 WJC.

17. Barret Jackman. Penalty minutes provide a rugged picture of Jackman's two years with Regina in the WHL. The 6-foot, 200-pound defenseman out of British Columbia totaled 224 and 259 PIMs. The St. Louis Blues tabbed him as their first pick.

18. Konstantin Kaltsov. Described by a scout as the fastest player in the draft, the right wing from Belarus will display his speed and scoring talents with the Pittsburgh Penguins. They went for him in the draft after seeing his four goals and seven assists in the 1999 WJC.

19. Kiril Safranov. He's a Russian import whose English is impeccable and whose defensive prowess made him Phoenix's second pick in the first round. The Coyotes traded with Anaheim to obtain Scott Kelman as the fifteenth pick in the draft.

20. Barrett Heisten. An Alaskan-born left wing, Heisten is a physical force who helped make the U. of Maine the NCAA champion. He excelled in the 1999 WJC and was Buffalo's choice to help in its perennial pursuit of the Stanley Cup.

21. Nick Boynton. Another U. of Maine product, Boynton has twice been an NHL first-round pick; he was Washington's No. 9 selection from Ottawa in the OHL in 1997. Boynton's an offensive-oriented defenseman who could find a place in Boston.

22. Maxime Ouellet. It will be a while before Maxime Ouellet makes his way into Philadelphia's lineup. The patient goalie out of Quebec in the QMJHL has to contend with veteran John Vanbiesbrouck and prospects Brian Boucher and Jean-Marc Pelletier. Ouellet was 14-12-6 in 1998–99.

23. Steve McCarthy. Chicago used the pick obtained in the Chris Chelios deal with Detroit to secure this offensive defenseman. McCarthy played for the Kootenay Ice in the WHL and he's expected to play another year in the juniors before getting his shot at the NHL.

24. Luca Cereda. A promising center from the Swiss League, Cereda packs 200 pounds on his 6-foot-2 frame. Unlike most Swiss stars who remain home with their big salaries, Cereda appears eager to try life in the NHL.

25. Mikhail Kuleshov. "He really teases you with his talent," said one scout of Kuleshov. "But it's going to be hit or miss with him. He's a treat to watch, but a high risk." This Russian left wing is considered a wild card with Colorado.

26. Martin Havlat. A high-scoring center/wing from Czechoslovakia, Havlat gets high grades for his talent, but one scout claims "he doesn't always bust his tail." That may be the case, but the Ottawa Senators see him as a powerful prospect.

27. Ari Ahonen. New Jersey opted for the 18-year-old who helped Finland win the gold medal in the 1999 World Junior Championships. Ahonen had a 2.90 goals against average for Jyvaskyla in the Finnish Junior League. "We couldn't pass him up," said the Devils' GM Lou Lamoriello.

28. Kristian Kudroc. A 6-foot-6 Slovak defenseman, Kudroc was the last pick in the first round. The height-conscious Islanders got him from Dallas for second- and third-round picks. He hopes to join 6-foot-4 defenseman Branislav Mezei, tenth pick in the draft, and 6-foot-9 defenseman Zdeno Chara, who appeared in 59 games in 1998–99.

29. Michal Sivek. The first pick in the second round, Sivek played in the Czech Senior League with Kladno Jr. He's a 6-foot-3, 209-pound center chosen by Washington.

30. Luke Sellers. A defenseman with Ottawa in the OHL in 1998–99, Sellers is a superb skater from Pickering, Ontario.

31. Charlie Stephens. This 6-foot-3, 225-pound center/right wing has had two seasons in the OHL, first with St. Michael's, then with Guelph. He lands with Washington via transactions with Vancouver and Colorado.

32. Michael Ryan. You won't see him soon, but follow him on the way up. Ryan is a 19-year-old center out of Boston College H.S. who was picked by Dallas. He's a 6-foot-1, 170-pounder described as a skater who can fly. He's committed to playing for Northeastern University in 1999–2000.

33. Jonas Anderrson. A Swedish hopeful at right wing, he got the second-round call from Nashville. He's 6-foot-2, 189 pounds.

34. Ross Lupaschuck. A 6-foot-1, 211-pound defenseman, Lupaschuk had 8 goals, 19 assists for 27 points with Prince Albert in the WHL. Washington got him with its fourth pick.

35. Milan Bartovec. He's a Slovakian right wing who starred for Trencin Jr. with 35 goals and 24 assists for 59 points. He was Buffalo's second selection.

36. Alexei Semenov. "He'll be a monster. He's 6-foot-6, 210 pounds, and he has speed, skill, and the smarts to go with it," says the scouting report on Semenov, a Russian import. The brawny defenseman displayed his talents on joining the OHL's Sudbury Wolves in 1998–99. The Edmonton Oilers grabbed him up in the draft.

37. Nolan Yonkman. Featuring mobility for a big man, Yonkman has been called "a young colt full of energy and enthusiasm." At 6-foot-5 and 218 pounds, this appealing defenseman displayed his potential for two years with Kelowna in the WHL. Looking to the future, Washington chose him.

38. Dan Cavanaugh. Considered effective as a face-off specialist, Cavanaugh drew high marks off his play as a freshman at Boston University. He proved a good skater with strong acceleration. It added up to Calgary's making this center/right wing a second-round pick.

39. Alexander Buturlin. Montreal was impressed by his play with Central Army in Russia. The 5-foot-11, 183-pound left wing ranked high among the Europeans, close to Daniel and Henrik Sedin and Martin Havlat. He starred at the Five Nations and European junior tourneys.

40. Alexander Auld. His GAA, 3.36 with North Bay in the OHL, isn't as impressive as his size for a goalie (6-foot-3, 196 pounds). But Florida thought enough of his potential to select Auld in the second round.

41. Tony Salmelainen. A Finnish left wing, Salmelainen is one of the smallest players in the draft as a 5-foot-9, 176-pounder. Salmelainen played in the Finnish Elite League. Edmonton tabbed him as its third entry.

42. Mike Commodore. A punishing defenseman who has mobility and size (6-foot-4, 225 pounds), Commodore drew the scouts to the U. of North Dakota. In his two seasons with the Fighting Sioux, he showed enough to ensure second-round selection in the draft.

43. Andrei Shefer. Los Angeles's first draft pick is a left wing from Russia who had 31 goals and 18 assists in 82 games with Cherepovec.

44. Jordan Leopold. A native of Minnesota, where he figured prominently as a U. of Minnesota blueliner as a freshman, the 6-foot 193-pound Leopold makes up for his size with offensive flair that appealed to Anaheim.

45. Martin Grenier. Nobody in the draft amassed as many penalty minutes, 479, as the Quebec Ramparts' defenseman. Grenier, Colorado's second-round selection, is, according to one scout, "a nice person and a nasty player. He's meaner and tougher than the whole lot of them."

46. Dmtri Levinski. In Russia they play more than 80 games a season. In 1998–99 Levinski, a right wing with Cherepovec, had 47 goals and 23 assists in 85 games. Chicago took the 6-foot-1, 183-pounder in the second round.

47. Sheldon Keefe. A 5-foot-10, 176-pound right wing, Keefe makes up for his size with his competitive play. He mounted 116 points on 51 goals and 65 assists for Barrie in the OHL in 1998–99. Chicago expressed no reservations as they opted for this gifted native of Brampton, Ont.

48. Simon Lajeunesse. A goaltender from Quebec City, Lajeunesse had a GAA of 2.79 with Moncton in the QMJHL, where he displayed enough promise to draw a second-round call from Ottawa.

49. Brett Lysak. He was 16 when he began life as a center in the WHL with Regina. Lysak has played three years there, his best one in 1998–99 when he posted 30 goals and 49 assists. Carolina picked him in the second round.

50. Brent Clouthier. Fearless and aggressive, this 6-foot-3, 215-pound left wing makes maximum use of his bulk. He's tough to clear in front of the opposition's net. New Jersey views him as a rough hombre ready for polishing.

24

NHL
COACH REGISTER

On your feet all game, pacing back and forth in cramped quarters. Coast-to-coast road trips. Countless practices. And little, if any, job security. That's the lot of the coach in the National Hockey League.

Still, some have thrived on it. Scotty Bowman, for example. Entering the 1999–2000 season, Bowman led all coaches with 1,895 regular-season games and 1,096 victories with St. Louis, Montreal, Buffalo, Pittsburgh, and Detroit. He was tied with Montreal's Toe Blake for most Stanley Cups, eight.

Al Arbour, who began at St. Louis and won four consecutive Stanley Cups with the New York Islanders, is runner-up in games with 1,606.

Billy Reay, known for the hat he wore behind the bench, coached for 16 years (1,102 games) with the Chicago Blackhawks and Toronto Maple Leafs and held on to his job despite the fact that he never guided a Stanley Cup winner.

Other coaches have not been so fortunate. As the saying goes, "Coaches are hired to be fired," and it's as true in hockey as it is in other major sports.

In exceptional cases—as it was with baseball's legendary Billy Martin and the Yankees—hockey coaches sometimes resurface with their old teams. Art Ross coached the Boston Bruins four separate times between 1924 and 1945, and Emile Francis took over the coaching reins of the New York Rangers three times in the 1960s and '70s.

Roger Neilson holds the league's "suitcase award," having served as coach in six different cities—Toronto, Buffalo, Vancouver, Los Angeles, New York, Florida, and Philadelphia. Bowman has been head coach in five cities.

Detroit Red Wings coach Scotty Bowman hoists the Stanley Cup after his team swept the Washington Capitals in 1998.

The following chapter includes the record of every player who has ever coached in an NHL game. In addition, NHL coaches who were behind the bench in the World Hockey Association also have their WHA records listed.

Where information is missing, it was unavailable.

The following are the abbreviations used for the various teams, Canadian provinces, column headings, and playoff performance:

Indicates Hall of Fame

na	Mighty Ducks of Anaheim
Atl	Atlanta Flames
Balt (WHA)	Baltimore Blades
Birm (WHA)	Birmingham Bulls
Bos	Boston Bruins
Brk	Brooklyn Americans
Buf	Buffalo Sabres
Cal	California Golden Seals
Calg	Calgary Flames
Calg (WHA)	Calgary Cowboys
Chi	Chicago Blackhawks
Chi (WHA)	Chicago Cougars
Cin (WHA)	Cincinnati Stingers
Clev	Cleveland Barons
Clev (WHA)	Cleveland Crusaders
Col	Colorado Rockies
Col A	Colorado Avalanche
Dal	Dallas Stars
Den (WHA)	Denver Spurs
Det	Detroit Cougars, Falcons, Red Wings

Edm or Edm (WHA)	Edmonton Oilers
Fla	Florida Panthers
Ham	Hamilton Tigers
Hart or Hart (WHA)	Hartford Whalers
Hou (WHA)	Houston Aeros
Ind (WHA)	Indianapolis Racers
KC	Kansas City Scouts
LA	Los Angeles Kings
LA (WHA)	Los Angeles Sharks
Mich (WHA)	Michigan Stags
Minn	Minnesota North Stars
Minn (WHA)	Minnesota Fighting Saints
Mont	Montreal Canadiens
Mont M	Montreal Maroons
Mont W	Montreal Wanderers
Nash	Nashville Predators
NE (WHA)	New England Whalers
NJ	New Jersey Devils
NJ (WHA)	New Jersey Knights
NYA	New York Americans
NYI	New York Islanders
NYR	New York Rangers
NY (WHA)	New York Golden Blades, Raiders
Oak	Oakland Seals
Ott	Ottawa Senators
Ott (WHA)	Ottawa Nationals
Phil	Philadelphia Flyers
Phil Q	Philadelphia Quakers
Phil (WHA)	Philadelphia Blazers
Phoe (WHA)	Phoenix Roadrunners
Pitt	Pittsburgh Penguins
Pitt Pi	Pittsburgh Pirates
Que	Quebec Bulldogs, Nordiques
Que (WHA)	Quebec Nordiques
SD (WHA)	San Diego Mariners
SJ	San Jose Sharks
StL	St. Louis Blues
StL E	St. Louis Eagles

TB	Tampa Bay Lightning
Tor	Toronto Arenas, Maple Leafs, St. Pats
Tor (WHA)	Toronto Toros
Van	Vancouver Canucks
Van (WHA)	Vancouver Blazers
Wash	Washington Capitals
WHA	World Hockey Association
Winn or Winn (WHA)	Winnipeg Jets

CANADIAN PROVINCES

Alta.	Alberta
B.C.	British Columbia
Man.	Manitoba
N.B.	New Brunswick
Nfld.	Newfoundland
N.S.	Nova Scotia
Ont.	Ontario
P.E.I.	Prince Edward Island
Que.	Quebec
Sask.	Saskatchewan
Yuk.	The Yukon
N.W.T.	Northwest Territories

COLUMN HEADINGS

L	Losses
PLY.	Playoffs
T	Ties
W	Wins

PLAYOFF PERFORMANCE

LCF	Lost Cup Finals
LFR	Lost First Round
LLF	Lost League Finals
LQF	Lost Quarterfinals
LSF	Lost Semifinals
LSR	Lost Second Round
WAC	Won Avco Cup (WHA)
WSC	Won Stanley Cup

COACHES REGISTER

SEASON	TEAM	GC	W	L	T	PLY.

*ABEL, Sid
B. Melville, Sask., Feb. 22, 1918

52–53	Chi	70	27	28	15	LFR
53–54	Chi	70	12	51	7	
57–58	Det	33	16	12	5	LFR
58–59	Det	70	25	37	8	
59–60	Det	70	26	29	15	LFR
60–61	Det	70	25	29	16	LCF
61–62	Det	70	23	33	14	
62–63	Det	70	32	25	13	LCF
63–64	Det	70	30	29	11	LCF
64–65	Det	70	40	23	7	LFR
65–66	Det	70	31	27	12	LCF
66–67	Det	70	27	39	4	
67–68	Det	74	27	35	12	
69–70	Det	73	38	20	15	LFR
71–72	StL	10	3	6	1	
75–76	KC	3	0	3	0	
Totals		**963**	**382**	**426**	**155**	
Playoff Totals		**76**	**32**	**44**	**0**	

*ADAMS, Jack
B. Fort William, Ont., June 14, 1895

22–23	Tor	18	10	7	1	
27–28	Det	44	19	19	6	
28–29	Det	44	19	16	9	LFR
29–30	Det	44	14	24	6	
30–31	Det	44	16	21	7	
31–32	Det	48	18	20	10	LFR
32–33	Det	48	25	15	8	LSF

33–34	Det	48	24	14	10	LCF
34–35	Det	48	19	22	7	
35–36	Det	48	24	16	8	WSC
36–37	Det	48	25	14	9	WSC
37–38	Det	48	12	25	11	
38–39	Det	48	18	24	6	LSF
39–40	Det	48	16	26	6	LSF
40–41	Det	48	21	16	11	LCF
41–42	Det	48	19	25	4	LCF
42–43	Det	50	25	14	11	WSC
43–44	Det	50	26	18	6	LSF
44–45	Det	50	31	14	5	LCF
45–46	Det	50	20	20	10	LFR
46–47	Det	60	22	27	11	LFR
Totals		**982**	**423**	**397**	**162**	
Playoff Totals		**105**	**52**	**52**	**1**	

ALLEN, Keith
B. Saskatoon, Sask., Aug. 21, 1923

97–98	Phil	74	31	32	11	LFR
68–69	Phil	76	20	35	21	LFR
Totals		**150**	**51**	**67**	**32**	
Playoff Totals		**11**	**3**	**8**	**0**	

ALLISON, Dave
B. Fort Frances, Ont., Apr. 14, 1959

95–96	Ott	25	2	22	1	

ANDERSON, Jim
B. Pembroke, Ont., Dec. 1, 1930

74–75	Wash	54	4	45	5	

ANGOTTI, Lou
B. Toronto, Ont., Jan. 16, 1938

73–74	StL	23	4	15	4	
74–75	StL	9	2	5	2	
83–84	Pitt	80	16	58	6	
Totals		**112**	**22**	**78**	**12**	

ARBOUR, Al
B. Sudbury, Ont., Nov. 1, 1932

70–71	StL	50	21	15	14	
71–72	StL	44	19	19	6	LSF
72–73	StL	13	2	6	5	
73–74	NYI	78	19	41	18	
74–75	NYI	80	33	25	22	LSF
75–76	NYI	80	42	21	17	LSF
76–77	NYI	80	47	21	12	LSF
77–78	NYI	80	48	17	15	LFR
78–79	NYI	80	51	15	14	LSF
79–80	NYI	80	39	28	13	WSC
80–81	NYI	80	48	18	14	WSC
81–82	NYI	80	54	16	10	WSC
82–83	NYI	80	42	26	12	WSC
83–84	NYI	80	50	26	4	LF
84–85	NYI	80	40	34	6	LSR
85–86	NYI	80	39	29	12	LFR
88–89	NYI	53	21	29	3	
89–90	NYI	80	31	38	11	LFR
90–91	NYI	80	25	45	10	
91–92	NYI	80	34	35	11	
92–93	NYI	84	40	37	7	LSF
93–94	NYI	48	15	28	5	LFR
Totals		**1606**	**781**	**577**	**248**	
Playoff Totals		**209**	**123**	**86**	**0**	

SEASON TEAM GC W L T PLY.

ARMSTRONG, George
B. Skead, Ont., July 6, 1930

Season	Team	GC	W	L	T	PLY.
88-89	Tor	47	17	26	4	

BARKLEY, Doug
B. Lethbridge, Alta., Jan. 6, 1937

Season	Team	GC	W	L	T	PLY.
70-71	Det	40	10	23	7	
71-72	Det	11	3	8	0	
75-76	Det	26	7	15	4	
Totals		**77**	**20**	**46**	**11**	

*BATHGATE, Andy
B. Winnipeg, Man., Aug. 28, 1932

Season	Team	GC	W	L	T	PLY.
73-74	Van (WHA)	59	21	37	1	

BAUN, Bob
B. Lanigan, Sask., Sept. 9, 1936

Season	Team	GC	W	L	T	PLY.
75-76	Tor (WHA)	55	15	35	5	

BEAULIEU, Andre
B. Shawinigan Falls, Que., July 30, 1942

Season	Team	GC	W	L	T	PLY.
77-78	Minn	32	6	23	3	

BELISLE, Danny
B. South Porcupine, Ont., May 9, 1937

Season	Team	GC	W	L	T	PLY.
78-79	Wash	80	24	41	15	
79-80	Wash	16	4	10	2	
Totals		**96**	**28**	**51**	**17**	

BERENSON, Red
B. Regina, Sask., Dec. 8, 1939

Season	Team	GC	W	L	T	PLY.
79-80	StL	55	27	20	9	LFR
80-81	StL	80	45	18	17	LSR
81-82	StL	69	28	35	6	
Totals		**204**	**100**	**72**	**32**	
Playoff Totals		**15**	**5**	**9**	**0**	

BERGERON, Michel
B. Chicoutimi, Que., Nov. 11, 1954

Season	Team	GC	W	L	T	PLY.
80-81	Que	74	29	29	16	LFR
81-82	Que	80	33	31	16	LSF
82-83	Que	80	34	34	12	LFR
83-84	Que	80	42	28	10	LSF
84-85	Que	80	41	30	9	LCF
85-86	Que	80	43	31	6	LFR
86-87	Que	80	31	39	10	LSR
87-88	NYR	80	36	34	10	
88-89	NYR	78	37	33	8	
89-90	Que	80	12	61	7	
Totals		**792**	**338**	**350**	**104**	
Playoff Totals		**68**	**31**	**37**	**0**	

BERRY, Bob
B. Montreal, Que., Nov. 29, 1943

Season	Team	GC	W	L	T	PLY.
78-79	LA	80	34	34	12	LFR
79-80	LA	80	31	36	14	LFR
80-81	LA	80	43	24	13	LFR
81-82	Mont	80	46	17	17	LFR
82-83	Mont	80	42	24	14	LFR
83-84	Mont	63	28	30	5	
84-85	Pitt	80	21	54	5	
85-86	Pitt	80	34	38	8	
86-87	Pitt	80	30	38	12	
92-93	StL	73	33	30	10	.LSR
93-94	StL	84	40	33	11	LFR
Totals		**860**	**384**	**355**	**121**	
Playoff Totals		**33**	**11**	**22**	**0**	

BEVERLY, Nick
B. Toronto, Ont., Apr. 21, 1947

Season	Team	GC	W	L	T	PLY.
95-96	Tor	17	9	6	2	

BLACKBURN, Don
B. Kirkland Lake, Ont., May 14, 1938

Season	Team	GC	W	L	T	PLY.
75-76	NE (WHA)	35	14	18	3	
79-80	Hart	80	27	34	19	LFR
80-81	Hart	60	15	29	16	
NHL Totals		**140**	**42**	**63**	**35**	
Playoff Totals		**3**	**0**	**3**	**0**	
WHA Totals		**35**	**14**	**18**	**3**	

BLAIR, Wren
B. Lindsay, Ont., Oct. 2, 1925

Season	Team	GC	W	L	T	PLY.
67-68	Minn	74	27	32	15	LSF
68-69	Minn	41	12	21	8	
69-70	Minn	32	9	13	10	
Totals		**147**	**48**	**66**	**33**	
Playoff Totals		**14**	**7**	**7**	**0**	

BLAKE, Toe
B. Victoria Mines, Ont., Aug. 21, 1912

Season	Team	GC	W	L	T	PLY.
55-56	Mont	70	45	15	10	WSC
56-57	Mont	70	35	23	12	WSC
57-58	Mont	70	43	17	10	WSC
58-59	Mont	70	39	18	13	WSC
59-60	Mont	70	40	18	12	WSC
60-61	Mont	70	41	19	10	LFR
61-62	Mont	70	42	14	14	LFR
62-63	Mont	70	28	19	23	LFR
63-64	Mont	70	36	21	13	LFR
64-65	Mont	70	36	23	11	WSC
65-66	Mont	70	41	21	8	WSC
66-67	Mont	70	32	25	13	LCF
67-68	Mont	74	42	22	10	WSC
Totals		**914**	**500**	**255**	**159**	
Playoff Totals		**119**	**82**	**37**	**0**	

BOILEAU, Marc
B. Pointe Claire, Que., Sept. 3, 1932

Season	Team	GC	W	L	T	PLY.
73-74	Pitt	28	14	10	4	
74-75	Pitt	80	37	28	15	LSR
75-76	Pitt	43	15	23	5	
76-77	Que (WHA)	81	47	31	3	WAC
77-78	Que (WHA)	59	27	30	2	
NHL Totals		**151**	**66**	**61**	**24**	
Playoff Totals		**9**	**5**	**4**	**0**	
WHA Totals		**140**	**74**	**61**	**5**	
Playoff Totals		**17**	**12**	**5**	**0**	

BOIVIN, Leo
B. Prescott, Ont., Aug. 2, 1932

Season	Team	GC	W	L	T	PLY.
75-76	StL	43	17	17	9	LFR
77-78	StL	54	11	36	7	
Totals		**97**	**28**	**53**	**16**	
Playoff Totals		**3**	**1**	**2**	**0**	

*BOUCHER, Frank
B. Ottawa, Ont., Oct. 7, 1901

Season	Team	GC	W	L	T	PLY.
39-40	NYR	48	27	11	10	WSC
40-41	NYR	48	21	19	8	LFR
41-42	NYR	48	29	17	2	LFR
42-43	NYR	50	11	31	8	
43-44	NYR	50	6	39	5	
44-45	NYR	50	11	29	10	
45-46	NYR	50	13	28	9	
46-47	NYR	60	22	32	6	
47-48	NYR	60	21	26	13	LFR
48-49	NYR	23	6	11	6	
53-54	NYR	27	12	20	6	
Totals		**525**	**179**	**263**	**83**	
Playoff Totals		**27**	**13**	**14**	**0**	

*BOUCHER, George
B. Ottawa, Ont.

Season	Team	GC	W	L	T	PLY.
30-31	Mont	12	6	5	1	LFR
33-34	Ott	48	13	29	6	
34-35	StL	35	9	20	6	
49-50	Bos	70	22	32	16	
Totals		**165**	**50**	**86**	**29**	
Playoff Totals		**2**	**0**	**2**	**0**	

BOWMAN, Scotty
B. Montreal, Que., Sept. 18, 1933

Season	Team	GC	W	L	T	PLY.
67-68	StL	58	23	21	14	LCF
68-69	StL	76	37	25	14	LCF
69-70	StL	76	37	27	12	LCF
70-71	StL	28	13	10	5	LFR
71-72	Mont	78	46	16	16	LFR
72-73	Mont	78	52	10	16	WSC
73-74	Mont	78	45	24	9	LFR
74-75	Mont	80	47	14	19	LSF
75-76	Mont	80	58	11	11	WSC
76-77	Mont	80	60	8	12	WSC
77-78	Mont	80	59	10	11	WSC
78-79	Mont	80	52	17	11	WSC
79-80	Buf	80	47	17	16	LSF
81-82	Buf	35	18	10	7	LFR
82-83	Buf	80	38	29	13	LSR
83-84	Buf	80	48	25	7	LFR
84-85	Buf	80	38	28	14	LFR
85-86	Buf	37	18	18	1	
86-87	Buf	12	3	7	2	
91-92	Pitt	80	39	32	9	WSC
92-93	Pitt	84	56	21	7	LSR
93-94	Det	84	46	30	8	LFR
94-95	Det	48	33	11	4	LCF
95-96	Det	82	62	13	7	LSF
96-97	Det	82	38	26	18	WSC
97-98	Det	82	44	23	15	WSC
98-99	Det	77	39	31	7	LSR
Totals		**1895**	**1096**	**514**	**285**	
Playoff Totals		**315**	**200**	**115**	**0**	

BOWNESS, Rick
B. Moncton, N.B., Jan. 25, 1955

Season	Team	GC	W	L	T	PLY.
88-89	Winn	28	8	17	3	
91-92	Bos	80	36	32	12	
92-93	Ott	84	10	70	4	
93-94	Ott	84	14	61	9	
94-95	Ott	48	9	34	5	
95-96	Ott	19	6	13	0	
96-97	NYI	37	16	18	3	
97-98	NYI	63	22	32	9	
Totals		**443**	**121**	**277**	**45**	

BROOKS, Herb
B. St. Paul, Minn., Aug. 5, 1937

Season	Team	GC	W	L	T	PLY.
81-82	NYR	80	39	27	14	LQF
82-83	NYR	80	39	27	14	LQF
83-84	NYR	80	42	29	9	LFR
84-85	NYR	45	15	22	8	
87-88	Minn	80	19	48	13	
92-93	NJ	84	40	37	7	LFR
Totals		**449**	**190**	**198**	**61**	
Playoff Totals		**29**	**13**	**16**	**0**	

BROPHY, John
B. Halifax, N.S., Jan. 20, 1933

Season	Team	GC	W	L	T	PLY.
78-79	Birm (WHA)	80	32	42	6	
86-87	Tor	80	32	42	6	LSR
87-88	Tor	80	21	49	10	
NHL Totals		**160**	**53**	**91**	**16**	
WHA Totals		**80**	**32**	**42**	**6**	
NHL Playoff Totals		**13**	**7**	**6**	**0**	

BURNETT, George
B. Port Perry, Ont., Mar. 25, 1962

Season	Team	GC	W	L	T	PLY.
94-95	Edm	35	12	20	3	

BURNS, Charlie
B. Detroit, Mich., Feb. 14, 1936

Season	Team	GC	W	L	T	PLY.
69-70	Minn	44	10	22	12	LFR
74-75	Minn	42	12	28	2	
Totals		**86**	**22**	**50**	**14**	
Playoff Totals		**6**	**2**	**4**	**0**	

BURNS, Pat
B. St. Henri, Que., Apr. 4, 1952

Season	Team	GC	W	L	T	PLY.
88-89	Mont	80	53	18	9	WSC
89-90	Mont	80	41	28	11	LSR
90-91	Mont	80	39	30	11	LSR
91-92	Mont	80	41	28	11	LSR
92-93	Tor	84	44	29	11	LSF
93-94	Tor	84	43	29	12	LSF
94-95	Tor	48	21	19	8	LFR
95-96	Tor	65	25	30	10	
96-97	Bos	82	39	30	13	LFR
98-99	Bos	82	39	30	13	LSR
Totals		**765**	**385**	**271**	**109**	
Playoff Totals		**120**	**61**	**59**	**0**	

BUSH, Eddie
B. Collingwood, Que., July 11, 1948

Season	Team	GC	W	L	T	PLY.
75-76	KC	32	1	23	8	

CAMPBELL, Colin
B. London, Ont., Jan. 28, 1953

Season	Team	GC	W	L	T	PLY.
94-95	NYR	48	22	23	3	LSR
95-96	NYR	82	41	27	14	LSR

SEASON	TEAM	GC	W	L	T	PLY.
96–97	NYR	82	38	34	10	LSF
97–98	NYR	57	17	24	16	
Totals		269	118	108	43	
Playoff Totals		36	18	18	0	

CARPENTER, Doug
B. Cornwall, Ont., July 1, 1942

SEASON	TEAM	GC	W	L	T	PLY.
84–85	NJ	80	22	48	10	
85–86	NJ	80	28	49	3	
86–87	NJ	80	29	45	6	
87–88	NJ	50	21	24	5	
89–90	Tor	80	38	38	4	LSR
90–91	Tor	11	1	9	1	
Totals		381	139	213	29	
Playoff Totals		5	1	4	0	

CARROLL, Dick

SEASON	TEAM	GC	W	L	T	PLY.
17–18	Tor	22	13	9	0	WSC
18–19	Tor	18	5	13	0	
20–21	Tor	24	15	9	0	LSF
Totals		64	33	31	0	
Playoff Totals		7	3	4	0	

CASHMAN, Wayne
B. Kingston, Ont., June 24, 1945

SEASON	TEAM	GC	W	L	T	PLY.
86–87	NYR	2	0	2	0	
97–98	Phil	61	32	20	9	
Totals		63	32	22	9	

CHAMBERS, Dave
B. Leaside, Ont., May 7, 1940

SEASON	TEAM	GC	W	L	T	PLY.
90–91	Que	80	16	50	14	
91–92	Que	18	3	14	1	
Totals		98	19	64	15	

CHARRON, Guy
B. Verdun, Que., Jan. 24, 1949

SEASON	TEAM	GC	W	L	T	PLY.
91–92	Calg	16	6	7	3	

CHEEVERS, Gerry
B. St. Catharines, Que., Dec. 7, 1940

SEASON	TEAM	GC	W	L	T	PLY.
80–81	Bos	80	49	25	6	LFR
84–85	Bos	56	25	24	7	
Totals		376	204	126	46	
Playoff Totals		32	15	17	0	

CHERRY, Don
B. Kingston, Ont., Feb. 5, 1934

SEASON	TEAM	GC	W	L	T	PLY.
74–75	Bos	80	40	26	14	LFR
75–76	Bos	80	48	15	17	LSF
76–77	Bos	80	49	23	8	LCF
77–78	Bos	80	51	18	11	LCF
78–79	Bos	80	19	48	13	LSF
79–80	Col	80	19	48	13	
Totals		480	250	153	77	
Playoff Totals		55	31	24	0	

*CLANCY, King
B. Ottawa, Ont., Feb. 25, 1903

SEASON	TEAM	GC	W	L	T	PLY.
37–38	MontM	18	6	11	1	
53–54	Tor	70	32	24	14	LFR
54–55	Tor	70	24	33	13	LFR
55–56	Tor	70	24	33	13	LFR
66–67	Tor	10	7	1	2	
71–72	Tor	15	9	3	3	LFR
Totals		253	102	105	46	
Playoff Totals		19	3	16	0	

*CLAPPER, Dit
B. Newmarket, Ont., Feb. 9, 1907

SEASON	TEAM	GC	W	L	T	PLY.
45–46	Bos	50	24	18	8	LCF
46–47	Bos	60	26	23	11	LFR
47–48	Bos	60	23	24	13	LFR
48–49	Bos	60	29	23	8	LFR
Totals		230	102	88	40	
Playoff Totals		25	8	17	0	

CLEGHORN, Odie
B. Montreal, Que.

SEASON	TEAM	GC	W	L	T	PLY.
25–26	PittPi	36	19	16	1	LFR
26–27	PittPi	44	15	26	3	
27–28	PittPi	44	19	17	8	LFR
28–29	PittPi	44	9	27	8	
Totals		168	62	86	20	
Playoff Totals		4	1	3	0	

*CLEGHORN, Sprague
B. Montreal, Que.

SEASON	TEAM	GC	W	L	T	PLY.
31–32	MontM	48	19	22	7	LSF
Playoff Totals		4	1	1	2	

COLVILLE, Neil
B. Edmonton, Alta., Aug. 4, 1914

SEASON	TEAM	GC	W	L	T	PLY.
50–51	NYR	70	20	29	21	
51–52	NYR	23	6	12	5	
Totals		162	56	84	22	

*CONACHER, Charlie
B. Toronto, Ont., Dec. 20, 1910

SEASON	TEAM	GC	W	L	T	PLY.
47–48	Chi	32	13	15	4	
48–49	Chi	60	21	31	8	
49–50	Chi	70	22	38	10	
Totals		162	56	84	22	

CONACHER, Lionel
B. Toronto, Ont., May 24, 1901

SEASON	TEAM	GC	W	L	T	PLY.
29–30	NYA	44	14	25	5	

CONSTANTINE, Kevin
B. International Falls, Minn., Dec. 27, 1958

SEASON	TEAM	GC	W	L	T	PLY.
93–94	SJ	84	33	35	16	LSR
94–95	SJ	48	19	25	4	LSR
95–96	SJ	25	3	18	4	
98–99	Pitt	82	38	30	14	LSR
Totals		239	93	108	38	
Playoff Totals		38	17	21	0	

*COOK, Bill
B. Brantford, Ont., Oct. 9, 1896

SEASON	TEAM	GC	W	L	T	PLY.
51–52	NYR	47	17	22	8	
52–53	NYR	70	17	37	16	
Totals		117	34	59	24	

CRAWFORD, Marc
B. Belleville, Ont., Feb. 13, 1961

SEASON	TEAM	GC	W	L	T	PLY.
94–95	Que	48	30	13	5	LFR
95–96	Col	82	47	25	10	WSC
96–97	Col	82	49	24	9	LSF
97–98	Col	82	39	26	17	LFR
98–99	Van	37	8	23	6	
Totals		331	173	111	47	
Playoff Totals		52	31	21	0	

CREAMER, Pierre
B. Chomedy, Que., July 6, 1944

SEASON	TEAM	GC	W	L	T	PLY.
87–88	Pitt	80	36	35	9	LFR
Playoff Totals		5	2	3	0	

CREIGHTON, Fred
B. Hammota, Man., July 14, 1933

SEASON	TEAM	GC	W	L	T	PLY.
74–75	Atl	28	12	11	5	
75–76	Atl	80	35	33	12	LFR
76–77	Atl	80	34	34	12	LFR
77–78	Atl	80	34	27	19	LFR
78–79	Atl	80	41	31	8	LFR
79–80	Bos	73	40	20	13	
Totals		421	196	156	69	
Playoff Totals		9	1	8	0	

CRISP, Terry
B. Parry Sound, Ont., May 28, 1943

SEASON	TEAM	GC	W	L	T	PLY.
87–88	Calg	80	48	23	9	LSR
88–89	Calg	80	54	17	9	WSC
89–90	Calg	80	42	23	15	LFR
92–93	TB	84	23	54	7	
93–94	TB	84	30	43	11	
94–95	TB	48	17	28	3	
95–96	TB	82	38	32	12	LFR
96–97	TB	82	32	40	10	
97–98	TB	11	2	7	2	
Totals		631	286	267	78	
Playoff Totals		43	24	19	0	

CROZIER, Joe
B. Winnipeg, Man., Feb. 19, 1929

SEASON	TEAM	GC	W	L	T	PLY.
71–72	Buf	36	8	19	9	
72–73	Buf	78	37	27	14	LFR
73–74	Buf	78	32	34	12	
74–75	Van	78	37	39	2	
75–76	Calg (WHA)	80	41	35	4	LSF
76–77	Calg (WHA)	80	31	42	7	
80–81	Tor	40	13	22	5	
NHL Totals		232	90	102	40	
WHA Totals		238	109	116	13	
NHL Playoff Totals		6	2	4	0	

CROZIER, Roger
B. Bracebridge, Ont., Mar. 16, 1942

SEASON	TEAM	GC	W	L	T	PLY.
81–82	Wash	1	0	1	0	

CUNNIFF, John
B. South Boston, Mass., July 9, 1944

SEASON	TEAM	GC	W	L	T	PLY.
82–83	Hart	13	3	9	1	
89–90	NJ	66	31	28	7	LFR
90–91	NJ	67	28	28	11	
Totals		146	62	65	19	
Playoff Totals		6	2	4	0	

DANDURAND, Leo
B. Bourbonnais, Ill., July 9, 1889

SEASON	TEAM	GC	W	L	T	PLY.
20–21	Mont	24	13	11	0	
21–22	Mont	24	12	11	1	
22–23	Mont	24	13	9	2	LSF
23–24	Mont	24	13	11	0	WSC
24–25	Mont	30	17	11	2	LCF
34–35	Mont	32	14	15	3	LFR
Totals		158	82	68	8	
Playoff Totals		16	10	5	1	

*DAY, Hap
B. Owen Sound, Ont., June 1, 1901

SEASON	TEAM	GC	W	L	T	PLY.
40–41	Tor	48	28	14	6	LFR
41–42	Tor	48	27	18	3	WSC
42–43	Tor	50	22	19	9	LFR
43–44	Tor	50	23	23	4	LFR
44–45	Tor	50	24	22	4	WSC
45–46	Tor	50	19	24	7	
46–47	Tor	60	31	19	10	WSC
47–48	Tor	60	32	15	13	WSC
48–49	Tor	60	22	25	13	WSC
49–50	Tor	70	31	27	12	LFR
Totals		546	259	206	81	
Playoff Totals		80	49	31	0	

DEA, Billy
B. Edmonton, Alta., Apr. 3, 1933

SEASON	TEAM	GC	W	L	T	PLY.
81–82	Det	11	3	8	0	

*DELVECCHIO, Alex
B. Fort William, Ont., Dec. 4, 1931

SEASON	TEAM	GC	W	L	T	PLY.
73–74	Det	66	27	30	9	
74–75	Det	80	23	45	12	
75–76	Det	54	19	29	6	
76–77	Det	44	13	26	6	
Totals		244	82	130	32	

DEMERS, Jacques
B. Montreal, Que., Aug. 25, 1944

SEASON	TEAM	GC	W	L	T	PLY.
75–76	Ind (WHA)	80	35	39	6	LFR
76–77	Ind (WHA)	81	36	37	8	LSF
77–78	Cinn (WHA)	80	35	42	3	
78–79	Que (WHA)	80	41	34	5	LFR
83–84	StL	80	32	41	7	LSR
84–85	StL	80	37	31	12	LFR
85–86	StL	80	37	34	9	LSF
86–87	Det	80	34	36	10	LSF
87–88	Det	80	41	28	11	LSF
88–89	Det	80	34	34	12	LFR
89–90	Det	80	28	38	14	
92–93	Mont	84	48	30	6	WSC
93–94	Mont	84	41	29	14	LFR
94–95	Mont	48	18	23	7	
95–96	Mont	4	0	4	0	
97–98	TB	65	15	42	8	
98–99	TB	82	19	54	9	
NHL Totals		1007	309	468	130	
Playoff Totals		98	55	43	0	

SEASON	TEAM	GC	W	L	T	PLY.
WHA Totals		321	147	152	22	
Playoff Totals		20	8	12	0	

DENNENY, Cy
B. Farran's Point, Ont., Dec. 23, 1897

28–29	Bos	44	26	13	5	WSC
32–33	Ott	48	11	27	10	
Totals		92	37	40	15	
Playoff Totals		5	5	0	0	

DINEEN, Bill
B. Arvida, Que., Sept. 18, 1932

72–73	Hous (WHA)	78	39	35	4	LSF
73–74	Hous (WHA)	78	48	25	5	Won WHA Finals
74–75	Hous (WHA)	78	53	25	0	Won WHA Finals
75–76	Hous (WHA)	80	53	27	0	LLF
76–77	Hous (WHA)	80	50	24	6	LSF
77–78	Hous (WHA)	80	42	34	4	LFR
78–79	NE (WHA)	80	37	34	9	LSF
91–92	Phil	56	24	23	9	
92–93	Phil	84	36	37	11	
NHL Totals		140	60	60	20	
WHA Totals		554	332	204	28	
WHA Playoff Totals		71	44	27	0	

DUDLEY, Rick
B. Toronto, Ont., Jan. 31, 1949

89–90	Buf	80	45	27	8	LFR
90–91	Buf	80	31	30	19	LFR
91–92	Buf	28	9	15	4	
Totals		188	85	72	31	
Playoff Totals		12	4	8	0	

DRAKE, Clare
B. Yorkton, Sask., Oct. 9, 1928

75–76	Edm (WHA)	48	18	28		

DUFF, Dick
B. Kirkland Lake, Ont., Feb. 18, 1936

79–80	Tor	2	0	2	0	

DUGAL, Jules
B. Montreal, Que.

38–39	Mont	18	9	6	3	LFR
Playoff Totals		3	1	2	0	

DUNCAN, Art

26–27	Det	44	12	28	4	
30–31	Tor	42	21	13	8	LFR
31–32	Tor	5	0	3	2	
Totals		91	33	44	14	
Playoff Totals		2	0	1	1	

*DUTTON, Red
B. Russell, Man., Jan. 3, 1898

35–36	NYA	48	16	25	7	LSF
36–37	NYA	48	15	29	4	
37–38	NYA	48	19	18	11	LSF
38–39	NYA	48	17	21	10	LFR
39–40	NYA	48	15	29	4	LFR
40–41	NYA	48	8	29	11	
41–42	NYA	48	16	29	3	
Totals		336	106	180	50	
Playoff Totals		24	10	14	0	

EDDOLLS, Frank
B. Lachine, Que., July 5, 1921

54–55	Chi	70	13	40	17	

ESPOSITO, Phil
B. Sault Ste. Mari, Feb. 20, 1942

86–87	NYR	43	24	19	0	LFR
88–89	NYR	2	0	2	0	LFR
Totals		45	24	21	0	
Playoff Totals		10	2	8	0	

EVANS, Jack
B. Garnant, South Wales, Apr. 21, 1928

75–76	Cal	80	27	42	11	
76–77	Clev	80	25	42	13	
77–78	Clev	80	22	45	13	
83–84	Hart	80	28	42	10	
84–85	Hart	80	30	41	9	
85–86	Hart	80	40	36	4	LSR
86–87	Hart	80	43	30	7	LFR
87–88	Hart	54	22	25	7	
Totals		614	237	303	74	
Playoff Totals		16	8	8	0	

FASHOWAY, Gordie
B. Portage La Prairie, Man., June 16, 1926

67–68	Oak	10	4	5	1	

FERGUSON, John
B. Vancouver, B.C., Sept. 5, 1938

75–76	NYR	41	14	22	5	
76–77	NYR	80	29	37	14	
85–86	Winn	14	7	6	1	LFR
Totals		135	50	65	20	
Playoff Totals		3	0	3	0	

FILION, Maurice
B. Montreal, Que., Feb. 12, 1932

72–73	Que (WHA)	76	32	39	5	
77–78	Que (WHA)	21	13	7	1	LSF
80–81	Que	6	1	3	2	
NHL Totals		6	1	3	2	
WHA Totals		97	45	46	6	

FRANCIS, Emile
B. North Battleford, Sask., Sept. 13, 1926

65–66	NYR	50	13	31	6	
66–67	NYR	70	30	28	12	LFR
67–68	NYR	74	39	23	12	LFR
68–69	NYR	33	19	8	6	LFR
69–70	NYR	76	38	22	16	LFR
70–71	NYR	78	49	18	11	LSF
71–72	NYR	78	48	17	13	LCF
72–73	NYR	78	47	23	8	LSF
73–74	NYR	37	22	10	5	LSF
74–75	NYR	80	37	29	14	LFR
76–77	StL	80	32	39	9	LFR
81–82	StL	12	4	6	2	LQF
82–83	StL	32	10	19	3	
Totals		778	393	273	112	
Playoff Totals		93	40	53	0	

*FREDERICKSON, Frank
B. Winnipeg, Man.

29–30	PittPi	44	5	36	3	

FTOREK, Robbie
B. Needham, Mass., Jan. 2, 1952

87–88	LA	52	23	25	4	LFR
88–89	LA	80	42	31	7	LSR
98–99	NJ	82	47	24	11	LFR
Totals		214	112	80	22	
Playoff Totals		23	8	15	0	

*GADSBY, Bill
B. Calgary, Alta., Aug. 8, 1927

68–69	Det	76	33	31	12	
69–70	Det	2	2	0	0	
Totals		78	35	31	12	

GAINEY, Bob
B. Peterborough, Ont., Dec. 13, 1953

90–91	Minn	80	27	39	14	LCF
91–92	Minn	80	32	42	6	LFR
92–93	Minn	84	36	38	10	
93–94	Dall	84	42	29	13	LSR
94–95	Dall	48	17	23	8	LFR
95–96	Dall	39	11	19	9	
Totals		415	165	190	60	
Playoff Totals		44	23	21	0	

*GARDINER, Herb
B. Winnipeg, Man.

28–29	Chi	44	7	29	8	

*GARDNER, Jimmy

24–25	Ham	30	19	10	1	

GARVIN, Ted
B. Sarnia, Ont., Aug. 30, 1920

73–74	Det	11	2	8	1	

GENDRON, Jean Guy
B. Montreal, Que., Aug. 30, 1934

74–75	Que (WHA)	78	46	32	0	LF
75–76	Que (WHA)	81	50	27	4	LFR
Totals		159	96	59	4	

*GEOFFRION, Bernie
B. Montreal, Que., Aug. 30, 1934

68–69	NYR	43	22	18	3	
72–73	Atl	78	25	38	15	
73–74	Atl	78	30	34	14	LFR
74–75	Atl	52	22	20	10	
79–80	Mont	30	15	9	6	
Totals		281	114	119	48	
Playoff Totals		4	0	4	0	

*GERARD, Eddie
B. Feb. 22, 1890

17–18	Ott	22	9	13	0	
24–25	MontM	30	9	19	2	
25–26	MontM	36	20	11	5	WSC
26–27	MontM	44	20	20	4	LFR
27–28	MontM	44	24	14	6	LCF
28–29	MontM	44	15	20	9	
30–31	NYA	44	18	16	10	
31–32	NYA	48	16	24	8	
32–33	MontM	48	22	20	6	LFR
33–34	MontM	48	19	18	11	LSF
34–35	StL	13	2	11	0	
Totals		421	174	186	61	
Playoff Totals		23	10	10	3	

GILL, Dave

26–27	Ott	44	30	10	4	WSC
27–28	Ott	44	20	14	10	LFR
28–29	Ott	44	14	17	13	
Totals		132	64	41	27	
Playoff Totals		8	3	2	3	

GLOVER, Fred
B. Toronto, Ont., Jan. 5, 1928

68–69	Cal	76	29	36	11	LFR
69–70	Cal	76	22	40	14	LFR
70–71	Cal	78	20	53	5	
71–72	Cal	3	0	1	2	
72–73	Cal	66	14	39	13	
73–74	Cal	57	14	38	8	
Totals		424	114	249	61	
Playoff Totals		11	3	8	0	

GOLDSWORTHY, Bill
B. Kitchener, Ont., Aug. 24, 1944

77–78	Ind (WHA)	30	8	17	5	

*GOODFELLOW, Ebbie
B. Ottawa, Ont., Apr. 9, 1907

50–51	Chi	70	13	47	10	
51–52	Chi	70	17	44	9	
Totals		140	30	91	19	

GORDON, Jackie
B. Winnipeg, Man., Mar. 3, 1928

GORING, Butch
B. St. Boniface, Man., Oct. 22, 1949

85–86	Bos	80	37	31	12	LFR
86–87	Bos	13	5	7	1	
Totals		93	42	38	13	
Playoff Totals		3	0	3	0	

*GORMAN, Tommy
B. Ottawa, Ont., July 9, 1886

25–26	NYA	36	12	20	4	
28–29	NYA	44	19	13	12	LFR
32–33	Chi	25	8	11	6	
33–34	Chi	48	20	17	11	WSC
34–35	MontM	48	24	19	5	WSC
35–36	MontM	48	22	16	10	LFR
36–37	MontM	48	22	17	9	LSF

SEASON	TEAM	GC	W	L	T	PLY.
37–38	MontM	30	6	19	5	
Totals		327	133	132	62	
Playoff Totals		24	13	8	3	

GOTTSELIG, Johnny
B. Odessa, Russia, June 24, 1905

SEASON	TEAM	GC	W	L	T	PLY.
44–45	Chi	49	13	29	7	
45–46	Chi	50	23	20	7	LFR
46–47	Chi	60	19	37	4	
47–48	Chi	28	7	18	3	
Totals		187	62	104	21	
Playoff Totals		4	0	4	0	

GOYETTE, Phil
B. Lachine, Que., Oct. 31, 1933

SEASON	TEAM	GC	W	L	T	PLY.
72–73	NYI	50	6	40	4	

GRAHAM, Dirk
B. Regina, Sask., July 29, 1959

SEASON	TEAM	GC	W	L	T	PLY.
98–99	Chi	59	16	35	8	

GREEN, Gary
B. Tillsonburg, Ont., Aug. 23, 1953

SEASON	TEAM	GC	W	L	T	PLY.
79–80	Wash	64	23	30	11	
80–81	Wash	80	26	36	18	
81–82	Wash	13	1	12	0	
Totals		157	50	78	29	

GREEN, Peter

SEASON	TEAM	GC	W	L	T	PLY.
19–20	Ott	24	19	5	0	WSC
20–21	Ott	24	13	11	0	WSC
21–22	Ott	24	14	8	2	LLF
22–23	Ott	24	14	9	1	WSC
23–24	Ott	24	16	8	0	LLF
24–25	Ott	30	17	12	1	
25–26	Ott	36	24	8	4	LSF
Totals		186	117	61	8	
Playoff Totals		26	14	9	3	

GREEN, Wilf
B. Sudbury, Ont., July 17, 1896

SEASON	TEAM	GC	W	L	T	PLY.
27–28	NYA	44	11	27	6	

GREEN, Ted
B. Eriksdale, Man., Mar. 23, 1940

SEASON	TEAM	GC	W	L	T	PLY.
91–92	Edm	80	36	34	10	LSF
92–93	Edm	84	26	50	8	
93–94	Edm	24	3	18	3	
Totals		188	65	102	21	
Playoff Totals		16	8	8	0	

GUIDOLIN, Aldo
B. Forks of Credit, Ont., June 6, 1932

SEASON	TEAM	GC	W	L	T	PLY.
78–79	Col	59	12	39	8	

GUIDOLIN, Bep
B. Thorold, Ont., Dec. 9 1925

SEASON	TEAM	GC	W	L	T	PLY.
72–73	Bos	26	20	6	0	LFR
73–74	Bos	78	52	17	9	LCF
74–75	KC	80	15	54	11	
75–76	KC	45	11	30	4	
76–77	Edm (WHA)	63	25	36	2	
NHL Totals		229	98	107	24	
WHA Totals		63	25	36	2	
Playoff Totals		21	11	10	0	

HANNA, John
B. Sydney, N.S., Apr. 5, 1935

SEASON	TEAM	GC	W	L	T	PLY.
74–75	Clev (WHA)	33	14	18	1	

HARKNESS, Ned
B. Ottawa, Ont., Sept. 19, 1921

SEASON	TEAM	GC	W	L	T	PLY.
70–71	Det	19	9	7	3	

HARRIS, Billy
B. Toronto, Ont., July 29, 1935

SEASON	TEAM	GC	W	L	T	PLY.
72–73	Ott (WHA)	78	35	39	4	LFR
73–74	Tor (WHA)	78	41	33	4	LSF
74–75	Tor (WHA)	40	22	17	1	
Totals		196	98	89	9	

HARRIS, Ted
B. Winnipeg, Man., July 18, 1936

SEASON	TEAM	GC	W	L	T	PLY.
75–76	Minn	80	20	53	7	
76–77	Minn	80	23	39	18	LFR
77–78	Minn	19	5	12	2	
Totals		179	48	104	27	
Playoff Totals		2	0	2	0	

HART, Cecil
B. Montreal, Que

SEASON	TEAM	GC	W	L	T	PLY.
25–26	Mont	36	11	24	1	
26–27	Mont	44	28	14	2	LSF
27–28	Mont	44	26	11	7	LSF
28–29	Mont	44	22	7	15	LFR
29–30	Mont	44	21	14	9	WSC
30–31	Mont	44	26	10	8	WSC
31–32	Mont	48	25	16	7	LFR
36–37	Mont	48	24	18	6	LFR
37–38	Mont	48	18	17	13	LFR
38–39	Mont	30	6	18	6	
Totals		430	207	149	74	
Playoff Totals		35	15	17	3	

HARTLEY, Bob
B. Hawkesbury, Ont., Sept. 7, 1960

SEASON	TEAM	GC	W	L	T	PLY.
98–99	Col A	82	44	28	10	LSF
Playoff Totals		19	11	8	0	

HARTSBURG, Craig
B. Stratford, Ont., June 29, 1959

SEASON	TEAM	GC	W	L	T	PLY.
95–96	Chi	82	40	28	14	LSR
96–97	Chi	82	34	35	13	LFR
97–98	Chi	82	30	39	13	
98–99	Ana	82	35	34	13	LFR
Totals		328	139	136	53	
Playoff Totals		20	8	12	0	

HARVEY, Doug
B. Montreal, Que., Dec. 19, 1924

SEASON	TEAM	GC	W	L	T	PLY.
61–62	NYR	70	26	32	12	LFR
Playoff Totals		6	2	4	0	

HAY, Don
B. Kamloops, B.C., Feb. 13, 1954

SEASON	TEAM	GC	W	L	T	PLY.
96–97	Phoe	82	38	37	7	LFR
Playoff Totals		7	3	4	0	

HEFFERNAN, Frank

SEASON	TEAM	GC	W	L	T	PLY.
19–20	Tor	12	5	7	0	

HENNING, Lorne

SEASON	TEAM	GC	W	L	T	PLY.
85–86	Minn	80	38	33	9	LFR
86–87	Minn	78	30	39	9	
94–95	NYI	48	15	28	5	
Totals		206	83	100	23	
Playoff Totals		5	2	3	0	

HENRY, Camille
B. Quebec City, Que., Jan. 31, 1933

SEASON	TEAM	GC	W	L	T	PLY.
72–73	NY (WHA)	78	33	43	2	
73–74	NY–NJ (WHA)	20	6	12	2	
Totals		98	39	55	4	

HILLMAN, Larry
B. Kirkland Lake, Ont., Feb. 5, 1937

SEASON	TEAM	GC	W	L	T	PLY.
77–78	Winn (WHA)	80	50	28	2	WAC
78–79	Winn (WHA)	80	39	35	6	WAC
Totals		160	89	63	8	

HITCHCOCK, Ken
B. Edmonton, Alta., Dec. 17, 1951

SEASON	TEAM	GC	W	L	T	PLY.
95–96	Dall	43	15	23	5	
96–97	Dall	82	48	26	8	LFR
97–98	Dall	82	49	22	11	LSF
98–99	Dal	82	51	19	12	WSC
Totals		289	163	90	36	
Playoff Totals		47	29	18	0	

HOLMGREN, Paul
B. St. Paul, Minn., Dec. 2, 1955

SEASON	TEAM	GC	W	L	T	PLY.
88–89	Phil	80	36	36	8	LSF
89–90	Phil	80	30	39	11	
90–91	Phil	80	33	37	10	
91–92	Phil	24	8	14	2	
92–93	Hart	84	26	52	6	
93–94	Hart	17	4	11	2	
94–95	Hart	48	19	24	5	
95–96	Hart	12	5	6	1	
Totals		425	161	219	45	
Playoff Totals		19	10	9	0	

*HOWELL, Harry
B. Hamilton, Ont., Dec. 28, 1932

SEASON	TEAM	GC	W	L	T	PLY.
73–74	NY–NJ (WHA)	58	26	30	2	
74–75	SD (WHA)	78	43	31	4	LSF
78–79	Minn	11	3	6	2	
NHL Totals		11	3	6	2	
WHA Totals		136	69	61	6	

HUCUL, Sandy
B. Eston, Sask., Dec. 5, 1933

SEASON	TEAM	GC	W	L	T	PLY.
74–75	Phoe (WHA)	78	39	31	8	LFR
75–76	Phoe (WHA)	80	39	35	6	LFR
Totals		158	78	66	14	

*HULL, Bobby
B. Pointe Anne, Ont., Jan. 3, 1939

SEASON	TEAM	GC	W	L	T	PLY.
72–73	Winn (WHA)	78	43	31	4	LF
73–74	Winn (WHA)	78	34	39	5	LFR
74–75	Winn (WHA)	13	4	9	0	
Totals		169	81	79	9	

HUNTER, Bill

SEASON	TEAM	GC	W	L	T	PLY.
74–75	Edm (WHA)	19	6	12	1	
75–76	Edm (WHA)	33	9	21	3	LFR
Totals		52	15	33	4	

*IMLACH, Punch
B. Toronto, Ont., Mar. 15, 1918

SEASON	TEAM	GC	W	L	T	PLY.
58–59	Tor	50	22	20	8	LCF
59–60	Tor	70	35	26	9	LCF
60–61	Tor	70	39	19	12	LFR
61–62	Tor	70	37	22	11	WSC
62–63	Tor	70	35	23	12	WSC
63–64	Tor	70	33	25	12	WSC
64–65	Tor	70	30	26	14	LFR
65–66	Tor	70	34	25	11	LFR
66–67	Tor	60	25	26	9	
67–68	Tor	74	33	31	10	
68–69	Tor	76	35	26	15	LFR
70–71	Buff	78	24	39	15	
71–72	Buff	41	8	23	10	
79–80	Tor	10	5	5	0	LFR
Totals		879	395	336	148	
Playoff Totals		92	44	48	0	

INGERFIELD, Earl
B. Lethbridge, Alta., Oct. 25, 1934

SEASON	TEAM	GC	W	L	T	PLY.
72–73	NYI	30	6	22	2	

INGLIS, Bill
B. Ottawa, Ont., May 11, 1943

SEASON	TEAM	GC	W	L	T	PLY.
78–79	Buff	56	28	18	10	LFR
Playoff Totals		3	1	2	0	

INGRAM, Ron
B. Toronto, Ont., July 5, 1933

SEASON	TEAM	GC	W	L	T	PLY.
75–76	SD (WHA)	80	36	38	6	LFR
76–77	SD (WHA)	81	40	37	4	LFR
77–78	Ind (WHA)	51	16	31	4	
Totals		212	92	106	14	

*IRVIN, Dick
B. Limestone Ridge, Ont., July 19, 1892

SEASON	TEAM	GC	W	L	T	PLY.
30–31	Chi	44	24	17	3	LCF
31–32	Tor	43	23	15	5	WSC
32–33	Tor	48	24	18	6	LCF
33–34	Tor	48	26	13	9	LFR
34–35	Tor	48	30	14	4	LCF
35–36	Tor	48	23	19	6	LCF
36–37	Tor	48	22	21	5	LFR
37–38	Tor	48	24	15	9	LCF
38–39	Tor	48	19	20	9	LCF
39–40	Tor	48	25	17	6	LCF
40–41	Mont	48	16	26	6	LFR
41–42	Mont	48	18	27	3	LFR

SEASON	TEAM	GC	W	L	T	PLY.
42–43	Mont	50	19	19	12	LFR
43–44	Mont	50	38	5	7	WSC
44–45	Mont	50	38	8	4	LFR
45–46	Mont	50	28	17	5	WSC
46–47	Mont	60	34	16	10	LCF
47–48	Mont	60	20	29	11	
48–49	Mont	60	28	23	9	LFR
49–50	Mont	70	29	22	19	LFR
50–51	Mont	70	25	30	15	LCF
51–52	Mont	70	34	26	10	LCF
52–53	Mont	70	28	23	19	WSC
53–54	Mont	70	35	24	11	LCF
54–55	Mont	70	41	18	11	LCF
55–56	Chi	70	19	39	12	
Totals		1437	690	521	226	
Playoff Totals		190	100	88	2	

IVAN, Tommy
B. Toronto, Ont., Jan. 31, 1911

SEASON	TEAM	GC	W	L	T	PLY.
47–48	Det	60	30	18	12	LCF
48–49	Det	60	34	19	7	LCF
49–50	Det	70	37	19	14	WSC
50–51	Det	70	44	13	13	LFR
51–52	Det	70	44	14	12	WSC
52–53	Det	70	36	16	18	LFR
53–54	Det	70	37	19	14	WSC
56–57	Chi	70	16	39	15	
Totals		540	278	157	105	
Playoff Totals		67	36	31	0	

IVERSON, Emil

SEASON	TEAM	GC	W	L	T	PLY.
31–32	Chi	48	18	19	11	LFR
32–33	Chi	23	8	9	6	
Totals		71	26	28	17	
Playoff Totals		2	1	1	0	

JOHNSON, Bob
B. Minneapolis, Minn., Mar. 4, 1931

SEASON	TEAM	GC	W	L	T	PLY.
82–83	Calg	80	32	34	14	LSR
83–84	Calg	80	34	32	14	LSR
84–85	Calg	80	41	27	12	LFR
85–86	Calg	80	40	31	9	LF
86–87	Calg	80	46	31	3	LFR
90–91	Pitt	80	41	33	6	WSC
Totals		480	234	188	58	
Playoff Totals		78	42	36	0	

*JOHNSON, Tom
B. Baldur, Man., Feb. 18, 1928

SEASON	TEAM	GC	W	L	T	PLY.
70–71	Bos	78	57	14	7	LFR
71–72	Bos	78	54	13	11	WSC
72–73	Bos	52	31	16	5	
Totals		208	142	43	23	
Playoff Totals		22	15	7	0	

JOHNSTON, Eddie
B. Montreal, Que., Nov. 24, 1935

SEASON	TEAM	GC	W	L	T	PLY.
79–80	Chi	80	34	27	19	LQF
80–81	Pitt	80	30	37	13	LFR
81–82	Pitt	80	31	36	13	LFR
82–83	Pitt	80	18	53	9	
93–94	Pitt	84	44	27	19	LFR
94–95	Pitt	48	29	16	3	LSR
95–96	Pitt	82	49	29	4	LSF
96–97	Pitt	62	31	26	5	
Totals		596	266	251	79	
Playoff Totals		53	25	28	0	

JOHNSTON, Marshall
B. Birch Hills, Sask., June 6, 1941

SEASON	TEAM	GC	W	L	T	PLY.
73–74	Col	21	2	17	2	
74–75	Col	48	11	28	9	
81–82	Col	56	15	32	9	
Totals		125	28	77	20	

KASPER, Steve
B. Montreal, Que., Sept. 28, 1961

SEASON	TEAM	GC	W	L	T	PLY.
95–96	Bos	82	40	31	11	LFR
96–97	Bos	82	26	47	9	
Totals		164	66	78	20	
Playoff Totals		5	1	4	0	

KEATS, Duke

SEASON	TEAM	GC	W	L	T	PLY.
26–27	Det	11	2	7	2	

KEENAN, Mike
B. Toronto, Ont., Oct. 21, 1949

SEASON	TEAM	GC	W	L	T	PLY.
84–85	Phil	80	53	20	7	LF
85–86	Phil	80	53	23	4	LFR
86–87	Phil	80	46	26	8	LF
87–88	Phil	80	38	33	9	LFR
88–89	Chi	80	27	41	12	LSF
89–90	Chi	80	41	33	6	LSF
90–91	Chi	80	49	23	8	LFR
91–92	Chi	80	36	29	15	LF
93–94	NYR	84	52	24	8	WSC
94–95	StL	48	28	15	5	LFR
95–96	StL	82	32	34	16	LSR
96–97	StL	33	15	17	1	
97–98	Van	63	21	30	12	
98–99	Van	45	15	24	6	
Totals		995	506	372	117	
Playoff Totals		160	91	69	0	

KELLEY, Jack
B. Medford, Mass., July 10, 1927

SEASON	TEAM	GC	W	L	T	PLY.
72–73	NE (WHA)	78	46	30	2	WAC
74–75	NE (WHA)	5	3	2	0	LFR
75–76	NE (WHA)	33	14	16	3	
Totals		116	63	48	5	

KELLY, Pat
B. Sioux Lookout, Ont., Sept. 8, 1935

SEASON	TEAM	GC	W	L	T	PLY.
76–77	Birm (WHA)	59	24	32	3	
77–78	Col	80	19	40	21	LFR
78–79	Col	21	3	14	4	
Totals		101	22	54	25	
Playoff Totals		2	0	2	0	
WHA Totals		59	24	32	3	

*KELLY, Red
B. Simcoe, Ont., July 9, 1927

SEASON	TEAM	GC	W	L	T	PLY.
67–68	LA	76	31	33	10	LFR
68–69	LA	76	24	42	10	LSF
69–70	Pitt	76	26	38	12	LSF
70–71	Pitt	78	21	37	20	
71–72	Pitt	78	26	38	14	LFR
72–73	Pitt	42	17	19	6	
73–74	Tor	80	31	33	16	LFR
74–75	Tor	80	31	33	16	LSR
75–76	Tor	80	34	31	15	LSR
76–77	Tor	80	33	32	15	LSR
Totals		744	274	336	134	
Playoff Totals		55	21	34	0	

KENNEDY, George

SEASON	TEAM	GC	W	L	T	PLY.
17–18	Mont	22	13	9	0	LSF
18–19	XXX	18	10	8	0	
19–20	XXX	24	13	11	0	
Totals		64	36	28	0	

KINASEWICK, Ray
B. Smokey Lake, Alta., Sept. 12, 1933

SEASON	TEAM	GC	W	L	T	PLY.
72–73	Alb (WHA)	78	38	37	3	

KING, Dave
B. Saskatoon, Sask., Dec. 22, 1947

SEASON	TEAM	GC	W	L	T	PLY.
92–93	Calg	84	43	30	11	LFR
93–94	Calg	84	42	29	13	LFR
94–95	Calg	48	24	17	7	LFR
Totals		216	109	76	31	
Playoff Totals		20	8	12	0	

KINGSTON, George
B. Bigger, Sask., Aug. 20, 1939

SEASON	TEAM	GC	W	L	T	PLY.
91–92	SJ	80	17	58	5	
92–93	SJ	84	11	71	2	
Totals		164	28	129	7	

KISH, Larry
B. Welland, Ont., Dec. 11, 1941

SEASON	TEAM	GC	W	L	T	PLY.
82–83	Hart	49	12	32	·5	

KROMM, Bobby
B. Calgary, Alta., June 8, 1928

SEASON	TEAM	GC	W	L	T	PLY.
75–76	Winn (WHA)	81	52	27	2	WAC

SEASON	TEAM	GC	W	L	T	PLY.
76–77	Winn (WHA)	80	46	32	2	LLF
77–78	Det	80	32	34	14	LSR
78–79	Det	80	23	41	16	
79–80	Det	71	24	36	11	
NHL Totals		231	79	111	41	
WHA Totals		161	98	59	4	
NHA Playoff Totals		7	3	4	0	

KURTENBACH, Orland
B. Culworth, Sask., Sept. 7, 1936

SEASON	TEAM	GC	W	L	T	PLY.
76–77	Van	45	16	19	10	
77–78	Van	80	20	43	17	
Totals		125	36	62	27	

LAFORGE, Bill

SEASON	TEAM	GC	W	L	T	PLY.
84–85	Van	20	4	14	2	

*LALONDE, Newsy
B. Cornwall, Ont., Oct. 31, 1887

SEASON	TEAM	GC	W	L	T	PLY.
26–27	NYA	44	17	25	2	
29–30	Ott	44	21	15	8	LFR
30–31	Ott	44	10	30	4	
32–33	Mont	48	18	25	5	LFR
33–34	Mont	48	22	20	6	LFR
34–35	Mont	16	5	8	3	
Totals		244	93	123	28	
Playoff Totals		6	0	3	3	

LAPERRIERE, Jacques
B. Rouyn, Que., Nov. 22, 1941

SEASON	TEAM	GC	W	L	T	PLY.
95–96	Mont	1	0	1	0	

LAPOINTE, Ron
B. Verdun, Que., Nov. 12, 1949

SEASON	TEAM	GC	W	L	T	PLY.
87–88	Que	56	22	30	4	
88–89	Que	33	11	20	2	
Totals		89	33	50	6	

LAYCOE, Hal
B. Sutherland, Sask., June 23, 1922

SEASON	TEAM	GC	W	L	T	PLY.
69–70	LA	24	5	18	1	
70–71	Van	78	24	46	8	
71–72	Van	78	20	50	8	
Totals		180	49	114	17	

LEDUC, Bob
B. Sudbury, Ont., May 24, 1944

SEASON	TEAM	GC	W	L	T	PLY.
74–75	Tor (WHA)	38	21	16	1	LFR

LEGER, Gilles
B. Cornwall, Ont., July 16, 1941

SEASON	TEAM	GC	W	L	T	PLY.
75–76	Tor (WHA)	26	9	17	0	
76–77	Birm (WHA)	24	7	16	1	
Totals		50	16	33	1	

*LEHMAN, Hugh
B. Pembroke, Ont., Oct. 27, 1885

SEASON	TEAM	GC	W	L	T	PLY.
27–28	Chi	21	3	17	1	

*LEMAIRE, Jacques
B. LaSalle, Que., Sept. 7, 1945

SEASON	TEAM	GC	W	L	T	PLY.
83–84	Mont	17	7	10	0	LSF
84–85	Mont	80	41	27	12	LSF
93–94	NJ	84	47	25	12	LSF
94–95	NJ	48	22	18	8	WSC
95–96	NJ	82	37	33	12	
96–97	NJ	82	45	23	14	LSR
97–98	NJ	82	48	23	11	LFR
Totals		475	247	159	69	
Playoff Totals		83	49	34	0	

LEPINE, Pit
B. Ste. Anne Bellevue, Que., July 30, 1901

SEASON	TEAM	GC	W	L	T	PLY.
39–40	Mont	48	10	33	5	

LESUEUR, Percy

SEASON	TEAM	GC	W	L	T	PLY.
23–24	Ham	24	9	15	0	

LEY, Rick
B. Orillia, Ont., Nov. 2, 1948

SEASON	TEAM	GC	W	L	T	PLY.
89–90	Hart	80	38	33	9	LFR
90–91	Hart	80	31	38	11	LFR
94–95	Van	48	18	18	12	LSR

SEASON TEAM	GC	W	L	T	PLY.
~~95-96 Van~~	~~76~~	~~29~~	~~32~~	~~15~~	
Totals	**284**	**116**	**121**	**47**	
Playoff Totals	**24**	**9**	**15**	**0**	

*LINDSAY, Ted
B. Renfrew, Ont., July 29, 1925

80-81 Det	20	3	14	3	

LONG, Barry
B. Brantford, Ont., Jan. 3, 1949

83-84 Winn	59	25	25	9	LFR
84-85 Winn	80	43	27	10	LSR
85-86 Winn	66	19	41	6	
Totals	**205**	**87**	**93**	**25**	
Playoff Totals	**11**	**3**	**8**	**0**	

LOUGHLIN, Clem
B. Carroll, Man., Nov. 15, 1894

34-35 Chi	48	26	17	5	LFR
35-36 Chi	48	21	19	8	LFR
36-37 Chi	48	14	27	7	
Totals	**144**	**61**	**63**	**20**	
Playoff Totals	**4**	**0**	**3**	**1**	

LOW, Ron
B. Birtie, Man., June 21, 1950

94-95 Edm	13	5	7	1	
95-96 Edm	82	30	44	8	
96-97 Edm	82	36	37	9	LSR
97-98 Edm	82	35	37	10	LSR
98-99 Edm	82	33	37	12	LFR
Totals	**341**	**139**	**162**	**40**	
Playoff Totals	**28**	**10**	**18**	**0**	

MacDONALD, Parker
B. Sydney, N.S., June 14, 1933

73-74 Minn	61	20	30	11	
81-82 LA	42	13	24	5	
Totals	**103**	**33**	**52**	**16**	

MacLEAN, Doug
B. Summerside, P.E.I., Apr. 12, 1954

95-96 Flor	82	41	31	10	LF
96-97 Flor	82	35	28	19	LFR
97-98 Flor	23	7	12	4	
Totals	**187**	**83**	**71**	**33**	
Playoff Totals	**27**	**13**	**14**	**0**	

MacMILLAN, Billy
B. Charlottetown, P.E.I., Mar. 7, 1943

80-81 Col	80	22	45	13	
82-83 NJ	80	17	49	14	
83-84 NJ	20	2	18	0	
Totals	**180**	**41**	**112**	**27**	

MacNEIL, Al
B. Sydney, N.S., Sept. 27, 1935

70-71 Mont	55	31	15	9	WSC
79-80 Atl	80	35	32	13	LFR
80-81 Calg	80	39	27	14	LSF
81-82 Calg	80	29	34	17	LFR
Totals	**295**	**134**	**108**	**53**	
Playoff Totals	**43**	**22**	**21**	**0**	

MAHONEY, Bill
B. Peterborough, Ont., June 23, 1939

83-84 Minn	80	39	31	10	LSF
84-85 Minn	13	3	8	2	
Totals	**93**	**42**	**39**	**12**	
Playoff Totals	**16**	**7**	**9**	**0**	

MAGNUSON, Keith
B. Saskatoon, Sask., Apr. 27, 1947

80-81 Chi	80	31	33	16	LFR
81-82 Chi	52	18	24	10	
Totals	**132**	**49**	**57**	**26**	
Playoff Totals	**3**	**0**	**3**	**0**	

MAGUIRE, Pierre

93-94 Hart	67	23	37	7	

MALONEY, Dan
B. Barrie, Ont., Sept. 24, 1950

84-85 Tor	80	20	52	8	
85-86 Tor	80	25	48	7	LSR
86-87 Winn	80	40	32	8	LSR
87-88 Winn	80	33	36	11	LFR
88-89 Winn	52	18	25	9	
Totals	**372**	**136**	**193**	**43**	
Playoff Totals	**25**	**11**	**14**	**0**	

MALONEY, Phil
B. Ottawa, Ont.

73-74 Van	37	15	18	4	
74-75 Van	80	38	32	10	LFR
75-76 Van	80	33	32	15	LFR
76-77 Van	35	9	23	3	
Totals	**232**	**95**	**105**	**32**	
Playoff Totals	**7**	**1**	**6**	**0**	

*MANTHA, Sylvio
B. Montreal, Que., Apr. 14, 1902

35-36 Mont	48	11	26	11	

MARSHALL, Bert
B. Kamloops, B.C., Nov. 22, 1943

81-82 Col	24	3	17	4	

MARSHALL, Jacques
B. St. Pascal, Ont., Oct. 1, 1952

86-87 StL	80	32	33	15	LFR
87-88 StL	80	34	38	8	LSR
95-96 Ott	38	10	24	4	
96-97 Ott	82	31	36	15	LFR
97-98 Ott	82	34	33	15	LSR
Totals	**362**	**141**	**164**	**57**	
Playoff Totals	**34**	**15**	**19**	**0**	

MARTIN, Jacques
B. St. Pascal, Ont., Oct. 1, 1952

86-87 StL	80	32	33	15	LFR
87-88 StL	80	34	38	8	LSR
95-96 Ott	38	10	24	4	
96-97 Ott	82	31	36	15	LFR
97-98 Ott	82	34	33	15	LSR
98-99 Ott	82	44	23	15	LFR
Totals	**444**	**185**	**187**	**72**	
Playoff Totals	**38**	**15**	**23**	**0**	

MAURICE, Paul
B. Jan. 30, 1967

95-96 Hart	70	29	33	8	
96-97 Hart	82	32	39	11	
97-98 Car	82	33	41	8	
98-99 Car	82	34	30	18	LFR
Totals	**316**	**128**	**143**	**45**	
Playoff Totals	**6**	**2**	**4**	**0**	

MAXNER, Wayne
B. Halifax, N.S., Sept. 27, 1942

80-81 Det	60	16	29	15	
81-82 Det	69	18	39	12	
Totals	**129**	**34**	**68**	**27**	

McCAMMON, Bob
B. Kenora, Ont., Apr. 1941

78-79 Phil	50	22	17	11	
81-82 Phil	8	4	2	2	LFR
82-83 Phil	80	49	23	8	LFR
83-84 Phil	80	44	26	12	LFR
87-88 Van	80	25	46	9	
88-89 Van	80	33	39	8	
89-90 Van	80	25	41	14	LFR
90-91 Van	54	19	30	5	
Totals	**511**	**221**	**223**	**67**	
Playoff Totals	**17**	**4**	**13**	**0**	

McCASKILL, Ted
B. Kapuskasing, Ont., Dec. 2, 1934

73-74 LA (WHA)	59	20	39	0	

McCREARY, Bill
B. Sundridge, Ont., Dec. 2, 1934

71-72 StL	24	6	14	4	
73-74 Van	41	9	25	7	
74-75 Cal	32	8	20	4	
Totals	**97**	**23**	**59**	**15**	

McKENZIE, John
B. High River, Alta., Dec. 12, 1937

72-73 Phil (WHA)	7	1	6	0	
73-74 Van (WHA)	7	3	4	0	
Totals	**14**	**4**	**10**	**0**	

McLELLAN, John
B. South Porcupine, Ont., Aug. 6, 1928

69-70 Tor	76	29	34	13	
70-71 Tor	78	37	33	8	
71-72 Tor	63	24	28	11	
72-73 Tor	78	27	41	10	
Totals	**295**	**117**	**136**	**42**	
Playoff Totals	**6**	**2**	**4**	**0**	

McVIE, Tom
B. Trail, B.C., June 6, 1935

75-76 Wash	44	8	31	5	
76-77 Wash	80	24	42	14	
77-78 Wash	80	17	49	14	
78-79 Winn (WHA)	19	11	8	0	
79-80 Winn	77	19	47	11	
80-81 Winn	28	1	20	7	
83-84 NJ	60	15	38	7	
90-91 NJ	13	4	5	4	LFR
91-92 NJ	80	38	31	11	LFR
NHL Totals	**462**	**126**	**263**	**73**	
Playoff Totals	**14**	**6**	**8**	**0**	
WHA Totals	**19**	**11**	**8**	**0**	

MEEKER, Howie
B. Kitchener, Ont., Nov. 4, 1924

56-57 Tor	70	21	34	15	

MELROSE, Barry
B. Kelvington, Sask., July 15, 1956

92-93 LA	84	39	35	10	LF
93-94 LA	84	27	45	12	
94-95 LA	41	13	21	7	
Totals	**209**	**79**	**101**	**29**	
Playoff Totals	**24**	**13**	**11**	**0**	

MILBURY, Mike
B. Walpole, Mass., June 17, 1952

89-90 Bos	80	46	25	9	LF
90-91 Bos	80	44	24	12	LSF
95-96 NYI	82	22	50	10	
96-97 NYI	45	13	23	9	
97-98 NYI	19	8	9	2	
98-99 NYI	45	13	29	3	
Totals	**351**	**146**	**160**	**45**	
Playoff Totals	**40**	**23**	**17**	**0**	

MOLLEKEN, Lorne
B. Regina, Sask., June 11, 1956

98-99 Chi	23	13	6	4	

MOORE, Gerry
B. Ottawa, Ont., Nov. 23, 1931

74-75 Ind (WHA)	78	18	57	3	

MUCKLER, John
B. Midland, Ont., Apr. 3, 1934

68-69 Minn	35	6	23	6	
89-90 Edm	80	38	28	14	WSC
90-91 Edm	80	37	37	6	LSF
91-92 Buf	52	22	22	8	LFR
92-93 Buf	84	38	36	10	LSR
93-94 Buf	84	43	32	9	LFR
94-95 Buf	48	22	19	7	LFR
97-98 NYR	25	8	15	2	
98-99 NYR	82	33	38	11	
Totals	**570**	**247**	**250**	**63**	
Playoff Totals	**51**	**24**	**27**	**0**	

SEASON	TEAM	GC	W	L	T	PLY.
MULDOON, Pete						
26–27	Chi	44	19	22	3	LFR
Playoff Totals		**2**	**0**	**1**	**1**	
MUNRO, Dunc						
B. Toronto, Ont.						
29–30	MontM	44	23	16	5	LFR
30–31	MontM	32	14	13	5	
Totals		**76**	**37**	**29**	**10**	
Playoff Totals		**4**	**1**	**3**	**0**	
MURDOCH, Bob						
87–88	Chi	80	30	41	9	LFR
89–90	Winn	80	37	32	11	LFR
90–91	Winn	80	26	43	11	
Totals		**240**	**93**	**116**	**31**	
Playoff Totals		**12**	**4**	**8**	**0**	
MURPHY, Mike						
B. Toronto, Ont., Sept. 12, 1950						
86–87	LA	38	13	21	4	LFR
87–88	LA	27	7	16	4	
96–97	Tor	82	30	44	8	
97–98	Tor	82	30	43	9	
Totals		**229**	**80**	**124**	**25**	
Playoff Totals		**5**	**1**	**4**	**0**	
MURRAY, Bryan						
B. Shawville, Que., Dec. 5, 1942						
81–82	Wash	76	25	28	13	
82–83	Wash	80	39	25	16	LFR
83–84	Wash	80	48	27	5	LSR
84–85	Wash	80	46	25	9	LSR
85–86	Wash	80	50	23	7	LSR
86–87	Wash	80	38	32	10	LFR
87–88	Wash	80	38	33	9	LSF
88–89	Wash	80	41	29	10	LFR
89–90	Wash	46	18	24	4	
90–91	Det	80	34	38	8	LFR
91–92	Det	80	43	25	12	LSR
92–93	Det	84	47	28	9	LFR
97–98	Flor	59	17	31	11	
Totals		**975**	**484**	**368**	**123**	
Playoff Totals		**78**	**34**	**44**	**0**	
MURRAY, Terry						
B. Shawville, Que., July 20, 1950						
89–90	Wash	34	18	14	2	LSF
90–91	Wash	80	37	36	7	LSR
91–92	Wash	80	45	27	8	LFR
92–93	Wash	84	43	34	7	LFR
93–94	Wash	47	20	23	4	
94–95	Phil	48	28	16	4	LSF
95–96	Phil	82	45	24	13	LSR
96–97	Phil	82	45	24	13	LF
98–99	Flor	82	30	34	18	
Totals		**619**	**311**	**232**	**76**	
Playoff Totals		**85**	**46**	**39**	**0**	
NANNE, Lou						
B. Sault Ste. Marie, Ont., June 2, 1941						
77–78	Minn	29	7	18	4	
NEALE, Harry						
B. Sarnia, Ont., Mar. 9, 1937						
73–74	Minn (WHA)	78	44	32	2	LSF
74–75	Minn (WHA)	78	42	33	3	LSF
75–76	Minn (WHA)	59	30	25	4	
	NE (WHA)	12	5	6	1	LSF
76–77	NE (WHA)	81	35	40	6	LFR
77–78	NE (WHA)	80	44	31	5	LLF
78–79	Van	80	25	42	13	LFR
79–80	Van	80	27	37	16	LFR
80–81	Van	80	28	32	20	LFR
81–82	Van	75	26	33	16	
83–84	Van	32	15	13	4	
84–85	Van	60	21	32	7	
85–86	Det	35	8	23	4	
NHL Totals		**442**	**150**	**212**	**80**	
Playoff Totals		**14**	**3**	**11**	**0**	
WHA Totals		**388**	**200**	**167**	**21**	

SEASON	TEAM	GC	W	L	T	PLY.
NEEDHAM, Bill						
B. Kirkland Lake, Ont., Jan. 12, 1932						
72–73	Clev (WHA)	78	43	32	3	
73–74	Clev (WHA)	78	37	32	9	
Totals		**156**	**80**	**64**	**12**	
NEILSON, Roger						
B. Toronto, Ont., June 16, 1934						
77–78	Tor	80	41	29	10	LSF
78–79	Tor	80	34	33	13	LQF
80–81	Buf	80	39	20	21	LQF
81–82	Van	5	4	0	1	LCF
82–83	Van	80	30	35	15	LFR
83–84	Van	48	17	26	5	
	LA	28	8	17	3	
89–90	NYR	80	36	31	13	LSR
90–91	NYR	80	36	31	13	LFR
91–92	NYR	80	50	25	5	LSR
92–93	NYR	40	19	17	4	
93–94	Flor	84	33	34	17	
94–95	Flor	48	20	22	6	
97–98	Phil	21	10	9	2	
98–99	Phil	82	37	26	19	LFR
Totals		**916**	**414**	**355**	**147**	
Playoff Totals		**73**	**34**	**39**	**0**	
NOLAN, Ted						
B. Sault Ste. Marie, Ont., Apr. 7, 1958						
95–96	Buf	82	33	42	7	
96–96	Buf	82	40	30	12	LSR
Totals		**164**	**73**	**72**	**19**	
Playoff Totals		**12**	**5**	**7**	**0**	
NYKOLUK, Mike						
B. Toronto, Ont., Dec. 11, 1934						
80–81	Tor	40	15	15	10	LFR
81–82	Tor	80	20	44	16	
82–83	Tor	80	28	40	12	LFR
83–84	Tor	80	26	45	9	
Totals		**280**	**89**	**144**	**47**	
Playoff Totals		**7**	**1**	**6**	**0**	
OLIVER, Murray						
B. Hamilton, Ont., Nov. 14, 1937						
82–83	Minn	36	18	11	7	LSR
OLMSTEAD, Bert						
B. Scepter, Sask., Sept. 4, 1926						
67–68	Oak	64	11	37	16	
O'REILLY, Terry						
B. Niagara Falls, Ont., June 7, 1951						
86–87	Bos	80	39	34	7	LFR
87–88	Bos	80	44	30	6	LF
88–89	Bos	67	32	22	13	
Totals		**227**	**115**	**86**	**26**	
Playoff Totals		**26**	**12**	**14**	**0**	
PADDOCK, John						
B. Brandon, Man., June 9, 1954						
91–92	Winn	80	33	32	15	LFR
92–93	Winn	84	40	37	7	LFR
93–94	Winn	84	24	51	9	
94–95	Winn	33	9	18	6	
Totals		**281**	**106**	**138**	**37**	
Playoff Totals		**13**	**5**	**8**	**0**	
PAGE, Pierre						
B. St. Hermas, Que., Apr. 30, 1948						
88–89	Minn	80	27	37	16	LFR
89–90	Minn	80	36	40	4	LFR
91–92	Que	62	17	34	11	
92–93	Que	84	47	27	10	LFR
93–94	Que	84	34	42	8	
95–96	Calg	82	34	37	11	LFR
96–97	Calg	82	32	41	9	
97–98	Ana	82	26	43	13	
Totals		**636**	**253**	**301**	**82**	
Playoff Totals		**22**	**6**	**16**	**0**	
PARK, Brad						
B. Toronto, Ont., July 6, 1948						
85–86	Det	45	9	34	2	

SEASON	TEAM	GC	W	L	T	PLY.
PATRICK, Craig						
B. Detroit, Mich., May 20, 1946						
80–81	NYR	59	26	23	10	LSF
84–85	NYR	35	11	22	2	LFR
89–90	Pitt	54	22	26	6	
96–97	Pitt	20	7	10	3	LFR
Totals		**168**	**66**	**81**	**21**	
Playoff Totals		**22**	**8**	**14**	**0**	
PATRICK, Frank						
B. Ottawa, Ont., Dec. 21, 1885						
34–35	Bos	48	26	16	6	LFR
35–36	Bos	48	22	20	6	LFR
Totals		**96**	**48**	**36**	**12**	
Playoff Totals		**6**	**2**	**4**	**0**	
*PATRICK, Lester						
B. Drummondville, Que., Dec. 30, 1883						
26–27	NYR	44	25	13	6	LSF
27–28	NYR	44	19	16	9	WSC
28–29	NYR	44	21	13	10	LCF
29–30	NYR	44	17	17	10	LSF
30–31	NYR	44	19	16	9	LSF
31–32	NYR	48	23	17	8	LCF
32–33	NYR	48	23	17	8	WSC
33–34	NYR	48	21	19	8	LFR
34–35	NYR	48	22	20	6	LSF
35–36	NYR	48	19	17	12	
36–37	NYR	48	19	20	9	LCF
37–38	NYR	48	27	15	6	LFR
38–39	NYR	48	26	16	6	LFR
Totals		**604**	**281**	**216**	**107**	
Playoff Totals		**65**	**31**	**26**	**8**	
*PATRICK, Lynn						
B. Victoria, B.C., Feb. 3, 1912						
78–49	NYR	37	12	20	5	
49–50	NYR	70	28	31	11	LCF
50–51	Bos	70	22	30	18	LFR
51–52	Bos	70	25	29	16	LCF
52–53	Bos	70	28	19	13	LCF
53–54	Bos	70	32	28	10	LFR
54–55	Bos	20	10	14	6	
67–68	StL	16	4	10	2	
74–75	StL	2	1	0	1	
75–76	StL	8	3	5	0	
Totals		**443**	**165**	**186**	**82**	
Playoff Totals		**40**	**16**	**23**	**1**	
PATRICK, Muzz						
B. Victoria, B.C., June 28, 1915						
53–54	NYR	32	17	11	4	
54–55	NYR	70	17	35	18	
62–63	NYR	34	11	19	4	
Totals		**136**	**45**	**65**	**26**	
PERRON, Jean						
B. St. Isidore d'Auckland, Que., Oct. 5, 1946						
85–86	Mont	80	40	33	7	WSC
86–87	Mont	80	41	29	10	LSF
87–88	Mont	80	45	22	13	LSR
88–89	Que	47	16	26	5	
Totals		**287**	**142**	**110**	**35**	
Playoff Totals		**48**	**30**	**18**	**0**	
PERRY, Don						
B. Edmonton, Alta., Mar. 16, 1930						
81–82	LA	38	11	17	10	LSR
82–83	LA	80	27	41	12	
83–84	LA	50	14	27	9	
Totals		**168**	**52**	**85**	**31**	
Playoff Totals		**10**	**4**	**6**	**0**	
PIKE, Alf						
B. Winnipeg, Man., Sept. 15, 1917						
59–60	NYR	55	14	29	12	
60–61	NYR	70	22	38	10	
Totals		**125**	**36**	**67**	**22**	
PILOUS, Rudy						
B. Winnipeg, Man., Aug. 11, 1914						
57–58	Chi	70	24	39	7	
58–59	Chi	70	28	29	13	LFR

SEASON	TEAM	GC	W	L	T	PLY.
59–60	Chi	70	28	29	13	LFR
60–61	Chi	70	29	24	17	WSC
61–62	Chi	70	31	26	13	LCF
62–63	Chi	70	32	21	17	LFR
74–75	Winn (WHA)	65	34	26	5	
NHL Totals		**420**	**172**	**168**	**80**	
Playoff Totals		**41**	**19**	**22**	**0**	
WHA Totals		**65**	**34**	**26**	**5**	

PLAGER, Barclay
B. Kirkland Lake, Ont., Mar. 26, 1941

77–78	StL	26	9	11	6	
78–79	StL	80	18	50	12	
79–80	StL	28	8	16	4	
82–83	StL	48	15	21	12	LFR
Totals		**182**	**50**	**98**	**34**	
Playoff Totals		**4**	**1**	**3**	**0**	

PLAGER, Bob
B. Kirkland Lake, Ont., Mar. 11, 1943

92–93	StL	11	4	6	1	

*PLANTE, Jacques
B. Mount Carmel, Que., Jan. 17, 1929

73–74	Que (WHA)	78	38	36	4	

PLEAU, Larry
B. Lynn, Mass., Jan. 29, 1947

80–81	Hart	20	6	12	2	LFR
81–82	Hart	80	21	41	18	
82–83	Hart	18	4	13	1	
87–88	Hart	26	13	13	0	LFR
88–89	Hart	80	37	38	5	LFR
Totals		**224**	**81**	**117**	**26**	
Playoff Totals		**13**	**2**	**11**	**0**	

POLANO, Nick
B. Sudbury, Ont., Mar. 25, 1941

82–83	Det	80	21	44	15	
83–84	Det	80	31	42	7	LFR
84–85	Det	80	27	41	12	LFR
Totals		**240**	**79**	**127**	**34**	
Playoff Totals		**7**	**1**	**6**	**0**	

POPEIN, Larry
B. Yorkson, Sask., Aug. 11, 1930

73–74	NYR	41	18	14	9	

POWERS, Eddie

21–22	Tor	24	13	10	1	WSC
23–24	Tor	24	10	14	0	
24–25	Tor	30	19	11	0	LFR
25–26	Tor	36	12	21	3	
Totals		**114**	**54**	**56**	**4**	
Playoff Totals		**11**	**5**	**4**	**2**	

*PRIMEAU, Joe
B. Lindsay, Ont., Jan. 24, 1906

50–51	Tor	70	41	16	13	WSC
51–52	Tor	70	29	25	16	LFR
52–53	Tor	70	27	30	13	
Totals		**210**	**97**	**71**	**42**	
Playoff Totals		**15**	**8**	**6**	**1**	

*PRONOVOST, Marcel
B. Lac la Torque, Que., June 15, 1930

72–73	Chi (WHA)	78	26	50	2	
77–78	Buf	80	44	19	17	Lost Second
78–79	Buf	24	8	10	6	
NHL Totals		**104**	**52**	**29**	**23**	
Playoff Totals		**8**	**4**	**4**	**0**	
WHA Totals		**78**	**26**	**50**	**2**	

PULFORD, Bob
B. Newton Robinson, Ont., Mar. 31, 1936

72–73	LA	78	31	36	11	
73–74	LA	78	33	33	12	LFR
74–75	LA	80	42	17	21	LFR
75–76	LA	80	38	33	9	LQF
76–77	LA	80	34	31	15	LQF
77–78	Chi	80	32	29	19	LFR
78–79	Chi	80	29	36	15	LFR
81–82	Chi	28	12	14	2	LSF
84–85	Chi	27	16	7	4	LSF
85–86	Chi	80	39	33	8	LFR
86–87	Chi	80	29	37	14	LFR
Totals		**771**	**336**	**305**	**130**	
Playoff Totals		**71**	**28**	**43**	**0**	

QUERRIE, Charlie

22–23	Tor	6	3	3	0	

QUENNEVILLE, Joel
B. Windsor, Ont., Sept. 15, 1958

96–97	StL	40	18	15	7	LFR
97–98	StL	82	45	29	8	LSR
98–99	StL	82	37	32	13	LSR
Totals		**204**	**100**	**76**	**28**	
Playoff Totals		**29**	**14**	**15**	**0**	

QUINN, Mike

19–20	Que	24	4	20	0	

QUINN, Pat
B. Hamilton, Ont., Jan. 29, 1943

78–79	Phil	30	18	8	4	LQF
79–80	Phil	80	48	12	20	LCF
80–81	Phil	80	41	24	15	LQF
81–82	Phil	72	34	29	9	
84–85	LA	80	34	32	14	LFR
85–86	LA	80	23	49	8	
86–87	LA	42	18	20	4	
90–91	Van	26	9	13	4	
91–92	Van	80	42	26	12	LSR
92–93	Van	84	46	29	9	LSR
93–94	Van	84	41	40	3	LCF
95–96	Van	6	3	3	0	LFR
98–99	Tor	82	45	30	7	LSF
Totals		**826**	**402**	**315**	**109**	
Playoff Totals		**120**	**62**	**58**	**0**	

RAMSAY, Craig
B. Weston, Ont., Mar. 17, 1951

86–87	Buf	21	4	15	2	

REAY, Billy
B. Winnipeg, Man., Aug. 21, 1918

57–58	Tor	70	21	38	11	
58–59	Tor	20	5	12	3	
63–64	Chi	70	36	22	12	LFR
64–65	Chi	70	34	28	8	LCF
65–66	Chi	70	37	25	8	LFR
66–67	Chi	70	41	17	12	LFR
67–68	Chi	74	32	26	16	LSF
68–69	Chi	76	34	33	9	
69–70	Chi	76	45	22	9	LSF
70–71	Chi	78	49	20	9	LCF
71–72	Chi	78	46	17	15	LSF
72–73	Chi	78	42	27	9	LCF
73–74	Chi	78	41	14	23	LSF
74–75	Chi	80	37	35	8	LQF
75–76	Chi	80	32	30	18	LFR
76–77	Chi	34	10	10	5	
Totals		**1102**	**542**	**376**	**175**	
Playoff Totals		**117**	**57**	**60**	**0**	

REGAN, Larry
B. North Bay, Ont., Aug. 9, 1930

70–71	LA	78	25	40	13	
71–72	LA	10	2	7	1	
Totals		**88**	**27**	**47**	**14**	

RENNEY, Tom
B. Cranbrook, B.C., Mar. 1, 1955

96–97	Van	82	35	40	7	
97–98	Van	19	4	13	2	
Totals		**101**	**39**	**53**	**9**	

*RICHARD, Maurice
B. Montreal, Que., Aug. 4, 1921

72–73	Que (WHA)	2	1	1	0	

RIESBROUGH, Doug
B. Guelph, Ont., Jan. 29, 1954

90–91	Calg	80	46	26	8	LFR
91–92	Calg	64	25	30	9	
Totals		**144**	**71**	**56**	**17**	
Playoff Totals		**7**	**3**	**4**	**0**	

ROBERTS, Jim
B. Toronto, Ont., Apr. 9, 1940

81–82	Buf	45	21	15	9	
91–92	Hart	80	26	41	13	
96–97	StL	9	3	3	3	
Totals		**134**	**50**	**60**	**24**	

*ROBINSON, Larry
B. Winchester, Ont., June 2, 1951

95–96	LA	82	24	40	18	
96–97	LA	82	28	43	11	
97–98	LA	82	38	33	11	
98–99	LA	82	32	45	5	
Totals		**328**	**122**	**161**	**45**	
Playoff Totals		**4**	**0**	**4**	**0**	

*ROSS, Art
B. Naughton, Ont., Jan. 13, 1886

17–18	MontW	6	1	5	0	
22–23	Ham	24	6	18	0	
24–25	Bos	30	6	24	0	
25–26	Bos	36	17	15	4	
26–27	Bos	44	21	20	3	LCF
27–28	Bos	44	20	13	11	LQF
29–30	Bos	44	38	5	1	LCF
30–31	Bos	44	28	10	6	LFR
31–32	Bos	48	15	21	12	
32–33	Bos	48	25	15	8	LFR
33–34	Bos	48	18	25	5	
36–37	Bos	48	23	18	7	LFR
37–38	Bos	48	30	11	7	LFR
38–39	Bos	48	36	10	2	WSC
41–42	Bos	48	25	17	6	LSF
42–43	Bos	50	24	17	9	LSF
43–44	Bos	50	19	26	5	
44–45	Bos	50	16	30	4	LFR
Totals		**758**	**368**	**300**	**90**	
Playoff Totals		**70**	**32**	**33**	**5**	

RUEL, Claude
B. Sherbrooke, Ont., Sept. 12, 1938

68–69	Mont	76	46	19	11	WSC
69–70	Mont	76	38	22	16	
70–71	Mont	23	11	8	4	
79–80	Mont	50	32	11	7	LSR
80–81	Mont	80	45	22	13	LFR
Totals		**305**	**172**	**82**	**51**	
Playoff Totals		**27**	**15**	**12**	**0**	

RUFF, Lindy
B. Warburg, Alta., Feb. 17, 1960

97–98	Buf	82	36	29	17	LSF
98–99	Buf	82	37	28	17	LCF
Totals		**164**	**73**	**57**	**34**	
Playoff Totals		**36**	**24**	**12**	**0**	

RYAN, Ron
B. Welland, Ont., July 11, 1938

73–74	NE (WHA)	78	43	31	4	LFR
74–75	NE (WHA)	73	40	28	5	
Totals		**151**	**83**	**59**	**9**	

*SATHER, Glen
B. High River, Alta., Sept. 2, 1943

76–77	Edm (WHA)	18	9	7	2	LFR
77–78	Edm (WHA)	80	38	39	3	LFR
78–79	Edm (WHA)	80	48	30	2	LLF
79–80	Edm	80	28	39	13	LFR
80–81	Edm	62	25	26	11	LQF
81–82	Edm	80	48	17	15	LFR
82–83	Edm	80	47	21	12	LCF
83–84	Edm	80	57	18	5	WSC
84–85	Edm	80	49	20	11	WSC
85–86	Edm	80	56	17	7	LSR
86–87	Edm	80	50	24	6	WSC
87–88	Edm	80	44	25	11	WSC
88–89	Edm	80	38	34	8	LFR
93–94	Edm	60	22	27	11	
NHL Totals		**842**	**464**	**268**	**110**	
Playoff Totals		**126**	**89**	**37**	**0**	

SEASON	TEAM	GC	W	L	T	PLY.
WHA Totals		**178**	**95**	**76**	**7**	

SATOR, Ted
B. Utica, N.Y., Nov. 18, 1949

SEASON	TEAM	GC	W	L	T	PLY.
85–86	NYR	80	36	38	6	LSF
86–87	NYR	19	5	10	4	
	Buf	47	21	22	4	
87–88	Buf	80	37	32	11	LFR
88–89	Buf	80	38	35	7	LFR
Totals		**306**	**137**	**137**	**32**	
Playoff Totals		**27**	**11**	**16**	**0**	

SAVARD, Andre
B. Temiscamingue, Que., Feb. 9, 1953

SEASON	TEAM	GC	W	L	T	PLY.
87–88	Que	24	10	13	1	

SCHINKEL, Ken
B. Jansen, Sask., Nov. 27, 1932

SEASON	TEAM	GC	W	L	T	PLY.
72–73	Pitt	36	15	18	3	
73–74	Pitt	50	14	31	5	
75–76	Pitt	37	20	10	7	LFR
76–77	Pitt	80	34	33	13	LFR
Totals		**203**	**83**	**92**	**28**	
Playoff Totals		**6**	**2**	**4**	**0**	

*SCHMIDT, Milt
B. Kitchener, Ont., Mar. 5, 1918

SEASON	TEAM	GC	W	L	T	PLY.
54–55	Bos	40	13	12	15	LFR
55–56	Bos	70	23	34	13	
56–57	Bos	70	34	24	12	LCF
57–58	Bos	70	27	28	15	LCF
58–59	Bos	70	32	29	9	LFR
59–60	Bos	70	28	34	8	
60–61	Bos	70	15	42	13	
62–63	Bos	56	13	31	12	
63–64	Bos	70	18	40	12	
64–65	Bos	70	21	43	6	
65–66	Bos	70	21	43	6	
74–75	Wash	7	2	5	0	
75–76	Wash	36	3	28	5	
Totals		**769**	**250**	**393**	**126**	
Playoff Totals		**34**	**15**	**19**	**0**	

SCHOENFELD, Jim
B. Galt, Ont., Sept. 4, 1952

SEASON	TEAM	GC	W	L	T	PLY.
85–86	Buf	43	19	19	5	
87–88	NJ	30	17	12	1	LSF
88–89	NJ	80	27	41	12	
89–90	NJ	14	6	6	2	
93–94	Wash	37	19	12	6	LSR
94–95	Wash	48	22	18	8	LFR
95–96	Wash	82	39	32	11	LFR
96–97	Wash	82	33	40	9	
97–98	Phoe	82	35	35	12	
98–99	Phoe	82	39	31	12	LFR
Totals		**580**	**256**	**246**	**78**	
Playoff Totals		**57**	**26**	**31**	**0**	

SHAUGHNESSY, Tom

SEASON	TEAM	GC	W	L	T	PLY.
29–30	Chi	21	10	8	3	

SHAW, Brian

SEASON	TEAM	GC	W	L	T	PLY.
73–74	Edm (WHA)	78	38	37	3	LFR
74–75	Edm (WHA)	59	30	26	3	
Totals		**137**	**68**	**63**	**6**	

SHERO, Fred
B. Winnipeg, Man., Oct. 23, 1925

SEASON	TEAM	GC	W	L	T	PLY.
71–72	Phil	78	26	38	14	
72–73	Phil	78	37	30	11	LSF
73–74	Phil	78	50	16	12	WSC
74–75	Phil	80	51	18	11	WSC
75–76	Phil	80	51	13	16	LCF
76–77	Phil	80	48	16	16	LSF
77–78	Phil	80	45	20	15	LSF
78–79	NYR	80	40	29	11	LCF
79–80	NYR	80	38	32	10	LQF
80–81	NYR	21	4	13	4	
Totals		**735**	**390**	**225**	**120**	
Playoff Totals		**108**	**61**	**47**	**0**	

*SIMPSON, Joe
B. Selkirk, Man., Aug. 18, 1893

SEASON	TEAM	GC	W	L	T	PLY.
32–33	NYA	48	15	22	11	
33–34	NYA	48	15	23	10	
34–35	NYA	48	12	27	9	
Totals		**144**	**42**	**72**	**30**	

SIMPSON, Terry
B. Brantford, Ont., Aug. 30, 1943

SEASON	TEAM	GC	W	L	T	PLY.
86–87	NYI	80	35	33	12	LSR
87–88	NYI	80	39	31	10	LFR
88–89	NYI	27	7	18	2	
93–94	Phil	84	35	39	10	
94–95	Winn	15	7	7	1	
95–96	Winn	82	36	40	6	LFR
Totals		**358**	**159**	**168**	**41**	
Playoff Totals		**26**	**11**	**15**	**0**	

SIMS, Al
B. Toronto, Ont., Apr. 18, 1953

SEASON	TEAM	GC	W	L	T	PLY.
96–97	SJ	82	27	47	8	

SINDEN, Harry
B. Collins Bay, Ont., Sept. 14, 1932

SEASON	TEAM	GC	W	L	T	PLY.
66–67	Bos	70	17	43	10	
67–68	Bos	74	37	27	10	LFR
68–69	Bos	76	42	18	16	LSF
69–70	Bos	76	40	17	19	WSC
79–80	Bos	7	6	1	0	LQF
84–85	Bos	27	9	15	3	
Totals		**330**	**151**	**121**	**58**	
Playoff Totals		**43**	**24**	**19**	**0**	

SKINNER, Jimmy
B. Selkirk, Mass., Jan. 12, 1917

SEASON	TEAM	GC	W	L	T	PLY.
54–55	Det	70	42	17	11	WSC
55–56	Det	70	30	24	16	LCF
56–57	Det	70	38	20	12	LFR
57–58	Det	37	13	17	7	
Totals		**247**	**123**	**78**	**46**	
Playoff Totals		**26**	**14**	**12**	**0**	

SLATER, Terry
B. Kirkland Lake, Ont., Dec. 5, 1937

SEASON	TEAM	GC	W	L	T	PLY.
72–73	LA (WHA)	78	37	35	6	LFR
73–74	LA (WHA)	19	5	14	0	
75–76	Cin (WHA)	80	35	44	1	
76–77	Cin (WHA)	81	39	37	5	LFR
Totals		**258**	**116**	**130**	**12**	

*SMEATON, Cooper
B. Carlton Place, Ont., July 22, 1890

SEASON	TEAM	GC	W	L	T	PLY.
30–31	Phil	44	4	36	4	

SMITH, Alf

SEASON	TEAM	GC	W	L	T	PLY.
18–19	Ott	18	12	6	0	LSF

SMITH, Floyd
B. Perth, Ont., May 16, 1935

SEASON	TEAM	GC	W	L	T	PLY.
71–72	Buf	1	0	1	0	
74–75	Buf	80	49	16	15	LCF
75–76	Buf	80	46	21	13	LQF
76–77	Buf	80	48	24	8	LQF
78–79	Cin (WHA)	80	33	41	6	LFR
79–80	Tor	68	30	33	5	
NHL Totals		**309**	**173**	**95**	**41**	
Playoff Totals		**32**	**16**	**16**	**0**	
WHA Totals		**80**	**33**	**41**	**6**	

SMITH, Mike

SEASON	TEAM	GC	W	L	T	PLY.
80–81	Winn	23	2	17	4	

SMITH, Ron

SEASON	TEAM	GC	W	L	T	PLY.
92–93	NYR	44	15	22	7	

*SMYTHE, Conn
B. Toronto, Ont., Feb. 1, 1895

SEASON	TEAM	GC	W	L	T	PLY.
26–27	Tor	44	15	24	5	
27–28	Tor	44	18	18	8	
28–29	Tor	44	21	18	5	LSF
29–30	Tor	44	17	21	6	
30–31	Tor	2	1	0	1	
Totals		**178**	**72**	**81**	**25**	
Playoff Totals		**4**	**2**	**2**	**0**	

SONMOR, Glen
B. Moose Jaw, Sask., Apr. 22, 1929

SEASON	TEAM	GC	W	L	T	PLY.
72–73	Minn (WHA)	79	39	37	3	LFR
76–77	Minn (WHA)	42	19	18	5	
77–78	Birm (WHA)	80	36	41	3	LFR
78–79	Minn	69	25	34	10	
79–80	Minn	80	36	28	16	LSF
80–81	Minn	80	35	28	17	LCF
81–82	Minn	80	37	23	20	LFR
82–83	Minn	44	22	13	9	
NHL Totals		**353**	**155**	**126**	**72**	
Playoff Totals		**44**	**23**	**21**	**0**	
WHA Totals		**201**	**94**	**96**	**11**	

SPROULE, Harry

SEASON	TEAM	GC	W	L	T	PLY.
19–20	Tor	12	7	5	0	

STANLEY, Barney
B. Paisley, Ont., Jan. 1 1893

SEASON	TEAM	GC	W	L	T	PLY.
27–28	Chi	23	4	17	2	

STAPLETON, Pat
B. Sarnia, Ont., July 4, 1940

SEASON	TEAM	GC	W	L	T	PLY.
73–74	Chi (WHA)	78	38	35	5	LF
74–75	Chi (WHA)	78	30	47	1	
78–79	Ind (WHA)	25	5	18	2	
Totals		**181**	**73**	**100**	**8**	

STASIUK, Vic
B. Lethbridge, Alta., May 23, 1929

SEASON	TEAM	GC	W	L	T	PLY.
69–70	Phil	76	17	35	24	
70–71	Phil	78	28	33	17	LFR
71–72	Cal	75	21	38	16	
72–73	Van	78	22	47	9	
Totals		**307**	**88**	**153**	**66**	
Playoff Totals		**4**	**0**	**4**	**0**	

STEWART, Bill

SEASON	TEAM	GC	W	L	T	PLY.
37–38	Chi	48	14	25	9	WSC
38–39	Chi	21	8	10	3	
Totals		**69**	**22**	**35**	**12**	
Playoff Totals		**7**	**5**	**2**	**0**	

STEWART, Bill
B. Toronto, Ont., Oct. 6, 1957

SEASON	TEAM	GC	W	L	T	PLY.
98–99	NYI	37	11	19	7	

STEWART, Ron
B. Calgary, Alta., July 11, 1932

SEASON	TEAM	GC	W	L	T	PLY.
75–76	NYR	39	15	20	4	
77–78	LA	80	31	34	15	LFR
Totals		**119**	**46**	**54**	**19**	
Playoff Totals		**2**	**0**	**2**	**0**	

SULLIVAN, Red
B. Peterborough, Ont., Dec. 24, 1929

SEASON	TEAM	GC	W	L	T	PLY.
62–63	NYR	36	11	17	8	
63–64	NYR	70	22	38	10	
64–65	NYR	70	20	38	12	
65–66	NYR	20	5	10	5	
67–68	Pitt	74	27	34	13	
68–69	Pitt	76	20	45	11	
74–75	Wash	19	2	17	0	
Totals		**365**	**107**	**199**	**59**	

SUTHERLAND, Bill
B. Regina, Sask., Nov. 10, 1934

SEASON	TEAM	GC	W	L	T	PLY.
80–81	Winn	32	7	22	3	

SUTTER, Brian
B. Viking, Alta., Oct. 7, 1956

SEASON	TEAM	GC	W	L	T	PLY.
88–89	StL	80	33	35	12	LSR
89–90	StL	80	37	34	9	LSR
90–91	StL	80	47	22	11	LSR
91–92	StL	80	36	33	11	LFR
92–93	Bos	84	51	26	7	LFR
93–94	Bos	84	42	29	13	LSR
94–95	Bos	48	27	18	3	LFR
97–98	Calg	82	26	41	15	
98–99	Calg	82	30	40	12	
Totals		**700**	**329**	**278**	**93**	
Playoff Totals		**63**	**27**	**36**	**0**	

SUTTER, Darryl
B. Viking, Alta., Aug. 19, 1958

Season	Team	GC	W	L	T	PLY.
92–93	Chi	84	47	25	12	LFR
93–94	Chi	84	39	36	9	LFR
94–95	Chi	48	24	19	5	LSF
97–98	SJ	82	34	38	10	LFR
98–99	SJ	82	31	33	18	LFR
Totals		**380**	**175**	**151**	**54**	
Playoff Totals		**38**	**15**	**23**	**0**	

TALBOT, Jean–Guy
B. Cap Madelaine, Que., July 11, 1942

Season	Team	GC	W	L	T	PLY.
72–73	StL	65	30	28	7	LFR
73–74	StL	55	22	25	8	
75–76	Ott (WHA)	41	14	26	1	
77–78	NYR	80	30	37	13	LFR
NHL Totals		**200**	**82**	**90**	**28**	
Playoff Totals		**8**	**2**	**6**	**0**	
WHA Totals		**41**	**14**	**26**	**1**	

TESSIER, Orval
B. Cornwall, Ont., June 30, 1933

Season	Team	GC	W	L	T	PLY.
82–83	Chi	80	47	23	10	LSF
83–84	Chi	80	30	42	8	LFR
84–85	Chi	53	22	28	3	
Totals		**213**	**99**	**93**	**21**	
Playoff Totals		**18**	**9**	**9**	**0**	

THOMPSON, Paul
B. Calgary, Alta., Nov. 2, 1906

Season	Team	GC	W	L	T	PLY.
38–39	Chi	27	4	18	5	
39–40	Chi	48	23	19	6	LFR
40–41	Chi	48	16	25	7	LSF
41–42	Chi	48	22	23	3	LFR
42–43	Chi	50	17	18	15	
43–44	Chi	50	22	23	5	LCF
44–45	Chi	1	0	1	0	
Totals		**272**	**104**	**127**	**41**	
Playoff Totals		**19**	**7**	**12**	**0**	

THOMPSON, Percy
Season	Team	GC	W	L	T	PLY.
20–21	Ham	24	7	17	0	
21–22	Ham	24	7	17	0	
Totals		**48**	**14**	**34**	**0**	

TOBIN, Bill
Season	Team	GC	W	L	T	PLY.
29–30	Chi	23	11	10	2	LFR
Playoff Totals		**2**	**0**	**1**	**1**	

TREMBLAY, Mario
B. Alma, Que., Sept. 2, 1956

Season	Team	GC	W	L	T	PLY.
95–96	Mont	77	40	27	10	LFR
96–97	Mont	82	31	36	15	LFR
Totals		**159**	**71**	**63**	**25**	
Playoff Totals		**11**	**3**	**8**	**0**	

TROTZ, Barry
B. Winnipeg, Man., July 15, 1962

Season	Team	GC	W	L	T	PLY.
98–99	Nash	82	28	47	7	

UBRIACO, Gene
B. Sault Ste. Marie, Ont., Dec. 26, 1937

Season	Team	GC	W	L	T	PLY.
88–89	Pitt	80	40	33	7	LSR
89–90	Pitt	26	10	14	2	
Totals		**106**	**50**	**47**	**9**	
Playoff Totals		**11**	**7**	**4**	**0**	

VACHON, Rogie
B. Palmorelle, Que., Sept. 8, 1945

Season	Team	GC	W	L	T	PLY.
83–84	LA	2	1	0	1	
87–88	LA	1	0	1	0	
94–95	LA	7	3	2	2	
Totals		**10**	**4**	**3**	**3**	

VIGNEAULT, Alain
B. Quebec City, Que., May 14, 1961

Season	Team	GC	W	L	T	PLY.
97–98	Mont	82	37	32	13	LSR
98–99	Mont	82	32	39	11	
Totals		**164**	**69**	**71**	**24**	
Playoff Totals		**10**	**4**	**6**	**0**	

VIVIAN, Jack
B. Strathroy, Ont., May 14, 1941

Season	Team	GC	W	L	T	PLY.
74–75	Clev	45	21	22	2	LFR

WATSON, Bryan
B. Bancroft, Ont., Nov. 14, 1942

Season	Team	GC	W	L	T	PLY.
80–81	Edm	18	4	9	5	

WATSON, Phil
B. Montreal, Que., Apr. 24, 1914

Season	Team	GC	W	L	T	PLY.
55–56	NYR	70	32	28	10	LFR
56–57	NYR	70	26	30	14	LFR
57–58	NYR	70	32	25	13	LFR
58–59	NYR	70	26	32	12	
59–60	NYR	15	3	9	3	
61–62	Bos	70	15	47	8	
62–63	Bos	14	1	8	5	
72–73	Phil (WHA)	71	37	34	0	LFR
73–74	Van (WHA)	12	3	9	0	
NHL Totals		**379**	**135**	**179**	**65**	
Playoff Totals		**16**	**4**	**12**	**0**	
WHA Totals		**83**	**40**	**43**	**0**	

WATT, Tom
B. Toronto, Ont., June 17, 1935

Season	Team	GC	W	L	T	PLY.
81–82	Winn	80	33	33	14	LFR
82–83	Winn	80	33	39	8	LFR
83–84	Winn	21	6	13	2	
85–86	Van	80	23	44	13	LFR
86–87	Van	80	29	43	8	
90–91	Tor	69	22	37	10	
91–92	Tor	80	30	43	7	
Totals		**490**	**176**	**252**	**62**	
Playoff Totals		**10**	**1**	**9**	**0**	

WEBSTER, Tom
B. Kirkland Lake, Ont., Oct. 4, 1948

Season	Team	GC	W	L	T	PLY.
86–87	NYR	16	5	7	4	
89–90	LA	80	34	39	7	LSR

Season	Team	GC	W	L	T	PLY.
90–91	LA	80	46	24	10	LSR
91–92	LA	80	35	31	14	LFR
Totals		**256**	**120**	**101**	**35**	
Playoff Totals		**28**	**12**	**16**	**0**	

*WELLAND, Cooney
B. Seaforth, Ont., Nov. 5, 1904

Season	Team	GC	W	L	T	PLY.
39–40	Bos	48	31	12	5	LFR
40–41	Bos	48	27	8	13	WSC
Totals		**96**	**58**	**20.**	**18**	
Playoff Totals		**17**	**10**	**7**	**0**	

WHITE, Bill
B. Toronto, Ont., Aug. 26, 1939

Season	Team	GC	W	L	T	PLY.
76–77	Chi	46	16	24	6	LFR
Playoff Totals		**2**	**0**	**2**	**0**	

WILEY, Jim
B. Sault Ste. Marie, Ont., Apr. 28, 1950

Season	Team	GC	W	L	T	PLY.
95–96	SJ	57	17	37	3	

WILSON, Johnny
B. Kincardine, Ont., June 14, 1929

Season	Team	GC	W	L	T	PLY.
69–70	LA	52	9	34	9	
71–72	Det	67	30	27	10	
72–73	Det	78	37	29	12	
74–75	Balt (WHA)	78	21	53	4	
75–76	Clev (WHA)	80	35	40	5	LFR
76–77	Col	80	20	46	14	
77–78	Pitt	80	25	37	18	
78–79	Pitt	80	36	31	13	LQF
79–80	Pitt	80	30	37	13	LFR
NHL Totals		**517**	**178**	**241**	**89**	
Playoff Totals		**12**	**4**	**8**	**0**	
WHA Totals		**158**	**56**	**93**	**9**	

WILSON, Larry
B. Kincardine, Ont., Oct. 23, 1930

Season	Team	GC	W	L	T	PLY.
76–77	Det	36	3	29	4	

WILSON, Ron
B. Windsor, Ont., May 28, 1955

Season	Team	GC	W	L	T	PLY.
93–94	Ana	84	33	46	5	
94–95	Ana	48	16	27	5	
95–96	Ana	82	35	39	8	
96–97	Ana	82	36	33	13	LSR
97–98	Wash	82	40	30	12	
98–99	Wash	82	31	45	6	
Totals		**460**	**191**	**220**	**49**	
Playoff Totals		**32**	**16**	**16**	**0**	

YOUNG, Gary
B. Toronto, Ont., Jan. 2, 1936

Season	Team	GC	W	L	T	PLY.
72–73	Cal	12	2	7	3	
74–75	StL	69	32	26	11	LFR
75–76	StL	29	9	15	5	
Totals		**110**	**43**	**48**	**19**	
Playoff Totals		**2**	**0**	**2**	**0**	

25

ALL-TIME NHL PLAYER REGISTER

The following sections (the first covering forwards and defensemen; the second, goalies) include the record of every player who has ever appeared in an NHL game. In addition, NHL players who performed in the World Hockey Association also have their WHA records listed.

Where information is missing, it was unavailable.

The following are the abbreviations used for the various teams, Canadian provinces and column headings:

*Indicates deceased

Alb (WHA)	Alberta Oilers
Ana	Mighty Ducks of Anaheim
Atl	Atlanta Flames
Balt (WHA)	Baltimore Blades
Birm (WHA)	Birmingham Bulls
Bos	Boston Bruins
Brk	Brooklyn Americans
Buf	Buffalo Sabres
Cal	California Golden Seals
Calg	Calgary Flames
Calg (WHA)	Calgary Cowboys
Chi	Chicago Blackhawks
Chi (WHA)	Chicago Cougars
Cin (WHA)	Cincinnati Stingers
Clev	Cleveland Barons
Clev (WHA)	Cleveland Crusaders
Col	Colorado Rockies
Col A	Colorado Avalanche
Dal	Dallas Stars
Den (WHA)	Denver Spurs
Det	Detroit Cougars, Falcons, Red Wings

Edm or Edm (WHA)	Edmonton Oilers
Fla	Florida Panthers
Ham	Hamilton Tigers
Hart or Hart (WHA)	Hartford Whalers
Hou (WHA)	Houston Aeros
Ind (WHA)	Indianapolis Racers
KC	Kansas City Scouts
LA	Los Angeles Kings
LA (WHA)	Los Angeles Sharks
Mich (WHA)	Michigan Stags
Minn	Minnesota North Stars
Minn (WHA)	Minnesota Fighting Saints
Mont	Montreal Canadiens
Mont M	Montreal Maroons
Mont W	Montreal Wanderers
Nash	Nashville Predators
NE (WHA)	New England Whalers
NJ	New Jersey Devils
NJ (WHA)	New Jersey Knights
NYA	New York Americans
NYI	New York Islanders
NYR	New York Rangers
NY (WHA)	New York Golden Blades, Raiders
Oak	Oakland Seals
Ott	Ottawa Senators
Ott (WHA)	Ottawa Nationals
Phil	Philadelphia Flyers
Phil Q	Philadelphia Quakers
Phil (WHA)	Philadelphia Blazers
Phoe	Phoenix Coyotes
Phoe (WHA)	Phoenix Roadrunners
Pitt	Pittsburgh Penguins
Pitt Pi	Pittsburgh Pirates
Que	Quebec Bulldogs, Nordiques
Que (WHA)	Quebec Nordiques
SD (WHA)	San Diego Mariners
SJ	San Jose Sharks

StL	St. Louis Blues
StL E	St. Louis Eagles
TB	Tampa Bay Lightning
Tor	Toronto Arenas, Maple Leafs, St. Pats
Tor (WHA)	Toronto Toros
Van	Vancouver Canucks
Van (WHA)	Vancouver Blazers
Wash	Washington Capitals
Winn or Winn (WHA)	Winnipeg Jets

CANADIAN PROVINCES

Alta.	Alberta
B.C.	British Columbia
Man.	Manitoba
N.B.	New Brunswick
Nfld.	Newfoundland
N.S.	Nova Scotia
Ont.	Ontario
P.E.I.	Prince Edward Island
Que.	Quebec
Sask.	Saskatchewan
Yuk.	The Yukon
N.W.T.	Northwest Territories

COLUMN HEADINGS

A	Assists
Avg.	Average
G	Goals
GA	Goals against
GP	Games played
Min.	Minutes played
NHL	National Hockey League
PIM	Penalties in minutes
Pts.	Points
SO	Shutouts
SSN	Season
WHA	World Hockey Association
+/-	Plus/Minus

FORWARDS and DEFENSEMEN

SSN	TEAM	GP	G	A	PTS.	PIM	+/-

AALTO, Antti *6–2 190 C*
B. Lappentanta, Finland, Mar. 4, 1975

SSN	TEAM	GP	G	A	PTS.	PIM	+/-
97–98	Ana	3	0	0	0	0	-1
98–99	Ana	73	3	5	8	24	-12
Totals		76	3	5	8	24	-13

Playoffs

| 98–99 | Ana | 4 | 0 | 0 | 0 | 2 | |

ABBOTT, Reginald *5–10 155 C*
B. Winnipeg, Man., Feb. 4, 1930

| 52–53 | Mont | 3 | 0 | 0 | 0 | 0 | |

***ABEL, Clarence John (Taffy)** 6–1 225 D*
B. Sault Ste. Marie, Mich., May 28, 1900

26–27	NYR	44	8	4	12	78	
27–28	NYR	22	0	1	1	28	
28–29	NYR	33	2	1	3	41	
29–30	Chi	38	3	3	6	42	
30–31	Chi	43	0	1	1	45	
31–32	Chi	48	3	3	6	34	
32–33	Chi	47	0	4	4	63	
33–34	Chi	46	2	1	3	28	
Totals		321	18	18	36	359	

Playoffs

26–27	NYR	2	0	1	1	8	
27–28	NYR	9	1	0	1	14	
28–29	NYR	6	0	0	0	8	
29–30	Chi	2	0	0	0	10	
30–31	Chi	9	0	0	0	8	
31–32	Chi	2	0	0	0	2	
33–34	Chi	8	0	0	0	8	
Totals		38	1	1	2	58	

ABEL, Gerald Scott *6–2 168 LW*
B. Detroit, Mich., Dec. 25, 1944

| 66–67 | Det | 1 | 0 | 0 | 0 | 0 | |

ABEL, Sidney Gerald *5–11 190 C*
B. Melville, Sask., Feb. 22, 1918

38–39	Det	15	1	1	2	0	
39–40	Det	24	1	5	6	4	
40–41	Det	47	11	22	33	29	
41–42	Det	48	18	31	49	45	
42–43	Det	49	18	24	42	33	
45–46	Det	7	0	2	2	0	
46–47	Det	60	19	29	48	29	
47–48	Det	60	14	30	44	69	
48–49	Det	60	28	26	54	49	
49–50	Det	70	34	35	69	46	
50–51	Det	69	23	38	61	30	
51–52	Det	62	17	36	53	32	
52–53	Chi	39	5	4	9	6	
53–54	Chi	3	0	0	0	4	
Totals		613	189	283	472	376	

Playoffs

38–39	Det	3	1	1	2	2	
39–40	Det	5	0	3	3	21	
40–41	Det	9	2	2	4	2	
41–42	Det	12	4	2	6	6	
42–43	Det	10	5	8	13	4	
45–46	Det	3	0	0	0	0	
46–47	Det	5	1	1	2	2	
47–48	Det	10	0	3	3	16	
48–49	Det	11	3	3	6	6	
49–50	Det	14	6	2	8	6	
50–51	Det	6	4	3	7	0	
51–52	Det	7	2	2	4	12	
52–53	Chi	1	0	0	0	0	
Totals		96	28	30	58	77	

ABGRALL, Dennis Harvey *6–1 180 RW*
B. Mooseomin, Sask., Apr. 24, 1953

75–76	LA	13	0	2	2	4	
76–77	Cin (WHA)	80	23	39	62	22	
77–78	Cin (WHA)	65	13	11	24	13	
NHL Totals		13	0	2	2	4	
WHA Totals		145	36	50	86	35	

Playoffs

SSN	TEAM	GP	G	A	PTS.	PIM	+/-
76–77	Cin (WHA)	4	2	0	2	5	

ABRAHAMSSON, Thommy *6–2 190 D*
B. Ulmea, Sweden, Apr. 12, 1947

74–75	NE (WHA)	76	8	22	30	46	
75–76	NE (WHA)	63	14	21	35	47	
76–77	NE (WHA)	64	6	24	30	33	
80–81	Hart	32	6	11	17	16	
NHL Totals		32	6	11	17	16	
WHA Totals		203	28	67	95	126	

Playoffs

75–76	NE (WHA)	17	2	4	6	15	
76–77	NE (WHA)	5	0	3	3	0	
Totals		22	2	7	9	15	

ACHTYMICHUK, Eugene Edward *5–11 170 C*
B. Lamont, Alta., Sept. 7, 1932

51–52	Mont	1	0	0	0	0	
56–57	Mont	3	0	0	0	0	
57–58	Mont	16	3	5	8	2	
58–59	Det	12	0	0	0	0	
Totals		32	3	5	8	2	

ACOMB, Douglas Raymond *5–10 165 C*
B. Toronto, Ont., May 15, 1949

| 69–70 | Tor | 2 | 0 | 1 | 1 | 0 | |

ACTON, Keith Edward *5–8 167 C*
B. Newmarket, Ont., Apr. 15, 1958

79–80	Mont	2	0	1	1	0	0
80–81	Mont	61	15	24	39	74	+48
81–82	Mont	78	36	52	88	88	-6
82–83	Mont	78	24	26	50	63	-5
83–84	Mont–Minn	71	20	45	65	64	+2
84–85	Minn	78	20	38	58	90	-3
85–86	Minn	79	26	32	58	100	-11
86–87	Minn	78	16	29	45	56	-15
87–88	Minn–Edm	72	11	17	28	95	-19
88–89	Edm–Phil	71	14	25	39	111	+10
89–90	Phil	69	13	14	27	80	-2
90–91	Phil	76	14	23	37	131	-9
91–92	Phil	50	7	10	17	98	-4
92–93	Phil	83	8	15	23	51	-10
93–94	Wash–NYI	77	2	7	9	71	-5
Totals		1023	226	358	584	1172	-19

Playoffs

80–81	Mont	2	0	0	0	6	
81–82	Mont	5	0	4	4	16	
82–83	Mont	3	0	0	0	0	
83–84	Minn	15	4	7	11	12	
84–85	Minn	9	4	4	8	6	
85–86	Minn	5	0	3	3	6	
87–88	Edm	7	2	0	2	16	
88–89	Phil	16	2	3	5	18	
93–94	NYI	4	0	0	0	8	
Totals		66	12	21	33	88	

ADAM, Douglas Patrick *5–10 165 LW*
B. Toronto, Ont., Sept. 7, 1923

| 49–50 | NYR | 4 | 0 | 1 | 1 | 0 | |

ADAM, Russell Norm *5–10 185 C*
B. Windsor, Ont., May 5, 1961

| 82–83 | Tor | 8 | 1 | 2 | 3 | 11 | -3 |

ADAMS, Greg *6–3 198 LW*
B. Nelson, B.C., Aug. 1, 1963

84–85	NJ	36	12	9	21	14	-14
85–86	NJ	78	35	42	77	30	-7
86–87	NJ	72	20	27	47	19	-16
87–88	Van	80	36	40	76	30	-24
88–89	Van	61	19	14	33	24	-8
89–90	Van	65	30	20	50	18	-5
90–91	Van	55	21	24	45	10	+8
91–92	Van	76	30	27	57	26	+21
92–93	Van	53	25	31	56	14	-1
93–94	Van	68	13	24	37	20	+1
94–95	Van–Dal	43	8	13	21	16	-4
95–96	Dal	66	22	21	43	33	-21
96–97	Dal	50	21	15	36	2	+7
97–98	Dal	49	14	18	32	20	+11
98–99	Phoe	75	19	24	43	26	-1
Totals		927	325	349	674	302	-33

Playoffs

SSN	TEAM	GP	G	A	PTS.	PIM	+/-
88–89	Van	7	2	3	5	2	
90–91	Van	5	0	0	0	2	
91–92	Van	6	0	2	2	4	
92–93	Van	12	7	6	13	6	
93–94	Van	23	6	8	14	2	
94–95	Dal	5	2	0	2	0	
96–97	Dal	3	0	1	1	0	
97–98	Dal	12	2	2	4	0	
98–99	Phoe	3	1	0	1	0	
Totals		76	20	22	42	16	

ADAMS, Gregory Charles *6–1 190 LW*
B. Duncan, B.C., May 31, 1960

80–81	Phil	6	3	0	3	8	0
81–82	Phil	33	4	15	19	105	+7
82–83	Hart	79	10	13	23	216	-46
83–84	Wash	57	2	6	8	133	+1
84–85	Wash	51	6	12	18	72	+8
85–86	Wash	78	18	38	56	152	+24
86–87	Wash	67	14	30	44	184	+9
87–88	Wash	78	15	12	27	153	-3
88–89	Edm–Van	61	8	7	15	117	+1
89–90	Que–Det	35	4	10	14	33	-2
Totals		545	84	143	227	1173	-1

Playoffs

83–84	Wash	1	0	0	0	0	
84–85	Wash	5	0	0	0	9	
85–86	Wash	9	1	3	4	27	
86–87	Wash	7	1	3	4	38	
87–88	Wash	14	0	5	5	58	
88–89	Van	7	0	0	0	21	
Totals		43	2	11	13	153	

ADAMS, John Ellis (Jack) *5–10 163 LW*
B. Calgary, Alta., May 5, 1920

| 40–41 | Mont | 42 | 6 | 12 | 18 | 11 | |

Playoffs

| 40–41 | Mont | 3 | 0 | 0 | 0 | 0 | |

***ADAMS, John James (Jack)** C*
B. Ft. William, Ont., June 14, 1895

17–18	Tor	8	0	0	0	15	
18–19	Tor	17	3	3	6	17	
22–23	Tor	23	19	9	28	42	
23–24	Tor	22	13	3	16	49	
24–25	Tor	27	21	8	29	66	
25–26	Tor	36	21	5	26	52	
26–27	Ott	40	5	1	6	66	
Totals		173	82	29	111	307	

Playoffs

17–18	Tor	2	2	0	2	3	
24–25	Tor	2	1	0	1	7	
26–27	Tor	6	0	0	0	2	
Totals		10	3	0	3	12	

ADAMS, Kevyn *6–1 162 C*
B. Washington, D.C., Oct. 8, 1974

97–98	Tor	5	0	0	0	7	0
98–99	Tor	1	0	0	0	0	0
Totals		6	0	0	0	7	0

Playoffs

| 98–99 | Tor | 7 | 0 | 2 | 2 | 14 | |

***ADAMS, Stewart** *LW*
B. 1904

29–30	Chi	24	4	6	10	16	
30–31	Chi	37	5	13	18	18	
31–32	Chi	26	0	5	5	26	
32–33	Tor	19	0	2	2	0	
Totals		106	9	26	35	60	

Playoffs

29–30	Chi	2	0	0	0	6	
30–31	Chi	9	3	3	6	8	
Totals		11	3	3	6	14	

ADDUONO, Rick *5–11 182 C*
B. Thunder Bay, Ont., Dec. 5, 1955

75–76	Bos	1	0	0	0	0	-1
78–79	Birm (WHA)	80	20	33	53	67	
79–80	Atl	3	0	0	0	2	-1

SSN	TEAM	GP	G	A	PTS.	PIM	+/-
NHL Totals		4	0	0	0	2	-2
WHA Totals		80	20	33	53	67	

AFFLECK, Robert (Bruce) *6–0 205 D*
B. Salmon Arm, B.C., May 5, 1954

SSN	TEAM	GP	G	A	PTS.	PIM	+/-
74–75	StL	13	0	2	2	4	+7
75–76	StL	80	4	26	30	20	+3
76–77	StL	80	5	20	25	24	-22
77–78	StL	75	4	14	18	26	-56
78–79	StL	26	1	3	4	12	-11
79–80	Van	5	0	1	1	0	0
83–84	NYI	1	0	0	0	0	-1
Totals		280	14	66	80	86	-81

Playoffs

SSN	TEAM	GP	G	A	PTS.	PIM
74–75	StL	1	0	0	0	0
75–76	StL	3	0	0	0	0
76–77	StL	4	0	0	0	0
Totals		8	0	0	0	0

AGNEW, Jim *6–1 190 D*
B. Hartney, Man., Mar. 21, 1966

SSN	TEAM	GP	G	A	PTS.	PIM	+/-
86–87	Van	4	0	0	0	0	0
87–88	Van	10	0	1	1	16	+1
89–90	Van	7	0	0	0	36	-1
90–91	Van	20	0	0	0	81	-11
91–92	Van	24	0	0	0	56	-1
92–93	Hart	16	0	0	0	68	+3
Totals		81	0	1	1	257	-9

Playoffs

SSN	TEAM	GP	G	A	PTS.	PIM
91–92	Van	4	0	0	0	6

AHERN, Frederick Vincent Jr. *6–0 180 RW*
B. Boston, Mass., Feb. 12, 1952

SSN	TEAM	GP	G	A	PTS.	PIM	+/-
74–75	Cal	3	2	1	3	0	-1
75–76	Cal	44	17	8	25	43	-2
76–77	Clev	25	4	4	8	20	-12
77–78	Clev–Col	74	8	17	25	67	-32
Totals		146	31	30	61	130	-47

Playoffs

SSN	TEAM	GP	G	A	PTS.	PIM
77–78	Col	2	0	1	1	2

AHLIN *F*

SSN	TEAM	GP	G	A	PTS.	PIM
37–38	Chi	1	0	0	0	0

AHOLA, Peter *6–3 205 D*
B. Espoo, Finland, May 14, 1968

SSN	TEAM	GP	G	A	PTS.	PIM	+/-
91–92	LA	71	7	12	19	101	+12
92–93	LA–Pitt–SJ	50	3	5	8	36	-10
93–94	Calg	2	0	0	0	0	0
Totals		123	10	17	27	137	+2

Playoffs

SSN	TEAM	GP	G	A	PTS.	PIM
91–92	LA	6	0	0	0	2

AHRENS, Chris Alfred *5–10 162 D*
B. San Bernardino, Calif., July 31, 1952

SSN	TEAM	GP	G	A	PTS.	PIM	+/-
73–74	Minn	3	0	1	1	0	+1
74–75	Minn	44	0	2	2	7	-27
75–76	Minn	2	0	0	0	2	-1
76–77	Minn	2	0	0	0	5	+1
77–78	Minn	1	0	0	0	0	0
77–78	Edm (WHA)	4	0	0	0	15	
NHL Totals		52	0	3	3	14	-26
WHA Totals		4	0	0	0	15	

Playoffs

SSN	TEAM	GP	G	A	PTS.	PIM
91–92	Minn	1	0	0	0	0

AILSBY, Lloyd Harold *5–11 194 D*
B. Lac Pelletier, Sask., May 11, 1917

SSN	TEAM	GP	G	A	PTS.	PIM
51–52	NYR	3	0	0	0	2

AITKEN, Brad *6–3 200 LW*
B. Scarborough, Ont., Oct. 30, 1967

SSN	TEAM	GP	G	A	PTS.	PIM	+/-
87–88	Pitt	5	1	1	2	0	+1
90–91	Pitt–Edm	9	0	2	2	25	-3
Totals		14	1	3	4	25	-2

AIVAZOFF, Micah *6–0 195 C*
B. Powell River, B.C., May 4, 1969

SSN	TEAM	GP	G	A	PTS.	PIM	+/-
93–94	Det	59	4	4	8	38	-1
94–95	Edm	21	0	1	1	2	-2
95–96	NYI	12	0	1	1	6	-6

SSN	TEAM	GP	G	A	PTS.	PIM	+/-
Totals		92	4	6	10	46	-9

ALBELIN, Tommy *6–1 190 D*
B. Stockholm, Sweden, May 21, 1964

SSN	TEAM	GP	G	A	PTS.	PIM	+/-
87–88	Que	60	3	23	26	47	-7
88–89	Que–NJ	60	9	28	37	67	+12
89–90	NJ	68	6	23	29	63	-1
90–91	NJ	47	2	12	14	44	+1
91–92	NJ	19	0	4	4	4	+7
92–93	NJ	36	1	5	6	14	0
93–94	NJ	62	2	17	19	36	+20
94–95	NJ	48	5	10	15	20	+9
95–96	NJ–Calg	73	1	13	14	18	+1
96–97	Calg	72	4	11	15	14	-8
97–98	Calg	69	2	17	19	32	+9
98–99	Calg	60	1	5	6	8	-11
Totals		674	36	168	204	367	+32

Playoffs

SSN	TEAM	GP	G	A	PTS.	PIM
90–91	NJ	3	0	1	1	2
91–92	NJ	1	1	1	2	0
92–93	NJ	5	2	0	2	0
93–94	NJ	20	2	5	7	14
94–95	NJ	20	1	7	8	2
95–96	Calg	4	0	0	0	0
Totals		52	6	14	20	18

ALBRIGHT, Clinton Howard *6–2 180 C*
B. Winnipeg, Man., Feb. 28, 1926

SSN	TEAM	GP	G	A	PTS.	PIM
48–49	NYR	59	14	5	19	19

ALDCORN, Gary William *5–11 180 F*
B. Shaunavon, Sask., Mar. 7, 1935

SSN	TEAM	GP	G	A	PTS.	PIM
56–57	Tor	22	5	1	6	4
57–58	Tor	59	10	14	24	12
58–59	Tor	5	0	3	3	2
59–60	Det	70	22	29	51	32
60–61	Det–Bos	70	4	9	13	28
Totals		226	41	56	97	78

Playoffs

SSN	TEAM	GP	G	A	PTS.	PIM
59–60	Det	6	1	2	3	4

ALEXANDER, Claire Arthur *6–1 175 D*
B. Collingwood, Ont., June 16, 1945

SSN	TEAM	GP	G	A	PTS.	PIM
74–75	Tor	42	7	11	18	12
75–76	Tor	33	2	6	8	6
76–77	Tor	48	1	12	13	12
77–78	Van	32	8	18	26	6
78–79	Edm (WHA)	54	8	23	31	16
NHL Totals		155	18	47	65	36
WHA Totals		54	8	23	31	16

Playoffs

SSN	TEAM	GP	G	A	PTS.	PIM
74–75	Tor	7	0	0	0	0
75–76	Tor	9	2	4	6	4
Totals		16	2	4	6	4

*ALEXANDRE, Arthur *F*

SSN	TEAM	GP	G	A	PTS.	PIM
31–32	Mont	10	0	2	2	8
32–33	Mon	1	0	0	0	0
Totals		11	0	2	2	8

Playoffs

SSN	TEAM	GP	G	A	PTS.	PIM
31–32	Mont	4	0	0	0	0

ALFREDSSON, Daniel *5–11 187 C–RW*
B. Grums, Sweden, Dec. 11, 1972

SSN	TEAM	GP	G	A	PTS.	PIM	+/-
95–96	Ott	82	26	35	61	28	-18
96–97	Ott	76	24	47	71	30	+5
97–98	Ott	55	17	28	45	18	+7
98–99	Ott	58	11	22	33	14	+8
Totals		271	78	132	270	90	+2

Playoffs

SSN	TEAM	GP	G	A	PTS.	PIM
96–97	Ott	7	5	2	7	6
97–98	Ott	11	7	2	9	20
98–99	Ott	4	1	2	3	4
Totals		22	13	6	19	30

ALLAN, Jeffrey *D*
B. Hull, Que., May 17, 1957

SSN	TEAM	GP	G	A	PTS.	PIM
77–78	Cin (WHA)	2	0	0	0	0
77–78	Clev	4	0	0	0	2

SSN	TEAM	GP	G	A	PTS.	PIM	+/-

ALLEN, Chris *6–2 193 D*
B. Chatham, Ont., May 8, 1978

SSN	TEAM	GP	G	A	PTS.	PIM	+/-
97–98	Fla	1	0	0	0	2	0
98–99	Fla	1	0	0	0	0	+1
Totals		2	0	0	0	2	+1

ALLEN, Courtney Keith (Keith and Bingo) *5–11 190 D*
B. Saskatoon, Sask., Aug. 21, 1923

SSN	TEAM	GP	G	A	PTS.	PIM
53–54	Det	10	0	4	4	2
54–55	Det	18	0	0	0	6
Totals		28	0	4	4	8

Playoffs

SSN	TEAM	GP	G	A	PTS.	PIM
53–54	Det	5	0	0	0	0

ALLEN, George Trenholme *5–10 162 D*
B. Bayfield, N.B., July 27, 1914

SSN	TEAM	GP	G	A	PTS.	PIM
38–39	NYR	19	6	6	12	10
39–40	Chi	48	10	12	22	26
40–41	Chi	44	14	17	31	22
41–42	Chi	43	7	13	20	31
42–43	Chi	47	10	14	24	26
43–44	Chi	45	17	24	41	36
45–46	Chi	44	11	15	26	16
46–47	Mont	49	7	14	21	12
Totals		339	82	115	197	179

Playoffs

SSN	TEAM	GP	G	A	PTS.	PIM
38–39	NYR	7	0	0	0	4
39–40	Chi	2	0	0	0	0
40–41	Chi	5	2	2	4	10
41–42	Chi	3	1	1	2	0
43–44	Chi	9	5	4	9	8
45–46	Chi	4	0	0	0	4
46–47	Mont	11	1	3	4	6
Totals		41	9	10	19	32

ALLEN, Peter *6–2 185 D*
B. Calgary, Alta., Mar. 6, 1970

SSN	TEAM	GP	G	A	PTS.	PIM	+/-
95–96	Pitt	8	0	0	0	8	+2

ALLEN, Vivan Mariner (Squee) *5–6 140 RW*
B. Bayfield, N.B., Sept. 9, 1916

SSN	TEAM	GP	G	A	PTS.	PIM
40–41	NYA	6	0	1	1	0

ALLEY, Steve *6–0 185 LW*
B. Anoka, Minn., Dec. 29, 1953

SSN	TEAM	GP	G	A	PTS.	PIM	+/-
77–78	Birm (WHA)	27	8	12	20	11	
78–79	Birm (WHA)	78	17	24	41	36	
79–80	Hart	7	1	1	2	0	-4
80–81	Hart	8	2	2	4	11	+1
NHL Totals		15	3	3	6	11	-3
WHA Totals		105	25	36	61	47	

Playoffs

SSN	TEAM	GP	G	A	PTS.	PIM
77–78	Birm	5	1	0	1	5
79–80	Hart	3	0	1	1	0
NHL Totals		8	1	1	2	5
WHA Totals		5	1	0	1	5

ALLISON, David Bryan *6–1 200 D*
B. Fort Frances, Ont., Apr. 14, 1959

SSN	TEAM	GP	G	A	PTS.	PIM	+/-
83–84	Mont	3	0	0	0	12	-2

ALLISON, Jamie *6–1 190 D*
B. Lindsay, Ont., May 13, 1975

SSN	TEAM	GP	G	A	PTS.	PIM	+/-
94–95	Calg	1	0	0	0	0	0
96–97	Calg	20	0	0	0	35	-4
97–98	Calg	43	3	8	11	104	+3
98–99	Chi	39	2	2	4	62	0
Totals		103	5	10	15	201	-1

ALLISON, Jason *6–3 205 C*
B. North York, Ont., May 29, 1975

SSN	TEAM	GP	G	A	PTS.	PIM	+/-
93–94	Wash	2	0	1	1	0	+1
94–95	Wash	12	2	1	3	6	-3
95–96	Wash	19	0	3	3	2	-3
96–97	Wash–Bos	72	8	26	34	34	-6
97–98	Bos	81	33	50	83	60	+33
98–99	Bos	82	23	53	76	68	+5
Totals		268	66	134	200	170	+27

Playoffs

SSN	TEAM	GP	G	A	PTS.	PIM
97–98	Bos	6	2	6	8	4

SSN	TEAM	GP	G	A	PTS.	PIM	+/-
98–99	Bos	12	2	9	11	6	
Totals		18	4	15	19	10	

ALLISON, Michael Earnest 6–0 200 LW
B. Fort Frances, Ont., Mar. 28, 1961

SSN	TEAM	GP	G	A	PTS.	PIM	+/-
80–81	NYR	75	26	38	64	83	+12
81–82	NYR	48	7	15	22	74	-3
82–83	NYR	39	11	9	20	37	+8
83–84	NYR	45	8	12	20	64	+5
84–85	NYR	31	9	15	24	17	0
85–86	NYR	28	2	13	15	22	+4
86–87	Tor	71	7	16	23	66	+1
87–88	Tor–LA	52	16	15	31	67	+3
88–89	LA	55	14	22	36	122	+7
89–90	LA	55	2	11	13	78	-6
Totals		499	102	166	268	630	+31

Playoffs

80–81	NYR	14	3	1	4	20	
81–82	NYR	10	1	3	4	18	
82–83	NYR	8	0	5	5	10	
83–84	NYR	5	0	1	1	6	
85–86	NYR	16	0	2	2	38	
86–87	Tor	13	3	5	8	15	
87–88	LA	5	0	0	0	16	
88–89	LA	7	1	0	1	10	
89–90	LA	4	1	0	1	2	
Totals		82	9	17	26	135	

ALLISON, Raymond Peter 5–10 195 RW
B. Cranbrook, B.C., Mar. 4, 1959

79–80	Hart	64	16	12	28	13	-3
80–81	Hart	6	1	0	1	0	-1
81–82	Phil	51	17	37	54	104	+13
82–83	Phil	67	21	30	51	57	+30
83–84	Phil	37	8	13	21	47	+11
84–85	Phil	11	1	1	2	2	+3
86–87	Phil	2	0	0	0	0	-2
Totals		238	64	93	157	223	+51

Playoffs

79–80	Hart	2	0	1	1	0	
81–82	Phil	3	2	0	2	2	
82–83	Phil	3	0	1	1	12	
83–84	Phil	3	0	1	1	4	
84–85	Phil	1	0	0	0	2	
Totals		12	2	3	5	20	

ALLUM, William James Douglas 5–11 194 D
B. Winnipeg, Man., Oct. 9, 1916

40–41	NYR	1	0	1	1	0	

*AMADIO, David A. 6–1 205 D
B. Glace Bay, N.S., Apr. 23, 1939

57–58	Det	2	0	0	0	2	
67–68	LA	58	4	6	10	101	
68–69	LA	65	1	5	6	60	
Totals		125	5	11	16	163	

Playoffs

67–68	LA	7	0	2	2	8	
68–69	LA	9	1	0	1	10	
Totals		16	1	2	3	18	

AMBROZIAK, Peter 6–0 206 LW
B. Toronto, Ont., Sept. 15, 1971

94–95	Buf	12	0	1	1	0	+1

AMODEO, Michael 5–10 190 D
B. Toronto, Ont., June 22, 1952

72–73	Ott (WHA)	61	1	14	15	77	
73–74	Tor (WHA)	77	0	11	11	82	
74–75	Tor (WHA)	64	1	13	14	50	
75–76	Tor (WHA)	31	4	8	12	35	
77–78	Winn (WHA)	3	1	1	2	0	
78–79	Winn (WHA)	64	4	18	22	29	
79–80	Winn	19	0	0	0	2	
NHL Totals		19	0	0	0	2	
WHA Totals		300	11	65	76	273	

Playoffs

72–73	Ott (WHA)	5	0	1	1	10	
73–74	Tor (WHA)	12	0	2	2	26	
74–75	Tor (WHA)	3	0	1	1	4	
77–78	Winn (WHA)	7	1	3	4	19	
Totals		27	1	7	8	59	

AMONTE, Anthony (Tony) 6–0 190 RW
B. Hingham, Mass., Aug. 2, 1970

SSN	TEAM	GP	G	A	PTS.	PIM	+/-
91–92	NYR	79	35	34	69	55	+12
92–93	NYR	83	33	43	76	49	0
93–94	NYR–Chi	79	17	25	42	37	0
94–95	Chi	48	15	20	35	41	+7
95–96	Chi	81	31	32	63	62	+10
96–97	Chi	81	41	36	77	64	+35
97–98	Chi	82	31	42	73	66	+21
98–99	Chi	82	44	31	75	60	0
Totals		615	247	263	510	434	+85

Playoffs

90–91	NYR	2	0	2	2	2	
91–92	NYR	13	3	6	9	2	
93–94	Chi	6	4	2	6	4	
94–95	Chi	16	3	3	6	10	
95–96	Chi	7	2	4	6	6	
96–97	Chi	6	4	2	6	8	
Totals		50	16	19	35	32	

ANDERSON, Dale Norman 6–3 190 D
B. Regina, Sask., Mar. 5, 1932

56–57	Det	13	0	0	0	6	

Playoffs

56–57	Det	2	0	0	0	0	

ANDERSON, Douglas 5–7 157 C
B. Edmonton, Alta., Oct. 20, 1927

52–53	Mont	0	0	0	0	0	

Playoffs

		2	0	0	0	0	

ANDERSON, Earl Orlin 6–0 185 RW
B. Roseau, Minn., Feb. 24, 1951

74–75	Det–Bos	64	9	7	16	16	+6
75–76	Bos	5	0	1	1	2	-2
76–77	Bos	40	10	11	21	4	+4
Totals		109	19	19	38	22	+8

Playoffs

74–75	Bos	3	0	1	1	0	
76–77	Bos	2	0	0	0	0	
Totals		5	0	1	1	0	

ANDERSON, Glenn Chris 6–1 190 RW
B. Vancouver, B.C., Oct. 2, 1960

80–81	Edm	58	30	23	53	24	+4
81–82	Edm	80	38	67	105	71	+46
82–83	Edm	72	48	56	104	70	+41
83–84	Edm	80	54	45	99	65	+41
84–85	Edm	80	42	39	81	69	+24
85–86	Edm	72	54	48	102	90	+38
86–87	Edm	80	35	38	73	65	+27
87–88	Edm	80	38	50	88	58	+5
88–89	Edm	79	16	48	64	93	-16
89–90	Edm	73	34	38	72	107	-1
90–91	Edm	74	24	31	55	59	-7
91–92	Tor	72	24	33	57	100	-13
92–93	Tor	76	22	43	65	117	+19
93–94	Tor–NYR	85	21	20	41	62	-5
94–95	StL	36	12	14	26	37	+9
95–96	Edm–StL	32	6	8	14	33	-11
Totals		1129	498	601	1099	1120	+204

Playoffs

80–81	Edm	9	5	7	12	12	
81–82	Edm	5	2	5	7	8	
82–83	Edm	16	10	10	20	32	
83–84	Edm	19	6	11	17	33	
84–85	Edm	18	10	16	26	38	
85–86	Edm	10	8	3	11	14	
86–87	Edm	21	14	13	27	59	
87–88	Edm	19	9	16	25	49	
88–89	Edm	7	1	2	3	8	
89–90	Edm	22	10	12	22	20	
90–91	Edm	18	6	7	13	41	
92–93	Tor	21	7	11	18	31	
93–94	NYR	23	3	3	6	42	
94–95	StL	6	1	1	2	49	
95–96	StL	11	1	4	5	6	
Totals		225	93	121	214	442	

ANDERSON, James William 5–9 170 LW
B. Pembroke, Ont., Dec. 1, 1930

SSN	TEAM	GP	G	A	PTS.	PIM	+/-
67–68	LA	7	1	2	3	2	

Playoffs

68–69	LA	4	0	0	0	2	

ANDERSON, John Murray 5–11 190 RW
B. Toronto, Ont., Mar. 28, 1957

77–78	Tor	17	1	2	3	2	+1
78–79	Tor	71	15	11	26	10	+2
79–80	Tor	74	25	28	53	22	+5
80–81	Tor	75	17	26	43	31	-11
81–82	Tor	69	31	26	57	30	+8
82–83	Tor	80	31	49	80	24	-6
83–84	Tor	73	37	31	68	22	-12
84–85	Tor	75	32	31	63	27	-20
85–86	Que–Hart	79	29	45	74	28	+17
86–87	Hart	76	31	44	75	19	+11
87–88	Hart	63	17	32	49	20	-5
88–89	Hart	62	16	24	40	28	+15
Totals		814	282	349	631	263	+5

Playoffs

77–78	Tor	2	0	0	0	0	
78–79	Tor	6	0	2	2	0	
79–80	Tor	3	1	1	2	0	
80–81	Tor	2	0	0	0	0	
82–83	Tor	4	2	4	6	0	
85–86	Hart	10	5	8	13	0	
86–87	Hart	6	1	2	3	0	
88–89	Hart	4	0	1	1	2	
Totals		37	9	18	27	2	

ANDERSON, Murray Craig 5–10 175 D
B. Dauphin, Man., Aug. 28, 1949

74–75	Wash	40	0	1	1	68	-40

ANDERSON, Perry Lynn 6–0 195 LW
B. Barrie, Ont., Oct. 14, 1961

81–82	StL	5	1	2	3	0	+1
82–83	StL	18	5	2	7	14	-6
83–84	StL	50	7	5	12	195	-13
84–85	StL	71	9	9	18	146	+2
85–86	NJ	51	7	12	19	91	-7
86–87	NJ	57	10	9	19	107	-13
87–88	NJ	60	4	6	10	222	-8
88–89	NJ	39	3	6	9	128	+5
90–91	NJ	1	0	0	0	5	0
91–92	SJ	48	4	8	12	141	-17
Totals		400	56	59	109	1049	-56

Playoffs

81–82	StL	10	2	0	2	4	
83–84	StL	9	0	0	0	27	
84–85	StL	3	0	0	0	7	
87–88	NJ	10	0	0	0	113	
90–91	NJ	4	0	1	1	10	
Totals		36	2	1	3	161	

ANDERSON, Ronald Chester (Goings) 6–0 180 RW
B. Red Deer, Alta., July 29, 1945

67–68	Det	18	2	0	2	13	-4
68–69	Det–LA	63	3	5	8	34	-12
69–70	StL	59	9	9	18	36	+11
70–71	Buf	74	14	12	26	44	-11
71–72	Buf	37	0	4	4	19	-10
72–73	Alb (WHA)	73	14	15	29	43	
73–74	Edm (WHA)	19	5	2	7	6	
NHL Totals		251	28	30	58	146	-26
WHA Totals		92	19	17	36	49	

Playoffs

69–70	StL	5	0	0	0	4	

ANDERSON, Ronald Henry 5–10 165 RW
B. Moncton, N.B., Jan. 21, 1950

74–75	Wash	28	9	7	16	8	-20

ANDERSON, Russell Vincent 6–3 210 D
B. Des Moines, Iowa, Feb. 12, 1955

76–77	Pitt	66	2	11	13	81	+5
77–78	Pitt	74	2	16	18	150	-5
78–79	Pitt	72	3	13	16	93	+1
79–80	Pitt	76	5	22	27	150	+11
80–81	Pitt	34	3	14	17	112	+8

SSN	TEAM	GP	G	A	PTS.	PIM	+/-
81–82	Pitt–Hart	56	1	4	5	183	-17
82–83	Hart	57	0	6	6	171	-33
83–84	LA	70	5	12	17	126	-30
84–85	LA	14	1	1	2	20	-2
Totals		519	22	99	121	1086	-62

Playoffs

SSN	TEAM	GP	G	A	PTS.	PIM	
76–77	Pitt	3	0	1	1	14	
78–79	Pitt	2	0	0	0	0	
79–80	Pitt	5	0	2	2	14	
Totals		10	0	3	3	28	

ANDERSON, Shawn 6-1 200 D
B. Montreal, Que., Feb. 7, 1968

SSN	TEAM	GP	G	A	PTS.	PIM	+/-
86–87	Buf	41	2	11	13	23	0
87–88	Buf	23	1	2	3	17	-3
88–89	Buf	33	2	10	12	18	+3
89–90	Buf	16	1	3	4	8	+2
90–91	Que	31	3	10	13	21	+2
92–93	Wash	60	2	6	8	18	-2
93–94	Wash	50	0	9	9	12	-1
94–95	Phil	1	0	0	0	0	0
Totals		255	11	51	62	117	+1

Playoffs

SSN	TEAM	GP	G	A	PTS.	PIM	
88–89	Buf	5	0	1	1	4	
92–93	Wash	6	0	0	0	0	
93–94	Wash	8	1	0	1	12	
Totals		19	1	1	2	16	

*ANDERSON, Thomas Linton (Cowboy) 5-10 180 LW
B. Edinburgh, Scotland, July 9, 1911

SSN	TEAM	GP	G	A	PTS.	PIM	
34–35	Det	27	5	2	7	16	
35–36	NYA	24	3	2	5	20	
36–37	NYA	45	10	15	25	24	
37–38	NYA	45	4	21	25	22	
38–39	NYA	47	13	27	40	14	
39–40	NYA	48	12	19	31	22	
40–41	NYA	35	3	12	15	8	
41–42	NYA	48	12	29	41	64	
Totals		319	62	127	189	190	

Playoffs

SSN	TEAM	GP	G	A	PTS.	PIM	
35–36	NYA	5	0	0	0	60	
37–38	NYA	6	1	4	5	2	
38–39	NYA	2	0	0	0	0	
39–40	NYA	3	1	3	4	0	
Totals		16	2	7	9	62	

ANDERSON, William D
B. Tilsonberg, Ont., Dec. 13, 1912

SSN	TEAM	GP	G	A	PTS.	PIM	
42–43	Bos	0	0	0	0	0	

Playoffs

SSN	TEAM	GP	G	A	PTS.	PIM	
42–43	Bos	1	0	0	0	0	

ANDERSSON, Bo Mikael 5-11 185 LW
B. Malmo, Sweden, May 10, 1966

SSN	TEAM	GP	G	A	PTS.	PIM	+/-
85–86	Buf	32	1	9	10	4	0
86–87	Buf	16	0	3	3	0	-2
87–88	Buf	37	3	20	23	10	+7
88–89	Buf	14	0	1	1	4	-1
89–90	Hart	50	13	24	37	6	0
90–91	Hart	41	4	7	11	8	0
91–92	Hart	74	18	29	47	14	+18
92–93	TB	77	16	11	27	14	-14
93–94	TB	76	13	12	25	23	+8
94–95	TB	36	4	7	11	4	-3
95–96	TB	64	8	11	19	2	0
96–97	TB	70	5	14	19	8	+1
97–98	TB	72	6	11	17	29	-4
98–99	TB-Phil	47	2	4	6	4	-7
Totals		706	93	163	256	130	+3

Playoffs

SSN	TEAM	GP	G	A	PTS.	PIM	
87–88	Buf	1	1	0	1	0	
89–90	Hart	5	0	3	3	2	
91–92	Hart	7	0	2	2	6	
95–96	TB	6	1	1	2	0	
98–99	Phil	6	0	1	1	2	
Totals		25	2	7	9	10	

ANDERSSON, Kent-Erik 6-2 185 RW
B. Orebro, Sweden, May 24, 1951

SSN	TEAM	GP	G	A	PTS.	PIM	+/-
77–78	Minn	73	15	18	33	4	-17
78–79	Minn	41	9	4	13	4	-6
79–80	Minn	61	9	10	19	8	-3
80–81	Minn	77	17	24	41	22	+8
81–82	Minn	70	9	12	21	18	-5
82–83	NYR	71	8	20	28	14	+6
83–84	NYR	63	5	15	20	8	+5
Totals		456	72	103	175	78	-18

Playoffs

SSN	TEAM	GP	G	A	PTS.	PIM	
79–80	Minn	13	2	4	6	2	
80–81	Minn	19	2	4	6	2	
81–82	Minn	4	0	2	2	0	
82–83	NYR	9	0	0	0	0	
83–84	NYR	5	0	1	1	0	
Totals		50	4	11	15	4	

ANDERSSON, Niclas 5-9 175 LW
B. Kungalv, Sweden, May 20, 1971

SSN	TEAM	GP	G	A	PTS.	PIM	+/-
92–93	Que	3	0	1	1	2	0
95–96	NYI	48	14	12	26	12	-3
96–97	NYI	74	12	31	43	57	+4
97–98	SJ	5	0	0	0	2	-1
Totals		130	26	44	70	73	0

ANDERSSON, Peter 6-2 200 D
B. Ferdertaive, Sweden, Mar. 2, 1962

SSN	TEAM	GP	G	A	PTS.	PIM	+/-
83–84	Wash	42	3	7	10	20	+12
84–85	Wash	57	0	10	10	20	+5
85–86	Wash–Que	73	7	24	31	40	0
Totals		172	10	41	51	80	+17

Playoffs

SSN	TEAM	GP	G	A	PTS.	PIM	
83–84	Wash	3	0	1	1	2	
84–85	Wash	2	0	0	0	0	
85–86	Que	2	0	1	1	0	
Totals		7	0	2	2	2	

ANDERSSON, Peter 6-0 196 D
B. Orebro, Sweden, Aug. 29, 1965

SSN	TEAM	GP	G	A	PTS.	PIM	+/-
92–93	NYR	31	4	11	15	18	+4
93–94	NYR-Fla	16	2	2	4	2	-8
Totals		47	6	13	19	20	-4

ANDRASCIK, Steve George 5-11 200 RW
B. Sherridon, Man., Nov. 6, 1948

SSN	TEAM	GP	G	A	PTS.	PIM	
74–75	Ind (WHA)	77	6	11	17	58	
75–76	Cin (WHA)	20	3	2	5	21	
WHA Totals		97	9	13	22	79	

Playoffs

SSN	TEAM	GP	G	A	PTS.	PIM	
71–72	NYR	1	0	0	0	0	

ANDREA, Paul Lawrence 5-10 174 RW
B. North Sydney, N.S., July 31, 1941

SSN	TEAM	GP	G	A	PTS.	PIM	+/-
65–66	NYR	4	1	1	2	0	
67–68	Pitt	65	11	21	32	2	-2
68–69	Pitt	25	7	6	13	2	-10
70–71	Cal-Buf	56	12	21	33	8	-22
72–73	Clev (WHA)	66	21	30	51	12	
73–74	Clev (WHA)	69	15	18	33	14	
NHL Totals		150	31	49	80	12	-34
WHA Totals		135	36	48	84	26	

Playoffs

SSN	TEAM	GP	G	A	PTS.	PIM	
72–73	Clev (WHA)	9	2	8	10	2	
73–74	Clev (WHA)	5	1	0	1	0	
Totals		14	3	8	11	2	

ANDREWS, Lloyd F

SSN	TEAM	GP	G	A	PTS.	PIM	
21–22	Tor	11	0	0	0	0	
22–23	Tor	23	5	4	9	10	
23–24	Tor	12	2	1	3	0	
24–25	Tor	7	1	0	1	0	
Totals		53	8	5	13	10	

Playoffs

SSN	TEAM	GP	G	A	PTS.	PIM	
21–22	Tor	7	2	0	2	5	

ANDREYCHUK, David 6-3 220 LW
B. Hamilton, Ont., Sept. 29, 1963

SSN	TEAM	GP	G	A	PTS.	PIM	+/-
82–83	Buf	43	14	23	37	16	+6
83–84	Buf	78	38	42	80	42	+20
84–85	Buf	64	31	30	61	54	-4
85–86	Buf	80	36	51	87	61	+3
86–87	Buf	77	25	48	73	46	+2
87–88	Buf	80	30	48	78	112	+1
88–89	Buf	56	28	24	52	40	0
89–90	Buf	73	40	42	82	42	+6
90–91	Buf	80	36	33	69	32	+11
91–92	Buf	80	41	50	91	71	-9
92–93	Buf-Tor	83	54	45	99	56	+4
93–94	Tor	83	53	46	99	98	+22
94–95	Tor	48	22	16	38	34	-7
95–96	Tor-NJ	76	28	29	57	64	-9
96–97	NJ	82	27	34	61	48	+38
97–98	NJ	75	14	34	48	26	+19
98–99	NJ	52	15	13	28	20	+1
Totals		1210	532	608	1140	862	+104

Playoffs

SSN	TEAM	GP	G	A	PTS.	PIM	
82–83	Buf	4	1	0	1	4	
83–84	Buf	2	0	1	1	2	
84–85	Buf	5	4	2	6	4	
87–88	Buf	6	2	4	6	0	
88–89	Buf	5	0	3	3	0	
89–90	Buf	6	2	5	7	2	
90–91	Buf	6	2	2	4	8	
91–92	Buf	7	1	3	4	12	
92–93	Tor	21	12	7	19	35	
93–94	Tor	18	5	5	10	16	
94–95	Tor	7	3	2	5	25	
96–97	NJ	1	0	0	0	0	
97–98	NJ	6	1	0	1	4	
98–99	NJ	4	2	0	2	4	
Totals		98	35	34	69	116	

ANDRIJEVSKI, Alexander 6-5 211 RW
B. Moscow, USSR, Aug. 10, 1968

SSN	TEAM	GP	G	A	PTS.	PIM	+/-
92–93	Chi	1	0	0	0	0	0

ANDRUFF, Ronald Nicholas 6-0 185 C
B. Chemainus, B.C., July 10, 1953

SSN	TEAM	GP	G	A	PTS.	PIM	+/-
74–75	Mont	5	0	0	0	2	-1
75–76	Mont	1	0	0	0	0	0
76–77	Col	66	4	18	22	21	-18
77–78	Col	78	15	18	33	31	-16
78–79	Col	3	0	0	0	0	-4
Totals		153	19	36	55	54	-40

Playoffs

SSN	TEAM	GP	G	A	PTS.	PIM	
77–78	Col	2	0	0	0	0	

ANDRUSAK, Greg Frederick 6-1 190 D
B. Cranbrook, B.C., Nov. 14, 1969

SSN	TEAM	GP	G	A	PTS.	PIM	+/-
93–94	Pitt	3	0	0	0	2	-1
94–95	Pitt	7	0	4	4	6	-1
95–96	Pitt	2	0	0	0	0	-1
98–99	Pitt	7	0	1	1	4	+4
Totals		19	0	5	5	12	+1

Playoffs

SSN	TEAM	GP	G	A	PTS.	PIM	
98–99	Pitt	12	1	0	1	6	

ANGOTTI, Louis Frederick 5-8 170 C
B. Toronto, Ont., Jan. 16, 1938

SSN	TEAM	GP	G	A	PTS.	PIM	+/-
64–65	NYR	70	9	8	17	20	
65–66	NYR-Chi	51	6	12	18	14	
66–67	Chi	63	6	12	18	21	
67–68	Phil	70	12	37	49	35	+4
68–69	Pitt	71	17	20	37	36	+21
69–70	Chi	70	12	26	38	25	+2
70–71	Chi	65	9	16	25	19	+17
71–72	Chi	65	5	10	15	23	0
72–73	Chi	77	15	22	37	26	-3
73–74	StL	51	12	23	35	9	-3
74–75	Chi (WHA)	26	2	5	7	9	
NHL Totals		653	103	186	289	228	+38
WHA Totals		26	2	5	7	9	

Playoffs

SSN	TEAM	GP	G	A	PTS.	PIM	
65–66	Chi	6	0	0	0	2	
97–98	Phi	7	0	0	0	2	
69–70	Chi	8	0	0	0	0	
70–71	Chi	16	3	3	6	9	
71–72	Chi	6	0	0	0	0	
72–73	Chi	16	3	4	7	2	
Totals		65	8	8	16	17	

ANHOLT, Darrel 6-2 230 D
B. Hardisty, Alta., Nov. 23, 1962

SSN	TEAM	GP	G	A	PTS.	PIM	+/-
83–84	Chi	1	0	0	0	0	+2

ANSLOW, Hubert Wallace (Hub) 5–11 173 LW
B. Pembroke, Ont., Mar. 23, 1926

SSN	TEAM	GP	G	A	PTS.	PIM	+/-
47-48	NYR	2	0	0	0	0	

ANTONOVICH, Michael J. 5–6 155 C
B. Calumet, Minn., Oct. 18, 1951

SSN	TEAM	GP	G	A	PTS.	PIM	+/-
72-73	Minn (WHA)	75	20	19	39	46	
73-74	Minn (WHA)	68	21	29	50	4	
74-75	Minn (WHA)	67	24	26	50	20	
75-76	Minn (WHA)	57	25	21	46	18	
75-76	Minn	12	0	2	2	8	
76-77	Minn–Edm–NE (WHA)	75	40	31	71	38	
77-78	NE (WHA)	75	32	35	67	32	
78-79	NE (WHA)	69	20	27	47	35	
79-80	Hart	5	0	1	1	2	0
81-82	Minn	2	0	0	0	0	
82-83	NJ	30	7	7	14	11	-7
83-84	NJ	38	3	5	8	16	-15
NHL Totals		87	10	15	25	37	-23
WHA Totals		486	182	188	370	193	

Playoffs

SSN	TEAM	GP	G	A	PTS.	PIM	+/-
72-73	Minn (WHA)	5	2	0	2	0	
73-74	Minn (WHA)	11	1	4	5	4	
74-75	Minn (WHA)	12	1	4	5	2	
76-77	NE (WHA)	5	2	2	4	4	
77-78	NE (WHA)	14	10	7	17	4	
78-79	NE (WHA)	10	5	3	8	14	
Totals		57	21	20	41	28	

ANTOSKI, Shawn 6–4 235 LW
B. Brantford, Ont., Mar. 25, 1970

SSN	TEAM	GP	G	A	PTS.	PIM	+/-
90-91	Van	2	0	0	0	0	-2
91-92	Van	4	0	0	0	29	-1
92-93	Van	2	0	0	0	0	0
93-94	Van	55	1	2	3	190	-11
94-95	Van–Phil	32	0	0	0	107	-4
95-96	Phil	64	1	3	4	204	+4
96-97	Pitt–Ana	15	0	0	0	51	+1
97-98	Ana	9	1	0	1	18	+1
Totals		183	3	5	8	599	-20

Playoffs

SSN	TEAM	GP	G	A	PTS.	PIM	+/-
93-94	Van	16	0	1	1	36	
94-95	Phil	13	0	1	1	10	
95-96	Phil	7	1	1	2	28	
Totals		36	1	3	4	74	

APPS, Charles Joseph Sylvanus (Syl) 6–0 173 C
B. Paris, Ont., Jan. 18, 1915

SSN	TEAM	GP	G	A	PTS.	PIM	+/-
36-37	Tor	48	16	29	45	10	
37-38	Tor	47	21	29	50	9	
38-39	Tor	44	15	25	40	4	
39-40	Tor	27	13	17	30	5	
40-41	Tor	41	20	24	44	6	
41-42	Tor	38	18	23	41	0	
42-43	Tor	29	23	17	40	2	
45-46	Tor	40	24	16	40	2	
46-47	Tor	54	25	24	49	6	
47-48	Tor	55	26	27	53	12	
Totals		423	201	231	432	56	

Playoffs

SSN	TEAM	GP	G	A	PTS.	PIM	+/-
36-37	Tor	2	0	1	1	0	
37-38	Tor	7	1	4	5	0	
38-39	Tor	10	2	6	8	10	
39-40	Tor	10	5	2	7	2	
40-41	Tor	7	3	2	5	2	
41-42	Tor	13	5	8	13	2	
46-47	Tor	11	5	1	6	0	
47-48	Tor	9	4	4	8	0	
Totals		69	25	28	53	16	

APPS, Sylvanus Marshall (Syl) 6–0 195 C
B. Toronto, Ont., Aug. 1, 1947

SSN	TEAM	GP	G	A	PTS.	PIM	+/-
70-71	NYR–Pitt	62	10	18	28	32	+3
71-72	Pitt	72	15	44	59	78	+18
72-73	Pitt	77	29	56	85	18	+25
73-74	Pitt	75	24	61	85	37	+21
74-75	Pitt	79	24	55	79	43	+8
75-76	Pitt	80	32	67	99	24	+17
76-77	Pitt	72	18	43	61	20	+2
77-78	Pitt–LA	79	19	33	52	18	-11
78-79	LA	80	7	30	37	29	-25

SSN	TEAM	GP	G	A	PTS.	PIM	+/-
79-80	LA	51	5	16	21	12	-17
Totals		727	183	423	606	311	+41

Playoffs

SSN	TEAM	GP	G	A	PTS.	PIM	+/-
71-72	Pitt	4	1	0	1	2	
74-75	Pitt	9	2	3	5	9	
75-76	Pitt	3	0	1	1	0	
76-77	Pitt	3	1	0	1	12	
77-78	LA	2	0	1	1	0	
78-79	LA	2	1	0	1	0	
Totals		23	5	5	10	23	

ARBOUR, Alger Joseph (Al) 6–1 180 D
B. Sudbury, Ont., Nov. 1, 1932

SSN	TEAM	GP	G	A	PTS.	PIM	+/-
53-54	Det	36	0	1	1	18	
56-57	Det	44	1	6	7	38	
57-58	Det	69	1	6	7	104	
58-59	Chi	70	2	10	12	86	
59-60	Chi	57	1	5	6	66	
60-61	Chi	53	3	2	5	40	
61-62	Tor	52	1	5	6	68	
62-63	Tor	4	1	0	1	4	
63-64	Tor	6	0	1	1	0	
65-66	Tor	4	1	0	1	2	
67-68	StL	74	1	10	11	50	
68-69	StL	67	1	6	7	50	
69-70	StL	68	0	3	3	85	
70-71	StL	22	0	2	2	6	
Totals		626	12	58	70	617	

Playoffs

SSN	TEAM	GP	G	A	PTS.	PIM	+/-
55-56	Det	4	0	1	1	0	
56-57	Det	5	0	0	0	6	
57-58	Det	4	0	1	1	4	
58-59	Chi	6	1	2	3	26	
59-60	Chi	4	0	0	0	4	
60-61	Chi	7	0	0	0	2	
61-62	Tor	8	0	0	0	6	
64-65	Tor	1	0	0	0	2	
67-68	StL	14	0	3	3	10	
68-69	StL	12	0	0	0	10	
69-70	StL	14	0	1	1	16	
70-71	StL	6	0	0	0	6	
Totals		85	1	8	9	92	

*ARBOUR, Amos F

SSN	TEAM	GP	G	A	PTS.	PIM	+/-
18-19	Mont	1	0	0	0	0	
19-20	Mont	20	22	4	26	10	
20-21	Mont	22	14	3	17	40	
21-22	Ham	23	8	3	11	6	
22-23	Ham	23	6	1	7	6	
23-24	Tor	20	1	2	3	4	
Totals		109	51	13	64	66	

ARBOUR, Ernest (Ty) F

SSN	TEAM	GP	G	A	PTS.	PIM	+/-
26-27	Pitt Pi	41	7	8	15	10	
27-28	Pitt Pi–Chi	39	5	5	10	32	
28-29	Chi	44	3	4	7	32	
29-30	Chi	42	10	8	18	26	
30-31	Chi	41	3	3	6	12	
Totals		207	28	28	56	112	

Playoffs

SSN	TEAM	GP	G	A	PTS.	PIM	+/-
29-30	Chi	2	1	0	1	0	
30-31	Chi	9	1	0	1	6	
Totals		11	2	0	2	6	

ARBOUR, John A. (Jack) F

SSN	TEAM	GP	G	A	PTS.	PIM	+/-
26-27	Det	37	4	1	5	46	
28-29	Tor	10	1	0	1	10	
Totals		47	5	1	6	56	

ARBOUR, John Gilbert (Jack) 5–11 195 D
B. Niagara Falls, Ont., Sept. 28, 1945

SSN	TEAM	GP	G	A	PTS.	PIM	+/-
65-66	Bos	2	0	0	0	0	
67-68	Bos	4	0	1	1	11	
68-69	Pitt	17	0	2	2	35	
70-71	Van–StL	66	1	6	7	93	
71-72	Stl	17	0	0	0	10	
72-73	Minn (WHA)	76	6	27	33	188	
73-74	Minn (WHA)	77	6	43	49	192	
74-75	Minn (WHA)	70	11	43	54	67	
75-76	Den–Minn (WHA)	42	2	17	19	63	
76-77	Minn–Calg (WHA)	70	4	34	38	60	
NHL Totals		106	1	9	10	149	

SSN	TEAM	GP	G	A	PTS.	PIM	+/-
WHA Totals		335	29	164	193	570	

Playoffs

SSN	TEAM	GP	G	A	PTS.	PIM	+/-
70-71	StL	5	0	0	0	0	
72-73	Minn (WHA)	5	0	1	1	12	
73-74	Minn (WHA)	11	3	6	9	27	
74-75	Minn (WHA)	12	0	6	6	23	
NHL Totals		5	0	0	0	0	
WHA Totals		28	3	13	16	62	

ARCHAMBAULT, Michel Joseph 5–8 160 LW
B. St. Hyacinthe, Que., Sept. 27, 1950

SSN	TEAM	GP	G	A	PTS.	PIM	+/-
72-73	Que (WHA)	57	12	25	37	36	
76-77	Chi	3	0	0	0	0	-3

ARCHIBALD, David 6–1 210 C
B. Chilliwack, B.C., Apr. 14, 1969

SSN	TEAM	GP	G	A	PTS.	PIM	+/-
87-88	Minn	78	13	20	33	26	-17
88-89	Minn	72	14	19	33	14	-11
89-90	Minn–NYR	31	3	8	11	12	+1
92-93	Ott	44	9	6	15	32	-16
93-94	Ott	33	10	8	18	14	-7
94-95	Ott	14	2	2	4	19	-7
95-96	Ott	44	6	4	10	18	-14
96-97	NYI	7	0	0	0	4	-4
Totals		323	57	67	124	139	-75

Playoffs

SSN	TEAM	GP	G	A	PTS.	PIM	+/-
88-89	Minn	5	0	1	1	0	

ARCHIBALD, James 5–11 175 RW
B. Craik, Sask., June 6, 1961

SSN	TEAM	GP	G	A	PTS.	PIM	+/-
84-85	Minn	4	1	2	3	11	0
85-86	Minn	11	0	0	0	32	-3
86-87	Minn	1	0	0	0	2	-1
Totals		16	1	2	3	45	-4

ARESHENKOFF, Ronald 6–0 175 C
B. Grand Forks, B.C., June 13, 1957

SSN	TEAM	GP	G	A	PTS.	PIM	+/-
79-80	Edm	4	0	0	0	0	-4

ARMSTRONG, Derek 5–11 180 C
B. Ottawa, Ont., Apr. 23, 1973

SSN	TEAM	GP	G	A	PTS.	PIM	+/-
93-94	NYI	1	0	0	0	0	0
95-96	NYI	19	1	3	4	14	-6
96-97	NYI	50	6	7	13	33	-8
97-98	Ott	9	2	0	2	9	+1
98-99	NYR	3	0	0	0	0	0
Totals		82	9	10	19	56	-13

ARMSTRONG, George Edward (Chief) 6–1 194 RW
B. Skead, Ont., July 6, 1930

SSN	TEAM	GP	G	A	PTS.	PIM	+/-
49-50	Tor	2	0	0	0	0	
51-52	Tor	20	3	3	6	30	
52-53	Tor	52	14	11	25	54	
53-54	Tor	63	17	15	32	60	
54-55	Tor	66	10	18	28	80	
55-56	Tor	67	16	32	48	97	
56-57	Tor	54	18	26	44	37	
57-58	Tor	59	17	25	42	93	
58-59	Tor	59	20	16	36	37	
59-60	Tor	70	23	28	51	60	
60-61	Tor	47	14	19	33	21	
61-62	Tor	70	21	32	53	27	
62-63	Tor	70	19	24	43	27	
63-64	Tor	66	20	17	37	14	
64-65	Tor	59	15	22	37	14	
65-66	Tor	70	16	35	51	12	
66-67	Tor	70	9	24	33	26	
67-68	Tor	62	13	21	34	4	+8
68-69	Tor	53	11	16	27	10	-9
69-70	Tor	49	13	15	28	12	+9
70-71	Tor	59	7	18	25	6	+7
Totals		1187	296	417	713	721	+15

Playoffs

SSN	TEAM	GP	G	A	PTS.	PIM	+/-
51-52	Tor	4	0	0	0	2	
53-54	Tor	5	1	0	1	2	
54-55	Tor	4	1	0	1	40	
55-56	Tor	5	4	2	6	0	
58-59	Tor	12	0	4	4	10	
59-60	Tor	10	1	4	5	4	
60-61	Tor	5	1	1	2	0	
61-62	Tor	12	7	5	12	2	
62-63	Tor	10	3	6	9	4	
63-64	Tor	14	5	8	13	10	

SSN	TEAM	GP	G	A	PTS.	PIM	+/-
64–65	Tor	6	1	0	1	4	
65–66	Tor	4	0	1	1	4	
66–67	Tor	9	2	1	3	6	
68–69	Tor	4	0	0	0	0	
70–71	Tor	6	0	2	2	0	
Totals		110	26	34	60	88	

ARMSTRONG, Murray Alexander 5–10 170 C
B. Manor, Sask., Jan. 1, 1916

37–38	Tor	9	0	0	0	0	
38–39	Tor	3	0	1	1	0	
39–40	NYA	48	16	20	36	12	
40–41	NYA	47	10	14	24	6	
41–42	NYA	45	6	22	28	15	
43–44	Det	28	12	22	34	4	
44–45	Det	50	15	24	39	31	
45–46	Det	40	8	18	26	4	
Totals		270	67	121	188	72	

Playoffs

37–38	Tor	3	0	0	0	0	
39–40	NYA	3	0	0	0	0	
43–44	Det	5	0	2	2	0	
44–45	Det	14	4	2	6	2	
45–46	Det	5	0	2	2	0	
Totals		30	4	6	10	2	

*ARMSTRONG, Norman Gerrard (Red) 5–11 205 D
B. Owen Sound, Ont., Oct. 17, 1938

62–63	Tor	7	1	1	2	2	

ARMSTRONG, Robert Richard 6–1 180 D
B. Toronto, Ont., Apr. 17, 1931

50–51	Bos	2	0	0	0	2	
52–53	Bos	55	0	8	8	45	
53–54	Bos	64	2	10	12	81	
54–55	Bos	57	1	3	4	38	
55–56	Bos	68	0	12	12	122	
56–57	Bos	57	1	15	16	79	
57–58	Bos	47	1	4	5	66	
58–59	Bos	60	1	9	10	50	
59–60	Bos	69	5	14	19	96	
60–61	Bos	54	0	10	10	72	
61–62	Bos	9	2	1	3	20	
Totals		542	13	86	99	671	

Playoffs

51–52	Bos	5	0	0	0	2	
52–53	Bos	11	1	1	2	10	
53–54	Bos	4	0	1	1	0	
54–55	Bos	5	0	0	0	2	
56–57	Bos	10	0	3	3	10	
58–59	Bos	7	0	2	2	4	
Totals		42	1	7	8	28	

ARMSTRONG, Tim 5–11 170 C
B. Toronto, Ont., May 12, 1967

88–89	Tor	11	1	0	1	6	-2

ARMSTRONG, William 6–2 195 C
B. London, Ont., June 25, 1966

90–91	Phil	1	0	1	1	1	+1

ARNASON, Ernest Charles (Chuck) 5–10 185 RW
B. Dauphin, Man., July 15, 1951

71–72	Mont	17	3	0	3	4	-1
72–73	Mont	19	1	1	2	2	-1
73–74	Atl-Pitt	74	20	11	31	17	-1
74–75	Pitt	78	26	32	58	32	0
75–76	Pitt-KC	69	21	13	34	35	-39
76–77	Col	61	13	10	23	10	-23
77–78	Col-Clev	69	25	21	46	18	-5
78–79	Minn-Wash	14	0	2	2	4	-1
Totals		401	109	90	199	122	-71

Playoffs

74–75	Pitt	9	2	4	6	4	

ARNIEL, Scott 6–1 188 C
B. Cornwall, Ont., Sept. 17, 1962

81–82	Winn	17	1	8	9	14	+2
82–83	Winn	75	13	5	18	46	-16
83–84	Winn	80	21	35	56	68	-10
84–85	Winn	79	22	22	44	81	+7
85–86	Winn	80	18	25	43	40	-8
86–87	Buf	63	11	14	25	69	-1
87–88	Buf	73	17	23	40	61	+8
88–89	Buf	80	18	23	41	46	+10
89–90	Buf	79	18	14	32	77	+4
90–91	Winn	75	5	17	22	87	-12
91–92	Bos	29	5	3	8	20	+5
Totals		730	149	189	338	599	-11

Playoffs

81–82	Winn	3	0	0	0	0	
82–83	Winn	2	0	0	0	0	
83–84	Winn	2	0	0	0	5	
84–85	Winn	8	1	2	3	9	
85–86	Winn	3	0	0	0	12	
87–88	Buf	6	0	1	1	5	
88–89	Buf	5	1	0	1	4	
89–90	Buf	5	1	0	1	4	
Totals		34	3	3	6	39	

ARNOTT, Jason 6–3 220 C
B. Collingwood, Ont., Oct. 11, 1974

93–94	Edm	78	33	35	68	104	+1
94–95	Edm	42	15	22	37	128	-14
95–96	Edm	64	28	31	59	87	-6
96–97	Edm	67	19	38	57	92	-21
97–98	Edm-NJ	70	10	23	33	99	-24
98–99	NJ	74	27	27	54	79	+10
Totals		395	132	176	308	589	-54

Playoffs

96–97	Edm	12	3	6	9	18	
97–98	NJ	5	0	2	2	0	
98–99	NJ	7	2	2	4	4	
Totals		24	5	10	15	22	

ARTHUR, Frederick Edward 6–5 210 D
B. Toronto, Ont., Mar. 6, 1961

80–81	Hart	3	0	0	0	0	-5
81–82	Phil	74	1	7	8	47	-8
82–83	Phil	3	0	1	1	2	-1
Totals		80	1	8	9	49	-14

Playoffs

81–82	Phil	4	0	0	0	2	

ARUNDEL, John O'Gorman 5–11 181 D
B. Winnipeg, Man., Nov. 4, 1927

49–50	Tor	3	0	0	0	0	

ARVEDSON, Magnus 6–2 198 LW
B. Karlstad, Sweden, Nov. 25, 1971

97–98	Ott	61	11	15	26	36	+2
98–99	Ott	80	21	26	47	50	+33
Totals		141	32	41	73	86	+35

Playoffs

97–98	Ott	11	0	1	1	6	
98–99	Ott	3	0	1	1	2	
Totals		14	0	2	2	8	

ASHAM, Aaron 5–11 176 RW
B. Portage, La Prairie, Man., Apr. 13, 1978

98–99	Mont	7	0	0	0	0	-4

*ASHBEE, William Barry (Barry) 5–10 180 D
B. Weston, Ont., July 28, 1939

65–66	Bos	14	0	3	3	14	
70–71	Phil	64	4	23	27	44	+3
71–72	Phil	73	6	14	20	75	+2
72–73	Phil	64	1	17	18	106	-2
73–74	Phil	69	4	13	17	52	+52
Totals		284	15	70	85	291	+55

Playoffs

72–73	Phil	11	0	4	4	20	
73–74	Phil	6	0	0	0	2	
Totals		17	0	4	4	22	

*ASHBY, Donald Alan (Ash) 6–1 185 C
B. Kamloops, B.C., Mar. 8, 1955

75–76	Tor	50	6	15	21	10	+5
76–77	Tor	76	19	23	42	24	-14
77–78	Tor	12	1	2	3	0	-4
78–79	Tor-Col	15	2	3	5	0	-6
79–80	Col-Edm	29	10	10	20	4	-1
80–81	Col	6	2	3	5	2	-1
Totals		188	40	56	96	40	-21

Playoffs

76–77	Tor	9	1	0	1	4	
79–80	Edm	3	0	0	0	0	
Totals		12	1	0	1	4	

ASHTON, Brent Kenneth 6–1 210 LW
B. Saskatoon, Sask., May 18, 1960

79–80	Van	47	5	14	19	11	+4
80–81	Van	77	18	11	29	57	-10
81–82	Col	80	24	36	60	26	-31
82–83	NJ	76	14	19	33	47	-23
83–84	Minn	68	7	10	17	54	-13
84–85	Minn-Que	78	31	31	62	53	+19
85–86	Que	77	26	32	58	64	+7
86–87	Que-Det	81	40	35	75	39	-15
87–88	Det	73	26	27	53	50	-10
88–89	Winn	75	31	37	68	36	-5
89–90	Winn	79	22	34	56	37	+4
90–91	Winn	61	12	24	36	58	-10
91–92	Winn-Bos	68	18	22	40	51	-7
92–93	Bos-Calg	58	10	13	23	52	+11
Totals		998	284	345	629	635	-59

Playoffs

79–80	Van	4	1	0	1	6	
80–81	Van	3	0	0	0	2	
83–84	Minn	12	1	2	3	22	
84–85	Que	18	6	4	10	13	
85–86	Que	3	2	1	3	9	
86–87	Det	16	4	9	13	6	
87–88	Det	16	7	5	12	10	
89–90	Winn	7	3	1	4	2	
92–93	Calg	6	0	3	3	2	
Totals		85	24	25	49	70	

ASHWORTH, Frank 5–9 165 C
B. Moose Jaw, Sask., Oct. 16, 1927

46–47	Chi	18	5	4	9	2	

ASMUNDSON, Oscar 5–11 170 C
B. Red Deer, Alta., Nov. 17, 1908

32–33	NYR	48	5	10	15	20	
33–34	NYR	46	2	6	8	8	
34–35	Det-StLE	14	4	7	11	2	
36–37	NYA	2	0	0	0	0	
37–38	Mont	2	0	0	0	0	
Totals		112	11	23	34	30	

Playoffs

32–33	NYR	8	0	2	2	4	
33–34	NYR	1	0	0	0	0	
Totals		9	0	2	2	4	

ASTLEY, Mark 5–11 185 D
B. Calgary, Alta., Mar. 30, 1969

93–94	Buf	1	0	0	0	0	-1
94–95	Buf	14	2	1	3	12	-2
95–96	Buf	60	2	18	20	80	-12
Totals		75	4	19	23	92	-15

Playoffs

94–95	Buf	2	0	0	0	0	

ATANAS, Walter (Ants) 5–8 168 RW
B. Hamilton, Ont., Dec. 22, 1922

44–45	NYR	49	13	8	21	40	

ATCHEYNUM, Blair 6–2 190 RW
B. Estevan, Sask., Apr. 20, 1969

92–93	Ott	4	0	1	1	0	-3
97–98	StL	61	11	15	26	10	+5
98–99	Nash-StL	65	10	8	18	18	-8
Totals		130	21	24	45	28	-6

Playoffs

97–98	StL	10	0	0	0	2	
98–99	StL	13	1	3	4	6	
Totals		23	1	3	4	8	

ATKINSON, Steven John 5–11 170 RW
B. Toronto, Ont., Oct. 16, 1948

68–69	Bos	1	0	0	0	0	-1

SSN	TEAM	GP	G	A	PTS.	PIM	+/-
70–71	Buf	57	20	18	38	12	+1
71–72	Buf	67	14	10	24	26	-22
72–73	Buf	61	9	9	18	36	-5
73–74	Buf	70	6	10	16	22	+1
74–75	Wash	44	11	4	15	8	-26
75–76	Tor (WHA)	52	2	6	8	22	
NHL Totals		302	60	51	111	104	-52
WHA Totals		52	2	6	8	22	

Playoffs

| 72–73 | Buf | 1 | 0 | 0 | 0 | 0 | |

ATTWELL, Robert Allan 6–0 192 RW
B. Spokane, Wash., Dec. 26, 1959

79–80	Col	7	1	1	2	0	-5
80–81	Col	15	0	4	4	0	+1
Totals		22	1	5	6	0	-4

ATTWELL, Ronald Allan 6–2 208 C
B. Humber Summit, Ont., Feb. 9, 1935

| 67–68 | StL–NYR | 21 | 1 | 7 | 8 | 8 | |

AUBIN, Normand 6–0 185 C
B. St.–Leonard, Que., July 26, 1960

81–82	Tor	43	14	12	26	22	-16
82–83	Tor	26	4	1	5	8	-9
Totals		69	18	13	31	30	-25

Playoffs

| 82–83 | Tor | 1 | 0 | 0 | 0 | 0 | |

AUBIN, Serge 6–0 190 C
B. Val D'Or, Que, Feb 15, 1975

| 98–99 | Col A | 1 | 0 | 0 | 0 | 0 | 0 |

AUBRY, Pierre 5–10 175 LW
B. Cap–de–la–Madeleine, Que., Apr. 15, 1960

80–81	Que	1	0	0	0	0	0
81–82	Que	62	10	13	23	27	-9
82–83	Que	77	9	16	48	46	-6
83–84	Que–Det	37	5	2	7	25	-4
84–85	Det	25	2	2	4	33	-1
Totals		202	24	26	50	133	-20

Playoffs

81–82	Que	15	1	1	2	30	
82–83	Que	2	0	0	0	0	
83–84	Det	3	0	0	0	2	
Totals		20	1	1	2	32	

AUBUCHON, Oscar (Ossie) 5–10 175 LW
B. St. Hyacinthe, Que., Jan. 1, 1917

42–43	Bos	3	3	0	3	0	
43–44	Bos–NYR	47	16	12	28	4	
Totals		50	19	12	31	4	

Playoffs

| 42–43 | Bos | 6 | 1 | 0 | 1 | 0 | |

AUCOIN, Adrian 6–1 194 D
B. Ottawa, Ont., July 3, 1973

94–95	Van	1	1	0	1	0	+1
95–96	Van	49	4	14	18	34	+8
96–97	Van	70	5	16	21	63	0
97–98	Van	35	3	3	6	21	-4
98–99	Van	82	23	11	34	77	-14
Totals		237	36	44	80	195	-9

Playoffs

94–95	Van	4	1	0	1	0	
95–96	Van	6	0	0	0	2	
Totals		10	1	0	1	2	

AUDET, Phillippe 6–2 175 LW
B. Ottawa, Ont., June 4, 1977

| 98–99 | Det | 4 | 0 | 0 | 0 | 0 | -2 |

AUDETTE, Donald 5–8 180 RW
B. Laval, Que., Sept. 23, 1969

90–91	Buf	8	4	3	7	4	-1
91–92	Buf	63	31	17	48	75	-1
92–93	Buf	44	12	7	19	51	-8
93–94	Buf	77	29	30	59	41	+2
94–95	Buf	46	24	13	37	27	-3
95–96	Buf	23	12	13	25	18	0

SSN	TEAM	GP	G	A	PTS.	PIM	+/-
96–97	Buf	73	28	22	50	48	-6
97–98	Buf	75	24	20	44	59	+10
98–99	LA	49	18	18	36	51	+7
Totals		458	182	143	325	394	0

Playoffs

89–90	Buf	2	0	0	0	0	
92–93	Buf	8	2	2	4	6	
93–94	Buf	7	0	1	1	6	
94–95	Buf	5	1	1	2	4	
96–97	Buf	11	4	5	9	6	
97–98	Buf	15	5	8	13	10	
Totals		48	12	17	29	32	

AUGE, Les 6–1 190 D
B. St. Paul, Minn., May 16, 1953

| 80–81 | Col | 6 | 0 | 3 | 3 | 4 | -3 |

AUGUSTA, Patrik 5–10 170 RW
B. Jihlava, Czechoslovakia, Nov. 13, 1969

93–94	Tor	2	0	0	0	0	0
98–99	Wash	2	0	0	0	0	0
Totals		4	0	0	0	0	0

*AURIE, Harry Lawrence (Larry) 5–6 148 RW
B. Sudbury, Ont., Feb. 8, 1905

27–28	Det	44	13	3	16	43	
28–29	Det	35	1	1	2	26	
29–30	Det	43	14	5	19	28	
30–31	Det	41	12	6	18	23	
31–32	Det	48	12	8	20	18	
32–33	Det	45	12	11	23	25	
33–34	Det	48	16	19	35	36	
34–35	Det	48	17	29	46	24	
35–36	Det	44	16	18	34	17	
36–37	Det	45	23	20	43	20	
37–38	Det	47	10	9	19	19	
38–39	Det	1	1	0	1	0	
Totals		489	147	129	276	279	

Playoffs

28–29	Det	2	1	0	1	2	
31–32	Det	2	0	0	0	0	
32–33	Det	4	1	0	1	4	
33–34	Det	9	3	7	10	2	
35–36	Det	7	1	2	3	2	
Totals		24	6	9	15	10	

AWREY, Donald William 6–0 195 D
B. Kitchener, Ont., July 18, 1943

63–64	Bos	16	1	0	1	4	
64–65	Bos	47	2	3	5	41	
65–66	Bos	70	4	3	7	74	
66–67	Bos	4	1	0	1	6	
67–68	Bos	74	3	12	15	150	+18
68–69	Bos	73	0	13	13	149	+25
69–70	Bos	73	3	10	13	120	+27
70–71	Bos	74	4	21	25	141	+40
71–72	Bos	34	1	8	9	52	+20
72–73	Bos	78	2	17	19	90	+29
73–74	StL	55	5	16	21	51	-7
74–75	StL–Mont	76	1	19	20	62	+13
75–76	Mont	72	0	12	12	29	+30
76–77	Pitt	79	1	12	13	40	-2
77–78	NYR	78	2	8	10	38	-14
78–79	Col	56	1	4	5	18	-33
Totals		979	31	158	189	1065	+146

Playoffs

67–68	Bos	4	0	1	1	4	
68–69	Bos	10	0	1	1	28	
69–70	Bos	14	0	5	5	32	
70–71	Bos	7	0	0	0	17	
71–72	Bos	15	0	4	4	45	
72–73	Bos	4	0	0	0	6	
74–75	Mont	11	0	6	6	12	
76–77	Pitt	3	0	1	1	0	
77–78	NYR	3	0	0	0	6	
Totals		71	0	18	18	150	

AXELSSON, Per–Johan 6–1 174 LW
B. Kingali, Sweden, Feb. 26, 1975

97–98	Bos	82	8	19	27	38	-14
98–99	Bos	77	7	10	17	18	-14
Totals		159	15	29	44	56	-28

Playoffs

97–98	Bos	6	1	0	1	0	
98–99	Bos	12	1	1	2	4	
Totals		18	2	1	3	4	

AYERS, Thomas Vernon (Vern) 6–2 220 D
B. Toronto, Ont., Apr. 27, 1909

30–31	NYA	26	2	1	3	54	
31–32	NYA	45	2	4	6	82	
32–33	NYA	48	0	3	3	97	
33–34	Mont M	17	0	0	0	19	
34–35	StLE	47	2	2	4	60	
35–36	NYR	28	0	4	4	38	
Totals		211	6	14	20	350	

BABANDO, Peter Joseph 5–9 187 LW
B. Braeburn, Pa., May 10, 1925

47–48	Bos	60	23	11	34	52	
48–49	Bos	58	19	14	33	34	
49–50	Det	56	6	6	12	25	
50–51	Chi	70	18	19	37	36	
51–52	Chi	49	11	14	25	29	
52–53	Chi–NYR	58	9	9	18	18	
Totals		351	86	73	159	194	

Playoffs

47–48	Bos	5	1	1	2	2	
48–49	Bos	4	0	0	0	2	
49–50	Det	8	2	2	4	2	
Totals		17	3	3	6	6	

BABCOCK, Bob 6–1 225 D
B. Agincourt, Ont., Aug. 3, 1968

90–91	Wash	1	0	0	0	0	0
92–93	Wash	1	0	0	0	2	0
Totals		2	0	0	0	2	0

BABE, Warren 6–3 200 LW
B. Medicine Hat, Alta., Sept. 7, 1968

87–88	Minn	6	0	1	1	4	-1
88–89	Minn	14	2	3	5	19	+3
90–91	Minn	1	0	1	1	0	+1
Totals		21	2	5	7	23	+3

Playoffs

| 88–89 | Minn | 2 | 0 | 0 | 0 | 0 | |

BABIN, Mitch 6–2 195 C
B. Kapuskasing, Ont., Dec. 1, 1954

| 75–76 | StL | 8 | 0 | 0 | 0 | 0 | -2 |

BABY, John George 6–0 195 D
B. Sudbury, Ont., May 18, 1957

77–78	Clev	24	2	7	9	26	-10
78–79	Minn	2	0	1	1	0	-2
Totals		26	2	8	10	26	-12

BABYCH, David Michael 6–2 215 D
B. Edmonton, Alta., May 23, 1961

80–81	Winn	69	6	38	44	90	-61
81–82	Winn	79	19	49	68	92	-11
82–83	Winn	79	13	61	74	56	-10
83–84	Winn	66	18	39	57	62	-31
84–85	Winn	78	13	49	62	78	-6
85–86	Winn–Hart	81	14	55	69	50	+1
86–87	Hart	66	8	33	41	44	-18
87–88	Hart	71	14	36	50	54	-25
88–89	Hart	70	6	41	47	54	-5
89–90	Hart	72	6	37	43	62	-16
90–91	Hart	8	0	6	6	4	-4
91–92	Van	75	5	24	29	63	-2
92–93	Van	43	3	16	19	44	+6
93–94	Van	73	4	28	32	52	0
94–95	Van	40	3	11	14	18	-13
95–96	Van	53	3	21	24	38	-5
96–97	Van	78	5	22	27	38	-2
97–98	Van–Phil	53	0	9	9	49	-9
98–99	Phil–LA	41	2	6	8	22	-2
Totals		1195	142	571	723	970	-223

Playoffs

81–82	Winn	4	1	2	3	29	
82–83	Winn	3	0	0	0	0	
83–84	Winn	3	1	1	2	0	
84–85	Winn	8	2	7	9	6	

SSN	TEAM	GP	G	A	PTS.	PIM	+/-
85–86	Hart	8	1	3	4	14	
86–87	Hart	6	1	1	2	14	
87–88	Hart	6	3	2	5	2	
88–89	Hart	4	1	5	6	2	
89–90	Hart	7	1	2	3	0	
91–92	Van	13	2	6	8	10	
92–93	Van	12	2	5	7	6	
93–94	Van	24	3	5	8	12	
94–95	Van	11	2	2	4	14	
97–98	Phil	5	1	0	1	4	
Totals		114	21	41	62	113	

BABYCH, Wayne Joseph 5–11 191 RW
B. Edmonton, Alta., June 6, 1958

SSN	TEAM	GP	G	A	PTS.	PIM	+/-
78–79	Stl	67	27	36	63	75	–11
79–80	Stl	59	26	35	61	49	+11
80–81	Stl	78	54	42	96	93	+14
81–82	Stl	51	19	25	44	51	–12
82–83	Stl	71	16	23	39	62	–24
83–84	Stl	70	13	29	42	52	+1
84–85	Pitt	65	20	34	54	35	–7
85–86	Pitt–Que–Hart	54	17	22	39	77	+5
86–87	Hart	4	0	0	0	4	–5
Totals		519	192	246	438	498	–28

Playoffs

79–80	Stl	3	1	2	3	2	
80–81	Stl	11	2	0	2	8	
81–82	Stl	7	3	2	5	8	
83–84	Stl	10	1	4	5	4	
85–86	Hart	10	0	1	1	2	
Totals		41	7	9	16	24	

BACA, Jergus 6–2 210 D
B. Kosice, Czechoslovakia, Jan. 4, 1965

90–91	Hart	9	0	2	2	14	–3
91–92	Hart	1	0	0	0	0	–1
Totals		10	0	2	2	14	–4

BACKMAN, Michael Charles 5–10 175 RW
B. Halifax, N.S., Feb. 2, 1955

81–82	NYR	3	0	2	2	4	+7
82–83	NYR	7	1	3	4	6	–5
83–84	NYR	8	0	1	1	8	–1
Totals		18	1	6	7	18	+1

Playoffs

81–82	NYR	1	0	0	0	2	
82–83	NYR	9	2	2	4	0	
Totals		10	2	2	4	2	

BACKOR, Peter 6–0 185 D
B. Ft. William, Ont., Apr. 29, 1919

44–45	Tor	36	4	5	9	6	

BACKSTROM, Ralph Gerald 5–10 170 C
B. Kirkland Lake, Ont., Sept. 18, 1937

56–57	Mont	3	0	0	0	0	
57–58	Mont	2	0	1	1	0	
58–59	Mont	64	18	22	40	19	
59–60	Mont	64	13	15	28	24	
60–61	Mont	69	12	20	32	44	
61–62	Mont	66	27	38	65	29	
62–63	Mont	70	23	12	35	51	
63–64	Mont	70	8	21	29	41	
64–65	Mont	70	25	30	55	41	
65–66	Mont	67	22	20	42	10	
66–67	Mont	69	14	27	41	39	
67–68	Mont	70	20	25	45	14	+4
68–69	Mont	72	13	28	41	16	+20
69–70	Mont	72	19	24	43	20	+4
70–71	Mont–LA	49	15	17	32	8	–7
71–72	LA	76	23	29	52	22	–22
72–73	LA–Chi	79	26	32	58	8	–12
73–74	Chi (WHA)	78	33	50	83	26	
74–75	Chi (WHA)	70	15	24	39	28	
75–76	Ott–NE (WHA)	79	35	48	83	20	
76–77	NE (WHA)	77	17	31	48	30	
NHL Totals		1032	278	361	639	386	–13
WHA Totals		304	100	153	253	104	

Playoffs

58–59	Mont	11	3	5	8	12	
59–60	Mont	7	0	3	3	2	
60–61	Mont	5	0	0	0	4	
61–62	Mont	5	0	1	1	6	
62–63	Mont	5	0	0	0	2	
63–64	Mont	7	2	1	3	8	
64–65	Mont	13	2	3	5	10	
65–66	Mont	10	3	4	7	4	
66–67	Mont	10	5	2	7	6	
67–68	Mont	13	4	3	7	4	
68–69	Mont	14	3	4	7	10	
72–73	Chi	16	5	6	11	0	
73–74	Chi (WHA)	18	5	14	19	4	
75–76	NE (WHA)	3	0	0	0	0	
NHL Totals		116	27	32	59	68	
WHA Totals		38	10	18	28	12	

BAILEY, Garnet Edward (Ace) 5–11 192 LW
B. Lloydminster, Sask., June 13, 1948

68–69	Bos	8	3	3	6	10	+5
69–70	Bos	58	11	11	22	82	+17
70–71	Bos	36	0	6	6	44	+4
71–72	Bos	73	9	13	22	64	+11
72–73	Bos–Det	70	10	24	34	105	+9
73–74	Det–StL	67	16	17	33	53	–13
74–75	StL–Wash	71	19	39	58	121	–33
75–76	Wash	67	13	19	32	75	–42
76–77	Wash	78	19	27	46	51	–21
77–78	Wash	40	7	12	19	28	–12
78–79	Edm (WHA)	38	5	4	9	22	
NHL Totals		568	107	171	278	633	–75
WHA Totals		38	5	4	9	22	

Playoffs

68–69	Bos	1	0	0	0	2	
70–71	Bos	1	0	0	0	10	
71–72	Bos	13	2	4	6	16	
78–79	Edm (WHA)	2	0	0	0	4	
NHL Totals		15	2	4	6	28	
WHA Totals		2	0	0	0	4	

*BAILEY, Irvine Wallace (Ace) 5–10 160 RW
B. Bracebridge, Ont., July 3, 1903

26–27	Tor	42	15	13	28	82	
27–28	Tor	43	9	3	12	72	
28–29	Tor	44	22	10	32	78	
29–30	Tor	43	22	21	43	69	
30–31	Tor	40	23	19	42	46	
31–32	Tor	41	8	5	13	62	
32–33	Tor	47	10	8	18	52	
33–34	Tor	13	2	3	5	11	
Totals		313	111	82	193	472	

Playoffs

28–29	Tor	4	2	1	3	4	
30–31	Tor	2	1	1	2	0	
31–32	Tor	7	0	1	1	4	
32–33	Tor	8	0	1	1	4	
Totals		21	3	4	7	12	

BAILEY, Reid 6–2 200 D
B. Toronto, Ont., May 28, 1956

80–81	Phil	17	1	3	4	55	+8
81–82	Phil	10	0	0	0	23	–5
82–83	Tor	1	0	0	0	2	–2
83–84	Hart	12	0	0	0	25	–2
Totals		40	1	3	4	105	–1

Playoffs

80–81	Phil	12	0	2	2	23	
81–82	Phil	2	0	0	0	0	
82–83	Tor	2	0	0	0	2	
Totals		16	0	2	2	25	

BAILEY, Robert Allan 6–0 197 RW
B. Kenora, Ont., May 29, 1931

53–54	Tor	48	2	7	9	70	
54–55	Tor	32	4	2	6	52	
55–56	Tor	6	0	0	0	6	
57–58	Chi–Det	64	9	12	21	79	
Totals		150	15	21	36	207	

Playoffs

53–54	Tor	5	0	2	2	4	
54–55	Tor	1	0	0	0	0	
56–57	Det	5	0	2	2	2	
57–58	Det	4	0	0	0	16	
Totals		15	0	4	4	22	

BAILLARGEON, Joel 6–1 205 LW
B. Quebec City, Que., Oct. 6, 1964

86–87	Winn	11	0	1	1	15	–3
87–88	Winn	4	0	1	1	12	0
88–89	Que	5	0	0	0	4	–3
Totals		20	0	2	2	31	–6

BAIRD, Kenneth Stewart 6–0 190 D
B. Flin Flon, Man., Feb. 1, 1951

71–72	Cal	10	0	2	2	15	
72–73	Alb (WHA)	75	14	15	29	112	
73–74	Edm (WHA)	68	17	19	36	115	
74–75	Edm (WHA)	77	30	28	58	151	
75–76	Edm (WHA)	48	13	24	37	87	
76–77	Edm–Calg (WHA)	9	1	2	3	2	
77–78	Winn (WHA)	55	16	11	27	31	
NHL Totals		10	0	2	2	15	
WHA Totals		332	91	99	190	498	

Playoffs

73–74	Edm (WHA)	5	1	1	2	7	
75–76	Edm (WHA)	4	3	1	4	16	
77–78	Winn (WHA)	7	0	4	4	7	
WHA Totals		16	4	6	10	30	

BAKER, Jamie 6–0 190 C
B. Ottawa, Ont., Aug. 31, 1966

89–90	Que	.1	0	0	0	0	–1
90–91	Que	18	2	0	2	8	–4
91–92	Que	52	7	10	17	32	–5
92–93	Ott	76	19	29	48	54	–20
93–94	SJ	65	12	5	17	38	+2
94–95	SJ	43	7	4	11	22	–7
95–96	SJ	77	16	17	33	79	–19
96–97	Tor	58	8	8	16	28	+2
97–98	Tor	13	0	5	5	10	+1
98–99	SJ	1	0	1	1	0	+1
Totals		404	71	79	150	271	–50

Playoffs

93–94	SJ	14	3	2	5	30	
94–95	SJ	11	2	2	4	12	
Totals		25	5	4	9	42	

BAKER, William Robert 6–1 195 D
B. Grand Rapids, Mich., Nov. 29, 1956

80–81	Mont–Col	24	0	3	3	44	–1
81–82	Col–StL	49	3	8	11	67	–21
82–83	NYR	70	4	14	18	64	–8
Totals		143	7	25	32	175	–30

Playoffs

81–82	StL	4	0	0	0	0	
82–83	NYR	2	0	0	0	0	
Totals		6	0	0	0	0	

BAKOVIC, Peter George 6–2 200 RW
B. Thunder Bay, Ont., Jan. 31, 1965

87–88	Van	10	2	0	2	48	–1

BALDERIS, Helmut 5–11 190 RW
B. Riga, Latvia, June 30, 1952

89–90	Minn	26	3	6	9	2	0

BALDWIN, Douglas 6–0 175 D
B. Winnipeg, Man., Nov. 2, 1922

45–46	Tor	15	0	1	1	6	
46–47	Det	4	0	0	0	0	
47–48	Chi	5	0	0	0	2	
Totals		24	0	1	1	8	

BALFOUR, Earl Frederick 6–1 180 LW
B. Toronto, Ont., Jan. 4, 1933

51–52	Tor	3	0	0	0	2	
53–54	Tor	17	0	1	1	6	
55–56	Tor	59	14	5	19	40	
57–58	Tor	1	0	0	0	0	
58–59	Chi	70	10	8	18	10	
59–60	Chi	70	3	5	8	16	
60–61	Chi	68	3	3	6	4	
Totals		288	30	22	52	78	

Playoffs

51–52	Tor	1	0	0	0	0	
55–56	Tor	3	0	1	1	2	

SSN	TEAM	GP	G	A	PTS.	PIM	+/-
58–59	Chi	6	0	2	2	0	
59–60	Chi	4	0	0	0	0	
61–61	Chi	12	0	0	0	2	
Totals		26	0	3	3	4	

*BALFOUR, Murray 5–9 178 RW
B. Regina, Sask., Aug. 24, 1936

SSN	TEAM	GP	G	A	PTS.	PIM	+/-
56–57	Mont	2	0	0	0	2	
57–58	Mont	3	1	1	2	4	
59–60	Chi	61	18	12	30	55	
60–61	Chi	70	21	27	48	123	
61–62	Chi	49	15	15	30	72	
62–63	Chi	65	10	23	33	35	
63–64	Chi	41	2	10	12	36	
64–65	Bos	15	0	2	2	26	
Totals		306	67	90	157	353	

Playoffs

SSN	TEAM	GP	G	A	PTS.	PIM
59–60	Chi	3	1	0	1	0
60–61	Chi	12	5	5	10	12
61–62	Chi	12	1	1	2	15
62–63	Chi	6	0	2	2	12
63–64	Chi	7	2	2	4	6
Totals		40	9	10	19	45

BALL, Terry James 5–8 165 D
B. Selkirk, Man., Nov. 29, 1944

SSN	TEAM	GP	G	A	PTS.	PIM	+/-
67–68	Phil	1	0	0	0	0	-1
69–70	Phil	61	7	18	25	20	-7
70–71	Buf	2	0	0	0	0	0
71–72	Buf	10	0	1	1	6	-7
72–73	Minn (WHA)	76	6	34	40	66	
73–74	Minn (WHA)	71	8	28	36	34	
74–75	Minn (WHA)	76	8	37	45	36	
75–76	Clev-Cin (WHA)	59	5	29	34	30	
76–77	Birm (WHA)	23	1	6	7	8	
NHL Totals		74	7	19	26	26	-16
WHA Totals		305	28	134	162	174	

Playoffs

SSN	TEAM	GP	G	A	PTS.	PIM
72–73	Minn (WHA)	5	1	2	3	4
73–74	Minn (WHA)	11	1	2	3	6
74–75	Minn (WHA)	12	3	4	7	4
WHA Totals		28	5	8	13	14

BALON, David Alexander 5–10 172 LW
B. Wakaw, Sask., Aug. 2, 1937

SSN	TEAM	GP	G	A	PTS.	PIM	+/-
59–60	NYR	3	0	0	0	0	
60–61	NYR	13	1	2	3	8	
61–62	NYR	30	4	11	15	11	
62–63	NYR	70	11	13	24	72	
63–64	Mont	70	24	18	42	80	
64–65	Mont	63	18	23	41	61	
65–66	Mont	45	3	7	10	24	
66–67	Mont	48	11	8	19	31	
67–68	Minn	73	15	32	47	84	-10
68–69	NYR	75	10	21	31	57	+5
69–70	NYR	76	33	37	70	100	+40
70–71	NYR	78	36	24	60	34	+14
71–72	NYR-Van	75	23	24	47	23	-10
72–73	Van	57	3	2	5	22	-16
73–74	Que (WHA)	9	0	0	0	0	
NHL Totals		776	192	222	414	607	+33
WHA Totals		9	0	0	0	2	

Playoffs

SSN	TEAM	GP	G	A	PTS.	PIM
61–62	NYR	6	2	3	5	2
63–64	Mont	7	1	1	2	25
64–65	Mont	10	0	0	0	10
65–66	Mont	9	2	3	5	8
66–67	Mont	9	0	2	2	6
67–68	Minn	14	4	9	13	14
68–69	NYR	4	1	0	1	0
69–70	NYR	6	1	1	2	32
70–71	NYR	13	3	2	5	4
Totals		78	14	21	35	109

BALTIMORE, Byron Don 6–2 200 D
B. Whitehorse, Yuk., Aug. 26, 1952

SSN	TEAM	GP	G	A	PTS.	PIM	+/-
74–75	Chi (WHA)	77	8	12	20	110	
75–76	Ott-Ind (WHA)	78	2	18	20	62	
76–77	Ind (WHA)	55	0	15	15	63	
77–78	Ind-Cin (WHA)	50	3	16	19	70	
78–79	Ind-Cin (WHA)	71	5	11	16	85	
79–80	Edm	2	0	0	0	4	+4
NHL Totals		2	0	0	0	4	+4

SSN	TEAM	GP	G	A	PTS.	PIM	+/-
WHA Totals		331	18	72	90	390	

Playoffs

SSN	TEAM	GP	G	A	PTS.	PIM
75–76	Ind (WHA)	7	0	1	1	4
76–77	Ind (WHA)	9	0	0	0	5
78–79	Cin (WHA)	3	0	0	0	2
WHA Totals		19	0	1	1	11

BALUIK, Stanley 5–8 160 C
B. Port Arthur, Ont., Oct. 5, 1935

SSN	TEAM	GP	G	A	PTS.	PIM
59–60	Bos	7	0	0	0	2

BANCROFT, Steve 6–1 214 D
B. Toronto, Ont., Oct. 6, 1970

SSN	TEAM	GP	G	A	PTS.	PIM	+/-
92–93	Chi	1	0	0	0	0	0

BANDURA, Jeffrey Mitchell Joseph 6–1 195 D
B. White Rock, B.C., Apr. 4, 1957

SSN	TEAM	GP	G	A	PTS.	PIM	+/-
80–81	NYR	2	0	1	1	0	-3

BANHAM, Frank 6–0 187 RW
B. Calahoo, Alta., April 14, 1975

SSN	TEAM	GP	G	A	PTS.	PIM	+/-
96–97	Ana	3	0	0	0	0	-2
97–98	Ana	21	9	2	11	12	-6
Totals		24	9	2	11	12	-8

BANKS, Darren Alexander 6–2 215 LW
B. Toronto, Ont., Mar. 18, 1966

SSN	TEAM	GP	G	A	PTS.	PIM	+/-
92–93	Bos	16	2	1	3	64	+5
93–94	Bos	4	0	1	1	9	0
Totals		20	2	2	4	73	+5

BANNISTER, Drew 6–1 193 D
B. Belleville, Ont., Sept. 4, 1974

SSN	TEAM	GP	G	A	PTS.	PIM	+/-
95–96	TB	13	0	1	1	4	-1
96–97	TB-Edm	65	4	14	18	44	-23
97–98	Edm-Ana	61	0	8	8	89	-9
98–99	TB	21	1	2	3	24	-4
Totals		160	5	25	30	161	-37

Playoffs

SSN	TEAM	GP	G	A	PTS.	PIM
96–97	Edm	12	0	0	0	30

BARAHONA, Ralph J. 5–10 180 C
B. Long Beach, Cal., Nov. 16, 1965

SSN	TEAM	GP	G	A	PTS.	PIM	+/-
90–91	Bos	3	2	1	3	0	+2
91–92	Bos	3	0	1	1	0	+1
Totals		6	2	2	4	0	+3

BARBE, Andre Joseph (Andy) 6–0 175 RW
B. Coniston, Ont., July 27, 1923

SSN	TEAM	GP	G	A	PTS.	PIM
50–51	Tor	1	0	0	0	2

BARBER, Donald 6–1 205 LW
B. Victoria, B.C., Dec. 2, 1964

SSN	TEAM	GP	G	A	PTS.	PIM	+/-
88–89	Minn	23	8	5	13	8	+2
89–90	Minn	44	15	19	34	32	+4
90–91	Minn-Winn	23	1	2	3	18	-6
91–92	Winn-Que-SJ	25	1	6	7	6	-6
Totals		115	25	32	57	64	-6

Playoffs

SSN	TEAM	GP	G	A	PTS.	PIM
88–89	Minn	4	1	1	2	7
89–90	Minn	7	3	3	6	8
Totals		11	4	4	8	15

BARBER, William Charles 6–0 190 LW
B. Callander, Ont., July 11, 1952

SSN	TEAM	GP	G	A	PTS.	PIM	+/-
72–73	Phil	69	30	34	64	46	+10
73–74	Phil	75	34	35	69	54	+34
74–75	Phil	79	34	37	71	66	+46
75–76	Phil	80	50	62	112	104	+74
76–77	Phil	73	20	35	55	62	+32
77–78	Phil	80	41	31	72	34	+31
78–79	Phil	79	34	46	80	22	+19
79–80	Phil	79	40	32	72	17	+39
80–81	Phil	80	43	42	85	69	+6
81–82	Phil	80	45	44	89	85	+4
82–83	Phil	66	27	33	60	28	+17
83–84	Phil	63	22	32	54	36	+4
Totals		903	420	463	883	623	+316

Playoffs

SSN	TEAM	GP	G	A	PTS.	PIM
72–73	Phil	11	3	2	5	22
73–74	Phil	17	3	6	9	18

SSN	TEAM	GP	G	A	PTS.	PIM	+/-
74–75	Phil	17	6	9	15	8	
75–76	Phil	16	6	7	13	18	
76–77	Phil	10	1	4	5	2	
77–78	Phil	12	6	3	9	2	
78–79	Phil	8	3	4	7	10	
79–80	Phil	19	12	9	21	23	
80–81	Phil	12	11	5	16	0	
81–82	Phil	4	1	5	6	4	
82–83	Phil	3	1	1	2	2	
Totals		129	53	55	108	109	

*BARILKO, William 5–11 184 D
B. Timmins, Ont., Mar. 25, 1927

SSN	TEAM	GP	G	A	PTS.	PIM
46–47	Tor	18	3	7	10	33
47–48	Tor	57	5	9	14	147
48–49	Tor	60	5	4	9	95
49–50	Tor	59	7	10	17	85
50–51	Tor	58	6	6	12	96
Totals		252	26	36	62	456

Playoffs

SSN	TEAM	GP	G	A	PTS.	PIM
46–47	Tor	11	0	3	3	18
47–48	Tor	9	1	0	1	17
48–49	Tor	9	0	1	1	20
49–50	Tor	7	1	1	2	18
50–51	Tor	11	3	2	5	31
Totals		47	5	7	12	104

BARKLEY, Douglas 6–2 185 D
B. Lethbridge, Alta., Jan. 6, 1937

SSN	TEAM	GP	G	A	PTS.	PIM
57–58	Chi	3	0	0	0	0
59–60	Chi	3	0	0	0	2
62–63	Det	70	3	24	27	78
63–64	Det	67	11	21	32	115
64–65	Det	67	5	20	25	122
65–66	Det	43	5	15	20	65
Totals		253	24	80	104	382

Playoffs

SSN	TEAM	GP	G	A	PTS.	PIM
62–63	Det	11	0	3	3	16
63–64	Det	14	0	5	5	33
64–65	Det	5	0	1	1	14
Totals		30	0	9	9	63

BARLOW, Robert George 5–10 175 F
B. Hamilton, Ont., June 17, 1935

SSN	TEAM	GP	G	A	PTS.	PIM	+/-
69–70	Minn	70	16	17	33	10	-3
70–71	Minn	7	0	0	0	0	0
74–75	Phoe (WHA)	51	6	20	26	8	
NHL Totals		77	16	17	33	10	-3
WHA Totals		51	6	20	26	8	

Playoffs

SSN	TEAM	GP	G	A	PTS.	PIM
69–70	Minn	6	2	2	4	6

BARNABY, Matthew 6–0 170 LW
B. Ottawa, Ont., May 4, 1973

SSN	TEAM	GP	G	A	PTS.	PIM	+/-
92–93	Buf	2	1	0	1	10	0
93–94	Buf	35	2	4	6	106	7
94–95	Buf	23	1	1	2	116	-2
95–96	Buf	73	15	16	31	335	-2
96–97	Buf	68	19	24	43	249	+16
97–98	Buf	72	5	20	25	289	+8
98–99	Buf-Pitt	62	6	16	22	177	-12
Totals		335	49	81	130	1282	+1

Playoffs

SSN	TEAM	GP	G	A	PTS.	PIM
92–93	Buf	1	0	1	1	4
93–94	Buf	3	0	0	0	17
96–97	Buf	8	0	4	4	36
97–98	Buf	15	7	6	13	22
98–99	Pitt	13	0	0	0	35
Totals		40	7	11	18	114

BARNES, Blair 5–11 190 RW
B. Windsor, Ont., Sept. 21, 1960

SSN	TEAM	GP	G	A	PTS.	PIM	+/-
82–83	LA	1	0	0	0	0	0

BARNES, Norman Leonard Charles 6–0 190 D
B. Toronto, Ont., Aug. 24, 1953

SSN	TEAM	GP	G	A	PTS.	PIM	+/-
76–77	Phil	1	0	0	0	0	0
79–80	Phil	59	4	21	25	59	+23
80–81	Phil-Hart	76	1	13	14	100	-33
81–82	Hart	20	1	4	5	19	-4
Totals		156	6	38	44	178	-14

SSN	TEAM	GP	G	A	PTS.	PIM	+/-

Playoffs

SSN	TEAM	GP	G	A	PTS.	PIM	+/-
78–79	Phil	2	0	0	0	0	
79–80	Phil	10	0	0	0	8	
Totals		12	0	0	0	8	

BARNES, Stu 5–11 175 C
B. Edmonton, Alta., Dec. 25, 1970

SSN	TEAM	GP	G	A	PTS.	PIM	+/-
91–92	Winn	46	8	9	17	26	-2
92–93	Winn	38	12	10	22	10	-3
93–94	Winn–Fla	77	23	24	47	38	+4
94–95	Fla	41	10	19	29	8	+7
95–96	Fla	72	19	25	44	46	-12
96–97	Fla–Pitt	81	19	30	49	26	-23
97–98	Pitt	78	30	35	65	30	+15
98–99	Pitt–Buf	81	20	16	36	30	-11
Totals		514	141	168	309	215	-25

Playoffs

SSN	TEAM	GP	G	A	PTS.	PIM	+/-
92–93	Winn	6	1	3	4	2	
95–96	Fla	22	6	10	16	4	
96–97	Pitt	5	0	1	1	0	
97–98	Pitt	6	3	3	6	2	
98–99	Buf	21	7	4	11	6	
Totals		54	14	18	32	12	

BARON, Murray 6–3 215 D
B. Prince George, B.C., June 1, 1967

SSN	TEAM	GP	G	A	PTS.	PIM	+/-
89–90	Phil	16	2	2	4	12	-1
90–91	Phil	67	8	8	16	74	-3
91–92	StL	67	3	8	11	94	-3
92–93	StL	53	2	2	4	59	-5
93–94	StL	77	5	9	14	123	-14
94–95	StL	39	0	5	5	93	+9
95–96	StL	82	2	9	11	190	+3
96–97	StL–Mont–Phoe	79	1	7	8	122	-20
97–98	Phoe	45	1	5	6	106	-10
98–99	Van	81	2	6	8	115	-23
Totals		606	26	61	87	988	-67

Playoffs

SSN	TEAM	GP	G	A	PTS.	PIM	+/-
91–92	StL	2	0	0	0	2	
92–93	StL	11	0	0	0	12	
93–94	StL	4	0	0	0	10	
94–95	StL	7	1	1	2	2	
95–96	StL	13	1	0	1	20	
96–97	Phoe	1	0	0	0	0	
97–98	Phoe	6	0	2	2	6	
Totals		44	2	3	5	52	

BARON, Normand 6–0 205 LW
B. Verdun, Que., Dec. 15, 1957

SSN	TEAM	GP	G	A	PTS.	PIM	+/-
83–84	Mont	4	0	0	0	12	-2
85–86	StL	23	2	0	2	39	-2
Totals		27	2	0	2	51	-4

Playoffs

SSN	TEAM	GP	G	A	PTS.	PIM	+/-
83–84	Mont	3	0	0	0	22	

BARR, David 6–1 195 RW
B. Toronto, Ont., Nov. 30, 1960

SSN	TEAM	GP	G	A	PTS.	PIM	+/-
81–82	Bos	2	0	0	0	0	0
82–83	Bos	10	1	1	2	7	+1
83–84	NYR–StL	7	0	0	0	2	0
84–85	StL	75	16	18	34	32	-1
85–86	StL	72	13	38	51	70	+5
86–87	StL–Hart–Det	69	15	17	32	68	+11
87–88	Det	51	14	26	40	58	+7
88–89	Det	73	27	32	59	69	+20
89–90	Det	62	10	25	35	45	+12
90–91	Det	70	18	22	40	55	+5
91–92	NJ	41	6	12	18	32	+9
92–93	NJ	62	6	8	14	61	+1
93–94	Dal	20	2	5	7	21	-6
Totals		614	128	204	332	520	+64

Playoffs

SSN	TEAM	GP	G	A	PTS.	PIM	+/-
81–82	Bos	5	1	0	1	0	
82–83	Bos	10	0	0	0	2	
84–85	StL	2	0	0	0	2	
85–86	StL	11	1	1	2	14	
86–87	Det	13	1	0	1	14	
87–88	Det	16	5	7	12	22	
88–89	Det	6	3	1	4	6	
92–93	NJ	5	1	0	1	6	
93–94	Dal	3	0	1	1	4	
Totals		71	12	10	22	70	

BARRAULT, Doug 6–2 205 RW
B. Golden, B.C., Apr. 21, 1970

SSN	TEAM	GP	G	A	PTS.	PIM	+/-
92–93	Minn	2	0	0	0	2	-1
93–94	Fla	2	0	0	0	0	-2
Totals		4	0	0	0	2	-3

BARRETT, Frederick William 6–0 194 D
B. Ottawa, Ont., Dec. 6, 1950

SSN	TEAM	GP	G	A	PTS.	PIM	+/-
70–71	Minn	57	0	13	13	75	+2
72–73	Minn	46	2	4	6	21	+14
73–74	Minn	40	0	7	7	12	-1
74–75	Minn	62	3	18	21	82	-21
75–76	Minn	79	2	9	11	66	-25
76–77	Minn	60	1	8	9	46	-31
77–78	Minn	79	0	15	15	59	-35
78–79	Minn	45	1	9	10	48	-4
79–80	Minn	80	8	14	22	71	+17
80–81	Minn	62	4	8	12	72	+1
81–82	Minn	69	1	15	16	89	-12
82–83	Minn	51	1	3	4	22	-19
83–84	LA	15	2	0	2	8	-2
Totals		745	25	123	148	671	-116

Playoffs

SSN	TEAM	GP	G	A	PTS.	PIM	+/-
72–73	Minn	6	0	0	0	4	
76–77	Minn	2	0	0	0	2	
79–80	Minn	14	0	0	0	22	
80–81	Minn	14	0	1	1	16	
81–82	Minn	4	0	1	1	16	
82–83	Minn	4	0	0	0	0	
Totals		44	0	2	2	60	

BARRETT, John David 6–1 210 D
B. Ottawa, Ont., July 1, 1958

SSN	TEAM	GP	G	A	PTS.	PIM	+/-
80–81	Det	56	3	10	13	60	-21
81–82	Det	69	1	12	13	93	-31
82–83	Det	79	4	10	14	74	-18
83–84	Det	78	2	8	10	78	0
84–85	Det	71	6	19	25	117	-15
85–86	Det–Wash	79	2	15	17	137	-26
86–87	Wash	55	2	2	4	43	-15
87–88	Minn	1	0	1	1	2	-3
Totals		488	20	77	97	604	-129

Playoffs

SSN	TEAM	GP	G	A	PTS.	PIM	+/-
83–84	Det	4	0	0	0	4	
84–85	Det	3	0	1	1	11	
85–86	Wash	9	2	1	3	35	
Totals		16	2	2	4	50	

BARRIE, Douglas Robert 5–9 175 D
B. Edmonton, Alta., Oct. 2, 1946

SSN	TEAM	GP	G	A	PTS.	PIM	+/-
68–69	Pitt	8	1	1	2	8	-2
70–71	Buf	75	4	23	27	168	-19
71–72	Buf–LA	75	5	18	23	92	-31
72–73	Alb (WHA)	54	9	22	31	111	
73–74	Edm (WHA)	69	4	27	31	214	
74–75	Edm (WHA)	78	12	33	45	122	
75–76	Edm (WHA)	79	4	21	25	81	
76–77	Edm (WHA)	70	8	19	27	92	
NHL Totals		158	10	42	52	268	-52
WHA Totals		350	37	122	159	620	

Playoffs

SSN	TEAM	GP	G	A	PTS.	PIM	+/-
73–74	Edm (WHA)	4	1	0	1	16	
75–76	Edm (WHA)	4	0	1	1	6	
76–77	Edm (WHA)	4	0	0	0	0	
WHA Totals		12	1	1	2	22	

BARRIE, Len 5–11 200 C
B. Kelowna, B.C., June 4, 1969

SSN	TEAM	GP	G	A	PTS.	PIM	+/-
89–90	Phil	1	0	0	0	0	-2
92–93	Phil	8	2	2	4	9	+2
93–94	Fla	2	0	0	0	0	-2
94–95	Pitt	48	3	11	14	66	-4
95–96	Pitt	5	0	0	0	18	-1
Totals		64	5	13	18	93	-7

Playoffs

SSN	TEAM	GP	G	A	PTS.	PIM	+/-
94–95	Pitt	4	1	0	1	8	

BARRY, Edward Thomas 5–10 180 LW
B. Wellesley, Mass., Oct. 9, 1919

SSN	TEAM	GP	G	A	PTS.	PIM	+/-
46–47	Bos	19	1	3	4	2	

*BARRY, Martin J. 5–11 175 C
B. Quebec City, Que., Dec. 8, 1905

SSN	TEAM	GP	G	A	PTS.	PIM	+/-
27–28	NYA	7	1	0	1	2	
29–30	Bos	44	18	15	33	8	
30–31	Bos	44	20	11	31	26	
31–32	Bos	48	21	17	38	22	
32–33	Bos	48	24	13	37	40	
33–34	Bos	48	27	12	39	12	
34–35	Bos	48	20	20	40	33	
35–36	Bos	48	21	19	40	16	
36–37	Det	48	17	27	44	6	
37–38	Det	48	9	20	29	34	
38–39	Det	48	13	28	41	4	
39–40	Mont	30	4	10	14	2	
Totals		509	195	192	387	205	

Playoffs

SSN	TEAM	GP	G	A	PTS.	PIM	+/-
29–30	Bos	6	3	3	6	14	
30–31	Bos	5	1	1	2	4	
32–33	Bos	5	2	2	4	6	
34–35	Bos	4	0	0	0	2	
35–36	Det	7	2	4	6	4	
36–37	Det	10	4	7	11	2	
38–39	Det	6	3	1	4	0	
Totals		43	15	18	33	34	

BARRY, William Raymond (Ray) 5–11 170 C
B. Boston, Mass., Oct. 4, 1928

SSN	TEAM	GP	G	A	PTS.	PIM	+/-
51–52	Bos	18	1	2	3	6	

BARTECKO, Lubos 6–1 200 C
B. Kezmaroc, Czech, July 14, 1976

SSN	TEAM	GP	G	A	PTS.	PIM	+/-
98–99	StL	32	5	11	16	4	+6

Playoffs

SSN	TEAM	GP	G	A	PTS.	PIM	+/-
98–99	StL	5	0	0	0	2	

BARTEL, Robin Dale 6–0 200 D
B. Drake, Sask., May 16, 1961

SSN	TEAM	GP	G	A	PTS.	PIM	+/-
85–86	Calg	1	0	0	0	0	-1
86–87	Van	40	0	1	1	14	+2
Totals		41	0	1	1	14	+1

Playoffs

SSN	TEAM	GP	G	A	PTS.	PIM	+/-
85–86	Calg	6	0	0	0	16	

BARTLETT, James Baker (Rocky) 5–9 165 LW
B. Verdun, Que., May 27, 1932

SSN	TEAM	GP	G	A	PTS.	PIM	+/-
54–55	Mont	2	0	0	0	4	
55–56	NYR	12	0	1	1	8	
58–59	NYR	70	11	9	20	118	
59–60	NYR	44	8	4	12	48	
60–61	Bos	63	15	9	24	95	
Totals		191	34	23	57	273	

Playoffs

SSN	TEAM	GP	G	A	PTS.	PIM	+/-
54–55	Mont	2	0	0	0	0	

*BARTON, Clifford John 5–7 155 RW
B. Sault Ste. Marie, Mich., Sept. 3, 1907

SSN	TEAM	GP	G	A	PTS.	PIM	+/-
29–30	Pitt Pi	39	4	2	6	4	
30–31	PhilQ	43	6	7	13	18	
39–40	NYR	3	0	0	0	0	
Totals		85	10	9	19	22	

BASHKIROV, Andrei 6–0 198 RW
B. Shelekhov, USSR, June 22, 1970

SSN	TEAM	GP	G	A	PTS.	PIM	+/-
98–99	Mont	10	0	0	0	0	-3

BASSEN, Bob 5–10 180 C
B. Calgary, Alta., May 6, 1965

SSN	TEAM	GP	G	A	PTS.	PIM	+/-
85–86	NYI	11	2	1	3	6	0
86–87	NYI	77	7	10	17	89	-17
87–88	NYI	77	6	16	22	99	+8
88–89	NYI–Chi	68	5	16	21	83	+5
89–90	Chi	6	1	1	2	8	+1
90–91	StL	79	16	18	34	183	+17
91–92	StL	79	7	25	32	167	+12
92–93	StL	53	9	10	19	63	0
93–94	StL–Que	83	13	15	28	99	-17
94–95	Que	47	12	15	27	33	+14
95–96	Dal	13	0	1	1	15	-6
96–97	Dal	46	5	7	12	41	+5
97–98	Dal	58	3	4	7	57	-4
Totals		738	87	141	228	878	+5

Playoffs

85–86	NYI	3	0	1	1	0
86–87	NYI	14	1	2	3	21
87–88	NYI	6	0	1	1	23
88–89	Chi	10	1	1	2	34
89–90	Chi	1	0	0	0	2
90–91	StL	13	1	3	4	24
91–92	StL	6	0	2	2	4
92–93	StL	11	0	0	0	10
94–95	Que	5	2	4	6	0
96–97	Dal	7	3	1	4	4
97–98	Dal	17	1	0	1	12
Totals		**93**	**9**	**15**	**24**	**134**

BAST, Ryan *6–2 190 D*
B. Spruce Grove, Alta., Aug. 27, 1975

98–99	Phil	2	0	1	1	0	0

BATES, Shawn *5–11 205 C*
B. Melrose, Mass., Apr. 3, 1975

97–98	Bos	13	2	0	2	2	-3
98–99	Bos	33	5	4	9	2	+3
Totals		**46**	**7**	**4**	**11**	**4**	**0**

Playoffs

98–99	Bos	12	0	0	0	4

BATHE, Francis Lenard *6–1 190 D*
B. Oshawa, Ont., Sept. 27, 1954

74–75	Det	19	0	3	3	31	-5
75–76	Det	7	0	1	1	9	-1
77–78	Phil	1	0	0	0	0	0
78–79	Phil	21	1	3	4	76	+9
79–80	Phil	47	0	7	7	111	+7
80–81	Phil	44	0	3	3	175	-3
81–82	Phil	28	1	3	4	68	+11
82–83	Phil	57	1	8	9	72	+4
Totals		**224**	**3**	**28**	**31**	**542**	**+22**

Playoffs

78–79	Phil	6	1	0	1	12
79–80	Phil	1	0	0	0	0
80–81	Phil	12	0	3	3	16
81–82	Phil	4	0	0	0	2
82–83	Phil	4	0	0	0	12
Totals		**27**	**1**	**3**	**4**	**42**

*BATHGATE, Andrew James *6–0 180 RW*
B. Winnipeg, Man., Aug. 28, 1932

52–53	NYR	18	0	1	1	6	
53–54	NYR	20	2	2	4	18	
54–55	NYR	70	20	20	40	37	
55–56	NYR	70	19	47	66	59	
56–57	NYR	70	27	50	77	60	
57–58	NYR	65	30	48	78	42	
58–59	NYR	70	40	48	88	48	
59–60	NYR	70	26	48	74	28	
60–61	NYR	70	29	48	77	22	
61–62	NYR	70	28	56	84	44	
62–63	NYR	70	35	46	81	54	
63–64	NYR–Tor	71	19	58	77	34	
64–65	Tor	55	16	29	45	34	
65–66	Det	70	15	32	47	25	
66–67	Det	60	8	23	31	24	
67–68	Pitt	74	20	39	59	55	-11
70–71	Pitt	76	15	29	44	34	-11
74–75	Van (WHA)	11	1	6	7	2	
NHL Totals		**1069**	**349**	**624**	**973**	**624**	**-22**
WHA Totals		**11**	**1**	**6**	**7**	**2**	

Playoffs

55–56	NYR	5	1	2	3	2
56–57	NYR	5	2	0	2	7
57–58	NYR	6	5	3	8	6
61–62	NYR	6	1	2	3	4
63–64	Tor	14	5	4	9	25
64–65	Tor	6	1	0	1	6
65–66	Det	12	6	3	9	6
Totals		**54**	**21**	**14**	**35**	**76**

BATHGATE, Frank Douglas *5–10 162 C*
B. Winnipeg, Man., Feb. 14, 1930

52–53	NYR	2	0	0	0	2

BATTAGLIA, Jon *6–2 185 LW*
B. Chicago, Ill., Dec. 13, 1975

97–98	Car	33	2	4	6	10	-1
98–99	Car	60	7	11	18	22	+7
Totals		**93**	**9**	**15**	**24**	**32**	**+6**

Playoffs

98–99	Car	6	0	3	3	8

BATTERS, Jeffrey William *6–2 215 D*
B. Victoria, B.C., Oct. 23, 1970

93–94	StL	6	0	0	0	7	+1
94–95	Stl	10	0	0	0	21	-5
Totals		**16**	**0**	**0**	**0**	**28**	**-4**

BATYRSHIN, Ruslan *6–1 160 D*
B. Moscow, U.S.S.R., Feb. 19, 1975

95–96	LA	2	0	0	0	6	0

*BAUER, Robert Theodore *5–6 150 RW*
B. Waterloo, Ont., Feb. 16, 1915

35–36	Bos	1	0	0	0	0
36–37	Bos	1	1	0	1	0
37–38	Bos	48	20	14	34	9
38–39	Bos	48	13	18	31	4
39–40	Bos	48	17	26	43	2
40–41	Bos	48	17	22	39	2
41–42	Bos	36	13	22	35	11
45–46	Bos	39	11	10	21	4
46–47	Bos	58	30	24	54	4
51–52	Bos	1	1	1	2	0
Totals		**328**	**123**	**137**	**260**	**36**

Playoffs

36–37	Bos	1	0	0	0	0
37–38	Bos	3	0	0	0	2
38–39	Bos	12	3	2	5	0
39–40	Bos	6	1	0	1	2
40–41	Bos	11	2	2	4	0
45–46	Bos	10	4	3	7	2
46–47	Bos	5	1	1	2	0
Totals		**48**	**11**	**8**	**19**	**6**

BAUMGARTNER, Ken *6–1 200 LW*
B. Flin Flon, Man., Mar. 11, 1966

87–88	LA	30	2	3	5	189	+5
88–89	LA	49	1	3	4	288	-9
89–90	LA–NYI	65	1	5	6	222	-4
89–90	NYI	78	1	6	7	282	-14
91–92	NYI–Tor	55	0	1	1	225	-9
92–93	Tor	63	1	0	1	155	-11
93–94	Tor	64	4	4	8	185	-6
94–95	Tor	2	0	0	0	5	0
95–96	Tor–Ana	72	2	4	6	193	-5
96–97	Ana	67	0	11	11	182	0
97–98	Bos	82	0	1	1	199	-14
98–99	Bos	69	1	3	4	119	-6
Totals		**697**	**13**	**41**	**54**	**2244**	**-73**

Playoffs

87–88	LA	5	0	1	1	28
88–89	LA	5	0	0	0	8
89–90	NYI	4	0	0	0	27
92–93	Tor	7	1	0	1	0
93–94	Tor	10	0	0	0	18
96–97	Ana	11	0	1	1	11
97–98	Bos	6	0	0	0	14
98–99	Bos	3	0	0	0	0
Totals		**51**	**1**	**2**	**3**	**106**

BAUMGARTNER, Michael Edward *6–1 195 D*
B. Roseau, Minn., Jan. 30, 1949

74–75	KC	17	0	0	0	0	-9

BAUMGARTNER, Nolan *6–1 200 D*
B. Calgary, Alta., Mar. 23, 1976

95–96	Wash	1	0	0	0	0	-1
97–98	Wash	4	0	1	1	0	0
98–99	Wash	5	0	0	0	0	-3
Totals		**10**	**0**	**1**	**1**	**0**	**-4**

Playoffs

95–96	Wash	1	0	0	0	10

BAUN, Robert Neil *5–9 182 D*
B. Lanigan, Sask., Sept. 9, 1936

56–57	Tor	20	0	5	5	37	
57–58	Tor	67	1	9	10	91	
58–59	Tor	51	1	8	9	87	
59–60	Tor	61	8	9	17	59	
60–61	Tor	70	1	14	15	70	
61–62	Tor	65	4	11	15	94	
62–63	Tor	48	4	8	12	65	
63–64	Tor	52	4	14	18	113	
64–65	Tor	70	0	18	18	160	
65–66	Tor	44	0	6	6	68	
66–67	Tor	54	2	8	10	83	
67–68	Oak	67	3	10	13	81	-18
68–69	Det	76	4	16	20	121	+24
69–70	Det	71	1	18	19	112	+7
70–71	Det–Tor	69	1	20	21	147	+15
71–72	Tor	74	2	12	14	101	+8
72–73	Tor	5	1	1	2	4	-5
Totals		**964**	**37**	**187**	**224**	**1493**	**+31**

Playoffs

58–59	Tor	12	0	0	0	24
59–60	Tor	10	1	0	1	17
60–61	Tor	3	0	0	0	8
61–62	Tor	12	0	3	3	19
62–63	Tor	10	0	3	3	6
63–64	Tor	14	2	3	5	42
64–65	Tor	6	0	1	1	14
65–66	Tor	4	0	1	1	8
66–67	Tor	10	0	0	0	4
69–70	Det	4	0	0	0	6
70–71	Tor	6	0	1	1	19
71–72	Tor	5	0	0	0	4
Totals		**96**	**3**	**12**	**15**	**171**

BAUTIN, Sergei *6–3 200 D*
B. Rogachev, USSR, Mar. 11, 1967

92–93	Winn	71	5	18	23	96	-2
93–94	Winn–Det	60	0	7	7	78	-12
95–96	SJ	1	0	0	0	2	-1
Totals		**132**	**5**	**25**	**30**	**176**	**-15**

Playoffs

92–93	Winn	6	0	0	0	2

BAWA, Robin *6–2 214 RW*
B. Chemainus, B.C., Mar. 26, 1966

89–90	Wash	5	1	0	1	6	-3
91–92	Van	2	0	0	0	0	0
92–93	SJ	42	5	0	5	47	-25
93–94	Ana	12	0	1	1	7	-3
Totals		**61**	**6**	**1**	**7**	**60**	**-31**

Playoffs

91–92	Van	1	0	0	0	0

BAXTER, Paul Gordon *5–11 200 D*
B. Winnipeg, Man., Oct. 25, 1955

74–75	Clev (WHA)	5	0	0	0	37	
75–76	Clev (WHA)	67	3	7	10	201	
76–77	Que (WHA)	66	6	17	23	244	
77–78	Que (WHA)	76	6	29	35	240	
78–79	Que (WHA)	76	10	36	46	240	
79–80	Que	61	7	13	20	145	-27
80–81	Pitt	51	5	14	19	204	-11
81–82	Pitt	76	9	34	43	409	-9
82–83	Pitt	75	11	21	32	238	-49
83–84	Calg	74	7	20	27	182	-1
84–85	Calg	70	5	14	19	126	+39
85–86	Calg	47	4	3	7	194	+5
86–87	Calg	18	0	2	2	66	-5
NHL Totals		**472**	**48**	**121**	**169**	**1564**	**-58**
WHA Totals		**290**	**25**	**89**	**114**	**962**	

Playoffs

75–76	Clev (WHA)	3	0	0	0	10
76–77	Que (WHA)	12	2	2	4	35
77–78	Que (WHA)	11	4	7	11	42
78–79	Que (WHA)	4	0	2	2	7
80–81	Pitt	5	0	1	1	28
81–82	Pitt	5	0	0	0	14
83–84	Calg	11	0	2	2	37
84–85	Calg	4	0	1	1	18
85–86	Calg	13	0	1	1	55
86–87	Calg	2	0	0	0	10
NHL Totals		**40**	**0**	**5**	**5**	**162**

SSN	TEAM	GP	G	A	PTS.	PIM	+/-
WHA Totals		30	6	11	17	94	

BEADLE, Sandy James 6–2 185 LW
B. Regina, Sask., July 12, 1960

SSN	TEAM	GP	G	A	PTS.	PIM	+/-
80–81	Winn	6	1	0	1	2	-2

BEATON, Alexander Francis (Frank, Seldom) 5–10 200 LW
B. Antigonish, N.S., Apr. 28, 1953

SSN	TEAM	GP	G	A	PTS.	PIM	+/-
75–76	Cin (WHA)	29	2	3	5	61	
76–77	Edm (WHA)	68	4	9	13	274	
77–78	Birm (WHA)	56	6	9	15	279	
78–79	NYR	2	0	0	0	0	-1
79–80	NYR	23	1	1	2	43	-5
NHL Totals		25	1	1	2	43	-6
WHA Totals		153	12	21	33	614	

Playoffs

SSN	TEAM	GP	G	A	PTS.	PIM	+/-
76–77	Edm (WHA)	5	0	2	2	21	
77–78	Birm (WHA)	5	2	0	2	10	
Totals		10	2	2	4	31	

BEATTIE, John (Red) 5–9 170 LW
B. Ibstock, England, Oct. 7, 1907

SSN	TEAM	GP	G	A	PTS.	PIM
30–31	Bos	32	10	11	21	25
31–32	Bos	2	0	0	0	0
32–33	Bos	48	8	12	20	12
33–34	Bos	48	9	13	22	26
34–35	Bos	48	9	18	27	27
35–36	Bos	48	14	18	32	27
36–37	Bos	48	8	7	15	10
37–38	Bos–Det–NYA	44	4	6	10	5
38–39	NYA	17	0	0	0	5
Totals		335	62	85	147	137

Playoffs

SSN	TEAM	GP	G	A	PTS.	PIM
30–31	Bos	4	0	0	0	0
32–33	Bos	5	0	0	0	2
34–35	Bos	4	1	0	1	2
36–37	Bos	3	1	0	1	0
37–38	NYA	6	2	2	4	2
Totals		22	4	2	6	6

BEAUDIN, Norman Joseph Andrew 5–8 170 RW
B. Montmartre, Sask., Nov. 28, 1941

SSN	TEAM	GP	G	A	PTS.	PIM	+/-
67–68	StL	13	1	1	2	4	-4
70–71	Minn	12	0	1	1	0	-3
72–73	Winn (WHA)	78	38	65	103	15	
73–74	Winn (WHA)	74	27	28	55	8	
74–75	Winn (WHA)	77	16	31	47	8	
75–76	Winn (WHA)	80	16	31	47	38	
NHL Totals		25	1	2	3	4	-7
WHA Totals		309	97	155	252	69	

Playoffs

SSN	TEAM	GP	G	A	PTS.	PIM
72–72	Winn (WHA)	14	13	15	28	2
73–74	Winn (WHA)	4	3	1	4	2
75–76	WINN (WHA)	13	2	3	5	10
Totals		31	18	19	37	14

BEAUDOIN, Serge 6–2 215 D
B. Montreal, Que., Nov. 30, 1952

SSN	TEAM	GP	G	A	PTS.	PIM	+/-
73–74	Van (WHA)	26	1	11	12	37	
74–75	Van (WHA)	4	0	0	0	2	
75–76	Phoe (WHA)	76	0	21	21	102	
76–77	Phoe (WHA)	77	6	24	30	136	
77–78	Birm (WHA)	77	8	26	34	115	
78–79	Birm (WHA)	72	5	21	26	127	
79–80	Atl	3	0	0	0	0	-1
NHL Totals		3	0	0	0	0	-1
WHA Totals		332	20	103	123	519	

Playoffs

SSN	TEAM	GP	G	A	PTS.	PIM
75–76	Phoe (WHA)	3	1	0	1	10
77–78	Birm (WHA)	5	1	0	1	46
Totals		8	2	0	2	56

BEAUDOIN, Yves 5–11 180 D
B. Pointe–aux–Trembles, Que., Jan. 7, 1965

SSN	TEAM	GP	G	A	PTS.	PIM	+/-
85–86	Wash	4	0	0	0	0	-4
86–87	Wash	6	0	0	0	5	-4
87–88	Wash	1	0	0	0	0	-1
Totals		11	0	0	0	5	-9

BEAUFAIT, Mark 5–9 170 C
B. Livonia, Mich., May 13, 1970

SSN	TEAM	GP	G	A	PTS.	PIM	+/-
92–93	SJ	5	1	0	1	0	-1

BEAUPRE, Donald William 5–8 150
B. Waterloo, Ont., Sept. 19, 1961

Playoffs

SSN	TEAM	GP	G	A	PTS.	PIM
80–81	Minn	6	0	0	0	0

BECK, Barry David 6–3 215 D
B. Vancouver, B.C., June 3, 1957

SSN	TEAM	GP	G	A	PTS.	PIM	+/-
77–78	Col	75	22	38	60	89	-14
78–79	Col	63	14	28	42	91	-30
79–80	Col–NYR	71	15	50	65	106	+14
80–81	NYR	75	11	23	34	231	+9
81–82	NYR	60	9	29	38	111	+19
82–83	NYR	66	12	22	34	112	+22
83–84	NYR	72	9	27	36	134	+12
84–85	NYR	56	7	19	26	65	-11
85–86	NYR	25	4	8	12	24	+7
89–90	LA	52	1	7	8	53	+3
Totals		615	104	251	355	1016	+31

Playoffs

SSN	TEAM	GP	G	A	PTS.	PIM
77–78	Col	2	0	1	1	0
79–80	NYR	9	1	4	5	6
80–81	NYR	14	5	8	13	32
81–82	NYR	10	1	5	6	14
82–83	NYR	9	2	4	6	8
83–84	NYR	4	1	0	1	6
84–85	NYR	3	0	1	1	11
Totals		51	10	23	33	77

BECKETT, Robert Owen 6–0 185 C
B. Unionville, Ont., Apr. 8, 1936

SSN	TEAM	GP	G	A	PTS.	PIM
56–57	Bos	18	0	3	3	2
57–58	Bos	9	0	0	0	2
61–62	Bos	34	7	2	9	14
63–64	Bos	7	0	1	1	0
Totals		68	7	6	13	18

BEDARD, James Arthur 5–10 181
B. Niagara Falls, Ont., Nov. 14, 1956

SSN	TEAM	GP	G	A	PTS.	PIM
77–78	Wash	43	0	2	2	4

BEDARD, James Leo 6–0 180 D
B. Admiral, Sask., Nov. 19, 1927

SSN	TEAM	GP	G	A	PTS.	PIM
49–50	Chi	5	0	0	0	2
50–51	Chi	17	1	1	2	6
Totals		22	1	1	2	8

BEDDOES, Clayton 5–10 180 C
B. Bentley, Alta., Nov. 10, 1970

SSN	TEAM	GP	G	A	PTS.	PIM	+/-
95–96	Bos	39	1	6	7	44	-5
96–97	Bos	21	1	2	3	13	-1
Totals		60	2	8	10	57	-6

BEDNARSKI, John Severn 5–10 195 D
B. Thunder Bay, Ont., July 4, 1952

SSN	TEAM	GP	G	A	PTS.	PIM	+/-
74–75	NYR	35	1	10	11	37	-1
75–76	NYR	59	1	8	9	77	-15
76–77	NYR	5	0	0	0	0	-3
79–80	Edm	1	0	0	0	0	
Totals		100	2	18	20	114	-19

Playoffs

SSN	TEAM	GP	G	A	PTS.	PIM
75–76	NYR	1	0	0	0	17

BEERS, Bob 6–2 200 D
B. Cheektowaga, N.Y., May 20, 1967

SSN	TEAM	GP	G	A	PTS.	PIM	+/-
89–90	Bos	3	0	1	1	6	+2
90–91	Bos	16	0	1	1	10	-8
91–92	Bos	31	0	5	5	29	-13
92–93	TB	64	12	24	36	70	-25
93–94	TB–Edm	82	11	32	43	86	-22
94–95	NYI	22	2	7	9	6	-8
95–96	NYI	13	0	5	5	10	-2
96–97	Bos	27	3	4	7	8	0
Totals		258	28	79	107	225	-76

Playoffs

SSN	TEAM	GP	G	A	PTS.	PIM
89–90	Bos	14	1	1	2	18
90–91	Bos	6	0	0	0	4
91–92	Bos	1	0	0	0	0

SSN	TEAM	GP	G	A	PTS.	PIM
Totals		21	1	1	2	22

BEERS, Edward Joseph 6–2 200 LW
B. Merritt, B.C., Oct. 12, 1959

SSN	TEAM	GP	G	A	PTS.	PIM	+/-
81–82	Calg	5	1	1	2	21	0
82–83	Calg	41	11	15	26	21	+11
83–84	Calg	73	36	39	75	88	+7
84–85	Calg	74	28	40	68	94	+7
85–86	Calg–StL	57	18	21	39	32	-6
Totals		250	94	116	210	256	+19

Playoffs

SSN	TEAM	GP	G	A	PTS.	PIM
82–83	Calg	8	1	1	2	27
83–84	Calg	11	2	5	7	12
84–85	Calg	3	1	0	1	0
85–86	StL	19	3	4	7	8
Totals		41	7	10	17	47

BEGIN, Steve 5–11 180 C
B. Trois–Rivieres, Que., June 14, 1978

SSN	TEAM	GP	G	A	PTS.	PIM	+/-
97–98	Calg	5	0	0	0	23	0

BEHLING, Richard Clarence D
B. Kitchener, Ont., Mar. 16, 1916

SSN	TEAM	GP	G	A	PTS.	PIM
40–41	Det	3	0	0	0	0
42–43	Det	2	1	0	1	2
Totals		5	1	0	1	2

BEISLER, Frank D
B. New Haven, Conn.

SSN	TEAM	GP	G	A	PTS.	PIM
36–37	NYA	1	0	0	0	0
39–40	NYA	1	0	0	0	0
Totals		2	0	0	0	0

BELAK, Wade 6–4 213 D
B. Saskatoon, Sask., July 3, 1976

SSN	TEAM	GP	G	A	PTS.	PIM	+/-
96–97	Col A	5	0	0	0	11	-1
97–98	Col A	8	1	1	2	27	-3
98–99	Col A–Calg	31	0	1	1	94	+1
Totals		44	1	2	3	132	-3

BELANGER, Alain 6–1 190 RW
B. St. Janvier, Que., Jan. 18, 1956

SSN	TEAM	GP	G	A	PTS.	PIM
77–78	Tor	9	0	1	1	6	0

BELANGER, Jesse 6–0 186 C
B. St. Georges de Beauce, Que., June 15, 1969

SSN	TEAM	GP	G	A	PTS.	PIM	+/-
91–92	Mont	4	0	0	0	0	-1
92–93	Mont	19	4	2	6	4	+1
93–94	Fla	70	17	33	50	16	-4
94–95	Fla	47	15	14	29	18	-5
95–96	Fla–Van	72	20	21	41	14	-5
96–97	Edm	6	0	0	0	0	-3
Totals		218	56	70	126	52	-17

Playoffs

SSN	TEAM	GP	G	A	PTS.	PIM
92–93	Mont	9	0	1	1	0
95–96	Van	3	0	2	2	2
Totals		12	0	3	3	2

BELANGER, Ken 6–4 225 LW
B. Sault Ste. Marie, Ont., May 14, 1974

SSN	TEAM	GP	G	A	PTS.	PIM	+/-
94–95	Tor	3	0	0	0	9	0
95–96	NYI	7	0	0	0	27	-2
96–97	NYI	18	0	2	2	102	-1
97–98	NYI	37	3	1	4	101	+1
98–99	NYI–Bos	54	2	5	7	182	-1
Totals		119	5	8	13	421	-3

Playoffs

SSN	TEAM	GP	G	A	PTS.	PIM
98–99	Bos	12	1	0	1	16

BELANGER, Roger 6–0 190 C
B. St. Catharines, Ont., Dec. 1, 1965

SSN	TEAM	GP	G	A	PTS.	PIM	+/-
84–85	Pitt	44	3	5	8	32	-13

BELISLE, Daniel George 5–10 175 RW
B. South Porcupine, Ont., May 9, 1937

SSN	TEAM	GP	G	A	PTS.	PIM
60–61	NYR	4	2	0	2	0

*BELIVEAU, Jean Arthur 6–3 205 C
B. Trois Rivieres, Que., Aug. 31, 1931

SSN	TEAM	GP	G	A	PTS.	PIM
50–51	Mont	2	1	1	2	0
52–53	Mont	3	5	0	5	0

SSN	TEAM	GP	G	A	PTS.	PIM	+/-
53–54	Mont	44	13	21	34	22	
54–55	Mont	70	37	36	73	58	
55–56	Mont	70	47	41	88	143	
56–57	Mont	69	33	51	84	105	
57–58	Mont	55	27	32	59	93	
58–59	Mont	64	45	46	91	67	
59–60	Mont	60	34	40	74	57	
60–61	Mont	69	32	58	90	57	
61–62	Mont	43	18	23	41	36	
62–63	Mont	69	18	49	67	68	
63–64	Mont	68	28	50	78	42	
64–65	Mont	58	20	23	43	76	
65–66	Mont	67	29	48	77	50	
66–67	Mont	53	12	26	38	22	
67–68	Mont	59	31	37	68	28	+27
68–69	Mont	69	33	49	82	55	+15
69–70	Mont	63	19	30	49	10	+1
70–71	Mont	70	25	51	76	40	+24
Totals		1125	507	712	1219	1029	+67

Playoffs

SSN	TEAM	GP	G	A	PTS.	PIM	+/-
53–54	Mont	10	2	8	10	4	
54–55	Mont	12	6	7	13	18	
55–56	Mont	10	12	7	19	22	
56–57	Mont	10	6	6	12	15	
57–58	Mont	10	4	8	12	10	
58–59	Mont	3	1	4	5	4	
59–60	Mont	8	5	2	7	6	
60–61	Mont	6	0	5	5	0	
61–62	Mont	6	2	1	3	4	
62–63	Mont	5	2	1	3	2	
63–64	Mont	5	2	0	2	18	
64–65	Mont	13	8	8	16	34	
65–66	Mont	10	5	5	10	6	
66–67	Mont	10	6	5	11	26	
67–68	Mont	10	7	4	11	6	
68–69	Mont	14	5	10	15	8	
70–71	Mont	20	6	16	22	28	
Totals		162	79	97	176	211	

BELL, Bruce 6–0 190 D
B. Toronto, Ont., Feb. 15, 1965

SSN	TEAM	GP	G	A	PTS.	PIM	+/-
84–85	Que	75	6	31	37	44	+32
85–86	StL	75	2	18	20	43	+2
86–87	StL	45	3	13	16	18	+3
87–88	NYR	13	1	2	3	8	-10
89–90	Edm	1	0	0	0	0	0
Totals		209	12	64	76	113	+28

Playoffs

SSN	TEAM	GP	G	A	PTS.	PIM
84–85	Que	16	2	2	4	21
85–86	StL	14	0	2	2	13
86–87	Stl	4	1	1	2	7
Totals		34	3	5	8	41

BELL, Harry 5–8 180 D
B. Regina, Sask., Oct. 31, 1925

SSN	TEAM	GP	G	A	PTS.	PIM
46–47	NYR	1	0	1	1	0

BELL, Joseph Alexander 5–10 170 LW
B. Portage la Prairie, Man., Nov. 27, 1923

SSN	TEAM	GP	G	A	PTS.	PIM
42–43	NYR	15	2	5	7	6
46–47	NYR	47	6	4	10	12
Totals		62	8	9	17	18

*BELL, William C/D
B. Lachine, Que., June 10, 1891

SSN	TEAM	GP	G	A	PTS.	PIM
17–18	Mont W–Mont	8	1	0	1	3
18–19	Mont	1	0	0	0	0
20–21	Mont	4	0	0	0	0
21–22	Mont–Ott	23	2	1	3	4
22–23	Mont	15	0	0	0	0
23–24	Mont	10	0	0	0	0
Totals		61	3	1	4	7

Playoffs

SSN	TEAM	GP	G	A	PTS.	PIM
21–22	Ott	1	0	0	0	0
22–23	Mont	2	0	0	0	0
23–24	Mont	5	0	0	0	0
Totals		8	0	0	0	0

BELLAND, Neil 5–11 175 D
B. Parry Sound, Ont., Apr. 3, 1961

SSN	TEAM	GP	G	A	PTS.	PIM	+/-
81–82	Van	28	3	6	9	16	-1
82–23	Van	14	2	4	6	4	-4
83–84	Van	44	7	13	20	24	-8
84–85	Van	13	0	6	6	6	-4
85–86	Van	7	1	2	3	4	-2

SSN	TEAM	GP	G	A	PTS.	PIM	+/-
86–87	Pitt	3	0	1	1	0	0
Totals		109	13	32	45	54	-19

Playoffs

SSN	TEAM	GP	G	A	PTS.	PIM
81–82	Van	17	1	7	8	16
83–84	Van	4	1	2	3	7
Totals		21	2	9	11	23

BELLEFEUILLE, Peter RW

SSN	TEAM	GP	G	A	PTS.	PIM
25–26	Tor	36	14	2	16	22
26–27	Tor–Det	31	6	0	6	26
28–29	Det	1	1	0	1	0
29–30	Det	24	5	2	7	10
Totals		92	26	4	30	58

*BELLEMER, Andrew D
B. Penetang, Ont., July 3, 1904

SSN	TEAM	GP	G	A	PTS.	PIM
32–33	Mont M	15	0	0	0	0

BELLOWS, Brian 5–11 210 RW
B. St. Catharines, Ont., Sept. 1, 1964

SSN	TEAM	GP	G	A	PTS.	PIM	+/-
82–83	Minn	78	35	30	65	27	-12
83–84	Minn	78	41	42	83	66	-2
84–85	Minn	78	26	36	62	72	-18
85–86	Minn	77	31	48	79	46	+16
86–87	Minn	65	26	27	53	34	-13
87–88	Minn	77	40	41	81	81	-8
88–89	Minn	60	23	27	50	55	-14
89–90	Minn	80	55	44	99	72	-3
90–91	Minn	80	35	40	75	43	-13
91–92	Minn	80	30	45	75	41	-20
92–93	Mont	82	40	48	88	44	+4
93–94	Mont	77	33	38	71	36	+9
94–95	Mont	41	8	8	16	8	-7
95–96	TB	79	23	26	49	39	-14
96–97	TB–Ana	69	16	15	31	22	-4
97–98	Wash	11	6	3	9	6	-11
98–99	Wash	76	17	19	36	26	-12
Totals		1188	485	537	1022	718	-122

Playoffs

SSN	TEAM	GP	G	A	PTS.	PIM
82–83	Minn	9	5	4	9	18
83–84	Minn	16	2	12	14	6
84–85	Minn	9	2	4	6	9
85–86	Minn	5	5	0	5	16
88–89	Minn	5	2	3	5	8
89–90	Minn	7	4	3	7	10
90–91	Minn	23	10	19	29	30
91–92	Minn	7	4	4	8	14
92–93	Mont	18	6	9	15	18
93–94	Mont	6	1	2	3	2
95–96	TB	6	2	0	2	4
96–97	Ana	11	2	4	6	2
97–98	Wash	21	6	7	13	6
Totals		143	51	71	122	143

BEND, John Linthwaite (Lin) 5–9 165 C
B. Poplar Point, Man., Dec. 20, 1922

SSN	TEAM	GP	G	A	PTS.	PIM
42–43	NYR	8	3	1	4	2

BENDA, Jan 6–2 208 C
B. Reef, Belgium, March 28, 1972

SSN	TEAM	GP	G	A	PTS.	PIM	+/-
97–98	Wash	9	0	3	3	6	0

BENNETT, Adam 6–4 206 D
B. Georgetown, Ont., Mar. 30, 1971

SSN	TEAM	GP	G	A	PTS.	PIM	+/-
91–92	Chi	5	0	0	0	12	+1
92–93	Chi	16	0	2	2	8	-2
93–94	Edm	48	3	6	9	49	-8
Totals		69	3	8	11	69	-9

BENNETT, Curt Alexander 6–3 195 C
B. Regina, Sask., Mar. 27, 1948

SSN	TEAM	GP	G	A	PTS.	PIM	+/-
70–71	StL	4	2	0	2	0	0
71–72	StL	31	3	5	8	30	-4
72–73	NYR–Atl	68	18	18	36	20	-15
73–74	Atl	71	17	24	41	34	+3
74–75	Atl	80	31	33	64	40	+10
75–76	Atl	80	34	31	65	61	+1
76–77	Atl	76	22	25	47	36	-14
77–78	Atl–StL	75	10	24	34	64	-26
78–79	StL	74	14	19	33	62	-23
79–80	Atl	21	1	3	4	0	-6
Totals		580	152	182	334	347	-74

Playoffs

SSN	TEAM	GP	G	A	PTS.	PIM
70–71	StL	2	0	0	0	0
71–72	StL	10	0	0	0	12
73–74	Atl	4	0	1	1	34
75–76	Atl	2	0	0	0	4
76–77	Atl	3	1	0	1	7
Totals		21	1	1	2	57

BENNETT, Eric (Ric) 6–3 200 LW
B. Springfield, Mass., July 24, 1967

SSN	TEAM	GP	G	A	PTS.	PIM	+/-
89–90	NYR	6	0	1	1	5	-4
90–91	NYR	6	0	0	0	6	-2
91–92	NYR	3	0	1	1	2	0
Totals		15	1	1	2	13	-6

BENNETT, Frank F
B. Toronto, Ont.

SSN	TEAM	GP	G	A	PTS.	PIM
43–44	Det	7	0	1	1	2

BENNETT, Harvey A., Jr. 6–4 215 C
B. Cranston, R.I., Aug. 9, 1952

SSN	TEAM	GP	G	A	PTS.	PIM	+/-
74–75	Pitt	7	0	0	0	0	-2
75–76	Pitt–Wash	74	15	13	28	92	-23
76–77	Wash–Phil	69	14	14	28	94	-18
77–78	Phil–Minn	66	12	10	22	91	-31
78–79	StL	52	3	9	12	63	-18
Totals		268	44	46	90	340	-92

Playoffs

SSN	TEAM	GP	G	A	PTS.	PIM
76–77	Phil	4	0	0	0	2

*BENNETT, Maxwell RW
B. Cobalt, Ont., Nov. 4, 1912

SSN	TEAM	GP	G	A	PTS.	PIM
35–36	Mont	1	0	0	0	0

BENNETT, William 6–5 235 LW
B. Warwick, R.I., May 31, 1953

SSN	TEAM	GP	G	A	PTS.	PIM	+/-
78–79	Bos	7	1	4	5	2	+4
79–80	Hart	24	3	3	6	63	+1
Totals		31	4	7	11	65	+5

BENNING, Brian 6–0 195 D
B. Edmonton, Alta., June 10, 1966

SSN	TEAM	GP	G	A	PTS.	PIM	+/-
84–85	StL	4	0	2	2	0	-6
86–87	StL	78	13	36	49	110	0
87–88	StL	77	8	29	37	107	+2
88–89	StL	66	8	26	34	102	-5
89–90	StL–LA	55	6	19	25	106	-26
90–91	LA	61	7	24	31	127	+1
91–92	LA–Phil	75	4	42	46	134	-5
92–93	Phil–Edm	55	10	24	34	152	-1
93–94	Fla	73	6	24	30	107	-7
94–95	Fla	24	1	7	8	18	-6
Totals		568	63	233	296	963	-53

Playoffs

SSN	TEAM	GP	G	A	PTS.	PIM
85–86	StL	6	1	2	3	13
86–87	StL	6	0	4	4	9
87–88	StL	10	1	6	7	25
88–89	StL	7	1	1	2	11
89–90	LA	7	0	2	2	10
90–91	LA	12	0	5	5	6
Totals		48	3	20	23	74

BENNING, James 6–0 183 D
B. Edmonton, Alta., Apr. 29, 1963

SSN	TEAM	GP	G	A	PTS.	PIM	+/-
81–82	Tor	74	7	24	31	46	-27
82–83	Tor	74	5	17	22	47	-8
83–84	Tor	79	12	39	51	66	-4
84–85	Tor	80	9	35	44	55	-39
85–86	Tor	52	4	21	25	71	-4
86–87	Tor–Van	59	2	11	13	44	+9
87–88	Van	77	7	26	33	58	0
88–89	Van	65	3	9	12	48	-4
89–90	Van	45	3	9	12	26	+4
Totals		605	52	191	243	461	-73

Playoffs

SSN	TEAM	GP	G	A	PTS.	PIM
82–83	Tor	4	1	1	2	2
88–89	Van	3	0	0	0	0
Totals		7	1	1	2	2

*BENOIT, Joseph 5–9 160 RW
B. St. Albert, Alta., Feb. 27, 1916

SSN	TEAM	GP	G	A	PTS.	PIM
40–41	Mont	45	16	16	32	32
41–42	Mont	46	20	16	36	27

SSN	TEAM	GP	G	A	PTS.	PIM	+/-
42–43	Mont	49	30	27	57	23	
45–46	Mont	39	9	10	19	8	
46–47	Mont	6	0	0	0	4	
Totals		185	75	69	144	94	

Playoffs

SSN	TEAM	GP	G	A	PTS.	PIM	+/-
40–41	Mont	3	4	0	4	2	
41–42	Mont	3	1	0	1	5	
42–43	Mont	5	1	3	4	4	
Totals		11	6	3	9	11	

BENSON, Robert *D*
B. Buffalo, N.Y.

SSN	TEAM	GP	G	A	PTS.	PIM
24–25	Bos	8	0	1	1	4

BENSON, William Lloyd *5–11 165 C*
B. Winnipeg, Man., July 29, 1920

SSN	TEAM	GP	G	A	PTS.	PIM
40–41	NYA	22	3	4	7	4
41–42	NYA	45	8	21	29	31
Totals		67	11	25	36	35

*BENTLEY, Douglas Wagner *5–8 145 LW*
B. Delisle, Sask., Sept. 3, 1916

SSN	TEAM	GP	G	A	PTS.	PIM
39–40	Chi	39	12	7	19	12
40–41	Chi	47	8	20	28	12
41–42	Chi	38	12	14	26	11
42–43	Chi	50	33	40	73	18
43–44	Chi	50	38	39	77	22
45–46	Chi	36	19	21	40	16
46–47	Chi	52	21	34	55	18
47–48	Chi	60	20	37	57	16
48–49	Chi	58	23	43	66	38
49–50	Chi	64	20	33	53	28
50–51	Chi	44	9	23	32	20
51–52	Chi	8	2	3	5	4
53–54	NYR	20	2	10	12	2
Totals		566	219	324	543	217

Playoffs

SSN	TEAM	GP	G	A	PTS.	PIM
39–40	Chi	2	0	0	0	0
40–41	Chi	5	1	1	2	4
41–42	Chi	3	0	1	1	4
43–44	Chi	9	8	4	12	4
45–46	Chi	4	0	2	2	0
Totals		23	9	8	17	12

*BENTLEY, Maxwell Herbert Lloyd *5–8 158 C*
B. Delisle, Sask., Mar. 1, 1920

SSN	TEAM	GP	G	A	PTS.	PIM
40–41	Chi	36	7	10	17	6
41–42	Chi	39	13	17	30	19
42–43	Chi	47	26	44	70	2
45–46	Chi	47	31	30	61	6
46–47	Chi	60	29	43	72	12
47–48	Chi–Tor	59	26	28	54	10
48–49	Tor	60	19	22	41	18
49–50	Tor	69	23	18	41	14
50–51	Tor	67	21	41	62	34
51–52	Tor	69	24	17	41	40
52–53	Tor	36	12	11	23	16
53–54	NYR	57	14	18	32	15
Totals		646	245	299	544	192

Playoffs

SSN	TEAM	GP	G	A	PTS.	PIM
40–41	Chi	5	1	3	4	2
41–42	Chi	3	2	0	2	0
45–46	Chi	4	1	0	1	4
47–48	Tor	9	4	7	11	0
48–49	Tor	9	4	3	7	2
49–50	Tor	7	3	3	6	0
50–51	Tor	11	2	11	13	4
51–52	Tor	4	1	0	1	2
Totals		52	18	27	45	14

BENTLEY, Reginald *RW*
B. Delisle, Sask., May 3, 1914

SSN	TEAM	GP	G	A	PTS.	PIM
42–43	Chi	11	1	2	3	2

BENYSEK, Ladislav *6–2 190 D*
B. Olomovc, Czech., Mar. 24, 1975

SSN	TEAM	GP	G	A	PTS.	PIM	+/-
97–98	Edm	2	0	0	0	0	0

BERALDO, Paul *5–11 175 RW*
B. Hamilton, Ont., Oct. 5, 1967

SSN	TEAM	GP	G	A	PTS.	PIM
87–88	Bos	3	0	0	0	0
88–89	Bos	7	0	0	0	4

SSN	TEAM	GP	G	A	PTS.	PIM
Totals		10	0	0	0	4

BERANEK, Josef *6–2 180 LW*
B. Litvinov, Czechoslovakia, Oct. 25, 1969

SSN	TEAM	GP	G	A	PTS.	PIM	+/-
91–92	Edm	58	12	16	28	18	-2
92–93	Edm–Phil	66	15	18	33	78	-8
93–94	Phil	80	28	21	49	85	-2
94–95	Phil–Van	51	13	18	31	30	-7
95–96	Van	61	6	14	20	60	-11
96–97	Pitt	8	3	1	4	4	-1
98–99	Edm	66	19	30	49	23	+6
Totals		390	96	188	214	298	-25

Playoffs

SSN	TEAM	GP	G	A	PTS.	PIM
91–92	Edm	12	2	1	3	0
94–95	Van	11	1	1	2	12
95–96	Van	3	2	1	3	0
96–97	Pitt	5	0	0	0	2
98–99	Edm	2	0	0	0	4
Totals		31	5	3	8	14

BERARD, Bryan *6–1 190 D*
B. Woonsocket, R.I., March 5, 1977

SSN	TEAM	GP	G	A	PTS.	PIM	+/-
96–97	NYI	82	8	40	48	86	+1
97–98	NYI	75	14	32	46	89	-32
98–99	NYI–Tor	69	9	25	34	48	+1
Totals		226	31	97	128	193	-30

Playoffs

SSN	TEAM	GP	G	A	PTS.	PIM
98–99	Tor	17	1	8	9	8

BEREHOWSKY, Drake *6–1 210 D*
B. Toronto, Ont., Jan. 3, 1972

SSN	TEAM	GP	G	A	PTS.	PIM	+/-
90–91	Tor	8	0	1	1	25	-6
91–92	Tor	1	0	0	0	0	0
92–93	Tor	41	4	15	19	61	+1
93–94	Tor	49	2	8	10	63	-3
94–95	Tor–Pitt	29	0	2	2	28	-9
95–96	Pitt	1	0	0	0	0	+1
97–98	Edm	67	1	6	7	169	+1
98–99	Nash	74	2	15	17	140	-9
Totals		270	9	47	56	486	-24

Playoffs

SSN	TEAM	GP	G	A	PTS.	PIM
94–95	Pitt	1	0	0	0	0
97–98	Edm	12	1	2	3	14
Totals		13	1	2	3	14

BERENSON, Gordon Arthur (Red) *6–0 195 C*
B. Regina, Sask., Dec. 8, 1939

SSN	TEAM	GP	G	A	PTS.	PIM	+/-
61–62	Mont	4	1	2	3	4	
62–63	Mont	37	2	6	8	15	
63–64	Mont	69	7	9	16	12	
64–65	Mont	3	1	2	3	0	
65–66	Mont	23	3	4	7	12	
66–67	NYR	30	0	5	5	2	
67–68	NYR–StL	74	24	30	54	24	-9
68–69	StL	76	35	47	82	43	+26
69–70	StL	67	33	39	72	38	-3
70–71	StL–Det	69	21	38	59	16	-14
71–72	Det	78	28	41	69	16	-8
72–73	Det	78	13	30	43	8	-14
73–74	Det	76	24	42	66	28	-22
74–75	Det–StL	71	15	22	37	20	-17
75–76	StL	72	20	27	47	47	-11
76–77	StL	80	21	28	49	8	-28
77–78	StL	80	13	25	38	12	-20
Totals		987	261	397	658	305	-119

Playoffs

SSN	TEAM	GP	G	A	PTS.	PIM
61–62	Mont	5	2	0	2	0
62–63	Mont	5	0	0	0	0
63–64	Mont	7	0	0	0	4
64–65	Mont	9	0	1	1	2
66–67	NYR	4	0	1	1	2
67–68	StL	18	5	2	7	9
68–69	StL	12	7	3	10	20
69–70	StL	16	7	5	12	8
74–75	StL	2	1	0	1	0
75–76	StL	3	1	2	3	0
76–77	StL	4	0	0	0	4
Totals		85	23	14	37	49

BEREZAN, Perry Edmund *6–2 190 C*
B. Edmonton, Alta., Dec. 5, 1964

SSN	TEAM	GP	G	A	PTS.	PIM	+/-
84–85	Calg	9	3	2	5	4	+5

SSN	TEAM	GP	G	A	PTS.	PIM	+/-
85–86	Calg	55	12	21	33	39	+19
86–87	Calg	24	5	3	8	24	+4
87–88	Calg	29	7	12	19	66	+11
88–89	Calg–Minn	51	5	8	13	27	+6
89–90	Minn	64	3	12	15	31	-4
90–91	Minn	52	11	6	17	30	-2
91–92	SJ	66	12	7	19	30	-26
92–93	SJ	28	3	4	7	28	-18
Totals		378	61	75	136	279	-5

Playoffs

SSN	TEAM	GP	G	A	PTS.	PIM
84–85	Calg	2	1	0	1	4
85–86	Calg	8	1	1	2	6
86–87	Calg	2	0	2	2	7
87–88	Calg	8	0	2	2	13
88–89	Minn	5	1	2	3	4
89–90	Minn	5	1	0	1	0
90–91	Minn	1	0	0	0	0
Totals		31	4	7	11	34

BEREZIN, Sergei *5–10 187 RW*
B. Voskreserisk, USSR, Nov. 5, 1971

SSN	TEAM	GP	G	A	PTS.	PIM	+/-
96–97	Tor	73	25	16	41	2	-3
97–98	Tor	68	16	15	31	10	-3
98–99	Tor	76	37	22	59	12	+16
Totals		217	78	53	131	24	+10

Playoffs

SSN	TEAM	GP	G	A	PTS.	PIM
98–99	Tor	17	6	6	12	4

BERG, Aki–Petteri *6–3 196 D*
B. Turku, Finland, July 28, 1977

SSN	TEAM	GP	G	A	PTS.	PIM	+/-
95–96	LA	51	0	7	7	29	-13
96–97	LA	41	2	6	8	24	-9
97–98	LA	72	0	8	8	61	+3
Totals		164	2	21	23	114	-19

Playoffs

SSN	TEAM	GP	G	A	PTS.	PIM
97–98	LA	4	0	3	3	0

BERG, Bill *6–1 205 LW*
B. St. Catharines, Ont., Oct. 21, 1967

SSN	TEAM	GP	G	A	PTS.	PIM	+/-
88–89	NYI	7	1	2	3	10	-2
90–91	NYI	78	9	14	23	67	-3
91–92	NYI	47	5	9	14	28	-18
92–93	NYI–Tor	80	13	11	24	103	+3
93–94	Tor	83	8	11	19	93	-3
94–95	Tor	32	5	1	6	26	-11
95–96	Tor–NYR	41	3	2	5	41	-6
96–97	NYR	67	8	6	14	37	+2
97–98	NYR	67	1	9	10	55	-15
98–99	Ott	44	2	2	4	28	+4
Totals		546	55	67	122	508	-49

Playoffs

SSN	TEAM	GP	G	A	PTS.	PIM
92–93	Tor	21	1	1	2	18
93–94	Tor	18	1	2	3	10
94–95	Tor	7	0	1	1	4
95–96	NYR	10	1	0	1	0
96–97	NYR	3	0	0	0	2
98–99	Ott	2	0	0	0	0
Totals		61	3	4	7	34

BERGDINON, Fred *F*
B. Quebec City, Que.

SSN	TEAM	GP	G	A	PTS.	PIM
25–26	Bos	2	0	0	0	0

BERGEN, Todd *6–3 185 C*
B. Prince Albert, Sask., July 11, 1963

SSN	TEAM	GP	G	A	PTS.	PIM	+/-
84–85	Phil	14	11	5	16	4	+9

Playoffs

SSN	TEAM	GP	G	A	PTS.	PIM
84–85	Phil	17	4	9	13	8

BERGER, Michael *6–0 200 D*
B. Edmonton, Alta., June 2, 1967

SSN	TEAM	GP	G	A	PTS.	PIM	+/-
87–88	Minn	29	3	1	4	65	-19
88–89	Minn	1	0	0	0	2	-1
Totals		30	3	1	4	67	-20

BERGERON, Michel *5–10 170 RW*
B. Chicoutimi, Que., Nov. 11, 1954

SSN	TEAM	GP	G	A	PTS.	PIM	+/-
74–75	Det	25	10	7	17	10	+5
75–76	Det	72	32	27	59	48	+2
76–77	Det	74	21	12	33	98	-40
77–78	Det–NYI	28	10	6	16	2	+14

SSN	TEAM	GP	G	A	PTS.	PIM	+/-
78–79	Wash	30	7	6	13	7	-18
Totals		229	80	58	138	165	-37

BERGERON, Yves 5–9 165 RW
B. Malartic, Que., Jan. 11, 1952

		GP	G	A	PTS.	PIM	+/-
72–73	Que (WHA)	65	14	19	33	32	
74–75	Pitt	2	0	0	0	0	-3
76–77	Pitt	1	0	0	0	0	-0
NHL Totals		3	0	0	0	0	-3
WHA Totals		65	14	19	33	32	

BERGEVIN, Marc 6–0 197 D
B. Montreal, Que., Aug. 11, 1965

		GP	G	A	PTS.	PIM	+/-
84–85	Chi	60	0	6	6	54	-9
85–86	Chi	71	7	7	14	60	0
86–87	Chi	66	4	10	14	66	+4
87–88	Chi	58	1	6	7	85	-19
88–89	Chi–NYI	69	2	13	15	80	-1
89–90	NYI	18	0	4	4	30	-8
90–91	Hart	4	0	0	0	4	-3
91–92	Hart	75	7	17	24	64	-13
92–93	TB	78	2	12	14	66	-15
93–94	TB	83	1	15	16	87	-5
94–95	TB	44	2	4	6	51	-6
95–96	Det	70	1	9	10	33	+7
96–97	StL	82	0	4	4	53	-9
97–98	StL	81	3	7	10	90	-2
98–99	StL	52	1	1	2	99	-14
Totals		911	31	115	146	922	-93

Playoffs

		GP	G	A	PTS.	PIM	
84–85	Chi	6	0	3	3	2	
85–86	Chi	3	0	0	0	0	
86–87	Chi	3	1	0	1	2	
91–92	Hart	5	0	0	0	2	
95–96	Det	17	1	0	1	14	
96–97	StL	6	1	0	1	8	
97–98	StL	10	0	1	1	8	
Totals		50	3	4	7	36	

BERGLAND, Tim 6–3 194 C
B. Crookston, Minn., Jan. 11, 1965

		GP	G	A	PTS.	PIM	+/-
89–90	Wash	32	2	5	7	31	+2
90–91	Wash	47	5	9	14	21	-1
91–92	Wash	22	1	4	5	2	-3
92–93	TB	27	3	3	6	11	-5
93–94	TB–Wash	54	6	5	11	10	-15
Totals		182	17	26	43	75	-22

Playoffs

		GP	G	A	PTS.	PIM	
89–90	Wash	15	1	1	2	10	
90–91	Wash	11	1	1	2	12	
Totals		26	2	2	4	22	

BERGLOFF, Robert Kane 6–1 185 D
B. Dickinson, N.D., July 26, 1958

		GP	G	A	PTS.	PIM	+/-
82–83	Minn	2	0	0	0	5	-1

BERGLUND, Bo 5–10 175 RW
B. Sjalevad, Sweden, Apr. 6, 1955

		GP	G	A	PTS.	PIM	+/-
83–84	Que	75	16	27	43	20	+6
84–85	Que–Minn	45	10	10	20	14	-1
85–86	Minn–Phil	10	2	2	4	6	0
Totals		130	28	39	67	40	+5

Playoffs

		GP	G	A	PTS.	PIM	
83–84	Que	7	2	0	2	4	
84–85	Minn	2	0	0	0	2	
Totals		9	2	0	2	6	

BERGMAN, Gary Gunnar 5–11 185 D
B. Kenora, Ont., Oct. 7, 1938

		GP	G	A	PTS.	PIM	+/-
64–65	Det	58	4	7	11	85	
65–66	Det	61	3	16	19	96	
66–67	Det	70	5	30	35	129	
67–68	Det	74	13	28	41	109	-1
68–69	Det	76	7	30	37	80	+45
69–70	Det	69	6	17	23	122	+4
70–71	Det	68	8	25	33	149	-28
71–72	Det	75	6	31	37	138	+7
72–73	Det	68	3	28	31	71	+10
73–74	Det–Minn	68	3	29	32	84	-18
74–75	Det	76	5	25	30	104	-25
75–76	KC	75	5	33	38	82	-52
Totals		838	68	299	367	1249	-58

Playoffs

		GP	G	A	PTS.	PIM	
64–65	Det	5	0	1	1	4	
65–66	Det	12	0	3	3	14	
69–70	Det	4	0	1	1	2	
Totals		21	0	5	5	20	

BERGMAN, Thommie Lars Rudolph 6–2 200 D
B. Munkfors, Sweden, Dec. 10, 1947

		GP	G	A	PTS.	PIM	+/-
72–73	Det	75	9	12	21	70	+6
73–74	Det	43	0	3	3	21	-15
74–75	Det	18	0	1	1	27	-7
74–75	Winn (WHA)	49	4	15	19	70	
75–76	Winn (WHA)	81	11	30	41	111	
76–77	Winn (WHA)	42	2	24	26	37	
77–78	Winn (WHA)	65	5	28	33	43	
77–78	Det	14	1	6	7	16	+1
78–79	Det	68	10	17	27	64	-25
79–80	Det	28	1	5	6	45	+4
NHL Totals		246	21	44	65	243	-36
WHA Totals		237	22	97	119	261	

Playoffs

		GP	G	A	PTS.	PIM	
75–76	Winn (WHA)	13	3	10	13	8	
77–78	Det	7	0	2	2	2	
NHL Totals		7	0	2	2	2	
WHA Totals		13	3	10	13	8	

BERGQVIST, Jonas 6–0 185 RW
B. Hassleholm, Sweden, Sept. 26, 1962

		GP	G	A	PTS.	PIM	+/-
89–90	Calg	22	2	5	7	10	+10

BERGQVIST, Stefan 6–3 216 D
B. Leksand, Sweden, Mar. 10, 1975

		GP	G	A	PTS.	PIM	+/-
95–96	Pitt	2	0	0	0	2	0
96–97	Pitt	5	0	0	0	7	-1
Totals		7	0	0	0	9	-1

Playoffs

		GP	G	A	PTS.	PIM	
95–96	Pitt	4	0	0	0	0	2

*BERLINQUETTE, Louis LW

		GP	G	A	PTS.	PIM	
17–18	Mont	20	2	0	2	9	
18–19	Mont	18	5	3	8	9	
19–20	Mont	24	7	7	14	36	
20–21	Mont	24	12	9	21	24	
21–22	Mont	24	12	5	17	8	
22–23	Mont	24	2	3	5	4	
24–25	Mont M	29	4	2	6	22	
25–26	Pitt Pi	30	0	0	0	8	
Totals		193	44	29	73	120	

Playoffs

		GP	G	A	PTS.	PIM	
17–18	Mont	2	0	0	0	0	
18–19	Mont	2	1	0	1	9	
22–23	Mont	2	0	1	1	0	
25–26	Pitt	2	0	0	0	0	
Totals		8	1	1	2	9	

BERNIER, Serge Joseph 6–1 190 C
B. Padoue, Que., Apr. 29, 1947

		GP	G	A	PTS.	PIM	+/-
68–69	Phil	1	0	0	0	2	0
69–70	Phil	1	0	1	1	0	-1
70–71	Phil	77	23	28	51	77	-7
71–72	Phil–LA	70	23	22	45	63	-17
72–73	LA	75	22	46	68	43	-3
73–74	Que (WHA)	74	37	49	86	107	
74–75	Que (WHA)	76	54	68	122	75	
75–76	Que (WHA)	70	34	68	102	91	
76–77	Que (WHA)	74	43	53	96	94	
77–78	Que (WHA)	58	26	52	78	48	
78–79	Que (WHA)	65	36	46	82	71	
79–80	Que	32	8	14	22	31	-5
80–81	Que	46	2	8	10	18	-8
NHL Totals		302	78	119	197	234	-41
WHA Totals		417	230	336	566	486	

Playoffs

		GP	G	A	PTS.	PIM	
70–71	Phil	4	1	1	2	0	
74–75	Que (WHA)	16	8	8	16	6	
75–76	Que (WHA)	5	2	6	8	6	
76–77	Que (WHA)	17	14	22	36	10	
77–78	Que (WHA)	11	4	10	14	17	
78–79	Que (WHA)	1	0	0	0	2	
80–81	Que	1	0	0	0	0	
NHL Totals		5	1	1	2	0	

		GP	G	A	PTS.	PIM	+/-
WHA Totals		50	28	46	74	41	

BERRY, Brad 6–2 190 D
B. Bashaw, Alta., Apr. 1, 1965

		GP	G	A	PTS.	PIM	+/-
85–86	Winn	13	1	0	1	10	+1
86–87	Winn	52	2	8	10	60	+6
87–88	Winn	48	0	6	6	75	-11
88–89	Winn	38	0	9	9	45	-8
89–90	Winn	12	1	2	3	6	-2
91–92	Minn	7	0	0	0	6	-1
92–93	Minn	63	0	3	3	109	+2
93–94	Dal	8	0	0	0	12	-2
Totals		241	4	28	32	323	-15

Playoffs

		GP	G	A	PTS.	PIM	
85–86	Winn	3	0	0	0	0	
86–87	Winn	7	0	1	1	14	
89–90	Winn	1	0	0	0	0	
91–92	Minn	2	0	0	0	2	
Totals		13	0	1	1	16	

BERRY, Douglas Alan 6–1 190 C
B. New Westminster, B.C., June 3, 1957

		GP	G	A	PTS.	PIM	+/-
78–79	Edm (WHA)	29	6	3	9	4	
79–80	Col	75	7	23	30	16	-23
80–81	Col	46	3	10	13	8	-15
NHL Totals		121	10	33	43	24	-38
WHA Totals		29	6	3	9	4	

BERRY, Frederick Allan 5–9 175 C
B. Stoney Plains, Alta., Mar. 26, 1956

		GP	G	A	PTS.	PIM	+/-
76–77	Det	3	0	0	0	0	-3

BERRY, Kenneth E. 5–8 175 LW
B. Burnaby, B.C., June 21, 1960

		GP	G	A	PTS.	PIM	+/-
81–82	Edm	15	2	3	5	9	-6
83–84	Edm	13	2	3	5	10	+6
87–88	Van	14	2	3	5	6	-1
88–89	Van	13	2	1	3	5	+2
Totals		55	8	10	18	30	+1

BERRY, Robert Victor 6–0 190 LW
B. Montreal, Que., Nov. 29, 1943

		GP	G	A	PTS.	PIM	+/-
68–69	LA	2	0	0	0	0	0
70–71	LA	77	25	38	63	52	-5
71–72	LA	78	17	22	39	44	-23
72–73	LA	78	36	28	64	75	-13
73–74	LA	77	23	33	56	56	0
74–75	LA	80	25	23	48	60	+21
75–76	LA	80	20	22	42	37	+2
76–77	LA	69	13	25	38	20	+12
Totals		541	159	191	350	344	-6

Playoffs

		GP	G	A	PTS.	PIM	
73–74	LA	5	0	0	0	0	
74–75	LA	3	1	2	3	2	
75–76	LA	9	1	1	2	0	
76–77	LA	9	0	3	3	4	
Totals		26	2	6	8	6	

BERTUZZI, Todd 6–3 227 LW
B. Sudbury, Ont., Feb. 2, 1975

		GP	G	A	PTS.	PIM	+/-
95–96	NYI	76	18	21	39	83	-14
96–97	NYI	64	10	13	23	68	-3
97–98	NYI–Van	74	13	20	33	121	-17
98–99	Van	32	8	8	16	44	-6
Totals		246	49	62	111	316	-40

BERUBE, Craig 6–2 205 LW
B. Calihoo, Alta., Dec. 17, 1965

		GP	G	A	PTS.	PIM	+/-
86–87	Phil	7	0	0	0	57	+2
87–88	Phil	27	3	2	5	108	+1
88–89	Phil	53	1	1	2	199	-15
89–90	Phil	74	4	14	18	291	-7
90–91	Phil	74	8	9	17	293	-6
91–92	Tor–Calg	76	6	11	17	264	-5
92–93	Calg	77	4	8	12	209	-6
93–94	Wash	84	7	7	14	305	-4
94–95	Wash	43	2	4	6	173	-5
95–96	Wash	50	2	10	12	151	+1
96–97	Wash	80	4	3	7	218	-11
97–98	Wash	74	6	9	15	189	-3
98–99	Wash Phil	77	5	4	9	194	-10
Totals		796	52	82	134	2651	-68

Playoffs

SSN	TEAM	GP	G	A	PTS.	PIM	+/-
86–87	Phil	5	0	0	0	17	
88–89	Phil	16	0	0	0	56	
92–93	Calg	6	0	1	1	21	
93–94	Wash	8	0	0	0	21	
94–95	Wash	7	0	0	0	29	
95–96	Wash	2	0	0	0	19	
97–98	Wash	21	1	0	1	21	
98–99	Phil	6	1	0	1	4	
Totals		71	2	1	3	188	

BESLER, Phillip Rudolph *RW*
B. Melville, Sask., Dec. 9, 1913

SSN	TEAM	GP	G	A	PTS.	PIM	+/-
35–36	Bos	8	0	0	0	0	
38–39	Chi–Det	22	1	4	5	18	
Totals		30	1	4	5	18	

BESSONE, Peter *5–10 200 D*
B. New Bedford, Mass., Jan. 13, 1913

SSN	TEAM	GP	G	A	PTS.	PIM	+/-
37–38	Det	6	0	1	1	6	

BETHEL, John Charles *5–11 185 LW*
B. Montreal, Que., Apr. 15, 1957

SSN	TEAM	GP	G	A	PTS.	PIM	+/-
79–80	Winn	17	0	2	2	4	–3

BETIK, Karel *6–2 208 D*
B. Karvina, Czech, Oct. 28, 1978

SSN	TEAM	GP	G	A	PTS.	PIM	+/-
98–99	TB	3	0	2	2	2	–3

BETS, Maxim *6–1 185 LW*
B. Chelyabinsk, USSR, Jan. 31, 1974

SSN	TEAM	GP	G	A	PTS.	PIM	+/-
93–94	Ana	3	0	0	0	0	–3

BETTIO, Silvio Angelo (Sam) *5–8 175 LW*
B. Copper Cliff, Ont., Dec. 1, 1928

SSN	TEAM	GP	G	A	PTS.	PIM	+/-
49–50	Bos	44	9	12	21	32	

BEUKEBOOM, Jeff *6–5 230 D*
B. Ajax, Ont., Mar. 28, 1965

SSN	TEAM	GP	G	A	PTS.	PIM	+/-
86–87	Edm	44	3	8	11	124	+7
87–88	Edm	73	5	20	25	201	+27
88–89	Edm	36	0	5	5	94	+2
89–90	Edm	46	1	12	13	86	+5
90–91	Edm	67	3	7	10	150	+6
91–92	Edm–NYR	74	1	15	16	200	+23
92–93	NYR	82	2	17	19	153	+9
93–94	NYR	68	8	8	16	170	+18
94–95	NYR	44	1	3	4	70	+3
95–96	NYR	82	3	11	14	220	+19
96–97	NYR	80	3	9	12	167	+22
97–98	NYR	63	0	5	5	195	–25
98–99	NYR	45	0	9	9	60	–2
Totals		804	30	129	159	1890	+114

Playoffs

SSN	TEAM	GP	G	A	PTS.	PIM	+/-
85–86	Edm	1	0	0	0	4	
87–88	Edm	7	0	0	0	16	
88–89	Edm	1	0	0	0	2	
89–90	Edm	2	0	0	0	0	
90–91	Edm	18	1	3	4	28	
91–92	NYR	13	2	3	5	47	
93–94	NYR	22	0	6	6	50	
94–95	NYR	9	0	0	0	10	
95–96	NYR	11	0	3	3	6	
96–97	NYR	15	0	1	1	34	
Totals		99	3	16	19	197	

BEVERLEY, Nicholas Gerald (Nick) *6–2 185 D*
B. Toronto, Ont., Apr. 21, 1947

SSN	TEAM	GP	G	A	PTS.	PIM	+/-
66–67	Bos	2	0	0	0	0	
69–40	Bos	2	0	0	0	2	0
71–72	Bos	1	0	0	0	0	0
72–73	Bos	76	1	10	11	26	+7
73–74	Bos–Pitt	77	2	14	16	21	–17
74–75	NYR	54	3	15	18	19	+13
75–76	NYR	63	1	8	9	46	–9
76–77	NYR–Minn	61	2	17	19	8	0
77–78	Minn	57	7	14	21	18	–1
78–79	LA–Col	59	2	7	9	6	–14
79–80	Col	46	0	9	9	10	–4
Totals		498	18	94	112	156	–25

Playoffs

SSN	TEAM	GP	G	A	PTS.	PIM	+/-
72–73	Bos	4	0	0	0	0	
74–75	NYR	3	0	1	1	0	
Totals		7	0	1	1	0	

BIALOWAS, Dwight Joseph *6–0 185 D*
B. Regina, Sask., Sept. 8, 1952

SSN	TEAM	GP	G	A	PTS.	PIM	+/-
73–74	Atl	11	0	0	0	2	–6
74–75	Atl–Minn	77	5	19	24	22	–2
75–76	Minn	58	5	18	23	22	–9
76–77	Minn	18	1	9	10	0	–3
Totals		164	11	46	57	46	–20

BIALOWAS, Frank *5–11 220 D*
B. Winnipeg, Man., Sept. 25, 1970

SSN	TEAM	GP	G	A	PTS.	PIM	+/-
93–94	Tor	3	0	0	0	12	0

BIANCHIN, Wayne Richard *5–10 180 LW*
B. Nanaimo, B.C., Sept. 6, 1953

SSN	TEAM	GP	G	A	PTS.	PIM	+/-
73–74	Pitt	69	12	13	25	38	–15
74–75	Pitt	2	0	0	0	0	–1
75–76	Pitt	14	1	5	6	4	–4
76–77	Pitt	79	28	6	34	28	–1
77–78	Pitt	61	20	13	33	40	–14
78–79	Pitt	40	7	4	11	20	–2
79–80	Edm	11	0	0	0	7	–4
Totals		276	68	41	109	137	–41

Playoffs

SSN	TEAM	GP	G	A	PTS.	PIM	+/-
76–77	Pitt	3	0	1	1	6	

BICANEK, Radim *6–1 195 D*
B. Uherske Hradiste, Czechoslovakia, Jan. 18, 1975

SSN	TEAM	GP	G	A	PTS.	PIM	+/-
94–95	Ott	6	0	0	0	0	+3
96–97	Ott	21	0	1	1	8	–4
97–98	Ott	1	0	0	0	0	0
98–99	Ott–Chi	14	0	0	0	10	–4
Totals		41	0	1	1	18	–5

Playoffs

SSN	TEAM	GP	G	A	PTS.	PIM	+/-
96–97	Ott	7	0	0	0	8	

BIDNER, Richard Todd (Todd) *6–2 205 LW*
B. Petrolia, Ont., July 4, 1961

SSN	TEAM	GP	G	A	PTS.	PIM	+/-
81–82	Wash	12	2	1	3	7	0

BIGGS, Don *5–8 175 C*
B. Mississauga, Ont., Apr. 7, 1965

SSN	TEAM	GP	G	A	PTS.	PIM	+/-
84–85	Minn	1	0	0	0	0	0
89–90	Phil	11	2	0	2	8	–4
Totals		12	2	0	2	8	–4

BIGNELL, Larry Irvin *6–0 170 D*
B. Edmonton, Alta., Jan. 7, 1950

SSN	TEAM	GP	G	A	PTS.	PIM	+/-
73–74	Pitt	20	0	3	3	2	–3
75–76	Ott (WHA)	41	5	5	10	43	

Playoffs

SSN	TEAM	GP	G	A	PTS.	PIM	+/-
74–75	Pitt	3	0	0	0	2	

BILODEAU, Gilles *6–1 220 LW*
B. St. Prime, Que., July 31, 1955

SSN	TEAM	GP	G	A	PTS.	PIM	+/-
75–76	Tor (WHA)	14	0	1	1	38	
76–77	Birm (WHA)	34	2	6	8	133	
77–78	Birm (WHA)	59	2	2	4	258	
78–79	Que (WHA)	36	3	6	9	141	
79–80	Que	9	0	1	1	25	–1
NHL Totals		9	0	1	1	25	–1
WHA Totals		143	7	15	22	570	

Playoffs

SSN	TEAM	GP	G	A	PTS.	PIM	+/-
77–78	Birm (WHA)	3	0	0	0	27	
78–79	Que (WHA)	3	0	0	0	25	
WHA Totals		6	0	0	0	52	

BIONDA, Jack Arthur *6–0 175 D*
B. Huntsville, Ont., Sept. 18, 1933

SSN	TEAM	GP	G	A	PTS.	PIM	+/-
55–56	Tor	13	0	1	1	18	
56–57	Bos	35	2	3	5	43	
57–58	Bos	42	1	4	5	50	
58–59	Bos	3	0	1	1	2	
Totals		93	3	9	12	113	

Playoffs

SSN	TEAM	GP	G	A	PTS.	PIM	+/-
56–57	Bos	10	0	1	1	14	
58–59	Bos	1	0	0	0	0	
Totals		11	0	1	1	14	

BISSETT, Thomas *6–0 180 C*
B. Seattle, Wash., Mar. 13, 1966

SSN	TEAM	GP	G	A	PTS.	PIM	+/-
90–91	Det	5	0	0	0	0	–4

BJUGSTAD, Scott *6–1 185 RW*
B. St. Paul, Minn., June 2, 1961

SSN	TEAM	GP	G	A	PTS.	PIM	+/-
83–84	Minn	5	0	0	0	2	–1
84–85	Minn	72	11	4	15	32	–21
85–86	Minn	80	43	33	76	24	+5
86–87	Minn	39	4	9	13	43	–6
87–88	Minn	33	10	12	22	15	+2
88–89	Pitt	24	3	0	3	4	–12
89–90	LA	11	1	2	3	2	+2
90–91	LA	31	2	4	6	12	–5
91–92	LA	22	2	4	6	10	–1
Totals		317	76	68	144	144	–37

Playoffs

SSN	TEAM	GP	G	A	PTS.	PIM	+/-
85–86	Minn	5	0	1	1	0	
89–90	LA	2	0	0	0	2	
90–91	LA	2	0	0	0	0	
Totals		9	0	1	1	2	

BLACK, James *5–11 185 C*
B. Regina, Sask., Aug. 15, 1969

SSN	TEAM	GP	G	A	PTS.	PIM	+/-
89–90	Hart	1	0	0	0	0	0
90–91	Hart	1	0	0	0	0	0
91–92	Hart	30	4	6	10	10	–4
92–93	Minn	10	2	1	3	4	0
93–94	Dal–Buf	15	2	3	5	2	–4
95–96	Chi	13	3	3	6	16	+1
96–97	Chi	64	12	11	23	20	+6
97–98	Chi	52	10	5	15	8	–8
98–99	Wash	75	16	14	30	14	+5
Totals		261	49	43	92	74	–4

Playoffs

SSN	TEAM	GP	G	A	PTS.	PIM	+/-
95–96	Chi	8	1	0	1	2	
96–97	Chi	5	1	1	2	2	
Totals		13	1	2	3	4	

BLACK, Stephen *6–0 185 LW*
B. Fort William, Ont., Mar. 31, 1927

SSN	TEAM	GP	G	A	PTS.	PIM	+/-
49–50	Det	69	7	14	21	53	
50–51	Det–Chi	44	4	6	10	24	
Totals		113	11	20	31	77	

Playoffs

SSN	TEAM	GP	G	A	PTS.	PIM	+/-
49–50	Det	13	0	0	0	13	

BLACKBURN, John Donald (Don) *6–0 190 LW*
B. Kirkland Lake, Ont., May 14, 1938

SSN	TEAM	GP	G	A	PTS.	PIM	+/-
62–63	Bos	6	0	5	5	4	
67–68	Phil	67	9	20	29	23	–2
68–69	Phil	48	7	9	16	36	–13
69–70	NYR	3	0	0	0	0	0
70–71	NYR	1	0	0	0	0	0
72–73	NYI–Minn	60	7	10	17	24	–33
73–74	NE (WHA)	75	20	39	59	18	
74–75	NE (WHA)	50	18	32	50	10	
75–76	NE (WHA)	21	2	3	5	6	
NHL Totals		185	23	44	67	87	–48
WHA Totals		146	40	74	114	34	

Playoffs

SSN	TEAM	GP	G	A	PTS.	PIM	+/-
67–68	Phil	7	3	0	3	8	
68–69	Phil	4	0	0	0	0	
69–70	NYR	1	0	0	0	0	
73–74	NE (WHA)	7	2	4	6	4	
74–75	NE (WHA)	5	1	2	3	2	
NHL Totals		12	3	0	3	8	
WHA Totals		12	3	6	9	6	

BLACKBURN, Robert John *5–11 198 D*
B. Rouyn, Que., Feb. 1, 1938

SSN	TEAM	GP	G	A	PTS.	PIM	+/-
68–69	NYR	11	0	0	0	0	+4
69–70	Pitt	60	4	7	11	51	–14
70–71	Pitt	64	4	5	9	54	0
Totals		135	8	12	20	105	–10

Playoffs

SSN	TEAM	GP	G	A	PTS.	PIM	+/-
69–70	Pitt	6	0	0	0	4	

BLADE, Henry Gordon (Hank) 6-0 182 C
B. Peterborough, Ont., Apr. 28, 1921

SSN	TEAM	GP	G	A	PTS.	PIM	+/-
46-47	Chi	18	1	3	4	2	
47-48	Chi	6	1	0	1	0	
Totals		24	2	3	5	2	

BLADON, Thomas George (Bomber) 6-1 195 D
B. Edmonton, Alta., Dec. 29, 1952

SSN	TEAM	GP	G	A	PTS.	PIM	+/-
72-73	Phil	78	11	31	42	26	+9
73-74	Phil	70	12	22	34	37	+24
74-75	Phil	76	9	20	29	54	+42
75-76	Phil	80	14	23	37	68	+45
76-77	Phil	80	10	43	53	39	+34
77-78	Phil	79	11	24	35	57	+32
78-79	Pitt	78	4	23	27	64	-17
79-80	Pitt	57	2	6	8	35	-25
80-81	Edm-Winn-Det	12	0	5	5	12	-11
Totals		610	73	197	270	392	+133

Playoffs

SSN	TEAM	GP	G	A	PTS.	PIM	+/-
72-73	Phil	11	0	4	4	2	
73-74	Phil	16	4	6	10	25	
74-75	Phil	13	1	3	4	4	
75-76	Phil	16	2	6	8	14	
76-77	Phil	10	1	3	4	4	
77-78	Phil	12	0	2	2	11	
78-79	Pitt	7	0	4	4	2	
79-80	Pitt	1	0	1	1	0	
Totals		86	8	29	37	70	

BLAINE, Gary James 5-11 190 D
B. St. Boniface, Man., Feb. 27, 1908

SSN	TEAM	GP	G	A	PTS.	PIM	+/-
54-55	Mont	1	0	0	0	0	

*BLAIR, Andrew Dryden 6-1 180 C
B. Winnipeg, Man., Feb. 27,1908

SSN	TEAM	GP	G	A	PTS.	PIM	+/-
28-29	Tor	44	12	15	27	41	
29-30	Tor	42	11	10	21	27	
30-31	Tor	44	11	8	19	32	
31-32	Tor	48	9	14	23	35	
32-33	Tor	43	6	9	15	38	
33-34	Tor	47	14	9	23	35	
34-35	Tor	45	6	14	20	22	
35-36	Tor	45	5	4	9	60	
36-37	Chi	44	0	3	3	33	
Totals		402	74	86	160	323	

Playoffs

SSN	TEAM	GP	G	A	PTS.	PIM	+/-
28-29	Tor	4	3	0	3	2	
30-31	Tor	2	1	0	1	0	
31-32	Tor	7	2	2	4	6	
32-33	Tor	9	0	2	2	4	
33-34	Tor	5	0	2	2	16	
34-35	Tor	2	0	0	0	2	
35-36	Tor	9	0	0	0	2	
Totals		38	6	6	12	32	

BLAIR, Charles (Chuck) 5-10 175 RW
B. Edinburgh, Scotland, July 23, 1928

SSN	TEAM	GP	G	A	PTS.	PIM	+/-
48-49	Tor	1	0	0	0	0	
50-51	Tor	2	0	0	0	0	
Totals		3	0	0	0	0	

BLAIR, George (Dusty) 5-8 160 C
B. South Porcupine, Ont., Sept. 15, 1929

SSN	TEAM	GP	G	A	PTS.	PIM	+/-
50-51	Tor	2	0	0	0	0	

BLAISDELL, Michael Walter 6-1 195 RW
B. Moose Jaw, Sask., Jan. 18, 1960

SSN	TEAM	GP	G	A	PTS.	PIM	+/-
80-81	Det	32	3	6	9	10	-7
81-82	Det	80	23	32	55	48	-15
82-83	Det	80	18	23	41	22	-6
83-84	NYR	36	5	6	11	31	0
84-85	NYR	12	1	0	1	11	-4
85-86	Pitt	66	15	14	29	36	+15
86-87	Pitt	10	1	1	2	2	+2
87-88	Tor	18	3	2	5	2	-5
88-89	Tor	9	1	0	1	4	-5
Totals		343	70	84	154	166	-25

Playoffs

SSN	TEAM	GP	G	A	PTS.	PIM	+/-
87-88	Tor	6	1	2	3	10	

BLAKE, Francis Joseph (Mickey) 5-10 186 D
B. Barriefield, Ont., Oct. 31, 1912

SSN	TEAM	GP	G	A	PTS.	PIM	+/-
34-35	StL E	8	1	1	2	2	
35-36	Bos-Tor	8	0	0	0	2	
Totals		16	1	1	2	4	

*BLAKE, Hector (Toe) 5-9 165 LW
B. Victoria Mines, Ont., Aug. 21, 1912

SSN	TEAM	GP	G	A	PTS.	PIM	+/-
32-33	Mont M	1	0	0	0	0	
34-35	Mont M	8	0	0	0	0	
35-36	Mont	11	1	2	3	28	
36-37	Mont	43	10	12	22	12	
37-38	Mont	43	17	16	33	33	
38-39	Mont	48	24	23	47	10	
39-40	Mont	48	17	19	36	48	
40-41	Mont	48	12	20	32	49	
41-42	Mont	48	17	28	45	19	
42-43	Mont	48	23	36	59	26	
43-44	Mont	41	26	33	59	10	
44-45	Mont	49	29	38	67	25	
45-46	Mont	50	29	21	50	2	
46-47	Mont	60	21	29	50	6	
47-48	Mont	32	9	15	24	4	
Totals		578	235	292	527	272	

Playoffs

SSN	TEAM	GP	G	A	PTS.	PIM	+/-
36-37	Mont	5	1	0	1	0	
37-38	Mont	3	3	1	4	2	
38-39	Mont	3	1	1	2	2	
40-41	Mont	3	0	3	3	5	
41-42	Mont	3	0	3	3	2	
42-43	Mont	5	4	3	7	0	
43-44	Mont	9	7	11	18	2	
44-45	Mont	6	0	2	2	5	
45-46	Mont	9	7	6	13	5	
46-47	Mont	11	2	7	9	0	
Totals		57	25	37	62	23	

BLAKE, Jason 5-10 180 C
B. Moorhead, Minn, Sept. 2, 1973

SSN	TEAM	GP	G	A	PTS.	PIM	+/-
98-99	LA	1	1	0	1	0	+1

BLAKE, Robert (Rob) 6-3 215 D
B. Simcoe, Ont., Dec. 10, 1969

SSN	TEAM	GP	G	A	PTS.	PIM	+/-
89-90	LA	4	0	0	0	4	0
90-91	LA	75	12	34	46	125	+3
91-92	LA	57	7	13	20	102	-5
92-93	LA	76	16	43	59	152	+18
93-94	LA	84	20	48	68	137	-7
94-95	LA	24	4	7	11	38	-16
95-96	LA	6	1	2	3	8	0
96-97	LA	62	8	23	31	82	-28
97-98	LA	81	23	27	50	94	-3
98-99	LA	62	12	23	35	128	-7
Totals		531	103	220	323	870	-45

Playoffs

SSN	TEAM	GP	G	A	PTS.	PIM	+/-
89-90	LA	8	1	3	4	4	
90-91	LA	12	1	4	5	26	
91-92	LA	6	2	1	3	12	
92-93	LA	23	4	6	10	46	
97-98	LA	4	0	0	0	6	
Totals		53	8	14	22	94	

BLIGHT, Richard Derek 6-2 195 RW
B. Portage La Prairie, Man., Oct. 17, 1955

SSN	TEAM	GP	G	A	PTS.	PIM	+/-
75-76	Van	74	25	31	56	29	-4
76-77	Van	78	28	40	68	32	0
77-78	Van	80	25	38	63	33	-32
78-79	Van	56	5	10	15	16	-28
79-80	Van	33	12	6	18	54	+7
80-81	Van	3	1	0	1	4	-1
82-83	LA	2	0	0	0	2	-3
Totals		326	96	125	221	170	-61

Playoffs

SSN	TEAM	GP	G	A	PTS.	PIM	+/-
75-76	Van	2	0	1	1	0	
78-79	Van	3	0	4	4	2	
Totals		5	0	5	5	2	

BLINCO, Russell Percival (Beaver) 5-10 171 C
B. Grand Mere, Que., Mar. 12, 1908

SSN	TEAM	GP	G	A	PTS.	PIM	+/-
33-34	Mont M	31	14	9	23	2	
34-35	Mont M	48	13	14	27	4	
35-36	Mont M	46	13	10	23	10	
36-37	Mont M	48	6	12	18	2	
37-38	Mont M	47	10	9	19	4	
38-39	Chi	48	3	12	15	2	
Totals		268	59	66	125	24	

Playoffs

SSN	TEAM	GP	G	A	PTS.	PIM	+/-
33-34	MontM	4	0	1	1	0	
34-35	MontM	7	2	2	4	2	
35-36	MontM	3	0	0	0	0	
36-37	MontM	5	1	0	1	2	
Totals		19	3	3	6	4	

BLOCK, Kenneth Richard 5-10 184 D
B. Grunthal, Man., Mar. 18, 1944

SSN	TEAM	GP	G	A	PTS.	PIM	+/-
70-71	Van	1	0	0	0	0	-1
72-73	NY (WHA)	78	5	53	58	43	
73-74	NY-NJ (WHA)	74	3	43	46	22	
74-75	SD-Ind (WHA)	73	1	28	29	30	
75-76	Ind (WHA)	79	1	25	26	28	
76-77	Ind (WHA)	52	0	13	13	25	
77-78	Ind (WHA)	77	1	25	26	34	
78-79	Ind (WHA)	22	2	3	5	10	
NHL Totals		1	0	0	0	0	-1
WHA Totals		455	16	187	203	192	

Playoffs

SSN	TEAM	GP	G	A	PTS.	PIM	+/-
76-77	Ind (WHA)	9	0	2	2	6	

BLOEMBERG, Jeff 6-1 205 D
B. Listowel, Ont., Jan. 31, 1968

SSN	TEAM	GP	G	A	PTS.	PIM	+/-
88-89	NYR	9	0	0	0	0	+2
89-90	NYR	28	3	3	6	25	-8
90-91	NYR	3	0	2	2	0	+3
91-92	NYR	3	0	1	1	0	+1
Totals		43	3	6	9	25	-2

Playoffs

SSN	TEAM	GP	G	A	PTS.	PIM	+/-
89-90	NYR						
Totals		7	0	3	3	5	

BLOMSTEN, Arto 6-3 210 D
B. Vaasa, Finland, Mar. 16, 1965

SSN	TEAM	GP	G	A	PTS.	PIM	+/-
93-94	Winn	18	0	2	2	6	-6
94-95	Winn-LA	5	0	1	1	2	+2
95-96	LA	2	0	1	1	0	+1
Totals		25	0	4	4	8	-3

BLOMQVIST, Timo 6-0 198 D
B. Helsinki, Finland, Jan. 23, 1961

SSN	TEAM	GP	G	A	PTS.	PIM	+/-
81-82	Wash	44	1	11	12	62	-17
82-83	Wash	61	1	17	18	67	+15
83-84	Wash	65	1	19	20	84	+17
84-85	Wash	53	1	4	5	51	+11
86-87	NJ	20	0	2	2	29	-3
Totals		243	4	53	57	293	+23

Playoffs

SSN	TEAM	GP	G	A	PTS.	PIM	+/-
82-83	Wash	3	0	0	0	16	
83-84	Wash	8	0	0	0	8	
84-85	Wash	2	0	0	0	0	
Totals		13	0	0	0	24	

BLOOM, Michael Carroll 6-3 205 LW
B. Ottawa, Ont., Apr. 12, 1952

SSN	TEAM	GP	G	A	PTS.	PIM	+/-
73-74	SD (WHA)	76	25	44	69	—	
74-75	Wash-Det	80	11	27	38	94	-52
75-76	Det	76	13	17	30	99	-19
76-77	Det	45	6	3	9	22	-10
NHL Totals		201	30	47	77	215	-81
WHA Totals		76	25	44	69	0	

BLOUIN, Sylvain 6-2 225 LW
B. Montreal, Que., May 21, 1974

SSN	TEAM	GP	G	A	PTS.	PIM	+/-
96-97	NYR	6	0	0	0	18	-1
97-98	NYR	1	0	0	0	5	0
98-99	Mont	5	0	0	0	19	0
Totals		12	0	0	0	42	-1

BLUM, John Joseph 6-3 205 D
B. Detroit, Mich., Oct. 8, 1959

SSN	TEAM	GP	G	A	PTS.	PIM	+/-
82-83	Edm	5	0	3	3	24	+2
83-84	Edm-Bos	16	1	2	3	32	+5
84-85	Bos	75	3	13	16	263	0
85-86	Bos	61	1	7	8	80	+8
86-87	Wash	66	2	8	10	133	+1

SSN	TEAM	GP	G	A	PTS.	PIM	+/-
87–88	Bos	19	0	1	1	70	-5
88–89	Det	6	0	0	0	8	-2
89–90	Bos	2	0	0	0	0	-1
Totals		250	7	34	41	610	+8

Playoffs

83–84	Bos	3	0	0	0	4	
84–85	Bos	5	0	0	0	13	
85–86	Bos	3	0	0	0	6	
86–87	Wash	6	0	1	1	4	
87–88	Bos	3	0	1	1	0	
Totals		20	0	2	2	27	

BODAK, Robert Peter *6-2 195 LW*
B. Thunder Bay, Ont., May 28, 1961

87–88	Calg	3	0	0	0	22	-2
89–90	Hart	1	0	0	0	7	0
Totals		4	0	0	0	29	-2

BODDY, Gregg Allen *6-2 200 D*
B. Ponoka, Alta., Mar. 19, 1949

71–72	Van	40	2	5	7	45	+2
72–73	Van	74	3	11	14	50	-35
73–74	Van	53	2	10	12	59	-4
74–75	Van	72	11	12	23	56	-5
75–76	Van	34	5	6	11	33	-2
76–77	SD–Edm (WHA)	64	2	19	21	60	
NHL Totals		273	23	44	67	243	-44
WHA Totals		64	2	19	21	60	

Playoffs

74–75	Van	3	0	0	0	0	
76–77	Edm (WHA)	4	1	2	3	14	
NHL Totals		3	0	0	0	0	
WHA Totals		4	1	2	3	14	

BODGER, Doug *6-2 210 D*
B. Chemainus, B.C., June 18, 1966

84–85	Pitt	65	5	26	31	67	-24
85–86	Pitt	79	4	33	37	63	+3
86–87	Pitt	76	11	38	49	52	+6
87–88	Pitt	69	14	31	45	103	-4
88–89	Pitt-Buf	71	8	44	52	59	+15
89–90	Buf	71	12	36	48	64	0
90–91	Buf	58	5	23	28	54	-8
91–92	Buf	73	11	35	46	108	+1
92–93	Buf	81	9	45	54	87	+14
93–94	Buf	75	7	32	39	76	+8
94–95	Buf	44	3	17	20	47	-3
95–96	Buf-SJ	73	4	24	28	68	-24
96–97	SJ	81	1	15	16	64	-14
97–98	SJ–NJ	77	9	11	20	57	-1
98–99	LA	45	2	6	8	48	-12
Totals		1038	105	416	521	1017	-39

Playoffs

88–89	Buf	5	1	1	2	11	
89–90	Buf	6	1	5	6	8	
90–91	Buf	4	0	1	1	0	
91–92	Buf	7	2	1	3	2	
92–93	Buf	8	2	3	5	0	
93–94	Buf	7	0	3	3	6	
94–95	Buf	5	0	4	4	0	
97–98	NJ	5	0	0	0	0	
Totals		47	6	18	24	25	

BODNAR, August (Gus) *5-10 160 C*
B. Fort William, Ont., Aug. 24, 1925

43–44	Tor	50	22	40	62	18	
44–45	Tor	49	8	36	44	18	
45–46	Tor	49	14	23	37	14	
46–47	Tor	39	4	6	10	10	
47–48	Chi	46	13	22	35	23	
48–49	Chi	59	19	26	45	14	
49–50	Chi	70	11	28	39	6	
50–51	Chi	44	8	12	20	8	
51–52	Chi	69	14	26	40	26	
52–53	Chi	66	16	13	29	26	
53–54	Chi-Bos	59	9	18	27	30	
54–55	Bos	67	4	4	8	14	
Totals		667	142	254	396	207	

Playoffs

43–44	Tor	5	0	0	0	0	
44–45	Tor	13	3	1	4	4	
46–47	Tor	1	0	0	0	0	

SSN	TEAM	GP	G	A	PTS.	PIM	+/-
52–53	Chi	7	1	1	2	2	
53–54	Bos	1	0	0	0	0	
54–55	Bos	5	0	1	1	4	
Totals		32	4	3	7	10	

BOEHM, Ronald John *5-7 160 LW*
B. Saskatoon, Sask., Aug. 14, 1943

| 67–68 | Oak | 16 | 2 | 1 | 3 | 10 | -5 |

BOESCH, Garth Vernon *6-0 180 D*
B. Milestone, Sask., Oct. 7, 1920

46–47	Tor	35	4	5	9	47	
47–48	Tor	45	2	7	9	52	
48–49	Tor	59	1	10	11	43	
49–50	Tor	58	2	6	8	63	
Totals		197	9	28	37	205	

Playoffs

46–47	Tor	11	0	2	2	6	
47–48	Tor	8	2	1	3	2	
48–49	Tor	9	0	2	2	6	
49–50	Tor	6	0	0	0	4	
Totals		34	2	5	7	18	

BOH, Rick *5-10 185 C*
B. Kamloops, B.C., May 18, 1964

| 87–88 | Minn | 8 | 2 | 1 | 3 | 4 | +1 |

BOHONOS, Lonny *5-11 190 RW*
B. Winnipeg, Man., May 20, 1973

95–96	Van	3	0	1	1	0	+1
96–97	Van	36	11	11	22	10	+3
97–98	Van-Tor	37	5	4	9	8	+8
98–99	Tor	7	3	0	3	4	+3
Totals		83	19	16	35	22	+15

Playoffs

| 98–99 | Tor | 9 | 3 | 6 | 9 | 2 | |

BOILEAU, Marc Claude *5-11 170 C*
B. Pointe Claire, Que., Sept. 3, 1932

| 61–62 | Det | 54 | 5 | 6 | 11 | 8 | |

BOILEAU, Patrick *6-0 190 D*
B. Montreal, Que., Feb. 22, 1975

96–97	Wash	1	0	0	0	0	0
98–99	Wash	4	0	1	1	2	-4
Totals		5	0	1	1	2	-4

BOILEAU, Rene *F*

| 25–26 | NYA | 7 | 0 | 0 | 0 | 0 | |

BOIMISTRUCK, Frederick *5-11 191 D*
B. Sudbury, Ont., Nov. 4, 1962

81–82	Tor	57	2	11	13	32	+9
82–83	Tor	26	2	3	5	13	-3
Totals		83	4	14	18	45	+6

BOISVERT, Serge *5-9 172 RW*
B. Drummondville, Ont., June 1, 1959

82–83	Tor	17	0	2	2	4	-10
84–85	Mont	14	2	2	4	0	+3
85–86	Mont	9	2	2	4	2	+1
86–87	Mont	1	0	0	0	0	0
87–88	Mont	5	1	1	2	2	0
Totals		46	5	7	12	8	-6

Playoffs

84–85	Mont	12	3	5	8	2	
85–86	Mont	8	0	1	1	0	
87–88	Mont	3	0	1	1	2	
Totals		23	3	7	10	4	

BOIVIN, Claude *6-2 200 LW*
B. Ste. Foy, Que., Mar. 1, 1970

91–92	Phil	58	5	13	18	187	-2
92–93	Phil	30	5	4	9	76	-5
93–94	Phil-Ott	41	2	1	3	95	-17
94–95	Ott	3	0	1	1	6	-1
Totals		132	12	19	31	364	-25

BOIVIN, Leo Joseph *5-7 190 D*
B. Prescott, Ont., Aug. 2, 1932

| 51–52 | Tor | 2 | 0 | 1 | 1 | 4 | |

SSN	TEAM	GP	G	A	PTS.	PIM	+/-
52–53	Tor	70	2	13	15	97	
53–54	Tor	58	1	6	7	81	
54–55	Tor-Bos	66	6	11	17	113	
55–56	Bos	68	4	16	20	80	
56–57	Bos	55	2	8	10	55	
57–58	Bos	33	0	4	4	54	
58–59	Bos	70	5	16	21	94	
59–60	Bos	70	4	21	25	66	
60–61	Bos	57	6	17	23	50	
61–62	Bos	65	5	18	23	89	
62–63	Bos	62	2	24	26	48	
63–64	Bos	65	10	14	24	42	
64–65	Bos	67	3	10	13	68	
65–66	Bos-Det	62	0	10	10	50	
66–67	Det	69	4	17	21	55	
67–68	Pitt	73	9	13	22	74	-15
68–69	Pitt-Minn	69	6	19	25	42	-25
69–70	Minn	69	3	12	15	30	-2
Totals		1150	72	250	322	1192	-42

Playoffs

53–54	Tor	5	0	0	0	2	
54–55	Bos	5	0	1	1	4	
56–57	Bos	10	2	3	5	12	
57–58	Bos	12	0	3	3	21	
58–59	Bos	7	1	2	3	4	
65–66	Det	12	0	1	1	16	
69–70	Pitt	3	0	0	0	0	
Totals		54	3	10	13	59	

BOLAND, Michael Anthony *5-10 185 RW*
B. Montreal, Que., Dec. 16, 1949

| 72–73 | Ott (WHA) | 41 | 1 | 15 | 16 | 44 | |
| 74–75 | Phil | 2 | 0 | 0 | 0 | 0 | 0 |

Playoffs

| 72–73 | Ott (WHA) | 1 | 0 | 0 | 0 | 0 | |

BOLAND, Michael John *6-0 190 D*
B. London, Ont., Oct. 29, 1954

74–75	KC	1	0	0	0	0	0
78–79	Buf	22	1	2	3	29	+6
Totals		23	1	2	3	29	+6

Playoffs

| 78–79 | Buf | 3 | 1 | 0 | 1 | 2 | |

BOLDIREV, Ivan *6-0 190 C*
B. Zranjanin, Yugoslavia, Aug. 15, 1949

70–71	Bos	2	0	0	0	0	0
71–72	Bos-Cal	68	16	25	41	60	-12
72–73	Cal	56	11	23	34	58	-23
73–74	Cal	78	25	31	56	22	-51
74–75	Chi	80	24	43	67	54	-3
75–76	Chi	78	28	34	62	33	-23
76–77	Chi	80	24	38	62	40	-15
77–78	Chi	80	35	45	80	34	-3
78–79	Chi-Atl	79	35	43	78	31	+8
79–80	Atl-Van	79	32	35	67	34	-2
80–81	Van	72	26	33	59	34	-12
81–82	Van	78	33	40	73	45	-17
82–83	Van-Det	72	18	37	55	26	-17
83–84	Det	75	35	48	83	20	+3
84–85	Det	75	19	30	49	16	-25
Totals		1052	361	505	866	507	-192

Playoffs

74–75	Chi	8	4	2	6	2	
75–76	Chi	4	0	1	1	0	
76–77	Chi	2	0	1	1	0	
77–78	Chi	4	0	2	2	2	
78–79	Atl	2	0	2	2	2	
79–80	Van	4	0	2	2	0	
80–81	Van	1	1	1	2	0	
81–82	Van	17	8	3	11	4	
83–84	Det	4	0	5	5	4	
84–85	Det	2	0	1	1	0	
Totals		48	13	20	33	14	

BOLDUC, Daniel George *5-9 180 LW*
B. Waterville, Maine, Apr. 6, 1953

75–76	NE (WHA)	14	2	5	7	14	
76–77	NE (WHA)	33	8	3	11	15	
77–78	NE (WHA)	41	5	5	10	22	
78–79	Det	56	16	13	29	14	-9
79–80	Det	44	6	5	11	19	-14
83–84	Calg	2	0	1	1	0	+1

SSN	TEAM	GP	G	A	PTS.	PIM	+/-
NHL Totals		102	22	19	41	33	-22
WHA Totals		88	15	13	28	51	

Playoffs

SSN	TEAM	GP	G	A	PTS.	PIM	+/-
75-76	NE (WHA)	16	1	6	7	4	
77-78	NE (WHA)	14	2	4	6	4	
83-84	Calg	1	0	0	0	0	
NHL Totals		1	0	0	0	0	
WHA Totals		30	3	10	13	8	

BOLDUC, Michel 6-2 210 D
B. Angegardien, Que., Mar. 13, 1961

SSN	TEAM	GP	G	A	PTS.	PIM	+/-
81-82	Que	3	0	0	0	0	0
82-83	Que	7	0	0	0	6	+2
Totals		10	0	0	0	6	+2

BOLL, Frank Thurman (Buzz) 5-10 166 LW
B. Filmore, Sask., Mar. 6, 1911

SSN	TEAM	GP	G	A	PTS.	PIM	+/-
33-34	Tor	42	12	8	20	21	
34-35	Tor	47	14	4	18	4	
35-36	Tor	44	15	13	28	14	
36-37	Tor	25	6	3	9	12	
37-38	Tor	44	14	11	25	18	
38-39	Tor	11	0	0	0	0	
39-40	NYA	47	5	10	15	18	
40-41	NYA	46	12	14	26	16	
41-42	NYA	48	11	15	26	23	
42-43	Bos	43	25	27	52	20	
43-44	Bos	39	19	25	44	2	
Totals		436	133	130	263	148	

Playoffs

SSN	TEAM	GP	G	A	PTS.	PIM	+/-
33-34	Tor	5	0	0	0	9	
34-35	Tor	5	0	0	0	0	
35-36	Tor	9	7	3	10	2	
36-37	Tor	2	0	0	0	0	
37-38	Tor	7	0	0	0	2	
39-40	NYA	1	0	0	0	0	
Totals		29	7	3	10	13	

BOLONCHUK, Larry Kenneth Mitchell 5-10 190 D
B. Winnipeg, Man., Feb. 26, 1952

SSN	TEAM	GP	G	A	PTS.	PIM	+/-
72-73	Van	15	0	0	0	6	-11
75-76	Wash	1	0	1	1	0	-1
76-77	Wash	9	0	0	0	12	-12
77-78	Wash	49	3	8	11	79	-19
Totals		74	3	9	12	97	-43

BOLTON, Hugh Edward 6-3 190 D
B. Toronto, Ont., Apr. 15, 1929

SSN	TEAM	GP	G	A	PTS.	PIM	+/-
49-50	Tor	2	0	0	0	2	
50-51	Tor	13	1	3	4	2	
51-52	Tor	60	3	13	16	73	
52-53	Tor	9	0	0	0	10	
53-54	Tor	9	0	0	0	10	
54-55	Tor	69	2	19	21	55	
55-56	Tor	67	4	16	20	65	
56-57	Tor	6	0	0	0	0	
Totals		235	10	51	61	217	

Playoffs

SSN	TEAM	GP	G	A	PTS.	PIM	+/-
51-52	Tor	3	0	0	0	4	
53-54	Tor	5	0	1	1	4	
54-55	Tor	4	0	3	3	6	
55-56	Tor	5	0	1	1	0	
Totals		17	0	5	5	14	

BOMBARDIR, Brad 6-2 190 D
B. Powell River, B.C., May 5, 1972

SSN	TEAM	GP	G	A	PTS.	PIM	+/-
97-98	NJ	43	1	5	6	8	+11
98-99	NJ	56	1	7	8	16	-4
Totals		99	2	12	14	24	+7

Playoffs

SSN	TEAM	GP	G	A	PTS.	PIM	+/-
98-99	NJ	5	0	0	0	0	

BONAR, Daniel 5-9 175 C
B. Brandon, Man., Sept. 23, 1956

SSN	TEAM	GP	G	A	PTS.	PIM	+/-
80-81	LA	71	11	15	26	57	0
81-82	LA	79	13	23	36	111	-4
82-83	LA	20	1	1	2	40	-7
Totals		170	25	39	64	208	-11

Playoffs

SSN	TEAM	GP	G	A	PTS.	PIM	+/-
80-81	LA	4	1	1	2	11	

SSN	TEAM	GP	G	A	PTS.	PIM	+/-
81-82	LA	10	2	3	5	11	
Totals		14	3	4	7	22	

BONDRA, Peter 6-1 200 RW
B. Luck, Soviet Union, Feb. 7, 1966

SSN	TEAM	GP	G	A	PTS.	PIM	+/-
90-91	Wash	54	12	16	28	47	-10
91-92	Wash	71	28	28	56	42	+16
92-93	Wash	83	37	48	85	70	+8
93-94	Wash	69	24	19	43	40	+22
94-95	Wash	47	34	9	43	24	+9
95-96	Wash	67	52	28	80	40	+18
96-97	Wash	77	46	31	77	72	+7
97-98	Wash	76	52	26	78	44	+14
98-99	Wash	66	31	24	55	56	-1
Totals		610	316	229	545	435	+83

Playoffs

SSN	TEAM	GP	G	A	PTS.	PIM	+/-
90-91	Wash	4	0	1	1	2	
91-92	Wash	7	6	2	8	4	
92-93	Wash	6	0	6	6	0	
93-94	Wash	9	2	4	6	4	
94-95	Wash	7	5	3	8	10	
95-96	Wash	6	3	2	5	8	
97-98	Wash	17	7	5	12	12	
Totals		56	23	23	46	40	

BONIN, Brian 5-10 185 C
B. St. Paul, Minn, Nov. 28, 1973

SSN	TEAM	GP	G	A	PTS.	PIM	+/-
98-99	Pitt	5	0	0	0	0	-2

Playoffs

SSN	TEAM	GP	G	A	PTS.	PIM	+/-
98-99	Pitt	3	0	0	0	0	

BONIN, Marcel 5-9 175 LW
B. Montreal, Que., Sept. 12, 1932

SSN	TEAM	GP	G	A	PTS.	PIM	+/-
52-53	Det	37	4	9	13	14	
53-54	Det	1	0	0	0	0	
54-55	Det	69	16	20	36	53	
55-56	Bos	67	9	9	18	49	
57-58	Mont	66	15	24	39	37	
58-59	Mont	57	13	30	43	38	
59-60	Mont	59	17	34	51	59	
60-61	Mont	65	16	35	51	45	
61-62	Mont	33	7	14	21	41	
Totals		454	97	175	272	336	

Playoffs

SSN	TEAM	GP	G	A	PTS.	PIM	+/-
52-53	Det	5	0	1	1	0	
54-55	Det	11	0	2	2	4	
57-58	Mont	9	0	1	1	12	
58-59	Mont	11	10	5	15	4	
59-60	Mont	8	1	4	5	12	
60-61	Mont	6	0	1	1	29	
Totals		50	11	14	25	61	

BONK, Radek 6-3 215 C
B. Krnov, Czechoslovakia, Jan. 9, 1976

SSN	TEAM	GP	G	A	PTS.	PIM	+/-
94-95	Ott	42	3	8	11	28	-5
95-96	Ott	76	16	19	35	36	-5
96-97	Ott	53	5	13	18	14	-4
97-98	Ott	65	7	9	16	16	-13
98-99	Ott	81	16	16	32	48	+15
Totals		317	47	65	112	132	-12

Playoffs

SSN	TEAM	GP	G	A	PTS.	PIM	+/-
96-97	Ott	7	0	1	1	4	
97-98	Ott	5	0	0	0	2	
98-99	Ott	4	0	0	0	6	
Totals		16	0	1	1	12	

BONSIGNORE, Jason 6-4 208 C
B. Rochester, N.Y., Apr. 15, 1976

SSN	TEAM	GP	G	A	PTS.	PIM	+/-
94-95	Edm	1	1	0	1	0	-1
95-96	Edm	20	0	2	2	4	-6
97-98	TB	35	2	8	10	22	-11
98-99	TB	23	0	3	3	8	-4
Totals		79	3	13	16	34	-22

BONVIE, Dennis 5-11 210 D
B. Antigonish, N.S., July 23, 1973

SSN	TEAM	GP	G	A	PTS.	PIM	+/-
94-95	Edm	2	0	0	0	0	0
95-96	Edm	8	0	0	0	47	-3
97-98	Edm	4	0	0	0	27	0
98-99	Chi	11	0	0	0	44	-4
Totals		25	0	0	0	118	-7

BOO, James McQuaid 6-1 200 D
B. Rolla, Mo., Nov. 12, 1954

SSN	TEAM	GP	G	A	PTS.	PIM	+/-
77-78	Minn	6	0	0	0	22	-6

BOONE, Carl George (Buddy) 5-7 158 RW
B. Kirkland Lake, Ont., Sept. 11, 1932

SSN	TEAM	GP	G	A	PTS.	PIM	+/-
57-58	Bos	34	5	3	8	28	

Playoffs

SSN	TEAM	GP	G	A	PTS.	PIM	+/-
56-57	Bos	10	1	0	1	12	
57-58	Bos	12	1	1	2	13	
Totals		22	2	1	3	25	

BOOTHMAN, George Edward 6-2 175 D
B. Calgary, Alta., Sept. 25, 1916

SSN	TEAM	GP	G	A	PTS.	PIM	+/-
42-43	Tor	9	1	1	2	4	
43-44	Tor	49	16	18	34	14	
Totals		58	17	19	36	18	

Playoffs

SSN	TEAM	GP	G	A	PTS.	PIM	+/-
43-44	Tor	5	2	1	3	2	

BORDELEAU, Christian Gerard 5-8 172 C
B. Noranda, Que., Sept. 23, 1947

SSN	TEAM	GP	G	A	PTS.	PIM	+/-
68-69	Mont	13	1	3	4	4	+1
69-40	Mont	48	2	13	15	18	+2
70-71	StL	78	21	32	53	48	+14
71-72	StL-Chi	66	14	17	31	12	-8
72-73	Winn (WHA)	78	47	54	101	12	
73-74	Winn (WHA)	75	26	49	75	22	
74-75	Winn-Que (WHA)	71	23	41	64	24	
75-76	Que (WHA)	74	37	72	109	42	
76-77	Que (WHA)	72	32	75	107	34	
77-78	Que (WHA)	26	9	22	31	28	
78-79	Que (WHA)	16	5	12	17	0	
NHL Totals		205	38	65	103	82	+9
WHA Totals		412	179	325	504	162	

Playoffs

SSN	TEAM	GP	G	A	PTS.	PIM	+/-
68-69	Mont	6	1	0	1	0	
70-71	StL	5	0	1	1	17	
71-72	Chi	8	3	6	9	0	
72-73	Winn (WHA)	12	5	8	13	4	
73-74	Winn (WHA)	3	3	2	5	0	
74-75	Que (WHA)	15	2	13	15	2	
75-76	Que (WHA)	5	1	1	2	4	
76-77	Que (WHA)	8	4	5	9	0	
77-78	Que (WHA)	10	1	5	6	6	
NHL Totals		19	4	7	11	17	
WHA Totals		53	16	34	50	16	

BORDELEAU, Jean-Pierre (J.P.) 6-0 170 RW
B. Noranda, Que., June 13, 1949

SSN	TEAM	GP	G	A	PTS.	PIM	+/-
71-72	Chi	3	0	2	2	2	+1
72-73	Chi	73	15	15	30	6	+7
73-74	Chi	64	11	9	20	11	+11
74-75	Chi	59	7	8	15	4	-5
75-76	Chi	76	12	18	30	6	-9
76-77	Chi	60	15	14	29	20	-14
77-78	Chi	76	15	25	40	32	+9
78-79	Chi	63	15	21	36	34	-7
79-80	Chi	45	7	14	21	28	+3
Totals		519	97	126	223	143	-4

Playoffs

SSN	TEAM	GP	G	A	PTS.	PIM	+/-
69-70	Chi	1	0	0	0	0	
72-73	Chi	14	1	0	1	4	
73-74	Chi	11	0	2	2	2	
74-75	Chi	7	2	2	4	2	
75-76	Chi	4	0	0	0	0	
76-77	Chi	2	0	0	0	2	
77-78	Chi	4	0	1	1	0	
78-79	Chi	4	0	1	1	2	
79-80	Chi	1	0	0	0	0	
Totals		48	3	6	9	12	

BORDELEAU, Paulin Joseph (Paul) 5-9 162 RW
B. Noranda, Que., Jan. 29, 1953

SSN	TEAM	GP	G	A	PTS.	PIM	+/-
73-74	Van	68	11	13	24	20	-16
74-75	Van	67	17	31	48	21	+9
75-76	Van	48	5	12	17	6	-1
76-77	Que (WHA)	80	42	41	83	52	
77-78	Que (WHA)	77	42	23	65	29	
78-79	Que (WHA)	77	17	12	29	44	

SSN	TEAM	GP	G	A	PTS.	PIM	+/-
NHL Totals		183	33	56	89	47	-8
WHA Totals		234	101	76	177	125	

Playoffs

74-75	Que (WHA)	5	2	1	3	0	
76-77	Que (WHA)	16	12	9	21	12	
77-78	Que (WHA)	11	4	6	10	2	
78-79	Que (WHA)	4	1	0	1	0	
NHL Totals		5	2	1	3	0	
WHA Totals		31	17	15	32	14	

BORDELEAU, Sebastien *5-10 180 C*
B. Vancouver, B.C., Feb. 15, 1975

95-96	Mont	4	0	0	0	0	-1
96-97	Mont	28	2	9	11	2	-3
97-98	Mont	53	6	8	14	36	+5
98-99	Nash	72	16	24	40	26	-14
Totals		157	24	41	65	64	-13

Playoffs

97-98	Mont	5	0	0	0	2	

BOROTSIK, John Nicholas (Jack) *5-9 178 C*
B. Brandon, Man., Nov. 26, 1949

74-75	StL	1	0	0	0	0	0

BORSATO, Luciano *5-11 190 C*
B. Richmond Hill, Ont., Jan. 7, 1966

90-91	Winn	1	0	1	1	2	0
91-92	Winn	56	15	21	36	45	-6
92-93	Winn	67	15	20	35	38	-1
93-94	Winn	75	5	13	18	28	-11
94-95	Winn	4	0	0	0	0	-1
Totals		203	35	55	90	113	-19

Playoffs

91-92	Winn	1	0	0	0	0	
92-93	Winn	6	1	0	1	4	
Totals		7	1	0	1	4	

BORSCHEVSKY, Nikolai *5-9 180 RW*
B. Tomsk, USSR, Jan. 12, 1965

92-93	Tor	78	34	40	74	28	+33
93-94	Tor	45	14	20	34	10	+6
94-95	Tor-Calg	27	0	10	10	0	+3
95-96	Dal	12	1	3	4	6	+7
Totals		162	49	73	122	44	+49

Playoffs

92-93	Tor	16	2	7	9	0	
93-94	Tor	15	2	2	4	4	
Totals		31	4	9	13	4	

BOSCHMAN, Laurie Joseph *6-0 185 C*
B. Major, Sask., June 4, 1960

79-80	Tor	80	16	32	48	78	+2
80-81	Tor	53	14	19	33	178	-10
81-82	Tor-Edm	65	11	22	33	187	-1
82-83	Edm-Winn	74	11	17	28	219	+6
83-84	Winn	61	28	46	74	234	-4
84-85	Winn	80	32	44	76	180	-8
85-86	Winn	77	27	42	69	241	-29
86-87	Winn	80	17	24	41	152	-17
87-88	Winn	80	25	23	48	229	-24
88-89	Winn	70	10	26	36	163	-17
89-90	Winn	66	10	17	27	103	-11
90-91	NJ	78	11	9	20	79	-1
91-92	NJ	75	8	20	28	121	+9
92-93	Ott	70	9	7	16	101	-26
Totals		1009	229	348	577	2265	-141

Playoffs

79-80	Tor	3	1	1	2	18	
80-81	Tor	3	0	0	0	7	
81-82	Edm	3	0	1	1	4	
82-83	Winn	3	0	1	1	12	
83-84	Winn	3	0	1	1	5	
84-85	Winn	8	2	1	3	21	
85-86	Winn	3	0	1	1	6	
86-87	Winn	10	2	3	5	32	
87-88	Winn	5	1	3	4	9	
89-90	Winn	2	0	0	0	2	
90-91	NJ	7	1	1	2	16	
91-92	NJ	7	1	0	1	8	
Totals		57	8	13	21	140	

BOSSY, Michel (Mike) *6-0 186 RW*
B. Montreal, Que., Jan. 22, 1957

77-78	NYI	73	53	38	91	6	+31
78-79	NYI	80	69	57	126	25	+63
79-80	NYI	75	51	41	92	12	+28
80-81	NYI	79	68	51	119	32	+37
81-82	NYI	80	64	83	147	22	+69
82-83	NYI	79	60	58	118	20	+27
83-84	NYI	67	51	67	118	8	+66
84-85	NYI	76	58	59	117	38	+37
85-86	NYI	80	61	62	123	14	+30
86-87	NYI	63	38	37	75	33	-7
Totals		752	573	553	1126	210	+381

Playoffs

77-78	NYI	7	2	2	4	2	
78-79	NYI	10	6	2	8	2	
79-80	NYI	16	10	13	23	8	
80-81	NYI	18	17	18	35	4	
81-82	NYI	19	17	10	27	0	
82-83	NYI	19	17	9	26	10	
83-84	NYI	21	8	10	18	4	
84-85	NYI	10	5	6	11	4	
85-86	NYI	3	1	2	3	4	
86-87	NYI	6	2	3	5	0	
Totals		129	85	75	160	38	

BOSTROM, Helge *5-7 185 D*
B. Winnipeg, Man., Jan. 9, 1894

29-30	Chi	20	0	1	1	8	
30-31	Chi	42	2	2	4	32	
31-32	Chi	14	0	0	0	4	
32-33	Chi	20	1	0	1	14	
Totals		96	3	3	6	58	

Playoffs

29-30	Chi	2	0	0	0	0	
30-31	Chi	9	0	0	0	16	
31-32	Chi	2	0	0	0	0	
Totals		13	0	0	0	16	

BOTELL, Mark *6-4 212 D*
B. Scarborough, Ont., Aug. 27, 1961

81-82	Phil	32	4	10	14	31	+8

BOTHWELL, Timothy *6-3 190 D*
B. Vancouver, B.C., May 6, 1955

78-79	NYR	1	0	0	0	2	-1
79-80	NYR	45	4	6	10	20	-3
80-81	NYR	3	0	1	1	0	0
81-82	NYR	13	0	3	3	10	-5
82-83	StL	61	4	11	15	34	-8
83-84	StL	62	2	13	15	65	+22
84-85	StL	79	4	22	26	62	+27
85-86	Hart	62	2	8	10	53	+13
86-87	Hart-StL	76	6	16	22	46	-19
87-88	StL	78	6	13	19	76	+6
88-89	StL	22	0	0	0	14	+4
Totals		502	28	93	121	382	+36

Playoffs

79-80	NYR	9	0	0	0	8	
83-84	StL	11	0	2	2	14	
84-85	StL	3	0	0	0	2	
85-86	Hart	10	0	0	0	8	
86-87	StL	6	0	0	0	6	
87-88	StL	10	0	1	1	18	
Totals		49	0	3	3	56	

BOTTERIL, Jason *6-3 205 LW*
B. Edmonton, Alta., May 19, 1976

97-98	Dal	4	0	0	0	19	-1
98-99	Dal	17	0	0	0	23	-2
Totals		21	0	0	0	42	-3

BOTTING, Cameron Allen (Cam) *6-2 205 RW*
B. Kingston, Ont., Mar. 10, 1954

75-76	Atl	2	0	1	1	0	+1

BOUCHA, Henry Charles *6-0 185 C*
B. Warroad, Minn., June 1, 1951

71-72	Det	16	1	0	1	2	-3
72-43	Det	73	14	14	28	82	-2
73-74	Det	70	19	12	31	32	-22
74-75	Minn	51	15	14	29	23	-12
75-76	KC	28	4	7	11	14	-13
75-76	Minn (WHA)	36	15	20	35	47	
76-77	Col	9	0	2	2	4	0
NHL Totals		247	53	49	102	157	-52
WHA Totals		36	15	20	35	47	

BOUCHARD, Edmond *F*
B. Trois Rivieres, Que.

21-22	Mont	18	1	4	5	4	
22-23	Ham	24	5	12	17	32	
23-24	Ham-Mont	24	5	0	5	2	
24-25	Ham	29	2	2	4	14	
25-26	NYA	34	3	1	4	10	
26-27	NYA	38	2	1	3	12	
27-28	NYA	39	1	0	1	27	
28-29	NYA-Pitt	17	0	0	0	4	
Totals		223	19	20	39	105	

BOUCHARD, Emile Joseph (Butch) *6-2 205 D*
B. Montreal, Que., Sept. 11, 1920

41-42	Mont	44	0	6	6	38	
42-43	Mont	45	2	16	18	47	
43-44	Mont	39	5	14	19	52	
44-45	Mont	50	11	23	34	34	
45-46	Mont	45	7	10	17	52	
46-47	Mont	60	5	7	12	60	
47-48	Mont	60	4	6	10	78	
48-49	Mont	27	3	3	6	42	
49-50	Mont	69	1	7	8	88	
50-51	Mont	52	3	10	13	80	
51-52	Mont	60	3	9	12	45	
52-53	Mont	58	2	8	10	55	
53-54	Mont	70	1	10	11	89	
54-55	Mont	70	2	15	17	81	
55-56	Mont	36	0	0	0	22	
Totals		785	49	144	193	863	

Playoffs

41-42	Mont	3	1	1	2	0	
42-43	Mont	5	0	1	1	4	
43-44	Mont	9	1	3	4	4	
44-45	Mont	6	3	4	7	4	
45-46	Mont	9	2	1	3	17	
46-47	Mont	11	0	3	3	21	
48-49	Mont	7	0	0	0	6	
49-50	Mont	5	0	2	2	2	
50-51	Mont	11	1	1	2	2	
51-52	Mont	11	0	2	2	14	
52-53	Mont	12	1	1	2	6	
53-54	Mont	11	2	1	3	4	
54-55	Mont	12	0	1	1	37	
55-56	Mont	1	0	0	0	0	
Totals		113	11	21	32	121	

BOUCHARD, Joel *6-0 190 D*
B. Montreal, Que., Jan. 23, 1974

94-95	Calg	2	0	0	0	0	0
95-96	Calg	4	0	0	0	4	0
96-97	Calg	76	4	5	9	49	-23
97-98	Calg	44	5	7	12	57	0
98-99	Nash	64	4	11	15	60	-10
Totals		190	13	23	36	170	-33

BOUCHARD, Pierre *6-2 205 D*
B. Longueuil, Que., Feb. 20, 1948

70-71	Mont	51	0	3	3	50	+3
71-72	Mont	60	3	5	8	39	+10
72-73	Mont	41	0	7	7	69	+11
73-74	Mont	60	1	14	15	25	+8
74-75	Mont	79	3	9	12	65	+24
75-76	Mont	66	1	11	12	50	+20
76-77	Mont	73	4	11	15	52	+33
77-78	Mont	59	4	6	10	29	+27
78-79	Wash	1	0	0	0	0	+1
79-80	Wash	54	5	9	14	16	-7
80-81	Wash	50	3	7	10	28	-18
81-82	Wash	1	0	0	0	10	-2
Totals		595	24	82	106	433	+110

Playoffs

70-71	Mont	13	0	1	1	10	
71-72	Mont	1	0	0	0	0	
72-73	Mont	17	1	3	4	2	
73-74	Mont	6	0	2	2	4	
74-75	Mont	10	0	2	2	10	
75-76	Mont	13	2	0	2	8	
76-77	Mont	6	0	1	1	6	

SSN	TEAM	GP	G	A	PTS.	PIM	+/-
77–78	Mont	10	0	1	1	5	
Totals		76	3	10	13	45	

BOUCHARD, Richard Joseph (Dick) 5–8 155 RW
B. Lettelier, Man., Dec. 2, 1934

SSN	TEAM	GP	G	A	PTS.	PIM	+/-
54–55	NYR	1	0	0	0	0	

*BOUCHER, Francois X. (Frank, Raffles) 5–8 185 RW
B. Ottawa, Ont., Oct. 7, 1901

SSN	TEAM	GP	G	A	PTS.	PIM	+/-
21–22	Ott	24	9	1	10	4	
26–27	NYR	44	13	15	28	17	
27–28	NYR	44	23	12	35	14	
28–29	NYR	44	10	16	26	8	
29–30	NYR	42	26	36	62	16	
30–31	NYR	44	12	27	39	20	
31–32	NYR	48	12	23	35	18	
32–33	NYR	46	7	28	35	4	
33–34	NYR	48	14	30	44	4	
34–35	NYR	48	13	32	45	2	
35–36	NYR	48	11	18	29	2	
36–37	NYR	44	7	13	20	5	
37–38	NYR	18	0	1	1	2	
43–44	NYR	15	4	10	14	2	
Totals		557	161	262	423	118	

Playoffs

SSN	TEAM	GP	G	A	PTS.	PIM	+/-
21–22	Ott	2	0	0	0	0	
26–27	NYR	2	0	0	0	4	
27–28	NYR	9	7	1	8	2	
28–29	NYR	6	1	0	1	0	
29–30	NYR	3	1	1	2	0	
30–31	NYR	4	0	2	2	0	
31–32	NYR	7	3	6	9	0	
32–33	NYR	8	2	2	4	6	
33–34	NYR	2	0	0	0	0	
34–35	NYR	4	0	3	3	0	
36–37	NYR	9	2	3	5	0	
Totals		56	16	18	34	12	

*BOUCHER, George (Buck) F
B. Ottawa, Ont., 1896

SSN	TEAM	GP	G	A	PTS.	PIM	+/-
17–18	Ott	22	9	0	9	27	
18–19	Ott	17	5	2	7	21	
19–20	Ott	22	10	4	14	34	
20–21	Ott	23	12	5	17	43	
21–22	Ott	23	12	8	20	10	
22–23	Ott	23	15	9	24	44	
23–24	Ott	21	14	5	19	28	
24–25	Ott	28	15	4	19	80	
25–26	Ott	36	8	4	12	64	
26–27	Ott	44	8	3	11	115	
27–28	Ott	44	7	5	12	78	
28–29	Ott–Mont M	41	4	2	6	70	
29–30	Mont M	39	2	6	8	50	
30–31	Mont M	31	0	0	0	25	
31–32	Chi	43	1	5	6	50	
Totals		457	122	62	184	739	

Playoffs

SSN	TEAM	GP	G	A	PTS.	PIM	+/-
18–19	Ott	5	2	1	3	9	
19–20	Ott	5	2	0	2	0	
20–21	Ott	7	5	0	5	18	
21–22	Ott	2	0	0	0	4	
22–23	Ott	8	2	1	3	8	
23–24	Ott	2	0	1	1	4	
25–26	Ott	2	0	0	0	10	
26–27	Ott	6	0	0	0	26	
27–28	Ott	2	0	0	0	4	
29–30	MontM	3	0	0	0	2	
31–32	Chi	2	0	1	1	0	
Totals		44	11	4	15	84	

BOUCHER, Philippe 6–2 189 D
B. St. Apollinaire, Que., Mar. 24, 1973

SSN	TEAM	GP	G	A	PTS.	PIM	+/-
92–93	Buf	18	0	4	4	14	+1
93–94	Buf	38	6	8	14	29	-1
94–95	Buf–LA	15	2	4	6	4	+3
95–96	LA	53	7	16	23	31	-26
96–97	LA	60	7	18	25	25	0
97–98	LA	45	6	10	16	49	+6
98–99	LA	45	2	6	8	32	-12
Totals		274	30	66	96	184	-29

Playoffs

SSN	TEAM	GP	G	A	PTS.	PIM	+/-
93–94	Buf	7	1	1	2	2	

*BOUCHER, Robert F
B. Ottawa, Ont.

SSN	TEAM	GP	G	A	PTS.	PIM	+/-
23–24	Mont	12	0	0	0	0	

*BOUCHER, William RW
B. Ottawa, Ont.

SSN	TEAM	GP	G	A	PTS.	PIM	+/-
21–22	Mont	24	17	5	22	18	
22–23	Mont	24	23	4	27	52	
23–24	Mont	23	16	6	22	33	
24–25	Mont	30	18	13	31	92	
25–26	Mont	34	8	5	13	112	
26–27	Mont–Bos	35	6	0	6	26	
27–28	NYA	43	5	2	7	58	
Totals		213	93	35	128	391	

Playoffs

SSN	TEAM	GP	G	A	PTS.	PIM	+/-
22–23	Mont	2	1	0	1	2	
23–24	Mont	5	6	2	8	14	
24–25	Mont	6	2	1	3	17	
26–27	Bos	8	0	0	0	2	
Totals		21	9	3	12	35	

BOUDREAU, Bruce Allan 5–9 175 C
B. Toronto, Ont., Jan. 9, 1955

SSN	TEAM	GP	G	A	PTS.	PIM	+/-
76–77	Tor	15	2	5	7	4	+2
77–78	Tor	40	11	18	29	12	+8
78–79	Tor	26	4	3	7	2	-3
79–80	Tor	2	0	0	0	2	0
80–81	Tor	39	10	14	24	18	-7
81–82	Tor	12	0	2	2	6	-6
85–86	Chi	7	1	0	1	2	+1
Totals		141	28	42	70	46	-5

Playoffs

SSN	TEAM	GP	G	A	PTS.	PIM	+/-
76–77	Tor	3	0	0	0	0	
80–81	Tor	2	1	0	1	0	
82–83	Tor	4	1	0	1	4	
Totals		9	2	0	2	4	

BOUDRIAS, Andre G. 5–8 165 LW
B. Montreal, Que., Sept. 19, 1943

SSN	TEAM	GP	G	A	PTS.	PIM	+/-
63–44	Mont	4	1	4	5	2	
64–65	Mont	1	0	0	0	2	
66–67	Mont	2	0	1	1	0	
67–68	Minn	74	18	35	53	42	+3
68–69	Minn–Chi	73	8	19	27	10	-19
69–70	StL	50	3	14	17	20	+7
70–71	Van	77	25	41	66	16	+15
71–72	Van	78	27	34	61	26	-34
72–73	Van	77	30	40	70	24	-20
73–74	Van	78	16	59	75	18	-6
74–75	Van	77	16	62	78	46	+8
75–76	Van	71	7	31	38	10	-7
76–77	Que (WHA)	74	12	31	43	12	
77–78	Que (WHA)	66	10	17	27	22	
NHL Totals		662	151	340	491	216	-59
WHA Totals		140	22	48	70	34	

Playoffs

SSN	TEAM	GP	G	A	PTS.	PIM	+/-
67–68	Minn	14	3	6	9	8	
69–70	StL	14	2	4	6	4	
74–75	Van	5	1	0	1	0	
75–76	Van	1	0	0	0	0	
76–77	Que (WHA)	17	3	12	15	6	
77–78	Que (WHA)	11	0	2	2	4	
NHL Totals		34	6	10	16	12	
WHA Totals		28	3	14	17	10	

BOUGHNER, Barry Michael 5–10 180 LW
B. Delhi, Ont., Jan. 29, 1948

SSN	TEAM	GP	G	A	PTS.	PIM	+/-
69–70	Oak	4	0	0	0	2	0
70–71	Cal	16	0	0	0	9	-3
Totals		20	0	0	0	11	-3

BOUGHNER, Bob 6–1 200 D
B. Windsor, Ont., Mar. 8, 1971

SSN	TEAM	GP	G	A	PTS.	PIM	+/-
95–96	Buf	31	0	1	1	104	+3
96–97	Buf	77	1	7	8	225	+12
97–98	Buf	69	1	3	4	165	+5
98–99	Nash	79	3	10	13	137	-6
Totals		256	5	21	26	631	+14

Playoffs

SSN	TEAM	GP	G	A	PTS.	PIM	+/-
96–97	Buf	11	0	1	1	9	
97–98	Buf	14	0	4	4	15	
Totals		25	0	5	5	24	

BOURBONNAIS, Dan 5–10 181 LW
B. Winnipeg, Man., Mar. 3, 1962

SSN	TEAM	GP	G	A	PTS.	PIM	+/-
81–82	Hart	24	3	9	12	11	-8
83–84	Hart	35	0	16	16	0	+3
Totals		59	3	25	28	11	-5

BOURBONNAIS, Rick 6–0 186 RW
B. Toronto, Ont., Apr. 20, 1955

SSN	TEAM	GP	G	A	PTS.	PIM	+/-
75–76	StL	7	0	0	0	8	-1
76–77	StL	33	6	8	14	10	-6
77–78	StL	31	3	7	10	11	-12
Totals		71	9	15	24	29	-19

Playoffs

SSN	TEAM	GP	G	A	PTS.	PIM	+/-
76–77	StL	4	0	1	1	0	

BOURCIER, Conrad 5–7 145 C
B. Montreal, Que., May 28, 1916

SSN	TEAM	GP	G	A	PTS.	PIM	+/-
35–36	Mont	6	0	0	0	0	

BOURCIER, Jean–Louis 5–11 175 LW
B. Montreal, Que., Jan. 3, 1912

SSN	TEAM	GP	G	A	PTS.	PIM	+/-
35–36	Mont	9	0	1	1	0	

*BOURGEAULT, Leo A. 5–6 165 D
B. Sturgeon Falls, Ont., Jan. 17, 1903

SSN	TEAM	GP	G	A	PTS.	PIM	+/-
26–27	Tor–NYR	42	2	1	3	72	
27–28	NYR	37	7	0	7	7	
28–29	NYR	44	2	3	5	59	
29–30	NYR	44	7	6	13	54	
30–31	NYR–Ott	38	0	5	5	40	
32–33	Ott–Mont	50	2	2	4	27	
33–34	Mont	48	4	3	7	10	
34–35	Mont	4	0	0	0	0	
Totals		307	24	20	44	269	

Playoffs

SSN	TEAM	GP	G	A	PTS.	PIM	+/-
26–27	NYR	2	0	0	0	4	
27–28	NYR	9	0	0	0	8	
28–29	NYR	6	0	0	0	0	
29–30	NYR	3	1	1	2	6	
32–33	Mont	2	0	0	0	0	
33–34	Mont	2	0	0	0	0	
Totals		24	1	1	2	18	

BOURGEOIS, Charles Marc 6–4 205 D
B. Moncton, N.B., Nov. 11, 1959

SSN	TEAM	GP	G	A	PTS.	PIM	+/-
81–82	Calg	54	2	13	15	112	+5
82–83	Calg	15	2	3	5	21	-4
83–84	Calg	17	1	3	4	35	0
84–85	Calg	47	2	10	12	134	+14
85–86	Calg–StL	60	7	12	19	244	+18
86–87	StL	66	2	12	14	164	+16
87–88	StL–Hart	31	0	1	1	78	-3
Totals		290	16	54	70	788	+46

Playoffs

SSN	TEAM	GP	G	A	PTS.	PIM	+/-
81–82	Calg	3	0	0	0	7	
83–84	Calg	8	0	1	1	27	
84–85	Calg	4	0	0	0	17	
85–86	StL	19	2	2	4	116	
86–87	StL	6	0	0	0	27	
Totals		40	2	3	5	194	

BOURNE, Robert Glen 6–3 200 C
B. Kindersley, Sask., June 21, 1954

SSN	TEAM	GP	G	A	PTS.	PIM	+/-
74–75	NYI	77	16	23	39	12	+9
75–76	NYI	14	2	3	5	13	-2
76–77	NYI	75	16	19	35	30	+27
77–78	NYI	80	30	33	63	31	+15
78–79	NYI	80	30	31	61	48	+34
79–80	NYI	73	15	25	40	52	+5
80–81	NYI	78	35	41	76	62	+34
81–82	NYI	76	27	26	53	77	+27
82–83	NYI	77	20	42	62	55	+14
83–84	NYI	78	22	34	56	75	+12
84–85	NYI	44	8	12	20	51	-8
85–86	NYI	62	17	15	32	36	-7
86–87	LA	78	13	9	22	35	-13
87–88	LA	72	7	11	18	28	-31
Totals		964	258	324	582	605	+106

Playoffs

SSN	TEAM	GP	G	A	PTS.	PIM	+/-
74–75	NYI	9	1	2	3	4	
76–77	NYI	8	2	0	2	4	
77–78	NYI	7	2	3	5	2	

SSN	TEAM	GP	G	A	PTS.	PIM	+/-
78–79	NYI	10	1	3	4	6	
79–80	NYI	21	10	10	20	10	
80–81	NYI	14	4	6	10	19	
81–82	NYI	19	9	7	16	36	
82–83	NYI	20	8	20	28	14	
83–84	NYI	8	1	1	2	7	
84–85	NYI	10	0	2	2	6	
85–86	NYI	3	0	0	0	0	
86–87	LA	5	2	1	3	0	
87–88	LA	5	0	1	1	0	
Totals		139	40	56	96	108	

BOURQUE, Phillippe Richard *6–1 200 LW*
B. Chelmsford, Mass., June 8, 1962

SSN	TEAM	GP	G	A	PTS.	PIM	+/-
83–84	Pitt	5	0	1	1	12	-2
85–86	Pitt	4	0	0	0	2	-2
86–87	Pitt	22	2	3	5	32	-2
87–88	Pitt	21	4	12	16	20	+3
88–89	Pitt	80	17	26	43	97	-22
89–90	Pitt	76	22	17	39	108	-7
90–91	Pitt	78	20	14	34	106	+7
91–92	Pitt	58	10	16	26	58	-6
92–93	NYR	55	6	14	20	39	-9
93–94	NYR–Ott	27	2	4	6	8	-4
94–95	Ott	38	4	3	7	20	-17
95–96	Ott	13	1	1	2	14	-3
Totals		477	88	111	199	516	-64

Playoffs

SSN	TEAM	GP	G	A	PTS.	PIM	+/-
88–89	Pitt	11	4	1	5	66	
90–91	Pitt	24	6	7	13	16	
91–92	Pitt	21	3	4	7	25	
Totals		56	13	12	25	107	

BOURQUE, Raymond Jean *5–11 215 D*
B. Montreal, Que., Dec. 28, 1960

SSN	TEAM	GP	G	A	PTS.	PIM	+/-
79–80	Bos	80	17	48	65	73	+52
80–81	Bos	67	27	29	56	96	+29
81–82	Bos	65	17	49	66	51	+22
82–83	Bos	65	22	51	73	20	+49
83–84	Bos	78	31	65	96	57	+51
84–85	Bos	73	20	66	86	53	+30
85–86	Bos	74	19	58	77	68	+17
86–87	Bos	78	23	72	95	36	+44
87–88	Bos	78	17	64	81	72	+34
88–89	Bos	60	18	43	61	52	+20
89–90	Bos	76	19	65	84	50	+31
90–91	Bos	76	21	73	94	75	+33
91–92	Bos	80	21	60	81	56	+11
92–93	Bos	78	19	63	82	40	+38
93–94	Bos	72	20	71	91	58	+26
94–95	Bos	46	12	31	43	20	+3
95–96	Bos	82	20	62	82	58	+31
96–97	Bos	62	19	31	50	18	-11
97–98	Bos	82	13	35	48	80	+2
98–99	Bos	81	10	47	57	34	-7
Totals		1453	385	1083	1468	1087	+505

Playoffs

SSN	TEAM	GP	G	A	PTS.	PIM	+/-
79–80	Bos	10	2	9	11	27	
80–81	Bos	3	0	1	1	2	
81–82	Bos	9	1	5	6	16	
82–83	Bos	17	8	15	23	10	
83–84	Bos	3	0	2	2	0	
84–85	Bos	5	0	3	3	4	
85–86	Bos	3	0	0	0	0	
86–87	Bos	4	1	2	3	0	
87–88	Bos	23	3	18	21	26	
88–89	Bos	10	0	4	4	6	
89–90	Bos	17	5	12	17	16	
90–91	Bos	19	7	18	25	12	
91–92	Bos	12	3	6	9	12	
92–93	Bos	4	1	0	1	2	
93–94	Bos	13	2	8	10	0	
94–95	Bos	5	0	3	3	0	
95–96	Bos	5	1	6	7	2	
97–98	Bos	6	1	4	5	2	
98–99	Box	12	1	9	10	14	
Totals		180	36	125	161	151	

BOUTETTE, Patrick Michael *5–8 175 RW*
B. Windsor, Ont., Mar. 1, 1952

SSN	TEAM	GP	G	A	PTS.	PIM	+/-
75–76	Tor	77	10	22	32	140	-1
76–77	Tor	80	18	18	36	107	+13
77–78	Tor	80	17	19	36	120	0
78–79	Tor	80	14	19	33	136	+3
79–80	Tor–Hart	79	13	35	48	92	+11
80–81	Hart	80	28	52	80	160	-13

SSN	TEAM	GP	G	A	PTS.	PIM	+/-
91–82	Pitt	80	23	51	74	230	-23
82–83	Pitt	80	27	29	56	152	-33
83–84	Pitt	73	14	26	40	142	-58
84–85	Pitt–Hart	47	7	11	18	75	-11
Totals		756	171	282	453	1354	-112

Playoffs

SSN	TEAM	GP	G	A	PTS.	PIM	+/-
75–76	Tor	10	1	4	5	16	
76–77	Tor	9	0	4	4	17	
77–78	Tor	13	3	3	6	40	
78–79	Tor	6	2	2	4	29	
78–79	Hart	3	1	0	1	6	
81–82	Pitt	5	3	1	4	8	
Totals		46	10	14	24	109	

BOUTILIER, Paul Andre *5–11 188 D*
B. Sydney, N.S., May 3, 1963

SSN	TEAM	GP	G	A	PTS.	PIM	+/-
81–82	NYI	1	0	0	0	0	
82–83	NYI	29	4	5	9	24	-5
83–84	NYI	28	0	11	11	36	+18
84–85	NYI	78	12	23	35	90	0
85–86	NYI	77	4	30	34	100	-5
86–87	Bos–Minn	62	7	13	20	92	-1
87–88	NYR–Winn	10	0	1	1	12	-3
88–89	Winn	3	0	0	0	4	+2
Totals		288	27	83	110	358	+6

Playoffs

SSN	TEAM	GP	G	A	PTS.	PIM	+/-
82–83	NYI	2	0	0	0	2	
83–84	NYI	21	1	7	8	10	
84–85	NYI	10	0	2	2	16	
85–86	NYI	3	0	0	0	2	
87–88	Winn	5	0	0	0	15	
Totals		41	1	9	10	45	

BOWCHER, Clarence *D*
B. Sudbury, Ont.

SSN	TEAM	GP	G	A	PTS.	PIM	+/-
26–27	NYA	11	0	1	1	4	
27–28	NYA	36	2	1	3	106	
Totals		47	2	2	4	110	

BOWEN, Jason *6–4 215 D*
B. Port Alice, B.C., Nov. 9, 1973

SSN	TEAM	GP	G	A	PTS.	PIM	+/-
92–93	Phil	7	1	0	1	2	+1
93–94	Phil	56	1	5	6	87	+12
94–95	Phil	4	0	0	0	0	-2
95–96	Phil	2	0	0	0	2	0
96–97	Phil	4	0	1	1	8	+1
97–98	Edm	77	2	6	8	109	0
Totals		77	2	6	8	109	+12

*BOWMAN, Ralph B. (Scotty) *5–11 190 D*
B. Winnipeg, Man., June 20, 1911

SSN	TEAM	GP	G	A	PTS.	PIM	+/-
33–34	Ott	46	0	2	2	64	
34–35	StL E–Det	44	3	5	8	72	
35–36	Det	48	3	2	5	44	
36–37	Det	37	0	1	1	24	
37–38	Det	45	2	2	2	26	
38–39	Det	43	2	3	5	26	
39–40	Det	11	0	2	2	4	
Totals		274	8	17	25	260	

Playoffs

SSN	TEAM	GP	G	A	PTS.	PIM	+/-
35–36	Det	7	2	1	3	2	
36–37	Det	10	0	1	1	4	
38–39	Det	5	0	0	0	0	
Totals		22	2	2	4	6	

BOWMAN, Robert (Kirk) *5–9 178 LW*
B. Leamington, Ont., Sept. 30, 1952

SSN	TEAM	GP	G	A	PTS.	PIM	+/-
73–74	LA (WHA)	10	0	2	2	0	
76–77	Chi	55	10	13	23	6	-7
77–78	Chi	33	1	4	5	13	0
NHL Totals		88	11	17	28	19	-7
WHA Totals		10	0	2	2	0	

Playoffs

SSN	TEAM	GP	G	A	PTS.	PIM	+/-
76–77	Chi	2	1	0	1	0	
77–78	Chi	3	0	0	0	0	
78–79	Chi	2	0	0	0	0	
NHL Totals		7	1	0	1	0	

BOWNASS, John (Jack) *6–1 200 D*
B. Winnipeg, Man., July 27, 1930

SSN	TEAM	GP	G	A	PTS.	PIM	+/-
57–58	Mont	4	0	1	1	0	

SSN	TEAM	GP	G	A	PTS.	PIM	+/-
58–59	NYR	35	1	2	3	20	
59–60	NYR	37	2	5	7	34	
61–62	NYR	4	0	0	0	4	
Totals		80	3	8	11	58	

BOWNESS, Richard Gary (Rick) *6–1 185 RW*
B. Moncton, N.B., Jan. 25, 1955

SSN	TEAM	GP	G	A	PTS.	PIM	+/-
75–76	Atl	5	0	0	0	0	-5
76–77	Atl	28	0	4	4	29	-9
77–78	Det	61	8	11	19	76	-8
78–79	StL	24	1	3	4	30	-17
79–80	StL	10	1	2	3	11	-2
80–81	Winn	45	8	17	25	45	-35
Totals		173	18	37	55	191	-76

Playoffs

SSN	TEAM	GP	G	A	PTS.	PIM	+/-
77–78	Det	4	0	0	0	2	
81–82	Winn	1	0	0	0	0	
Totals		5	0	0	0	2	

BOYD, Irwin (Yank) *5–10 152 RW*
B. Ardmore, Pa., Nov. 13, 1908

SSN	TEAM	GP	G	A	PTS.	PIM	+/-
31–32	Bos	30	10	10	20	31	
34–35	Det	42	2	3	5	14	
42–43	Bos	20	6	5	11	6	
43–44	Bos	5	0	1	1	0	
Totals		97	18	19	37	51	

Playoffs

SSN	TEAM	GP	G	A	PTS.	PIM	+/-
31–32	Bos	10	0	0	0	0	
42–43	Bos	5	0	1	1	4	
Totals		15	0	1	1	4	

BOYD, Randy Keith *5–11 192 D*
B. Coniston, Ont., Jan. 23, 1962

SSN	TEAM	GP	G	A	PTS.	PIM	+/-
81–82	Pitt	23	0	2	2	49	-5
82–83	Pitt	56	4	14	18	71	-36
83–84	Pitt–Chi	28	0	5	5	22	-2
84–85	Chi	3	0	0	0	6	0
85–86	NYI	55	2	12	14	79	+9
86–87	NYI	30	7	17	24	37	0
87–88	Van	60	7	16	23	64	-9
88–89	Van	2	0	1	1	0	-1
Totals		257	20	67	87	328	-44

Playoffs

SSN	TEAM	GP	G	A	PTS.	PIM	+/-
81–82	Pitt	3	0	0	0	11	
84–85	Chi	3	0	1	1	7	
85–86	NYI	3	0	0	0	2	
86–87	NYI	4	0	1	1	6	
Totals		13	0	2	2	26	

*BOYD, William G. *5–10 185 RW*
B. Belleville, Ont., May 15, 1898

SSN	TEAM	GP	G	A	PTS.	PIM	+/-
26–27	NYR	41	4	1	5	40	
27–28	NYR	43	4	0	4	11	
28–29	NYR	11	0	0	0	5	
29–30	NYA	43	7	6	13	16	
Totals		138	15	7	22	72	

Playoffs

SSN	TEAM	GP	G	A	PTS.	PIM	+/-
27–28	NYR	9	0	0	0	2	

BOYER, Walter (Wally) *5–8 165 C*
B. Cowan, Man., Sept. 27, 1937

SSN	TEAM	GP	G	A	PTS.	PIM	+/-
65–66	Tor	46	4	17	21	23	
66–67	Chi	42	5	6	11	15	
67–68	Oak	74	13	20	33	44	0
68–69	Pitt	62	10	19	29	17	-21
69–70	Pitt	72	11	12	23	34	-5
70–71	Pitt	68	11	30	41	30	+10
71–72	Pitt	1	0	1	1	0	-1
72–73	Winn (WHA)	69	6	28	34	27	
NHL Totals		365	54	105	159	163	-17
WHA Totals		69	6	28	34	27	

Playoffs

SSN	TEAM	GP	G	A	PTS.	PIM	+/-
65–66	Tor	4	0	1	1	0	
66–67	Chi	1	0	0	0	0	
69–70	Pitt	10	1	2	3	0	
72–73	Winn (WHA)	14	4	2	6	4	
NHL Totals		15	1	3	4	0	
WHA Totals		14	4	2	6	4	

BOYER, Zac 6–1 199 RW
B. Inuvik, N.W.T., Oct. 25, 1971

94–95	Dal	1	0	0	0	0	0
95–96	Dal	2	0	0	0	0	0
Totals		3	0	0	0	0	0

Playoffs

| 94–95 | Dal | 2 | 0 | 0 | 0 | 0 |

BOYKO, Darren 5–9 170 C
B. Winnipeg, Man., Jan. 16, 1964

| 88–89 | Winn | 1 | 0 | 0 | 0 | 0 | -1 |

BOYLE, Dan 5–11 190 D
B. Ottawa, Ont., July 12, 1976

| 98–99 | Fla | 22 | 3 | 5 | 8 | 6 | 0 |

BOZEK, Steven Michael 5–11 170 C
B. Kelowna, B.C., Nov. 26, 1960

81–82	LA	71	33	23	56	68	-6
82–83	LA	53	13	13	26	14	-18
83–84	Calg	46	10	10	20	16	-16
84–85	Calg	54	13	22	35	6	+11
85–86	Calg	64	21	22	43	24	+24
86–87	Calg	71	17	18	35	22	+3
87–88	Calg–StL	33	3	7	10	14	-5
88–89	Van	71	17	18	35	64	+1
89–90	Van	58	14	9	23	32	-3
90–91	Van	62	15	17	32	22	-6
91–92	SJ	58	8	8	16	27	-30
Totals		641	164	167	331	309	-45

Playoffs

81–82	LA	10	4	1	5	6
83–84	Calg	10	3	1	4	15
84–85	Calg	3	1	0	1	4
85–86	Calg	14	2	6	8	32
86–87	Calg	4	1	0	1	2
87–88	StL	7	1	1	2	6
88–89	Van	7	0	2	2	4
90–91	Van	3	0	0	0	0
Totals		58	12	11	23	69

BOZON, Philippe 5–10 185 LW
B. Charmonix, France, Nov. 30, 1966

91–92	StL	9	1	3	4	4	+5
92–93	StL	54	6	6	12	55	+3
93–94	StL	80	9	16	25	42	+4
94–95	StL	1	0	0	0	0	0
Totals		144	16	25	41	101	+6

Playoffs

91–92	StL	6	1	0	1	27
92–93	StL	9	1	0	1	0
93–94	StL	4	0	0	0	4
Totals		19	2	0	2	31

*BRACKENBOROUGH, John C

| 25–26 | Bos | 7 | 0 | 0 | 0 | 0 |

BRACKENBURY, John Curtis (Curt) 5–10 197 RW
B. Kapuskasing, Ont., Jan. 31, 1952

73–74	Chi (WHA)	4	0	1	1	11
74–75	Minn (WHA)	7	0	0	0	22
75–76	Minn–Que (WHA)	74	8	14	22	365
76–77	Que (WHA)	77	16	13	29	146
77–78	Que (WHA)	33	4	9	13	54
78–79	Que (WHA)	70	13	13	26	155
79–80	Que	63	6	8	14	55	-21
80–81	Edm	58	2	7	9	153	-3
81–82	Edm	14	0	2	2	12	+2
82–83	StL	6	1	0	1	6	-8
NHL Totals		141	9	17	26	226	-30
WHA Totals		265	41	50	91	753

Playoffs

74–75	Minn (WHA)	12	0	2	2	59
75–76	Que (WHA)	5	0	0	0	18
76–77	Que (WHA)	17	3	5	8	51
77–78	Que (WHA)	10	1	1	2	31
78–79	Que (WHA)	4	1	1	2	2
80–81	Edm	2	0	0	0	0
NHL Totals		2	0	0	0	0
WHA Totals		48	5	9	14	161

BRADLEY, Barton William 5–7 150 C
B. Ft. William, Ont., July 29, 1930

| 49–50 | Bos | 1 | 0 | 0 | 0 | 0 |

BRADLEY, Brian Walter Richard 5–10 170 C
B. Kitchener, Ont., Jan. 21, 1965

85–86	Calg	5	0	1	1	0	-3
86–87	Calg	40	10	18	28	16	+6
87–88	Van	11	3	5	8	6	-3
88–89	Van	71	18	27	45	42	-6
89–90	Van	67	19	29	48	65	+5
90–91	Van–Tor	70	11	31	42	62	-9
91–92	Tor	59	10	21	31	48	-3
92–93	TB	80	42	44	86	92	-24
93–94	TB	78	24	40	64	56	-8
94–95	TB	46	13	27	40	42	-6
95–96	TB	75	23	56	79	77	-11
96–97	TB	35	7	17	24	16	+2
97–98	TB	14	2	5	7	6	-9
Totals		651	182	321	503	528	-68

Playoffs

85–86	Calg	1	0	0	0	0
88–89	Van	7	3	4	7	10
95–96	TB	5	0	3	3	6
Totals		13	3	7	10	16

BRADLEY, Walter Lyle 5–9 160 C
B. Lloydminster, Sask., July 31, 1943

73–74	Cal	4	1	0	1	2	-2
76–77	Clev	2	0	0	0	0	0
Totals		6	1	0	1	2	-2

BRADY, Neil 6–2 200 C
B. Montreal, Que., Apr. 12, 1968

89–90	NJ	19	1	4	5	13	-1
90–91	NJ	3	0	0	0	0	0
91–92	NJ	7	1	0	1	4	+1
92–93	Ott	55	7	17	24	57	-25
93–94	Dal	5	0	1	1	21	-1
Totals		89	9	22	31	95	-26

BRAGNALO, Richard James (Rick) 5–8 160 C
B. Thunder Bay, Ont., Dec. 1, 1951

75–76	Wash	19	2	10	12	8	-4
76–77	Wash	80	11	12	23	16	-16
77–78	Wash	44	2	13	15	22	-6
78–79	Wash	2	0	0	0	0	-1
Totals		145	15	35	50	46	-27

BRANNIGAN, Andrew John 5–11 190 D
B. Winnipeg, Man., Apr. 11, 1922

40–41	NYA	6	1	0	1	5
41–42	NYA	20	0	2	2	26
Totals		26	1	2	3	31

BRASAR, Per–Olov 5–10 180 LW
B. Falun, Sweden, Sept. 30, 1950

77–78	Minn	77	20	37	57	6	-7
78–79	Minn	68	6	28	34	6	-4
79–80	Minn–Van	70	10	24	34	7	-3
80–81	Van	80	22	41	63	8	+12
81–82	Van	53	6	12	18	6	-9
Totals		348	64	142	206	33	-11

Playoffs

79–80	Van	4	1	2	3	0
80–81	Van	3	0	0	0	0
81–82	Van	6	0	0	0	0
Totals		13	1	2	3	0

BRASHEAR, Donald 6–2 220 LW
B. Bedford, Ind., Jan. 7, 1972

93–94	Mont	14	2	2	4	34	0
94–95	Mont	20	1	1	2	63	-5
95–96	Mont	67	0	4	4	223	-10
96–97	Mont–Van	69	8	5	13	245	-8
97–98	Van	77	9	9	18	372	-9
98–99	Van	82	8	10	18	209	-25
Totals		329	28	31	59	1146	-57

Playoffs

94–95	Mont	2	0	0	0	0
95–96	Mont	6	0	0	0	2
Totals		8	0	0	0	2

BRAYSHAW, Russell Ambrose 5–10 170 LW
B. Saskatoon, Sask., Jan. 17, 1918

| 44–45 | Chi | 43 | 5 | 9 | 14 | 24 |

BREAULT, Frank 5–11 185 RW
B. Acton Vale, Que., May 11, 1967

90–91	LA	17	1	4	5	6	-1
91–92	LA	6	1	0	1	30	0
92–93	LA	4	0	0	0	6	-1
Totals		27	2	4	6	42	-2

BREITENBACH, Ken 6–1 190 D
B. Welland, Ont., Jan. 9, 1955

75–76	Buf	7	0	0	0	6	+4
76–77	Buf	31	0	5	5	18	-2
78–79	Buf	30	1	8	9	25	+5
Totals		68	1	13	14	49	+7

Playoffs

75–76	Buf	1	0	0	0	0
76–77	Buf	4	0	0	0	0
78–79	Buf	3	0	1	1	4
Totals		8	0	1	1	4

BRENNAN, Daniel 6–3 210 LW
B. Dawson Creek, B.C., Oct. 1, 1962

83–84	LA	2	0	0	0	0	-1
85–86	LA	6	0	1	1	9	-1
Totals		8	0	1	1	9	-2

BRENNAN, Douglas R. 5–10 180 D
B. Peterborough, Ont., Jan. 10, 1905

31–32	NYR	38	4	3	7	40
32–33	NYR	48	5	4	9	94
33–34	NYR	37	0	0	0	18
Totals		123	9	7	16	152

Playoffs

31–32	NYR	7	1	0	1	10
32–33	NYR	8	0	0	0	11
33–34	NYR	1	0	0	0	0
Totals		16	1	0	1	21

BRENNAN, Richard 6–2 200 D
B. Schenectady, N.Y., Nov. 26, 1972

96–97	Col	2	0	0	0	0	0
97–98	SJ	11	1	2	3	2	-4
98–99	NYR	24	1	3	4	23	-4
Totals		37	2	5	7	25	-8

BRENNAN, Thomas E. 5–8 155 RW
B. Philadelphia, Pa., Jan. 22, 1922

43–44	Bos	21	2	1	3	2
44–45	Bos	1	0	1	1	0
Totals		22	2	2	4	2

BRENNEMAN, John Gary 5–10 175 LW
B. Fort Erie, Ont., Jan. 5, 1943

64–65	Chi–NYR	39	4	3	7	8
65–66	NYR	11	0	0	0	14
66–67	Tor	41	6	4	10	4
67–68	Det–Oak	40	10	10	20	14	-7
68–69	Oak	21	1	2	3	6	-4
Totals		152	21	19	40	46	-11

BRETTO, Joseph 6–1 248 D
B. Hibbing, Minn., Nov. 29, 1912

| 44–45 | Chi | 3 | 0 | 0 | 0 | 4 |

BREWER, Carl Thomas 5–10 180 D
B. Toronto, Ont., Oct. 21, 1938

57–58	Tor	2	0	0	0	0
58–59	Tor	69	3	21	24	125
59–60	Tor	67	4	19	23	150
60–61	Tor	51	1	14	15	92
61–62	Tor	67	1	22	23	89
62–63	Tor	70	2	23	25	168
63–64	Tor	57	4	9	13	114
64–65	Tor	70	4	23	27	177
69–70	Det	70	2	37	39	51	+44
70–71	StL	19	2	9	11	29	-1
71–72	StL	42	2	16	18	40	-6
73–74	Tor (WHA)	77	2	23	25	42

SSN	TEAM	GP	G	A	PTS.	PIM	+/-
79–80	Tor	20	0	5	5	2	-6
NHL Totals		604	25	198	223	1037	+31
WHA Totals		77	2	23	25	42	

Playoffs

58–59	Tor	12	0	6	6	40	
59–60	Tor	10	2	3	5	16	
60–61	Tor	5	0	0	0	4	
61–62	Tor	8	0	2	2	22	
62–63	Tor	10	0	1	1	12	
63–64	Tor	12	0	1	1	30	
64–65	Tor	6	1	2	3	12	
69–70	Det	4	0	0	0	2	
70–71	StL	5	0	2	2	8	
73–74	Tor (WHA)	12	0	4	4	11	
NHL Totals		72	3	17	20	146	
WHA Totals		12	0	4	4	11	

BREWER, Eric 6–3 195 D
B. Vernon, B.C., April 17, 1979

98–99	NYI	63	5	6	11	32	-14

BRICKLEY, Andy 5–11 195 C
B. Melrose, Mass., Aug. 9, 1961

82–83	Phil	3	1	1	2	0	-1
83–84	Pitt	50	18	20	38	9	-7
84–85	Pitt	45	7	15	22	10	-14
86–87	NJ	51	11	12	23	8	-15
87–88	NJ	45	8	14	22	14	+1
88–89	Bos	71	13	22	35	20	+4
89–90	Bos	43	12	28	40	8	+11
90–91	Bos	40	2	9	11	8	-4
91–92	Bos	23	10	17	27	2	+6
92–93	Winn	12	0	2	2	2	0
93–94	Winn	2	0	0	0	0	-2
Totals		385	82	140	222	81	-21

Playoffs

87–88	NJ	4	0	1	1	4	
88–89	Bos	10	0	2	2	0	
89–90	Bos	2	0	0	0	0	
92–93	Winn	1	1	1	2	0	
Totals		17	1	4	5	4	

BRIDEN, E. Archibald (Archie) F

26–27	Det	42	5	2	7	36	
29–30	Pitt Pi	30	4	3	7	20	
Totals		72	9	5	14	56	

BRIDGMAN, Melvin John 6–0 190 C
B. Trenton, Ont., Apr. 28, 1955

75–76	Phil	80	23	27	50	86	+22
76–77	Phil	70	19	38	57	120	+35
77–78	Phil	76	16	32	48	203	+26
78–79	Phil	76	24	35	59	184	+14
79–80	Phil	74	16	31	47	136	+13
80–81	Phil	77	14	37	51	195	+28
81–82	Phil–Calg	72	33	54	87	141	+16
82–83	Calg	79	19	31	50	103	-1
83–84	NJ	79	23	38	61	121	-27
84–85	NJ	80	22	39	61	105	-16
85–86	NJ	78	23	40	63	80	-1
86–87	NJ–Det	64	10	33	43	99	-7
87–88	Det	57	6	11	17	42	+4
88–89	Van	15	4	3	7	10	-4
Totals		977	252	449	701	1625	+102

Playoffs

75–76	Phil	16	6	8	14	31	
76–77	Phil	7	1	0	1	8	
77–78	Phil	12	1	7	8	36	
78–79	Phil	8	1	2	3	17	
79–80	Phil	19	2	9	11	70	
80–81	Phil	12	2	4	6	39	
81–82	Cal	3	2	0	2	14	
82–83	Calg	9	3	4	7	33	
86–87	Det	16	5	2	7	28	
87–88	Det	16	4	1	5	12	
88–89	Van	7	1	2	3	10	
Totals		125	28	39	67	298	

BRIERE, Daniel 5–9 160 C
B. Gatineau, Que., Oct. 6, 1977

97–98	Phoe	5	1	0	1	2	+1
98–99	Phoe	64	8	14	22	30	-3
Totals		69	9	14	23	32	-2

*BRIERE, Michel Edouard 5–10 165 C
B. Malartic, Que., Oct. 21, 1949

69–70	Pitt	76	12	32	44	20	-15

Playoffs

69–70	Pitt	10	5	3	8	17	

BRIGLEY, Travis 6–1 190 LW
B. Coronation, Alb., June 16, 1977

97–98	Calg	2	0	0	0	2	0

BRIMANIS, Aris 6–3 210 D
B. Cleveland, Ohio, Mar. 14, 1972

93–94	Phil	1	0	0	0	0	-1
95–96	Phil	17	0	2	2	12	-1
96–97	Phil	3	0	1	1	0	0
Totals		21	0	3	3	12	-2

BRIND'AMOUR, Rod 6–1 200 LW/C
B. Ottawa, Ont., Aug. 9, 1970

89–90	StL	79	26	35	61	46	+23
90–91	StL	78	17	32	49	93	+2
91–92	Phil	80	33	44	77	100	-3
92–93	Phil	81	37	49	86	89	-8
93–94	Phil	84	35	62	97	85	-9
94–95	Phil	48	12	27	39	33	-4
95–96	Phil	82	26	61	87	110	+20
96–97	Phil	82	27	32	59	41	+2
97–98	Phil	82	36	38	74	54	-2
98–99	Phil	82	24	50	74	47	+3
Totals		778	273	430	704	698	+24

Playoffs

88–89	StL	5	2	0	2	4	
89–90	StL	12	5	8	13	6	
90–91	StL	13	2	5	7	10	
94–95	Phil	15	6	9	15	8	
95–96	Phil	12	2	5	7	6	
96–97	Phil	19	13	8	21	10	
97–98	Phil	5	2	2	4	7	
98–99	Phil	6	1	3	4	0	
Totals		87	33	40	73	51	

BRINDLEY, Douglas Allen 6–1 175 C
B. Walkerton, Ont., June 8, 1949

70–71	Tor	3	0	0	0	0	
72–73	Clev (WHA)	73	15	11	26	6	
73–74	Clev (WHA)	30	13	9	22	13	
NHL Totals		3	0	0	0	0	
WHA Totals		103	28	20	48	19	

Playoffs

73–74	Clev (WHA)	5	0	1	1	2	

BRINK, Milton F

36–37	Chi	5	0	0	0	0	

BRISEBOIS, Patrice 6–1 188 D
B. Montreal, Que., Jan. 27, 1971

90–91	Mont	10	0	2	2	4	+1
91–92	Mont	26	2	8	10	20	+9
92–93	Mont	70	10	21	31	79	+6
93–94	Mont	53	2	21	23	63	+5
94–95	Mont	35	4	8	12	26	-2
95–96	Mont	69	9	27	36	65	+10
96–97	Mont	49	2	13	15	24	-7
97–98	Mont	79	10	27	37	67	+16
98–99	Mont	54	3	9	12	28	-8
Totals		445	42	136	178	376	+30

Playoffs

91–92	Mont	11	2	4	6	6	
92–93	Mont	20	0	4	4	18	
93–94	Mont	7	0	4	4	6	
95–96	Mont	6	1	2	3	6	
96–97	Mont	3	1	1	2	24	
97–98	Mont	10	1	0	1	0	
Totals		57	5	15	20	60	

BRISSON, Gerald (Gerry) 5–9 155 RW
B. Boniface, Man., Sept. 3, 1937

62–63	Mont	4	0	2	2	4	

BRITZ, Greg 6–0 190 RW
B. Buffalo, N.Y., Jan. 3, 1961

83–84	Tor	6	0	0	0	2	-1

84–85	Tor	1	0	0	0	2	0
86–87	Hart	1	0	0	0	0	0
Totals		8	0	0	0	4	-1

*BROADBENT, Harry L. (Punch) RW
B. Ottawa, Ont., July 13, 1892

18–19	Ott	8	4	2	6	12	
19–20	Ott	20	19	4	23	39	
20–21	Ott	9	4	1	5	6	
21–22	Ott	24	32	14	46	24	
22–23	Ott	24	14	0	14	32	
23–24	Ott	22	9	4	13	44	
24–25	Mont M	30	15	4	19	75	
25–26	Mont M	36	12	5	17	112	
26–27	Mont M	42	9	5	14	42	
27–28	Ott	43	3	2	5	62	
28–29	NYA	44	1	4	5	59	
Totals		302	122	45	167	507	

Playoffs

18–19	Ott	5	2	0	2	12	
19–20	Ott	4	0	0	0	0	
20–21	Ott	7	3	2	5	6	
21–22	Ott	2	0	0	0	6	
22–23	Ott	8	6	1	7	12	
23–24	Ott	2	0	0	0	2	
25–26	MontM	8	2	0	2	36	
26–27	MontM	2	0	0	0	0	
27–28	Ott	2	0	0	0	0	
28–29	NYA	2	0	0	0	2	
Totals		42	13	3	16	76	

BROCHU, Stephane 6–1 185 D
B. Sherbrooke, Que., Aug. 15, 1967

88–89	NYR	1	0	0	0	0	+1

BRODEN, Connell (Connie) 5–8 160 C
B. Montreal, Que., Apr. 6, 1932

55–56	Mont	3	0	0	0	2	
57–58	Mont	3	2	1	3	0	
Totals		6	2	1	3	2	

Playoffs

56–57	Mont	6	0	1	1	0	
57–58	Mont	1	0	0	0	0	
Totals		7	0	1	1	0	

BROOKE, Robert W. 6–1 200 C
B. Melrose, Mass., Dec. 18, 1960

83–84	NYR	9	1	2	3	4	+1
84–85	NYR	72	7	9	16	79	-18
85–86	NYR	79	24	20	44	111	+6
86–87	NYR–Minn	80	13	23	36	98	-9
87–88	Minn	77	5	20	25	108	-6
88–89	Minn	57	7	9	16	57	-12
89–90	Minn–NJ	73	12	14	26	63	-2
Totals		447	69	97	166	520	-40

Playoffs

83–84	NYR	5	0	0	0	7	
84–85	NYR	3	0	0	0	8	
85–86	NYR	16	6	9	15	28	
88–89	Minn	5	3	0	3	2	
89–90	NJ	5	0	0	0	14	
Totals		34	9	9	18	59	

BROOKS, Gordon John (Gord) 5–8 168 RW
B. Cobourg, Ont., Sept. 11, 1950

71–72	StL	2	0	0	0	0	0
73–74	StL	30	6	8	14	12	0
74–75	Wash	38	1	10	11	25	-19
Totals		70	7	18	25	37	-19

*BROPHY, Bernard F
B. Collingwood, Ont.

25–26	Mont M	10	0	0	0	0	
28–29	Det	37	2	4	6	23	
29–30	Det	15	2	0	2	2	
Totals		62	4	4	8	25	

Playoffs

28–29	Det	2	0	0	0	2	

BROSSART, William (Willie) *6–0 190 D*
B. Allan, Sask., May 29, 1949

SSN	TEAM	GP	G	A	PTS.	PIM	+/-
70–71	Phil	1	0	0	0	0	-2
71–72	Phil	42	0	4	4	12	-7
72–73	Phil	4	0	1	1	0	-5
73–74	Tor	17	0	1	1	20	+2
74–75	Tor–Wash	16	1	0	1	16	-14
75–76	Wash	49	0	8	8	40	-49
Totals		129	1	14	15	88	-75

Playoffs

73–74	Tor	1	0	0	0	0	

BROTEN, Aaron *5–10 175 LW*
B. Roseau, Minn., Nov. 14, 1960

SSN	TEAM	GP	G	A	PTS.	PIM	+/-
80–81	Col	2	0	0	0	0	0
81–82	Col	58	15	24	39	6	-11
82–83	NJ	73	16	39	55	28	-20
83–84	NJ	80	13	23	36	36	-28
84–85	NJ	80	22	37	57	38	-18
85–86	NJ	66	18	25	43	26	+2
86–87	NJ	80	26	53	79	36	+5
87–88	NJ	80	26	57	83	80	+20
88–89	NJ	80	16	43	59	81	-7
89–90	NJ–Minn	77	18	18	36	58	-23
90–91	Que–Tor	47	11	8	19	38	+9
91–92	Winn	25	4	5	9	14	+2
Totals		748	185	330	515	441	-69

Playoffs

87–88	NJ	20	5	11	16	20	
89–90	Minn	7	0	5	5	8	
91–92	Winn	7	2	2	4	12	
Totals		34	7	18	25	40	

BROTEN, Neal Lemoy *5–9 175 C*
B. Roseau, Minn., Nov. 29, 1959

SSN	TEAM	GP	G	A	PTS.	PIM	+/-
80–81	Minn	3	2	0	2	12	+1
81–82	Minn	73	38	60	98	42	+14
82–83	Minn	79	32	45	77	43	+24
83–84	Minn	76	28	61	89	43	+16
84–85	Minn	80	19	37	56	39	-18
85–86	Minn	80	29	76	105	47	+14
86–87	Minn	46	18	35	53	33	+12
87–88	Minn	54	9	30	39	32	-23
88–89	Minn	68	18	38	56	57	+1
89–90	Minn	80	23	62	85	45	-16
90–91	Minn	79	13	56	69	26	-3
91–92	Minn	76	8	26	34	16	-15
92–93	Minn	82	12	21	33	22	+7
93–94	Dal	79	17	35	52	62	+10
94–95	Dal–NJ	47	8	24	32	24	+1
95–96	NJ	55	7	16	23	14	-3
96–97	NJ–LA–Dal	42	8	12	20	12	-4
Totals		1099	289	634	923	569	+18

Playoffs

80–81	Minn	19	1	7	8	9	
81–82	Minn	4	0	2	2	0	
82–83	Minn	9	1	6	7	10	
83–84	Minn	16	5	5	10	4	
84–85	Minn	9	2	5	7	10	
85–86	Minn	5	3	2	5	2	
88–89	Minn	5	2	2	4	4	
89–90	Minn	7	2	2	4	18	
90–91	Minn	23	9	13	22	6	
91–92	Minn	7	1	5	6	2	
93–94	Dal	9	2	1	3	6	
94–95	NJ	20	7	12	19	6	
96–97	Dal	2	0	1	1	0	
Totals		135	35	63	98	77	

BROTEN, Paul *5–11 188 RW*
B. Roseau, Minn., Oct. 27, 1965

SSN	TEAM	GP	G	A	PTS.	PIM	+/-
89–90	NYR	32	5	3	8	26	-4
90–91	NYR	28	4	6	10	18	+7
91–92	NYR	74	13	15	28	102	+14
92–93	NYR	60	5	9	14	48	-6
93–94	Dal	64	12	12	24	30	+18
94–95	Dal	47	7	9	16	36	-7
95–96	StL	17	0	1	1	4	-1
Totals		322	46	55	101	264	+21

Playoffs

89–90	NYR	6	1	1	2	2	
90–91	NYR	5	0	0	0	2	
91–92	NYR	13	1	2	3	10	

BROUSSEAU, Paul *6–1 203 RW*
B. Montreal, Que., Sept. 18, 1973

SSN	TEAM	GP	G	A	PTS.	PIM	+/-
93–94	Dal	9	1	1	2	2	
94–95	Dal	5	1	2	3	2	
Totals		38	4	6	10	18	

BROUSSEAU, Paul *6–1 203 RW*
B. Montreal, Que., Sept. 18, 1973

SSN	TEAM	GP	G	A	PTS.	PIM	+/-
95–96	Col A	8	1	1	2	2	+1
96–97	TB	6	0	0	0	0	-4
97–98	TB	11	0	2	2	27	0
Totals		25	1	3	4	29	-3

*BROWN, Adam *5–10 175 LW*
B. Johnstone, Scotland, Feb. 4, 1920

SSN	TEAM	GP	G	A	PTS.	PIM	+/-
41–42	Det	28	6	9	15	15	
43–44	Det	50	24	18	42	56	
45–46	Det	48	20	11	31	27	
46–47	Det–Chi	64	19	30	49	87	
47–48	Chi	32	7	10	17	41	
48–49	Chi	58	8	12	20	69	
49–50	Chi	25	2	2	4	16	
50–51	Chi	53	10	12	22	16	
51–52	Bos	33	8	9	17	6	
Totals		391	104	113	217	333	

Playoffs

41–42	Det	12	0	2	2	4	
42–43	Det	6	1	1	2	2	
43–44	Det	5	1	1	2	0	
45–46	Det	5	1	1	2	0	
Totals		28	3	5	8	6	

BROWN, Brad *6–3 220 D*
B. Baie Verte, Nfld., Dec. 27, 1975

SSN	TEAM	GP	G	A	PTS.	PIM	+/-
96–97	Mont	8	0	0	0	22	-1
98–99	Mont–Chi	66	1	7	8	205	-4

BROWN, Cam *6–1 205 LW*
B. Saskatoon, Sask., May 15, 1969

SSN	TEAM	GP	G	A	PTS.	PIM	+/-
90–91	Van	1	0	0	0	7	0

BROWN, Curtis *6–0 182 C*
B. Unity, Sask., Feb. 12, 1976

SSN	TEAM	GP	G	A	PTS.	PIM	+/-
94–95	Buf	1	1	1	2	2	+2
95–96	Buf	4	0	0	0	0	0
96–97	Buf	28	4	3	7	18	+4
97–98	Buf	63	12	12	24	34	+11
98–99	Buf	78	16	31	47	56	+23
Totals		174	33	47	80	110	+40

Playoffs

97–98	Buf	13	1	2	3	10	
98–99	Buf	21	7	6	13	10	
Totals		34	8	8	16	20	

BROWN, David *6–5 222 RW*
B. Saskatoon, Sask., Oct. 12, 1962

SSN	TEAM	GP	G	A	PTS.	PIM	+/-
82–83	Phil	2	0	0	0	5	-1
83–84	Phil	19	1	5	6	98	+4
84–85	Phil	57	3	6	9	165	-3
85–86	Phil	76	10	7	17	277	+7
86–87	Phil	62	7	3	10	274	-7
87–88	Phil	47	12	5	17	114	+10
88–89	Phil–Edm	72	0	5	5	156	-12
89–90	Edm	60	0	6	6	145	-3
90–91	Edm	58	3	4	7	160	-7
91–92	Phil	70	4	2	6	81	-11
92–93	Phil	70	0	2	2	78	-5
93–94	Phil	71	1	4	5	137	-12
94–95	Phil	28	1	2	3	53	-1
95–96	SJ	37	3	1	4	46	+4
Totals		729	45	52	97	1789	-37

Playoffs

83–84	Phil	2	0	0	0	12	
84–85	Phil	11	0	0	0	59	
85–86	Phil	5	0	0	0	16	
86–87	Phil	26	1	2	3	59	
87–88	Phil	7	1	0	1	27	
88–89	Edm	7	0	0	0	6	
89–90	Edm	3	0	0	0	0	
90–91	Edm	16	0	1	1	30	
94–95	Phil	3	0	0	0	0	
Totals		80	2	3	5	209	

BROWN, Doug *5–10 180 RW*
B. Southboro, Mass., July 12, 1964

SSN	TEAM	GP	G	A	PTS.	PIM	+/-
86–87	NJ	4	0	1	1	0	-4
87–88	NJ	70	14	11	25	20	+7
88–89	NJ	63	15	10	25	15	-7
89–90	NJ	69	14	20	34	16	+7
90–91	NJ	58	14	16	30	4	+18
91–92	NJ	71	11	17	28	27	+17
92–93	NJ	15	0	5	5	2	+3
93–94	Pitt	77	18	37	55	18	+19
94–95	Det	45	9	12	21	16	+14
95–96	Det	62	12	15	27	4	+11
96–97	Det	49	6	7	13	8	-3
97–98	Det	80	19	23	42	12	+17
98–99	Det	80	9	19	28	42	+5
Totals		743	141	193	334	184	+104

Playoffs

87–88	NJ	19	5	1	6	6	
89–90	NJ	6	0	1	1	2	
90–91	NJ	7	2	2	4	2	
93–94	Pitt	6	0	0	0	2	
94–95	Det	18	4	8	12	2	
95–96	Det	13	3	3	6	4	
96–97	Det	14	3	3	6	0	
97–98	Det	9	4	2	6	0	
98–99	Det	10	2	2	4	4	
Totals		102	23	22	45	24	

BROWN, Frederick *F*
B. Kingston, Ont.

SSN	TEAM	GP	G	A	PTS.	PIM	+/-
27–28	Mont M	19	1	0	1	0	
Playoff Totals		9	0	0	0	0	

BROWN, George Allan *5–11 185 C*
B. Winnipeg, Man., May 17, 1912

SSN	TEAM	GP	G	A	PTS.	PIM	+/-
36–37	Mont	27	4	6	10	10	
37–38	Mont	34	1	7	8	14	
38–39	Mont	18	1	9	10	10	
Totals		79	6	22	28	34	

Playoffs

36–37	Mont	4	0	0	0	0	
37–38	Mont	3	0	0	0	2	
Totals		7	0	0	0	2	

BROWN, Gerald William Joseph (Gerry) *5–10 176 LW*
B. Edmonton, Alta., July 7, 1917

SSN	TEAM	GP	G	A	PTS.	PIM	+/-
41–42	Det	13	4	4	8	0	
45–46	Det	10	0	1	1	2	
Totals		23	4	5	9	2	

Playoffs

41–42	Det	12	2	1	3	4	

BROWN, Greg *6–0 180 D*
B. Hartford, Conn., Mar. 7, 1968

SSN	TEAM	GP	G	A	PTS.	PIM	+/-
90–91	Buf	39	1	2	3	35	-20
92–93	Buf	10	0	1	1	6	-5
93–94	Pitt	36	3	8	11	28	0
94–95	Winn	9	0	3	3	17	+1
Totals		94	4	14	18	86	-24

Playoffs

92–93	Pitt	6	0	1	1	4	

BROWN, Harold Fraser *5–10 160 RW*
B. Brandon, Man., Sept. 14, 1920

SSN	TEAM	GP	G	A	PTS.	PIM	+/-
45–46	NYR	13	2	1	3	2	

BROWN, Jeff *6–1 202 D*
B. Ottawa, Ont., Apr. 30, 1966

SSN	TEAM	GP	G	A	PTS.	PIM	+/-
85–86	Que	8	3	2	5	6	+5
86–87	Que	44	7	22	29	16	+11
87–88	Que	78	16	36	52	64	-25
88–89	Que	78	21	47	68	62	-22
89–90	Que–StL	77	16	38	54	55	-26
90–91	StL	67	12	47	59	39	+4
91–92	StL	80	20	39	59	38	+8
92–93	StL	71	25	53	78	58	-6
93–94	StL–Van	74	14	52	66	56	-11
94–95	Van	33	8	23	31	16	-2
95–96	Van–Hart	76	8	47	55	56	+8
96–97	Hart	1	0	0	0	0	0
97–98	Car–Tor–Wash	60	4	24	28	32	+5
Totals		747	154	430	584	498	-49

SSN	TEAM	GP	G	A	PTS.	PIM	+/-
Playoffs							
86–87	Que	13	3	3	6	2	
89–90	StL	12	2	10	12	6	
90–91	StL	13	3	9	12	6	
91–92	StL	6	2	1	3	2	
92–93	StL	11	3	8	11	6	
93–94	Van	24	6	9	15	37	
94–95	Van	5	1	3	4	2	
97–98	Wash	2	0	2	2	0	
Totals		87	20	45	65	59	

BROWN, Jim 6–4 210 D
B. Phoenix, Ariz., Mar. 1, 1960

82–83	LA	3	0	1	1	5	-2

BROWN, Keith Jeffrey 6–1 195 D
B. Corner Brook, Nfld., May 6, 1960

79–80	Chi	76	2	18	20	27	+7
80–81	Chi	80	9	34	43	80	+5
81–82	Chi	33	4	20	24	26	+4
82–83	Chi	50	4	27	31	20	+8
83–84	Chi	74	10	25	35	94	-18
84–85	Chi	56	1	22	23	55	+2
85–86	Chi	70	11	29	40	87	-6
86–87	Chi	73	4	23	27	86	+5
87–88	Chi	24	3	6	9	45	+5
88–89	Chi	74	2	16	18	84	-5
89–90	Chi	67	5	20	25	87	+26
90–91	Chi	45	1	10	11	55	+9
91–92	Chi	57	6	10	16	69	+7
92–93	Chi	33	2	6	8	39	+3
93–94	Fla	51	4	8	12	60	+11
94–95	Fla	13	0	0	0	2	+1
Totals		876	68	274	342	916	+64

Playoffs

79–80	Chi	6	0	0	0	4	
80–81	Chi	3	0	2	2	2	
81–82	Chi	4	0	2	2	5	
82–83	Chi	7	0	0	0	11	
83–84	Chi	5	0	1	1	10	
84–85	Chi	11	2	7	9	31	
85–86	Chi	3	0	1	1	9	
86–87	Chi	4	0	1	1	6	
87–88	Chi	5	0	2	2	10	
88–89	Chi	13	1	3	4	25	
89–90	Chi	18	0	4	4	43	
90–91	Chi	6	1	0	1	8	
91–92	Chi	14	0	8	8	18	
92–93	Chi	4	0	1	1	2	
Totals		103	4	32	36	184	

BROWN, Kevin 6–1 212 RW
B. Birmingham, England, May 11, 1974

94–95	LA	23	2	3	5	18	-7
95–96	LA	7	1	0	1	4	-2
96–97	Hart	11	0	4	4	6	-6
97–98	Car	4	0	0	0	0	-2
98–99	Edm	12	4	2	6	0	-2
Totals		57	7	9	16	28	-19

BROWN, Larry Wayne 6–2 210 D
B. Brandon, Man., Apr. 14, 1947

69–70	NYR	15	0	3	3	8	+6
70–71	Det–NYR	64	2	5	7	18	-7
71–72	Phil	12	0	0	0	2	-3
72–73	LA	55	0	7	7	46	-4
73–74	LA	45	0	4	4	14	+4
74–75	LA	78	1	15	16	50	+31
75–76	LA	74	2	5	7	33	-27
76–77	LA	55	1	6	7	24	-17
77–78	LA	57	1	8	9	23	-13
Totals		455	7	53	60	218	-28

Playoffs

70–71	NYR	11	0	1	1	0	
73–74	LA	2	0	0	0	0	
74–75	LA	3	0	2	2	0	
75–76	LA	9	0	0	0	2	
76–77	LA	9	0	1	1	6	
77–78	LA	1	0	0	0	2	
Totals		35	0	4	4	10	

BROWN, Patrick Cornelius (Connie) 5–7 168 C
B. Van Kleek Hill, Ont., Jan. 11, 1917

38–39	Det	20	1	0	1	0	

SSN	TEAM	GP	G	A	PTS.	PIM	+/-
39–40	Det	36	8	3	11	2	
40–41	Det	3	1	2	3	0	
41–42	Det	9	0	3	3	4	
42–43	Det	23	5	16	21	6	
Totals		91	15	24	39	12	

Playoffs

39–40	Det	5	2	1	3	0	
40–41	Det	9	0	2	2	0	
Totals		14	2	3	5	0	

BROWN, Rob 5–11 185 RW
B. Kingston, Ont., Apr. 10, 1968

87–88	Pitt	51	24	20	44	56	+8
88–89	Pitt	68	49	66	115	118	+27
89–90	Pitt	80	33	47	80	102	-10
90–91	Pitt–Hart	69	24	34	58	132	-7
91–92	Hart–Chi	67	21	26	47	73	-15
92–93	Chi	15	1	6	7	33	+6
93–94	Dal	1	0	0	0	0	-1
94–95	LA	2	0	0	0	0	-2
97–98	Pitt	82	15	25	40	59	-1
98–99	Pitt	58	13	11	24	16	-15
Totals		493	180	235	415	589	-10

Playoffs

88–89	Pitt	11	5	3	8	22	
90–91	Hart	5	1	0	1	7	
91–92	Chi	8	2	4	6	4	
97–98	Pitt	6	1	0	1	4	
98–99	Pitt	13	2	5	7	8	
Totals		43	11	12	23	45	

BROWN, Sean 6–2 205 D
B. Oshawa, Ont., Nov. 5, 1976

96–97	Edm	5	0	0	0	4	-1
97–98	Edm	18	0	1	1	43	-1
98–99	Edm	51	0	7	7	188	+1
Totals		74	0	8	8	235	-1

Playoffs

98–99	Edm	1	0	0	0	10	

BROWN, Stanley 5–9 150 F
B. North Bay, Ont., May 9, 1898

26–27	NYR	24	6	2	8	14	
27–28	Det	24	2	0	2	4	
Totals		48	8	2	10	18	

Playoffs

26–27	NYR	2	0	0	0	0	

BROWN, Stewart Arnold (Arnie) 5–11 185 D
B. Apsley, Ont., Jan. 28, 1942

61–62	Tor	2	0	0	0	0	
63–64	Tor	4	0	0	0	6	
64–65	NYR	58	1	11	12	145	
65–66	NYR	64	1	7	8	106	
66–67	NYR	69	2	10	12	61	
67–68	NYR	74	1	25	26	83	+17
68–69	NYR	74	10	12	22	48	+1
69–70	NYR	73	15	21	36	78	+28
70–71	NYR–Det	75	5	18	23	54	0
71–72	Det	77	2	23	25	84	0
72–73	NYI–Atl	63	5	8	13	44	-57
73–74	Atl	48	2	6	8	29	-14
74–75	Mich–Van (WHA)	60	3	5	8	40	
NHL Totals		681	44	141	185	738	-25
WHA Totals		60	3	5	8	40	

Playoffs

66–67	NYR	4	0	0	0	6	
67–68	NYR	6	0	1	1	8	
68–69	NYR	4	0	1	1	0	
69–70	NYR	4	0	4	4	9	
70–71	NYR	11	0	1	1	0	
73–74	Atl	4	0	0	0	0	
NHL Totals		33	0	7	7	23	

BROWN, Wayne Hewetson 5–8 150 RW
B. Deloro, Ont., Nov. 16, 1930

Playoffs

53–54	Bos	4	0	0	0	2	

SSN	TEAM	GP	G	A	PTS.	PIM	+/-
***BROWNE, Cecil** LW*							
27–28	CHI	13	2	0	2	4	

BROWNSCHIDLE, Jeffrey Paul 6–2 205 D
B. Buffalo, N.Y., Mar. 1, 1959

81–82	Hart	3	0	1	1	2	-3
82–83	Hart	4	0	0	0	0	-6
Totals		7	0	1	1	2	-9

BROWNSCHIDLE, John J. (Jack) 6–2 195 D
B. Buffalo, N.Y., Oct. 2, 1955

77–78	StL	40	2	15	17	23	-11
78–79	StL	64	10	24	34	14	-21
79–80	StL	77	12	32	44	8	+16
80–81	StL	71	5	23	28	12	+5
81–82	StL	80	5	33	38	26	-5
82–83	StL	72	1	22	23	30	-3
83–84	StL–Hart	64	3	9	12	29	-26
84–85	Hart	17	1	4	5	5	0
85–86	Hart	9	0	0	0	4	-4
Totals		494	39	162	201	151	-49

Playoffs

79–80	StL	3	0	0	0	0	
80–81	StL	11	0	3	3	2	
81–82	StL	8	0	2	2	14	
82–83	StL	4	0	0	0	2	
Totals		26	0	5	5	18	

BRUBAKER, Jeffery J. 6–2 210 LW
B. Hagerstown, Md., Feb. 24, 1958

78–79	NE (WHA)	12	0	0	0	19	
79–80	Hart	3	0	1	1	2	-2
80–81	Hart	43	5	3	8	93	-5
81–82	Mont	3	0	1	1	32	+1
83–84	Calg	4	0	0	0	19	-1
84–85	Tor	68	8	4	12	209	-18
85–86	Tor–Edm	25	1	0	1	79	+1
87–88	NYR	31	2	0	2	78	0
88–89	Det	1	0	0	0	0	0
Totals		178	16	9	25	512	-24

Playoffs

78–79	NE (WHA)	3	0	0	0	12	
81–82	Mont	2	0	0	0	27	
NHL Totals		2	0	0	0	27	
WHA Totals		3	0	0	0	12	

BRUCE, Arthur Gordon (Gordie) 5–11 195 LW
B. Ottawa, Ont., May 9, 1919

40–41	Bos	8	0	1	1	2	
41–42	Bos	15	4	8	12	11	
45–46	Bos	5	0	0	0	0	
Totals		28	4	9	13	13	

Playoffs

40–41	Bos	2	0	0	0	0	
41–42	Bos	5	2	3	5	4	
Totals		7	2	3	5	4	

BRUCE, David 5–11 187 LW
B. Thunder Bay, Ont., Oct. 7, 1964

85–86	Van	12	0	1	1	14	-2
86–87	Van	50	9	7	16	109	-4
87–88	Van	28	7	3	10	57	-6
88–89	Van	53	7	7	14	65	-16
90–91	StL	12	1	2	3	14	+1
91–92	SJ	60	22	16	38	46	-20
92–93	SJ	17	2	3	5	33	-14
93–94	SJ	2	0	0	0	0	-2
Totals		234	48	39	87	338	-57

Playoffs

85–86	Van	1	0	0	0	0	
90–91	StL	2	0	0	0	2	
Totals		3	0	0	0	2	

BRUCE, Morley D

17–18	Ott	7	0	0	0	0	
19–20	Ott	21	1	0	1	2	
20–21	Ott	21	3	1	4	23	
21–22	Ott	23	4	0	4	2	
Totals		72	8	1	9	27	

Playoffs

SSN	TEAM	GP	G	A	PTS.	PIM	+/-
19-20	Ott	5	0	0	0	0	
20-21	Ott	7	0	0	0	3	
21-22	Ott	1	0	0	0	0	
Totals		13	0	0	0	3	

BRUMWELL, James (Murray) 6-2 190 D
B. Calgary, Alta., Mar. 31, 1960

SSN	TEAM	GP	G	A	PTS.	PIM	+/-
80-81	Minn	1	0	0	0	0	+1
81-82	Minn	21	0	3	3	18	0
82-83	NJ	59	5	14	19	34	-20
83-84	NJ	42	7	13	20	14	-5
85-86	NJ	1	0	0	0	0	-1
86-87	NJ	1	0	0	0	2	+1
87-88	NJ	3	0	1	1	2	0
Totals		128	12	31	43	70	-24

Playoffs

81-82	Minn	2	0	0	0	2	

BRUNET, Benoit 5-11 195 LW
B. Ste.–Anne de Bellevue, Que., Aug. 24, 1968

SSN	TEAM	GP	G	A	PTS.	PIM	+/-
88-89	Mont	2	0	1	1	0	0
90-91	Mont	17	1	3	4	0	-1
91-92	Mont	18	4	6	10	14	+4
92-93	Mont	47	10	15	25	19	+13
93-94	Mont	71	10	20	30	20	+14
94-95	Mont	45	7	18	25	16	+7
95-96	Mont	26	7	8	15	17	-4
96-97	Mont	39	10	13	23	14	+6
97-98	Mont	68	12	20	32	61	+11
98-99	Mont	60	14	17	31	31	-1
Totals		393	75	121	196	192	+49

Playoffs

92-93	Mont	20	2	8	10	8	
93-94	Mont	7	1	4	5	16	
95-96	Mont	3	0	2	2	0	
96-97	Mont	4	1	3	4	4	
97-98	Mont	8	1	0	1	4	
Totals		42	5	17	22	32	

BRUNETEAU, Edward Ernest Henry 5-9 172 RW
B. St. Boniface, Man., Aug. 1, 1919

SSN	TEAM	GP	G	A	PTS.	PIM	+/-
40-41	Det	12	1	1	2	2	
43-44	Det	2	0	1	1	0	
44-45	Det	42	12	13	25	6	
45-46	Det	46	17	12	29	11	
46-47	Det	60	9	14	23	14	
47-48	Det	18	1	1	2	2	
48-49	Det	1	0	0	0	0	
Totals		181	40	42	82	35	

Playoffs

44-45	Det	14	5	2	7	0	
45-46	Det	4	1	0	1	0	
46-47	Det	4	1	4	5	0	
47-48	Det	6	0	0	0	5	
Totals		28	7	6	13	5	

*BRUNETEAU, Modere (Mud) 5-11 185 RW
B. St. Boniface, Man., Nov. 28, 1914

SSN	TEAM	GP	G	A	PTS.	PIM	+/-
35-36	Det	24	2	0	2	2	
36-37	Det	42	9	7	16	18	
37-38	Det	24	3	6	9	16	
38-39	Det	20	3	7	10	0	
39-40	Det	48	10	14	24	10	
40-41	Det	45	11	17	28	12	
41-42	Det	48	14	19	33	8	
42-43	Det	50	23	22	45	2	
43-44	Det	39	35	18	53	4	
44-45	Det	43	23	24	47	6	
45-46	Det	28	6	4	10	2	
Totals		411	139	138	277	80	

Playoffs

35-36	Det	7	2	2	4	4	
36-37	Det	10	2	0	2	6	
38-39	Det	6	0	0	0	0	
39-40	Det	5	3	2	5	0	
40-41	Det	9	2	1	3	2	
41-42	Det	12	5	1	6	6	
42-43	Det	9	5	4	9	0	
43-44	Det	5	1	2	3	2	
44-45	Det	14	3	2	5	2	
Totals		77	23	14	37	22	

BRUNETTE, Andrew 6-0 212 LW
B. Sudbury, Ont., Aug. 24, 1973

SSN	TEAM	GP	G	A	PTS.	PIM	+/-
95-96	Wash	11	3	3	6	0	+5
96-97	Wash	23	4	7	11	12	-3
97-98	Wash	28	11	12	23	12	+2
98-99	Nash	77	11	20	31	26	-10
Totals		139	29	42	71	50	-6

Playoffs

95-96	Wash	6	1	3	4	0	

*BRYDGE, William H. 5-9 195 D
B. Renfrew, Ont., 1901

SSN	TEAM	GP	G	A	PTS.	PIM	+/-
26-27	Tor	41	6	3	9	76	
28-29	Det	31	2	2	4	59	
29-30	NYA	41	2	6	8	64	
30-31	NYA	43	2	5	7	70	
31-32	NYA	48	2	8	10	77	
32-33	NYA	48	4	15	19	60	
33-34	NYA	48	6	7	13	44	
34-35	NYA	47	2	6	8	29	
35-36	NYA	21	0	0	0	27	
Totals		368	26	52	78	506	

Playoffs

28-29	Det	2	0	0	0	4	

BRYDGES, Paul 5-11 180 C
B. Guelph, Ont., June 21, 1965

86-87	Buf	15	2	2	4	6	+4

*BRYDSON, Glenn 5-9 170 RW
B. Swansea, Ont., Nov. 7, 1910

SSN	TEAM	GP	G	A	PTS.	PIM	+/-
30-31	Mont M	14	0	0	0	4	
31-32	Mont M	47	12	13	25	44	
32-33	Mont M	48	11	17	28	26	
33-34	Mont M	37	4	5	9	19	
34-35	StL E	48	11	18	29	45	
35-36	NYR–Chi	52	10	16	26	39	
36-37	Chi	34	7	7	14	20	
37-38	Chi	19	1	3	4	6	
Totals		299	56	79	135	203	

Playoffs

30-31	MontM	2	0	0	0	0	
31-32	MontM	4	0	0	0	4	
32-33	MontM	2	0	0	0	0	
33-34	MontM	1	0	0	0	0	
35-36	Chi	2	0	0	0	4	
Totals		11	0	0	0	8	

BRYDSON, Gordon (Gord) F
B. Toronto, Ont.

29-30	Tor	8	2	0	2	8	

BRYLIN, Sergei 5-9 175 C
B. Moscow, USSR, Jan. 13, 1974

SSN	TEAM	GP	G	A	PTS.	PIM	+/-
94-95	NJ	26	6	8	14	8	+12
95-96	NJ	50	4	5	9	26	-2
96-97	NJ	29	2	2	4	20	-13
97-98	NJ	18	2	3	5	0	+4
98-99	NJ	47	5	10	15	28	+8
Totals		170	19	28	47	82	+9

Playoffs

94-95	NJ	12	1	2	3	4	
98-99	NJ	5	3	1	4	4	
Totals		17	4	3	7	8	

BUBLA, Jiri 5-11 200 D
B. Usti Nad Labem, Czechoslovakia, Jan. 27, 1950

SSN	TEAM	GP	G	A	PTS.	PIM	+/-
81-82	Van	23	1	1	2	16	+8
82-83	Van	72	2	28	30	59	-9
83-84	Van	62	6	33	39	43	-10
84-85	Van	56	2	15	17	54	-15
85-86	Van	43	6	24	30	30	-25
Totals		256	17	101	118	202	-51

Playoffs

82-83	Van	1	0	0	0	5	

BUCHANAN, Allaster William (Al) 5-8 160 LW
B. Winnipeg, Man., May 17, 1927

SSN	TEAM	GP	G	A	PTS.	PIM	+/-
48-49	Tor	3	0	1	1	2	
49-50	Tor	1	0	0	0	0	
Totals		4	0	1	1	2	

BUCHANAN, Jeff 6-2 200 D
B. Swift Current, Sask., May 23, 1971

98-99	Col A	6	0	0	0	6	+1

BUCHANAN, Michael Murray 6-1 185 D
B. Sault Ste. Marie, Ont., Mar. 1, 1932

51-52	Chi	1	0	0	0	0	

BUCHANAN, Ralph Leonard (Bucky) 5-8 172 C
B. Montreal, Que., Dec. 28, 1922

48-49	NYR	2	0	0	0	0	

BUCHANAN, Ronald Leonard 6-3 178 C
B. Montreal, Que., Nov. 15, 1944

SSN	TEAM	GP	G	A	PTS.	PIM	+/-
66-67	Bos	3	0	0	0	0	
69-70	StL	2	0	0	0	0	-1
72-73	Clev (WHA)	75	37	44	81	20	
73-74	Clev (WHA)	49	18	27	45	2	
74-75	Clev–Edm–Ind (WHA)	58	24	24	48	22	
75-76	Ind (WHA)	23	4	7	11	4	
NHL Totals		5	0	0	0	0	-1
WHA Totals		205	83	102	185	48	

Playoffs

72-73	Clev (WHA)	9	7	3	10	0	
73-74	Clev (WHA)	5	0	0	0	2	
Totals		14	7	3	10	2	

BUCHBERGER, Kelly 6-2 200 LW
B. Langenburg, Sask., Dec. 2, 1966

SSN	TEAM	GP	G	A	PTS.	PIM	+/-
87-88	Edm	19	1	0	1	81	-1
88-89	Edm	66	5	9	14	234	-14
89-90	Edm	55	2	6	8	168	-8
90-91	Edm	64	3	1	4	160	-6
91-92	Edm	79	20	24	44	157	+9
92-93	Edm	83	12	18	30	133	-27
93-94	Edm	84	3	18	21	199	-20
94-95	Edm	48	7	17	24	82	0
95-96	Edm	82	11	14	25	184	-20
96-97	Edm	81	8	30	38	159	+4
97-98	Edm	82	6	17	23	122	-10
98-99	Edm	52	4	4	8	68	-6
Totals		795	82	158	240	1747	-99

Playoffs

86-87	Edm	3	0	1	1	5	
89-90	Edm	19	0	5	5	13	
90-91	Edm	12	2	1	3	25	
91-92	Edm	16	1	4	5	32	
96-97	Edm	12	5	2	7	16	
97-98	Edm	12	1	2	3	25	
98-99	Edm	4	0	0	0	0	
Totals		78	9	15	24	116	

*BUCYK, John Paul (Chief) 6-0 215 LW
B. Edmonton, Alta., May 12, 1935

SSN	TEAM	GP	G	A	PTS.	PIM	+/-
55-56	Det	38	1	8	9	20	
56-57	Det	66	10	11	21	41	
57-58	Bos	68	21	31	52	57	
58-59	Bos	69	24	36	60	36	
59-60	Bos	56	16	36	52	26	
60-61	Bos	70	19	20	39	48	
61-62	Bos	67	20	40	60	32	
62-63	Bos	69	27	39	66	36	
63-64	Bos	62	18	36	54	36	
64-65	Bos	68	26	29	55	24	
65-66	Bos	63	27	30	57	12	
66-67	Bos	59	18	30	48	12	
67-68	Bos	72	30	39	69	8	+18
68-69	Bos	70	24	42	66	18	-3
69-70	Bos	76	31	38	69	13	+19
70-71	Bos	78	51	65	116	8	+36
71-72	Bos	78	32	51	83	4	+16
72-73	Bos	78	40	53	93	12	+18
73-74	Bos	76	31	44	75	8	+13
74-75	Bos	78	29	52	81	10	+11
75-76	Bos	77	36	47	83	20	+22
76-77	Bos	49	20	23	43	12	+2
77-78	Bos	53	5	13	18	4	-2
Totals		1540	556	813	1369	497	+146

SSN	TEAM	GP	G	A	PTS.	PIM	+/-

Playoffs

SSN	TEAM	GP	G	A	PTS.	PIM	+/-
55–56	Det	10	1	1	2	8	
56–57	Det	5	0	1	1	0	
57–58	Bos	12	0	4	4	16	
58–59	Bos	7	2	4	6	6	
67–68	Bos	3	0	2	2	0	
68–69	Bos	10	5	6	11	0	
69–70	Bos	14	11	8	19	2	
70–71	Bos	7	2	5	7	0	
71–72	Bos	15	9	11	20	6	
72–73	Bos	5	0	3	3	0	
73–74	Bos	16	8	10	18	4	
74–75	Bos	3	1	0	1	0	
75–76	Bos	12	2	7	9	0	
76–77	Bos	5	0	0	0	0	
Totals		124	41	62	103	42	

BUCYK, Randy *5–11 185 C*
B. Edmonton, Alta., Nov. 9, 1962

SSN	TEAM	GP	G	A	PTS.	PIM	+/-
85–86	Mont	17	4	2	6	8	+5
87–88	Calg	2	0	0	0	0	-1
Totals		19	4	2	6	8	+4

Playoffs

SSN	TEAM	GP	G	A	PTS.	PIM	+/-
85–86	Mont	2	0	0	0	0	

BUHR, Douglas Leonard *6–3 215 LW*
B. Vancouver, B.C., June 29, 1949

SSN	TEAM	GP	G	A	PTS.	PIM	+/-
74–75	KC	6	0	2	2	4	0

BUKOVICH, Anthony John (Tony) *5–11 160 C*
B. Painesdale, Mich., Aug. 30, 1918

SSN	TEAM	GP	G	A	PTS.	PIM	+/-
43–44	Det	30	0	1	1	0	
44–45	Det	14	7	2	9	6	
Totals		44	7	3	10	6	

Playoffs

SSN	TEAM	GP	G	A	PTS.	PIM	+/-
44–45	Det	6	0	1	1	0	

BULIS, Jan *6–0 194 C*
B. Pardubice, Czech., Mar. 18, 1978

SSN	TEAM	GP	G	A	PTS.	PIM	+/-
97–98	Wash	48	5	11	16	18	-5
98–99	Wash	38	7	16	23	6	+3
Totals		86	12	27	39	24	-2

BULLARD, Michael Brian *5–10 185 C*
B. Ottawa, Ont., Mar. 10, 1961

SSN	TEAM	GP	G	A	PTS.	PIM	+/-
80–81	Pitt	15	1	2	3	19	-1
81–82	Pitt	75	36	27	63	91	-1
82–83	Pitt	57	22	22	44	60	-21
83–84	Pitt	76	51	41	92	57	-33
84–85	Pitt	68	32	31	63	75	-43
85–86	Pitt	77	41	42	83	69	-16
86–87	Pitt–Calg	71	30	36	66	51	+5
87–88	Calg	79	48	55	103	68	+25
88–89	StL–Phil	74	27	38	65	106	+2
89–90	Phil	70	27	37	64	67	0
91–92	Tor	65	14	14	28	42	-19
Totals		727	329	345	674	705	-102

Playoffs

SSN	TEAM	GP	G	A	PTS.	PIM	+/-
80–81	Pitt	4	3	3	6	0	
81–82	Pitt	5	1	1	2	4	
86–87	Calg	6	4	3	7	2	
87–88	Calg	6	0	2	2	6	
88–89	Phil	19	3	9	12	32	
Totals		40	11	18	29	44	

***BULLER, Hyman (Hy)** *5–11 185 D*
B. Montreal, Que., Mar. 15, 1926

SSN	TEAM	GP	G	A	PTS.	PIM	+/-
43–44	Det	7	0	3	3	4	
44–45	Det	2	0	0	0	2	
51–52	NYR	68	12	23	35	96	
52–53	NYR	70	7	18	25	73	
53–54	NYR	41	3	14	17	40	
Totals		188	22	58	80	215	

BULLEY, Edward H. (Ted) *6–1 192 LW*
B. Windsor, Ont., Mar. 25, 1955

SSN	TEAM	GP	G	A	PTS.	PIM	+/-
76–77	Chi	2	0	0	0	0	-2
77–78	Chi	79	23	28	51	141	+4
78–79	Chi	75	27	23	50	153	+18
79–80	Chi	66	14	17	31	136	-12
80–81	Chi	68	18	16	34	95	+18
81–82	Chi	59	12	18	30	120	-1
82–83	Chi	39	4	9	13	47	-3
83–84	Pitt	26	3	2	5	12	-14
Totals		414	101	113	214	704	+8

Playoffs

SSN	TEAM	GP	G	A	PTS.	PIM	+/-
77–78	Chi	4	1	1	2	2	
78–79	Chi	2	0	0	0	0	
79–80	Chi	7	2	3	5	10	
81–82	Chi	15	2	1	3	12	
82–83	Wash	1	0	0	0	0	
Totals		29	5	5	10	24	

BURAKOVSKY, Robert *5–10 185 RW*
B. Malmo, Sweden, Nov. 24, 1966

SSN	TEAM	GP	G	A	PTS.	PIM	+/-
93–94	Ott	23	2	3	5	6	-7

***BURCH, William** *6–0 200 C*
B. Yonkers, N.Y., Nov. 20, 1900

SSN	TEAM	GP	G	A	PTS.	PIM	+/-
22–23	Ham	10	6	2	8	2	
23–24	Ham	24	16	2	18	4	
24–25	Ham	27	20	4	24	10	
25–26	NYA	36	22	3	25	33	
26–27	NYA	43	19	8	27	40	
27–28	NYA	32	10	2	12	34	
28–29	NYA	44	11	5	16	45	
29–30	NYA	35	7	3	10	22	
30–31	NYA	44	14	8	22	35	
31–32	NYA	48	7	15	22	71	
32–33	Bos–Chi	47	5	1	6	6	
Totals		390	137	53	190	302	

Playoffs

SSN	TEAM	GP	G	A	PTS.	PIM	+/-
28–29	NYA	2	0	0	0	0	

BURCHELL, Frederick (Skippy) *5–6 145 C*
B. Montreal, Que., Jan. 9, 1931

SSN	TEAM	GP	G	A	PTS.	PIM	+/-
50–51	Mont	2	0	0	0	0	
53–54	Mont	2	0	0	0	2	
Totals		4	0	0	0	2	

BURDON, Glen William *6–2 178 C*
B. Regina, Sask., Aug. 4, 1954

SSN	TEAM	GP	G	A	PTS.	PIM	+/-
74–75	KC	11	0	2	2	0	-3

BURE, Pavel *5–10 189 RW*
B. Moscow, USSR, Mar. 31, 1971

SSN	TEAM	GP	G	A	PTS.	PIM	+/-
91–92	Van	65	34	26	60	30	0
92–93	Van	83	60	50	110	69	+35
93–94	Van	76	60	47	107	86	+1
94–95	Van	44	20	23	43	47	-8
95–96	Van	15	6	7	13	8	-2
96–97	Van	63	23	32	55	40	-14
97–98	Van	82	51	39	90	48	+5
98–99	Fla	11	13	3	16	4	+3
Totals		439	267	224	491	332	+20

Playoffs

SSN	TEAM	GP	G	A	PTS.	PIM	+/-
91–92	Van	13	6	4	10	14	
92–93	Van	12	5	7	12	8	
93–94	Van	24	16	15	31	40	
94–95	Van	11	7	6	13	10	
Totals		60	34	32	66	72	

BURE, Valeri *5–10 168 RW*
B. Moscow, USSR, June 13, 1974

SSN	TEAM	GP	G	A	PTS.	PIM	+/-
94–95	Mont	24	3	1	4	6	-1
95–96	Mont	77	22	20	42	28	+10
96–97	Mont	64	14	21	35	6	+4
97–98	Mont–Calg	66	12	26	38	35	-5
98–99	Calg	80	26	27	53	22	0
Totals		311	77	95	172	97	+8

Playoffs

SSN	TEAM	GP	G	A	PTS.	PIM	+/-
95–96	Mont	6	0	1	1	6	
96–97	Mont	5	0	1	1	2	
Totals		11	0	2	2	8	

BUREAU, Marc *6–1 198 C*
B. Trois–Rivieres, Que., May 19, 1966

SSN	TEAM	GP	G	A	PTS.	PIM	+/-
89–90	Calg	5	0	0	0	4	-1
90–91	Calg–Minn	14	0	6	6	6	-7
91–92	Minn	46	6	4	10	50	-5
92–93	TB	63	10	21	31	111	-12
93–94	TB	75	8	7	15	30	-9
94–95	TB	48	2	12	14	30	-8
95–96	Mont	65	3	7	10	46	-3
96–97	Mont	43	16	9	15	16	+4
97–98	Mont	74	13	6	19	12	0
98–99	Phil	71	4	6	10	10	-2
Totals		504	52	78	130	315	-43

Playoffs

SSN	TEAM	GP	G	A	PTS.	PIM	+/-
90–91	Minn	23	3	2	5	20	
91–92	Minn	5	0	0	0	14	
95–96	Mont	6	1	1	2	4	
97–98	Mont	10	1	2	3	6	
98–99	Phil	6	0	2	2	2	
Totals		50	5	7	12	46	

BUREGA, William *6–1 200 D*
B. Winnipeg, Man., Mar. 13, 1932

SSN	TEAM	GP	G	A	PTS.	PIM	+/-
55–56	Bos	4	0	1	1	4	

BURKE, Edward A. *F*
B. Toronto, Ont., June 3, 1907

SSN	TEAM	GP	G	A	PTS.	PIM	+/-
31–32	Bos	16	3	0	3	12	
32–33	NYA	15	2	0	2	4	
33–34	NYA	46	20	10	30	24	
34–35	NYA	29	4	10	14	15	
Totals		106	29	20	49	55	

***BURKE, Martin Alphonsus** *5–7 160 D*
B. Toronto, Ont., Jan. 28, 1903

SSN	TEAM	GP	G	A	PTS.	PIM	+/-
27–28	Mont–Pitt Pi	46	2	1	3	61	
28–29	Mont	44	4	2	6	68	
29–30	Mont	44	2	11	13	71	
30–31	Mont	44	2	5	7	91	
31–32	Mont	48	3	6	9	50	
32–33	Mont–Ott	45	2	5	7	46	
33–34	Mont	45	1	4	5	28	
34–35	Chi	47	2	2	4	29	
35–36	Chi	40	0	3	3	49	
36–37	Chi	41	1	3	4	28	
37–38	Chi–Mont	50	0	5	5	39	
Totals		494	19	47	66	560	

Playoffs

SSN	TEAM	GP	G	A	PTS.	PIM	+/-
27–28	Pitt	2	1	0	1	2	
28–29	Mont	3	0	0	0	8	
29–30	Mont	6	0	1	1	6	
30–31	Mont	10	1	2	3	10	
31–32	Mont	4	0	0	0	12	
33–34	Mont	2	0	1	1	2	
34–35	Chi	2	0	0	0	2	
35–36	Chi	2	0	0	0	2	
Totals		31	2	4	6	44	

BURMEISTER, Roy *5–10 155 LW*
B. Collingwood, Ont., 1909

SSN	TEAM	GP	G	A	PTS.	PIM	+/-
29–30	NYA	40	1	1	2	0	
30–31	NYA	11	0	0	0	0	
31–32	NYA	16	3	2	5	2	
Totals		67	4	3	7	2	

BURNETT, James Kelvin (Kelly) *5–10 160 C*
B. Lachine, Que., June 16, 1926

SSN	TEAM	GP	G	A	PTS.	PIM	+/-
52–53	NYR	3	1	0	1	0	

BURNS, Charles Frederick *5–11 170 C*
B. Detroit, Mich., Feb. 14, 1936

SSN	TEAM	GP	G	A	PTS.	PIM	+/-
58–59	Det	70	9	11	20	32	
59–60	Bos	62	10	17	27	46	
60–61	Bos	62	15	26	41	16	
61–62	Bos	70	11	17	28	43	
62–63	Bos	68	12	10	22	13	
67–68	Oak	73	9	26	35	20	-14
68–69	Pitt	76	13	38	51	22	-9
69–70	Minn	50	3	13	16	10	-4
70–71	Minn	76	9	19	28	13	0
71–72	Minn	77	11	14	25	24	+5
72–73	Minn	65	4	7	11	13	-3
Totals		749	106	198	304	252	-25

Playoffs

SSN	TEAM	GP	G	A	PTS.	PIM	+/-
69–70	Minn	6	1	0	1	2	
70–71	Minn	12	3	3	6	2	
71–72	Minn	7	1	1	2	2	
72–73	Minn	6	0	0	0	0	
Totals		31	5	4	9	4	

BURNS, Gary 6-1 190 C
B. Cambridge, Mass., Jan. 16, 1955

SSN	TEAM	GP	G	A	PTS.	PIM	+/-
80-81	NYR	11	2	2	4	18	-9

Playoffs

SSN	TEAM	GP	G	A	PTS.	PIM	+/-
80-81	NYR	1	0	0	0	2	
81-82	NYR	4	0	0	0	4	
Totals		5	0	0	0	6	

*BURNS, Norman 6-0 195 C
B. Youngstown, Alta., Feb. 20, 1918

SSN	TEAM	GP	G	A	PTS.	PIM	+/-
41-42	NYR	11	0	4	4	2	

BURNS, Robert 5-9 155 LW
B. Gore Bay, Ont., Apr. 4, 1905

SSN	TEAM	GP	G	A	PTS.	PIM	+/-
27-28	Chi	1	0	0	0	0	
28-29	Chi	7	0	0	0	6	
29-30	Chi	12	1	0	1	2	
Totals		20	1	0	1	8	

BURNS, Robert Arthur (Robin) 6-0 195 LW
B. Montreal, Que., Aug. 27, 1946

SSN	TEAM	GP	G	A	PTS.	PIM	+/-
70-71	Pitt	10	0	3	3	4	+1
71-72	Pitt	5	0	0	0	8	-4
72-73	Pitt	26	0	2	2	20	-6
74-75	KC	71	18	15	33	70	-40
75-76	KC	78	13	18	31	37	-40
Totals		190	31	38	69	139	-89

BURR, Shawn 6-1 195 LW/C
B. Sarnia, Ont., July 1, 1966

SSN	TEAM	GP	G	A	PTS.	PIM	+/-
84-85	Det	9	0	0	0	2	-4
85-86	Det	5	1	0	1	4	+1
86-87	Det	80	22	25	47	107	+42
87-88	Det	78	17	23	40	97	+7
88-89	Det	79	19	27	46	78	+5
89-90	Det	76	24	32	56	82	+14
90-91	Det	80	20	30	50	112	+14
91-92	Det	79	19	32	51	118	+26
92-93	Det	80	10	25	35	74	+18
93-94	Det	51	10	12	22	31	+12
94-95	Det	42	6	8	14	60	+13
95-96	TB	81	13	15	28	119	+4
96-97	TB	74	14	21	35	106	+5
97-98	SJ	42	6	6	12	50	+2
98-99	SJ	18	0	1	1	29	-3
Totals		874	181	257	438	1069	+117

Playoffs

SSN	TEAM	GP	G	A	PTS.	PIM	+/-
86-87	Det	16	7	2	9	20	
87-88	Det	9	3	1	4	14	
88-89	Det	6	1	2	3	6	
90-91	Det	7	0	4	4	15	
91-92	Det	11	1	5	6	10	
92-93	Det	7	2	1	3	2	
93-94	Det	7	2	0	2	6	
94-95	Det	16	0	2	2	6	
95-96	TB	6	0	2	2	8	
97-98	SJ	6	0	0	0	8	
Totals		91	16	19	35	95	

BURRIDGE, Randy 5-9 180 LW
B. Fort Erie, Ont., Jan. 7, 1966

SSN	TEAM	GP	G	A	PTS.	PIM	+/-
85-86	Bos	52	17	25	42	28	+17
86-87	Bos	23	1	4	5	16	-6
87-88	Bos	79	27	28	55	105	0
88-89	Bos	80	31	30	61	39	+19
89-90	Bos	63	17	15	32	47	+9
90-91	Bos	62	15	13	28	40	+17
91-92	Wash	66	23	44	67	50	-4
92-93	Wash	4	0	0	0	0	+1
93-94	Wash	78	25	17	42	73	-1
94-95	Wash-LA	40	4	15	19	10	-4
95-96	Buf	74	25	33	58	30	0
96-97	Buf	55	10	21	31	20	+17
97-98	Buf	30	4	6	10	0	0
Totals		706	199	251	450	458	+65

Playoffs

SSN	TEAM	GP	G	A	PTS.	PIM	+/-
85-86	Bos	3	0	4	4	12	
86-87	Bos	2	1	0	1	2	
87-88	Bos	23	2	10	12	16	
88-89	Bos	10	5	2	7	6	
89-90	Bos	21	4	11	15	14	
90-91	Bos	19	0	3	3	39	
91-92	Wash	2	0	1	1	0	
92-93	Wash	4	1	0	1	0	
93-94	Wash	11	0	2	2	12	
96-97	Buf	12	5	1	6	2	
Totals		107	18	34	52	103	

BURROWS, David James 6-1 190 D
B. Toronto, Ont., Jan. 11, 1949

SSN	TEAM	GP	G	A	PTS.	PIM	+/-
71-72	Pitt	77	2	10	12	48	-7
72-73	Pitt	78	3	24	27	46	-4
73-74	Pitt	71	3	14	17	30	-13
74-75	Pitt	78	2	15	17	49	+3
75-76	Pitt	80	7	22	29	51	+27
76-77	Pitt	69	3	6	9	29	-15
77-78	Pitt	67	4	15	19	24	-30
78-79	Tor	65	2	11	13	28	-10
79-80	Tor	80	3	16	19	42	0
80-81	Tor-Pitt	59	0	2	2	30	-17
Totals		724	29	135	164	377	-66

Playoffs

SSN	TEAM	GP	G	A	PTS.	PIM	+/-
71-72	Pitt	4	0	0	0	4	
74-75	Pitt	9	1	1	2	12	
75-76	Pitt	3	0	0	0	0	
76-77	Pitt	3	0	2	2	0	
78-79	Tor	6	0	1	1	7	
79-80	Tor	3	0	1	1	2	
80-81	Pitt	1	0	0	0	0	
Totals		29	1	5	6	25	

BURRY, Berthold (Bert) D

SSN	TEAM	GP	G	A	PTS.	PIM	+/-
32-33	Ott	4	0	0	0	0	

BURT, Adam 6-0 195 D
B. Detroit, Mich., Jan. 15, 1969

SSN	TEAM	GP	G	A	PTS.	PIM	+/-
88-89	Hart	5	0	0	0	6	-1
89-90	Hart	63	4	8	12	105	+3
90-91	Hart	42	2	7	9	63	-4
91-92	Hart	66	9	15	24	93	-16
92-93	Hart	65	6	14	20	116	-11
93-94	Hart	63	1	17	18	75	-4
94-95	Hart	46	7	11	18	65	0
95-96	Hart	78	4	9	13	121	-4
96-97	Hart	71	2	11	13	79	-13
97-98	Car	76	1	11	12	106	-6
98-99	Car-Phil	68	0	4	4	60	+4
Totals		643	36	107	143	889	-52

Playoffs

SSN	TEAM	GP	G	A	PTS.	PIM	+/-
89-90	Hart	2	0	0	0	0	
91-92	Hart	2	0	0	0	0	
98-99	Phil	6	0	0	0	4	
Totals		10	0	0	0	4	

BURTON, Cumming Scott (Cummy) 5-10 175 RW
B. Sudbury, Ont., May 12, 1936

SSN	TEAM	GP	G	A	PTS.	PIM	+/-
55-56	Det	3	0	0	0	0	
57-58	Det	26	0	1	1	12	
58-59	Det	14	0	1	1	9	
Totals		43	0	2	2	21	

Playoffs

SSN	TEAM	GP	G	A	PTS.	PIM	+/-
55-56	Det	3	0	0	0	0	

BURTON, Nelson Keith 6-0 205 LW
B. Sydney, N.S., Nov. 6, 1957

SSN	TEAM	GP	G	A	PTS.	PIM	+/-
77-78	Wash	5	1	0	1	8	-3
78-79	Wash	3	0	0	0	13	-2
Totals		8	1	0	1	21	-5

*BUSH, Edward Webster 6-1 195 D
B. Collingwood, Ont., July 11, 1918

SSN	TEAM	GP	G	A	PTS.	PIM	+/-
38-39	Det	9	0	0	0	0	
41-42	Det	18	4	6	10	50	
Totals		27	4	6	10	50	

Playoffs

SSN	TEAM	GP	G	A	PTS.	PIM	+/-
41-42	Det	12	1	6	7	23	

BUSKAS, Rod 6-1 206 D
B. Wetaskiwin, Alta., Jan. 7, 1961

SSN	TEAM	GP	G	A	PTS.	PIM	+/-
82-83	Pitt	41	2	2	4	102	-15
83-84	Pitt	47	2	4	6	60	-18
84-85	Pitt	69	2	7	9	191	-21
85-86	Pitt	72	2	7	9	159	-9
86-87	Pitt	68	3	15	18	123	+2
87-88	Pitt	76	4	8	12	206	+6
88-89	Pitt	52	1	5	6	105	-2
89-90	Van-Pitt	23	0	3	3	49	-3
90-91	LA	57	3	8	11	182	+14
91-92	LA-Chi	47	0	4	4	91	-13
92-93	Chi	4	0	0	0	26	+2
Totals		556	19	63	82	1294	-57

Playoffs

SSN	TEAM	GP	G	A	PTS.	PIM	+/-
88-89	Pitt	10	0	0	0	23	
90-91	LA	2	0	2	2	22	
91-92	Chi	6	0	1	1	0	
Totals		18	0	3	3	45	

BUSNIUK, Michael 6-3 200 D
B. Thunder Bay, Ont., Dec. 13, 1951

SSN	TEAM	GP	G	A	PTS.	PIM	+/-
79-80	Phil	71	2	18	20	93	+39
80-81	Phil	72	1	5	6	204	+27
Totals		143	3	23	26	297	+66

Playoffs

SSN	TEAM	GP	G	A	PTS.	PIM	+/-
79-80	Phil	19	2	4	6	23	
80-81	Phil	6	0	1	1	11	
Totals		25	2	5	7	34	

BUSNIUK, Ronald Edward 5-11 180 RW
B. Fort William, Ont. Aug. 13, 1948

SSN	TEAM	GP	G	A	PTS.	PIM	+/-
72-73	Buf	1	0	0	0	0	0
73-74	Buf	5	0	3	3	4	-1
74-75	Minn (WHA)	73	2	21	23	176	
75-76	Minn-NE (WHA)	71	2	14	16	205	
76-77	Edm (WHA)	84	3	11	14	224	
77-78	Edm (WHA)	59	2	18	20	157	
NHL Totals		6	0	3	3	4	-1
WHA Totals		287	9	64	73	762	

Playoffs

SSN	TEAM	GP	G	A	PTS.	PIM	+/-
74-75	Minn (WHA)	12	2	1	3	63	
75-76	NE (WHA)	17	0	2	2	14	
76-77	Edm (WHA)	5	0	2	2	37	
77-78	Edm (WHA)	5	0	0	0	18	
WHA Totals		39	2	5	7	132	

*BUSWELL, Walter Gerard 5-11 170 D
B. Montreal, Que., Nov. 6, 1907

SSN	TEAM	GP	G	A	PTS.	PIM	+/-
32-33	Det	46	2	4	6	16	
33-34	Det	47	1	2	3	8	
34-35	Det	47	1	3	4	32	
35-36	Mont	44	0	2	2	34	
36-37	Mont	44	0	4	4	30	
37-38	Mont	48	2	15	17	24	
38-39	Mont	46	3	7	10	10	
39-40	Mont	46	1	3	4	10	
Totals		368	10	40	50	164	

Playoffs

SSN	TEAM	GP	G	A	PTS.	PIM	+/-
32-33	Det	4	0	0	0	4	
33-34	Det	9	0	1	1	2	
36-37	Mont	5	0	0	0	2	
37-38	Mont	3	0	0	0	0	
38-39	Mont	3	2	0	2	2	
Totals		24	2	1	3	10	

BUTCHER, Garth 6-0 200 D
B. Regina, Sask., Jan. 8, 1963

SSN	TEAM	GP	G	A	PTS.	PIM	+/-
81-82	Van	5	0	0	0	9	+4
82-83	Van	55	1	13	14	104	-7
83-84	Van	28	2	0	2	34	-12
84-85	Van	75	3	9	12	152	-31
85-86	Van	70	4	7	11	188	-25
86-87	Van	70	5	15	20	207	-12
87-88	Van	80	6	17	23	285	-14
88-89	Van	78	0	20	20	227	+4
89-90	Van	67	6	14	20	205	-10
90-91	Van-StL	82	6	16	22	289	-14
91-92	StL	68	5	15	20	189	+5
92-93	StL	84	5	10	15	211	0
93-94	StL-Que	77	4	15	19	143	-7
94-95	Tor	45	1	7	8	59	-5
Totals		897	48	158	206	2302	-124

Playoffs

SSN	TEAM	GP	G	A	PTS.	PIM	+/-
81-82	Van	1	0	0	0	0	
82-83	Van	3	1	0	1	2	
85-86	Van	3	0	0	0	0	
88-89	Van	7	1	1	2	22	
90-91	StL	13	2	1	3	54	
91-92	StL	5	1	2	3	16	

SSN	TEAM	GP	G	A	PTS.	PIM	+/-
92–93	StL	11	1	1	2	20	
94–95	Tor	7	0	0	0	8	
Totals		50	6	5	11	122	

BUTENSCHON, Sven *6–5 201 D*
B. Itzehoe, W. Germany, Mar. 22, 1976

SSN	TEAM	GP	G	A	PTS.	PIM	+/-
97–98	Pitt	8	0	0	0	6	-1
98–99	Pitt	17	0	0	0	6	-7
Totals		25	0	0	0	12	-8

BUTLER, Jerome Patrick *6–0 180 RW*
B. Sarnia, Ont., Feb. 27, 1951

SSN	TEAM	GP	G	A	PTS.	PIM	+/-
72–73	NYR	8	1	0	1	4	+1
73–74	NYR	26	6	10	16	24	+7
74–75	NYR	78	17	16	33	102	-5
75–76	StL	66	17	24	41	75	0
76–77	StL	80	12	20	32	65	-31
77–78	StL–Tor	82	9	9	18	54	-16
78–79	Tor	76	8	7	15	52	-2
79–80	Tor–Van	78	11	12	23	50	-8
80–81	Van	80	12	15	27	60	+2
81–82	Van	25	3	1	4	15	-5
82–83	Winn	42	3	6	9	14	-5
Totals		641	99	120	219	515	-62

Playoffs

SSN	TEAM	GP	G	A	PTS.	PIM	+/-
73–74	NYR	12	0	2	2	25	
74–75	NYR	3	1	0	1	16	
75–76	StL	3	0	0	0	0	
76–77	StL	4	0	0	0	14	
77–78	Tor	13	1	1	2	18	
78–79	Tor	6	0	0	0	4	
79–80	Van	4	0	0	0	2	
80–81	Van	3	1	0	1	0	
Totals		48	3	3	6	79	

BUTLER, John Richard (Dick) *5–7 175 RW*
B. Delisle, Sask., June 2, 1926

SSN	TEAM	GP	G	A	PTS.	PIM	+/-
47–48	Chi	7	2	0	2	0	

BUTSAYEV, Viacheslav *6–2 200 C*
B. Togliatti, USSR, June 13, 1970

SSN	TEAM	GP	G	A	PTS.	PIM	+/-
92–93	Phil	52	2	14	16	61	+3
93–94	Phil–SJ	59	12	11	23	68	0
94–95	SJ	6	2	0	2	0	-2
95–96	Ana	7	1	0	1	0	-4
98–99	Fla–Ott	3	0	1	1	4	-1
Totals		127	17	26	43	133	-4

BUTTERS, William Joseph *5–9 192 D*
B. St. Paul Minn., Jan. 10, 1951

SSN	TEAM	GP	G	A	PTS.	PIM	+/-
74–75	Minn (WHA)	24	2	2	4	58	
75–76	Minn–Hou (WHA)	73	0	19	19	138	
76–77	Minn–Edm–NE (WHA)	75	1	17	18	215	
77–78	NE (WHA)	45	1	13	14	69	
77–78	Minn	23	1	0	1	30	-3
78–79	Minn	49	0	4	4	47	-12
NHL Totals		72	1	4	5	77	-15
WHA Totals		217	4	51	55	480	

Playoffs

SSN	TEAM	GP	G	A	PTS.	PIM	+/-
74–75	Minn (WHA)	12	1	0	1	21	
75–76	Hous (WHA)	17	0	3	3	51	
76–77	NE (WHA)	5	0	1	1	15	
WHA Totals		34	1	4	5	87	

BUTTREY, Gordon (Gord) *5–7 167 F*
B. Regina, Sask., Mar. 17, 1926

SSN	TEAM	GP	G	A	PTS.	PIM	+/-
43–44	Chi	10	0	0	0	0	

BUYNAK, Gordon *6–1 180 D*
B. Detroit, Mich., Mar. 19, 1954

SSN	TEAM	GP	G	A	PTS.	PIM	+/-
74–75	StL	4	0	0	0	2	+3

BUZEK, Petr *6–0 205 D*
B. Jhiava, Czech., Apr. 26, 1977

SSN	TEAM	GP	G	A	PTS.	PIM	+/-
97–98	Dal	2	0	0	0	2	+1
98–99	Dal	2	0	0	0	2	0
Totals		4	0	0	0	4	+1

BYAKIN, Ilya *5–9 185 D*
B. Sverdlovsk, USSR, Feb. 2, 1963

SSN	TEAM	GP	G	A	PTS.	PIM	+/-
93–94	Edm	44	8	20	28	30	-3
94–95	SJ	13	0	5	5	14	-9
Totals		57	8	25	33	44	-12

BYCE, John *6–1 180 RW*
B. Madison, Wisc., Aug. 9, 1967

SSN	TEAM	GP	G	A	PTS.	PIM	+/-
90–91	Bos	18	1	3	4	6	+1
91–92	Bos	3	1	0	1	0	-1
Totals		21	2	3	5	6	0

Playoffs

SSN	TEAM	GP	G	A	PTS.	PIM	+/-
89–90	Bos	8	2	0	2	2	

BYERS, Gordon Charles (Gord) *5–9 182 D*
B. Eganville, Ont., Mar. 11, 1930

SSN	TEAM	GP	G	A	PTS.	PIM	+/-
49–50	Bos	1	0	1	1	0	

BYERS, Jerry William *5–11 170 LW*
B. Kentville, N.S., Mar. 29, 1952

SSN	TEAM	GP	G	A	PTS.	PIM	+/-
72–73	Minn	14	0	2	2	6	-2
73–74	Minn	10	0	0	0	0	-5
74–75	Atl	12	1	1	2	4	-4
77–78	NYR	7	2	1	3	0	-1
Totals		43	3	4	7	10	-12

BYERS, Lyndon *6–1 200 RW*
B. Nipawin, Sask., Feb. 29, 1964

SSN	TEAM	GP	G	A	PTS.	PIM	+/-
83–84	Bos	10	2	4	6	32	+3
84–85	Bos	33	3	8	11	41	0
85–86	Bos	5	0	2	2	9	+1
86–87	Bos	18	2	3	5	53	-1
87–88	Bos	53	10	14	24	236	+10
88–89	Bos	49	0	4	4	218	-8
89–90	Bos	43	4	4	8	159	0
90–91	Bos	19	2	2	4	82	-2
91–92	Bos	31	1	1	2	129	-5
92–93	SJ	18	4	1	5	122	-2
Totals		279	28	43	71	1081	-4

Playoffs

SSN	TEAM	GP	G	A	PTS.	PIM	+/-
86–87	Bos	1	0	0	0	0	
87–88	Bos	11	1	2	3	62	
88–89	Bos	2	0	0	0	0	
89–90	Bos	17	1	0	1	12	
90–91	Bos	1	0	0	0	10	
91–92	Bos	5	0	0	0	12	
Totals		37	2	2	4	96	

BYERS, Michael Arthur *5–10 185 RW*
B. Toronto, Ont., Sept. 11, 1946

SSN	TEAM	GP	G	A	PTS.	PIM	+/-
67–68	Tor	10	2	2	4	0	+2
68–69	Tor–Phil	10	0	2	2	2	-1
70–71	LA	72	27	18	45	14	-5
71–72	LA–Buf	74	13	12	25	23	-33
72–73	LA–NE (WHA)	75	25	21	46	24	
73–74	NE (WHA)	78	29	21	50	6	
74–75	NE (WHA)	72	22	26	48	10	
75–76	NE–Cin (WHA)	41	7	6	13	0	
NHL Totals		166	42	34	76	39	-37
WHA Totals		266	83	74	157	40	

Playoffs

SSN	TEAM	GP	G	A	PTS.	PIM	+/-
68–69	Phil	4	0	1	1	0	
72–73	NE (WHA)	12	6	5	11	6	
73–74	NE (WHA)	7	2	4	6	12	
74–75	NE (WHA)	6	2	2	4	2	
NHL Totals		4	0	1	1	0	
WHA Totals		25	10	11	21	20	

BYLSMA, Daniel *6–2 205 LW*
B. Grand Rapids, Mich., Sept. 19, 1970

SSN	TEAM	GP	G	A	PTS.	PIM	+/-
95–96	LA	4	0	0	0	0	0
96–97	LA	79	3	6	9	32	-15
97–98	LA	65	3	9	12	33	+9
98–99	LA	8	0	0	0	2	-1
Totals		156	6	15	21	67	-7

Playoffs

SSN	TEAM	GP	G	A	PTS.	PIM	+/-
97–98	LA	2	0	0	0	0	

BYRAM, Shawn *6–2 204 LW*
B. Neepawa, Man., Sept. 12, 1968

SSN	TEAM	GP	G	A	PTS.	PIM	+/-
90–91	NYI	4	0	0	0	14	-2
91–92	Chi	1	0	0	0	0	0
Totals		5	0	0	0	14	-2

*CAFFERY, John (Jack) *6–0 175 C*
B. Kingston, Ont., June 30, 1934

SSN	TEAM	GP	G	A	PTS.	PIM	+/-
54–55	Tor	3	0	0	0	0	
56–57	Bos	47	2	2	4	20	
57–58	Bos	7	1	0	1	2	
Totals		57	3	2	5	22	

Playoffs

SSN	TEAM	GP	G	A	PTS.	PIM	+/-
56–57	Bos	10	1	0	1	4	

CAFFERY, Terrance Michael *5–9 165 C*
B. Toronto, Ont., Apr. 1, 1949

SSN	TEAM	GP	G	A	PTS.	PIM	+/-
69–70	Chi	6	0	0	0	0	0
70–71	Minn	8	0	0	0	0	-2
72–73	Ne (WHA)	74	39	61	100	14	
74–75	NE (WHA)	67	15	37	52	12	
75–76	NE–Calg (WHA)	23	5	13	18	4	
NHL Totals		14	0	0	0	0	-2
WHA Totals		164	59	111	170	30	

Playoffs

SSN	TEAM	GP	G	A	PTS.	PIM	+/-
70–71	Minn	1	0	0	0	0	
72–73	NE (WHA)	8	3	7	10	0	
NHL Totals		1	0	0	0	0	
WHA Totals		8	3	7	10	0	

*CAHAN, Lawrence Louis *6–0 195 D*
B. Ft. William, Ont., Dec. 25, 1933

SSN	TEAM	GP	G	A	PTS.	PIM	+/-
54–55	Tor	58	0	6	6	64	
55–56	Tor	21	0	2	2	46	
56–57	NYR	61	5	4	9	65	
57–58	NYR	34	1	1	2	20	
58–59	NYR	16	1	0	1	8	
61–62	NYR	57	2	7	9	85	
62–63	NYR	56	6	14	20	47	
63–64	NYR	53	4	8	12	80	
64–65	NYR	26	0	5	5	32	
67–68	Oak	74	9	15	24	80	-29
68–69	LA	72	3	11	14	76	-20
69–70	LA	70	4	8	12	50	-25
70–71	LA	67	3	11	14	45	-29
72–73	Chi (WHA)	75	1	10	11	44	
73–74	Chi (WHA)	3	0	0	0	2	
NHL Totals		665	38	92	130	698	-103
WHA Totals		78	1	10	11	46	

Playoffs

SSN	TEAM	GP	G	A	PTS.	PIM	+/-
54–55	Tor	4	0	0	0	0	
56–57	NYR	3	0	0	0	2	
57–58	NYR	5	0	0	0	4	
61–62	NYR	6	0	0	0	10	
68–69	LA	11	1	1	2	22	
Totals		29	1	1	2	38	

CAHILL, Charles (Chuck) *F*

SSN	TEAM	GP	G	A	PTS.	PIM	+/-
25–26	Bos	31	0	1	1	4	
26–27	Bos	1	0	0	0	0	
Totals		32	0	1	1	4	

CAIN, Herbert *5–11 180 LW*
B. Newmarket, Ont., Dec. 24, 1913

SSN	TEAM	GP	G	A	PTS.	PIM	+/-
33–34	Mont M	31	4	5	9	14	
34–35	Mont M	44	20	7	27	13	
35–36	Mont M	47	5	13	18	16	
36–37	Mont M	43	13	17	30	18	
37–38	Mont M	47	11	19	30	10	
38–39	Mont	45	13	14	27	26	
39–40	Bos	48	21	10	31	30	
40–41	Bos	40	8	10	18	6	
41–42	Bos	35	8	10	18	2	
42–43	Bos	45	18	18	36	19	
43–44	Bos	48	36	46	82	4	
44–45	Bos	50	32	13	45	16	
45–46	Bos	48	17	12	29	4	
Totals		571	206	194	400	178	

Playoffs

SSN	TEAM	GP	G	A	PTS.	PIM	+/-
33–34	MontM	4	0	0	0	0	
34–35	MontM	4	1	0	1	2	
35–36	MontM	3	0	1	1	0	
36–37	MontM	5	1	1	2	0	
38–39	Mont	3	0	0	0	2	
39–40	Bos	6	1	3	4	2	
40–41	Bos	11	3	2	5	5	
41–42	Bos	5	1	0	1	0	
42–43	Bos	7	4	2	6	0	
44–45	Bos	7	5	2	7	0	

SSN	TEAM	GP	G	A	PTS.	PIM	+/-
45–46	Bos	9	0	2	2	2	
Totals		64	16	13	29	13	

CAIN, James F. (Dutch) D
B. Newmarket, Ont.

SSN	TEAM	GP	G	A	PTS.	PIM	+/-
24–25	Mont M	28	4	0	4	27	
25–26	Mont M–Tor	33	0	0	0	8	
Totals		61	4	0	4	35	

CAIRNS, Donald 6–1 195 LW
B. Calgary, Alta., Oct. 8, 1955

SSN	TEAM	GP	G	A	PTS.	PIM	+/-
75–76	KC	7	0	0	0	0	-1
76–77	Col	2	0	1	1	2	+1
Totals		9	0	1	1	2	0

CAIRNS, Eric 6–5 225 D
B. Oakville, Ont., June 27, 1974

SSN	TEAM	GP	G	A	PTS.	PIM	+/-
96–97	NYR	40	0	1	1	147	-7
97–98	NYR	39	0	3	3	92	-3
98–99	NYI	9	0	3	3	23	+1
Totals		88	0	7	7	262	-9

Playoffs

SSN	TEAM	GP	G	A	PTS.	PIM
96–97	NYR	3	0	0	0	0

CALDER, Eric 6–1 180 D
B. Kitchener, Ont., July 26, 1963

SSN	TEAM	GP	G	A	PTS.	PIM	+/-
81–82	Wash	1	0	0	0	0	0
82–83	Wash	1	0	0	0	0	0
Totals		2	0	0	0	0	0

CALLADINE, Norman 5–9 155 C
B. Peterborough, Ont., 1916

SSN	TEAM	GP	G	A	PTS.	PIM
42–43	Bos	3	0	1	1	0
43–44	Bos	49	16	27	43	8
44–45	Bos	11	3	1	4	0
Totals		63	19	29	48	8

CALLANDER, John (Jock) 6–1 185 RW
B. Regina, Sask., Apr. 23, 1961

SSN	TEAM	GP	G	A	PTS.	PIM	+/-
87–88	Pitt	41	11	16	27	45	-13
88–89	Pitt	30	6	5	11	20	-3
89–90	Pitt	30	4	7	11	49	0
92–93	TB	8	1	1	2	2	-5
Totals		109	22	29	51	116	-21

Playoffs

SSN	TEAM	GP	G	A	PTS.	PIM
88–89	Pitt	10	2	5	7	10
91–92	Pitt	12	1	2	3	4
Totals		22	3	8	11	12

CALLANDER, Leonard Drew 6–2 188 C
B. Regina, Sask., Aug. 17, 1956

SSN	TEAM	GP	G	A	PTS.	PIM	+/-
76–77	Phil	2	1	0	1	0	+1
77–78	Phil	1	0	0	0	0	0
78–79	Phil–Van	32	4	1	5	7	-10
79–80	Van	4	1	1	2	0	-2
Totals		39	6	2	8	7	-11

CALLIGHEN, Brett 5–11 182 C
B. Toronto, Ont., May 15, 1953

SSN	TEAM	GP	G	A	PTS.	PIM	+/-
76–77	NE–Edm (WHA)	62	15	26	41	89	
77–78	Edm (WHA)	80	20	30	50	112	
78–79	Edm (WHA)	71	31	39	70	79	
79–80	Edm	59	23	35	58	72	-1
80–81	Edm	55	25	35	60	32	+13
81–82	Edm	46	8	19	27	28	+16
NHL Totals		160	56	89	145	132	+28
WHA Totals		213	66	95	161	280	

Playoffs

SSN	TEAM	GP	G	A	PTS.	PIM
76–77	Edm (WHA)	5	4	1	5	7
77–78	Edm (WHA)	5	0	2	2	16
78–79	Edm (WHA)	13	5	10	15	15
79–80	Edm	3	0	2	2	0
80–81	Edm	9	4	4	8	6
81–82	Edm	2	0	0	0	2
NHL Totals		14	4	6	10	8
WHA Totals		23	9	13	22	38

CALLIGHEN, Francis Charles Winslow (Patsy) 5–6 175 LW
B. Toronto, Ont., Feb. 13, 1906

SSN	TEAM	GP	G	A	PTS.	PIM
27–28	NYR	36	0	0	0	32

Playoffs

SSN	TEAM	GP	G	A	PTS.	PIM
27–28	NYR	9	0	0	0	0

CALOUN, Jan 5–10 175 RW
B. Usti–Nad–Labern, Czech., Dec. 20, 1972

SSN	TEAM	GP	G	A	PTS.	PIM	+/-
95–96	SJ	11	8	3	11	0	+4
96–97	SJ	2	0	0	0	0	-2
Totals		13	8	3	11	0	+2

CAMAZZOLA, Anthony Bert (Tony) 6–2 210 D
B. Vancouver, B.C., Sept. 11, 1962

SSN	TEAM	GP	G	A	PTS.	PIM	+/-
81–82	Wash	3	0	0	0	0	0

CAMAZZOLA, James 5–11 190 LW
B. Vancouver, B.C., Jan. 5, 1964

SSN	TEAM	GP	G	A	PTS.	PIM	+/-
83–84	Chi	1	0	0	0	0	0
86–87	Chi	2	0	0	0	0	0
Totals		3	0	0	0	0	0

CAMERON, Alan Richard 6–0 205 D
B. Edmonton, Alta., Oct. 21, 1955

SSN	TEAM	GP	G	A	PTS.	PIM	+/-
75–76	Det	38	2	8	10	49	-7
76–77	Det	80	3	13	16	112	-43
77–78	Det	63	2	7	9	94	-12
78–79	Det	9	0	3	3	8	+1
79–80	Winn	63	3	11	14	72	-26
80–81	Winn	29	1	2	3	21	-19
Totals		282	11	44	55	356	-106

Playoffs

SSN	TEAM	GP	G	A	PTS.	PIM
77–78	Det	7	0	1	1	2

CAMERON, Angus (Scotty) 6–1 175 C
B. Prince Albert, Sask., Nov. 5, 1921

SSN	TEAM	GP	G	A	PTS.	PIM
42–43	NYR	35	8	11	19	0

CAMERON, Craig Lauder 6–0 200 RW
B. Edmonton, Alta., July 19, 1945

SSN	TEAM	GP	G	A	PTS.	PIM	+/-
66–67	Det	1	0	0	0	0	
67–68	StL	32	7	2	9	8	+2
68–69	StL	72	11	5	16	40	-8
70–71	StL	78	14	6	20	32	-11
71–72	Minn	64	2	1	3	11	-1
72–73	NYI	72	19	14	33	27	-38
73–74	NYI	78	15	14	29	28	-15
74–75	NYI–Minn	77	11	13	24	22	+5
75–76	Minn	78	8	10	18	34	-27
Totals		552	87	65	152	202	-93

Playoffs

SSN	TEAM	GP	G	A	PTS.	PIM
67–68	StL	14	1	0	1	11
68–69	StL	2	0	0	0	0
70–71	StL	6	2	0	2	4
71–72	Minn	5	0	1	1	0
Totals		27	3	1	4	15

CAMERON, David William 6–0 185 C
B. Charlottetown, P.E.I., July 29, 1958

SSN	TEAM	GP	G	A	PTS.	PIM	+/-
81–82	Col	66	11	12	23	103	-14
82–83	NJ	35	5	4	9	50	-8
83–84	NJ	67	9	12	21	85	-11
Totals		168	25	28	53	238	-33

*CAMERON, Harold Hugh (Harry) D
B. Pembroke, Ont., Feb. 6, 1890

SSN	TEAM	GP	G	A	PTS.	PIM
17–18	Tor	20	17	0	17	17
18–19	Tor	14	11	3	14	35
19–20	Tor–Mont	23	16	1	17	11
20–21	Tor	24	18	9	27	55
21–22	Tor	24	19	8	27	18
22–23	Tor	22	9	6	15	18
Totals		127	90	27	117	154

Playoffs

SSN	TEAM	GP	G	A	PTS.	PIM
17–18	Tor	7	3	0	3	4
18–19	Tor	5	4	0	4	6
20–21	Tor	2	0	0	0	0
21–22	Tor	7	0	3	3	19
Totals		21	7	3	10	29

CAMERON, William RW
B. Timmins, Ont., 1904

SSN	TEAM	GP	G	A	PTS.	PIM
23–24	Mont	18	0	0	0	2
25–26	NYA	21	0	0	0	0
Totals		39	0	0	0	2

Playoffs

SSN	TEAM	GP	G	A	PTS.	PIM
23–24	Mont	6	0	0	0	0

CAMPBELL, Bryan Albert 6–0 175 C
B. Sudbury, Ont., Mar. 27, 1944

SSN	TEAM	GP	G	A	PTS.	PIM	+/-
67–68	LA	44	6	15	21	16	+2
68–69	LA	18	2	1	3	4	-7
69–70	LA–Chi	45	5	5	10	6	-13
70–71	Chi	78	17	37	54	26	+26
71–72	Chi	75	5	13	18	22	+2
72–73	Phil (WHA)	75	25	48	73	85	
73–74	Van (WHA)	76	27	62	89	50	
74–75	Van (WHA)	78	29	34	63	24	
75–76	Cin (WHA)	77	22	50	72	24	
76–77	Ind–Edm (WHA)	74	13	46	59	24	
77–78	Edm (WHA)	53	7	13	20	12	
NHL Totals		260	35	71	106	74	+10
WHA Totals		433	123	253	376	219	

Playoffs

SSN	TEAM	GP	G	A	PTS.	PIM
68–69	LA	6	2	1	3	0
69–70	Chi	8	1	2	3	0
70–71	Chi	4	0	1	1	0
71–72	Chi	4	0	0	0	2
72–73	Phil (WHA)	3	0	1	1	8
76–77	Edm (WHA)	5	3	1	4	0
NHL Totals		22	3	4	7	2
WHA Totals		8	3	2	5	8

CAMPBELL, Colin John 5–9 190 D
B. London, Ont., Jan. 28, 1953

SSN	TEAM	GP	G	A	PTS.	PIM	+/-
73–74	Van (WHA)	78	3	20	23	191	
74–75	Pitt	59	4	15	19	172	+28
75–76	Pitt	64	7	10	17	105	-4
76–77	Pitt	54	3	8	11	67	-22
77–78	Pitt	55	1	9	10	103	-19
78–79	Pitt	65	2	18	20	137	+14
79–80	Edm	72	2	11	13	196	-18
80–81	Van	42	1	8	9	75	+10
81–82	Van	47	0	8	8	131	+4
82–83	Det	53	1	7	8	74	+2
83–84	Det	8	3	4	7	108	0
84–85	Det	57	1	5	6	124	-14
NHL Totals		636	25	103	128	1292	-19
WHA Totals		78	3	20	23	191	

Playoffs

SSN	TEAM	GP	G	A	PTS.	PIM
74–75	Pitt	9	1	3	4	21
75–76	Pitt	3	0	0	0	0
78–79	Pitt	7	1	4	5	30
79–80	Edm	3	0	0	0	11
81–82	Van	16	2	2	4	89
83–84	Det	4	0	0	0	21
Totals		45	4	10	14	181

*CAMPBELL, David D
B. Lachute, Que., Apr. 27, 1896

SSN	TEAM	GP	G	A	PTS.	PIM
20–21	Mont	3	0	0	0	0

CAMPBELL, Donald William F
B. Drumheller, Alta., July 12, 1925

SSN	TEAM	GP	G	A	PTS.	PIM
43–44	Chi	1	1	3	4	8

CAMPBELL, Earl (Spiff) F

SSN	TEAM	GP	G	A	PTS.	PIM
23–24	Ott	18	4	1	5	6
24–25	Ott	30	0	0	0	0
25–26	NYA	29	1	0	1	6
Totals		77	5	1	6	12

Playoffs

SSN	TEAM	GP	G	A	PTS.	PIM
23–24	Ott	2	0	0	0	0

CAMPBELL, Jim 6–1 175 C
B. Worcester, Mass., Feb. 3, 1973

SSN	TEAM	GP	G	A	PTS.	PIM	+/-
95–96	Ana	16	2	3	5	36	0
96–97	StL	68	23	20	43	68	+3
97–98	StL	76	22	19	41	55	0
98–99	StL	55	4	21	25	41	-8
Totals		215	51	63	114	132	-5

Playoffs

SSN	TEAM	GP	G	A	PTS.	PIM
96–97	StL	4	1	0	1	6
97–98	StL	10	7	3	10	12
Totals		14	8	3	11	18

SSN	TEAM	GP	G	A	PTS.	PIM	+/-

CAMPBELL, Scott *6–3 205 D*
B. Toronto, Ont., June 22, 1957

SSN	TEAM	GP	G	A	PTS.	PIM	+/-
77–78	Hou (WHA)	75	8	29	37	116	
78–79	Winn (WHA)	74	3	15	18	248	
79–80	Winn	63	3	17	20	136	-39
80–81	Winn	14	1	4	5	55	+3
81–82	StL	3	0	0	0	52	-1
NHL Totals		80	4	21	25	243	-37
WHA Totals		149	11	44	55	364	

Playoffs

77–78	Hous (WHA)	6	1	1	2	8	
78–79	Winn (WHA)	10	0	2	2	25	
WHA Totals		16	1	3	4	33	

CAMPBELL, Wade Allan *6–4 220 D*
B. Peace River, Alta., Jan. 2, 1961

82–83	Winn	42	1	2	3	50	-12
83–84	Winn	79	7	14	21	147	-2
84–85	Winn	40	1	6	7	21	+1
85–86	Winn–Bos	32	0	1	1	42	-11
86–87	Bos	14	0	3	3	24	-1
87–88	Bos	6	0	1	1	21	+1
Totals		213	9	27	36	305	-24

Playoffs

83–84	Winn	3	0	0	0	7	
84–85	Winn	3	0	0	0	2	
86–87	Bos	4	0	0	0	11	
Totals		10	0	0	0	20	

CAMPEAU, Jean Claude (Tod) *5–11 175 C*
B. St. Jerome, Que., June 4, 1923

43–44	Mont	2	0	0	0	0	
47–48	Mont	14	2	2	4	4	
48–49	Mont	26	3	7	10	12	
Totals		42	5	9	14	16	

Playoffs

| 48–49 | Mont | 1 | 0 | 0 | 0 | 0 | |

CAMPEDELLI, Dom *6–1 185 D*
B. Cohasset, Mass., Apr. 3, 1964

| 85–86 | Mont | 2 | 0 | 0 | 0 | 0 | -2 |

CAPUANO, David *6–2 190 C*
B. Warwick, R.I., July 27, 1968

89–90	Pitt–Van	33	3	5	8	12	-7
90–91	Van	61	13	31	44	42	+1
92–93	TB	6	1	1	2	2	-4
93–94	SJ	4	0	1	1	0	-5
Totals		104	17	38	55	56	-15

Playoffs

| 90–91 | Van | 6 | 1 | 1 | 2 | 5 | |

CAPUANO, Jack *6–2 210 D*
B. Cranston, R.I., July 7, 1966

89–90	Tor	1	0	0	0	0	-1
90–91	Van	3	0	0	0	0	
91–92	Bos	2	0	0	0	0	-1
Totals		6	0	0	0	0	-2

CARBOL, Leo *5–10 170 D*
B. Ottawa, Ont., June 5, 1912

| 42–43 | Chi | 6 | 0 | 1 | 1 | 4 | |

CARBONNEAU, Guy *5–11 180 C*
B. Sept Iles, Que., Mar. 18, 1960

80–81	Mont	2	0	1	1	0	0
82–83	Mont	77	18	29	47	68	+18
83–84	Mont	78	24	30	54	75	+5
84–85	Mont	79	23	34	57	43	+28
85–86	Mont	80	20	36	56	57	+18
86–87	Mont	79	18	27	45	68	+9
87–88	Mont	80	17	21	38	61	+14
88–89	Mont	79	26	30	56	44	+37
89–90	Mont	68	19	36	55	37	+21
90–91	Mont	78	20	24	44	63	-1
91–92	Mont	72	18	21	39	39	+2
92–93	Mont	61	4	13	17	20	-9
93–94	Mont	79	14	24	38	48	+16
94–95	StL	42	5	11	16	16	+11
95–96	Dal	71	8	15	23	38	-2
96–97	Dal	73	5	16	21	36	+9
97–98	Dal	77	7	17	24	40	+3

98–99	Dal	74	4	12	16	31	-3
Totals		1249	250	397	647	784	+176

Playoffs

82–83	Mont	3	0	0	0	2	
83–84	Mont	15	4	3	7	12	
84–85	Mont	12	4	3	7	8	
85–86	Mont	20	7	5	12	35	
86–87	Mont	17	3	8	11	20	
88–89	Mont	11	0	4	4	2	
89–90	Mont	21	4	5	9	10	
90–91	Mont	11	2	3	5	6	
91–92	Mont	13	1	5	6	10	
92–93	Mont	11	1	1	2	6	
93–94	Mont	20	3	3	6	10	
94–95	StL	7	1	2	3	6	
96–97	Dal	7	0	1	1	6	
97–98	Dal	16	3	1	4	6	
98–99	Dal	17	2	4	6	6	
Totals		208	36	51	87	149	

CARDIN, Claude *5–7 160 LW*
B. Sorel, Que., May 28, 1943

| 67–68 | StL | 1 | 0 | 0 | 0 | 0 | -1 |

CARDWELL, Stephen Michael *5–11 190 LW*
B. Toronto, Ont., Aug. 13, 1950

70–71	Pitt	5	0	1	1	15	-4
71–72	Pitt	28	7	8	15	18	0
72–73	Pitt	20	2	2	4	2	-2
73–74	Minn (WHA)	77	23	23	46	100	
74–75	Clev (WHA)	75	9	13	22	127	
NHL Totals		53	9	11	20	35	-6
WHA Totals		152	32	36	68	227	

Playoffs

71–72	Pitt	4	0	0	0	2	
73–74	Minn (WHA)	10	0	0	0	20	
74–75	Clev (WHA)	5	0	1	1	14	
NHL Totals		4	0	0	0	2	
WHA Totals		15	0	1	1	34	

***CAREY, George** *RW*

19–20	Que	20	11	5	16	4	
20–21	Ham	20	7	1	8	8	
21–22	Ham	23	3	2	5	2	
22–23	Ham	5	1	0	1	0	
23–24	Tor	4	0	0	0	0	
Totals		72	22	8	30	14	

CARKNER, Terry *6–3 210 D*
B. Smiths Falls, Ont., Mar. 7, 1966

86–87	NYR	52	2	13	15	118	-1
87–88	Que	63	3	24	27	159	-8
88–89	Phil	78	11	32	43	149	-6
89–90	Phil	63	4	18	22	169	-8
90–91	Phil	79	7	25	32	204	-15
91–92	Phil	73	4	12	16	195	-14
92–93	Phil	83	3	16	19	150	+18
93–94	Det	68	1	6	7	130	+13
94–95	Det	20	1	2	3	21	+7
95–96	Fla	73	3	10	13	80	+10
96–97	Fla	70	0	14	14	96	-4
97–98	Fla	74	1	7	8	63	+6
98–99	Fla	62	2	9	11	54	0
Totals		858	42	188	230	1588	-2

Playoffs

86–87	NYR	1	0	0	0	0	
88–89	Phil	19	1	5	6	28	
93–94	Det	7	0	0	0	4	
95–96	Fla	22	0	4	4	10	
96–97	Fla	5	0	0	0	6	
Totals		54	1	9	10	48	

CARLETON, Kenneth Wayne *6–2 215 LW*
B. Sudbury, Ont., Aug. 4, 1946

65–66	Tor	2	0	1	1	0	
66–67	Tor	5	1	0	1	4	
67–68	Tor	65	8	11	19	34	+5
68–69	Tor	12	1	3	4	6	-8
69–70	Tor–Bos	49	6	20	26	29	+7
70–71	Bos	69	22	24	46	44	+35
71–72	Cal	76	17	14	31	45	-23
72–73	Ott (WHA)	75	42	49	91	42	
73–74	Tor (WHA)	78	37	55	92	31	
74–75	NE (WHA)	73	35	39	74	50	

75–76	NE–Edm (WHA)	61	17	37	54	12	
76–77	Birm (WHA)	3	1	0	1	0	
NHL Totals		278	55	73	128	172	+16
WHA Totals		290	132	180	312	135	

Playoffs

69–70	Bos	14	2	4	6	14	
70–71	Bos	4	0	0	0	0	
72–73	Ott (WHA)	3	3	3	6	4	
73–74	Tor (WHA)	12	2	12	14	4	
74–75	NE (WHA)	6	2	5	7	14	
75–76	Edm (WHA)	4	1	1	2	2	
NHL Totals		18	2	4	6	14	
WHA Totals		25	8	21	29	24	

CARLIN, Brian John *5–10 175 LW*
B. Calgary, Alta., June 13, 1950

71–72	LA	5	1	0	1	0	0
72–73	Alb (WHA)	65	12	22	34	6	
73–74	Edm (WHA)	5	1	0	1	0	
NHL Totals		5	1	0	1	0	0
WHA Totals		70	13	22	35	6	

CARLSON, Jack Anthony *6–3 205 LW*
B. Virginia, Minn., Aug. 23, 1954

74–75	Minn (WHA)	32	5	5	10	85	
75–76	Minn–Edm (WHA)	68	9	11	20	220	
76–77	Minn–Edm (WHA)	71	11	8	19	136	
77–78	NE (WHA)	34	2	7	9	61	
78–79	NE (WHA)	67	9	20	29	192	
78–79	Minn	16	3	0	3	40	+2
80–81	Minn	43	7	2	9	108	-5
81–82	Minn	57	8	4	12	103	-5
82–83	StL	54	6	1	7	58	-3
83–84	StL	58	6	8	14	95	+9
86–87	Minn	8	0	0	0	13	0
NHL Totals		236	30	15	45	417	-2
WHA Totals		272	36	51	87	694	

Playoffs

74–75	Minn (WHA)	10	1	2	3	41	
75–76	Edm (WHA)	4	0	0	0	4	
76–77	NE (WHA)	5	1	1	2	9	
77–78	NE (WHA)	9	1	1	2	14	
80–81	Minn	15	1	2	3	50	
81–82	StL	0	0	0	0	15	
82–83	StL	4	0	0	0	5	
NHL Totals		20	1	2	3	70	
WHA Totals		28	3	4	7	68	

CARLSON, Kent *6–3 200 D*
B. Concord, N.H., Jan. 11, 1962

83–84	Mont	65	3	7	10	73	-15
84–85	Mont	18	1	1	2	33	+1
85–86	Mont–StL	28	2	3	5	42	+2
88–89	Wash	2	1	0	1	0	+2
Totals		113	7	11	18	148	-10

Playoffs

85–86	StL	5	0	0	0	11	
87–88	StL	3	0	0	0	2	
Totals		8	0	0	0	13	

CARLSON, Steven Edward *6–3 180 C*
B. Virginia, Minn., Aug. 26, 1955

75–76	Minn (WHA)	10	0	1	1	23	
76–77	Minn–NE (WHA)	52	9	17	26	48	
77–78	NE (WHA)	38	6	7	13	11	
78–79	Edm (WHA)	73	18	22	40	50	
79–80	LA	52	9	12	21	23	-7
NHL Totals		52	9	12	21	23	-7
WHA Totals		173	33	47	80	132	

Playoffs

76–77	NE (WHA)	5	0	0	0	9	
77–78	NE (WHA)	13	2	7	9	2	
78–79	Edm (WHA)	11	1	1	2	12	
79–80	LA	4	1	1	2	7	
NHL Totals		4	1	1	2	7	
WHA Totals		29	3	8	11	23	

CARLSSON, Anders *5–11 185 C*
B. Gavie, Sweden, Nov. 25, 1960

| 86–87 | NJ | 48 | 2 | 18 | 20 | 14 | -11 |

SSN	TEAM	GP	G	A	PTS.	PIM	+/-
87–88	NJ	9	1	0	1	0	-5
88–89	NJ	47	4	8	12	20	+3
Totals		104	7	26	33	34	-13

Playoffs

		GP	G	A	PTS.	PIM
87–88	NJ	3	1	0	1	2

CARLYLE, Randy Robert 5–10 200 D
B. Sudbury, Ont., Apr. 19, 1956

SSN	TEAM	GP	G	A	PTS.	PIM	+/-
76–77	Tor	45	0	5	5	51	-19
77–78	Tor	49	2	11	13	31	+4
78–79	Pitt	70	13	34	47	78	+4
79–80	Pitt	67	8	28	36	45	-23
80–81	Pitt	76	16	67	83	136	-16
81–82	Pitt	73	11	64	75	131	-16
82–83	Pitt	61	15	41	56	110	-26
83–84	Pitt–Winn	55	3	26	29	84	-21
84–85	Winn	71	13	38	51	98	+23
85–86	Winn	68	16	33	49	93	-12
86–87	Winn	71	16	26	42	93	-6
87–88	Winn	78	15	44	59	210	-20
88–89	Winn	78	6	38	44	78	-19
89–90	Winn	53	3	15	18	50	+8
90–91	Winn	52	9	19	28	44	+6
91–92	Winn	66	1	9	10	54	+4
92–93	Winn	22	1	1	2	14	-6
Totals		1055	148	499	647	1400	-135

Playoffs

		GP	G	A	PTS.	PIM
76–77	Tor	9	0	1	1	20
77–78	Tor	7	0	1	1	8
78–79	Pitt	7	0	0	0	12
79–80	Pitt	5	1	0	1	4
80–81	Pitt	5	4	5	9	9
81–82	Pitt	5	1	3	4	16
83–84	Winn	3	0	2	2	4
84–85	Winn	8	1	5	6	13
86–87	Winn	10	1	5	6	18
87–88	Winn	5	0	2	2	10
91–92	Winn	5	1	0	1	6
Totals		69	9	24	33	120

CARNBACK, Patrik 6–0 187 C
B. Goteborg, Sweden, Feb. 1, 1968

SSN	TEAM	GP	G	A	PTS.	PIM	+/-
92–93	Mont	6	0	0	0	2	-4
93–94	Ana	73	12	11	23	54	-8
94–95	Ana	41	6	15	21	32	-8
95–96	Ana	34	6	12	18	34	+3
Totals		154	24	38	62	122	-17

CARNEY, Keith E. 6–1 199 D
B. Pawtucket, R.I., Feb. 3, 1970

SSN	TEAM	GP	G	A	PTS.	PIM	+/-
91–92	Buf	14	1	2	3	18	-3
92–93	Buf	30	2	4	6	55	+3
93–94	Buf–Chi	37	4	8	12	39	+14
94–95	Chi	18	1	0	1	11	-1
95–96	Chi	82	5	14	19	94	+31
96–97	Chi	81	3	15	18	62	+25
97–98	Chi–Phoe	80	3	19	22	91	-2
98–99	Phoe	82	2	14	16	62	+15
Totals		424	21	76	97	432	+82

Playoffs

		GP	G	A	PTS.	PIM
91–92	Buf	7	0	3	3	0
92–93	Buf	8	0	3	3	6
93–94	Chi	6	0	1	1	4
94–95	Chi	4	0	1	1	0
95–96	Chi	10	0	3	3	4
96–97	Chi	6	1	1	2	2
97–98	Phoe	6	0	0	0	4
98–99	Phoe	7	1	2	3	10
Totals		48	2	14	16	30

*CARON, Alain Luc (Boom Boom) 5–10 175 RW
B. Dolbeau, Que., Apr. 27, 1938

SSN	TEAM	GP	G	A	PTS.	PIM	+/-
67–68	Oak	58	9	13	22	18	-22
68–69	Mont	2	0	0	0	0	0
72–73	Que (WHA)	68	36	27	63	14
73–74	Que (WHA)	59	31	15	46	10
74–75	Que–Balt (WHA)	68	15	8	23	6
NHL Totals		60	9	13	22	18	-22
WHA Totals		195	82	50	132	30

*CARPENTER, Everard Lorne (Eddie) D
B. Hartford, Mich.

SSN	TEAM	GP	G	A	PTS.	PIM	+/-
19–20	Que	24	8	3	11	19
20–21	Ham	20	2	1	3	4
Totals		44	10	4	14	23

CARPENTER, Robert 6–0 200 C/LW
B. Beverly, Mass., July 13, 1963

SSN	TEAM	GP	G	A	PTS.	PIM	+/-
81–82	Wash	80	32	35	67	69	-23
82–83	Wash	80	32	37	69	64	0
83–84	Wash	80	28	40	68	51	0
84–85	Wash	80	53	42	95	87	+20
85–86	Wash	80	27	29	56	105	-12
86–87	Wash–NYR–LA	60	9	18	27	47	-27
87–88	LA	71	19	33	52	84	-21
88–89	LA–Bos	57	16	24	40	26	+7
89–90	Bos	80	25	31	56	97	-3
90–91	Bos	29	8	8	16	22	+2
91–92	Bos	60	25	23	48	46	-3
92–93	Wash	68	11	17	28	65	-16
93–94	NJ	76	10	23	33	51	+7
94–95	NJ	41	5	11	16	19	-1
95–96	NJ	52	5	5	10	14	-10
96–97	NJ	62	4	15	19	14	+6
97–98	NJ	66	9	18	27	22	-4
98–99	NJ	56	2	8	10	36	-3
Totals		1178	320	408	728	919	-81

Playoffs

		GP	G	A	PTS.	PIM
82–83	Wash	4	1	0	1	2
83–84	Wash	8	2	1	3	25
84–85	Wash	5	1	4	5	8
85–86	Wash	9	5	4	9	12
86–87	LA	5	1	2	3	2
87–88	LA	5	1	1	2	0
88–89	Bos	8	1	1	2	4
89–90	Bos	21	4	6	10	39
90–91	Bos	1	0	1	1	2
91–92	Bos	8	0	1	1	6
92–93	Wash	6	1	4	5	6
93–94	NJ	20	1	7	8	20
94–95	NJ	17	1	4	5	6
96–97	NJ	10	1	2	3	2
97–98	NJ	6	1	0	1	0
98–99	NJ	7	0	0	0	2
Totals		140	21	38	59	136

*CARR
19–20 | Que | 1 | 0 | 0 | 0 | 0

CARR, Alfred George Robert (Red) 5–8 178 LW
B. Winnipeg, Man.

		GP	G	A	PTS.	PIM
43–44	Tor	5	0	1	1	4

CARR, Eugene William (Gene) 5–11 185 C
B. Nanaimo, B.C., Sept. 17, 1951

SSN	TEAM	GP	G	A	PTS.	PIM	+/-
71–72	StL–NYR	74	11	10	21	34	+16
72–73	NYR	50	9	10	19	50	-4
73–74	NYR–LA	50	7	16	23	51	-6
74–75	LA	80	7	32	39	103	+19
75–76	LA	38	8	11	19	16	-1
76–77	LA	68	15	12	27	25	+5
77–78	LA–Pitt	75	19	37	56	80	-15
78–79	Atl	30	3	8	11	6	-4
Totals		465	79	136	215	365	+10

Playoffs

		GP	G	A	PTS.	PIM
71–72	NYR	16	1	3	4	21
72–73	NYR	1	0	1	1	0
73–74	LA	5	2	1	3	14
74–75	LA	3	1	2	3	29
76–77	LA	9	1	1	2	2
78–79	Atl	1	0	0	0	0
Totals		35	5	8	13	66

CARR, Lorne Bell 5–8 161 RW
B. Stoughton, Sask., July 2, 1910

SSN	TEAM	GP	G	A	PTS.	PIM
33–34	NYR	14	0	0	0	0
34–35	NYA	48	17	14	31	14
35–36	NYA	44	8	10	18	4
36–37	NYA	47	18	16	34	22
37–38	NYA	48	16	7	23	12
38–39	NYA	47	19	18	37	16
39–40	NYA	48	8	17	25	17
40–41	NYA	48	13	19	32	10
41–42	Tor	47	16	17	33	4
42–43	Tor	50	27	33	60	15
43–44	Tor	50	36	38	74	9
44–45	Tor	47	11	25	36	7
45–46	Tor	42	5	8	13	2
Totals		580	194	222	416	132

Playoffs

		GP	G	A	PTS.	PIM
35–36	NYA	5	1	1	2	0
37–38	NYA	6	3	1	4	2
38–39	NYA	2	0	0	0	0
39–40	NYA	3	0	0	0	0
41–42	Tor	13	3	2	5	6
42–43	Tor	6	1	2	3	0
43–44	Tor	5	0	1	1	0
44–45	Tor	13	2	2	4	5
Totals		53	10	9	19	13

CARRIERE, Larry 6–1 190 D
B. Montreal, Que., Jan. 30, 1952

SSN	TEAM	GP	G	A	PTS.	PIM	+/-
72–73	Buf	40	2	8	10	52	-1
73–74	Buf	77	6	24	30	103	+3
74–75	Buf	80	1	11	12	111	+12
75–76	Atl	75	4	15	19	96	+5
76–77	Atl–Van	74	3	12	15	71	-8
77–78	Van–LA–Buf	18	0	3	3	30	-1
79–80	Tor	2	0	1	1	0	-1
Totals		366	16	74	90	463	+9

Playoffs

		GP	G	A	PTS.	PIM
72–73	Buf	6	0	1	1	8
74–75	Buf	17	0	2	2	32
75–76	Atl	2	0	0	0	2
79–80	Tor	2	0	0	0	0
Totals		27	0	3	3	42

*CARRIGAN, Eugene (Gene) 6–1 200 C
B. Edmonton, Alta., July 5, 1907

SSN	TEAM	GP	G	A	PTS.	PIM
30–31	NYR	33	2	0	2	13
34–35	StL E	4	0	1	1	0
Totals		37	2	1	3	13

Playoffs

		GP	G	A	PTS.	PIM
33–34	Det	4	0	0	0	0

CARROLL, George D

		GP	G	A	PTS.	PIM
24–25	Mont M–Bos	15	0	0	0	9

CARROLL, Gregory John 6–0 185 C
B. Gimli, Man., Nov. 10, 1956

SSN	TEAM	GP	G	A	PTS.	PIM	+/-
76–77	Cin (WHA)	77	15	39	54	53
77–78	NE–Cin (WHA)	74	15	27	42	63
78–79	Wash–Det	60	7	15	22	20	-8
79–80	Hart	71	13	19	32	24	-5
NHL Totals		131	20	34	54	44	-13
WHA Totals		151	30	66	96	116

Playoffs

		GP	G	A	PTS.	PIM
76–77	Cin (WHA)	4	1	2	3	0

CARROLL, William Allan 5–10 190 C
B. Toronto, Ont., Jan. 19, 1959

SSN	TEAM	GP	G	A	PTS.	PIM	+/-
80–81	NYI	18	4	4	8	6	+3
81–82	NYI	72	9	20	29	32	+12
82–83	NYI	71	1	11	12	24	+3
83–84	NYI	39	5	2	7	12	-1
84–85	Edm	65	8	9	17	22	0
85–86	Edm–Det	26	2	6	8	11	-4
86–87	Det	31	1	2	3	6	-9
Totals		322	30	54	84	113	+4

Playoffs

		GP	G	A	PTS.	PIM
80–81	NYI	18	3	9	12	4
81–82	NYI	19	2	2	4	8
82–83	NYI	20	1	1	2	2
83–84	NYI	5	0	0	0	0
84–85	Edm	9	0	0	0	4
Totals		71	6	12	18	18

CARRUTHERS, Gordon (Dwight) 5–9 185 D
B. Lashburn, Sask., Nov. 7, 1944

SSN	TEAM	GP	G	A	PTS.	PIM	+/-
65–66	Det	1	0	0	0	0
67–68	Phil	1	0	0	0	0	0
Totals		2	0	0	0	0

CARSE, Robert Allison 5-9 170 LW
B. Edmonton, Alta., July 19, 1919

SSN	TEAM	GP	G	A	PTS.	PIM	+/-
39–40	Chi	22	3	5	8	11	
40–41	Chi	43	9	9	18	9	
41–42	Chi	33	7	16	23	10	
42–43	Chi	47	10	22	32	6	
47–48	Mont	22	3	3	6	16	
Totals		167	32	55	87	52	

Playoffs

39–40	Chi	2	0	0	0	0	
40–41	Chi	5	0	0	0	2	
41–42	Chi	3	0	2	2	0	
Totals		10	0	2	2	2	

CARSE, William Alexander 5-8 165 C
B. Edmonton, Alta., May 29, 1914

38–39	NYR	1	0	1	1	0	
39–40	Chi	48	10	13	23	10	
40–41	Chi	32	5	15	20	12	
41–42	Chi	43	13	14	27	16	
Totals		124	28	43	71	38	

Playoffs

38–39	NYR	6	1	1	2	0	
39–40	Chi	2	1	0	1	0	
40–41	Chi	5	0	0	0	0	
41–42	Chi	3	1	1	2	0	
Totals		16	3	2	5	0	

CARSON, Frank R. 5-7 165 RW
B. Parry Sound, Ont., Jan. 12, 1902

25–26	Mont M	16	2	1	3	6	
26–27	Mont M	44	2	3	5	12	
27–28	Mont M	21	0	1	1	10	
30–31	NYA	44	6	7	13	36	
31–32	Det	31	10	14	24	31	
32–33	Det	45	12	13	25	35	
33–34	Det	47	10	9	19	36	
Totals		248	42	48	90	166	

Playoffs

25–26	MontM	8	0	0	0	0	
26–27	MontM	2	0	0	0	2	
31–32	Det	2	0	0	0	2	
32–33	Det	4	0	1	1	0	
33–34	Det	7	0	1	1	5	
Totals		22	0	2	2	9	

CARSON, Gerald (Stub) 5-10 175 D
B. Parry Sound, Ont., Oct. 10, 1905

28–29	Mont–NYR	40	0	0	0	9	
29–30	Mont	35	1	0	1	8	
32–33	Mont	48	5	2	7	53	
33–34	Mont	48	5	1	6	51	
34–35	Mont	48	0	5	5	56	
36–37	Mont M	42	1	3	4	28	
Totals		261	12	11	23	205	

Playoffs

28–29	NYR	5	0	0	0	0	
29–30	Mont	6	0	0	0	0	
32–33	Mont	2	0	0	0	2	
33–34	Det	2	0	0	0	2	
34–35	Mont	2	0	0	0	4	
36–37	MontM	5	0	0	0	4	
Totals		22	0	0	0	12	

CARSON, Jimmy 6-1 200 C
B. Southfield, Mich., July 20, 1968

86–87	LA	80	37	42	79	22	-5
87–88	LA	80	55	52	107	45	-19
88–89	Edm	80	49	51	100	36	+3
89–90	Edm–Det	48	21	18	39	8	-8
90–91	Det	64	21	25	46	28	+3
91–92	Det	80	34	35	69	30	+17
92–93	Det–LA	86	37	36	73	32	-2
93–94	LA–Van	59	11	17	28	24	-15
94–95	Hart	38	9	10	19	29	+5
95–96	Hart	11	1	0	1	0	+1
Totals		626	275	286	561	254	-20

Playoffs

86–87	LA	5	1	2	3	6	
87–88	LA	5	5	3	8	4	
88–89	Edm	7	2	1	3	6	
90–91	Det	7	2	1	3	4	
91–92	Det	11	2	3	5	0	
92–93	LA	18	5	4	9	2	
93–94	Van	2	0	1	1	0	
Totals		55	17	15	32	22	

CARSON, Lindsay Warren 6-2 195 C
B. Oxbow, Sask., Nov. 21, 1960

81–82	Phil	18	0	1	1	32	-15
82–83	Phil	78	18	19	37	67	+20
83–84	Phil	16	1	3	4	10	-7
84–85	Phil	77	20	19	39	123	0
85–86	Phil	50	9	12	21	84	+10
86–87	Phil	71	11	15	26	141	-2
87–88	Phil–Hart	63	7	11	18	67	-4
Totals		373	66	80	146	524	+2

Playoffs

82–83	Phil	1	0	0	0	0	

*CARSON, William Joseph F
B. Bracebridge, Ont., Nov. 25, 1900

26–27	Tor	40	16	6	22	41
27–28	Tor	32	20	6	26	36
28–29	Tor–Bos	43	11	8	19	55
29–30	Bos	44	7	4	11	24
Totals		159	54	24	78	156

Playoffs

28–29	Bos	5	2	0	2	8
29–30	Bos	6	1	0	1	6
Totals		11	3	0	3	14

CARTER, Anson 6-1 175 C
B. Toronto, Ont., June 6, 1974

96–97	Wash–Bos	38	11	7	18	9	-7
97–98	Bos	78	16	27	43	31	+7
98–99	Bos	55	24	16	40	22	+7
Totals		171	51	50	101	62	+7

Playoffs

97–98	Bos	6	1	1	2	0
98–99	Bos	12	4	3	7	0
Totals		13	5	4	9	0

CARTER, John 5-10 175 LW
B. Winchester, Mass., May 3, 1963

85–86	Bos	3	0	0	0	0	0
86–87	Bos	8	0	1	1	0	+3
87–88	Bos	4	0	1	1	2	+3
88–89	Bos	44	12	10	22	24	-1
89–90	Bos	76	17	22	39	26	+17
90–91	Bos	50	4	7	11	68	-13
91–92	SJ	4	0	0	0	0	-2
92–93	SJ	55	7	9	16	81	-25
Totals		244	40	50	90	201	-18

Playoffs

88–89	Bos	10	1	2	3	6
89–90	Bos	21	6	3	9	45
Totals		31	7	5	12	51

CARTER, Lyle Dwight 6-1 185 F
B. Truro, N.S., Apr. 29, 1945

71–72	Cal	15	0	0	0	2	0

CARTER, Ronald 6-1 205 RW
B. Montreal, Que., Mar. 14, 1958

79–80	Edm	2	0	0	0	0	0

CARTER, William 5-11 155 C
B. Cornwall, Ont., Dec. 2, 1937

57–58	Mont	1	0	0	0	0
60–61	Bos	8	0	0	0	2
61–62	Mont	7	0	0	0	4
Totals		16	0	0	0	6

*CARVETH, Joseph Gordon 5-10 180 RW
B. Regina, Sask., Mar. 21, 1918

40–41	Det	19	2	1	3	2
41–42	Det	29	6	11	17	2
42–43	Det	43	18	18	36	6
43–44	Det	46	21	35	56	6
44–45	Det	50	26	28	54	10
45–46	Det	48	17	18	35	18
46–47	Bos	51	21	15	36	10
47–48	Bos–Mont	57	9	19	28	8
48–49	Mont	60	15	22	37	8
49–50	Mont–Det	71	14	18	32	15
50–51	Det	30	1	4	5	0
Totals		504	150	189	339	85

Playoffs

41–42	Det	9	4	0	4	0
42–43	Det	10	6	2	8	4
43–44	Det	5	2	1	3	8
44–45	Det	14	5	6	11	2
45–46	Det	5	0	1	1	0
46–47	Bos	5	2	1	3	0
48–49	Mont	7	0	1	1	8
49–50	Det	14	2	4	6	6
Totals		69	21	16	37	28

CASHMAN, Wayne John 6-1 208 LW
B. Kingston, Ont., June 24, 1945

64–65	Bos	1	0	0	0	0	
67–68	Bos	12	0	4	4	2	-6
68–69	Bos	51	8	23	31	49	+19
69–70	Bos	70	9	26	35	79	+22
70–71	Bos	77	21	58	79	100	+59
71–72	Bos	74	23	29	52	103	+42
72–73	Bos	76	29	39	68	100	+5
73–74	Bos	78	30	59	89	111	+49
74–75	Bos	42	11	22	33	24	+7
75–76	Bos	80	28	43	71	87	+30
76–77	Bos	65	15	37	52	76	+4
77–78	Bos	76	24	38	62	69	+34
78–79	Bos	75	27	40	67	63	+16
79–80	Bos	44	11	21	32	19	-3
80–81	Bos	77	25	35	60	80	+17
81–82	Bos	64	12	31	43	59	-17
82–83	Bos	65	4	11	15	20	+2
Totals		1027	277	516	793	1041	+288

Playoffs

67–68	Bos	1	0	0	0	0
68–69	Bos	6	0	1	1	0
69–70	Bos	14	5	4	9	50
70–71	Bos	7	3	2	5	15
71–72	Bos	15	4	7	11	42
72–73	Bos	5	1	1	2	4
73–74	Bos	16	5	9	14	46
74–75	Bos	1	0	2	2	0
75–76	Bos	11	1	5	6	16
76–77	Bos	14	1	8	9	18
77–78	Bos	15	4	6	10	13
78–79	Bos	10	4	5	9	8
79–80	Bos	10	3	3	6	32
80–81	Bos	3	0	1	1	0
81–82	Bos	9	0	2	2	6
82–83	Bos	8	0	1	1	0
Totals		145	31	57	88	250

CASSELMAN, Mike 5-11 190 C
B. Morrisburg, Ont., Aug. 23, 1968

95–96	Fla	3	0	0	0	0	-1

CASSELS, Andrew 6-0 192 C
B. Bramalea, Ont., July 23, 1969

89–90	Mont	6	2	0	2	2	+1
90–91	Mont	54	6	19	25	20	+2
91–92	Hart	67	11	30	41	18	+3
92–93	Hart	84	21	64	85	62	-11
93–94	Hart	79	16	42	58	37	-21
94–95	Hart	46	7	30	37	18	-3
95–96	Hart	81	20	43	63	39	+8
96–97	Hart	81	22	44	66	46	-16
97–98	Calg	81	17	24	44	32	-7
98–99	Calg	70	12	25	37	18	-12
Totals		649	134	324	458	292	-56

Playoffs

90–91	Mont	8	0	2	2	2
91–92	Hart	7	2	4	6	6
Totals		15	2	6	8	8

CASSIDY, Bruce 5-11 175 D
B. Ottawa, Ont., May 20, 1965

83–84	Chi	1	0	0	0	0	0
85–86	Chi	1	0	0	0	0	0
86–87	Chi	2	0	0	0	0	-1
87–88	Chi	21	3	10	13	6	-3
88–89	Chi	9	0	2	2	4	-5
89–90	Chi	2	1	1	2	0	-1

SSN	TEAM	GP	G	A	PTS.	PIM	+/-
Totals		36	4	13	17	10	-10

Playoffs

SSN	TEAM	GP	G	A	PTS.	PIM	+/-
89–90	Chi	1	0	0	0	0	

CASSIDY, Thomas E. J. *5–11 180 C*
B. Blind River, Ont., Mar. 15, 1952

SSN	TEAM	GP	G	A	PTS.	PIM	+/-
77–78	Pitt	26	3	4	7	15	-4

CASSOLATO, Anthony Gerald *5–11 183 RW*
B. Guelph, Ont., May 7, 1956

SSN	TEAM	GP	G	A	PTS.	PIM	+/-
76–77	SD (WHA)	43	13	12	25	26	
77–78	Birm (WHA)	77	18	25	43	59	
78–79	Birm (WHA)	64	13	7	20	62	
79–80	Wash	9	0	2	2	0	+2
80–81	Wash	2	0	0	0	0	0
81–82	Wash	12	1	4	5	4	+1
NHL Totals		23	1	6	7	4	+3
WHA Totals		184	44	44	88	147	

Playoffs

SSN	TEAM	GP	G	A	PTS.	PIM	+/-
76–77	SD (WHA)	3	0	0	0	4	
77–78	Birm (WHA)	4	0	0	0	4	
WHA Totals		7	0	0	0	8	

CAUFIELD, Jay *6–4 230 RW*
B. Philadelphia, Pa., July 17, 1960

SSN	TEAM	GP	G	A	PTS.	PIM	+/-
86–87	NYR	13	2	1	3	45	-2
87–88	Minn	1	0	0	0	0	0
88–89	Pitt	58	1	4	5	285	-4
89–90	Pitt	37	1	2	3	123	0
90–91	Pitt	23	1	1	2	71	-2
91–92	Pitt	50	0	0	0	175	-6
92–93	Pitt	26	0	0	0	60	-1
Totals		208	5	8	13	759	-15

Playoffs

SSN	TEAM	GP	G	A	PTS.	PIM	+/-
86–87	NYR	3	0	0	0	12	
88–89	Pitt	9	0	0	0	28	
91–92	Pitt	5	0	0	0	2	
Totals		17	0	0	0	42	

CAVALLINI, Gino John *6–1 215 LW*
B. Toronto, Ont., Nov. 24, 1962

SSN	TEAM	GP	G	A	PTS.	PIM	+/-
84–85	Calg	27	6	10	16	14	+11
85–86	Calg-StL	57	13	12	25	62	-9
86–87	StL	80	18	26	44	54	+4
87–88	StL	64	15	17	32	62	-4
88–89	StL	74	20	23	43	79	+2
89–90	StL	80	15	15	30	77	-8
90–91	StL	78	8	27	35	81	+4
91–92	StL-Que	66	10	14	24	44	-9
92–93	Que	67	9	15	24	34	+10
Totals		593	114	159	273	507	-5

Playoffs

SSN	TEAM	GP	G	A	PTS.	PIM	+/-
84–85	Calg	3	0	0	0	4	
85–86	StL	17	4	5	9	10	
86–87	StL	6	3	1	4	2	
87–88	StL	10	5	5	10	19	
88–89	StL	9	0	2	2	17	
89–90	StL	12	1	3	4	12	
90–91	StL	13	1	3	4	2	
92–93	Que	4	0	0	0	0	
Totals		74	14	19	33	66	

CAVALLINI, Paul *6–1 210 D*
B. Toronto, Ont., Oct. 13, 1965

SSN	TEAM	GP	G	A	PTS.	PIM	+/-
86–87	Wash	6	0	2	2	8	-4
87–88	Wash-StL	72	6	10	16	152	+7
88–89	StL	65	4	20	24	128	+25
89–90	StL	80	8	39	47	106	+38
90–91	StL	67	10	25	35	89	+19
91–92	StL	66	10	25	35	95	+7
92–93	StL-Wash	82	6	12	18	56	+6
93–94	Dal	74	11	33	44	82	+13
94–95	Dal	44	1	11	12	28	+8
95–96	Dal	8	0	0	0	6	-3
Totals		564	56	177	233	750	+116

Playoffs

SSN	TEAM	GP	G	A	PTS.	PIM	+/-
87–88	StL	10	1	6	7	26	
88–89	StL	10	2	2	4	14	
89–90	StL	12	2	3	5	20	
90–91	StL	13	2	3	5	20	
91–92	StL	4	0	1	1	6	
92–93	Wash	6	0	2	2	18	
93–94	Dal	9	1	8	9	4	
94–95	Dal	5	0	2	2	6	
Totals		69	8	27	35	114	

CERESINO, Raymond *5–8 160 RW*
B. Port Arthur, Ont., Apr. 24, 1929

SSN	TEAM	GP	G	A	PTS.	PIM	+/-
48–49	Tor	12	1	1	2	2	

CERNIK, Frantisek *5–10 189 LW/RW*
B. Novy Jicin, Czechoslovakia, June 3, 1953

SSN	TEAM	GP	G	A	PTS.	PIM	+/-
84–85	Det	49	5	4	9	13	-7

CHABOT, John David *6–2 200 C*
B. Summerside, P.E.I., May 18, 1962

SSN	TEAM	GP	G	A	PTS.	PIM	+/-
83–84	Mont	56	18	25	43	13	-2
84–85	Mont-Pitt	77	9	51	60	14	-34
85–86	Pitt	77	14	31	45	6	-1
86–87	Pitt	72	14	22	36	8	-7
87–88	Det	78	13	44	57	10	+12
88–89	Det	52	2	10	12	6	-18
89–90	Det	69	9	40	49	24	+5
90–91	Det	27	5	5	10	4	+6
Totals		508	84	228	312	85	-39

Playoffs

SSN	TEAM	GP	G	A	PTS.	PIM	+/-
83–84	Mont	11	1	4	5	0	
87–88	Det	16	4	15	19	2	
88–89	Det	6	1	1	2	0	
Totals		33	6	20	26	2	

CHAD, John *5–10 167 RW*
B. Provost, Alta., Sept. 16, 1919

SSN	TEAM	GP	G	A	PTS.	PIM	+/-
39–40	Chi	22	8	3	11	11	
40–41	Chi	45	7	18	25	16	
45–46	Chi	13	0	1	1	2	
Totals		80	15	22	37	29	

Playoffs

SSN	TEAM	GP	G	A	PTS.	PIM	+/-
39–40	Chi	2	0	0	0	0	
40–41	Chi	5	0	0	0	2	
45–46	Chi	3	0	1	1	0	
Totals		10	0	1	1	2	

CHALMERS, William (Chick) *6–0 180 C*
B. Stratford, Ont., Jan. 24, 1934

SSN	TEAM	GP	G	A	PTS.	PIM	+/-
53–54	NYR	1	0	0	0	0	

CHALUPA, Milan *5–10 183 D*
B. Oudolen, Czechoslovakia, July 4, 1953

SSN	TEAM	GP	G	A	PTS.	PIM	+/-
84–85	Det	14	0	5	5	6	+4

*CHAMBERLAIN, Erwin Groves (Murph) *5–11 172 C*
B. Shawville, Que., Feb. 14, 1915

SSN	TEAM	GP	G	A	PTS.	PIM	+/-
37–38	Tor	43	4	12	16	51	
38–39	Tor	48	10	16	26	32	
39–40	Tor	40	5	17	22	63	
40–41	Mont	45	10	15	25	75	
41–42	Mont–NYA	37	12	12	24	46	
42–43	Bos	45	9	24	33	67	
43–44	Mont	47	15	32	47	85	
44–45	Mont	32	2	12	14	38	
45–46	Mont	40	12	14	26	42	
46–47	Mont	49	10	10	20	97	
47–48	Mont	30	6	3	9	62	
48–49	Mont	54	5	8	13	111	
Totals		510	100	175	275	769	

Playoffs

SSN	TEAM	GP	G	A	PTS.	PIM	+/-
37–38	Tor	5	0	0	0	2	
38–39	Tor	10	2	5	7	4	
39–40	Tor	3	0	0	0	0	
40–41	Mont	3	0	2	2	11	
42–43	Bos	6	1	1	2	12	
43–44	Mont	9	5	3	8	12	
44–45	Mont	6	1	1	2	10	
45–46	Mont	9	4	2	6	18	
46–47	Mont	11	1	3	4	19	
48–49	Mont	4	0	0	0	8	
Totals		66	14	17	31	96	

CHAMBERS, Shawn *6–2 200 D*
B. Sterling Heights, Mich., Oct. 11, 1966

SSN	TEAM	GP	G	A	PTS.	PIM	+/-
87–88	Minn	19	1	7	8	21	-6
88–89	Minn	72	5	19	24	80	-4
89–90	Minn	78	8	18	26	81	-2
90–91	Minn	29	1	3	4	24	+2
91–92	Wash	2	0	0	0	2	-3
92–93	TB	55	10	29	39	36	-21
93–94	TB	66	11	23	34	23	-6
94–95	TB-NJ	45	4	17	21	12	+2
95–96	NJ	64	2	21	23	18	+1
96–97	NJ	73	4	17	21	19	+17
97–98	Dal	57	2	22	24	26	+11
98–99	Dal	61	2	9	11	18	+6
Totals		621	52	185	237	360	-3

Playoffs

SSN	TEAM	GP	G	A	PTS.	PIM	+/-
88–89	Minn	3	0	2	2	0	
89–90	Minn	7	2	1	3	10	
90–91	Minn	23	0	7	7	16	
94–95	NJ	20	4	5	9	2	
96–97	NJ	10	1	6	7	6	
97–98	Dal	14	0	3	3	20	
98–99	Dal	17	0	2	2	18	
Totals		94	7	26	33	72	

CHAMPAGNE, Andre Joseph Orius *6–0 190 LW*
B. Eastview, Ont., Sept. 19, 1943

SSN	TEAM	GP	G	A	PTS.	PIM	+/-
62–63	Tor	2	0	0	0	0	

CHAPDELAINE, Rene *6–1 195 D*
B. Weyburn, Sask., Sept. 27, 1966

SSN	TEAM	GP	G	A	PTS.	PIM	+/-
90–91	LA	3	0	1	1	10	+1
91–92	LA	16	0	1	1	10	0
92–93	LA	13	0	0	0	12	-6
Totals		32	0	2	2	32	-5

*CHAPMAN, Arthur V. *5–10 170 C*
B. Winnipeg, Man., May 29, 1906

SSN	TEAM	GP	G	A	PTS.	PIM	+/-
30–31	Bos	44	7	7	14	22	
31–32	Bos	48	11	14	25	18	
32–33	Bos	46	3	6	9	19	
33–34	Bos–NYA	46	5	10	15	15	
34–35	NYA	47	9	34	43	4	
35–36	NYA	48	10	28	38	14	
36–37	NYA	43	8	23	31	36	
37–38	NYA	45	2	27	29	8	
38–39	NYA	45	3	19	22	2	
39–40	NYA	26	4	6	10	2	
Totals		438	62	174	236	140	

Playoffs

SSN	TEAM	GP	G	A	PTS.	PIM	+/-
30–31	Bos	5	0	1	1	7	
32–33	Bos	5	0	0	0	2	
35–36	NYA	5	0	3	3	0	
37–38	NYA	6	0	1	1	0	
38–39	NYA	2	0	0	0	0	
39–40	NYA	2	1	0	1	0	
Totals		25	1	5	6	9	

CHAPMAN, Blair Douglas *6–1 190 RW*
B. Lloydminster, Sask., June 13, 1956

SSN	TEAM	GP	G	A	PTS.	PIM	+/-
76–77	Pitt	80	14	23	37	16	-12
77–78	Pitt	75	24	20	44	37	-11
78–79	Pitt	71	10	8	18	18	-12
79–80	Pitt-StL	64	25	26	51	28	-5
80–81	StL	55	20	26	46	41	+3
81–82	StL	18	6	11	17	8	+1
82–83	StL	39	7	11	18	10	-8
Totals		402	106	125	231	158	-44

Playoffs

SSN	TEAM	GP	G	A	PTS.	PIM	+/-
76–77	Pitt	3	1	1	2	7	
78–79	Pitt	7	1	0	1	2	
79–80	StL	3	0	0	0	0	
80–81	StL	9	2	5	7	6	
81–82	StL	3	0	0	0	0	
Totals		25	4	6	10	15	

CHAPMAN, Brian *6–0 195 D*
B. Brockville, Ont., Feb. 10, 1968

SSN	TEAM	GP	G	A	PTS.	PIM	+/-
90–91	Hart	3	0	0	0	29	0

CHARA, Zdeno *6–9 240 D*
B. Trencin, Slovakia, Mar. 18, 1977

SSN	TEAM	GP	G	A	PTS.	PIM	+/-
97–98	NYI	25	0	1	1	50	1
98–99	NYI	59	2	6	8	83	-8
Totals		84	2	7	9	133	-7

CHARBONNEAU, Jose (Joe) 6-0 195 RW
B. Ferme-Neuve, Que., Nov. 21, 1966

SSN	TEAM	GP	G	A	PTS.	PIM	+/-
87-88	Mont	16	0	2	2	6	+1
88-89	Mont-Van	22	1	4	5	12	-4
93-94	Van	30	7	7	14	49	-3
94-95	Van	3	1	0	1	0	0
Totals		71	9	13	22	67	-6

Playoffs

SSN	TEAM	GP	G	A	PTS.	PIM
87-88	Mont	8	0	0	0	4
93-94	Van	3	1	0	1	4
Totals		11	1	0	1	8

CHARBONNEAU, Stephane 6-0 195 RW
B. Ste-Adele, Que., June 27, 1970

SSN	TEAM	GP	G	A	PTS.	PIM	+/-
91-92	Que	2	0	0	0	0	-2

CHARLEBOIS, Robert Richard (Chuck) 6-0 175 LW
B. Cornwall, Ont., May 27, 1944

SSN	TEAM	GP	G	A	PTS.	PIM	+/-
67-68	Minn	7	1	0	1	0	-3
72-73	Ott (WHA)	78	24	40	64	28	
73-74	NE (WHA)	74	4	7	11	6	
74-75	NE (WHA)	8	1	0	1	0	
75-76	NE (WHA)	28	3	3	6	0	
NHL Totals		7	1	0	1	0	-3
WHA Totals		188	32	50	82	34	

Playoffs

SSN	TEAM	GP	G	A	PTS.	PIM
72-73	Ott (WHA)	5	1	1	2	4
73-74	NE (WHA)	7	0	0	0	4
74-75	NE (WHA)	4	1	0	1	0
WHA Totals		16	2	1	3	8

CHARLESWORTH, Todd 6-1 190 D
B. Calgary, Alta., Mar. 22, 1965

SSN	TEAM	GP	G	A	PTS.	PIM	+/-
83-84	Pitt	10	0	0	0	8	-7
84-85	Pitt	67	1	8	9	31	-23
85-86	Pitt	2	0	1	1	0	-1
86-87	Pitt	1	0	0	0	0	0
87-88	Pitt	6	2	0	2	2	0
89-90	NYR	7	0	0	0	6	-3
Totals		93	3	9	12	47	-34

CHARRON, Eric 6-3 192 D
B. Verdun, Que., Jan. 14, 1970

SSN	TEAM	GP	G	A	PTS.	PIM	+/-
92-93	Mont	3	0	0	0	2	0
93-94	TB	4	0	0	0	2	0
94-95	TB	45	1	4	5	26	+1
95-96	TB-Wash	18	0	1	1	22	-3
96-97	Wash	25	1	1	2	20	+1
97-98	Calg	2	0	0	0	4	0
98-99	Calg	12	0	1	1	14	-6
Totals		109	2	7	9	86	-7

Playoffs

SSN	TEAM	GP	G	A	PTS.	PIM
95-96	Wash	6	0	0	0	8

CHARRON, Guy Joseph Jean 5-10 180 C
B. Verdun, Que., Jan. 24, 1949

SSN	TEAM	GP	G	A	PTS.	PIM	+/-
69-70	Mont	5	0	0	0	0	-2
70-71	Mont-Det	39	10	6	16	8	-2
71-72	Det	64	9	16	25	12	-8
72-73	Det	75	18	18	36	23	+9
73-74	Det	76	25	30	55	10	-31
74-75	Det-KC	77	14	39	53	27	-50
75-76	KC	78	27	44	71	12	-51
76-77	Wash	80	36	46	82	10	-28
77-78	Wash	80	38	35	73	12	-25
78-79	Wash	80	28	42	70	24	-14
79-80	Wash	33	11	20	31	6	-2
80-81	Wash	47	5	13	18	2	-4
Totals		734	221	309	530	146	-208

CHARTIER, David 5-9 170 C
B. St. Lazare, Man., Feb. 15, 1961

SSN	TEAM	GP	G	A	PTS.	PIM	+/-
80-81	Winn	1	0	0	0	0	0

CHARTRAW, Raymond Richard (Rick) 6-2 210 D
B. Caracas, Venezuela, July 13, 1954

SSN	TEAM	GP	G	A	PTS.	PIM	+/-
74-75	Mont	12	0	0	0	6	-4
75-76	Mont	16	1	3	4	25	+12
76-77	Mont	43	3	4	7	59	+27
77-78	Mont	68	4	12	16	64	+16
78-79	Mont	62	5	11	16	29	+14
79-80	Mont	66	5	7	12	35	+6
80-81	Mont-LA	35	1	6	7	32	-4
81-82	LA	33	2	8	10	56	-11
82-83	LA-NYR	57	5	7	12	68	-12
83-84	NYR-Edm	28	2	6	8	25	+2
Totals		420	28	64	92	399	+46

Playoffs

SSN	TEAM	GP	G	A	PTS.	PIM
75-76	Mont	2	0	0	0	0
76-77	Mont	13	2	1	3	17
77-78	Mont	10	1	1	2	10
78-79	Mont	16	2	1	3	24
79-80	Mont	10	2	2	4	0
80-81	LA	4	0	1	1	4
81-82	LA	10	0	2	2	17
82-83	NYR	9	0	2	2	6
Totals		75	7	9	16	80

CHASE, Kelly Wayne 5-11 192 RW
B. Porcupine Plain, Sask., Oct. 25, 1967

SSN	TEAM	GP	G	A	PTS.	PIM	+/-
89-90	StL	43	1	3	4	244	-1
90-91	StL	2	1	0	1	15	+1
91-92	StL	46	1	2	3	264	-6
92-93	StL	49	2	5	7	204	-9
93-94	StL	68	2	5	7	278	-5
94-95	Hart	28	0	4	4	141	+1
95-96	Hart	55	2	4	6	220	-4
96-97	Hart-Tor	30	1	2	3	149	+2
97-98	StL	67	4	3	7	231	+10
98-99	StL	45	3	7	10	143	+2
Totals		433	17	35	52	1889	-9

Playoffs

SSN	TEAM	GP	G	A	PTS.	PIM
89-90	StL	9	1	0	1	46
90-91	StL	6	0	0	0	18
91-92	StL	1	0	0	0	7
93-94	StL	4	0	1	1	6
97-98	StL	7	0	0	0	23
Totals		27	1	1	2	100

CHASSE, Denis 6-2 200 RW
B. Montreal, Que., Feb. 7, 1970

SSN	TEAM	GP	G	A	PTS.	PIM	+/-
93-94	StL	3	0	1	1	15	+1
94-95	StL	47	7	9	16	133	+12
95-96	StL-Wash-Winn	60	3	0	3	125	-14
96-97	Ott	22	1	4	5	19	+3
Totals		132	11	14	25	292	+2

Playoffs

SSN	TEAM	GP	G	A	PTS.	PIM
94-95	StL	7	1	7	8	23

CHEBATURKIN, Vladimir 6-2 213 D
B. Tyumen, Russia, Apr. 23, 1975

SSN	TEAM	GP	G	A	PTS.	PIM	+/-
97-98	NYI	2	0	2	2	0	-1
98-99	NYI	8	0	0	0	12	+6
Totals		10	0	2	2	12	+5

CHECK, Ludic (Lude) 154 F
B. Brandon, Man., May 22, 1919

SSN	TEAM	GP	G	A	PTS.	PIM
43-44	Det	1	0	0	0	0
44-45	Chi	26	6	2	8	4
Totals		27	6	2	8	4

CHELIOS, Chris 6-1 186 D
B. Chicago, Ill., Jan. 25, 1962

SSN	TEAM	GP	G	A	PTS.	PIM	+/-
83-84	Mont	12	0	2	2	12	-5
84-85	Mont	74	9	55	64	87	+11
85-86	Mont	41	8	26	34	67	+4
86-87	Mont	71	11	33	44	124	-5
87-88	Mont	71	20	41	61	172	+14
88-89	Mont	80	15	58	73	185	+35
89-90	Mont	53	9	22	31	136	+20
90-91	Chi	77	12	52	64	192	+23
91-92	Chi	80	9	47	56	245	+24
92-93	Chi	84	15	58	73	282	+14
93-94	Chi	76	16	44	60	212	+12
94-95	Chi	48	5	33	38	72	+17
95-96	Chi	81	14	58	72	140	+25
96-97	Chi	72	10	38	48	112	+16
97-98	Chi	81	3	39	42	151	-7
98-99	Chi-Det	75	9	27	36	93	+1
Totals		1076	165	633	798	2282	+199

Playoffs

SSN	TEAM	GP	G	A	PTS.	PIM
83-84	Mont	15	1	9	10	17
84-85	Mont	9	2	8	10	17
85-86	Mont	20	2	9	11	49
86-87	Mont	17	4	9	13	38
87-88	Mont	11	3	1	4	29
88-89	Mont	21	4	15	19	28
89-90	Mont	5	0	1	1	8
90-91	Chi	6	1	7	8	46
91-92	Chi	18	6	15	21	37
92-93	Chi	4	0	2	2	14
93-94	Chi	6	1	1	2	8
94-95	Chi	16	4	7	11	12
95-96	Chi	9	0	3	3	8
96-97	Chi	6	0	1	1	8
98-99	Det	10	0	4	4	14
Totals		173	28	92	120	333

CHERNOFF, Michael Terence 5-9 175 LW
B. Yorkton, Sask., May 13, 1946

SSN	TEAM	GP	G	A	PTS.	PIM	+/-
68-69	Minn	1	0	0	0	0	0
73-74	Van (WHA)	36	11	10	21	4	
74-75	Van (WHA)	3	0	0	0	0	
NHL Totals		1	0	0	0	0	0
WHA Totals		39	11	10	21	4	

CHERNOMAZ, Richard 5-8 185 RW
B. Selkirk, Man., Sept. 1, 1963

SSN	TEAM	GP	G	A	PTS.	PIM	+/-
81-82	Col	2	0	0	0	0	-2
83-84	NJ	7	2	1	3	2	-3
84-85	NJ	3	0	2	2	2	+2
86-87	NJ	25	6	4	10	8	-11
87-88	Calg	2	1	0	1	0	+1
88-89	Calg	1	0	0	0	0	-1
91-92	Calg	11	0	0	0	6	-9
Totals		51	9	7	16	18	-23

CHERRY, Donald Stewart (Grapes) 5-11 180 D
B. Kingston, Ont., Feb. 5, 1934

SSN	TEAM	GP	G	A	PTS.	PIM
54-55	Bos	1	0	0	0	0

CHERRY, Richard John (Dick) 6-0 200 D
B. Kingston, Ont., Mar. 18, 1937

SSN	TEAM	GP	G	A	PTS.	PIM	+/-
56-57	Bos	6	0	0	0	4	
68-69	Phil	71	9	6	15	18	-11
69-70	Phil	68	3	4	7	23	-24
Totals		145	12	10	22	45	-35

Playoffs

SSN	TEAM	GP	G	A	PTS.	PIM
68-69	Phil	4	1	0	1	4

CHERVYAKOV, Denis 6-0 185 D
B. Leningrad, USSR, Apr. 20, 1970

SSN	TEAM	GP	G	A	PTS.	PIM	+/-
92-93	Bos	2	0	0	0	2	-1

*CHEVREFILS, Real 5-10 175 LW
B. Timmins, Ont., May 2, 1932

SSN	TEAM	GP	G	A	PTS.	PIM
51-52	Bos	33	8	17	25	8
52-53	Bos	69	19	14	33	44
53-54	Bos	14	4	1	5	2
54-55	Bos	64	18	22	40	30
55-56	Det-Bos	63	14	12	26	34
56-57	Bos	70	31	17	48	38
57-58	Bos	44	9	9	18	21
58-69	Bos	30	1	5	6	8
Totals		387	104	97	201	185

Playoffs

SSN	TEAM	GP	G	A	PTS.	PIM
51-52	Bos	7	1	1	2	6
52-53	Bos	7	0	1	1	6
54-55	Bos	5	2	1	3	4
56-57	Bos	10	2	1	3	4
57-58	Bos	1	0	0	0	0
Totals		30	5	4	9	20

*CHIASSON, Steve 6-1 205 D
B. Barrie, Ont., Apr. 14, 1967

SSN	TEAM	GP	G	A	PTS.	PIM	+/-
86-87	Det	45	1	4	5	73	-7
87-88	Det	29	2	9	11	57	+15
88-89	Det	65	12	35	47	149	-6
89-90	Det	67	14	28	42	114	-16
90-91	Det	42	3	17	20	80	+9
91-92	Det	62	10	24	34	136	+22
92-93	Det	79	12	50	62	155	+14
93-94	Det	82	13	33	46	122	+17
94-95	Calg	45	2	23	25	39	+10
95-96	Calg	76	8	25	33	62	+3
96-97	Calg-Hart	65	8	22	30	39	-21
97-98	Car	66	7	27	34	65	-2

SSN	TEAM	GP	G	A	PTS.	PIM	+/-
98–99	Car	28	1	8	9	16	+7
Totals		751	93	305	398	1107	+36

Playoffs

86–87	Det	2	0	0	0	19	
87–88	Det	9	2	2	4	31	
88–89	Det	5	2	1	3	6	
90–91	Det	5	3	1	4	19	
91–92	Det	11	1	5	6	12	
92–93	Det	7	2	2	4	19	
93–94	Det	7	2	3	5	2	
94–95	Calg	7	1	2	3	9	
95–96	Calg	4	2	1	3	0	
98–99	Car	6	1	2	3	2	
Totals		63	16	19	35	119	

CHIBIREV, Igor 6–0 180 C
B. Kiev, USSR, Apr. 19, 1968

93–94	Hart	37	4	11	15	2	+7
94–95	Hart	8	3	1	4	0	+1
Totals		45	7	12	19	2	+8

CHICOINE, Daniel 5–11 192 RW
B. Sherbrooke, Que., Nov. 30, 1957

77–78	Clev	6	0	0	0	0	-2
78–79	Minn	1	0	0	0	0	
79–80	Minn	24	1	2	3	12	-10
Totals		31	1	2	3	12	-12

Playoffs

79–80	Minn	1	0	0	0	0	

CHINNICK, Richard Vaughn (Rick) 5–11 180 RW
B. Chatham, Ont., Aug. 15, 1953

73–74	Minn	1	0	1	1	0	0
74–75	Minn	3	0	1	1	0	0
Totals		4	0	2	2	0	0

CHIPPERFIELD, Ronald James 5–11 180 C
B. Brandon, Man., Mar. 28, 1954

74–75	Van (WHA)	78	19	20	39	30	
75–76	Calg (WHA)	75	42	41	83	32	
76–77	Calg (WHA)	81	27	27	54	32	
77–78	Edm (WHA)	80	33	52	85	48	
78–79	Edm (WHA)	55	32	37	69	47	
79–80	Edm–Que	79	22	23	45	32	-24
80–81	Que	4	0	1	1	2	-1
NHL Totals		83	22	24	46	34	-25
WHA Totals		369	153	177	330	189	

Playoffs

75–76	Calg (WHA)	10	5	4	9	6	
77–78	Edm (WHA)	5	1	1	2	0	
78–79	Edm (WHA)	13	9	10	19	8	
Totals		28	15	15	30	14	

*CHISHOLM, Alexander (Lex) C
B. Galt, Ont., Apr. 1, 1915

39–40	Tor	28	6	8	14	11	
40–41	Tor	26	4	0	4	8	
Totals		54	10	8	18	19	

Playoffs

40–41	Tor	3	1	0	1	0	

CHISHOLM, Arthur C

60–61	Bos	3	0	0	0	0	

CHISHOLM, Colin 6–2 185 D
B. Edmonton, Alta., Feb. 25, 1963

86–87	Minn	1	0	0	0	0	0

CHORNEY, Marc 6–0 200 D
B. Sudbury, Ont., Nov. 8, 1959

80–81	Pitt	8	1	6	7	14	+1
81–82	Pitt	60	1	6	7	63	-11
82–83	Pitt	67	3	5	8	66	-30
83–84	Pitt–LA	75	3	10	13	66	-28
Totals		210	8	27	35	209	-68

Playoffs

80–81	Pitt	2	0	1	1	2	
81–82	Pitt	5	0	0	0	0	
Totals		7	0	1	1	2	

CHORSKE, Tom 6–1 204 RW
B. Minneapolis, Minn., Sept. 18, 1966

89–90	Mont	14	3	1	4	2	+2
90–91	Mont	57	9	11	20	32	-8
91–92	NJ	76	19	17	36	32	+8
92–93	NJ	50	7	12	19	25	-1
93–94	NJ	76	21	20	41	32	+14
94–95	NJ	42	10	8	18	16	-4
95–96	Ott	72	15	14	29	21	-9
96–97	Ott	68	18	8	26	16	-1
97–98	NYI	82	12	23	35	39	+7
98–99	NYI–Wash–Calg	26	0	3	3	8	-8
Totals		563	114	117	231	223	0

Playoffs

91–92	NJ	7	0	3	3	4	
92–93	NJ	1	0	0	0	0	
93–94	NJ	20	4	3	7	0	
94–95	NJ	17	1	5	6	4	
96–97	Ott	5	0	1	1	2	
Totals		50	5	12	17	10	

*CHOUINARD, Eugene (Gene) D

27–28	Ott	8	0	0	0	0	

CHOUINARD, Guy Camil 5–11 180 C
B. Quebec City, Que., Oct. 20, 1956

74–75	Atl	5	0	0	0	2	-2
75–76	Atl	4	0	2	2	2	+2
76–77	Atl	80	17	33	50	8	-12
77–78	Atl	73	28	30	58	8	+8
78–79	Atl	80	50	57	107	14	+23
79–80	Atl	76	31	46	77	22	+5
80–81	Calg	52	31	52	83	24	+18
81–82	Calg	64	23	57	80	12	-5
82–83	Calg	80	13	59	72	18	-24
83–84	StL	64	12	34	46	10	-15
Totals		578	205	370	575	120	-2

Playoffs

75–76	Atl	2	0	0	0	0	
76–77	Atl	3	2	0	2	0	
77–78	Atl	2	1	0	1	0	
78–79	Atl	2	1	2	3	0	
79–80	Atl	4	1	3	4	4	
80–81	Calg	16	3	14	17	4	
81–82	Calg	3	0	1	1	0	
82–83	Calg	9	1	6	7	4	
83–84	AtL	5	0	2	2	0	
Totals		46	9	28	37	12	

CHRISTIAN, David 5–11 175 RW
B. Warroad, Minn., May 12, 1959

79–80	Winn	15	8	10	18	2	-5
80–81	Winn	80	28	43	71	22	-54
81–82	Winn	80	25	51	76	28	-41
82–83	Winn	55	18	26	44	23	-5
83–84	Wash	80	29	52	81	28	+26
84–85	Wash	80	26	43	69	14	+20
85–86	Wash	80	41	42	83	15	+3
86–87	Wash	76	23	27	50	8	-5
87–88	Wash	80	37	21	58	26	-14
88–89	Wash	80	34	31	65	12	+2
89–90	Wash–Bos	78	15	25	40	12	-8
90–91	Bos	78	32	21	53	41	+8
91–92	StL	78	20	24	44	41	+2
92–93	Chi	60	4	14	18	12	+6
93–94	Chi	9	0	3	3	0	0
Totals		1009	340	433	773	284	-67

Playoffs

81–82	Winn	4	0	1	1	2	
82–83	Winn	3	0	0	0	0	
83–84	Winn	8	5	4	9	5	
84–85	Wash	5	1	1	2	0	
85–86	Wash	9	4	4	8	0	
86–87	Wash	7	1	3	4	6	
87–88	Wash	14	5	6	11	6	
88–89	Wash	6	1	1	2	0	
89–90	Bos	21	4	1	5	4	
90–91	Bos	19	8	4	12	4	
91–92	StL	4	3	0	3	0	
92–93	Chi	1	0	0	0	0	
93–94	Chi	1	0	0	0	0	
Totals		102	32	25	57	27	

CHRISTIAN, Jeff 6–1 195 LW
B. Burlington, Ont., July 3, 1970

91–92	NJ	2	0	0	0	2	0
94–95	Pitt	1	0	0	0	0	0
95–96	Pitt	3	0	0	0	2	0
96–97	Pitt	11	2	2	4	13	-3
97–98	Phoe	1	0	0	0	0	-1
Totals		18	2	2	4	17	-4

CHRISTIE, Michael Hunt 6–0 190 D
B. Big Spring, Tex., Dec. 20, 1949

74–75	Cal	34	0	14	14	76	-13
75–76	Cal	78	3	18	21	152	-18
76–77	Clev	79	6	27	33	79	+18
77–78	Clev–Col	69	3	14	17	77	-20
78–79	Col	68	1	10	11	88	-44
79–80	Col	74	1	17	18	78	-30
80–81	Col–Van	10	1	1	2	0	+10
Totals		412	15	101	116	550	-77

Playoffs

77–78	Col	2	0	0	0	0	

CHRISTOFF, Steve 6–1 180 C
B. Richfield, Minn., Jan. 23, 1958

79–80	Minn	20	8	7	15	19	+3
80–81	Minn	56	26	13	39	58	-9
81–82	Minn	69	26	29	55	14	+9
82–83	Calg	45	9	8	17	4	-3
83–84	LA	58	8	7	15	13	-19
Totals		248	77	64	141	108	-19

Playoffs

79–80	Minn	14	8	4	12	7	
80–81	Minn	18	8	8	16	16	
81–82	Minn	2	0	0	0	2	
82–83	Calg	1	0	0	0	0	
Totals		35	16	12	28	25	

CHRYSTAL, Robert Harry 6–0 180 D
B. Winnipeg, Man., Apr. 30, 1930

53–54	NYR	64	5	5	10	44	
54–55	NYR	68	6	9	15	68	
Totals		132	11	14	25	112	

CHURCH, Brad 6–1 210 LW
B. Dauphin, Man., Nov. 14, 1976

97–98	Wash	2	0	0	0	0	0

CHURCH, John (Jack) 5–11 180 D
B. Kamsack, Sask., May 24, 1915

38–39	Tor	3	0	2	2	2	
39–40	Tor	31	1	4	5	62	
40–41	Tor	11	0	1	1	22	
41–42	Tor–NYA	42	1	6	7	40	
42–43	NYA	15	1	3	4	10	
45–46	Bos	43	2	6	8	28	
Totals		145	5	22	27	164	

Playoffs

38–39	Tor	1	0	0	0	0	
39–40	Tor	10	1	1	2	6	
40–41	Tor	5	0	0	0	8	
45–46	Bos	9	0	0	0	4	
Totals		25	1	1	2	18	

CHURLA, Shane 6–1 200 RW
B. Fernie, B.C., June 24, 1965

86–87	Hart	20	0	1	1	78	-1
87–88	Hart–Calg	31	1	5	6	146	+1
88–89	Calg–Minn	18	1	0	1	79	-3
89–90	Minn	53	2	3	5	292	-4
90–91	Minn	40	2	2	4	286	+1
91–92	Minn	57	4	1	5	278	-12
92–93	Minn	73	5	16	21	286	-8
93–94	Dal	69	6	7	13	333	-8
94–95	Dal	27	1	3	4	186	0
95–96	Dal–LA–NYR	55	4	6	10	231	-8
96–97	NYR	45	0	1	1	106	-10
Totals		488	26	45	71	2301	-52

Playoffs

86–87	Hart	2	0	0	0	42	
87–88	Calg	7	0	1	1	17	
89–90	Minn	7	0	0	0	44	
90–91	Minn	22	2	1	3	90	

SSN	TEAM	GP	G	A	PTS.	PIM	+/-
93–94	Dal	9	1	3	4	35	
94–95	Dal	5	0	0	0	20	
95–96	NYR	11	2	2	4	14	
96–97	NYR	15	0	0	0	20	
Totals		78	5	7	12	282	

CHYCHRUN, Jeff *6–4 215 D*
B. LaSalle, Que., May 3, 1966

86–87	Phil	1	0	0	0	4	0
87–88	Phil	3	0	0	0	4	-1
88–89	Phil	80	1	4	5	245	+11
89–90	Phil	79	2	7	9	250	-12
90–91	Phil	36	0	6	6	105	+1
91–92	LA–Pitt	43	0	4	4	111	-12
92–93	Pitt–LA	18	0	1	1	25	-2
93–94	Edm	2	0	0	0	0	+1
Totals		262	3	22	25	744	-14

Playoffs

88–89	Phil	19	0	2	2	65	

CHYNOWETH, Dean *6–2 190 D*
B. Calgard, Alta., Oct. 30, 1968

88–89	NYI	6	0	0	0	48	-4
89–90	NYI	20	2	2	2	39	0
90–91	NYI	25	1	1	2	59	-6
91–92	NYI	11	1	0	1	23	-3
93–94	NYI	39	0	4	4	122	+3
94–95	NYI	32	0	2	2	77	+9
95–96	NYI–Bos	49	2	6	8	128	-5
96–97	Bos	57	0	3	3	171	-12
97–98	Bos	2	0	0	0	0	-4
Totals		241	4	18	22	667	-22

Playoffs

93–94	NYI	2	0	0	0	2	
95–96	Bos	4	0	0	0	24	
Totals		6	0	0	0	26	

CHYZOWSKI, David *6–1 190 LW*
B. Edmonton, Alta., July 11, 1971

89–90	NYI	34	8	6	14	45	-4
90–91	NYI	56	5	9	14	61	-19
91–92	NYI	12	1	1	2	17	-4
93–94	NYI	3	1	0	1	4	-1
94–95	NYI	13	0	0	0	11	-2
96–97	Chi	8	0	0	0	6	+1
Totals		126	15	16	31	144	-29

Playoffs

93–94	NYI	2	0	0	0	0	

CIAVAGLIA, Peter *5–10 175 C*
B. Albany, N.Y., July 15, 1969

91–92	Buf	2	0	0	0	0	+1
92–93	Buf	3	0	0	0	0	0
Totals		5	0	0	0	0	+1

CICCARELLI, Dino *5–10 185 RW*
B. Sarnia, Ont., Feb. 8, 1960

80–81	Minn	32	18	12	30	29	+2
81–82	Minn	76	55	51	106	138	+14
82–83	Minn	77	37	38	75	94	+16
83–84	Minn	79	38	33	71	58	+1
84–85	Minn	51	15	17	32	41	-10
85–86	Minn	75	44	45	89	51	+12
86–87	Minn	80	52	51	103	88	+10
87–88	Minn	67	41	45	86	79	-29
88–89	Minn–Wash	76	44	30	74	76	-6
89–90	Wash	80	41	38	79	122	-5
90–91	Wash	54	21	18	39	66	-17
91–92	Wash	78	38	38	76	78	-10
92–93	Det	82	41	56	97	81	+12
93–94	Det	66	28	29	57	73	+10
94–95	Det	42	16	27	43	39	+12
95–96	Det	64	22	21	43	99	+14
96–97	TB	77	35	25	60	116	-11
97–98	TB–Fla	62	16	17	33	70	-16
98–99	Fla	14	6	1	7	27	-1
Totals		1232	608	592	1200	1425	-2

Playoffs

80–81	Minn	19	14	7	21	25	
81–82	Minn	4	3	1	4	2	
82–83	Minn	9	4	6	10	11	
83–84	Minn	16	4	5	9	27	
84–85	Minn	9	3	3	6	8	

85–86	Minn	5	0	1	1	6	
88–89	Wash	6	3	3	6	12	
89–90	Wash	8	8	3	11	6	
90–91	Wash	11	5	4	9	22	
91–92	Wash	7	5	4	9	14	
93–94	Det	7	5	2	7	14	
94–95	Det	16	9	2	11	22	
95–96	Det	17	6	2	8	26	
Totals		141	73	45	118	211	

CICCONE, Enrico *6–4 210 D*
B. Montreal, Que., Apr. 10, 1970

91–92	Minn	11	0	0	0	48	-2
92–93	Minn	31	0	1	1	115	+2
93–94	Wash–TB	57	1	2	3	226	-4
94–95	TB	41	2	4	6	225	+3
95–96	TB–Chi	66	2	4	6	306	+1
96–97	Chi	67	2	2	4	233	-1
97–98	Car–Van–TB	39	0	4	4	175	-2
98–99	TB–Wash	59	3	1	4	127	-7
Totals		371	10	18	28	1455	-10

Playoffs

95–96	Chi	9	1	0	1	30	
96–97	Chi	4	0	0	0	18	
Totals		13	1	0	1	48	

CICHOCKI, Chris *5–11 185 RW*
B. Detroit, Mich., Sept. 17, 1963

85–86	Det	59	10	11	21	21	-8
86–87	Det	2	0	0	0	2	-2
87–88	NJ	5	1	0	1	2	+1
88–89	NJ	2	0	1	1	2	0
Totals		68	11	12	23	27	-9

CIERNIK, Ivan *6–1 198 LW*
B. Nitra, Slovakia, Oct. 30, 1977

97–98	Ott	0	0	0	0	0	0

CIERNY, Jozef *6–2 185 LW*
B. Zvolen, Czechoslovakia, May 13, 1974

93–94	Edm	1	0	0	0	0	-1

*CIESLA, Henry Edward (Hank) *6–2 190 C*
B. St. Catharines, Ont., Oct. 15, 1934

55–56	Chi	70	8	23	31	22	
56–57	Chi	70	10	8	18	28	
57–58	NYR	60	2	6	8	16	
58–59	NYR	69	6	14	20	21	
Totals		269	26	51	77	87	

Playoffs

57–58	NYR	6	0	2	2	0	

CIGER, Zdeno *6–1 190 LW*
B. Martin, Czechoslovakia, Oct. 19, 1969

90–91	NJ	45	8	17	25	8	+3
91–92	NJ	20	6	5	11	10	-2
92–93	NJ–Edm	64	13	23	36	8	-13
93–94	Edm	84	22	35	57	8	-11
94–95	Edm	5	2	2	4	0	-1
95–96	Edm	78	31	39	70	41	-15
Totals		296	82	121	203	75	-42

Playoffs

90–91	NJ	6	0	2	2	4	
91–92	NJ	7	2	4	6	0	
Totals		13	2	6	8	4	

CIMELLARO, Tony *5–11 180 C*
B. Kingston, Ont., June 14, 1971

92–93	Ott	2	0	0	0	0	-2

CIMETTA, Robert *6–0 190 LW*
B. Toronto, Ont., Feb. 15, 1970

88–89	Bos	7	2	0	2	0	-4
89–90	Bos	47	8	9	17	33	+4
90–91	Tor	25	2	4	6	21	-5
91–92	Tor	24	4	3	7	12	+5
Totals		103	16	16	32	66	

Playoffs

88–89	Bos	1	0	0	0	15	

CIRELLA, Joe *6–3 210 D*
B. Hamilton, Ont., May 9, 1963

81–82	Col	65	7	12	19	52	-36
82–83	NJ	2	0	1	1	4	-7
83–84	NJ	79	11	33	44	137	-43
84–85	NJ	66	6	18	24	141	-45
85–86	NJ	66	6	23	29	147	-12
86–87	NJ	65	9	22	31	111	-20
87–88	NJ	80	8	31	39	191	+15
88–89	NJ	80	3	19	22	155	-14
89–90	Que	56	4	14	18	67	-27
90–91	Que–NYR	58	3	10	13	111	-27
91–92	NYR	67	3	12	15	121	+11
92–93	NYR	55	3	6	9	85	+1
93–94	Fla	63	1	9	10	99	+8
94–95	Fla	20	0	1	1	21	-7
95–96	Ott	6	0	0	0	4	-21
Totals		828	64	211	275	1446	-203

Playoffs

87–88	NJ	19	0	7	7	49	
90–91	NYR	6	0	2	2	26	
91–92	NYR	13	0	4	4	23	
Totals		38	0	13	13	98	

CIRONE, Jason *5–9 185 C*
B. Toronto, Ont., Feb. 21, 1971

91–92	Winn	3	0	0	0	2	0

CLACKSON, Kimble Gerald (Kim) *5–11 195 D*
B. Saskatoon, Sask., Feb. 13, 1955

75–76	Ind (WHA)	77	1	12	13	351	
76–77	Ind (WHA)	71	3	8	11	168	
77–78	Winn (WHA)	52	2	7	9	203	
78–79	Winn (WHA)	71	0	12	12	210	
79–80	Pitt	45	0	3	3	166	-8
80–81	Que	61	0	5	5	204	-3
NHL Totals		106	0	8	8	370	-11
WHA Totals		271	6	39	45	932	

Playoffs

75–76	Ind (WHA)	6	0	0	0	25	
76–77	Ind (WHA)	9	0	1	1	24	
77–78	Winn (WHA)	9	0	1	1	61	
78–79	Winn (WHA)	9	0	5	5	28	
79–80	Pitt	3	0	0	0	37	
80–81	Que	5	0	0	0	33	
NHL Totals		8	0	0	0	70	
WHA Totals		33	0	7	7	138	

*CLANCY, Francis Michael (King) *5–9 184 D*
B. Ottawa, Ont., Feb. 25, 1903

21–22	Ott	24	4	5	9	19	
22–23	Ott	24	3	1	4	20	
23–24	Ott	24	9	8	17	18	
24–25	Ott	29	14	5	19	61	
25–26	Ott	35	8	4	12	80	
26–27	Ott	43	9	10	19	78	
27–28	Ott	39	8	7	15	73	
28–29	Ott	44	13	2	15	89	
29–30	Ott	44	17	23	40	83	
30–31	Tor	44	7	14	21	63	
31–32	Tor	48	10	9	19	61	
32–33	Tor	48	13	12	25	79	
33–34	Tor	46	11	17	28	62	
34–35	Tor	47	5	16	21	53	
35–36	Tor	47	5	10	15	61	
36–37	Tor	6	1	0	1	4	
Totals		592	137	143	280	904	

Playoffs

21–22	Ott	2	0	0	0	2	
22–23	Ott	8	1	0	1	4	
23–24	Ott	2	0	0	0	6	
25–26	Ott	2	1	0	1	4	
26–27	Ott	6	1	1	2	14	
27–28	Ott	2	0	0	0	0	
29–30	Ott	2	0	1	1	2	
30–31	Tor	2	1	0	1	2	
31–32	Tor	7	2	1	3	14	
32–33	Tor	9	0	3	3	14	
33–34	Tor	3	0	0	0	0	
34–35	Tor	7	1	0	1	8	
35–36	Tor	9	2	2	4	10	
Totals		61	9	8	17	80	

CLANCY, Terrance John 6-0 195 RW
B. Ottawa, Ont., Apr. 2, 1943

SSN	TEAM	GP	G	A	PTS.	PIM	+/-
67–68	Oak	7	0	0	0	2	-4
68–69	Tor	2	0	0	0	0	-1
69–70	Tor	52	6	5	11	31	+4
72–73	Tor	32	0	1	1	6	-10
Totals		93	6	6	12	39	-11

*CLAPPER, Aubrey Victor (Dit) 6-2 195 RW
B. Newmarket, Ont., Feb. 9, 1907

SSN	TEAM	GP	G	A	PTS.	PIM
27–28	Bos	40	4	1	5	20
28–29	Bos	40	9	2	11	48
29–30	Bos	44	41	20	61	48
30–31	Bos	43	22	8	30	50
31–32	Bos	48	17	22	39	21
32–33	Bos	48	14	14	28	42
33–34	Bos	48	10	12	22	6
34–35	Bos	48	21	16	37	21
35–36	Bos	44	12	13	25	14
36–37	Bos	48	17	8	25	25
37–38	Bos	46	6	9	15	24
38–39	Bos	42	13	13	26	22
39–40	Bos	44	10	18	28	25
40–41	Bos	48	8	18	26	24
41–42	Bos	32	3	12	15	31
42–43	Bos	38	5	18	23	12
43–44	Bos	50	6	25	31	13
44–45	Bos	48	8	14	22	16
45–46	Bos	30	2	3	5	0
46–47	Bos	6	0	0	0	0
Totals		833	228	246	474	462

Playoffs

SSN	TEAM	GP	G	A	PTS.	PIM
27–28	Bos	2	0	0	0	2
28–29	Bos	5	1	0	1	0
29–30	Bos	6	4	0	4	4
30–31	Bos	5	2	4	6	4
32–33	Bos	5	1	1	2	2
34–35	Bos	3	1	0	1	0
35–36	Bos	2	0	1	1	0
36–37	Bos	3	2	0	2	5
37–38	Bos	3	0	0	0	12
38–39	Bos	11	0	1	1	6
39–40	Bos	5	0	2	2	2
40–41	Bos	11	0	5	5	4
41–42	Bos	5	0	0	0	0
42–43	Bos	9	2	3	5	9
44–45	Bos	7	0	0	0	0
45–46	Bos	4	0	0	0	0
Totals		86	13	17	30	50

CLARK, Andrew D

SSN	TEAM	GP	G	A	PTS.	PIM
27–28	Bos	5	0	0	0	0

CLARK, Brett 6-0 175 D
B. Moosimon, Sask., Dec. 23, 1976

SSN	TEAM	GP	G	A	PTS.	PIM	+/-
97–98	Mont	41	1	0	1	20	-3
98–99	Mont	61	2	2	4	16	-3
Totals		102	3	2	5	36	-6

CLARK, Daniel 6-1 195 D
B. Toronto, Ont., Nov. 3, 1957

SSN	TEAM	GP	G	A	PTS.	PIM	+/-
78–79	NYR	4	0	1	1	6	+1

CLARK, Dean 6-1 180 D
B. Edmonton, Alta., Jan. 10, 1964

SSN	TEAM	GP	G	A	PTS.	PIM	+/-
83–84	Edm	1	0	0	0	0	0

CLARK, Gordon Corson (Gordie) 5-10 180 RW
B. Glasgow, Scotland, May 31, 1952

SSN	TEAM	GP	G	A	PTS.	PIM	+/-
74–75	Bos	1	0	0	0	0	0
75–76	Bos	7	0	1	1	0	-5
78–79	Cin (WHA)	21	3	3	6	2	
NHL Totals		8	0	1	1	0	-5
WHA Totals		21	3	3	6	2	

Playoffs

SSN	TEAM	GP	G	A	PTS.	PIM
75–76	Bos	1	0	0	0	0

CLARK, Wendel 5-11 194 LW
B. Kelvington, Sask., Oct. 25, 1966

SSN	TEAM	GP	G	A	PTS.	PIM	+/-
85–86	Tor	66	34	11	45	227	-27
86–87	Tor	80	37	23	60	271	-23
87–88	Tor	28	12	11	23	80	-13
88–89	Tor	15	7	4	11	66	-3
89–90	Tor	38	18	8	26	116	+2
90–91	Tor	63	18	16	34	152	-5
91–92	Tor	43	19	21	40	123	-14
92–93	Tor	66	17	22	39	193	+2
93–94	Tor	64	46	30	76	115	+10
94–95	Que	37	12	18	30	45	-1
95–96	NYI–Tor	71	32	26	58	76	-5
96–97	Tor	65	30	19	49	75	-2
97–98	Tor	47	12	7	19	80	-21
98–99	TB–Det	77	32	16	48	37	-24
Totals		760	326	232	558	1656	-124

Playoffs

SSN	TEAM	GP	G	A	PTS.	PIM
85–86	Tor	10	5	1	6	47
86–87	Tor	13	6	5	11	38
89–90	Tor	5	1	1	2	19
92–93	Tor	21	10	10	20	51
93–94	Tor	18	9	7	16	24
94–95	Que	6	1	2	3	6
95–96	Tor	6	2	2	4	2
98–99	Det	10	2	3	5	10
Totals		89	36	31	67	197

*CLARKE, Robert Earle (Bobby) 5-10 185 C
B. Flin Flon, Man., Aug. 13, 1949

SSN	TEAM	GP	G	A	PTS.	PIM	+/-
69–70	Phil	76	15	31	46	68	+1
70–71	Phil	77	27	36	63	78	+9
71–72	Phil	78	35	46	81	87	+22
72–73	Phil	78	37	67	104	80	+32
73–74	Phil	77	35	52	87	113	+35
74–75	Phil	80	27	89	116	125	+79
75–76	Phil	76	30	89	119	136	+83
76–77	Phil	80	27	63	90	71	+39
77–78	Phil	71	21	68	89	83	+47
78–79	Phil	80	16	57	73	68	+12
79–80	Phil	76	12	57	69	65	+42
80–81	Phil	80	19	46	65	140	+17
81–82	Phil	62	17	46	63	154	+28
82–83	Phil	80	23	62	85	115	+37
83–84	Phil	73	17	43	60	70	+23
Totals		1144	358	852	1210	1453	+506

Playoffs

SSN	TEAM	GP	G	A	PTS.	PIM
70–71	Phil	4	0	0	0	2
72–73	Phil	11	2	6	8	6
73–74	Phil	17	5	11	16	42
74–75	Phil	17	4	12	16	16
75–76	Phil	16	2	14	16	28
76–77	Phil	10	5	5	10	8
77–78	Phil	12	4	7	11	8
78–79	Phil	8	2	4	6	8
79–80	Phil	19	8	12	20	16
80–81	Phil	12	3	3	6	6
81–82	Phil	4	4	2	6	4
82–83	Phil	3	1	0	1	2
83–84	Phil	3	2	1	3	6
Totals		136	42	77	119	152

CLEARY, Daniel 6-0 203 LW
B. Carbonear, Nfld., Dec. 18, 1978

SSN	TEAM	GP	G	A	PTS.	PIM	+/-
97–98	Chi	6	0	0	0	0	-2
98–99	Chi-Edm	35	4	5	9	24	-1
Totals		41	4	5	9	24	-3

*CLEGHORN, Ogilvie (Odie) RW
B. Montreal, Que., 1891

SSN	TEAM	GP	G	A	PTS.	PIM
18–19	Mont	17	23	6	29	22
19–20	Mont	21	19	3	22	30
20–21	Mont	21	5	4	9	8
21–22	Mont	23	21	3	24	26
22–23	Mont	24	19	7	26	14
23–24	Mont	22	3	3	6	14
24–25	Mont	30	3	2	5	14
25–26	Pitt Pi	17	3	1	4	4
26–27	Pitt Pi	3	0	0	0	0
27–28	Pitt Pi	2	0	0	0	0
Totals		180	96	29	125	132

Playoffs

SSN	TEAM	GP	G	A	PTS.	PIM
18–19	Mont	10	9	1	10	11
22–23	Mont	2	0	0	0	2
23–24	Mont	6	0	1	1	0
24–25	Mont	5	0	1	1	0
25–26	PittPi	1	0	0	0	0
Totals		24	9	3	12	13

*CLEGHORN, Sprague D
B. Montreal, Que., 1890

SSN	TEAM	GP	G	A	PTS.	PIM
18–19	Ott	18	6	6	12	27
19–20	Ott	21	16	5	21	62
20–21	Ott–Tor	16	5	5	10	35
21–22	Mont	24	17	7	24	63
22–23	Mont	24	9	4	13	34
23–24	Mont	23	8	3	11	39
24–25	Mont	27	8	1	9	82
25–26	Bos	28	6	5	11	49
26–27	Bos	44	7	1	8	84
27–28	Bos	37	2	2	4	14
Totals		262	84	39	123	489

Playoffs

SSN	TEAM	GP	G	A	PTS.	PIM
18–19	Ott	5	2	2	4	5
19–20	Ott	5	0	1	1	9
20–21	Ott	6	1	2	3	21
22–23	Mont	1	0	0	0	0
23–24	Mont	6	2	1	3	2
24–25	Mont	6	1	2	3	4
26–27	Bos	8	0	1	1	8
27–28	Bos	2	0	0	0	0
Totals		39	6	9	15	49

CLEMENT, William H. 6-1 194 C
B. Buckingham, Que., Dec. 20, 1950

SSN	TEAM	GP	G	A	PTS.	PIM	+/-
71–72	Phil	49	9	14	23	39	-14
72–73	Phil	73	14	14	28	51	-11
73–74	Phil	39	9	8	17	34	+15
74–75	Phil	68	21	16	37	42	+21
75–76	Wash–Atl	77	23	31	54	49	-27
76–77	Atl	67	17	26	43	27	-4
77–78	Atl	70	20	30	50	34	+18
78–79	Atl	65	12	23	35	14	-5
79–80	Atl	64	7	14	21	32	+3
80–81	Calg	78	12	20	32	33	-16
81–82	Calg	69	4	12	16	28	-2
Totals		719	148	208	356	383	-22

Playoffs

SSN	TEAM	GP	G	A	PTS.	PIM
72–73	Phil	2	0	0	0	0
73–74	Phil	4	1	0	1	4
74–75	Phil	12	1	0	1	8
75–76	Phil	2	0	1	1	0
76–77	Atl	3	1	1	2	0
77–78	Atl	2	0	0	0	2
78–79	Atl	2	0	0	0	0
79–80	Atl	4	0	0	0	4
80–81	Calg	16	2	1	3	6
81–82	Calg	3	0	0	0	2
Totals		50	5	3	8	26

CLINE, Bruce 5-7 137 RW
B. Massawippi, Que., Nov. 14, 1931

SSN	TEAM	GP	G	A	PTS.	PIM
56–57	NYR	30	2	3	5	10

CLIPPINGDALE, Steve 6-2 195 LW
B. Vancouver, B.C., Apr. 29, 1956

SSN	TEAM	GP	G	A	PTS.	PIM	+/-
76–77	LA	16	1	2	3	9	+3
79–80	Wash	3	0	0	0	0	-0
Totals		19	1	2	3	9	+3

Playoffs

SSN	TEAM	GP	G	A	PTS.	PIM
76–77	LA	1	0	0	0	0

CLOUTIER, Real 5-10 185 RW
B. St. Emile, Que., July 30, 1956

SSN	TEAM	GP	G	A	PTS.	PIM	+/-
74–75	Que (WHA)	63	26	27	53	36	
75–76	Que (WHA)	80	60	54	114	27	
76–77	Que (WHA)	76	66	75	141	39	
77–78	Que (WHA)	73	56	73	129	19	
78–79	Que (WHA)	77	75	54	129	48	
79–80	Que	67	42	47	89	12	-6
80–81	Que	34	15	16	31	18	+2
81–82	Que	67	37	60	97	34	+26
82–83	Que	68	28	39	67	30	-4
83–84	Buf	77	24	36	60	25	-1
84–85	Buf	4	0	0	0	0	-2
NHL Totals		317	146	198	344	119	+15
WHA Totals		369	283	283	566	169	

Playoffs

SSN	TEAM	GP	G	A	PTS.	PIM
74–75	Que (WHA)	12	4	8	7	2
75–76	Que (WHA)	5	4	5	9	0
76–77	Que (WHA)	17	14	13	27	10
77–78	Que (WHA)	10	9	7	16	15

SSN	TEAM	GP	G	A	PTS.	PIM	+/-
78–79	Que (WHA)	4	2	2	4	4	
80–81	Que	3	0	0	0	10	
81–82	Que	16	7	5	12	10	
82–83	Que	4	0	0	0	0	
83–84	Buf	2	0	0	0	0	
NHL Totals		25	7	5	12	20	
WHA Totals		48	33	30	63	31	

CLOUTIER, Rejean 6–0 180 D
B. Windsor, Ont., Feb. 15, 1960

SSN	TEAM	GP	G	A	PTS.	PIM	+/-
79–80	Det	3	0	1	1	0	+2
81–82	Det	2	0	1	1	2	0
Totals		5	0	2	2	2	+2

CLOUTIER, Roland 5–8 157 C
B. Rouyn–Noranda, Que., Oct. 6, 1957

77–78	Det	1	0	0	0	0	-2
78–79	Det	19	6	6	12	2	0
79–80	Que	14	2	3	5	0	+1
Totals		34	8	9	17	2	-1

CLOUTIER, Sylvain 6–0 195 C
B. Mont-Lourier, Que., Feb. 13, 1974

98–99	Chi	7	0	0	0	0	-1

CLUNE, Walter James (Wally) 5–9 150 D
B. Toronto, Ont., Feb. 29, 1930

55–56	Mont	5	0	0	0	6	

COALTER, Gary Merritt Charles 5–10 185 RW
B. Toronto, Ont., July 8, 1950

73–74	Cal	4	0	0	0	0	-4
74–75	KC	30	2	4	6	2	-8
Totals		34	2	4	6	2	-12

COATES, Stephen John 5–9 172 RW
B. Toronto, Ont., July 2, 1950

76–77	Det	5	1	0	1	24	-1

COCHRANE, Glen Macleod 6–2 205 D
B. Cranbrook, B.C., Jan. 29, 1958

78–79	Phil	1	0	0	0	0	-2
80–81	Phil	31	1	8	9	219	+3
81–82	Phil	63	6	12	18	329	+19
82–83	Phil	77	2	22	24	237	+42
83–84	Phil	67	7	16	23	225	+16
84–85	Phil	18	0	3	3	100	-4
85–86	Van	49	0	3	3	125	-5
86–87	Van	14	0	0	0	52	0
87–88	Chi	73	1	8	9	204	-7
88–89	Chi–Edm	18	0	0	0	65	-3
Totals		411	17	72	89	1556	+59

Playoffs

80–81	Phil	6	1	1	2	18	
81–82	Phil	2	0	0	0	2	
82–83	Phil	3	0	0	0	4	
85–86	Van	2	0	0	0	5	
87–88	Chi	5	0	0	0	2	
Totals		18	1	1	2	31	

COFFEY, Paul Douglas 6–0 190 D
B. Weston, Ont., June 1, 1961

80–81	Edm	74	9	23	32	130	+4
81–82	Edm	80	29	60	89	106	+35
82–83	Edm	80	29	67	96	87	+52
83–84	Edm	80	40	86	126	104	+52
84–85	Edm	80	37	84	121	97	+55
85–86	Edm	79	48	90	138	120	+61
86–87	Edm	59	17	50	67	49	+12
87–88	Pitt	46	15	52	67	93	-1
88–89	Pitt	75	30	83	113	195	-10
89–90	Pitt	80	29	74	103	95	-25
90–91	Pitt	76	24	69	93	128	-18
91–92	Pitt–LA	64	11	58	69	87	+1
92–93	LA–Det	80	12	75	87	77	+16
93–94	Det	80	14	63	77	106	+28
94–95	Det	45	14	44	58	72	+18
95–96	Det	76	14	60	74	90	+19
96–97	Hart–Phil	57	9	25	34	38	+11
97–98	Phil	57	2	27	29	30	+3
98–99	Chi–Car	54	2	12	14	28	-7
Totals		1322	385	1102	1487	1732	+306

Playoffs

SSN	TEAM	GP	G	A	PTS.	PIM	
80–81	Edm	9	4	3	7	22	
81–82	Edm	5	1	1	2	6	
82–83	Edm	16	7	7	14	15	
83–84	Edm	19	8	14	22	21	
84–85	Edm	18	12	25	37	44	
85–86	Edm	10	1	9	10	30	
86–87	Edm	17	3	8	11	30	
88–89	Pitt	11	2	13	15	31	
90–91	Pitt	12	2	9	11	6	
91–92	LA	6	4	3	7	2	
92–93	Det	7	2	9	11	2	
93–94	Det	7	1	6	7	8	
94–95	Det	18	6	12	18	10	
95–96	Det	17	5	9	14	30	
96–97	Phil	17	1	8	9	6	
98–99	Car	5	0	1	1	2	
Totals		194	59	137	196	264	

COFLIN, Hugh Alexander 6–0 190 D
B. Blaine Lake, Sask., Dec. 15, 1928

50–51	Chi	31	0	3	3	33	

COLE, Danton 5–11 189 RW
B. Pontiac, Mich., Jan. 10, 1967

89–90	Winn	2	1	1	2	0	-1
90–91	Winn	66	13	11	24	24	-14
91–92	Winn	52	7	5	12	32	-15
92–93	TB	67	12	15	27	23	-2
93–94	TB	81	20	23	43	32	+7
94–95	TB–NJ	38	4	5	9	14	-1
95–96	NYI–Chi	12	1	0	1	0	0
Totals		318	58	60	118	125	-26

Playoffs

94–95	NJ	1	0	0	0	0	

COLLEY, Thomas 5–9 162 C
B. Toronto, Ont., Aug. 21, 1953

74–75	Minn	1	0	0	0	2	-3

COLLINGS, Norman (Dodger) F
B. Bradford, Ont.

34–35	Mont	1	0	1	1	0	

COLLINS, Ranleigh (Gary) 5–11 190 C
B. Toronto, Ont., Sept. 27, 1935

58–59	Tor	0	0	0	0	0	

Playoffs

58–59	Tor	2	0	0	0	0	

COLLINS, William Earl 6–0 178 RW
B. Ottawa, Ont., July 13, 1943

67–68	Minn	71	9	11	20	41	-16
68–69	Minn	75	9	10	19	24	-26
69–70	Minn	74	29	9	38	48	+4
70–71	Mont–Det	76	11	18	29	29	0
71–72	Det	71	15	25	40	38	+3
72–73	Det	78	21	21	42	44	-1
73–74	Det–StL	66	15	17	32	51	-30
74–75	StL	70	22	15	37	34	+4
75–76	NYR	50	4	4	8	38	-19
76–77	Phil–Wash	63	12	15	27	30	-8
77–78	Wash	74	10	9	19	18	-32
Totals		768	157	154	311	415	-121

Playoffs

67–68	Minn	10	2	4	6	4	
69–70	Minn	6	0	1	1	8	
74–75	StL	2	1	0	1	0	
Totals		18	3	5	8	12	

COLLYARD, Robert Leander 5–9 170 C
B. Hibbing, Minn., Oct. 16, 1949

73–74	StL	10	1	3	4	4	+1

*COLMAN, Mike 6–3 218 D
B. Stoneham, Mass., Aug. 4, 1968

91–92	SJ	15	0	1	1	32	-8

COLVILLE, Matthew Lamont (Mac) 5–8 175 RW
B. Edmonton, Alta., Jan. 8, 1916

35–36	NYR	18	1	4	5	6	
36–37	NYR	46	7	12	19	10	

SSN	TEAM	GP	G	A	PTS.	PIM	+/-
37–38	NYR	48	14	14	28	18	
38–39	NYR	48	7	21	28	26	
39–40	NYR	47	7	14	21	12	
40–41	NYR	47	14	17	31	18	
41–42	NYR	46	14	16	30	26	
45–46	NYR	39	7	6	13	8	
46–47	NYR	14	0	0	0	8	
Totals		353	71	104	175	132	

Playoffs

36–37	NYR	9	1	2	3	2	
37–38	NYR	3	0	2	2	0	
38–39	NYR	7	1	2	3	4	
39–40	NYR	12	3	2	5	6	
40–41	NYR	3	1	1	2	2	
41–42	NYR	6	3	1	4	0	
Totals		40	9	10	19	14	

*COLVILLE, Neil McNeil 6–0 175 C
B. Edmonton, Alta., Aug. 4, 1914

35–36	NYR	1	0	0	0	0	
36–37	NYR	45	10	18	28	33	
37–38	NYR	45	17	19	36	11	
38–39	NYR	47	18	19	37	12	
39–40	NYR	48	19	19	38	22	
40–41	NYR	48	14	28	42	28	
41–42	NYR	48	8	25	33	37	
44–45	NYR	4	0	1	1	2	
45–46	NYR	49	5	4	9	25	
46–47	NYR	60	4	16	20	16	
47–48	NYR	55	4	12	16	25	
48–49	NYR	14	0	5	5	2	
Totals		464	99	166	265	213	

Playoffs

36–37	NYR	9	3	3	6	0	
37–38	NYR	3	0	1	1	0	
38–39	NYR	7	0	2	2	2	
39–40	NYR	12	2	7	9	19	
40–41	NYR	3	1	1	2	0	
41–42	NYR	6	0	5	5	6	
47–48	NYR	6	1	0	1	6	
Totals		46	7	19	26	33	

COLWILL, Leslie John 5–11 170 RW
B. Divide, Sask., Jan. 1, 1935

58–59	NYR	69	7	6	13	16	

COMEAU, Reynald Xavier (Rey) 5–8 173 C
B. Montreal, Que., Oct. 25, 1948

71–72	Mont	4	0	0	0	0	0
72–73	Atl	77	21	21	42	19	0
73–74	Atl	78	11	23	34	16	-15
74–75	Atl	75	14	20	34	40	+9
75–76	Atl	79	17	22	39	42	+9
76–77	Atl	80	15	18	33	16	+7
77–78	Atl	79	10	22	32	20	0
78–79	Col	70	8	10	18	16	-20
79–80	Col	22	2	5	7	6	0
Totals		564	98	141	239	175	-10

Playoffs

73–74	Atl	4	2	1	3	6	
76–77	Atl	3	0	0	0	2	
77–78	Atl	2	0	0	0	0	
Totals		9	2	1	3	8	

CONACHER, Brian Kennedy 6–3 197 LW
B. Toronto, Ont., Aug. 31, 1941

61–62	Tor	1	0	0	0	0	
65–66	Tor	2	0	0	0	2	
66–67	Tor	66	14	13	27	47	
67–68	Tor	64	11	14	25	31	+7
71–72	Det	22	3	1	4	4	-3
72–73	Ott (WHA)	69	8	19	27	32	
NHL Totals		155	28	28	56	84	+4
WHA Totals		69	8	19	27	32	

Playoffs

66–67	Tor	12	3	2	5	21	
72–73	Ott (WHA)	5	1	3	4	4	
NHL Totals		12	3	2	5	21	
WHA Totals		5	1	3	4	4	

CONACHER, Charles William, Jr. (Pete) 5–10 165 LW
B. Toronto, Ont., July 29, 1932

SSN	TEAM	GP	G	A	PTS.	PIM	+/-
51–52	Chi	2	0	1	1	0	
52–53	Chi	41	5	6	11	7	
53–54	Chi	70	19	9	28	23	
54–55	Chi–NYR	70	12	11	23	12	
55–56	NYR	41	11	11	22	10	
57–58	Tor	5	0	1	1	5	
Totals		229	47	39	86	57	

Playoffs

SSN	TEAM	GP	G	A	PTS.	PIM	+/-
52–53	Chi	2	0	0	0	0	
55–56	NYR	5	0	0	0	0	
Totals		7	0	0	0	0	

*CONACHER, Charles William (The Bomber) 6–1 195 RW
B. Toronto, Ont., Dec. 20, 1910

SSN	TEAM	GP	G	A	PTS.	PIM	+/-
29–30	Tor	38	20	9	29	48	
30–31	Tor	37	31	12	43	78	
31–32	Tor	44	34	14	48	66	
32–33	Tor	40	14	19	33	64	
33–34	Tor	42	32	20	52	38	
34–35	Tor	47	36	21	57	24	
35–36	Tor	44	23	15	38	74	
36–37	Tor	15	3	5	8	16	
37–38	Tor	19	7	9	16	6	
38–39	Det	40	8	15	23	29	
39–40	NYA	48	10	18	28	41	
40–41	NYA	46	7	16	23	32	
Totals		460	225	173	398	516	

Playoffs

SSN	TEAM	GP	G	A	PTS.	PIM	+/-
30–31	Tor	2	0	1	1	4	
31–32	Tor	7	6	2	8	6	
32–33	Tor	9	1	1	2	10	
33–34	Tor	5	3	2	5	0	
34–35	Tor	7	1	4	5	6	
35–36	Tor	9	3	2	5	12	
36–37	Tor	2	0	0	0	5	
38–39	Det	5	2	5	7	2	
39–40	NYA	3	1	1	2	8	
Totals		49	17	18	35	53	

CONACHER, James 5–10 155 C
B. Motherwell, Scotland, May 5, 1921

SSN	TEAM	GP	G	A	PTS.	PIM	+/-
45–46	Det	20	1	5	6	6	
46–47	Det	33	16	13	29	2	
47–48	Det	60	17	23	40	2	
48–49	Det–Chi	59	26	23	49	43	
49–50	Chi	66	13	20	33	14	
50–51	Chi	52	10	27	37	16	
51–52	Chi–NYR	21	1	2	3	2	
52–53	NYR	17	1	4	5	2	
Totals		328	85	117	202	87	

Playoffs

SSN	TEAM	GP	G	A	PTS.	PIM	+/-
45–46	Det	5	1	1	2	0	
46–47	Det	5	2	1	3	2	
47–48	Det	9	2	0	2	2	
Totals		19	5	2	7	4	

*CONACHER, Lionel Pretoria (Big Train) 6–1 195 D
B. Toronto, Ont., May 24, 1901

SSN	TEAM	GP	G	A	PTS.	PIM	+/-
25–26	Pitt Pi	33	9	4	13	64	
26–27	Pitt Pi–NYA	40	8	9	17	93	
27–28	NYA	36	11	6	17	82	
28–29	NYA	44	5	2	7	132	
29–30	NYA	39	4	6	10	73	
30–31	Mont M	35	4	3	7	57	
31–32	Mont M	46	7	9	16	60	
32–33	Mont M	47	7	21	28	61	
33–34	Chi	48	10	13	23	87	
34–35	Mont M	40	2	6	8	44	
35–36	Mont M	47	7	7	14	65	
36–37	Mont M	45	6	19	25	64	
Totals		500	80	105	185	882	

Playoffs

SSN	TEAM	GP	G	A	PTS.	PIM	+/-
25–26	PittPi	2	0	0	0	0	
28–29	NYA	2	0	0	0	10	
30–31	Mont M	2	0	0	0	2	
31–32	Mont M	4	0	0	0	8	
32–33	Mont M	2	0	1	1	0	
33–34	Chi	8	2	0	2	4	
34–35	Mont M	7	0	0	0	14	
35–36	Mont M	3	0	0	0	0	
36–37	Mont M	5	0	1	1	2	
Totals		35	2	2	4	40	

CONACHER, Patrick John 5–8 190 LW
B. Edmonton, Alta., May 1, 1959

SSN	TEAM	GP	G	A	PTS.	PIM	+/-
79–80	NYR	17	0	5	5	4	-10
82–83	NYR	5	0	1	1	4	0
83–84	Edm	45	2	8	10	31	-2
85–86	NJ	2	0	2	2	2	0
87–88	NJ	24	2	5	7	12	+8
88–89	NJ	55	7	5	12	14	-7
89–90	NJ	19	3	3	6	4	+2
90–91	NJ	49	5	11	16	27	+9
91–92	NJ	44	7	3	10	16	0
92–93	LA	81	9	8	17	20	-16
93–94	LA	77	15	13	28	71	0
94–95	LA	48	7	9	16	12	-9
95–96	LA–Calg–NYI	55	6	3	9	18	-13
Totals		521	63	76	139	235	-38

Playoffs

SSN	TEAM	GP	G	A	PTS.	PIM	+/-
79–80	NYR	3	0	1	1	2	
83–84	Edm	3	1	0	1	2	
87–88	NJ	17	2	2	4	14	
89–90	NJ	5	1	0	1	10	
90–91	NJ	7	0	2	2	2	
91–92	NJ	7	1	1	2	4	
92–93	LA	24	6	4	10	6	
Totals		66	11	10	21	40	

CONACHER, Roy Gordon 6–1 175 LW
B. Toronto, Ont., Oct. 5, 1916

SSN	TEAM	GP	G	A	PTS.	PIM	+/-
38–39	Bos	47	26	11	37	12	
39–40	Bos	31	18	12	30	9	
40–41	Bos	41	24	14	38	7	
41–42	Bos	43	24	13	37	12	
45–46	Bos	4	2	1	3	0	
46–47	Det	60	30	24	54	6	
47–48	Chi	52	22	27	49	4	
48–49	Chi	60	26	42	68	8	
49–50	Chi	70	25	31	56	16	
50–51	Chi	70	26	24	50	16	
51–52	Chi	12	3	1	4	0	
Totals		490	226	200	426	90	

Playoffs

SSN	TEAM	GP	G	A	PTS.	PIM	+/-
38–39	Bos	12	6	4	10	12	
39–40	Bos	6	2	1	3	0	
40–41	Bos	11	1	5	6	0	
41–42	Bos	5	2	1	3	0	
45–46	Bos	3	0	0	0	0	
46–47	Det	5	4	4	8	2	
Totals		42	15	15	30	14	

*CONN, Hugh Maitland (Red) 170 F
B. Hartley, Man., Oct. 25, 1908

SSN	TEAM	GP	G	A	PTS.	PIM	+/-
33–34	NYA	48	4	17	21	12	
34–35	NYA	48	5	11	16	10	
Totals		96	9	28	37	22	

CONN, Rob 6–2 200 LW/RW
B. Calgary, Alb., Sept. 3, 1968

SSN	TEAM	GP	G	A	PTS.	PIM	+/-
91–92	Chi	2	0	0	0	2	+1
95–96	Buf	28	2	5	7	18	-9
Totals		30	2	5	7	20	-8

CONNELLY, Wayne Francis 5–10 170 RW
B. Rouyn, Que., Dec. 16, 1939

SSN	TEAM	GP	G	A	PTS.	PIM	+/-
60–61	Mont	3	0	0	0	0	
61–62	Bos	61	8	12	20	34	
62–63	Bos	18	2	6	8	2	
63–64	Bos	26	2	3	5	12	
66–67	Bos	64	13	17	30	12	
67–68	Minn	74	35	21	56	40	-32
68–69	Minn–Det	74	18	25	43	11	-32
69–70	Det	76	23	36	59	10	+27
70–71	Det–StL	79	13	29	42	21	-29
71–72	StL–Van	68	19	25	44	14	-21
72–73	Minn (WHA)	78	40	30	70	16	
73–74	Minn (WHA)	78	42	53	95	16	
74–75	Minn (WHA)	76	38	33	71	16	
75–76	Minn–Clev (WHA)	71	29	25	54	23	
76–77	Calg–Edm (WHA)	63	18	21	39	22	
NHL Totals		543	133	174	307	156	-87
WHA Totals		366	167	162	329	93	

Playoffs

SSN	TEAM	GP	G	A	PTS.	PIM	+/-
67–68	Minn	14	8	3	11	2	
69–70	Det	4	1	3	4	2	
70–71	StL	2	1	2	3	0	
72–73	Minn (WHA)	5	1	3	4	0	
73–74	Minn (WHA)	11	6	7	13	4	
74–75	Minn (WHA)	12	8	4	12	10	
75–76	Clev (WHA)	3	1	0	1	2	
76–77	Edm (WHA)	5	0	1	1	0	
NHL Totals		24	11	7	18	4	
WHA Totals		36	16	15	31	16	

CONNOLLY, Albert Patrick (Bert) 5–11 174 LW
B. Montreal, Que., Apr. 22, 1909

SSN	TEAM	GP	G	A	PTS.	PIM	+/-
34–35	NYR	47	10	11	21	23	
35–36	NYR	25	2	2	4	10	
37–38	Chi	15	1	2	3	4	
Totals		87	13	15	28	37	

Playoffs

SSN	TEAM	GP	G	A	PTS.	PIM	+/-
34–35	NYR	4	1	0	1	0	
37–38	Chi	10	0	0	0	0	
Totals		14	1	0	1	0	

CONNOR, Cameron Duncan 6–2 200 RW
B. Winnipeg, Man., Aug. 10, 1954

SSN	TEAM	GP	G	A	PTS.	PIM	+/-
74–75	Phoe (WHA)	57	9	19	28	168	
75–76	Phoe (WHA)	73	18	21	39	295	
76–77	Hou (WHA)	76	35	32	67	224	
77–78	Hou (WHA)	68	21	16	37	217	
78–79	Mont	23	1	3	4	39	+2
79–80	Edm–NYR	50	7	16	23	173	+5
80–81	NYR	15	1	3	4	44	+6
82–83	NYR	1	0	0	0	0	0
NHL Totals		89	9	22	31	256	+13
WHA Totals		274	83	88	171	904	

Playoffs

SSN	TEAM	GP	G	A	PTS.	PIM	+/-
74–75	Phoe (WHA)	5	0	0	0	2	
75–76	Phoe (WHA)	5	1	0	1	21	
76–77	Hous (WHA)	11	3	4	7	47	
77–78	Hous (WHA)	2	1	0	1	22	
78–79	Mont	8	1	0	1	0	
79–80	NYR	2	0	0	0	2	
81–82	NYR	10	4	0	4	16	
NHL Totals		20	5	0	5	18	
WHA Totals		23	5	4	9	92	

CONNOR, Harold (Harry) F
B. Ottawa, Ont.

SSN	TEAM	GP	G	A	PTS.	PIM	+/-
27–28	Bos	42	9	1	10	26	
28–29	NYA	43	6	2	8	83	
29–30	Ott–Bos	38	1	2	3	26	
30–31	Ott	11	0	0	0	4	
Totals		134	16	5	21	139	

Playoffs

SSN	TEAM	GP	G	A	PTS.	PIM	+/-
27–28	Bos	2	0	0	0	0	
28–29	NYA	2	0	0	0	2	
29–30	Bos	6	0	0	0	0	
Totals		10	0	0	0	2	

CONNORS, Robert D

SSN	TEAM	GP	G	A	PTS.	PIM	+/-
26–27	NYA	6	1	0	1	0	
28–29	Det	41	13	3	16	68	
29–30	Det	31	3	7	10	42	
Totals		78	17	10	27	110	

Playoffs

SSN	TEAM	GP	G	A	PTS.	PIM	+/-
28–29	Det	2	0	0	0	10	

CONROY, Allan 5–8 170 C
B. Calgary, Alta., Jan. 17, 1966

SSN	TEAM	GP	G	A	PTS.	PIM	+/-
91–92	Phil	31	2	9	11	74	+1
92–93	Phil	21	3	2	5	17	-1
93–94	Phil	62	4	3	7	65	-12
Totals		114	9	14	23	156	-12

CONROY, Craig 6–2 198 C
B. Potsdam, N.Y., Sept. 4, 1971

SSN	TEAM	GP	G	A	PTS.	PIM	+/-
94–95	Mont	6	1	0	1	0	-1
95–96	Mont	7	0	0	0	2	-4

SSN	TEAM	GP	G	A	PTS.	PIM	+/-
96–97	StL	61	6	11	17	43	0
97–98	StL	81	14	29	43	46	+20
98–99	StL	69	14	25	39	38	+14
Totals		224	35	65	100	129	+29

Playoffs

96–97	StL	6	0	0	0	8	
97–98	StL	10	1	2	3	8	
98–99	StL	13	1	2	3	6	
Totals		29	2	4	6	22	

CONTINI, Joseph Mario 5–10 178 C
B. Galt, Ont., Jan. 29, 1957

77–78	Col	37	12	9	21	28	-2
78–79	Col	30	5	12	17	6	-19
80–81	Minn	1	0	0	0	0	0
Totals		68	17	21	38	34	-21

Playoffs

77–78	Col	2	0	0	0	0	

CONVERY, Brandon 6–1 182 C
B. Kingston, Ont., Feb. 4, 1974

95–96	Tor	11	5	2	7	4	-7
96–97	Tor	39	2	8	10	20	-9
97–98	Van	7	0	2	2	0	0
98–99	Van-LA	15	2	7	9	12	+4
Totals		72	9	19	28	36	-12

Playoffs

95–96	Tor	5	0	0	0	2	

CONVEY, Edward F
B. Toronto, Ont.

30–31	NYA	2	0	0	0	0	
31–32	NYA	21	1	0	1	21	
32–33	NYA	13	0	1	1	12	
Totals		36	1	1	2	33	

*COOK, Alexander Leone Lally (Bud) 5–9 160 C
B. Kingston, Ont., Nov. 15, 1907

31–32	Bos	28	4	4	8	14	
33–34	Ott	19	1	0	1	8	
34–35	StL	4	0	0	0	0	
Totals		51	5	4	9	22	

*COOK, Frederick Joseph (Bun) 5–11 180 LW
B. Kingston, Ont., Sept. 18, 1903

26–27	NYR	44	14	9	23	42	
27–28	NYR	44	14	14	28	28	
28–29	NYR	43	13	5	18	70	
29–30	NYR	43	24	18	42	55	
30–31	NYR	44	18	17	35	72	
31–32	NYR	45	14	20	34	43	
32–33	NYR	48	22	15	37	35	
33–34	NYR	48	18	15	33	36	
34–35	NYR	48	13	21	34	26	
35–36	NYR	26	4	5	9	12	
36–37	Bos	40	4	5	9	8	
Totals		473	158	144	302	427	

Playoffs

26–27	NYR	2	0	0	0	6	
27–28	NYR	9	2	1	3	10	
28–29	NYR	6	1	0	1	8	
29–30	NYR	4	2	0	2	4	
30–31	NYR	4	0	0	0	11	
31–32	NYR	7	6	2	8	12	
32–33	NYR	8	2	0	2	4	
33–34	NYR	2	0	0	0	2	
34–35	NYR	4	2	0	2	0	
Totals		46	15	3	18	57	

*COOK, Lloyd D

24–25	Bos	4	1	0	1	0	

*COOK, Robert Arthur 6–0 190 RW
B. Sudbury, Ont., Jan. 6, 1946

70–71	Van	2	0	0	0	0	0
72–73	Det–NYI	46	11	7	18	18	-20
73–74	NYI	22	2	1	3	4	+3
74–75	Minn	2	0	1	1	0	-1
Totals		72	13	9	22	22	-18

*COOK, Thomas John 5–7 140 C
B. Ft. William, Ont., May 7, 1907

29–30	Chi	41	14	16	30	16	
30–31	Chi	44	15	14	29	34	
31–32	Chi	48	12	13	25	36	
32–33	Chi	47	12	14	26	30	
34–35	Chi	47	13	18	31	33	
35–36	Chi	47	4	8	12	20	
36–37	Chi	17	0	2	2	0	
37–38	Mont M	20	2	4	6	0	
Totals		311	72	89	161	169	

Playoffs

29–30	Chi	2	0	1	1	4	
30–31	Chi	9	1	3	4	9	
31–32	Chi	2	0	0	0	2	
33–34	Chi	8	1	0	1	0	
34–35	Chi	2	0	0	0	2	
35–36	Chi	1	0	0	0	0	
Totals		24	2	4	6	17	

*COOK, William Osser 5–10 170 RW
B. Brantford, Ont., Oct. 9, 1896

26–27	NYR	44	33	4	37	58	
27–28	NYR	43	18	6	24	42	
28–29	NYR	43	15	8	23	41	
29–30	NYR	44	29	30	59	56	
30–31	NYR	44	30	12	42	39	
31–32	NYR	48	34	14	48	33	
32–33	NYR	48	28	22	50	51	
33–34	NYR	48	13	13	26	21	
34–35	NYR	48	21	15	36	23	
35–36	NYR	21	1	4	5	16	
36–37	NYR	21	1	4	5	6	
Totals		452	223	132	355	386	

Playoffs

26–27	NYR	2	1	0	1	10	
27–28	NYR	9	2	3	5	24	
28–29	NYR	6	0	0	0	6	
29–30	NYR	4	0	1	1	9	
30–31	NYR	4	3	0	3	2	
31–32	NYR	7	3	4	7	2	
32–33	NYR	8	3	2	5	4	
33–34	NYR	2	0	0	0	2	
34–35	NYR	4	1	2	3	7	
Totals		46	13	12	25	66	

COOKE, Matt 5–11 200 LW
B. Belleville, Ont., Sept. 7, 1978

98–99	Van	30	0	2	2	27	-12

COOPER, Carson E. F
B. Cornwall, Ont.

24–25	Bos	12	5	3	8	4	
25–26	Bos	36	28	3	31	10	
26–27	Bos–Mont	24	9	3	12	16	
27–28	Det	43	15	2	17	32	
28–29	Det	44	18	9	27	14	
29–30	Det	44	18	18	36	14	
30–31	Det	43	14	14	28	10	
31–32	Det	48	3	5	8	11	
Totals		294	110	57	167	111	

Playoffs

26–27	Mont	3	0	0	0	0	
28–29	Det	2	0	0	0	2	
31–32	Det	2	0	0	0	0	
Totals		7	0	0	0	2	

COOPER, David 6–2 204 D
B. Ottawa, Ont., Nov. 2, 1973

96–97	Tor	19	3	3	6	16	-3
97–98	Tor	9	0	4	4	8	+2
Totals		28	3	7	10	24	-1

COOPER, Edward William 5–10 188 LW
B. Loon Lake, Sask., Aug. 28, 1960

80–81	Col	47	7	7	14	46	-6
81–82	Col	2	1	0	1	0	0
Totals		49	8	7	15	46	-6

COOPER, Harold Wallace (Hal) 5–5 155 RW
B. New Liskeard, Ont., Aug. 29, 1915

44–45	NYR	8	0	0	0	2	

*COOPER, Joseph 6–1 200 D
B. Winnipeg, Man., Dec. 14, 1914

35–36	NYR	1	0	0	0	0	
36–37	NYR	48	0	3	3	42	
37–38	NYR	46	3	2	5	56	
38–39	Chi	17	3	3	6	10	
39–40	Chi	44	4	7	11	59	
40–41	Chi	45	5	5	10	66	
41–42	Chi	47	6	14	20	58	
43–44	Chi	13	1	0	1	17	
44–45	Chi	50	4	17	21	50	
45–46	Chi	50	2	7	9	46	
46–47	NYR	59	2	8	10	38	
Totals		420	30	66	96	442	

Playoffs

36–37	NYR	9	1	1	2	12	
39–40	Chi	2	0	0	0	6	
40–41	Chi	5	1	0	1	8	
41–42	Chi	3	0	2	2	2	
43–44	Chi	9	1	1	2	18	
45–46	Chi	4	0	1	1	14	
Totals		32	3	5	8	60	

COPP, Robert Alonzo 5–11 180 D
B. Port Elgin, N.B., Nov. 15, 1918

42–43	Tor	38	3	9	12	24	
50–51	Tor	2	0	0	0	2	
Totals		40	3	9	12	26	

*CORBEAU, Albert (Bert) D

17–18	Mont	20	8	0	8	22	
18–19	Mont	16	2	1	3	51	
19–20	Mont	23	11	5	16	59	
20–21	Mont	24	12	1	13	86	
21–22	Mont	22	4	7	11	26	
22–23	Ham	21	10	3	13	36	
23–24	Tor	24	8	6	14	55	
24–25	Tor	30	4	3	7	67	
25–26	Tor	36	5	5	10	121	
26–27	Tor	41	1	2	3	88	
Totals		257	65	33	98	611	

Playoffs

17–18	Mont	2	1	0	1	5	
18–19	Mont	10	1	0	1	5	
24–25	Tor	2	0	0	0	6	
Totals		14	2	0	2	10	

CORBET, Rene 6–0 187 LW
B. Victoriaville, Que., June 25, 1973

93–94	Que	9	1	1	2	0	+1
94–95	Que	8	0	3	3	2	+3
95–96	Col A	33	3	6	9	33	+10
96–97	Col A	76	12	15	27	67	+14
97–98	Col A	68	16	12	28	133	+8
98–99	Col A–Calg	73	13	18	31	68	+1
Totals		267	45	55	100	303	+37

Playoffs

94–95	Que	2	0	1	1	0	
95–96	Col-A	8	3	2	5	2	
96–97	Col-A	17	2	2	4	27	
97–98	Col-A	2	0	0	0	2	
Totals		29	5	5	10	31	

CORBETT, Michael Charles 6–2 200 RW
B. Toronto, Ont., Oct. 4, 1942

Playoffs

67–68	LA	2	0	1	1	2	

CORCORAN, Norman 6–0 165 C
B. Toronto, Ont., Aug. 15, 1931

49–50	Bos	1	0	0	0	0	
52–53	Bos	1	0	0	0	0	
54–55	Bos	2	0	0	0	2	
55–56	Det–Chi	25	1	3	4	19	
Totals		29	1	3	4	21	

Playoffs

54–55	Bos	4	0	0	0	6	

CORKUM, Bob 6–2 185 C
B. Salisbury, Mass., Dec. 18, 1967

89–90	Buf	8	2	0	2	4	+2

SSN	TEAM	GP	G	A	PTS.	PIM	+/-
91–92	Buf	20	2	4	6	21	-9
92–93	Buf	68	6	4	10	38	-3
93–94	Ana	76	23	28	51	18	+4
94–95	Ana	44	10	9	19	25	-7
95–96	Ana–Phil	76	9	10	19	34	+3
96–97	Phoe	80	9	11	20	40	-7
97–98	Phoe	76	12	9	21	28	-7
98–99	Phoe	77	9	10	19	17	-9
Totals		525	82	85	167	225	-33

Playoffs

89–90	Buf	5	1	0	1	4	
91–92	Buf	4	1	0	1	0	
92–93	Buf	5	0	0	0	2	
95–96	Phil	12	1	2	3	6	
96–97	Phoe	7	2	2	4	4	
97–98	Phoe	6	1	0	1	4	
98–99	Phoe	7	0	1	1	4	
Totals		46	6	5	11	24	

CORMIER, Roger *F*

| 25–26 | Mont | 1 | 0 | 0 | 0 | 0 | |

CORNFORTH, Mark *6-1 185 D*
B. Montreal, Que., Nov. 13, 1972

| 95–96 | Bos | 6 | 0 | 0 | 0 | 4 | +4 |

CORRIGAN, Charles Hubert Patrick (Chuck) *6-1 192 RW*
B. Moosomin, Sask., May 22, 1916

37–38	Tor	3	0	0	0	0	
40–41	NYA	16	2	2	4	2	
Totals		19	2	2	4	2	

CORRIGAN, Michael Douglas *5-10 175 LW*
B. Ottawa, Ont., Jan. 11, 1946

67–68	LA	5	0	0	0	2	-2
69–70	LA	36	6	4	10	30	-17
70–71	Van	76	21	28	49	103	-20
71–72	Van–LA	75	15	26	41	120	-15
72–73	LA	78	37	30	67	146	-17
73–74	LA	75	16	26	42	119	-10
74–75	LA	80	13	21	34	61	+9
75–76	LA	71	22	21	43	71	-2
76–77	Pitt	73	14	27	41	36	-13
77–78	Pitt	25	8	12	20	10	-7
Totals		594	152	195	347	698	-94

Playoffs

73–74	LA	3	0	1	1	4	
74–75	LA	3	0	0	0	4	
75–76	LA	9	2	2	4	12	
76–77	Pitt	2	0	0	0	0	
Totals		17	2	3	5	20	

CORRIVEAU, Fred Andre (Andre) *5-8 135 RW*
B. Grand Mere, Que., May 15, 1928

| 53–54 | Mont | 3 | 0 | 1 | 1 | 0 | |

CORRIVEAU, Yvon *6-2 195 LW*
B. Welland, Ont., Feb. 8, 1967

85–86	Wash	2	0	0	0	0	-1
86–87	Wash	17	1	1	2	24	-4
87–88	Wash	44	10	9	19	84	+17
88–89	Wash	33	3	2	5	62	0
89–90	Wash–Hart	63	13	7	20	72	+2
90–91	Hart	23	1	1	2	18	-8
91–92	Hart	38	12	8	20	36	+5
92–93	SJ–Hart	57	8	12	20	14	-20
93–94	Hart	3	0	0	0	0	0
Totals		280	48	40	88	310	-9

Playoffs

85–86	Wash	4	0	3	3	2	
87–88	Wash	13	1	2	3	30	
88–89	Wash	1	0	0	0	0	
89–90	Wash	4	1	0	1	0	
91–92	Hart	7	3	2	5	18	
Totals		29	5	7	12	50	

CORSON, Shayne *6-0 201 LW*
B. Barrie, Ont., Aug. 13, 1966

85–86	Mont	3	0	0	0	2	-3
86–87	Mont	55	12	11	23	144	+10
87–88	Mont	71	12	27	39	152	+22

SSN	TEAM	GP	G	A	PTS.	PIM	+/-
88–89	Mont	80	26	24	50	193	-1
89–90	Mont	76	31	44	75	144	+33
90–91	Mont	71	23	24	47	138	+9
91–92	Mont	64	17	36	53	118	+15
92–93	Edm	80	16	31	47	209	-19
93–94	Edm	64	25	29	54	118	-8
94–95	Edm	48	12	24	36	86	-17
95–96	StL	77	18	28	46	192	+3
96–97	StL–Mont	58	8	16	24	104	-9
97–98	Mont	62	21	34	55	108	+2
98–99	Mont	63	12	20	32	147	-10
Totals		872	233	348	581	1855	+27

Playoffs

86–87	Mont	17	6	5	11	30	
87–88	Mont	3	1	0	1	12	
88–89	Mont	21	4	5	9	65	
89–90	Mont	11	2	8	10	20	
90–91	Mont	13	9	6	15	36	
91–92	Mont	10	2	5	7	15	
95–96	StL	13	8	6	14	22	
96–97	Mont	5	1	0	1	4	
97–98	Mont	10	3	6	9	26	
Totals		103	36	41	77	230	

CORY, Keith Ross *6-2 195 D*
B. Calgary, Alta., Feb. 4, 1957

79–80	Winn	46	2	9	11	32	-16
80–81	Winn	5	0	1	1	9	-8
Totals		51	2	10	12	41	-24

COSSETE, Jacques *5-9 185 RW*
B. Rouyn–Noranda, Que., June 20, 1954

75–76	Pitt	7	0	2	2	9	-2
77–78	Pitt	19	1	2	3	4	-5
78–79	Pitt	38	7	2	9	16	-1
Totals		64	8	6	14	29	-8

Playoffs

| 78–79 | Pitt | 3 | 0 | 1 | 1 | 4 | |

COSTELLO, Lester John Thomas *5-8 158 LW*
B. South Porcupine, Ont., Feb. 16, 1928

| 48–49 | Tor | 15 | 2 | 3 | 5 | 11 | |

Playoffs

| 47–48 | Tor | 6 | 2 | 2 | 4 | 2 | |

COSTELLO, Murray *6-3 190 C*
B. South Porcupine, Ont., Feb. 24, 1934

53–54	Chi	40	3	2	5	6	
54–55	Bos	54	4	11	15	25	
55–56	Bos–Det	65	6	6	12	23	
56–57	Det	3	0	0	0	0	
Totals		162	13	19	32	54	

Playoffs

54–55	Bos	1	0	0	0	2	
55–56	Det	4	0	0	0	0	
Totals		5	0	0	0	2	

COSTELLO, Richard *6-0 175 C*
B. Farmington, Mass., June 27, 1963

83–84	Tor	10	2	1	3	2	-5
85–86	Tor	2	0	1	1	0	0
Totals		12	2	2	4	2	-5

COTCH, Charles *F*

| 24–25 | Ham | 11 | 1 | 0 | 1 | 0 | |

COTE, Alain *5-10 205 LW*
B. Matane, Que., May 3, 1957

77–78	Que (WHA)	27	3	5	8	8	
78–79	Que (WHA)	79	14	13	27	23	
79–80	Que	41	5	11	16	13	-8
80–81	Que	51	8	18	26	64	+9
81–82	Que	79	15	16	31	82	-11
82–83	Que	79	12	28	40	45	-1
83–84	Que	77	19	24	43	41	+21
84–85	Que	80	13	22	35	31	+12
85–86	Que	78	13	21	34	29	-3
86–87	Que	80	12	24	36	38	-4
87–88	Que	76	4	18	22	26	+3
88–89	Que	55	2	8	10	14	-1
NHL Totals		696	103	190	293	383	+17

SSN	TEAM	GP	G	A	PTS.	PIM	+/-
WHA Totals		106	17	18	35	31	

Playoffs

77–78	Que (WHA)	11	1	2	3	0	
78–79	Que (WHA)	4	0	0	0	2	
80–81	Que	4	0	0	0	6	
81–82	Que	16	1	2	3	8	
82–83	Que	4	0	3	3	0	
83–84	Que	9	0	2	2	17	
84–85	Que	18	5	5	10	11	
85–86	Que	3	1	0	1	0	
86–87	Que	13	2	3	5	2	
NHL Totals		67	9	15	24	44	
WHA Totals		15	1	2	3	2	

COTE, Alain Gabriel *6-0 200 D*
B. Montmagny, Que., Apr. 14, 1967

85–86	Bos	32	0	6	6	14	+5
86–87	Bos	3	0	0	0	0	-1
87–88	Bos	2	0	0	0	0	-1
88–89	Bos	31	2	3	5	51	-9
89–90	Wash	2	0	0	0	7	-2
90–91	Mont	28	0	6	6	26	+8
91–92	Mont	13	0	3	3	22	+7
92–93	TB	2	0	0	0	0	-1
93–94	Que	6	0	0	0	0	-2
Totals		119	2	18	20	124	+4

Playoffs

| 90–91 | Mont | 11 | 0 | 2 | 2 | 6 | |

COTE, Patrick *6-3 199 LW*
B. Lasalle, Que., Jan. 24, 1975

95–96	Dal	2	0	0	0	5	-2
96–97	Dal	3	0	0	0	27	0
97–98	Dal	3	0	0	0	15	-1
98–99	Nash	70	1	2	3	242	-7
Totals		78	1	2	3	289	-10

COTE, Raymond *5-11 170 C*
B. Pincher Creek, Alta., May 31, 1961

83–84	Edm	13	0	0	0	2	-5
84–85	Edm	2	0	0	0	2	0
Totals		15	0	0	0	4	-5

Playoffs

| 82–83 | Edm | 14 | 3 | 2 | 5 | 0 | |

COTE, Sylvain *6-0 185 D*
B. Quebec City, Que., Jan. 19, 1966

84–85	Hart	67	3	9	12	17	-30
85–86	Hart	2	0	0	0	0	+1
86–87	Hart	67	2	8	10	20	+11
87–88	Hart	67	7	21	28	30	-8
88–89	Hart	78	8	9	17	49	-7
89–90	Hart	28	4	2	6	14	+2
90–91	Hart	73	7	12	19	17	-17
91–92	Wash	78	11	29	40	31	+7
92–93	Wash	77	21	29	50	34	+28
93–94	Wash	84	16	35	51	66	+30
94–95	Wash	47	5	14	19	53	+2
95–96	Wash	81	5	33	38	40	+5
96–97	Wash	57	6	18	24	28	+11
97–98	Wash–Tor	71	4	21	25	42	-3
98–99	Tor	79	5	24	29	28	+22
Totals		956	104	264	368	469	+54

Playoffs

86–87	Hart	2	0	0	0	2	
87–88	Hart	6	1	1	2	4	
88–89	Hart	3	0	1	1	4	
89–90	Hart	5	0	0	0	2	
90–91	Hart	6	0	2	2	2	
91–92	Wash	7	1	2	3	4	
92–93	Wash	6	1	1	2	4	
93–94	Wash	9	1	8	9	6	
94–95	Wash	7	1	3	4	2	
96–97	Wash	6	2	0	2	12	
98–99	Tor	17	2	1	3	10	
Totals		74	9	21	30	52	

*COTTON, Harold (Baldy) *5-10 155 LW*
B. Nanticoke, Ont., Nov. 5, 1902

25–26	Pitt Pi	33	7	1	8	22	
26–27	Pitt Pi	35	5	0	5	17	
27–28	Pitt Pi	42	9	3	12	40	
28–29	Pitt Pi–Tor	43	4	4	8	46	

SSN	TEAM	GP	G	A	PTS.	PIM	+/-
29–30	Tor	41	21	17	38	47	
30–31	Tor	43	12	17	29	45	
31–32	Tor	47	5	13	18	41	
32–33	Tor	48	10	11	21	29	
33–34	Tor	47	8	14	22	46	
34–35	Tor	47	11	14	25	36	
35–36	NYA	45	7	9	16	23	
36–37	NYA	29	2	0	2	23	
Totals		500	101	103	204	415	

Playoffs

SSN	TEAM	GP	G	A	PTS.	PIM	+/-
25–26	PittPi	1	1	0	1	0	
27–28	PittPi	2	1	1	2	2	
28–29	Tor	4	0	0	0	2	
30–31	Tor	2	0	0	0	2	
31–32	Tor	7	2	2	4	8	
32–33	Tor	9	0	3	3	6	
33–34	Tor	5	0	2	2	0	
34–35	Tor	7	0	0	0	17	
35–36	NYA	5	0	1	1	9	
Totals		43	4	9	13	46	

*COUGHLIN, James (Jack) F

SSN	TEAM	GP	G	A	PTS.	PIM	+/-
17–18	Tor	6	2	0	2	0	
19–20	Que–Mont	11	0	0	0	0	
20–21	Ham	2	0	0	0	0	
Totals		19	2	0	2	0	

COULIS, Tim *6–0 200 LW*
B. Kenora, Ont., Feb. 24, 1958

SSN	TEAM	GP	G	A	PTS.	PIM	+/-
79–80	Wash	19	1	2	3	27	-6
83–84	Minn	2	0	0	0	4	-1
84–85	Minn	7	1	1	2	34	-1
85–86	Minn	19	2	2	4	73	-5
Totals		47	4	5	9	138	-13

Playoffs

SSN	TEAM	GP	G	A	PTS.	PIM	+/-
84–85	Minn	3	1	0	1	2	

COULSON, D'Arcy D

SSN	TEAM	GP	G	A	PTS.	PIM	+/-
30–31	Phil Q	28	0	0	0	103	

*COULTER, Arthur Edmond *5–11 185 D*
B. Winnipeg, Man., May 31, 1909

SSN	TEAM	GP	G	A	PTS.	PIM	+/-
31–32	Chi	13	0	1	1	23	
32–33	Chi	46	3	2	5	53	
33–34	Chi	46	5	2	7	59	
34–35	Chi	48	4	8	12	68	
35–36	Chi–NYR	48	1	7	8	44	
36–37	NYR	47	1	5	6	27	
37–38	NYR	43	5	10	15	90	
38–39	NYR	44	4	8	12	58	
39–40	NYR	48	1	9	10	68	
40–41	NYR	35	5	14	19	42	
41–42	NYR	47	1	16	17	31	
Totals		465	30	82	112	563	

Playoffs

SSN	TEAM	GP	G	A	PTS.	PIM	+/-
31–32	Chi	2	1	0	1	0	
33–34	Chi	8	1	0	1	10	
34–35	Chi	2	0	0	0	5	
36–37	NYR	9	0	3	3	15	
38–39	NYR	7	1	1	2	6	
39–40	NYR	12	1	0	1	21	
40–41	NYR	3	0	0	0	0	
41–42	NYR	6	0	1	1	4	
Totals		49	4	5	9	61	

COULTER, Neal *6–2 180 RW*
B. London, Ont., Jan. 2, 1963

SSN	TEAM	GP	G	A	PTS.	PIM	+/-
85–86	NYI	16	3	4	7	4	-1
86–87	NYI	9	2	1	3	7	-2
87–88	NYI	1	0	0	0	0	-1
Totals		26	5	5	10	11	-4

Playoffs

SSN	TEAM	GP	G	A	PTS.	PIM	+/-
85–86	NYI	1	0	0	0	0	

COULTER, Thomas F

SSN	TEAM	GP	G	A	PTS.	PIM	+/-
33–34	Chi	2	0	0	0	0	

COURNOYER, Yvan Serge (Roadrunner) *5–7 178 RW*
B. Drummondville, Que., Nov. 22, 1943

SSN	TEAM	GP	G	A	PTS.	PIM	+/-
63–64	Mont	5	4	0	4	0	
64–65	Mont	55	7	10	17	10	
65–66	Mont	65	18	11	29	8	
66–67	Mont	69	25	15	40	14	
67–68	Mont	64	28	32	60	23	+19
68–69	Mont	76	43	44	87	31	+19
69–70	Mont	72	27	36	63	23	+1
70–71	Mont	65	37	36	73	21	+20
71–72	Mont	73	47	36	83	15	+23
72–73	Mont	67	40	39	79	18	+50
73–74	Mont	67	40	33	73	18	+16
74–75	Mont	76	29	45	74	32	+16
75–76	Mont	71	32	36	68	20	+37
76–77	Mont	60	25	28	53	8	+27
77–78	Mont	68	24	29	53	12	+39
78–79	Mont	15	2	5	7	2	+5
Totals		968	428	435	863	255	+272

Playoffs

SSN	TEAM	GP	G	A	PTS.	PIM	+/-
64–65	Mont	12	3	1	4	0	
65–66	Mont	10	2	3	5	2	
66–67	Mont	10	2	3	5	6	
67–68	Mont	13	6	8	14	4	
68–69	Mont	14	4	7	11	5	
70–71	Mont	20	10	12	22	6	
71–72	Mont	6	2	1	3	2	
72–73	Mont	17	15	10	25	2	
73–74	Mont	6	5	2	7	2	
74–75	Mont	11	5	6	11	4	
75–76	Mont	13	3	6	9	4	
77–78	Mont	15	7	4	11	10	
Totals		147	64	63	127	47	

COURTEAU, Yves *5–10 185 RW*
B. Montreal, Que., Apr. 25, 1964

SSN	TEAM	GP	G	A	PTS.	PIM	+/-
84–85	Calg	14	1	4	5	4	+2
85–86	Calg	4	1	1	2	0	+1
86–87	Hart	4	0	0	0	0	-6
Totals		22	2	5	7	4	-3

Playoffs

SSN	TEAM	GP	G	A	PTS.	PIM	+/-
85–86	Calg	1	0	0	0	0	

COURTENAY, Edward *6–4 215 RW*
B. Verdun, Que., Feb. 2, 1968

SSN	TEAM	GP	G	A	PTS.	PIM	+/-
91–92	SJ	5	0	0	0	0	-6
92–93	SJ	39	7	13	20	10	-15
Totals		44	7	13	20	10	-21

COURTNALL, Geoff *6–1 190 LW*
B. Victoria, B.C., Aug. 18, 1962

SSN	TEAM	GP	G	A	PTS.	PIM	+/-
83–84	Bos	4	0	0	0	0	-1
84–85	Bos	64	12	16	28	82	-3
85–86	Bos	64	21	16	37	61	+1
86–87	Bos	65	13	23	36	117	-4
87–88	Bos–Edm	74	36	30	66	123	+25
88–89	Wash	79	42	38	80	112	+11
89–90	Wash	80	35	39	74	104	+27
90–91	StL–Van	77	33	32	65	64	+16
91–92	Van	70	23	34	57	118	-6
92–93	Van	84	31	46	77	167	+27
93–94	Van	82	26	44	70	123	+15
94–95	Van	45	16	18	34	81	+2
95–96	StL	69	24	16	40	101	-9
96–97	StL	82	17	40	57	86	+3
97–98	StL	79	31	31	62	94	+12
98–99	StL	24	5	7	12	28	+2
Totals		1042	365	430	795	1459	+120

Playoffs

SSN	TEAM	GP	G	A	PTS.	PIM	+/-
84–85	Bos	5	0	2	2	7	
85–86	Bos	3	0	0	0	2	
86–87	Bos	1	0	0	0	0	
87–88	Edm	19	0	3	3	23	
88–89	Wash	6	2	5	7	12	
89–90	Wash	15	4	9	13	32	
90–91	Van	6	3	5	8	4	
91–92	Van	12	6	8	14	20	
92–93	Van	12	4	10	14	12	
93–94	Van	24	9	10	19	51	
94–95	Van	11	4	2	6	34	
95–96	StL	13	0	3	3	14	
96–97	StL	6	3	1	4	23	
97–98	StL	10	2	8	10	18	
98–99	StL	13	2	4	6	10	
Totals		156	39	70	109	262	

COURTNALL, Russell *5–11 183 C/RW*
B. Duncan, B.C., June 2, 1965

SSN	TEAM	GP	G	A	PTS.	PIM	+/-
83–84	Tor	14	3	9	12	6	0
84–85	Tor	69	12	10	22	44	-23
85–86	Tor	73	22	38	60	52	0
86–87	Tor	79	29	44	73	90	-20
87–88	Tor	65	23	26	49	47	-16
88–89	Tor–Mont	73	23	18	41	19	+9
89–90	Mont	80	27	32	59	27	+14
90–91	Mont	79	26	50	76	29	+5
91–92	Mont	27	7	14	21	6	+6
92–93	Minn	84	36	43	79	49	+1
93–94	Dal	84	23	57	80	59	+6
94–95	Dal–Van	45	11	24	35	17	+2
95–96	Van	81	26	39	65	40	+25
96–97	Van–NYR	61	11	24	35	26	+1
97–98	LA	58	12	6	18	27	-2
98–99	LA	57	6	13	19	19	-9
Totals		1029	297	447	744	557	-1

Playoffs

SSN	TEAM	GP	G	A	PTS.	PIM	+/-
85–86	Tor	10	3	6	9	8	
86–87	Tor	13	3	4	7	11	
87–88	Tor	6	2	1	3	0	
88–89	Mont	21	8	5	13	18	
89–90	Mont	11	5	1	6	10	
90–91	Mont	13	8	3	11	7	
91–92	Mont	10	1	1	2	4	
93–94	Dal	9	1	8	9	0	
94–95	Van	11	4	8	12	21	
95–96	Van	6	1	3	4	2	
96–97	NYR	15	3	4	7	0	
97–98	LA	4	0	0	0	2	
Totals		129	39	44	83	83	

COURTURIER, Sylvain *6–2 205 C*
B. Greenfield Park, Que., Apr. 23, 1968

SSN	TEAM	GP	G	A	PTS.	PIM	+/-
88–89	LA	16	1	3	4	2	-3
90–91	LA	3	0	1	1	0	0
91–92	LA	14	3	1	4	2	-3
Totals		33	4	5	9	4	-6

COURVILLE, Larry *6–1 180 LW*
B. Timmins, Ont., Apr. 2, 1975

SSN	TEAM	GP	G	A	PTS.	PIM	+/-
95–96	Van	3	1	0	1	0	+1
96–97	Van	19	0	2	2	11	-4
97–98	Van	11	0	0	0	5	-7
Totals		33	1	2	3	16	-10

*COUTURE, Billy D
B. Sault Ste. Marie, Ont.

SSN	TEAM	GP	G	A	PTS.	PIM	+/-
17–18	Mont	19	2	0	2	30	
18–19	Mont	15	1	1	2	18	
19–20	Mont	17	4	0	4	30	
20–21	Ham	24	8	4	12	74	
21–22	Mont	23	4	3	7	4	
22–23	Mont	24	5	2	7	37	
23–24	Mont	16	3	1	4	8	
24–25	Mont	28	3	2	5	49	
25–26	Mont	33	2	4	6	95	
26–27	Bos	41	1	1	2	25	
Totals		240	33	18	51	370	

Playoffs

SSN	TEAM	GP	G	A	PTS.	PIM	+/-
17–18	Mont	2	0	0	0	0	
18–19	Mont	10	0	0	0	6	
22–23	Mont	1	0	0	0	2	
23–24	Mont	6	0	0	0	2	
24–25	Mont	6	1	0	1	14	
26–27	Bos	7	1	0	1	4	
Totals		32	2	0	2	28	

*COUTURE, Gerald Joseph Wilfred Arthur (Doc) *6–2 185 C*
B. Saskatoon, Sask., Aug. 6, 1925

SSN	TEAM	GP	G	A	PTS.	PIM	+/-
45–46	Det	43	3	7	10	18	
46–47	Det	30	5	10	15	0	
47–48	Det	19	3	6	9	2	
48–49	Det	51	19	10	29	6	
49–50	Det	70	24	7	31	21	
50–51	Det	53	7	6	13	2	
51–52	Mont	10	0	1	1	4	
52–53	Chi	70	19	18	37	22	
53–54	Chi	40	6	5	11	14	
Totals		386	86	70	156	89	

Playoffs

SSN	TEAM	GP	G	A	PTS.	PIM	+/-
44–45	Det	2	0	0	0	0	
45–46	Det	5	0	2	2	0	
46–47	Det	1	0	0	0	0	

SSN	TEAM	GP	G	A	PTS.	PIM	+/-
48–49	Det	10	2	0	2	2	
49–50	Det	14	5	4	9	2	
50–51	Det	6	1	1	2	0	
52–53	Chi	7	1	0	1	0	
Totals		45	9	7	16	4	

*COUTURE, Rosario (Rosie, Lolo) 5-11 164 RW
B. St. Boniface, Man., July 24, 1905

SSN	TEAM	GP	G	A	PTS.	PIM	+/-
28–29	Chi	43	1	3	4	22	
29–30	Chi	43	8	8	16	63	
30–31	Chi	44	8	11	19	30	
31–32	Chi	48	9	9	18	8	
32–33	Chi	46	10	7	17	26	
33–34	Chi	48	5	8	13	21	
34–35	Chi	27	7	9	16	14	
35–36	Mont	10	0	1	1	0	
Totals		309	48	56	104	184	

Playoffs

29–30	Chi	2	0	0	0	2	
30–31	Chi	9	0	3	3	2	
31–32	Chi	2	0	0	0	2	
33–34	Chi	8	1	2	3	4	
34–35	Chi	2	0	0	0	5	
Totals		23	1	5	6	15	

COWAN, Thomas D
30–31 Phil 1 0 0 0 0

COWICK, Robert Bruce (Bruce) 6-1 200 LW
B. Victoria, B.C., Aug. 18, 1951

74–75	Wash	65	5	6	11	41	-42
75–76	StL	5	0	0	0	2	+1
Totals		70	5	6	11	43	-41

Playoffs
73–74 Phil 8 0 0 0 9

COWIE, Rob 6-0 195 D
B. Toronto, Ont., Nov. 3, 1967

94–95	LA	32	2	7	9	20	-6
95–96	LA	46	5	5	10	32	-16
Totals		78	7	12	19	52	-22

*COWLEY, William Mailes 5-10 165 C
B. Bristol, Que., June 12, 1912

34–35	StLE	41	5	7	12	10	
35–36	Bos	48	11	10	21	17	
36–37	Bos	46	13	22	35	35	
37–38	Bos	48	17	22	39	8	
38–39	Bos	34	8	34	42	2	
39–40	Bos	48	13	27	40	24	
40–41	Bos	46	17	45	62	16	
41–42	Bos	28	4	23	27	6	
42–43	Bos	48	27	45	72	10	
43–44	Bos	36	30	41	71	12	
44–45	Bos	49	25	40	65	12	
45–46	Bos	26	12	12	24	6	
46–47	Bos	51	13	25	38	16	
Totals		549	195	353	548	174	

Playoffs

35–36	Bos	2	2	1	3	2	
36–37	Bos	3	0	3	3	0	
37–38	Bos	3	2	0	2	0	
38–39	Bos	12	3	11	14	2	
39–40	Bos	6	1	0	1	7	
40–41	Bos	2	0	0	0	0	
41–42	Bos	5	0	3	3	5	
42–43	Bos	9	1	7	8	4	
44–45	Bos	7	3	3	6	0	
45–46	Bos	10	1	3	4	2	
46–47	Bos	5	0	2	2	0	
Totals		64	13	33	46	22	

*COX, Daniel Smith 5-10 180 LW
B. Little Current, Ont., Oct. 12, 1903

26–27	Tor	14	0	1	1	4	
27–28	Tor	41	9	6	15	27	
28–29	Tor	42	12	7	19	14	
29–30	Tor-Ott	42	4	6	10	20	
30–31	Ott	44	9	12	21	12	
31–32	Det	47	4	6	10	23	
32–33	Ott	47	4	7	11	8	
33–34	Ott-NYR	42	5	4	9	2	
34–35	StLE	10	0	0	0	0	
Totals		329	47	49	96	110	

Playoffs

28–29	Tor	4	0	1	1	4	
29–30	Ott	2	0	0	0	0	
31–32	Det	2	0	0	0	2	
33–34	NYR	2	0	0	0	0	
Totals		10	0	1	1	6	

COXE, Craig 6-4 200 C
B. Chula Vista, Cal., Jan. 21, 1964

84–85	Van	9	0	0	0	49	-5
85–86	Van	57	3	5	8	176	-13
86–87	Van	15	0	1	1	31	-3
87–88	Van-Calg	71	7	15	22	218	+2
88–89	StL	41	0	7	7	127	+3
89–90	Van	25	1	4	5	66	-4
90–91	Van	7	0	0	0	27	-3
91–92	SJ	10	2	0	2	19	-4
Totals		235	14	31	45	713	-27

Playoffs

85–86	Van	3	0	0	0	2	
87–88	Calg	2	1	0	1	16	
Totals		5	1	0	1	18	

CRAIG, Mike 6-1 180 RW
B. London, Ont., June 6, 1971

90–91	Minn	39	8	4	12	32	-11
91–92	Minn	67	15	16	31	155	-12
92–93	Minn	70	15	23	38	106	-11
93–94	Dal	72	13	24	37	139	-14
94–95	Tor	37	5	5	10	12	-21
95–96	Tor	70	8	12	20	42	-8
96–97	Tor	65	7	13	20	62	-20
98–99	SJ	1	0	0	0	0	-1
Totals		421	71	97	168	548	-98

Playoffs

90–91	Minn	10	1	1	2	20	
91–92	Minn	4	1	0	1	7	
93–94	Dal	4	0	0	0	2	
94–95	Tor	2	0	1	1	2	
95–96	Tor	6	0	0	0	18	
Totals		26	2	2	4	49	

CRAIGHEAD, John 6-0 195 RW
B. Vancouver, B.C., Nov. 13, 1971
96–97 Tor 5 0 0 0 10

CRAIGWELL, Dale 5-11 178 C
B. Toronto, Ont., Apr. 24, 1971

91–92	SJ	32	5	11	16	8	-3
92–93	SJ	8	3	1	4	4	-4
93–94	SJ	58	3	6	9	16	-13
Totals		98	11	18	29	28	-20

CRASHLEY, William Barton (Bart) 6-0 180 D
B. Toronto, Ont., June 15, 1946

65–66	Det	1	0	0	0	0	
66–67	Det	2	0	0	0	2	
67–68	Det	57	2	14	16	18	+6
68–69	Det	1	0	0	0	0	0
72–73	LA (WHA)	70	18	27	45	10	
73–74	LA (WHA)	78	4	26	30	16	
74–75	KC-Det	75	5	21	26	24	-26
75–76	LA	4	0	1	1	6	-10
NHL Totals		140	7	36	43	50	-30
WHA Totals		148	22	53	75	26	

Playoffs
72–73 LA (WHA) 6 0 2 2 2

CRAVEN, Murray 6-2 190 LW
B. Medicine Hat, Alta., July 20, 1964

82–83	Det	31	4	7	11	6	+4
83–84	Det	15	0	4	4	6	+2
84–85	Phil	80	26	35	61	30	+45
85–86	Phil	78	21	33	54	34	+24
86–87	Phil	77	19	30	49	38	+1
87–88	PHil	72	30	46	76	58	+25
88–89	Phil	51	9	28	37	52	+4
89–90	Phil	76	25	50	75	42	+2
90–91	Phil	77	19	47	66	53	-2
91–92	Phil-Hart	73	27	33	60	46	-8
92–93	Hart-Van	77	25	52	77	32	-1
93–94	Van	78	15	40	55	30	+5
94–95	Chi	16	4	3	7	2	+2
95–96	Chi	66	18	29	47	36	+20
96–97	Chi	75	8	27	35	12	0
97–98	SJ	67	12	17	29	25	+4
98–99	SJ	43	4	10	14	18	-3
Totals		1052	266	491	757	520	+124

Playoffs

84–85	Phil	19	4	6	10	11	
85–86	Phil	5	0	3	3	4	
86–87	Phil	12	3	1	4	9	
87–88	Phil	7	2	5	7	4	
88–89	Phil	1	0	0	0	0	
91–92	Hart	7	3	3	6	6	
92–93	Van	12	4	6	10	4	
93–94	Van	22	4	9	13	18	
94–95	Chi	16	5	5	10	4	
95–96	Chi	9	1	4	5	2	
96–97	Chi	2	0	0	0	2	
97–98	SJ	6	1	1	2	0	
Totals		118	27	43	70	64	

*CRAWFORD, Jack Shea (John) 5-11 200 D
B. Dublin, Ont., Oct. 26, 1916

37–38	Bos	2	0	0	0	0	
38–39	Bos	38	4	8	12	12	
39–40	Bos	36	1	4	5	26	
40–41	Bos	45	2	8	10	27	
41–42	Bos	43	2	9	11	37	
42–43	Bos	49	5	18	23	24	
43–44	Bos	34	4	16	20	8	
44–45	Bos	40	5	19	24	10	
45–46	Bos	48	7	9	16	10	
46–47	Bos	58	1	17	18	16	
47–48	Bos	45	3	11	14	10	
48–49	Bos	55	2	13	15	14	
49–50	Bos	46	2	8	10	8	
Totals		539	38	140	178	202	

Playoffs

38–39	Bos	12	1	1	2	9	
39–40	Bos	6	0	0	0	0	
40–41	Bos	11	0	2	2	7	
41–42	Bos	5	0	1	1	4	
42–43	Bos	6	1	1	2	10	
44–45	Bos	7	0	5	5	0	
45–46	Bos	10	1	2	3	4	
46–47	Bos	2	1	0	1	0	
47–48	Bos	4	0	1	1	2	
48–49	Bos	3	0	0	0	0	
Totals		66	4	13	17	36	

CRAWFORD, Louis 6-0 185 LW
B. Belleville, Ont., Nov. 5, 1962

89–90	Bos	7	0	0	0	20	+1
91–92	Bos	19	2	1	3	9	-6
Totals		26	2	1	3	29	-5

CRAWFORD, Marc Joseph 5-11 185 LW
B. Belleville, Ont., Feb. 13, 1961

81–82	Van	40	4	8	12	29	0
82–83	Van	41	4	5	9	28	-3
83–84	Van	19	0	1	1	9	0
84–85	Van	1	0	0	0	4	-4
85–86	Van	54	11	14	25	92	-7
86–87	Van	21	0	3	3	67	-8
Totals		176	19	31	50	229	-22

Playoffs

81–82	Van	14	1	0	1	11	
82–83	Van	3	0	1	1	25	
85–86	Van	3	0	1	1	8	
Totals		20	1	2	3	44	

CRAWFORD, Robert (Bobby) 5-8 180 RW
B. Long Island, N.Y., May 27, 1960

80–81	Col	15	1	3	4	6	+4
82–83	Det	1	0	0	0	0	0
Totals		16	1	3	4	6	+4

CRAWFORD, Robert Remi (Bob) 5-11 180 RW
B. Belleville, Ont., Apr. 6, 1959

79–80	StL	8	1	0	1	2	-6
81–82	StL	3	0	1	1	0	-4
82–83	StL	27	5	9	14	2	-5

SSN	TEAM	GP	G	A	PTS.	PIM	+/-
83–84	Hart	80	36	25	61	32	-1
84–85	Hart	45	14	14	28	8	-3
85–86	Hart–NYR	68	15	22	37	26	-14
86–87	NYR–Wash	15	0	0	0	2	-1
Totals		246	71	71	142	72	-34

Playoffs

82–83	StL	4	0	0	0	0	
85–86	NYR	7	0	1	1	8	
Totals		11	0	1	1	8	

CRAWFORD, Samuel Russell (Rusty) *LW*
B. Cardinal, Ont., Nov. 7, 1884

17–18	Ott–Tor	20	3	0	3	33	
18–19	Tor	18	7	3	10	18	
Totals		38	10	3	13	51	

Playoffs

| 17–18 | Tor | 2 | 2 | 1 | 3 | 0 | |

CREIGHTON, Adam *6–5 214 C*
B. Burlington, Ont., June 2, 1965

83–84	Buf	7	2	2	4	4	0
84–85	Buf	30	2	8	10	33	-7
85–86	Buf	19	1	1	2	2	-2
86–87	Buf	56	18	22	40	26	+4
87–88	Buf	36	10	17	27	87	+7
88–89	Buf–Chi	67	22	24	46	136	-9
89–90	Chi	80	34	36	70	224	+4
90–91	Chi	72	22	29	51	135	0
91–92	Chi–NYI	77	21	15	36	118	-5
92–93	TB	83	19	20	39	110	-19
93–94	TB	53	10	10	20	37	-7
94–95	StL	48	14	20	34	74	+17
95–96	StL	61	11	10	21	78	0
96–97	Chi	19	1	2	3	13	-2
Totals		708	187	216	403	1077	-19

Playoffs

88–89	Chi	15	5	6	11	44	
89–90	Chi	20	3	6	9	59	
90–91	Chi	6	0	1	1	10	
94–95	StL	7	2	0	2	16	
95–96	StL	13	1	1	2	8	
Totals		61	11	14	25	137	

CREIGHTON, David Theodore *6–1 181 C*
B. Port Arthur, Ont., June 24, 1930

48–49	Bos	12	1	3	4	0	
49–50	Bos	64	18	13	31	13	
50–51	Bos	56	5	4	9	4	
51–52	Bos	49	20	17	37	18	
52–53	Bos	45	8	8	16	14	
53–54	Bos	69	20	20	40	27	
54–55	Tor–Chi	63	9	8	17	14	
55–56	NYR	70	20	31	51	43	
56–57	NYR	70	18	21	39	42	
57–58	NYR	70	17	35	52	40	
58–59	Tor	34	3	9	12	4	
59–60	Tor	14	1	5	6	4	
Totals		616	140	174	314	223	

Playoffs

48–49	Bos	3	0	0	0	0	
50–51	Bos	5	0	1	1	0	
51–52	Bos	7	2	1	3	2	
52–53	Bos	11	4	5	9	10	
53–54	Bos	4	0	0	0	0	
55–56	NYR	5	0	0	0	4	
56–57	NYR	5	2	2	4	2	
57–58	NYR	6	3	3	6	2	
58–59	Tor	5	0	1	1	0	
Totals		51	11	13	24	20	

*CREIGHTON, James *F*

| 30–31 | Det | 11 | 1 | 0 | 1 | 2 | |

CRESSMAN, David Gregory *6–1 180 LW*
B. Kitchener, Ont., Jan. 2, 1950

74–75	Minn	5	2	0	2	4	+2
75–76	Minn	80	4	8	12	33	-4
Totals		85	6	8	14	37	-2

CRESSMAN, Glen *5–8 155 C*
B. Peterborough, Ont., Aug. 29, 1934

| 56–57 | Mont | 4 | 0 | 0 | 0 | 2 | |

CRISP, Terrance Arthur (Terry) *5–10 180 C*
B. Parry Sound, Ont., May 28, 1943

65–66	Bos	3	0	0	0	0	
67–68	StL	73	9	20	29	10	+9
68–69	StL	57	6	9	15	14	+8
69–70	StL	26	5	6	11	2	0
70–71	StL	54	5	11	16	13	+3
71–72	StL	75	13	18	31	12	+7
72–73	NYI–Phil	66	5	21	26	8	-18
73–74	Phil	71	10	21	31	28	+12
74–75	Phil	71	8	19	27	20	+11
75–76	Phil	38	6	9	15	28	+6
76–77	Phil	2	0	0	0	0	0
Totals		536	67	134	201	135	+32

Playoffs

67–68	StL	18	1	5	6	6	
68–69	StL	12	3	4	7	20	
69–70	StL	16	2	3	5	2	
70–71	StL	6	1	0	1	2	
71–72	StL	11	1	3	4	2	
72–73	Phil	11	3	2	5	2	
73–74	Phil	17	2	2	4	4	
74–75	Phil	9	2	4	6	0	
75–76	Phil	10	0	5	5	2	
Totals		110	15	28	43	40	

CRISTOFOLI, Ed *6–2 205 C*
B. Trail, B.C., May 14, 1967

| 89–90 | Mont | 9 | 0 | 1 | 1 | 4 | -1 |

CROGHEN, Maurice *F*
B. Montreal, Que., Nov. 19, 1914

| 37–38 | Mont M | 16 | 0 | 0 | 0 | 4 | |

CROMBEEN, Michael Joseph *5–11 190 RW*
B. Sarnia, Ont., Apr. 16, 1957

77–78	Clev	48	3	4	7	13	-26
78–79	StL	37	3	8	11	34	-13
79–80	StL	71	10	12	22	20	-14
80–81	StL	66	9	14	23	58	+1
81–82	StL	71	19	8	27	32	-10
82–83	StL	80	6	11	17	20	-5
83–84	Hart	56	1	4	5	25	-13
84–85	Hart	46	4	7	11	16	0
Totals		475	55	68	123	218	-80

Playoffs

79–80	StL	2	0	0	0	0	
80–81	StL	11	3	0	3	8	
81–82	StL	10	3	1	4	20	
82–83	StL	4	0	1	1	4	
Totals		27	6	2	8	32	

CRONIN, Shawn *6–2 225 D*
B. Flushing, Mich., Aug. 20, 1963

88–89	Wash	1	0	0	0	0	0
89–90	Winn	61	0	4	4	243	-16
90–91	Winn	67	1	5	6	189	-10
91–92	Winn	65	0	4	4	271	-11
92–93	Phil	35	2	1	3	37	0
93–94	SJ	34	0	2	2	76	+2
94–95	SJ	29	0	2	2	61	0
Totals		292	3	18	21	877	-35

Playoffs

89–90	Winn	5	0	0	0	7	
91–92	Winn	4	0	0	0	6	
93–94	SJ	14	1	0	1	20	
94–95	SJ	9	0	0	0	5	
Totals		32	1	0	1	38	

CROSS, Cory James *6–5 212 D*
B. Lloydminster, Alta., Jan. 3, 1971

93–94	TB	5	0	0	0	6	-3
94–95	TB	43	1	5	6	41	-6
95–96	TB	75	2	14	16	66	+4
96–97	TB	72	4	5	9	95	+6
97–98	TB	74	3	6	9	77	-24
98–99	TB	67	2	16	18	92	-25
Totals		336	12	46	58	377	-48

Playoffs

| 95–96 | TB | 6 | 0 | 0 | 0 | 22 | |

CROSSETT, Stanley *F*

| 30–31 | Phil Q | 21 | 0 | 0 | 0 | 10 | |

CROSSMAN, Douglas *6–2 190 D*
B. Peterborough, Ont., June 30, 1960

80–81	Chi	9	0	2	2	2	-5
81–82	Chi	70	12	28	40	24	-19
82–83	Chi	80	13	40	53	46	+21
83–84	Phil	78	7	28	35	63	+23
84–85	Phil	80	4	33	37	65	+31
85–86	Phil	80	6	37	43	55	-5
86–87	Phil	78	9	31	40	29	+18
87–88	Phil	76	9	29	38	43	-1
88–89	LA	74	10	15	25	53	-11
89–90	NYI	80	15	44	59	54	+3
90–91	NYI–Hart–Det	74	8	29	37	48	-23
91–92	Det	26	0	8	8	14	+8
92–93	TB–StL	59	10	28	38	28	-7
93–94	StL	50	2	7	9	10	+1
Totals		914	105	359	464	534	+34

Playoffs

81–82	Chi	11	0	3	3	4	
82–83	Chi	13	3	7	10	6	
83–84	Phil	3	0	0	0	0	
84–85	Phil	19	4	6	10	38	
85–86	Phil	5	0	1	1	4	
86–87	Phil	26	4	14	18	31	
87–88	Phil	7	1	1	2	8	
88–89	LA	2	0	1	1	2	
89–90	NYI	5	0	1	1	6	
90–91	Det	6	0	5	5	6	
Totals		97	12	39	51	105	

CROTEAU, Gary Paul *6–0 202 LW*
B. Sudbury, Ont., June 20, 1946

68–69	LA	11	5	1	6	6	-1
69–70	LA–Det	13	0	2	2	2	-1
70–71	Cal	74	15	28	43	12	-22
71–72	Cal	73	12	12	24	11	-18
72–73	Cal	47	6	15	21	8	-13
73–74	Cal	76	14	21	35	16	-47
74–75	KC	77	8	11	19	16	-36
75–76	KC	79	19	14	33	24	-24
76–77	Col	78	24	27	51	14	-18
77–78	Col	62	17	22	39	24	-15
78–79	Col	79	23	18	41	18	-28
79–80	Col	15	1	4	5	4	-4
Totals		684	144	175	319	143	-227

Playoffs

| 68–69 | LA | 11 | 3 | 2 | 5 | 8 | |

CROWDER, Bruce *6–0 180 RW*
B. Essex, Ont., Mar. 25, 1957

81–82	Bos	63	16	11	27	31	+7
82–83	Bos	80	21	19	40	58	-30
83–84	Bos	74	6	14	20	44	+1
84–85	Pitt	26	4	7	11	23	-9
Totals		243	47	51	98	156	-31

Playoffs

81–82	Bos	11	5	3	8	9	
82–83	Bos	17	3	1	4	32	
83–84	Bos	3	0	0	0	0	
Totals		31	8	4	12	41	

CROWDER, Keith Scott *6–0 190 RW*
B. Windsor, Ont., Jan. 6, 1959

78–79	Birm (WHA)	5	1	0	1	17	
80–81	Bos	47	13	12	25	172	+9
81–82	Bos	71	23	21	44	101	0
82–83	Bos	74	35	39	74	105	+22
83–84	Bos	63	24	28	52	128	+12
84–85	Bos	79	32	38	70	142	+31
85–86	Bos	78	38	46	84	177	+14
86–87	Bos	58	22	30	52	106	+20
87–88	Bos	68	17	26	43	173	+14
88–89	Bos	69	15	18	33	147	+6
89–90	LA	55	4	13	17	93	+2
NHL Totals		662	223	271	494	1346	+130
WHA Totals		5	1	0	1	17	

Playoffs

80–81	Bos	3	2	0	2	9	
81–82	Bos	11	2	2	4	14	
82–83	Bos	17	1	6	7	54	

SSN	TEAM	GP	G	A	PTS.	PIM	+/-
83–84	Bos	3	0	0	0	7	
84–85	Bos	4	3	2	5	19	
85–86	Bos	3	2	0	2	21	
86–87	Bos	4	0	1	1	4	
87–88	Bos	23	3	9	12	44	
88–89	Bos	10	0	2	2	37	
89–90	LA	7	1	0	1	9	
Totals		85	14	22	36	218	

CROWDER, Troy *6–4 215 RW*
B. Sudbury, Ont., May 3, 1968

SSN	TEAM	GP	G	A	PTS.	PIM	+/-
89–90	NJ	10	0	0	0	23	0
90–91	NJ	59	6	3	9	182	-10
91–92	Det	7	0	0	0	35	0
94–95	LA	29	1	2	3	99	0
95–96	LA	15	1	0	1	42	-3
96–97	Van	30	1	2	3	52	-6
Totals		150	9	7	16	433	-19

Playoffs

88–89	NJ	1	0	0	0	12	
89–90	NJ	2	0	0	0	10	
91–92	Det	1	0	0	0	0	
Totals		4	0	0	0	22	

CROWE, Philip *6–2 220 LW*
B. Nanton, Alta., Apr. 14, 1970

93–94	LA	31	0	2	2	77	+4
95–96	Phil	16	1	1	2	28	0
96–97	Ott	26	0	1	1	30	0
97–98	Ott	9	3	0	3	24	+3
98–99	Ott	8	0	1	1	4	+1
Totals		90	4	5	9	163	+8

Playoffs

96–97	Ott	3	0	0	0	16	

CROWLEY, Mike *5–11 190 D*
B. Bloomington, Minn., July 4, 1975

97–98	Ana	8	2	2	4	8	0
98–99	Ana	20	2	3	5	16	-10
Totals		28	4	5	9	24	-10

CROWLEY, Ted *6–2 188 D*
B. Concord, Mass., May 3, 1970

93–94	Hart	21	1	2	3	10	-1
98–99	Col A-NYI	13	1	2	3	2	-1
Totals		34	2	4	6	12	-2

CROZIER, Joseph Richard *6–0 180 D*
B. Winnipeg, Man., Feb. 19, 1929

59–60	Tor	5	0	3	3	2	

CRUTCHFIELD, Nelson (Nels) *6–1 175 C*
B. Knowlton, Que., July 12, 1911

34–35	Mont	41	5	5	10	20	

Playoffs

34–35	Mont	2	0	1	1	22	

CULHANE, Jim *6–0 195 D*
B. Halleybury, Ont., Mar. 13, 1965

89–90	Hart	6	0	1	1	4	+3

CULLEN, Brian Joseph *5–10 164 C*
B. Ottawa, Ont., Nov. 11, 1933

54–55	Tor	27	3	5	8	6	
55–56	Tor	21	2	6	8	8	
56–57	Tor	46	8	12	20	27	
57–58	Tor	67	20	23	43	29	
58–59	Tor	59	4	14	18	10	
59–60	NYR	64	8	21	29	6	
60–61	NYR	42	11	19	30	6	
Totals		326	56	100	156	92	

Playoffs

54–55	Tor	4	1	0	1	0	
55–56	Tor	5	1	0	1	2	
58–59	Tor	10	1	0	1	0	
Totals		19	3	0	3	2	

CULLEN, Charles Francis (Barry) *6–0 175 RW*
B. Ottawa, Ont., June 16, 1935

55–56	Tor	3	0	0	0	4	

SSN	TEAM	GP	G	A	PTS.	PIM	+/-
56–57	Tor	51	6	10	16	30	
57–58	Tor	70	16	25	41	37	
58–59	Tor	40	6	8	14	17	
59–60	Det	55	4	9	13	23	
Totals		219	32	52	84	111	

Playoffs

58–59	Tor	2	0	0	0	0	
59–60	Det	4	0	0	0	2	
Totals		6	0	0	0	2	

CULLEN, John *5–10 185 C*
B. Puslinch, Ont., Aug. 2, 1964

88–89	Pitt	79	12	37	49	112	-25
89–90	Pitt	72	32	60	92	138	-13
90–91	Pitt-Hart	78	39	71	110	101	-6
91–92	Hart	77	26	51	77	141	-28
92–93	Hart-Tor	66	18	32	50	111	-23
93–94	Tor	53	13	17	30	67	-2
94–95	Tor	46	13	24	37	66	-4
95–96	TB	76	16	34	50	65	+1
96–97	TB	70	18	37	55	95	-14
98–99	TB	4	0	0	0	2	-1
Totals		621	187	363	550	898	-116

Playoffs

88–89	Pitt	11	3	6	9	28	
90–91	Hart	6	2	7	9	10	
91–92	Hart	7	2	1	3	12	
92–93	Tor	12	2	3	5	0	
93–94	Tor	3	0	0	0	0	
94–95	Pitt	9	0	2	2	8	
95–96	TB	5	3	3	6	0	
Totals		53	12	22	34	58	

CULLEN, Matt *6–1 195 C*
B. Virginia, Minn., Nov. 2, 1976

97–98	Ana	61	6	21	27	23	-4
98–99	Ana	75	11	14	25	47	-12
Totals		136	17	35	52	70	-16

Playoffs

98–99	Ana	4	0	0	0	0	

CULLEN, Raymond Murray *5–11 180 C*
B. Ottawa, Ont., Sept. 20, 1941

65–66	NYR	8	1	3	4	0	
66–67	Det	27	8	8	16	8	
67–68	Minn	67	28	25	53	18	-24
68–69	Minn	67	26	38	64	44	-27
69–70	Minn	74	17	28	45	8	+19
70–71	Van	70	12	21	33	42	-24
Totals		313	92	123	215	120	-56

Playoffs

67–68	Minn	14	2	6	8	2	
69–70	Minn	6	1	4	5	0	
Totals		20	3	10	13	2	

CULLIMORE, Jassen *6–5 225 D*
B. Simcoe, Ont., Dec. 4, 1972

94–95	Van	34	1	2	3	39	-2
95–96	Van	27	1	1	2	21	+4
96–97	Van-Mont	52	2	6	8	44	+2
97–98	Mont-TB	28	1	2	3	26	-4
98–99	TB	78	5	12	17	81	-22
Totals		219	10	23	33	211	-22

Playoffs

94–95	Van	11	0	0	0	12	
96–97	Mont	2	0	0	0	2	
Totals		13	0	0	0	14	

CUMMINS, Barry Kenneth *5–9 175 D*
B. Regina, Sask., Jan. 25, 1949

73–74	Cal	36	1	2	3	39	-35

CUMMINS, Jim *6–2 203 RW*
B. Dearborn, Mich., May 17, 1970

91–92	Det	1	0	0	0	7	0
92–93	Det	7	1	1	2	58	0
93–94	Phil-TB	26	1	2	3	84	-1
94–95	TB-Chi	37	4	1	5	158	-6
95–96	Chi	52	2	4	6	180	-1
96–97	Chi	65	6	6	12	199	+4
97–98	Chi-Phoe	75	0	2	2	225	-16

SSN	TEAM	GP	G	A	PTS.	PIM	+/-
98–99	Phoe	55	1	7	8	190	+3
Totals		338	15	23	38	1101	-17

Playoffs

94–95	Chi	14	1	1	2	4	
95–96	Chi	10	0	0	0	2	
96–97	Chi	6	0	0	0	24	
97–98	Phoe	3	0	0	0	4	
98–99	Phoe	3	0	1	1	0	
Totals		36	1	2	3	34	

CUNNEYWORTH, Randy William *6–0 180 LW*
B. Etobicoke, Ont., May 10, 1961

80–81	Buf	1	0	0	0	2	0
81–82	Buf	20	2	4	6	47	-3
85–86	Pitt	75	15	30	45	74	+12
86–87	Pitt	79	26	27	53	142	+14
87–88	Pitt	71	35	39	74	141	+13
88–89	Pitt	70	25	19	44	156	-22
89–90	Winn-Hart	71	14	15	29	75	-11
90–91	Hart	32	9	5	14	49	-6
91–92	Hart	39	7	10	17	71	-5
92–93	Hart-Chi	39	5	4	9	63	-1
93–94	Hart-Chi	79	13	11	24	100	-1
94–95	Ott	48	5	5	10	68	-19
95–96	Ott	81	17	19	36	130	-31
96–97	Ott	76	12	24	36	99	-7
97–98	Ott	71	2	11	13	63	-14
98–99	Buf	14	2	2	4	0	+1
Totals		866	189	225	414	1280	-80

Playoffs

88–89	Pitt	11	3	5	8	26	
89–90	Hart	4	0	0	0	2	
90–91	Hart	1	0	0	0	0	
91–92	Hart	7	3	0	3	9	
93–94	Chi	6	0	0	0	0	
96–97	Ott	7	1	1	2	10	
97–98	Ott	6	0	1	1	6	
98–99	Buf	3	0	0	0	0	
Totals		45	7	7	14	61	

CUNNINGHAM, James *5–11 185 LW*
B. St. Paul, Minn., Aug. 15, 1956

77–78	Phil	1	0	0	0	4	+1

CUNNINGHAM, Leslie Roy *5–8 165 C*
B. Calgary, Alta., Oct. 4, 1913

36–37	NYA	23	1	8	9	19	
39–40	Chi	37	6	11	17	2	
Totals		60	7	19	26	21	

Playoffs

39–40	Chi	1	0	0	0	2	

CUNNINGHAM, Robert Gordon *5–11 168 C*
B. Welland, Ont., Feb. 26, 1941

60–61	NYR	3	0	1	1	0	
61–62	NYR	1	0	0	0	0	
NHL Totals		4	0	1	1	0	

Playoffs

72–73	Ott (WHA)	5	1	1	2	2	

CUPOLO, William Donald *5–8 170 RW*
B. Niagara Falls, Ont., Jan. 8, 1924

44–45	Bos	47	11	13	24	10	

Playoffs

44–45	Bos	7	1	2	3	0	

CURRAN, Brian *6–5 215 D*
B. Toronto, Ont., Nov. 5, 1963

83–84	Bos	16	1	1	2	57	0
84–85	Bos	56	0	1	1	158	-8
85–86	Bos	43	2	5	7	192	+6
86–87	NYI	68	0	10	10	356	+3
87–88	NYI-Tor	29	0	2	2	87	-6
88–89	Tor	47	1	4	5	185	0
89–90	Tor	72	2	9	11	301	-2
90–91	Tor-Buf	21	0	1	1	50	-5
91–92	Buf	3	0	0	0	14	0
93–94	Wash	26	1	0	1	61	-2
Totals		381	7	33	40	1461	-14

Playoffs

SSN	TEAM	GP	G	A	PTS.	PIM	+/-
83–84	Bos	3	0	0	0	7	
85–86	Bos	2	0	0	0	4	
86–87	NYI	8	0	0	0	51	
87–88	Tor	6	0	0	0	41	
89–90	Tor	5	0	1	1	19	
Totals		24	0	1	1	122	

CURRIE, Dan 6–2 198 LW
B. Burlington, Ont., Mar. 15, 1968

SSN	TEAM	GP	G	A	PTS.	PIM	+/-
90–91	Edm	5	0	0	0	0	0
91–92	Edm	7	1	0	1	0	-1
92–93	Edm	5	0	0	0	4	-4
93–94	LA	5	1	1	2	0	-1
Totals		22	2	1	3	4	-6

CURRIE, Glen 6–2 180 C
B. Montreal, Que., July 18, 1958

SSN	TEAM	GP	G	A	PTS.	PIM	+/-
79–80	Wash	32	2	0	2	2	-2
80–81	Wash	40	5	13	18	16	-5
81–82	Wash	43	7	7	14	14	-2
82–83	Wash	68	11	28	39	20	+18
83–84	Wash	80	12	24	36	20	+9
84–85	Wash	44	1	5	6	19	+2
85–86	LA	12	1	2	3	9	0
87–88	LA	7	0	0	0	0	-2
Totals		326	39	79	118	100	+18

Playoffs

SSN	TEAM	GP	G	A	PTS.	PIM	+/-
82–83	Wash	4	0	3	3	4	
83–84	Wash	8	1	0	1	4	
Totals		12	1	3	4	4	

CURRIE, Hugh Roy 6–0 190 D
B. Saskatoon, Sask., Oct. 22, 1925

SSN	TEAM	GP	G	A	PTS.	PIM	+/-
50–51	Mont	1	0	0	0	0	

CURRIE, Tony 5–11 165 RW
B. Sydney Mines, N.S., Nov. 12, 1957

SSN	TEAM	GP	G	A	PTS.	PIM	+/-
77–78	StL	22	4	5	9	4	-10
78–79	StL	36	4	15	19	0	-9
79–80	StL	40	19	14	33	4	+9
80–81	StL	61	23	32	55	38	+32
81–82	StL-Van	60	23	25	48	19	-6
82–83	Van	8	1	1	2	0	-3
83–84	Van-Hart	50	15	19	34	6	-4
84–85	Hart	13	3	8	11	12	-4
Totals		290	92	119	211	83	+5

Playoffs

SSN	TEAM	GP	G	A	PTS.	PIM	+/-
79–80	StL	2	0	0	0	0	
80–81	StL	11	4	12	16	4	
81–82	Van	3	0	0	0	10	
Totals		16	4	12	16	14	

CURRY, Floyd James (Busher) 5–11 175 RW
B. Chapleau, Ont., Aug. 11, 1925

SSN	TEAM	GP	G	A	PTS.	PIM	+/-
47–48	Mont	31	1	5	6	0	
49–50	Mont	49	8	8	16	8	
50–51	Mont	69	13	14	27	23	
51–52	Mont	64	20	18	38	10	
52–53	Mont	68	16	6	22	10	
53–54	Mont	70	13	8	21	22	
54–55	Mont	68	11	10	21	36	
55–56	Mont	70	14	18	32	10	
56–57	Mont	70	7	9	16	20	
57–58	Mont	42	2	3	5	8	
Totals		601	105	99	204	147	

Playoffs

SSN	TEAM	GP	G	A	PTS.	PIM	+/-
48–49	Mont	2	0	0	0	2	
49–50	Mont	5	1	0	1	2	
50–51	Mont	11	0	2	2	2	
51–52	Mont	11	4	3	7	6	
52–53	Mont	12	2	1	3	2	
53–54	Mont	11	4	0	4	4	
54–55	Mont	12	8	4	12	4	
55–56	Mont	10	1	5	6	12	
56–57	Mont	10	3	2	5	2	
57–58	Mont	7	0	0	0	2	
Totals		91	23	17	40	38	

CURTALE, Tony 6–0 183 D
B. Detroit, Mich., Jan. 29, 1962

SSN	TEAM	GP	G	A	PTS.	PIM	+/-
80–81	Calg	2	0	0	0	0	-1

CURTIS, Paul Edwin 6–0 185 D
B. Peterborough, Ont., Sept. 29, 1947

SSN	TEAM	GP	G	A	PTS.	PIM	+/-
69–70	Mont	1	0	0	0	0	-1
70–71	LA	64	1	13	14	82	-18
71–72	LA	64	1	12	13	57	-32
72–73	LA-StL	56	1	9	10	22	0
74–75	Balt (WHA)	76	4	15	19	32	
NHL Totals		185	3	34	37	161	-51
WHA Totals		76	4	15	19	32	

Playoffs

SSN	TEAM	GP	G	A	PTS.	PIM	+/-
72–73	StL	5	0	0	0	2	

CUSHENAN, Ian Robertson 6–1 195 D
B. Hamilton, Ont., Nov. 29, 1933

SSN	TEAM	GP	G	A	PTS.	PIM	+/-
56–57	Chi	11	0	0	0	13	
57–58	Chi	61	2	8	10	67	
58–59	Mont	35	1	2	3	28	
59–60	NYR	17	0	1	1	12	
63–64	Det	5	0	0	0	4	
Totals		129	3	11	14	124	

CUSSON, Jean 5–10 175 LW
B. Verdon, Que., Oct. 5, 1942

SSN	TEAM	GP	G	A	PTS.	PIM	+/-
67–68	Oak	2	0	0	0	0	-1

CYR, Denis 5–10 180 RW
B. Verdun, Que., Feb. 4, 1961

SSN	TEAM	GP	G	A	PTS.	PIM	+/-
80–81	Calg	10	1	4	5	0	+2
81–82	Calg	45	12	10	22	13	+5
82–83	Calg-Chi	52	8	9	17	2	+7
83–84	Chi	46	12	13	25	19	0
84–85	StL	9	5	3	8	0	+1
85–86	StL	31	3	4	7	2	-11
Totals		193	41	43	84	36	+4

Playoffs

SSN	TEAM	GP	G	A	PTS.	PIM	+/-
82–83	Chi	1	0	0	0	0	
84–85	StL	3	0	0	0	0	
Totals		4	0	0	0	0	

CYR, Paul 5–10 185 LW
B. Port Alberni, B.C., Oct. 31, 1963

SSN	TEAM	GP	G	A	PTS.	PIM	+/-
82–83	Buf	36	15	12	27	59	-6
83–84	Buf	71	16	27	43	52	-3
84–85	Buf	71	22	24	46	63	-7
85–86	Buf	71	20	31	51	120	+4
86–87	Buf	73	11	16	27	122	-16
87–88	Buf-NYR	60	5	14	19	79	-7
88–89	NYR	1	0	0	0	2	0
90–91	Hart	70	12	13	25	107	-8
91–92	Hart	17	0	3	3	19	-4
Totals		470	101	140	241	623	-47

Playoffs

SSN	TEAM	GP	G	A	PTS.	PIM	+/-
82–83	Buf	10	1	3	4	6	
84–85	Buf	3	0	1	1	0	
84–85	Buf	5	2	2	4	15	
90–91	Hart	6	1	0	1	10	
Totals		24	4	6	10	31	

CZERKAWSKI, Mariusz 6–0 195 RW
B. Radomsko, Poland, Apr. 13, 1972

SSN	TEAM	GP	G	A	PTS.	PIM	+/-
93–94	Bos	4	2	1	3	0	-2
94–95	Bos	47	12	14	26	31	+4
95–96	Bos-Edm	70	17	23	40	18	-4
96–97	Edm	76	26	21	47	16	0
97–98	NYI	68	12	13	25	23	+11
98–99	NYI	78	21	17	38	14	-10
Totals		343	90	89	179	102	-1

Playoffs

SSN	TEAM	GP	G	A	PTS.	PIM	+/-
93–94	Bos	13	3	3	6	4	
94–95	Bos	5	1	0	1	0	
96–97	Edm	12	2	1	3	10	
Totals		30	6	4	10	14	

DACKELL, Andreas 5–10 191 RW
B. Gavle, Sweden, Dec. 29, 1972

SSN	TEAM	GP	G	A	PTS.	PIM	+/-
96–97	Ott	79	12	19	31	8	
97–98	Ott	82	15	18	33	24	-11
98–99	Ott	77	15	35	50	30	+9
Totals>		238	42	72	114	62	-8

Playoffs

SSN	TEAM	GP	G	A	PTS.	PIM	+/-
96–97	Ott	7	1	0	1	0	
97–98	Ott	11	1	1	2	2	
98–99	Ott	4	0	1	1	0	
Totals		22	2	2	4	2	

DAHL, Kevin 5–11 190 D
B. Regina, Sask., Dec. 30, 1968

SSN	TEAM	GP	G	A	PTS.	PIM	+/-
92–93	Calg	61	2	9	11	56	
93–94	Calg	33	0	3	3	23	
94–95	Calg	34	4	8	12	38	
95–96	Calg	32	1	1	2	26	
96–97	Phoe	2	0	0	0	0	
97–98	Tor	19	0	1	1	6	-3
Totals		181	7	22	29	149	+10

Playoffs

SSN	TEAM	GP	G	A	PTS.	PIM	+/-
92–93	Calg	6	0	2	2	8	
93–94	Calg	6	0	0	0	4	
94–95	Calg	3	0	0	0	0	
95–96	Calg	1	0	0	0	0	
Totals		16	0	2	2	12	

DAHLEN, Ulf 6–2 195 RW
B. Ostersund, Sweden, Jan. 12, 1967

SSN	TEAM	GP	G	A	PTS.	PIM	+/-
87–88	NYR	70	29	23	52	26	
88–89	NYR	56	24	19	43	50	
89–90	NYR-Minn	76	20	22	42	30	
90–91	Minn	66	21	18	39	6	
91–92	Minn	79	36	30	66	10	
92–93	Minn	83	35	39	74	6	
93–94	Dal-SJ	78	25	44	69	10	
94–95	SJ	46	11	23	34	11	
95–96	SJ	59	16	12	28	27	
96–97	SJ-Chi	73	14	19	33	18	
Totals		686	231	249	480	194	

Playoffs

SSN	TEAM	GP	G	A	PTS.	PIM	+/-
88–89	NYR	4	0	0	0	0	
89–90	Minn	7	1	4	5	2	
90–91	Minn	15	2	6	8	4	
91–92	Minn	7	0	3	3	2	
93–94	SJ	14	6	2	8	0	
94–95	SJ	11	5	4	9	0	
96–97	Chi	5	0	1	1	0	
Totals		63	14	20	34	8	

DAHLIN, Kjell 6–0 175 RW
B. Timra, Sweden, Mar. 2, 1963

SSN	TEAM	GP	G	A	PTS.	PIM	+/-
85–86	Mont	77	32	39	71	4	
86–87	Mont	41	12	8	20	0	
87–88	Mont	48	13	12	25	6	
Totals		166	57	59	116	10	

Playoffs

SSN	TEAM	GP	G	A	PTS.	PIM	+/-
85–86	Mont	16	2	3	5	4	
86–87	Mont	8	2	4	6	0	
87–88	Mont	11	2	4	6	2	
Totals		35	6	11	17		

DAHLQUIST, Chris 6–1 190 D
B. Fridley, Minn., Dec. 14, 1962

SSN	TEAM	GP	G	A	PTS.	PIM	+/-
85–86	Pitt	5	1	2	3	2	
86–87	Pitt	19	0	1	1	20	
87–88	Pitt	44	3	6	9	69	
88–89	Pitt	43	1	5	6	42	
89–90	Pitt	62	4	10	14	56	
90–91	Pitt-Minn	64	3	8	11	63	
91–92	Minn	74	1	13	14	68	
92–93	Calg	74	3	7	10	66	
93–94	Calg	77	1	11	12	52	
94–95	Ott	46	1	7	8	36	
95–96	Ott	24	1	1	2	14	
Totals		532	19	71	90	488	

Playoffs

SSN	TEAM	GP	G	A	PTS.	PIM	+/-
88–89	Pitt	2	0	0	0	0	
90–91	Minn	23	1	6	7	20	
91–92	Minn	7	0	0	0	6	
92–93	Calg	6	3	1	4	4	
93–94	Calg	1	0	0	0	0	
Totals		39	4	7	11	30	

DAHLSTROM, Carl S. (Cully) 5–1 175 C
B. Minneapolis, Minn., July 3, 1913

SSN	TEAM	GP	G	A	PTS.	PIM	+/-
37–38	Chi	48	10	9	19	11	

SSN	TEAM	GP	G	A	PTS.	PIM	+/-
38-39	Chi	48	6	14	20	2	
39-40	Chi	45	11	19	30	15	
40-41	Chi	40	11	14	25	6	
41-42	Chi	33	13	14	27	6	
42-43	Chi	38	11	13	24	10	
43-44	Chi	50	20	22	42	8	
44-45	Chi	40	6	13	19	0	
Totals		342	88	118	206	58	

Playoffs

SSN	TEAM	GP	G	A	PTS.	PIM	
37-38	Chi	10	3	1	4	2	
39-40	Chi	2	0	0	0	0	
40-41	Chi	5	3	3	6	2	
41-42	Chi	3	0	0	0	0	
43-44	Chi	9	0	4	4	0	
Totals		29	6	8	14	4	

DAIGLE, Alexandre 6-0 185 C
B. Montreal, Que., Feb. 7, 1975

SSN	TEAM	GP	G	A	PTS.	PIM	+/-
93-94	Ott	84	20	31	51	40	-45
94-95	Ott	47	16	21	37	14	-22
95-96	Ott	50	5	12	17	24	-30
96-97	Ott	82	26	25	51	33	-33
97-98	Ott-Phil	75	16	26	42	14	-8
98-99	Phil-TB	63	9	8	17	4	-13
Totals		401	92	123	215	129	-151

Playoffs

SSN	TEAM	GP	G	A	PTS.	PIM	
96-97	Ott	7	0	0	0	2	
97-98	Phil	5	0	2	2	0	
Totals		12	0	2	2	2	

DAIGLE, Roland Alain (Alain) 5-10 180 RW
B. Cap-de-la-Madeleine, Que., Aug. 24, 1954

SSN	TEAM	GP	G	A	PTS.	PIM	+/-
74-75	Chi	52	5	4	9	6	-6
75-76	Chi	71	15	9	24	15	-18
76-77	Chi	73	12	8	20	11	-1
77-78	Chi	53	6	6	12	95	-12
78-79	Chi	74	11	14	25	55	+2
79-80	Chi	66	7	9	16	22	-6
Totals		389	56	50	106	204	-41

Playoffs

SSN	TEAM	GP	G	A	PTS.	PIM	
74-75	Chi	2	0	0	0	0	
75-76	Chi	4	0	0	0	0	
76-77	Chi	1	0	0	0	0	
77-78	Chi	4	0	1	1	0	
78-79	Chi	4	0	0	0	0	
79-80	Chi	2	0	0	0	0	
Totals		17	0	1	1	0	

DAIGNEAULT, Jean-Jacques 5-10 185 D
B. Montreal, Que., Oct. 12, 1965

SSN	TEAM	GP	G	A	PTS.	PIM	+/-
84-85	Van	67	4	23	27	69	-14
85-86	Van	64	5	23	28	45	-20
86-87	Phil	77	6	16	22	56	+12
87-88	Phil	28	2	2	4	12	-8
89-90	Mont	36	2	10	12	14	+11
90-91	Mont	51	3	16	19	31	-2
91-92	Mont	79	4	14	18	36	+16
92-93	Mont	66	8	10	18	57	+25
93-94	Mont	68	2	12	14	73	+16
94-95	Mont	45	3	5	8	40	+2
95-96	Mont-StL-Pitt	57	4	7	11	53	-6
96-97	Pitt-Ana	66	5	23	28	58	0
97-98	Ana-NYI	71	2	21	23	49	-9
98-99	Nash-Phoe	70	2	9	11	70	-12
Totals		845	52	191	243	663	+11

Playoffs

SSN	TEAM	GP	G	A	PTS.	PIM	
85-86	Van	3	0	2	2	0	
86-87	Phil	9	1	0	1	0	
89-90	Mont	9	0	0	0	2	
90-91	Mont	5	0	1	1	0	
91-92	Mont	11	0	3	3	4	
92-93	Mont	20	1	3	4	22	
93-94	Mont	7	0	1	1	12	
95-96	Pitt	17	1	9	10	36	
96-97	Ana	11	2	7	9	16	
98-99	Phoe	6	0	0	0	8	
Totals		109	7	33	40	116	

DAILEY, Robert Scott 6-5 220 D
B. Kingston, Ont., May 3, 1953

SSN	TEAM	GP	G	A	PTS.	PIM	+/-
73-74	Van	76	7	17	24	143	-32
74-75	Van	70	12	36	48	103	-9
75-76	Van	67	15	24	39	119	-5
76-77	Van-Phil	76	9	30	39	90	0
77-78	Phil	76	21	36	57	62	+45
78-79	Phil	70	9	30	39	63	+21
79-80	Phil	61	13	26	39	71	+30
80-81	Phil	53	7	27	34	141	+8
81-82	Phil	12	1	5	6	22	+4
Totals		561	94	231	325	814	+63

Playoffs

SSN	TEAM	GP	G	A	PTS.	PIM	
74-75	Van	5	1	3	4	14	
75-76	Van	2	1	1	2	0	
76-77	Phil	10	4	9	13	15	
77-78	Phil	12	1	5	6	22	
78-79	Phil	8	1	2	3	14	
79-80	Phil	19	4	13	17	22	
80-81	Phil	7	0	1	1	18	
Totals		63	12	34	46	105	

DALEY, Franklin D

SSN	TEAM	GP	G	A	PTS.	PIM	
28-29	Det	5	0	0	0	0	

Playoffs

SSN	TEAM	GP	G	A	PTS.	PIM	
28-29	Det	2	0	0	0	0	

DALEY, Patrick Lloyd 6-1 176 LW
B. Marieville, France, Mar. 27, 1959

SSN	TEAM	GP	G	A	PTS.	PIM	+/-
79-80	Winn	5	1	0	1	4	-2
80-81	Winn	7	0	0	0	9	-3
Totals		12	1	0	1	13	-5

DALGARNO, Brad 6-3 215 RW
B. Vancouver, B.C., Aug. 11, 1967

SSN	TEAM	GP	G	A	PTS.	PIM	+/-
85-86	NYI	2	1	0	1	0	+1
87-88	NYI	38	2	8	10	58	+4
88-89	NYI	55	11	10	21	86	-8
90-91	NYI	41	3	12	15	24	-10
91-92	NYI	15	2	1	3	12	-8
92-93	NYI	57	15	17	32	62	+17
93-94	NYI	73	11	19	30	62	+14
94-95	NYI	22	3	2	5	14	-8
95-96	NYI	18	1	2	3	14	-2
Totals		321	49	71	120	332	0

Playoffs

SSN	TEAM	GP	G	A	PTS.	PIM	
86-87	NYI	1	0	1	1	0	
87-88	NYI	4	0	0	0	19	
92-93	NYI	18	2	2	4	14	
93-94	NYI	4	0	1	1	4	
Totals		27	2	4	6	37	

DALLMAN, Marty 5-10 180 C
B. Niagara Falls, Ont., Feb. 15, 1963

SSN	TEAM	GP	G	A	PTS.	PIM	+/-
87-88	Tor	2	0	1	1	0	+1
88-89	Tor	4	0	0	0	0	0
Totals		6	0	1	1	0	+1

DALLMAN, Rod 5-11 185 LW
B. Quesnal, B.C., Jan. 26, 1967

SSN	TEAM	GP	G	A	PTS.	PIM	+/-
87-88	NYI	3	1	0	1	6	+1
88-89	NYI	1	0	0	0	15	-1
91-92	Phil	2	0	0	0	5	0
Totals		6	1	0	1	26	0

Playoffs

SSN	TEAM	GP	G	A	PTS.	PIM	
89-90	NYI	1	0	1	1	0	

DAME, Aurelia N. (Bunny) LW
B. Edmonton, Alta.

SSN	TEAM	GP	G	A	PTS.	PIM	
41-42	Mont	34	2	5	7	4	

DAMPHOUSSE, Vincent 6-1 200 LW
B. Montreal, Que., Dec. 17, 1967

SSN	TEAM	GP	G	A	PTS.	PIM	+/-
86-87	Tor	80	21	25	46	26	-6
87-88	Tor	75	12	36	48	40	+2
88-89	Tor	80	26	42	68	75	-8
89-90	Tor	80	33	61	94	56	+2
90-91	Tor	79	26	47	73	65	-31
91-92	Edm	80	38	51	89	53	+10
92-93	Mont	84	39	58	97	98	+5
93-94	Mont	84	40	51	91	75	0
94-95	Mont	48	10	30	40	42	+15
95-96	Mont	80	38	56	94	158	+5
96-97	Mont	82	27	54	81	82	-6
97-98	Mont	76	18	41	59	58	+14
98-99	Mont-SJ	77	19	30	49	50	-4
Totals		705	347	582	929	878	-2

Playoffs

SSN	TEAM	GP	G	A	PTS.	PIM	
86-87	Tor	12	1	5	6	8	
87-88	Tor	6	0	1	1	10	
89-90	Tor	5	0	2	2	2	
91-92	Edm	16	6	8	14	8	
92-93	Mont	20	11	12	23	16	
93-94	Mont	7	1	2	3	8	
95-96	Mont	6	4	4	8	0	
96-97	Mont	5	0	0	0	2	
97-98	Mont	10	3	6	9	22	
98-99	SJ	6	3	2	5	6	
Totals		93	29	42	71	82	

DAMORE, Henry John (Hank, Lou Costello)
5-5 200 C
B. Niagara Falls, Ont., July 17, 1919

SSN	TEAM	GP	G	A	PTS.	PIM	
43-44	NYR	4	1	0	1	2	

DANDENAULT, Mathieu 6-0 174 RW
B. Magog, Que., Feb. 3, 1976

SSN	TEAM	GP	G	A	PTS.	PIM	+/-
95-96	Det	34	5	7	12	6	+6
96-97	Det	65	3	9	12	28	-10
97-98	Det	68	5	12	17	43	+5
98-99	Det	75	4	10	14	59	+17
Totals		242	17	38	55	136	+18

Playoffs

SSN	TEAM	GP	G	A	PTS.	PIM	
97-98	Det	3	1	0	1	0	
98-99	Det	10	0	1	1	0	
Totals		13	1	1	2	0	

DANEYKO, Kenneth 6-0 210 D
B. Windsor, Ont., Apr. 17, 1964

SSN	TEAM	GP	G	A	PTS.	PIM	+/-
83-84	NJ	11	1	4	5	17	-1
84-85	NJ	1	0	0	0	10	-1
85-86	NJ	44	0	10	10	100	0
86-87	NJ	79	2	12	14	183	-13
87-88	NJ	80	5	7	12	239	-3
88-89	NJ	80	5	5	10	283	-22
89-90	NJ	74	6	15	21	216	+15
90-91	NJ	80	4	16	20	249	-10
91-92	NJ	80	1	7	8	170	+7
92-93	NJ	84	2	11	13	236	+4
93-94	NJ	78	1	9	10	176	+27
94-95	NJ	25	1	2	3	54	+4
95-96	NJ	80	2	4	6	115	-10
96-97	NJ	77	2	7	9	70	+24
97-98	NJ	37	0	1	1	56	+3
98-99	NJ	82	2	9	11	63	+27
Totals		992	34	119	153	2237	+51

Playoffs

SSN	TEAM	GP	G	A	PTS.	PIM	
87-88	NJ	20	1	6	7	83	
89-90	NJ	6	2	0	2	21	
90-91	NJ	7	0	1	1	10	
91-92	NJ	7	0	3	3	16	
92-93	NJ	5	0	0	0	8	
93-94	NJ	20	0	1	1	45	
94-95	NJ	20	1	0	1	22	
96-97	NJ	10	0	0	0	28	
97-98	NJ	6	0	1	1	10	
98-99	NJ	7	0	0	0	8	
Totals		108	4	12	16	251	

DANIELS, Jeff 6-1 195 LW
B. Oshawa, Ont., June 24, 1968

SSN	TEAM	GP	G	A	PTS.	PIM	+/-
90-91	Pitt	11	0	2	2	0	
91-92	Pitt	2	0	0	0	0	0
92-93	Pitt	58	5	4	9	14	-5
93-94	Pitt-Fla	70	3	5	8	20	-1
94-95	Fla	3	0	0	0	0	0
96-97	Hart	10	0	2	2	0	+2
97-98	Car	2	0	0	0	0	0
98-99	Nash	9	1	3	4	2	-9
Totals		165	9	16	25	38	-13

Playoffs

SSN	TEAM	GP	G	A	PTS.	PIM	
92-93	Pitt	12	3	2	5	0	

DANIELS, Kimbi 5-11 175 C
B. Brandon, Man., Jan. 19, 1972

SSN	TEAM	GP	G	A	PTS.	PIM	+/-
90-91	Phil	2	0	1	1	0	-2
91-92	Phil	25	1	1	2	4	-4
Totals		27	1	2	3	4	-6

DANIELS, Scott 6-3 200 LW
B. Prince Albert, Sask., Sept. 19, 1969

SSN	TEAM	GP	G	A	PTS.	PIM	+/-
92–93	Hart	1	0	0	0	19	0
94–95	Hart	12	0	2	2	55	+1
95–96	Hart	53	3	4	7	254	-4
96–97	Phil	56	5	3	8	237	+2
97–98	NJ	26	0	3	3	102	+1
98–99	NJ	1	0	0	0	0	0
Totals		149	8	12	20	667	0

Playoffs

97–98	NJ	1	0	0	0	0

DAOUST, Daniel 5-11 170 C
B. Montreal, Que., Feb. 29, 1960

SSN	TEAM	GP	G	A	PTS.	PIM	+/-
82–83	Mont-Tor	52	18	34	52	35	-3
83–84	Tor	78	18	56	74	88	-16
84–85	Tor	79	17	37	54	98	-27
85–86	Tor	80	7	13	20	88	-21
86–87	Tor	33	4	3	7	35	0
87–88	Tor	67	9	8	17	57	-7
88–89	Tor	68	7	5	12	54	-20
89–90	Tor	65	7	11	18	89	+1
Totals		522	87	167	254	544	-93

Playoffs

85–86	Tor	10	2	2	4	19
86–87	Tor	13	5	2	7	42
87–88	Tor	4	0	0	0	2
89–90	Tor	5	0	1	1	20
Totals		32	7	5	12	83

DARBY, Craig 6-3 180 C
B. Oneida, N.Y., Sept. 26, 1972

SSN	TEAM	GP	G	A	PTS.	PIM	+/-
94–95	Mont–NYI	13	0	2	2	0	-6
95–96	NYI	10	0	2	2	0	-1
96–97	Phil	9	1	4	5	2	+2
97–98	Phil	3	1	0	1	0	0
Totals		35	2	8	10	2	-5

DARK, Michael 6-3 210 D
B. Sarnia, Ont., Sept. 17, 1963

SSN	TEAM	GP	G	A	PTS.	PIM	+/-
86–87	StL	13	2	0	2	2	0
87–88	StL	30	3	6	9	12	+6
Totals		43	5	6	11	14	+6

*DARRAGH, Harold Edward (Harry and Howl) 5-1 145 F
B. Ottawa, Ont., Sept. 13, 1902

SSN	TEAM	GP	G	A	PTS.	PIM
25–26	Pitt Pi	35	10	7	17	6
26–27	Pitt Pi	42	12	3	15	4
27–28	Pitt Pi	44	13	2	15	16
28–29	Pitt Pi	43	9	3	12	6
29–30	Pitt Pi	42	15	17	32	6
30–31	Phil Q-Bos	35	3	5	8	6
31–32	Tor	48	5	10	15	6
32–33	Tor	19	1	2	3	0
Totals		308	68	49	117	50

Playoffs

25–26	PittPi	2	1	0	1	0
27–28	PittPi	2	0	1	1	0
30–31	Bos	5	0	1	1	2
31–32	Tor	7	0	1	1	2
Totals		16	1	3	4	4

*DARRAGH, John Proctor (Jack) RW
B. Ottawa, Ont., Dec. 4, 1890

SSN	TEAM	GP	G	A	PTS.	PIM
17–18	Ott	18	14	0	14	3
18–19	Ott	14	12	1	13	27
19–20	Ott	22	22	5	27	22
20–21	Ott	24	11	8	19	20
22–23	Ott	24	7	7	14	14
23–24	Ott	18	2	0	2	2
Totals		120	68	21	89	88

Playoffs

18–19	Ott	5	3	0	3	0
19–20	Ott	5	5	2	7	3
20–21	Ott	7	5	0	5	6
22–23	Ott	2	1	0	1	2
23–24	Ott	2	0	0	0	2
Totals		21	14	2	16	13

DAVID, Richard 6-0 195 LW
B. Notre Dame de la Salette, Que., Apr. 8, 1958

SSN	TEAM	GP	G	A	PTS.	PIM	+/-
78–79	Que (WHA)	14	0	4	4	4	
79–80	Que	10	0	0	0	2	-2
81–82	Que	5	1	1	2	4	-3
82–83	Que	16	3	3	6	4	-2
NHL Totals		31	4	4	8	10	-7
WHA Totals		14	0	4	4	4	

Playoffs

81–82	Que	1	0	0	0	0

DAVIDSON, Gordon John (Gord) 5-11 188 D
B. Stratton, Ont., Aug. 5, 1918

SSN	TEAM	GP	G	A	PTS.	PIM
42–43	NYR	35	2	3	5	4
43–44	NYR	16	1	3	4	4
Totals		51	3	6	9	8

DAVIDSON, Robert E. 5-11 185 F
B. Toronto, Ont., Feb. 10, 1912

SSN	TEAM	GP	G	A	PTS.	PIM
34–35	Tor	5	0	0	0	6
35–36	Tor	35	4	4	8	32
36–37	Tor	46	8	7	15	43
37–38	Tor	48	3	17	20	52
38–39	Tor	47	4	10	14	29
39–40	Tor	48	8	18	26	56
40–41	Tor	37	3	6	9	39
41–42	Tor	37	6	20	26	39
42–43	Tor	50	13	23	36	20
43–44	Tor	47	19	28	47	21
44–45	Tor	50	17	18	35	49
45–46	Tor	41	9	9	18	12
Totals		491	94	160	254	398

Playoffs

35–36	Tor	9	1	3	4	2
36–37	Tor	2	0	0	0	5
37–38	Tor	7	0	2	2	10
38–39	Tor	10	1	1	2	6
39–40	Tor	10	0	3	3	16
40–41	Tor	7	0	2	2	7
41–42	Tor	13	1	2	3	20
42–43	Tor	6	1	2	3	7
43–44	Tor	5	0	0	0	4
44–45	Tor	13	1	2	3	2
Totals		82	5	17	22	79

DAVIDSSON, Johan 6-1 190 C
B. Jonkoping, Sweden, Jan. 6, 1976

SSN	TEAM	GP	G	A	PTS.	PIM	+/-
98–99	Ana	64	3	5	8	14	-9

Playoffs

98–99	Ana	1	0	0	0	0

*DAVIE, Robert Howard (Pinkie) 6-0 170 D
B. Beausejour, Man., Sept. 12, 1912

SSN	TEAM	GP	G	A	PTS.	PIM
33–34	Bos	9	0	0	0	6
34–35	Bos	30	0	1	1	17
35–36	Bos	2	0	0	0	2
Totals		41	0	1	1	25

DAVIES, Kenneth George (Buck) 5-6 160 C
B. Bowmanville, Ont., Aug. 10, 1922

SSN	TEAM	GP	G	A	PTS.	PIM
47–48	NYR	0	0	0	0	0

Playoffs

47–48	NYR	1	0	0	0	0

DAVIS, Kim 5-11 170 C
B. Flin Flon, Man., Oct. 31, 1957

SSN	TEAM	GP	G	A	PTS.	PIM	+/-
77–78	Pitt	1	0	0	0	0	0
78–79	Pitt	1	1	0	1	0	0
79–80	Pitt	24	3	7	10	4	-7
80–81	Pitt-Tor	10	1	0	1	8	-3
Totals		36	5	7	12	12	-10

Playoffs

79–80	Pitt	4	0	0	0	0

DAVIS, Lorne Austin 5-11 190 RW
B. Regina, Sask., July 20, 1930

SSN	TEAM	GP	G	A	PTS.	PIM
51–52	Mont	3	1	1	2	2
53–54	Mont	37	6	4	10	2
54–55	Chi-Det	30	0	5	5	6
55–56	Bos	15	0	1	1	0
59–60	Bos	10	1	1	2	10
Totals		95	8	12	20	20

Playoffs

52–53	Mont	7	1	1	2	2
53–54	Mont	11	2	0	2	8
Totals		18	3	1	4	10

DAVIS, Malcolm Sterling 5-11 180 LW
B. Lockeport, N.S., Oct. 10, 1956

SSN	TEAM	GP	G	A	PTS.	PIM	+/-
78–79	Det	6	0	0	0	0	-2
80–81	Det	5	2	0	2	0	+5
82–83	Buf	24	8	12	20	0	-6
83–34	Buf	11	2	1	3	4	-1
84–85	Buf	47	17	9	26	26	+1
85–86	Buf	7	2	0	2	4	-1
Totals		100	31	22	53	34	-4

Playoffs

82–83	Buf	6	1	0	1	0
84–85	Buf	1	0	0	0	0
Totals		7	1	0	1	0

DAVIS, Robert F
B. Lachine, Que.

SSN	TEAM	GP	G	A	PTS.	PIM
32–33	Det	3	0	0	0	0

DAVISON, Murray 6-2 190 D
B. Brantford, Ont., June 10, 1938

SSN	TEAM	GP	G	A	PTS.	PIM
65–66	Bos	1	0	0	0	0

DAVYDOV, Evgeny 6-0 200 LW
B. Chelyabinsk, Soviet Union, May 27, 1967

SSN	TEAM	GP	G	A	PTS.	PIM	+/-
91–92	Winn	12	4	3	7	8	+7
92–93	Winn	79	28	21	49	66	-2
93–94	Fla-Ott	61	7	13	20	46	-9
94–95	Ott	3	1	2	3	0	+2
Totals		155	40	39	79	120	-2

Playoffs

91–92	Winn	7	2	2	4	2
92–93	Winn	4	0	0	0	0
Totals		11	2	2	4	2

DAWE, Jason 5-10 195 LW
B. North York, Ont., May 29, 1973

SSN	TEAM	GP	G	A	PTS.	PIM	+/-
93–94	Buf	32	6	7	13	12	1
94–95	Buf	42	7	4	11	19	-6
95–96	Buf	67	25	25	50	33	-8
96–97	Buf	81	22	26	48	32	+14
97–98	Buf–NYI	81	20	19	39	42	+4
98–99	NYI–Mont	59	6	8	14	22	0
Totals		362	86	89	175	160	+9

Playoffs

93–94	Buf	6	0	1	1	6
94–95	Buf	5	2	1	3	6
96–97	Buf	11	2	1	3	6
Totals		22	4	3	7	18

DAWES, Robert James 6-1 170 D
B. Saskatoon, Sask., Nov. 29, 1924

SSN	TEAM	GP	G	A	PTS.	PIM
46–47	Tor	1	0	0	0	0
48–49	Tor	5	1	0	1	0
49–50	Tor	11	1	2	3	2
50–51	Mont	15	0	5	5	4
Totals		32	2	7	9	6

Playoffs

48–49	Tor	9	0	0	0	2
50–51	Tor	1	0	0	0	0
Totals		10	0	0	0	2

*DAY, Clarence Henry (Hap) 5-11 175 LW
B. Owen Sound, Ont., June 14, 1901

SSN	TEAM	GP	G	A	PTS.	PIM
24–25	Tor	26	10	12	22	33
25–26	Tor	36	14	2	16	26
26–27	Tor	44	11	5	16	50
27–28	Tor	22	9	8	17	48
28–29	Tor	44	6	6	12	84
29–30	Tor	43	7	14	21	77
30–31	Tor	44	1	13	14	56
31–32	Tor	47	7	8	15	33
32–33	Tor	47	6	14	20	46
33–34	Tor	48	9	10	19	35

SSN	TEAM	GP	G	A	PTS.	PIM	+/-
34-35	Tor	45	2	4	6	38	
35-36	Tor	44	1	13	14	41	
36-37	Tor	48	3	4	7	20	
37-38	NYA	43	0	3	3	14	
Totals		581	86	116	202	601	

Playoffs

SSN	TEAM	GP	G	A	PTS.	PIM	+/-
24-25	Tor	2	0	0	0	0	
28-29	Tor	4	1	0	1	2	
30-31	Tor	2	0	3	3	7	
31-32	Tor	7	3	3	6	6	
32-33	Tor	9	0	1	1	21	
33-34	Tor	5	0	0	0	6	
34-35	Tor	7	0	0	0	4	
35-36	Tor	9	0	0	0	8	
36-37	Tor	2	0	0	0	0	
37-38	NYA	6	0	0	0	0	
Totals		53	4	7	11	54	

DAY, Joseph 5-11 180 LW
B. Chicago, Ill., May 11, 1968

SSN	TEAM	GP	G	A	PTS.	PIM	+/-
91-92	Hart	24	0	3	3	10	-2
92-93	Hart	24	1	7	8	47	-8
93-94	NYI	24	0	0	0	30	-7
Totals		72	1	10	11	87	-17

DAZE, Eric 6-4 215 LW
B. Montreal, Que., July 2, 1975

SSN	TEAM	GP	G	A	PTS.	PIM	+/-
94-95	Chi	4	1	1	2	2	+2
95-96	Chi	80	30	23	53	18	+16
96-97	Chi	71	22	19	41	16	-4
97-98	Chi	80	31	11	42	22	+4
98-99	Chi	72	22	20	42	22	-13
Totals		307	106	74	180	80	+5

Playoffs

SSN	TEAM	GP	G	A	PTS.	PIM	+/-
94-95	Chi	16	0	1	1	4	
95-96	Chi	10	3	5	8	11	
96-97	Chi	6	2	1	3	2	
Totals		32	5	7	12	17	

DEA, William Fraser 5-8 175 LW
B. Edmonton, Alta., Apr. 3, 1933

SSN	TEAM	GP	G	A	PTS.	PIM	+/-
53-54	NYR	14	1	1	2	2	
56-57	Det	69	15	15	30	14	
57-58	Det-Chi	63	9	12	21	10	
67-68	Pitt	73	16	12	28	6	-15
68-69	Pitt	66	10	8	18	4	-32
69-70	Det	70	10	3	13	6	+3
70-71	Det	42	6	3	9	2	-5
Totals		397	67	54	121	44	-49

Playoffs

SSN	TEAM	GP	G	A	PTS.	PIM	+/-
56-57	Det	5	2	0	2	2	
66-67	Chi	2	0	0	0	2	
69-70	Det	4	0	1	1	2	
Totals		11	2	1	3	6	

DEACON, Donald John 5-9 190 LW
B. Regina, Sask., June 2, 1913

SSN	TEAM	GP	G	A	PTS.	PIM	+/-
36-37	Det	4	0	0	0	2	
38-39	Det	8	1	3	4	2	
39-40	Det	18	5	1	6	2	
Totals		30	6	4	10	6	

Playoffs

SSN	TEAM	GP	G	A	PTS.	PIM	+/-
38-39	Det	2	2	1	3	0	

DEADMARSH, Adam 6-0 195 C
B. Trail, B.C., May 10, 1975

SSN	TEAM	GP	G	A	PTS.	PIM	+/-
94-95	Que	48	9	8	17	56	+16
95-96	Col A	78	21	27	48	142	+20
96-97	Col A	78	33	27	60	136	+8
97-98	Col A	73	22	21	43	125	0
98-99	Col A	66	22	27	49	99	-2
Totals		343	107	110	217	558	+42

Playoffs

SSN	TEAM	GP	G	A	PTS.	PIM	+/-
94-95	Que	6	0	1	1	0	
95-96	Col A	22	5	12	17	25	
96-97	Col A	17	3	6	9	24	
97-98	Col A	7	2	0	2	4	
98-99	Col A	19	8	4	12	20	
Totals		71	18	23	41	73	

DEADMARSH, Ernest Charles (Butch) 5-10 185 LW
B. Trail, B.C., Apr. 5, 1950

SSN	TEAM	GP	G	A	PTS.	PIM	+/-
70-71	Buf	10	0	0	0	9	-3
71-72	Buf	12	1	1	2	4	-10
72-73	Buf-Atl	53	2	1	3	34	-7
73-74	Atl	42	6	1	7	89	+1
74-75	KC	20	3	2	5	19	-5
74-75	Van (WHA)	38	7	8	15	128	
75-76	Calg (WHA)	79	26	28	54	196	
76-77	Minn-Calg (WHA)	73	22	21	43	128	
77-78	Cin (WHA)	65	8	9	17	118	
NHL Totals		137	12	5	17	155	-24
WHA Totals		255	63	66	129	570	

Playoffs

SSN	TEAM	GP	G	A	PTS.	PIM	+/-
73-74	Atl	4	0	0	0	17	
75-76	Calg (WHA)	8	0	1	1	14	
NHL Totals		4	0	0	0	17	
WHA Totals		8	0	1	1	14	

DEAN, Barry James 6-1 195 LW
B. Maple Creek, Sask., Feb. 26, 1955

SSN	TEAM	GP	G	A	PTS.	PIM	+/-
75-76	Phoe (WHA)	71	9	25	34	110	
76-77	Col	79	14	25	39	92	-26
77-78	Phil	56	7	18	25	34	+12
78-79	Phil	30	4	13	17	20	-1
NHL Totals		165	25	56	81	146	-15
WHA Totals		71	9	25	34	110	

DEAN, Kevin 6-2 195 D
B. Madison, Wis., Apr. 1, 1969

SSN	TEAM	GP	G	A	PTS.	PIM	+/-
94-95	NJ	17	0	1	1	4	+6
95-96	NJ	41	0	6	6	28	+4
96-97	NJ	28	2	4	6	6	+2
97-98	NJ	50	1	8	9	12	+12
98-99	NJ	62	1	10	11	22	+4
Totals		198	4	29	33	72	+28

Playoffs

SSN	TEAM	GP	G	A	PTS.	PIM	+/-
94-95	NJ	3	0	2	2	0	
96-97	NJ	1	1	0	1	0	
97-98	NJ	5	1	0	1	2	
98-99	NJ	7	0	0	0	0	
Totals		16	2	2	4	2	

DEBENEDET, Nelson Flavio 6-1 195 LW
B. Cardenona, Italy, Dec. 31, 1947

SSN	TEAM	GP	G	A	PTS.	PIM	+/-
73-74	Det	15	4	1	5	2	+1
74-75	Pitt	31	6	3	9	11	-3
Totals		46	10	4	14	13	-2

DeBLOIS, Lucien 5-11 200 LW
B. Joliette, Que., June 21, 1957

SSN	TEAM	GP	G	A	PTS.	PIM	+/-
77-78	NYR	71	22	8	30	27	-11
78-79	NYR	62	11	17	28	26	-10
79-80	NYR-Col	76	27	20	47	43	-19
80-81	Col	74	26	16	42	78	-42
81-82	Winn	65	25	27	52	87	-10
82-83	Winn	79	27	27	54	69	-25
83-84	Winn	80	34	45	79	50	-15
84-85	Mont	51	12	11	23	20	+9
85-86	Mont	61	14	17	31	48	+3
86-87	NYR	40	3	8	11	27	-7
87-88	NYR	74	9	21	30	103	-3
88-89	NYR	73	9	24	33	107	-6
89-90	Que	70	9	8	17	45	-29
90-91	Que-Tor	52	12	14	26	43	-3
91-92	Tor-Winn	65	9	13	22	41	-2
Totals		993	249	276	525	814	-170

Playoffs

SSN	TEAM	GP	G	A	PTS.	PIM	+/-
77-78	NYR	3	0	0	0	2	
78-79	NYR	9	2	0	2	4	
81-82	Winn	4	2	1	3	4	
82-83	Winn	3	0	0	0	5	
Totals		52	7	6	13	38	

DEBOL, David 5-11 175 C
B. Clair Shores, Mich., Mar. 27, 1956

SSN	TEAM	GP	G	A	PTS.	PIM	+/-
77-78	Cin (WHA)	9	3	2	5	2	
78-79	Cin (WHA)	59	10	27	37	9	
79-80	Hart	48	12	14	26	4	-5
80-81	Hart	44	14	12	26	0	-12
NHL Totals		92	26	26	52	4	-17
WHA Totals		68	13	29	42	11	

Playoffs

SSN	TEAM	GP	G	A	PTS.	PIM	+/-
79-80	Hart	3	0	0	0	0	

DeBRUSK, Louis 6-1 215 LW
B. Dunnville, Ont., June 13, 1968

SSN	TEAM	GP	G	A	PTS.	PIM	+/-
91-92	Edm	25	2	1	3	124	4
92-93	Edm	51	8	2	10	205	-16
93-94	Edm	48	4	6	10	185	-9
94-95	Edm	34	2	0	2	93	-4
95-96	Edm	38	1	3	4	96	-7
96-97	Edm	32	2	0	2	94	-6
97-98	TB	6	0	0	0	4	-2
98-99	Phoe	15	0	0	0	34	-2
Totals		243	19	12	31	831	-42

Playoffs

SSN	TEAM	GP	G	A	PTS.	PIM	+/-
96-97	Edm	6	0	0	0	4	
98-99	Phoe	6	2	0	2	6	
Totals		12	2	0	2	10	

DEFAZIO, Dean 5-11 185 LW
B. Ottawa, Ont., Apr. 16, 1963

SSN	TEAM	GP	G	A	PTS.	PIM	+/-
83-84	Pitt	22	0	2	2	28	-11

DEGRAY, Dale Edward 6-0 200 D
B. Oshawa, Ont., Sept. 1, 1963

SSN	TEAM	GP	G	A	PTS.	PIM	+/-
85-86	Calg	1	0	0	0	0	-1
86-87	Calg	27	6	7	13	29	-3
87-88	Tor	56	6	18	24	63	+4
88-89	LA	63	6	22	28	97	+3
89-90	Buf	6	0	0	0	6	-4
Totals		153	18	47	65	195	-1

Playoffs

SSN	TEAM	GP	G	A	PTS.	PIM	+/-
87-88	Tor	5	0	1	1	16	
88-89	LA	8	1	2	3	12	
Totals		13	1	3	4	28	

DELISLE, Jonathan 5-10 193 RW
B. Ste.-Anne-des-Plaines, Que., June 30, 1977

SSN	TEAM	GP	G	A	PTS.	PIM	+/-
98-99	Mont	1	0	0	0	0	0

DELISLE, Xavier 5-11 182 C
B. Quebec City, Que., May 24, 1977

SSN	TEAM	GP	G	A	PTS.	PIM	+/-
98-99	TB	2	0	0	0	0	0

DELMONTE, Armond Romeo (Dutch) 5-10 190 C
B. Timmins, Ont., Jan. 4, 1925

SSN	TEAM	GP	G	A	PTS.	PIM	+/-
45-46	Bos	1	0	0	0	0	

DELMORE, Andy 6-1 192 D
B. LaSalle, Ont., Dec. 26, 1976

SSN	TEAM	GP	G	A	PTS.	PIM	+/-
98-99	Phil	2	0	1	1	0	-1

DELORME, Gilbert 6-1 205 D
B. Boucherville, Que., Nov. 25, 1962

SSN	TEAM	GP	G	A	PTS.	PIM	+/-
81-82	Mont	60	3	8	11	55	+19
82-83	Mont	78	12	21	33	89	+27
83-84	Mont-StL	71	2	12	14	49	-11
84-85	StL	74	2	12	14	53	+7
85-86	Que	64	2	18	20	51	-1
86-87	Que-Det	43	2	5	7	47	-2
87-88	Det	55	2	8	10	81	+9
88-89	Det	42	1	3	4	51	-11
89-90	Pitt	54	3	7	10	44	+3
Totals		541	31	92	123	520	+40

Playoffs

SSN	TEAM	GP	G	A	PTS.	PIM	+/-
82-83	Mont	3	0	0	0	2	
83-84	StL	11	1	3	4	11	
84-85	StL	3	0	0	0	0	
85-86	Que	2	0	0	0	5	
86-87	Det	16	0	2	2	14	
87-88	Det	15	0	3	3	22	
88-89	Det	6	0	1	1	2	
Totals		56	1	9	10	56	

DELORME, Ronald Elmer 6-2 185 C
B. North Battleford, Sask., Sept. 3, 1955

SSN	TEAM	GP	G	A	PTS.	PIM	+/-
75-76	Den (WHA)	22	1	3	4	28	
76-77	Col	29	6	4	10	23	-11
77-78	Col	68	10	11	21	47	-20
78-79	Col	77	20	8	28	68	-30

SSN	TEAM	GP	G	A	PTS.	PIM	+/-
79–80	Col	75	19	24	43	76	-24
80–81	Col	65	11	16	27	70	-11
81–82	Van	59	9	8	17	177	-8
82–83	Van	56	5	8	13	87	-6
83–84	Van	64	2	2	4	68	-2
84–85	Van	31	1	2	3	51	-8
NHL Totals		524	83	83	166	667	-120
WHA Totals		22	1	3	4	28	

Playoffs

SSN	TEAM	GP	G	A	PTS.	PIM	
77–78	Col	2	0	0	0	10	
81–82	Van	15	0	2	2	31	
82–83	Van	4	0	0	0	10	
83–84	Van	4	1	0	1	8	
Totals		25	1	2	3	59	

DELORY, Valentine Arthur *5–10 160 LW*
B. Toronto, Ont., Feb. 14, 1927

SSN	TEAM	GP	G	A	PTS.	PIM	
48–49	NYR	1	0	0	0	0	

DELPARTE, Guy Philipp *5–9 178 LW*
B. Prince Albert, Sask., Aug. 30, 1949

SSN	TEAM	GP	G	A	PTS.	PIM	+/-
76–77	Col	48	1	8	9	18	-10

DELVECCHIO, Alexander Peter (Alex) *6–0 195 C*
B. Ft. William, Ont., Dec. 4, 1931

SSN	TEAM	GP	G	A	PTS.	PIM	+/-
50–51	Det	1	0	0	0	0	
51–52	Det	65	15	22	37	22	
52–53	Det	70	16	43	59	28	
53–54	Det	69	11	18	29	34	
54–55	Det	69	17	31	48	37	
55–56	Det	70	25	26	51	24	
56–57	Det	48	16	25	41	8	
57–58	Det	70	21	38	59	22	
58–59	Det	70	19	35	54	6	
59–60	Det	70	19	28	47	8	
60–61	Det	70	27	35	62	26	
61–62	Det	70	26	43	69	18	
62–63	Det	70	20	44	64	8	
63–64	Det	70	23	30	53	11	
64–65	Det	68	25	42	67	16	
65–66	Det	70	31	38	69	16	
66–67	Det	70	17	38	55	10	
67–68	Det	74	22	48	70	14	+8
68–69	Det	72	25	58	83	8	+43
69–70	Det	73	21	47	68	24	+26
70–71	Det	77	21	34	55	6	-18
71–72	Det	75	20	45	65	22	-19
72–73	Det	77	18	53	71	13	+6
73–74	Det	11	1	4	5	2	-13
Totals		1549	456	825	1281	383	+33

Playoffs

SSN	TEAM	GP	G	A	PTS.	PIM	
51–52	Det	8	0	3	3	4	
52–53	Det	6	2	4	6	2	
53–54	Det	12	2	7	9	7	
54–55	Det	11	7	8	15	2	
55–56	Det	10	7	3	10	2	
56–57	Det	5	3	2	5	2	
57–58	Det	4	0	1	1	0	
59–60	Det	6	2	6	8	0	
60–61	Det	11	4	5	9	0	
62–63	Det	11	3	6	9	2	
63–64	Det	14	3	8	11	0	
64–65	Det	7	2	3	5	4	
65–66	Det	12	0	11	11	4	
69–70	Det	4	0	2	2	0	
Totals		121	35	69	104	29	

DEMARCO, Albert George (Ab) *6–0 168 C*
B. North Bay, Ont., May 10,1916

SSN	TEAM	GP	G	A	PTS.	PIM	
38–39	Chi	2	1	0	1	0	
39–40	Chi	17	0	5	5	17	
42–43	Tor–Bos	7	4	2	6	0	
43–44	Bos–NYR	39	14	19	33	2	
44–45	NYR	50	24	30	54	10	
45–46	NYR	50	20	27	47	20	
46–47	NYR	44	9	10	19	4	
Totals		209	72	93	165	53	

Playoffs

SSN	TEAM	GP	G	A	PTS.	PIM	
39–40	Chi	2	0	0	0	0	
42–43	Bos	9	3	0	3	2	
Totals		11	3	0	3	2	

*DEMARCO, Albert Thomas (Ab) *6–0 170 D*
B. North Bay, Ont., Feb. 27, 1949

SSN	TEAM	GP	G	A	PTS.	PIM	+/-
69–70	NYR	3	0	0	0	0	-1
70–71	NYR	2	0	1	1	0	+1
71–72	NYR	48	4	7	11	4	+18
72–73	NYR–StL	65	8	22	30	17	+20
73–74	StL–Pitt	57	10	21	31	15	+11
74–75	Pitt–Van	69	12	15	27	25	-6
75–76	Van–LA	64	7	11	18	8	-6
76–77	LA	33	3	3	6	6	-8
77–78	Edm (WHA)	47	6	8	14	20	
78–79	Bos	3	0	0	0	0	0
NHL Totals		344	44	80	124	75	+29
WHA Totals		47	6	8	14	20	

Playoffs

SSN	TEAM	GP	G	A	PTS.	PIM	
69–70	NYR	5	0	0	0	2	
71–72	NYR	4	0	1	1	0	
72–73	StL	4	1	1	2	2	
74–75	Van	2	0	0	0	0	
75–76	LA	9	0	0	0	11	
76–77	LA	1	0	0	0	2	
77–78	Edm (WHA)	1	0	0	0	0	
NHL Totals		25	1	2	3	17	
WHA Totals		1	0	0	0	0	

DEMERS, Antonio (Tony) *5–9 180 RW*
B. Chambly Basin, Que., July 22,1917

SSN	TEAM	GP	G	A	PTS.	PIM	
37–38	Mont	6	0	0	0	0	
39–40	Mont	14	2	3	5	2	
40–41	Mont	46	13	10	23	17	
41–42	Mont	7	3	4	7	4	
42–43	Mont	9	2	5	7	0	
43–44	NYR	1	0	0	0	0	
Totals		83	20	22	42	23	

Playoffs

SSN	TEAM	GP	G	A	PTS.	PIM	
40–41	Mont	3	0	0	0	0	

DEMITRA, Pavol *6–0 189 LW*
B. Dubnica, Czechoslovakia, Nov. 29, 1974

SSN	TEAM	GP	G	A	PTS.	PIM	+/-
93–94	Ott	12	1	1	2	4	-7
94–95	Ott	16	4	3	7	0	-4
95–96	Ott	31	7	10	17	6	-3
96–97	StL	8	3	0	3	2	0
97–98	StL	61	22	30	52	22	+11
98–99	StL	82	37	52	89	16	+13
Totals		210	74	96	170	50	+10

Playoffs

SSN	TEAM	GP	G	A	PTS.	PIM	
96–97	StL	6	1	3	4	6	
97–98	StL	10	3	3	6	2	
98–99	StL	13	5	4	9	4	
Totals		29	9	10	19	12	

DEMPSEY, Nathan *6–0 170 LW*
B. Spruce Grove, Alta., July 14, 1974

SSN	TEAM	GP	G	A	PTS.	PIM	+/-
96–97	Tor	14	1	1	2	2	-2

DENIS, Jean Paul (Johnny) *5–8 170 RW*
B. Montreal, Que., Feb. 28, 1924

SSN	TEAM	GP	G	A	PTS.	PIM	
46–47	NYR	6	0	1	1	0	
49–50	NYR	4	0	1	1	2	
Totals		10	0	2	2	2	

DENIS, Louis Gilbert (Lulu) *5–8 140 RW*
B. Vonda, Sask., June 7, 1928

SSN	TEAM	GP	G	A	PTS.	PIM	
49–50	Mont	2	0	1	1	0	
50–51	Mont	1	0	0	0	0	
Totals		3	0	1	1	0	

*DENNENY, Corbett *LW*
B. Cornwall, Ont., 1894

SSN	TEAM	GP	G	A	PTS.	PIM	
17–18	Tor	21	20	0	20	8	
18–19	Tor	16	7	3	10	15	
19–20	Tor	23	23	12	35	18	
20–21	Tor	20	17	6	23	27	
21–22	Tor	24	19	7	26	28	
22–23	Tor	1	1	0	1	0	
23–34	Ham	23	0	0	0	6	
26–27	Tor	29	7	1	8	24	
27–28	Chi	18	5	0	5	12	
Totals		175	99	29	128	138	

Playoffs

SSN	TEAM	GP	G	A	PTS.	PIM	
17–18	Tor	7	3	2	5	3	

SSN	TEAM	GP	G	A	PTS.	PIM	+/-
20–21	Tor	2	0	0	0	0	
21–22	Tor	7	3	2	5	2	
Totals		16	6	4	10	5	

*DENNENY, Cyril Joseph (Cy) *LW*
B. Farran's Point, Ont., Dec. 23, 1897

SSN	TEAM	GP	G	A	PTS.	PIM	
17–18	Ott	22	36	0	36	34	
18–19	Ott	18	18	4	22	43	
19–20	Ott	22	16	2	18	21	
20–21	Ott	24	34	5	39	0	
21–22	Ott	22	27	12	39	18	
22–23	Ott	24	21	10	31	20	
23–24	Ott	21	22	1	23	10	
24–25	Ott	28	27	15	42	16	
25–26	Ott	36	24	12	36	18	
26–27	Ott	42	17	6	23	16	
27–28	Ott	44	3	0	3	12	
28–29	Bos	23	1	2	3	2	
Totals		326	246	69	315	210	

Playoffs

SSN	TEAM	GP	G	A	PTS.	PIM	
18–19	Ott	5	2	0	2	0	
19–20	Ott	5	0	0	0	3	
20–21	Ott	7	4	2	6	20	
21–22	Ott	2	0	2	2	4	
22–23	Ott	8	3	1	4	6	
23–24	Ott	2	0	2	2	2	
25–26	Ott	2	0	0	0	4	
26–27	Ptt	6	5	0	5	0	
27–28	Bos	2	0	0	0	0	
28–29	Bos	2	0	0	0	0	
Totals		41	18	3	21	39	

DENNIS, Norman Marshall *5–10 175 C*
B. Aurora, Ont., Dec. 10, 1942

SSN	TEAM	GP	G	A	PTS.	PIM	+/-
68–69	StL	2	0	0	0	2	+1
69–70	StL	5	3	0	3	5	0
70–71	StL	4	0	0	0	0	-4
71–72	StL	1	0	0	0	4	-1
Totals		12	3	0	3	11	-4

Playoffs

SSN	TEAM	GP	G	A	PTS.	PIM	
69–70	StL	2	0	0	0	2	
70–71	StL	3	0	0	0	0	
Totals		5	0	0	0	2	

DENOIRD, Gerald (Gerry) *F*

SSN	TEAM	GP	G	A	PTS.	PIM	
22–23	Tor	15	0	0	0	0	

DePALMA, Larry *6–0 195 LW*
B. Trenton, Mich., Oct. 27, 1965

SSN	TEAM	GP	G	A	PTS.	PIM	+/-
85–86	Minn	1	0	0	0	0	0
86–87	Minn	56	9	6	15	219	-7
87–88	Minn	7	1	1	2	15	-2
88–89	Minn	43	5	7	12	102	-14
90–91	Minn	14	3	0	3	26	-5
92–93	SJ	20	2	6	8	41	-14
93–94	Pitt	7	1	0	1	5	+1
Totals		148	21	20	41	408	-41

Playoffs

SSN	TEAM	GP	G	A	PTS.	PIM	
88–89	Minn	2	0	0	0	6	
93–94	Pitt	1	0	0	0	0	
Totals		3	0	0	0	6	

DERLAGO, William Anthony *5–10 195 C*
B. Birtle, Man., Aug. 25, 1958

SSN	TEAM	GP	G	A	PTS.	PIM	+/-
78–79	Van	9	4	4	8	2	-2
79–80	Van–Tor	77	16	27	43	40	-7
80–81	Tor	80	35	39	74	26	-11
81–82	Tor	75	34	50	84	42	+5
82–83	Tor	58	13	24	37	27	-19
83–84	Tor	79	40	20	60	50	-8
84–85	Tor	62	31	31	62	21	-15
85–86	Tor–Bos–Winn	67	10	21	31	21	-9
86–87	Winn–Que	48	6	11	17	18	-7
Totals		555	189	227	416	247	-89

Playoffs

SSN	TEAM	GP	G	A	PTS.	PIM	
79–80	Tor	3	0	0	0	4	
80–81	Tor	3	1	0	1	2	
82–83	Tor	4	3	0	3	2	
85–86	Winn	3	1	0	1	0	
Totals		13	5	0	5	8	

DESAULNIERS, Gerard *5–11 152 C*
B. Shawinigan Falls, Quebec, Dec 31, 1928

SSN	TEAM	GP	G	A	PTS.	PIM	+/-
50–51	Mont	3	0	1	1	2	
52–53	Mont	2	0	1	1	2	
53–54	Mont	3	0	0	0	0	
Totals		8	0	2	2	4	

DESILETS, Joffre Wilfred *5–10 170 RW*
B. Capreal, Ont., Apr. 16, 1915

35–36	Mont	38	7	6	13	0	
36–37	Mont	48	7	12	19	17	
37–38	Mont	32	6	7	13	6	
38–39	Chi	48	11	13	24	28	
39–40	Chi	26	6	7	13	6	
Totals		192	37	45	82	57	

Playoffs

36–37	Mont	5	1	0	1	0	
37–38	Mont	2	0	0	0	7	
Totals		7	1	0	1	7	

DESJARDINS, Eric *6–1 200 D*
B. Rouyn, Que., June 14, 1969

88–89	Mont	36	2	12	14	26	+9
89–90	Mont	55	3	13	16	51	+1
90–91	Mont	62	7	18	25	27	+7
91–92	Mont	77	6	32	38	50	+17
92–93	Mont	82	13	32	45	98	+20
93–94	Mont	84	12	23	35	97	-1
94–95	Mont–Phil	43	5	24	29	14	+12
95–96	Phil	80	7	40	47	45	+19
96–97	Phil	82	12	34	46	50	+25
97–98	Phil	77	6	27	33	36	+11
98–99	Phil	68	15	36	51	38	+18
Totals		746	88	291	379	532	+128

Playoffs

88–89	Mont	14	1	1	2	6	
89–90	Mont	6	0	0	0	10	
90–91	Mont	13	1	4	5	8	
91–92	Mont	11	3	3	6	4	
92–93	Mont	20	4	10	14	23	
93–94	Mont	7	0	2	2	4	
94–95	Phil	15	4	4	8	10	
95–96	Phil	12	0	6	6	2	
96–97	Phil	19	2	8	10	12	
97–98	Phil	5	0	1	1	0	
98–99	Phil	6	2	2	4	4	
Totals		128	17	41	58	83	

DESJARDINS, Martin *5–11 179 C*
B. Ste.–Rose, Que., Jan. 28, 1967

| 89–90 | Mont | 8 | 0 | 2 | 2 | 2 | -4 |

DESJARDINS, Victor Arthur *5–9 160 C*
B. Sault Ste. Marie, Mich., July 4, 1900

30–31	Chi	39	3	12	15	11	
31–32	NYR	48	3	3	6	16	
Totals		87	6	15	21	27	

Playoffs

30–31	Chi	9	0	0	0	0	
31–32	NYR	7	0	0	0	0	
Totals		16	0	0	0	0	

DESLAURIERS, Jacques *6–0 170 D*
B. Montreal, Que., Sept. 3, 1928

| 55–56 | Mont | 2 | 0 | 0 | 0 | 0 | |

DEULING, Jarrett *5–11 194 LW*
B. Vernon, B.C., Mar. 4, 1974

95–96	NYI	14	0	1	1	11	-1
96–97	NYI	1	0	0	0	0	0
Totals		15	0	1	1	11	-1

DEVEREAUX, Boyd *6–2 195 C*
B. Seaforth, Ont., Apr. 16, 1978

97–98	Edm	38	1	4	5	6	-5
98–99	Edm	61	6	8	14	23	+2
Totals		99	7	12	19	29	-3

Playoffs

| 98–99 | Edm | 1 | 0 | 0 | 0 | 0 | |

DEVINE, Kevin *5–8 165 LW*
B. Toronto, Ont., Dec. 9, 1954

| 82–83 | NYI | 2 | 0 | 1 | 1 | 8 | +1 |

DE VRIES, Greg *6–3 218 D*
B. Sundridge, Ont., Jan. 4, 1973

95–96	Edm	13	1	1	2	12	-2
96–97	Edm	37	0	4	4	52	-2
97–98	Edm	65	7	4	11	80	-17
98–99	Nash–Col A	73	1	3	4	64	-7
Totals		188	9	12	21	208	-28

Playoffs

96–97	Edm	12	0	1	1	8	
97–98	Edm	7	0	0	0	21	
98–99	Col A	19	0	2	2	22	
Totals		38	0	3	3	51	

DEWAR, Thomas *D*
B. Frobisher, Sask., June 10, 1913

| 43–44 | NYR | 9 | 0 | 2 | 2 | 4 | |

DEWSBURY, Albert Percy *6–2 202 D*
B. Goderich, Ont., Apr. 12, 1926

46–47	Det	23	2	1	3	12	
49–50	Det	11	2	2	4	2	
50–51	Chi	67	5	14	19	79	
51–52	Chi	69	7	17	24	99	
52–53	Chi	69	5	16	21	97	
53–54	Chi	69	6	15	21	44	
54–55	Chi	2	0	1	1	10	
55–56	Chi	37	3	12	15	22	
Totals		347	30	78	108	365	

Playoffs

46–47	Det	2	0	0	0	4	
47–48	Det	1	0	0	0	0	
49–50	Det	4	0	3	3	8	
52–53	Chi	7	1	2	3	4	
Totals		14	1	5	6	16	

DEZIEL, Michael *5–11 180 D*
B. Sorel, Que., Jan. 13, 1954

| 74–75 | Buf | 0 | 0 | 0 | 0 | 0 | |

Playoffs

| 74–75 | Buf | 1 | 0 | 0 | 0 | 0 | |

DHEERE, Marcel Albert (Ching) *5–7 175 LW*
B. St. Boniface, Man., Dec. 19, 1920

| 42–43 | Mont | 11 | 1 | 2 | 3 | 2 | |

Playoffs

| 42–43 | Mont | 5 | 0 | 0 | 0 | 6 | |

DIACHUK, Edward *6–1 195 LW*
B. Vergreville, Alta., Aug. 16, 1936

| 60–61 | Det | 12 | 0 | 0 | 0 | 19 | |

DICK, Harry *5–11 210 D*
B. Port Colborne, Ont., Nov. 22, 1922

| 46–47 | Chi | 12 | 0 | 1 | 1 | 12 | |

DICKENS, Ernest Leslie *6–10 175 D*
B. Winnipeg, Man., June 25, 1921

41–42	Tor	10	2	2	4	6	
45–46	Tor	15	1	3	4	6	
47–48	Chi	54	5	15	20	30	
48–49	Chi	59	2	3	5	14	
49–50	Chi	70	0	13	13	22	
50–51	Chi	70	2	8	10	20	
Totals		278	12	44	56	98	

Playoffs

| 41–42 | Tor | 13 | 0 | 0 | 0 | 4 | |

DICKENSON, John Herbert (Herb) *5–11 175 LW*
B. Mount Hope, Ont., June 11, 1931

51–52	NYR	37	14	13	27	8	
52–53	NYR	11	4	4	8	2	
Totals		48	18	17	35	10	

DIDUCK, Gerald *6–2 207 D*
B. Edmonton, Alta., Apr. 6, 1965

84–85	NYI	65	2	8	10	80	+2
85–86	NYI	10	1	2	3	2	+5
86–87	NYI	30	2	3	5	67	-3
87–88	NYI	68	7	12	19	113	+22
88–89	NYI	65	11	21	32	155	+9
89–90	NYI	76	3	17	20	163	+2
90–91	Mont–Van	63	4	9	13	105	-5
91–92	Van	77	6	21	27	229	-3
92–93	Van	80	6	14	20	171	+32
93–94	Van	55	1	10	11	72	-2
94–95	Van–Chi	35	2	3	5	63	-5
95–96	Hart	79	1	9	10	88	+7
96–97	Hart–Phoe	67	2	12	14	63	-7
97–98	Phoe	78	8	10	18	118	+14
98–99	Phoe	44	0	2	2	72	+9
Totals		892	56	153	209	1561	+77

Playoffs

86–87	NYI	14	0	1	1	35	
87–88	NYI	6	1	0	1	42	
89–90	NYI	5	0	0	0	12	
90–91	Van	6	1	0	1	11	
91–92	Van	5	0	0	0	10	
92–93	Van	12	4	2	6	12	
93–94	Van	24	1	7	8	22	
94–95	Chi	16	1	3	4	22	
96–97	Phoe	7	0	0	0	10	
97–98	Phoe	6	0	2	2	20	
98–99	Phoe	3	0	0	0	2	
Totals		104	8	15	23	198	

DIETRICH, Don Armond *6–1 195 D*
B. Deloraine, Man., Apr. 5, 1961

83–84	Chi	17	0	5	5	0	-1
85–86	NJ	11	0	2	2	10	-8
Totals		28	0	7	7	10	-9

*DILL, Robert Edward *5–8 185 D*
B. St. Paul, Minn., Apr. 25, 1920

43–44	NYR	28	6	10	16	66	
44–45	NYR	48	9	5	14	69	
Totals		76	15	15	30	135	

DILLABOUGH, Robert Wellington *5–10 180 C*
B. Belleville, Ont., Apr. 14, 1941

61–62	Det	5	0	0	0	2	
64–65	Det	4	0	0	0	2	
65–66	Bos	53	7	13	20	18	
66–67	Bos	60	6	12	18	14	
67–68	Pitt	47	7	12	19	18	-7
68–69	Pitt-Oak	62	7	12	19	6	-10
69–70	Oak	52	5	5	10	16	-18
72–73	Clev (WHA)	72	8	8	16	8	
NHL Totals		283	32	54	86	76	-35
WHA Totals		72	8	8	16	8	

Playoffs

62–63	Det	1	0	0	0	0	
63–64	Det	1	0	0	0	0	
64–65	Det	4	0	0	0	0	
68–69	Cal	7	3	0	3	0	
69–70	Oak	4	0	0	0	0	
72–73	Clev (WHA)	9	1	0	1	0	
NHL Totals		17	3	0	3	0	
WHA Totals		9	1	0	1	0	

*DILLON, Cecil Graham (Ceece) *5–10 173 F*
B. Toledo, Ohio, Apr. 26, 1908

30–31	NYR	25	7	3	10	8	
31–32	NYR	48	23	15	38	22	
32–33	NYR	48	21	10	31	12	
33–34	NYR	48	13	26	39	10	
34–35	NYR	48	25	9	34	4	
35–36	NYR	48	18	14	32	12	
36–37	NYR	48	20	11	31	13	
37–38	NYR	48	21	18	39	6	
38–39	NYR	48	12	15	27	6	
39–40	Det	44	7	10	17	12	
Totals		453	167	131	298	105	

Playoffs

| 30–31 | NYR | 4 | 0 | 1 | 1 | 2 | |
| 31–32 | NYR | 7 | 2 | 1 | 3 | 4 | |

SSN	TEAM	GP	G	A	PTS.	PIM	+/-
32–33	NYR	8	8	2	10	6	
33–34	NYR	2	0	1	1	2	
34–35	NYR	4	2	1	3	0	
36–37	NYR	9	0	3	3	0	
37–38	NYR	3	1	0	1	0	
38–39	NYR	1	0	0	0	0	
39–40	Det	5	1	0	1	0	
Totals		43	14	9	23	14	

DILLON, Gary Kevin *5–10 173 C*
B. Toronto, Ont., Feb. 28, 1959

SSN	TEAM	GP	G	A	PTS.	PIM	+/-
80–81	Col	13	1	1	2	29	-6

DILLON, Gerald Wayne (Wayne) *6–0 185 C*
B. Toronto, Ont., May 25, 1955

SSN	TEAM	GP	G	A	PTS.	PIM	+/-
73–74	Tor (WHA)	71	30	35	65	13	
74–75	Tor (WHA)	77	29	66	95	22	
75–76	NYR	79	21	24	45	10	-11
76–77	NYR	78	17	29	46	33	-14
77–78	NYR	59	5	13	18	15	-8
78–79	Birm (WHA)	64	12	27	39	43	
79–80	Winn	13	0	0	0	2	-6
NHL Totals		229	43	66	109	60	-39
WHA Totals		212	71	128	199	78	

Playoffs

SSN	TEAM	GP	G	A	PTS.	PIM	+/-
73–74	Tor (WHA)	12	5	6	11	9	
74–75	Tor (WHA)	6	4	4	8	4	
77–78	NYR	3	0	1	1	0	
NHL Totals		3	0	1	1	0	
WHA Totals		18	9	10	19	13	

DiMAIO, Robert (Rob) *5–10 190 C*
B. Calgary, Alta., Feb. 19, 1968

SSN	TEAM	GP	G	A	PTS.	PIM	+/-
88–89	NYI	16	1	0	1	30	-6
89–90	NYI	7	0	0	0	2	0
90–91	NYI	1	0	0	0	0	0
91–92	NYI	50	5	2	7	43	-23
92–93	TB	54	9	15	24	62	0
93–94	TB–Phil	53	11	12	23	46	-4
94–95	Phil	36	3	1	4	53	+8
95–96	Phil	59	6	15	21	58	0
96–97	Bos	72	13	15	28	82	-21
97–98	Bos	79	10	17	27	82	-13
98–99	Bos	71	7	14	21	95	-14
Totals		498	65	91	156	553	-73

Playoffs

SSN	TEAM	GP	G	A	PTS.	PIM	+/-
89–90	NYI	1	1	0	1	4	
94–95	Phil	15	2	4	6	4	
95–96	Phil	3	0	0	0	0	
97–98	Bos	6	1	0	1	8	
98–99	Bos	12	2	0	2	8	
Totals		37	6	4	10	24	

DINEEN, Gary Daniel Patrick *5–10 175 C*
B. Montreal, Que., Dec. 24, 1943

SSN	TEAM	GP	G	A	PTS.	PIM	+/-
68–69	Minn	4	0	1	1	0	-2

DINEEN, Gordon *6–0 195 D*
B. Quebec City, Que., Sept. 21, 1962

SSN	TEAM	GP	G	A	PTS.	PIM	+/-
82–83	NYI	2	0	0	0	4	-2
83–84	NYI	43	1	11	12	32	+10
84–85	NYI	48	1	12	13	89	+10
85–86	NYI	57	1	8	9	81	+15
86–87	NYI	71	4	10	14	110	-8
87–88	NYI–Minn	70	5	13	18	83	+4
88–89	Minn–Pitt	40	1	3	4	44	-9
89–90	Pitt	69	1	8	9	125	+6
90–91	Pitt	9	0	0	0	4	-4
91–92	Pitt	1	0	0	0	0	-2
92–93	Ott	32	2	4	6	30	-19
93–94	Ott	77	0	21	21	89	-52
94–95	NYI	9	0	0	0	2	-5
Totals		528	16	90	106	693	-56

Playoffs

SSN	TEAM	GP	G	A	PTS.	PIM	+/-
83–84	NYI	9	1	1	2	28	
84–85	NYI	10	0	0	0	26	
85–86	NYI	3	0	0	0	2	
86–87	NYI	7	0	4	4	4	
88–89	Pitt	11	0	2	2	8	
Totals		40	1	7	8	68	

DINEEN, Kevin *5–11 195 RW*
B. Quebec City, Que., Oct. 28, 1963

SSN	TEAM	GP	G	A	PTS.	PIM	+/-
84–85	Hart	57	25	16	41	120	-6
85–86	Hart	57	33	35	68	124	+16
86–87	Hart	78	40	39	79	110	+7
87–88	Hart	74	25	25	50	217	-14
88–89	Hart	79	45	44	89	167	-6
89–90	Hart	67	25	41	66	164	+7
90–91	Hart	61	17	30	47	104	-15
91–92	Hart–Phil	80	30	32	62	153	-5
92–93	Phil	83	35	28	63	201	+14
93–94	Phil	71	19	23	42	113	-9
94–95	Phil	40	8	5	13	39	-1
95–96	Phil–Hart	46	2	9	11	117	-1
96–97	Hart	78	19	29	48	141	-6
97–98	Car	54	7	16	23	105	-7
98–99	Car	67	8	10	18	97	5
Totals		982	338	382	720	1982	-21

Playoffs

SSN	TEAM	GP	G	A	PTS.	PIM	+/-
85–86	Hart	10	6	7	13	18	
86–87	Hart	6	2	1	3	31	
87–88	Hart	6	4	4	8	8	
88–89	Hart	4	1	0	1	10	
89–90	Hart	6	3	2	5	18	
90–91	Hart	6	1	0	1	16	
94–95	Phil	15	6	4	10	18	
98–99	Car	6	0	0	0	8	
Totals		59	23	18	41	127	

DINEEN, Peter Kevin *5–11 190 D*
B. Kingston, Ont., Nov. 19, 1960

SSN	TEAM	GP	G	A	PTS.	PIM	+/-
86–87	LA	11	0	2	2	8	-9
89–90	Det	2	0	0	0	5	0
Totals		13	0	2	2	13	-9

DINEEN, William Patrick *5–11 180 RW*
B. Arvida, Que., Sept. 18, 1932

SSN	TEAM	GP	G	A	PTS.	PIM	+/-
53–54	Det	70	17	8	25	34	
54–55	Det	69	10	9	19	36	
55–56	Det	70	12	7	19	30	
56–57	Det	51	6	7	13	12	
57–58	Det–Chi	63	6	13	19	12	
Totals		323	51	44	95	124	

Playoffs

SSN	TEAM	GP	G	A	PTS.	PIM	+/-
53–54	Det	12	0	0	0	2	
54–55	Det	11	0	1	1	8	
55–56	Det	10	1	0	1	8	
56–57	Det	4	0	0	0	0	
Totals		37	1	1	2	18	

DINGMAN, Chris *6–4 225 LW*
B. Edmonton, Alta., July 6, 1976

SSN	TEAM	GP	G	A	PTS.	PIM	+/-
97–98	Calg	70	3	3	6	149	-11
98–99	Calg–Col A	3	0	0	0	24	-2
Totals		73	3	3	6	173	-13

DINSMORE, Charles A. (Chuck, Dinny) *F*
B. Toronto, Ont., July 23, 1903

SSN	TEAM	GP	G	A	PTS.	PIM	+/-
24–25	Mont M	30	2	1	3	26	
25–26	Mont M	33	3	1	4	18	
26–27	Mont M	28	1	0	1	6	
29–30	Mont M	9	0	0	0	0	
Totals		100	6	2	8	50	

Playoffs

SSN	TEAM	GP	G	A	PTS.	PIM	+/-
25–26	MontM	8	0	0	0	4	
29–30	MontM	4	0	0	0	0	
Totals		12	0	0	0	4	

DIONNE, Gilbert *6–0 194 LW*
B. Drummondville, Que., Sept. 19, 1970

SSN	TEAM	GP	G	A	PTS.	PIM	+/-
90–91	Mont	2	0	0	0	0	-2
91–92	Mont	39	21	13	34	10	+7
92–93	Mont	75	20	28	48	63	+5
93–94	Mont	74	19	26	45	31	-9
94–95	Mont–Phil	26	0	9	9	4	-4
95–96	Phil–Fla	7	1	3	4	0	0
Totals		223	61	79	140	108	-3

Playoffs

SSN	TEAM	GP	G	A	PTS.	PIM	+/-
91–92	Mont	11	3	4	7	10	
92–93	Mont	20	6	6	12	20	
93–94	Mont	5	1	2	3	0	
94–95	Phil	3	0	0	0	4	
Totals		39	10	12	22	34	

DIONNE, Marcel Elphege *5–8 185 C*
B. Drummondville, Que., Aug. 3, 1951

SSN	TEAM	GP	G	A	PTS.	PIM	+/-
71–72	Det	78	28	49	77	14	0
72–73	Det	77	40	50	90	21	-4
73–74	Det	74	24	54	78	10	-31
74–75	Det	80	47	74	121	14	-15
75–76	LA	80	40	54	94	38	+2
76–77	LA	80	53	69	122	12	+10
77–78	LA	70	36	43	79	37	-8
78–79	LA	80	59	71	130	30	+23
79–80	LA	80	53	84	137	32	+35
80–81	LA	80	58	77	135	70	+55
81–82	LA	78	50	67	117	50	-10
82–83	LA	80	56	51	107	22	+10
83–84	LA	66	39	53	92	28	+8
84–85	LA	80	46	80	126	46	+11
85–86	LA	80	36	58	94	42	-22
86–87	LA–NYR	81	28	56	84	60	-16
87–88	NYR	67	31	34	65	54	-14
88–89	NYR	37	7	16	23	20	-6
Totals		1348	731	1040	1771	600	+28

Playoffs

SSN	TEAM	GP	G	A	PTS.	PIM	+/-
75–76	LA	9	6	1	7	0	
76–77	LA	9	5	9	14	2	
77–78	LA	2	0	0	0	0	
78–79	LA	2	0	1	1	0	
79–80	LA	4	0	3	3	4	
80–81	LA	4	1	3	4	7	
81–82	LA	10	7	4	11	0	
84–85	LA	3	1	2	3	2	
86–87	NYR	6	1	1	2	2	
Totals		49	21	24	45	17	

DI PIETRO, Paul *5–8 181 C*
B. Sault Ste. Marie, Ont., Sept 8, 1970

SSN	TEAM	GP	G	A	PTS.	PIM	+/-
91–92	Mont	33	4	6	10	25	
92–93	Mont	29	4	13	17	14	
93–94	Mont	70	13	20	33	37	
94–95	Mont–Tor	34	5	6	11	10	
95–96	Tor	20	4	4	8	4	
96–97	LA	6	1	0	1	6	
Totals		192	31	49	80	96	

Playoffs

SSN	TEAM	GP	G	A	PTS.	PIM	+/-
92–93	Mont	17	8	5	13	8	
93–94	Mont	7	2	4	6	2	
94–95	Tor	7	1	1	2	0	
Totals		31	11	10	21	10	

DIRK, Robert *6–4 205 D*
B. Regina, Sask., Aug. 20, 1966

SSN	TEAM	GP	G	A	PTS.	PIM	+/-
87–88	StL	7	0	1	1	16	0
88–89	StL	9	0	1	1	11	-3
89–90	StL	37	1	1	2	128	+9
90–91	StL–Van	52	2	3	5	120	-5
91–92	Van	72	2	7	9	126	+6
92–93	Van	69	4	8	12	150	+25
93–94	Van–Chi	71	2	3	5	131	+18
94–95	Ana	38	1	3	4	56	-3
95–96	Ana–Mont	47	1	2	3	48	+8
Totals		402	13	29	42	786	+55

Playoffs

SSN	TEAM	GP	G	A	PTS.	PIM	+/-
87–88	StL	6	0	1	1	2	
89–90	StL	3	0	0	0	0	
90–91	Van	6	0	0	0	13	
91–92	Van	13	0	1	1	20	
92–93	Van	9	0	0	0	6	
93–94	Chi	2	0	0	0	15	
Totals		39	0	1	1	56	

DJOOS, Per *5–11 170 D*
B. Mora, Sweden, May 11, 1968

SSN	TEAM	GP	G	A	PTS.	PIM	+/-
90–91	Det	26	0	12	12	16	-2
91–92	NYR	50	1	18	19	40	+7
92–93	NYR	6	1	1	2	2	0
Totals		82	2	31	33	58	+5

DOAK, Gary Walter *5–11 191 D*
B. Goderich, Ont., Feb. 26, 1946

SSN	TEAM	GP	G	A	PTS.	PIM	+/-
65–66	Det–Bos	24	0	8	8	40	
66–67	Bos	29	0	1	1	50	
67–68	Bos	59	2	10	12	100	+13
68–69	Bos	22	3	3	6	37	+11

SSN	TEAM	GP	G	A	PTS.	PIM	+/-
69–70	Bos	44	1	7	8	63	+7
70–71	Van	77	2	10	12	112	-5
71–72	Van–NYR	55	1	11	12	46	+15
72–73	Det–Bos	49	0	5	5	53	+4
73–74	Bos	69	0	4	4	44	-2
74–75	Bos	40	0	0	0	30	-3
75–76	Bos	58	1	6	7	60	+25
76–77	Bos	76	3	13	16	107	+15
77–78	Bos	61	4	13	17	50	+37
78–79	Bos	63	6	11	17	28	+12
79–80	Bos	52	0	5	5	45	+14
80–81	Bos	11	0	0	0	12	-3
Totals		789	23	107	130	877	+140

Playoffs

SSN	TEAM	GP	G	A	PTS.	PIM
67–68	Bos	4	0	0	0	4
69–70	Bos	8	0	0	0	9
71–72	NYR	12	0	0	0	46
72–73	Bos	2	0	0	0	2
74–75	Bos	3	0	0	0	4
75–76	Bos	12	1	0	1	22
76–77	Bos	14	0	2	2	26
77–78	Bos	12	1	0	1	4
78–79	Bos	7	0	2	2	4
79–80	Bos	4	0	0	0	0
Totals		78	2	4	6	121

DOAN, Shane 6–1 215 RW
B. Eston, Sask., Oct. 10, 1976

SSN	TEAM	GP	G	A	PTS.	PIM	+/-
95–96	Winn	74	7	10	17	101	-9
96–97	Phoe	63	4	8	12	49	-3
97–98	Phoe	33	5	6	11	35	-3
98–99	Phoe	79	6	16	22	54	-5
Totals		249	22	40	62	239	-20

Playoffs

SSN	TEAM	GP	G	A	PTS.	PIM
95–96	Winn	6	0	0	0	6
96–97	Phoe	4	0	0	0	2
97–98	Phoe	6	1	0	1	6
98–99	Phoe	7	2	2	4	6
Totals		23	3	2	5	20

DOBBIN, Brian 5–11 205 RW
B. Petrolia, Ont., Aug. 18, 1966

SSN	TEAM	GP	G	A	PTS.	PIM	+/-
86–87	Phil	12	2	1	3	14	+2
87–88	Phil	21	3	5	8	6	-1
88–89	Phil	14	0	1	1	8	-6
89–90	Phil	9	1	1	2	11	+1
91–92	Bos	7	1	0	1	22	0
Totals		63	7	8	15	61	-4

Playoffs

SSN	TEAM	GP	G	A	PTS.	PIM
88–89	Phil	2	0	0	0	17

DOBSON, James 6–1 176 RW
B. Winnipeg, Man., Feb. 29, 1960

SSN	TEAM	GP	G	A	PTS.	PIM	+/-
79–80	Minn	1	0	0	0	0	0
80–81	Minn	1	0	0	0	0	0
81–82	Minn–Col	9	0	0	0	6	-2
Totals		11	0	0	0	6	-2

DOHERTY, Fredrick F
SSN	TEAM	GP	G	A	PTS.	PIM
18–19	Mont M	3	0	0	0	0

DOIG, Jason 6–3 216 D
B. Montreal, Que., Jan. 29, 1977

SSN	TEAM	GP	G	A	PTS.	PIM	+/-
95–96	Winn	15	1	1	2	28	-2
97–98	Phoe	4	0	1	1	12	-4
98–99	Phoe–NYR	9	0	1	1	10	+2
Totals		28	1	3	4	50	-4

DOLLAS, Bobby 6–2 212 D
B. Montreal, Que., Jan. 31, 1965

SSN	TEAM	GP	G	A	PTS.	PIM	+/-
83–84	Winn	1	0	0	0	0	-2
84–85	Winn	9	0	0	0	0	+4
85–86	Winn	46	0	5	5	66	-3
87–88	Que	9	0	0	0	2	-4
88–89	Que	16	0	3	3	16	-11
90–91	Det	56	3	5	8	20	+6
91–92	Det	27	3	1	4	20	+4
92–93	Det	6	0	0	0	2	-1
93–94	Ana	77	9	11	20	55	+20
94–95	Ana	45	7	13	20	12	-3
95–96	Ana	82	8	22	30	64	+9
96–97	Ana	79	4	14	18	55	+17
97–98	Ana–Edm	52	2	6	8	49	-6
98–99	Pitt	70	2	8	10	60	-3

SSN	TEAM	GP	G	A	PTS.	PIM	+/-
Totals		575	38	88	126	421	+27

Playoffs

SSN	TEAM	GP	G	A	PTS.	PIM
85–86	Winn	3	0	0	0	2
90–91	Det	7	1	0	1	13
91–92	Det	2	0	1	1	0
96–97	Ana	11	0	0	0	4
98–99	Pitt	13	1	0	1	6
Totals		36	2	1	3	25

DOME, Robert 6–0 205 C
B. Skalica, Slovakia, Jan. 29, 1979

SSN	TEAM	GP	G	A	PTS.	PIM
97–98	Pitt	30	5	2	7	12

DOMENICHELLI, Hnat 6–0 175 C
B. Edmonton, Alta., Feb. 17, 1976

SSN	TEAM	GP	G	A	PTS.	PIM	+/-
96–97	Hart–Calg	23	3	3	6	9	-3
97–98	Calg	31	9	7	16	6	+4
98–99	Calg	23	5	5	10	11	-4
Totals		77	17	15	32	26	-3

DOMI, Tahir (Tie) 5–10 200 RW
B. Windsor, Ont., Nov. 1 1969

SSN	TEAM	GP	G	A	PTS.	PIM	+/-
89–90	Tor	2	0	0	0	42	0
90–91	NYR	28	1	0	1	185	-5
91–92	NYR	42	2	4	6	246	-4
92–93	NYR–Winn	61	5	10	15	344	+1
93–94	Winn	81	8	11	19	347	-8
94–95	Winn–Tor	40	4	5	9	159	-5
95–96	Tor	72	7	6	13	297	-3
96–97	Tor	80	11	17	28	275	-17
97–98	Tor	80	4	10	14	365	-5
98–99	Tor	72	8	14	22	198	+5
Totals		558	50	77	127	2458	-41

Playoffs

SSN	TEAM	GP	G	A	PTS.	PIM
91–92	NYR	6	1	1	2	32
92–93	Winn	6	1	0	1	23
94–95	Tor	7	1	0	1	0
95–96	Tor	6	0	2	2	4
98–99	Tor	14	0	2	2	24
Totals		39	3	5	8	83

DONALDSON, Robert Gary (Gary) F
B. Trail, B.C., July 15, 1952

SSN	TEAM	GP	G	A	PTS.	PIM	+/-
73–74	Chi	1	0	0	0	0	+1
76–77	Hou (WHA)	5	0	0	0	6	

DONATELLI, Clark 5–10 190 LW
B. Providence, R.I., Nov. 22, 1965

SSN	TEAM	GP	G	A	PTS.	PIM	+/-
89–90	Minn	25	3	3	6	17	-11
91–92	Bos	10	0	1	1	22	-8
Totals		35	3	4	7	39	-19

Playoffs

SSN	TEAM	GP	G	A	PTS.	PIM
91–92	Bos	2	0	0	0	0

DONATO, Ted 5–10 181 LW
B. Dedham, Mass., Apr. 18, 1968

SSN	TEAM	GP	G	A	PTS.	PIM	+/-
91–92	Bos	10	1	2	3	8	-1
92–93	Bos	82	15	20	35	61	+2
93–94	Bos	84	22	32	54	59	0
94–95	Bos	47	10	10	20	10	+3
95–96	Bos	82	23	26	49	46	+6
96–97	Bos	67	25	26	51	37	-9
97–98	Bos	79	16	23	39	54	+6
98–99	Bos–NYI–Ott	82	11	16	27	41	-8
Totals		533	123	155	278	316	

Playoffs

SSN	TEAM	GP	G	A	PTS.	PIM
91–92	Bos	15	3	4	7	4
92–93	Bos	4	0	1	1	0
93–94	Bos	11	4	2	6	10
94–95	Bos	5	0	0	0	4
95–96	Bos	5	1	2	3	2
97–98	Bos	5	0	0	0	2
98–99	Ott	1	0	0	0	0
Totals		48	8	9	17	22

*DONNELLY, Babe D
B. Sault Ste. Marie, Ont., Dec. 22, 1895

SSN	TEAM	GP	G	A	PTS.	PIM
26–27	Mont M	34	0	1	1	14

Playoffs

SSN	TEAM	GP	G	A	PTS.	PIM
26–27	Mont M	2	0	0	0	0

DONNELLY, David 5–11 185 C
B. Edmonton, Alta., Feb. 2, 1962

SSN	TEAM	GP	G	A	PTS.	PIM	+/-
83–84	Bos	16	3	4	7	2	+13
84–85	Bos	38	6	8	14	46	-1
85–86	Bos	8	0	0	0	17	+3
86–87	Chi	71	6	12	18	81	-7
87–88	Edm	4	0	0	0	4	0
Totals		137	15	24	39	150	+8

Playoffs

SSN	TEAM	GP	G	A	PTS.	PIM
83–84	Bos	3	0	0	0	0
84–85	Bos	1	0	0	0	0
86–87	Chi	1	0	0	0	0
Totals		5	0	0	0	0

DONNELLY, Gordon 6–1 202 D
B. Montreal, Que., Apr. 5, 1962

SSN	TEAM	GP	G	A	PTS.	PIM	+/-
83–84	Que	38	0	5	5	60	-1
84–85	Que	22	0	0	0	33	+1
85–86	Que	36	2	2	4	85	0
86–87	Que	38	0	2	2	143	-3
87–88	Que	63	4	3	7	301	-16
88–89	Que–Winn	73	10	10	20	274	-20
89–90	Winn	55	3	3	6	222	+3
90–91	Winn	57	3	4	7	265	-13
91–92	Winn–Buf	71	2	3	5	316	-12
92–93	Buf	60	3	8	11	221	+5
93–94	Buf–Dal	25	0	1	1	97	-3
94–95	Dal	16	1	0	1	52	+1
Totals		554	28	41	69	2069	-58

Playoffs

SSN	TEAM	GP	G	A	PTS.	PIM
85–86	Que	1	0	0	0	0
86–87	Que	13	0	0	0	53
89–90	Winn	6	0	1	1	8
91–92	Buf	6	0	1	1	0
Totals		26	0	1	1	61

DONNELLY, Mike 5–11 185 LW
B. Detroit, Mich., Oct. 10, 1963

SSN	TEAM	GP	G	A	PTS.	PIM	+/-
86–87	NYR	5	1	1	2	0	0
87–88	NYR–Buf	57	8	10	18	52	-6
88–89	Buf	22	4	6	10	10	-1
89–90	Buf	12	1	2	3	8	-4
90–91	LA	53	7	5	12	41	+3
91–92	LA	80	29	16	45	20	+5
92–93	LA	84	29	40	69	45	+17
93–94	LA	81	21	21	42	34	+2
94–95	LA–Dal	44	12	15	27	33	-4
95–96	Dal	24	2	5	7	10	-2
96–97	NYI	3	0	0	0	2	0
Totals		465	114	121	235	255	+10

Playoffs

SSN	TEAM	GP	G	A	PTS.	PIM
90–91	LA	12	5	4	9	6
91–92	LA	6	1	0	1	4
92–93	LA	24	6	7	13	14
94–95	Dal	5	0	1	1	6
Totals		47	12	12	24	30

DONOVAN, Shean 6–2 190 RW
B. Timmins, Ont., Jan. 22, 1975

SSN	TEAM	GP	G	A	PTS.	PIM	+/-
94–95	SJ	14	0	0	0	6	-6
95–96	SJ	74	13	8	21	39	-17
96–97	SJ	73	9	6	15	42	+18
97–98	SJ–Col A	67	8	10	18	70	+6
98–99	Col A	68	7	12	19	37	+4
Totals		296	37	36	73	194	-31

Playoffs

SSN	TEAM	GP	G	A	PTS.	PIM
94–95	SJ	7	0	1	1	6
98–99	Col A	5	0	0	0	2
Totals		12	0	1	1	8

*DORAN, John Michael (Red) 6–0 195 D
B. Belleville, Ont., May 24, 1911

SSN	TEAM	GP	G	A	PTS.	PIM
33–34	NYA	39	1	4	5	40
35–36	NYA	25	4	2	6	44
36–37	NYA	21	0	1	1	10
37–38	Det	7	0	0	0	10
39–40	Mont	6	0	3	3	6
Totals		98	5	10	15	110

Playoffs

SSN	TEAM	GP	G	A	PTS.	PIM
35–36	NYA	3	0	0	0	0

DORAN, Lloyd George (Red) 6-0 175 C
B. South Porcupine, Ont., Jan. 10, 1921

SSN	TEAM	GP	G	A	PTS.	PIM	+/-
46-47	Det	24	3	2	5	10	

*DORATY, Kenneth Edward 5-7 133 F
B. Stittsville, Ont., June 23, 1906

SSN	TEAM	GP	G	A	PTS.	PIM	+/-
26-27	Chi	18	0	0	0	0	
32-33	Tor	38	5	11	16	16	
33-34	Tor	34	9	10	19	6	
34-35	Tor	11	1	4	5	0	
37-38	Det	2	0	1	1	2	
Totals		103	15	26	41	24	

Playoffs

32-33	Tor	9	5	0	5	2	
33-34	Tor	5	2	2	4	0	
34-35	Tor	1	0	0	0	0	
Totals		15	7	2	9	2	

DORE, Andre Hector 6-2 200 D
B. Montreal, Que., Feb. 11, 1958

78-79	NYR	2	0	0	0	0	0
79-80	NYR	2	0	0	0	0	-1
80-81	NYR	15	1	3	4	15	-1
81-82	NYR	56	4	16	20	64	+10
82-83	NYR-StL	77	5	27	32	64	+23
83-84	StL-Que	80	4	28	32	83	+4
84-85	NYR	25	0	7	7	35	-2
Totals		257	14	81	95	261	+36

Playoffs

81-82	NYR	10	1	1	2	16	
82-83	StL	4	0	1	1	8	
83-84	Que	9	0	0	0	8	
Totals		23	1	2	3	32	

DORE, Daniel 6-3 202 RW
B. Ferme-Neuve, Que., Apr. 9, 1970

89-90	Que	16	2	3	5	59	-8
90-91	Que	1	0	0	0	0	+1
Totals		17	2	3	5	59	-7

DOREY, Robert James (Jim) 6-1 190 D
B. Kingston, Ont., Aug. 17, 1947

68-69	Tor	61	8	22	30	200	+9
69-70	Tor	46	6	11	17	99	+9
70-71	Tor	74	7	22	29	198	+6
71-72	Tor-NYR	51	4	19	23	56	+10
72-73	NE (WHA)	75	7	56	63	95	
73-74	NE (WHA)	77	6	40	46	134	
74-75	NE-Tor (WHA)	74	16	40	56	112	
75-76	Tor (WHA)	74	9	51	60	134	
76-77	Que (WHA)	73	13	34	47	102	
77-78	Que (WHA)	26	1	9	10	23	
78-79	Que (WHA)	32	0	2	2	17	
NHL Totals		232	25	74	99	553	+34
WHA Totals		431	52	232	284	617	

Playoffs

68-69	Tor	4	0	1	1	21	
70-71	Tor	6	0	1	1	19	
71-72	NYR	1	0	0	0	0	
72-73	NE (WHA)	15	3	16	19	41	
73-74	NE (WHA)	6	0	6	6	26	
74-75	Tor (WHA)	6	2	6	8	2	
76-77	Que (WHA)	10	0	2	2	28	
77-78	Que (WHA)	11	0	3	3	34	
78-79	Que (WHA)	3	0	0	0	0	
NHL Totals		11	0	2	2	40	
WHA Totals		51	5	33	38	131	

DORION, Dan 5-9 180 C
B. Astoria, N.Y., Mar. 2, 1963

85-86	NJ	3	1	1	2	0	-1
87-88	NJ	1	0	0	0	2	0
Totals		4	1	1	2	2	-1

DORNHOEFER, Gerhardt Otto (Gary) 6-1 190 RW
B. Kitchener, Ont., Feb. 2, 1943

63-64	Bos	32	12	10	22	20	
64-65	Bos	20	0	1	1	13	
65-66	Bos	10	0	1	1	2	
67-68	Phil	65	13	30	43	134	+6
68-69	Phil	60	8	16	24	80	-20
69-70	Phil	65	26	29	55	96	+2

SSN	TEAM	GP	G	A	PTS.	PIM	+/-
70-71	Phil	57	20	20	40	93	+3
71-72	Phil	75	17	32	49	183	-15
72-73	Phil	77	30	49	79	168	+17
73-74	Phil	57	11	39	50	125	+13
74-75	Phil	69	17	27	44	102	+23
75-76	Phil	74	28	35	63	128	+14
76-77	Phil	79	25	34	59	85	+47
77-78	Phil	47	7	5	12	62	-3
Totals		787	214	328	542	1291	+87

Playoffs

67-68	Phil	3	0	0	0	15	
68-69	Phil	4	0	1	1	20	
70-71	Phil	2	0	0	0	4	
72-73	Phil	11	3	3	6	16	
73-74	Phil	14	5	6	11	43	
74-75	Phil	17	5	5	10	33	
75-76	Phil	16	3	4	7	43	
76-77	Phil	9	1	0	1	22	
77-78	Phil	4	0	0	0	7	
Totals		80	17	19	36	203	

DOROHOY, Edward 5-9 150 C
B. Medicine Hat, Alta., Mar. 13, 1929

48-49	Mont	16	0	0	0	6	

DOUGLAS, Jordy Paul 6-0 200 LW
B. Winnipeg, Man., Jan. 20, 1958

78-79	NE (WHA)	51	6	10	16	15	
79-80	Hart	77	33	24	57	39	-11
80-81	Hart	55	13	9	22	29	-23
81-82	Hart	30	10	7	17	44	-11
82-83	Minn	68	13	14	27	30	-11
83-84	Minn-Winn	31	7	6	13	18	-7
84-85	Winn	7	0	2	2	0	-6
NHL Totals		268	76	62	138	160	-69
WHA Totals		51	6	10	16	15	

Playoffs

78-79	NE (WHA)	10	4	0	4	23	
82-83	Minn	6	0	0	0	4	
NHL Totals		6	0	0	0	4	
WHA Totals		10	4	0	4	23	

DOUGLAS, Kent Gemmell 5-10 189 D
B. Cobalt, Ont., Feb 6, 1936

62-63	Tor	70	7	15	22	105	
63-64	Tor	43	0	1	1	29	
64-65	Tor	67	5	23	28	129	
65-66	Tor	64	6	14	20	97	
66-67	Tor	39	2	12	14	48	
67-68	Oak-Det	76	11	21	32	126	-12
68-69	Det	69	2	29	31	97	+4
72-73	NY (WHA)	60	3	15	18	74	
NHL Totals		428	33	115	148	631	-8
WHA Totals		60	3	15	18	74	

Playoffs

62-63	Tor	10	1	1	2	2	
64-65	Tor	5	0	1	1	19	
65-66	Tor	4	0	1	1	12	
Totals		19	1	3	4	33	

DOUGLAS, Leslie Gordon (Les) 5-9 165 C
B. Perth, Ont., Dec. 5, 1918

40-41	Det	18	1	2	3	2	
42-43	Det	21	5	8	13	4	
45-46	Det	1	0	0	0	0	
46-47	Det	12	0	2	2	2	
Totals		52	6	12	18	8	

Playoffs

42-43	Det	10	3	2	5	0	

DOURIS, Peter 6-1 195 RW
B. Toronto, Ont., Feb. 19, 1966

85-86	Winn	11	0	0	0	0	-1
86-87	Winn	6	0	0	0	0	-1
87-88	Winn	4	0	2	2	0	-1
89-90	Bos	36	5	6	11	15	+8
90-91	Bos	39	5	2	7	9	-12
91-92	Bos	54	10	13	23	10	+9
92-93	Bos	19	4	4	8	4	+5
93-94	Ana	74	12	22	34	21	-5
94-95	Ana	46	10	11	21	12	+4
95-96	Ana	31	8	7	15	9	-3
97-98	Dal	1	0	0	0	0	-1

SSN	TEAM	GP	G	A	PTS.	PIM	+/-
Totals		321	54	67	121	80	+2

Playoffs

87-88	Winn	1	0	0	0	0	
89-90	Bos	8	0	1	1	8	
90-91	Bos	7	0	1	1	6	
91-92	Bos	7	2	3	5	0	
92-93	Bos	4	1	0	1	0	
Totals		27	3	5	8	14	

DOWD, James 6-1 185 C
B. Brick, N.J., Dec. 25, 1968

91-92	NJ	1	0	0	0	0	0
92-93	NJ	1	0	0	0	0	-1
93-94	NJ	15	5	10	15	0	+8
94-95	NJ	10	1	4	5	0	-5
95-96	NJ-Van	66	5	15	20	23	-9
96-97	NYI	3	0	0	0	0	-1
97-98	Calg	48	6	8	14	12	+10
98-99	Edm	1	0	0	0	0	0
Totals		145	17	37	54	35	+18

Playoffs

93-94	NJ	19	2	6	8	8	
94-95	NJ	11	2	1	3	8	
95-96	Van	1	0	0	0	0	
Totals		31	4	7	11	16	

DOWNIE, David M. 5-7 168 C
B. Burke's Falls, Ont., Mar. 11, 1909

32-33	Tor	11	0	1	1	2	

DOYON, Mario 6-0 174 D
B. Quebec City, Que., Aug. 27, 1968

88-89	Chi	7	1	1	2	6	+2
89-90	Que	9	2	3	5	6	-1
90-91	Que	12	0	0	0	4	-3
Totals		28	3	4	7	16	-2

DRAKE, Dallas James 6-0 180 C
B. Trail, B.C., Feb. 4, 1969

92-93	Det	72	18	26	44	93	+15
93-94	Det-Winn	62	13	27	40	49	-1
94-95	Winn	43	8	18	26	30	-6
95-96	Winn	69	19	20	39	36	-7
96-97	Phoe	63	17	19	36	52	-11
97-98	Phoe	60	11	29	40	71	+17
98-99	Phoe	53	9	22	31	65	+17
Totals		422	95	161	256	396	+24

Playoffs

92-93	Dal	7	3	3	6	6	
95-96	Winn	3	0	0	0	0	
96-97	Phoe	7	0	1	1	2	
97-98	Phoe	4	0	1	1	2	
98-99	Phoe	7	4	3	7	4	
Totals		28	7	8	15	14	

*DRAPER, Bruce 5-10 157 F
B. Toronto, Ont., Oct. 2, 1940

62-63	Tor	1	0	0	0	0	

DRAPER, Kris 5-11 190 C
B. Toronto, Ont., May 24, 1971

90-91	Winn	3	1	0	1	5	0
91-92	Winn	10	2	0	2	2	0
92-93	Winn	7	0	0	0	2	-6
93-94	Det	39	5	8	13	31	+11
94-95	Det	36	2	6	8	22	+1
95-96	Det	52	7	9	16	32	+2
96-97	Det	76	8	5	13	73	-11
97-98	Det	64	13	10	23	45	+5
98-99	Det	80	4	14	18	79	+2
Totals		367	42	52	94	291	+4

Playoffs

91-92	Winn	2	0	0	0	0	
93-94	Det	7	2	2	4	4	
94-95	Det	18	4	1	5	12	
95-96	Det	18	4	2	6	18	
96-97	Det	20	2	4	6	12	
97-98	Det	19	1	3	4	12	
98-99	Det	10	0	1	1	6	
Totals		94	13	13	26	64	

*DRILLON, Gordon Arthur 6–2 178 LW
B. Moncton, N.B., Oct. 23, 1914

SSN	TEAM	GP	G	A	PTS.	PIM	+/-
36–37	Tor	41	16	17	33	2	
37–38	Tor	48	26	26	52	4	
38–39	Tor	40	18	16	34	15	
39–40	Tor	43	21	19	40	13	
40–41	Tor	42	23	21	44	2	
41–42	Tor	48	23	18	41	6	
42–43	Mont	49	28	22	50	14	
Totals		311	155	139	294	56	

Playoffs

SSN	TEAM	GP	G	A	PTS.	PIM	+/-
36–37	Tor	2	0	0	0	0	
37–38	Tor	7	7	1	8	2	
38–39	Tor	10	7	6	13	4	
39–40	Tor	10	3	1	4	0	
40–41	Tor	7	3	2	5	2	
41–42	Tor	9	2	3	5	2	
42–43	Mont	5	4	2	6	0	
Totals		50	26	15	41	10	

DRISCOLL, Peter John (Drisk) 6–0 190 LW
B. Kingston, Ont., Oct 27, 1954

SSN	TEAM	GP	G	A	PTS.	PIM	+/-
74–75	Van (WHA)	21	3	2	5	40	
75–76	Calg (WHA)	75	16	18	34	127	
76–77	Calg (WHA)	76	23	29	52	120	
77–78	Que–Ind (WHA)	77	28	28	56	158	
78–79	Ind–Edm (WHA)	77	20	24	44	132	
79–80	Edm	39	1	5	6	54	-11
80–81	Edm	21	2	3	5	43	+1
NHL Totals		60	3	8	11	97	-10
WHA Totals		326	90	101	191	577	

Playoffs

SSN	TEAM	GP	G	A	PTS.	PIM	+/-
75–76	Calg (WHA)	10	2	5	7	41	
78–79	Edm (WHA)	13	1	6	7	8	
79–80	Edm	3	0	0	0	0	
NHL Totals		3	0	0	0	0	
WHA Totals		23	3	11	14	49	

DRIVER, Bruce 6–0 185 D
B. Toronto, Ont., Apr. 29, 1962

SSN	TEAM	GP	G	A	PTS.	PIM	+/-
83–84	NJ	4	0	2	2	0	-2
84–85	NJ	67	9	23	32	36	-22
85–86	NJ	40	3	15	18	32	+9
86–87	NJ	74	6	28	34	36	-26
87–88	NJ	74	15	40	55	68	+7
88–89	NJ	27	1	15	16	24	0
89–90	NJ	75	7	46	53	63	+6
90–91	NJ	73	9	36	45	62	+11
91–92	NJ	78	7	35	42	66	+5
92–93	NJ	83	14	40	54	66	-10
93–94	NJ	66	8	24	32	63	+29
94–95	NJ	41	4	12	16	18	-1
95–96	NYR	66	3	34	37	42	+2
96–97	NYR	79	5	25	30	48	+8
97–98	NYR	75	5	15	20	46	-3
Totals		922	96	390	486	670	+13

Playoffs

SSN	TEAM	GP	G	A	PTS.	PIM	+/-
87–88	NJ	20	3	7	10	14	
89–90	NJ	6	1	5	6	6	
90–91	NJ	7	1	2	3	12	
91–92	NJ	7	0	4	4	2	
92–93	NJ	5	1	3	4	4	
93–94	NJ	20	3	5	8	12	
94–95	NJ	17	1	6	7	8	
95–96	NYR	11	0	7	7	4	
96–97	NYR	15	0	1	1	2	
Totals		108	10	40	50	64	

DROLET, Rene Georges 5–7 155 RW
B. Quebec City, Que., Nov. 13, 1944

SSN	TEAM	GP	G	A	PTS.	PIM	+/-
71–72	Phil	1	0	0	0	0	0
74–75	Det	1	0	0	0	0	0
Totals		2	0	0	0	0	0

DROPPA, Ivan 6–2 209 D
B. Liptovsky Mikulas, Czechoslovakia, Feb. 1, 1972

SSN	TEAM	GP	G	A	PTS.	PIM	+/-
93–94	Chi	12	0.	1	1	12	+2
95–96	Chi	7	0	0	0	2	+2
Totals		19	0	1	1	14	+4

DROUILLARD, Clarence Joseph (Clare) 5–7 150 C
B. Windsor, Ont., Mar. 2, 1914

SSN	TEAM	GP	G	A	PTS.	PIM	+/-
37–38	Det	10	0	1	1	0	

DROUIN, Jude 5–9 165 C
B. Mont–Louis, Que., Oct. 28, 1948

SSN	TEAM	GP	G	A	PTS.	PIM	+/-
68–69	Mont	9	0	1	1	0	+1
69–70	Mont	3	0	0	0	2	-2
70–71	Minn	75	16	52	68	49	+5
71–72	Minn	63	13	43	56	31	+4
72–73	Minn	78	27	46	73	61	+12
73–74	Minn	65	19	24	43	30	-11
74–75	Minn–NYI	78	18	36	54	22	-11
75–76	NYI	76	21	41	62	58	+18
76–77	NYI	78	24	29	53	27	+18
77–78	NYI	56	5	17	22	12	+14
79–80	Winn	78	8	16	24	50	-38
80–81	Winn	7	0	0	0	4	-2
Totals		666	151	305	456	346	+8

Playoffs

SSN	TEAM	GP	G	A	PTS.	PIM	+/-
70–71	Minn	12	5	7	12	10	
71–72	Minn	7	4	4	8	6	
72–73	Minn	6	1	3	4	0	
74–75	NYI	17	6	12	18	6	
75–76	NYI	13	6	9	15	0	
76–77	NYI	12	5	6	11	6	
77–78	NYI	5	0	0	0	5	
Totals		72	27	41	68	33	

DROUIN, Emile Paul (Polly) 5–7 160 LW
B. Verdun, Que., Jan. 1916

SSN	TEAM	GP	G	A	PTS.	PIM	+/-
35–36	Mont	30	1	8	9	19	
36–37	Mont	4	0	0	0	0	
37–38	Mont	31	7	13	20	8	
38–39	Mont	28	7	11	18	2	
39–40	Mont	42	4	11	15	51	
40–41	Mont	21	4	7	11	0	
Totals		156	23	50	73	80	

Playoffs

SSN	TEAM	GP	G	A	PTS.	PIM	+/-
37–38	Mont	1	0	0	0	0	
38–39	Mont	3	0	1	1	5	
40–41	Mont	1	0	0	0	0	
Totals		5	0	1	1	5	

DROUIN, P.C. 6–2 208 LW
B. St. Lambert, Que., April 22, 1974

SSN	TEAM	GP	G	A	PTS.	PIM	+/-
96–97	Bos	3	0	0	0	0	+1

DRUCE, John 6–2 200 RW
B. Peterbrough, Ont., Feb. 23, 1966

SSN	TEAM	GP	G	A	PTS.	PIM	+/-
88–89	Wash	48	8	7	15	62	+7
89–90	Wash	45	8	3	11	52	-3
90–91	Wash	80	22	36	58	46	+4
91–92	Wash	67	19	18	37	39	+14
92–93	Winn	50	6	14	20	37	-4
93–94	LA	55	14	17	31	50	+16
94–95	LA	43	15	5	20	20	-3
95–96	LA–Phil	77	13	16	29	27	-20
96–97	Phil	43	7	8	15	12	-5
97–98	Phil	23	1	2	3	2	0
Totals		531	113	126	239	347	+6

Playoffs

SSN	TEAM	GP	G	A	PTS.	PIM	+/-
88–89	Wash	1	0	0	0	0	
89–90	Wash	15	14	3	17	23	
90–91	Wash	11	1	1	2	7	
91–92	Wash	7	1	0	1	2	
92–93	Winn	2	0	0	0	0	
95–96	Phil	2	0	2	2	2	
96–97	Phil	13	1	0	1	2	
97–98	Phil	2	0	0	0	2	
Totals		53	17	6	23	38	

DRULIA, Stan 5–11 190 RW
B. Elmira, N.Y., Jan. 5, 1968

SSN	TEAM	GP	G	A	PTS.	PIM	+/-
92–93	TB	24	2	1	3	10	+1

DRUMMOND, John S. D
B. Toronto, Ont., Oct. 20, 1918

SSN	TEAM	GP	G	A	PTS.	PIM	+/-
44–45	NYR	2	0	1	1	0	

DRURY, Chris 5–10 180 C
B. Trumbull, Conn., Aug. 20, 1976

SSN	TEAM	GP	G	A	PTS.	PIM	+/-
98–99	Col A	79	20	24	44	62	+9

Playoffs

SSN	TEAM	GP	G	A	PTS.	PIM	+/-
98–99	Col A	19	6	2	8	4	

DRURY, Herbert 5–7 165 F
B. 1895

SSN	TEAM	GP	G	A	PTS.	PIM	+/-
25–26	Pitt Pi	33	6	2	8	40	
26–27	Pitt Pi	42	5	1	6	48	
27–28	Pitt Pi	43	6	4	10	44	
28–29	Pitt Pi	44	5	4	9	49	
29–30	Pitt Pi	27	2	0	2	12	
30–31	Phil Q	24	0	2	2	10	
Totals		213	24	13	37	203	

Playoffs

SSN	TEAM	GP	G	A	PTS.	PIM	+/-
25–26	PittPi	2	1	0	1	0	
27–28	PittPi	2	0	1	1	0	
Totals		4	1	1	2	0	

DRURY, Theodore Evans 6–0 185 C
B. Boston, Mass., Sept. 13, 1971

SSN	TEAM	GP	G	A	PTS.	PIM	+/-
93–94	Calg–Hart	50	6	12	18	36	-15
94–95	Hart	34	3	6	9	21	-3
95–96	Ott	42	9	7	16	54	-19
96–97	Ana	73	9	9	18	54	-9
97–98	Ana	73	6	10	16	82	-10
98–99	Ana	75	5	6	11	83	+2
Totals		347	38	50	88	330	-54

Playoffs

SSN	TEAM	GP	G	A	PTS.	PIM	+/-
96–97	Ana	10	1	0	1	4	
98–99	Ana	4	0	0	0	0	
Totals		14	1	0	1	4	

DUBE, Christian 5–11 170 C
B. Sherbrooke, Que., April 25, 1977

SSN	TEAM	GP	G	A	PTS.	PIM	+/-
96–97	NYR	27	1	1	2	4	-4
98–99	NYR	6	0	0	0	0	0
Totals		33	1	1	2	4	-4

Playoffs

SSN	TEAM	GP	G	A	PTS.	PIM	+/-
96–97	NYR	3	0	0	0	0	

DUBE, Joseph Gilles (Gilles) 5–10 165 LW
B. Sherbrooke, Que., June 2, 1927

SSN	TEAM	GP	G	A	PTS.	PIM	+/-
49–50	Mont	12	1	2	3	2	

Playoffs

SSN	TEAM	GP	G	A	PTS.	PIM	+/-
53–54	Det	2	0	0	0	0	

DUBE, Normand G. (Norm) 5–11 185 LW
B. Sherbrooke, Que., Sept. 12, 1951

SSN	TEAM	GP	G	A	PTS.	PIM	+/-
74–75	KC	56	8	10	18	54	-12
75–76	KC	1	0	0	0	0	0
76–77	Que (WHA)	39	15	18	33	8	
77–78	Que (WHA)	73	16	31	47	17	
78–79	Que (WHA)	36	2	13	15	4	
NHL Totals		57	8	10	18	54	-12
WHA Totals		148	33	62	95	29	

Playoffs

SSN	TEAM	GP	G	A	PTS.	PIM	+/-
76–77	Que (WHA)	14	3	12	15	11	
77–78	Que (WHA)	10	2	2	4	6	
WHA Totals		24	5	14	19	17	

DUBERMAN, Justin 6–1 185 RW
B. New Haven, Conn., Mar. 23, 1970

SSN	TEAM	GP	G	A	PTS.	PIM	+/-
93–94	Pitt	4	0	0	0	0	0

DUBINSKY, Steve 6–0 190 C
B. Montreal, Que., July 9, 1970

SSN	TEAM	GP	G	A	PTS.	PIM	+/-
93–94	Chi	27	2	6	8	16	+1
94–95	Chi	16	0	0	0	8	-5
95–96	Chi	43	2	3	5	14	+3
96–97	Chi	5	0	0	0	0	+2
97–98	Chi	82	5	13	18	57	-6
98–99	Chi–Calg	62	4	10	14	14	-7
Totals		235	13	32	45	109	-12

Playoffs

SSN	TEAM	GP	G	A	PTS.	PIM	+/-
93–94	Chi	6	0	0	0	10	
96–97	Chi	4	1	0	1	4	

SSN	TEAM	GP	G	A	PTS.	PIM	+/-
Totals		10	1	0	1	14	

DUCHESNE, Gaetan 5-11 197 LW
B. Quebec City, Que., July 11, 1962

SSN	TEAM	GP	G	A	PTS.	PIM	+/-
81-82	Wash	74	9	14	23	46	-6
82-83	Wash	77	18	19	37	52	+15
83-84	Wash	79	17	19	36	29	+15
84-85	Wash	67	15	23	38	32	+16
85-86	Wash	80	11	28	39	39	+10
86-87	Wash	74	17	35	52	53	+18
87-88	Que	80	24	23	47	83	+8
88-89	Que	70	8	21	29	56	0
89-90	Minn	72	12	8	20	33	+5
90-91	Minn	68	9	9	18	18	+4
91-92	Minn	73	8	15	23	102	+6
92-93	Minn	84	16	13	29	30	+6
93-94	SJ	84	12	18	30	28	+8
94-95	SJ-Fla	46	3	9	12	16	-3
Totals		1028	179	254	433	617	+102

Playoffs

SSN	TEAM	GP	G	A	PTS.	PIM	
82-83	Wash	4	1	1	2	4	
83-84	Wash	8	2	1	3	2	
84-85	Wash	5	0	1	1	7	
85-86	Wash	9	4	3	7	12	
86-87	Wash	7	3	0	3	14	
89-90	Minn	7	0	0	0	6	
90-91	Minn	23	2	3	5	34	
91-92	Minn	7	1	0	1	6	
93-94	SJ	14	1	4	5	12	
Totals		84	14	13	27	97	

DUCHESNE, Steve 5-11 195 D
B. Sept-Iles, Que., June 30, 1965

SSN	TEAM	GP	G	A	PTS.	PIM	+/-
86-87	LA	75	13	25	38	74	+8
87-88	LA	71	16	39	55	109	0
88-89	LA	79	25	50	75	92	+31
89-90	LA	79	20	42	62	36	-3
90-91	LA	78	21	41	62	66	+19
91-92	Phil	78	18	38	56	86	-7
92-93	Que	82	20	62	82	57	+15
93-94	StL	36	12	19	31	14	+1
94-95	StL	47	12	26	38	36	+29
95-96	Ott	62	12	24	36	42	-23
96-97	Ott	78	19	28	47	38	-9
97-98	StL	80	14	42	56	32	+9
98-99	LA-Phil	71	6	24	30	24	-6
Totals		916	208	460	668	706	+64

Playoffs

SSN	TEAM	GP	G	A	PTS.	PIM	
86-87	LA	5	2	2	4	4	
87-88	LA	5	1	3	4	14	
88-89	LA	11	4	4	8	12	
89-90	LA	10	2	9	11	6	
90-91	LA	12	4	8	12	8	
92-93	Que	6	0	5	5	6	
93-94	StL	4	0	2	2	2	
94-95	StL	7	0	4	4	2	
96-97	Ott	7	1	4	5	6	
97-98	StL	10	0	4	4	6	
98-99	Phil	6	0	2	2	2	
Totals		83	14	47	61	62	

DUDLEY, Richard Clarence (Rick And Duds)
6-0 190 LW
B. Toronto, Ont., Jan. 31, 1949

SSN	TEAM	GP	G	A	PTS.	PIM	+/-
72-73	Buf	6	0	1	1	7	-2
73-74	Buf	67	13	13	26	71	0
74-75	Buf	78	31	39	70	116	+29
75-76	Cin (WHA)	74	43	38	81	156	
76-77	Cin (WHA)	77	41	47	88	102	
77-78	Cin (WHA)	72	30	41	71	156	
78-79	Cin (WHA)	47	17	20	37	102	
78-79	Buf	24	5	6	11	2	+11
79-80	Buf	66	11	22	33	58	+11
80-81	Buf-Winn	68	15	18	33	38	-5
NHL Totals		309	75	99	174	292	+44
WHA Totals		270	131	146	277	516	

Playoffs

SSN	TEAM	GP	G	A	PTS.	PIM	
74-75	Buf	10	3	1	4	26	
76-77	Cin (WHA)	4	0	1	1	7	
78-79	Buf	3	1	1	2	2	
79-80	Buf	12	3	0	3	41	
NHL Totals		25	7	2	9	69	
WHA Totals		4	0	1	1	7	

DUFF, Terrance Richard (Dick) 5-9 166 LW
B. Kirkland Lake, Ont., Feb. 18, 1936

SSN	TEAM	GP	G	A	PTS.	PIM	+/-
54-55	Tor	3	0	0	0	2	
55-56	Tor	69	18	19	37	74	
56-57	Tor	70	26	14	40	50	
57-58	Tor	65	26	23	49	79	
58-59	Tor	69	29	24	53	73	
59-60	Tor	67	19	22	41	51	
60-61	Tor	67	16	17	33	54	
61-62	Tor	51	17	20	37	37	
62-63	Tor	69	16	19	35	56	
63-64	Tor-NYR	66	11	14	25	61	
64-65	NYR-Mont	69	12	16	28	36	
65-66	Mont	63	21	24	45	78	
66-67	Mont	51	12	11	23	23	
67-68	Mont	66	25	21	46	21	+6
68-69	Mont	68	19	21	40	55	-13
69-70	Mont-LA	49	6	9	15	12	-20
70-71	LA-Buf	60	8	13	21	12	-18
71-72	Buf	8	2	2	4	0	-2
Totals		1030	283	289	572	774	-47

Playoffs

SSN	TEAM	GP	G	A	PTS.	PIM	
55-56	Tor	5	1	4	5	2	
58-59	Tor	12	4	3	7	8	
59-60	Tor	10	2	4	6	6	
60-61	Tor	5	0	1	1	2	
61-62	Tor	12	3	10	13	20	
62-63	Tor	10	4	1	5	2	
64-65	Mont	13	3	6	9	17	
65-66	Mont	10	2	5	7	2	
66-67	Mont	10	2	3	5	4	
67-68	Mont	13	3	4	7	4	
68-69	Mont	14	6	8	14	11	
Totals		114	30	49	79	78	

DUFOUR, Luc 5-11 180 LW
B. Chicoutimi, Que., Feb. 13, 1963

SSN	TEAM	GP	G	A	PTS.	PIM	+/-
82-83	Bos	73	14	11	25	107	+19
83-84	Bos	41	6	4	10	47	+2
84-85	Que-StL	53	3	6	9	45	-13
Totals		167	23	21	44	199	+8

Playoffs

SSN	TEAM	GP	G	A	PTS.	PIM	
82-83	Bos	17	1	0	1	30	
84-85	StL	1	0	0	0	2	
Totals		18	1	0	1	32	

DUFOUR, Marc 6-0 175 RW
B. Trois Rivieres, Que., Sept. 11, 1941

SSN	TEAM	GP	G	A	PTS.	PIM	+/-
63-64	NYR	10	1	0	1	2	
64-65	NYR	2	0	0	0	0	
68-69	LA	2	0	0	0	0	-1
Totals		14	1	0	1	2	-1

DUFRESNE, Donald 6-1 206 D
B. Rimouski, Que., Apr. 10, 1967

SSN	TEAM	GP	G	A	PTS.	PIM	+/-
88-89	Mont	13	0	1	1	43	+3
89-90	Mont	18	0	4	4	23	+1
90-91	Mont	53	2	13	15	55	+5
91-92	Mont	3	0	0	0	0	+2
92-93	Mont	32	1	2	3	32	0
93-94	TB-LA	60	2	6	8	58	-7
94-95	StL	22	0	3	3	10	+2
95-96	StL-Edm	45	1	6	7	20	-4
96-97	Edm	22	0	1	1	15	-1
Totals		268	6	36	42	258	+1

Playoffs

SSN	TEAM	GP	G	A	PTS.	PIM	
88-89	Mont	6	1	1	2	4	
89-90	Mont	10	0	1	1	18	
90-91	Mont	10	0	1	1	21	
92-93	Mont	2	0	0	0	0	
94-95	StL	3	0	1	1	4	
96-97	Edm	3	0	0	0	0	
Totals		34	1	3	4	47	

DUGGAN, James (Jack) D

SSN	TEAM	GP	G	A	PTS.	PIM	
25-26	Ott	27	0	0	0	0	

Playoffs

SSN	TEAM	GP	G	A	PTS.	PIM	
25-26	Ott	2	0	0	0	0	

DUGGAN, Ken 6-3 210 D
B. Toronto, Ont., Feb. 21, 1963

SSN	TEAM	GP	G	A	PTS.	PIM	+/-
87-88	Minn	1	0	0	0	0	0

DUGUAY, Ronald 6-2 210 C
B. Sudbury, Ont., July 6, 1957

SSN	TEAM	GP	G	A	PTS.	PIM	+/-
77-78	NYR	71	20	20	40	43	-17
78-79	NYR	79	27	36	63	35	+10
79-80	NYR	73	28	22	50	37	-6
80-81	NYR	50	17	21	38	83	+2
81-82	NYR	72	40	36	76	82	+18
82-83	NYR	72	19	25	44	58	-13
83-84	Det	80	33	47	80	34	-26
84-85	Det	80	38	51	89	51	-16
85-86	Det-Pitt	80	24	36	61	32	-44
86-87	Pitt-NYR	74	14	25	39	39	-16
87-88	Det-LA	63	6	10	16	40	-14
88-89	LA	70	7	17	24	48	+23
Totals		864	274	346	620	582	-101

Playoffs

SSN	TEAM	GP	G	A	PTS.	PIM	
77-78	NYR	3	1	1	2	2	
78-79	NYR	18	5	4	9	11	
79-80	NYR	9	5	2	7	11	
80-81	NYR	14	8	9	17	16	
81-82	NYR	10	5	1	6	31	
82-83	NYR	9	2	2	4	28	
83-84	Det	4	2	3	5	2	
84-85	Det	2	1	0	1	7	
86-87	NYR	2	2	0	2	4	
87-88	LA	2	0	0	0	0	
88-89	LA	11	0	0	0	6	
Totals		89	31	22	53	118	

*DUGUID, Lorne Wallace 5-11 185 LW
B. Bolton, Ont., Apr. 4, 1910

SSN	TEAM	GP	G	A	PTS.	PIM	
31-32	Mont M	13	0	0	0	6	
32-33	Mont M	48	4	7	11	38	
33-34	Mont M	5	0	1	1	0	
34-35	Det	34	3	3	6	9	
35-36	Det-Bos	34	1	4	5	2	
36-37	Bos	1	1	0	1	2	
Totals		135	9	15	24	57	

Playoffs

SSN	TEAM	GP	G	A	PTS.	PIM	
32-33	Mont M	2	0	0	0	4	

*DUMART, Woodrow Wilson Clarence (Woody, Porky) 6-1 200 LW
B. Kitchener, Ont., Dec. 23, 1916

SSN	TEAM	GP	G	A	PTS.	PIM	
35-36	Bos	1	0	0	0	0	
36-37	Bos	17	4	4	8	2	
37-38	Bos	48	13	14	27	6	
38-39	Bos	45	14	15	29	2	
39-40	Bos	48	22	21	43	16	
40-41	Bos	40	18	15	33	2	
41-42	Bos	35	14	15	29	8	
45-46	Bos	50	22	12	34	2	
46-47	Bos	60	24	28	52	12	
47-48	Bos	59	21	16	37	14	
48-49	Bos	59	11	12	23	6	
49-50	Bos	69	14	25	39	14	
50-51	Bos	70	20	21	41	7	
51-52	Bos	39	5	8	13	0	
52-53	Bos	62	5	9	14	2	
53-54	Bos	69	4	3	7	6	
Totals		771	211	218	429	99	

Playoffs

SSN	TEAM	GP	G	A	PTS.	PIM	
36-37	Bos	3	0	0	0	0	
37-38	Bos	3	0	0	0	0	
38-39	Bos	12	1	3	4	6	
39-40	Bos	6	1	0	1	0	
40-41	Bos	11	1	3	4	9	
45-46	Bos	10	4	3	7	0	
46-47	Bos	5	1	1	2	8	
47-48	Bos	5	0	0	0	0	
48-49	Bos	5	3	0	3	0	
50-51	Bos	6	1	2	3	0	
51-52	Bos	7	0	1	1	0	
52-53	Bos	11	0	2	2	0	
53-54	Bos	4	0	0	0	0	
Totals		88	12	15	27	23	

DUMONT, Jean-Pierre 6-1 187 RW
B. Montreal, Que., April 1, 1978

SSN	TEAM	GP	G	A	PTS.	PIM	+/-
98-99	Chi	25	9	6	15	10	+7

DUNBAR, Dale 6-0 200 D
B. Winthrop, Mass., Oct. 14, 1961

SSN	TEAM	GP	G	A	PTS.	PIM	+/-
85-86	Van	1	0	0	0	2	0

SSN	TEAM	GP	G	A	PTS.	PIM	+/-
88–89	Bos	1	0	0	0	0	0
Totals		2	0	0	0	2	0

*DUNCAN, Arthur D

SSN	TEAM	GP	G	A	PTS.	PIM	+/-
26–27	Det	34	3	2	5	26	
27–28	Tor	43	7	5	12	97	
28–29	Tor	39	4	4	8	53	
29–30	Tor	38	4	5	9	49	
30–31	Tor	2	0	0	0	0	
Totals		156	18	16	34	225	

Playoffs

28–29	Tor	4	0	0	0	4	
30–31	Tor	1	0	0	0	0	
Totals		5	0	0	0	4	

DUNCAN, Iain 6-1 200 LW
B. Weston, Ont., Aug. 4, 1963

SSN	TEAM	GP	G	A	PTS.	PIM	+/-
86–87	Winn	6	1	2	3	0	+1
87–88	Winn	62	19	23	42	73	-2
88–89	Winn	57	14	30	44	74	-17
90–91	Winn	2	0	0	0	2	-1
Totals		127	34	55	89	149	-19

Playoffs

86–87	Winn	7	0	2	2	6	
87–88	Winn	4	0	1	1	0	
Totals		11	0	3	3	6	

DUNCANSON, Craig 6-0 190 LW
B. Sudbury, Ont., Mar. 17, 1967

SSN	TEAM	GP	G	A	PTS.	PIM	+/-
85–86	LA	2	0	1	1	0	-1
86–87	LA	2	0	0	0	24	0
87–88	LA	9	0	0	0	12	-5
88–89	LA	5	0	0	0	0	-1
89–90	LA	10	3	2	5	9	+1
90–91	Winn	7	2	0	2	16	-5
92–93	NYR	3	0	1	1	0	0
Totals		38	5	4	9	61	-11

DUNDAS, Rocky 6-0 195 RW
B. Regina, Sask., Jan. 30, 1967

89–90	Tor	5	0	0	0	14	-1

DUNLOP, Blake Robert 5-10 170 C
B. Hamilton, Ont., Apr. 4, 1953

SSN	TEAM	GP	G	A	PTS.	PIM	+/-
73–74	Minn	12	0	0	0	2	-3
74–75	Minn	52	9	18	27	8	-9
75–76	Minn	33	9	11	20	8	-9
76–77	Minn	3	0	1	1	0	-2
77–78	Phil	3	0	1	1	0	+1
78–79	Phil	66	20	28	48	16	+27
79–80	StL	72	18	27	45	28	-6
80–81	StL	80	20	67	87	40	+16
81–82	StL	77	25	53	78	32	-9
82–83	StL	78	22	44	66	14	-6
83–84	StL–Det	74	7	24	31	24	-14
Totals		550	130	274	404	172	-12

Playoffs

78–79	Phil	8	1	1	2	4	
79–80	StL	3	0	2	2	2	
80–81	StL	11	0	3	3	4	
81–82	StL	10	2	2	4	4	
82–83	StL	4	1	1	2	0	
83–84	Det	4	0	1	1	4	
Totals		40	4	10	14	18	

DUNLOP, Frank F

43–44	Tor	15	0	1	1	2	

DUNN, David George 6-2 200 D
B. Wapella, Sask., Aug. 19, 1948

SSN	TEAM	GP	G	A	PTS.	PIM	+/-
73–74	Van	68	11	22	33	76	-13
74–75	Van–Tor	73	3	11	14	153	-10
75–76	Tor	43	0	8	8	84	-5
76–77	Winn (WHA)	40	3	11	14	129	
77–78	Winn (WHA)	66	6	20	26	79	
NHL Totals		184	14	41	55	313	-28
WHA Totals		106	9	31	40	208	

Playoffs

74–75	Tor	7	1	1	2	24	
75–76	Tor	3	0	0	0	17	
76–77	Winn (WHA)	20	4	4	8	23	
77–78	Winn (WHA)	9	1	2	3	0	

NHL Totals		10	1	1	2	41	
WHA Totals		29	5	6	11	23	

DUNN, Richard L. 6-0 200 D
B. Boston, Mass., May 12, 1957

SSN	TEAM	GP	G	A	PTS.	PIM	+/-
77–78	Buf	25	0	3	3	16	-3
78–79	Buf	24	0	3	3	14	-2
79–80	Buf	80	7	31	38	61	+25
80–81	Buf	79	7	42	49	34	+21
81–82	Buf	72	7	19	26	73	+6
82–83	Calg	80	3	11	14	47	-4
83–84	Hart	63	5	20	25	30	-20
84–85	Buf	13	1	4	5	2	-3
85–86	Buf	29	4	5	9	25	-5
86–87	Buf	2	0	1	1	2	+2
87–88	Buf	12	2	0	2	8	-7
88–89	Buf	4	0	1	1	2	-1
Totals		483	36	140	176	314	+9

Playoffs

77–78	Buf	1	0	0	0	2	
79–80	Buf	14	2	8	10	8	
80–81	Buf	8	0	5	5	6	
81–82	Buf	4	0	1	1	0	
82–83	Calg	9	1	1	2	8	
Totals		36	3	15	18	24	

DUPERE, Denis Gilles 6-1 200 LW
B. Jonquiere, Que., June 21, 1948

SSN	TEAM	GP	G	A	PTS.	PIM	+/-
70–71	Tor	20	1	2	3	4	-1
71–72	Tor	77	7	10	17	4	+5
72–73	Tor	61	13	23	36	10	-4
73–74	Tor	34	8	9	17	8	+3
74–75	Wash–StL	75	23	21	44	16	-37
75–76	KC	43	6	8	14	16	-8
76–77	Col	57	7	11	18	4	+3
77–78	Col	54	15	15	30	4	+9
Totals		421	80	99	179	66	-30

Playoffs

70–71	Tor	6	0	0	0	0	
71–72	Tor	5	0	0	0	0	
73–74	Tor	3	0	0	0	0	
77–78	Col	2	1	0	1	0	
Totals		16	1	0	1	0	

DUPONT, Andre (Moose) 6-0 200 D
B. Trois-Rivieres, Que., July 27, 1949

SSN	TEAM	GP	G	A	PTS.	PIM	+/-
70–71	NYR	7	1	2	3	21	+1
71–72	StL	60	3	10	13	147	+11
72–73	StL–Phil	71	4	26	30	215	+9
73–74	Phil	75	3	20	23	216	+34
74–75	Phil	80	11	21	32	276	+41
75–76	Phil	75	9	27	36	214	+40
76–77	Phil	69	10	19	29	168	+57
77–78	Phil	69	2	12	14	225	+31
78–79	Phil	77	3	9	12	135	+21
79–80	Phil	58	1	7	8	107	+37
80–81	Que	63	5	8	13	93	+6
81–82	Que	60	4	12	16	100	+3
82–83	Que	46	3	12	15	69	+11
Totals		810	59	185	244	1986	+298

Playoffs

71–72	StL	11	1	0	1	20	
72–73	StL	11	1	2	3	29	
73–74	Phil	16	4	3	7	67	
74–75	Phil	17	3	2	5	49	
75–76	Phil	15	2	2	4	46	
76–77	Phil	10	1	1	2	35	
77–78	Phil	12	2	1	3	13	
78–79	Phil	8	0	0	0	17	
79–80	Phil	19	0	4	4	50	
80–81	Que	1	0	0	0	0	
81–82	Que	16	0	3	3	18	
82–83	Que	4	0	0	0	8	
Totals		140	14	18	32	352	

DUPONT, Jerome 6-3 190 D
B. Ottawa, Ont., Feb. 21, 1962

SSN	TEAM	GP	G	A	PTS.	PIM	+/-
81–82	Chi	34	0	4	4	51	-2
82–83	Chi	1	0	0	0	0	0
83–84	Chi	36	2	2	4	116	-11
84–85	Chi	55	3	10	13	105	+5
85–86	Chi	75	2	13	15	173	-17
86–87	Tor	13	0	0	0	23	-5
Totals		214	7	29	36	468	-30

Playoffs

83–84	Chi	4	0	0	0	15	
84–85	Chi	15	0	2	2	41	
85–86	Chi	1	0	0	0	0	
Totals		20	0	2	2	56	

DUPONT, Normand 5-10 185 LW
B. Montreal, Que., Feb. 5, 1957

SSN	TEAM	GP	G	A	PTS.	PIM	+/-
79–80	Mont	35	1	3	4	4	+2
80–81	Winn	80	27	26	53	8	-57
81–82	Winn	62	13	25	38	22	-24
82–83	Winn	39	7	16	23	6	-16
83–84	Hart	40	7	15	22	12	-16
Totals		256	55	85	140	52	-111

Playoffs

79–80	Mont	8	1	1	2	0	
81–82	Winn	4	2	0	2	0	
82–83	Winn	1	1	1	2	0	
Totals		13	4	2	6	0	

DUPRE, Yanic 6-0 189 LW
B. Montreal, Que., Nov. 20, 1972

SSN	TEAM	GP	G	A	PTS.	PIM	+/-
91–92	Phil	1	0	0	0	0	0
94–95	Phil	22	0	0	0	8	-7
95–96	Phil	12	2	0	2	8	0
Totals		35	2	0	2	16	-7

DURBANO, Harry Steven (Steve) 6-1 210 D
B. Toronto, Ont., Dec. 12, 1951

SSN	TEAM	GP	G	A	PTS.	PIM	+/-
72–73	StL	49	3	18	21	231	-3
73–74	StL–Pitt	69	8	19	27	284	+16
74–75	Pitt	1	0	1	1	10	0
75–76	Pitt–KC	69	1	19	20	370	-21
76–77	Col	19	0	2	2	129	-6
77–78	Birm (WHA)	45	6	4	10	284	
78–79	Col	13	1	1	2	103	-7
NHL Totals		220	13	60	73	1127	-47
WHA Totals		45	6	4	10	284	

Playoffs

72–73	StL	5	0	2	2	8	
77–78	Birm (WHA)	4	0	2	2	16	
NHL Totals		5	0	2	2	8	
WHA Totals		4	0	2	2	16	

DURIS, Vitezslav 6-1 185 D
B. Pizen, Czechoslovakia, Jan. 5, 1954

SSN	TEAM	GP	G	A	PTS.	PIM	+/-
80–81	Tor	57	1	12	13	50	+13
82–83	Tor	32	2	8	10	12	+3
Totals		89	3	20	23	62	+16

Playoffs

80–81	Tor	3	0	1	1	2	

DUSSAULT, Joseph Normand (Norm) 5-7 165 C
B. Springfield, Mass., Sept. 26, 1925

SSN	TEAM	GP	G	A	PTS.	PIM	+/-
47–48	Mont	28	5	10	15	4	
48–49	Mont	47	9	8	17	6	
49–50	Mont	67	13	24	37	22	
50–51	Mont	64	4	20	24	15	
Totals		206	31	62	93	47	

Playoffs

48–49	Mont	2	0	0	0	0	
49–50	Mont	5	3	1	4	0	
Totals		7	3	1	4	0	

*DUTKOWSKI, Laudas Joseph (Duke) 5-10 185 D
B. Regina, Sask., Aug. 30, 1902

SSN	TEAM	GP	G	A	PTS.	PIM	+/-
26–27	Chi	28	3	2	5	16	
29–30	Chi	44	7	10	17	42	
30–31	Chi–NYA	37	2	4	6	40	
32–33	NYA	48	4	7	11	43	
33–34	NYA–Chi–NYR	43	0	7	7	31	
Totals		200	16	30	46	172	

Playoffs

26–27	Chi	2	0	0	0	0	
29–30	Chi	2	0	0	0	6	
33–34	NYR	2	0	0	0	0	
Totals		6	0	0	0	6	

*DUTTON, Mervyn A. (Red) 6-0 185 D
B. Russell, Man., July 23, 1898

SSN	TEAM	GP	G	A	PTS.	PIM	+/-
26-27	Mont M	44	4	4	8	108	
27-28	Mont M	42	7	6	13	94	
28-29	Mont M	44	1	3	4	139	
29-30	NYA	43	3	13	16	98	
30-31	NYA	44	1	11	12	71	
31-32	NYA	47	3	5	8	107	
32-33	NYA	43	0	2	2	74	
33-34	NYA	48	2	8	10	65	
34-35	NYA	48	3	7	10	46	
35-36	NYA	46	5	8	13	69	
Totals		449	29	67	96	871	

Playoffs

SSN	TEAM	GP	G	A	PTS.	PIM	+/-
26-27	Mont M	2	0	0	0	4	
27-28	Mont M	9	1	0	1	27	
29-30	Mont M	4	0	0	0	2	
35-36	NYA	3	0	0	0	0	
Totals		18	1	0	1	33	

DVORAK, Miroslav 5-10 195 D
B. Htuboka nad Vitavou, Czech., Oct. 11, 1951

SSN	TEAM	GP	G	A	PTS.	PIM	+/-
82-83	Phil	80	4	33	37	20	+27
83-84	Phil	66	4	27	31	27	+19
84-85	Phil	47	3	14	17	4	+12
Totals		193	11	74	85	51	+58

Playoffs

SSN	TEAM	GP	G	A	PTS.	PIM	+/-
82-83	Phil	3	0	1	1	0	
83-84	Phil	2	0	0	0	2	
84-85	Phil	13	0	1	1	4	
Totals		18	0	2	2	6	

DVORAK, Radek 6-2 185 LW
B. Ceske Budejovice, Czech., Mar. 9, 1977

SSN	TEAM	GP	G	A	PTS.	PIM	+/-
95-96	Fla	77	13	14	27	20	+5
96-97	Fla	78	18	21	39	30	-2
97-98	Fla	64	12	24	36	33	-1
98-99	Fla	82	19	24	43	29	+7
Totals		301	62	83	145	112	+9

Playoffs

SSN	TEAM	GP	G	A	PTS.	PIM	+/-
95-96	Fla	16	1	3	4	0	
96-97	Fla	3	0	0	0	0	
Totals		19	1	3	4	0	

DWYER, Michael 5-11 172 LW
B. Brampton, Ont., Sept. 16, 1957

SSN	TEAM	GP	G	A	PTS.	PIM	+/-
78-79	Col	12	2	3	5	2	-4
79-80	Col	10	0	0	0	19	-5
80-81	Calg	4	0	1	1	4	-1
81-82	Calg	5	0	2	2	0	0
Totals		31	2	6	8	25	-10

Playoffs

SSN	TEAM	GP	G	A	PTS.	PIM	+/-
80-81	Calg	1	1	0	1	0	

DYCK, Henry Richard 5-7 155 C
B. Saskatoon, Sask., Sept. 5, 1911

SSN	TEAM	GP	G	A	PTS.	PIM	+/-
43-44	NYR	1	0	0	0	0	

*DYE, Cecil Henry (Babe) RW
B. Hamilton, Ont., May 13, 1898

SSN	TEAM	GP	G	A	PTS.	PIM	+/-
19-20	Tor	21	12	3	15	0	
20-21	Ham-Tor	24	35	2	37	32	
21-22	Tor	24	30	7	37	18	
22-23	Tor	22	26	11	37	19	
23-24	Tor	19	17	2	19	23	
24-25	Tor	29	38	6	44	41	
25-26	Tor	31	18	5	23	26	
26-27	Chi	41	25	5	30	14	
27-28	Chi	11	0	0	0	0	
28-29	NYA	42	1	0	1	17	
30-31	Tor	6	0	0	0	0	
Totals		270	202	41	243	190	

Playoffs

SSN	TEAM	GP	G	A	PTS.	PIM	+/-
20-21	Tor	2	0	0	0	9	
21-22	Tor	7	9	2	11	7	
24-25	Tor	2	0	0	0	0	
26-27	Chi	2	0	0	0	2	
28-29	NYA	2	0	0	0	0	
Totals		15	9	2	11	18	

DYKHUIS, Karl 6-3 195 D
B. Sept-Iles, Que., July 8, 1972

SSN	TEAM	GP	G	A	PTS.	PIM	+/-
91-92	Chi	6	1	3	4	4	-1
92-93	Chi	12	0	5	5	0	+2
94-95	Phil	33	2	6	8	37	+7
95-96	Phil	82	5	15	20	101	+12
96-97	Phil	62	4	15	19	35	+6
97-98	TB	78	5	9	14	110	-8
98-99	TB-Phil	78	4	5	9	50	-23
Totals		351	21	58	79	337	-5

Playoffs

SSN	TEAM	GP	G	A	PTS.	PIM	+/-
94-95	Phil	15	4	4	8	14	
95-96	Phil	12	2	2	4	22	
96-97	Phil	18	0	3	3	2	
98-99	Phil	5	1	0	1	4	
Totals		50	7	9	16	42	

DYKSTRA, Steven 6-2 210 D
B. Edmonton, Alta., Dec. 1, 1962

SSN	TEAM	GP	G	A	PTS.	PIM	+/-
85-86	Buf	64	4	21	25	108	+1
86-87	Buf	37	0	1	1	179	-7
87-88	Buf-Edm	42	3	4	7	130	+1
88-89	Pitt	65	1	6	7	126	-12
89-90	Hart	9	0	0	0	2	+2
Totals		217	8	32	40	545	-17

Playoffs

SSN	TEAM	GP	G	A	PTS.	PIM	+/-
88-89	Pitt	1	0	0	0	2	

DYTE, John Leonard (Jack) 6-0 D
B. Kingston, Ont., Oct. 13, 1918

SSN	TEAM	GP	G	A	PTS.	PIM	+/-
43-44	Chi	27	1	0	1	31	

DZIEDZIC, Joe 6-3 220 LW
B. Minneapolis, Minn., Dec. 18, 1971

SSN	TEAM	GP	G	A	PTS.	PIM	+/-
95-96	Pitt	69	5	5	10	68	-5
96-97	Pitt	59	9	9	18	63	-4
98-99	Phoe	2	0	0	0	0	-2
Totals		130	14	14	28	131	-11

Playoffs

SSN	TEAM	GP	G	A	PTS.	PIM	+/-
95-96	Pitt	16	1	2	3	19	
96-97	Pitt	5	0	1	1	4	
Totals		21	1	3	4	23	

EAGLES, Michael 5-10 190 C
B. Sussex, N.B., Mar. 7, 1963

SSN	TEAM	GP	G	A	PTS.	PIM	+/-
82-83	Que	2	0	0	0	2	-1
85-86	Que	73	11	12	23	49	+3
86-87	Que	73	13	19	32	55	-15
87-88	Que	76	10	10	20	74	-18
88-89	Chi	47	5	11	16	44	-8
89-90	Chi	23	1	2	3	34	-4
90-91	Winn	44	0	9	9	79	-10
91-92	Winn	65	7	10	17	118	-17
92-93	Winn	84	8	18	26	131	-1
93-94	Winn	73	4	8	12	96	-20
94-95	Winn-Wash	40	3	4	7	48	-11
95-96	Wash	70	4	7	11	75	-1
96-97	Wash	70	1	7	8	42	-4
97-98	Wash	36	1	3	4	16	-2
98-99	Wash	52	4	2	6	50	-5
Totals		828	72	122	194	913	-115

Playoffs

SSN	TEAM	GP	G	A	PTS.	PIM	+/-
85-86	Que	3	0	0	0	2	
86-87	Que	4	1	0	1	10	
91-92	Winn	7	0	0	0	8	
92-93	Winn	5	0	1	1	6	
94-95	Wash	7	0	2	2	4	
95-96	Wash	6	1	1	2	2	
97-98	Wash	12	0	2	2	2	
Totals		44	2	6	8	34	

EAKIN, Bruce Glen 5-11 190 C
B. Winnipeg, Man., Sept. 18, 1962

SSN	TEAM	GP	G	A	PTS.	PIM	+/-
81-82	Calg	1	0	0	0	0	-2
83-84	Calg	7	2	1	3	4	-1
84-85	Calg	1	0	0	0	0	0
85-86	Det	4	0	1	1	0	-4
Totals		13	2	2	4	4	-7

EAKINS, Dallas 6-2 195 D
B. Dade City, Fla., Feb. 27, 1967

SSN	TEAM	GP	G	A	PTS.	PIM	+/-
92-93	Winn	14	0	2	2	38	+2
93-94	Fla	1	0	0	0	0	0
94-95	Fla	17	0	1	1	35	+2
95-96	StL-Winn	18	0	1	1	34	-1
96-97	Phoe-NYR	7	0	0	0	16	-4
97-98	Fla	23	0	1	1	44	+1
98-99	Tor	18	0	2	2	24	+3
Totals		98	0	7	7	191	+3

Playoffs

SSN	TEAM	GP	G	A	PTS.	PIM	+/-
96-97	NYR	4	0	0	0	4	
98-99	Tor	1	0	0	0	0	
Totals		5	0	0	0	4	

EASTWOOD, Michael 6-3 205 C
B. Ottawa, Ont., July 1, 1967

SSN	TEAM	GP	G	A	PTS.	PIM	+/-
91-92	Tor	9	0	2	2	4	-4
92-93	Tor	12	1	6	7	21	-2
93-94	Tor	54	8	10	18	28	+2
94-95	Tor-Winn	49	8	11	19	36	-9
95-96	Winn	80	14	14	28	20	-14
96-97	Phoe-NYR	60	2	10	12	14	-1
97-98	NYR-StL	58	6	5	11	22	-2
98-99	StL	82	9	21	30	36	+6
Totals		404	48	79	127	181	-24

Playoffs

SSN	TEAM	GP	G	A	PTS.	PIM	+/-
92-93	Tor	10	1	2	3	8	
93-94	Tor	18	3	2	5	12	
94-95	Winn	6	0	1	1	2	
96-97	NYR	15	1	2	3	22	
97-98	StL	3	1	0	1	0	
98-99	StL	13	1	1	2	6	
Totals		65	7	8	15	50	

EATOUGH, Jeff 5-9 168 RW
B. Toronto, Ont., June 2, 1963

SSN	TEAM	GP	G	A	PTS.	PIM	+/-
81-82	Buf	1	0	0	0	0	-1

EAVES, Michael Gordon 5-10 180 C
B. Denver, Colo., June 10, 1956

SSN	TEAM	GP	G	A	PTS.	PIM	+/-
78-79	Minn	3	0	0	0	0	-1
79-80	Minn	56	18	28	46	11	+3
80-81	Minn	48	10	24	34	18	+1
81-82	Minn	25	11	10	21	0	+2
82-83	Minn	75	16	16	32	21	-3
83-84	Calg	61	14	36	50	20	+9
84-85	Calg	56	14	29	43	10	+14
Totals		324	83	143	226	80	+25

Playoffs

SSN	TEAM	GP	G	A	PTS.	PIM	+/-
79-80	Minn	15	2	5	7	4	
82-83	Minn	9	0	0	0	0	
83-84	Calg	11	4	4	8	2	
84-85	Calg	5	1	1	2	8	
Totals		40	7	10	17	14	

EAVES, Murray 5-10 185 C
B. Calgary, Alta., May 10, 1960

SSN	TEAM	GP	G	A	PTS.	PIM	+/-
80-81	Winn	12	1	2	3	5	-7
81-82	Winn	2	0	0	0	0	0
82-83	Winn	26	2	7	9	2	-6
83-84	Winn	2	0	0	0	0	0
84-85	Winn	3	0	3	3	0	+3
85-86	Winn	4	1	0	1	0	-2
87-88	Det	7	0	1	1	2	-1
89-90	Det	1	0	0	0	0	-2
Totals		57	4	13	17	9	-15

Playoffs

SSN	TEAM	GP	G	A	PTS.	PIM	+/-
83-84	Winn	2	0	0	0	2	
84-85	Winn	2	0	1	1	0	
Totals		4	0	1	1	2	

ECCLESTONE, Timothy James 5-10 195 RW
B. Toronto, Ont., Sept. 24, 1947

SSN	TEAM	GP	G	A	PTS.	PIM	+/-
67-68	StL	50	6	8	14	36	+1
68-69	StL	68	11	23	34	31	+20
69-70	StL	65	16	21	37	59	+7
70-71	StL-Det	74	19	34	53	47	-22
71-72	Det	72	18	35	53	33	-21
72-73	Det	78	18	30	48	28	+6
73-74	Det-Tor	60	9	19	28	38	+2
74-75	Tor-Atl	67	14	22	36	34	+8
75-76	Atl	69	6	21	27	30	+7
76-77	Atl	78	9	18	27	26	+10

SSN	TEAM	GP	G	A	PTS.	PIM	+/-
77–78	Atl	11	0	2	2	2	+1
Totals		692	126	233	359	364	+19

Playoffs

SSN	TEAM	GP	G	A	PTS.	PIM
67–68	StL	12	1	2	3	2
68–69	StL	12	2	2	4	20
69–70	StL	16	3	4	7	48
73–74	Tor	4	0	1	1	0
76–77	Atl	3	0	2	2	6
77–78	Atl	1	0	0	0	0
Totals		48	6	11	17	76

EDBERG, Rolf Arne *5–10 175 C*
B. Stockholm, Sweden, Sept. 29, 1950

SSN	TEAM	GP	G	A	PTS.	PIM	+/-
78–79	Wash	76	14	27	41	6	+11
79–80	Wash	63	23	56	46	12	-5
80–81	Wash	45	8	8	16	6	+1
Totals		184	45	58	103	24	+7

*EDDOLLS, Frank Herbert *5–8 180 D*
B. Lachine, Que., July 5, 1921

SSN	TEAM	GP	G	A	PTS.	PIM
44–45	Mont	43	5	8	13	20
45–46	Mont	8	0	1	1	6
46–47	Mont	6	0	0	0	0
47–48	NYR	58	6	13	19	16
48–49	NYR	34	4	2	6	10
49–50	NYR	58	2	6	8	20
50–51	NYR	68	3	8	11	24
51–52	NYR	42	3	5	8	18
Totals		317	23	43	66	114

Playoffs

SSN	TEAM	GP	G	A	PTS.	PIM
44–45	Mont	3	0	0	0	0
45–46	Mont	8	0	1	1	2
46–47	Mont	6	0	0	0	4
47–48	Mont	2	0	0	0	0
49–50	NYR	11	0	1	1	4
Totals		30	0	2	2	10

EDESTRAND, Darryl *5–11 185 D*
B. Strathroy, Ont., Nov. 6, 1945

SSN	TEAM	GP	G	A	PTS.	PIM	+/-
67–68	StL	12	0	0	0	2	-2
69–70	Phil	2	0	0	0	6	-1
71–72	Pitt	77	10	23	33	52	-12
72–73	Pitt	78	15	24	39	88	+3
73–74	Pitt–Bos	55	3	8	11	20	+17
74–75	Bos	68	1	9	10	56	+8
75–76	Bos	77	4	17	21	103	+7
76–77	Bos	17	0	3	3	16	+4
77–78	Bos–LA	14	0	2	2	21	-9
78–79	LA	55	1	4	5	46	-8
Totals		455	34	90	124	410	+7

Playoffs

SSN	TEAM	GP	G	A	PTS.	PIM
71–72	Pitt	4	0	2	2	0
73–74	Bos	16	1	2	3	15
74–76	Bos	3	0	1	1	7
75–76	Bos	12	1	3	4	23
76–77	Bos	3	0	0	0	2
77–78	LA	2	1	1	2	4
78–79	LA	2	0	0	0	6
Totals		42	3	9	12	57

EDMUNDSON, Garry Frank *6–0 173 LW*
B. Sexsmith, Alta., May 6, 1932

SSN	TEAM	GP	G	A	PTS.	PIM
51–52	Mont	1	0	0	0	0
59–60	Tor	39	4	6	10	47
60–61	Tor	3	0	0	0	0
Totals		43	4	6	10	47

Playoffs

SSN	TEAM	GP	G	A	PTS.	PIM
51–52	Mont	2	0	0	0	4
59–60	Tor	9	0	1	1	4
Totals		11	0	1	1	8

EDUR, Thomas *6–1 185·D*
B. Toronto, Ont., Nov. 18, 1954

SSN	TEAM	GP	G	A	PTS.	PIM	+/-
73–74	Clev (WHA)	76	7	31	38	26	
74–75	Clev (WHA)	61	3	20	23	28	
75–76	Clev (WHA)	80	7	28	35	62	
76–77	Col	80	7	25	32	39	+14
77–78	Col–Pitt	78	10	45	55	28	+1
NHL Totals		158	17	70	87	67	+15
WHA Totals		217	17	79	96	116	

Playoffs

SSN	TEAM	GP	G	A	PTS.	PIM
73–74	Clev (WHA)	5	1	2	3	0
74–75	Clev (WHA)	5	2	0	2	0
75–76	Clev (WHA)	3	0	3	3	0
Totals		13	3	5	8	0

EGAN, Martin Joseph (Pat) *5–10 190 D*
B. Blackie, Alta., Apr. 25, 1918

SSN	TEAM	GP	G	A	PTS.	PIM
39–40	NYA	10	4	3	7	6
40–41	NYA	39	4	9	13	51
41–42	NYA	48	8	20	28	124
42–43	Det–Bos	48	15	28	43	95
44–45	Bos	48	7	15	22	86
45–46	Bos	41	8	10	18	32
46–47	Bos	60	7	18	25	89
47–48	Bos	60	8	11	19	81
48–49	Bos	60	6	18	24	92
49–50	NYR	70	5	11	16	50
50–51	NYR	70	5	10	15	70
Totals		554	77	153	230	776

Playoffs

SSN	TEAM	GP	G	A	PTS.	PIM
39–40	NYA	2	0	0	0	4
44–45	Bos	7	2	0	2	6
45–46	Bos	10	3	0	3	8
46–47	Bos	5	0	2	2	6
47–48	Bos	5	1	1	2	2
48–49	Bos	5	0	0	0	16
49–50	NYR	12	3	1	4	6
Totals		46	9	4	13	48

EGELAND, Allan *6–0 184 C*
B. Lethbridge, Alta., Jan. 31, 1973

SSN	TEAM	GP	G	A	PTS.	PIM	+/-
95–96	TB	5	0	0	0	2	0
96–97	TB	4	0	0	0	5	-3
97–98	TB	8	0	0	0	9	0
Totals		17	0	0	0	16	-3

EGERS, John Richard (Jack) *6–1 175 RW*
B. Sudbury, Ont., Jan. 28, 1949

SSN	TEAM	GP	G	A	PTS.	PIM	+/-
69–70	NYR	6	3	0	3	2	0
70–71	NYR	60	7	10	17	50	+8
71–72	NYR–StL	80	23	26	49	48	+7
72–73	StL	78	24	24	48	26	+1
73–74	StL–NYR	34	1	4	5	12	+2
74–75	Wash	14	3	2	5	8	-14
75–76	Wash	12	3	3	6	8	-2
Totals		284	64	69	133	154	+2

Playoffs

SSN	TEAM	GP	G	A	PTS.	PIM
69–70	NYR	5	3	1	4	10
70–71	NYR	3	0	0	0	2
71–72	StL	11	1	4	5	14
72–73	StL	5	0	1	1	2
73–74	NYR	8	1	0	1	4
Totals		32	5	6	11	32

EHMAN, Gerald Joseph *6–0 190 RW*
B. Cudworth, Sask., Nov. 3, 1932

SSN	TEAM	GP	G	A	PTS.	PIM	+/-
57–58	Bos	1	1	0	1	0	
58–59	Det–Tor	44	12	14	26	16	
59–60	Tor	69	12	16	28	26	
60–61	Tor	14	1	1	2	2	
63–64	Tor	4	1	1	2	0	
67–68	Oak	73	19	25	44	20	-5
68–69	Oak	70	21	24	45	12	-13
69–70	Oak	76	11	19	30	8	-25
70–71	Cal	78	18	18	36	16	-40
Totals		429	96	118	214	100	-83

Playoffs

SSN	TEAM	GP	G	A	PTS.	PIM
58–59	Tor	12	6	7	13	8
59–60	Tor	9	0	0	0	0
63–64	Tor	9	1	0	1	4
68–69	Cal	7	2	2	4	0
69–70	Oak	4	1	1	2	0
Totals		41	10	10	20	12

EISENHUT, Neil *6–1 190 C*
B. Osoyoos, B.C., Feb. 9, 1967

SSN	TEAM	GP	G	A	PTS.	PIM	+/-
93–94	Van	13	1	3	4	21	0
94–95	Calg	3	0	0	0	0	0
Totals		16	1	3	4	21	0

EKLUND, Per–Erik (Pelle) *5–10 175 C*
B. Stockholm, Sweden, Mar. 22, 1963

SSN	TEAM	GP	G	A	PTS.	PIM	+/-
85–86	Phil	70	15	51	66	12	-4
86–87	Phil	72	14	41	55	2	-2
87–88	Phil	71	10	32	42	12	+5
88–89	Phil	79	18	51	69	23	+7
89–90	Phil	70	23	39	62	16	+7
90–91	Phil	73	19	50	69	14	-2
91–92	Phil	51	7	16	23	4	0
92–93	Phil	55	11	38	49	16	+12
93–94	Phil–Dal	53	3	17	20	10	-2
Totals		594	120	335	455	109	+8

Playoffs

SSN	TEAM	GP	G	A	PTS.	PIM
85–86	Phil	5	0	2	2	0
86–87	Phil	26	7	20	27	2
87–88	Phil	7	0	3	3	0
88–89	Phil	19	3	8	11	2
93–94	Dal	9	0	3	3	4
Totals		66	10	36	46	8

ELDEBRINK, Anders *5–11 190 D*
B. Kalix, Sweden, Dec. 11, 1960

SSN	TEAM	GP	G	A	PTS.	PIM	+/-
81–82	Van	38	1	8	9	21	-2
82–83	Van–Que	17	2	3	5	8	-2
Totals		55	3	11	14	29	-4

Playoffs

SSN	TEAM	GP	G	A	PTS.	PIM
81–82	Van	13	0	0	0	10
82–83	Que	1	0	0	0	0
Totals		14	0	0	0	10

ELIAS, Patrik *6–0 176 LW*
B. Trebic, Czech., Apr. 13, 1976

SSN	TEAM	GP	G	A	PTS.	PIM	+/-
95–96	NJ	1	0	0	0		-1
96–97	NJ	17	2	3	5	2	-4
97–98	NJ	74	18	19	37	28	+18
98–99	NJ	74	17	33	50	34	+19
Totals		166	37	55	92	64	+32

Playoffs

SSN	TEAM	GP	G	A	PTS.	PIM
96–97	NJ	8	2	3	5	4
97–98	NJ	4	0	1	1	0
98–99	NJ	7	0	5	5	6
Totals		19	2	9	11	10

ELIK, Boris (Bo) *5–10 190 LW*
B. Geraldton, Ont., Oct. 17, 1929

SSN	TEAM	GP	G	A	PTS.	PIM
62–63	Det	3	0	0	0	0

ELIK, Todd *6–2 190 C*
B. Brampton, Ont., Apr. 15, 1966

SSN	TEAM	GP	G	A	PTS.	PIM	+/-
89–90	LA	48	10	23	33	41	+4
90–91	LA	74	21	37	58	58	+20
91–92	Minn	62	14	32	46	125	0
92–93	Minn–Edm	60	14	27	41	56	+4
93–94	Edm–SJ	79	25	41	66	95	-3
94–95	SJ–StL	35	9	14	23	22	+8
95–96	Bos	59	13	33	46	40	+2
96–97	Bos	31	4	12	16	16	-12
Totals		448	110	219	329	453	+23

Playoffs

SSN	TEAM	GP	G	A	PTS.	PIM
89–90	LA	10	3	9	12	10
90–91	LA	12	2	7	9	6
91–92	LA	5	1	1	2	2
93–94	SJ	14	5	5	10	12
94–95	StL	7	4	3	7	2
95–96	Bos	4	0	2	2	16
Totals		52	15	27	42	48

ELLETT, David *6–2 200 D*
B. Cleveland, Ohio, Mar. 30, 1964

SSN	TEAM	GP	G	A	PTS.	PIM	+/-
84–85	Winn	80	11	27	38	85	+20
85–86	Winn	80	15	31	46	96	-38
86–87	Winn	78	13	31	44	53	+19
87–88	Winn	68	13	45	58	106	-8
88–89	Winn	75	22	34	56	62	-18
89–90	Winn	77	17	29	46	96	-15
90–91	Winn–Tor	77	12	37	49	75	-8
91–92	Tor	79	18	33	51	95	-13
92–93	Tor	70	6	34	40	46	+19
93–94	Tor	68	7	36	43	42	+6
94–95	Tor	33	5	10	15	26	-6
95–96	Tor	80	3	19	22	59	-10
96–97	Tor–NJ	76	6	15	21	40	-6

SSN	TEAM	GP	G	A	PTS.	PIM	+/-
97–98	Bos	82	3	20	23	67	+3
98–99	Bos	54	0	6	6	25	+11
Totals		1077	151	407	558	973	-44

Playoffs

84–85	Winn	8	1	5	6	4	
85–86	Winn	3	0	1	1	0	
86–87	Winn	10	0	8	8	2	
87–88	Winn	5	1	2	3	10	
89–90	Winn	7	2	0	2	6	
92–93	Tor	21	4	8	12	8	
93–94	Tor	18	3	15	18	31	
94–95	Tor	7	0	2	2	0	
95–96	Tor	6	0	0	0	0	
96–97	NJ	10	0	3	3	10	
97–98	NJ	6	0	1	1	6	
98–99	Bos	8	0	0	0	4	
Totals		109	11	45	56	85	

ELLIOT, Fred H F

28–29	Ott	43	2	0	2	6	

ELLIS, Ronald John Edward 5–9 195 RW
B. Lindsay, Ont., Jan. 8, 1945

63–64	Tor	1	0	0	0	0	
64–65	Tor	62	23	16	39	14	
65–66	Tor	70	19	23	42	24	
66–67	Tor	67	22	23	45	14	
67–68	Tor	74	28	20	48	8	+6
68–69	Tor	72	25	21	46	12	+5
69–70	Tor	76	35	19	54	14	+11
70–71	Tor	78	24	29	53	10	+17
71–72	Tor	78	23	24	47	17	+7
72–73	Tor	78	22	29	51	22	-1
73–74	Tor	70	23	25	48	12	+8
74–75	Tor	79	32	29	61	25	+9
77–78	Tor	80	26	24	50	17	+8
78–79	Tor	63	16	12	28	10	+7
79–80	Tor	59	12	11	23	6	-9
80–81	Tor	27	2	3	5	2	-1
Totals		1034	332	308	640	207	+67

Playoffs

64–65	Tor	6	3	0	3	2	
65–66	Tor	4	0	0	0	2	
66–67	Tor	12	2	1	3	4	
68–69	Tor	4	2	1	3	2	
70–71	Tor	6	1	1	2	2	
71–72	Tor	5	1	1	2	4	
73–74	Tor	4	2	1	3	0	
74–75	Tor	7	3	0	3	2	
77–78	Tor	13	3	2	5	0	
78–79	Tor	6	1	1	2	2	
79–80	Tor	3	0	0	0	0	
Totals		70	18	8	26	20	

ELORANTA, Karl 6–2 200 D
B. Lahti, Finland, Feb. 29, 1956

81–82	Calg–StL	31	1	12	13	20	-9
82–83	Calg	80	4	40	44	43	+13
83–84	Calg	78	5	34	39	44	-12
84–85	Calg	65	2	11	13	39	+1
86–87	Calg	13	1	6	7	9	+3
Totals		267	13	103	116	155	+20

Playoffs

81–82	StL	5	0	0	0	0	
82–83	Calg	9	1	3	4	17	
83–84	Calg	6	0	2	2	2	
84–85	Calg	6	0	2	2	0	
Totals		26	1	7	8	19	

ELYNUIK, Pat 6–0 185 RW
B. Foam Lake, Sask., Oct. 30, 1967

87–88	Winn	13	1	3	4	12	+2
88–89	Winn	56	26	25	51	29	+5
89–90	Winn	80	32	42	74	83	+2
90–91	Winn	80	31	34	65	73	-13
91–92	Winn	60	25	25	50	65	-2
92–93	Wash	80	22	35	57	66	+3
93–94	Wash–TB	67	13	15	28	64	-21
94–95	Ott	41	3	7	10	51	-11
95–96	Ott	29	1	2	3	16	+2
Totals		506	154	188	342	459	-33

Playoffs

89–90	Winn	7	2	4	6	2	

SSN	TEAM	GP	G	A	PTS.	PIM	+/-
91–92	Winn	7	2	2	4	4	
92–93	Wash	6	2	3	5	19	
Totals		20	6	9	15	25	

EMBERG, Edward F
B. Montreal, Que., Nov. 18, 1921

44–45	Mont	0	0	0	0	0	

Playoffs

44–45	Mont	2	1	0	1	0	

EMERSON, Nelson 5–11 175 C
B. Hamilton, Ont., Aug. 17, 1967

90–91	StL	4	0	3	3	2	-2
91–92	StL	79	23	36	59	66	-5
92–93	StL	82	22	51	73	62	+2
93–94	Winn	83	33	41	74	80	-38
94–95	Winn	48	14	23	37	26	-12
95–96	Hart	81	29	29	58	78	-7
96–97	Hart	66	9	29	38	34	-21
97–98	Car	81	21	24	45	50	-17
98–99	Car–Chi–Ott	65	13	24	37	51	+8
Totals		589	164	260	424	449	-92

Playoffs

91–92	StL	6	3	3	6	21	
92–93	StL	11	1	6	7	6	
98–99	Ott	4	1	3	4	0	
Totals		21	5	12	17	27	

EMMA, David Anaclethe 5–11 180 C
B. Cranston, R.I., Jan. 14, 1969

92–93	NJ	2	0	0	0	0	0
93–94	NJ	15	5	5	10	2	0
94–95	NJ	6	0	1	1	0	-2
96–97	Bos	5	0	0	0	0	-1
Totals		28	5	6	11	2	-3

EMMONS, Gary 6–0 185 C
B. Winnipeg, Man., Dec. 30, 1963

93–94	SJ	3	1	0	1	0	-4

EMMS, Leighton (Hap) 6–0 190 LW
B. Barrie, Ont., Jan. 12, 1905

26–27	Mont M	8	0	0	0	0	
27–28	Mont M	8	0	1	1	10	
30–31	NYA	44	5	4	9	56	
31–32	NYA–Det	33	7	9	16	38	
32–33	Det	41	9	13	22	63	
33–34	Det	47	7	7	14	51	
34–35	Bos–NYA	39	3	3	6	27	
35–36	NYA	31	1	5	6	12	
36–37	NYA	47	4	8	12	48	
37–38	NYA	22	1	3	4	6	
Totals		320	37	53	90	311	

Playoffs

31–32	Det	2	0	0	0	2	
32–33	Det	4	0	0	0	8	
33–34	Det	8	0	0	0	2	
Totals		14	0	0	0	12	

ENDEAN, Craig 5–11 170 LW
B. Kamloops, B.C., Apr. 13, 1968

86–87	Winn	2	0	1	1	0	+1

ENGBLOM, Brian Paul 6–2 190 D
B. Winnipeg, Man., Jan. 27, 1955

77–78	Mont	28	1	2	3	23	+9
78–79	Mont	62	3	11	14	60	+21
79–80	Mont	70	3	20	23	43	+22
80–81	Mont	80	3	25	28	96	+63
81–82	Mont	76	4	29	33	76	+78
82–83	Wash	73	5	22	27	59	-4
83–84	Wash–LA	80	2	28	30	67	-13
84–85	LA	79	4	19	23	70	-2
85–86	LA–Buf	79	4	17	21	77	-10
86–87	Calg	32	0	4	4	28	-7
Totals		659	29	177	206	599	+157

Playoffs

76–77	Mont	2	0	0	0	2	
77–78	Mont	5	0	0	0	2	
78–79	Mont	16	0	1	1	11	
79–80	Mont	10	2	4	6	6	
80–81	Mont	3	1	0	1	4	

SSN	TEAM	GP	G	A	PTS.	PIM	+/-
81–82	Mont	5	0	2	2	14	
82–83	Wash	4	0	2	2	2	
Totals		48	3	9	12	41	

ENGELE, Jerome Wilfred (Jerry) 6–0 197 D
B. Humboldt, Sask., Nov. 26, 1950

75–76	Minn	17	0	1	1	16	-12
76–77	Minn	31	1	7	8	41	+13
77–78	Minn	52	1	5	6	105	-10
Totals		100	2	13	15	162	-19

Playoffs

76–77	Minn	2	0	1	1	0	

ENGLISH, John 6–2 190 D
B. Toronto, Ont., May 13, 1966

87–88	LA	3	1	3	4	4	+2

ENNIS, Jim 6–0 200 D
B. Sherwood Park, Alta., July 10, 1967

87–88	Edm	5	1	0	1	10	0

ERICKSON, Autry Raymond (Aut) 6–0 188 D
B. Lethbridge, Alta., Jan. 25, 1938

59–60	Bos	58	1	6	7	29	
60–61	Bos	68	2	6	8	65	
62–63	Chi	3	0	0	0	8	
63–64	Chi	31	0	1	1	34	
67–68	Oak	66	4	11	15	46	-17
69–70	Oak	1	0	0	0	0	-1
Totals		227	7	24	31	182	-18

Playoffs

63–64	Chi	6	0	0	0	0	
66–67	Tor	1	0	0	0	2	
Totals		7	0	0	0	2	

ERICKSON, Bryan 5–9 170 RW
B. Roseau, Minn., Mar. 7, 1960

83–84	Wash	45	12	17	29	16	+10
84–85	Wash	57	15	13	28	23	+11
85–86	LA	55	20	23	43	36	+1
86–87	LA	68	20	30	50	26	-12
87–88	LA–Pitt	53	7	19	26	20	-12
90–91	Winn	6	0	7	7	0	+1
91–92	Winn	10	2	4	6	0	+9
92–93	Winn	41	4	12	16	14	+2
93–94	Winn	16	0	0	0	6	-7
Totals		351	80	125	205	141	+3

Playoffs

83–84	Wash	8	2	3	5	7	
86–87	LA	3	1	1	2	0	
92–93	Winn	3	0	0	0	0	
Totals		14	3	4	7	7	

ERICKSON, Grant Charles 5–9 165 LW
B. Pierceland, Sask., Apr. 28, 1947

68–69	Bos	2	1	0	1	0	+2
69–70	Minn	4	0	0	0	4	-3
72–73	Clev (WHA)	77	15	29	44	23	
73–74	Clev (WHA)	78	23	27	50	26	
74–75	Clev (WHA)	78	12	15	27	24	
75–76	Phoe (WHA)	33	4	4	8	6	
NHL Totals		6	1	0	1	4	-1
WHA Totals		266	54	75	129	79	

Playoffs

72–73	Clev (WHA)	9	2	1	3	2	
73–74	Clev (WHA)	5	0	2	2	0	
75–76	Phoe (WHA)	5	0	2	2	0	
WHA Totals		19	2	5	7	2	

ERIKSSON, Anders 6–3 218 D
B. Vastervik, Sweden, Feb. 17, 1969

95–96	Det	1	0	0	0	2	+1
96–97	Det	23	0	6	6	10	+5
97–98	Det	66	7	14	21	32	+21
98–99	Det–Chi	72	2	18	20	34	+11
Totals		162	9	38	47	78	+38

Playoffs

95–96	Det	3	0	0	0	0	
97–98	Det	18	0	5	5	16	
Totals		21	0	5	5	16	

ERIKSSON, Bengt Roland (Rolie) 6–3 190 C
B. Storatuna, Sweden, Mar. 1, 1954

SSN	TEAM	GP	G	A	PTS.	PIM	+/-
76–77	Minn	80	25	44	69	10	-29
77–78	Minn	78	21	39	60	12	-29
78–79	Van	35	2	12	14	4	-12
78–79	Winn (WHA)	33	5	10	15	2	
NHL Totals		193	48	95	143	26	-70
WHA Totals		33	5	10	15	2	

Playoffs

SSN	TEAM	GP	G	A	PTS.	PIM	+/-
76–77	Minn	2	1	0	1	0	
78–79	Winn (WHA)	10	1	4	5	0	
NHL Totals		2	1	0	1	0	
WHA Totals		10	1	4	5	0	

ERIKSSON, Peter 6–4 224 LW
B. Kramfors, Sweden, July 12, 1965

SSN	TEAM	GP	G	A	PTS.	PIM	+/-
89–90	Edm	20	3	3	6	24	-1

ERIKSSON, Thomas 6–2 180 D
B. Stockholm, Sweden, Oct. 16, 1959

SSN	TEAM	GP	G	A	PTS.	PIM	+/-
80–81	Phil	24	1	10	11	14	+4
81–82	Phil	1	0	0	0	4	-1
83–84	Phil	68	11	33	44	37	+28
84–85	Phil	72	10	29	39	36	+24
85–86	Phil	43	0	4	4	16	-12
Totals		208	22	76	98	107	+43

Playoffs

SSN	TEAM	GP	G	A	PTS.	PIM	+/-
80–81	Phil	7	0	2	2	6	
83–84	Phil	3	0	1	1	0	
85–86	Phil	9	0	0	0	0	
Totals		19	0	3	3	6	

ERIXON, Jan 6–0 190 LW
B. Skelleftea, Sweden, July 8, 1962

SSN	TEAM	GP	G	A	PTS.	PIM	+/-
83–84	NYR	75	5	25	30	16	+14
84–85	NYR	66	7	22	29	33	-11
85–86	NYR	31	2	17	19	4	+12
86–87	NYR	68	8	18	26	24	+3
87–88	NYR	70	7	19	26	33	+3
88–89	NYR	44	4	11	15	27	-3
89–90	NYR	58	4	9	13	8	-17
90–91	NYR	53	7	18	25	8	+13
91–92	NYR	46	8	9	17	4	+13
92–93	NYR	45	5	11	16	10	+11
Totals		556	57	159	216	167	+38

Playoffs

SSN	TEAM	GP	G	A	PTS.	PIM	+/-
83–84	NYR	5	2	0	2	4	
84–85	NYR	2	0	0	0	2	
85–86	NYR	12	0	1	1	4	
86–87	NYR	6	1	0	1	0	
88–89	NYR	4	0	1	1	2	
89–90	NYR	10	1	0	1	2	
90–91	NYR	6	1	2	3	0	
91–92	NYR	13	2	3	5	2	
Totals		58	7	7	14	16	

ERREY, Bob 5–10 180 LW
B. Montreal, Que., Sept. 21, 1964

SSN	TEAM	GP	G	A	PTS.	PIM	+/-
83–84	Pitt	65	9	13	22	29	-20
84–85	Pitt	16	0	2	2	7	-8
85–86	Pitt	37	11	6	17	8	+1
86–87	Pitt	72	16	18	34	46	-6
87–88	Pitt	17	3	6	9	18	+6
88–89	Pitt	76	26	32	58	124	+40
89–90	Pitt	78	20	19	39	109	+3
90–91	Pitt	79	20	22	42	115	+11
91–92	Pitt	78	19	16	35	119	+1
92–93	Pitt–Buf	62	9	9	18	80	0
93–94	SJ	64	12	18	30	126	-11
94–95	SJ–Det	43	8	13	21	58	+13
95–96	Det	71	11	21	32	66	+30
96–97	Det–SJ	66	4	8	12	47	-5
97–98	Dal–NYR	71	2	9	11	53	+2
Totals		895	170	212	382	1005	+57

Playoffs

SSN	TEAM	GP	G	A	PTS.	PIM	+/-
88–89	Pitt	11	1	2	3	12	
90–91	Pitt	24	5	2	7	29	
91–92	Pitt	14	3	0	3	10	
92–93	Buf	4	0	1	1	10	
93–94	SJ	14	3	2	5	10	
94–95	Det	18	1	5	6	30	
95–96	Det	14	0	4	4	8	

SSN	TEAM	GP	G	A	PTS.	PIM	+/-
Totals		99	13	16	29	109	

ESAU, Leonard 6–3 190 D
B. Meadow Lake, Sask., June 3, 1968

SSN	TEAM	GP	G	A	PTS.	PIM	+/-
91–92	Tor	2	0	0	0	0	0
92–93	Que	4	0	1	1	2	+1
93–94	Calg	6	0	3	3	7	-1
94–95	Edm–Calg	15	0	6	6	15	-10
Totals		27	0	10	10	24	-10

ESPOSITO, Phillip Anthony (Espo) 6–1 205 C
B. Sault Ste. Marie, Ont., Feb. 20, 1942

SSN	TEAM	GP	G	A	PTS.	PIM	+/-
63–64	Chi	27	3	2	5	2	
64–65	Chi	70	23	32	55	44	
65–66	Chi	69	27	26	53	49	
66–67	Chi	69	21	40	61	40	
67–68	Bos	74	35	49	84	21	-19
68–69	Bos	74	49	77	126	79	+56
69–70	Bos	76	43	56	99	50	+28
70–71	Bos	78	76	76	152	71	+71
71–72	Bos	76	66	67	133	76	+55
72–73	Bos	78	55	75	130	87	+16
73–74	Bos	78	68	77	145	58	+51
74–75	Bos	79	61	66	127	62	+18
75–76	Bos–NYR	74	35	48	83	36	-40
76–77	NYR	80	34	46	80	52	-28
77–78	NYR	79	38	43	81	53	-22
78–79	NYR	80	42	36	78	14	-1
79–80	NYR	80	34	44	78	73	-13
80–81	NYR	41	7	13	20	20	-13
Totals		1282	717	873	1590	887	+197

Playoffs

SSN	TEAM	GP	G	A	PTS.	PIM	+/-
63–64	Chi	4	0	0	0	0	
64–65	Chi	13	3	3	6	15	
65–66	Chi	6	1	1	2	2	
66–67	Chi	6	0	0	0	4	
67–68	Bos	4	0	3	3	0	
68–69	Bos	10	8	10	18	8	
69–70	Bos	14	13	14	27	16	
70–71	Bos	7	3	7	10	6	
71–72	Bos	15	9	15	24	24	
72–73	Bos	2	0	1	1	2	
73–74	Bos	16	9	5	14	25	
74–75	Bos	3	4	1	5	0	
77–78	NYR	3	0	1	1	5	
78–79	NYR	18	8	12	20	20	
79–80	NYR	9	3	3	6	8	
Totals		130	61	76	137	135	

EVANS, Christopher Bruce 5–9 180 D
B. Toronto, Ont., Sept. 14, 1946

SSN	TEAM	GP	G	A	PTS.	PIM	+/-
69–70	Tor	2	0	0	0	0	-5
71–72	Buf–StL	63	6	18	24	98	-20
72–73	StL	77	9	12	21	31	-2
73–74	StL–Det	77	4	9	13	10	+1
74–75	KC–StL	22	0	3	3	4	-2
75–76	Calg (WHA)	75	3	20	23	50	
76–77	Calg (WHA)	81	7	27	34	60	
77–78	Que (WHA)	48	1	4	5	26	
NHL Totals		241	19	42	61	143	-28
WHA Totals		204	11	51	62	136	

Playoffs

SSN	TEAM	GP	G	A	PTS.	PIM	+/-
71–72	StL	7	1	0	1	4	
72–73	StL	5	0	1	1	4	
75–76	Calg (WHA)	10	5	5	10	4	
NHL Totals		12	1	1	2	8	
WHA Totals		10	5	5	10	4	

EVANS, Daryl Thomas 5–8 185 LW
B. Toronto, Ont., Jan. 12, 1961

SSN	TEAM	GP	G	A	PTS.	PIM	+/-
81–82	LA	14	2	6	8	2	+2
82–83	LA	80	18	22	40	21	-10
83–84	LA	4	0	1	1	0	+1
84–85	LA	7	1	0	1	2	+2
85–86	Wash	6	0	1	1	0	-1
86–87	Tor	2	1	0	1	0	-2
Totals		113	22	30	52	25	-8

Playoffs

SSN	TEAM	GP	G	A	PTS.	PIM	+/-
81–82	LA	10	5	8	13	12	
86–87	Tor	1	0	0	0	0	
Totals		11	5	8	13	12	

EVANS, Doug 5–9 185 LW
B. Peterborough, Ont., June 2, 1963

SSN	TEAM	GP	G	A	PTS.	PIM	+/-
85–86	StL	13	1	0	1	2	0
86–87	StL	53	3	13	16	91	+2
87–88	StL	41	5	7	12	49	-7
88–89	StL	53	7	12	19	81	+3
89–90	StL–Winn	30	10	8	18	33	+7
90–91	Winn	70	7	27	34	108	-1
91–92	Winn	30	7	7	14	68	+2
92–93	Phil	65	8	13	21	70	-9
Totals		355	48	87	135	502	-3

Playoffs

SSN	TEAM	GP	G	A	PTS.	PIM	+/-
86–87	StL	5	0	0	0	10	
87–88	StL	2	0	0	0	0	
88–89	StL	7	1	2	3	16	
89–90	Winn	7	2	2	4	10	
91–92	Winn	1	0	0	0	2	
Totals		22	3	4	7	38	

EVANS, John (Paul) 5–9 185 C
B. Toronto, Ont., May 2, 1954

SSN	TEAM	GP	G	A	PTS.	PIM	+/-
78–79	Phil	44	6	5	11	12	-3
80–81	Phil	1	0	0	0	2	0
82–83	Phil	58	5	20	28	20	+16
Totals		103	14	25	39	34	+13

Playoffs

SSN	TEAM	GP	G	A	PTS.	PIM	+/-
82–83	Phil	1	0	0	0	0	

EVANS, Kevin Robert 5–9 185 LW
B. Peterborough, Ont., July 10, 1965

SSN	TEAM	GP	G	A	PTS.	PIM	+/-
90–91	Minn	4	0	1	1	19	-3
91–92	SJ	5	0	1	1	25	0
Totals		9	0	1	1	44	-3

EVANS, Paul Edward Vincent 5–11 175 C
B. Peterborough, Ont., Feb. 24, 1955

SSN	TEAM	GP	G	A	PTS.	PIM	+/-
76–77	Tor	7	1	1	2	19	+3
77–78	Tor	4	0	0	0	2	-1
Totals		11	1	1	2	21	+2

Playoffs

SSN	TEAM	GP	G	A	PTS.	PIM	+/-
76–77	Tor	2	0	0	0	0	

EVANS, Shawn 6–3 195 D
B. Kingston, Ont., Sept. 7, 1965

SSN	TEAM	GP	G	A	PTS.	PIM	+/-
85–86	StL	7	0	0	0	2	-1
89–90	NYI	2	1	0	1	0	-1
Totals		9	1	0	1	2	-2

*EVANS, Stewart (Stu) 5–10 170 D
B. Ottawa, Ont., June 19, 1908

SSN	TEAM	GP	G	A	PTS.	PIM	+/-
30–31	Det	43	1	4	5	14	
32–33	Det	48	2	6	8	74	
33–34	Det–Mont M	44	4	2	6	55	
34–35	Mont M	46	5	7	12	54	
35–36	Mont M	47	3	5	8	57	
36–37	Mont M	48	6	7	13	54	
37–38	Mont M	48	5	11	16	59	
38–39	Mont	43	2	7	9	58	
Totals		367	28	49	77	425	

Playoffs

SSN	TEAM	GP	G	A	PTS.	PIM	+/-
32–33	Det	4	0	0	0	6	
33–34	Mont M	4	0	0	0	4	
34–35	Mont M	7	0	0	0	8	
35–36	Mont M	3	0	0	0	0	
36–37	Mont M	5	0	0	0	0	
38–39	Mont	3	0	0	0	2	
Totals		26	0	0	0	20	

*EVANS, William John (Jack, Tex) 6–1 194 D
B. Garnant, South Wales, Apr. 21, 1928

SSN	TEAM	GP	G	A	PTS.	PIM	+/-
48–49	NYR	3	0	0	0	4	
49–50	NYR	2	0	0	0	2	
50–51	NYR	49	1	0	1	95	
51–52	NYR	52	1	6	7	83	
53–54	NYR	44	4	4	8	73	
54–55	NYR	47	0	5	5	91	
55–56	NYR	70	2	9	11	104	
56–57	NYR	70	3	6	9	110	
57–58	NYR	70	4	8	12	108	
58–59	Chi	70	1	8	9	75	
59–60	Chi	68	0	4	4	60	
60–61	Chi	69	0	8	8	58	

SSN	TEAM	GP	G	A	PTS.	PIM	+/-
61–62	Chi	70	3	14	17	80	
62–63	Chi	68	0	8	8	46	
Totals		752	19	80	99	989	

Playoffs

SSN	TEAM	GP	G	A	PTS.	PIM	+/-
55–56	NYR	5	1	0	1	18	
56–57	NYR	5	0	1	1	4	
57–58	NYR	6	0	0	0	17	
58–59	Chi	6	0	0	0	10	
59–60	Chi	4	0	0	0	4	
60–61	Chi	12	1	1	2	14	
61–62	Chi	12	0	0	0	26	
62–63	Chi	6	0	0	0	4	
Totals		56	2	2	4	97	

EVASON, Dean 5–10 180 C
B. Flin Flon, Man., Aug. 22, 1964

SSN	TEAM	GP	G	A	PTS.	PIM	+/-
83–84	Wash	2	0	0	0	2	0
84–85	Wash–Hart	17	3	4	7	2	+15
85–86	Hart	55	20	28	48	65	+3
86–87	Hart	80	22	37	59	67	+5
87–88	Hart	77	10	18	28	115	-29
88–89	Hart	67	11	17	28	60	-9
89–90	Hart	78	18	25	43	138	+7
90–91	Hart	75	6	23	29	170	-6
91–92	SJ	74	11	15	26	99	-22
92–93	SJ	84	12	19	31	132	-35
93–94	Dal	80	11	33	44	66	-12
94–95	Dal	47	8	7	15	48	+3
95–96	Calg	67	7	7	14	38	-6
Totals		803	139	233	372	1002	-86

Playoffs

SSN	TEAM	GP	G	A	PTS.	PIM	+/-
85–86	Hart	10	1	4	5	10	
86–87	Hart	5	3	2	5	35	
87–88	Hart	6	1	1	2	2	
88–89	Hart	4	1	2	3	10	
89–90	Hart	7	2	2	4	22	
90–91	Hart	6	0	4	4	29	
93–94	Dal	9	0	2	2	12	
94–95	Dal	5	1	2	3	12	
95–96	Calg	3	0	1	1	0	
Totals		55	9	20	29	132	

EWEN, Todd 6–2 220 RW
B. Saskatoon, Sask., Mar. 22, 1966

SSN	TEAM	GP	G	A	PTS.	PIM	+/-
86–87	StL	23	2	0	2	84	-1
87–88	StL	64	4	2	6	227	-5
88–89	StL	34	4	5	9	171	+4
89–90	StL–Mont	44	4	6	10	169	-1
90–91	Mont	28	3	2	5	128	+4
91–92	Mont	46	1	2	3	130	+3
92–93	Mont	75	5	9	14	193	+6
93–94	Ana	76	9	9	18	272	-7
94–95	Ana	24	0	0	0	90	-2
95–96	Ana	53	4	3	7	285	-5
96–97	SJ	51	0	2	2	162	-5
Totals		518	36	40	76	1911	-9

Playoffs

SSN	TEAM	GP	G	A	PTS.	PIM	+/-
86–87	StL	4	0	0	0	23	
87–88	StL	6	0	0	0	21	
88–89	StL	2	0	0	0	21	
89–90	Mont	10	0	0	0	4	
91–92	Mont	3	0	0	0	18	
92–93	Mont	1	0	0	0	0	
Totals		26	0	0	0	87	

EZINICKI, William (Wild Bill) 5–10 170 RW
B. Winnipeg, Man., Mar. 11, 1924

SSN	TEAM	GP	G	A	PTS.	PIM	+/-
44–45	Tor	8	1	4	5	17	
45–46	Tor	24	4	8	12	29	
46–47	Tor	60	17	20	37	93	
47–48	Tor	60	11	20	31	97	
48–49	Tor	52	13	15	28	145	
49–50	Tor	67	10	12	22	144	
50–51	Bos	53	16	19	35	119	
51–52	Bos	28	5	5	10	47	
54–55	NYR	16	2	2	4	22	
Totals		368	79	105	184	713	

Playoffs

SSN	TEAM	GP	G	A	PTS.	PIM	+/-
46–47	Tor	11	0	2	2	30	
47–48	Tor	9	3	1	4	6	
48–49	Tor	9	1	4	5	20	
49–50	Tor	5	0	0	0	13	
50–51	Bos	6	1	1	2	18	

SSN	TEAM	GP	G	A	PTS.	PIM	+/-
Totals		40	5	8	13	87	

FAHEY, John (Trevor) 6–0 180 LW
B. New Waterford, N.S., Jan. 4, 1944

SSN	TEAM	GP	G	A	PTS.	PIM	+/-
64–65	NYR	1	0	0	0	0	

FAIRBAIRN, William John 5–10 195 RW
B. Brandon, Man., Jan. 7, 1947

SSN	TEAM	GP	G	A	PTS.	PIM	+/-
68–69	NYR	1	0	0	0	0	-1
69–70	NYR	76	23	33	56	23	+24
70–71	NYR	56	7	23	30	32	-4
71–72	NYR	78	22	37	59	53	+36
72–73	NYR	78	30	33	63	23	+36
73–74	NYR	78	18	44	62	12	+11
74–75	NYR	80	24	37	61	10	+13
75–76	NYR	80	13	15	28	8	-14
76–77	NYR–Minn	60	10	22	32	2	0
77–78	Minn–StL	66	14	17	31	10	-24
78–79	StL	5	1	0	1	0	-2
Totals		658	162	261	423	173	+75

Playoffs

SSN	TEAM	GP	G	A	PTS.	PIM	+/-
69–70	NYR	6	0	1	1	10	
70–71	NYR	4	0	0	0	0	
71–72	NYR	16	5	7	12	11	
72–73	NYR	10	1	8	9	2	
73–74	NYR	13	3	5	8	6	
74–75	NYR	3	4	0	4	13	
76–77	Minn	2	0	1	1	0	
Totals		54	13	22	35	42	

FAIRCHILD, Kelly 5–11 180 C
B. Hibbing, Minn., April 9, 1973

SSN	TEAM	GP	G	A	PTS.	PIM	+/-
95–96	Tor	1	0	1	1	2	+1
96–97	Tor	22	0	2	2	2	-5
98–99	Dal	1	0	0	0	0	0
Totals		24	0	3	3	4	-4

FALKENBERG, Robert Arthur (Steady) 6–0 205 D
B. Stettler, Alta., Jan. 1, 1946

SSN	TEAM	GP	G	A	PTS.	PIM	+/-
66–67	Det	16	1	1	2	10	
67–68	Det	20	0	3	3	10	-2
68–69	Det	5	0	0	0	0	-3
70–71	Det	9	0	1	1	6	-3
71–72	Det	4	0	0	0	0	+2
72–73	Alb (WHA)	76	6	23	29	44	
73–74	Edm (WHA)	78	3	14	17	32	
74–75	SD (WHA)	78	2	18	20	42	
75–76	SD (WHA)	79	3	13	16	31	
76–77	SD (WHA)	64	0	6	6	34	
77–78	Edm (WHA)	2	0	0	0	0	
NHL Totals		54	1	5	6	26	-6
WHA Totals		377	14	74	88	183	

Playoffs

SSN	TEAM	GP	G	A	PTS.	PIM	+/-
73–74	Edm (WHA)	5	0	2	2	14	
74–75	SD (WHA)	10	0	1	1	4	
75–76	SD (WHA)	11	1	2	3	6	
76–77	SD (WHA)	2	0	0	0	0	
Totals		28	1	5	6	24	

FALLOON, Pat 5–11 192 RW
B. Birtle, Man., Sept. 22, 1972

SSN	TEAM	GP	G	A	PTS.	PIM	+/-
91–92	SJ	79	25	34	59	16	-32
92–93	SJ	41	14	14	28	12	-25
93–94	SJ	83	22	31	53	18	-3
94–95	SJ	46	12	7	19	25	-4
95–96	SJ–Phil	71	25	26	51	10	+14
96–97	Phil	52	11	12	23	10	-8
97–98	Phil–Ott	58	8	10	18	16	-8
98–99	Edm	82	17	23	40	20	-8
Totals		512	134	157	291	127	-70

Playoffs

SSN	TEAM	GP	G	A	PTS.	PIM	+/-
93–94	SJ	14	1	2	3	6	
94–95	SJ	11	3	1	4	0	
95–96	Phil	12	3	2	5	2	
96–97	Phil	14	3	1	4	2	
97–98	Ott	1	0	0	0	0	
98–99	Edm	4	0	1	1	4	
Totals		56	10	7	17	14	

FARRANT, Walter Leslie (Whitey) 5–10 155 RW
B. Toronto, Ont., Aug. 12, 1912

SSN	TEAM	GP	G	A	PTS.	PIM	+/-
43–44	Chi	1	0	0	0	0	

FARRISH, David Allan 6–1 195 D
B. Wingham, Ont., Aug. 1, 1956

SSN	TEAM	GP	G	A	PTS.	PIM	+/-
76–77	NYR	80	2	17	19	102	-16
77–78	NYR	66	3	5	8	62	-13
78–79	NYR	71	1	19	20	61	-3
79–80	Que–Tor	24	1	8	9	30	+5
80–81	Tor	74	2	18	20	90	-7
82–83	Tor	56	4	24	28	38	+1
83–84	Tor	59	4	19	23	57	-13
Totals		430	17	110	127	440	-46

Playoffs

SSN	TEAM	GP	G	A	PTS.	PIM	+/-
77–78	NYR	3	0	0	0	0	
78–79	NYR	7	0	2	2	14	
79–80	Tor	3	0	0	0	10	
80–81	Tor	1	0	0	0	0	
Totals		14	0	2	2	24	

FASHOWAY, Gordon 5–11 180 F
B. Portage La Prairie, Man., June 16, 1926

SSN	TEAM	GP	G	A	PTS.	PIM	+/-
50–51	Chi	13	3	2	5	14	

FATA, Rico 5–11 202 C
B. Sault Ste. Marie, Ont. Feb. 12, 1980

SSN	TEAM	GP	G	A	PTS.	PIM	+/-
98–99	Calg	20	0	1	1	4	0

FAUBERT, Mario 6–1 175 D
B. Valleyfield, Que., Dec. 2, 1954

SSN	TEAM	GP	G	A	PTS.	PIM	+/-
74–75	Pitt	10	1	0	1	0	-2
75–76	Pitt	21	1	8	9	10	+6
76–77	Pitt	47	2	11	13	32	-4
77–78	Pitt	18	0	6	6	11	+2
79–80	Pitt	49	5	13	18	31	-19
80–81	Pitt	72	8	44	52	118	-18
81–82	Pitt	14	4	8	12	14	-2
Totals		231	21	90	111	216	-37

Playoffs

SSN	TEAM	GP	G	A	PTS.	PIM	+/-
76–77	Pitt	3	1	0	1	2	
79–80	Pitt	2	0	1	1	0	
80–81	Pitt	5	1	1	2	4	
Totals		10	2	2	4	6	

FAULKNER, Alexander Selm 5–8 165 C
B. Bishops Falls, Nfld., May 21, 1936

SSN	TEAM	GP	G	A	PTS.	PIM	+/-
61–62	Tor	1	0	0	0	0	
62–63	Det	70	10	10	20	6	
63–64	Det	30	5	7	12	9	
Totals		101	15	17	32	15	

Playoffs

SSN	TEAM	GP	G	A	PTS.	PIM	+/-
62–63	Det	8	5	0	5	2	
63–64	Det	4	0	0	0	0	
Totals		12	5	0	5	2	

FAUSS, Ted 6–2 205 D
B. Clark Mills, N.Y., June 30, 1961

SSN	TEAM	GP	G	A	PTS.	PIM	+/-
86–87	Tor	15	0	1	1	11	+4
87–88	Tor	13	0	1	1	4	+6
Totals		28	0	2	2	15	+10

FAUST, Andre 5–11 191 C
B. Joliette, Que., Oct. 7, 1969

SSN	TEAM	GP	G	A	PTS.	PIM	+/-
92–93	Phil	10	2	2	4	4	+5
93–94	Phil	37	8	5	13	10	-1
Totals		47	10	7	14	14	+4

FEAMSTER, David Allan 5–11 180 D
B. Detroit, Mich., Sept. 10, 1958

SSN	TEAM	GP	G	A	PTS.	PIM	+/-
81–82	Chi	29	0	2	2	29	-6
82–83	Chi	78	6	12	18	69	+15
83–84	Chi	46	6	7	13	42	-8
84–85	Chi	16	1	3	4	14	+5
Totals		169	13	24	37	155	+6

Playoffs

SSN	TEAM	GP	G	A	PTS.	PIM	+/-
81–82	Chi	15	2	4	6	53	
82–83	Chi	13	1	0	1	4	
83–84	Chi	5	0	1	1	4	

SSN	TEAM	GP	G	A	PTS.	PIM	+/-
Totals		33	3	5	8	61	

FEATHERSTONE, Anthony James (Tony) *5–11 187 RW*
B. Toronto, Ont., July 31, 1949

SSN	TEAM	GP	G	A	PTS.	PIM	+/-
69–70	Oak	9	0	1	1	17	-7
70–71	Cal	67	8	8	16	44	-4
73–74	Minn	54	9	12	21	4	-9
74–75	Tor (WHA)	76	25	38	63	26	
75–76	Tor (WHA)	32	4	7	11	5	
NHL Totals		130	17	21	38	65	-20
WHA Totals		108	29	45	74	31	

Playoffs

SSN	TEAM	GP	G	A	PTS.	PIM	+/-
69–70	Oak	2	0	0	0	0	
74–75	Tor (WHA)	6	2	1	3	2	
NHL Totals		2	0	0	0	0	
WHA Totals		6	2	1	3	2	

FEATHERSTONE, Glen *6–4 216 D*
B. Toronto, Ont., July 8, 1968

SSN	TEAM	GP	G	A	PTS.	PIM	+/-
88–89	StL	18	0	2	2	22	-3
89–90	StL	58	0	12	12	145	-1
90–91	StL	68	5	15	20	204	+19
91–92	Bos	7	1	0	1	20	-2
92–93	Bos	34	5	5	10	102	+6
93–94	Bos	58	1	8	9	152	-5
94–95	NYR–Hart	19	2	1	3	50	-7
95–96	Hart	68	2	10	12	138	+10
96–97	Hart–Calg	54	3	8	11	106	-1
Totals		384	19	61	80	939	+16

Playoffs

SSN	TEAM	GP	G	A	PTS.	PIM	+/-
88–89	StL	6	0	0	0	25	
89–90	StL	12	0	2	2	47	
90–91	StL	9	0	0	0	31	
93–94	Bos	1	0	0	0	0	
Totals		28	0	2	2	103	

FEDERKO, Bernard Allan *6–0 190 C*
B. Foam Lake, Sask., May 12, 1956

SSN	TEAM	GP	G	A	PTS.	PIM	+/-
76–77	StL	31	14	9	23	15	-6
77–78	StL	72	17	24	41	27	-35
78–79	StL	74	31	64	95	14	-15
79–80	StL	79	38	56	94	24	+3
80–81	StL	78	31	73	104	47	+9
81–82	StL	74	30	62	92	70	-10
82–83	StL	75	24	60	84	24	-10
83–84	StL	79	41	66	107	43	-3
84–85	StL	76	30	73	103	27	-10
85–86	StL	80	34	68	102	34	+10
86–87	StL	64	20	52	72	32	-25
87–88	StL	79	20	69	89	52	-12
88–89	StL	66	22	45	67	54	-20
89–90	StL	73	17	40	57	24	-8
Totals		1000	369	761	1130	487	-132

Playoffs

SSN	TEAM	GP	G	A	PTS.	PIM	+/-
76–77	StL	4	1	1	2	2	
79–80	StL	3	1	0	1	2	
80–81	StL	11	8	10	18	2	
81–82	StL	10	3	15	18	10	
82–83	StL	4	2	3	5	0	
Totals		91	35	66	101	83	

FEDEROV, Sergei *6–1 200 C*
B. Moscow, USSR, Dec. 13, 1969

SSN	TEAM	GP	G	A	PTS.	PIM	+/-
90–91	Det	77	31	48	79	66	+11
91–92	Det	80	32	54	86	72	+26
92–93	Det	73	34	53	87	72	+33
93–94	Det	82	56	64	120	34	+48
94–95	Det	42	20	30	50	24	+6
95–96	Det	78	39	68	107	48	+49
96–97	Det	74	30	33	63	30	+29
97–98	Det	21	6	11	17	25	+10
98–99	Det	77	26	37	63	66	+9
Totals		606	274	398	672	675	+221

Playoffs

SSN	TEAM	GP	G	A	PTS.	PIM	+/-
90–91	Det	7	1	5	6	4	
91–92	Det	11	5	5	10	8	
92–93	Det	7	3	6	9	23	
93–94	Det	7	1	7	8	6	
94–95	Det	17	7	17	24	6	
95–96	Det	19	2	18	20	10	
96–97	Det	20	8	12	20	12	
97–98	Det	22	10	10	20	12	
98–99	Det	10	1	8	9	8	
Totals		120	38	88	126	89	

FEDOTOV, Anatoli *5–11 178 D*
B. Saratov, USSR, May 11, 1966

SSN	TEAM	GP	G	A	PTS.	PIM	+/-
92–93	Winn	1	0	2	2	0	+1
93–94	Ana	3	0	0	0	0	-1
Totals		4	0	2	2	0	0

FEDYK, Brent *6–0 195 LW*
B. Yorkton, Sask., Mar. 8, 1967

SSN	TEAM	GP	G	A	PTS.	PIM	+/-
87–88	Det	2	0	1	1	2	-1
88–89	Det	5	2	0	2	0	-1
89–90	Det	27	1	4	5	6	-1
90–91	Det	67	16	19	35	38	+20
91–92	Det	61	5	8	13	42	-5
92–93	Phil	74	21	38	59	48	+14
93–94	Phil	72	20	18	38	74	-14
94–95	Phil	30	8	4	12	14	-2
95–96	Phil–Dal	65	20	14	34	54	-16
97–98	NYR	67	4	6	10	30	-11
Totals		470	97	112	209	308	-17

Playoffs

SSN	TEAM	GP	G	A	PTS.	PIM	+/-
90–91	Det	6	1	0	1	2	
91–92	Det	1	0	0	0	2	
94–95	Phil	9	2	2	4	8	
Totals		16	3	2	5	12	

FELIX, Chris *5–10 191 D*
B. Bramalea, Ont., May 27, 1964

SSN	TEAM	GP	G	A	PTS.	PIM	+/-
88–89	Wash	21	0	8	8	8	+7
89–90	Wash	6	1	0	1	2	-6
90–91	Wash	8	0	4	4	0	0
Totals		35	1	12	13	10	+1

Playoffs

SSN	TEAM	GP	G	A	PTS.	PIM	+/-
87–88	Wash	1	0	0	0	0	
88–89	Wash	1	0	1	1	0	
Totals		2	0	1	1	0	

FELSNER, Brian *5–11 189 LW*
B. Mt. Clemens, Mich., Nov. 11, 1972

SSN	TEAM	GP	G	A	PTS.	PIM	+/-
97–98	Chi	12	1	3	4	12	0

FELSNER, Denny *6–0 195 LW*
B. Warren, Mich., Apr. 29, 1970

SSN	TEAM	GP	G	A	PTS.	PIM	+/-
91–92	StL	3	0	1	1	0	0
92–93	StL	6	0	3	3	2	+4
93–94	StL	6	1	0	1	2	-1
94–95	StL	3	0	0	0	2	-1
Totals		18	1	4	5	6	+2

Playoffs

SSN	TEAM	GP	G	A	PTS.	PIM	+/-
91–92	StL	1	0	0	0	0	
92–93	StL	9	2	3	5	2	
Totals		10	2	3	5	2	

FELTRIN, Anthony Louis (Tony) *5–11 185 D*
B. Ladysmith, B.C., Dec. 6, 1961

SSN	TEAM	GP	G	A	PTS.	PIM	+/-
80–81	Pitt	2	0	0	0	0	-3
81–82	Pitt	4	0	0	0	4	-3
82–83	Pitt	32	3	3	6	40	-11
85–86	NYR	10	0	0	0	21	-3
Totals		48	3	3	6	65	-20

FENTON, Paul John *5–11 180 LW*
B. Springfield, Mass., Dec. 22, 1959

SSN	TEAM	GP	G	A	PTS.	PIM	+/-
84–85	Hart	33	7	5	12	10	+6
85–86	Hart	1	0	0	0	0	+1
86–87	NYR	8	0	0	0	2	-5
87–88	LA	71	20	23	43	46	-14
88–89	LA–Winn	80	16	12	28	39	-16
89–90	Winn	80	32	18	50	40	+2
90–91	Winn–Tor–Calg	78	14	21	35	28	-5
91–92	SJ	60	11	4	15	33	-39
Totals		411	100	83	183	198	-70

Playoffs

SSN	TEAM	GP	G	A	PTS.	PIM	+/-
87–88	LA	5	2	1	3	2	
89–90	Winn	7	2	0	2	23	
90–91	Calg	5	0	0	0	2	
Totals		17	4	1	5	27	

FENYVES, David *5–11 195 D*
B. Dunnville, Ont., Apr. 29, 1960

SSN	TEAM	GP	G	A	PTS.	PIM	+/-
82–83	Buf	24	0	8	8	14	-10
83–84	Buf	10	0	4	4	9	+7
84–85	Buf	60	1	8	9	27	0
85–86	Buf	47	0	7	7	37	-12
86–87	Buf	7	1	0	1	0	-3
87–88	Phil	5	0	0	0	0	-1
88–89	Phil	1	0	1	1	0	0
89–90	Phil	12	0	0	0	4	-6
90–91	Phil	40	1	4	5	28	+1
Totals		206	3	32	35	119	-24

Playoffs

SSN	TEAM	GP	G	A	PTS.	PIM	+/-
82–83	Buf	4	0	0	0	0	
83–84	Buf	2	0	0	0	7	
84–85	Buf	5	0	0	0	2	
Totals		11	0	0	0	9	

FERGUS, Thomas Joseph *6–3 210 C*
B. Chicago, Ill., June 16, 1962

SSN	TEAM	GP	G	A	PTS.	PIM	+/-
81–82	Bos	61	15	24	39	12	+15
82–83	Bos	80	28	35	63	39	+26
83–84	Bos	69	25	36	61	12	+8
84–85	Bos	79	30	43	73	75	+14
85–86	Tor	78	31	42	73	64	-24
86–87	Tor	57	21	28	49	57	+1
87–88	Tor	63	19	31	50	81	+5
88–89	Tor	80	22	45	67	48	-38
89–90	Tor	54	19	26	45	62	-18
90–91	Tor	14	5	4	9	8	-5
91–92	Tor–Van	55	15	23	38	21	-10
92–93	Van	36	5	9	14	20	+1
Totals		726	235	346	581	499	-25

Playoffs

SSN	TEAM	GP	G	A	PTS.	PIM	+/-
81–82	Bos	6	3	0	3	0	
82–83	Bos	15	2	2	4	15	
83–84	Bos	3	2	0	2	9	
84–85	Bos	5	0	0	0	4	
85–86	Tor	10	5	7	12	6	
86–87	Tor	2	0	1	1	2	
87–88	Tor	6	2	3	5	2	
89–90	Tor	5	2	1	3	4	
91–92	Van	13	5	3	8	6	
Totals		65	21	17	38	48	

FERGUSON *F*

SSN	TEAM	GP	G	A	PTS.	PIM	+/-
39–40	Chi	1	0	0	0	0	

FERGUSON, Craig *5–11 190 RW*
B. Castro Valley, Cal., Apr. 8, 1970

SSN	TEAM	GP	G	A	PTS.	PIM	+/-
93–94	Mont	2	0	1	1	0	+1
94–95	Mont	1	0	0	0	0	0
95–96	Mont–Calg	18	1	0	1	6	-9
96–97	Fla	3	0	0	0	0	-1
Totals		24	1	1	2	6	-9

FERGUSON, George Stephen *6–0 195 C*
B. Trenton, Ont., Aug. 22, 1952

SSN	TEAM	GP	G	A	PTS.	PIM	+/-
72–73	Tor	72	10	13	23	34	-17
73–74	Tor	16	0	4	4	4	+1
74–75	Tor	69	19	30	49	61	+5
75–76	Tor	79	12	32	44	76	+11
76–77	Tor	50	9	15	24	24	0
77–78	Tor	73	7	16	23	37	-9
78–79	Pitt	80	21	29	50	37	+10
79–80	Pitt	73	21	28	49	36	0
80–81	Pitt	79	25	18	43	42	-30
81–82	Pitt	71	22	31	53	45	-6
82–83	Pitt–Minn	72	8	12	20	16	-8
83–84	Minn	63	6	10	16	19	-6
Totals		797	160	238	398	431	-49

Playoffs

SSN	TEAM	GP	G	A	PTS.	PIM	+/-
73–74	Tor	3	0	1	1	2	
74–75	Tor	7	1	0	1	7	
75–76	Tor	10	2	4	6	2	
76–77	Tor	9	0	3	3	7	
77–78	Tor	13	5	1	6	7	
78–79	Pitt	7	2	1	3	0	
79–80	Pitt	5	0	3	3	4	
80–81	Pitt	5	2	6	8	9	
81–82	Pitt	5	0	1	1	0	
82–83	Minn	9	0	3	3	4	
83–84	Minn	13	2	0	2	2	
Totals		86	14	23	37	44	

FERGUSON, John Bowie (Fergie) *5-11 190 LW*
B. Vancouver, B.C., Sept. 5, 1938

SSN	TEAM	GP	G	A	PTS.	PIM	+/-
63-64	Mont	59	18	27	45	125	
64-65	Mont	69	17	27	44	156	
65-66	Mont	65	11	14	25	153	
66-67	Mont	67	20	22	42	177	
67-68	Mont	61	15	18	33	117	+18
68-69	Mont	71	29	23	52	45	+30
69-70	Mont	48	19	13	32	139	+11
70-71	Mont	60	16	14	30	32	+2
Totals		500	145	158	303	944	+61

Playoffs

SSN	TEAM	GP	G	A	PTS.	PIM	+/-
63-64	Mont	7	0	1	1	25	
64-65	Mont	13	3	1	4	28	
65-66	Mont	10	2	0	2	44	
66-67	Mont	10	4	2	6	22	
67-68	Mont	13	3	5	8	25	
68-69	Mont	14	4	3	7	80	
70-71	Mont	18	4	6	10	36	
Totals		85	20	18	38	260	

FERGUSON, Lorne Robert (Fergie) *6-0 185 LW*
B. Palmerston, Ont., May 26, 1930

SSN	TEAM	GP	G	A	PTS.	PIM	+/-
49-50	Bos	3	1	1	2	0	
50-51	Bos	70	16	17	33	31	
51-52	Bos	27	3	4	7	14	
54-55	Bos	69	20	14	34	24	
55-56	Bos-Det	63	15	12	27	30	
56-57	Det	70	13	10	23	26	
57-58	Det-Chi	53	7	12	19	24	
58-59	Chi	67	7	10	17	44	
Totals		422	82	80	162	193	

Playoffs

SSN	TEAM	GP	G	A	PTS.	PIM	+/-
50-51	Bos	6	1	0	1	2	
54-55	Bos	4	1	0	1	2	
55-56	Det	10	1	2	3	12	
56-57	Det	5	1	0	1	6	
58-59	Chi	6	2	1	3	2	
Totals		31	6	3	9	24	

FERGUSON, Norman Gerard *5-8 165 RW*
B. Sydney, N.S., Oct. 16, 1945

SSN	TEAM	GP	G	A	PTS.	PIM	+/-
68-69	Oak	76	34	20	54	31	-9
69-70	Oak	72	11	9	20	19	-15
70-71	Cal	54	14	17	31	9	-21
71-72	Cal	77	14	20	34	13	-5
72-73	NY (WHA)	56	28	40	68	8	
73-74	NY-NJ (WHA)	75	15	21	36	12	
74-75	SD (WHA)	78	36	33	69	6	
75-76	SD (WHA)	79	37	37	74	12	
76-77	SD (WHA)	77	39	32	71	5	
77-78	Edm (WHA)	71	26	21	47	2	
NHL Totals		279	73	66	139	72	-50
WHA Totals		436	181	184	365	45	

Playoffs

SSN	TEAM	GP	G	A	PTS.	PIM	+/-
68-69	Cal	7	1	4	5	7	
69-70	Oak	3	0	0	0	0	
74-75	SD (WHA)	10	6	5	11	0	
75-76	SD (WHA)	4	2	0	2	9	
76-77	SD (WHA)	7	2	4	6	0	
77-78	Edm (WHA)	5	0	0	0	0	
NHL Totals		10	1	4	5	7	
WHA Totals		26	10	9	19	9	

FERGUSON, Scott *6-1 195 D*
B. Camrose, Alta., Jan. 6, 1973

SSN	TEAM	GP	G	A	PTS.	PIM	+/-
97-98	Edm	1	0	0	0	0	+1
98-99	Ana	2	0	1	1	0	0
Totals		3	0	1	1	0	+1

FERNER, Mark *6-0 193 D*
B. Regina, Sask., Sept. 5, 1965

SSN	TEAM	GP	G	A	PTS.	PIM	+/-
86-87	Buf	13	0	3	3	9	+2
88-89	Buf	2	0	0	0	2	-2
89-90	Wash	2	0	0	0	0	-1
90-91	Wash	7	0	1	1	4	-2
93-94	Ana	50	3	5	8	30	-20
94-95	Ana-Det	17	0	1	1	6	0
Totals		91	3	10	13	51	-23

FERRARO, Chris *5-10 175 RW*
B. Port Jefferson, N.Y., Jan. 24, 1973

SSN	TEAM	GP	G	A	PTS.	PIM	+/-
95-96	NYR	2	1	0	1	0	-3
96-97	NYR	12	1	1	2	6	+1
97-98	Pitt	46	3	4	7	43	-2
98-99	Edm	2	1	0	1	0	+1
Totals		62	6	5	11	49	-3

FERRARO, Peter *5-10 175 C*
B. Port Jefferson, N.Y., Jan. 24, 1973

SSN	TEAM	GP	G	A	PTS.	PIM	+/-
95-96	NYR	5	0	1	1	0	-6
96-97	NYR	2	0	0	0	0	0
97-98	Pitt-NYR	30	3	4	7	14	-4
98-99	Bos	46	6	8	14	44	+10
Totals		83	9	13	22	58	0

Playoffs

SSN	TEAM	GP	G	A	PTS.	PIM	+/-
96-97	NYR	2	0	0	0	0	

FERRARO, Ray *5-10 185 C*
B. Trail, B.C., Aug. 23, 1964

SSN	TEAM	GP	G	A	PTS.	PIM	+/-
84-85	Hart	44	11	17	28	40	-1
85-86	Hart	76	30	47	77	57	+10
86-87	Hart	80	27	32	59	42	-9
87-88	Hart	68	21	29	50	81	+1
88-89	Hart	80	41	35	76	86	+1
89-90	Hart	79	25	29	54	109	-15
90-91	Hart-NYI	76	21	21	42	70	-12
91-92	NYI	80	40	40	80	92	+25
92-93	NYI	46	14	13	27	40	0
93-94	NYI	82	21	32	53	83	+1
94-95	NYI	47	22	21	43	30	+1
95-96	NYR-LA	76	29	31	60	92	0
96-97	LA	81	25	21	46	112	-22
97-98	LA	40	6	9	15	42	-10
98-99	LA	65	13	18	31	59	0
Totals		1020	346	395	741	1035	-30

Playoffs

SSN	TEAM	GP	G	A	PTS.	PIM	+/-
85-86	Hart	10	3	6	9	4	
86-87	Hart	6	1	1	2	8	
87-88	Hart	6	1	1	2	6	
88-89	Hart	4	2	0	2	4	
89-90	Hart	7	0	3	3	2	
92-93	NYI	18	13	7	20	18	
93-94	NYI	4	1	0	1	6	
97-98	LA	3	0	1	1	2	
Totals		58	21	19	40	50	

FETISOV, Viacheslav *6-1 220 D*
B. Moscow, USSR, May 20, 1958

SSN	TEAM	GP	G	A	PTS.	PIM	+/-
89-90	NJ	72	8	34	42	52	+9
90-91	NJ	67	3	16	19	62	+5
91-92	NJ	70	3	23	26	108	+11
92-93	NJ	76	4	23	27	158	+7
93-94	NJ	52	1	14	15	30	+14
94-95	NJ-Det	18	3	12	15	2	+1
95-96	Det	69	7	35	42	96	+37
96-97	Det	64	5	23	28	76	+26
97-98	Det	58	2	12	14	72	+4
Totals		546	36	192	228	656	+114

Playoffs

SSN	TEAM	GP	G	A	PTS.	PIM	+/-
88-89	NJ	6	0	2	2	10	
89-90	NJ	7	0	0	0	17	
91-92	NJ	6	0	3	3	8	
92-93	NJ	5	0	2	2	4	
93-94	NJ	14	1	0	1	8	
94-95	Det	18	0	8	8	14	
95-96	Det	19	1	4	5	34	
96-97	Det	20	0	4	4	42	
97-98	Det	21	0	3	3	10	
Totals		116	2	26	28	147	

FIDLER, Michael Edward *5-11 195 LW*
B. Everett, Mass., Aug. 19, 1956

SSN	TEAM	GP	G	A	PTS.	PIM	+/-
76-77	Clev	46	17	16	33	17	-5
77-78	Clev	78	23	28	51	38	-13
78-79	Minn	59	23	26	49	42	-25
79-80	Minn	24	5	4	9	13	+3
80-81	Minn-Hart	58	14	21	35	10	-10
81-82	Hart	2	0	1	1	0	
82-83	Chi	4	2	1	3	4	-1
Totals		271	84	97	181	124	-51

FIELD, Wilfred Spence *5-11 185 D*
B. Winnipeg, Man., Apr. 29, 1915

SSN	TEAM	GP	G	A	PTS.	PIM	+/-
36-37	NYA	1	0	0	0	0	
38-39	NYA	43	1	3	4	37	
39-40	NYA	45	1	3	4	28	
40-41	NYA	36	5	6	11	31	
41-42	Brk	41	6	9	15	23	
44-45	Mont-Chi	48	4	4	8	32	
Totals		214	17	25	42	151	

Playoffs

SSN	TEAM	GP	G	A	PTS.	PIM	+/-
38-39	NYA	2	0	0	0	2	
39-40	NYA	3	0	0	0	0	
Totals		5	0	0	0	2	

FIELDER, Guyle Abner (Guy) *5-9 165 C*
B. Potlatch, Idaho, Nov. 21, 1930

SSN	TEAM	GP	G	A	PTS.	PIM	+/-
50-51	Chi	30	0	0	0	0	
57-58	Det	6	0	0	0	2	
Totals		36	0	0	0	2	

Playoffs

SSN	TEAM	GP	G	A	PTS.	PIM	+/-
52-53	Det	4	0	0	0	0	
53-54	Bos	2	0	0	0	2	
Totals		6	0	0	0	2	

FILIMONOV, Dmitri *6-4 220 D*
B. Perm, USSR, Oct. 14, 1971

SSN	TEAM	GP	G	A	PTS.	PIM	+/-
93-94	Ott	30	1	4	5	18	-10

FILLION, Louis Robert (Bob) *5-9 170 LW*
B. Thetford Mines, Que., July 12, 1921

SSN	TEAM	GP	G	A	PTS.	PIM	+/-
43-44	Mont	41	7	23	30	14	
44-45	Mont	31	6	8	14	12	
45-46	Mont	50	10	6	16	12	
46-47	Mont	57	6	3	9	16	
47-48	Mont	32	4	9	13	8	
48-49	Mont	59	3	9	12	14	
49-50	Mont	57	1	3	4	8	
Totals		327	37	61	98	84	

Playoffs

SSN	TEAM	GP	G	A	PTS.	PIM	+/-
43-44	Mont	3	0	0	0	0	
44-45	Mont	1	3	0	3	0	
45-46	Mont	9	4	3	7	6	
46-47	Mont	8	0	0	0	0	
48-49	Mont	7	0	1	1	4	
49-50	Mont	5	0	0	0	0	
Totals		33	7	4	11	10	

FILLION, Marcel *5-7 175 LW*
B. Thetford Mines, Que., May 28, 1923

SSN	TEAM	GP	G	A	PTS.	PIM	+/-
44-45	Bos	1	0	0	0	0	

FILMORE, Thomas *5-11 189 RW*
B. Thamesford, Ont., 1906

SSN	TEAM	GP	G	A	PTS.	PIM	+/-
30-31	Det	40	6	2	8	10	
31-32	Det-NYA	40	8	6	14	14	
32-33	NYA	33	1	4	5	9	
33-34	Bos	3	0	0	0	0	
Totals		116	15	12	27	33	

FINKBEINER, Lloyd *F*
B. Guelph, Ont., Mar. 12, 1920

SSN	TEAM	GP	G	A	PTS.	PIM	+/-
40-41	NYA	1	0	0	0	0	

FINLEY, Jeff *6-2 204 D*
B. Edmonton, Alta., Apr. 14. 1967

SSN	TEAM	GP	G	A	PTS.	PIM	+/-
87-88	NYI	10	0	5	5	15	+5
88-89	NYI	4	0	0	0	6	+1
89-90	NYI	11	0	1	1	0	0
90-91	NYI	11	0	0	0	4	-1
91-92	NYI	51	1	10	11	26	-6
93-94	Phil	55	1	8	9	24	+16
95-96	Winn	65	1	5	6	81	-2
96-97	Phoe	65	3	7	10	40	-8
97-98	NYR	63	1	6	7	55	-3
98-99	NYR-StL	32	1	2	3	20	+11
Totals		367	8	44	52	271	+13

Playoffs

SSN	TEAM	GP	G	A	PTS.	PIM	+/-
87-88	NYI	1	0	0	0	2	
89-90	NYI	5	0	2	2	2	
95-96	Winn	6	0	0	0	4	
96-97	Phoe	1	0	0	0	2	

SSN	TEAM	GP	G	A	PTS.	PIM	+/-
98–99	StL	13	1	2	3	8	
Totals		26	1	4	5	18	

FINN, Steven 6–0 198 D
B. Laval, Que., Aug. 20, 1966

SSN	TEAM	GP	G	A	PTS.	PIM	+/-
85–86	Que	17	0	1	1	28	0
86–87	Que	36	2	5	7	40	-8
87–88	Que	75	3	7	10	198	-4
88–89	Que	77	2	6	8	235	-21
89–90	Que	64	3	9	12	208	-33
90–91	Que	71	6	13	19	228	-26
91–92	Que	65	4	7	11	194	-9
92–93	Que	80	5	9	14	160	-3
93–94	Que	80	4	13	17	159	-9
94–95	Que	40	0	3	3	64	+1
95–96	TB–LA	66	3	2	5	126	-12
96–97	LA	54	2	3	5	84	-8
Totals		725	34	78	112	1724	-132

Playoffs

86–87	Que	13	0	2	2	29	
92–93	Que	6	0	1	1	8	
94–95	Que	4	0	1	1	2	
Totals		23	0	3	3	39	

FINNEY, Joseph Sidney (Sid) 5–10 160 C
B. Banbridge, Ireland, May 1, 1929

51–52	Chi	35	6	5	11	0	
52–53	Chi	18	4	2	6	4	
53–54	Chi	6	0	0	0	0	
Totals		59	10	7	17	4	

Playoffs

| 52–53 | Chi | 7 | 0 | 0 | 0 | 2 | |

*FINNIGAN, Edward F
B. Shawville, Que.

| 35–36 | Bos | 3 | 0 | 0 | 0 | 0 | |

*FINNIGAN, Frank 5–9 165 RW
B. Shawville, Que., July 9, 1903

23–24	Ott	4	0	0	0	0	
24–25	Ott	29	0	0	0	20	
25–26	Ott	36	2	0	2	24	
26–27	Ott	36	15	1	16	52	
27–28	Ott	38	20	5	25	34	
28–29	Ott	44	15	4	19	71	
29–30	Ott	43	21	15	36	46	
30–31	Ott	44	9	8	17	40	
31–32	Tor	47	8	13	21	45	
32–33	Tor	45	4	14	18	37	
33–34	Tor	48	10	10	20	10	
34–35	StL–Tor	45	7	5	12	12	
35–36	Tor	48	2	6	8	10	
36–37	Tor	48	2	7	9	4	
Totals		555	115	88	203	405	

Playoffs

25–26	Ott	2	0	0	0	0	
26–27	Ott	6	3	0	3	2	
27–28	Ott	2	0	1	1	4	
29–30	Ott	2	0	0	0	2	
31–32	Tor	7	2	3	5	8	
34–35	Tor	7	1	2	3	2	
35–36	Tor	9	0	3	3	0	
36–37	Tor	2	0	0	0	0	
Totals		37	6	9	15	18	

FIORENTINO, Peter 6–1 200 D
B. Niagara Falls, Ont., Dec. 22, 1968

| 91–92 | NYR | 1 | 0 | 0 | 0 | 0 | 0 |

FISCHER, Ronald Alexander 6–2 195 D
B. Merritt, B.C., Apr. 12, 1959

81–82	Buf	15	0	7	7	6	-3
82–83	Buf	3	0	0	0	0	0
Totals		18	0	7	7	6	-3

*FISHER, Alvin F

| 24–25 | Tor | 9 | 1 | 0 | 1 | 4 | |

FISHER, Craig 6–3 185 C
B. Oshawa, Ont., June 30, 1970

89–90	Phil	2	0	0	0	0	0
90–91	Phil	2	0	0	0	0	0
93–94	Winn	4	0	0	0	2	-1

| 96–97 | Fla | 4 | 0 | 0 | 0 | 0 | -2 |
| **Totals** | | 12 | 0 | 0 | 0 | 2 | -3 |

FISHER, Duncan Robert (Dunc) 5–8 165 RW
B. Regina, Sask., Aug. 30, 1927

48–49	NYR	60	9	16	25	40	
49–50	NYR	70	12	21	33	42	
50–51	NYR–Bos	65	9	20	29	20	
51–52	Bos	65	15	12	27	2	
52–53	Bos	7	0	1	1	0	
58–59	Det	8	0	0	0	0	
Totals		275	45	70	115	104	

Playoffs

47–48	NYR	1	0	1	1	0	
49–50	NYR	12	3	3	6	14	
50–51	Bos	6	1	0	1	0	
51–52	Bos	2	0	0	0	0	
Totals		21	4	4	8	14	

FISHER, Joseph H. 6–0 175 RW
B. Medicine Hat, Alta., July 4, 1916

39–40	Det	34	2	4	6	2	
40–41	Det	28	5	8	13	11	
41–42	Det	3	0	0	0	0	
42–43	Det	1	1	0	1	0	
Totals		66	8	12	20	13	

Playoffs

39–40	Det	5	1	1	2	0	
40–41	Det	9	1	0	1	6	
42–43	Det	1	0	0	0	0	
Totals		15	2	1	3	6	

FITCHNER, Robert Douglas 6–0 190 C
B. Sudbury, Ont., Dec. 22, 1950

73–74	Edm (WHA)	31	1	2	3	21	
74–75	Ind (WHA)	78	11	19	30	96	
75–76	Ind–Que (WHA)	73	22	25	47	134	
76–77	Que (WHA)	81	9	30	39	105	
77–78	Que (WHA)	72	15	28	43	76	
78–79	Que (WHA)	79	10	35	45	69	
79–80	Que	70	11	20	31	59	-24
80–81	Que	8	1	0	1	0	-1
NHL Totals		78	12	20	32	59	-25
WHA Totals		414	68	139	207	501	

Playoffs

75–76	Que (WHA)	5	1	0	1	8	
76–77	Que (WHA)	17	3	3	6	16	
77–78	Que (WHA)	11	1	6	7	10	
78–79	Que (WHA)	4	1	3	4	0	
80–81	Que	3	0	0	0	10	
NHL Totals		3	0	0	0	10	
WHA Totals		37	6	12	18	34	

FITZGERALD, Rusty 6–1 190 C
B. Minneapolis, Minn., Oct. 4, 1972

94–95	Pitt	4	1	0	1	0	+2
95–96	Pitt	21	1	2	3	12	+7
Totals		25	2	2	4	12	+9

Playoffs

| 94–95 | Pitt | 5 | 0 | 0 | 0 | 4 | |

FITZGERALD, Tom 6–1 195 C
B. Melrose, Mass., Aug. 28, 1968

88–89	NYI	23	3	5	8	10	+1
89–90	NYI	19	2	5	7	4	-3
90–91	NYI	41	5	5	10	24	-9
91–92	NYI	45	6	11	17	28	-3
92–93	NYI	77	9	18	27	34	-2
93–94	Fla	83	18	14	32	54	-3
94–95	Fla	48	3	13	16	31	-3
95–96	Fla	82	13	21	34	75	-3
96–97	Fla	71	10	14	24	64	+7
97–98	Fla–Col A	80	12	6	18	79	-4
98–99	Nash	80	13	19	32	48	-18
Totals		649	94	131	225	451	-40

Playoffs

89–90	NYI	4	1	0	1	4	
92–93	NYI	18	2	5	7	18	
95–96	Fla	22	4	4	8	34	
96–97	Fla	5	0	1	1	0	

| 97–98 | Col A | 7 | 0 | 1 | 1 | 20 | |
| **Totals** | | 56 | 7 | 11 | 18 | 76 | |

FITZPATRICK, Alexander Stewart (Sandy)
6–1 195 C
B. Paisley, Scotland, Dec. 22, 1944

64–65	NYR	4	0	0	0	2	
67–68	Minn	18	3	6	9	6	0
Totals		22	3	6	9	8	0

Playoffs

| 67–68 | Minn | 12 | 0 | 0 | 0 | 0 | |

FITZPATRICK, Rory 6–1 195 D
B. Rochester, N.Y., Jan. 11, 1975

95–96	Mont	42	0	2	2	18	-7
96–97	Mont–StL	8	0	1	1	8	-4
98–99	StL	1	0	0	0	2	-3
Totals		51	0	3	3	28	-14

Playoffs

| 95–96 | Mont | 6 | 1 | 1 | 2 | 0 | |

FITZPATRICK, Ross 6–0 190 C
B. Penticton, B.C., Oct. 7, 1960

82–83	Phil	1	0	0	0	0	-1
83–84	Phil	12	4	2	6	0	+4
84–85	Phil	5	1	0	1	0	-3
85–86	Phil	2	0	0	0	0	-1
Totals		20	5	2	7	0	-1

FLAMIN, Ferdinand Charles (Fernie) 5–10
190 D
B. Dysart, Sask., Jan. 25, 1927

44–45	Bos	1	0	0	0	0	
45–46	Bos	1	0	0	0	0	
46–47	Bos	23	1	4	5	41	
47–48	Bos	56	4	6	10	69	
48–49	Bos	60	4	12	16	62	
49–50	Bos	69	2	5	7	122	
50–51	Bos–Tor	53	3	7	10	101	
51–52	Tor	61	0	7	7	110	
52–53	Tor	66	2	6	8	110	
53–54	Tor	62	0	8	8	84	
54–55	Bos	70	4	14	18	150	
55–56	Bos	62	4	17	21	70	
56–57	Bos	68	6	25	31	108	
57–58	Bos	66	0	15	15	71	
58–59	Bos	70	0	21	21	101	
59–60	Bos	60	2	18	20	112	
60–61	Bos	62	2	9	11	59	
Totals		910	34	174	208	1370	

Playoffs

46–47	Bos	5	0	0	0	8	
47–48	Bos	5	0	0	0	12	
48–49	Bos	5	0	1	1	8	
50–51	Tor	9	1	0	1	8	
51–52	Tor	4	0	2	2	18	
53–54	Tor	2	0	0	0	0	
54–55	Bos	4	1	0	1	2	
56–57	Bos	10	0	3	3	19	
57–58	Bos	12	2	2	4	10	
58–59	Bos	7	0	0	0	8	
Totals		63	4	8	12	93	

FLATLEY, Patrick 6–2 197 RW
B. Toronto, Ont., Oct. 3, 1963

83–84	NYI	16	2	7	9	6	+3
84–85	NYI	78	20	31	51	106	-8
85–86	NYI	73	18	34	52	66	+20
86–87	NYI	63	16	35	51	81	+17
87–88	NYI	40	9	15	24	28	+7
88–89	NYI	41	10	15	25	31	-5
89–90	NYI	62	17	32	49	101	+10
90–91	NYI	56	20	25	45	74	-2
91–92	NYI	38	8	28	36	31	+14
92–93	NYI	80	13	47	60	63	+5
93–94	NYI	64	12	30	42	40	+12
94–95	NYI	45	7	20	27	12	+9
95–96	NYI	56	8	9	17	21	-24
96–97	NYR	68	10	12	22	26	+6
Totals		780	170	340	510	686	+64

Playoffs

| 83–84 | NYI | 21 | 9 | 6 | 15 | 14 | |
| 84–85 | NYI | 4 | 1 | 0 | 1 | 6 | |

SSN	TEAM	GP	G	A	PTS.	PIM	+/-
85–86	NYI	3	0	0	0	21	
86–87	NYI	11	3	2	5	6	
89–90	NYI	5	3	0	3	2	
92–93	NYI	15	2	7	9	12	
96–97	NYR	11	0	0	0	14	
Totals		70	18	15	33	75	

FLEMING, Gerry 6–5 253 LW
B. Montreal, Que., Oct. 16, 1967

SSN	TEAM	GP	G	A	PTS.	PIM	+/-
93–94	Mont	5	0	0	0	25	-4
94–95	Mont	6	0	0	0	17	-1
Totals		11	0	0	0	42	-5

FLEMING, Reginald Stephen (Reggie) 5–10 185 LW
B. Montreal, Que., Apr. 21, 1936

SSN	TEAM	GP	G	A	PTS.	PIM	+/-
59–60	Mont	3	0	0	0	2	
60–61	Chi	66	4	4	8	145	
61–62	Chi	70	7	9	16	71	
62–63	Chi	64	7	7	14	99	
63–64	Chi	61	3	6	9	140	
64–65	Bos	67	18	23	41	136	
65–66	Bos–NYR	69	14	20	34	166	
66–67	NYR	61	15	16	31	146	
67–68	NYR	73	17	7	24	132	+1
68–69	NYR	72	8	12	20	138	-13
69–70	Phil	65	9	18	27	134	-4
70–71	Buf	78	6	10	16	159	-8
72–73	Chi (WHA)	74	23	45	68	93	
73–74	Chi (WHA)	45	2	12	14	49	
NHL Totals		749	108	132	240	1468	-24
WHA Totals		119	25	57	82	142	

Playoffs

SSN	TEAM	GP	G	A	PTS.	PIM	+/-
60–61	Chi	12	1	0	1	12	
61–62	Chi	12	2	2	4	27	
62–63	Chi	6	0	0	0	27	
63–64	Chi	7	0	0	0	18	
66–67	NYR	4	0	2	2	11	
67–68	NYR	6	0	2	2	4	
68–69	NYR	3	0	0	0	7	
73–74	Chi (WHA)	12	0	4	4	12	
NHL Totals		50	3	6	9	106	
WHA Totals		12	0	4	4	12	

*FLESCH F

SSN	TEAM	GP	G	A	PTS.	PIM
20–21	Ham	1	0	0	0	0

FLESCH, John Patrick 6–2 200 LW
B. Sudbury, Ont., July 15, 1953

SSN	TEAM	GP	G	A	PTS.	PIM	+/-
74–75	Minn	57	8	15	23	47	-19
75–76	Minn	33	3	2	5	47	-8
77–78	Pitt	29	7	5	12	19	-7
79–80	Col	5	0	1	1	4	-1
Totals		124	18	23	41	117	-35

FLETCHER, Steven 6–3 205 LW
B. Montreal, Que., Mar. 31, 1962

SSN	TEAM	GP	G	A	PTS.	PIM	+/-
88–89	Winn	3	0	0	0	5	-1

Playoffs

SSN	TEAM	GP	G	A	PTS.	PIM
97–98	Mont	1	0	0	0	5

*FLETT, William Myer (Cowboy) 6–1 205 RW
B. Vermillion, Alta., July 21, 1943

SSN	TEAM	GP	G	A	PTS.	PIM	+/-
67–68	LA	73	26	20	46	97	+4
68–69	LA	72	24	25	49	53	-24
69–70	LA	69	14	18	32	70	-27
70–71	LA	64	13	24	37	57	-30
71–72	LA–Phil	76	18	22	40	44	-25
72–73	Phil	69	43	31	74	53	+31
73–74	Phil	67	17	27	44	51	+20
74–75	Tor	77	15	25	40	38	0
75–76	Atl	78	23	17	40	30	+9
76–77	Atl	24	4	4	8	6	+1
76–77	Edm (WHA)	48	34	20	54	20	
77–78	Edm (WHA)	74	41	28	69	34	
78–79	Edm (WHA)	73	28	36	64	14	
79–80	Edm	20	5	2	7	2	-17
NHL Totals		689	202	215	417	501	-58
WHA Totals		195	103	84	187	68	

Playoffs

SSN	TEAM	GP	G	A	PTS.	PIM
67–68	LA	7	1	2	3	8
68–69	LA	10	3	4	7	11
72–73	Phil	11	3	4	7	0
73–74	Phil	17	0	6	6	21

SSN	TEAM	GP	G	A	PTS.	PIM	+/-
74–75	Tor	5	0	0	0	2	
75–76	Atl	2	0	0	0	0	
76–77	Edm (WHA)	5	0	2	2	2	
78–79	Edm (WHA)	10	5	2	7	2	
NHL Totals		52	7	16	23	42	
WHA Totals		15	5	4	9	4	

FLEURY, Theoren 5–6 160 RW
B. Oxbow, Sask., June 29, 1968

SSN	TEAM	GP	G	A	PTS.	PIM	+/-
88–89	Calg	36	14	20	34	46	+5
89–90	Calg	80	31	35	66	157	+22
90–91	Calg	79	51	53	104	136	+48
91–92	Calg	80	33	40	73	133	0
92–93	Calg	83	34	66	100	88	+14
93–94	Calg	83	40	45	85	186	+30
94–95	Calg	47	29	29	58	112	+6
95–96	Calg	80	46	50	96	112	+17
96–97	Calg	81	29	38	67	104	-12
97–98	Calg	82	27	51	78	197	0
98–99	Calg–Col A	75	40	53	93	86	+26
Totals		806	374	480	854	1357	+156

Playoffs

SSN	TEAM	GP	G	A	PTS.	PIM
88–89	Calg	22	5	6	11	24
89–90	Calg	6	2	3	5	10
90–91	Calg	7	2	5	7	14
92–93	Calg	6	5	7	12	27
93–94	Calg	7	6	4	10	5
94–95	Calg	7	7	7	14	2
95–96	Calg	4	2	1	3	14
98–99	Col A	18	5	12	17	20
Totals		77	34	45	79	116

FLICHEL, Todd 6–3 195 D
B. Osgoode, Ont., Sept. 14, 1964

SSN	TEAM	GP	G	A	PTS.	PIM	+/-
87–88	Winn	2	0	0	0	2	-4
88–89	Winn	1	0	0	0	0	-1
89–90	Winn	3	0	1	1	2	0
Totals		6	0	1	1	4	-5

FLOCKHART, Robert Walter (Rob) 6–0 185 RW
B. Sicamous, B.C., Feb. 6, 1956

SSN	TEAM	GP	G	A	PTS.	PIM	+/-
76–77	Van	5	0	0	0	0	+1
77–78	Van	24	0	1	1	9	-14
78–79	Van	14	1	1	2	0	-3
79–80	Minn	10	1	3	4	2	-4
80–81	Minn	2	0	0	0	0	-2
Totals		55	2	5	7	11	-22

Playoffs

SSN	TEAM	GP	G	A	PTS.	PIM
79–80	Minn	1	1	0	1	2

FLOCKHART, Ronald 5–11 185 C
B. Smithers, B.C., Oct. 10, 1960

SSN	TEAM	GP	G	A	PTS.	PIM	+/-
80–81	Phil	14	3	7	10	11	+6.
81–82	Phil	72	33	39	72	44	+18
82–83	Phil	73	29	31	60	49	+3
83–84	Phil–Pitt	76	27	21	48	44	-18
84–85	Pitt–Mont	54	10	17	27	18	+7
85–86	StL	79	22	45	67	26	+8
86–87	StL	60	16	19	35	12	-9
87–88	StL	21	5	4	9	4	+5
88–89	Bos	4	0	0	0	0	-3
Totals		453	145	183	328	208	+17

Playoffs

SSN	TEAM	GP	G	A	PTS.	PIM
80–81	Phil	3	1	0	1	2
81–82	Phil	4	0	1	1	2
82–83	Phil	2	1	1	2	2
84–85	Mont	2	1	1	2	2
85–86	StL	8	1	3	4	6
Totals		19	4	6	10	14

FLOYD, Larry David 5–8 180 C
B. Peterborough, Ont., May 1, 1961

SSN	TEAM	GP	G	A	PTS.	PIM	+/-
82–83	NJ	5	1	0	1	2	-4
83–84	NJ	7	1	3	4	7	-4
Totals		12	2	3	5	9	-8

FOGARTY, Bryan 6–2 206 D
B. Brantford, Ont., June 11, 1969

SSN	TEAM	GP	G	A	PTS.	PIM	+/-
89–90	Que	45	4	10	14	31	-47
90–91	Que	45	9	22	31	24	-11
91–92	Que	20	3	12	15	16	-15
92–93	Pitt	12	0	4	4	4	-3

SSN	TEAM	GP	G	A	PTS.	PIM	+/-
93–94	Mont	13	1	2	3	10	-4
94–95	Mont	21	5	2	7	34	-3
Totals		156	22	52	74	119	-83

FOGOLIN, Lee Joseph 6–0 205 D
B. Chicago, Ill., Feb. 7, 1955

SSN	TEAM	GP	G	A	PTS.	PIM	+/-
74–75	Buf	50	2	2	4	59	0
75–76	Buf	58	0	9	9	64	+15
76–77	Buf	71	3	15	18	100	+9
77–78	Buf	76	0	23	23	98	+7
78–79	Buf	74	3	19	22	103	-4
79–80	Edm	80	5	10	15	104	-8
80–81	Edm	80.	13	17	30	139	+2
81–82	Edm	80	4	25	29	154	+40
82–83	Edm	72	0	18	18	92	+24
83–84	Edm	80	5	16	21	125	+33
84–85	Edm	79	4	14	18	126	+16
85–86	Edm	80	4	22	26	129	+47
86–87	Edm–Buf	44	1	5	6	25	-7
Totals		924	44	195	239	1318	+177

Playoffs

SSN	TEAM	GP	G	A	PTS.	PIM
74–75	Buf	8	0	0	0	6
75–76	Buf	9	0	4	4	23
76–77	Buf	4	0	0	0	2
77–78	Buf	6	0	2	2	23
78–79	Buf	3	0	0	0	4
79–80	Edm	3	0	0	0	4
80–81	Edm	9	0	0	0	12
81–82	Edm	5	1	1	2	14
82–83	Edm	16	0	5	5	36
83–84	Edm	19	1	4	5	23
84–85	Edm	18	3	1	4	16
85–86	Edm	8	0	2	2	10
Totals		108	5	19	24	173

FOGOLIN, Lidio John (Lee) 5–11 200 D
B. Fort William, Ont., Feb. 27, 1926

SSN	TEAM	GP	G	A	PTS.	PIM
48–49	Det	43	1	2	3	59
49–50	Det	64	4	8	12	63
50–51	Det–Chi	54	3	11	14	79
51–52	Chi	69	0	9	9	96
52–53	Chi	70	2	8	10	79
53–54	Chi	68	0	1	1	95
54–55	Chi	9	0	1	1	16
55–56	Chi	51	0	8	8	88
Totals		428	10	48	58	575

Playoffs

SSN	TEAM	GP	G	A	PTS.	PIM
47–48	Det	2	0	1	1	6
48–49	Det	9	0	0	0	4
49–50	Det	10	0	0	0	16
52–53	Chi	7	0	1	1	4
Totals		28	0	2	2	30

FOLCO, Peter Kevin 6–0 185 D
B. Montreal, Que., Aug. 13, 1953

SSN	TEAM	GP	G	A	PTS.	PIM	+/-
73–74	Van	2	0	0	0	0	-1
75–76	Tor (WHA)	19	1	8	9	15	
76–77	Birm (WHA)	2	0	0	0	0	
NHL Totals		2	0	0	0	0	-1
WHA Totals		21	1	8	9	15	

FOLEY, Gerald James 6–0 172 RW
B. Ware, Mass., Sept. 22, 1932

SSN	TEAM	GP	G	A	PTS.	PIM	+/-
54–55	Tor	4	0	0	0	8	
56–57	NYR	69	7	9	16	48	
57–58	NYR	68	2	5	7	43	
68–69	LA	1	0	0	0	0	-1
Totals		142	9	14	23	99	-1

Playoffs

SSN	TEAM	GP	G	A	PTS.	PIM
56–57	NYR	3	0	0	0	0
57–58	NYR	6	0	1	1	2
Totals		9	0	1	1	2

FOLEY, Gilbert Anthony (Rick) 6–4 225 D
B. Niagara Falls, Ont., Sept. 22, 1945

SSN	TEAM	GP	G	A	PTS.	PIM	+/-
70–71	Chi	2	0	1	1	8	+1
71–72	Phil	58	11	25	36	168	-16
73–74	Det	7	0	0	0	4	-7
75–76	Tor (WHA)	11	1	2	3	6	
NHL Totals		67	11	26	37	180	-22
WHA Totals		11	1	2	3	6	

SSN	TEAM	GP	G	A	PTS.	PIM	+/-

Playoffs

SSN	TEAM	GP	G	A	PTS.	PIM
70–71	Chi	4	0	1	1	4

FOLIGNO, Mike Anthony *6–2 195 RW*
B. Sudbury, Ont., Jan. 29, 1959

SSN	TEAM	GP	G	A	PTS.	PIM	+/-
79–80	Det	80	36	35	71	109	-2
80–81	Det	80	28	35	63	210	-13
81–82	Det–Buf	82	33	44	77	177	+19
82–83	Buf	66	22	25	47	135	+9
83–84	Buf	70	32	31	63	151	+32
84–85	Buf	77	27	29	56	154	+16
85–86	Buf	79	41	39	80	168	+25
86–87	Buf	75	30	29	59	176	+13
87–88	Buf	74	29	28	57	220	-11
88–89	Buf	75	27	22	49	156	-7
89–90	Buf	61	15	25	40	99	+13
90–91	Buf–Tor	68	12	12	24	107	-7
91–92	Tor	33	6	8	14	50	-3
92–93	Tor	55	13	5	18	84	+2
93–94	Tor–Fla	43	4	5	9	53	+7
Totals		1018	355	372	727	2049	+93

Playoffs

SSN	TEAM	GP	G	A	PTS.	PIM
81–82	Buf	4	2	0	2	9
82–83	Buf	10	2	3	5	39
83–84	Buf	3	2	1	3	19
84–85	Buf	5	1	3	4	12
87–88	Buf	6	3	2	5	31
88–89	Buf	5	3	1	4	21
89–90	Buf	6	0	1	1	12
92–93	Tor	18	2	6	8	42
Totals		57	15	17	32	185

FOLK, William Joseph *6–0 190 D*
B. Regina, Sask., July 11, 1927

SSN	TEAM	GP	G	A	PTS.	PIM
51–52	Det	8	0	0	0	2
52–53	Det	4	0	0	0	2
Totals		12	0	0	0	4

FONTAINE, Leonard Joseph *5–7 165 RW*
B. Quebec City, Que., Feb. 25, 1948

SSN	TEAM	GP	G	A	PTS.	PIM	+/-
72–73	Det	39	8	10	18	6	-2
73–74	Det	7	0	1	1	4	-2
74–75	Mich (WHA)	21	1	8	9	6	
NHL Totals		46	8	11	19	10	-4
WHA Totals		21	1	8	9	6	

FONTAS, Jon *5–10 185 C*
B. Arlington, Mass., Apr. 16, 1955

SSN	TEAM	GP	G	A	PTS.	PIM	+/-
79–80	Minn	1	0	0	0	0	-1
80–81	Minn	1	0	0	0	0	0
Totals		2	0	0	0	0	-1

FONTEYNE, Valere Ronald (Val) *5–9 155 LW*
B. Wetaskiwin, Alta., Dec. 2, 1933

SSN	TEAM	GP	G	A	PTS.	PIM	+/-
59–60	Det	69	4	7	11	2	
60–61	Det	66	6	11	17	4	
61–62	Det	70	5	5	10	4	
62–63	Det	67	6	14	20	2	
63–64	NYR	69	7	18	25	4	
64–65	NYR–Det	43	2	6	8	8	
65–66	Det	59	5	10	15	0	
66–67	Det	28	1	1	2	0	
67–68	Pitt	69	6	28	34	0	-23
68–69	Pitt	74	12	17	29	2	-25
69–70	Pitt	68	11	15	26	2	-4
70–71	Pitt	70	4	9	13	0	-8
71–72	Pitt	68	6	13	19	0	-1
72–73	Alb (WHA)	77	7	32	39	2	
73–74	Edm (WHA)	72	9	13	22	2	
NHL Totals		820	75	154	229	28	-61
WHA Totals		149	16	45	61	4	

Playoffs

SSN	TEAM	GP	G	A	PTS.	PIM
59–60	Det	6	0	4	4	0
60–61	Det	11	2	3	5	0
62–63	Det	11	0	0	0	2
64–65	Det	5	0	1	1	0
65–66	Det	12	1	0	1	4
69–70	Pitt	10	0	2	2	0
71–72	Pitt	4	0	0	0	2
73–74	Edm (WHA)	5	1	0	1	0
NHL Totals		59	3	10	13	8
WHA Totals		5	1	0	1	0

FONTINATO, Louis (Louie, The Leaper) *6–1 195 D*
B. Guelph, Ont., Jan. 20, 1932

SSN	TEAM	GP	G	A	PTS.	PIM
54–55	NYR	27	2	2	4	60
55–56	NYR	70	3	15	18	202
56–57	NYR	70	3	12	15	139
57–58	NYR	70	3	8	11	152
58–59	NYR	64	7	6	13	149
59–60	NYR	64	2	11	13	137
60–61	NYR	53	2	3	5	100
61–62	Mont	54	2	13	15	167
62–63	Mont	63	2	8	10	141
Totals		535	26	78	104	1247

Playoffs

SSN	TEAM	GP	G	A	PTS.	PIM
55–56	NYR	4	0	0	0	6
56–57	NYR	5	0	0	0	7
57–58	NYR	6	0	1	1	6
61–62	Mont	6	0	1	1	23
Totals		21	0	2	2	42

FOOTE, Adam *6–1 202 D*
B. Toronto, Ont., July 10, 1971

SSN	TEAM	GP	G	A	PTS.	PIM	+/-
91–92	Que	46	2	5	7	44	-4
92–93	Que	81	4	12	16	168	+6
93–94	Que	45	2	6	8	67	+3
94–95	Que	35	0	7	7	52	+17
95–96	Col A	73	5	11	16	88	+27
96–97	Col A	78	2	19	21	135	+16
97–98	Col A	77	3	14	17	124	-3
98–99	Col A	64	5	16	21	92	+20
Totals		499	23	90	113	768	+82

Playoffs

SSN	TEAM	GP	G	A	PTS.	PIM
92–93	Que	6	0	1	1	2
94–95	Que	6	0	1	1	14
95–96	Col A	22	1	3	4	36
96–97	Col A	17	0	4	4	62
97–98	Col A	7	0	0	0	23
98–99	Col A	19	2	3	5	24
Totals		77	3	12	15	161

FORBES, Colin *6–3 205 LW*
B. New Westminster, B.C., Feb. 16, 1976

SSN	TEAM	GP	G	A	PTS.	PIM	+/-
96–97	Phil	3	1	0	1	0	0
97–98	Phil	63	12	7	19	59	-2
98–99	Phil–TB	80	12	8	20	61	-5
Totals		146	25	15	40	110	-7

Playoffs

SSN	TEAM	GP	G	A	PTS.	PIM
96–97	Phil	3	0	0	0	0
97–98	Phil	5	0	0	0	2
Totals		8	0	0	0	2

FORBES, David Stephen *5–10 180 LW*
B. Montreal, Que., Nov. 6, 1948

SSN	TEAM	GP	G	A	PTS.	PIM	+/-
73–74	Bos	63	10	16	26	41	+9
74–75	Bos	69	18	12	30	80	+22
75–76	Bos	79	16	13	29	52	+15
76–77	Bos	73	9	11	20	47	+13
77–78	Wash	77	11	11	22	119	-34
78–79	Wash	2	0	1	1	2	0
78–79	Cin (WHA)	73	6	5	11	83	
NHL Totals		363	64	64	128	341	+25
WHA Totals		73	6	5	11	83	

Playoffs

SSN	TEAM	GP	G	A	PTS.	PIM
73–74	Bos	16	0	2	2	6
74–75	Bos	3	0	0	0	0
75–76	Bos	12	1	1	2	5
76–77	Bos	14	0	1	1	2
78–79	Cin (WHA)	3	0	1	1	7
NHL Totals		45	1	4	5	13
WHA Totals		3	0	1	1	7

FORBES, Michael D. *6–2 200 D*
B. Brampton, Ont., Sept. 20, 1957

SSN	TEAM	GP	G	A	PTS.	PIM	+/-
77–78	Bos	32	0	4	4	15	-5
79–80	Edm	2	0	0	0	0	-4
81–82	Edm	16	1	7	8	26	+14
Totals		50	1	11	12	41	+5

FOREY, Conley Michael (Connie) *6–2 185 LW*
B. Montreal, Que., Oct. 18, 1950

SSN	TEAM	GP	G	A	PTS.	PIM	+/-
73–74	StL	4	0	0	0	2	-1

FORSBERG, Peter *6–0 190 C*
B. Ornsköldsvik, Sweden, July 20, 1973

SSN	TEAM	GP	G	A	PTS.	PIM	+/-
94–95	Que	47	15	35	50	16	+17
95–96	Col A	82	30	86	116	47	+25
96–97	Col A	65	28	58	86	73	+31
97–98	Col A	72	25	66	91	94	-6
98–99	Col A	78	30	67	97	108	+27
Totals		344	128	312	440	338	+94

Playoffs

SSN	TEAM	GP	G	A	PTS.	PIM
94–95	Que	6	2	4	6	4
95–96	Col A	22	10	11	21	18
96–97	Col A	14	5	12	17	10
97–98	Col A	7	6	5	11	12
98–99	Col A	19	8	16	24	31
Totals		68	31	48	79	75

*FORSEY, John (Jack) *F*

SSN	TEAM	GP	G	A	PTS.	PIM
42–43	Tor	19	7	9	16	10

Playoffs

SSN	TEAM	GP	G	A	PTS.	PIM
42–43	Tor	3	0	1	1	0

*FORSLUND, Gustav (Gus) *150 F*
B. Sweden, Apr. 25, 1908

SSN	TEAM	GP	G	A	PTS.	PIM
32–33	Ott	48	4	9	13	2

FORSLUND, Thomas *5–11 200 RW*
B. Falun, Sweden, Nov. 24, 1968

SSN	TEAM	GP	G	A	PTS.	PIM	+/-
91–92	Calg	38	5	9	14	12	-6
92–93	Calg	6	0	2	2	0	0
Totals		44	5	11	16	12	-6

FORSYTH, Alex *6–2 195 C*
B. Galt, Ont., Jan. 6, 1955

SSN	TEAM	GP	G	A	PTS.	PIM	+/-
76–77	Wash	1	0	0	0	0	0

FORTIER, Charles *F*

SSN	TEAM	GP	G	A	PTS.	PIM
23–24	Mont	1	0	0	0	0

FORTIER, David Edward *5–11 190 D*
B. Sudbury, Ont., June 17, 1951

SSN	TEAM	GP	G	A	PTS.	PIM	+/-
72–73	Tor	23	1	4	5	63	-10
74–75	NYI	65	6	12	18	79	+14
75–76	NYI	59	0	2	2	68	+9
76–77	Van	58	1	3	4	125	-15
77–78	Ind (WHA)	54	1	15	16	86	
NHL Totals		205	8	21	29	335	-2
WHA Totals		54	1	15	16	86	

Playoffs

SSN	TEAM	GP	G	A	PTS.	PIM
74–75	NYI	14	0	2	2	33
75–76	NYI	6	0	0	0	0
Totals		20	0	2	2	33

FORTIER, Marc *6–0 192 C*
B. Windsor, Que., Feb. 26, 1966

SSN	TEAM	GP	G	A	PTS.	PIM	+/-
87–88	Que	27	4	10	14	12	-17
88–89	Que	57	20	19	39	45	-18
89–90	Que	59	13	17	30	28	-16
90–91	Que	14	0	4	4	6	-3
91–92	Que	39	5	9	14	33	-7
92–93	Ott–LA	16	0	1	1	11	-9
Totals		212	42	60	102	135	-70

FORTIN, Raymond Henri *5–8 180 D*
B. Brummondville, Que., Mar. 11, 1941

SSN	TEAM	GP	G	A	PTS.	PIM	+/-
67–68	StL	24	0	2	2	8	-3
68–69	StL	11	1	0	1	6	+4
69–70	StL	57	1	4	5	19	+3
Totals		92	2	6	8	33	+4

Playoffs

SSN	TEAM	GP	G	A	PTS.	PIM
67–68	StL	3	0	0	0	2
69–70	StL	3	0	0	0	6
Totals		6	0	0	0	8

FOSTER, Corey *6–3 200 D*
B. Ottawa, Ont., Oct. 27, 1969

SSN	TEAM	GP	G	A	PTS.	PIM	+/-
88–89	NJ	2	0	0	0	0	-2
91–92	Phil	25	3	4	7	20	-14
95–96	Pitt	11	2	2	4	2	-2
96–97	NYI	7	0	0	0	2	-2
Totals		45	5	6	11	24	-20

Playoffs

SSN	TEAM	GP	G	A	PTS.	PIM	+/-
95–96	Pitt	3	0	0	0	4	

FOSTER, Dwight Alexander *5–11 195 C*
B. Toronto, Ont., Apr. 2, 1957

SSN	TEAM	GP	G	A	PTS.	PIM	+/-
77–78	Bos	14	2	1	3	6	+1
78–79	Bos	44	11	13	24	14	-1
79–80	Bos	57	10	28	38	42	+23
80–81	Bos	77	24	28	52	62	+4
81–82	Col	70	12	19	31	41	-63
82–83	NJ-Det	62	17	22	39	60	-9
83–84	Det	52	9	12	21	50	-4
84–85	Det	50	16	16	32	56	+12
85–86	Det–Bos	68	6	12	18	52	+18
86–87	Bos	47	4	12	16	37	+1
Totals		541	111	163	274	420	-18

Playoffs

78–79	Bos	11	1	3	4	0	
79–80	Bos	9	3	5	8	2	
80–81	Bos	3	1	1	2	0	
83–84	Det	3	0	1	1	0	
84–85	Det	3	0	0	0	0	
85–86	Bos	3	0	2	2	0	
86–87	Bos	3	0	0	0	0	
Totals		35	5	12	17	4	

*FOSTER, Harold C. (Harry, Yip) *198 D*
B. Guelph, Ont., Nov. 25, 1907

29–30	NYR	31	0	0	0	10	
31–32	Bos	34	1	2	3	12	
33–34	Det	6	0	0	0	2	
34–35	Det	12	2	0	2	8	
Totals		83	3	2	5	32	

FOSTER, Herbert Stanley *5–9 168 LW*
B. Brockville, Ont., Aug. 9, 1913

40–41	NYR	4	1	0	1	5	
47–48	NYR	1	0	0	0	0	
Totals		5	1	0	1	5	

FOTIU, Nicholas Evlampios *6–2 210 LW*
B. Staten Island, N.Y., May 25, 1952

74–75	NE (WHA)	61	2	2	4	144	
75–76	NE (WHA)	49	3	2	5	94	
76–77	NYR	70	4	8	12	174	-23
77–78	NYR	59	2	7	9	105	-14
78–79	NYR	71	3	5	8	190	+3
79–80	Hart	74	10	8	18	107	+2
80–81	Hart–NYR	69	9	9	18	170	-13
81–82	NYR	70	8	10	18	151	-7
82–83	NYR	72	8	13	21	90	+6
83–84	NYR	40	7	6	13	115	+8
84–85	NYR	46	4	7	11	54	-7
85–86	Calg	9	0	1	1	21	-3
86–87	Calg	42	5	3	8	145	-3
87–88	Phil	23	0	0	0	40	-9
88–89	Edm	1	0	0	0	0	+1
NHL Totals		646	60	77	137	1362	-56
WHA Totals		110	5	4	9	238	

Playoffs

74–75	NE (WHA)	4	2	0	2	27	
75–76	NE (WHA)	16	3	2	5	57	
77–78	NYR	3	0	0	0	5	
78–79	NYR	4	0	0	0	6	
79–80	Hart	3	0	0	0	6	
80–81	NYR	2	0	0	0	4	
81–82	NYR	10	0	2	2	6	
82–83	NYR	5	0	1	1	6	
85–86	Calg	11	0	1	1	34	
NHL Totals		38	0	4	4	67	
WHA Totals		20	5	2	7	84	

*FOWLER, James William *5–11 168 D*
B. Toronto, Ont., Apr. 6, 1915

36–37	Tor	48	7	11	18	22	
37–38	Tor	48	10	12	22	8	
38–39	Tor	39	1	6	7	9	
Totals		135	18	29	47	39	

Playoffs

36–37	Tor	2	0	0	0	0	
37–38	Tor	7	0	2	2	0	
38–39	Tor	9	0	1	1	2	
Totals		18	0	3	3	2	

FOWLER, Thomas *5–11 165 C*
B. Winnipeg, Man., May 18, 1924

SSN	TEAM	GP	G	A	PTS.	PIM	+/-
46–47	Chi	24	0	1	1	18	

FOX, Gregory Brent *6–2 190 D*
B. Port McNeil, B.C., Aug. 12, 1953

77–78	Atl	16	1	2	3	25	+5
78–79	Atl-Chi	78	0	17	17	86	+34
79–80	Chi	71	4	11	15	73	-13
80–81	Chi	75	3	16	19	112	-10
81–82	Chi	79	2	19	21	137	-13
82–83	Chi	76	0	12	12	81	+11
83–84	Chi-Pitt	73	2	10	12	97	-42
84–85	Pitt	26	2	5	7	26	-6
Totals		494	14	92	106	637	-34

Playoffs

77–78	Atl	2	0	1	1	8	
78–79	Chi	4	0	1	1	0	
79–80	Chi	7	0	0	0	8	
80–81	Chi	3	0	1	1	2	
81–82	Chi	15	1	3	4	27	
82–83	Chi	13	0	3	3	22	
Totals		44	1	9	10	67	

FOX, James Charles *5–8 185 RW*
B. Coniston, Ont., May 18, 1960

80–81	LA	71	18	25	43	8	0
81–82	LA	77	30	38	68	23	-15
82–83	LA	77	28	40	68	8	-11
83–84	LA	80	30	42	72	26	-12
84–85	LA	79	30	53	83	10	+4
85–86	LA	39	14	17	31	2	-9
86–87	LA	76	19	42	61	48	-10
87–88	LA	68	16	35	51	18	-7
89–90	LA	11	1	1	2	0	-1
Totals		578	186	293	479	143	-61

Playoffs

80–81	LA	4	0	1	1	0	
81–82	LA	9	1	4	5	0	
84–85	LA	3	0	1	1	0	
86–87	LA	5	3	2	5	0	
87–88	LA	1	0	0	0	0	
Totals		22	4	8	12	0	

*FOYSTON, Frank C. *C*
B. Minesing, Ont., Feb. 2, 1891

26–27	Det	41	10	5	15	16	
27–28	Det	23	7	2	9	16	
Totals		64	17	7	24	32	

FRAMPTON, Robert Percy James *5–10 175 LW*
B. Toronto, Ont., Jan. 20, 1929

| 49–50 | Mont | 2 | 0 | 0 | 0 | 0 | |

Playoffs

| 49–50 | Mont | 3 | 0 | 0 | 0 | 0 | |

FRANCESCHETTI, Lou *6–0 190 LW*
B. Toronto, Ont., Mar. 28, 1958

81–82	Wash	30	2	10	12	23	-4
83–84	Wash	2	0	0	0	0	-2
84–85	Wash	22	4	7	11	45	+1
85–86	Wash	76	7	14	21	131	-4
86–87	Wash	75	12	9	21	127	-9
87–88	Wash	59	4	8	12	113	+2
88–89	Wash	63	7	10	17	123	-4
89–90	Tor	80	21	15	36	127	-12
90–91	Tor-Buf	51	2	8	10	58	0
91–92	Buf	1	0	0	0	0	0
Totals		459	59	81	140	747	-32

Playoffs

83–84	Wash	3	0	0	0	8	
84–85	Wash	5	1	1	2	15	
85–86	Wash	8	0	0	0	15	
86–87	Wash	7	0	0	0	23	
87–88	Wash	4	0	0	0	14	
88–89	Wash	6	1	0	1	8	
89–90	Tor	5	0	1	1	26	
90–91	Buf	6	1	0	1	2	
Totals		44	3	2	5	111	

FRANCIS, Robert (Bobby) *5–9 175 C*
B. North Battleford, Sask., Dec. 5, 1958

SSN	TEAM	GP	G	A	PTS.	PIM	+/-
82–83	Det	14	2	0	2	0	-1

FRANCIS, Ronald *6–2 200 C*
B. Sault Ste. Marie, Ont., Mar. 1, 1963

81–82	Hart	59	25	43	68	51	-13
82–83	Hart	79	31	59	90	60	-25
83–84	Hart	72	23	60	83	45	-10
84–85	Hart	80	24	57	81	66	-23
85–86	Hart	53	24	53	77	24	+8
86–87	Hart	75	30	63	93	45	-10
87–88	Hart	80	25	50	75	87	-8
88–89	Hart	69	29	48	77	36	+4
89–90	Hart	80	32	69	101	73	+13
90–91	Hart–Pitt	81	23	64	87	72	-2
91–92	Pitt	70	21	33	54	30	-7
92–93	Pitt	84	24	76	100	68	+6
93–94	Pitt	82	27	66	93	62	-3
94–95	Pitt	44	11	48	59	18	+30
95–96	Pitt	77	27	92	119	56	+25
96–97	Pitt	81	27	63	90	20	+7
97–98	Pitt	81	25	62	87	20	+12
98–99	Car	82	21	31	52	34	-2
Totals		1329	449	1037	1486	867	+22

Playoffs

85–86	Hart	10	1	2	3	4	
86–87	Hart	6	2	2	4	6	
87–88	Hart	6	2	5	7	2	
88–89	Hart	4	0	2	2	0	
89–90	Hart	7	3	3	6	6	
90–91	Pitt	24	7	10	17	24	
91–92	Pitt	21	8	19	27	6	
92–93	Pitt	12	6	11	17	19	
93–94	Pitt	6	0	2	2	6	
94–95	Pitt	12	6	13	19	4	
95–96	Pitt	11	3	6	9	4	
96–97	Pitt	5	1	2	3	2	
97–98	Pitt	6	1	5	6	2	
98–99	Car	3	0	1	1	0	
Totals		133	40	83	123	87	

*FRASER, Archibald McKay (Archie) *F*
B. Souris, Man., Feb. 9, 1914

| 43–44 | NYR | 3 | 0 | 1 | 1 | 0 | |

FRASER, Curt M. *6–1 200 LW*
B. Cincinnati, Ohio, Jan. 12, 1958

78–79	Van	78	16	19	35	116	-7
79–80	Van	78	17	25	42	143	+7
80–81	Van	77	25	24	49	118	-19
81–82	Van	79	28	39	67	175	+2
82–83	Van–Chi	74	12	20	32	176	-5
83–84	Chi	29	5	12	17	28	+9
84–85	Chi	73	25	25	50	109	+3
85–86	Chi	61	29	39	68	84	+11
86–87	Chi	75	25	25	50	182	+5
87–88	Chi–Minn	37	5	7	12	77	-20
88–89	Minn	35	5	5	10	76	-15
89–90	Minn	8	1	0	1	22	-5
Totals		704	193	240	433	1306	-34

Playoffs

78–79	Van	3	0	2	2	6	
79–80	Van	4	0	0	0	2	
80–81	Van	3	1	0	1	2	
81–82	Van	17	3	7	10	98	
82–83	Chi	13	4	4	8	18	
83–84	Chi	5	0	0	0	14	
84–85	Chi	15	6	3	9	36	
85–86	Chi	3	0	1	1	12	
86–87	Chi	2	1	1	2	10	
Totals		65	15	18	33	198	

*FRASER, Gordon (Gord) *D*
B. Pembroke, Ont.

26–27	Chi	43	14	6	20	89	
27–28	Chi-Det	41	4	2	6	60	
28–29	Det	13	0	0	0	12	
29–30	Mont–Pitt Pi	40	6	4	10	41	
30–31	Phil Q	7	0	0	0	22	
Totals		144	24	12	36	224	

Playoffs

| 26–27 | Chi | 2 | 1 | 0 | 1 | 6 | |

FRASER, Iain *5–10 175 C*
B. Scarborough, Ont., Aug. 10, 1969

SSN	TEAM	GP	G	A	PTS.	PIM	+/-
92–93	NYI	7	2	2	4	2	-1
93–94	Que	60	17	20	37	23	-5
94–95	Dal–Edm	13	3	0	3	0	0
95–96	Winn	12	1	1	2	4	+1
96–97	SJ	2	0	0	0	2	-1
Totals		94	23	23	46	31	-6

Playoffs

95–96	Winn	4	0	0	0	0	

*FRASER, Jack *F*

23–24	Ham	1	0	0	0	0	

FRASER, James Harvey (Harry) *5–10 168 C*
B. Souris, Man., Oct. 14, 1918

44–45	Chi	21	5	4	9	0	

FRASER, Scott *6–1 178 C*
B. Moncton, N.B., May 3, 1972

95–96	Mont	14	2	0	2	4	+1
97–98	Edm	29	12	11	23	6	+6
98–99	NYR	28	2	4	6	14	-12
Totals		71	16	15	31	24	-17

Playoffs

97–98	Edm	11	1	1	2	0	

FRAWLEY, William Daniel (Dan) *6–1 190 RW*
B. Sturgeon Falls, Ont., June 2, 1962

83–84	Chi	3	0	0	0	0	-1
84–85	Chi	30	4	3	7	64	-2
85–86	Pitt	69	10	11	21	174	-19
86–87	Pitt	78	14	14	28	218	-10
87–88	Pitt	47	6	8	14	152	0
88–89	Pitt	46	3	4	7	66	-1
Totals		273	37	40	77	674	-33

Playoffs

84–85	Chi	1	0	0	0	0	

*FREDERICKSON, Frank *5–11 175 C*
B. Winnipeg, Man., 1895

26–27	Det–Bos	44	18	13	31	45	
27–28	Bos	44	10	4	14	83	
28–29	Bos–Pitt Pi	43	6	8	14	52	
29–30	Pitt Pi	9	4	7	11	20	
30–31	Det	25	1	2	3	6	
Totals		165	39	34	73	206	

Playoffs

26–27	Bos	8	2	4	6	22	
27–28	Bos	2	0	1	1	4	
Totals		10	2	5	7	26	

FREER, Mark *5–10 180 C*
B. Peterborough, Ont., July 14, 1968

86–87	Phil	1	0	1	1	0	+1
87–88	Phil	1	0	0	0	0	-2
88–89	Phil	5	0	1	1	0	0
89–90	Phil	2	0	0	0	0	0
91–92	Phil	50	6	7	13	18	-1
92–93	Ott	63	10	14	24	39	-35
93–94	Calg	2	0	0	0	4	0
Totals		124	16	23	39	61	-37

FREW, Irvine (Irv) *5–9 180 D*
B. Kilsyth, Scotland, Aug. 16, 1907

33–34	Mont M	30	2	1	3	41	
34–35	StLE	47	0	2	2	89	
35–36	Mont	18	0	2	2	16	
Totals		95	2	5	7	146	

Playoffs

33–34	Mont M	4	0	0	0	6	

FRIDAY, Tim *6–0 190 D*
B. Burbank, Cal., Mar. 5, 1961

85–86	Det	23	0	3	3	6	-9

FRIDGEN, Dan *5–11 175 LW*
B. Arnprior, Ont., May 18, 1959

81–82	Hart	2	0	1	1	0	-2
82–83	Hart	11	2	2	4	2	+2

Totals		13	2	3	5	2	0

FRIEDMAN, Doug *6–1 195 LW*
B. Cape Elizabeth, Me, Sept. 1, 1971

97–98	Edm	16	0	0	0	20	0
98–99	Nash	2	0	1	1	14	0
Totals		18	0	1	1	34	0

FRIESEN, Jeff *6–0 185 C*
B. Meadow Lake, Sask., Aug. 5, 1976

94–95	SJ	48	15	10	25	14	-8
95–96	SJ	79	15	31	46	42	-19
96–97	SJ	82	28	34	62	75	-8
97–98	SJ	79	31	32	63	40	+8
98–99	SJ	78	22	35	57	42	+3
Totals		366	111	142	253	213	-24

Playoffs

94–95	SJ	11	1	5	6	4	
97–98	SJ	6	0	1	1	2	
98–99	SJ	6	2	2	4	14	
Totals		23	3	8	11	20	

FRIEST, Ronald *5–11 185 LW*
B. Windsor, Ont., Nov. 4, 1958

80–81	Minn	4	1	0	1	10	-2
81–82	Minn	10	0	0	0	31	-4
82–83	Minn	50	6	7	13	150	-4
Totals		64	7	7	14	191	-10

Playoffs

81–82	Minn	2	0	0	0	5	
82–83	Minn	4	1	0	1	2	
Totals		6	1	0	1	7	

FRIG, Leonard Elroy (Len) *5–11 190 D*
B. Lethbridge, Alta., Oct. 23, 1950

73–74	Chi	66	4	10	14	35	+16
74–75	Cal	80	3	17	20	127	-28
75–76	Cal	62	3	12	15	55	-5
76–77	Clev	66	2	7	9	213	-31
77–78	StL	30	1	3	4	45	-13
79–80	StL	7	0	2	2	2	-5
Totals		311	13	51	64	479	-66

Playoffs

72–73	Chi	4	1	1	2	0	
73–74	Chi	7	1	0	1	0	
79–80	StL	3	0	0	0	0	
Totals		14	2	1	3	0	

FROST, Harold (Harry) *5–11 165 RW*
B. Kerr Lake, Ont., Aug. 17, 1914

38–39	Bos	3	0	0	0	0	

Playoffs

38–39	Bos	1	0	0	0	0	

FRYCER, Miroslav *6–0 200 RW*
B. Ostrava, Czechoslovakia, Sept. 27, 1959

81–82	Que–Tor	59	24	23	47	78	-19
82–83	Tor	67	25	30	55	90	+2
83–84	Tor	47	10	16	26	55	-24
84–85	Tor	65	25	30	55	55	-7
85–86	Tor	73	32	43	75	74	-24
86–87	Tor	29	7	8	15	28	-15
87–88	Tor	38	12	20	32	41	+8
88–89	Det–Edm	37	12	13	25	65	-2
Totals		415	147	183	330	486	-81

Playoffs

82–83	Tor	4	2	5	7	0	
85–86	Tor	10	1	3	4	10	
87–88	Tor	3	0	0	0	6	
Totals		17	3	8	11	16	

FRYDAY, Robert George *5–10 155 RW*
B. Toronto, Ont., Dec. 5, 1928

49–50	Mont	2	1	0	1	0	
51–52	Mont	3	0	0	0	0	
Totals		5	1	0	1	0	

FTOREK, Robert Brian *5–10 155 C*
B. Needham, Mass., Jan. 2, 1952

72–73	Det	3	0	0	0	0	0

73–74	Det	12	2	5	7	4	+1
74–75	Phoe (WHA)	53	31	37	68	29	
75–76	Phoe (WHA)	80	41	72	113	109	
76–77	Phoe (WHA)	80	46	71	117	86	
77–78	Cin (WHA)	80	59	50	109	54	
78–79	Cin (WHA)	80	39	77	116	87	
79–80	Que	52	18	33	51	28	+6
80–81	Que	78	24	49	73	104	-19
81–82	Que–NYR	49	9	32	41	28	+6
82–83	NYR	61	12	19	31	41	+11
83–84	NYR	31	3	2	5	22	+2
84–85	NYR	48	9	10	19	35	-7
NHL Totals		334	77	150	227	262	0
WHA Totals		373	216	307	523	365	

Playoffs

74–75	Phoe (WHA)	5	2	5	7	2	
75–76	Phoe (WHA)	5	1	3	4	2	
78–79	Chi (WHA)	3	3	2	5	6	
80–81	Que	5	1	2	3	17	
81–82	NYR	10	7	4	11	11	
82–83	NYR	4	1	0	1	0	
NHL Totals		19	9	6	15	28	
WHA Totals		13	6	10	16	10	

FULLAN, Lawrence *5–11 185 LW*
B. Toronto, Ont., Aug. 11, 1949

74–75	Wash	4	1	0	1	0	-2

FUSCO, Mark *5–9 175 D*
B. Burlington, Mass., Mar. 12, 1961

83–84	Hart	17	0	4	4	2	-6
84–85	Hart	63	3	8	11	40	-15
Totals		80	3	12	15	42	-21

GADSBY, William Alexander *6–0 185 D*
B. Calgary, Alta., Aug. 8, 1927

46–47	Chi	48	8	10	18	31	
47–48	Chi	60	6	10	16	66	
48–49	Chi	50	3	10	13	85	
49–50	Chi	70	10	24	34	138	
50–51	Chi	25	3	7	10	32	
51–52	Chi	59	7	15	22	87	
52–53	Chi	68	2	20	22	84	
53–54	Chi	70	12	29	41	108	
54–55	Chi–NYR	70	11	13	24	61	
55–56	NYR	70	9	42	51	84	
56–57	NYR	70	4	37	41	72	
57–58	NYR	65	14	32	46	48	
58–59	NYR	70	5	46	51	56	
59–60	NYR	65	9	22	31	60	
60–61	NYR	65	9	26	35	49	
61–62	Det	70	7	30	37	88	
62–63	Det	70	4	24	28	116	
63–64	Det	64	2	16	18	80	
64–65	Det	61	0	12	12	122	
65–66	Det	58	5	12	17	72	
Totals		1248	130	437	567	1539	

Playoffs

52–53	Chi	7	0	1	1	4	
55–56	NYR	5	1	3	4	4	
56–57	NYR	5	1	2	3	2	
57–58	NYR	6	0	3	3	4	
62–63	Det	11	1	4	5	36	
63–64	Det	14	0	4	4	22	
64–65	Det	7	0	3	3	8	
65–66	Det	12	1	3	4	12	
Totals		67	4	23	27	92	

GAETZ, Link *6–4 210 D*
B. Vancouver, B.C., Oct. 2, 1968

88–89	Minn	12	0	2	2	53	-3
89–90	Minn	5	0	0	0	33	-5
91–92	SJ	48	6	6	12	326	-27
Totals		65	6	8	14	412	-35

GAGE, Joseph William (Jody) *6–0 190 RW*
B. Toronto, Ont., Nov. 29, 1959

80–81	Det	16	2	2	4	22	-10
81–82	Det	31	9	10	19	2	-1
83–84	Det	3	0	0	0	0	0
85–86	Buf	7	3	2	5	0	-3
87–88	Buf	2	0	0	0	0	-2
91–92	Buf	9	0	1	1	2	-1
Totals		68	14	15	29	26	-20

GAGNE, Arthur E. *5–7 160 RW*
B. Ottawa, Ont., Oct. 11, 1897

SSN	TEAM	GP	G	A	PTS.	PIM	+/-
26–27	Mont	44	14	3	17	42	
27–28	Mont	44	20	10	30	75	
28–29	Mont	44	7	3	10	52	
29–30	Bos–Ott	39	6	5	11	38	
30–31	Ott	44	19	11	30	50	
31–32	Det	13	1	1	2	0	
Totals		228	67	33	100	257	

Playoffs

SSN	TEAM	GP	G	A	PTS.	PIM	+/-
26–27	Mont	4	0	0	0	0	
27–28	Mont	2	1	1	2	4	
28–29	Mont	3	0	0	0	12	
29–30	Ott	2	1	0	1	4	
Totals		11	2	1	3	20	

GAGNE, Paul *5–10 180 LW*
B. Iroquois Falls, Ont., Feb. 6, 1962

SSN	TEAM	GP	G	A	PTS.	PIM	+/-
80–81	Col	61	25	16	41	12	-24
81–82	Col	59	10	12	22	17	-27
82–83	NJ	63	14	15	29	13	-2
83–84	NJ	66	14	18	32	33	-22
84–85	NJ	79	24	19	43	28	-11
85–86	NJ	47	19	19	38	14	-15
88–89	Tor	16	3	2	5	6	-8
89–90	NYI	9	1	0	1	4	-1
Totals		400	110	101	211	127	-110

GAGNE, Pierre Reynald *6–0 180 LW*
B. North Bay, Ont., June 5, 1940

SSN	TEAM	GP	G	A	PTS.	PIM	+/-
59–60	Bos	2	0	0	0	0	

GAGNER, Dave *5–10 180 C*
B. Chatham, Ont., Dec. 11, 1964

SSN	TEAM	GP	G	A	PTS.	PIM	+/-
84–85	NYR	38	6	6	12	16	-16
85–86	NYR	32	4	6	10	19	-1
86–87	NYR	10	1	4	5	12	-1
87–88	Minn	51	8	11	19	55	-14
88–89	Minn	75	35	43	78	104	+13
89–90	Minn	79	40	38	78	54	-1
90–91	Minn	73	40	42	82	114	+9
91–92	Minn	78	31	40	71	107	-4
92–93	Minn	84	33	43	76	143	-13
93–94	Dal	76	32	29	61	83	+13
94–95	Dal	48	14	28	42	42	+2
95–96	Dal–Tor	73	21	28	49	103	-19
96–97	Calg	82	27	33	60	48	+2
97–98	Fla	78	20	28	48	55	-21
98–99	Fla–Van	69	6	22	28	63	-16
Totals		946	318	401	719	1018	-65

Playoffs

SSN	TEAM	GP	G	A	PTS.	PIM	+/-
89–90	Minn	7	2	3	5	16	
90–91	Minn	23	12	15	27	28	
91–92	Minn	7	2	4	6	8	
93–94	Dal	9	5	1	6	2	
94–95	Dal	5	1	1	2	4	
95–96	Tor	6	0	2	2	6	
Totals		57	22	26	48	64	

GAGNON, Germain *6–0 172 LW*
B. Chicoutimi, Que., Dec. 9, 1942

SSN	TEAM	GP	G	A	PTS.	PIM	+/-
71–72	Mont	4	0	0	0	0	0
72–73	NYI	63	12	29	41	31	-24
73–74	NYI–Chi	76	11	28	39	12	+12
74–75	Chi	80	16	35	51	21	+5
75–76	Chi–KC	36	1	9	10	8	-15
Totals		259	40	101	141	72	-22

Playoffs

SSN	TEAM	GP	G	A	PTS.	PIM	+/-
73–74	Chi	11	2	2	4	2	
74–75	Chi	8	0	1	1	0	
Totals		19	2	3	5	2	

*GAGNON, Johnny (Black Cat) *5–5 140 RW*
B. Chicoutimi, Que., June 8, 1905

SSN	TEAM	GP	G	A	PTS.	PIM	+/-
30–31	Mont	41	18	7	25	43	
31–32	Mont	48	19	18	37	40	
32–33	Mont	48	12	23	35	64	
33–34	Mont	48	9	15	24	25	
34–35	Bos–Mont	47	2	6	8	11	
35–36	Mont	48	7	9	16	42	
36–37	Mont	48	20	16	36	38	
37–38	Mont	47	13	17	30	9	
38–39	Mont	45	12	22	34	23	

SSN	TEAM	GP	G	A	PTS.	PIM	+/-
39–40	Mont–NYA	34	8	8	16	0	
Totals		454	120	141	261	295	

Playoffs

SSN	TEAM	GP	G	A	PTS.	PIM	+/-
30–31	Mont	10	6	2	8	8	
31–32	Mont	4	1	1	2	4	
32–33	Mont	2	0	2	2	0	
33–34	Mont	2	1	0	1	2	
34–35	Mont	2	0	1	1	2	
36–37	Mont	5	2	1	3	9	
37–38	Mont	3	1	3	4	2	
38–39	Mont	3	0	2	2	10	
39–40	NYA	1	1	0	1	0	
Totals		32	12	12	24	37	

GAGNON, Sean *6–2 210 D*
B. Sault Ste. Marie, Ont., Sept. 11, 1973

SSN	TEAM	GP	G	A	PTS.	PIM	+/-
97–98	Phoe	5	0	1	1	14	+1
98–99	Phoe	2	0	0	0	7	-2
Totals		7	0	1	1	21	-1

GAINEY, Robert Michael *6–2 200 LW*
B. Peterborough, Ont., Dec. 13, 1953

SSN	TEAM	GP	G	A	PTS.	PIM	+/-
73–74	Mont	66	3	7	10	34	-9
74–75	Mont	80	17	20	37	49	+23
75–76	Mont	78	15	13	28	57	+20
76–77	Mont	80	14	19	33	41	+31
77–78	Mont	66	15	16	31	57	+11
78–79	Mont	79	20	18	38	44	+11
79–80	Mont	64	14	19	33	32	-2
80–81	Mont	78	23	24	47	36	+13
81–82	Mont	79	21	24	45	24	+37
82–83	Mont	80	12	18	30	43	+7
83–84	Mont	77	17	22	39	41	+10
84–85	Mont	79	19	13	32	40	+13
85–86	Mont	80	20	23	43	20	+10
86–87	Mont	47	8	8	16	19	0
87–88	Mont	78	11	11	22	14	+8
88–89	Mont	49	10	7	17	34	+13
Totals		1160	239	262	501	585	+196

Playoffs

SSN	TEAM	GP	G	A	PTS.	PIM	+/-
73–74	Mont	6	0	0	0	6	
74–75	Mont	11	2	4	6	4	
75–76	Mont	13	1	3	4	20	
76–77	Mont	14	4	1	5	25	
77–78	Mont	15	2	7	9	14	
78–79	Mont	16	6	10	16	10	
79–80	Mont	10	1	1	2	4	
80–81	Mont	3	0	0	0	2	
81–82	Mont	5	0	1	1	8	
82–83	Mont	3	0	0	0	4	
83–84	Mont	15	1	5	6	9	
84–85	Mont	12	1	3	4	13	
85–86	Mont	20	5	5	10	12	
86–87	Mont	17	1	3	4	6	
87–88	Mont	6	0	1	1	6	
88–89	Mont	16	1	4	5	8	
Totals		182	25	48	73	151	

*GAINOR, Norman (Dutch) *6–1 170 C*
B. Calgary, Alta., Apr. 10, 1904

SSN	TEAM	GP	G	A	PTS.	PIM	+/-
27–28	Bos	41	8	4	12	35	
28–29	Bos	39	14	5	19	30	
29–30	Bos	43	18	31	49	39	
30–31	Bos	32	8	3	11	14	
31–32	NYR	46	3	9	12	9	
32–33	Ott	2	0	0	0	0	
34–35	Mont M	40	0	4	4	2	
Totals		243	51	56	107	129	

Playoffs

SSN	TEAM	GP	G	A	PTS.	PIM	+/-
27–28	Bos	2	0	0	0	6	
28–29	Bos	5	2	0	2	4	
29–30	Bos	6	0	0	0	0	
30–31	Bos	5	0	1	1	2	
31–32	NYR	7	0	0	0	2	
Totals		25	2	1	3	14	

GALANOV, Maxim *6–1 195 D*
B. Krasnoyarsk, USSR, Mar. 13, 1974

SSN	TEAM	GP	G	A	PTS.	PIM	+/-
97–98	NYR	6	0	1	1	2	+1
98–99	Pitt	51	4	3	7	14	-8
Totals		57	4	4	8	16	-7

Playoffs

SSN	TEAM	GP	G	A	PTS.	PIM	+/-
98–99	Pitt	1	0	0	0	0	

GALARNEAU, Michel *6–2 180 C*
B. Montreal, Que., Mar. 1, 1961

SSN	TEAM	GP	G	A	PTS.	PIM	+/-
80–81	Hart	30	2	6	8	9	-12
81–82	Hart	10	0	0	0	4	-7
82–83	Hart	38	5	4	9	21	-8
Totals		78	7	10	17	34	-27

*GALBRAITH, Percival (Perk) *5–10 162 LW*
B. Toronto, Ont., 1899

SSN	TEAM	GP	G	A	PTS.	PIM	+/-
26–27	Bos	42	9	8	17	26	
27–28	Bos	42	6	5	11	26	
28–29	Bos	38	2	1	3	44	
29–30	Bos	44	7	9	16	38	
30–31	Bos	43	2	3	5	28	
31–32	Bos	47	2	1	3	28	
32–33	Bos	47	1	2	3	28	
33–34	Ott–Bos	44	0	2	2	5	
Totals		347	29	31	60	223	

Playoffs

SSN	TEAM	GP	G	A	PTS.	PIM	+/-
26–27	Bos	8	3	3	6	2	
27–28	Bos	2	0	1	1	6	
28–29	Bos	5	0	0	0	2	
29–30	Bos	6	1	3	4	8	
30–31	Bos	5	0	0	0	6	
32–33	Bos	5	0	0	0	0	
Totals		31	4	7	11	24	

*GALLAGHER, John James Patrick *5–11 188 D*
B. Kenora, Ont., Jan. 19, 1909

SSN	TEAM	GP	G	A	PTS.	PIM	+/-
30–31	Mont M	35	4	2	6	35	
31–32	Mont M	19	1	0	1	18	
32–33	Mont M–Det	41	4	6	10	48	
33–34	Det	1	0	0	0	0	
36–37	NYA–Det	20	1	0	1	12	
37–38	NYA	47	3	6	9	18	
38–39	NYA	41	1	5	6	22	
Totals		204	14	19	33	153	

Playoffs

SSN	TEAM	GP	G	A	PTS.	PIM	+/-
30–31	Mont M	2	0	0	0	0	
32–33	Det	4	1	1	2	4	
36–37	Det	10	1	0	1	17	
37–38	NYA	6	0	2	2	6	
Totals		22	2	3	5	27	

GALLANT, Gerard *5–10 185 LW*
B. Summerside, P.E.I., Sept. 2, 1963

SSN	TEAM	GP	G	A	PTS.	PIM	+/-
84–85	Det	32	6	12	18	66	+9
85–86	Det	52	20	19	39	106	-14
86–87	Det	80	38	34	72	216	-5
87–88	Det	73	34	39	73	242	+24
88–89	Det	76	39	54	93	230	+4
89–90	Det	69	36	44	80	254	-6
90–91	Det	45	10	16	26	111	+6
91–92	Det	69	14	22	36	187	+16
92–93	Det	67	10	20	30	188	+20
93–94	TB	51	4	9	13	74	-6
94–95	TB	1	0	0	0	0	0
Totals		615	211	269	480	1674	+55

Playoffs

SSN	TEAM	GP	G	A	PTS.	PIM	+/-
84–85	Det	3	0	0	0	11	
86–87	Det	16	8	6	14	43	
87–88	Det	16	6	9	15	55	
88–89	Det	6	1	2	3	40	
91–92	Det	11	2	2	4	25	
92–93	Det	6	1	2	3	4	
Totals		58	18	21	39	178	

GALLEY, Garry *6–0 204 D*
B. Montreal, Que., Apr. 16, 1963

SSN	TEAM	GP	G	A	PTS.	PIM	+/-
84–85	LA	78	8	30	38	82	+3
85–86	LA	49	9	13	22	46	-9
86–87	LA–Wash	48	6	21	27	67	-6
87–88	Wash	58	7	23	30	44	+11
88–89	Bos	78	8	21	29	80	-7
89–90	Bos	71	8	27	35	75	+2
90–91	Bos	70	6	21	27	84	0
91–92	Bos–Phil	77	5	27	32	117	-2
92–93	Phil	83	13	49	62	115	-18
93–94	Phil	81	10	60	70	91	-11
94–95	Phil–Buf	47	3	29	32	30	+4
95–96	Buf	78	10	44	54	81	-2
96–97	Buf	71	4	34	38	102	+10
97–98	LA	74	9	28	37	63	-5

SSN	TEAM	GP	G	A	PTS.	PIM	+/-
98–99	LA	60	4	12	16	30	-9
Totals		1023	110	439	549	1107	-3
Playoffs							
84–85	LA	3	1	0	1	2	
86–87	Wash	2	0	0	0	0	
87–88	Wash	12	2	4	6	13	
88–89	Bos	9	0	1	1	33	
89–90	Bos	21	3	3	6	34	
90–91	Bos	16	1	5	6	17	
94–95	Buf	5	0	3	3	4	
96–97	Buf	12	0	6	6	14	
97–98	LA	4	0	1	1	2	
Totals		85	7	23	30	119	

GALLIMORE, James (Jamie) 6–0 180 RW
B. Edmonton, Alta., Nov. 28, 1957

77–78	Minn	2	0	0	0	0	0

*GALLINGER, Donald C. 6–0 170 C
B. Port Colborne, Ont., Apr. 10, 1925

42–43	Bos	48	14	20	34	16	
43–44	Bos	23	13	5	18	6	
45–46	Bos	50	17	23	40	18	
46–47	Bos	47	11	19	30	12	
47–48	Bos	54	10	21	31	37	
Totals		222	65	88	153	89	
Playoffs							
42–43	Bos	9	3	1	4	10	
45–46	Bos	10	2	4	6	2	
46–47	Bos	4	0	0	0	7	
Totals		23	5	5	10	19	

GAMBLE, Richard Frank (Dick) 6–0 178 LW
B. Moncton, N.B., Nov. 16, 1928

50–51	Mont	1	0	0	0	0	
51–52	Mont	64	23	17	40	8	
52–53	Mont	69	11	13	24	26	
53–54	Mont	32	4	8	12	18	
54–55	Chi	14	2	0	2	6	
55–56	Mont	12	0	3	3	8	
65–66	Tor	2	1	0	1	0	
66–67	Tor	1	0	0	0	0	
Totals		195	41	41	82	66	
Playoffs							
51–52	Mont	7	0	2	2	0	
52–53	Mont	5	1	0	1	2	
54–55	Mont	2	0	0	0	2	
Totals		14	1	2	3	4	

GAMBUCCI, Gary Allan 5–9 175 C
B. Hibbing, Minn., Sept. 27, 1946

71–72	Minn	9	1	0	1	0	+2
73–74	Minn	42	1	7	8	9	+5
74–75	Minn (WHA)	67	19	18	37	19	
75–76	Minn (WHA)	45	10	6	16	14	
NHL Totals		51	2	7	9	9	+7
WHA Totals		112	29	24	53	33	
Playoffs							
74–75	Minn (WHA)	12	4	0	4	6	

GANCHAR, Perry 5–9 180 RW
B. Saskatoon, Sask., Oct. 28, 1963

83–84	StL	1	0	0	0	0	+1
84–85	StL	7	0	2	2	0	0
87–88	Mont-Pitt	31	3	5	8	36	-1
88–89	Pitt	3	0	0	0	0	-3
Totals		42	3	7	10	36	-3
Playoffs							
83–84	StL	7	3	1	4	0	

GANS, David 5–10 180 C
B. Brantford, Ont., June 6, 1964

82–83	LA	3	0	0	0	0	-1
85–86	LA	3	0	0	0	2	0
Totals		6	0	0	0	2	-1

GARDINER, Bruce 6–1 185 C
B. Barrie, Ont., Feb. 11, 1971

96–97	Ott	67	11	10	21	49	+4
97–98	Ott	55	7	11	18	50	+2

SSN	TEAM	GP	G	A	PTS.	PIM	+/-
98–99	Ott	59	4	8	12	43	+6
Totals		181	22	29	51	142	+12
Playoffs							
96–97	Ott	7	0	1	1	2	
97–98	Ott	11	1	3	4	2	
98–99	Ott	3	0	0	0	4	
Totals		21	1	4	5	8	

*GARDINER, Herbert Martin D
B. Winnipeg, Man., May 8, 1891

26–27	Mont	44	6	6	12	26	
27–28	Mont	44	4	3	7	26	
28–29	Chi-Mont	13	0	0	0	0	
Totals		101	10	9	19	52	
Playoffs							
26–27	Mont	2	0	0	0	10	
27–28	Mont	2	0	1	1	4	
28–29	Mont	3	0	0	0	0	
Totals		7	0	1	1	14	

GARDNER, Calvin Pearly (Finger) 6–1 175 C
B. Transcona, Man., Oct. 30, 1924

45–46	NYR	16	8	2	10	2	
46–47	NYR	52	13	16	29	30	
47–48	NYR	58	7	18	25	71	
48–49	Tor	53	13	22	35	35	
49–50	Tor	30	7	19	26	12	
50–51	Tor	66	23	28	51	42	
51–52	Tor	70	15	26	41	40	
52–53	Chi	70	11	24	35	60	
53–54	Bos	70	14	20	34	62	
54–55	Bos	70	16	22	38	40	
55–56	Bos	70	15	21	36	57	
56–57	Bos	70	12	20	32	66	
Totals		695	154	238	392	517	
Playoffs							
47–48	NYR	5	0	0	0	0	
48–49	Tor	9	2	5	7	0	
49–50	Tor	7	1	0	1	4	
50–51	Tor	11	1	1	2	4	
51–52	Tor	3	0	0	0	2	
52–53	Chi	7	0	2	2	4	
53–54	Bos	4	1	1	2	0	
54–55	Bos	5	0	0	0	4	
56–57	Bos	10	2	1	3	2	
Totals		61	7	10	17	20	

GARDNER, David Calvin 6–0 183 C
B. Toronto, Ont., Aug. 23, 1952

72–73	Mont	5	1	1	2	0	0
73–74	Mont–StL	46	6	12	18	8	-2
74–75	StL–Cal	72	16	22	38	6	-22
75–76	Cal	74	16	32	48	8	-4
76–77	Clev	76	16	22	38	9	-20
77–78	Clev	75	19	25	44	10	-16
79–80	Phil	2	1	1	2	0	+1
Totals		350	75	115	190	41	-63

GARDNER, Paul Malone 6–0 195 C
B. Fort Erie, Ont., Mar. 5. 1956

76–77	Col	60	30	29	59	25	-28
77–78	Col	46	30	22	52	29	-17
78–79	Col-Tor	75	30	28	58	32	-25
79–80	Tor	45	11	13	24	10	-8
80–81	Pitt	62	34	40	74	59	-6
81–82	Pitt	59	36	33	69	28	-7
82–83	Pitt	70	28	27	55	12	-23
83–84	Pitt	16	0	5	5	6	-4
84–85	Wash	12	2	4	6	6	-1
85–86	Buf	2	0	0	0	0	-3
Totals		447	201	201	402	207	-122
Playoffs							
78–79	Tor	6	0	1	1	4	
80–81	Pitt	5	1	0	1	8	
81–82	Pitt	5	1	5	6	2	
Totals		16	2	6	8	14	

GARDNER, William Scott 5–10 180 C
B. Toronto, Ont., Mar. 18, 1960

80–81	Chi	1	0	0	0	0	0
81–82	Chi	69	8	15	23	20	-9
82–83	Chi	77	15	25	40	12	+10

SSN	TEAM	GP	G	A	PTS.	PIM	+/-
83–84	Chi	79	27	21	48	12	+1
84–85	Chi	74	17	34	51	12	+7
85–86	Chi–Hart	64	4	18	22	10	-14
86–87	Hart	8	0	1	1	0	-2
87–88	Chi	2	1	0	1	2	-1
88–89	Chi	6	1	1	2	0	+2
Totals		380	73	115	188	68	-6
Playoffs							
81–82	Chi	15	1	4	5	6	
82–83	Chi	13	1	0	1	9	
83–84	Chi	5	0	1	1	0	
84–85	Chi	12	1	3	4	2	
Totals		45	3	8	11	17	

GARE, Daniel Mirl 5–9 175 RW
B. Nelson, B.C., May 14, 1954

74–75	Buf	78	31	31	62	75	+40
75–76	Buf	79	50	23	73	129	+32
76–77	Buf	35	11	15	26	73	+7
77–78	Buf	69	39	38	77	95	+32
78–79	Buf	71	27	40	67	90	+18
79–80	Buf	76	56	33	89	90	+49
80–81	Buf	73	46	39	85	109	+12
81–82	Buf–Det	58	20	23	43	99	-4
82–83	Det	79	26	35	61	107	-16
83–84	Det	63	13	13	26	147	+3
84–85	Det	71	27	29	56	163	+5
85–86	Det	57	7	9	16	102	-19
86–87	Edm	18	1	3	4	6	+2
Totals		827	354	331	685	1285	+169
Playoffs							
74–75	Buf	17	7	6	13	19	
75–76	Buf	9	5	2	7	21	
76–77	Buf	4	0	0	0	18	
77–78	Buf	8	4	6	10	37	
78–79	Buf	3	0	0	0	9	
79–80	Buf	14	4	7	11	35	
80–81	Buf	3	3	0	3	8	
83–84	Det	4	2	0	2	38	
84–85	Det	2	0	0	0	10	
Totals		64	25	21	46	195	

GARIEPY, Raymond 5–8 180 D
B. Toronto, Ont., Sept. 4, 1928

53–54	Bos	35	1	6	7	39	
55–56	Tor	1	0	0	0	4	
Totals		36	1	6	7	43	

*GARLAND, Stephen (Scott) 6–1 185 C
B. Regina, Sask., May 16, 1952

75–76	Tor	16	4	3	7	8	0
76–77	Tor	69	9	20	29	83	-18
78–79	LA	6	0	1	1	24	-4
Totals		91	13	24	37	115	-22
Playoffs							
75–76	Tor	7	1	2	3	35	

GARNER, Robert William 5–11 180 C
B. Weston, Ont., Aug. 17, 1958

82–83	Pitt	1	0	0	0	0	0

GARPENLOV, Johan 5–11 183 LW
B. Stockholm, Sweden, Mar. 21, 1968

90–91	Det	71	18	22	40	18	-4
91–92	Det–SJ	28	6	7	13	8	0
92–93	SJ	79	22	44	66	56	-26
93–94	SJ	80	18	35	53	28	+9
94–95	SJ–Fla	40	4	10	14	2	+1
95–96	Fla	82	23	28	51	36	-10
96–97	Fla	53	11	25	36	47	+10
97–98	Fla	39	2	3	5	8	-6
98–99	Fla	64	8	9	17	42	-9
Totals		536	112	183	295	245	-35
Playoffs							
90–91	Det	6	0	1	1	4	
93–94	SJ	14	4	6	10	6	
95–96	Fla	20	4	2	6	8	
96–97	Fla	4	2	0	2	4	
Totals		44	10	9	19	22	

GARRETT, Dudley (Red) 5-11 190 D
B. Toronto, Ont., July 24, 1924

SSN	TEAM	GP	G	A	PTS.	PIM	+/-
42-43	NYR	23	1	1	2	18	

GARTNER, Michael Alfred 6-0 190 RW
B. Ottawa, Ont., Oct. 29, 1959

SSN	TEAM	GP	G	A	PTS.	PIM	+/-
78-79	Cin (WHA)	78	27	25	52	123	
79-80	Wash	77	36	32	68	66	+15
80-81	Wash	80	48	46	94	100	-5
81-82	Wash	80	35	45	80	121	-11
82-83	Wash	73	38	38	76	54	-2
83-84	Wash	80	40	45	85	90	+22
84-85	Wash	80	50	52	102	71	+17
85-86	Wash	74	35	40	75	63	-5
86-87	Wash	78	41	32	73	61	+1
87-88	Wash	80	48	33	81	73	+20
88-89	Wash–Minn	69	33	36	69	73	+11
89-90	Minn–NYR	79	45	41	86	38	-4
90-91	NYR	79	49	20	69	53	-9
91-92	NYR	76	40	41	81	55	+11
92-93	NYR	84	45	23	68	59	-4
93-94	NYR–Tor	81	34	28	62	40	+20
94-95	Tor	38	12	8	20	6	0
95-96	Tor	82	35	19	54	52	+5
96-97	Phoe	82	32	31	63	38	-11
97-98	Phoe	60	12	15	27	24	-4
	NHL Totals	1432	708	627	1335	1159	+67
	WHA Totals	78	27	25	52	123	

Playoffs

SSN	TEAM	GP	G	A	PTS.	PIM
78-79	Cin (WHA)	3	0	0	0	2
82-83	Wash	4	0	0	0	4
83-84	Wash	8	3	7	10	16
84-85	Wash	5	4	3	7	9
85-86	Wash	9	2	10	12	4
86-87	Wash	7	4	3	7	14
87-88	Wash	14	3	4	7	14
88-89	Minn	5	0	0	0	6
89-90	NYR	10	5	3	8	12
90-91	NYR	6	1	1	2	0
91-92	NYR	13	8	8	16	4
93-94	Tor	18	5	6	11	14
94-95	Tor	5	2	2	4	2
95-96	Tor	6	4	1	5	4
96-97	Phoe	7	1	2	3	4
97-98	Phoe	5	1	0	1	18
	NHL Totals	122	43	50	93	125
	WHA Totals	3	0	2	2	2

*GASSOFF, Robert Allen 5-10 195 D
B. Quesnel, B.C., Apr. 17, 1953

SSN	TEAM	GP	G	A	PTS.	PIM	+/-
73-74	StL	28	0	3	3	84	-16
74-75	StL	60	4	14	18	222	+11
75-76	StL	80	1	12	13	306	-8
76-77	StL	77	6	18	24	254	-2
	Totals	245	11	47	58	866	-15

Playoffs

SSN	TEAM	GP	G	A	PTS.	PIM
74-75	StL	2	0	0	0	0
75-76	StL	3	0	0	0	6
76-77	StL	4	0	1	1	10
	Totals	9	0	1	1	16

GASSOFF, Howard Bradley (Brad) 5-11 195 LW
B. Quesnel, B.C., Nov. 13, 1955

SSN	TEAM	GP	G	A	PTS.	PIM	+/-
75-76	Van	4	0	0	0	5	-2
76-77	Van	37	6	4	10	35	-24
77-78	Van	47	9	6	15	70	-6
78-79	Van	34	4	7	11	53	-11
	Totals	122	19	17	36	163	-43

Playoffs

SSN	TEAM	GP	G	A	PTS.	PIM
78-79	Van	3	0	0	0	0

GATZOS, Steve 5-11 185 RW
B. Toronto, Ont., June 22, 1961

SSN	TEAM	GP	G	A	PTS.	PIM	+/-
81-82	Pitt	16	6	8	14	14	0
82-83	Pitt	44	6	7	13	52	-16
83-84	Pitt	23	3	3	6	15	-9
84-85	Pitt	6	0	2	2	2	-6
	Totals	89	15	20	35	83	-31

Playoffs

SSN	TEAM	GP	G	A	PTS.	PIM
81-82	Pitt	1	0	0	0	0

GAUDREAU, Robert Rene 5-11 185 RW
B. Lincoln, R.i., Jan. 20, 1970

SSN	TEAM	GP	G	A	PTS.	PIM	+/-
92-93	SJ	59	23	20	43	18	-18
93-94	SJ	84	15	20	35	28	-10
94-95	Ott	36	5	9	14	8	-16
95-96	Ott	52	8	5	13	15	-19
	Totals	231	51	54	105	69	-63

Playoffs

SSN	TEAM	GP	G	A	PTS.	PIM
93-94	SJ	14	2	0	2	0

GAUDREAULT, Armand Gerard 5-9 155 LW
B. Lac St. Jean, Que., July 14, 1921

SSN	TEAM	GP	G	A	PTS.	PIM
44-45	Bos	44	15	9	24	27

Playoffs

SSN	TEAM	GP	G	A	PTS.	PIM
44-45	Bos	7	0	2	2	8

*GAUDREAULT, Leonard (Leo) 5-9 152 LW
B. Chicoutimi, Que.

SSN	TEAM	GP	G	A	PTS.	PIM
27-28	Mont	32	6	2	8	24
28-29	Mont	11	0	0	0	4
32-33	Mont	24	2	2	4	2
	Totals	67	8	4	12	30

GAUL, Michael 6-1 200 D
B. Lachine, Que., April 22, 1973

SSN	TEAM	GP	G	A	PTS.	PIM	+/-
98-99	Col A	1	0	0	0	0	0

GAULIN, Jean–Marc 5-10 180 RW
B. Balve, Germany, Mar. 3, 1962

SSN	TEAM	GP	G	A	PTS.	PIM	+/-
82-83	Que	1	0	0	0	0	0
83-84	Que	2	0	0	0	0	-1
84-85	Que	22	3	3	6	8	+2
85-86	Que	1	1	0	1	0	0
	Totals	26	4	3	7	8	+1

Playoffs

SSN	TEAM	GP	G	A	PTS.	PIM
84-85	Que	1	0	0	0	0

GAUME, Dallas 5-10 185 C
B. Innisfal, Alta., Aug. 27, 1963

SSN	TEAM	GP	G	A	PTS.	PIM	+/-
88-89	Hart	4	1	1	2	0	+1

GAUTHIER, Arthur F

SSN	TEAM	GP	G	A	PTS.	PIM
26-27	Mont	13	0	0	0	0

Playoffs

SSN	TEAM	GP	G	A	PTS.	PIM
26-27	Mont	1	0	0	0	0

GAUTHIER, Daniel 6-1 190 LW
B. Charlemagne, Que., May 17, 1970

SSN	TEAM	GP	G	A	PTS.	PIM	+/-
94-95	Chi	5	0	0	0	0	0

GAUTHIER, Denis 6-2 195 D
B. Montreal, Que., Oct. 1, 1976

SSN	TEAM	GP	G	A	PTS.	PIM	+/-
97-98	Calg	5	0	0	0	23	-5
98-99	Calg	55	3	4	7	68	+3
	Totals	60	3	4	7	91	-2

GAUTHIER, Jean Philippe 6-1 200 D
B. Montreal, Que., Mar. 29, 1937

SSN	TEAM	GP	G	A	PTS.	PIM	+/-
60-61	Mont	4	0	1	1	8	
61-62	Mont	12	0	1	1	10	
62-63	Mont	65	1	17	18	46	
63-64	Mont	1	0	0	0	2	
65-66	Mont	2	0	0	0	0	
66-67	Mont	2	0	0	0	2	
67-68	Phil	65	5	7	12	74	0
68-69	Bos	11	0	2	2	8	-2
69-70	Mont	4	0	1	1	0	0
72-73	NY (WHA)	31	2	1	3	21	
	NHL Totals	166	6	29	35	150	-2
	WHA Totals	31	2	1	3	21	

Playoffs

SSN	TEAM	GP	G	A	PTS.	PIM
62-63	Mont	5	0	0	0	12
64-65	Mont	2	0	0	0	4
67-68	Phil	7	1	3	4	6
	NHL Totals	14	1	3	4	22

GAUTHIER, Luc 5-9 205 D
B. Longueuil, Que., Apr. 19, 1964

SSN	TEAM	GP	G	A	PTS.	PIM	+/-
90-91	Mont	3	0	0	0	2	+1

*GAUTHIER, Rene Fernand (Fern) 5-11 175 RW
B. Chicoutimi, Que., Aug. 31, 1919

SSN	TEAM	GP	G	A	PTS.	PIM
43-44	NYR	33	14	10	24	0
44-45	Mont	50	18	13	31	23
45-46	Det	30	9	8	17	6
46-47	Det	40	1	12	13	2
47-48	Det	35	1	5	6	2
48-49	Det	41	3	2	5	2
	Totals	229	46	50	96	35

Playoffs

SSN	TEAM	GP	G	A	PTS.	PIM
44-45	Mont	4	0	0	0	0
45-46	Det	5	3	0	3	2
46-47	Det	3	1	0	1	0
47-48	Det	10	1	1	2	5
	Totals	22	5	1	6	7

GAUVREAU, Jocelyn 5-11 180 D
B. Masham, Que., Mar. 4, 1964

SSN	TEAM	GP	G	A	PTS.	PIM	+/-
83-84	Mont	2	0	0	0	0	-2

GAVEY, Aaron 6-1 169 C
B. Sudburg, Ont., Feb. 22, 1974

SSN	TEAM	GP	G	A	PTS.	PIM	+/-
95-96	TB	73	8	4	12	56	-6
96-97	TB–Calg	57	8	11	19	46	-12
97-98	Calg	26	2	3	5	24	-5
98-99	Dal	7	0	0	0	10	-1
	Totals	163	18	18	36	136	-24

Playoffs

SSN	TEAM	GP	G	A	PTS.	PIM
95-96	TB	6	0	0	0	4

GAVIN, Robert (Stewart) 6-0 190 LW/RW
B. Ottawa, Ont., Mar. 15, 1960

SSN	TEAM	GP	G	A	PTS.	PIM	+/-
80-81	Tor	14	1	2	3	13	0
81-82	Tor	38	5	6	11	29	-6
82-83	Tor	63	6	5	11	44	-7
83-84	Tor	80	10	22	32	90	-6
84-85	Tor	73	12	13	25	38	-22
85-86	Hart	76	26	29	55	51	+12
86-87	Hart	79	20	21	41	28	+10
87-88	Hart	56	11	10	21	59	-17
88-89	Minn	73	8	18	26	34	+3
89-90	Minn	80	12	13	25	76	+9
90-91	Minn	38	4	4	8	36	-3
91-92	Minn	35	5	4	9	27	0
92-93	Minn	63	10	8	18	59	-4
	Totals	768	130	155	285	584	-31

Playoffs

SSN	TEAM	GP	G	A	PTS.	PIM
82-83	Tor	4	0	0	0	0
85-86	Hart	10	4	1	5	13
86-87	Hart	6	2	4	6	10
87-88	Hart	6	2	2	4	4
88-89	Minn	5	3	1	4	10
89-90	Minn	7	0	2	2	12
90-91	Minn	21	3	10	13	20
91-92	Minn	7	0	0	0	6
	Totals	66	14	20	34	75

GEALE, Robert Charles 5-11 175 C
B. Edmonton, Alta., Apr. 17, 1962

SSN	TEAM	GP	G	A	PTS.	PIM	+/-
84-85	Pitt	1	0	0	0	2	-1

*GEE, George 5-11 180 C
B. Stratford, Ont., June 28, 1922

SSN	TEAM	GP	G	A	PTS.	PIM
45-46	Chi	35	14	15	29	12
46-47	Chi	60	20	20	40	26
47-48	Chi	60	14	25	39	18
48-49	Chi–Det	51	7	14	21	31
49-50	Det	69	17	21	38	42
50-51	Det	70	17	20	37	19
51-52	Chi	70	18	31	49	39
52-53	Chi	67	18	21	39	99
53-54	Chi	69	10	16	26	59
	Totals	551	135	183	318	345

Playoffs

SSN	TEAM	GP	G	A	PTS.	PIM
45-46	Chi	4	1	1	2	4
48-49	Det	10	1	3	4	22
49-50	Det	14	3	6	9	0
50-51	Chi	6	0	1	1	0
52-53	Chi	7	1	2	3	6
	Totals	41	6	13	19	32

GELDART, Gary Daniel 5–8 155 D
B. Moncton, N.B., June 14, 1950

SSN	TEAM	GP	G	A	PTS.	PIM	+/-
70–71	Minn	4	0	0	0	5	+1

GELINAS, Martin 5–11 195 LW
B. Shawinigan, Que., June 5, 1970

SSN	TEAM	GP	G	A	PTS.	PIM	+/-
88–89	Edm	6	1	2	3	0	-1
89–90	Edm	46	17	8	25	30	0
90–91	Edm	73	20	20	40	34	-7
91–92	Edm	68	11	18	29	62	+14
92–93	Edm	65	11	12	23	30	+3
93–94	Que-Van	64	14	14	28	34	-8
94–95	Van	46	13	10	23	36	+8
95–96	Van	81	30	26	56	59	+8
96–97	Van	74	35	33	68	42	+6
97–98	Van-Car	64	16	18	34	40	-5
98–99	Car	76	13	15	28	67	+3
Totals		663	181	176	357	434	+21

Playoffs

88–89	Edm	20	2	3	5	6	
89–90	Edm	18	3	6	9	25	
90–91	Edm	15	1	3	4	10	
93–94	Van	24	5	4	9	14	
94–95	Van	3	0	1	1	0	
95–96	Van	6	1	1	2	12	
98–99	Car	6	0	3	3	2	
Totals		92	12	21	33	69	

GENDRON, Jean Guy (Smitty) 5–9 165 LW
B. Montreal, Que., Aug. 30, 1934

55–56	NYR	63	5	7	12	38	
56–57	NYR	70	9	6	15	40	
57–58	NYR	70	10	17	27	68	
58–59	Bos	60	15	9	24	57	
59–60	Bos	67	24	11	35	64	
60–61	Bos-Mont	66	10	19	29	75	
61–62	NYR	69	14	11	25	71	
62–63	Bos	66	21	22	43	42	
63–64	Bos	54	5	13	18	43	
67–68	Phil	1	0	1	1	2	+1
68–69	Phil	74	20	35	55	65	-8
69–70	Phil	71	23	21	44	54	+8
70–71	Phil	76	20	16	36	46	-9
71–72	Phil	56	6	13	19	36	-2
72–73	Que (WHA)	63	17	33	50	113	
73–74	Que (WHA)	64	11	8	19	42	
NHL Totals		863	182	201	383	701	-10
WHA Totals		127	28	41	69	155	

Playoffs

55–56	NYR	5	2	1	3	2	
56–57	NYR	5	0	1	1	6	
57–58	NYR	6	1	0	1	11	
58–59	Bos	7	1	0	1	18	
60–61	Mont	5	0	0	0	2	
61–62	NYR	6	3	1	4	2	
68–69	Phil	4	0	0	0	6	
70–71	Phil	4	0	1	1	0	
Totals		42	7	4	11	47	

GENDRON, Martin 5–9 190 RW
B. Valleyfield, Que., Feb. 15, 1974

94–95	Wash	8	2	1	3	2	+3
95–96	Wash	20	2	1	3	8	-5
97–98	Chi	2	0	0	0	0	-1
Totals		20	4	2	6	10	-3

GEOFFRION, Bernard Joseph Andre (Boom Boom) 5–11 185 RW
B. Montreal, Que., Feb. 16, 1931

50–51	Mont	18	8	6	14	9	
51–52	Mont	67	30	24	54	66	
52–53	Mont	65	22	17	39	37	
53–54	Mont	54	29	25	54	87	
54–55	Mont	70	38	37	75	57	
55–56	Mont	59	29	33	62	66	
56–57	Mont	41	19	21	40	18	
57–58	Mont	42	27	23	50	51	
58–59	Mont	59	22	44	66	30	
59–60	Mont	59	30	41	71	36	
60–61	Mont	64	50	45	95	29	
61–62	Mont	62	23	36	59	36	
62–63	Mont	51	23	18	41	73	
63–64	Mont	55	21	18	39	41	
66–67	NYR	58	17	25	42	42	
67–68	NYR	59	5	16	21	11	+1
Totals		883	393	429	822	689	+1

Playoffs

50–51	Mont	11	1	1	2	6	
51–52	Mont	11	3	1	4	6	
52–53	Mont	12	6	4	10	12	
53–54	Mont	11	6	5	11	18	
54–55	Mont	12	8	5	13	8	
55–56	Mont	10	5	9	14	6	
56–57	Mont	10	11	7	18	2	
57–58	Mont	10	6	5	11	2	
58–59	Mont	11	5	8	13	10	
59–60	Mont	8	2	10	12	4	
60–61	Mont	4	2	1	3	0	
61–62	Mont	5	0	1	1	6	
62–63	Mont	5	0	1	1	4	
63–64	Mont	7	1	1	2	4	
66–67	NYR	4	2	0	2	0	
67–68	NYR	1	0	1	1	0	
Totals		132	58	60	118	88	

GEOFFRION, Daniel 5–10 185 RW
B. Montreal, Que., Jan. 24, 1958

78–79	Que (WHA)	77	12	14	26	74	
79–80	Mont	32	0	6	6	12	+1
80–81	Winn	78	20	26	46	82	-32
81–82	Winn	1	0	0	0	5	-2
NHL Totals		111	20	32	52	99	-31
WHA Totals		77	12	14	26	74	

Playoffs

78–79	Que (WHA)	4	1	2	3	2	
79–80	Mont	2	0	0	0	7	
NHL Totals		2	0	0	0	7	
WHA Totals		4	1	2	3	2	

*GERAN, Gerald Pierce F
B. Holyoke, Mass., Aug. 3, 1896

17–18	Mont W	4	0	0	0	0	
25–26	Bos	33	5	1	6	6	
Totals		37	5	1	6	6	

*GERARD, Edward George F
B. Ottawa, Ont., Feb. 22, 1890

17–18	Ott	21	13	0	13	12	
18–19	Ott	18	4	6	10	17	
19–20	Ott	21	9	3	12	19	
20–21	Ott	24	11	4	15	18	
21–22	Ott	21	7	9	16	16	
22–23	Ott	23	6	8	14	24	
Totals		128	50	30	80	106	

Playoffs

18–19	Ott	5	3	0	3	3	
19–20	Ott	5	2	1	3	6	
20–21	Ott	7	1	0	1	33	
21–22	Ott	3	0	0	0	8	
22–23	Ott	7	1	0	1	2	
Totals		26	7	3	10	51	

GERMAIN, Eric 6–1 195 D
B. Quebec City, Que., June 26, 1966

87–88	LA	4	0	1	1	13	-2

GERNANDER, Ken 5–10 180 C
B. Coleraine, Minn., June 30, 1969

95–96	NYR	10	2	3	5	4	-3

Playoffs

95–96	NYR	6	0	0	0	0	
96–97	NYR	9	0	0	0	0	
Totals		15	0	0	0	0	

GETLIFFE, Raymond 5–11 175 C
B. Galt, Ont., Apr. 3, 1914

35–36	Bos	1	0	0	0	2	
36–37	Bos	48	16	15	31	28	
37–38	Bos	36	11	13	24	16	
38–39	Bos	43	10	12	22	11	
39–40	Mont	46	11	12	23	29	
40–41	Mont	39	15	10	25	25	
41–42	Mont	45	11	15	26	35	
42–43	Mont	50	18	28	46	56	
43–44	Mont	44	28	25	53	44	
44–45	Mont	41	16	7	23	34	
Totals		393	136	137	273	280	

Playoffs

35–36	Bos	2	0	0	0	0	
36–37	Bos	3	2	1	3	2	
37–38	Bos	3	0	1	1	2	
38–39	Bos	11	1	1	2	2	
40–41	Mont	3	1	1	2	0	
41–42	Mont	3	0	0	0	0	
42–43	Mont	5	0	1	1	8	
43–44	Mont	9	5	4	9	16	
44–45	Mont	6	0	1	1	0	
Totals		45	9	10	19	30	

GIALLONARDO, Mario 5–11 201 D
B. Toronto, Ont., Sept. 27, 1957

79–80	Col	8	0	1	1	2	-3
80–81	Col	15	0	2	2	4	+1
Totals		23	0	3	3	6	-2

GIBBS, Barry Paul 5–11 195 D
B. Lloydminster, Sask., Sept. 28, 1948

67–68	Bos	16	0	0	0	2	-1
68–69	Bos	8	0	0	0	2	-3
69–70	Minn	56	3	13	16	182	-12
70–71	Minn	68	5	15	20	132	-10
71–72	Minn	75	4	20	24	128	+4
72–73	Minn	63	10	24	34	54	+14
73–74	Minn	76	9	29	38	82	-17
74–75	Minn–Atl	76	7	33	40	61	-19
75–76	Atl	76	8	21	29	92	+1
76–77	Atl	66	1	16	17	63	-5
77–78	Atl-StL	78	7	17	24	69	-13
78–79	StL	76	2	27	29	46	-42
79–80	LA	63	2	9	11	32	-13
Totals		797	58	224	282	945	-106

Playoffs

69–70	Minn	6	1	0	1	7	
70–71	Minn	12	0	1	1	47	
71–72	Minn	7	1	1	2	9	
72–73	Minn	5	1	0	1	0	
75–76	Atl	2	1	0	1	2	
76–77	Atl	3	0	0	0	2	
79–80	LA	1	0	0	0	0	
Totals		36	4	2	6	67	

GIBSON, Don 6–1 210 D
B. Deloraine, Man., Dec. 29, 1967

90–91	Van	14	0	3	3	20	-1

GIBSON, Douglas John 5–10 175 C
B. Peterborough, Ont., Sept. 28, 1953

73–74	Bos	2	0	0	0	0	-1
75–76	Bos	50	7	18	25	0	+8
77–78	Wash	11	2	1	3	0	-3
Totals		63	9	19	28	0	+4

Playoffs

73–74	Bos	1	0	0	0	0	

GIBSON, John William 6–3 210 D
B. St. Catharines, Ont., June 2, 1959

78–79	Winn (WHA)	9	0	1	1	5	
80–81	LA	4	0	0	0	21	-5
81–82	LA-Tor	33	0	2	2	85	-9
83–84	Winn	11	0	0	0	14	+2
NHL Totals		48	0	2	2	120	-12
WHA Totals		9	0	1	1	5	

GIESEBRECHT, Roy (Gus) 6–0 177 C
B. Pembroke, Ont., Sept. 16, 1918

38–39	Det	28	10	10	20	2	
39–40	Det	30	4	7	11	2	
40–41	Det	43	7	18	25	7	
41–42	Det	34	6	16	22	2	
Totals		135	27	51	71	13	

Playoffs

38–39	Det	6	0	2	2	0	
40–41	Det	9	2	1	3	0	
41–42	Det	2	0	0	0	0	
Totals		17	2	3	5	0	

GIFFIN, Lee 6–0 188 RW
B. Chatham, Ont., Apr. 1, 1967

86–87	Pitt	8	1	1	2	0	+2

SSN	TEAM	GP	G	A	PTS.	PIM	+/-
87–88	Pitt	19	0	2	2	9	-2
Totals		27	1	3	4	9	0

GILBERT, Edward Ferguson *6–0 185 C*
B. Hamilton, Ont., Mar. 12, 1952

74–75	KC	80	16	22	38	14	-45
75–76	KC–Pitt	79	5	9	14	8	-30
76–77	Pitt	7	0	0	0	0	-3
78–79	Cin (WHA)	29	3	3	6	40	
NHL Totals		166	21	31	52	22	-78
WHA Totals		29	3	3	6	40	

GILBERT, Gregory Scott *6–1 191 LW*
B. Mississauga, Ont., Jan. 22, 1962

81–82	NYI	1	1	0	1	0	0
82–83	NYI	45	8	11	19	30	+1
83–84	NYI	79	31	35	66	59	+51
84–85	NYI	58	13	25	38	36	+4
85–86	NYI	60	9	19	28	82	-5
86–87	NYI	51	6	7	13	26	-12
87–88	NYI	76	17	28	45	46	+14
88–89	NYI–Chi	59	8	13	21	45	+2
89–90	Chi	70	12	25	37	54	+27
90–91	Chi	72	10	15	25	58	+6
91–92	Chi	50	7	5	12	35	-4
92–93	Chi	77	13	19	32	57	+5
93–94	NYR	76	4	11	15	29	-3
94–95	StL	46	11	14	25	11	+22
95–96	StL	17	0	1	1	8	-1
Totals		837	150	228	378	576	+107

Playoffs

81–82	NYI	4	1	1	2	2	
82–83	NYI	10	1	0	1	14	
83–84	NYI	21	5	7	12	39	
85–86	NYI	2	0	0	0	0	
86–87	NYI	10	2	2	4	6	
87–88	NYI	4	0	0	0	6	
88–89	Chi	15	1	5	6	20	
89–90	Chi	19	5	8	13	34	
90–91	Chi	5	0	1	1	2	
91–92	Chi	10	1	3	4	16	
92–93	Chi	3	0	0	0	0	
93–94	NYR	23	1	3	4	8	
94–95	StL	7	0	3	3	6	
Totals		133	17	33	50	162	

GILBERT, Jeannot Elmourt (Jean) *5–9 170 C*
B. Port Alfred, Que., Dec. 29, 1940

62–63	Bos	5	0	0	0	4	
64–65	Bos	4	0	0	0	0	
73–74	Que (WHA)	75	17	39	56	20	
74–75	Que (WHA)	58	7	21	28	12	
NHL Totals		9	0	0	0	4	
WHA Totals		133	24	60	84	32	

Playoffs

74–75	Que (WHA)	11	3	6	9	2	

GILBERT, Rodrique Gabriel (Rod) *5–9 180 RW*
B. Montreal, Que., July 1, 1941

60–61	NYR	1	0	1	1	2	
61–62	NYR	1	0	0	0	0	
62–63	NYR	70	11	20	31	20	
63–64	NYR	70	24	40	64	62	
64–65	NYR	70	25	36	61	52	
65–66	NYR	34	10	15	25	20	
66–67	NYR	64	28	18	46	12	
67–68	NYR	73	29	48	77	12	+13
68–69	NYR	66	28	49	77	22	+12
69–70	NYR	72	16	37	53	22	+2
70–71	NYR	78	30	31	61	65	+22
71–72	NYR	73	43	54	97	64	+51
72–73	NYR	76	25	59	84	25	+12
73–74	NYR	75	36	41	77	20	+11
74–75	NYR	76	36	61	97	22	+1
75–76	NYR	70	36	50	86	32	-8
76–77	NYR	77	27	48	75	50	-17
77–78	NYR	19	2	7	9	6	-10
Totals		1065	406	615	1021	508	+89

Playoffs

61–62	NYR	4	2	3	5	4	
66–67	NYR	4	2	2	4	6	
67–68	NYR	6	5	0	5	4	

SSN	TEAM	GP	G	A	PTS.	PIM	+/-
68–69	NYR	4	1	0	1	2	
69–70	NYR	6	4	5	9	0	
70–71	NYR	13	4	6	10	8	
71–72	NYR	16	7	8	15	11	
72–73	NYR	10	5	1	6	2	
73–74	NYR	13	3	5	8	4	
74–75	NYR	3	1	3	4	2	
Totals		79	34	33	67	43	

GILBERTSON, Stanley Frank *6–0 175 LW*
B. Duluth, Minn., Oct. 29, 1944

71–72	Cal	78	16	16	32	47	-6
72–73	Cal	66	6	15	21	19	-34
73–74	Cal	76	18	12	30	39	-41
74–75	Cal–StL–Wash	62	13	15	28	18	-50
75–76	Wash–Pitt	79	26	22	48	12	-28
76–77	Pitt	67	6	9	15	13	-9
Totals		428	85	89	174	148	-168

Playoffs

75–76	Pitt	3	1	1	2	2	

GILCHRIST, Brent *5–11 181 LW*
B. Moose Jaw, Sask., Apr. 3, 1967

88–89	Mont	49	8	16	24	16	+9
89–90	Mont	57	9	15	24	28	+3
90–91	Mont	51	6	9	15	10	-3
91–92	Mont	79	23	27	50	57	+29
92–93	Edm–Minn	68	10	11	21	49	-12
93–94	Dal	76	17	14	31	31	0
94–95	Dal	32	9	4	13	16	-3
95–96	Dal	77	20	22	42	36	-11
96–97	Dal	67	10	20	30	24	+6
97–98	Dal	61	13	14	27	40	+4
98–99	Det	5	1	0	1	0	-1
Totals		622	126	152	278	307	+21

Playoffs

88–89	Mont	9	1	1	2	10	
89–90	Mont	8	2	0	2	2	
90–91	Mont	13	5	3	8	6	
91–92	Mont	11	2	4	6	6	
93–94	Dal	9	3	1	4	2	
94–95	Dal	5	0	1	1	2	
96–97	Dal	6	2	2	4	2	
97–98	Dal	15	2	1	3	12	
98–99	Det	3	0	0	0	0	
Totals		79	17	13	30	42	

GILES, Curt *5–8 175 D*
B. The Pas, Man., Nov. 30, 1958

79–80	Minn	37	2	7	9	31	-9
80–81	Minn	67	5	22	27	56	+9
81–82	Minn	74	3	12	15	87	+15
82–83	Minn	76	2	21	23	70	+11
83–84	Minn	70	6	22	28	59	+2
84–85	Minn	77	5	25	30	49	+3
85–86	Minn	69	6	21	27	30	+19
86–87	Minn–NYR	72	2	20	22	54	+5
87–88	NYR–Minn	72	1	12	13	76	-33
88–89	Minn	76	5	10	15	77	+2
89–90	Minn	74	1	12	13	48	+3
90–91	Minn	70	4	10	14	48	+3
91–92	StL	13	1	1	2	8	-3
92–93	StL	48	0	4	4	40	-2
Totals		895	43	199	242	733	+25

Playoffs

79–80	Minn	12	2	4	6	10	
80–81	Minn	19	1	4	5	14	
81–82	Minn	4	0	0	0	2	
82–83	Minn	5	0	2	2	6	
83–84	Minn	16	1	3	4	25	
84–85	Minn	9	0	0	0	17	
85–86	Minn	5	0	1	1	10	
86–87	NYR	5	0	0	0	6	
88–89	Minn	5	0	0	0	4	
89–90	Minn	7	0	1	1	6	
90–91	Minn	10	1	0	1	16	
91–92	StL	3	1	1	2	0	
92–93	StL	3	0	0	0	2	
Totals		103	6	16	22	118	

GILHEN, Randy *6–0 190 C*
B. Zweibrucken, West Germany, June 13, 1963

SSN	TEAM	GP	G	A	PTS.	PIM	+/-
82–83	Hart	2	0	1	1	0	0
86–87	Winn	2	0	0	0	0	-2
87–88	Winn	13	3	2	5	15	+5
88–89	Winn	64	5	3	8	38	-24
89–90	Winn	61	5	11	16	54	-8
90–91	Pitt	72	15	10	25	51	+3
91–92	LA–NYR	73	10	13	23	28	+2
92–93	NYR–TB	44	3	4	7	14	-14
93–94	Fla–Winn	60	7	7	14	50	-12
94–95	Winn	44	5	6	11	52	-17
95–96	Winn	22	2	3	5	12	+1
Totals		457	55	60	115	314	-66

Playoffs

87–88	Winn	4	1	0	1	10	
90–91	Pitt	16	1	0	1	14	
91–92	NYR	13	1	2	3	2	
Totals		33	3	2	5	26	

GILL, Hal *6–6 200 D*
B. Concord, Mass., Apr. 6, 1975

97–98	Bos	68	2	4	6	47	+4
98–99	Bos	80	3	7	10	63	-10
Totals		148	5	11	16	110	-6

Playoffs

97–98	Bos	6	0	0	0	4	
98–99	Bos	12	0	0	0	14	
Totals		18	0	0	0	18	

GILL, Todd *6–0 185 D*
B. Brockville, Ont., Nov. 9, 1965

84–85	Tor	10	1	0	1	13	-1
85–86	Tor	15	1	2	3	28	0
86–87	Tor	61	4	27	31	92	-3
87–88	Tor	65	8	17	25	131	-20
88–89	Tor	59	11	14	25	72	-3
89–90	Tor	48	1	14	15	92	-8
90–91	Tor	72	2	22	24	113	-4
91–92	Tor	74	2	15	17	91	-22
92–93	Tor	69	11	32	43	66	+4
93–94	Tor	45	4	24	28	44	+8
94–95	Tor	47	7	25	32	64	-8
95–96	Tor	74	7	18	25	116	-15
96–97	SJ	79	0	21	21	101	-20
97–98	SJ–StL	75	13	17	30	41	-11
98–99	StL–Det	51	4	5	9	27	-10
Totals		844	76	253	329	1091	-113

Playoffs

85–86	Tor	1	0	0	0	0	
86–87	Tor	13	2	2	4	42	
87–88	Tor	6	1	3	4	20	
89–90	Tor	5	0	3	3	16	
92–93	Tor	21	1	10	11	26	
93–94	Tor	18	1	5	6	37	
94–95	Tor	7	0	3	3	6	
95–96	Tor	6	0	0	0	24	
97–98	StL	10	2	2	4	10	
98–99	Det	2	0	1	1	0	
Totals		89	7	29	36	181	

GILLEN, Donald *6–3 222 RW*
B. Dodsland, Sask., Dec. 24, 1960

79–80	Phil	1	1	0	1	0	+1
81–82	Hart	34	1	4	5	22	-11
Totals		35	2	4	6	22	-10

GILLIE, Ferrand *F*
B. Cornwall, Ont.

28–29	Det	1	0	0	0	0	

GILLIES, Clark *6–3 215 LW*
B. Moose Jaw, Sask., Apr. 7, 1954

74–75	NYI	80	25	22	47	66	-4
75–76	NYI	80	34	27	61	96	+20
76–77	NYI	70	33	22	55	93	-18
77–78	NYI	80	35	50	85	76	+49
78–79	NYI	75	35	56	91	68	+57
79–80	NYI	73	19	35	54	49	+29
80–81	NYI	80	33	45	78	99	+26
81–82	NYI	79	38	39	77	75	+39
82–83	NYI	70	21	20	41	76	+9
83–84	NYI	76	12	16	28	65	+5

SSN	TEAM	GP	G	A	PTS.	PIM	+/-
84-85	NYI	54	15	17	32	73	0
85-86	NYI	55	4	10	14	55	-8
86-87	Buf	61	10	17	27	81	0
87-88	Buf	25	5	2	7	51	+1
Totals		958	319	378	697	1023	+239

Playoffs

SSN	TEAM	GP	G	A	PTS.	PIM
74-75	NYI	17	4	2	6	36
75-76	NYI	13	2	4	6	16
76-77	NYI	12	4	4	8	15
77-78	NYI	7	2	0	2	15
78-79	NYI	10	1	2	3	11
79-80	NYI	21	6	10	16	63
80-81	NYI	18	6	9	15	28
81-82	NYI	19	8	6	14	34
82-83	NYI	8	0	2	2	10
83-84	NYI	21	12	7	19	19
84-85	NYI	10	1	0	1	9
85-86	NYI	3	1	0	1	6
87-88	Buf	5	0	1	1	25
Totals		164	47	47	94	284

GILLIS, Jere Alan 6-0 190 LW
B. Bend, Ore., Jan. 18, 1957

SSN	TEAM	GP	G	A	PTS.	PIM	+/-
77-78	Van	79	23	18	41	35	-24
78-79	Van	78	13	12	25	33	-31
79-80	Van	67	13	17	30	108	0
80-81	Van-NYR	46	10	14	24	8	+6
81-82	NYR-Que	38	5	10	15	16	0
82-83	Buf	3	0	0	0	0	6
83-84	Van	37	9	13	22	7	+2
84-85	Van	37	5	11	16	23	-7
86-87	Phil	1	0	0	0	0	0
Totals		386	78	95	173	230	-60

Playoffs

SSN	TEAM	GP	G	A	PTS.	PIM
78-79	Van	1	0	1	1	0
80-81	NYR	14	2	5	7	9
83-84	Van	4	2	1	3	0
Totals		19	4	7	11	9

GILLIS, Michael David 6-1 195 LW
B. Sudbury, Ont., Dec. 1, 1958

SSN	TEAM	GP	G	A	PTS.	PIM	+/-
78-79	Col	30	1	7	8	6	-18
79-80	Col	40	4	5	9	22	-18
80-81	Col-Bos	68	13	11	24	69	-23
81-82	Bos	53	9	8	17	54	+10
82-83	Bos	5	0	1	1	0	+1
83-84	Bos	50	6	11	17	35	-7
Totals		246	33	43	76	186	-55

Playoffs

SSN	TEAM	GP	G	A	PTS.	PIM
80-81	Bos	1	0	0	0	0
81-82	Bos	11	1	2	3	6
82-83	Bos	12	1	3	4	2
83-84	Bos	3	0	0	0	2
Totals		27	2	5	7	10

GILLIS, Paul 5-11 198 C
B. Toronto, Ont., Dec. 31, 1963

SSN	TEAM	GP	G	A	PTS.	PIM	+/-
82-83	Que	7	0	2	2	2	-1
83-84	Que	57	8	9	17	59	+10
84-85	Que	77	14	28	42	168	+12
85-86	Que	80	19	24	43	203	-2
86-87	Que	76	13	26	39	267	-5
87-88	Que	80	7	10	17	164	-29
88-89	Que	79	15	25	40	163	-14
89-90	Que	71	8	14	22	234	-24
90-91	Que-Chi	62	3	13	16	144	-18
91-92	Chi-Hart	14	0	2	2	54	-3
92-93	Hart	21	1	1	2	40	-2
Totals		624	88	154	242	1498	-76

Playoffs

SSN	TEAM	GP	G	A	PTS.	PIM
83-84	Que	1	0	0	0	2
84-85	Que	18	1	7	8	73
85-86	Que	3	0	2	2	14
86-87	Que	13	2	4	6	65
90-91	Chi	2	0	0	0	2
91-92	Hart	5	0	1	1	0
Totals		42	3	14	17	156

GILMOUR, Douglas 5-11 170 C
B. Kingston, Ont., June 25, 1963

SSN	TEAM	GP	G	A	PTS.	PIM	+/-
83-84	StL	80	25	28	53	57	+6
84-85	StL	78	21	36	57	49	+3
85-86	StL	74	25	28	53	41	-3
86-87	StL	80	42	63	105	58	-2
87-88	StL	72	36	50	86	59	-13
88-89	Calg	72	26	59	85	44	+45
89-90	Calg	78	24	67	91	54	+20
90-91	Calg	78	20	61	81	144	+27
91-92	Calg-Tor	78	26	61	87	78	+25
92-93	Tor	83	32	95	127	100	+32
93-94	Tor	83	27	84	111	105	+25
94-95	Tor	44	10	23	33	26	-5
95-96	Tor	81	32	40	72	77	-5
96-97	Tor-NJ	81	22	60	82	68	+2
97-98	NJ	63	13	40	53	68	+10
98-99	Chi	72	16	40	56	56	-16
Totals		1197	397	835	1232	1084	+151

Playoffs

SSN	TEAM	GP	G	A	PTS.	PIM
83-84	StL	11	2	9	11	10
84-85	StL	3	1	1	2	2
85-86	StL	19	9	12	21	25
86-87	StL	6	2	2	4	16
87-88	StL	10	3	14	17	18
88-89	Calg	22	11	11	22	20
89-90	Calg	6	3	1	4	8
90-91	Calg	7	1	1	2	0
92-93	Tor	21	10	25	35	30
93-94	Tor	18	6	22	28	42
94-95	Tor	7	0	6	6	6
95-96	Tor	6	1	7	8	12
96-97	NJ	10	0	4	4	4
97-98	NJ	6	5	2	7	4
Totals		152	54	117	171	207

GINGRAS, Gaston Reginald 6-0 190 D
B. Temiscamingue, Que., Feb. 13, 1959

SSN	TEAM	GP	G	A	PTS.	PIM	+/-
78-79	Birm (WHA)	60	13	21	34	35	
79-80	Mont	34	3	7	10	18	+11
80-81	Mont	55	5	16	21	22	+5
81-82	Mont	34	6	18	24	28	+10
82-83	Mont-Tor	67	11	26	37	18	+17
83-84	Tor	59	7	20	27	16	-30
84-85	Tor	5	0	2	2	0	-7
85-86	Mont	34	8	18	26	12	-10
86-87	Mont	66	11	34	45	21	+2
87-88	Mont-StL	70	7	23	30	20	+1
88-89	StL	52	3	10	13	6	+1
NHL Totals		476	61	174	235	161	-4
WHA Totals		60	13	21	34	35	

Playoffs

SSN	TEAM	GP	G	A	PTS.	PIM
79-80	Mont	10	1	6	7	8
80-81	Mont	1	1	0	1	0
81-82	Mont	5	0	1	1.	0
82-83	Tor	3	1	2	3	2
85-86	Mont	11	2	3	5	4
86-87	Mont	5	0	2	2	0
87-88	StL	10	1	3	4	4
88-89	StL	7	0	1	1	2
NHL Totals		52	6	18	24	20

GIRARD, Jonathan 5-11 192 D
B. Joliette, Que,. May 27, 1980

SSN	TEAM	GP	G	A	PTS.	PIM	+/-
98-99	Bos	3	0	0	0	0	+1

GIRARD, Kenneth 6-0 184 RW
B. Toronto, Ont., Dec. 8, 1936

SSN	TEAM	GP	G	A	PTS.	PIM
56-57	Tor	3	0	1	1	2
57-58	Tor	3	0	0	0	0
59-60	Tor	1	0	0	0	0
Totals		7	0	1	1	2

GIRARD, Robert 6-0 180 LW
B. Montreal, Que., Apr. 12, 1949

SSN	TEAM	GP	G	A	PTS.	PIM	+/-
75-76	Cal	80	16	26	42	54	-3
76-77	Clev	68	11	10	21	33	-24
77-78	Clev-Wash	77	9	18	27	17	-11
78-79	Wash	79	9	15	24	36	-15
79-80	Wash	1	0	0	0	0	0
Totals		305	45	69	114	140	-53

***GIROUX, Arthur Joseph** 5-1 165 RW
B. Strathmore, Alta., June 6, 1907

SSN	TEAM	GP	G	A	PTS.	PIM
32-33	Mont	40	5	2	7	14
34-35	Bos	10	1	0	1	0
35-36	Det	4	0	2	2	0
Totals		54	6	4	10	14

Playoffs

SSN	TEAM	GP	G	A	PTS.	PIM
32-33	Mont	2	0	0	0	0

GIROUX, Larry Douglas 6-0 190 D
B. Weyburn, Sask., Aug. 28, 1951

SSN	TEAM	GP	G	A	PTS.	PIM	+/-
73-74	StL	74	5	17	22	59	-14
74-75	KC-Det	60	2	26	28	84	-30
75-76	Det	10	1	1	2	25	-10
76-77	Det	2	0	0	0	2	0
77-78	Det	5	0	3	3	4	-5
78-79	StL	73	5	22	27	111	-25
79-80	StL-Hart	50	2	5	7	48	-2
Totals		274	15	74	89	333	-86

Playoffs

SSN	TEAM	GP	G	A	PTS.	PIM
77-78	Det	2	0	0	0	2
79-80	Hart	3	0	0	0	0
Totals		5	0	0	0	4

GIROUX, Pierre Yves Richard 5-11 185 C
B. Brownsburg, Que., Nov. 17, 1955

SSN	TEAM	GP	G	A	PTS.	PIM	+/-
82-83	LA	6	1	0	1	17	-1

GLADNEY, Robert Lawrence 5-11 185 D
B. Come-by-Chance, Nfld., Aug. 27, 1957

SSN	TEAM	GP	G	A	PTS.	PIM	+/-
82-83	LA	1	0	0	0	2	-2
83-84	Pitt	13	1	5	6	2	-1
Totals		14	1	5	6	4	-3

GLADU, Joseph Jean Paul 5-10 180 LW
B. St. Hyacinthe, Que., June 20, 1921

SSN	TEAM	GP	G	A	PTS.	PIM
44-45	Bos	40	6	14	20	2

Playoffs

SSN	TEAM	GP	G	A	PTS.	PIM
44-45	Bos	7	2	2	4	0

GLENNIE, Brian Alexander 6-1 200 D
B. Toronto, Ont., Aug. 29, 1946

SSN	TEAM	GP	G	A	PTS.	PIM	+/-
69-70	Tor	52	1	14	15	50	-4
70-71	Tor	54	0	8	8	31	-1
71-72	Tor	61	2	8	10	44	+11
72-73	Tor	44	1	10	11	54	+2
73-74	Tor	65	4	18	22	100	+27
74-75	Tor	63	1	7	8	110	-5
75-76	Tor	69	0	8	8	75	+10
76-77	Tor	69	1	10	11	73	-1
77-78	Tor	77	2	15	17	62	+24
78-79	LA	18	2	2	4	22	+2
Totals		572	14	100	114	621	+65

Playoffs

SSN	TEAM	GP	G	A	PTS.	PIM
70-71	Tor	3	0	0	0	0
71-72	Tor	5	0	0	0	25
73-74	Tor	3	0	0	0	10
75-76	Tor	6	0	1	1	15
76-77	Tor	2	0	0	0	0
77-78	Tor	13	0	0	0	16
Totals		32	0	1	1	66

GLENNON, Matthew 6-0 185 LW
B. Hull, Mass., Sept. 20, 1968

SSN	TEAM	GP	G	A	PTS.	PIM	+/-
91-92	Bos	3	0	0	0	2	0

GLOECKNER, Lorry 6-2 210 D
B. Kindersley, Sask., Jan. 25, 1956

SSN	TEAM	GP	G	A	PTS.	PIM	+/-
78-79	Det	13	0	2	2	6	-7

GLOOR, Daniel Harold 5-9 170 C
B. Stratford, Ont., Dec. 4, 1952

SSN	TEAM	GP	G	A	PTS.	PIM	+/-
73-74	Van	2	0	0	0	0	-2

GLOVER, Frederick Austin 5-9 175 RW
B. Toronto, Ont., Jan. 5, 1928

SSN	TEAM	GP	G	A	PTS.	PIM
49-50	Det	7	0	0	0	0
51-52	Det	54	9	9	18	25
52-53	Chi	31	4	2	6	37
Totals		92	13	11	24	62

Playoffs

SSN	TEAM	GP	G	A	PTS.	PIM
48-49	Det	1	0	0	0	0
50-51	Det	2	0	0	0	0
Totals		3	0	0	0	0

GLOVER, Howard Edward *5-11 195 RW*
B. Toronto, Ont., Feb. 14, 1935

SSN	TEAM	GP	G	A	PTS.	PIM	+/-
58-59	Chi	13	0	1	1	2	
60-61	Det	66	21	8	29	46	
61-62	Det	39	7	8	15	44	
63-64	NYR	25	1	0	1	9	
68-69	Mont	1	0	0	0	0	0
Totals		144	29	17	46	101	0

Playoffs

60-61	Det	11	1	2	3	2	

GLYNN, Brian *6-4 224 D*
B. Iserlohn, West Germany, Nov. 23, 1967

87-88	Calg	67	5	14	19	87	-2
88-89	Calg	9	0	1	1	19	+1
89-90	Calg	1	0	0	0	0	-1
90-91	Minn	66	8	11	19	83	-5
91-92	Minn-Edm	62	4	18	22	30	-5
92-93	Edm	64	4	12	16	60	-13
93-94	Ott-Van	64	2	13	15	53	-19
94-95	Hart	43	1	6	7	32	-2
95-96	Hart	54	0	4	4	44	-15
96-97	Hart	1	1	0	1	2	+2
Totals		431	25	79	104	410	-59

Playoffs

87-88	Calg	1	0	0	0	0	
90-91	Minn	23	2	6	8	18	
91-92	Edm	16	4	1	5	12	
93-94	Van	17	0	3	3	10	
Totals		57	6	10	16	40	

GODDEN, Ernie Alfred *5-7 154 C*
B. Keswick, Ont., Mar. 13, 1961

81-82	Tor	5	1	1	2	6	+1

GODFREY, Warren Edward (Rocky) *6-1 190 D*
B. Toronto, Ont., Mar. 23, 1931

52-53	Bos	60	1	13	14	40	
53-54	Bos	70	5	9	14	71	
54-55	Bos	62	1	17	18	58	
55-56	Det	67	2	6	8	86	
56-57	Det	69	1	8	9	103	
57-58	Det	67	2	16	18	56	
58-59	Det	69	6	4	10	44	
59-60	Det	69	5	9	14	60	
60-61	Det	63	3	16	19	62	
61-62	Bos	69	4	13	17	84	
62-63	Bos	66	2	9	11	56	
63-64	Det	4	0	0	0	2	
64-65	Det	11	0	0	0	8	
65-66	Det	26	0	4	4	22	
66-67	Det	2	0	0	0	0	
67-68	Det	12	0	1	1	0	+11
Totals		786	32	125	157	752	+11

Playoffs

52-53	Bos	11	0	1	1	2	
53-54	Bos	4	0	0	0	4	
54-55	Bos	3	0	0	0	0	
56-57	Det	5	0	0	0	6	
57-58	Det	4	0	0	0	0	
59-60	Det	6	1	0	1	10	
60-61	Det	11	0	2	2	18	
64-65	Det	4	0	1	1	2	
65-66	Det	4	0	0	0	0	
Totals		52	1	4	5	42	

*GODIN, Hogomer Gabriel (Sammy) *5-9 156 RW*
B. Rockland, Ont., Sept. 20, 1909

27-28	Ott	24	0	0	0	0	
28-29	Ott	23	2	1	3	21	
33-34	Mont	36	2	2	4	15	
Totals		83	4	3	7	36	

GODIN, Joseph Alain (Eddy) *5-10 187 RW*
B. Donnacona, Que., Mar. 29, 1957

77-78	Wash	18	3	3	6	6	-14
78-79	Wash	9	0	3	3	6	-2
Totals		27	3	6	9	12	-16

GODYNYUK, Alexander *6-0 207 D*
B. Kiev, Soviet Union, Jan. 27, 1970

90-91	Tor	18	0	3	3	16	-3

SSN	TEAM	GP	G	A	PTS.	PIM	+/-
91-92	Tor-Calg	37	3	7	10	63	-14
92-93	Calg	27	3	4	7	19	+6
93-94	Fla-Hart	69	3	19	22	75	+13
94-95	Hart	14	0	0	0	8	+1
95-96	Hart	3	0	0	0	2	-1
96-97	Hart	55	1	6	7	41	-10
Totals		223	10	39	49	224	-8

GOEGAN, Peter John *6-1 200 D*
B. Fort William, Ont., Mar. 6, 1934

57-58	Det	14	0	2	2	28	
58-59	Det	67	1	11	12	109	
59-60	Det	21	3	0	3	6	
60-61	Det	67	5	29	34	48	
61-62	Det-NYR	46	5	7	12	30	
62-63	Det	62	1	8	9	48	
63-64	Det	12	0	0	0	8	
64-65	Det	4	1	0	1	2	
65-66	Det	13	0	2	2	14	
66-67	Det	31	2	6	8	12	
67-68	Minn	46	1	2	3	30	-16
Totals		383	19	67	86	335	-16

Playoffs

57-58	Det	4	0	0	0	18	
59-60	Det	6	1	0	1	13	
60-61	Det	11	0	1	1	18	
62-63	Det	11	0	2	2	12	
65-66	Det	1	0	0	0	0	
Totals		33	1	3	4	61	

GOERTZ, Dave *5-11 199 D*
B. Edmonton, Alta., Mar. 28, 1965

87-88	Pitt	2	0	0	0	2	-1

*GOLDHAM, Robert John *6-1 195 D*
B. Georgetown, Ont., May 12, 1922

41-42	Tor	19	4	7	11	25	
45-46	Tor	49	7	14	21	44	
46-47	Tor	11	1	1	2	10	
47-48	Chi	38	2	9	11	38	
48-49	Chi	60	1	10	11	43	
49-50	Chi	67	2	10	12	57	
50-51	Chi	61	5	18	23	31	
51-52	Det	69	0	14	14	24	
52-53	Det	70	1	13	14	32	
53-54	Det	69	1	15	16	50	
54-55	Det	69	1	16	17	14	
55-56	Det	68	3	16	19	32	
Totals		650	28	143	171	400	

Playoffs

41-42	Tor	13	2	2	4	31	
50-51	Det	6	0	1	1	0	
51-52	Det	8	0	1	1	8	
52-53	Det	6	1	1	2	2	
53-54	Det	12	0	2	2	2	
54-55	Det	11	0	4	4	4	
55-56	Det	10	0	3	3	4	
Totals		66	3	14	17	53	

*GOLDSWORTHY, Leroy D. *6-0 190 RW*
B. Two Harbors, Minn., Oct. 18, 1908

29-30	NYR	44	4	1	5	16	
30-31	Det	13	1	0	1	2	
32-33	Det	26	3	6	9	6	
33-34	Chi	28	3	3	6	0	
34-35	Chi-Mont	40	20	9	29	15	
35-36	Mont	47	15	11	26	8	
36-37	Bos	47	8	6	14	8	
37-38	Bos	45	9	10	19	14	
38-39	NYA	47	3	11	14	10	
Totals		337	66	57	123	79	

Playoffs

29-30	NYR	4	0	0	0	2	
32-33	Det	2	0	0	0	0	
33-34	Chi	8	0	0	0	0	
34-35	Mont	2	1	0	1	0	
36-37	Bos	3	0	0	0	0	
37-38	Bos	3	0	0	0	2	
Totals		22	1	0	1	4	

*GOLDSWORTHY, William Alfred *6-0 190 RW*
B. Kitchener, Ont., Aug. 24, 1944

64-65	Bos	2	0	0	0	0	

SSN	TEAM	GP	G	A	PTS.	PIM	+/-
65-66	Bos	13	3	1	4	6	
66-67	Bos	18	3	5	8	21	
67-68	Minn	68	14	19	33	68	-8
68-69	Minn	68	14	10	24	110	-27
69-70	Minn	75	36	29	65	89	-9
70-71	Minn	77	34	31	65	85	-13
71-72	Minn	78	31	31	62	59	+11
72-73	Minn	75	27	33	60	97	+24
73-74	Minn	74	48	26	74	73	+3
74-75	Minn	71	37	35	72	77	-37
75-76	Minn	68	24	22	46	47	-19
76-77	Minn-NYR	77	12	15	27	49	-25
77-78	NYR	7	0	1	1	12	+1
77-78	Ind (WHA)	32	8	10	18	10	
78-79	Edm (WHA)	17	4	2	6	14	
NHL Totals		771	283	258	541	793	-99
WHA Totals		49	12	12	24	24	

Playoffs

67-68	Minn	14	8	7	15	12	
69-70	Minn	6	4	3	7	6	
70-71	Minn	7	2	4	6	6	
71-72	Minn	7	2	3	5	6	
72-73	Minn	6	2	2	4	0	
78-79	Edm (WHA)	4	1	1	2	11	
NHL Totals		40	18	19	37	30	
WHA Totals		4	1	1	2	11	

GOLDUP, Glenn Michael *6-0 190 RW*
B. St. Catharines, Ont., Apr. 26, 1953

73-74	Mont	6	0	0	0	0	-1
74-75	Mont	9	0	1	1	2	-1
75-76	Mont	3	0	0	0	2	-1
76-77	LA	28	7	6	13	29	+5
77-78	LA	66	14	18	32	66	-8
78-79	LA	73	15	22	37	89	-7
79-80	LA	55	10	11	21	78	-4
80-81	LA	49	6	9	15	35	-2
81-82	LA	2	0	0	0	0	0
Totals		291	52	67	119	301	-19

Playoffs

76-77	LA	8	2	2	4	2	
77-78	LA	2	1	0	1	11	
78-79	LA	2	0	1	1	9	
79-80	LA	4	1	0	1	0	
Totals		16	4	3	7	22	

GOLDUP, Henry G. (Hank) *5-11 175 LW*
B. Kingston, Ont., Oct. 29, 1918

40-41	Tor	26	10	5	15	9	
41-42	Tor	44	12	18	30	13	
42-43	Tor-NYR	44	12	27	39	37	
44-45	NYR	48	17	25	42	25	
45-46	NYR	19	6	1	7	11	
Totals		181	57	76	133	95	

Playoffs

39-40	Tor	10	5	1	6	4	
40-41	Tor	7	0	0	0	0	
41-42	Tor	9	0	0	0	2	
Totals		26	5	1	6	6	

GOLUBOVSKY, Yan *6-4 204 D*
B. Novosibirsk, Russia, Mar. 9, 1976

97-98	Det	12	0	2	2	6	+1
98-99	Det	17	0	1	1	16	+4
Totals		29	0	3	3	22	+5

GONCHAR, Sergei *6-2 212 D*
B. Chelyabinsk, USSR, Apr. 13, 1974

94-95	Wash	31	2	5	7	22	+4
95-96	Wash	78	15	26	41	60	+25
96-97	Wash	57	13	17	30	36	-11
97-98	Wash	72	5	16	21	66	+2
98-99	Wash	53	21	10	31	57	+1
Totals		291	56	74	130	241	+21

Playoffs

94-95	Wash	7	2	2	4	2	
95-96	Wash	6	2	4	6	4	
97-98	Wash	21	7	4	11	30	
Totals		34	11	10	21	36	

GONEAU, Daniel *6-1 196 LW*
B. Montreal, Que., Jan. 16, 1976

96-97	NYR	41	10	3	13	10	-5

SSN	TEAM	GP	G	A	PTS.	PIM	+/-
97–98	NYR	11	2	0	2	4	-4
Totals		51	12	3	15	14	-9

GOODEN, William Francis Charles 5–9 175 LW
B. Winnipeg, Man., Sept. 8, 1924

SSN	TEAM	GP	G	A	PTS.	PIM	+/-
42–43	NYR	12	0	3	3	0	
43–44	NYR	41	9	8	17	15	
Totals		53	9	11	20	15	

GOODENOUGH, Larry J. 6–0 195 D
B. Toronto, Ont., Jan. 19, 1953

SSN	TEAM	GP	G	A	PTS.	PIM	+/-
74–75	Phil	20	3	9	12	0	+12
75–76	Phil	77	8	34	42	83	+45
76–77	Phil–Van	62	6	17	23	48	+10
77–78	Van	42	1	6	7	28	-16
78–79	Van	36	4	9	13	18	-14
79–80	Van	5	0	2	2	2	0
Totals		242	22	77	99	179	+37

Playoffs

SSN	TEAM	GP	G	A	PTS.	PIM	
74–75	Phil	5	0	4	4	2	
75–76	Phil	16	3	11	14	6	
78–79	Van	1	0	0	0	2	
Totals		22	3	15	18	10	

*GOODFELLOW, Ebenezer Ralston (Ebbie) 6–0 180 C
B. Ottawa, Ont., Apr. 9, 1907

SSN	TEAM	GP	G	A	PTS.	PIM	
29–30	Det	44	17	17	34	54	
30–31	Det	44	25	23	48	32	
31–32	Det	48	14	16	30	56	
32–33	Det	40	12	8	20	47	
33–34	Det	48	13	13	26	45	
34–35	Det	48	12	24	36	44	
35–36	Det	48	5	18	23	69	
36–37	Det	48	9	16	25	43	
37–38	Det	29	0	7	7	18	
38–39	Det	48	8	8	16	36	
39–40	Det	43	11	17	28	31	
40–41	Det	47	5	17	22	35	
41–42	Det	8	2	2	4	2	
42–43	Det	11	1	4	5	4	
Totals		554	134	190	324	516	

Playoffs

SSN	TEAM	GP	G	A	PTS.	PIM	
31–32	Det	2	0	0	0	0	
32–33	Det	4	1	0	1	11	
33–34	Det	9	4	3	7	12	
35–36	Det	7	1	0	1	4	
36–37	Det	9	2	2	4	12	
38–39	Det	6	0	0	0	8	
39–40	Det	5	0	2	2	9	
40–41	Det	3	0	1	1	9	
Totals		45	8	8	16	65	

GORDIOUK, Viktor 5–10 176 LW
B. Odintsovo, USSR, Apr. 11, 1970

SSN	TEAM	GP	G	A	PTS.	PIM	+/-
92–93	Buf	16	3	6	9	0	+4
94–95	Buf	10	0	2	2	0	-3
Totals		26	3	8	11	0	+1

GORDON, Frederick F

SSN	TEAM	GP	G	A	PTS.	PIM	
26–27	Det	36	5	5	10	28	
27–28	Bos	41	3	2	5	40	
Totals		77	8	7	15	68	

Playoffs

SSN	TEAM	GP	G	A	PTS.	PIM	
27–28	Bos	1	0	0	0	0	

GORDON, John (Jackie) 5–8 154 C
B. Winnipeg, Man., Mar. 3, 1928

SSN	TEAM	GP	G	A	PTS.	PIM	
48–49	NYR	31	3	9	12	0	
49–50	NYR	1	0	0	0	0	
50–51	NYR	4	0	1	1	0	
Totals		36	3	10	13	0	

Playoffs

SSN	TEAM	GP	G	A	PTS.	PIM	
49–50	NYR	9	1	1	2	7	

GORDON, Robb 5–11 190 C
B. Murrayville, B.C., Jan 13, 1976

SSN	TEAM	GP	G	A	PTS.	PIM	+/-
98–99	Van	4	0	0	0	2	0

GORENCE, Thomas 6–0 190 RW
B. St. Paul, Minn., Mar. 11, 1957

SSN	TEAM	GP	G	A	PTS.	PIM	+/-
78–79	Phil	42	13	6	19	10	+16
79–80	Phil	51	8	13	21	15	+7
80–81	Phil	79	24	18	42	46	+17
81–82	Phil	66	5	8	13	8	-17
82–83	Phil	53	7	7	14	10	+4
83–84	Edm	12	1	1	2	0	0
Totals		303	58	53	111	89	+27

Playoffs

SSN	TEAM	GP	G	A	PTS.	PIM	
78–79	Phil	7	3	1	4	0	
79–80	Phil	15	3	3	6	18	
80–81	Phil	12	3	2	5	29	
81–82	Phil	3	0	0	0	0	
Totals		37	9	6	15	47	

GORING, Robert Thomas (Butch) 5–9 170 C
B. St. Boniface, Man., Oct. 22, 1949

SSN	TEAM	GP	G	A	PTS.	PIM	+/-
69–70	LA	59	13	23	36	8	-15
70–71	LA	19	2	5	7	2	+4
71–72	LA	74	21	29	50	2	-10
72–73	LA	67	28	31	59	2	0
73–74	LA	70	28	33	61	2	+2
74–75	LA	60	27	33	60	6	+26
75–76	LA	80	33	40	73	8	0
76–77	LA	78	30	55	85	6	+10
77–78	LA	80	37	36	73	2	-4
78–79	LA	80	36	51	87	16	-20
79–80	LA–NYI	81	26	53	79	14	-14
80–81	NYI	78	23	37	60	0	+4
81–82	NYI	67	15	17	32	10	-3
82–83	NYI	75	19	20	39	8	+10
83–84	NYI	71	22	24	46	8	+9
84–85	NYI–Bos	68	15	26	41	8	-19
Totals		1107	375	513	888	102	-20

Playoffs

SSN	TEAM	GP	G	A	PTS.	PIM	
73–74	LA	5	0	1	1	0	
74–75	LA	3	0	0	0	0	
75–76	LA	9	2	3	5	4	
76–77	LA	9	7	5	12	0	
77–78	LA	2	0	0	0	2	
78–79	LA	2	0	0	0	0	
79–80	NYI	21	7	12	19	2	
80–81	NYI	18	10	10	20	6	
81–82	NYI	19	6	5	11	12	
82–83	NYI	20	4	8	12	4	
83–84	NYI	21	1	5	6	2	
84–85	Bos	5	1	1	2	0	
Totals		134	38	50	88	32	

GORMAN, David Peter 5–11 185 RW
B. Oshawa, Ont., Apr. 8, 1955

SSN	TEAM	GP	G	A	PTS.	PIM	+/-
74–75	Phoe (WHA)	13	3	5	8	10	
75–76	Phoe (WHA)	67	11	20	31	28	
76–77	Phoe–Birm (WHA)	57	9	13	22	38	
77–78	Birm (WHA)	63	19	21	40	93	
78–79	Birm (WHA)	60	14	24	38	18	
79–80	Atl	3	0	0	0	0	-1
NHL Totals		3	0	0	0	0	-1
WHA Totals		260	56	83	139	187	-1

Playoffs

SSN	TEAM	GP	G	A	PTS.	PIM	
75–76	Phoe (WHA)	5	0	2	2	24	
77–78	Birm (WHA)	4	1	1	2	0	
WHA Totals		9	1	3	4	24	

GORMAN, Edwin D

SSN	TEAM	GP	G	A	PTS.	PIM	
24–25	Ott	30	11	3	14	49	
25–26	Ott	23	2	1	3	12	
26–27	Ott	39	1	0	1	17	
27–28	Tor	19	0	1	1	30	
Totals		111	14	5	19	108	

Playoffs

SSN	TEAM	GP	G	A	PTS.	PIM	
25–26	Ott	2	0	0	0	2	
26–27	Ott	6	0	0	0	0	
Totals		8	0	0	0	2	

GOSSELIN, Benoit 5–11 190 LW
B. Montreal, Que., July 19, 1957

SSN	TEAM	GP	G	A	PTS.	PIM	+/-
77–78	NYR	7	0	0	0	33	-3

GOSSELIN, Guy 5–10 185 D
B. Rochester, Minn., Jan. 6, 1964

SSN	TEAM	GP	G	A	PTS.	PIM	+/-
87–88	Winn	5	0	0	0	6	-1

GOTAAS, Steve 5–10 180 C
B. Camrose, Alta., May 10, 1967

SSN	TEAM	GP	G	A	PTS.	PIM	+/-
87–88	Pitt	36	5	6	11	45	-11
88–89	Minn	12	1	3	4	6	-1
90–91	Minn	1	0	0	0	2	-1
Totals		49	6	9	15	53	-13

Playoffs

SSN	TEAM	GP	G	A	PTS.	PIM	
88–89	Minn	3	0	1	1	5	

*GOTTSELIG, John P. 5–11 158 LW
B. Odessa, Russia, June 24, 1905

SSN	TEAM	GP	G	A	PTS.	PIM	
28–29	Chi	42	5	3	8	26	
29–30	Chi	39	21	4	25	28	
30–31	Chi	42	20	12	32	14	
31–32	Chi	43	14	15	29	50	
32–33	Chi	42	11	11	22	6	
33–34	Chi	48	16	14	30	4	
34–35	Chi	48	19	18	37	16	
35–36	Chi	40	14	15	29	4	
36–37	Chi	47	9	21	30	10	
37–38	Chi	48	13	19	32	22	
38–39	Chi	48	16	23	39	15	
39–40	Chi	38	8	15	23	7	
40–41	Chi	8	1	4	5	5	
42–43	Chi	10	2	6	8	12	
43–44	Chi	45	8	15	23	6	
44–45	Chi	1	0	0	0	0	
Totals		589	177	195	372	225	

Playoffs

SSN	TEAM	GP	G	A	PTS.	PIM	
29–30	Chi	2	0	0	0	4	
30–31	Chi	9	3	3	6	4	
31–32	Chi	2	0	0	0	2	
33–34	Chi	8	4	3	7	4	
34–35	Chi	2	0	0	0	0	
35–36	Chi	2	0	2	2	0	
37–38	Chi	10	5	3	8	4	
39–40	Chi	2	0	1	1	0	
43–44	Chi	6	1	1	2	2	
Totals		43	13	13	26	20	

GOULD, John Milton 5–11 197 RW
B. Beeton, Ont., Apr. 11, 1949

SSN	TEAM	GP	G	A	PTS.	PIM	+/-
71–72	Buf	2	1	0	1	0	-1
72–73	Buf	8	0	1	1	0	0
73–74	Buf–Van	75	13	12	25	10	-11
74–75	Van	78	34	31	65	27	+7
75–76	Van	70	32	27	59	16	+9
76–77	Van–Atl	79	15	23	38	10	-11
77–78	Atl	79	19	28	47	21	+7
78–79	Atl	61	8	7	15	18	-4
79–80	Buf	52	9	9	18	11	+9
Totals		504	131	138	269	113	+5

Playoffs

SSN	TEAM	GP	G	A	PTS.	PIM	
74–75	Van	5	2	2	4	0	
75–76	Van	2	1	0	1	0	
76–77	Atl	3	0	0	0	2	
77–78	Atl	2	0	0	0	2	
78–79	Atl	2	0	0	0	0	
Totals		14	3	2	5	4	

GOULD, Robert (Bobby) 6–0 195 RW
B. Petrolia, Ont., Sept. 2, 1957

SSN	TEAM	GP	G	A	PTS.	PIM	+/-
79–80	Atl	1	0	0	0	0	-1
80–81	Calg	3	0	0	0	0	0
81–82	Calg–Wash	76	21	13	34	73	-5
82–83	Wash	80	22	18	40	43	+16
83–84	Wash	78	21	19	40	74	-2
84–85	Wash	78	14	19	33	69	+10
85–86	Wash	79	19	19	38	26	+7
86–87	Wash	78	23	27	50	74	+18
87–88	Wash	72	12	14	26	56	-1
88–89	Wash	75	5	13	18	65	-2
89–90	Bos	77	8	17	25	92	-3
Totals		697	145	159	304	572	+37

Playoffs

SSN	TEAM	GP	G	A	PTS.	PIM	
80–81	Calg	11	3	1	4	4	
82–83	Wash	4	5	0	5	4	
83–84	Wash	5	0	2	2	4	
84–85	Wash	5	0	1	1	2	

SSN	TEAM	GP	G	A	PTS.	PIM	+/-
85–86	Wash	9	4	3	7	11	
86–87	Wash	7	0	3	3	8	
87–88	Wash	14	3	1	4	21	
88–89	Wash	6	0	2	2	0	
89–90	Bos	17	0	0	0	4	
Totals		78	15	13	28	58	

GOULD, Larry Stephen *5–9 170 LW*
B. Alliston, Ont., Aug. 16, 1952

SSN	TEAM	GP	G	A	PTS.	PIM	+/-
73–74	Van	2	0	0	0	0	-2

GOULET, Michel *6–1 195 LW*
B. Peribonka, Que., Apr. 21, 1960

SSN	TEAM	GP	G	A	PTS.	PIM	+/-
78–79	Birm (WHA)	78	28	30	58	65	
79–80	Que	77	22	32	54	48	-10
80–81	Que	76	32	39	71	45	0
81–82	Que	80	42	42	84	48	+35
82–83	Que	80	57	48	105	51	+31
83–84	Que	75	56	65	121	76	+62
84–85	Que	69	55	40	95	55	+10
85–86	Que	75	53	51	104	64	+6
86–87	Que	75	49	47	96	61	-12
87–88	Que	80	48	58	106	56	-31
88–89	Que	69	26	38	64	67	-20
89–90	Que–Chi	65	20	30	50	51	-32
90–91	Chi	74	27	38	65	65	+27
91–92	Chi	75	22	41	63	69	+20
92–93	Chi	63	23	21	44	43	+10
93–94	Chi	56	16	14	30	26	+1
NHL Totals		1089	548	604	1152	825	+97
WHA Totals		78	28	30	58	65	

Playoffs

SSN	TEAM	GP	G	A	PTS.	PIM	+/-
80–81	Que	4	3	4	7	7	
81–82	Que	16	8	5	13	6	
82–83	Que	4	0	0	0	6	
83–84	Que	9	2	4	6	17	
84–85	Que	17	11	10	21	17	
85–86	Que	3	1	2	3	10	
86–87	Que	13	9	5	14	35	
89–90	Chi	14	2	4	6	6	
91–92	Chi	9	3	4	7	6	
92–93	Chi	3	0	1	1	0	
Totals		92	39	39	78	110	

GUOLLA, Stephen *6–0 180 LW*
B. Scarborough, Ont., Mar. 15, 1963

SSN	TEAM	GP	G	A	PTS.	PIM	+/-
96–97	SJ	43	13	8	21	14	
97–98	SJ	7	1	1	2	0	
Totals		50	14	9	23	14	

GOUPILLE, Clifford (Red) *6–0 190 D*
B. Trois Rivieres, Que., Sept. 2, 1915

SSN	TEAM	GP	G	A	PTS.	PIM	+/-
35–36	Mont	4	0	0	0	0	
36–37	Mont	4	0	0	0	0	
37–38	Mont	47	4	5	9	44	
38–39	Mont	18	0	2	2	24	
39–40	Mont	48	2	10	12	48	
40–41	Mont	48	3	6	9	81	
41–42	Mont	47	1	5	6	51	
42–43	Mont	6	2	0	2	8	
Totals		222	12	28	40	256	

Playoffs

SSN	TEAM	GP	G	A	PTS.	PIM	+/-
37–38	Mont	3	2	0	2	4	
40–41	Mont	2	0	0	0	0	
41–42	Mont	3	0	0	0	2	
Totals		8	2	0	2	6	

GOVEDARIS, Chris *6–0 200 LW*
B. Toronto, Ont., Feb. 2, 1970

SSN	TEAM	GP	G	A	PTS.	PIM	+/-
89–90	Hart	12	0	1	1	6	0
90–91	Hart	14	1	3	4	4	-4
92–93	Hart	7	1	0	1	0	-2
93–94	Tor	12	2	2	4	14	+4
Totals		45	4	6	10	24	-2

Playoffs

SSN	TEAM	GP	G	A	PTS.	PIM	+/-
89–90	Hart	2	0	0	0	2	
93–94	Tor	2	0	0	0	0	
Totals		4	0	0	0	2	

GOYER, Gerald Francis *6–1 196 C*
B. Belleville, Ont., Oct. 20, 1936

SSN	TEAM	GP	G	A	PTS.	PIM	+/-
67–68	Chi	40	1	2	3	4	-18

Playoffs

SSN	TEAM	GP	G	A	PTS.	PIM	+/-
67–68	Chi	3	0	0	0	2	

GOYETTE, Joseph Georges Philipe (Phil) *5–11 170 C*
B. Lachine, Que., Oct. 31, 1933

SSN	TEAM	GP	G	A	PTS.	PIM	+/-
56–57	Mont	14	3	4	7	0	
57–58	Mont	70	9	37	46	8	
58–59	Mont	63	10	18	28	8	
59–60	Mont	65	21	22	43	4	
60–61	Mont	62	7	4	11	4	
61–62	Mont	69	7	27	34	18	
62–63	Mont	32	5	8	13	2	
63–64	NYR	67	24	41	65	15	
64–65	NYR	52	12	34	46	6	
65–66	NYR	60	11	31	42	6	
66–67	NYR	70	12	49	61	6	
67–68	NYR	73	25	40	65	10	+18
68–69	NYR	67	13	32	45	8	+9
69–70	StL	72	29	49	78	16	+3
70–71	Buf	60	15	46	61	6	-15
71–72	Buf–NYR	45	4	25	29	14	-11
Totals		941	207	467	674	131	+4

Playoffs

SSN	TEAM	GP	G	A	PTS.	PIM	+/-
56–57	Mont	10	2	1	3	4	
57–58	Mont	10	4	1	5	4	
58–59	Mont	10	0	4	4	0	
59–60	Mont	8	2	1	3	4	
60–61	Mont	6	3	3	6	0	
61–62	Mont	6	1	4	5	2	
62–63	Mont	2	0	0	0	0	
66–67	NYR	4	1	0	1	0	
67–68	NYR	6	0	1	1	4	
68–69	NYR	3	0	0	0	0	
69–70	StL	16	3	11	14	6	
71–72	NYR	13	1	3	4	2	
Totals		94	17	29	46	26	

GRABOSKI, Anthony Rudel (Tony) *5–10 170 F*
B. Timmins, Ont., May 9, 1916

SSN	TEAM	GP	G	A	PTS.	PIM	+/-
40–41	Mont	34	4	3	7	6	
41–42	Mont	23	2	5	7	8	
42–43	Mont	9	0	2	2	4	
Totals		66	6	10	16	18	

Playoffs

SSN	TEAM	GP	G	A	PTS.	PIM	+/-
40–41	Mont	2	0	0	0	0	

*GRACIE, Robert J. *5–8 155 LW*
B. North Bay, Ont., Nov. 8, 1910

SSN	TEAM	GP	G	A	PTS.	PIM	+/-
30–31	Tor	8	4	2	6	4	
31–32	Tor	48	13	8	21	29	
32–33	Tor	48	9	13	22	27	
33–34	Bos–NYA	48	6	12	18	20	
34–35	NYA–Mont M	46	12	9	21	15	
35–36	Mont M	46	11	14	25	31	
36–37	Mont M	48	11	25	36	18	
37–38	Mont M	48	12	19	31	32	
38–39	Mont–Chi	38	4	7	11	31	
Totals		378	82	109	191	207	

Playoffs

SSN	TEAM	GP	G	A	PTS.	PIM	+/-
30–31	Tor	2	0	0	0	0	
31–32	Tor	7	3	1	4	0	
32–33	Tor	9	0	1	1	0	
34–35	Mont M	7	0	2	2	2	
35–36	Mont M	3	0	1	1	0	
36–37	Mont M	5	1	2	3	2	
Totals		33	4	7	11	4	

GRADIN, Thomas *5–11 170 C*
B. Solleftea, Sweden, Feb. 18, 1956

SSN	TEAM	GP	G	A	PTS.	PIM	+/-
78–79	Van	76	20	31	51	22	-12
79–80	Van	80	30	45	75	22	+14
80–81	Van	79	21	48	69	34	+2
81–82	Van	76	37	49	86	32	+15
82–83	Van	80	32	54	86	61	-17
83–84	Van	75	21	57	78	32	-2
84–85	Van	76	22	42	64	43	-22
85–86	Van	71	14	27	41	34	-16
86–87	Bos	64	12	31	43	18	+4
Totals		677	209	384	593	298	-34

Playoffs

SSN	TEAM	GP	G	A	PTS.	PIM	+/-
78–79	Van	3	4	1	5	4	
79–80	Van	4	0	2	2	0	

SSN	TEAM	GP	G	A	PTS.	PIM	+/-
80–81	Van	3	1	3	4	0	
81–82	Van	17	9	10	19	10	
82–83	Van	4	1	3	4	2	
83–84	Van	4	0	1	1	2	
85–86	Van	3	2	1	3	2	
86–87	Bos	4	0	4	4	0	
Totals		42	17	25	42	20	

GRAHAM, Dirk Milton *5–11 198 LW/RW*
B. Regina, Sask., July 29, 1959

SSN	TEAM	GP	G	A	PTS.	PIM	+/-
83–84	Minn	6	1	1	2	0	+1
84–85	Minn	36	12	11	23	23	-15
85–86	Minn	80	22	33	55	87	-6
86–87	Minn	76	25	29	54	142	-2
87–88	Minn–Chi	70	24	24	48	71	-7
88–89	Chi	80	33	45	78	89	+8
89–90	Chi	73	22	32	54	102	+1
90–91	Chi	80	24	21	45	88	+12
91–92	Chi	80	17	30	47	89	-5
92–93	Chi	84	20	17	37	139	0
93–94	Chi	67	15	18	33	45	+13
94–95	Chi	40	4	9	13	42	+2
Totals		772	219	270	489	917	+2

Playoffs

SSN	TEAM	GP	G	A	PTS.	PIM	+/-
83–84	Minn	1	0	0	0	2	
84–85	Minn	9	0	4	4	7	
85–86	Minn	5	3	1	4	2	
87–88	Chi	4	1	2	3	4	
88–89	Chi	16	2	4	6	38	
89–90	Chi	5	1	5	6	2	
90–91	Chi	6	1	2	3	17	
91–92	Chi	18	7	5	12	8	
92–93	Chi	4	0	0	0	0	
93–94	Chi	6	0	1	1	4	
94–95	Chi	16	2	3	5	8	
Totals		90	17	27	44	92	

*GRAHAM, Edward Dixon (Ted) *5–10 173 D*
B. Owen Sound, Ont., June 30, 1906

SSN	TEAM	GP	G	A	PTS.	PIM	+/-
27–28	Chi	16	1	0	1	8	
29–30	Chi	26	1	2	3	23	
30–31	Chi	42	0	7	7	38	
31–32	Chi	48	0	3	3	40	
32–33	Chi	47	3	8	11	57	
33–34	Mont M–Det	47	3	1	4	39	
34–35	Det–StL E	37	0	2	2	28	
35–36	Bos	48	4	1	5	37	
36–37	Bos–NYA	32	2	1	3	30	
Totals		343	14	25	39	300	

Playoffs

SSN	TEAM	GP	G	A	PTS.	PIM	+/-
29–30	Chi	2	0	0	0	8	
30–31	Chi	8	0	0	0	14	
31–32	Chi	2	0	0	0	2	
33–34	Det	9	3	1	4	8	
35–36	Bos	2	0	0	0	2	
Totals		23	3	1	4	34	

*GRAHAM, Leth *LW*
B. 1894

SSN	TEAM	GP	G	A	PTS.	PIM	+/-
20–21	Ott	13	0	0	0	0	
21–22	Ott	2	2	0	2	0	
22–23	Ham	4	1	0	1	0	
23–24	Ott	3	0	0	0	0	
24–25	Ott	3	0	0	0	0	
25–26	Ott	1	0	0	0	0	
Totals		26	3	0	3	0	

Playoffs

SSN	TEAM	GP	G	A	PTS.	PIM	+/-
20–21	Ott	1	0	0	0	0	

GRAHAM, Patrick Thomas *6–1 190 LW*
B. Toronto, Ont., May 25, 1961

SSN	TEAM	GP	G	A	PTS.	PIM	+/-
81–82	Pitt	42	6	8	14	55	-1
82–83	Pitt	20	1	5	6	16	-6
83–84	Tor	41	4	4	8	65	-9
Totals		103	11	17	28	136	-16

Playoffs

SSN	TEAM	GP	G	A	PTS.	PIM	+/-
81–82	Pitt	4	0	0	0	2	

GRAHAM, Rodney Douglas (Rod) *5–11 185 LW*
B. London, Ont., Aug. 19, 1946

SSN	TEAM	GP	G	A	PTS.	PIM	+/-
74–75	Bos	14	2	1	3	7	0

GRANATO, Tony 5–10 185 LW
B. Downers Grove, Ill., July 25, 1964

SSN	TEAM	GP	G	A	PTS.	PIM	+/-
88–89	NYR	78	36	27	63	140	+17
89–90	NYR–LA	56	12	24	36	122	-1
90–91	LA	68	30	34	64	154	+22
91–92	LA	80	39	29	68	187	+4
92–93	LA	81	37	45	82	171	-1
93–94	LA	50	7	14	21	150	-2
94–95	LA	33	13	11	24	68	+9
95–96	LA	49	17	18	35	46	-5
96–97	SJ	76	25	15	40	159	-7
97–98	SJ	59	16	9	25	70	+3
98–99	SJ	35	6	6	12	54	+4
Totals		665	238	232	470	1321	+43

Playoffs

SSN	TEAM	GP	G	A	PTS.	PIM
88–89	NYR	4	1	1	2	21
89–90	LA	10	5	4	9	12
90–91	LA	12	1	4	5	28
91–92	LA	6	1	5	6	10
92–93	LA	24	6	11	17	50
97–98	SJ	1	0	0	0	0
98–99	SJ	6	1	1	2	2
Totals		63	15	26	41	123

GRAND-PIERRE, Jean-Luc 6–3 207 D
B. Montreal, Que., Feb. 2, 1977

SSN	TEAM	GP	G	A	PTS.	PIM	+/-
98–99	Buf	15	0	1	1	17	0

GRANT, Daniel Frederick 5–10 188 LW
B. Fredericton, N.B., Feb. 21, 1946

SSN	TEAM	GP	G	A	PTS.	PIM	+/-
65–66	Mont	1	0	0	0	0	
67–68	Mont	22	3	4	7	10	+3
68–69	Minn	75	34	31	65	46	-12
69–70	Minn	76	29	28	57	23	-13
70–71	Minn	78	34	23	57	46	+7
71–72	Minn	78	18	25	43	18	0
72–73	Minn	78	32	35	67	12	+23
73–74	Minn	78	29	35	64	16	-1
74–75	Det	80	50	37	87	28	-11
75–76	Det	39	10	13	23	20	-17
76–77	Det	42	2	10	12	4	-34
77–78	Det–LA	54	12	21	33	2	-4
78–79	LA	35	10	11	21	8	+5
Totals		736	263	273	536	233	-54

Playoffs

SSN	TEAM	GP	G	A	PTS.	PIM
67–68	Mont	10	0	3	3	5
69–70	Minn	6	0	2	2	4
70–71	Minn	12	5	5	10	8
71–72	Minn	7	2	1	3	0
72–73	Minn	6	3	1	4	0
77–78	LA	2	0	2	2	2
Totals		43	10	14	24	19

GRATTON, Benoit 5–10 163 LW
B. Montreal, Que., Dec. 28, 1976

SSN	TEAM	GP	G	A	PTS.	PIM	+/-
97–98	Wash	6	0	1	1	6	+1
98–99	Wash	16	4	3	7	16	-1
Totals		22	4	4	8	22	0

GRATTON, Chris 6–3 212 C
B. Brantford, Ont., July 5, 1975

SSN	TEAM	GP	G	A	PTS.	PIM	+/-
93–94	TB	84	13	29	42	123	-25
94–95	TB	46	7	20	27	89	-2
95–96	TB	82	17	21	38	105	-13
96–97	TB	82	30	32	62	201	-28
97–98	Phil	82	22	40	62	159	+11
98–99	Phil–TB	78	8	26	34	143	-28
Totals		354	97	168	265	820	-85

Playoffs

SSN	TEAM	GP	G	A	PTS.	PIM
95–96	TB	6	0	2	2	27
97–98	Phil	5	2	0	2	10
Totals		11	2	2	4	37

GRATTON, Dan 6–0 185 C
B. Brantford, Ont., Dec. 7, 1966

SSN	TEAM	GP	G	A	PTS.	PIM	+/-
87–88	LA	7	1	0	1	5	+1

GRATTON, Normand Lionel (Norm) 5–11 165 LW
B. LaSalle, Que., Dec. 22, 1950

SSN	TEAM	GP	G	A	PTS.	PIM	+/-
71–72	NYR	3	0	1	1	0	+1
72–73	Atl–Buf	50	9	11	20	24	+1
73–74	Buf	57	6	11	17	16	-10
74–75	Buf–Minn	59	17	18	35	10	-9
75–76	Minn	32	7	3	10	14	-12
Totals		201	39	44	83	64	-29

Playoffs

SSN	TEAM	GP	G	A	PTS.	PIM
72–73	Buf	6	0	1	1	2

GRAVELLE, Joseph Gerard (Leo, The Gazelle) 5–8 158 RW
B. Aylmer, Que., June 10, 1925

SSN	TEAM	GP	G	A	PTS.	PIM
46–47	Mont	53	16	14	30	12
47–48	Mont	15	0	0	0	0
48–49	Mont	36	4	6	10	6
49–50	Mont	70	19	10	29	18
50–51	Mont–Det	49	5	4	9	6
Totals		223	44	34	78	42

Playoffs

SSN	TEAM	GP	G	A	PTS.	PIM
46–47	Mont	6	2	0	2	2
48–49	Mont	7	2	1	3	0
49–50	Mont	4	0	0	0	0
Totals		17	4	1	5	2

GRAVES, Adam 6–0 205 C
B. Toronto, Ont., Apr. 12, 1968

SSN	TEAM	GP	G	A	PTS.	PIM	+/-
87–88	Det	9	0	1	1	8	-2
88–89	Det	56	7	5	12	60	-5
89–90	Det–Edm	76	9	13	22	136	0
90–91	Edm	76	7	18	25	127	-21
91–92	NYR	80	26	33	59	139	+19
92–93	NYR	84	36	29	65	148	-4
93–94	NYR	84	52	27	79	127	+27
94–95	NYR	47	17	14	31	51	+9
95–96	NYR	82	22	36	58	100	+18
96–97	NYR	82	33	28	61	66	+10
97–98	NYR	72	23	12	35	41	-30
98–99	NYR	82	38	15	53	47	-12
Totals		830	270	231	501	1050	+9

Playoffs

SSN	TEAM	GP	G	A	PTS.	PIM
88–89	Det	5	0	0	0	4
89–90	Edm	22	5	6	11	17
90–91	Edm	18	2	4	6	22
91–92	NYR	10	5	3	8	22
93–94	NYR	23	10	7	17	24
94–95	NYR	10	4	4	8	8
95–96	NYR	10	7	1	8	4
96–97	NYR	15	2	1	3	12
Totals		113	35	26	61	113

GRAVES, Hilliard Donald 5–11 175 RW
B. Saint John, N.B., Oct. 18, 1950

SSN	TEAM	GP	G	A	PTS.	PIM	+/-
70–71	Cal	14	0	0	0	0	-2
72–73	Cal	75	27	25	52	34	-15
73–74	Cal	64	11	18	29	48	-32
74–75	Atl	67	10	19	29	30	+3
75–76	Atl	80	19	30	49	16	+3
76–77	Atl–Van	79	18	25	43	34	-1
77–78	Van	80	21	26	47	18	-17
78–79	Van	62	11	15	26	14	-15
79–80	Winn	35	1	5	6	15	-13
Totals		556	118	163	281	209	-89

Playoffs

SSN	TEAM	GP	G	A	PTS.	PIM
75–76	Atl	2	0	0	0	0

GRAVES, Steve 5–10 175 LW
B. Trenton, Ont., Apr. 7, 1964

SSN	TEAM	GP	G	A	PTS.	PIM	+/-
83–84	Edm	2	0	0	0	0	0
86–87	Edm	12	2	0	2	0	-2
87–88	Edm	21	3	4	7	10	+13
Totals		35	5	4	9	10	+11

GRAY, Alexander 5–10 170 RW
B. Glasgow, Scotland, June 21, 1899

SSN	TEAM	GP	G	A	PTS.	PIM
27–28	NYR	43	7	0	7	28
28–29	Tor	7	0	0	0	2
Totals		50	7	0	7	30

Playoffs

SSN	TEAM	GP	G	A	PTS.	PIM
27–28	NYR	9	1	0	1	0
28–29	Tor	4	0	0	0	0
Totals		13	1	0	1	0

GRAY, Terrence Stanley (Terry) 6–0 175 RW
B. Montreal, Que., Mar. 21, 1938

SSN	TEAM	GP	G	A	PTS.	PIM	+/-
61–62	Bos	42	8	7	15	15	
63–64	Mont	4	0	0	0	6	
67–68	LA	65	12	16	28	22	-3
68–69	StL	8	4	0	4	4	0
69–70	StL	28	2	5	7	17	+2
Totals		147	26	28	54	64	-1

Playoffs

SSN	TEAM	GP	G	A	PTS.	PIM
67–68	LA	7	0	2	2	10
68–69	StL	11	3	2	5	8
69–70	StL	16	2	1	3	4
70–71	StL	1	0	0	0	0
Totals		35	5	5	10	22

*GREEN LW

SSN	TEAM	GP	G	A	PTS.	PIM
28–29	Det	2	0	0	0	0

GREEN, Edward Joseph (Ted) 5–10 200 D
B. Eriksdale, Man., Mar. 23, 1940

SSN	TEAM	GP	G	A	PTS.	PIM	+/-
60–61	Bos	1	0	0	0	2	
61–62	Bos	66	3	8	11	116	
62–63	Bos	70	1	11	12	117	
63–64	Bos	70	4	10	14	145	
64–65	Bos	70	8	27	35	156	
65–66	Bos	27	5	13	18	113	
66–67	Bos	47	6	10	16	67	
67–68	Bos	72	7	36	43	133	+14
68–69	Bos	65	8	38	46	99	+9
69–70	Bos	78	5	37	42	60	+37
70–71	Bos	54	1	16	17	21	+10
72–73	NE (WHA)	78	16	30	46	47	
73–74	NE (WHA)	75	7	26	33	42	
74–75	NE (WHA)	57	6	14	20	29	
75–76	Winn (WHA)	79	5	23	28	73	
76–77	Winn (WHA)	70	4	21	25	45	
77–78	Winn (WHA)	73	4	22	26	52	
78–79	Winn (WHA)	20	0	2	2	16	
NHL Totals		620	48	206	254	1029	+70
WHA Totals		452	42	138	180	304	

Playoffs

SSN	TEAM	GP	G	A	PTS.	PIM
67–68	Bos	4	1	1	2	11
68–69	Bos	10	2	7	9	18
70–71	Bos	7	1	0	1	25
71–72	Bos	10	0	0	0	0
72–73	NE (WHA)	12	1	5	6	25
73–74	NE (WHA)	7	0	4	4	7
75–76	Winn (WHA)	11	0	2	2	16
76–77	Winn (WHA)	20	1	3	4	12
77–78	Winn (WHA)	8	0	2	2	2
NHL Totals		31	4	8	12	54
WHA Totals		58	2	16	18	62

GREEN, Josh 6–4 212 LW
B. Camrose, Atlanta, Nov. 16, 1977

SSN	TEAM	GP	G	A	PTS.	PIM	+/-
98–99	LA	27	1	3	4	8	-5

GREEN, Redvers (Red) LW
B. Sudbury, Ont.

SSN	TEAM	GP	G	A	PTS.	PIM
23–24	Ham	23	11	0	11	20
24–25	Ham	30	19	4	23	63
25–26	NYA	35	13	4	17	42
26–27	NYA	44	10	4	14	53
27–28	NYA	40	6	1	7	67
28–29	Bos	25	0	0	0	16
Totals		197	59	13	72	261

GREEN, Richard Douglas (Rick) 6–3 220 D
B. Belleville, Ont., Feb. 20, 1956

SSN	TEAM	GP	G	A	PTS.	PIM	+/-
76–77	Wash	45	3	12	15	16	-20
77–78	Wash	60	5	14	19	67	-35
78–79	Wash	71	8	33	41	62	-45
79–80	Wash	71	4	20	24	52	-10
80–81	Wash	65	8	23	31	91	-15
81–82	Wash	65	3	25	28	93	-12
82–83	Mont	66	2	24	26	58	+23
83–84	Mont	7	0	1	1	7	-5
84–85	Mont	77	1	18	19	30	-11
85–86	Mont	46	3	2	5	20	-9
86–87	Mont	72	1	9	10	10	-1
87–88	Mont	59	2	11	13	33	+21
88–89	Mont	72	1	14	15	25	+19
90–91	Det	65	2	14	16	24	+10
91–92	NYI	4	0	0	0	0	-1
Totals		845	43	220	263	588	-93

SSN	TEAM	GP	G	A	PTS.	PIM	+/-

Playoffs

SSN	TEAM	GP	G	A	PTS.	PIM	+/-
82–83	Mont	3	0	0	0	2	
83–84	Mont	15	1	2	3	33	
84–85	Mont	12	0	3	3	14	
85–86	Mont	18	1	4	5	8	
86–87	Mont	17	0	4	4	8	
87–88	Mont	11	0	2	2	2	
88–89	Mont	21	1	1	2	6	
90–91	Det	3	0	0	0	0	
Totals		100	3	16	19	73	

GREEN, Travis *6–2 200 C*
B. Castlegar, B.C. Dec. 20, 1970

SSN	TEAM	GP	G	A	PTS.	PIM	+/-
92–93	NYI	61	7	18	25	43	+4
93–94	NYI	83	18	22	40	44	+16
94–95	NYI	42	5	7	12	25	-10
95–96	NYI	69	24	45	69	42	-20
96–97	NYI	79	23	41	64	38	-5
97–98	NYI–Ana	76	19	23	42	82	-29
98–99	Ana	79	13	17	30	81	-7
Totals		489	109	173	282	355	-51

Playoffs

SSN	TEAM	GP	G	A	PTS.	PIM	+/-
92–93	NYI	12	3	1	4	6	
93–94	NYI	4	0	0	0	2	
98–99	Ana	4	0	1	1	4	
Totals		20	3	2	5	12	

***GREEN, Wilfred Thomas (Wilf, Shorty)** *RW*
B. Sudbury, Ont., July 17, 1896

SSN	TEAM	GP	G	A	PTS.	PIM	+/-
23–24	Ham	22	7	2	9	19	
24–25	Ham	28	18	1	19	75	
25–26	NYA	32	6	4	10	40	
26–27	NYA	21	2	1	3	17	
Totals		103	33	8	41	151	

GREENLAW, Jeff *6–1 230 LW*
B. Toronto, Ont., Feb. 28, 1968

SSN	TEAM	GP	G	A	PTS.	PIM	+/-
86–87	Wash	22	0	3	3	44	+2
90–91	Wash	10	2	0	2	10	+1
91–92	Wash	5	0	1	1	34	-1
92–93	Wash	16	1	1	2	18	-3
93–94	Fla	4	0	1	1	2	-1
Totals		57	3	6	9	108	-2

Playoffs

SSN	TEAM	GP	G	A	PTS.	PIM	+/-
87–88	Wash	1	0	0	0	19	
90–91	Wash	1	0	0	0	2	
Totals		2	0	0	0	21	

GREGG, Randall John *6–4 215 D*
B. Edmonton, Alta., Feb. 19, 1956

SSN	TEAM	GP	G	A	PTS.	PIM	+/-
82–83	Edm	80	6	22	28	54	+15
83–84	Edm	80	13	27	40	56	+40
84–85	Edm	57	3	20	23	32	+27
85–86	Edm	64	2	26	28	47	+20
86–87	Edm	52	8	16	24	42	+36
87–88	Edm	15	1	2	3	8	+4
88–89	Edm	57	3	15	18	28	-9
89–90	Edm	48	4	20	24	42	+24
91–92	Van	21	1	4	5	24	-2
Totals		474	41	152	193	333	+155

Playoffs

SSN	TEAM	GP	G	A	PTS.	PIM	+/-
81–82	Edm	4	0	2	2	12	
82–83	Edm	16	2	4	6	13	
83–84	Edm	19	3	7	10	21	
84–85	Edm	17	0	6	6	12	
85–86	Edm	10	1	0	1	12	
87–88	Edm	18	3	6	9	17	
88–89	Edm	19	1	8	9	24	
89–90	Edm	7	1	0	1	4	
91–92	Van	7	0	1	1	8	
Totals		137	13	38	51	127	

GREIG, Bruce *6–2 220 LW*
B. High River, Alta., May 9, 1953

SSN	TEAM	GP	G	A	PTS.	PIM	+/-
73–74	Cal	1	0	0	0	4	0
74–75	Cal	8	0	1	1	42	-3
76–77	Calg (WHA)	7	1	1	2	10	
77–78	Cin (WHA)	32	3	1	4	57	
78–79	Ind (WHA)	21	3	7	10	64	
NHL Totals		9	1	2	3	46	-3
WHA Totals		60	7	9	16	131	

GREIG, Mark *5–11 190 RW*
B. High River, Alta., Jan. 25, 1970

SSN	TEAM	GP	G	A	PTS.	PIM	+/-
90–91	Hart	4	0	0	0	0	+1
91–92	Hart	17	0	5	5	6	+7
92–93	Hart	22	1	7	8	27	-11
93–94	Hart–Tor	44	6	7	13	41	-5
94–95	Calg	8	1	1	2	2	+1
98–99	Phil	7	1	2	2	4	+1
Totals		102	9	22	31	80	-8

Playoffs

SSN	TEAM	GP	G	A	PTS.	PIM	+/-
98–99	Phil	2	0	1	1	0	

GRENIER, Lucien S. J. *5–10 163 RW*
B. Malartic, Que., Nov. 3, 1946

SSN	TEAM	GP	G	A	PTS.	PIM	+/-
69–70	Mont	23	2	3	5	2	+1
70–71	LA	68	9	7	16	12	-1
71–72	LA	60	3	4	7	4	-6
Totals		151	14	14	28	18	-6

Playoffs

SSN	TEAM	GP	G	A	PTS.	PIM	+/-
68–69	Mont	2	0	0	0	0	

GRENIER, Richard *5–11 170 C*
B. Montreal, Que., Sept. 18, 1952

SSN	TEAM	GP	G	A	PTS.	PIM	+/-
72–73	NYI	10	1	1	2	2	-2
76–77	Que (WHA)	34	11	9	20	4	

GRESCHNER, Ronald John *6–2 185 D*
B. Goodsoil, Sask., Dec. 22, 1954

SSN	TEAM	GP	G	A	PTS.	PIM	+/-
74–75	NYR	70	8	37	45	93	+8
75–76	NYR	77	6	21	27	93	51
76–77	NYR	80	11	36	47	89	0
77–78	NYR	78	24	48	72	100	+3
78–79	NYR	60	17	36	53	66	0
79–80	NYR	76	21	37	58	103	-11
80–81	NYR	74	27	41	68	112	0
81–82	NYR	29	5	11	16	16	-11
82–83	NYR	10	3	5	8	0	0
83–84	NYR	77	12	44	56	117	+5
84–85	NYR	48	16	29	45	42	-19
85–86	NYR	78	20	28	48	104	+9
86–87	NYR	61	6	34	40	62	-6
87–88	NYR	51	1	5	6	82	-9
88–89	NYR	58	1	10	11	94	+9
89–90	NYR	55	1	9	10	53	-7
Totals		982	179	431	610	1226	-80

Playoffs

SSN	TEAM	GP	G	A	PTS.	PIM	+/-
74–75	NYR	3	0	1	1	2	
77–78	NYR	3	0	0	0	2	
78–79	NYR	18	7	5	12	16	
79–80	NYR	9	0	6	6	10	
80–81	NYR	14	4	8	12	17	
82–83	NYR	8	2	2	4	12	
83–84	NYR	2	1	0	1	2	
84–85	NYR	2	0	3	3	12	
85–86	NYR	5	3	1	4	11	
86–87	NYR	6	0	5	5	0	
88–89	NYR	4	0	1	1	6	
89–90	NYR	10	0	0	0	16	
Totals		84	17	32	49	106	

GRETZKY, Brent *5–10 160 C*
B. Brantford, Ont., Feb. 20, 1972

SSN	TEAM	GP	G	A	PTS.	PIM	+/-
93–94	TB	10	1	2	3	2	0
94–95	TB	3	0	1	1	0	-2
Totals		13	1	3	4	2	-2

GRETZKY, Wayne (The Great) *6–0 180 C*
B. Brantford, Ont., Jan. 26, 1961

SSN	TEAM	GP	G	A	PTS.	PIM	+/-
78–79	Ind–Edm (WHA)	80	46	64	110	19	
79–80	Edm	79	51	86	137	21	+15
80–81	Edm	80	55	109	164	28	+41
81–82	Edm	80	92	120	212	26	+81
82–83	Edm	80	71	125	196	59	+60
83–84	Edm	74	87	118	205	39	+75
84–85	Edm	80	73	135	208	52	+98
85–86	Edm	80	52	163	215	46	+71
86–87	Edm	79	62	121	183	28	+70
87–88	Edm	64	40	109	149	24	+39
88–89	LA	78	54	114	168	26	+15
89–90	LA	73	40	102	142	42	+8
90–91	LA	78	41	122	163	16	+30
91–92	LA	74	31	90	121	34	-12
92–93	LA	45	16	49	65	6	+6
93–94	LA	81	38	92	130	20	-25
94–95	LA	48	11	37	48	6	-20
95–96	LA–StL	80	23	79	102	34	-13
96–97	NYR	82	25	72	97	28	+12
97–98	NYR	82	23	67	90	28	-11
98–99	NYR	70	9	53	62	14	-23
NHL Totals		1484	894	1963	2857	577	+517
WHA Totals		80	46	64	110	19	

Playoffs

SSN	TEAM	GP	G	A	PTS.	PIM	+/-
78–79	Edm (WHA)	13	10	10	20	2	
80–81	Edm	9	7	14	21	4	
81–82	Edm	5	5	7	12	8	
82–83	Edm	16	12	26	38	4	
83–84	Edm	19	13	22	35	12	
84–85	Edm	18	17	30	47	4	
85–86	Edm	10	8	11	19	2	
86–87	Edm	21	5	29	34	6	
87–88	Edm	19	12	31	43	16	
88–89	LA	11	5	17	22	0	
89–90	LA	7	3	7	10	0	
90–91	LA	12	4	11	15	2	
91–92	LA	6	2	5	7	2	
92–93	LA	24	15	25	40	4	
95–96	StL	13	2	14	16	0	
96–97	NYR	15	10	10	20	2	
NHL Totals		208	122	260	382	66	
WHA Totals		13	10	10	20	2	

GRIER, Michael *6–1 232 RW*
B. Detroit, Mich., Jan. 5, 1975

SSN	TEAM	GP	G	A	PTS.	PIM	+/-
96–97	Edm	79	15	17	32	45	+7
97–98	Edm	66	9	6	15	73	-3
98–99	Edm	82	20	24	44	54	+5
Totals		227	44	47	91	172	+9

Playoffs

SSN	TEAM	GP	G	A	PTS.	PIM	+/-
96–97	Edm	12	3	1	4	4	
97–98	Edm	12	2	2	4	13	
98–99	Edm	4	1	1	2	6	
Totals		28	6	4	10	23	

GRIEVE, Brent *6–1 202 LW*
B. Oshawa, Ont., May 9, 1969

SSN	TEAM	GP	G	A	PTS.	PIM	+/-
93–94	NYI–Edm	27	13	5	18	21	+4
94–95	Chi	28	2	4	6	28	+2
95–96	Chi	28	2	4	6	28	+5
96–97	LA	18	4	2	6	15	-2
Totals		97	20	16	36	87	+9

GRIGOR, George (Shorty) *F*
B. Edinburgh, Scotland

SSN	TEAM	GP	G	A	PTS.	PIM	+/-
43–44	Chi	2	1	0	1	0	

Playoffs

SSN	TEAM	GP	G	A	PTS.	PIM	+/-
43–44	Chi	1	0	0	0	0	

GRIMSON, Stu *6–5 220 LW*
B. Kamloops, B.C., May 20, 1965

SSN	TEAM	GP	G	A	PTS.	PIM	+/-
88–89	Calg	1	0	0	0	5	0
89–90	Calg	3	0	0	0	17	-1
90–91	Chi	35	0	1	1	183	-3
91–92	Chi	54	2	2	4	234	-2
92–93	Chi	78	1	1	2	193	+2
93–94	Ana	77	1	5	6	199	-6
94–95	Ana–Det	42	0	1	1	147	-11
95–96	Det	56	0	1	1	128	-10
96–97	Det–Hart	76	2	2	4	218	-8
97–98	Car	82	3	4	7	304	0
98–99	Ana	73	3	0	3	158	0
Totals		577	12	17	29	1784	-39

Playoffs

SSN	TEAM	GP	G	A	PTS.	PIM	+/-
90–91	Chi	5	0	0	0	46	
91–92	Chi	14	0	1	1	10	
92–93	Chi	2	0	0	0	4	
94–95	Det	11	1	0	1	26	
95–96	Det	2	0	0	0	0	
98–99	Ana	3	0	0	0	30	
Totals		64	1	1	2	116	

GRISDALE, John Russell *6–0 195 D*
B. Geraldton, Ont., Aug. 23, 1948

SSN	TEAM	GP	G	A	PTS.	PIM	+/-
72–73	Tor	49	1	7	8	76	-22
74–75	Tor–Van	60	1	12	13	95	+3
75–76	Van	38	2	6	8	54	+4
76–77	Van	20	0	2	2	20	-13

SSN	TEAM	GP	G	A	PTS.	PIM	+/-
77–78	Van	42	0	9	9	47	+2
78–79	Van	41	0	3	3	54	-23
Totals		250	4	39	43	346	-49

Playoffs

74–75	Van	5	0	1	1	13	
75–76	Van	2	0	0	0	0	
78–79	Van	3	0	0	0	2	
Totals		10	0	1	1	15	

GROLEAU, Francois 6–0 195 D
B. Longvueil, Que., Jan. 23, 1973

95–96	Mont	2	0	1	1	2	+2
96–97	Mont	5	0	0	0	4	0
97–98	Mont	1	0	0	0	0	+1
Totals		8	0	1	1	6	+3

GRONMAN, Tuomas 6–3 198 D
B. Vitasaari, Finland, March 22, 1974

96–97	Chi	16	0	1	1	13	-4
97–98	Pitt	22	1	2	3	25	+3
Totals		38	1	3	4	38	-1

Playoffs

97–98	Pitt	1	0	0	0	0	

GRONSDAHL, Lloyd Gilford (Gabby) 5–9 170 RW
B. Norquay, Sask., May 10, 1921

41–42	Bos	10	1	2	3	0	

GRONSTRAND, Jari 6–3 195 D
B. Tampere, Finland, Nov. 14, 1962

86–87	Minn	47	1	6	7	27	+4
87–88	NYR	62	3	11	14	63	+8
88–89	Que	25	1	3	4	14	-9
89–90	Que–NYI	48	3	5	8	29	-1
90–91	NYI	3	0	1	1	2	-2
Totals		185	8	26	34	135	0

Playoffs

89–90	NYI	3	0	0	0	4	

GROSEK, Michal 6–2 180 LW
B. Vyskov, Czechoslovakia, June 1, 1975

93–94	Winn	3	1	0	1	0	-1
94–95	Winn	24	2	2	4	21	-3
95–96	Winn–Buf	23	6	4	10	31	-1
96–97	Buf	82	15	21	36	71	+25
97–98	Buf	67	10	20	30	60	+9
98–99	Buf	76	20	30	50	102	+21
Totals		275	54	77	131	285	+50

Playoffs

96–97	Buf	12	3	3	6	8	
97–98	Buf	15	6	4	10	28	
98–99	Buf	13	0	4	4	28	
Totals		40	9	11	20	64	

***GROSS, Lloyd George** 5–8 175 LW
B. Kitchener, Ont., Oct. 15, 1907

26–27	Tor	16	1	1	2	0	
33–34	NYA–Bos–Det	40	9	4	13	18	
34–35	Det	6	1	0	1	2	
Totals		62	11	5	16	20	

Playoffs

33–34	Det	1	0	0	0	0	

***GROSSO, Donald (Count)** 5–11 170 LW
B. Sault Ste. Marie, Ont., Apr. 12, 1915

39–40	Det	28	2	3	5	11	
40–41	Det	45	8	7	15	14	
41–42	Det	48	23	30	53	13	
42–43	Det	50	15	17	32	10	
43–44	Det	42	16	31	47	13	
44–45	Det–Chi	41	15	16	31	10	
45–46	Chi	47	7	10	17	17	
46–47	Bos	33	0	2	2	2	
Totals		334	86	116	202	90	

Playoffs

38–39	Det	5	0	0	0	0	
39–40	Det	5	0	0	0	0	
40–41	Det	9	1	4	5	0	

SSN	TEAM	GP	G	A	PTS.	PIM	+/-
41–42	Det	12	8	6	14	19	
42–43	Det	10	4	2	6	10	
43–44	Det	5	1	0	1	0	
45–46	Chi	4	0	0	0	17	
Totals		50	14	12	26	46	

GROSVENAR, Leonard (Len) F
B. Ottawa, Ont.

27–28	Ott	41	1	2	3	18	
28–29	Ott	42	3	2	5	16	
29–30	Ott	14	0	3	3	19	
30–31	Ott	34	5	4	9	25	
31–32	NYA	12	0	0	0	0	
32–33	Mont	4	0	0	0	0	
Totals		147	9	11	20	78	

Playoffs

27–28	Ott	2	0	0	0	2	
32–33	Mont	2	0	0	0	0	
Totals		4	0	0	0	2	

GROULX, Wayne 6–1 185 C
B. Welland, Ont., Feb. 2, 1965

84–85	Que	1	0	0	0	0	

GRUDEN, John 6–0 189 D
B. Hastings, Minn., Apr. 6, 1970

93–94	Bos	7	0	1	1	2	-3
94–95	Bos	38	0	6	6	22	+3
95–96	Bos	14	0	0	0	4	-3
98–99	Ott	13	0	1	1	8	0
Totals		72	0	8	8	36	-3

Playoffs

95–96	Bos	3	0	1	1	0	

GRUEN, Daniel Patrick 5–11 190 LW
B. Thunder Bay, Ont., June 26, 1952

72–73	Det	2	0	0	0	0	0
73–74	Det	18	1	3	4	7	0
74–75	Mich–Winn (WHA)	66	19	28	47	94	
75–76	Clev (WHA)	80	26	24	50	72	
76–77	Minn–Calg (WHA)	35	11	9	20	19	
76–77	Col	29	8	10	18	12	-6
NHL Totals		49	9	13	22	19	-6
WHA Totals		181	56	61	117	185	

Playoffs

75–76	Clev (WHA)	3	0	1	1	0	

GRUHL, Scott Kenneth 5–11 185 LW
B. Port Colborne, Ont., Sept. 13, 1959

81–82	LA	7	2	1	3	2	+1
82–83	LA	7	0	2	2	4	-5
87–88	Pitt	6	1	0	1	0	0
Totals		20	3	3	6	6	-4

GRYP, Robert Douglas 6–1 190 LW
B. Chatham, Ont., May 6, 1950

73–74	Bos	1	0	0	0	0	-2
74–75	Wash	27	5	8	13	21	-24
75–76	Wash	46	6	5	11	12	-18
Totals		74	11	13	24	33	-44

GUAY, Francois 6–0 190 C
B. Gatineau, Que., June 8, 1968

89–90	Buf	1	0	0	0	0	0

GUAY, Paul 5–11 185 RW
B. Providence, R.I., Sept. 2, 1963

83–84	Phil	14	2	6	8	14	+1
84–85	Phil	2	0	1	1	0	+2
85–86	LA	23	3	3	6	18	-6
86–87	LA	35	2	5	7	16	-14
87–88	LA	33	4	4	8	40	-7
88–89	LA–Bos	7	0	2	2	2	-2
90–91	NYI	3	0	2	2	2	+2
Totals		117	11	23	34	92	-24

Playoffs

83–84	Phil	3	0	0	0	4	
86–87	LA	2	0	0	0	0	
87–88	LA	4	0	1	1	8	

SSN	TEAM	GP	G	A	PTS.	PIM	+/-
Totals		9	0	1	1	12	

GUERARD, Daniel 6–4 215 RW
B. LaSalle, Que., Apr. 9, 1974

94–95	Que	2	0	0	0	0	0

GUERARD, Stephane 6–2 198 D
B. Ste. Elizabeth, Que., Apr. 12, 1968

87–88	Que	30	0	0	0	34	-7
88–89	Que	4	0	0	0	6	-5
Totals		34	0	0	0	40	-12

GUERIN, Bill 6–2 200 RW
B. Wilbraham, Mass., Nov. 9, 1970

91–92	NJ	5	0	1	1	9	+1
92–93	NJ	65	14	20	34	63	+14
93–94	NJ	81	25	19	44	101	+14
94–95	NJ	48	12	13	25	72	+6
95–96	NJ	80	23	30	53	116	+7
96–97	NJ	82	29	18	47	95	-2
97–98	NJ–Edm	59	18	21	39	93	+1
98–99	Edm	80	30	34	64	133	+7
Totals		500	151	156	307	682	+48

Playoffs

91–92	NJ	6	3	0	3	4	
92–93	NJ	5	1	1	2	4	
93–94	NJ	17	2	1	3	35	
94–95	NJ	20	3	8	11	30	
96–97	NJ	8	2	1	3	18	
97–98	Edm	12	7	1	8	17	
98–99	Edm	3	0	2	2	2	
Totals		71	18	14	32	110	

GUEVREMONT, Jocelyn Marcel Josh 6–2 200 D
B. Montreal, Que., Mar. 1, 1951

71–72	Van	75	13	38	51	44	-28
72–73	Van	78	16	26	42	46	-42
73–74	Van	72	15	24	39	34	-37
74–75	Van–Buf	66	7	25	32	32	+31
75–76	Buf	80	12	40	52	57	+47
76–77	Buf	80	9	29	38	46	+26
77–78	Buf	66	7	28	35	46	+25
78–79	Buf	34	3	8	11	8	+12
79–80	NYR	20	2	5	7	6	-12
Totals		571	84	223	307	319	+22

Playoffs

74–75	Buf	17	0	6	6	14	
75–76	Buf	9	0	5	5	2	
76–77	Buf	6	3	4	7	0	
77–78	Buf	8	1	2	3	2	
Totals		40	4	17	21	18	

GUIDOLIN, Aldo Reno 6–0 180 D
B. Forks of Credit, Ont., June 6, 1932

52–53	NYR	30	4	4	8	24	
53–54	NYR	68	2	6	8	51	
54–55	NYR	70	2	5	7	34	
55–56	NYR	14	1	0	1	8	
Totals		182	9	15	24	117	

GUIDOLIN, Armand (Bep) 5–8 175 LW
B. Thorold, Ont., Dec. 9, 1925

42–43	Bos	42	7	15	22	43	
43–44	Bos	47	17	25	42	58	
45–46	Bos	50	15	17	32	62	
46–47	Bos	56	10	13	23	73	
47–48	Det	58	12	10	22	78	
48–49	Det–Chi	60	4	17	21	116	
49–50	Chi	70	17	34	51	42	
50–51	Chi	69	12	22	34	56	
51–52	Chi	67	13	18	31	78	
Totals		519	107	171	278	606	

Playoffs

42–43	Bos	9	0	4	4	12	
45–46	Bos	10	5	2	7	13	
46–47	Bos	3	0	1	1	6	
47–48	Det	2	0	0	0	4	
Totals		24	5	7	12	35	

GUINDON, Robert Pierre 5–9 175 LW
B. Labelle, Que., Nov. 19, 1950

72–73	Que (WHA)	71	28	28	56	31	

SSN	TEAM	GP	G	A	PTS.	PIM	+/-
73–74	Que (WHA)	77	31	39	70	30	
74–75	Que (WHA)	69	12	18	30	23	
75–76	Winn (WHA)	39	3	3	6	14	
76–77	Winn (WHA)	69	10	17	27	19	
77–78	Winn (WHA)	77	20	22	42	18	
78–79	Winn (WHA)	71	8	18	26	21	
79–80	Winn	6	0	1	1	0	+2
NHL Totals		6	0	1	1	0	+2
WHA Totals		473	112	145	257	156	

Playoffs

SSN	TEAM	GP	G	A	PTS.	PIM	+/-
74–75	Que (WHA)	15	7	6	13	10	
75–76	Winn (WHA)	13	3	3	6	9	
76–77	Winn (WHA)	20	4	4	8	9	
77–78	Winn (WHA)	9	8	5	13	5	
78–79	Winn (WHA)	7	2	1	3	0	
WHA Totals		64	24	19	43	33	

GUOLLA, Stephen 6–0 180 LW
B. Scarborough, Ont., March 15, 1973

SSN	TEAM	GP	G	A	PTS.	PIM	+/-
96–97	SJ	43	13	8	21	14	-10
97–98	SJ	7	1	1	2	0	-2
98–99	SJ	14	2	2	4	6	+3
Totals		64	16	11	27	20	-9

GUREN, Miloslav 6–2 210 D
B. Uherske Hradiste, Czech., Sept. 24, 1976

SSN	TEAM	GP	G	A	PTS.	PIM	+/-
98–99	Mont	12	0	1	1	4	-1

GUSAROV, Alexei 6–3 183 D
B. Leningrad, Soviet Union, July 8, 1964

SSN	TEAM	GP	G	A	PTS.	PIM	+/-
90–91	Que	36	3	9	12	12	-4
91–92	Que	68	5	18	23	22	-9
92–93	Que	79	8	22	30	57	+18
93–94	Que	76	5	20	25	38	+3
94–95	Que	14	1	2	3	6	-1
95–96	Col A	65	5	15	20	56	+29
96–97	Col A	58	2	12	14	28	+4
97–98	Col A	72	4	10	14	42	+9
98–99	Col A	54	3	10	13	24	+12
Totals		522	36	118	154	285	+61

Playoffs

SSN	TEAM	GP	G	A	PTS.	PIM	+/-
92–93	Que	5	0	0	0	2	
95–96	Col A	21	0	9	9	12	
96–97	Col A	17	0	3	3	14	
97–98	Col A	7	0	1	1	6	
98–99	Col A	5	0	0	0	2	
Totals		55	0	14	14	34	

GUSEV, Sergey 6–1 195 D
B. Nizhny Tagil, USSR, July 31, 1975

SSN	TEAM	GP	G	A	PTS.	PIM	+/-
97–98	Dal	9	0	0	0	2	-5
98–99	Dal–TB	36	1	7	8	16	-3
Totals		45	1	7	8	18	-8

GUSMANOV, Ravil 6–3 185 LW
B. Naberezhyne Chelny, U.S.S.R., July 25, 1972

SSN	TEAM	GP	G	A	PTS.	PIM	+/-
95–96	Winn	4	0	0	0	0	-3

GUSTAFSSON, Bengt–Ake 5–11 198 C
B. Kariskoga, Sweden, Mar. 23, 1958

SSN	TEAM	GP	G	A	PTS.	PIM	+/-
79–80	Wash	80	22	38	60	17	-17
80–81	Wash	72	21	34	55	26	+11
81–82	Wash	70	26	34	60	40	-20
82–83	Wash	67	22	42	64	16	+9
83–84	Wash	69	32	43	75	16	+29
84–85	Wash	51	14	29	43	8	+13
85–86	Wash	70	23	52	75	26	-9
87–88	Wash	78	18	36	54	29	+2
88–89	Wash	72	18	51	69	18	+13
Totals		629	196	359	555	196	+31

Playoffs

SSN	TEAM	GP	G	A	PTS.	PIM	+/-
78–79	Edm (WHA)	2	1	2	3	0	
82–83	Wash	4	0	1	1	4	
83–84	Wash	5	2	3	5	0	
84–85	Wash	5	1	3	4	0	
87–88	Wash	14	4	9	13	6	
88–89	Wash	4	2	3	5	6	
NHL Totals		32	9	19	28	16	
WHA Totals		2	1	2	3	0	

GUSTAFSSON, Per 6–2 190 D
B. Osterham, Sweden, June 6, 1970

SSN	TEAM	GP	G	A	PTS.	PIM	+/-
96–97	Fla	58	7	22	29	22	+11
97–98	Tor–Ott	31	1	5	6	16	-2
Totals		89	8	27	35	38	+9

Playoffs

SSN	TEAM	GP	G	A	PTS.	PIM	+/-
97–98	Ott	1	0	0	0	0	

GUSTAVSSON, Peter 6–1 188 LW
B. Bollebygd, Sweden, Mar. 30, 1958

SSN	TEAM	GP	G	A	PTS.	PIM	+/-
81–82	Col	2	0	0	0	0	-1

GUY, Kevan 6–3 202 D
B. Edmonton, Alta., July 16, 1965

SSN	TEAM	GP	G	A	PTS.	PIM	+/-
86–87	Calg	24	0	4	4	19	+8
87–88	Calg	11	0	3	3	8	+1
88–89	Van	45	2	2	4	34	-14
89–90	Van	30	2	5	7	32	-12
90–91	Van–Calg	43	1	6	7	43	-5
91–92	Calg	3	0	0	0	2	+2
Totals		156	5	20	25	138	-20

Playoffs

SSN	TEAM	GP	G	A	PTS.	PIM	+/-
86–87	Calg	4	0	1	1	23	
88–89	Van	1	0	0	0	0	
Totals		5	0	1	1	23	

HAANPAA, Ari 6–1 190 RW
B. Nokia, Finland, Nov. 29, 1965

SSN	TEAM	GP	G	A	PTS.	PIM	+/-
85–86	NYI	18	0	7	7	20	0
86–87	NYI	41	6	4	10	17	+8
87–88	NYI	1	0	0	0	0	-2
Totals		60	6	11	17	37	+6

Playoffs

SSN	TEAM	GP	G	A	PTS.	PIM	+/-
86–87	NYI	6	0	0	0	10	

HAAS, David 6–2 196 LW
B. Toronto, Ont., June 23, 1968

SSN	TEAM	GP	G	A	PTS.	PIM	+/-
90–91	Edm	5	1	0	1	0	-2
93–94	Calg	2	1	1	2	7	+2
Totals		7	2	1	3	7	0

HABSCHEID, Marc Joseph 6–0 185 RW/C
B. Swift Current, Sask., Mar. 1, 1963

SSN	TEAM	GP	G	A	PTS.	PIM	+/-
81–82	Edm	7	1	3	4	2	+5
82–83	Edm	32	3	10	13	14	+14
83–84	Edm	9	1	0	1	6	-3
84–85	Edm	26	5	3	8	4	-2
85–86	Minn	6	2	3	5	0	-2
86–87	Minn	15	2	0	2	6	-6
87–88	Minn	16	4	11	15	6	-4
88–89	Minn	76	23	31	54	40	+2
89–90	Det	66	15	11	26	33	+1
90–91	Det	46	9	8	17	22	-10
91–92	Calg	46	7	11	18	42	-11
Totals		345	72	91	163	171	-16

Playoffs

SSN	TEAM	GP	G	A	PTS.	PIM	+/-
85–86	Minn	2	0	0	0	0	
88–89	Minn	5	1	3	4	13	
90–91	Det	5	0	0	0	0	
Totals		12	1	3	4	13	

HACHBORN, Leonard 5–10 175 C
B. Brantford, Ont., Sept. 4, 1961

SSN	TEAM	GP	G	A	PTS.	PIM	+/-
83–84	Phil	38	11	21	32	4	+8
84–85	Phil	40	5	17	22	23	+16
85–86	LA	24	4	1	5	2	-9
Totals		102	20	39	59	25	+15

Playoffs

SSN	TEAM	GP	G	A	PTS.	PIM	+/-
83–84	Phil	3	0	0	0	7	
84–85	Phil	4	0	3	3	0	
Totals		7	0	3	3	7	

HADDON, Lloyd Ward 6–0 195 D
B. Sarnia, Ont., Aug. 10, 1938

SSN	TEAM	GP	G	A	PTS.	PIM	+/-
59–60	Det	8	0	0	0	2	

Playoffs

SSN	TEAM	GP	G	A	PTS.	PIM	+/-
59–60	Det	1	0	0	0	0	

HADFIELD, Victor Edward 6–0 190 LW
B. Oakville, Ont., Oct. 4, 1940

SSN	TEAM	GP	G	A	PTS.	PIM	+/-
61–62	NYR	44	3	1	4	22	
62–63	NYR	36	5	6	11	32	
63–64	NYR	69	14	11	25	151	
64–65	NYR	70	18	20	38	102	
65–66	NYR	67	16	19	35	112	
66–67	NYR	69	13	20	33	80	
67–68	NYR	59	20	19	39	45	-2
68–69	NYR	73	26	40	66	108	+12
69–70	NYR	71	20	34	54	69	-3
70–71	NYR	63	22	22	44	38	+14
71–72	NYR	78	50	56	106	142	+60
72–73	NYR	63	28	34	62	60	+13
73–74	NYR	77	27	28	55	75	+1
74–75	Pitt	78	31	42	73	72	+5
75–76	Pitt	76	30	35	65	46	-3
76–77	Pitt	9	0	2	2	0	+1
Totals		1002	323	389	712	1154	+98

Playoffs

SSN	TEAM	GP	G	A	PTS.	PIM	+/-
61–62	NYR	4	0	0	0	2	
66–67	NYR	4	1	0	1	17	
67–68	NYR	6	1	2	3	6	
68–69	NYR	4	2	1	3	2	
70–71	NYR	13	8	5	13	46	
71–72	NYR	16	7	9	16	22	
72–73	NYR	9	2	2	4	11	
73–74	NYR	6	1	0	1	0	
74–75	Pitt	9	4	2	6	0	
75–76	Pitt	3	1	0	1	11	
Totals		74	27	21	48	117	

HAGGARTY, James 5–11 167 LW
B. Port Arthur, Ont., Apr. 14, 1914

SSN	TEAM	GP	G	A	PTS.	PIM	+/-
41–42	Mont	5	1	1	2	0	

Playoffs

SSN	TEAM	GP	G	A	PTS.	PIM	+/-
41–42	Mont	3	2	1	3	0	

HAGGERTY, Sean 6–1 186 C
B. Greenwich, Conn., Feb. 11, 1976

SSN	TEAM	GP	G	A	PTS.	PIM	+/-
95–96	Tor	1	0	0	0	0	0
97–98	NYI	5	0	0	0	0	-3
Totals		6	0	0	0	0	-3

*HAGGLUND, Roger 6–1 175 D
B. Umea, Sweden, July 2, 1961

SSN	TEAM	GP	G	A	PTS.	PIM	+/-
84–85	Que	3	0	0	0	0	0

HAGMAN, Matti Risto Tapio (Hakki) 6–1 184 C
B. Helsinki, Finland, Sept. 21, 1955

SSN	TEAM	GP	G	A	PTS.	PIM	+/-
76–77	Bos	75	11	17	28	0	+6
77–78	Bos	15	4	1	5	6	-1
77–78	Que (WHA)	53	25	31	56	16	
80–81	Edm	75	20	33	53	16	+44
81–82	Edm	72	21	38	59	18	+15
NHL Totals		237	56	89	145	40	+24
WHA Totals		53	25	31	56	16	

Playoffs

SSN	TEAM	GP	G	A	PTS.	PIM	+/-
76–77	Bos	9	0	1	1	0	
80–81	Edm	8	4	1	5	6	
81–82	Edm	3	1	0	1	0	
Totals		20	5	2	7	6	

HAIDY, Gordon Adam (Adam) 5–10 185 RW
B. Winnipeg, Man., Apr. 11, 1928

Playoffs

SSN	TEAM	GP	G	A	PTS.	PIM	+/-
49–50	Det	1	0	0	0	0	

HADJU, Richard 6–1 185 LW
B. Victoria, B.C., May 10, 1965

SSN	TEAM	GP	G	A	PTS.	PIM	+/-
85–86	Buf	3	0	0	0	4	+1
86–87	Buf	2	0	0	0	0	+1
Totals		5	0	0	0	4	+2

HAJT, William Albert 6–3 205 D
B. Borden, Sask., Nov. 18, 1951

SSN	TEAM	GP	G	A	PTS.	PIM	+/-
73–74	Buf	6	0	2	2	0	-1
74–75	Buf	76	3	26	29	68	+47
75–76	Buf	80	6	21	27	48	+39
76–77	Buf	79	6	20	26	56	+39
77–78	Buf	76	4	18	22	30	+36
78–79	Buf	40	3	8	11	20	-4
79–80	Buf	75	4	12	16	24	+36
80–81	Buf	68	2	19	21	42	+38
81–82	Buf	65	2	9	11	44	+11

SSN	TEAM	GP	G	A	PTS.	PIM	+/-
82–83	Buf	72	3	12	15	26	+6
83–84	Buf	79	3	24	27	32	+25
84–85	Buf	57	5	13	18	14	+32
85–86	Buf	58	1	16	17	25	+17
86–87	Buf	23	0	2	2	4	0
Totals		854	42	202	244	433	+321

Playoffs

74–75	Buf	17	1	4	5	18
75–76	Buf	9	0	1	1	15
76–77	Buf	6	0	1	1	4
77–78	Buf	8	0	0	0	2
79–80	Buf	14	0	5	5	4
80–81	Buf	8	0	2	2	17
81–82	Buf	2	0	0	0	0
82–83	Buf	10	0	0	0	4
83–84	Buf	3	0	0	0	0
84–85	Buf	3	1	3	4	6
Totals		80	2	16	18	70

HAKANSSON, Anders *6–2 190 LW*
B. Munkfors, Sweden, Apr. 27, 1956

81–82	Minn	72	12	4	16	29	-12
82–83	Minn–Pitt	67	9	12	21	35	-10
83–84	LA	80	15	17	32	41	-7
84–85	LA	73	12	12	24	28	-4
85–86	LA	38	4	1	5	8	-8
Totals		330	52	46	98	141	-41

Playoffs

81–82	Minn	3	0	0	0	2
84–85	LA	3	0	0	0	0
Totals		6	0	0	0	2

*HALDERSON, Harold (Slim) *6–3 200 D*
B. Winnipeg, Man., Jan. 6, 1900

26–27	Det–Tor	44	3	2	5	65

HALE, Larry James *6–1 180 D*
B. Summerland, B.C., Oct. 9, 1941

68–69	Phil	67	3	16	19	28	-24
69–70	Phil	53	1	9	10	28	-4
70–71	Phil	70	1	11	12	34	-18
71–72	Phil	6	0	1	1	0	-5
72–73	Hou (WHA)	68	4	26	30	65	
73–74	Hou (WHA)	69	2	14	16	39	
74–75	Hou (WHA)	76	2	18	20	40	
75–76	Hou (WHA)	77	2	12	14	30	
76–77	Hou (WHA)	67	0	14	14	18	
77–78	Hou (WHA)	56	2	11	13	22	
NHL Totals		196	5	37	42	90	-51
WHA Totals		413	12	95	107	214	

Playoffs

68–69	Phil	4	0	0	0	10
70–71	Phil	4	0	0	0	2
72–73	Hou (WHA)	10	1	2	3	2
73–74	Hou (WHA)	14	3	2	5	6
74–75	Hou (WHA)	13	0	4	4	0
75–76	Hou (WHA)	17	0	5	5	8
76–77	Hou (WHA)	11	0	2	2	6
NHL Totals		8	0	0	0	12
WHA Totals		65	4	15	19	22

HALEY, Leonard Frank (Len) *5–7 168 RW*
B. Edmonton, Alta., Sept. 15, 1931

59–60	Det	27	1	2	3	12
60–61	Det	3	1	0	1	2
Totals		30	2	2	4	14

Playoffs

59–60	Det	6	1	3	4	6

HALKIDIS, Bob *5–11 200 D*
B. Toronto, Ont., Mar. 5, 1966

85–86	Buf	37	1	9	10	115	-3
86–87	Buf	6	1	1	2	19	+3
87–88	Buf	30	0	3	3	115	+6
88–89	Buf	16	0	1	1	66	-1
89–90	LA	20	0	4	4	56	+4
90–91	LA	34	1	3	4	133	+8
91–92	Tor	46	3	3	6	145	+9
93–94	Det	28	1	4	5	93	-1
94–95	Det–TB	31	1	4	5	46	-10
95–96	TB–NYI	8	0	0	0	37	-4
Totals		256	8	32	40	825	-7

Playoffs

84–85	Buf	4	0	0	0	19
87–88	Buf	4	0	0	0	22
89–90	LA	8	0	1	1	8
90–91	LA	3	0	0	0	0
93–94	Det	1	0	0	0	2
Totals		20	0	1	1	51

HALKO, Steven *6–1 195 D*
B. Etobicoke, Ont., Mar. 8, 1974

97–98	Car	18	0	2	2	10	-1
98–99	Car	20	0	3	3	24	+5
Totals		38	0	5	5	34	+4

Playoffs

98–99	Car	4	0	0	0	2

HALL, Del Allison *5–10 170 C*
B. Peterborough, Ont., May 7, 1949

71–72	Cal	1	0	0	0	0	-1
72–73	Cal	6	0	0	0	0	0
73–74	Cal	2	2	0	2	2	+1
75–76	Phoe (WHA)	80	47	44	91	10	
76–77	Phoe (WHA)	80	38	41	79	30	
77–78	Edm (WHA)	26	4	3	7	4	
NHL Totals		9	2	0	2	2	0
WHA Totals		186	89	88	177	44	

Playoffs

75–76	Phoe (WHA)	5	2	3	5	0

HALL, Gary Wayne *5–8 170 LW*
B. Melita, Man., May 22, 1939

60–61	NYR	4	0	0	0	0

*HALL, Joseph Henry (Bad Joe) *F*
B. Stratfordshire, England, May 3, 1882

17–18	Mont	20	8	0	8	60
18–19	Mont	17	7	1	8	85
Totals		37	15	1	16	145
Playoff Totals		12	0	2	2	31

HALL, Murray Winston *6–0 175 C*
B. Kirkland Lake, Ont., Nov. 24, 1940

61–62	Chi	2	0	0	0	0	
63–64	Chi	23	2	0	2	4	
65–66	Det	1	0	0	0	0	
66–67	Det	12	4	3	7	4	
67–68	Minn	17	2	1	3	10	-7
70–71	Van	77	21	38	59	22	-16
71–72	Van	32	6	6	12	6	-12
72–73	Hou (WHA)	76	28	42	70	84	
73–74	Hou (WHA)	78	30	28	58	25	
74–75	Hou (WHA)	78	18	29	47	28	
75–76	Hou (WHA)	80	20	26	46	18	
NHL Totals		164	35	48	83	46	-35
WHA Totals		312	96	125	221	155	

Playoffs

62–63	Chi	4	0	0	0	0
64–65	Det	1	0	0	0	0
72–73	Hou (WHA)	10	4	4	8	18
73–74	Hou (WHA)	14	9	6	15	6
74–75	Hou (WHA)	13	7	3	10	8
75–76	Hou (WHA)	17	1	4	5	0
NHL Totals		5	0	0	0	0
WHA Totals		54	21	17	38	32

HALL, Robert *F*

25–26	NYA	8	0	0	0	0

HALL, Taylor *5–11 180 LW*
B. Regina, Sask., Feb. 20, 1964

83–84	Van	4	1	0	1	0	-2
84–85	Van	7	1	4	5	19	0
85–86	Van	19	5	5	10	6	-11
86–87	Van	4	0	0	0	0	-2
87–88	Bos	7	0	0	0	4	-3
Totals		41	7	9	16	29	-18

HALLER, Kevin *6–2 183 D*
B. Trochu, Alta., Dec. 5, 1970

89–90	Buf	2	0	0	0	0	
90–91	Buf	21	1	8	9	20	+9
91–92	Buf–Mont	66	8	17	25	92	-9
92–93	Mont	73	11	14	25	117	+7

93–94	Mont	68	4	9	13	118	+13
94–95	Phil	36	2	8	10	48	+16
95–96	Phil	69	5	9	14	92	+18
96–97	Phil–Hart	62	2	11	13	85	-12
97–98	Car	65	3	5	8	94	-5
98–99	Ana	82	1	6	7	122	-1
Totals		544	37	87	124	788	+36

Playoffs

90–91	Buf	6	1	4	5	10
91–92	Mont	9	0	0	0	6
92–93	Mont	17	1	6	7	16
93–94	Mont	7	1	1	2	19
94–95	Phil	15	4	4	8	10
95–96	Phil	6	0	1	1	8
98–99	Ana	4	0	0	0	2
Totals		64	7	16	23	71

HALLIDAY, Milton *F-D*
B. Ottawa, Ont.

26–27	Ott	38	1	0	1	4
27–28	Ott	13	0	0	0	2
28–29	Ott	16	0	0	0	0
Totals		67	1	0	1	6

Playoffs

26–27	Ott	6	0	0	0	0

HALLIN, Mats *6–2 200 LW*
B. Eskilstuna, Sweden, Mar. 9, 1958

82–83	NYI	30	7	7	14	26	+4
83–84	NYI	40	2	5	7	27	-2
84–85	NYI	38	5	0	5	50	-7
85–86	Minn	38	3	2	5	86	-3
86–87	Minn	6	0	0	0	4	-3
Totals		152	17	14	31	193	-11

Playoffs

82–83	NYI	7	1	0	1	6
83–84	NYI	6	0	0	0	7
84–85	NYI	1	0	0	0	0
85–86	Minn	1	0	0	0	0
Totals		15	1	0	1	13

HALVERSON, Trevor *6–2 203 LW*
B. White River, Ont., Apr. 6, 1971

98–99	Wash	17	0	4	4	28	-5

HALWARD, Douglas Robert *6–1 200 D*
B. Toronto, Ont., Nov. 1, 1955

75–76	Bos	22	1	5	6	6	-4
76–77	Bos	18	2	2	4	6	+9
77–78	Bos	25	0	2	2	2	+1
78–79	LA	27	1	5	6	13	-4
79–80	LA	63	11	45	56	52	+14
80–81	LA–Van	58	4	16	20	100	-7
81–82	Van	37	4	13	17	40	-11
82–83	Van	75	19	33	52	83	-18
83–84	Van	54	7	16	23	35	+1
84–85	Van	71	7	27	34	82	-42
85–86	Van	70	8	25	33	111	-19
86–87	Van–Det	21	0	6	6	53	-4
87–88	Det	70	5	21	26	130	+6
88–89	Det–Edm	42	0	8	8	61	-13
Totals		653	69	224	293	774	-91

Playoffs

75–76	Bos	1	0	0	0	0
76–77	Bos	6	0	0	0	4
78–79	LA	1	0	0	0	12
80–81	Van	2	0	1	1	6
81–82	Van	15	2	4	6	44
82–83	Van	4	1	0	1	21
83–84	Van	4	3	1	4	2
85–86	Van	3	0	0	0	4
87–88	Det	8	1	4	5	18
88–89	Edm	2	0	0	0	0
Totals		47	7	10	17	113

HAMEL, Gilles *6–0 185 LW*
B. Asbestos, Que., Mar. 18, 1960

80–81	Buf	51	10	9	19	53	-8
81–82	Buf	16	2	7	9	2	-1
82–83	Buf	66	22	20	42	26	+4
83–84	Buf	75	21	23	44	37	+4
84–85	Buf	80	18	30	48	36	-3
85–86	Buf	77	19	25	44	61	-27

SSN	TEAM	GP	G	A	PTS.	PIM	+/-
86–87	Winn	79	27	21	48	24	+3
87–88	Winn	63	8	11	19	35	-16
88–89	Winn–LA	12	0	1	1	2	-3
Totals		519	127	147	274	276	-50

Playoffs

80–81	Buf	5	0	1	1	4	
82–83	Buf	9	2	2	4	2	
83–84	Buf	3	0	2	2	2	
84–85	Buf	1	0	0	0	0	
86–87	Winn	8	2	0	2	2	
87–88	Winn	1	0	0	0	0	
Totals		27	4	5	9	10	

HAMEL, Herbert (Hap) F

| 30–39 | Tor | 2 | 0 | 0 | 0 | 14 | |

HAMEL, Jean 5–11 195 D
B. Asbestos, Que., June 6, 1952

72–73	StL	55	2	7	9	24	-5
73–74	StL–Det	45	1	4	5	46	-15
74–75	Det	80	5	19	24	136	-40
75–76	Det	77	3	9	12	129	-13
76–77	Det	71	1	10	11	63	-18
77–78	Det	32	2	6	8	34	+3
78–79	Det	52	2	4	6	72	-9
79–80	Det	49	1	4	5	43	-2
80–81	Det	68	5	7	12	57	-1
81–82	Que	40	1	6	7	32	+3
82–83	Que	51	2	7	9	38	+11
83–84	Mont	79	1	12	13	92	+7
Totals		699	26	95	121	766	-79

Playoffs

72–73	StL	2	0	0	0	0	
77–78	Det	7	0	0	0	10	
81–82	Que	5	0	0	0	16	
82–83	Que	4	0	0	0	2	
83–84	Mont	15	0	2	2	16	
Totals		33	0	2	2	44	

*HAMILL, Robert George (Red) 5–11 180 LW
B. Toronto, Ont., 11, 1917

37–38	Bos	6	0	1	1	2	
38–39	Bos	7	0	1	1	0	
39–40	Bos	28	10	8	18	16	
40–41	Bos	8	0	1	1	0	
41–42	Bos–Chi	43	24	12	36	23	
42–43	Chi	50	28	16	44	44	
45–46	Chi	38	20	17	37	23	
46–47	Chi	60	21	19	40	12	
47–48	Chi	60	11	13	24	18	
48–49	Chi	57	8	4	12	16	
49–50	Chi	59	6	2	8	6	
50–51	Chi	2	0	0	0	0	
Totals		418	128	94	222	160	

Playoffs

38–39	Bos	11	0	0	0	8	
39–40	Bos	5	0	1	1	5	
41–42	Chi	3	0	1	1	0	
45–46	Chi	4	1	0	1	7	
Totals		23	1	2	3	20	

HAMILTON, Allan Guy 6–1 195 D
B. Flin Flon, Man., Aug. 20, 1946

65–66	NYR	4	0	0	0	0	
67–68	NYR	2	0	0	0	0	0
68–69	NYR	16	0	0	0	0	0
69–70	NYR	59	0	5	5	54	-8
70–71	Buf	69	2	28	30	71	-23
71–72	Buf	76	4	30	34	105	-12
72–73	Alb (WHA)	78	11	50	61	124	
73–74	Edm (WHA)	77	14	45	59	104	
74–75	Edm (WHA)	25	1	13	14	42	
75–76	Edm (WHA)	54	2	32	34	78	
76–77	Edm (WHA)	81	8	37	45	60	
77–78	Edm (WHA)	59	11	43	54	46	
78–79	Edm (WHA)	80	6	38	44	38	
79–80	Edm	31	4	15	19	20	-2
NHL Totals		257	10	78	88	250	-45
WHA Totals		454	53	258	311	492	

Playoffs

68–69	NYR	1	0	0	0	0	
69–70	NYR	5	0	0	0	2	
73–74	Edm (WHA)	4	1	1	2	15	
75–76	Edm (WHA)	4	0	1	1	6	
76–77	Edm (WHA)	5	0	4	4	4	
78–79	Edm (WHA)	13	4	5	9	4	
79–80	Edm	1	0	0	0	0	
NHL Totals		7	0	0	0	2	
WHA Totals		26	5	11	16	29	

HAMILTON, Charles (Chuck) 5–11 175 LW
B. Kirkland Lake, Ont., Jan. 18, 1939

61–62	Mont	1	0	0	0	0	
72–73	StL	3	0	2	2	2	+4
Totals		4	0	2	2	2	+4

HAMILTON, James 6–0 180 RW
B. Barrie, Ont., Jan. 18, 1957

77–78	Pitt	25	2	4	6	2	-3
78–79	Pitt	2	0	0	0	0	0
79–80	Pitt	10	2	0	2	0	-6
80–81	Pitt	20	1	6	7	18	+2
81–82	Pitt	11	5	3	8	2	+2
82–83	Pitt	5	0	2	2	2	-2
83–84	Pitt	11	2	2	4	4	+2
84–85	Pitt	11	2	1	3	0	-6
Totals		95	14	18	32	28	-10

Playoffs

78–79	Pitt	5	3	0	3	0	
80–81	Pitt	1	0	0	0	0	
Totals		6	3	0	3	0	

*HAMILTON, John McIvor (Jack) 5–7 170 C
B. Trenton, Ont., June 2, 1925

42–43	Tor	49	4	22	26	60	
43–44	Tor	49	20	17	37	4	
45–46	Tor	40	7	9	16	12	
Totals		138	31	48	79	76	

Playoffs

42–43	Tor	6	1	1	2	0	
43–44	Tor	5	1	0	1	0	
Totals		11	2	1	3	0	

*HAMILTON, Reginald (Reg) 5–11 180 D
B. Toronto, Ont., Apr. 29, 1914

35–36	Tor	7	0	0	0	0	
36–37	Tor	39	3	7	10	32	
37–38	Tor	45	1	4	5	43	
38–39	Tor	48	0	7	7	54	
39–40	Tor	23	2	2	4	23	
40–41	Tor	45	3	12	15	59	
41–42	Tor	22	0	4	4	27	
42–43	Tor	11	1	1	2	68	
43–44	Tor	39	4	12	16	32	
44–45	Tor	50	3	12	15	41	
45–46	Chi	48	1	7	8	31	
46–47	Chi	10	0	3	3	2	
Totals		387	18	71	89	412	

Playoffs

36–37	Tor	2	0	1	1	2	
37–38	Tor	7	0	1	1	2	
38–39	Tor	10	0	0	0	4	
39–40	Tor	10	0	0	0	0	
40–41	Tor	7	1	2	3	13	
42–43	Tor	6	1	1	2	9	
43–44	Tor	5	1	0	1	8	
44–45	Tor	13	3	0	3	14	
45–46	Chi	4	0	1	1	2	
Totals		64	6	6	12	54	

HAMMARSTROM, Hans Inge 6–0 180 LW
B. Sundsvall, Sweden, Jan. 20, 1948

73–74	Tor	66	20	23	43	14	+17
74–75	Tor	69	21	20	41	23	-14
75–76	Tor	76	19	21	40	21	0
76–77	Tor	78	24	17	41	16	+8
77–78	Tor–StL	73	20	20	40	10	-20
78–79	StL	65	12	22	34	8	-13
Totals		427	116	123	239	92	-22

Playoffs

73–74	Tor	4	1	0	1	0	
74–75	Tor	7	1	3	4	4	
76–77	Tor	2	0	0	0	0	
Totals		13	2	3	5	4	

HAMMOND, Ken 6–1 190 D
B. Port Credit, Ont., Aug. 22, 1963

84–85	LA	3	1	0	1	0	+2
85–86	LA	3	0	1	1	2	-1
86–87	LA	10	0	2	2	11	0
87–88	LA	46	7	9	16	69	-1
88–89	Edm–NYR–Tor	22	0	3	3	20	-18
90–91	Bos	1	1	0	1	2	+2
91–92	SJ–Van	46	5	10	15	82	-17
92–93	Ott	62	4	4	8	104	-42
Totals		193	18	29	47	290	-75

Playoffs

84–85	LA	3	0	0	0	4	
87–88	LA	2	0	0	0	4	
90–91	Bos	8	0	0	0	10	
91–92	Van	2	0	0	0	6	
Totals		15	0	0	0	24	

HAMPSON, Edward George (Ted) 5–8 173 C
B. Togo, Sask., Dec. 11, 1936

59–60	Tor	41	2	8	10	17	
60–61	NYR	69	6	14	20	4	
61–62	NYR	68	4	24	28	10	
62–63	NYR	46	4	2	6	2	
63–64	Det	7	0	1	1	0	
64–65	Det	1	0	0	0	0	
66–67	Det	65	13	35	48	4	
67–68	Det–Oak	71	17	37	54	14	-2
68–69	Oak	76	26	49	75	6	-15
69–70	Oak	76	17	35	52	10	-17
70–71	Cal–Minn	78	14	26	40	18	-22
71–72	Minn	78	5	14	19	6	-1
72–73	Minn (WHA)	77	17	45	62	20	
73–74	Minn (WHA)	77	17	38	55	9	
74–75	Minn (WHA)	78	17	36	53	6	
75–76	Minn–Que (WHA)	73	9	25	34	16	
NHL Totals		676	108	245	353	91	-57
WHA Totals		305	60	144	204	51	

Playoffs

61–62	NYR	6	0	1	1	0	
68–69	Oak	7	3	4	7	2	
69–70	Oak	4	1	1	2	0	
70–71	Minn	11	3	3	6	0	
71–72	Minn	7	0	1	1	2	
72–73	Minn (WHA)	5	3	1	4	0	
73–74	Minn (WHA)	11	4	4	8	8	
74–75	Minn (WHA)	12	1	7	8	0	
75–76	Que (WHA)	5	0	2	2	10	
NHL Totals		35	7	10	17	4	
WHA Totals		33	8	14	22	18	

HAMPSON, Gordon 6–3 210 LW
B. Vancouver, B.C., Feb. 13, 1959

| 82–83 | Calg | 4 | 0 | 0 | 0 | 5 | -2 |

HAMPTON, Richard Charles (Rick) 6–0 190 D
B. King, Ont., June 14, 1956

74–75	Cal	78	8	17	25	59	-40
75–76	Cal	73	14	37	51	54	-12
76–77	Clev	57	16	24	40	13	-11
77–78	Clev	77	18	18	36	19	-24
78–79	LA	49	3	17	20	22	0
79–80	LA	3	0	0	0	0	+3
Totals		337	59	113	172	167	-84

Playoffs

| 78–79 | LA | 2 | 0 | 0 | 0 | 0 | |

HAMR, Radek 5–11 175 D
B. Usti–Nad–Labem, Czechoslovakia, June 15, 1974

92–93	Ott	4	0	0	0	0	-4
93–94	Ott	7	0	0	0	0	-10
Totals		11	0	0	0	0	-14

HAMRLIK, Roman 6–2 202 D
B. Gottwaldov, Czechoslovakia, Apr. 12, 1974

92–93	TB	67	6	15	21	71	-21
93–94	TB	64	3	18	21	135	-14
94–95	TB	48	12	11	23	86	-18
95–96	TB	82	16	49	65	103	-24
96–97	TB	79	12	28	40	57	-29

SSN	TEAM	GP	G	A	PTS.	PIM	+/-
97–98	TB–Edm	78	9	32	41	70	-15
98–99	Edm	75	8	24	32	70	+9
Totals		493	66	177	243	592	-112

Playoffs

95–96	TB	5	0	1	1	4	
97–98	Edm	12	0	6	6	12	
98–99	Edm	3	0	0	0	2	
Totals		20	0	7	7	18	

HAMWAY, Mark 6–0 190 RW
B. Detroit, Mich., Aug. 9, 1961

84–85	NYI	2	0	0	0	0	0
85–86	NYI	49	5	12	17	9	-5
86–87	NYI	2	0	1	1	0	-1
Totals		53	5	13	18	9	-6

Playoffs

85–86	NYI	1	0	0	0	0	

HANDY, Ronald 5–11 175 LW
B. Toronto, Ont., Jan. 5, 1963

85–85	NYI	10	0	2	2	0	-1
87–88	StL	4	0	1	1	0	-1
Totals		14	0	3	3	0	-2

HANDZUS, Michal 6–3 191 C
B. Banska Bystrica, Czech., March 11, 1977

98–99	StL	66	4	12	16	30	-9

Playoffs

98–99	StL	11	0	2	2	8	

HANGSLEBEN, Alan (Hank) 6–1 195 D
B. Warroad, Minn., Feb. 22, 1953

74–75	NE (WHA)	26	0	4	4	8	
75–76	NE (WHA)	78	2	23	25	62	
76–77	NE (WHA)	74	13	9	22	79	
77–78	NE (WHA)	79	11	18	29	140	
78–79	NE (WHA)	77	10	19	29	148	
79–80	Hart–Wash	74	13	22	35	114	+10
80–81	Wash	76	5	19	24	198	-7
81–82	Wash–LA	35	3	7	10	84	0
NHL Totals		185	21	48	69	396	+3
WHA Totals		334	36	73	109	437	

Playoffs

74–75	NE (WHA)	6	0	3	3	19	
75–76	NE (WHA)	13	2	3	5	20	
76–77	NE (WHA)	4	0	0	0	9	
77–78	NE (WHA)	14	1	4	5	37	
78–79	NE (WHA)	10	1	2	3	12	
WHA Totals		47	4	12	16	97	

HANKINSON, Benjamin John 6–2 210 RW
B. Edina, Minn., May 1, 1969

92–93	NJ	4	2	1	3	9	+2
93–94	NJ	13	1	0	1	23	0
94–95	NJ–TB	26	0	2	2	13	-5
Totals		43	3	3	6	45	-3

Playoffs

93–94	NJ	2	1	0	1	4	

HANNA, John 6–0 195 D
B. Sydney, N. S., Apr. 5, 1935

58–59	NYR	70	1	10	11	83	
59–60	NYR	61	4	8	12	87	
60–61	NYR	46	1	8	9	34	
63–64	Mont	6	0	0	0	2	
67–68	Phil	15	0	0	0	0	+1
72–73	Clev (WHA)	66	6	20	26	68	
NHL Totals		198	6	26	32	206	+1
WHA Totals		66	6	20	26	68	

HANNAN, David 5–10 185 C
B. Sudbury, Ont., Nov. 26, 1961

81–82	Pitt	1	0	0	0	0	-2
82–83	Pitt	74	11	22	33	127	-28
83–84	Pitt	24	2	3	5	33	-2
84–85	Pitt	30	6	7	13	43	-8
85–86	Pitt	75	17	18	35	91	-4
86–87	Pitt	58	10	15	25	56	-2
87–88	Pitt–Edm	72	13	14	27	66	+10
88–89	Pitt	72	10	20	30	157	-12
89–90	Tor	39	6	9	15	55	-12
90–91	Tor	74	11	23	34	82	-9
91–92	Tor–Buf	47	4	6	10	64	-9
92–93	Buf	55	5	15	20	43	+8
93–94	Buf	83	6	15	21	53	+10
94–95	Buf	42	4	12	16	32	+3
95–96	Buf–Col A	61	7	10	17	32	+3
96–97	Ott	34	2	2	4	8	-1
Totals		841	114	191	305	942	-56

Playoffs

87–88	Edm	12	1	1	2	8	
88–89	Pitt	8	0	1	1	4	
89–90	Tor	3	1	0	1	4	
91–92	Buf	7	2	0	2	2	
92–93	Buf	8	1	1	2	18	
93–94	Buf	7	1	0	1	6	
94–95	Buf	5	0	2	2	2	
95–96	Col A	13	0	2	2	2	
Totals		63	6	7	13	46	

HANNAN, Scott 6–2 210 D
B. Richmond, B.C., Jan. 23, 1979

98–99	SJ	5	0	2	2	6	0

HANNIGAN, John Gordon (Gord) 5–7 163 C
B. Schumacher, Ont., Jan. 19, 1929

52–53	Tor	65	17	18	35	51	
53–54	Tor	35	4	4	8	18	
54–55	Tor	13	0	2	2	8	
55–56	Tor	48	8	7	15	40	
Totals		161	29	31	60	117	

Playoffs

53–54	Tor	5	2	0	2	4	
55–56	Tor	4	0	0	0	4	
Totals		9	2	0	2	8	

HANNIGAN, Patrick Edward 5–10 190 RW
B. Timmins, Ont., Mar. 5, 1936

59–60	Tor	1	0	0	0	0	
60–61	NYR	53	11	9	20	24	
61–62	NYR	56	8	14	22	34	
67–68	Phil	65	11	15	26	36	+6
68–69	Phil	7	0	1	1	22	-4
Totals		182	30	39	69	116	+2

Playoffs

61–62	NYR	4	0	0	0	2	
67–68	Phil	7	1	2	3	9	
Totals		11	1	2	3	11	

HANNIGAN, Raymond James F
B. Schumacher, Ont., July 14, 1927

48–49	Tor	3	0	0	0	2	

HANSEN, Richard John 5–10 197 C
B. Bronx, N.Y., Oct. 30, 1955

76–77	NYI	4	1	0	1	0	-1
77–78	NYI	2	0	0	0	0	0
78–79	NYI	12	1	6	7	4	+9
81–82	StL	2	0	2	2	2	+2
Totals		20	2	8	10	6	+10

HANSEN, Tavis 6–1 180 C
B. Prince Albert, Sask., June 17, 1975

94–95	Winn	1	0	0	0	0	0
96–97	Phoe	1	0	0	0	0	0
98–99	Phoe	20	2	1	3	12	-4
Totals		22	2	1	3	12	-4

Playoffs

98–99	Phoe	2	0	0	0	0	

HANSON, David 6–0 190 D
B. Cumberland, Wis., Apr. 12, 1954

76–77	Minn–NE (WHA)	8	0	2	2	44	
77–78	Birm (WHA)	42	7	16	23	241	
78–79	Birm (WHA)	53	6	22	28	212	
78–79	Det	11	0	0	0	26	-1
79–80	Minn	22	1	1	2	39	-6
NHL Totals		33	1	1	2	65	-7
WHA Totals		103	13	40	53	497	

Playoffs

76–77	NE (WHA)	1	0	0	0	0	
77–78	Birm (WHA)	5	0	1	1	48	
WHA Totals		6	0	1	1	48	

*HANSON, Emil 5–10 180 D
B. Centerville, S.D., Nov. 18, 1907

32–33	Det	7	0	0	0	6	

HANSON, Keith 6–5 210 D
B. Ada, Minn., Apr. 26, 1957

83–84	Calg	25	0	2	2	77	-13

*HANSON, Oscar (Ossie) D
B. U.S.A.

37–38	Chi	7	0	0	0	0	

HARBARUK, Mikolaj Nickolas (Nick) 6–0 195 RW
B. Drohiczyn, Poland, Aug. 16, 1943

69–70	Pitt	74	5	17	22	56	-7
70–71	Pitt	78	13	12	25	108	-9
71–72	Pitt	78	12	17	29	46	-13
72–73	Pitt	78	10	15	25	47	-11
73–74	StL	56	5	14	19	16	+4
74–75	Ind (WHA)	78	20	23	43	52	
75–76	Ind (WHA)	76	23	19	42	24	
76–77	Ind (WHA)	27	2	2	4	2	
NHL Totals		364	45	75	120	273	-36
WHA Totals		181	45	44	89	78	

Playoffs

69–70	Pitt	10	3	0	3	20	
71–72	Pitt	4	0	1	1	0	
75–76	Ind (WHA)	7	2	0	2	10	
76–77	Ind (WHA)	6	1	1	2	0	
NHL Totals		14	3	1	4	20	
WHA Totals		13	3	1	4	10	

HARDING, Jeff 6–3 200 RW
B. Toronto, Ont., Apr. 6, 1969

88–89	Phil	6	0	0	0	29	+1
89–90	Phil	9	0	0	0	18	-1
Totals		15	0	0	0	47	0

HARDY, Jocelyn Joseph (Joe) 6–0 175 C
B. Kenogami, Que., Dec. 5, 1945

69–70	Oak	23	5	4	9	20	-8
70–71	Cal	40	4	10	14	31	-14
72–73	Clev (WHA)	72	17	33	50	80	
73–74	Chi (WHA)	77	24	35	59	55	
74–75	Chi–Ind–SD (WHA)	61	5	26	31	66	
NHL Totals		63	9	14	23	51	-22
WHA Totals		210	46	94	140	201	

Playoffs

69–70	Oak	4	0	0	0	0	
72–73	Clev (WHA)	7	0	2	2	0	
73–74	Chi (WHA)	17	4	8	12	13	
NHL Totals		4	0	0	0	0	
WHA Totals		24	4	10	14	13	

HARDY, Mark Lea 5–11 195 D
B. Semaden, Switzerland, Feb. 1, 1959

79–80	LA	15	0	1	1	10	-7
80–81	LA	77	5	20	25	77	+14
81–82	LA	77	6	39	45	130	-12
82–83	LA	74	5	34	39	101	-30
83–84	LA	79	8	41	49	122	-30
84–85	LA	78	14	39	53	97	-20
85–86	LA	55	6	21	27	71	-11
86–87	LA	73	3	27	30	120	+16
87–88	LA–NYR	80	8	24	32	130	-33
88–89	Minn–NYR	60	4	16	20	71	-9
89–90	NYR	54	0	15	15	94	+4
90–91	NYR	70	1	5	6	89	-1
91–92	NYR	52	1	8	9	65	+33
92–93	NYR–LA	55	1	13	14	89	-2
93–94	LA	16	0	3	3	27	-6
Totals		915	62	306	368	1293	-94

Playoffs

79–80	LA	4	1	1	2	9	
80–81	LA	4	1	2	3	4	
81–82	LA	10	1	2	3	9	

(continued)

SSN	TEAM	GP	G	A	PTS.	PIM	+/-
84–85	LA	3	0	1	1	2	
86–87	LA	5	1	2	3	10	
88–89	NYR	4	0	1	1	31	
89–90	NYR	3	0	1	1	2	
90–91	NYR	6	0	1	1	30	
91–92	NYR	13	0	3	3	31	
92–93	LA	15	1	2	3	30	
Totals		67	5	16	21	158	

HARGREAVES, James Albert (Cement Head) 5-11 185 D
B. Winnipeg, Man., May 2, 1950

SSN	TEAM	GP	G	A	PTS.	PIM	+/-
70–71	Van	7	0	1	1	33	-3
72–73	Van	59	1	6	7	72	-31
73–74	Winn (WHA)	53	1	4	5	50	
74–75	Ind–SD (WHA)	78	10	15	25	75	
75–76	SD (WHA)	43	1	1	2	26	
NHL Totals		66	1	7	8	105	-34
WHA Totals		174	12	20	32	151	

Playoffs

SSN	TEAM	GP	G	A	PTS.	PIM	+/-
74–75	SD (WHA)	10	1	0	1	6	
75–76	SD (WHA)	5	0	0	0	2	
WHA Totals		15	1	0	1	8	

HARKINS, Brett Alan 6-1 185 LW
B. North Ridgeville, Ohio, July 2, 1970

SSN	TEAM	GP	G	A	PTS.	PIM	+/-
94–95	Bos	1	0	1	1	0	0
95–96	Fla	8	0	3	3	6	-2
96–97	Bos	44	4	14	18	8	-3
Totals		53	4	18	22	14	-5

HARKINS, Todd 6-3 210 C
B. Cleveland, Ohio, Oct. 8, 1968

SSN	TEAM	GP	G	A	PTS.	PIM	+/-
91–92	Calg	5	0	0	0	7	-2
92–93	Calg	15	2	3	5	22	-4
93–94	Hart	28	1	0	1	49	-4
Totals		48	3	3	6	78	-10

HARLOCK, David Alan 6-2 205 D
B. Toronto, Ont., Mar. 16, 1971

SSN	TEAM	GP	G	A	PTS.	PIM	+/-
93–94	Tor	6	0	0	0	0	-2
94–95	Tor	1	0	0	0	0	-1
95–96	Tor	1	0	0	0	0	0
97–98	Wash	6	0	0	0	4	+2
98–99	NYI	70	2	6	8	68	-16
Totals		84	2	6	8	72	-17

HARLOW, Scott 6-1 185 LW
B. East Bridgewater, Mass., Oct. 11, 1963

SSN	TEAM	GP	G	A	PTS.	PIM	+/-
87–88	StL	1	0	1	1	0	-1

HARMON, David Glen (Glen) 5-8 165 D
B. Holland, Man., Jan. 2, 1921

SSN	TEAM	GP	G	A	PTS.	PIM	+/-
42–43	Mont	27	5	9	14	25	
43–44	Mont	43	5	16	21	36	
44–45	Mont	42	5	8	13	41	
45–46	Mont	49	7	10	17	28	
46–47	Mont	57	5	9	14	53	
47–48	Mont	56	10	4	14	52	
48–49	Mont	59	8	12	20	44	
49–50	Mont	62	3	16	19	28	
50–51	Mont	57	2	12	14	27	
Totals		452	50	96	146	334	

Playoffs

SSN	TEAM	GP	G	A	PTS.	PIM	+/-
42–43	Mont	5	0	1	1	2	
43–44	Mont	9	1	2	3	4	
44–45	Mont	6	1	0	1	2	
45–46	Mont	9	1	4	5	0	
46–47	Mont	11	1	1	2	4	
48–49	Mont	7	1	1	2	4	
49–50	Mont	5	0	1	1	21	
50–51	Mont	1	0	0	0	0	
Totals		53	5	10	15	37	

HARMS, John 5-8 160 RW
B. Saskatoon, Sask., Apr. 29, 1925

SSN	TEAM	GP	G	A	PTS.	PIM	+/-
43–44	Chi	1	0	0	0	0	
44–45	Chi	43	5	5	10	21	
Totals		44	5	5	10	21	

Playoffs

SSN	TEAM	GP	G	A	PTS.	PIM	+/-
43–44	Chi	3	3	0	3	2	

HARNOTT, Walter Herbert (Happy) 5-7 170 F
B. Montreal, Que., Sept. 24, 1909

SSN	TEAM	GP	G	A	PTS.	PIM	+/-
33–34	Bos	6	0	0	0	6	

HARPER, Terrance Victor (Terry) 6-1 197 D
B. Regina, Sask., Jan. 27, 1940

SSN	TEAM	GP	G	A	PTS.	PIM	+/-
62–63	Mont	14	1	1	2	10	
63–64	Mont	70	2	15	17	149	
64–65	Mont	62	0	7	7	93	
65–66	Mont	69	1	11	12	91	
66–67	Mont	56	0	16	16	99	
67–68	Mont	57	3	8	11	66	+21
68–69	Mont	21	0	3	3	37	+7
69–70	Mont	75	4	18	22	109	+27
70–71	Mont	78	1	21	22	116	+35
71–72	Mont	52	2	12	14	35	+8
72–73	LA	77	1	8	9	74	+6
73–74	LA	77	0	17	17	119	+25
74–75	LA	80	5	21	26	120	+38
75–76	Det	69	8	25	33	59	+6
76–77	Det	52	4	8	12	28	-23
77–78	Det	80	2	17	19	85	+19
78–79	Det	51	0	6	6	58	-3
79–80	StL	11	1	5	6	6	+5
80–81	Col	15	0	2	2	8	-3
Totals		1066	35	221	256	1362	+174

Playoffs

SSN	TEAM	GP	G	A	PTS.	PIM	+/-
62–63	Mont	5	1	0	1	8	
63–64	Mont	7	0	0	0	6	
64–65	Mont	13	0	0	0	19	
65–66	Mont	10	2	3	5	18	
66–67	Mont	10	0	1	1	15	
67–68	Mont	13	0	1	1	8	
68–69	Mont	11	0	0	0	8	
70–71	Mont	20	0	6	6	28	
71–72	Mont	5	1	1	2	6	
73–74	LA	5	0	0	0	16	
74–75	LA	3	0	0	0	2	
77–78	Det	7	0	1	1	4	
79–80	StL	3	0	0	0	2	
Totals		112	4	13	17	140	

HARRER, Tim 6-0 185 RW
B. Bloomington, Minn., May 10, 1957

SSN	TEAM	GP	G	A	PTS.	PIM	+/-
82–83	Calg	3	0	0	0	2	0

*HARRINGTON, Leland K. (Hago) 5-8 163 LW
B. Melrose, Mass.

SSN	TEAM	GP	G	A	PTS.	PIM	+/-
25–26	Bos	26	7	2	9	6	
27–28	Bos	22	1	0	1	7	
32–33	Mont	24	1	1	2	2	
Totals		72	9	3	12	15	
Playoff Totals		4	1	0	1	2	

HARRIS, Edward Alexander (Ted) 6-2 183 D
B. Winnipeg, Man., July 18, 1936

SSN	TEAM	GP	G	A	PTS.	PIM	+/-
63–64	Mont	4	0	1	1	0	
64–65	Mont	68	1	14	15	107	
65–66	Mont	53	0	13	13	81	
66–67	Mont	65	2	16	18	86	
67–68	Mont	67	5	16	21	78	+23
68–69	Mont	76	7	18	25	102	+24
69–70	Mont	74	3	17	20	116	+9
70–71	Minn	78	2	13	15	130	0
71–72	Minn	78	2	15	17	77	0
72–73	Minn	78	7	23	30	89	+25
73–74	Minn–Det–StL	77	0	16	16	86	-14
74–75	Phil	70	1	6	7	48	+27
Totals		788	30	168	198	1000	+94

Playoffs

SSN	TEAM	GP	G	A	PTS.	PIM	+/-
64–65	Mont	13	0	5	5	45	
65–66	Mont	10	0	0	0	38	
66–67	Mont	10	0	1	1	19	
67–68	Mont	13	0	4	4	22	
68–69	Mont	14	1	2	3	34	
70–71	Minn	12	0	4	4	36	
71–72	Minn	7	0	1	1	17	
72–73	Minn	5	0	1	1	15	
74–75	Phil	16	0	4	4	4	
Totals		100	1	22	23	230	

*HARRIS, Frederick Henry (Smokey) LW
B. ...

SSN	TEAM	GP	G	A	PTS.	PIM	+/-
24–25	Bos	6	3	1	4	8	
30–31	Bos	34	2	4	6	20	
Totals		40	5	5	10	28	

Playoffs

SSN	TEAM	GP	G	A	PTS.	PIM	+/-
30–31	Bos	2	0	0	0	0	

HARRIS, George Francis (Duke) 6-0 204 RW
B. Sarnia, Ont., Feb. 25, 1942

SSN	TEAM	GP	G	A	PTS.	PIM	+/-
67–68	Minn–Tor	26	1	4	5	4	-14
72–73	Hou (WHA)	75	30	12	42	14	
73–74	Chi (WHA)	64	14	16	30	20	
74–75	Chi (WHA)	54	9	19	28	18	
NHL Totals		26	1	4	5	4	-14
WHA Totals		193	53	47	100	52	

Playoffs

SSN	TEAM	GP	G	A	PTS.	PIM	+/-
72–73	Hou (WHA)	10	1	1	2	4	
73–74	Chi (WHA)	18	6	6	12	2	
Totals		28	7	7	14	6	

HARRIS, Hugh Thomas 6-1 195 C
B. Toronto, Ont., June 7, 1948

SSN	TEAM	GP	G	A	PTS.	PIM	+/-
72–73	Buf	60	12	26	38	17	+8
73–74	NE (WHA)	75	24	28	52	78	
74–75	Phoe–Van (WHA)	80	33	44	77	34	
75–76	Calg–Ind (WHA)	71	17	36	53	42	
76–77	Ind (WHA)	46	21	35	56	21	
77–78	Ind–Cin (WHA)	64	12	30	42	36	
NHL Totals		60	12	26	38	17	+8
WHA Totals		336	107	173	280	211	

Playoffs

SSN	TEAM	GP	G	A	PTS.	PIM	+/-
72–73	Buf	3	0	0	0	0	
73–74	NE (WHA)	7	0	4	4	11	
75–76	Ind (WHA)	7	2	5	7	8	
76–77	Ind (WHA)	2	0	0	0	0	
NHL Totals		3	0	0	0	0	
WHA Totals		9	2	9	11	19	

HARRIS, Ronald Thomas 5-9 190 D
B. Verdun, Que., June 30, 1942

SSN	TEAM	GP	G	A	PTS.	PIM	+/-
62–63	Det	1	0	1	1	0	
63–64	Det	3	0	0	0	7	
67–68	Oak	54	4	6	10	60	-27
68–69	Det	73	3	13	16	91	+6
69–70	Det	72	2	19	21	99	+14
70–71	Det	42	2	8	10	65	-29
71–72	Det	61	1	10	11	80	-15
72–73	Atl–NYR	70	5	14	19	25	-3
73–74	NYR	63	2	12	14	25	-2
74–75	NYR	34	1	7	8	22	0
75–76	NYR	3	0	1	1	0	-1
Totals		476	20	91	111	474	-57

Playoffs

SSN	TEAM	GP	G	A	PTS.	PIM	+/-
69–70	Det	4	0	0	0	8	
72–73	NYR	10	0	3	3	2	
73–74	NYR	11	3	0	3	14	
74–75	NYR	3	1	0	1	9	
Totals		28	4	3	7	33	

HARRIS, William Edward 6-0 165 C
B. Toronto, Ont., July 29, 1935

SSN	TEAM	GP	G	A	PTS.	PIM	+/-
55–56	Tor	70	9	13	22	8	
56–57	Tor	23	4	6	10	6	
57–58	Tor	68	16	28	44	32	
58–59	Tor	70	22	30	52	29	
59–60	Tor	70	13	25	38	29	
60–61	Tor	66	12	27	39	30	
61–62	Tor	67	15	10	25	14	
62–63	Tor	65	8	24	32	22	
63–64	Tor	63	6	12	18	17	
64–65	Tor	48	1	6	7	0	
65–66	Det	24	1	4	5	6	
67–68	Oak	62	12	17	29	2	-6
68–69	Oak–Pitt	73	7	17	24	10	-19
Totals		769	126	219	345	205	-25

Playoffs

SSN	TEAM	GP	G	A	PTS.	PIM	+/-
55–56	Tor	5	1	1	4	0	
58–59	Tor	12	3	4	7	16	
59–60	Tor	9	0	3	3	4	
60–61	Tor	5	1	0	1	0	
61–62	Tor	12	2	1	3	2	

SSN	TEAM	GP	G	A	PTS.	PIM	+/-
62-63	Tor	10	0	1	1	0	
63-64	Tor	9	1	1	2	4	
64-65	Tor	9	1	1	2	4	
Totals		71	9	12	23	30	

HARRIS, William Edward 6-2 195 RW
B. Toronto, Ont., Jan. 29, 1952

SSN	TEAM	GP	G	A	PTS.	PIM	+/-
72-73	NYI	78	28	22	50	35	-44
73-74	NYI	78	23	27	50	34	-11
74-75	NYI	80	25	37	62	34	+4
75-76	NYI	80	32	38	70	54	+22
76-77	NYI	80	24	43	67	44	+18
77-78	NYI	80	22	38	60	40	+27
78-79	NYI	80	15	39	54	18	+26
79-80	NYI–LA	78	19	18	37	43	+4
80-81	LA	80	20	29	49	36	-1
81-82	LA–Tor	36	3	3	6	10	-25
82-83	Tor	76	11	19	30	26	-15
83-84	Tor–LA	71	9	14	23	20	-23
Totals		897	231	327	558	394	-16

Playoffs

SSN	TEAM	GP	G	A	PTS.	PIM
74-75	NYI	17	3	7	10	12
75-76	NYI	13	5	2	7	10
76-77	NYI	12	7	7	14	8
77-78	NYI	7	0	0	0	4
78-79	NYI	10	2	1	3	10
79-80	LA	4	0	0	0	2
80-81	LA	4	2	1	3	0
82-83	Tor	4	0	1	1	2
Totals		71	19	19	38	48

HARRISON, Edward Francis (Fran) 6-0 170 LW
B. Mimico, Ont., July 25, 1927

SSN	TEAM	GP	G	A	PTS.	PIM
47-48	Bos	52	6	7	13	8
48-49	Bos	59	5	5	10	20
49-50	Bos	70	14	12	26	23
50-51	Bos–NYR	13	2	0	2	2
Totals		194	27	24	51	53

Playoffs

SSN	TEAM	GP	G	A	PTS.	PIM
47-48	Bos	5	1	0	1	2
48-49	Bos	4	0	0	0	0
Totals		9	1	0	1	2

HARRISON, James David 5-11 185 C
B. Bonnyville, Alta., July 9, 1947

SSN	TEAM	GP	G	A	PTS.	PIM	+/-
68-69	Bos	16	1	2	3	21	-5
69-70	Bos-Tor	54	10	11	21	52	+8
70-71	Tor	78	13	20	33	108	+6
71-72	Tor	66	19	17	36	104	-4
72-73	Alb (WHA)	66	39	47	86	93	
73-74	Edm (WHA)	46	24	45	69	99	
74-75	Clev (WHA)	60	20	22	42	106	
75-76	Clev (WHA)	59	34	38	72	62	
76-77	Chi	60	18	23	41	97	-26
77-78	Chi	26	2	8	10	13	-3
78-79	Chi	21	4	5	9	22	-6
79-80	Edm	3	0	0	0	0	-1
NHL Totals		324	67	86	153	417	-31
WHA Totals		231	117	152	269	360	

Playoffs

SSN	TEAM	GP	G	A	PTS.	PIM
70-71	Tor	6	0	1	1	33
71-72	Tor	5	1	0	1	10
74-75	Clev (WHA)	5	1	2	3	4
75-76	Clev (WHA)	3	0	1	1	9
76-77	Chi	2	0	0	0	0
NHL Totals		13	1	1	2	43
WHA Totals		8	1	3	4	13

HART, Gerald William 5-9 190 D
B. Flin Flon, Man., Jan. 1, 1948

SSN	TEAM	GP	G	A	PTS.	PIM	+/-
68-69	Det	1	0	0	0	2	0
69-70	Det	3	0	0	0	2	0
70-71	Det	64	2	7	9	148	-3
71-72	Det	3	0	0	0	0	-2
72-73	NYI	47	1	11	12	158	-18
73-74	NYI	70	1	10	11	61	+17
74-75	NYI	71	4	14	18	143	+28
75-76	NYI	80	6	18	24	151	+35
76-77	NYI	80	4	18	22	98	+29
77-78	NYI	78	2	23	25	94	+44
78-79	NYI	50	2	14	16	78	+30
79-80	Que	71	3	23	26	59	-13
80-81	Que–StL	69	4	11	15	142	+7

SSN	TEAM	GP	G	A	PTS.	PIM	+/-
81-82	StL	35	0	1	1	102	-5
82-83	StL	8	0	0	0	2	-3
Totals		730	29	150	179	1240	+146

Playoffs

SSN	TEAM	GP	G	A	PTS.	PIM
74-75	NYI	17	2	2	4	42
75-76	NYI	13	1	3	4	24
76-77	NYI	12	0	2	2	23
77-78	NYI	7	0	0	0	6
78-79	NYI	9	0	2	2	10
80-81	StL	10	0	0	0	27
81-82	StL	10	0	3	3	33
Totals		78	3	12	15	175

*HART, Wilfred Harold (Gizzy) 5-9 171 LW
B. Weyburn, Sask., June 1, 1903

SSN	TEAM	GP	G	A	PTS.	PIM
26-27	Det–Mont	38	3	3	6	8
27-28	Mont	44	3	2	5	4
32-33	Mont	18	0	3	3	0
Totals		100	6	8	14	12

Playoffs

SSN	TEAM	GP	G	A	PTS.	PIM
26-27	Mont	4	0	0	0	0
27-28	Mont	2	0	0	0	0
32-33	Mont	2	0	1	1	0
Totals		8	0	1	1	0

HARTMAN, Mike 6-0 190 LW
B. Detroit, Mich., Feb. 7, 1967

SSN	TEAM	GP	G	A	PTS.	PIM	+/-
86-87	Buf	17	3	3	6	69	+2
87-88	Buf	18	3	1	4	90	-3
88-89	Buf	70	8	9	17	316	+9
89-90	Buf	60	11	10	21	211	-10
90-91	Buf	60	9	3	12	204	-10
91-92	Winn	75	4	4	8	264	-10
92-93	TB-NYR	61	4	4	8	160	-7
93-94	NYR	35	1	1	2	70	-5
94-95	NYR	1	0	0	0	4	0
Totals		397	43	35	78	1388	-34

Playoffs

SSN	TEAM	GP	G	A	PTS.	PIM
87-88	Buf	6	0	0	0	35
88-89	Buf	5	0	0	0	34
89-90	Buf	6	0	0	0	18
90-91	Buf	2	0	0	0	17
91-92	Winn	2	0	0	0	2
Totals		21	0	0	0	106

HARTSBURG, Craig 6-1 200 D
B. Stratford, Ont., June 29, 1959

SSN	TEAM	GP	G	A	PTS.	PIM	+/-
79-80	Minn	79	14	30	44	81	-2
80-81	Minn	74	13	30	43	124	-9
81-82	Minn	76	17	60	77	117	+11
82-83	Minn	78	12	50	62	109	+7
83-84	Minn	26	7	7	14	37	-2
84-85	Minn	32	7	11	18	54	-5
85-86	Minn	75	10	47	57	127	+7
86-87	Minn	73	11	50	61	93	-2
87-88	Minn	27	3	16	19	29	-2
88-89	Minn	30	4	14	18	47	-8
Totals		570	98	315	413	818	-5

Playoffs

SSN	TEAM	GP	G	A	PTS.	PIM
79-80	Minn	15	3	1	4	17
80-81	Minn	19	3	12	15	16
81-82	Minn	4	1	2	3	14
82-83	Minn	9	3	8	11	7
84-85	Minn	9	5	3	8	14
85-86	Minn	5	0	1	1	2
Totals		61	15	27	42	70

*HARVEY, Douglas Norman 5-11 180 D
B. Montreal, Que., Dec. 19, 1924

SSN	TEAM	GP	G	A	PTS.	PIM
47-48	Mont	35	4	4	8	32
48-49	Mont	55	3	13	16	87
49-50	Mont	70	4	20	24	76
50-51	Mont	70	5	24	29	93
51-52	Mont	68	6	23	29	82
52-53	Mont	69	4	30	34	67
53-54	Mont	68	8	29	37	110
54-55	Mont	70	6	43	49	58
55-56	Mont	62	5	39	44	60
56-57	Mont	70	6	44	50	92
57-58	Mont	68	9	32	41	131
58-59	Mont	61	4	16	20	61
59-60	Mont	66	6	21	27	45
60-61	Mont	58	6	33	39	48

SSN	TEAM	GP	G	A	PTS.	PIM	+/-
61-62	NYR	69	6	24	30	42	
62-63	NYR	68	4	35	39	92	
63-64	NYR	14	0	2	2	10	
66-67	Det	2	0	0	0	0	
68-69	StL	70	2	20	22	30	+11
Totals		1113	88	452	540	1216	+11

Playoffs

SSN	TEAM	GP	G	A	PTS.	PIM
48-49	Mont	7	0	1	1	10
49-50	Mont	5	0	2	2	10
50-51	Mont	11	0	5	5	12
51-52	Mont	11	0	3	3	8
52-53	Mont	12	0	5	5	8
53-54	Mont	10	0	2	2	12
54-55	Mont	12	0	8	8	6
55-56	Mont	10	2	5	7	10
56-57	Mont	10	0	7	7	10
57-58	Mont	10	2	9	11	16
58-59	Mont	11	1	11	12	22
59-60	Mont	8	3	0	3	6
60-61	Mont	6	0	1	1	8
61-62	NYR	6	0	1	1	2
67-68	StL	8	0	4	4	12
Totals		137	8	64	72	152

HARVEY, Frederic John Charles (Buster) 6-0 185 RW
B. Fredericton, N.B., Apr. 2, 1950

SSN	TEAM	GP	G	A	PTS.	PIM	+/-
70-71	Minn	59	12	8	20	36	-13
72-73	Minn	68	21	34	55	16	+23
73-74	MInn	72	16	17	33	14	-11
74-75	Atl	79	17	27	44	16	+4
75-76	Atl–KC–Det	75	13	21	34	31	-39
76-77	Det	54	11	11	22	18	-13
Totals		407	90	118	208	131	-49

Playoffs

SSN	TEAM	GP	G	A	PTS.	PIM
70-71	Minn	7	0	0	0	4
71-72	Minn	1	0	1	1	17
72-73	Minn	6	0	2	2	4
Totals		14	0	2	2	8

HARVEY, Lionel Hugh 6-0 175 LW
B. Kingston, Ont., June 25, 1949

SSN	TEAM	GP	G	A	PTS.	PIM	+/-
74-75	KC	8	0	0	0	2	-1
75-76	KC	10	1	1	2	2	-5
Totals		18	1	1	2	4	-6

HARVEY, Todd 6-0 195 C
B. Hamilton, Ont., Feb. 17, 1975

SSN	TEAM	GP	G	A	PTS.	PIM	+/-
94-95	Dal	40	11	9	20	67	-3
95-96	Dal	69	9	20	29	136	-13
96-97	Dal	71	9	22	31	142	+19
97-98	Dal-NYR	59	9	10	19	104	+5
98-99	NYR	37	11	17	28	72	-1
Totals		276	49	78	127	521	+7

Playoffs

SSN	TEAM	GP	G	A	PTS.	PIM
94-95	Dal	5	0	0	0	8
96-97	Dal	7	0	1	1	10
Totals		12	0	1	1	18

HASSARD, Robert Harry 6-0 165 C
B. Lloydminster, Sask., Mar. 26, 1929

SSN	TEAM	GP	G	A	PTS.	PIM
49-50	Tor	1	0	0	0	0
50-51	Tor	12	0	1	1	0
52-53	Tor	70	8	23	31	14
53-54	Tor	26	1	4	5	4
54-55	Chi	17	0	0	0	4
Totals		126	9	28	37	22

HATCHER, Derian 6-5 225 D
B. Sterling Heights, Mich., June 4, 1972

SSN	TEAM	GP	G	A	PTS.	PIM	+/-
91-92	Minn	43	8	4	12	88	+7
92-93	Minn	67	4	15	19	178	-27
93-94	Dal	83	12	19	31	211	+19
94-95	Dal	43	5	11	16	105	+3
95-96	Dal	79	8	23	31	129	-12
96-97	Dal	63	3	19	22	97	+8
97-98	Dal	70	6	25	31	132	+9
98-99	Dal	80	9	21	30	102	+21
Totals		528	55	137	192	1042	+28

Playoffs

SSN	TEAM	GP	G	A	PTS.	PIM
91-92	Minn	5	0	2	2	8
93-94	Dal	9	0	2	2	14

SSN	TEAM	GP	G	A	PTS.	PIM	+/-
96–97	Dal	7	0	2	2	20	
97–98	Dal	17	3	3	6	39	
98–99	Dal	18	1	6	7	24	
Totals		56	4	15	19	105	

HATCHER, Kevin *6–4 225 D*
B. Detroit, Mich., Sept. 9, 1966

SSN	TEAM	GP	G	A	PTS.	PIM	+/-
84–85	Wash	2	1	0	1	0	+1
85–86	Wash	79	9	10	19	119	+6
86–87	Wash	78	8	16	24	144	-29
87–88	Wash	71	14	27	41	137	+1
88–89	Wash	62	13	27	40	101	+19
89–90	Wash	80	13	41	54	102	+4
90–91	Wash	79	24	50	74	69	-10
91–92	Wash	79	17	37	54	105	+18
92–93	Wash	83	34	45	79	114	-7
93–94	Wash	72	16	24	40	108	-13
94–95	Dal	47	10	19	29	66	-4
95–96	Dal	74	15	26	41	58	-24
96–97	Pitt	80	15	39	54	103	+11
97–98	Pitt	74	19	29	48	66	-3
98–99	Pitt	66	11	27	38	24	+11
Totals		1026	219	417	636	1316	-19

Playoffs

SSN	TEAM	GP	G	A	PTS.	PIM	
84–85	Wash	1	0	0	0	0	
85–86	Wash	9	1	1	2	19	
86–87	Wash	7	1	0	1	20	
87–88	Wash	14	5	7	12	55	
88–89	Wash	6	1	4	5	20	
89–90	Wash	11	0	8	8	32	
90–91	Wash	11	3	3	6	8	
91–92	Wash	7	2	4	6	19	
92–93	Wash	6	0	1	1	14	
93–94	Wash	11	3	4	7	37	
94–95	Dal	5	2	1	3	2	
96–97	Pitt	5	1	1	2	4	
97–98	Pitt	6	1	0	1	12	
98–99	Pitt	13	2	3	5	4	
Totals		112	22	37	59	246	

HATOUM, Edward *5–10 185 RW*
B. Beirut, Lebanon, Dec. 7, 1947

SSN	TEAM	GP	G	A	PTS.	PIM	+/-
68–69	Det	16	2	1	3	2	+1
69–70	Det	5	0	2	2	2	+1
70–71	Van	26	1	3	4	21	-14
72–73	Chi (WHA)	15	1	1	2	2	
73–74	Van (WHA)	37	3	12	15	8	
NHL Totals		47	3	6	9	25	-12
WHA Totals		52	4	13	17	10	

HAUER, Brett *6–2 210 D*
B. Richfield, Minn., July 11, 1971

SSN	TEAM	GP	G	A	PTS.	PIM	+/-
95–96	Edm	29	4	2	6	30	-11

HAWERCHUK, Dale *5–11 185 C*
B. Toronto, Ont., Apr. 4, 1963

SSN	TEAM	GP	G	A	PTS.	PIM	+/-
81–82	Winn	80	45	58	103	47	-4
82–83	Winn	79	40	51	91	31	-17
83–84	Winn	80	37	65	102	73	-14
84–85	Winn	80	53	77	130	74	+22
85–86	Winn	80	46	59	105	44	-27
86–87	Winn	80	47	53	100	52	+3
87–88	Winn	80	44	77	121	59	-9
88–89	Winn	75	41	55	96	28	-30
89–90	Winn	79	26	55	81	60	-11
90–91	Buf	80	31	58	89	32	+2
91–92	Buf	77	23	75	98	27	-22
92–93	Buf	81	16	80	96	52	-17
93–94	Buf	81	35	51	86	91	+10
94–95	Buf	23	5	11	16	2	-2
95–96	StL–Phil	82	17	44	61	26	+15
96–97	Phil	51	12	22	34	32	+9
Totals		1188	518	891	1409	730	-92

Playoffs

SSN	TEAM	GP	G	A	PTS.	PIM	
81–82	Winn	4	1	7	8	5	
82–83	Winn	3	1	4	5	8	
83–84	Winn	3	1	1	2	0	
84–85	Winn	3	2	1	3	4	
85–86	Winn	3	0	3	3	0	
86–87	Winn	10	5	8	13	4	
87–88	Winn	5	3	4	7	16	
89–90	Winn	7	3	5	8	2	
90–91	Buf	6	2	4	6	10	
91–92	Buf	7	2	5	7	0	
92–93	Buf	8	5	9	14	2	
93–94	Buf	7	0	7	7	4	
94–95	Buf	2	0	0	0	0	
95–96	Phil	12	3	6	9	12	
96–97	Phil	17	2	5	7	0	
Totals		97	30	69	99	67	

HAWGOOD, Greg *5–10 190 LW/D*
B. Edmonton, Alta., Aug. 10, 1968

SSN	TEAM	GP	G	A	PTS.	PIM	+/-
87–88	Bos	1	0	0	0	0	-1
88–89	Bos	56	16	24	40	84	+4
89–90	Bos	77	11	27	38	76	+12
90–91	Edm	6	0	1	1	6	-2
91–92	Edm	20	2	11	13	22	+19
92–93	Edm–Phil	69	11	35	46	74	-8
93–94	Phil–Fla–Pitt	64	6	28	34	36	+9
94–95	Pitt	21	1	4	5	25	+2
96–97	SJ	63	6	12	18	69	-22
Totals		377	53	142	195	392	+13

Playoffs

SSN	TEAM	GP	G	A	PTS.	PIM	
88–89	Bos	10	0	2	2	2	
89–90	Bos	15	1	3	4	12	
91–92	Edm	13	0	3	3	23	
93–94	Pitt	1	0	0	0	0	
Totals		42	2	8	10	37	

HAWKINS, Todd *6–1 195 LW/RW*
B. Kingston, Ont., Aug. 2, 1966

SSN	TEAM	GP	G	A	PTS.	PIM	+/-
88–89	Van	4	0	0	0	9	-1
89–90	Van	4	0	0	0	6	-1
91–92	Tor	2	0	0	0	0	
Totals		10	0	0	0	15	-2

HAWORTH, Alan Joseph *5–10 190 C*
B. Drummondville, Ont., Sept. 1, 1960

SSN	TEAM	GP	G	A	PTS.	PIM	+/-
80–81	Buf	49	16	20	36	34	-6
81–82	Buf	57	21	18	39	30	+6
82–83	Wash	74	23	27	50	34	-5
83–84	Wash	75	24	31	55	52	+14
84–85	Wash	76	23	26	49	48	+19
85–86	Wash	71	34	39	73	72	+36
86–87	Wash	50	25	16	41	43	+3
87–88	Que	72	23	34	57	112	-5
Totals		524	189	211	400	425	+62

Playoffs

SSN	TEAM	GP	G	A	PTS.	PIM	
80–81	Buf	7	4	4	8	2	
81–82	Buf	3	0	1	1	2	
82–83	Wash	4	0	0	0	2	
83–84	Wash	8	3	2	5	4	
84–85	Wash	5	1	0	1	0	
85–86	Wash	9	4	6	10	11	
86–87	Wash	6	0	3	3	7	
Totals		42	12	16	28	0	

HAWORTH. Gordon Joseph *5–10 165 C*
B. Drummondville, Que., Feb. 20, 1932

SSN	TEAM	GP	G	A	PTS.	PIM	
52–53	NYR	2	0	1	1	0	

HAWRYLIW, Neil *5–11 185 RW*
B. Fielding, Sask., Nov. 9, 1955

SSN	TEAM	GP	G	A	PTS.	PIM	+/-
81–82	NYI	1	0	0	0	0	0

HAY, Dwayne *6–1 183 LW*
B. London, Ont., Feb. 11, 1977

SSN	TEAM	GP	G	A	PTS.	PIM	+/-
97–98	Wash	2	0	0	0	2	0
98–99	Fla	9	0	0	0	0	-1
Totals		11	0	0	0	2	-1

*HAY, George William *LW*
B. Listowel, Ont., Jan. 10, 1898

SSN	TEAM	GP	G	A	PTS.	PIM	
26–27	Chi	37	14	8	22	12	
27–28	Det	42	22	13	35	20	
28–29	Det	42	11	8	19	14	
29–80	Det	42	18	15	33	8	
30–31	Det	44	8	10	18	24	
32–33	Det	34	1	6	7	6	
33–34	Det	1	0	0	0	0	
Totals		242	74	60	134	84	

Playoffs

SSN	TEAM	GP	G	A	PTS.	PIM	
26–27	Chi	2	1	2	3	12	
28–29	Det	2	1	0	1	2	
32–33	Det	4	0	1	1	0	
Totals		8	2	3	5	14	

HAY, James Alexander (Red Eye) *5–11 185 D*
B. Saskatoon, Sask., May 15, 1931

SSN	TEAM	GP	G	A	PTS.	PIM	
52–53	Det	42	1	4	5	2	
53–54	Det	12	0	0	0	0	
54–55	Det	21	0	1	1	20	
Totals		75	1	5	6	22	

Playoffs

SSN	TEAM	GP	G	A	PTS.	PIM	
52–53	Det	4	0	0	0	0	
54–55	Det	5	1	0	1	0	
Totals		9	1	0	1	2	

HAY, William Charles (Red) *6–3 197 C*
B. Saskatoon, Sask., Dec. 8, 1935

SSN	TEAM	GP	G	A	PTS.	PIM	
59–60	Chi	70	18	37	55	31	
60–61	Chi	69	11	48	59	45	
61–62	Chi	60	11	52	63	34	
62–63	Chi	64	12	33	45	36	
63–64	Chi	70	23	33	56	30	
64–65	Chi	69	11	26	37	36	
65–66	Chi	68	20	31	51	20	
66–67	Chi	36	7	13	20	33	
Totals		506	113	273	386	265	

Playoffs

SSN	TEAM	GP	G	A	PTS.	PIM	
59–60	Chi	4	1	2	3	2	
60–61	Chi	12	2	5	7	20	
61–62	Chi	12	3	7	10	18	
62–63	Chi	6	3	2	5	6	
63–64	Chi	7	3	1	4	4	
64–65	Chi	14	3	1	4	4	
65–66	Chi	6	0	2	2	4	
66–67	Chi	6	0	1	1	4	
Totals		67	15	21	36	62	

HAYEK, Peter *5–10 198 D*
B. Minneapolis, Minn., Nov. 16, 1957

SSN	TEAM	GP	G	A	PTS.	PIM	+/-
81–82	Minn	1	0	0	0	0	-1

HAYES, Christopher Joseph *5–10 180 LW*
B. Rouyn, Que., Aug. 24, 1946

Playoffs

SSN	TEAM	GP	G	A	PTS.	PIM	
71–72	Bos	1	0	0	0	0	

HAYNES, Paul *5–10 160 C*
B. Montreal, Que., Mar. 1, 1910

SSN	TEAM	GP	G	A	PTS.	PIM	
30–31	Mont M	19	1	0	1	0	
31–32	Mont M	11	1	0	1	0	
32–33	Mont M	47	16	25	41	18	
33–34	Mont	45	5	4	9	18	
34–35	Mont M–Bos	48	5	5	10	8	
35–36	Mont	48	5	19	24	24	
36–37	Mont	47	8	18	26	24	
37–38	Mont	48	13	22	35	25	
38–39	Mont	47	5	33	38	27	
39–40	Mont	23	2	8	10	8	
40–41	Mont	7	0	0	0	12	
Totals		390	61	134	195	164	

Playoffs

SSN	TEAM	GP	G	A	PTS.	PIM	
31–32	Mont M	4	0	0	0	0	
32–33	Mont M	2	0	0	0	2	
33–34	Mont	4	0	1	1	2	
34–35	Bos	4	0	0	0	0	
36–37	Mont	5	2	3	5	0	
37–38	Mont	3	0	4	4	5	
38–39	Mont	3	0	0	0	4	
Totals		25	2	8	10	13	

HAYWARD, Rick *6–0 180 D*
B. Toledo, Ohio, Feb. 25, 1966

SSN	TEAM	GP	G	A	PTS.	PIM	+/-
90–91	LA	4	0	0	0	5	0

HAZLETT, Steven *5–9 170 LW*
B. Sarnia, Ont., Dec. 12, 1957

SSN	TEAM	GP	G	A	PTS.	PIM	+/-
79–80	Van	1	0	0	0	0	-1

HEAD, Galen Russell *5–10 170 RW*
B. Grand Prairie, Alta., Apr. 6, 1947

SSN	TEAM	GP	G	A	PTS.	PIM	+/-
67–68	Det	1	0	0	0	0	-1

HEADLEY, Fern James (Curley) *5–11 175 D*
B. Christie. N.D., Mar. 2, 1901

SSN	TEAM	GP	G	A	PTS.	PIM	
24–25	Bos–Mont	27	1	1	2	6	

Playoffs

SSN	TEAM	GP	G	A	PTS.	PIM	+/-
24–25	Mont	5	0	0	0	0	

HEALEY, Paul *6–2 196 RW*
B. Edmonton, Alta., March 20, 1975

SSN	TEAM	GP	G	A	PTS.	PIM	+/-
96–97	Phil	2	0	0	0	0	0
97–98	Phil	4	0	0	0	12	0
Totals		6	0	0	0	12	0

HEALEY, Richard Thomas (Dick) *5–10 170 D*
B. Vancouver, B.C., Mar. 12, 1938

SSN	TEAM	GP	G	A	PTS.	PIM
60–61	Det	1	0	0	0	2

HEAPHY, Shawn *5–8 180 C*
B. Sudbury, Ont., Nov. 27, 1968

SSN	TEAM	GP	G	A	PTS.	PIM	+/-
92–93	Calg	1	0	0	0	0	0

HEASLIP, Mark Patrick *5–10 190 RW*
B. Duluth, Minn., Dec. 26, 1951

SSN	TEAM	GP	G	A	PTS.	PIM	+/-
76–77	NYR	19	1	0	1	31	-3
77–78	NYR	29	5	10	15	34	+3
78–79	LA	69	4	9	13	45	-10
Totals		117	10	19	29	110	-10

Playoffs

SSN	TEAM	GP	G	A	PTS.	PIM
77–78	NYR	3	0	0	0	0
78–79	LA	2	0	0	0	2
Totals		5	0	0	0	2

HEATH, Randy *5–8 160 LW*
B. Vancouver, B.C., Nov. 11, 1964

SSN	TEAM	GP	G	A	PTS.	PIM	+/-
84–85	NYR	12	2	3	5	15	-1
85–86	NYR	1	0	1	1	0	+1
Totals		13	2	4	6	15	0

HEBENTON, Andrew Alexander *5–9 182 RW*
B. Winnipeg, Man., Oct, 3, 1929

SSN	TEAM	GP	G	A	PTS.	PIM
55–56	NYR	70	24	14	38	8
56–57	NYR	70	21	23	44	10
57–58	NYR	70	21	24	45	17
58–59	NYR	70	33	29	62	8
59–60	NYR	70	19	27	46	4
60–61	NYR	70	26	28	54	10
61–62	NYR	70	18	24	42	10
62–63	NYR	70	15	22	37	8
63–64	Bos	70	12	11	23	8
Totals		630	189	202	391	83

Playoffs

SSN	TEAM	GP	G	A	PTS.	PIM
55–56	NYR	5	1	0	1	2
56–57	NYR	5	2	0	2	2
57–58	NYR	6	2	3	5	4
61–62	NYR	6	1	2	3	0
Totals		22	6	5	11	8

HECHT, Jochen *6–1 180 C*
B. Mannheim, Germany, June 21, 1977

SSN	TEAM	GP	G	A	PTS.	PIM	+/-
98–99	StL	3	0	0	0	0	-2

Playoffs

SSN	TEAM	GP	G	A	PTS.	PIM
98–99	StL	5	2	0	2	0

HEDBERG, Anders *5–11 175 RW*
B. Ornskoldsvik, Sweden, Feb. 25, 1951

SSN	TEAM	GP	G	A	PTS.	PIM	+/-
74–75	Winn (WHA)	65	53	47	100	45	
75–76	Winn (WHA)	76	50	55	105	48	
76–77	Winn (WHA)	68	70	61	131	48	
77–78	Winn (WHA)	77	63	59	122	60	
78–79	NYR	80	33	45	78	33	+19
79–80	NYR	80	32	39	71	21	+13
80–81	NYR	80	30	40	70	52	0
81–82	NYR	4	0	1	1	0	-2
82–83	NYR	78	25	34	59	12	+17
83–84	NYR	79	32	35	67	16	+18
84–85	NYR	64	20	31	51	10	-15
NHL Totals		465	172	225	397	144	+50
WHA Totals		286	236	222	458	201	

Playoffs

SSN	TEAM	GP	G	A	PTS.	PIM
75–76	Winn (WHA)	13	13	6	19	15
76–77	Winn (WHA)	20	13	16	29	13
77–78	Winn (WHA)	18	4	5	9	12
78–79	NYR	18	4	5	9	12
79–80	NYR	9	3	2	5	7
80–81	NYR	14	8	8	16	6
82–83	NYR	9	4	8	12	4
83–84	NYR	5	1	0	1	0
84–85	NYR	3	2	1	3	2
NHL Totals		58	22	24	46	31
WHA Totals		42	35	28	63	30

HEDICAN, Brett *6–2 195 D*
B. St. Paul, Minn., Aug. 10, 1970

SSN	TEAM	GP	G	A	PTS.	PIM	+/-
91–92	StL	4	1	0	1	0	+1
92–93	StL	42	0	8	8	30	-2
93–94	StL–Van	69	0	12	12	64	-7
94–95	Van	45	2	11	13	34	-3
95–96	Van	77	6	23	29	83	+8
96–97	Van	67	4	15	19	51	-3
97–98	Van	71	3	24	27	79	+3
98–99	Van–Fla	67	5	18	23	51	+5
Totals		442	21	111	132	392	+2

Playoffs

SSN	TEAM	GP	G	A	PTS.	PIM
91–92	StL	5	0	0	0	0
92–93	StL	10	0	0	0	14
93–94	Van	24	1	6	7	16
94–95	Van	11	0	2	2	6
95–96	Van	6	0	1	1	10
Totals		56	1	9	10	46

*HEFFERNAN, Frank *F*

SSN	TEAM	GP	G	A	PTS.	PIM
19–20	Tor	17	0	0	0	4

HEFFERNAN, Gerald J. *5–9 160 RW*
B. Montreal, Que., July 24, 1916

SSN	TEAM	GP	G	A	PTS.	PIM
41–42	Mont	40	5	15	20	15
43–44	Mont	43	28	20	48	12
Totals		83	33	35	68	27

Playoffs

SSN	TEAM	GP	G	A	PTS.	PIM
41–42	Mont	2	2	1	3	0
42–43	Mont	2	0	0	0	0
43–44	Mont	7	1	2	3	8
Totals		11	3	3	6	8

HEIDT, Michael *6–1 190 D*
B. Calgary, Alta., Nov. 4, 1963

SSN	TEAM	GP	G	A	PTS.	PIM	+/-
83–84	LA	6	0	1	1	7	-1

HEINDL, William Wayne *5–10 175 LW*
B. Sherbrooke, Que., May 13, 1946

SSN	TEAM	GP	G	A	PTS.	PIM	+/-
70–71	Minn	12	1	1	2	0	-1
71–72	Minn	2	0	0	0	0	0
72–73	NYR	4	1	0	1	0	+1
73–74	Clev (WHA)	67	4	14	18	4	0
NHL Totals		18	2	1	3	0	
WHA Totals		67	4	14	18	4	

Playoffs

SSN	TEAM	GP	G	A	PTS.	PIM
73–74	Clev (WHA)	5	0	1	1	2

HEINRICH, Lionel Grant *5–10 180 LW*
B. Churchbridge, Sask., Apr. 20, 1934

SSN	TEAM	GP	G	A	PTS.	PIM
55–56	Bos	35	1	1	2	33

HEINS, Shawn *6–4 215 D*
B. Eganville, Ont., Dec. 24, 1973

SSN	TEAM	GP	G	A	PTS.	PIM	+/-
98–99	SJ	5	0	0	0	13	0

HEINZE, Stephen *5–11 193 RW*
B. Lawrence, Mass., Jan. 30, 1970

SSN	TEAM	GP	G	A	PTS.	PIM	+/-
91–92	Bos	14	3	4	7	6	-1
92–93	Bos	73	18	13	31	24	+20
93–94	Bos	77	10	11	21	32	-2
94–95	Bos	36	7	9	16	23	0
95–96	Bos	76	16	12	28	43	-3
96–97	Bos	30	17	8	25	27	-8
97–98	Bos	61	26	20	46	54	+8
98–99	Bos	73	22	18	40	30	+7
Totals		440	119	95	214	239	+21

Playoffs

SSN	TEAM	GP	G	A	PTS.	PIM
91–92	Bos	7	0	3	3	17
92–93	Bos	4	1	1	2	2
93–94	Bos	13	2	3	5	7
94–95	Bos	5	0	0	0	0
95–96	Bos	5	1	1	2	4
97–98	Bos	6	0	0	0	6
98–99	Bos	12	4	3	7	0
Totals		52	8	11	19	36

HEISKALA, Earl Waldemar *6–0 185 LW*
B. Kirkland lake, Ont., Nov. 30, 1942

SSN	TEAM	GP	G	A	PTS.	PIM	+/-
68–69	Phil	21	3	3	6	51	-4
69–70	Phil	65	8	7	15	171	-15
70–71	Phil	41	2	1	3	72	-9
72–73	LA (WHA)	70	12	17	29	150	
73–74	LA (WHA)	24	2	6	8	45	
NHL Totals		127	13	11	24	294	-28
WHA Totals		94	14	23	37	195	

Playoffs

SSN	TEAM	GP	G	A	PTS.	PIM
72–73	LA (WHA)	5	1	1	2	4

HEJDUK, Milan *5–11 165 RW*
B. Usti-nad-Labem, Czech., Feb. 14, 1976

SSN	TEAM	GP	G	A	PTS.	PIM	+/-
98–99	Col A	82	14	34	48	26	+8

Playoffs

SSN	TEAM	GP	G	A	PTS.	PIM
98–99	Col A	16	6	6	12	4

HELANDER, Peter *6–1 185 D*
B. Stockholm, Sweden, Dec. 4, 1951

SSN	TEAM	GP	G	A	PTS.	PIM	+/-
82–83	LA	7	0	1	1	0	-2

HELENIUS, Sami *6–5 225 D*
B. Helsinki, Finland, Jan. 22, 1974

SSN	TEAM	GP	G	A	PTS.	PIM	+/-
96–97	Calg	3	0	1	1	0	+1
98–99	Calg-TB-Col A	8	1	0	1	23	-5
Totals		11	1	1	2	23	-4

*HELLER, Ehrhardt Henry (Ott) *6–0 195 D*
B. Kitchener, Ont., June 2, 1910

SSN	TEAM	GP	G	A	PTS.	PIM
31–32	NYR	21	2	2	4	9
32–33	NYR	40	5	7	12	31
33–34	NYR	48	2	5	7	29
34–35	NYR	47	3	11	14	31
35–36	NYR	43	2	11	13	40
36–37	NYR	48	5	12	17	42
37–38	NYR	48	2	14	16	68
38–39	NYR	48	0	23	23	42
39–40	NYR	47	5	14	19	26
40–41	NYR	48	2	16	18	42
41–42	NYR	35	6	5	11	22
42–43	NYR	45	4	14	18	14
43–44	NYR	50	8	27	35	29
44–45	NYR	45	7	12	19	26
45–46	NYR	34	2	3	5	14
Totals		647	55	176	231	465

Playoffs

SSN	TEAM	GP	G	A	PTS.	PIM
31–32	NYR	7	3	1	4	8
33–34	NYR	2	0	0	0	0
34–35	NYR	4	0	1	1	4
36–37	NYR	9	0	0	0	11
37–38	NYR	3	0	1	1	2
38–39	NYR	7	0	1	1	10
39–40	NYR	12	0	3	3	12
40–41	NYR	3	0	1	1	4
41–42	NYR	6	0	0	0	0
Totals		53	3	8	11	51

*HELMAN, Harold (Harry) *D*

SSN	TEAM	GP	G	A	PTS.	PIM
22–23	Ott	24	0	0	0	5
23–24	Ott	17	1	0	1	2
24–26	Ott	1	0	0	0	0
Totals		42	1	0	1	7

Playoffs

SSN	TEAM	GP	G	A	PTS.	PIM
22–23	Ott	5	0	0	0	0

HELMER, Bryan *6–1 200 D*
B. Sault Ste. Marie, Ont., July 15, 1972

SSN	TEAM	GP	G	A	PTS.	PIM	+/-
98–99	Phoe-StL	40	0	4	4	42	+5

HELMINEN, Raimo Ilmari *6–0 183 C*
B. Tampere, Finland, Mar. 11, 1964

SSN	TEAM	GP	G	A	PTS.	PIM	+/-
85–86	NYR	66	10	30	40	10	-1
86–87	NYR–Minn	27	2	5	7	2	-11
88–89	NYI	24	1	11	12	4	-15
Totals		117	13	46	59	16	-27

Playoffs

SSN	TEAM	GP	G	A	PTS.	PIM
85–86	NYR	2	0	0	0	0

SSN | TEAM | GP | G | A | PTS. | PIM | +/-

HEMMERLING, Elmer Charles (Tony) *5–11 178 LW*
B. Landis, Sask., May 11, 1913

SSN	TEAM	GP	G	A	PTS.	PIM	+/-
35–36	NYA	6	0	0	0	0	
36–37	NYA	18	3	3	6	4	
Totals		24	3	3	6	4	

HENDERSON, Archie *6–6 220 RW*
B. Calgary, Alta., Feb. 17, 1957

SSN	TEAM	GP	G	A	PTS.	PIM	+/-
80–81	Wash	7	1	0	1	28	-1
81–82	Minn	1	0	0	0	0	0
82–83	Hart	15	2	1	3	64	-2
Totals		23	3	1	4	92	-3

HENDERSON, Jay *5–11 188 LW*
B. Edmonton, Alta., Sept. 17, 1978

SSN	TEAM	GP	G	A	PTS.	PIM	+/-
98–99	Bos	4	0	0	0	2	-1

HENDERSON, John Murray (Murray, Moe) *6–0 180 D*
B. Toronto, Ont., Sept. 5, 1921

SSN	TEAM	GP	G	A	PTS.	PIM	+/-
44–45	Bos	5	0	1	1	4	
45–46	Bos	48	4	11	15	30	
46–47	Bos	57	5	12	17	63	
47–48	Bos	49	6	8	14	50	
48–49	Bos	60	2	9	11	28	
49–50	Bos	64	3	8	11	42	
50–51	Bos	66	4	7	11	37	
51–52	Bos	56	0	6	6	51	
Totals		405	24	62	86	305	

Playoffs

SSN	TEAM	GP	G	A	PTS.	PIM	+/-
44–45	Bos	7	0	1	1	2	
45–46	Bos	10	1	1	2	4	
46–47	Bos	4	0	0	0	4	
47–48	Bos	3	1	0	1	5	
48–49	Bos	5	0	1	1	2	
50–51	Bos	5	0	0	0	2	
51–52	Bos	7	0	0	0	4	
Totals		41	2	3	5	23	

HENDERSON, Matt *6–1 200 RW*
B. White Bear Lake, Minn., June 22, 1974

SSN	TEAM	GP	G	A	PTS.	PIM	+/-
98–99	Nash	2	0	0	0	2	-1

HENDERSON, Paul Garnet *5–11 180 LW*
B. Kincardine, Ont., Jan. 28, 1943

SSN	TEAM	GP	G	A	PTS.	PIM	+/-
62–63	Det	2	0	0	0	9	
63–64	Det	32	3	3	6	6	
64–65	Det	70	8	13	21	30	
65–66	Det	69	22	24	46	34	
66–67	Det	46	21	19	40	10	
67–68	Det–Tor	63	18	26	44	43	+13
68–69	Tor	74	27	32	59	16	+18
69–70	Tor	67	20	22	42	18	+14
70–71	Tor	72	30	30	60	34	+14
71–72	Tor	73	38	19	57	32	+14
72–73	Tor	40	18	16	34	18	+2
73–74	Tor	69	24	31	55	40	+9
74–75	Tor (WHA)	58	30	33	63	18	
75–76	Tor (WHA)	65	26	29	55	22	
76–77	Birm (WHA)	81	23	25	48	30	
77–78	Birm (WHA)	80	37	29	66	22	
78–79	Birm (WHA)	76	24	27	51	20	
79–80	Atl	30	7	6	13	6	+5
NHL Totals		707	236	241	477	296	+89
WHA Totals		360	140	143	283	112	

Playoffs

SSN	TEAM	GP	G	A	PTS.	PIM	+/-
63–64	Det	14	2	3	5	6	
64–65	Det	7	0	2	2	0	
65–66	Det	12	3	3	6	10	
68–69	Tor	4	0	1	1	0	
70–71	Tor	6	5	1	6	4	
71–72	Tor	5	1	2	3	6	
73–74	Tor	4	0	2	2	2	
77–78	Birm (WHA)	5	1	1	2	0	
79–80	Atl	4	0	0	0	0	
NHL Totals		56	11	14	25	28	
WHA Totals		5	1	1	2	0	

HENDRICKSON, Darby *6–0 185 C*
B. Richfield, Minn., Aug. 28, 1972

SSN	TEAM	GP	G	A	PTS.	PIM	+/-
94–95	Tor	8	0	1	1	4	0
95–96	Tor–NYI	62	7	10	17	80	-8
96–97	Tor	64	11	6	17	47	-20
97–98	Tor	80	8	4	12	67	-20
98–99	Tor–Van	62	4	5	9	52	-19
Totals		274	30	26	56	250	-67

Playoffs

SSN	TEAM	GP	G	A	PTS.	PIM	+/-
93–94	Tor	2	0	0	0	0	

HENDRICKSON, John Gunnard *5–11 175 D*
B. Kingston, Ont., Dec. 5, 1936

SSN	TEAM	GP	G	A	PTS.	PIM	+/-
57–58	Det	1	0	0	0	0	
58–59	Det	3	0	0	0	2	
61–62	Det	1	0	0	0	2	
Totals		5	0	0	0	4	

HENNING, Lorne Edward *5–11 185 C*
B. Melfort, Sask., Feb. 22, 1952

SSN	TEAM	GP	G	A	PTS.	PIM	+/-
72–73	NYI	63	7	19	26	14	-28
73–74	NYI	60	12	15	27	6	-7
74–75	NYI	61	5	6	11	6	+7
75–76	NYI	80	7	10	17	16	+6
76–77	NYI	80	13	18	31	10	+21
77–78	NYI	79	12	15	27	16	+10
78–79	NYI	73	13	20	33	14	+17
79–80	NYI	39	3	6	9	6	-10
80–81	NYI	9	1	2	3	14	+4
Totals		544	73	111	184	102	+20

Playoffs

SSN	TEAM	GP	G	A	PTS.	PIM	+/-
74–75	NYI	17	0	2	2	0	
75–76	NYI	13	2	0	2	2	
76–77	NYI	12	0	1	1	0	
77–78	NYI	7	0	0	0	4	
78–79	NYI	10	2	0	2	0	
79–80	NYI	21	3	4	7	2	
80–81	NYI	1	0	0	0	0	
Totals		81	7	7	14	8	

HENRY, Camille Joseph Wilfred (Eel) *5–8 152 C*
B. Quebec City, Que., Jan. 31, 1933

SSN	TEAM	GP	G	A	PTS.	PIM	+/-
53–54	NYR	66	24	15	39	10	
54–55	NYR	21	5	2	7	4	
56–57	NYR	36	14	15	29	2	
57–58	NYR	70	32	24	56	2	
58–59	NYR	70	23	35	58	2	
59–60	NYR	49	12	15	27	6	
60–61	NYR	53	28	25	53	8	
61–62	NYR	60	23	15	38	8	
62–63	NYR	60	37	23	60	8	
63–64	NYR	68	29	26	55	8	
64–65	NYR–Chi	70	26	18	44	22	
67–68	NYR	36	8	12	20	0	+8
68–69	StL	64	17	22	39	8	+14
69–70	StL	4	1	2	3	0	-2
Totals		727	279	249	528	88	+20

Playoffs

SSN	TEAM	GP	G	A	PTS.	PIM	+/-
56–57	NYR	5	2	3	5	0	
57–58	NYR	6	1	4	5	5	
61–62	NYR	5	0	0	0	0	
64–65	Chi	14	1	0	1	2	
67–68	NYR	6	0	0	0	0	
68–69	StL	11	2	5	7	0	
Totals		47	6	12	18	7	

HENRY, Dale *6–0 205 LW*
B. Prince Albert, Sask., Sept. 24, 1964

SSN	TEAM	GP	G	A	PTS.	PIM	+/-
84–85	NYI	16	2	1	3	19	+1
85–86	NYI	7	1	3	4	15	0
86–87	NYI	19	3	3	6	46	+2
87–88	NYI	48	5	15	20	115	+8
88–89	NYI	22	2	2	4	66	-4
89–90	NYI	20	0	2	2	2	-4
Totals		132	13	26	39	263	+3

Playoffs

SSN	TEAM	GP	G	A	PTS.	PIM	+/-
86–87	NYI	8	0	0	0	2	
87–88	NYI	6	1	0	1	17	
Totals		14	1	0	1	19	

HEPPLE, Alan *5–9 200 D*
B. Blaydon-on-Tyne, England, Aug. 16, 1963

SSN	TEAM	GP	G	A	PTS.	PIM	+/-
83–84	NJ	1	0	0	0	7	-1
84–85	NJ	1	0	0	0	0	-2
85–86	NJ	1	0	0	0	0	0
Totals		3	0	0	0	7	-3

HERBERS, Ian *6–4 225 D*
B. Jasper, Alta., July 18, 1967

SSN	TEAM	GP	G	A	PTS.	PIM	+/-
93–94	Edm	22	0	2	2	32	-6

HERBERTS, James *F*
B. Collingwood, Ont., 1897

SSN	TEAM	GP	G	A	PTS.	PIM	+/-
24–25	Bos	30	17	5	22	50	
25–26	Bos	36	26	5	31	47	
26–27	Bos	34	15	7	22	51	
27–28	Tor	43	15	4	19	64	
28–29	Det	40	9	5	14	34	
29–30	Det	23	1	3	4	4	
Totals		206	83	29	112	250	

Playoffs

SSN	TEAM	GP	G	A	PTS.	PIM	+/-
26–27	Bos	8	3	0	3	33	
28–29	Det	1	0	0	0	2	
Totals		9	3	0	3	35	

HERCHENRATTER, Arthur *6–0 185 LW*
B. Kitchener, Ont., Nov. 24, 1917

SSN	TEAM	GP	G	A	PTS.	PIM	+/-
40–41	Det	10	1	2	3	2	

HERGERTS, Frederick *6–0 190 C*
B. Calgary, Alta., Jan. 29, 1913

SSN	TEAM	GP	G	A	PTS.	PIM	+/-
34–35	NYA	18	2	4	6	2	
35–36	NYA	1	0	0	0	0	
Totals		19	2	4	6	2	

HERGESHEIMER, Phillip *5–10 175 RW*
B. Winnipeg, Man., July 9, 1914

SSN	TEAM	GP	G	A	PTS.	PIM	+/-
39–40	Chi	41	9	11	20	6	
40–41	Chi	47	8	16	24	9	
41–42	Chi–Bos	26	3	11	14	4	
42–43	Chi	9	1	3	4	0	
Totals		123	21	41	62	19	

Playoffs

SSN	TEAM	GP	G	A	PTS.	PIM	+/-
39–40	Chi	2	0	0	0	0	
40–41	Chi	5	0	0	0	2	
Totals		7	0	0	0	2	

HERGESHEIMER, Walter Edgar (Wally, Hergie) *5–8 155 RW*
B. Winnipeg, Man., Jan. 8, 1927

SSN	TEAM	GP	G	A	PTS.	PIM	+/-
51–52	NYR	68	26	12	38	6	
52–53	NYR	70	30	29	59	10	
53–54	NYR	66	27	16	43	42	
54–55	NYR	14	4	2	6	4	
55–56	NYR	70	22	18	40	26	
56–57	Chi	41	2	8	10	12	
58–59	NYR	22	3	0	3	6	
Totals		351	114	85	199	106	

Playoffs

SSN	TEAM	GP	G	A	PTS.	PIM	+/-
55–56	NYR	5	1	0	1	0	

HERON, Robert Geatrex (Red) *5–11 170 C*
B. Tornoto, Ont., Dec. 31, 1917

SSN	TEAM	GP	G	A	PTS.	PIM	+/-
38–39	Tor	6	0	0	0	0	
39–40	Tor	42	11	12	23	12	
40–41	Tor	35	9	5	14	12	
41–42	NYA–Mont	23	1	2	3	14	
Totals		106	21	19	40	38	

Playoffs

SSN	TEAM	GP	G	A	PTS.	PIM	+/-
39–40	Tor	9	2	0	2	55	
40–41	Tor	7	0	2	2	0	
Totals		16	2	2	4	55	

HEROUX, Yves *5–11 185 RW*
B. Terrebonne, Que., Apr. 27, 1965

SSN	TEAM	GP	G	A	PTS.	PIM	+/-
86–87	Que	1	0	0	0	0	0

HERR, Matt *6–1 180 C*
B. Hackensack, N.J., May 26, 1976

SSN	TEAM	GP	G	A	PTS.	PIM	+/-
98–99	Wash	30	2	2	4	8	-7

HERTER, Jason *6–1 190 D*
B. Hafford, Sask., Oct. 2, 1970

SSN	TEAM	GP	G	A	PTS.	PIM	+/-
95–96	NYI	1	0	1	1	0	+1

SSN	TEAM	GP	G	A	PTS.	PIM	+/-

HERVEY, Matt *5–11 205 D*
B. Whittier, Cal., May 16, 1966

SSN	TEAM	GP	G	A	PTS.	PIM	+/-
88–89	Winn	2	0	0	0	4	+2
91–92	Bos	16	0	1	1	55	-5
92–93	TB	17	0	4	4	38	-6
Totals		35	0	5	5	97	-9

Playoffs

| 91–92 | Bos | 5 | 0 | 0 | 0 | 6 | |

HESS, Robert George *5–11 180 D*
B. Middleton, N.S., May 19, 1955

74–75	StL	79	9	30	39	58	+7
75–76	StL	78	9	23	32	58	+3
76–77	StL	53	4	18	22	14	-2
77–78	StL	55	2	12	14	16	0
78–79	StL	27	3	4	7	14	0
80–81	StL–Buf	4	0	0	0	4	-23
81–82	Buf	33	0	8	8	14	+6
83–84	Hart	3	0	0	0	0	+1
Totals		329	27	95	122	178	-8

Playoffs

74–75	StL	10	0	0	0	2	
75–76	StL	1	0	1	1	0	
76–77	StL	1	0	0	0	0	
80–81	Buf	1	1	0	1	0	
Totals		13	1	1	2	2	

HEWARD, Jamie *6–2 207 D*
B. Regina, Sask., Mar. 30, 1971

95–96	Tor	5	0	0	0	0	-1
96–97	Tor	20	1	4	5	6	-6
98–99	Nash	63	6	12	18	44	-24
Totals		88	7	16	23	50	-31

HEXIMER, Orville Russell (Obs) *5–7 159 LW*
B. Niagara Falls, Ont., Feb. 16, 1910

29–30	NYR	19	1	0	1	4	
32–33	Bos	48	7	5	12	24	
34–35	NYA	18	5	2	7	0	
Totals		85	13	7	20	28	

Playoffs

| 32–33 | Bos | 5 | 0 | 0 | 0 | 2 | |

*HEXTALL, Bryan Aldwyn *5–10 180 RW*
B. Grenfell, Sask., July 31, 1913

36–37	NYR	1	0	1	1	0	
37–38	NYR	48	17	4	21	6	
38–39	NYR	48	20	15	35	18	
39–40	NYR	48	24	15	39	52	
40–41	NYR	48	26	18	44	16	
41–42	NYR	48	24	32	56	30	
42–43	NYR	50	27	32	59	28	
43–44	NYR	50	21	33	54	41	
45–46	NYR	3	0	1	1	0	
46–47	NYR	60	21	10	31	12	
47–48	NYR	43	8	14	22	18	
Totals		447	188	175	363	221	

Playoffs

37–38	NYR	3	2	0	2	0	
38–39	NYR	7	0	1	1	4	
39–40	NYR	12	4	3	7	11	
40–41	NYR	3	0	1	1	0	
41–42	NYR	6	1	1	2	4	
47–48	NYR	6	1	3	4	0	
Totals		37	8	9	17	19	

HEXTALL, Bryan Lee *5–11 185 C*
B. Winnipeg, Man., May 23, 1941

62–63	NYR	21	0	2	2	10	
69–70	Pitt	66	12	19	31	87	-22
70–71	Pitt	76	16	32	48	133	-23
71–72	Pitt	78	20	24	44	126	-26
72–73	Pitt	78	21	33	54	113	-23
73–74	Pitt–Atl	77	4	11	15	94	-13
74–75	Atl	74	18	16	34	62	-13
75–76	Det–Minn	79	8	24	32	113	-20
Totals		549	99	161	260	738	-140

Playoffs

69–70	Pitt	10	0	1	1	34	
71–72	Pitt	4	0	2	2	9	
73–74	Atl	4	0	1	1	16	
Totals		18	0	4	4	59	

HEXTALL, Dennis Harold *5–11 175 C*
B. Winnipeg, Man., Apr. 17, 1943

68–69	NYR	13	1	4	5	25	+1
69–70	LA	28	5	7	12	40	-23
70–71	Cal	78	21	31	52	217	-20
71–72	Minn	33	6	10	16	49	+1
72–73	Minn	78	30	52	82	140	+29
73–74	Minn	78	20	62	82	138	+4
74–75	Minn	80	17	57	74	147	-44
75–76	Minn–Det	76	16	44	60	164	-27
76–77	Det	78	14	32	46	158	-35
77–78	Det	78	16	33	49	195	-5
78–79	Det–Wash	46	6	17	23	76	-10
79–80	Wash	15	1	1	2	49	-5
Totals		681	153	350	503	1398	-134

Playoffs

67–68	NYR	2	0	0	0	0	
71–72	Minn	7	0	2	2	19	
72–73	Minn	6	2	0	2	16	
77–78	Det	7	1	1	2	10	
Totals		22	3	3	6	45	

HEYLIGER, Victor *5–8 175 C*
B. Boston, Mass., Sept. 26, 1919

37–38	Chi	8	0	0	0	0	
43–44	Chi	26	2	3	5	2	
Totals		34	2	3	5	2	

HICKE, Ernest Allan *5–11 180 LW*
B. Regina, Sask., Nov. 7, 1947

70–71	Cal	78	22	25	47	62	-36
71–72	Cal	68	11	12	23	55	-13
72–73	Atl–NYI	59	14	23	37	37	-2
73–74	NYI	55	6	7	13	26	-19
74–75	NYI–Minn	62	17	19	36	91	-19
75–76	Minn	80	23	19	42	77	-31
76–77	Minn	77	30	20	50	41	-32
77–78	LA	41	9	15	24	18	+7
Totals		520	132	140	272	407	-145

Playoffs

| 76–77 | Minn | 2 | 1 | 0 | 1 | 0 | |

HICKE, William Lawrence *5–8 170 RW*
B. Regina, Sask., Mar. 31, 1938

59–60	Mont	43	3	10	13	17	
60–61	Mont	70	18	27	45	31	
61–62	Mont	70	20	31	51	42	
62–63	Mont	70	17	22	39	39	
63–64	Mont	48	11	9	20	41	
64–65	Mont–NYR	57	6	12	18	32	
65–66	NYR	49	9	18	27	21	
66–67	NYR	48	3	4	7	11	
67–68	Oak	52	21	19	40	32	-22
68–69	Oak	67	25	36	61	68	-11
69–70	Oak	69	15	29	44	14	-10
70–71	Cal	74	18	17	35	41	-29
71–72	Pitt	12	2	0	2	6	-6
72–73	Alb (WHA)	73	14	24	38	20	
NHL Totals		729	168	234	402	395	-78
WHA Totals		73	14	24	38	20	

Playoffs

58–59	Mont	1	0	0	0	0	
59–60	Mont	7	1	2	3	0	
60–61	Mont	5	2	0	2	19	
61–62	Mont	6	0	2	2	14	
62–63	Mont	5	0	0	0	0	
63–64	Mont	7	0	2	2	2	
68–69	Cal	7	0	3	3	4	
69–70	Oak	4	0	1	1	2	
NHL Totals		42	3	10	13	41	

HICKEY, Greg *5–10 160 LW*
B. Toronto, Ont., Mar. 8, 1955

| 77–78 | NYR | 1 | 0 | 0 | 0 | 0 | -1 |

HICKEY, Patrick Joseph *6–1 190 LW*
B. Brantford, Ont., May 15, 1953

73–74	Tor (WHA)	78	26	29	55	52	
74–75	Tor (WHA)	74	34	34	68	50	
75–76	NYR	70	14	22	36	36	-29
76–77	NYR	80	23	17	40	35	-11
77–78	NYR	80	40	33	73	47	-19
78–79	NYR	80	34	41	75	56	+8
79–80	NYR–Col–Tor	76	31	27	58	36	-2
80–81	Tor	72	16	33	49	49	-16
81–82	Tor–NYR–Que	61	15	15	30	36	-16
82–83	StL	1	0	0	0	0	0
83–84	StL	69	9	11	20	24	-3
84–85	StL	57	10	13	23	32	-4
NHL Totals		646	192	212	404	351	-92
WHA Totals		152	60	63	123	102	

Playoffs

73–74	Tor (WHA)	12	3	3	6	12	
74–75	Tor (WHA)	5	0	1	1	4	
77–78	NYR	3	2	0	2	0	
78–79	NYR	18	1	7	8	6	
79–80	Tor	3	0	0	0	2	
80–81	Tor	2	0	0	0	0	
81–82	Que	15	1	3	4	21	
83–84	StL	11	1	1	2	6	
84–85	StL	3	0	0	0	2	
NHL Totals		55	5	11	16	37	
WHA Totals		17	3	4	7	16	

HICKS, Alex *6–1 195 LW*
B. Calgary, Alta., Sept. 4, 1969

95–96	Ana	64	10	11	21	37	+11
96–97	Ana–Pitt	73	7	21	28	90	-5
97–98	Pitt	58	7	13	20	54	+4
98–99	SJ–Fla	55	0	7	7	62	-5
Totals		250	24	52	76	243	+5

Playoffs

96–97	Pitt	5	0	1	1	2	
97–98	Pitt	6	0	0	0	2	
Totals		11	0	1	1	4	

HICKS, Douglas Allan *6–0 185 D*
B. Cold Lake, Alta., May 28, 1955

74–75	Minn	80	6	12	18	51	-25
75–76	Minn	80	5	13	18	54	-17
76–77	Minn	79	5	14	19	68	-31
77–78	Minn–Chi	74	3	16	19	53	-23
78–79	Chi	44	1	8	9	15	-12
79–80	Edm	78	9	31	40	52	+18
80–81	Edm	59	5	16	21	76	+21
81–82	Edm–Wash	61	3	21	24	66	-1
82–83	Wash	6	0	0	0	7	-3
Totals		561	37	131	168	442	-73

Playoffs

76–77	Minn	2	0	0	0	7	
77–78	Chi	4	1	0	1	2	
79–80	Edm	3	0	0	0	2	
80–81	Edm	9	1	1	2	4	
Totals		18	2	1	3	15	

HICKS, Glenn *5–10 177 LW*
B. Red Deer, Alta., Aug. 28, 1958

78–79	Winn (WHA)	69	6	10	16	48	
79–80	Det	50	1	2	3	43	-21
80–81	Det	58	5	10	15	84	0
NHL Totals		108	6	12	18	127	-21
WHA Totals		69	6	10	16	48	

Playoffs

| 78–79 | Minn (WHA) | 7 | 1 | 1 | 2 | 4 | |

*HICKS, Harold H. (Hal) *D*
B. Ottawa, Ont., Dec. 10, 1900

28–29	Mont M	44	2	0	2	27	
29–80	Det	44	3	2	5	35	
30–31	Det	22	2	0	2	10	
Totals		110	7	2	9	72	

HICKS, Wayne Wilson *5–10 190 RW*
B. Aberdeen, Wash., Apr. 9, 1937

60–61	Chi	1	0	0	0	0	
62–63	Bos	65	7	9	16	14	
63–64	Mont	2	0	0	0	0	
67–68	Phil–Pitt	47	6	14	20	8	-3
Totals		115	13	23	36	22	-3

Playoffs

59–60	Chi	1	0	1	1	0	
60–61	Chi	1	0	0	0	2	
Totals		2	0	1	1	2	

HIDI, Andre Lawrence 6–2 205 LW
B. Toronto, Ont., June 5, 1960

SSN	TEAM	GP	G	A	PTS.	PIM	+/-
83–84	Wash	1	0	0	0	0	0
84–85	Wash	6	2	1	3	9	+2
Totals		7	2	1	3	9	+2

Playoffs

SSN	TEAM	GP	G	A	PTS.	PIM
83–84	Wash	2	0	0	0	0

HIEMER, Ullrich (Uli) 6–1 190 D
B. Fussen, W. Germany, Sept. 21, 1962

SSN	TEAM	GP	G	A	PTS.	PIM	+/-
84–85	NJ	53	5	24	29	70	-14
85–86	NJ	50	8	16	24	61	-1
86–87	NJ	40	6	14	20	45	-6
Totals		143	19	54	73	176	-21

HIGGINS, Matt 6–2 170 C
B. Calgary, Alta., Oct. 29, 1977

SSN	TEAM	GP	G	A	PTS.	PIM	+/-
97–98	Mont	1	0	0	0	0	-1
98–99	Mont	25	1	0	1	0	-2
Totals		26	1	0	1	0	-3

HIGGINS, Paul 6–1 195 RW
B. St. John, N.B., Jan. 13, 1962

SSN	TEAM	GP	G	A	PTS.	PIM	+/-
81–82	Tor	3	0	0	0	17	-1
82–83	Tor	22	0	0	0	135	-3
Totals		25	0	0	0	152	-4

Playoffs

SSN	TEAM	GP	G	A	PTS.	PIM
82–83	Tor	1	0	0	0	0

HIGGINS, Tim Ray 6–1 185 RW
B. Ottawa, Ont., Feb. 7, 1958

SSN	TEAM	GP	G	A	PTS.	PIM	+/-
78–79	Chi	36	7	16	23	30	+6
79–80	Chi	74	13	12	25	50	-15
80–81	Chi	78	24	35	59	86	+20
81–82	Chi	74	20	30	50	85	-6
82–83	Chi	64	14	9	23	63	-4
83–84	Chi–NJ	69	19	14	33	48	-3
84–85	NJ	71	19	29	48	30	-10
85–86	NJ	59	9	17	26	47	+7
86–87	Det	77	12	14	26	124	-2
87–88	Det	62	12	13	25	94	+5
88–89	Det	42	5	9	14	62	0
Totals		706	154	198	352	719	-2

Playoffs

SSN	TEAM	GP	G	A	PTS.	PIM
78–79	Chi	4	0	0	0	0
79–80	Chi	7	0	3	3	10
80–81	Chi	3	0	0	0	0
81–82	Chi	12	3	1	4	15
82–83	Chi	13	1	3	4	10
86–87	Det	12	0	1	1	16
87–88	Det	13	1	0	1	26
88–89	Det	1	0	0	0	0
Totals		65	5	8	13	77

HILDEBRAND, Isaac Bruce (Ike) 5–8 155 RW
B. Winnipeg, Man., May 27, 1927

SSN	TEAM	GP	G	A	PTS.	PIM
53–54	NYR–Chi	38	7	11	18	16
54–55	Chi	3	0	0	0	0
Totals		41	7	11	18	16

HILL, Alan Douglas 6–1 175 LW/C
B. Nanaimo, B.C., Apr. 22, 1955

SSN	TEAM	GP	G	A	PTS.	PIM	+/-
76–77	Phil	9	2	4	6	27	+6
77–78	Phil	3	0	0	0	2	0
78–79	Phil	31	5	11	16	28	+5
79–80	Phil	61	16	10	26	53	+14
80–81	Phil	57	10	15	25	45	+11
81–82	Phil	41	6	13	19	58	-4
86–87	Phil	7	0	2	2	4	+1
87–88	Phil	12	1	0	1	10	0
Totals		221	40	55	95	227	+33

Playoffs

SSN	TEAM	GP	G	A	PTS.	PIM
78–79	Phil	7	1	0	1	2
79–80	Phil	19	3	5	8	19
80–81	Phil	12	2	4	6	18
81–82	Phil	3	0	0	0	0
86–87	Phil	9	2	1	3	0
87–88	Phil	1	0	1	1	4
Totals		51	8	11	19	43

HILL, Brian Nelson 6–0 175 RW
B. Regina, Sask., Jan. 12, 1957

SSN	TEAM	GP	G	A	PTS.	PIM	+/-
79–80	Hart	19	1	1	2	4	-1

HILL, John Melvin (Mel, Sudden Death) 5–10 175 RW
B. Glenboro, Man., Feb. 15, 1914

SSN	TEAM	GP	G	A	PTS.	PIM
37–38	Bos	8	2	0	2	2
38–39	Bos	44	10	10	20	16
39–40	Bos	37	9	11	20	19
40–41	Bos	41	5	4	9	4
41–42	Brk	47	14	23	37	10
42–43	Tor	49	17	27	44	47
43–44	Tor	17	9	10	19	6
44–45	Tor	45	18	17	35	14
45–46	Tor	35	5	7	12	10
Totals		323	89	109	198	128

Playoffs

SSN	TEAM	GP	G	A	PTS.	PIM
38–39	Bos	12	6	3	9	12
39–40	Bos	2	0	0	0	0
40–41	Bos	10	1	1	2	0
42–43	Tor	6	3	0	3	0
44–45	Tor	13	2	3	5	6
Totals		43	12	7	19	18

HILL, Sean 6–0 195 D
B. Duluth, Minn., Feb. 14, 1970

SSN	TEAM	GP	G	A	PTS.	PIM	+/-
92–93	Mont	31	2	6	8	54	-5
93–94	Ana	68	7	20	27	78	-12
94–95	Ott	45	1	14	15	30	-11
95–96	Ott	80	7	14	21	94	-26
96–97	Ott	5	0	0	0	4	+1
97–98	Ott–Car	55	1	6	7	54	-5
98–99	Car	54	0	10	10	48	+9
Totals		338	18	70	88	362	-49

Playoffs

SSN	TEAM	GP	G	A	PTS.	PIM
90–91	Mont	1	0	0	0	0
91–92	Mont	4	1	0	1	2
92–93	Mont	3	0	0	0	4
Totals		8	1	0	1	6

HILLER, Jim 6–0 190 RW
B. Port Alberni, B.C., May 15, 1969

SSN	TEAM	GP	G	A	PTS.	PIM	+/-
92–93	LA–Det	61	8	12	20	109	+7
93–94	NYR	2	0	0	0	7	+1
Totals		63	8	12	20	116	+8

Playoffs

SSN	TEAM	GP	G	A	PTS.	PIM
92–93	Det	2	0	0	0	4

HILLER, Wilbert Carl (Dutch) 5–8 170 LW
B. Kitchener, Ont., May 11, 1915

SSN	TEAM	GP	G	A	PTS.	PIM
37–38	NYR	9	0	1	1	2
38–39	NYR	48	10	19	29	22
39–40	NYR	48	13	18	31	57
40–41	NYR	45	8	10	18	20
41–42	Det–Bos	50	7	10	17	19
42–43	Mont	48	8	6	14	4
43–44	NYR	50	18	22	40	15
44–45	Mont	48	20	16	36	20
45–46	Mont	45	7	11	18	4
Totals		385	91	113	204	163

Playoffs

SSN	TEAM	GP	G	A	PTS.	PIM
37–38	NYR	1	0	0	0	0
38–39	NYR	7	1	0	1	9
39–40	NYR	12	2	4	6	2
40–41	NYR	3	0	0	0	0
41–42	Bos	5	0	1	1	0
42–43	Mont	5	1	0	1	4
44–45	Mont	6	1	1	2	4
45–46	Mont	9	4	2	6	2
Totals		48	9	8	17	21

HILLIER, Randy George 6–1 192 D
B. Toronto, Ont., Mar. 30, 1960

SSN	TEAM	GP	G	A	PTS.	PIM	+/-
81–82	Bos	25	0	8	8	29	+6
82–83	Bos	70	0	10	10	99	+10
83–84	Bos	69	3	12	15	125	-5
84–85	Pitt	45	2	19	21	56	-12
85–86	Pitt	28	0	3	3	53	-3
86–87	Pitt	55	4	8	12	97	+12
87–88	Pitt	55	1	12	13	144	-6
88–89	Pitt	68	1	23	24	141	-4
89–90	Pitt	61	3	12	15	71	+11
90–91	Pitt	31	2	2	4	32	-3
91–92	NYI–Buf	36	0	1	1	59	-17
Totals		543	16	110	126	906	-11

Playoffs

SSN	TEAM	GP	G	A	PTS.	PIM
81–82	Bos	8	0	1	1	16
82–83	Bos	3	0	0	0	4
88–89	Pitt	9	0	1	1	49
90–91	Pitt	8	0	0	0	24
Totals		28	0	2	2	93

HILLMAN, Floyd Arthur 5–11 170 D
B. Ruthven, Ont., Nov. 19, 1933

SSN	TEAM	GP	G	A	PTS.	PIM
56–57	Bos	6	0	0	0	10

HILLMAN, Larry Morley 6–0 181 D
B. Kirkland Lake, Ont., Feb. 5, 1937

SSN	TEAM	GP	G	A	PTS.	PIM	+/-
54–55	Det	6	0	0	0	2	
55–56	Det	47	0	3	3	53	
56–57	Det	16	1	2	3	4	
57–58	Bos	70	3	19	22	60	
58–59	Bos	55	3	10	13	19	
59–60	Bos	2	0	1	1	2	
60–61	Tor	62	3	10	13	59	
61–62	Tor	5	0	0	0	4	
62–63	Tor	5	0	0	0	2	
63–64	Tor	33	0	4	4	31	
64–65	Tor	2	0	0	0	2	
65–66	Tor	48	3	25	28	34	
66–67	Tor	55	4	19	23	40	
67–68	Tor	55	3	17	20	13	+7
68–69	Minn–Mont	37	1	10	11	17	-10
69–70	Phil	76	5	26	31	73	+2
70–71	Phil	73	3	13	16	39	+9
71–72	LA–Buf	65	2	13	15	69	-28
72–73	Buf	78	5	24	29	56	-3
73–74	Clev (WHA)	44	5	21	26	37	
74–75	Clev (WHA)	77	0	16	16	83	
75–76	Winn (WHA)	71	1	12	13	62	
NHL Totals		790	36	196	232	579	-23
WHA Totals		192	6	49	55	182	

Playoffs

SSN	TEAM	GP	G	A	PTS.	PIM
54–55	Det	3	0	0	0	0
55–56	Det	10	0	1	1	6
57–58	Bos	11	0	2	2	6
58–59	Bos	7	0	1	1	0
60–61	Tor	5	0	0	0	2
63–64	Tor	11	0	0	0	2
65–66	Tor	4	1	1	2	6
66–67	Tor	12	1	2	3	0
68–69	Mont	1	0	0	0	0
70–71	Phil	4	0	2	2	2
72–73	Buf	6	0	0	0	8
74–75	Clev (WHA)	5	1	3	4	4
75–76	Winn (WHA)	12	0	2	2	32
NHL Totals		74	2	9	11	30
WHA Totals		17	1	5	6	40

HILLMAN, Wayne James 6–1 205 D
B. Kirkland Lake, Ont., Nov. 13, 1938

SSN	TEAM	GP	G	A	PTS.	PIM	+/-
61–62	Chi	19	0	2	2	14	
62–63	Chi	67	3	5	8	74	
63–64	Chi	59	1	4	5	31	
64–65	Chi–NYR	41	1	8	9	34	
65–66	NYR	68	3	17	20	70	
66–67	NYR	67	2	12	14	43	
67–68	NYR	62	0	5	5	46	+9
68–69	Minn	50	0	8	8	32	-25
69–70	Phil	68	3	5	8	69	-9
70–71	Phil	69	5	7	12	47	+12
71–72	Phil	47	0	3	3	21	-16
72–73	Phil	74	0	10	10	33	+16
73–74	Clev (WHA)	66	1	7	8	51	
74–75	Clev (WHA)	60	2	9	11	37	
NHL Totals		691	18	86	104	514	-13
WHA Totals		126	3	16	19	88	

Playoffs

SSN	TEAM	GP	G	A	PTS.	PIM
60–61	Chi	1	0	0	0	0
62–63	Chi	6	0	2	2	2
63–64	Chi	7	0	1	1	15
66–67	NYR	4	0	0	0	2
67–68	NYR	2	0	0	0	0
72–73	Phil	8	0	0	0	0
73–74	Clev (WHA)	5	0	0	0	16
74–75	Clev (WHA)	5	0	2	2	2

SSN	TEAM	GP	G	A	PTS.	PIM	+/-
NHL Totals		28	0	3	3	19	
WHA Totals		10	0	2	2	18	

HILWORTH, John 6-4 205 D
B. Jasper, Alta., May 23, 1957

SSN	TEAM	GP	G	A	PTS.	PIM	+/-
77-78	Det	5	0	0	0	12	0
78-79	Det	37	1	1	2	66	-13
79-80	Det	15	0	0	0	11	-2
Totals		57	1	1	2	89	-15

*HIMES, Norman 5-9 145 F
B. Galt, Ont., Apr. 13, 1903

SSN	TEAM	GP	G	A	PTS.	PIM
26-27	NYA	42	9	2	11	14
27-28	NYA	44	14	5	19	22
28-29	NYA	44	10	0	10	25
29-30	NYA	44	28	22	50	15
30-31	NYA	44	15	9	24	18
31-32	NYA	48	7	21	28	9
32-33	NYA	48	9	25	34	12
33-34	NYA	48	9	16	25	10
34-35	NYA	40	5	13	18	2
Totals		402	106	113	219	127

Playoffs

SSN	TEAM	GP	G	A	PTS.	PIM
28-29	NYA	2	0	0	0	0

HINDMARCH, David 5-11 180 RW
B. Vancouver, B.C., Oct. 15, 1958

SSN	TEAM	GP	G	A	PTS.	PIM	+/-
80-81	Calg	1	1	0	1	0	0
81-82	Calg	9	3	0	3	0	-4
82-83	Calg	60	11	12	23	23	-8
83-84	Calg	29	6	5	11	2	-2
Totals		99	21	17	38	25	-14

Playoffs

SSN	TEAM	GP	G	A	PTS.	PIM
80-81	Calg	6	0	0	0	2
82-83	Calg	4	0	0	0	4
Totals		10	0	0	0	6

HINSE, Andre Joseph Charles 5-9 172 LW
B. Trois Rivieres, Que., Apr. 19, 1945

SSN	TEAM	GP	G	A	PTS.	PIM	+/-
67-68	Tor	4	0	0	0	0	-2
73-74	Hou (WHA)	69	24	56	80	39	
74-75	Hou (WHA)	75	39	47	86	12	
75-76	Hou (WHA)	70	35	38	73	6	
76-77	Phoe (WHA)	42	4	10	14	12	
NHL Totals		4	0	0	0	0	-2
WHA Totals		256	102	151	253	69	

Playoffs

SSN	TEAM	GP	G	A	PTS.	PIM
73-74	Hou (WHA)	14	8	9	17	18
74-75	Hou (WHA)	11	5	4	9	8
75-76	Hou (WHA)	17	2	3	5	2
WHA Totals		42	15	16	31	28

HINTON, Daniel Anthony 6-1 175 LW
B. Toronto, Ont., May 24, 1953

SSN	TEAM	GP	G	A	PTS.	PIM	+/-
76-77	Chi	14	0	0	0	16	-5

HIRSCH, Tom 6-4 210 D
B. Minneapolis, Minn., Jan 27, 1963

SSN	TEAM	GP	G	A	PTS.	PIM	+/-
83-84	Minn	15	1	3	4	20	-3
84-85	Minn	15	0	4	4	10	-13
87-88	Minn	1	0	0	0	0	+1
Totals		31	1	7	8	30	-15

Playoffs

SSN	TEAM	GP	G	A	PTS.	PIM
83-84	Minn	12	0	0	0	6

*HIRSCHFELD, John Albert (Bert) 5-10 165 LW
B. Halifax, N.S., Mar. 1, 1929

SSN	TEAM	GP	G	A	PTS.	PIM
49-50	Mont	13	1	2	3	2
50-51	Mont	20	0	2	2	0
Totals		33	1	4	5	2

Playoffs

SSN	TEAM	GP	G	A	PTS.	PIM
49-50	Mont	5	1	0	1	0

HISLOP, James Donald (Jamie) 5-10 180 RW
B. Sarnia, Ont., Jan. 20, 1954

SSN	TEAM	GP	G	A	PTS.	PIM	+/-
76-77	Cin (WHA)	46	7	9	16	26	
77-78	Cin (WHA)	80	24	43	67	17	
78-79	Chi (WHA)	80	30	40	70	45	
79-80	Que	80	19	20	39	6	-13

SSN	TEAM	GP	G	A	PTS.	PIM	+/-
80-81	Que-Calg	79	25	31	56	26	-7
81-82	Calg	80	16	25	41	35	+1
82-83	Calg	79	14	19	33	17	-5
83-84	Calg	27	1	8	9	2	0
NHL Totals		345	75	103	178	86	-24
WHA Totals		206	61	102	163	68	

Playoffs

SSN	TEAM	GP	G	A	PTS.	PIM
76-77	Cin (WHA)	4	0	1	1	5
78-79	Chi (WHA)	3	2	4	6	0
80-81	Calg	16	3	0	3	5
81-82	Calg	3	0	0	0	0
82-83	Calg	9	0	2	2	6
NHL Totals		28	3	2	5	11
WHA Totals		7	2	5	7	5

HITCHMAN, Lionel 6-0 167 D
B. Toronto, Ont., 1903

SSN	TEAM	GP	G	A	PTS.	PIM
22-23	Ott	3	0	1	1	12
23-24	Ott	24	2	6	8	24
24-25	Ott-Bos	30	3	0	3	24
25-26	Bos	36	7	4	11	70
26-27	Bos	40	3	6	9	70
27-28	Bos	43	5	3	8	87
28-29	Bos	37	1	0	1	64
29-30	Bos	39	2	7	9	39
30-31	Bos	43	0	2	2	40
31-32	Bos	48	4	3	7	36
32-33	Bos	41	0	1	1	34
33-34	Bos	29	1	0	1	4
Totals		413	28	33	61	504

Playoffs

SSN	TEAM	GP	G	A	PTS.	PIM
22-23	Ott	7	1	0	1	4
23-24	Ott	2	0	0	0	4
26-27	Bos	8	1	0	1	16
27-28	Bos	2	0	0	0	2
28-29	Bos	5	0	1	1	22
29-30	Bos	6	1	0	1	12
30-31	Bos	5	0	0	0	0
32-33	Bos	5	1	0	1	0
Totals		40	4	1	5	60

HLINKA, Ivan 6-2 220 C
B. Most, Czechoslovakia, Jan. 26, 1950

SSN	TEAM	GP	G	A	PTS.	PIM	+/-
81-82	Van	72	23	37	60	16	+21
82-83	Van	65	19	44	63	12	-3
Totals		137	42	81	123	28	+18

Playoffs

SSN	TEAM	GP	G	A	PTS.	PIM
81-82	Van	12	2	6	8	4
82-83	Van	4	1	4	5	4
Totals		16	3	10	13	8

HLUSHKO, Todd 5-11 185 C
B. Toronto, Ont., Feb. 7, 1970

SSN	TEAM	GP	G	A	PTS.	PIM	+/-
93-94	Phil	2	1	0	1	0	+1
94-95	Calg	2	0	1	1	2	+1
95-96	Calg	4	0	0	0	6	0
96-97	Calg	58	7	11	18	49	-2
97-98	Calg	13	0	1	1	27	0
Totals		79	8	13	21	84	0

Playoffs

SSN	TEAM	GP	G	A	PTS.	PIM
94-95	Calg	1	0	0	0	2
98-99	Pitt	2	0	0	0	0
Totals		3	0	0	0	2

HOCKING, Justin 6-4 205 D
B. Stettler, Alta., Jan. 9, 1974

SSN	TEAM	GP	G	A	PTS.	PIM	+/-
93-94	LA	1	0	0	0	0	0

HODGE, Kenneth Jr. 6-1 200 C/RW
B. Windsor, Ont., Apr. 13, 1966

SSN	TEAM	GP	G	A	PTS.	PIM	+/-
88-89	Minn	5	1	1	2	0	+1
90-91	Bos	70	30	29	59	20	+11
91-92	Bos	42	6	11	17	10	-8
92-93	TB	25	2	7	9	2	-6
Totals		142	39	48	87	32	-2

Playoffs

SSN	TEAM	GP	G	A	PTS.	PIM
90-91	Bos	15	4	6	10	6

HODGE, Kenneth Raymond 6-2 210 RW
B. Birmingham, England, June 25, 1944

SSN	TEAM	GP	G	A	PTS.	PIM
64-65	Chi	1	0	0	0	2

SSN	TEAM	GP	G	A	PTS.	PIM	+/-
65-66	Chi	63	6	17	23	47	
66-67	Chi	69	10	25	35	59	
67-68	Bos	74	25	31	56	31	+13
68-69	Bos	75	45	45	90	75	+49
69-70	Bos	72	25	29	54	87	+15
70-71	Bos	78	43	62	105	113	+71
71-72	Bos	60	16	40	56	81	+41
72-73	Bos	73	37	44	81	58	+10
73-74	Bos	76	50	55	105	43	+40
74-75	Bos	72	23	43	66	90	+7
75-76	Bos	72	25	36	61	42	+19
76-77	NYR	78	21	41	62	43	-18
77-78	NYR	18	2	4	6	8	-6
Totals		881	328	472	800	779	+241

Playoffs

SSN	TEAM	GP	G	A	PTS.	PIM
65-66	Chi	5	0	0	0	8
66-67	Chi	6	0	0	0	4
67-68	Bos	4	3	0	3	2
68-69	Bos	10	5	7	12	4
69-70	Bos	14	3	10	13	17
70-71	Bos	7	2	5	7	6
71-72	Bos	15	9	8	17	62
72-73	Bos	5	1	0	1	7
73-74	Bos	16	6	10	16	16
74-75	Bos	3	1	1	2	0
75-76	Bos	12	4	6	10	4
Totals		97	34	47	81	130

HODGSON, Daniel 5-10 165 C
B. Fort Vermillion, Alta., Aug. 29, 1965

SSN	TEAM	GP	G	A	PTS.	PIM	+/-
85-86	Tor	40	13	12	25	12	-5
86-87	Van	43	9	13	22	25	-9
87-88	Van	8	3	7	10	2	+1
88-89	Van	23	4	13	17	25	+3
Totals		114	29	45	74	64	-10

HODGSON, Edward James (Ted) 5-11 175 RW
B. Hobbema, Alta., June 30, 1945

SSN	TEAM	GP	G	A	PTS.	PIM
66-67	Bos	4	0	0	0	0
72-73	Clev (WHA)	74	15	23	38	93
73-74	Clev-LA (WHA)	33	3	11	14	28
NHL Totals		4	0	0	0	0
WHA Totals		107	18	34	52	121

Playoffs

SSN	TEAM	GP	G	A	PTS.	PIM
72-73	Clev (WHA)	9	1	3	4	13

HODGSON, Richard (Rick) 6-0 175 RW
B. Medicine Hat, Alta., May 23, 1956

SSN	TEAM	GP	G	A	PTS.	PIM	+/-
79-80	Hart	6	0	0	0	6	-5

Playoffs

SSN	TEAM	GP	G	A	PTS.	PIM
79-80	Hart	1	0	0	0	0

HOEKSTRA, Cecil Thomas 6-1 175 C
B. Winnipeg, Man., Apr. 2, 1935

SSN	TEAM	GP	G	A	PTS.	PIM
59-60	Mont	4	0	0	0	0

HOEKSTRA, Edward Adrian 5-11 170 C
B. Winnipeg, Man., Nov. 4, 1937

SSN	TEAM	GP	G	A	PTS.	PIM	+/-
67-68	Phil	70	15	21	36	6	+6
72-73	Hou (WHA)	78	11	28	39	12	
73-74	Hou (WHA)	19	2	0	2	0	
NHL Totals		70	15	21	36	6	+6
WHA Totals		97	13	28	41	12	

Playoffs

SSN	TEAM	GP	G	A	PTS.	PIM
67-68	Phil	7	0	1	1	0
72-73	Hous (WHA)	9	1	2	3	0
NHL Totals		7	0	1	1	0
WHA Totals		9	1	2	3	0

HOENE, Phil George 5-9 175 LW
B. Duluth, Minn., Mar. 15, 1949

SSN	TEAM	GP	G	A	PTS.	PIM	+/-
72-73	LA	4	0	1	1	0	+1
73-74	LA	31	2	3	5	22	-5
74-75	LA	2	0	0	0	0	0
Totals		37	2	4	6	22	-4

*HOFFINGER, Victor D

SSN	TEAM	GP	G	A	PTS.	PIM
27-28	Chi	18	0	1	1	18
28-29	Chi	10	0	0	0	12
Totals		28	0	1	1	30

HOFFMAN, Micheal 5-11 180 LW
B. Barrie, Ont., Feb. 26, 1963

SSN	TEAM	GP	G	A	PTS.	PIM	+/-
82-83	Hart	2	0	1	1	0	-2
84-85	Hart	1	0	0	0	0	0
85-86	Hart	6	1	2	3	2	-2
Totals		9	1	3	4	2	-4

HOFFMEYER, Robert Frank 6-0 180 D
B. Dodsland, Sask., July 27, 1955

SSN	TEAM	GP	G	A	PTS.	PIM	+/-
77-78	Chi	5	0	1	1	12	-2
78-79	Chi	6	0	2	2	5	-4
81-82	Phil	57	7	20	27	142	+13
82-83	Phil	35	2	11	13	40	+7
83-84	NJ	58	4	12	16	61	-20
84-85	NJ	37	1	6	7	65	-15
Totals		198	14	52	66	325	-21

Playoffs

SSN	TEAM	GP	G	A	PTS.	PIM	+/-
81-82	Phil	2	0	1	1	25	
82-83	Phil	1	0	0	0	0	
Totals		3	0	1	1	25	

HOFFORD, James 6-0 190 D
B. Sudbury, Ont., Oct. 4, 1964

SSN	TEAM	GP	G	A	PTS.	PIM	+/-
85-86	Buf	5	0	0	0	5	-1
86-87	Buf	12	0	0	0	40	-1
88-89	LA	1	0	0	0	2	+2
Totals		18	0	0	0	47	0

HOGABOAM, William Harold 5-11 170 C
B. Swift Current, Sask., Sept. 5, 1949

SSN	TEAM	GP	G	A	PTS.	PIM	+/-
72-73	Atl-Det	6	1	0	1	2	-1
73-74	Det	47	18	23	41	12	-3
74-75	Det	60	14	27	41	16	-34
75-76	Det-Minn	68	28	23	51	36	-12
76-77	Minn	73	10	15	25	16	-17
77-78	Minn	8	1	2	3	4	-5
78-79	Minn-Det	28	5	7	12	4	-6
79-80	Det	42	3	12	15	10	-8
Totals		332	80	109	189	100	-86

Playoffs

SSN	TEAM	GP	G	A	PTS.	PIM	+/-
76-77	Minn	2	0	0	0	0	

HOGANSON, Dale Gordon (Red) 5-10 190 D
B. North Battleford, Sask., July 8, 1949

SSN	TEAM	GP	G	A	PTS.	PIM	+/-
69-70	LA	49	1	7	8	37	-21
70-71	LA	70	4	10	14	52	-16
71-72	LA-Mont	31	1	2	3	16	+3
72-73	Mont	25	0	2	2	2	+4
73-74	Que (WHA)	62	8	33	41	27	
74-75	Que (WHA)	78	9	35	44	47	
75-76	Que (WHA)	45	3	14	17	18	
76-77	Birm (WHA)	81	7	48	55	48	
77-78	Birm (WHA)	43	1	12	13	29	
78-79	Que (WHA)	69	2	19	21	17	
79-80	Que	77	4	36	40	31	-42
80-81	Que	61	3	14	17	32	-8
81-82	Que	30	0	6	6	16	-24
NHL Totals		343	13	77	90	186	-104
WHA Totals		378	30	161	191	186	

Playoffs

SSN	TEAM	GP	G	A	PTS.	PIM	+/-
74-75	Que (WHA)	13	1	3	4	4	
75-76	Que (WHA)	5	1	3	4	2	
77-78	Birm (WHA)	5	0	0	0	7	
78-79	Que (WHA)	4	0	0	0	2	
80-81	Que	5	0	3	3	10	
81-82	Que	6	0	0	0	2	
NHL Totals		11	0	3	3	12	
WHA Totals		27	2	6	8	15	

HOGLUND, Jonas 6-3 200 RW
B. Hammond, Sweden, Aug. 29, 1972

SSN	TEAM	GP	G	A	PTS.	PIM	+/-
96-97	Calg	68	19	16	35	12	-4
97-98	Calg-Mont	78	12	13	25	22	-7
98-99	Mont	74	8	10	18	16	-5
Totals		218	39	39	78	50	-16

Playoffs

SSN	TEAM	GP	G	A	PTS.	PIM	+/-
97-98	Mont	10	2	0	2	0	

HOGUE, Benoit 5-10 190 C
B. Repentigny, Que., Oct. 28, 1966

SSN	TEAM	GP	G	A	PTS.	PIM	+/-
87-88	Buf	3	1	1	2	0	+3
88-89	Buf	69	14	30	44	120	-5
89-90	Buf	45	11	7	18	79	0
90-91	Buf	76	19	28	47	76	-8
91-92	Buf-NYI	75	30	46	76	67	+30
92-93	NYI	70	33	42	75	108	+13
93-94	NYI	83	36	33	69	73	-7
94-95	NYI-Tor	45	9	7	16	34	0
95-96	Tor-Dal	78	19	45	64	104	+10
96-97	Dal	73	19	24	43	54	+8
97-98	Dal	53	6	16	22	35	+7
98-99	TB-Dal	74	12	17	29	54	-10
Totals		744	209	296	505	804	+41

Playoffs

SSN	TEAM	GP	G	A	PTS.	PIM	+/-
88-89	Buf	5	0	0	0	17	
89-90	Buf	3	0	0	0	10	
90-91	Buf	5	3	1	4	10	
92-93	NYI	18	6	6	12	31	
93-94	NYI	4	0	1	1	4	
94-95	Tor	7	0	0	0	6	
96-97	Dal	7	2	2	4	6	
97-98	Dal	17	4	2	6	16	
98-99	Dal	14	0	2	2	16	
Totals		80	15	14	29	116	

HOLAN, Milos 5-11 191 D
B. Bilovec, Czechoslovakia, Apr. 22, 1971

SSN	TEAM	GP	G	A	PTS.	PIM	+/-
93-94	Phil	8	1	1	2	4	-4
94-95	Ana	25	2	8	10	14	+4
95-96	Ana	16	2	2	4	24	-12
Totals		49	5	11	16	42	-12

HOLBROOK, Terry Eugene 6-0 185 RW
B. Petrolia, Ont., July 11, 1950

SSN	TEAM	GP	G	A	PTS.	PIM	+/-
72-73	Minn	21	2	3	5	0	-4
73-74	Minn	22	1	3	4	4	-3
74-75	Clev (WHA)	78	10	13	23	7	
75-76	Clev (WHA)	15	1	2	3	6	
NHL Totals		43	3	6	9	4	-7
WHA Totals		93	11	15	26	13	

Playoffs

SSN	TEAM	GP	G	A	PTS.	PIM	+/-
72-73	Minn	6	0	0	0	0	
74-75	Clev (WHA)	5	0	1	1	0	
75-76	Clev (WHA)	3	0	0	0	0	
NHL Totals		6	0	0	0	0	
WHA Totals		8	0	1	1	0	

HOLDEN, Josh 6-0 190 C
B. Calgary, Alta., Jan. 18, 1978

SSN	TEAM	GP	G	A	PTS.	PIM	+/-
98-99	Van	30	2	4	6	10	-10

HOLIK, Robert (Bobby) 6-3 220 LW
B. Jihlava, Czechoslovakia, Jan. 1, 1971

SSN	TEAM	GP	G	A	PTS.	PIM	+/-
90-91	Hart	78	21	22	43	113	-3
91-92	Hart	76	21	24	45	44	+4
92-93	NJ	61	20	19	39	76	-6
93-94	NJ	70	13	20	33	72	+28
94-95	NJ	48	10	10	20	18	+9
95-96	NJ	63	13	17	30	58	+9
96-97	NJ	82	23	39	62	54	+24
97-98	NJ	82	29	36	65	100	+23
98-99	NJ	78	27	37	64	119	+16
Totals		638	177	224	401	654	+104

Playoffs

SSN	TEAM	GP	G	A	PTS.	PIM	+/-
90-91	Hart	6	0	0	0	7	
91-92	Hart	7	0	1	1	6	
92-93	NJ	5	1	1	2	6	
93-94	NJ	20	0	3	3	6	
94-95	NJ	20	4	4	8	22	
96-97	NJ	10	2	3	5	4	
97-98	NJ	5	0	0	0	8	
98-99	NJ	7	0	7	7	6	
Totals		80	7	19	26	65	

HOLLAND, Jason 6-2 193 D
B. Morinville, Alta., April 30, 1976

SSN	TEAM	GP	G	A	PTS.	PIM	+/-
96-97	NYI	4	1	0	1	0	+1
97-98	NYI	8	0	0	0	4	-4
98-99	Buf	3	0	0	0	8	-1
Totals		15	1	0	1	12	-4

HOLLAND, Jerry Allan 5-10 190 LW
B. Bearverlodge, Alta., Aug. 25, 1954

SSN	TEAM	GP	G	A	PTS.	PIM	+/-
74-75	NYR	1	1	0	1	0	+1
75-76	NYR	36	7	4	11	6	-5
77-78	Edm (WHA)	22	2	1	3	14	
NHL Totals		37	8	4	12	6	-4
WHA Totals		22	2	1	3	14	

*HOLLETT, Frank William (Flash) 6-0 180 D
B. North Sydney, N.S., Apr. 13, 1912

SSN	TEAM	GP	G	A	PTS.	PIM	+/-
33-34	Tor-Ott	34	7	4	11	25	
34-35	Tor	48	10	16	26	38	
35-36	Tor-Bos	17	2	6	8	10	
36-37	Bos	47	3	7	10	22	
37-38	Bos	48	4	10	14	54	
38-39	Bos	47	10	17	27	35	
39-40	Bos	44	10	18	28	18	
40-41	Bos	42	9	15	24	23	
41-42	Bos	48	19	14	33	41	
42-43	Bos	50	19	25	44	19	
43-44	Bos-Det	52	15	19	34	38	
44-45	Det	50	20	21	41	39	
45-46	Det	38	4	9	13	16	
Totals		565	132	181	313	378	

Playoffs

SSN	TEAM	GP	G	A	PTS.	PIM	+/-
34-35	Tor	7	0	0	0	6	
36-37	Tor	3	0	0	0	2	
37-38	Bos	3	0	1	1	0	
38-39	Bos	12	1	3	4	2	
39-40	Bos	5	1	2	3	2	
40-41	Bos	11	3	4	7	8	
41-42	Bos	5	0	1	1	2	
42-43	Bos	9	0	9	9	4	
43-44	Det	5	0	0	0	6	
44-45	Det	14	3	4	7	6	
45-46	Det	5	0	2	2	0	
Totals		79	8	26	34	38	

HOLLINGER, Terry 6-1 200 D
B. Regina, Sask., Feb. 24, 1971

SSN	TEAM	GP	G	A	PTS.	PIM	+/-
93-94	StL	2	0	0	0	0	+1
94-95	StL	5	0	0	0	2	-1
Totals		7	0	0	0	2	0

*HOLLINGWORTH, Gordon (Bucky) 5-11 185 D
B. Verdun, Que., July 24, 1933

SSN	TEAM	GP	G	A	PTS.	PIM	+/-
54-55	Chi	70	3	9	12	135	
55-56	Chi	41	0	2	2	28	
56-57	Det	25	0	1	1	16	
57-58	Det	27	1	2	3	22	
Totals		163	4	14	18	201	

Playoffs

SSN	TEAM	GP	G	A	PTS.	PIM	+/-
55-56	Det	3	0	0	0	2	

HOLLOWAY, Bruce 6-0 200 D
B. Revelstoke, B.C., June 27, 1963

SSN	TEAM	GP	G	A	PTS.	PIM	+/-
84-85	Van	2	0	0	0	0	-1

HOLMES, Charles Frank (Chuck) 6-0 185 RW
B. Edmonton, Alta., Sept. 21, 1934

SSN	TEAM	GP	G	A	PTS.	PIM	+/-
58-59	Det	15	0	3	3	6	
61-62	Det	8	1	0	1	4	
Totals		23	1	3	4	10	

HOLMES, Louis 5-10 150 F
B. England, Jan. 29, 1911

SSN	TEAM	GP	G	A	PTS.	PIM	+/-
31-32	Chi	41	1	4	5	6	
32-33	Chi	18	0	0	0	0	
Totals		59	1	4	5	6	

Playoffs

SSN	TEAM	GP	G	A	PTS.	PIM	+/-
31-32	Chi	2	0	0	0	2	

HOLMES, Warren 6-1 195 C
B. Beeton, Ont., Feb. 18, 1957

SSN	TEAM	GP	G	A	PTS.	PIM	+/-
81-82	LA	3	0	2	2	0	+1
82-83	LA	39	8	16	24	7	-8
83-84	LA	3	0	0	0	0	-3
Totals		45	8	18	26	7	-10

*HOLMES, William F
B. Weyburn, Sask., 1899

SSN	TEAM	GP	G	A	PTS.	PIM	+/-
25-26	Mont	9	1	0	1	2	
26-27	NYA	1	0	0	0	0	
29-30	NYA	42	5	4	9	33	

SSN	TEAM	GP	G	A	PTS.	PIM	+/-
Totals		52	6	4	10	35	

HOLMGREN, Paul Howard 6–3 210 RW
B. St. Paul, Minn., Dec. 22, 1955

SSN	TEAM	GP	G	A	PTS.	PIM	+/-
75–76	Minn (WHA)	51	14	16	30	121	
75–76	Phil	1	0	0	0	2	0
76–77	Phil	59	14	12	26	201	+10
77–78	Phil	62	16	18	34	190	+23
78–79	Phil	57	19	10	29	168	+2
79–80	Phil	74	30	35	65	267	+35
80–81	Phil	77	22	37	59	306	+12
81–82	Phil	41	9	22	31	183	+10
82–83	Phil	77	19	24	43	178	+18
83–84	Phil–Minn	63	11	18	29	151	-1
84–85	Minn	16	4	3	7	38	-4
NHL Totals		527	144	179	323	1684	+105
WHA Totals		51	14	16	30	121	

Playoffs

SSN	TEAM	GP	G	A	PTS.	PIM
76–77	Phil	10	1	1	2	25
77–78	Phil	12	1	4	5	26
78–79	Phil	8	1	5	6	22
79–80	Phil	18	10	10	20	47
80–81	Phil	12	5	9	14	49
81–82	Phil	4	1	2	3	6
82–83	Phil	3	0	0	0	6
83–84	Minn	12	0	1	1	6
84–85	Minn	3	0	0	0	8
Totals		82	19	32	51	195

HOLMSTROM, Tomas 6–0 200 LW
B. Pitea, Sweden, Jan. 23, 1973

SSN	TEAM	GP	G	A	PTS.	PIM	+/-
96–97	Det	47	6	3	9	33	-10
97–98	Det	57	5	17	22	44	+6
98–99	Det	82	13	21	34	69	-11
Totals		186	24	41	65	146	-15

Playoffs

SSN	TEAM	GP	G	A	PTS.	PIM
96–97	Det	1	0	0	0	0
97–98	Det	22	7	12	19	16
98–99	Det	10	4	3	7	4
Totals		33	11	15	26	20

*HOLOTA, John Paul 5–6 160 C
B. Hamilton, Ont., Feb. 25, 1921

SSN	TEAM	GP	G	A	PTS.	PIM
42–43	Det	12	2	0	2	0
45–46	Det	3	0	0	0	0
Totals		15	2	0	2	0

HOLST, Greg 5–10 170 C
B. Montreal, Que., Feb. 21, 1954

SSN	TEAM	GP	G	A	PTS.	PIM	+/-
75–76	NYR	2	0	0	0	0	-3
76–77	NYR	5	0	0	0	0	-2
77–78	NYR	4	0	0	0	0	-1
Totals		11	0	0	0	0	-6

HOLT, Gareth Ray (Gary) 5–9 175 LW
B. Sarnia, Ont., Nov. 1, 1952

SSN	TEAM	GP	G	A	PTS.	PIM	+/-
73–74	Cal	1	0	0	0	0	0
74–75	Cal	1	0	1	1	0	+1
75–76	Cal	48	6	5	11	50	-10
76–77	Clev	2	0	1	1	2	-1
77–78	StL	49	7	4	11	81	-6
Totals		101	13	11	24	133	-16

HOLT, Stewart Randall (Randy) 5–11 185 D
B. Pembroke, Ont., Jan. 15, 1953

SSN	TEAM	GP	G	A	PTS.	PIM	+/-
74–75	Chi	12	0	1	1	13	-1
75–76	Chi	12	0	0	0	13	-12
76–77	Chi	12	0	3	3	14	-4
77–78	Chi–Clev	54	1	4	5	24	-28
78–79	Van–LA	58	1	9	10	282	-3
79–80	LA	42	0	1	1	94	-3
80–81	Calg	48	0	5	5	165	-6
81–82	Calg–Wash	61	2	6	8	259	-11
82–83	Wash	70	0	8	8	275	-7
83–84	Phil	26	0	0	0	74	-1
Totals		395	4	37	41	1438	-76

Playoffs

SSN	TEAM	GP	G	A	PTS.	PIM
76–77	Chi	2	0	0	0	7
78–79	LA	2	0	0	0	4
80–81	Calg	13	2	2	4	52
82–83	Wash	4	0	1	1	20
Totals		21	2	3	5	83

HOLWAY, Albert Robert (Toots) 6–1 190 D
B. Toronto, Ont., Sept. 24, 1902

SSN	TEAM	GP	G	A	PTS.	PIM
23–24	Tor	6	1	0	1	0
24–25	Tor	25	2	2	4	20
25–26	Tor–Mont M	29	0	0	0	6
26–27	Mont M	13	0	0	0	10
28–29	Pitt Pi	44	4	0	4	20
Totals		117	7	2	9	56

Playoffs

SSN	TEAM	GP	G	A	PTS.	PIM
24–25	Tor	2	0	0	0	0
25–26	Mont M	6	0	0	0	2
Totals		8	0	0	0	2

HOLZINGER, Brian 5–11 180 C
B. Parma, Ohio, Oct. 10, 1972

SSN	TEAM	GP	G	A	PTS.	PIM	+/-
94–95	Buf	4	0	3	3	0	+2
95–96	Buf	58	10	10	20	37	-21
96–97	Buf	81	22	29	51	54	+9
97–98	Buf	69	14	21	35	36	-2
98–99	Buf	81	17	17	34	45	+2
Totals		293	63	80	143	172	-10

Playoffs

SSN	TEAM	GP	G	A	PTS.	PIM
94–95	Buf	4	2	1	3	2
96–97	Buf	12	2	5	7	8
97–98	Buf	15	4	7	11	18
98–99	Buf	21	3	5	8	33
Totals		52	11	18	29	61

HOMENUKE, Ronald Wayne 5–10 180 RW
B. Hazelton, B.C., Jan. 5, 1952

SSN	TEAM	GP	G	A	PTS.	PIM	+/-
72–73	Van	1	0	0	0	0	-3

HOOVER, Ron 6–1 185 C/LW
B. Oakville, Ont., Oct. 28, 1966

SSN	TEAM	GP	G	A	PTS.	PIM	+/-
89–90	Bos	2	0	0	0	0	-2
90–91	Bos	15	4	0	4	31	0
91–92	StL	1	0	0	0	0	0
Totals		18	4	0	4	31	-2

Playoffs

SSN	TEAM	GP	G	A	PTS.	PIM
90–91	Bos	8	0	0	0	18

HOPKINS, Dean Robert 6–1 210 RW
B. Cobourg, Ont., June 6, 1959

SSN	TEAM	GP	G	A	PTS.	PIM	+/-
79–80	LA	60	8	6	14	39	-16
80–81	LA	67	8	18	26	118	+6
81–82	LA	41	2	13	15	102	-20
82–83	LA	49	5	12	17	43	-5
85–86	Edm	1	0	0	0	0	0
88–89	Que	5	0	2	2	4	+1
Totals		223	23	51	74	306	-34

Playoffs

SSN	TEAM	GP	G	A	PTS.	PIM
79–80	LA	4	0	1	1	5
80–81	LA	4	1	0	1	9
81–82	LA	10	0	4	4	15
Totals		18	1	5	6	29

HOPKINS, Larry Harold 6–1 215 LW
B. Oshawa, Ont., Mar. 17, 1954

SSN	TEAM	GP	G	A	PTS.	PIM	+/-
77–78	Tor	2	0	0	0	0	0
79–80	Winn	5	0	0	0	0	-3
81–82	Winn	41	10	15	25	22	+8
82–83	Winn	12	3	1	4	4	+5
Totals		60	13	16	29	26	+10

Playoffs

SSN	TEAM	GP	G	A	PTS.	PIM
81–82	Winn	4	0	0	0	2
82–83	Winn	2	0	0	0	0
Totals		6	0	0	0	2

HORACEK, Tony 6–4 210 LW
B. Vancouver, B.C., Feb. 3, 1967

SSN	TEAM	GP	G	A	PTS.	PIM	+/-
89–90	Phil	48	5	5	10	117	+6
90–91	Phil	34	3	6	9	49	+6
91–92	Phil–Chi	46	2	7	9	72	-7
93–94	Chi	7	0	0	0	53	+1
94–95	Chi	19	0	1	1	25	-4
Totals		154	10	19	29	316	+2

Playoffs

SSN	TEAM	GP	G	A	PTS.	PIM
91–92	Chi	2	1	0	1	2

HORAVA, Miloslav 6–0 193 D
B. Kladno, Czechoslovakia, Aug. 14, 1961

SSN	TEAM	GP	G	A	PTS.	PIM	+/-
88–89	NYR	6	0	1	1	0	-2
89–90	NYR	45	4	10	14	26	+10
90–91	NYR	29	1	6	7	12	+2
Totals		80	5	17	22	38	+10

Playoffs

SSN	TEAM	GP	G	A	PTS.	PIM
89–90	NYR	2	0	1	1	0

HORBUL, Douglas George 5–9 170 LW
B. Nokomis, Sask., July 27, 1952

SSN	TEAM	GP	G	A	PTS.	PIM	+/-
74–75	KC	4	1	0	1	2	-3

HORDY, Michael 5–10 180 D
B. Thunder Bay, Ont., Oct. 10, 1956

SSN	TEAM	GP	G	A	PTS.	PIM	+/-
78–79	NYI	2	0	0	0	0	0
79–80	NYI	9	0	0	0	7	0
Totals		11	0	0	0	7	0

HORECK, Peter 5–9 160 RW
B. Massey, Ont., June 15, 1923

SSN	TEAM	GP	G	A	PTS.	PIM
44–45	Chi	50	20	16	36	44
45–46	Chi	50	20	21	41	34
46–47	Chi–Det	56	16	19	35	61
47–48	Det	50	12	17	29	44
48–49	Det	60	14	16	30	46
49–50	Bos	34	5	5	10	22
50–51	Bos	66	10	13	23	57
51–52	Chi	60	9	11	20	22
Totals		426	106	118	224	330

Playoffs

SSN	TEAM	GP	G	A	PTS.	PIM
45–46	Chi	4	0	0	0	2
46–47	Det	5	2	0	2	6
47–48	Det	10	3	7	10	12
48–49	Det	11	1	1	2	10
50–51	Bos	4	0	0	0	13
Totals		34	6	8	14	43

*HORNE, George (Shorty) F

SSN	TEAM	GP	G	A	PTS.	PIM
25–26	Mont M	13	0	0	0	2
26–27	Mont M	2	0	0	0	0
28–29	Tor	39	9	3	12	32
Totals		54	9	3	12	34

Playoffs

SSN	TEAM	GP	G	A	PTS.	PIM
28–29	Tor	4	0	0	0	4

HORNER, George Reginald (Red) 6–0 190 D
B. Lynden, Ont., May 29, 1909

SSN	TEAM	GP	G	A	PTS.	PIM
28–29	Tor	22	0	0	0	30
29–30	Tor	33	2	7	9	96
30–31	Tor	42	1	11	12	71
31–32	Tor	42	7	9	16	97
32–33	Tor	48	3	8	11	144
33–34	Tor	40	11	10	21	146
34–35	Tor	46	4	8	12	125
35–36	Tor	43	2	9	11	167
36–37	Tor	48	3	9	12	124
37–38	Tor	47	4	20	24	92
38–39	Tor	48	4	10	14	85
39–40	Tor	31	1	9	10	87
Totals		490	42	110	152	1264

Playoffs

SSN	TEAM	GP	G	A	PTS.	PIM
28–29	Tor	4	1	0	1	2
30–31	Tor	2	0	0	0	0
31–32	Tor	7	2	2	4	20
32–33	Tor	9	1	0	1	10
33–34	Tor	5	1	0	1	6
34–35	Tor	7	0	1	1	4
35–36	Tor	9	1	2	3	22
36–37	Tor	2	0	0	0	7
37–38	Tor	7	0	1	1	14
38–39	Tor	10	1	2	3	26
39–40	Tor	9	0	2	2	55
Totals		71	7	10	17	166

HORNUNG, Lawrence John 6–0 190 D
B. Gravelburg, Sask., Oct. 10, 1945

SSN	TEAM	GP	G	A	PTS.	PIM	+/-
70–71	StL	1	0	0	0	0	+1
71–72	StL	47	2	9	11	10	-1
72–73	Winn (WHA)	77	13	45	58	28	
73–74	Winn (WHA)	51	4	19	23	18	
74–75	Winn (WHA)	69	7	25	32	21	

SSN	TEAM	GP	G	A	PTS.	PIM	+/-
75–76	Winn (WHA)	76	3	18	21	26	
76–77	Edm–SD (WHA)	79	6	10	16	8	
77–78	Winn (WHA)	19	1	4	5	2	
NHL Totals		48	2	9	11	10	0
WHA Totals		371	34	121	155	103	

Playoffs

SSN	TEAM	GP	G	A	PTS.	PIM	
71–72	StL	11	0	2	2	2	
72–73	Winn (WHA)	14	2	9	11	0	
73–74	Winn (WHA)	4	0	0	0	0	
75–76	Winn (WHA)	13	0	3	3	6	
76–77	SD (WHA)	6	0	0	0	0	
NHL Totals		11	0	2	2	2	
WHA Totals		37	2	12	14	6	

*HORTON, Miles Gilbert (Tim) *5–10 180 D*
B. Cochrane, Ont., Jan. 12, 1930

SSN	TEAM	GP	G	A	PTS.	PIM	+/-
49–50	Tor	1	0	0	0	2	
51–52	Tor	4	0	0	0	8	
52–53	Tor	70	2	14	16	85	
53–54	Tor	70	7	24	31	94	
54–55	Tor	67	5	9	14	84	
55–56	Tor	35	0	5	5	36	
56–57	Tor	66	6	19	25	72	
57–58	Tor	53	6	20	26	39	
58–59	Tor	70	5	21	26	76	
59–60	Tor	70	3	29	32	69	
60–61	Tor	57	6	15	21	75	
61–62	Tor	70	10	28	38	88	
62–63	Tor	70	6	19	25	69	
63–64	Tor	70	9	20	29	71	
64–65	Tor	70	12	16	28	95	
65–66	Tor	70	6	22	28	76	
66–67	Tor	70	8	17	25	70	
67–68	Tor	69	4	23	27	82	+20
68–69	Tor	74	11	29	40	107	+14
69–70	Tor–NYR	74	4	24	28	107	-3
70–71	NYR	78	2	18	20	57	+28
71–72	Pitt	44	2	9	11	40	+5
72–73	Buf	69	1	16	17	56	+12
73–74	Buf	55	0	6	6	53	+5
Totals		1446	115	403	518	1611	+81

Playoffs

SSN	TEAM	GP	G	A	PTS.	PIM	
49–50	Tor	1	0	0	0	2	
53–54	Tor	5	1	1	2	4	
55–56	Tor	2	0	1	1	4	
58–59	Tor	12	0	3	3	16	
59–60	Tor	10	0	1	1	6	
60–61	Tor	5	0	0	0	0	
61–62	Tor	12	3	13	16	16	
62–63	Tor	10	1	3	4	10	
63–64	Tor	14	0	4	4	20	
64–65	Tor	6	0	2	2	13	
65–66	Tor	4	1	0	1	12	
66–67	Tor	12	3	5	8	25	
68–69	Tor	4	0	0	0	7	
69–70	NYR	6	1	1	2	28	
70–71	NYR	13	1	4	5	14	
71–72	Pitt	4	0	1	1	2	
72–73	Buf	6	0	1	1	4	
Totals		126	11	39	50	183	

HORVATH, Bronco Joseph *5–10 185 C*
B. Port Colborne, Ont., Mar. 12, 1930

SSN	TEAM	GP	G	A	PTS.	PIM	+/-
55–56	NYR	66	12	17	29	40	
56–57	NYR–Mont	8	1	2	3	4	
57–58	Bos	67	30	36	66	71	
58–59	Bos	45	19	20	39	58	
59–60	Bos	68	39	41	80	60	
60–61	Bos	47	15	15	30	15	
61–62	Chi	69	17	29	46	21	
62–63	NYR–Tor	50	7	19	26	46	
67–68	Minn	14	1	6	7	4	-6
Totals		434	141	185	326	319	-6

Playoffs

SSN	TEAM	GP	G	A	PTS.	PIM	
55–56	NYR	5	1	2	3	4	
57–58	Bos	12	5	3	8	8	
58–59	Bos	7	2	3	5	0	
61–62	Chi	12	4	1	5	6	
Totals		36	12	9	21	18	

HOSPODAR, Edward David *6–2 210 D*
B. Bowling Green, Ohio, Feb. 9, 1959

SSN	TEAM	GP	G	A	PTS.	PIM	+/-
79–80	NYR	20	0	1	1	76	-2
80–81	NYR	61	5	14	19	214	+10
81–82	NYR	41	3	8	11	152	-8
82–83	Hart	72	1	9	10	199	-32
83–84	Hart	59	0	9	9	163	-17
84–85	Phil	50	3	4	7	130	+7
85–86	Phil–Minn	60	3	3	6	146	+8
86–87	Phil	45	2	2	4	136	-8
87–88	Buf	42	0	1	1	98	-1
Totals		450	17	51	68	1314	-43

Playoffs

SSN	TEAM	GP	G	A	PTS.	PIM	
79–80	NYR	7	1	0	1	42	
80–81	NYR	12	2	0	2	93	
84–85	Phil	18	1	1	2	69	
85–86	Minn	2	0	0	0	0	
86–87	Phil	5	0	0	0	2	
Totals		44	4	1	5	206	

HOSSA, Marian *6–1 194 LW*
B. Stara Lubovna, Slovakia, Jan. 12, 1979

SSN	TEAM	GP	G	A	PTS.	PIM	+/-
97–98	Ott	7	0	1	1	0	-1
98–99	Ott	60	15	15	30	37	+18
Totals		67	15	16	31	37	+17

Playoffs

SSN	TEAM	GP	G	A	PTS.	PIM	
98–99	Ott	4	0	2	2	4	

HOSTAK, Martin *6–3 198 C*
B. Hradec Kralove, Czech., Nov. 11, 1967

SSN	TEAM	GP	G	A	PTS.	PIM	+/-
90–91	Phil	50	3	10	13	22	+1
91–92	Phil	5	0	1	1	2	-1
Totals		55	3	11	14	24	0

HOTHAM, Gregory *5–11 185 D*
B. London, Ont., Mar. 7, 1956

SSN	TEAM	GP	G	A	PTS.	PIM	+/-
79–80	Tor	46	3	10	13	10	-4
80–81	Tor	11	1	1	2	11	+4
81–82	Tor–Pitt	28	4	6	10	16	-11
82–83	Pitt	58	2	30	32	39	-14
83–84	Pitt	76	5	25	30	59	-25
84–85	Pitt	11	0	2	2	4	-3
Totals		230	15	74	89	139	-53

Playoffs

SSN	TEAM	GP	G	A	PTS.	PIM	
81–82	Pitt	5	0	3	3	6	

HOUCK, Paul *5–11 185 RW*
B. North Vancouver, B.C., Aug. 12, 1963

SSN	TEAM	GP	G	A	PTS.	PIM	+/-
85–86	Minn	3	1	0	1	0	+1
86–87	Minn	12	0	2	2	2	-2
87–88	Minn	1	0	0	0	0	0
Totals		16	1	2	3	2	-1

HOUDA, Doug *6–2 190 D*
B. Blairmore, Alta., June 3, 1966

SSN	TEAM	GP	G	A	PTS.	PIM	+/-
85–86	Det	6	0	0	0	4	-7
87–88	Det	11	1	1	2	10	0
88–89	Det	57	2	11	13	67	+17
89–90	Det	73	2	9	11	127	-5
90–91	Det–Hart	41	1	6	7	84	-5
91–92	Hart	56	3	6	9	125	-2
92–93	Hart	60	2	6	8	167	-19
93–94	Hart–LA	61	2	6	8	188	-19
94–95	Buf	28	1	2	3	68	+1
95–96	Buf	38	1	3	4	52	+3
96–97	NYI	70	2	8	10	99	+1
97–98	NYI–Ana	55	2	4	6	99	-11
98–99	Det	3	0	1	1	0	-2
Totals		559	19	63	82	1090	-48

Playoffs

SSN	TEAM	GP	G	A	PTS.	PIM	
88–89	Det	6	0	1	1	0	
90–91	Hart	6	0	0	0	8	
91–92	Hart	6	0	2	2	13	
Totals		18	0	3	3	21	

HOUDE, Claude Daniel *6–1 190 D*
B. Drummondville, Que., Nov. 8, 1947

SSN	TEAM	GP	G	A	PTS.	PIM	+/-
74–75	KC	34	3	4	7	20	-31
75–76	KC	25	0	2	2	20	-13
Totals		59	3	6	9	40	-44

HOUDE, Eric *5–11 190 C*
B. Montreal, Que., Dec. 19, 1976

SSN	TEAM	GP	G	A	PTS.	PIM	+/-
96–97	Mont	13	0	2	2	2	+1
97–98	Mont	9	1	0	1	0	-3
98–99	Mont	8	1	1	2	2	-2
Totals		30	2	3	5	4	-4

HOUGH, Mike *6–1 192 LW*
B. Montreal, Que., Feb. 6, 1963

SSN	TEAM	GP	G	A	PTS.	PIM	+/-
86–87	Que	56	6	8	14	79	-8
87–88	Que	17	3	2	5	2	-8
88–89	Que	46	9	10	19	39	-7
89–90	Que	43	13	13	26	84	-24
90–91	Que	63	13	20	33	111	-7
91–92	Que	61	16	22	38	77	-1
92–93	Que	77	8	22	30	69	-11
93–94	Fla	78	6	23	29	62	+3
94–95	Fla	48	6	7	13	38	+1
95–96	Fla	64	7	16	23	37	+4
96–97	Fla	69	8	6	14	48	+12
97–98	NYI	74	5	7	12	27	-4
98–99	NYI	11	0	0	0	2	-2
Totals		707	100	156	256	675	-52

Playoffs

SSN	TEAM	GP	G	A	PTS.	PIM	
86–87	Que	9	0	3	3	26	
92–93	Que	6	0	1	1	2	
95–96	Fla	22	4	1	5	8	
96–97	Fla	5	1	0	1	2	
Totals		42	5	5	10	38	

HOULDER, Bill *6–3 212 D*
B. Thunder Bay, Ont., Mar. 11, 1967

SSN	TEAM	GP	G	A	PTS.	PIM	+/-
87–88	Wash	30	1	2	3	10	-2
88–89	Wash	8	0	3	3	4	+7
89–90	Wash	41	1	11	12	28	+8
90–91	Buf	7	0	2	2	4	-2
91–92	Buf	10	1	0	1	8	-2
92–93	Buf	15	3	5	8	6	+5
93–94	Ana	80	14	25	39	40	-18
94–95	StL	41	5	13	18	20	+16
95–96	TB	61	5	23	28	22	+1
96–97	TB	79	4	21	25	30	+16
97–98	SJ	82	7	25	32	48	+13
98–99	SJ	76	9	23	32	40	+8
Totals		530	50	153	203	260	+50

Playoffs

SSN	TEAM	GP	G	A	PTS.	PIM	
92–93	Buf	8	0	2	2	4	
94–95	StL	4	1	1	2	0	
95–96	TB	6	0	1	1	4	
97–98	SJ	6	1	2	3	2	
98–99	SJ	6	3	0	3	4	
Totals		30	5	6	11	14	

HOULE, Rejean *5–11 170 LW/RW*
B. Rouyn, Que., Oct. 25, 1949

SSN	TEAM	GP	G	A	PTS.	PIM	+/-
69–70	Mont	9	0	1	1	0	+1
70–71	Mont	66	10	9	19	28	+7
71–72	Mont	77	11	17	28	21	+9
72–73	Mont	72	13	35	48	36	+24
73–74	Que (WHA)	69	27	35	62	17	
74–75	Que (WHA)	64	40	52	92	37	
75–76	Que (WHA)	81	51	52	103	61	
76–77	Mont	65	22	30	52	24	+39
77–78	Mont	76	30	28	58	50	+39
78–79	Mont	66	17	34	51	43	+16
79–80	Mont	60	18	27	45	68	+3
80–81	Mont	77	27	31	58	83	+20
81–82	Mont	51	11	32	43	34	+18
82–83	Mont	16	2	3	5	8	+4
NHL Totals		635	161	247	408	395	+180
WHA Totals		214	118	139	257	115	

Playoffs

SSN	TEAM	GP	G	A	PTS.	PIM	
70–71	Mont	20	2	5	7	20	
71–72	Mont	6	0	0	0	2	
72–73	Mont	17	3	6	9	0	
74–75	Que (WHA)	15	10	6	16	2	
75–76	Que (WHA)	5	2	0	2	8	
76–77	Mont	6	0	1	1	4	
77–78	Mont	15	3	8	11	14	
78–79	Mont	7	1	5	6	2	
79–80	Mont	10	4	5	9	12	
80–81	Mont	3	1	0	1	6	
81–82	Mont	5	0	4	4	6	
82–83	Mont	1	0	0	0	0	
NHL Totals		90	14	34	48	66	
WHA Totals		20	12	6	18	10	

HOUSLEY, Phil 5-10 179 D
B. St. Paul, Minn., Mar. 9, 1964

SSN	TEAM	GP	G	A	PTS.	PIM	+/-
82–83	Buf	77	19	47	66	39	-4
83–84	Buf	75	31	46	77	33	+3
84–85	Buf	73	16	53	69	28	+15
85–86	Buf	79	15	47	62	54	-9
86–87	Buf	78	21	46	67	57	-2
87–88	Buf	74	29	37	66	96	-17
88–89	Buf	72	26	44	70	47	+6
89–90	Buf	80	21	60	81	32	+11
90–91	Winn	78	23	53	76	24	-13
91–92	Winn	74	23	63	86	92	-5
92–93	Winn	80	18	79	97	52	-14
93–94	StL	26	7	15	22	12	-5
94–95	Calg	43	8	35	43	18	+17
95–96	Calg–NJ	81	17	51	68	30	-6
96–97	Wash	77	11	29	40	24	-10
97–98	Wash	64	6	25	31	24	-10
98–99	Calg	79	11	43	54	52	+14
Totals		1210	302	773	1075	714	-29

Playoffs

SSN	TEAM	GP	G	A	PTS.	PIM
82–83	Buf	10	3	4	7	2
83–84	Buf	3	0	0	0	6
84–85	Buf	5	3	2	5	2
87–88	Buf	6	2	4	6	6
88–89	Buf	5	1	3	4	2
89–90	Buf	6	1	4	5	4
91–92	Winn	7	1	4	5	0
92–93	Winn	6	0	7	7	2
93–94	StL	4	2	1	3	4
94–95	Calg	7	0	9	9	0
97–98	Wash	18	0	4	4	4
Totals		77	13	42	55	32

HOUSTON, Kenneth Lyle 6-2 210 RW
B. Desden, Ont., Sept. 15, 1953

SSN	TEAM	GP	G	A	PTS.	PIM	+/-
75–76	Atl	38	5	6	11	11	-3
76–77	Atl	78	20	24	44	35	+5
77–78	Atl	74	22	16	38	51	+4
78–79	Atl	80	21	31	52	135	+4
79–80	Atl	80	23	31	54	100	-1
80–81	Calg	42	15	15	30	93	0
81–82	Calg	70	22	22	44	91	-2
82–83	Wash	71	25	14	39	93	-8
83–84	Wash–LA	37	8	8	16	15	-5
Totals		570	161	167	328	624	-6

Playoffs

SSN	TEAM	GP	G	A	PTS.	PIM
75–76	Atl	2	0	0	0	0
76–77	Atl	3	0	0	0	4
77–78	Atl	2	0	0	0	0
78–79	Atl	1	1	0	1	16
79–80	Atl	4	1	1	2	10
80–81	Calg	16	7	8	15	28
81–82	Calg	3	1	0	1	4
82–83	Wash	4	1	0	1	4
Totals		35	11	9	20	66

HOWARD, Jack Francis (Frank) D
B. London, Ont., Oct. 15, 1915

SSN	TEAM	GP	G	A	PTS.	PIM
36–37	Tor	1	0	0	0	0

HOWATT, Garry Robert Charles 5-9 175 LW
B. Grand Center, Alta., Sept. 26, 1952

SSN	TEAM	GP	G	A	PTS.	PIM	+/-
72–73	NYI	8	0	1	1	18	-5
73–74	NYI	78	6	11	17	204	-13
74–75	NYI	77	18	30	48	121	+32
75–76	NYI	80	21	13	34	197	+26
76–77	NYI	70	13	15	28	182	+14
77–78	NYI	61	7	12	19	146	+7
78–79	NYI	75	16	12	28	205	+6
79–80	NYI	77	8	11	19	219	-3
80–81	NYI	70	4	15	19	174	+12
81–82	Hart	80	18	32	50	242	-5
82–83	NJ	38	1	4	5	114	-29
83–84	NJ	6	0	0	0	14	-1
Totals		720	112	156	268	1836	+41

Playoffs

SSN	TEAM	GP	G	A	PTS.	PIM
74–75	NYI	17	3	3	6	59
75–76	NYI	13	5	5	10	23
76–77	NYI	12	1	1	2	28
77–78	NYI	7	0	1	1	62
78–79	NYI	9	0	1	1	18
79–80	NYI	21	3	1	4	84
80–81	NYI	8	0	2	2	15

SSN	TEAM	GP	G	A	PTS.	PIM
Totals		87	12	14	26	289

HOWE, Gordon (Gordie) 6-0 205 RW
B. Floral, Sask., Mar. 31, 1928

SSN	TEAM	GP	G	A	PTS.	PIM	+/-
46–47	Det	58	7	15	22	52	
47–48	Det	60	16	28	44	63	
48–49	Det	40	12	25	37	57	
49–50	Det	70	35	33	68	69	
50–51	Det	70	43	43	86	74	
51–52	Det	70	47	39	86	78	
52–53	Det	70	49	46	95	57	
53–54	Det	70	33	48	81	109	
54–55	Det	64	29	33	62	68	
55–56	Det	70	38	41	79	100	
56–57	Det	70	44	45	89	72	
57–58	Det	64	33	44	77	40	
58–59	Det	70	32	46	78	57	
59–60	Det	70	28	45	73	46	
60–61	Det	64	23	49	72	30	
61–62	Det	70	33	44	77	54	
62–63	Det	70	38	48	86	100	
63–64	Det	69	26	47	73	70	
64–65	Det	70	29	47	76	104	
65–66	Det	70	29	46	75	83	
66–67	Det	69	25	40	65	53	
67–68	Det	74	39	43	82	53	+12
68–69	Det	76	44	59	103	58	+45
69–70	Det	76	31	40	71	58	+23
70–71	Det	63	23	29	52	38	-2
73–74	Hou (WHA)	70	31	69	100	46	
74–75	Hou (WHA)	75	34	65	99	84	
75–76	Hou (WHA)	78	32	70	102	76	
76–77	Hou (WHA)	62	24	44	68	57	
77–78	NE (WHA)	76	34	62	96	85	
78–79	NE (WHA)	58	19	24	43	51	
79–80	Hart	80	15	26	41	42	+9
NHL Totals		1767	801	1049	1850	1685	+87
WHA Totals		419	174	334	508	399	

Playoffs

SSN	TEAM	GP	G	A	PTS.	PIM
46–47	Det	5	0	0	0	18
47–48	Det	10	1	1	2	11
48–49	Det	11	8	3	11	19
49–50	Det	1	0	0	0	7
50–51	Det	6	4	3	7	4
51–52	Det	8	2	5	7	2
52–53	Det	6	2	5	7	2
53–54	Det	12	4	5	9	31
54–55	Det	11	9	11	20	24
55–56	Det	10	3	9	12	8
56–57	Det	5	2	5	7	6
57–58	Det	4	1	1	2	0
59–60	Det	6	1	5	6	4
60–61	Det	11	4	11	15	10
62–63	Det	11	7	9	16	22
63–64	Det	14	9	10	19	16
64–65	Det	7	4	2	6	20
65–66	Det	12	4	6	10	12
69–70	Det	4	2	0	2	2
73–74	Hou (WHA)	13	3	14	17	34
74–75	Hou (WHA)	13	8	12	20	20
75–76	Hou (WHA)	17	4	8	12	31
76–77	Hou (WHA)	11	5	3	8	11
77–78	NE (WHA)	14	5	5	10	15
78–79	NE (WHA)	10	3	1	4	4
79–80	Hart	3	1	1	2	2
NHL Totals		157	68	92	160	220
WHA Totals		78	24	43	71	115

HOWE, Mark Steven 5-11 185 D
B. Detroit, Mich., May 28, 1955

SSN	TEAM	GP	G	A	PTS.	PIM	+/-
73–74	Hou (WHA)	76	38	41	79	20	
74–75	Hou (WHA)	74	36	40	76	30	
75–75	Hou (WHA)	72	39	37	76	38	
76–77	Hou (WHA)	57	23	52	75	46	
77–78	NE (WHA)	70	30	61	91	32	
78–79	NE (WHA)	77	42	65	107	32	
79–80	Hart	74	24	56	80	20	+14
80–81	Hart	63	19	46	65	54	+10
81–82	Hart	76	8	45	53	18	-6
82–83	Phil	76	20	47	67	18	+47
83–84	Phil	71	19	34	53	44	+30
84–85	Phil	73	18	39	57	31	+51
85–86	Phil	77	24	58	82	36	+85
86–87	Phil	69	15	43	58	37	+57
87–88	Phil	75	19	43	62	62	+23
88–89	Phil	52	9	29	38	45	+7
89–90	Phil	40	7	21	28	24	+22
90–91	Phil	19	0	10	10	8	+9
91–92	Phil	42	7	18	25	18	+18
92–93	Det	60	3	31	34	22	+22
93–94	Det	44	4	20	24	8	+16
94–95	Det	18	1	5	6	10	-3
NHL Totals		929	197	545	742	455	+403
WHA Totals		426	208	296	504	198	

Playoffs

SSN	TEAM	GP	G	A	PTS.	PIM
73–74	Hou (WHA)	14	9	10	19	4
74–75	Hou (WHA)	13	10	12	22	0
75–76	Hou (WHA)	17	6	10	16	18
76–77	Hou (WHA)	11	4	10	14	2
77–78	NE (WHA)	14	8	7	15	18
78–79	NE (WHA)	6	4	2	6	6
79–80	Hart	3	1	2	3	2
82–83	Phil	3	0	2	2	4
83–84	Phil	3	0	0	0	2
84–85	Phil	19	3	8	11	6
85–86	Phil	5	0	4	4	0
86–87	Phil	26	2	10	12	4
87–88	Phil	7	3	6	9	4
88–89	Phil	19	0	15	15	10
92–93	Det	7	1	3	4	2
93–94	Det	6	0	1	1	0
94–95	Det	3	0	0	0	0
NHL Totals		101	10	51	61	34
WHA Totals		74	41	51	92	48

HOWE, Marty Gordon 6-1 195 D
B. Detroit, Mich., Feb. 18, 1954

SSN	TEAM	GP	G	A	PTS.	PIM	+/-
73–74	Hou (WHA)	73	4	20	24	90	
74–75	Hou (WHA)	75	13	21	34	89	
75–76	Hou (WHA)	80	14	23	37	81	
76–77	Hou (WHA)	80	17	28	45	103	
77–78	NE (WHA)	75	10	10	20	66	
78–79	NE (WHA)	66	9	15	24	31	
79–80	Hart	6	0	1	1	4	-2
80–81	Hart	12	0	1	1	25	-6
81–82	Hart	13	0	4	4	2	-4
82–83	Bos	78	1	11	12	24	+21
83–84	Hart	69	0	11	11	34	+1
84–85	Hart	19	1	1	2	10	-4
NHL Totals		197	2	29	31	99	+6
WHA Totals		449	67	117	184	460	

Playoffs

SSN	TEAM	GP	G	A	PTS.	PIM
73–74	Hou (WHA)	14	1	5	6	31
74–75	Hou (WHA)	11	0	2	2	11
75–76	Hou (WHA)	16	4	4	8	12
76–77	Hou (WHA)	11	3	1	4	10
77–78	NE (WHA)	14	1	1	2	13
78–79	NE (WHA)	9	0	1	1	8
79–80	Hart	3	1	1	2	0
82–83	Bos	12	0	1	1	9
NHL Totals		15	1	2	3	9
WHA Totals		75	9	14	23	85

*HOWE, Sydney Harris 5-9 165 C
B. Ottawa, Ont., Sept. 18, 1911

SSN	TEAM	GP	G	A	PTS.	PIM
29–30	Ott	14	1	1	2	2
30–31	Phil Q	44	9	11	20	20
31–32	Tor	3	0	0	0	0
32–33	Ott	48	12	12	24	17
33–34	Ott	41	13	7	20	18
34–35	StL–Det	50	22	25	47	34
35–36	Det	48	16	14	30	26
36–37	Det	42	17	10	27	10
37–38	Det	47	8	19	27	14
38–39	Det	48	16	20	36	11
39–40	Det	48	14	23	37	17
40–41	Det	48	20	24	44	8
41–42	Det	48	16	19	35	6
42–43	Det	50	20	35	55	10
43–44	Det	40	32	28	60	6
44–45	Det	46	17	36	53	6
45–46	Det	26	4	7	11	9
Totals		691	237	291	528	214

Playoffs

SSN	TEAM	GP	G	A	PTS.	PIM
29–30	Ott	2	0	0	0	0
35–36	Det	7	3	3	6	2
36–37	Det	10	2	5	7	0
38–39	Det	6	3	1	4	4
39–40	Det	5	2	2	4	2
40–41	Det	9	1	7	8	0
41–42	Det	12	3	5	8	0
42–43	Det	7	1	2	3	0
43–44	Det	5	2	2	4	0
44–45	Det	7	0	0	0	2

SSN	TEAM	GP	G	A	PTS.	PIM	+/-
Totals		70	17	27	44	10	

HOWE, Victor Stanley *6-0 172 RW*
B. Saskatoon, Sask., Nov. 2, 1929

SSN	TEAM	GP	G	A	PTS.	PIM	+/-
50-51	NYR	3	1	0	1	0	
53-54	NYR	1	0	0	0	0	
54-55	NYR	29	2	4	6	10	
Totals		33	3	4	7	10	

*HOWELL, Henry Vernon (Harry) *6-1 200 D*
B. Hamilton, Ont., Dec. 28, 1932

SSN	TEAM	GP	G	A	PTS.	PIM	+/-
52-53	NYR	67	3	8	11	46	
53-54	NYR	67	7	9	16	58	
54-55	NYR	70	2	14	16	87	
55-56	NYR	70	3	15	18	77	
56-57	NYR	65	2	10	12	70	
57-58	NYR	70	4	7	11	62	
58-59	NYR	70	4	10	14	101	
59-60	NYR	67	7	6	13	58	
60-61	NYR	70	7	10	17	62	
61-62	NYR	66	6	15	21	89	
62-63	NYR	70	5	20	25	55	
63-64	NYR	70	5	31	36	75	
64-65	NYR	68	2	20	22	63	
65-66	NYR	70	4	29	33	92	
66-67	NYR	70	12	28	40	54	
67-68	NYR	74	5	24	29	62	+12
68-69	NYR	56	4	7	11	36	+2
69-70	Oak	55	4	16	20	52	-14
70-71	Cal-LA	46	3	17	20	18	-19
71-72	LA	77	1	17	18	53	-34
72-73	LA	73	4	11	15	28	-4
73-74	NY-NJ (WHA)	65	3	23	26	24	
74-75	SD (WHA)	74	4	10	14	28	
75-76	Calg (WHA)	31	0	3	3	6	
NHL Totals		1411	94	324	418	1298	-57
WHA Totals		170	7	36	43	58	

Playoffs

55-56	NYR	5	0	1	1	4	
56-57	NYR	5	1	0	1	6	
57-58	NYR	6	1	0	1	8	
61-62	NYR	6	0	1	1	8	
66-67	NYR	4	0	0	0	4	
67-68	NYR	6	1	0	1	0	
68-69	NYR	2	0	0	0	0	
69-70	Oak	4	0	1	1	2	
74-75	SD (WHA)	5	1	0	1	10	
75-76	Calg (WHA)	2	0	0	0	2	
NHL Totals		38	3	3	6	32	
WHA Totals		7	1	0	1	12	

HOWELL, Ronald *D*
B. Hamilton, Ont., Dec. 4, 1935

54-55	NYR	3	0	0	0	4	
55-56	NYR	1	0	0	0	0	
Totals		4	0	0	0	4	

HOWSE, Donald Gordon *6-0 182 LW*
B. Grand Falls, Nfld., July 28, 1952

79-80	LA	33	2	5	7	6	-16

Playoffs

79-80	LA	2	0	0	0	0	

HOWSON, Donald (Scott) *5-11 160 C*
B. Toronto, Ont., Apr. 9, 1960

84-85	NYI	8	4	1	5	2	+4
85-86	NYI	10	1	2	3	2	+2
Totals		18	5	3	8	4	+6

HOYDA, David Allan *6-0 206 LW*
B. Edmonton, Alta., May 20, 1957

77-78	Phil	41	1	3	4	119	-5
78-79	Phil	67	3	13	16	138	+2
79-80	Winn	15	1	1	2	35	-4
80-81	Winn	9	1	0	1	7	0
Totals		132	6	17	23	299	-7

Playoffs

77-78	Phil	9	0	0	0	17	
78-79	Phil	3	0	0	0	0	
Totals		12	0	0	0	17	

HRDINA, Jan *6-0 197 C*
B. Hradec Kralove, Czech., Feb. 5, 1976

SSN	TEAM	GP	G	A	PTS.	PIM	+/-
98-99	Pitt	82	13	29	42	40	-2

Playoffs

98-99	Pitt	13	4	1	5	12	

HRDINA, Jiri *6-0 195 C*
B. Prague, Czechoslovakia, Jan. 5, 1958

87-88	Calg	9	2	5	7	2	+7
88-89	Calg	70	22	32	54	26	+19
89-90	Calg	64	12	18	30	31	+10
90-91	Calg-Pitt	51	6	17	23	17	-6
91-92	Pitt	56	3	13	16	16	+4
Totals		250	45	85	130	92	+34

Playoffs

87-88	Calg	1	0	0	0	0	
88-89	Calg	4	0	0	0	0	
89-90	Calg	6	0	1	1	2	
90-91	Pitt	14	2	2	4	6	
91-92	Pitt	21	0	2	2	16	
Totals		46	2	5	7	24	

HRECHKOSY, David John *6-2 216 LW*
B. Winnipeg, Man., Nov. 1, 1951

73-74	Cal	2	0	0	0	0	+1
74-75	Cal	72	29	14	43	25	-17
75-76	Cal-StL	51	12	8	20	14	-13
76-77	StL	15	1	2	3	2	0
Totals		140	42	24	66	41	-29

Playoffs

75-76	StL	3	1	0	1	2	

HRKAC, Anthony *5-11 170 C*
B. Thunder Bay, Ont., July 7, 1966

87-88	StL	67	11	37	48	22	+5
88-89	StL	70	17	28	45	8	-10
89-90	StL-Que	50	9	20	29	10	-4
90-91	Que	70	16	32	48	16	-22
91-92	SJ-Chi	40	3	12	15	10	+2
93-94	StL	36	6	5	11	8	-11
97-98	Dal-Edm	49	13	14	27	10	+2
98-99	Dal	69	13	14	27	26	+2
Totals		451	88	162	250	110	-36

Playoffs

86-87	StL	3	0	0	0	0	
87-88	StL	10	6	1	7	4	
88-89	StL	4	1	1	2	0	
91-92	Chi	3	0	0	0	2	
93-94	StL	4	0	0	0	0	
97-98	Edm	12	0	3	3	2	
98-99	Dal	5	0	2	2	4	
Totals		41	7	7	14	12	

HRYNEWICH, Tim *5-11 190 LW*
B. Leamington, Ont., Oct. 2, 1963

82-83	Pitt	30	2	3	5	48	-6
83-84	Pitt	25	4	5	9	34	-10
Totals		55	6	8	14	82	-16

HRYCUIK, James Peter *5-10 178 C*
B. Rosthern, Sask., Oct. 7, 1949

74-75	Wash	21	5	5	10	12	

HRYMNAK, Stefan (Steve) *5-10 178 D*
B. Port Arthur, Ont., Mar. 3, 1926

51-52	Chi	18	2	1	3	4	

Playoffs

52-53	Det	2	0	0	0	0	

HUARD, Bill *6-1 215 LW*
B. Welland, Ont., June 24, 1967

92-93	Bos	2	0	0	0	0	0
93-94	Ott	63	2	2	4	162	-19
94-95	Ott-Que	33	3	3	6	77	0
95-96	Dal	51	6	6	12	176	+3
96-97	Dal	40	5	6	11	105	+5
97-98	Edm	3	0	1	1	72	-5
98-99	Edm	3	0	0	0	0	0
Totals		192	16	17	33	520	-16

SSN	TEAM	GP	G	A	PTS.	PIM	+/-

Playoffs

94-95	Que	1	0	0	0	0	
97-98	Edm	4	0	0	0	2	
Totals		5	0	0	0	2	

HUARD, Roland (Rolly) *F*

30-31	Tor	1	1	0	1	0	

HUBER, Wilhelm Heinrich (Willie) *6-5 230 D*
B. Strasskirchen, W. Germany, Jan. 15, 1958

78-79	Det	68	7	24	31	114	-25
79-80	Det	76	17	23	40	164	-26
80-81	Det	80	15	34	49	130	-28
81-82	Det	74	15	30	45	98	-16
82-83	Det	74	14	29	43	106	-34
83-84	NYR	42	9	14	23	60	-14
84-85	NYR	49	3	11	14	55	-20
85-86	NYR	70	7	8	15	85	-11
86-87	NYR	66	8	22	30	68	-13
87-88	NYR-Van–Phil	56	9	22	31	70	-16
Totals		655	104	217	321	950	-203

Playoffs

83-84	NYR	4	1	1	2	9	
84-85	NYR	2	1	0	1	2	
85-86	NYR	16	3	2	5	16	
86-87	NYR	6	0	2	2	6	
87-88	Phil	5	0	0	0	2	
Totals		33	5	5	10	35	

HUBICK, Gregory Wayne *5-11 183 D*
B. Strasbourg, Sask., Nov. 12, 1951

75-76	Tor	72	6	8	14	10	0
79-80	Van	5	0	1	1	0	-1
Totals		77	6	9	15	10	-1

HUCK, Anthony Francis (Fran) *5-7 165 C*
B. Regina, Sask., Dec. 4, 1945

69-70	Mont	2	0	0	0	0	0
70-71	Mont-StL	34	8	10	18	18	+4
72-73	StL	58	16	20	36	20	-1
73-74	Winn (WHA)	74	26	48	74	68	
74-75	Minn (WHA)	78	22	45	67	26	
75-76	Winn (WHA)	59	17	32	49	27	
76-77	Winn (WHA)	12	2	2	4	10	
77-78	Winn (WHA)	5	0	0	0	2	
NHL Totals		94	24	30	54	38	+3
WHA Totals		228	67	127	194	133	

Playoffs

70-71	StL	6	1	2	3	2	
72-73	StL	5	2	2	4	0	
73-74	Winn (WHA)	4	0	0	0	2	
74-75	Winn (WHA)	12	3	13	16	6	
76-77	Winn (WHA)	7	0	2	2	6	
NHL Totals		11	3	4	7	2	
WHA Totals		23	3	15	18	14	

HUCUL, Frederick Albert *5-11 188 D*
B. Tubrose, Sask., Dec. 5, 1931

50-51	Chi	3	1	0	1	2	
51-52	Chi	34	3	7	10	37	
52-53	Chi	57	5	7	12	25	
53-54	Chi	27	0	3	3	19	
67-68	StL	43	2	13	15	30	-3
Totals		164	11	30	41	113	-3

Playoffs

52-53	Chi	6	1	0	1	10	

HUDDY, Charles William *6-0 210 D*
B. Oshawa, Ont., June 2, 1959

80-81	Edm	12	2	5	7	6	+1
81-82	Edm	41	4	11	15	46	+17
82-83	Edm	76	20	37	57	58	+62
83-84	Edm	75	8	34	42	43	+50
84-85	Edm	80	7	44	51	46	+50
85-86	Edm	76	6	35	41	55	+30
86-87	Edm	58	4	15	19	35	+27
87-88	Edm	77	13	28	41	71	+23
88-89	Edm	76	11	33	44	52	0
89-90	Edm	70	1	23	24	56	-13
90-91	Edm	53	5	22	27	32	+4
91-92	LA	56	4	19	23	43	-10
92-93	LA	82	2	25	27	64	+16

SSN	TEAM	GP	G	A	PTS.	PIM	+/-
93–94	LA	79	5	13	18	71	+4
94–95	LA–Buf	41	2	5	7	42	-7
95–96	Buf–StL	64	5	5	10	65	-12
96–97	Buf	1	0	0	0	0	-1
Totals		1017	99	354	453	785	+241

Playoffs

SSN	TEAM	GP	G	A	PTS.	PIM	+/-
81–82	Edm	5	1	2	3	14	
82–83	Edm	15	1	6	7	10	
83–84	Edm	12	1	9	10	8	
84–85	Edm	18	3	17	20	17	
85–86	Edm	7	0	2	2	0	
86–87	Edm	21	1	7	8	21	
87–88	Edm	13	4	5	9	10	
88–89	Edm	7	2	0	2	4	
89–90	Edm	22	0	6	6	11	
90–91	Edm	18	3	7	10	10	
91–92	LA	6	1	1	2	10	
92–93	LA	23	1	4	5	12	
94–95	Buf	3	0	0	0	0	
95–96	StL	13	1	0	1	8	
Totals		183	19	66	85	135	

HUDSON, Alexander (Lex) *6–3 184 D*
B. Winnipeg, Man., Dec. 31, 1955

SSN	TEAM	GP	G	A	PTS.	PIM	+/-
78–79	Pitt	2	0	0	0	0	0

HUDSON, David Richard *6–0 175 C*
B. St. Thomas, Ont., Dec. 28, 1949

SSN	TEAM	GP	G	A	PTS.	PIM	+/-
72–73	NYI	69	12	19	31	17	-39
73–74	NYI	63	2	10	12	7	-6
74–75	KC	70	9	32	41	27	-19
75–76	KC	74	11	20	31	12	-28
76–77	Col	73	15	21	36	14	-3
77–78	Col	60	10	22	32	12	-5
Totals		409	59	124	183	89	-100

Playoffs

SSN	TEAM	GP	G	A	PTS.	PIM	+/-
77–78	Col	2	1	1	2	0	

HUDSON, Mike *6–1 201 C/LW*
B. Guelph, Ont., Feb. 6, 1967

SSN	TEAM	GP	G	A	PTS.	PIM	+/-
88–89	Chi	41	7	16	23	20	-12
89–90	Chi	49	9	12	21	56	-3
90–91	Chi	55	7	9	16	62	+5
91–92	Chi	76	14	15	29	92	-11
92–93	Chi–Edm	41	1	7	8	46	-7
93–94	NYR	48	4	7	11	47	-5
94–95	Pitt	40	2	9	11	34	-1
95–96	Tor–StL	59	5	12	17	55	+2
96–97	Phoe	7	0	0	0	2	-4
Totals		416	49	87	136	414	-36

Playoffs

SSN	TEAM	GP	G	A	PTS.	PIM	+/-
88–89	Chi	10	1	2	3	18	
89–90	Chi	4	0	0	0	2	
90–91	Chi	6	0	2	2	8	
91–92	Chi	16	3	5	8	26	
94–95	Pitt	11	0	0	0	6	
95–96	StL	2	0	1	1	4	
Totals		49	4	10	14	64	

HUDSON, Ronald *5–10 175 RW*
B. Timmins, Ont., Apr. 18, 1914

SSN	TEAM	GP	G	A	PTS.	PIM	+/-
37–38	Det	33	5	2	7	2	
39–40	Det	1	0	0	0	0	
Totals		34	5	2	7	2	

HUFFMAN, Kerry *6–2 200 D*
B. Peterborough, Ont., Jan. 3, 1968

SSN	TEAM	GP	G	A	PTS.	PIM	+/-
86–87	Phil	9	0	0	0	2	+5
87–88	Phil	52	6	17	23	34	-11
88–89	Phil	29	0	11	11	31	0
89–90	Phil	43	1	12	13	34	-3
90–91	Phil	10	1	2	3	10	+1
91–92	Phil	60	14	18	32	41	+1
92–93	Que	52	4	18	22	54	0
93–94	Que–Ott	62	4	14	18	4	-28
94–95	Ott	37	2	4	6	46	-17
95–96	Ott–Phil	47	5	12	17	69	-18
Totals		401	37	108	145	361	-70

Playoffs

SSN	TEAM	GP	G	A	PTS.	PIM	+/-
87–88	Phil	2	0	0	0	0	
92–93	Que	3	0	0	0	0	
95–96	Phil	6	0	0	0	2	
Totals		11	0	0	0	2	

HUGGINS, Allan *F*
B. Toronto, Ont.

SSN	TEAM	GP	G	A	PTS.	PIM	+/-
30–31	Mont M	20	1	1	2	2	

HUGHES, Albert *F*
B. Collingwood, Ont.

SSN	TEAM	GP	G	A	PTS.	PIM	+/-
30–31	NYA	42	5	7	12	14	
31–32	NYA	18	1	1	2	8	
Totals		60	6	8	14	22	

HUGHES, Brent Allen *5–11 195 LW*
B. New Westminster, B.C., Apr. 5, 1966

SSN	TEAM	GP	G	A	PTS.	PIM	+/-
88–89	Winn	28	3	2	5	82	-7
89–90	Winn	11	1	2	3	33	-4
91–92	Bos	8	1	1	2	38	+1
92–93	Bos	62	5	4	9	191	-4
93–94	Bos	77	13	11	24	143	+10
94–95	Bos	44	6	6	12	139	+6
95–96	Buf	76	5	10	15	148	-9
96–97	NYI	51	7	3	10	57	-4
Totals		357	41	39	80	831	-11

Playoffs

SSN	TEAM	GP	G	A	PTS.	PIM	+/-
91–92	Bos	10	2	0	2	20	
92–93	Bos	1	0	0	0	2	
93–94	Bos	13	2	1	3	27	
94–95	Bos	5	0	0	0	4	
Totals		29	4	1	5	53	

HUGHES, Brenton Alexander (Brent) *6–0 205 D*
B. Bowmanville, Ont., June 17, 1943

SSN	TEAM	GP	G	A	PTS.	PIM	+/-
67–68	LA	44	4	10	14	36	+15
68–69	LA	72	2	19	21	73	-16
69–70	LA	52	1	7	8	108	-33
70–71	Phil	30	1	10	11	21	-6
71–72	Phil	63	2	20	22	35	+6
72–73	Phil–StL	37	3	12	15	32	-7
73–74	StL–Det	71	1	21	22	92	-28
74–75	KC	66	1	18	19	43	-51
75–76	SD (WHA)	78	7	28	35	63	
76–77	SD (WHA)	62	4	13	17	48	
77–78	Birm (WHA)	80	9	35	44	48	
78–79	Birm (WHA)	48	3	3	6	21	
NHL Totals		435	15	117	132	440	-120
WHA Totals		268	23	79	102	180	

Playoffs

SSN	TEAM	GP	G	A	PTS.	PIM	+/-
67–68	LA	7	0	0	0	10	
68–69	LA	7	0	0	0	2	
70–71	Phil	4	0	0	0	6	
75–76	SD (WHA)	10	1	5	6	6	
76–77	SD (WHA)	7	1	4	5	0	
77–78	Birm (WHA)	5	0	0	0	12	
NHL Totals		18	0	0	0	18	
WHA Totals		22	2	9	11	18	

HUGHES, Frank *5–10 180 LW*
B. Fernie, B.C., Oct. 1, 1949

SSN	TEAM	GP	G	A	PTS.	PIM	+/-
71–72	Cal	5	0	0	0	0	-2
72–73	Hou (WHA)	76	22	19	41	41	
73–74	Hou (WHA)	73	42	42	84	47	
74–75	Hou (WHA)	76	48	35	83	35	
75–76	Hou (WHA)	80	31	45	76	26	
76–77	Hou–Phoe (WHA)	75	27	37	64	22	
77–78	Hou (WHA)	11	3	2	5	2	
NHL Totals		5	0	0	0	0	-2
WHA Totals		391	173	180	353	173	

Playoffs

SSN	TEAM	GP	G	A	PTS.	PIM	+/-
72–73	Hou (WHA)	10	4	4	8	2	
73–74	Hou (WHA)	14	9	5	14	9	
74–75	Hou (WHA)	13	6	6	12	2	
75–76	Hou (WHA)	17	5	1	6	20	
WHA Totals		54	24	16	40	33	

HUGHES, Howard Duncan *5–9 180 RW*
B. St. Boniface, Man., Apr. 4, 1939

SSN	TEAM	GP	G	A	PTS.	PIM	+/-
67–68	LA	74	9	14	23	20	+1
68–69	LA	73	16	14	30	10	-3
69–70	LA	21	0	4	4	0	-6
Totals		168	25	32	57	30	-8

Playoffs

SSN	TEAM	GP	G	A	PTS.	PIM	+/-
67–68	LA	7	2	0	2	0	
68–69	LA	7	0	0	0	2	
Totals		14	2	0	2	2	

HUGHES, J. Rusty *D*

SSN	TEAM	GP	G	A	PTS.	PIM	+/-
29–30	Det	40	0	1	1	48	

HUGHES, John F. (Jack) *6–1 205 D*
B. Somerville, Mass., July 20, 1957

SSN	TEAM	GP	G	A	PTS.	PIM	+/-
80–81	Col	38	2	5	7	91	-22
81–82	Col	8	0	0	0	13	-7
Totals		46	2	5	7	104	-29

HUGHES, John Spencer *5–11 200 D*
B. Charlottetown, P.E.I., Mar. 18, 1954

SSN	TEAM	GP	G	A	PTS.	PIM	+/-
74–75	Phoe (WHA)	72	4	25	29	201	
75–76	Cin (WHA)	79	3	34	37	204	
76–77	Cin (WHA)	79	3	27	30	113	
77–78	Hou (WHA)	79	3	25	28	130	
78–79	Ind–Edm (WHA)	63	5	19	24	130	
79–80	Van	52	2	11	13	181	0
80–81	Edm	18	0	3	3	30	-6
NHL Totals		70	2	14	16	211	-6
WHA Totals		372	18	130	148	778	

Playoffs

SSN	TEAM	GP	G	A	PTS.	PIM	+/-
76–77	Cin (WHA)	4	0	0	0	8	
77–78	Hou (WHA)	6	1	1	2	6	
78–79	Edm (WHA)	13	1	0	1	35	
79–80	Van	4	0	0	0	10	
80–81	NYR	3	0	1	1	6	
NHL Totals		7	0	1	1	16	
WHA Totals		23	2	1	3	49	

HUGHES, Patrick *6–1 180 RW*
B. Calgary, Alta., Mar. 25, 1955

SSN	TEAM	GP	G	A	PTS.	PIM	+/-
77–78	Mont	3	0	0	0	2	-2
78–79	Mont	41	9	8	17	22	+7
79–80	Pitt	76	18	14	32	78	-38
80–81	Pitt–Edm	60	10	9	19	161	-12
81–82	Edm	68	24	22	46	99	+21
82–83	Edm	80	25	20	45	85	0
83–84	Edm	77	27	28	55	61	+18
84–85	Edm	73	12	13	25	85	-7
85–86	Buf	50	4	9	13	25	-6
86–87	StL–Hart	45	1	5	6	28	-7
Totals		573	130	128	258	653	-26

Playoffs

SSN	TEAM	GP	G	A	PTS.	PIM	+/-
78–79	Mont	8	1	2	3	4	
79–80	Pitt	5	0	0	0	21	
80–81	Edm	5	0	0	0	4	
81–82	Edm	5	2	1	3	6	
82–83	Edm	16	2	5	7	14	
83–84	Edm	19	2	11	13	12	
84–85	Edm	10	1	1	2	4	
86–87	Hart	3	0	0	0	0	
Totals		71	8	25	33	77	

HUGHES, Ryan *6–1 180 C*
B. Montreal, Que., Jan. 17, 1972

SSN	TEAM	GP	G	A	PTS.	PIM	+/-
95–96	Bos	3	0	0	0	0	0

HULBIG, Joe *6–3 215 LW*
B. Norwood, Mass., Sept. 29, 1973

SSN	TEAM	GP	G	A	PTS.	PIM	+/-
96–97	Edm	6	0	0	0	0	-1
97–98	Edm	17	2	2	4	2	-1
98–99	Edm	1	0	0	0	2	+1
Totals		24	2	2	4	6	-1

Playoffs

SSN	TEAM	GP	G	A	PTS.	PIM	+/-
96–97	Edm	6	0	1	1	2	

HULL, Brett *5–10 201 RW*
B. Belleville, Ont., Aug. 9, 1964

SSN	TEAM	GP	G	A	PTS.	PIM	+/-
86–87	Calg	5	1	0	1	0	-1
87–88	Calg–StL	65	32	32	64	16	+14
88–89	StL	78	41	43	84	33	-17
89–90	StL	80	72	41	113	24	-1
90–91	StL	78	86	45	131	22	+23
91–92	StL	73	70	39	109	48	-2
92–93	StL	80	54	47	101	41	-27
93–94	StL	81	57	40	97	38	-3
94–95	StL	48	29	21	50	10	+13

SSN	TEAM	GP	G	A	PTS.	PIM	+/-
95–96	StL	70	43	40	83	30	+4
96–97	StL	77	42	40	82	10	-9
97–98	StL	66	27	45	72	26	-1
98–99	Dal	60	32	26	58	30	+19
Totals		861	586	459	1045	328	+12

Playoffs

SSN	TEAM	GP	G	A	PTS.	PIM	+/-
85–86	Calg	2	0	0	0	0	
86–87	Calg	4	2	1	3	0	
87–88	StL	10	7	2	9	4	
88–89	StL	10	5	5	10	6	
89–90	StL	12	13	8	21	17	
90–91	StL	13	11	8	19	4	
91–92	StL	6	4	4	8	4	
92–93	StL	11	8	5	13	2	
93–94	StL	4	2	1	3	0	
94–95	StL	7	6	2	8	0	
95–96	StL	13	6	5	11	10	
96–97	StL	6	2	7	9	2	
97–98	StL	10	3	3	6	2	
98–99	Dal	22	8	7	15	4	
Totals		130	77	58	135	55	

HULL, Dennis William 5–11 195 LW
B. Pointe Anne, Ont., Nov. 19, 1944

SSN	TEAM	GP	G	A	PTS.	PIM	+/-
64–65	Chi	55	10	4	14	18	
65–66	Chi	25	1	5	6	6	
66–67	Chi	70	25	17	42	33	
67–68	Chi	74	18	15	33	34	-20
68–69	Chi	72	30	34	64	25	+7
69–70	Chi	76	17	35	52	31	+4
70–71	Chi	78	40	26	66	16	+28
71–72	Chi	78	30	39	69	10	+12
72–73	Chi	78	39	51	90	27	+28
73–74	Chi	74	29	39	68	15	+25
74–75	Chi	69	16	21	37	10	-14
75–76	Chi	80	27	39	66	28	-17
76–77	Chi	75	16	17	33	2	-20
77–78	Det	55	5	9	14	6	-20
Totals		959	303	351	654	261	+13

Playoffs

SSN	TEAM	GP	G	A	PTS.	PIM	+/-
64–65	Chi	6	0	0	0	0	
67–68	Chi	11	1	3	4	6	
69–70	Chi	8	5	2	7	0	
70–71	Chi	18	7	6	13	2	
71–72	Chi	8	4	2	6	4	
72–73	Chi	16	9	15	24	4	
73–74	Chi	10	6	3	9	0	
74–75	Chi	5	0	2	2	0	
75–76	Chi	4	0	0	0	0	
76–77	Chi	2	1	0	1	0	
77–78	Det	7	0	0	0	2	
Totals		95	33	33	66	18	

HULL, Jody 6–2 200 RW
B. Cambridge, Ont., Feb. 2, 1969

SSN	TEAM	GP	G	A	PTS.	PIM	+/-
88–89	Hart	60	16	18	34	10	+6
89–90	Hart	38	7	10	17	21	-6
90–91	NYR	47	5	8	13	10	+2
91–92	NYR	3	0	0	0	2	-4
92–93	Ott	69	13	21	34	14	-24
93–94	Fla	69	13	13	26	8	+6
94–95	Fla	46	11	8	19	8	-1
95–96	Fla	78	20	17	37	25	+5
96–97	Fla	67	10	6	16	4	+1
97–98	Fla–TB	49	4	4	8	8	+3
98–99	Phil	72	3	11	14	12	-2
Totals		568	102	116	218	122	-14

Playoffs

SSN	TEAM	GP	G	A	PTS.	PIM	+/-
88–89	Hart	1	0	0	0	2	
89–90	Hart	5	0	1	1	2	
95–96	Fla	14	3	2	5	0	
96–97	Fla	5	0	0	0	0	
98–99	Phil	6	0	0	0	4	
Totals		31	3	3	6	8	

HULL, Robert Marvin (Golden Jet) 5–10 193 LW
B. Pointe Anne, Ont., Jan. 3, 1939

SSN	TEAM	GP	G	A	PTS.	PIM	+/-
57–58	Chi	70	13	34	47	62	
58–59	Chi	70	18	32	50	50	
59–60	Chi	70	39	42	81	68	
60–61	Chi	67	31	25	56	43	
61–62	Chi	70	50	34	84	35	
62–63	Chi	65	31	31	62	27	
63–64	Chi	70	43	44	87	50	
64–65	Chi	61	39	32	71	32	
65–66	Chi	65	54	43	97	70	
66–67	Chi	66	52	28	80	52	
67–68	Chi	71	44	31	75	39	+14
68–69	Chi	74	58	49	107	48	-7
69–70	Chi	61	38	29	67	8	+20
70–71	Chi	78	44	52	96	32	+34
71–72	Chi	78	50	43	93	24	+54
72–73	Winn (WHA)	63	51	52	103	37	
73–74	Winn (WHA)	75	53	42	95	38	
74–75	Winn (WHA)	78	77	65	142	41	
75–76	Winn (WHA)	80	53	70	123	30	
76–77	Winn (WHA)	34	21	32	53	14	
77–78	Winn (WHA)	77	46	71	117	23	
78–79	Winn (WHA)	4	2	3	5	0	
79–80	Winn–Hart	27	6	11	17	0	
NHL Totals		1063	610	560	1170	640	+115
WHA Totals		411	303	335	638	183	

Playoffs

SSN	TEAM	GP	G	A	PTS.	PIM	+/-
58–59	Chi	6	1	1	2	2	
59–60	Chi	3	1	0	1	2	
60–61	Chi	12	4	10	14	4	
61–62	Chi	12	8	6	14	12	
62–63	Chi	5	8	2	10	4	
63–64	Chi	7	2	5	7	2	
64–65	Chi	14	10	7	17	27	
65–66	Chi	3	2	2	4	10	
66–67	Chi	6	4	2	6	0	
67–68	Chi	11	4	6	10	15	
69–70	Chi	8	3	8	11	2	
70–71	Chi	18	11	14	25	16	
71–72	Chi	8	4	4	8	6	
72–73	Winn (WHA)	14	9	16	25	16	
73–74	Winn (WHA)	4	1	1	2	4	
75–76	Winn (WHA)	13	12	8	20	4	
76–77	Winn (WHA)	20	13	9	22	2	
77–78	Winn (WHA)	9	8	3	11	12	
79–80	Hart	3	0	0	0	0	
NHL Totals		116	62	67	129	102	
WHA Totals		60	43	37	80	38	

HULSE, Cale 6–3 210 D
B. Edmonton, Alta., Nov. 10, 1973

SSN	TEAM	GP	G	A	PTS.	PIM	+/-
95–96	NJ–Calg	11	0	0	0	20	+1
96–97	Calg	63	1	6	7	91	-2
97–98	Calg	79	5	22	27	169	+1
98–99	Calg	79	3	9	12	117	-8
Totals		232	9	37	46	397	-8

Playoffs

SSN	TEAM	GP	G	A	PTS.	PIM	+/-
95–96	Calg	1	0	0	0	0	

HUNT, Fredrick Tennyson (Fritz) 5–8 160 RW
B. Brantford, Ont., Jan. 17, 1918

SSN	TEAM	GP	G	A	PTS.	PIM	+/-
40–41	NYA	15	2	5	7	0	
44–45	NYR	44	13	9	22	6	
Totals		59	15	14	29	6	

HUNTER, Dale Robert 5–10 198 C
B. Petrolia, Ont., July 31, 1960

SSN	TEAM	GP	G	A	PTS.	PIM	+/-
80–81	Que	80	19	44	63	226	+5
81–82	Que	80	22	50	72	272	+26
82–83	Que	80	17	46	63	206	+10
83–84	Que	77	24	55	79	232	+35
84–85	Que	80	20	52	72	209	+23
85–86	Que	80	28	42	70	265	+6
86–87	Que	46	10	29	39	135	+4
87–88	Wash	79	22	37	59	240	+7
88–89	Wash	80	20	37	57	219	-3
89–90	Wash	80	23	39	62	233	+17
90–91	Wash	76	16	30	46	234	-22
91–92	Wash	80	28	50	78	205	-2
92–93	Wash	84	20	59	79	198	+3
93–94	Wash	52	9	29	38	131	-4
94–95	Wash	45	8	15	23	101	-4
95–96	Wash	82	13	24	37	112	+5
96–97	Wash	82	14	32	46	125	-2
97–98	Wash	82	8	18	26	103	+1
98–99	Wash-Col A	62	2	9	11	119	-7
Totals		1409	323	697	1020	3565	+97

Playoffs

SSN	TEAM	GP	G	A	PTS.	PIM	+/-
80–81	Que	5	4	2	6	34	
81–82	Que	16	3	7	10	52	
82–83	Que	4	2	1	3	24	
83–84	Que	9	2	3	5	41	
84–85	Que	17	4	6	10	97	
85–86	Que	3	0	0	0	15	
86–87	Que	13	1	7	8	56	
87–88	Wash	14	7	5	12	98	
88–89	Wash	6	0	4	4	29	
89–90	Wash	15	4	8	12	61	
90–91	Wash	11	1	9	10	41	
91–92	Wash	7	1	4	5	16	
92–93	Wash	6	7	1	8	35	
93–94	Wash	7	0	3	3	14	
94–95	Wash	7	4	4	8	24	
95–96	Wash	6	1	5	6	24	
97–98	Wash	21	0	4	4	30	
98–99	Wash-Col A	19	1	3	4	38	
Totals		186	42	76	118	729	

HUNTER, David 5–11 195 LW
B. Petrolia, Ont., Jan. 1, 1958

SSN	TEAM	GP	G	A	PTS.	PIM	+/-
78–79	Edm (WHA)	72	7	25	32	134	
79–80	Edm	80	12	31	43	103	+7
80–81	Edm	78	12	16	28	98	-12
81–82	Edm	63	16	22	38	63	+33
82–83	Edm	80	13	18	31	120	+12
83–84	Edm	80	22	26	48	90	+25
84–85	Edm	80	17	19	36	122	-1
85–86	Edm	62	15	22	37	77	+37
86–87	Edm	77	6	9	15	79	+1
87–88	Edm–Pitt	80	14	21	35	83	+9
88–89	Winn–Edm	66	6	6	12	83	-8
NHL Totals		746	133	190	323	918	+103
WHA Totals		72	7	25	32	134	

Playoffs

SSN	TEAM	GP	G	A	PTS.	PIM	+/-
78–79	Edm (WHA)	13	2	3	5	32	
79–80	Edm	3	0	0	0	7	
80–81	Edm	9	0	0	0	28	
81–82	Edm	5	0	1	1	26	
82–83	Edm	16	4	7	11	60	
83–84	Edm	17	5	5	10	14	
84–85	Edm	18	2	5	7	33	
85–86	Edm	10	2	3	5	23	
86–87	Edm	21	3	3	6	20	
88–89	Edm	6	0	0	0	0	
NHL Totals		105	16	24	40	211	
WHA Totals		13	2	3	5	32	

HUNTER, Mark 6–0 200 RW
B. Petrolia, Ont., Nov. 12, 1962

SSN	TEAM	GP	G	A	PTS.	PIM	+/-
81–82	Mont	71	18	11	29	143	+10
82–83	Mont	31	8	8	16	73	+5
83–84	Mont	22	6	4	10	42	-2
84–85	Mont	72	21	12	33	123	-13
85–86	StL	78	44	30	74	171	+15
86–87	StL	74	36	33	69	167	-19
87–88	StL	66	32	31	63	136	-6
88–89	Calg	66	22	8	30	194	+4
89–90	Calg	10	2	3	5	39	0
90–91	Calg–Hart	68	14	18	32	165	+2
91–92	Hart	63	10	13	23	159	-8
92–93	Wash	7	0	0	0	14	+1
Totals		628	213	171	384	1426	-11

Playoffs

SSN	TEAM	GP	G	A	PTS.	PIM	+/-
81–82	Mont	5	0	0	0	20	
83–84	Mont	14	2	1	3	69	
84–85	Mont	11	0	3	3	13	
85–86	StL	19	7	7	14	48	
86–87	StL	5	0	3	3	10	
87–88	StL	5	2	3	5	24	
88–89	Calg	10	2	2	4	23	
90–91	Hart	6	5	1	6	17	
91–92	Hart	4	0	0	0	6	
Totals		79	18	20	38	230	

HUNTER, Timothy Robert 6–2 202 RW
B. Calgary, Alta., Sept. 10, 1960

SSN	TEAM	GP	G	A	PTS.	PIM	+/-
81–82	Calg	2	0	0	0	9	0
82–83	Calg	16	1	0	1	54	-2
83–84	Calg	43	4	4	8	130	0
84–85	Calg	71	11	11	22	259	+14
85–86	Calg	66	8	7	15	291	-9
86–87	Calg	73	6	15	21	361	-1
87–88	Calg	68	8	5	13	337	-8
88–89	Calg	75	3	9	12	375	+22
89–90	Calg	67	2	3	5	279	-9
90–91	Calg	34	5	2	7	143	+1
91–92	Calg	30	1	3	4	167	+2
92–93	Que–Van	74	5	7	12	19	-3

SSN	TEAM	GP	G	A	PTS.	PIM	+/-
93-94	Van	56	3	4	7	171	-7
94-95	Van	34	3	2	5	120	+1
95-96	Van	60	2	0	2	122	-8
96-97	SJ	46	0	4	4	135	0
Totals		815	62	76	138	3146	-7

Playoffs

82-83	Calg	9	1	0	1	70	
83-84	Calg	7	0	0	0	21	
84-85	Calg	4	0	0	0	24	
85-86	Calg	19	0	3	3	108	
86-87	Calg	6	0	0	0	51	
87-88	Calg	9	4	0	4	32	
88-89	Calg	19	0	4	4	32	
89-90	Calg	6	0	0	0	4	
90-91	Calg	7	0	0	0	10	
92-93	Van	11	0	0	0	26	
93-94	Van	24	0	0	0	26	
94-95	Van	11	0	0	0	22	
Totals		132	5	7	12	426	

HURAS, Larry Robert 6-2 200 D
B. Listowel, Ont., July 8, 1955

| 76-77 | NYR | 1 | 0 | 0 | 0 | 0 | 0 |

HURLBURT, Robert George 5-11 185 LW
B. Toronto, Ont., May 1, 1950

| 74-75 | Van | 1 | 0 | 0 | 0 | 2 | 0 |

HURLBUT, Michael Ray 6-2 200 D
B. Massena, N.Y., Oct. 7, 1966

92-93	NYR	23	1	8	9	16	+4
93-94	Que	1	0	0	0	0	-1
97-98	Buf	3	0	0	0	2	-1
98-99	Buf	1	0	0	0	0	+2
Totals		28	1	8	9	18	+4

HURLEY, Paul Michael 5-11 185 D
B. Melrose, Mass., July 12, 1946

68-69	Bos	1	0	1	1	0	+1
72-73	NE (WHA)	78	3	15	18	58	
73-74	NE (WHA)	52	3	11	14	21	
74-75	NE (WHA)	75	3	26	29	36	
75-76	NE-Edm (WHA)	72	1	18	19	34	
76-77	Calg (WHA)	34	0	6	6	32	
NHL Totals		1	0	1	1	0	+1
WHA Totals		311	10	76	86	181	

Playoffs

72-73	NE (WHA)	15	0	7	7	14	
74-75	NE (WHA)	6	0	1	1	4	
75-76	Edm (WHA)	4	0	0	0	0	
WHA Totals		25	0	8	8	18	

HURST, Ronald 5-9 175 RW
B. Toronto, Ont., May 18, 1931

55-56	Tor	50	7	5	12	62	
56-57	Tor	14	2	2	4	8	
Totals		64	9	7	16	70	

Playoffs

| 55-56 | Tor | 3 | 0 | 2 | 2 | 4 | |

HUSCROFT, Jamie 6-2 200 D
B. Creston, B.C., Jan. 9, 1967

88-89	NJ	15	0	2	2	51	-3
89-90	NJ	42	2	3	5	149	-2
90-91	NJ	8	0	1	1	27	+1
93-94	Bos	36	0	1	1	144	-2
94-95	Bos	34	0	6	6	103	-3
95-96	Calg	70	3	9	12	162	+14
96-97	Calg-TB	52	0	5	5	151	-2
97-98	TB-Van	51	0	4	4	177	-2
98-99	Van-Phoe	37	0	2	2	90	-4
Totals		345	5	33	38	1054	-3

Playoffs

89-90	NJ	5	0	0	0	16	
90-91	NJ	3	0	0	0	6	
93-94	Bos	4	0	0	0	9	
94-95	Bos	5	0	0	0	11	
95-96	Calg	4	0	1	1	4	
Totals		21	0	1	1	46	

HUSKA, Ryan 6-2 194 LW
B. Cranbrook, B.C., July 2, 1975

| 97-98 | Chi | 1 | 0 | 0 | 0 | 0 | 0 |

HUSTON, Ronald Earle 5-9 170 C
B. Manitou, Man., Apr. 8, 1945

73-74	Cal	23	3	10	13	0	-12
74-75	Cal	56	12	21	33	8	-15
75-76	Phoe (WHA)	79	22	44	66	4	
76-77	Phoe (WHA)	80	20	39	59	10	
NHL Totals		79	15	31	46	8	-27
WHA Totals		159	42	83	125	14	

Playoffs

| 75-76 | Phoe (WHA) | 5 | 1 | 1 | 2 | 0 | |

HUTCHINSON, Ronald Wayne 5-10 175 C
B. Flin Flon, Man., Oct. 24, 1936

| 60-61 | NYR | 9 | 0 | 0 | 0 | 0 | |

HUTCHISON, David Joseph 6-3 205 D
B. London, Ont., May 2, 1952

72-73	Phil (WHA)	28	0	2	2	34	
73-74	Van (WHA)	69	0	13	13	151	
74-75	LA	68	0	6	6	133	+5
75-76	LA	50	0	10	10	181	+4
76-77	LA	70	6	11	17	220	+7
77-78	LA	44	0	10	10	71	+11
78-79	Tor	79	4	15	19	235	+36
79-80	Tor-Chi	69	1	11	12	101	+1
80-81	Chi	59	2	9	11	124	+12
81-82	Chi	66	5	18	23	246	+4
82-83	NJ	32	1	4	5	102	-20
83-84	Tor	47	0	3	3	137	+5
NHL Totals		584	19	97	116	1550	+65
WHA Totals		97	0	15	15	185	

Playoffs

74-75	LA	2	0	0	0	22	
75-76	LA	9	0	3	3	29	
76-77	LA	9	1	4	5	17	
78-79	Tor	6	0	3	3	23	
79-80	Tor	6	0	0	0	12	
80-81	Chi	2	0	0	0	2	
81-82	Chi	14	1	2	3	44	
Totals		48	2	12	14	149	

HUTTON, William David 5-10 165 D
B. Calgary, Alta., Jan. 28, 1910

29-30	Bos-Ott	34	2	1	3	2	
30-31	Bos-Phil Q	30	1	1	2	6	
Totals		64	3	2	5	8	

Playoffs

| 29-30 | Ott | 2 | 0 | 0 | 0 | 0 | |

*__HYLAND, Harold M. (Harry)__ RW
B. Montreal, Que., Jan. 2, 1889

| 17-18 | Mont W-Ott | 16 | 14 | 0 | 14 | 9 | |

HYNES, David E. 5-9 182 LW
B. Cambridge, Mass., Apr. 17, 1951

73-74	Bos	3	0	0	0	0	0
74-75	Bos	19	4	0	4	2	+3
76-77	NE (WHA)	22	5	4	9	4	
NHL Totals		22	4	0	4	2	+3
WHA Totals		22	5	4	9	4	

HYNES, Gord 6-1 170 D
B. Montreal, Que., July 22, 1966

91-92	Bos	15	0	5	5	6	+8
92-93	Phil	37	3	4	7	16	-3
Totals		52	3	9	12	22	+5

Playoffs

| 91-92 | Bos | 12 | 1 | 2 | 3 | 6 | |

IAFRATE, Al 6-3 235 D
B. Dearborn, Mich., Mar. 21, 1966

84-85	Tor	68	5	16	21	51	-19
85-86	Tor	65	8	25	33	40	-10
86-87	Tor	80	9	21	30	55	-18
87-88	Tor	77	22	30	52	80	-21
88-89	Tor	65	13	20	33	72	+3
89-90	Tor	75	21	42	63	135	-4
90-91	Tor-Wash	72	9	23	32	237	-16
91-92	Wash	78	17	34	51	180	+1
92-93	Wash	81	25	41	66	169	+15
93-94	Wash-Bos	79	15	43	58	163	+16
96-97	SJ	38	6	9	15	91	-10
97-98	SJ	21	2	7	9	28	-1
Totals		799	152	311	463	1301	-64

Playoffs

85-86	Tor	10	0	3	3	4	
86-87	Tor	13	1	3	4	11	
87-88	Tor	6	3	4	7	6	
90-91	Tor	10	1	3	4	22	
91-92	Wash	7	4	2	6	14	
92-93	Wash	6	6	0	6	4	
93-94	Bos	13	3	1	4	6	
97-98	SJ	6	1	0	1	10	
Totals		71	19	16	35	77	

IGINLA, Jarome 6-1 193 RW
B. Edmonton, Alta., July 1, 1977

96-97	Calg	82	21	29	50	37	-4
97-98	Calg	70	13	19	32	29	-10
98-99	Calg	82	28	23	51	58	+1
Totals		234	62	71	134	124	-13

Playoffs

| 95-96 | Calg | 2 | 1 | 1 | 2 | 0 | |

IGNATIEV, Victor 6-4 215 D
B. Riga, USSR, April 26, 1970

| 98-99 | Pitt | 11 | 0 | 1 | 1 | 6 | -3 |

Playoffs

| 98-99 | Pitt | 1 | 0 | 0 | 0 | 2 | |

IHNACAK, Miroslav 5-11 175 LW
B. Poprad, Czechoslovakia, Nov. 19, 1962

85-86	Tor	21	2	4	6	27	-6
86-87	Tor	34	6	5	11	12	+3
88-89	Det	1	0	0	0	0	
Totals		56	8	9	17	39	-3

Playoffs

| 86-87 | Tor | 1 | 0 | 0 | 0 | 0 | |

IHNACAK, Peter 5-11 180 C
B. Poprad, Czechoslovakia, May 3, 1957

82-83	Tor	80	28	38	66	44	+6
83-84	Tor	47	10	13	23	24	-21
84-85	Tor	70	22	22	44	24	-26
85-86	Tor	63	18	27	45	16	-9
86-87	Tor	58	12	27	39	16	+5
87-88	Tor	68	10	20	30	41	-6
88-89	Tor	26	2	16	18	10	+3
89-90	Tor	5	0	2	2	0	+3
Totals		417	102	165	267	175	-45

Playoffs

85-86	Tor	10	2	3	5	12	
86-87	Tor	13	2	4	6	9	
87-88	Tor	5	0	3	3	4	
Totals		28	4	10	14	25	

IMLACH, Brent F
B. Toronto, Ont., Nov. 16, 1946

65-66	Tor	2	0	0	0	2	
66-67	Tor	1	0	0	0	0	
Totals		3	0	0	0	2	

INGARFIELD, Earl Thompson 5-11 185 C
B. Lethbridge, Alta., Oct. 25, 1934

58-59	NYR	35	1	2	3	10	
59-60	NYR	20	1	2	3	2	
60-61	NYR	66	13	21	34	18	
61-62	NYR	70	26	31	57	18	
62-63	NYR	69	19	24	43	40	
63-64	NYR	63	15	11	26	26	
64-65	NYR	69	15	13	28	40	
65-66	NYR	68	20	16	36	35	
66-67	NYR	67	12	22	34	12	
67-68	Pitt	50	15	22	37	12	-7
68-69	Pitt-Oak	66	16	30	46	12	-18
69-70	Oak	54	21	24	45	10	-7
70-71	Cal	49	5	8	13	4	-8
Totals		746	179	226	405	239	-40

SSN	TEAM	GP	G	A	PTS.	PIM	+/-
Playoffs							
61–62	NYR	6	3	2	5	2	
66–67	NYR	4	1	0	1	2	
68–69	Cal	7	4	6	10	2	
69–70	Oak	4	1	0	1	4	
Totals		21	9	8	17	10	

INGARFIELD, Earl Thompson, Jr. *5–10 175 C*
B. Manhasset, N.Y., Jan. 30, 1959

SSN	TEAM	GP	G	A	PTS.	PIM	+/-
79–80	Atl	1	0	0	0	0	-1
80–81	Calg–Det	38	4	4	8	22	+3
Totals		39	4	4	8	22	+2

Playoffs

| 79–80 | Atl | 2 | 0 | 1 | 1 | 0 | |

INGLIS, William John *5–9 160 C*
B. Ottawa, Ont., May 11, 1943

SSN	TEAM	GP	G	A	PTS.	PIM	+/-
67–68	LA	12	1	1	2	0	-6
68–69	LA	10	0	1	1	0	-2
70–71	Buf	14	0	1	1	4	-4
Totals		36	1	3	4	4	-12

Playoffs

| 68–69 | LA | 11 | 1 | 2 | 3 | 4 | |

***INGOLDSBY, John Gordon (Jack, Ding)** 6–2
210 RW*
B. Toronto, Ont., June 21, 1924

SSN	TEAM	GP	G	A	PTS.	PIM
42–43	Tor	8	0	1	1	0
43–44	Tor	21	5	0	5	15
Totals		29	5	1	6	15

INGRAM, Frank *5–7 185 RW*
B. Graven, Sask., Sept. 17, 1907

SSN	TEAM	GP	G	A	PTS.	PIM
29–30	Chi	37	6	10	16	28
30–31	Chi	43	17	4	21	37
31–32	Chi	21	1	2	3	4
Totals		101	24	16	40	69

Playoffs

29–30	Chi	2	0	0	0	0
30–31	Chi	9	0	1	1	2
Totals		11	0	1	1	2

INGRAM, John *5–11 170 C*
B. Halifax, N.S., 1894

| 24–25 | Bos | 1 | 0 | 0 | 0 | 0 |

INGRAM, Ronald Walter *5–11 185 D*
B. Toronto, Ont., July 5, 1933

SSN	TEAM	GP	G	A	PTS.	PIM
56–57	Chi	45	1	6	7	21
63–64	Det–NYR	66	4	9	13	58
64–65	NYR	3	0	0	0	2
Totals		114	5	15	20	81

Playoffs

| 62–63 | Chi | 2 | 0 | 0 | 0 | 0 |

INTRANUOVO, Ralph *5–8 185 C*
B. East York, Ont., Dec. 11, 1973

SSN	TEAM	GP	G	A	PTS.	PIM	+/-
94–95	Edm	1	0	1	1	0	+1
95–96	Edm	13	1	2	3	4	-3
96–97	Tor–Edm	8	1	1	2	0	-1
Totals		22	2	4	6	4	-3

***IRVIN, James Dickinson (Dick)** F*
B. Limestone Ridge, Ont., July 19, 1892

SSN	TEAM	GP	G	A	PTS.	PIM
26–27	Chi	44	18	18	36	34
27–28	Chi	14	5	4	9	12
28–29	Chi	36	6	1	7	30
Totals		94	29	23	52	76

Playoffs

| 26–27 | Chi | 2 | 2 | 0 | 2 | 4 |

IRVINE, Edward Amos (Ted) *6–2 195 LW*
B. Winnipeg, Man., Dec. 8, 1944

SSN	TEAM	GP	G	A	PTS.	PIM	+/-
63–64	Bos	1	0	0	0	0	
67–68	LA	73	18	22	40	26	-10
68–69	LA	76	15	24	39	47	-17
69–70	LA–NYR	75	11	16	27	38	-26
70–71	NYR	76	20	18	38	137	+18
71–72	NYR	78	15	21	36	66	+8

SSN	TEAM	GP	G	A	PTS.	PIM	+/-
72–73	NYR	53	8	12	20	54	+4
73–74	NYR	75	26	20	46	105	+2
74–75	NYR	79	17	17	34	66	-15
75–76	StL	69	10	13	23	80	-12
76–77	StL	69	14	14	28	38	-16
Totals		724	154	177	331	657	-64

Playoffs

SSN	TEAM	GP	G	A	PTS.	PIM
67–68	LA	6	1	3	4	2
68–69	LA	11	5	1	6	7
69–70	NYR	6	1	2	3	8
70–71	NYR	12	1	2	3	28
71–72	NYR	16	4	5	9	19
72–73	NYR	10	1	3	4	20
73–74	NYR	13	3	5	8	16
74–75	NYR	3	0	1	1	11
75–76	StL	3	0	2	2	2
76–77	StL	3	0	0	0	2
Totals		83	16	24	40	115

IRWIN, Ivan Duane (Ivan the Terrible) *6–2
185 D*
B. Chicago, Ill., Mar. 13, 1927

SSN	TEAM	GP	G	A	PTS.	PIM
52–53	Mont	4	0	1	1	0
53–54	NYR	56	2	12	14	109
54–55	NYR	60	0	13	13	85
55–56	NYR	34	0	1	1	20
57–58	NYR	1	0	0	0	0
Totals		155	2	27	29	214

Playoffs

| 55–56 | NYR | 5 | 0 | 0 | 0 | 8 |

ISAKSSON, Ulf *6–1 185 LW*
B. Norfunda, Sweden, Mar. 19, 1954

| 82–83 | LA | 50 | 7 | 15 | 22 | 10 | +1 |

ISBISTER, Brad *6–2 198 RW*
B. Edmonton, Alta., May 7, 1977

SSN	TEAM	GP	G	A	PTS.	PIM	+/-
97–98	Phoe	66	9	8	17	102	+4
98–99	Phoe–NYI	32	4	4	8	46	+1
Totals		98	13	12	25	148	+5

Playoffs

| 97–98 | Phoe | 5 | 0 | 0 | 0 | 2 |

ISSEL, Kim *6–4 196 RW*
B. Regina, Sask., Sept. 25, 1967

| 88–89 | Edm | 4 | 0 | 0 | 0 | 0 | -1 |

***JACKSON, Arthur M.** 5–7 165 C*
B. Toronto, Ont., Dec. 15, 1915

SSN	TEAM	GP	G	A	PTS.	PIM
34–35	Tor	20	1	3	4	4
35–36	Tor	48	5	15	20	14
36–37	Tor	14	2	0	2	2
37–38	Bos	48	9	3	12	24
38–39	NYA	48	12	13	25	15
39–40	Bos	45	7	18	25	6
40–41	Bos	47	17	15	32	10
41–42	Bos	47	6	18	24	25
42–43	Bos	50	22	31	53	20
43–44	Bos	49	21	38	59	8
44–45	Bos–Tor	50	14	21	35	16
Totals		466	116	175	291	144

Playoffs

SSN	TEAM	GP	G	A	PTS.	PIM
35–36	Tor	8	0	3	3	2
37–38	Bos	3	0	0	0	0
38–39	NYA	2	0	0	0	2
39–40	Bos	5	1	2	3	0
40–41	Bos	11	1	3	4	16
41–42	Bos	5	0	1	1	0
42–43	Bos	9	6	3	9	7
44–45	Tor	8	0	0	0	0
Totals		51	8	12	20	27

JACKSON, Dane *6–1 200 RW*
B. Castlegar, B.C., May 17, 1970

SSN	TEAM	GP	G	A	PTS.	PIM	+/-
93–94	Van	12	5	1	6	9	+3
94–95	Van	3	1	0	1	4	0
95–96	Buf	22	5	4	9	41	+3
97–98	NYI	8	1	1	2	4	+1
Totals		45	12	6	18	58	+7

Playoffs

| 94–95 | Van | 6 | 0 | 0 | 0 | 10 |

JACKSON, Donald Clinton *6–3 210 D*
B. Minneapolis, Minn., Sept. 2, 1956

SSN	TEAM	GP	G	A	PTS.	PIM	+/-
77–78	Minn	2	0	0	0	2	+1
78–79	Minn	5	0	0	0	2	-1
79–80	Minn	10	0	4	4	18	+4
80–81	Edm	10	0	3	3	19	+3
81–82	Edm	8	0	0	0	18	
82–83	Edm	71	2	8	10	136	+12
83–84	Edm	60	8	12	20	120	+28
84–85	Edm	78	3	17	20	141	+27
85–86	Edm	45	2	8	10	93	+2
86–87	NYR	22	1	0	1	91	-1
Totals		311	16	52	68	640	+75

Playoffs

SSN	TEAM	GP	G	A	PTS.	PIM
79–80	Minn	1	0	0	0	0
82–83	Edm	16	3	3	6	30
83–84	Edm	19	1	2	3	32
84–85	Edm	9	0	0	0	64
85–86	Edm	8	0	0	0	21
Totals		53	4	5	9	147

***JACKSON, Harold Russell (Hal)** 5–11 175 D*
B. Cedar Springs, Ont., Aug. 1, 1917

SSN	TEAM	GP	G	A	PTS.	PIM
36–37	Chi	40	1	3	4	6
37–38	Chi	4	0	0	0	0
40–41	Det	1	0	0	0	0
42–43	Det	4	0	4	4	6
43–44	Det	50	7	12	19	76
44–45	Det	50	5	6	11	45
45–46	Det	36	3	4	7	36
46–47	Det	37	1	5	6	39
Totals		222	17	34	51	208

Playoffs

SSN	TEAM	GP	G	A	PTS.	PIM
37–38	Chi	1	0	0	0	2
42–43	Det	6	0	1	1	4
43–44	Det	5	0	0	0	11
44–45	Det	14	1	1	2	10
45–46	Det	5	0	0	0	6
Totals		31	1	2	3	33

JACKSON, James Kenneth *5–9 190 LW*
B. Oshawa, Ont., Feb. 1, 1960

SSN	TEAM	GP	G	A	PTS.	PIM	+/-
82–83	Calg	48	8	12	20	7	+9
83–84	Calg	49	6	14	20	13	+1
84–85	Calg	10	1	4	5	0	+1
87–88	Buf	5	2	0	2	0	0
Totals		112	17	30	47	20	+11

Playoffs

SSN	TEAM	GP	G	A	PTS.	PIM
82–83	Calg	8	2	1	3	2
83–84	Calg	6	1	1	2	4
Totals		14	3	2	5	6

JACKSON, Jeff *6–1 195 LW*
B. Dresden, Ont., Apr. 24, 1965

SSN	TEAM	GP	G	A	PTS.	PIM	+/-
84–85	Tor	17	0	1	1	24	-4
85–86	Tor	5	1	2	3	2	+3
86–87	Tor–NYR	64	13	8	21	79	+4
87–88	Que	68	9	18	27	103	+5
88–89	Que	33	4	6	10	28	-15
89–90	Que	65	8	12	20	71	-21
90–91	Que	10	3	1	4	4	+3
91–92	Chi	1	0	0	0	2	0
Totals		263	38	48	86	313	-43

Playoffs

| 86–87 | NYR | 6 | 1 | 1 | 2 | 16 |

JACKSON, John Alexander *5–10 185 D*
B. Windsor, Ont., May 3, 1925

| 46–47 | Chi | 48 | 2 | 5 | 7 | 38 |

JACKSON, Lloyd Edgar *5–9 150 C*
B. Ottawa, Ont., Jan. 7, 1912

| 36–37 | NYA | 14 | 1 | 1 | 2 | 0 |

***JACKSON, Ralph Harvey (Busher)** 5–11 195
F*
B. Toronto, Ont., Jan. 19, 1911

SSN	TEAM	GP	G	A	PTS.	PIM
29–30	Tor	32	12	6	18	29
30–31	Tor	43	18	13	31	81
31–32	Tor	48	28	25	53	63
32–33	Tor	48	27	17	44	43
33–34	Tor	38	20	18	38	38

SSN	TEAM	GP	G	A	PTS.	PIM	+/-
34–35	Tor	42	22	22	44	27	
35–36	Tor	47	11	11	22	19	
36–37	Tor	46	21	19	40	12	
37–38	Tor	48	17	17	34	18	
38–39	Tor	42	10	17	27	12	
39–40	NYA	43	12	8	20	10	
40–41	NYA	46	8	18	26	4	
41–42	Bos	27	5	7	12	18	
42–43	Bos	44	19	15	34	38	
43–44	Bos	42	11	21	32	25	
Totals		636	241	234	475	437	

Playoffs

SSN	TEAM	GP	G	A	PTS.	PIM	+/-
30–31	Tor	2	0	0	0	0	
31–32	Tor	7	5	2	7	13	
32–33	Tor	9	3	1	4	2	
33–34	Tor	5	1	0	1	8	
34–35	Tor	7	3	2	5	2	
35–36	Tor	9	3	2	5	4	
36–37	Tor	2	1	0	1	2	
37–38	Tor	6	1	0	1	8	
38–39	Tor	7	0	1	1	2	
39–40	NYA	3	0	1	1	2	
41–42	Bos	5	0	1	1	0	
42–43	Bos	9	1	2	3	10	
Totals		71	18	12	30	53	

*JACKSON, Stanton (Stan) LW

SSN	TEAM	GP	G	A	PTS.	PIM	+/-
21–22	Tor	1	0	0	0	0	
23–24	Tor	21	1	1	2	6	
24–25	Tor–Bos	27	5	0	5	36	
25–26	Bos	28	3	3	6	30	
26–27	Ott	7	0	0	0	2	
Totals		84	9	4	13	74	

JACKSON, Walter (Red) 160 F
B. Instock, England, June 3, 1908

SSN	TEAM	GP	G	A	PTS.	PIM	+/-
32–33	NYA	35	10	2	12	6	
33–34	NYA	46	6	9	15	12	
34–35	NYA	1	0	0	0	0	
Totals		82	16	11	27	18	

*JACOBS, Paul F

SSN	TEAM	GP	G	A	PTS.	PIM	+/-
18–19	Tor	1	0	0	0	0	

JACOBS, Timothy James 5–10 180 D
B. Espanola, Ont., Mar. 28, 1952

SSN	TEAM	GP	G	A	PTS.	PIM	+/-
75–76	Cal	46	0	10	10	35	-2

JAGR, Jaromir 6–2 208 RW
B. Kladno, Czechoslovakia, Feb. 15, 1972

SSN	TEAM	GP	G	A	PTS.	PIM	+/-
90–91	Pitt	80	27	30	57	42	-4
91–92	Pitt	70	32	37	69	34	+12
92–93	Pitt	81	34	60	94	61	+30
93–94	Pitt	80	32	67	99	61	+15
94–95	Pitt	48	32	38	70	37	+23
95–96	Pitt	82	62	87	149	96	+31
96–97	Pitt	63	47	48	95	40	+22
97–98	Pitt	77	35	67	102	64	+17
98–99	Pitt	81	44	83	127	66	+17
Totals		662	345	517	862	501	+162

Playoffs

SSN	TEAM	GP	G	A	PTS.	PIM	+/-
90–91	Pitt	24	3	10	13	6	
91–92	Pitt	21	11	13	24	6	
92–93	Pitt	12	5	4	9	23	
93–94	Pitt	6	2	4	6	16	
94–95	Pitt	12	10	5	15	6	
95–96	Pitt	18	11	12	23	18	
96–97	Pitt	5	4	4	8	4	
97–98	Pitt	6	4	5	9	2	
98–99	Pitt	9	5	7	12	16	
Totals		113	55	64	119	97	

JAKOPIN, John 6–5 220 D
B. Toronto, Ont., May 16, 1975

SSN	TEAM	GP	G	A	PTS.	PIM	+/-
97–98	Fla	2	0	0	0	4	-3
98–99	Fla	3	0	0	0	0	-1
Totals		5	0	0	0	4	-4

JALO, Risto 5–11 185 C
B. Tampere, Finland, July 18, 1962

SSN	TEAM	GP	G	A	PTS.	PIM	+/-
85–86	Edm	3	0	3	3	0	+2

JALONEN, Kari 6–3 190 C
B. Oulu, Finland, Jan. 6, 1960

SSN	TEAM	GP	G	A	PTS.	PIM	+/-
82–83	Calg	25	9	3	12	4	+8
83–84	Calg–Edm	12	0	3	3	0	-3
Totals		37	9	6	15	4	+5

Playoffs

SSN	TEAM	GP	G	A	PTS.	PIM	+/-
82–83	Calg	5	1	0	1	0	

JAMES, Gerald Edwin (Gerry) 5–11 191 RW
B. Regina, Sask., Oct. 22, 1934

SSN	TEAM	GP	G	A	PTS.	PIM	+/-
54–55	Tor	1	0	0	0	0	
55–56	Tor	46	3	3	6	50	
56–57	Tor	53	4	12	16	90	
57–58	Tor	15	3	2	5	61	
59–60	Tor	34	4	9	13	56	
Totals		149	14	26	40	257	

Playoffs

SSN	TEAM	GP	G	A	PTS.	PIM	+/-
55–56	Tor	5	1	0	1	8	
59–60	Tor	10	0	0	0	0	
Totals		15	1	0	1	8	

JAMES, Valmore (Val) 6–2 205 LW
B. Ocala, Fla., Feb. 14, 1957

SSN	TEAM	GP	G	A	PTS.	PIM	+/-
81–82	Buf	7	0	0	0	16	-1
86–87	Tor	4	0	0	0	14	0
Totals		11	0	0	0	30	-1

JAMIESON, James 5–8 170 D
B. Brantford, Ont., Mar. 21, 1922

SSN	TEAM	GP	G	A	PTS.	PIM	+/-
43–44	NYR	1	0	1	1	0	

JANKOWSKI, Louis Casimer 6–0 184 LW
B. Regina, Sask., June 27, 1931

SSN	TEAM	GP	G	A	PTS.	PIM	+/-
50–51	Det	1	0	1	1	0	
52–53	Det	22	1	2	3	0	
53–54	Chi	68	15	13	28	7	
54–55	Chi	36	3	2	5	8	
Totals		127	19	18	37	15	

Playoffs

SSN	TEAM	GP	G	A	PTS.	PIM	+/-
52–53	Det	1	0	0	0	0	

JANNEY, Craig 6–1 190 C
B. Hartford, Conn., Sept. 26, 1967

SSN	TEAM	GP	G	A	PTS.	PIM	+/-
87–88	Bos	15	7	9	16	0	+6
88–89	Bos	62	16	46	62	12	+20
89–90	Bos	55	24	38	62	4	+3
90–91	Bos	77	26	66	92	8	+15
91–92	Bos–StL	78	18	69	87	22	+6
92–93	StL	84	24	82	106	12	-4
93–94	StL	69	16	68	84	24	-14
94–95	StL–SJ	35	7	20	27	10	-1
95–96	SJ–Winn	84	20	62	82	26	-33
96–97	Phoe	77	15	38	53	26	-1
97–98	Phoe	68	10	43	53	12	+5
98–99	TB–NYI	56	5	22	27	14	-15
Totals		760	188	563	751	170	-13

Playoffs

SSN	TEAM	GP	G	A	PTS.	PIM	+/-
87–88	Bos	23	6	10	16	11	
88–89	Bos	10	4	9	13	21	
89–90	Bos	18	3	19	22	2	
90–91	Bos	18	4	18	22	11	
91–92	StL	6	0	6	6	0	
92–93	StL	11	2	9	11	0	
93–94	StL	4	1	3	4	0	
94–95	SJ	11	3	4	7	4	
95–96	Winn	6	1	2	3	0	
96–97	Phoe	7	0	3	3	4	
97–98	Phoe	6	0	3	3	0	
Totals		120	24	86	110	53	

JANSSENS, Mark 6–3 216 C
B. Surrey, B.C., May 19, 1968

SSN	TEAM	GP	G	A	PTS.	PIM	+/-
87–88	NYR	1	0	0	0	0	0
88–89	NYR	5	0	0	0	0	-4
89–90	NYR	80	5	8	13	161	-25
90–91	NYR	67	9	7	16	172	-1
91–92	NYR–Minn	7	0	0	0	5	-2
92–93	Hart	76	12	17	29	237	-15
93–94	Hart	84	2	10	12	137	-13
94–95	Hart	46	2	5	7	93	-8
95–96	Hart	81	2	7	9	155	-13
96–97	Hart–Ana	66	2	6	8	137	-13
97–98	Ana–NYI–Phoe	74	5	7	12	154	-21
98–99	Chi	60	1	0	1	65	-11
Totals		647	40	67	107	1316	-126

Playoffs

SSN	TEAM	GP	G	A	PTS.	PIM	+/-
89–90	NYR	9	2	1	3	10	
90–91	NYR	6	3	0	3	6	
96–97	Ana	11	0	0	0	15	
97–98	Phoe	1	0	0	0	2	
Totals		27	5	1	6	33	

JANTUNEN, Marko 5–10 185 C
B. Lahti, Finland, Feb. 14, 1971

SSN	TEAM	GP	G	A	PTS.	PIM	+/-
96–97	Calg	3	0	0	0	0	-1

JARRETT, Douglas William 6–1 205 D
B. London, Ont., Apr. 22, 1944

SSN	TEAM	GP	G	A	PTS.	PIM	+/-
64–65	Chi	46	2	15	17	34	
65–66	Chi	66	4	12	16	71	
66–67	Chi	70	5	21	26	76	
67–68	Chi	74	4	19	23	48	-15
68–69	Chi	69	0	13	13	58	+7
69–70	Chi	72	4	20	24	78	+33
70–71	Chi	51	1	12	13	46	+10
71–72	Chi	78	6	23	29	68	+39
72–73	Chi	49	2	11	13	18	+9
73–74	Chi	67	5	11	16	45	+5
74–75	Chi	79	5	21	26	66	+13
75–76	NYR	45	0	4	4	19	-25
76–77	NYR	9	0	0	0	4	-6
Totals		775	38	182	220	631	+70

Playoffs

SSN	TEAM	GP	G	A	PTS.	PIM	+/-
64–65	Chi	11	1	0	1	10	
65–66	Chi	5	0	1	1	9	
66–67	Chi	6	0	3	3	8	
67–68	Chi	11	4	0	4	9	
69–70	Chi	8	1	0	1	4	
70–71	Chi	18	1	6	7	14	
71–72	Chi	8	0	2	2	16	
72–73	Chi	15	0	3	3	2	
73–74	Chi	10	0	1	1	6	
74–75	Chi	7	0	0	0	4	
Totals		99	7	16	23	82	

JARRETT, Gary Walter 5–8 170 LW
B. Toronto, Ont., Sept. 3, 1942

SSN	TEAM	GP	G	A	PTS.	PIM	+/-
60–61	Tor	1	0	0	0	0	
66–67	Det	4	0	0	0	0	
67–68	Det	68	18	21	39	20	+4
68–69	Oak	63	22	23	45	22	-8
69–70	Oak	75	12	19	31	31	-24
70–71	Cal	75	15	19	34	40	-27
71–72	Cal	55	5	10	15	18	0
72–73	Clev (WHA)	77	40	39	79	79	
73–74	Clev (WHA)	75	31	39	70	68	
74–75	Clev (WHA)	77	17	24	41	70	
75–76	Clev (WHA)	69	16	17	33	22	
NHL Totals		341	72	92	164	131	-55
WHA Totals		298	104	119	223	239	

Playoffs

SSN	TEAM	GP	G	A	PTS.	PIM	+/-
68–69	Cal	7	2	1	3	4	
69–70	Oak	4	1	0	1	5	
72–73	Clev (WHA)	9	8	3	11	19	
73–74	Clev (WHA)	5	1	1	2	13	
74–75	Clev (WHA)	5	0	1	1	0	
75–76	Clev (WHA)	3	0	3	3	2	
NHL Totals		11	3	1	4	9	
WHA Totals		22	9	8	17	34	

JARRY, Pierre Joseph Reynald 5–11 182 LW
B. Montreal, Que., Mar. 30, 1949

SSN	TEAM	GP	G	A	PTS.	PIM	+/-
71–72	NYR–Tor	52	6	7	13	33	-1
72–73	Tor	74	19	18	37	42	-13
73–74	Tor–Det	64	17	31	48	27	-3
74–75	Det	39	8	13	21	4	-12
75–76	Minn	59	21	18	39	32	-7
76–77	Minn	21	8	13	21	2	-6
77–78	Minn	35	9	17	26	2	-9
77–78	Edm (WHA)	18	4	10	14	4	
NHL Totals		344	88	117	205	142	-51
WHA Totals		18	4	10	14	4	

Playoffs

SSN	TEAM	GP	G	A	PTS.	PIM	+/-
71–72	Tor	5	0	1	1	0	
77–78	Edm (WHA)	5	1	0	1	4	
NHL Totals		5	0	1	1	0	
WHA Totals		5	1	0	1	4	

JARVENPAA, Hannu *6–0 194 RW*
B. Ii, Finland, May 19, 1963

86–87	Winn	20	1	8	9	8	-4
87–88	Winn	41	6	11	17	34	0
88–89	Winn	53	4	7	11	41	-14
Totals		**114**	**11**	**26**	**37**	**83**	**-18**

JARVI, Iiro *6–1 198 LW*
B. Helsinki, Finland, Mar. 23, 1965

88–89	Que	75	11	30	41	40	-13
89–90	Que	41	7	13	20	18	-11
Totals		**116**	**18**	**43**	**61**	**58**	**-24**

JARVIS, Douglas *5–9 170 C*
B. Brantford, Ont., Mar. 24, 1955

75–76	Mont	80	5	30	35	16	+17
76–77	Mont	80	16	22	38	14	+30
77–78	Mont	80	11	28	39	23	+12
78–79	Mont	80	10	13	23	16	+5
79–80	Mont	80	13	11	24	28	-5
80–81	Mont	80	16	22	38	34	+12
81–82	Mont	80	20	28	48	20	+34
82–83	Wash	80	8	22	30	10	-12
83–84	Wash	80	13	29	42	12	+7
84–85	Wash	80	9	28	37	32	+19
85–86	Wash–Hart	82	9	18	27	36	+2
86–87	Hart	80	9	13	22	20	0
87–88	Hart	2	0	0	0	2	0
Totals		**964**	**139**	**264**	**403**	**263**	**+121**

Playoffs

75–76	Mont	13	2	1	3	2	
76–77	Mont	14	0	7	7	2	
77–78	Mont	15	3	5	8	12	
78–79	Mont	12	1	3	4	4	
79–80	Mont	10	4	4	8	2	
80–81	Mont	3	0	0	0	0	
81–82	Mont	5	1	0	1	4	
82–83	Wash	4	0	1	1	0	
83–84	Wash	8	2	3	5	6	
84–85	Wash	5	1	0	1	2	
85–86	Hart	10	0	3	3	4	
86–87	Hart	6	0	0	0	4	
Totals		**105**	**14**	**27**	**41**	**42**	

JARVIS, James (Bud) *5–6 165 LW*
B. Fort William, Ont., Dec. 7, 1907

29–30	Pitt Pi	41	11	8	19	32
30–31	Phil Q	43	5	7	12	30
36–37	Tor	24	1	0	1	0
Totals		**108**	**17**	**15**	**32**	**62**

JARVIS, Wesley Herbert *5–11 185 C*
B. Toronto, Ont., May 30, 1958

79–80	Wash	63	11	15	26	8	-3
80–81	Wash	55	9	14	23	20	-9
81–82	Wash	26	1	12	13	18	+5
82–83	Minn	3	0	0	0	2	-2
83–84	LA	61	9	13	22	36	-7
84–85	Tor	26	0	1	1	2	-6
85–86	Tor	2	1	0	1	2	-1
87–88	Tor	1	0	0	0	0	0
Totals		**237**	**31**	**55**	**86**	**98**	**-23**

Playoffs

86–87	Tor	2	0	0	0	2

JAVANAINEN, Arto *6–0 185 LW*
B. Pori, Finland, Apr. 8, 1959

84–85	Pitt	14	4	1	5	2	+1

JAY, Bob *5–11 190 D*
B. Burlington, Mass., Nov. 18, 1965

93–94	LA	3	0	1	1	0	-2

JEFFREY, Lawrence Joseph *5–11 189 LW*
B. Zurich, Ont., Oct. 12, 1940

61–62	Det	18	5	3	8	20	
62–63	Det	53	5	11	16	62	
63–64	Det	58	10	18	28	87	
64–65	Det	41	4	2	6	48	
65–66	Tor	20	1	1	2	22	
66–67	Tor	56	11	17	28	27	
67–68	NYR	47	2	4	6	15	-13
68–69	NYR	75	1	6	7	12	0
Totals		**368**	**39**	**62**	**101**	**293**	**13**

Playoffs

62–63	Det	9	3	3	6	8	
63–64	Det	14	1	6	7	28	
64–65	Det	2	0	0	0	0	
66–67	Tor	6	0	1	1	4	
67–68	NYR	4	0	0	0	2	
Totals		**38**	**4**	**10**	**14**	**42**	

JELINEK, Tomas *5–9 189 RW*
B. Prague, Czechoslovakia, Apr. 29, 1962

92–93	Ott	49	7	6	13	52	-24

JENKINS, Dean *6–0 190 RW*
B. Billerica, Mass., Nov. 21, 1959

83–84	LA	5	0	0	0	2	-1

JENKINS, Roger *5–11 173 D*
B. Appleton, Wis., Nov. 18, 1911

30–31	Tor–Chi	31	0	1	1	14
32–33	Chi	45	3	10	13	42
33–34	Chi	48	2	2	4	63
34–35	Mont	45	4	6	10	63
35–36	Bos	42	2	6	8	51
36–37	Mont–					
	Mont M–NYA	37	1	4	5	14
37–38	Chi	39	1	8	9	26
38–39	Chi–NYA	41	2	2	4	6
Totals		**328**	**15**	**39**	**54**	**279**

Playoffs

30–31	Chi	3	0	0	0	0
33–34	Chi	8	0	0	0	0
34–35	Mont	2	1	0	1	2
35–36	Bos	2	0	1	1	2
37–38	Chi	10	0	6	6	8
Totals		**25**	**1**	**7**	**8**	**12**

JENNINGS, Grant *6–3 210 D*
B. Hudson Bay, Sask., May 5, 1965

88–89	Hart	55	3	10	13	159	+17
89–90	Hart	64	3	6	9	171	-4
90–91	Hart–Pitt	57	2	7	9	108	-11
91–92	Pitt	53	4	5	9	104	-1
92–93	Pitt	58	0	5	5	65	+6
93–94	Pitt	61	2	4	6	126	-10
94–95	Pitt–Tor	35	0	6	6	43	-4
95–96	Buf	6	0	0	0	28	+1
Totals		**389**	**14**	**43**	**57**	**804**	**-6**

Playoffs

87–88	Wash	1	0	0	0	0	
88–89	Hart	4	1	0	1	17	
89–90	Hart	7	0	0	0	13	
90–91	Pitt	13	1	1	2	16	
91–92	Pitt	10	0	0	0	12	
92–93	Pitt	12	0	0	0	8	
93–94	Pitt	3	0	0	0	2	
94–95	Tor	4	0	0	0	0	
Totals		**54**	**2**	**1**	**3**	**68**	

JENNINGS, Joseph William (Bill) *5–9 165 RW*
B. Toronto, Ont., June 28, 1917

40–41	Det	12	1	5	6	2
41–42	Det	16	2	1	3	6
42–43	Det	8	3	3	6	2
43–44	Det	33	6	11	17	10
44–45	Bos	39	20	13	33	25
Totals		**108**	**32**	**33**	**65**	**45**

Playoffs

40–41	Det	9	2	2	4	0
43–44	Det	4	0	0	0	0
44–45	Bos	7	2	2	4	6
Totals		**20**	**4**	**4**	**8**	**6**

JENSEN, Chris *5–11 180 RW*
B. Fort St. John, B.C., Oct. 28, 1963

85–86	NYR	9	1	3	4	0	+1
86–87	NYR	37	6	7	13	21	-1
87–88	NYR	7	0	1	1	2	-1
89–90	Phil	1	0	0	0	2	-1
90–91	Phil	18	2	1	3	2	-5
91–92	Phil	2	0	0	0	0	-1
Totals		**74**	**9**	**12**	**21**	**27**	**-8**

JENSEN, David A. *6–1 195 C*
B. Newton, Mass., Aug. 19, 1965

84–85	Hart	13	0	4	4	6	-1
85–86	Wash	5	1	0	1	0	+1
86–87	Wash	46	8	8	16	12	-10
87–88	Wash	5	0	1	1	4	0
Totals		**69**	**9**	**13**	**22**	**22**	**-10**

Playoffs

85–86	Wash	4	0	0	0	0	
86–87	Wash	7	0	0	0	2	
Totals		**11**	**0**	**0**	**0**	**2**	

JENSEN, David Henry *6–1 185 D*
B. Minneapolis, Minn., May 3, 1961

83–84	Minn	8	0	1	1	0	+2
84–85	Minn	5	0	1	1	4	-5
85–86	Minn	5	0	0	0	7	-2
Totals		**18**	**0**	**2**	**2**	**11**	**-5**

JENSEN, Steven Allan *6–2 190 LW*
B. Minneapolis, Minn., Apr. 14, 1955

75–76	Minn	19	7	6	13	6	-5
76–77	Minn	78	22	23	45	62	-6
77–78	Minn	74	13	17	30	73	-30
78–79	LA	72	23	8	31	57	-28
79–80	LA	76	21	15	36	13	-39
80–81	LA	74	19	19	38	88	-6
81–82	LA	45	8	19	27	19	-14
Totals		**438**	**113**	**107**	**220**	**318**	**-128**

Playoffs

76–77	Minn	2	0	1	1	0
78–79	LA	2	0	0	0	0
79–80	LA	4	0	0	0	2
80–81	LA	4	0	2	2	7
Totals		**12**	**0**	**3**	**3**	**9**

*JEREMIAH, Edward J. *D*
B. Worcester, Mass., Nov. 4, 1905

31–32	NYA–Bos	1	0	1	1	0

JERRARD, Paul *5–10 185 D*
B. Winnipeg, Man., Apr. 20, 1965

88–89	Minn	5	0	0	0	4	+1

JERWA, Frank *6–1 179 LW*
B. Bankhead, Alta., Feb. 28, 1910

31–32	Bos	29	4	5	9	14
32–33	Bos	34	3	4	7	23
33–34	Bos	7	0	0	0	2
34–35	Bos–StL E	21	4	7	11	14
Totals		**91**	**11**	**16**	**27**	**53**

*JERWA, Joseph *5–2 185 D*
B. Bankhead, Alta., Jan. 22, 1909

30–31	NYR	33	4	7	11	72
31–32	Bos	6	0	0	0	8
33–34	Bos	3	0	0	0	8
35–36	NYA	48	9	12	21	65
36–37	Bos–NYA	48	9	13	22	57
37–38	NYA	47	3	14	17	53
38–39	NYA	48	4	12	16	52
Totals		**233**	**29**	**58**	**87**	**315**

Playoffs

30–31	NYR	4	0	0	0	8
35–36	NYA	5	2	3	5	2
37–38	NYA	6	0	0	0	8
38–39	NYA	2	0	0	0	2
Totals		**17**	**2**	**3**	**5**	**20**

JIRIK, Jaroslav *5–11 170 RW*
B. Vojnuv Mestac, Czechoslovakia, Dec. 10, 1939

69–70	StL	3	0	0	0	0	+1

JOANETTE, Rosario (Kit) *5–11 168 C*
B. Valleyfield, Que., July 27, 1919

44–45	Mont	2	0	1	1	4

JODZIO, Richard Joseph (Rick) *6–1 190 LW*
B. Edmonton, Alta., June 3, 1954

74–75	Van (WHA)	44	1	3	4	159
75–76	Calg (WHA)	47	10	7	17	137

Playoffs

SSN	TEAM	GP	G	A	PTS.	PIM	+/-
98–99	Tor	17	3	2	5	4	

JOHNSON, Norman B. F
B. Moose Jaw, Sask., Nov. 27, 1932

SSN	TEAM	GP	G	A	PTS.	PIM	+/-
57–58	Bos	15	2	3	5	8	
58–59	Bos–Chi	46	3	17	20	33	
Totals		61	5	20	25	41	

Playoffs

57–58	Bos	12	4	0	4	6	
59–60	Chi	2	0	0	0	0	
Totals		14	4	0	4	6	

JOHNSON, Norman James (Jim, J.J.) 5–9 190 C
B. Winnipeg, Man., Nov. 7, 1942

SSN	TEAM	GP	G	A	PTS.	PIM	+/-
64–65	NYR	1	0	0	0	0	
65–66	NYR	5	1	0	1	0	
66–67	NYR	2	0	0	0	0	
67–68	Phil	13	2	1	3	2	-1
68–69	Phil	69	17	27	44	20	-5
69–70	Phil	72	18	30	48	17	+1
70–71	Phil	66	16	29	45	16	-10
71–72	Phil–LA	74	21	24	45	18	-22
72–73	Minn (WHA)	33	9	14	23	12	
73–74	Minn (WHA)	71	15	39	54	30	
74–75	Minn–Ind (WHA)	53	8	18	26	12	
NHL Totals		302	75	111	186	73	-37
WHA Totals		157	32	71	103	54	

Playoffs

68–69	Phil	3	0	0	0	2	
70–71	Phil	4	0	2	2	0	
72–73	Minn (WHA)	5	2	1	3	2	
73–74	Minn (WHA)	11	1	4	5	4	
NHL Totals		7	0	2	2	2	
WHA Totals		16	3	5	8	6	

JOHNSON, Ryan 6–2 185 C
B. Thunder Bay, Ont., June 14, 1976

SSN	TEAM	GP	G	A	PTS.	PIM	+/-
97–98	Fla	10	0	2	2	0	-4
98–99	Fla	1	1	0	1	0	0
Totals		11	1	2	3	0	-4

JOHNSON, Terrance 6–3 210 D
B. Calgary, Alta., Nov. 28, 1958

SSN	TEAM	GP	G	A	PTS.	PIM	+/-
79–80	Que	3	0	0	0	2	0
80–81	Que	13	0	1	1	46	-1
81–82	Que	6	0	1	1	5	-1
82–83	Que	3	0	0	0	2	0
83–84	StL	65	2	6	8	143	+5
84–85	StL	74	0	7	7	120	-6
85–86	StL–Calg	73	1	8	9	158	-3
86–87	Tor	48	0	1	1	104	-5
Totals		285	3	24	27	580	-11

Playoffs

80–81	Que	2	0	0	0	0	
83–84	StL	11	0	1	1	25	
84–85	StL	3	0	0	0	19	
85–86	Calg	17	0	3	3	64	
86–87	Tor	2	0	0	0	0	
Totals		35	0	4	4	108	

***JOHNSON, Thomas Christian** 6–0 180 D
B. Baldur, Man., Feb. 18, 1928

SSN	TEAM	GP	G	A	PTS.	PIM	+/-
47–48	Mont	1	0	0	0	0	
50–51	Mont	70	2	8	10	128	
51–52	Mont	67	0	7	7	76	
52–53	Mont	70	3	8	11	63	
53–54	Mont	70	7	11	18	85	
54–55	Mont	70	6	19	25	74	
55–56	Mont	64	3	10	13	75	
56–57	Mont	70	4	11	15	59	
57–58	Mont	66	3	18	21	75	
58–59	Mont	70	10	29	39	76	
59–60	Mont	64	4	25	29	59	
60–61	Mont	70	1	15	16	54	
61–62	Mont	62	1	17	18	45	
62–63	Mont	43	3	5	8	28	
63–64	Bos	70	4	21	25	33	
64–65	Bos	51	0	9	9	30	
Totals		978	51	213	264	960	

Playoffs

SSN	TEAM	GP	G	A	PTS.	PIM	+/-
49–50	Mont	1	0	0	0	0	
50–51	Mont	11	0	0	0	6	
51–52	Mont	11	1	0	1	2	
52–53	Mont	12	2	3	5	8	
53–54	Mont	11	1	2	3	30	
54–55	Mont	12	2	0	2	22	
55–56	Mont	10	0	2	2	8	
56–57	Mont	10	0	2	2	13	
57–58	Mont	2	0	0	0	0	
58–59	Mont	11	2	3	5	8	
59–60	Mont	8	0	1	1	4	
60–61	Mont	6	0	1	1	8	
61–62	Mont	6	0	1	1	0	
Totals		111	8	15	23	109	

JOHNSON, Virgil 5–8 165 D
B. Minneapolis, Minn., Mar. 4, 1912

37–38	Chi	25	1	0	1	2	
43–44	Chi	48	1	8	9	23	
44–45	Chi	2	0	1	1	2	
Totals		75	2	9	11	27	

Playoffs

37–38	Chi	10	0	0	0	0	
43–44	Chi	9	0	3	3	4	
Totals		19	0	3	3	4	

JOHNSON, William Odd 6–0 163 C
B. Port Aurthur, Ont., July 27, 1928

49–50	Tor	1	0	0	0	0	

JOHNSTON, Bernard 5–11 185 C
B. Toronto, Ont., Sept. 15, 1956

79–80	Hart	32	8	13	21	8	+9
80–81	Hart	25	4	11	15	8	-4
Totals		57	12	24	36	16	+5

Playoffs

79–80	Hart	3	0	1	1	0	

JOHNSTON, George Joseph (Wingy) 5–8 160 RW
B. St. Charles, Man., July 30, 1920

41–42	Chi	2	2	0	2	0	
42–43	Chi	30	10	7	17	0	
45–46	Chi	16	5	4	9	2	
46–47	Chi	10	3	1	4	0	
Totals		58	20	12	32	2	

JOHNSTON, Greg 6–1 205 RW
B. Barrie, Ont., Jan. 14, 1965

83–84	Bos	15	2	1	3	2	-3
84–85	Bos	6	0	0	0	0	-1
85–86	Bos	20	0	2	2	0	-1
86–87	Bos	76	12	15	27	79	-7
88–89	Bos	57	11	10	21	32	+7
89–90	Bos	9	1	1	2	6	-1
90–91	Tor	1	0	0	0	0	0
91–92	Tor	3	0	1	1	5	-1
Totals		187	26	30	56	124	-7

Playoffs

86–87	Bos	4	0	0	0	0	
87–88	Bos	3	0	1	1	2	
88–89	Bos	10	1	0	1	6	
89–90	Bos	5	1	0	1	4	
Totals		22	2	1	3	12	

JOHNSTON, John (Jay) 5–11 180 D
B. Hamilton, Ont., Feb. 28, 1958

80–81	Wash	2	0	0	0	9	0
81–82	Wash	6	0	0	0	0	-2
Totals		8	0	0	0	9	-2

JOHNSTON, Joseph John (Joey) 5–10 180 LW
B. Peterborough, Ont., Mar. 3, 1949

68–69	Minn	12	1	0	1	6	-1
71–72	Cal	77	15	17	32	107	-28
72–73	Cal	71	28	21	49	62	-19
73–74	Cal	78	27	40	67	67	-37
74–75	Cal	62	14	23	37	72	-30
75–76	Chi	32	0	5	5	6	-5
Totals		332	85	106	191	320	-120

JOHNSTON, Lawrence Marshall (Marsh)
5–11 175 D
B. Birch Hills, Sask., June 6, 1941

SSN	TEAM	GP	G	A	PTS.	PIM	+/-
67–68	Minn	7	0	0	0	6	+1
68–69	Minn	13	0	0	0	2	-2
69–70	Minn	28	0	5	5	14	+1
70–71	Minn	1	0	0	0	0	0
71–72	Cal	74	2	11	13	4	-27
72–73	Cal	78	10	20	30	14	-1
73–74	Cal	50	2	16	18	24	-45
Totals		251	14	52	66	64	-73

Playoffs

69–70	Minn	6	0	0	0	2	

JOHNSTON, Lawrence Roy 5–11 195 D
B. Kitchener, Ont., July 20, 1943

67–68	LA	4	0	0	0	4	-7
71–72	Det	65	4	20	24	111	+20
72–73	Det	73	1	12	13	169	+61
73–74	Det	65	2	12	14	139	-26
74–75	Mich (WHA)	49	0	9	9	93	
74–75	KC	16	0	7	7	10	-17
75–76	KC	72	2	10	12	112	-61
76–77	Col	25	0	3	3	35	-25
NHL Totals		320	9	64	73	580	-110
WHA Totals		49	0	9	9	93	

JOHNSTON, Randy John 6–0 190 D
B. Brampton, Ont., June 2, 1958

79–80	NYI	4	0	0	0	4	-2

JOHNSTONE, Edward Lavern 5–9 175 RW
B. Brandon, Man., Mar. 2, 1954

74–75	Mich (WHA)	23	4	4	8	43	
75–76	NYR	10	2	1	3	4	+4
77–78	NYR	53	13	13	26	44	-3
78–79	NYR	30	5	3	8	27	-5
79–80	NYR	78	14	21	35	60	+3
80–81	NYR	80	30	38	68	100	+15
81–82	NYR	68	30	28	58	57	-5
82–83	NYR	52	15	21	36	27	-4
83–84	Det	46	12	11	23	54	+3
85–86	Det	3	1	0	1	2	0
86–87	Det	6	0	0	0	0	+1
NHL Totals		426	122	136	258	375	+9
WHA Totals		23	4	4	8	43	

Playoffs

78–79	NYR	17	5	0	5	10	
79–80	NYR	9	0	1	1	25	
80–81	NYR	8	2	2	4	4	
81–82	NYR	10	2	6	8	25	
82–83	NYR	9	4	1	5	19	
83–84	Det	2	0	0	0	0	
Totals		55	13	10	23	83	

JOHNSTONE, Robert Ross (Ross) 6–0 185 D
B. Montreal, Que., Apr. 7, 1926

43–44	Tor	18	2	0	2	6	
44–45	Tor	24	3	4	7	8	
Totals		42	5	4	9	14	

Playoffs

43–44	Tor	3	0	0	0	0	

JOKINEN, Olli 6–2 198 C
B. Kuopio, Finland, Dec. 5, 1978

97–98	LA	8	0	0	0	6	-5
98–99	LA	66	9	12	21	44	-10
Totals		74	9	12	21	50	-15

***JOLIAT, Aurel Emile** 5–6 136 LW
B. Ottawa, Ont., Aug. 29, 1901

22–23	Mont	24	13	9	22	31	
23–24	Mont	24	15	5	20	19	
24–25	Mont	24	29	11	40	85	
25–26	Mont	35	17	9	26	52	
26–27	Mont	43	14	4	18	79	
27–28	Mont	44	28	11	39	105	
28–29	Mont	44	12	5	17	59	
29–30	Mont	42	19	12	31	40	
30–31	Mont	43	13	22	35	73	
31–32	Mont	48	15	24	39	46	
32–33	Mont	48	18	21	39	53	

SSN	TEAM	GP	G	A	PTS.	PIM	+/-
33–34	Mont	48	22	15	37	27	
34–35	Mont	48	17	12	29	18	
35–36	Mont	48	15	8	23	16	
36–37	Mont	47	17	15	32	30	
37–38	Mont	44	6	7	13	24	
Totals		654	270	190	460	757	

Playoffs

22–23	Mont	2	1	1	2	8	
23–24	Mont	6	4	4	8	10	
24–25	Mont	5	2	2	4	21	
26–27	Mont	4	1	0	1	10	
27–28	Mont	2	0	0	0	4	
28–29	Mont	3	1	1	2	10	
29–30	Mont	6	0	2	2	6	
30–31	Mont	10	0	4	4	12	
31–32	Mont	4	2	0	2	4	
32–33	Mont	2	2	1	3	2	
33–34	Mont	3	0	1	1	0	
34–35	Mont	2	1	0	1	0	
36–37	Mont	5	0	3	3	2	
Totals		54	14	19	33	89	

*JOLIAT, Rene (Bobby) *F*

24–25	Mont	1	0	0	0	0	

JOLY, Gregory James *6–1 190 D*
B. Calgary, Alta., May 30, 1954

74–75	Wash	44	1	7	8	44	-68
75–76	Wash	54	8	17	25	28	-46
76–77	Det	53	1	11	12	14	-22
77–78	Det	79	7	20	27	73	-4
78–79	Det	20	0	4	4	6	-8
79–80	Det	59	3	10	13	45	-2
80–81	Det	17	0	2	2	10	-8
81–82	Det	37	1	5	6	30	-5
82–83	Det	2	0	0	0	0	0
Totals		365	21	76	97	250	-163

Playoffs

77–78	Det	5	0	0	0	8	

JOLY, Yvan Rene *5–11 175 RW*
B. Hawkesbury, Ont., Feb. 6, 1960

80–81	Mont	1	0	0	0	0	0
82–83	Mont	1	0	0	0	0	-1
Totals		2	0	0	0	0	-1

Playoffs

79–80	Mont	10	0	0	0	0	

JOMPHE, Jean–Francois *6–1 195 C*
B. Harve St. Pierre, Que., Dec. 28, 1972

95–96	Ana	31	2	12	14	39	+7
96–97	Ana	64	7	14	21	53	-9
97–98	Ana	9	1	3	4	8	+1
98–99	Ana-Mont	7	0	0	0	2	0
Totals		111	10	29	39	102	-1

JONATHAN, Stanley Carl *5–8 175 LW*
B. Oshweken, Ont., Sept. 5, 1955

75–76	Bos	1	0	0	0	0	0
76–77	Bos	69	17	13	30	69	+1
77–78	Bos	68	27	25	52	116	+34
78–79	Bos	33	6	9	15	96	+8
79–80	Bos	79	21	19	40	208	+20
80–81	Bos	74	14	24	38	192	+5
81–82	Bos	67	6	17	23	57	+6
82–83	Bos-Pitt	20	0	3	3	13	-8
Totals		411	91	110	201	751	+66

Playoffs

76–77	Bos	14	4	2	6	24	
77–78	Bos	15	0	1	1	36	
78–79	Bos	11	4	1	5	12	
79–80	Bos	9	0	0	0	29	
80–81	Bos	3	0	0	0	30	
81–82	Bos	11	0	0	0	6	
Totals		63	8	4	12	137	

JONES, Alvin Bernard (Buck) *6–0 180 D*
B. Owen Sound, Ont., Aug. 17, 1918

38–39	Det	11	0	1	1	6	
39–40	Det	2	0	0	0	0	
41–42	Det	21	2	1	3	8	
42–43	Tor	16	0	0	0	22	

Totals		50	2	2	4	36	

Playoffs

38–39	Det	6	0	1	1	10	
42–43	Det	6	0	0	0	8	
Totals		12	0	1	1	18	

JONES, Brad *6–0 195 LW*
B. Sterling Heights, Mich., June 26, 1965

86–87	Winn	4	1	0	1	0	+2
87–88	Winn	19	2	5	7	15	+2
88–89	Winn	22	6	5	11	6	0
89–90	Winn	2	0	0	0	0	-2
90–91	LA	53	9	11	20	57	+11
91–92	Phil	48	7	10	17	44	-2
Totals		148	25	31	56	122	+11

Playoffs

87–88	Winn	1	0	0	0	0	
90–91	LA	8	1	1	2	2	
Totals		9	1	1	2	2	

JONES, James Harrison *5–9 177 C*
B. Woodbridge, Ont., Jan. 2, 1953

73–74	Van (WHA)	18	3	2	5	23	
74–75	Van (WHA)	63	11	7	18	39	
77–78	Tor	78	4	9	13	23	+1
78–79	Tor	69	9	9	18	45	+2
79–80	Tor	1	0	0	0	0	-1
NHL Totals		148	13	18	31	68	+2
WHA Totals		81	14	9	23	62	

Playoffs

77–78	Tor	13	1	5	6	7	
78–79	Tor	6	0	0	0	4	
Totals		19	1	5	6	11	

JONES, James William *5–10 185 D*
B. Espanola, Ont., July 27, 1949

71–72	Cal	2	0	0	0	0	0
73–74	Chi (WHA)	1	0	0	0	0	

JONES, Keith *6–0 200 RW*
B. Brantford, Ont., Nov. 8, 1968

92–93	Wash	71	12	14	26	124	+18
93–94	Wash	68	16	19	35	149	+4
94–95	Wash	40	14	6	20	65	-2
95–96	Wash	68	18	23	41	103	+8
96–97	Wash-Col A	78	25	23	48	118	+3
97–98	Col A	23	3	7	10	22	-4
98–99	Col A-Phil	78	20	33	53	98	+23
Totals		426	108	125	233	679	+50

Playoffs

92–93	Wash	6	0	0	0	10	
93–94	Wash	11	0	1	1	36	
94–95	Wash	7	4	4	8	22	
95–96	Wash	2	0	0	0	7	
96–97	Col A	6	3	3	6	4	
97–98	Col A	7	0	0	0	13	
98–99	Phil	6	2	1	3	14	
Totals		45	9	9	18	106	

JONES, Robert Charles *6–1 192 LW*
B. Espanola, Ont., Nov. 27, 1945

68–69	NYR	2	0	0	0	0	0
72–73	LA-NY (WHA)	76	13	19	32	32	
73–74	NJ (WHA)	78	17	28	45	20	
74–75	Balt (WHA)	5	0	1	1	8	
75–76	Ind (WHA)	2	0	0	0	0	
NHL Totals		2	0	0	0	0	0
WHA Totals		161	30	48	78	60	

JONES, Ronald Perry *6–1 190 D*
B. Vermillion, Alta., Apr. 11, 1951

71–72	Bos	1	0	0	0	0	+1
72–73	Bos	7	0	0	0	2	+1
73–74	Pitt	25	0	3	3	15	-14
74–75	Wash	19	1	1	2	16	-14
75–76	Wash	2	0	0	0	0	-1
Totals		54	1	4	5	33	-27

JONES, Ty *6–3 218 RW*
B. Richland, Wash., Feb. 22, 1979

98–99	Chi	8	0	0	0	12	-1

JONSSON, Kenny *6–3 195 D*
B. Angelholm, Sweden, Oct. 6, 1974

94–95	Tor	39	2	7	9	16	-8
95–96	Tor–NYI	66	4	26	30	32	+7
96–97	NYI	81	3	18	21	24	+10
97–98	NYI	81	14	26	40	58	-2
98–99	NYI	63	8	18	26	34	-18
Totals		330	31	95	126	164	-11

Playoffs

94–95	Tor	4	0	0	0	0	

JONSSON, Tomas *5–11 183 D*
B. Falun, Sweden, Apr. 12, 1960

81–82	NYI	70	9	25	34	51	+26
82–83	NYI	72	13	35	48	50	+40
83–84	NYI	72	11	36	47	54	+12
84–85	NYI	69	16	34	50	58	-1
85–86	NYI	77	14	30	44	62	+16
86–87	NYI	47	6	25	31	36	-8
87–88	NYI	72	6	41	47	115	+6
88–89	NYI–Edm	73	10	33	43	56	-25
Totals		552	85	259	344	482	+66

Playoffs

81–82	NYI	10	0	2	2	21	
82–83	NYI	20	2	10	12	18	
83–84	NYI	21	3	5	8	22	
84–85	NYI	7	1	2	3	10	
85–86	NYI	3	0	1	1	4	
86–87	NYI	10	1	4	5	6	
87–88	NYI	5	2	2	4	10	
88–89	Edm	4	2	0	2	6	
Totals		80	11	26	37	97	

JOSEPH, Anthony *6–4 203 RW*
B. Cornwall, Ont., Mar. 1, 1969

88–89	Winn	2	1	0	1	0	+1

JOSEPH, Chris *6–2 210 D*
B. Burnaby, B.C., Sept. 10, 1969

87–88	Pitt–Edm	24	0	8	8	18	-1
88–89	Edm	44	4	5	9	54	-9
89–90	Edm	4	0	2	2	2	-2
90–91	Edm	49	5	17	22	59	+3
91–92	Edm	7	0	0	0	8	-1
92–93	Edm	33	2	10	12	48	-9
93–94	Edm–TB	76	11	20	31	136	-21
94–95	Pitt	33	5	10	15	46	+3
95–96	Pitt	70	5	14	19	71	+6
96–97	Van	63	3	13	16	62	+21
97–98	Phil	15	1	0	1	19	+1
98–99	Phil	2	0	0	0	2	0
Totals		420	36	99	135	525	-9

Playoffs

91–92	Edm	5	1	3	4	2	
94–95	Pitt	10	1	1	2	12	
95–96	Pitt	15	1	0	1	8	
97–98	Phil	1	0	0	0	2	
Totals		31	3	4	7	24	

JOVANOVSKI, Ed *6–2 210 D*
B. Windsor, Ont., June 26, 1976

95–96	Fla	70	10	11	21	137	-3
96–97	Fla	61	7	16	23	172	-1
97–98	Fla	81	9	14	23	158	-12
98–99	Fla-Van	72	5	22	27	126	-9
Totals		284	31	63	94	593	-25

Playoffs

95–96	Fla	22	1	8	9	52	
96–97	Fla	5	0	0	0	4	
Totals		27	1	8	9	56	

JOYAL, Edward Abel *6–0 180 C*
B. Edmonton, Alta., May 8, 1940

62–63	Det	14	2	8	10	0	
63–64	Det	47	10	7	17	17	
64–65	Det	46	8	14	22	4	
65–66	Tor	14	0	2	2	2	
67–68	LA	74	23	34	57	20	-2
68–69	LA	73	33	19	52	24	-30
69–70	LA	59	18	22	40	8	-17
70–71	LA	69	20	21	41	14	-10
71–72	LA-Phil	70	14	7	21	35	-43

SSN	TEAM	GP	G	A	PTS.	PIM	+/-
72–73	Alb (WHA)	71	22	16	38	16	
73–74	Edm (WHA)	45	8	10	18	2	
74–75	Edm (WHA)	78	22	25	47	2	
75–76	Edm (WHA)	45	5	4	9	6	
NHL Totals		466	128	134	262	124	-102
WHA Totals		239	57	55	112	26	

Playoffs

62–63	Det	11	1	0	1	2	
63–64	Det	14	2	3	5	10	
64–65	Det	7	1	1	2	4	
67–68	LA	7	4	1	5	2	
68–69	LA	11	3	3	6	0	
73–74	Edm (WHA)	5	2	0	2	4	
NHL Totals		50	11	8	19	18	
WHA Totals		5	2	0	2	4	

JOYCE, Duane 6–2 203 D
B. Pembroke, Mass., May 5, 1965

93–94	Dal	3	0	0	0	0	0

JOYCE, Robert Thomas 6–0 195 LW
B. St. John, N.B., July 11, 1966

87–88	Bos	15	7	5	12	10	+4
88–89	Bos	77	18	31	49	46	+8
89–90	Bos–Wash	47	6	10	16	26	-6
90–91	Wash	17	3	3	6	8	+3
91–92	Winn	1	0	0	0	0	
92–93	Winn	1	0	0	0	0	
Totals		158	34	49	83	90	+9

Playoffs

87–88	Bos	23	8	6	14	18	
88–89	Bos	9	5	2	7	2	
89–90	Wash	14	2	1	3	9	
Totals		46	15	9	24	29	

JUCKES, Winston Bryan (Bing) 5–10 165 LW
B. Hamiota, Man., June 14, 1926

47–48	NYR	2	0	0	0	0	
49–50	NYR	14	2	1	3	6	
Totals		16	2	1	3	6	

JUHLIN, Patrik 6–0 194 LW
B. Huddinge, Sweden, Apr. 24, 1970

94–95	Phil	42	4	3	7	6	-13
95–96	Phil	14	3	3	6	17	+4
Totals		56	7	6	13	23	-9

Playoffs

94–95	Phil	13	1	0	1	2	

JULIEN, Claude 6–0 198 D
B. Blind River, Ont., Apr. 23, 1960

84–85	Que	1	0	0	0	0	0
85–86	Que	13	0	1	1	25	+2
Totals		14	0	1	1	25	+2

JUNEAU, Joseph 6–0 195 C/LW
B. Pont–Rouge, Que., Jan. 5, 1968

91–92	Bos	14	5	14	19	4	+6
92–93	Bos	84	32	70	102	33	+23
93–94	Bos–Wash	74	19	66	85	41	+11
94–95	Wash	44	5	38	43	8	-1
95–96	Wash	80	14	50	64	30	-3
96–97	Wash	58	15	27	42	8	-11
97–98	Wash	56	9	22	31	26	-8
98–99	Wash-Buf	72	15	28	43	22	-4
Totals		482	114	315	429	172	+13

Playoffs

91–92	Bos	15	4	8	12	21	
92–93	Bos	4	2	4	6	6	
93–94	Wash	11	4	5	9	6	
94–95	Wash	7	2	6	8	2	
95–96	Wash	5	0	7	7	6	
97–98	Wash	21	7	10	17	8	
98–99	Buf	20	3	8	11	10	
Totals		83	22	48	70	59	

JUNKER, Steve 6–0 184 LW
B. Castlegar, B.C., June 26, 1972

93–94	NYI	5	0	0	0	0	0

Playoffs

92–93	NYI	3	0	1	1	0	

JUTILA, Timo 5–7 175 D
B. Finland, Dec. 24, 1963

84–85	Buf	10	1	5	6	13	-5

JUZDA, William (Fireman, Beast) 5–8 203 D
B. Winnipeg, Man., Oct. 29, 1920

40–41	NYR	5	0	0	0	2	
41–42	NYR	45	4	8	12	29	
45–46	NYR	32	1	3	4	17	
46–47	NYR	45	3	5	8	60	
47–48	NYR	60	3	9	12	70	
48–49	Tor	38	1	2	3	23	
49–50	Tor	62	1	14	15	23	
50–51	Tor	65	0	9	9	64	
51–52	Tor	46	1	4	5	65	
Totals		398	14	54	68	353	

Playoffs

41–42	NYR	6	0	1	1	4	
47–48	NYR	6	0	0	0	9	
48–49	Tor	9	0	2	2	8	
49–50	Tor	7	0	0	0	16	
50–51	Tor	11	0	0	0	7	
51–52	Tor	3	0	0	0	2	
Totals		42	0	3	3	46	

KABEL, Robert Gerald 6–0 183 C
B. Dauphin, Minn., Dec. 11, 1934

59–60	NYR	44	5	11	16	32	
60–61	NYR	4	0	2	2	2	
Totals		48	5	13	18	34	

KABERLE, Tomas 6–1 195 D
B. Rakovnic, Czech., March 2, 1978

98–99	Tor	57	4	18	22	12	+3

Playoffs

98–99	Tor	14	0	3	3	2	

KACHOWSKI, Mark Edward 5–11 200 LW
B. Edmonton, Alta., Feb. 20, 1965

87–88	Pitt	38	5	3	8	126	+1
88–89	Pitt	12	1	1	2	43	+1
89–90	Pitt	14	0	1	1	40	+1
Totals		64	6	5	11	209	+3

KACHUR, Edward Charles 5–8 170 RW
B. Fort William, Ont., Apr. 22, 1934

56–57	Chi	34	5	7	12	21	
57–58	Chi	62	5	7	12	14	
Totals		96	10	14	24	35	

KAESE, Trent 5–11 205 RW
B. Nanaimo, B.C., Sept. 9, 1967

88–89	Buf	1	0	0	0	0	0

KAISER, Vernon Charles 6–0 180 LW
B. Preston, Ont., Sept. 28, 1925

50–51	Mont	50	7	5	12	33	

Playoffs

50–51	Mont	2	0	0	0	0	

*KALBFLEISH, Walter Morris (Jeff) 5–10 175 D
B. New Hamburg, Ont., Dec. 18, 1911

33–34	Ott	22	0	4	4	20	
34–35	StL E	3	0	0	0	6	
35–36	NYA	4	0	0	0	2	
36–37	NYA–Bos	7	0	0	0	4	
Totals		36	0	4	4	32	

Playoffs

35–36	NYA	5	0	0	0	2	

*KALETA, Alexander (Killer) 5–11 175 LW
B. Canmore, Alta., Nov. 29, 1919

41–42	Chi	48	7	21	28	24	
45–46	Chi	49	19	27	46	17	
46–47	Chi	57	24	20	44	37	
47–48	Chi	52	10	16	26	40	
48–49	NYR	56	12	19	31	18	
49–50	NYR	67	17	14	31	40	
50–51	NYR	58	3	4	7	26	
Totals		387	92	121	213	202	

Playoffs

41–42	Chi	3	1	2	3	0	
45–46	Chi	4	0	1	1	2	
49–50	NYR	10	0	3	3	0	
Totals		17	1	6	7	2	

KALLUR, Anders 5–11 185 RW
B. Ludvika, Sweden, July 6, 1952

79–80	NYI	76	22	30	52	18	+12
80–81	NYI	78	36	28	64	32	+25
81–82	NYI	58	18	22	40	18	+5
82–83	NYI	55	6	8	14	33	+9
83–84	NYI	65	9	14	23	24	0
84–85	NYI	51	10	8	18	26	-9
Totals		383	101	110	211	149	+42

Playoffs

80–81	NYI	12	4	3	7	10	
81–82	NYI	19	1	6	7	8	
82–83	NYI	20	3	12	15	12	
83–84	NYI	17	2	2	4	2	
84–85	NYI	10	2	0	2	0	
Totals		78	12	23	35	32	

KAMENSKY, Valeri 6–2 198 LW
B. Voskresensk, Soviet Union, Apr. 18, 1966

91–92	Que	23	7	14	21	14	-1
92–93	Que	32	15	22	37	14	+13
93–94	Que	76	28	37	65	42	+12
94–95	Que	40	10	20	30	22	+3
95–96	Col A	81	38	47	85	85	+14
96–97	Col A	68	28	38	66	38	+5
97–98	Col A	75	26	40	66	60	-2
98–99	Col A	65	14	30	44	28	+1
Totals		460	166	248	414	303	+45

Playoffs

92–93	Que	6	0	1	1	6	
94–95	Que	2	1	0	1	0	
95–96	Col A	22	10	12	22	28	
96–97	Col A	17	8	14	22	16	
97–98	Col A	7	2	3	5	18	
98–99	Col A	10	4	5	9	4	
Totals		64	25	35	60	72	

KAMINSKI, Kevin 5–10 190 C
B. Churchbridge, Sask., Mar. 13, 1969

88–89	Minn	1	0	0	0	0	0
89–90	Que	1	0	0	0	0	-1
91–92	Que	5	0	0	0	45	-2
93–94	Wash	13	0	5	5	87	+2
94–95	Wash	27	1	1	2	102	-6
95–96	Wash	54	1	2	3	164	-1
96–97	Wash	38	1	2	3	130	0
Totals		139	3	10	13	528	-8

Playoffs

94–95	Wash	5	0	0	0	36	
95–96	Wash	3	0	0	0	16	
Totals		8	0	0	0	52	

KAMINSKY, Max 5–10 160 C
B. Niagara Falls, Ont., Apr. 19, 1913

33–34	Ott	38	9	17	26	14	
34–35	StL E–Bos	49	12	15	27	4	
35–36	Bos	37	1	2	3	20	
36–37	Mont M	6	0	0	0	0	
Totals		130	22	34	56	38	

Playoffs

34–35	Bos	4	0	0	0	0	

KAMINSKY, Yan 6–1 176 RW
B. Penza, USSR, July 28, 1971

93–94	Winn–NYI	24	2	1	3	4	+5
94–95	NYI	2	1	1	2	0	+2
Totals		26	3	2	5	4	+7

Playoffs

93–94	NYI	2	0	0	0	4	

*KAMPMAN, Rudolph (Bingo) *5–9 187 D*
B. Kitchener, Ont., Mar. 12, 1914

SSN	TEAM	GP	G	A	PTS.	PIM	+/-
37–38	Tor	32	1	2	3	56	
38–39	Tor	41	2	8	10	52	
39–40	Tor	39	6	9	15	59	
40–41	Tor	39	1	4	5	53	
41–42	Tor	38	4	7	11	67	
Totals		189	14	30	44	287	

Playoffs

SSN	TEAM	GP	G	A	PTS.	PIM
37–38	Tor	7	0	1	1	6
38–39	Tor	10	1	1	2	20
39–40	Tor	10	0	0	0	0
40–41	Tor	7	0	0	0	0
41–42	Tor	13	0	2	2	12
Totals		47	1	4	5	38

KANE, Francis Joseph (Red) *5–11 190 D*
B. Stratford, Ont., Jan. 19, 1923

SSN	TEAM	GP	G	A	PTS.	PIM
43–44	Det	2	0	0	0	0

KANNEGIESSER, Gordon Cameron *6–0 190 D*
B. North Bay, Ont., Dec. 21, 1945

SSN	TEAM	GP	G	A	PTS.	PIM	+/-
67–68	StL	19	0	1	1	13	-3
71–72	StL	4	0	0	0	2	-1
72–73	Hou (WHA)	45	0	10	10	32	
73–74	Hou (WHA)	78	0	20	20	26	
74–75	Ind (WHA)	4	1	4	5	4	
NHL Totals		23	0	1	1	15	-4
WHA Totals		127	1	34	35	62	

Playoffs

SSN	TEAM	GP	G	A	PTS.	PIM
72–73	Hou (WHA)	9	0	1	1	11
73–74	Hou (WHA)	3	0	2	2	2
WHA Totals		12	0	3	3	13

KANNEGIESSER, Sheldon Bruce *6–0 198 D*
B. North Bay, Ont., Aug. 15, 1947

SSN	TEAM	GP	G	A	PTS.	PIM	+/-
70–71	Pitt	18	0	2	2	29	-9
71–72	Pitt	54	2	4	6	47	-14
72–73	Pitt–NYR	6	0	1	1	0	+2
73–74	NYR–LA	63	4	20	24	55	+7
74–75	LA	74	2	23	25	57	+41
75–76	LA	70	4	9	13	36	+10
76–77	LA	39	1	1	2	28	-7
77–78	Van	42	1	7	8	36	-7
Totals		366	14	67	81	288	+23

Playoffs

SSN	TEAM	GP	G	A	PTS.	PIM
72–73	NYR	1	0	0	0	2
73–74	LA	5	0	1	1	0
74–75	LA	3	0	1	1	4
75–76	LA	9	0	0	0	4
Totals		18	0	2	2	10

KAPANEN, Sami *5–10 169 LW*
B. Vantaa, Finland, June 14, 1973

SSN	TEAM	GP	G	A	PTS.	PIM	+/-
95–96	Hart	35	5	4	9	6	0
96–97	Hart	45	13	12	25	2	+6
97–98	Car	81	26	37	63	16	+9
98–99	Car	81	24	35	59	10	-1
Totals		242	68	88	156	34	+14

Playoffs

SSN	TEAM	GP	G	A	PTS.	PIM
98–99	Car	5	1	1	2	0

KARABIN, Ladislav *6–1 189 LW*
B. Spisska Nova Ves, Czechoslovakia, Feb. 16, 1970

SSN	TEAM	GP	G	A	PTS.	PIM	+/-
93–94	Pitt	9	0	0	0	2	0

KARAMNOV, Vitali *6–2 185 LW*
B. Moscow, USSR, July 6, 1968

SSN	TEAM	GP	G	A	PTS.	PIM	+/-
92–93	StL	7	0	1	1	0	-2
93–94	StL	59	9	12	21	51	-3
94–95	StL	26	3	7	10	14	+7
Totals		92	12	20	32	65	+2

Playoffs

SSN	TEAM	GP	G	A	PTS.	PIM
94–95	StL	2	0	0	0	2

KARIYA, Paul *5–11 175 LW*
B. Vancouver, B.C., Oct. 16, 1974

SSN	TEAM	GP	G	A	PTS.	PIM	+/-
94–95	Ana	47	18	21	39	4	-17
95–96	Ana	82	50	58	108	20	+9
96–97	Ana	69	44	55	99	6	+36
97–98	Ana	22	17	14	31	23	+12
98–99	Ana	82	39	62	101	40	+17
Totals		302	168	210	378	93	+57

Playoffs

SSN	TEAM	GP	G	A	PTS.	PIM
96–97	Ana	11	7	6	13	4
98–99	Ana	3	1	3	4	0
Totals		14	8	9	17	4

KARJALAINEN, Kyosti *6–1 190 RW*
B. Gavle, Sweden, June 19, 1967

SSN	TEAM	GP	G	A	PTS.	PIM	+/-
91–92	LA	28	1	8	9	12	+4

Playoffs

SSN	TEAM	GP	G	A	PTS.	PIM
91–92	LA	3	0	1	1	2

KARLANDER, Allan David *5–8 170 C*
B. Lac la Hache, B.C., Nov. 5, 1946

SSN	TEAM	GP	G	A	PTS.	PIM	+/-
69–70	Det	41	5	10	15	6	+8
70–71	Det	23	1	4	5	10	+5
71–72	Det	71	15	20	35	29	+14
72–73	Det	77	15	22	37	25	+2
73–74	NE (WHA)	77	20	41	61	46	
74–75	NE (WHA)	48	7	14	21	2	
75–76	Ind (WHA)	79	19	26	45	36	
76–77	Ind (WHA)	65	17	28	45	23	
NHL Totals		212	36	56	92	70	+29
WHA Totals		269	63	109	172	107	

Playoffs

SSN	TEAM	GP	G	A	PTS.	PIM
69–70	Det	4	0	1	1	0
73–74	NE (WHA)	7	1	3	4	2
74–75	NE (WHA)	5	0	3	3	0
75–76	Ind (WHA)	3	0	0	0	4
76–77	Ind (WHA)	6	2	1	3	0
NHL Totals		4	0	1	1	0
WHA Totals		21	3	7	10	6

KARPA, David *6–1 202 D*
B. Regina, Sask., May 7, 1971

SSN	TEAM	GP	G	A	PTS.	PIM	+/-
91–92	Que	4	0	0	0	14	+2
92–93	Que	12	0	1	1	13	-6
93–94	Que	60	5	12	17	148	0
94–95	Que–Ana	28	1	5	6	91	-1
95–96	Ana	72	3	16	19	270	-3
96–97	Ana	69	2	11	13	210	+11
97–98	Ana	78	1	11	12	217	-3
98–99	Car	33	0	2	2	55	+1
Totals		356	12	58	70	1018	+1

Playoffs

SSN	TEAM	GP	G	A	PTS.	PIM
92–93	Que	3	0	0	0	0
96–97	Ana	8	1	1	2	20
98–99	Car	2	0	0	0	2
Totals		13	1	1	2	22

KARPOV, Valeri *5–10 176 RW*
B. Chelyabinsk, USSR, Aug. 5, 1971

SSN	TEAM	GP	G	A	PTS.	PIM	+/-
94–95	Ana	30	4	7	11	6	-4
95–96	Ana	37	9	8	17	10	-1
96–97	Ana	9	1	0	1	16	-2
Totals		76	14	15	29	32	-7

KARPOVTSEV, Alexander *6–1 200 D*
B. Moscow, USSR, Apr. 7, 1970

SSN	TEAM	GP	G	A	PTS.	PIM	+/-
93–94	NYR	67	3	15	18	58	+12
94–95	NYR	47	4	8	12	30	-4
95–96	NYR	40	2	16	18	26	+12
96–97	NYR	77	9	29	38	59	+1
97–98	NYR	47	3	7	10	38	-1
98–99	NYR–Tor	58	3	25	28	52	+39
Totals		336	24	100	124	263	+59

Playoffs

SSN	TEAM	GP	G	A	PTS.	PIM
93–94	NYR	17	0	4	4	12
94–95	NYR	8	1	0	1	0
95–96	NYR	6	0	1	1	4
96–97	NYR	13	1	3	4	20
98–99	Tor	14	1	3	4	12
Totals		58	3	11	14	48

KASATONOV, Alexei *6–1 215 D*
B. Leningrad, Soviet Union, Oct. 14, 1959

SSN	TEAM	GP	G	A	PTS.	PIM	+/-
89–90	NJ	39	6	15	21	16	+15
90–91	NJ	78	10	31	41	76	+23
91–92	NJ	76	12	28	40	70	+14
92–93	NJ	64	3	14	17	57	+4
93–94	Ana–StL	63	4	20	24	62	-3
94–95	Bos	44	2	14	16	33	-2
95–96	Bos	19	1	0	1	12	+1
Totals		383	38	122	160	326	+52

Playoffs

SSN	TEAM	GP	G	A	PTS.	PIM
89–90	NJ	6	0	3	3	14
90–91	NJ	7	1	3	4	10
91–92	NJ	7	1	1	2	12
92–93	NJ	4	0	0	0	0
93–94	StL	4	2	0	2	2
94–95	Bos	5	0	0	0	2
Totals		33	4	7	11	40

KASPARAITIS, Darius *5–11 195 D*
B. Elektrenai, USSR, Oct. 16, 1972

SSN	TEAM	GP	G	A	PTS.	PIM	+/-
92–93	NYI	79	4	17	21	166	+15
93–94	NYI	76	1	10	11	142	-6
94–95	NYI	13	0	1	1	22	-11
95–96	NYI	46	1	7	8	93	-12
96–97	NYI–Pitt	75	2	21	23	100	+17
97–98	Pitt	81	4	8	12	127	+3
98–99	Pitt	48	1	4	5	70	+12
Totals		418	13	68	81	720	+18

Playoffs

SSN	TEAM	GP	G	A	PTS.	PIM
92–93	NYI	18	0	5	5	81
93–94	NYI	4	0	0	0	8
96–97	Pitt	5	0	0	0	6
97–98	Pitt	5	0	0	0	8
Totals		32	0	5	5	53

KASPER, Stephen Neil *5–8 175 C*
B. Montreal, Que., Sept. 28, 1961

SSN	TEAM	GP	G	A	PTS.	PIM	+/-
80–81	Bos	76	21	35	56	94	+9
81–82	Bos	73	20	31	51	72	-18
82–83	Bos	24	2	6	8	24	-8
83–84	Bos	27	3	11	14	19	+3
84–85	Bos	77	16	24	40	33	-12
85–86	Bos	80	17	23	40	73	-10
86–87	Bos	79	20	30	50	51	-4
87–88	Bos	79	26	44	70	35	-1
88–89	Bos–LA	78	19	31	50	63	-2
89–90	LA	77	17	28	45	27	+4
90–91	LA	67	9	19	28	33	+3
91–92	Phil	16	3	2	5	10	-3
92–93	Phil–TB	68	4	7	11	20	-17
Totals		821	177	291	468	554	-56

Playoffs

SSN	TEAM	GP	G	A	PTS.	PIM
80–81	Bos	3	0	1	1	0
81–82	Bos	11	3	6	9	22
82–83	Bos	12	2	1	3	10
83–84	Bos	3	0	0	0	7
84–85	Bos	5	1	0	1	9
85–86	Bos	3	1	0	1	4
86–87	Bos	3	0	2	2	0
87–88	Bos	23	7	6	13	10
88–89	LA	11	1	5	6	10
89–90	LA	10	1	1	2	2
90–91	LA	10	4	6	10	8
Totals		94	20	28	48	82

KASTELIC, Edward *6–4 215 RW*
B. Toronto, Ont., Jan. 29, 1964

SSN	TEAM	GP	G	A	PTS.	PIM	+/-
85–86	Wash	15	0	0	0	73	0
86–87	Wash	23	1	1	2	83	-3
87–88	Wash	35	1	0	1	78	-3
88–89	Hart	10	0	2	2	15	0
89–90	Hart	67	6	2	8	198	-3
90–91	Hart	45	2	2	4	211	-7
91–92	Hart	25	1	3	4	61	-4
Totals		220	11	10	21	719	-20

Playoffs

SSN	TEAM	GP	G	A	PTS.	PIM
86–87	Wash	5	1	0	1	13
87–88	Wash	1	0	0	0	19
89–90	Hart	2	0	0	0	0
Totals		8	1	0	1	32

KASZYCKI, Michael *5–9 190 C*
B. Milton, Ont., Feb. 27, 1956

SSN	TEAM	GP	G	A	PTS.	PIM	+/-
77–78	NYI	58	13	29	42	24	+15
78–79	NYI	71	16	18	34	37	+7
79–80	NYI–Wash–						

SSN	TEAM	GP	G	A	PTS.	PIM	+/-
	Tor	69	12	18	30	35	-6
80–81	Tor	6	0	2	2	2	+2
82–83	Tor	22	1	13	14	10	0
Totals		226	42	80	122	108	+18

Playoffs

SSN	TEAM	GP	G	A	PTS.	PIM
77–78	NYI	7	1	3	4	4
78–79	NYI	10	1	3	4	4
79–80	Tor	2	0	0	0	2
Totals		19	2	6	8	10

KEA, Adrian Joseph (Ed) *6–3 200 D*
B. Weesp, Holland, Jan. 19, 1948

SSN	TEAM	GP	G	A	PTS.	PIM	+/-
73–74	Atl	3	0	2	2	0	+2
74–75	Atl	50	1	9	10	39	+7
75–76	Atl	78	8	19	27	101	+21
76–77	Atl	72	4	21	25	63	0
77–78	Atl	60	3	23	26	40	+25
78–79	Atl	53	6	18	24	40	-2
79–80	StL	69	3	16	19	79	+9
80–81	StL	74	3	18	21	60	+15
81–82	StL	78	2	14	16	62	+19
82–83	StL	46	0	5	5	24	-7
Totals		583	30	145	175	508	+89

Playoffs

SSN	TEAM	GP	G	A	PTS.	PIM
75–76	Atl	2	0	0	0	7
76–77	Atl	3	0	1	1	2
77–78	Atl	1	0	0	0	0
78–79	Atl	2	0	0	0	0
79–80	StL	3	0	0	0	2
80–81	StL	11	1	2	3	12
81–82	StL	10	1	1	2	16
Totals		32	2	4	6	39

KEANE, Mike *5–10 185 RW*
B. Winnipeg, Man., May 29, 1967

SSN	TEAM	GP	G	A	PTS.	PIM	+/-
88–89	Mont	69	16	19	35	69	+9
89–90	Mont	74	9	15	24	78	0
90–91	Mont	73	13	23	36	50	+6
91–92	Mont	67	11	30	41	64	+16
92–93	Mont	77	15	45	60	95	+29
93–94	Mont	80	16	30	46	119	+6
94–95	Mont	48	10	10	20	15	+5
95–96	Mont–Col A	73	10	17	27	46	-5
96–97	Col A	81	10	17	27	63	+2
97–98	NYR–Dal	83	10	13	23	52	-12
98–99	Dal	81	6	23	29	62	-2
Totals		806	126	242	368	713	+54

Playoffs

SSN	TEAM	GP	G	A	PTS.	PIM
88–89	Mont	21	4	3	7	17
89–90	Mont	11	0	1	1	8
90–91	Mont	12	3	2	5	6
91–92	Mont	8	1	1	2	16
92–93	Mont	19	2	13	15	6
93–94	Mont	6	3	1	4	4
95–96	Col A	22	3	2	5	16
96–97	Col A	17	3	1	4	24
97–98	Dal	17	4	4	8	0
98–99	Dal	23	5	2	7	6
Totals		156	28	30	58	103

KEANS, Douglas Frederick *5–7 174*
B. Pembroke, Ont., Jan. 7, 1958

Playoffs

SSN	TEAM	GP	G	A	PTS.	PIM
79–80	LA	1	0	0	0	0

KEARNS, Dennis McAleer *5–9 185 D*
B. Kingston, Ont., Sept. 27, 1945

SSN	TEAM	GP	G	A	PTS.	PIM	+/-
71–72	Van	73	3	26	29	59	-27
72–73	Van	72	4	33	37	51	-26
73–74	Van	52	4	13	17	30	-11
74–75	Van	49	1	11	12	31	+5
75–76	Van	80	5	46	51	48	-6
76–77	Van	80	5	55	60	60	-25
77–78	Van	80	4	43	47	27	-40
78–79	Van	78	3	31	34	28	-23
79–80	Van	67	1	18	19	24	+2
80–81	Van	46	1	14	15	28	-7
Totals		677	31	290	321	386	-158

Playoffs

SSN	TEAM	GP	G	A	PTS.	PIM
74–75	Van	4	0	0	0	4
75–76	Van	2	0	1	1	0
78–79	Van	3	1	1	2	2
79–80	Van	2	0	0	0	2
Totals		11	1	2	3	8

***KEATING, John R. (Jack)** *F*
B. St. John, N.B.

SSN	TEAM	GP	G	A	PTS.	PIM
31–32	NYA	22	5	3	8	6
32–33	NYA	13	0	2	2	11
Totals		35	5	5	10	17

KEATING, John Thomas (Red) *6–0 180 LW*
B. Kitchener, Ont., Oct. 9, 1916

SSN	TEAM	GP	G	A	PTS.	PIM
38–39	Det	1	0	1	1	2
39–40	Det	10	2	0	2	2
Totals		11	2	1	3	4

KEATING, Michael Joseph *6–0 185 LW*
B. Toronto, Ont., Jan. 21, 1957

SSN	TEAM	GP	G	A	PTS.	PIM	+/-
77–78	NYR	1	0	0	0	0	-1

***KEATS, Gordon Blanchard (Duke)** *C*
B. Montreal, Que., Mar. 1, 1895

SSN	TEAM	GP	G	A	PTS.	PIM
26–27	Det	40	16	8	24	52
27–28	Det–Chi	37	14	10	24	61
28–29	Chi	3	0	1	1	0
Totals		80	30	19	49	113

KECZMER, Dan *6–1 190 D*
B. Mt. Clemens, Mich., May 25, 1968

SSN	TEAM	GP	G	A	PTS.	PIM	+/-
90–91	Minn	9	0	1	1	6	0
91–92	Hart	1	0	0	0	0	-1
92–93	Hart	23	4	4	8	28	-3
93–94	Hart–Calg	69	1	21	22	60	-8
94–95	Calg	28	2	3	5	10	+7
95–96	Calg	13	0	0	0	14	-6
96–97	Dal	13	0	1	1	6	+3
97–98	Dal	17	1	2	3	26	+5
98–99	Dal–Nash	38	0	1	1	34	-5
Totals		211	8	33	41	184	-8

Playoffs

SSN	TEAM	GP	G	A	PTS.	PIM
93–94	Calg	3	0	0	0	4
94–95	Calg	7	0	1	1	2
97–98	Dal	2	0	0	0	2
Totals		12	0	1	1	8

***KEELING, Melville Sidney (Butch)** *6–0 180 LW*
B. Owen Sound, Ont., Aug. 10, 1905

SSN	TEAM	GP	G	A	PTS.	PIM
26–27	Tor	30	11	2	13	29
27–28	Tor	43	10	6	16	52
28–29	NYR	43	6	3	9	35
29–30	NYR	44	19	7	26	34
30–31	NYR	44	13	9	22	35
31–32	NYR	48	17	3	20	38
32–33	NYR	47	8	6	14	22
33–34	NYR	48	15	5	20	20
34–35	NYR	47	15	4	19	14
35–36	NYR	47	13	5	18	22
36–37	NYR	48	22	4	26	18
37–38	NYR	39	8	9	17	12
Totals		528	157	63	220	331

Playoffs

SSN	TEAM	GP	G	A	PTS.	PIM
28–29	NYR	6	3	0	3	2
29–30	NYR	4	0	3	3	8
30–31	NYR	4	1	1	2	0
31–32	NYR	7	2	1	3	12
32–33	NYR	8	0	2	2	8
33–34	NYR	2	0	0	0	0
34–35	NYR	4	2	1	3	0
36–37	NYR	9	3	2	5	2
37–38	NYR	3	0	1	1	0
Totals		47	11	11	22	32

KEENAN, Lawrence Christopher *5–10 177 LW*
B. North Bay, Ont., Oct. 1, 1940

SSN	TEAM	GP	G	A	PTS.	PIM	+/-
61–62	Tor	2	0	0	0	0	
67–68	StL	40	12	8	20	4	-7
68–69	StL	47	5	9	14	6	+19
69–70	StL	56	10	23	33	8	-8
70–71	StL–Buf	60	8	23	31	6	-7
71–72	Buf–Phil	29	3	1	4	4	-7
Totals		234	38	64	102	28	-10

Playoffs

SSN	TEAM	GP	G	A	PTS.	PIM
67–68	StL	18	4	5	9	4
68–69	StL	13	4	5	9	8
69–70	StL	16	7	6	13	0
Totals		47	15	16	31	12

KEHOE, Rick Thomas *5–11 180 RW*
B. Windsor, Ont., July 15, 1951

SSN	TEAM	GP	G	A	PTS.	PIM	+/-
71–72	Tor	38	8	8	16	4	-1
72–73	Tor	77	33	42	75	20	-11
73–74	Tor	69	18	22	40	8	+19
74–75	Pitt	76	32	31	63	22	+18
75–76	Pitt	71	29	47	76	6	+9
76–77	Pitt	80	30	27	57	10	-5
77–78	Pitt	70	29	21	50	10	-18
78–79	Pitt	57	27	18	45	2	+14
79–80	Pitt	79	30	30	60	4	-3
80–81	Pitt	80	55	33	88	6	-9
81–82	Pitt	71	33	52	85	8	-27
82–83	Pitt	75	29	36	65	12	-45
83–84	Pitt	57	18	27	45	8	-20
84–85	Pitt	6	0	2	2	0	0
Totals		906	371	396	767	120	-79

Playoffs

SSN	TEAM	GP	G	A	PTS.	PIM
71–72	Tor	2	0	0	0	2
74–75	Pitt	9	0	2	2	0
75–76	Pitt	3	0	0	0	0
76–77	Pitt	3	0	2	2	0
78–79	Pitt	7	0	2	2	0
79–80	Pitt	5	2	5	7	0
80–81	Pitt	5	0	3	3	0
81–82	Pitt	5	2	3	5	2
Totals		39	4	17	21	4

KEKALAINEN, Jarmo *6–0 190 LW*
B. Tampere, Finland, July 3, 1966

SSN	TEAM	GP	G	A	PTS.	PIM	+/-
89–90	Bos	11	2	2	4	8	+2
90–91	Bos	16	2	1	3	6	0
93–94	Ott	28	1	5	6	14	-8
Totals		55	5	8	13	28	-6

KELLER, Ralph *5–9 175 D*
B. Wilkie, Sask., Feb. 6, 1936

SSN	TEAM	GP	G	A	PTS.	PIM
62–63	NYR	3	1	0	1	6

KELLGREN, Christer *6–0 173 RW*
B. Goteborg, Sweden, Aug. 15, 1958

SSN	TEAM	GP	G	A	PTS.	PIM	+/-
81–82	Col	5	0	0	0	0	-4

KELLY, David Leslie *6–2 205 RW*
B. Chatham, Ont., Sept. 20, 1952

SSN	TEAM	GP	G	A	PTS.	PIM	+/-
76–77	Det	16	2	0	2	4	-8

KELLY, John Paul *6–1 215 LW*
B. Edmonton, Alta., Nov. 15, 1959

SSN	TEAM	GP	G	A	PTS.	PIM	+/-
79–80	LA	40	2	5	7	28	-6
80–81	LA	19	3	6	9	8	+4
81–82	LA	70	12	11	23	100	-21
82–83	LA	65	16	15	31	52	-14
83–84	LA	72	7	14	21	73	-34
84–85	LA	73	8	10	18	55	-9
85–86	LA	61	6	9	15	50	-17
Totals		400	54	70	124	366	-97

Playoffs

SSN	TEAM	GP	G	A	PTS.	PIM
79–80	LA	3	0	0	0	2
80–81	LA	4	0	1	1	25
81–82	LA	10	1	0	1	14
84–85	LA	1	0	0	0	0
Totals		18	1	1	2	41

KELLY, John Robert (Battleship) *6–2 195 LW*
B. Fort William, Ont., June 6, 1946

SSN	TEAM	GP	G	A	PTS.	PIM	+/-
73–74	StL–Pitt	67	16	18	34	123	-4
74–75	Pitt	69	27	24	51	120	+6
75–76	Pitt	77	25	30	55	149	+6
76–77	Pitt	74	10	21	31	115	+13
77–78	Chi	75	7	11	18	95	-26
78–79	Chi	63	2	5	7	85	-10
Totals		425	87	109	196	687	-17

Playoffs

SSN	TEAM	GP	G	A	PTS.	PIM
74–75	Pitt	9	5	3	8	17
75–76	Pitt	3	0	0	0	2
76–77	Pitt	3	1	0	1	4
77–78	Chi	4	0	0	0	8

SSN	TEAM	GP	G	A	PTS.	PIM	+/-
78–79	Chi	4	0	0	0	9	
Totals		23	6	3	9	40	

*KELLY, Leonard Patrick (Red) *6–0 195 C*
B. Simcoe, Ont., July 9, 1927

SSN	TEAM	GP	G	A	PTS.	PIM	+/-
47–48	Det	60	6	14	20	13	
48–49	Det	59	5	11	16	10	
49–50	Det	70	15	25	40	9	
50–51	Det	70	17	37	54	24	
51–52	Det	67	16	31	47	16	
52–53	Det	70	19	27	46	8	
53–54	Det	62	16	33	49	18	
54–55	Det	70	15	30	45	28	
55–56	Det	70	16	34	50	39	
56–57	Det	70	10	25	35	18	
57–58	Det	61	13	18	31	26	
58–59	Det	67	8	13	21	34	
59–60	Det–Tor	68	12	17	29	18	
60–61	Tor	64	20	50	70	12	
61–62	Tor	58	22	27	49	6	
62–63	Tor	66	20	40	60	8	
63–64	Tor	70	11	34	45	16	
64–65	Tor	70	18	28	46	8	
65–66	Tor	63	8	24	32	12	
66–67	Tor	61	14	24	38	4	
Totals		1316	281	542	823	327	

Playoffs

SSN	TEAM	GP	G	A	PTS.	PIM	+/-
47–48	Det	10	3	2	5	2	
48–49	Det	11	1	1	2	6	
49–50	Det	14	1	3	4	2	
50–51	Det	6	0	1	1	0	
51–52	Det	5	1	0	1	0	
52–53	Det	6	0	4	4	0	
53–54	Det	12	5	1	6	4	
54–55	Det	11	2	4	6	17	
55–56	Det	10	2	4	6	2	
56–57	Det	5	1	0	1	0	
57–58	Det	4	0	1	1	2	
59–60	Tor	10	3	8	11	2	
60–61	Tor	2	1	0	1	0	
61–62	Tor	12	4	6	10	0	
62–63	Tor	10	2	6	8	6	
63–64	Tor	14	4	9	13	4	
64–65	Tor	6	3	2	5	2	
65–66	Tor	4	0	2	2	0	
66–67	Tor	12	0	5	5	2	
Totals		164	33	59	92	51	

KELLY, Peter Cameron *5–10 170 RW*
B. St. Vital, Man., May 22, 1913

SSN	TEAM	GP	G	A	PTS.	PIM	+/-
34–35	StL E	25	3	10	13	14	
35–36	Det	48	6	8	14	30	
36–37	Det	48	5	4	9	12	
37–38	Det	9	0	1	1	2	
38–39	Det	32	4	9	13	4	
40–41	NYA	10	3	5	8	2	
41–42	Brk	8	0	1	1	4	
Totals		180	21	38	59	68	

Playoffs

SSN	TEAM	GP	G	A	PTS.	PIM	+/-
35–36	Det	7	1	1	2	2	
36–37	Det	8	2	0	2	6	
38–39	Det	4	0	0	0	0	
Totals		19	3	1	4	8	

*KELLY, Regis J. (Pep) *5–6 152 F*
B. North Bay, Ont., Jan. 9, 1914

SSN	TEAM	GP	G	A	PTS.	PIM	+/-
34–35	Tor	47	11	8	19	14	
35–36	Tor	42	11	8	19	24	
36–37	Tor–Chi	45	15	4	19	8	
37–38	Tor	43	9	10	19	25	
38–39	Tor	48	11	11	22	12	
39–40	Tor	34	11	9	20	15	
40–41	Chi	22	5	3	8	7	
41–42	Brk	8	1	0	1	0	
Totals		289	74	53	127	105	

Playoffs

SSN	TEAM	GP	G	A	PTS.	PIM	+/-
34–35	Tor	7	2	0	2	4	
35–36	Tor	9	2	3	5	4	
37–38	Tor	7	2	2	4	2	
38–39	Tor	10	1	0	1	0	
39–40	Tor	6	0	1	1	0	
Totals		39	7	6	13	10	

KELLY, Robert James (Hound) *5–10 200 LW*
B. Oakville, Ont., Nov. 25, 1950

SSN	TEAM	GP	G	A	PTS.	PIM	+/-
70–71	Phil	76	14	18	32	70	+7
71–72	Phil	78	14	15	29	157	+16
72–73	Phil	77	10	11	21	238	+1
73–74	Phil	65	4	10	14	130	+10
74–75	Phil	67	11	18	29	99	+21
75–76	Phil	79	12	8	20	125	+3
76–77	Phil	73	22	24	46	117	+27
77–78	Phil	74	19	13	32	95	+15
78–79	Phil	77	7	31	38	132	+15
79–80	Phil	75	15	20	35	122	+19
80–81	Wash	80	26	36	62	157	–13
81–82	Wash	16	0	4	4	12	–12
Totals		837	154	208	362	1454	+109

Playoffs

SSN	TEAM	GP	G	A	PTS.	PIM	+/-
70–71	Phil	4	1	0	1	2	
72–73	Phil	11	0	1	1	8	
73–74	Phil	5	0	0	0	0	
74–75	Phil	16	3	3	6	15	
75–76	Phil	16	0	2	2	44	
76–77	Phil	10	0	1	1	18	
77–78	Phil	12	3	5	8	26	
78–79	Phil	8	1	1	2	10	
79–80	Phil	19	1	1	2	38	
Totals		101	9	14	23	172	

KELLY, Steve *6–3 190 C*
B. Vancouver, B.C., Oct. 26, 1975

SSN	TEAM	GP	G	A	PTS.	PIM	+/-
96–97	Edm	8	1	0	1	6	–1
97–98	Edm–TB	43	2	3	5	23	–13
98–99	TB	34	1	3	4	27	–15
Totals		85	4	6	10	56	–29

Playoffs

SSN	TEAM	GP	G	A	PTS.	PIM	+/-
96–97	Edm	6	0	0	0	2	

KEMP, Kevin Glen *6–0 188 D*
B. Ottawa, Ont., May 3, 1954

SSN	TEAM	GP	G	A	PTS.	PIM	+/-
80–81	Hart	3	0	0	0	4	–1

KEMP, Stanley *5–9 165 D*
B. Hamilton, Ont., Mar. 2, 1924

SSN	TEAM	GP	G	A	PTS.	PIM	+/-
48–49	Tor	1	0	0	0	2	

KENADY, Chris *6–2 195 RW*
B. Mound, Minn., Apr. 10, 1973

SSN	TEAM	GP	G	A	PTS.	PIM	+/-
97–98	StL	5	0	2	2	0	+1

*KENDALL, William *5–8 168 F*
B. Winnipeg, Man., Apr. 1, 1910

SSN	TEAM	GP	G	A	PTS.	PIM	+/-
33–34	Chi	20	3	0	3	0	
34–35	Chi	47	6	4	10	16	
35–36	Chi	23	2	1	3	0	
36–37	Chi–Tor	32	5	4	9	10	
37–38	Chi	10	0	1	1	2	
Totals		132	16	10	26	28	

Playoffs

SSN	TEAM	GP	G	A	PTS.	PIM	+/-
33–34	Chi	1	0	0	0	0	
34–35	Chi	2	0	0	0	0	
35–36	Chi	2	0	0	0	0	
Totals		5	0	0	0	0	

KENNEDY, Edward (Dean) *6–2 205 D*
B. Redver, Sask., Jan. 18, 1963

SSN	TEAM	GP	G	A	PTS.	PIM	+/-
82–83	LA	55	0	12	12	97	–17
83–84	LA	37	1	5	6	50	–5
85–86	LA	78	2	10	12	132	–10
86–87	LA	66	6	14	20	91	+9
87–88	LA	58	1	11	12	158	–22
88–89	NYR–LA	67	3	11	14	103	+17
89–90	Buf	80	2	12	14	53	–12
90–91	Buf	64	4	8	12	119	+5
91–92	Winn	18	2	4	6	21	+2
92–93	Winn	78	1	7	8	105	–3
93–94	Winn	76	2	8	10	164	–22
94–95	Edm	40	2	8	10	25	+2
Totals		717	26	110	136	1118	–56

Playoffs

SSN	TEAM	GP	G	A	PTS.	PIM	+/-
86–87	LA	5	0	2	2	10	
87–88	LA	4	0	1	1	10	
88–89	LA	11	0	2	2	8	
89–90	Buf	6	1	1	2	12	

SSN	TEAM	GP	G	A	PTS.	PIM	+/-
90–91	Buf	2	0	1	1	17	
91–92	Winn	2	0	0	0	0	
92–93	Winn	6	0	0	0	2	
Totals		36	1	7	8	59	

KENNEDY, Forbes Taylor *5–8 185 C*
B. Dorchester, N.B., Aug. 18, 1935

SSN	TEAM	GP	G	A	PTS.	PIM	+/-
56–57	Chi	69	8	13	21	102	
57–58	Det	70	11	16	27	135	
58–59	Det	67	1	4	5	49	
59–60	Det	17	1	2	3	8	
61–62	Det	14	1	0	1	8	
62–63	Bos	49	12	18	30	46	
63–64	Bos	70	8	17	25	95	
64–65	Bos	52	6	4	10	41	
65–66	Bos	50	4	6	10	55	
67–68	Phil	73	10	18	28	130	+4
68–69	Phil–Tor	72	8	10	18	219	–26
Totals		603	70	108	178	888	–22

Playoffs

SSN	TEAM	GP	G	A	PTS.	PIM	+/-
57–58	Det	4	1	0	1	12	
67–68	Phil	7	1	4	5	14	
68–69	Tor	1	0	0	0	38	
Totals		12	2	4	6	64	

KENNEDY, Mike *6–1 170 C*
B. Vancouver, B.C., Apr. 13, 1972

SSN	TEAM	GP	G	A	PTS.	PIM	+/-
94–95	Dal	44	6	12	18	33	+4
95–96	Dal	61	9	17	26	48	–7
96–97	Dal	24	1	6	7	13	+3
97–98	Tor–Dal	15	0	1	1	16	–1
98–99	NYI	1	0	0	0	2	0
Totals		145	16	36	52	112	–1

Playoffs

SSN	TEAM	GP	G	A	PTS.	PIM	+/-
94–95	Dal	5	0	0	0	9	

KENNEDY, Sheldon *5–10 180 RW*
B. Brandon, Man., June 15, 1969

SSN	TEAM	GP	G	A	PTS.	PIM	+/-
89–90	Det	20	2	7	9	10	0
90–91	Det	7	1	0	1	12	–1
91–92	Det	27	3	8	11	24	–2
92–93	Det	68	19	11	30	46	–1
93–94	Det	61	6	7	13	30	–2
94–95	Calg	30	7	8	15	45	+5
95–96	Calg	41	3	7	10	36	+3
96–97	Bos	56	8	10	18	30	–17
Totals		310	49	58	107	233	–15

Playoffs

SSN	TEAM	GP	G	A	PTS.	PIM	+/-
92–93	Det	7	1	1	2	2	
93–94	Det	7	1	2	3	0	
94–95	Calg	7	3	1	4	16	
95–96	Calg	3	1	0	1	2	
Totals		24	6	4	10	20	

KENNEDY, Theodore (Teeder) *5–11 180 C*
B. Humberstone, Ont., Dec. 12, 1925

SSN	TEAM	GP	G	A	PTS.	PIM	+/-
42–43	Tor	2	0	1	1	0	
43–44	Tor	49	26	23	49	2	
44–45	Tor	49	29	25	54	14	
45–46	Tor	21	3	2	5	4	
46–47	Tor	60	28	32	60	27	
47–48	Tor	60	25	21	46	32	
48–49	Tor	59	18	21	39	25	
49–50	Tor	53	20	24	44	34	
50–51	Tor	63	18	43	61	32	
51–52	Tor	70	19	33	52	33	
52–53	Tor	43	14	23	37	42	
53–54	Tor	67	15	23	38	78	
54–55	Tor	70	10	42	52	74	
56–57	Tor	30	6	16	22	35	
Totals		696	231	329	560	432	

Playoffs

SSN	TEAM	GP	G	A	PTS.	PIM	+/-
43–44	Tor	5	1	1	2	4	
44–45	Tor	13	7	2	9	12	
46–47	Tor	11	4	5	9	4	
47–48	Tor	9	8	6	14	0	
48–49	Tor	9	2	6	8	2	
49–50	Tor	7	1	2	3	8	
50–51	Tor	11	4	5	9	6	
51–52	Tor	4	0	0	0	4	
53–54	Tor	5	1	1	2	2	
54–55	Tor	4	1	3	4	0	

SSN	TEAM	GP	G	A	PTS.	PIM	+/-
Totals		78	29	31	60	42	

*KENNY, William Ernest (Eddie) *6–2 195 D*
B. Vermillion, Alta., Aug. 20, 1907

SSN	TEAM	GP	G	A	PTS.	PIM	+/-
30–31	NYR	6	0	0	0	0	
34–35	Chi	5	0	0	0	18	
Totals		11	0	0	0	18	

KEON, David Michael *5–9 167 C*
B. Noranda, Que., Mar. 22, 1940

SSN	TEAM	GP	G	A	PTS.	PIM	+/-
60–61	Tor	70	20	25	45	6	
61–62	Tor	64	26	35	61	2	
62–63	Tor	68	28	28	56	2	
63–64	Tor	70	23	37	60	6	
64–65	Tor	65	21	29	50	10	
65–66	Tor	69	24	30	54	4	
66–67	Tor	66	19	33	52	2	
67–68	Tor	67	11	37	48	4	+16
68–69	Tor	75	27	34	61	12	+17
69–70	Tor	72	32	30	62	6	-15
70–71	Tor	76	38	38	76	4	+24
71–72	Tor	72	18	30	48	4	+1
72–73	Tor	76	37	36	73	2	+4
73–74	Tor	74	25	28	53	7	+13
74–75	Tor	78	16	43	59	4	+3
75–76	Minn–Ind (WHA)	69	29	45	74	6	
76–77	Minn–NE (WHA)	76	27	63	90	10	
77–78	NE (WHA)	77	24	38	62	2	
78–79	NE (WHA)	79	22	43	65	2	
79–80	Hart	76	10	52	62	10	-13
80–81	Hart	80	13	34	47	26	-31
81–82	Hart	78	8	11	19	6	-31
NHL Totals		1296	396	590	986	117	-12
WHA Totals		301	102	189	291	20	

Playoffs

SSN	TEAM	GP	G	A	PTS.	PIM	+/-
60–61	Tor	5	1	1	2	0	
61–62	Tor	12	5	3	8	0	
62–63	Tor	10	7	5	12	0	
63–64	Tor	14	7	2	9	2	
64–65	Tor	6	2	2	4	2	
65–66	Tor	4	0	2	2	0	
66–67	Tor	12	3	5	8	0	
68–69	Tor	4	1	3	4	2	
70–71	Tor	6	3	2	5	0	
71–72	Tor	5	2	3	5	0	
73–74	Tor	4	1	2	3	0	
74–75	Tor	7	0	5	5	0	
75–76	Ind (WHA)	7	2	2	4	2	
76–77	NE (WHA)	5	3	1	4	0	
77–78	NE (WHA)	14	5	11	16	4	
78–79	NE (WHA)	10	3	9	12	2	
79–80	Hart	3	0	1	1	0	
NHL Totals		92	32	36	68	6	
WHA Totals		36	13	23	36	8	

KERCH, Alexander *5–10 190 LW*
B. Arkhangelsk, USSR, Mar. 16, 1967

SSN	TEAM	GP	G	A	PTS.	PIM	+/-
93–94	Edm	5	0	0	0	2	-8

KERR, Alan *5–11 195 RW*
B. Hazelton, B.C., Mar. 28, 1964

SSN	TEAM	GP	G	A	PTS.	PIM	+/-
84–85	NYI	19	3	1	4	24	-7
85–86	NYI	7	0	1	1	16	+1
86–87	NYI	72	7	10	17	175	-10
87–88	NYI	80	24	34	58	198	+30
88–89	NYI	71	20	18	38	144	-5
89–90	NYI	75	15	21	36	129	-1
90–91	NYI	2	0	0	0	5	0
91–92	Det	58	3	8	11	133	+1
92–93	Winn	7	0	1	1	2	-4
Totals		391	72	94	166	826	+5

Playoffs

SSN	TEAM	GP	G	A	PTS.	PIM	+/-
84–85	NYI	4	1	0	1	4	
85–86	NYI	1	0	0	0	0	
86–87	NYI	14	1	4	5	25	
87–88	NYI	6	1	0	1	14	
89–90	NYI	4	0	0	0	10	
91–92	Det	9	2	0	2	17	
Totals		38	5	4	9	70	

KERR, Reginald John (Reg) *5–10 180 LW/C*
B. Oxbow, Sask., Oct. 16, 1957

SSN	TEAM	GP	G	A	PTS.	PIM	+/-
77–78	Clev–Chi	9	0	4	4	7	+2
78–79	Chi	73	16	24	40	50	-7

SSN	TEAM	GP	G	A	PTS.	PIM	+/-
79–80	Chi	49	9	8	17	17	-10
80–81	Chi	70	30	30	60	56	+10
81–82	Chi	59	11	28	39	39	-10
83–84	Edm	3	0	0	0	0	-3
Totals		263	66	94	160	169	-18

Playoffs

SSN	TEAM	GP	G	A	PTS.	PIM	+/-
78–79	Chi	4	1	0	1	5	
80–81	Chi	3	0	0	0	2	
Totals		7	1	0	1	7	

KERR, Tim *6–3 225 C/RW*
B. Windsor, Ont., Jan. 5, 1960

SSN	TEAM	GP	G	A	PTS.	PIM	+/-
80–81	Phil	68	22	23	45	84	+3
81–82	Phil	61	21	30	51	138	+6
82–83	Phil	24	11	8	19	6	+4
83–84	Phil	79	54	39	93	29	+30
84–85	Phil	74	54	44	98	57	+29
85–86	Phil	76	58	26	84	79	-5
86–87	Phil	75	58	37	95	57	+38
87–88	Phil	8	3	2	5	12	0
88–89	Phil	69	48	40	88	73	-4
89–90	Phil	40	24	24	48	34	-3
90–91	Phil	27	10	14	24	8	-8
91–92	NYR	32	7	11	18	12	-5
92–93	Hart	22	0	6	6	7	-11
Totals		655	370	304	674	596	+74

Playoffs

SSN	TEAM	GP	G	A	PTS.	PIM	+/-
80–81	Phil	10	1	3	4	2	
81–82	Phil	4	0	2	2	2	
82–83	Phil	2	2	0	2	0	
83–84	Phil	3	0	0	0	0	
84–85	Phil	12	10	4	14	13	
85–86	Phil	5	3	3	6	8	
86–87	Phil	12	8	5	13	2	
87–88	Phil	6	1	3	4	4	
88–89	Phil	19	14	11	25	27	
91–92	NYR	8	1	0	1	0	
Totals		81	40	31	71	58	

KESA, Dan *6–0 198 RW*
B. Vancouver, B.C., Nov. 23, 1971

SSN	TEAM	GP	G	A	PTS.	PIM	+/-
93–94	Van	19	2	4	6	18	-3
95–96	Dal	3	0	0	0	0	-1
98–99	Pitt	67	2	8	10	27	-9
Totals		89	4	12	16	45	-13

Playoffs

SSN	TEAM	GP	G	A	PTS.	PIM	+/-
98–99	Pitt	13	1	0	1	0	

KESSELL, Richard John (Rick) *5–10 175 C*
B. Toronto, Ont., July 27, 1949

SSN	TEAM	GP	G	A	PTS.	PIM	+/-
69–70	Pitt	8	1	2	3	2	0
70–71	Pitt	6	0	2	2	2	+1
71–72	Pitt	3	0	1	1	0	-1
72–73	Pitt	67	1	13	14	0	-9
73–74	Cal	51	2	6	8	4	-4
Totals		135	4	24	28	8	-13

KETOLA, Veli–Pekka *6–3 220 C*
B. Pori, Finland, Mar. 28, 1948

SSN	TEAM	GP	G	A	PTS.	PIM	+/-
74–75	Winn (WHA)	74	23	28	51	25	
75–76	Winn (WHA)	80	32	36	68	32	
76–77	Winn–Calg (WHA)	81	29	35	64	61	
81–82	Col	44	9	5	14	4	-17
NHL Totals		44	9	5	14	4	-17
WHA Totals		235	84	99	183	118	

Playoffs

SSN	TEAM	GP	G	A	PTS.	PIM	+/-
75–76	Winn (WHA)	13	7	5	12	2	

KETTER, Kerry Kenneth *6–1 202 D*
B. Prince George, B.C., Sept. 20, 1947

SSN	TEAM	GP	G	A	PTS.	PIM	+/-
72–73	Atl	41	0	2	2	58	-6
75–76	Edm (WHA)	48	1	9	10	20	
NHL Totals		41	0	2	2	58	-6
WHA Totals		48	1	9	10	20	

KHARIN, Sergei *5–11 180 RW*
B. Odintsovo, Soviet Union, Feb. 20, 1963

SSN	TEAM	GP	G	A	PTS.	PIM	+/-
90–91	Winn	7	2	3	5	2	+2

KHMYLEV, Yuri *6–1 189 LW*
B. Moscow, USSR, Aug. 9, 1964

SSN	TEAM	GP	G	A	PTS.	PIM	+/-
92–93	Buf	68	20	19	39	28	+6
93–94	Buf	72	27	31	58	49	+13
94–95	Buf	48	8	17	25	14	+8
95–96	Buf–StL	73	8	21	29	40	-17
96–97	StL	2	1	0	1	2	-1
Totals		263	64	88	152	133	+9

Playoffs

SSN	TEAM	GP	G	A	PTS.	PIM	+/-
92–93	Buf	8	4	3	7	4	
93–94	Buf	7	3	1	4	8	
94–95	Buf	5	0	1	1	8	
95–96	StL	6	1	1	2	4	
Totals		26	8	6	14	24	

KHRISTICH, Dmitri *6–2 195 LW/C*
B. Kiev, Soviet Union, July 23, 1969

SSN	TEAM	GP	G	A	PTS.	PIM	+/-
90–91	Wash	40	13	14	27	21	-1
91–92	Wash	80	36	37	73	35	+24
92–93	Wash	64	31	35	66	28	+29
93–94	Wash	83	29	29	58	73	-2
94–95	Wash	48	12	14	26	41	0
95–96	LA	76	27	37	64	44	0
96–97	LA	75	19	37	56	38	+8
97–98	Bos	82	29	37	66	42	+25
98–99	Bos	79	29	42	71	48	+11
Totals		627	225	282	507	370	+94

Playoffs

SSN	TEAM	GP	G	A	PTS.	PIM	+/-
90–91	Wash	11	1	3	4	6	
91–92	Wash	7	3	2	5	15	
92–93	Wash	6	2	5	7	2	
93–94	Wash	11	2	3	5	10	
94–95	Wash	7	1	4	5	0	
97–98	Bos	6	2	2	4	2	
98–99	Bos	12	3	4	7	6	
Totals		60	14	23	37	41	

KIDD, Ian *5–11 195 D*
B. Gresham, Ore., May 11, 1964

SSN	TEAM	GP	G	A	PTS.	PIM	+/-
87–88	Van	19	4	7	11	25	-3
88–89	Van	1	0	0	0	0	-1
Totals		20	4	7	11	25	-4

KIESSLING, Udo *5–10 180 D*
B. Crimmitschau, Germany, May 21, 1955

SSN	TEAM	GP	G	A	PTS.	PIM	+/-
81–82	Minn	1	0	0	0	2	0

KILGER, Chad *6–3 204 C*
B. Cornwall, Ont., Nov. 27, 1976

SSN	TEAM	GP	G	A	PTS.	PIM	+/-
95–96	Ana–Winn	74	7	10	17	34	-4
96–97	Phoe	24	4	3	7	13	-5
97–98	Phoe–Chi	32	3	9	12	10	0
98–99	Chi–Edm	77	15	12	27	34	-4
Totals		207	29	34	63	91	-13	-1

Playoffs

SSN	TEAM	GP	G	A	PTS.	PIM	+/-
95–96	Winn	4	1	0	1	0	
98–99	Edm	4	0	0	0	4	
Totals		8	1	0	1	4	

KILREA, Brian Blair *5–11 182 C*
B. Ottawa, Ont., Oct. 21, 1934

SSN	TEAM	GP	G	A	PTS.	PIM	+/-
57–58	Det	1	0	0	0	0	
67–68	LA	25	3	5	8	12	-4
Totals		26	3	5	8	12	-4

*KILREA, Hector J. (Hec) *5–7 175 LW*
B. Blackburn, Ont., June 11, 1907

SSN	TEAM	GP	G	A	PTS.	PIM	+/-
25–26	Ott	35	5	0	5	12	
26–27	Ott	42	11	7	18	48	
27–28	Ott	43	19	4	23	66	
28–29	Ott	38	5	7	12	36	
29–30	Ott	44	36	22	58	72	
30–31	Ott	44	14	8	22	44	
31–32	Det	47	13	3	16	28	
32–33	Ott	47	14	8	22	26	
33–34	Tor	43	10	13	23	15	
34–35	Tor	46	11	13	24	16	
35–36	Det	48	6	17	23	37	
36–37	Det	48	6	9	15	20	
37–38	Det	48	9	9	18	10	
38–39	Det	48	8	9	17	8	
39–40	Det	12	0	0	0	0	
Totals		633	167	129	296	438	

Playoffs

SSN	TEAM	GP	G	A	PTS.	PIM	+/-
25–26	Ott	2	0	0	0	0	
26–27	Ott	6	1	1	2	4	
27–28	Ott	2	1	0	1	0	
29–30	Ott	2	0	0	0	4	
31–32	Det	2	0	0	0	0	
33–34	Tor .	5	2	0	2	2	
34–35	Tor	6	0	0	0	4	
35–36	Det	7	0	3	3	2	
36–37	Det	10	3	1	4	2	
38–39	Det	6	1	2	3	0	
Totals		48	8	7	15	18	

KILREA, Kenneth Armstrong 6–0 170 LW
B. Ottawa, Ont., Jan. 16, 1919

38–39	Det	1	0	0	0	0	
39–40	Det	40	10	8	18	4	
40–41	Det	12	2	0	2	0	
41–42	Det	21	3	12	15	4	
43–44	Det	14	1	3	4	0	
Totals		88	16	23	39	8	

Playoffs

38–39	Det	3	1	1	2	4	
39–40	Det	5	1	1	2	0	
43–44	Det	2	0	0	0	0	
Totals		10	2	2	4	4	

KILREA, Walter Charles (Wally) 5–7 150 F
B. Ottawa, Ont., Feb. 18, 1909

29–30	Ott	42	4	2	6	4	
30–31	Phil Q	44	8	12	20	22	
31–32	NYA	48	3	8	11	18	
32–33	Ott–Mont M	38	5	12	17	16	
33–34	Mont M	44	3	1	4	7	
34–35	Det	2	0	0	0	0	
35–36	Det	44	4	10	14	10	
36–37	Det	48	8	13	21	6	
37–38	Det	5	0	0	0	4	
Totals		315	35	58	93	87	

Playoffs

29–30	Ott	2	0	0	0	0	
32–33	Mont M	2	0	0	0	0	
33–34	Mont M	4	0	0	0	0	
35–36	Det	7	2	2	4	2	
36–37	Det	10	2	2	4	4	
Totals		25	2	4	6	6	

KIMBLE, Darin 6–2 205 RW
B. Lucky Lake, Sask., Nov. 22, 1968

88–89	Que	26	3	1	4	149	-5
89–90	Que	44	5	5	10	185	-20
90–91	Que–StL	61	3	6	9	242	-3
91–92	StL	46	1	3	4	166	-3
92–93	Bos	55	7	3	10	177	+4
93–94	Chi	65	4	2	6	133	+2
94–95	Chi	14	0	0	0	30	-5
Totals		311	23	20	43	1082	-30

Playoffs

90–91	StL	13	0	0	0	38	
91–92	StL	5	0	0	0	7	
92–93	Bos	4	0	0	0	2	
93–94	Chi	1	0	0	0	5	
Totals		23	0	0	0	52	

KINDRACHUK, Orest 5–10 175 C
B. Nanton, Alta., Sept. 14, 1950

72–73	Phil	2	0	0	0	0	0
73–74	Phil	71	11	30	41	85	+19
74–75	Phil	60	10	21	31	72	+8
75–76	Phil	76	26	49	75	101	+32
76–77	Phil	78	15	36	51	79	+22
77–78	Phil	73	17	45	62	128	+35
78–79	Pitt	79	18	42	60	84	+3
79–80	Pitt	52	17	29	46	63	+4
80–81	Pitt	13	3	9	12	34	+3
81–82	Wash	4	1	0	1	2	-4
Totals		508	118	261	379	648	+122

Playoffs

73–74	Phil	17	5	4	9	17	
74–75	Phil	14	0	2	2	12	
75–76	Phil	16	4	7	11	4	
76–77	Phil	10	2	1	3	0	
77–78	Phil	12	5	5	10	13	

78–79	Pitt	7	4	1	5	7	
Totals		76	20	20	40	53	

KING, Derek 6–1 203 LW
B. Hamilton, Ont., Feb. 11, 1967

86–87	NYI	2	0	0	0	0	0
87–88	NYI	55	12	24	36	30	+7
88–89	NYI	60	14	29	43	14	+10
89–90	NYI	46	13	27	40	20	+2
90–91	NYI	66	19	26	45	44	+1
91–92	NYI	80	40	38	78	46	-10
92–93	NYI	77	38	38	76	47	-4
93–94	NYI	78	30	40	70	59	+18
94–95	NYI	43	10	16	26	41	-5
95–96	NYI	61	12	20	32	23	-10
96–97	NYI–Hart	82	26	33	59	22	-6
97–98	Tor	77	21	25	46	43	-7
98–99	Tor	81	24	28	52	20	+15
Totals		808	259	344	603	409	+11

Playoffs

87–88	NYI	5	0	2	2	2	
89–90	NYI	4	0	0	0	4	
92–93	NYI	18	3	11	14	14	
93–94	NYI	4	0	1	1	0	
98–99	Tor	16	1	3	4	4	
Totals		47	4	17	21	24	

KING, Frank Edward 5–11 185 C
B. Toronto, Ont., Mar. 7, 1929

50–51	Mont	10	1	0	1	2	

KING, Kris 5–11 210 LW
B. Bracebridge, Ont., Feb. 18, 1966

87–88	Det	3	1	0	1	2	+1
88–89	Det	55	2	3	5	168	-7
89–90	NYR	68	6	7	13	286	+2
90–91	NYR	72	11	14	25	154	-1
91–92	NYR	79	10	9	19	224	+13
92–93	NYR–Winn	78	8	11	19	+43	
93–94	Winn	83	4	8	12	205	-22
94–95	Winn	48	4	2	6	85	0
95–96	Winn	81	9	11	20	151	-7
96–97	Phoe	81	3	11	14	185	-7
97–98	Tor	82	3	3	6	199	-13
98–99	Tor	67	2	2	4	105	-16
Totals		797	63	81	144	1967	-53

Playoffs

88–89	Det	2	0	0	0	2	
89–90	NYR	10	0	1	1	38	
90–91	NYR	6	2	0	2	36	
91–92	NYR	13	4	1	5	14	
92–93	Winn	6	1	1	2	4	
95–96	Winn	5	0	1	1	4	
96–97	Phoe	7	0	0	0	17	
98–99	Tor	17	1	1	2	25	
Totals		66	8	5	13	140	

KING, Steven 6–0 195 RW
B. Greenwich, R.I., July 22, 1969

92–93	NYR	24	7	5	12	16	+4
93–94	Ana	36	8	3	11	44	-7
95–96	Ana	7	2	0	2	15	-1
Totals		67	17	8	25	75	-4

KING, Wayne Gordon 5–10 185 C
B. Midland, Ont., Sept. 4, 1951

73–74	Cal	2	0	0	0	0	0
74–75	Cal	25	4	7	11	8	-10
75–76	Cal	46	1	11	12	26	-3
Totals		73	5	18	23	34	-13

KINSELLA, Brian Edward 5–11 180 C
B. Barrie, Ont., Feb. 11, 1954

75–76	Wash	4	0	1	1	0	-2
76–77	Wash	6	0	0	0	0	-2
Totals		10	0	1	1	0	-4

*KINSELLA, Thomas Raymond (Ray) F
B. Ottawa, Ont., Jan. 27, 1911

30–31	Ott	14	0	0	0	0	

KIPRUSOFF, Marko 6–0 194 D
B. Turku, Finland, June 6, 1972

95–96	Mont	24	0	4	4	8	-3

*KIRK, Robert Hunter 5–9 180 RW
B. Belfast, Ireland, Aug. 8, 1910

37–38	NYR	39	4	8	12	14	

KIRKPATRICK, Robert Drynan 5–10 165 C
B. Regina, Sask., Dec. 1, 1915

42–43	NYR	49	12	12	24	6	

KIRTON, Mark Robert 5–10 170 C
B. Regina, Sask., Feb. 3, 1958

79–80	Tor	2	1	0	1	2	0
80–81	Tor–Det	61	18	13	31	24	-31
81–82	Det	74	14	28	42	62	-18
82–83	Det–Van	41	5	7	12	10	+4
83–84	Van	26	2	3	5	2	-8
84–85	Van	62	17	5	22	21	-22
Totals		266	57	56	113	121	-75

Playoffs

82–83	Van	4	1	2	3	7	

KISIO, Kelly W. 5–10 185 C
B. Peace River, Alta. Sept. 18, 1959

82–83	Det	15	4	3	7	0	-2
83–84	Det	70	23	37	60	34	+16
84–85	Det	75	20	41	61	56	+4
85–86	Det	76	21	48	69	85	-21
86–87	NYR	70	24	40	64	73	-5
87–88	NYR	77	23	55	78	88	+8
88–89	NYR	70	26	36	62	91	+14
89–90	NYR	68	22	44	66	105	+11
90–91	NYR	51	15	20	35	58	+3
91–92	SJ	48	11	26	37	54	-7
92–93	SJ	78	26	52	78	90	-15
93–94	Calg	51	7	23	30	28	-5
94–95	Calg	12	7	4	11	6	+2
Totals		761	229	429	658	768	0

Playoffs

83–84	Det	4	1	0	1	4	
84–85	Det	3	0	2	2	2	
86–87	NYR	4	0	1	1	2	
88–89	NYR	4	0	0	0	9	
89–90	NYR	10	2	8	10	8	
93–94	Calg	7	0	2	2	8	
94–95	Calg	7	3	2	5	19	
Totals		39	6	15	21	52	

*KITCHEN, Chapman Hobie (Hobie) D
B. Toronto, Ont.

25–26	Mont M	30	5	2	7	16	
26–27	Det	17	0	2	2	42	
Totals		47	5	4	9	58	

KITCHEN, Michael Elwin 5–10 180 D
B. Newmarket, Ont., Feb. 1, 1956

76–77	Col	60	1	8	9	36	-2
77–78	Col	61	2	17	19	45	-12
78–79	Col	53	1	4	5	28	-19
79–80	Col	42	1	6	7	25	-10
80–81	Col	75	1	7	8	100	-38
81–82	Col	63	1	8	9	60	-18
82–83	NJ	77	4	8	12	52	-25
83–84	NJ	43	1	4	5	24	-15
Totals		474	12	62	74	370	-139

Playoffs

77–78	Col	2	0	0	0	2	

KITCHEN, William 6–1 200 D
B. Schomburg, Ont., Oct. 2, 1960

81–82	Mont	1	0	0	0	7	0
82–83	Mont	8	0	0	0	4	-2
83–84	Mont	3	0	0	0	2	0
84–85	Tor	29	1	4	5	27	-6
Totals		41	1	4	5	40	-8

Playoffs

81–82	Mont	3	0	1	1	0	

KJELLBERG, Patrik 6–2 196 LW
B. Falun, Sweden, June 17, 1969

92–93	Mont	7	0	0	0	2	-3
98–99	Nash	71	11	20	31	24	-13
Totals		78	11	20	31	26	-16

KLATT, Trent *6–1 208 RW*
B. Robbinsdale, Minn., Jan. 30, 1971

SSN	TEAM	GP	G	A	PTS.	PIM	+/-
91–92	Minn	1	0	0	0	0	0
92–93	Minn	47	4	19	23	38	+2
93–94	Dal	61	14	24	38	30	+13
94–95	Dal	47	12	10	22	26	-2
95–96	Dal–Phil	71	7	12	19	44	+2
96–97	Phil	76	24	21	45	20	+9
97–98	Phil	82	14	28	42	16	+2
98–99	Phil-Van	75	4	10	14	12	-3
Totals		460	79	124	203	186	+19

Playoffs

SSN	TEAM	GP	G	A	PTS.	PIM
91–92	Minn	6	0	0	0	2
93–94	Dal	9	2	1	3	4
95–96	Phil	12	4	1	5	0
96–97	Phil	19	4	3	7	12
97–98	Phil	5	0	0	0	0
Totals		51	10	5	15	18

KLEE, Kenneth William *6–1 205 D*
B. Indianapolis, Ind., Apr. 24, 1971

SSN	TEAM	GP	G	A	PTS.	PIM	+/-
94–95	Wash	23	3	1	4	41	+2
95–96	Wash	66	8	3	11	60	-1
96–97	Wash	80	3	8	11	115	-5
97–98	Wash	51	4	2	6	46	-3
98–99	Wash	78	7	13	20	80	-9
Totals		298	25	27	52	342	-16

Playoffs

SSN	TEAM	GP	G	A	PTS.	PIM
94–95	Wash	7	0	0	0	4
95–96	Wash	1	0	0	0	0
97–98	Wash	9	1	0	1	10
Totals		17	1	0	1	14

KLEIN, James Lloyd (Dede) *6–0 185 LW*
B. Saskatoon, Sask., Jan. 13, 1910

SSN	TEAM	GP	G	A	PTS.	PIM
28–29	Bos	14	1	0	1	5
31–32	Bos	6	1	0	1	0
32–33	NYA	15	2	2	4	4
33–34	NYA	48	13	9	22	34
34–35	NYA	30	7	3	10	9
35–36	NYA	42	4	8	12	14
36–37	NYA	11	2	1	3	2
37–38	NYA	3	0	1	1	0
Totals		169	30	24	54	68

Playoffs

SSN	TEAM	GP	G	A	PTS.	PIM
35–36	NYA	5	0	0	0	2

KLEINENDORST, Scot *6–2 215 D*
B. Grand Rapids, Mich., Jan. 16, 1960

SSN	TEAM	GP	G	A	PTS.	PIM	+/-
82–83	NYR	30	2	9	11	8	+7
83–84	NYR	23	0	2	2	35	-10
84–85	Hart	35	1	8	9	69	-10
85–86	Hart	41	2	7	9	62	+8
86–87	Hart	66	3	9	12	130	+4
87–88	Hart	44	3	6	9	86	-5
88–89	Hart-Wash	27	0	2	2	46	-11
89–90	Wash	15	1	3	4	16	+4
Totals		281	12	46	58	452	-13

Playoffs

SSN	TEAM	GP	G	A	PTS.	PIM
82–83	NYR	6	0	2	2	2
85–86	Hart	10	0	1	1	18
86–87	Hart	4	1	3	4	20
87–88	Hart	3	1	1	2	0
89–90	Wash	3	0	0	0	0
Totals		26	2	7	9	40

KLEMM, Jon *6–3 200 D*
B. Cranbrook, B.C., Jan. 8, 1970

SSN	TEAM	GP	G	A	PTS.	PIM	+/-
91–92	Que	4	0	1	1	0	+2
93–94	Que	7	0	0	0	4	-1
94–95	Que	4	1	0	1	2	+3
95–96	Col A	56	3	12	15	20	+12
96–97	Col A	80	9	15	24	37	+12
97–98	Col A	67	6	8	14	30	-3
98–99	Col A	39	1	2	3	31	+4
Totals		257	20	38	58	124	+29

Playoffs

SSN	TEAM	GP	G	A	PTS.	PIM
95–96	Col A	15	2	1	3	0
96–97	Col A	17	1	1	2	6
97–98	Col A	4	0	0	0	0
98–99	Col A	19	0	1	1	10
Totals		55	3	3	6	16

KLIMA, Petr *6–0 190 LW*
B. Chomutov, Czechoslovakia, Dec. 23, 1964

SSN	TEAM	GP	G	A	PTS.	PIM	+/-
85–86	Det	74	32	24	56	16	-39
86–87	Det	77	30	23	53	42	-9
87–88	Det	78	37	25	62	46	+4
88–89	Det	51	25	16	41	44	+5
89–90	Det–Edm	76	30	33	63	72	
90–91	Edm	70	40	28	68	113	+24
91–92	Edm	57	21	13	34	52	-18
92–93	Edm	68	32	16	48	100	-15
93–94	TB	75	28	27	55	76	-15
94–95	TB	47	13	13	26	26	-13
95–96	TB	67	22	30	52	68	-25
96–97	LA–Pitt–Edm	33	2	12	14	12	-12
98–99	Det	13	1	0	1	4	-3
Totals		786	313	260	573	671	-125

Playoffs

SSN	TEAM	GP	G	A	PTS.	PIM
86–87	Det	13	1	2	3	4
87–88	Det	12	10	8	18	10
88–89	Det	6	2	4	6	19
89–90	Edm	21	5	0	5	8
90–91	Edm	18	7	6	13	16
91–92	Edm	15	1	4	5	8
95–96	TB	4	2	0	2	14
96–97	Edm	6	0	0	0	4
Totals		95	28	24	52	83

KLIMOVICH, Sergei *6–3 189 C*
B. Novosibirsk, USSR, March 8, 1974

SSN	TEAM	GP	G	A	PTS.	PIM	+/-
96–97	Chi	1	0	0	0	2	0

KLINGBELL, Ernest (Ike) *F*

SSN	TEAM	GP	G	A	PTS.	PIM
36–37	Chi	5	1	2	3	2

KLUKAY, Joseph Francis (Duke of Paducah)
6–0 175 LW
B. Sault Ste. Marie, Ont., Nov. 6, 1922

SSN	TEAM	GP	G	A	PTS.	PIM
46–47	Tor	55	9	20	29	12
47–48	Tor	59	15	15	30	28
48–49	Tor	45	11	10	21	11
49–50	Tor	70	15	16	31	11
50–51	Tor	70	14	16	30	16
51–52	Tor	43	4	8	12	6
52–53	Bos	70	13	16	29	20
53–54	Bos	70	20	17	37	27
54–55	Bos–Tor	66	8	8	16	48
55–56	Tor	18	0	1	1	2
Totals		566	109	127	236	181

Playoffs

SSN	TEAM	GP	G	A	PTS.	PIM
42–43	Tor	1	0	0	0	0
46–47	Tor	11	1	0	1	0
47–48	Tor	9	1	1	2	2
48–49	Tor	9	2	3	5	4
49–50	Tor	7	3	0	3	4
50–51	Tor	11	3	4	7	0
51–52	Tor	4	1	1	2	0
52–53	Bos	11	1	2	3	9
53–54	Bos	4	0	0	0	0
54–55	Tor	4	0	0	0	4
Totals		71	12	11	23	23

KLUZAK, Gordon *6–4 215 D*
B. Climax, Sask., Mar. 4, 1964

SSN	TEAM	GP	G	A	PTS.	PIM	+/-
82–83	Bos	70	1	6	7	105	+6
83–84	Bos	80	10	27	37	135	+9
85–86	Bos	70	8	31	39	155	+3
87–88	Bos	66	6	31	37	135	+18
88–89	Bos	3	0	1	1	2	-2
89–90	Bos	8	0	2	2	11	+4
90–91	Bos	2	0	0	0	0	+2
Totals		299	25	98	123	543	+40

Playoffs

SSN	TEAM	GP	G	A	PTS.	PIM
82–83	Bos	17	1	4	5	54

KNIBBS, William Arthur *6–1 180 C*
B. Toronto, Ont., Jan. 24, 1942

SSN	TEAM	GP	G	A	PTS.	PIM
64–65	Bos	53	7	10	17	4

KNIPSCHEER, Fred *5–11 185 C*
B. Ft. Wayne, Ind., Sept. 3, 1969

SSN	TEAM	GP	G	A	PTS.	PIM	+/-
93–94	Bos	11	3	2	5	14	+3
94–95	Bos	16	3	1	4	2	+1
95–96	StL	1	0	0	0	2	0
Totals		28	6	3	9	18	+4

Playoffs

SSN	TEAM	GP	G	A	PTS.	PIM
93–94	Bos	12	2	1	3	6
94–95	Bos	4	0	0	0	0
Totals		16	2	1	3	6

***KNOTT, William Earl (Nick)** *6–1 200 D*
B. Kingston, Ont., July 23, 1920

SSN	TEAM	GP	G	A	PTS.	PIM
41–42	Brk	14	3	1	4	9

KNOX, Paul William (Bill) *RW*

SSN	TEAM	GP	G	A	PTS.	PIM
54–55	Tor	1	0	0	0	0

KNUBLE, Michael *6–3 208 RW*
B. Toronto, Ont., July 4, 1972

SSN	TEAM	GP	G	A	PTS.	PIM	+/-
96–97	Det	9	1	0	1	0	-1
97–98	Det	53	7	6	13	16	+2
98–99	NYR	82	15	20	35	26	-7
Totals		144	23	26	49	42	-6

Playoffs

SSN	TEAM	GP	G	A	PTS.	PIM
97–98	Det	3	0	1	1	0

KNUTSEN, Espen *5–11 180 C*
B. Oslo, Norway, Jan. 12, 1972

SSN	TEAM	GP	G	A	PTS.	PIM	+/-
97–98	Ana	19	3	0	3	6	-10

KOCUR, Joe *6–0 205 RW*
B. Calgary, Alta., Dec. 21, 1964

SSN	TEAM	GP	G	A	PTS.	PIM	+/-
84–85	Det	17	1	0	1	64	-4
85–86	Det	59	9	6	15	377	-24
86–87	Det	77	9	9	18	276	-10
87–88	Det	63	7	7	14	263	-11
88–89	Det	60	9	9	18	213	-4
89–90	Det	71	16	20	36	268	-4
90–91	Det–NYR	57	5	4	9	28	-79
91–92	NYR	51	7	4	11	121	-4
92–93	NYR	65	3	6	9	131	-9
93–94	NYR	71	2	1	3	129	-9
94–95	NYR	48	1	2	3	71	-4
95–96	NYR–Van	45	1	3	4	68	-7
96–97	Det	34	2	1	3	70	-7
97–98	Det	63	6	5	11	92	-7
98–99	Det	39	2	5	7	87	0
Totals		820	80	82	162	2519	-111

Playoffs

SSN	TEAM	GP	G	A	PTS.	PIM
84–85	Bos	3	1	0	1	5
86–87	Det	16	2	3	5	71
87–88	Det	10	0	1	1	13
88–89	Det	3	0	1	1	6
90–91	NYR	6	0	2	2	21
91–92	NYR	12	1	1	2	38
93–94	NYR	20	1	1	2	17
94–95	NYR	10	0	0	0	8
95–96	Van	1	0	0	0	0
96–97	Det	19	1	3	4	22
97–98	Det	18	4	0	4	30
Totals		118	10	12	22	231

KOHN, Ladislav *5–10 175 RW*
B. Uherske Hradste, Czech., Mar. 4, 1975

SSN	TEAM	GP	G	A	PTS.	PIM	+/-
95–96	Calg	5	1	0	1	2	-1
97–98	Calg	4	0	1	1	0	+2
98–99	Tor	16	1	3	4	4	+1
Totals		25	2	5	7	6	+2

Playoffs

SSN	TEAM	GP	G	A	PTS.	PIM
98–99	Tor	2	0	0	0	5

KOIVU, Saku *5–9 163 C*
B. Turku, Finland, Nov. 23, 1974

SSN	TEAM	GP	G	A	PTS.	PIM	+/-
95–96	Mont	82	20	25	45	40	-7
96–97	Mont	50	17	39	56	38	+7
97–98	Mont	69	14	43	57	48	+8
98–99	Mont	65	14	30	44	38	-7
Totals		266	65	137	202	164	+1

Playoffs

SSN	TEAM	GP	G	A	PTS.	PIM
95–96	Mont	6	3	1	4	8
96–97	Mont	5	1	3	4	10
97–98	Mont	6	2	3	5	2
Totals		17	6	7	13	20

SSN	TEAM	GP	G	A	PTS.	PIM	+/-

KOLESAR, Mark 6–1 188 LW
B. Brampton, Ont., Jan. 23, 1973

SSN	TEAM	GP	G	A	PTS.	PIM	+/-
95–96	Tor	21	2	2	4	14	0
96–97	Tor	7	0	0	0	0	-3
Totals		28	2	2	4	14	-3

Playoffs

| 95–96 | Tor | 3 | 1 | 0 | 1 | 2 | |

KOLSTAD, Dean 6–6 210 D
B. Edmonton, Alta., June 16, 1968

88–89	Minn	25	1	5	6	42	-5
90–91	Minn	5	0	0	0	15	-2
92–93	SJ	10	0	2	2	12	-9
Totals		40	1	7	8	69	-16

KOMADOSKI, Neil George 6–0 200 D
B. Winnipeg, Man., Nov. 5, 1951

72–73	LA	62	1	8	9	67	-22
73–74	LA	68	2	4	6	43	-4
74–75	LA	75	4	12	16	69	+10
75–76	LA	80	3	15	18	165	+7
76–77	LA	68	3	9	12	109	+17
77–78	LA–StL	58	2	14	16	97	-20
78–79	StL	42	1	2	3	30	0
79–80	StL	49	0	12	12	52	-22
Totals		502	16	76	92	632	-34

Playoffs

73–74	LA	2	0	0	0	12	
74–75	LA	3	0	0	0	2	
75–76	LA	9	0	0	0	18	
76–77	LA	9	0	2	2	15	
Totals		23	0	2	2	47	

KONIK, George Samuel 5–10 200 LW
B. Flin Flon, Man., May 4, 1938

67–68	Pitt	52	7	8	15	26	-9
72–73	Minn (WHA)	54	4	12	16	34	

KONOWALCHUK, Steve 6–1 195 C
B. Salt Lake City, Utah, Nov. 11, 1972

91–92	Wash	1	0	0	0	0	0
92–93	Wash	36	4	7	11	16	+4
93–94	Wash	62	12	14	26	33	+9
94–95	Wash	46	11	14	25	44	+7
95–96	Wash	70	23	22	45	92	+13
96–97	Wash	78	17	25	42	67	-3
97–98	Wash	80	10	24	34	80	+9
98–99	Wash	45	12	12	24	26	0
Totals		418	89	118	207	358	+39

Playoffs

92–93	Wash	2	0	1	1	0	
93–94	Wash	11	0	1	1	10	
94–95	Wash	7	2	5	7	12	
95–96	Wash	2	0	2	2	0	
Totals		22	2	9	11	22	

KONROYD, Stephen Mark 6–1 195 D
B. Scarborough, Ont., Feb. 10, 1961

80–81	Calg	4	0	0	0	4	0
81–82	Calg	63	3	14	17	78	-6
82–83	Calg	79	4	13	17	73	+3
83–84	Calg	80	1	13	14	94	-8
84–85	Calg	64	3	23	26	73	+12
85–86	Calg–NYI	73	7	25	32	80	+24
86–87	NYI	72	5	16	21	70	-4
87–88	NYI	62	2	15	17	99	+16
88–89	NYI–Chi	78	6	12	18	42	-16
89–90	Chi	75	3	14	17	34	+6
90–91	Chi	70	0	12	12	40	+11
91–92	Chi–Hart	82	4	24	28	97	-1
92–93	Hart–Det	65	3	12	15	67	-15
93–94	Det–Ott	27	0	2	2	12	-3
94–95	Calg	1	0	0	0	0	0
Totals		895	41	195	236	863	+19

Playoffs

81–82	Calg	3	0	0	0	12	
82–83	Calg	9	2	1	3	18	
83–84	Calg	8	1	2	3	8	
84–85	NYI	4	1	4	5	2	
85–86	NYI	3	0	0	0	6	
86–87	NYI	14	1	4	5	10	
87–88	NYI	6	1	0	1	4	
88–89	Chi	16	2	0	2	10	
89–90	Chi	20	1	3	4	19	
90–91	Chi	6	1	0	1	8	
91–92	Hart	7	0	1	1	2	
92–93	Det	1	0	0	0	0	
Totals		97	10	15	25	99	

KONSTANTINOV, Vladimir 5–11 190 D
B. Murmansk, Soviet Union, Mar. 19, 1967

91–92	Det	79	8	26	34	172	+25
92–93	Det	82	5	17	22	137	+22
93–94	Det	80	12	21	33	138	+30
94–95	Det	47	3	11	14	101	+10
95–96	Det	81	14	20	34	139	+60
96–97	Det	77	5	33	38	151	+38
Totals		446	47	128	175	838	+185

Playoffs

91–92	Det	11	0	1	1	16	
92–93	Det	7	0	1	1	8	
93–94	Det	7	0	2	2	4	
94–95	Det	18	1	1	2	22	
95–96	Det	19	4	5	9	28	
96–97	Det	20	0	4	4	29	
Totals		82	5	14	19	107	

KONTOS, Christopher 6–1 195 LW/C
B. Toronto, Ont., Dec. 10, 1963

82–83	NYR	44	8	7	15	33	+1
83–84	NYR	6	0	1	1	8	0
84–85	NYR	28	4	8	12	24	-12
86–87	Pitt	31	8	9	17	6	-6
87–88	Pitt–LA	42	3	17	20	14	-2
88–89	LA	7	2	1	3	2	+2
89–90	LA	6	2	2	4	4	+3
92–93	TB	66	27	24	51	12	-7
Totals		230	54	69	123	103	-21

Playoffs

87–88	LA	4	1	0	1	4	
88–89	LA	11	9	0	9	8	
89–90	LA	5	1	0	1	0	
Totals		20	11	0	11	12	

KOPAK, Russell 5–10 158 C
B. Edmonton, Alta., Apr. 26, 1924

| 43–44 | Bos | 24 | 7 | 9 | 16 | 0 | |

KORAB, Jerry (Kong) 6–3 218 D
B. Sault Ste. Marie, Ont. Sept. 15, 1948

70–71	Chi	46	4	14	18	152	+14
71–72	Chi	73	9	5	14	95	+1
72–73	Chi	77	12	15	27	94	+5
73–74	Van–Buf	76	10	19	29	13	-447
74–75	Buf	79	12	44	56	184	+41
75–76	Buf	65	13	28	41	85	+18
76–77	Buf	77	14	33	47	120	+22
77–78	Buf	77	7	34	41	119	+19
78–79	Buf	78	11	40	51	104	+5
79–80	Buf–LA	54	2	12	14	108	-3
80–81	LA	78	9	43	52	139	+10
81–82	LA	50	5	13	18	91	-19
82–83	LA	72	3	26	29	90	-6
83–84	Buf	48	2	9	11	82	+4
84–85	Buf	25	1	6	7	29	-9
Totals		975	114	341	455	1629	+58

Playoffs

70–71	Chi	7	1	0	1	20	
71–72	Chi	8	0	1	1	20	
72–73	Chi	15	0	0	0	22	
74–75	Buf	16	3	2	5	32	
75–76	Buf	9	1	3	4	12	
76–77	Buf	6	2	4	6	8	
77–78	Buf	8	0	5	5	6	
78–79	Buf	3	1	0	1	4	
79–80	LA	3	0	1	1	11	
80–81	LA	4	0	0	0	33	
81–82	LA	10	0	2	2	26	
Totals		93	8	18	26	201	

KORDIC, Dan 6–5 220 D
B. Edmonton, Alta., Apr. 18, 1971

91–92	Phil	46	1	3	4	126	+1
93–94	Phil	4	0	0	0	5	0
95–96	Phil	9	1	0	1	31	+1
96–97	Phil	75	1	4	5	210	-1
97–98	Phil	61	1	1	2	210	-4
98–99	Phil	2	0	0	0	2	-1
Totals		197	4	8	12	584	-4

Playoffs

| 96–97 | Phil | 12 | 1 | 0 | 1 | 22 | |

*KORDIC, John 6–2 210 RW
B. Edmonton, Alta., Mar. 22, 1965

85–86	Mont	5	0	1	1	12	+1
86–87	Mont	44	5	3	8	151	-7
87–88	Mont	60	2	6	8	159	0
88–89	Mont–Tor	52	1	2	3	198	-14
89–90	Tor	55	9	4	13	252	-8
90–91	Tor–Wash	10	0	0	0	110	+1
91–92	Que	19	0	2	2	115	-3
Totals		245	17	18	35	997	-30

Playoffs

85–86	Mont	18	0	0	0	53	
86–87	Mont	11	2	0	2	19	
87–88	Mont	7	2	2	4	26	
89–90	Tor	5	0	1	1	33	
Totals		41	4	3	7	131	

KORN, Jim 6–3 210 D
B. Hopkins, Minn., July 28, 1957

79–80	Det	63	5	13	18	108	-4
80–81	Det	63	5	15	20	246	-5
81–82	Det–Tor	70	2	10	12	14	-18
82–83	Tor	80	8	21	29	246	-27
83–84	Tor	65	12	14	26	257	-33
84–85	Tor	41	5	5	10	171	-17
86–87	Buf	52	4	10	14	158	-3
87–88	NJ	52	8	13	21	140	-22
88–89	NJ	65	15	16	31	212	-3
89–90	NJ–Calg	46	2	5	7	125	0
Totals		597	66	122	188	1801	-135

Playoffs

82–83	Tor	3	0	0	0	26	
87–88	NJ	9	0	2	2	71	
89–90	Calg	4	1	0	1	12	
Totals		16	1	2	3	109	

KORNEY, Michael Wayne 6–3 195 RW
B. Dauphin, Man., Sept. 15, 1953

73–74	Det	2	0	0	0	0	-3
74–75	Det	30	8	2	10	18	-9
75–76	Det	27	1	7	8	23	-8
78–79	NYR	18	0	1	1	18	+4
Totals		77	9	10	19	59	-16

KOROLEV, Igor 6–1 187 RW
B. Moscow, USSR, Sept. 6, 1970

92–93	StL	74	4	23	27	20	-1
93–94	StL	73	6	10	16	40	-12
94–95	Winn	45	8	22	30	10	+1
95–96	Winn	72	22	29	51	42	+1
96–97	Phoe	41	3	7	10	28	-5
97–98	Tor	78	17	22	39	22	-18
98–99	Tor	66	13	34	47	46	+11
Totals		450	73	147	220	208	-23

Playoffs

92–93	StL	3	0	0	0	0	
93–94	StL	2	0	0	0	0	
95–96	Winn	6	0	3	3	0	
96–97	Phoe	1	0	0	0	0	
98–99	Tor	1	0	0	0	0	
Totals		13	0	3	3	0	

KOROLL, Clifford Eugene 6–0 195 RW
B. Canora, Sask., Oct. 1, 1946

69–70	Chi	73	18	19	37	44	+15
70–71	Chi	72	16	34	50	85	+28
71–72	Chi	76	22	23	45	51	+20
72–73	Chi	77	33	24	57	38	+17
73–74	Chi	78	21	25	46	32	+27
74–75	Chi	80	27	32	59	27	+20
75–76	Chi	80	25	33	58	29	+6
76–77	Chi	80	15	26	41	18	-25
77–78	Chi	73	16	15	31	19	+8
78–79	Chi	78	12	19	31	20	+3
79–80	Chi	47	3	4	7	6	-10
Totals		814	208	254	462	359	+109

SSN	TEAM	GP	G	A	PTS.	PIM	+/-
Playoffs							
69–70	Chi	8	1	4	5	9	
70–71	Chi	18	7	9	16	18	
71–72	Chi	8	0	0	0	11	
72–73	Chi	16	4	6	10	6	
73–74	Chi	11	2	5	7	13	
74–75	Chi	8	3	5	8	8	
75–76	Chi	4	1	0	1	0	
76–77	Chi	2	0	0	0	0	
77–78	Chi	4	1	0	1	0	
78–79	Chi	4	0	0	0	0	
79–80	Chi	2	0	0	0	2	
Totals		85	19	29	48	67	

KOROLYUK, Alex *5–9 190 RW*
B. Moscow, USSR, Jan. 15, 1976

SSN	TEAM	GP	G	A	PTS.	PIM	+/-
97–98	SJ	19	2	3	5	6	-5
98–99	SJ	55	12	18	30	26	+3
Totals		74	14	21	35	32	-2
Playoffs							
98–99	SJ	6	1	3	4	2	

KOTANEN, Elno Richard (Dick) *5–11 190 D*
B. Strathmore, Alta., Nov. 18, 1925

SSN	TEAM	GP	G	A	PTS.	PIM	+/-
48–49	Det	1	0	1	1	0	
50–51	NYR	1	0	0	0	0	
Totals		2	0	1	1	0	

KOVALENKO, Andrei *5–10 200 RW*
B. Balakovo, USSR, June 7, 1970

SSN	TEAM	GP	G	A	PTS.	PIM	+/-
92–93	Que	81	27	41	68	57	+13
93–94	Que	58	16	17	33	46	-5
94–95	Que	45	14	10	24	31	-4
95–96	Col A–Mont	77	28	28	56	49	+20
96–97	Edm	74	32	27	59	81	-5
97–98	Edm	59	6	17	23	28	-14
98–99	Edm–Phil–Car	74	19	21	40	32	-6
Totals		468	142	161	303	324	-1
Playoffs							
92–93	Que	4	1	0	1	2	
94–95	Que	6	0	1	1	2	
95–96	Mont	6	0	0	0	6	
96–97	Edm	12	4	3	7	6	
97–98	Edm	1	0	0	0	0	
98–99	Car	4	0	2	2	2	
Totals		33	5	6	11	18	

KOVALEV, Alexei *6–0 205 RW*
B. Togliatti, USSR, Feb. 24, 1973

SSN	TEAM	GP	G	A	PTS.	PIM	+/-
92–93	NYR	65	20	18	38	79	-10
93–94	NYR	76	23	33	56	154	+18
94–95	NYR	48	13	15	28	30	-6
95–96	NYR	81	24	34	58	98	+5
96–97	NYR	45	13	22	35	42	+11
97–98	NYR	73	23	30	53	44	-22
98–99	NYR–Pitt	77	23	30	53	49	+2
Totals		465	139	182	321	496	-2
Playoffs							
93–94	NYR	23	9	12	21	18	
94–95	NYR	10	4	7	11	10	
95–96	NYR	11	3	4	7	14	
98–99	Pitt	10	5	7	12	14	
Totals		54	21	30	51	56	

KOWAL, Joseph Douglas *6–5 212 LW*
B. Toronto, Ont., Feb. 3, 1956

SSN	TEAM	GP	G	A	PTS.	PIM	+/-
76–77	Buf	16	0	5	5	6	+3
77–78	Buf	6	0	0	0	7	0
Totals		22	0	5	5	13	+3
Playoffs							
77–78	Buf	2	0	0	0	0	

KOZAK, Donald *5–9 184 RW*
B. Saskatoon, Sask., Feb. 2, 1952

SSN	TEAM	GP	G	A	PTS.	PIM	+/-
72–73	LA	72	14	6	20	104	-25
73–74	LA	76	21	14	35	54	+7
74–75	LA	77	16	15	31	64	+5
75–76	LA	62	20	24	44	94	-4
76–77	LA	79	15	17	32	89	-9
77–78	LA	43	8	5	13	45	+4
78–79	Van	28	2	5	7	30	-15
Totals		437	96	86	182	480	-37

SSN	TEAM	GP	G	A	PTS.	PIM	+/-
Playoffs							
73–74	LA	5	0	0	0	33	
74–75	LA	3	1	1	2	7	
75–76	LA	9	1	0	1	12	
76–77	LA	9	4	1	5	17	
78–79	Van	3	1	0	1	0	
Totals		29	7	2	9	69	

KOZAK, Leslie Paul *6–0 185 F*
B. Yorkton, Sask., Oct. 28, 1940

SSN	TEAM	GP	G	A	PTS.	PIM	+/-
61–62	Tor	12	1	0	1	2	

KOZLOV, Viktor *6–5 225 LW*
B. Togliatti, USSR, Feb. 14, 1975

SSN	TEAM	GP	G	A	PTS.	PIM	+/-
94–95	SJ	16	2	0	2	2	-5
95–96	SJ	62	6	13	19	6	-15
96–97	SJ	78	16	25	41	40	-16
97–98	SJ–Fla	64	17	13	30	16	-3
98–99	Fla	65	16	35	51	24	+13
Totals		285	57	86	143	88	-26

KOZLOV, Vyacheslav *5–10 180 C*
B. Voskresensk, USSR, May 3, 1972

SSN	TEAM	GP	G	A	PTS.	PIM	+/-
91–92	Det	7	0	2	2	2	-2
92–93	Det	17	4	1	5	14	-1
93–94	Det	77	34	39	73	50	+27
94–95	Det	46	13	20	33	45	+12
95–96	Det	82	36	37	73	70	+33
96–97	Det	75	23	22	45	46	+21
97–98	Det	80	25	27	52	46	+14
98–99	Det	79	29	29	58	45	+10
Totals		463	164	177	341	318	+114
Playoffs							
92–93	Det	4	0	2	2	2	
93–94	Det	7	2	5	7	12	
94–95	Det	18	9	7	16	10	
95–96	Det	19	5	7	12	10	
96–97	Det	20	8	5	13	14	
97–98	Det	22	6	8	14	10	
98–99	Det	10	6	1	7	4	
Totals		100	36	35	71	62	

KRAFTCHECK, Stephen *5–10 185 D*
B. Tinturn, Ont., Mar. 3, 1929

SSN	TEAM	GP	G	A	PTS.	PIM	+/-
50–51	Bos	22	0	0	0	8	
51–52	NYR	58	8	9	17	30	
52–53	NYR	69	2	9	11	45	
58–59	Tor	8	1	0	1	0	
Totals		157	11	18	29	83	
Playoffs							
50–51	Bos	6	0	0	0	7	

KRAKE, Philip Gordon (Skip) *5–11 170 C*
B. North Battleford, Sask., Oct. 14, 1943

SSN	TEAM	GP	G	A	PTS.	PIM	+/-
63–64	Bos	2	0	0	0	0	
65–66	Bos	2	0	0	0	0	
66–67	Bos	15	6	2	8	4	
67–68	Bos	68	5	7	12	13	+9
68–69	LA	30	3	9	12	11	-10
69–70	LA	58	5	17	22	86	-25
70–71	Buf	74	4	5	9	68	-21
72–73	Clev (WHA)	26	9	10	19	61	
73–74	Clev (WHA)	69	20	36	56	94	
74–75	Clev (WHA)	71	15	23	38	108	
75–76	Edm (WHA)	41	8	8	16	55	
NHL Totals		249	23	40	63	182	-47
WHA Totals		207	52	77	129	318	
Playoffs							
67–68	Bos	4	0	0	0	2	
68–69	LA	6	1	0	1	15	
72–73	Clev (WHA)	9	1	2	3	27	
73–74	Clev (WHA)	5	0	1	1	39	
74–75	Clev (WHA)	5	1	1	2	0	
NHL Totals		10	1	0	1	17	
WHA Totals		19	2	4	6	66	

KRAVCHUK, Igor *6–1 200 D*
B. Ufa, Soviet Union, Sept. 13, 1966

SSN	TEAM	GP	G	A	PTS.	PIM	+/-
91–92	Chi	18	1	8	9	4	-3
92–93	Chi–Edm	50	10	17	27	32	+3
93–94	Edm	81	12	38	50	16	-12
94–95	Edm	36	7	11	18	29	-15
95–96	Edm–StL	66	7	16	23	34	-19

SSN	TEAM	GP	G	A	PTS.	PIM	+/-
96–97	StL	82	4	24	28	35	+7
97–98	Ott	81	8	27	35	8	-19
98–99	Ott	79	4	21	25	32	+14
Totals		498	53	162	215	190	-44
Playoffs							
91–92	Chi	18	2	6	8	8	
95–96	StL	10	1	5	6	4	
96–97	StL	2	0	0	0	2	
97–98	Ott	11	2	3	5	4	
98–99	Ott	4	0	0	0	0	
Totals		45	5	14	19	18	

KRAVETS, Mikhail *5–10 176 LW*
B. Leningrad, Soviet Union, Nov. 11, 1963

SSN	TEAM	GP	G	A	PTS.	PIM	+/-
91–92	SJ	1	0	0	0	0	0
92–93	SJ	1	0	0	0	0	-1
Totals		2	0	0	0	0	-1

KRENTZ, Dale *5–11 190 LW*
B. Steinbach, Man., Dec. 19, 1961

SSN	TEAM	GP	G	A	PTS.	PIM	+/-
86–87	Det	8	0	0	0	0	
87–88	Det	6	2	0	2	5	
88–89	Det	16	3	3	6	4	
Totals		30	5	3	8	9	
Playoffs							
87–88	Det	2	0	0	0	0	

KRIVOKRASOV, Sergei *5–10 195 RW*
B. Angarsk, USSR, Apr. 15, 1974

SSN	TEAM	GP	G	A	PTS.	PIM	+/-
92–93	Chi	4	0	0	0	2	-2
93–94	Chi	9	1	0	1	4	-2
94–95	Chi	41	12	7	19	33	+9
95–96	Chi	46	6	10	16	32	+10
96–97	Chi	67	13	11	24	42	-1
97–98	Chi	58	10	13	23	33	-1
98–99	Nash	70	25	23	48	42	-5
Totals		237	57	51	108	155	+8
Playoffs							
94–95	Chi	10	0	0	0	8	
95–96	Chi	5	1	0	1	2	
96–97	Chi	6	1	0	1	4	
Totals		21	2	0	2	14	

*KROL, Joseph *5–11 173 LW*
B. Winnipeg, Man., Aug. 13, 1915

SSN	TEAM	GP	G	A	PTS.	PIM	+/-
36–37	NYR	1	0	0	0	0	
38–39	NYR	1	1	1	2	0	
41–42	Brk	24	9	3	12	8	
Totals		26	10	4	14	8	

KROMM, Richard Gordon (Rich) *5–11 180 LW*
B. Trail, B.C., Mar. 29, 1964

SSN	TEAM	GP	G	A	PTS.	PIM	+/-
83–84	Calg	53	11	12	23	27	+14
84–85	Calg	73	20	32	52	32	+19
85–86	Calg–NYI	77	19	24	43	35	+17
86–87	NYI	70	12	17	29	20	+2
87–88	NYI	71	5	10	15	20	+2
88–89	NYI	20	1	6	7	4	-3
90–91	NYI	6	1	0	1	0	-2
91–92	NYI	1	0	0	0	0	0
92–93	NYI	1	1	2	3	0	+3
Totals		372	70	103	173	138	+52
Playoffs							
82–83	Calg	11	1	1	2	9	
83–84	Calg	3	0	1	1	4	
85–86	NYI	3	0	1	1	0	
86–87	NYI	14	1	3	4	4	
87–88	NYI	5	0	0	0	5	
Totals		36	2	6	8	22	

KRON, Robert *5–10 180 LW*
B. Brno, Czechoslovakia, Feb. 27, 1967

SSN	TEAM	GP	G	A	PTS.	PIM	+/-
90–91	Van	76	12	20	32	21	-11
91–92	Van	36	2	2	4	2	-9
92–93	Van–Hart	45	14	13	27	18	+5
93–94	Hart	77	24	26	50	8	0
94–95	Hart	37	10	8	18	10	-3
95–96	Hart	77	22	28	50	6	-1
96–97	Hart	68	10	12	22	10	-18
97–98	Car	81	16	20	36	12	-8
98–99	Car	75	9	16	25	10	-13

SSN	TEAM	GP	G	A	PTS.	PIM	+/-
Totals		572	119	145	264	97	-58

Playoffs

91–92	Van	11	1	2	3	2	
98–99	Car	5	2	0	2	0	
Totals		16	3	2	5	2	

KROOK, Kevin Bradley *5–11 187 D*
B. Cold Lake, Alta., Apr. 5, 1958

78–79	Col	3	0	0	0	2	0

KROUPA, Vlastimil *6–3 210 D*
B. Most, Czechoslovakia, Apr. 27, 1975

93–94	SJ	27	1	3	4	20	-6
94–95	SJ	14	0	2	2	16	-7
95–96	SJ	27	1	7	8	18	-17
96–97	SJ	35	2	6	8	12	-17
97–98	NJ	2	0	1	1	0	+1
Totals		105	4	19	23	66	-46

Playoffs

93–94	SJ	14	1	2	3	21	
94–95	SJ	6	0	0	0	4	
Totals		20	1	2	3	25	

KRULICKI, James John *5–11 180 LW*
B. Kitchener, Ont., Mar. 9, 1948

70–71	NYR–Det	41	0	3	3	6	-7

KRUPP, Uwe *6–6 235 D*
B. Cologne, W. Germany, June 24, 1965

86–87	Buf	26	1	4	5	23	-9
87–88	Buf	75	2	9	11	151	-1
88–89	Buf	70	5	13	18	55	0
89–90	Buf	74	3	20	23	85	+15
90–91	Buf	74	12	32	44	66	+14
91–92	Buf–NYI	67	8	29	37	49	+13
92–93	NYI	80	9	29	38	67	+6
93–94	NYI	41	7	14	21	30	+11
94–95	Que	44	6	17	23	20	+14
95–96	Col A	6	0	3	3	4	+4
96–97	Col A	60	4	17	21	48	+12
97–98	Col A	78	9	22	31	38	+21
98–99	Det	22	3	2	5	6	0
Totals		717	69	211	280	642	+90

Playoffs

87–88	Buf	6	0	0	0	15	
88–89	Buf	5	0	1	1	4	
89–90	Buf	6	0	0	0	4	
90–91	Buf	6	1	1	2	6	
92–93	NYI	18	1	5	6	12	
93–94	NYI	4	0	1	1	4	
94–95	Que	5	0	2	2	2	
95–96	Col A	22	4	12	16	33	
97–98	Col A	7	0	1	1	4	
Totals		79	6	23	29	84	

KRUPPKE, Gord *6–1 215 D*
B. Slave Lake, Alta., Apr. 2, 1969

90–91	Det	4	0	0	0	0	+1
92–93	Det	10	0	0	0	20	+1
93–94	Det	9	0	0	0	12	-4
Totals		23	0	0	0	32	-2

KRUSE, Paul *6–0 202 LW*
B. Merritt, B.C., Mar. 15, 1970

90–91	Calg	1	0	0	0	7	-1
91–92	Calg	16	3	1	4	65	+1
92–93	Calg	27	2	3	5	41	+2
93–94	Calg	68	3	8	11	185	-6
94–95	Calg	45	11	5	16	141	+13
95–96	Calg	75	3	12	15	145	-5
96–97	Calg–NYI	62	6	2	8	14	-9
97–98	NYI–Buf	74	7	2	9	187	-11
98–99	Buf	43	3	0	3	114	0
Totals		414	38	33	71	1026	-34

Playoffs

93–94	Calg	7	0	0	0	14	
94–95	Calg	7	4	2	6	10	
95–96	Calg	3	0	0	0	4	
97–98	Buf	1	1	0	1	4	
98–99	Buf	10	0	0	0	4	
Totals		28	5	2	7	36	

KRUSHELNYSKI, Michael *6–2 200 LW/C*
B. Montreal, Que., Apr. 27, 1960

81–82	Bos	17	3	3	6	2	0
82–83	Bos	79	23	42	65	43	+38
83–84	Bos	66	25	20	45	55	+9
84–85	Edm	80	43	45	88	60	+56
85–86	Edm	54	16	24	40	22	+11
86–87	Edm	80	16	35	51	67	+26
87–88	Edm	76	20	27	47	64	+26
88–89	LA	78	26	36	62	110	+9
89–90	LA	63	16	25	41	50	+7
90–91	LA–Tor	74	18	27	45	58	+1
91–92	Tor	72	9	15	24	72	-5
92–93	Tor	84	19	20	39	62	+3
93–94	Tor	54	5	6	11	28	-5
94–95	Det	20	2	3	5	6	+3
Totals		897	241	328	569	699	+179

Playoffs

81–82	Bos	1	0	0	0	2	
82–83	Bos	17	8	6	14	12	
83–84	Bos	2	0	0	0	0	
84–85	Edm	18	5	8	13	22	
85–86	Edm	10	4	5	9	16	
86–87	Edm	21	3	4	7	18	
87–88	Edm	19	4	6	10	12	
88–89	LA	11	1	4	5	4	
89–90	LA	10	1	3	4	12	
92–93	Tor	16	3	7	10	8	
93–94	Tor	6	0	0	0	0	
94–95	Det	8	0	0	0	0	
Totals		139	29	43	72	106	

KRUTOV, Vladimir *5–9 195 LW*
B. Moscow, June 1, 1960

89–90	Van	61	11	23	34	20	-5

KRYGIER, Todd *6–0 180 LW*
B. Northville, Mich., Oct. 12, 1965

89–90	Hart	58	18	12	30	52	+4
90–91	Hart	72	13	17	30	95	+1
91–92	Wash	67	13	17	30	107	-1
92–93	Wash	77	11	12	23	60	-13
93–94	Wash	66	12	18	30	60	-4
94–95	Ana	35	11	11	22	10	+1
95–96	Ana–Wash	76	15	33	48	82	-1
96–97	Wash	47	5	11	16	37	-10
97–98	Wash	45	2	12	14	30	-3
Totals		543	100	143	243	533	-26

Playoffs

89–90	Hart	7	2	1	3	4	
90–91	Hart	6	0	2	2	0	
91–92	Wash	5	2	1	3	4	
92–93	Wash	6	1	1	2	4	
93–94	Wash	5	2	0	2	10	
95–96	Wash	6	2	0	2	12	
97–98	Wash	13	1	2	3	6	
Totals		48	10	7	17	40	

KRYSKOW, David Roy *5–10 175 LW*
B. Edmonton, Alta., Dec. 25, 1951

72–73	Chi	11	1	0	1	0	-1
73–74	Chi	72	7	12	19	22	+5
74–75	Wash–Det	69	10	19	29	87	-30
75–76	Atl	79	15	25	40	65	-6
76–77	Calg (WHA)	45	16	17	33	47	
77–78	Winn (WHA)	71	20	21	41	16	
NHL Totals		231	33	56	89	174	-32
WHA Totals		116	36	38	74	63	

Playoffs

72–73	Chi	3	2	0	2	0	
73–74	Chi	7	0	0	0	2	
75–76	Atl	2	0	0	0	2	
77–78	Winn (WHA)	9	4	4	8	2	
NHL Totals		12	2	0	2	4	
WHA Totals		9	4	4	8	2	

KRYZANOWSKI, Edward Lloyd *5–10 178 D*
B. Fort Francis, Ont., Nov. 14, 1925

48–49	Bos	36	1	3	4	10	
49–50	Bos	59	6	10	16	12	
50–51	Bos	69	3	6	9	10	
51–52	Bos	70	5	3	8	33	
52–53	Chi	5	0	0	0	0	
Totals		239	15	22	37	65	

Playoffs

48–49	Bos	5	0	1	1	2	
50–51	Bos	6	0	0	0	2	
51–52	Bos	7	0	0	0	0	
Totals		18	0	1	1	4	

KUBA, Filip *6–3 202 D*
B. Ostrava, Czech., Dec. 29, 1976

98–99	Fla	5	0	1	1	0	+2

KUBINA, Pavel *6–3 213 D*
B. Celedna, Czech., Apr. 15, 1977

97–98	TB	10	1	2	3	22	-1
98–99	TB	68	9	12	21	80	-33
Totals		78	10	14	23	102	-34

KUCERA, Frantisek *6–2 205 D*
B. Prague, Czechoslovakia, Feb. 3, 1968

90–91	Chi	40	2	12	14	32	+3
91–92	Chi	61	3	10	13	36	+3
92–93	Chi	71	5	14	19	59	+7
93–94	Chi–Hart	76	5	16	21	48	-3
94–95	Hart	48	3	17	20	30	+3
95–96	Hart–Van	54	3	6	9	20	+2
96–97	Van–Phil	4	0	0	0	2	-2
Totals		354	21	75	96	227	+13

Playoffs

91–92	Chi	6	0	0	0	0	
95–96	Van	6	0	1	1	0	
Totals		12	0	1	1	0	

KUDASHOV, Alexei *6–0 183 C*
B. Elektrostal, USSR, July 21, 1971

93–94	Tor	25	1	0	1	4	-3

KUDELSKI, Bob *6–1 200 RW*
B. Springfield, Mass., Mar. 3, 1964

87–88	LA	26	0	1	1	8	-10
88–89	LA	14	1	3	4	17	-5
89–90	LA	62	22	13	36	49	-7
90–91	LA	72	22	13	36	46	+9
91–92	LA	80	22	21	43	42	-15
92–93	LA–Ott	63	24	17	41	30	-25
93–94	Ott–Fla	86	40	30	70	24	-33
94–95	Fla	26	6	3	9	2	+2
95–96	Fla	13	0	1	1	0	+1
Totals		442	139	102	241	218	-83

Playoffs

89–90	LA	8	1	2	3	2	
90–91	LA	8	3	2	5	2	
91–92	LA	6	0	0	0	0	
Totals		22	4	4	8	4	

*KUHN, Gordon (Doggie) *F*
B. Truro, N.S.

32–33	NYA	12	1	1	2	4	

KUKULOWICZ, Adolph Frank (Aggie) *6–2 175 C*
B. Winnipeg, Man., Apr. 2, 1933

52–53	NYR	3	1	0	1	0	
53–54	NYR	1	0	0	0	0	
Totals		4	1	0	1	0	

KULAK, Stuart *5–10 180 RW*
B. Edmonton, Alta., Mar. 10, 1963

82–83	Van	4	1	1	2	0	+1
86–87	Van–Edm–NYR	54	4	2	6	78	-9
87–88	Que	14	1	1	2	28	-5
88–89	Winn	18	2	0	2	24	-6
Totals		90	8	4	12	130	-19

Playoffs

88–89	Winn	3	0	0	0	2	

KULLMAN, Arnold Edwin *5–6 175 C*
B. Winnipeg, Man., Oct. 9, 1927

47–48	Bos	1	0	0	0	0	
49–50	Bos	12	0	1	1	11	
Totals		13	0	1	1	11	

KULLMAN, Edward George 5-7 170 RW
B. Winnipeg, Man., Dec. 12, 1923

SSN	TEAM	GP	G	A	PTS.	PIM	+/-
47–48	NYR	51	15	17	32	32	
48–49	NYR	18	4	5	9	14	
50–51	NYR	70	14	18	32	88	
51–52	NYR	64	11	10	21	59	
52–53	NYR	70	8	10	18	61	
53–54	NYR	70	4	10	14	44	
Totals		343	56	70	126	298	

Playoffs

47–48	NYR	6	1	0	1	2	

KUMPEL, Mark 6-0 190 RW
B. Wakefield, Mass., Mar. 7, 1961

SSN	TEAM	GP	G	A	PTS.	PIM	+/-
84–85	Que	42	8	7	15	26	+4
85–86	Que	47	10	12	22	17	+10
86–87	Que–Det	45	1	9	10	16	-10
87–88	Det–Winn	45	4	6	10	23	+4
89–90	Winn	56	8	9	17	21	-5
90–91	Winn	53	7	3	10	10	-10
Totals		288	38	46	84	113	-7

Playoffs

84–85	Que	18	3	4	7	4	
85–86	Que	2	1	0	1	0	
86–87	Det	8	0	0	0	4	
88–89	Winn	4	0	0	0	4	
89–90	Winn	7	2	0	2	2	
Totals		39	6	4	10	14	

KUNTZ, Alan Robert 5-11 165 LW
B. Toronto, Ont., June 4, 1919

SSN	TEAM	GP	G	A	PTS.	PIM	+/-
41–42	NYR	31	10	11	21	10	
45–46	NYR	14	0	1	1	2	
Totals		45	10	12	22	12	

Playoffs

41–42	NYR	6	1	0	1	2	

KUNTZ, Murray Robert 5-10 180 LW
B. Ottawa, Ont., Dec. 19, 1945

SSN	TEAM	GP	G	A	PTS.	PIM	+/-
74–75	StL	7	1	2	3	0	+6

KURRI, Jari 6-1 195 RW
B. Helsinki, Finland, May 18, 1960

SSN	TEAM	GP	G	A	PTS.	PIM	+/-
80–81	Edm	75	32	43	75	40	+26
81–82	Edm	71	32	54	86	32	+38
82–83	Edm	80	45	59	104	22	+47
83–84	Edm	64	52	61	113	14	+38
84–85	Edm	73	71	64	135	30	+76
85–86	Edm	78	68	63	131	22	+45
86–87	Edm	79	54	54	108	41	+19
87–88	Edm	80	43	53	96	30	+25
88–89	Edm	76	44	58	102	69	+19
89–90	Edm	78	33	60	93	48	+18
91–92	LA	73	23	37	60	24	-24
92–93	LA	82	27	60	87	38	+19
93–94	LA	81	31	46	77	48	-24
94–95	LA	38	10	19	29	24	-17
95–96	LA–NYR	71	18	27	45	39	-16
96–97	Ana	82	13	22	35	12	-13
97–98	Col A	70	5	17	22	12	+6
Totals		1251	601	797	1398	545	+282

Playoffs

80–81	Edm	9	5	7	12	4	
81–82	Edm	5	2	5	7	10	
82–83	Edm	16	8	15	23	8	
83–84	Edm	19	14	14	28	13	
84–85	Edm	18	19	12	31	6	
85–86	Edm	10	2	10	12	4	
86–87	Edm	21	15	10	25	20	
87–88	Edm	19	14	17	31	12	
88–89	Edm	7	3	5	8	6	
91–92	LA	4	1	2	3	4	
92–93	LA	24	9	8	17	4	
95–96	NYR	11	3	5	8	2	
96–97	Ana	11	1	2	3	4	
97–98	Col A	4	0	0	0	0	
Totals		200	106	127	233	123	

KURTENBACH, Orland John 6-2 195 C
B. Cudworth, Sask., Sept. 7, 1936

SSN	TEAM	GP	G	A	PTS.	PIM	+/-
60–61	NYR	10	0	6	6	2	
61–62	Bos	8	0	0	0	6	
63–64	Bos	70	12	25	37	91	
64–65	Bos	64	6	20	26	86	
65–66	Tor	70	9	6	15	54	
66–67	NYR	60	11	25	36	58	
67–68	NYR	73	15	20	35	82	+5
68–69	NYR	2	0	0	0	2	0
69–70	NYR	53	4	10	14	47	+4
70–71	Van	52	21	32	53	84	-1
71–72	Van	78	24	37	61	48	-2
72–73	Van	47	9	19	28	38	-14
73–74	Van	52	8	13	21	30	-30
Totals		639	119	213	332	628	-38

Playoffs

65–66	Tor	4	0	0	0	20	
66–67	NYR	3	0	2	2	0	
67–68	NYR	6	1	0	1	26	
69–70	NYR	6	1	2	3	24	
Totals		19	2	4	6	70	

KURVERS, Tom 6-2 195 D
B. Minneapolis, Minn., Sept. 14, 1962

SSN	TEAM	GP	G	A	PTS.	PIM	+/-
84–85	Mont	75	10	35	45	30	-3
85–86	Mont	62	7	23	30	36	+9
86–87	Mont–Buf	56	6	17	23	22	-9
87–88	NJ	56	5	29	34	46	+6
88–89	NJ	74	16	50	66	38	+11
89–90	NJ–Tor	71	15	37	52	29	-9
90–91	Tor–Van	51	4	26	30	28	-25
91–92	NYI	74	9	47	56	30	-18
92–93	NYI	52	8	30	38	38	+9
93–94	NYI	66	9	31	40	47	+7
94–95	Ana	22	4	3	7	6	-13
Totals		659	93	328	421	350	-35

Playoffs

84–85	Mont	12	0	6	6	6	
87–88	NJ	19	6	9	15	38	
89–90	Tor	5	0	3	3	4	
90–91	Van	6	2	2	4	12	
92–93	NYI	12	0	2	2	6	
93–94	NYI	3	0	0	0	2	
Totals		57	8	22	30	68	

KURYLUK, Mervin 5-11 185 LW
B. Yorkton, Sask., Aug. 10, 1937

SSN	TEAM	GP	G	A	PTS.	PIM	+/-
61–62	Chi	0	0	0	0	0	

Playoffs

61–62	Chi	2	0	0	0	0	

KUSHNER, Dale 6-1 195 LW
B. Terrace, B.C., June 13, 1966

SSN	TEAM	GP	G	A	PTS.	PIM	+/-
89–90	NYI	2	0	0	0	2	0
90–91	Phil	63	7	11	18	195	-4
91–92	Phil	19	3	2	5	18	-5
Totals		84	10	13	23	215	-9

KUZYK, Kenneth Michael 6-1 195 RW
B. Toronto, Ont., Aug. 11, 1953

SSN	TEAM	GP	G	A	PTS.	PIM	+/-
76–77	Clev	13	0	5	5	2	+1
77–78	Clev	28	5	4	9	6	-1
Totals		41	5	9	14	8	0

KVASHA, Oleg 6-5 205 LW
B. Moscow, USSR, July 26, 1978

SSN	TEAM	GP	G	A	PTS.	PIM	+/-
98–99	Fla	68	12	13	25	45	+5

KVARTALNOV, Dmitri 5-11 180 LW
B. Voskresensk, USSR, Mar. 25, 1966

SSN	TEAM	GP	G	A	PTS.	PIM	+/-
92–93	Bos	73	30	42	72	16	+9
93–94	Bos	39	12	7	19	10	-9
Totals		112	42	49	91	26	0

Playoffs

92–93	Bos	4	0	0	0	0	

KWONG, Lawrence (King) 5-6 150 RW
B. Vernon, B.C., June 17, 1923

SSN	TEAM	GP	G	A	PTS.	PIM	+/-
47–48	NYR	1	0	0	0	0	

*KYLE, Walter Lawrence (Gus) 6-1 202 D
B. Dysart, Sask., Sept. 11, 1923

SSN	TEAM	GP	G	A	PTS.	PIM	+/-
49–50	NYR	70	3	5	8	143	
50–51	NYR	64	2	3	5	92	
51–52	Bos	69	1	12	13	127	
Totals		203	6	20	26	362	

Playoffs

49–50	NYR	12	1	2	3	30	
51–52	Bos	2	0	0	0	4	
Totals		14	1	2	3	34	

*KYLE, William Miller 6-1 175 C
B. Dysart, Sask., Dec. 23, 1924

SSN	TEAM	GP	G	A	PTS.	PIM	+/-
49–50	NYR	2	0	0	0	0	
50–51	NYR	1	0	3	3	0	
Totals		3	0	3	3	0	

KYLLONEN, Markku 5-11 187 LW
B. Joensuu, Finland, Feb. 15, 1962

SSN	TEAM	GP	G	A	PTS.	PIM	+/-
88–89	Winn	9	0	2	2	2	-3

KYPREOS, Nicholas 6-0 205 LW
B. Toronto, Ont., June 4, 1966

SSN	TEAM	GP	G	A	PTS.	PIM	+/-
89–90	Wash	31	5	4	9	82	+2
90–91	Wash	79	9	9	18	196	-4
91–92	Wash	65	4	6	10	206	-3
92–93	Hart	75	17	10	27	325	-5
93–94	Hart–NYR	56	3	5	8	139	-16
94–95	NYR	40	1	3	4	93	0
95–96	NYR–Tor	61	4	5	9	107	+1
96–97	Tor	35	3	2	5	62	+1
Totals		442	46	44	90	1210	-24

Playoffs

89–90	Wash	7	1	0	1	15	
90–91	Wash	9	0	1	1	38	
93–94	NYR	3	0	0	0	2	
94–95	NYR	10	0	2	2	6	
95–96	Tor	5	0	0	0	4	
Totals		34	1	3	4	65	

KYTE, James (Jim) 6-5 210 D
B. Ottawa, Ont., Mar. 21, 1964

SSN	TEAM	GP	G	A	PTS.	PIM	+/-
82–83	Winn	2	0	0	0	0	-1
83–84	Winn	58	1	2	3	55	-7
84–85	Winn	71	0	3	3	111	-26
85–86	Winn	71	1	3	4	126	-21
86–87	Winn	72	5	5	10	162	+4
87–88	Winn	51	1	3	4	128	+1
88–89	Winn	74	3	9	12	190	-25
89–90	Pitt	56	3	1	4	125	-10
90–91	Pitt–Calg	43	0	9	9	155	+10
91–92	Calg	21	0	1	1	107	+2
92–93	Ott	4	0	1	1	4	0
94–95	SJ	18	2	5	7	33	-7
95–96	SJ	57	1	7	8	146	-12
Totals		598	17	49	66	1342	-92

Playoffs

83–84	Winn	3	0	0	0	11	
84–85	Winn	8	0	0	0	14	
85–86	Winn	3	0	0	0	12	
86–87	Winn	10	0	4	4	36	
90–91	Calg	7	0	0	0	7	
94–95	SJ	11	0	2	2	14	
Totals		42	0	6	6	94	

LAAKSONEN, Antti 6-0 180 LW
B. Tammela, Finland, Oct. 3, 1973

SSN	TEAM	GP	G	A	PTS.	PIM	+/-
98–99	Bos	11	1	2	3	2	-1

LABADIE, Joseph Michel (Mike) 5-11 170 RW
B. St. Francis Assisi, Que., Aug. 17, 1932

SSN	TEAM	GP	G	A	PTS.	PIM	+/-
52–53	NYR	3	0	0	0	0	

LABATTE, Neil Joseph Henry 6-2 178 D
B. Toronto, Ont., Apr. 24, 1957

SSN	TEAM	GP	G	A	PTS.	PIM	+/-
78–79	StL	22	0	2	2	13	-1
81–82	StL	4	0	0	0	6	-3
Totals		26	0	2	2	19	-4

L'ABBE, Maurice Joseph (Moe) 5-9 170 RW
B. Montreal, Que., Aug. 12, 1947

SSN	TEAM	GP	G	A	PTS.	PIM	+/-
72–73	Chi	5	0	1	1	0	+1

LABELLE, Marc 6-1 215 LW
B. Maniwaki, Que., Dec. 20, 1969

SSN	TEAM	GP	G	A	PTS.	PIM	+/-
96–97	Dal	9	0	0	0	46	-4

LABINE, Leo Gerald 5-10 178 RW
B. Haileybury, Ont., July 22, 1931

SSN	TEAM	GP	G	A	PTS.	PIM	+/-
51-52	Bos	15	2	4	6	9	
52-53	Bos	51	8	15	23	69	
53-54	Bos	68	16	19	35	57	
54-55	Bos	67	24	18	42	75	
55-56	Bos	68	16	18	34	104	
56-57	Bos	67	18	29	47	128	
57-58	Bos	62	7	14	21	60	
58-59	Bos	70	9	23	32	74	
59-60	Bos	63	16	28	44	58	
60-61	Bos-Det	64	9	21	30	66	
61-62	Det	48	3	4	7	30	
Totals		643	128	193	321	730	

Playoffs

51-52	Bos	5	0	1	1	4	
52-53	Bos	7	2	1	3	19	
53-54	Bos	4	0	1	1	28	
54-55	Bos	5	2	1	3	11	
56-57	Bos	10	2	3	5	14	
57-58	Bos	11	0	2	2	10	
58-59	Bos	7	2	1	3	12	
60-61	Det	11	3	2	5	4	
Totals		60	11	12	23	102	

LABOSSIERRE, Gordon William 6-1 180 C
B. St. Boniface, Man., Jan. 2, 1940

SSN	TEAM	GP	G	A	PTS.	PIM	+/-
63-64	NYR	15	0	0	0	12	
64-65	NYR	1	0	0	0	0	
67-68	LA	68	13	27	40	31	+6
68-69	LA	48	10	18	28	12	-7
70-71	LA-Minn	74	19	14	33	20	-25
71-72	Minn	9	2	3	5	0	+2
72-73	Hou (WHA)	77	36	60	96	56	
73-74	Hou (WHA)	67	19	36	55	30	
74-75	Hou (WHA)	76	23	34	57	40	
75-76	Hou (WHA)	80	24	32	56	18	
NHL Totals		215	44	62	106	75	-24
WHA Totals		300	102	162	264	144	

Playoffs

67-68	LA	7	2	3	5	24	
70-71	Minn	3	0	0	0	4	
72-73	Hou (WHA)	6	1	4	5	8	
73-74	Hou (WHA)	14	7	9	16	20	
74-75	Hou (WHA)	13	6	7	13	4	
75-76	Hou (WHA)	17	2	8	10	14	
NHL Totals		10	2	3	5	28	
WHA Totals		50	16	28	44	46	

LABOVITCH, Maxwell 5-10 165 RW
B. Winnipeg, Man., Jan. 18, 1924

43-44	NYR	5	0	0	0	4	

LABRAATEN, Daniel 6-0 190 LW
B. Leksland, Sweden, June 9, 1951

SSN	TEAM	GP	G	A	PTS.	PIM	+/-
76-77	Winn (WHA)	64	24	27	51	21	
77-78	Winn (WHA)	47	18	16	34	30	
78-79	Det	78	19	19	38	8	-17
79-80	Det	76	30	27	57	8	+5
80-81	Det-Calg	71	12	15	27	25	-18
81-82	Calg	43	10	12	22	6	-4
NHL Totals		268	71	73	144	47	-34
WHA Totals		111	42	43	85	51	

Playoffs

76-77	Winn (WHA)	20	7	17	24	15	
77-78	Winn (WHA)	4	1	1	2	8	
80-81	Calg	5	1	0	1	4	
81-82	Calg	3	0	0	0	0	
NHL Totals		8	1	0	1	4	
WHA Totals		24	8	18	26	23	

LABRE, Yvon Jules 5-10 190 D
B. Sudbury, Ont., Nov. 29, 1949

SSN	TEAM	GP	G	A	PTS.	PIM	+/-
70-71	Pitt	21	1	1	2	19	+2
73-74	Pitt	16	1	2	3	13	-7
74-75	Wash	76	4	23	27	182	-54
75-76	Wash	80	2	20	22	146	-38
76-77	Wash	62	3	11	14	169	-5
77-78	Wash	22	0	8	8	41	0
78-79	Wash	51	1	13	14	80	+7
79-80	Wash	18	0	5	5	38	+3
80-81	Wash	25	2	4	6	100	-2
Totals		371	14	87	101	788	-94

LABRIE, Guy 6-0 185 D
B. St. Charles Bellechase, Que., Aug. 11, 1920

SSN	TEAM	GP	G	A	PTS.	PIM	+/-
43-44	Bos	15	2	7	9	2	
44-45	NYR	27	2	2	4	14	
Totals		42	4	9	13	16	

LACH, Elmer James 5-10 170 C
B. Nokomis, Sask., Jan. 22, 1918

SSN	TEAM	GP	G	A	PTS.	PIM	+/-
40-41	Mont	43	7	14	21	16	
41-42	Mont	1	0	1	1	0	
42-43	Mont	45	18	40	58	14	
43-44	Mont	48	24	48	72	23	
44-45	Mont	50	26	54	80	37	
45-46	Mont	50	13	34	47	34	
46-47	Mont	31	14	16	30	22	
47-48	Mont	60	30	31	61	72	
48-49	Mont	36	11	18	29	59	
49-50	Mont	64	15	33	48	33	
50-51	Mont	65	21	24	45	45	
51-52	Mont	70	15	50	65	36	
52-53	Mont	53	16	25	41	56	
53-54	Mont	48	5	20	25	28	
Totals		664	215	406	623	475	

Playoffs

40-41	Mont	3	1	0	1	0	
42-43	Mont	5	2	4	6	6	
43-44	Mont	9	2	11	13	4	
44-45	Mont	6	4	4	8	2	
45-46	Mont	9	5	12	17	4	
48-49	Mont	1	0	0	0	4	
49-50	Mont	5	1	2	3	4	
50-51	Mont	11	2	2	4	2	
51-52	Mont	11	1	2	3	4	
52-53	Mont	12	1	6	7	6	
53-54	Mont	4	0	2	2	0	
Totals		76	19	45	64	36	

*LACHANCE, Earl F

26-27	Mont	1	0	0	0	0	

LACHANCE, Michel 6-0 190 D
B. Quebec City, Que., Apr. 11, 1955

78-79	Col	21	0	4	4	22	-9

LACHANCE, Scott 6-1 197 D
B. Charlottesville, Va., Oct. 22, 1972

SSN	TEAM	GP	G	A	PTS.	PIM	+/-
91-92	NYI	17	1	4	5	9	+13
92-93	NYI	75	7	17	24	67	-1
93-94	NYI	74	3	11	14	70	-5
94-95	NYI	26	6	7	13	46	-2
95-96	NYI	55	3	10	13	54	-19
96-97	NYI	81	3	11	14	47	-7
97-98	NYI	63	2	11	13	45	-11
98-99	NYI-Mont	76	2	9	11	41	-21
Totals		467	27	80	107	359	-49

Playoffs

93-94	NYI	3	0	0	0	0	

LACOMBE, Francois 5-10 175 D
B. Lachine, Que., Feb. 24, 1948

SSN	TEAM	GP	G	A	PTS.	PIM	+/-
68-69	Oak	72	2	16	18	50	-10
69-70	Oak	2	0	0	0	0	+1
70-71	Buf	1	0	1	1	2	-2
72-73	Que (WHA)	61	10	18	28	123	
73-74	Que (WHA)	71	9	26	35	41	
74-75	Que (WHA)	55	7	17	24	54	
75-76	Calg (WHA)	71	3	28	31	62	
76-77	Que (WHA)	81	5	22	27	86	
77-78	Que (WHA)	22	1	7	8	12	
78-79	Que (WHA)	78	3	21	24	44	
79-80	Que	3	0	0	0	2	
NHL Totals		78	2	17	19	54	-11
WHA Totals		439	38	139	177	422	

Playoffs

68-69	Cal	3	1	0	1	0	
74-75	Que (WHA)	15	0	2	2	14	
75-76	Calg (WHA)	8	0	0	0	2	
76-77	Que (WHA)	17	4	3	7	16	
77-78	Que (WHA)	10	1	4	5	2	
78-79	Que (WHA)	4	0	1	1	2	
NHL Totals		3	1	0	1	0	
WHA Totals		54	5	10	15	36	

LACOMBE, Normand 6-0 210 RW
B. Pierrefonds, Que., Oct. 18, 1964

SSN	TEAM	GP	G	A	PTS.	PIM	+/-
84-85	Buf	30	2	4	6	25	-3
85-86	Buf	25	6	7	13	13	+9
86-87	Buf-Edm	40	4	7	11	10	-10
87-88	Edm	53	8	9	17	36	-3
88-89	Edm	64	17	11	28	57	+2
89-90	Edm-Phil	33	5	4	9	28	+4
90-91	Phil	74	11	20	31	27	-1
Totals		319	53	62	115	196	-2

Playoffs

87-88	Edm	19	3	0	3	28	
88-89	Edm	7	2	1	3	21	
Totals		26	5	1	6	49	

LACOUTURE, Dan 6-3 210 LW
B. Hyannis, Mass., April 18, 1977

98-99		3	0	0	0	0	+1

LACROIX, Andre Joseph 5-8 175 C
B. Lauzon, Que., June 5, 1945

SSN	TEAM	GP	G	A	PTS.	PIM	+/-
67-68	Phil	18	6	8	14	6	0
68-69	Phil	75	24	32	56	4	-12
69-70	Phil	74	22	36	58	14	-6
70-71	Phil	78	20	22	42	12	-9
71-72	Chi	51	4	7	11	6	+4
72-73	Phil (WHA)	78	50	74	124	83	
73-74	NY-NJ (WHA)	78	31	80	111	54	
74-75	SD (WHA)	78	41	106	147	63	
75-76	SD (WHA)	80	29	72	101	42	
76-77	SD (WHA)	81	32	82	114	79	
77-78	Hou (WHA)	78	36	77	113	57	
78-79	NE (WHA)	78	32	56	88	34	
79-80	Hart	29	3	14	17	2	-6
NHL Totals		325	79	119	198	44	-29
WHA Totals		551	251	547	798	412	

Playoffs

67-68	Phil	7	2	3	5	0	
68-69	Phil	4	0	0	0	0	
70-71	Phil	4	0	2	2	0	
71-72	Chi	1	0	0	0	0	
72-73	Phil (WHA)	4	0	2	2	18	
74-75	SD (WHA)	10	3	9	12	2	
75-76	SD (WHA)	11	4	6	10	4	
76-77	SD (WHA)	7	1	6	7	6	
77-78	Hou (WHA)	6	2	2	4	0	
78-79	NE (WHA)	10	4	4	8	0	
NHL Totals		16	2	5	7	0	
WHA Totals		48	14	29	43	30	

LACROIX, Daniel 6-2 195 LW
B. Montreal, Que., Mar. 11, 1969

SSN	TEAM	GP	G	A	PTS.	PIM	+/-
93-94	NYR	4	0	0	0	0	0
94-95	Bos-NYR	34	1	0	1	38	-2
95-96	NYR	25	2	2	4	30	-1
96-97	Phil	74	7	1	8	163	-1
97-98	Phil	56	1	4	5	135	0
98-99	Edm	4	0	0	0	13	0
Totals		197	11	7	18	379	-4

Playoffs

96-97	Phil	12	0	1	1	22	
97-98	Phil	4	0	0	0	4	
Totals		16	0	1	1	26	

LACROIX, Eric 6-1 205 LW
B. Montreal, Que., July 15, 1971

SSN	TEAM	GP	G	A	PTS.	PIM	+/-
93-94	Tor	3	0	0	0	2	0
94-95	LA	45	9	7	16	54	+2
95-96	LA	72	16	16	32	110	-11
96-97	Col A	81	18	18	36	26	+16
97-98	Col A	82	16	15	31	84	0
98-99	Col-LA-NYR	64	2	2	4	18	-12
Totals		347	61	58	119	294	-5

Playoffs

96-97	Col A	17	1	4	5	19	
97-98	Col A	7	0	0	0	6	
Totals		24	1	4	5	25	

LACROIX, Pierre 5-11 185 D
B. Quebec City, Que., Apr. 11, 1959

79-80	Que	76	9	21	30	45	-6
80-81	Que	61	5	34	39	54	+9

| --- | --- | --- | --- | --- | --- | --- | --- |
81–82	Que	68	4	23	27	74	+1
82–83	Que–Hart	69	6	30	36	24	-15
Totals		274	24	108	132	197	-11

Playoffs

80–81	Que	5	0	2	2	10	
81–82	Que	3	0	0	0	0	
Totals		8	0	2	2	10	

LADOUCEUR, Randy 6–2 220 D
B. Brockville, Ont., June 30, 1960

82–83	Det	27	0	4	4	16	-10
83–84	Det	71	3	17	20	58	-12
84–85	Det	80	3	27	30	108	+3
85–86	Det	78	5	13	18	196	-54
86–87	Det–Hart	70	5	9	14	121	+2
87–88	Hart	67	1	7	8	91	+7
88–89	Hart	75	2	5	7	95	-23
89–90	Hart	71	3	12	15	126	-6
90–91	Hart	67	1	3	4	118	-10
91–92	Hart	74	1	9	10	127	-1
92–93	Hart	62	2	4	6	109	-18
93–94	Ana	81	1	9	10	74	+7
94–95	Ana	44	2	4	6	36	+2
95–96	Ana	63	1	3	4	47	+5
Totals		930	30	126	156	1322	-110

Playoffs

83–84	Det	4	1	0	1	6	
84–85	Det	3	1	0	1	0	
86–87	Hart	6	0	2	2	12	
87–88	Hart	6	1	1	2	4	
88–89	Hart	1	0	0	0	10	
89–90	Hart	7	1	0	1	10	
90–91	Hart	6	1	4	5	6	
91–92	Hart	7	0	1	1	11	
Totals		40	5	8	13	59	

LAFAYETTE, Nathan 6–1 194 C
B. New Westminster, B.C., Feb. 17, 1973

93–94	StL–Van	49	3	4	7	18	-7
94–95	Van–NYR	39	4	4	8	2	+3
95–96	NYR–LA	17	2	4	6	8	-4
96–97	LA	15	1	3	4	8	-8
97–98	LA	34	5	3	8	32	+2
98–99	LA	33	2	2	4	35	0
Totals		187	17	20	37	103	-14

Playoffs

93–94	Van	20	2	7	9	4	
94–95	NYR	8	0	0	0	2	
97–98	LA	4	0	0	0	2	
Totals		32	2	7	9	8	

LAFLAMME, Christian 6–1 195 D
B. St. Charles, Que., Nov. 24, 1976

96–97	Chi	4	0	1	1	2	+3
97–98	Chi	72	0	11	11	59	+14
98–99	Chi–Edm	73	2	12	14	70	-3
Totals		149	2	24	26	131	+14

Playoffs

| 98–99 | Edm | 4 | 0 | 1 | 1 | 0 | |

LAFLEUR, Guy Damien 6–0 185 RW
B. Thurso, Que., Sept. 20, 1951

71–72	Mont	73	29	35	64	48	+27
72–73	Mont	69	28	27	55	51	+16
73–74	Mont	73	21	35	56	29	+10
74–75	Mont	70	53	66	119	37	+52
75–76	Mont	80	56	69	125	36	+68
76–77	Mont	80	56	80	136	20	+89
77–78	Mont	78	60	72	132	26	+73
78–79	Mont	80	52	77	129	28	+56
79–80	Mont	74	50	75	125	12	+40
80–81	Mont	51	27	43	70	29	+24
81–82	Mont	66	27	57	84	24	+33
82–83	Mont	68	27	49	76	12	+6
83–84	Mont	80	30	40	70	19	-14
84–85	Mont	19	2	3	5	10	-3
88–89	NYR	67	18	27	45	12	+1
89–90	Que	39	12	22	34	4	-15
90–91	Que	59	12	16	28	2	-10
Totals		1126	560	793	1353	399	+463

Playoffs

71–72	Mont	6	1	4	5	2	
72–73	Mont	17	3	5	8	9	
73–74	Mont	6	0	1	1	4	
74–75	Mont	11	12	7	19	15	
75–76	Mont	13	7	10	17	2	
76–77	Mont	14	9	17	26	6	
77–78	Mont	15	10	11	21	16	
78–79	Mont	16	10	13	23	0	
79–80	Mont	3	3	1	4	0	
80–81	Mont	3	0	1	1	2	
81–82	Mont	5	2	1	3	4	
82–83	Mont	3	0	2	2	2	
83–84	Mont	12	0	3	3	5	
88–89	NYR	4	1	0	1	0	
Totals		128	58	76	134	67	

*LAFLEUR, Rene F
| 24–25 | Mont | 1 | 0 | 0 | 0 | 0 | |

LaFONTAINE, Pat 5–10 180 C
B. St. Louis, Mo., Feb. 22, 1965

83–84	NYI	15	13	6	19	6	+9
84–85	NYI	67	19	35	54	32	+9
85–86	NYI	65	30	23	53	43	+16
86–87	NYI	80	38	32	70	70	-10
87–88	NYI	75	47	45	92	52	+12
88–89	NYI	79	45	43	88	26	-8
89–90	NYI	74	54	51	105	38	-13
90–91	NYI	75	41	44	85	42	-6
91–92	Buf	57	46	47	93	98	+10
92–93	Buf	84	53	95	148	63	+11
93–94	Buf	16	5	13	18	2	-4
94–95	Buf	22	12	15	27	4	+2
95–96	Buf	76	40	51	91	36	-8
96–97	Buf	13	2	6	8	4	-8
97–98	NYR	67	23	39	62	36	-16
Totals		865	468	545	1013	552	-4

Playoffs

83–84	NYI	16	3	6	9	8	
84–85	NYI	9	1	2	3	4	
85–86	NYI	3	1	0	1	0	
86–87	NYI	14	5	7	12	10	
87–88	NYI	6	4	5	9	8	
89–90	NYI	2	0	1	1	0	
91–92	Buf	7	8	3	11	4	
92–93	Buf	7	2	10	12	0	
94–95	Buf	5	2	2	4	2	
Totals		69	26	36	62	36	

LAFORCE, Ernest D
B. Montreal, Que., June 23, 1916
| 42–43 | Mont | 1 | 0 | 0 | 0 | 0 | |

LaFOREST, Robert 5–10 195 RW
B. Sault Ste. Marie, Ont., May 19, 1963
| 83–84 | LA | 5 | 1 | 0 | 1 | 2 | -3 |

LaFORGE, Claude Roger 5–9 172 LW
B. Sorel, Que., July 1, 1936

57–58	Mont	4	0	0	0	0	
58–59	Det	57	2	5	7	18	
60–61	Det	10	1	0	1	2	
61–62	Det	38	10	9	19	20	
63–64	Det	17	2	3	5	4	
64–65	Det	1	0	0	0	2	
67–68	Phil	63	9	16	25	36	+8
68–69	Phil	2	0	0	0	0	-2
Totals		192	24	33	57	82	+6

Playoffs

| 67–68 | Phil | 5 | 1 | 2 | 3 | 15 | |

LaFORGE, Marc 6–2 210 LW
B. Sudbury, Ont., Jan. 3, 1968
89–90	Hart	9	0	0	0	43	-1
93–94	Edm	5	0	0	0	21	-2
Totals		14	0	0	0	64	-3

LAFRAMBOISE, Peter Alfred 6–2 185 C
B. Ottawa, Ont., Jan. 18, 1950
71–72	Cal	5	0	0	0	0	-5
72–73	Cal	77	16	25	41	26	-24
73–74	Cal	71	7	7	14	14	-28
74–75	Wash–Pitt	80	10	23	33	30	-34
76–77	Edm (WHA)	17	0	5	5	12	
NHL Totals		227	33	55	88	70	-91
WHA Totals		17	0	5	5	12	

Playoffs

| 74–75 | Pitt | 9 | 1 | 0 | 1 | 0 | |

LAFRANCE, Adelard (Adie) F
B. Chapleau, Ont., Jan. 13, 1912
| 33–34 | Mont | 3 | 0 | 0 | 0 | 2 | |

Playoffs

| 33–34 | Mont | 2 | 0 | 0 | 0 | 0 | |

LAFRANCE, Leo F
26–27	Mont	4	0	0	0	0	
27–28	Mont–Chi	29	2	0	2	6	
Totals		33	2	0	2	6	

LAFRENIERE, Jason 5–11 185 C
B. St. Catharines, Ont., Dec. 6, 1966
86–87	Que	56	13	15	28	8	-3
87–88	Que	40	10	19	29	4	-1
88–89	NYR	38	8	16	24	6	-3
92–93	TB	11	3	3	6	4	-6
93–94	TB	1	0	0	0	0	-1
Totals		146	34	53	87	22	-14

Playoffs

86–87	Que	12	1	5	6	2	
88–89	NYR	3	0	0	0	17	
Totals		15	1	5	6	19	

LAFRENIERE, Roger Joseph 6–0 190 LW
B. Montreal, Que., July 24, 1942
62–63	Det	3	0	0	0	4	
72–73	StL	10	0	0	0	0	-1
Totals		13	0	0	0	4	-1

LAGACE, Jean–Guy 5–10 185 D
B. L'Abord a Plouffe, Que., Feb. 5, 1945
68–69	Pitt	13	0	1	1	14	-8
70–71	Buf	3	0	0	0	2	0
72–73	Pitt	31	1	5	6	32	-8
73–74	Pitt	31	2	6	8	34	-12
74–75	Pitt–KC	40	3	17	20	61	-15
75–76	KC	69	3	10	13	108	-38
Totals		187	9	39	48	251	-81

LAGACE, Michel F
| 68–69 | Pitt | 17 | 0 | 1 | 1 | 14 | 0 |

LAIDLAW, Thomas 6–1 205 D
B. Brampton, Ont., Apr. 15, 1958
80–81	NYR	80	6	23	29	100	0
81–82	NYR	79	3	18	21	104	+7
82–83	NYR	80	0	10	10	75	-11
83–84	NYR	79	3	15	18	62	-10
84–85	NYR	61	1	11	12	52	-12
85–86	NYR	68	6	12	18	103	-3
86–87	NYR–LA	74	1	13	14	69	-17
87–88	LA	57	1	12	13	47	+3
88–89	LA	70	3	17	20	63	+30
89–90	LA	57	1	8	9	42	+4
Totals		705	25	139	164	717	-9

Playoffs

80–81	NYR	14	1	4	5	18	
81–82	NYR	10	0	3	3	14	
82–83	NYR	9	1	1	2	10	
83–84	NYR	5	0	0	0	8	
84–85	NYR	3	0	2	2	4	
85–86	NYR	7	0	2	2	12	
86–87	LA	5	0	0	0	2	
87–88	LA	5	0	2	2	4	
88–89	LA	11	2	3	5	6	
Totals		69	4	17	21	78	

LAIRD, Robbie 5–9 165 LW
B. Regina, Sask., Dec. 29, 1954
| 79–80 | Minn | 1 | 0 | 0 | 0 | 0 | -2 |

LAJEUNESSE, Serge 5–10 185 RW
B. Montreal, Que., June 11, 1950
70–71	Det	62	1	3	4	55	-28
71–72	Det	7	0	0	0	20	-1
72–73	Det	28	0	1	1	26	-15
73–74	Phil	1	0	0	0	0	0
74–75	Phil	5	0	0	0	2	+1

SSN	TEAM	GP	G	A	PTS.	PIM	+/-
Totals		103	1	4	5	103	-43

Playoffs

SSN	TEAM	GP	G	A	PTS.	PIM
70-71	Det	7	1	2	3	4

LAKOVIC, Sasha *6-0 207 LW*
B. Vancouver, B.C., Sept. 7, 1971

SSN	TEAM	GP	G	A	PTS.	PIM	+/-
96-97	Calg	19	0	1	1	54	-1
97-98	NJ	2	0	0	0	5	0
98-99	NJ	16	0	3	3	59	0
Totals		37	0	4	4	118	-1

LALANDE, Hector *5-9 157 C*
B. North Bay, Ont., Nov. 24, 1934

SSN	TEAM	GP	G	A	PTS.	PIM
53-54	Chi	2	0	0	0	2
55-56	Chi	65	8	18	26	70
56-57	Chi	50	11	17	28	38
57-58	Chi-Det	34	2	4	6	12
Totals		151	21	39	60	122

*LALONDE, Edouard C. (Newsy) *C*
B. Cornwall, Ont., Oct. 31, 1887

SSN	TEAM	GP	G	A	PTS.	PIM
17-18	Mont	14	23	0	23	16
18-19	Mont	17	23	9	32	40
19-20	Mont	23	36	6	42	33
20-21	Mont	24	33	8	41	36
21-22	Mont	20	9	4	13	11
26-27	NYA	1	0	0	0	2
Totals		99	124	27	151	138

Playoffs

SSN	TEAM	GP	G	A	PTS.	PIM
17-18	Mont	2	5	0	5	11
18-19	Mont	10	17	1	18	8
Totals		12	22	1	23	19

LALONDE, Robert Patrick *5-5 155 C*
B. Montreal, Que., Mar. 27, 1951

SSN	TEAM	GP	G	A	PTS.	PIM	+/-
71-72	Van	27	1	5	6	2	-8
72-73	Van	77	20	27	47	32	-32
73-74	Van	36	3	4	7	18	-3
74-75	Van	74	17	30	47	48	0
75-76	Van	71	14	36	50	46	-4
76-77	Van	68	17	15	32	39	-12
77-78	Atl	73	14	23	37	28	+5
78-79	Atl	78	24	32	56	24	-3
79-80	Atl-Bos	74	10	26	36	30	+13
80-81	Bos	62	4	12	16	31	+3
81-82	Calg	1	0	0	0	0	+2
Totals		641	124	210	334	298	-39

Playoffs

SSN	TEAM	GP	G	A	PTS.	PIM
74-75	Van	5	0	0	0	0
75-76	Van	1	0	0	0	2
77-78	Atl	1	1	0	1	0
78-79	Atl	2	1	0	1	0
79-80	Bos	4	0	1	1	2
80-81	Bos	3	2	1	3	2
Totals		16	4	2	6	6

LALONDE, Ronald Leo *5-10 170 C*
B. Toronto, Ont., Oct. 30, 1952

SSN	TEAM	GP	G	A	PTS.	PIM	+/-
72-73	Pitt	9	0	0	0	2	0
73-74	Pitt	73	10	17	27	14	+2
74-75	Pitt-Wash	74	12	17	29	27	-38
75-76	Wash	80	9	19	28	19	-26
76-77	Wash	76	12	17	29	24	-20
77-78	Wash	67	1	5	6	16	-18
78-79	Wash	18	1	3	4	4	-1
Totals		397	45	78	123	106	-101

LALOR, Mike *6-0 200 D*
B. Buffalo, N.Y., Mar. 8, 1963

SSN	TEAM	GP	G	A	PTS.	PIM	+/-
85-86	Mont	62	3	5	8	56	-4
86-87	Mont	57	0	10	10	47	+5
87-88	Mont	66	1	10	11	113	+4
88-89	Mont-StL	48	2	18	20	69	+14
89-90	StL	78	0	16	16	81	-6
90-91	Wash	68	1	5	6	61	-23
91-92	Wash-Winn	79	7	10	17	78	+25
92-93	Winn	64	1	8	9	76	-10
93-94	SJ-Dal	35	0	3	3	14	-10
94-95	Dal	12	0	0	0	9	0
95-96	Dal	63	1	2	3	31	-10
96-97	Dal	55	1	1	2	42	+3
Totals		687	17	88	105	677	-12

Playoffs

SSN	TEAM	GP	G	A	PTS.	PIM
85-86	Mont	17	1	2	3	29
86-87	Mont	13	2	1	3	29
87-88	Mont	11	0	0	0	11
88-89	StL	10	1	1	2	14
89-90	StL	12	0	2	2	31
90-91	Wash	10	1	2	3	22
91-92	Winn	7	0	0	0	19
92-93	Winn	4	0	2	2	4
93-94	Dal	5	0	0	0	6
94-95	Dal	3	0	0	0	2
Totals		92	5	10	15	167

*LAMB, Joseph Gordon *5-9 170 RW*
B. Sussex, N.B., June 18, 1906

SSN	TEAM	GP	G	A	PTS.	PIM
27-28	Mont M	21	8	5	13	39
28-29	Mont M-Ott	35	4	1	5	52
29-30	Ott	44	29	20	49	119
30-31	Ott	44	11	14	25	91
31-32	NYA	48	14	11	25	71
32-33	Bos	42	11	8	19	68
33-34	Bos	48	10	15	25	47
34-35	Mont-StLE	38	14	14	28	23
35-36	Mont M	35	0	3	3	12
36-37	NYA	48	3	9	12	53
37-38	NYA-Det	41	4	1	5	26
Totals		444	108	101	209	601

Playoffs

SSN	TEAM	GP	G	A	PTS.	PIM
27-28	Mont M	8	1	0	1	32
29-30	Ott	2	0	0	0	11
32-33	Bos	5	0	1	1	6
35-36	Mont M	3	0	0	0	2
Totals		18	1	1	2	51

LAMB, Mark *5-9 180 C*
B. Ponteix, Sask., Aug. 3, 1964

SSN	TEAM	GP	G	A	PTS.	PIM	+/-
85-86	Calg	1	0	0	0	0	0
86-87	Det	22	2	1	3	8	0
87-88	Edm	2	0	0	0	0	0
88-89	Edm	20	2	8	10	14	+4
89-90	Edm	58	12	16	28	42	+10
90-91	Edm	37	4	8	12	25	-2
91-92	Edm	59	6	22	28	46	+4
92-93	Ott	71	7	19	26	64	-40
93-94	Ott-Phil	85	12	24	36	72	-44
94-95	Phil-Mont	47	1	2	3	20	-12
95-96	Mont	1	0	0	0	0	0
Totals		403	46	100	146	291	-80

Playoffs

SSN	TEAM	GP	G	A	PTS.	PIM
86-87	Det	11	0	0	0	11
88-89	Edm	6	0	2	2	8
89-90	Edm	22	6	11	17	2
90-91	Edm	15	0	5	5	20
91-92	Edm	16	1	1	2	10
Totals		70	7	19	26	51

LAMBERT, Dan *5-8 177 D*
B. St. Boniface, Man., Jan. 12, 1970

SSN	TEAM	GP	G	A	PTS.	PIM	+/-
90-91	Que	1	0	0	0	0	0
91-92	Que	28	6	9	15	22	-5
Totals		29	6	9	15	22	-5

LAMBERT, Denny *5-11 200 LW*
B. Wawa, Ont., Jan. 7, 1970

SSN	TEAM	GP	G	A	PTS.	PIM	+/-
94-95	Ana	13	1	3	4	4	+3
95-96	Ana	33	0	8	8	55	-2
96-97	Ott	80	4	16	20	217	-4
97-98	Ott	72	9	10	19	250	+4
98-99	Nash	76	5	11	16	218	-3
Totals		274	19	48	67	744	-2

Playoffs

SSN	TEAM	GP	G	A	PTS.	PIM
96-97	Ott	6	0	1	1	9
97-98	Ott	11	0	0	0	19
Totals		17	0	1	1	28

LAMBERT, Lane *6-0 185 RW*
B. Melfort, Sask., Nov. 18, 1964

SSN	TEAM	GP	G	A	PTS.	PIM	+/-
83-84	Det	73	20	15	35	115	-5
84-85	Det	69	14	11	25	104	-3
85-86	Det	34	2	3	5	130	-11
86-87	NYR-Que	33	7	7	14	51	+1
87-88	Que	61	13	28	41	98	0
88-89	Que	13	2	2	4	23	-2
Totals		283	58	66	124	521	-20

Playoffs

SSN	TEAM	GP	G	A	PTS.	PIM
83-84	Det	4	0	0	0	10
86-87	Que	13	2	4	6	30
Totals		17	2	4	6	40

LAMBERT, Yvon Pierre *6-0 195 LW*
B. Drummondville, Que., May 20, 1950

SSN	TEAM	GP	G	A	PTS.	PIM	+/-
72-73	Mont	1	0	0	0	0	0
73-74	Mont	60	6	10	16	42	+5
74-75	Mont	80	32	35	67	74	+26
75-76	Mont	80	32	35	67	28	+10
76-77	Mont	79	24	28	52	50	+30
77-78	Mont	77	18	22	40	20	+10
78-79	Mont	79	26	40	66	26	+30
79-80	Mont	77	21	32	53	23	+3
80-81	Mont	73	22	32	54	39	+7
81-82	Buf	77	25	39	64	38	+22
Totals		683	206	273	479	340	+143

Playoffs

SSN	TEAM	GP	G	A	PTS.	PIM
73-74	Mont	5	0	0	0	7
74-75	Mont	11	4	2	6	0
75-76	Mont	12	2	3	5	18
76-77	Mont	14	3	3	6	12
77-78	Mont	15	2	4	6	6
78-79	Mont	16	5	6	11	16
79-80	Mont	10	8	4	12	4
80-81	Mont	3	0	0	0	2
81-82	Buf	4	3	0	3	2
Totals		90	27	22	49	67

LAMBY, Richard A. (Dick) *6-1 200 D*
B. Auburn, Mass., May 3, 1955

SSN	TEAM	GP	G	A	PTS.	PIM	+/-
78-79	StL	9	0	4	4	12	+5
79-80	StL	12	0	1	1	10	-7
80-81	StL	1	0	0	0	0	-1
Totals		22	0	5	5	22	-3

*LAMIRANDE, Jean-Paul *5-8 170 D*
B. Shawinigan Falls, Que., Aug. 21, 1923

SSN	TEAM	GP	G	A	PTS.	PIM
46-47	NYR	14	1	1	2	14
47-48	NYR	18	0	1	1	6
49-50	NYR	16	4	3	7	6
54-55	Mont	1	0	0	0	0
Totals		49	5	5	10	26

Playoffs

SSN	TEAM	GP	G	A	PTS.	PIM
47-48	NYR	6	0	0	0	4
49-50	NYR	2	0	0	0	0
Totals		8	0	0	0	4

LAMMENS, Hank *6-2 210 D*
B. Brockville, Ont., Feb. 21, 1966

SSN	TEAM	GP	G	A	PTS.	PIM	+/-
93-94	Ott	27	1	2	3	22	-20

*LAMOUREUX, Leo Peter *5-11 175 D*
B. Espanola, Ont., Oct. 1, 1916

SSN	TEAM	GP	G	A	PTS.	PIM
41-42	Mont	1	0	0	0	0
42-43	Mont	46	2	16	18	43
43-44	Mont	44	8	23	31	32
44-45	Mont	49	2	22	24	38
45-46	Mont	45	5	7	12	18
46-47	Mont	50	2	11	13	14
Totals		235	19	79	98	145

Playoffs

SSN	TEAM	GP	G	A	PTS.	PIM
43-44	Mont	9	0	3	3	8
44-45	Mont	6	1	1	2	2
45-46	Mont	9	0	2	2	2
46-47	Mont	4	0	0	0	4
Totals		28	1	6	7	16

LAMOUREUX, Mitch *5-6 175 C*
B. Ottawa, Ont., Aug. 22, 1962

SSN	TEAM	GP	G	A	PTS.	PIM	+/-
83-84	Pitt	8	1	1	2	6	-6
84-85	Pitt	62	10	8	18	53	-9
87-88	Phil	3	0	0	0	0	-1
Totals		73	11	9	20	59	-16

LAMPMAN, Michael David *6-2 195 LW*
B. Hamilton, Ont., Apr. 20, 1950

SSN	TEAM	GP	G	A	PTS.	PIM	+/-
72-73	StL	18	2	3	5	2	+4
73-74	StL-Van	29	2	0	2	0	-9

SSN	TEAM	GP	G	A	PTS.	PIM	+/-
75–76	Wash	27	7	12	19	28	-6
76–77	Wash	22	6	5	11	4	-4
Totals		96	17	20	37	34	-15

LANCIEN, John Gordon (Jack) 6–0 188 D
B. Regina, Sask., June 14, 1923

SSN	TEAM	GP	G	A	PTS.	PIM	+/-
46–47	NYR	1	0	0	0	0	
49–50	NYR	43	1	4	5	27	
50–51	NYR	19	0	1	1	8	
Totals		63	1	5	6	35	

Playoffs

47–48	NYR	2	0	0	0	2	
49–50	NYR	4	0	1	1	0	
Totals		6	0	1	1	2	

LANDON, Larry 6–0 191 RW
B. Niagara Falls, Ont., May 4, 1958

83–84	Mont	2	0	0	0	0	+2
84–85	Tor	7	0	0	0	2	-4
Totals		9	0	0	0	2	-2

LANDRY, Eric 5–11 185 C
B. Gatineau, Que., Jan. 20, 1975

97–98	Calg	12	1	0	1	4	-2
98–99	Calg	3	0	1	1	0	+1
Totals		15	1	1	2	4	-1

LANE, Gordon 6–1 190 D
B. Brandon, Man., Mar. 31, 1953

75–76	Wash	3	1	0	1	12	-5
76–77	Wash	80	2	15	17	207	-25
77–78	Wash	69	2	9	11	195	-19
78–79	Wash	64	3	15	18	147	-15
79–80	Wash–NYI	74	4	18	22	205	+11
80–81	NYI	60	3	9	12	124	-6
81–82	NYI	51	0	13	13	98	+26
82–83	NYI	44	3	4	7	87	+1
83–84	NYI	37	0	3	3	70	+6
84–85	NYI	57	1	8	9	83	+10
Totals		539	19	94	113	1228	-16

Playoffs

79–80	NYI	21	1	3	4	85	
80–81	NYI	12	1	5	6	32	
81–82	NYI	19	0	4	4	61	
82–83	NYI	18	1	2	3	32	
Totals		75	3	14	17	214	

*LANE, Myles J. 6–0 180 D
B. Melrose, Mass., Oct. 2, 1905

28–29	NYR–Bos	29	2	0	2	24	
29–30	Bos	3	0	0	0	0	
33–34	Bos	28	2	1	3	17	
Totals		60	4	1	5	41	

Playoffs

28–29	Bos	4	0	0	0	0	
29–30	Bos	6	0	0	0	0	
Totals		10	0	0	0	0	

LANG, Robert 6–2 189 C
B. Teplice, Czechoslovakia, Dec. 19, 1970

92–93	LA	11	0	5	5	2	-3
93–94	LA	32	9	10	19	10	+7
94–95	LA	36	4	8	12	4	-7
95–96	LA	68	6	16	22	10	-15
97–98	Bos-Pitt	54	9	13	22	16	+7
98–99	Pitt	72	21	23	44	24	-10
Totals		273	49	75	124	66	-21

Playoffs

97–98	Pitt	6	0	3	3	2	
98–99	Pitt	12	0	2	2	0	
Totals		18	0	5	5	2	

LANGDON, Darren 6–1 205 LW
B. Deer Lake, Nfld., Jan. 8, 1971

94–95	NYR	18	1	1	2	62	0
95–96	NYR	64	7	4	11	175	+2
96–97	NYR	60	3	6	9	195	-1
97–98	NYR	70	3	3	6	197	0
98–99	NYR	44	0	0	0	80	-3
Totals		256	14	14	28	709	-2

Playoffs

95–96	NYR	2	0	0	0	0	
96–97	NYR	10	0	0	0	2	
Totals		12	0	0	0	2	

LANGDON, Stephen Murray 5–11 175 LW
B. Toronto, Ont., Dec. 23, 1953

74–75	Bos	1	0	1	1	0	+1
75–76	Bos	4	0	0	0	2	-1
77–78	Bos	2	0	0	0	0	-1
Totals		7	0	1	1	2	-1

Playoffs

75–76	Bos	4	0	0	0	0	

LANGELLE, Peter 5–10 170 C
B. Winnipeg, Man., Nov. 4, 1917

38–39	Tor	2	1	0	1	0	
39–40	Tor	39	7	14	21	2	
40–41	Tor	48	4	15	19	0	
41–42	Tor	48	10	22	32	9	
Totals		137	22	51	73	11	

Playoffs

38–39	Tor	11	1	2	3	2	
39–40	Tor	10	0	3	3	0	
40–41	Tor	7	1	1	2	0	
41–42	Tor	13	3	3	6	2	
Totals		41	5	9	14	4	

LANGENBRUNNER, Jamie 5–11 185 C
B. Duluth, Minn., July 24, 1975

94–95	Dal	2	0	0	0	2	0
95–96	Dal	12	2	2	4	6	-2
96–97	Dal	76	13	26	39	76	-2
97–98	Dal	81	23	29	52	61	+9
98–99	Dal	75	12	33	45	62	+10
Totals		246	50	90	140	182	+15

Playoffs

96–97	Dal	5	1	1	2	14	
97–98	Dal	16	1	4	5	14	
98–99	Dal	23	10	7	17	16	
Totals		44	12	12	24	44	

LANGEVIN, Chris 6–0 190 LW
B. Montreal, Que., Nov. 27, 1959

83–85	Buf	6	1	0	1	2	-2
85–86	Buf	16	2	1	3	20	+3
Totals		22	3	1	4	22	+1

LANGEVIN, David 6–2 200 D
B. St. Paul, Minn., May 15, 1954

76–77	Edm (WHA)	77	7	16	23	94	
77–78	Edm (WHA)	62	6	22	28	90	
78–79	Edm (WHA)	77	6	21	27	76	
79–80	NYI	76	3	13	16	109	+11
80–81	NYI	75	1	16	17	122	+40
81–82	NYI	73	1	20	21	82	+34
82–83	NYI	73	4	17	21	64	+22
83–84	NYI	69	3	16	19	53	+26
84–85	NYI	56	0	13	13	35	-6
85–86	Minn	80	0	8	8	58	-17
86–87	LA	11	0	4	4	7	-3
NHL Totals		513	12	107	119	530	+107
WHA Totals		216	19	59	78	260	

Playoffs

76–77	Edm (WHA)	5	2	1	3	9	
77–78	Edm (WHA)	5	0	2	2	10	
78–79	Edm (WHA)	13	0	1	1	25	
79–80	NYI	21	0	3	3	32	
80–81	NYI	18	0	3	3	25	
81–82	NYI	19	2	4	6	16	
82–83	NYI	8	0	2	2	2	
83–84	NYI	12	0	4	4	18	
84–85	NYI	4	0	0	0	4	
85–86	Minn	5	0	1	1	9	
NHL Totals		87	2	15	17	106	
WHA Totals		23	2	4	6	44	

LANGKOW, Daymond 5–10 170 C
B. Edmonton, Alta., Sept. 27, 1976

95–96	TB	4	0	1	1	0	-1
96–97	TB	79	15	13	28	35	+1
97–98	TB	68	8	14	22	62	-9
98–99	TB-Phil	78	14	19	33	39	-8
Totals		229	37	47	84	136	-17

Playoffs

98–99	Phil	6	0	2	2	2	

LANGLAIS, Joseph Alfred Alain (Alain) 5–10 175 LW
B. Chicoutimi, Que., Oct. 9, 1950

73–74	Minn	14	3	3	6	8	-6
74–75	Minn	11	1	1	2	2	-3
Totals		25	4	4	8	10	-9

LANGLOIS, Albert (Junior) 6–0 205 D
B. Magog, Que., Nov. 6, 1934

57–58	Mont	1	0	0	0	0	
58–59	Mont	48	0	3	3	26	
59–60	Mont	67	1	14	15	48	
60–61	Mont	61	1	12	13	56	
61–62	NYR	69	7	18	25	90	
62–63	NYR	60	2	14	16	62	
63–64	NYR–Det	61	5	8	13	45	
64–65	Det	65	1	12	13	107	
65–66	Bos	65	4	10	14	54	
Totals		497	21	91	112	488	

Playoffs

57–58	Mont	7	0	1	1	4	
58–59	Mont	7	0	0	0	4	
59–60	Mont	8	0	3	3	18	
60–61	Mont	5	0	0	0	6	
61–62	NYR	6	0	1	1	2	
63–64	Det	14	0	0	0	12	
64–65	Det	6	1	0	1	4	
Totals		53	1	5	6	50	

*LANGLOIS, Charles D
B. Latbiniere, Que., Aug. 25, 1894

24–25	Ham	30	6	1	7	59	
25–26	NYA	36	9	1	10	76	
26–27	NYA–Pitt Pi	45	7	1	8	44	
27–28	Pitt Pi–Mont	40	0	0	0	22	
Totals		151	22	3	25	201	

Playoffs

27–28	Mont	2	0	0	0	0	

LANGWAY, Rod Corry 6–3 218 D
B. Formosa, Taiwan, May 3, 1957

77–78	Birm (WHA)	52	3	18	21	52	
78–79	Mont	45	3	4	7	30	+5
79–80	Mont	77	7	29	36	81	+36
80–81	Mont	80	11	34	45	120	+53
81–82	Mont	66	5	34	39	116	+66
82–83	Wash	80	3	29	32	75	0
83–84	Wash	80	9	24	33	61	+14
84–85	Wash	79	4	22	26	54	+35
85–86	Wash	71	1	17	18	61	+27
86–87	Wash	78	2	25	27	53	+11
87–88	Wash	63	3	13	16	28	+1
88–89	Wash	76	2	19	21	65	+12
89–90	Wash	58	0	8	8	39	+7
90–91	Wash	56	1	7	8	24	+12
91–92	Wash	64	0	13	13	22	+11
92–93	Wash	21	0	0	0	20	-13
NHL Totals		994	51	278	329	849	+277
WHA Totals		52	3	18	21	52	

Playoffs

77–78	Birm (WHA)	4	0	0	0	9	
78–79	Mont	8	0	0	0	16	
79–80	Mont	10	3	3	6	2	
80–81	Mont	3	0	0	0	6	
81–82	Mont	5	0	3	3	18	
82–83	Wash	4	0	0	0	0	
83–84	Wash	8	0	5	5	7	
84–85	Wash	5	0	1	1	6	
85–86	Wash	9	1	2	3	6	
86–87	Wash	7	0	1	1	2	
87–88	Wash	6	0	0	0	8	
88–89	Wash	6	0	0	0	6	
89–90	Wash	15	1	4	5	12	
90–91	Wash	11	0	2	2	6	
91–92	Wash	7	0	1	1	2	
NHL Totals		104	5	22	27	97	
WHA Totals		4	0	0	0	9	

LANTHIER, Jean–Marc 6–2 195 RW
B. Montreal, Que., Mar. 27, 1963

SSN	TEAM	GP	G	A	PTS.	PIM	+/-
83–84	Van	11	2	1	3	2	-2
84–85	Van	27	6	4	10	13	-16
85–86	Van	62	7	10	17	12	-17
87–88	Van	5	1	1	2	1	-1
Totals		105	16	16	32	29	-36

LANYON, Edward George (Ted) 5–11 170 D
B. Winnipeg, Man., June 11, 1939

SSN	TEAM	GP	G	A	PTS.	PIM	+/-
67–68	Pitt	5	0	0	0	4	+1

LANZ, Rick Roman 6–2 203 D
B. Karlouy Vary, Czech., Sept. 16, 1961

SSN	TEAM	GP	G	A	PTS.	PIM	+/-
80–81	Van	76	7	22	29	40	+1
81–82	Van	39	3	11	14	48	-13
82–83	Van	74	10	38	48	46	-5
83–84	Van	79	18	39	57	45	-3
84–85	Van	57	2	17	19	69	-22
85–86	Van	75	15	38	53	73	-26
86–87	Van–Tor	61	3	25	28	42	-9
87–88	Tor	75	6	22	28	65	-12
88–89	Tor	32	1	9	10	18	-17
91–92	Chi	1	0	0	0	2	0
Totals		569	65	221	286	448	-106

Playoffs

SSN	TEAM	GP	G	A	PTS.	PIM	
80–81	Van	3	0	0	0	4	
82–83	Van	4	2	1	3	0	
83–84	Van	4	0	4	4	2	
85–86	Van	3	0	0	0	0	
86–87	Tor	13	1	3	4	27	
87–88	Tor	1	0	0	0	2	
Totals		28	3	8	11	35	

LAPERRIERE, Daniel Jacques 6–1 195 D
B. Laval, Que., Mar. 28, 1969

SSN	TEAM	GP	G	A	PTS.	PIM	+/-
92–93	StL	5	0	1	1	0	-3
93–94	StL	20	1	3	4	8	-1
94–95	StL–Ott	17	1	1	2	15	-3
95–96	Ott	6	0	0	0	4	+2
Totals		48	2	5	7	27	-5

LAPERRIERE, Ian 6–1 195 C
B. Montreal, Que., Jan. 19, 1974

SSN	TEAM	GP	G	A	PTS.	PIM	+/-
93–94	StL	1	0	0	0	0	0
94–95	StL	37	13	14	27	85	+12
95–96	StL–NYR–LA	71	6	11	17	155	-11
96–97	LA	62	8	15	23	102	-25
97–98	LA	77	6	15	21	131	0
98–99	LA	72	3	10	13	138	-5
Totals		320	36	65	101	611	-29

Playoffs

SSN	TEAM	GP	G	A	PTS.	PIM	
94–95	StL	7	0	4	4	21	
97–98	LA	4	1	0	1	6	
Totals		11	1	4	5	27	

LAPERRIERE, Joseph Jacques Hughes (Jacques) 6–2 190 D
B. Rouyn, Que., Nov. 22, 1941

SSN	TEAM	GP	G	A	PTS.	PIM	+/-
62–63	Mont	6	0	2	2	2	
63–64	Mont	65	2	28	30	102	
64–65	Mont	67	5	22	27	92	
65–66	Mont	57	6	25	31	85	
66–67	Mont	61	0	20	20	48	
67–68	Mont	72	4	21	25	84	+23
68–69	Mont	69	5	26	31	45	+37
69–70	Mont	73	6	31	37	98	+28
70–71	Mont	49	0	16	16	20	+24
71–72	Mont	73	3	25	28	50	+36
72–73	Mont	57	7	16	23	34	+78
73–74	Mont	42	2	10	12	14	+15
Totals		691	40	242	282	674	+241

Playoffs

SSN	TEAM	GP	G	A	PTS.	PIM	
62–63	Mont	5	0	1	1	4	
63–64	Mont	7	1	1	2	8	
64–65	Mont	6	1	1	2	16	
66–67	Mont	9	0	1	1	9	
67–68	Mont	13	1	3	4	20	
68–69	Mont	14	1	3	4	28	
70–71	Mont	20	4	9	13	12	
71–72	Mont	4	0	0	0	2	
72–73	Mont	10	1	3	4	2	
Totals		88	9	22	31	101	

LAPLANTE, Darryl 6–0 185 C
B. Calgary, Alta., Mar. 28, 1977

SSN	TEAM	GP	G	A	PTS.	PIM	+/-
97–98	Det	2	0	0	0	0	0
98–99	Det	3	0	0	0	0	0
Totals		5	0	0	0	0	0

LAPOINTE, Claude 5–9 181 C
B. Lachine, Que., Oct. 11, 1968

SSN	TEAM	GP	G	A	PTS.	PIM	+/-
90–91	Que	13	2	2	4	4	+3
91–92	Que	78	13	20	33	86	-8
92–93	Que	74	10	26	36	98	+5
93–94	Que	59	11	17	28	70	+2
94–95	Que	29	4	8	12	41	+5
95–96	Col A–Calg	35	4	5	9	20	+1
96–97	NYI	73	13	5	18	49	-12
97–98	NYI	78	10	10	20	40	-9
98–99	NYI	82	14	23	37	62	-19
Totals		521	81	116	197	470	-32

Playoffs

SSN	TEAM	GP	G	A	PTS.	PIM	
92–93	Que	6	2	4	6	8	
94–95	Que	5	0	0	0	8	
95–96	Calg	2	0	0	0	0	
Totals		13	2	4	6	16	

LAPOINTE, Guy Gerard 6–0 205 D
B. Montreal, Que., Mar. 18, 1948

SSN	TEAM	GP	G	A	PTS.	PIM	+/-
68–69	Mont	1	0	0	0	2	0
69–70	Mont	5	0	0	0	4	0
70–71	Mont	78	15	29	44	107	+28
71–72	Mont	69	11	38	49	58	+15
72–73	Mont	76	19	35	54	117	+51
73–74	Mont	71	13	40	53	63	+12
74–75	Mont	80	28	47	75	88	+46
75–76	Mont	77	21	47	68	78	+64
76–77	Mont	77	25	51	76	53	+69
77–78	Mont	49	13	29	42	19	+46
78–79	Mont	69	13	42	55	43	+27
79–80	Mont	45	6	20	26	29	-2
80–81	Mont	33	1	9	10	79	-6
81–82	Mont–StL	55	1	25	26	76	-6
82–83	StL	54	3	23	26	43	-12
83–84	Bos	45	2	16	18	34	-3
Totals		884	171	451	622	893	+329

Playoffs

SSN	TEAM	GP	G	A	PTS.	PIM	
70–71	Chi	20	4	5	9	34	
71–72	Mont	6	0	1	1	0	
72–73	Mont	17	6	7	13	20	
73–74	Mont	6	0	2	2	4	
74–75	Mont	11	6	4	10	4	
75–76	Mont	13	3	3	6	12	
76–77	Mont	12	3	9	12	4	
77–78	Mont	14	1	6	7	16	
78–79	Mont	10	2	6	8	10	
79–80	Mont	2	0	0	0	0	
80–81	Mont	1	0	0	0	17	
81–82	StL	7	1	0	1	8	
82–83	StL	4	0	1	1	9	
Totals		123	26	44	70	138	

LAPOINTE, Martin 5–11 197 RW
B. Lachine, Que., Sept. 12, 1973

SSN	TEAM	GP	G	A	PTS.	PIM	+/-
91–92	Det	4	0	1	1	5	+2
92–93	Det	3	0	0	0	0	-2
93–94	Det	50	8	8	16	55	+7
94–95	Det	39	4	6	10	73	+1
95–96	Det	58	6	3	9	93	0
96–97	Det	78	16	17	33	167	-14
97–98	Det	79	15	19	34	106	0
98–99	Det	77	15	13	28	141	+7
Totals		388	64	67	131	640	+1

Playoffs

SSN	TEAM	GP	G	A	PTS.	PIM	
93–94	Det	4	0	0	0	6	
94–95	Det	2	0	1	1	8	
95–96	Det	11	1	2	3	12	
96–97	Det	20	4	8	12	60	
97–98	Det	21	9	6	15	20	
98–99	Det	10	0	2	2	20	
Totals		71	14	20	34	126	

LAPOINTE, Richard Paul 6–2 200 D
B. Victoria, B.C., Aug. 2, 1955

SSN	TEAM	GP	G	A	PTS.	PIM	+/-
75–76	Det	80	10	23	33	95	-3
76–77	Det–Phil	71	3	19	22	119	+3
77–78	Phil	47	4	16	20	91	+35

LAPLANTE column 3 — continued

SSN	TEAM	GP	G	A	PTS.	PIM	+/-
78–79	Phil	77	3	18	21	53	+15
79–80	StL	80	6	19	25	87	-24
80–81	StL	80	8	25	33	124	+36
81–82	StL	71	2	20	22	127	-6
82–83	Que	43	2	9	11	59	+14
83–84	Que	22	2	10	12	12	+9
84–85	LA	73	4	13	17	46	-10
85–86	LA	20	0	4	4	18	-13
Totals		664	44	176	220	831	+56

Playoffs

SSN	TEAM	GP	G	A	PTS.	PIM	
76–77	Phil	10	0	0	0	7	
77–78	Phil	12	0	3	3	19	
78–79	Phil	7	0	1	1	14	
79–80	StL	3	0	1	1	6	
80–81	StL	8	2	2	4	12	
81–82	StL	3	0	0	0	6	
83–84	Que	3	0	0	0	0	
Totals		46	2	7	9	64	

LAPPIN, Peter 5–11 180 RW
B. St. Charles, Ill., Dec. 31, 1965

SSN	TEAM	GP	G	A	PTS.	PIM	+/-
89–90	Minn	6	0	0	0	2	-5
91–92	SJ	1	0	0	0	0	0
Totals		7	0	0	0	2	-5

LAPRADE, Edgar Louis 5–8 157 C
B. Mine Center, Ont., Oct. 10, 1919

SSN	TEAM	GP	G	A	PTS.	PIM	
45–46	NYR	49	15	19	34	0	
46–47	NYR	58	15	25	40	9	
47–48	NYR	59	13	34	47	7	
48–49	NYR	56	18	12	30	12	
49–50	NYR	60	22	22	44	2	
50–51	NYR	42	10	13	23	0	
51–52	NYR	70	9	29	38	8	
52–53	NYR	11	2	1	3	2	
53–54	NYR	35	1	6	7	2	
54–55	NYR	60	3	11	14	0	
Totals		500	108	172	280	42	

Playoffs

SSN	TEAM	GP	G	A	PTS.	PIM	
47–48	NYR	6	1	4	5	0	
49–50	NYR	12	3	5	8	4	
Totals		18	4	9	13	4	

LaPRAIRIE, Benjamin (Bun) D
SSN	TEAM	GP	G	A	PTS.	PIM	
36–37	Chi	7	0	0	0	0	

LARAQUE, Georges 6–3 225 RW
B. Montreal, Que., Dec. 7, 1976

SSN	TEAM	GP	G	A	PTS.	PIM	+/-
97–98	Edm	11	0	0	0	59	-4
98–99	Edm	39	3	2	5	57	-1
Totals		50	3	2	5	116	-5

Playoffs

SSN	TEAM	GP	G	A	PTS.	PIM	
98–99	Edm	4	0	0	0	2	

LARIONOV, Igor 5–9 165 C
B. Voskresensk, Soviet Union, Dec. 3, 1960

SSN	TEAM	GP	G	A	PTS.	PIM	+/-
89–90	Van	74	17	27	44	20	-5
90–91	Van	64	13	21	34	14	-3
91–92	Van	72	21	44	65	54	+7
93–94	SJ	60	18	38	56	40	+20
94–95	SJ	33	4	20	24	14	-3
95–96	SJ–Det	73	22	51	73	34	+31
96–97	Det	64	12	42	54	26	+31
97–98	Det	69	8	39	47	40	+14
98–99	Det	75	14	49	63	48	+13
Totals		584	129	331	460	290	+105

Playoffs

SSN	TEAM	GP	G	A	PTS.	PIM	
90–91	Van	6	1	0	1	6	
91–92	Van	13	3	7	10	4	
93–94	SJ	14	5	13	18	10	
94–95	SJ	11	1	8	9	2	
95–96	Det	19	6	7	13	6	
96–97	Det	20	4	8	12	8	
97–98	Det	22	3	10	13	12	
98–99	Det	7	0	2	2	0	
Totals		112	23	55	78	46	

LARIVIERE, Garry Joseph 6–0 190 D
B. St. Catharines, Ont., Dec. 6, 1954

SSN	TEAM	GP	G	A	PTS.	PIM	
74–75	Phoe (WHA)	4	0	1	1	28	
75–76	Phoe (WHA)	79	7	17	24	100	
76–77	Phoe–Que						

SSN	TEAM	GP	G	A	PTS.	PIM	+/-
	(WHA)	76	7	26	33	56	
77–78	Que (WHA)	80	7	49	56	78	
78–79	Que (WHA)	50	5	33	38	54	
79–80	Que	75	2	19	21	56	-10
80–81	Que–Edm	65	3	15	18	56	+7
81–82	Edm	62	1	21	22	41	+27
82–83	Edm	17	0	2	2	14	+13
NHL Totals		219	6	57	63	167	+37
WHA Totals		289	26	126	152	316	

Playoffs

SSN	TEAM	GP	G	A	PTS.	PIM	+/-
74–75	Phoe (WHA)	1	0	0	0	0	
75–76	Phoe (WHA)	5	0	2	2	2	
76–77	Que (WHA)	17	0	10	10	10	
77–78	Que (WHA)	11	3	2	5	4	
78–79	Que (WHA)	4	0	1	1	2	
80–81	Edm	9	0	3	3	8	
81–82	Edm	4	0	1	1	0	
82–83	Edm	1	0	1	1	0	
NHL Totals		14	0	5	5	8	
WHA Totals		38	3	15	18	18	

LARMER, Jeff 5–10 175 LW
B. Peterborough, Ont., Nov. 10, 1962

SSN	TEAM	GP	G	A	PTS.	PIM	+/-
81–82	Col	8	1	1	2	8	-3
82–83	NJ	65	21	24	45	21	-6
83–84	NJ–Chi	76	15	26	41	28	-14
84–85	Chi	7	0	0	0	0	+1
85–86	Chi	2	0	0	0	0	+1
Totals		158	37	51	88	57	-21

Playoffs

SSN	TEAM	GP	G	A	PTS.	PIM	+/-
83–84	Chi	5	1	0	1	2	

LARMER, Steve Donald 5–11 195 RW
B. Peterborough, Ont., June 16, 1961

SSN	TEAM	GP	G	A	PTS.	PIM	+/-
80–81	Chi	4	0	1	1	0	+1
81–82	Chi	3	0	0	0	0	0
82–83	Chi	80	43	47	90	28	+44
83–84	Chi	80	35	40	75	34	-1
84–85	Chi	80	46	40	86	16	+17
85–86	Chi	80	31	45	76	47	+9
86–87	Chi	80	28	56	84	22	+20
87–88	Chi	80	41	48	89	42	-5
88–89	Chi	80	43	44	87	54	+2
89–90	Chi	80	31	59	90	40	+25
90–91	Chi	80	44	57	101	79	+37
91–92	Chi	80	29	45	74	65	+10
92–93	Chi	84	35	35	70	48	+23
93–94	NYR	68	21	39	60	41	+14
94–95	NYR	47	14	15	29	16	+8
Totals		1006	441	571	1012	532	+204

Playoffs

SSN	TEAM	GP	G	A	PTS.	PIM	+/-
82–83	Chi	11	5	7	12	8	
83–84	Chi	5	2	2	4	7	
85–86	Chi	15	9	13	22	14	
86–87	Chi	3	0	3	3	4	
87–88	Chi	4	0	0	0	2	
88–89	Chi	5	1	6	7	0	
89–90	Chi	16	8	9	17	22	
90–91	Chi	20	7	15	22	2	
91–92	Chi	6	5	1	6	4	
92–93	Chi	18	8	7	15	6	
93–94	NYR	23	9	7	16	14	
94–95	NYR	10	2	2	4	6	
Totals		140	56	75	131	89	

*LAROCHELLE, Wildor 5–8 158 F
B. Sorel, Que., Oct. 23, 1906

SSN	TEAM	GP	G	A	PTS.	PIM	+/-
25–26	Mont	33	2	1	3	10	
26–27	Mont	41	0	1	1	6	
27–28	Mont	40	3	1	4	30	
28–29	Mont	2	0	0	0	0	
29–30	Mont	44	14	11	25	28	
30–31	Mont	40	8	5	13	35	
31–32	Mont	48	18	8	26	16	
32–33	Mont	47	11	4	15	27	
33–34	Mont	48	16	11	27	27	
34–35	Mont	48	9	19	28	12	
35–36	Mont–Chi	40	2	3	5	14	
36–37	Chi	43	9	10	19	6	
Totals		474	92	74	166	211	

Playoffs

SSN	TEAM	GP	G	A	PTS.	PIM	+/-
26–27	Mont	4	0	0	0	0	
27–28	Mont	2	0	0	0	0	
29–30	Mont	6	1	0	1	12	
30–31	Mont	10	1	2	3	8	
31–32	Mont	4	2	1	3	4	
32–33	Mont	2	1	0	1	0	
33–34	Mont	2	1	1	2	0	
34–35	Mont	2	0	0	0	0	
35–36	Chi	2	0	0	0	0	
Totals		34	6	4	10	24	

LAROCQUE, Denis 6–1 205 D
B. Hawkesbury, Ont., Oct. 5, 1967

SSN	TEAM	GP	G	A	PTS.	PIM	+/-
87–88	LA	8	0	1	1	18	

LAROCQUE, Mario 6–2 182 D
B. Montreal, Que., April 24, 1978

SSN	TEAM	GP	G	A	PTS.	PIM	+/-
98–99	TB	5	0	0	0	16	-4

LAROSE, Charles Bonner F

SSN	TEAM	GP	G	A	PTS.	PIM	+/-
25–26	Bos	6	0	0	0	0	

LAROSE, Claude 5–10 170 LW
B. St. Jean, Que., May 17, 1955

SSN	TEAM	GP	G	A	PTS.	PIM	+/-
75–76	Cin (WHA)	79	28	24	52	19	
76–77	Cin (WHA)	81	30	46	76	8	
77–78	Cin–Ind (WHA)	79	25	36	61	18	
78–79	Ind (WHA)	13	5	8	13	0	
79–80	NYR	25	4	7	11	2	-5
NHL Totals		25	4	7	11	2	-5
WHA Totals		252	88	114	202	45	

Playoffs

SSN	TEAM	GP	G	A	PTS.	PIM	+/-
76–77	Cin (WHA)	4	2	1	3	0	
81–82	NYR	2	0	0	0	0	
NHL Totals		2	0	0	0	0	
WHA Totals		4	2	1	3	0	

LAROSE, Claude David 6–0 170 RW
B. Hearst, Ont., Mar. 2, 1942

SSN	TEAM	GP	G	A	PTS.	PIM	+/-
62–63	Mont	4	0	0	0	0	
63–64	Mont	21	1	1	2	43	
64–65	Mont	68	21	16	37	82	
65–66	Mont	64	15	18	33	67	
66–67	Mont	69	19	16	35	82	
67–68	Mont	42	2	9	11	28	0
68–69	Minn	67	25	37	62	106	-10
69–70	Minn	75	24	23	47	109	-17
70–71	Mont	64	10	13	23	90	-8
71–72	Mont	77	20	18	38	64	+9
72–73	Mont	73	11	23	34	30	+29
73–74	Mont	39	17	7	24	52	+11
74–75	Mont–StL	64	11	19	30	44	+4
75–76	StL	67	13	25	38	48	+7
76–77	StL	80	29	19	48	22	+5
77–78	StL	69	8	13	21	20	-19
Totals		943	226	257	483	887	+11

Playoffs

SSN	TEAM	GP	G	A	PTS.	PIM	+/-
63–64	Mont	2	1	0	1	0	
64–65	Mont	13	0	1	1	14	
65–66	Mont	6	0	1	1	31	
66–67	Mont	10	1	5	6	15	
67–68	Mont	12	3	2	5	8	
69–70	Mont	1	1	1	2	25	
70–71	Mont	11	1	0	1	10	
71–72	Mont	6	2	1	3	23	
72–73	Mont	17	3	4	7	6	
73–74	Mont	5	0	2	2	11	
74–75	StL	2	1	1	2	0	
75–76	StL	3	0	0	0	0	
76–77	StL	4	1	0	1	0	
Totals		97	14	18	32	143	

LAROSE, Guy 5–9 175 C
B. Hull, Que., Aug. 31, 1967

SSN	TEAM	GP	G	A	PTS.	PIM	+/-
88–89	Winn	3	0	1	1	6	-1
90–91	Winn	7	0	0	0	8	-1
91–92	Tor	34	9	5	14	27	-8
92–93	Tor	9	0	0	0	8	-3
93–94	Tor–Calg	17	1	3	4	14	-5
Totals		70	10	9	19	63	-18

Playoffs

SSN	TEAM	GP	G	A	PTS.	PIM	+/-
93–94	Calg	4	0	0	0	0	

LAROUCHE, Pierre 5–11 175 C
B. Taschereau, Que., Nov. 16, 1955

SSN	TEAM	GP	G	A	PTS.	PIM	+/-
74–75	Pitt	79	31	37	68	52	+2
75–76	Pitt	76	53	58	111	33	+4
76–77	Pitt	65	29	34	63	14	-10
77–78	Pitt–Mont	64	23	37	60	11	+19
78–79	Mont	36	9	13	22	4	+3
79–80	Mont	73	50	41	91	16	+36
80–81	Mont	61	25	28	53	28	+13
81–82	Mont–Hart	67	34	37	71	12	-20
82–83	Hart	38	18	22	40	8	-24
83–84	NYR	77	48	33	81	22	-15
84–85	NYR	65	24	36	60	8	-17
85–86	NYR	28	20	7	27	4	-6
86–87	NYR	73	28	35	63	12	-7
87–88	NYR	10	3	9	12	13	-3
Totals		812	395	427	822	237	-25

Playoffs

SSN	TEAM	GP	G	A	PTS.	PIM	+/-
74–75	Pitt	9	2	5	7	2	
75–76	Pitt	3	0	1	1	0	
76–77	Pitt	3	0	3	3	0	
77–78	Mont	5	2	1	3	4	
78–79	Mont	6	1	3	4	0	
79–80	Mont	9	1	7	8	2	
80–81	Mont	2	0	2	2	0	
83–84	NYR	5	3	1	4	2	
85–86	NYR	16	8	9	17	2	
86–87	NYR	6	3	2	5	4	
Totals		64	20	34	54	16	

LAROUCHE, Steve 6–0 180 C
B. Rouyn, Que., Apr. 14, 1971

SSN	TEAM	GP	G	A	PTS.	PIM	+/-
94–95	Ott	18	8	7	15	6	-5
95–96	NYR–LA	8	1	2	3	4	0
Totals		26	9	9	18	10	-5

LARSEN, Brad 5–11 212 LW
B. Nakusp, B.C., Jan. 28, 1977

SSN	TEAM	GP	G	A	PTS.	PIM	+/-
97–98	Col A	1	0	0	0	0	0

LARSON, Norman Lyle 6–0 175 RW
B. Moose Jaw, Sask., Oct. 13, 1920

SSN	TEAM	GP	G	A	PTS.	PIM	+/-
40–41	NYA	48	9	9	18	6	
41–42	NYA	40	16	9	25	6	
46–47	NYR	1	0	0	0	0	
Totals		89	25	18	43	12	

LARSON, Reed David 6–0 195 D
B. Minneapolis, Minn., July 30, 1956

SSN	TEAM	GP	G	A	PTS.	PIM	+/-
76–77	Det	14	0	1	1	23	-2
77–78	Det	75	19	41	60	95	+3
78–79	Det	79	18	49	67	169	-20
79–80	Det	80	22	44	66	101	-7
80–81	Det	78	27	31	58	153	-35
81–82	Det	80	21	39	60	112	-17
82–83	Det	80	22	52	74	104	-7
83–84	Det	78	23	39	62	122	-10
84–85	Det	77	17	45	62	139	+7
85–86	Det–Bos	80	22	45	67	117	-31
86–87	Bos	66	12	24	36	95	-9
87–88	Bos	62	10	24	34	93	-3
88–89	Edm–NYI–Minn	54	9	29	38	68	-10
89–90	Buf	1	0	0	0	0	+1
Totals		904	222	463	685	1391	-151

Playoffs

SSN	TEAM	GP	G	A	PTS.	PIM	+/-
77–78	Det	7	0	2	2	4	
83–84	Det	4	2	0	2	21	
84–85	Det	3	1	2	3	20	
85–86	Bos	3	1	0	1	6	
86–87	Bos	4	0	2	2	2	
87–88	Bos	8	0	1	1	6	
88–89	Minn	3	0	0	0	4	
Totals		32	4	7	11	63	

LARTER, Tyler 5–10 185 C
B. Charlottetown, P.E.I., Mar. 12, 1968

SSN	TEAM	GP	G	A	PTS.	PIM	+/-
89–90	Wash	1	0	0	0	0	-1

LATAL, Jiri 6–0 190 D
B. Olomouc, Czechoslovakia, Feb. 2, 1967

SSN	TEAM	GP	G	A	PTS.	PIM	+/-
89–90	Phil	32	6	13	19	6	+4
90–91	Phil	50	5	21	26	14	-19
91–92	Phil	10	1	2	3	4	+1
Totals		92	12	36	48	24	-14

LATOS, James 6–1 200 RW
B. Wakaw, Sask., Jan. 4, 1966

SSN	TEAM	GP	G	A	PTS.	PIM	+/-
88–89	NYR	1	0	0	0	0	-1

LATREILLE, Philippe J. (Phil) F
B. Montreal, Que., Apr. 20, 1938

SSN	TEAM	GP	G	A	PTS.	PIM	+/-
60–61	NYR	4	0	0	0	2	

LATTA, David 6–1 190 LW
B. Thunder Bay, Ont., Jan. 3, 1967

SSN	TEAM	GP	G	A	PTS.	PIM	+/-
85–86	Que	1	0	0	0	0	0
87–88	Que	10	0	0	0	0	-4
88–89	Que	24	4	8	12	4	-8
90–91	Que	1	0	0	0	0	0
Totals		36	4	8	12	4	-12

*LAUDER, Martin D

SSN	TEAM	GP	G	A	PTS.	PIM	+/-
27–28	Bos	3	0	0	0	2	

LAUEN, Michael Arthur 6–1 185 RW
B. Edina, Minn., Feb. 9, 1961

SSN	TEAM	GP	G	A	PTS.	PIM	+/-
83–84	Winn	3	0	1	1	0	0

LAUER, Brad 6–0 195 LW
B. Humboldt, Sask., Oct. 27, 1966

SSN	TEAM	GP	G	A	PTS.	PIM	+/-
86–87	NYI	61	7	14	21	65	0
87–88	NYI	69	17	18	35	67	+13
88–89	NYI	14	3	2	5	2	-2
89–90	NYI	63	6	18	24	19	+5
90–91	NYI	44	4	8	12	45	-6
91–92	NYI–Chi	14	1	0	1	6	-5
92–93	Chi	7	0	1	1	2	-1
93–94	Ott	30	2	5	7	6	-15
95–96	Pitt	21	4	1	5	6	-5
Totals		323	44	67	111	218	-16

Playoffs

SSN	TEAM	GP	G	A	PTS.	PIM
86–87	NYI	6	2	0	2	4
87–88	NYI	5	3	1	4	4
89–90	NYI	4	0	2	2	10
91–92	Chi	7	1	1	2	2
95–96	Pitt	12	1	1	2	4
Totals		34	7	5	12	24

LAUGHLIN, Craig 6–0 190 RW
B. Toronto, Ont., Sept. 19, 1957

SSN	TEAM	GP	G	A	PTS.	PIM	+/-
81–82	Mont	36	12	11	23	33	+10
82–83	Wash	75	17	27	44	41	-7
83–84	Wash	80	20	32	52	69	+4
84–85	Wash	78	16	34	50	38	+12
85–86	Wash	75	30	45	75	43	+24
86–87	Wash	80	22	30	52	67	-3
87–88	Wash–LA	59	9	13	22	32	-16
88–89	Tor	66	10	13	23	41	-22
Totals		549	136	205	341	364	+2

Playoffs

SSN	TEAM	GP	G	A	PTS.	PIM
81–82	Mont	3	0	1	1	0
82–83	Wash	4	1	0	1	0
83–84	Wash	8	4	2	6	6
84–85	Wash	5	0	0	0	2
85–86	Wash	9	1	2	3	10
86–87	Wash	1	0	0	0	0
87–88	LA	3	0	1	1	2
Totals		33	6	6	12	20

LAUGHTON, Michael Frederic 6–2 185 C
B. Nelson, B.C., Feb. 21, 1944

SSN	TEAM	GP	G	A	PTS.	PIM	+/-
67–68	Oak	35	2	6	8	38	-17
68–69	Oak	53	20	23	43	12	0
69–70	Oak	76	16	19	35	39	-28
70–71	Cal	25	1	0	1	2	-12
72–73	NY (WHA)	67	16	20	36	44	
73–74	NY–NJ (WHA)	71	20	18	38	34	
74–75	SD (WHA)	65	7	9	16	22	
NHL Totals		189	39	48	87	91	-57
WHA Totals		203	43	47	90	100	

Playoffs

SSN	TEAM	GP	G	A	PTS.	PIM
68–69	Cal	7	3	2	5	0
69–70	Oak	4	0	1	1	0
74–75	SD (WHA)	10	4	1	5	0
NHL Totals		11	3	3	6	0
WHA Totals		10	4	1	5	0

LAUKKANEN, Janne 6–0 180 D
B. Lahti, Finland, Mar. 19, 1970

SSN	TEAM	GP	G	A	PTS.	PIM	+/-
94–95	Que	11	0	3	3	4	+3
95–96	Col A–Ott	23	1	2	3	14	-1
96–97	Ott	76	3	18	21	76	-14
97–98	Ott	60	4	17	21	64	-15
98–99	Ott	50	1	11	12	40	+18
Totals		220	9	51	60	198	-9

Playoffs

SSN	TEAM	GP	G	A	PTS.	PIM
94–95	Que	6	1	0	1	2
96–97	Ott	7	0	1	1	6
97–98	Ott	11	2	2	4	8
98–99	Ott	4	0	0	0	4
Totals		28	3	3	6	20

LAURENCE, Donald (Red) 5–9 173 C
B. Galt, Ont., June 27, 1957

SSN	TEAM	GP	G	A	PTS.	PIM	+/-
78–79	Atl	59	14	20	34	6	+8
79–80	StL	20	1	2	3	8	-7
Totals		79	15	22	37	14	+1

LAUS, Paul 6–1 216 D
B. Beamsville, Ont., Sept. 26, 1970

SSN	TEAM	GP	G	A	PTS.	PIM	+/-
93–94	Fla	39	2	0	2	109	+9
94–95	Fla	37	0	7	7	138	+12
95–96	Fla	78	3	6	9	236	-2
96–97	Fla	77	0	12	12	313	+13
97–98	Fla	77	0	11	11	293	-5
98–99	Fla	75	1	9	10	238	-1
Totals		383	6	45	51	1327	+26

Playoffs

SSN	TEAM	GP	G	A	PTS.	PIM
95–96	Fla	21	2	6	8	62
96–97	Fla	5	0	1	1	4
Totals		26	2	7	9	66

LaVALLEE, Kevin A. 5–8 180 LW
B. Sudbury, Ont., Sept. 16, 1961

SSN	TEAM	GP	G	A	PTS.	PIM	+/-
80–81	Calg	77	15	20	35	16	-4
81–82	Calg	75	32	29	61	30	-9
82–83	Calg	60	19	16	35	17	-6
83–84	LA	19	3	3	6	2	-5
84–85	StL	38	15	17	32	8	+2
85–86	StL	64	18	20	38	8	+8
86–87	Pitt	33	8	20	28	4	-2
Totals		366	110	125	235	85	-16

Playoffs

SSN	TEAM	GP	G	A	PTS.	PIM
80–81	Calg	8	2	3	5	4
81–82	Calg	3	0	0	0	7
82–83	Calg	8	1	3	4	4
85–86	StL	13	2	2	4	6
Totals		32	5	8	13	21

LaVARRE, Mark 5–11 170 RW
B. Evanston, Ill., Feb. 21, 1965

SSN	TEAM	GP	G	A	PTS.	PIM	+/-
85–86	Chi	2	0	0	0	0	-2
86–87	Chi	58	8	15	23	33	+11
87–88	Chi	18	1	1	2	25	-8
Totals		78	9	16	25	58	+1

Playoffs

SSN	TEAM	GP	G	A	PTS.	PIM
87–88	Chi	1	0	0	0	2

LAVENDER, Brian James 6–0 180 LW
B. Edmonton, Alta., Apr. 20, 1947

SSN	TEAM	GP	G	A	PTS.	PIM	+/-
71–72	StL	46	5	11	16	54	-2
72–73	NYI–Det	69	8	8	16	61	-40
73–74	Det	4	0	0	0	11	-4
74–75	Cal	65	3	7	10	48	-10
75–76	Den (WHA)	37	2	0	2	7	
NHL Totals		184	16	26	42	174	-56
WHA Totals		37	2	0	2	7	

Playoffs

SSN	TEAM	GP	G	A	PTS.	PIM	+/-
71–72	StL	3	0	0	0	2	-1

LAVIGNE, Eric 6–3 195 D
B. Victoriaville, Que., Nov. 4, 1972

SSN	TEAM	GP	G	A	PTS.	PIM
94–95	LA	1	0	0	0	0

*LAVIOLETTE, Jean-Baptiste (Jack) D
B. Belleville, Ont., July 27, 1879

SSN	TEAM	GP	G	A	PTS.	PIM
17–18	Mont	18	2	0	2	0

Playoffs

SSN	TEAM	GP	G	A	PTS.	PIM
17–18	Mont	2	0	0	0	0

LAVIOLETTE, Peter 6–2 200 D
B. Norwood, Mass., Dec. 7, 1964

SSN	TEAM	GP	G	A	PTS.	PIM	+/-
88–89	NYR	12	0	0	0	6	+2

LAVOIE, Dominic 6–2 205 D
B. Montreal, Que., Nov. 21, 1967

SSN	TEAM	GP	G	A	PTS.	PIM	+/-
88–89	StL	1	0	0	0	0	+2
89–90	StL	13	1	1	2	16	-5
90–91	StL	6	1	2	3	2	+4
91–92	StL	6	0	1	1	10	-3
92–93	Ott–Bos	4	0	1	1	2	-1
93–94	LA	8	3	3	6	2	-2
Totals		38	5	8	13	32	-4

LAWLESS, Paul 5–11 185 LW
B. Scarborough, Ont., July 2, 1964

SSN	TEAM	GP	G	A	PTS.	PIM	+/-
82–83	Hart	47	6	9	15	4	-31
83–84	Hart	6	0	3	3	0	-5
85–86	Hart	64	17	21	38	20	-3
86–87	Hart	60	22	32	54	14	+24
87–88	Hart–Phil–Van	49	4	11	15	16	-11
88–89	Tor	7	0	0	0	0	-2
89–90	Tor	6	0	1	1	0	-4
Totals		239	49	77	126	54	-32

Playoffs

SSN	TEAM	GP	G	A	PTS.	PIM
85–86	Hart	1	0	0	0	0
86–87	Hart	2	0	2	2	2
Totals		3	0	2	2	2

LAWRENCE, Mark 6–4 215 RW
B. Burlington, Ont., Jan. 27, 1972

SSN	TEAM	GP	G	A	PTS.	PIM	+/-
94–95	Dal	2	0	0	0	0	0
95–96	Dal	13	0	1	1	17	0
97–98	NYI	2	0	0	0	2	0
98–99	NYI	60	14	16	30	38	-8
Totals		77	14	17	31	57	-8

LAWSON, Daniel Michael 5–11 180 RW
B. Toronto, Ont., Oct. 30, 1947

SSN	TEAM	GP	G	A	PTS.	PIM	+/-
67–68	Det	1	0	0	0	0	0
68–69	Det–Minn	62	8	10	18	25	-9
69–70	Minn	45	9	8	17	19	-3
70–71	Minn	33	1	5	6	2	+3
71–72	Buf	78	10	6	16	15	-23
72–73	Phil (WHA)	78	61	45	106	35	
73–74	Van (WHA)	78	55	33	88	14	
74–75	Van (WHA)	78	33	43	76	19	
75–76	Calg (WHA)	80	44	52	96	46	
76–77	Calg–Winn (WHA)	78	30	26	56	28	
NHL Totals		219	28	29	57	61	-32
WHA Totals		392	223	199	422	142	

Playoffs

SSN	TEAM	GP	G	A	PTS.	PIM
69–70	Minn	6	0	1	1	2
70–71	Minn	10	0	0	0	0
72–73	Phil (WHA)	4	0	1	1	0
75–76	Calg (WHA)	9	4	4	8	19
76–77	Winn (WHA)	13	2	4	6	6
NHL Totals		16	0	1	1	2
WHA Totals		26	6	9	15	25

LAWTON, Brian 6–0 180 LW
B. New Brunswick, N.J., June 29, 1965

SSN	TEAM	GP	G	A	PTS.	PIM	+/-
83–84	Minn	58	10	21	31	33	0
84–85	Minn	40	5	6	11	24	-2
85–86	Minn	65	18	17	35	36	+10
86–87	Minn	66	21	23	44	86	+20
87–88	Minn	74	17	24	41	71	-10
88–89	NYR–Hart	65	17	26	43	67	-11
89–90	Hart–Que–Bos	35	7	7	14	30	-13
91–92	SJ	59	15	22	37	42	-25
92–93	SJ	21	2	8	10	12	-9
Totals		483	112	154	266	401	-41

Playoffs

SSN	TEAM	GP	G	A	PTS.	PIM
83–84	Minn	5	0	0	0	10
85–86	Minn	3	0	1	1	2
88–89	Hart	3	1	0	1	0
Totals		11	1	1	2	12

LAXDAL, Derek *6–1 175 RW*
B. St. Boniface, Man., Feb. 21, 1966

SSN	TEAM	GP	G	A	PTS.	PIM	+/-
84–85	Tor	3	0	0	0	6	-1
86–87	Tor	2	0	0	0	7	-1
87–88	Tor	5	0	0	0	6	0
88–89	Tor	41	9	6	15	65	-11
89–90	NYI	12	3	1	4	6	-4
90–91	NYI	4	0	0	0	0	-1
Totals		67	12	7	19	90	-18

Playoffs

SSN	TEAM	GP	G	A	PTS.	PIM
89–90	NYI	1	0	2	2	2

*LAYCOE, Harold Richardson (Hal) *6–1 175 D*
B. Sutherland, Sask., June 23, 1922

SSN	TEAM	GP	G	A	PTS.	PIM
45–46	NYR	17	0	2	2	6
46–47	NYR	58	1	12	13	25
47–48	Mont	14	1	2	3	4
48–49	Mont	51	3	5	8	31
49–50	Mont	30	0	2	2	21
50–51	Mont–Bos	44	1	3	4	29
51–52	Bos	70	5	7	12	61
52–53	Bos	54	2	10	12	36
53–54	Bos	58	3	16	19	29
54–55	Bos	70	4	13	17	34
55–56	Bos	65	5	5	10	16
Totals		531	25	77	102	292

Playoffs

SSN	TEAM	GP	G	A	PTS.	PIM
48–49	Mont	7	0	1	1	13
49–50	Mont	2	0	0	0	0
50–51	Bos	6	0	1	1	5
51–52	Bos	7	1	1	2	11
52–53	Bos	11	0	2	2	10
53–54	Bos	2	0	0	0	0
54–55	Bos	5	1	0	1	0
Totals		40	2	5	7	39

LAZARO, Jeff *5–10 180 LW*
B. Waltham, Mass., Mar. 21, 1968

SSN	TEAM	GP	G	A	PTS.	PIM	+/-
90–91	Bos	49	5	13	18	67	+7
91–92	Bos	27	3	6	9	31	+4
92–93	Ott	26	6	4	10	16	-8
Totals		102	14	23	37	114	+3

Playoffs

SSN	TEAM	GP	G	A	PTS.	PIM
90–91	Bos	19	3	2	5	30
91–92	Bos	9	0	1	1	2
Totals		28	3	3	6	32

LEACH, Jamie *6–1 205 RW*
B. Winnipeg, Man., Aug. 25, 1969

SSN	TEAM	GP	G	A	PTS.	PIM	+/-
89–90	Pitt	10	0	3	3	0	+3
90–91	Pitt	7	2	0	2	0	-1
91–92	Pitt	38	5	4	9	8	-2
92–93	Pitt–Hart	24	3	2	5	4	-7
93–94	Fla	2	1	0	1	0	-2
Totals		81	11	9	20	12	-9

LEACH, Lawrence Raymond *6–2 180 C*
B. Lloydminster, Sask., June 18, 1936

SSN	TEAM	GP	G	A	PTS.	PIM
58–59	Bos	29	4	12	16	26
59–60	Bos	69	7	12	19	47
61–62	Bos	28	2	5	7	18
Totals		126	13	29	42	91

Playoffs

SSN	TEAM	GP	G	A	PTS.	PIM
58–59	Bos	7	1	1	2	8

LEACH, Reginald Joseph *6–0 180 RW*
B. Riverton, Man., Apr. 23, 1950

SSN	TEAM	GP	G	A	PTS.	PIM	+/-
70–71	Bos	23	2	4	6	0	+7
71–72	Bos–Cal	73	13	20	33	19	+7
72–73	Cal	76	23	12	35	45	-41
73–74	Cal	78	22	24	46	34	-61
74–75	Phil	80	45	33	78	63	+53
75–76	Phil	80	61	30	91	41	+73
76–77	Phil	77	32	14	46	23	+6
77–78	Phil	72	24	28	52	24	+20
78–79	Phil	76	34	20	54	20	-3
79–80	Phil	76	50	26	76	28	+40
80–81	Phil	79	34	36	70	59	+21
81–82	Phil	66	26	21	47	18	+2
82–83	Det	78	15	17	32	13	-1
Totals		934	381	285	666	387	+133

Playoffs

SSN	TEAM	GP	G	A	PTS.	PIM	+/-
70–71	Bos	3	0	0	0	0	
74–75	Phil	17	8	2	10	6	
75–76	Phil	16	19	5	24	8	
76–77	Phil	10	4	5	9	0	
77–78	Phil	12	2	2	4	0	
78–79	Phil	8	5	1	6	0	
79–80	Phil	19	9	7	16	6	
80–81	Phil	9	0	0	0	2	
Totals		94	47	22	69	22	

LEACH, Stephen *5–11 197 RW*
B. Cambridge, Mass., Jan. 16, 1966

SSN	TEAM	GP	G	A	PTS.	PIM	+/-
85–86	Wash	11	1	1	2	2	0
86–87	Wash	15	1	0	1	6	-4
87–88	Wash	8	1	1	2	17	+2
88–89	Wash	74	11	19	30	94	-4
89–90	Wash	70	18	14	32	104	+10
90–91	Wash	68	11	19	30	99	-9
91–92	Bos	78	31	29	60	147	-8
92–93	Bos	79	26	25	51	126	-6
93–94	Bos	42	5	10	15	74	-10
94–95	Bos	35	5	6	11	68	-3
95–96	Bos–StL	73	11	17	28	108	-7
96–97	StL	17	2	1	3	24	-2
97–98	Car	45	4	5	9	42	-19
98–99	Ott-Phoe	31	1	3	4	43	-7
Totals		646	128	150	278	954	-70

Playoffs

SSN	TEAM	GP	G	A	PTS.	PIM
85–86	Wash	6	0	1	1	0
87–88	Wash	9	2	1	3	0
88–89	Wash	6	1	0	1	12
89–90	Wash	14	2	2	4	8
90–91	Wash	9	1	2	3	8
91–92	Bos	15	4	0	4	10
92–93	Bos	4	1	1	2	2
93–94	Bos	5	0	1	1	2
95–96	StL	11	3	2	5	10
96–97	StL	6	0	0	0	33
98–99	Phoe	7	1	1	2	2
Totals		92	15	11	26	87

LEAVINS, Jim *5–11 185 D*
B. Dinsmore, Sask., July 28, 1960

SSN	TEAM	GP	G	A	PTS.	PIM	+/-
85–86	Det	37	2	11	13	26	-23
86–87	NYR	4	0	1	1	4	0
Totals		41	2	12	14	30	-23

LEBEAU, Patrick *5–10 172 LW*
B. St. Jerome, Que., Mar. 17, 1970

SSN	TEAM	GP	G	A	PTS.	PIM	+/-
90–91	Mont	2	1	1	2	0	0
92–93	Calg	1	0	0	0	0	0
93–94	Fla	4	1	1	2	4	0
98–99	Pitt	8	1	0	1	2	-2
Totals		15	3	2	5	6	-2

LEBEAU, Stephan *5–10 172 C*
B. St. Jerome, Que., Feb. 28, 1968

SSN	TEAM	GP	G	A	PTS.	PIM	+/-
88–89	Mont	1	0	1	1	2	+1
89–90	Mont	57	15	20	35	11	+13
90–91	Mont	73	22	31	53	24	+4
91–92	Mont	77	27	31	58	14	+18
92–93	Mont	71	31	49	80	20	+23
93–94	Mont–Ana	56	15	11	26	22	-4
94–95	Ana	38	8	16	24	12	+8
Totals		373	118	159	277	105	+63

Playoffs

SSN	TEAM	GP	G	A	PTS.	PIM
89–90	Mont	2	3	0	3	0
90–91	Mont	7	2	1	3	2
91–92	Mont	8	1	3	4	4
92–93	Mont	13	3	3	6	6
Totals		30	9	7	16	12

LeBLANC, Fernand (Fern) *5–9 170 C*
B. Gaspesie, Que., Jan. 12, 1956

SSN	TEAM	GP	G	A	PTS.	PIM	+/-
76–77	Det	3	0	0	0	0	-3
77–78	Det	2	0	0	0	0	-2
78–79	Det	29	5	6	11	0	+1
Totals		34	5	6	11	0	-4

LeBLANC, Jean–Paul (J.P.) *5–10 175 C*
B. South Durham, Que., Oct. 20, 1946

SSN	TEAM	GP	G	A	PTS.	PIM	+/-
68–69	Chi	6	1	2	3	0	+1
72–73	LA (WHA)	77	19	50	69	49	

SSN	TEAM	GP	G	A	PTS.	PIM	+/-
73–74	LA (WHA)	78	20	46	66	58	
74–75	Balt (WHA)	78	16	33	49	100	
75–76	Denver (WHA)	15	1	5	6	25	
75–76	Det	46	4	9	13	39	-5
76–77	Det	74	7	11	18	40	-16
77–78	Det	3	0	2	2	4	+1
78–79	Det	24	2	6	8	4	-7
NHL Totals		153	14	30	44	87	-26
WHA Totals		248	56	134	190	232	

Playoffs

SSN	TEAM	GP	G	A	PTS.	PIM
72–73	LA (WHA)	6	0	5	5	2
77–78	Det	2	0	0	0	0
NHL Totals		2	0	0	0	0
WHA Totals		6	0	5	5	2

LeBLANC, John Glenn *6–1 190 RW*
B. Campbellton, N.B., Jan. 21, 1964

SSN	TEAM	GP	G	A	PTS.	PIM	+/-
86–87	Van	2	1	0	1	0	+1
87–88	Van	41	12	10	22	18	-12
88–89	Edm	2	1	0	1	0	0
91–92	Winn	16	6	1	7	6	-6
92–93	Winn	3	0	0	0	2	0
93–94	Winn	17	6	2	8	2	-2
94–95	Winn	2	0	0	0	0	0
Totals		83	26	13	39	28	-19

Playoffs

SSN	TEAM	GP	G	A	PTS.	PIM
88–89	Edm	1	0	0	0	0

LEBOUTILIER, Peter *6–1 198 RW*
B. Minnedosa, Man., Jan. 11, 1975

SSN	TEAM	GP	G	A	PTS.	PIM	+/-
96–97	Ana	1	0	1	1	21	0
97–98	Ana	12	1	1	2	55	-1
Totals		13	1	2	3	76	-1

LeBRUN, Albert Ivan *6–0 195 D*
B. Timmins, Ont., Dec. 1, 1940

SSN	TEAM	GP	G	A	PTS.	PIM
60–61	NYR	4	0	2	2	4
65–66	NYR	2	0	0	0	0
Totals		6	0	2	2	4

LECAINE, William Joseph *6–0 172 LW*
B. Moose Jaw, Sask., Mar. 11, 1940

SSN	TEAM	GP	G	A	PTS.	PIM	+/-
68–69	Pitt	4	0	0	0	0	0

LECAVALIER, Vincent *6–4 180 C*
B. Ile Bizard, Que., April 21, 1980

SSN	TEAM	GP	G	A	PTS.	PIM	+/-
98–99	TB	82	13	15	28	23	-19

LeCLAIR, John *6–2 215 LW*
B. St. Albans, Vt., July 5, 1969

SSN	TEAM	GP	G	A	PTS.	PIM	+/-
90–91	Mont	10	2	5	7	2	+1
91–92	Mont	59	8	11	19	14	+5
92–93	Mont	72	19	25	44	33	+11
93–94	Mont	74	19	24	43	32	+17
94–95	Mont-Phil	46	26	28	54	30	+20
95–96	Phil	82	51	46	97	64	+21
96–97	Phil	82	50	47	97	58	+44
97–98	Phil	82	51	36	87	32	+30
98–99	Phil	76	43	47	90	30	+36
Totals		583	269	269	538	295	+185

Playoffs

SSN	TEAM	GP	G	A	PTS.	PIM
90–91	Mont	3	0	0	0	0
91–92	Mont	8	1	1	2	4
92–93	Mont	20	4	6	10	14
93–94	Mont	7	2	1	3	8
94–95	Phil	15	5	7	12	4
95–96	Phil	11	6	5	11	6
96–97	Phil	19	9	12	21	10
97–98	Phil	5	1	1	2	8
98–99	Phil	6	3	0	3	12
Totals		94	31	33	64	66

LECLAIR, John Louis (Jackie) *5–10 175 C*
B. Quebec City, Que., May 30, 1929

SSN	TEAM	GP	G	A	PTS.	PIM
54–55	Mont	59	11	22	33	12
55–56	Mont	54	6	8	14	30
56–57	Mont	47	3	10	13	14
Totals		160	20	40	60	56

Playoffs

SSN	TEAM	GP	G	A	PTS.	PIM
54–55	Mont	12	5	0	5	2
55–56	Mont	8	1	1	2	4

SSN	TEAM	GP	G	A	PTS.	PIM	+/-
Totals		20	6	1	7	6	

LECLERC, Mike 6-1 205 LW
B. Winnipeg, Man., Nov. 10, 1976

SSN	TEAM	GP	G	A	PTS.	PIM	+/-
96-97	Ana	5	1	1	2	0	+2
97-98	Ana	7	0	0	0	6	-6
98-99	Ana	7	0	0	0	4	-2
Totals		19	1	1	2	10	-6

Playoffs

SSN	TEAM	GP	G	A	PTS.	PIM	+/-
96-97	Ana	1	0	0	0	0	
98-99	Ana	1	0	0	0	0	
Totals		2	0	0	0	0	

LECLERC, Renald (Rene) 5-11 165 RW
B. Ville-de-Vanier, Que., Nov. 12, 1947

SSN	TEAM	GP	G	A	PTS.	PIM	+/-
68-69	Det	43	2	3	5	62	-8
70-71	Det	44	8	8	16	30	-3
72-73	Que (WHA)	60	24	28	52	111	
73-74	Que (WHA)	58	17	27	44	84	
74-75	Que (WHA)	73	18	32	50	85	
75-76	Que-Ind (WHA)	82	33	38	71	87	
76-77	Ind (WHA)	68	25	30	55	43	
77-78	Ind (WHA)	60	12	15	27	31	
78-79	Ind-Que (WHA)	45	5	7	12	20	
NHL Totals		87	10	11	21	92	-11
WHA Totals		446	134	177	311	461	

Playoffs

SSN	TEAM	GP	G	A	PTS.	PIM	+/-
74-75	Que (WHA)	14	7	7	14	41	
75-76	Ind (WHA)	7	2	5	7	7	
76-77	Ind (WHA)	9	1	1	2	4	
78-79	Que (WHA)	4	0	0	0	0	
WHA Totals		34	10	13	23	52	

LECUYER, Douglas J. 5-9 180 LW
B. Wainwright, Alta., Mar. 10, 1958

SSN	TEAM	GP	G	A	PTS.	PIM	+/-
78-79	Chi	2	0	1	1	0	-1
79-80	Chi	53	3	10	13	59	-7
80-81	Chi-Winn	59	6	17	23	107	-29
82-83	Pitt	12	1	4	5	12	-2
Totals		126	11	31	42	178	-39

LEDINGHAM, Walter Norman 5-11 180 LW
B. Weyburn, Sask., Oct. 26, 1950

SSN	TEAM	GP	G	A	PTS.	PIM	+/-
72-73	Chi	9	0	1	1	4	0
74-75	NYI	2	0	1	1	0	-3
76-77	NYI	4	0	0	0	0	-1
Totals		15	0	2	2	4	-4

***LeDUC, Albert (Battleship)** 5-9 180 D
B. Valleyfield, Que., Nov. 22, 1902

SSN	TEAM	GP	G	A	PTS.	PIM	+/-
25-26	Mont	32	10	3	13	62	
26-27	Mont	43	5	2	7	62	
27-28	Mont	43	8	5	13	73	
28-29	Mont	43	9	2	11	79	
29-30	Mont	44	6	8	14	90	
30-31	Mont	44	8	6	14	82	
31-32	Mont	41	5	3	8	60	
32-33	Mont	48	5	3	8	62	
33-34	Ott-NYR	42	1	3	4	40	
34-35	Mont	4	0	0	0	4	
Totals		384	57	35	92	614	

Playoffs

SSN	TEAM	GP	G	A	PTS.	PIM	+/-
26-27	Mont	4	0	0	0	2	
27-28	Mont	2	1	0	1	5	
28-29	Mont	3	1	0	1	4	
29-30	Mont	6	1	3	4	8	
30-31	Mont	7	0	2	2	9	
31-32	Mont	4	1	1	2	2	
32-33	Mont	2	1	0	1	2	
33-34	NYR	2	0	0	0	0	
Totals		30	5	6	11	32	

LeDUC, Richard Henri 5-11 170 C
B. Ile Perrot, Que., Aug. 24, 1951

SSN	TEAM	GP	G	A	PTS.	PIM	+/-
72-73	Bos	5	1	1	2	2	-1
73-74	Bos	28	3	3	6	12	+3
74-75	Clev (WHA)	78	34	31	65	122	
75-76	Clev (WHA)	79	36	22	58	76	
76-77	Cin (WHA)	81	52	55	107	75	
77-78	Cin-Ind (WHA)	82	37	46	83	82	
78-79	Ind-Que (WHA)	74	35	41	76	44	
79-80	Que	75	21	27	48	49	-35
80-81	Que	22	3	7	10	6	+2
NHL Totals		130	28	38	66	69	-31
WHA Totals		394	194	195	389	399	

Playoffs

SSN	TEAM	GP	G	A	PTS.	PIM	+/-
73-74	Bos	5	0	0	0	9	
74-75	Clev (WHA)	5	0	2	2	2	
75-76	Clev (WHA)	3	2	1	3	2	
76-77	Cin (WHA)	4	1	3	4	16	
78-79	Que (WHA)	4	0	2	2	0	
NHL Totals		5	0	0	0	9	
WHA Totals		16	3	8	11	20	

LEDYARD, Grant 6-2 200 D
B. Winnipeg, Man., Nov. 19, 1961

SSN	TEAM	GP	G	A	PTS.	PIM	+/-
84-85	NYR	42	8	12	20	53	+8
85-86	NYR-LA	79	9	27	36	98	-29
86-87	LA	67	14	23	37	93	-40
87-88	LA-Wash	44	5	10	16	66	-11
88-89	Wash-Buf	74	4	16	20	51	+2
89-90	Buf	67	2	13	15	37	+2
90-91	Buf	60	8	23	31	46	+13
91-92	Buf	50	5	16	21	45	-4
92-93	Buf	50	2	14	16	45	-2
93-94	Dal	84	9	37	46	42	+7
94-95	Dal	38	5	13	18	20	+6
95-96	Dal	73	5	19	24	20	-15
96-97	Dal	67	1	15	16	61	+31
97-98	Van-Bos	71	4	20	24	20	-4
98-99	Bos	47	4	8	12	33	-8
Totals		914	85	266	351	730	-43

Playoffs

SSN	TEAM	GP	G	A	PTS.	PIM	+/-
84-85	NYR	3	0	2	2	4	
86-87	LA	5	0	0	0	10	
87-88	Wash	14	1	0	1	30	
88-89	Buf	5	1	2	3	2	
90-91	Buf	6	3	3	6	10	
92-93	Buf	8	0	0	0	8	
93-94	Dal	9	1	2	3	6	
94-95	Dal	3	0	0	0	2	
96-97	Dal	7	0	2	2	0	
97-98	Bos	6	0	0	0	2	
98-99	Bos	2	0	0	0	2	
Totals		68	6	11	17	76	

LEE, Edward 6-2 180 RW
B. Rochester, N.Y., Dec. 17, 1961

SSN	TEAM	GP	G	A	PTS.	PIM	+/-
84-85	Que	2	0	0	0	5	-4

LEE, Peter John 5-9 180 RW
B. Ellesmere, England, Jan. 2, 1956

SSN	TEAM	GP	G	A	PTS.	PIM	+/-
77-78	Pitt	60	5	13	18	19	-11
78-79	Pitt	80	32	26	58	24	-13
79-80	Pitt	74	16	29	45	20	-13
80-81	Pitt	80	30	34	64	86	0
81-82	Pitt	74	18	16	34	98	-8
82-83	Pitt	63	13	13	26	10	-9
Totals		431	114	131	245	257	-54

Playoffs

SSN	TEAM	GP	G	A	PTS.	PIM	+/-
78-79	Pitt	7	0	3	3	0	
79-80	Pitt	4	0	1	1	0	
80-81	Pitt	5	0	4	4	4	
81-82	Pitt	3	0	0	0	0	
Totals		19	0	8	8	4	

***LEE, Robert** D

SSN	TEAM	GP	G	A	PTS.	PIM	+/-
42-43	Mont	1	0	0	0	0	

LEEMAN, Gary 5-11 175 RW
B. Toronto, Ont., Feb. 19, 1964

SSN	TEAM	GP	G	A	PTS.	PIM	+/-
83-84	Tor	52	4	8	12	31	-14
84-85	Tor	53	5	26	31	72	-12
85-86	Tor	53	9	23	32	20	-1
86-87	Tor	80	21	31	52	66	-26
87-88	Tor	80	30	31	61	62	-6
88-89	Tor	61	32	43	75	66	+4
89-90	Tor	80	51	44	95	63	+4
90-91	Tor	52	17	12	29	39	-25
91-92	Tor-Calg	63	9	20	29	71	-12
92-93	Calg-Mont	50	15	17	32	24	+14
93-94	Mont	31	4	11	15	17	+5
94-95	Van	10	2	0	2	0	-3
96-97	StL	2	0	1	1	0	0
Totals		667	199	267	466	531	-70

Playoffs

SSN	TEAM	GP	G	A	PTS.	PIM	+/-
82-83	Tor	2	0	0	0	0	
85-86	Tor	10	2	10	12	2	
86-87	Tor	5	0	1	1	14	
87-88	Tor	2	2	0	2	2	
89-90	Tor	5	3	3	6	16	
92-93	Mont	11	1	2	3	2	
93-94	Mont	1	0	0	0	0	
Totals		36	8	16	24	36	

LEETCH, Brian 5-11 190 D
B. Corpus Christi, Tex., Mar. 3, 1968

SSN	TEAM	GP	G	A	PTS.	PIM	+/-
87-88	NYR	17	2	12	14	0	+5
88-89	NYR	68	23	48	71	50	+8
89-90	NYR	72	11	45	56	26	-18
90-91	NYR	80	16	72	88	42	+2
91-92	NYR	80	22	80	102	26	+25
92-93	NYR	36	6	30	36	26	+2
93-94	NYR	84	23	56	79	67	+28
94-95	NYR	48	9	32	41	18	0
95-96	NYR	82	15	70	85	30	+12
96-97	NYR	82	20	58	78	40	+31
97-98	NYR	76	17	33	50	32	-36
98-99	NYR	82	13	42	55	42	-7
Totals		807	177	578	755	399	+52

Playoffs

SSN	TEAM	GP	G	A	PTS.	PIM	+/-
88-89	NYR	4	3	2	5	2	
90-91	NYR	6	1	3	4	0	
91-92	NYR	13	4	11	15	4	
93-94	NYR	23	11	23	34	6	
94-95	NYR	10	6	8	14	8	
95-96	NYR	11	1	6	7	4	
96-97	NYR	15	2	8	10	6	
Totals		82	28	61	89	30	

LEFEVRE, Patrice 5-6 160 RW
B. Montreal, Que., June 28, 1967

SSN	TEAM	GP	G	A	PTS.	PIM	+/-
98-99	Wash	3	0	0	0	2	-2

LEFEBVRE, Sylvain 6-2 204 D
B. Richmond, Que., Oct. 14, 1967

SSN	TEAM	GP	G	A	PTS.	PIM	+/-
89-90	Mont	68	3	10	13	61	+18
90-91	Mont	63	5	18	23	30	-11
91-92	Mont	69	3	14	17	91	+9
92-93	Tor	81	2	12	14	90	+8
93-94	Tor	84	2	9	11	79	+33
94-95	Que	48	2	11	13	17	+13
95-96	Col A	75	5	11	16	49	+26
96-97	Col A	71	2	11	13	30	+12
97-98	Col A	81	0	10	10	48	+2
98-99	Col A	76	2	18	20	48	+18
Totals		716	26	124	150	543	+128

Playoffs

SSN	TEAM	GP	G	A	PTS.	PIM	+/-
89-90	Mont	6	0	0	0	2	
90-91	Mont	11	1	0	1	6	
91-92	Mont	2	0	0	0	2	
92-93	Tor	21	3	3	6	20	
93-94	Tor	18	0	3	3	16	
94-95	Que	6	0	2	2	2	
95-96	Col A	22	0	5	5	12	
96-97	Col A	17	0	0	0	25	
97-98	Col A	7	0	0	0	4	
Totals		110	4	13	17	89	

LEFLEY, Bryan Andrew 6-0 184 D
B. Grosse Isle, Man., Oct. 18, 1948

SSN	TEAM	GP	G	A	PTS.	PIM	+/-
72-73	NYI	63	3	7	10	56	-39
73-74	NYI	7	0	0	0	0	0
74-75	KC	29	0	3	3	6	-23
76-77	Col	58	0	6	6	27	-15
77-78	Col	71	4	13	17	12	-4
Totals		228	7	29	36	101	-81

Playoffs

SSN	TEAM	GP	G	A	PTS.	PIM	+/-
77-78	Col	2	0	0	0	0	

LEFLEY, Charles Thomas (Chuck) 6-2 185 LW
B. Winnipeg, Man., Jan. 20, 1950

SSN	TEAM	GP	G	A	PTS.	PIM	+/-
70-71	Mont	1	0	0	0	0	-1
71-72	Mont	16	0	2	2	0	-1
72-73	Mont	65	21	25	46	22	+35

SSN	TEAM	GP	G	A	PTS.	PIM	+/-
73–74	Mont	74	23	31	54	34	+9
74–75	Mont–StL	75	24	28	52	28	+6
75–76	StL	75	43	42	85	41	+15
76–77	StL	71	11	30	41	12	-15
79–80	StL	28	6	6	12	0	+5
80–81	StL	2	0	0	0	0	0
Totals		407	128	164	292	137	+53

Playoffs

70–71	Mont	20	0	1	1	0	
72–73	Mont	17	3	5	8	6	
73–74	Mont	6	0	1	1	0	
74–75	StL	2	0	0	0	2	
75–76	StL	2	2	1	3	0	
76–77	StL	1	0	1	1	2	
Totals		48	5	9	14	10	

*LEGER, Roger 5–11 210 D
B. L'Annonciation, Que., Mar. 26, 1919

43–44	NYR	7	1	2	3	2	
46–47	Mont	49	4	18	22	12	
47–48	Mont	48	4	14	18	26	
48–49	Mont	28	6	7	13	10	
49–50	Mont	55	3	12	15	21	
Totals		187	18	53	71	71	

Playoffs

46–47	Mont	11	0	6	6	10	
48–49	Mont	5	0	1	1	2	
49–50	Mont	4	0	0	0	2	
Totals		20	0	7	7	14	

LEGGE, Barry Graham 6–0 186 D
B. Winnipeg, Man., Oct. 22, 1954

74–75	Balt (WHA)	36	3	18	21	20	
75–76	Ott–Clev (WHA)	75	6	15	21	37	
76–77	Minn–Cin (WHA)	76	7	22	29	39	
77–78	Cin (WHA)	78	7	17	24	114	
78–79	Cin (WHA)	80	3	8	11	131	
79–80	Que	31	0	3	3	18	+2
80–81	Winn	38	0	6	6	69	-33
81–82	Winn	38	1	2	3	57	-6
NHL Totals		107	1	11	12	144	-37
WHA Totals		345	26	80	106	341	

Playoffs

75–76	Clev (WHA)	3	0	1	1	12	
76–77	Cin (WHA)	4	0	0	0	0	
78–79	Cin (WHA)	3	0	4	4	0	
WHA Totals		10	0	5	5	12	

LEGGE, Norman Randall (Randy) 5–11 184 D
B. Newmarket, Ont., Dec. 16, 1945

72–73	NYR	12	0	2	2	2	0
74–75	Balt (WHA)	78	1	14	15	69	
75–76	Winn–Clev (WHA)	45	1	8	9	28	
76–77	SD (WHA)	69	1	9	10	69	
NHL Totals		12	0	2	2	2	0
WHA Totals		192	3	31	34	166	

Playoffs

75–76	Clev (WHA)	3	0	0	0	0	
76–77	SD (WHA)	7	0	0	0	18	
WHA Totals		10	0	0	0	18	

LEGWAND, David 6–1 175 C
B. Detroit, Mich., Aug. 17, 1980

98–99	Nash	1	0	0	0	0	0

LEHMANN, Tommy 6–1 185 C
B. Solna, Sweden, Feb. 3, 1964

87–88	Bos	9	1	3	4	6	0
88–89	Bos	26	4	2	6	10	-7
89–90	Edm	1	0	0	0	0	+1
Totals		36	5	5	10	16	-6

LEHTINEN, Jere 6–0 185 RW
B. Espoo, Finland, June 24, 1973

95–96	Dal	57	6	22	28	16	+5
96–97	Dal	63	16	27	43	2	+26
97–98	Dal	72	23	19	42	20	+19
98–99	Dal	74	20	32	52	18	+29
Totals		266	65	100	165	56	+79

Playoffs

96–97	Dal	7	2	2	4	0	
97–98	Dal	12	3	5	8	2	
98–99	Dal	23	10	3	13	2	
Totals		42	15	10	25	4	

LEHTO, Petteri 5–11 195 D
B. Turku, Finland, Mar. 23, 1961

84–85	Pitt	6	0	0	0	4	-4

LEHTONEN, Antero 6–0 185 LW
B. Tampere, Finland, Apr. 12, 1954

79–80	Wash	65	9	12	21	14	-4

LEHVONEN, Henri 6–0 185 D
B. Sarnia, Ont., Aug. 26, 1950

74–75	KC	4	0	0	0	0	+4

LEIER, Edward 5–11 165 C
B. Poland, Nov. 3, 1927

49–50	Chi	5	0	1	1	0	
50–51	Chi	11	2	0	2	2	
Totals		16	2	1	3	2	

LEINONEN, Mikko 6–0 175 C
B. Tampere, Finland, July 15, 1955

81–82	NYR	53	11	20	31	18	+2
82–83	NYR	78	17	34	51	23	+12
83–84	NYR	28	3	23	26	28	+4
84–85	Wash	3	0	1	1	2	+1
Totals		162	31	78	109	71	+19

Playoffs

81–82	NYR	7	1	6	7	20	
82–83	NYR	7	1	3	4	4	
83–84	NYR	5	0	2	2	4	
84–85	Wash	1	0	0	0	0	
Totals		20	2	11	13	28	

LEITER, Ken 6–1 195 D
B. Detroit, Mich., Apr. 19, 1961

84–85	NYI	5	0	2	2	2	0
85–86	NYI	9	1	1	2	6	+1
86–87	NYI	74	9	20	29	30	+2
87–88	NYI	51	4	13	17	24	+18
89–90	Minn	4	0	0	0	0	-2
Totals		143	14	36	50	62	+19

Playoffs

86–87	NYI	11	0	5	5	6	
87–88	NYI	4	0	1	1	2	
Totals		15	0	6	6	8	

LEITER, Robert Edward 5–9 164 C
B. Winnipeg, Man., Mar. 22, 1941

62–63	Bos	51	9	13	22	34	
63–64	Bos	56	6	13	19	43	
64–65	Bos	18	3	1	4	6	
65–66	Bos	9	2	1	3	2	
68–69	Bos	1	0	0	0	0	0
71–72	Pitt	78	14	17	31	18	-25
72–73	Atl	78	26	34	60	19	-12
73–74	Atl	78	26	26	52	10	-4
74–75	Atl	52	10	18	28	8	-15
75–76	Atl	26	2	3	5	4	-9
75–76	Calg (WHA)	51	17	17	34	8	
NHL Totals		447	98	126	224	144	-56
WHA Totals		51	17	17	34	8	

Playoffs

71–72	Pitt	4	3	0	3	0	
73–74	Stl	4	0	0	0	2	
75–76	Calg (WHA)	3	2	0	2	0	
NHL Totals		8	3	0	3	2	
WHA Totals		3	2	0	2	0	

LEMAIRE, Jacques Gerard 5–10 180 C
B. LaSalle, Que., Sept. 7, 1945

67–68	Mont	69	22	20	42	16	+15
68–69	Mont	75	29	34	63	29	+31
69–70	Mont	69	32	28	60	16	+19
70–71	Mont	78	28	28	56	18	0
71–72	Mont	77	32	49	81	26	+37
72–73	Mont	77	44	51	95	16	+59
73–74	Mont	66	29	38	67	10	+4
74–75	Mont	80	36	56	92	20	+25
75–76	Mont	61	20	32	52	20	+26
76–77	Mont	75	34	41	75	22	+70
77–78	Mont	76	36	61	97	14	+54
78–79	Mont	50	24	31	55	10	+9
Totals		853	366	469	835	217	+349

Playoffs

67–68	Mont	13	7	6	13	6	
68–69	Mont	14	4	2	6	6	
70–71	Mont	20	9	10	19	17	
71–72	Mont	6	2	1	3	2	
72–73	Mont	17	7	13	20	2	
73–74	Mont	6	0	4	4	2	
74–75	Mont	11	5	7	12	4	
75–76	Mont	13	3	3	6	2	
76–77	Mont	14	7	12	19	6	
77–78	Mont	15	6	8	14	10	
78–79	Mont	16	11	12	23	6	
Totals		145	61	78	139	63	

LEMAY, Maurice (Moe) 5–11 185 LW
B. Saskatoon, Sask., Feb. 18, 1962

81–82	Van	5	1	2	3	0	+1
82–83	Van	44	11	9	20	41	-6
83–84	Van	56	12	18	30	38	+4
84–85	Van	74	21	31	52	68	-11
85–86	Van	48	16	15	31	92	-14
86–87	Van–Edm	62	10	19	29	164	0
87–88	Edm–Bos	6	0	0	0	2	-3
88–89	Bos–Winn	22	1	0	1	37	-8
Totals		317	72	94	166	442	-37

Playoffs

83–84	Van	4	0	0	0	12	
86–87	Edm	9	2	1	3	11	
87–88	Bos	15	4	2	6	32	
Totals		28	6	3	9	55	

LEMELIN, Roger Marcel 6–3 215 D
B. Iroquois Falls, Ont., Feb. 6, 1954

74–75	KC	8	0	1	1	6	-9
75–76	KC	11	0	0	0	0	-1
76–77	Col	14	1	1	2	21	-6
77–78	Col	3	0	0	0	0	0
Totals		37	1	2	3	27	-16

LEMIEUX, Alain 6–0 185 C
B. Montreal, Que., May 24, 1961

81–82	StL	3	0	1	1	0	-1
82–83	StL	42	9	25	34	18	-10
83–84	StL	17	4	5	9	6	0
84–85	StL–Que	49	15	13	28	12	+1
85–86	Que	7	0	0	0	2	-1
86–87	Pitt	1	0	0	0	0	-1
Totals		119	28	44	72	38	-12

Playoffs

82–83	StL	4	0	1	1	0	
84–85	Que	14	3	3	6	0	
85–86	Que	1	1	2	3	0	
Totals		19	4	6	10	0	

LEMIEUX, Claude 6–1 215 RW
B. Buckingham, Que., July 16, 1965

83–84	Mont	8	1	1	2	12	-2
84–85	Mont	1	0	1	1	7	+1
85–86	Mont	10	1	2	3	22	-6
86–87	Mont	76	27	26	53	156	0
87–88	Mont	78	31	30	61	137	+16
88–89	Mont	69	29	22	51	136	+14
89–90	Mont	39	8	10	18	106	-8
90–91	NJ	78	30	17	47	105	-8
91–92	NJ	74	41	27	68	109	+9
92–93	NJ	77	30	51	81	155	+3
93–94	NJ	79	18	26	44	86	+13
94–95	NJ	45	6	13	19	86	+2
95–96	Col A	79	39	32	71	117	+14
96–97	Col A	45	11	17	28	43	-4
97–98	Col A	78	26	27	53	115	-7
98–99	Col A	82	27	24	51	102	0
Totals		918	325	326	651	1494	+37

Playoffs

85–86	Mont	20	10	6	16	68	

SSN	TEAM	GP	G	A	PTS.	PIM	+/-
86–87	Mont	17	4	9	13	41	
87–88	Mont	11	3	2	5	20	
88–89	Mont	18	4	3	7	58	
89–90	Mont	11	1	3	4	38	
90–91	NJ	7	4	0	4	34	
91–92	NJ	7	4	3	7	26	
92–93	NJ	5	2	0	2	19	
93–94	NJ	20	7	11	18	44	
94–95	NJ	20	13	3	16	20	
95–96	Col A	19	5	7	12	55	
96–97	Col A	17	13	10	23	32	
97–98	Col A	7	3	3	6	8	
98–99	Col A	19	3	11	14	26	
Totals		198	76	71	147	489	

LEMIEUX, Jacques *6–2 185 F*
B. Matane, Que., Apr. 8, 1943

SSN	TEAM	GP	G	A	PTS.	PIM	+/-
67–68	LA	16	0	3	3	8	+3
69–70	LA	3	0	1	1	0	0
Totals		19	0	4	4	8	+3

Playoffs

SSN	TEAM	GP	G	A	PTS.	PIM
68–69	LA	1	0	0	0	0

LEMIEUX, Jean Louis *6–1 180 D*
B. Noranda, Que., May 31, 1952

SSN	TEAM	GP	G	A	PTS.	PIM	+/-
73–74	Atl	32	3	5	8	6	-4
74–75	Atl	75	3	24	27	19	-3
75–76	Atl–Wash	66	10	23	33	12	-17
76–77	Wash	15	4	4	8	2	-9
77–78	Wash	16	3	7	10	0	-12
Totals		204	23	63	86	39	-45

Playoffs

SSN	TEAM	GP	G	A	PTS.	PIM
73–74	Atl	3	1	1	2	0

LEMIEUX, Jocelyn *5–10 200 RW*
B. Mont–Laurier, Que., Nov. 18, 1967

SSN	TEAM	GP	G	A	PTS.	PIM	+/-
86–87	StL	53	10	8	18	94	+1
87–88	StL	23	1	0	1	42	-5
88–89	Mont	1	0	1	1	0	-1
89–90	Mont–Chi	73	14	13	27	108	-1
90–91	Chi	67	6	7	13	119	-7
91–92	Chi	78	6	10	16	80	-2
92–93	Chi	81	10	21	31	111	+5
93–94	Chi–Hart	82	18	9	27	82	-3
94–95	Hart	41	6	5	11	32	-7
95–96	Hart–NJ–Calg	67	5	7	12	45	-19
96–97	Phoe	2	1	0	1	0	0
97–98	Phoe	30	3	3	6	27	0
Totals		598	80	84	164	740	-39

Playoffs

SSN	TEAM	GP	G	A	PTS.	PIM
86–87	StL	5	0	1	1	6
87–88	StL	5	0	0	0	15
89–90	Chi	18	1	8	9	28
90–91	Chi	4	0	0	0	0
91–92	Chi	18	3	1	4	33
92–93	Chi	4	1	0	1	2
95–96	Calg	4	0	0	0	0
96–97	Phoe	2	0	0	0	4
Totals		60	5	10	15	88

LEMIEUX, Mario *6–4 210 C*
B. Montreal, Que., Oct. 5, 1965

SSN	TEAM	GP	G	A	PTS.	PIM	+/-
84–85	Pitt	73	43	57	100	54	-35
85–86	Pitt	79	48	93	141	43	-6
86–87	Pitt	63	54	53	107	57	+13
87–88	Pitt	77	70	98	168	92	+23
88–89	Pitt	76	85	114	199	100	+41
89–90	Pitt	59	45	78	123	78	-18
90–91	Pitt	26	19	26	45	30	+8
91–92	Pitt	64	44	87	131	94	+27
92–93	Pitt	60	69	91	160	38	+55
93–94	Pitt	22	17	20	37	32	-2
95–96	Pitt	70	69	92	161	54	+10
96–97	Pitt	76	50	72	122	65	+27
Totals		745	613	881	1494	737	+143

Playoffs

SSN	TEAM	GP	G	A	PTS.	PIM
88–89	Pitt	11	12	7	19	16
90–91	Pitt	23	16	28	44	16
91–92	Pitt	15	16	18	34	2
92–93	Pitt	11	8	10	18	10
93–94	Pitt	6	4	3	7	2
95–96	Pitt	18	11	16	27	33
96–97	Pitt	5	3	3	6	4
Totals		89	70	85	155	83

***LEMIEUX, Real Gaston** *5–11 180 LW*
B. Victoriaville, Que., Jan. 3, 1945

SSN	TEAM	GP	G	A	PTS.	PIM	+/-
66–67	Det	1	0	0	0	0	
67–68	LA	74	12	23	35	60	-2
68–69	LA	75	11	29	40	78	-22
69–70	NYR–LA	73	6	10	16	51	0
70–71	LA	43	3	6	9	22	-7
71–72	LA	78	13	25	38	28	-40
72–73	LA	74	5	10	15	19	-1
73–74	LA–NYR–Buf	38	1	1	2	4	-1
Totals		456	51	104	155	262	-73

Playoffs

SSN	TEAM	GP	G	A	PTS.	PIM
67–68	LA	7	1	1	2	0
68–69	LA	11	1	3	4	10
Totals		18	2	4	6	10

LEMIEUX, Richard Bernard (Dick) *5–8 160 C*
B. Temiscamingue So., Que., Apr. 19, 1951

SSN	TEAM	GP	G	A	PTS.	PIM	+/-
71–72	Van	42	7	9	16	4	-13
72–73	Van	78	17	35	52	41	-25
73–74	Van	72	5	17	22	23	-24
74–75	KC	79	10	20	30	64	-35
75–76	KC–Atl	3	0	1	1	0	+2
76–77	Calg (WHA)	33	6	11	17	9	
NHL Totals		274	39	82	121	132	-95
WHA Totals		33	6	11	17	9	

Playoffs

SSN	TEAM	GP	G	A	PTS.	PIM
75–76	Atl	2	0	0	0	0

LEMIEUX, Robert *D*
B. Rochester, NY, Dec. 16, 1944

SSN	TEAM	GP	G	A	PTS.	PIM	+/-
67–68	Oak	19	0	1	1	12	0

LENARDON, Tim *6–2 185 C/LW*
B. Trail, B.C., May 11, 1962

SSN	TEAM	GP	G	A	PTS.	PIM	+/-
86–87	NJ	7	1	1	2	0	-2
89–90	Van	8	1	0	1	4	-2
Totals		15	2	1	3	4	-4

***LEPINE, Alfred (Pit)** *C*
B. St. Anne de Bellevue, Que., July 31, 1901

SSN	TEAM	GP	G	A	PTS.	PIM
25–26	Mont	27	9	1	10	18
26–27	Mont	44	16	1	17	20
27–28	Mont	20	4	1	5	6
28–29	Mont	44	6	1	7	48
29–30	Mont	44	24	9	33	47
30–31	Mont	44	17	7	24	63
31–32	Mont	48	19	11	30	32
32–33	Mont	46	8	8	16	45
33–34	Mont	48	10	8	18	44
34–35	Mont	48	12	19	31	16
35–36	Mont	32	6	10	16	4
36–37	Mont	34	7	8	15	15
37–38	Mont	47	5	14	19	24
Totals		526	143	98	241	382

Playoffs

SSN	TEAM	GP	G	A	PTS.	PIM
26–27	Mont	4	0	0	0	2
27–28	Mont	1	0	0	0	0
28–29	Mont	3	0	0	0	2
29–30	Mont	6	2	2	4	6
30–31	Mont	10	4	2	6	6
31–32	Mont	3	1	0	1	4
32–33	Mont	2	0	0	0	0
33–34	Mont	2	0	0	0	0
34–35	Mont	2	0	0	0	2
36–37	Mont	5	0	1	1	0
37–38	Mont	3	0	0	0	0
Totals		41	7	5	12	26

***LEPINE, Hector (Hec)** *F*

SSN	TEAM	GP	G	A	PTS.	PIM
25–26	Mont	33	5	2	7	2

LEROUX, Francois *6–5 221 D*
B. Ste.–Adele, Que., Apr. 18, 1970

SSN	TEAM	GP	G	A	PTS.	PIM	+/-
88–89	Edm	2	0	0	0	0	+1
89–90	Edm	3	0	1	1	0	-2
90–91	Edm	1	0	2	2	0	+1
91–92	Edm	4	0	0	0	7	-1
92–93	Edm	1	0	0	0	4	0
93–94	Ott	23	0	1	1	70	-4
94–95	Pitt	40	0	2	2	114	+7
95–96	Pitt	66	2	9	11	161	+2
96–97	Pitt	59	0	3	3	81	-3
97–98	Col A	50	1	2	3	140	-3
Totals		249	3	20	23	577	-2

Playoffs

SSN	TEAM	GP	G	A	PTS.	PIM
94–95	Pitt	12	0	2	2	14
95–96	Pitt	18	1	1	2	20
96–97	Pitt	3	0	0	0	0
Totals		33	1	3	4	34

LEROUX, Gaston *F*

SSN	TEAM	GP	G	A	PTS.	PIM
35–36	Mont	2	0	0	0	0

LEROUX, Jean–Yves *6–2 193 LW*
B. Montreal, Que., June 24, 1976

SSN	TEAM	GP	G	A	PTS.	PIM	+/-
96–97	Chi	1	0	1	1	5	+1
97–98	Chi	66	6	7	13	55	-2
98–99	Chi	40	3	5	8	21	-7
Totals		107	9	13	22	76	-8

LESCHYSHYN, Curtis *6–1 205 D*
B. Thompson, Man., Sept. 21, 1969

SSN	TEAM	GP	G	A	PTS.	PIM	+/-
88–89	Que	71	4	9	13	71	-32
89–90	Que	68	2	6	8	44	-41
90–91	Que	55	3	7	10	49	-19
91–92	Que	42	5	12	17	42	-28
92–93	Que	82	9	23	32	61	+25
93–94	Que	72	5	17	22	65	-2
94–95	Que	44	2	13	15	20	+29
95–96	Col A	77	4	15	19	73	+32
96–97	Col A–Wash–Hart	77	4	18	22	38	-18
97–98	Car	73	2	10	12	45	-2
98–99	Car	65	2	7	9	50	-1
Totals		726	42	137	179	558	-67

Playoffs

SSN	TEAM	GP	G	A	PTS.	PIM
92–93	Que	6	1	1	2	6
94–95	Que	3	0	1	1	4
95–96	Col A	17	1	2	3	8
98–99	Car	6	0	0	0	6
Totals		33	2	4	6	24

LESIEUR, Arthur *5–10 191 D*
B. Fall River, Mass., Sept. 13, 1907

SSN	TEAM	GP	G	A	PTS.	PIM
28–29	Mont–Chi	17	0	0	0	0
30–31	Mont	21	2	0	2	14
31–32	Mont	24	1	2	3	12
35–36	Mont	38	1	0	1	24
Totals		100	4	2	6	50

Playoffs

SSN	TEAM	GP	G	A	PTS.	PIM
30–31	Mont	10	0	0	0	4
31–32	Mont	4	0	0	0	0
Totals		14	0	0	0	4

LESSARD, Rick *6–2 200 D*
B. Timmins, Ont., Jan. 9, 1968

SSN	TEAM	GP	G	A	PTS.	PIM	+/-
88–89	Calg	6	0	1	1	2	-2
90–91	Calg	1	0	1	1	0	-1
91–92	SJ	8	0	2	2	16	-4
Totals		15	0	4	4	18	-7

LESUK, William Anton *5–9 187 LW*
B. Moose Jaw, Sask., Nov. 1, 1946

SSN	TEAM	GP	G	A	PTS.	PIM	+/-
68–69	Bos	5	0	1	1	0	+2
69–70	Bos	3	0	0	0	0	+1
70–71	Phil	78	17	19	36	81	-5
71–72	Phil–LA	72	11	16	27	45	-12
72–73	LA	67	6	14	20	90	-2
73–74	LA	35	2	1	3	32	-4
74–75	Wash	79	8	11	19	77	-34
75–76	Winn (WHA)	81	15	21	36	92	
76–77	Winn (WHA)	78	14	27	41	85	
77–78	Winn (WHA)	80	9	18	27	48	
78–79	Winn (WHA)	79	17	15	32	44	
79–80	Winn	49	0	1	1	43	-15
NHL Totals		388	44	63	107	368	-69
WHA Totals		318	55	81	136	269	

Playoffs

SSN	TEAM	GP	G	A	PTS.	PIM
68–69	Bos	1	0	0	0	0
69–70	Bos	2	0	0	0	0
70–71	Phil	4	1	0	1	8
73–74	LA	2	0	0	0	4
75–76	Winn (WHA)	13	2	2	4	8

SSN	TEAM	GP	G	A	PTS.	PIM	+/-
76–77	Winn (WHA)	18	2	1	3	22	
77–78	Winn (WHA)	9	2	5	7	12	
78–79	Winn (WHA)	10	1	3	4	6	
NHL Totals		9	1	0	1	12	
WHA Totals		50	7	11	18	48	

*LESWICK, Anthony Joseph (Tough Tony)
5–6 160 LW
B. Humboldt, Sask., Mar. 17, 1923

SSN	TEAM	GP	G	A	PTS.	PIM	+/-
45–46	NYR	50	15	9	24	9	
46–47	NYR	59	27	14	41	51	
47–48	NYR	60	24	16	40	76	
48–49	NYR	60	13	14	27	70	
49–50	NYR	69	19	25	44	70	
50–51	NYR	70	15	11	26	112	
51–52	Det	70	9	10	19	93	
52–53	Det	70	15	12	27	87	
53–54	Det	70	6	18	24	90	
54–55	Det	70	10	17	27	137	
55–56	Chi	70	11	11	22	71	
57–58	Det	22	1	2	3	2	
Totals		740	165	159	324	868	

Playoffs

47–48	NYR	6	3	2	5	8	
49–50	NYR	12	2	4	6	12	
51–52	Det	8	3	1	4	22	
52–53	Det	6	1	0	1	11	
53–54	Det	12	3	1	4	18	
54–55	Det	11	1	2	3	20	
57–58	Det	4	0	0	0	0	
Totals		59	13	10	23	91	

LESWICK, Jack F

33–34	Chi	47	1	7	8	16	

LESWICK, Peter John 5–6 145 RW
B. Saskatoon, Sask., July 12, 1918

36–37	NYA	1	1	0	1	0	
44–45	Bos	2	0	0	0	0	
Totals		3	1	0	1	0	

LETOWSKI, Trevor 5–10 170 C
B. Thunder Bay, Ont., April 5, 1977

98–99	Phoe	14	2	2	4	2	+1

LEVANDOSKI, Joseph Thomas 5–10 185 RW
B. Cobalt, Ont., Mar. 17, 1921

46–47	NYR	8	1	1	2	0	

LEVEILLE, Normand 5–10 175 LW
B. Montreal, Que., Jan. 10, 1963

81–82	Bos	66	14	19	33	49	+16
82–83	Bos	9	3	6	9	0	+1
Totals		75	17	25	42	49	+17

LEVEQUE, Guy Scott 5–11 180 C
B. Kingston, Ont., Dec. 28, 1972

92–93	LA	12	2	1	3	19	-4
93–94	LA	5	0	1	1	2	+1
Totals		17	2	2	4	21	-3

LEVER, Donald Richard 5–11 185 C
B. South Porcupine, Ont., Nov. 14, 1952

72–73	Van	78	10	26	38	49	-27
73–74	Van	78	23	25	48	28	-16
74–75	Van	80	38	30	68	49	-13
75–76	Van	80	25	40	65	93	-2
76–77	Van	80	27	30	57	28	-8
77–78	Van	75	17	32	49	58	-29
78–79	Van	71	23	21	44	17	-41
79–80	Van–Atl	79	35	33	68	36	-8
80–81	Calg	62	26	31	57	56	+21
81–82	Calg–Col	82	30	39	69	26	-24
82–83	NJ	79	23	30	53	68	-25
83–84	NJ	70	14	19	33	44	-21
84–85	NJ	67	10	8	18	31	-29
85–86	Buf	29	7	1	8	6	-5
86–87	Buf	10	3	2	5	4	-3
Totals		1020	313	367	680	593	-228

Playoffs

74–75	Van	5	0	1	1	4	
75–76	Van	2	0	0	0	0	
78–79	Van	3	2	1	3	2	
79–80	Atl	4	1	1	2	0	
80–81	Calg	16	4	7	11	20	
Totals		30	7	10	17	26	

LEVIE, Craig Dean 5–11 190 D
B. Calgary, Alta., Aug. 17, 1959

81–82	Winn	40	4	9	13	48	+4
82–83	Winn	22	4	5	9	31	-3
83–84	Minn	37	6	13	19	44	+9
84–85	StL	61	6	23	29	33	+2
85–86	Minn	14	2	2	4	8	-5
86–87	Van	9	0	1	1	13	+3
Totals		183	22	53	75	177	+10

Playoffs

83–84	Minn	15	2	3	5	32	
84–85	StL	1	0	0	0	0	
Totals		16	2	3	5	32	

LEVINS, Scott 6–4 210 C/RW
B. Spokane, Wash., Jan. 30, 1970

92–93	Winn	9	0	1	1	18	-2
93–94	Fla–Ott	62	8	11	19	162	-26
94–95	Ott	24	5	6	11	51	+4
95–96	Ott	27	0	2	2	80	-3
97–98	Phoe	2	0	0	0	5	-1
Totals		124	13	20	33	316	-28

*LEVINSKY, Alexander (Mine Boy) 5–10 184 D
B. Syracuse, N.Y., Feb. 2, 1910

30–31	Tor	8	0	1	1	2	
31–32	Tor	47	5	5	10	29	
32–33	Tor	48	5	11	16	61	
33–34	Tor	47	5	11	16	38	
34–35	NYR–Chi	44	3	8	11	22	
35–36	Chi	48	1	7	8	69	
36–37	Chi	48	0	8	8	32	
37–38	Chi	48	3	2	5	18	
38–39	Chi	29	1	3	4	16	
Totals		367	23	56	79	287	

Playoffs

30–31	Tor	2	0	0	0	0	
31–32	Tor	7	0	0	0	6	
32–33	Tor	9	1	0	1	14	
33–34	Tor	5	0	0	0	0	
34–35	Chi	2	0	0	0	0	
35–36	Chi	2	0	1	1	0	
37–38	Chi	7	1	0	1	0	
Totals		34	2	1	3	20	

LEVO, Tapio 6–2 200 D
B. Pori, Finland, Sept. 24, 1955

81–82	Col	34	9	13	22	14	-13
82–83	NJ	73	7	40	47	22	-41
Totals		107	16	53	69	36	-54

LEWICKI, Daniel 5–9 165 LW
B. Fort William, Ont., Mar. 12, 1931

50–51	Tor	61	16	18	34	26	
51–52	Tor	51	4	9	13	26	
52–53	Tor	4	1	3	4	2	
53–54	Tor	7	0	1	1	12	
54–55	NYR	70	29	24	53	8	
55–56	NYR	70	18	27	45	26	
56–57	NYR	70	18	20	38	47	
57–58	NYR	70	11	19	30	26	
58–59	Chi	58	8	14	22	4	
Totals		461	105	135	240	177	

Playoffs

50–51	Tor	9	0	0	0	0	
55–56	NYR	5	0	3	3	0	
56–57	NYR	5	0	1	1	2	
57–58	NYR	6	0	0	0	6	
58–59	Chi	3	0	0	0	0	
Totals		28	0	4	4	8	

LEWIS, David Rodney 6–2 205 D
B. Kindersley, Sask., July 3, 1953

73–74	NYI	66	2	15	17	58	-7
74–75	NYI	78	5	14	19	98	+8
75–76	NYI	73	0	19	19	54	+29
76–77	NYI	79	4	24	28	44	+29
77–78	NYI	77	3	11	14	58	+32
78–79	NYI	79	5	18	23	43	+43
79–80	NYI–LA	73	6	17	23	66	+13
80–81	LA	67	1	12	13	98	+25
81–82	LA	64	1	13	14	75	-19
82–83	LA	79	2	10	12	53	-22
83–84	NJ	66	2	5	7	63	-19
84–85	NJ	74	3	9	12	78	-29
85–86	NJ	69	0	15	15	81	0
86–87	Det	58	2	5	7	66	+12
87–88	Det	6	0	0	0	18	-3
Totals		1008	36	187	223	953	+92

Playoffs

74–75	NYI	17	0	1	1	28	
75–76	NYI	13	0	1	1	44	
76–77	NYI	12	1	6	7	4	
77–78	NYI	7	0	1	1	11	
78–79	NYI	10	0	0	0	4	
79–80	LA	4	0	1	1	2	
80–81	LA	4	0	2	2	4	
81–82	LA	10	0	4	4	36	
86–87	Det	14	0	4	4	10	
Totals		91	1	20	21	143	

LEWIS, Douglas 5–8 155 LW
B. Winnipeg, Man., Mar. 3, 1921

46–47	Mont	3	0	0	0	0	

*LEWIS, Herbert A. 5–9 160 LW
B. Calgary, Alta., Apr. 17, 1907

28–29	Det	37	9	5	14	33	
29–30	Det	44	20	11	31	36	
30–31	Det	44	15	6	21	38	
31–32	Det	48	5	14	19	21	
32–33	Det	48	20	14	34	20	
33–34	Det	43	16	15	31	15	
34–35	Det	48	16	27	43	26	
35–36	Det	45	14	23	37	25	
36–37	Det	45	14	18	32	14	
37–38	Det	42	13	18	31	12	
38–39	Det	39	6	10	16	8	
Totals		483	148	161	309	248	

Playoffs

31–32	Det	2	0	0	0	0	
32–33	Det	4	1	0	1	0	
33–34	Det	9	5	2	7	2	
35–36	Det	7	2	3	5	0	
36–37	Det	10	4	3	7	4	
38–39	Det	6	1	2	3	0	
Totals		38	13	10	23	6	

LEWIS, Robert Dale 6–0 190 LW
B. Edmonton, Alta., July 28, 1952

75–76	NYR	8	0	0	0	0	0

LEY, Richard Norman (Rick) 5–9 185 D
B. Orillia, Ont., Nov. 2, 1948

68–69	Tor	38	1	11	12	39	+2
69–70	Tor	48	2	13	15	102	-16
70–71	Tor	76	4	16	20	151	+11
71–72	Tor	67	1	14	15	124	+3
72–73	NE (WHA)	76	3	27	30	108	
73–74	NE (WHA)	72	6	35	41	148	
74–75	NE (WHA)	62	6	36	42	50	
75–76	NE (WHA)	67	8	30	38	78	
76–77	NE (WHA)	55	2	21	23	102	
77–78	NE (WHA)	73	3	41	44	95	
78–79	NE (WHA)	73	7	20	27	135	
79–80	Hart	65	4	16	20	92	+2
80–81	Hart	16	0	2	2	20	-13
NHL Totals		310	12	72	84	528	-11
WHA Totals		478	35	210	245	716	

Playoffs

68–69	Tor	3	0	0	0	9	
70–71	Tor	6	0	2	2	4	
71–72	Tor	5	0	0	0	7	
72–73	NE (WHA)	15	3	7	10	24	
73–74	NE (WHA)	7	1	5	6	18	
74–75	NE (WHA)	6	1	1	2	32	
75–76	NE (WHA)	17	1	4	5	49	
76–77	NE (WHA)	5	0	4	4	4	
77–78	NE (WHA)	14	1	8	9	4	
78–79	NE (WHA)	9	0	4	4	11	
NHL Totals		14	0	2	2	20	
WHA Totals		73	7	33	40	142	

SSN	TEAM	GP	G	A	PTS.	PIM	+/-

LIBA, Igor *6–0 192 LW*
B. Kosice, Czechoslovakia, Nov. 4, 1960

SSN	TEAM	GP	G	A	PTS.	PIM	+/-
88–89	NYR-LA	37	7	18	25	36	-3

Playoffs

| 88–89 | LA | 2 | 0 | 0 | 0 | 2 | |

LIBBY, Jeff *6–3 215 D*
B. Waterville, Me., Mar. 1, 1974

| 97–98 | NYI | 1 | 0 | 0 | 0 | 0 | 0 |

LIBETT, Lynn Nicholas (Nick) *6–1 195 LW*
B. Stratford, Ont., Dec. 9, 1945

67–68	Det	22	2	1	3	12	-13
68–69	Det	75	10	14	24	34	-16
69–70	Det	76	20	20	40	39	+9
70–71	Det	78	16	13	29	25	-38
71–72	Det	77	31	22	53	50	+7
72–73	Det	78	19	34	53	54	+1
73–74	Det	67	24	24	48	37	-25
74–75	Det	80	23	28	51	39	-41
75–76	KC	80	20	26	46	71	-9
76–77	Det	80	14	27	41	25	-25
77–78	Det	80	23	22	45	46	-3
78–79	Det	68	15	19	34	20	+4
79–80	Pitt	78	14	12	26	14	-19
80–81	Pitt	43	6	6	12	14	+2
Totals		982	237	268	505	472	-168

Playoffs

69–70	Det	4	2	0	2	2	
77–78	Det	7	3	1	4	0	
79–80	Pitt	5	1	1	2	0	
Totals		16	6	2	8	2	

LICARI, Anthony *5–7 147 RW*
B. Ottawa, Ont., Apr. 9, 1921

| 46–47 | Det | 9 | 0 | 1 | 1 | 0 | |

LIDDINGTON, Robert Allen *6–0 175 LW*
B. Calgary, Alta., Sept. 15, 1948

70–71	Tor	11	0	1	1	2	-2
72–73	Chi (WHA)	78	20	11	31	24	
73–74	Chi (WHA)	73	26	21	47	20	
74–75	Chi (WHA)	78	23	18	41	27	
75–76	Ott-Hou (WHA)	37	7	8	15	16	
76–77	Phoe (WHA)	80	20	24	44	28	
NHL Totals		11	0	1	1	2	-2
WHA Totals		346	96	82	178	115	

Playoffs

| 73–74 | Chi (WHA) | 18 | 6 | 5 | 11 | 11 | |

LIDSTER, Doug *6–1 190 D*
B. Kamloops, B.C., Oct. 18, 1960

83–84	Van	8	0	0	0	4	-7
84–85	Van	78	6	24	30	55	-11
85–86	Van	78	12	16	28	56	-12
86–87	Van	80	12	51	63	40	-35
87–88	Van	64	4	32	36	105	-19
88–89	Van	63	5	17	22	78	-4
89–90	Van	80	8	28	36	36	-16
90–91	Van	78	6	32	38	77	-6
91–92	Van	66	6	23	29	39	+9
92–93	Van	71	6	19	25	36	+9
93–94	NYR	34	0	2	2	33	-12
94–95	StL	37	2	7	9	12	+9
95–96	NYR	59	5	9	14	50	+11
96–97	NYR	48	3	4	7	24	+10
97–98	NYR	36	0	4	4	24	+2
98–99	Dal	17	0	0	0	10	0
Totals		897	75	268	343	679	-72

Playoffs

83–85	Van	2	0	1	1	0	
85–86	Van	3	0	1	1	2	
88–89	Van	7	1	1	2	9	
90–91	Van	6	0	2	2	6	
91–92	Van	11	1	2	3	11	
92–93	Van	12	0	3	3	8	
93–94	NYR	9	2	0	2	10	
94–95	StL	4	0	0	0	2	
95–96	NYR	7	1	0	1	6	
96–97	NYR	15	1	5	6	8	
98–99	Dal	4	0	0	0	2	
Totals		80	6	15	21	64	

LIDSTROM, Nicklas *6–2 185 D*
B. Vasteras, Sweden, Apr. 28, 1970

91–92	Det	80	11	49	60	22	+36
92–93	Det	84	7	34	41	28	+7
93–94	Det	84	10	46	56	26	+43
94–95	Det	43	10	16	26	6	+15
95–96	Det	81	17	50	67	20	+29
96–97	Det	79	15	42	57	30	+11
97–98	Det	80	17	42	59	18	+22
98–99	Det	81	14	43	57	14	+14
Totals		612	101	322	423	164	+177

Playoffs

91–92	Det	11	1	2	3	0	
92–93	Det	7	1	0	1	0	
93–94	Det	7	3	2	5	0	
94–95	Det	18	4	12	16	8	
95–96	Det	19	5	9	14	10	
96–97	Det	20	2	6	8	2	
97–98	Det	22	6	13	19	8	
98–99	Det	10	2	9	11	4	
Totals		114	24	53	77	32	

LILLEY, John *5–9 170 RW*
B. Wakefield, Mass., Aug. 3, 1972

93–94	Ana	13	1	6	7	8	+1
94–95	Ana	9	2	2	4	5	+2
95–96	Ana	1	0	0	0	0	-1
Totals		23	3	8	11	13	+2

LIND, Juha *5–11 180 LW*
B. Helsinki, Finland, Jan. 22, 1974

| 97–98 | Dal | 39 | 2 | 3 | 5 | 6 | +4 |

Playoffs

| 97–98 | Dal | 15 | 2 | 2 | 4 | 8 | |

LINDBERG, Chris *6–1 190 LW*
B. Fort Frances, Ont., Apr. 16, 1967

91–92	Calg	17	2	5	7	17	+3
92–93	Calg	62	9	12	21	18	-3
93–94	Que	37	6	8	14	12	-1
Totals		116	17	25	42	47	-1

Playoffs

| 92–93 | Calg | 2 | 0 | 1 | 1 | 2 | |

LINDBOM, Johan *6–2 216 LW*
B. Alverta, Sweden, July 8, 1971

| 97–98 | NYI | 38 | 1 | 3 | 4 | 28 | +4 |

LINDEN, Jamie *6–3 185 RW*
B. Medicine Hat, Alta., July 19, 1972

| 94–95 | Fla | 4 | 0 | 0 | 0 | 17 | -1 |

LINDEN, Trevor *6–4 210 C/RW*
B. Medicine Hat, Alta., Apr. 11, 1970

88–89	Van	80	30	29	59	41	-10
89–90	Van	73	21	30	51	43	-17
90–91	Van	80	33	37	70	65	-25
91–92	Van	80	31	44	75	101	+3
92–93	Van	84	33	39	72	64	+19
93–94	Van	84	32	29	61	73	+6
94–95	Van	48	18	22	40	40	-5
95–96	Van	82	33	47	80	42	+6
96–97	Van	49	9	31	40	27	+5
97–98	Van–NYI	67	17	21	38	82	-14
98–99	NYI	82	18	29	47	32	-14
Totals		809	275	358	633	610	-46

Playoffs

88–89	Van	7	3	4	7	8	
90–91	Van	6	0	7	7	2	
91–92	Van	13	4	8	12	6	
92–93	Van	12	5	8	13	16	
93–94	Van	24	12	13	25	18	
94–95	Van	11	2	6	8	12	
95–96	Van	6	4	4	8	6	
Totals		79	30	50	80	68	

LINDGREN, Lars *6–1 210 D*
B. Pitea, Sweden, Oct. 12, 1952

78–79	Van	64	2	19	21	68	-32
79–80	Van	73	5	30	35	66	-8
80–81	Van	52	4	18	22	32	+16
81–82	Van	75	5	16	21	74	+2

82–83	Van	64	6	14	20	48	+3
83–84	Van-Minn	66	3	16	19	37	-3
Totals		394	25	113	138	325	-22

Playoffs

78–79	Van	3	0	0	0	6	
79–80	Van	2	0	1	1	0	
81–82	Van	16	2	4	6	6	
82–83	Van	4	1	1	2	2	
83–84	Van	15	2	0	2	6	
Totals		40	5	6	11	20	

LINDGREN, Mats *6–2 200 C*
B. Skelleftea, Sweden, Oct. 1, 1974

96–97	Edm	69	11	14	25	12	-7
97–98	Edm	82	13	13	26	42	0
98–99	Edm-NYI	60	10	15	25	24	+6
Totals		211	34	42	76	78	-1

Playoffs

96–97	Edm	12	0	4	4	0	
97–98	Edm	12	1	1	2	10	
Totals		24	1	5	6	10	

LINDHOLM, Mikael *6–1 194 C*
B. Gavle, Sweden, Dec. 19, 1964

| 89–90 | LA | 18 | 2 | 2 | 4 | 2 | +2 |

LINDQUIST, Fredrik *6–0 190 C*
B. Sodertalje, Sweden, June 21, 1973

| 98–99 | Edm | 8 | 0 | 0 | 0 | 2 | -2 |

LINDROS, Brett *6–4 215 RW*
B. London, Ont., Dec. 2, 1975

94–95	NYI	33	1	3	4	100	-8
95–96	NYI	18	1	2	3	47	-6
Totals		51	2	5	7	147	-14

LINDROS, Eric *6–4 229 C*
B. London, Ont., Feb. 28, 1973

92–93	Phil	61	41	34	75	147	+28
93–94	Phil	65	44	53	97	103	+16
94–95	Phil	46	29	41	70	60	+27
95–96	Phil	73	47	68	115	163	+26
96–97	Phil	52	32	47	79	136	+31
97–98	Phil	63	30	41	71	134	+14
98–99	Phil	71	40	53	93	120	+35
Totals		431	263	337	600	863	+177

Playoffs

94–95	Phil	12	4	11	15	18	
95–96	Phil	12	6	6	12	43	
96–97	Phil	19	12	14	26	40	
97–98	Phil	5	1	2	3	17	
Totals		48	23	33	56	118	

LINDSAY, Bill *5–11 190 LW*
B. Big Fork, Man., May 17, 1971

91–92	Que	23	2	4	6	14	-6
92–93	Que	44	4	9	13	16	0
93–94	Fla	84	6	6	12	97	-2
94–95	Fla	48	10	9	19	46	+1
95–96	Fla	73	12	22	34	57	+13
96–97	Fla	81	11	23	34	120	+1
97–98	Fla	82	12	16	28	80	-2
98–99	Fla	75	12	15	27	92	-1
Totals		510	69	104	173	522	+4

Playoffs

95–96	Fla	22	5	5	10	18	
96–97	Fla	3	0	1	1	8	
Totals		25	5	6	11	26	

LINDSAY, Robert Blake Theodore (Ted) *5–8 160 LW*
B. Renfrew, Ont., July 29, 1925

44–45	Det	45	17	6	23	43	
45–46	Det	47	7	10	17	14	
46–47	Det	59	27	15	42	57	
47–48	Det	60	33	19	52	95	
48–49	Det	50	26	28	54	97	
49–50	Det	69	23	55	78	141	
50–51	Det	67	24	35	59	110	
51–52	Det	70	30	39	69	123	
52–53	Det	70	32	39	71	111	

SSN	TEAM	GP	G	A	PTS.	PIM	+/-
53–54	Det	70	26	36	62	110	
54–55	Det	49	19	19	38	85	
55–56	Det	67	27	23	50	161	
56–57	Det	70	30	55	85	103	
57–58	Chi	68	15	24	39	110	
58–59	Chi	70	22	36	58	184	
59–60	Det	68	7	19	26	91	
64–65	Det	69	14	14	28	173	
Totals		1068	379	472	851	1808	

Playoffs

SSN	TEAM	GP	G	A	PTS.	PIM	
44–45	Det	14	2	0	2	6	
45–46	Det	5	0	1	1	0	
46–47	Det	5	2	2	4	10	
47–48	Det	10	3	1	4	6	
48–49	Det	11	2	6	8	31	
49–50	Det	13	4	4	8	16	
50–51	Det	6	0	1	1	8	
51–52	Det	8	5	2	7	8	
52–53	Det	6	4	4	8	6	
53–54	Det	12	4	4	8	14	
54–55	Det	11	7	12	19	12	
55–56	Det	10	6	3	9	22	
56–57	Det	5	2	4	6	8	
58–59	Chi	6	2	4	6	13	
59–60	Chi	4	1	1	2	0	
64–65	Det	7	3	0	3	34	
Totals		133	47	49	96	194	

LINDSTROM, Bo Morgan (Willy) *6–0 180 RW*
B. Grunns, Sweden, May 5, 1951

SSN	TEAM	GP	G	A	PTS.	PIM	+/-
75–76	Winn (WHA)	81	23	36	59	32	
76–77	Winn (WHA)	79	44	36	80	37	
77–78	Winn (WHA)	77	30	30	60	42	
78–79	Winn (WHA)	79	26	36	62	22	
79–80	Winn	79	23	26	49	20	-19
80–81	Winn	72	22	13	35	45	-28
81–82	Winn	74	32	27	59	33	+11
82–83	Winn–Edm	73	26	30	56	10	0
83–84	Edm	73	22	16	38	38	+17
84–85	Edm	80	12	20	32	18	+5
85–86	Pitt	71	14	17	31	30	0
86–87	Pitt	60	10	13	23	6	+9
NHL Totals		582	161	162	323	200	-5
WHA Totals		316	123	138	261	133	

Playoffs

SSN	TEAM	GP	G	A	PTS.	PIM	
75–76	Winn (WHA)	13	4	7	11	2	
76–77	Winn (WHA)	20	9	6	15	22	
77–78	Winn (WHA)	8	3	4	7	17	
78–79	Winn (WHA)	10	10	5	15	9	
81–82	Winn	4	2	1	3	2	
82–83	Edm	16	2	11	13	4	
83–84	Edm	19	5	5	10	10	
84–85	Edm	18	5	1	6	8	
NHL Totals		57	14	18	32	24	
WHA Totals		51	26	22	48	50	

LING, David *5–9 185 RW*
B. Halifax, N.S., Jan. 9, 1975

SSN	TEAM	GP	G	A	PTS.	PIM	+/-
96–97	Mont	2	0	0	0	0	0
97–98	Mont	1	0	0	0	0	-1
Totals		3	0	0	0	0	-1

LINSEMAN, Ken *5–11 180 C*
B. Kingston, Ont., Aug. 11, 1958

SSN	TEAM	GP	G	A	PTS.	PIM	+/-
77–78	Birm (WHA)	71	38	38	76	126	
78–79	Phil	30	5	20	25	23	+16
79–80	Phil	80	22	57	79	107	+26
80–81	Phil	51	17	30	47	150	+9
81–82	Phil	79	24	68	92	275	+6
82–83	Edm	72	33	42	75	181	+16
83–84	Edm	72	18	49	67	119	+30
84–85	Bos	75	24	49	73	126	+22
85–86	Bos	64	23	58	81	97	+15
86–87	Bos	64	15	34	49	126	+15
87–88	Bos	77	29	45	74	167	+36
88–89	Bos	78	27	45	72	164	+15
89–90	Bos–Phil	61	11	25	36	96	+5
90–91	Edm	56	7	29	36	94	+15
91–92	Tor	2	0	0	0	2	-2
NHL Totals		860	256	551	807	1727	+224
WHA Totals		71	38	38	76	126	

Playoffs

SSN	TEAM	GP	G	A	PTS.	PIM	
77–78	Birm (WHA)	5	2	2	4	15	
78–79	Phil	8	2	6	8	22	
79–80	Phil	17	4	18	22	40	
80–81	Phil	12	4	16	20	67	
81–82	Phil	11	1	2	3	6	
82–83	Edm	16	6	8	14	22	
83–84	Edm	19	10	4	14	65	
84–85	Bos	5	4	6	10	8	
85–86	Bos	3	0	1	1	17	
86–87	Bos	4	1	1	2	22	
87–88	Bos	23	11	14	25	56	
90–91	Edm	2	0	1	1	0	
NHL Totals		113	43	77	120	325	
WHA Totals		5	2	2	4	15	

LIPUMA, Chris *6–0 183 D*
B. Bridgeview, IL, Mar. 23, 1971

SSN	TEAM	GP	G	A	PTS.	PIM	+/-
92–93	TB	15	0	5	5	34	+1
93–94	TB	27	0	4	4	77	+1
94–95	TB	1	0	0	0	0	+2
95–96	TB	21	0	0	0	13	-7
96–97	SJ	8	0	0	0	22	-2
Totals		72	0	9	9	146	-5

LISCOMBE, Harry Carlyle (Carl) *5–8 170 LW*
B. Perth, Ont., May 17, 1915

SSN	TEAM	GP	G	A	PTS.	PIM	
37–38	Det	42	14	10	24	30	
38–39	Det	47	8	18	26	13	
39–40	Det	30	2	7	9	4	
40–41	Det	31	10	10	20	0	
41–42	Det	47	13	17	30	30	
42–43	Det	50	19	23	42	19	
43–44	Det	50	36	37	73	17	
44–45	Det	42	23	9	32	18	
45–46	Det	44	12	9	21	2	
Totals		383	137	140	277	133	

Playoffs

SSN	TEAM	GP	G	A	PTS.	PIM	
38–39	Det	6	0	0	0	2	
40–41	Det	8	4	3	7	12	
41–42	Det	12	6	6	12	2	
42–43	Det	10	6	8	14	2	
43–44	Det	5	1	0	1	2	
44–45	Det	14	4	2	6	0	
45–46	Det	4	1	0	1	0	
Totals		59	22	19	41	20	

LITZENBERGER, Edward C. J. *6–3 194 RW*
B. Neudorf, Sask., July 15, 1932

SSN	TEAM	GP	G	A	PTS.	PIM	
52–53	Mont	2	1	0	1	2	
53–54	Mont	3	0	0	0	0	
54–55	Mont–Chi	73	23	28	51	40	
55–56	Chi	70	10	29	39	36	
56–57	Chi	70	32	32	64	48	
57–58	Chi	70	32	30	62	63	
58–59	Chi	70	33	44	77	37	
59–60	Chi	52	12	18	30	15	
60–61	Chi	62	10	22	32	14	
61–62	Det–Tor	69	18	22	40	18	
62–63	Tor	58	5	13	18	10	
63–64	Tor	19	2	0	2	0	
Totals		618	178	238	416	283	

Playoffs

SSN	TEAM	GP	G	A	PTS.	PIM	
58–59	Chi	6	3	5	8	8	
59–60	Chi	4	0	1	1	4	
60–61	Chi	10	1	3	4	2	
61–62	Tor	10	0	2	2	4	
62–63	Tor	9	1	2	3	6	
63–64	Tor	1	0	0	0	10	
Totals		40	5	13	18	34	

LOACH, Lonnie *5–10 181 LW*
B. New Liskeard, Ont., Apr. 14, 1968

SSN	TEAM	GP	G	A	PTS.	PIM	+/-
92–93	Ott–LA	53	10	13	23	27	+3
93–94	Ana	3	0	0	0	2	-2
Totals		56	10	13	23	29	+1

Playoffs

SSN	TEAM	GP	G	A	PTS.	PIM	
92–93	LA	1	0	0	0	0	

***LOCAS, Jacques** *5–11 175 C*
B. Pointe aux Trembles, Que., Feb. 12, 1926

SSN	TEAM	GP	G	A	PTS.	PIM	
47–48	Mont	56	7	8	15	66	
48–49	Mont	3	0	0	0	0	
Totals		59	7	8	15	66	

LOCHEAD, William Alexander *6–1 190 LW*
B. Forest, Ont., Oct. 13, 1954

SSN	TEAM	GP	G	A	PTS.	PIM	+/-
74–75	Det	65	16	12	28	34	-30
75–76	Det	53	9	11	20	22	-15
76–77	Det	61	16	14	30	39	-11
77–78	Det	77	20	16	36	47	+6
78–79	Det–Col	67	8	9	17	34	-19
79–80	NYR	7	0	0	0	4	-5
Totals		330	69	62	131	180	-74

Playoffs

SSN	TEAM	GP	G	A	PTS.	PIM	
77–78	Det	7	3	0	3	6	

***LOCKING, Norman Wesley** *6–0 165 LW*
B. Owen Sound, Ont., May 24, 1911

SSN	TEAM	GP	G	A	PTS.	PIM	
34–35	Chi	35	2	5	7	19	
35–36	Chi	13	0	1	1	7	
Totals		48	2	6	8	26	

Playoffs

SSN	TEAM	GP	G	A	PTS.	PIM	
34–35	Chi	1	0	0	0	0	

LOEWEN, Darcy *5–10 185 LW*
B. Calgary, Alta., Feb. 26, 1969

SSN	TEAM	GP	G	A	PTS.	PIM	+/-
89–90	Buf	4	0	0	0	4	-3
90–91	Buf	6	0	0	0	8	-4
91–92	Buf	2	0	0	0	2	0
92–93	Ott	79	4	5	9	145	-26
93–94	Ott	44	0	3	3	52	-11
Totals		135	4	8	12	211	-44

LOFTHOUSE, Mark *6–2 195 RW/C*
B. New Westminster, B.C., Apr. 21, 1957

SSN	TEAM	GP	G	A	PTS.	PIM	+/-
77–78	Wash	18	2	1	3	8	-5
78–79	Wash	52	13	10	23	10	-11
79–80	Wash	68	15	18	33	20	-9
80–81	Wash	3	1	1	2	4	0
81–82	Det	12	3	4	7	13	-7
82–83	Det	28	8	4	12	18	+8
Totals		181	42	38	80	73	-24

LOGAN, David George *5–10 190 D*
B. Montreal, Que., July 2, 1954

SSN	TEAM	GP	G	A	PTS.	PIM	+/-
75–76	Chi	2	0	0	0	0	-1
76–77	Chi	34	0	2	2	61	22
77–78	Chi	54	1	5	6	77	-14
78–79	Chi	76	1	14	15	176	-9
79–80	Chi–Van	45	3	8	11	14	-4
80–81	Van	7	0	0	0	13	+1
Totals		218	5	29	34	470	-49

Playoffs

SSN	TEAM	GP	G	A	PTS.	PIM	
77–78	Chi	4	0	0	0	8	
78–79	Chi	4	0	0	0	2	
79–80	Van	4	0	0	0	0	
Totals		12	0	0	0	10	

LOGAN, Robert *6–0 190 RW*
B. Montreal, Que., Feb. 22, 1964

SSN	TEAM	GP	G	A	PTS.	PIM	+/-
86–87	Buf	22	7	3	10	0	+5
87–88	Buf	16	3	2	5	0	+1
88–89	LA	4	0	0	0	0	0
Totals		42	10	5	15	0	+6

LOISELLE, Claude *5–11 195 C*
B. Ottawa, Ont., May 29, 1963

SSN	TEAM	GP	G	A	PTS.	PIM	+/-
81–82	Det	4	1	0	1	2	-2
82–83	Det	18	2	0	2	15	-14
83–84	Det	28	4	6	10	32	+4
84–85	Det	30	8	1	9	45	-5
85–86	Det	48	7	15	22	142	-27
86–87	NJ	75	16	24	40	137	-7
87–88	NJ	68	17	18	35	121	+1
88–89	NJ	74	7	14	21	209	-10
89–90	Que	72	11	14	25	104	-27
90–91	Que–Tor	66	6	11	17	88	-20
91–92	Tor–NYI	75	7	10	17	115	-24
92–93	NYI	41	5	3	8	90	-5
93–94	NYI	17	1	1	2	49	-2
Totals		616	92	117	209	1149	-132

Playoffs

SSN	TEAM	GP	G	A	PTS.	PIM	
84–85	Det	3	0	2	2	0	
87–88	NJ	20	4	6	10	50	
92–93	NY	18	0	3	3	10	

SSN	TEAM	GP	G	A	PTS.	PIM	+/-
Totals		41	4	11	15	60	

LOMAKIN, Andrei *5-10 176 RW*
B. Voskresensk, Soviet Union, Apr. 3, 1964

SSN	TEAM	GP	G	A	PTS.	PIM	+/-
91-92	Phil	57	14	16	30	26	-6
92-93	Phil ·	51	8	12	20	34	+15
93-94	Fla	76	19	28	47	26	+1
94-95	Fla	31	1	6	7	6	-5
Totals		215	42	62	104	92	+5

LONEY, Brian *6-2 195 RW*
B. Winnipeg, Man., Aug. 9, 1972

SSN	TEAM	GP	G	A	PTS.	PIM	+/-
95-96	Van	12	2	3	5	6	+2

LONEY, Troy *6-3 209 LW*
B. Bow Island, Alta., Sept. 21, 1963

SSN	TEAM	GP	G	A	PTS.	PIM	+/-
83-84	Pitt	13	0	0	0	9	-7
84-85	Pitt	46	10	8	18	59	-11
85-86	Pitt	47	3	9	12	95	-8
86-87	Pitt	23	8	7	15	22	0
87-88	Pitt	65	5	13	18	151	-3
88-89	Pitt	69	10	6	16	165	-5
89-90	Pitt	67	11	16	27	168	-9
90-91	Pitt	44	7	9	16	85	+10
91-92	Pitt	76	10	16	26	127	-5
92-93	Pitt	82	5	16	21	99	+1
93-94	Ana	62	13	6	19	88	-5
94-95	NYI-NYR	30	5	4	9	23	-2
Totals		624	87	110	197	1091	-44

Playoffs

SSN	TEAM	GP	G	A	PTS.	PIM	
88-89	Pitt	11	1	3	4	24	
90-91	Pitt	24	2	2	4	41	
91-92	Pitt	21	4	5	9	32	
92-93	Pitt	10	1	4	5	0	
94-95	NYR	1	0	0	0	0	
Totals		67	8	14	22	97	

LONG, Barry Kenneth *6-2 210 D*
B. Brantford, Ont., Jan. 3, 1949

SSN	TEAM	GP	G	A	PTS.	PIM	+/-
72-72	LA	70	2	13	15	48	-7
73-74	LA	60	3	19	22	118	+25
74-75	Edm (WHA)	78	20	40	60	116	
75-76	Edm (WHA)	78	10	32	42	66	
76-77	Edm-Winn (WHA)	73	9	39	48	56	
77-78	Winn (WHA)	78	7	24	31	42	
78-79	Winn (WHA)	79	5	36	41	42	
79-80	Det	80	0	17	17	38	-28
80-81	Winn	65	6	17	23	42	-47
81-82	Winn	5	0	2	2	4	-1
NHL Totals		280	11	68	79	250	-58
WHA Totals		386	51	171	222	322	

Playoffs

SSN	TEAM	GP	G	A	PTS.	PIM	
73-74	LA	5	0	1	1	18	
75-76	Edm (WHA)	4	0	0	0	4	
76-77	Winn (WHA)	20	1	5	6	10	
77-78	Winn (WHA)	9	0	5	5	6	
78-79	Winn (WHA)	10	2	3	5	0	
NHL Totals		5	0	1	1	18	
WHA Totals		43	3	13	16	20	

***LONG, Stanley Gordon** *5-11 190 D'*
B. Owen Sound, Ont., Nov. 6, 1929

SSN	TEAM	GP	G	A	PTS.	PIM	
51-52	Mont	0	0	0	0	0	

Playoffs

SSN	TEAM	GP	G	A	PTS.	PIM	
51-52	Mont	3	0	0	0	0	

LONSBERRY, David Ross (Ross) *5-11 195 LW*
B. Humboldt, Sask., Feb. 7, 1947

SSN	TEAM	GP	G	A	PTS.	PIM	+/-
66-67	Bos	8	0	1	1	2	
67-68	Bos	19	2	2	4	12	+2
68-69	Bos	6	0	0	0	2	0
69-70	LA	76	20	22	42	118	-18
70-71	LA	76	25	28	53	80	-35
71-72	LA-Phil	82	16	21	37	61	-27
72-73	Phil	77	21	29	50	59	+6
73-74	Phil	75	32	19	51	48	+16
74-75	Phil	80	24	25	49	99	+28
75-76	Phil	80	19	28	47	87	+29
76-77	Phil	75	23	32	55	43	+42
77-78	Phil	78	18	30	48	45	+41
78-79	Pitt	80	24	22	46	38	+7
79-80	Pitt	76	15	18	33	36	-4

SSN	TEAM	GP	G	A	PTS.	PIM	+/-
80-81	Pitt	80	17	33	50	76	-3
Totals		968	256	310	566	806	+84

Playoffs

SSN	TEAM	GP	G	A	PTS.	PIM	
72-73	Phil	11	4	3	7	9	
73-74	Phil	17	4	9	13	18	
74-75	Phil	17	4	3	7	10	
75-76	Phil	16	4	3	7	2	
76-77	Phil	10	1	2	3	29	
77-78	Phil	12	2	2	4	6	
78-79	Pitt	7	0	2	2	9	
79-80	Pitt	5	2	1	3	2	
80-81	Pitt	5	0	0	0	2	
Totals		100	21	25	46	87	

LOOB, Hakan *5-10 174 RW*
B. Visby, Sweden, July 3, 1960

SSN	TEAM	GP	G	A	PTS.	PIM	+/-
83-84	Calg	77	30	25	55	22	+11
84-85	Calg	78	37	35	72	14	+14
85-86	Calg	68	31	36	67	36	+22
86-87	Calg	68	18	26	44	26	-13
87-88	Calg	80	50	56	106	47	+41
88-89	Calg	79	27	58	85	44	+28
Totals		450	193	236	429	189	+103

Playoffs

SSN	TEAM	GP	G	A	PTS.	PIM	
83-84	Calg	11	2	3	5	2	
84-85	Calg	4	3	3	6	0	
85-86	Calg	22	4	10	14	6	
86-87	Calg	5	1	2	3	0	
87-88	Calg	9	8	1	9	4	
88-89	Calg	22	8	9	17	4	
Totals		73	26	28	54	16	

LOOB, Peter *6-3 190 D*
B. Karlstad, Sweden, July 23, 1957

SSN	TEAM	GP	G	A	PTS.	PIM	+/-
84-85	Que	8	1	2	3	0	+5

LORENTZ, James Peter *6-0 180 C*
B. Waterloo, Ont., May 1, 1947

SSN	TEAM	GP	G	A	PTS.	PIM	+/-
68-69	Bos	11	1	3	4	6	-3
69-70	Bos	68	7	16	23	30	+14
70-71	StL	76	19	21	40	34	+2
71-72	StL-NYR-Buf	52	10	15	25	24	-20
72-73	Buf	78	27	35	62	30	+6
73-74	Buf	78	23	31	54	28	-19
74-75	Buf	72	25	45	70	18	+17
75-76	Buf	75	17	24	41	18	+3
76-77	Buf	79	23	33	56	8	+3
77-78	Buf	70	9	15	24	12	-4
Totals		359	161	238	399	208	-1

Playoffs

SSN	TEAM	GP	G	A	PTS.	PIM	
69-70	Bos	11	1	0	1	4	
70-71	StL	6	0	1	1	4	
72-73	Buf	6	0	3	3	2	
74-75	Buf	16	6	4	10	6	
75-76	Buf	9	1	2	3	6	
76-77	Buf	6	4	0	4	8	
Totals		54	12	10	22	30	

LORIMER, Robert Roy *6-1 200 D*
B. Toronto, Ont., Aug. 25, 1953

SSN	TEAM	GP	G	A	PTS.	PIM	+/-
76-77	NYI	1	0	1	1	0	+1
77-78	NYI	5	1	0	1	0	0
78-79	NYI	67	3	18	21	42	+27
79-80	NYI	74	3	16	19	53	+32
80-81	NYI	73	1	12	13	77	+45
81-82	Col	79	5	15	20	68	-19
82-83	NJ	66	3	10	13	42	-20
83-84	NJ	72	2	10	12	62	-28
84-85	NJ	46	2	6	8	35	+6
85-86	NJ	46	2	2	4	52	-13
Totals		529	22	90	112	431	+31

Playoffs

SSN	TEAM	GP	G	A	PTS.	PIM	
78-79	NYI	10	1	3	4	15	
79-80	NYI	21	1	3	5	41	
80-81	NYI	18	1	4	5	27	
Totals		49	3	10	13	83	

***LORRAIN, Rodrique (Rod)** *5-5 156 RW*
B. Buckingham, Que., July 1915

SSN	TEAM	GP	G	A	PTS.	PIM	
35-36	Mont	1	0	0	0	2	
36-37	Mont	47	3	6	9	8	
37-38	Mont	48	13	19	32	14	

SSN	TEAM	GP	G	A	PTS.	PIM	+/-
38-39	Mont	38	10	9	19	0	
39-40	Mont	41	1	5	6	6	
41-42	Mont	4	1	0	1	0	
Totals		179	28	39	67	30	

Playoffs

SSN	TEAM	GP	G	A	PTS.	PIM	
36-37	Mont	5	0	0	0	0	
37-38	Mont	3	0	0	0	0	
38-39	Mont	3	0	3	3	0	
Totals		11	0	3	3	0	

***LOUGHLIN, Clement (Clem)** *6-0 180 D*
B. Carroll, Man., Nov. 15, 1894

SSN	TEAM	GP	G	A	PTS.	PIM	
26-27	Det	34	7	3	10	40	
27-28	Det	43	1	2	3	21	
28-29	Chi	24	0	1	1	16	
Totals		101	8	6	14	77	

***LOUGHLIN, Wilfred** *D*

SSN	TEAM	GP	G	A	PTS.	PIM	
23-24	Tor	14	0	0	0	2	

LOVSIN, Ken *6-0 195 D*
B. Peace River, Alta., Dec. 3, 1966

SSN	TEAM	GP	G	A	PTS.	PIM	+/-
90-91	Wash	1	0	0	0	0	-2

LOWDERMILK, Dwayne, Kenneth *6-0 201 D*
B. Burnaby, B.C., Jan. 9, 1958

SSN	TEAM	GP	G	A	PTS.	PIM	+/-
80-81	Wash	2	0	1	1	2	-1

LOWE, Darren *5-10 185 RW*
B. Toronto, Ont., Oct. 13, 1960

SSN	TEAM	GP	G	A	PTS.	PIM	+/-
83-84	Pitt	8	1	2	3	0	-5

LOWE, Kevin Hugh *6-2 190 D*
B. Lachute, Que., Apr. 15, 1959

SSN	TEAM	GP	G	A	PTS.	PIM	+/-
79-80	Edm	64	2	19	21	70	+1
80-81	Edm	79	10	24	34	94	-10
81-82	Edm	80	9	31	40	63	+46
82-83	Edm	80	6	34	40	43	+39
83-84	Edm	80	4	42	46	59	+37
84-85	Edm	80	4	21	25	104	+9
85-86	Edm	74	2	16	18	90	+24
86-87	Edm	77	8	29	37	94	+41
87-88	Edm	70	9	15	24	89	+18
88-89	Edm	76	7	18	25	98	+26
89-90	Edm	78	7	26	33	140	+18
90-91	Edm	73	3	13	16	113	-9
91-92	Edm	55	2	8	10	107	-4
92-93	NYR	49	3	12	15	58	-2
93-94	NYR	71	5	14	19	70	+4
94-95	NYR	44	1	7	8	58	-2
95-96	NYR	53	1	5	6	76	+20
96-97	Edm	64	1	13	14	50	-1
97-98	Edm	7	0	0	0	22	-3
Totals		1254	84	347	431	1498	+258

Playoffs

SSN	TEAM	GP	G	A	PTS.	PIM	
79-80	Edm	3	0	1	1	0	
80-81	Edm	9	0	2	2	11	
81-82	Edm	5	0	3	3	0	
82-83	Edm	16	1	8	9	10	
83-84	Edm	19	3	7	10	16	
84-85	Edm	16	0	5	5	8	
85-86	Edm	10	1	3	4	15	
86-87	Edm	21	2	4	6	22	
87-88	Edm	10	0	2	2	26	
88-89	Edm	7	1	2	3	4	
89-90	Edm	20	0	2	2	10	
90-91	Edm	14	1	1	2	14	
91-92	Edm	11	0	3	3	16	
93-94	NYR	22	1	0	1	20	
94-95	NYR	10	0	1	1	12	
95-96	NYR	10	0	4	4	4	
96-97	Edm	1	0	0	0	0	
97-98	Edm	1	0	0	0	4	
Totals		214	10	48	58	192	

LOWE, Norman E. (Odie) *5-8 140 C*
B. Winnipeg, Man., Apr. 15, 1928

SSN	TEAM	GP	G	A	PTS.	PIM	
48-49	NYR	1	0	0	0	0	
49-50	NYR	3	1	1	2	0	
Totals		4	1	1	2	0	

***LOWE, Ross Robert** *6-1 180 F*
B. Oshawa, Ont., Sept. 21, 1928

SSN	TEAM	GP	G	A	PTS.	PIM	
49-50	Bos	3	0	0	0	0	
50-51	Bos-Mont	43	5	3	8	40	

SSN	TEAM	GP	G	A	PTS.	PIM	+/-
51–52	Mont	31	1	5	6	42	
Totals		77	6	8	14	82	

*LOWERY, Frederick John (Frock) D
B. Ottawa, Ont.

SSN	TEAM	GP	G	A	PTS.	PIM	+/-
24–25	Mont M	28	0	0	0	6	
25–26	Mont M–Pitt Pi	26	1	0	1	4	
Totals		54	1	0	1	10	

Playoffs

SSN	TEAM	GP	G	A	PTS.	PIM	+/-
25–26	Pitt	2	0	0	0	6	

*LOWREY, Eddie F
B. 1894

SSN	TEAM	GP	G	A	PTS.	PIM	+/-
17–18	Ott	11	0	0	0	3	
18–19	Ott	10	0	0	0	3	
20–21	Ham	3	0	0	0	0	
Totals		24	0	0	0	6	

*LOWREY, Gerald 5-8 150 LW
B. Ottawa, Ont.

SSN	TEAM	GP	G	A	PTS.	PIM	+/-
27–28	Tor	25	6	5	11	29	
28–29	Tor–Pitt Pi	44	5	12	17	30	
29–30	Pitt Pi	44	16	14	30	30	
30–31	Phil Q	42	13	14	27	27	
31–32	Chi	48	8	3	11	32	
32–33	Ott	6	0	0	0	0	
Totals		209	48	48	96	148	

Playoffs

SSN	TEAM	GP	G	A	PTS.	PIM	+/-
31–32	Chi	2	1	0	1	2	

LOWRY, Dave 6-1 200 LW
B. Sudbury, Ont., Feb. 14, 1965

SSN	TEAM	GP	G	A	PTS.	PIM	+/-
85–86	Van	73	10	8	18	143	-21
86–87	Van	70	8	10	18	176	-23
87–88	Van	22	1	3	4	38	-2
88–89	StL	21	3	3	6	11	+1
89–90	StL	78	19	6	25	75	+1
90–91	StL	79	19	21	40	168	+19
91–92	StL	75	7	13	20	77	-11
92–93	StL	58	5	8	13	101	-18
93–94	Fla	80	15	22	37	64	-4
94–95	Fla	45	10	10	20	25	-3
95–96	Fla	63	10	14	24	36	-2
96–97	Fla	77	15	14	29	51	+2
97–98	Fla–SJ	57	4	4	8	53	-1
98–99	SJ	61	6	9	15	24	-5
Totals		859	132	145	277	1042	-67

Playoffs

SSN	TEAM	GP	G	A	PTS.	PIM	+/-
85–86	Van	3	0	0	0	0	
88–89	StL	10	0	5	5	4	
89–90	StL	12	2	1	3	39	
90–91	StL	13	1	4	5	35	
91–92	StL	6	0	1	1	20	
92–93	StL	11	2	0	2	14	
95–96	Fla	22	10	7	17	39	
96–97	Fla	5	0	0	0	0	
97–98	SJ	6	0	0	0	18	
98–99	SJ	1	0	0	0	0	
Totals		89	15	18	33	169	

LUCAS, Daniel Kenneth 6-1 197 RW
B. Powell River, B.C., Feb. 28, 1958

SSN	TEAM	GP	G	A	PTS.	PIM	+/-
78–79	Phil	6	1	0	1	0	-2

LUCAS, David Charles D
B. Downeyville, Ont., Mar. 22, 1932

SSN	TEAM	GP	G	A	PTS.	PIM	+/-
62–63	Det	1	0	0	0	0	

LUCE, Donald Harold 6-2 185 C
B. London, Ont., Oct. 2, 1948

SSN	TEAM	GP	G	A	PTS.	PIM	+/-
69–70	NYR	12	1	2	3	8	-2
70–71	NYR–Det	67	3	12	15	18	-6
71–72	Buf	78	11	8	19	38	-18
72–73	Buf	78	18	25	43	32	+7
73–74	Buf	75	26	31	57	44	+3
74–75	Buf	80	33	43	76	45	+61
75–76	Buf	77	21	49	70	42	+37
76–77	Buf	80	26	43	69	16	+38
77–78	Buf	78	26	35	61	24	+32
78–79	Buf	79	26	35	61	14	+20
79–80	Buf	80	14	29	43	30	+22
80–81	Buf–LA	71	16	13	29	21	+10
81–82	Tor	39	4	4	8	32	-7
Totals		894	225	329	554	364	+197

Playoffs

SSN	TEAM	GP	G	A	PTS.	PIM	+/-
69–70	NYR	5	0	1	1	4	
72–73	Buf	6	1	1	2	2	
74–75	Buf	16	5	8	13	19	
75–76	Buf	9	4	3	7	6	
76–77	Buf	6	3	1	4	2	
77–78	Buf	8	0	2	2	6	
78–79	Buf	3	1	1	2	0	
79–80	Buf	14	3	3	6	11	
80–81	LA	4	0	2	2	2	
Totals		71	17	22	39	52	

LUDVIG, Jan 5-10 190 RW
B. Liberec, Czechoslovakia, Sept. 17, 1961

SSN	TEAM	GP	G	A	PTS.	PIM	+/-
82–83	NJ	51	7	10	17	30	-27
83–84	NJ	74	22	32	54	70	-18
84–85	NJ	74	12	19	31	53	-19
85–86	NJ	42	5	9	14	63	-16
86–87	NJ	47	7	9	16	98	-5
87–88	Buf	13	1	6	7	65	+1
88–89	Buf	13	0	2	2	39	-1
Totals		314	54	87	141	418	-85

LUDWIG, Craig Lee 6-3 217 D
B. Rhinelander, Wisc., Mar. 15, 1961

SSN	TEAM	GP	G	A	PTS.	PIM	+/-
82–83	Mont	80	0	25	25	59	+4
83–84	Mont	80	7	18	25	52	-10
84–85	Mont	72	5	14	19	90	+5
85–86	Mont	69	2	4	6	63	+7
86–87	Mont	75	4	12	16	105	+3
87–88	Mont	74	4	10	14	69	+17
88–89	Mont	74	3	13	16	73	+33
89–90	Mont	73	1	15	16	108	+24
90–91	NYI	75	1	8	9	77	-24
91–92	Minn	73	2	9	11	54	0
92–93	Minn	78	1	10	11	153	+1
93–94	Dal	84	1	13	14	123	-1
94–95	Dal	47	2	7	9	61	-6
95–96	Dal	65	1	2	3	70	-17
96–97	Dal	77	2	11	13	62	+17
97–98	Dal	80	0	7	7	131	+21
98–99	Dal	80	2	6	8	87	+5
Totals		1256	38	184	222	1437	+79

Playoffs

SSN	TEAM	GP	G	A	PTS.	PIM	+/-
82–83	Mont	3	0	0	0	2	
83–84	Mont	15	0	3	3	23	
84–85	Mont	12	0	2	2	6	
85–86	Mont	20	0	1	1	48	
86–87	Mont	17	2	3	5	30	
87–88	Mont	11	1	1	2	6	
88–89	Mont	21	0	2	2	24	
89–90	Mont	11	0	1	1	16	
91–92	Minn	7	0	1	1	19	
93–94	Dal	9	0	3	3	8	
94–95	Dal	4	0	1	1	2	
96–97	Dal	7	0	2	2	18	
97–98	Dal	17	0	1	1	22	
98–99	Dal	23	1	4	5	20	
Totals		177	4	25	29	244	

LUDZIK, Steve 5-11 185 C
B. Toronto, Ont., Apr. 3, 1962

SSN	TEAM	GP	G	A	PTS.	PIM	+/-
81–82	Chi	8	2	1	3	2	+1
82–83	Chi	66	6	19	25	68	+7
83–84	Chi	80	9	20	29	73	-5
84–85	Chi	79	11	20	31	86	+5
85–86	Chi	49	6	5	11	21	-2
86–87	Chi	52	5	12	17	34	-3
87–88	Chi	73	6	15	21	40	-14
88–89	Buf	6	1	0	1	8	0
89–90	Buf	11	0	1	1	6	-2
Totals		424	46	93	139	333	-13

Playoffs

SSN	TEAM	GP	G	A	PTS.	PIM	+/-
82–83	Chi	13	3	5	8	20	
83–84	Chi	4	0	1	1	9	
84–85	Chi	15	1	1	2	16	
85–86	Chi	3	0	0	0	12	
86–87	Chi	4	0	0	0	0	
87–88	Chi	5	0	1	1	13	
Totals		44	4	8	12	70	

LUHNING, Warren 6-2 185 RW
B. Edmonton, Alta., July 3, 1975

SSN	TEAM	GP	G	A	PTS.	PIM	+/-
97–98	NYI	8	0	0	0	0	-4
98–99	NYI	11	0	0	0	8	-4
Totals		19	0	0	0	8	-8

LUKOWICH, Bernard Joseph 6-0 190 RW
B. North Battleford, Sask., Mar. 18, 1952

SSN	TEAM	GP	G	A	PTS.	PIM	+/-
73–74	Pitt	53	9	10	19	32	-4
74–75	StL	26	4	5	9	2	+4
75–76	Calg (WHA)	15	5	2	7	18	
NHL Totals		79	13	15	28	34	0
WHA Totals		15	5	2	7	18	

Playoffs

SSN	TEAM	GP	G	A	PTS.	PIM	+/-
74–75	StL	2	0	0	0	0	
75–76	Calg (WHA)	10	4	3	7	8	
NHL Totals		2	0	0	0	0	
WHA Totals		10	4	3	7	8	

LUKOWICH, Brad 6-1 170 D
B. Cranbrook, B.C., Aug. 12, 1976

SSN	TEAM	GP	G	A	PTS.	PIM	+/-
97–98	Dal	4	0	1	1	2	-2
98–99	Dal	14	1	2	3	19	+3
Totals		18	1	3	4	21	+1

Playoffs

SSN	TEAM	GP	G	A	PTS.	PIM	+/-
98–99	Dal	8	0	1	1	4	

LUKOWICH, Eugene (Morris) 5-9 170 LW
B. Speers, Sask., June 1, 1956

SSN	TEAM	GP	G	A	PTS.	PIM	+/-
76–77	Hou (WHA)	62	27	18	45	67	
77–78	Hou (WHA)	80	40	35	75	131	
78–79	Winn (WHA)	80	65	34	99	119	
79–80	Winn	78	35	39	74	77	-16
80–81	Winn	80	33	34	67	90	-39
81–82	Winn	77	43	49	92	102	-4
82–83	Winn	69	22	21	43	67	-28
83–84	Winn	80	30	25	55	71	+10
84–85	Winn–Bos	69	10	17	27	52	-6
85–86	Bos–LA	69	12	13	25	61	-17
86–87	LA	60	14	21	35	64	0
NHL Totals		582	199	219	418	584	-100
WHA Totals		222	132	87	219	317	

Playoffs

SSN	TEAM	GP	G	A	PTS.	PIM	+/-
76–77	Hou (WHA)	11	6	4	10	19	
77–78	Hou (WHA)	6	1	2	3	17	
78–79	Winn (WHA)	10	8	7	15	21	
81–82	Winn	4	0	2	2	16	
83–84	Winn	3	0	0	0	0	
84–85	Bos	1	0	0	0	0	
86–87	LA	3	0	0	0	8	
NHL Totals		11	0	2	2	24	
WHA Totals		27	15	13	28	57	

LUKSA, Charles (Chuck) 6-1 197 D
B. Toronto, Ont., July 15, 1954

SSN	TEAM	GP	G	A	PTS.	PIM	+/-
78–79	Cin (WHA)	78	8	12	20	116	
79–80	Hart	8	0	1	1	4	0
NHL Totals		8	0	1	1	4	0
WHA Totals		78	8	12	20	116	

Playoffs

SSN	TEAM	GP	G	A	PTS.	PIM	+/-
78–79	Cin (WHA)	3	0	0	0	7	

LUMLEY, David 6-0 185 RW
B. Toronto, Ont., Sept. 1, 1954

SSN	TEAM	GP	G	A	PTS.	PIM	+/-
78–79	Mont	3	0	0	0	0	0
79–80	Edm	80	20	38	58	138	+15
80–81	Edm	53	7	9	16	74	-15
81–82	Edm	66	32	42	74	96	+12
82–83	Edm	72	13	24	37	158	+19
83–84	Edm	56	6	15	21	68	+14
84–85	Hart–Edm	60	9	23	32	111	-18
85–86	Edm	46	11	9	20	35	+13
86–87	Edm	1	0	0	0	0	0
Totals		437	98	160	258	680	+40

Playoffs

SSN	TEAM	GP	G	A	PTS.	PIM	+/-
79–80	Edm	3	1	0	1	12	
80–81	Edm	7	1	0	1	4	
81–82	Edm	5	2	1	3	21	
82–83	Edm	16	0	0	0	19	
Totals		31	4	1	5	56	

LUMME, Jyrki 6-1 205 D
B. Tampere, Finland, July 16, 1966

SSN	TEAM	GP	G	A	PTS.	PIM	+/-
88-89	Mont	21	1	3	4	10	+3
89-90	Mont-Van	65	4	26	30	49	+17
90-91	Van	80	5	27	32	59	-15
91-92	Van	75	12	32	44	65	+25
92-93	Van	74	8	36	44	55	+30
93-94	Van	83	13	42	55	50	+43
94-95	Van	36	5	12	17	26	+4
95-96	Van	80	17	37	54	50	-9
96-97	Van	66	11	24	35	32	+8
97-98	Van	74	9	21	30	34	-25
98-99	Phoe	60	7	21	28	34	+5
Totals		714	92	281	273	464	+46

Playoffs

SSN	TEAM	GP	G	A	PTS.	PIM	
90-91	Van	6	2	3	5	0	
91-92	Van	13	2	3	5	4	
92-93	Van	12	0	5	5	6	
93-94	Van	24	2	11	13	16	
94-95	Van	11	2	6	8	8	
95-96	Van	6	1	3	4	2	
98-99	Phoe	7	0	1	1	6	
Totals		79	9	32	41	42	

LUND, Pentti Alexander (Penny) 6-0 185 RW
B. Helsinki, Finland, Dec. 6, 1925

SSN	TEAM	GP	G	A	PTS.	PIM
48-49	NYR	59	14	16	30	16
49-50	NYR	64	18	9	27	16
50-51	NYR	59	4	16	20	6
51-52	Bos	23	0	5	5	0
52-53	Bos	54	8	9	17	2
Totals		259	44	55	99	40

Playoffs

SSN	TEAM	GP	G	A	PTS.	PIM
46-47	Bos	1	0	0	0	0
47-48	Bos	2	0	0	0	0
49-50	NYR	12	6	5	11	0
51-52	Bos	2	1	0	1	0
52-53	Bos	2	0	0	0	0
Totals		19	7	5	12	0

LUNDBERG, Brian Frederick 5-10 190 D
B. Burnaby, B.C., June 5, 1960

SSN	TEAM	GP	G	A	PTS.	PIM	+/-
82-83	Pitt	1	0	0	0	2	-1

LUNDE, Leonard Melvin 6-1 194 C
B. Campbell River, B.C., Nov. 13, 1936

SSN	TEAM	GP	G	A	PTS.	PIM	+/-
58-59	Det	68	14	12	26	15	
59-60	Det	66	6	17	23	10	
60-61	Det	53	6	12	18	10	
61-62	Det	23	2	9	11	4	
62-63	Chi	60	6	22	28	30	
65-66	Chi	24	4	7	11	4	
67-68	Minn	7	0	1	1	0	-7
70-71	Van	20	1	3	4	2	-3
73-74	Edm (WHA)	71	26	22	48	8	
NHL Totals		321	39	83	122	75	-10
WHA Totals		71	26	22	48	8	

Playoffs

SSN	TEAM	GP	G	A	PTS.	PIM
59-60	Det	6	1	2	3	0
60-61	Det	10	2	0	2	0
62-63	Chi	4	0	0	0	2
73-74	Edm (WHA)	5	0	1	1	0
NHL Totals		20	3	2	5	2
WHA Totals		5	0	1	1	0

LUNDHOLM, Bengt 6-0 180 LW
B. Falun, Sweden, Aug. 4, 1955

SSN	TEAM	GP	G	A	PTS.	PIM	+/-
81-82	Winn	66	14	30	44	10	+5
82-83	Winn	58	14	28	42	16	+10
83-84	Winn	57	5	14	19	20	-7
84-85	Winn	78	12	18	30	20	+8
85-86	Winn	16	3	5	8	6	-4
Totals		275	48	95	143	72	+12

Playoffs

SSN	TEAM	GP	G	A	PTS.	PIM
81-82	Winn	4	1	1	2	2
82-83	Winn	3	0	1	1	2
84-85	Winn	5	2	2	4	8
85-86	Winn	2	0	0	0	2
Totals		14	3	4	7	14

LUNDRIGAN, Joseph Roche 5-11 180 D
B. Corner Brook, Nfld., Sept. 12, 1948

SSN	TEAM	GP	G	A	PTS.	PIM	+/-
72-73	Tor	49	2	8	10	20	+4
74-75	Wash	3	0	0	0	2	-3
Totals		52	2	8	10	22	+1

LUNDSTROM, Tord 5-11 176 LW
B. Kiruna, Sweden, Mar. 4, 1945

SSN	TEAM	GP	G	A	PTS.	PIM	+/-
73-74	Det	11	1	1	2	0	-2

LUNDY, Patrick Anthony 5-10 168 C
B. Saskatoon, Sask., May 31, 1924

SSN	TEAM	GP	G	A	PTS.	PIM
45-46	Det	4	3	2	5	2
46-47	Det	59	17	17	34	10
47-48	Det	11	4	1	5	6
48-49	Det	15	4	3	7	4
50-51	Chi	61	9	9	18	9
Totals		150	37	32	69	31

Playoffs

SSN	TEAM	GP	G	A	PTS.	PIM
45-46	Det	2	1	0	1	0
47-48	Det	5	1	1	2	0
48-49	Det	4	0	0	0	0
Totals		11	2	1	3	0

LUONGO, Christopher John 6-0 199 D
B. Detroit, Mich., Mar. 17, 1967

SSN	TEAM	GP	G	A	PTS.	PIM	+/-
90-91	Det	4	0	1	1	4	0
92-93	Ott	76	3	9	12	68	-47
93-94	NYI	17	1	3	4	13	-1
94-95	NYI	47	1	3	4	36	-2
95-96	NYI	74	3	7	10	55	-23
Totals		218	8	23	31	176	-73

LUPIEN, Gilles 6-6 210 D
B. Lachute, Que., Apr. 20, 1954

SSN	TEAM	GP	G	A	PTS.	PIM	+/-
77-78	Mont	46	1	3	4	108	+19
78-79	Mont	72	1	9	10	124	+33
79-80	Mont	56	1	7	8	109	+13
80-81	Pitt-Hart	51	2	5	7	73	-21
81-82	Hart	1	0	1	1	2	0
Totals		226	5	25	30	416	+44

Playoffs

SSN	TEAM	GP	G	A	PTS.	PIM
77-78	Mont	8	0	0	0	17
78-79	Mont	13	0	0	0	2
79-80	Mont	4	0	0	0	2
Totals		25	0	0	0	21

LUPUL, Gary John 5-8 175 C/LW
B. Powell River, B.C., Apr. 4, 1959

SSN	TEAM	GP	G	A	PTS.	PIM	+/-
79-80	Van	51	9	11	20	24	-12
80-81	Van	7	0	2	2	2	-1
81-82	Van	41	10	7	17	26	-2
82-83	Van	40	18	10	28	46	+1
83-84	Van	69	17	27	44	51	-6
84-85	Van	66	12	17	29	82	-15
85-86	Van	19	4	1	5	12	0
Totals		293	70	75	145	243	-45

Playoffs

SSN	TEAM	GP	G	A	PTS.	PIM
79-80	Van	4	1	0	1	0
81-82	Van	10	2	3	5	4
82-83	Van	4	1	3	4	0
83-84	Van	4	0	1	1	7
85-86	Van	3	0	0	0	0
Totals		25	4	7	11	11

LYLE, George 6-2 205 LW
B. North Vancouver, B.C., Nov. 24, 1953

SSN	TEAM	GP	G	A	PTS.	PIM	+/-
76-77	NE (WHA)	75	39	33	72	62	
77-78	NE (WHA)	68	30	24	54	74	
78-79	NE (WHA)	59	17	18	35	54	
79-80	Det	27	7	4	11	2	-2
80-81	Det	31	10	14	24	28	0
81-82	Det-Hart	25	3	14	17	13	-5
82-83	Hart	16	4	6	10	8	+5
NHL Totals		99	24	38	62	51	-2
WHA Totals		202	86	75	161	190	

Playoffs

SSN	TEAM	GP	G	A	PTS.	PIM
76-77	NE (WHA)	5	1	0	1	4
77-78	NE (WHA)	12	2	1	3	13
78-79	NE (WHA)	9	3	5	8	25
WHA Totals		26	6	6	12	42

LYNCH, John Alan (Jack) 6-2 180 D
B. Toronto, Ont., May 25, 1952

SSN	TEAM	GP	G	A	PTS.	PIM	+/-
72-73	Pitt	47	1	18	19	40	-21
73-74	Pitt-Det	52	3	16	19	48	-29
74-75	Det-Wash	70	3	20	23	62	-69
75-76	Wash	79	9	13	22	78	-52
76-77	Wash	75	5	25	30	90	-15
77-78	Wash	29	1	8	9	4	-13
78-79	Wash	30	2	6	8	14	+2
Totals		382	24	106	130	336	-197

LYNN, Victor Ivan 5-9 185 D
B. Saskatoon, Sask., Jan. 26, 1925

SSN	TEAM	GP	G	A	PTS.	PIM
43-44	Det	3	0	0	0	4
45-46	Mont	2	0	0	0	0
46-47	Tor	31	6	14	20	44
47-48	Tor	60	12	22	34	53
48-49	Tor	52	7	9	16	36
49-50	Tor	70	7	13	20	36
50-51	Bos	56	14	6	20	69
51-52	Bos	12	2	2	4	4
52-53	Chi	29	0	10	10	23
53-54	Chi	11	1	0	1	2
Totals		326	49	76	125	271

Playoffs

SSN	TEAM	GP	G	A	PTS.	PIM
46-47	Tor	11	4	1	5	16
47-48	Tor	9	2	5	7	20
48-49	Tor	8	0	1	1	2
49-50	Tor	7	0	2	2	2
50-51	Bos	5	0	0	0	2
52-53	Chi	7	1	1	2	4
Totals		47	7	10	17	46

LYON, Steven 5-10 169 D
B. Toronto, Ont., May 16, 1952

SSN	TEAM	GP	G	A	PTS.	PIM	+/-
76-77	Pitt	3	0	0	0	2	0

LYONS, Ronald (Peaches) 5-11 170 LW
B. Portage in Prairie, Man., Feb. 15, 1909

SSN	TEAM	GP	G	A	PTS.	PIM
30-31	Bos-Phil Q	36	2	4	6	29

Playoffs

SSN	TEAM	GP	G	A	PTS.	PIM
30-31	Bos	5	0	0	0	0

LYSIAK, Thomas James 6-1 195 C
B. High Prairie, Alta., Apr. 22, 1953

SSN	TEAM	GP	G	A	PTS.	PIM	+/-
73-74	Atl	77	19	45	64	54	-15
74-75	Atl	77	25	52	77	73	+23
75-76	Atl	80	31	51	82	60	+2
76-77	Atl	79	30	51	81	52	+3
77-78	Atl	80	27	42	69	54	-3
78-79	Atl-Chi	66	23	45	68	50	+19
79-80	Chi	77	26	43	69	31	-7
80-81	Chi	72	21	55	76	20	+7
81-82	Chi	71	32	50	82	84	-8
82-83	Chi	61	23	38	61	27	+13
83-84	Chi	54	17	30	47	35	-13
84-85	Chi	74	16	30	46	13	-16
85-86	Chi	51	2	19	21	14	-19
Totals		919	292	551	843	567	-14

Playoffs

SSN	TEAM	GP	G	A	PTS.	PIM
73-74	Atl	4	0	2	2	0
75-76	Atl	2	0	0	0	2
76-77	Atl	3	1	3	4	8
77-78	Atl	2	1	0	1	2
78-79	Chi	4	0	0	0	2
79-80	Chi	7	4	4	8	0
80-81	Chi	3	0	3	3	0
81-82	Chi	15	6	9	15	13
82-83	Chi	13	6	7	13	8
83-84	Chi	5	1	1	2	2
84-85	Chi	15	4	8	12	10
85-86	Chi	3	2	1	3	2
Totals		78	25	38	63	49

MacADAM, Reginald Alan (Al) 6-0 180 RW
B. Charlottetown, P.E.I., Mar. 16, 1952

SSN	TEAM	GP	G	A	PTS.	PIM	+/-
73-74	Phil	5	0	0	0	0	-2
74-75	Cal	80	18	25	43	55	-23
75-76	Cal	80	32	31	63	49	-9
76-77	Clev	80	22	41	63	68	-2
77-78	Clev	80	16	32	48	42	-19
78-79	Minn	69	24	34	58	30	0
79-80	Minn	80	42	51	93	24	+36
80-81	Minn	78	21	39	60	94	-6

SSN	TEAM	GP	G	A	PTS.	PIM	+/-
81–82	Minn	79	18	43	61	37	+9
82–83	Minn	73	11	22	33	60	+3
83–84	Minn	80	22	13	35	23	-5
84–85	Van	80	14	20	34	27	-29
Totals		864	240	351	591	509	-47

Playoffs

73–74	Phil	1	0	0	0	0	
79–80	Minn	15	7	9	16	4	
80–81	Minn	19	9	10	19	4	
81–82	Minn	4	1	0	1	4	
82–83	Minn	9	2	1	3	2	
83–84	Minn	16	1	4	5	7	
Totals		64	20	24	44	21	

MacDERMID, Paul 6-1 205 RW
B. Chesley, Ont., Apr. 14, 1963

81–82	Hart	3	1	0	1	2	0
82–83	Hart	7	0	0	0	2	-6
83–84	Hart	3	0	1	1	0	+1
84–85	Hart	31	4	7	11	29	+3
85–86	Hart	74	13	10	23	160	+1
86–87	Hart	72	7	11	18	202	+3
87–88	Hart	80	20	15	35	139	+3
88–89	Hart	74	17	27	44	141	+1
89–90	Hart–Winn	73	13	22	35	169	+5
90–91	Winn	69	15	21	36	128	-6
91–92	Winn–Wash	74	12	16	28	194	-6
92–93	Wash	72	9	8	17	80	-13
93–94	Que	44	2	3	5	35	-3
94–95	Que	14	3	1	4	22	+3
Totals		690	116	142	258	1303	-14

Playoffs

85–86	Hart	10	2	1	3	20	
86–87	Hart	6	2	1	3	34	
87–88	Hart	6	0	5	5	14	
88–89	Hart	4	1	1	2	16	
89–90	Winn	7	0	2	2	8	
91–92	Wash	7	0	1	1	22	
94–95	Que	3	0	0	0	2	
Totals		43	5	11	16	116	

MacDONALD, Blair Joseph 5-10 180 RW
B. Cornwall, Ont., Nov. 17, 1953

73–74	Edm (WHA)	78	21	24	45	34	
74–75	Edm (WHA)	72	22	24	46	14	
75–76	Edm–Ind (WHA)	85	27	16	43	22	
76–77	Ind (WHA)	81	34	30	64	28	
77–78	Edm (WHA)	80	34	34	68	11	
78–79	Edm (WHA)	80	34	37	71	44	
79–80	Edm	80	46	48	94	6	+1
80–81	Edm–Van	63	24	33	57	37	-7
81–82	Van	59	18	15	33	20	0
82–83	Van	17	3	4	7	2	-1
NHL Totals		219	91	100	191	65	-7
WHA Totals		476	172	165	337	153	

Playoffs

73–74	Edm (WHA)	5	4	2	6	2	
75–76	Ind (WHA)	7	0	0	0	0	
76–77	Ind (WHA)	9	7	8	15	4	
77–78	Edm (WHA)	5	1	1	2	0	
78–79	Edm (WHA)	13	8	10	18	6	
79–80	Edm	3	0	3	3	0	
80–81	Van	3	0	1	1	2	
81–82	Van	3	0	0	0	0	
82–83	Van	2	0	2	2	0	
NHL Totals		11	0	6	6	2	
WHA Totals		39	20	21	41	12	

MacDONALD, Brett 6-0 195 D
B. Bothwell, Ont., Jan. 5, 1966

87–88	Van	1	0	0	0	0	-1

MacDONALD, Calvin Parker (Parker) 5-11 184 LW
B. Sydney, N.S., June 14, 1933

52–53	Tor	1	0	0	0	0	
54–55	Tor	62	8	3	11	36	
56–57	NYR	45	7	8	15	24	
57–58	NYR	70	8	10	18	30	
59–60	NYR	4	0	0	0	0	
60–61	Det	70	14	12	26	6	
61–62	Det	32	5	7	12	8	
62–63	Det	69	33	28	61	32	

SSN	TEAM	GP	G	A	PTS.	PIM	+/-
63–64	Det	68	21	25	46	25	
64–65	Det	69	13	33	46	38	
65–66	Bos–Det	66	11	16	27	30	
66–67	Det	16	3	5	8	2	
67–68	Minn	69	19	23	42	22	
68–69	Minn	35	2	9	11	0	
Totals		676	144	179	323	253	

Playoffs

54–55	Tor	4	0	0	0	4	
56–57	NYR	1	1	1	2	0	
57–58	NYR	6	1	2	3	2	
60–61	Det	9	1	0	1	0	
62–63	Det	11	3	2	5	2	
63–64	Det	14	3	3	6	2	
64–65	Det	7	1	1	2	6	
65–66	Det	9	0	0	0	2	
67–68	Minn	14	4	5	9	2	
Totals		75	14	14	28	20	

MacDONALD, Craig 6-2 180 C
B. Antigonish, N.S., April 7, 1977

98–99	Car	11	0	0	0	0	0

Playoffs

98–99	Car	1	0	0	0	0	

MacDONALD, Douglas Bruce 6-0 192 LW
B. Assiniboia, Sask., Feb. 8, 1969

92–93	Buf	5	1	0	1	2	0
93–94	Buf	4	0	0	0	0	-2
94–95	Buf	2	0	0	0	0	-1
Totals		11	1	0	1	2	-3

*MacDONALD, James Allen (Kilby) 5-11 178 LW
B. Ottawa, Ont., Sept. 6, 1914

39–40	NYR	44	15	13	28	19	
40–41	NYR	47	5	6	11	12	
43–44	NYR	24	7	9	16	4	
44–45	NYR	36	9	6	15	12	
Totals		151	36	34	70	47	

Playoffs

39–40	NYR	12	0	2	2	4	
40–41	NYR	3	1	0	1	0	
Totals		15	1	2	3	4	

MacDONALD, Kevin 6-0 200 D
B. Prescott, Ont., Feb. 24, 1966

93–94	Ott	1	0	0	0	2	0

MacDONALD, Lowell Wilson 5-11 185 RW
B. New Glasgow, N.S., Aug. 30, 1941

61–62	Det	1	0	0	0	2	
62–63	Det	26	2	1	3	8	
63–64	Det	10	1	4	5	0	
64–65	Det	9	2	1	3	0	
67–68	LA	74	21	24	45	12	-11
68–69	LA	58	14	14	28	10	-11
70–71	Pitt	10	0	1	1	0	-6
72–73	Pitt	78	34	41	75	8	+37
73–74	Pitt	78	43	39	82	14	+17
74–75	Pitt	71	27	33	60	24	+16
75–76	Pitt	69	30	43	73	12	+14
76–77	Pitt	3	1	1	2	0	-1
77–78	Pitt	19	5	8	13	2	0
Totals		506	180	210	390	92	+55

Playoffs

67–68	LA	7	3	4	7	2	
68–69	LA	7	2	3	5	0	
74–75	Pitt	9	4	2	6	4	
75–76	Pitt	3	1	0	1	0	
76–77	Pitt	3	1	2	3	4	
Totals		29	11	11	22	10	

MacDOUGALL, Kim 5-11 180 D
B. Regina, Sask., Aug. 29, 1954

74–75	Minn	1	0	0	0	0	-1

MacEACHERN, Shane 5-11 180 C
B. Charlottetown, P.E.I., Dec. 14, 1967

87–88	StL	1	0	0	0	0	0

SSN	TEAM	GP	G	A	PTS.	PIM	+/-

MACEY, Hubert (Hub) 5-8 178 C
B. Big River, Sask., Apr. 13, 1921

41–42	NYR	9	3	5	8	0	
42–43	NYR	9	3	3	6	0	
46–47	Mont	12	0	1	1	0	
Totals		30	6	9	15	0	

Playoffs

41–42	NYR	1	0	0	0	0	
46–47	Mont	7	0	0	0	0	
Totals		8	0	0	0	0	

MacGREGOR, Bruce Cameron 5-10 180 RW
B. Edmonton, Alta., Apr. 26, 1941

60–61	Det	12	0	1	1	0	
61–62	Det	65	6	12	18	16	
62–63	Det	67	11	11	22	12	
63–64	Det	63	11	21	32	15	
64–65	Det	66	21	20	41	19	
65–66	Det	70	20	14	34	28	
66–67	Det	70	28	19	47	14	
67–68	Det	71	15	24	39	13	-19
68–69	Det	69	18	23	41	14	+6
69–70	Det	73	15	23	38	24	-1
70–71	Det–NYR	74	18	29	47	22	+1
71–72	NYR	75	19	21	40	22	+23
72–73	NYR	52	14	12	26	12	+14
73–74	NYR	66	17	27	44	6	-1
74–75	Edm (WHA)	72	24	28	52	10	
75–76	Edm (WHA)	63	13	10	23	13	
NHL Totals		893	213	257	470	217	+23
WHA Totals		135	37	38	75	23	

Playoffs

60–61	Det	8	1	2	3	6	
62–63	Det	10	1	4	5	40	
63–64	Det	14	5	2	7	12	
64–65	Det	7	0	2	2	2	
65–66	Det	12	1	4	5	2	
69–70	Det	4	1	0	1	2	
70–71	NYR	13	0	4	4	2	
71–72	NYR	16	2	6	8	4	
72–73	NYR	10	2	2	4	2	
73–74	NYR	13	6	2	8	2	
NHL Totals		107	19	28	47	44	

MacGREGOR, Randy Kenneth 5-9 175 RW
B. Cobourg, Ont., July 9, 1953

81–82	Hart	2	1	1	2	2	+2

MacGUIGAN, Garth Leslie 6-0 191 C
B. Charlottetown, P.E.I., Feb. 16, 1956

79–80	NYI	2	0	0	0	0	+1
83–84	NYI	3	0	1	1	0	0
Totals		5	0	1	1	0	+1

MacINNIS, Allan 6-2 196 D
B. Inverness, N.S., July 11, 1963

81–82	Calg	2	0	0	0	0	0
82–83	Calg	14	1	3	4	9	0
83–84	Calg	51	11	34	45	42	0
84–85	Calg	67	14	52	66	75	+7
85–86	Calg	77	11	57	68	76	+38
86–87	Calg	79	20	56	76	97	+20
87–88	Calg	80	25	58	83	114	+13
88–89	Calg	79	16	58	74	126	+38
89–90	Calg	79	28	62	90	82	+20
90–91	Calg	78	28	75	103	90	+42
91–92	Calg	72	20	57	77	83	+13
92–93	Calg	50	11	43	54	61	+15
93–94	Calg	75	28	54	82	95	+35
94–95	StL	32	8	20	28	43	+19
95–96	StL	82	17	44	61	88	+5
96–97	StL	72	13	30	43	65	+2
97–98	StL	71	19	30	49	80	+6
98–99	StL	82	20	42	62	70	+33
Totals		1142	290	775	1065	1296	+306

Playoffs

83–84	Calg	11	2	12	14	13	
84–85	Calg	4	1	2	3	8	
85–86	Calg	21	4	15	19	30	
86–87	Calg	4	1	0	1	0	
87–88	Calg	7	3	6	9	18	
88–89	Calg	22	7	24	31	46	
89–90	Calg	6	2	3	5	8	

SSN	TEAM	GP	G	A	PTS.	PIM	+/-
90-91	Calg	7	2	3	5	8	
92-93	Calg	6	1	6	7	10	
93-94	Calg	7	2	6	8	12	
94-95	StL	7	1	5	6	10	
95-96	StL	13	3	4	7	20	
96-97	StL	6	1	2	3	4	
97-98	StL	8	2	6	8	12	
98-99	StL	13	4	8	12	20	
Totals		142	36	102	138	219	

MacINTOSH, Ian *F*

| 52-53 | NYR | 4 | 0 | 0 | 0 | 4 | |

MacIVER, Donald *6-0 200 D*
B. Montreal, Que., May 3, 1955

| 79-80 | Winn | 6 | 0 | 0 | 0 | 2 | -5 |

MacIVER, Norman Steven *5-11 180 D*
B. Thunder Bay, Ont., Sept. 8, 1964

86-87	NYR	3	0	1	1	0	-5
87-88	NYR	37	9	15	24	14	+10
88-89	NYR-Hart	63	1	32	33	38	-3
89-90	Edm	1	0	0	0	0	-1
90-91	Edm	21	2	5	7	14	+1
91-92	Edm	57	6	34	40	38	+20
92-93	Ott	80	17	46	63	84	-46
93-94	Ott	53	3	20	23	26	-26
94-95	Ott-Pitt	41	4	16	20	16	-2
95-96	Pitt-Winn	71	7	46	53	58	+6
96-97	Phoe	32	4	9	13	24	-11
97-98	Phoe	41	2	6	8	38	-11
Totals		500	55	230	285	350	-68

Playoffs

88-89	Hart	1	0	0	0	2	0
90-91	Edm	18	0	4	4	8	
91-92	Edm	13	1	2	3	10	
94-95	Pitt	12	1	4	5	8	
95-96	Winn	6	1	0	1	2	
97-98	Phoe	6	0	1	1	2	
Totals		56	3	11	14	32	

MacKASEY, Blair *6-2 200 D*
B. Hamilton, Ont., Dec. 13, 1955

| 76-77 | Tor | 1 | 0 | 0 | 0 | 2 | 0 |

MacKAY, Calum (Baldy) *5-9 185 LW*
B. Toronto, Ont., Jan. 1, 1927

46-47	Det	5	0	0	0	0	
48-49	Det	1	0	0	0	0	
49-50	Mont	52	8	10	18	44	
50-51	Mont	70	18	10	28	69	
51-52	Mont	12	0	1	1	8	
53-54	Mont	47	10	13	23	54	
54-55	Mont	50	14	21	35	39	
Totals		237	50	55	105	214	

Playoffs

49-50	Mont	5	0	1	1	2	
50-51	Mont	11	1	0	1	0	
52-53	Mont	7	1	3	4	10	
53-54	Mont	3	0	1	1	0	
54-55	Mont	12	3	8	11	8	
Totals		38	5	13	18	20	

MacKAY, David *D*
B. Edmonton, Alta.

| 40-41 | Chi | 29 | 3 | 0 | 3 | 26 | |

Playoffs

| 40-41 | Chi | 5 | 0 | 1 | 1 | 2 | |

***MacKAY, Duncan (Mickey)** C*
B. Chesley, Ont., May 21, 1894

26-27	Chi	36	14	8	22	23	
27-28	Chi	35	17	4	21	23	
28-29	Pitt Pi-Bos	40	9	2	11	20	
29-30	Bos	40	4	5	9	13	
Totals		151	44	19	63	79	

Playoffs

26-27	Chi	2	0	0	0	0	
28-29	Bos	3	0	0	0	2	
29-30	Bos	6	0	0	0	4	
Totals		11	0	0	0	6	

MacKAY, Murdo John *5-11 175 C*
B. Fort William, Ont., Aug. 8, 1917

45-46	Mont	5	0	1	1	0	
47-48	Mont	14	0	2	2	0	
Totals		19	0	3	3	0	

Playoffs

46-47	Mont	9	0	1	1	0	
47-48	Mont	6	1	1	2	0	
Totals		15	1	2	3	0	

MACKELL, Fleming David *5-8 167 C*
B. Montreal, Que., Apr. 30, 1929

47-48	Tor	3	0	0	0	2	
48-49	Tor	11	1	1	2	0	
49-50	Tor	36	7	13	20	0	
50-51	Tor	70	12	13	25	40	
51-52	Tor-Bos	62	3	16	19	40	
52-53	Bos	65	27	17	44	63	
53-54	Bos	67	15	32	47	60	
54-55	Bos	60	11	24	35	76	
55-56	Bos	52	7	9	16	59	
56-57	Bos	65	22	17	39	73	
57-58	Bos	70	20	40	60	72	
58-59	Bos	57	17	23	40	28	
59-60	Bos	47	7	15	22	19	
Totals		665	149	220	369	532	

Playoffs

48-49	Tor	9	2	4	6	2	
49-50	Tor	7	1	1	2	11	
50-51	Tor	11	2	3	5	9	
51-52	Bos	5	2	1	3	12	
52-53	Bos	11	2	7	9	7	
53-54	Bos	4	1	1	2	8	
54-55	Bos	4	0	1	1	0	
56-57	Bos	10	5	3	8	4	
57-58	Bos	12	5	14	19	12	
58-59	Bos	7	2	6	8	8	
Totals		80	22	41	63	73	

MacKENZIE, John Barry (Barry) *6-0 190 D*
B. Toronto, Ont., Aug. 16, 1941

| 68-69 | Minn | 6 | 0 | 1 | 1 | 6 | -2 |

***MacKENZIE, William Kenneth** 5-11 175 D*
B. Winnipeg, Man., Dec. 12, 1911

32-33	Chi	35	4	4	8	13	
33-34	Mont M	48	4	3	7	20	
34-35	Mont M-NYR	20	1	0	1	10	
36-37	Mont M-Mont	44	4	4	8	38	
37-38	Mont-Chi	46	1	2	3	24	
38-39	Chi	48	1	0	1	14	
39-40	Chi	20	0	1	1	14	
Totals		266	15	14	29	133	

Playoffs

33-34	Mont M	4	0	0	0	0	
34-35	NYR	3	0	0	0	0	
36-37	Mont	5	1	0	1	0	
37-38	Chi	7	0	1	1	11	
Totals		19	1	1	2	11	

MACKEY, David *6-4 200 LW*
B. Richmond, B.C., July 24, 1966

87-88	Chi	23	1	3	4	71	-14
88-89	Chi	23	1	2	3	78	-1
89-90	Minn	16	2	0	2	28	-3
91-92	StL	19	1	0	1	49	-4
92-93	StL	15	1	4	5	23	-3
93-94	StL	30	2	3	5	56	-4
Totals		126	8	12	20	305	-29

Playoffs

91-92	StL	1	0	0	0	0	
93-94	StL	2	0	0	0	2	
Totals		3	0	0	0	2	

***MACKEY, Reginald** 5-7 155 D*
B. Ottawa, Ont., May 7, 1900

| 26-27 | NYR | 34 | 0 | 0 | 0 | 16 | |

Playoffs

| 26-27 | NYR | 1 | 0 | 0 | 0 | 0 | |

***MACKIE, Howard** 5-8 175 D*
B. Kitchener, Ont., Aug. 30, 1913

36-37	Det	13	1	0	1	4	
37-38	Det	7	0	0	0	0	
Totals		20	1	0	1	4	

Playoffs

| 36-37 | Det | 8 | 0 | 0 | 0 | 0 | |

MacKINNON, Paul *6-0 195 D*
B. Brantford, Ont., Nov. 6, 1958

78-79	Winn (WHA)	73	2	15	17	70	
79-80	Wash	63	1	11	12	22	-1
80-81	Wash	14	0	0	0	22	+5
81-82	Wash	39	2	9	11	35	-10
82-83	Wash	19	2	2	4	8	+1
83-84	Wash	12	0	1	1	4	-7
NHL Totals		147	5	23	28	91	-12
WHA Totals		73	2	15	17	70	

Playoffs

| 78-79 | Winn (WHA) | 10 | 2 | 5 | 7 | 4 | |

MacLEAN, Donald *6-2 174 C*
B. Sydney, N.S., Jan. 14, 1977

| 97-98 | LA | 22 | 5 | 2 | 7 | 4 | -1 |

MacLEAN, John *6-0 200 RW*
B. Oshawa, Ont., Nov. 20, 1964

83-84	NJ	23	1	0	1	10	-7
84-85	NJ	61	13	20	33	44	-11
85-86	NJ	74	21	36	57	112	-3
86-87	NJ	80	31	36	67	120	-23
87-88	NJ	76	23	16	39	147	-10
88-89	NJ	74	42	45	87	122	+26
89-90	NJ	80	41	38	79	80	+17
90-91	NJ	78	45	33	78	150	+8
92-93	NJ	80	24	24	48	102	-6
93-94	NJ	80	37	33	70	95	+30
94-95	NJ	46	17	12	29	32	+13
95-96	NJ	76	20	28	48	91	+3
96-97	NJ	80	29	25	54	49	+11
97-98	NJ-SJ	77	16	27	43	42	-6
98-99	NYR	82	28	27	55	46	+5
Totals		1067	388	400	788	1242	+47

Playoffs

87-88	NJ	20	7	11	18	60	
89-90	NJ	6	4	1	5	12	
90-91	NJ	7	5	3	8	20	
92-93	NJ	5	0	1	1	10	
93-94	NJ	20	6	10	16	22	
94-95	NJ	20	5	13	18	14	
96-97	NJ	10	4	5	9	4	
97-98	SJ	6	2	3	5	4	
Totals		94	33	47	80	146	

MacLEAN, Paul *6-2 218 RW*
B. Grostenquin, France, Mar. 9, 1958

80-81	StL	1	0	0	0	0	+1
81-82	Winn	74	36	25	61	106	-9
82-83	Winn	80	32	44	76	121	-5
83-84	Winn	76	40	31	71	155	-15
84-85	Winn	79	41	60	101	119	+5
85-86	Winn	69	27	29	56	74	-14
86-87	Winn	72	32	42	74	75	+12
87-88	Winn	77	40	39	79	76	-17
88-89	Det	76	36	35	71	118	+7
89-90	Det	78	34	33	67	100	+2
90-91	StL	37	6	11	17	24	-2
Totals		719	324	349	673	968	-35

Playoffs

81-82	Winn	4	3	2	5	20	
82-83	Winn	3	1	2	3	6	
83-84	Winn	3	1	0	1	0	
84-85	Winn	8	3	4	7	4	
85-86	Winn	2	1	0	1	7	
86-87	Winn	10	5	2	7	16	
87-88	Winn	5	2	0	2	23	
88-89	Det	5	1	1	2	8	
89-90	StL	12	4	3	7	20	
Totals		52	21	14	35	104	

MacLEISH, Richard George *5-11 185 C*
B. Lindsay, Ont., Jan. 3, 1950

| 70-71 | Phil | 26 | 2 | 4 | 6 | 19 | -4 |

SSN	TEAM	GP	G	A	PTS.	PIM	+/-
71–72	Phil	17	1	2	3	9	-9
72–73	Phil	78	50	50	100	69	+15
73–74	Phil	78	32	45	77	42	+21
74–75	Phil	80	38	41	79	50	+29
75–76	Phil	51	22	23	45	16	+6
76–77	Phil	79	49	48	97	42	+46
77–78	Phil	76	31	39	70	33	+24
78–79	Phil	71	26	32	58	47	+4
79–80	Phil	78	31	35	66	28	+23
80–81	Phil	78	38	36	74	25	+22
81–82	Hart–Pitt	74	19	28	47	44	-20
82–83	Pitt	6	0	5	5	2	-5
83–84	Phil–Det	54	10	22	32	8	0
Totals		846	349	410	759	434	+152

Playoffs

70–71	Phil	4	1	0	1	0	
72–73	Phil	10	3	4	7	2	
73–74	Phil	17	13	9	22	20	
74–75	Phil	17	11	9	20	8	
76–77	Phil	10	4	9	13	2	
77–78	Phil	12	7	9	16	4	
78–79	Phil	7	0	1	1	0	
79–80	Phil	19	9	6	15	2	
80–81	Phil	12	5	5	10	0	
81–82	Pitt	5	1	1	2	0	
83–84	Det	1	0	0	0	0	
Totals		114	54	53	107	38	

MacLELLAN, Brian 6–3 215 LW
B. Guelph, Ont., Oct. 27, 1958

82–83	LA	8	0	3	3	7	-5
83–84	LA	72	25	29	54	45	-21
84–85	LA	80	31	54	85	53	+2
85–86	LA–NYR	78	16	29	45	66	-33
86–87	Minn	76	32	31	63	69	-12
87–88	Minn	75	16	32	48	74	-44
88–89	Minn–Calg	72	18	26	44	118	+3
89–90	Calg	65	20	18	38	26	-3
90–91	Calg	57	13	14	27	55	+15
91–92	Det	23	1	5	6	28	+4
Totals		606	172	241	413	541	-94

Playoffs

84–85	LA	3	0	1	1	0	
85–86	NYR	16	2	4	6	15	
88–89	Calg	21	3	2	5	19	
89–90	Calg	6	0	2	2	8	
90–91	Calg	1	0	0	0	0	
Totals		47	5	9	14	42	

MacLEOD, Pat 5–11 190 D
B. Melfort, Sask., June 15, 1969

90–91	Minn	1	0	1	1	0	+1
91–92	SJ	37	5	11	16	4	-32
92–93	SJ	13	0	1	1	10	-19
95–96	Dal	2	0	0	0	0	0
Totals		53	5	13	18	14	-50

MacMILLAN, John 5–9 185 RW
B. Lethbridge, Alta., Oct. 25, 1935

60–61	Tor	31	3	5	8	8	
61–62	Tor	32	1	0	1	8	
62–63	Tor	6	1	1	2	6	
63–64	Tor–Det	33	0	3	3	16	
64–65	Det	3	0	1	1	0	
Totals		105	5	10	15	38	

Playoffs

60–61	Tor	4	0	0	0	0	
61–62	Tor	3	0	0	0	0	
62–63	Tor	1	0	0	0	0	
63–64	Det	4	0	1	1	2	
Totals		12	0	1	1	2	

MacMILLAN, Robert Lea 5–11 185 RW
B. Charlottetown, P.E.I., Dec. 3, 1952

72–73	Minn (WHA)	75	13	27	40	48	
73–74	Minn (WHA)	78	14	34	48	81	
74–75	NYR	22	1	2	3	4	+3
75–76	StL	80	20	32	52	41	+13
76–77	StL	80	19	39	58	11	+1
77–78	StL–Atl	80	38	33	71	49	+17
78–79	Atl	79	37	71	108	14	+34
79–80	Atl	77	22	39	61	10	+3
80–81	Calg	77	28	35	63	47	+18
81–82	Calg–Col	80	22	39	61	41	-20
82–83	NJ	71	19	29	48	8	-35
83–84	NJ	71	17	23	40	23	-21
84–85	Chi	36	5	7	12	12	-16
NHL Totals		753	228	349	577	260	-3
WHA Totals		153	27	61	88	129	

Playoffs

72–73	Minn (WHA)	5	0	3	3	0	
73–74	Minn (WHA)	11	2	3	5	4	
75–76	StL	3	0	1	1	0	
76–77	StL	4	0	1	1	0	
77–78	Atl	2	0	2	2	0	
78–79	Atl	2	0	1	1	0	
79–80	Atl	4	0	0	0	9	
80–81	Calg	16	8	6	14	7	
NHL Totals		31	8	11	19	16	
WHA Totals		16	2	6	8	4	

MacMILLAN, William Stewart 5–10 180 RW
B. Charlottetown, P.E.I., Mar. 7, 1943

70–71	Tor	76	22	19	41	42	+10
71–72	Tor	61	10	7	17	39	-1
72–73	Atl	78	10	15	25	52	-10
73–74	NYI	55	4	9	13	16	-6
74–75	NYI	69	13	12	25	12	0
75–76	NYI	64	9	7	16	10	+5
76–77	NYI	43	6	8	14	13	+4
Totals		446	74	77	151	184	+2

Playoffs

70–71	Tor	6	0	3	3	2	
71–72	Tor	5	0	0	0	0	
74–75	NYI	17	0	1	1	23	
75–76	NYI	13	4	2	6	8	
76–77	NYI	12	2	0	2	7	
Totals		53	6	6	12	40	

MacNEIL, Allister Wences 5–10 180 D
B. Sydney, N.S., Sept. 27, 1935

55–56	Tor	1	0	0	0	2	
56–57	Tor	53	4	8	12	84	
57–58	Tor	13	0	0	0	9	
59–60	Tor	4	0	0	0	2	
61–62	Mont	61	1	7	8	74	
62–63	Chi	70	2	19	21	100	
63–64	Chi	70	5	19	24	91	
64–65	Chi	69	3	7	10	119	
65–66	Chi	51	0	1	1	34	
66–67	NYR	58	0	4	4	44	
67–68	Pitt	74	2	10	12	58	-6
Totals		524	17	75	92	617	-6

Playoffs

61–62	Mont	5	0	0	0	2	
62–63	Chi	4	0	1	1	4	
63–64	Chi	7	0	2	2	25	
64–65	Chi	14	0	1	1	34	
65–66	Chi	3	0	0	0	0	
66–67	NYR	4	0	0	0	2	
Totals		37	0	4	4	67	

MacNEIL, Stephen Bernard (Bernie) 5–11 190 LW
B. Sudbury, Ont., Mar. 7, 1950

72–73	LA (WHA)	42	4	7	11	48	
73–74	StL	4	0	0	0	0	+1
75–76	Cin (WHA)	77	15	12	27	83	
NHL Totals		4	0	0	0	0	+1
WHA Totals		119	19	19	38	131	

MACOUN, Jamie 6–2 197 D
B. Newmarket, Ont., Aug. 17, 1961

82–83	Calg	22	1	4	5	25	+3
83–84	Calg	72	9	23	32	97	+3
84–85	Calg	70	9	30	39	67	+44
85–86	Calg	77	11	21	32	81	+14
86–87	Calg	79	7	33	40	111	+33
88–89	Calg	72	8	19	27	76	+40
89–90	Calg	78	8	27	35	70	+34
90–91	Calg	79	7	15	22	84	+29
91–92	Calg–Tor	76	5	25	30	71	+10
92–93	Tor	77	4	15	19	55	+3
93–94	Tor	82	3	27	30	115	-5
94–95	Tor	46	2	8	10	75	-6
95–96	Tor	82	0	8	8	87	+2
96–97	Tor	73	1	10	11	93	-14
97–98	Tor–Det	74	0	7	7	65	-17
98–99	Det	69	1	10	11	36	-1
Totals		1128	76	282	358	1208	+174

Playoffs

82–83	Calg	9	0	2	2	8	
83–84	Calg	11	1	0	1	0	
84–85	Calg	4	1	0	1	4	
85–86	Calg	22	1	6	7	23	
86–87	Calg	3	0	1	1	8	
88–89	Calg	22	3	6	9	30	
89–90	Calg	6	0	3	3	10	
90–91	Calg	7	0	1	1	4	
92–93	Tor	21	0	6	6	36	
93–94	Tor	18	1	1	2	12	
94–95	Tor	7	1	2	3	8	
95–96	Tor	6	0	2	2	8	
97–98	Det	22	2	2	4	18	
98–99	Det	1	0	0	0	0	
Totals		159	10	32	42	169	

*MacPHERSON, James Albert (Bud) 6–3 205 D
B. Edmonton, Alta., Mar. 21, 1927

48–49	Mont	3	0	0	0	2	
50–51	Mont	62	0	16	16	40	
51–52	Mont	54	2	1	3	24	
52–53	Mont	59	2	3	5	67	
53–54	Mont	41	0	5	5	41	
54–55	Mont	30	1	8	9	55	
56–57	Mont	10	0	0	0	4	
Totals		259	5	33	38	233	

Playoffs

50–51	Mont	11	0	2	2	8	
51–52	Mont	11	0	0	0	0	
52–53	Mont	4	0	1	1	9	
53–54	Mont	3	0	0	0	4	
Totals		29	0	3	3	21	

*MacSWEYN, Donald Ralph 5–11 195 D
B. Hawkesbury, Ont., Sept. 8, 1942

67–68	Phil	4	0	0	0	0	+1
68–69	Phil	24	0	4	4	6	+4
69–70	Phil	17	0	0	0	4	-7
71–72	Phil	2	0	1	1	0	0
72–73	LA (WHA)	78	0	23	23	39	
73–74	LA–Van (WHA)	69	2	21	23	58	
NHL Totals		47	0	5	5	10	-2
WHA Totals		147	2	44	46	97	

Playoffs

68–69	Phil	4	0	0	0	4	
70–71	Phil	4	0	0	0	2	
72–73	LA (WHA)	6	1	2	3	4	
NHL Totals		8	0	0	0	6	
WHA Totals		6	1	2	3	4	

MacTAVISH, Craig 6–1 195 C
B. London, Ont., Aug. 15, 1958

79–80	Bos	46	11	17	28	8	+16
80–81	Bos	24	3	5	8	13	-1
81–82	Bos	2	0	1	1	0	0
82–83	Bos	75	10	20	30	18	+15
83–84	Bos	70	20	23	43	35	+9
85–86	Edm	74	23	24	47	70	+17
86–87	Edm	79	20	19	39	55	+9
87–88	Edm	80	15	17	32	47	-3
88–89	Edm	80	21	31	52	55	+10
89–90	Edm	80	21	22	43	89	+13
90–91	Edm	80	17	15	32	76	-1
91–92	Edm	80	12	18	30	98	-1
92–93	Edm	82	10	20	30	110	-16
93–94	Edm–NYR	78	20	12	32	91	-14
94–95	Phil	45	3	9	12	23	+2
95–96	Phil–StL	668	5	9	14	70	-9
96–97	StL	50	2	5	7	33	-12
Totals		1093	213	267	480	891	+34

Playoffs

79–80	Bos	10	3	2	5	7	
82–83	Bos	17	3	1	4	18	
83–84	Bos	1	0	0	0	0	
85–86	Edm	10	4	4	8	11	
86–87	Edm	21	1	9	10	16	
87–88	Edm	19	0	1	1	31	
88–89	Edm	7	0	1	1	8	

SSN	TEAM	GP	G	A	PTS.	PIM	+/-

MAKELA, Mikko 6–1 194 *LW*
B. Tampere, Finland, Feb. 28, 1965

SSN	TEAM	GP	G	A	PTS.	PIM	+/-
85–86	NYI	58	16	20	36	28	+12
86–87	NYI	80	24	33	57	24	+3
87–88	NYI	73	36	40	76	22	+14
88–89	NYI	76	17	28	45	22	-16
89–90	NYI–LA	65	9	17	26	18	-14
90–91	Buf	60	15	7	22	25	-2
94–95	Bos	11	1	2	3	0	0
Totals		423	118	147	265	139	-3

Playoffs

86–87	NYI	11	2	4	6	8	
87–88	NYI	6	1	4	5	6	
89–90	LA	1	0	0	0	0	
Totals		18	3	8	11	14	

MAKI, Ronald Patrick (Chico) 5–10 170 *RW*
B. Sault Ste. Marie, Ont., Aug. 17, 1939

61–62	Chi	16	4	6	10	2	
62–63	Chi	65	7	17	24	35	
63–64	Chi	68	8	14	22	70	
64–65	Chi	65	16	24	40	58	
65–66	Chi	68	17	31	48	41	
66–67	Chi	56	9	29	38	14	
67–68	Chi	60	8	16	24	4	-10
68–69	Chi	66	7	21	28	30	-1
69–70	Chi	75	10	24	34	27	+9
70–71	Chi	72	22	26	48	18	+31
71–72	Chi	62	13	34	47	22	+44
72–73	Chi	77	13	19	32	10	+5
73–74	Chi	69	9	25	34	12	+13
75–76	Chi	22	0	6	6	2	-9
Totals		841	143	292	435	345	+82

Playoffs

60–61	Chi	1	0	0	0	0	
62–63	Chi	6	0	1	1	2	
63–64	Chi	7	0	0	0	15	
64–65	Chi	14	3	9	12	8	
65–66	Chi	3	1	1	2	0	
66–67	Chi	6	0	0	0	0	
67–68	Chi	2	1	0	1	2	
69–70	Chi	8	2	2	4	2	
70–71	Chi	18	6	5	11	6	
71–72	Chi	8	1	4	5	4	
72–73	Chi	16	2	8	10	0	
73–74	Chi	11	0	1	1	2	
75–76	Chi	4	0	0	0	0	
Totals		104	16	31	47	41	

*MAKI, Wayne 5–11 185 *LW*
B. Sault Ste. Marie, Ont., Nov. 10, 1944

67–68	Chi	49	5	5	10	32	-4
68–69	Chi	1	0	0	0	0	0
69–70	StL	16	2	1	3	4	-4
70–71	Van	78	25	38	63	99	-13
71–72	Van	76	22	25	47	43	-4
72–73	Van	26	3	10	13	6	-11
Totals		246	57	79	136	184	-36

Playoffs

| 69–70 | StL | 2 | 1 | 0 | 1 | 2 | |

MAKKONEN, Karl 6–0 190 *RW*
B. Pori, Finland, Jan. 20, 1955

| 79–80 | Edm | 9 | 2 | 2 | 4 | 0 | -2 |

MALAKHOV, Vladimir 6–3 220 *D*
B. Sverdlovsk, USSR, Aug. 30, 1968

92–93	NYI	64	14	38	52	59	+14
93–94	NYI	76	10	47	57	80	+29
94–95	NYI–Mont	40	4	17	21	46	-3
95–96	Mont	61	5	23	28	79	+7
96–97	Mont	65	10	20	30	43	+3
97–98	Mont	74	13	31	44	70	+16
98–99	Mont	62	13	21	34	77	-7
Totals		442	69	197	266	454	+59

Playoffs

92–93	NYI	17	3	6	9	12	
93–94	NYI	4	0	0	0	6	
96–97	Mont	5	0	0	0	6	
97–98	Mont	9	3	4	7	10	
Totals		35	6	10	16	34	

MALEY, David 6–2 195 *LW*
B. Beaver Dam, Wis., Apr. 24, 1963

85–86	Mont	3	0	0	0	0	
86–87	Mont	48	6	12	18	55	-1
87–88	NJ	44	4	2	6	65	-13
88–89	NJ	68	5	6	11	249	-27
89–90	NJ	67	8	17	25	160	-2
90–91	NJ	64	8	14	22	151	+9
91–92	NJ–Edm	60	10	17	27	104	+8
92–93	Edm–SJ	56	2	7	9	155	-28
93–94	SJ–NYI	56	0	6	6	104	-7
Totals		466	43	81	124	1043	-61

Playoffs

85–86	Mont	7	1	3	4	2	
87–88	NJ	20	3	1	4	80	
89–90	NJ	6	0	0	0	25	
91–92	Edm	10	1	1	2	4	
93–94	NYI	3	0	0	0	0	
Totals		46	5	5	10	111	

MALGUNAS, Stewart 6–0 200 *D*
B. Prince George, B.C., Apr. 21, 1970

93–94	Phil	67	1	3	4	86	+2
94–95	Phil	4	0	0	0	4	-1
95–96	Winn–Van	30	0	1	1	32	-10
96–97	Wash	6	0	0	0	2	+2
97–98	Wash	8	0	0	0	12	+1
98–99	Wash	10	0	0	0	6	-5
Totals		125	1	4	5	142	-11

MALIK, Marek 6–5 190 *D*
B. Ostrava, Czechoslovakia, June 24, 1975

94–95	Hart	1	0	1	1	0	+1
95–96	Hart	7	0	0	0	4	-3
96–97	Hart	47	1	5	6	50	+5
98–99	Car	52	2	9	11	36	-6
Totals		107	3	15	18	90	-9

Playoffs

| 98–99 | Car | 4 | 0 | 0 | 0 | 4 | |

MALINOWSKI, Merlin Trevis 6–0 190 *C*
B. North Battleford, Sask., Sept. 27, 1958

78–79	Col	54	6	17	23	10	-17
79–80	Col	10	2	4	6	2	-1
80–81	Col	69	25	37	62	61	-24
81–82	Col	69	13	28	41	32	-22
82–83	NJ–Hart	80	8	25	33	16	-40
Totals		282	54	111	165	121	-104

MALKOC, Dean 6–3 200 *D*
B. Vancouver, B.C., Jan. 26, 1970

95–96	Van	41	0	2	2	136	-10
96–97	Bos	33	0	0	0	70	-14
97–98	Bos	40	1	0	1	86	-12
98–99	NYI	2	0	1	1	7	+3
Totals		116	1	3	4	299	-33

MALLETTE, Troy Matthew 6–2 210 *LW*
B. Sudbury, Ont., Feb. 25, 1970

89–90	NYR	79	13	16	29	305	-8
90–91	NYR	71	12	10	22	252	-8
91–92	Edm–NJ	32	4	7	11	79	+6
92–93	NJ	34	4	3	7	56	+3
93–94	Ott	82	7	16	23	166	-33
94–95	Ott	23	3	5	8	35	+6
95–96	Ott	64	2	3	5	171	-7
96–97	Bos	68	6	8	14	155	-8
97–98	TB	3	0	0	0	7	0
Totals		456	51	68	119	1226	-49

Playoffs

89–90	NYR	10	2	2	4	81	
90–91	NYR	5	0	0	0	18	
Totals		15	2	2	4	99	

MALONE, Clifford 5–10 155 *RW*
B. Quebec City, Que., Sept. 4, 1925

| 51–52 | Mont | 3 | 0 | 0 | 0 | 0 | |

*MALONE, Maurice Joseph (Joe) *F*
B. Sillery, Que., Feb. 28, 1890

17–18	Mont	20	44	0	44	12	
18–19	Mont	8	7	1	8	3	
19–20	Que	24	39	6	45	12	
20–21	Ham	20	30	4	34	2	
21–22	Ham	24	25	7	32	4	
22–23	Mont	20	1	0	1	2	
23–24	Mont	9	0	0	0	0	
Totals		125	146	18	164	35	

Playoffs

17–18	Mont	2	1	0	1	0	
18–19	Mont	5	6	1	7	0	
22–23	Mont	2	0	0	0	0	
Totals		9	7	1	8	0	

MALONE, William Gregory (Greg) 6–0 190 *C*
B. Fredericton, N.B., Mar. 8, 1956

76–77	Pitt	66	18	19	37	43	+3
77–78	Pitt	78	18	43	61	80	-16
78–79	Pitt	80	35	30	65	52	+16
79–80	Pitt	51	19	32	51	46	+4
80–81	Pitt	62	21	29	50	68	-14
81–82	Pitt	78	15	24	39	125	-24
82–83	Pitt	80	17	44	61	82	-29
83–84	Hart	78	17	37	54	56	-10
84–85	Hart	76	22	39	61	67	-16
85–86	Hart–Que	49	9	12	21	42	-8
86–87	Que	6	0	1	1	0	0
Totals		704	191	310	501	661	-104

Playoffs

76–77	Pitt	3	1	1	2	2	
78–79	Pitt	7	0	1	1	10	
80–81	Pitt	5	2	3	5	16	
81–82	Pitt	3	0	0	0	4	
85–86	Que	1	0	0	0	0	
86–87	Que	1	0	0	0	0	
Totals		20	3	5	8	32	

MALONEY, Daniel Charles 6–2 195 *LW*
B. Barrie, Ont., Sept. 24, 1950

70–71	Chi	74	12	14	26	174	+7
72–73	Chi–LA	71	17	24	41	81	+17
73–74	LA	65	15	17	32	113	+6
74–75	LA	80	27	39	66	165	+29
75–76	Det	77	27	39	66	203	0
76–77	Det	34	13	13	26	64	+3
77–78	Det–Tor	79	19	33	52	176	-1
78–79	Tor	77	17	36	53	157	+19
79–80	Tor	71	17	16	33	102	-13
80–81	Tor	65	20	21	41	183	-10
81–82	Tor	44	8	7	15	71	-11
Totals		737	192	259	451	1489	+46

Playoffs

70–71	Chi	10	0	1	1	8	
73–74	LA	5	0	0	0	2	
74–75	LA	3	0	0	0	2	
77–78	Tor	13	1	3	4	17	
78–79	Tor	6	3	0	3	6	
80–81	Tor	3	0	0	0	4	
Totals		40	4	7	11	35	

MALONEY, David Wilfred 6–1 195 *D*
B. Kitchener, Ont., July 31, 1956

74–75	NYR	4	0	2	2	0	+2
75–76	NYR	21	1	3	4	66	-7
76–77	NYR	66	3	18	21	100	-8
77–78	NYR	56	2	19	21	63	+18
78–79	NYR	76	11	17	28	151	+17
79–80	NYR	77	12	25	37	186	+16
80–81	NYR	79	11	36	47	132	+24
81–82	NYR	64	13	36	49	105	+2
82–83	NYR	78	8	42	50	132	-3
83–84	NYR	68	7	26	33	168	+11
84–85	NYR–Buf	68	3	22	25	51	+23
Totals		657	71	246	317	1154	+89

Playoffs

77–78	NYR	3	0	0	0	11	
78–79	NYR	17	3	4	7	45	
79–80	NYR	8	2	1	3	8	
80–81	NYR	2	0	2	2	9	
81–82	NYR	10	1	4	5	6	
82–83	NYR	7	1	6	7	10	
83–84	NYR	1	0	0	0	0	
84–85	Buf	1	0	0	0	0	
Totals		49	7	17	24	91	

MALONEY, Donald Michael 6-1 190 LW
B. Lindsay, Ont., Sept. 5, 1958

SSN	TEAM	GP	G	A	PTS.	PIM	+/-
78-79	NYR	28	9	17	26	39	+4
79-80	NYR	79	25	48	73	97	-15
80-81	NYR	61	29	23	52	99	+17
81-82	NYR	54	22	36	58	73	+9
82-83	NYR	78	29	40	69	88	-5
83-84	NYR	79	24	42	66	62	-5
84-85	NYR	37	11	16	27	32	-9
85-86	NYR	68	11	17	28	56	+18
86-87	NYR	72	19	38	57	117	+7
87-88	NYR	66	12	21	33	60	+12
88-89	NYR-Hart	52	7	20	27	39	+3
89-90	NYI	79	16	27	43	47	+6
90-91	NYI	12	0	5	5	6	-3
Totals		765	214	350	564	815	+39

Playoffs

SSN	TEAM	GP	G	A	PTS.	PIM
78-79	NYR	18	7	13	20	19
79-80	NYR	9	0	4	4	10
80-81	NYR	19	1	6	7	13
81-82	NYR	10	5	5	10	10
82-83	NYR	5	0	1	1	0
83-84	NYR	5	1	4	5	0
84-85	NYR	3	4	0	4	2
85-86	NYR	16	2	1	3	31
86-87	NYR	6	2	1	3	6
88-89	Hart	4	0	0	0	8
89-90	NYI	5	0	0	0	2
Totals		94	22	35	57	101

MALONEY, Philip Francis 5-9 170 C
B. Ottawa, Ont., Oct. 6, 1927

SSN	TEAM	GP	G	A	PTS.	PIM
49-50	Bos	70	15	31	46	6
50-51	Bos-Tor	14	3	0	3	2
52-53	Tor	29	2	6	8	2
58-59	Chi	24	2	2	4	6
59-60	Chi	21	6	4	10	0
Totals		158	28	43	71	16

Playoffs

SSN	TEAM	GP	G	A	PTS.	PIM
58-59	Chi	6	0	0	0	0

MALTAIS, Steve 6-2 205 LW
B. Arvida, Que., Jan. 25, 1969

SSN	TEAM	GP	G	A	PTS.	PIM	+/-
89-90	Wash	8	0	0	0	2	-2
90-91	Wash	7	0	0	0	2	-1
91-92	Minn	12	2	1	3	2	-1
92-93	TB	63	7	13	20	35	-20
93-94	Det	4	0	1	1	0	-1
Totals		94	9	15	24	41	-25

Playoffs

SSN	TEAM	GP	G	A	PTS.	PIM
88-89	Wash	1	0	0	0	0

MALTBY, Kirk 6-0 180 RW
B. Guelph, Ont., Dec. 22, 1972

SSN	TEAM	GP	G	A	PTS.	PIM	+/-
93-94	Edm	68	11	8	19	74	-2
94-95	Edm	47	8	3	11	49	-11
95-96	Edm-Det	55	3	6	9	67	-16
96-97	Det	66	3	5	8	75	+3
97-98	Det	65	14	9	23	89	+11
98-99	Det	53	8	6	14	34	-6
Totals		354	47	37	84	388	-21

Playoffs

SSN	TEAM	GP	G	A	PTS.	PIM
95-96	Det	8	0	1	1	4
96-97	Det	20	5	2	7	24
97-98	Det	22	3	1	4	30
98-99	Det	10	1	0	1	8
Totals		60	9	4	13	66

MALUTA, Raymond William 5-8 173 D
B. Flin Flon, Man., July 24, 1954

SSN	TEAM	GP	G	A	PTS.	PIM	+/-
75-76	Bos	2	0	0	0	2	-3
76-77	Bos	23	2	3	5	4	+4
Totals		25	2	3	5	6	+1

Playoffs

SSN	TEAM	GP	G	A	PTS.	PIM
75-76	Bos	2	0	0	0	0

MANASTERSKY, Timothy (Tom) 5-9 185 D
B. Montreal, Que., Mar. 7, 1929

SSN	TEAM	GP	G	A	PTS.	PIM
50-51	Mont	6	0	0	0	11

*MANCUSO, Felix (Gus) F
B. Niagara Falls, Ont., Apr. 11, 1914

SSN	TEAM	GP	G	A	PTS.	PIM
37-38	Mont	17	1	1	2	4
38-39	Mont	2	0	0	0	0
39-40	Mont	2	0	0	0	0
42-43	NYR	21	6	8	14	13
Totals		42	7	9	16	17

MANDERVILLE, Kent Stephen 6-3 207 LW
B. Edmonton, Alta., Apr. 12, 1971

SSN	TEAM	GP	G	A	PTS.	PIM	+/-
91-92	Tor	15	0	4	4	0	+1
92-93	Tor	18	1	1	2	17	-9
93-94	Tor	67	7	9	16	63	+5
94-95	Tor	36	0	1	1	22	-2
95-96	Edm	37	3	5	8	38	-5
96-97	Hart	44	6	5	11	18	+3
97-98	Car	77	4	4	8	31	-6
98-99	Car	81	5	11	16	38	+9
Totals		375	26	40	66	227	-4

Playoffs

SSN	TEAM	GP	G	A	PTS.	PIM
92-93	Tor	18	1	0	1	8
93-94	Tor	12	1	0	1	4
94-95	Tor	7	0	0	0	6
98-99	Car	6	0	0	0	2
Totals		43	2	0	2	20

MANDICH, Daniel 6-3 205 D
B. Brantford, Ont., June 12, 1960

SSN	TEAM	GP	G	A	PTS.	PIM	+/-
82-83	Minn	67	3	4	7	169	0
83-84	Minn	31	2	7	9	77	-6
84-85	Minn	10	0	0	0	32	-3
85-86	Minn	3	0	0	0	25	0
Totals		111	5	11	16	303	-9

Playoffs

SSN	TEAM	GP	G	A	PTS.	PIM
82-83	Minn	7	0	0	0	2

MANELUK, Mike 5-11 198 LW
B. Winnipeg, Man., Oct. 1, 1973

SSN	TEAM	GP	G	A	PTS.	PIM	+/-
98-99	Phil-Chi-NYR	45	6	9	15	20	+5

MANERY, Kris Franklin 6-0 185 RW
B. Leamington, Ont., Sept. 24, 1954

SSN	TEAM	GP	G	A	PTS.	PIM	+/-
77-78	Clev	78	22	27	49	14	-15
78-79	Minn	60	17	19	36	16	-13
79-80	Minn-Van-Winn	65	11	9	20	37	-19
80-81	Winn	47	13	9	22	24	-15
Totals		250	63	64	127	91	-62

MANERY, Randy Neal 6-0 185 D
B. Leamington, Ont., Jan. 10, 1949

SSN	TEAM	GP	G	A	PTS.	PIM	+/-
70-71	Det	2	0	0	0	0	+1
71-72	Det	1	0	0	0	0	0
72-73	Atl	78	5	30	35	44	-2
73-74	Atl	78	8	29	37	75	+15
74-75	Atl	68	5	27	32	48	+18
75-76	Atl	80	7	32	39	42	+2
76-77	Atl	73	5	24	29	33	-2
77-78	LA	79	6	27	33	61	-12
78-79	LA	71	8	27	35	64	+6
79-80	LA	52	6	10	16	48	-13
Totals		582	50	206	256	415	+13

Playoffs

SSN	TEAM	GP	G	A	PTS.	PIM
73-74	Atl	4	0	2	2	4
75-76	Atl	2	0	0	0	0
76-77	Atl	3	0	0	0	0
77-78	LA	2	0	0	0	2
78-79	LA	2	0	0	0	6
Totals		13	0	2	2	12

MANN, Cameron 6-0 194 RW
B. Thompson, Man., Apr. 20, 1977

SSN	TEAM	GP	G	A	PTS.	PIM	+/-
97-98	Bos	9	0	1	1	4	+1
98-99	Bos	33	5	2	7	17	0
Totals		42	5	3	8	21	+1

Playoffs

SSN	TEAM	GP	G	A	PTS.	PIM
98-99	Bos	1	0	0	0	0

MANN, James Edward 6-0 205 RW
B. Montreal, Que., Apr. 17, 1959

SSN	TEAM	GP	G	A	PTS.	PIM	+/-
79-80	Winn	72	3	5	8	287	-20
80-81	Winn	37	3	3	6	105	-18
81-82	Winn	37	3	2	5	79	-8
82-83	Winn	40	0	1	1	73	-7
83-84	Winn-Que	38	1	2	3	96	-3
84-85	Que	25	0	4	4	54	+1
85-86	Que	35	0	3	3	148	-2
87-88	Pitt	9	0	0	0	53	0
Totals		293	10	20	30	895	-57

Playoffs

SSN	TEAM	GP	G	A	PTS.	PIM
81-82	Winn	3	0	0	0	7
82-83	Winn	1	0	0	0	0
83-84	Que	3	0	0	0	22
84-85	Que	13	0	0	0	41
85-86	Que	2	0	0	0	19
Totals		22	0	0	0	89

MANN, John Edward Kingsley (Jack) 5-7 180 C
B. Winnipeg, Man., July 27, 1919

SSN	TEAM	GP	G	A	PTS.	PIM
43-44	NYR	3	0	0	0	0
44-45	NYR	6	3	4	7	0
Totals		9	3	4	7	0

MANN, Kenneth Ross 5-11 200 RW
B. Hamilton, Ont., Sept. 5, 1953

SSN	TEAM	GP	G	A	PTS.	PIM	+/-
75-76	Det	1	0	0	0	0	-1

MANN, Norman Thomas 5-10 155 RW
B. Bradford, England, Mar. 3, 1914

SSN	TEAM	GP	G	A	PTS.	PIM
38-39	Tor	16	0	0	0	2
40-41	Tor	15	0	3	3	2
Totals		31	0	3	4	4

Playoffs

SSN	TEAM	GP	G	A	PTS.	PIM
40-41	Tor	1	0	0	0	0

*MANNERS, Rennison (Ren) F

SSN	TEAM	GP	G	A	PTS.	PIM
29-30	Pitt Pi	33	3	2	5	14
30-31	Phil Q	4	0	0	0	0
Totals		37	3	2	5	14

MANNO, Robert 6-0 185 D/LW
B. Niagara Falls, Ont., Oct. 31, 1956

SSN	TEAM	GP	G	A	PTS.	PIM	+/-
76-77	Van	2	0	0	0	0	-2
77-78	Van	49	5	14	19	29	-23
78-79	Van	52	5	16	21	42	-17
79-80	Van	40	3	14	17	14	+5
80-81	Van	20	0	11	11	30	-6
81-82	Tor	72	9	41	50	67	+5
83-84	Det	62	9	13	22	60	-11
84-85	Det	74	10	22	32	32	0
Totals		371	41	131	172	274	-39

Playoffs

SSN	TEAM	GP	G	A	PTS.	PIM
78-79	Van	3	0	1	1	4
79-80	Van	4	1	0	1	6
80-81	Van	3	0	0	0	2
83-84	Det	4	0	3	3	0
84-85	Det	3	1	0	1	0
Totals		17	2	4	6	12

MANSON, Dave 6-2 202 D
B. Prince Albert, Sask., Jan. 27, 1967

SSN	TEAM	GP	G	A	PTS.	PIM	+/-
86-87	Chi	63	1	8	9	146	-2
87-88	Chi	54	1	6	7	185	-12
88-89	Chi	79	18	36	54	352	+5
89-90	Chi	59	5	23	28	301	+4
90-91	Chi	75	14	15	29	191	+20
91-92	Edm	79	15	32	47	220	+9
92-93	Edm	83	15	30	45	210	-28
93-94	Edm-Winn	70	4	17	21	191	-14
94-95	Winn	44	3	15	18	139	-20
95-96	Winn	82	7	23	30	205	+8
96-97	Phoe-Mont	75	4	18	22	187	-26
97-98	Mont	81	4	30	34	122	+22
98-99	Mont-Chi	75	6	17	23	155	+1
Totals		919	97	270	367	2604	-33

Playoffs

SSN	TEAM	GP	G	A	PTS.	PIM
86-87	Chi	3	0	0	0	10
87-88	Chi	5	0	0	0	27
88-89	Chi	16	0	8	8	84
89-90	Chi	20	2	4	6	46
90-91	Chi	6	0	1	1	36
91-92	Edm	16	3	9	12	44
95-96	Winn	6	2	1	3	30
96-97	Mont	5	0	0	0	17
97-98	Mont	10	0	1	1	14

SSN	TEAM	GP	G	A	PTS.	PIM	+/-
Totals		97	7	24	31	308	

MANSON, Raymond Clifton *5-11 180 LW*
B. St. Boniface, Man., Dec. 3, 1926

SSN	TEAM	GP	G	A	PTS.	PIM	+/-
47-48	Bos	1	0	0	0	0	
48-49	NYR	1	0	1	1	0	
Totals		2	0	1	1	0	

*MANTHA, Leon–Georges (George) *5-8 162 LW*
B. Lachine, Que., Nov. 29, 1908

SSN	TEAM	GP	G	A	PTS.	PIM
28-29	Mont	31	0	0	0	8
29-30	Mont	44	5	2	7	16
30-31	Mont	44	11	6	17	25
31-32	Mont	48	1	7	8	8
32-33	Mont	43	3	6	9	10
33-34	Mont	44	6	9	15	12
34-35	Mont	42	12	10	22	14
35-36	Mont	35	1	12	13	14
36-37	Mont	47	13	14	27	17
37-38	Mont	47	23	19	42	12
38-39	Mont	25	5	5	10	6
39-40	Mont	42	9	11	20	6
40-41	Mont	6	0	1	1	0
Totals		498	89	102	191	148

Playoffs

SSN	TEAM	GP	G	A	PTS.	PIM
28-29	Mont	3	0	0	0	0
29-30	Mont	6	0	0	0	0
30-31	Mont	10	5	1	6	4
31-32	Mont	4	0	1	1	8
34-35	Mont	2	0	0	0	4
36-37	Mont	5	0	0	0	0
37-38	Mont	3	1	0	1	0
38-39	Mont	3	0	0	0	0
Totals		36	6	2	8	16

MANTHA, Maurice William (Moe) *6-2 210 D*
B. Lakewood, Ohio, Jan. 21, 1961

SSN	TEAM	GP	G	A	PTS.	PIM	+/-
80-81	Winn	58	2	23	25	35	-33
81-82	Winn	25	0	12	12	28	-10
82-83	Winn	21	2	7	9	6	0
83-84	Winn	72	16	38	54	67	-14
84-85	Pitt	71	11	40	51	54	-35
85-86	Pitt	78	15	52	67	102	-4
86-87	Pitt	62	9	31	40	44	-6
87-88	Pitt-Edm–Minn	76	11	27	38	53	-1
88-89	Minn–Phil	46	4	14	18	43	-4
89-90	Winn	73	2	26	28	28	+8
90-91	Winn	57	9	15	24	33	-20
91-92	Winn–Phil	17	0	4	4	8	0
Totals		656	81	289	370	501	-119

Playoffs

SSN	TEAM	GP	G	A	PTS.	PIM
81-82	Winn	4	1	3	4	16
82-83	Winn	2	2	2	4	0
83-84	Winn	3	1	0	1	0
88-89	Phil	1	0	0	0	0
89-90	Winn	7	1	5	6	2
Totals		17	5	10	15	18

*MANTHA, Sylvio *5-10 178 D*
B. Montreal, Que., Apr. 14, 1902

SSN	TEAM	GP	G	A	PTS.	PIM
23-24	Mont	24	1	0	1	9
24-25	Mont	30	2	0	2	16
25-26	Mont	34	2	1	3	66
26-27	Mont	43	10	5	15	77
27-28	Mont	43	4	11	15	61
28-29	Mont	44	9	4	13	56
29-30	Mont	44	13	11	24	108
30-31	Mont	44	4	7	11	75
31-32	Mont	47	5	5	10	62
32-33	Mont	48	4	7	11	50
33-34	Mont	48	4	6	10	24
34-35	Mont	47	3	11	14	36
35-36	Mont	42	2	4	6	25
36-37	Bos	5	0	0	0	2
Totals		543	63	72	135	667

Playoffs

SSN	TEAM	GP	G	A	PTS.	PIM
23-24	Mont	5	0	0	0	0
24-25	Mont	6	0	0	0	2
26-27	Mont	4	1	0	1	4
27-28	Mont	2	0	0	0	6
28-29	Mont	6	2	1	3	18
30-31	Mont	10	2	1	3	26
31-32	Mont	4	0	1	1	8
32-33	Mont	2	0	1	1	2
33-34	Mont	2	0	0	0	2
34-35	Mont	2	0	0	0	2
Totals		46	5	4	9	70

MARA, Paul *6-4 202 D*
B. Ridgewood, N.J., Sept. 7, 1979

SSN	TEAM	GP	G	A	PTS.	PIM	+/-
98-99	TB	1	1	1	2	0	-3

*MARACLE, Henry Elmer (Buddy) *F*
B. Ayr, Ont., Sept. 8, 1904

SSN	TEAM	GP	G	A	PTS.	PIM
30-31	NYR	11	1	3	4	4

Playoffs

SSN	TEAM	GP	G	A	PTS.	PIM
30-31	NYR	4	0	0	0	0

MARCETTA, Milan (Mike) *6-1 195 C*
B. Cadomin, Alta., Sept. 19, 1936

SSN	TEAM	GP	G	A	PTS.	PIM	+/-
67-68	Minn	36	4	12	16	6	-10
68-69	Minn	18	3	2	5	4	-4
Totals		54	7	14	21	10	-14

Playoffs

SSN	TEAM	GP	G	A	PTS.	PIM
66-67	Tor	3	0	0	0	0
67-68	Minn	14	7	7	14	4
Totals		17	7	7	14	4

*MARCH, Harold C. (Mush) *5-5 154 RW*
B. Silton, Sask., Oct. 18, 1908

SSN	TEAM	GP	G	A	PTS.	PIM
28-29	Chi	35	3	3	6	6
29-30	Chi	43	8	7	15	48
30-31	Chi	44	11	6	17	36
31-32	Chi	48	12	13	25	36
32-33	Chi	48	9	11	20	38
33-34	Chi	48	4	13	17	26
34-35	Chi	47	13	17	30	48
35-36	Chi	48	16	19	35	48
36-37	Chi	37	11	6	17	31
37-38	Chi	41	11	17	28	16
38-39	Chi	46	10	11	21	29
39-40	Chi	45	9	14	23	49
40-41	Chi	44	8	9	17	16
41-42	Chi	48	6	26	32	22
42-43	Chi	50	7	29	36	46
43-44	Chi	48	10	27	37	16
44-45	Chi	38	5	5	10	12
Totals		758	153	233	386	523

Playoffs

SSN	TEAM	GP	G	A	PTS.	PIM
30-31	Chi	9	3	1	4	11
31-32	Chi	2	0	0	0	2
33-34	Chi	8	2	2	4	6
34-35	Chi	2	0	0	0	0
35-36	Bos	2	2	3	5	0
37-38	Chi	10	2	4	6	12
39-40	Chi	2	1	0	1	2
40-41	Chi	5	2	3	5	0
41-42	Chi	3	0	2	2	4
43-44	Chi	5	0	0	0	4
Totals		48	12	15	27	41

MARCHANT, Todd *6-0 180 C*
B. Buffalo, N.Y., Aug. 12, 1973

SSN	TEAM	GP	G	A	PTS.	PIM	+/-
93-94	NYR–Edm	4	0	1	1	2	-2
94-95	Edm	45	13	14	27	32	-3
95-96	Edm	81	19	19	38	66	-19
96-97	Edm	79	14	19	33	44	+11
97-98	Edm	76	14	21	35	71	+9
98-99	Edm	82	14	22	36	63	+3
Totals		367	74	96	170	280	-1

Playoffs

SSN	TEAM	GP	G	A	PTS.	PIM
96-97	Edm	12	4	2	6	12
97-98	Edm	12	1	1	2	10
98-99	Edm	4	1	1	2	12
Totals		28	6	4	10	34

MARCHINKO, Brian Nicholas Wayne *6-0 180 C*
B. Weyburn, Sask., Aug. 2, 1948

SSN	TEAM	GP	G	A	PTS.	PIM	+/-
70-71	Tor	2	0	0	0	0	
71-72	Tor	3	0	0	0	0	
72-73	NYI	36	2	6	8	0	-10
73-74	NYI	6	0	0	0	0	
Totals		47	2	6	8	0	-10

MARCHMENT, Bryan *6-1 205 D*
B. Scarborough, Ont., May 1, 1969

SSN	TEAM	GP	G	A	PTS.	PIM	+/-
88-89	Winn	2	0	0	0	2	0
89-90	Winn	7	0	2	2	28	0
90-91	Winn	28	2	2	4	91	-5
91-92	Chi	58	5	10	15	168	-4
92-93	Chi	78	5	15	20	313	+15
93-94	Chi-Hart	55	4	11	15	166	-14
94-95	Edm	40	1	5	6	184	-11
95-96	Edm	78	3	15	18	202	-7
96-97	Edm	71	3	13	16	132	+13
97-98	Edm-TB-SJ	61	2	11	13	144	-3
98-99	SJ	59	2	6	8	101	+7
Totals		537	27	90	117	1531	-9

Playoffs

SSN	TEAM	GP	G	A	PTS.	PIM
91-92	Chi	16	1	0	1	36
92-93	Chi	4	0	0	0	12
96-97	Edm	3	0	0	0	4
97-98	SJ	6	0	0	0	10
98-99	SJ	6	0	0	0	4
Totals		35	1	0	1	66

MARCINYSHYN, David *6-3 210 D*
B. Edmonton, Alta., Feb. 4, 1967

SSN	TEAM	GP	G	A	PTS.	PIM	+/-
90-91	NJ	9	0	1	1	21	-1
91-92	Que	5	0	0	0	26	-1
92-93	NYR	2	0	0	0	2	-1
Totals		16	0	1	1	49	-3

MARCON, Louis Angelo *5-9 178 D*
B. Fort William, Ont., May 28, 1935

SSN	TEAM	GP	G	A	PTS.	PIM
58-59	Det	31	0	1	1	12
59-60	Det	38	0	3	3	30
62-63	Det	1	0	0	0	0
Totals		70	0	4	4	42

MARCOTTE, Donald Michel *5-10 185 LW*
B. Asbestos, Que., Apr. 15, 1947

SSN	TEAM	GP	G	A	PTS.	PIM	+/-
65-66	Bos	1	0	0	0	0	
68-69	Bos	7	1	0	1	2	0
69-70	Bos	35	9	3	12	14	-3
70-71	Bos	75	15	13	28	30	+20
71-72	Bos	47	6	4	10	12	0
72-73	Bos	78	24	31	55	49	+32
73-74	Bos	78	24	26	50	18	+44
74-75	Bos	80	31	33	64	76	+24
75-76	Bos	58	16	20	36	24	+15
76-77	Bos	80	27	18	45	20	+28
77-78	Bos	77	20	34	54	16	+32
78-79	Bos	79	20	27	47	10	+6
79-80	Bos	32	4	11	15	0	+4
80-81	Bos	72	20	13	33	32	+3
81-82	Bos	69	13	21	34	14	-2
Totals		868	230	254	484	317	+203

Playoffs

SSN	TEAM	GP	G	A	PTS.	PIM
69-70	Bos	14	2	0	2	11
70-71	Bos	4	0	0	0	0
71-72	Bos	14	3	0	3	6
72-73	Bos	5	1	1	2	0
73-74	Bos	16	4	2	6	8
74-75	Bos	3	1	0	1	0
75-76	Bos	12	4	2	6	8
76-77	Bos	14	5	6	11	10
77-78	Bos	15	5	4	9	8
78-79	Bos	11	5	3	8	10
79-80	Bos	10	2	3	5	4
80-81	Bos	3	2	2	4	6
81-82	Bos	11	0	4	4	10
Totals		132	34	27	61	81

MARHA, Josef *6-0 176 C*
B. Havlickuv Brod, Czech., June 2, 1976

SSN	TEAM	GP	G	A	PTS.	PIM	+/-
95-96	Col A	2	0	1	1	0	+1
96-97	Col A	6	0	1	1	0	0
97-98	Col A-Ana	23	9	9	18	4	+4
98-99	Ana-Chi	32	2	6	8	4	+1
Totals		63	11	17	28	8	+6

MARINI, Hector *6-1 200 RW*
B. Timmins, Ont., Jan. 27, 1957

SSN	TEAM	GP	G	A	PTS.	PIM	+/-
78-79	NYI	1	0	0	0	2	-2
80-81	NYI	14	4	7	11	39	+4
81-82	NYI	30	4	9	13	53	+3
82-83	NJ	77	17	28	45	105	-15

SSN	TEAM	GP	G	A	PTS.	PIM	+/-
83–84	NJ	32	2	2	4	47	-2
Totals		154	27	46	73	246	-7

Playoffs

SSN	TEAM	GP	G	A	PTS.	PIM	+/-
78–79	NYI	1	0	0	0	0	
80–81	NYI	9	3	6	9	14	
Totals		10	3	6	9	14	

MARINUCCI, Christopher Jon *6–0 175 C*
B. Grand Rapids, Minn., Dec. 29, 1971

SSN	TEAM	GP	G	A	PTS.	PIM	+/-
94–95	NYI	12	1	4	5	2	-1
96–97	LA	1	0	0	0	0	
Totals		13	1	4	5	2	-3

*MARIO, Frank George *5–8 170 C*
B. Esterhazy, Sask., Feb. 25, 1921

SSN	TEAM	GP	G	A	PTS.	PIM	+/-
41–42	Bos	9	1	1	2	0	
44–45	Bos	44	8	18	26	24	
Totals		53	9	19	28	24	

*MARIUCCI, John *5–10 200 D*
B. Eveleth, Minn., May 8, 1916

SSN	TEAM	GP	G	A	PTS.	PIM	+/-
40–41	Chi	23	0	5	5	33	
41–42	Chi	47	5	8	13	44	
45–46	Chi	50	3	8	11	58	
46–47	Chi	52	2	9	11	110	
47–48	Chi	51	1	4	5	63	
Totals		223	11	34	45	308	

Playoffs

SSN	TEAM	GP	G	A	PTS.	PIM	+/-
40–41	Chi	4	0	2	2	16	
41–42	Chi	3	0	0	0	0	
45–46	Chi	4	0	1	1	10	
Totals		11	0	3	3	26	

MARK, Gordon *6–4 210 D*
B. Edmonton, Alta., Sept. 10, 1964

SSN	TEAM	GP	G	A	PTS.	PIM	+/-
86–87	NJ	36	3	5	8	82	4
87–88	NJ	19	0	2	2	27	-21
93–94	Edm	12	0	1	1	43	-2
Totals		67	3	8	11	152	-19

MARKELL, John Richard *5–11 185 LW*
B. Cornwall, Ont., Mar. 10, 1956

SSN	TEAM	GP	G	A	PTS.	PIM	+/-
79–80	Winn	38	10	7	17	21	-12
80–81	Winn	14	1	3	4	15	-11
83–84	StL	2	0	0	0	0	-4
84–85	Minn	1	0	0	0	0	
Totals		55	11	10	21	36	-27

*MARKER, August Solberg (Gus) *F*
B. Wetaskewin, Alta., Aug. 1, 1907

SSN	TEAM	GP	G	A	PTS.	PIM	+/-
32–33	Det	15	1	1	2	8	
33–34	Det	7	1	0	1	2	
34–35	Mont M	42	11	4	15	18	
35–36	Mont M	47	7	12	19	10	
36–37	Mont M	48	10	12	22	22	
37–38	Mont M	48	9	15	24	35	
38–39	Tor	43	9	6	15	14	
39–40	Tor	42	10	9	19	15	
40–41	Tor	27	4	5	9	10	
41–42	Brk	17	2	5	7	2	
Totals		336	64	69	133	136	

Playoffs

SSN	TEAM	GP	G	A	PTS.	PIM	+/-
33–34	Det	3	1	1	2	2	
34–35	Mont M	7	1	1	2	4	
35–36	Mont M	3	1	0	1	2	
36–37	Mont M	5	0	1	1	0	
38–39	Tor	10	2	2	4	0	
39–40	Tor	10	1	3	4	23	
40–41	Tor	7	0	0	0	5	
Totals		45	6	8	14	36	

MARKHAM, Raymond Joseph *6–3 220 C*
B. Windsor, Ont., Jan. 23, 1958

SSN	TEAM	GP	G	A	PTS.	PIM	+/-
79–80	NYR	14	1	1	2	21	-3

Playoffs

SSN	TEAM	GP	G	A	PTS.	PIM	+/-
79–80	NYR	7	1	0	1	24	

*MARKLE, John A. (Jack) *F*
B. Thessalon, Ont., 1909

SSN	TEAM	GP	G	A	PTS.	PIM	+/-
35–36	Tor	8	0	1	1	0	

MARKOV, Daniil *5–11 176 D*
B. Moscow, USSR, July 11, 1976

SSN	TEAM	GP	G	A	PTS.	PIM	+/-
97–98	Tor	25	2	5	7	28	0
98–99	Tor	57	4	8	12	47	+5
Totals		82	6	13	19	75	+5

Playoffs

SSN	TEAM	GP	G	A	PTS.	PIM	+/-
98–99	Tor	17	0	6	6	18	

*MARKS, John (Jack) *F*

SSN	TEAM	GP	G	A	PTS.	PIM	+/-
17–18	Mont W–Tor	6	0	0	0	0	
19–20	Que	1	0	0	0	4	
Totals		7	0	0	0	4	

MARKS, John Garrison *6–2 200 LW*
B. Hamiota, Man., Mar. 22, 1948

SSN	TEAM	GP	G	A	PTS.	PIM	+/-
72–73	Chi	55	3	10	13	21	+5
73–74	Chi	76	13	18	31	22	+22
74–75	Chi	80	17	30	47	56	+27
75–76	Chi	80	21	23	44	43	-4
76–77	Chi	80	7	15	22	41	-21
77–78	Chi	80	15	22	37	26	+27
78–79	Chi	80	21	24	45	35	+2
79–80	Chi	74	6	15	21	51	-16
80–81	Chi	39	8	6	14	28	-3
81–82	Chi	13	1	0	1	7	0
Totals		657	112	163	275	330	+39

Playoffs

SSN	TEAM	GP	G	A	PTS.	PIM	+/-
72–73	Chi	16	1	2	3	2	
73–74	Chi	11	2	0	2	8	
74–75	Chi	8	2	6	8	34	
75–76	Chi	4	0	0	0	10	
76–77	Chi	2	0	0	0	4	
77–78	Chi	4	0	1	1	0	
78–79	Chi	4	0	0	0	2	
79–80	Chi	4	0	0	0	0	
80–81	Chi	3	0	0	0	0	
81–82	Chi	1	0	0	0	0	
Totals		57	5	9	14	60	

MARKWART, Nevin *5–10 180 LW*
B. Toronto, Ont., Dec. 9, 1964

SSN	TEAM	GP	G	A	PTS.	PIM	+/-
83–84	Bos	70	14	16	30	121	+2
84–85	Bos	26	0	4	4	36	-1
85–86	Bos	65	7	15	22	207	-2
86–87	Bos	64	10	9	19	225	-6
87–88	Bos	25	1	12	13	85	+4
89–90	Bos	8	1	2	3	15	-2
90–91	Bos	23	3	3	6	36	0
91–92	Bos–Calg	28	5	7	12	69	0
Totals		309	41	68	109	794	-5

Playoffs

SSN	TEAM	GP	G	A	PTS.	PIM	+/-
84–85	Bos	1	0	0	0	0	
86–87	Bos	4	0	0	0	9	
87–88	Bos	2	0	0	0	2	
90–91	Bos	12	1	0	1	22	
Totals		19	1	0	1	33	

MARLEAU, Patrick *6–2 200 C*
B. Swift Current, Alta., Sept. 15, 1979

SSN	TEAM	GP	G	A	PTS.	PIM	+/-
97–98	SJ	74	13	19	32	14	+5
98–99	SJ	81	21	24	45	24	+10
Totals		155	34	43	77	38	+15

Playoffs

SSN	TEAM	GP	G	A	PTS.	PIM	+/-
97–98	SJ	5	0	1	1	0	
98–99	SJ	6	2	1	3	4	
Totals		11	2	2	4	4	

MAROIS, Daniel *6–0 190 RW*
B. Montreal, Que., Oct. 3, 1968

SSN	TEAM	GP	G	A	PTS.	PIM	+/-
88–89	Tor	76	31	23	54	76	-4
89–90	Tor	68	39	37	76	82	+1
90–91	Tor	78	21	9	30	112	-16
91–92	Tor–NYI	75	17	16	33	94	-34
92–93	NYI	28	2	5	7	35	-3
93–94	Bos	22	7	3	10	18	-4
95–96	Dal	3	0	0	0	2	0
Totals		350	117	93	210	419	-60

Playoffs

SSN	TEAM	GP	G	A	PTS.	PIM	+/-
87–88	Tor	3	1	0	1	0	
89–90	Tor	5	2	2	4	12	
93–94	Bos	11	0	1	1	16	

SSN	TEAM	GP	G	A	PTS.	PIM	+/-
Totals		19	3	3	6	28	

MAROIS, Mario *5–11 190 D*
B. Quebec City, Que., Dec. 15, 1957

SSN	TEAM	GP	G	A	PTS.	PIM	+/-
77–78	NYR	8	1	1	2	15	-3
78–79	NYR	71	5	26	31	153	+18
79–80	NYR	79	8	23	31	142	0
80–81	NYR– Van–Que	69	5	21	26	181	+6
81–82	Que	71	11	32	43	161	+19
82–83	Que	36	2	12	14	108	+5
83–84	Que	80	13	36	49	151	+51
84–85	Que	76	6	37	43	91	+2
85–86	Que–Winn	76	5	40	45	152	-32
86–87	Winn	79	4	40	44	106	-1
87–88	Winn	79	7	44	51	11	+5
88–89	Winn–Que	49	3	12	15	148	-21
89–90	Que	67	3	15	18	104	-45
90–91	StL	64	2	14	16	81	+17
91–92	StL–Winn	51	1	4	5	72	-11
Totals		955	76	357	433	1746	+10

Playoffs

SSN	TEAM	GP	G	A	PTS.	PIM	+/-
77–78	NYR	1	0	0	0	5	
78–79	NYR	18	0	6	6	29	
79–80	NYR	9	0	2	2	8	
80–81	Que	5	0	1	1	6	
81–82	Que	13	1	2	3	44	
83–84	Que	9	1	4	5	6	
84–85	Que	18	0	8	8	12	
85–86	Winn	3	1	4	5	6	
86–87	Winn	10	1	3	4	23	
87–88	Winn	5	0	4	4	6	
90–91	StL	9	0	0	0	37	
Totals		100	4	34	38	182	

MAROTTE, Jean Gilles (Gilles) *5–9 205 D*
B. Montreal, Que., June 7, 1945

SSN	TEAM	GP	G	A	PTS.	PIM	+/-
65–66	Bos	51	3	17	20	52	
66–67	Bos	67	7	8	15	65	
67–68	Chi	73	0	21	21	122	+4
68–69	Chi	68	5	29	34	120	+23
69–70	Chi–LA	75	5	19	24	52	-11
70–71	LA	78	6	27	33	96	-9
71–72	LA	72	10	24	34	83	-33
72–73	LA	78	6	39	45	102	-21
73–74	LA–NYR	68	3	28	31	51	-12
74–75	NYR	77	4	32	36	69	0
75–76	NYR	57	4	17	21	34	-3
76–77	NYR	47	3	4	7	26	-13
77–78	Ind (WHA)	73	3	20	23	76	
NHL Totals		808	56	265	321	872	-75
WHA Totals		73	3	20	23	76	

Playoffs

SSN	TEAM	GP	G	A	PTS.	PIM	+/-
67–68	Chi	11	3	1	4	14	
73–74	NYR	12	0	1	1	6	
74–75	NYR	3	0	1	1	4	
76–77	StL	3	0	0	0	2	
Totals		29	3	3	6	26	

MARQUESS, Clarence Emmett (Mark) *5–8 160 RW*
B. Bassano, Alta., Mar. 26, 1925

SSN	TEAM	GP	G	A	PTS.	PIM	+/-
46–47	Bos	27	5	4	9	27	

Playoffs

SSN	TEAM	GP	G	A	PTS.	PIM	+/-
46–47	Bos	4	0	0	0	0	

MARSH, Charles Bradley (Brad) *6–3 220 D*
B. London, Ont., Mar. 31, 1958

SSN	TEAM	GP	G	A	PTS.	PIM	+/-
78–79	Atl	80	0	19	19	101	+23
79–80	Atl	80	2	9	11	119	-15
80–81	Calg	80	1	12	13	87	-2
81–82	Calg–Phil	83	2	23	25	116	+1
82–83	Phil	68	2	11	13	52	+20
83–84	Phil	77	3	14	17	83	+24
84–85	Phil	77	2	18	20	91	+42
85–86	Phil	79	0	13	13	123	0
86–87	Phil	77	2	9	11	124	+9
87–88	Phil	70	3	9	12	57	-13
88–89	Tor	80	1	15	16	79	-16
89–90	Tor	79	1	13	14	95	+14
90–91	Tor–Det	42	1	3	4	31	-9
91–92	Det	55	3	4	7	53	+8
92–93	Ott	59	0	3	3	30	-29
Totals		1086	23	175	198	1241	+57

SSN	TEAM	GP	G	A	PTS.	PIM	+/-

Playoffs

SSN	TEAM	GP	G	A	PTS.	PIM	+/-
78–79	Atl	2	0	0	0	17	
79–80	Atl	4	0	1	1	2	
80–81	Calg	16	0	5	5	8	
81–82	Phil	4	0	0	0	2	
82–83	Phil	2	0	1	1	0	
83–84	Phil	3	1	1	2	2	
84–85	Phil	19	0	6	6	65	
85–86	Phil	5	0	0	0	2	
86–87	Phil	26	3	4	7	16	
87–88	Phil	7	1	0	1	8	
89–90	Tor	5	1	0	1	2	
90–91	Det	1	0	0	0	0	
91–92	Det	3	0	0	0	0	
Totals		97	6	18	24	124	

MARSH, Gary Arthur *5–9 172 LW*
B. Toronto, Ont., Mar. 9, 1946

67–68	Det	6	1	3	4	4	+2
68–69	Tor	1	0	0	0	0	0
Totals		7	1	3	4	4	+2

MARSH, Peter *6–1 180 RW*
B. Halifax, N.S., Dec. 21, 1956

76–77	Cin (WHA)	76	23	28	51	52	
77–78	Cin (WHA)	74	25	25	50	123	
78–79	Cin (WHA)	80	43	23	66	95	
79–80	Winn	57	18	20	38	59	-38
80–81	Winn–Chi	53	10	13	23	19	-17
81–82	Chi	57	10	18	28	47	+3
82–83	Chi	68	6	14	20	55	-8
83–84	Chi	43	4	6	10	44	-11
NHL Totals		279	48	71	119	224	-71
WHA Totals		230	91	76	167	270	

Playoffs

76–77	Cin (WHA)	4	2	0	2	0	
78–79	Cin (WHA)	3	1	0	1	0	
80–81	Chi	2	1	1	2	2	
81–82	Chi	12	0	2	2	31	
82–83	Chi	12	0	2	2	0	
NHL Totals		26	1	5	6	33	
WHA Totals		7	3	0	3	0	

MARSHALL, Albert Leroy (Bert) *6–3 205 D*
B. Kamloops, B.C., Nov. 22, 1943

65–66	Det	61	0	19	19	45	
66–67	Det	57	0	10	10	68	
67–68	Det–Oak	57	1	9	10	74	+4
68–69	Oak	68	3	15	18	81	-24
69–70	Oak	72	1	15	16	109	-21
70–71	Cal	32	2	6	8	48	-20
71–72	Cal	66	0	14	14	68	-5
72–73	Cal–NYR	63	2	6	8	85	-39
73–74	NYI	69	1	7	8	84	+5
74–75	NYI	77	2	28	30	58	+18
75–76	NYI	71	0	16	16	72	+37
76–77	NYI	72	4	21	25	61	+48
77–78	NYI	58	0	7	7	44	+10
78–79	NYI	45	1	8	9	29	+9
Totals		868	17	181	198	926	+22

Playoffs

65–66	Det	12	1	3	4	16	
68–69	Cal	7	0	7	7	20	
69–70	Oak	4	0	1	1	12	
72–73	NYR	6	0	1	1	8	
74–75	NYI	17	2	5	7	16	
75–76	NYI	13	1	3	4	12	
76–77	NYI	6	0	0	0	6	
77–78	NYI	7	0	2	2	9	
Totals		72	4	22	26	99	

MARSHALL, Donald Robert *5–10 166 LW*
B. Verdun, Que., Mar. 23, 1932

51–52	Mont	1	0	0	0	0	
54–55	Mont	39	5	3	8	9	
55–56	Mont	66	4	1	5	10	
56–57	Mont	70	12	8	20	6	
57–58	Mont	68	22	19	41	14	
58–59	Mont	70	10	22	32	12	
59–60	Mont	70	16	22	38	4	
60–61	Mont	70	14	17	31	8	
61–62	Mont	66	18	28	46	12	
62–63	Mont	65	13	20	33	6	
63–64	NYR	70	11	12	23	8	
64–65	NYR	69	20	15	35	2	
65–66	NYR	69	26	28	54	6	
66–67	NYR	70	24	22	46	4	
67–68	NYR	70	19	30	49	2	+19
68–69	NYR	74	20	19	39	12	+15
69–70	NYR	57	9	15	24	6	+6
70–71	Buf	62	20	29	49	6	-13
71–72	Tor	50	2	14	16	0	+2
Totals		1176	265	324	589	127	+29

Playoffs

54–55	Mont	12	1	1	2	2	
55–56	Mont	10	1	0	1	0	
56–57	Mont	10	1	3	4	2	
57–58	Mont	10	0	2	2	4	
58–59	Mont	11	0	2	2	2	
59–60	Mont	8	2	2	4	0	
60–61	Mont	6	0	2	2	0	
61–62	Mont	6	0	1	1	2	
62–63	Mont	5	0	1	1	0	
66–67	NYR	4	0	1	1	2	
67–68	NYR	6	2	1	3	0	
68–69	NYR	4	1	0	1	0	
69–70	NYR	1	0	0	0	0	
71–72	Tor	1	0	0	0	0	
Totals		94	8	15	23	14	

MARSHALL, Grant *6–1 185 RW*
B. Mississauga, Ont., June 9, 1973

94–95	Dal	2	0	1	1	0	+1
95–96	Dal	70	9	19	28	111	0
96–97	Dal	56	6	4	10	98	+5
97–98	Dal	72	9	10	19	96	-2
98–99	Dal	82	13	18	31	85	+1
Totals		282	37	52	89	390	+5

Playoffs

96–97	Dal	5	0	2	2	8	
97–98	Dal	17	0	2	2	47	
98–99	Dal	14	0	3	3	20	
Totals		36	0	7	7	75	

MARSHALL, Jason *6–2 195 D*
B. Cranbrook, B.C., Feb. 22, 1972

91–92	StL	2	1	0	1	4	0
94–95	Ana	1	0	0	0	0	-2
95–96	Ana	24	0	1	1	42	+3
96–97	Ana	73	1	9	10	140	+6
97–98	Ana	72	3	6	9	189	-8
98–99	Ana	72	1	7	8	142	-5
Totals		244	6	23	29	517	-6

Playoffs

96–97	Ana	7	0	1	1	4	
98–99	Ana	4	1	0	1	10	
Totals		11	1	1	2	14	

MARSHALL, Paul A. *6–2 180 LW*
B. Toronto, Ont., Sept. 7, 1960

79–80	Pitt	46	9	12	21	9	-2
80–81	Pitt–Tor	26	3	2	5	6	-9
81–82	Tor	10	2	2	4	2	-4
82–83	Hart	13	1	2	3	0	-2
Totals		95	15	18	33	17	-17

Playoffs

79–80	Pitt	1	0	0	0	0	

MARSHALL, Willmott Charles (Willie) *5–10 160 C*
B. Kirkland Lake, Ont., Dec. 1, 1931

52–53	Tor	2	0	0	0	0	
54–55	Tor	16	1	14	15	0	
55–56	Tor	6	0	0	0	0	
58–59	Tor	9	0	1	1	2	
Totals		33	1	15	16	2	

MARSON, Michael Robert *5–9 200 LW*
B. Scarborough, Ont., July 24, 1955

74–75	Wash	76	16	12	28	59	-65
75–76	Wash	57	4	7	11	50	-19
76–77	Wash	10	0	1	1	18	-1
77–78	Wash	46	4	4	8	101	+1
78–79	Wash	4	0	0	0	0	-3
79–80	LA	3	0	0	0	5	-2
Totals		196	24	24	48	233	-89

*MARTIN, Clare George *5–11 180 D*
B. Waterloo, Ont., Feb. 25, 1922

41–42	Bos	13	0	1	1	4	
46–47	Bos	6	3	0	3	0	
47–48	Bos	59	5	13	18	34	
49–50	Det	64	2	5	7	14	
50–51	Det	50	1	6	7	12	
51–52	Chi–NYR	45	1	3	4	14	
Totals		237	12	28	40	78	

Playoffs

41–42	Bos	5	0	0	0	0	
46–47	Bos	5	0	1	1	0	
47–48	Bos	5	0	0	0	6	
49–50	Det	10	0	1	1	0	
50–51	Det	2	0	0	0	0	
Totals		27	0	2	2	6	

MARTIN, Craig *6–2 215 RW*
B. Amherst, N.S., Jan. 21, 1971

94–95	Winn	20	0	1	1	19	-4
96–97	Fla	1	0	0	0	5	0
Totals		21	0	1	1	24	-4

MARTIN, Francis William (Frank) *6–1 194 D*
B. Cayuga, Ont., May 1, 1933

52–53	Bos	14	0	2	2	6	
53–54	Bos	68	3	17	20	38	
54–55	Chi	66	4	8	12	35	
55–56	Chi	61	3	11	14	21	
56–57	Chi	70	1	8	9	12	
57–58	Chi	3	0	0	0	10	
Totals		282	11	46	57	122	

Playoffs

52–53	Bos	6	0	1	1	2	
53–54	Bos	4	0	1	1	0	
Totals		10	0	2	2	2	

MARTIN, Grant Michael *5–10 190 LW*
B. Smooth Rock Falls, Ont., Mar. 13, 1962

83–84	Van	12	0	2	2	6	-2
84–85	Van	12	0	1	1	39	-8
85–86	Wash	11	0	1	1	6	-5
86–87	Wash	9	0	0	0	4	-1
Totals		44	0	4	4	55	-16

Playoffs

86–87	Wash	1	1	0	1	2	

MARTIN, Hubert Jacques (Pit) *5–9 170 C*
B. Noranda, Que., Dec. 9, 1943

61–62	Det	1	0	1	1	0	
63–64	Det	50	9	12	21	21	
64–65	Det	58	8	9	17	32	
65–66	Det–Bos	51	17	12	29	10	
66–67	Bos	70	20	22	42	40	
67–68	Chi	63	16	19	35	36	+9
68–69	Chi	76	23	38	61	73	+9
69–70	Chi	73	30	33	63	61	+22
70–71	Chi	62	22	33	55	40	+18
71–72	Chi	78	24	51	75	56	+44
72–73	Chi	78	29	61	90	30	+29
73–74	Chi	78	30	47	77	43	+29
74–75	Chi	70	19	26	45	34	-3
75–76	Chi	80	32	39	71	44	+6
76–77	Chi	75	17	36	53	22	-4
77–78	Chi–Van	74	16	32	48	48	-27
78–79	Van	64	12	14	26	24	-3
Totals		1101	324	485	809	614	+127

Playoffs

63–64	Det	14	1	4	5	14	
64–65	Det	3	0	1	1	2	
67–68	Chi	11	3	6	9	2	
69–70	Chi	8	3	3	6	4	
70–71	Chi	17	2	7	9	12	
71–72	Chi	8	4	2	6	4	
72–73	Chi	15	10	6	16	6	
73–74	Chi	7	2	0	2	4	
74–75	Chi	8	1	1	2	2	
75–76	Chi	4	1	0	1	4	
76–77	Chi	2	0	0	0	0	
78–79	Van	3	0	1	1	2	
Totals		100	27	31	58	56	

MARTIN, Jack 5–11 184 F
B. St. Catharines, Ont., Nov. 29, 1940

SSN	TEAM	GP	G	A	PTS.	PIM	+/-
60–61	Tor	1	0	0	0	0	

MARTIN, Matt 6–3 205 D
B. Hamden, Conn., Apr. 30, 1971

SSN	TEAM	GP	G	A	PTS.	PIM	+/-
93–94	Tor	12	0	1	1	6	0
94–95	Tor	15	0	0	0	13	+2
95–96	Tor	13	0	0	0	14	-1
96–97	Tor	36	0	4	4	38	-12
Totals		76	0	5	5	71	-11

MARTIN, Richard Lionel 5–11 179 LW
B. Verdun, Que., July 26, 1951

SSN	TEAM	GP	G	A	PTS.	PIM	+/-
71–72	Buf	73	44	30	74	36	-38
72–73	Buf	75	37	36	73	79	+4
73–74	Buf	78	52	34	86	38	-22
74–75	Buf	68	52	43	95	72	+5
75–76	Buf	80	49	37	86	67	+23
76–77	Buf	66	36	29	65	58	+10
77–78	Buf	65	28	35	63	16	+16
78–79	Buf	73	32	21	53	35	-7
79–80	Buf	80	45	34	79	16	+18
80–81	Buf–LA	24	8	15	23	20	+5
81–82	LA	3	1	3	4	2	+1
Totals		685	384	317	701	439	+15

Playoffs

SSN	TEAM	GP	G	A	PTS.	PIM
72–73	Buf	6	3	2	5	12
74–75	Buf	17	7	8	15	20
75–76	Buf	9	4	7	11	12
76–77	Buf	6	2	1	3	9
77–78	Buf	7	2	4	6	13
78–79	Buf	3	0	3	3	0
79–80	Buf	14	6	4	10	8
80–81	LA	1	0	0	0	0
Totals		63	24	29	53	74

*MARTIN, Ronald D. 130 F
B. Calgary, Alta., Aug. 22, 1909

SSN	TEAM	GP	G	A	PTS.	PIM
32–33	NYA	47	5	7	12	6
33–34	NYA	47	8	9	17	30
Totals		94	13	16	29	36

MARTIN, Terry George 5–11 195 LW
B. Barrie, Ont., Oct. 25, 1955

SSN	TEAM	GP	G	A	PTS.	PIM	+/-
75–76	Buf	1	0	0	0	0	0
76–77	Buf	62	11	12	23	8	+6
77–78	Buf	21	3	2	5	9	-1
78–79	Buf	64	6	8	14	33	-17
79–80	Que–Tor	40	6	15	21	2	+1
80–81	Tor	69	23	14	37	32	+15
81–82	Tor	72	25	24	49	39	-18
82–83	Tor	76	14	13	27	28	-29
83–84	Tor	63	15	10	25	51	-8
84–85	Edm–Minn	11	1	3	4	0	+3
Totals		479	104	101	205	202	-48

Playoffs

SSN	TEAM	GP	G	A	PTS.	PIM
76–77	Buf	3	0	2	2	5
77–78	Buf	8	2	0	2	5
79–80	Tor	3	2	0	2	7
80–81	Tor	3	0	0	0	0
82–83	Tor	4	0	0	0	9
Totals		21	4	2	6	26

MARTIN, Thomas Raymond 5–9 170 RW
B. Toronto, Ont., Oct. 16, 1947

SSN	TEAM	GP	G	A	PTS.	PIM	+/-
67–68	Tor	3	1	0	1	0	0
72–73	Ott (WHA)	75	19	27	46	27	
73–74	Tor (WHA)	74	25	32	57	14	
74–75	Tor (WHA)	64	14	17	31	18	
NHL Totals		3	1	0	1	0	0
WHA Totals		213	58	76	134	59	

Playoffs

SSN	TEAM	GP	G	A	PTS.	PIM
72–73	Ott (WHA)	5	0	5	5	2
73–74	Tor (WHA)	12	7	3	10	2
74–75	Tor (WHA)	5	1	5	6	0
WHA Totals		22	8	13	21	4

MARTIN, Tom 6–2 200 LW
B. Kelowna, B.C., May 11, 1965

SSN	TEAM	GP	G	A	PTS.	PIM	+/-
84–85	Winn	8	1	0	1	42	+1
85–86	Winn	5	0	0	0	0	0
86–87	Winn	11	1	0	1	49	+1
87–88	Hart	5	1	2	3	14	-1
88–89	Minn–Hart	42	8	7	15	140	+9
89–90	Hart	21	1	2	3	27	0
Totals		92	12	11	23	249	+10

Playoffs

SSN	TEAM	GP	G	A	PTS.	PIM
84–85	Winn	3	0	0	0	2
88–89	Hart	1	0	0	0	4
Totals		4	0	0	0	6

MARTINEAU, Donald Jean 6–0 190 RW
B. Kimberley, B.C., Apr. 25, 1952

SSN	TEAM	GP	G	A	PTS.	PIM	+/-
73–74	Atl	4	0	0	0	2	-3
74–75	Minn	76	6	9	15	61	-13
75–76	Det	9	0	1	1	0	-1
76–77	Det	1	0	0	0	0	0
Totals		90	6	10	16	63	-17

MARTINI, Darcy 6–4 220 D
B. Castlegar, B.C., Jan. 30, 1969

SSN	TEAM	GP	G	A	PTS.	PIM	+/-
93–94	Edm	2	0	0	0	0	-1

MARTINS, Steve 5–9 175 C
B. Gatineau, Que., Apr. 13, 1972

SSN	TEAM	GP	G	A	PTS.	PIM	+/-
95–96	Hart	23	1	3	4	8	-3
96–97	Hart	2	0	1	1	0	0
97–98	Car	3	0	0	0	0	0
98–99	Ott	36	4	3	7	10	+4
Totals		64	5	7	12	18	+1

MARTINSON, Steven 6–1 205 LW
B. Minnetonka, Minn., June 21, 1959

SSN	TEAM	GP	G	A	PTS.	PIM	+/-
87–88	Det	10	1	1	2	84	+3
88–89	Mont	25	1	0	1	87	-1
89–90	Mont	13	0	0	0	64	-2
91–92	Minn	1	0	0	0	9	0
Totals		49	2	1	3	244	0

Playoffs

SSN	TEAM	GP	G	A	PTS.	PIM
88–89	Mont	1	0	0	0	10

MARUK, Dennis John 5–8 175 C
B. Toronto, Ont., Nov. 17, 1955

SSN	TEAM	GP	G	A	PTS.	PIM	+/-
75–76	Cal	80	30	32	62	44	-6
76–77	Clev	80	28	50	78	68	+4
77–78	Clev	76	36	35	71	50	-26
78–79	Minn–Wash	78	31	59	90	71	-15
79–80	Wash	27	10	17	27	8	0
80–81	Wash	80	50	47	97	87	-7
81–82	Wash	80	60	76	136	128	+4
82–83	Wash	80	31	50	81	71	-21
83–84	Minn	71	17	43	60	42	-17
84–85	Minn	71	19	41	60	56	-2
85–86	Minn	70	21	37	58	67	+13
86–87	Minn	67	16	30	46	52	+5
87–88	Minn	22	7	4	11	15	+1
88–89	Minn	6	0	1	1	2	0
Totals		888	356	522	878	761	-75

Playoffs

SSN	TEAM	GP	G	A	PTS.	PIM
82–83	Wash	4	1	1	2	2
83–84	Minn	16	5	5	10	8
84–85	Minn	9	4	7	11	12
85–86	Minn	5	4	9	13	4
Totals		34	14	22	36	26

MASNICK, Paul Andrew 5–9 165 C
B. Regina, Sask., Apr. 14, 1931

SSN	TEAM	GP	G	A	PTS.	PIM
50–51	Mont	43	4	1	5	14
51–52	Mont	15	1	2	3	2
52–53	Mont	53	5	7	12	44
53–54	Mont	50	5	21	26	57
54–55	Mont–Chi	30	1	1	2	8
57–58	Tor	41	2	9	11	14
Totals		232	18	41	59	139

Playoffs

SSN	TEAM	GP	G	A	PTS.	PIM
50–51	Mont	11	2	1	3	4
51–52	Mont	6	1	0	1	12
52–53	Mont	6	1	0	1	7
53–54	Mont	10	0	4	4	4
Totals		33	4	5	9	27

*MASON, Charles C. (Dutch) 5–10 160 F
B. Seaforth, Ont., Feb. 1, 1912

SSN	TEAM	GP	G	A	PTS.	PIM	+/-
34–35	NYR	46	5	9	14	14	
35–36	NYR	28	1	5	6	30	
37–38	NYA	2	0	0	0	0	
38–39	Det–Chi	19	1	4	5	0	
Totals		95	7	18	25	44	

Playoffs

SSN	TEAM	GP	G	A	PTS.	PIM
34–35	NYR	4	0	1	1	0

*MASSECAR, George LW
B. Waterford, Ont., July 10, 1904

SSN	TEAM	GP	G	A	PTS.	PIM
29–30	NYA	43	7	3	10	18
30–31	NYA	43	4	7	11	16
31–32	NYA	14	1	1	2	12
Totals		100	12	11	23	46

MASTERS, James Edward (Jamie) 6–1 195 D
B. Toronto, Ont., Apr. 14, 1955

SSN	TEAM	GP	G	A	PTS.	PIM	+/-
75–76	StL	7	0	0	0	0	+4
76–77	StL	16	1	7	8	2	-7
78–79	StL	10	0	6	6	0	-6
Totals		33	1	13	14	2	-9

Playoffs

SSN	TEAM	GP	G	A	PTS.	PIM
75–76	StL	1	0	0	0	0
76–77	StL	1	0	0	0	0
Totals		2	0	0	0	0

*MASTERTON, William (Bat) 6–0 189 C
B. Winnipeg, Man., Aug. 13, 1938

SSN	TEAM	GP	G	A	PTS.	PIM	+/-
67–68	Minn	38	4	8	12	4	-4

MATHERS, Frank Sydney 6–0 182 D
B. Winnipeg, Man., Mar. 29, 1924

SSN	TEAM	GP	G	A	PTS.	PIM
48–49	Tor	15	1	2	3	2
49–50	Tor	6	0	1	1	2
51–52	Tor	2	0	0	0	0
Totals		23	1	3	4	4

MATHIASON, Dwight 6–1 190 RW
B. Brandon, Man., May 12, 1963

SSN	TEAM	GP	G	A	PTS.	PIM	+/-
85–86	Pitt	4	1	0	1	2	-4
86–87	Pitt	6	0	1	1	2	-1
87–88	Pitt	23	0	6	6	14	-7
Totals		33	1	7	8	18	-12

MATHIESON, Jim 6–1 209 D
B. Kindersley, Sask., Jan. 24, 1970

SSN	TEAM	GP	G	A	PTS.	PIM	+/-
89–90	Wash	2	0	0	0	4	0

MATHIEU, Marquis 5–11 190 C
B. Hartford, Conn., May 31, 1973

SSN	TEAM	GP	G	A	PTS.	PIM	+/-
98–99	Bos	9	0	0	0	8	-1

MATTE, Christian 5–11 166 RW
B. Hull, Que., Jan. 20, 1975

SSN	TEAM	GP	G	A	PTS.	PIM	+/-
96–97	Col A	5	1	1	2	0	+1
97–98	Col A	5	0	0	0	6	0
98–99	Col A	7	1	1	2	0	-2
Totals		17	2	2	4	6	-1

*MATTE, Joseph D
B. Bourget, Ont., 1893

SSN	TEAM	GP	G	A	PTS.	PIM
19–20	Tor	16	8	2	10	12
20–21	Ham	19	7	9	16	27
21–22	Ham	20	3	3	6	4
25–26	Bos–Mont	9	0	0	0	0
Totals		64	18	14	32	43

MATTE, Joseph D
B. Ottawa, Ont., Mar. 3, 1909

SSN	TEAM	GP	G	A	PTS.	PIM
42–43	Chi	12	0	2	2	8

*MATTE, Roland 5–10 178 D
B. Bourget, Ont., Mar. 15, 1909

SSN	TEAM	GP	G	A	PTS.	PIM
29–30	Det	12	0	1	1	0

MATTEAU, Stephane 6–3 210 LW
B. Rouyn–Noranda, Que., Sept. 2, 1969

SSN	TEAM	GP	G	A	PTS.	PIM	+/-
90–91	Calg	78	15	19	34	93	+17
91–92	Calg–Chi	24	6	8	14	64	+5

SSN	TEAM	GP	G	A	PTS.	PIM	+/-
92–93	Chi	79	15	18	33	98	+6
33–94	Chi–NYR	77	19	19	38	57	+15
94–95	NYR	41	3	5	8	25	-6
95–96	NYR–StL	78	11	15	26	87	-8
96–97	StL	74	16	20	36	50	+11
97–98	SJ	73	15	14	29	60	+4
98–99	SJ	68	8	15	23	73	+2
Totals		592	108	133	241	607	+46

Playoffs

SSN	TEAM	GP	G	A	PTS.	PIM	
90–91	Calg	5	0	1	1	0	
91–92	Chi	18	4	6	10	24	
92–93	Chi	3	0	1	1	2	
93–94	NYR	23	6	3	9	20	
94–95	NYR	9	0	1	1	10	
95–96	StL	11	0	2	2	8	
96–97	StL	5	0	0	0	0	
97–98	SJ	4	0	1	1	0	
98–99	SJ	5	0	0	0	6	
Totals		83	10	15	25	70	

MATTIUSSI, Richard Arthur (Dick) *5-10 185 D*
B. Smooth Rock Falls, Ont., May 1, 1938

SSN	TEAM	GP	G	A	PTS.	PIM	+/-
67–68	Pitt	32	0	2	2	18	-9
68–69	Pitt-Oak	36	4	11	12	30	+1
69–70	Oak	65	4	10	14	38	-21
70–71	Cal	67	3	8	11	38	-34
Totals		200	8	31	39	124	-63

Playoffs

SSN	TEAM	GP	G	A	PTS.	PIM	
68–69	Cal	7	0	1	1	6	
69–70	Oak	1	0	0	0	0	
Totals		8	0	1	1	6	

MATVICHUK, Richard *6-2 190 D*
B. Edmonton, Alta., Feb. 5, 1973

SSN	TEAM	GP	G	A	PTS.	PIM	+/-
92–93	Minn	53	2	3	5	26	-6
93–94	Dal	25	0	3	3	22	+1
94–95	Dal	14	0	2	2	14	-7
95–96	Dal	73	6	16	22	71	+4
96–97	Dal	57	5	7	12	87	+1
97–98	Dal	74	3	15	18	63	+7
98–99	Dal	64	3	9	12	51	+23
Totals		360	19	55	74	334	+23

Playoffs

SSN	TEAM	GP	G	A	PTS.	PIM	
93–94	Dal	7	1	1	2	12	
94–95	Dal	5	0	2	2	4	
96–97	Dal	7	0	1	1	20	
97–98	Dal	16	1	1	2	14	
98–99	Dal	22	1	5	6	20	
Totals		57	3	10	13	70	

*MATZ, Jean (Johnny) *F*

24–25	Mont	30	3	2	5	0	

Playoffs

24–25	Mont	5	0	0	0	2	

MAXNER, Wayne Douglas *5-11 170 LW*
B. Halifax, N.S., Sept. 27, 1942

SSN	TEAM	GP	G	A	PTS.	PIM	
64–65	Bos	54	7	6	13	42	
65–66	Bos	8	1	3	4	6	
Totals		62	8	9	17	48	

MAXWELL, Brad Robert *6-2 195 D*
B. Brandon, Man., July 8, 1957

SSN	TEAM	GP	G	A	PTS.	PIM	+/-
77–78	Minn	75	18	29	47	100	-57
78–79	Minn	70	9	28	37	145	-13
79–80	Minn	58	7	30	37	126	+9
80–81	Minn	27	3	13	16	98	-1
81–82	Minn	51	10	21	31	96	+6
82–83	Minn	77	11	28	39	157	-1
83–84	Minn	78	19	54	73	225	-7
84–85	Minn–Que	68	10	31	41	172	+14
85–86	Tor	52	8	18	26	108	-27
86–87	Van–NYR–Minn	56	3	18	21	43	-7
Totals		612	98	270	368	1270	-80

Playoffs

SSN	TEAM	GP	G	A	PTS.	PIM	
79–80	Minn	11	0	8	8	20	
80–81	Minn	18	3	11	14	35	
81–82	Minn	4	0	3	3	13	
82–83	Minn	9	5	6	11	23	
83–84	Minn	16	2	11	13	40	
84–85	Que	18	2	9	11	35	
85–86	Tor	3	0	1	1	12	
Totals		79	12	49	61	178	

MAXWELL, Bryan Clifford *6-2 200 D*
B. North Bay, Ont., Sept. 7, 1955

SSN	TEAM	GP	G	A	PTS.	PIM	+/-
75–76	Clev (WHA)	73	3	14	17	177	
76–77	Cin (WHA)	34	1	8	9	29	
77–78	NE (WHA)	17	2	1	3	11	
77–78	Minn	18	2	5	7	41	+2
78–79	Minn	25	1	6	7	46	-13
79–80	StL	57	1	11	12	112	-13
80–81	StL	40	3	10	13	137	+7
81–82	Winn	45	1	9	10	110	-11
82–83	Winn	54	7	13	20	131	+6
83–84	Winn-Pitt	48	3	15	18	111	+3
84–85	Pitt	44	0	8	8	57	-23
NHL Totals		331	18	77	95	745	-42
WHA Totals		124	6	23	29	217	

Playoffs

SSN	TEAM	GP	G	A	PTS.	PIM	
75–76	Clev (WHA)	2	0	0	0	4	
76–77	Cin (WHA)	4	0	0	0	29	
79–80	StL	1	0	0	0	9	
80–81	StL	11	0	1	1	54	
82–83	Winn	3	1	0	1	23	
NHL Totals		15	1	1	2	86	
WHA Totals		6	0	0	0	33	

MAXWELL, Kevin *5-9 165 C*
B. Edmonton, Alta., Mar. 30, 1960

SSN	TEAM	GP	G	A	PTS.	PIM	+/-
80–81	Minn	6	0	3	3	7	-1
81–82	Minn-Col	46	6	9	15	52	-17
83–84	NJ	14	0	3	3	2	-9
Totals		66	6	15	21	61	-27

Playoffs

80–81	Minn	16	3	4	7	24	

MAXWELL, Walter (Wally) *F*
B. Ottawa, Ont., Aug. 24, 1933

52–53	Tor	2	0	0	0	0	

MAY, Alan Randy *6-1 200 RW*
B. Barrhead, Alta., Jan. 14, 1965

SSN	TEAM	GP	G	A	PTS.	PIM	+/-
87–88	Bos	3	0	0	0	15	-1
88–89	Edm	3	1	0	1	7	0
89–90	Wash	77	7	10	17	339	-1
90–91	Wash	67	4	6	10	264	-10
91–92	Wash	75	6	9	15	221	-7
92–93	Wash	83	6	10	16	268	+1
93–94	Wash-Dal	51	5	7	12	115	-3
94–95	Dal–Calg	34	2	3	5	119	+3
Totals		393	31	45	76	1348	-18

Playoffs

SSN	TEAM	GP	G	A	PTS.	PIM	
89–90	Wash	15	0	0	0	37	
90–91	Wash	11	1	1	2	37	
91–92	Wash	7	0	0	0	0	
92–93	Wash	6	0	1	1	6	
93–94	Dal	1	0	0	0	0	
Totals		40	1	2	3	80	

MAY, Brad *6-1 210 LW*
B. Toronto, Ont., Nov. 29, 1971

SSN	TEAM	GP	G	A	PTS.	PIM	+/-
91–92	Buf	69	11	6	17	309	-12
92–93	Buf	82	13	13	26	242	+3
93–94	Buf	84	18	27	45	171	-6
94–95	Buf	33	3	3	6	87	+5
95–96	Buf	79	15	29	44	295	+6
96–97	Buf	42	3	4	7	106	-8
97–98	Buf–Van	63	13	10	23	154	+2
98–99	Van	66	6	11	17	102	-14
Totals		518	82	103	185	1466	-24

Playoffs

SSN	TEAM	GP	G	A	PTS.	PIM	
91–92	Buf	7	1	4	5	2	
92–93	Buf	8	1	1	2	14	
93–94	Buf	7	0	2	2	9	
94–95	Buf	4	0	0	0	2	
96–97	Buf	10	1	1	2	32	
Totals		36	3	8	11	59	

MAYER, Derek *6-0 200 D*
B. Rossland, B.C., May 21, 1967

93–94	Ott	17	2	2	4	8	-16

MAYER, Patrick *6-3 225 D*
B. Royal Oak, Mich., July 24, 1961

87–88	Pitt	1	0	0	0	4	0

MAYER, James Patrick *6-0 190 RW*
B. Capreol, Ont., Oct. 30, 1954

SSN	TEAM	GP	G	A	PTS.	PIM	+/-
76–77	Calg (WHA)	21	2	3	5	0	
77–78	NE (WHA)	51	11	9	20	21	
78–79	Edm (WHA)	2	0	0	0	0	
79–80	NYR	4	0	0	0	0	+1
NHL Totals		4	0	0	0	0	+1
WHA Totals		74	13	12	25	21	

MAYER, Sheppard E. (Shep) *F*
B. Sturgeon Falls, Ont.

42–43	Tor	12	1	2	3	4	

MAYERS, Jamal *6-0 190 C*
B. Toronto, Ont., Oct. 24, 1974

SSN	TEAM	GP	G	A	PTS.	PIM	+/-
96–97	StL	6	0	1	1	2	-3
98–99	StL	34	4	5	9	40	-3
Totals		40	4	6	10	42	-6

Playoffs

98–99	StL	11	0	1	1	8	

*MAZUR, Edward Joseph (Spider) *6-2 186 LW*
B. Winnipeg, Man., July 25, 1929

SSN	TEAM	GP	G	A	PTS.	PIM	
53–54	Mont	67	7	14	21	95	
54–55	Mont	25	1	5	6	21	
56–57	Chi	15	0	1	1	4	
Totals		107	8	20	28	120	

Playoffs

SSN	TEAM	GP	G	A	PTS.	PIM	
50–51	Mont	2	0	0	0	0	
51–52	Mont	5	2	0	2	4	
52–53	Mont	7	2	2	4	11	
53–54	Mont	11	0	3	3	7	
Totals		25	4	5	9	22	

MAZUR, Jay *6-2 205 C/RW*
B. Hamilton, Ont., Jan. 22, 1965

SSN	TEAM	GP	G	A	PTS.	PIM	+/-
88–89	Van	1	0	0	0	0	0
89–90	Van	5	0	0	0	4	-2
90–91	Van	36	11	7	18	14	+3
91–92	Van	5	0	0	0	2	-2
Totals		47	11	7	18	20	-1

Playoffs

90–91	Van	6	0	1	1	8	

McADAM, Gary *5-11 175 LW*
B. Smiths Falls, Ont., Dec. 31, 1955

SSN	TEAM	GP	G	A	PTS.	PIM	+/-
75–76	Buf	31	1	2	3	2	0
76–77	Buf	73	13	16	29	17	+17
77–78	Buf	79	19	22	41	44	+3
78–79	Buf–Pitt	68	11	14	25	15	-2
79–80	Pitt	78	19	22	41	63	-17
80–81	Pitt–Det	74	8	23	31	57	-30
81–82	Calg	46	12	15	27	18	-6
82–83	Buf	4	1	0	1	0	-4
83–84	Wash–NJ	62	10	11	21	27	-4
84–85	NJ	4	1	1	2	0	-0
85–86	Tor	15	1	6	7	0	-11
Totals		534	96	132	228	243	-54

Playoffs

SSN	TEAM	GP	G	A	PTS.	PIM	
75–76	Buf	1	0	0	0	0	
76–77	Buf	6	1	0	1	0	
77–78	Buf	8	2	2	4	7	
78–79	Pitt	7	2	1	3	0	
79–80	Pitt	5	1	2	3	9	
81–82	Calg	3	0	0	0	0	
Totals		30	6	5	11	16	

*McADAM, Samuel *5-8 175 C*
B. Sterling, Scotland, May 31, 1908

30–31	NYR	5	0	0	0	0	

McALLISTER, Chris *7-7 225 D*
B. Saskatoon, Sask., June 6, 1975

SSN	TEAM	GP	G	A	PTS.	PIM	+/-
97–98	Van	36	1	2	3	106	-12
98–99	Van-Tor	48	1	3	4	102	-3
Totals		84	2	5	7	208	-15

Playoffs

SSN	TEAM	GP	G	A	PTS.	PIM	+/-
98–99	Tor	6	0	1	1	4	

McALPINE, Chris *6–0 190 D*
B. Roseville, Minn., Dec. 1, 1971

94–95	NJ	24	0	3	3	17	+4
96–97	StL	15	0	0	0	24	-2
97–98	StL	54	3	7	10	36	+14
98–99	StL	51	1	1	2	50	-10
Totals		144	4	11	15	127	+6

Playoffs

96–97	StL	4	0	1	1	0	
97–98	StL	10	0	0	0	16	
98–99	StL	13	0	0	0	2	
Totals		27	0	1	1	18	

McAMMOND, Dean *5–11 185 C*
B. Grand Cache, B.C., June 15, 1973

91–92	Chi	5	0	2	2	0	-2
93–94	Edm	45	6	21	27	16	+12
94–95	Edm	6	0	0	0	0	-1
95–96	Edm	53	15	15	30	23	+6
96–97	Edm	57	12	17	29	28	-15
97–98	Edm	77	19	31	50	46	+9
98–99	Edm-Chi	77	10	20	30	38	+8
Totals		320	62	106	168	151	+17

Playoffs

91–92	Chi	3	0	0	0	2	
97–98	Edm	12	1	4	5	12	
Totals		15	1	4	5	14	

*McANDREW, Hazen Bernard *5–9 175 D*
B. Mayo, Que., Aug. 7, 1917

41–42	Brk	7	0	1	1	6	

McANEELEY, Edward Joseph (Ted) *5–9 185 D*
B. Cranbrook, B.C., Nov. 7, 1950

72–73	Cal	77	4	13	17	75	-29
73–74	Cal	72	4	20	24	62	-24
74–75	Cal	9	0	2	2	4	-6
75–76	Edm (WHA)	79	2	17	19	71	
NHL Totals		158	8	35	43	141	-59
WHA Totals		79	2	17	19	71	

Playoffs

75–76	Edm (WHA)	4	0	0	0	0	

McATEE, Jerome F. (Jud) *5–9 170 LW*
B. Stratford, Ont., Feb. 5, 1920

42–43	Det	1	0	0	0	0	
43–44	Det	1	0	2	2	0	
44–45	Det	44	15	11	26	6	
Totals		46	15	13	28	6	

Playoffs

44–45	Det	14	2	1	3	0	

McATEE, Norman Jerome *5–8 165 C*
B. Stratford, Ont., June 28, 1921

46–47	Bos	13	0	1	1	0	

McAVOY, George *6–0 190 D*
B. Edmonton, Alta., June 21, 1931
@statplayoff:Playoffs

54–55	Mont	4	0	0	0	0	

McBAIN, Andrew *6–1 205 RW*
B. Scarborough, Ont., Jan. 18, 1965

83–84	Winn	78	11	19	30	37	-6
84–85	Winn	77	7	15	22	45	-2
85–86	Winn	28	3	3	6	17	-11
86–87	Winn	71	11	21	32	106	+6
87–88	Winn	74	32	31	63	145	-10
88–89	Winn	80	37	40	77	71	-35
89–90	Pitt-Van	67	9	14	23	73	-11
90–91	Van	13	0	5	5	32	-4
91–92	Van	6	1	0	1	0	-1
92–93	Ott	59	7	16	23	43	-37
93–94	Ott	55	11	8	19	64	-41
Totals		608	129	172	301	633	-151

Playoffs

83–84	Winn	3	2	0	2	0	
84–85	Winn	7	1	0	1	0	
86–87	Winn	9	0	2	2	10	
87–88	Winn	5	2	5	7	29	
Totals		24	5	7	12	39	

McBAIN, Jason *6–2 178 D*
B. Ilion, N.Y., April 12, 1974

95–96	Hart	3	0	0	0	0	-1
96–97	Hart	6	0	0	0	0	-4
Totals		9	0	0	0	0	-5

McBAIN, Mike *6–1 191 D*
B. Kimberley, B.C., Jan. 12, 1977

97–98	TB	27	0	1	1	8	-10
98–99	TB	37	0	6	6	14	-11
Totals		64	0	7	7	22	-21

McBEAN, Wayne *6–2 185 D*
B. Calgary, Alta., Feb. 21, 1969

87–88	LA	27	0	1	1	26	-14
88–89	LA–NYI	52	0	6	6	35	-13
89–90	NYI	5	0	1	1	2	-1
90–91	NYI	52	5	14	19	47	-21
91–92	NYI	25	2	4	6	18	+11
93–94	NYI–Winn	50	3	13	16	40	-34
Totals		211	10	39	49	168	-72

Playoffs

89–90	NYI	2	1	1	2	0	

McBRIDE, Clifford *D*

28–29	Mont M	1	0	0	0	0	
29–30	Tor	1	0	0	0	0	
Totals		2	0	0	0	0	

McBURNEY, James *F*
B. Sault Ste. Marie, Ont., Jan. 3, 1933

52–53	Chi	1	0	1	1	0	

McCABE, Bryan *6–1 200 D*
B. St. Catharines, Ont., June 8, 1975

95–96	NYI	82	7	16	23	156	-24
96–97	NYI	82	8	20	28	165	-2
97–98	NYI–Van	82	4	20	24	209	+19
98–99	Van	69	7	14	21	120	-11
Totals		315	26	70	96	650	-18

*McCABE, Stanley *D*
B. Ottawa, Ont.

29–30	Det	25	7	3	10	23	
30–31	Det	44	2	1	3	22	
32–33	Mont M	1	0	0	0	0	
33–34	Mont M	8	0	0	0	4	
Totals		78	9	4	13	49	

*McCAFFREY, Albert (Bert) *D*
B. Listowel, Ont.

24–25	Tor	30	9	6	15	12	
25–26	Tor	36	14	7	21	42	
26–27	Tor	43	5	5	10	43	
27–28	Tor–Pitt Pi	44	7	4	11	23	
28–29	Pitt Pi	42	1	0	1	34	
29–30	Pitt Pi–Mont	43	4	7	11	38	
30–31	Mont	22	2	1	3	10	
Totals		260	42	30	72	202	

Playoffs

24–25	Tor	2	1	0	1	6	
27–28	Pitt	2	0	0	0	0	
29–30	Mont	6	1	1	2	6	
Totals		10	2	1	3	12	

McCAHILL, John Walter *6–1 215 D*
B. Sarnia, Ont., Dec. 2, 1955

77–78	Col	1	0	0	0	0	0

McCAIG, Douglas *6–0 180 D*
B. Guelph, Ont., Feb. 24, 1919

41–42	Det	9	0	1	1	6	
45–46	Det	6	0	1	1	12	
46–47	Det	47	2	4	6	64	
47–48	Det	29	3	3	6	37	
48–49	Det-Chi	56	1	3	4	60	
49–50	Chi	64	0	4	4	49	
50–51	Chi	53	2	5	7	29	
Totals		264	8	21	29	257	

Playoffs

41–42	Det	2	0	0	0	6	
46–47	Det	5	0	1	1	4	
Totals		7	0	1	1	10	

*McCALLUM, Duncan Selbie *6–1 193 D*
B. Flin Flon, Man., Mar. 29, 1940

65–66	NYR	2	0	0	0	2	
67–68	Pitt	32	0	2	2	36	-2
68–69	Pitt	62	5	13	18	81	-35
69–70	Pitt	14	0	0	0	16	-4
70–71	Pitt	77	9	20	29	95	-13
72–73	Hou (WHA)	69	9	20	29	112	
74–75	Chi (WHA)	31	0	10	10	24	
NHL Totals		187	14	35	49	230	-54
WHA Totals		100	9	30	39	136	

Playoffs

69–70	Pitt	10	1	2	3	12	
72–73	Hou (WHA)	10	2	3	5	6	
NHL Totals		10	1	2	3	12	
WHA Totals		10	2	3	5	6	

McCALMON, Edward *RW*

27–28	Chi	23	2	0	2	8	
30–31	Phil Q	16	3	0	3	6	
Totals		39	5	0	5	14	

McCANN, Richard Leo (Rick) *5–9 178 C*
B. Hamilton, Ont., May 27, 1944

67–68	Det	3	0	0	0	0	0
68–69	Det	3	0	0	0	0	-1
69–70	Det	18	0	1	1	4	-2
70–71	Det	5	0	0	0	0	-2
71–72	Det	1	0	0	0	0	0
74–75	Det	13	1	3	4	2	-4
Totals		43	1	4	5	6	-9

McCARTHY, Daniel *5–9 189 C*
B. St. Mary's, Ont., Apr. 7, 1958

80–81	NYR	5	4	0	4	4	+3

McCARTHY, Kevin *5–11 195 D*
B. Winnipeg, Man., July 14, 1957

77–78	Phil	62	2	15	17	32	+29
78–79	Phil–Van	23	1	2	3	21	0
79–80	Van	79	15	30	45	70	-5
80–81	Van	80	16	37	53	85	-11
81–82	Van	71	6	39	45	84	+12
82–83	Van	74	12	28	40	88	-1
83–84	Van–Pitt	78	6	30	36	113	-40
84–85	Pitt	64	9	10	19	30	-20
85–86	Phil	4	0	0	0	4	0
86–87	Phil	2	0	0	0	0	-1
Totals		537	67	191	258	527	-66

Playoffs

77–78	Phil	10	0	1	1	8	
79–80	Van	4	1	0	1	0	
80–81	Van	3	0	1	1	0	
82–83	Van	4	1	1	2	12	
Totals		21	2	3	5	20	

McCARTHY, Sandy *6–3 225 RW*
B. Toronto, Ont., June 15, 1972

93–94	Calg	79	5	5	10	173	-3
94–95	Calg	37	5	3	8	101	+1
95–96	Calg	75	9	7	16	173	-8
96–97	Calg	33	3	5	8	113	-8
97–98	Calg–TB	66	8	10	18	241	-19
98–99	TB–Phil	80	5	8	13	160	-24
Totals		370	35	38	73	981	-61

Playoffs

93–94	Calg	7	0	0	0	34	
94–95	Calg	6	0	1	1	17	
95–96	Calg	4	0	0	0	10	
98–99	Phil	6	0	1	1	0	
Totals		23	0	2	2	61	

SSN	TEAM	GP	G	A	PTS.	PIM	+/-

*McCARTHY, Thomas *RW*

SSN	TEAM	GP	G	A	PTS.	PIM	+/-
19-20	Que	12	11	2	13	0	
20-21	Ham	22	8	1	9	10	
Totals		34	19	3	22	10	

McCARTHY, Thomas Joseph (Jug) *6-2 200 LW*
B. Toronto, Ont., July 31, 1960

SSN	TEAM	GP	G	A	PTS.	PIM	+/-
79-80	Minn	68	16	20	36	39	-7
80-81	Minn	62	23	25	48	62	+3
81-82	Minn	40	12	30	42	36	+10
82-83	Minn	80	28	48	76	59	+18
83-84	Minn	66	39	31	70	49	+17
84-85	Minn	44	16	21	37	36	+3
85-86	Minn	25	12	12	24	12	-3
86-87	Bos	68	30	29	59	31	+10
87-88	Bos	7	2	5	7	6	+3
Totals		460	178	221	399	330	+54

Playoffs

SSN	TEAM	GP	G	A	PTS.	PIM	+/-
79-80	Minn	15	5	6	11	20	
80-81	Minn	8	0	3	3	6	
81-82	Minn	4	0	2	2	4	
82-83	Minn	9	2	4	6	9	
83-84	Minn	8	1	4	5	6	
84-85	Minn	7	0	2	2	0	
86-87	Bos	4	1	1	2	4	
87-88	Bos	13	3	4	7	18	
Totals		68	12	26	38	67	

McCARTHY, Thomas Patrick Francis *6-1 190 LW*
B. Toronto, Ont., Sept. 15, 1934

SSN	TEAM	GP	G	A	PTS.	PIM	+/-
56-57	Det	3	0	0	0	0	
57-58	Det	18	2	1	3	4	
58-59	Det	15	2	3	5	4	
60-61	Bos	24	4	5	9	0	
Totals		60	8	9	17	8	

*McCARTNEY, Walter *D*

SSN	TEAM	GP	G	A	PTS.	PIM	+/-
32-33	Mont	2	0	0	0	0	

McCARTY, Darren *6-1 210 RW*
B. Burnaby, B.C., Apr. 1, 1972

SSN	TEAM	GP	G	A	PTS.	PIM	+/-
93-94	Det	67	9	17	26	181	+12
94-95	Det	31	5	8	13	88	+5
95-96	Det	63	15	14	29	158	+14
96-97	Det	68	19	30	49	126	+14
97-98	Det	71	15	22	37	157	0
98-99	Det	69	14	26	40	108	+10
Totals		369	77	117	194	818	+55

Playoffs

SSN	TEAM	GP	G	A	PTS.	PIM	+/-
93-94	Det	7	2	2	4	8	
94-95	Det	18	3	2	5	18	
95-96	Det	19	3	2	5	20	
96-97	Det	20	3	4	7	34	
97-98	Det	22	3	8	11	34	
98-99	Det	10	1	1	2	23	
Totals		96	15	19	34	133	

McCASKILL, Edward Joel (Ted) *6-1 195 C*
B. Kapuskasing, Ont., Oct. 29, 1936

SSN	TEAM	GP	G	A	PTS.	PIM	+/-
67-68	Minn	4	0	2	2	0	-2
72-73	LA (WHA)	73	11	11	22	150	
73-74	LA (WHA)	18	2	2	4	63	
NHL Totals		4	0	2	2	0	-2
WHA Totals		91	13	13	26	213	

Playoffs

SSN	TEAM	GP	G	A	PTS.	PIM	+/-
72-73	LA (WHA)	6	2	3	5	12	

McCAULEY, Alyn *5-11 185 C*
B. Brookville, Ont., May 29, 1977

SSN	TEAM	GP	G	A	PTS.	PIM	+/-
97-98	Tor	60	6	10	16	6	-7
98-99	Tor	39	9	15	24	2	+7
Totals		99	15	25	40	8	0

McCLANAHAN, Rob *5-10 180 C*
B. St. Paul, Minn., Jan. 9, 1958

SSN	TEAM	GP	G	A	PTS.	PIM	+/-
79-80	Buf	13	2	5	7	0	+8
80-81	Buf	53	3	12	15	38	-19
81-82	Hart-NYR	39	5	12	17	21	0
82-83	NYR	78	22	26	48	46	+12
83-84	NYR	41	6	8	14	21	0
Totals		224	38	63	101	126	+1

Playoffs

SSN	TEAM	GP	G	A	PTS.	PIM	+/-
79-80	Buf	10	0	1	1	4	
80-81	Buf	5	0	1	1	13	
81-82	NYR	10	2	5	7	2	
82-83	NYR	9	2	5	7	12	
Totals		34	4	12	16	31	

McCLEARY, Trent *6-0 183 RW*
B. Swift Current, Sask., Oct. 10, 1972

SSN	TEAM	GP	G	A	PTS.	PIM	+/-
95-96	Ott	75	4	10	14	68	-15
96-97	Bos	59	3	5	8	33	-16
98-99	Mont	46	0	0	0	29	-1
Totals		180	7	15	22	130	-32

McCLELLAND, Kevin William *6-2 205 RW*
B. Oshawa, Ont., July 4, 1962

SSN	TEAM	GP	G	A	PTS.	PIM	+/-
81-82	Pitt	10	1	4	5	4	+6
82-83	Pitt	38	5	4	9	73	-18
83-84	Pitt-Edm	76	10	24	34	189	+2
84-85	Edm	62	8	15	23	205	-11
85-86	Edm	79	11	25	36	266	+9
86-87	Edm	72	12	13	25	238	-4
87-88	Edm	74	10	6	16	281	+1
88-89	Edm	79	6	14	20	161	-10
89-90	Edm-Det	71	5	6	11	196	-6
90-91	Det	3	0	0	0	7	-4
91-92	Tor	18	0	1	1	33	-3
93-94	Winn	6	0	0	0	19	0
Totals		588	68	112	180	1672	-38

Playoffs

SSN	TEAM	GP	G	A	PTS.	PIM	+/-
81-82	Pitt	5	1	1	2	5	
83-84	Edm	18	4	6	10	42	
84-85	Edm	18	1	3	4	75	
85-86	Edm	10	1	0	1	32	
86-87	Edm	21	2	3	5	43	
87-88	Edm	19	2	3	5	68	
88-89	Edm	7	0	2	2	16	
Totals		98	11	18	29	281	

McCORD, Dennis Frederick *5-10 190 D*
B. Chatham, Ont., July 28, 1951

SSN	TEAM	GP	G	A	PTS.	PIM	+/-
73-74	Van	3	0	0	0	0	

McCORD, Robert Lomer *6-1 202 D*
B. Matheson, Ont., Mar. 30, 1934

SSN	TEAM	GP	G	A	PTS.	PIM	+/-
63-64	Bos	65	1	9	10	49	
64-65	Bos	43	0	6	6	26	
65-66	Det	9	0	2	2	16	
66-67	Det	14	1	2	3	27	
67-68	Det-Minn	73	3	9	12	41	-13
68-69	Minn	69	4	17	21	70	-33
72-73	StL	43	1	13	14	33	-5
Totals		316	10	58	68	262	-51

Playoffs

SSN	TEAM	GP	G	A	PTS.	PIM	+/-
67-68	Minn	14	2	5	7	10	

McCORMACK, John Ronald (Goose) *6-0 185 C*
B. Edmonton, Alta., Aug. 2, 1925

SSN	TEAM	GP	G	A	PTS.	PIM	+/-
47-48	Tor	3	0	1	1	0	
48-49	Tor	1	0	0	0	0	
49-50	Tor	34	6	5	11	0	
50-51	Tor	46	6	7	13	2	
51-52	Mont	54	2	10	12	4	
52-53	Mont	59	1	9	10	9	
53-54	Mont	51	5	10	15	12	
54-55	Chi	63	5	7	12	8	
Totals		311	25	49	74	35	

Playoffs

SSN	TEAM	GP	G	A	PTS.	PIM	+/-
49-50	Tor	6	1	0	1	0	
52-53	Mont	9	0	0	0	0	
53-54	Mont	7	0	1	1	0	
Totals		22	1	1	2	0	

McCOSH, Shawn *6-0 188 C*
B. Oshawa, Ont., June 5, 1969

SSN	TEAM	GP	G	A	PTS.	PIM	+/-
91-92	LA	4	0	0	0	4	0
94-95	NYR	5	1	0	1	2	+1
Totals		9	1	0	1	6	+1

McCOURT, Dale Allen *5-10 180 C*
B. Falconbridge, Ont., Jan. 26, 1957

SSN	TEAM	GP	G	A	PTS.	PIM	+/-
77-78	Det	76	33	39	72	10	+10
78-79	Det	79	28	43	71	14	-27
79-80	Det	80	30	51	81	12	+12
80-81	Det	80	30	56	86	50	-17
81-82	Det-Buf	78	33	36	69	18	-4
82-83	Buf	62	20	32	52	10	-12
83-84	Buf-Tor	77	20	27	47	10	-16
Totals		532	194	284	478	124	-75

Playoffs

SSN	TEAM	GP	G	A	PTS.	PIM	+/-
77-78	Det	7	4	2	6	2	
81-82	Buf	4	2	3	5	0	
82-83	Buf	10	3	2	5	4	
Totals		21	9	7	16	6	

McCREARY, Vernon Keith *5-10 180 RW*
B. Sundridge, Ont., June 19, 1940

SSN	TEAM	GP	G	A	PTS.	PIM	+/-
64-65	Mont	9	0	3	3	4	
67-68	Pitt	70	14	12	26	44	-3
68-69	Pitt	70	25	23	48	42	-23
69-70	Pitt	60	18	8	26	67	-6
70-71	Pitt	59	21	12	33	24	+7
71-72	Pitt	33	4	4	8	22	-10
72-73	Atl	77	20	21	41	21	-22
73-74	Atl	76	18	19	37	62	-8
74-75	Atl	78	11	10	21	8	+12
Totals		532	131	112	243	294	-53

Playoffs

SSN	TEAM	GP	G	A	PTS.	PIM	+/-
69-70	Pitt	10	0	4	4	4	
71-72	Pitt	2	0	0	0	2	
73-74	Atl	4	0	0	0	0	
Totals		16	0	4	4	6	

McCREARY, William *6-0 190 RW*
B. Springfield, Mass., Apr. 15, 1960

SSN	TEAM	GP	G	A	PTS.	PIM	+/-
80-81	Tor	12	1	0	1	4	

McCREARY, William Edward *5-10 172 LW*
B. Sundridge, Ont., Dec. 2, 1934

SSN	TEAM	GP	G	A	PTS.	PIM	+/-
53-54	NYR	2	0	0	0	2	
54-55	NYR	8	0	2	2	0	
57-58	Det	3	1	0	1	2	
62-63	Mont	14	2	3	5	0	
67-68	StL	70	13	13	26	22	+2
68-69	StL	71	13	17	30	50	+4
69-70	StL	73	15	17	32	16	-43
70-71	StL	68	9	10	19	16	+7
Totals		309	53	62	115	108	-30

Playoffs

SSN	TEAM	GP	G	A	PTS.	PIM	+/-
61-62	Mont	1	0	0	0	0	
67-68	StL	15	3	2	5	0	
68-69	StL	12	1	5	6	14	
69-70	StL	15	1	7	8	0	
70-71	StL	6	1	2	3	0	
Totals		49	6	16	22	14	

*McCREEDY, John *5-8 160 RW*
B. Winnipeg, Man., Mar. 23, 1911

SSN	TEAM	GP	G	A	PTS.	PIM	+/-
41-42	Tor	47	15	8	23	14	
44-45	Tor	17	2	4	6	11	
Totals		64	17	12	29	25	

Playoffs

SSN	TEAM	GP	G	A	PTS.	PIM	+/-
41-42	Tor	13	4	3	7	6	
44-45	Tor	8	0	0	0	10	
Totals		21	4	3	7	16	

McCRIMMON, Byron (Brad) *5-11 197 D*
B. Dodsland, Sask., Mar. 29, 1959

SSN	TEAM	GP	G	A	PTS.	PIM	+/-
79-80	Bos	72	5	11	16	94	-3
80-81	Bos	78	11	18	29	148	+27
81-82	Bos	78	1	8	9	83	+4
82-83	Phil	79	4	21	25	61	+24
83-84	Phil	71	0	24	24	76	+19
84-85	Phil	66	8	35	43	81	+52
85-86	Phil	80	13	43	56	85	+83
86-87	Phil	71	10	29	39	52	+45
87-88	Calg	80	7	35	42	98	+48
88-89	Calg	72	5	17	22	96	+43
89-90	Calg	79	4	15	19	78	+18
90-91	Det	64	0	13	13	81	+7
91-92	Det	79	7	22	29	118	+39

SSN	TEAM	GP	G	A	PTS.	PIM	+/-
92–93	Det	60	1	14	15	71	+21
93–94	Hart	65	1	5	6	72	-7
94–95	Hart	33	0	1	1	42	+7
95–96	Hart	58	3	6	9	62	+15
96–97	Phoe	37	1	5	6	18	+2
Totals		1222	81	322	403	1416	+424

Playoffs

SSN	TEAM	GP	G	A	PTS.	PIM
79–80	Bos	10	1	1	2	28
80–81	Bos	3	0	1	1	2
81–82	Bos	2	0	0	0	2
82–83	Phil	3	0	0	0	4
83–84	Phil	1	0	0	0	4
84–85	Phil	11	2	1	3	15
85–86	Phil	5	2	0	2	2
86–87	Phil	26	3	5	8	30
87–88	Calg	9	2	3	5	22
88–89	Calg	22	0	3	3	30
89–90	Calg	6	0	2	2	8
90–91	Det	7	1	1	2	21
91–92	Det	11	0	1	1	8
Totals		116	11	18	29	176

McCRIMMON, John James (Jim) 6–1 210 D
B. Ponoka, Alta., May 29, 1953

SSN	TEAM	GP	G	A	PTS.	PIM	+/-
73–74	Edm (WHA)	75	2	3	5	106	
74–75	Edm (WHA)	34	1	5	6	50	
74–75	StL	2	0	0	0	0	0
75–76	Calg (WHA)	5	0	0	0	2	
NHL Totals		2	0	0	0	0	0
WHA Totals		114	3	8	11	158	

McCULLEY, Robert F

SSN	TEAM	GP	G	A	PTS.	PIM
34–35	Mont	1	0	0	0	0

McCUTCHEON, Brian Kenneth 5–10 180 LW
B. Toronto, Ont., Aug. 3, 1949

SSN	TEAM	GP	G	A	PTS.	PIM	+/-
74–75	Det	17	3	1	4	2	-3
75–76	Det	8	0	0	0	5	-2
76–77	Det	12	0	0	0	0	0
Totals		37	3	1	4	7	-5

McCUTCHEON, Darwin 6–4 190 D
B. Listowel, Ont., Apr. 19, 1962

SSN	TEAM	GP	G	A	PTS.	PIM	+/-
81–82	Tor	1	0	0	0	2	-1

McDILL, Jeffrey Donald 5–11 190 RW
B. Thunder Bay, Ont., Mar. 16, 1956

SSN	TEAM	GP	G	A	PTS.	PIM	+/-
76–77	Chi	1	0	0	0	0	0

McDONAGH, William James 5–9 150 LW
B. Rouyn, Que., Apr. 30, 1928

SSN	TEAM	GP	G	A	PTS.	PIM
49–50	NYR	4	0	0	0	2

McDONALD, Albert John (John) 5–11 205 RW
B. Swan River, Man., Nov. 24, 1941

SSN	TEAM	GP	G	A	PTS.	PIM
43–44	NYR	43	10	9	19	6

McDONALD, Alvin Brian (Ab) 6–2 194 LW
B. Winnipeg, Man., Feb. 18, 1936

SSN	TEAM	GP	G	A	PTS.	PIM	+/-
58–59	Mont	69	13	23	36	35	
59–60	Mont	68	9	13	22	26	
60–61	Chi	61	17	16	33	22	
61–62	Chi	65	22	18	40	8	
62–63	Chi	69	20	41	61	12	
63–64	Chi	70	14	32	46	19	
64–65	Bos	60	9	9	18	6	
65–66	Det	43	6	16	22	6	
66–67	Det	12	2	0	2	2	
67–68	Pitt	74	22	21	43	38	-4
68–69	StL	68	21	21	42	12	+19
69–70	StL	64	25	30	55	8	+11
70–71	StL	20	0	5	5	6	-3
71–72	Det	19	2	3	5	0	-8
72–73	Winn (WHA)	77	17	24	41	16	
73–74	Winn (WHA)	70	12	17	29	8	
NHL Totals		762	182	248	430	200	+15
WHA Totals		147	29	41	70	24	

Playoffs

SSN	TEAM	GP	G	A	PTS.	PIM
57–58	Mont	2	0	0	0	2
58–59	Mont	11	1	1	2	6
60–61	Chi	8	2	2	4	0
61–62	Chi	12	6	6	12	0
62–63	Chi	6	2	3	5	9
63–64	Chi	7	2	2	4	0

SSN	TEAM	GP	G	A	PTS.	PIM
65–66	Det	10	1	4	5	2
68–69	StL	12	2	1	3	10
69–70	StL	16	5	10	15	13
72–73	Winn (WHA)	14	2	5	7	2
73–74	Winn (WHA)	4	0	1	1	2
NHL Totals		84	21	29	50	42
WHA Totals		18	2	6	8	4

McDONALD, Brian Harold 5–11 190 RW
B. Toronto, Ont., Mar. 23, 1945

SSN	TEAM	GP	G	A	PTS.	PIM	+/-
70–71	Buf	12	0	0	0	29	-8
72–73	Hou (WHA)	71	20	20	40	78	
73–74	LA (WHA)	56	22	30	52	54	
74–75	Mich–Ind (WHA)	65	17	20	37	34	
75–76	Ind (WHA)	62	15	18	33	54	
76–77	Ind (WHA)	50	15	13	28	48	
NHL Totals		12	0	0	0	29	-8
WHA Totals		304	89	101	190	268	

Playoffs

SSN	TEAM	GP	G	A	PTS.	PIM
67–68	Chi	8	0	0	0	2
72–73	Hou (WHA)	10	3	0	3	16
75–76	Ind (WHA)	7	0	1	1	12
76–77	Ind (WHA)	9	3	4	7	33
NHL Totals		8	0	0	0	2
WHA Totals		26	6	5	11	61

McDONALD, Byron Russell (Butch) 6–0 185 LW
B. Moose Jaw, Sask., Nov. 21, 1916

SSN	TEAM	GP	G	A	PTS.	PIM
39–40	Det	37	1	6	7	2
44–45	Det–Chi	29	7	14	21	0
Totals		66	8	20	28	2

Playoffs

SSN	TEAM	GP	G	A	PTS.	PIM
39–40	Det	5	0	2	2	10

McDONALD, Girard J. (Gerry) 6–3 190 D
B. Weymouth, Mass., Mar. 18, 1958

SSN	TEAM	GP	G	A	PTS.	PIM	+/-
81–82	Hart	3	0	0	0	0	-2
83–84	Hart	5	0	0	0	4	-3
Totals		8	0	0	0	4	-5

McDONALD, John (Jack) LW

SSN	TEAM	GP	G	A	PTS.	PIM
17–18	Mont W–Mont	12	12	0	12	9
18–19	Mont	18	8	4	12	9
19–20	Que	24	7	6	13	4
20–21	Mont–Tor	17	0	1	1	0
21–22	Mont	2	0	0	0	0
Totals		73	27	11	38	22

Playoffs

SSN	TEAM	GP	G	A	PTS.	PIM
17–18	Mont	2	1	0	1	0
18–19	Mont	10	1	0	1	5
Totals		12	2	0	2	5

McDONALD, Lanny King 6–0 194 RW
B. Hanna, Alta., Feb. 16, 1953

SSN	TEAM	GP	G	A	PTS.	PIM	+/-
73–74	Tor	70	14	16	30	43	+3
74–75	Tor	64	17	27	44	86	+5
75–76	Tor	75	37	56	93	70	+24
76–77	Tor	80	46	44	90	77	+12
77–78	Tor	74	47	40	87	54	+34
78–79	Tor	79	43	42	85	32	+12
79–80	Tor–Col	81	40	35	75	53	-16
80–81	Col	80	35	46	81	56	-27
81–82	Col–Calg	71	40	42	82	57	+19
82–83	Calg	80	66	32	98	90	-2
83–84	Calg	65	33	33	66	64	-15
84–85	Calg	43	19	18	37	36	-4
85–86	Calg	80	28	43	71	44	-2
86–87	Calg	58	14	12	26	54	-3
87–88	Calg	60	10	13	23	57	+2
88–89	Calg	51	11	7	18	26	-1
Totals		1111	500	506	1006	899	+41

Playoffs

SSN	TEAM	GP	G	A	PTS.	PIM
74–75	Tor	7	0	0	0	2
75–76	Tor	10	4	4	8	4
76–77	Tor	9	10	7	17	6
77–78	Tor	13	3	4	7	10
78–79	Tor	6	3	2	5	0
81–82	Calg	3	0	1	1	6
82–83	Calg	7	3	4	7	19
83–84	Calg	11	6	7	13	6
84–85	Calg	1	0	0	0	0

SSN	TEAM	GP	G	A	PTS.	PIM
85–86	Calg	22	11	7	18	30
86–87	Calg	5	0	0	0	2
87–88	Calg	9	3	1	4	6
88–89	Calg	14	1	3	4	29
Totals		117	44	40	84	120

*McDONALD, Robert F
B. Toronto, Ont., Jan. 4, 1923

SSN	TEAM	GP	G	A	PTS.	PIM
43–44	NYR	1	0	0	0	0

McDONALD, Terry Grant 6–1 180 D
B. Coquitlam, B.C., June 17, 1955

SSN	TEAM	GP	G	A	PTS.	PIM	+/-
75–76	KC	8	0	1	1	6	-5

*McDONALD, Wilfred Kennedy (Bucko) 5–9 205 D
B. Fergus, Ont., Oct. 31, 1911

SSN	TEAM	GP	G	A	PTS.	PIM
34–35	Det	16	1	2	3	8
35–36	Det	48	4	6	10	32
36–37	Det	47	3	5	8	20
37–38	Det	47	3	7	10	14
38–39	Det–Tor	47	3	3	6	22
39–40	Tor	34	2	5	7	13
40–41	Tor	31	6	11	17	12
41–42	Tor	48	2	19	21	24
42–43	Tor	40	2	11	13	39
43–44	Tor–NYR	50	7	10	17	22
44–45	NYR	40	2	9	11	0
Totals		448	35	88	123	206

Playoffs

SSN	TEAM	GP	G	A	PTS.	PIM
35–36	Det	7	3	0	3	10
36–37	Det	10	0	0	0	2
38–39	Tor	10	0	0	0	4
39–40	Tor	10	0	0	0	0
40–41	Tor	7	2	0	2	2
41–42	Tor	13	0	1	1	2
42–43	Tor	6	1	0	1	4
Totals		63	6	1	7	24

McDONNELL, Joseph Patrick 6–2 200 D
B. Kitchener, Ont., May 11, 1961

SSN	TEAM	GP	G	A	PTS.	PIM	+/-
81–82	Van	7	0	1	1	12	-2
84–85	Pitt	40	2	9	11	20	-19
85–86	Pitt	3	0	0	0	2	-3
Totals		50	2	10	12	34	-24

McDONNELL, Moylan D

SSN	TEAM	GP	G	A	PTS.	PIM
20–21	Ham	20	1	1	2	0

McDONOUGH, Hubie 5–9 180 C
B. Manchester, N.H., July 8, 1963

SSN	TEAM	GP	G	A	PTS.	PIM	+/-
88–89	LA	4	0	1	1	0	+2
89–90	LA–NYI	76	21	15	36	36	+14
90–91	NYI	52	6	6	12	10	-14
91–92	NYI	33	7	2	9	15	-4
92–93	SJ	30	6	2	8	6	-21
Totals		195	40	26	66	67	-23

Playoffs

SSN	TEAM	GP	G	A	PTS.	PIM
89–90	NYI	5	1	0	1	4

McDONOUGH, James Allison (Al) 6–1 175 RW
B. Hamilton, Ont., June 6, 1950

SSN	TEAM	GP	G	A	PTS.	PIM	+/-
70–71	LA	6	2	1	3	0	+2
71–72	LA–Pitt	68	10	13	23	16	-14
72–73	Pitt	78	35	41	76	26	+20
73–74	Pitt–Atl	72	24	31	55	27	-7
74–75	Clev (WHA)	78	34	30	64	27	
75–76	Clev (WHA)	80	23	22	45	19	
76–77	Minn (WHA)	42	9	21	30	6	
77–78	Det	13	2	2	4	4	+2
NHL Totals		237	73	88	161	73	+3
WHA Totals		200	66	73	139	52	

Playoffs

SSN	TEAM	GP	G	A	PTS.	PIM
71–72	Pitt	4	0	1	1	0
73–74	Atl	4	0	0	0	2
74–75	Clev (WHA)	5	2	1	3	2
75–76	Clev (WHA)	3	1	0	1	0
NHL Totals		8	0	1	1	2
WHA Totals		8	3	1	4	2

SSN	TEAM	GP	G	A	PTS.	PIM	+/-

McDOUGAL, Michael George 6-2 200 RW
B. Port Huron, Mich., Apr. 30, 1958

SSN	TEAM	GP	G	A	PTS.	PIM	+/-
78-79	NYR	1	0	0	0	0	0
80-81	NYR	2	0	0	0	0	+1
81-82	Hart	3	0	0	0	0	0
82-83	Hart	55	8	10	18	43	-33
Totals		61	8	10	18	43	-32

McDOUGALL, William Henry 6-0 185 C
B. Mississauga, Ont., Aug. 10, 1966

90-91	Det	2	0	1	1	0	0
92-93	Edm	4	2	1	3	4	+2
93-94	TB	22	3	3	6	8	-4
Totals		28	5	5	10	12	-2

Playoffs

| 90-91 | Det | 1 | 0 | 0 | 0 | 0 | |

McEACHERN, Shawn 5-11 195 C
B. Waltham, Mass., Feb. 28, 1969

91-92	Pitt	15	0	4	4	0	+1
92-93	Pitt	84	28	33	61	46	+21
93-94	LA-Pitt	76	20	22	42	34	+14
94-95	Pitt	44	13	13	26	22	+4
95-96	Bos	82	24	29	53	34	-5
96-97	Ott	65	11	20	31	18	-5
97-98	Ott	81	24	24	48	42	+1
98-99	Ott	77	31	25	56	46	+8
Totals		524	151	170	321	243	+39

Playoffs

91-92	Pitt	19	2	7	9	4	
92-93	Pitt	12	3	2	5	10	
93-94	Pitt	6	1	0	1	2	
94-95	Pitt	11	0	2	2	8	
95-96	Bos	5	2	1	3	8	
96-97	Ott	7	2	0	2	8	
97-98	Ott	11	0	4	4	8	
98-99	Ott	4	2	0	2	6	
Totals		75	12	16	28	54	

McELMURY, James Donald 6-0 190 D
B. St. Paul, Minn., Oct. 3, 1949

72-73	Minn	7	0	1	1	2	+1
74-75	KC	78	5	17	22	25	-48
75-76	KC	38	2	6	8	6	-13
76-77	Col	55	7	23	30	16	-15
77-78	Col	2	0	0	0	0	+1
Totals		180	14	47	61	49	-74

McEWEN, Michael Todd 6-1 185 D
B. Hornepayne, Ont., Aug. 10, 1956

76-77	NYR	80	14	29	43	38	-24
77-78	NYR	57	5	13	18	52	-11
78-79	NYR	80	20	38	58	35	+10
79-80	NYR-Col	76	12	47	59	41	-10
80-81	Col-NYI	78	11	38	49	94	-30
81-82	NYI	73	10	39	49	50	+30
82-83	NYI	42	2	11	13	16	+11
83-84	NYI-LA	62	10	26	36	20	-17
84-85	Wash	56	11	27	38	42	+22
85-86	Det-NYR-Hart	55	5	17	22	30	-7
86-87	Hart	48	8	8	16	32	-9
87-88	Hart	9	0	3	3	10	-1
Totals		716	108	296	404	460	-36

Playoffs

78-79	NYR	18	2	11	13	8	
80-81	NYI	17	6	8	14	6	
81-82	NYI	15	3	7	10	18	
82-83	NYI	12	0	2	2	4	
84-85	Wash	5	0	1	1	4	
85-86	Hart	8	0	4	4	6	
86-87	Hart	1	1	1	2	0	
87-88	Hart	2	0	2	2	2	
Totals		78	12	36	48	48	

McFADDEN, James Alexander 5-7 178 C
B. Belfast, Ireland, Apr. 15, 1920

47-48	Det	60	24	24	48	12	
48-49	Det	55	12	20	32	10	
49-50	Det	68	14	16	30	8	
50-51	Det	70	14	18	32	10	
51-52	Chi	70	10	24	34	14	
52-53	Chi	70	23	21	44	29	
53-54	Chi	19	3	3	6	6	
Totals		412	100	126	226	89	

Playoffs

47-48	Det	10	5	3	8	10	
48-49	Det	8	0	1	1	6	
49-50	Det	14	2	3	5	8	
50-51	Det	6	0	2	2	2	
52-53	Chi	7	3	0	3	4	
Totals		45	10	9	19	30	

McFADYEN, Donald P. 5-9 163 F
B. Grossfield, Alta., Mar. 24, 1907

32-33	Chi	48	5	9	14	20	
33-34	Chi	46	1	3	4	20	
34-35	Chi	37	2	5	7	4	
35-36	Chi	48	4	16	20	33	
Totals		179	12	33	45	77	

Playoffs

33-34	Chi	8	2	2	4	5	
34-35	Chi	2	0	0	0	0	
35-36	Chi	2	0	0	0	0	
Totals		12	2	2	4	5	

McFALL, Dan 6-0 180 D
B. Kenmore, N.Y., Apr. 8, 1963

84-85	Winn	2	0	0	0	0	-3
85-86	Winn	7	0	1	1	0	-3
Totals		9	0	1	1	0	-6

***McFARLAN, George** D

| 26-27 | Chi | 2 | 0 | 0 | 0 | 0 | |

McGEOUGH, James 5-8 170 C
B. Regina, Sask., Apr. 13, 1963

81-82	Wash	4	0	0	0	0	-2
84-85	Wash-Pitt	15	3	4	7	16	-4
85-86	Pitt	17	3	2	5	8	-4
86-87	Pitt	11	1	4	5	8	-5
Totals		57	7	10	17	32	-15

***McGIBBON, John Irving** F

| 42-43 | Mont | 1 | 0 | 0 | 0 | 0 | |

***McGILL, John (Jack)** 5-10 150 F
B. Ottawa, Ont., Nov. 3, 1910

34-35	Mont	44	9	1	10	34	
35-36	Mont	46	13	7	20	28	
36-37	Mont	44	5	2	7	9	
Totals		134	27	10	37	71	

Playoffs

34-35	Mont	2	2	0	2	0	
36-37	Mont	1	0	0	0	0	
Totals		3	2	0	2	0	

McGILL, John George (Big Jack) 6-1 180 C
B. Edmonton, Alta., Sept. 19, 1921

41-42	Bos	13	8	11	19	2	
44-45	Bos	14	4	2	6	0	
45-46	Bos	46	6	14	20	21	
46-47	Bos	24	5	9	14	19	
Totals		97	23	36	59	42	

Playoffs

41-42	Bos	5	4	1	5	6	
44-45	Bos	7	3	3	6	0	
45-46	Bos	10	0	0	0	0	
46-47	Bos	5	0	0	0	11	
Totals		27	7	4	11	17	

McGILL, Robert Paul 6-1 193 D
B. Edmonton, Alta., Apr. 27, 1962

81-82	Tor	68	1	10	11	263	-9
82-83	Tor	30	0	0	0	146	-24
83-84	Tor	11	0	2	2	51	+1
84-85	Tor	72	0	5	5	250	0
85-86	Tor	61	1	4	5	141	-17
86-87	Tor	56	1	4	5	103	-2
87-88	Chi	67	4	7	11	131	-19
88-89	Chi	68	0	4	4	155	+9
89-90	Chi	69	2	10	12	204	-7
90-91	Chi	77	4	5	9	151	+8
91-92	SJ-Det	74	3	1	4	91	-37
92-93	Tor	19	1	0	1	34	+5
93-94	NYI-Hart	33	0	3	3	46	-7
Totals		705	17	55	72	1766	-65

Playoffs

85-86	Tor	9	0	0	0	35	
86-87	Tor	3	0	0	0	0	
87-88	Chi	3	0	0	0	2	
88-89	Chi	16	0	0	0	33	
89-90	Chi	5	0	0	0	2	
90-91	Chi	5	0	0	0	2	
91-92	Det	8	0	0	0	14	
Totals		49	0	0	0	88	

McGILL, Ryan 6-2 210 D
B. Sherwood Park, Alta., Feb. 28, 1969

91-92	Phil	9	0	2	2	20	+1
92-93	Phil	72	3	10	13	238	+9
93-94	Phil	50	1	3	4	112	-5
94-95	Phil-Edm	20	0	0	0	21	-4
Totals		151	4	15	19	391	+1

McGILLIS, Daniel 6-2 220 D
B. Hawkesbury, Ont., July 1, 1972

96-97	Edm	73	6	16	22	52	+2
97-98	Edm-Phil	80	11	20	31	109	-21
98-99	Phil	78	8	37	45	61	+16
Totals		231	25	73	98	222	-3

Playoffs

96-97	Edm	12	0	5	5	24	
97-98	Phil	5	1	2	3	10	
98-99	Phil	6	0	1	1	12	
Totals		23	1	8	9	46	

McGREGOR, Donald Alexander (Sandy) 5-11 165 RW
B. Toronto, Ont., Mar. 30, 1939

| 63-64 | NYR | 2 | 0 | 0 | 0 | 2 | |

***McGUIRE, Frank S. (Mickey)** F

26-27	Pitt Pi	32	3	0	3	6	
27-28	Pitt Pi	4	0	0	0	0	
Totals		36	3	0	3	6	

McHUGH, Michael 5-10 190 LW
B. Bowdoin, Mass., Aug. 16, 1965

88-89	Minn	3	0	0	0	2	-1
89-90	Minn	3	0	0	0	0	-1
90-91	Minn	6	0	0	0	0	-3
91-92	SJ	8	1	0	1	14	-3
Totals		20	1	0	1	16	-8

McILHARGEY, John Cecil (Jack) 6-0 190 D
B. Edmonton, Alta., Mar. 7, 1952

74-75	Phil	2	0	0	0	11	-1
75-76	Phil	57	1	2	3	205	+11
76-77	Phil-Van	61	3	8	11	225	+9
77-78	Van	69	3	5	8	172	-45
78-79	Van	53	2	4	6	129	-16
79-80	Van-Phil	50	0	6	6	136	+2
80-81	Phil-Hart	51	1	6	7	164	-1
81-82	Hart	50	1	5	6	60	-8
Totals		393	11	36	47	1102	-49

Playoffs

75-76	Phil	15	0	3	3	41	
78-79	Phil	3	0	0	0	2	
79-80	Phil	9	0	0	0	25	
Totals		27	0	3	3	68	

***McINENLY, Bertram H.** 5-9 160 D
B. Quebec City, Que., May 6, 1906

30-31	Det	44	3	5	8	48	
31-32	Det-NYA	47	12	7	19	60	
32-33	Ott	30	2	2	4	8	
33-34	Ott-Bos	9	0	0	0	4	
34-35	Bos	33	2	1	3	24	
35-36	Bos	3	0	0	0	0	
Totals		166	19	15	34	144	

Playoffs

| 34-35 | Bos | 4 | 0 | 0 | 0 | 2 | |

SSN	TEAM	GP	G	A	PTS.	PIM	+/-

McINNIS, Martin Edward *6–0 185 C*
B. Weymouth, Mass., June 2, 1970

SSN	TEAM	GP	G	A	PTS.	PIM	+/-
91–92	NYI	15	3	5	8	0	+6
92–93	NYI	56	10	20	30	24	+7
93–94	NYI	81	25	31	56	24	+31
94–95	NYI	41	9	7	16	8	-1
95–96	NYI	74	12	34	46	39	-11
96–97	NYI–Calg	80	23	26	49	22	-8
97–98	Calg	75	19	25	44	34	+1
98–99	Calg-Ana	81	19	35	54	42	-15
Totals		503	120	183	303	193	+10

Playoffs

SSN	TEAM	GP	G	A	PTS.	PIM
92–93	NYI	3	0	1	1	0
93–94	NYI	4	0	0	0	0
98–99	Ana	4	2	0	2	2
Totals		11	2	1	3	2

McINTOSH, Bruce *6–0 178 D*
B. Minneapolis, Minn., Mar. 17, 1949

SSN	TEAM	GP	G	A	PTS.	PIM	+/-
72–73	Minn	2	0	0	0	0	0

McINTOSH, Paul *5–10 177 D*
B. Listowel, Ont., Mar. 13, 1954

SSN	TEAM	GP	G	A	PTS.	PIM	+/-
74–75	Buf	6	0	1	1	5	+2
75–76	Buf	42	0	1	1	61	-5
Totals		48	0	2	2	66	-3

Playoffs

SSN	TEAM	GP	G	A	PTS.	PIM
74–75	Buf	1	0	0	0	0
75–76	Buf	1	0	0	0	7
Totals		2	0	0	0	7

McINTYRE, John *6–1 190 C*
B. Ravenswood, Ont., Apr. 29, 1969

SSN	TEAM	GP	G	A	PTS.	PIM	+/-
89–90	Tor	59	5	12	17	117	-12
90–91	Tor–LA	69	8	8	16	140	+6
91–92	LA	73	5	19	24	100	0
92–93	LA–NYR	60	3	5	8	84	-14
93–94	Van	62	3	6	9	38	-9
94–95	Van	28	0	4	4	37	-3
Totals		351	24	54	78	516	-32

Playoffs

SSN	TEAM	GP	G	A	PTS.	PIM
89–90	Tor	2	0	0	0	2
90–91	LA	12	0	1	1	24
91–92	LA	6	0	4	4	12
93–97	Van	24	0	1	1	16
Totals		44	0	6	6	54

McINTYRE, John Archibald (Jack) *5–11 190 LW*
B. Brussels, Ont., Sept. 8, 1930

SSN	TEAM	GP	G	A	PTS.	PIM
49–50	Bos	1	0	1	1	0
51–52	Bos	52	12	19	31	18
52–53	Bos	70	7	15	22	31
53–54	Chi	23	8	3	11	4
54–55	Chi	65	16	13	29	40
55–56	Chi	46	10	5	15	14
56–57	Chi	70	18	14	32	32
57–58	Chi–Det	68	15	11	26	14
58–59	Det	55	15	14	29	14
59–60	Det	49	8	7	15	6
Totals		499	109	102	211	173

Playoffs

SSN	TEAM	GP	G	A	PTS.	PIM
50–51	Bos	2	0	0	0	0
51–52	Bos	7	1	2	3	2
52–53	Bos	10	4	2	6	2
57–58	Det	4	1	1	2	0
59–60	Det	6	1	1	2	0
Totals		29	7	6	13	4

McINTYRE, Lawrence Albert *6–1 190 D*
B. Moose Jaw, Sask., July 13, 1949

SSN	TEAM	GP	G	A	PTS.	PIM	+/-
69–70	Tor	1	0	0	0	0	+3
72–73	Tor	40	0	3	3	26	+6
Totals		41	0	3	3	26	+9

McKAY, Alvin Douglas (Doug) *5–9 165 LW*
B. Hamilton, Ont., May 28, 1929

Playoffs

SSN	TEAM	GP	G	A	PTS.	PIM
49–50	Det	1	0	0	0	0

McKAY, Hugh Randall (Randy) *6–1 205 RW*
B. Montreal, Que., Jan. 25, 1967

SSN	TEAM	GP	G	A	PTS.	PIM	+/-
88–89	Det	3	0	0	0	0	-1
89–90	Det	33	3	6	9	51	+1
90–91	Det	47	1	7	8	183	-15
91–92	NJ	80	17	16	33	246	+6
92–93	NJ	73	11	11	22	206	0
93–94	NJ	78	12	15	27	244	+24
94–95	NJ	33	5	7	12	44	+10
95–96	NJ	76	11	10	21	145	+7
96–97	NJ	77	9	18	27	109	+15
97–98	NJ	74	24	24	48	86	+30
98–99	NJ	70	17	20	37	143	+10
Totals		644	110	134	244	1457	+87

Playoffs

SSN	TEAM	GP	G	A	PTS.	PIM
88–89	Det	2	0	0	0	2
90–91	Det	5	0	1	1	41
91–92	NJ	7	1	3	4	10
92–93	NJ	5	0	0	0	16
93–94	NJ	20	1	2	3	24
94–95	NJ	19	8	4	12	11
96–97	NJ	10	1	1	2	0
97–98	NJ	6	0	1	1	0
98–99	NJ	7	3	2	5	2
Totals		81	14	14	28	106

McKAY, Raymond Owen *6–4 183 D*
B. Edmonton, Alta., Aug. 22, 1946

SSN	TEAM	GP	G	A	PTS.	PIM	+/-
68–69	Chi	9	0	1	1	12	+3
69–70	Chi	17	0	0	0	23	-8
70–71	Chi	2	0	0	0	0	0
71–72	Buf	39	0	3	3	18	-12
72–73	Buf	1	0	0	0	0	0
73–74	Cal	72	2	12	14	49	-31
74–75	Edm (WHA)	69	8	20	28	47	
75–76	Clev (WHA)	68	3	10	13	44	
76–77	Minn–Birm (WHA)	61	0	12	12	39	
77–78	Edm (WHA)	14	1	4	5	4	
NHL Totals		140	2	16	18	102	-48
WHA Totals		212	14	44	58	134	

Playoffs

SSN	TEAM	GP	G	A	PTS.	PIM
69–70	Chi	1	0	0	0	0
75–76	Clev (WHA)	3	0	0	0	4
77–78	Edm (WHA)	4	0	1	1	4
NHL Totals		1	0	0	0	0
WHA Totals		7	0	1	1	8

McKAY, Scott *5–11 200 C*
B. Burlington, Ont., Jan. 26, 1972

SSN	TEAM	GP	G	A	PTS.	PIM
93–94	Ana	1	0	0	0	0

McKECHNIE, Walter Thomas John *6–2 200 C*
B. London, Ont., June 19, 1947

SSN	TEAM	GP	G	A	PTS.	PIM	+/-
67–68	Minn	4	0	0	0	0	-3
68–69	Minn	58	5	9	14	22	-10
69–70	Minn	20	1	3	4	21	-5
70–71	Minn	30	3	1	4	34	-7
71–72	Cal	56	11	20	31	40	+2
72–73	Cal	78	16	38	54	58	-25
73–74	Cal	63	23	29	52	14	-14
74–75	Bos–Det	76	9	14	23	14	-9
75–76	Det	80	26	56	82	85	+9
76–77	Det	80	25	34	59	50	-24
77–78	Wash–Clev	69	16	23	39	12	-22
78–79	Tor	79	25	36	61	18	+21
79–80	Tor–Col	71	7	40	47	6	-20
80–81	Col	53	15	23	38	18	-7
81–82	Det	74	18	37	55	35	-1
82–83	Det	64	14	29	43	42	+1
Totals		955	214	392	606	469	-114

Playoffs

SSN	TEAM	GP	G	A	PTS.	PIM
67–68	Minn	9	3	2	5	0
78–79	Tor	6	4	3	7	9
Totals		15	7	5	12	9

McKEE, Jay *6–2 175 D*
B. Kingston, Ont., Sept. 8, 1977

SSN	TEAM	GP	G	A	PTS.	PIM	+/-
95–96	Buf	1	0	1	1	2	+1
96–97	Buf	43	1	9	10	35	+3
97–98	Buf	56	1	13	14	42	-1
98–99	Buf	72	0	6	6	75	+20
Totals		172	2	29	31	154	+23

Playoffs

SSN	TEAM	GP	G	A	PTS.	PIM
96–97	Buf	3	0	0	0	0
97–98	Buf	1	0	0	0	0
98–99	Buf	21	0	3	3	24
Totals		25	0	3	3	24

McKEE, Mike *6–3 203 LW*
B. Toronto, Ont., June 18, 1969

SSN	TEAM	GP	G	A	PTS.	PIM	+/-
93–94	Que	48	3	12	15	41	+5

McKEGNEY, Anthony *6–1 200 LW*
B. Montreal, Que., Feb. 15, 1958

SSN	TEAM	GP	G	A	PTS.	PIM	+/-
78–79	Buf	52	8	14	22	10	-2
79–80	Buf	80	23	29	52	24	+40
80–81	Buf	80	37	32	69	24	+11
81–82	Buf	73	23	29	52	41	-12
82–83	Buf	78	36	37	73	18	+2
83–84	Que	75	24	27	51	23	+4
84–85	Que–Minn	57	23	22	45	16	+11
85–86	Minn	70	15	25	40	48	-5
86–87	Minn–NYR	75	31	20	51	72	+1
87–88	StL	80	40	38	78	82	+13
88–89	StL	71	25	17	42	58	-1
89–90	Det–Que	62	18	12	30	53	-29
90–91	Que–Chi	59	17	17	34	48	-27
Totals		912	320	319	639	517	+6

Playoffs

SSN	TEAM	GP	G	A	PTS.	PIM
78–79	Buf	2	0	1	1	0
79–80	Buf	14	3	4	7	2
80–81	Buf	8	5	3	8	2
81–82	Buf	4	0	0	0	2
82–83	Buf	10	3	1	4	4
83–84	Que	7	0	0	0	0
84–85	Minn	9	8	6	14	0
85–86	Minn	5	2	1	3	22
86–87	NYR	6	0	0	0	12
87–88	StL	9	3	6	9	8
88–89	StL	3	0	1	1	0
90–91	Chi	2	0	0	0	4
Totals		79	24	23	47	56

McKEGNEY, Ian Robert *5–11 165 D*
B. Sarnia, Ont., May 7, 1947

SSN	TEAM	GP	G	A	PTS.	PIM	+/-
76–77	Chi	3	0	0	0	2	-8
Playoff Totals		9	0	0	0	0	

McKENDRY, Alexander *6–4 200 LW*
B. Midland, Ont., Nov. 21, 1956

SSN	TEAM	GP	G	A	PTS.	PIM	+/-
77–78	NYI	4	0	0	0	2	0
78–79	NYI	5	0	0	0	0	-1
79–80	NYI	2	0	0	0	2	-1
80–81	Calg	36	3	6	9	19	-6
Totals		47	3	6	9	23	-8

Playoffs

SSN	TEAM	GP	G	A	PTS.	PIM
79–80	NYI	6	2	2	4	0

McKENNA, Sean Michael *6–0 190 RW*
B. Asbestos, Que., Mar. 7, 1962

SSN	TEAM	GP	G	A	PTS.	PIM	+/-
81–82	Buf	3	0	1	1	2	+3
82–83	Buf	46	10	14	24	4	-4
83–84	Buf	78	20	10	30	45	0
84–85	Buf	65	20	16	36	41	-6
85–86	Buf–LA	75	10	12	22	35	-23
86–87	LA	69	14	19	33	10	+11
87–88	LA–Tor	70	8	7	15	24	-25
88–89	Tor	3	0	1	1	0	-1
89–90	Tor	5	0	0	0	20	-3
Totals		414	82	80	162	181	-48

Playoffs

SSN	TEAM	GP	G	A	PTS.	PIM
83–84	Buf	3	1	0	1	2
84–85	Buf	5	0	1	1	0
85–86	LA	5	0	1	1	0
89–89	LA	2	0	0	0	0
Totals		10	1	2	3	2

McKENNA, Steve *6–8 247 D*
B. Toronto, Ont., Aug. 21, 1973

SSN	TEAM	GP	G	A	PTS.	PIM	+/-
96–97	LA	9	0	0	0	37	+1
97–98	LA	62	4	8	150		-9
98–99	LA	20	1	0	1	36	-3
Totals		91	5	4	9	223	-11

SSN	TEAM	GP	G	A	PTS.	PIM	+/-

Playoffs

SSN	TEAM	GP	G	A	PTS.	PIM
97–98	LA	3	0	1	1	8

McKENNEY, Donald Hamilton 6–0 175 C
B. Smith Falls, Ont., Apr. 30, 1934

SSN	TEAM	GP	G	A	PTS.	PIM	+/-
54–55	Bos	69	22	20	42	34	
55–56	Bos	65	10	24	34	20	
56–57	Bos	69	21	39	60	31	
57–58	Bos	70	28	30	58	59	
58–59	Bos	70	32	30	62	20	
59–60	Bos	70	20	49	69	28	
60–61	Bos	68	26	23	49	22	
61–62	Bos	70	22	33	55	10	
62–63	Bos–NYR	62	22	35	57	6	
63–64	NYR–Tor	70	18	23	41	8	
64–65	Tor	52	6	13	19	6	
65–66	Det	24	1	6	7	0	
67–68	StL	39	9	20	29	4	+1
Totals		798	237	345	582	248	+1

Playoffs

SSN	TEAM	GP	G	A	PTS.	PIM
54–55	Bos	5	1	2	3	4
56–57	Bos	10	1	5	6	4
57–58	Bos	12	9	8	17	0
58–59	Bos	7	2	5	7	0
63–64	Tor	12	4	8	12	0
64–65	Tor	6	0	0	0	0
67–68	StL	6	1	1	2	2
Totals		38	11	9	20	10

McKENNY, James Claude 6–0 185 D
B. Ottawa, Ont., Dec. 1, 1946

SSN	TEAM	GP	G	A	PTS.	PIM	+/-
65–66	Tor	2	0	0	0	2	
66–67	Tor	1	1	0	1	0	
67–68	Tor	5	1	0	1	0	-2
68–69	Tor	7	0	0	2	+1	
69–70	Tor	73	11	33	44	34	-2
70–71	Tor	68	4	26	30	42	+11
71–72	Tor	76	5	31	36	27	+1
72–73	Tor	77	11	41	52	55	+6
73–74	Tor	77	14	28	42	36	+16
74–75	Tor	66	8	35	43	31	-4
75–76	Tor	46	10	19	29	19	-7
76–77	Tor	76	14	31	45	36	-26
77–78	Tor	15	2	2	4	8	+4
78–79	Tor	10	1	1	2	2	-3
Totals		604	82	247	329	294	-59

Playoffs

SSN	TEAM	GP	G	A	PTS.	PIM
70–71	Tor	6	2	1	3	2
71–72	Tor	5	3	0	3	2
73–74	Tor	4	0	2	2	0
74–75	Tor	7	0	1	1	2
75–76	Tor	6	2	3	5	2
76–77	Tor	9	0	2	2	2
Totals		37	7	9	16	10

McKENZIE, Brian Stewart 5–10 165 LW
B. St. Catherines, Ont., Mar. 16, 1951

SSN	TEAM	GP	G	A	PTS.	PIM	+/-
71–72	Pitt	6	1	1	2	4	-2
73–74	Edm (WHA)	78	18	20	38	66	
74–75	Ind (WHA)	9	1	0	1	6	
NHL Totals		6	1	1	2	4	-2
WHA Totals		87	19	20	39	72	

Playoffs

SSN	TEAM	GP	G	A	PTS.	PIM
73–74	Edm (WHA)	5	0	1	1	0

McKENZIE, Jim 6–3 205 LW/D
B. Gull Lake, Sask., Nov. 3, 1969

SSN	TEAM	GP	G	A	PTS.	PIM	+/-
89–90	Hart	5	0	0	0	4	0
90–91	Hart	41	4	3	7	108	-7
91–92	Hart	67	5	1	6	87	-6
92–93	Hart	64	3	6	9	202	-10
93–94	Hart–Del–Pitt	71	3	5	8	146	-7
94–95	Pitt	39	2	1	3	63	-7
95–96	Winn	73	2	4	6	202	-4
96–97	Phoe	65	5	3	8	200	-5
97–98	Phoe	64	3	4	7	146	-7
98–99	Ana	73	5	4	9	99	-18
Totals		562	32	31	63	1257	-71

Playoffs

SSN	TEAM	GP	G	A	PTS.	PIM
90–91	Hart	6	0	0	0	8
93–94	Pitt	3	0	0	0	0
94–95	Pitt	5	0	0	0	4
95–96	Winn	1	0	0	0	2

SSN	TEAM	GP	G	A	PTS.	PIM	+/-
96–97	Phoe	7	0	0	0	2	
97–98	Phoe	1	0	0	0	0	
98–99	Ana	4	0	0	0	4	
Totals		27	0	0	0	20	

McKENZIE, John Albert 5–9 175 RW
B. High River, Alta., Dec. 12, 1937

SSN	TEAM	GP	G	A	PTS.	PIM	+/-
58–59	Chi	32	3	4	7	22	
59–60	Det	59	8	12	20	50	
60–61	Det	16	3	1	4	13	
63–64	Chi	45	9	9	18	50	
64–65	Chi	51	8	10	18	46	
65–66	NYR–Bos	71	19	14	33	72	
66–67	Bos	69	17	19	36	98	
67–68	Bos	74	28	38	66	107	+14
68–69	Bos	60	29	27	56	99	+13
69–70	Bos	72	29	41	70	114	+20
70–71	Bos	65	31	46	77	120	+27
71–72	Bos	77	22	47	69	126	+19
72–73	Phil (WHA)	60	28	50	78	157	
73–74	Van (WHA)	45	14	38	52	71	
74–75	Van (WHA)	74	23	37	60	82	
75–76	Minn–Cin (WHA)	69	24	36	60	54	
76–77	Minn–NE (WHA)	74	28	32	60	77	
77–78	NE (WHA)	79	27	29	56	61	
78–79	NE (WHA)	76	19	28	47	115	
NHL Totals		691	206	268	474	917	+93
WHA Totals		477	163	250	413	617	

Playoffs

SSN	TEAM	GP	G	A	PTS.	PIM
58–59	Chi	2	0	0	0	2
59–60	Det	2	0	0	0	0
63–64	Chi	4	0	1	1	6
64–65	Chi	11	0	1	1	6
67–68	Bos	4	1	1	2	8
68–69	Bos	10	2	2	4	17
69–70	Bos	14	5	12	17	35
70–71	Bos	7	2	3	5	22
72–73	Phil (WHA)	4	3	1	4	8
76–77	NE (WHA)	5	2	1	3	8
77–78	NE (WHA)	14	6	6	12	16
78–79	NE (WHA)	10	3	7	10	10
NHL Totals		69	15	32	47	133
WHA Totals		33	14	15	29	42

McKIM, Andrew Harry 5–8 175 C
B. St. John, N.B., July 6, 1970

SSN	TEAM	GP	G	A	PTS.	PIM	+/-
92–93	Bos	7	1	3	4	0	+2
93–94	Bos	29	0	1	1	4	-10
94–95	Det	2	0	0	0	2	0
Totals		38	1	4	5	6	-8

McKINNON, Alexander D
B. Sudbury, Ont.

SSN	TEAM	GP	G	A	PTS.	PIM
24–25	Ham	30	8	2	10	45
25–26	NYA	35	5	3	8	34
26–27	NYA	42	2	1	3	29
27–28	NYA	43	3	3	6	71
28–29	Chi	44	1	1	2	56
Totals		194	19	10	29	235

*McKINNON, John Douglas 5–8 170 D
B. Guysborough, N.S., July 15, 1902

SSN	TEAM	GP	G	A	PTS.	PIM
25–26	Mont	2	0	0	0	0
26–27	Pitt Pi	44	13	0	13	46
27–28	Pitt Pi	43	3	3	6	46
28–29	Pitt Pi	39	1	0	1	44
29–30	Pitt Pi	41	10	7	17	42
30–31	Phil Q	39	1	1	2	46
Totals		208	28	11	39	224

Playoffs

SSN	TEAM	GP	G	A	PTS.	PIM
27–28	Pitt	2	0	0	0	4

McKINNON, Robert F
B.

SSN	TEAM	GP	G	A	PTS.	PIM
28–29	Chi	2	0	0	0	0

McLAREN, Kyle 6–4 210 D
B. Coaldale, Atla., June 18, 1977

SSN	TEAM	GP	G	A	PTS.	PIM	+/-
95–96	Bos	74	5	12	17	73	+16
96–97	Bos	58	5	9	14	54	-9
97–98	Bos	66	5	20	25	56	+13
98–99	Bos	52	6	18	24	48	+1
Totals		250	21	59	80	231	+21

Playoffs

SSN	TEAM	GP	G	A	PTS.	PIM
95–96	Bos	5	0	0	0	14
97–98	Bos	6	1	0	1	4
98–99	Bos	12	0	3	3	10
Totals		23	1	3	4	28

*McLEAN, Fred F

SSN	TEAM	GP	G	A	PTS.	PIM
19–20	Que	7	0	0	0	2
20–21	Ham	2	0	0	0	0
Totals		9	0	0	0	2

McLEAN, Jack 5–8 165 C
B. Winnipeg, Man., Jan. 1, 1923

SSN	TEAM	GP	G	A	PTS.	PIM
42–43	Tor	27	9	8	17	33
43–44	Tor	32	3	15	18	30
44–45	Tor	8	2	1	3	13
Totals		67	14	24	38	76

Playoffs

SSN	TEAM	GP	G	A	PTS.	PIM
42–43	Tor	6	2	2	4	2
43–44	Tor	3	0	0	0	6
44–45	Tor	4	0	0	0	0
Totals		13	2	2	4	8

McLEAN, Jeff 5–10 190 C
B. Port Moody, B.C., Oct. 6, 1969

SSN	TEAM	GP	G	A	PTS.	PIM	+/-
93–94	SJ	6	0	1	1	0	+1

McLEAN, Robert Donald (Don) 6–1 200 D
B. Niagara Falls, Ont., Jan. 19, 1954

SSN	TEAM	GP	G	A	PTS.	PIM	+/-
75–76	Wash	9	0	0	0	6	-3

McLELLAN, Daniel (Scott) 6–0 170 RW
B. Burlington, Ont., Feb. 10, 1963

SSN	TEAM	GP	G	A	PTS.	PIM
82–83	Bos	2	0	0	0	0

*McLELLAN, Daniel John (John) 5–11 150 C
B. South Porcupine, Ont., Aug. 6, 1928

SSN	TEAM	GP	G	A	PTS.	PIM
51–52	Tor	2	0	0	0	0

McLELLAN, Todd 5–11 185 C
B. Melville, Sask., Oct. 3, 1967

SSN	TEAM	GP	G	A	PTS.	PIM	+/-
87–88	NYI	5	1	1	2	0	-1

*McLENAHAN, Roland Joseph (Roly) 5–7 170 D
B. Fredericton, N.B., Oct. 26, 1921

SSN	TEAM	GP	G	A	PTS.	PIM
45–46	Det	9	2	1	3	10

Playoffs

SSN	TEAM	GP	G	A	PTS.	PIM
45–46	Det	2	0	0	0	0

McLEOD, Allan Sidney 5–11 200 D
B. Medicine Hat, Alta., June 17, 1949

SSN	TEAM	GP	G	A	PTS.	PIM	+/-
73–74	Det	26	2	2	4	24	-7
74–75	Phoe (WHA)	77	3	16	19	98	
75–76	Phoe (WHA)	80	2	17	19	82	
76–77	Phoe–Hou (WHA)	80	8	26	34	55	
77–78	Hou (WHA)	80	2	22	24	54	
78–79	Ind (WHA)	25	0	11	11	22	
NHL Totals		26	2	2	4	24	-7
WHA Totals		342	15	92	107	311	

Playoffs

SSN	TEAM	GP	G	A	PTS.	PIM
74–75	Phoe (WHA)	5	0	4	4	4
75–76	Phoe (WHA)	5	0	2	2	4
76–77	Hou (WHA)	10	1	3	4	9
77–78	Hou (WHA)	6	1	0	1	2
WHA Totals		26	2	9	11	19

McLEOD, Robert John (Jackie) 5–8 150 RW
B. Regina, Sask., Apr. 30, 1930

SSN	TEAM	GP	G	A	PTS.	PIM
49–50	NYR	38	6	9	15	2
50–51	NYR	41	5	10	15	2
51–52	NYR	13	2	3	5	2
52–53	NYR	3	0	0	0	2
54–55	NYR	11	1	1	2	2
Totals		106	14	23	37	10

Playoffs

SSN	TEAM	GP	G	A	PTS.	PIM
49–50	Det	7	0	0	0	0

McLLWAIN, Dave 6-0 185 C/RW
B. Seaforth, Ont., Jan. 9, 1967

SSN	TEAM	GP	G	A	PTS.	PIM	+/-
87-88	Pitt	66	11	8	19	40	-1
88-89	Pitt	24	1	2	3	4	-11
89-90	Winn	80	25	26	51	60	-1
90-91	Winn	60	14	11	25	46	-13
91-92	Winn–Buf–NYI–Tor	73	10	18	28	36	-9
92-93	Tor	66	14	4	18	30	-18
93-94	Ott	66	17	26	43	48	-40
94-95	Ott	43	5	6	11	22	-26
95-96	Ott–Pitt	19	2	5	7	6	-5
96-97	NYI	4	1	1	2	0	-2
Totals		501	100	107	207	292	-126

Playoffs

SSN	TEAM	GP	G	A	PTS.	PIM
88-89	Pitt	3	0	1	1	0
89-90	Winn	7	0	1	1	2
92-93	Tor	4	0	0	0	0
95-96	Pitt	6	0	0	0	0
Totals		20	0	2	2	2

*McMAHON, Michael Clarence 5-8 215 D
B. Brockville, Ont., Feb. 1, 1915

SSN	TEAM	GP	G	A	PTS.	PIM
43-44	Mont	42	7	17	24	98
45-46	Mont–Bos	15	0	1	1	4
Totals		57	7	18	25	102

Playoffs

SSN	TEAM	GP	G	A	PTS.	PIM
42-43	Mont	5	0	0	0	14
43-44	Mont	8	1	2	3	16
Totals		13	1	2	3	30

McMAHON, Michael William 5-11 175 D
B. Quebec City, Que., Aug. 30, 1941

SSN	TEAM	GP	G	A	PTS.	PIM	+/-
63-64	NYR	18	0	1	1	16	
64-65	NYR	1	0	0	0	0	
65-66	NYR	41	0	12	12	34	
67-68	Minn	74	14	33	47	71	-13
68-69	Minn–Chi	63	0	19	19	6	-11
69-70	Det–Pitt	14	1	3	4	19	+2
70-71	Buf	12	0	0	0	4	-8
71-72	NYR	1	0	0	0	0	+1
72-73	Minn (WHA)	75	12	39	51	87	
73-74	Minn (WHA)	71	10	35	45	82	
74-75	Minn (WHA)	54	5	15	20	42	
75-76	SD (WHA)	69	2	12	14	38	
NHL Totals		224	15	68	83	150	-29
WHA Totals		269	29	101	130	249	

Playoffs

SSN	TEAM	GP	G	A	PTS.	PIM
67-68	Minn	14	3	7	10	4
72-73	Minn (WHA)	5	0	5	5	2
73-74	Minn (WHA)	11	1	7	8	9
74-75	Minn (WHA)	7	0	1	1	0
75-76	SD (WHA)	9	0	1	1	2
NHL Totals		14	3	7	10	4
WHA Totals		32	1	14	15	13

McMANAMA, Robert S. 6-0 180 C
B. Belmont, Mass., Oct. 7, 1951

SSN	TEAM	GP	G	A	PTS.	PIM	+/-
73-74	Pitt	47	5	14	19	18	-12
74-75	Pitt	40	5	9	14	6	+6
75-76	Pitt	12	1	2	3	4	0
75-76	NE (WHA)	37	3	10	13	28	-6
NHL Totals		99	11	25	36	28	
WHA Totals		37	3	10	13	28	

Playoffs

SSN	TEAM	GP	G	A	PTS.	PIM
74-75	Pitt	8	0	1	1	6
75-76	NE (WHA)	12	4	3	7	4
NHL Totals		8	0	1	1	6
WHA Totals		12	4	3	7	4

*McMANUS, A. Samuel (Sammy) LW
B. Belfast, Ireland, 1909

SSN	TEAM	GP	G	A	PTS.	PIM
34-35	Mont M	25	0	1	1	8
36-37	Bos	1	0	0	0	0
Totals		26	0	1	1	8

Playoffs

SSN	TEAM	GP	G	A	PTS.	PIM
34-35	Mont M	1	0	0	0	0

McMURCHY, Thomas 5-9 165 RW
B. New Westminster, B.C., Dec. 2, 1963

SSN	TEAM	GP	G	A	PTS.	PIM	+/-
83-84	Chi	27	3	1	4	42	-7
84-85	Chi	15	1	2	3	13	-1
85-86	Chi	4	0	0	0	2	-1
87-88	Edm	9	4	1	5	8	+2
Totals		55	8	4	12	65	-7

McNAB, Maxwell Douglas 6-2 170 C
B. Watson, Sask., June 21, 1924

SSN	TEAM	GP	G	A	PTS.	PIM
47-48	Det	12	2	2	4	2
48-49	Det	51	10	13	23	14
49-50	Det	65	4	4	8	8
Totals		128	16	19	35	24

Playoffs

SSN	TEAM	GP	G	A	PTS.	PIM
47-48	Det	3	0	0	0	2
48-49	Det	10	0	1	1	2
49-50	Det	10	0	0	0	0
50-51	Det	2	0	0	0	0
Totals		25	0	1	1	4

McNAB, Peter Maxwell 6-3 205 C
B. Vancouver, B.C., May 8, 1952

SSN	TEAM	GP	G	A	PTS.	PIM	+/-
73-74	Buf	22	3	6	9	2	-3
74-75	Buf	53	22	21	43	8	+13
75-76	Buf	79	24	32	56	16	+18
76-77	Bos	80	38	48	86	11	+26
77-78	Bos	79	41	39	80	4	+35
78-79	Bos	76	35	45	80	10	+29
79-80	Bos	74	40	38	78	10	+24
80-81	Bos	80	37	46	83	24	+12
81-82	Bos	80	36	40	76	19	0
82-83	Bos	74	22	52	74	23	+16
83-84	Bos–Van	65	15	22	37	20	+5
84-85	Van	75	23	25	48	10	-20
85-86	NJ	71	19	24	43	14	-11
86-87	NJ	46	8	12	20	8	-14
Totals		954	363	450	813	179	+130

Playoffs

SSN	TEAM	GP	G	A	PTS.	PIM
74-75	Buf	17	2	6	8	4
75-76	Buf	8	0	0	0	0
76-77	Bos	14	5	3	8	2
77-78	Bos	15	8	11	19	2
78-79	Bos	11	5	3	8	0
79-80	Bos	10	8	6	14	2
80-81	Bos	3	3	0	3	0
81-82	Bos	11	6	8	14	6
82-83	Bos	15	3	5	8	4
83-84	Van	3	0	0	0	0
Totals		107	40	42	82	20

McNABNEY, Sidney 5-7 150 C
B. Toronto, Ont., Jan. 15, 1929

Playoffs

SSN	TEAM	GP	G	A	PTS.	PIM
50-51	Mont	5	0	1	1	2

McNAMARA, Howard 240 D

SSN	TEAM	GP	G	A	PTS.	PIM
19-20	Mont	11	1	0	1	2

McNAUGHTON, George F

SSN	TEAM	GP	G	A	PTS.	PIM
19-20	Que	1	0	0	0	0

McNEILL, Michael 6-0 195 LW
B. Winona, Minn., July 22, 1966

SSN	TEAM	GP	G	A	PTS.	PIM	+/-
90-91	Chi–Que	37	4	7	11	10	+4
91-92	Que	26	1	4	5	8	-8
Totals		63	5	11	16	18	-4

McNEILL, Stuart (Stu) 5-10 170 C
B. Port Arthur, Ont., Sept. 25, 1938

SSN	TEAM	GP	G	A	PTS.	PIM
57-58	Det	2	0	0	0	0
58-59	Det	3	1	1	2	2
59-60	Det	5	0	0	0	0
Totals		10	1	1	2	2

McNEILL, William Ronald 5-10 185 RW
B. Edmonton, Alta., Jan. 26, 1936

SSN	TEAM	GP	G	A	PTS.	PIM
56-57	Det	64	5	10	15	34
57-58	Det	35	5	10	15	29
58-59	Det	54	2	5	7	32
59-60	Det	47	5	13	18	33
62-63	Det	42	3	7	10	12
63-64	Det	15	1	1	2	2
Totals		257	21	46	67	142

SSN	TEAM	GP	G	A	PTS.	PIM
57-58	Det	4	1	1	2	4

McPHEE, George 5-9 170 LW
B. Guelph, Ont., July 2, 1958

SSN	TEAM	GP	G	A	PTS.	PIM	+/-
83-84	NYR	9	1	1	2	11	0
84-85	NYR	49	12	15	27	139	-9
85-86	NYR	30	4	4	8	63	+5
86-87	NYR	21	4	4	8	34	-2
87-88	NJ	5	3	0	3	8	+2
88-89	NJ	1	0	1	1	2	+1
Totals		115	24	25	49	257	-3

Playoffs

SSN	TEAM	GP	G	A	PTS.	PIM
82-83	NYR	9	3	3	6	2
84-85	NYR	3	1	0	1	7
85-86	NYR	11	0	0	0	32
86-87	NYR	1	0	1	1	28
Totals		29	5	3	8	69

McPHEE, Michael Joseph 6-1 203 LW
B. Sydney, N.S., July 14, 1960

SSN	TEAM	GP	G	A	PTS.	PIM	+/-
83-84	Mont	14	5	2	7	41	+4
84-85	Mont	70	17	22	39	120	+1
85-86	Mont	70	19	21	40	69	+8
86-87	Mont	79	18	21	39	58	+7
87-88	Mont	77	23	20	43	53	+19
88-89	Mont	73	19	22	41	74	+14
89-90	Mont	56	23	18	41	47	+28
90-91	Mont	64	22	21	43	56	+6
91-92	Mont	78	16	15	31	63	+6
92-93	Minn	84	18	22	40	44	-2
93-94	Dal	79	20	15	35	36	+8
Totals		744	200	199	399	661	+99

Playoffs

SSN	TEAM	GP	G	A	PTS.	PIM
83-84	Mont	15	1	0	1	31
84-85	Mont	12	4	1	5	32
85-86	Mont	20	3	4	7	45
86-87	Mont	17	7	2	9	13
87-88	Mont	11	4	3	7	8
88-89	Mont	20	4	7	11	30
89-90	Mont	9	1	1	2	16
90-91	Mont	13	1	7	8	12
91-92	Mont	8	1	1	2	4
93-94	Dal	9	2	1	3	2
Totals		134	28	27	55	193

McRAE, Basil Paul 6-2 210 LW
B. Beaverton, Ont., Jan. 5, 1961

SSN	TEAM	GP	G	A	PTS.	PIM	+/-
81-82	Que	20	4	3	7	69	-3
82-83	Que	22	1	1	2	59	-1
83-84	Tor	3	0	0	0	19	-3
84-85	Tor	1	0	0	0	0	0
85-86	Det	4	0	0	0	5	-4
86-87	Det–Que	69	11	7	18	342	-2
87-88	Minn	80	5	11	16	382	-28
88-89	Minn	78	12	19	31	365	-8
89-90	Minn	66	9	17	26	351	-5
90-91	Minn	40	1	3	4	224	-8
91-92	Minn	59	5	8	13	245	-14
92-93	TB–StL	47	3	6	9	169	-16
93-94	StL	40	1	2	3	103	-7
94-95	StL	21	0	5	5	72	+4
95-96	StL	18	1	1	2	40	-5
96-97	Chi	8	0	0	0	12	-2
Totals		576	53	83	136	2457	-103

Playoffs

SSN	TEAM	GP	G	A	PTS.	PIM
81-82	Que	9	1	0	1	34
86-87	Que	13	3	1	4	99
88-89	Minn	5	0	0	0	58
89-90	Minn	7	1	0	1	24
90-91	Minn	22	1	1	2	94
92-93	StL	11	0	1	1	24
93-94	StL	2	0	0	0	12
94-95	StL	7	2	1	3	4
95-96	StL	2	0	0	0	0
Totals		78	8	4	12	349

McRAE, Chris 6-0 200 LW
B. Beaverton, Ont., Aug. 26, 1965

SSN	TEAM	GP	G	A	PTS.	PIM	+/-
87-88	Tor	11	0	0	0	65	0
88-89	Tor	3	0	0	0	12	0
89-90	Det	7	1	0	1	45	0
Totals		21	1	0	1	122	0

McRAE, Ken *6–1 195 C*
B. Winchester, Ont., Apr. 23, 1968

SSN	TEAM	GP	G	A	PTS.	PIM	+/-
87–88	Que	1	0	0	0	0	
88–89	Que	37	6	11	17	68	-9
89–90	Que	66	7	8	15	191	-38
90–91	Que	12	0	0	0	36	-7
91–92	Que	10	0	1	1	31	-5
92–93	Tor	2	0	0	0	2	-1
93–94	Tor	9	1	1	2	36	+1
Totals		137	14	21	35	364	-59

Playoffs

| 93–94 | Tor | 6 | 0 | 0 | 0 | 4 | |

McREYNOLDS, Brian *6–1 192 C*
B. Penetanguishene, Ont., Jan. 5, 1965

89–90	Winn	9	0	2	2	4	-4
90–91	NYR	1	0	0	0	0	-1
93–94	LA	20	1	3	4	4	-2
Totals		30	1	5	6	8	-7

McSHEFFREY, Bryan Gerald *6–2 205 RW*
B. Ottawa, Ont., Sept. 25, 1952

72–73	Van	33	4	4	8	10	-32
73–74	Van	54	9	3	12	34	-14
74–75	Buf	3	0	0	0	0	+1
Totals		90	13	7	20	44	-45

McSORLEY, Martin James *6–1 225 D*
B. Hamilton, Ont., May 18, 1963

83–84	Pitt	72	2	7	9	224	-39
84–85	Pitt	15	0	0	0	15	-3
85–86	Edm	59	11	12	23	265	+9
86–87	Edm	41	2	4	6	159	-4
87–88	Edm	60	9	17	26	223	+23
88–89	LA	66	10	17	27	350	+3
89–90	LA	75	15	21	36	322	+4
90–91	LA	61	7	32	39	221	+48
91–92	LA	71	7	22	29	268	-13
92–93	LA	81	15	26	41	399	+1
93–94	Pitt–LA	65	7	24	31	194	-12
94–95	LA	41	3	18	21	83	-14
95–96	LA–NYR	68	10	23	33	169	-20
96–97	SJ	57	4	12	16	186	-6
97–98	SJ	56	2	10	12	140	+10
98–99	Edm	46	2	3	5	101	-5
Totals		934	106	248	354	3317	-20

Playoffs

85–86	Edm	8	0	2	2	50	
86–87	Edm	21	4	3	7	65	
87–88	Edm	16	0	3	3	67	
88–89	LA	11	0	2	2	33	
89–90	LA	10	1	3	4	18	
90–94	LA	12	0	0	0	58	
91–92	LA	6	1	0	1	21	
92–93	LA	24	4	6	10	60	
95–96	NYR	4	0	0	0	0	
98–99	Edm	3	0	0	0	2	
Totals		115	10	19	29	374	

McSWEEN, Donald Kennedy *5–11 195 D*
B. Detroit, Mich., June 9, 1964

87–88	Buf	5	0	1	1	6	+1
89–90	Buf	4	0	0	0	6	-3
93–94	Ana	32	3	9	12	39	+4
94–95	Ana	2	0	0	0	0	0
95–96	Ana	4	0	0	0	4	0
Totals		47	3	10	13	55	+2

McTAGGART, James *5–11 197 D*
B. Weyburn, Sask., Mar. 31, 1960

80–81	Wash	52	1	6	7	185	-5
81–82	Wash	19	2	4	6	20	-2
Totals		71	3	10	13	205	-7

McTAVISH, Dale *6–1 200 LW*
B. Eganville, Ont., Feb. 28, 1972

| 96–97 | Calg | 9 | 1 | 2 | 3 | 2 | -4 |

McTAVISH, Gordon *6–4 200 C*
B. Guelph, Ont., June 3, 1954

78–79	StL	1	0	0	0	0	-2
79–80	Winn	10	1	3	4	2	+4
Totals		11	1	3	4	2	+2

***McVEIGH, Charles (Rabbit)** *5–6 145 LW*
B. Kenora, Ont., Mar. 29, 1898

26–27	Chi	43	12	4	16	23	
27–28	Chi	43	6	7	13	10	
28–29	NYA	44	6	2	8	16	
29–30	NYA	40	14	14	28	32	
30–31	NYA	44	5	11	16	23	
31–32	NYA	48	12	15	27	16	
32–33	NYA	40	7	12	19	10	
33–34	NYA	48	15	12	27	4	
34–35	NYA	47	7	11	18	4	
Totals		397	84	88	172	138	

Playoffs

26–27	Chi	2	0	0	0	0	
28–29	NYA	2	0	0	0	2	
Totals		4	0	0	0	2	

***McVICAR, John (Slim)** *D*

30–31	Mont M	40	2	4	6	35	
31–32	Mont M	48	0	0	0	28	
Totals		88	2	4	6	63	

Playoffs

| 30–31 | Mont M | 2 | 0 | 0 | 0 | 2 | |

MEAGHER, Richard *5–8 192 C*
B. Belleville, Ont., Nov. 2, 1953

79–80	Mont	2	0	0	0	0	0
80–81	Hart	27	7	10	17	19	+2
81–82	Hart	65	24	19	43	51	-4
82–83	Hart–NJ	61	15	14	29	11	-24
83–84	NJ	52	14	14	28	16	-9
84–85	NJ	71	11	20	31	22	-13
85–86	StL	79	11	19	30	28	-1
86–87	StL	80	18	21	39	54	-9
87–88	StL	76	18	16	34	76	0
88–89	StL	78	15	14	29	53	+9
89–90	StL	76	8	17	25	47	+4
90–91	StL	24	3	1	4	6	0
Totals		691	144	165	309	383	-45

Playoffs

85–86	StL	19	4	4	8	12	
86–87	StL	6	0	0	0	11	
87–88	StL	10	0	0	0	8	
88–89	StL	10	3	2	5	8	
89–90	StL	8	1	0	1	2	
90–91	StL	9	0	1	1	2	
Totals		62	8	7	15	41	

MEEHAN, Gerald Marcus (Gerry) *6–2 200 C*
B. Toronto, Ont., Sept. 3, 1946

68–69	Tor–Phil	37	0	5	5	6	-2
70–71	Buf	77	24	31	55	8	-12
71–72	Buf	77	19	27	46	12	-28
72–73	Buf	77	31	29	60	21	+4
73–74	Buf	72	20	26	46	17	-7
74–75	Buf–Van–Atl	74	14	26	40	6	-8
75–76	Atl–Wash	80	23	35	58	18	-8
76–77	Wash	80	28	36	64	13	-11
77–78	Wash	78	19	24	43	10	-41
78–79	Wash	18	2	4	6	0	-3
78–79	Cin (WHA)	2	0	0	0	0	
NHL Totals		670	180	243	423	111	-116
WHA Totals		2	0	0	0	0	

Playoffs

68–69	Phil	4	0	0	0	0	
72–73	Buf	6	0	1	1	0	
Totals		10	0	1	1	0	

MEEKE, Brent Alan *5–11 172 D*
B. Toronto, Ont., Apr. 10, 1952

72–73	Cal	3	0	0	0	0	0
73–74	Cal	18	1	9	10	4	-11
74–75	Cal	4	0	0	0	0	+1
75–76	Cal	1	0	0	0	0	0
76–77	Clev	49	8	13	21	4	-15
Totals		75	9	22	31	8	-25

MEEKER, Howard William *5–8 165 RW*
B. Kitchener, Ont., Nov. 4, 1924

46–47	Tor	55	27	18	45	76	
47–48	Tor	58	14	20	34	62	
48–49	Tor	30	7	7	14	56	

49–50	Tor	70	18	22	40	35	
50–51	Tor	49	6	14	20	24	
51–52	Tor	54	9	14	23	50	
52–53	Tor	25	1	7	8	26	
53–54	Tor	5	1	0	1	0	
Totals		346	83	102	185	329	

Playoffs

46–47	Tor	11	3	3	6	6	
47–48	Tor	9	2	4	6	15	
49–50	Tor	7	0	1	1	4	
50–51	Tor	11	1	1	2	14	
51–52	Tor	4	0	0	0	11	
Totals		42	6	9	15	50	

MEEKER, Michael Thomas *5–11 195 RW*
B. Kingston Ont., Feb 23, 1958

| 78–79 | Pitt | 4 | 0 | 0 | 0 | 5 | -1 |

***MEEKING, Harry** *LW*
B. Kitchener, Ont., Nov. 4, 1894

17–18	Tor	20	10	0	10	19	
18–19	Tor	14	7	3	10	22	
26–27	Det–Bos	29	1	0	1	6	
Totals		63	18	3	21	47	

Playoffs

17–18	Tor	7	1	2	3	24	
26–27	Bos	8	0	0	0	0	
Totals		15	1	2	3	24	

MEGER, Paul Carl *5–7 160 LW*
B. Watrous, Sask., Feb. 17, 1929

50–51	Mont	17	2	4	6	6	
51–52	Mont	69	24	18	42	44	
52–53	Mont	69	9	17	26	38	
53–54	Mont	44	4	9	13	24	
54–55	Mont	13	0	4	4	6	
Totals		212	39	52	91	118	

Playoffs

49–50	Mont	2	0	0	0	2	
50–51	Mont	11	1	3	4	4	
51–52	Mont	11	0	3	3	2	
52–53	Mont	5	1	2	3	4	
53–54	Mont	6	1	0	1	4	
Totals		35	3	8	11	16	

MEIGHAN, Ron James *6–3 195 D*
B. Montreal, Que., May 26, 1963

81–82	Minn	7	1	1	2	2	-2
82–83	Pitt	41	2	6	8	16	-10
Totals		48	3	7	10	18	-12

MEISSNER, Barrie Michael *5–9 165 LW*
B. Unity, Sask., July 26, 1946

67–68	Minn	1	0	0	0	2	-1
68–69	Minn	5	0	1	1	2	+1
Totals		6	0	1	1	4	0

MEISSNER, Richard Donald (Dick) *5–11 200 RW*
B. Kindersley, Sask., Jan. 6, 1940

59–60	Bos	60	5	6	11	22	
60–61	Bos	9	0	1	1	2	
61–62	Bos	66	3	6	13		
63–64	NYR	35	3	5	8	0	
64–65	NYR	1	0	0	0	0	
Totals		171	11	15	26	37	

MELAMETSA, Anssi *6–0 190 LW*
B. Jyvaskyla, Finland, June 21, 1961

| 85–86 | Winn | 27 | 0 | 3 | 3 | 2 | -5 |

MELANSON, Dean *5–11 211 D*
B. Antigonish, N.S., Nov. 19, 1973

| 94–95 | Buf | 5 | 0 | 0 | 0 | 4 | -1 |

MELIN, Roger Alf *6–4 198 LW*
B. Enkoping, Sweden, Apr. 25, 1956

80–81	Minn	1	0	0	0	0	-1
81–82	Minn	2	0	0	0	0	0
Totals		3	0	0	0	0	-1

SSN	TEAM	GP	G	A	PTS.	PIM	+/-

MELLANBY, Scott Edgar *6–1 199 RW*
B. Montreal, Que., June 11, 1966

SSN	TEAM	GP	G	A	PTS.	PIM	+/-
85–86	Phil	2	0	0	0	0	-1
86–87	Phil	71	11	21	32	94	+8
87–88	Phil	75	25	26	51	185	-7
88–89	Phil	76	21	29	50	183	-13
89–90	Phil	57	6	17	23	77	-4
90–91	Phil	74	20	21	41	155	+8
91–92	Edm	80	23	27	50	197	+5
92–93	Edm	69	15	17	32	147	-4
93–94	Fla	80	30	30	60	149	0
94–95	Fla	48	13	12	25	90	-16
95–96	Fla	79	32	38	70	160	+4
96–97	Fla	82	27	29	56	170	+7
97–98	Fla	79	15	24	39	127	-14
98–99	Fla	67	18	27	45	85	+5
Totals		939	256	318	574	1819	-22

Playoffs

86–87	Phil	24	5	5	10	46	
87–88	Phil	7	0	1	1	16	
88–89	Phil	19	4	5	9	28	
91–92	Edm	16	2	1	3	29	
95–96	Fla	22	3	6	9	44	
96–97	Fla	5	0	2	2	4	
Totals		93	14	20	34	167	

MELLOR, Thomas Robert *6–1 185 D*
B. Cranston, R.I., Jan. 27, 1950

73–74	Det	25	2	4	6	25	-9
74–75	Det	1	0	0	0	0	0
Totals		26	2	4	6	25	-9

MELNYK, Larry Joseph *6–0 195 D*
B. Saskatoon, Sask., Feb. 21, 1960

80–81	Bos	26	0	4	4	39	-7
81–82	Bos	48	0	8	8	84	+3
82–83	Bos	1	0	0	0	0	-2
84–85	Edm	28	0	11	11	25	+12
85–86	Edm–NYR	52	3	11	14	76	+10
86–87	NYR	73	3	12	15	182	-13
87–88	NYR–Van	63	2	4	6	107	-19
88–89	Van	74	3	11	14	82	+3
89–90	Van	67	0	2	2	91	-27
Totals		432	11	63	74	686	-40

Playoffs

81–82	Bos	11	0	3	3	40	
82–83	Bos	11	0	0	0	9	
83–84	Edm	6	0	1	1	0	
84–85	Edm	12	1	3	4	26	
85–86	NYR	16	1	2	3	46	
86–87	NYR	6	0	0	0	4	
88–89	Van	4	0	0	0	2	
Totals		66	2	9	11	127	

MELNYK, Michael Gerald (Gerry) *5–10 180 C*
B. Edmonton, Alta., Sept. 16, 1934

59–60	Det	63	10	10	20	12	
60–61	Det	70	9	16	25	2	
61–62	Chi	63	5	16	21	6	
67–68	StL	73	15	35	50	14	-11
Totals		269	39	77	116	34	-11

Playoffs

55–56	Det	6	0	0	0	0	
59–60	Det	6	3	0	3	0	
60–61	Det	11	1	0	1	2	
61–62	Chi	7	0	0	0	2	
64–65	Chi	6	0	0	0	0	
67–68	StL	17	2	6	8	2	
Totals		53	6	6	12	6	

MELROSE, Barry *6–0 205 D*
B. Kelvington, Sask., July 15, 1956

76–77	Cin (WHA)	29	1	4	5	8	
77–78	Cin (WHA)	69	2	9	11	113	
78–79	Cin (WHA)	80	2	14	16	222	
79–80	Winn	74	4	6	10	124	-41
80–81	Winn–Tor	75	3	6	9	206	-30
81–82	Tor	64	1	5	6	186	-26
82–83	Tor	52	2	5	7	68	-16
83–84	Det	21	0	1	1	74	0
85–86	Det	14	0	0	0	70	-6
NHL Totals		300	10	23	33	728	-119
WHA Totals		178	5	27	32	343	

Playoffs

76–77	Cin (WHA)	2	0	0	0	2	
78–79	Cin (WHA)	3	0	1	1	8	
80–81	Tor	3	0	1	1	15	
82–83	Tor	4	0	1	1	23	
NHL Totals		7	0	2	2	38	
WHA Totals		5	0	1	1	10	

MENARD, Hillary (Hill) *D*
B. Timmins, Ont., Jan. 15, 1934

53–54	Chi	1	0	0	0	0	

MENARD, Howard Hubert *5–8 160 C*
B. Timmins, Ont., Apr. 28, 1942

63–64	Det	3	0	0	0	0	
67–68	LA	35	9	15	24	32	+4
68–69	LA	56	10	17	27	31	0
69–70	Chi–Oak	57	4	10	14	24	0
Totals		151	23	42	65	87	+4

Playoffs

67–68	LA	7	0	5	5	24	
68–69	LA	11	3	2	5	12	
69–70	Oak	1	0	0	0	0	
Totals		19	3	7	10	36	

MERCREDI, Victor Dennis *5–11 185 C*
B. Yellowknife, N.W.T., Mar. 31, 1953

74–75	Atl	2	0	0	0	0	0
75–76	Calg (WHA)	3	0	0	0	29	

MEREDITH, Gregory Paul *6–1 210 RW*
B. Toronto, Ont., Feb. 23, 1958

80–81	Calg	3	1	0	1	0	+1
82–83	Calg	35	5	4	9	8	-5
Totals		38	6	4	10	8	-4

Playoffs

83–83	Calg	5	3	1	4	4	

MERKOSKY, Glenn *5–10 175 C*
B. Edmonton, Alta., Apr. 8, 1959

81–82	Hart	7	0	0	0	2	-1
82–83	NJ	34	4	10	14	20	-10
83–84	NJ	5	1	0	1	0	0
85–86	Det	17	0	2	2	0	-12
89–90	Det	3	0	0	0	0	0
Totals		66	5	12	17	22	-23

MERONEK, William (Smiley) *F*
B. Stoney Mountain, Man., Apr. 15, 1917

39–40	Mont	7	2	2	4	0	
42–43	Mont	12	3	6	9	0	
Totals		19	5	8	13	0	

Playoffs

42–43	Mont	1	0	0	0	0	

MERRICK, Leonard (Wayne) *6–1 195 C*
B. Sarnia, Ont., Apr. 23, 1952

72–73	StL	50	10	11	21	10	-2
73–74	StL	64	20	23	43	32	-11
74–75	StL	76	28	37	65	57	+29
75–76	StL–Cal	75	32	35	67	36	-3
76–77	Clev	80	18	38	56	25	-21
77–78	Clev–NYI	55	12	19	31	16	-8
78–79	NYI	75	20	21	41	24	+13
79–80	NYI	70	13	22	35	16	+12
80–81	NYI	71	16	15	31	30	+12
81–82	NYI	68	12	27	39	20	+4
82–83	NYI	59	4	12	16	27	-3
83–84	NYI	31	6	5	11	10	+2
Totals		774	191	265	456	303	+24

Playoffs

72–73	StL	5	0	1	1	2	
74–75	StL	2	1	1	2	0	
77–78	NYI	7	1	0	1	0	
78–79	NYI	10	2	3	5	2	
79–80	NYI	21	2	4	6	2	
80–81	NYI	18	6	12	18	8	
81–82	NYI	19	6	6	12	6	
82–83	NYI	19	1	3	4	10	
83–84	NYI	1	0	0	0	0	
Totals		102	19	30	49	30	

*MERRILL, Horace *D*
B. 1885

17–18	Ott	4	0	0	0	0	
19–20	Ott	7	0	0	0	0	
Totals		11	0	0	0	0	

MERTZIG, Jan *6–4 218 D*
B. Huddinge, Sweden, July 18, 1970

98–99	NYR	23	0	2	2	8	-5

MESSIER, Eric *6–2 200 D*
B. Drummondville, Que., Oct. 29, 1973

96–97	Col A	21	0	0	0	4	+7
97–98	Col A	62	4	12	16	20	+4
98–99	Col A	31	4	2	6	14	0
Totals		114	8	14	22	38	+11

Playoffs

96–97	Col A	6	0	0	0	4	
98–99	Col A	3	0	0	0	0	
Totals		9	0	0	0	4	

MESSIER, Marcus Cyril (Joby) *6–0 193 D*
B. Regina, Sask., Mar. 2, 1970

92–93	NYR	11	0	0	0	6	0
93–94	NYR	4	0	2	2	0	-1
94–95	NYR	10	0	2	2	18	+2
Totals		25	0	4	4	24	+1

MESSIER, Mark Douglas *6–1 205 C*
B. Edmonton, Alta., Jan. 18, 1961

78–79	Ind–Cin (WHA)	52	1	10	11	58	
79–80	Edm	75	12	21	33	120	-12
80–81	Edm	72	23	40	63	102	+21
81–82	Edm	78	50	38	88	119	+19
82–83	Edm	77	48	58	106	72	+40
83–84	Edm	73	37	64	101	165	+8
84–85	Edm	55	23	31	54	57	+36
85–86	Edm	63	35	49	84	68	+21
86–87	Edm	77	37	70	107	73	+21
87–88	Edm	77	37	74	111	103	-6
88–89	Edm	72	33	61	94	130	+19
89–90	Edm	79	45	84	129	79	+15
90–91	Edm	53	12	52	64	34	+31
91–92	NYR	79	35	72	107	76	-6
92–93	NYR	75	25	66	91	72	+25
93–94	NYR	76	26	58	84	76	+8
94–95	NYR	46	14	39	53	40	+8
95–96	NYR	74	47	52	99	122	+29
96–97	NYR	71	36	48	84	88	+12
97–98	Van	82	22	38	60	58	-10
98–99	Van	59	13	35	48	33	-12
NHL Totals		1413	610	1050	1660	1687	+249
WHA Totals		52	1	10	11	58	

Playoffs

79–80	Edm	3	1	2	3	2	
80–81	Edm	9	2	5	7	13	
81–82	Edm	5	1	2	3	8	
82–83	Edm	15	15	6	21	14	
83–84	Edm	19	8	18	26	19	
84–85	Edm	18	12	13	25	12	
85–86	Edm	10	4	6	10	18	
86–87	Edm	21	12	16	28	16	
87–88	Edm	19	11	23	34	29	
88–89	Edm	7	1	11	12	8	
89–90	Edm	22	9	22	31	20	
90–91	Edm	18	4	11	15	16	
91–92	NYR	11	7	7	14	6	
93–94	NYR	23	12	18	30	33	
94–95	NYR	10	3	10	13	8	
95–96	NYR	11	4	7	11	16	
96–97	NYR	15	3	9	12	6	
Totals		236	109	186	295	244	

MESSIER, Mitch *6–2 200 C*
B. Regina, Sask., Aug. 21, 1965

87–88	Minn	13	0	1	1	11	-5
88–89	Minn	3	0	1	1	0	-1
89–90	Minn	2	0	0	0	0	-2
90–91	Minn	2	0	0	0	0	-2
Totals		20	0	2	2	11	-10

SSN	TEAM	GP	G	A	PTS.	PIM	+/-

MESSIER, Paul Edmond *6-1 184 C*
B. Nottingham, England, Jan. 27, 1958

		GP	G	A	PTS.	PIM	+/-
78-79	Col	9	0	0	0	4	-6

METCALFE, Scott *6-0 200 LW*
B. Toronto, Ont., Jan. 6, 1967

87-88	Edm-Buf	3	0	1	1	0	-2
88-89	Buf	9	1	1	2	13	-1
89-90	Buf	7	0	0	0	5	0
Totals		19	1	2	3	18	-3

METZ, Donald Maurice *5-9 165 RW*
B. Wilcox, Sask., Jan. 10, 1916

39-40	Tor	10	1	1	2	4	
40-41	Tor	31	4	10	14	6	
41-42	Tor	25	2	3	5	8	
45-46	Tor	7	1	0	1	0	
46-47	Tor	40	4	9	13	10	
47-48	Tor	26	4	6	10	2	
48-49	Tor	33	4	6	10	12	
Totals		172	20	35	55	42	

Playoffs

39-40	Tor	2	0	0	0	0	
40-41	Tor	5	1	1	2	2	
41-42	Tor	13	4	3	7	0	
44-45	Tor	11	0	1	1	4	
46-47	Tor	11	2	3	5	4	
47-48	Tor	2	0	0	0	0	
48-49	Tor	3	0	0	0	0	
Totals		47	7	8	15	10	

*METZ, Nicholas J. (Nick) *5-11 160 LW*
B. Wilcox, Sask., Feb. 16, 1914

34-35	Tor	18	2	2	4	4	
35-36	Tor	38	14	6	20	14	
36-37	Tor	48	9	11	20	19	
37-38	Tor	48	15	7	22	12	
38-39	Tor	47	11	10	21	15	
39-40	Tor	31	6	5	11	2	
40-41	Tor	47	14	21	35	10	
41-42	Tor	30	11	9	20	20	
44-45	Tor	50	22	13	35	26	
45-46	Tor	41	11	11	22	4	
46-47	Tor	60	12	16	28	15	
47-48	Tor	60	4	8	12	8	
Totals		518	131	119	250	149	

Playoffs

34-35	Tor	6	1	1	2	0	
36-37	Tor	2	0	0	0	0	
37-38	Tor	7	0	2	2	0	
38-39	Tor	10	3	3	6	6	
39-40	Tor	9	1	3	4	9	
40-41	Tor	7	3	4	7	0	
41-42	Tor	13	4	4	8	12	
44-45	Tor	7	1	1	2	2	
46-47	Tor	6	4	2	6	0	
47-48	Tor	9	2	0	2	2	
Totals		76	19	20	39	31	

MICHALUK, Arthur *6-0 182 D*
B. Canmore, Alta., May 4, 1923

| 47-48 | Chi | 5 | 0 | 0 | 0 | 0 | |

MICHALUK, John *5-10 155 F*
B. Canmore, Alta., Nov. 2, 1928

| 50-51 | Chi | 1 | 0 | 0 | 0 | 0 | |

MICHALYUK, David *5-10 189 LW*
B. Wakaw, Sask., May 18, 1962

81-82	Phil	1	0	0	0	0	-2
82-83	Phil	13	2	6	8	8	+1
Totals		14	2	6	8	8	-1

Playoffs

| 82-83 | Phil | 7 | 1 | 1 | 2 | 0 | |

MICHELETTI, Joseph Robert *6-1 185 D*
B. Hibbing, Minn., Oct. 24, 1954

76-77	Calg (WHA)	14	3	3	6	10	
77-78	Edm (WHA)	56	14	34	48	56	
78-79	Edm (WHA)	72	14	33	47	85	
79-80	StL	54	2	16	18	29	-5
80-81	StL	63	4	27	31	53	+12
81-82	StL-Col	41	5	17	22	32	-6
NHL Totals		158	11	60	71	114	+1
WHA Totals		142	31	70	101	151	

Playoffs

77-78	Edm (WHA)	5	0	2	2	4	
78-79	Edm (WHA)	13	0	9	9	2	
80-81	StL	11	1	11	12	10	
NHL Totals		11	1	11	12	10	
WHA Totals		18	0	11	11	6	

MICHELETTI, Patrick *5-9 175 C*
B. Hibbing, Minn., Dec. 11, 1963

| 87-88 | Minn | 12 | 2 | 0 | 2 | 8 | +2 |

*MICKEY, Robert Lawrence (Larry) *5-11 180 RW*
B. Lacombe, Alta., Oct. 21, 1943

64-65	Chi	1	0	0	0	0	
65-66	NYR	7	0	0	0	2	
66-67	NYR	8	0	0	0	0	
67-68	NYR	4	0	2	2	0	+2
68-69	Tor	55	8	19	27	43	0
69-70	Mont	21	4	4	8	4	-10
70-71	LA	65	6	12	18	46	-15
71-72	Phil-Buf	18	1	3	4	8	-6
72-73	Buf	77	15	9	24	47	-6
73-74	Buf	13	3	4	7	8	+5
74-75	Buf	23	2	0	2	2	+1
Totals		292	39	53	92	160	-29

Playoffs

68-69	Tor	3	0	0	0	5	
72-73	Buf	6	1	0	1	5	
Totals		9	1	0	1	10	

MICKOSKI, Nicholas (Nick) *6-1 193 LW*
B. Winnipeg, Man., Dec. 7, 1927

48-49	NYR	54	13	9	22	20	
49-50	NYR	45	10	10	20	10	
50-51	NYR	64	20	15	35	12	
51-52	NYR	43	7	13	20	20	
52-53	NYR	70	19	16	35	39	
53-54	NYR	68	19	16	35	22	
54-55	NYR-Chi	70	10	33	43	48	
55-56	Chi	70	19	20	39	52	
56-57	Chi	70	16	20	36	24	
57-58	Chi-Det	65	13	18	31	50	
58-59	Det	66	11	15	26	20	
59-60	Bos	18	1	0	1	2	
Totals		703	158	185	343	319	

Playoffs

47-48	NYR	2	0	1	1	0	
49-50	NYR	12	1	5	6	2	
57-58	Det	4	0	0	0	4	
Totals		18	1	6	7	6	

MIDDENDORF, Max *6-4 210 RW*
B. Syracuse, N.Y., Aug. 18, 1967

86-87	Que	6	1	4	5	4	-2
87-88	Que	1	0	0	0	0	0
89-90	Que	3	0	0	0	0	-9
90-91	Edm	3	1	0	1	2	0
Totals		13	2	4	6	6	-11

MIDDLETON, Richard David *5-11 180 RW*
B. Toronto, Ont., Dec. 4, 1953

74-75	NYR	47	22	18	40	19	-6
75-76	NYR	77	24	26	50	14	-38
76-77	Bos	72	20	22	42	2	+2
77-78	Bos	79	25	35	60	8	+40
78-79	Bos	71	38	48	86	7	+33
79-80	Bos	80	40	52	92	24	+31
80-81	Bos	80	44	59	103	16	+15
81-82	Bos	75	51	43	94	12	+15
82-83	Bos	80	49	47	96	8	+33
83-84	Bos	80	47	58	105	14	+26
84-85	Bos	80	30	46	76	6	+2
85-86	Bos	49	14	30	44	10	+17
86-87	Bos	76	31	37	68	6	+7
87-88	Bos	59	13	19	32	11	+3
Totals		1005	448	540	988	157	+180

Playoffs

74-75	NYR	3	0	0	0	2	
76-77	Bos	13	5	4	9	0	
77-78	Bos	15	5	2	7	0	
78-79	Bos	11	4	8	12	0	
79-80	Bos	10	4	2	6	5	
80-81	Bos	3	0	1	1	2	
81-82	Bos	11	6	9	15	0	
82-83	Bos	17	11	22	33	6	
83-84	Bos	3	0	0	0	0	
84-85	Bos	5	3	0	3	2	
86-87	Bos	4	2	2	4	0	
87-88	Bos	19	5	5	10	4	
Totals		114	45	55	100	19	

MIEHM, Kevin *6-2 200 C*
B. Kitchener, Ont., Sept. 10, 1969

92-93	StL	8	1	3	4	4	+1
93-94	StL	14	0	1	1	4	-3
Totals		22	1	4	5	8	-2

Playoffs

| 92-93 | StL | 2 | 0 | 1 | 1 | 0 | |

MIGAY, Rudolph Joseph *5-10 175 C*
B. Fort William Ont., Nov. 18, 1928

49-50	Tor	18	1	5	6	8	
51-52	Tor	19	2	1	3	12	
52-53	Tor	40	5	4	9	22	
53-54	Tor	70	8	15	23	60	
54-55	Tor	67	8	16	24	66	
55-56	Tor	70	12	16	28	52	
56-57	Tor	66	15	20	35	51	
57-58	Tor	48	7	14	21	18	
58-59	Tor	19	1	1	2	4	
59-60	Tor	1	0	0	0	0	
Totals		418	59	92	151	293	

Playoffs

53-54	Tor	5	1	0	1	4	
54-55	Tor	3	0	0	0	10	
55-56	Tor	5	0	0	0	6	
58-59	Tor	2	0	0	0	0	
Totals		15	1	0	1	20	

MIKITA, Stanley (Stosh) *5-9 169 C*
B. Skolce, Czechoslovakia, May 20, 1940

58-59	Chi	3	0	1	1	4	
59-60	Chi	67	8	18	26	119	
60-61	Chi	66	19	34	53	100	
61-62	Chi	70	25	52	77	97	
62-63	Chi	65	31	45	76	69	
63-64	Chi	70	39	50	89	149	
64-65	Chi	70	28	59	87	154	
65-66	Chi	68	30	48	78	58	
66-67	Chi	70	35	62	97	12	
67-68	Chi	72	40	47	87	14	-3
68-69	Chi	74	30	67	97	52	+17
69-70	Chi	76	39	47	86	50	+19
70-71	Chi	74	24	48	72	85	+21
71-72	Chi	74	26	39	65	46	+16
72-73	Chi	57	27	56	83	32	+31
73-74	Chi	76	30	50	80	46	+24
74-75	Chi	79	36	50	86	48	+14
75-76	Chi	48	16	41	57	37	-4
76-77	Chi	57	19	30	49	20	-9
77-78	Chi	76	18	41	59	35	+18
78-79	Chi	65	19	36	55	34	+3
79-80	Chi	17	2	5	7	12	+2
Totals		1394	541	926	1467	1273	+159

Playoffs

59-60	Chi	3	0	1	1	2	
60-61	Chi	12	6	5	11	21	
61-62	Chi	12	6	15	21	19	
62-63	Chi	6	3	2	5	2	
63-64	Chi	7	3	6	9	8	
64-65	Chi	14	3	7	10	53	
65-66	Chi	6	1	2	3	2	
66-67	Chi	6	2	2	4	2	
67-68	Chi	11	5	7	12	6	
69-70	Chi	8	4	6	10	2	
70-71	Chi	18	5	13	18	16	
71-72	Chi	8	3	1	4	2	
72-73	Chi	15	7	13	20	8	
73-74	Chi	11	5	6	11	8	
74-75	Chi	8	3	4	7	12	
75-76	Chi	4	0	0	0	4	
77-78	Chi	4	3	0	3	0	
Totals		155	59	91	150	169	

MIKKELSON, William Robert 6–0 190 D
B. Neepawa, Man., May 21, 1948

SSN	TEAM	GP	G	A	PTS.	PIM	+/-
71–72	LA	15	0	1	1	6	-11
72–73	NYI	72	1	10	11	45	-54
74–75	Wash	59	3	7	10	52	-82
76–77	Wash	1	0	0	0	2	0
Totals		147	4	18	22	105	-137

MIKOL, John Stanley (Jim) 6–0 175 D
B. Kitchener, Ont., June 11, 1938

SSN	TEAM	GP	G	A	PTS.	PIM
62–63	Tor	4	0	1	1	2
64–65	NYR	30	1	3	4	6
Totals		34	1	4	5	8

MIKULCHIK, Oleg 6–2 200 D
B. Minsk, USSR, June 27, 1964

SSN	TEAM	GP	G	A	PTS.	PIM	+/-
93–94	Winn	4	0	1	1	17	-2
94–95	Winn	25	0	2	2	12	+10
95–96	Ana	8	0	0	0	4	-2
Totals		37	0	3	3	33	+6

MILBURY, Michael James 6–1 200 D
B. Brighton, Mass., June 17, 1952

SSN	TEAM	GP	G	A	PTS.	PIM	+/-
75–76	Bos	3	0	0	0	9	+1
76–77	Bos	77	6	18	24	166	+25
77–78	Bos	80	8	30	38	151	+52
78–79	Bos	74	1	34	35	149	+23
79–80	Bos	72	10	13	23	59	+7
80–81	Bos	77	0	18	18	222	+14
81–82	Bos	51	2	10	12	71	+10
82–83	Bos	78	9	15	24	216	+22
83–84	Bos	74	2	17	19	159	+2
84–85	Bos	78	3	13	16	152	-6
85–86	Bos	22	2	5	7	102	+1
86–87	Bos	68	6	16	22	96	+22
Totals		754	49	189	238	1552	+173

Playoffs

SSN	TEAM	GP	G	A	PTS.	PIM
75–76	Bos	11	0	0	0	290
76–77	Bos	31	2	2	4	47
77–78	Bos	15	1	8	9	27
78–79	Bos	11	1	7	8	7
79–80	Bos	10	0	2	2	50
80–81	Bos	2	0	1	1	10
81–82	Bos	11	0	4	4	6
83–84	Bos	3	0	0	0	12
84–85	Bos	5	0	0	0	10
85–86	Bos	1	0	0	0	17
86–87	Bos	4	0	0	0	4
Totals		86	4	24	28	219

*MILKS, Herbert (Hib) 5–11 165 LW
B. Eardley, Ont., Apr. 1, 1902

SSN	TEAM	GP	G	A	PTS.	PIM
25–26	Pitt Pi	36	14	5	19	17
26–27	Pitt Pi	44	16	6	22	18
27–28	Pitt Pi	44	18	3	21	34
28–29	Pitt Pi	44	9	3	12	22
29–30	Pitt Pi	41	13	11	24	36
30–31	Phil Q	44	17	6	23	42
31–32	NYR	45	0	4	4	12
32–33	Ott	16	0	3	3	0
Totals		314	87	41	128	181

Playoffs

SSN	TEAM	GP	G	A	PTS.	PIM
25–26	Pitt	2	0	0	0	0
27–28	Pitt	2	0	0	0	2
31–32	NYR	6	0	0	0	0
Totals		10	0	0	0	2

MILLAR, Craig 6–2 200 D
B. Winnipeg, Man., July 12, 1976

SSN	TEAM	GP	G	A	PTS.	PIM	+/-
96–97	Edm	1	0	0	0	2	0
97–98	Edm	11	4	0	4	8	-3
98–99	Edm	24	0	2	2	19	-6
Totals		36	4	2	6	29	-9

MILLAR, Hugh Alexander 5–8 200 D
B. Edmonton, Alta., Apr. 3, 1921

SSN	TEAM	GP	G	A	PTS.	PIM
46–47	Det	4	0	0	0	0

Playoffs

SSN	TEAM	GP	G	A	PTS.	PIM
46–47	Det	1	0	0	0	0

MILLAR, Mike 5–10 170 RW
B. St. Catharines, Ont., Apr. 28, 1965

SSN	TEAM	GP	G	A	PTS.	PIM	+/-
86–87	Hart	10	2	2	4	0	+3
87–88	Hart	28	7	7	14	6	-5
88–89	Wash	18	6	3	9	4	-4
89–90	Bos	15	1	4	5	0	-2
90–91	Tor	7	2	2	4	2	-1
Totals		78	18	18	36	12	-9

MILLEN, Corey 5–7 168 C
B. Cloquet, Minn., Apr. 29, 1964

SSN	TEAM	GP	G	A	PTS.	PIM	+/-
89–90	NYR	4	0	0	0	2	-2
90–91	NYR	4	3	1	4	0	+1
91–92	NYR–LA	57	21	25	46	54	+2
92–93	LA	42	23	16	39	42	+16
93–94	NJ	78	20	30	50	52	+24
94–95	NJ–Dal	45	5	18	23	36	+6
95–96	Dal–Calg	44	7	14	21	18	+8
96–97	Calg	61	11	15	26	32	-19
Totals		335	90	119	209	236	+36

Playoffs

SSN	TEAM	GP	G	A	PTS.	PIM
90–91	NYR	6	1	2	3	0
91–92	LA	6	0	1	1	6
92–93	LA	23	2	4	6	12
93–94	NJ	7	1	0	1	2
94–95	Dal	5	1	0	1	2
Totals		47	5	7	12	22

MILLER, Aaron Michael 6–3 197 D
B. Buffalo, N.Y., Aug. 11, 1971

SSN	TEAM	GP	G	A	PTS.	PIM	+/-
93–94	Que	1	0	0	0	0	-1
94–95	Que	9	0	3	3	6	+2
95–96	Col A	5	0	0	0	0	0
96–97	Col A	56	5	12	17	15	+15
97–98	Col A	55	2	2	4	51	0
98–99	Col A	76	5	13	18	42	+3
Totals		202	12	30	42	114	+19

Playoffs

SSN	TEAM	GP	G	A	PTS.	PIM
96–97	Col A	17	1	2	3	10
97–98	Col A	7	0	0	0	8
98–99	Col A	19	1	5	6	10
Totals		43	2	7	9	28

MILLER, Brad 6–4 220 D
B. Edmonton, Alta., July 23, 1969

SSN	TEAM	GP	G	A	PTS.	PIM	+/-
88–89	Buf	7	0	0	0	6	-1
89–90	Buf	1	0	0	0	0	+1
90–91	Buf	13	0	0	0	67	-1
91–92	Buf	42	1	4	5	192	-5
92–93	Ott	11	0	0	0	42	-5
93–94	Calg	8	0	1	1	14	-2
Totals		82	1	5	6	321	-13

*MILLER, Earl F
B. Regina, Sask.

SSN	TEAM	GP	G	A	PTS.	PIM
27–28	Chi	22	1	1	2	32
28–29	Chi	15	1	1	2	24
29–30	Chi	38	11	5	16	50
30–31	Chi	17	3	4	7	8
31–32	Chi–Tor	24	3	3	6	10
Totals		116	19	14	33	124

Playoffs

SSN	TEAM	GP	G	A	PTS.	PIM
29–30	Chi	2	1	0	1	6
30–31	Chi	1	0	0	0	0
31–32	Tor	7	0	0	0	0
Totals		10	1	0	1	6

MILLER, Jack Leslie 5–8 155 LW
B. Delisle, Sask., Sept. 16, 1925

SSN	TEAM	GP	G	A	PTS.	PIM
49–50	Chi	6	0	0	0	0
50–51	Chi	11	0	0	0	4
Totals		17	0	0	0	4

MILLER, Jason 6–1 190 LW
B. Edmonton, Alta., Mar. 1, 1971

SSN	TEAM	GP	G	A	PTS.	PIM	+/-
90–91	NJ	1	0	0	0	0	+1
91–92	NJ	3	0	0	0	0	0
92–93	NJ	2	0	0	0	0	-1
Totals		6	0	0	0	0	0

MILLER, Jay 6–2 210 LW
B. Wellesley, Mass., July 16, 1960

SSN	TEAM	GP	G	A	PTS.	PIM	+/-
85–86	Bos	46	3	0	3	178	-3
86–87	Bos	55	1	4	5	208	-11
87–88	Bos	78	7	12	19	304	-5
88–89	Bos–LA	66	7	7	14	301	-9
89–90	LA	68	10	2	12	224	-6
90–91	LA	66	8	12	20	259	+9
91–92	LA	67	4	7	11	237	-8
Totals		446	40	44	84	1711	-33

Playoffs

SSN	TEAM	GP	G	A	PTS.	PIM
85–86	Bos	2	0	0	0	17
87–88	Bos	12	0	0	0	124
88–89	LA	11	0	1	1	63
89–90	LA	10	1	1	2	10
90–91	LA	8	0	0	0	17
91–92	LA	5	1	1	2	12
Totals		48	2	3	5	243

MILLER, Kelly David 5–11 196 LW
B. Lansing, Mich., Mar. 3, 1963

SSN	TEAM	GP	G	A	PTS.	PIM	+/-
84–85	NYR	5	0	2	2	2	-2
85–86	NYR	74	13	20	33	52	+3
86–87	NYR–Wash	77	16	26	42	48	+5
87–88	Wash	80	9	23	32	35	+9
88–89	Wash	78	19	21	40	45	+13
89–90	Wash	80	18	22	40	49	-2
90–91	Wash	80	24	26	50	29	+10
91–92	Wash	78	14	38	52	49	+20
92–93	Wash	84	18	27	45	32	+2
93–94	Wash	84	14	25	39	32	+8
94–95	Wash	48	10	13	23	6	+5
95–96	Wash	74	7	13	20	30	+7
96–97	Wash	77	10	14	24	33	+4
97–98	Wash	76	7	7	14	41	-2
98–99	Wash	62	2	5	7	29	-5
Totals		1057	181	282	463	512	+71

Playoffs

SSN	TEAM	GP	G	A	PTS.	PIM
84–85	NYR	3	0	0	0	2
85–86	NYR	16	3	4	7	4
86–87	Wash	7	2	2	4	0
87–88	Wash	14	4	4	8	10
88–89	Wash	6	1	0	1	2
89–90	Wash	15	3	5	8	23
90–91	Wash	11	4	2	6	6
91–92	Wash	7	1	2	3	4
92–93	Wash	6	0	3	3	2
93–94	Wash	11	2	7	9	0
94–95	Wash	7	0	3	3	4
95–96	Wash	6	0	1	1	4
97–98	Wash	10	0	1	1	4
Totals		119	20	34	54	65

MILLER, Kevin Bradley 5–11 191 C
B. Lansing, Mich., Sept. 9, 1965

SSN	TEAM	GP	G	A	PTS.	PIM	+/-
88–89	NYR	24	3	5	8	2	-1
89–90	NYR	16	0	5	5	2	-1
90–91	NYR–Det	74	22	29	51	67	-3
91–92	Det	80	20	26	46	53	+6
92–93	Wash–StL	82	24	25	49	100	+2
93–94	StL	75	23	25	48	83	+6
94–95	StL–SJ	36	8	12	20	13	+4
95–96	SJ–Pitt	81	26	24	50	45	-4
96–97	Chi	69	14	17	31	41	-10
97–98	Chi	37	4	7	11	8	-4
98–99	NYI	33	1	5	6	13	-5
Totals		607	147	181	328	427	-10

Playoffs

SSN	TEAM	GP	G	A	PTS.	PIM
89–90	NYR	1	0	0	0	0
90–91	Det	7	3	2	5	20
91–92	Det	9	0	2	2	4
92–93	StL	10	0	3	3	11
93–94	StL	3	1	0	1	4
94–95	SJ	6	0	0	0	2
95–96	Pitt	18	3	2	5	8
96–97	Chi	6	0	1	1	0
Totals		60	7	10	17	49

MILLER, Kip Charles 5–10 190 C
B. Lansing, Mich., June 11, 1969

SSN	TEAM	GP	G	A	PTS.	PIM	+/-
90–91	Que	13	4	3	7	7	-1
91–92	Que–Minn	39	6	12	18	14	-22
93–94	SJ	11	2	2	4	6	-1
94–95	NYI	8	0	1	1	0	+1

SSN	TEAM	GP	G	A	PTS.	PIM	+/-
95–96	Chi	10	1	4	5	2	+1
97–98	NYI	9	1	3	4	2	-2
98–99	Pitt	77	19	23	42	22	+1
Totals		167	33	48	81	53	-23

Playoffs

| 98–99 | Pitt | 13 | 2 | 7 | 9 | 19 | |

MILLER, Paul Edward 5-10 170 C
B. Billerica, Mass., Aug. 21, 1959

81–82	Col	3	0	3	3	0	+2

MILLER, Perry Elvin 6-1 194 D
B. Winnipeg, Man., June 24, 1952

74–75	Winn (WHA)	67	9	19	28	133	
75–76	Winn–Minn (WHA)	60	8	10	18	48	
76–77	Winn (WHA)	74	14	31	45	124	
77–78	Det	62	4	17	21	120	-5
78–79	Det	75	5	23	28	156	-13
79–80	Det	16	0	3	3	41	-4
80–81	Det	64	1	8	9	70	-18
NHL Totals		217	10	51	61	387	-40
WHA Totals		201	31	60	91	305	

Playoffs

| 76–77 | Winn (WHA) | 20 | 4 | 6 | 10 | 27 | |

MILLER, Robert 5-11 180 C
B. Medford, Mass., Sept. 28, 1956

77–78	Bos	76	20	20	40	41	+16
78–79	Bos	77	15	33	48	30	+20
79–80	Bos	80	16	25	41	53	+9
80–81	Bos-Col	52	9	5	14	34	-24
81–82	Col	56	11	20	31	27	-24
84–85	LA	63	4	16	20	35	-17
Totals		404	75	119	294	220	-20

Playoffs

77–78	Bos	13	0	3	3	15	
78–79	Bos	11	1	1	2	8	
79–80	Bos	10	3	2	5	4	
84–85	LA	2	0	1	1	0	
Totals		36	4	7	11	27	

MILLER, Thomas William 6-0 187 C
B. Kitchener, Ont., Mar. 31, 1947

70–71	Det	29	1	7	8	9	-18
72–73	NYI	69	13	17	30	21	-29
73–74	NYI	19	2	1	3	4	3
74–75	NYI	1	0	0	0	0	0
Totals		118	16	25	41	34	-50

MILLER, Warren 6-0 180 RW
B. South St. Paul, Minn., Jan. 1, 1954

75–76	Calg (WHA)	3	0	0	0	0	
76–77	Calg (WHA)	80	23	32	55	51	
77–78	Edm-Que (WHA)	78	16	28	44	68	
78–79	NE (WHA)	77	26	23	49	44	
79–80	NYR	55	7	6	13	17	-6
80–81	Hart	77	22	22	44	37	-31
81–82	Hart	74	10	12	22	68	-14
82–83	Hart	56	1	10	11	15	-13
NHL Totals		262	40	50	90	137	-64
WHA Totals		238	65	83	148	163	

Playoffs

75–76	Calg (WHA)	10	1	0	1	28	
77–78	Que (WHA)	11	0	2	2	0	
78–79	NE (WHA)	10	0	8	8	28	
79–80	NYR	6	1	0	1	0	
NHL Totals		6	1	0	1	0	
WHA Totals		31	1	10	11	56	

MILLER, William 6-0 160 C
B. Campbellton, N.B., Aug. 1, 1911

34–35	Mont M	22	3	0	3	2	
35–36	Mont M–Mont	25	1	2	3	2	
36–37	Mont	48	3	1	4	12	
Totals		95	7	3	10	16	

Playoffs

| 34–35 | Mont M | 7 | 0 | 0 | 0 | 0 | |
| 36–37 | Mont | 5 | 0 | 0 | 0 | 0 | |

Totals		12	0	0	0	0	

MILLS, Craig 5-11 174 RW
B. Toronto, Ont., Aug. 27, 1976

95–96	Winn	4	0	2	2	0	0
97–98	Chi	20	0	3	3	34	+1
98–99	Chi	7	0	0	0	2	-2
Totals		31	0	5	5	36	-3

Playoffs

| 95–96 | Winn | 1 | 0 | 0 | 0 | 0 | |

MINER, John 5-10 180 D
B. Moose Jaw, Sask., Aug. 28, 1965

87–88	Edm	14	2	3	5	16	-4

MINOR, Gerald 5-8 175 C
B. Regina, Sask. Oct. 27, 1958

79–80	Van	5	0	1	1	2	0
80–81	Van	74	10	14	24	108	+4
81–82	Van	13	0	1	1	6	-6
82–83	Van	39	1	5	6	57	-6
83–84	Van	9	0	0	0	0	0
Totals		140	11	21	32	173	-8

Playoffs

80–81	Van	3	0	0	0	8	
81–82	Van	9	1	3	4	17	
Totals		12	1	3	4	25	

MIRONOV, Boris 6-3 220 D
B. Moscow, USSR, Mar. 21, 1972

93–94	Winn–Edm	79	7	24	31	110	-33
94–95	Edm	29	1	7	8	40	-9
95–96	Edm	78	8	24	32	101	-23
96–97	Edm	55	6	26	32	85	+2
97–98	Edm	81	16	30	46	100	+8
98–99	Edm-Chi	75	11	38	49	131	+13
Totals		397	49	149	198	567	-58

Playoffs

96–97	Edm	12	2	8	10	16	
97–98	Edm	12	3	3	6	27	
Totals		24	5	11	16	43	

MIRONOV, Dmitri 6-2 214 D
B. Moscow, USSR, Dec. 25, 1965

91–92	Tor	7	1	0	1	0	-4
92–93	Tor	59	7	24	31	40	-1
93–94	Tor	76	9	27	36	78	+5
94–95	Tor	33	5	12	17	28	+6
95–96	Pitt	72	3	31	34	88	+19
96–97	Pitt–Ana	77	13	39	52	101	+16
97–98	Ana–Det	77	8	35	43	119	-7
98–99	Wash	46	2	14	16	80	-5
Totals		447	48	182	230	534	+29

Playoffs

92–93	Tor	14	1	2	3	2	
93–94	Tor	18	6	9	15	6	
94–95	Tor	6	2	1	3	2	
95–96	Pitt	15	0	1	1	10	
96–97	Ana	11	1	10	11	10	
97–98	Det	7	0	3	3	14	

MISZUK, John Stanley 6-0 200 D
B. Naliboki, Poland, Sept. 29, 1940

63–64	Det	42	0	2	2	30	
65–66	Chi	2	1	1	2	2	
66–67	Chi	3	0	0	0	0	
67–68	Phil	74	5	17	22	79	+1
68–69	Phil	66	1	13	14	70	-6
69–70	Minn	50	0	6	6	51	-3
74–75	Balt (WHA)	66	2	19	21	56	
75–76	Calg (WHA)	69	2	21	23	66	
76–77	Calg (WHA)	79	2	26	28	57	
NHL Totals		237	7	39	46	232	-8
WHA Totals		214	6	66	72	179	

Playoffs

63–64	Det	3	0	0	0	2	
65–66	Chi	3	0	0	0	4	
66–67	Chi	2	0	0	0	2	
67–68	Phil	7	0	3	3	11	
68–69	Phil	4	0	0	0	0	
75–76	Calg (WHA)	10	0	1	1	10	

NHL Totals		19	0	3	3	19	
WHA Totals		10	0	1	1	10	

*MITCHELL, Herbert F

24–25	Bos	27	3	0	3	24	
25–26	Bos	26	3	0	3	14	
Totals		53	6	0	6	38	

MITCHELL, Jeff 6-1 175 RW
B. Wayne, Mich., May 16, 1975

97–98	Dal	7	0	0	0	7	0

MITCHELL, Roy 6-1 199 D
B. Edmonton, Alta., Mar. 14, 1969

92–93	Minn	3	0	0	0	0	0

MITCHELL, William Dickie (Red) 5-10 185 D
B. Port Dalhousie, Ont., Feb. 22, 1930

41–42	Chi	1	0	0	0	4	
42–43	Chi	42	1	1	2	47	
44–45	Chi	40	3	4	7	16	
Totals		83	4	5	9	67	

MITCHELL, William Lawson 5-10 185 D
B. Toronto, Ont., Sept. 6, 1912

63–64	Det	1	0	0	0	0	

MODANO, Michael 6-3 190 C
B. Livonia, Mich., June 7, 1970

89–90	Minn	80	29	46	75	63	-7
90–91	Minn	79	28	36	64	65	+2
91–92	Minn	76	33	44	77	46	-9
92–93	Minn	82	33	60	93	83	-7
93–94	Dal	76	50	43	93	54	-8
94–95	Dal	30	12	17	29	8	+7
95–96	Dal	78	36	45	81	63	-12
96–97	Dal	80	35	48	83	42	+43
97–98	Dal	52	21	38	59	32	+25
98–99	Dal	77	34	47	81	44	+29
Totals		710	311	424	735	520	+63

Playoffs

88–89	Minn	2	0	0	0	0	
89–90	Minn	7	1	1	2	12	
90–91	Minn	23	8	12	20	16	
91–92	Minn	7	3	2	5	4	
93–94	Dal	9	7	3	10	16	
96–97	Dal	7	4	1	5	0	
97–98	Dal	17	4	10	14	12	
98–99	Dal	23	5	18	23	16	
Totals		95	32	47	79	76	

MODIN, Fredrik 6-3 202 LW
B. Sundsvall, Sweden, Oct. 8, 1974

96–97	Tor	76	6	7	13	24	-14
97–98	Tor	74	16	16	32	32	-5
98–99	Tor	67	16	15	31	35	+14
Totals		217	38	38	76	91	-5

Playoffs

| 98–99 | Tor | 8 | 0 | 0 | 0 | 6 | |

MODRY, Jaroslav 6-2 195 D
B. Ceske–Budejovice, Czechoslovakia, Feb. 27, 1971

93–94	NJ	41	2	15	17	18	+10
94–95	NJ	11	0	0	0	0	-1
95–96	Ott-LA	73	4	17	21	44	-21
96–97	LA	30	3	3	6	25	-13
98–99	LA	5	0	1	1	0	+1
Totals		160	9	36	45	87	-24

MOE, William Carl 5-11 185 D
B. Danvers, Mass., Oct. 2, 1916

44–45	NYR	35	2	4	6	14	
45–46	NYR	48	4	4	8	14	
46–47	NYR	59	4	10	14	44	
47–48	NYR	59	1	15	16	31	
48–49	NYR	60	0	9	9	60	
Totals		261	11	42	53	163	

Playoffs

| 47–48 | NYR | 1 | 0 | 0 | 0 | 0 | |

MOFFAT, Lyle Gordon *5–10 180 LW*
B. Calgary, Alta., Mar, 19, 1948

SSN	TEAM	GP	G	A	PTS.	PIM	+/-
72–73	Tor	1	0	0	0	0	-1
74–75	Tor	22	2	7	9	13	-2
75–76	Clev–Winn (WHA)	75	17	16	33	77	
76–77	Winn (WHA)	74	13	11	24	90	
77–78	Winn (WHA)	57	9	16	25	39	
78–79	Winn (WHA)	70	14	18	32	38	
79–80	Winn	74	10	9	19	38	-24
NHL Totals		97	12	16	28	51	-27
WHA Totals		276	53	61	114	244	

Playoffs

SSN	TEAM	GP	G	A	PTS.	PIM	+/-
75–76	Winn (WHA)	13	3	3	6	9	
76–77	Winn (WHA)	17	2	0	2	6	
77–78	Winn (WHA)	9	5	7	12	9	
78–79	Winn (WHA)	10	3	1	4	22	
Totals		49	13	11	24	46	

*MOFFATT, Ronald *F*
B. West Hope, N.D.

SSN	TEAM	GP	G	A	PTS.	PIM	+/-
32–33	Det	24	1	1	2	6	
33–34	Det	5	0	0	0	2	
34–35	Det	7	0	0	0	0	
Totals		36	1	1	2	8	

Playoffs

SSN	TEAM	GP	G	A	PTS.	PIM	+/-
32–33	Det	4	0	0	0	0	
33–34	Det	3	0	0	0	0	
Totals		7	0	0	0	0	

MOGER, Alexander Sandy *6–3 215 C*
B. 100 Mile House, B.C., Mar. 21, 1969

SSN	TEAM	GP	G	A	PTS.	PIM	+/-
94–95	Bos	18	2	6	8	6	-1
95–96	Bos	80	15	14	29	65	-9
96–97	Bos	34	10	3	13	45	-12
97–98	LA	62	11	13	24	70	+4
98–99	LA	42	3	2	5	26	-9
Totals		236	41	38	79	214	-27

Playoffs

SSN	TEAM	GP	G	A	PTS.	PIM	+/-
95–96	Bos	5	2	2	4	12	

MOGILNY, Alexander *5–11 187 RW*
B. Khabarovsk, Soviet Union, Feb. 18, 1969

SSN	TEAM	GP	G	A	PTS.	PIM	+/-
89–90	Buf	65	15	28	43	16	+8
90–91	Buf	62	30	34	64	16	+14
91–92	Buf	67	39	45	84	73	+7
92–93	Buf	77	76	51	127	40	+7
93–94	Buf	66	32	47	79	22	+8
94–95	Buf	44	19	28	47	36	0
95–96	Van	79	55	52	107	16	+14
96–97	Van	76	31	42	73	18	+9
97–98	Van	51	18	27	45	36	-6
98–99	Van	59	14	31	45	58	0
Totals		646	329	385	714	331	+61

Playoffs

SSN	TEAM	GP	G	A	PTS.	PIM	+/-
89–90	Buf	4	0	1	1	2	
90–91	Buf	6	0	6	6	2	
91–92	Buf	2	0	2	2	0	
92–93	Buf	7	7	3	10	6	
93–94	Buf	7	4	2	6	6	
94–95	Buf	5	3	2	5	2	
95–96	Van	6	1	8	9	6	
Totals		36	15	24	39	26	

MOHER, Mike *5–10 180 RW*
B. Manitouwadge, Ont., Mar. 26, 1962

SSN	TEAM	GP	G	A	PTS.	PIM	+/-
82–83	NJ	9	0	1	1	28	-3

MOHNS, Douglas Allen *6–0 184 D*
B. Capreol, Ont., Dec. 13, 1933

SSN	TEAM	GP	G	A	PTS.	PIM	+/-
53–54	Bos	70	13	14	27	27	
54–55	Bos	70	14	18	32	82	
55–56	Bos	64	10	8	18	48	
56–57	Bos	68	6	34	40	89	
57–58	Bos	54	5	16	21	28	
58–59	Bos	47	6	24	30	40	
59–60	Bos	65	12	21	33	62	
60–61	Bos	65	12	21	33	63	
61–62	Bos	69	16	29	45	74	
62–63	Bos	68	7	23	30	63	
63–64	Bos	70	9	17	26	95	
64–65	Chi	49	13	20	33	84	
65–66	Chi	70	22	27	49	63	
66–67	Chi	61	25	35	60	58	
67–68	Chi	65	24	29	53	33	+7
68–69	Chi	65	22	19	41	47	+8
69–70	Chi	66	6	27	33	46	+29
70–71	Chi–Minn	56	6	11	17	30	+8
71–72	Minn	78	6	30	36	82	+6
72–73	Minn	67	4	13	17	52	+11
73–74	Atl	28	0	3	3	10	-7
74–75	Wash	75	2	19	21	54	-52
Totals		1390	248	462	710	1230	+10

Playoffs

SSN	TEAM	GP	G	A	PTS.	PIM	+/-
53–54	Bos	4	1	0	1	4	
54–55	Bos	5	0	0	0	4	
56–57	Bos	10	2	3	5	2	
57–58	Bso	12	3	10	13	18	
58–59	Bso	4	0	2	2	12	
64–65	Chi	14	3	4	7	21	
65–66	Chi	5	1	0	1	4	
66–67	Chi	5	0	5	5	8	
67–68	Chi	11	1	5	6	12	
69–70	Chi	8	0	2	2	15	
70–71	Minn	6	2	2	4	10	
71–72	Minn	4	1	2	3	10	
72–73	Minn	6	0	1	1	2	
Totals		94	14	36	50	122	

MOHNS, Warren Lloyd *5–9 185 D*
B. Petawawa, Ont., July 31, 1921

SSN	TEAM	GP	G	A	PTS.	PIM	+/-
43–44	NYR	1	0	0	0	0	

MOKOSAK, Carl *6–1 200 LW*
B. Fort Saskatchewan, Alta., Sept. 22, 1962

SSN	TEAM	GP	G	A	PTS.	PIM	+/-
81–82	Calg	1	0	1	1	0	+1
82–83	Calg	41	7	6	13	87	-5
84–85	LA	30	4	8	12	43	-8
85–86	Phil	1	0	0	0	5	0
86–87	Pitt	3	0	0	0	4	-4
88–89	Bos	7	0	0	0	31	-2
Totals		83	11	15	26	170	-18

Playoffs

SSN	TEAM	GP	G	A	PTS.	PIM	+/-
88–89	Bos	1	0	0	0	0	

MOKOSAK, John *5–11 200 D*
B. Edmonton, Alta., Sept. 7, 1963

SSN	TEAM	GP	G	A	PTS.	PIM	+/-
88–89	Det	8	0	1	1	14	0
89–90	Det	33	0	1	1	82	-9
Totals		41	0	2	2	96	-9

MOLIN, Lars *6–0 180 LW*
B. Ornskoldsvik, Sweden, May 7, 1956

SSN	TEAM	GP	G	A	PTS.	PIM	+/-
81–82	Van	72	15	31	46	10	0
82–83	Van	58	12	27	39	23	-20
83–84	Van	42	6	7	13	4	-9
Totals		172	33	65	98	37	-29

Playoffs

SSN	TEAM	GP	G	A	PTS.	PIM	+/-
81–82	Van	17	2	9	11	7	
83–84	Van	2	0	0	0	0	
Totals		19	2	9	11	7	

MOLLER, Michael John *6–0 190 RW*
B. Calgary, Alta., June 16, 1962

SSN	TEAM	GP	G	A	PTS.	PIM	+/-
80–81	Buf	5	2	2	4	0	+3
81–82	Buf	9	0	0	0	0	-7
82–83	Buf	49	6	12	18	14	+2
83–84	Buf	59	5	11	16	27	+2
84–85	Buf	5	0	2	2	0	0
85–86	Edm	1	0	0	0	0	0
86–87	Edm	6	2	1	3	0	+2
Totals		134	15	28	43	41	+2

Playoffs

SSN	TEAM	GP	G	A	PTS.	PIM	+/-
80–81	Buf	3	0	1	1	0	

MOLLER, Randy *6–2 207 D*
B. Red Deer, Alta., Aug. 23, 1963

SSN	TEAM	GP	G	A	PTS.	PIM	+/-
82–83	Que	75	2	12	14	145	+11
83–84	Que	74	4	14	18	147	+26
84–85	Que	79	7	22	29	120	+29
85–86	Que	69	5	18	23	141	+9
86–87	Que	71	5	9	14	144	-11
87–88	Que	66	3	22	25	169	-11
88–89	Que	74	7	22	29	136	+2
89–90	NYR	60	1	12	13	139	-1
90–91	NYR	61	4	19	23	161	+13
91–92	NYR–Buf	56	3	9	12	137	-14
92–93	Buf	35	2	7	9	83	+6
93–94	Buf	78	2	11	13	154	-5
94–95	Fla	17	0	3	3	16	-5
Totals		815	45	180	225	1692	+49

Playoffs

SSN	TEAM	GP	G	A	PTS.	PIM	+/-
81–82	Que	1	0	0	0	2	
82–83	Que	4	1	0	1	4	
83–84	Que	9	1	0	1	45	
84–85	Que	18	2	2	4	40	
85–86	Que	3	0	0	0	26	
86–87	Que	13	1	4	5	23	
89–90	NYR	10	1	6	7	32	
90–91	NYR	6	0	2	2	11	
91–92	Buf	7	0	0	0	8	
93–94	Buf	7	0	2	2	8	
Totals		78	6	16	22	197	

MOLLOY, Mitchell Dennis *6–3 212 LW*
B. Red Lake, Ont., Oct. 10, 1966

SSN	TEAM	GP	G	A	PTS.	PIM	+/-
89–90	Buf	2	0	0	0	10	0

MOLYNEAUX, Laurence S. *5–11 208 D*
B. West Sutton, Ont., July 8, 1912

SSN	TEAM	GP	G	A	PTS.	PIM	+/-
37–38	NYR	2	0	0	0	2	
38–39	NYR	43	0	1	1	18	
Totals		45	0	1	1	20	

Playoffs

SSN	TEAM	GP	G	A	PTS.	PIM	+/-
37–38	NYR	3	0	0	0	8	

MOMESSO, Sergio *6–3 215 LW*
B. Montreal, Que., Sept. 4, 1965

SSN	TEAM	GP	G	A	PTS.	PIM	+/-
83–84	Mont	1	0	0	0	0	+1
85–86	Mont	24	8	7	15	46	-4
86–87	Mont	59	14	17	31	96	+1
87–88	Mont	53	7	14	21	101	+9
88–89	StL	53	9	17	26	139	-1
89–90	StL	79	24	32	56	199	-15
90–91	StL–Van	70	16	20	36	174	+13
91–92	Van	58	20	23	43	198	+16
92–93	Van	84	18	20	38	200	+11
93–94	Van	68	14	13	27	149	-2
94–95	Van	48	10	15	25	65	-2
95–96	Tor–NYR	73	11	12	23	142	-13
96–97	NYR–StL	40	1	3	4	48	-6
Totals		710	152	193	345	1557	+8

Playoffs

SSN	TEAM	GP	G	A	PTS.	PIM	+/-
86–87	Mont	11	1	3	4	31	
87–88	Mont	6	0	2	2	16	
88–89	StL	10	2	5	7	24	
89–90	StL	12	3	2	5	63	
90–91	StL	6	0	3	3	25	
91–92	Van	13	0	5	5	30	
92–93	Van	12	3	0	3	30	
93–94	Van	24	3	4	7	56	
94–95	Van	11	3	1	4	16	
95–96	NYR	11	3	1	4	14	
96–97	StL	3	0	0	0	6	
Totals		119	18	26	44	311	

MONAHAN, Garry Michael *6–0 185 LW*
B. Barrie, Ont., Oct. 20, 1946

SSN	TEAM	GP	G	A	PTS.	PIM	+/-
67–68	Mont	11	0	0	0	8	-2
68–69	Mont	3	0	0	0	0	0
69–70	Det–LA	72	3	7	10	37	-12
70–71	Tor	78	15	22	37	79	+11
71–72	Tor	78	14	17	31	47	+2
72–73	Tor	78	13	18	31	53	-3
73–74	Tor	78	9	16	25	70	+4
74–75	Tor–Van	79	14	20	34	51	-10
75–76	Van	66	16	17	33	39	+1
76–77	Van	76	18	26	44	48	-1
77–78	Van	67	10	19	29	28	+2
78–79	Tor	62	4	7	11	25	+4
Totals		748	116	169	285	485	-4

Playoffs

SSN	TEAM	GP	G	A	PTS.	PIM	+/-
70–71	Tor	6	2	0	2	2	
71–72	Tor	5	0	0	0	0	
73–74	Tor	4	0	1	1	7	
74–75	Van	5	1	0	1	2	
75–76	Van	2	0	0	0	2	

SSN	TEAM	GP	G	A	PTS.	PIM	+/-
Totals		22	3	1	4	13	

MONAHAN, Hartland Patrick 5-11 197 RW
B. Montreal, Que., Mar. 29, 1951

SSN	TEAM	GP	G	A	PTS.	PIM	+/-
73–74	Cal	1	0	0	0	0	0
74–75	NYR	6	0	1	1	4	-2
75–76	Wash	80	17	29	46	35	-49
76–77	Wash	79	23	27	50	37	-28
77–78	Pitt–LA	71	12	9	21	45	-20
79–80	StL	72	5	12	17	36	-32
80–81	StL	25	4	2	6	4	+2
Totals		334	61	80	141	161	-129

Playoffs

SSN	TEAM	GP	G	A	PTS.	PIM	+/-
77–78	LA	2	0	0	0	0	
79–80	StL	3	0	0	0	0	
80–81	StL	1	0	0	0	4	
Totals		6	0	0	0	4	

*MONDOU, Armand 5-10 175 LW
B. Yanaska, Que., June 27, 1905

SSN	TEAM	GP	G	A	PTS.	PIM	+/-
28–29	Mont	32	3	4	7	6	
29–30	Mont	44	3	5	8	24	
30–31	Mont	40	5	4	9	10	
31–32	Mont	47	6	12	18	22	
32–33	Mont	24	1	3	4	15	
33–34	Mont	48	5	3	8	4	
34–35	Mont	45	9	15	24	6	
35–36	Mont	36	7	11	18	10	
36–37	Mont	7	1	1	2	0	
37–38	Mont	7	2	4	6	0	
38–39	Mont	34	3	7	10	2	
39–40	Mont	21	2	2	4	0	
Totals		385	47	71	118	99	

Playoffs

SSN	TEAM	GP	G	A	PTS.	PIM	+/-
28–29	Mont	3	0	0	0	2	
29–30	Mont	6	1	1	2	6	
30–31	Mont	8	0	0	0	0	
31–32	Mont	4	1	2	3	2	
33–34	Mont	4	0	1	1	0	
34–35	Mont	2	0	1	1	0	
36–37	Mont	5	0	0	0	0	
38–39	Mont	3	1	0	1	2	
Totals		35	3	5	8	12	

MONDOU, Pierre 5-10 185 C
B. Sorel, Que., Nov. 27, 1955

SSN	TEAM	GP	G	A	PTS.	PIM	+/-
77–78	Mont	71	19	30	49	8	+32
78–79	Mont	77	31	41	72	26	+59
79–80	Mont	75	30	36	66	12	+26
80–81	Mont	57	17	24	41	16	+24
81–82	Mont	73	35	33	68	57	+18
82–83	Mont	76	29	37	66	31	+32
83–84	Mont	52	15	22	37	8	+9
84–85	Mont	67	18	39	57	21	+15
Totals		548	194	262	456	179	+215

Playoffs

SSN	TEAM	GP	G	A	PTS.	PIM	+/-
76–77	Mont	3	0	0	0	0	
77–78	Mont	15	3	7	10	4	
78–79	Mont	16	3	6	9	4	
79–80	Mont	4	1	4	5	4	
80–81	Mont	3	0	1	1	0	
81–82	Mont	5	2	5	7	8	
82–83	Mont	3	0	1	1	2	
83–84	Mont	14	6	3	9	2	
84–85	Mont	5	2	1	3	2	
Totals		69	17	28	45	26	

MONGEAU, Michel 5-9 190 C
B. Nun's Island, Que., Feb. 9, 1965

SSN	TEAM	GP	G	A	PTS.	PIM	+/-
89–90	StL	7	1	5	6	2	+4
90–91	StL	7	1	1	2	0	+1
91–92	StL	36	3	12	15	6	-2
92–93	TB	4	1	1	2	2	-2
Totals		54	6	19	25	10	+1

Playoffs

SSN	TEAM	GP	G	A	PTS.	PIM	+/-
89–90	StL	2	0	1	1	0	

MONGRAIN, Robert 5-10 165 C
B. La Sarre, Que., Aug. 31, 1959

SSN	TEAM	GP	G	A	PTS.	PIM	+/-
79–80	Buf	34	4	6	10	4	+6
80–81	Buf	4	0	0	0	2	-2
81–82	Buf	24	6	4	10	6	-3
84–85	Buf	8	1	1	2	0	+1
85–86	LA	11	2	3	5	2	3
Totals		83	13	14	27	14	-1

Playoffs

SSN	TEAM	GP	G	A	PTS.	PIM	+/-
79–80	Buf	9	1	2	3	2	
81–82	Buf	1	0	0	0	0	
83–84	Buf	1	0	0	0	0	
Totals		11	1	2	3	2	

MONTEITH, Henry George (Hank) 5-10 180 LW
B. Stratford, Ont., Oct. 2, 1945

SSN	TEAM	GP	G	A	PTS.	PIM	+/-
68–69	Det	34	1	9	10	6	+4
69–70	Det	9	0	0	0	4	-1
70–71	Det	34	4	3	7	0	-5
Totals		77	5	12	17	10	-2

Playoffs

SSN	TEAM	GP	G	A	PTS.	PIM	+/-
69–70	Det	4	0	0	0	0	

MONTGOMERY, Jim 5-10 185 C
B. Montreal, Que., June 30, 1969

SSN	TEAM	GP	G	A	PTS.	PIM	+/-
93–94	StL	67	6	14	20	44	-1
94–95	Mont–Phil	13	1	1	2	8	-4
95–96	Phil	5	1	2	3	9	+1
Totals		85	8	17	25	61	-4

Playoffs

SSN	TEAM	GP	G	A	PTS.	PIM	+/-
94–95	Phil	7	1	0	1	2	
95–96	Phil	1	0	0	0	0	
Totals		8	1	0	1	2	

MOORE, Barrie 5-11 175 LW
B. London, Ont., May 22, 1975

SSN	TEAM	GP	G	A	PTS.	PIM	+/-
95–96	Buf	3	0	0	0	0	0
96–97	Buf–Edm	35	2	6	8	18	+1
Totals		38	2	6	8	18	+1

MOORE, Richard Winston (Dickie) 5-10 185 RW
B. Montreal, Que., Jan. 6, 1931

SSN	TEAM	GP	G	A	PTS.	PIM	+/-
51–52	Mont	33	18	15	33	44	
52–53	Mont	18	2	6	8	19	
53–54	Mont	13	1	4	5	12	
54–55	Mont	67	16	20	36	32	
55–56	Mont	70	11	39	50	55	
56–57	Mont	70	29	29	58	56	
57–58	Mont	70	36	48	84	65	
58–59	Mont	70	41	55	96	61	
59–60	Mont	62	22	42	64	54	
60–61	Mont	57	35	34	69	62	
61–62	Mont	57	19	22	41	54	
62–63	Mont	67	24	26	50	61	
64–65	Tor	38	2	4	6	68	
67–68	StL	27	5	3	8	9	-8
Totals		719	261	347	608	652	-8

Playoffs

SSN	TEAM	GP	G	A	PTS.	PIM	+/-
51–52	Mont	11	1	1	2	12	
52–53	Mont	12	3	2	5	13	
53–54	Mont	11	5	8	13	8	
54–55	Mont	12	1	5	6	22	
55–56	Mont	10	3	6	9	12	
56–57	Mont	10	3	7	10	4	
57–58	Mont	10	4	7	11	4	
58–59	Mont	11	5	12	17	8	
59–60	Mont	8	6	4	10	4	
60–61	Mont	6	3	1	4	4	
61–62	Mont	6	4	2	6	8	
62–63	Mont	5	0	1	1	2	
64–65	Tor	5	1	1	2	6	
67–68	StL	18	7	7	14	15	
Totals		135	46	64	110	122	

*MORAN, Ambrose Jason (Amby) D

SSN	TEAM	GP	G	A	PTS.	PIM	+/-
26–27	Mont	12	0	0	0	10	
27–28	Chi	23	1	1	2	14	
Totals		35	1	1	2	24	

MORAN, Ian 5-11 180 D
B. Cleveland, Ohio, Aug. 24, 1972

SSN	TEAM	GP	G	A	PTS.	PIM	+/-
95–96	Pitt	51	1	1	2	47	-1
96–97	Pitt	36	4	5	9	22	-11
97–98	Pitt	37	1	6	7	19	0
98–99	Pitt	62	4	5	9	37	+1
Totals		186	10	17	27	125	-11

Playoffs

SSN	TEAM	GP	G	A	PTS.	PIM	+/-
94–95	Pitt	8	0	0	0	0	
96–97	Pitt	5	1	2	3	4	
97–98	Pitt	6	0	0	0	2	
98–99	Pitt	13	0	2	2	8	
Totals		32	1	4	5	14	

MORE, Jayson 6-1 200 D
B. Souris, Man., Jan. 12, 1969

SSN	TEAM	GP	G	A	PTS.	PIM	+/-
88–89	NYR	1	0	0	0	0	-1
89–90	Minn	5	0	0	0	16	+1
91–92	SJ	46	4	13	17	85	-32
92–93	SJ	73	5	6	11	179	-35
93–94	SJ	49	1	6	7	63	-5
94–95	SJ	45	0	6	6	71	+7
95–96	SJ	74	2	7	9	147	-32
96–97	NYR–Phoe	37	1	7	8	62	+10
97–98	Phoe–Chi	58	5	7	12	61	+7
98–99	Nash	18	0	2	2	18	+2
Totals		388	18	52	70	724	+78

Playoffs

SSN	TEAM	GP	G	A	PTS.	PIM	+/-
93–94	SJ	13	0	2	2	32	
94–95	SJ	11	0	4	4	6	
96–97	Phoe	7	0	0	0	7	
Totals		31	0	6	6	45	

MOREAU, Ethan 6-2 205 LW
B. Huntsville, Ont., Sept. 22, 1975

SSN	TEAM	GP	G	A	PTS.	PIM	+/-
95–96	Chi	8	0	1	1	4	+1
96–97	Chi	82	15	16	31	123	+13
97–98	Chi	54	9	9	18	73	0
98–99	Chi–Edm	80	10	11	21	92	-3
Totals		224	34	37	71	292	+11

Playoffs

SSN	TEAM	GP	G	A	PTS.	PIM	+/-
96–97	Chi	6	1	0	1	9	
98–99	Edm	4	0	3	3	6	
Totals		10	1	3	4	15	

*MORENZ, Howarth William (Howie) 5-9 165 C
B. Mitchell, Ont., June 21, 1902

SSN	TEAM	GP	G	A	PTS.	PIM	+/-
23–24	Mont	24	13	3	16	20	
24–25	Mont	30	27	7	34	31	
25–26	Mont	31	23	3	26	39	
26–27	Mont	44	25	7	32	49	
27–28	Mont	43	33	18	51	66	
28–29	Mont	42	17	10	27	47	
29–30	Mont	44	40	10	50	72	
30–31	Mont	39	28	23	51	49	
31–32	Mont	48	24	25	49	46	
32–33	Mont	46	14	21	35	32	
33–34	Mont	39	8	13	21	21	
34–35	Chi	48	8	26	34	21	
35–36	Chi–NYR	42	6	15	21	26	
36–37	Mont	30	4	16	20	12	
Totals		550	270	197	467	531	

Playoffs

SSN	TEAM	GP	G	A	PTS.	PIM	+/-
23–24	Mont	6	7	2	9	10	
24–25	Mont	6	7	1	8	10	
26–27	Mont	4	1	0	1	4	
27–28	Mont	2	0	0	0	12	
28–29	Mont	3	0	0	0	6	
29–30	Mont	6	3	0	3	10	
30–31	Mont	10	1	4	5	10	
31–32	Mont	4	1	0	1	4	
32–33	Mont	2	0	3	3	2	
33–34	Mont	2	1	1	2	0	
34–35	Chi	2	0	0	0	0	
Totals		47	21	11	32	68	

MORETTO, Angelo Joseph 6-3 212 C
B. Toronto, Ont., Sept. 18, 1953

SSN	TEAM	GP	G	A	PTS.	PIM	+/-
76–77	Clev	5	1	2	3	2	0
78–79	Ind (WHA)	18	3	1	4	2	

MORGAN, Jason 6-1 185 C
B. St. John's, Nfld., Oct. 9, 1976

SSN	TEAM	GP	G	A	PTS.	PIM	+/-
96–97	LA	3	0	0	0	0	-3
97–98	LA	11	1	0	1	4	-7
Totals		14	1	0	1	4	-10

SSN	TEAM	GP	G	A	PTS.	PIM	+/-

*MORIN, Pierre (Pete) *F*
B. Lachine, Que., Dec. 8, 1915

41–42	Mont	31	10	12	22	7	

Playoffs

| 41–42 | Mont | 1 | 0 | 0 | 0 | 0 | |

MORIN, Stephane *6–0 174 C*
B. Montreal, Que., Mar. 27, 1969

89–90	Que	6	0	2	2	2	+1
90–91	Que	48	13	27	40	30	+6
91–92	Que	30	2	8	10	14	-2
92–93	Van	1	0	1	1	0	-1
93–94	Van	5	1	1	2	6	0
Totals		90	16	39	55	52	+4

MORISSETTE, Dave *6–1 220 LW*
B. Baie Comeau, Que., Dec. 24, 1971

| 98–99 | Mont | 10 | 0 | 0 | 0 | 52 | +1 |

MORO, Marc *6–1 220 D*
B. Toronto, Ont., July 17, 1977

| 97–98 | Ana | 1 | 0 | 0 | 0 | 0 | 0 |

MOROZOV, Alexei *6–1 180 RW*
B. Moscow, USSR, Feb. 16, 1977

97–98	Pitt	76	13	13	26	8	-4
98–99	Pitt	67	9	10	19	14	+5
Totals		143	22	23	45	22	+1

Playoffs

97–98	Pitt	6	0	1	1	2	
98–99	Pitt	10	1	1	2	0	
Totals		16	1	2	3	2	

*MORRIS, Bernard *D*

| 24–25 | Bos | 6 | 2 | 0 | 2 | 0 | |

MORRIS, Derek *5–11 180 D*
B. Edmonton, Alta., Aug. 24, 1978

97–98	Calg	82	9	20	29	88	+1
98–99	Calg	71	7	27	34	73	+4
Totals		153	16	47	63	161	+5

MORRIS, Elwin Gordon (Moe) *5–7 185 D*
B. Toronto, Ont., Jan. 3, 1921

43–44	Tor	50	12	21	33	22	
44–45	Tor	29	0	2	2	18	
45–46	Tor	38	1	5	6	10	
48–49	NYR	18	0	1	1	8	
Totals		135	13	29	42	58	

Playoffs

43–44	Tor	5	1	2	3	2	
44–45	Tor	13	3	0	3	14	
Totals		18	4	2	6	16	

MORRIS, Jon *6–0 175 C*
B. Lowell, Mass., May 6, 1966

88–89	NJ	4	0	2	2	0	0
89–90	NJ	20	6	7	13	8	+12
90–91	NJ	53	9	19	28	27	+9
91–92	NJ	7	1	2	3	6	-6
92–93	NJ–SJ	15	0	3	3	6	-11
93–94	Bos	4	0	0	0	0	-2
Totals		103	16	33	49	47	+2

Playoffs

89–90	NJ	6	1	3	4	23	
90–91	NJ	5	0	4	4	2	
Totals		11	1	7	8	25	

MORRISON, Brendan *5–11 175 C*
B. N. Vancouver, B.C., Aug. 12, 1975

97–98	NJ	11	5	4	9	0	+3
98–99	NJ	76	13	33	46	18	-4
Totals		87	18	37	55	18	-1

Playoffs

97–98	NJ	3	0	1	1	0	
98–99	NJ	7	0	2	2	0	
Totals		10	0	3	3	0	

MORRISON, David Stuart *6–0 190 RW*
B. Toronto, Ont., June 12, 1962

80–81	LA	3	0	0	0	0	-1
81–82	LA	4	0	0	0	0	-1
82–83	LA	24	3	3	6	4	-7
84–85	Van	8	0	0	0	0	-6
Totals		39	3	3	6	4	-15

MORRISON, Donald MacRae *5–10 165 C*
B. Saskatoon, Sask., July 14, 1923

47–48	Det	40	10	15	25	6	
48–49	Det	13	0	1	1	0	
50–51	Chi	59	8	12	20	6	
Totals		112	18	28	46	12	

Playoffs

| 47–48 | Det | 3 | 0 | 1 | 1 | 0 | |

MORRISON, Douglas *5–11 185 RW*
B. Vancouver, B.C., Feb. 1, 1960

79–80	Bos	1	0	0	0	0	0
80–81	Bos	18	7	3	10	13	+5
81–82	Bos	6	0	0	0	0	-2
84–85	Bos	1	0	0	0	2	0
Totals		23	7	3	10	15	+3

MORRISON, Gary *6–2 200 RW*
B. Detroit, Mich., Nov. 8, 1955

79–80	Phil	3	0	2	2	0	0
80–81	Phil	33	1	13	14	68	+10
81–82	Phil	7	0	0	0	2	-6
Totals		43	1	15	16	70	+4

Playoffs

| 79–80 | Phil | 5 | 0 | 1 | 1 | 2 | |

MORRISON, George Harold *6–1 170 LW*
B. Toronto, Ont., Dec. 24, 1948

70–71	StL	73	15	10	25	6	-2
71–72	StL	42	2	11	13	7	-11
72–73	Minn (WHA)	70	16	24	40	20	
73–74	Minn (WHA)	73	40	38	78	37	
74–75	Minn (WHA)	76	31	29	60	30	
75–76	Calg (WHA)	79	25	32	57	13	
76–77	Calg (WHA)	63	11	19	30	10	
NHL Totals		115	17	21	38	13	-13
WHA Totals		361	123	142	265	110	

Playoffs

70–71	StL	3	0	0	0	0	
72–73	Minn (WHA)	5	1	1	2	2	
73–74	Minn (WHA)	11	5	5	10	12	
74–75	Minn (WHA)	12	5	9	14	0	
75–76	Calg (WHA)	10	3	2	5	0	
NHL Totals		3	0	0	0	0	
WHA Totals		38	14	17	31	14	

MORRISON, James Stuart Hunter *5–10 183 D*
B. Montreal, Que., Oct. 11, 1931

51–52	Bos–Tor	31	0	3	3	6	
52–53	Tor	56	1	8	9	36	
53–54	Tor	60	9	11	20	51	
54–55	Tor	70	5	12	17	84	
55–56	Tor	63	2	17	19	77	
56–57	Tor	63	3	17	20	44	
57–58	Tor	70	3	21	24	62	
58–59	Bos	70	8	17	25	42	
59–60	Det	70	3	23	26	62	
60–61	NYR	19	1	6	7	6	
69–70	Pitt	59	5	15	20	40	-20
70–71	Pitt	73	0	10	10	32	-12
Totals		704	40	160	200	542	-32

Playoffs

51–52	Tor	2	0	0	0	0	
53–54	Tor	5	0	0	0	4	
54–55	Tor	4	0	1	1	4	
55–56	Tor	5	0	0	0	4	
58–59	Bos	6	0	6	6	13	
59–60	Det	6	0	2	2	0	
69–70	Pitt	8	0	3	3	10	
Totals		36	0	12	12	35	

*MORRISON, John W. (Crutchy) *F*
B. Selkirk, Man.

| 25–26 | NYA | 18 | 0 | 0 | 0 | 0 | |

MORRISON, Kevin Gregory Joseph *5–11 202 D*
B. Sydney, N.S., Oct. 28, 1949

73–74	NY–NJ (WHA)	78	24	43	67	132	
74–75	SD (WHA)	78	20	61	81	143	
75–76	SD (WHA)	80	22	43	65	56	
76–77	SD (WHA)	75	8	30	38	68	
77–78	Ind (WHA)	75	17	40	57	49	
78–79	Ind–Que (WHA)	32	2	7	9	14	
79–80	Col	41	4	11	15	23	-6
NHL Totals		41	4	11	15	23	-6
WHA Totals		418	93	224	317	462	

Playoffs

74–75	SD (WHA)	10	0	7	7	2	
75–76	SD (WHA)	11	1	5	6	12	
76–77	SD (WHA)	7	1	3	4	8	
WHA Totals		28	2	15	17	22	

MORRISON, Henry Lewis (Lew) *6–0 185 RW*
B. Gainsborough, Sask., Feb. 11, 1948

69–70	Phil	66	9	10	19	19	-3
70–71	Phil	78	5	7	12	25	-12
71–72	Phil	58	5	5	10	26	-18
72–73	Atl	78	6	9	15	19	-11
73–74	Atl	52	1	4	5	0	-1
74–75	Wash–Pitt	70	7	9	16	10	-19
75–76	Pitt	78	4	5	9	8	+7
76–77	Pitt	76	2	1	3	0	-6
77–78	Pitt	8	0	2	2	0	+3
Totals		564	39	52	91	107	-60

Playoffs

70–71	Phil	4	0	0	0	2	
74–75	Pitt	9	0	0	0	0	
75–76	Pitt	3	0	0	0	0	
76–77	Pitt	1	0	0	0	0	
Totals		17	0	0	0	2	

MORRISON, Mark *5–8 150 C*
B. Prince George, B.C., Mar. 11, 1963

81–82	NYR	9	1	1	2	0	-5
83–84	NYR	1	0	0	0	0	0
Totals		10	1	1	2	0	-5

MORRISON, Roderick Finlay *5–9 160 RW*
B. Saskatoon, Sask., Oct. 7, 1925

| 47–48 | Det | 34 | 8 | 7 | 15 | 4 | |

Playoffs

| 47–48 | Det | 3 | 0 | 0 | 0 | 0 | |

MORROW, Ken *6–4 210 D*
B. Flint, Mich., Oct. 17, 1956

79–80	NYI	18	0	3	3	4	+4
80–81	NYI	80	2	11	13	20	+19
81–82	NYI	75	1	18	19	56	+53
82–83	NYI	79	5	11	16	44	+18
83–84	NYI	63	3	11	14	45	+26
84–85	NYI	15	1	7	8	14	+5
85–86	NYI	69	0	12	12	22	+24
86–87	NYI	64	3	8	11	32	+7
87–88	NYI	53	1	4	5	40	0
88–89	NYI	34	1	3	4	32	-7
Totals		490	17	88	105	309	+149

Playoffs

79–80	NYI	20	1	2	3	12	
80–81	NYI	18	3	4	7	8	
81–82	NYI	19	0	4	4	8	
82–83	NYI	19	5	7	12	18	
83–84	NYI	20	1	2	3	20	
84–85	NYI	10	0	0	0	17	
85–86	NYI	2	0	0	0	4	
86–87	NYI	13	1	3	4	2	
87–88	NYI	6	0	0	0	8	
Totals		127	11	22	33	97	

MORROW, Scott *6–1 185 LW*
B. Chicago, IL, June 18, 1969

| 94–95 | Calg | 4 | 0 | 0 | 0 | 0 | 0 |

MORTON, Dean 6–1 196 D
B. Peterborough, Ont., Feb. 27, 1968

SSN	TEAM	GP	G	A	PTS.	PIM	+/-
89–90	Det	1	1	0	1	2	-1

MORTSON, James Angus Gerald (Gus) 5–11 190 D
B. New Liskeard, Ont., Jan. 24, 1925

SSN	TEAM	GP	G	A	PTS.	PIM
46–47	Tor	60	5	13	18	133
47–48	Tor	58	7	11	18	118
48–49	Tor	60	2	13	15	85
49–50	Tor	68	3	14	17	85
50–51	Tor	60	3	10	13	142
51–52	Tor	65	1	10	11	106
52–53	Chi	68	5	18	23	88
53–54	Chi	68	5	13	18	132
54–55	Chi	65	2	11	13	133
55–56	Chi	52	5	10	15	87
56–57	Chi	70	5	18	23	147
57–58	Chi	67	3	10	13	62
58–59	Chi	36	0	1	1	22
Totals		**797**	**46**	**152**	**198**	**1340**

Playoffs

46–47	Tor	11	1	3	4	22
47–48	Tor	5	1	2	3	2
48–49	Tor	9	2	1	3	5
49–50	Tor	7	0	0	0	18
50–51	Tor	11	0	1	1	4
51–52	Tor	4	0	0	0	8
52–53	Chi	7	1	1	2	6
Totals		**54**	**5**	**8**	**13**	**65**

MOSDELL, Kenneth 6–1 170 C
B. Montreal, Que., July 13, 1922

SSN	TEAM	GP	G	A	PTS.	PIM
41–42	Brk	41	7	9	16	16
44–45	Mont	31	12	6	18	16
45–46	Mont	13	2	1	3	8
46–47	Mont	54	5	10	15	50
47–48	Mont	23	1	0	1	19
48–49	Mont	60	17	9	26	59
49–50	Mont	67	15	12	27	42
50–51	Mont	66	13	18	31	24
51–52	Mont	44	5	11	16	19
52–53	Mont	63	5	14	19	27
53–54	Mont	67	22	24	46	64
54–55	Mont	70	22	32	54	82
55–56	Mont	67	13	17	30	48
56–57	Chi	25	2	4	6	10
57–58	Mont	2	0	1	1	0
Totals		**693**	**141**	**168**	**309**	**484**

Playoffs

45–46	Mont	9	4	1	5	6
46–47	Mont	4	2	0	2	4
48–49	Mont	7	1	1	2	4
49–50	Mont	5	0	0	0	12
50–51	Mont	11	1	1	2	4
51–52	Mont	2	1	0	1	0
52–53	Mont	7	3	2	5	4
53–54	Mont	11	1	0	1	4
54–55	Mont	12	2	7	9	8
55–56	Mont	9	1	1	2	2
58–59	Mont	2	0	0	0	0
Totals		**79**	**16**	**13**	**29**	**48**

*MOSIENKO, William (Mosi) 5–8 160 RW
B. Winnipeg, Man., Nov. 2, 1921

SSN	TEAM	GP	G	A	PTS.	PIM
41–42	Chi	12	6	8	14	4
42–43	Chi	2	2	0	2	0
43–44	Chi	50	32	38	70	10
44–45	Chi	50	28	26	54	0
45–46	Chi	40	18	30	48	12
46–47	Chi	59	25	27	52	2
47–48	Chi	40	16	9	25	0
48–49	Chi	60	17	25	42	6
49–50	Chi	69	18	28	46	10
50–51	Chi	65	21	15	36	18
51–52	Chi	70	31	22	53	10
52–53	Chi	65	17	20	37	8
53–54	Chi	65	15	19	34	17
54–55	Chi	64	12	15	27	24
Totals		**711**	**258**	**282**	**540**	**121**

Playoffs

41–42	Chi	3	2	0	2	0
43–44	Chi	8	2	2	4	6
45–46	Chi	4	2	0	2	2
52–53	Chi	7	4	2	6	4

MOTT, Morris Kenneth 5–10 165 RW
B. Creelman, Sask., May 25, 1946

SSN	TEAM	GP	G	A	PTS.	PIM	+/-
	Totals	**22**	**10**	**4**	**14**	**15**	
72–73	Cal	70	6	7	13	8	-17
73–74	Cal	77	9	17	26	33	-19
74–75	Cal	52	3	8	11	8	-10
76–77	Winn (WHA)	2	0	1	1	5	
NHL Totals		**199**	**18**	**32**	**50**	**49**	**-46**
WHA Totals		**2**	**0**	**1**	**1**	**5**	

*MOTTER, Alexander Everett 6–0 175 C
B. Melville, Sask., June 20, 1913

SSN	TEAM	GP	G	A	PTS.	PIM
34–35	Bos	5	0	0	0	0
35–36	Bos	23	1	4	5	4
37–38	Det	33	5	17	22	6
38–39	Det	42	5	11	16	17
39–40	Det	37	7	12	19	28
40–41	Det	47	13	12	25	18
41–42	Det	30	2	4	6	20
42–43	Det	50	6	4	10	42
Totals		**267**	**39**	**64**	**103**	**135**

Playoffs

34–35	Bos	4	0	0	0	0
35–36	Bos	2	0	0	0	0
38–39	Det	4	0	1	1	0
39–40	Det	5	1	1	2	15
40–41	Det	9	1	3	4	4
41–42	Det	11	1	3	4	20
42–43	Det	5	0	1	1	2
Totals		**40**	**3**	**9**	**12**	**41**

MOWERS, Mark 5–11 188 RW
B. Whitesboro, N.Y., Jan. 6, 1974

SSN	TEAM	GP	G	A	PTS.	PIM	+/-
98–99	Nash	30	0	6	6	4	-4

MOXEY, James George 6–1 190 RW
B. Toronto, Ont., May 28, 1953

SSN	TEAM	GP	G	A	PTS.	PIM	+/-
74–75	Cal	47	5	4	9	14	-4
75–76	Cal	44	10	16	26	33	-10
76–77	Clev–LA	36	7	7	14	22	-15
Totals		**127**	**22**	**27**	**49**	**69**	**-29**

MUIR, Bryan 6–4 220 D
B. Winnipeg, Man., June 8, 1973

SSN	TEAM	GP	G	A	PTS.	PIM	+/-
95–96	Edm	5	0	0	0	6	-4
97–98	Edm	7	0	0	0	17	0
98–99	NJ-Chi	54	1	4	5	50	+1
Totals		**66**	**1**	**4**	**5**	**73**	**-3**

Playoffs

96–97	Edm	5	0	0	0	4

MUCKALT, Bill 6–0 190 RW
B. Surrey, B.C., July 15, 1974

SSN	TEAM	GP	G	A	PTS.	PIM	+/-
98–99	Van	73	16	20	36	98	-9

MULHERN, Richard Sydney 6–1 188 D
B. Edmonton, Alta., Mar. 1, 1955

SSN	TEAM	GP	G	A	PTS.	PIM	+/-
75–76	Atl	12	1	0	1	4	-8
76–77	Atl	79	12	32	44	80	+6
77–78	Atl	79	9	23	32	47	+11
78–79	Atl–LA	73	5	21	26	45	+3
79–80	LA–Tor	41	0	13	13	27	0
80–81	Winn	19	0	4	4	14	-9
Totals		**303**	**27**	**93**	**120**	**217**	**+3**

Playoffs

76–77	Atl	3	0	2	2	5
77–78	Atl	2	0	1	1	0
78–79	LA	1	0	0	0	0
79–80	Tor	1	0	0	0	0
Totals		**7**	**0**	**3**	**3**	**5**

MULHERN, Ryan 6–1 180 C
B. Philadelphia, Pa., Jan. 11, 1973

SSN	TEAM	GP	G	A	PTS.	PIM	+/-
97–98	Wash	3	0	0	0	0	0

MULLEN, Brian 5–10 185 RW
B. New York, N.Y., Mar. 16, 1962

SSN	TEAM	GP	G	A	PTS.	PIM	+/-
82–83	Winn	80	24	26	50	14	+11
83–84	Winn	75	21	41	62	28	-12
84–85	Winn	69	32	39	71	32	+15
85–86	Winn	79	28	34	62	38	-17

MULLEN, Joseph Patrick 5–9 180 RW
B. New York, N.Y., Feb. 26, 1957

SSN	TEAM	GP	G	A	PTS.	PIM	+/-
86–87	Winn	69	19	32	51	20	-2
87–88	NYR	74	25	29	54	42	-2
88–89	NYR	78	29	35	64	60	+7
89–90	NYR	76	27	41	68	42	+7
90–91	NYR	79	19	43	62	44	+12
91–92	SJ	72	18	28	46	66	-14
92–93	NYI	81	18	14	32	28	+5
Totals		**832**	**260**	**362**	**622**	**414**	**+10**

Playoffs

82–83	Winn	3	1	0	1	0
83–84	Winn	3	0	3	3	6
84–85	Winn	8	1	2	3	4
85–86	Winn	3	1	2	3	6
86–87	Winn	9	4	2	6	0
88–89	NYR	3	0	1	1	4
89–90	NYR	10	2	2	4	8
90–91	NYR	6	0	2	2	0
92–93	NYI	18	3	4	7	2
Totals		**63**	**12**	**18**	**30**	**30**

81–82	StL	45	25	34	59	4	+6
82–83	StL	49	17	30	47	6	-8
83–84	StL	80	41	44	85	19	+5
84–85	StL	79	40	52	92	6	-7
85–86	StL–Calg	77	44	46	90	21	+2
86–87	Calg	79	47	40	87	14	+18
87–88	Calg	80	40	44	84	30	+28
88–89	Calg	79	51	59	110	16	+51
89–90	Calg	78	36	33	69	24	+6
90–91	Pitt	47	17	22	39	6	+9
91–92	Pitt	77	42	45	87	30	+12
92–93	Pitt	72	33	37	70	14	+19
93–94	Pitt	84	38	32	70	41	+9
94–95	Pitt	45	16	21	37	6	+15
95–96	Bos	37	8	7	15	0	-2
96–97	Pitt	54	7	15	22	4	0
Totals		**1062**	**502**	**561**	**1063**	**241**	**+163**

Playoffs

79–80	StL	1	0	0	0	0
81–82	StL	10	7	11	18	4
83–84	StL	6	2	0	2	0
84–85	StL	3	0	0	0	0
85–86	Calg	21	12	7	19	4
86–87	Calg	6	2	1	3	0
87–88	Calg	7	2	4	6	10
88–89	Calg	21	16	8	24	4
89–90	Calg	6	3	0	3	0
90–91	Pitt	22	8	9	17	4
91–92	Pitt	9	3	1	4	4
92–93	Pitt	12	4	2	6	6
93–94	Pitt	6	1	0	1	2
94–95	Pitt	12	0	3	3	4
96–97	Pitt	1	0	0	0	0
Totals		**143**	**60**	**46**	**106**	**42**

MULLER, Kirk 6–0 205 LW
B. Kingston, Ont., Feb. 8, 1966

SSN	TEAM	GP	G	A	PTS.	PIM	+/-
84–85	NJ	80	17	37	54	69	-31
85–86	NJ	77	25	41	66	45	-20
86–87	NJ	79	26	50	76	75	-7
87–88	NJ	80	37	57	94	114	+19
88–89	NJ	80	31	43	74	119	-23
89–90	NJ	80	30	56	86	74	-1
90–91	NJ	80	19	51	70	76	+1
91–92	Mont	78	36	41	77	86	+15
92–93	Mont	80	37	57	94	77	+8
93–94	Mont	76	23	34	57	96	-1
94–95	Mont–NYI	45	11	16	27	47	-18
95–96	NYI–Tor	51	13	19	32	57	-13
96–97	Tor–Fla	76	21	19	40	89	-25
97–98	Fla	70	8	21	29	54	-14
98–99	Fla	82	4	11	15	49	-11
Totals		**1114**	**338**	**553**	**891**	**1127**	**-121**

Playoffs

87–88	NJ	20	4	8	12	37
89–90	NJ	6	1	3	4	11
90–91	NJ	7	0	2	2	10
91–92	Mont	11	4	3	7	31
92–93	Mont	20	10	7	17	18
93–94	Mont	7	6	2	8	4
95–96	Tor	6	2	3	5	0
96–97	Fla	5	1	2	3	4
Totals		**82**	**29**	**29**	**58**	**115**

MULOIN, John Wayne *5–8 176 D*
B. Toronto, Ont., Dec. 24, 1941

SSN	TEAM	GP	G	A	PTS.	PIM	+/-
63–64	Det	3	0	1	1	2	
69–70	Oak	71	3	6	9	53	-21
70–71	Cal–Minn	73	0	14	14	38	-36
72–73	Clev (WHA)	70	2	13	15	62	
73–74	Clev (WHA)	76	3	7	10	39	
74–75	Clev (WHA)	78	4	17	21	5	
75–76	Clev–Edm (WHA)	37	1	6	7	12	
NHL Totals		147	3	21	24	93	-57
WHA Totals		261	10	43	53	118	

Playoffs

SSN	TEAM	GP	G	A	PTS.	PIM	+/-
69–70	Oak	4	0	0	0	0	
70–71	Minn	7	0	0	0	2	
72–73	Clev (WHA)	9	1	3	4	14	
73–74	Clev (WHA)	5	1	0	1	0	
74–75	Clev (WHA)	5	0	1	1	4	
75–76	Edm (WHA)	1	0	0	0	0	
NHL Totals		11	0	0	0	2	
WHA Totals		20	2	4	6	18	

MULVENNA, Glenn *5–11 187 C*
B. Calgary, Alta., Feb. 18, 1967

SSN	TEAM	GP	G	A	PTS.	PIM	+/-
91–92	Pitt	1	0	0	0	2	-1
92–93	Phil	1	0	0	0	2	0
Totals		2	0	0	0	4	-1

MULVEY, Grant Michael *6–4 200 RW*
B. Sudbury, Ont., Sept. 17, 1956

SSN	TEAM	GP	G	A	PTS.	PIM	+/-
74–75	Chi	74	7	4	11	36	-3
75–76	Chi	64	11	17	28	72	-5
76–77	Chi	80	10	14	24	111	-17
77–78	Chi	78	14	24	38	135	-1
78–79	Chi	80	19	15	34	99	-14
79–80	Chi	80	39	26	65	122	+3
80–81	Chi	42	18	14	32	81	-18
81–82	Chi	73	30	19	49	141	-9
82–83	Chi	3	0	0	0	0	0
83–84	NJ	12	1	2	3	19	-5
Totals		586	149	135	284	816	-69

Playoffs

SSN	TEAM	GP	G	A	PTS.	PIM	+/-
74–75	Chi	6	2	0	2	6	
75–76	Chi	4	0	0	0	2	
76–77	Chi	2	1	0	1	2	
77–78	Chi	4	2	2	4	0	
78–79	Chi	1	0	0	0	2	
79–80	Chi	7	1	1	2	8	
80–81	Chi	3	0	0	0	0	
81–82	Chi	15	4	2	6	50	
Totals		42	10	5	15	70	

MULVEY, Paul Joseph *6–4 200 LW*
B. Sudbury, Ont., Sept. 27, 1958

SSN	TEAM	GP	G	A	PTS.	PIM	+/-
78–79	Wash	55	7	4	11	81	-18
79–80	Wash	77	15	19	34	240	-8
80–81	Wash	55	7	14	21	166	-9
81–82	Pitt–LA	38	1	14	15	126	-7
Totals		225	30	51	81	613	-42

***MUMMERY, Harry** *245 D*

SSN	TEAM	GP	G	A	PTS.	PIM	+/-
17–18	Tor	18	3	0	3	24	
18–19	Tor	13	2	0	2	27	
19–20	Que	24	9	6	15	42	
20–21	Mont	24	15	5	20	68	
21–22	Ham	20	4	2	6	20	
22–23	Ham	7	0	0	0	4	
Totals		106	33	13	46	185	

Playoffs

SSN	TEAM	GP	G	A	PTS.	PIM	+/-
17–18	Tor	7	0	4	4	18	

MUNI, Craig Douglas *6–3 208 D*
B. Toronto, Ont., July 19, 1962

SSN	TEAM	GP	G	A	PTS.	PIM	+/-
81–82	Tor	3	0	0	0	2	-4
82–83	Tor	2	0	1	1	0	-3
84–85	Tor	8	0	0	0	0	0
85–86	Tor	6	0	1	1	4	-3
86–87	Edm	79	7	22	29	85	+45
87–88	Edm	72	4	15	19	77	+32
88–89	Edm	69	5	13	18	71	+43
89–90	Edm	71	5	12	17	81	+22
90–91	Edm	76	1	9	10	77	+10
91–92	Edm	54	2	5	7	34	+11
92–93	Edm–Chi	81	0	11	11	75	-14
93–94	Chi–Buf	82	2	12	14	66	+31
94–95	Buf	40	0	6	6	36	-4
95–96	Buf–Winn	72	1	7	8	106	-6
96–97	Pitt	64	0	4	4	36	-6
97–98	Dal	40	1	1	2	25	0
Totals		819	28	119	147	775	+174

Playoffs

SSN	TEAM	GP	G	A	PTS.	PIM	+/-
86–87	Edm	14	0	2	2	17	
87–88	Edm	19	0	4	4	31	
88–89	Edm	7	0	3	3	8	
89–90	Edm	22	0	3	3	16	
90–91	Edm	18	0	3	3	20	
91–92	Edm	3	0	0	0	2	
92–93	Chi	4	0	0	0	3	
93–94	Buf	7	0	0	0	4	
94–95	Buf	5	0	1	1	2	
95–96	Winn	6	0	1	1	2	
96–97	Pitt	3	0	0	0	0	
97–98	Dal	5	0	0	0	4	
Totals		113	0	17	17	108	

***MUNRO, Duncan B. (Dunc)** *D*
B. Toronto, Ont.

SSN	TEAM	GP	G	A	PTS.	PIM	+/-
24–25	Mont M	27	5	1	6	14	
25–26	Mont M	33	4	6	10	55	
26–27	Mont M	43	6	5	11	42	
27–28	Mont M	43	5	2	7	35	
28–29	Mont M	1	0	0	0	0	
29–30	Mont M	40	7	2	9	10	
30–31	Mont M	4	0	1	1	0	
31–32	Mont	48	1	1	2	14	
Totals		239	28	18	46	170	

Playoffs

SSN	TEAM	GP	G	A	PTS.	PIM	+/-
25–26	Mont M	6	1	0	1	6	
26–27	Mont M	2	0	0	0	4	
27–28	Mont M	9	0	2	2	8	
29–30	Mont M	4	2	0	2	4	
31–32	Mont	2	0	0	0	2	
Totals		23	3	2	5	24	

MUNRO, Gerald (Gerry) *D*
B. Sault Ste. Marie, Ont., Nov. 20, 1897

SSN	TEAM	GP	G	A	PTS.	PIM	+/-
24–25	Mont M	29	1	0	1	22	
25–26	Tor	4	0	0	0	0	
Totals		33	1	0	1	22	

***MURDOCH, Donald Walter (Murder)** *5–11 180 RW*
B. Cranbrook, B.C., Oct. 25, 1956

SSN	TEAM	GP	G	A	PTS.	PIM	+/-
76–77	NYR	59	32	24	56	47	+5
77–78	NYR	66	27	28	55	41	-5
78–79	NYR	40	15	22	37	6	-6
79–80	NYR–Edm	66	28	21	49	20	-11
80–81	Edm	40	10	9	19	18	-16
81–82	Det	49	9	13	22	23	+1
Totals		320	121	117	238	155	-32

Playoffs

SSN	TEAM	GP	G	A	PTS.	PIM	+/-
77–78	NYR	3	1	3	4	4	
78–79	NYR	18	7	5	12	12	
79–80	Edm	3	2	0	2	0	
Totals		24	10	8	18	16	

MURDOCH, John Murray *5–10 180 LW*
B. Lucknow, Ont., May 19, 1904

SSN	TEAM	GP	G	A	PTS.	PIM	+/-
26–27	NYR	44	6	4	10	12	
27–28	NYR	44	7	3	10	14	
28–29	NYR	44	8	6	14	18	
29–30	NYR	44	13	13	26	22	
30–31	NYR	44	7	7	14	8	
31–32	NYR	48	5	16	21	32	
32–33	NYR	48	5	11	16	23	
33–34	NYR	48	17	10	27	29	
34–35	NYR	48	14	15	29	14	
35–36	NYR	48	2	9	11	9	
36–37	NYR	48	0	14	14	16	
Totals		508	84	108	192	197	

Playoffs

SSN	TEAM	GP	G	A	PTS.	PIM	+/-
26–27	NYR	2	0	0	0	0	
27–28	NYR	9	2	1	3	12	
28–29	NYR	6	0	0	0	2	
29–30	NYR	4	3	0	3	6	
30–31	NYR	4	0	2	2	0	
31–32	NYR	7	0	2	2	0	
32–33	NYR	8	3	4	7	2	
33–34	NYR	4	0	2	2	4	
34–35	NYR	4	0	2	2	4	
35–36	NYR	9	1	1	2	0	
36–37	NYR	9	1	1	2	0	
Totals		66	10	15	25	30	

MURDOCH, Robert John *6–0 190 D*
B. Kirkland Lake, Ont., Nov. 20, 1946

SSN	TEAM	GP	G	A	PTS.	PIM	+/-
70–71	Mont	1	0	2	2	2	0
71–72	Mont	11	1	1	2	8	+8
72–73	Mont	69	2	22	24	55	+39
73–74	LA	76	8	20	28	85	-11
74–75	LA	80	13	29	42	116	+39
75–76	LA	80	6	29	35	103	+13
76–77	LA	70	9	23	32	79	+36
77–78	LA	76	2	17	19	68	+2
78–79	LA–Atl	67	8	23	31	70	+2
79–80	Atl	80	5	16	21	48	+2
80–81	Calg	74	3	19	22	54	+22
81–82	Calg	73	3	17	20	76	+5
Totals		757	60	218	278	764	+157

Playoffs

SSN	TEAM	GP	G	A	PTS.	PIM	+/-
70–71	Mont	2	0	0	0	0	
71–72	Mont	1	0	0	0	0	
72–73	Mont	13	0	3	3	10	
73–74	LA	5	0	0	0	2	
74–75	LA	3	0	1	1	4	
75–76	LA	9	0	5	5	15	
76–77	LA	9	2	3	5	14	
77–78	LA	2	0	1	1	5	
78–79	Atl	2	0	0	0	4	
79–80	Atl	4	1	1	2	2	
80–81	Calg	16	1	4	5	36	
81–82	Calg	3	0	0	0	0	
Totals		69	4	18	22	92	

MURDOCH, Robert Lovell *5–11 191 RW*
B. Cranbrook, B.C., Jan. 29, 1954

SSN	TEAM	GP	G	A	PTS.	PIM	+/-
75–76	Cal	78	22	27	49	53	-13
76–77	Clev	57	23	19	42	30	-5
77–78	Clev	71	14	26	40	27	-18
78–79	StL	54	13	13	26	17	-6
Totals		260	72	85	157	127	-42

MURPHY, Brian *6–3 195 C*
B. Toronto, Ont., Aug. 20, 1947

SSN	TEAM	GP	G	A	PTS.	PIM	+/-
74–75	Det	1	0	0	0	0	0

MURPHY, Gordon *6–2 195 D*
B. Willowdale, Ont., Mar. 23, 1967

SSN	TEAM	GP	G	A	PTS.	PIM	+/-
88–89	Phil	75	4	31	35	68	-3
89–90	Phil	75	14	27	41	95	-7
90–91	Phil	80	11	31	42	58	-7
91–92	Phil–Bos	73	5	14	19	84	-2
92–93	Bos	49	5	12	17	62	-13
93–94	Fla	84	14	29	43	71	-11
94–95	Fla	46	6	16	22	24	-14
95–96	Fla	70	8	22	30	30	+5
96–97	Fla	80	8	15	23	51	+3
97–98	Fla	79	6	11	17	46	-3
98–99	Fla	51	0	7	7	16	+4
Totals		762	81	215	296	605	-48

Playoffs

SSN	TEAM	GP	G	A	PTS.	PIM	+/-
88–89	Phil	19	2	7	9	13	
91–92	Bos	15	1	0	1	12	
95–96	Fla	14	0	4	4	6	
96–97	Fla	5	0	5	5	4	
Totals		53	3	16	19	35	

MURPHY, Joseph Patrick *6–1 190 RW*
B. London, Ont., Oct. 16, 1967

SSN	TEAM	GP	G	A	PTS.	PIM	+/-
86–87	Det	5	0	1	1	2	0
87–88	Det	50	10	9	19	37	-4
88–89	Det	26	1	7	8	28	-7
89–90	Det–Edm	71	10	19	29	60	+5
90–91	Edm	80	27	35	62	35	+2
91–92	Edm	80	35	47	82	52	+17
92–93	Chi	19	7	10	17	18	-3
93–94	Chi	81	31	39	70	111	+1
94–95	Chi	40	23	18	41	89	+7
95–96	Chi	70	22	29	51	86	-3
96–97	StL	75	20	25	45	69	-1
97–98	StL–SJ	37	9	13	22	36	+9
98–99	SJ	76	25	23	48	73	+10

SSN	TEAM	GP	G	A	PTS.	PIM	+/-
Totals		710	220	275	495	696	+33

Playoffs

SSN	TEAM	GP	G	A	PTS.	PIM
87–88	Det	8	0	1	1	6
89–90	Edm	22	6	8	14	16
90–91	Edm	15	2	5	7	14
91–92	Edm	16	8	16	24	12
92–93	Chi	4	0	0	0	8
93–94	Chi	6	1	3	4	25
94–95	Chi	16	9	3	12	29
95–96	Chi	6	1	1	2	10
97–98	SJ	6	1	1	2	20
98–99	SJ	6	0	3	3	4
Totals		115	34	43	77	177

MURPHY, Lawrence Thomas (Larry) *6–2 210 D*
B. Scarborough, Ont., Mar. 8, 1961

SSN	TEAM	GP	G	A	PTS.	PIM	+/-
80–81	LA	80	16	60	76	79	+17
81–82	LA	79	22	44	66	95	-13
82–83	LA	77	14	48	62	81	+2
83–84	LA–Wash	78	13	36	49	50	+8
84–85	Wash	79	13	42	55	51	+21
85–86	Wash	78	21	44	65	50	+2
86–87	Wash	80	23	58	81	39	+25
87–88	Wash	79	8	53	61	72	+2
88–89	Wash–Minn	78	11	35	46	82	0
89–90	Minn	77	10	58	68	44	-13
90–91	Minn–Pitt	75	9	34	43	68	-6
91–92	Pitt	77	21	56	77	48	+33
92–93	Pitt	83	22	63	85	73	+45
93–94	Pitt	84	17	56	73	44	+10
94–95	Pitt	48	13	25	38	18	+12
95–96	Tor	82	12	49	61	34	-2
96–97	Tor–Det	81	9	36	45	20	+3
97–98	Det	82	11	41	52	37	+35
98–99	Det	80	10	42	52	42	+21
Totals		1477	275	880	1155	1027	+202

Playoffs

SSN	TEAM	GP	G	A	PTS.	PIM
80–81	LA	4	3	0	3	2
81–82	LA	10	2	8	10	12
83–84	Wash	8	0	3	3	6
84–85	Wash	5	2	3	5	0
85–86	Wash	9	1	5	6	6
86–87	Wash	7	2	2	4	6
87–88	Wash	13	4	4	8	33
88–89	Minn	5	0	2	2	8
89–90	Minn	7	1	2	3	31
90–91	Pitt	23	5	18	23	44
91–92	Pitt	21	6	10	16	19
92–93	Pitt	12	2	11	13	10
93–94	Pitt	6	0	5	5	0
94–95	Pitt	12	2	13	15	0
95–96	Tor	6	0	2	2	4
96–97	Det	20	2	9	11	8
97–98	Det	22	3	12	15	2
98–99	Det	10	0	2	2	8
Totals		200	35	111	146	198

MURPHY, Michael John *6–0 190 RW*
B. Toronto, Ont., Sept. 12, 1950

SSN	TEAM	GP	G	A	PTS.	PIM	+/-
71–72	StL	63	20	23	43	19	-4
72–73	StL–NYR	79	22	31	53	53	+8
73–74	NYR–LA	69	15	17	32	38	0
74–75	LA	78	30	38	68	44	+32
75–76	LA	80	26	42	68	61	-3
76–77	LA	76	25	36	61	58	+15
77–78	LA	72	20	36	56	48	-1
78–79	LA	64	16	29	45	38	-12
79–80	LA	80	27	22	49	29	-12
80–81	LA	68	16	23	39	54	-7
81–82	LA	28	5	10	15	20	0
82–83	LA	74	16	11	27	52	-11
Totals		831	238	318	556	514	+5

Playoffs

SSN	TEAM	GP	G	A	PTS.	PIM
71–72	StL	11	2	3	5	6
72–73	NYR	10	0	0	0	0
73–74	LA	5	0	4	4	0
74–75	LA	3	3	0	3	4
75–76	LA	9	1	4	5	6
76–77	LA	9	4	9	13	4
77–78	LA	2	0	0	0	0
78–79	LA	2	0	1	1	0
79–80	LA	4	1	0	1	2
80–81	LA	1	0	1	1	0
81–82	LA	10	2	1	3	32

SSN	TEAM	GP	G	A	PTS.	PIM
Totals		66	13	23	36	54

MURPHY, Rob *6–3 205 LW/C*
B. Hull, Que., Apr. 7, 1969

SSN	TEAM	GP	G	A	PTS.	PIM	+/-
87–88	Van	5	0	0	0	2	-1
88–89	Van	8	0	1	1	2	-1
89–90	Van	12	1	1	2	0	-13
90–91	Van	42	5	1	6	90	-11
91–92	Van	6	0	1	1	6	-2
92–93	Ott	44	3	7	10	30	-23
93–94	LA	8	0	1	1	22	-3
Totals		125	9	12	21	152	-54

Playoffs

SSN	TEAM	GP	G	A	PTS.	PIM
90–91	Van	4	0	0	0	2

MURPHY, Robert Ronald (Ron) *5–11 185 LW*
B. Hamilton, Ont., Apr. 10, 1933

SSN	TEAM	GP	G	A	PTS.	PIM	+/-
52–53	NYR	15	3	1	4	0	
53–54	NYR	27	1	3	4	20	
54–55	NYR	66	14	16	30	36	
55–56	NYR	66	16	28	44	71	
56–57	NYR	33	7	12	19	14	
57–58	Chi	69	11	17	28	32	
58–59	Chi	59	17	30	47	52	
59–60	Chi	63	15	21	36	18	
60–61	Chi	70	21	19	40	30	
61–62	Chi	60	12	16	28	41	
62–63	Chi	68	18	16	34	28	
63–64	Chi	70	11	8	19	32	
64–65	Chi	58	20	19	39	32	
65–66	Det–Bos	34	10	8	18	10	
66–67	Bos	39	11	16	27	6	
67–68	Bos	12	0	1	1	4	-2
68–69	Bos	60	16	38	54	26	+23
69–70	Bos	20	2	5	7	8	+1
Totals		889	205	274	479	460	+22

Playoffs

SSN	TEAM	GP	G	A	PTS.	PIM
55–56	NYR	5	0	1	1	2
56–57	NYR	5	0	0	0	0
59–60	Chi	4	1	0	1	0
60–61	Chi	12	2	1	3	0
62–63	Chi	1	0	0	0	0
63–64	Chi	7	0	1	1	8
64–65	Det	5	0	1	1	4
67–68	Bos	4	0	0	0	0
68–69	Bos	10	4	4	8	12
Totals		53	7	8	15	26

MURRAY, Allan *5–7 165 D*
B. Stratford, Ont., Nov. 10, 1908

SSN	TEAM	GP	G	A	PTS.	PIM
33–34	NYA	48	1	1	2	20
34–35	NYA	43	2	1	3	36
35–36	NYA	48	1	0	1	33
36–37	NYA	39	0	2	2	22
37–38	NYA	46	0	1	1	34
38–39	NYA	19	0	0	0	8
39–40	NYA	34	1	4	5	10
Totals		277	5	9	14	163

Playoffs

SSN	TEAM	GP	G	A	PTS.	PIM
35–36	NYA	5	0	0	0	2
37–38	NYA	6	0	0	0	6
39–40	NYA	3	0	0	0	0
Totals		14	0	0	0	8

MURRAY, Chris *6–2 209 RW*
B. Port Hardy, B.C., Oct. 25, 1974

SSN	TEAM	GP	G	A	PTS.	PIM	+/-
94–95	Mont	3	0	0	0	4	0
95–96	Mont	48	3	4	7	163	+5
96–97	Mont–Hart	64	5	3	8	124	-7
97–98	Car–Ott	53	5	4	9	118	+3
98–99	Ott–Chi	42	1	6	7	79	-2
Totals		210	14	17	31	488	-1

Playoffs

SSN	TEAM	GP	G	A	PTS.	PIM
95–96	Mont	4	0	0	0	4
97–98	Ott	11	1	0	1	8
Totals		15	1	0	1	12

MURRAY, Glen *6–2 213 RW*
B. Halifax, N.S., Nov. 1, 1972

SSN	TEAM	GP	G	A	PTS.	PIM	+/-
91–92	Bos	5	3	1	4	0	+2
92–93	Bos	27	3	4	7	8	-6
93–94	Bos	81	18	13	31	48	-1
94–95	Bos	35	5	2	7	46	-11
95–96	Pitt	69	14	15	29	57	+4
96–97	Pitt–LA	77	16	14	30	32	-21
97–98	LA	81	29	31	60	54	+6
98–99	LA	61	16	15	31	36	-14
Totals		436	104	95	199	281	-41

Playoffs

SSN	TEAM	GP	G	A	PTS.	PIM
91–92	Bos	15	4	2	6	10
93–94	Bos	13	4	5	9	14
94–95	Bos	2	0	0	0	2
95–96	Pitt	18	2	6	8	10
97–98	LA	4	2	0	2	6
Totals		52	12	13	25	42

MURRAY, James Arnold *6–1 165 D*
B. Virden, Man., Nov. 25, 1943

SSN	TEAM	GP	G	A	PTS.	PIM	+/-
67–68	LA	30	0	2	2	14	-4

MURRAY, Kenneth Richard *6–0 180 D*
B. Toronto, Ont., Jan. 22, 1948

SSN	TEAM	GP	G	A	PTS.	PIM	+/-
69–70	Tor	1	0	1	1	2	+1
70–71	Tor	4	0	0	0	0	+1
72–73	NYI–Det	70	1	5	6	95	-22
74–75	KC	8	0	2	2	14	+3
75–76	KC	23	0	2	2	24	-1
Totals		106	1	10	11	135	-18

*MURRAY, Leonard (Leo) *C*
B. Portage La Prairie, Man., Feb. 15, 1902

SSN	TEAM	GP	G	A	PTS.	PIM
32–33	Mont	6	0	0	0	2

MURRAY, Marty *5–9 170 C*
B. Deloraine, Man., Feb. 16, 1975

SSN	TEAM	GP	G	A	PTS.	PIM	+/-
95–96	Calg	15	3	3	6	0	-4
96–97	Calg	2	0	0	0	4	0
97–98	Calg	2	0	0	0	2	+1
Totals		19	3	3	6	6	-3

MURRAY, Mike *6–0 180 C*
B. Kingston, Ont., Aug. 29, 1966

SSN	TEAM	GP	G	A	PTS.	PIM	+/-
87–88	Phil	1	0	0	0	0	0

MURRAY, Pat *6–2 185 LW*
B. Stratford, Ont., Aug. 20, 1969

SSN	TEAM	GP	G	A	PTS.	PIM	+/-
90–91	Phil	16	2	1	3	15	-5
91–92	Phil	9	1	0	1	0	+3
Totals		25	3	1	4	15	-2

MURRAY, Randall (Randy) *6–1 195 D*
B. Chatham, Ont., Aug. 24, 1945

SSN	TEAM	GP	G	A	PTS.	PIM	+/-
69–70	Tor	3	0	0	0	2	0

MURRAY, Rem *6–1 183 LW*
B. Stratford, Ont., Oct. 9, 1972

SSN	TEAM	GP	G	A	PTS.	PIM	+/-
96–97	Edm	82	11	20	31	16	+9
97–98	Edm	61	9	9	18	39	-9
98–99	Edm	78	21	18	39	20	+4
Totals		241	41	47	88	75	+4

Playoffs

SSN	TEAM	GP	G	A	PTS.	PIM
96–97	Edm	12	1	2	3	4
97–98	Edm	11	1	4	5	2
98–99	Edm	4	1	1	2	2
Totals		27	3	7	10	8

MURRAY, Rob *6–1 180 C*
B. Toronto, Ont., Apr. 4, 1967

SSN	TEAM	GP	G	A	PTS.	PIM	+/-
89–90	Wash	41	2	7	9	58	-10
90–91	Wash	17	0	3	3	19	0
91–92	Winn	9	0	1	1	18	-2
92–93	Winn	10	1	0	1	6	0
93–94	Winn	6	0	0	0	2	0
94–95	Winn	10	0	2	2	4	+1
95–96	Winn	1	0	0	0	2	-1
98–99	Phoe	13	1	2	3	4	+2
Totals		107	4	15	19	111	-10

Playoffs

SSN	TEAM	GP	G	A	PTS.	PIM
89–90	Wash	9	0	0	0	18

MURRAY, Robert Frederick *5–10 183 D*
B. Kingston, Ont., Nov. 26, 1954

SSN	TEAM	GP	G	A	PTS.	PIM	+/-
75–76	Chi	64	1	2	3	44	-6
76–77	Chi	77	10	11	21	71	-7

SSN	TEAM	GP	G	A	PTS.	PIM	+/-
77–78	Chi	70	14	17	31	41	+11
78–79	Chi	79	19	32	51	38	+4
79–80	Chi	74	16	34	50	60	-16
80–81	Chi	77	13	47	60	93	+6
81–82	Chi	45	8	22	30	48	+1
82–83	Chi	79	7	32	39	71	+24
83–84	Chi	78	11	37	48	78	+1
84–85	Chi	80	5	38	43	56	+13
85–86	Chi	80	9	29	38	75	+6
86–87	Chi	79	6	20	26	44	-7
87–88	Chi	62	6	20	26	44	-7
88–89	Chi	15	2	4	6	27	-4
89–90	Chi	49	5	19	24	45	+3
Totals		1008	132	382	514	873	+22

Playoffs

SSN	TEAM	GP	G	A	PTS.	PIM	
76–77	Chi	2	0	1	1	2	
77–78	Chi	4	1	4	5	2	
78–79	Chi	4	1	0	1	6	
79–80	Chi	7	2	4	6	6	
80–81	Chi	3	0	0	0	2	
81–82	Chi	15	1	6	7	16	
82–83	Chi	13	2	3	5	10	
83–84	Chi	5	3	1	4	6	
84–85	Chi	15	3	6	9	20	
85–86	Chi	3	0	2	2	0	
86–87	Chi	4	1	0	1	4	
87–88	Chi	5	1	3	4	2	
88–89	Chi	16	2	3	5	22	
89–90	Chi	16	2	4	6	8	
Totals		112	19	37	56	106	

MURRAY, Robert John 6–1 195 D
B. Burlington, Ont., July 16, 1948

SSN	TEAM	GP	G	A	PTS.	PIM	+/-
73–74	Atl	62	0	3	3	34	-20
74–75	Atl–Van	55	4	8	12	30	+11
75–76	Van	65	2	5	7	28	
76–77	Van	12	0	0	0	6	-1
Totals		194	6	16	22	98	-7

Playoffs

SSN	TEAM	GP	G	A	PTS.	PIM	
73–74	Atl	4	1	0	1	2	
74–75	Van	5	0	1	1	13	
75–76	Van	5	0	1	1	13	
Totals		14	1	2	3	28	

MURRAY, Terrence Rodney (Terry) 6–2 190 D
B. Shawville, Que., July 20, 1950

SSN	TEAM	GP	G	A	PTS.	PIM	+/-
72–73	Cal	23	0	3	3	4	-14
73–74	Cal	58	0	12	12	48	-43
74–75	Cal	9	0	2	2	8	+2
75–76	Phil	3	0	0	0	2	0
76–77	Phil–Det	59	0	20	20	24	+3
78–79	Phil	5	0	0	0	0	0
80–81	Phil	71	1	17	18	53	+46
81–82	Wash	74	3	22	25	60	-14
Totals		302	4	76	80	199	-20

Playoffs

SSN	TEAM	GP	G	A	PTS.	PIM	
75–76	Phil	6	0	1	1	0	
80–81	Phil	12	2	1	3	10	
Totals		18	2	2	4	10	

MURRAY, Troy Norman 6–1 195 C
B. Calgary, Alta., July 31, 1962

SSN	TEAM	GP	G	A	PTS.	PIM	+/-
81–82	Chi	1	0	0	0	0	0
82–83	Chi	54	8	8	16	27	-4
83–84	Chi	61	15	15	30	45	+10
84–85	Chi	80	26	40	66	82	+16
85–86	Chi	80	45	54	99	94	+32
86–87	Chi	77	28	43	71	59	+14
87–88	Chi	79	22	36	58	96	-17
88–89	Chi	79	21	30	51	113	0
89–90	Chi	68	17	38	55	86	-2
90–91	Chi	75	14	23	37	74	+13
91–92	Winn	74	17	30	47	69	-13
92–93	Winn–Chi	51	4	7	11	59	-15
93–94	Chi–Ott	27	2	4	6	10	+2
94–95	Ott–Pitt	46	4	12	16	39	-2
95–96	Col A	63	7	14	21	22	+15
Totals		915	230	354	584	875	+49

Playoffs

SSN	TEAM	GP	G	A	PTS.	PIM	
81–82	Chi	7	1	0	1	5	
82–83	Chi	2	0	0	0	0	
83–84	Chi	5	1	0	1	7	
84–85	Chi	15	5	14	19	24	
85–86	Chi	2	0	0	0	2	
86–87	Chi	4	0	0	0	5	
87–88	Chi	5	1	0	1	8	
88–89	Chi	16	3	6	9	25	
89–90	Chi	20	4	4	8	22	
90–91	Chi	6	0	1	1	12	
91–92	Winn	7	0	0	0	2	
92–93	Chi	4	0	0	0	2	
94–95	Pitt	12	2	1	3	12	
95–96	Col A	6	0	0	0	19	
Totals		113	17	26	43	145	

MURZYN, Dana 6–2 200 D
B. Calgary, Alta., Dec. 9, 1966

SSN	TEAM	GP	G	A	PTS.	PIM	+/-
85–86	Hart	78	3	23	26	125	+1
86–87	Hart	74	9	19	28	95	+17
87–88	Hart–Calg	74	7	11	18	139	+1
88–89	Calg	63	3	19	22	142	+26
89–90	Calg	78	7	13	20	140	+19
90–91	Calg–Van	29	1	2	3	38	-7
91–92	Van	70	3	11	14	147	+15
92–93	Van	79	5	11	16	196	+34
93–94	Van	80	6	14	20	109	+4
94–95	Van	40	0	8	8	129	+14
95–96	Van	69	2	10	12	130	+9
96–97	Van	61	1	7	8	118	+7
97–98	Van	31	5	2	7	42	-3
98–99	Van	12	0	2	2	21	+1
Totals		838	52	152	204	1571	+138

Playoffs

SSN	TEAM	GP	G	A	PTS.	PIM	
85–86	Hart	4	0	0	0	10	
86–87	Hart	6	2	1	3	29	
87–88	Calg	5	2	0	2	13	
88–89	Calg	21	0	3	3	20	
89–90	Calg	6	2	2	4	2	
90–91	Calg	1	0	1	1	8	
91–92	Van	1	0	0	0	15	
92–93	Van	12	3	2	5	18	
93–94	Van	7	0	0	0	4	
94–95	Van	8	0	1	1	22	
95–96	Van	6	0	0	0	25	
Totals		82	9	10	19	166	

MUSIL, Frantisek 6–3 215 D
B. Pardubice, Czechoslovakia, Dec. 17, 1964

SSN	TEAM	GP	G	A	PTS.	PIM	+/-
86–87	Minn	72	2	9	11	148	0
87–88	Minn	80	9	8	17	213	-2
88–89	Minn	55	1	19	20	54	+4
89–90	Minn	56	2	8	10	109	0
90–91	Minn–Calg	75	7	16	23	183	+12
91–92	Calg	78	4	8	12	103	+12
92–93	Calg	80	6	10	16	131	+28
93–94	Calg	75	1	8	9	50	+38
94–95	Calg	35	0	5	5	61	+6
95–96	Ott	65	1	3	4	85	-10
96–97	Ott	57	0	5	5	58	+6
97–98	Edm	17	1	2	3	8	+1
98–99	Edm	39	0	3	3	34	0
Totals		784	34	104	138	1237	+105

Playoffs

SSN	TEAM	GP	G	A	PTS.	PIM	
88–89	Minn	5	1	1	2	4	
89–90	Minn	4	0	0	0	14	
90–91	Calg	7	0	0	0	10	
92–93	Calg	6	1	1	2	7	
93–94	Calg	7	0	1	1	4	
94–95	Calg	5	0	1	1	0	
97–98	Edm	7	0	0	0	6	
98–99	Edm	1	0	0	0	2	
Totals		42	2	4	6	47	

MYERS, Harold Robert (Hap) 5–11 195 D
B. Edmonton, Alta., July 28, 1947

SSN	TEAM	GP	G	A	PTS.	PIM	+/-
70–71	Buf	13	0	0	0	6	-11

MYHRES, Brantt 6–3 220 LW
B. Edmonton, Alta., Mar. 18, 1974

SSN	TEAM	GP	G	A	PTS.	PIM	+/-
94–95	TB	15	2	0	2	81	-2
96–97	TB	47	3	1	4	136	+1
97–98	Phil	23	0	0	0	169	-1
98–99	SJ	30	1	0	1	116	-2
Totals		115	6	1	7	502	-4

MYLES, Victor Robert 6–1 208 D
B. Fairlight, Sask., Nov. 12, 1915

SSN	TEAM	GP	G	A	PTS.	PIM	
42–43	NYR	45	6	9	15	57	

MYRVOLD, Anders 6–1 178 D
B. Lorenskog, Norway, Aug. 12, 1975

SSN	TEAM	GP	G	A	PTS.	PIM	+/-
95–96	Col A	4	0	1	1	6	-2
96–97	Bos	9	0	2	2	4	-1
Totals		13	0	3	3	10	-3

NABAKOV, Dmitri 6–2 209 C
B. Novosibirsk, USSR, Jan. 4, 1977

SSN	TEAM	GP	G	A	PTS.	PIM	
97–98	Chi	25	7	4	11	10	

NACHBAUR, Donald Kenneth 6–2 195 C
B. Kitimat, B.C., Jan. 30, 1959

SSN	TEAM	GP	G	A	PTS.	PIM	+/-
80–81	Hart	77	16	17	33	139	-1
81–82	Hart	77	5	21	26	117	-21
82–83	Edm	4	0	0	0	17	-1
85–86	Phil	5	1	1	2	7	+3
86–87	Phil	23	0	2	2	87	+2
87–88	Phil	20	0	4	4	61	-1
88–89	Phil	15	1	0	1	37	+1
89–90	Phil	2	0	1	1	0	
Totals		223	23	46	69	465	-17

Playoffs

SSN	TEAM	GP	G	A	PTS.	PIM	
82–83	Edm	2	0	0	0	7	
86–87	Phil	7	1	1	2	15	
87–88	Phil	2	0	0	0	2	
Totals		11	1	1	2	24	

NAHRGANG, James Herbert 6–0 185 D
B. Millbank, Ont., Apr. 17, 1951

SSN	TEAM	GP	G	A	PTS.	PIM	+/-
74–75	Det	1	0	1	1	0	0
75–76	Det	3	0	1	1	0	-5
76–77	Det	53	5	11	16	34	-12
Totals		57	5	12	17	34	-17

NAMESTNIKOV, Yevgeny 5–11 190 D
B. Arzamis–Ig, USSR, Oct. 9, 1971

SSN	TEAM	GP	G	A	PTS.	PIM	+/-
93–94	Van	17	0	5	5	10	-2
94–95	Van	16	0	3	3	4	+2
96–97	Van	2	0	0	0	4	-1
97–98	NYI	6	0	1	1	4	-1
Totals		41	0	9	9	22	-2

Playoffs

SSN	TEAM	GP	G	A	PTS.	PIM	
94–95	Van	1	0	0	0	2	
95–96	Van	1	0	0	0	0	
Totals		2	0	0	0	2	

NANNE, Louis Vincent (Lou) 6–0 185 D
B. Sault Ste. Marie, Ont., June 2, 1941

SSN	TEAM	GP	G	A	PTS.	PIM	+/-
67–68	Minn	2	0	1	1	0	0
68–69	Minn	41	2	12	14	47	-9
69–70	Minn	74	3	20	23	75	-8
70–71	Minn	68	5	11	16	22	-6
71–72	Minn	78	21	28	49	27	-5
72–73	Minn	74	15	20	35	39	+19
73–74	Minn	76	11	21	32	46	-1
74–75	Minn	49	6	9	15	35	-24
75–76	Minn	79	3	14	17	45	-34
76–77	Minn	68	2	20	22	12	-24
77–78	Minn	26	0	1	1	8	-14
Totals		635	68	157	225	356	-96

Playoffs

SSN	TEAM	GP	G	A	PTS.	PIM	
69–70	Minn	5	0	2	2	2	
70–71	Minn	12	3	6	9	4	
71–72	Minn	7	0	0	0	2	
72–73	Minn	6	1	2	3	0	
76–77	Minn	2	0	0	0	2	
Totals		32	4	10	14	10	

NANTAIS, Richard Francois 5–11 188 LW
B. Repentigny, Que., Oct. 27, 1954

SSN	TEAM	GP	G	A	PTS.	PIM	+/-
74–75	Minn	18	4	1	5	9	+1
75–76	Minn	5	0	0	0	17	-1
76–77	Minn	40	1	3	4	53	-8
Totals		63	5	4	9	79	-8

NAPIER, Robert Mark 5–10 183 RW
B. Toronto, Ont., Jan. 28, 1957

SSN	TEAM	GP	G	A	PTS.	PIM	
75–76	Tor (WHA)	78	43	50	93	20	

SSN	TEAM	GP	G	A	PTS.	PIM	+/-
76–77	Birm (WHA)	80	60	36	96	24	
77–78	Birm (WHA)	79	33	32	65	9	
78–79	Mont	54	11	20	31	11	+17
79–80	Mont	76	16	33	49	7	+11
80–81	Mont	79	35	36	71	24	+34
81–82	Mont	80	40	41	81	14	+49
82–83	Mont	73	40	27	67	6	+20
83–84	Mont–Minn	63	16	30	46	17	+2
84–85	Minn–Edm	72	19	44	63	21	+6
85–86	Edm	80	24	32	56	14	+13
86–87	Edm–Buf	77	13	18	31	2	-2
87–88	Buf	47	10	8	18	18	-3
88–89	Buf	66	11	17	28	33	-3
NHL Totals		767	265	306	571	157	+154
WHA Totals		237	136	118	254	53	

Playoffs

SSN	TEAM	GP	G	A	PTS.	PIM	+/-
77–78	Birm (WHA)	5	0	2	2	14	
78–79	Mont	12	3	2	5	2	
79–80	Mont	10	2	6	8	0	
80–81	Mont	3	0	0	0	2	
81–82	Mont	5	3	2	5	0	
82–83	Mont	3	0	0	0	0	
83–84	Minn	12	3	2	5	0	
84–85	Edm	18	5	5	10	7	
85–86	Edm	10	1	4	5	0	
87–88	Buf	6	0	3	3	0	
88–89	Buf	3	1	0	1	0	
NHL Totals		82	18	24	42	11	
WHA Totals		5	0	2	2	14	

NASH, Tyson 6–0 185 LW
B. Edmonton, Alta., March 11, 1975

SSN	TEAM	GP	G	A	PTS.	PIM	+/-
98–99	StL	2	0	0	0	5	-1

Playoffs

SSN	TEAM	GP	G	A	PTS.	PIM	+/-
98–99	StL	1	0	0	0	2	

NASLUND, Markus 6–0 186 RW
B. Ornskoldsvik, Sweden, July 30, 1973

SSN	TEAM	GP	G	A	PTS.	PIM	+/-
93–94	Pitt	71	4	7	11	27	-3
94–95	Pitt	14	2	2	4	2	0
95–96	Pitt–Van	76	22	33	55	42	+20
96–97	Van	78	21	20	41	30	-15
97–98	Van	76	14	20	34	56	+5
98–99	Van	80	36	30	66	74	-13
Totals		395	99	112	211	231	-6

Playoffs

SSN	TEAM	GP	G	A	PTS.	PIM	+/-
95–96	Van	6	1	2	3	8	

NASLUND, Mats 5–7 160 LW
B. Timra, Sweden, Oct. 31, 1959

SSN	TEAM	GP	G	A	PTS.	PIM	+/-
82–83	Mont	74	26	45	71	10	+34
83–84	Mont	77	29	35	64	4	+5
84–85	Mont	80	42	37	79	14	+19
85–86	Mont	80	43	67	110	16	+11
86–87	Mont	79	25	55	80	16	+3
87–88	Mont	78	24	59	83	14	+17
88–89	Mont	77	33	51	84	14	+34
89–90	Mont	72	21	20	41	19	+3
94–95	Bos	34	8	14	22	4	-4
Totals		651	251	383	634	111	+116

Playoffs

SSN	TEAM	GP	G	A	PTS.	PIM	+/-
82–83	Mont	3	1	0	1	0	
83–84	Mont	15	6	8	14	4	
84–85	Mont	12	7	4	11	6	
85–86	Mont	20	8	11	19	4	
86–87	Mont	17	7	15	22	11	
87–88	Mont	6	0	7	7	2	
88–89	Mont	21	4	11	15	6	
89–90	Mont	3	1	1	2	0	
94–95	Bos	5	1	0	1	0	
Totals		102	35	57	92	33	

NASREDDINE, Alain 6–1 201 D
B. Montreal, Que., July 10, 1975

SSN	TEAM	GP	G	A	PTS.	PIM	+/-
98–99	Chi–Mont	15	0	0	0	52	-1

NATTRASS, Ralph William 6–0 200 D
B. Gainsboro, Sask., May 26, 1925

SSN	TEAM	GP	G	A	PTS.	PIM	+/-
46–47	Chi	35	4	5	9	34	
47–48	Chi	60	5	12	17	79	
48–49	Chi	60	4	10	14	99	
49–50	Chi	68	5	11	16	96	
Totals		223	18	38	56	308	

NATTRESS, Eric (Ric) 6–2 210 D
B. Hamilton, Ont., May 25, 1962

SSN	TEAM	GP	G	A	PTS.	PIM	+/-
82–83	Mont	40	1	3	4	19	+8
83–84	Mont	34	0	12	12	15	-11
84–85	Mont	5	0	1	1	2	-2
85–86	StL	78	4	20	24	52	-8
86–87	StL	73	6	22	28	24	-34
87–88	Calg	63	2	13	15	37	+14
88–89	Calg	38	1	8	9	47	+12
89–90	Calg	49	1	14	15	26	+14
90–91	Calg	58	5	13	18	63	-1
91–92	Calg–Tor	54	2	19	21	63	-1
92–93	Phil	44	7	10	17	29	+1
Totals		536	29	135	164	377	-8

Playoffs

SSN	TEAM	GP	G	A	PTS.	PIM	+/-
82–83	Mont	3	0	0	0	10	
84–85	Mont	2	0	0	0	2	
85–86	StL	18	1	4	5	24	
86–87	StL	6	0	0	0	2	
87–88	Calg	6	1	3	4	0	
88–89	Calg	19	0	3	3	20	
89–90	Calg	6	2	0	2	0	
90–91	Calg	7	1	0	1	2	
Totals		67	5	10	15	60	

NATYSHAK, Mike 6–2 201 RW
B. Belle River, Ont., Nov. 29, 1963

SSN	TEAM	GP	G	A	PTS.	PIM	+/-
87–88	Que	4	0	0	0	0	-1

NAZAROV, Andrei 6–5 230 LW
B. Chelyabinsk, USSR, May 22, 1974

SSN	TEAM	GP	G	A	PTS.	PIM	+/-
93–94	SJ	1	0	0	0	0	0
94–95	SJ	26	3	5	8	94	-1
95–96	SJ	42	7	7	14	62	-15
96–97	SJ	60	12	15	27	222	-4
97–98	SJ–TB	54	2	2	4	170	-13
98–99	TB–Calg	62	7	9	16	73	-4
Totals		245	31	38	69	621	-37

Playoffs

SSN	TEAM	GP	G	A	PTS.	PIM	+/-
94–95	SJ	6	0	0	0	9	

NDUR, Roman 6–2 200 D
B. Zaria, Nigeria, July 7, 1975

SSN	TEAM	GP	G	A	PTS.	PIM	+/-
96–97	Buf	2	0	0	0	2	+1
97–98	Buf	1	0	0	0	2	-1
98–99	StL–NYR	39	1	3	4	62	-1
Totals		42	1	3	4	66	-1

NEATON, Pat 6–0 180 D
B. Redford, Mich., May 21, 1971

SSN	TEAM	GP	G	A	PTS.	PIM	+/-
93–94	Pitt	9	1	1	2	12	+3

NECHAEV, Victor 6–1 183 C
B. Kuib.–Vost, Siberia, Jan. 28, 1955

SSN	TEAM	GP	G	A	PTS.	PIM	+/-
82–83	LA	3	1	0	1	0	+1

NECKAR, Stanislav 6–1 196 D
B. Ceske Budejovice, Czechoslovakia, Dec. 22, 1975

SSN	TEAM	GP	G	A	PTS.	PIM	+/-
94–95	Ott	48	1	3	4	37	-20
95–96	Ott	82	3	9	12	54	-16
96–97	Ott	5	0	0	0	2	+2
97–98	Ott	60	2	2	4	31	-14
98–99	Ott–NYR–Phoe	32	0	3	3	18	+1
Totals		227	6	17	23	142	-47

Playoffs

SSN	TEAM	GP	G	A	PTS.	PIM	+/-
97–98	Ott	9	0	0	0	2	
98–99	Phoe	6	0	1	1	4	
Totals		15	0	1	1	6	

NEDOMANSKY, Vaclav 6–2 205 RW
B. Hodonin, Czechoslovakia, Mar. 14, 1944

SSN	TEAM	GP	G	A	PTS.	PIM	+/-
74–75	Tor (WHA)	78	41	40	81	19	
75–76	Tor (WHA)	81	56	42	98	8	
76–77	Birm (WHA)	81	36	33	69	10	
77–78	Birm (WHA)	12	2	3	5	6	
77–78	Det	63	11	17	28	2	-17
78–79	Det	80	38	35	73	19	-13
79–80	Det	79	35	39	74	13	-5
80–81	Det	74	12	20	32	30	-35
81–82	Det	68	12	28	40	22	-15
82–83	StL–NYR	57	14	17	31	2	-7
NHL Totals		421	122	156	278	88	-92
WHA Totals		252	135	118	253	43	

Playoffs

SSN	TEAM	GP	G	A	PTS.	PIM	+/-
74–75	Tor (WHA)	6	3	1	4	9	
77–78	Det	7	3	5	8	0	
NHL Totals		7	3	5	8	0	
WHA Totals		6	3	1	4	9	

NEDVED, Petr 6–3 195 C
B. Liberec, Czechoslovakia, Dec. 9, 1971

SSN	TEAM	GP	G	A	PTS.	PIM	+/-
90–91	Van	61	10	6	16	20	-21
91–92	Van	77	15	22	37	36	-3
92–93	Van	84	38	33	71	96	+20
93–94	StL	19	6	14	20	8	+2
94–95	NYR	46	11	12	23	26	-1
95–96	Pitt	80	45	54	99	68	+37
96–97	Pitt	74	33	38	71	66	-2
98–99	NYR	56	20	27	47	50	-6
Totals		497	178	206	384	370	+26

Playoffs

SSN	TEAM	GP	G	A	PTS.	PIM	+/-
90–91	Van	6	0	1	1	0	
91–92	Van	10	1	4	5	16	
92–93	Van	12	2	3	5	2	
93–94	StL	4	0	1	1	4	
94–95	NYR	10	3	2	5	6	
95–96	Pitt	18	10	10	20	16	
96–97	Pitt	5	1	2	3	12	
Totals		65	17	23	40	56	

NEDVED, Zdenek 6–0 180 RW
B. Lany, Czechoslovakia, Mar. 3, 1975

SSN	TEAM	GP	G	A	PTS.	PIM	+/-
94–95	Tor	1	0	0	0	2	0
95–96	Tor	7	1	1	2	6	-1
96–97	Tor	23	3	5	8	6	+4
Totals		31	4	6	10	14	+3

NEEDHAM, Michael 5–10 185 RW
B. Calgary, Alta., Apr. 4, 1970

SSN	TEAM	GP	G	A	PTS.	PIM	+/-
91–92	Pitt	0	0	0	0	0	-1
92–93	Pitt	56	8	5	13	14	0
93–94	Pitt–Dal	30	1	0	1	2	-2
Totals		86	9	5	14	16	-3

Playoffs

SSN	TEAM	GP	G	A	PTS.	PIM	+/-
91–92	Pitt	5	1	0	1	2	
92–93	Pitt	9	1	0	1	2	
Totals		14	2	0	2	4	

NEELY, Cameron Michael (Cam) 6–1 218 RW
B. Comox, B.C., June 6, 1965

SSN	TEAM	GP	G	A	PTS.	PIM	+/-
83–84	Van	56	16	15	31	57	0
84–85	Van	72	21	18	39	137	-26
85–86	Van	73	14	20	34	126	-30
86–87	Bos	75	36	36	72	143	+23
87–88	Bos	69	42	27	69	175	+30
88–89	Bos	74	37	38	75	190	+14
89–90	Bos	76	55	37	92	117	+10
90–91	Bos	69	51	40	91	98	+26
91–92	Bos	9	9	3	12	16	+9
92–93	Bos	13	11	7	18	25	+4
93–94	Bos	49	50	24	74	54	+12
94–95	Bos	42	27	14	41	72	+7
95–96	Bos	49	26	20	46	31	+3
Totals		726	395	299	694	1241	+82

Playoffs

SSN	TEAM	GP	G	A	PTS.	PIM	+/-
83–84	Van	4	2	0	2	2	
85–86	Van	3	0	0	0	6	
86–87	Bos	4	5	1	6	8	
87–88	Bos	23	9	8	17	51	
88–89	Bos	10	7	2	9	8	
89–90	Bos	21	12	16	28	51	
90–91	Bos	19	16	4	20	36	
92–93	Bos	4	4	1	5	4	
94–95	Bos	5	2	0	2	2	
Totals		93	57	32	89	168	

NEELY, Robert Barry 6–1 210 LW
B. Sarnia, Ont., Nov. 9, 1953

SSN	TEAM	GP	G	A	PTS.	PIM	+/-
73–74	Tor	54	5	7	12	98	-14
74–75	Tor	57	5	16	21	61	-18
75–76	Tor	69	9	13	22	89	-15
76–77	Tor	70	17	16	33	16	-17
77–78	Tor–Col	33	3	7	10	2	-13

SSN	TEAM	GP	G	A	PTS.	PIM	+/-
Totals		283	39	59	98	266	-77

Playoffs

SSN	TEAM	GP	G	A	PTS.	PIM
73–74	Tor	4	1	3	4	0
74–75	Tor	3	0	0	0	2
75–76	Tor	10	3	1	4	7
76–77	Tor	9	1	3	4	6
Totals		26	5	7	12	15

NEILSON, James Anthony (Chief) *6–2 205 D*
B. Big River, Sask., Nov. 28, 1941

SSN	TEAM	GP	G	A	PTS.	PIM	+/-
62–63	NYR	69	5	11	16	38	
63–64	NYR	69	5	24	29	93	
64–65	NYR	62	0	13	13	58	
65–66	NYR	65	4	19	23	84	
66–67	NYR	61	4	11	15	65	
67–68	NYR	67	6	29	35	60	+29
68–69	NYR	76	10	34	44	95	+6
69–70	NYR	62	3	20	23	75	+24
70–71	NYR	77	8	24	32	69	+31
71–72	NYR	78	7	30	37	56	+38
72–73	NYR	52	4	16	20	35	+22
73–74	NYR	72	4	7	11	38	-4
74–75	Cal	72	3	17	20	56	-46
75–76	Cal	26	1	6	7	20	-6
76–77	Clev	47	3	17	20	42	-5
77–78	Clev	68	2	21	23	20	-25
78–79	Edm (WHA)	35	0	5	5	18	
NHL Totals		1023	69	299	368	904	+74
WHA Totals		35	0	5	5	18	

Playoffs

SSN	TEAM	GP	G	A	PTS.	PIM
66–67	NYR	4	1	0	1	0
67–68	NYR	6	1	1	2	4
68–69	NYR	4	0	3	3	5
69–70	NYR	6	0	1	1	8
70–71	NYR	13	0	3	3	30
71–72	NYR	10	0	3	3	8
72–73	NYR	10	0	4	4	2
73–74	NYR	12	0	1	1	4
NHL Totals		65	2	16	18	61

NELSON, Gordon William *5–7 180 D*
B. Kinistino, Sask., May 10, 1947

SSN	TEAM	GP	G	A	PTS.	PIM	+/-
69–70	Tor	3	0	0	0	11	+2

NELSON, Jeffrey Arthur *6–0 190 C*
B. Prince Albert, Sask., Dec. 18, 1972

SSN	TEAM	GP	G	A	PTS.	PIM	+/-
94–95	Wash	10	1	0	1	2	-2
95–96	Wash	33	0	7	7	16	+3
98–99	Nash	9	2	1	3	2	-1
Totals		52	3	8	11	20	0

Playoffs

SSN	TEAM	GP	G	A	PTS.	PIM
95–96	Wash	3	0	0	0	4

NELSON, Todd *6–0 201 D*
B. Prince Albert, Sask., May 15, 1969

SSN	TEAM	GP	G	A	PTS.	PIM	+/-
91–92	Pitt	1	0	0	0	0	0
93–94	Wash	2	1	0	1	2	+1
Totals		3	1	0	1	2	+1

Playoffs

SSN	TEAM	GP	G	A	PTS.	PIM
93–94	Wash	4	0	0	0	0

NEMCHINOV, Sergei *6–0 200 C*
B. Moscow, Soviet Union, Jan. 14, 1964

SSN	TEAM	GP	G	A	PTS.	PIM	+/-
91–92	NYR	73	30	28	58	15	+19
92–93	NYR	81	23	31	54	34	+15
93–94	NYR	76	22	27	49	36	+13
94–95	NYR	47	7	6	13	16	-6
95–96	NYR	78	17	15	32	38	+9
96–97	NYR–Van	69	8	16	24	16	+9
97–98	NYI	74	10	19	29	24	+3
98–99	NYI-NJ	77	12	8	20	28	-13
Totals		575	129	150	279	207	+49

Playoffs

SSN	TEAM	GP	G	A	PTS.	PIM
91–92	NYR	13	1	4	5	8
93–94	NYR	23	2	5	7	6
94–95	NYR	10	4	5	9	2
95–96	NYR	6	0	1	1	2
98–99	NJ	4	0	0	0	0
Totals		56	7	15	22	18

NEMETH, Steve *5–8 170 C*
B. Calgary, Alta., Feb. 11, 1967

SSN	TEAM	GP	G	A	PTS.	PIM	+/-
87–88	NYR	12	2	0	2	2	-4

NEMIROVSKY, David *6–1 176 RW*
B. Toronto, Ont., Aug. 1, 1976

SSN	TEAM	GP	G	A	PTS.	PIM	+/-
95–96	Fla	9	0	2	2	2	-1
96–97	Fla	39	7	7	14	32	+1
97–98	Fla	41	9	12	21	8	-3
98–99	Fla	2	0	0	0	0	+1
Totals		91	16	21	37	42	-2

Playoffs

SSN	TEAM	GP	G	A	PTS.	PIM
96–97	Fla	3	1	0	1	0

NESTERENKO, Eric Paul *6–2 197 RW*
B. Flin Flon, Man., Oct. 31, 1933

SSN	TEAM	GP	G	A	PTS.	PIM	+/-
51–52	Tor	1	0	0	0	0	
52–53	Tor	35	10	6	16	27	
53–54	Tor	68	14	9	23	70	
54–55	Tor	62	15	15	30	99	
55–56	Tor	40	4	6	10	65	
56–57	Chi	24	8	15	23	32	
57–58	Chi	70	20	18	38	104	
58–59	Chi	70	16	18	34	81	
59–60	Chi	61	13	23	36	71	
60–61	Chi	68	19	19	38	125	
61–62	Chi	68	15	14	29	97	
62–63	Chi	67	12	15	27	103	
63–64	Chi	70	7	19	26	93	
64–65	Chi	56	14	16	30	63	
65–66	Chi	67	15	25	40	58	
66–67	Chi	68	14	23	37	38	
67–68	Chi	71	11	25	36	37	+3
68–69	Chi	72	15	17	32	29	+5
69–70	Chi	67	16	18	34	26	+17
70–71	Chi	76	8	15	23	28	+13
71–72	Chi	38	4	8	12	27	+7
73–74	LA (WHA)	29	2	5	7	8	
NHL Totals		1219	250	324	574	1273	+45
WHA Totals		29	2	5	7	8	

Playoffs

SSN	TEAM	GP	G	A	PTS.	PIM
53–54	Tor	5	0	1	1	9
54–55	Tor	4	0	1	1	6
58–59	Chi	6	2	2	4	8
59–60	Chi	4	0	0	0	2
60–61	Chi	11	2	3	5	6
61–62	Chi	12	0	5	5	22
62–63	Chi	6	2	3	5	8
63–64	Chi	7	2	1	3	8
64–65	Chi	14	2	2	4	16
65–66	Chi	6	1	0	1	4
66–67	Chi	6	1	2	3	2
67–68	Chi	10	0	1	1	2
69–70	Chi	7	1	2	3	4
70–71	Chi	18	0	1	1	19
71–72	Chi	8	0	0	0	11
Totals		124	13	24	37	127

NETHERY, Lance *6–1 185 C*
B. Toronto, Ont., June 28, 1957

SSN	TEAM	GP	G	A	PTS.	PIM	+/-
80–81	NYR	33	11	12	23	12	0
81–82	NYR–Edm	8	0	2	2	2	0
Totals		41	11	14	25	14	0

Playoffs

SSN	TEAM	GP	G	A	PTS.	PIM
80–81	NYR	14	5	3	8	9

NEUFELD, Ray Matthew *6–3 210 RW*
B. St. Boniface, Man., Apr. 15, 1959

SSN	TEAM	GP	G	A	PTS.	PIM	+/-
79–80	Hart	8	1	0	1	0	-2
80–81	Hart	52	5	10	15	44	+1
81–82	Hart	19	4	3	7	4	-7
82–83	Hart	80	26	31	57	86	-34
83–84	Hart	80	27	42	69	97	-18
84–85	Hart	76	27	35	62	129	-29
85–86	Hart–Winn	76	25	38	63	102	-20
86–87	Winn	80	18	18	36	105	-13
87–88	Winn	78	18	18	36	169	-29
88–89	Winn-Bos	45	6	5	11	80	-11
89–90	Bos	1	0	0	0	0	0
Totals		595	157	200	357	816	-162

Playoffs

SSN	TEAM	GP	G	A	PTS.	PIM
79–80	Hart	2	1	0	1	0
85–86	Winn	3	2	0	2	10
86–87	Winn	8	1	1	2	30

SSN	TEAM	GP	G	A	PTS.	PIM
87–88	Winn	5	2	2	4	6
88–89	Bos	10	2	3	5	9
Totals		28	8	6	14	55

*NEVILLE, Michael R. *F*
B. Toronto, Ont.

SSN	TEAM	GP	G	A	PTS.	PIM
17–18	Tor	1	1	0	1	0
24–25	Tor	12	1	0	1	0
25–26	Tor	33	3	3	6	8
30–31	NYA	16	1	0	1	2
Totals		62	6	3	9	14

Playoffs

SSN	TEAM	GP	G	A	PTS.	PIM
24–25	Tor	2	0	0	0	0

NEVIN, Robert Frank *6–0 190 RW*
B. South Porcupine, Ont., Mar. 18, 1938

SSN	TEAM	GP	G	A	PTS.	PIM	+/-
57–58	Tor	4	0	0	0	0	
58–59	Tor	2	0	0	0	2	
60–61	Tor	68	21	37	58	13	
61–62	Tor	69	15	30	45	10	
62–63	Tor	58	12	21	33	4	
63–64	Tor–NYR	63	12	16	28	35	
64–65	NYR	64	16	14	30	28	
65–66	NYR	69	29	33	62	10	
66–67	NYR	67	20	24	44	6	
67–68	NYR	74	28	30	58	20	+15
68–69	NYR	71	31	25	56	14	+13
69–70	NYR	68	18	19	37	8	+1
70–71	NYR	78	21	25	46	10	+17
71–72	Minn	72	15	19	34	6	+7
72–73	Minn	66	5	13	18	0	-12
73–74	LA	78	20	30	50	12	+8
74–75	LA	80	31	41	72	19	+36
75–76	LA	77	13	42	55	14	+10
76–77	Edm (WHA)	13	3	2	5	0	
NHL Totals		1128	307	419	726	211	+95
WHA Totals		13	3	2	5	0	

Playoffs

SSN	TEAM	GP	G	A	PTS.	PIM
60–61	Tor	5	1	0	1	2
61–62	Tor	12	2	4	6	6
62–63	Tor	10	3	0	3	2
66–67	NYR	4	0	3	3	2
67–68	NYR	6	0	3	3	4
68–69	NYR	4	0	2	2	0
69–70	NYR	6	1	1	2	2
70–71	NYR	13	5	3	8	0
71–72	Minn	7	1	1	2	0
73–74	LA	5	1	0	1	2
74–75	LA	3	0	0	0	0
75–76	LA	9	2	1	3	4
Totals		84	16	18	34	24

NEWBERRY, John *6–0 190 C*
B. Port Alberni, B.C., Apr. 8, 1962

SSN	TEAM	GP	G	A	PTS.	PIM	+/-
83–84	Mont	3	0	0	0	0	0
84–85	Mont	16	0	4	4	6	+3
85–86	Hart	3	0	0	0	0	-4
Totals		22	0	4	4	6	-1

Playoffs

SSN	TEAM	GP	G	A	PTS.	PIM
82–83	Mont	2	0	0	0	0

NEWELL, Gordon Richard (Rick) *5–11 180 D*
B. Winnipeg, Man., Feb. 18, 1948

SSN	TEAM	GP	G	A	PTS.	PIM	+/-
72–73	Det	3	0	0	0	0	-1
73–74	Det	4	0	0	0	0	-1
74–75	Phoe (WHA)	25	0	4	4	39	
NHL Totals		7	0	0	0	0	-2
WHA Totals		25	0	4	4	39	

Playoffs

SSN	TEAM	GP	G	A	PTS.	PIM
74–75	Phoe (WHA)	5	0	1	1	2

NEWMAN, Daniel Kenneth *6–1 195 LW*
B. Windsor, Ont., Jan. 26, 1952

SSN	TEAM	GP	G	A	PTS.	PIM	+/-
76–77	NYR	41	9	8	17	37	-4
77–78	NYR	59	5	13	18	22	-11
78–79	Mont	16	0	2	2	4	-1
79–80	Edm	10	3	1	4	0	-1
Totals		126	17	24	41	63	-17

Playoffs

SSN	TEAM	GP	G	A	PTS.	PIM
.77–78	NYR	3	0	0	0	4

*NEWMAN, John D

SSN	TEAM	GP	G	A	PTS.	PIM	+/-
30–31	Det	8	1	1	2	0	

NICHOL, Scott 5–8 160 C
B. Edmonton, Alta., Dec. 31, 1974

SSN	TEAM	GP	G	A	PTS.	PIM	+/-
95–96	Buf	2	0	0	0	10	0
97–98	Buf	3	0	0	0	4	0
Totals		5	0	0	0	14	0

NICHOLLS, Bernie Irvine 6–1 185 C
B. Haliburton, Ont., June 24, 1961

SSN	TEAM	GP	G	A	PTS.	PIM	+/-
81–82	LA	22	14	18	32	27	+2
82–83	LA	71	28	22	50	124	-23
83–84	LA	78	41	54	95	83	-21
84–85	LA	80	46	54	100	76	-4
85–86	LA	80	36	61	97	78	-5
86–87	LA	80	33	48	81	101	-16
87–88	LA	65	32	46	78	114	+2
88–89	LA	79	70	80	150	96	+30
89–90	LA–NYR	79	39	73	112	86	-9
90–91	NYR	71	25	48	73	96	+5
91–92	NYR–Edm	50	20	29	49	60	+4
92–93	Edm–NJ	69	13	47	60	80	-13
93–94	NJ	61	19	27	46	86	+24
94–95	Chi	48	22	29	51	32	+4
95–96	Chi	59	19	41	60	60	+11
96–97	SJ	65	12	33	45	63	-21
97–98	SJ	60	6	22	28	38	-4
98–99	SJ	10	0	2	2	4	-4
Totals		1127	475	734	1209	1294	-38

Playoffs

SSN	TEAM	GP	G	A	PTS.	PIM
81–82	LA	10	4	0	4	23
84–85	LA	3	1	1	2	9
86–87	LA	5	2	5	7	6
87–88	LA	5	2	6	8	11
88–89	LA	11	7	9	16	12
89–90	NYR	10	7	5	12	16
90–91	NYR	5	4	3	7	8
91–92	Edm	16	8	11	19	25
92–93	NJ	5	0	0	0	6
93–94	NJ	16	4	9	13	28
94–95	Chi	16	1	11	12	8
95–96	Chi	10	2	7	9	4
97–98	SJ	6	0	5	5	8
Totals		118	42	72	114	164

NICHOLSON, Allan Douglas 6–1 180 LW
B. Estevan, Sask., Apr. 26, 1936

SSN	TEAM	GP	G	A	PTS.	PIM
55–56	Bos	14	0	0	0	4
56–57	Bos	5	0	1	1	0
Totals		19	0	1	1	4

NICHOLSON, Edward George 5–7 171 D
B. Portsmouth, Ont., Sept. 9, 1923

SSN	TEAM	GP	G	A	PTS.	PIM
47–48	Det	1	0	0	0	0

NICHOLSON, Graeme Butte 6–0 185 D
B. North Bay, Ont., Jan. 13, 1958

SSN	TEAM	GP	G	A	PTS.	PIM	+/-
78–79	Bos	1	0	0	0	0	0
81–82	Col	41	2	7	9	51	-16
82–83	NYR	10	0	0	0	9	-5
Totals		52	2	7	9	60	-21

*NICHOLSON, John Ivan 5–9 170 LW
B. Charlottetown, P.E.I., Sept. 9, 1914

SSN	TEAM	GP	G	A	PTS.	PIM
37–38	Chi	2	1	0	1	0

NICHOLSON, Neil Andrews 5–11 180 D
B. Saint John, N.B., Sept. 12, 1949

SSN	TEAM	GP	G	A	PTS.	PIM	+/-
72–73	NYI	30	3	1	4	23	-22
73–74	NYI	8	0	0	0	0	+2
77–78	NYI	1	0	0	0	0	+2
Totals		39	3	1	4	23	-18

Playoffs

SSN	TEAM	GP	G	A	PTS.	PIM
69–70	Oak	2	0	0	0	0

NICHOLSON, Paul 6–0 190 LW
B. London, Ont., Feb. 16, 1954

SSN	TEAM	GP	G	A	PTS.	PIM	+/-
74–75	Wash	39	4	5	9	7	-29
75–76	Wash	14	0	2	2	9	-4
76–77	Wash	9	0	1	1	2	-6
Totals		62	4	8	12	18	-39

NICKULAS, Eric 5–11 190 C
B. Cape Cod, Mass., Mar. 25, 1975

SSN	TEAM	GP	G	A	PTS.	PIM	+/-
98–99	Bos	2	0	0	0	0	0

Playoffs

SSN	TEAM	GP	G	A	PTS.	PIM
98–99	Bos	1	0	0	0	2

NIECKAR, Barry 6–3 200 LW
B. Rama, Sask., Dec. 16, 1967

SSN	TEAM	GP	G	A	PTS.	PIM	+/-
92–93	Hart	2	0	0	0	2	-2
94–95	Calg	3	0	0	0	12	0
96–97	Ana	2	0	0	0	5	0
97–98	Ana	1	0	0	0	2	0
Totals		8	0	0	0	21	-2

NIEDERMAYER, Rob 6–2 201 C
B. Cassiar, B.C., Dec. 28, 1974

SSN	TEAM	GP	G	A	PTS.	PIM	+/-
93–94	Fla	65	9	17	26	51	-11
94–95	Fla	48	4	6	10	36	-13
95–96	Fla	82	26	35	61	107	+1
96–97	Fla	60	14	24	38	54	+4
97–98	Fla	33	8	7	15	41	-9
98–99	Fla	82	18	33	51	50	-13
Totals		370	79	122	201	339	-41

Playoffs

SSN	TEAM	GP	G	A	PTS.	PIM
96–97	Fla	22	5	3	8	12
97–98	Fla	5	2	1	3	6
Totals		27	7	4	11	18

NIEDERMAYER, Scott 6–0 200 D
B. Edmonton, Alta., Aug. 31, 1973

SSN	TEAM	GP	G	A	PTS.	PIM	+/-
91–92	NJ	4	0	1	1	2	+1
92–93	NJ	80	11	29	40	47	+8
93–94	NJ	81	10	36	46	42	+34
94–95	NJ	48	4	15	19	18	+19
95–96	NJ	79	8	25	33	46	+5
96–97	NJ	81	5	30	35	64	-4
97–98	NJ	81	14	43	57	27	+5
98–99	NJ	72	11	35	46	26	+16
Totals		526	63	214	277	272	+84

Playoffs

SSN	TEAM	GP	G	A	PTS.	PIM
92–93	NJ	5	0	3	3	2
93–94	NJ	20	2	2	4	8
94–95	NJ	20	4	7	11	10
96–97	NJ	10	2	4	6	6
97–98	NJ	6	0	2	2	4
98–99	NJ	7	1	3	4	18
Totals		68	9	21	30	48

NIEKAMP, James Lawrence 6–0 170 D
B. Detroit, Mich., Mar. 11, 1946

SSN	TEAM	GP	G	A	PTS.	PIM	+/-
70–71	Det	24	0	2	2	27	-14
71–72	Det	5	0	0	0	0	-3
72–73	LA (WHA)	78	7	22	29	155	
73–74	LA (WHA)	76	2	19	21	95	
74–75	Phoe (WHA)	71	2	26	28	66	
75–76	Phoe (WHA)	79	4	14	18	77	
76–77	Phoe (WHA)	79	1	15	16	91	
NHL Totals		29	0	2	2	27	-17
WHA Totals		383	16	96	112	484	

Playoffs

SSN	TEAM	GP	G	A	PTS.	PIM
72–73	LA (WHA)	6	2	1	3	10
75–76	Phoe (WHA)	5	1	0	1	0
WHA Totals		11	3	1	4	10

NIELSEN, Jeff 6–0 200 RW
B. Grand Rapids, Mich., Sept. 20, 1971

SSN	TEAM	GP	G	A	PTS.	PIM	+/-
96–97	NYR	2	0	0	0	2	-1
97–98	Ana	32	4	5	9	16	-1
98–99	Ana	80	5	4	9	34	-12
Totals		114	9	9	18	52	-14

Playoffs

SSN	TEAM	GP	G	A	PTS.	PIM
98–99	Ana	4	0	0	0	2

NIELSEN, Kirk 6–1 205 RW
B. Grand Rapids, Mich., Oct. 19, 1973

SSN	TEAM	GP	G	A	PTS.	PIM	+/-
97–98	Bos	6	0	0	0	0	-1

NIENHUIS, Kraig 6–2 205 LW
B. Sarnia, Ont., May 9, 1961

SSN	TEAM	GP	G	A	PTS.	PIM	+/-
85–86	Bos	70	16	14	30	37	-10
86–87	Bos	16	4	2	6	2	-5
87–88	Bos	1	0	0	0	0	-1
Totals		87	20	16	36	39	-16

Playoffs

SSN	TEAM	GP	G	A	PTS.	PIM
85–86	Bos	2	0	0	0	14

NIEUWENDYK, Joe 6–1 195 C
B. Oshawa, Ont., Sept. 10, 1966

SSN	TEAM	GP	G	A	PTS.	PIM	+/-
86–87	Calg	9	5	1	6	0	0
87–88	Calg	75	51	41	92	23	+20
88–89	Calg	77	51	31	82	40	+25
89–90	Calg	79	45	50	95	40	+32
90–91	Calg	79	45	40	85	36	+19
91–92	Calg	69	22	34	56	55	-1
92–93	Calg	79	38	37	75	52	+9
93–94	Calg	64	36	39	75	51	+19
94–95	Calg	46	21	29	50	33	+11
95–96	Dal	52	14	18	32	41	-17
96–97	Dal	66	30	21	51	32	-5
97–98	Dal	73	39	30	69	30	+16
98–99	Dal	67	28	27	55	34	+11
Totals		769	395	377	772	435	+139

Playoffs

SSN	TEAM	GP	G	A	PTS.	PIM
86–87	Calg	6	2	2	4	0
87–88	Calg	8	3	4	7	2
88–89	Calg	22	10	4	14	10
89–90	Calg	6	4	6	10	4
90–91	Calg	7	4	1	5	10
92–93	Calg	6	3	6	9	10
93–94	Calg	6	2	2	4	0
94–95	Calg	5	4	3	7	0
96–97	Dal	7	2	2	4	6
97–98	Dal	1	1	0	1	0
98–99	Dal	23	11	10	21	19
Totals		97	46	40	86	61

*NIGHBOR, Frank (Dutch) C
B. Pembroke, Ont., Jan. 26, 1893

SSN	TEAM	GP	G	A	PTS.	PIM
17–18	Ott	9	11	0	11	3
18–19	Ott	18	18	4	22	27
19–20	Ott	23	26	7	33	18
20–21	Ott	24	18	3	21	10
21–22	Ott	20	7	9	16	16
22–23	Ott	22	11	5	16	16
23–24	Ott	20	10	3	13	14
24–25	Ott	26	5	2	7	18
25–26	Ott	35	12	13	25	40
26–27	Ott	38	6	6	12	26
27–28	Ott	42	8	5	13	46
28–29	Ott	30	1	4	5	22
29–30	Ott–Tor	41	2	0	2	10
Totals		348	135	61	196	266

Playoffs

SSN	TEAM	GP	G	A	PTS.	PIM
18–19	Ott	2	0	3	3	0
19–20	Ott	5	6	1	7	3
20–21	Ott	7	1	3	4	2
21–22	Ott	2	2	0	2	4
22–23	Ott	8	1	2	3	10
23–24	Ott	2	0	1	1	2
25–26	Ott	2	0	0	0	2
26–27	Ott	6	1	0	1	2
27–28	Ott	2	0	0	0	2
Totals		36	11	10	21	27

NIGRO, Frank 5–9 180 C
B. Richmond Hill, Ont., Feb. 11, 1960

SSN	TEAM	GP	G	A	PTS.	PIM	+/-
82–83	Tor	51	6	15	21	23	-1
83–84	Tor	17	2	3	5	16	-4
Totals		68	8	18	26	39	-5

Playoffs

SSN	TEAM	GP	G	A	PTS.	PIM
82–83	Tor	3	0	0	0	2

NIINIMAA, Janne 6–1 196 D
B. Raahe, Finland, May 22, 1975

SSN	TEAM	GP	G	A	PTS.	PIM	+/-
96–97	Phil	77	4	40	44	58	+12
97–98	Phil–Edm	77	4	39	43	62	+13
98–99	Edm	81	4	24	28	88	+7
Totals		235	12	103	115	208	+32

Playoffs

SSN	TEAM	GP	G	A	PTS.	PIM
96–97	Phil	19	1	12	13	16
97–98	Edm	11	1	1	2	12
98–99	Edm	4	0	0	0	0
Totals		34	2	13	15	30

NIKOLISHIN, Andrei 5–11 180 LW
B. Vorkuta, USSR, Mar. 25, 1973

SSN	TEAM	GP	G	A	PTS.	PIM	+/-
94–95	Hart	39	8	10	18	10	+7
95–96	Hart	61	14	37	51	34	-2
96–97	Hart–Wash	71	9	19	28	32	+3
97–98	Wash	38	6	10	16	14	+1
98–99	Wash	73	8	27	35	28	0
Totals		282	45	103	148	118	+9

Playoffs

| 97–98 | Wash | 21 | 1 | 13 | 14 | 12 | |

NIKULIN, Igor 6–1 190 RW
B. Cherepovets, USSR, Aug. 26, 1972

@statplayoff:**Playoffs**

| 96–97 | Ana | 1 | 0 | 0 | 0 | 0 | |

NILAN, Christopher John 6–0 205 RW
B. Boston, Mass., Feb. 9, 1958

79–80	Mont	15	0	2	2	50	-1
80–81	Mont	57	7	8	15	262	+7
81–82	Mont	49	7	4	11	204	+6
82–83	Mont	66	6	8	14	213	-10
83–84	Mont	76	16	10	26	338	-4
84–85	Mont	77	21	16	37	358	+3
85–86	Mont	72	19	15	34	274	+10
86–87	Mont	44	4	16	20	266	+2
87–88	Mont–NYR	72	10	10	20	305	-2
88–89	NYR	38	7	7	14	177	-8
89–90	NYR	25	1	2	3	59	-8
90–91	Bos	41	6	9	15	277	+4
91–92	Bos–Mont	56	6	8	14	260	-6
Totals		688	110	115	225	3043	-7

Playoffs

79–80	Mont	5	0	0	0	2	
80–81	Mont	2	0	0	0	0	
81–82	Mont	5	1	1	2	22	
82–83	Mont	3	0	0	0	5	
83–84	Mont	15	1	0	1	81	
84–85	Mont	12	2	1	3	81	
85–86	Mont	18	1	2	3	141	
86–87	Mont	17	3	0	3	75	
88–89	NYR	4	0	1	1	38	
89–90	NYR	4	0	1	1	19	
90–91	Bos	19	0	2	2	62	
91–92	Mont	9	0	1	1	15	
Totals		111	8	9	17	541	

NILL, James Edward 6–0 185 RW
B. Hanna, Alta., Apr. 11, 1958

81–82	StL–Van	69	10	14	24	132	-13
82–83	Van	65	7	15	22	136	-18
83–84	Van–Bos	78	12	8	20	159	-12
84–85	Bos–Winn	69	9	17	26	100	-9
85–86	Winn	61	6	8	14	75	-6
86–87	Winn	36	3	4	7	52	+1
87–88	Winn–Det	60	3	12	15	99	-5
88–89	Det	71	8	7	15	83	-1
89–90	Det	15	0	2	2	18	-3
Totals		524	58	87	145	854	-66

Playoffs

81–82	Van	16	4	3	7	67	
82–83	Van	4	0	0	0	6	
83–84	Bos	3	0	0	0	4	
84–85	Winn	8	0	1	1	28	
85–86	Winn	3	0	0	0	4	
86–87	Winn	3	0	0	0	7	
87–88	Det	16	6	1	7	62	
88–89	Det	6	0	0	0	25	
Totals		59	10	5	15	203	

NILSON, Marcus 6–1 183 RW
B. Stockholm, Sweden, March 1, 1978

| 98–99 | Fla | 8 | 1 | 1 | 2 | 5 | +2 |

NILSSON, Kent 6–1 195 C
B. Nynasham, Sweden, Aug. 31, 1956

77–78	Winn (WHA)	80	42	65	107	8	
78–79	Winn (WHA)	78	39	68	107	8	
79–80	Atl	80	40	53	93	10	-3
80–81	Calg	80	49	82	131	26	+15
81–82	Calg	41	26	29	55	8	-20
82–83	Calg	80	46	58	104	10	+5
83–84	Calg	67	31	49	80	22	-24
84–85	Calg	77	37	62	99	14	-4

85–86	Minn	61	16	44	60	10	+4
86–87	Minn–Edm	61	18	45	63	16	+12
94–95	Edm	6	1	0	1	0	-5
NHL Totals		553	264	422	686	116	-20
WHA Totals		158	81	133	214	16	

Playoffs

77–78	Winn (WHA)	9	2	8	10	10	
78–79	Winn (WHA)	10	3	11	14	4	
79–80	Atl	4	0	0	0	2	
80–81	Calg	14	3	9	12	2	
81–82	Calg	3	0	3	3	2	
82–83	Calg	9	1	11	12	2	
84–85	Calg	3	0	1	1	0	
85–86	Minn	5	1	4	5	0	
86–87	Edm	21	6	13	19	6	
NHL Totals		59	11	41	52	14	
WHA Totals		19	5	19	23	14	

NILSSON, Ulf Gosta 5–11 175 C
B. Nynasham, Sweden, May 11, 1950

74–75	Winn (WHA)	78	26	94	120	79	
75–76	Winn (WHA)	78	38	76	114	84	
76–77	Winn (WHA)	71	39	85	124	89	
77–78	Winn (WHA)	73	37	89	126	89	
78–79	NYR	59	27	39	66	21	+17
79–80	NYR	50	14	44	58	20	+15
80–81	NYR	51	14	25	39	42	-3
82–83	NYR	10	2	4	6	2	-1
NHL Totals		170	57	112	169	85	+28
WHA Totals		300	140	344	484	341	

Playoffs

75–76	Winn (WHA)	13	7	19	26	6	
76–77	Winn (WHA)	20	6	21	27	33	
77–78	Winn (WHA)	9	1	13	14	12	
78–79	NYR	2	0	0	0	2	
79–80	NYR	9	0	6	6	2	
80–81	NYR	14	8	8	16	23	
NHL Totals		25	8	14	22	27	
WHA Totals		42	14	53	67	51	

NISTICO, Louis Charles 5–7 170 C
B. Thunder Bay, Ont., Jan. 25, 1953

73–74	Tor (WHA)	13	1	3	4	14	
74–75	Tor (WHA)	29	11	11	22	75	
75–76	Tor (WHA)	65	12	22	34	120	
76–77	Birm (WHA)	79	20	36	56	166	
77–78	Col	3	0	0	0	0	0
NHL Totals		3	0	0	0	0	0
WHA Totals		186	44	72	116	375	

Playoffs

| 74–75 | Tor (WHA) | 6 | 6 | 1 | 7 | 19 | |

*NOBLE, Reginald (Reg) 5–8 180 LW
B. Collingwood, Ont., June 23, 1895

17–18	Tor	20	28	0	28	23	
18–19	Tor	17	11	3	14	35	
19–20	Tor	24	24	7	31	51	
20–21	Tor	24	20	6	26	54	
21–22	Tor	24	17	8	25	10	
22–23	Tor	24	12	10	22	41	
23–24	Tor	23	12	3	15	23	
24–25	Tor–Mont M	30	8	6	14	62	
25–26	Mont M	30	9	9	18	36	
26–27	Mont M	44	3	3	6	12	
27–28	Det	44	6	8	14	63	
28–29	Det	44	6	4	10	52	
29–30	Det	43	6	4	10	72	
30–31	Det	44	2	5	7	42	
31–32	Det	48	3	3	6	72	
32–33	Det–Mont M	32	0	0	0	22	
Totals		515	167	79	246	670	

Playoffs

17–18	Tor	7	2	1	3	3	
20–21	Tor	2	0	0	0	0	
21–22	Tor	7	0	2	2	20	
25–26	Mont M	8	0	0	0	10	
26–27	Mont M	2	0	0	0	2	
28–29	Det	2	0	0	0	0	
31–32	Det	2	0	0	0	0	
Totals		30	2	3	5	37	

NOEL, Claude 5–11 165 C
B. Kirkland Lake, Ont., Oct. 31, 1955

| 79–80 | Wash | 7 | 0 | 0 | 0 | 0 | -3 |

NOLAN, Owen 6–1 201 RW
B. Belfast, N. Ireland, Feb. 12, 1972

90–91	Que	59	3	10	13	109	-19
91–92	Que	75	42	31	73	183	-9
92–93	Que	73	36	41	77	185	-1
93–94	Que	6	2	2	4	8	+2
94–95	Que	46	30	19	49	46	+21
95–96	Col A–SJ	81	33	36	69	146	-33
96–97	SJ	72	31	32	63	155	-19
97–98	SJ	75	14	27	41	144	-2
98–99	SJ	78	19	26	45	129	+16
Totals		565	210	224	434	1105	-44

Playoffs

92–93	Que	5	1	0	1	2	
94–95	Que	6	2	3	5	6	
97–98	SJ	6	2	2	4	26	
98–99	SJ	6	1	1	2	6	
Totals		23	6	6	12	40	

*NOLAN, Patrick F

| 21–22 | Tor | 2 | 0 | 0 | 0 | 0 | |

NOLAN, Theodore John (Ted) 6–0 185 C
B. Sault Ste. Marie, Ont., Apr. 7, 1958

81–82	Det	41	4	13	17	45	-6
83–84	Det	19	1	2	3	26	-11
85–86	Pitt	18	1	1	2	34	-1
Totals		78	6	16	22	105	-18

NOLET, Simon Laurent 5–9 185 RW
B. St. Odilon, Que., Nov. 23, 1941

67–68	Phil	4	0	0	0	2	-1
68–69	Phil	35	4	10	14	8	-10
69–70	Phil	56	22	22	44	36	+12
70–71	Phil	74	9	19	28	42	-1
71–72	Phil	67	23	20	43	22	+6
72–73	Phil	70	16	20	36	6	-3
73–74	Phil	52	19	17	36	13	+28
74–75	KC	72	26	32	58	30	-52
75–76	KC–Pitt	80	19	23	42	18	-2
76–77	Col	52	12	19	31	10	0
Totals		562	150	182	332	187	-23

Playoffs

67–68	Phil	1	0	0	0	0	
70–71	Phil	4	2	1	3	0	
72–73	Phil	11	3	1	4	4	
73–74	Phil	15	1	1	2	4	
75–76	Pitt	3	0	0	0	0	
Totals		34	6	3	9	8	

NOONAN, Brian 6–1 200 RW
B. Boston, Mass., May 29, 1965

87–88	Chi	77	10	20	30	44	-27
88–89	Chi	45	4	12	16	28	-2
89–90	Chi	8	0	2	2	6	0
90–91	Chi	7	0	4	4	2	-1
91–92	Chi	65	19	12	31	81	+9
92–93	Chi	63	16	14	30	82	+3
93–94	Chi–NYR	76	18	23	41	69	+7
94–95	NYR	45	14	13	27	26	-3
95–96	StL	81	13	22	35	84	+2
96–97	StL–NYR–Van	73	12	22	-3	34	34
97–98	Van	82	10	15	25	62	-19
98–99	Phoe	7	0	0	0	0	-3
Totals		629	116	159	275	518	-37

Playoffs

87–88	Chi	3	0	0	0	4	
88–89	Chi	1	0	0	0	0	
91–92	Chi	18	6	9	15	30	
92–93	Chi	4	3	0	3	4	
93–94	NYR	22	4	7	11	17	
94–95	NYR	5	0	0	0	8	
95–96	StL	13	4	1	5	10	
98–99	Phoe	5	0	2	2	4	
Totals		71	17	19	36	77	

NORDMARK, Robert 6–1 200 D
B. Lulea, Sweden, Aug. 20, 1962

| 87–88 | StL | 67 | 3 | 18 | 21 | 60 | -6 |

SSN	TEAM	GP	G	A	PTS.	PIM	+/-
88–89	Van	80	6	35	41	97	-4
89–90	Van	44	2	11	13	34	-16
90–91	Van	45	2	6	8	63	-10
Totals		236	13	70	83	254	-36

Playoffs

SSN	TEAM	GP	G	A	PTS.	PIM	+/-
88–89	Van	7	3	2	5	8	

NORDSTROM, Peter 6–1 200 C
B. Munkfors, Sweden, July 26, 1974

SSN	TEAM	GP	G	A	PTS.	PIM	+/-
98–99	Bos	2	0	0	0	0	-1

NORIS, Joseph S. 6–0 185 D
B. Denver, Colo., Oct. 26, 1951

SSN	TEAM	GP	G	A	PTS.	PIM	+/-
71–72	Pitt	35	2	5	7	20	-8
72–73	StL	2	0	0	0	0	-2
73–74	Buf	18	0	0	0	2	-4
75–76	SD (WHA)	80	28	40	68	24	
76–77	SD (WHA)	73	35	57	92	30	
77–78	Birm (WHA)	45	9	19	28	6	
NHL Totals		55	2	5	7	22	-14
WHA Totals		198	72	116	188	60	

Playoffs

SSN	TEAM	GP	G	A	PTS.	PIM	+/-
75–76	SD (WHA)	11	2	4	6	6	
76–77	SD (WHA)	7	2	1	3	6	
WHA Totals		18	4	5	9	12	

NORRIS, Dwayne Carl 5–10 175 RW
B. St. John's, Nfld., Jan. 8, 1970

SSN	TEAM	GP	G	A	PTS.	PIM	+/-
93–94	Que	4	1	1	2	4	+1
94–95	Que	13	1	2	3	2	+1
95–96	Ana	3	0	1	1	2	0
Totals		20	2	4	6	8	+2

NORRISH, Rod 5–10 185 LW
B. Saskatoon, Sask., Nov. 27, 1951

SSN	TEAM	GP	G	A	PTS.	PIM	+/-
73–74	Minn	9	2	1	3	0	-3
74–75	Minn	12	1	2	3	2	-2
Totals		21	3	3	6	2	-5

NORSTROM, Mattias 6–1 205 D
B. Mora, Sweden, Jan. 2, 1972

SSN	TEAM	GP	G	A	PTS.	PIM	+/-
93–94	NYR	9	0	2	2	6	0
94–95	NYR	9	0	3	3	2	+2
95–96	NYR–LA	36	2	2	4	40	-3
96–97	LA	80	1	21	22	84	-4
97–98	LA	73	1	12	13	90	+14
98–99	LA	78	2	5	7	36	-10
Totals		285	6	45	51	258	-1

Playoffs

SSN	TEAM	GP	G	A	PTS.	PIM	+/-
94–95	NYR	3	0	0	0	0	
97–98	LA	4	0	0	0	2	
Totals		7	0	0	0	2	

*NORTHCOTT, Lawrence (Baldy) 6–0 184 LW
B. Calgary, Alta., Sept. 7, 1908

SSN	TEAM	GP	G	A	PTS.	PIM	+/-
28–29	Mont M	6	0	0	0	0	
29–30	Mont M	41	10	1	11	6	
30–31	Mont M	22	7	3	10	15	
31–32	Mont M	47	19	6	25	33	
32–33	Mont M	47	22	21	43	30	
33–34	Mont M	47	20	13	33	27	
34–35	Mont M	47	9	14	23	44	
35–36	Mont M	48	15	21	36	41	
36–37	Mont M	48	15	14	29	18	
37–38	Mont M	47	11	12	23	50	
38–39	Chi	46	5	7	12	9	
Totals		446	133	112	245	273	

Playoffs

SSN	TEAM	GP	G	A	PTS.	PIM	+/-
29–30	Mont M	4	0	0	0	4	
30–31	Mont M	2	0	1	1	0	
31–32	Mont M	4	1	2	3	4	
32–33	Mont M	2	0	0	0	4	
33–34	Mont M	4	2	0	2	0	
34–35	Mont M	7	4	1	5	0	
35–36	Mont M	3	0	0	0	0	
36–37	Mont M	5	1	1	2	2	
Totals		31	8	5	13	14	

NORTON, Jeffrey Zaccari 6–2 200 D
B. Acton, Mass., Nov. 25, 1965

SSN	TEAM	GP	G	A	PTS.	PIM	+/-
87–88	NYI	15	1	6	7	14	+3
88–89	NYI	69	1	30	31	74	-24
89–90	NYI	60	4	49	53	65	-9
90–91	NYI	44	3	25	28	16	-13
91–92	NYI	28	1	18	19	18	+2
92–93	NYI	66	12	38	50	45	-3
93–94	SJ	64	7	33	40	36	+16
94–95	SJ-StL	48	3	27	30	72	+22
95–96	StL-Edm	66	8	23	31	42	+9
96–97	Edm-TB	75	2	16	18	58	-7
97–98	TB-Fla	56	4	13	17	44	-32
98–99	Fla-SJ	72	4	18	22	44	+2
Totals		663	50	296	346	528	-34

Playoffs

SSN	TEAM	GP	G	A	PTS.	PIM	+/-
87–88	NYI	3	0	2	2	13	
89–90	NYI	4	1	3	4	17	
92–93	NYI	10	1	1	2	4	
93–94	SJ	14	1	5	6	20	
94–95	StL	7	1	1	2	11	
98–99	SJ	6	0	7	7	10	
Totals		44	4	19	23	75	

NORWICH, Craig Richard 5–11 175 D
B. New York, N.Y., Dec. 15, 1955

SSN	TEAM	GP	G	A	PTS.	PIM	+/-
77–78	Cin (WHA)	65	7	23	30	48	
78–79	Cin (WHA)	80	6	51	57	73	
79–80	Winn	70	10	35	45	36	-11
80–81	StL–Col	34	7	23	30	24	+5
NHL Totals		104	17	58	75	60	-6
WHA Totals		145	13	74	87	121	

Playoffs

SSN	TEAM	GP	G	A	PTS.	PIM	+/-
78–79	Cin (WHA)	3	0	1	1	4	

NORWOOD, Lee Charles 6–1 198 D
B. Oakland, Cal., Feb. 2, 1960

SSN	TEAM	GP	G	A	PTS.	PIM	+/-
80–81	Que	11	1	1	2	9	-3
81–82	Que–Wash	28	7	10	17	127	+8
82–83	Wash	8	0	1	1	14	-3
85–86	StL	71	5	24	29	134	+7
86–87	Det	57	6	21	27	163	-23
87–88	Det	51	9	22	31	131	+4
88–89	Det	66	10	32	42	100	+6
89–90	Det	64	8	14	22	95	+14
90–91	Det-NJ	49	6	9	15	137	+5
91–92	Hart-StL	50	3	11	14	110	+14
92–93	StL	32	3	7	10	63	-5
93–94	Calg	16	0	1	1	16	+3
Totals		503	58	153	211	1099	+27

Playoffs

SSN	TEAM	GP	G	A	PTS.	PIM	+/-
80–81	Que	3	0	0	0	2	
85–86	StL	19	2	7	9	64	
86–87	Det	16	1	6	7	31	
87–88	Det	16	2	6	8	40	
88–89	Det	6	1	2	3	12	
90–91	NJ	4	0	0	0	18	
91–92	StL	1	0	1	1	0	
Totals		65	6	22	28	171	

NOUR, Rumun 6–2 200 D
B. Zaria, Nigeria, July 7, 1975

SSN	TEAM	GP	G	A	PTS.	PIM	+/-
96–97	Buf	2	0	0	0	2	
97–98	Buf	1	0	0	0	2	
Totals		3	0	0	0	4	

NOVY, Milan 5–10 196 C
B. Kladno, Czechoslovakia, Sept. 23, 1951

SSN	TEAM	GP	G	A	PTS.	PIM	+/-
82–83	Wash	73	18	30	48	16	+1

Playoffs

SSN	TEAM	GP	G	A	PTS.	PIM	+/-
82–83	Wasj	2	0	0	0	0	

NOWAK, Henry Stanley (Hank) 6–1 195 LW
B. Oshawa, Ont., Nov. 24, 1950

SSN	TEAM	GP	G	A	PTS.	PIM	+/-
73–74	Pitt	13	0	0	0	11	-14
74–75	Det-Bos	77	12	21	33	95	-26
75–76	Bos	66	7	3	10	41	-1
76–77	Bos	24	7	5	12	14	+4
Totals		180	26	29	55	161	-37

Playoffs

SSN	TEAM	GP	G	A	PTS.	PIM	+/-
74–75	Bos	3	1	0	1	0	
75–76	Bos	10	0	0	0	8	
Totals		13	1	0	1	8	

NUMMINEN, Teppo 6–1 190 D
B. Tampere, Finland, July 3, 1968

SSN	TEAM	GP	G	A	PTS.	PIM	+/-
88–89	Winn	69	1	14	15	36	-11
89–90	Winn	79	11	32	43	20	-4
90–91	Winn	80	8	25	33	28	-15
91–92	Winn	80	5	34	39	32	+15
92–93	Winn	66	7	30	37	33	+4
93–94	Winn	57	5	18	23	28	-23
94–95	Winn	42	5	16	21	16	+13
95–96	Winn	74	11	43	54	22	-4
96–97	Phoe	82	2	25	27	28	-3
97–98	Phoe	82	11	40	51	30	+25
98–99	Phoe	82	10	30	40	30	+3
Totals		792	76	307	383	303	+3

Playoffs

SSN	TEAM	GP	G	A	PTS.	PIM	+/-
89–90	Winn	7	1	2	3	10	
91–92	Winn	7	0	0	0	0	
92–93	Winn	6	1	1	2	2	
95–96	Winn	6	0	0	0	2	
96–97	Phoe	7	3	3	6	0	
97–98	Phoe	1	0	0	0	0	
98–99	Phoe	7	2	1	3	4	
Totals		41	7	7	14	18	

NYKOLUK, Michael 5–11 212 RW
B. Toronto, Ont., Dec. 11, 1934

SSN	TEAM	GP	G	A	PTS.	PIM	+/-
56–57	Tor	32	3	1	4	20	

NYLANDER, Michael 5–11 190 C
B. Stockholm, Sweden, Oct. 3, 1972

SSN	TEAM	GP	G	A	PTS.	PIM	+/-
92–93	Hart	59	11	22	33	36	-7
93–94	Hart-Calg	73	13	42	55	30	+8
94–95	Calg	6	0	1	1	2	+1
95–96	Calg	73	17	38	55	20	0
97–98	Calg	65	13	23	36	24	+10
98–99	Calg-TB	33	4	10	14	8	-9
Totals		309	58	136	194	120	+3

Playoffs

SSN	TEAM	GP	G	A	PTS.	PIM	+/-
93–94	Calg	3	0	0	0	0	
94–95	Calg	6	0	6	6	2	
95–96	Calg	4	0	0	0	0	
Totals		13	0	6	6	2	

NYLUND, Gary 6–4 210 D
B. Surrey, B.C., Oct. 28, 1963

SSN	TEAM	GP	G	A	PTS.	PIM	+/-
82–83	Tor	16	0	3	3	16	0
83–84	Tor	47	2	14	16	103	-27
84–85	Tor	76	3	17	20	99	-37
85–86	Tor	79	2	16	18	180	-32
86–87	Chi	80	7	20	27	190	-9
87–88	Chi	76	4	15	19	208	-9
88–89	Chi-NYI	69	7	10	17	137	-19
89–90	NYI	64	4	21	25	144	+8
90–91	NYI	72	2	21	23	105	-8
91–92	NYI	7	0	1	1	10	-3
92–93	NYI	22	1	1	2	43	-2
Totals		608	32	139	171	1235	-138

Playoffs

SSN	TEAM	GP	G	A	PTS.	PIM	+/-
85–86	Tor	10	0	2	2	25	
86–87	Chi	4	0	2	2	11	
87–88	Chi	5	0	0	0	10	
89–90	NYI	5	0	2	2	17	
Totals		24	0	6	6	63	

*NYROP, William D. 6–2 205 D
B. Washington, D.C., July 23, 1952

SSN	TEAM	GP	G	A	PTS.	PIM	+/-
75–76	Mont	19	0	3	3	8	+21
76–77	Mont	74	3	19	22	21	+42
77–78	Mont	72	5	21	26	37	+56
81–82	Minn	42	4	8	12	35	+14
Totals		207	12	51	63	101	+133

Playoffs

SSN	TEAM	GP	G	A	PTS.	PIM	+/-
75–76	Mont	13	0	3	3	12	
76–77	Mont	8	1	0	1	4	
77–78	Mont	12	0	4	4	6	
81–82	Minn	2	0	0	0	0	
Totals		35	1	7	8	22	

NYSTROM, Thore Robert (Bobby) 6–1 200 RW
B. Stockholm, Sweden, Oct. 10, 1952

SSN	TEAM	GP	G	A	PTS.	PIM	+/-
72–73	NYI	11	1	1	2	10	-11

SSN	TEAM	GP	G	A	PTS.	PIM	+/-
73–74	NYI	77	21	20	41	118	-17
74–75	NYI	76	27	28	55	122	+17
75–76	NYI	80	23	25	48	106	+24
76–77	NYI	80	29	27	56	91	+22
77–78	NYI	80	30	29	59	94	+19
78–79	NYI	78	19	20	39	113	+19
79–80	NYI	67	21	18	39	94	+4
80–81	NYI	79	14	30	44	145	+6
81–82	NYI	74	22	25	47	103	+13
82–83	NYI	74	10	20	30	98	+6
83–84	NYI	74	15	29	44	80	+9
84–85	NYI	36	2	5	7	58	+6
85–86	NYI	14	1	1	2	16	-4
Totals		900	235	278	513	1248	+113

Playoffs

74–75	NYI	17	1	3	4	27	
75–76	NYI	13	3	6	9	30	
76–77	NYI	12	0	2	2	7	
77–78	NYI	7	3	1	4	14	
78–79	NYI	10	3	2	5	4	
79–80	NYI	20	9	9	18	50	
80–81	NYI	18	6	6	12	20	
81–82	NYI	15	5	5	10	32	
82–83	NYI	20	7	6	13	15	
83–84	NYI	15	0	2	2	8	
84–85	NYI	10	2	2	4	29	
Totals		157	39	44	83	236	

OATES, Adam 5–11 189 C
B. Weston, Ont., Aug. 27, 1962

85–86	Det	38	9	11	20	10	-24
86–87	Det	76	15	32	47	21	0
87–88	Det	63	14	40	54	20	+16
88–89	Det	69	16	62	78	14	-1
89–90	StL	80	23	79	102	30	+9
90–91	StL	61	25	90	115	29	+15
91–92	StL–Bos	80	20	79	99	22	-9
92–93	Bos	84	45	97	142	32	+15
93–94	Bos	77	32	80	112	45	+10
94–95	Bos	48	12	41	53	8	-11
95–96	Bos	70	25	67	92	18	+16
96–97	Bos–Wash	80	22	60	82	14	-5
97–98	Wash	82	18	58	76	36	+6
98–99	Wash	59	12	42	54	22	-1
Totals		967	278	838	1126	321	+36

Playoffs

86–87	Det	16	4	7	11	6	
87–88	Det	16	8	12	20	6	
88–89	Det	6	0	8	8	2	
89–90	StL	12	2	12	14	4	
90–91	StL	13	7	13	20	10	
91–92	Bos	15	5	14	19	4	
92–93	Bos	4	0	9	9	4	
93–94	Bos	13	3	9	12	8	
94–95	Bos	5	1	0	1	2	
95–96	Bos	5	2	5	7	2	
97–98	Wash	21	6	11	17	8	
Totals		126	38	100	138	56	

*OATMAN, Warren Russell 5–10 195 F
B. Tilsonburg, Ont., Feb. 19, 1905

26–27	Det–Mont M	42	11	4	15	42	
27–28	Mont M	44	7	4	11	36	
28–29	Mont M–NYR	38	2	1	3	22	
Totals		124	20	9	29	100	

Playoffs

26–27	Mont M	2	0	0	0	0	
27–28	Mont M	9	1	0	1	18	
28–29	NYR	6	0	0	0	0	
Totals		17	1	0	1	18	

O'BRIEN, Dennis Francis 6–0 195 D
B. Port Hope, Ont., June 10, 1949

70–71	Minn	27	3	2	5	29	-2
71–72	Minn	70	3	6	9	108	+11
72–73	Minn	74	3	11	14	75	+11
73–74	Minn	77	5	12	17	166	+10
74–75	Minn	56	6	10	16	125	-11
75–76	Minn	78	1	14	15	187	-26
76–77	Minn	75	6	18	24	114	-35
77–78	Minn–Col–Clev–Bos	68	2	10	12	77	-22
78–79	Bos	64	2	8	10	107	+16
79–80	Bos	3	0	0	0	2	-4
Totals		592	31	91	122	990	-52

Playoffs

70–71	Minn	9	0	0	0	200	
71–72	Minn	3	0	0	0	11	
72–73	Minn	6	1	0	1	38	
76–77	Minn	2	0	0	0	4	
77–78	Bos	14	0	0	0	28	
Totals		34	1	0	1	281	

O'BRIEN, Ellard John (Obie) 6–3 183 LW
B. St. Catherines, Ont., May 27, 1930

55–56	Bos	2	0	0	0	0	

O'CALLAHAN, Jack 6–1 190 D
B. Charlestown, Mass., July 24, 1957

82–83	Chi	39	0	11	11	46	+9
83–84	Chi	70	4	13	17	67	-6
84–85	Chi	66	6	8	14	105	+6
85–86	Chi	80	4	19	23	116	+5
86–87	Chi	48	1	13	14	59	+10
87–88	NJ	50	7	19	26	97	-3
88–89	NJ	36	5	21	26	51	0
Totals		389	27	104	131	541	+21

Playoffs

82–83	Chi	5	0	2	2	2	
83–84	Chi	2	0	0	0	2	
84–85	Chi	15	3	5	8	25	
85–86	Chi	3	0	1	1	4	
86–87	Chi	2	0	0	0	2	
87–88	NJ	5	1	3	4	6	
Totals		32	4	11	15	41	

O'CONNELL, Michael Thomas 5–9 180 D
B. Chicago, Ill., Nov. 25, 1955

77–78	Chi	6	1	1	2	2	0
78–79	Chi	48	4	22	26	20	-1
79–80	Chi	78	8	22	30	52	-2
80–81	Chi–Bos	82	15	38	53	74	+4
81–82	Bos	80	5	34	39	75	+8
82–83	Bos	80	14	39	53	42	+44
83–84	Bos	75	18	42	60	42	+18
84–85	Bos	78	15	40	55	64	+3
85–86	Bos–Det	76	9	28	37	63	-14
86–87	Det	77	5	26	31	70	-25
87–88	Det	48	6	13	19	38	+24
88–89	Det	66	1	15	16	41	-8
89–90	Det	66	4	14	18	22	-12
Totals		860	105	334	439	605	+39

Playoffs

78–79	Chi	4	0	0	0	4	
79–80	Chi	7	0	1	1	0	
80–81	Bos	3	1	3	4	2	
81–82	Bos	11	2	2	4	20	
82–83	Bos	17	3	5	8	12	
83–84	Bos	3	0	0	0	0	
84–85	Bos	5	1	5	6	0	
86–87	Det	16	1	4	5	14	
87–88	Det	10	0	4	4	8	
88–89	Det	6	0	0	0	4	
Totals		82	8	24	32	64	

*O'CONNOR, Herbert William (Buddy) 5–7 145 F
B. Montreal, Que., June 21, 1916

41–42	Mont	36	9	16	25	4	
42–43	Mont	50	15	43	58	2	
43–44	Mont	44	12	42	54	6	
44–45	Mont	50	21	23	44	2	
45–46	Mont	45	11	11	22	2	
46–47	Mont	46	10	20	30	6	
47–48	NYR	60	24	36	60	8	
48–49	NYR	46	11	24	35	0	
49–50	NYR	66	11	22	33	4	
50–51	NYR	66	16	20	36	0	
Totals		509	140	257	397	34	

Playoffs

41–42	Mont	3	0	1	1	0	
42–43	Mont	5	4	5	9	0	
43–44	Mont	8	1	2	3	2	
44–45	Mont	2	0	0	0	0	
45–46	Mont	9	2	3	5	0	
46–47	Mont	8	3	4	7	0	
47–48	NYR	6	1	4	5	0	
49–50	NYR	12	4	2	6	4	
Totals		53	15	21	36	6	

O'CONNOR, Myles 5–11 190 D
B. Calgary, Alta., Apr. 2, 1967

90–91	NJ	22	3	1	4	41	+3
91–92	NJ	9	0	2	2	13	-2
92–93	NJ	7	0	0	0	9	-4
93–94	Ana	5	0	1	1	6	0
Totals		43	3	4	7	69	-3

ODDLEIFSON, Christopher Roy 6–2 185 C
B. Brandon, Man., Sept. 7, 1950

72–73	Bos	6	0	0	0	0	-1
73–74	Bos–Van	70	13	16	29	44	+16
74–75	Van	60	16	35	51	54	+17
75–76	Van	80	16	46	62	88	+17
76–77	Van	80	14	26	40	81	-18
77–78	Van	78	17	22	39	64	-18
78–79	Van	67	11	26	37	51	-15
79–80	Van	75	8	20	28	76	-9
80–81	Van	8	0	0	0	6	-1
Totals		524	95	191	286	464	-12

Playoffs

74–75	Van	5	0	3	3	2	
75–76	Van	2	1	2	3	0	
78–79	Van	3	0	1	1	2	
79–80	Van	4	0	0	0	4	
Totals		14	1	6	7	8	

ODELEIN, Lyle 5–11 210 D
B. Quill Lake, Sask., July 21, 1968

89–90	Mont	8	0	2	2	33	-1
90–91	Mont	52	0	2	2	259	+7
91–92	Mont	71	1	7	8	212	+15
92–93	Mont	83	2	14	16	205	+35
93–94	Mont	79	11	29	40	276	+8
94–95	Mont	48	3	7	10	152	-13
95–96	Mont	79	3	14	17	230	+8
96–97	NJ	79	3	13	16	110	+16
97–98	NJ	79	4	19	23	171	+11
98–99	NJ	70	5	26	31	114	+6
Totals		648	32	133	165	1762	+92

Playoffs

90–91	Mont	12	0	0	0	54	
91–92	Mont	7	0	0	0	11	
92–93	Mont	20	1	5	6	30	
93–94	Mont	7	0	0	0	17	
95–96	Mont	6	1	1	2	6	
96–97	NJ	10	2	2	4	19	
97–98	NJ	6	1	1	2	21	
98–99	NJ	7	0	3	3	10	
Totals		75	5	12	17	168	

ODELEIN, Selmar 6–0 205 D
B. Quill Lake, Sask., Apr. 11, 1966

85–86	Edm	4	0	0	0	0	+1
87–88	Edm	12	0	2	2	33	-2
88–89	Edm	2	0	0	0	2	-1
Totals		18	0	2	2	35	-2

ODGERS, Jeff 6–0 195 RW
B. Spy Hill, Sask., May 31, 1969

91–92	SJ	61	7	4	11	217	-21
92–93	SJ	66	12	15	27	253	-26
93–94	SJ	81	13	8	21	222	-13
94–95	SJ	48	4	3	7	117	-8
95–96	SJ	78	12	4	16	192	-4
96–97	Bos	80	7	8	15	197	-15
97–98	Col A	68	5	8	13	213	+5
98–99	Col A	75	2	3	5	259	-3
Totals		857	62	53	115	1670	-79

Playoffs

93–94	SJ	11	0	0	0	11	
94–95	SJ	11	1	1	2	23	
97–98	Col A	6	0	0	0	25	
98–99	Col A	15	1	0	1	14	
Totals		43	2	1	3	73	

ODJICK, Gino 6–3 210 LW
B. Maniwaki, Que., Sept. 7, 1970

90–91	Van	45	7	1	8	296	-6
91–92	Van	65	4	6	10	348	-1

SSN	TEAM	GP	G	A	PTS.	PIM	+/-
92–93	Van	75	4	13	17	370	+3
93–94	Van	76	16	13	29	271	+13
94–95	Van	23	4	5	9	109	-3
95–96	Van	55	3	4	7	181	-16
96–97	Van	70	5	8	13	371	-5
97–98	Van–NYI	48	3	2	5	212	-2
98–99	NYI	23	4	3	7	133	-2
Totals		480	50	55	105	2291	-16

Playoffs

90–91	Van	6	0	0	0	18	
91–92	Van	4	0	0	0	6	
92–93	Van	1	0	0	0	0	
93–94	Van	10	0	0	0	18	
94–95	Van	5	0	0	0	47	
95–96	Van	6	3	1	4	6	
Totals		32	3	1	4	95	

O'DONNELL, Frederick James 5–10 175 RW
B. Kingston, Ont., Dec. 6, 1949

72–73	Bos	72	10	4	14	55	+3
73–74	Bos	43	5	7	12	43	+3
74–75	NE (WHA)	76	21	15	36	84	
75–76	NE (WHA)	79	11	11	22	81	
NHL Totals		115	15	11	26	98	+6
WHA Totals		155	32	26	58	165	

Playoffs

72–73	Bos	5	0	1	1	5	
75–76	NE (WHA)	17	2	5	7	20	
NHL Totals		5	0	1	1	5	
WHA Totals		17	2	5	7	20	

O'DONNELL, Sean 6–2 224 D
B. Ottawa, Ont., Oct. 13, 1971

94–95	LA	15	0	2	2	49	-2
95–96	LA	71	2	5	7	127	+3
96–97	LA	55	5	12	17	144	-13
97–98	LA	80	2	15	17	179	+7
98–99	LA	80	1	13	14	186	+1
Totals		301	10	47	57	685	-4

Playoffs

| 97–98 | LA | 4 | 1 | 0 | 1 | 36 | |

O'DONOGHUE, Donald Francis 5–10 180 RW
B. Kingston, Ont., Sept. 27, 1949

69–70	Oak	68	5	6	11	21	-26
70–71	Cal	43	11	9	20	10	-20
71–72	Cal	14	2	2	4	4	-4
72–73	Phil (WHA)	74	16	23	39	43	
73–74	Van (WHA)	49	8	6	14	20	
74–75	Van (WHA)	4	0	0	0	0	
75–76	Cin (WHA)	20	1	8	9	0	
NHL Totals		125	18	17	35	35	-50
WHA Totals		147	25	37	62	63	

Playoffs

69–70	Oak	3	0	0	0	0	
72–73	Phil (WHA)	4	0	1	1	0	
NHL Totals		3	0	0	0	0	
WHA Totals		4	0	1	1	0	

ODROWSKI, Gerald Bernard (Gerry) 5–11 190 D
B. Trout Creek, Ont., Oct. 4, 1938

60–61	Det	68	1	4	5	45	
61–62	Det	69	1	6	7	24	
62–63	Det	1	0	0	0	0	
67–68	Oak	42	4	6	10	10	0
68–69	Oak	74	5	1	6	24	+4
71–72	StL	55	1	2	3	8	-1
72–73	LA (WHA)	78	6	31	37	89	
73–74	LA (WHA)	77	4	32	36	48	
74–75	Phoe (WHA)	77	5	38	43	77	
75–76	Minn–Winn (WHA)	50	1	13	14	16	
NHL Totals		309	12	19	31	111	+3
WHA Totals		282	16	114	130	230	

Playoffs

60–61	Det	10	0	0	0	4	
62–63	Det	2	0	0	0	2	
68–69	Cal	7	0	1	1	2	
71–72	StL	11	0	0	0	8	
72–73	LA (WHA)	6	1	2	3	6	

74–75	Phoe (WHA)	5	0	2	2	0	
NHL Totals		30	0	1	1	16	
WHA Totals		11	1	4	5	6	

O'DWYER, Bill 6–0 190 C
B. Boston, Mass., Jan. 25, 1960

83–84	LA	5	0	0	0	0	+1
84–85	LA	13	1	0	1	15	0
87–88	Bos	77	7	10	17	83	-3
88–89	Bos	19	1	2	3	8	-4
89–90	Bos	6	0	1	1	7	-2
Totals		126	11	14	25	115	-8

Playoffs

87–88	Bos	9	0	0	0	0	
89–90	Bos	1	0	0	0	2	
Totals		10	0	0	0	2	

O'FLAHERTY, Gerard Joseph (Gerry) 5–10 182 LW
B. Pittsburgh, Pa., Aug. 31, 1950

71–72	Tor	2	0	0	0	0	
72–73	Van	78	13	17	30	29	-17
73–74	Van	78	22	20	42	18	-5
74–75	Van	80	25	17	42	37	+6
75–76	Van	68	20	18	38	47	+11
76–77	Van	72	12	12	24	20	-24
77–78	Van	59	6	11	17	15	-5
78–79	Atl	1	1	0	1	2	0
Totals		438	99	95	194	168	-34

Playoffs

74–75	Van	5	2	2	4	6	
75–76	Van	2	0	0	0	0	
Totals		7	2	2	4	6	

O'FLAHERTY, John Benedict (Peanuts) 5–7 154 RW
B. Toronto, Ont., Apr. 10, 1918

40–41	NYA	10	4	0	4	0	
41–42	Brk	11	1	1	2	0	
Totals		21	5	1	6	0	

OGLIVIE, Brian Hugh 5–11 186 C
B. Stettler, Alta., Jan. 30, 1952

72–73	Chi	12	1	2	3	18	-2
74–75	StL	20	5	5	10	4	-4
75–76	StL	9	2	1	3	2	-1
76–77	StL	3	0	0	0	0	-1
77–78	StL	32	6	8	14	12	-12
78–79	StL	14	1	5	6	7	-3
Totals		90	15	21	36	43	-23

*O'GRADY, George F
| 17–18 | Mont W | 4 | 0 | 0 | 0 | 0 | |

OGRODNICK, John Alexander 6–0 204 LW
B. Ottawa, Ont., June 20, 1959

79–80	Det	41	8	24	32	8	-4
80–81	Det	80	35	35	70	14	-17
81–82	Det	80	28	26	54	28	+5
82–83	Det	80	41	44	85	30	+11
83–84	Det	64	42	36	78	14	-15
84–85	Det	79	55	50	105	30	+1
85–86	Det	76	38	32	70	18	-30
86–87	Det–Que	71	23	44	67	10	-8
87–88	NYR	64	22	32	54	16	-3
88–89	NYR	60	13	29	42	14	0
89–90	NYR	80	43	31	74	44	+11
90–91	NYR	79	31	23	54	10	+15
91–92	NYR	55	17	13	30	22	+6
92–93	Det	19	6	6	12	2	-2
Totals		928	402	425	827	260	-50

Playoffs

83–84	Det	4	0	0	0	0	
84–85	Det	3	1	1	2	0	
86–87	Que	13	9	4	13	6	
88–89	NYR	3	2	0	2	0	
89–90	NYR	10	6	3	9	0	
90–91	NYR	4	0	0	0	0	
91–92	NYR	3	0	0	0	0	
92–93	Det	1	0	0	0	0	
Totals		41	18	8	26	6	

OHLUND, Mattias 6–3 209 D
B. Pitea, Sweden, Sept. 9, 1976

97–98	Van	77	7	23	30	76	+3
98–99	Van	74	9	26	35	83	-19
Totals		151	16	49	65	159	-16

OJANEN, Janne 6–2 200 C
B. Tampere, Finland, Apr. 9, 1968

88–89	NJ	3	0	1	1	2	-1
89–90	NJ	64	17	13	30	12	-5
92–93	NJ	31	4	9	13	14	-2
Totals		98	21	23	44	28	-8

Playoffs

| 91–92 | NJ | 3 | 0 | 2 | 2 | 0 | |

OKERLUND, Todd 5–11 200 RW
B. Burnsville, Minn., Sept. 6, 1964

| 87–88 | NYI | 4 | 0 | 0 | 0 | 2 | 0 |

OKSIUTA, Roman 6–3 229 RW
B. Murmansk, USSR, Aug. 21, 1970

93–94	Edm	10	1	2	3	4	-1
94–95	Edm–Van	38	16	4	20	10	-12
95–96	Van–Ana	70	23	28	51	60	+4
96–97	Ana–Pitt	35	6	7	13	26	-16
Totals		153	46	41	87	100	-25

Playoffs

| 94–95 | Van | 10 | 2 | 3 | 5 | 0 | |

OLAUSSON, Fredrik 6–2 195 D
B. Vaxsjo, Sweden, Oct. 5, 1966

86–87	Winn	72	7	29	36	24	-3
87–88	Winn	38	5	10	15	18	+3
88–89	Winn	75	15	47	62	32	+6
89–90	Winn	77	9	46	55	32	-1
90–91	Winn	71	12	29	41	24	-22
91–92	Winn	77	20	42	62	34	-31
92–93	Winn	68	16	41	57	22	-4
93–94	Winn–Edm	73	11	24	35	30	-7
94–95	Edm	33	0	10	10	20	-4
95–96	Edm–Ana	56	2	22	24	38	-7
96–97	Ana–Pitt	71	9	29	38	32	+16
97–98	Pitt	76	6	27	33	42	+13
98–99	Ana	74	16	40	56	30	+17
Totals		861	128	396	524	378	-32

Playoffs

86–87	Winn	10	2	3	5	4	
87–88	Winn	5	1	1	2	0	
89–90	Winn	7	0	2	2	2	
91–92	Winn	7	1	5	6	4	
92–93	Winn	6	0	2	2	2	
96–97	Pitt	4	0	1	1	0	
97–98	Pitt	6	0	3	3	2	
98–99	Ana	4	0	2	2	4	
Totals		49	4	19	23	18	

OLCZYK, Ed 6–1 200 C
B. Chicago, Ill., Aug. 16, 1966

84–85	Chi	70	20	30	50	67	+11
85–86	Chi	79	29	50	79	47	+2
86–87	Chi	79	16	35	51	119	-4
87–88	Tor	80	42	33	75	55	-22
88–89	Tor	80	38	52	90	75	0
89–90	Tor	79	32	56	88	78	0
90–91	Tor–Winn	79	30	41	71	82	-27
91–92	Winn	64	32	33	65	67	+11
92–93	Winn–NYR	71	21	28	49	52	-2
93–94	NYR	37	3	5	8	28	-1
94–95	NYR–Winn	33	4	9	13	12	-1
95–96	Winn	51	27	22	49	65	0
96–97	LA–Pitt	79	25	30	55	51	-14
97–98	Pitt	56	11	11	22	35	-9
98–99	Chi	61	10	15	25	29	-5
Totals		998	340	450	790	862	-59

Playoffs

84–85	Chi	15	6	5	11	11	
85–86	Chi	3	0	0	0	0	
86–87	Chi	4	1	1	2	4	
87–88	Chi	6	5	4	9	2	
89–90	Tor	5	1	2	3	14	
91–92	Winn	6	2	1	3	4	
93–94	NYR	1	0	0	0	0	
95–96	Winn	6	1	2	3	6	

SSN	TEAM	GP	G	A	PTS.	PIM	+/-
96–97	Pitt	5	1	0	1	12	
97–98	Pitt	6	2	0	2	4	
Totals		57	19	15	34	57	

OLIVER, David 6–0 190 RW
B. Sechelt, B.C., Apr. 17, 1971

SSN	TEAM	GP	G	A	PTS.	PIM	+/-
94–95	Edm	44	16	14	30	20	-11
95–96	Edm	80	20	19	39	34	-22
96–97	Edm–NYR	31	3	3	6	8	-5
98–99	Ott	17	2	5	7	4	+1
Totals		172	41	41	82	66	-37

Playoffs
| 96–97 | NYR | 3 | 0 | 0 | 0 | 0 | |

*OLIVER, Harold (Harry) 5–8 155 RW
B. Selkirk, Man., Oct. 26, 1898

SSN	TEAM	GP	G	A	PTS.	PIM
26–27	Bos	44	18	6	24	17
27–28	Bos	44	13	5	18	20
28–29	Bos	43	17	6	23	24
29–30	Bos	42	16	5	21	12
30–31	Bos	43	16	14	30	18
31–32	Bos	44	13	7	20	22
32–33	Bos	47	11	7	18	10
33–34	Bos	48	5	9	14	6
34–35	NYA	48	7	9	16	4
35–36	NYA	58	9	16	25	12
36–37	NYA	22	2	1	3	2
Totals		473	127	85	212	147

Playoffs
26–27	Bos	8	4	2	6	4
27–28	Bos	2	2	0	2	2
28–29	Bos	5	1	1	2	8
29–30	Bos	6	2	1	3	6
30–31	Bos	4	0	0	0	2
32–33	Bos	5	0	0	0	0
35–36	NYA	5	1	2	3	0
Totals		35	10	6	16	22

OLIVER, Murray Clifford 5–9 170 C
B. Hamilton, Ont., Nov. 14, 1937

SSN	TEAM	GP	G	A	PTS.	PIM	+/-
57–58	Det	1	0	1	1	0	
59–60	Det	54	20	19	39	6	
60–61	Det–Bos	70	17	22	39	16	
61–62	Bos	70	17	29	46	21	
62–63	Bos	65	22	40	62	38	
63–64	Bos	70	24	44	68	41	
64–65	Bos	65	20	23	43	76	
65–66	Bos	70	18	42	60	30	
66–67	Bos	65	9	26	35	16	
67–68	Tor	74	16	21	37	18	+8
68–69	Tor	76	14	36	50	16	+12
69–70	Tor	76	14	33	47	16	-19
70–71	Minn	61	9	23	32	8	0
71–72	Minn	77	27	29	56	16	+9
72–73	Minn	75	11	31	42	10	+4
73–74	Minn	78	17	20	37	4	-13
74–75	Minn	80	19	15	34	24	-19
Totals		1127	274	454	728	356	-18

Playoffs
59–60	Det	6	1	0	1	4
68–69	Tor	4	1	2	3	0
70–71	Minn	12	7	4	11	0
71–72	Minn	7	0	6	6	4
72–73	Minn	6	0	4	4	2
Totals		35	9	16	25	10

OLIWA, Krzysztof 6–5 235 LW
B. Tychy, Poland, April 12, 1973

SSN	TEAM	GP	G	A	PTS.	PIM	+/-
96–97	NJ	1	0	0	0	5	-1
97–98	NJ	73	2	3	5	295	+3
98–99	NJ	64	5	7	12	240	+4
Totals		138	7	10	17	540	+6

Playoffs
97–98	NJ	6	0	0	0	23
98–99	NJ	1	0	0	0	2
Totals		7	0	0	0	25

OLMSTEAD, Murray Bert (Bert) 6–2 183 LW
B. Scepter, Sask., Sept. 4, 1926

SSN	TEAM	GP	G	A	PTS.	PIM
48–49	Chi	9	0	2	2	4
49–50	Chi	70	20	29	49	40
50–51	Chi–Mont	54	18	23	41	40
51–52	Mont	69	7	28	35	49
52–53	Mont	69	17	28	45	83
53–54	Mont	70	15	37	52	85
54–55	Mont	70	10	48	58	103
55–56	Mont	70	14	56	70	94
56–57	Mont	64	15	33	48	74
57–58	Mont	57	9	28	37	71
58–59	Tor	70	10	31	41	74
59–60	Tor	53	15	21	36	63
60–61	Tor	67	18	34	52	84
61–62	Tor	56	13	23	36	10
Totals		848	181	421	602	874

Playoffs
50–51	Mont	11	2	3	5	9
51–52	Mont	11	0	1	1	4
52–53	Mont	12	2	2	4	4
53–54	Mont	11	0	1	1	19
54–55	Mont	12	0	4	4	21
55–56	Mont	10	4	10	14	8
56–57	Mont	10	0	9	9	13
57–58	Mont	9	0	3	3	0
58–59	Tor	12	4	2	6	13
59–60	Tor	10	3	4	7	0
60–61	Tor	3	1	2	3	10
61–62	Tor	4	0	1	1	0
Totals		115	16	42	58	101

OLSEN, Darryl 6–0 180 D
B. Calgary, Alta., Oct. 7, 1966

SSN	TEAM	GP	G	A	PTS.	PIM	+/-
91–92	Calg	1	0	0	0	0	-2

OLSON, Dennis 6–0 182 C
B. Kenora, Ont., Nov. 9, 1934

SSN	TEAM	GP	G	A	PTS.	PIM
57–58	Det	4	0	0	0	0

OLSSON, Christer 6–0 196 D
B. Arboga, Sweden, June 24, 1970

SSN	TEAM	GP	G	A	PTS.	PIM	+/-
95–96	StL	26	2	8	10	14	-6
96–97	StL–Ott	30	2	4	6	10	-4
Totals		56	4	12	16	24	-10

Playoffs
| 95–96 | StL | 3 | 0 | 0 | 0 | 0 |

O'NEIL, Paul Joseph 6–1 177 C
B. Charlestown, Mass., Aug. 24, 1953

SSN	TEAM	GP	G	A	PTS.	PIM	+/-
73–74	Van	5	0	0	0	0	-2
75–76	Bos	1	0	0	0	0	0
78–79	Birm (WHA)	1	0	0	0	0	-2
NHL Totals		6	0	0	0	0	
WHA Totals		1	0	0	0	0	

*O'NEILL, James Beaton (Peggy) 5–8 160 C
B. Semans, Sask., Apr. 3, 1913

SSN	TEAM	GP	G	A	PTS.	PIM
33–34	Bos	25	2	2	4	15
34–35	Bos	48	2	11	13	35
35–36	Bos	48	2	11	13	49
36–37	Bos	20	0	2	2	6
40–41	Mont	12	0	3	3	0
41–42	Mont	12	0	1	1	4
Totals		165	6	30	36	109

Playoffs
34–35	Bos	4	0	0	0	9
35–36	Bos	1	1	1	2	4
40–41	Mont	3	0	0	0	0
41–42	Mont	3	0	0	0	0
Totals		11	1	1	2	13

O'NEILL, Jeff 6–0 176 C
B. Richmond Hill, Ont., Feb. 23, 1976

SSN	TEAM	GP	G	A	PTS.	PIM	+/-
95–96	Hart	65	8	19	27	40	-3
96–97	Hart	72	14	16	30	40	-24
97–98	Car	74	19	20	39	67	-8
98–99	Car	75	16	15	31	66	+3
Totals		286	57	70	127	213	-32

Playoffs
| 98–99 | Car | 6 | 0 | 1 | 1 | 0 |

*O'NEILL, Thomas (Windy) 5–10 155 RW
B. Deseronto, Ont., Sept. 28, 1923

SSN	TEAM	GP	G	A	PTS.	PIM
43–44	Tor	33	8	7	15	29
44–45	Tor	33	2	5	7	24
Totals		66	10	12	22	53

Playoffs
SSN	TEAM	GP	G	A	PTS.	PIM
43–44	Tor	4	0	0	0	6

ORBAN, William Terrence 6–0 175 LW
B. Regina, Sask., Feb. 20, 1944

SSN	TEAM	GP	G	A	PTS.	PIM	+/-
67–68	Chi	39	3	2	5	17	-11
68–69	Chi–Minn	66	5	11	16	43	-4
69–70	Minn	9	0	2	2	7	-2
Totals		114	8	15	23	67	-17

Playoffs
| 67–68 | Chi | 3 | 0 | 0 | 0 | 0 |

O'REE, William Eldon (Willie) 5–10 175 LW
B. Fredericton, N.B., Oct. 15, 1935

SSN	TEAM	GP	G	A	PTS.	PIM
57–58	Bos	2	0	0	0	0
60–61	Bos	43	4	10	14	26
Totals		45	4	10	14	26

O'REGAN, Thomas Patrick 5–10 180 C
B. Cambridge, Mass., Dec. 29, 1961

SSN	TEAM	GP	G	A	PTS.	PIM	+/-
83–84	Pitt	51	4	10	14	8	-22
84–85	Det	1	0	0	0	0	-1
85–86	Det	9	1	2	3	2	+1
Totals		61	5	12	17	10	-22

O'REILLY, Joseph James Terence (Terry) 6–1 200 RW
B. Niagara Falls, Ont., June 7, 1951

SSN	TEAM	GP	G	A	PTS.	PIM	+/-
71–72	Bos	1	0	1	1	0	+3
72–73	Bos	72	5	22	27	109	+27
73–74	Bos	76	11	24	35	94	+30
74–75	Bos	68	15	20	35	146	+15
75–76	Bos	80	23	27	50	150	+3
76–77	Bos	79	14	41	55	147	+38
77–78	Bos	77	29	61	90	211	+40
78–79	Bos	80	26	51	77	205	+7
79–80	Bos	71	19	42	61	265	+17
80–81	Bos	77	8	35	43	223	+2
81–82	Bos	70	22	30	52	213	+23
82–83	Bos	19	6	14	20	40	+16
83–84	Bos	58	12	18	30	124	+9
84–85	Bos	63	13	17	30	168	-18
Totals		891	204	402	606	2095	+212

Playoffs
72–73	Bos	5	0	0	0	2
73–74	Bos	16	2	5	7	38
74–75	Bos	3	0	0	0	17
75–76	Bos	12	3	1	4	25
76–77	Bos	14	5	6	11	28
77–78	Bos	15	5	10	15	40
78–79	Bos	11	0	6	6	25
79–80	Bos	10	3	6	9	69
80–81	Bos	3	1	2	3	12
81–82	Bos	11	5	4	9	56
83–84	Bos	3	0	0	0	14
84–85	Bos	5	1	2	3	9
Totals		108	25	42	67	335

ORLANDO, Gaetano (Gates) 5–8 180 C
B. Montreal, Que., Nov. 13, 1962

SSN	TEAM	GP	G	A	PTS.	PIM	+/-
84–85	Buf	11	3	6	9	6	+3
85–86	Buf	60	13	12	25	29	-7
86–87	Buf	27	2	8	10	16	-6
Totals		98	18	26	44	51	-10

Playoffs
| 84–85 | Buf | 5 | 0 | 4 | 4 | 14 |

ORLANDO, James V. 5–11 185 D
B. Montreal, Que., Feb. 27, 1916

SSN	TEAM	GP	G	A	PTS.	PIM
36–37	Det	10	0	1	1	8
37–38	Det	6	0	0	0	4
39–40	Det	48	1	3	4	54
40–41	Det	48	1	10	11	99
41–42	Det	48	1	7	8	111
42–43	Det	40	4	3	7	99
Totals		200	7	24	31	375

Playoffs
39–40	Det	5	0	0	0	15
40–41	Det	9	0	2	2	31
41–42	Det	12	0	4	4	45
42–43	Det	10	1	3	3	14
Totals		36	0	9	9	105

SSN	TEAM	GP	G	A	PTS.	PIM	+/-

ORLESKI, David Eugene *6–3 210 LW*
B. Edmonton, Alta., Dec. 26, 1959

SSN	TEAM	GP	G	A	PTS.	PIM	+/-
80–81	Mont	1	0	0	0	0	0
81–82	Mont	1	0	0	0	0	0
Totals		2	0	0	0	0	0

ORR, Robert Gordon (Bobby) *6–0 199 D*
B. Parry Sound, Ont., Mar. 20, 1948

SSN	TEAM	GP	G	A	PTS.	PIM	+/-
66–67	Bos	61	13	28	41	102	
67–68	Bos	46	11	20	31	63	+30
68–69	Bos	67	21	43	64	133	+65
69–70	Bos	76	33	87	120	125	+54
70–71	Bos	78	37	102	139	91	+124
71–72	Bos	76	37	80	117	106	+86
72–73	Bos	63	29	72	101	99	+56
73–74	Bos	74	32	90	122	82	+84
74–75	Bos	80	46	89	135	101	+80
75–76	Bos	10	5	13	18	22	+10
76–77	Chi	20	4	19	23	25	+6
78–79	Chi	6	2	2	4	4	+2
Totals		657	270	645	915	953	+517

Playoffs

SSN	TEAM	GP	G	A	PTS.	PIM	+/-
67–68	Bos	4	0	2	2	2	
68–69	Bos	10	1	7	8	10	
69–70	Bos	14	9	11	20	14	
70–71	Bos	7	5	7	12	25	
71–72	Bos	15	5	19	24	19	
72–73	Bos	5	1	1	2	7	
73–74	Bos	16	4	14	18	28	
74–75	Bos	3	1	5	6	2	
Totals		74	26	66	92	107	

ORSZAGH, Vladimir *5–11 175 RW*
B. Banska Bysterica, Czech., May 27, 1977

SSN	TEAM	GP	G	A	PTS.	PIM	+/-
97–98	NYI	11	0	1	1	2	+3
98–99	NYI	12	1	0	1	6	+2
Totals		23	1	1	2	8	-1

OSBORNE, Keith *6–1 180 RW*
B. Toronto, Ont., Apr. 2, 1969

SSN	TEAM	GP	G	A	PTS.	PIM	+/-
89–90	StL	5	0	2	2	8	-2
92–93	TB	11	1	1	2	8	-1
Totals		16	1	3	4	16	-3

OSBORNE, Mark Anatole *6–2 205 LW*
B. Toronto, Ont., Aug. 13, 1961

SSN	TEAM	GP	G	A	PTS.	PIM	+/-
81–82	Det	80	26	41	67	61	-7
82–83	Det	80	19	24	43	83	-41
83–84	NYR	73	23	28	51	88	+1
84–85	NYR	23	4	4	8	33	-2
85–86	NYR	62	16	24	40	80	+5
86–87	NYR–Tor	74	22	25	47	113	-16
87–88	Tor	79	23	37	60	102	-3
88–89	Tor	75	16	30	46	112	-5
89–90	Tor	78	23	50	73	91	+2
90–91	Tor–Winn	55	11	11	22	63	-11
91–92	Winn–Tor	54	7	13	20	73	-10
92–93	Tor	76	12	14	26	89	-7
93–94	Tor	73	9	15	24	145	+2
94–95	NYR	37	1	3	4	19	-2
Totals		919	212	319	531	1152	-94

Playoffs

SSN	TEAM	GP	G	A	PTS.	PIM	+/-
83–84	NYR	5	0	1	1	7	
84–85	NYR	3	0	0	0	4	
85–86	NYR	15	2	3	5	26	
86–87	Tor	9	1	3	4	6	
97–88	Tor	6	1	3	4	16	
89–90	Tor	5	2	3	5	12	
92–93	Tor	19	1	1	2	16	
93–94	Tor	18	4	2	6	52	
94–95	NYR	7	1	0	1	2	
Totals		87	12	16	28	141	

OSBURN, Randoulf Allan (Randy) *6–0 190 LW*
B. Collingwood, Ont., Nov. 26, 1952

SSN	TEAM	GP	G	A	PTS.	PIM	+/-
72–73	Tor	26	0	2	2	0	-5
74–75	Phil	1	0	0	0	0	0
Totals		27	0	2	2	0	-5

O'SHEA, Daniel Patrick *6–1 190 C*
B. Toronto, Ont., June 15, 1945

SSN	TEAM	GP	G	A	PTS.	PIM	+/-
68–69	Minn	74	15	34	49	57	-26
69–70	Minn	75	10	24	34	82	-4
70–71	Minn–Chi	77	18	19	37	26	+2
71–72	Chi–StL	68	9	12	21	39	-4
72–73	StL	75	12	26	38	30	-5
74–75	Minn (WHA)	76	16	25	41	47	
NHL Totals		369	64	115	179	234	-37
WHA Totals		76	16	25	41	47	

Playoffs

SSN	TEAM	GP	G	A	PTS.	PIM	+/-
69–70	Minn	6	1	0	1	8	
70–71	Chi	18	2	5	7	15	
71–72	StL	18	0	2	2	36	
72–73	StL	5	0	0	0	2	
Totals		39	3	7	10	61	

O'SHEA, Kevin William *6–2 205 RW*
B. Toronto, Ont., May 28, 1947

SSN	TEAM	GP	G	A	PTS.	PIM	+/-
70–71	Buf	41	4	4	8	8	-11
71–72	Buf–StL	56	6	9	15	46	-20
72–73	StL	36	3	5	8	31	-13
74–75	Minn (WHA)	68	10	10	20	42	
NHL Totals		133	13	18	31	85	-44
WHA Totals		68	10	10	20	42	

Playoffs

SSN	TEAM	GP	G	A	PTS.	PIM	+/-
71–72	StL	11	2	1	3	6	
72–73	StL	1	0	0	0	0	
Totals		12	2	1	3	6	

OSIECKI, Mark *6–2 200 D*
B. St. Paul, Minn., July 23, 1968

SSN	TEAM	GP	G	A	PTS.	PIM	+/-
91–92	Calg	50	2	7	9	24	-4
92–93	Ott–Winn–Minn	43	1	4	5	19	-20
Totals		93	3	11	14	43	-24

O'SULLIVAN, Chris *6–2 185 D*
B. Dorchester, Mass., May 15, 1974

SSN	TEAM	GP	G	A	PTS.	PIM	+/-
96–97	Calg	27	2	8	10	2	0
97–98	Calg	12	0	2	2	10	+4
98–99	Calg-NYR	10	0	1	1	2	-1
Totals		49	2	11	13	14	+3

OTEVREL, Jaroslav *6–3 215 LW*
B. Gottwaldov, Czechoslovakia, Sept. 16, 1968

SSN	TEAM	GP	G	A	PTS.	PIM	+/-
92–93	SJ	7	0	2	2	0	-6
93–94	SJ	9	3	2	5	2	-5
Totals		16	3	4	7	2	-11

OTTO, Joel Stuart *6–4 220 C*
B. Elk River, Minn., Oct. 29, 1961

SSN	TEAM	GP	G	A	PTS.	PIM	+/-
84–85	Calg	17	4	8	12	30	+3
85–86	Calg	79	25	34	59	188	+23
86–87	Calg	68	19	31	50	185	+8
87–88	Calg	62	13	39	52	194	+16
88–89	Calg	72	23	30	53	213	+12
89–90	Calg	75	13	20	33	116	+4
90–91	Calg	76	19	20	39	183	-4
91–92	Calg	78	13	21	34	161	-10
92–93	Calg	75	19	33	52	150	+2
93–94	Calg	81	11	12	23	92	-17
94–95	Calg	47	8	13	21	130	+8
95–96	Phil	67	12	29	41	115	+11
96–97	Phil	78	13	19	32	99	+12
97–98	Phil	68	3	4	7	78	-2
Totals		943	195	313	508	1934	+66

Playoffs

SSN	TEAM	GP	G	A	PTS.	PIM	+/-
84–85	Calg	3	2	1	3	10	
84–86	Calg	22	5	10	15	80	
86–87	Calg	2	0	2	2	6	
87–88	Calg	9	3	2	5	26	
88–89	Calg	22	6	13	19	46	
89–90	Calg	6	2	2	4	2	
90–91	Calg	7	1	2	3	8	
92–93	Calg	6	4	2	6	4	
93–94	Calg	3	0	1	1	4	
94–95	Calg	7	0	3	3	2	
95–96	Phil	12	3	4	7	11	
96–97	Phil	18	1	5	6	8	
97–98	Phil	5	0	0	0	0	
Totals		122	27	47	74	207	

OUELETTE, Adelard Edward (Eddie) *5–8 172 C*
B. Ottawa, Ont., Mar. 11, 1911

SSN	TEAM	GP	G	A	PTS.	PIM	+/-
35–36	Chi	43	3	2	5	11	

Playoffs

SSN	TEAM	GP	G	A	PTS.	PIM	+/-
35–36	Chi	1	0	0	0	0	

OUELETTE, Gerald Adrian (Gerry) *5–8 170 RW*
B. Grand Falls, N.B., Nov. 1, 1938

SSN	TEAM	GP	G	A	PTS.	PIM	+/-
60–61	Bos	34	5	4	9	0	

OWCHAR, Dennis *5–11 190 D*
B. Dryden, Ont., Mar. 28, 1953

SSN	TEAM	GP	G	A	PTS.	PIM	+/-
74–75	Pitt	46	6	11	17	67	+12
75–76	Pitt	54	5	12	17	19	+13
76–77	Pitt	46	5	18	23	37	-7
77–78	Pitt–Col	82	10	31	41	48	-61
78–79	Col	50	3	13	16	27	-33
79–80	Col	10	1	0	1	2	-3
Totals		288	30	85	115	200	-79

Playoffs

SSN	TEAM	GP	G	A	PTS.	PIM	+/-
75–75	Pitt	6	0	1	1	4	
75–76	Pitt	2	0	0	0	2	
77–78	Col	2	1	0	1	2	
Totals		10	1	1	2	8	

***OWEN, George** *5–11 190 D*
B. Hamilton, Ont.

SSN	TEAM	GP	G	A	PTS.	PIM	+/-
28–29	Bos	26	5	4	9	48	
29–30	Bos	42	9	4	13	31	
30–31	Bos	37	12	13	25	33	
31–32	Bos	45	12	10	22	29	
32–33	Bos	42	6	2	8	10	
Totals		192	44	33	77	151	

Playoffs

SSN	TEAM	GP	G	A	PTS.	PIM	+/-
28–29	Bos	5	0	0	0	0	
29–30	Bos	6	0	2	2	6	
30–31	Bos	5	2	3	5	13	
32–33	Bos	5	0	0	0	6	
Totals		21	2	5	7	25	

OZOLINSH, Sandis *6–1 195 D*
B. Riga, Latvia, Aug. 3, 1972

SSN	TEAM	GP	G	A	PTS.	PIM	+/-
92–93	SJ	37	7	16	23	40	-9
93–94	SJ	81	26	38	64	24	+16
94–95	SJ	48	9	16	25	30	-6
95–96	SJ–Col A	73	14	40	54	54	+2
96–97	Col A	80	23	45	68	88	+4
97–98	Col A	66	13	38	51	65	-12
98–99	Col A	39	7	25	32	22	+10
Totals		424	99	218	317	323	+5

Playoffs

SSN	TEAM	GP	G	A	PTS.	PIM	+/-
93–94	SJ	14	0	10	10	8	
94–95	SJ	11	3	2	5	6	
95–96	Col A	22	5	14	19	16	
96–97	Col A	17	4	13	17	24	
97–98	Col A	7	0	7	7	14	
98–99	Col A	19	4	8	12	22	
Totals		90	16	54	70	90	

PACHAL, Clayton *5–10 185 LW*
B. Yorkton, Sask., Apr. 21, 1956

SSN	TEAM	GP	G	A	PTS.	PIM	+/-
76–77	Bos	1	0	0	0	12	0
77–78	Bos	10	0	0	0	14	-1
78–79	Col	24	2	3	5	69	-11
Totals		35	2	3	5	95	-12

PADDOCK, Alvin (John) *6–3 190 RW*
B. Brandon, Man., June 9, 1954

SSN	TEAM	GP	G	A	PTS.	PIM	+/-
75–76	Wash	8	1	1	2	12	-5
76–77	Phil	5	0	0	0	9	0
79–80	Phil	32	3	7	10	36	-4
80–81	Que	32	2	5	7	25	-7
82–83	Phil	10	2	1	3	4	-6
Totals		87	8	14	22	86	-22

Playoffs

SSN	TEAM	GP	G	A	PTS.	PIM	+/-
79–80	Phil	3	2	0	2	0	
80–81	Que	2	0	0	0	0	
Totals		5	2	0	2	0	

PAEK, Jim *6–1 194 D*
B. Seoul, Korea, Apr. 7, 1967

SSN	TEAM	GP	G	A	PTS.	PIM	+/-
90–91	Pitt	3	0	0	0	9	+2
91–92	Pitt	49	1	7	8	36	0

SSN	TEAM	GP	G	A	PTS.	PIM	+/-
92–93	Pitt	77	3	15	18	64	+13
93–94	Pitt–LA	59	1	5	6	18	-5
94–95	Ott	29	0	2	2	28	-5
Totals		217	5	29	34	155	+2

Playoffs

SSN	TEAM	GP	G	A	PTS.	PIM	+/-
90–91	Pitt	8	1	0	1	2	
91–92	Pitt	19	0	4	4	6	
Totals		27	1	4	5	8	

PAIEMENT, Joseph Wilfred Rosaire (Rosey)
5–11 170 RW
B. Earlton, Ont., Aug. 12, 1945

SSN	TEAM	GP	G	A	PTS.	PIM	+/-
67–68	Phil	7	1	0	1	11	+1
68–69	Phil	27	2	4	6	52	-14
69–70	Phil	9	1	1	2	11	-4
70–71	Van	78	34	28	62	152	+12
71–72	Van	69	10	19	29	117	-37
72–73	Chi (WHA)	78	33	36	69	135	
73–74	Chi (WHA)	78	30	43	73	87	
74–75	Chi (WHA)	78	26	48	74	97	
75–76	NE (WHA)	80	28	43	71	89	
76–77	NE–Ind (WHA)	80	23	27	50	103	
77–78	Ind (WHA)	61	6	24	30	81	
NHL Totals		190	48	52	100	343	-42
WHA Totals		455	146	221	367	592	

Playoffs

SSN	TEAM	GP	G	A	PTS.	PIM	+/-
67–68	Phil	3	3	0	3	0	
73–74	Chi (WHA)	18	9	6	15	16	
75–76	NE (WHA)	17	4	11	15	41	
76–77	Ind (WHA)	9	0	5	5	15	
NHL Totals		3	3	0	3	0	
WHA Totals		44	13	22	35	72	

PAIEMENT, Wilfrid Jr. (Wilf) *6–1 210 RW*
B. Earlton, Ont., Oct. 16, 1955

SSN	TEAM	GP	G	A	PTS.	PIM	+/-
74–75	KC	78	26	13	39	101	-42
75–76	KC	57	21	22	43	121	-37
76–77	Col	78	41	40	81	101	-13
77–78	Col	80	31	56	87	114	-14
78–79	Col	65	24	36	60	80	-30
79–80	Col–Tor	75	30	44	74	113	-5
80–81	Tor	77	40	57	97	145	+7
81–82	Tor–Que	77	25	46	71	221	-22
82–83	Que	80	26	38	64	100	-10
83–84	Que	80	39	37	76	121	+28
84–85	Que	68	23	28	51	165	+12
85–86	Que–NYR	52	8	18	26	158	+2
86–87	Buf	56	20	17	37	108	+2
87–88	Pitt	23	2	6	8	39	-4
Totals		946	356	458	814	1757	-140

Playoffs

SSN	TEAM	GP	G	A	PTS.	PIM	+/-
77–78	Col	2	0	0	0	7	
79–80	Tor	3	0	2	2	17	
80–81	Tor	3	0	0	0	2	
81–82	Que	14	6	6	12	28	
82–83	Que	4	0	1	1	4	
83–84	Que	9	3	1	4	24	
84–85	Que	18	4	2	6	58	
85–86	NYR	16	5	5	10	45	
Totals		69	18	17	35	185	

PALANGIO, Peter Albert *5–11 175 LW*
B. North Bay, Ont., Oct. 10, 1908

SSN	TEAM	GP	G	A	PTS.	PIM	+/-
26–27	Mont	6	0	0	0	0	
27–28	Det	14	3	0	3	8	
28–29	Mont	2	0	0	0	0	
36–37	Chi	30	8	9	17	16	
37–38	Chi	19	2	1	3	4	
Totals		71	13	10	23	28	

Playoffs

SSN	TEAM	GP	G	A	PTS.	PIM	+/-
26–27	Mont	4	0	0	0	0	
37–38	Chi	3	0	0	0	0	
Totals		7	0	0	0	0	

PALAZZARI, Aldo *5–7 168 RW*
B. Eveleth, Minn., July 25, 1918

SSN	TEAM	GP	G	A	PTS.	PIM	+/-
43–44	Bos–NYR	35	8	3	11	4	

PALAZZARI, Douglas John *5–5 170 C*
B. Eveleth, Minn., Nov. 3, 1952

SSN	TEAM	GP	G	A	PTS.	PIM	+/-
74–75	StL	73	14	17	31	19	+5
76–77	StL	12	1	0	1	0	-3
77–78	StL	3	1	0	1	0	-2
78–79	StL	20	2	3	5	4	-5

SSN	TEAM	GP	G	A	PTS.	PIM	+/-
Totals		108	18	20	38	23	-2

Playoffs

SSN	TEAM	GP	G	A	PTS.	PIM	+/-
74–75	StL	2	0	0	0	0	

PALFFY, Zigmund *5–10 169 LW*
B. Skalica, Czechoslovakia, May 5, 1972

SSN	TEAM	GP	G	A	PTS.	PIM	+/-
93–94	NYI	5	0	0	0	0	-6
94–95	NYI	33	10	7	17	6	+3
95–96	NYI	81	43	44	87	56	-17
96–97	NYI	80	48	42	90	43	+21
97–98	NYI	82	45	42	87	34	-2
98–99	NYI	50	22	28	50	34	-6
Totals		331	168	163	331	173	-7

PALMER, Brad Donald *6–0 185 LW*
B. Duncan, B.C., Sept. 14, 1961

SSN	TEAM	GP	G	A	PTS.	PIM	+/-
80–81	Minn	23	4	4	8	22	-6
81–82	Minn	72	22	23	45	18	-13
82–83	Bos	73	6	11	17	18	-7
Totals		168	32	38	70	58	-26

Playoffs

SSN	TEAM	GP	G	A	PTS.	PIM	+/-
80–81	Minn	19	8	5	13	4	
81–82	Minn	3	0	0	0	12	
82–83	Bos	7	1	0	1	0	
Totals		29	9	5	14	16	

PALMER, Robert Hazen *6–0 190 C*
B. Detroit, Mich., Oct. 2, 1952

SSN	TEAM	GP	G	A	PTS.	PIM	+/-
73–74	Chi	1	0	0	0	0	0
74–75	Chi	13	0	2	2	2	+1
75–76	Chi	2	0	1	1	0	+1
Totals		16	0	3	3	2	+2

PALMER, Robert Ross *5–11 190 D*
B. Sarnia, Ont., Sept. 10, 1956

SSN	TEAM	GP	G	A	PTS.	PIM	+/-
77–78	LA	48	0	3	3	27	-8
78–79	LA	78	4	41	45	26	-13
79–80	LA	78	4	36	40	18	+29
80–81	LA	13	0	4	4	13	+5
81–82	LA	5	0	2	2	0	+1
82–83	NJ	60	1	10	11	21	-6
83–84	NJ	38	0	5	5	10	-10
Totals		320	9	101	110	115	-2

Playoffs

SSN	TEAM	GP	G	A	PTS.	PIM	+/-
77–78	LA	2	0	0	0	0	
78–79	LA	2	0	0	0	2	
79–80	LA	4	1	2	3	4	
Totals		8	1	2	3	6	

*PANAGABKO, Edwin Arnold *5–8 170 C*
B. Norquay, Sask., May 17, 1934

SSN	TEAM	GP	G	A	PTS.	PIM	+/-
55–56	Bos	28	0	3	3	38	
56–57	Bos	1	0	0	0	0	
Totals		29	0	3	3	38	

PANDOLFO, Jay *6–1 195 LW*
B. Winchester, Mass., Dec. 27, 1974

SSN	TEAM	GP	G	A	PTS.	PIM	+/-
96–97	NJ	46	6	8	14	6	-1
97–98	NJ	23	1	3	4	4	-4
98–99	NJ	70	14	13	27	10	+3
Totals		122	15	19	34	52	-2

Playoffs

SSN	TEAM	GP	G	A	PTS.	PIM	+/-
96–97	NJ	6	0	1	1	0	
97–98	NJ	3	0	2	2	0	
98–99	NJ	7	1	0	1	0	
Totals		16	1	3	4	0	

PANKEWICZ, Greg *6–0 185 RW*
B. Drayton Valley, Alta., Oct. 6, 1970

SSN	TEAM	GP	G	A	PTS.	PIM	+/-
93–94	Ott	3	0	0	0	2	-1
98–99	Calg	18	0	3	3	20	0
Totals		21	0	3	3	22	-1

PANTELEEV, Grigori *5–9 190 LW*
B. Gastello, USSR, Nov. 3, 1972

SSN	TEAM	GP	G	A	PTS.	PIM	+/-
92–93	Bos	39	8	6	14	12	-6
93–94	Bos	10	0	0	0	0	-2
94–95	Bos	1	0	0	0	0	0
95–96	NYI	4	0	0	0	0	-3
Totals		54	8	6	14	12	-11

*PAPIKE, Joseph *6–0 175 RW*
B. Eveleth, Minn., Mar. 28, 1915

SSN	TEAM	GP	G	A	PTS.	PIM	+/-
40–41	Chi	10	2	2	4	2	
41–42	Chi	9	1	0	1	0	
44–45	Chi	2	0	1	1	2	
Totals		21	3	3	6	4	

Playoffs

SSN	TEAM	GP	G	A	PTS.	PIM	+/-
40–41	Chi	5	0	2	2	0	

PAPPIN, James Joseph *6–1 190 RW*
B. Copper Cliff, Ont., Sept. 10, 1939

SSN	TEAM	GP	G	A	PTS.	PIM	+/-
63–64	Tor	50	11	8	19	33	
64–65	Tor	44	9	9	18	33	
65–66	Tor	7	0	3	3	8	
66–67	Tor	64	21	11	32	89	
67–68	Tor	58	13	15	28	37	0
68–69	Chi	75	30	40	70	49	+7
69–70	Chi	66	28	25	53	68	+17
70–71	Chi	58	22	23	45	40	+9
71–72	Chi	64	27	21	48	38	+3
72–73	Chi	76	41	51	92	82	+25
73–74	Chi	78	32	41	73	76	+25
74–75	Chi	71	36	27	63	94	-1
75–76	Cal	32	6	13	19	12	-16
76–77	Clev	24	2	8	10	8	+5
Totals		767	278	295	573	667	+74

Playoffs

SSN	TEAM	GP	G	A	PTS.	PIM	+/-
63–64	Tor	11	0	0	0	0	
66–67	Tor	12	7	8	15	12	
69–70	Chi	8	3	2	5	6	
70–71	Chi	18	10	4	14	24	
71–72	Chi	8	2	5	7	4	
72–73	Chi	16	8	7	15	24	
73–74	Chi	11	3	6	9	29	
74–75	Chi	8	0	2	2	2	
Totals		92	33	34	67	101	

PARADISE, Robert Harvey *6–1 205 D*
B. St. Paul, Minn., Apr. 22, 1944

SSN	TEAM	GP	G	A	PTS.	PIM	+/-
71–72	Minn	6	0	0	0	6	+1
72–73	Atl	71	1	7	8	103	-20
73–74	Atl–Pitt	56	2	8	10	52	-10
74–75	Pitt	78	3	15	18	109	-2
75–76	Pitt–Wash	57	0	8	8	46	-48
76–77	Wash	22	0	5	5	20	-3
77–78	Pitt	64	2	10	12	53	-30
78–79	Pitt	14	0	1	1	4	-4
Totals		368	8	54	62	393	-116

Playoffs

SSN	TEAM	GP	G	A	PTS.	PIM	+/-
71–72	Minn	4	0	0	0	0	
74–75	Pitt	6	0	1	1	17	
78–79	Pitt	2	0	0	0	0	
Totals		12	0	1	1	17	

PARGETER, George William *5–7 168 LW*
B. Calgary, Alta., Feb. 24, 1923

SSN	TEAM	GP	G	A	PTS.	PIM	+/-
46–47	Mont	4	0	0	0	0	

PARISE, Jean Paul (J.P.) *5–9 175 LW*
B. Smooth Rock Falls, Ont., Dec. 11, 1941

SSN	TEAM	GP	G	A	PTS.	PIM	+/-
65–66	Bos	3	0	0	0	0	
66–67	Bos	18	2	2	4	10	
67–68	Tor–Minn	44	11	17	28	27	-10
68–69	Minn	76	22	27	49	53	-44
69–70	Minn	74	24	48	72	72	-3
70–71	Minn	73	11	23	34	60	-15
71–72	Minn	71	19	18	37	70	+10
72–73	Minn	78	27	48	75	96	+18
73–74	Minn	78	18	37	55	42	-8
74–75	Minn–NYI	79	23	32	55	62	-8
75–76	NYI	80	22	35	57	80	+12
76–77	NYI	80	25	31	56	46	+26
77–78	NYI–Clev	79	21	29	50	39	+4
78–79	Minn	57	13	9	22	45	-12
Totals		890	238	356	594	702	-30

Playoffs

SSN	TEAM	GP	G	A	PTS.	PIM	+/-
67–68	Minn	14	2	5	7	10	
69–70	Minn	6	3	2	5	2	
70–71	Minn	12	3	3	6	22	
71–72	Minn	7	3	3	6	6	
72–73	Minn	6	0	0	0	9	
74–75	NYI	17	8	8	16	22	
75–76	NYI	13	4	6	10	10	

SSN	TEAM	GP	G	A	PTS.	PIM	+/-
76–77	NYI	11	4	4	8	6	
Totals		86	17	31	58	87	

PARIZEAU, Michel Gerard (Mike) 5–10 165 C
B. Montreal, Que., Apr. 9, 1948

SSN	TEAM	GP	G	A	PTS.	PIM	+/-
71–72	StL–Phil	58	3	14	17	18	-7
72–73	Que (WHA)	75	25	48	73	50	
73–74	Que (WHA)	78	26	34	60	39	
74–75	Que (WHA)	78	28	46	74	69	
75–76	Que–Ind (WHA)	81	25	42	67	42	
76–77	Ind (WHA)	75	18	37	55	39	
77–78	Ind (WHA)	70	13	27	40	47	
78–79	Ind–Cin (WHA)	52	7	18	25	32	
NHL Totals		58	3	14	17	18	-7
WHA Totals		509	142	252	394	318	

Playoffs

SSN	TEAM	GP	G	A	PTS.	PIM	
74–75	Que (WHA)	15	2	4	6	10	
75–76	Ind (WHA)	7	4	4	8	6	
76–77	Ind (WHA)	8	3	6	9	8	
78–79	Cin (WHA)	3	1	0	1	0	
WHA Totals		33	10	14	24	24	

PARK, Douglas Bradford (Brad) 6–0 200 D
B. Toronto, Ont., July 6, 1948

SSN	TEAM	GP	G	A	PTS.	PIM	+/-
68–69	NYR	54	3	23	26	70	+12
69–70	NYR	60	11	26	37	98	+23
70–71	NYR	68	7	37	44	114	+25
71–72	NYR	75	24	49	73	130	+62
72–73	NYR	52	10	43	53	51	+31
73–74	NYR	78	25	57	82	148	+18
74–75	NYR	65	13	44	57	104	+6
75–76	NYR–Bos	56	18	41	59	118	+19
76–77	Bos	77	12	55	67	67	+47
77–78	Bos	80	22	57	79	79	+68
78–79	Bos	40	7	32	39	10	+28
79–80	Bos	32	5	16	21	27	+11
80–81	Bos	78	14	52	66	111	+21
81–82	Bos	75	14	42	56	82	+11
82–83	Bos	76	10	26	36	82	+20
83–84	Det	80	5	53	58	85	-29
84–85	Det	67	13	30	43	53	-15
Totals		1113	213	683	896	1429	+358

Playoffs

SSN	TEAM	GP	G	A	PTS.	PIM	
68–69	NYR	4	0	2	2	7	
69–70	NYR	5	1	2	3	11	
70–71	NYR	13	0	4	4	42	
71–72	NYR	16	4	7	11	21	
72–73	NYR	10	2	5	7	8	
73–74	NYR	13	4	8	12	38	
74–75	NYR	3	1	4	5	2	
75–76	Bos	11	3	8	11	14	
76–77	Bos	14	2	10	12	4	
77–78	Bos	15	9	11	20	14	
78–79	Bos	11	1	4	5	8	
79–80	Bos	10	3	6	9	4	
80–81	Bos	3	1	3	4	11	
81–82	Bos	11	1	4	5	4	
82–83	Bos	16	3	9	12	18	
83–84	Det	3	0	3	3	0	
84–85	Det	3	0	0	0	11	
Totals		101	35	90	125	217	

PARK, Richard 5–11 176 C
B. Seoul, South Korea, May 27, 1976

SSN	TEAM	GP	G	A	PTS.	PIM	+/-
94–95	Pitt	1	0	1	1	2	+1
95–96	Pitt	56	4	6	10	36	+3
96–97	Pitt–Ana	12	1	1	2	10	-1
97–98	Ana	15	0	2	2	8	-3
98–99	Phil	7	0	0	0	0	-1
Totals		91	5	10	15	56	-1

Playoffs

SSN	TEAM	GP	G	A	PTS.	PIM	
94–95	Pitt	3	0	0	0	2	
95–96	Pitt	1	0	0	0	0	
96–97	Ana	11	0	1	1	2	
Totals		15	0	1	1	4	

PARKER, Jeff 6–3 194 RW
B. St. Paul, Minn., Sept. 7, 1964

SSN	TEAM	GP	G	A	PTS.	PIM	+/-
86–87	Buf	15	3	3	6	7	+1
87–88	Buf	4	0	2	2	2	-1
88–89	Buf	57	9	9	18	82	+3
89–90	Buf	61	4	5	9	70	-9
90–91	Hart	4	0	0	0	2	-2
Totals		141	16	19	35	163	-8

Playoffs

SSN	TEAM	GP	G	A	PTS.	PIM	
88–89	Buf	5	0	0	0	26	

PARKER, Scott 6–4 220 D
B. Hanford, Conn., Jan. 29, 1978

SSN	TEAM	GP	G	A	PTS.	PIM	+/-
98–99	Col A	27	0	0	0	71	-3

*PARKES, Ernest RW

SSN	TEAM	GP	G	A	PTS.	PIM	
24–25	Mont M	17	0	0	0	2	

PARKS, Greg 5–9 180 C
B. Edmonton, Alta., Mar. 25, 1967

SSN	TEAM	GP	G	A	PTS.	PIM	+/-
90–91	NYI	20	1	2	3	4	0
91–92	NYI	1	0	0	0	2	0
92–93	NYI	2	0	0	0	0	0
Totals		23	1	2	3	6	0

Playoffs

SSN	TEAM	GP	G	A	PTS.	PIM	
92–93	NYI	2	0	0	0	0	

PARRISH, Mark 6–0 185 LW
B. Edina, Minn., Feb. 2, 1977

SSN	TEAM	GP	G	A	PTS.	PIM	+/-
98–99	Fla	73	24	13	37	25	-6

*PARSONS, George Henry 5–11 174 LW
B. Toronto, Ont., June 28, 1914

SSN	TEAM	GP	G	A	PTS.	PIM	
36–37	Tor	5	0	0	0	0	
37–38	Tor	30	5	6	11	6	
38–39	Tor	29	7	7	14	11	
Totals		64	12	13	25	17	

Playoffs

SSN	TEAM	GP	G	A	PTS.	PIM	
37–38	Tor	7	3	2	5	11	

*PASEK, Dusan 6–1 200 C
B. Bratislava, Czechoslovakia, Sept. 7, 1960

SSN	TEAM	GP	G	A	PTS.	PIM	+/-
88–89	Minn	48	4	10	14	30	-8

Playoffs

SSN	TEAM	GP	G	A	PTS.	PIM	
88–89	Minn	2	1	0	1	0	

PASIN, Dave 6–1 205 RW
B. Edmonton, Alta., July 8, 1966

SSN	TEAM	GP	G	A	PTS.	PIM	+/-
85–86	Bos	71	18	19	37	50	-1
88–89	LA	5	0	0	0	0	-1
Totals		76	18	19	37	50	-2

Playoffs

SSN	TEAM	GP	G	A	PTS.	PIM	
85–86	Bos	3	0	1	1	0	

PASLAWSKI, Gregory Stephen 5–11 190 RW
B. Kindersley, Sask., Aug. 25, 1961

SSN	TEAM	GP	G	A	PTS.	PIM	+/-
83–84	Mont–StL	60	9	10	19	21	-1
84–85	StL	72	22	20	42	21	+6
85–86	StL	56	22	11	33	18	-12
86–87	StL	76	29	35	64	27	+1
87–88	StL	17	2	1	3	4	-14
88–89	StL	75	26	26	52	18	+8
89–90	Winn	71	18	30	48	14	-4
90–91	Winn–Buf	55	11	11	22	14	-6
91–92	Que	80	28	17	45	18	-12
92–93	Phil–Calg	73	18	24	42	12	+3
93–94	Calg	15	2	0	2	2	-4
Totals		650	187	185	372	169	-35

Playoffs

SSN	TEAM	GP	G	A	PTS.	PIM	
83–84	StL	9	1	0	1	2	
84–85	StL	3	0	0	0	2	
85–86	StL	17	10	7	17	13	
86–87	StL	6	1	1	2	4	
87–88	StL	3	1	1	2	2	
88–89	StL	9	2	1	3	2	
89–90	Winn	7	1	3	4	0	
92–93	Calg	6	3	0	3	0	
Totals		60	19	13	32	25	

PATERSON, Joseph 6–2 207 LW
B. Toronto, Ont., June 25, 1960

SSN	TEAM	GP	G	A	PTS.	PIM	+/-
80–81	Det	38	2	5	7	53	+4
81–82	Det	3	0	0	0	0	+1
82–83	Det	33	2	1	3	14	-8
83–84	Det	41	2	5	7	148	0
84–85	Phil	6	0	0	0	31	-1
85–86	Phil–LA	52	9	18	27	165	-6
86–87	LA	45	2	1	3	158	-15
87–88	LA–NYR	53	2	6	8	176	-14
88–89	NYR	20	0	1	1	84	-3
Totals		291	19	37	56	829	-42

Playoffs

SSN	TEAM	GP	G	A	PTS.	PIM	
83–84	Det	3	0	0	0	7	
84–85	Det	17	3	4	7	70	
86–87	LA	2	0	0	0	0	
Totals		22	3	4	7	77	

PATERSON, Mark 5–11 180 D
B. Ottawa, Ont., Feb. 22, 1964

SSN	TEAM	GP	G	A	PTS.	PIM	+/-
82–83	Hart	2	0	0	0	0	-1
83–84	Hart	9	2	0	2	4	+4
84–85	Hart	13	1	3	4	24	+6
85–86	Hart	5	0	0	0	5	-5
Totals		29	3	3	6	33	+4

PATERSON, Richard David 5–9 190 C
B. Kingston, Ont., Feb. 10, 1958

SSN	TEAM	GP	G	A	PTS.	PIM	+/-
79–80	Chi	11	0	2	2	0	0
80–81	Chi	49	8	2	10	18	-2
81–82	Chi	48	4	7	11	8	-2
82–83	Chi	79	14	9	23	14	-1
83–84	Chi	72	7	6	13	41	-13
84–85	Chi	79	7	12	19	25	+6
85–86	Chi	70	9	3	12	24	-1
86–87	Chi	22	1	2	3	6	+1
Totals		430	50	43	93	136	-12

Playoffs

SSN	TEAM	GP	G	A	PTS.	PIM	
78–79	Chi	1	0	1	1	0	
79–80	Chi	7	0	0	0	5	
80–81	Chi	2	1	0	1	0	
81–82	Chi	15	3	2	5	21	
82–83	Chi	13	1	1	2	4	
83–84	Chi	5	1	1	2	6	
84–85	Chi	15	1	5	6	15	
85–86	Chi	3	0	0	0	0	
Totals		61	7	10	17	51	

PATEY, Douglas Edward 5–11 180 RW
B. Toronto, Ont., Dec. 28, 1956

SSN	TEAM	GP	G	A	PTS.	PIM	+/-
76–77	Wash	37	3	1	4	6	-15
77–78	Wash	2	0	1	1	0	+1
78–79	Wash	6	1	0	1	2	-2
Totals		45	4	2	6	8	-16

PATEY, Larry James 6–1 185 C
B. Toronto, Ont., Mar. 19, 1953

SSN	TEAM	GP	G	A	PTS.	PIM	+/-
73–74	Cal	1	0	0	0	0	0
74–75	Cal	79	25	20	45	68	-20
75–76	Cal–StL	71	12	10	22	49	-20
76–77	StL	80	21	29	50	41	+11
77–78	StL	80	17	17	34	29	-20
78–79	StL	78	15	19	34	60	-27
79–80	StL	78	17	17	34	76	-18
80–81	StL	80	22	23	45	107	+2
81–82	StL	70	14	12	26	97	-10
82–83	StL	67	9	12	21	80	-6
83–84	StL–NYR	26	1	3	4	12	-12
84–85	NYR	7	0	1	1	12	-6
Totals		717	153	163	316	631	-126

Playoffs

SSN	TEAM	GP	G	A	PTS.	PIM	
75–76	StL	3	1	1	2	2	
76–77	StL	4	1	0	1	0	
79–80	StL	3	1	0	1	2	
80–81	StL	11	2	4	6	30	
81–82	StL	10	2	4	6	13	
82–83	StL	4	1	0	1	4	
83–84	NYR	4	0	1	1	6	
84–85	NYR	1	0	0	0	0	
Totals		40	8	10	18	57	

PATRICK, Craig 6–0 185 RW
B. Detroit, Mich., May 20, 1946

SSN	TEAM	GP	G	A	PTS.	PIM	+/-
71–72	Cal	59	8	3	11	12	-24
72–73	Cal	71	20	22	42	6	-32
73–74	Cal	59	10	20	30	17	-30
74–75	Cal–StL	57	8	10	18	6	-2
75–76	KC	80	17	18	35	14	-24
76–77	Minn (WHA)	30	6	11	17	6	

SSN	TEAM	GP	G	A	PTS.	PIM	+/-
76–77	Wash	28	7	10	17	2	-10
77–78	Wash	44	1	7	8	4	-6
78–79	Wash	3	1	1	2	0	-1
NHL Totals		401	72	91	163	61	-129
WHA Totals		30	6	11	17	6	

Playoffs

| 74–75 | StL | 2 | 0 | 1 | 1 | 0 | |

*PATRICK, Frederick Murray (Muzz) *6–2 200 D*
B. Victoria, B.C., June 28, 1915

37–38	NYR	1	0	2	2	0	
38–39	NYR	48	1	10	11	64	
39–40	NYR	46	2	4	6	44	
40–41	NYR	47	2	8	10	21	
45–46	NYR	24	0	2	2	4	
Totals		166	5	26	31	133	

Playoffs

37–38	NYR	3	0	0	0	2	
38–39	NYR	7	1	0	1	17	
39–40	NYR	12	3	0	3	13	
40–41	NYR	3	0	0	0	2	
Totals		25	4	0	4	34	

PATRICK, Glenn Curtiss *6–2 195 D*
B. New York, N.Y., Apr. 26, 1950

73–74	StL	1	0	0	0	2	-1
74–75	Cal	2	0	0	0	0	-2
76–77	Clev	35	2	3	5	70	-11
76–77	Edm (WHA)	23	0	4	4	62	
NHL Totals		38	2	3	5	72	-14
WHA Totals		23	0	4	4	62	

Playoffs

| 76–77 | Edm (WHA) | 2 | 0 | 0 | 0 | 0 | |

PATRICK, James *6–2 198 D*
B. Winnipeg, Man., June 14, 1963

83–84	NYR	12	1	7	8	2	+6
84–85	NYR	75	8	28	36	71	-17
85–86	NYR	75	14	29	43	88	+14
86–87	NYR	78	10	45	55	62	+13
87–88	NYR	70	17	45	62	52	+16
88–89	NYR	68	11	36	47	41	+3
89–90	NYR	73	14	43	57	50	+4
90–91	NYR	74	10	49	59	58	-5
91–92	NYR	80	14	57	71	54	+34
92–93	NYR	60	5	21	26	61	+1
93–94	NYR–Hart–Calg	68	10	25	35	40	-5
94–95	Calg	43	0	10	10	14	-3
95–96	Calg	80	3	32	35	30	+3
96–97	Calg	19	3	1	4	6	+2
97–98	Calg	60	6	11	17	26	-2
98–99	Buf	45	1	7	8	16	+12
Totals		980	127	446	573	671	+81

Playoffs

83–84	NYR	5	0	3	3	2	
84–85	NYR	3	0	0	0	4	
85–86	NYR	16	1	5	6	34	
86–87	NYR	6	1	2	3	2	
88–89	NYR	4	0	1	1	2	
89–90	NYR	10	3	8	11	0	
90–91	NYR	6	0	0	0	6	
91–92	NYR	13	0	7	7	12	
93–94	Calg	7	0	1	1	6	
94–95	Calg	5	0	1	1	0	
95–96	Calg	4	0	0	0	2	
98–99	Buf	20	0	1	1	12	
Totals		99	5	29	34	82	

*PATRICK, Lester *6–1 180 D*
B. Drummondville, Que., Dec. 30, 1883

| 26–27 | NYR | 1 | 0 | 1 | 0 | 2 | |

*PATRICK, Lynn *6–1 192 LW*
B. Victoria, B.C., Feb. 3, 1912

34–35	NYR	48	9	13	22	17	
35–36	NYR	48	11	14	25	29	
36–37	NYR	45	8	16	24	23	
37–38	NYR	48	15	19	34	24	
38–39	NYR	35	8	21	29	25	
39–40	NYR	48	12	16	28	34	
40–41	NYR	48	20	24	44	12	
41–42	NYR	47	32	22	54	18	
42–43	NYR	50	22	39	61	58	
45–46	NYR	38	8	6	14	30	
Totals		455	145	190	335	270	

Playoffs

34–35	NYR	4	2	2	4	0	
36–37	NYR	9	3	0	3	2	
37–38	NYR	3	0	1	1	2	
38–39	NYR	7	1	1	2	0	
39–40	NYR	12	2	2	4	4	
40–41	NYR	3	1	0	1	14	
41–42	NYR	6	1	0	1	0	
Totals		44	10	6	16	22	

PATRICK, Stephen Gary *6–4 205 RW*
B. Winnipeg, Man., Feb. 4, 1961

80–81	Buf	30	1	7	8	25	+1
81–82	Buf	41	8	8	16	64	+3
82–83	Buf	56	9	13	22	26	+4
83–84	Buf	11	1	4	5	6	-2
84–85	Buf–NYR	57	13	20	33	67	-8
85–86	NYR–Que	55	8	16	24	54	-6
Totals		250	40	68	108	242	-8

Playoffs

80–81	Buf	5	0	1	1	6	
81–83	Buf	2	0	0	0	0	
83–84	Buf	1	0	0	0	0	
84–85	NYR	1	0	0	0	0	
85–86	Que	3	0	0	0	6	
Totals		12	0	1	1	12	

PATTERSON, Colin *6–2 195 RW/LW*
B. Rexdale, Ont., May 11, 1960

83–84	Calg	56	13	14	27	15	+17
84–85	Calg	57	22	21	43	5	+20
85–86	Calg	61	14	13	27	22	+8
86–87	Calg	68	13	13	26	41	+7
87–88	Calg	39	7	11	18	28	+7
88–89	Calg	74	14	24	38	56	+44
89–90	Calg	61	5	3	8	20	-4
91–92	Buf	52	4	8	12	30	-4
92–93	Buf	36	4	2	6	22	-2
Totals		504	96	109	205	239	+93

Playoffs

83–84	Calg	11	1	1	2	6	
84–85	Calg	4	0	0	0	5	
85–86	Calg	19	6	3	9	10	
86–87	Calg	6	0	2	2	2	
87–88	Calg	9	1	0	1	8	
88–89	Calg	22	3	10	13	24	
90–91	Calg	1	0	0	0	0	
91–92	Buf	5	1	0	1	0	
92–93	Buf	8	0	1	1	2	
Totals		85	12	17	29	57	

PATTERSON, Dennis G. *5–8 175 D*
B. Peterborough, Ont., Jan. 9, 1950

74–75	KC	66	1	5	6	39	-57
75–76	KC	69	5	16	21	28	-28
76–77	Edm (WHA)	23	0	2	2	2	
79–80	Phil	3	0	1	1	0	-1
NHL Totals		138	6	22	28	67	-86
WHA Totals		23	0	2	2	2	

PATTERSON, Ed *6–2 213 RW*
B. Delta, B.C., Nov. 14, 1972

93–94	Pitt	27	3	1	4	10	-5
95–96	Pitt	35	0	2	2	38	-5
96–97	Pitt	6	0	0	0	8	0
Totals		68	3	3	6	56	-10

*PATTERSON, George F. (Paddy) *6–1 176 RW*
B. Kingston, Ont., May 22, 1906

26–27	Tor	17	4	2	6	17	
27–28	Tor–Mont	28	1	1	2	17	
28–29	Mont	44	4	5	9	34	
29–30	NYA	44	13	4	17	24	
30–31	NYA	44	8	6	14	67	
31–32	NYA	20	6	0	6	26	
32–33	NYA	48	12	7	19	26	
33–34	NYA–Bos	23	3	1	4	8	
34–35	Det–StL E	21	0	1	1	2	
Totals		289	51	27	78	221	

Playoffs

| 28–29 | Mont | 3 | 0 | 0 | 0 | 2 | |

*PAUL, Arthur Stewart (Butch) *5–11 160*
B. Rocky Mtn. House, Alta., Sept. 11, 1943

| 64–65 | Det | 3 | 0 | 0 | 0 | 0 | |

*PAULHUS, Roland (Rollie) *D*

| 25–26 | Mont | 33 | 0 | 0 | 0 | 0 | |

PAVELICH, Mark *5–8 170 C*
B. Eveleth, Minn., Feb. 28, 1958

81–82	NYR	79	33	43	76	67	+21
82–83	NYR	78	37	38	75	52	+20
83–84	NYR	77	29	53	82	96	+11
84–85	NYR	48	14	31	45	29	+1
85–86	NYR	59	20	20	40	82	-3
86–87	Minn	12	4	6	10	10	+7
91–92	SJ	2	0	1	1	4	-2
Totals		355	137	192	329	340	+55

Playoffs

81–82	NYR	6	1	5	6	0	
82–83	NYR	9	4	5	9	12	
83–84	NYR	5	2	4	6	0	
84–85	NYR	3	0	3	3	2	
Totals		23	7	17	24	14	

PAVELICH, Martin Nicholas *5–10 170 LW*
B. Sault Ste. Marie, Ont., Nov. 6, 1927

47–48	Det	41	4	8	12	10	
48–49	Det	60	10	16	26	40	
49–50	Det	65	8	15	23	58	
50–51	Det	67	9	20	29	41	
51–52	Det	68	17	19	36	54	
52–53	Det	64	13	20	33	49	
53–54	Det	65	9	20	29	57	
54–55	Det	70	15	15	30	59	
55–56	Det	70	5	13	18	38	
56–57	Det	64	3	16	19	48	
Totals		634	93	159	252	454	

Playoffs

47–48	Det	10	2	2	4	6	
48–49	Det	9	0	1	1	8	
49–50	Det	14	4	2	6	13	
50–51	Det	6	0	1	1	2	
51–52	Det	8	2	2	4	2	
52–53	Det	6	2	1	3	7	
53–54	Det	12	2	2	4	4	
54–55	Det	11	1	3	4	12	
55–56	Det	10	0	1	1	14	
56–57	Det	5	0	0	0	6	
Totals		91	13	15	28	74	

PAVESE, James Peter *6–2 205 D*
B. New York, N.Y., May 8, 1962

81–82	StL	42	2	9	11	101	-14
82–83	StL	42	0	2	2	45	-11
83–84	StL	4	0	1	1	19	-1
84–85	StL	51	2	5	7	69	-4
85–86	StL	69	4	7	11	116	-3
86–87	StL	69	2	9	11	127	-21
87–88	StL–NYR–Det	25	0	5	5	77	-5
88–89	Det–Hart	44	3	6	9	135	-2
Totals		328	13	44	57	689	-61

Playoffs

81–82	StL	3	0	3	3	2	
82–83	StL	4	0	0	0	6	
Totals		7	0	3	3	8	

*PAYER, Evariste P. *F*

| 17–18 | Mont | 1 | 0 | 0 | 0 | 0 | |

PAYNE, Davis *6–1 190 LW*
B. King City, Ont., Oct. 24, 1970

95–96	Bos	7	0	0	0	7	0
96–97	Bos	15	0	1	1	7	-4
Totals		22	0	1	1	14	-4

PAYNE, Steven John *6–2 210 LW*
B. Toronto, Ont., Aug. 16, 1958

| 78–79 | Minn | 70 | 23 | 17 | 40 | 29 | -5 |

SSN	TEAM	GP	G	A	PTS.	PIM	+/-
79–80	Minn	80	42	43	85	40	+37
80–81	Minn	76	30	28	58	88	+14
81–82	Minn	74	33	45	78	76	+20
82–83	Minn	80	30	39	69	53	-9
83–84	Minn	78	28	31	59	49	-2
84–85	Minn	76	29	22	51	61	-14
85–86	Minn	22	8	4	12	8	0
86–87	Minn	48	4	6	10	19	-12
87–88	Minn	9	1	3	4	12	-1
Totals		613	228	238	466	435	+28

Playoffs

79–80	Minn	15	7	7	14	9	
80–81	Minn	19	17	12	29	6	
81–82	Minn	4	4	2	6	2	
82–83	Minn	9	3	6	9	19	
83–84	Minn	15	3	6	9	18	
84–85	Minn	9	1	2	3	6	
Totals		71	35	35	70	60	

PAYNTER, Kent 6–0 183 D
B. Summerside, P.E.I., Apr. 17, 1965

87–88	Chi	2	0	0	0	2	0
88–89	Chi	1	0	0	0	2	-1
89–90	Wash	13	1	2	3	18	-7
90–91	Wash	1	0	0	0	15	0
91–92	Winn	5	0	0	0	4	-1
92–93	Ott	6	0	0	0	20	-7
93–94	Ott	9	0	1	1	8	-6
Totals		37	1	3	4	69	-22

Playoffs

89–90	Wash	3	0	0	0	10	
90–91	Wash	1	0	0	0	0	
Totals		4	0	0	0	10	

PEAKE, Patrick Michael 6–1 195 C
B. Rochester, Mich., May 28, 1973

93–94	Wash	49	11	18	29	39	+1
94–95	Wash	18	0	4	4	12	-6
95–96	Wash	62	17	19	36	46	+7
96–97	Wash	4	0	0	0	4	+1
97–98	Wash	1	0	0	0	4	0
Totals		134	28	41	69	105	+3

Playoffs

93–94	Wash	8	0	1	1	8	
95–96	Wash	5	2	1	3	12	
Totals		13	2	2	4	20	

PEARSON, George Alexander Melvin (Mel) 5–10 175 LW
B. Flin Flon, Man., Apr. 29, 1938

59–60	NYR	23	1	5	6	13	
61–62	NYR	3	0	0	0	2	
62–63	NYR	5	1	0	1	6	
64–65	NYR	5	0	0	0	4	
67–68	Pitt	2	0	1	1	0	-1
72–73	Minn (WHA)	70	8	12	20	12	
NHL Totals		38	2	6	8	25	-1
WHA Totals		70	8	12	20	12	

Playoffs

| 72–73 | Minn (WHA) | 5 | 2 | 0 | 2 | 0 | |

PEARSON, Rob 6–3 198 RW
B. Oshawa, Ont., Aug. 3, 1971

91–92	Tor	47	14	10	24	58	-16
92–93	Tor	78	23	14	37	211	-2
93–94	Tor	67	12	18	30	189	-6
94–95	Wash	32	0	6	6	96	-6
95–96	StL	27	6	4	10	54	+4
96–97	StL	18	1	2	3	37	-5
Totals		269	56	54	110	645	-31

Playoffs

92–93	Tor	14	2	2	4	31	
93–94	Tor	14	1	0	1	32	
94–95	Wash	3	1	0	1	17	
95–96	StL	2	0	0	0	14	
Totals		33	4	2	6	94	

PEARSON, Scott 6–1 205 LW
B. Cornwall, Ont., Dec. 19, 1969

| 88–89 | Tor | 9 | 0 | 1 | 1 | 2 | 0 |
| 89–90 | Tor | 41 | 5 | 10 | 15 | 90 | -7 |

SSN	TEAM	GP	G	A	PTS.	PIM	+/-
90–91	Tor–Que	47	11	4	15	100	-9
91–92	Que	10	1	2	3	14	-5
92–93	Que	41	13	1	14	95	+3
93–94	Edm	72	19	18	37	165	-4
94–95	Edm–Buf	42	3	5	8	74	-14
95–96	Buf	27	4	0	4	67	-4
96–97	Tor	1	0	0	0	2	0
Totals		290	56	41	97	615	-39

Playoffs

89–90	Tor	2	2	0	2	10	
92–93	Que	3	0	0	0	0	
94–95	Buf	5	0	0	0	4	
Totals		10	2	0	2	14	

PECA, Michael 5–11 180 RW
B. Toronto, Ont., Mar. 26, 1974

93–94	Van	4	0	0	0	2	-1
94–95	Van	33	6	6	12	30	-6
95–96	Buf	68	11	20	31	67	-1
96–97	Buf	79	20	29	49	80	+26
97–98	Buf	61	18	22	40	57	+12
98–99	Buf	82	27	29	56	81	+7
Totals		327	82	106	188	317	+27

Playoffs

94–95	Van	5	0	1	1	8	
96–97	Buf	10	0	2	2	8	
97–98	Buf	13	3	2	5	8	
98–99	Buf	21	5	8	13	18	
Totals		49	8	13	21	42	

PEDERSEN, Allen 6–3 210 D
B. Fort Saskatchewan, Alta., Jan. 13, 1965

86–87	Bos	79	1	11	12	71	-15
87–88	Bos	78	0	6	6	90	+6
88–89	Bos	51	0	6	6	69	-3
89–90	Bos	68	1	2	3	71	-5
90–91	Bos	57	2	6	8	107	+15
91–92	Minn	29	0	1	1	10	-1
92–93	Hart	59	1	4	5	60	0
93–94	Hart	7	0	0	0	9	-1
Totals		428	5	36	41	487	-4

Playoffs

86–87	Bos	4	0	0	0	4	
87–88	Bos	21	0	0	0	34	
88–89	Bos	10	0	0	0	2	
89–90	Bos	21	0	0	0	41	
90–91	Bos	8	0	0	0	10	
Totals		64	0	0	0	91	

PEDERSON, Barry Alan 5–11 185 C
B. Big River, Sask., Mar. 13, 1961

80–81	Bos	9	1	4	5	6	-5
81–82	Bos	80	44	48	92	53	+27
82–83	Bos	77	46	61	107	47	+38
83–84	Bos	80	39	77	116	64	+27
84–85	Bos	22	4	8	12	10	-11
85–86	Bos	79	29	47	76	60	+19
86–87	Van	79	24	52	76	50	-13
87–88	Van	76	19	52	71	92	+2
88–89	Van	62	15	26	41	22	+5
89–90	Van–Pitt	54	6	25	31	39	-13
90–91	Pitt	46	6	8	14	21	+2
91–92	Hart–Bos	37	5	8	13	8	-7
Totals		701	238	416	654	472	+71

Playoffs

81–82	Bos	11	7	11	18	2	
82–83	Bos	17	14	18	32	21	
83–84	Bos	3	0	1	1	2	
85–86	Bos	3	1	0	1	0	
Totals		34	22	30	52	25	

PEDERSON, Denis 6–2 190 C
B. Prince Albert, Sask., Sept. 10, 1975

95–96	NJ	10	3	1	4	0	-1
96–97	NJ	70	12	20	32	62	+7
97–98	NJ	80	15	13	28	97	-6
98–99	NJ	76	11	12	23	66	-10
Totals		236	41	46	87	225	-10

Playoffs

96–97	NJ	9	0	0	0	2	
97–98	NJ	6	1	1	2	2	
98–99	NJ	3	0	1	1	0	

SSN	TEAM	GP	G	A	PTS.	PIM	+/-
Totals		18	1	2	3	4	

PEDERSON, Mark 6–2 196 LW
B. Prelate, Sask., Jan. 14, 1968

89–90	Mont	9	0	2	2	2	0
90–91	Mont–Phil	59	10	16	26	23	-5
91–92	Phil	58	15	25	40	22	+14
92–93	Phil–SJ	41	10	7	17	28	-22
93–94	Det	2	0	0	0	0	-1
Totals		169	35	50	85	77	-14

Playoffs

| 89–90 | Mont | 2 | 0 | 0 | 0 | 0 | |

PEDERSON, Thomas Stuart 5–9 175 D
B. Bloomington, Minn., Jan. 14, 1970

92–93	SJ	44	7	13	20	31	-16
93–94	SJ	74	6	19	25	31	+3
94–95	SJ	47	5	11	16	31	-14
95–96	SJ	60	1	4	5	40	-9
96–97	Tor	15	1	2	3	9	0
Totals		240	20	49	69	142	-36

Playoffs

93–94	SJ	14	1	6	7	2	
94–95	SJ	10	0	5	5	8	
Totals		24	1	11	12	10	

PEER, Bertram (Bert) D
| 39–40 | Det | 1 | 0 | 0 | 0 | 0 | |

PEIRSON, John Frederick 5–11 170 RW
B. Winnipeg, Man., July 21, 1925

46–47	Bos	5	0	0	0	0	
47–48	Bos	15	4	2	6	0	
48–49	Bos	59	22	21	43	45	
49–50	Bos	57	27	25	52	49	
50–51	Bos	70	19	19	38	43	
51–52	Bos	68	20	30	50	30	
52–53	Bos	49	14	15	29	32	
53–54	Bos	68	21	19	40	55	
55–56	Bos	33	11	14	25	10	
56–57	Bos	68	13	26	39	41	
57–58	Bos	53	2	2	4	10	
Totals		545	153	173	326	315	

Playoffs

47–48	Bos	4	2	3	5	0	
48–49	Bos	5	3	1	4	4	
50–51	Bos	2	1	1	2	2	
51–52	Bos	7	0	2	2	4	
52–53	Bos	11	3	6	9	2	
53–54	Bos	4	0	0	0	2	
56–57	Bos	10	0	3	3	12	
57–58	Bos	5	0	1	1	0	
Totals		48	9	17	26	26	

PELENSKY, Perry 5–11 180 RW
B. Edmonton, Alta., May 22, 1962

| 83–84 | Chi | 4 | 0 | 0 | 0 | 5 | 0 |

PELLERIN, Jaque–Frederick Scott 5–11 180 LW
B. Shediac, N.B., Jan. 9, 1970

92–93	NJ	45	10	11	21	41	-1
93–94	NJ	1	0	0	0	2	0
95–96	NJ	6	2	1	3	0	+1
96–97	StL	54	8	10	18	35	+12
97–98	StL	80	8	21	29	62	+14
98–99	StL	80	20	21	41	42	+1
Totals		266	48	64	112	192	+27

Playoffs

96–97	StL	6	0	0	0	6	
97–98	StL	10	0	2	2	10	
98–99	StL	8	1	0	1	4	
Totals		24	1	2	3	20	

PELLETIER, Joseph Georges (Roger) D
B. Montreal, Que., June 22, 1945

| 67–68 | Phil | 1 | 0 | 0 | 0 | 0 | 0 |

PELOFFY, Andre Charles 5–8 160 C
B. Sete, France, Feb. 25, 1951

| 74–75 | Wash | 9 | 0 | 0 | 0 | 2 | -8 |
| 77–78 | NE (WHA) | 10 | 2 | 0 | 2 | 2 | |

SSN	TEAM	GP	G	A	PTS.	PIM	+/-

Playoffs

SSN	TEAM	GP	G	A	PTS.	PIM	+/-
77–78	NE (WHA)	2	0	0	0	0	

PELTONEN, Ville *5–11 172 LW*
B. Vantaa, Finland, May 24, 1973

SSN	TEAM	GP	G	A	PTS.	PIM	+/-
95–96	SJ	31	2	11	13	14	-7
96–97	SJ	28	2	3	5	0	-8
98–99	Nash	14	5	5	10	2	+1
Totals		73	9	19	28	16	-14

PELUSO, Michael David *6–4 220 LW*
B. Pengilly, Minn., Nov. 8, 1965

SSN	TEAM	GP	G	A	PTS.	PIM	+/-
89–90	Chi	2	0	0	0	15	0
90–91	Chi	53	6	1	7	320	-3
91–92	Chi	63	6	3	9	408	+1
92–93	Ott	81	15	10	25	318	-35
93–94	NJ	69	4	16	20	238	+19
94–95	NJ	46	2	9	11	167	+5
95–96	NJ	57	3	8	11	146	+4
96–97	NJ–StL	64	2	5	7	226	0
97–98	Calg	23	0	0	0	113	-6
Totals		458	38	52	90	1951	-15

Playoffs

SSN	TEAM	GP	G	A	PTS.	PIM	+/-
90–91	Chi	3	0	0	0	2	
91–92	Chi	17	1	2	3	8	
93–94	NJ	17	1	0	1	64	
94–95	NJ	20	1	2	3	8	
96–97	StL	5	0	0	0	25	
Totals		62	3	4	7	107	

PELYK, Michael Joseph *6–1 188 D*
B. Toronto, Ont., Sept. 29, 1947

SSN	TEAM	GP	G	A	PTS.	PIM	+/-
67–68	Tor	24	0	3	3	55	+3
68–69	Tor	65	3	9	12	146	-2
69–70	Tor	36	1	3	4	37	-10
70–71	Tor	73	5	21	26	54	+17
71–72	Tor	46	1	4	5	44	-2
72–73	Tor	72	3	16	19	118	-20
73–74	Tor	71	12	19	31	94	+5
74–75	Van (WHA)	75	14	26	40	121	
75–76	Cin (WHA)	75	10	23	33	117	
76–77	Tor	13	0	2	2	4	-4
77–78	Tor	41	1	11	12	14	+1
NHL Totals		441	26	88	114	566	-12
WHA Totals		150	24	49	73	238	

Playoffs

SSN	TEAM	GP	G	A	PTS.	PIM	+/-
68–69	Tor	4	0	0	0	8	
70–71	Tor	6	0	0	0	10	
71–72	Tor	5	0	0	0	8	
73–74	Tor	4	0	0	0	4	
76–77	Tor	9	0	2	2	4	
77–78	Tor	12	0	1	1	7	
Totals		40	0	3	3	41	

PENNEY, Chadwick Paul *6–0 195 LW*
B. Labrador City, Nfld., Sept. 18, 1973

SSN	TEAM	GP	G	A	PTS.	PIM	+/-
93–94	Ott	3	0	0	0	2	-2

PENNINGTON, Clifford *6–0 170 C*
B. Winnipeg, Man., Apr. 18, 1940

SSN	TEAM	GP	G	A	PTS.	PIM	+/-
60–61	Mont	4	1	0	1	0	
61–62	Bos	70	9	32	41	2	
62–63	Bos	27	7	10	17	4	
Totals		101	17	42	59	6	

PEPLINSKI, James Desmond *6–3 209 RW*
B. Renfrew, Ont., Oct. 24, 1960

SSN	TEAM	GP	G	A	PTS.	PIM	+/-
80–81	Calg	80	13	25	38	108	-2
81–82	Calg	74	30	37	67	115	0
82–83	Calg	80	15	26	41	134	-5
83–84	Calg	74	11	22	33	114	-21
84–85	Calg	80	16	29	45	111	+12
85–86	Calg	77	24	35	59	214	+31
86–87	Calg	80	18	32	50	181	+13
87–88	Calg	75	20	31	51	234	+20
88–89	Calg	79	13	25	38	241	+6
89–90	Calg	6	1	0	1	4	-1
94–95	Calg	6	0	1	1	11	-2
Totals		711	161	263	424	1467	+51

Playoffs

SSN	TEAM	GP	G	A	PTS.	PIM	+/-
80–81	Calg	16	2	3	5	41	
81–82	Calg	3	1	0	1	13	
82–83	Calg	8	1	1	2	45	
83–84	Calg	11	3	4	7	21	
84–85	Calg	4	1	3	4	11	
85–86	Calg	22	5	9	14	107	
86–87	Calg	6	1	0	1	24	
87–88	Calg	9	0	5	5	45	
88–89	Calg	20	1	6	7	75	
Totals		99	15	31	46	382	

PERLINI, Fred *6–2 175 C*
B. Sault Ste. Marie, Ont., Apr. 12, 1962

SSN	TEAM	GP	G	A	PTS.	PIM	+/-
81–82	Tor	7	2	3	5	0	-2
83–84	Tor	1	0	0	0	0	0
Totals		8	2	3	5	0	-2

PERREAULT, Fernand (Fern) *6–0 180 LW*
B. Chambly Basin, Que., Mar. 31, 1927

SSN	TEAM	GP	G	A	PTS.	PIM	+/-
47–48	NYR	2	0	0	0	0	
49–50	NYR	1	0	0	0	0	
Totals		3	0	0	0	0	

PERREAULT, Gilbert (Gil) *6–0 200 C*
B. Victoriaville, Que., Nov. 13, 1950

SSN	TEAM	GP	G	A	PTS.	PIM	+/-
70–71	Buf	78	38	34	72	19	-39
71–72	Buf	76	26	48	74	24	-40
72–73	Buf	78	28	60	88	10	+11
73–74	Buf	55	18	33	51	10	-8
74–75	Buf	68	39	57	96	36	+1
75–76	Buf	80	44	69	113	36	+17
76–77	Buf	80	39	56	95	30	+10
77–78	Buf	79	41	48	89	20	+18
78–79	Buf	79	27	58	85	20	+12
79–80	Buf	80	40	66	106	57	+32
80–81	Buf	56	20	39	59	56	+3
81–82	Buf	62	31	42	73	40	+19
82–83	Buf	77	30	46	76	34	-10
83–84	Buf	73	31	59	90	32	+19
84–85	Buf	78	30	53	83	42	+9
85–86	Buf	72	21	39	60	28	-10
86–87	Buf	20	9	7	16	6	-2
Totals		1191	512	814	1326	500	+42

Playoffs

SSN	TEAM	GP	G	A	PTS.	PIM	+/-
72–73	Buf	6	3	7	10	2	
74–75	Buf	17	6	9	15	10	
75–76	Buf	9	4	4	8	4	
76–77	Buf	6	1	8	9	4	
77–78	Buf	8	3	2	5	0	
78–79	Buf	3	1	0	1	2	
79–80	Buf	14	10	11	21	8	
80–81	Buf	8	2	10	12	2	
81–82	Buf	4	0	7	7	0	
82–83	Buf	10	0	7	7	8	
84–85	Buf	5	3	5	8	4	
Totals		90	33	70	103	44	

PERREAULT, Yanic *5–11 182 C*
B. Sherbrooke, Que., Apr. 4, 1971

SSN	TEAM	GP	G	A	PTS.	PIM	+/-
93–94	Tor	13	3	3	6	0	+1
94–95	LA	26	2	5	7	20	+3
95–96	LA	78	25	24	49	16	-11
96–97	LA	41	11	14	25	20	0
97–98	LA	79	28	20	48	32	+6
98–99	LA-Tor	76	17	25	42	42	+7
Totals		313	86	91	177	130	+6

Playoffs

SSN	TEAM	GP	G	A	PTS.	PIM	+/-
97–98	LA	4	1	2	3	6	
98–99	Tor	17	3	6	9	6	
Totals		21	4	8	12	12	

PERRY, Brian Thomas *5–11 180 C*
B. Aldershot, England, Apr. 6, 1944

SSN	TEAM	GP	G	A	PTS.	PIM	+/-
68–69	Oak	61	10	21	31	10	-6
69–70	Oak	34	6	8	14	14	-3
70–71	Buf	1	0	0	0	0	0
72–73	NY (WHA)	74	13	20	33	30	
73–74	NY–NJ (WHA)	71	20	11	31	19	
NHL Totals		96	16	29	45	24	-9
WHA Totals		145	33	31	64	49	
68–69	Cal	6	1	1	2	4	
69–70	Oak	2	0	0	0	0	
74–75	SD (WHA)	6	1	2	3	6	
NHL Totals		8	1	1	2	4	
WHA Totals		6	1	2	3	6	

PERSSON, Ricard *6–2 205 D*
B. Ostersund, Sweden, Aug. 24, 1969

SSN	TEAM	GP	G	A	PTS.	PIM	+/-
95–96	NJ	12	2	1	3	8	+5
96–97	NJ–StL	54	4	8	12	45	-2
97–98	StL	1	0	0	0	0	0
98–99	StL	54	1	12	13	94	+4
Totals		121	7	21	28	147	+7

Playoffs

SSN	TEAM	GP	G	A	PTS.	PIM	+/-
96–97	StL	6	0	0	0	27	
98–99	StL	13	0	3	3	17	
Totals		19	0	3	3	44	

PERSSON, Stefan *6–1 190 D*
B. Umea, Sweden, Dec. 22, 1954

SSN	TEAM	GP	G	A	PTS.	PIM	+/-
77–78	NYI	66	6	50	56	54	+19
78–79	NYI	78	10	56	66	57	+38
79–80	NYI	73	4	35	39	76	+13
80–81	NYI	80	9	52	61	82	+24
81–82	NYI	70	6	37	43	99	+35
82–83	NYI	70	4	25	29	71	+12
83–84	NYI	75	9	24	33	65	+30
84–85	NYI	54	3	19	22	30	+8
85–86	NYI	56	1	19	20	40	-3
Totals		622	52	317	369	574	+176

Playoffs

SSN	TEAM	GP	G	A	PTS.	PIM	+/-
77–78	NYI	7	0	2	2	6	
78–79	NYI	10	0	4	4	8	
79–80	NYI	21	5	10	15	16	
80–81	NYI	7	0	5	5	6	
81–82	NYI	13	1	14	15	9	
82–83	NYI	18	1	5	6	18	
83–84	NYI	16	0	6	6	2	
84–85	NYI	10	0	4	4	4	
Totals		102	7	50	57	69	

PESUT, George Mathew *6–1 185 D*
B. Saskatoon, Sask., June 17, 1953

SSN	TEAM	GP	G	A	PTS.	PIM	+/-
74–75	Cal	47	0	13	13	73	-16
75–76	Cal	45	3	9	12	57	-8
76–77	Calg (WHA)	17	2	0	2	2	
NHL Totals		92	3	22	25	130	-24
WHA Totals		17	2	0	2	2	

***PETERS, Franklin J. (Frank)** *D*
B. Rouses Point, N.Y., June 5, 1905

SSN	TEAM	GP	G	A	PTS.	PIM	+/-
30–31	NYR	43	0	0	0	59	

Playoffs

SSN	TEAM	GP	G	A	PTS.	PIM	+/-
30–31	NYR	4	0	0	0	2	

PETERS, Garry Lorne *5–10 180 C*
B. Regina, Sask., Oct. 9, 1942

SSN	TEAM	GP	G	A	PTS.	PIM	+/-
64–65	Mont	13	0	2	2	6	
65–66	NYR	63	7	3	10	42	
66–67	Mont	4	0	1	1	2	
67–68	Phil	31	7	5	12	22	-2
68–69	Phil	66	8	6	14	49	-20
69–70	Phil	59	6	10	16	69	-9
70–71	Phil	73	6	7	13	69	-14
71–72	Bos	2	0	0	0	2	0
72–73	NY (WHA)	23	2	7	9	24	
73–74	NY–NJ (WHA)	34	2	5	7	18	
NHL Totals		311	34	34	68	261	-45
WHA Totals		57	4	12	16	42	

Playoffs

SSN	TEAM	GP	G	A	PTS.	PIM	+/-
68–69	Phil	4	1	1	2	16	
70–71	Phil	4	1	1	2	15	
71–72	Bos	1	0	0	0	0	
Totals		9	2	2	4	31	

PETERS, James Meldrum *5–11 165 RW*
B. Verdun, Que., Oct. 2, 1922

SSN	TEAM	GP	G	A	PTS.	PIM	+/-
45–46	Mont	47	11	19	30	10	
46–47	Mont	60	11	13	24	27	
47–48	Mont–Bos	59	13	18	31	44	
48–49	Bos	60	16	15	31	8	
49–50	Det	70	14	16	30	20	
50–51	Det	68	17	21	38	14	
51–52	Chi	70	15	21	36	15	
52–53	Chi	69	22	19	41	16	
53–54	Chi–Det	71	6	8	14	31	
Totals		574	125	150	275	185	

SSN	TEAM	GP	G	A	PTS.	PIM	+/-
Playoffs							
45–46	Mont	9	3	1	4	6	
46–47	Mont	11	1	2	3	10	
47–48	Bos	5	1	2	3	2	
48–49	Bos	4	0	1	1	0	
49–50	Det	8	2	2	0	0	
50–51	Det	6	0	0	0	0	
52–53	Chi	7	0	1	1	4	
53–54	Det	10	0	0	0	0	
Totals		60	5	9	14	22	

PETERS, James Stephen, Jr. *6–2 185 C*
B. Montreal, Que., June 20, 1944

SSN	TEAM	GP	G	A	PTS.	PIM	+/-
64–65	Det	1	0	0	0	0	
65–66	Det	6	1	1	2	2	
66–67	Det	2	0	0	0	0	
67–68	Det	45	5	6	11	8	-10
68–69	LA	76	10	15	25	28	-10
69–70	LA	74	15	9	24	10	-13
72–73	LA	77	4	5	9	0	-3
73–74	LA	25	2	0	2	0	-2
74–75	LA	3	0	0	0	0	0
Totals		309	37	36	73	48	-38
Playoffs							
68–69	LA	11	0	2	2	2	

PETERS, Steven Alan *5–11 186 C*
B. Peterborough, Ont., Jan. 23, 1960

SSN	TEAM	GP	G	A	PTS.	PIM	+/-
79–80	Col	2	0	1	1	0	+1

PETERSON, Brent Ronald *6–0 190 C*
B. Calgary, Alta., Feb. 15, 1958

SSN	TEAM	GP	G	A	PTS.	PIM	+/-
79–80	Det	18	1	2	3	2	0
80–81	Det	53	6	18	24	24	-1
81–82	Det–Buf	61	10	5	15	49	+2
82–83	Buf	75	13	24	37	38	-9
83–84	Buf	70	9	12	21	52	+10
84–85	Buf	74	12	22	34	47	+3
85–86	Van	77	8	23	31	94	+18
86–87	Van	69	7	15	22	77	-10
87–88	Hart	52	2	7	9	40	-14
88–89	Hart	66	4	13	17	61	-7
Totals		620	72	141	213	484	-8
Playoffs							
81–82	Buf	4	1	0	1	12	
82–83	Buf	10	1	2	3	28	
83–84	Buf	3	0	1	1	4	
84–85	Buf	5	0	0	0	6	
85–86	Van	3	2	0	2	9	
87–88	Hart	4	0	0	0	2	
88–89	Hart	2	0	1	1	4	
Totals		31	4	4	8	65	

PETERSON, Brent *6–3 200 LW*
B. Calgary, Alta., July 20, 1972

SSN	TEAM	GP	G	A	PTS.	PIM	+/-
96–97	TB	17	2	0	2	4	-4
97–98	TB	19	5	0	5	2	-2
98–99	TB	20	2	1	3	0	-2
Totals		56	9	1	10	4	-8

PETIT, Michel *6–1 205 D*
B. St. Malo, Que., Feb. 12, 1964

SSN	TEAM	GP	G	A	PTS.	PIM	+/-
82–83	Van	2	0	0	0	0	-4
83–84	Van	44	6	9	15	53	-6
84–85	Van	69	5	26	31	127	-26
85–86	Van	32	1	6	7	27	-6
86–87	Van	69	12	13	25	131	-5
87–88	Van–NYR	74	9	27	36	258	-1
88–89	NYR	69	8	25	33	154	-15
89–90	Que	63	12	24	36	215	-38
90–91	Que–Tor	73	13	26	39	179	-34
91–92	Tor–Calg	70	4	23	27	164	-15
92–93	Calg	35	3	9	12	54	-5
93–94	Calg	63	2	21	23	110	+5
94–95	LA	40	5	12	17	84	+4
95–96	LA–TB	54	4	8	12	135	-11
96–97	Edm–Phil	38	2	7	9	71	-11
97–98	Phoe	32	4	2	6	77	-4
Totals		827	90	238	328	1839	-172
Playoffs							
83–84	Van	1	0	0	0	0	
88–89	NYR	4	0	2	2	27	
95–96	TB	6	0	0	0	20	
96–97	Phil	3	0	0	0	6	

SSN	TEAM	GP	G	A	PTS.	PIM	+/-
97–98	Phoe	5	0	0	0	8	
Totals		19	0	2	2	61	

PETRENKO, Sergei *6–0 176 LW*
B. Kharkov, USSR, Sept. 10, 1968

SSN	TEAM	GP	G	A	PTS.	PIM	+/-
93–94	Buf	14	0	4	4	0	-3

PETROV, Oleg *5–8 175 RW*
B. Moscow, USSR, Apr. 18, 1971

SSN	TEAM	GP	G	A	PTS.	PIM	+/-
92–93	Mont	9	2	1	3	10	+2
93–94	Mont	55	12	15	27	2	+7
94–95	Mont	12	2	3	5	4	-7
95–96	Mont	36	4	7	11	23	-9
Totals		112	20	26	46	39	-7
Playoffs							
92–93	Mont	1	0	0	0	0	
93–94	Mont	2	0	0	0	0	
95–96	Mont	5	0	1	1	0	
Totals		8	0	1	1	0	

PETROVICKY, Robert *5–11 172 C*
B. Kosice, Czechoslovakia, Oct. 26, 1973

SSN	TEAM	GP	G	A	PTS.	PIM	+/-
92–93	Hart	42	3	6	9	45	-10
93–94	Hart	33	6	5	11	39	-1
94–95	Hart	2	0	0	0	0	0
95–96	Dal	5	1	1	2	0	+1
96–97	StL	44	7	12	19	10	+2
98–99	TB	28	3	4	7	6	-8
Totals		164	20	28	48	100	-16
Playoffs							
96–97	StL	2	0	0	0	0	

PETTERSSON, Jorgen *6–2 185 LW*
B. Gothenburg, Sweden, July 11, 1956

SSN	TEAM	GP	G	A	PTS.	PIM	+/-
80–81	StL	62	37	36	73	24	+14
81–82	StL	77	38	31	69	28	-8
82–83	StL	74	35	38	73	4	-10
83–84	StL	77	28	34	62	29	-2
84–85	StL	75	23	32	55	20	+8
85–86	Hart–Wash	70	13	21	34	12	-16
Totals		435	174	192	366	117	-14
Playoffs							
80–81	StL	11	4	3	7	0	
81–82	StL	7	1	2	3	0	
82–83	StL	4	1	1	2	0	
83–84	StL	11	7	3	10	2	
84–85	StL	3	1	1	2	0	
85–86	Wash	8	1	2	3	2	
Totals		44	15	12	27	4	

*PETTINGER, Eric (Cowboy) *6–0 175 LW*
B. Regina, Sask.

SSN	TEAM	GP	G	A	PTS.	PIM	+/-
28–29	Bos–Tor	42	3	3	6	41	
29–30	Tor	43	4	9	13	40	
30–31	Ott	12	0	0	0	2	
Totals		97	7	12	19	83	
Playoffs							
28–29	Tor	4	1	0	1	8	

*PETTINGER, Gordon Robinson *6–0 175 C*
B. Regina, Sask., Nov. 17, 1911

SSN	TEAM	GP	G	A	PTS.	PIM	+/-
32–33	NYR	35	1	2	3	18	
33–34	Det	48	3	14	17	14	
34–35	Det	13	2	3	5	2	
35–36	Det	33	8	7	15	6	
36–37	Det	48	7	15	22	13	
37–38	Det–Bos	46	8	13	21	14	
38–39	Bos	48	11	14	25	8	
39–40	Bos	21	2	6	8	2	
Totals		292	42	74	116	77	
Playoffs							
32–33	NYR	8	0	0	0	0	
33–34	Det	9	1	0	1	2	
35–36	Det	7	2	2	4	0	
36–37	Det	10	0	2	2	2	
37–38	Bos	3	0	0	0	0	
38–39	Bos	12	1	1	2	7	
Totals		49	4	5	9	11	

PHAIR, Lyle *6–1 190 LW*
B. Pilot Mount, Man., Aug. 31, 1961

SSN	TEAM	GP	G	A	PTS.	PIM	+/-
85–86	LA	15	0	1	1	2	-12
86–87	LA	5	2	0	2	2	-1
87–88	LA	28	4	6	10	8	-5
Totals		48	6	7	13	12	-18
Playoffs							
89–88	LA	1	0	0	0	0	

PHILLIPOFF, Harold *6–3 220 LW*
B. Kamsack, Sask., July 15, 1956

SSN	TEAM	GP	G	A	PTS.	PIM	+/-
77–78	Atl	67	17	36	53	128	+27
78–79	Atl–Chi	65	9	21	30	119	+1
79–80	Chi	9	0	0	0	20	-3
Totals		141	26	57	83	267	+25
Playoffs							
77–78	Atl	2	0	1	1	2	
78–79	Chi	4	0	1	1	7	
Totals		6	0	2	2	9	

PHILLIPS, Charles *D*
B. Toronto, Ont., May 10, 1917

SSN	TEAM	GP	G	A	PTS.	PIM	+/-
42–43	Mont	17	0	0	0	6	

PHILLIPS, Chris *6–0 210 D*
B. Minneapolis, Minn., Nov. 5, 1967

SSN	TEAM	GP	G	A	PTS.	PIM	+/-
97–98	Ott	72	5	11	16	38	+2
98–99	Ott	34	3	3	6	32	-5
Totals		106	8	14	22	70	-3
Playoffs							
97–98	Ott	11	0	2	2	2	
98–99	Ott	3	0	0	0	0	
Totals		14	0	2	2	2	

*PHILLIPS, Merlyn J. (Bill) *5–7 160 F*
B. Thesselon, Ont., 1896

SSN	TEAM	GP	G	A	PTS.	PIM	+/-
25–26	Mont M	12	3	1	4	6	
26–27	Mont M	43	15	1	16	45	
27–28	Mont M	40	7	5	12	33	
28–29	Mont M	42	6	5	11	41	
29–30	Mont M	44	13	10	23	38	
30–31	Mont M	43	6	1	7	38	
31–32	Mont M	46	1	1	2	11	
32–33	Mont M–NYA	32	1	7	8	10	
Totals		302	52	31	83	222	
Playoffs							
25–26	Mont M	8	1	1	2	4	
26–27	Mont M	2	0	0	0	0	
27–28	Mont M	9	2	1	3	13	
29–30	Mont M	4	0	0	0	6	
30–31	Mont M	1	0	0	0	2	
31–32	Mont M	4	0	0	0	2	
Totals		28	3	2	5	27	

*PHILLIPS, W. J. (Bat) *RW*
B. Carleton Place, Ont.

SSN	TEAM	GP	G	A	PTS.	PIM	+/-
29–30	Mont M	27	1	1	2	6	
Playoffs							
29–30	Mont M	4	0	0	0	2	

PICARD, Adrien Roger (Roger) *6–0 200 RW*
B. Montreal, Que., Jan. 13, 1935

SSN	TEAM	GP	G	A	PTS.	PIM	+/-
67–68	StL	15	2	2	4	21	-4

PICARD, Jean–Noel Yves (Noel) *6–1 185 D*
B. Montreal, Que., Dec. 25, 1938

SSN	TEAM	GP	G	A	PTS.	PIM	+/-
64–65	Mont	16	0	7	7	33	
67–68	StL	66	1	10	11	142	-4
68–69	StL	67	5	19	24	131	+19
69–70	StL	39	1	4	5	88	0
70–71	StL	75	3	8	11	119	+2
71–72	StL	15	1	5	6	50	+4
72–73	StL–Atl	57	1	10	11	53	-8
Totals		335	12	63	75	616	+10
Playoffs							
64–65	Mont	3	0	1	1	0	
67–68	StL	13	0	3	3	46	
68–69	StL	12	1	4	5	30	
69–70	StL	16	0	2	2	65	

SSN	TEAM	GP	G	A	PTS.	PIM	+/-
70–71	StL	6	1	1	2	26	
Totals		50	2	11	13	167	

PICARD, Michel *5–11 190 LW*
B. Beauport, Que., Nov. 7, 1969

SSN	TEAM	GP	G	A	PTS.	PIM	+/-
90–91	Hart	5	1	0	1	2	-2
91–92	Hart	25	3	5	8	6	-2
92–93	SJ	25	4	0	4	24	-17
94–95	Ott	24	5	8	13	14	-1
95–96	Ott	17	2	6	8	10	-1
97–98	StL	16	1	8	9	29	+3
98–99	StL	45	11	11	22	16	+5
Totals		157	27	38	65	101	-15

Playoffs

SSN	TEAM	GP	G	A	PTS.	PIM	+/-
98–99	StL	5	0	0	0	2	

PICARD, Robert Rene Joseph *6–2 207 D*
B. Montreal, Que., May 25, 1957

SSN	TEAM	GP	G	A	PTS.	PIM	+/-
77–78	Wash	75	10	27	37	101	-25
78–79	Wash	77	21	44	65	85	+3
79–80	Wash	78	11	43	54	122	-21
80–81	Tor–Mont	67	8	21	29	74	-33
81–82	Mont	62	2	26	28	106	+17
82–83	Mont	64	7	31	38	60	+31
83–84	Mont–Winn	69	6	18	24	34	+8
84–85	Winn	78	12	22	34	107	+31
85–86	Winn–Que	68	9	32	41	53	-4
86–87	Que	78	8	20	28	71	-17
87–88	Que	65	3	13	16	103	-1
88–89	Que	74	7	14	21	61	-28
89–90	Que–Det	44	0	8	8	48	-3
Totals		899	104	319	423	1025	-43

Playoffs

SSN	TEAM	GP	G	A	PTS.	PIM	+/-
80–81	Mont	1	0	0	0	0	
81–82	Mont	5	1	1	2	7	
82–83	Mont	3	0	0	0	0	
83–84	Winn	3	0	0	0	12	
84–85	Winn	8	2	2	4	8	
85–86	Que	3	0	2	2	2	
86–87	Que	13	2	10	12	10	
Totals		36	5	15	20	39	

PICHETTE, Dave *6–3 190 D*
B. Grand Falls, Nfld., Feb. 4, 1960

SSN	TEAM	GP	G	A	PTS.	PIM	+/-
80–81	Que	46	4	16	20	62	+3
81–82	Que	67	7	30	37	152	-1
82–83	Que	53	3	21	24	49	+9
83–84	Que–StL	46	2	18	20	18	-3
84–85	NJ	71	17	40	57	41	-20
85–86	NJ	33	7	12	19	22	-11
87–88	NYR	6	1	3	4	4	-3
Totals		322	41	140	181	348	-26

Playoffs

SSN	TEAM	GP	G	A	PTS.	PIM	+/-
80–81	Que	1	0	0	0	14	
81–82	Que	16	2	4	6	22	
82–83	Que	2	0	1	1	0	
83–84	StL	9	1	2	3	18	
Totals		28	3	7	10	54	

PICKETTS, Frederic Harold (Hal) *180 F*
B. Asquith, Sask., Apr. 22, 1909

SSN	TEAM	GP	G	A	PTS.	PIM	+/-
33–34	NYA	48	3	1	4	32	

PIDHIRNY, Harry *5–11 155 C*
B. Toronto, Ont., Mar. 5, 1928

SSN	TEAM	GP	G	A	PTS.	PIM	+/-
57–58	Bos	2	0	0	0	0	

PIERCE, Randy Stephen *5–11 185 RW*
B. Arnprior, Ont., Nov. 23, 1957

SSN	TEAM	GP	G	A	PTS.	PIM	+/-
77–78	Col	35	9	10	19	15	0
78–79	Col	70	19	17	36	35	-21
79–80	Col	75	16	23	39	100	-11
80–81	Col	55	9	21	30	52	-28
81–82	Col	5	0	0	0	4	-1
82–83	NJ	3	0	0	0	0	0
83–84	Hart	17	6	3	9	9	+5
84–85	Hart	17	3	2	5	8	-4
Totals		277	62	76	138	223	-60

Playoffs

SSN	TEAM	GP	G	A	PTS.	PIM	+/-
77–78	Col	2	0	0	0	0	

PIKE, Alfred G. (Alf) *6–0 187 C*
B. Winnipeg, Man., Sept. 15, 1917

SSN	TEAM	GP	G	A	PTS.	PIM	+/-
39–40	NYR	47	8	9	17	38	
40–41	NYR	48	6	13	19	23	
41–42	NYR	34	8	19	27	16	
42–43	NYR	41	6	16	22	48	
45–46	NYR	33	7	9	16	18	
46–47	NYR	31	7	11	18	2	
Totals		234	42	77	119	145	

Playoffs

SSN	TEAM	GP	G	A	PTS.	PIM	+/-
39–40	NYR	12	3	1	4	6	
40–41	NYR	3	0	1	1	2	
41–42	NYR	6	1	0	1	4	
Totals		21	4	2	6	12	

PILON, Richard *6–0 202 D*
B. Saskatoon, Sask., Apr. 30, 1968

SSN	TEAM	GP	G	A	PTS.	PIM	+/-
88–89	NYI	62	0	14	14	242	-9
89–90	NYI	14	0	2	2	31	+2
90–91	NYI	60	1	4	5	126	-12
91–92	NYI	65	1	6	7	183	-1
92–93	NYI	44	1	3	4	164	-4
93–94	NYI	28	1	4	5	75	-4
94–95	NYI	20	1	1	2	40	-3
95–96	NYI	27	0	3	3	72	-9
96–97	NYI	52	1	4	5	179	+4
97–98	NYI	76	0	7	7	291	+1
98–99	NYI	52	0	4	4	88	-8
Totals		500	6	52	58	1491	-43

Playoffs

SSN	TEAM	GP	G	A	PTS.	PIM	+/-
92–93	NYI	15	0	0	0	50	

PILOTE, Joseph Albert Pierre Paul (Pierre) *5–10 178 D*
B. Kenogami, Que., Dec. 11, 1931

SSN	TEAM	GP	G	A	PTS.	PIM	+/-
55–56	Chi	20	3	5	8	34	
56–57	Chi	70	3	14	17	117	
57–58	Chi	70	6	24	30	91	
58–59	Chi	70	7	30	37	79	
59–60	Chi	70	7	38	45	100	
60–61	Chi	70	6	29	35	165	
61–62	Chi	59	7	35	42	97	
62–63	Chi	59	8	18	26	57	
63–64	Chi	70	7	46	53	84	
64–65	Chi	68	14	45	59	162	
65–66	Chi	51	2	34	36	60	
66–67	Chi	70	6	46	52	90	
67–68	Chi	74	1	36	37	69	-8
68–69	Tor	69	3	18	21	46	+5
Totals		890	80	418	498	1251	-3

Playoffs

SSN	TEAM	GP	G	A	PTS.	PIM	+/-
58–59	Chi	6	0	2	2	10	
59–60	Chi	4	0	1	1	8	
60–61	Chi	12	3	12	15	8	
61–62	Chi	12	0	7	7	8	
62–63	Chi	6	0	8	8	8	
63–64	Chi	7	2	6	8	6	
64–65	Chi	12	0	7	7	22	
65–66	Chi	6	0	2	2	10	
66–67	Chi	6	2	4	6	6	
67–68	Chi	11	1	3	4	12	
68–69	Tor	4	0	1	1	4	
Totals		86	8	53	61	102	

PINDER, Allen Gerald (Gerry) *5–8 165 LW*
B. Saskatoon, Sask., Sept. 15, 1948

SSN	TEAM	GP	G	A	PTS.	PIM	+/-
69–70	Chi	75	19	20	39	41	+23
70–71	Chi	74	13	18	31	35	-2
71–72	Cal	74	23	31	54	59	-18
72–73	Clev (WHA)	78	30	36	66	21	
73–74	Clev (WHA)	73	23	33	56	90	
74–75	Clev (WHA)	74	13	28	41	71	
75–76	Clev (WHA)	79	21	30	51	118	
76–77	SD (WHA)	44	6	13	19	36	
77–78	Edm (WHA)	5	0	1	1	0	
NHL Totals		223	55	69	124	135	+3
WHA Totals		353	93	141	234	336	

Playoffs

SSN	TEAM	GP	G	A	PTS.	PIM	+/-
69–70	Chi	8	0	4	4	4	
70–71	Chi	9	0	0	0	2	
72–73	Clev (WHA)	9	2	9	11	30	
73–74	Clev (WHA)	1	0	0	0	0	
74–75	Clev (WHA)	5	3	1	4	6	
75–76	Clev (WHA)	3	0	0	0	4	
NHL Totals		17	0	4	4	6	
WHA Totals		18	5	10	15	40	

PIRUS, Joseph Alexander (Alex) *6–1 205 RW*
B. Toronto, Ont., Jan. 12, 1955

SSN	TEAM	GP	G	A	PTS.	PIM	+/-
76–77	Minn	79	20	17	37	47	-20
77–78	Minn	61	9	6	15	38	-25
78–79	Minn	15	1	3	4	9	-8
79–80	Det	4	0	2	2	0	0
Totals		159	30	28	58	94	-53

Playoffs

SSN	TEAM	GP	G	A	PTS.	PIM	+/-
76–77	Minn	2	0	1	1	2	

PITLICK, Lance *6–0 180 D*
B. Minneapolis, Minn., Nov. 5, 1967

SSN	TEAM	GP	G	A	PTS.	PIM	+/-
94–95	Ott	15	0	1	1	6	-5
95–96	Ott	28	1	6	7	20	-8
96–97	Ott	66	5	5	10	91	+2
97–98	Ott	69	2	7	9	50	+8
98–99	Ott	50	3	6	9	33	+7
Totals		228	11	25	36	200	+4

Playoffs

SSN	TEAM	GP	G	A	PTS.	PIM	+/-
96–97	Ott	7	0	0	0	4	
97–98	Ott	11	0	1	1	17	
98–99	Ott	2	0	0	0	0	
Totals		20	0	1	1	21	

*PITRE, Didier (Cannonball) *200 F*
B. Sault Ste. Marie, Ont., 1884

SSN	TEAM	GP	G	A	PTS.	PIM	+/-
17–18	Mont	19	17	0	17	9	
18–19	Mont	17	14	4	18	9	
19–20	Mont	22	15	7	22	6	
20–21	Mont	23	15	1	16	23	
21–22	Mont	23	2	3	5	12	
22–23	Mont	23	1	2	3	0	
Totals		127	64	17	81	59	

Playoffs

SSN	TEAM	GP	G	A	PTS.	PIM	+/-
17–18	Mont	2	0	0	0	10	
18–19	Mont	10	2	2	4	3	
22–23	Mont	2	0	0	0	0	
Totals		14	2	2	4	13	

PITTIS, Domenic *5–11 185 C*
B. Calgary, Alta., Oct. 1, 1974

SSN	TEAM	GP	G	A	PTS.	PIM	+/-
96–97	Pitt	1	0	0	0	0	-1
98–99	Buf	3	0	0	0	2	0
Totals		4	0	0	0	2	-1

PIVONKA, Michal *6–2 198 C*
B. Kladno, Czechoslovakia, Jan. 28, 1966

SSN	TEAM	GP	G	A	PTS.	PIM	+/-
86–87	Wash	73	18	25	43	41	-19
87–88	Wash	71	11	23	34	28	+1
88–89	Wash	52	8	19	27	30	+9
89–90	Wash	77	25	39	64	54	-7
90–91	Wash	79	20	50	70	34	+3
91–92	Wash	80	23	57	80	47	+10
92–93	Wash	69	21	53	74	66	+14
93–94	Wash	82	14	36	50	38	+2
94–95	Wash	46	10	23	33	50	+3
95–96	Wash	73	16	65	81	36	+18
96–97	Wash	54	7	16	23	22	-15
97–98	Wash	33	3	6	9	20	+5
98–99	Wash	36	5	6	11	12	-6
Totals		825	181	418	599	498	+18

Playoffs

SSN	TEAM	GP	G	A	PTS.	PIM	+/-
86–87	Wash	7	1	1	2	2	
87–88	Wash	14	4	9	13	4	
88–89	Wash	6	3	1	4	10	
89–90	Wash	11	0	2	2	6	
90–91	Wash	11	2	3	5	8	
91–92	Wash	7	1	5	6	13	
92–93	Wash	6	0	2	2	0	
93–94	Wash	7	4	4	8	4	
94–95	Wash	7	1	4	5	21	
95–96	Wash	6	3	2	5	18	
97–98	Wash	13	0	3	3	0	
Totals		95	19	36	55	86	

PLAGER, Barclay Graham 5-11 175 D
*PLAGER, Barclay Graham *5-11 175 D*
B. Kirkland Lake, Ont., Mar. 26, 1941

SSN	TEAM	GP	G	A	PTS.	PIM	+/-
67-68	StL	49	5	15	20	153	+4
68-69	StL	61	4	26	30	120	+21
69-70	StL	75	6	26	32	128	+2
70-71	StL	69	4	20	24	172	+11
71-72	StL	78	7	22	29	176	+6
72-73	StL	68	8	25	33	102	0
73-74	StL	72	6	20	26	99	-11
74-75	StL	76	4	24	28	96	+20
75-76	StL	64	0	8	8	67	-6
76-77	StL	2	0	1	1	2	+1
Totals		614	44	187	231	1115	+48

Playoffs

67-68	StL	18	2	5	7	73
68-69	StL	12	0	4	4	31
69-70	StL	13	0	2	2	20
70-71	StL	6	0	3	3	10
71-72	StL	11	1	4	5	21
72-73	StL	5	0	1	1	0
74-75	StL	2	0	1	1	14
75-76	StL	1	0	0	0	13
Totals		68	3	20	23	182

PLAGER, Robert Bryan *5-11 195 D*
B. Kirkland Lake, Ont., Mar. 11, 1943

64-65	NYR	10	0	0	0	18	
65-66	NYR	18	0	5	5	5	
66-67	NYR	1	0	0	0	0	
67-68	StL	53	2	5	7	86	-11
68-69	StL	32	0	7	7	43	+10
69-70	StL	64	3	11	14	113	+2
70-71	StL	70	1	19	20	114	+9
71-72	StL	50	4	7	11	81	-1
72-73	StL	77	2	31	33	107	-1
73-74	StL	61	3	10	13	48	+9
74-75	StL	73	1	14	15	53	+10
75-76	StL	63	3	8	11	90	+17
76-77	StL	54	1	9	10	23	-9
77-78	StL	18	0	0	0	4	-8
Totals		644	20	126	146	802	+27

Playoffs

67-68	StL	18	1	2	3	69
68-69	StL	9	0	4	4	47
69-70	StL	16	0	3	3	46
70-71	StL	6	0	2	2	4
71-72	StL	11	1	4	5	5
72-73	StL	5	0	2	2	2
74-75	StL	2	0	0	0	20
75-76	StL	3	0	0	0	2
76-77	StL	4	0	0	0	0
Totals		74	2	17	19	195

PLAGER, William Ronald *5-9 175 D*
B. Kirkland Lake, Ont., July 6, 1945

67-68	Minn	32	0	2	2	30	-16
68-69	StL	2	0	0	0	2	0
69-70	StL	24	1	4	5	30	-5
70-71	StL	36	0	3	3	45	0
71-72	StL	65	1	11	12	64	-15
72-73	Atl	76	2	11	13	92	-18
73-74	Minn	1	0	0	0	2	-1
74-75	Minn	7	0	0	0	8	-3
75-76	Minn	20	0	3	3	21	-5
Totals		263	4	34	38	294	-63

Playoffs

67-68	Minn	12	0	2	2	8
68-69	StL	4	0	0	0	4
69-70	StL	3	0	0	0	0
70-71	StL	1	0	0	0	2
71-72	StL	11	0	0	0	12
Totals		31	0	2	2	26

PLAMANDON, Gerard Roger (Gerry) *5-7 170 LW*
B. Sherbrooke, Que., Jan. 5, 1925

45-46	Mont	6	0	2	2	2
47-48	Mont	3	1	1	2	0
48-49	Mont	27	5	5	10	8
49-50	Mont	37	1	5	6	0
50-51	Mont	1	0	0	0	0
Totals		74	7	13	20	10

Playoffs

45-46	Mont	1	0	0	0	0
48-49	Mont	7	5	1	6	0
49-50	Mont	3	0	1	1	2
Totals		11	5	2	7	2

PLANTE, Cam *6-1 195 D*
B. Brandon, Man., Mar. 12, 1964

84-85	Tor	2	0	0	0	0	0

PLANTE, Daniel Leon *5-11 198 RW*
B. St. Louis, Mo., Oct. 5, 1971

93-94	NYI	12	0	1	1	4	-2
95-96	NYI	73	5	3	8	50	-22
96-97	NYI	67	4	9	13	75	-6
97-98	NYI	7	0	1	1	6	-1
Totals		159	9	14	23	135	-31

Playoffs

93-94	NYR	1	1	0	1	2

PLANTE, Derek John *5-11 180 C*
B. Cloquet, Minn., Jan. 17, 1971

93-94	Buf	77	21	35	56	24	+4
94-95	Buf	47	3	19	22	12	-4
95-96	Buf	76	23	33	56	28	-4
96-97	Buf	82	27	26	53	24	+14
97-98	Buf	72	13	21	34	26	+8
98-99	Buf-Dal	51	6	14	20	16	+4
Totals		405	93	148	241	130	+22

Playoffs

93-94	Buf	7	1	0	1	0
96-97	Buf	12	4	6	10	4
97-98	Buf	11	0	3	3	10
98-99	Dal	6	1	0	1	4
Totals		36	6	9	15	18

PLANTE, Pierre Renald *6-1 190 RW*
B. Valleyfield, Que., May 14, 1951

71-72	Phil	24	1	0	1	15	-11
72-73	Phil-StL	51	12	16	28	56	+11
73-74	StL	78	26	28	54	85	-14
74-75	StL	80	34	32	66	125	+16
75-76	StL	74	14	19	33	77	-22
76-77	StL	76	18	20	38	77	-4
77-78	Chi	77	10	18	28	59	-2
78-79	NYR	70	6	25	31	37	+11
79-80	Que	69	4	14	18	68	-14
Totals		599	125	172	297	599	-29

Playoffs

72-73	StL	5	2	0	2	15
74-75	StL	2	0	0	0	8
75-76	StL	3	0	0	0	6
76-77	StL	4	0	0	0	2
77-78	Chi	1	0	0	0	0
78-79	NYR	18	0	6	6	20
Totals		33	2	6	8	51

PLANTERY, Mark P. *6-1 185 D*
B. St. Catherines, Ont., Aug. 14, 1959

80-81	Winn	25	1	5	6	14	-10

PLAVSIC, Adrien *6-1 200 D*
B. Montreal, Que., Jan. 13, 1970

89-90	StL-Van	15	3	3	6	10	+1
90-91	Van	48	2	10	12	62	-23
91-92	Van	16	1	9	10	14	+4
92-93	Van	57	6	21	27	53	+28
93-94	Van	47	1	9	10	6	-5
94-95	Van-TB	18	2	2	4	8	+8
95-96	TB	7	1	2	3	6	+5
96-97	Ana	6	0	0	0	2	-5
Totals		214	16	56	72	161	+13

Playoffs

91-92	Van	13	1	7	8	4

*PLAXTON, Hugh John *184 LW*
B. Barrie, Ont., May 16, 1904

32-33	Mont M	15	1	2	3	4

PLAYFAIR, James *6-4 220 D*
B. Fort St. James, B.C., May 22, 1964

83-84	Edm	2	1	1	2	2	+4
87-88	Chi	12	1	3	4	21	+4
88-89	Chi	7	0	0	0	28	+1
Totals		21	2	4	6	51	+9

PLAYFAIR, Larry William *6-4 205 D*
B. Fort St. James, B.C., June 23, 1958

78-79	Buf	26	0	3	3	60	+1
79-80	Buf	79	2	10	12	145	+13
80-81	Buf	75	3	9	12	169	+4
81-82	Buf	77	6	10	16	258	-5
82-83	Buf	79	4	13	17	180	+5
83-84	Buf	76	5	11	16	211	+4
84-85	Buf	72	3	14	17	157	-3
85-86	Buf-LA	61	1	3	4	126	-22
86-87	LA	37	2	7	9	181	-1
87-88	LA	54	0	7	7	197	-13
88-89	LA-Buf	48	0	6	6	126	-7
89-90	Buf	4	0	1	1	2	-2
Totals		688	26	94	120	1812	-26

Playoffs

79-80	Buf	14	0	2	2	29
80-81	Buf	8	0	0	0	26
81-82	Buf	4	0	0	0	22
82-83	Buf	5	0	1	1	11
83-84	Buf	3	0	0	0	0
84-85	Buf	5	0	3	3	9
87-88	LA	3	0	0	0	14
88-89	Buf	1	0	0	0	0
Totals		43	0	6	6	111

PLEAU, Lawrence Winslow *6-1 190 C*
B. Lynn, Mass., June 29, 1947

69-70	Mont	20	0	1	1	0	-1
70-71	Mont	19	1	5	6	8	-8
71-72	Mont	55	7	12	19	14	+4
72-73	NE (WHA)	78	39	48	87	42	
73-74	NE (WHA)	77	26	43	69	35	
74-75	NE (WHA)	78	30	34	64	50	
75-76	NE (WHA)	75	29	45	74	21	
76-77	NE (WHA)	78	11	21	32	22	-5
77-78	NE (WHA)	54	16	18	34	4	
78-79	NE (WHA)	28	6	6	12	6	
NHL Totals		94	9	15	24	22	-10
WHA Totals		468	157	215	372	180	

Playoffs

71-72	Mont	4	0	0	0	0
72-73	NE (WHA)	15	12	7	19	15
73-74	NE (WHA)	2	2	0	2	0
74-75	NE (WHA)	6	2	3	5	14
75-76	NE (WHA)	14	5	7	12	0
76-77	NE (WHA)	5	1	0	1	0
77-78	NE (WHA)	14	5	4	9	8
78-79	NE (WHA)	10	2	1	3	0
NHL Totals		4	0	0	0	0
WHA Totals		66	29	22	51	37

PLETT, Willi *6-3 205 RW*
B. Paraguay, June 7, 1955

75-76	Atl	4	0	0	0	0	0
76-77	Atl	64	33	23	56	123	+15
77-78	Atl	78	22	21	43	171	-6
78-79	Atl	74	23	20	43	213	+13
79-80	Atl	76	13	19	32	231	-4
80-81	Calg	78	38	30	68	239	+5
81-82	Calg	78	21	36	57	288	-22
82-83	Minn	71	25	14	39	170	-12
83-84	Minn	73	15	23	38	316	-6
84-85	Minn	47	14	14	28	157	+4
85-86	Minn	59	10	7	17	231	-20
86-87	Minn	67	6	5	11	263	+1
87-88	Bos	65	2	3	5	170	-10
Totals		834	222	215	437	2572	-42

Playoffs

76-77	Atl	3	1	0	1	19
78-79	Atl	2	1	0	1	29
79-80	Atl	4	1	0	1	15
80-81	Calg	15	8	4	12	89
81-82	Calg	3	1	2	3	39
82-83	Minn	9	1	3	4	38
83-84	Minn	16	6	2	8	51
84-85	Minn	9	3	6	9	67
85-86	Minn	5	0	1	1	45
87-88	Boss	17	2	4	6	74
Totals		83	24	22	46	466

PLUMB, Robert Edwin (Rob) 5-8 166 LW
B. Kingston, Ont., Aug. 29, 1957

SSN	TEAM	GP	G	A	PTS.	PIM	+/-
77-78	Det	7	2	1	3	0	-4
78-79	Det	7	1	1	2	2	-1
Totals		14	3	2	5	2	-5

PLUMB, Ronald William 5-10 175 D
B. Kingston, Ont., July 17, 1950

SSN	TEAM	GP	G	A	PTS.	PIM	+/-
72-73	Phil (WHA)	78	10	41	51	66	
73-74	Van (WHA)	75	6	32	38	40	
74-75	SD (WHA)	78	10	38	48	56	
75-76	Cin (WHA)	80	10	36	46	31	
76-77	Cin (WHA)	79	11	58	69	52	
77-78	Cin-NE (WHA)	81	14	43	57	63	
78-79	NE (WHA)	78	4	16	20	33	
79-80	Hart	26	3	4	7	14	+10
NHL Totals		26	3	4	7	14	+10
WHA Totals		549	65	264	329	341	

Playoffs

SSN	TEAM	GP	G	A	PTS.	PIM	+/-
72-73	Phil (WHA)	4	0	2	2	13	
74-75	SD (WHA)	10	2	3	5	19	
76-77	Cin (WHA)	4	1	2	3	0	
77-78	NE (WHA)	14	1	5	6	16	
78-79	NE (WHA)	9	1	3	4	0	
WHA Totals		41	5	15	20	48	

POAPST, Steve 6-0 200 D
B. Cornwall, Ont., Jan. 3, 1969

SSN	TEAM	GP	G	A	PTS.	PIM	+/-
95-96	Wash	3	1	0	1	0	-1
98-99	Wash	22	0	0	0	8	-8
Totals		25	1	0	1	8	-9

Playoffs

SSN	TEAM	GP	G	A	PTS.	PIM	+/-
95-96	Wash	6	0	0	0	0	

POCZA, Harvie D. 6-2 198 LW
B. Lethbridge, Alta., Sept. 22, 1959

SSN	TEAM	GP	G	A	PTS.	PIM	+/-
79-80	Wash	1	0	0	0	0	0
81-82	Wash	2	0	0	0	0	-2
Totals		3	0	0	0	0	-2

PODDUBNY, Walter Michael 6-1 210 LW
B. Thunder Bay, Ont., Feb. 14, 1960

SSN	TEAM	GP	G	A	PTS.	PIM	+/-
81-82	Edm-Tor	15	3	4	7	8	-1
82-83	Tor	72	28	31	59	71	+8
83-84	Tor	38	11	14	25	48	-13
84-85	Tor	32	5	15	20	26	+1
85-86	Tor	33	12	22	34	25	+6
86-87	NYR	75	40	47	87	49	+16
87-88	NYR	77	38	50	88	76	+2
88-89	Que	72	38	37	75	107	-18
89-90	NJ	33	4	10	14	28	-4
90-91	NJ	14	4	6	10	10	+8
91-92	NJ	7	1	2	3	6	-1
Totals		468	184	238	422	454	+4

Playoffs

SSN	TEAM	GP	G	A	PTS.	PIM	+/-
82-83	Tor	4	3	1	4	0	
85-86	Tor	9	4	1	5	4	
86-87	NYR	6	0	0	0	8	
Totals		19	7	2	9	12	

PODEIN, Shjon 6-2 200 C
B. Rochester, Minn., Mar. 5, 1968

SSN	TEAM	GP	G	A	PTS.	PIM	+/-
92-93	Edm	40	13	6	19	25	-2
93-94	Edm	28	3	5	8	8	+3
94-95	Phil	44	3	7	10	33	-2
95-96	Phil	79	15	10	25	89	+25
96-97	Phil	82	14	18	32	41	+7
97-98	Phil	82	11	13	14	53	+8
98-99	Phil-Col A	55	3	6	9	24	-5
Totals		410	62	65	127	273	+34

Playoffs

SSN	TEAM	GP	G	A	PTS.	PIM	+/-
94-95	Phil	15	1	3	4	10	
95-96	Phil	12	1	2	3	50	
96-97	Phil	19	4	3	7	16	
97-98	Phil	5	0	0	0	10	
98-99	Col A	19	1	1	2	12	
Totals		70	7	9	16	98	

PODLOSKI, Ray 6-2 210 C
B. Edmonton, Alta., Jan. 5, 1966

SSN	TEAM	GP	G	A	PTS.	PIM	+/-
88-89	Bos	8	0	1	1	22	-1

PODOLLAN, Jason 6-1 192 RW
B. Vernon, B.C., Feb. 18, 1976

SSN	TEAM	GP	G	A	PTS.	PIM	+/-
96-97	Fla-Tor	29	1	4	5	10	-5
98-99	Tor-LA	10	0	0	0	5	-3
Totals		39	1	4	5	15	-8

PODOLSKY, Nelson (Nellie) 5-10 170 LW
B. Winnipeg, Man., Dec. 19, 1925

SSN	TEAM	GP	G	A	PTS.	PIM	+/-
48-49	Det	1	0	0	0	0	

Playoffs

SSN	TEAM	GP	G	A	PTS.	PIM	+/-
48-49	Det	7	0	0	0	4	

POESCHEK, Rudolph Leopold 6-2 210 RW/D
B. Kamloops, B.C., Sept. 29, 1966

SSN	TEAM	GP	G	A	PTS.	PIM	+/-
87-88	NYR	1	0	0	0	2	0
88-89	NYR	52	0	2	2	199	-8
89-90	NYR	15	0	0	0	55	-1
90-91	Winn	1	0	0	0	5	0
91-92	Winn	4	0	0	0	17	-5
93-94	TB	71	3	6	9	118	+3
94-95	TB	25	1	1	2	92	0
95-96	TB	57	1	3	4	88	-2
96-97	TB	60	0	6	6	120	-3
97-98	StL	50	1	7	8	64	-5
98-99	StL	16	0	0	0	33	0
Totals		352	6	25	31	793	-21

Playoffs

SSN	TEAM	GP	G	A	PTS.	PIM	+/-
95-96	TB	3	0	0	0	12	
97-98	StL	2	0	0	0	6	
Totals		5	0	0	0	18	

POETA, Anthony Joseph 5-5 168 RW
B. North Bay, Ont., Mar. 4, 1933

SSN	TEAM	GP	G	A	PTS.	PIM	+/-
51-52	Chi	1	0	0	0	0	

POILE, Donald B. C
B. Fort William, Ont., June 1, 1932

SSN	TEAM	GP	G	A	PTS.	PIM	+/-
54-55	Det	4	0	0	0	0	
57-58	Det	62	7	9	16	12	
Totals		66	7	9	16	12	

Playoffs

SSN	TEAM	GP	G	A	PTS.	PIM	+/-
57-58	Det	4	0	0	0	0	

POILE, Norman Robert (Bud) 6-0 185 C
B. Fort William, Ont., Feb. 10, 1924

SSN	TEAM	GP	G	A	PTS.	PIM	+/-
42-43	Tor	48	16	19	35	24	
43-44	Tor	11	6	8	14	9	
45-46	Tor	9	1	8	9	0	
46-47	Tor	59	19	17	36	19	
47-48	Tor-Chi	58	25	29	54	14	
48-49	Chi-Det	60	21	21	42	8	
49-50	NYR-Bos	66	19	20	39	14	
Totals		311	107	122	229	88	

Playoffs

SSN	TEAM	GP	G	A	PTS.	PIM	+/-
42-43	Tor	6	2	4	6	4	
46-47	Tor	7	2	0	2	2	
48-49	Det	10	0	1	1	2	
Totals		23	4	5	9	8	

POIRIER, Gordon Arthur C
B. Maple Creek, Sask., Oct. 27, 1913

SSN	TEAM	GP	G	A	PTS.	PIM	+/-
39-40	Mont	10	0	1	1	0	

POLANIC, Thomas Joseph 6-3 205 D
B. Toronto, Ont., Apr. 2, 1943

SSN	TEAM	GP	G	A	PTS.	PIM	+/-
69-70	Minn	16	0	2	2	53	-5
70-71	Minn	3	0	0	0	0	0
Totals		19	0	2	2	53	-5

Playoffs

SSN	TEAM	GP	G	A	PTS.	PIM	+/-
69-70	Minn	5	1	1	2	4	

POLICH, John 6-1 200 RW
B. Hibbing, Minn., July 8, 1916

SSN	TEAM	GP	G	A	PTS.	PIM	+/-
39-40	NYR	1	0	0	0	0	
40-41	NYR	2	0	1	1	0	
Totals		3	0	1	1	0	

POLICH, Michael D. 5-8 165 LW
B. Hibbing, Minn., Dec. 19, 1952

SSN	TEAM	GP	G	A	PTS.	PIM	+/-
77-78	Mont	1	0	0	0	0	0
78-79	Minn	73	6	10	16	18	-13
79-80	Minn	78	10	14	24	20	0
80-81	Minn	74	8	5	13	19	-2
Totals		226	24	29	53	57	-15

Playoffs

SSN	TEAM	GP	G	A	PTS.	PIM	+/-
76-77	Mont	5	0	0	0	0	
79-80	Minn	15	2	1	3	2	
80-81	Minn	3	0	0	0	0	
Totals		23	2	1	3	2	

POLIS, Gregory Linn 6-0 195 LW
B. Westlock, Alta., Aug. 8, 1950

SSN	TEAM	GP	G	A	PTS.	PIM	+/-
70-71	Pitt	61	18	15	33	40	-6
71-72	Pitt	76	30	19	49	38	-4
72-73	Pitt	78	26	23	49	36	-32
73-74	Pitt-StL	78	22	25	47	56	-25
74-75	NYR	76	26	15	41	55	+3
75-76	NYR	79	15	21	36	77	-8
76-77	NYR	77	16	23	39	44	0
77-78	NYR	37	7	16	23	12	-3
78-79	NYR-Wash	25	13	7	20	14	+4
79-80	Wash	28	1	5	6	19	-6
Totals		615	174	169	343	391	-77

Playoffs

SSN	TEAM	GP	G	A	PTS.	PIM	+/-
71-72	Pitt	4	0	2	2	0	
74-75	NYR	3	0	0	0	6	
Totals		7	0	2	2	6	

POLIZIANI, Daniel 5-11 160 RW
B. Sydney, N.S., Jan. 8, 1935

SSN	TEAM	GP	G	A	PTS.	PIM	+/-
58-59	Bos	1	0	0	0	0	

Playoffs

SSN	TEAM	GP	G	A	PTS.	PIM	+/-
58-59	Bos	3	0	0	0	0	

POLONICH, Dennis Daniel 5-6 165 C/RW
B. Foam Lake, Sask., Dec. 4, 1953

SSN	TEAM	GP	G	A	PTS.	PIM	+/-
74-75	Det	4	0	0	0	0	-1
75-76	Det	57	11	12	23	302	-9
76-77	Det	79	18	28	46	274	-20
77-78	Det	79	16	19	35	254	-5
78-79	Det	62	10	12	22	208	-10
79-80	Det	66	2	8	10	127	-15
80-81	Det	32	2	2	4	77	-14
82-83	Det	11	0	1	1	0	-4
Totals		390	59	82	141	1242	-78

Playoffs

SSN	TEAM	GP	G	A	PTS.	PIM	+/-
77-78	Det	7	1	0	1	19	

POOLEY, Paul 6-0 177 C
B. Exeter, Ont., Aug. 2, 1960

SSN	TEAM	GP	G	A	PTS.	PIM	+/-
84-85	Winn	12	0	2	2	0	+1
85-86	Winn	3	0	1	1	0	+1
Totals		15	0	3	3	0	+2

POPEIN, Lawrence Thomas (Pope) 5-9 165 C
B. Yorkton, Sask., Aug. 11, 1930

SSN	TEAM	GP	G	A	PTS.	PIM	+/-
54-55	NYR	70	11	17	28	27	
55-56	NYR	64	14	25	39	37	
56-57	NYR	67	11	19	30	20	
57-58	NYR	70	12	22	34	22	
58-59	NYR	61	13	21	34	28	
59-60	NYR	66	14	22	36	16	
60-61	NYR	4	0	1	1	0	
67-68	Oak	47	5	14	19	12	-17
Totals		449	80	141	221	162	-17

Playoffs

SSN	TEAM	GP	G	A	PTS.	PIM	+/-
55-56	NYR	5	0	1	1	2	
56-57	NYR	5	0	3	3	0	
57-58	NYR	6	1	0	1	4	
Totals		16	1	4	5	6	

POPIEL, Poul Peter (Paul) 5-8 170 D
B. Sollested, Denmark, Feb. 28, 1943

SSN	TEAM	GP	G	A	PTS.	PIM	+/-
65-66	Bos	3	0	1	1	2	
67-68	LA	1	0	0	0	0	-1
68-69	Det	62	2	13	15	82	+10
69-70	Det	32	0	4	4	31	+5

SSN	TEAM	GP	G	A	PTS.	PIM	+/-
70–71	Van	78	10	22	32	61	+9
71–72	Van	38	1	1	2	36	-11
72–73	Hou (WHA)	74	16	48	64	158	
73–74	Hou (WHA)	78	7	41	48	126	
74–75	Hou (WHA)	78	11	53	64	22	
75–76	Hou (WHA)	78	10	36	46	71	
76–77	Hou (WHA)	80	12	56	68	87	
77–78	Hou (WHA)	80	6	31	37	53	
79–80	Edm	10	0	0	0	0	-5
NHL Totals		224	13	41	54	212	+7
WHA Totals		468	62	265	327	517	

Playoffs

67–68	LA	3	1	0	1	4	
69–70	Det	1	0	0	0	0	
72–73	Hou (WHA)	10	2	9	11	23	
73–74	Hou (WHA)	14	1	14	15	22	
74–75	Hou (WHA)	13	1	10	11	34	
75–76	Hou (WHA)	17	3	5	8	16	
76–77	Hou (WHA)	11	0	7	7	10	
77–78	Hou (WHA)	6	0	2	2	13	
NHL Totals		4	1	0	1	4	
WHA Totals		71	7	47	54	118	

POPOVIC, Peter 6–6 235 D
B. Koping, Sweden, Feb. 10, 1968

93–94	Mont	47	2	12	14	26	+10
94–95	Mont	33	0	5	5	8	-10
95–96	Mont	76	2	12	14	69	+21
96–97	Mont	78	1	13	14	32	+9
97–98	Mont	69	2	6	8	38	-6
98–99	NYR	68	1	4	5	40	-12
Totals		371	8	52	60	213	+12

Playoffs

93–94	Mont	6	0	1	1	0	
95–96	Mont	6	0	2	2	4	
96–97	Mont	3	0	0	0	2	
97–98	Mont	10	1	1	2	2	
Totals		25	1	4	5	8	

*PORTLAND, John Frederick (Jack) 6–2 185 D
B. Waubaushene, Ont., July 30, 1912

33–34	Mont	31	0	2	2	10	
34–35	Mont–Bos	20	1	1	2	4	
35–36	Bos	2	0	0	0	0	
36–37	Bos	46	2	4	6	58	
37–38	Bos	48	0	5	5	26	
38–39	Bos	48	4	5	9	46	
39–40	Bos–Chi	44	1	9	10	36	
40–41	Chi–Mont	47	2	7	9	38	
41–42	Mont	46	2	9	11	53	
42–43	Mont	49	3	14	17	52	
Totals		381	15	56	71	323	

Playoffs

33–34	Mont	2	0	0	0	0	
36–37	Bos	3	0	0	0	4	
37–38	Bos	3	0	0	0	4	
38–39	Bos	12	0	0	0	11	
39–40	Chi	2	0	0	0	2	
40–41	Mont	3	0	1	1	2	
41–42	Mont	3	0	0	0	0	
42–43	Mont	5	1	2	3	2	
Totals		33	1	3	4	25	

PORVARI, Jukka 5–11 175 RW
B. Tampere, Finland, Jan. 19, 1954

81–82	Col	31	2	6	8	0	-22
82–83	NJ	8	1	3	4	4	-1
Totals		39	3	9	12	4	-23

POSA, Victor 6–0 195 LW/D
B. Bari, Italy, Nov. 5, 1966

85–86	Chi	2	0	0	0	2	0

POSAVAD, Mike 5–11 195 D
B. Brantford, Ont., Jan. 3, 1964

85–86	StL	6	0	0	0	0	-1
86–87	StL	2	0	0	0	0	+1
Totals		8	0	0	0	0	0

POTI, Tom 6–3 215 D
B. Worcester, Mass., March 27, 1977

98–99	Edm	73	5	16	21	42	+10

Playoffs

SSN	TEAM	GP	G	A	PTS.	PIM	+/-
98–99	Edm	4	0	1	1	2	

POTOMSKI, Barry 6–2 215 LW
B. Windsor, Ont., Nov. 24, 1972

95–96	LA	33	3	2	5	104	-7
96–97	LA	26	3	2	5	93	-8
97–98	SJ	9	0	1	1	30	+1
Totals		68	6	5	11	227	-14

POTVIN, Denis Charles 6–0 205 D
B. Ottawa, Ont., Oct. 29, 1953

73–74	NYI	77	17	37	54	175	-16
74–75	NYI	79	21	55	76	105	+28
75–76	NYI	78	31	67	98	100	+12
76–77	NYI	80	25	55	80	103	+42
77–78	NYI	80	30	64	94	81	+57
78–79	NYI	73	31	70	101	58	+71
79–80	NYI	31	8	33	41	44	+13
80–81	NYI	74	20	56	76	104	+38
81–82	NYI	60	24	37	61	83	+38
82–83	NYI	69	12	54	66	60	+32
83–84	NYI	78	22	63	85	87	+55
84–85	NYI	77	17	51	68	96	+36
85–86	NYI	74	21	38	59	76	+34
86–87	NYI	58	12	30	42	70	-6
87–88	NYI	72	19	32	51	112	+25
Totals		1060	310	742	1052	1354	+459

Playoffs

74–75	NYI	17	5	9	14	30	
75–76	NYI	13	5	14	19	32	
76–77	NYI	12	6	4	10	20	
77–78	NYI	7	2	2	4	6	
78–79	NYI	10	4	7	11	8	
79–80	NYI	21	6	13	19	24	
80–81	NYI	18	8	17	25	16	
81–82	NYI	19	5	16	21	30	
82–83	NYI	20	8	12	20	22	
83–84	NYI	20	1	5	6	28	
84–85	NYI	10	3	2	5	10	
85–86	NYI	3	0	1	1	0	
86–87	NYI	10	2	2	4	21	
87–88	NYI	5	1	4	5	6	
Totals		185	56	108	164	253	

POTVIN, Jean Rene 5–11 188 D
B. Ottawa, Ont., Mar. 25, 1949

70–71	LA	4	1	3	4	2	+5
71–72	LA–Phil	68	5	15	20	41	-45
72–73	Phil–NYI	45	3	12	15	22	-4
73–74	NYI	78	5	23	28	100	-26
74–75	NYI	73	9	24	33	59	-3
75–76	NYI	78	17	55	72	74	+16
76–77	NYI	79	10	36	46	26	-14
77–78	NYI–Clev	74	4	24	28	60	+7
78–79	Minn	64	5	16	21	65	-10
79–80	NYI	32	2	13	15	26	-12
80–81	NYI	18	2	3	5	25	-4
Totals		613	63	224	287	500	-62

Playoffs

74–75	NYI	15	2	4	6	9	
75–76	NYI	13	0	1	1	2	
76–77	NYI	11	0	4	4	6	
Totals		39	2	9	11	17	

POTVIN, Marc Richard 6–1 200 RW
B. Ottawa, Ont., Jan. 29, 1967

90–91	Det	9	0	0	0	55	-4
91–92	Det	5	1	0	1	52	-2
92–93	LA	20	0	1	1	61	-10
93–94	LA–Hart	54	2	3	5	272	-8
94–95	Bos	6	0	1	1	4	+1
95–96	Bos	27	0	0	0	12	-2
Totals		121	3	5	8	456	-25

Playoffs

90–91	Det	6	0	0	0	32	
91–92	Det	1	0	0	0	0	
92–93	LA	1	0	0	0	0	
95–96	Bos	5	0	1	1	18	
Totals		13	0	1	1	50	

POUDRIER, Daniel 6–2 175 D
B. Thetford Mines, Que., Feb. 15, 1964

SSN	TEAM	GP	G	A	PTS.	PIM	+/-
85–86	Que	13	1	5	6	10	+2
86–87	Que	6	0	0	0	0	-2
87–88	Que	6	0	0	0	0	-1
Totals		25	1	5	6	10	-1

POULIN, Daniel 5–11 185 D
B. Robertsville, Que., Sept. 19, 1957

81–82	Minn	3	1	1	2	2	+1
82–83	Phil	2	2	0	2	2	
Totals		5	3	1	4	4	

POULIN, David James 5–11 190 C
B. Timmins, Ont., Dec. 17, 1958

82–83	Phil	2	2	0	2	2	+1
83–84	Phil	73	31	45	76	47	+31
84–85	Phil	73	30	44	74	59	+43
85–86	Phil	79	27	42	69	49	+20
86–87	Phil	75	25	45	70	53	+47
87–88	Phil	68	19	32	51	32	+17
88–89	Phil–Bos	69	18	17	35	49	+4
89–90	Phil–Bos	60	15	27	42	24	+16
90–91	Bos	31	8	12	20	25	+5
91–92	Bos	18	4	4	8	18	-2
92–93	Bos	84	16	33	49	62	+29
93–94	Wash	63	6	19	25	52	-1
94–95	Wash	29	4	5	9	10	+2
Totals		724	205	325	530	482	+212

Playoffs

82–83	Phil	3	1	3	4	9	
83–84	Phil	3	0	0	0	2	
84–85	Phil	11	3	5	8	6	
85–86	Phil	5	2	0	2	2	
86–87	Phil	15	3	3	6	14	
87–88	Phil	7	2	0	2	4	
88–89	Phil	19	6	5	11	16	
89–90	Bos	18	8	5	13	8	
90–91	Bos	16	0	9	9	20	
91–92	Bos	15	3	3	6	22	
92–93	Bos	4	1	1	2	10	
93–94	Wash	11	2	2	4	19	
94–95	Wash	2	0	0	0	0	
Totals		129	31	42	73	132	

POULIN, Patrick 6–1 208 LW
B. Vanier, Que., Apr. 23, 1973

91–92	Hart	1	0	0	0	2	-1
92–93	Hart	81	20	31	51	37	-19
93–94	Hart–Chi	67	14	14	28	51	-8
94–95	Chi	45	15	15	30	53	+13
95–96	Chi–TB	46	7	9	16	16	+7
96–97	TB	73	12	14	26	56	-16
97–98	TB–Mont	78	6	13	19	27	-4
98–99	Mont	81	8	17	25	21	+6
Totals		472	82	113	195	263	-22

Playoffs

91–92	Hart	7	2	1	3	0	
93–94	Chi	4	0	0	0	0	
94–95	Chi	16	4	1	5	8	
95–96	TB	2	0	0	0	0	
97–98	Mont	3	0	0	0	0	
Totals		32	6	2	8	8	

POUZAR, Jaroslav 5–11 202 LW
B. Czechoslovakia, Jan. 23, 1952

82–83	Edm	74	15	18	33	57	+17
83–84	Edm	67	13	19	32	44	+17
84–85	Edm	33	4	8	12	28	+3
86–87	Edm	12	2	3	5	6	+3
Totals		186	34	48	82	135	+40

Playoffs

82–83	Edm	1	2	0	2	0	
83–84	Edm	14	1	2	3	12	
84–85	Edm	9	2	1	3	2	
86–87	Edm	5	1	1	2	2	
Totals		29	6	4	10	16	

POWELL, Raymond Henry 6–0 170 C
B. Timmins, Ont., Nov. 16, 1925

50–51	Chi	31	7	15	22	2	

POWIS, Geoffrey Charles 6-0 179 C
B. Winnipeg, Man., June 14, 1945

SSN	TEAM	GP	G	A	PTS.	PIM	+/-
67-68	Chi	2	0	0	0	0	0

POWIS, Trevor Lynn (Lynn) 6-0 176 C
B. Saskatoon, Sask., Apr. 19, 1949

SSN	TEAM	GP	G	A	PTS.	PIM	+/-
73-74	Chi	57	8	13	21	6	+10
74-75	KC	73	11	20	31	19	-54
75-76	Calg (WHA)	21	4	10	14	2	
76-77	Calg (WHA)	63	30	30	60	40	
77-78	Winn (WHA)	69	16	25	41	18	
NHL Totals		130	19	33	52	25	-44
WHA Totals		153	50	65	115	60	

Playoffs

SSN	TEAM	GP	G	A	PTS.	PIM	+/-
73-74	Chi	1	0	0	0	0	
75-76	Calg (WHA)	10	5	4	9	2	
77-78	Winn (WHA)	3	2	1	3	7	
NHL Totals		1	0	0	0	0	
WHA Totals		13	7	5	12	9	

PRAJSLER, Petr 6-2 200 D
B. Hradec Kralove, Czech., Sept. 21, 1965

SSN	TEAM	GP	G	A	PTS.	PIM	+/-
87-88	LA	7	0	0	0	2	+2
88-89	LA	2	0	3	3	0	+4
89-90	LA	34	3	7	10	47	-9
91-92	Bos	3	0	0	0	2	-1
Totals		46	3	10	13	51	-4

Playoffs

SSN	TEAM	GP	G	A	PTS.	PIM	+/-
88-89	LA	1	0	0	0	0	
89-90	LA	3	0	0	0	0	
Totals		4	0	0	0	0	

PRATT, John (Jack) D
B. Edinburgh, Scotland

SSN	TEAM	GP	G	A	PTS.	PIM	+/-
30-31	Bos	32	2	0	2	36	
31-32	Bos	5	0	0	0	6	
Totals		37	2	0	2	42	

Playoffs

SSN	TEAM	GP	G	A	PTS.	PIM	+/-
30-31	Bos	4	0	0	0	0	

PRATT, Kelly Edward 5-9 170 RW
B. High Prairie, Alta., Feb. 8, 1953

SSN	TEAM	GP	G	A	PTS.	PIM	+/-
73-74	Winn (WHA)	46	4	6	10	50	
74-75	Pitt	22	0	6	6	15	+1

PRATT, Nolan 6-2 195 D
B. Fort McMurray, Alta., Aug. 14, 1975

SSN	TEAM	GP	G	A	PTS.	PIM	+/-
96-97	Hart	9	0	2	2	6	0
97-98	Car	23	0	2	2	44	-2
98-99	Car	61	1	14	15	95	+15
Totals		93	1	18	19	145	+13

Playoffs

SSN	TEAM	GP	G	A	PTS.	PIM	+/-
98-99	Car	3	0	0	0	2	

PRATT, Tracy Arnold 6-2 195 D
B. New York, N.Y., Mar. 8, 1943

SSN	TEAM	GP	G	A	PTS.	PIM	+/-
67-68	Oak	34	0	5	5	90	-18
68-69	Pitt	18	0	5	5	34	+6
69-70	Pitt	65	5	7	12	124	-29
70-71	Buf	76	1	7	8	179	-17
71-72	Buf	27	0	10	10	52	0
72-73	Buf	74	1	15	16	116	+9
73-74	Buf-Van	78	3	15	18	96	-2
74-75	Van	79	5	17	22	145	+6
75-76	Van	52	1	5	6	72	-7
76-77	Col-Tor	77	1	11	12	118	-34
Totals		580	17	97	114	1026	-86

Playoffs

SSN	TEAM	GP	G	A	PTS.	PIM	+/-
69-70	Pitt	10	0	1	1	51	
72-73	Buf	6	0	0	0	6	
74-75	Van	3	0	0	0	5	
75-76	Van	2	0	0	0	0	
76-77	Tor	4	0	0	0	0	
Totals		25	0	1	1	62	

*PRATT, Walter (Babe) 6-3 210 D
B. Stony Mountain, Man., Jan. 7, 1916

SSN	TEAM	GP	G	A	PTS.	PIM	+/-
35-36	NYR	17	1	1	2	16	
36-37	NYR	47	8	7	15	23	
37-38	NYR	47	5	14	19	56	
38-39	NYR	48	2	19	21	20	
39-40	NYR	48	4	13	17	61	
40-41	NYR	47	3	17	20	52	
41-42	NYR	47	4	24	28	45	
42-43	NYR-Tor	50	17	22	39	50	
43-44	Tor	50	17	40	57	30	
44-45	Tor	50	18	23	41	39	
45-46	Tor	41	5	20	25	36	
46-47	Bos	31	4	4	8	25	
Totals		517	83	209	292	453	

Playoffs

SSN	TEAM	GP	G	A	PTS.	PIM	+/-
36-37	NYR	9	3	1	4	11	
37-38	NYR	2	0	0	0	2	
38-39	NYR	7	1	2	3	9	
39-40	NYR	12	3	1	4	18	
40-41	NYR	3	1	1	2	6	
41-42	NYR	6	1	3	4	24	
42-43	Tor	6	1	2	3	8	
43-44	Tor	5	0	3	3	4	
44-45	Tor	13	2	4	6	8	
Totals		63	12	17	29	90	

PRENTICE, Dean Sutherland 5-11 180 LW
B. Schumacher, Ont., Oct. 5, 1932

SSN	TEAM	GP	G	A	PTS.	PIM	+/-
52-53	NYR	55	6	3	9	20	
53-54	NYR	52	4	13	17	18	
54-55	NYR	70	16	15	31	21	
55-56	NYR	70	24	18	42	44	
56-57	NYR	68	19	23	42	38	
57-58	NYR	38	13	9	22	14	
58-59	NYR	70	17	33	50	11	
59-60	NYR	70	32	34	66	43	
60-61	NYR	56	20	25	45	17	
61-62	NYR	68	22	38	60	20	
62-63	NYR-Bos	68	19	34	53	22	
63-64	Bos	70	23	16	39	37	
64-65	Bos	31	14	9	23	12	
65-66	Bos-Det	69	13	31	44	18	
66-67	Det	68	23	22	45	18	
67-68	Det	69	17	38	55	42	+7
68-69	Det	74	14	20	34	18	-8
69-70	Pitt	75	26	25	51	14	-20
70-71	Pitt	69	21	17	38	18	-8
71-72	Minn	71	20	27	47	14	+4
72-73	Minn	73	26	16	42	22	+3
73-74	Minn	24	2	3	5	4	-11
Totals		1378	391	469	860	485	-33

Playoffs

SSN	TEAM	GP	G	A	PTS.	PIM	+/-
55-56	NYR	5	1	0	1	2	
56-57	NYR	5	0	2	2	4	
57-58	NYR	6	1	3	4	4	
61-62	NYR	3	0	2	2	0	
65-66	Det	12	5	5	10	4	
69-70	Pitt	10	2	5	7	8	
71-72	Minn	7	3	0	3	0	
72-73	Minn	6	1	0	1	16	
Totals		54	13	17	30	38	

PRENTICE, Eric Dayton D
B. Schumacher, Ont., Aug. 22, 1926

SSN	TEAM	GP	G	A	PTS.	PIM	+/-
43-44	Tor	5	0	0	0	4	

PRESLEY, Wayne 5-11 180 RW
B. Detroit, Mich., Mar. 23, 1965

SSN	TEAM	GP	G	A	PTS.	PIM	+/-
84-85	Chi	3	0	1	1	0	+1
85-86	Chi	38	7	8	15	38	-6
86-87	Chi	80	32	29	61	114	-18
87-88	Chi	42	12	10	22	52	-13
88-89	Chi	72	21	19	40	100	-3
89-90	Chi	49	6	7	13	69	-19
90-91	Chi	71	15	19	34	122	+11
91-92	SJ-Buf	59	10	16	26	133	-27
92-93	Buf	79	15	17	32	96	+5
93-94	Buf	65	17	8	25	103	+18
94-95	Buf	46	14	5	19	41	+5
95-96	NYR-Tor	80	6	8	14	85	+3
Totals		684	155	147	302	953	-43

Playoffs

SSN	TEAM	GP	G	A	PTS.	PIM	+/-
85-86	Chi	3	0	0	0	0	
86-87	Chi	4	1	0	1	9	
87-88	Chi	5	0	0	0	4	
88-89	Chi	14	7	5	12	18	
89-90	Chi	19	9	6	15	29	
90-91	Chi	6	0	1	1	38	
91-92	Buf	7	3	3	6	14	
92-93	Buf	8	1	0	1	6	
93-94	Buf	7	2	1	3	14	
94-95	Buf	5	3	1	4	8	
95-96	Tor	5	0	0	0	2	
Totals		83	26	17	43	142	

PRESTON, Richard John 5-11 185 RW
B. Regina, Sask., May 22, 1952

SSN	TEAM	GP	G	A	PTS.	PIM	+/-
74-75	Hou (WHA)	78	20	21	41	10	
75-76	Hou (WHA)	77	22	33	55	33	
76-77	Hou (WHA)	80	38	41	79	54	
77-78	Hou (WHA)	73	25	25	50	52	
78-79	Winn (WHA)	80	28	32	60	88	
79-80	Chi	80	31	30	61	70	+16
80-81	Chi	47	7	14	21	24	-15
81-82	Chi	75	15	28	43	30	0
82-83	Chi	79	25	28	53	64	+14
83-84	Chi	75	10	18	28	50	-21
84-85	NJ	75	12	15	27	26	-24
85-86	NJ	76	19	22	41	65	+3
86-87	Chi	73	8	9	17	19	-8
NHL Totals		580	127	164	291	348	-35
WHA Totals		388	133	152	285	237	

Playoffs

SSN	TEAM	GP	G	A	PTS.	PIM	+/-
74-75	Hou (WHA)	13	1	6	7	6	
75-76	Hou (WHA)	17	4	6	10	8	
76-77	Hou (WHA)	11	3	5	8	10	
78-79	Winn (WHA)	10	8	5	13	15	
79-80	Chi	7	0	3	3	2	
80-81	Chi	3	0	1	1	0	
81-82	Chi	15	2	4	6	21	
82-83	Chi	13	2	7	9	25	
83-84	Chi	5	0	1	1	4	
86-87	Chi	4	0	2	2	4	
NHL Totals		47	4	18	22	56	
WHA Totals		51	16	22	38	39	

PRESTON, Yves 5-11 180 LW
B. Montreal, Que., June 14, 1956

SSN	TEAM	GP	G	A	PTS.	PIM	+/-
78-79	Phil	9	3	1	4	0	-2
80-81	Phil	19	4	2	6	4	+1
Totals		28	7	3	10	4	-1

PRIAKHIN, Sergei 6-3 210 RW
B. Moscow, Soviet Union, Dec. 7, 1963

SSN	TEAM	GP	G	A	PTS.	PIM	+/-
88-89	Calg	2	0	0	0	2	+1
89-90	Calg	20	2	2	4	0	-7
90-91	Calg	24	1	6	7	0	-3
Totals		46	3	8	11	2	-9

Playoffs

SSN	TEAM	GP	G	A	PTS.	PIM	+/-
88-89	Calg	1	0	0	0	0	

PRICE, Bob F

SSN	TEAM	GP	G	A	PTS.	PIM	+/-
19-20	Ott	1	0	0	0	0	

PRICE, Garry Noel (Noel) 6-0 185 D
B. Brockville, Ont., Dec. 9, 1935

SSN	TEAM	GP	G	A	PTS.	PIM	+/-
57-58	Tor	1	0	0	0	5	
58-59	Tor	28	0	0	0	4	
59-60	NYR	6	0	0	0	0	
60-61	NYR	1	0	0	0	2	
61-62	Det	20	0	1	1	6	
65-66	Mont	15	0	6	6	8	
66-67	Mont	24	0	3	3	8	
67-68	Pitt	70	6	27	33	48	-7
68-69	Pitt	73	2	18	20	79	-30
70-71	LA	62	1	19	20	29	-15
72-73	Atl	54	1	13	14	38	-7
73-74	Atl	62	0	13	13	38	-11
74-75	Atl	80	4	14	18	82	0
75-76	Atl	3	0	0	0	2	0
Totals		499	14	114	128	349	-70

Playoffs

SSN	TEAM	GP	G	A	PTS.	PIM	+/-
58-59	Tor	5	0	0	0	2	
65-66	Mont	3	0	1	1	0	
73-74	Atl	4	0	0	0	6	
Totals		12	0	1	1	8	

PRICE, John Rees (Jack) 5-9 185 D
B. Goderich, Ont., May 8, 1932

SSN	TEAM	GP	G	A	PTS.	PIM	+/-
51-52	Chi	1	0	0	0	0	
52-53	Chi	10	0	0	0	2	
53-54	Chi	46	4	6	10	22	

SSN	TEAM	GP	G	A	PTS.	PIM	+/-
Totals		57	4	6	10	24	

Playoffs

SSN	TEAM	GP	G	A	PTS.	PIM	+/-
52–53	Chi	4	0	0	0	0	

PRICE, Shaun Patrick (Pat) 6-2 195 D
B. Nelson, B.C., Mar. 24, 1955

SSN	TEAM	GP	G	A	PTS.	PIM	+/-
74–75	Van (WHA)	68	5	29	34	15	
75–76	NYI	4	0	2	2	2	+4
76–77	NYI	71	3	22	25	25	+26
77–78	NYI	52	2	10	12	27	+25
78–79	NYI	55	3	11	14	50	+18
79–80	Edm	75	11	21	32	193	+4
80–81	Edm-Pitt	72	8	34	42	226	-5
81–82	Pitt	77	7	31	38	322	+2
82–83	Pitt-Que	52	2	13	15	132	-22
83–84	Que	72	3	25	28	188	+20
84–85	Que	68	1	26	27	118	+17
85–86	Que	54	3	13	16	82	0
86–87	Que–NYR	60	0	8	8	130	-15
87–88	Minn	14	0	2	2	20	-3
NHL Totals		726	43	218	261	1456	+71
WHA Totals		68	5	29	34	15	

Playoffs

SSN	TEAM	GP	G	A	PTS.	PIM
76–77	NYI	10	0	1	1	2
77–78	NYI	5	0	1	1	2
78–79	NYI	7	0	1	1	25
79–80	Edm	3	0	0	0	11
80–81	Pitt	5	1	1	2	21
81–82	Pitt	5	0	0	0	28
82–83	Que	4	0	0	0	14
83–84	Que	9	1	0	1	10
84–85	Que	17	0	4	4	51
85–86	Que	3	0	1	1	4
86–87	NYR	6	0	1	1	27
Totals		74	2	10	12	195

PRICE, Thomas Edward 6-1 190 D
B. Toronto, Ont., July 12, 1954

SSN	TEAM	GP	G	A	PTS.	PIM	+/-
74–75	Cal	3	0	0	0	4	-1
75–76	Cal	5	0	0	0	0	-9
76–77	Clev-Pitt	9	0	2	2	4	-4
77–78	Pitt	10	0	0	0	0	-4
78–79	Pitt	2	0	0	0	4	-2
Totals		29	0	2	2	12	-20

PRIESTLAY, Ken 5-10 190 C
B. Richmond, B.C., Aug. 24, 1967

SSN	TEAM	GP	G	A	PTS.	PIM	+/-
86–87	Buf	34	11	6	17	8	+3
87–88	Buf	33	5	12	17	35	-4
88–89	Buf	15	2	0	2	2	-8
89–90	Buf	35	7	7	14	14	-1
90–91	Buf	2	0	1	1	0	0
91–92	Pitt	49	2	8	10	4	+5
Totals		168	27	34	61	63	-5

Playoffs

SSN	TEAM	GP	G	A	PTS.	PIM
87–88	Buf	6	0	0	0	11
88–89	Buf	3	0	0	0	2
89–90	Buf	5	0	0	0	8
Totals		14	0	0	0	21

*PRIMEAU, A. Joseph (Joe) 5-11 153 C
B. Lindsay, Ont., Jan. 29, 1906

SSN	TEAM	GP	G	A	PTS.	PIM
27–28	Tor	2	0	0	0	0
28–29	Tor	6	0	1	1	2
29–30	Tor	43	5	21	26	28
30–31	Tor	38	9	32	41	18
31–32	Tor	46	13	37	50	25
32–33	Tor	48	11	21	32	4
33–34	Tor	45	14	32	46	8
34–35	Tor	37	10	20	30	16
35–36	Tor	45	4	13	17	10
Totals		310	66	177	243	111

Playoffs

SSN	TEAM	GP	G	A	PTS.	PIM
30–31	Tor	2	0	0	0	0
31–32	Tor	7	0	6	6	2
32–33	Tor	8	0	1	1	4
33–34	Tor	5	2	4	6	6
34–35	Tor	7	0	3	3	0
35–36	Tor	9	3	4	7	0
Totals		38	5	18	23	12

PRIMEAU, Keith 6-4 210 C
B. Toronto, Ont., Nov. 24, 1971

SSN	TEAM	GP	G	A	PTS.	PIM	+/-
90–91	Det	58	3	12	15	106	-12
91–92	Det	35	6	10	16	83	+9
92–93	Det	73	15	17	32	152	-6
93–94	Det	78	31	42	73	173	+34
94–95	Det	45	15	27	42	99	+17
95–96	Det	74	27	25	52	168	+19
96–97	Hart	75	26	25	51	161	-3
97–98	Car	81	26	37	63	110	+19
98–99	Car	78	30	32	62	75	+8
Totals		597	179	227	406	1127	+85

Playoffs

SSN	TEAM	GP	G	A	PTS.	PIM
90–91	Det	5	1	1	2	25
91–92	Det	11	0	0	0	14
92–93	Det	7	0	2	2	26
93–94	Det	7	0	2	2	6
94–95	Det	17	4	5	9	45
95–96	Det	17	1	4	5	28
98–99	Car	6	0	3	3	6
Totals		70	6	17	23	150

PRIMEAU, Kevin 6-0 180 RW
B. Edmonton, Alta., Jan. 3, 1956

SSN	TEAM	GP	G	A	PTS.	PIM	+/-
77–78	Edm (WHA)	7	0	1	1	2	
80–81	Van	2	0	0	0	4	0

Playoffs

SSN	TEAM	GP	G	A	PTS.	PIM
77–78	Edm (WHA)	2	0	0	0	2

PRIMEAU, Wayne 6-3 193 C
B. Scarborough, Ont., June 4, 1976

SSN	TEAM	GP	G	A	PTS.	PIM	+/-
94–95	Buf	1	1	0	1	0	-2
95–96	Buf	2	0	0	0	0	0
96–97	Buf	45	2	4	6	64	-2
97–98	Buf	69	6	6	12	87	+9
98–99	Buf	67	5	8	13	38	-6
Totals		184	14	18	32	189	-1

Playoffs

SSN	TEAM	GP	G	A	PTS.	PIM
96–97	Buf	9	0	0	0	6
97–98	Buf	14	1	3	4	6
98–99	Buf	19	3	4	7	6
Totals		42	4	7	11	18

*PRINGLE, Ellis (Ellie) D
B. Toronto, Ont.

SSN	TEAM	GP	G	A	PTS.	PIM
30–31	NYA	6	0	0	0	0

PROBERT, Bob 6-3 225 RW
B. Windsor, Ont., June 5, 1965

SSN	TEAM	GP	G	A	PTS.	PIM	+/-
85–86	Det	44	8	13	21	186	-14
86–87	Det	63	13	11	24	221	-6
87–88	Det	74	29	33	62	398	+34
88–89	Det	25	4	2	6	106	-11
89–90	Det	4	3	0	3	21	0
90–91	Det	55	16	23	39	315	-3
91–92	Det	63	20	24	44	276	+16
92–93	Det	80	14	29	43	292	-9
93–94	Det	66	7	10	17	275	-1
95–96	Chi	78	19	21	40	237	+15
96–97	Chi	82	9	14	23	326	-3
97–98	Chi	14	2	1	3	48	-7
98–99	Chi	78	7	14	21	206	-11
Totals		726	151	195	346	2907	-18

Playoffs

SSN	TEAM	GP	G	A	PTS.	PIM
86–87	Det	16	3	4	7	63
87–88	Det	16	8	13	21	51
90–91	Det	6	1	2	3	50
91–92	Det	11	1	6	7	28
92–93	Det	7	0	3	3	10
93–94	Det	7	1	1	2	8
95–96	Chi	10	0	2	2	23
96–97	Chi	6	2	1	3	41
Totals		79	16	32	48	274

PROCHAZKA, Martin 5-11 180 RW
B. Slany, Czech., Mar. 3, 1972

SSN	TEAM	GP	G	A	PTS.	PIM	+/-
97–98	Tor	29	2	4	6	8	-1

*PRODGERS, George (Goldie) F
B. 1892

SSN	TEAM	GP	G	A	PTS.	PIM
19–20	Tor	16	8	6	14	2
20–21	Ham	23	18	8	26	8
21–22	Ham	24	15	4	19	4
22–23	Ham	23	13	3	16	13
23–24	Ham	23	9	1	10	6
24–25	Ham	1	0	0	0	0
25–26	Mont	24	0	0	0	0
Totals		134	63	22	85	33

PROKHOROV, Vitali 5-9 185 LW
B. Moscow, USSR, Dec. 25, 1966

SSN	TEAM	GP	G	A	PTS.	PIM	+/-
92–93	StL	26	4	1	5	15	-4
93–94	StL	55	15	10	25	20	-6
94–95	StL	2	0	0	0	0	+1
Totals		83	19	11	30	35	-9

Playoffs

SSN	TEAM	GP	G	A	PTS.	PIM
93–94	StL	4	0	0	0	0

PROKOPEC, Mike 6-2 190 RW
B. Toronto, Ont., May 17, 1974

SSN	TEAM	GP	G	A	PTS.	PIM	+/-
95–96	Chi	9	0	0	0	5	-4
96–97	Chi	6	0	0	0	6	-1
Totals		15	0	0	0	11	-5

PRONGER, Chris 6-5 220 D
B. Dryden, Ont., Oct. 10, 1974

SSN	TEAM	GP	G	A	PTS.	PIM	+/-
93–94	Hart	81	5	25	30	113	-3
94–95	Hart	43	5	9	14	54	-12
95–96	StL	78	7	18	25	110	-18
96–97	StL	79	11	24	35	143	+15
97–98	StL	81	9	27	36	180	+47
98–99	StL	67	13	33	46	113	+3
Totals		429	50	136	186	713	+32

Playoffs

SSN	TEAM	GP	G	A	PTS.	PIM
95–96	StL	13	1	5	6	16
96–97	StL	6	1	1	2	22
97–98	StL	10	1	9	10	26
98–99	StL	13	1	4	5	28
Totals		42	4	19	23	92

PRONGER, Sean 6-2 205 C
B. Dryden, Ont., Nov. 30, 1972

SSN	TEAM	GP	G	A	PTS.	PIM	+/-
95–96	Ana	7	0	1	1	6	0
96–97	Ana	39	7	7	14	20	+6
97–98	Ana-Pitt	67	6	15	21	32	-10
98–99	Pitt-NYR-LA	29	0	4	4	8	-1
Totals		142	13	27	40	66	-5

Playoffs

SSN	TEAM	GP	G	A	PTS.	PIM
96–97	Ana	9	0	2	2	4
97–98	Pitt	5	0	0	0	4
Totals		14	0	2	2	8

PRONOVOST, Joseph Armand (Andre) 5-9 165 LW
B. Shawinigan Falls, Que., July 9, 1936

SSN	TEAM	GP	G	A	PTS.	PIM	+/-
56–57	Mont	64	10	11	21	58	
57–58	Mont	66	16	12	28	55	
58–59	Mont	70	9	14	23	48	
59–60	Mont	69	12	19	31	61	
60–61	Mont–Bos	68	12	16	28	34	
61–62	Bos	70	15	8	23	70	
62–63	Bos–Det	68	13	7	20	24	
63–64	Det	70	7	16	23	23	
64–65	Det	3	0	1	1	0	
67–68	Minn	8	0	0	0	0	0
Totals		556	94	104	198	373	0

Playoffs

SSN	TEAM	GP	G	A	PTS.	PIM
56–57	Mont	8	1	0	1	4
57–58	Mont	10	2	0	2	16
58–59	Mont	11	2	1	3	6
59–60	Mont	8	1	2	3	0
62–63	Det	11	1	4	5	6
63–64	Det	14	4	3	7	26
67–68	Minn	8	0	1	1	0
Totals		70	11	11	22	58

PRONOVOST, Joseph Jean Dinis (Jean) 5-11 185 RW
B. Shawinigan Falls, Que., Dec. 18, 1945

SSN	TEAM	GP	G	A	PTS.	PIM	+/-
68–69	Pitt	76	16	25	41	41	-4
69–70	Pitt	72	20	21	41	45	-2
70–71	Pitt	78	21	24	45	35	+8
71–72	Pitt	68	30	23	53	12	+15
72–73	Pitt	66	21	22	43	16	-15

SSN	TEAM	GP	G	A	PTS.	PIM	+/-
73–74	Pitt	77	40	32	72	22	+9
74–75	Pitt	78	43	32	75	37	+13
75–76	Pitt	80	52	52	104	24	+16
76–77	Pitt	79	33	31	64	24	+8
77–78	Pitt	79	40	25	65	50	-16
78–79	Atl	75	28	39	67	30	+21
79–80	Atl	80	24	19	43	12	+12
80–81	Wash	80	22	36	58	67	-8
81–82	Wash	10	1	2	3	4	-7
Totals		998	391	383	774	419	+50

Playoffs

SSN	TEAM	GP	G	A	PTS.	PIM
69–70	Pitt	10	3	4	7	2
71–72	Pitt	4	1	1	2	0
74–75	Pitt	9	3	3	6	6
76–77	Pitt	3	2	1	3	2
78–79	Atl	2	2	0	2	0
79–80	Atl	4	0	0	0	2
Totals		35	11	9	20	14

PRONOVOST, Rene Marcel 6–0 190 D
B. Lac la Tortue, Que., June 15, 1930

SSN	TEAM	GP	G	A	PTS.	PIM	+/-
50–51	Det	37	1	6	7	20	
51–52	Det	69	7	11	18	50	
52–53	Det	68	8	19	27	72	
53–54	Det	57	6	12	18	50	
54–55	Det	70	9	25	34	90	
55–56	Det	68	4	13	17	46	
56–57	Det	70	7	9	16	38	
57–58	Det	62	2	18	20	52	
58–59	Det	69	11	21	32	44	
59–60	Det	69	7	17	24	38	
60–61	Det	70	6	11	17	44	
61–62	Det	70	4	14	18	30	
62–63	Det	69	4	9	13	48	
63–64	Det	67	3	17	20	20	
64–65	Det	68	1	15	16	45	
65–66	Tor	54	2	8	10	34	
66–67	Tor	58	2	12	14	28	
67–68	Tor	70	3	17	20	48	0
68–69	Tor	34	1	2	3	20	-2
69–70	Tor	7	0	1	1	4	+5
Totals		1206	88	257	345	821	+3

Playoffs

SSN	TEAM	GP	G	A	PTS.	PIM
49–50	Det	9	0	1	1	10
50–51	Det	6	0	0	0	0
51–52	Det	8	0	1	1	10
52–53	Det	6	0	0	0	6
53–54	Det	12	2	3	5	12
54–55	Det	11	1	3	4	6
55–56	Det	10	0	2	2	8
56–57	Det	5	0	0	0	6
57–58	Det	4	0	1	1	4
59–60	Det	6	1	1	2	2
60–61	Det	9	2	3	5	0
62–63	Det	11	1	4	5	8
64–65	Det	7	0	3	3	4
65–66	Tor	4	0	0	0	6
66–67	Tor	12	1	0	1	8
Totals		134	12	25	37	116

PROPP, Brian Philip 5–10 195 LW
B. Lanigan, Sask., Feb. 15, 1959

SSN	TEAM	GP	G	A	PTS.	PIM	+/-
79–80	Phil	80	34	41	75	54	+45
80–81	Phil	79	26	40	66	110	+27
81–82	Phil	80	44	47	91	117	+19
82–83	Phil	80	40	42	82	72	+35
83–84	Phil	79	39	53	92	37	+49
84–85	Phil	76	43	54	97	43	+46
85–86	Phil	72	40	57	97	47	+24
86–87	Phil	53	31	36	67	45	+39
87–88	Phil	74	27	49	76	76	+8
88–89	Phil	77	32	46	78	37	+16
89–90	Phil–Bos	54	16	24	40	41	+5
90–91	Minn	79	26	47	73	58	+7
91–92	Minn	51	12	23	35	49	-3
92–93	Minn	17	3	3	6	0	-10
93–94	Hart	65	12	17	29	44	+3
Totals		1016	425	579	1004	830	+310

Playoffs

SSN	TEAM	GP	G	A	PTS.	PIM
79–80	Phil	19	5	10	15	29
80–81	Phil	12	6	6	12	32
81–82	Phil	4	2	2	4	4
82–83	Phil	3	1	2	3	8
83–84	Phil	3	0	1	1	6
84–85	Phil	19	8	10	18	6

SSN	TEAM	GP	G	A	PTS.	PIM	+/-
85–86	Phil	5	0	2	2	4	
86–87	Phil	26	12	16	28	10	
87–88	Phil	7	4	2	6	8	
88–89	Phil	18	14	9	23	14	
89–90	Bos	20	4	9	13	2	
90–91	Minn	23	8	15	23	28	
91–92	Minn	1	0	0	0	0	
Totals		160	64	84	148	151	

PROSPAL, Vaclav 6–2 185 C
B. Ceske–Budejovice, Czech., Feb. 17, 1975

SSN	TEAM	GP	G	A	PTS.	PIM	+/-
96–97	Phil	18	5	10	15	4	+3
97–98	Phil–Ott	56	6	19	25	21	-11
98–99	Ott	79	10	26	36	58	+8
Totals		153	21	55	76	83	0

Playoffs

SSN	TEAM	GP	G	A	PTS.	PIM
96–97	Phil	5	1	3	4	4
97–98	Ott	6	0	0	0	0
98–99	Ott	4	0	0	0	0
Totals		15	1	3	4	4

PROULX, Christian 6–0 185 D
B. Sherbrooke, Que., Dec. 10, 1973

SSN	TEAM	GP	G	A	PTS.	PIM	+/-
93–94	Mont	7	1	2	3	20	0

*PROVOST, Joseph Antoine (Claude) 5–9, 175 RW
B. Montreal, Que., Sept. 17, 1933

SSN	TEAM	GP	G	A	PTS.	PIM
55–56	Mont	60	13	16	29	30
56–57	Mont	67	16	14	30	24
57–58	Mont	70	19	32	51	71
58–59	Mont	69	16	22	38	37
59–60	Mont	70	17	29	46	42
60–61	Mont	49	11	4	15	32
61–62	Mont	70	33	29	62	22
62–63	Mont	67	20	30	50	26
63–64	Mont	68	15	17	32	37
64–65	Mont	70	27	37	64	28
65–66	Mont	70	19	36	55	38
66–67	Mont	64	11	13	24	16
67–68	Mont	73	14	30	44	26
68–69	Mont	73	13	15	28	18
69–70	Mont	65	10	11	21	22
Totals		1005	254	335	589	469

Playoffs

SSN	TEAM	GP	G	A	PTS.	PIM
55–56	Mont	10	3	3	6	12
56–57	Mont	10	0	1	1	8
57–58	Mont	10	1	3	4	8
58–59	Mont	11	6	2	8	2
59–60	Mont	8	1	1	2	0
60–61	Mont	6	1	3	4	4
61–62	Mont	6	2	2	4	2
62–63	Mont	5	0	1	1	2
63–64	Mont	7	2	2	4	22
64–65	Mont	13	2	6	8	12
65–66	Mont	10	2	3	5	2
66–67	Mont	7	1	1	2	0
67–68	Mont	13	2	8	10	10
68–69	Mont	10	2	2	4	2
Totals		126	25	38	63	86

PRPIC, Joel 6–6 200 C
B. Sudbury, Ont., Sept. 25, 1974

SSN	TEAM	GP	G	A	PTS.	PIM	+/-
97–98	Bos	1	0	0	0	2	0

PRYOR, Chris 5–11 210 D
B. St. Paul, Minn., Jan. 23, 1961

SSN	TEAM	GP	G	A	PTS.	PIM	+/-
84–85	Minn	4	0	0	0	16	-2
85–86	Minn	7	0	1	1	0	0
86–87	Minn	50	1	3	4	49	-6
87–88	Minn–NYI	4	0	0	0	8	0
88–89	NYI	7	0	0	0	25	-6
89–90	NYI	10	0	0	0	24	-7
Totals		82	1	4	5	122	-21

PRYSTAI, Metro 5–9 170 C
B. Yorkton, Sask., Nov. 7, 1927

SSN	TEAM	GP	G	A	PTS.	PIM
47–48	Chi	54	7	11	18	25
48–49	Chi	59	12	7	19	19
49–50	Chi	65	29	22	51	31
50–51	Det	62	20	17	37	27
51–52	Det	69	21	22	43	16
52–53	Det	70	16	34	50	12
53–54	Det	70	12	15	27	26
54–55	Det–Chi	69	13	16	29	37

SSN	TEAM	GP	G	A	PTS.	PIM
55–56	Chi–Det	71	13	19	32	18
56–57	Det	70	7	15	22	16
57–58	Det	15	1	1	2	4
Totals		674	151	179	330	231

Playoffs

SSN	TEAM	GP	G	A	PTS.	PIM
50–51	Det	3	1	0	1	0
51–52	Det	8	2	5	7	0
52–53	Det	6	4	4	8	2
53–54	Det	12	2	3	5	0
55–56	Det	9	1	2	3	6
56–57	Det	5	2	0	2	0
Totals		43	12	14	26	8

*PUDAS, Albert LW

SSN	TEAM	GP	G	A	PTS.	PIM
26–27	Tor	3	0	0	0	0

PULFORD, Robert Jesse 5–11 188 LW
B. Newton Robinson, Ont., Mar. 31, 1936

SSN	TEAM	GP	G	A	PTS.	PIM	+/-
56–57	Tor	65	11	11	22	32	
57–58	Tor	70	14	17	31	48	
58–59	Tor	70	23	14	37	53	
59–60	Tor	70	24	28	52	81	
60–61	Tor	40	11	18	29	41	
61–62	Tor	70	18	21	39	98	
62–63	Tor	70	19	25	44	49	
63–64	Tor	70	18	30	48	73	
64–65	Tor	65	19	20	39	46	
65–66	Tor	70	28	28	56	51	
66–67	Tor	67	17	28	45	28	
67–68	Tor	74	20	30	50	40	-7
68–69	Tor	72	11	23	34	20	-9
69–70	Tor	74	18	19	37	31	-24
70–71	LA	59	17	26	43	53	-15
71–72	LA	73	13	24	37	48	-25
Totals		1079	281	362	643	792	-80

Playoffs

SSN	TEAM	GP	G	A	PTS.	PIM
58–59	Tor	12	4	4	8	8
59–60	Tor	10	4	1	5	10
60–61	Tor	5	0	0	0	8
61–62	Tor	12	7	1	8	24
62–63	Tor	10	2	5	7	14
63–64	Tor	14	5	3	8	20
64–65	Tor	6	1	1	2	16
65–66	Tor	4	1	1	2	12
66–67	Tor	12	1	10	11	12
68–69	Tor	4	0	0	0	2
Totals		89	25	26	51	126

PULKKINEN, David Joel John 6–0 175 D
B. Kapuskasing, Ont., May 18, 1949

SSN	TEAM	GP	G	A	PTS.	PIM	+/-
72–73	NYI	2	0	0	0	0	-1

PURPUR, Clifford (Fido) F
B. Grand Forks, N.D., Sept. 26, 1916

SSN	TEAM	GP	G	A	PTS.	PIM
34–35	StL E	25	2	1	3	8
41–42	Chi	8	0	0	0	0
42–43	Chi	50	13	16	29	14
43–44	Chi	40	9	10	19	13
44–45	Chi	21	2	7	9	11
Totals		144	26	34	60	46

Playoffs

SSN	TEAM	GP	G	A	PTS.	PIM
43–44	Chi	9	1	1	2	0
44–45	Det	7	0	1	1	4
Totals		16	1	2	3	4

PURVES, John 6–1 201 RW
B. Toronto, Ont., Feb. 12, 1968

SSN	TEAM	GP	G	A	PTS.	PIM	+/-
90–91	Wash	7	1	0	1	0	-3

PUSHOR, Jamie 6–3 192 D
B. Lethbridge, Alta., Feb. 11, 1973

SSN	TEAM	GP	G	A	PTS.	PIM	+/-
95–96	Det	5	0	1	1	17	+2
96–97	Det	75	4	7	11	129	+1
97–98	Det–Ana	64	2	7	9	81	+3
98–99	Ana	70	1	2	3	112	-20
Totals		214	7	17	24	339	-14

Playoffs

SSN	TEAM	GP	G	A	PTS.	PIM
96–97	Det	5	0	1	1	5
98–99	Ana	4	0	0	0	6
Totals		9	0	1	1	11

*PUSIE, Jean Baptiste *6-0 205 D*
B. Montreal, Que., Oct. 15, 1910

SSN	TEAM	GP	G	A	PTS.	PIM	+/-
30–31	Mont	6	0	0	0	0	
31–32	Mont	1	0	0	0	0	
33–34	NYR	19	0	2	2	17	
34–35	Bos	4	1	0	1	0	
35–36	Mont	31	0	2	2	11	
Totals		61	1	4	5	28	

Playoffs

30–31	Mont	3	0	0	0	0	
34–35	Bos	4	0	0	0	0	
Totals		7	0	0	0	0	

PYATT, Frederick (Nelson) *6-0 175 C*
B. Port Arthur, Ont., Sept. 9, 1953

73–74	Det	5	0	0	0	0	-2
74–75	Det–Wash	25	6	4	10	21	-16
75–76	Wash	77	26	23	49	14	-56
76–77	Col	77	23	22	45	20	-17
77–78	Col	71	9	12	21	8	-23
78–79	Col	28	2	2	4	2	-17
79–80	Col	13	5	0	5	2	-5
Totals		296	71	63	134	67	-136

QUACKENBUSH, Hubert George (Bill) *5-11 180 D*
B. Toronto, Ont., Mar. 2, 1922

42–43	Det	10	1	1	2	4	
43–44	Det	43	4	14	18	6	
44–45	Det	50	7	14	21	10	
45–46	Det	48	11	10	21	6	
46–47	Det	44	5	17	22	6	
47–48	Det	58	6	16	22	17	
48–49	Det	60	6	17	23	0	
49–50	Bos	70	8	17	25	4	
50–51	Bos	70	5	24	29	12	
51–52	Bos	69	2	17	19	6	
52–53	Bos	69	2	16	18	6	
53–54	Bos	45	0	17	17	6	
54–55	Bos	68	2	20	22	8	
55–56	Bos	70	3	22	25	4	
Totals		774	62	222	284	95	

Playoffs

43–44	Det	2	1	0	1	0	
44–45	Det	14	0	2	2	2	
45–46	Det	5	0	1	1	0	
46–47	Det	5	0	0	0	6	
47–48	Det	10	0	2	2	0	
48–49	Det	11	1	1	2	0	
50–51	Bos	6	0	1	1	0	
51–52	Bos	7	0	3	3	0	
52–53	Bos	11	0	4	4	4	
53–54	Bos	4	0	0	0	0	
54–55	Bos	5	0	5	5	0	
Totals		80	2	19	21	12	

QUACKENBUSH, Maxwell Joseph *6-2 180 D*
B. Toronto, Ont., Aug. 29, 1928

50–51	Bos	47	4	6	10	26	
51–52	Chi	14	0	1	1	4	
Totals		61	4	7	11	30	

Playoffs

50–51	Bos	6	0	0	0	4	

*QUENNEVILLE, Joel Norman *6-1 200 D*
B. Windsor, Ont., Sept. 15, 1958

78–79	Tor	61	2	9	11	60	+7
79–80	Tor–Col	67	6	11	17	50	-23
80–81	Col	71	10	24	34	86	-21
81–82	Col	64	5	10	15	55	-29
82–83	NJ	74	5	12	17	46	-13
83–84	Hart	80	5	8	13	95	-11
84–85	Hart	79	6	16	22	96	-15
85–86	Hart	71	5	20	25	83	+21
86–87	Hart	37	3	7	10	24	-7
87–88	Hart	77	1	8	9	44	-13
88–89	Hart	69	4	7	11	32	+3
89–90	Hart	44	1	4	5	34	+9
90–91	Wash	9	1	0	1	0	-8
Totals		803	54	136	190	705	-100

Playoffs

78–79	Tor	6	0	1	1	4	
85–86	Hart	10	0	2	2	12	
86–87	Hart	6	0	0	0	0	
87–88	Hart	6	0	2	2	2	
88–89	Hart	4	0	3	3	4	
Totals		26	0	8	8	22	

QUENNEVILLE, Leonard (Leo) *5-10 170 F*
B. St. Anicet, Que., June 15, 1900

29–30	NYR	25	0	3	3	10	

Playoffs

29–30	NYR	3	0	0	0	0	

*QUILTY, John Francis *5-10 175 C*
B. Ottawa, Ont., Jan. 21, 1921

40–41	Mont	48	18	16	34	31	
41–42	Mont	48	12	12	24	44	
46–47	Mont	3	1	1	2	0	
47–48	Mont–Bos	26	5	5	10	6	
Totals		125	36	34	70	81	

Playoffs

40–41	Mont	3	0	2	2	0	
41–42	Mont	3	0	1	1	0	
46–47	Mont	7	3	2	5	9	
Totals		13	3	5	8	9	

QUINN, Dan *5-11 182 C*
B. Ottawa, Ont., June 1, 1965

83–84	Calg	54	19	33	52	20	-3
84–85	Calg	74	20	38	58	22	+9
85–86	Calg	78	30	42	72	44	-12
86–87	Calg–Pitt	80	31	49	80	54	+8
87–88	Pitt	70	40	39	79	50	-8
88–89	Pitt	79	34	60	94	102	-37
89–90	Pitt–Van	78	25	38	63	49	-17
90–91	Van–StL	78	22	38	60	66	-43
91–92	Phil	67	11	26	37	26	-13
92–93	Minn	11	0	4	4	6	-4
93–94	Ott	13	7	0	7	6	0
94–95	LA	44	14	17	31	32	-3
95–96	Ott–Phil	63	13	32	45	46	-6
96–97	Pitt	16	0	3	3	10	-6
Totals		805	266	419	685	533	-135

Playoffs

83–84	Calg	8	3	5	8	4	
84–85	Calg	3	0	0	0	0	
85–86	Calg	18	8	7	15	10	
88–89	Pitt	11	6	3	9	10	
90–91	StL	13	4	7	11	32	
95–96	Phil	12	1	4	5	6	
Totals		65	22	26	48	62	

QUINN, John Brian Patrick (Pat) *6-3 215 D*
B. Hamilton, Ont., Jan. 19, 1943

68–69	Tor	40	2	7	9	95	+10
69–70	Tor	59	0	5	5	88	-14
70–71	Van	76	2	11	13	149	+2
71–72	Van	57	2	3	5	63	-28
72–73	Atl	78	2	18	20	113	+2
73–74	Atl	77	5	27	32	94	+15
74–75	Atl	80	2	19	21	156	+12
75–76	Atl	80	2	11	13	134	+5
76–77	Atl	59	1	12	13	58	-7
Totals		606	18	113	131	950	-3

Playoffs

68–69	Tor	4	0	0	0	13	
73–74	Atl	4	0	0	0	6	
75–76	Atl	2	0	1	1	2	
76–77	Atl	1	0	0	0	0	
Totals		11	0	1	1	21	

QUINNEY, Ken *5-10 186 RW*
B. New Westminster, B.C., May 23, 1965

86–87	Que	25	2	7	9	16	+2
87–88	Que	15	2	2	4	5	-3
90–91	Que	19	3	4	7	2	-2
Totals		59	7	13	20	23	-3

QUINT, Deron *6-1 182 D*
B. Dover, N.H., Mar. 12, 1976

95–96	Winn	51	5	13	18	22	-2
96–97	Phoe	27	3	11	14	4	-4
97–98	Phoe	32	4	7	11	16	-6
98–99	Phoe	60	5	8	13	20	-10
Totals		170	17	39	56	62	-22

Playoffs

96–97	Phoe	7	0	2	2	0	

QUINTAL, Stephane *6-3 215 D*
B. Boucherville, Que., Oct. 22, 1968

88–89	Bos	26	0	1	1	29	-5
89–90	Bos	38	2	2	4	22	-11
90–91	Bos	45	2	6	8	89	+2
91–92	Bos–StL	75	4	16	20	109	-11
92–93	StL	75	1	10	11	100	-6
93–94	Winn	81	8	18	26	119	-25
94–95	Winn	43	6	17	23	78	0
95–96	Mont	68	2	14	16	117	-4
96–97	Mont	71	7	15	22	100	+1
97–98	Mont	71	6	10	16	97	+13
98–99	Mont	82	8	19	27	84	-23
Totals		675	46	128	174	944	-69

Playoffs

90–91	Bos	3	0	1	1	2	
91–92	StL	4	1	2	3	6	
92–93	StL	9	0	0	0	8	
95–96	Mont	6	0	1	1	6	
96–97	Mont	5	0	1	1	6	
97–98	Mont	9	0	2	2	4	
Totals		36	1	7	8	37	

QUINTIN, Jean–Francois *6-0 187 LW*
B. St. Jean, Que., May 28, 1969

91–92	SJ	8	3	0	3	0	+2
92–93	SJ	14	2	5	7	4	-4
Totals		22	5	5	10	4	-2

RACINE, Yves *6-0 205 D*
B. Matane, Que., Feb. 7, 1969

89–90	Det	28	4	9	13	23	-3
90–91	Det	62	7	40	47	33	+1
91–92	Det	61	2	22	24	94	-6
92–93	Det	80	9	31	40	80	+13
93–94	Phil	67	9	43	52	48	-11
94–95	Mont	47	4	7	11	42	-1
95–96	Mont–SJ	57	1	19	20	54	-10
96–97	Calg	46	1	15	16	24	+4
97–98	TB	60	0	8	8	41	-23
Totals		508	37	194	231	439	-39

Playoffs

89–90	Det	7	2	0	2	0	
91–92	Det	11	2	1	3	10	
92–93	Det	7	1	3	4	27	
Totals		25	5	4	9	37	

*RADLEY, Harry John (Yip) *5-11 198 D*
B. Ottawa, Ont., June 27, 1910

30–31	NYA	1	0	0	0	0	
36–37	Mont M	17	0	1	1	13	
Totals		18	0	1	1	13	

RAGLAN, Clarence Eldon (Rags) *6-1 177 D*
B. Pembroke, Ont., Sept. 4, 1927

50–51	Det	33	3	1	4	14	
51–52	Chi	35	0	5	5	28	
52–53	Chi	32	1	3	4	10	
Totals		100	4	9	13	52	

Playoffs

52–53	Chi	3	0	0	0	0	

RAGLAN, Herb *6-0 205 RW*
B. Peterborough, Ont., Aug. 5, 1967

85–86	StL	7	0	0	0	5	-3
86–87	StL	62	6	10	16	159	+6
87–88	StL	73	10	15	25	190	-10
88–89	StL	50	7	10	17	144	-8
89–90	StL	11	0	1	1	21	-5
90–91	StL–Que	47	4	6	10	82	+5
91–92	Que	62	6	14	20	120	-5
92–93	TB	2	0	0	0	2	0
93–94	Ott	29	0	0	0	52	-13
Totals		343	33	56	89	775	-33

Playoffs

85–86	StL	10	1	1	2	24	

SSN	TEAM	GP	G	A	PTS.	PIM	+/-
86-87	StL	4	0	0	0	2	
87-88	StL	10	1	3	4	11	
88-89	StL	8	1	2	3	13	
Totals		32	3	6	9	50	

RAGNARSSON, Marcus 6-1 200 D
B. Ostervala, Sweden, Aug. 13, 1971

SSN	TEAM	GP	G	A	PTS.	PIM	+/-
95-96	SJ	71	8	31	39	42	-24
96-97	SJ	69	3	14	17	63	-18
97-98	SJ	79	5	20	25	65	-11
98-99	SJ	74	0	13	13	66	+7
Totals		293	16	78	94	236	-46

Playoffs

SSN	TEAM	GP	G	A	PTS.	PIM
97-98	SJ	6	0	0	0	4
98-99	SJ	6	0	1	1	6
Totals		12	0	1	1	10

RALEIGH, James Donald (Don, Bones) 5-11 150 C
B. Kenora, Ont., June 27, 1926

SSN	TEAM	GP	G	A	PTS.	PIM
43-44	NYR	15	2	2	4	2
47-48	NYR	52	15	18	33	2
48-49	NYR	41	10	16	26	8
49-50	NYR	70	12	25	37	11
50-51	NYR	64	15	24	39	18
51-52	NYR	70	19	42	61	14
52-53	NYR	55	4	18	22	2
53-54	NYR	70	15	30	45	16
54-55	NYR	69	8	32	40	19
55-56	NYR	29	1	12	13	4
Totals		535	101	219	320	96

Playoffs

SSN	TEAM	GP	G	A	PTS.	PIM
47-48	NYR	6	2	0	2	2
49-50	NYR	12	4	5	9	4
Totals		18	6	5	11	6

RAMAGE, George (Rob) 6-2 200 D
B. Byron, Ont., Jan. 11, 1959

SSN	TEAM	GP	G	A	PTS.	PIM	+/-
78-79	Birm (WHA)	80	12	36	48	165	
79-80	Col	75	8	20	28	135	-40
80-81	Col	79	20	42	62	193	-46
81-82	Col	80	13	29	42	201	-47
82-83	StL	78	16	35	51	193	-9
83-84	StL	80	15	45	60	121	-11
84-85	StL	80	7	31	38	178	-7
85-86	StL	77	10	56	66	171	+18
86-87	StL	59	11	28	39	108	-12
87-88	StL-Calg	79	9	40	49	164	-4
88-89	Calg	68	3	13	16	156	+26
89-90	Tor	80	8	41	49	202	-1
90-91	Tor	80	10	25	35	173	+2
91-92	Minn	34	4	5	9	69	-4
92-93	TB-Mont	74	5	13	18	146	-24
93-94	Mont-Phil	21	0	2	2	16	-12
NHL Totals		1044	139	425	564	2226	-167
WHA Totals		80	12	36	48	165	

Playoffs

SSN	TEAM	GP	G	A	PTS.	PIM
82-83	StL	4	0	3	3	22
83-84	StL	11	1	8	9	32
84-85	StL	3	1	3	4	6
85-86	StL	19	1	10	11	66
86-87	StL	6	2	2	4	21
87-88	Calg	9	1	3	4	21
88-89	Calg	20	1	11	12	26
89-90	Tor	5	1	2	3	20
92-93	Mont	7	0	0	0	4
Totals		84	8	42	50	218

*RAMSAY, Beattie D

SSN	TEAM	GP	G	A	PTS.	PIM
27-28	Tor	43	0	2	2	10

RAMSAY, Craig Edward 5-10 175 LW
B. Weston, Ont., Mar. 17, 1951

SSN	TEAM	GP	G	A	PTS.	PIM	+/-
71-72	Buf	57	6	10	16	0	+5
72-73	Buf	76	11	17	28	15	+13
73-74	Buf	78	20	26	46	0	+17
74-75	Buf	80	26	38	64	26	+51
75-76	Buf	80	22	49	71	34	+44
76-77	Buf	80	20	41	61	20	+37
77-78	Buf	80	28	43	71	18	+38
78-79	Buf	80	26	31	57	10	+21
79-80	Buf	80	21	39	60	18	+15
80-81	Buf	80	24	35	59	12	+39
81-82	Buf	80	16	35	51	8	+14
82-83	Buf	64	11	18	29	7	+14
83-84	Buf	76	9	17	26	17	+3
84-85	Buf	79	12	21	33	16	+17
Totals		1070	252	420	672	201	+328

Playoffs

SSN	TEAM	GP	G	A	PTS.	PIM
72-73	Buf	6	1	1	2	0
74-75	Buf	17	5	7	12	2
75-76	Buf	9	1	2	3	2
76-77	Buf	6	0	4	4	0
77-78	Buf	8	3	1	4	9
78-79	Buf	3	1	0	1	2
79-80	Buf	10	0	6	6	4
80-81	Buf	8	2	4	6	4
81-82	Buf	4	1	1	2	0
82-83	Buf	10	2	3	5	4
83-84	Buf	3	0	1	1	0
84-85	Buf	5	1	1	2	0
Totals		89	17	31	48	27

RAMSEY, Les LW
B. Montreal, Que., July 1, 1920

SSN	TEAM	GP	G	A	PTS.	PIM
44-45	Chi	11	2	2	4	2

RAMSEY, Michael Allen 6-3 195 D
B. Minneapolis, Minn., Dec. 3, 1960

SSN	TEAM	GP	G	A	PTS.	PIM	+/-
79-80	Buf	13	1	6	7	6	+9
80-81	Buf	72	3	14	17	56	+16
81-82	Buf	80	7	23	30	56	+18
82-83	Buf	77	8	30	38	55	+20
83-84	Buf	72	9	22	31	82	+27
84-85	Buf	79	8	22	30	102	+31
85-86	Buf	76	7	21	28	117	+1
86-87	Buf	80	8	31	39	109	+1
87-88	Buf	63	5	16	21	77	+6
88-89	Buf	56	2	14	16	84	+5
89-90	Buf	73	4	21	25	47	+21
90-91	Buf	71	6	14	20	46	+14
91-92	Buf	66	3	14	17	67	+8
92-93	Buf-Pitt	45	3	10	13	28	+17
93-94	Pitt	65	2	2	4	22	-4
94-95	Det	33	1	2	3	23	+11
95-96	Det	47	2	4	6	35	+17
96-97	Det	2	0	0	0	0	0
Totals		1070	79	266	345	1012	+218

Playoffs

SSN	TEAM	GP	G	A	PTS.	PIM
79-80	Buf	13	1	2	3	12
80-81	Buf	8	0	3	3	20
81-82	Buf	4	1	1	2	14
82-83	Buf	10	4	4	8	15
83-84	Buf	3	0	1	1	6
84-85	Buf	5	0	1	1	23
87-88	Buf	6	0	3	3	29
88-89	Buf	5	1	0	1	11
89-90	Buf	6	0	1	1	8
90-91	Buf	5	1	0	1	12
91-92	Buf	7	0	2	2	8
92-93	Pitt	12	0	6	6	4
93-94	Pitt	1	0	0	0	0
94-95	Det	15	0	1	1	4
95-96	Det	15	0	4	4	10
Totals		115	8	29	37	176

RAMSEY, Wayne 6-0 185 D
B. Hamiota, Man., Jan. 31, 1957

SSN	TEAM	GP	G	A	PTS.	PIM	+/-
77-78	Buf	2	0	0	0	0	0

*RANDALL, Kenneth RW

SSN	TEAM	GP	G	A	PTS.	PIM
17-18	Tor	20	12	0	12	55
18-19	Tor	14	7	6	13	27
19-20	Tor	21	10	7	17	43
20-21	Tor	21	6	1	7	58
21-22	Tor	24	10	6	16	20
22-23	Tor	24	3	5	8	51
23-24	Ham	24	7	1	8	18
24-25	Ham	30	8	0	8	49
25-26	NYA	34	4	2	6	94
26-27	NYA	5	0	0	0	0
Totals		217	67	28	95	415

Playoffs

SSN	TEAM	GP	G	A	PTS.	PIM
17-18	Tor	7	1	0	1	24
20-21	Tor	2	0	0	0	24
21-22	Tor	5	1	0	1	11
Totals		14	2	0	2	49

RANHEIM, Paul Stephen 6-0 195 LW
B. St. Louis, Mo., Jan. 25, 1966

SSN	TEAM	GP	G	A	PTS.	PIM	+/-
88-89	Calg	5	0	0	0	0	-3
89-90	Calg	80	26	28	54	23	+27
90-91	Calg	39	14	16	30	4	+20
91-92	Calg	80	23	20	43	32	+16
92-93	Calg	83	21	22	43	26	-4
93-94	Calg-Hart	82	10	17	27	22	-18
94-95	Hart	47	6	14	20	10	-3
95-96	Hart	73	10	20	30	14	-2
96-97	Hart	67	10	11	21	18	-13
97-98	Car	73	5	9	14	28	-11
98-99	Car	78	9	10	19	39	+4
Totals		707	134	167	301	218	+13

Playoffs

SSN	TEAM	GP	G	A	PTS.	PIM
89-90	Calg	6	1	2	3	2
90-91	Calg	7	2	2	4	0
92-93	Calg	6	0	1	1	0
98-99	Car	6	0	0	0	2
Totals		25	3	5	8	4

RANIERI, George Dominic 5-8 190 LW
B. Toronto, Ont., Jan. 14, 1936

SSN	TEAM	GP	G	A	PTS.	PIM
56-57	Bos	2	0	0	0	0

RASMUSSEN, Erik 6-2 205 LW
B. Minneapolis, Minn., Mar. 28, 1977

SSN	TEAM	GP	G	A	PTS.	PIM	+/-
97-98	Buf	21	2	3	5	14	+2
98-99	Buf	42	3	7	10	37	+6
Totals		63	5	10	15	51	+8

Playoffs

SSN	TEAM	GP	G	A	PTS.	PIM
98-99	Buf	21	2	4	6	18

RATCHUK, Peter 6-1 180 D
B. Buffalo, N.Y., Sept. 10, 1977

SSN	TEAM	GP	G	A	PTS.	PIM	+/-
98-99	Fla	24	1	1	2	10	-1

RATELLE, Joseph Gilbert Yvon (Jean) 6-1 180 C
B. Lac St. Jean, Que., Oct. 3, 1940

SSN	TEAM	GP	G	A	PTS.	PIM	+/-
60-61	NYR	3	2	1	3	0	
61-62	NYR	31	4	8	12	4	
62-63	NYR	48	11	9	20	8	
63-64	NYR	15	0	7	7	6	
64-65	NYR	54	14	21	35	14	
65-66	NYR	67	21	30	51	10	
66-67	NYR	41	6	5	11	4	
67-68	NYR	74	32	46	78	18	+23
68-69	NYR	75	32	46	78	26	+16
69-70	NYR	75	32	42	74	28	+8
70-71	NYR	78	26	46	72	14	+28
71-72	NYR	63	46	63	109	4	+61
72-73	NYR	78	41	53	94	12	+24
73-74	NYR	68	28	39	67	16	+5
74-75	NYR	79	36	55	91	26	+1
75-76	NYR-Bos	80	36	69	105	18	+19
76-77	Bos	78	33	61	94	22	+19
77-78	Bos	80	25	59	84	10	+49
78-79	Bos	80	27	45	72	12	+17
79-80	Bos	67	28	45	73	8	+11
80-81	Bos	47	11	26	37	16	+18
Totals		1281	491	776	1267	276	+299

Playoffs

SSN	TEAM	GP	G	A	PTS.	PIM
66-67	NYR	4	0	0	0	2
67-68	NYR	6	0	4	4	2
68-69	NYR	4	1	0	1	0
69-70	NYR	6	1	3	4	0
70-71	NYR	13	2	9	11	8
71-72	NYR	6	0	1	1	0
72-73	NYR	10	2	7	9	0
73-74	NYR	13	2	4	6	0
74-75	NYR	3	1	5	6	2
75-76	Bos	12	8	8	16	4
76-77	Bos	14	5	12	17	4
77-78	Bos	15	3	7	10	0
78-79	Bos	11	7	6	13	2
79-80	Bos	3	0	0	0	0
80-81	Bos	3	0	0	0	0
Totals		123	32	66	98	24

RATHJE, Mike 6-6 220 D
B. Mannville, Alta., May 11, 1974

SSN	TEAM	GP	G	A	PTS.	PIM	+/-
93-94	SJ	47	1	9	10	59	-9
94-95	SJ	42	2	7	9	29	-1

SSN	TEAM	GP	G	A	PTS.	PIM	+/-
95–96	SJ	27	0	7	7	14	-16
96–97	SJ	31	0	8	8	21	-1
97–98	SJ	81	3	12	15	59	-4
98–99	SJ	82	5	9	14	36	+15
Totals		310	11	52	63	218	-16

Playoffs

93–94	SJ	1	0	0	0	0	
94–95	SJ	11	5	2	7	4	
98–99	SJ	6	0	0	0	4	
Totals		18	5	2	7	8	

RATHWELL, John Donald 6-0 190 RW
B. Temiscaming, Que., Aug. 12, 1947

74–75	Bos	1	0	0	0	0	0

RATUSHNY, Dan 6-1 205 D
B. Nepean, Ont., Oct. 29, 1970

92–93	Van	1	0	1	1	2	0

RAUSSE, Errol A. 5-10 181 LW
B. Quesnel, B.C., May 18, 1959

79–80	Wash	24	6	2	8	0	+4
80–81	Wash	5	1	1	2	0	+1
81–82	Wash	2	0	0	0	0	-2
Totals		31	7	3	10	0	+3

RAUTAKALLIO, Pekka 5-11 185 D
B. Pori, Finland, July 25, 1953

75–76	Phoe (WHA)	73	11	39	50	8	
76–77	Phoe (WHA)	78	4	31	35	8	
79–80	Atl	79	5	25	30	18	+22
80–81	Calg	76	11	45	56	64	-1
81–82	Calg	80	17	51	68	40	-8
NHL Totals		235	33	121	154	122	+13
WHA Totals		151	15	70	85	16	

Playoffs

75–76	Phoe (WHA)	5	0	2	2	0	
79–80	Atl	4	0	1	1	2	
80–81	Calg	16	2	4	6	6	
81–82	Calg	3	0	0	0	0	
NHL Totals		23	2	5	7	8	
WHA Totals		5	0	2	2	0	

RAVLICH, Matthew Joseph 5-10 185 D
B. Sault Ste. Marie, Ont., July 12, 1938

62–63	Bos	2	1	0	1	0	
64–65	Chi	61	3	16	19	80	
65–66	Chi	62	0	16	16	78	
66–67	Chi	62	0	3	3	39	
68–69	Chi	60	2	12	14	57	+20
69–70	Det–LA	67	3	13	16	67	-1
70–71	LA	66	3	16	19	41	-14
71–72	Bos	25	0	1	1	2	+4
72–73	Bos	5	0	1	1	0	-5
Totals		410	12	78	90	364	+4

Playoffs

64–65	Chi	14	1	4	5	14	
65–66	Chi	6	0	1	1	2	
67–68	Chi	4	0	0	0	0	
Totals		24	1	5	6	16	

RAY, Robert 6-0 203 LW
B. Stirling, Ont., June 8, 1968

89–90	Buf	27	2	1	3	99	-2
90–91	Buf	66	8	8	16	350	-11
91–92	Buf	63	5	3	8	354	-9
92–93	Buf	68	3	2	5	211	-3
93–94	Buf	82	3	4	7	274	+2
94–95	Buf	47	0	3	3	173	-4
95–96	Buf	71	3	6	9	287	-8
96–97	Buf	82	7	3	10	286	+3
97–98	Buf	63	2	4	6	234	+2
98–99	Buf	76	0	4	4	261	-2
Totals		645	33	38	71	2529	-32

Playoffs

90–91	Buf	6	1	1	2	56	
91–92	Buf	7	0	0	0	2	
93–94	Buf	7	1	0	1	43	
94–95	Buf	5	0	0	0	14	
96–97	Buf	12	0	1	1	28	
97–98	Buf	10	0	0	0	24	
98–99	Buf	5	1	0	1	0	

SSN	TEAM	GP	G	A	PTS.	PIM	+/-
Totals		52	3	2	5	167	

*RAYMOND, Armand D
B. Mechanicsville, N.Y., Jan. 12, 1913

37–38	Mont	11	0	1	1	10	
39–40	Mont	11	0	1	1	0	
Totals		22	0	2	2	10	

*RAYMOND, Paul Marcel 5-7 138 RW
B. Montreal, Que., Feb. 27, 1913

32–33	Mont	16	0	0	0	0	
33–34	Mont	29	1	0	1	2	
34–35	Mont	20	1	1	2	0	
37–38	Mont	11	0	2	2	4	
Totals		76	2	3	5	6	

Playoffs

33–34	Mont	2	0	0	0	0	
37–38	Mont	3	0	0	0	2	
Totals		5	0	0	0	2	

READ, Melvin Dean (Pee Wee) 5-6 165 C
B. Montreal, Que., Apr. 10, 1922

46–47	NYR	1	0	0	0	0	

*REARDON, Kenneth Joseph 5-10 180 D
B. Winnipeg, Man., Apr. 1, 1921

40–41	Mont	34	2	8	10	41	
41–42	Mont	41	3	12	15	93	
45–46	Mont	43	5	4	9	45	
46–47	Mont	52	5	17	22	84	
47–48	Mont	58	7	15	22	129	
48–49	Mont	46	3	13	16	103	
49–50	Mont	67	1	27	28	109	
Totals		341	26	96	122	604	

Playoffs

40–41	Mont	3	0	0	0	4	
41–42	Mont	3	0	0	0	4	
45–46	Mont	9	1	1	2	4	
46–47	Mont	7	1	2	3	20	
48–49	Mont	7	0	0	0	18	
49–50	Mont	2	0	2	2	12	
Totals		31	2	5	7	62	

REARDON, Terrance George 5-10 170 D
B. Winnipeg, Man., Apr. 6, 1919

38–39	Bos	4	0	0	0	0	
40–41	Bos	34	6	5	11	19	
41–42	Mont	33	17	17	34	14	
42–43	Mont	13	6	6	12	2	
45–46	Bos	49	12	11	23	21	
46–47	Bos	60	6	14	20	17	
Totals		193	47	53	100	73	

REASONER, Marty 6-1 185 C
B. Rochester, N.Y., Feb. 26, 1977

98–99	StL	22	3	7	10	8	+2

REAUME, Marc Avellin 6-1 185 D
B. Lasalle, Que., Feb. 7, 1934

54–55	Tor	1	0	0	0	4	
55–56	Tor	48	0	12	12	50	
56–57	Tor	63	6	14	20	81	
57–58	Tor	68	1	7	8	49	
58–59	Tor	51	1	5	6	57	
59–60	Tor–Det	45	0	2	2	8	
60–61	Det	38	0	1	1	8	
63–64	Mont	3	0	0	0	2	
70–71	Van	27	0	2	2	4	-6
Totals		344	8	43	51	263	-6

Playoffs

54–55	Tor	4	0	0	0	2	
55–56	Tor	5	0	2	2	6	
58–59	Tor	10	0	0	0	0	
59–60	Det	2	0	0	0	0	
Totals		21	0	2	2	8	

REAY, William Tulip 5-7 155 C
B. Winnipeg, Man., Aug. 21, 1918

43–44	Det	2	2	0	2	2	
44–45	Det	2	0	0	0	0	
45–46	Mont	44	17	12	29	10	
46–47	Mont	59	22	20	42	17	

SSN	TEAM	GP	G	A	PTS.	PIM	+/-
47–48	Mont	60	6	14	20	24	
48–49	Mont	60	22	23	45	33	
49–50	Mont	68	19	26	45	48	
50–51	Mont	60	6	18	24	24	
51–52	Mont	68	7	34	41	20	
52–53	Mont	56	4	15	19	26	
Totals		479	105	162	267	204	

Playoffs

45–46	Mont	9	1	2	3	4	
46–47	Mont	11	6	1	7	14	
48–49	Mont	7	1	5	6	4	
49–50	Mont	4	0	1	1	0	
50–51	Mont	11	3	3	6	10	
51–52	Mont	10	2	2	4	7	
52–53	Mont	11	0	2	2	4	
Totals		63	13	16	29	43	

RECCHI, Mark 5-10 185 RW
B. Kamloops, B.C., Feb. 1, 1968

88–89	Pitt	15	1	1	2	0	-2
89–90	Pitt	74	30	37	67	44	+6
90–91	Pitt	78	40	73	113	48	0
91–92	Pitt–Phil	80	43	54	97	96	-21
92–93	Phil	84	53	70	123	95	+1
93–94	Phil	84	40	67	107	46	-2
94–95	Phil–Mont	49	16	32	48	28	-2
95–96	Mont	82	28	50	78	69	+20
96–97	Mont	82	34	46	80	58	-1
97–98	Mont	82	32	42	74	51	+11
98–99	Mont-Phil	71	16	37	53	34	-7
Totals		781	333	509	842	569	-5

Playoffs

90–91	Pitt	24	10	24	34	33	
95–96	Mont	6	3	3	6	0	
96–97	Mont	5	4	2	6	2	
97–98	Mont	10	4	8	12	6	
98–99	Phil	6	0	1	1	2	
Totals		51	21	38	59	43	

REDAHL, Gordon 5-11 170 RW
B. Kinistino, Sask., Aug. 28, 1935

58–59	Bos	18	0	1	1	2	

REDDEN, Wade 6-2 193 D
B. Lloydminster, Sask., June 12, 1977

96–97	Ott	82	6	24	30	41	+1
97–98	Ott	80	8	14	22	27	+17
98–99	Ott	72	8	21	29	54	+7
Totals		234	22	59	81	122	+25

Playoffs

96–97	Ott	7	1	3	4	2	
97–98	Ott	9	0	2	2	2	
98–99	Ott	4	1	2	3	2	
Totals		20	2	7	9	6	

*REDDING, George D

24–25	Bos	27	3	2	5	10	
25–26	Bos	8	0	0	0	0	
Totals		35	3	2	5	10	

REDMOND, Craig 5-11 190 D
B. Dawson Creek, B.C., Sept. 22, 1965

84–85	LA	79	6	33	39	57	-8
85–86	LA	73	6	18	24	57	-34
86–87	LA	16	1	7	8	8	-1
87–88	LA	2	0	0	0	0	-4
88–89	Edm	21	3	10	13	12	-10
Totals		191	16	68	84	134	-57

Playoffs

84–85	LA	3	1	0	1	2	

REDMOND, Keith Christopher 6-3 208 LW
B. Richmond Hill, Ont., Oct. 25, 1972

93–94	LA	12	1	0	1	20	-3

REDMOND, Michael Edward (Mickey) 5-11 185 RW
B. Kirkland Lake, Ont., Dec. 27, 1947

67–68	Mont	41	6	5	11	4	+2
68–69	Mont	65	9	15	24	12	+16
69–70	Mont	75	27	27	54	61	+23
70–71	Mont–Det	61	20	24	44	42	+10

SSN	TEAM	GP	G	A	PTS.	PIM	+/-
71–72	Det	78	42	28	70	34	-13
72–73	Det	76	52	41	93	24	+6
73–74	Det	76	51	26	77	14	-21
74–75	Det	29	15	12	27	18	-12
75–76	Det	37	11	17	28	10	-17
Totals		538	233	195	428	219	-6

Playoffs

67–68	Mont	2	0	0	0	0	
68–69	Mont	14	2	3	5	2	
Totals		16	2	3	5	2	

REDMOND, Richard John (Dick) *5–11 178 D*
B. Kirkland Lake, Ont., Aug. 14, 1949

69–70	Minn	7	0	1	1	4	-1
70–71	Minn–Cal	20	2	6	8	28	-8
71–72	Cal	74	10	35	45	76	-10
72–73	Cal–Chi	76	12	32	44	26	-13
73–74	Chi	76	17	42	59	69	+26
74–75	Chi	80	14	43	57	90	+6
75–76	Chi	53	9	27	36	25	+1
76–77	Chi	80	22	25	47	30	-40
77–78	StL–Atl	70	11	22	33	32	-2
78–79	Bos	64	7	26	33	21	0
79–80	Bos	76	14	33	47	39	+37
80–81	Bos	78	15	20	35	60	+4
81–82	Bos	17	0	0	0	4	-7
Totals		771	133	312	445	504	-7

Playoffs

72–73	Chi	13	4	2	6	2	
73–74	Chi	11	1	7	8	8	
74–75	Chi	8	2	3	5	0	
75–76	Chi	4	0	2	2	4	
76–77	Chi	2	0	1	1	0	
77–78	Atl	2	1	0	1	0	
78–79	Bos	11	1	3	4	2	
79–80	Bos	10	0	3	3	9	
80–81	Bos	3	0	1	1	2	
81–82	Bos	2	0	0	0	0	
Totals		66	9	22	31	27	

REEDS, Mark *5–10 190 RW*
B. Burlington, Ont., Jan. 24, 1960

81–82	StL	9	1	3	4	0	+3
82–83	StL	20	5	14	19	6	+8
83–84	StL	65	11	14	25	23	-3
84–85	StL	80	9	30	39	25	+8
85–86	StL	78	10	28	38	28	+11
86–87	StL	68	9	16	25	16	-20
87–88	Hart	38	0	7	7	31	-13
88–89	Hart	7	0	2	2	6	-1
Totals		365	45	114	159	135	-7

Playoffs

81–82	StL	10	0	1	1	2	
82–83	StL	4	1	0	1	2	
83–84	StL	11	3	3	6	15	
84–85	StL	3	0	0	0	0	
85–86	StL	19	4	4	8	2	
86–87	StL	6	0	1	1	2	
Totals		53	8	9	17	23	

REEKIE, Joseph James *6–3 220 D*
B. Victoria, B.C., Feb. 22, 1965

85–86	Buf	3	0	0	0	14	-2
86–87	Buf	56	1	8	9	82	+6
87–88	Buf	30	1	4	5	68	-3
88–89	Buf	15	1	3	4	26	+1
89–90	NYI	31	1	8	9	43	+13
90–91	NYI	66	3	16	19	96	+17
91–92	NYI	54	4	12	16	85	+15
92–93	TB	42	2	11	13	69	+2
93–94	TB–Wash	85	1	16	17	156	+15
94–95	Wash	48	1	6	7	97	+10
95–96	Wash	78	3	7	10	149	+7
96–97	Wash	65	1	8	9	107	+8
97–98	Wash	68	2	8	10	70	+15
98–99	Wash	73	0	10	10	88	+11
Totals		714	21	117	138	1150	+120

Playoffs

87–88	Buf	2	0	0	0	4	
93–94	Wash	11	2	1	3	29	
94–95	Wash	7	0	0	0	2	
97–98	Wash	21	1	2	3	20	
Totals		41	3	3	6	55	

REGAN, Lawrence Emmett *5–9 178 RW*
B. North Bay, Ont., Aug. 9, 1930

56–57	Bos	69	14	19	33	29	
57–58	Bos	59	11	28	39	22	
58–59	Bos–Tor	68	9	27	36	12	
59–60	Tor	47	4	16	20	6	
60–61	Tor	37	3	5	8	2	
Totals		280	41	95	136	71	

Playoffs

56–57	Bos	8	0	2	2	10	
57–58	Bos	12	3	8	11	6	
58–59	Tor	8	1	1	2	2	
59–60	Tor	10	3	3	6	0	
60–61	Tor	4	0	0	0	0	
Totals		42	7	14	21	18	

REGAN, William Donald *D*
B. Creighton Mines, Ont., Dec. 11, 1908

29–30	NYR	10	0	0	0	4	
30–31	NYR	42	2	1	3	49	
32–33	NYA	15	1	1	2	14	
Totals		67	3	2	5	67	

Playoffs

29–30	NYR	4	0	0	0	0	
30–31	NYR	4	0	0	0	2	
Totals		8	0	0	0	2	

REGIER, Darcy John *5–11 190 D*
B. Swift Current, Sask., Nov. 27, 1956

77–78	Clev	15	0	1	1	28	-5
82–83	NYI	6	0	0	0	7	0
83–84	NYI	5	0	1	1	0	+2
Totals		26	0	2	2	35	-3

REIBEL, Earl (Dutch) *5–8 160 C*
B. Kitchener, Ont., July 21, 1930

53–54	Det	69	15	33	48	18	
54–55	Det	70	25	41	66	15	
55–56	Det	68	17	39	56	10	
56–57	Det	70	13	23	36	6	
57–58	Det–Chi	69	8	17	25	10	
58–59	Bos	63	6	8	14	16	
Totals		409	84	161	245	75	

Playoffs

53–54	Det	9	1	3	4	0	
54–55	Det	11	5	7	12	2	
55–56	Det	10	0	2	2	2	
56–57	Det	5	0	2	2	0	
58–59	Bos	4	0	0	0	0	
Totals		39	6	14	20	4	

REICHEL, Robert *5–10 185 C*
B. Litinov, Czechoslovakia, June 25, 1971

90–91	Calg	66	19	22	41	22	+17
91–92	Calg	77	20	34	54	32	+1
92–93	Calg	80	40	48	88	54	+25
93–94	Calg	84	40	53	93	58	+20
94–95	Calg	48	18	17	35	28	-2
96–97	Calg–NYI	82	21	41	62	26	+5
97–98	NYI	82	25	40	65	32	-11
98–99	NYI–Phoe	83	26	43	69	54	-13
Totals		602	209	298	507	306	+42

Playoffs

90–91	Calg	6	1	1	2	0	
92–93	Calg	6	2	4	6	2	
93–94	Calg	7	0	5	5	0	
94–95	Calg	7	2	4	6	4	
98–99	Phoe	7	1	3	4	2	
Totals		33	6	17	23	8	

REICHERT, Craig *6–1 196 RW*
B. Winnipeg, Man., May 11, 1974

96–97	Ana	3	0	0	0	0	-2

REID, Allan Thomas *6–1 200 D*
B. Fort Erie, Ont., June 24, 1946

67–68	Chi	56	0	4	4	25	+1
68–69	Chi–Minn	48	0	7	7	50	-17
69–70	Minn	66	1	7	8	51	-10
70–71	Minn	73	3	14	17	62	-6
71–72	Minn	78	6	15	21	107	+13

72–73	Minn	60	1	13	14	50	+15
73–74	Minn	76	4	19	23	81	-22
74–75	Minn	74	1	5	6	103	-39
75–76	Minn	69	0	15	15	52	-24
76–77	Minn	65	0	8	8	52	-16
77–78	Minn	36	1	6	7	21	-26
Totals		701	17	113	130	654	-131

Playoffs

67–68	Chi	9	0	0	0	2	
69–70	Minn	6	0	1	1	4	
70–71	Minn	12	0	6	6	20	
71–72	Minn	7	1	4	5	17	
72–73	Minn	6	0	2	2	4	
76–77	Minn	2	0	0	0	2	
Totals		42	1	13	14	49	

REID, David *F*
B. Toronto, Ont., Jan. 11, 1934

52–53	Tor	2	0	0	0	0	
54–55	Tor	1	0	0	0	0	
55–56	Tor	4	0	0	0	0	
Totals		7	0	0	0	0	

REID, David *6–1 217 LW*
B. Toronto, Ont., May 15, 1964

83–84	Bos	8	1	0	1	2	+1
84–85	Bos	35	14	13	27	27	-1
85–86	Bos	37	10	10	20	10	+2
86–87	Bos	12	3	3	6	0	-1
87–88	Bos	3	0	0	0	0	
88–89	Tor	77	9	21	30	22	+12
89–90	Tor	70	9	19	28	9	-8
90–91	Tor	69	15	13	28	18	-10
91–92	Bos	43	7	7	14	27	+5
92–93	Bos	65	20	16	36	10	+12
93–94	Bos	83	6	17	23	25	+10
94–95	Bos	38	5	5	10	10	+8
95–96	Bos	63	23	21	44	4	+14
96–97	Dal	82	19	20	39	10	+12
97–98	Dal	65	6	12	18	14	-15
98–99	Dal	73	6	11	17	16	0
Totals		823	153	188	341	204	+41

Playoffs

84–85	Bos	5	1	0	1	0	
86–87	Bos	2	0	0	0	0	
89–90	Tor	3	0	0	0	0	
91–92	Bos	15	2	5	7	4	
93–94	Bos	13	2	1	3	2	
94–95	Bos	5	0	0	0	0	
95–96	Bos	5	0	2	2	2	
96–97	Dal	7	1	0	1	4	
97–98	Dal	5	0	3	3	2	
98–99	Dal	23	2	8	10	14	
Totals		83	8	19	27	28	

REID, Gerald Roland *6–0 160 C*
B. Owen Sound, Ont., Oct. 13, 1928

Playoffs

48–49	Det	2	0	0	0	0	

REID, Gordon J. *D*
B. Mt. Albert, Ont., Feb. 19, 1912

36–37	NYA	1	0	0	0	2	

REID, Reginald S. *F*

24–25	Tor	28	2	0	2	2	
25–26	Tor	12	0	0	0	2	
Totals		40	2	0	2	4	

Playoffs

24–25	Bos	2	0	0	0	0	

REIERSON, David *6–0 185 D*
B. Bashaw, Alta., Aug. 30, 1964

88–89	Calg	2	0	0	0	2	

REIGLE, Edmond (Rags) *5–8 180 D*
B. Winnipeg, Man., June 19, 1924

50–51	Bos	17	0	2	2	25	

REINHART, Paul *5–11 200 D*
B. Kitchener, Ont., Jan. 6, 1960

79–80	Atl	79	9	38	47	31	+11

SSN	TEAM	GP	G	A	PTS.	PIM	+/-
80–81	Calg	74	18	49	67	52	+10
81–82	Calg	62	13	48	61	17	+1
82–83	Calg	78	17	58	75	28	+1
83–84	Calg	27	6	15	21	10	-10
84–85	Calg	75	23	46	69	18	+3
85–86	Calg	32	8	25	33	15	+4
86–87	Calg	76	15	53	68	22	+7
87–88	Calg	14	0	4	4	10	0
88–89	Van	64	7	50	57	44	-4
89–90	Van	67	17	40	57	30	+2
Totals		648	133	426	559	277	+25

Playoffs

80–81	Calg	16	1	14	15	16	
81–82	Calg	3	0	1	1	2	
82–83	Calg	9	6	3	9	2	
83–84	Calg	11	6	11	17	2	
84–85	Calg	4	1	1	2	0	
85–86	Calg	21	5	13	18	4	
86–87	Calg	4	0	1	1	6	
87–88	Calg	8	2	7	9	6	
88–89	Van	7	2	3	5	4	
Totals		83	23	54	77	42	

*REINIKKA, Oliver Mathias (Rocco) *F*
B. Shuswap, B.C., Aug. 2, 1901

| 26–27 | NYR | 16 | 0 | 0 | 0 | 0 | |

REISE, Leo Charles, Jr. *D*
B. Stoney Creek, Ont., June 7, 1922

45–46	Chi	6	0	0	0	6	
46–47	Chi–Det	48	4	6	10	32	
47–48	Det	58	5	4	9	30	
48–49	Det	59	3	7	10	60	
49–50	Det	70	4	17	21	46	
50–51	Det	68	5	16	21	46	
51–52	Det	54	0	11	11	34	
52–53	NYR	61	4	15	19	53	
53–54	NYR	70	3	5	8	71	
Totals		494	28	81	109	399	

Playoffs

46–47	Det	5	0	1	1	4	
47–48	Det	10	2	1	3	12	
48–49	Det	11	1	0	1	4	
49–50	Det	14	2	0	2	19	
50–51	Det	6	2	3	5	2	
51–52	Det	6	1	0	1	27	
Totals		52	8	5	13	68	

*REISE, Leo Charles, Sr. *5–11 175 D*
B. Pembroke, Ont., June 1, 1892

20–21	Ham	6	2	0	2	8	
21–22	Ham	24	9	14	23	8	
22–23	Ham	24	6	6	12	35	
23–24	Ham	4	0	0	0	0	
26–27	NYA	40	7	6	13	24	
27–28	NYA	43	8	1	9	62	
28–29	NYA	44	4	1	5	32	
29–30	NYR	14	0	1	1	8	
Totals		199	36	29	65	177	

Playoffs

28–29	NYA	2	0	0	0	0	
29–30	NYA	4	0	0	0	16	
Totals		6	0	0	0	16	

REIRDON, Todd *6–5 220 D*
B. Deerfield, Ill., June 25, 1971

| 98–99 | Edm | 17 | 2 | 3 | 5 | 20 | -1 |

RENAUD, Mark Joseph *6–0 185 D*
B. Windsor, Ont., Feb. 21, 1959

79–80	Hart	13	0	2	2	4	-1
80–81	Hart	4	1	0	1	0	0
81–82	Hart	48	1	17	18	39	-17
82–83	Hart	77	3	28	31	37	-42
83–84	Buf	10	1	3	4	6	+1
Totals		152	6	50	56	86	-59

RENBERG, Mikael *6–1 218 RW*
B. Pitea, Sweden, May 5, 1972

93–94	Phil	83	38	44	82	36	+8
94–95	Phil	47	26	31	57	20	+20
95–96	Phil	51	23	20	43	45	+8
96–97	Phil	77	22	37	59	65	+36

SSN	TEAM	GP	G	A	PTS.	PIM	+/-
97–98	TB	68	16	22	38	34	-37
98–99	TB-Phil	66	15	23	38	18	+5
Totals		392	140	177	317	218	+40

Playoffs

94–95	Phil	15	6	7	13	6	
95–96	Phil	11	3	6	9	14	
96–97	Phil	18	5	6	11	4	
98–99	Phil	6	0	1	1	0	
Totals		50	14	20	34	24	

REYNOLDS, Bobby *5–11 175 LW*
B. Flint, Mich., July 14, 1967

| 89–90 | Tor | 7 | 1 | 1 | 2 | 0 | -3 |

RHEAUME, Pascal *6–1 200 C*
B. Quebec City, Que., June 21, 1973

96–97	NJ	2	1	0	1	0	+1
97–98	StL	48	6	9	15	35	+4
98–99	StL	60	9	18	27	24	+10
Totals		110	16	27	43	59	+15

Playoffs

97–98	StL	10	1	3	4	8	
98–99	StL	5	1	0	1	4	
Totals		15	2	3	5	12	

RIBBLE, Patrick Wayne *6–4 210 D*
B. Leamington, Ont., Apr. 26, 1954

75–76	Atl	3	0	0	0	0	
76–77	Atl	23	2	2	4	31	-1
77–78	Atl	80	5	12	17	68	+4
78–79	Atl–Chi	78	6	19	25	77	+25
79–80	Chi–Tor–Wash	55	2	9	11	52	-15
80–81	Wash	67	3	15	18	103	-13
81–82	Wash–Calg	15	1	2	3	16	-2
82–83	Calg	28	0	1	1	18	-12
Totals		349	19	60	79	365	-14

Playoffs

76–77	Atl	2	0	0	0	6	
77–78	Atl	2	0	1	1	2	
78–79	Chi	4	0	0	0	4	
Totals		8	0	1	1	12	

RICCI, Mike *6–0 190 C*
B. Scarborough, Ont., Oct. 27, 1971

90–91	Phil	68	21	20	41	64	-8
91–92	Phil	78	20	36	56	93	-10
82–83	Que	77	27	51	78	123	+8
93–94	Que	83	30	21	51	113	-9
94–95	Que	48	15	21	36	40	+5
95–96	Col A	62	6	21	27	52	+1
96–97	Col A	63	13	19	32	59	-3
97–98	Col A–SJ	65	9	18	27	32	-4
98–99	SJ	82	13	26	39	68	+1
Totals		626	154	233	387	644	-19

Playoffs

92–93	Que	6	0	6	6	8	
94–95	Que	6	1	3	4	8	
95–96	Col A	22	6	11	17	18	
96–97	Col A	17	2	4	6	17	
97–98	SJ	6	1	3	4	6	
98–99	SJ	6	2	3	5	10	
Totals		63	12	30	42	67	

RICE, Steven *6–0 215 RW*
B. Kitchener, Ont., May 26, 1971

90–91	NYR	11	1	1	2	4	+2
91–92	Edm	3	0	0	0	2	-2
92–93	Edm	28	2	5	7	28	-4
93–94	Edm	63	17	15	32	36	-10
94–95	Hart	40	11	10	21	61	+2
95–96	Hart	59	10	12	22	47	-4
96–97	Hart	78	21	14	35	59	-11
97–98	Car	47	2	4	6	38	-16
Totals		329	64	61	125	265	-43

Playoffs

| 90–91 | NYR | 2 | 2 | 1 | 3 | 6 | |

RICHARD, Jacques *5–11 180 LW*
B. Quebec City, Que., Oct. 7, 1952

| 72–73 | Atl | 74 | 13 | 18 | 31 | 32 | -24 |

SSN	TEAM	GP	G	A	PTS.	PIM	+/-
73–74	Atl	78	27	16	43	45	-18
74–75	Atl	63	17	12	29	31	-16
75–76	Buf	73	12	23	35	31	+4
76–77	Buf	21	2	0	2	16	-3
78–79	Buf	61	10	15	25	26	+8
79–80	Que	14	3	12	15	4	-7
80–81	Que	78	52	51	103	39	-9
81–82	Que	59	15	26	41	77	-9
82–83	Que	35	9	14	23	6	0
Totals		556	160	187	347	307	-74

Playoffs

73–74	Atl	4	0	0	0	2	
75–76	Buf	9	1	1	2	7	
78–79	Buf	3	1	0	1	0	
80–81	Que	5	2	4	6	14	
81–82	Que	10	1	0	1	9	
82–83	Que	4	0	0	0	2	
Totals		35	5	5	10	34	

RICHARD, Jean–Marc *5–11 178 D*
B. St.—Raymond, Que., Oct. 8, 1966

87–88	Que	4	2	1	3	2	-3
88–89	Que	1	0	0	0	0	-1
Totals		5	2	1	3	2	-4

RICHARD, Joseph Henri (Pocket Rocket) *5–7 160 C*
B. Montreal, Que., Feb. 29, 1936

55–56	Mont	64	19	21	40	46	
56–57	Mont	63	18	36	54	71	
57–58	Mont	67	28	52	80	56	
58–59	Mont	63	21	30	51	33	
59–60	Mont	70	30	43	73	66	
60–61	Mont	70	24	44	68	91	
61–62	Mont	54	21	29	50	48	
62–63	Mont	67	23	50	73	57	
63–64	Mont	66	14	39	53	73	
64–65	Mont	53	23	29	52	43	
65–66	Mont	62	22	39	61	47	
66–67	Mont	65	21	34	55	28	
67–68	Mont	54	9	19	28	16	+4
68–69	Mont	64	15	37	52	45	+25
69–70	Buf	62	16	36	52	61	+24
70–71	Mont	75	12	37	49	46	+13
71–72	Mont	75	12	32	44	48	+10
72–73	Mont	71	8	35	43	21	+34
73–74	Mont	75	19	36	55	28	+7
74–75	Mont	16	3	10	13	4	+9
Totals		1256	358	688	1046	928	+126

Playoffs

55–56	Mont	10	4	4	8	21	
56–57	Mont	10	2	6	8	10	
57–58	Mont	10	1	7	8	11	
58–59	Mont	11	3	8	11	13	
59–60	Mont	9	3	9	12	9	
60–61	Mont	6	2	4	6	22	
62–63	Mont	5	1	1	2	2	
63–64	Mont	7	1	1	2	9	
64–65	Mont	13	7	4	11	24	
65–66	Mont	8	1	4	5	2	
66–67	Mont	10	4	6	10	2	
67–68	Mont	13	4	4	8	4	
68–69	Mont	14	2	4	6	8	
70–71	Mont	20	5	7	12	20	
71–72	Mont	6	0	3	3	4	
72–73	Mont	17	6	4	10	14	
73–74	Mont	6	2	2	4	2	
74–75	Mont	6	1	2	3	4	
Totals		180	49	80	129	181	

RICHARD, Joseph Henri Maurice (Rocket) *5–10 195 RW*
B. Montreal, Que., Aug. 4, 1921

42–43	Mont	16	5	6	11	4	
43–44	Mont	46	32	22	54	45	
44–45	Mont	50	50	23	73	46	
45–46	Mont	50	27	21	48	50	
46–47	Mont	60	45	26	71	69	
47–48	Mont	53	28	25	53	89	
48–49	Mont	59	20	18	38	110	
49–50	Mont	70	43	22	65	114	
50–51	Mont	65	42	24	66	97	
51–52	Mont	48	27	17	44	44	
52–53	Mont	70	28	33	61	112	
53–54	Mont	70	37	30	67	112	
54–55	Mont	67	38	36	74	125	

SSN	TEAM	GP	G	A	PTS.	PIM	+/-
55–56	Mont	70	38	33	71	89	
56–57	Mont	63	33	29	62	74	
57–58	Mont	28	15	19	34	28	
58–59	Mont	42	17	21	38	27	
59–60	Mont	51	19	16	35	50	
Totals		978	544	421	965	1285	

Playoffs

SSN	TEAM	GP	G	A	PTS.	PIM	+/-
43–44	Mont	9	12	5	17	10	
44–45	Mont	6	6	2	8	10	
45–46	Mont	9	7	4	11	15	
46–47	Mont	10	6	5	11	44	
48–49	Mont	7	2	1	3	14	
49–50	Mont	5	1	1	2	6	
50–51	Mont	11	9	4	13	13	
51–52	Mont	11	4	2	6	6	
52–53	Mont	12	7	1	8	2	
53–54	Mont	11	3	0	3	22	
55–56	Mont	10	5	9	14	24	
56–57	Mont	10	8	3	11	8	
57–58	Mont	10	11	4	15	10	
58–59	Mont	4	0	0	0	2	
59–60	Mont	8	1	3	4	2	
Totals		133	82	44	126	188	

RICHARD, Michael 5–10 190 C
B. Scarborough, Ont., July 9, 1966

SSN	TEAM	GP	G	A	PTS.	PIM	+/-
87–88	Wash	4	0	0	0	0	-1
89–90	Wash	3	0	2	2	0	0
Totals		7	0	2	2	0	-1

RICHARDS, Todd 6–0 194 D
B. Robindale, Minn., Oct. 20, 1966

SSN	TEAM	GP	G	A	PTS.	PIM	+/-
90–91	Hart	2	0	4	4	2	-4
91–92	Hart	6	0	0	0	2	-2
Totals		8	0	4	4	4	-6

Playoffs

SSN	TEAM	GP	G	A	PTS.	PIM	+/-
90–91	Hart	6	0	0	0	2	
91–92	Hart	5	0	3	3	4	
Totals		11	0	3	3	6	

RICHARDS, Travis 6–1 185 D
B. Crystal, Minn., Mar. 22, 1970

SSN	TEAM	GP	G	A	PTS.	PIM	+/-
94–95	Dal	2	0	0	0	0	0
95–96	Dal	1	0	0	0	2	-1
Totals		3	0	0	0	2	-1

RICHARDSON, David George 5–8 175 LW
B. Boniface, Man., Dec. 11, 1940

SSN	TEAM	GP	G	A	PTS.	PIM	+/-
63–64	NYR	34	3	1	4	21	
64–65	NYR	7	0	1	1	4	
65–66	Chi	3	0	0	0	2	
67–68	Det	1	0	0	0	0	0
Totals		45	3	2	5	27	0

RICHARDSON, Glen Gordon 6–2 200 LW
B. Barrie, Ont., Sept. 20, 1955

SSN	TEAM	GP	G	A	PTS.	PIM	+/-
75–76	Van	24	3	6	9	19	-1

RICHARDSON, Kenneth William 6–0 190 C
B. North Bay, Ont., Apr. 12, 1951

SSN	TEAM	GP	G	A	PTS.	PIM	+/-
74–75	StL	21	5	7	12	12	+4
77–78	StL	12	2	5	7	2	+4
78–79	StL	16	1	1	2	2	-5
Totals		49	8	13	21	16	+3

RICHARDSON, Luke Glen 6–4 210 D
B. Ottawa, Ont., March 26, 1969

SSN	TEAM	GP	G	A	PTS.	PIM	+/-
87–88	Tor	78	4	6	10	80	-25
88–89	Tor	55	2	7	9	106	-15
89–90	Tor	67	4	14	18	122	-1
90–91	Tor	78	1	9	10	238	-28
91–92	Edm	75	2	19	21	118	-9
92–93	Edm	82	3	10	13	142	-18
93–94	Edm	69	2	6	8	131	-13
94–95	Edm	46	3	10	13	40	-6
95–96	Edm	82	2	9	11	108	-27
96–97	Edm	82	1	11	12	91	+9
97–98	Phil	81	2	3	5	139	+7
98–99	Phil	76	0	6	6	106	-3
Totals		871	26	110	136	1431	-131

Playoffs

SSN	TEAM	GP	G	A	PTS.	PIM	+/-
87–88	Tor	2	0	0	0	0	

SSN	TEAM	GP	G	A	PTS.	PIM	+/-
89–90	Tor	5	0	0	0	22	
91–92	Edm	16	0	5	5	45	
96–97	Edm	12	0	2	2	14	
97–98	Phil	5	0	0	0	0	
Totals		40	0	7	7	81	

RICHER, Robert Roger 5–10 175 C
B. Cowansville, Que., Mar. 5, 1951

SSN	TEAM	GP	G	A	PTS.	PIM	+/-
72–73	Buf	3	0	0	0	0	0

RICHER, Stephane J. G. 5–11 190 D
B. Hull, Que., Apr. 28, 1966

SSN	TEAM	GP	G	A	PTS.	PIM	+/-
92–93	TB–Bos	24	1	4	5	18	-9
93–94	Fla	2	0	1	1	0	-1
94–95	Fla	1	0	0	0	2	0
Totals		27	1	5	6	20	-10

Playoffs

SSN	TEAM	GP	G	A	PTS.	PIM	+/-
92–93	Bos	3	0	0	0	0	

RICHER, Stephane J.J. 6–2 215 RW
B. Ripon, Que., June 7, 1966

SSN	TEAM	GP	G	A	PTS.	PIM	+/-
84–85	Mont	1	0	0	0	0	0
85–86	Mont	65	21	16	37	50	+1
86–87	Mont	57	20	19	39	80	+11
87–88	Mont	72	50	28	78	72	+12
88–89	Mont	68	25	35	60	61	+4
89–90	Mont	75	51	40	91	46	+35
90–91	Mont	75	31	30	61	53	0
91–92	NJ	74	29	35	64	25	-1
92–93	NJ	78	38	35	73	44	-1
93–94	NJ	80	36	36	72	16	+31
94–95	NJ	45	23	16	39	10	+8
95–96	NJ	73	20	12	32	30	-8
96–97	Mont	63	22	24	46	32	0
97–98	Mont–TB	40	14	15	29	41	-6
98–99	TB	64	12	21	33	22	-10
Totals		930	392	362	754	582	+86

Playoffs

SSN	TEAM	GP	G	A	PTS.	PIM	+/-
85–86	Mont	16	4	1	5	23	
86–87	Mont	5	3	2	5	0	
87–88	Mont	8	7	5	12	6	
88–89	Mont	21	6	5	11	14	
89–90	Mont	9	7	3	10	2	
90–91	Mont	13	9	5	14	6	
91–92	NJ	7	1	2	3	0	
92–93	NJ	5	2	2	4	2	
93–94	NJ	20	7	5	12	6	
94–95	NJ	19	6	15	21	2	
96–97	Mont	5	0	0	0	0	
Totals		128	52	45	97	61	

RICHMOND, Steve 6–1 205 D
B. Chicago, Ill., Dec. 11, 1959

SSN	TEAM	GP	G	A	PTS.	PIM	+/-
83–84	NYR	26	2	5	7	110	+6
84–85	NYR	34	0	5	5	90	-16
85–86	NYR–Det	46	1	4	5	145	-16
86–87	NJ	44	1	7	8	143	-12
88–89	LA	9	0	2	2	26	+2
Totals		159	4	23	27	514	-36

Playoffs

SSN	TEAM	GP	G	A	PTS.	PIM	+/-
83–84	NYR	4	0	0	0	12	

RICHTER, Barry 6–2 195 D
B. Madison, Wisc., Sept. 11, 1970

SSN	TEAM	GP	G	A	PTS.	PIM	+/-
95–96	NYR	4	0	1	1	0	+2
96–97	Bos	50	5	13	18	32	-12
98–99	NYI	72	6	18	24	34	-4
Totals		124	11	32	43	66	-9

RICHTER, David 6–5 225 D
B. St. Boniface, Man., Apr. 8, 1960

SSN	TEAM	GP	G	A	PTS.	PIM	+/-
81–82	Minn	3	0	0	0	11	0
82–83	Minn	6	0	0	0	4	0
83–84	Minn	42	2	3	5	132	-8
84–85	Minn	55	2	8	10	221	+3
85–86	Minn–Phil	64	0	5	5	167	-8
86–87	Van	78	2	15	17	172	-2
87–88	Van	49	2	4	6	224	-5
88–89	StL	66	1	5	6	99	-21
89–90	StL	2	0	0	0	0	-2
Totals		365	9	40	49	1030	-43

Playoffs

SSN	TEAM	GP	G	A	PTS.	PIM	+/-
83–84	Minn	8	0	0	0	20	

SSN	TEAM	GP	G	A	PTS.	PIM	+/-
84–85	Minn	9	1	0	1	39	
85–86	Phil	5	0	0	0	21	
Totals		22	1	0	1	80	

RIDLEY, Mike 6–0 195 C
B. Winnipeg, Man., July 8, 1963

SSN	TEAM	GP	G	A	PTS.	PIM	+/-
85–86	NYR	80	22	43	65	69	0
86–87	NYR–Wash	78	31	39	70	40	-11
87–88	Wash	70	28	31	59	22	+1
88–89	Wash	80	41	48	89	49	+17
89–90	Wash	74	30	43	73	27	0
90–91	Wash	79	23	48	71	26	+9
91–92	Wash	80	29	40	69	38	+3
92–93	Wash	84	26	56	82	44	+5
93–94	Wash	81	26	44	70	24	+15
94–95	Tor	48	10	27	37	14	+1
95–96	Van	37	6	15	21	29	-3
96–97	Van	75	20	32	52	42	0
Totals		866	292	466	758	424	+37

Playoffs

SSN	TEAM	GP	G	A	PTS.	PIM	+/-
85–86	NYR	16	6	8	14	26	
86–87	Wash	7	2	1	3	6	
87–88	Wash	14	6	5	11	10	
88–89	Wash	6	0	5	5	2	
89–90	Wash	14	3	4	7	8	
90–91	Wah	11	3	4	7	8	
91–92	Wash	7	0	11	11	0	
92–93	Wash	6	1	5	6	0	
93–94	Wash	11	4	6	10	6	
94–95	Tor	7	3	1	4	2	
95–96	Van	5	0	0	0	2	
Totals		104	28	50	78	70	

RILEY, Jack 5–10 160 C
B. Berckenia, Ireland, Dec. 29, 1910

SSN	TEAM	GP	G	A	PTS.	PIM	+/-
32–33	Det	1	0	0	0	0	
33–34	Det	48	6	11	17	4	
34–35	Mont	47	4	11	15	4	
35–36	Mont	8	0	0	0	0	
Totals		104	10	22	32	8	

Playoffs

SSN	TEAM	GP	G	A	PTS.	PIM	+/-
33–34	Mont	2	0	1	1	0	
34–35	Mont	2	0	2	2	0	
Totals		4	0	3	3	0	

RILEY, James Norman LW
B. Bayfield, N.B., May 25, 1897

SSN	TEAM	GP	G	A	PTS.	PIM	+/-
26–27	Det	17	0	2	2	14	

RILEY, James William (Bill) 5–11 195 RW
B. Amherst, N.S., Sept. 20, 1950

SSN	TEAM	GP	G	A	PTS.	PIM	+/-
74–75	Wash	1	0	0	0	0	-1
76–77	Wash	43	13	14	27	124	+4
77–78	Wash	57	13	12	25	125	-15
78–79	Wash	24	2	2	4	64	-6
79–80	Winn	14	3	2	5	7	0
Totals		139	31	30	61	320	-18

RIOPELLE, Howard Joseph (Rip) 5–11 165 LW
B. Ottawa, Ont., Jan. 30, 1922

SSN	TEAM	GP	G	A	PTS.	PIM	+/-
47–48	Mont	55	5	2	7	12	
48–49	Mont	48	10	6	16	34	
49–50	Mont	66	12	8	20	27	
Totals		169	27	16	43	73	

Playoffs

SSN	TEAM	GP	G	A	PTS.	PIM	+/-
48–49	Mont	7	1	1	2	2	
49–50	Mont	1	0	0	0	0	
Totals		8	1	1	2	2	

RIOUX, Gerard (Gerry) 5–11 195 RW
B. Iroquois Falls, Ont., Feb. 17, 1959

SSN	TEAM	GP	G	A	PTS.	PIM	+/-
79–80	Winn	8	0	0	0	6	-2

RIOUX, Pierre 5–9 165 RW
B. Quebec City, Que., Feb. 1, 1962

SSN	TEAM	GP	G	A	PTS.	PIM	+/-
82–83	Calg	14	1	2	3	4	-3

*RIPLEY, Victor Merrick 5–7 170 LW
B. Elgin, Ont., May 30, 1906

SSN	TEAM	GP	G	A	PTS.	PIM	+/-
28–29	Chi	34	11	2	13	31	
29–30	Chi	40	8	8	16	33	
30–31	Chi	37	8	4	12	9	

SSN	TEAM	GP	G	A	PTS.	PIM	+/-
31–32	Chi	46	12	6	18	47	
32–33	Chi–Bos	38	4	9	13	27	
33–34	Bos–NYR	48	7	13	20	16	
34–45	NYR–StL E	35	1	7	8	10	
Totals		278	51	49	100	173	

Playoffs

29–30	Chi	2	0	0	0	2	
30–31	Chi	9	2	1	3	4	
31–32	Chi	2	0	0	0	0	
32–33	Bos	5	1	0	1	0	
33–34	NYR	2	1	0	1	4	
Totals		20	4	1	5	10	

RISEBROUGH, Douglas *5–11 180 C*
B. Guelph, Ont., Jan. 29, 1954

74–75	Mont	64	15	32	47	198	+27
75–76	Mont	80	16	28	44	180	+18
76–77	Mont	78	22	38	60	132	+33
77–78	Mont	72	18	23	41	97	+30
78–79	Mont	48	10	15	25	62	+22
79–80	Mont	44	8	10	18	81	-2
80–81	Mont	48	13	21	34	93	+7
81–82	Mont	59	15	18	33	116	+23
82–83	Calg	71	21	37	58	138	+13
83–84	Calg	77	23	28	51	161	+11
84–85	Calg	15	7	5	12	49	+10
85–86	Calg	62	15	28	43	169	+22
86–87	Calg	22	2	3	5	66	-2
Totals		740	185	286	471	1542	+212

Playoffs

74–75	Mont	11	3	5	8	37	
75–76	Mont	13	0	3	3	20	
76–77	Mont	12	2	3	5	16	
77–78	Mont	15	2	2	4	17	
78–79	Mont	15	1	6	7	32	
80–81	Mont	3	1	0	1	0	
81–82	Mont	5	2	1	3	11	
82–83	Calg	9	1	3	4	18	
83–84	Calg	11	2	1	3	25	
84–85	Calg	4	0	3	3	12	
85–86	Calg	22	7	9	16	38	
86–87	Calg	4	0	1	1	2	
Totals		124	21	37	58	238	

RISSLING, Gary Daniel *5–9 175 LW*
B. Saskatoon, Sask., Aug. 8, 1956

78–79	Wash	26	3	3	6	127	-5
79–80	Wash	11	0	1	1	49	-6
80–81	Pitt	25	1	0	1	143	-4
81–82	Pitt	16	0	0	0	55	-2
82–83	Pitt	40	5	4	9	128	-17
83–84	Pitt	47	4	13	17	297	-9
84–85	Pitt	56	10	9	19	209	-6
Totals		221	23	30	53	1008	-49

Playoffs

80–81	Pitt	5	0	1	1	4	

RITCHIE, Byron *5–10 180 C*
B. Burnaby, B.C., April 24, 1977

98–99	Car	3	0	0	0	0	0

***RITCHIE, David** F*

17–18	Mont W–Ott	17	9	0	9	12	
18–19	Tor	4	0	0	0	9	
19–20	Que	21	6	3	9	18	
20–21	Mont	5	0	0	0	0	
24–25	Mont	5	0	0	0	0	
25–26	Mont	2	0	0	0	0	
Totals		54	15	3	18	39	

Playoffs

24–25	Mont	1	0	0	0	0	

RITCHIE, Robert *5–10 170 LW*
B. Laverlochere, Que., Feb. 20, 1955

76–77	Phil–Det	18	6	2	8	10	-13
77–78	Det	11	2	2	4	0	-1
Totals		29	8	4	12	10	-14

RITSON, Alexander Clive *5–11 172 C*
B. Peace River, Alta., Mar. 7, 1922

44–45	NYR	1	0	0	0	0	

RITTINGER, Alan Wilbur *5–9 155 LW*
B. Regina, Sask., Jan. 28, 1925

43–44	Bos	19	3	7	10	0	

RIVARD, Joseph Robert (Bob) *5–8 155 LW*
B. Sherbrooke, Que., Aug. 1, 1939

67–68	Pitt	27	5	12	17	4	0

***RIVERS, George (Gus)** F*
B. Winnipeg, Man., Nov. 19, 1909

29–30	Mont	19	1	0	1	2	
30–31	Mont	44	2	5	7	6	
31–32	Mont	25	1	0	1	4	
Totals		88	4	5	9	12	

Playoffs

29–30	Mont	6	1	0	1	2	
30–31	Mont	10	1	0	1	0	
Totals		16	2	0	2	2	

RIVERS, Jamie *6–0 190 D*
B. Ottawa, Ont., Mar. 16, 1975

95–96	StL	3	0	0	0	2	-1
96–97	StL	15	2	5	7	6	-4
97–98	StL	59	2	4	6	36	+5
98–99	StL	76	2	5	7	47	-3
Totals		153	6	14	20	91	-3

Playoffs

98–99	StL	9	1	1	2	2	

RIVERS, John Wayne *5–10 180 RW*
B. Hamilton, Ont., Feb. 1, 1942

61–62	Det	2	0	0	0	0	
63–64	Bos	12	2	7	9	6	
64–65	Bos	58	6	17	23	72	
65–66	Bos	2	1	1	2	2	
66–67	Bos	8	2	1	3	6	
67–68	StL	22	4	4	8	8	-2
68–69	NYR	4	0	0	0	0	-1
72–73	NY (WHA)	75	37	40	77	47	
73–74	NY–NJ (WHA)	73	30	27	57	20	
74–75	SD (WHA)	78	54	53	107	52	
75–76	SD (WHA)	71	19	25	44	24	
76–77	SD (WHA)	60	18	31	49	40	
NHL Totals		108	15	30	45	94	-3
WHA Totals		357	158	176	334	183	

Playoffs

74–75	SD (WHA)	5	3	1	4	8	
75–76	SD (WHA)	11	4	4	8	4	
76–77	SD (WHA)	7	1	1	2	2	
WHA Totals		23	8	6	14	14	

RIVERS, Shawn *5–10 185 D*
B. Ottawa, Ont., Jan. 30, 1971

92–93	TB	4	0	2	2	2	-2

RIVET, Craig *6–1 190 D*
B. North Bay, Ont., Sept. 13, 1974

94–95	Mont	5	0	1	1	5	+2
95–96	Mont	19	1	4	5	54	+4
96–97	Mont	35	0	4	4	54	+7
97–98	Mont	61	0	2	2	93	-3
98–99	Mont	66	2	8	10	66	-3
Totals		186	3	19	22	276	+7

Playoffs

96–97	Mont	50	0	1	1	14	
97–98	Mont	5	0	0	0	2	
Totals		10	0	1	1	16	

RIZZUTO, Garth Alexander *5–11 180 C*
B. Trail, B.C., Sept. 11, 1947

70–71	Van	37	3	4	7	16	-16
72–73	Winn (WHA)	61	10	10	20	32	
73–74	Winn (WHA)	41	3	4	7	8	
NHL Totals		37	3	4	7	16	-16
WHA Totals		102	13	14	27	40	

Playoffs

72–73	Winn (WHA)	14	0	1	1	14	

***ROACH, Mickey** C*
B. Boston, Mass., 1895

19–20	Tor	20	10	2	12	4	
20–21	Tor–Ham	22	9	7	16	2	
21–22	Ham	24	14	3	17	7	
22–23	Ham	23	17	8	25	8	
23–24	Ham	21	5	3	8	0	
24–25	Ham	30	6	4	10	4	
25–26	NYA	25	3	0	3	4	
26–27	NYA	44	11	0	11	14	
Totals		209	75	27	102	43	

ROBERGE, Mario *5–11 193 LW*
B. Quebec City, Que., Jan. 23, 1964

90–91	Mont	5	0	0	0	21	-2
91–92	Mont	20	2	1	3	62	+3
92–93	Mont	50	4	4	8	142	+2
93–94	Mont	28	1	2	3	55	-2
94–95	Mont	9	0	0	0	34	-2
Totals		112	7	7	14	314	-1

Playoffs

90–91	Mont	12	0	0	0	24	
92–93	Mont	3	0	0	0	0	
Totals		15	0	0	0	24	

ROBERGE, Serge *6–1 195 RW*
B. Quebec City, Que., Mar. 31, 1965

90–91	Que	9	0	0	0	24	0

ROBERT, Claude *5–11 175 LW*
B. Montreal, Que., Aug. 10, 1928

50–51	Mont	23	1	0	1	9	

ROBERT, Rene Paul *5–10 184 RW*
B. Trois–Rivieres, Que., Dec. 31, 1948

70–71	Tor	5	0	0	0	0	-2
71–72	Pitt–Buf	61	13	14	27	44	-16
72–73	Buf	75	40	43	83	83	+16
73–74	Buf	76	21	44	65	71	-16
74–75	Buf	74	40	60	100	75	+6
75–76	Buf	72	35	52	87	53	+17
76–77	Buf	80	33	40	73	46	+27
77–78	Buf	67	25	48	73	25	+19
78–79	Buf	68	22	40	62	46	-12
79–80	Col	69	28	35	63	79	-20
80–81	Col–Tor	42	14	18	32	38	-8
81–82	Tor	55	13	24	37	37	-11
Totals		744	284	418	702	597	0

Playoffs

72–73	Buf	6	5	3	8	2	
74–75	Buf	16	5	8	13	16	
75–76	Buf	9	3	2	5	6	
76–77	Buf	6	5	2	7	20	
77–78	Buf	7	2	0	2	23	
78–79	Buf	3	2	2	4	4	
80–81	Tor	3	0	2	2	2	
Totals		50	22	19	41	73	

ROBERT, Samuel *F*

17–18	Ott	1	0	0	0	0	

ROBERTO, Phillip Joseph *6–1 190 RW*
B. Niagara Falls, Ont., Jan. 1, 1949

69–70	Mont	8	0	1	1	8	+1
70–71	Mont	39	14	7	21	76	+10
71–72	Mont–StL	76	15	15	30	98	+2
72–73	StL	77	20	22	42	99	-12
73–74	StL	15	1	1	2	10	-4
74–75	StL–Det	53	13	29	42	32	-13
75–76	Det–KC	74	8	22	30	110	-13
76–77	Col–Clev	43	4	9	13	31	-18
77–78	Birm (WHA)	53	8	20	28	91	
NHL Totals		385	75	106	181	464	-47
WHA Totals		53	8	20	28	91	

Playoffs

70–71	Mont	15	0	1	1	36	
71–72	StL	11	7	6	13	29	
72–73	StL	5	2	1	3	4	
77–78	Birm (WHA)	4	1	0	1	20	
NHL Totals		31	9	8	17	69	
WHA Totals		4	1	0	1	20	

ROBERTS, David Lance 6–0 185 LW
B. Alameda, Cal., May 28, 1970

SSN	TEAM	GP	G	A	PTS.	PIM	+/-
93–94	StL	1	0	0	0	2	0
94–95	StL	19	6	5	11	10	+2
95–96	StL–Edm	34	3	10	13	18	-7
96–97	Van	58	10	17	27	51	+11
97–98	Van	13	1	1	2	4	-1
Totals		125	20	33	53	85	+5

Playoffs

94–95	StL	6	0	0	0	4	

ROBERTS, Douglas William 6–2 190 D
B. Detroit, Mich., Oct. 28, 1942

SSN	TEAM	GP	G	A	PTS.	PIM	+/-
65–66	Det	1	0	0	0	0	
66–67	Det	13	3	1	4	25	
67–68	Det	37	8	9	17	12	0
68–69	Oak	76	1	19	20	79	-13
69–70	Oak	76	6	25	31	107	-37
70–71	Cal	78	4	13	17	94	-56
71–72	Bos	3	1	0	1	0	+1
72–73	Bos	45	4	7	11	7	+13
73–74	Bos–Det	64	12	26	38	35	-7
74–75	Det	26	4	4	8	8	-7
75–76	NE (WHA)	76	4	13	17	51	
76–77	NE (WHA)	64	3	18	21	33	
NHL Totals		419	43	104	147	367	-106
WHA Totals		140	7	31	38	84	

Playoffs

68–69	Cal	7	0	1	1	34	
69–70	Oak	4	0	2	2	6	
72–73	Bos	5	2	0	2	6	
75–76	NE (WHA)	17	1	1	2	8	
76–77	NE (WHA)	2	0	0	0	0	
NHL Totals		16	2	3	5	46	
WHA Totals		19	1	1	2	8	

ROBERTS, Gary 6–1 190 LW
B. North York, Ont., May 23, 1966

SSN	TEAM	GP	G	A	PTS.	PIM	+/-
86–87	Calg	32	5	10	15	85	+6
87–88	Calg	74	13	15	28	282	+24
88–89	Calg	71	22	16	38	250	+32
89–90	Calg	78	39	33	72	222	+31
90–91	Calg	80	22	31	53	252	+15
91–92	Calg	76	53	37	90	207	+32
92–93	Calg	58	38	41	79	172	+32
93–94	Calg	73	41	43	84	145	+37
94–95	Calg	8	2	2	4	43	+1
95–96	Calg	35	22	20	42	78	+15
97–98	Car	61	20	29	49	103	+3
98–99	Car	77	14	28	42	178	+2
Totals		723	291	305	596	2017	+230

Playoffs

86–87	Calg	2	0	0	0	4	
87–88	Calg	9	2	3	5	29	
88–89	Calg	22	5	7	12	57	
89–90	Calg	6	2	5	7	41	
90–91	Calg	7	1	3	4	18	
92–93	Calg	5	1	6	7	43	
93–94	Calg	7	2	6	8	24	
98–99	Car	6	1	1	2	8	
Totals		64	14	31	45	224	

ROBERTS, Gordon (Gordie) 6–1 195 D
B. Detroit, Mich., Oct. 2, 1957

SSN	TEAM	GP	G	A	PTS.	PIM	+/-
75–76	NE (WHA)	77	3	19	22	102	
76–77	NE (WHA)	77	13	33	46	169	
77–78	NE (WHA)	78	15	46	61	118	
78–79	NE (WHA)	79	11	46	57	113	
79–80	Hart	80	8	28	36	89	+6
80–81	Hart–Minn	77	8	42	50	175	-13
81–82	Minn	79	4	30	34	119	-1
82–83	Minn	80	3	41	44	103	+18
83–84	Minn	77	8	45	53	132	+14
84–85	Minn	78	6	36	42	112	-12
85–86	Minn	76	2	21	23	101	+14
86–87	Minn	8	3	10	13	68	-7
87–88	Minn–Phil–StL	70	3	15	18	143	-10
88–89	StL	77	2	24	26	90	+7
89–90	StL	75	3	14	17	140	-12
90–91	StL–Pitt	64	3	13	16	78	+17
91–92	Pitt	73	2	22	24	87	+19
92–93	Bos	65	5	12	17	105	+23
93–94	Bos	59	1	6	7	40	-13
NHL Totals		1097	61	359	420	1582	+40

SSN	TEAM	GP	G	A	PTS.	PIM	+/-
WHA Totals		311	42	144	186	502	

Playoffs

75–76	NE (WHA)	17	2	9	11	36	
76–77	NE (WHA)	5	2	2	4	6	
77–78	NE (WHA)	14	0	5	5	29	
78–79	NE (WHA)	10	0	4	4	10	
79–80	Hart	3	1	1	2	2	
80–81	Minn	19	1	5	6	17	
81–82	Minn	4	0	3	3	27	
82–83	Minn	9	1	5	6	14	
83–84	Minn	15	3	7	10	23	
84–85	Minn	9	1	6	7	6	
85–86	Minn	5	0	4	4	8	
87–88	StL	10	1	2	3	33	
88–89	StL	10	1	7	8	8	
89–90	StL	10	0	2	2	26	
90–91	Pitt	24	1	2	3	63	
91–92	Pitt	19	0	2	2	32	
92–93	Bos	4	0	0	0	6	
93–94	Bos	12	0	1	1	8	
NHL Totals		153	10	47	57	273	
WHA Totals		46	4	20	24	81	

ROBERTS, James Drew 6–1 198 LW
B. Toronto, Ont., June 8, 1956

SSN	TEAM	GP	G	A	PTS.	PIM	+/-
76–77	Minn	53	11	8	19	14	-9
77–78	Minn	42	4	14	18	19	-14
78–79	Minn	11	2	1	3	0	-5
Totals		106	17	23	40	33	-28

Playoffs

76–77	Minn	2	0	0	0	0	

ROBERTS, James Wilfred 5–10 185 RW
B. Toronto, Ont., Apr. 9, 1940

SSN	TEAM	GP	G	A	PTS.	PIM	+/-
63–64	Mont	15	0	1	1	2	
64–65	Mont	70	3	10	13	40	
65–66	Mont	70	5	5	10	20	
66–67	Mont	63	3	0	3	16	
67–68	StL	74	14	23	37	66	-8
68–69	StL	72	14	19	33	81	+13
69–70	StL	76	13	17	30	51	+18
70–71	StL	72	13	18	31	77	+7
71–72	StL–Mont	77	12	22	34	57	+7
72–73	Mont	77	14	18	32	28	+33
73–74	Mont	67	8	16	24	39	+27
74–75	Mont	79	5	13	18	52	+18
75–76	Mont	74	13	8	21	35	+7
76–77	Mont	45	5	14	19	18	+22
77–78	StL	75	4	10	14	39	-20
Totals		1006	126	194	320	621	+124

Playoffs

63–64	Mont	7	0	1	1	14	
64–65	Mont	13	0	0	0	30	
65–66	Mont	10	1	1	2	10	
66–67	Mont	4	1	0	1	0	
67–68	StL	18	4	1	5	20	
68–69	StL	12	1	4	5	10	
69–70	StL	16	2	3	5	29	
70–71	StL	6	2	1	3	11	
71–72	Mont	6	1	0	1	0	
72–73	Mont	17	0	2	2	22	
73–74	Mont	6	0	0	0	4	
74–75	Mont	11	2	2	4	2	
75–76	Mont	13	3	1	4	2	
76–77	Mont	14	3	0	3	6	
Totals		153	20	16	36	160	

*ROBERTSON, Fred 5–10 198 D
B. Carlisle, England, Oct. 22, 1911

SSN	TEAM	GP	G	A	PTS.	PIM	+/-
31–32	Tor	8	0	0	0	23	
33–34	Tor–Det	26	1	0	1	12	
Totals		34	1	0	1	35	

Playoffs

31–32	Tor	7	0	0	0	0	

ROBERTSON, Geordie 6–0 165 RW
B. Victoria, B.C., Aug. 1, 1959

SSN	TEAM	GP	G	A	PTS.	PIM	+/-
82–83	Buf	5	1	2	3	7	-1

ROBERTSON, George Thomas (Robbie) C
B. Winnipeg, Man., May 11, 1928

SSN	TEAM	GP	G	A	PTS.	PIM	+/-
47–48	Mont	1	0	0	0	0	
48–49	Mont	30	2	5	7	6	

SSN	TEAM	GP	G	A	PTS.	PIM	+/-
Totals		31	2	5	7	6	

ROBERTSON, Torrie Andrew 5–11 200 LW
B. Victoria, B.C., Aug. 2, 1961

SSN	TEAM	GP	G	A	PTS.	PIM	+/-
80–81	Wash	3	0	0	0	0	-2
81–82	Wash	54	8	13	21	204	-2
82–83	Wash	5	2	0	2	4	-2
83–84	Hart	66	7	13	20	198	-9
84–85	Hart	74	11	30	41	337	-13
85–86	Hart	76	13	24	37	358	-11
86–87	Hart	20	1	0	1	98	-6
87–88	Hart	63	2	8	10	293	0
88–89	Hart–Det	39	4	6	10	147	-3
89–90	Det	42	1	5	6	112	-3
Totals		442	49	99	148	1751	-50

Playoffs

85–86	Hart	10	1	0	1	67	
87–88	Hart	6	0	1	1	6	
88–89	Hart	6	1	0	1	17	
Totals		22	2	1	3	90	

ROBERTSSON, Bert 6–3 205 D
B. Sodertalje, Sweden, June 30, 1974

SSN	TEAM	GP	G	A	PTS.	PIM	+/-
97–98	Van	30	2	4	6	24	+2
98–99	Van	39	2	2	4	13	-7
Totals		69	4	6	10	37	-5

ROBIDOUX, Florent 6–2 190 LW
B. Treheme, Man., May 5, 1960

SSN	TEAM	GP	G	A	PTS.	PIM	+/-
80–81	Chi	39	6	2	8	75	-6
81–82	Chi	4	1	2	3	0	+2
83–84	Chi	9	0	0	0	0	-3
Totals		52	7	4	11	75	-7

ROBINSON, Douglas Garnet 6–2 197 LW
B. Catharines, Ont., Aug. 27, 1940

SSN	TEAM	GP	G	A	PTS.	PIM	+/-
64–65	Chi–NYR	61	10	23	33	10	
65–66	NYR	51	8	12	20	8	
66–67	NYR	1	0	0	0	0	
67–68	LA	34	9	9	18	6	+4
68–69	LA	31	2	10	12	2	-4
70–71	LA	61	15	13	28	8	-8
Totals		239	44	67	111	34	-8

Playoffs

63–64	Chi	4	0	0	0	0	
67–68	LA	7	1	3	7	0	
Totals		11	4	3	7	0	

ROBINSON, Douglas Scott 6–2 180 RW
B. 100 Mile House, B.C., Mar. 29, 1964

SSN	TEAM	GP	G	A	PTS.	PIM	+/-
89–90	Minn	1	0	0	0	2	0

*ROBINSON, Earl Henry 5–10 160 RW
B. Montreal, Que., Mar. 11, 1907

SSN	TEAM	GP	G	A	PTS.	PIM	+/-
28–29	Mont M	33	2	1	3	2	
29–30	Mont M	35	1	2	3	10	
31–32	Mont M	28	0	3	3	2	
32–33	Mont M	43	15	9	24	6	
33–34	Mont M	47	12	16	28	14	
34–35	Mont M	47	17	18	35	23	
35–36	Mont M	40	6	14	20	27	
36–37	Mont M	48	16	18	34	19	
37–38	Mont M	38	4	7	11	13	
38–39	Chi	48	9	6	15	13	
39–40	Mont	11	1	4	5	4	
Totals		418	83	98	181	133	

Playoffs

29–30	Mont M	4	0	0	0	0	
32–33	Mont M	2	0	0	0	0	
33–34	Mont M	4	2	0	2	0	
34–35	Mont M	7	2	2	4	0	
35–36	Mont M	3	0	0	0	0	
36–37	Mont M	5	1	2	3	0	
Totals		25	5	4	9	0	

ROBINSON, Larry Clark 6–4 225 D
B. Winchester, Ont., June 2, 1951

SSN	TEAM	GP	G	A	PTS.	PIM	+/-
72–73	Mont	36	2	4	6	20	+3
73–74	Mont	78	6	20	26	66	+32
74–75	Mont	80	14	47	61	76	+61
75–76	Mont	80	10	30	40	59	+50
76–77	Mont	77	19	66	85	45	+120
77–78	Mont	80	13	52	65	39	+71

SSN	TEAM	GP	G	A	PTS.	PIM	+/-
78–79	Mont	67	16	45	61	33	+50
79–80	Mont	72	14	61	75	39	+38
80–81	Mont	65	12	38	50	37	+46
81–82	Mont	71	12	47	59	41	+57
82–83	Mont	71	14	49	63	33	+33
83–84	Mont	74	9	34	43	39	+4
84–85	Mont	76	14	33	47	44	+33
85–86	Mont	78	19	63	82	39	+29
86–87	Mont	70	13	37	50	44	+24
87–88	Mont	53	6	34	40	30	+26
88–89	Mont	74	4	26	30	22	+23
89–90	LA	64	7	32	39	34	+7
90–91	LA	62	1	22	23	16	+22
91–92	LA	56	3	10	13	37	+1
Totals		1384	208	750	958	793	+731

Playoffs

72–73	Mont	11	1	4	5	9	
73–74	Mont	6	0	1	1	26	
74–75	Mont	11	0	4	4	27	
75–76	Mont	13	3	3	6	10	
76–77	Mont	14	2	10	12	12	
77–78	Mont	15	4	17	21	6	
78–79	Mont	16	6	9	15	8	
79–80	Mont	10	0	4	4	2	
80–81	Mont	3	0	1	1	2	
81–82	Mont	5	0	1	1	8	
82–83	Mont	3	0	0	0	2	
83–84	Mont	15	0	5	5	22	
84–85	Mont	12	3	8	11	8	
85–86	Mont	20	0	13	13	22	
86–87	Mont	17	3	17	20	6	
87–88	Mont	11	1	4	5	4	
88–89	Mont	21	2	8	10	12	
89–90	LA	10	2	3	5	10	
90–91	LA	12	1	4	5	15	
91–92	LA	2	0	0	0	0	
Totals		227	28	116	144	211	

ROBINSON, Morris (Moe) *6–4 175 D*
B. Winchester, Ont., May 29, 1957

79–89	Mont	1	0	0	0	0	0

ROBINSON, Robert *6–1 214 D*
B. St. Catharines, Ont., Apr. 19, 1967

91–92	StL	22	0	1	1	8	-4

ROBINSON, Scott *6–2 180 RW*
B. Mile House, B.C., March 29, 1964

89–90	Minn	1	0	0	0	2	0

ROBITAILLE, Luc *6–1 195 LW*
B. Montreal, Que., Feb. 17, 1966

86–87	LA	79	45	39	84	28	-18
87–88	LA	80	53	58	111	82	-9
88–89	LA	78	46	52	98	65	+5
89–90	LA	80	52	49	101	38	+8
90–91	LA	76	45	46	91	68	+28
91–92	LA	80	44	63	107	95	-4
92–93	LA	84	63	62	125	100	+18
93–94	LA	83	44	42	86	86	-20
94–95	Pitt	46	23	19	42	37	+10
95–96	NYR	77	23	46	69	80	+13
96–97	NYR	69	24	24	48	48	+16
97–98	LA	57	16	24	40	66	+5
98–99	LA	82	39	35	74	54	-1
Totals		971	517	559	1076	847	+51

Playoffs

86–87	LA	5	1	4	5	2	
87–88	LA	5	2	5	7	18	
88–89	LA	11	2	6	8	10	
89–90	LA	10	5	5	10	10	
90–91	LA	12	12	4	16	22	
91–92	LA	6	3	4	7	12	
92–93	LA	24	9	13	22	28	
94–95	Pitt	12	7	4	11	26	
95–96	NYR	11	1	5	6	8	
96–97	NYR	15	4	7	11	4	
97–98	LA	4	1	2	3	6	
Totals		115	47	59	106	146	

ROBITAILLE, Michael James David *5–11 195 D*
B. Midland, Ont., Feb. 12, 1948

69–70	NYR	4	0	0	0	8	0
70–71	NYR–Det	34	5	9	14	29	-15
71–72	Buf	31	2	10	12	22	-14

SSN	TEAM	GP	G	A	PTS.	PIM	+/-
72–73	Buf	65	4	17	21	40	+6
73–74	Buf	71	2	18	20	60	+2
74–75	Buf–Van	66	2	23	25	31	+19
75–76	Van	71	8	19	27	69	+8
76–77	Van	40	0	9	9	21	-13
Totals		382	23	105	128	280	-5

Playoffs

72–73	Buf	6	0	0	0	0	
74–75	Van	5	0	1	1	2	
75–76	Van	2	0	0	0	2	
Totals		13	0	1	1	4	

ROBITAILLE, Randy *5–11 190 C*
B. Ottawa, Ont., Oct. 12, 1975

96–97	Bos	1	0	0	0	0	0
97–98	Bos	4	0	0	0	0	-2
98–99	Bos	4	0	2	2	0	-1
Totals		9	0	2	2	0	-3

Playoffs

98–99	Bos	1	0	0	0	0	

ROCHE, Dave *6–4 224 LW*
B. Lindsay, Ont., June 13, 1975

95–96	Pitt	71	7	7	14	130	-5
96–97	Pitt	61	5	5	10	155	-13
98–99	Calg	36	3	3	6	44	-1
Totals		168	15	15	30	329	-19

Playoffs

95–96	Pitt	16	2	7	9	26	

*ROCHE, Earl *5–11 175 LW*
B. Prescott, Ont., Feb. 22, 1910

30–31	Mont M	42	2	0	2	18
32–33	Mont M–					
	Bos–Ott	28	4	5	9	6
33–34	Ott	44	13	16	29	22
34–35	StL E–Det	32	6	6	12	2
Totals		146	25	27	52	48

Playoffs

30–31	Mont M	2	0	0	0	0

ROCHE, Ernest Charles *6–1 170 D*
B. Montreal, Que., Feb. 4, 1930

50–51	Mont	4	0	0	0	2

*ROCHE, Michael Patrick Desmond (Desse)
5–6 188 RW
B. Kemptville, Ont., Feb. 1, 1909

30–31	Mont M	20	0	1	1	6
32–33	Mont M–Ott	21	3	6	9	6
33–34	Ott	44	14	10	24	22
34–35	StL E–Mont–					
	Det	27	3	1	4	10
Totals		112	20	18	38	44

ROCHEFORT, David Joseph *6–0 180 C*
B. Red Deer, Alta., July 22, 1946

66–67	Det	1	0	0	0	0

ROCHEFORT, Leon Joseph Fernand *6–0 185 RW*
B. Cap–de–la–Madeleine, Que., May 4, 1939

60–61	NYR	1	0	0	0	0	
62–63	NYR	23	5	4	9	6	
63–64	NYR	3	0	0	0	0	
64–65	Mont	9	2	0	2	0	
65–66	Mont	1	0	1	1	0	
66–67	Mont	27	9	7	16	6	
67–68	Phil	74	21	21	42	16	-1
68–69	Phil	65	14	21	35	10	-7
69–70	LA	76	9	23	32	14	-30
70–71	Mont	57	5	10	15	4	+11
71–72	Det	64	17	12	29	10	+1
72–73	Det–Atl	74	11	22	33	12	-4
73–74	Atl	56	10	12	22	13	-12
74–75	Van	76	18	11	29	2	-5
75–76	Van	11	0	3	3	0	-4
Totals		617	121	147	268	93	-51

Playoffs

65–66	Mont	4	1	1	2	4
66–67	Mont	10	1	1	2	4

SSN	TEAM	GP	G	A	PTS.	PIM	+/-
67–68	Phil	7	2	0	2	2	
68–69	Phil	3	0	0	0	0	
70–71	Mont	10	0	0	0	6	
74–75	Van	5	0	2	2	0	
Totals		39	4	4	8	16	

ROCHEFORT, Normand *6–1 214 D*
B. Trois Rivieres, Que., Jan. 28, 1961

80–81	Que	56	3	7	10	51	-11
81–82	Que	72	4	14	18	115	+19
82–83	Que	62	6	17	23	40	+11
83–84	Que	75	2	22	24	47	+41
84–85	Que	73	3	21	24	74	+12
85–86	Que	26	5	4	9	30	+9
86–87	Que	70	6	9	15	46	+2
87–88	Que	46	3	10	13	49	-2
88–89	NYR	11	1	5	6	18	0
89–90	NYR	31	3	1	4	24	+2
90–91	NYR	44	3	7	10	35	+10
91–92	NYR	26	0	2	2	31	-10
93–94	TB	6	0	0	0	10	-1
Totals		598	39	119	158	570	+82

Playoffs

80–81	Que	5	0	0	0	4	
81–82	Que	16	0	2	2	10	
82–83	Que	1	0	0	0	2	
83–84	Que	6	1	0	1	6	
84–85	Que	18	2	1	3	8	
86–87	Que	13	2	1	3	26	
89–90	NYR	10	2	1	3	26	
Totals		69	7	5	12	82	

*ROCKBURN, Harvey *D*

29–30	Det	36	4	0	4	97
30–31	Det	42	0	1	1	118
32–33	Ott	16	0	1	1	39
Totals		94	4	2	6	254

*RODDEN, Edmund Anthony (Eddie) *F*
B. Toronto, Ont., Mar. 22, 1901

26–27	Chi	20	3	3	6	92
27–28	Chi–Tor	34	3	8	11	42
28–29	Bos	20	0	0	0	10
30–31	NYR	24	0	3	3	8
Totals		98	6	14	20	152

Playoffs

26–27	Chi	2	0	1	1	0

ROENICK, Jeremy *6–0 170 C*
B. Boston, Mass., Jan. 17, 1970

88–89	Chi	20	9	9	18	4	+5
89–90	Chi	78	26	40	66	54	+2
90–91	Chi	79	41	53	94	80	+38
91–92	Chi	80	53	50	103	98	+23
92–93	Chi	84	50	57	107	86	+15
93–94	Chi	84	46	61	107	125	+21
94–95	Chi	33	10	24	34	14	+5
95–96	Chi	66	32	35	67	109	+9
96–97	Phoe	72	29	40	69	115	-7
97–98	Phoe	79	24	32	56	103	+5
98–99	Phoe	78	24	48	72	130	+7
Totals		753	344	449	793	918	+122

Playoffs

88–89	Chi	10	1	3	4	7
89–90	Chi	20	11	7	18	8
90–91	Chi	6	3	5	8	4
91–92	Chi	18	12	10	22	12
92–93	Chi	4	1	2	3	2
93–94	Chi	6	1	6	7	2
94–95	Chi	8	1	2	3	16
95–96	Chi	10	5	7	12	2
96–97	Phoe	6	2	4	6	4
97–98	Phoe	6	5	3	8	4
98–99	Phoe	1	0	0	0	0
Totals		95	42	49	91	61

ROEST, Stacy *5–9 192 C*
B. Lethbridge, Alta., March 15, 1974

98–99	Det	59	4	8	12	14	-7

ROGERS, Alfred John *5–11 175 RW*
B. Paradise Hill, Alta., Apr. 10, 1953

73–74	Minn	10	2	4	6	0	+1
74–75	Minn	4	0	0	0	0	-1

SSN	TEAM	GP	G	A	PTS.	PIM	+/-
75–76	Edm (WHA)	44	9	8	17	34	
NHL Totals		14	2	4	6	0	0
WHA Totals		44	9	8	17	34	

ROGERS, Michael *6–9 170 C*
B. Calgary, Alta., Oct. 24, 1954

SSN	TEAM	GP	G	A	PTS.	PIM	+/-
74–75	Edm (WHA)	78	35	48	83	2	
75–76	EDM–NE (WHA)	80	30	29	59	20	
76–77	NE (WHA)	78	25	57	82	10	
77–78	NE (WHA)	80	28	43	71	46	
78–79	NE (WHA)	80	27	45	72	31	
79–80	Hart	80	44	61	105	10	+29
80–81	Hart	80	40	65	105	32	-22
81–82	NYR	80	38	65	103	43	+2
82–83	NYR	71	29	47	76	28	-10
83–84	NYR	78	23	38	61	45	-24
84–85	NYR	78	26	38	64	24	-25
85–86	NYR–Edm	17	2	3	5	2	0
NHL Totals		484	202	317	519	184	-50
WHA Totals		396	145	222	367	109	

Playoffs

75–76	NE (WHA)	17	5	8	13	2	
76–77	NE (WHA)	5	1	1	2	2	
77–78	NE (WHA)	14	5	6	11	8	
78–79	NE (WHA)	10	2	6	8	2	
79–80	Hart (WHA)	3	0	3	3	0	
80–81	NYR	9	1	6	7	2	
81–82	NYR	1	0	0	0	0	
83–84	NYR	1	0	0	0	0	
84–85	NYR	3	0	4	4	4	
NHL Totals		17	1	13	14	6	
WHA Totals		46	13	21	34	14	

ROHLICEK, Jeff *6–0 180 C*
B. Park Ridge, Ill., Jan. 27, 1966

87–88	Van	7	0	0	0	4	-4
88–89	Van	2	0	0	0	4	0
Totals		9	0	0	0	8	-4

ROHLIN, Leif *6–1 198 D*
B. Vasteras, Sweden, Feb. 26, 1968

95–96	Van	56	6	16	22	32	0
96–97	Van	40	2	8	10	8	+4
Totals		96	8	24	32	40	+4

Playoffs

95–96	Van	5	0	0	0	0	

ROHLOFF, Jon Richard *5–11 220 D*
B. Mankato, Minn., Oct. 3, 1969

94–95	Bos	34	3	8	11	39	+1
95–96	Bos	79	1	12	13	59	-8
96–97	Bos	37	3	5	8	31	-14
Totals		150	7	25	32	129	-21

Playoffs

94–95	Bos	5	0	0	0	6	
95–96	Bos	5	1	2	3	2	
Totals		10	1	2	3	8	

ROLFE, Dale Roland Carl *6–4 210 D*
B. Timmins, Ont., Apr. 30, 1940

59–60	Bos	3	0	0	0	0	
67–68	LA	68	3	13	16	84	-10
68–69	LA	75	3	19	22	85	-24
69–70	LA–Det	75	3	18	21	89	-16
70–71	Det–NYR	58	3	16	19	71	-2
71–72	NYR	68	2	14	16	67	+41
72–73	NYR	72	7	25	32	74	+41
73–74	NYR	48	3	12	15	56	+16
74–75	NYR	42	1	8	9	30	+12
Totals		509	25	125	150	556	+58

Playoffs

67–68	LA	7	0	1	1	14	
68–69	LA	10	0	4	4	8	
69–70	Det	4	0	2	2	8	
70–71	NYR	13	0	1	1	14	
71–72	NYR	16	4	3	7	16	
72–73	NYR	8	0	5	5	6	
73–74	NYR	13	1	8	9	23	
Totals		71	5	24	29	89	

ROLSTON, Brian *6–2 185 C*
B. Flint, Mich., Feb. 21, 1973

SSN	TEAM	GP	G	A	PTS.	PIM	+/-
94–95	NJ	40	7	11	18	17	+5
95–96	NJ	58	13	11	24	8	+9
96–97	NJ	81	18	27	45	20	+6
97–98	NJ	76	16	14	30	16	+7
98–99	NJ	82	24	33	57	14	+11
Totals		337	78	96	174	75	+38

Playoffs

94–95	NJ	6	2	1	3	4	
96–97	NJ	41	4	1	5	5	
97–98	NJ	6	1	0	4	2	
98–99	NJ	7	1	0	1	2	
Totals		29	8	2	10	14	

ROMANCHYCH, Larry Brian *6–1 180 RW*
B. Vancouver, B.C., Sept. 7, 1949

70–71	Chi	10	0	2	2	2	0
72–73	Atl	70	18	30	48	39	-11
73–74	Atl	73	22	29	51	33	-7
74–75	Atl	53	8	12	20	16	-9
75–76	Atl	67	16	19	35	8	-7
76–77	Atl	25	4	5	9	4	-3
Totals		298	68	97	165	102	-37

Playoffs

73–74	Atl	4	2	2	4	4	
75–76	Atl	2	0	0	0	0	
76–77	Atl	1	0	0	0	0	
Totals		7	2	2	4	4	

ROMANIUK, Russell James *6–0 195 LW*
B. Winnipeg, Man., June 9, 1970

91–92	Winn	27	3	5	8	18	+2
92–93	Winn	28	3	1	4	22	0
93–94	Winn	24	4	8	12	6	-11
94–95	Winn	6	0	0	0	0	-3
95–96	Phil	17	3	0	3	17	-2
Totals		102	13	14	27	63	-14

Playoffs

92–93	Winn	1	0	0	0	0	
95–96	Phil	1	0	0	0	0	
Totals		2	0	0	0	0	

ROMBOUGH, Douglas George *6–3 215 C*
B. Fergus, Ont., July 8, 1950

72–73	Buf	5	2	0	2	0	+2
73–74	Buf–NYI	58	9	10	19	35	+4
74–75	NYI–Minn	68	11	15	26	39	+7
75–76	Minn	19	2	2	4	6	-4
Totals		150	24	27	51	80	+8

*ROMNES, Elwin Nelson (Doc) *5–11 156 F*
B. White Bear, Minn., Jan. 1, 1909

30–31	Chi	30	5	7	12	8	
31–32	Chi	18	0	1	1	6	
32–33	Chi	47	10	12	22	2	
33–34	Chi	47	8	21	29	6	
34–35	Chi	35	10	14	24	8	
35–36	Chi	48	13	25	38	6	
36–37	Chi	28	4	14	18	2	
37–38	Chi	44	10	22	32	4	
38–39	Chi–Tor	48	7	20	27	0	
39–40	NYA	14	0	1	1	0*	
Totals		359	67	137	204	42	

Playoffs

30–31	Chi	9	1	1	2	2	
31–32	Chi	2	0	0	0	2	
33–34	Chi	8	2	7	9	0	
34–35	Chi	2	0	0	0	0	
35–36	Chi	2	1	2	3	0	
37–38	Chi	10	2	4	6	2	
38–39	Chi	10	1	4	5	0	
Totals		43	9	18	25	4	

*RONAN, Edward *6–0 197 RW*
B. Quincy, Mass., Mar. 21, 1968

91–92	Mont	3	0	0	0	0	0
92–93	Mont	53	5	7	12	20	+6
93–94	Mont	61	6	8	14	42	+3
94–95	Mont	30	1	4	5	12	-7
95–96	Winn	17	0	0	0	16	-3
96–97	Buf	18	1	4	5	11	+4
Totals		182	13	23	36	101	+3

Playoffs

92–93	Mont	14	2	3	5	10	
93–94	Mont	7	1	0	1	0	
96–97	Buf	6	1	0	1	6	
Totals		27	4	3	7	16	

RONAN, Erskine (Skene) *D*

18–19	Ott	11	0	0	0	0	

RONNING, Cliff *5–8 170 C*
B. Vancouver, B.C., Oct. 1, 1965

86–87	StL	42	11	14	25	6	-1
87–88	StL	26	5	8	13	12	+6
88–89	StL	64	24	31	55	18	+3
90–91	StL–Van	59	20	24	44	10	0
91–92	Van	80	24	47	71	42	+18
92–93	Van	79	29	56	85	30	+19
93–94	Van	76	25	43	68	42	+7
94–95	Van	41	6	19	25	27	-4
95–96	Van	79	22	45	67	42	+16
96–97	Phoe	69	19	32	51	26	-9
97–98	Phoe	80	11	44	55	36	+5
98–99	Phoe-Nash	79	20	40	60	42	-3
Totals		774	216	403	619	333	+54

Playoffs

85–86	StL	5	1	1	2	2	
86–87	StL	4	0	1	1	0	
87–88	StL	7	1	3	4	0	
90–91	Van	6	6	3	9	12	
91–92	Van	13	8	5	13	6	
92–93	Van	12	2	9	11	6	
93–94	Van	24	5	10	15	16	
94–95	Van	11	3	5	8	2	
95–96	Vam	6	0	2	2	6	
96–97	Phoe	7	0	7	7	12	
97–98	Phoe	6	1	3	4	4	
Totals		101	27	49	76	66	

RONSON, Leonard Keith (Len) *5–9 175 LW*
B. Brantford, Ont., July 8, 1936

60–61	NYR	13	2	1	3	10	
68–69	Oak	5	0	0	0	0	-3
Totals		18	2	1	3	10	-3

RONTY, Paul *6–0 160 C*
B. Toronto, Ont., June 12, 1928

47–48	Bos	24	3	11	14	0	
48–49	Bos	60	20	29	49	11	
49–50	Bos	70	23	36	59	8	
50–51	Bos	70	10	22	32	20	
51–52	NYR	65	12	31	43	16	
52–53	NYR	70	16	38	54	20	
53–54	NYR	70	13	33	46	18	
54–55	NYR–Mont	59	4	11	15	10	
Totals		488	101	211	312	103	

Playoffs

47–48	Bos	5	0	4	4	0	
48–49	Bos	5	1	2	3	2	
50–51	Bos	6	0	1	1	2	
54–55	Mont	5	0	0	0	2	
Totals		21	1	7	8	6	

ROONEY, Steve *6–2 195 LW*
B. Canton, Mass., June 28, 1962

84–85	Mont	3	1	0	1	7	-1
85–86	Mont	38	2	3	5	114	-4
86–87	Mont–Winn	32	2	3	5	79	-4
87–88	Winn	56	7	6	13	217	-2
88–89	NJ	25	3	1	4	79	-9
Totals		154	15	13	28	496	-16

Playoffs

84–85	Mont	11	2	2	4	19	
85–86	Mont	1	0	0	0	0	
86–87	Winn	8	0	0	0	34	
87–88	Winn	5	1	0	1	33	
Totals		25	3	2	5	86	

ROOT, William John *6–2 210 D*
B. Toronto, Ont., Sept. 6, 1959

82–83	Mont	46	2	3	5	24	+5
83–84	Mont	72	4	13	17	45	+26

SSN	TEAM	GP	G	A	PTS.	PIM	+/-
84-85	Tor	35	1	1	2	23	-25
85-86	Tor	27	0	1	1	29	-8
86-87	Tor	34	3	3	6	37	-9
87-88	StL-Phil	33	1	2	3	22	-4
Totals		247	11	23	34	180	-15

Playoffs

85-86	Tor	7	0	2	2	13	
86-87	Tor	13	1	0	1	12	
87-88	Phil	2	0	0	0	0	
Totals		22	1	2	3	25	

ROSA, Pavel 6-0 195 RW
B. Most, Czech., June 7, 1977

| 98-99 | LA | 29 | 4 | 12 | 16 | 6 | 0 |

*ROSS, Arthur Howey D
B. Naughton, Ont., Jan.13, 1886

| 17-18 | Mont W | 3 | 1 | 0 | 1 | 0 | |

ROSS, James 6-3 190 D
B. Edinburgh, Scotland, May 20, 1926

51-52	NYR	51	2	9	11	25	
52-53	NYR	11	0	2	2	4	
Totals		62	2	11	13	29	

ROSSIGNOL, Roland 168 RW
B. Edmundston, N.B., Oct. 18, 1921

43-44	Det	1	0	1	1	0	
44-45	Mont	5	2	2	4	2	
45-46	Det	8	1	2	3	4	
Totals		14	3	5	8	6	

Playoffs

| 44-45 | Mont | 1 | 0 | 0 | 0 | 2 | |

ROTA, Darcy Irwin 5-11 180 LW
B. Vancouver, B.C., Feb. 16, 1953

73-74	Chi	74	21	12	33	58	+16
74-75	Chi	78	22	22	44	93	+1
75-76	Chi	79	20	17	37	73	-8
76-77	Chi	76	24	22	46	82	-7
77-78	Chi	78	17	20	37	67	+5
78-79	Chi-Atl	76	22	22	44	98	-7
79-80	Atl-Van	70	15	14	29	78	-6
80-81	Van	80	25	31	56	124	+10
81-82	Van	51	20	20	40	139	+6
82-83	Van	73	42	39	81	88	+13
83-84	Van	59	28	20	48	73	-12
Totals		794	256	239	495	973	+11

Playoffs

73-74	Chi	11	3	0	3	11	
74-75	Chi	7	0	1	1	24	
76-77	Chi	2	0	0	0	0	
77-78	Chi	4	0	0	0	2	
78-79	Atl	2	0	1	1	26	
79-80	Van	4	2	0	2	8	
80-81	Van	3	2	1	3	14	
81-82	Van	17	6	3	9	54	
82-83	Van	3	0	0	0	6	
83-84	Van	3	0	1	1	0	
Totals		60	14	7	21	147	

ROTA, Randolph Frank (Randy) 5-8 170 LW
B. Creston, B.C., Aug. 16, 1950

72-73	Mont	2	1	1	2	0	+2
73-74	LA	58	10	6	16	16	-8
74-75	KC	80	15	18	33	30	-39
75-76	KC	71	12	14	26	14	-38
76-77	Col	1	0	0	0	0	0
76-77	Edm (WHA)	40	9	6	15	8	
77-78	Edm (WHA)	53	8	22	30	12	
NHL Totals		212	38	39	77	60	-83
WHA Totals		93	17	28	45	20	

Playoffs

73-74	LA	5	0	1	1	0	
76-77	Edm (WHA)	5	3	2	5	0	
77-78	Edm (WHA)	5	1	1	2	4	
NHL Totals		5	0	1	1	0	
WHA Totals		10	4	3	7	4	

*ROTHSCHILD, Samuel F
B. Sudbury, Ont., Oct. 16, 1899

24-25	Mont M	27	5	4	9	4	
25-26	Mont M	33	2	1	3	8	
26-27	Mont M	22	1	1	2	8	
27-28	NYA	17	0	0	0	4	
Totals		99	8	6	14	24	

Playoffs

25-26	Mont M	8	0	0	0	0	
26-27	Mont M	2	0	0	0	0	
Totals		10	0	0	0	0	

*ROULSTON, Thomas 6-1 185 C/RW
B. Winnipeg, Man., Nov. 20, 1957

80-81	Edm	11	1	1	2	2	-3
81-82	Edm	35	11	3	14	22	-6
82-83	Edm	67	19	21	40	24	+29
83-84	Edm-Pitt	77	16	24	40	24	-31
85-86	Pitt	5	0	0	0	2	-2
Totals		195	47	49	96	74	-13

Playoffs

81-82	Edm	5	1	0	1	2	
82-83	Edm	16	1	2	3	0	
Totals		21	2	2	4	2	

*ROULSTON, William Orville (Rolly) 6-0 180 D
B. Toronto, Ont., Apr. 12, 1911

35-36	Det	1	0	0	0	0	
36-37	Det	21	0	5	5	10	
37-38	Det	2	0	1	1	0	
Totals		24	0	6	6	10	

ROUPE, Magnus 6-0 189 LW
B. Gislaved, Sweden, Mar. 23, 1963

87-88	Phil	33	2	4	6	32	-6
88-89	Phil	7	1	1	2	10	+1
Totals		40	3	5	8	42	-5

ROUSE, Robert 6-1 210 D
B. Surrey, B.C., June 18, 1964

83-84	Minn	1	0	0	0	0	0
84-85	Minn	63	2	9	11	113	-14
85-86	Minn	75	1	14	15	151	+15
86-87	Minn	72	2	10	12	179	+6
87-88	Minn	74	0	12	12	168	-30
88-89	Minn-Wash	79	4	15	19	160	-3
89-90	Wash	70	4	16	20	123	-2
90-91	Wash-Tor	60	7	19	26	75	-18
91-92	Tor	79	3	19	22	97	-20
92-93	Tor	82	3	11	14	130	+7
93-94	Tor	63	5	11	16	101	+8
94-95	Det	48	1	7	8	36	+14
95-96	Det	58	0	6	6	48	+5
96-97	Det	70	4	9	13	58	+8
97-98	Det	71	1	11	12	57	-9
98-99	SJ	70	0	11	11	44	0
Totals		1035	37	179	216	1540	-33

Playoffs

85-86	Minn	3	0	0	0	0	
88-89	Wash	6	2	0	2	4	
89-90	Wash	15	2	3	5	47	
92-93	Tor	21	3	8	11	29	
93-94	Tor	18	0	3	3	19	
94-95	Det	18	0	3	3	9	
95-96	Det	7	0	1	1	4	
96-97	Det	20	0	0	0	55	
97-98	Det	22	0	3	3	16	
98-99	SJ	6	0	0	0	6	
Totals		136	7	21	28	198	

ROUSSEAU, Guy 5-5 140 LW
B. Montreal, Que., Dec. 21, 1934

54-55	Mont	2	0	1	1	0	
56-57	Mont	2	0	0	0	2	
Totals		4	0	1	1	2	

ROUSSEAU, Bobby 5-10 178 RW
B. Montreal, Que., July 26, 1940

60-61	Mont	15	1	2	3	4	
61-62	Mont	70	21	24	45	26	
62-63	Mont	62	19	18	37	15	
63-64	Mont	70	25	31	56	32	
64-65	Mont	66	12	35	47	26	
65-66	Mont	70	30	48	78	20	
66-67	Mont	68	19	44	63	58	
67-68	Mont	74	19	46	65	47	+12
68-69	Mont	76	30	40	70	59	+27
69-70	Mont	72	24	34	58	30	+3
70-71	Minn	63	4	20	24	12	+3
71-72	NYR	78	21	36	57	12	+8
72-73	NYR	78	8	37	45	14	+1
73-74	NYR	72	10	41	51	4	+2
74-75	NYR	8	2	2	4	0	-2
Totals		942	245	458	703	359	+54

Playoffs

61-62	Mont	6	0	2	2	0	
62-63	Mont	5	0	1	1	2	
63-64	Mont	7	1	1	2	2	
64-65	Mont	13	5	8	13	24	
65-66	Mont	10	4	4	8	6	
66-67	Mont	10	1	7	8	4	
67-68	Mont	13	2	4	6	8	
68-69	Mont	14	3	2	5	8	
70-71	Mont	12	2	6	8	0	
71-72	NYR	16	6	11	17	7	
72-73	NYR	10	2	3	5	4	
73-74	NYR	12	1	8	9	4	
Totals		128	27	57	84	69	

ROUSSEAU, Roland (Roly) 5-8 160 D
B. Montreal, Que., Dec. 1, 1929

| 52-53 | Mont | 2 | 0 | 0 | 0 | 0 | |

ROUTHIER, Jean-Marc 6-2 190 RW
B. Quebec City, Que., Feb. 2, 1968

| 89-90 | Que | 8 | 0 | 0 | 0 | 9 | -3 |

ROWE, Mike 6-1 210 D
B. Kingston, Ont., Mar. 8, 1965

84-85	Pitt	6	0	0	0	7	-7
85-86	Pitt	3	0	0	0	4	-1
86-87	Pitt	2	0	0	0	0	-2
Totals		11	0	0	0	11	-10

*ROWE, Robert D

| 24-25 | Bos | 4 | 1 | 0 | 1 | 0 | |

ROWE, Ronald Nickolas 5-8 170 LW
B. Toronto, Ont., Nov. 30, 1924

| 47-48 | NYR | 5 | 1 | 0 | 1 | 0 | |

ROWE, Thomas John 6-0 190 RW
B. Lynn, Mass., May 23, 1956

76-77	Wash	12	1	2	3	2	-6
77-78	Wash	63	13	8	21	82	-18
78-79	Wash	69	31	30	61	137	-8
79-80	Wash-Hart	61	16	21	37	106	-12
80-81	Hart	74	13	28	41	190	-10
81-82	Hart-Wash	27	5	1	6	54	-11
82-83	Det	51	6	10	16	44	-17
Totals		357	85	100	185	615	-80

Playoffs

| 79-80 | Hart | 3 | 2 | 0 | 2 | 0 | |
| **Totals** | | 3 | 2 | 0 | 2 | 0 | |

ROY, Andre 6-3 178 LW
B. Port Chester, N.Y., Feb. 8, 1975

95-96	Bos	3	0	0	0	0	0
96-97	Bos	10	0	2	2	12	-5
Totals		13	0	2	2	12	-5

ROY, Jean-Yves 5-10 180 RW
B. Rosemere, Que., Feb. 17, 1969

94-95	NYR	3	1	0	1	2	-1
95-96	Ott	4	1	1	2	2	+3
96-97	Bos	52	10	15	25	22	-8
97-98	Bos	2	0	0	0	0	
Totals		61	12	16	28	26	-6

ROY, Stephane 6-0 190 C
B. Ste. Foy, Que., June 29, 1967

| 87-88 | Minn | 12 | 1 | 0 | 1 | 0 | -6 |

ROYER, Remi 6-1 183 D
B. Donnacana, Que., Feb. 12, 1978

| 98-99 | Chi | 18 | 0 | 0 | 0 | 67 | -10 |

ROZZINI, Gino 5–8 150 C
B. Shawinigan Falls, Que., Oct. 24, 1918

SSN	TEAM	GP	G	A	PTS.	PIM	+/-
44–45	Bos	31	5	10	15	20	

Playoffs

SSN	TEAM	GP	G	A	PTS.	PIM	+/-
44–45	Bos	6	1	2	3	6	

RUCCHIN, Steve 6–3 210 C
B. London, Ont., July 4, 1971

SSN	TEAM	GP	G	A	PTS.	PIM	+/-
94–95	Ana	43	6	11	17	23	+7
95–96	Ana	64	19	25	44	12	+3
96–97	Ana	79	19	48	67	24	+26
97–98	Ana	72	17	36	53	13	+8
98–99	Ana	69	23	39	62	22	+11
Totals		327	84	159	243	94	+48

Playoffs

SSN	TEAM	GP	G	A	PTS.	PIM	+/-
96–97	Ana	8	1	2	3	10	
98–99	Ana	4	0	3	3	0	
Totals		12	1	5	6	10	

RUCINSKI, Mike 5–11 190 C
B. Wheeling, Ill., Dec. 12, 1963

SSN	TEAM	GP	G	A	PTS.	PIM	+/-
88–89	Chi	1	0	0	0	0	0

Playoffs

SSN	TEAM	GP	G	A	PTS.	PIM	+/-
87–88	Chi	2	0	0	0	0	

RUCINSKY, Mike 5–11 179 D
B. Trenton, Mich., Mar. 30, 1975

SSN	TEAM	GP	G	A	PTS.	PIM	+/-
97–98	Car	9	0	1	1	2	0
98–99	Car	15	0	1	1	8	+1
Totals		24	0	2	2	10	+1

RUCINSKY, Martin 6–0 178 LW
B. Most, Czechoslovakia, Mar. 11, 1971

SSN	TEAM	GP	G	A	PTS.	PIM	+/-
91–92	Edm–Que	6	1	1	2	2	-2
92–93	Que	77	18	30	48	51	+16
93–94	Que	60	9	23	32	58	+4
94–95	Que	20	3	6	9	14	+5
95–96	Col A–Mont	78	29	46	75	68	+18
96–97	Mont	70	28	27	55	62	+1
97–98	Mont	78	21	32	53	84	+13
98–99	Mont	73	17	17	34	50	-25
Totals		462	126	182	308	389	+30

Playoffs

SSN	TEAM	GP	G	A	PTS.	PIM	+/-
92–96	Que	6	1	1	2	4	
96–97	Mont	5	0	0	0	4	
97–98	Mont	10	3	0	3	4	
Totals		21	4	1	5	12	

RUELLE, Bernard Edward 5–9 165 LW
B. Houghton, Mich., Nov. 23, 1920

SSN	TEAM	GP	G	A	PTS.	PIM	+/-
43–44	Det	2	1	0	1	0	

RUFF, Jason 6–2 192 LW
B. Kelowna, B.C., Jan. 27, 1970

SSN	TEAM	GP	G	A	PTS.	PIM	+/-
92–93	StL–TB	8	2	1	3	8	-1
93–94	TB	6	1	2	3	2	+2
Totals		14	3	3	6	10	+1

RUFF, Lindy Cameron 6–2 201 D/LW
B. Warburg, Alta., Feb. 17, 1960

SSN	TEAM	GP	G	A	PTS.	PIM	+/-
79–80	Buf	63	5	14	19	38	-2
80–81	Buf	65	8	18	26	121	+3
81–82	Buf	79	16	32	48	194	+1
82–83	Buf	60	12	17	29	130	+15
83–84	Buf	58	14	31	45	101	+15
84–85	Buf	39	13	11	24	45	-1
85–86	Buf	54	20	12	32	158	+8
86–87	Buf	50	6	14	20	74	-12
87–88	Buf	77	2	23	25	179	-9
88–89	Buf–NYR	76	6	16	22	117	-23
89–90	NYR	56	3	6	9	80	-10
90–91	NYR	14	0	1	1	27	-2
Totals		691	105	195	300	1264	-17

Playoffs

SSN	TEAM	GP	G	A	PTS.	PIM	+/-
79–80	Buf	8	1	1	2	19	
80–81	Buf	6	3	1	4	23	
81–82	Buf	4	0	0	0	28	
82–83	Buf	10	4	2	6	47	
84–85	Buf	5	2	4	6	15	
Totals		33	10	8	18	132	

RUHNKE, Kent 6–1 180 RW
B. Toronto, Ont., Sept. 18, 1952

SSN	TEAM	GP	G	A	PTS.	PIM	+/-
75–76	Bos	2	0	1	1	0	+1
76–77	Winn (WHA)	51	11	11	22	2	
77–78	Winn (WHA)	21	8	9	17	2	
NHL Totals		2	0	1	1	0	+1
WHA Totals		72	19	20	39	4	

Playoffs

SSN	TEAM	GP	G	A	PTS.	PIM	+/-
77–78	Winn (WHA)	5	2	0	2	0	

RUMBLE, Darren 6–1 200 D
B. Barrie, Ont., Jan. 23, 1969

SSN	TEAM	GP	G	A	PTS.	PIM	+/-
90–91	Phil	3	1	0	1	0	+1
92–93	Ott	69	3	13	16	61	-24
93–94	Ott	70	6	9	15	116	-50
95–96	Phil	5	0	0	0	4	0
96–97	Phil	10	0	0	0	0	-2
Totals		157	10	22	32	181	-75

RUNDQVIST, Thomas 6–3 195 C
B. Vimmerby, Sweden, May 4, 1960

SSN	TEAM	GP	G	A	PTS.	PIM	+/-
84–85	Mont	2	0	1	1	0	+1

*RUNGE, Paul 5–11 167 LW
B. Edmonton, Alta., Sept. 10, 1908

SSN	TEAM	GP	G	A	PTS.	PIM	+/-
30–31	Bos	2	0	0	0	0	
31–32	Bos	14	0	1	1	8	
33–34	Mont M	4	0	0	0	0	
34–35	Mont	3	0	0	0	2	
35–36	Mont–Bos	45	8	4	12	18	
36–37	Mont–Mont M	34	5	10	15	8	
37–38	Mont M	41	5	7	12	21	
Totals		143	18	22	40	57	

Playoffs

SSN	TEAM	GP	G	A	PTS.	PIM	+/-
35–36	Bos	2	0	0	0	2	
36–37	Mont M	5	0	0	0	4	
Totals		7	0	0	0	6	

RUOTSALAINEN, Reijo 5–8 170 D
B. Oulu, Finland, Apr. 1, 1960

SSN	TEAM	GP	G	A	PTS.	PIM	+/-
81–82	NYR	78	18	38	56	27	+18
82–83	NYR	77	16	53	69	22	+27
83–84	NYR	74	20	39	59	26	+17
84–85	NYR	80	28	45	73	32	-27
85–86	NYR	80	17	42	59	47	+22
86–87	Edm	16	5	8	13	6	+8
89–90	NJ–Edm	41	3	12	15	20	-5
Totals		446	107	237	344	180	+60

Playoffs

SSN	TEAM	GP	G	A	PTS.	PIM	+/-
83–84	NYR	5	1	1	2	2	
84–85	NYR	3	2	0	2	6	
85–86	NYR	16	0	8	8	6	
86–87	Edm	21	2	5	7	10	
89–90	Edm	22	2	11	13	12	
Totals		86	15	32	47	44	

RUPP, Duane Edward Franklin 6–1 185 D
B. Macnutt, Sask., Mar. 29, 1938

SSN	TEAM	GP	G	A	PTS.	PIM	+/-
62–63	NYR	2	0	0	0	0	
64–65	Tor	2	0	0	0	0	
65–66	Tor	2	0	1	1	0	
66–67	Tor	3	0	0	0	0	
67–68	Tor	71	1	8	9	42	+16
68–69	Minn–Pitt	59	5	11	16	32	-22
69–70	Pitt	64	2	14	16	18	-11
70–71	Pitt	59	5	28	33	34	-10
71–72	Pitt	34	4	18	22	32	0
72–73	Pitt	78	7	13	20	68	-3
74–75	Van (WHA)	72	3	26	29	45	
75–76	Calg (WHA)	42	0	16	16	33	
NHL Totals		373	24	93	117	226	-30
WHA Totals		114	3	42	45	78	

Playoffs

SSN	TEAM	GP	G	A	PTS.	PIM	+/-
69–70	Pitt	6	2	2	4	2	
71–72	Pitt	4	0	0	0	6	
75–76	Calg (WHA)	7	0	2	2	0	
NHL Totals		10	2	2	4	8	
WHA Totals		7	0	2	2	0	

RUSKOWSKI, Terry Wallace 5–9 190 C
B. Prince Albert, Sask., Dec. 31, 1954

SSN	TEAM	GP	G	A	PTS.	PIM	+/-
74–75	Hou (WHA)	71	10	36	46	134	
75–76	Hou (WHA)	65	14	35	49	100	
76–77	Hou (WHA)	80	24	60	84	146	
77–78	Hou (WHA)	78	15	57	72	170	
78–79	Winn (WHA)	75	20	66	86	211	
79–80	Chi	74	15	55	70	252	+7
80–81	Chi	72	8	51	59	225	-19
81–82	Chi	60	7	30	37	120	-13
82–83	Chi–LA	76	14	32	46	139	-16
83–84	LA	77	7	25	32	89	-24
84–85	LA	78	16	33	49	144	+2
85–86	Pitt	73	26	37	63	162	+10
86–87	Pitt	70	14	37	51	145	+8
87–88	Minn	47	5	12	17	76	-15
88–89	Minn	3	1	1	2	2	+1
NHL Totals		630	113	313	426	1354	-59
WHA Totals		369	83	254	337	761	

Playoffs

SSN	TEAM	GP	G	A	PTS.	PIM	+/-
74–75	Hous (WHA)	13	4	2	6	15	
75–76	Hous (WHA)	16	6	10	16	64	
76–77	Hous (WHA)	11	6	11	17	67	
77–78	Hous (WHA)	4	1	1	2	5	
78–79	Winn (WHA)	8	1	12	13	23	
79–80	Chi	4	0	0	0	22	
80–81	Chi	3	0	2	2	11	
81–82	Chi	11	1	2	3	53	
NHL Totals		18	1	4	5	86	
WHA Totals		52	28	36	54	174	

RUSSELL, Cam 6–4 195 D
B. Halifax, N.S., Jan. 12, 1969

SSN	TEAM	GP	G	A	PTS.	PIM	+/-
89–90	Chi	19	0	1	1	27	-3
90–91	Chi	3	0	0	0	5	+1
91–92	Chi	19	0	0	0	34	+8
92–93	Chi	67	2	4	6	151	+5
93–94	Chi	67	1	7	8	200	+10
94–95	Chi	33	1	3	4	88	+4
95–96	Chi	61	2	2	4	129	+8
96–97	Chi	44	1	1	2	65	-8
97–98	Chi	41	1	1	2	79	+3
98–99	Chi-Col A	42	1	2	3	94	-4
Totals		396	9	21	30	872	+24

Playoffs

SSN	TEAM	GP	G	A	PTS.	PIM	+/-
89–90	Chi	1	0	0	0	0	
90–91	Chi	1	0	0	0	0	
91–92	Chi	12	0	2	2	2	
92–93	Chi	4	0	0	0	0	
94–95	Chi	16	0	3	3	8	
95–96	chi	6	0	0	0	2	
96–97	Chi	4	0	0	0	4	
Totals		44	0	5	5	16	

*RUSSELL, Churchill Davidson (Church) 5–11 175 LW
B. Winnipeg, Man., Mar. 16, 1923

SSN	TEAM	GP	G	A	PTS.	PIM	+/-
45–46	NYR	17	0	5	5	2	
46–47	NYR	54	20	8	28	8	
47–48	NYR	19	0	3	3	2	
Totals		90	20	16	36	12	

RUSSELL, Phillip Douglas 6–2 205 D
B. Edmonton, Alta., July 21, 1952

SSN	TEAM	GP	G	A	PTS.	PIM	+/-
72–73	Chi	76	6	19	25	156	+31
73–74	Chi	75	10	25	35	184	+47
74–75	Chi	80	5	24	29	260	+7
75–76	Chi	74	9	29	38	194	-20
76–77	Chi	76	9	36	45	233	+1
77–78	Chi	57	6	20	26	139	+19
78–79	Chi–Atl	79	9	29	38	150	-6
79–80	Atl	80	5	31	36	115	+14
80–81	Calg	80	6	23	29	104	+17
81–82	Calg	71	4	25	29	110	+6
82–83	Calg	78	13	18	31	112	+2
83–84	NJ	76	9	22	31	96	-27
84–85	NJ	66	4	16	20	110	-14
85–86	NJ–Buf	42	4	6	10	63	-25
86–87	Buf	6	0	2	2	12	0
Totals		1016	99	325	424	2038	+42

Playoffs

SSN	TEAM	GP	G	A	PTS.	PIM	+/-
72–73	Chi	16	0	3	3	49	
73–74	Chi	9	0	1	1	41	
74–75	Chi	8	1	3	4	23	
75–76	Chi	4	0	1	1	17	
76–77	Chi	2	0	1	1	2	
78–79	Atl	2	0	0	0	9	
79–80	Atl	4	0	1	1	6	

SSN	TEAM	GP	G	A	PTS.	PIM	+/-
80–81	Calg	16	2	7	9	29	
81–82	Calg	3	0	1	1	2	
82–83	Calg	9	1	4	5	24	
Totals		73	4	22	26	202	

RUUTTU, Christian *5–11 194 C*
B. Lappeenranta, Finland, Feb. 20, 1964

SSN	TEAM	GP	G	A	PTS.	PIM	+/-
86–87	Buf	76	22	43	65	62	+9
87–88	Buf	73	26	45	71	85	-3
88–89	Buf	67	14	46	60	98	+13
89–90	Buf	75	19	41	60	66	+9
90–91	Buf	77	16	34	50	96	-6
91–92	Buf	70	4	21	25	76	-7
92–93	Chi	84	17	37	54	134	+14
93–94	Chi	54	9	20	29	68	-4
94–95	Chi-Van	45	7	11	18	29	+14
Totals		621	134	298	432	714	+39

Playoffs

SSN	TEAM	GP	G	A	PTS.	PIM	
87–88	Buf	6	2	5	7	4	
88–89	Buf	2	0	0	0	0	
89–90	Buf	6	0	0	0	4	
90–91	Buf	6	1	3	4	29	
91–92	Buf	3	0	0	0	6	
92–93	Chi	4	0	0	0	2	
93–94	Chi	6	0	0	0	2	
Totals		42	4	9	13	49	

RUZICKA, Vladimir *6–3 212 C*
B. Most, Czechoslovakia, June 6, 1963

SSN	TEAM	GP	G	A	PTS.	PIM	+/-
89–90	Edm	25	11	6	17	10	-21
90–91	Bos	29	8	8	16	19	+1
91–92	Bos	77	39	36	75	48	-10
92–93	Bos	60	19	22	41	38	-6
93–94	Ott	42	5	13	18	14	-21
Totals		233	82	85	167	129	-57

Playoffs

SSN	TEAM	GP	G	A	PTS.	PIM	
90–91	Bos	17	2	11	13	0	
91–92	Bos	13	2	3	5	2	
Totals		30	4	14	18	2	

RYAN, Terry *6–1 205 LW*
B. St. John's, Nfld., Jan. 14, 1977

SSN	TEAM	GP	G	A	PTS.	PIM	+/-
96–97	Mont	3	0	0	0	0	0
97–98	Mont	4	0	0	0	31	0
98–99	Mont	1	0	0	0	5	0
Totals		8	0	0	0	36	0

RYCHEL, Warren Stanley *6–0 202 LW*
B. Tecumseh, Ont., May 12, 1967

SSN	TEAM	GP	G	A	PTS.	PIM	+/-
88–89	Chi	2	0	0	0	17	-1
92–93	LA	70	6	7	13	314	-15
93–94	LA	80	10	9	19	322	-19
94–95	LA–Tor	33	1	6	7	120	-4
95–96	Col A	52	6	2	8	147	+6
96–97	Ana	70	10	7	17	218	+6
97–98	Ana-Col A	71	5	6	11	221	-11
98–99	Col A	28	0	2	2	63	+3
Totals		396	38	39	77	1422	-35

Playoffs

SSN	TEAM	GP	G	A	PTS.	PIM	
90–91	Chi	3	1	3	4	2	
92–93	LA	23	6	7	13	39	
94–95	Tor	3	0	0	0	0	
95–96	Col A	12	1	0	1	23	
96–97	Ana	11	0	2	2	19	
97–98	Col A	6	0	0	0	24	
98–99	Col A	12	0	1	1	14	
Playoff Totals		70	8	13	21	121	

RYMSHA, Andrew *6–3 210 D*
B. St. Catharines, Ont., Dec. 10, 1968

SSN	TEAM	GP	G	A	PTS.	PIM	+/-
91–92	Que	6	0	0	0	23	-3

SAARINEN, Simo *5–8 185 D*
B. Helsinki, Finland, Feb. 14, 1963

SSN	TEAM	GP	G	A	PTS.	PIM	
84–85	NYR	8	0	0	0	0	

SABOL, Shaun *6–3 230 D*
B. Minneapolis, Minn., July 13, 1966

SSN	TEAM	GP	G	A	PTS.	PIM	+/-
89–90	Phil	2	0	0	0	0	0

SABOURIN, Gary Bruce *5–11 180 RW*
B. Parry Sound, Ont., Dec. 4, 1943

SSN	TEAM	GP	G	A	PTS.	PIM	+/-
67–68	StL	50	13	10	23	50	+11
68–69	StL	75	25	23	48	58	+23
69–70	StL	72	28	14	42	61	-9
70–71	StL	59	14	17	31	56	+4
71–72	StL	77	28	17	45	52	+3
72–73	StL	76	21	27	48	30	-5
73–74	StL	54	7	23	30	27	-9
74–75	Tor	55	5	18	23	26	-13
75–76	Cal	76	21	28	49	33	-7
76–77	Clev	33	7	11	18	4	-6
Totals		627	169	188	357	397	-8

Playoffs

SSN	TEAM	GP	G	A	PTS.	PIM	
67–68	StL	18	4	2	6	30	
68–69	StL	12	6	5	11	12	
69–70	StL	16	5	0	5	10	
71–72	StL	11	3	3	6	6	
72–73	StL	5	1	1	2	0	
Totals		62	19	11	30	58	

SABOURIN, Ken *6–3 205 D*
B. Scarborough, Ont., Apr. 28, 1966

SSN	TEAM	GP	G	A	PTS.	PIM	+/-
88–89	Calg	6	0	1	1	26	+3
89–90	Calg	5	0	0	0	10	+1
90–91	Calg-Wash	44	2	7	9	117	+15
91–92	Wash	19	0	0	0	48	-5
Totals		74	2	8	10	201	+14

Playoffs

SSN	TEAM	GP	G	A	PTS.	PIM	
88–89	Calg	1	0	0	0	0	
90–91	Wash	11	0	0	0	34	
Totals		12	0	0	0	34	

SABOURIN, Robert *5–9 205 RW*
B. Sudbury, Ont., Mar. 17, 1933

SSN	TEAM	GP	G	A	PTS.	PIM	
51–52	Tor	1	0	0	0	2	

SACCO, David Anthony *6–0 180 RW*
B. Malden, Mass., July 31, 1970

SSN	TEAM	GP	G	A	PTS.	PIM	+/-
93–94	Tor	4	1	1	2	4	-2
94–95	Ana	8	0	2	2	0	-3
95–96	Ana	23	4	10	14	18	+1
Totals		35	5	13	18	22	-4

SACCO, Joseph *6–1 195 LW*
B. Medford, Mass., Feb. 4, 1969

SSN	TEAM	GP	G	A	PTS.	PIM	+/-
90–91	Tor	20	0	5	5	2	-5
91–92	Tor	17	7	4	11	4	+8
92–93	Tor	23	4	4	8	8	-4
93–94	Ana	84	19	18	37	61	-11
94–95	Ana	41	10	8	18	23	-8
95–96	Ana	76	13	14	27	40	0
96–97	Ana	77	12	17	29	35	+1
97–98	Ana–NYI	80	11	14	25	34	0
98–99	NYI	73	3	0	3	45	-24
Totals		491	79	84	163	252	-43

Playoffs

SSN	TEAM	GP	G	A	PTS.	PIM	
96–97	Ana	11	2	0	2	2	

SACHARUK, Lawrence William (Satch) *6–0 200 D*
B. Saskatoon, Sask., Oct. 16, 1952

SSN	TEAM	GP	G	A	PTS.	PIM	+/-
72–73	NYR	8	1	0	1	0	-1
73–74	NYR	23	2	4	6	4	0
74–75	StL	76	20	22	42	24	+9
75–76	NYR	42	6	7	13	14	-14
76–77	NYR	2	0	0	0	0	-1
78–79	Ind (WHA)	15	2	9	11	25	
NHL Totals		151	29	33	62	42	-25
WHA Totals		15	2	9	11	25	

Playoffs

SSN	TEAM	GP	G	A	PTS.	PIM	
74–75	StL	2	1	1	2	2	

SAGANIUK, Rocky *5–8 185 RW/C*
B. Myrnam, Alta., Oct. 15, 1957

SSN	TEAM	GP	G	A	PTS.	PIM	+/-
78–79	Tor	16	3	5	8	9	+1
79–80	Tor	75	24	23	47	52	-5
80–81	Tor	71	12	18	30	52	-16
81–82	Tor	65	17	16	33	49	-16
82–83	Tor	3	0	0	0	2	-3
83–84	Pitt	29	1	3	4	37	-12
Totals		259	57	65	122	201	-51

Playoffs

SSN	TEAM	GP	G	A	PTS.	PIM	
78–79	Tor	3	1	0	1	5	
79–80	Tor	3	0	0	0	10	
Totals		6	1	0	1	15	

ST. AMOUR, Martin *6–3 194 LW*
B. Montreal, Que., Jan. 30, 1970

SSN	TEAM	GP	G	A	PTS.	PIM	+/-
92–93	Ott	1	0	0	0	2	0

ST. LAURENT, Andre *5–10 180 C*
B. Rouyn–Noranda, Que., Feb. 16, 1953

SSN	TEAM	GP	G	A	PTS.	PIM	+/-
73–74	NYI	42	5	9	14	18	+1
74–75	NYI	78	14	27	41	60	+22
75–76	NYI	67	9	17	26	56	+14
76–77	NYI	72	10	13	23	55	+8
77–78	NYI–Det	79	31	39	70	110	+7
78–79	Det	76	18	31	49	124	-31
79–80	LA	77	6	24	30	88	-18
80–81	LA	22	10	6	16	63	+8
81–82	LA–Pitt	34	10	9	19	32	+7
82–83	Pitt	70	13	9	22	105	0
83–84	Pitt–Det	27	3	3	6	38	0
Totals		644	129	187	316	749	+18

Playoffs

SSN	TEAM	GP	G	A	PTS.	PIM	
74–75	NYI	15	2	2	4	6	
75–76	NYI	13	1	5	6	15	
76–77	NYI	12	1	2	3	6	
77–78	Det	7	1	1	2	4	
79–80	LA	4	1	0	1	0	
80–81	LA	3	0	1	1	9	
81–82	Pitt	5	2	1	3	8	
Totals		59	8	12	20	48	

ST. LAURENT, Dollard Herve *5–11 180 D*
B. Verdun, Que., May 12, 1929

SSN	TEAM	GP	G	A	PTS.	PIM	
50–51	Mont	3	0	0	0	0	
51–52	Mont	40	3	10	13	30	
52–53	Mont	54	2	6	8	34	
53–54	Mont	53	3	12	15	43	
54–55	Mont	58	3	14	17	24	
55–56	Mont	46	4	9	13	58	
56–57	Mont	64	1	11	12	49	
57–58	Mont	65	3	20	23	68	
58–59	Chi	70	4	8	12	28	
59–60	Chi	68	4	13	17	60	
60–61	Chi	67	2	17	19	58	
61–62	Chi	64	0	13	13	44	
Totals		652	29	133	162	496	

Playoffs

SSN	TEAM	GP	G	A	PTS.	PIM	
51–52	Mont	9	0	3	3	6	
52–53	Mont	12	0	3	3	4	
53–54	Mont	10	1	2	3	8	
54–55	Mont	12	0	5	5	12	
55–56	Mont	4	0	0	0	2	
56–57	Mont	7	0	1	1	13	
57–58	Mont	5	0	0	0	10	
58–59	Mont	6	0	1	1	2	
59–60	Mont	4	0	1	1	0	
60–61	Chi	11	1	2	3	12	
61–62	Chi	12	0	4	4	18	
Totals		92	2	22	24	87	

ST. LOUIS, Martin *5–9 180 C.*
B. Laval, Que, Aug. 9, 1971

SSN	TEAM	GP	G	A	PTS.	PIM	+/-
98–99	Calg	13	1	1	2	10	-2

ST. MARSEILLE, Francis Leo (Frank) *5–11 180 RW*
B. Levack, Ont., Dec. 14, 1939

SSN	TEAM	GP	G	A	PTS.	PIM	+/-
67–68	StL	57	16	16	32	12	+11
68–69	StL	72	12	26	38	22	+20
69–70	StL	74	16	43	59	18	-3
70–71	StL	77	19	32	51	26	+4
71–72	StL	78	16	36	52	32	+5
72–73	StL–LA	74	14	22	36	10	-7
73–74	LA	78	14	36	50	40	+1
74–75	LA	80	17	36	53	46	+12
75–76	LA	68	10	16	26	20	-14
76–77	LA	49	6	22	28	16	+1
Totals		707	140	285	425	242	+30

Playoffs

SSN	TEAM	GP	G	A	PTS.	PIM	
67–68	StL	18	5	8	13	0	
68–69	StL	12	3	3	6	2	
69–70	StL	15	6	7	13	4	

SSN	TEAM	GP	G	A	PTS.	PIM	+/-
70–71	StL	6	2	1	3	4	
71–72	StL	11	3	5	8	6	
73–74	LA	5	0	0	0	0	
74–75	LA	3	0	1	1	0	
75–76	LA	9	0	0	0	0	
76–77	LA	9	1	0	1	2	
Totals		88	20	25	45	18	

ST. SAUVEUR, Claude *6–0 170 LW*
B. Sherbrooke, Que., Jan. 2, 1952

SSN	TEAM	GP	G	A	PTS.	PIM	+/-
72–73	Phil (WHA)	2	1	0	1	0	
73–74	Van (WHA)	70	38	30	68	55	
74–75	Van (WHA)	76	24	23	47	32	
75–76	Atl	79	24	24	48	23	-6
76–77	Calg–Edm (WHA)	32	5	10	15	4	
77–78	Ind (WHA)	72	36	42	78	24	
78–79	Ind–Cin (WHA)	33	8	7	15	16	
NHL Totals		79	24	24	48	23	-6
WHA Totals		285	112	112	224	131	

Playoffs

SSN	TEAM	GP	G	A	PTS.	PIM	+/-
75–76	Atl	2	0	0	0	0	
75–77	Edm (WHA)	5	1	0	1	0	
NHL Totals		2	0	0	0	0	
WHA Totals		5	1	0	1	0	

SAKIC, Joseph Steve *5–11 185 C*
B. Burnaby, B.C., July 7, 1969

SSN	TEAM	GP	G	A	PTS.	PIM	+/-
88–89	Que	70	23	39	62	24	-36
89–90	Que	80	39	63	102	27	-40
90–91	Que	80	48	61	109	24	-26
91–92	Que	69	29	65	94	20	+5
92–93	Que	78	48	57	105	40	-3
93–94	Que	84	28	64	92	18	-8
94–95	Que	47	19	43	62	30	+7
95–96	Col A	82	51	69	120	44	+14
96–97	Col A	65	22	52	74	34	-10
97–98	Col A	64	27	36	63	50	0
98–99	Col A	73	41	55	96	29	+23
Totals		792	375	604	979	340	-74

Playoffs

SSN	TEAM	GP	G	A	PTS.	PIM	+/-
92–93	Que	6	3	3	6	2	
94–95	Que	6	4	1	5	0	
95–96	Col A	22	18	16	34	14	
96–97	Col A	17	8	17	28	14	
97–98	Col A	6	2	3	5	6	
98–	Col A	19	6	13	19	8	
Totals		76	41	53	94	44	

SALEI, Ruslan *6–1 200 D*
B. Minsk, USSR, Nov. 2, 1974

SSN	TEAM	GP	G	A	PTS.	PIM	+/-
96–97	Ana	30	0	1	1	37	-8
97–98	Ana	66	5	10	15	70	+7
98–99	Ana	74	2	14	16	65	+1
Totals		170	7	25	32	172	0

Playoffs

SSN	TEAM	GP	G	A	PTS.	PIM	+/-
98–99	Ana	3	0	0	0	4	

SALESKI, Donald Patrick (Big Bird) *6–3 205 RW*
B. Moose Jaw, Sask., Oct. 10, 1949

SSN	TEAM	GP	G	A	PTS.	PIM	+/-
71–72	Phil	1	0	0	0	0	-1
72–73	Phil	78	12	9	21	205	-20
73–74	Phil	77	15	25	40	131	+21
74–75	Phil	63	10	18	28	107	+7
75–76	Phil	78	21	26	47	68	+33
76–77	Phil	74	22	16	38	33	+24
77–78	Phil	70	27	18	45	44	+34
78–79	Phil–Col	51	13	5	18	18	-7
79–80	Col	51	8	8	16	23	-17
Totals		543	128	125	253	629	+75

Playoffs

SSN	TEAM	GP	G	A	PTS.	PIM	+/-
72–73	Phil	11	1	2	3	4	
73–74	Phil	17	2	7	9	24	
74–75	Phil	17	2	3	5	25	
75–76	Phil	16	6	5	11	47	
76–77	Phil	10	0	0	0	12	
77–78	Phil	11	2	0	2	19	
Totals		82	13	17	30	131	

SALMING, Anders Borje *6–1 193 D*
B. Kiruna, Sweden, Apr. 17, 1951

SSN	TEAM	GP	G	A	PTS.	PIM	+/-
73–74	Tor	76	5	34	39	48	+38
74–75	Tor	60	12	25	37	34	+4
75–76	Tor	78	16	41	57	70	+33
76–77	Tor	76	12	66	78	46	+45
77–78	Tor	80	16	60	76	70	+30
78–79	Tor	78	17	56	73	76	+36
79–80	Tor	74	19	52	71	94	+4
80–81	Tor	72	5	61	66	154	0
81–82	Tor	69	12	44	56	170	+4
82–83	Tor	69	7	38	45	104	-3
83–84	Tor	68	5	38	43	92	-34
84–85	Tor	73	6	33	39	76	-26
85–86	Tor	41	7	15	22	48	-7
86–87	Tor	56	4	16	20	42	+17
87–88	Tor	66	2	24	26	82	+7
88–89	Tor	63	3	17	20	86	+7
89–90	Det	49	2	17	19	52	+20
Totals		1148	150	637	787	1344	+175

Playoffs

SSN	TEAM	GP	G	A	PTS.	PIM	+/-
73–74	Tor	4	0	1	1	4	
74–75	Tor	7	0	4	4	6	
75–76	Tor	10	3	4	7	9	
76–77	Tor	9	3	6	9	6	
77–78	Tor	6	2	4	6	4	
78–79	Tor	6	0	1	1	8	
79–80	Tor	3	1	1	2	2	
80–81	Tor	3	0	2	2	4	
82–83	Tor	4	1	4	5	10	
85–86	Tor	10	1	6	7	14	
86–87	Tor	13	0	3	3	14	
87–88	Tor	6	1	3	4	0	
Totals		81	12	37	49	91	

SALO, Sami *6–3 190 D*
B. Turku, Finland, Sept. 2, 1974

SSN	TEAM	GP	G	A	PTS.	PIM	+/-
98–99	Ott	61	7	12	19	24	+20

Playoffs

SSN	TEAM	GP	G	A	PTS.	PIM	+/-
98–99	Ott	4	0	0	0	0	

SALOVAARA, John Barry *5–8 175 D*
B. Cooksville, Ont., Jan. 7, 1948

SSN	TEAM	GP	G	A	PTS.	PIM	+/-
74–75	Det	27	0	2	2	18	-11
75–76	Det	63	2	11	13	52	-7
Totals		90	2	13	15	70	-18

SALVIAN, David Clifford *5–10 170 RW*
B. Toronto, Ont., Sept. 9, 1955

Playoffs

SSN	TEAM	GP	G	A	PTS.	PIM	+/-
76–77	NYI	1	0	1	1	2	

SAMIS, Philip Lawrence *5–10 180 D*
B. Edmonton, Alta., Dec. 28, 1927

SSN	TEAM	GP	G	A	PTS.	PIM	+/-
49–50	Tor	2	0	0	0	0	

Playoffs

SSN	TEAM	GP	G	A	PTS.	PIM	+/-
47–48	Phil	5	0	1	1	20	

SAMPSON, Gary Edward *6–0 190 LW*
B. Atikokan, Ont., Aug. 24, 1959

SSN	TEAM	GP	G	A	PTS.	PIM	+/-
83–84	Wash	15	1	1	2	6	+1
84–85	Wash	46	10	15	25	13	+20
85–86	Wash	19	1	4	5	2	-3
86–87	Wash	25	1	2	3	4	-9
Totals		105	13	22	35	25	+12

Playoffs

SSN	TEAM	GP	G	A	PTS.	PIM	+/-
83–84	Wash	8	1	0	1	0	
84–85	Wash	4	0	0	0	0	
Totals		12	1	0	1	0	

SAMSANOV, Sergei *5–8 194 LW*
B. Moscow, USSR, Oct. 27, 1978

SSN	TEAM	GP	G	A	PTS.	PIM	+/-
98–99	Bos	79	25	26	51	18	-6
97–98	Bos	81	22	25	47	8	+9
Totals		160	47	51	98	26	+3

Playoffs

SSN	TEAM	GP	G	A	PTS.	PIM	+/-
97–98	Bos	6	2	5	7	0	
98–99	Bos	11	3	1	4	0	
Totals		17	5	6	11	0	

SAMUELSSON, Kjell *6–6 235 D*
B. Tyngsryd, Sweden, Oct. 18, 1958

SSN	TEAM	GP	G	A	PTS.	PIM	+/-
85–86	NYR	9	0	0	0	10	-1
86–87	NYR–Phil	76	3	12	15	136	-11
87–88	Phil	74	6	24	30	184	+28
88–89	Phil	69	3	14	17	140	+13
89–90	Phil	66	5	17	22	91	+20
90–91	Phil	78	9	19	28	82	+4
91–92	Phil–Pitt	74	5	11	16	110	+1
92–93	Pitt	63	3	6	9	106	+25
93–94	Pitt	59	5	8	13	118	+18
94–95	Pitt	41	1	6	7	54	+8
95–96	Phil	75	3	11	14	81	+20
96–97	Phil	34	4	3	7	47	+17
97–98	Phil	49	0	3	3	28	+9
98–99	TB	46	1	4	5	38	-6
Totals		813	48	138	186	1225	+145

Playoffs

SSN	TEAM	GP	G	A	PTS.	PIM	+/-
85–86	NYR	9	0	1	1	8	
86–87	Phil	26	0	4	4	25	
87–88	Phil	7	2	5	7	23	
88–89	Phil	19	1	3	4	24	
91–92	Pitt	15	0	3	3	12	
92–93	Pitt	12	0	3	3	2	
93–94	Pitt	6	0	0	0	26	
94–95	Pitt	11	0	1	1	32	
95–96	Phil	12	1	0	1	24	
96–97	Phil	5	0	0	0	2	
97–98	Phil	1	0	0	0	0	
Totals		123	4	20	24	178	

SAMUELSSON, Ulf *6–1 195 D*
B. Fagersta, Sweden, Mar. 26, 1964

SSN	TEAM	GP	G	A	PTS.	PIM	+/-
84–85	Hart	41	2	6	8	83	-6
85–86	Hart	80	5	19	24	174	+7
86–87	Hart	78	2	31	33	162	+28
87–88	Hart	76	8	33	41	159	-10
88–89	Hart	71	9	26	35	181	+15
89–90	Hart	55	2	11	13	177	+15
90–91	Hart–Pitt	76	4	22	26	211	+17
91–92	Pitt	62	1	14	15	208	+2
92–93	Pitt	77	3	26	29	249	+36
93–94	Pitt	80	5	24	29	199	+23
94–95	Pitt	44	1	15	16	113	+11
95–96	NYR	74	1	18	19	122	+9
96–97	NYR	73	6	11	17	138	+3
97–98	NYR	76	3	9	12	122	+1
98–99	NYR–Det	71	4	8	12	99	+5
Totals		1031	56	273	329	2395	+164

Playoffs

SSN	TEAM	GP	G	A	PTS.	PIM	+/-
85–86	Hart	10	1	2	3	38	
86–87	Hart	5	0	1	1	41	
87–88	Hart	5	0	0	0	8	
88–89	Hart	4	0	2	2	4	
89–90	Hart	7	1	0	1	12	
90–91	Pitt	20	3	2	5	34	
91–92	Pitt	21	0	2	2	39	
92–93	Pitt	12	1	5	6	24	
93–94	Pitt	6	0	1	1	18	
94–95	Pitt	7	0	2	2	8	
95–96	NYR	11	1	5	6	16	
96–97	NYR	15	0	2	2	30	
98–99	Det	9	0	3	3	10	
Totals		132	7	27	34	272	

SANDELIN, Scott *6–0 200 D*
B. Hibbing, Minn., Aug. 8, 1964

SSN	TEAM	GP	G	A	PTS.	PIM	+/-
86–87	Mont	1	0	0	0	0	+1
87–88	Mont	8	0	1	1	2	0
90–91	Phil	15	0	3	3	0	-3
91–92	Minn	1	0	0	0	0	-1
Totals		25	0	4	4	2	-3

SANDERSON, Derek Michael (Turk) *6–0 185 C*
B. Niagara Falls, Ont., June 16, 1946

SSN	TEAM	GP	G	A	PTS.	PIM	+/-
65–66	Bos	2	0	0	0	0	
66–67	Bos	2	0	0	0	0	
67–68	Bos	71	24	25	49	98	+11
68–69	Bos	61	26	22	48	146	+35
69–70	Bos	50	18	23	41	118	+8
70–71	Bos	71	29	34	63	130	+39
71–72	Bos	78	25	33	58	108	+25
72–73	Phil (WHA)	8	3	3	6	69	
72–73	Bos	25	5	10	15	38	+11
73–74	Bos	29	8	12	20	48	+17

SSN	TEAM	GP	G	A	PTS.	PIM	+/-
74–75	NYR	75	25	25	50	106	+10
75–76	NYR–StL	73	24	43	67	63	+7
76–77	StL–Van	48	15	22	37	56	-3
77–78	Pitt	13	3	1	4	0	-6
NHL Totals		598	202	250	452	911	+138
WHA Totals		8	3	3	6	69	

Playoffs

SSN	TEAM	GP	G	A	PTS.	PIM	
67–68	Bos	4	0	2	2	9	
68–69	Bos	9	8	2	10	36	
69–70	Bos	14	5	4	9	72	
70–71	Bos	7	2	1	3	13	
71–72	Bos	11	1	1	2	44	
72–73	Bos	5	1	2	3	13	
74–75	NYR	3	0	0	0	0	
75–76	StL	3	1	0	1	0	
Totals		56	18	12	30	187	

SANDERSON, Geoff *6-0 185 C*
B. Hay River, Northwest Territory, Feb. 1, 1972

SSN	TEAM	GP	G	A	PTS.	PIM	+/-
90–91	Hart	2	1	0	1	0	-2
91–92	Hart	64	13	18	31	18	+5
92–93	Hart	82	46	43	89	28	-21
93–94	Hart	82	41	26	67	42	-13
94–95	Hart	46	18	14	32	24	-10
95–96	Hart	81	34	31	65	40	0
96–97	Hart	82	36	31	67	29	-9
97–98	Car–Van–Buf	75	11	18	29	38	+1
98–99	Buf	75	12	18	30	22	+8
Totals		589	212	199	411	241	-41

Playoffs

SSN	TEAM	GP	G	A	PTS.	PIM	
90–91	Hart	3	0	0	0	0	
91–92	Hart	7	0	1	1	2	
97–98	Buf	14	3	1	4	4	
98–99	Buf	19	4	6	10	14	
Totals		43	7	8	15	20	

SANDFORD, Edward Michael (Sandy) *6-1 190 LW*
B. New Toronto, Ont., Aug. 20, 1928

SSN	TEAM	GP	G	A	PTS.	PIM	
47–48	Bos	59	10	15	25	25	
48–49	Bos	56	16	20	36	57	
49–50	Bos	17	1	4	5	6	
50–51	Bos	51	10	13	23	33	
51–52	Bos	65	13	12	25	54	
52–53	Bos	61	14	21	35	44	
53–54	Bos	70	16	31	47	42	
54–55	Bos	60	14	20	34	38	
55–56	Det–Chi	61	12	9	21	56	
Totals		500	106	145	251	355	

Playoffs

SSN	TEAM	GP	G	A	PTS.	PIM	
47–48	Bos	5	1	0	1	0	
48–49	Bos	5	1	3	4	2	
50–51	Bos	6	0	1	1	40	
51–52	Bos	7	2	2	4	0	
52–53	Bos	11	8	3	11	11	
53–54	Bos	3	0	1	1	4	
54–55	Bos	5	1	1	2	6	
Totals		42	13	11	24	27	

SANDLAK, Jim *6-4 219 RW*
B. Kitchener, Ont., Dec. 12, 1966

SSN	TEAM	GP	G	A	PTS.	PIM	+/-
85–86	Van	23	1	3	4	10	-4
86–87	Van	78	15	21	36	66	-4
87–88	Van	49	16	15	31	81	-9
88–89	Van	72	20	20	40	99	+8
89–90	Van	70	15	8	23	104	-15
90–91	Van	59	7	6	13	125	-20
91–92	Van	66	16	24	40	176	+22
92–93	Van	59	10	18	28	122	+2
93–94	Hart	27	6	2	8	32	+6
94–95	Hart	13	0	0	0	0	-10
95–96	Van	33	4	2	6	6	-3
Totals		549	110	119	229	821	-27

Playoffs

SSN	TEAM	GP	G	A	PTS.	PIM	
85–86	Van	3	0	1	1	0	
88–89	Van	6	1	1	2	2	
91–92	Van	13	4	6	10	22	
92–93	Van	6	2	2	4	4	
95–96	Van	5	0	0	0	2	
Totals		33	7	10	17	30	

*SANDS, Charles Henry *5-9 160 C*
B. Fort William, Ont., Mar. 23, 1910

SSN	TEAM	GP	G	A	PTS.	PIM	+/-
32–33	Tor	3	0	3	3	0	
33–34	Tor	45	8	8	16	2	
34–35	Bos	43	15	12	27	0	
35–36	Bos	41	6	4	10	8	
36–37	Bos	46	18	5	23	6	
37–38	Bos	46	17	12	29	12	
38–39	Bos	39	7	5	12	10	
39–40	Mont	47	9	20	29	10	
40–41	Mont	43	5	13	18	4	
41–42	Mont	39	11	16	27	6	
42–43	Mont	31	3	9	12	0	
43–44	NYR	9	0	2	2	0	
Totals		432	99	109	208	58	

Playoffs

SSN	TEAM	GP	G	A	PTS.	PIM	
32–33	Tor	9	2	2	4	2	
33–34	Tor	4	1	0	1	0	
34–35	Bos	4	0	0	0	0	
35–36	Bos	2	0	0	0	0	
36–37	Bos	3	1	2	3	0	
37–38	Bos	3	1	1	2	0	
38–39	Bos	12	0	0	0	0	
40–41	Mont	2	1	0	1	0	
41–42	Mont	3	0	1	1	2	
42–43	Mont	2	0	0	0	0	
Totals		44	6	6	12	4	

SANDSTROM, Tomas *6-2 200 RW*
B. Jakobstad, Finland, Sept. 4, 1964

SSN	TEAM	GP	G	A	PTS.	PIM	+/-
84–85	NYR	74	29	29	58	51	+3
85–86	NYR	73	25	29	54	109	-4
86–87	NYR	64	40	34	74	60	+8
87–88	NYR	69	28	40	68	95	-6
88–89	NYR	79	32	56	88	148	+5
89–90	NYR–LA	76	32	39	71	128	-11
90–91	LA	68	45	44	89	106	+27
91–92	LA	49	17	22	39	70	-2
92–93	LA	39	25	27	52	57	+12
93–94	LA–Pitt	78	23	35	58	83	-7
94–95	Pitt	47	21	23	44	42	+1
95–96	Pitt	58	35	35	70	69	+4
96–97	Pitt–Det	74	18	24	42	69	+6
97–98	Ana	77	9	8	17	64	-25
98–99	Ana	58	15	17	32	42	-5
Totals		983	394	462	856	1193	+6

Playoffs

SSN	TEAM	GP	G	A	PTS.	PIM	
84–85	NYR	3	0	2	2	0	
85–86	NYR	16	4	6	10	20	
86–87	NYR	6	1	2	3	20	
88–89	NYR	4	3	2	5	12	
89–90	LA	10	5	4	9	19	
90–91	LA	10	4	4	8	14	
91–92	LA	6	0	3	3	8	
92–93	LA	24	8	17	25	12	
93–94	Pitt	6	0	0	0	4	
94–95	Pitt	12	3	3	6	16	
95–96	Pitt	18	4	2	6	30	
96–97	Det	20	0	4	4	24	
98–99	Ana	4	0	0	0	4	
Totals		139	32	49	81	183	

SANDWITH, Terran *6-4 210 D*
B. Edmonton, Alta., Apr. 17, 1972

SSN	TEAM	GP	G	A	PTS.	PIM	+/-
97–98	Edm	8	0	0	0	6	-4

SANIPASS, Everett *6-2 204 LW*
B. Big Cove, N.B., Feb. 13, 1968

SSN	TEAM	GP	G	A	PTS.	PIM	+/-
86–87	Chi	7	1	3	4	2	+3
87–88	Chi	57	8	12	20	126	-9
88–89	Chi	50	6	9	15	164	-7
89–90	Chi–Que	21	5	5	10	25	-4
90–91	Que	29	5	5	10	41	-15
Totals		164	25	34	59	358	-32

Playoffs

SSN	TEAM	GP	G	A	PTS.	PIM	
87–88	Chi	2	2	0	2	2	
88–89	Chi	3	0	0	0	2	
Totals		5	2	0	2	4	

SARAULT, Yves *6-1 170 LW*
B. Valleyfield, Que., Dec. 23, 1972

SSN	TEAM	GP	G	A	PTS.	PIM	+/-
94–95	Mont	8	0	1	1	0	-1
95–96	Mont–Calg	25	2	1	3	8	-9
96–97	Col A	28	2	1	3	6	0
97–98	Col A	2	1	0	1	0	+1
98–99	Ott	11	0	1	1	4	+1
Totals		74	5	4	9	28	-9

Playoffs

SSN	TEAM	GP	G	A	PTS.	PIM	
96–97	Col A	5	0	0	0	2	

SARGENT, Gary Alan *5-10 210 D*
B. Red Lake, Minn,. Feb. 8, 1954

SSN	TEAM	GP	G	A	PTS.	PIM	+/-
75–76	LA	63	8	16	24	36	-3
76–77	LA	80	14	40	54	65	+7
77–78	LA	72	7	34	41	52	+18
78–79	Minn	79	12	32	44	39	-10
79–80	Minn	52	13	21	34	22	+14
80–81	Minn	23	4	7	11	36	-1
81–82	Minn	15	0	5	5	18	+5
82–83	Minn	18	3	6	9	5	+5
Totals		402	61	161	222	273	+33

Playoffs

SSN	TEAM	GP	G	A	PTS.	PIM	
76–77	LA	9	3	4	7	6	
77–78	LA	2	0	0	0	0	
79–80	Minn	4	2	1	3	2	
82–83	Minn	5	0	2	2	0	
Totals		20	5	7	12	8	

SARICH, Cory *6-3 175 D*
B. Saskatoon, Sask., Aug. 16, 1978

SSN	TEAM	GP	G	A	PTS.	PIM	+/-
98–99	Buf	4	0	0	0	0	+3

SARNER, Craig Brian *5-11 185 RW*
B. St. Paul, Minn., June 20, 1949

SSN	TEAM	GP	G	A	PTS.	PIM	+/-
74–75	Bos	7	0	0	0	0	-3
75–75	Minn (WHA)	1	0	0	0	0	

SARRAZIN, Richard (Dick) *6-0 185 RW*
B. St. Gabriel de Brandon, Que., Jan. 22, 1946

SSN	TEAM	GP	G	A	PTS.	PIM	+/-
68–69	Phil	54	16	30	46	14	-7
69–70	Phil	18	1	1	2	4	-2
71–72	Phil	28	3	4	7	4	0
72–73	NE–Chi (WHA)	68	7	15	22	2	
NHL Totals		100	20	35	55	22	-9
WHA Totals		68	7	15	22	2	

Playoffs

SSN	TEAM	GP	G	A	PTS.	PIM	
68–69	Phil	4	0	0	0	0	

SASKAMOOSE, Fred *5-9 165 C*
B. Sandy Lake Reserve, Sask., Dec. 24, 1934

SSN	TEAM	GP	G	A	PTS.	PIM	
53–54	Chi	11	0	0	0	6	

SASSER, Grant *5-10 175 C*
B. Portland, Ore., Feb. 13, 1964

SSN	TEAM	GP	G	A	PTS.	PIM	+/-
83–84	Pitt	3	0	0	0	0	-2

SATAN, Miroslav *6-1 176 C*
B. Topolcany, Czech., Oct. 22, 1974

SSN	TEAM	GP	G	A	PTS.	PIM	+/-
95–96	Edm	62	18	17	35	22	0
96–97	Edm–Buf	76	25	13	38	26	-3
97–98	Buf	79	22	24	46	34	+2
98–99	Buf	81	40	26	66	44	+24
Totals		298	105	80	185	126	+23

Playoffs

SSN	TEAM	GP	G	A	PTS.	PIM	
96–97	Buf	7	0	0	0	0	
97–98	Buf	14	5	4	9	4	
98–99	Buf	12	3	5	8	2	
Totals		33	8	9	17	6	

SATHER, Glen Cameron (Slats) *5-11 180 LW*
B. High River, Alta., Sept. 2, 1943

SSN	TEAM	GP	G	A	PTS.	PIM	+/-
66–67	Bos	5	0	0	0	0	
67–68	Bos	65	8	12	20	34	+9
68–69	Bos	76	4	11	15	67	+4
69–70	Pitt	76	12	14	26	114	-3
70–71	Pitt–NYR	77	10	3	13	148	0
71–72	NYR	76	5	9	14	77	-2
72–73	NYR	77	11	15	26	64	+16
73–74	NYR–StL	71	15	29	44	82	-9
74–75	Mont	63	6	10	16	44	+14
75–76	Mont	19	9	10	19	94	-8
76–77	Edm (WHA)	81	19	34	53	77	
NHL Totals		658	80	113	193	724	+11
WHA Totals		81	19	34	53	77	

Playoffs

SSN	TEAM	GP	G	A	PTS.	PIM
67–68	Bos	3	0	0	0	0
68–69	Bos	10	0	0	0	18
69–70	Pitt	10	0	2	2	17
70–71	NYR	13	0	1	1	18
71–72	NYR	16	0	1	1	22
72–73	NYR	9	0	0	0	7
74–75	Mont	11	1	1	2	4
76–77	Edm (WHA)	5	1	1	2	2
NHL Totals		72	1	5	6	86
WHA Totals		5	1	1	2	2

SAUNDERS, Bernard 6–0 190 LW
B. Montreal, Que., June 21, 1956

SSN	TEAM	GP	G	A	PTS.	PIM	+/-
79–80	Que	4	0	0	0	0	-1
80–81	Que	6	0	1	1	8	-1
Totals		10	0	1	1	8	-2

SAUNDERS, David 6–1 195 LW
B. Ottawa, Ont., May 20, 1966

SSN	TEAM	GP	G	A	PTS.	PIM	+/-
87–88	Van	56	7	13	20	10	-15

SAUNDERS, Edward (Bud) 5–10 168 RW
B. Ottawa, Ont., Aug. 29, 1912

SSN	TEAM	GP	G	A	PTS.	PIM
33–34	Ott	19	1	3	4	4

SAUVE, Jean–François 5–6 175 C
B. Ste–Genevieve, Que., Jan. 23, 1960

SSN	TEAM	GP	G	A	PTS.	PIM	+/-
80–81	Buf	20	5	9	14	12	-2
81–82	Buf	69	19	36	55	49	+7
82–83	Buf	9	0	4	4	9	0
83–84	Que	39	10	17	27	2	+4
84–85	Que	64	13	29	42	21	+11
85–86	Que	75	16	40	56	20	-13
86–87	Que	14	2	3	5	4	-4
Totals		290	65	138	203	117	+3

Playoffs

SSN	TEAM	GP	G	A	PTS.	PIM
80–81	Buf	5	2	0	2	0
81–82	Buf	2	0	2	2	0
83–84	Que	9	2	5	7	2
84–85	Que	18	5	5	10	8
85–86	Que	2	0	0	0	0
Totals		36	9	12	21	10

SAVAGE, Andre 6–0 195 C
B. Ottawa, Ont., May 27; 1975

SSN	TEAM	GP	G	A	PTS.	PIM	+/-
98–99	Bos	6	1	0	1	0	+2

SAVAGE, Brian 6–1 195 C
B. Sudbury, Ont., Feb. 24, 1971

SSN	TEAM	GP	G	A	PTS.	PIM	+/-
93–94	Mont	3	1	0	1	0	0
94–95	Mont	37	12	7	19	27	+5
95–96	Mont	75	25	8	33	28	-8
96–97	Mont	81	23	37	60	39	-14
97–98	Mont	64	26	17	43	36	+11
98–99	Mont	54	16	10	26	20	-14
Totals		314	103	79	182	150	-20

Playoffs

SSN	TEAM	GP	G	A	PTS.	PIM
93–94	Mont	3	0	2	2	0
95–96	Mont	6	0	2	2	2
96–97	Mont	5	1	1	2	0
97–98	Mont	9	0	2	2	6
Totals		23	1	7	8	8

*SAVAGE, Gordon (Tony) 5–11 170 D
B. Calgary, Alta., July 18, 1906

SSN	TEAM	GP	G	A	PTS.	PIM
34–35	Bos–Mont	49	1	5	6	6

Playoffs

SSN	TEAM	GP	G	A	PTS.	PIM
34–35	Mont	2	0	0	0	0

SAVAGE, Joel 5–11 205 RW
B. Surrey, B.C., Dec. 25, 1969

SSN	TEAM	GP	G	A	PTS.	PIM	+/-
90–91	Buf	3	0	1	1	0	-2

SAVAGE, Reginald 5–10 192 C
B. Montreal, Que., May 1, 1970

SSN	TEAM	GP	G	A	PTS.	PIM	+/-
90–91	Wash	1	0	0	0	0	-1
92–93	Wash	16	2	3	5	12	-4
93–94	Que	17	3	4	7	16	+3
Totals		34	5	7	12	28	-2

SAVARD, Andre 6–1 185 C
B. Temiscamingue, Que., Feb. 9, 1953

SSN	TEAM	GP	G	A	PTS.	PIM	+/-
73–74	Bos	72	16	14	30	39	+16
74–75	Bos	77	19	25	44	45	+16
75–76	Bos	79	17	23	40	60	+4
76–77	Buf	80	25	35	60	30	+9
77–78	Buf	80	19	20	39	40	+1
78–79	Buf	65	18	22	40	20	-2
79–80	Buf	33	3	10	13	16	+4
80–81	Buf	79	31	43	74	63	+32
81–82	Buf	62	18	20	38	24	+5
82–83	Buf	68	16	25	41	28	+11
83–84	Que	60	20	24	44	38	+17
84–85	Que	35	9	10	19	8	-3
Totals		790	211	271	482	411	+110

Playoffs

SSN	TEAM	GP	G	A	PTS.	PIM
73–74	Bos	16	3	2	5	24
74–75	Bos	3	1	1	2	2
75–76	Bos	12	1	4	5	9
76–77	Buf	6	0	1	1	2
77–78	Buf	6	0	0	0	4
78–79	Buf	3	0	2	2	2
79–80	Buf	8	1	1	2	2
80–81	Buf	8	4	2	6	17
81–82	Buf	4	0	1	1	5
82–83	Buf	10	0	4	4	8
83–84	Que	9	3	0	3	2
Totals		85	13	118	31	77

SAVARD, Denis Joseph 5–10 175 C
B. Pointe Gatineau, Que., Feb. 4, 1961

SSN	TEAM	GP	G	A	PTS.	PIM	+/-
80–81	Chi	76	28	47	75	47	+27
81–82	Chi	80	32	87	119	82	0
82–83	Chi	78	35	86	121	99	+26
83–84	Chi	75	37	57	94	71	-13
84–85	Chi	79	38	67	105	56	+16
85–86	Chi	80	47	69	116	111	+7
86–87	Chi	70	40	50	90	108	+15
87–88	Chi	80	44	87	131	95	+4
88–89	Chi	58	23	59	82	110	-5
89–90	Chi	60	27	53	80	56	+8
90–91	Mont	70	28	31	59	52	-1
91–92	Mont	77	28	42	70	73	+6
92–93	Mont	63	16	34	50	90	+1
93–94	TB	74	18	28	46	106	-1
94–95	TB–Chi	43	10	15	25	18	-3
95–96	Chi	69	13	35	48	102	+20
96–97	Chi	64	9	18	27	60	-10
Totals		1196	473	865	1338	1336	+97

Playoffs

SSN	TEAM	GP	G	A	PTS.	PIM
80–81	Chi	3	0	0	0	0
81–82	Chi	15	11	7	18	52
82–83	Chi	13	8	9	17	22
83–84	Chi	5	1	3	4	9
84–85	Chi	13	9	20	29	20
85–86	Chi	3	4	1	5	6
86–87	Chi	4	1	0	1	12
87–88	Chi	5	4	3	7	17
88–89	Chi	16	8	11	19	10
89–90	Chi	20	7	15	22	41
90–91	Mont	13	2	11	13	35
91–92	Mont	11	3	9	12	8
92–93	Mont	14	0	5	5	4
94–95	Chi	16	7	11	18	10
95–96	Chi	10	1	2	3	8
96–97	Chi	6	0	2	2	2
Totals		169	66	109	175	256

SAVARD, Jean 5–11 172 C
B. Verdun, Que., Apr. 26, 1957

SSN	TEAM	GP	G	A	PTS.	PIM	+/-
77–78	Chi	31	7	11	18	2	-6
78–79	Chi	11	0	1	1	9	+2
79–80	Hart	1	0	0	0	2	0
Totals		43	7	12	19	13	-4

SAVARD, Marc 5–10 174 C
B. Ottawa, Ont., July 17; 1977

SSN	TEAM	GP	G	A	PTS.	PIM	+/-
97–98	NYR	28	1	5	6	4	-4
98–99	NYR	70	9	36	45	38	-7
Totals		98	10	41	51	42	-11

SAVARD, Serge 6–2 210 D
B. Montreal, Que., Jan. 22, 1946

SSN	TEAM	GP	G	A	PTS.	PIM	+/-
66–67	Mont	2	0	0	0	0	
67–68	Mont	67	2	13	15	34	+13
68–69	Mont	74	8	23	31	73	+33
69–70	Mont	64	12	19	31	38	+4
70–71	Mont	37	5	10	15	30	+11
71–72	Mont	23	1	8	9	16	+21
72–73	Mont	74	7	32	39	58	+70
73–74	Mont	67	4	14	18	49	+20
74–75	Mont	80	20	40	60	64	+71
75–76	Mont	71	8	39	47	38	+52
76–77	Mont	78	9	33	42	35	+79
77–78	Mont	77	8	34	42	24	+62
78–79	Mont	80	7	26	33	30	+40
79–80	Mont	46	5	8	13	18	-2
80–81	Mont	77	4	13	17	30	+12
81–82	Winn	47	2	5	7	26	-8
82–83	Winn	76	4	16	20	29	-24
Totals		1040	106	333	439	592	+462

Playoffs

SSN	TEAM	GP	G	A	PTS.	PIM
67–68	Mont	6	2	0	2	0
68–69	Mont	14	4	6	10	24
71–72	Mont	6	0	0	0	10
72–73	Mont	17	3	8	11	22
73–74	Mont	6	1	1	2	4
74–75	Mont	11	1	7	8	2
75–76	Mont	13	3	6	9	6
76–77	Mont	14	2	7	9	2
77–78	Mont	15	1	7	8	8
78–79	Mont	16	2	7	9	6
79–80	Mont	2	0	0	0	0
80–81	Mont	3	0	0	0	0
81–82	Winn	4	0	0	0	2
82–83	Winn	3	0	0	0	2
Totals		130	19	49	68	88

SAVOIA, Ryan 6–1 204 C
B. Throrold, Ont. May 6, 1973

SSN	TEAM	GP	G	A	PTS.	PIM	+/-
98–99	Pitt	3	0	0	0	0	-1

SAWYER, Kevin 6–2 205 LW
B. Christina Lake, B.C., Feb. 21, 1974

SSN	TEAM	GP	G	A	PTS.	PIM	+/-
95–96	StL–Bos	8	0	0	0	28	-1
96–97	Bos	2	0	0	0	0	0
Totals		10	0	0	0	28	-1

SCAMURRA, Peter Vincent 6–3 185 D
B. Buffalo, N.Y., Feb. 23, 1955

SSN	TEAM	GP	G	A	PTS.	PIM	+/-
75–76	Wash	58	2	13	15	33	-38
76–77	Wash	21	0	2	2	8	-6
78–79	Wash	30	3	5	8	12	-13
79–80	Wash	23	3	5	8	6	-1
Totals		132	8	25	33	59	-58

SCATCHARD, Dave 6–2 200 C
B. Hinton, Alta., Feb. 20, 1976

SSN	TEAM	GP	G	A	PTS.	PIM	+/-
97–98	Van	76	13	11	24	165	-4
98–99	Van	82	13	13	26	140	-12
Totals		158	26	24	50	305	-16

SCEVIOUR, Darin 5–10 185 RW
B. Lacombe, Alta., Nov. 30, 1965

SSN	TEAM	GP	G	A	PTS.	PIM	+/-
86–87	Chi	1	0	0	0	0	0

SCHAEFFER, Paul (Butch) D

SSN	TEAM	GP	G	A	PTS.	PIM
36–37	Chi	5	0	0	0	6

SCHAEFER, Peter 5–11 190 LW
B. Yellow Grass, Sask., July 12, 1977

SSN	TEAM	GP	G	A	PTS.	PIM	+/-
98–99	Van	25	4	4	8	8	-1

SCHAMEHORN, Kevin Dean 5–9 185 RW
B. Calgary, Alta., July 28, 1956

SSN	TEAM	GP	G	A	PTS.	PIM	+/-
76–77	Det	3	0	0	0	9	-1
79–80	Det	2	0	0	0	4	-2
80–81	LA	5	0	0	0	4	-1
Totals		10	0	0	0	17	-4

SCHELLA, John Edward 6–0 180 D
B. Port Arthur, Ont., May 9, 1947

SSN	TEAM	GP	G	A	PTS.	PIM	+/-
70–71	Van	38	0	5	5	58	-5
71–72	Van	77	2	13	15	166	-29
72–73	Hou (WHA)	77	2	24	26	239	
73–74	Hou (WHA)	73	12	19	31	170	
74–75	Hou (WHA)	78	10	42	52	176	
75–76	Hou (WHA)	74	6	32	38	106	
76–77	Hou (WHA)	20	0	6	6	28	

SSN	TEAM	GP	G	A	PTS.	PIM	+/-
77–78	Hou (WHA)	63	9	20	29	125	
NHL Totals		115	2	18	20	224	-34
WHA Totals		385	39	143	182	844	

Playoffs

SSN	TEAM	GP	G	A	PTS.	PIM	+/-
72–73	Hous (WHA)	10	0	2	2	12	
73–74	Hous (WHA)	14	2	6	8	42	
74–75	Hous (WHA)	13	0	8	8	12	
75–76	Hous (WHA)	17	1	6	7	38	
76–77	Hous (WHA)	6	1	2	3	6	
77–78	Hous (WHA)	6	0	1	1	33	
WHA Totals		66	4	25	29	143	

SCHERZA, Charles (Chuck) *5–10 190 C*
B. Brandon, Man., Feb. 15, 1923

SSN	TEAM	GP	G	A	PTS.	PIM	+/-
43–44	Bos–NYR	34	4	3	7	17	
44–45	NYR	22	2	3	5	18	
Totals		56	6	6	12	35	

SCHINKEL, Kenneth Calvin *5–10 172 RW*
B. Jansen, Sask., Nov. 27, 1932

SSN	TEAM	GP	G	A	PTS.	PIM	+/-
59–60	NYR	69	13	16	29	27	
60–61	NYR	38	2	6	8	18	
61–62	NYR	65	7	21	28	17	
62–63	NYR	69	6	9	15	15	
63–64	NYR	4	0	0	0	0	
66–67	NYR	20	6	3	9	0	
67–68	Pitt	57	14	25	39	19	-10
68–69	Pitt	76	18	34	52	18	-39
69–70	Pitt	72	20	25	45	19	-26
70–71	Pitt	50	15	19	34	6	-19
71–72	Pitt	74	15	30	45	10	-10
72–73	Pitt	42	11	10	21	16	-10
Totals		636	127	198	325	165	-114

Playoffs

SSN	TEAM	GP	G	A	PTS.	PIM	+/-
61–62	NYR	2	1	0	1	0	
66–67	NYR	4	0	1	1	0	
69–70	Pitt	10	4	1	5	4	
71–72	Pitt	3	2	0	2	0	
Totals		19	7	2	9	4	

SCHLEGEL, Brad *5–10 188 D*
B. Kitchener, Ont., July 22, 1968

SSN	TEAM	GP	G	A	PTS.	PIM	+/-
91–92	Wash	15	0	1	1	0	-4
92–93	Wash	7	0	1	1	6	+1
93–94	Calg	26	1	6	7	4	-4
Totals		48	1	8	9	10	-7

Playoffs

SSN	TEAM	GP	G	A	PTS.	PIM	+/-
91–92	Wash	7	0	1	1	2	

SCHLIEBENER, Andreas (Andy) *6–0 200 D*
B. Ottawa, Ont., Aug. 16, 1962

SSN	TEAM	GP	G	A	PTS.	PIM	+/-
81–82	Van	22	0	1	1	10	-11
83–84	Van	51	2	10	12	48	-9
84–85	Van	11	0	0	0	16	-11
Totals		84	2	11	13	74	-31

Playoffs

SSN	TEAM	GP	G	A	PTS.	PIM	+/-
81–82	Van	3	0	0	0	0	
83–84	Van	3	0	0	0	0	
Totals		6	0	0	0	0	

SCHMAUTZ, Clifford Harvey *5–7 161 RW*
B. Saskatoon, Sask., Mar. 17, 1939

SSN	TEAM	GP	G	A	PTS.	PIM	+/-
70–71	Buf–Phil	56	13	19	32	33	-8

SCHMAUTZ, Robert James *5–9 172 RW*
B. Saskatoon, Sask., Mar. 28, 1945

SSN	TEAM	GP	G	A	PTS.	PIM	+/-
67–68	Chi	13	3	2	5	6	+1
68–69	Chi	63	9	7	16	37	-5
70–71	Van	26	5	5	10	14	+2
71–72	Van	60	12	13	25	82	-10
72–73	Van	77	38	33	71	137	-17
73–74	Van–Bos	76	33	32	65	89	+6
74–75	Bos	56	21	30	51	63	+23
75–76	Bos	75	28	34	62	116	+13
76–77	Bos	57	23	29	52	62	+25
77–78	Bos	54	27	27	54	87	+24
78–79	Bos	65	20	22	42	77	-1
79–80	Bos–Edm–Col	69	25	18	43	81	-15
80–81	Van	73	27	34	61	137	-5
Totals		764	271	286	557	988	+18

Playoffs

SSN	TEAM	GP	G	A	PTS.	PIM	+/-
67–68	Chi	11	2	3	5	2	
73–74	Bos	16	3	6	9	44	
74–75	Bos	3	1	5	6	6	
75–76	Bos	11	2	8	10	13	
76–77	Bos	14	11	1	12	10	
77–78	Bos	15	7	8	15	11	
78–79	Bos	11	2	2	4	6	
80–81	Van	3	0	0	0	0	

SCHMIDT, Clarence *5–11 165 RW*
B. Williams, Minn., 1923

SSN	TEAM	GP	G	A	PTS.	PIM	+/-
43–44	Bos	7	1	0	1	2	

SCHMIDT, John R. (Jackie) *5–10 155 LW*
B. Odessa, Sask., Nov. 11, 1924

SSN	TEAM	GP	G	A	PTS.	PIM	+/-
42–43	Bos	45	6	7	13	6	

Playoffs

SSN	TEAM	GP	G	A	PTS.	PIM	+/-
42–43	Bos	5	0	0	0	0	

SCHMIDT, Joseph *5–9 157 LW*
B. Odessa, Sask., Nov. 5, 1926

SSN	TEAM	GP	G	A	PTS.	PIM	+/-
43–44	Bos	2	0	0	0	0	

SCHMIDT, Milton Conrad *5–11 180 C*
B. Kitchener, Ont., Mar. 5, 1918

SSN	TEAM	GP	G	A	PTS.	PIM	+/-
36–37	Bos	26	2	8	10	15	
37–38	Bos	44	13	14	27	15	
38–39	Bos	41	15	17	32	13	
39–40	Bos	48	22	30	52	37	
40–41	Bos	45	13	25	38	23	
41–42	Bos	36	14	21	35	34	
45–46	Bos	48	13	18	31	21	
46–47	Bos	59	27	35	62	40	
47–48	Bos	33	9	17	26	28	
48–49	Bos	44	10	22	32	25	
49–50	Bos	68	19	22	41	41	
50–51	Bos	62	22	39	61	33	
51–52	Bos	69	21	29	50	57	
52–53	Bos	68	11	23	34	30	
53–54	Bos	64	14	18	32	28	
54–55	Bos	23	4	8	12	26	
Totals		778	229	346	575	466	

Playoffs

SSN	TEAM	GP	G	A	PTS.	PIM	+/-
36–37	Bos	3	0	0	0	0	
37–38	Bos	3	0	0	0	0	
38–39	Bos	12	3	3	6	2	
39–40	Bos	6	0	0	0	0	
40–41	Bos	11	5	6	11	9	
45–46	Bos	10	3	5	8	2	
46–47	Bos	5	3	1	4	4	
47–48	Bos	5	2	5	7	2	
48–49	Bos	4	0	2	2	8	
50–51	Bos	6	0	1	1	7	
51–52	Bos	7	2	1	3	0	
52–53	Bos	10	5	1	6	6	
53–54	Bos	4	1	0	1	20	
Totals		86	24	25	49	60	

SCHMIDT, Norm *5–11 190 D*
B. Sault Ste. Marie, Ont., Jan. 24, 1963

SSN	TEAM	GP	G	A	PTS.	PIM	+/-
83–84	Pitt	34	6	12	18	12	-1
85–86	Pitt	66	15	14	29	57	+7
86–87	Pitt	20	1	5	6	4	-8
87–88	Pitt	5	1	2	3	0	+1
Totals		125	23	33	56	73	-1

*SCHNARR, Werner *F*

SSN	TEAM	GP	G	A	PTS.	PIM	+/-
24–25	Bos	24	0	0	0	0	
25–26	Bos	1	0	0	0	0	
Totals		25	0	0	0	0	

SCHNEIDER, Andy *5–9 170 LW*
B. Edmonton, Alta., Mar. 29. 1972

SSN	TEAM	GP	G	A	PTS.	PIM	+/-
93–94	Ott	10	0	0	0	15	-6

SCHNEIDER, Mathieu *5–11 189 D*
B. New York, N.Y., June 12, 1969

SSN	TEAM	GP	G	A	PTS.	PIM	+/-
87–88	Mont	4	0	0	0	2	-1
89–90	Mont	44	7	14	21	25	+2
90–91	Mont	69	10	20	30	63	+7
91–92	Mont	78	8	24	32	72	+10
92–93	Mont	60	13	31	44	91	+8
93–94	Mont	75	20	32	52	62	+15
94–95	Mont–NYI	43	8	21	29	79	-8
95–96	NYI–Tor	78	13	41	54	103	-20
96–97	Tor	26	5	7	12	20	+3
97–98	Tor	76	11	26	37	44	-12
98–99	NYR	75	10	24	34	71	-19
Totals		628	105	240	345	632	-15

Playoffs

SSN	TEAM	GP	G	A	PTS.	PIM	+/-
89–90	Mont	9	1	3	4	31	
90–91	Mont	13	2	7	9	18	
91–92	Mont	10	1	4	5	6	
92–93	Mont	11	1	2	3	16	
93–94	Mont	1	0	0	0	0	
95–96	Tor	6	0	4	4	8	
Totals		50	5	20	25	79	

SCHOCK, Daniel Patrick *5–11 180 LW*
B. Terrace Bay, Ont., Dec. 30, 1948

SSN	TEAM	GP	G	A	PTS.	PIM	+/-
70–71	Bos–Phil	20	1	2	3	0	0

Playoffs

SSN	TEAM	GP	G	A	PTS.	PIM	+/-
69–70	Bos	1	0	0	0	0	

SCHOCK, Ronald Lawrence *5–11 180 C*
B. Chapleau, Ont., Dec. 19, 1943

SSN	TEAM	GP	G	A	PTS.	PIM	+/-
63–64	Bos	1		2	3	0	
64–65	Bos	33	4	7	11	14	
65–66	Bos	24	2	2	4	6	
66–67	Bos	66	10	20	30	8	
67–68	StL	55	9	9	18	17	-17
68–69	StL	67	12	27	39	14	+3
69–70	Pitt	76	8	21	29	40	-2
70–71	Pitt	71	14	26	40	20	+2
71–72	Pitt	77	17	29	46	22	-10
72–73	Pitt	78	13	36	49	23	-12
73–74	Pitt	77	14	29	43	22	-27
74–75	Pitt	80	23	63	86	36	+22
75–76	Pitt	80	18	44	62	28	+2
76–77	Pitt	80	17	32	49	10	-6
77–78	Buf	40	4	4	8	0	-5
Totals		909	166	351	517	260	-55

Playoffs

SSN	TEAM	GP	G	A	PTS.	PIM	+/-
67–68	StL	12	1	2	3	0	
68–69	StL	12	1	2	3	6	
69–70	Pitt	10	1	6	7	7	
71–72	Pitt	4	1	0	1	6	
74–75	Pitt	9	0	4	4	10	
75–76	Pitt	3	0	1	1	0	
76–77	Pitt	3	0	1	1	0	
77–78	Buf	2	0	0	0	0	
Totals		55	4	16	20	29	

SCHOENFELD, James Grant *6–2 210 D*
B. Galt, Ont., Sept. 4, 1952

SSN	TEAM	GP	G	A	PTS.	PIM	+/-
72–73	Buf	66	4	15	19	178	+12
73–74	Buf	28	1	8	9	56	-9
74–75	Buf	68	1	19	20	184	+35
75–76	Buf	56	2	22	24	114	+40
76–77	Buf	65	7	25	32	97	+24
77–78	Buf	60	2	20	22	89	+24
78–79	Buf	46	8	17	25	67	+8
79–80	Buf	77	9	27	36	72	+60
80–81	Buf	71	8	25	33	110	+28
81–82	Buf–Det	52	8	11	19	99	+7
82–83	Det	57	1	10	11	18	-14
83–84	Bos	39	0	2	2	20	+18
84–85	Buf	34	0	3	3	28	0
Totals		719	51	204	255	1132	+237

Playoffs

SSN	TEAM	GP	G	A	PTS.	PIM	+/-
72–73	Buf	6	2	1	3	4	
74–75	Buf	17	1	4	5	38	
75–76	Buf	9	0	3	3	33	
76–77	Buf	6	0	0	0	12	
77–78	Buf	8	0	1	1	28	
78–79	Buf	3	0	1	1	0	
79–80	Buf	14	0	3	3	10	
80–81	Buf	8	0	0	0	14	
84–85	Buf	5	0	0	0	4	
Totals		75	3	13	16	151	

SCHOFIELD, Dwight Hamilton *6–3 195 D*
B. Waltham, Mass., Mar. 25, 1956

SSN	TEAM	GP	G	A	PTS.	PIM	+/-
76–77	Det	3	1	0	1	2	0
82–83	Mont	2	0	0	0	7	+1
83–84	StL	70	4	10	14	219	-3
84–85	StL	43	1	4	5	184	-4

SSN	TEAM	GP	G	A	PTS.	PIM	+/-
85–86	Wash	50	1	2	3	127	+5
86–87	Pitt	25	1	6	7	59	+4
87–88	Winn	18	0	0	0	33	-3
Totals		211	8	22	30	631	0

Playoffs

83–84	StL	4	0	0	0	26	
84–85	StL	2	0	0	015		
85–86	Wash	3	0	0	0	14	
Totals		9	0	0	0	55	

SCHREIBER, Wally 5–11 180 RW
B. Edmonton, Alta., Apr. 15, 1962

87–88	Minn	16	6	5	11	2	-4
88–89	Minn	25	2	5	7	10	-5
Totals		41	8	10	18	12	-9

*SCHRINER, David (Sweeney) LW
B. Calgary, Alta., Nov. 30, 1911

34–35	NYA	48	18	22	40	6	
35–36	NYA	48	19	26	45	8	
36–37	NYA	48	21	25	46	17	
37–38	NYA	48	21	17	38	22	
38–39	NYA	48	13	31	44	20	
39–40	Tor	39	11	15	26	10	
40–41	Tor	48	24	14	38	4	
41–42	Tor	47	20	16	36	21	
42–43	Tor	37	19	17	36	13	
44–45	Tor	26	27	15	42	10	
45–46	Tor	47	13	6	19	15	
Totals		484	206	204	410	148	

Playoffs

35–36	NYA	5	3	1	4	2	
37–38	NYA	6	1	0	1	0	
38–39	NYA	2	0	0	0	30	
39–40	Tor	10	1	3	4	4	
40–41	Tor	7	2	1	3	4	
41–42	Tor	13	6	3	9	10	
42–43	Tor	4	2	2	4	0	
44–45	Tor	13	3	1	4	4	
Totals		60	18	11	29	54	

SCHULTE, Paxton 6–2 217 LW
B. Ionaway, Alta., July 16, 1972

93–94	Que	1	0	0	0	2	0
96–97	Calg	1	0	0	0	4	+1
Totals		2	0	0	0	4	+1

SCHULTZ, David William (Hammer) 6–1 190 LW
B. Waldheim, Sask., Oct. 14, 1949

71–72	Phil	1	0	0	0	0	0
72–73	Phil	76	9	12	21	259	+4
73–74	Phil	73	20	16	36	348	+26
74–75	Phil	76	9	17	26	472	+16
75–76	Phil	71	13	19	32	307	+24
76–77	LA	76	10	20	30	232	-8
77–78	LA–Pitt	74	11	25	36	405	-8
78–79	Pitt–Buf	75	6	12	18	243	-14
79–80	Buf	13	1	0	1	28	0
Totals		535	79	121	200	2294	+40

Playoffs

72–73	Phil	11	1	0	1	51	
73–74	Phil	17	2	4	6	139	
74–75	Phil	17	2	3	5	83	
75–76	Phil	16	2	2	4	90	
76–77	LA	9	1	1	2	45	
78–79	Buf	3	0	2	2	4	
Totals		73	8	12	20	412	

SCHULTZ, Ray 6–2 200 D
B. Red Deer, Alta., Nov. 14, 1976

97–98	NYI	13	0	1	1	45	+3
98–99	NYI	4	0	0	0	7	-2
Totals		17	0	1	1	52	+1

SCHURMAN, Maynard F. 6–3 205 LW
B. Summerdale, P.E.I., July 16, 1957

79–80	Hart	7	0	0	0	0	-1

SCHUTT, Rodney 5–10 185 LW
B. Bancroft, Ont., Oct. 13, 1956

77–78	Mont	2	0	0	0	0	0

SSN	TEAM	GP	G	A	PTS.	PIM	+/-
78–79	Pitt	74	24	21	45	33	-9
79–80	Pitt	73	18	21	39	43	-8
80–81	Pitt	80	25	35	60	55	-13
81–82	Pitt	35	9	12	21	42	+3
82–83	Pitt	5	0	0	0	0	-2
83–84	Pitt	11	1	3	4	4	0
85–86	Tor	6	0	0	0	0	-2
Totals		286	77	92	169	177	-31

Playoffs

78–79	Pitt	7	2	0	2	4	
79–80	Pitt	5	2	1	3	6	
80–81	Pitt	5	3	3	6	16	
81–82	Pitt	5	1	2	3	0	
Totals		22	8	6	14	26	

SCISSONS, Scott 6–1 201 C
B. Saskatoon, Sask., Oct. 29, 1971

90–91	NYI	1	0	0	0	0	0
93–94	NYI	1	0	0	0	0	0
Totals		2	0	0	0	0	0

Playoffs

92–93	NYI	1	0	0	0	0

SCLISIZZI, Enio James 5–10 168 LW
B. Milton, Ont., Aug. 1, 1925

47–48	Det	4	1	0	1	0
48–49	Det	50	9	8	17	24
49–50	Det	4	0	0	0	2
51–52	Det	9	2	1	3	0
52–53	Chi	14	0	2	2	0
Totals		81	12	11	23	26

Playoffs

46–47	Det	1	0	0	0	0
47–48	Det	6	0	0	0	4
48–49	Det	6	0	0	0	2
Totals		13	0	0	0	6

*SCOTT, Ganton RW

22–23	Tor	17	0	0	0	0
23–24	Tor–Ham	8	0	0	0	0
24–25	Mont M	28	1	1	2	0
26–27	Tor	1	0	0	0	0
Totals		54	1	1	2	0

*SCOTT, Lawrence (Laurie) 5–6 155 F
B. South River, Ont., June 19, 1900

26–27	NYA	39	6	2	8	22
27–28	NYR	23	0	1	1	6
Totals		62	6	3	9	28

SCREMIN, Claudio 6–2 205 D
B. Burnaby, B.C., May 28, 1968

91–92	SJ	13	0	0	0	25	-4
92–93	SJ	4	0	1	1	4	-1
Totals		17	0	1	1	29	-5

SCRUTON, Howard 6–3 190 D
B. Toronto, Ont., Oct. 6, 1962

82–83	LA	4	0	4	4	9	-4

SEABROOKE, Glen 6–0 190 C
B. Peterborough, Ont., Sept. 11, 1967

86–87	Phil	10	1	4	5	2	+2
87–88	Phil	6	0	1	1	2	-1
88–89	Phil	3	0	1	1	0	-1
Totals		19	1	6	7	4	0

SECORD, Alan William 6–1 205 LW
B. Sudbury, Ont., Mar. 3, 1958

78–79	Bos	71	16	7	23	125	+7
79–80	Bos	77	23	16	39	170	+20
80–81	Bos–Chi	59	13	12	25	187	-2
81–82	Chi	80	44	31	75	303	-17
82–83	Chi	80	54	32	86	180	+34
83–84	Chi	14	4	4	8	77	+7
84–85	Chi	51	15	11	26	193	0
85–86	Chi	80	40	36	76	201	+8
86–87	Chi	77	29	29	58	196	-20
87–88	Tor	74	15	27	42	221	-21
88–89	Tor–Phil	60	6	10	16	109	-20
89–90	Chi	43	14	7	21	131	+5
Totals		766	273	222	495	2093	+1

SSN	TEAM	GP	G	A	PTS.	PIM	+/-

Playoffs

78–79	Bos	4	0	0	0	4
79–80	Bos	10	0	3	3	65
80–81	Chi	3	4	0	4	14
81–82	Chi	15	2	5	7	61
82–83	Chi	12	4	7	11	66
83–84	Chi	5	3	4	7	28
84–85	Chi	15	7	9	16	42
85–86	Chi	2	0	2	2	26
86–87	Chi	4	0	0	0	21
87–88	Tor	6	1	0	1	16
88–89	Phil	14	0	4	4	31
89–90	Chi	12	0	0	0	8
Totals		102	21	34	55	382

SEDLBAUER, Ronald Andrew 6–3 200 LW
B. Burlington, Ont., Oct. 22, 1954

74–75	Van	26	3	4	7	17	-4
75–76	Van	56	19	13	32	66	-4
76–77	Van	70	18	20	38	29	+12
77–78	Van	62	18	12	30	25	-16
78–79	Van	79	40	16	56	26	-34
79–80	Van–Chi	77	23	14	37	21	-4
80–81	Chi–Tor	60	22	7	29	26	-10
Totals		430	143	86	229	210	-50

Playoffs

74–75	Van	5	0	0	0	10
75–76	Van	2	0	0	0	0
78–79	Van	3	0	1	1	9
79–80	Chi	7	1	1	2	6
80–81	Tor	2	0	1	1	2
Totals		19	1	3	4	27

SEGUIN, Daniel G. 5–8 165 LW
B. Sudbury, Ont., June 7, 1948

70–71	Minn–Van	36	1	6	7	50	-9
73–74	Van	1	1	0	1	0	+1
Totals		37	2	6	8	50	-8

SEGUIN, Steve 6–2 200 RW
B. Cornwall, Ont., Apr. 10, 1964

84–85	LA	5	0	0	0	9	-5

*SEIBERT, Earl Walter 6–2 198 D
B. Kitchener, Ont., Dec. 7, 1911

31–32	NYR	44	4	6	10	88
32–33	NYR	45	2	3	5	92
33–34	NYR	48	13	10	23	66
34–35	NYR	48	6	19	25	86
35–36	NYR–Chi	44	5	9	14	27
36–37	Chi	43	9	6	15	46
37–38	Chi	48	8	13	21	38
38–39	Chi	48	4	11	15	57
39–40	Chi	36	3	7	10	35
40–41	Chi	46	3	17	20	52
41–42	Chi	46	7	14	21	52
42–43	Chi	44	5	27	32	48
43–44	Chi	50	8	25	33	40
44–45	Chi–Det	47	12	17	29	23
45–46	Det	18	0	3	3	18
Totals		655	89	187	276	768
31–32	NYR	7	1	2	3	4
32–33	NYR	8	1	0	1	14
33–34	NYR	2	0	0	0	4
34–35	NYR	4	0	0	0	6
35–36	Chi	2	2	0	2	0
37–38	Chi	10	5	2	7	12
39–40	Chi	2	0	1	1	8
40–41	Chi	5	0	0	0	12
41–42	Chi	3	0	0	0	0
43–44	Chi	9	0	2	2	2
44–45	Det	14	2	1	3	4
Totals		66	11	8	19	66

SEILING, Richard James (Ric) 6–1 180 RW/C
B. Elmira, Ont., Dec. 15, 1957

77–78	Buf	80	19	19	38	33	+13
78–79	Buf	78	20	22	42	56	+15
79–80	Buf	80	25	35	60	54	+30
80–81	Buf	74	30	27	57	80	+20
81–82	Buf	57	22	25	47	58	+7
82–83	Buf	75	19	22	41	41	+2
83–84	Buf	78	13	22	35	42	+10
84–85	Buf	73	16	15	31	86	+30
85–86	Buf	69	12	13	25	74	-5

SSN	TEAM	GP	G	A	PTS.	PIM	+/-
86–87	Det	74	3	8	11	49	-4
Totals		738	179	208	387	573	+118

Playoffs

SSN	TEAM	GP	G	A	PTS.	PIM	+/-
77–78	Buf	8	0	2	2	7	
78–79	Buf	3	0	1	1	2	
79–80	Buf	14	5	4	9	6	
80–81	Buf	8	2	2	4	2	
81–82	Buf	4	1	1	2	2	
82–83	Buf	10	2	3	5	6	
83–84	Buf	3	0	0	0	2	
84–85	Buf	5	4	1	5	4	
86–87	Det	7	0	0	0	5	
Totals		62	14	14	28	36	

SEILING, Rodney Albert (Rod) 6-0 195 D
B. Elmira, Ont., Nov. 14, 1944

SSN	TEAM	GP	G	A	PTS.	PIM	+/-
62–63	Tor	1	0	1	1	0	
63–64	NYR	2	0	1	1	0	
64–65	NYR	68	4	22	26	44	
65–66	NYR	52	5	10	15	24	
66–67	NYR	12	1	1	2	6	
67–68	NYR	71	5	11	16	44	+23
68–69	NYR	73	4	17	21	75	+6
69–70	NYR	76	5	21	26	68	+41
70–71	NYR	68	5	22	27	34	+30
71–72	NYR	78	5	36	41	62	+53
72–73	NYR	72	9	33	42	36	+43
73–74	NYR	68	7	23	30	32	+16
74–75	NYR–Wash–Tor	65	5	13	18	40	+4
75–76	Tor	77	3	16	19	46	+11
76–77	StL	79	3	26	29	36	+1
77–78	StL	78	1	11	12	40	-48
78–79	StL–Atl	39	0	5	5	16	+7
Totals		979	62	269	331	603	+187

Playoffs

SSN	TEAM	GP	G	A	PTS.	PIM	+/-
67–68	NYR	3	0	2	2	4	
68–69	NYR	4	1	0	1	2	
69–70	NYR	2	0	0	0	0	
70–71	NYR	13	1	0	1	12	
71–72	NYR	16	1	4	5	10	
73–74	NYR	13	0	2	2	19	
74–75	Tor	7	0	0	0	6	
75–76	Tor	10	0	1	1	6	
76–77	StL	4	0	0	0	2	
78–79	Atl	2	0	0	0	0	
Totals		77	3	9	12	55	

SEJBA, Jiri 5-10 185 LW
B. Pardubice, Czechoslovakia, July 22, 1962

SSN	TEAM	GP	G	A	PTS.	PIM	+/-
90–91	Buf	11	0	2	2	8	-5

SELANNE, Teemu 6-0 200 RW
B. Helsinki, Finland, July 3, 1970

SSN	TEAM	GP	G	A	PTS.	PIM	+/-
92–93	Winn	84	76	56	132	45	+8
93–94	Winn	51	25	29	54	22	-23
94–95	Winn	45	22	26	48	2	+1
95–96	Winn–Ana	79	40	68	108	22	+5
96–97	Ana	78	51	58	109	34	+28
97–98	Ana	73	52	34	86	30	+12
98–99	Ana	75	47	60	107	30	+18
Totals		485	313	331	646	185	+49

Playoffs

SSN	TEAM	GP	G	A	PTS.	PIM	+/-
92–93	Winn	6	2	4	6	2	
96–97	Ana	11	7	3	10	4	
98–99	Anaa	4	2	2	4	2	
Totals		21	11	9	20	8	

SELBY, Robert Briton (Brit) 5-10 175 LW
B. Kingston, Ont., Mar. 27, 1945

SSN	TEAM	GP	G	A	PTS.	PIM	+/-
64–65	Tor	3	2	0	2	2	
65–66	Tor	61	14	13	27	26	
66–67	Tor	6	1	1	2	0	
67–68	Phil	56	15	15	30	24	-3
68–69	Phil–Tor	77	12	15	27	42	-11
69–70	Tor	74	10	13	23	40	-5
70–71	Tor–StL	67	1	5	6	29	-13
71–72	StL	6	0	0	0	8	-2
72–73	Que–NE (WHA)	72	13	30	43	52	
73–74	Tor (WHA)	64	9	17	26	21	
74–75	Tor (WHA)	17	1	4	5	0	
NHL Totals		350	55	62	117	171	-34
WHA Totals		153	23	51	74	73	

Playoffs

SSN	TEAM	GP	G	A	PTS.	PIM	+/-
65–66	Tor	4	0	0	0	0	
67–68	Phil	7	1	1	2	4	
68–69	Tor	4	0	0	0	4	
70–71	StL	1	0	0	0	0	
72–73	NE (WHA)	13	3	4	7	13	
73–74	Tor (WHA)	10	1	3	4	2	
NHL Totals		16	1	1	2	8	
WHA Totals		23	4	7	11	15	

SELF, Steven 5-9 170 C
B. Peterborough, Ont., May 9, 1950

SSN	TEAM	GP	G	A	PTS.	PIM	+/-
76–77	Wash	3	0	0	0	0	-3

SELIVANOV, Alexander 6-1 187 RW
B. Moscow, USSR, Mar. 23, 1971

SSN	TEAM	GP	G	A	PTS.	PIM	+/-
94–95	TB	43	10	6	16	14	-2
95–96	TB	79	31	21	52	93	+3
96–97	TB	69	15	18	33	61	-3
97–98	TB	70	16	19	35	85	-38
98–99	TB–Edm	72	14	19	33	42	-8
Totals		333	86	83	169	295	-48

Playoffs

SSN	TEAM	GP	G	A	PTS.	PIM	+/-
95–96	TB	6	2	2	4	6	
98–99	Edm	2	0	1	1	2	
Totals		8	2	3	5	8	

SELWOOD, Bradley Wayne 6-1 200 D
B. Leamington, Ont., Mar. 18, 1948

SSN	TEAM	GP	G	A	PTS.	PIM	+/-
70–71	Tor	28	2	10	12	13	-7
71–72	Tor	72	4	17	21	58	+7
72–73	NE (WHA)	75	13	21	34	114	
73–74	NE (WHA)	76	9	28	37	91	
74–75	NE (WHA)	77	4	35	39	117	
75–76	NE (WHA)	40	2	10	12	58	
76–77	NE (WHA)	41	4	12	16	71	
77–78	NE (WHA)	80	6	25	31	88	
78–79	NE (WHA)	42	4	12	16	47	
79–80	LA	63	1	13	14	82	-14
NHL Totals		163	7	40	47	153	-14
WHA Totals		431	42	143	185	556	

Playoffs

SSN	TEAM	GP	G	A	PTS.	PIM	+/-
71–72	Tor	5	0	0	0	04	
72–73	NE (WHA)	15	3	5	8	22	
73–74	NE (WHA)	7	0	2	2	11	
74–75	NE (WHA)	5	1	0	1	11	
75–76	NE (WHA)	17	2	2	4	27	
76–77	NE (WHA)	5	0	0	0	2	
77–78	NE (WHA)	14	0	3	3	8	
79–80	LA	1	0	0	0	0	
NHL Totals		6	0	0	0	4	
WHA Totals		63	6	12	18	81	

SEMAK, Alexander 5-10 180 C
B. Ufa, Soviet Union, Feb. 11, 1966

SSN	TEAM	GP	G	A	PTS.	PIM	+/-
91–92	NJ	25	5	6	11	0	+5
92–93	NJ	82	37	42	79	70	+24
93–94	NJ	54	12	17	29	22	+6
94–95	NJ–TB	41	7	11	18	25	-7
95–96	NYI	69	20	14	34	68	-4
96–97	Van	18	2	1	3	2	-2
Totals		289	83	91	174	187	+22

Playoffs

SSN	TEAM	GP	G	A	PTS.	PIM	+/-
91–92	NJ	1	0	0	0	0	
92–93	NJ	5	1	1	2	0	
93–94	NJ	2	0	0	0	0	
Totals		8	1	1	2	0	

SEMCHUK, Thomas (Brendy) 6-1 185 RW
B. Calgary, Alta., Sept. 22, 1971

SSN	TEAM	GP	G	A	PTS.	PIM	+/-
92–93	LA	1	0	0	0	2	0

SEMENKO, David 6-3 200 LW
B. Winnipeg, Man., July 12, 1957

SSN	TEAM	GP	G	A	PTS.	PIM	+/-
77–78	Edm (WHA)	65	6	6	12	140	
78–79	Edm (WHA)	77	10	14	24	158	
79–80	Edm	67	6	7	13	135	-13
80–81	Edm	58	11	8	19	80	-4
81–82	Edm	59	12	12	24	194	+7
82–83	Edm	75	12	15	27	141	+19
83–84	Edm	52	6	11	17	118	+9
84–85	Edm	69	6	12	18	172	+5
85–86	Edm	69	6	12	18	141	-1
86–87	Edm–Hart	56	4	8	12	87	-7
87–88	Tor	70	2	3	5	107	-8
NHL Totals		575	65	88	153	1175	+7
WHA Totals		142	16	20	36	298	

Playoffs

SSN	TEAM	GP	G	A	PTS.	PIM	+/-
77–78	Edm (WHA)	5	0	0	0	8	
78–79	Edm (WHA)	11	4	2	6	29	
79–80	Edm	3	0	0	0	2	
80–81	Edm	8	0	0	0	5	
81–82	Edm	4	0	0	0	2	
82–83	Edm	15	1	1	2	69	
83–84	Edm	19	5	5	10	44	
84–85	Edm	14	0	0	0	039	
85–86	Edm	6	0	0	0	32	
86–87	Hart	4	0	0	0	15	
NHL Totals		73	6	6	12	208	
WHA Totals		16	4	2	6	37	

SEMENOV, Anatoli 6-2 190 C/LW
B. Moscow, Soviet Union, Mar. 5, 1962

SSN	TEAM	GP	G	A	PTS.	PIM	+/-
90–91	Edm	57	15	16	31	26	+17
91–92	Edm	59	20	22	42	16	+12
92–93	TB–Van	75	12	37	49	32	+16
93–94	Ana	49	11	19	30	12	-4
94–95	Ana–Phil	41	4	6	10	10	-12
95–96	Phil–Ana	56	4	22	26	24	-1
96–97	Buf	25	2	4	6	2	-3
Totals		362	68	126	194	122	+25

Playoffs

SSN	TEAM	GP	G	A	PTS.	PIM	+/-
89–90	Edm	2	0	0	0	0	
90–91	Edm	12	5	5	10	6	
91–92	Edm	8	1	1	2	6	
92–93	Van	12	1	3	4	0	
94–95	Phil	15	2	4	6	0	
Totals		49	9	13	22	12	

SENICK, George 5-10 175 LW
B. Saskatoon, Sask., Sept. 16, 1929

SSN	TEAM	GP	G	A	PTS.	PIM	+/-
52–53	NYR	13	2	3	5	8	

SEPPA, Jyrki 6-1 190 D
B. Tampere, Finland, Nov. 14, 1961

SSN	TEAM	GP	G	A	PTS.	PIM	+/-
83–84	Winn	10	0	2	2	6	-9

SERAFINI, Ronald William 5-11 185 D
B. Detroit, Mich., Oct. 31, 1953

SSN	TEAM	GP	G	A	PTS.	PIM	+/-
73–74	Cal	2	0	0	0	2	-2
75–76	Cin (WHA)	16	0	2	2	15	

SEROWIK, Jeff 6-1 210 D
B. Manchester, N.H., Oct. 1, 1967

SSN	TEAM	GP	G	A	PTS.	PIM	+/-
90–91	Tor	1	0	0	0	0	0
94–95	Bos	1	0	0	0	0	+1
98–99	Pitt	26	0	6	6	16	-4
Totals		28	0	6	6	16	-3

SERVINIS, George 5-11 180 LW
B. Toronto, Ont., Apr. 29, 1962

SSN	TEAM	GP	G	A	PTS.	PIM	+/-
87–88	Minn	5	0	0	0	0	-2

SEVCIK, Jaroslav 5-9 170 LW
B. Brno, Czechoslovakia, May 15, 1965

SSN	TEAM	GP	G	A	PTS.	PIM	+/-
89–90	Que	13	0	2	2	2	-5

SEVERYN, Brent Leonard 6-2 210 D
B. Vegreville, Alta., Feb. 22, 1966

SSN	TEAM	GP	G	A	PTS.	PIM	+/-
89–90	Que	35	0	2	2	42	-19
93–94	Fla	67	4	7	11	156	-1
94–95	Fla–NYI	28	2	4	6	71	-2
95–96	NYI	65	1	8	9	180	+3
96–97	Col A	66	1	4	5	193	-6
97–98	Ana	37	1	3	4	133	-3
98–99	Dal	30	1	2	3	50	-2
Totals		328	10	30	40	825	-30

Playoffs

SSN	TEAM	GP	G	A	PTS.	PIM	+/-
96–97	Col A	8	0	0	0	12	

SEVIGNY, Pierre 6-0 195 LW
B. Trois-Rivières, Que., Sept. 8, 1971

SSN	TEAM	GP	G	A	PTS.	PIM	+/-
93–94	Mont	43	4	5	9	42	+6
94–95	Mont	19	0	0	0	15	-5
96–97	Mont	13	0	0	0	5	0
97–98	NYR	3	0	0	0	2	0

SSN	TEAM	GP	G	A	PTS.	PIM	+/-
Totals		78	4	5	9	64	+1

Playoffs

SSN	TEAM	GP	G	A	PTS.	PIM	+/-
93–94	Mont	3	0	1	1	0	

SHACK, Edward Steven Phillip *6–1 200 RW*
B. Sudbury, Ont., Feb. 11, 1937

SSN	TEAM	GP	G	A	PTS.	PIM	+/-
58–59	NYR	67	7	14	21	109	
59–60	NYR	62	8	10	18	110	
60–61	NYR–Tor	67	15	16	31	107	
61–62	Tor	44	7	14	21	62	
62–63	Tor	63	16	9	25	97	
63–64	Tor	64	11	10	21	128	
64–65	Tor	67	5	9	14	68	
65–66	Tor	63	26	17	43	88	
66–67	Tor	63	11	14	25	58	
67–68	Bos	70	23	19	42	107	+1
68–69	Bos	50	11	11	22	74	+2
69–70	LA	73	22	12	34	113	-38
70–71	LA–Buf	67	27	19	46	101	-32
71–72	Buf–Pitt	68	16	23	39	46	-6
72–73	Pitt	74	25	20	45	84	-10
73–74	Tor	59	7	8	15	74	+1
74–75	Tor	26	2	1	3	11	-8
Totals		1047	239	226	465	1437	-90

Playoffs

SSN	TEAM	GP	G	A	PTS.	PIM	+/-
60–61	Tor	4	0	0	0	2	
61–62	Tor	9	0	0	0	18	
62–63	Tor	10	2	1	3	11	
63–64	Tor	13	0	1	1	25	
64–65	Tor	5	1	0	1	8	
65–66	Tor	4	2	1	3	33	
66–67	Tor	8	0	0	0	8	
67–68	Bos	4	0	1	1	6	
68–69	Bos	9	0	2	2	23	
71–72	Pitt	4	0	1	1	15	
73–74	Tor	4	1	0	1	2	
Totals		74	6	7	13	151	

*SHACK, Joseph *5–10 170 LW*
B. Winnipeg, Man., Dec. 3, 1915

SSN	TEAM	GP	G	A	PTS.	PIM	+/-
42–43	NYR	20	5	9	14	6	
44–45	NYR	50	18	4	22	14	
Totals		70	23	13	36	20	

SHAKES, Paul Steven *5–10 172 D*
B. Collingwood, Ont., Sept. 4, 1952

SSN	TEAM	GP	G	A	PTS.	PIM	+/-
73–74	Cal	21	0	4	4	12	-13

SHALDYBIN, Yevgeny *6–1 198 D*
B. Novasbrsk, USSR, July 29, 1975

SSN	TEAM	GP	G	A	PTS.	PIM	+/-
96–97	Bos	3	1	0	1	0	-2

SHANAHAN, Brendan Frederick *6–3 215 LW*
B. Mimico, Ont., Jan. 23, 1969

SSN	TEAM	GP	G	A	PTS.	PIM	+/-
87–88	NJ	65	7	19	26	131	-20
88–89	NJ	68	22	28	50	115	+2
89–90	NJ	73	30	42	72	137	+15
90–91	NJ	75	29	37	66	141	+4
91–92	StL	80	33	36	69	171	-3
92–93	StL	71	51	43	94	174	+10
93–94	StL	81	52	50	102	211	-9
94–95	StL	45	20	21	41	136	+7
95–96	Hart	74	44	34	78	125	+2
96–97	Hart–Det	81	47	41	88	131	+32
97–98	Det	75	28	29	57	154	+6
98–99	Det	81	31	27	58	123	+2
Totals		869	394	407	801	1749	+48

Playoffs

SSN	TEAM	GP	G	A	PTS.	PIM	+/-
87–88	NJ	12	2	1	3	44	
89–90	NJ	6	3	3	6	20	
90–91	NJ	7	3	5	8	12	
91–92	StL	6	2	3	5	14	
92–93	StL	11	4	3	7	18	
93–94	StL	4	2	5	7	4	
94–95	StL	5	4	5	9	14	
96–97	Det	20	9	8	17	43	
97–98	Det	20	5	4	9	22	
98–99	Det	10	3	7	10	6	
Totals		101	37	44	81	197	

SHANAHAN, Sean Bryan *6–3 210 LW*
B. Toronto, Ont., Feb. 8, 1951

SSN	TEAM	GP	G	A	PTS.	PIM	+/-
75–76	Mont	4	0	0	0	0	-1
76–77	Col	30	1	3	4	40	-11

SSN	TEAM	GP	G	A	PTS.	PIM	+/-
77–78	Bos	6	0	0	0	7	-1
78–79	Cin (WHA)	4	0	0	0	7	
NHL Totals		40	1	3	4	47	-13
WHA Totals		4	0	0	0	7	

SHAND, David Alistair *6–2 200 D*
B. Cold Lake, Alta., Aug. 11, 1956

SSN	TEAM	GP	G	A	PTS.	PIM	+/-
76–77	Atl	55	5	11	16	62	+21
77–78	Atl	80	2	23	25	94	+23
78–79	Atl	79	4	22	26	64	+23
79–80	Atl	74	3	7	10	104	+1
80–81	Tor	47	0	4	4	60	-14
82–83	Tor	1	0	1	1	2	+2
83–84	Wash	72	4	15	19	124	+23
84–85	Wash	13	1	1	2	34	+1
Totals		421	19	84	103	544	+80

Playoffs

SSN	TEAM	GP	G	A	PTS.	PIM	+/-
76–77	Atl	3	0	0	0	33	
77–78	Atl	2	0	0	0	4	
78–79	Atl	2	0	0	0	20	
79–80	Atl	4	0	1	1	0	
80–81	tor	3	0	0	0	0	
82–83	Tor	4	1	0	1	13	
83–84	Wash	8	0	1	1	13	
Totals		16	1	2	3	83	

SHANK, Daniel *5–10 190 RW*
B. Montreal, Que., May 12, 1967

SSN	TEAM	GP	G	A	PTS.	PIM	+/-
89–90	Det	57	11	13	24	143	+1
90–91	Det	7	0	1	1	14	0
91–92	Hart	13	2	0	2	18	-4
Totals		77	13	14	27	175	-3

Playoffs

SSN	TEAM	GP	G	A	PTS.	PIM	+/-
91–92	Hart	5	0	0	0	22	

SHANNON, Charles Kitchener *5–10 192 D*
B. Campbellford, Ont., Mar. 22, 1916

SSN	TEAM	GP	G	A	PTS.	PIM	+/-
39–40	NYA	7	0	0	0	2	

SHANNON, Darrin *6–2 210 LW*
B. Barrie, Ont., Dec. 8, 1969

SSN	TEAM	GP	G	A	PTS.	PIM	+/-
88–89	Buf	3	0	0	0	0	-2
89–90	Buf	17	2	7	9	4	+6
90–91	Buf	34	8	6	14	12	-11
91–92	Buf–Winn	69	13	27	40	41	+6
92–93	Winn	84	20	40	60	91	-4
93–94	Winn	77	21	37	58	87	-18
94–95	Winn	19	5	3	8	14	-6
95–96	Winn	63	5	18	23	28	-5
96–97	Phoe	82	11	13	24	41	+4
97–98	Phoe	58	2	12	14	26	+4
Totals		506	87	163	250	344	-26

Playoffs

SSN	TEAM	GP	G	A	PTS.	PIM	+/-
88–89	Buf	2	0	0	0	0	
89–90	Buf	6	0	1	1	4	
90–91	Buf	6	1	2	3	4	
91–92	Winn	7	0	1	1	10	
92–93	Winn	6	2	4	6	6	
95–96	Winn	6	1	0	1	0	
96–97	Phoe	7	3	1	4	4	
97–98	Phoe	5	0	1	1	4	
Totals		45	7	10	17		

SHANNON, Darryl *6–2 200 D*
B. Barrie, Ont., June 21, 1968

SSN	TEAM	GP	G	A	PTS.	PIM	+/-
88–89	Tor	14	1	3	4	6	+5
89–90	Tor	10	0	1	1	12	-10
90–91	Tor	10	0	1	1	0	+1
91–92	Tor	48	2	8	10	23	-17
92–93	Tor	16	0	0	0	11	-5
93–94	Winn	20	0	4	4	18	-6
94–95	Winn	40	5	9	14	44	+15
95–96	Winn–Buf	74	4	13	17	92	+15
96–97	Buf	82	4	19	23	112	+23
97–98	Buf	75	3	19	22	56	+26
98–99	Buf	71	3	12	15	52	+28
Totals		461	22	89	111	430	+61

Playoffs

SSN	TEAM	GP	G	A	PTS.	PIM	+/-
96–97	Buf	12	2	3	5	8	
97–98	Buf	15	2	4	6	8	
98–99	Buf	2	0	0	0	0	
Totals		29	4	7	11	16	

*SHANNON, Gerald Edmund (Gerry) *5–11 170 F*
B. Campbellford, Ont., Oct. 25, 1910

SSN	TEAM	GP	G	A	PTS.	PIM	+/-
33–34	Ott	48	11	15	26	0	
34–35	StL–Bos	42	3	3	6	15	
35–36	Bos	25	0	1	1	6	
36–37	Mont M	32	9	7	16	20	
37–38	Mont M	36	0	3	3	80	
Totals		183	23	29	52	121	

Playoffs

SSN	TEAM	GP	G	A	PTS.	PIM	+/-
34–35	Bos	4	0	0	0	2	
36–37	Mont M	5	0	1	1	0	
Totals		9	0	1	1	2	

SHANTZ, Jeff *6–0 184 C*
B. Duchess, Alta., Oct. 10, 1973

SSN	TEAM	GP	G	A	PTS.	PIM	+/-
93–94	Chi	52	3	13	16	30	-14
94–95	Chi	45	6	12	18	33	+11
95–96	Chi	78	6	14	20	24	+12
96–97	Chi	69	9	21	30	28	+11
97–98	Chi	61	11	20	31	36	0
98–99	Chi–Calg	76	13	17	30	44	+14
Totals		381	48	97	145	195	+34

Playoffs

SSN	TEAM	GP	G	A	PTS.	PIM	+/-
93–94	Chi	6	0	0	0	6	
94–95	Chi	16	3	1	4	2	
95–96	Chi	10	2	3	5	6	
96–97	Chi	6	0	4	4	6	
Totals		38	5	8	13	20	

SHARIFIJANOV, Vadim *5–11 210 RW*
B. Ufa, USSR, Dec. 23, 1975

SSN	TEAM	GP	G	A	PTS.	PIM	+/-
96–97	NJ	2	0	0	0	0	0
98–99	NJ	53	11	16	27	28	+11
Totals		55	11	16	27	28	+11

Playoffs

SSN	TEAM	GP	G	A	PTS.	PIM	+/-
98–99	NJ	4	0	0	0	0	

SHARPLES, Jeff *6–1 195 D*
B. Terrace, B.C., July 28, 1967

SSN	TEAM	GP	G	A	PTS.	PIM	+/-
86–87	Det	3	0	1	1	2	0
87–88	Det	56	10	25	35	42	+13
88–89	Det	46	4	9	13	26	+5
Totals		105	14	35	49	70	+18

Playoffs

SSN	TEAM	GP	G	A	PTS.	PIM	+/-
86–87	Det	2	0	0	0	2	
87–88	Det	4	0	3	3	4	
88–89	Det	1	0	0	0	0	
Totals		7	0	3	3	6	

SHARPLEY, Glen Stuart *6–0 187 C*
B. Yotk, Ont., Sept. 6, 1956

SSN	TEAM	GP	G	A	PTS.	PIM	+/-
76–77	Minn	80	25	32	57	48	-21
77–78	Minn	79	22	33	55	42	-33
78–79	Minn	80	19	34	53	30	-18
79–80	Minn	51	20	27	47	38	-1
80–81	Minn–Chi	63	22	28	50	30	+2
81–82	Chi	36	9	7	16	11	+2
Totals		389	117	161	278	199	-69

Playoffs

SSN	TEAM	GP	G	A	PTS.	PIM	+/-
76–77	Minn	2	0	0	0	4	
79–80	Minn	9	1	6	7	4	
80–81	Chi	1	0	2	2	0	
81–82	Chi	15	6	3	9	16	
Totals		27	7	11	18	24	

SHAUNESSY, Scott *6–4 220 D/LW*
B. Newport, R.I., Jan. 22, 1964

SSN	TEAM	GP	G	A	PTS.	PIM	+/-
86–87	Que	3	0	0	0	7	-1
88–89	Que	4	0	0	0	16	0
Totals		7	0	0	0	23	-1

SHAW, Brad William *6–0 190 D*
B. Cambridge, Ont., Apr. 28, 1964

SSN	TEAM	GP	G	A	PTS.	PIM	+/-
85–86	Hart	8	0	2	2	4	-1
86–87	Hart	2	0	0	0	0	0
87–88	Hart	1	0	0	0	0	-1
88–89	Hart	3	1	0	1	0	+1
89–90	Hart	64	3	32	35	30	+2
90–91	Hart	72	4	28	32	29	-10

SSN	TEAM	GP	G	A	PTS.	PIM	+/-
91–92	Hart	62	3	22	25	44	+1
92–93	Ott	81	7	34	41	34	-47
93–94	Ott	66	4	19	23	59	-41
94–95	Ott	2	0	0	0	0	+3
98–99	Wash–StL	16	0	0	0	8	0
Totals		377	22	137	159	208	-93

Playoffs

88–89	Hart	3	1	0	1	0	
89–90	Hart	7	2	5	7	0	
90–91	Hart	6	1	2	3	2	
91–92	Hart	3	0	1	1	4	
98–99	StL	4	0	0	0	0	
Totals		23	4	8	12	6	

SHAW, David 6–2 204 D
B. St. Thomas, Ont., May 25, 1964

82–83	Que	2	0	0	0	0	-1
83–84	Que	3	0	0	0	0	+2
84–85	Que	14	0	0	0	11	-5
85–86	Que	73	7	19	26	78	+14
86–87	Que	75	0	19	19	69	-35
87–88	NYR	68	7	25	32	100	-8
88–89	NYR	63	6	11	17	88	+14
89–90	NYR	22	2	10	12	22	-3
90–91	NYR	77	2	10	12	89	+8
91–92	NYR–Edm–Minn	59	1	9	10	72	-12
92–93	Bos	77	10	14	24	108	+10
93–94	Bos	55	1	9	10	85	-11
94–95	Bos	44	3	4	7	36	-9
95–96	TB	66	1	11	12	64	+5
96–97	TB	57	1	110	11	72	+1
97–98	TB	15	0	2	2	12	-2
Totals		769	41	153	194	906	-32

Playoffs

88–89	NYR	4	0	2	2	30	
90–91	NYR	6	0	0	0	11	
91–92	Minn	7	2	2	4	10	
92–93	Bos	4	0	1	1	6	
93–94	Bos	13	1	2	3	16	
94–95	Bos	5	0	1	1	4	
95–96	TB	6	0	1	1	4	
Totals		45	3	9	12	81	

*SHAY, Norman F

24–25	Bos	18	1	1	2	14	
25–26	Bos–Tor	35	4	1	5	20	
Totals		53	5	2	7	34	

*SHEA, Francis (Pat) D
B. Potlatch, Idaho, Oct. 29, 1912

31–32	Chi	14	0	1	1	0	

SHEDDEN, Douglas Arthur 6–0 185 C
B. Wallaceburg, Ont., Apr. 29, 1961

81–82	Pitt	38	10	15	25	12	-2
82–83	Pitt	80	24	43	67	54	-20
83–84	Pitt	67	22	35	57	20	-38
84–85	Pitt	80	35	32	67	30	-51
85–86	Pitt–Det	78	34	37	71	34	-8
86–87	Det–Que	49	6	14	20	14	-2
88–89	Tor	1	0	0	0	2	-1
90–91	Tor	23	8	10	18	10	+2
Totals		416	139	186	325	176	-120

SHEEHAN, Robert Richard 5–7 155 C
B. Weymouth, Mass., Jan. 11, 1949

69–70	Mont	16	2	1	3	2	0
70–71	Mont	29	6	5	11	2	+4
71–72	Cal	78	20	26	46	12	-17
72–73	NY (WHA)	75	35	53	88	17	
73–74	NY–NJ–Edm (WHA)	60	13	11	24	14	
74–75	Edm (WHA)	77	19	39	58	8	
75–76	Chi	78	11	20	31	18	-4
76–77	Det	34	5	4	9	2	-10
77–78	Ind (WHA)	29	8	7	15	6	
79–80	Col	30	3	4	7	2	0
80–81	Col	41	1	3	4	10	-7
81–82	LA	4	0	0	0	2	-2
NHL Totals		310	48	63	111	50	-36
WHA Totals		241	75	110	185	45	

Playoffs

70–71	Mont	6	0	0	0	0	
73–74	Edm (WHA)	5	1	3	4	3	

75–76	Chi	4	0	0	0	0	
78–79	NYR	15	4	3	7	8	
NHL Totals		25	4	3	7	8	
WHA Totals		5	1	3	4	0	

SHEEHY, Neil 6–2 214 D
B. International Falls, Minn., Feb. 9, 1960

83–84	Calg	1	1	0	1	2	0
84–85	Calg	31	3	4	7	109	+5
85–86	Calg	65	2	16	18	271	-1
86–87	Calg	54	4	6	10	151	+11
87–88	Calg–Hart	62	3	10	13	189	+13
88–89	Wash	72	3	4	7	179	-1
89–90	Wash	59	1	5	6	291	+8
91–92	Calg	35	1	2	3	119	-7
Totals		379	18	47	65	1311	+28

Playoffs

83–84	Calg	4	0	0	0	4	
85–86	Calg	22	0	2	2	79	
86–87	Calg	6	0	0	0	21	
87–88	Hart	1	0	0	0	7	
88–89	Wash	6	0	0	0	19	
89–90	Wash	13	0	1	1	92	
90–91	Wash	2	0	0	0	19	
Totals		54	0	3	3	241	

SHEEHY, Timothy Kane 6–1 185 RW
B. Fort Francis, Ont., Sept. 3, 1948

72–73	NE (WHA)	78	33	38	71	30	
73–74	NE (WHA)	77	29	29	58	22	
74–75	NE–Edm (WHA)	81	28	33	61	22	
75–76	Edm (WHA)	81	34	31	65	17	
76–77	Edm–Birm (WHA)	78	41	29	70	48	
77–78	Birm–NE (WHA)	38	12	13	25	17	
77–78	Det	15	0	0	0	0	-13
79–80	Hart	12	2	1	3	0	+6
NHL Totals		27	2	1	3	0	-7
WHA Totals		433	177	173	350	156	

Playoffs

72–73	NE (WHA)	15	9	14	23	13	
75–76	Edm (WHA)	7	4	2	6	4	
77–78	NE (WHA)	13	1	3	4	9	
WHA Totals		39	16	21	37	26	

SHELTON, Wayne Douglas (Doug) 5–9 175 RW
B. Woodstock, Ont., June 27, 1945

67–68	Chi	5	0	1	1	0	-3

*SHEPPARD, Joseph Francis Xavier (Frank) 5–6 157 C
B. Montreal, Que., Oct. 19, 1907

27–28	Det	8	1	1	2	0	

SHEPPARD, Gregory Wayne 5–8 170 C
B. North Battleford, Sask., Apr. 23, 1949

72–73	Bos	64	24	26	50	18	+37
73–74	Bos	75	16	31	47	21	+23
74–75	Bos	76	30	48	78	19	+43
75–76	Bos	70	31	43	74	28	+24
76–77	Bos	77	31	36	67	20	+3
77–78	Bos	54	23	36	59	24	+19
78–79	Pitt	60	15	22	37	9	+8
79–80	Pitt	76	13	24	37	20	-72
80–81	Pitt	47	11	17	28	49	-13
81–82	Pitt	58	11	10	21	35	+9
Totals		657	205	293	498	243	+131

Playoffs

72–73	Bos	5	2	1	3	0	
73–74	Bos	16	11	8	19	4	
74–75	Bos	3	3	1	4	5	
75–76	Bos	12	5	6	11	6	
76–77	Bos	14	5	7	12	8	
77–78	Bos	15	2	10	12	6	
78–79	Pitt	7	1	2	3	0	
79–80	Pitt	5	1	1	2	0	
80–81	Pitt	5	2	4	6	2	
Totals		82	32	40	82	31	

*SHEPPARD, Jake O. (Johnny) 5–7 165 LW
B. Montreal, Que., Oct. 19, 1907

26–27	Det	43	13	8	21	60	
27–28	Det	44	10	10	20	40	
28–29	NYA	43	5	4	9	38	
29–30	NYA	43	14	15	29	32	
30–31	NYA	42	5	8	13	16	
31–32	NYA	8	1	0	1	2	
32–33	NYA	46	17	9	26	32	
33–34	Bos–Chi	42	3	4	7	4	
Totals		311	68	58	126	224	

Playoffs

28–29	NYA	2	0	0	0	0	
33–34	Chi	8	0	0	0	0	
Totals		10	0	0	0	0	

SHEPPARD, Ray 6–1 195 RW
B. Pembroke, Ont., May 27, 1966

87–88	Buf	74	38	27	65	14	-6
88–89	Buf	67	22	21	43	15	-7
89–90	Buf	18	4	2	6	0	+3
90–91	NYR	59	24	23	47	21	+8
91–92	Det	74	36	26	62	27	+7
92–93	Det	70	32	34	66	29	+7
93–94	Det	82	52	41	93	26	+13
94–95	Det	43	30	10	40	17	+11
95–96	Det–SJ–Fla	70	37	23	60	16	-19
96–97	Fla	68	29	31	60	4	+4
97–98	Fla–Car	71	18	19	37	23	-11
98–99	Car	74	25	33	58	16	+4
Totals		770	347	290	637	208	+14

Playoffs

87–88	Buf	6	1	1	2	2	
88–89	Buf	1	0	1	1	0	
91–92	Det	11	6	2	8	4	
94–93	Det	7	2	3	5	0	
93–94	Det	7	2	1	3	4	
94–95	Det	17	4	3	7	5	
95–96	Fla	21	8	8	16	4	
96–97	Fla	5	2	0	2	0	
98–99	Carr	6	5	1	6	2	
Totals		81	30	20	50	21	

*SHERF, John Harold 5–11 178 LW
B. Calumet, Mich., Apr. 8, 1914

35–36	Det	1	0	0	0	0	
36–37	Det	1	0	0	0	0	
37–38	Det	6	0	0	0	2	
38–39	Det	3	0	0	0	0	
43–44	Det	8	0	0	0	6	
Totals		19	0	0	0	8	

Playoffs

36–37	Det	5	0	1	1	2	
38–39	Det	3	0	0	0	0	
Totals		8	0	1	1	2	

*SHERO, Frederick Alexander (Fog) 5–10 185 D
B. Winnipeg, Man., Oct. 23, 1925

47–48	NYR	19	1	0	1	2	
48–49	NYR	59	3	6	9	64	
49–50	NYR	67	2	8	10	71	
Totals		145	6	14	20	137	

Playoffs

47–48	NYR	6	0	1	1	6	
49–50	NYR	7	0	1	1	2	
Totals		13	0	2	2	8	

SHERRITT, Gordon Ephraim (Moose) 6–1 195 D
B. Oakville, Man., Apr. 8, 1922

43–44	Det	8	0	0	0	12	

SHERVEN, Gord 6–0 185 C
B. Gravelbourg, Sask., Aug. 21, 1963

83–84	Edm	2	1	0	1	0	+1
84–85	Edm–Minn	69	11	19	30	18	+1
85–86	Minn–Edm	18	1	3	4	15	+1
86–87	Hart	7	0	0	0	0	-6
87–88	Hart	1	0	0	0	0	0
Totals		97	13	22	35	33	-3

Playoffs

84–85	Minn	3	0	0	0	0	

SHEVALIER, Jeff 5–11 185 LW
B. Mississauga, Ont., Mar. 14, 1974

94–95	LA	1	1	0	1	0	+1
96–97	LA	26	4	9	13	6	-6
Totals		27	5	9	14	6	-5

*SHEWCHUK, John Michael (Jack) 6–1 190 D
B. Brantford, Ont., June 19, 1917

38–39	Bos	3	0	0	0	2	
39–40	Bos	47	2	4	6	55	
40–41	Bos	20	2	2	4	8	
41–42	Bos	22	2	0	2	14	
42–43	Bos	48	2	6	8	50	
44–45	Bos	47	1	7	8	31	
Totals		187	9	19	28	160	

Playoffs

39–40	Bos	6	0	0	0	0	
41–42	Bos	5	0	1	1	7	
42–43	Bos	9	0	0	0	12	
Totals		20	0	1	1	19	

SHIBICKY, Alexi (Alex) 6–0 180 RW
B. Winnipeg, Man., May 19, 1914

35–36	NYR	18	4	2	6	6	
36–37	NYR	47	14	8	22	30	
37–38	NYR	43	17	18	35	26	
38–39	NYR	48	24	9	33	24	
39–40	NYR	43	11	21	32	33	
40–41	NYR	40	10	14	24	14	
41–42	NYR	45	20	14	34	16	
45–46	NYR	33	10	5	15	12	
Totals		317	110	91	201	161	

Playoffs

36–37	NYR	9	1	4	5	0	
37–38	NYR	3	2	0	2	2	
38–39	NYR	7	3	1	4	2	
39–40	NYR	12	2	5	7	4	
40–41	NYR	3	1	0	1	2	
41–42	NYR	6	3	2	5	2	
Totals		40	12	12	24	12	

*SHIELDS, Allen 6–0 188 D
B. Ottawa, Ont., May 10, 1907

27–28	Ott	6	0	1	1	2	
28–29	Ott	42	0	1	1	10	
29–30	Ott	44	6	3	9	32	
30–31	Phil Q	43	7	3	10	98	
31–32	NYA	48	4	1	5	45	
32–33	Ott	48	4	7	11	119	
33–34	Ott	48	4	7	11	44	
34–35	Mont M	43	4	8	12	45	
35–36	Mont M	45	2	7	9	81	
36–37	NYA–Bos	45	3	4	7	94	
37–38	Mont M	48	5	7	12	67	
Totals		460	39	49	88	637	
27–28	Ott	2	0	0	0	0	
29–30	Ott	2	0	0	0	0	
34–35	Mont M	7	0	1	1	6	
35–36	Mont M	3	0	0	0	6	
36–37	Bos	3	0	0	0	2	
Totals		17	0	1	1	14	

*SHILL, John Walker (Jack) 5–8 175 D
B. Toronto, Ont., Jan. 12, 1913

33–34	Tor	7	0	1	1	0	
34–35	Bos	45	4	4	8	22	
35–36	Tor	3	0	1	1	0	
36–37	Tor	32	4	4	8	26	
37–38	NYA–Chi	48	5	6	11	18	
38–39	Chi	28	2	4	6	4	
Totals		163	15	20	35	70	

Playoffs

33–34	Tor	2	0	0	0	0	
34–35	Bos	4	0	0	0	0	
35–36	Tor	9	0	3	3	8	
36–37	Tor	2	0	0	0	0	
37–38	Chi	10	1	3	4	5	
Totals		27	1	6	7	13	

SHILL, William Roy 6–1 175 RW
B. Toronto, Ont., Mar. 6, 1923

42–43	Bos	7	4	1	5	4	
45–46	Bos	45	15	12	27	12	
46–47	Bos	27	2	0	2	2	
Totals		79	21	13	34	18	

Playoffs

45–46	Bos	7	1	2	3	2	

SHINSKE, Richard Charles (Rick) 5–11 165 C
B. Weyburn, Sask., May 31, 1955

76–77	Clev	5	0	0	0	2	-4
77–78	Clev	47	5	12	17	6	-12
78–79	StL	11	0	4	4	2	-3
Totals		63	5	16	21	10	-19

SHIRES, James Arthur 6–0 180 LW
B. Edmonton, Alta., Nov. 15, 1945

70–71	Det	20	2	1	3	22	-3
71–72	StL	18	0	3	3	8	-13
72–73	Pitt	18	1	2	3	2	-8
Totals		56	3	6	9	32	-24

SHMYR, Paul 5–11 170 D
B. Cudworth, Sask., Jan. 28, 1946

68–69	Chi	3	1	0	1	8	0
69–70	Chi	24	0	4	4	26	+11
70–71	Chi	57	1	12	13	41	+3
71–72	Cal	69	6	21	27	156	-27
72–73	Clev (WHA)	73	5	43	48	169	
73–74	Clev (WHA)	78	13	31	44	165	
74–75	Clev (WHA)	49	7	14	21	103	
75–76	Clev (WHA)	70	6	44	50	101	
76–77	SD (WHA)	81	13	37	50	103	
77–78	Edm (WHA)	80	9	40	49	100	
78–79	Edm (WHA)	80	8	39	47	119	
79–80	Minn	63	3	15	18	84	+25
80–81	Minn	61	1	9	10	79	+4
81–82	Hart	66	1	11	12	134	-11
NHL Totals		343	13	72	85	528	+5
WHA Totals		511	61	248	309	860	

Playoffs

69–70	Chi	8	1	2	3	0	
70–71	Chi	9	0	0	0	17	
72–73	Clev (WHA)	8	1	3	4	19	
73–74	Clev (WHA)	5	0	4	4	31	
74–75	Clev (WHA)	5	2	1	3	15	
76–77	SD (WHA)	7	0	2	2	8	
77–78	Edm (WHA)	5	1	3	4	11	
78–79	Edm (WHA)	13	1	5	6	23	
79–80	Minn	14	2	1	3	23	
80–81	Minn	3	0	0	0	4	
NHL Totals		34	3	3	6	44	
WHA Totals		43	5	18	23	107	

SHOEBOTTOM, Bruce 6–2 200 D
B. Windsor, Ont., Aug. 20, 1965

87–88	Bos	3	0	1	1	0	-3
88–89	Bos	29	1	3	4	44	+5
89–90	Bos	2	0	0	0	4	0
90–91	Bos	1	0	0	0	5	-1
Totals		35	1	4	5	53	+1

Playoffs

87–88	Bos	4	1	0	1	42	
88–89	Bos	10	0	2	2	35	
Totals		14	1	2	3	77	

*SHORE, Edward William 5–11 190 D
B. Ft. Qu'Appelle, Sask., Nov. 25, 1902

26–27	Bos	41	12	6	18	130	
27–28	Bos	44	11	6	17	165	
28–29	Bos	39	12	7	19	96	
29–30	Bos	43	12	19	31	105	
30–31	Bos	44	15	16	31	105	
31–32	Bos	44	9	13	22	80	
32–33	Bos	48	8	27	35	102	
33–34	Bos	30	2	10	12	57	
34–35	Bos	48	7	26	33	32	
35–36	Bos	46	3	16	19	61	
36–37	Bos	19	3	1	4	12	
37–38	Bos	47	3	14	17	42	
38–39	Bos	46	4	14	18	47	
39–40	Bos–NYA	14	4	4	8	13	
Totals		553	105	179	284	1047	

Playoffs

26–27	Bos	8	1	1	2	46	
27–28	Bos	2	0	0	0	8	
28–29	Bos	5	1	1	2	28	
29–30	Bos	6	1	0	1	26	
30–31	Bos	5	2	1	3	24	
32–33	Bos	5	0	1	1	14	
34–35	Bos	4	0	1	1	2	
35–36	Bos	2	1	1	2	12	
37–38	Bos	3	0	1	1	6	
38–39	Bos	12	0	4	4	19	
39–40	NYA	3	0	2	2	2	
Totals		55	6	13	19	187	

*SHORE, Sam Hamilton (Hamby) LW
B. Ottawa, Ont., 1886

17–18	Ott	18	3	0	3	0	

SHORES, Aubrey F

30–31	Phil Q	1	0	0	0	0	

SHORT, Steven 6–2 210 LW
B. Roseville, Minn., Apr. 6, 1954

77–78	LA	5	0	0	0	2	-5
78–79	Det	1	0	0	0	0	0
Totals		6	0	0	0	2	-5

SHUCHUK, Gary Robert 5–11 190 RW
B. Edmonton, Alta., Feb. 17, 1967

90–91	Det	6	1	2	3	6	+1
92–93	LA	25	2	4	6	16	0
93–94	LA	56	3	4	7	30	-8
94–95	LA	22	3	6	9	6	-2
95–96	LA	33	4	10	14	12	+3
Totals		142	13	26	39	70	-6

Playoffs

90–91	Det	3	0	0	0	0	
92–93	LA	17	2	2	4	12	
Totals		20	2	2	4	12	

SHUDRA, Ron 6–2 192 D
B. Winnipeg, Man., Nov. 28, 1967

87–88	Edm	10	0	5	5	6	+5

SHUTT, Stephen John 5–11 185 LW
B. Toronto, Ont., July 1, 1952

72–73	Mont	50	8	8	16	24	+5
73–74	Mont	70	15	20	35	17	+19
74–75	Mont	77	30	35	65	40	+40
75–76	Mont	80	45	34	79	47	+73
76–77	Mont	80	60	45	105	28	+88
77–78	Mont	80	49	37	86	24	+56
78–79	Mont	72	37	40	87	31	+37
79–80	Mont	77	47	42	89	34	+45
80–81	Mont	77	35	38	73	51	+30
81–82	Mont	57	31	24	55	40	+24
82–83	Mont	78	35	22	57	26	+8
83–84	Mont	63	14	23	37	29	-18
84–85	Mont–LA	69	18	25	43	19	-14
Totals		930	424	393	817	410	+393

Playoffs

72–73	Mont	1	0	0	0	0	
73–74	Mont	6	5	3	8	9	
74–75	Mont	9	1	6	7	4	
75–76	Mont	13	7	8	15	2	
76–77	Mont	14	8	10	18	2	
77–78	Mont	11	4	7	11	6	
78–79	Mont	10	6	3	9	6	
80–81	Mont	3	2	1	3	4	
82–83	Mont	3	1	0	1	0	
83–84	Mont	11	7	2	9	8	
84–85	LA	3	0	0	0	4	
Totals		99	50	48	98	65	

*SIEBERT, Albert Charles (Babe) 5–10 182 LW
B. Plattsville, Que., Jan. 14, 1904

25–26	Mont M	35	16	8	24	108	
26–27	Mont M	42	5	3	8	116	
27–28	Mont M	40	8	9	17	109	
28–29	Mont M	39	3	5	8	82	
29–30	Mont M	41	14	19	33	94	
30–31	Mont M	42	16	12	28	76	

SSN	TEAM	GP	G	A	PTS.	PIM	+/-
31–32	Mont M	48	21	18	39	64	
32–33	NYR	42	9	10	19	38	
33–34	NYR–Bos	45	5	7	12	49	
34–35	Bos	48	6	18	24	80	
35–36	Bos	46	12	9	21	66	
36–37	Mont	44	8	20	28	38	
37–38	Mont	37	8	11	19	56	
38–39	Mont	44	9	7	16	26	
Totals		593	140	156	296	1002	

Playoffs

SSN	TEAM	GP	G	A	PTS.	PIM	+/-
25–26	Mont M	8	2	2	4	6	
26–27	Mont M	2	1	0	1	2	
27–28	Mont M	9	2	0	2	28	
29–30	Mont M	2	0	0	0	0	
30–31	Mont M	2	0	0	0	4	
31–32	Mont M	4	0	1	1	4	
32–33	NYR	8	1	0	1	12	
34–35	Bos	4	0	0	0	6	
35–36	Bos	2	0	1	1	0	
36–37	Mont	5	1	2	3	2	
37–38	Mont	3	1	1	2	0	
38–39	Mont	3	0	0	0	0	
Totals		52	8	7	15	64	

SILK, David 5–11 190 RW
B. Scituate, Mass., Jan. 1, 1958

SSN	TEAM	GP	G	A	PTS.	PIM	+/-
79–80	NYR	2	0	0	0	0	+1
80–81	NYR	59	14	12	26	58	-24
81–82	NYR	64	15	20	35	39	+17
82–83	NYR	16	1	1	2	15	-3
83–84	Bos	35	13	17	30	64	+11
84–85	Bos–Det	41	9	5	14	32	-3
85–86	Winn	32	2	4	6	63	-6
Totals		249	54	59	113	271	-7

Playoffs

SSN	TEAM	GP	G	A	PTS.	PIM
81–82	NYR	9	2	4	6	4
83–84	Bos	3	0	0	0	7
85–86	Winn	1	0	0	0	2
Totals		13	2	4	6	13

SILLINGER, Mike 5–10 191 C
B. Regina, Sask., June 29, 1971

SSN	TEAM	GP	G	A	PTS.	PIM	+/-
90–91	Det	3	0	1	1	0	-2
92–93	Det	51	4	17	21	16	0
93–94	Det	62	8	21	29	10	+2
94–95	Det–Ana	28	4	11	15	8	+4
95–96	Ana–Van	74	14	24	38	38	-18
96–97	Van	78	17	20	37	25	-3
97–98	Van–Phil	75	21	20	41	50	-11
98–99	Phil–TB	79	8	5	13	36	-29
Totals		450	76	119	195	183	-57

Playoffs

SSN	TEAM	GP	G	A	PTS.	PIM
90–91	Det	3	0	1	1	0
91–92	Det	8	2	2	4	2
95–96	Van	6	0	0	0	2
97–98	Phil	3	1	0	1	0
Totals		20	3	3	6	4

SILTALA, Michael 5–9 170 RW
B. Toronto, Ont., Aug. 5, 1963

SSN	TEAM	GP	G	A	PTS.	PIM	+/-
81–82	Wash	3	1	0	1	2	-1
86–87	NYR	1	0	0	0	0	+1
87–88	NYR	3	0	0	0	2	0
Totals		7	1	0	1	2	0

SILTANEN, Risto 5–9 180 D
B. Tampere, Finland, Oct. 31, 1958

SSN	TEAM	GP	G	A	PTS.	PIM	+/-
78–79	Edm (WHA)	20	3	4	7	4	
79–80	Edm	64	6	29	35	26	-9
80–81	Edm	79	17	36	53	54	+5
81–82	Edm	63	15	48	63	26	+13
82–83	Hart	74	5	25	30	28	-39
83–84	Hart	75	15	38	53	34	-21
84–85	Hart	76	12	33	45	30	-24
85–86	Hart–Que	65	10	27	37	36	+1
86–87	Que	66	10	29	39	32	-2
NHL Totals		562	90	265	355	266	-76
WHA Totals		20	3	4	7	4	

Playoffs

SSN	TEAM	GP	G	A	PTS.	PIM
78–79	Edm (WHA)	11	0	9	9	4
79–80	Edm	2	0	0	0	2
80–81	Edm	9	2	0	2	8
81–82	Edm	5	3	2	5	10

SSN	TEAM	GP	G	A	PTS.	PIM	+/-
85–86	Que	3	0	1	1	2	
86–87	Que	13	1	9	10	8	
NHL Totals		32	3	12	18	30	
WHA Totals		11	0	9	9	4	

SIM, Jonathan 5–9 175 C
B. New Glasgow, N.S., Sept. 29, 1977

SSN	TEAM	GP	G	A	PTS.	PIM	+/-
98–99	Dal	7	1	0	1	12	+1

Playoffs

SSN	TEAM	GP	G	A	PTS.	PIM
98–99	Dal	4	0	0	0	0

SIM, Trevor 6–2 192 RW
B. Calgary, Alta., June 9, 1970

SSN	TEAM	GP	G	A	PTS.	PIM	+/-
89–90	Edm	3	0	1	1	2	0

SIMARD, Martin 6–1 215 RW
B. Montreal, Que., June 25, 1966

SSN	TEAM	GP	G	A	PTS.	PIM	+/-
90–91	Calg	16	0	2	2	53	0
91–92	Calg	21	1	3	4	119	-4
92–93	TB	7	0	0	0	11	-1
Totals		44	1	5	6	183	-5

SIMMER, Charles Robert 6–3 210 LW
B. Terrace Bay, Ont., Mar. 20, 1954

SSN	TEAM	GP	G	A	PTS.	PIM	+/-
74–75	Cal	35	8	13	21	26	-2
75–76	Cal	21	1	1	2	22	-9
76–77	Clev	24	2	0	2	16	-11
77–78	LA	3	0	0	0	2	0
78–79	LA	38	21	27	48	16	+9
79–80	LA	64	56	45	101	65	+47
80–81	LA	65	56	49	105	62	+31
81–82	LA	50	15	24	39	42	-7
82–83	LA	80	29	51	80	51	0
83–84	LA	79	44	48	92	78	+7
84–85	LA–Bos	68	34	30	64	39	+10
85–86	Bos	55	36	24	60	42	+12
86–87	Bos	80	29	40	69	59	+20
87–88	Pitt	50	11	17	28	24	+6
Totals		712	342	369	711	544	+113

Playoffs

SSN	TEAM	GP	G	A	PTS.	PIM
78–79	LA	2	1	0	1	2
79–80	LA	3	2	0	2	0
81–82	LA	10	4	7	11	22
84–85	Bos	5	2	2	4	2
85–86	Bos	3	0	0	0	4
86–87	Bos	1	0	0	0	2
Totals		24	9	9	18	32

SIMMONS, Allan Kenneth 6–0 170 D
B. Winnipeg, Man., Sept. 25, 1951

SSN	TEAM	GP	G	A	PTS.	PIM	+/-
71–72	Cal	1	0	0	0	0	-1
73–74	Bos	3	0	0	0	0	-1
75–76	Bos	7	0	1	1	21	0
Totals		11	0	1	1	21	-2

Playoffs

SSN	TEAM	GP	G	A	PTS.	PIM
73–74	Bos	1	0	0	0	0

SIMON, Chris 6–3 219 LW
B. Wawa, Ont., Jan. 30, 1972

SSN	TEAM	GP	G	A	PTS.	PIM	+/-
92–93	Que	16	1	1	2	67	-2
93–94	Que	37	4	4	8	132	-2
94–95	Que	29	3	9	12	106	+14
95–96	Col A	64	16	18	34	250	+10
96–97	Wash	42	9	13	22	165	-1
97–98	Wash	28	7	10	17	38	-1
98–99	Wash	23	3	7	10	48	-4
Totals		239	43	62	105	806	+14

Playoffs

SSN	TEAM	GP	G	A	PTS.	PIM
92–93	Que	5	0	0	0	26
94–95	Que	6	1	1	2	19
95–96	Col A	12	1	2	3	11
97–98	Wash	18	1	0	1	26
Totals		41	3	3	6	82

SIMON, Jason 6–1 190 LW
B. Sarnia, Ont., Mar. 21, 1969

SSN	TEAM	GP	G	A	PTS.	PIM	+/-
93–94	NYI	4	0	0	0	34	0
96–97	Phoe	1	0	0	0	0	-1
Totals		5	0	0	0	34	-1

*SIMON, John Cullen (Cully) 5–10 190 D
B. Brockville, Ont., May 8, 1918

SSN	TEAM	GP	G	A	PTS.	PIM
42–43	Det	34	1	1	2	34
43–44	Det	46	3	7	10	52
44–45	Det–Chi	50	0	3	3	35
Totals		130	4	11	15	21

Playoffs

SSN	TEAM	GP	G	A	PTS.	PIM
42–43	Det	9	0	1	1	4
43–44	Det	5	0	0	0	2
Totals		14	0	1	1	6

SIMON, Thain Andrew 6–0 200 D
B. Brockville, Ont., Apr. 24, 1922

SSN	TEAM	GP	G	A	PTS.	PIM
46–47	Det	3	0	0	0	0

SIMON, Todd 5–10 188 C
B. Toronto, Ont., Apr. 21, 1972

SSN	TEAM	GP	G	A	PTS.	PIM
93–94	Buf	15	0	1	1	0

Playoffs

SSN	TEAM	GP	G	A	PTS.	PIM
93–94	Buf	5	1	0	1	0

SIMONETTI, Frank 6–1 190 D
B. Melrose, Mass., Sept. 11, 1962

SSN	TEAM	GP	G	A	PTS.	PIM	+/-
84–85	Bos	43	1	5	6	26	-1
85–86	Bos	17	1	0	1	14	-1
86–87	Bos	25	1	0	1	17	-6
87–88	Bos	30	2	3	5	19	+1
Totals		115	5	8	13	76	-7

Playoffs

SSN	TEAM	GP	G	A	PTS.	PIM
84–85	Bos	5	0	1	1	2
85–86	Bos	3	0	0	0	0
86–87	Bos	4	0	0	0	6
Totals		12	0	1	1	8

*SIMPSON, Clifford Vernon 5–11 175 C
B. Toronto, Ont., Apr. 4, 1923

SSN	TEAM	GP	G	A	PTS.	PIM
46–47	Det	6	0	1	1	0

Playoffs

SSN	TEAM	GP	G	A	PTS.	PIM
46–47	Det	1	0	0	0	0
47–48	Det	1	0	0	0	2
Totals		2	0	0	0	2

SIMPSON, Craig Andrew 6–2 195 LW
B. London, Ont., Feb. 15, 1967

SSN	TEAM	GP	G	A	PTS.	PIM	+/-
85–86	Pitt	76	11	17	28	49	+1
86–87	Pitt	72	26	25	51	57	+1
87–88	Pitt–Edm	80	56	34	90	77	+20
88–89	Edm	66	35	41	76	80	-3
89–90	Edm	80	29	32	61	180	-2
90–91	Edm	75	30	27	57	66	-8
91–92	Edm	79	24	37	61	80	+8
92–93	Edm	60	24	22	46	36	-14
93–94	Buf	22	8	8	16	8	-3
94–95	Buf	24	4	7	11	26	-5
Totals		634	247	250	497	659	+5

Playoffs

SSN	TEAM	GP	G	A	PTS.	PIM
87–88	Edm	19	13	6	19	26
88–89	Edm	7	2	0	2	10
89–90	Edm	22	16	15	31	8
90–91	Edm	18	5	11	16	12
91–92	Edm	1	0	0	0	0
Totals		67	36	32	68	56

*SIMPSON, Harold Joseph (Bullet Joe) D
B. Selkirk, Man., Aug. 13, 1893

SSN	TEAM	GP	G	A	PTS.	PIM
25–26	NYA	32	2	2	4	2
26–27	NYA	43	4	2	6	39
27–28	NYA	24	2	0	2	32
28–29	NYA	43	3	2	5	29
29–30	NYA	44	8	13	21	41
30–31	NYA	42	2	0	2	13
Totals		228	21	19	40	156

Playoffs

SSN	TEAM	GP	G	A	PTS.	PIM
28–29	Bos	2	0	0	0	0

SIMPSON, Reid 6–1 211 LW
B. Flin Flon, Man., May 21, 1969

SSN	TEAM	GP	G	A	PTS.	PIM	+/-
91–92	Phil	1	0	0	0	0	0
92–93	Minn	1	0	0	0	5	0
94–95	NJ	9	0	0	0	27	

SSN	TEAM	GP	G	A	PTS.	PIM	+/-
95–96	NJ	23	1	5	6	79	+2
96–97	NJ	27	0	4	4	60	0
97–98	NJ–Chi	44	3	2	5	118	-3
98–99	Chi	53	5	4	9	145	+2
Totals		158	9	15	24	280	0

Playoffs

| 96–97 | NJ | 5 | 0 | 0 | 0 | 29 | |

SIMPSON, Robert (Bobby) 6–0 190 LW
B. Caughnawa, Que., Nov. 17, 1956

76–77	Atl	72	13	10	23	45	+2
77–78	Atl	55	10	8	18	49	0
79–80	StL	18	2	2	4	0	-2
81–82	Pitt	26	9	9	18	4	-3
82–83	Pitt	4	1	0	1	0	-1
Totals		175	35	29	64	98	-4

Playoffs

76–77	Atl	2	0	1	1	0	
77–78	Atl	2	0	0	0	2	
81–82	Pitt	2	0	0	0	0	
Totals		6	0	1	1	2	

SIMPSON, Todd 6–3 215 D
B. Edmonton, Alta., May 28, 1973

95–96	Calg	6	0	0	0	32	0
96–97	Calg	82	1	13	14	208	-14
97–98	Calg	53	1	5	6	109	-10
98–99	Calg	73	2	8	10	151	+18
Totals		214	4	26	30	500	-6

SIMMS, Allan Eugene 6–0 180 D
B. Toronto, Ont., Apr. 18, 1953

73–74	Bos	77	3	9	12	22	+64
74–75	Bos	75	4	8	12	73	+29
75–76	Bos	48	4	3	7	43	+6
76–77	Bos	1	0	0	0	0	0
77–78	Bos	43	2	8	10	6	+11
78–79	Bos	67	9	20	29	28	+22
79–80	Hart	76	10	31	41	30	+9
80–81	Hart	80	16	36	52	68	-20
81–82	LA	8	1	1	2	16	-3
82–83	LA	1	0	0	0	0	0
Totals		476	49	116	165	384	+119

Playoffs

73–74	Bos	16	0	0	0	12	
76–77	Bos	2	0	0	0	0	
77–78	Bos	8	0	0	0	0	
78–79	Bos	11	0	2	2	0	
79–80	Hart	3	0	0	0	2	
Totals		40	0	2	2	14	

SINCLAIR, Reginald Alexander (Reg) 6–0 165 RW
B. Lachine, Que., Mar. 6, 1925

50–51	NYR	70	18	21	39	70	
51–52	NYR	69	20	10	30	33	
52–53	Det	69	11	12	23	36	
Totals		208	49	43	92	139	

Playoffs

| 52–53 | Det | 3 | 1 | 0 | 1 | 0 | |

***SINGBUSH, E. Alexander (Alex)** D
B. Winnipeg, Man., 1915

| 40–41 | Mont | 32 | 0 | 5 | 5 | 15 | |

Playoffs

| 40–41 | Mont | 3 | 0 | 0 | 0 | 4 | |

SINISALO, Ilkka 6–0 185 RW
B. Valeakoski, Finland, July 10, 1958

81–82	Phil	66	15	22	37	22	+18
82–83	Phil	61	21	29	50	16	+18
83–84	Phil	73	29	17	46	29	+22
84–85	Phil	70	36	37	73	16	+32
85–86	Phil	74	39	37	76	31	+17
86–87	Phil	42	10	21	31	8	+14
87–88	Phil	68	25	17	42	30	+2
88–89	Phil	13	1	6	7	2	+6
89–90	Phil	59	23	23	46	26	+6
90–91	Minn–LA	53	5	12	17	26	-6
91–92	LA	3	0	1	1	2	0
Totals		582	204	222	426	208	+129

Playoffs

81–82	Phil	4	0	2	2	0	
82–83	Phil	3	1	1	2	0	
83–84	Phil	2	2	0	2	0	
84–85	Phil	19	6	1	7	0	
85–86	Phil	5	2	2	4	2	
86–87	Phil	18	5	1	6	4	
87–88	Phil	7	4	2	6	0	
88–89	Phil	8	1	1	2	0	
90–91	LA	2	0	1	1	0	
Totals		68	21	11	32	6	

SIREN, Ville 6–2 191 D
B. Tampere, Finland, Feb. 11, 1964

85–86	Pitt	60	4	8	12	32	-8
86–87	Pitt	69	5	17	22	50	+8
87–88	Pitt	58	1	20	21	62	+14
88–89	Pitt–Minn	50	3	10	13	72	0
89–90	Minn	53	1	13	14	60	+1
Totals		290	14	68	82	276	+15

Playoffs

88–89	Minn	4	0	0	0	4	
89–90	Minn	3	0	0	0	2	
Totals		7	0	0	0	6	

SIROIS, Robert 6–0 178 RW
B. Montreal, Que., Feb. 6, 1954

74–75	Phil	3	1	0	1	4	+2
75–76	Phil–Wash	44	10	19	29	6	-33
76–77	Wash	45	13	22	35	2	+1
77–78	Wash	72	24	37	61	6	-11
78–79	Wash	73	29	25	54	6	-6
79–80	Wash	49	15	17	32	18	-5
Totals		286	92	120	212	42	-53

SITTLER, Darryl Glen 6–0 190 C
B. Kitchener, Ont., Sept. 18, 1950

70–71	Tor	49	10	8	18	37	+3
71–72	Tor	74	15	17	32	44	-4
72–73	Tor	78	29	48	77	69	-11
73–74	Tor	78	38	46	84	55	+12
74–75	Tor	72	36	44	80	47	-10
75–76	Tor	79	41	59	100	90	+12
76–77	Tor	73	38	52	90	89	+8
77–78	Tor	80	45	72	117	100	+34
78–79	Tor	70	36	51	87	69	+9
79–80	Tor	73	40	57	97	62	+3
80–81	Tor	80	43	53	96	77	-8
81–82	Tor–Phil	73	32	38	70	74	-15
82–83	Phil	80	43	40	83	60	+17
83–84	Phil	76	27	36	63	38	+13
84–85	Det	61	11	16	27	37	-10
Totals		1096	484	637	1121	948	+53

Playoffs

70–71	Tor	6	2	1	3	31	
71–72	Tor	3	0	0	0	2	
73–74	Tor	4	2	1	3	6	
74–75	Tor	7	2	1	3	15	
75–76	Tor	10	5	7	12	19	
76–77	Tor	9	5	16	21	4	
77–78	Tor	13	3	8	11	12	
78–79	Tor	6	5	4	9	17	
79–80	Tor	3	1	2	3	10	
80–81	Tor	3	0	0	0	4	
81–82	Phil	4	3	1	4	6	
82–83	Phil	3	1	0	1	4	
83–84	Phil	3	0	2	2	7	
84–85	Det	2	0	2	2	0	
Totals		76	29	45	74	137	

***SJOBERG, Lars–Erik** 5–8 179 D
B. Falun, Sweden, Apr. 5, 1944

74–75	Winn (WHA)	75	7	53	60	30	
75–76	Winn (WHA)	81	5	36	41	12	
76–77	Winn (WHA)	52	2	38	40	31	
77–78	Winn (WHA)	78	11	39	50	72	
78–79	Winn (WHA)	9	0	3	3	2	
79–80	Winn	79	7	27	34	48	-35
NHL Totals		79	7	27	34	48	-35
WHA Totals		295	25	169	194	147	

Playoffs

75–76	Winn (WHA)	13	0	5	5	12	
76–77	Winn (WHA)	20	0	6	6	22	
77–78	Winn (WHA)	9	0	9	9	4	
78–79	Winn (WHA)	10	1	2	3	4	
WHA Totals		52	1	22	23	42	

SJODIN, Tommy 5–11 190 D
B. Timra, Sweden, Aug. 13, 1965

92–93	Minn	77	7	29	36	30	-25
93–94	Dal–Que	29	1	11	12	22	+4
Totals		106	8	40	48	52	-21

***SKAARE, Bjorne** 6–0 180 C
B. Oslo, Norway, Oct. 29, 1948

| 78–79 | Det | 1 | 0 | 0 | 0 | 0 | 0 |

SKALDE, Jarrod 6–0 170 C
B. Niagara Falls, Ont., Feb. 26, 1971

90–91	NJ	1	0	1	1	0	0
91–92	NJ	15	2	4	6	4	-1
92–93	NJ	11	0	2	2	4	-3
93–94	Ana	20	5	4	9	10	-3
95–96	Calg	1	0	0	0	0	0
97–98	Chi	30	4	7	11	18	-2
98–99	SJ	17	1	1	2	4	-6
Totals		95	12	19	31	40	-15

SKARDA, Randy 6–1 205 D
B. St. Paul, Minn., May 5, 1968

89–90	StL	25	0	5	5	11	+2
91–92	StL	1	0	0	0	0	0
Totals		26	0	5	5	11	+2

***SKILTON, Raymond (Raymie)** D

| 17–18 | Mont W | 1 | 1 | 0 | 1 | 0 | |

***SKINNER, Alfred (Alf)** RW

17–18	Tor	19	13	0	13	20	
18–19	Tor	17	12	3	15	26	
24–25	Bos–Mont M	27	1	1	2	28	
25–26	Pitt Pi	7	0	0	0	2	
Totals		70	26	4	30	76	

Playoffs

| 17–18 | Tor | 7 | 8 | 1 | 9 | 0 | |

SKINNER, Laurence Foster (Larry) 5–11 180 C
B. Vancouver, B.C., Apr. 21, 1956

76–77	Col	19	4	5	9	6	-13
77–78	Col	14	3	5	8	0	+2
78–79	Col	12	3	2	5	2	-5
79–80	Col	2	0	0	0	0	-2
Totals		47	10	12	22	8	-18

Playoffs

| 77–78 | Col | 2 | 0 | 0 | 0 | 0 | |

SKOPINTSEV, Andrei 6–0 185 D
B. Elekrostal, USSR, Sept. 28, 1971

| 98–99 | TB | 19 | 1 | 1 | 2 | 10 | +1 |

SKOV, Glen Frederick 6–1 185 C
B. Wheatley, Ont., Jan. 26, 1931

49–50	Det	2	0	0	0	0	
50–51	Det	19	7	6	13	13	
51–52	Det	70	12	14	26	48	
52–53	Det	70	12	15	27	54	
53–54	Det	70	17	10	27	95	
54–55	Det	70	14	16	30	53	
55–56	Chi	70	7	20	27	26	
56–57	Chi	67	14	28	42	69	
57–58	Chi	70	17	18	35	35	
58–59	Chi	70	3	5	8	4	
59–60	Chi	69	3	4	7	16	
60–61	Mont	3	0	0	0	0	
Totals		650	106	136	242	413	

Playoffs

50–51	Det	6	0	0	0	0	
51–52	Det	8	1	4	5	16	
52–53	Det	6	1	0	1	2	
53–54	Det	12	1	2	3	16	
54–55	Det	11	2	0	2	8	
58–59	Chi	6	2	1	3	4	
59–60	Chi	4	0	0	0	2	
Totals		53	7	7	14	48	

SKRASTINS H. Karlis *6–1 196 D*
B. Riga, Latvia, July 9, 1974

SSN	TEAM	GP	G	A	PTS.	PIM	+/-
98–99	Nash	2	0	1	1	0	0

SKRBEK, Pavel *6–3 191 D*
B. Kladno, Czech., Aug. 9, 1978

SSN	TEAM	GP	G	A	PTS.	PIM	+/-
98–99	Pitt	4	0	0	0	2	2

SKRIKO, Petri *5–10 175 LW*
B. Lappeenranta, Finland, Mar. 12, 1962

SSN	TEAM	GP	G	A	PTS.	PIM	+/-
84–85	Van	72	21	14	35	10	-26
85–86	Van	80	38	40	78	34	-17
86–87	Van	76	33	41	74	44	-4
87–88	Van	73	30	34	64	32	-12
88–89	Van	74	30	36	66	57	-3
89–90	Van	77	15	33	48	36	-21
90–91	Van–Bos	48	9	18	27	17	-5
91–92	Bos–Winn	24	3	3	6	10	-4
92–93	SJ	17	4	3	7	6	-8
Totals		541	183	222	405	246	-100

Playoffs

85–86	Van	3	0	0	0	0	
88–89	Van	7	1	5	6	0	
90–91	Bos	18	4	4	8	4	
Totals		28	5	9	14	4	

SKRUDLAND, Brian *6–0 196 C*
B. Peace River, Alta., July 31, 1963

85–86	Mont	65	9	13	22	57	+3
86–87	Mont	79	11	17	28	107	+18
87–88	Mont	79	12	24	36	112	+14
88–89	Mont	71	12	29	41	84	+22
89–90	Mont	59	11	31	42	56	+21
90–91	Mont	57	15	19	34	85	+12
91–92	Mont	42	3	3	6	36	-4
92–93	Mont–Calg	39	7	7	14	65	+4
93–94	Fla	79	15	25	40	136	+13
94–95	Fla	47	5	9	14	88	0
95–96	Fla	79	7	20	27	129	+6
96–97	Fla	51	5	13	18	48	+4
97–98	NYR–Dal	72	7	6	13	49	-6
98–99	Dall	40	4	1	5	33	+2
Totals		859	123	217	340	1085	+109

Playoffs

85–86	Mont	20	2	4	6	76	
86–87	Mont	14	1	5	6	29	
87–88	Mont	11	1	5	6	24	
88–89	Mont	21	3	7	10	40	
89–90	Mont	11	3	5	8	30	
90–91	Mont	13	3	10	13	42	
91–92	Mont	11	1	1	2	20	
92–93	Calg	6	0	3	3	12	
95–96	Fla	21	1	3	4	18	
97–98	Dal	17	0	1	1	16	
98–99	Dal	19	0	2	2	16	
Totals		164	15	46	61	323	

SLANEY, John *6–0 185 D*
B. St. John's, Nfld., Feb. 7, 1972

93–94	Wash	47	7	9	16	27	+3
94–95	Wash	16	0	3	3	6	-3
95–96	Col A–LA	38	6	14	20	14	+7
96–97	LA	32	3	11	14	4	-10
97–98	Phoe	55	3	14	17	24	-3
98–99	Nash	46	2	12	14	14	-12
Totals		234	21	63	84	89	-18

Playoffs

93–94	Wash	11	1	1	2	2	

SLEAVER, John *6–1 180 C*
B. Copper Cliff, Ont., Aug. 18, 1934

53–54	Chi	12	1	0	1	2	
56–57	Chi	12	1	0	1	4	
Totals		24	2	0	2	6	

SLEGR, Jiri *6–1 205 D*
B. Jihlava, Czechoslovakia, May 30, 1971

92–93	Van	41	4	22	26	109	+16
93–94	Van	78	5	33	38	86	0
94–95	Van–Edm	31	2	10	12	46	-5
95–96	Edm	57	4	13	17	74	-1
97–98	Pitt	73	5	12	17	109	+10
98–99	Pitt	63	3	20	23	86	+13

Totals		343	23	110	133	510	+33

Playoffs

92–93	Van	5	0	3	3	4	
97–98	Pitt	6	0	4	4	2	
98–99	Pitt	13	1	3	4	12	
Totals		24	1	10	11	18	

SLEIGHER, Louis *5–11 200 RW*
B. Nouvelle, Que., Oct. 23, 1958

78–79	Birm (WHA)	62	26	12	38	46	
79–80	Que	2	0	1	1	0	+1
81–82	Que	8	0	0	0	0	-2
82–83	Que	51	14	10	24	49	+8
83–84	Que	44	15	19	34	32	+23
84–85	Que–Bos	76	13	21	34	45	-3
85–86	Bos	13	4	2	6	20	-4
NHL Totals		194	46	53	99	146	+23
WHA Totals		62	26	12	38	46	

Playoffs

82–83	Que	4	0	0	0	4	
83–84	Que	7	1	1	2	42	
84–85	Bos	5	0	0	0	4	
85–86	Bos	1	0	0	0	14	
NHL Totals		17	1	1	2	64	

SLOAN, Aloysius Martin (Tod) *5–10 175 C*
B. Vinton, Que., Nov. 30, 1927

47–48	Tor	1	0	0	0	0	
48–49	Tor	29	3	4	7	0	
50–51	Tor	70	31	25	56	105	
51–52	Tor	68	25	23	48	89	
52–53	Tor	70	15	10	25	76	
53–54	Tor	67	11	32	43	100	
54–55	Tor	63	13	15	28	89	
55–56	Tor	70	37	29	66	100	
56–57	Tor	52	14	21	35	33	
57–58	Tor	59	13	25	38	58	
58–59	Chi	59	27	35	62	79	
59–60	Chi	70	20	20	40	54	
60–61	Chi	67	11	23	34	48	
Totals		745	220	262	482	831	

Playoffs

50–51	Tor	11	4	5	9	18	
51–52	Tor	4	0	0	0	10	
53–54	Tor	5	1	1	2	24	
54–55	Tor	4	0	0	0	2	
55–56	Tor	2	0	0	0	5	
58–59	Chi	6	3	5	8	0	
59–60	Chi	3	0	0	0	0	
60–61	Chi	12	1	1	2	8	
Totals		47	9	12	21	67	

SLOAN, Blake *5–10 193 RW*
B. Park Ridge, Ill., July 27, 1975

98–99	Dal	14	0	0	0	10	-1

Playoffs

98–99	Dal	19	0	2	2	8	

SLOBODIAN, Peter Paul *6–1 185 D*
B. Dauphin, Man., Apr. 24, 1918

40–41	NYA	41	3	2	5	54	

SLOWINSKI, Edward Stanley *6–0 200 RW*
B. Winnipeg, Man., Nov. 18, 1922

47–48	NYR	38	6	5	11	2	
48–49	NYR	20	1	1	2	2	
49–50	NYR	63	14	23	37	12	
50–51	NYR	69	14	18	32	15	
51–51	NYR	64	21	22	43	18	
52–53	NYR	37	2	5	7	14	
Totals		291	58	74	132	63	

Playoffs

47–48	NYR	4	0	0	0	0	
49–50	NYR	12	2	6	8	6	
Totals		16	2	6	8	6	

SLY, Darryl Hayward *5–10 185 D*
B. Collingwood, Ont., Apr. 3, 1939

65–66	Tor	2	0	0	0	0	
67–68	Tor	17	0	0	0	4	-1
69–70	Minn	29	1	0	1	6	-5

70–71	Van	31	0	2	2	10	-1
Totals		79	1	2	3	20	-7

SMAIL, Douglas *5–9 175 LW*
B. Moose Jaw, Sask., Sept. 2, 1957

80–81	Winn	30	10	8	18	45	-7
81–82	Winn	72	17	18	35	55	-22
82–83	Winn	80	15	29	44	32	0
83–84	Winn	66	20	17	37	62	-5
84–85	Winn	80	31	35	66	45	+12
85–86	Winn	73	16	26	42	32	-10
86–87	Winn	78	25	18	43	36	+18
87–88	Winn	71	15	16	31	34	+5
88–89	Winn	47	14	15	29	52	+12
89–90	Winn	79	25	24	49	63	+15
90–91	Winn–Minn	72	8	15	23	48	-8
91–92	Que	46	10	18	28	47	-11
92–93	Ott	51	4	10	14	51	-34
Totals		845	210	249	459	602	-35

Playoffs

81–82	Winn	4	0	0	0	0	
82–83	Winn	3	0	0	0	6	
83–84	Winn	3	0	1	1	7	
84–85	Winn	8	2	1	3	4	
85–86	Winn	3	1	0	1	0	
86–87	Winn	10	4	0	4	10	
87–88	Winn	5	1	0	1	22	
89–90	Winn	5	1	0	1	0	
90–91	Minn	1	0	0	0	0	
Totals		42	9	2	11	49	

SMART, Alexander (Alec) *F*
B. Brandon, Man., May 29, 1918

42–43	Mont	8	2	5	7	0	

SMEDSMO, Dale Darwin *6–1 195 LW*
B. Roseau, Minn., Apr. 23, 1951

72–73	Tor	4	0	0	0	0	0
75–76	Cin (WHA)	66	8	14	22	187	
76–77	NE–Cin (WHA)	38	2	5	7	197	
77–78	Ind (WHA)	6	0	3	3	7	
NHL Totals		4	0	0	0	0	0
WHA Totals		110	10	22	32	291	

Playoffs

76–77	Cin (WHA)	2	0	1	1	0	

SMEHLIK, Richard *6–3 208 D*
B. Ostrava, Czechoslovakia, Jan. 23, 1970

92–93	Buf	80	4	27	31	59	+9
93–94	Buf	84	14	27	41	69	+22
94–95	Buf	39	4	7	11	46	+5
96–97	Buf	62	11	19	30	43	+19
97–98	Buf	72	3	17	20	62	+11
98–99	Buf	72	3	11	14	44	-9
Totals		409	39	108	147	323	+57

Playoffs

92–93	Buf	8	0	4	4	2	
93–94	Buf	7	0	2	2	10	
94–95	Buf	5	0	0	0	2	
96–97	Buf	12	0	2	2	4	
97–98	Buf	15	0	2	2	6	
98–99	Buf	21	0	3	3	10	
Totals		68	0	13	13	34	

SMILLIE, Donald *F*
B. Bos

33–34	Bos	12	2	2	4	4	

*SMITH, Alexander (Alex) *5–11 176 D*
B. Liverpool, England, Apr. 2, 1902

24–25	Ott	7	0	0	0	2	
25–26	Ott	36	0	0	0	36	
26–27	Ott	42	4	1	5	58	
27–28	Ott	44	9	4	13	90	
28–29	Ott	44	1	7	8	36	
29–30	Ott	43	2	6	8	91	
30–31	Ott	37	5	6	11	73	
31–32	Det	48	6	8	14	47	
32–33	Ott–Bos	49	4	7	11	72	
33–34	Bos	45	4	6	10	32	
34–35	NYA	48	3	8	11	46	
Totals		443	41	50	91	583	

SSN	TEAM	GP	G	A	PTS.	PIM	+/-
Playoffs							
25–26	Ott	2	0	0	0	0	
26–27	Ott	6	0	0	0	8	
27–28	Ott	2	0	0	0	4	
29–30	Ott	2	0	0	0	4	
31–32	Det	2	0	0	0	4	
32–33	Bos	5	0	2	2	6	
Totals		19	0	2	2	26	

*SMITH, Arthur *F*
B. 1907

SSN	TEAM	GP	G	A	PTS.	PIM	+/-
27–28	Tor	15	5	3	8	22	
28–29	Tor	43	5	0	5	91	
29–30	Tor	43	3	3	6	75	
30–31	Ott	36	2	4	6	61	
Totals		137	15	10	25	249	
Playoffs							
28–29	Tor	4	1	1	2	8	

SMITH, Barry Edward *5–11 178 C*
B. Surrey, B.C., Apr. 25, 1955

SSN	TEAM	GP	G	A	PTS.	PIM	+/-
75–76	Bos	19	1	0	1	2	-5
79–80	Col	33	2	3	5	4	-11
80–81	Col	62	4	4	8	4	-2
Totals		114	7	7	14	10	-18

SMITH, Brad Allan *6–1 195 RW*
B. Windsor, Ont., Apr. 13, 1958

SSN	TEAM	GP	G	A	PTS.	PIM	+/-
78–79	Van	2	0	0	0	2	-3
79–80	Van–Atl	23	1	3	4	54	-3
80–81	Calg–Det	65	12	6	18	158	-20
81–82	Det	33	2	0	2	80	-7
82–83	Det	1	0	0	0	0	-1
83–84	Det	8	2	1	3	36	-2
84–85	Det	1	1	0	1	5	0
85–86	Tor	42	5	17	22	84	-8
86–87	Tor	47	5	7	12	172	+15
Totals		222	28	34	62	591	-29
Playoffs							
84–85	Det	3	0	1	1	5	
85–86	Tor	6	2	1	3	20	
86–87	Tor	11	1	1	2	24	
Totals		20	3	3	6	49	

SMITH, Brandon *6–1 196 D*
B. Hazelton, B.C., Feb. 25, 1973

SSN	TEAM	GP	G	A	PTS.	PIM	+/-
98–99	Bos	5	0	0	0	0	+2

*SMITH, Brian Desmond *6–0 180 LW*
B. Ottawa, Ont., Sept. 6, 1940

SSN	TEAM	GP	G	A	PTS.	PIM	+/-
67–68	LA	58	10	9	19	33	-2
68–69	Minn	9	0	1	1	0	-7
Totals		67	10	10	20	33	-9
Playoffs							
67–68	LA	7	0	0	0	0	

SMITH, Brian Stuart *6–0 180 LW*
B. Creighton Mine, Ont., Dec. 6, 1937

SSN	TEAM	GP	G	A	PTS.	PIM	+/-
57–58	Det	4	0	1	1	0	
59–60	Det	31	2	5	7	2	
60–61	Det	26	0	2	2	10	
Totals		61	2	8	10	12	
Playoffs							
59–60	Det	5	0	0	0	0	

*SMITH, Carl David *F*
B. Cache Bay, Ont., Sept. 18, 1917

SSN	TEAM	GP	G	A	PTS.	PIM	+/-
43–44	Det	7	1	1	2	2	

SMITH, Clinton James (Snuffy) *5–8 165 C*
B. Assiniboia, Sask., Dec. 12, 1913

SSN	TEAM	GP	G	A	PTS.	PIM	+/-
36–37	NYR	2	1	0	1	0	
37–38	NYR	48	14	23	37	0	
38–39	NYR	48	21	20	41	2	
39–40	NYR	41	8	16	24	2	
40–41	NYR	48	14	11	25	0	
41–42	NYR	47	10	24	34	4	
42–43	NYR	47	12	21	33	4	
43–44	Chi	50	23	49	72	4	
44–45	Chi	50	23	31	54	0	
45–46	Chi	50	26	24	50	2	
46–47	Chi	52	9	17	26	6	
Totals		483	161	236	397	24	
Playoffs							
37–38	NYR	3	2	0	2	0	
38–39	NYR	7	1	2	3	0	
39–40	NYR	12	1	3	4	2	
40–41	NYR	3	0	0	0	0	
41–42	NYR	3	0	0	0	0	
43–44	Chi	9	4	8	12	0	
45–46	Chi	4	2	1	3	0	
Totals		44	10	14	24	2	

SMITH, Dallas Earl *5–11 180 D*
B. Hamiota, Man., Oct. 10, 1941

SSN	TEAM	GP	G	A	PTS.	PIM	+/-
59–60	Bos	5	1	1	2	0	
60–61	Bos	70	1	9	10	79	
61–62	Bos	7	0	0	0	10	
65–66	Bos	2	0	0	0	0	
66–67	Bos	33	0	1	1	24	
67–68	Bos	74	4	23	27	65	+33
68–69	Bos	75	4	24	28	74	+44
69–70	Bos	75	7	17	24	119	+9
70–71	Bos	73	7	38	45	68	+94
71–72	Bos	78	8	22	30	132	+34
72–73	Bos	78	4	27	31	72	+38
73–74	Bos	77	6	21	27	64	+26
74–75	Bos	79	3	20	23	84	+30
75–76	Bos	77	7	25	32	103	+42
76–77	Bos	58	2	20	22	40	+16
77–78	NYR	29	1	4	5	23	-11
Totals		890	55	252	307	957	+355
Playoffs							
67–68	Bos	4	0	2	2	0	
68–69	Bos	10	0	3	3	16	
69–70	Bos	14	0	3	3	19	
70–71	Bos	7	0	3	3	26	
71–72	Bos	15	0	4	4	22	
72–73	Bos	5	0	2	2	2	
73–74	Bos	16	1	7	8	20	
74–75	Bos	3	0	2	2	4	
75–76	Bos	11	2	2	4	19	
77–78	NYR	1	0	1	1	0	
Totals		86	3	29	32	128	

SMITH, Dalton J. (Nakina) *5–10 150 C*
B. Cache Bay, Ont., June 26, 1915

SSN	TEAM	GP	G	A	PTS.	PIM	+/-
36–37	NYA	1	0	0	0	0	
43–44	Det	10	1	2	3	0	
Totals		11	1	2	3	0	

SMITH Dan *6–2 195 D*
B. Fernie, B.C., Oct. 19, 1976

SSN	TEAM	GP	G	A	PTS.	PIM	+/-
98–99	Col A	12	0	0	0	9	+5

SMITH, Denis (D.J.) *6–1 200 D*
B. Windsor, Ont., May 13, 1977

SSN	TEAM	GP	G	A	PTS.	PIM	+/-
96–97	Tor	8	0	1	1	7	-5

SMITH, Dennis *5–11 190 D*
B. Detroit, Mich., July 27, 1964

SSN	TEAM	GP	G	A	PTS.	PIM	+/-
89–90	Wash	4	0	0	0	0	0
90–91	LA	4	0	0	0	4	+3
Totals		8	0	0	0	4	+3

SMITH, Derek Robert *5–11 180 C/LW*
B. Quebec City, Que., July 31, 1954

SSN	TEAM	GP	G	A	PTS.	PIM	+/-
76–77	Buf	5	0	0	0	0	-1
77–78	Buf	36	3	3	6	0	-4
78–79	Buf	43	14	12	26	8	-5
79–80	Buf	79	24	39	63	16	+33
80–81	Buf	69	21	43	64	12	+14
81–82	Buf–Det	61	9	15	24	12	-4
82–83	Det	42	7	4	11	12	-7
Totals		335	78	116	194	60	+26
Playoffs							
75–76	Buf	1	0	0	0	0	
77–78	Buf	8	3	3	6	7	
79–80	Buf	13	5	7	12	4	
80–81	Buf	8	1	4	5	2	
Totals		30	9	14	23	13	

SMITH, Derrick *6–2 215 LW*
B. Scarborough, Ont., Jan. 22, 1965

SSN	TEAM	GP	G	A	PTS.	PIM	+/-
84–85	Phil	77	17	22	39	31	+28
85–86	Phil	69	6	6	12	57	+14
86–87	Phil	71	11	21	32	34	-4
87–88	Phil	76	16	8	24	104	-20
88–89	Phil	74	16	14	30	43	-4
89–90	Phil	55	3	6	9	32	-15
90–91	Phil	72	11	20	31	37	0
91–92	Minn	33	2	4	6	33	-8
92–93	Minn	9	0	1	1	2	-2
93–94	Dal	1	0	0	0	0	-1
Totals		537	82	92	174	373	-12
Playoffs							
84–85	Phil	19	2	5	7	16	
85–86	Phil	4	0	0	0	10	
86–87	Phil	26	6	4	10	26	
87–88	Phil	7	0	0	0	6	
88–89	Phil	19	5	2	7	12	
91–92	Minn	7	1	0	1	9	
Totals		82	14	11	25	79	

SMITH, Desmond Patrick (Des) *6–0 185 D*
B. Ottawa, Ont., Feb. 22, 1914

SSN	TEAM	GP	G	A	PTS.	PIM	+/-
37–38	Mont M	41	3	1	4	47	
38–39	Mont	16	3	3	6	8	
39–40	Chi–Bos	42	3	6	9	50	
40–41	Bos	48	6	8	14	61	
41–42	Bos	48	7	7	14	70	
Totals		195	22	25	47	236	
Playoffs							
38–39	Mont	3	0	0	0	4	
39–40	Mont	6	0	0	0	0	
40–41	Bos	11	0	2	2	12	
41–42	Bos	5	1	2	3	2	
Totals		25	1	4	5	18	

*SMITH, Donald *C*
B. 1889

SSN	TEAM	GP	G	A	PTS.	PIM	+/-
19–20	Mont	10	1	0	1	4	

SMITH, Donald Arthur *5–10 165 C*
B. Regina, Sask., May 4, 1929

SSN	TEAM	GP	G	A	PTS.	PIM	+/-
49–50	NYR	11	1	1	2	0	
Playoffs							
49–50	NYR	1	0	0	0	0	

SMITH, Douglas Eric *5–11 186 C*
B. Ottawa, Ont., May 17, 1963

SSN	TEAM	GP	G	A	PTS.	PIM	+/-
81–82	LA	80	16	14	30	64	-13
82–83	LA	42	11	11	22	12	-14
83–84	LA	72	16	20	36	28	-33
84–85	LA	62	21	20	41	58	-15
85–86	LA–Buf	78	18	20	38	129	-27
86–87	Buf	62	16	24	40	106	-20
87–88	Buf	70	9	19	28	117	-10
88–89	Edm–Van	29	4	5	9	13	+2
89–90	Van–Pitt	40	4	5	9	97	-1
Totals		535	115	138	253	624	-131
Playoffs							
81–82	LA	10	3	2	5	11	
84–85	LA	3	1	0	1	4	
87–88	Buf	1	0	0	0	0	
88–89	Van	4	0	0	0	6	
Totals		18	4	2	6	21	

SMITH, Floyd Robert Donald *5–10 180 RW*
B. Perth, Ont., May 16, 1935

SSN	TEAM	GP	G	A	PTS.	PIM	+/-
54–55	Bos	3	0	1	1	0	
56–57	Bos	23	0	0	0	6	
60–61	NYR	29	5	9	14	0	
62–63	Det	51	9	17	26	10	
63–64	Det	52	18	13	31	22	
64–65	Det	67	16	29	45	49	
65–66	Det	66	21	28	49	20	
66–67	Det	54	11	14	25	8	
67–68	Det–Tor	63	24	22	46	14	+11
68–69	Tor	64	15	19	34	22	+14
69–70	Tor	61	4	14	18	13	-3
70–71	Buf	77	6	11	17	46	-12
71–72	Buf	6	0	1	1	2	-4
Totals		616	129	178	307	207	+6

Playoffs

SSN	TEAM	GP	G	A	PTS.	PIM	+/-
62–63	Det	11	2	3	5	4	
63–64	Det	14	4	3	7	4	
64–65	Det	7	1	3	4	4	
65–66	Det	12	5	2	7	4	
68–69	Tor	4	0	0	0	0	
Totals		48	12	11	23	16	

SMITH, Geoff Arthur *6–3 194 D*
B. Edmonton, Alta., Mar. 7, 1969

SSN	TEAM	GP	G	A	PTS.	PIM	+/-
89–90	Edm	74	4	11	15	52	+13
90–91	Edm	59	1	12	13	55	+13
91–92	Edm	74	2	16	18	43	-5
92–93	Edm	78	4	14	18	30	-11
93–94	Edm–Fla	77	1	8	9	50	-13
94–95	Fla	47	2	4	6	22	-5
95–96	Fla	31	3	7	10	20	-4
96–97	Fla	3	0	0	0	2	+1
97–98	NYR	15	1	1	2	6	-4
98–99	NYR	4	0	0	0	2	-5
Totals		462	18	73	91	282	-20

Playoffs

SSN	TEAM	GP	G	A	PTS.	PIM	
89–90	Edm	3	0	0	0	0	
90–91	Edm	4	0	0	0	0	
91–92	Edm	5	0	1	1	6	
95–96	fla	1	0	0	0	2	
Totals		13	0	1	1	8	

SMITH, George *F*

SSN	TEAM	GP	G	A	PTS.	PIM	
21–22	Tor	9	0	0	0	0	

SMITH, Glen *F*

SSN	TEAM	GP	G	A	PTS.	PIM	
50–51	Chi	2	0	0	0	0	

*SMITH, Glenn *D*

SSN	TEAM	GP	G	A	PTS.	PIM	
22–23	Tor	9	0	0	0	0	

SMITH, Gordon Joseph *5–10 175 D*
B. Perth, Ont., Nov. 17, 1949

SSN	TEAM	GP	G	A	PTS.	PIM	+/-
74–75	Wash	63	3	8	11	56	-56
75–76	Wash	25	1	2	3	28	-22
76–77	Wash	79	1	12	13	92	-27
77–78	Wash	80	4	7	11	78	-20
78–79	Wash	39	0	1	1	22	-7
79–80	Winn	13	0	0	0	8	-5
Totals		299	9	30	39	284	-137

SMITH, Gregory James *6–0 195 D*
B. Ponoka, Alta., July 8, 1955

SSN	TEAM	GP	G	A	PTS.	PIM	+/-
75–76	Cal	1	0	1	1	2	-1
76–77	Clev	74	9	17	26	65	-31
77–78	Clev	80	7	30	37	92	-26
78–79	Minn	80	5	27	32	147	-21
79–80	Minn	55	5	13	18	103	-1
80–81	Minn	74	5	21	26	126	+7
81–82	Det	69	10	22	32	79	-22
82–83	Det	73	4	26	30	79	+7
83–84	Det	75	3	20	23	108	+6
84–85	Det	73	2	18	20	117	-26
85–86	Det–Wash	76	5	22	27	94	-11
86–87	Wash	45	0	9	9	31	-6
87–88	Wash	54	1	6	7	67	+5
Totals		829	56	232	288	1110	-120

Playoffs

SSN	TEAM	GP	G	A	PTS.	PIM	
79–80	Minn	12	0	1	1	9	
80–81	Minn	19	1	5	6	39	
83–84	Det	4	1	0	1	8	
84–85	Det	3	0	0	0	7	
85–86	Wash	9	2	1	3	9	
86–87	Wash	7	0	0	0	11	
87–88	Wash	9	0	0	0	23	
Totals		63	4	7	11	106	

SMITH, James Stephen (Steve) *6–4 215 D*
B. Glasgow, Scotland, Apr. 30, 1963

SSN	TEAM	GP	G	A	PTS.	PIM	+/-
84–85	Edm	2	0	0	0	2	-2
85–86	Edm	55	4	20	24	166	+30
86–87	Edm	62	7	15	22	165	+11
87–88	Edm	79	12	43	55	286	+40
88–89	Edm	35	3	19	22	97	+5
89–90	Edm	75	7	34	41	171	+6
90–91	Edm	77	13	41	54	193	+14
91–92	Chi	76	9	21	30	304	+23
92–93	Chi	78	10	47	57	214	+12
93–94	Chi	57	5	22	27	174	-5
94–95	Chi	48	1	12	13	128	+6
95–96	Chi	37	0	9	9	71	+12
96–97	Chi	21	0	0	0	29	+4
98–99	Calg	69	1	14	15	80	-3
Totals		771	72	297	369	2080	+153

Playoffs

SSN	TEAM	GP	G	A	PTS.	PIM	
85–86	Edm	6	0	1	1	14	
86–87	Edm	15	1	3	4	45	
87–88	Edm	19	1	11	12	55	
88–89	Edm	7	2	2	4	20	
89–90	Edm	22	5	10	15	37	
90–91	Edm	18	1	2	3	45	
91–92	Chi	18	1	11	12	16	
92–93	Chi	4	0	0	0	10	
94–95	Chi	16	0	1	1	26	
95–96	Chi	6	0	0	0	16	
96–97	Chi	3	0	0	0	4	
Totals		134	11	41	52	288	

SMITH, Jason *6–3 195 D*
B. Calgary, Alta., Nov. 2, 1973

SSN	TEAM	GP	G	A	PTS.	PIM	+/-
93–94	NJ	41	0	5	5	43	+7
94–95	NJ	2	0	0	0	0	-3
95–96	NJ	64	2	1	3	86	+5
96–97	NJ–Tor	78	1	7	8	54	-12
97–98	Tor	81	3	13	16	100	-5
98–99	Tor–Edm	72	3	12	15	51	-9
Totals		338	9	28	37	334	-17

Playoffs

SSN	TEAM	GP	G	A	PTS.	PIM	
93–94	NJ	6	0	0	0	7	
98–99	Edm	4	0	1	1	4	
Totals		10	0	1	1	11	

SMITH, Kenneth Alvin *5–7 150 LW*
B. Moose Jaw, Sask., May 8, 1924

SSN	TEAM	GP	G	A	PTS.	PIM	
44–45	Bos	49	20	14	34	2	
45–46	Bos	23	2	6	8	0	
46–47	Bos	60	14	7	21	4	
47–48	Bos	60	11	12	23	14	
48–49	Bos	59	20	20	40	6	
49–50	Bos	66	10	31	41	12	
50–51	Bos	14	1	3	4	11	
Totals		331	78	93	171	49	

Playoffs

SSN	TEAM	GP	G	A	PTS.	PIM	
44–45	Bos	7	3	4	7	0	
45–46	Bos	8	0	4	4	0	
46–47	bos	5	3	0	3	2	
47–48	Bos	5	2	3	5	0	
48–49	Bos	5	0	2	2	4	
Totals		30	8	13	21	6	

SMITH, Randy *6–4 200 C*
B. Saskatoon, Sask., July 7, 1965

SSN	TEAM	GP	G	A	PTS.	PIM	+/-
85–86	Minn	1	0	0	0	0	0
86–87	Minn	2	0	0	0	0	-2
Totals		3	0	0	0	0	-2

*SMITH, Reginald Joseph (Hooley) *D*
B. Toronto, Ont., Jan. 7, 1905

SSN	TEAM	GP	G	A	PTS.	PIM	
24–25	Ott	30	10	3	13	81	
25–26	Ott	28	16	9	25	53	
26–27	Ott	43	9	6	15	125	
27–28	Mont M	34	14	5	19	72	
28–29	Mont M	41	10	9	19	120	
29–30	Mont M	42	21	9	30	83	
30–31	Mont M	39	12	14	26	48	
31–32	Mont M	43	11	33	44	49	
32–33	Mont M	48	20	21	41	66	
33–34	Mont M	47	18	19	37	58	
34–35	Mont M	46	5	22	27	41	
35–36	Mont M	47	19	19	38	75	
36–37	Bos	44	8	10	18	36	
37–38	NYA	47	10	10	20	23	
38–39	NYA	48	8	11	19	18	
39–40	NYA	47	7	8	15	41	
40–41	NYA	41	2	7	9	4	
Totals		715	200	215	415	993	

Playoffs

SSN	TEAM	GP	G	A	PTS.	PIM	
25–26	Ott	2	0	0	0	14	
26–27	Ott	6	1	0	1	16	
27–28	Mont M	9	2	1	3	17	
29–30	Mont M	4	1	1	2	12	
31–32	Mont M	4	2	1	3	2	
32–33	Mont M	2	2	0	2	2	
33–34	Mont M	4	0	1	1	6	
34–35	Mont M	6	0	0	0	14	
35–36	Mont M	3	0	0	0	2	
36–37	Bos	3	0	0	0	0	
37–38	NYA	6	0	3	3	0	
38–39	NYA	2	0	0	0	14	
39–40	NYA	3	3	1	4	2	
Totals		54	11	8	19	101	

SMITH, Richard Allan (Rick) *5–11 200 D*
B. Kingston, Ont., June 29, 1948

SSN	TEAM	GP	G	A	PTS.	PIM	+/-
68–69	Bos	48	0	5	5	29	+14
69–70	Bos	69	2	8	10	65	+12
70–71	Bos	67	4	19	23	44	+30
71–72	Bos–Cal	78	3	16	19	72	+36
72–73	Cal	64	9	24	33	77	-43
73–74	Minn (WHA)	71	10	28	38	98	
74–75	Minn (WHA)	78	9	29	38	112	
75–76	Minn (WHA)	51	1	32	33	50	
75–76	StL	24	1	7	8	18	+2
76–77	StL–Bos	64	6	17	23	36	+20
77–78	Bos	79	7	29	36	69	+70
78–79	Bos	65	7	18	25	46	+20
79–80	Bos	78	8	18	26	62	+22
80–81	Det–Wash	51	5	6	11	42	+2
NHL Totals		687	52	167	219	560	+185
WHA Totals		200	20	89	109	260	

Playoffs

SSN	TEAM	GP	G	A	PTS.	PIM	
68–69	Bos	9	0	0	0	6	
69–70	Bos	14	1	3	4	17	
70–71	Bos	6	0	0	0	0	
73–74	Minn (WHA)	11	0	1	1	22	
74–75	Minn (WHA)	12	2	7	9	6	
75–76	StL	3	0	1	1	4	
76–77	Bos	14	0	9	9	14	
77–78	Bos	15	1	5	6	18	
78–79	Bos	11	0	4	4	12	
79–80	Bos	6	1	1	2	6	
NHL Totals		78	3	23	26	73	
WHA Totals		23	2	8	10	28	

SMITH, Robert David (Bobby) *6–4 210 C*
B. North Sydney, N.S., Feb. 12, 1958

SSN	TEAM	GP	G	A	PTS.	PIM	+/-
78–79	Minn	80	30	44	74	39	-8
79–80	Minn	61	27	56	83	24	+16
80–81	Minn	78	29	64	93	73	+1
81–82	Minn	80	43	71	114	82	+10
82–83	Minn	77	24	53	77	81	-20
83–84	Minn–Mont	80	29	43	72	71	-8
84–85	Mont	65	16	40	56	59	-9
85–86	Mont	79	31	55	86	55	+10
86–87	Mont	80	28	47	75	72	+6
87–88	Mont	78	27	66	93	78	+13
88–89	Mont	80	32	51	83	69	+25
89–90	Mont	53	12	14	26	35	-4
90–91	Mont	73	15	31	46	60	-9
91–92	Mont	68	9	37	46	109	-24
92–93	Mont	45	5	7	12	10	-9
Totals		1077	357	679	1036	917	-10

Playoffs

SSN	TEAM	GP	G	A	PTS.	PIM	
79–80	Minn	15	1	13	14	9	
80–81	Minn	19	8	17	25	13	
81–82	Minn	4	2	4	6	5	
82–83	Minn	9	6	4	10	17	
83–84	Mont	15	2	7	9	8	
84–85	Mont	12	5	6	11	30	
85–86	Mont	20	7	8	15	22	
86–87	Mont	17	9	9	18	19	
87–88	Mont	11	3	4	7	8	
88–89	Mont	21	11	8	19	46	
89–90	Mont	11	1	4	5	4	
90–91	Mont	23	8	8	16	56	
91–92	Minn	7	1	4	5	6	
Totals		184	64	96	160	245	

*SMITH, Roger *6–0 175 D*
B. 1898

SSN	TEAM	GP	G	A	PTS.	PIM	
25–26	Pitt Pi	36	9	1	10	22	
26–27	Pitt Pi	36	4	0	4	16	
27–28	Pitt Pi	43	1	0	1	30	
28–29	Pitt Pi	44	4	2	6	49	
29–30	Pitt Pi	42	2	1	3	55	
30–31	Phil Q	9	0	0	0	0	
Totals		210	20	4	24	172	

SSN	TEAM	GP	G	A	PTS.	PIM	+/-
Playoffs							
25–26	Pitt Pi	2	1	0	1	0	
27–28	Pitt Pi	2	2	0	2	0	
Totals		4	3	0	3	0	

SMITH, Ronald Robert 6–0 185 D
B. Port Hope, Ont., Nov. 19, 1952

72–73	NYI	11	1	1	2	14	-8

SMITH, Sidney James 5–10 177 LW
B. Toronto, Ont., July 11, 1925

46–47	Tor	14	2	1	3	0	
47–48	Tor	31	7	10	17	10	
48–49	Tor	1	0	0	0	0	
49–50	Tor	68	22	23	45	6	
50–51	Tor	70	30	21	51	10	
51–52	Tor	70	27	30	57	6	
52–53	Tor	70	20	19	39	6	
53–54	Tor	70	22	16	38	28	
54–55	Tor	70	33	21	54	14	
55–56	Tor	55	4	17	21	8	
56–57	Tor	70	17	24	41	4	
57–58	Tor	12	2	1	3	2	
Totals		601	186	183	369	94	

Playoffs

47–48	Tor	2	0	0	0	0	
48–49	Tor	6	5	2	7	0	
49–50	Tor	7	0	3	3	2	
50–51	Tor	11	7	3	10	0	
51–52	Tor	4	0	0	0	0	
53–54	Tor	5	1	1	2	0	
54–55	Tor	4	3	1	4	0	
55–56	Tor	5	1	0	1	0	
Totals		44	17	10	27	2	

SMITH, Stanford George (Stan) 5–10 165 C
B. Coal Creek, B.C., Aug. 13, 1917

39–40	NYR	1	0	0	0	0	
40–41	NYR	8	2	1	3	0	
Totals		9	2	1	3	0	

SMITH, Steve 5–9 215 D
B. Trenton, Ont., Apr. 4, 1963

81–82	Phil	8	0	1	1	0	-2
84–85	Phil	2	0	0	0	7	+2
85–86	Phil	2	0	0	0	2	-2
86–87	Phil	2	0	0	0	6	0
87–88	Phil	1	0	0	0	0	0
88–89	Buf	3	0	0	0	0	0
Totals		18	0	1	1	15	-2

SMITH, Stuart Ernest (Stu) RW

40–41	Mont	16	2	3	5	2	
41–42	Mont	1	0	1	1	0	
Totals		17	2	4	6	2	

SMITH, Stuart Gordon 6–1 205 D
B. Toronto, Ont., Mar. 17, 1960

79–80	Hart	4	0	0	0	0	-1
80–81	Hart	38	1	7	8	55	-14
81–82	Hart	17	0	3	3	15	-7
82–83	Hart	18	1	0	1	25	-16
Totals		77	2	10	12	95	-38

***SMITH, Thomas J.** LW
B. Ottawa, Ont., Sept. 27, 1885

19–20	Que	1	0	0	0	9	

SMITH, Vern 6–1 190 D
B. Winnipeg, Man., May 30, 1964

84–85	NYI	1	0	0	0	0	0

SMITH, Wayne Clifford 6–0 195 D
B. Kamsack, Sask., Feb. 12, 1943

66–67	Chi	2	1	1	2	2	

Playoffs

66–67	Chi	1	0	0	0	0	

SMOLINSKI, Bryan Anthony 6–1 200 C
B. Toledo, Ohio, Dec. 27, 1971

92–93	Bos	9	1	3	4	0	+3
93–94	Bos	83	31	20	51	82	+4
94–95	Bos	44	18	13	31	31	-3
95–96	Pitt	81	24	40	64	69	+6

SSN	TEAM	GP	G	A	PTS.	PIM	+/-
96–97	NYI	64	28	28	56	25	+9
97–98	NYI	81	13	30	43	34	-16
98–99	NYI	82	16	24	40	49	-7
Totals		446	131	158	289	290	-4

Playoffs

92–93	Bos	4	1	0	1	2	
93–94	Bos	13	5	4	9	4	
94–95	Bos	5	0	1	1	4	
95–96	Pitt	18	5	4	9	10	
Totals		40	11	9	20	20	

SMRKE, John 5–11 205 LW
B. Chicoutimi, Que., Feb. 25, 1956

77–78	StL	18	2	4	6	11	-7
78–79	StL	55	6	8	14	20	-24
79–80	Que	30	3	5	8	2	+3
Totals		103	11	17	28	33	-28

SMRKE, Stanley 5–11 180 LW
B. Belgrade, Yugoslavia, Sept. 2, 1928

56–57	Mont	4	0	0	0	0	
57–58	Mont	5	0	3	3	0	
Totals		9	0	3	3	0	

SMYL, Stanley Phillip 5–8 185 RW
B. Glendon, Alta., Jan. 28, 1958

78–79	Van	62	14	24	38	89	-6
79–80	Van	77	31	47	78	204	+28
80–81	Van	80	25	38	63	171	-9
81–82	Van	80	34	44	78	144	+18
82–83	Van	74	38	50	88	114	-6
83–84	Van	80	24	43	67	136	-21
84–85	Van	80	27	37	64	100	-18
85–86	Van	73	27	35	62	144	-20
86–87	Van	66	20	23	43	84	-20
87–88	Van	57	12	25	37	110	-5
88–89	Van	75	7	18	25	102	0
89–90	Van	47	1	15	16	71	-14
90–91	Van	45	2	12	14	87	-5
Totals		896	262	411	673	1556	-77

Playoffs

78–79	Van	2	1	1	2	0	
79–80	Van	4	0	2	2	14	
80–81	Van	3	1	2	3	0	
81–82	Van	17	9	9	18	25	
82–83	Van	4	3	2	5	12	
83–84	Van	4	2	1	3	4	
88–89	Van	7	0	0	0	9	
Totals		41	16	17	33	64	

***SMYLIE, Roderick (Rod)** LW

20–21	Tor	23	2	0	2	2	
21–22	Tor	21	0	0	0	2	
22–23	Tor	2	0	0	0	0	
23–24	Ott	14	1	1	2	6	
24–25	Tor	11	0	0	0	0	
25–26	Tor	5	0	0	0	0	
Totals		76	3	1	4	10	

Playoffs

20–21	Tor	2	0	0	0	0	
21–22	Tor	6	1	2	3	2	
24–25	Tor	2	0	0	0	0	
Totals		10	1	2	3	2	

SMYTH, Brad 6–0 200 RW
B. Ottawa, Ont., Mar. 13, 1973

95–96	Fla	7	1	1	2	4	-3
96–97	Fla–LA	52	9	8	17	76	-10
97–98	LA–NYR	10	1	3	4	4	-1
98–99	Nash	3	0	0	0	6	-1
Totals		72	11	12	23	90	-15

SMYTH, Greg 6–3 212 D
B. Oakville, Ont., Apr. 23, 1966

86–87	Phil	1	0	0	0	0	-2
87–88	Phil	48	1	6	7	192	-9
88–89	Que	10	0	1	1	70	-8
89–90	Que	13	0	0	0	57	0
90–91	Que	1	0	0	0	0	0
91–92	Que–Calg	36	1	3	4	153	-3
92–93	Calg	35	1	2	3	95	+2
93–94	Fla–Tor–Chi	61	1	1	2	183	-4
94–95	Chi	22	0	3	3	33	+2
96–97	Tor	2	0	0	0	0	0

SSN	TEAM	GP	G	A	PTS.	PIM	+/-
Totals		229	4	16	20	783	-22

Playoffs

86–87	Phil	1	0	0	0	2	
87–88	Phil	5	0	0	0	38	
93–94	Chi	6	0	0	0	0	
Totals		12	0	0	0	40	

SMYTH, Kevin 6–2 217 LW
B. Banff, Alta., Nov. 22, 1973

93–94	Hart	21	3	2	5	10	-1
94–95	Hart	16	1	5	6	13	-3
95–96	Hart	21	2	1	3	8	-5
Totals		58	6	8	14	31	-9

SMYTH, Ryan 6–1 185 LW
B. Banff, Alta., Feb. 21, 1976

94–95	Edm	3	0	0	0	0	-1
95–96	Edm	48	2	9	11	28	-10
96–97	Edm	82	39	22	61	76	-7
97–98	Edm	65	20	13	33	44	-24
98–99	Edm	71	13	18	31	62	0
Totals		269	74	62	136	210	-42

Playoffs

96–97	Edm	12	5	5	10	12	
97–98	Edm	12	1	3	4	16	
98–99	Edm	3	0	0	0	0	
Totals		27	9	8	17	28	

SNELL, Chris 5–11 200 D
B. Regina, Sask., May 12, 1971

93–94	Tor	2	0	0	0	2	-1
94–95	LA	32	2	7	9	22	-7
Totals		34	2	7	9	24	-8

SNELL, Harold Edward (Ted) 5–9 190 RW
B. Ottawa, Ont., May 28, 1946

73–74	Pitt	55	4	12	16	8	-22
74–75	KC–Det	49	3	6	9	14	-18
Totals		104	7	18	25	22	-40

SNELL, Ronald Wayne 5–10 158 RW
B. Regina, Sask., Aug. 11, 1948

68–69	Pitt	4	3	1	4	6	+4
69–70	Pitt	3	0	1	1	0	-2
73–74	Winn (WHA)	70	24	25	49	32	
74–75	Winn (WHA)	20	0	0	0	8	
NHL Totals		7	3	2	5	6	+2
WHA Totals		90	24	25	49	40	

Playoffs

73–74	Winn (WHA)	4	0	0	0	0	

SNEPSTS, Harold John 6–3 210 D
B. Demonton, Alta., Oct. 24, 1954

74–75	Van	27	1	2	3	30	0
75–76	Van	78	3	15	18	125	+10
76–77	Van	79	4	18	22	149	-5
77–78	Van	75	4	16	20	118	-16
78–79	Van	76	7	24	31	130	-27
79–80	Van	79	3	20	23	202	+7
80–81	Van	76	3	16	19	212	+3
81–82	Van	68	3	14	17	153	+22
82–83	Van	46	2	8	10	80	-17
83–84	Van	79	4	16	20	152	-19
84–85	Minn	71	0	7	7	232	-19
85–86	Det	35	0	6	6	75	-7
86–87	Det	54	1	13	14	129	+7
87–88	Det	31	1	4	5	67	+3
88–89	Det	59	0	8	8	69	-3
89–90	Van–StL	46	1	4	5	36	-1
90–91	StL	54	1	4	5	50	+3
Totals		1033	38	195	233	2009	-59

Playoffs

75–76	Van	2	0	0	0	4	
78–79	Van	3	0	0	0	0	
79–80	Van	4	0	2	2	8	
80–81	Van	3	0	0	0	8	
81–82	Van	17	0	4	4	50	
82–83	Van	4	1	1	2	8	
83–84	Van	4	0	1	1	5	
84–85	Minn	9	0	0	0	24	
86–87	Det	11	0	2	2	18	
87–88	Det	10	0	1	1	40	

SSN	TEAM	GP	G	A	PTS.	PIM	+/-
88–89	Van	7	0	1	1	6	
89–90	StL	11	0	3	3	38	
90–91	StL	8	0	0	0	12	
Totals		93	1	14	15	231	

SNOW, William Alexander (Sandy) 5–11 175 RW
B. Glace Bay, N.S., Nov. 11, 1946

68–69	Det	3	0	0	0	2	0

SNUGGERUD, Dave 6–0 190 RW
B. Minnetonka, Minn., June 20, 1966

89–90	Buf	80	14	16	30	41	+8
90–91	Buf	80	9	15	24	32	-13
91–92	Buf–SJ	66	3	16	19	40	-15
92–93	SJ–Phil	39	4	7	11	14	-3
Totals		265	30	54	84	127	-23

Playoffs

89–90	Buf	6	0	0	0	2	
90–91	Buf	6	1	3	4	4	
Totals		12	1	3	4	6	

SOBCHUK, Dennis James 6–2 180 C
B. Lang, Sask., Jan. 12, 1954

74–75	Phoe (WHA)	38	32	45	77	36	
75–76	Cin (WHA)	79	32	40	72	74	
76–77	Cin (WHA)	81	44	52	96	38	
77–78	Cin–Edm (WHA)	36	11	12	23	26	
78–79	Edm (WHA)	74	26	37	63	31	
79–80	Det	33	4	6	10	0	-11
82–83	Que	2	1	0	1	2	+1
NHL Totals		35	5	6	11	2	-10
WHA Totals		308	145	186	331	205	

Playoffs

74–75	Phoe (WHA)	5	4	1	5	2	
76–77	Cin (WHA)	3	0	1	1	2	
77–78	Edm (WHA)	5	1	0	1	4	
78–79	Edm (WHA)	12	6	6	12	4	
WHA Totals		25	11	8	19	12	

SOBCHUK, Eugene 5–9 160 LW
B. Lang, Sask., Jan. 2, 1951

73–74	Van	1	0	0	0	0	0
74–75	Phoe (WHA)	3	1	0	1	0	
75–76	Cin (WHA)	78	24	19	43	37	
NHL Totals		1	0	0	0	0	0
WHA Totals		81	25	19	44	37	

SOLHEIM, Kenneth Lawrence 6–3 210 LW
B. Hythe, Alta., Mar. 27, 1961

80–81	Chi–Minn	10	4	1	5	0	0
81–82	Minn	29	4	5	9	4	-8
82–83	Minn–Det	35	2	4	6	6	-1
84–85	Minn	55	8	10	18	19	-15
85–86	Edm	6	1	0	1	5	-2
Totals		135	19	20	39	34	-26

Playoffs

80–81	Minn	2	1	0	1	0	
81–82	Minn	1	0	1	1	2	
Totals		3	1	1	2	2	

SOLINGER, Robert Edward 5–10 190 LW
B. Star City, Sask., Dec. 23, 1925

51–52	Tor	24	5	3	8	4	
52–53	Tor	19	1	1	2	2	
53–54	Tor	39	3	2	5	2	
54–55	Tor	17	1	5	6	11	
59–60	Det	1	0	0	0	0	
Totals		100	10	11	21	19	

SOMERS, Arthur E. 5–5 167 F
B. Winnipeg, Man., Jan. 17, 1904

29–30	Chi	44	11	13	24	74	
30–31	Chi	33	3	6	9	33	
31–32	NYR	48	11	15	26	45	
32–33	NYR	48	7	15	22	28	
33–34	NYR	8	1	2	3	5	
34–35	NYR	41	0	5	5	4	
Totals		222	33	56	89	189	

Playoffs

29–30	Chi	2	0	0	0	2	
30–31	Chi	9	0	0	0	0	
31–32	NYR	7	0	1	1	8	
32–33	NYR	8	1	4	5	8	
33–34	NYR	2	0	0	0	0	
34–35	NYR	2	0	0	0	2	
Totals		30	1	5	6	20	

SOMMER, Roy 6–0 180 C
B. Oakland, Calif., Apr. 5, 1957

80–81	Edm	3	1	0	1	7	0

SONGIN, Thomas David 6–3 195 RW
B. Norwood, Mass., Dec. 20, 1953

78–79	Bos	17	3	1	4	0	-3
79–80	Bos	17	1	3	4	16	0
80–81	Bos	9	1	1	2	6	0
Totals		43	5	5	10	22	-3

SONMOR, Glen Robert 5–11 165 LW
B. Moose Jaw, Sask., Apr. 22, 1929

53–54	NYR	15	2	0	2	17	
54–55	NYR	13	0	0	0	4	
Totals		28	2	0	2	21	

SONNENBERG, Martin 6–0 184 C
B. Wetaskiwin, Alta., Jan. 23, 1978

98–99	Pitt	44	1	1	2	19	-2

Playoffs

98–99	Pitt	7	0	0	0	0	

SOPEL, Brent 6–1 190 D
B. Calgary, Alta., Jan. 7, 1977

98–99	Van	5	1	0	1	4	-1

SOROCHAN, Lee 5–11 210 D
B. Edmonton, Alta., Sept. 9, 1975

98–99	Calg	2	0	0	0	0	-3

***SORRELL, John Arthur** 6–0 152 LW
B. Chesterville, Ont., Jan. 16, 1906

30–31	Det	39	9	7	16	10	
31–32	Det	48	8	5	13	22	
32–33	Det	47	14	10	24	11	
33–34	Det	47	21	10	31	8	
34–35	Det	47	20	16	36	12	
35–36	Det	48	13	15	28	8	
36–37	Det	48	8	16	24	4	
37–38	Det–NYA	40	11	9	20	9	
38–39	NYA	48	13	9	22	10	
39–40	NYA	48	8	16	24	4	
40–41	NYA	30	2	6	8	2	
Totals		490	127	119	246	100	

Playoffs

31–32	Det	2	1	0	1	0	
32–33	Det	4	2	2	4	4	
33–34	Det	8	0	2	2	0	
35–36	Det	7	3	4	7	0	
36–37	Det	10	2	4	6	2	
37–38	NYA	6	4	0	4	2	
38–39	NYA	2	0	0	0	0	
39–40	NYA	3	0	3	3	2	
Totals		42	12	15	27	10	

SOURAY, Sheldon 6–2 210 D
B. Elk Point, Alta., July 13, 1976

97–98	NJ	60	3	7	10	85	+18
98–99	NJ	70	1	7	8	110	+5
Totals		130	4	14	18	195	+23

Playoffs

97–98	NJ	3	0	1	1	2	
98–99	NJ	2	0	1	1	0	
Totals		5	0	2	2	2	

SPACEK, Jaroslav 5–11 198 D
B. Rokycany, Czech., Feb. 11, 1974

98–99	Fla		3	12	15	28	+15

***SPARROW, Emory (Spunk)** F

24–25	Bos	6	0	0	0	4	

SPECK, Frederick Edmondstone 5–9 160 C
B. Thorold, Ont., July 22, 1947

68–69	Det	5	0	0	0	2	0
69–70	Det	5	0	0	0	0	-2
71–72	Van	18	1	2	3	0	-15
72–73	Minn–LA (WHA)	75	16	29	45	74	
73–74	LA (WHA)	18	2	5	7	4	
74–75	Balt (WHA)	30	4	8	12	18	
NHL Totals		28	1	2	3	2	-17
WHA Totals		123	22	42	64	96	

Playoffs

72–73	LA (WHA)	6	3	2	5	2	

***SPEER, Francis William (Bill)** 5–11 200 D
B. Lindsay, Ont., Mar. 20, 1942

67–68	Pitt	68	3	13	16	44	-14
68–69	Pitt	34	1	4	5	27	-16
69–70	Bos	27	1	3	4	4	+6
70–71	Bos	1	0	0	0	4	0
72–73	NY (WHA)	69	3	23	26	40	
73–74	NY–NJ (WHA)	66	1	3	4	30	
NHL Totals		130	5	20	25	79	-24
WHA Totals		135	4	26	30	70	

Playoffs

69–70	bos	8	1	0	1	4	

SPEERS, Ted 5–11 200 RW
B. Ann Arbor, Mich., Jan. 28, 1961

85–86	Det	4	1	1	2	0	+2

***SPENCER, Brian Roy** 5–11 185 LW
B. Fort St. James, B.C., Sept. 3, 1949

69–70	Tor	9	0	0	0	12	-4
70–71	Tor	50	9	15	24	115	+2
71–72	Tor	36	1	5	6	65	+2
72–73	NYI	78	14	24	38	90	-47
73–74	NYI–Buf	67	8	18	26	69	-19
74–75	Buf	73	12	29	41	77	+17
75–76	Buf	77	13	26	39	70	+14
76–77	Buf	77	14	15	29	55	0
77–78	Pitt	79	9	11	20	81	-18
78–79	Pitt	7	0	0	0	0	0
Totals		553	80	143	223	634	-53

Playoffs

70–71	Tor	6	0	1	1	17	
74–75	Buf	16	0	4	4	8	
75–76	buf	9	1	0	1	4	
76–77	Buf	6	0	0	0	0	
Totals		37	1	5	6	29	

SPENCER, Irvin James 5–10 180 D
B. Sudbury, Ont., Dec. 4, 1937

59–60	NYR	32	1	2	3	20	
60–61	NYR	56	1	8	9	30	
61–62	NYR	43	2	10	12	31	
62–63	Bos	69	5	17	22	34	
63–64	Det	25	3	0	3	8	
67–68	Det	5	0	1	1	4	-1
72–73	Phil (WHA)	54	2	27	29	43	
73–74	Van (WHA)	19	0	1	1	6	
NHL Totals		230	12	38	50	127	-1
WHA Totals		73	2	28	30	49	

Playoffs

61–62	NYR	1	0	0	0	2	
63–64	Det	11	0	0	0	0	
64–65	Det	1	0	0	0	4	
65–66	Det	3	0	0	0	2	
Totals		16	0	0	0	8	

***SPEYER, Christopher** D
B. Toronto, Ont., Feb. 6, 1907

23–24	Tor	3	0	0	0	0	
24–25	Tor	2	0	0	0	0	
33–34	NYA	9	0	0	0	0	
Totals		14	0	0	0	0	

SPRING, Corey 6–4 214 RW
B. Cranbrook, B.C., May 31, 1971

97–98	TB	8	1	0	1	10	-1
98–99	TB	8	0	1	1	2	0
Totals		16	1	1	2	12	-1

SSN	TEAM	GP	G	A	PTS.	PIM	+/-

SPRING, Donald Neil *5–11 195 D*
B. Maracaibo, Venezuela, June 15, 1959

80–81	Winn	80	1	18	19	18	-40
82–82	Winn	78	0	16	16	21	-13
82–83	Winn	80	0	16	16	16	0
83–84	Winn	21	0	4	4	4	-5
Totals		259	1	54	55	80	-58

Playoffs

81–82	Winn	4	0	0	0	4	
82–83	Winn	2	0	0	0	6	
Totals		6	0	0	0	10	

SPRING, Franklin Patrick *6–3 216 RW*
B. Cranbrook, B.C., Oct. 19, 1949

69–70	Bos	1	0	0	0	0	
73–74	StL	2	0	0	0	0	0
74–75	StL–Cal	31	3	8	11	6	0
75–67	Cal	1	0	2	2	0	+1
76–77	Clev	26	11	10	21	6	-8
NHL Totals		61	14	20	34	12	-7
WHA Totals		13	2	4	6	2	

*SPRING, Jesse *D*
B. Alba., Penn., Jan. 18, 1901

23–24	Ham	20	3	2	5	8	
24–25	Ham	29	2	0	2	11	
25–26	Pitt Pi	32	5	0	5	23	
26–27	Tor	2	0	0	0	0	
28–29	NYA–Pitt Pi	32	0	0	0	2	
29–30	Pitt Pi	22	1	0	1	18	
Totals		137	11	2	13	62	

Playoffs

25–26	Pitt Pi	2	0	2	2	2	

SPRUCE, Andrew William *5–11 177 LW*
B. London, Ont., Apr. 17, 1954

76–77	Van	51	9	6	15	37	-20
77–78	Col	74	19	21	40	43	-7
78–79	Col	47	3	15	18	31	-18
Totals		172	31	42	73	111	-45

Playoffs

77–78	Col	2	0	2	2	0	

SRSEN, Tomas *5–11 180 LW*
B. Olomouc, Czechoslovakia, Aug. 25, 1966

90–91	Edm	2	0	0	0	0	0

*STACKHOUSE, Ronald Lorne *6–3 210 D*
B. Haliburton, Ont., Aug. 26, 1949

70–71	Cal	78	8	24	32	73	-28
71–72	Cal–Det	79	6	28	34	89	-8
72–73	Det	78	5	29	34	82	+22
73–74	Det–Pitt	69	6	29	35	66	+13
74–75	Pitt	72	15	45	60	52	+13
75–76	Pitt	80	11	60	71	76	+19
76–77	Pitt	80	7	34	41	74	+11
77–78	Pitt	50	5	15	20	36	-16
78–79	Pitt	75	10	33	43	54	+21
79–80	Pitt	78	6	27	33	36	+16
80–81	Pitt	74	6	29	35	86	-11
81–82	Pitt	76	2	19	21	102	-11
Totals		889	87	372	459	824	+41

Playoffs

74–75	Pitt	9	2	6	8	10	
75–76	Pitt	3	0	0	0	0	
76–77	Pitt	3	2	1	3	0	
78–79	Pitt	7	0	0	0	4	
79–80	Pitt	5	1	0	1	18	
80–81	Pitt	4	0	1	1	6	
81–82	Pitt	1	0	0	0	0	
Totals		32	5	8	13	38	

STACKHOUSE, Theodore (Ted) *D*

21–22	Tor	12	0	0	0	2	

Playoffs

21–22	Tor	5	0	0	0	0	

*STAHAN, Frank Ralph (Butch) *D*
B. Minnedosa, Man., Oct. 29, 1915

Playoffs

44–45	Mont	3	0	1	1	2	

STAIOS, Steve *6–0 185 D*
B. Hamilton, Ont., July 28, 1973

95–96	Bos	12	0	0	0	4	-5
96–97	Bos–Van	63	3	14	17	91	-24
97–98	Van	77	3	4	7	134	-3
98–99	Van	57	0	2	2	54	-12
Totals		209	6	20	26	283	-44

Playoffs

95–96	Bos	3	0	0	0	0	

STAJDUHAR, Nick *6–2 195 D*
B. Kitchener, Ont., Dec. 6, 1974

95–96	Edm	2	0	0	0	4	+2

STALEY, Allan R. (Red) *6–0 160 C*
B. Regina, Sask., Sept. 21. 1928

48–49	NYR	1	0	1	1	0	

STAMLER, Lorne Alexander *6–0 190 LW*
B. Winnipeg, Man., Aug. 9, 1951

76–77	LA	7	2	1	3	2	0
77–78	LA	2	0	0	0	0	0
78–79	Tor	45	4	3	7	2	-6
79–80	Winn	62	8	7	15	12	-29
Totals		116	14	11	25	16	-35

STANDING, George Michael *5–10 175 RW*
B. Toronto, Ont., Aug. 3, 1941

67–68	Minn	2	0	0	0	0	-1

STANFIELD, Frederic William *5–10 185 C*
B. Toronto, Ont., May 4, 1944

64–65	Chi	58	7	10	17	14	
65–66	Chi	39	2	2	4	2	
66–67	Chi	10	1	0	1	0	
67–68	Bos	73	20	44	64	10	+9
68–69	Bos	71	25	29	54	22	-4
69–70	Bos	73	23	35	58	14	+7
70–71	Bos	75	24	52	76	12	+32
71–72	Bos	78	23	56	79	12	+20
72–73	Bos	78	20	58	78	10	+12
73–74	Minn	71	16	28	44	10	-14
74–75	Minn–Buf	72	20	39	59	16	-5
75–76	Buf	80	18	30	48	4	+5
76–77	Buf	79	9	14	23	6	-2
77–78	Buf	57	3	8	11	2	-8
Totals		914	211	405	616	134	+52

Playoffs

64–65	Chi	14	2	1	3	2	
65–66	Chi	5	0	0	0	2	
66–67	Chi	1	0	0	0	0	
67–68	Bos	4	0	1	1	0	
68–69	Bos	10	2	2	4	0	
69–70	Bos	14	4	12	16	6	
70–71	Bos	7	3	4	7	0	
71–72	Bos	15	7	9	16	0	
72–73	Bos	5	1	1	2	0	
74–75	Buf	9	0	1	1	0	
76–77	Buf	5	0	0	0	0	
Totals		106	21	35	56	10	

STANFIELD, James Boviard *5–10 165 C*
B. Toronto, Ont., Jan. 1, 1947

69–70	LA	1	0	0	0	0	0
70–71	LA	2	0	0	0	0	+1
71–72	LA	4	0	1	1	0	-1
Totals		7	0	1	1	0	0

STANFIELD, John Gordon (Jack) *5–11 176 LW*
B. Toronto, Ont., May 30, 1942

72–73	Hou (WHA)	71	8	12	20	8	
73–74	Hou (WHA)	41	1	3	4	2	
WHA Totals		112	9	15	24	10	

Playoffs

65–66	Chi	1	0	0	0	0	
72–73	Hous (WHA)	9	1	0	1	0	
73–74	Hous (WHA)	7	0	0	0	2	
NHL Totals		1	0	0	0	0	
WHA Totals		16	1	0	1	2	

STANKIEWICZ, Edward *5–9 175 RW*
B. Kitchener, Ont., Dec. 1, 1929

53–54	Det	1	0	0	0	2	
55–56	Det	5	0	0	0	0	
Totals		6	0	0	0	2	

STANKIEWICZ, Myron (Mike) *5–11 185 LW*
B. Kitchener, Ont., Dec. 4, 1935

68–69	StL–Phil	35	0	7	7	36	-13

Playoffs

68–69	Phil	1	0	0	0	0	

STANLEY, Allan Herbert *6–2 191 D*
B. Timmins, Ont., Mar. 1, 1926

48–49	NYR	40	2	8	10	22	
49–50	NYR	55	4	4	8	58	
50–51	NYR	70	7	14	21	75	
51–52	NYR	50	5	14	19	52	
52–53	NYR	70	5	12	17	52	
53–54	NYR–Chi	10	0	2	2	11	
54–55	NYR–Chi	64	10	16	26	24	
55–56	Chi	59	4	14	18	70	
56–57	Bos	60	6	25	31	45	
57–58	Bos	69	6	25	31	37	
58–59	Tor	70	1	22	23	47	
59–60	Tor	64	10	23	33	22	
60–61	Tor	68	9	25	34	42	
61–62	Tor	60	9	26	35	24	
62–63	Tor	61	4	15	19	22	
63–64	Tor	70	6	21	27	60	
64–65	Tor	64	2	15	17	30	
65–66	Tor	59	4	14	18	35	
66–67	Tor	53	1	12	13	20	
67–68	Tor	64	1	13	14	16	+6
68–69	Phil	64	4	13	17	28	-4
Totals		1244	100	333	433	792	+2

Playoffs

49–50	NYR	12	2	5	7	10	
57–58	Bos	12	1	3	4	6	
58–59	Tor	12	0	3	3	2	
59–60	Tor	10	2	3	5	2	
60–61	Tor	5	0	3	3	0	
61–62	Tor	12	0	3	3	6	
62–63	Tor	10	1	6	7	8	
63–64	Tor	14	1	6	7	20	
64–65	Tor	6	0	1	1	12	
65–66	Tor	1	0	0	0	0	
66–67	Tor	12	0	2	2	10	
68–69	Phil	3	0	1	1	4	
Totals		109	7	36	43	80	

STANLEY, Daryl *6–2 200 D/LW*
B. Winnipeg, Man., Dec. 2, 1962

83–84	Phil	23	1	4	5	71	+4
85–86	Phil	33	0	2	2	69	-5
86–87	Phil	33	1	2	3	76	+6
87–88	Van	57	2	7	9	151	-12
88–89	Van	20	3	1	4	14	+3
89–90	Van	23	1	1	2	27	-2
Totals		189	8	17	25	408	-6

Playoffs

83–84	Phil	3	0	0	0	19	
85–86	Phil	1	0	0	0	2	
86–87	Phil	13	0	0	0	9	
Totals		17	0	0	0	30	

*STANLEY, Russell (Barney) *F*
B. Paisley, Ont., June 1, 1893

27–28	Chi	1	0	0	0	0	

STANOWSKI, Walter Peter (Wally) *5–11 180 D*
B. Winnipeg, Man., Apr. 28, 1919

39–40	Tor	27	2	7	9	11	
40–41	Tor	47	7	14	21	35	
41–42	Tor	24	1	7	8	10	
44–45	Tor	34	2	9	11	16	
45–46	Tor	45	3	10	13	10	
46–47	Tor	51	3	16	19	12	
47–48	Tor	54	2	11	13	12	
48–49	NYR	60	1	8	9	16	
49–50	NYR	37	1	1	2	10	
50–51	NYR	49	1	5	6	28	
Totals		428	23	88	111	160	

Playoffs

SSN	TEAM	GP	G	A	PTS.	PIM	+/-
39–40	Tor	10	1	0	1	2	
40–41	Tor	7	0	3	3	2	
41–42	tor	13	2	8	10	2	
44–45	Tor	13	0	1	1	5	
46–47	Tor	8	0	0	0	0	
47–48	Tor	9	0	2	2	2	
Totals		60	3	14	17	13	

STANTON, Paul Frederick *6–1 193 D*
B. Boston, Mass., June 22, 1967

SSN	TEAM	GP	G	A	PTS.	PIM	+/-
90–91	Pitt	75	5	18	23	40	+11
91–92	Pitt	54	2	8	10	62	-8
92–93	Pitt	77	4	12	16	97	+7
93–94	Bos	71	3	7	10	54	-7
94–95	NYI	18	0	4	4	9	-6
Totals		295	14	49	63	262	-3

Playoffs

SSN	TEAM	GP	G	A	PTS.	PIM	+/-
90–91	Pitt	22	1	2	3	24	
91–92	Pitt	21	1	7	8	42	
92–93	Pitt	1	0	1	1	0	
Totals		44	2	10	12	66	

STAPLETON, Brian *6–2 190 D*
B. Fort Erie, Ont., Dec. 25, 1951

SSN	TEAM	GP	G	A	PTS.	PIM	+/-
75–76	Wash	1	0	0	0	0	-2

STAPLETON, Mike *5–10 183 C*
B. Sarnia, Ont., May 5, 1966

SSN	TEAM	GP	G	A	PTS.	PIM	+/-
86–87	Chi	39	3	6	9	6	-9
87–88	Chi	53	2	9	11	59	-10
88–89	Chi	7	0	1	1	7	-1
90–91	Chi	7	0	1	1	2	0
91–92	Chi	19	4	4	8	8	0
92–93	Pitt	78	4	9	13	10	-8
93–94	Pitt–Edm	81	12	13	25	46	-5
94–95	Edm	46	6	11	17	21	-12
95–96	Winn	58	10	14	24	37	-4
96–97	Phoe	55	4	11	15	36	-4
97–98	Phoe	64	5	5	10	36	-4
98–99	Phoe	76	9	9	18	34	-6
Totals		583	59	93	152	302	-63

Playoffs

SSN	TEAM	GP	G	A	PTS.	PIM	+/-
86–87	Chi	4	0	0	0	2	
92–93	Pitt	4	0	0	0	0	
95–96	Winn	6	0	0	0	21	
96–97	Phoe	7	0	0	0	14	
97–98	Phoe	6	0	0	0	2	
98–99	Phoe	7	1	0	1	0	
Totals		34	1	0	1	39	

STAPLETON, Patrick James (Pat) *5–8 185 D*
B. Sarnia, Ont., July 4, 1940

SSN	TEAM	GP	G	A	PTS.	PIM	+/-
61–62	Bos	69	2	5	7	42	
62–63	Bos	21	0	3	3	8	
65–66	Chi	55	4	30	34	52	
66–67	Chi	70	3	31	34	54	
67–68	Chi	67	4	34	38	34	+4
68–69	Chi	75	6	50	56	44	+23
69–70	Chi	49	4	38	42	28	+18
70–71	Chi	76	7	44	51	30	+49
71–72	Chi	78	3	38	41	47	+41
72–73	Chi	75	10	21	31	14	+19
73–74	Chi (WHA)	78	6	52	58	44	
74–75	Chi (WHA)	68	4	30	34	38	
75–76	Ind (WHA)	80	4	40	44	48	
76–77	Ind (WHA)	81	8	45	53	29	
77–78	Cin (WHA)	65	4	45	49	28	
NHL Totals		635	43	294	337	353	+154
WHA Totals		372	26	212	238	187	

Playoffs

SSN	TEAM	GP	G	A	PTS.	PIM	+/-
65–66	Chi	6	2	3	5	4	
66–67	Chi	6	1	1	2	12	
67–68	Chi	11	0	4	4	4	
70–71	Chi	18	3	14	17	4	
71–72	Chi	8	3	2	4	4	
72–73	Chi	16	2	15	17	10	
73–74	Chi (WHA)	18	0	13	13	36	
75–76	Ind (WHA)	7	0	2	2	2	
76–77	Ind (WHA)	9	2	6	8	0	
NHL Totals		65	10	39	49	38	
WHA Totals		34	2	21	23	38	

STARIKOV, Sergei *5–10 225 D*
B. Chelyabinsk, Soviet Union, Dec. 4, 1958

SSN	TEAM	GP	G	A	PTS.	PIM	+/-
89–90	NJ	16	0	1	1	8	-8

STARR, Harold *5–11 176 D*
B. Ottawa, Ont., July 6, 1906

SSN	TEAM	GP	G	A	PTS.	PIM	+/-
29–30	Ott	27	2	1	3	12	
30–31	Ott	36	2	1	3	48	
31–32	Mont M	46	1	2	3	47	
32–33	Ott–Mont	46	0	0	0	36	
33–34	Mont M	1	0	0	0	0	
34–35	NYR	32	1	1	2	31	
35–36	NYR	15	0	0	0	12	
Totals		203	6	5	11	186	

Playoffs

SSN	TEAM	GP	G	A	PTS.	PIM	+/-
29–30	Ott	2	1	0	1	0	
31–32	Mont M	4	0	0	0	0	
32–33	Mont	4	0	0	0	0	
33–34	Mont M	3	0	0	0	0	
34–35	NYR	4	0	0	0	2	
Totals		17	1	0	1	2	

STARR, Wilfred Peter (Wilf) *5–11 190 F*
B. St. Boniface, Man., July 22, 1909

SSN	TEAM	GP	G	A	PTS.	PIM	+/-
32–33	NYA	27	4	3	7	8	
33–34	Det	28	2	2	4	17	
34–35	Det	29	1	1	2	0	
35–36	Det	5	1	0	1	0	
Totals		89	8	6	14	25	

Playoffs

SSN	TEAM	GP	G	A	PTS.	PIM	+/-
33–34	Det	7	0	2	2	2	

STASIUK, Victor John *6–1 185 LW*
B. Lethbridge, Alta., May 23, 1929

SSN	TEAM	GP	G	A	PTS.	PIM	+/-
49–50	Chi	17	1	1	2	2	
50–51	Chi–Det	70	8	13	21	18	
51–52	Det	58	5	9	14	19	
52–53	Det	3	0	0	0	0	
53–54	Det	42	5	2	7	4	
54–55	Det	59	8	11	19	67	
55–56	Bos	59	19	18	37	118	
56–57	Bos	64	24	16	40	50	
57–58	Bos	70	21	35	56	55	
58–59	Bos	70	27	33	60	63	
59–60	Bos	69	29	39	68	121	
60–61	Bos–Det	69	15	38	53	51	
61–62	Det	59	15	28	43	45	
62–63	Det	36	6	11	17	37	
Totals		745	183	254	437	650	

Playoffs

SSN	TEAM	GP	G	A	PTS.	PIM	+/-
51–52	Det	7	0	2	2	0	
54–55	Det	11	5	3	8	6	
56–57	Bos	10	2	1	3	2	
57–58	Bos	12	0	5	5	13	
58–59	Bos	7	4	2	6	11	
60–61	Det	11	2	5	7	4	
62–63	Det	11	3	0	3	4	
Totals		69	16	18	34	40	

STASTNY, Anton *6–0 188 LW*
B. Bratislava, Czechoslovakia, Aug. 5, 1959

SSN	TEAM	GP	G	A	PTS.	PIM	+/-
80–81	Que	80	39	46	85	12	+4
81–82	Que	68	26	46	72	16	-29
82–83	Que	79	32	60	92	25	+25
83–84	Que	69	25	37	62	14	+12
84–85	Que	79	38	42	80	30	+18
85–86	Que	74	31	43	74	19	+8
86–87	Que	77	27	35	62	8	+3
87–88	Que	69	27	45	72	14	-9
88–89	Que	55	7	30	37	12	-19
Totals		650	252	384	636	150	+13

Playoffs

SSN	TEAM	GP	G	A	PTS.	PIM	+/-
80–81	Que	5	4	3	7	2	
81–82	Que	16	5	10	15	10	
82–83	Que	4	2	2	4	0	
83–84	Que	9	2	5	7	7	
84–85	Que	16	3	3	6	6	
85–86	Que	3	1	1	2	0	
86–87	Que	13	3	8	11	6	
Totals		66	20	32	52	31	

STASTNY, Marian *5–10 195 RW*
B. Bratislava, Czechoslovakia, Jan. 8, 1953

SSN	TEAM	GP	G	A	PTS.	PIM	+/-
81–82	Que	74	35	54	89	27	0
82–83	Que	60	36	43	79	32	+20
83–84	Que	68	20	32	52	26	+1
84–85	Que	50	7	14	21	4	+1
85–86	Tor	70	23	30	53	21	-6
Totals		322	121	173	294	110	+16

Playoffs

SSN	TEAM	GP	G	A	PTS.	PIM	+/-
81–82	Que	16	3	14	17	5	
82–83	Que	2	0	0	0	0	
83–84	Que	9	2	3	5	2	
84–85	Que	2	0	0	0	0	
85–86	Que	3	0	0	0	0	
Totals		32	5	17	22	7	

STASTNY, Peter *6–1 200 C*
B. Bratislava, Czechoslovakia, Sept, 18, 1956

SSN	TEAM	GP	G	A	PTS.	PIM	+/-
80–81	Que	77	39	70	109	37	+11
81–82	Que	80	46	93	139	91	-10
82–83	Que	75	47	77	124	78	+28
83–84	Que	80	46	73	119	73	+22
84–85	Que	75	32	68	100	95	+23
85–86	Que	76	41	81	122	60	+2
86–87	Que	64	24	53	77	43	-21
87–88	Que	76	46	65	111	69	+2
88–89	Que	72	35	50	85	117	-23
89–90	Que–NJ	74	29	44	73	40	-46
90–91	NJ	77	18	42	60	53	0
91–92	NJ	66	24	38	62	42	+6
92–93	NJ	62	17	23	40	22	-5
93–94	StL	17	5	11	16	4	-2
94–95	StL	6	1	1	2	0	+1
Totals		977	450	789	1239	824	-12

Playoffs

SSN	TEAM	GP	G	A	PTS.	PIM	+/-
80–81	Que	5	2	8	10	7	
81–82	Que	12	7	11	18	10	
82–83	Que	4	3	2	5	10	
83–84	Que	9	2	7	9	31	
84–85	Que	18	4	19	23	24	
85–86	Que	3	0	1	1	2	
86–87	Que	13	6	9	15	12	
89–90	NJ	6	3	2	5	2	
90–91	NJ	7	3	4	7	2	
91–92	NJ	7	3	7	10	19	
92–93	NJ	5	0	2	2	2	
93–94	StL	4	0	0	0	2	
Totals		93	33	72	105	123	

STASZAK, Ray *6–0 200 RW*
B. Philadelphia, Pa., Dec. 1, 1962

SSN	TEAM	GP	G	A	PTS.	PIM	+/-
85–86	Det	4	0	1	1	7	-3

***STEELE, Frank** *D*

SSN	TEAM	GP	G	A	PTS.	PIM	+/-
30–31	Det	1	0	0	0	0	

STEEN, Anders *F*
B. Nykoping, Sweden, Apr. 28, 1955

SSN	TEAM	GP	G	A	PTS.	PIM	+/-
80–81	Winn	42	5	11	16	22	-22

STEEN, Thomas *5–11 190 C*
B. Grums, Sweden, June 8, 1960

SSN	TEAM	GP	G	A	PTS.	PIM	+/-
81–82	Winn	73	15	29	44	42	+16
82–83	Winn	75	26	33	59	60	-6
83–84	Winn	78	20	45	65	69	-5
84–85	Winn	79	30	54	84	80	-1
85–86	Winn	78	17	47	64	76	-29
86–87	Winn	75	17	33	50	59	+7
87–88	Winn	76	16	38	54	53	-11
88–89	Winn	80	27	61	88	80	+14
89–90	Winn	53	18	48	66	35	+2
90–91	Winn	58	19	48	67	49	-3
91–92	Winn	38	13	25	38	29	+5
92–93	Winn	80	22	50	72	75	-8
93–94	Winn	76	19	32	51	32	-38
94–95	Winn	31	5	10	15	14	-13
Totals		950	264	553	817	753	-70

Playoffs

SSN	TEAM	GP	G	A	PTS.	PIM	+/-
81–82	Winn	4	0	4	4	2	
82–83	Winn	3	0	2	2	0	
83–84	Winn	3	0	1	1	9	
84–85	Winn	8	2	3	5	17	
85–86	Winn	3	1	1	2	4	
86–87	Winn	10	3	4	7	8	

SSN	TEAM	GP	G	A	PTS.	PIM	+/-
87-88	Winn	5	1	5	6	2	
89-90	Winn	7	2	5	7	16	
91-92	Winn	7	2	4	6	2	
92-93	Winn	6	1	3	4	2	
Totals		56	12	32	44	62	

STEFANIW, Morris Alexander *5-11 170 C*
B. North Battleford, Sask., Jan. 10, 1948

72-73	Atl	13	1	1	2	2	-3

STEFANSKI, Edward Stanley Michael (Bud)
5-10 170 C
B. South Porcupine, Ont., Apr. 28, 1955

77-78	NYR	1	0	0	0	0	-1

STEMKOWSKI, Peter David (Stemmer) *6-1 210 C*
B. Winnipeg, Man., Aug. 25, 1943

63-64	Tor	1	0	0	0	2	
64-65	Tor	36	5	15	20	33	
65-66	Tor	56	4	12	16	55	
66-67	Tor	68	13	22	35	75	
67-68	Tor-Det	73	10	21	31	86	-9
68-69	Det	71	21	31	52	81	+1
69-70	Det	76	25	24	49	114	+13
70-71	Det-NYR	78	18	31	49	69	+15
71-72	NYR	59	11	17	28	53	+2
72-73	NYR	78	22	37	59	71	+27
73-74	NYR	78	25	45	70	74	+3
74-75	NYR	77	24	35	59	63	-3
75-76	NYR	75	13	28	41	49	-7
76-77	NYR	61	2	13	15	8	-14
77-78	LA	80	13	18	31	33	+1
Totals		967	206	349	555	866	+30

Playoffs

64-65	Tor	6	0	3	3	7	
65-66	Tor	4	0	0	0	26	
66-67	Tor	12	5	7	12	20	
69-70	Det	4	1	1	2	6	
70-71	NYR	13	3	2	5	6	
71-72	NYR	16	4	8	12	18	
72-73	NYR	10	4	2	6	6	
73-74	NYR	13	6	6	12	35	
74-75	NYR	3	1	0	1	10	
77-78	LA	2	1	0	1	2	

STENLUND, Kenneth Vern (Vern) *6-1 178 C*
B. Thunder Bay, Ont., Nov. 4, 1956

76-77	Clev	4	0	0	0	0	-3

***STEPHENS, Philip** *D*
B. 1895

17-18	Mont W	4	1	0	1	0	
21-22	Mont	4	0	0	0	0	
Totals		8	1	0	1	0	

STEPHENSON, Robert *6-1 187 D*
B. Saskatoon, Sask., Feb. 1, 1954

77-78	Birm (WHA)	39	7	6	13	33	
78-79	Birm (WHA)	78	23	24	47	72	
79-80	Hart-Tor	18	2	3	5	4	-5
NHL Totals		18	2	3	5	4	-5
WHA Totals		117	30	30	60	105	

STERN, Ronald *6-0 195 RW*
B. Ste. Agathe, Que., Jan. 11, 1967

87-88	Van	15	0	0	0	52	-7
88-89	Van	17	1	0	1	49	-6
89-90	Van	34	2	3	5	208	-17
90-91	Van-Calg	44	3	6	9	240	-14
91-92	Calg	72	13	9	22	338	0
92-93	Calg	70	10	15	25	207	+4
93-94	Calg	71	9	20	29	243	+6
94-95	Calg	39	9	4	13	163	+4
95-96	Calg	52	10	5	15	111	+2
96-97	Calg	79	7	10	17	157	-4
98-99	SJ	78	7	9	16	158	-3
Totals		571	71	81	152	1926	-35

Playoffs

88-89	Van	3	0	1	1	17	
90-91	Calg	7	1	3	4	14	
92-93	Calg	6	0	0	0	43	
93-94	Calg	7	2	0	2	12	
94-95	Calg	7	3	1	4	8	
95-96	Calg	4	0	2	2	8	

SSN	TEAM	GP	G	A	PTS.	PIM	+/-
98-99	SJ	6	0	0	0	6	
Totals		40	6	7	13	108	

STERNER, Ulf *6-2 187 LW*
B. Deje, Sweden, Feb. 11, 1941

64-65	NYR	4	0	0	0	0	

STEVENS, John *6-1 195 D*
B. Campbellton, N.B., May 4, 1966

86-87	Phil	6	0	2	2	14	0
87-88	Phil	3	0	0	0	0	-1
90-91	Hart	14	0	1	1	11	0
91-92	Hart	21	0	4	4	19	-4
93-94	Hart	9	0	3	3	4	+4
Totals		53	0	10	10	48	-1

STEVENS, Kevin Michael *6-3 217 LW*
B. Brockton, Mass., Apr. 15, 1965

87-88	Pitt	16	5	2	7	8	-6
88-89	Pitt	24	12	3	15	19	-8
89-90	Pitt	76	29	41	70	171	-13
90-91	Pitt	80	40	46	86	133	-1
91-92	Pitt	80	54	69	123	254	+8
92-93	Pitt	72	55	56	111	177	+17
93-94	Pitt	83	41	47	88	155	-24
94-95	Pitt	27	15	12	27	51	0
95-96	Bos-LA	61	13	23	36	71	-10
96-97	LA	69	14	20	34	96	-27
97-98	NYR	80	14	27	41	130	-7
98-99	NYR	81	23	20	43	64	-10
Totals		749	315	366	681	1329	-81

Playoffs

88-89	Pitt	11	3	7	10	16	
90-91	Pitt	24	17	16	33	53	
91-92	Pitt	21	13	15	28	28	
92-93	Pitt	12	5	11	16	22	
93-94	Pitt	6	1	1	2	10	
94-95	Pitt	12	4	7	11	21	
Totals		86	43	57	100	171	

STEVENS, Mike *5-11 195 LW*
B. Kitchener, Ont., Dec. 30, 1965

84-85	Van	6	0	3	3	6	-2
87-88	Bos	7	0	1	1	9	0
88-89	NYI	9	1	0	1	14	-1
89-90	Tor	1	0	0	0	0	0
Totals		23	1	4	5	29	-3

STEVENS, Paul *D*

25-26	Bos	17	0	0	0	0	

STEVENS, Scott *6-2 215 D*
B. Kitchener, Ont., Apr. 1, 1964

82-83	Wash	77	9	16	25	195	+14
83-84	Wash	78	13	32	45	201	+26
84-85	Wash	80	21	44	65	221	+19
85-86	Wash	73	15	38	53	165	0
86-87	Wash	77	10	51	61	283	+13
87-88	Wash	80	12	60	72	184	+14
88-89	Wash	80	7	61	68	225	+1
89-90	Wash	56	11	29	40	154	+1
90-91	StL	78	5	44	49	150	+23
91-92	NJ	68	17	42	59	124	+24
92-93	NJ	81	12	45	57	120	+14
93-94	NJ	83	18	60	78	112	+53
94-95	NJ	48	2	20	22	56	+4
95-96	NJ	82	5	23	28	100	+7
96-97	NJ	79	5	19	24	70	+26
97-98	NJ	80	4	22	26	80	+19
98-99	NJ	75	5	22	27	64	+29
Totals		1275	171	628	799	2504	+277

Playoffs

82-83	Wash	4	1	0	1	26	
83-84	Wash	8	1	8	9	21	
84-85	Wash	5	0	1	1	20	
85-86	Wash	9	3	8	11	12	
86-87	Wash	7	0	5	5	19	
87-88	Wash	13	1	11	12	46	
88-89	Wash	6	1	4	5	11	
89-90	Wash	15	2	7	9	25	
90-91	StL	13	0	3	3	36	
91-92	NJ	7	2	1	3	29	
92-93	NJ	5	2	2	4	10	
93-94	NJ	20	2	9	11	42	
94-95	NJ	20	1	7	8	24	

SSN	TEAM	GP	G	A	PTS.	PIM	+/-
96-97	NJ	10	0	4	4	2	
97-98	NJ	6	1	0	1	8	
98-99	NJ	7	2	1	3	10	
Totals		155	19	71	90	341	

STEVENSON, Jeremy *6-2 215 LW*
B. San Bernadino, Cal., July 28, 1974

95-96	Ana	3	0	1	1	12	+1
96-97	Ana	5	0	0	0	14	-1
97-98	Ana	45	3	5	8	101	-4
Totals		53	3	6	9	127	-4

STEVENSON, Shayne *6-1 190 RW*
B. Newmarket, Ont., Oct. 28, 1970

90-91	Bos	14	0	0	0	26	-4
91-92	Bos	5	0	1	1	2	+1
92-93	TB	8	0	1	1	7	-5
Totals		27	0	2	2	35	-8

STEVENSON, Turner *6-3 220 RW*
B. Prince George, B.C., May 18, 1972

92-93	Mont	1	0	0	0	0	-1
93-94	Mont	2	0	0	0	2	-2
94-95	Mont	41	6	1	7	86	0
95-96	Mont	80	9	16	25	167	-2
96-97	Mont	65	8	13	21	97	-14
97-98	Mont	63	4	6	10	110	-8
98-99	Mont	69	10	17	27	88	+6
Totals		321	37	53	90	550	-21

Playoffs

93-94	Mont	3	0	2	2	0	
95-96	Mont	6	0	1	1	2	
96-97	Mont	5	1	1	2	2	
97-98	Mont	10	3	4	7	12	
Totals		24	4	8	12	16	

STEWART, Allan *6-0 195 LW*
B. Fort St. John, B.C., Jan. 31, 1964

85-86	NJ	4	0	0	0	21	-1
86-87	NJ	7	1	0	1	26	-4
87-88	NJ	1	0	0	0	0	+2
88-89	NJ	6	0	2	2	15	-2
90-91	NJ	41	5	2	7	159	-6
91-92	NJ-Bos	5	0	0	0	22	-1
Totals		64	6	4	10	243	-12

STEWART, Blair James *5-11 185 LW*
B. Winnipeg, Man., Mar. 15, 1953

73-74	Det	17	0	4	4	16	-6
74-75	Det-Wash	21	1	5	6	40	-7
75-76	Wash	74	13	14	27	113	-53
76-77	Wash	34	5	2	7	85	-6
77-78	Wash	8	0	1	1	9	-3
78-79	Wash	45	7	12	19	48	+1
79-80	Que	30	8	6	14	15	+2
Totals		229	34	44	78	326	-69

STEWART, Cameron *5-11 196 LW*
B. Kitchener, Ont., Sept. 18, 1971

93-94	Bos	57	3	6	9	66	-6
94-95	Bos	5	0	0	0	2	0
95-96	Bos	6	0	0	0	0	-2
96-97	Bos	15	0	1	1	4	-2
Totals		88	3	7	10	72	-10

Playoffs

93-94	Bos	8	0	3	3	7	
95-96	Bos	5	1	0	1	2	
Totals		13	1	3	4	9	

STEWART, James (Gaye) *5-11 175 LW*
B. Fort William, Ont., June 28, 1923

42-43	Tor	48	24	23	47	20	
45-46	Tor	50	37	15	52	8	
46-47	Tor	60	19	14	33	15	
47-48	Tor-Chi	61	27	29	56	83	
48-49	Chi	54	20	18	38	57	
49-50	Chi	70	24	19	43	43	
50-51	Det	67	18	13	31	18	
51-52	NYR	69	15	25	40	22	
52-53	NYR-Mont	23	1	3	4	8	
Totals		502	185	159	344	274	

Playoffs

41-42	Tor	3	0	0	0	0	

SSN	TEAM	GP	G	A	PTS.	PIM	+/-
42–43	Tor	4	0	2	2	4	
46–47	Tor	11	2	5	7	4	
50–51	Det	6	0	2	2	4	
53–54	Mont	3	0	0	0	0	
Totals		27	2	9	11	12	

STEWART, John Alexander *6–0 180 LW*
B. Eriksdale, Man., May 16, 1950

SSN	TEAM	GP	G	A	PTS.	PIM	+/-
70–71	Pitt	15	2	1	3	9	-9
71–72	Pitt	25	2	8	10	23	-6
72–73	Atl	68	17	17	34	30	-9
73–74	Atl	74	18	15	33	41	+3
74–75	Cal	76	19	19	38	55	-42
75–76	Clev (WHA)	79	12	21	33	43	
76–77	Minn–Birm (WHA)	16	3	3	6	2	
77–78	Birm (WHA)	48	13	26	39	52	
78–79	Birm (WHA)	70	24	26	50	108	
79–80	Que	2	0	0	0	0	0
NHL Totals		260	58	60	118	158	-63
WHA Totals		213	52	76	128	205	

Playoffs

SSN	TEAM	GP	G	A	PTS.	PIM	
73–74	Atl	4	0	0	0	10	
75–76	Clev (WHA)	3	0	0	0	0	
NHL Totals		4	0	0	0	10	
WHA Totals		3	0	0	0	0	

*STEWART, John Sherratt (Black Jack) *5–11 185 D*
B. Pilot Mound, Man., May 6, 1917

SSN	TEAM	GP	G	A	PTS.	PIM	
38–39	Det	32	0	1	1	18	
39–40	Det	48	1	0	1	40	
40–41	Det	47	2	6	8	56	
41–42	Det	44	4	7	11	93	
42–43	Det	44	2	9	11	68	
45–46	Det	47	4	11	15	73	
46–47	Det	55	5	9	14	83	
47–48	Det	60	5	14	19	83	
48–49	Det	60	4	11	15	96	
49–50	Det	65	3	11	14	86	
50–51	Chi	26	0	2	2	49	
51–52	Chi	37	1	3	4	12	
Totals		565	31	84	115	757	

Playoffs

SSN	TEAM	GP	G	A	PTS.	PIM	
39–40	Set	5	0	0	0	4	
40–41	Det	9	1	2	3	8	
41–42	Det	12	0	1	1	12	
42–43	Det	10	1	2	3	35	
45–46	Det	5	0	0	0	14	
46–47	Det	5	0	1	1	12	
47–48	Det	9	1	3	4	6	
48–49	Det	11	1	1	2	32	
49–50	Det	14	1	4	5	20	
Totals		80	5	14	19	143	

*STEWART, Kenneth *D*
B. Port Arthur, Ont., 1915

SSN	TEAM	GP	G	A	PTS.	PIM	
41–42	Chi	6	1	1	2	2	

*STEWART, Nelson Robert (Nels, Old Poison) *6–1 195 C*
B. Montreal, Que., Dec. 29, 1902

SSN	TEAM	GP	G	A	PTS.	PIM	
25–26	Mont M	36	34	8	42	119	
26–27	Mont M	43	17	4	21	133	
27–28	Mont M	41	27	7	34	104	
28–29	Mont M	44	21	8	29	74	
29–30	Mont M	44	39	16	55	81	
30–31	Mont M	43	25	14	39	75	
31–32	Mont M	38	22	11	33	61	
32–33	Bos	47	18	18	36	62	
33–34	Bos	48	21	17	38	68	
34–35	Bos	47	21	18	39	45	
35–36	NYA	48	14	15	29	16	
36–37	Bos–NYA	43	23	12	35	37	
37–38	NYA	48	19	17	36	29	
38–39	NYA	46	16	19	35	43	
39–40	NYA	35	7	7	14	6	
Totals		651	324	191	515	953	

Playoffs

SSN	TEAM	GP	G	A	PTS.	PIM	
25–26	Mont M	8	6	1	7	24	
26–27	Mont M	2	0	0	0	4	
27–28	Mont M	9	2	2	4	17	
29–30	Mont M	4	1	1	2	2	
30–31	Mont M	2	1	0	1	6	
31–32	Mont M	4	0	1	1	2	
32–33	Bos	5	2	0	2	4	
34–35	Bos	4	0	1	1	0	
35–36	NYA	5	1	2	3	4	
37–38	NYA	6	2	3	5	2	
38–39	NYA	2	0	0	0	0	
39–40	NYA	3	0	0	0	0	
Totals		54	15	11	26	65	

STEWART, Paul G. *6–1 205 LW*
B. Boston, Mass., Mar. 21, 1954

SSN	TEAM	GP	G	A	PTS.	PIM	+/-
76–77	Edm (WHA)	2	0	0	0	2	
77–78	Cin (WHA)	40	1	5	6	241	
78–79	Cin (WHA)	23	2	1	3	45	
79–80	Que	21	2	0	2	74	-1
NHL Totals		21	2	0	2	74	-1
WHA Totals		65	3	6	9	288	

Playoffs

SSN	TEAM	GP	G	A	PTS.	PIM	
78–79	Cin (WHA)	3	0	0	0	0	

STEWART, Ralph Donald *6–2 190 C*
B. Fort William, Ont., Dec. 2, 1948

SSN	TEAM	GP	G	A	PTS.	PIM	+/-
70–71	Van	3	0	1	1	0	-1
72–73	NYI	31	4	10	14	4	-11
73–74	NYI	67	23	20	43	6	-7
74–75	NYI	70	16	24	40	12	-9
75–76	NYI	31	6	7	13	2	+3
76–77	Van	34	6	8	14	4	+3
77–78	Van	16	2	3	5	0	-10
Totals		252	57	73	130	28	-32

Playoffs

SSN	TEAM	GP	G	A	PTS.	PIM	
74–75	NYI	13	3	3	6	2	
75–76	NYI	6	1	1	2	0	
Totals		19	4	4	8	2	

STEWART, Robert Harold *6–1 205 D*
B. Charlottetown, P.E.I., Nov. 10, 1950

SSN	TEAM	GP	G	A	PTS.	PIM	+/-
71–72	Bos–Cal	24	1	2	3	59	-8
72–73	Cal	63	4	17	21	181	-46
73–74	Cal	47	2	5	7	69	-42
74–75	Cal	67	5	12	17	93	-18
75–76	Cal	76	4	17	21	112	-34
76–77	Clev	73	1	12	13	108	-31
77–78	Clev	72	2	15	17	84	-25
78–79	StL	78	5	13	18	47	-28
79–80	StL–Pitt	75	3	8	11	56	-28
Totals		575	27	101	128	809	-260

Playoffs

SSN	TEAM	GP	G	A	PTS.	PIM	
79–80	Pitt	5	1	1	2	2	

STEWART, Ronald George *6–1 197 RW*
B. Calgary, Alta., July 11, 1932

SSN	TEAM	GP	G	A	PTS.	PIM	+/-
52–53	Tor	70	13	22	35	29	
53–54	Tor	70	14	11	25	72	
54–55	Tor	53	14	5	19	20	
55–56	Tor	69	13	14	27	35	
56–57	Tor	65	15	20	35	28	
57–58	Tor	70	15	24	39	51	
58–59	Tor	70	21	13	34	23	
59–60	Tor	67	14	20	34	28	
60–61	Tor	51	13	12	25	8	
61–62	Tor	60	8	9	17	14	
62–63	Tor	63	16	16	32	26	
63–64	Tor	65	14	5	19	46	
64–65	Tor	65	16	11	27	33	
65–66	Bos	70	20	16	36	17	
66–67	Bos	56	14	10	24	31	
67–68	StL–NYR	74	14	12	26	30	-11
68–69	NYR	75	18	11	29	20	-11
69–70	NYR	76	14	10	24	14	+7
70–71	NYR	76	5	6	11	19	+9
71–72	Van–NYR	55	3	3	6	12	-9
72–73	NYR–NYI	33	2	3	5	4	-17
Totals		1353	276	253	529	560	-32

Playoffs

SSN	TEAM	GP	G	A	PTS.	PIM	
53–54	Tor	5	0	1	1	10	
54–55	Tor	4	0	0	0	2	
55–56	tor	5	1	1	2	2	
58–59	Tor	12	3	3	6	6	
59–60	Tor	10	0	2	2	2	
60–61	Tor	5	1	0	1	2	
61–62	Tor	11	1	6	7	4	
62–63	Tor	10	4	0	4	2	
63–64	Tor	14	0	4	4	24	
64–65	Tor	6	0	1	1	2	
67–68	NYR	6	1	1	2	2	
68–69	NYR	4	0	1	1	0	
69–70	NYR	6	0	0	0	2	
70–71	NYR	13	1	0	1	0	
71–72	NYR	8	2	1	3	0	
Totals		119	14	21	35	60	

STEWART, Ryan *6–1 175 C*
B. Houston, B.C., June 1, 1967

SSN	TEAM	GP	G	A	PTS.	PIM	+/-
85–86	Winn	3	1	0	1	0	0

STEWART, William Donald (Bill) *6–2 180 D*
B. Toronto, Ont., Oct. 6, 1957

SSN	TEAM	GP	G	A	PTS.	PIM	+/-
77–78	Buf	13	2	0	2	15	+1
78–79	Buf	68	1	17	18	101	+4
80–81	StL	60	2	21	23	114	+19
81–82	StL	22	0	5	5	25	-5
82–83	StL	7	0	0	0	8	-1
83–84	Tor	56	2	17	19	116	-1
84–85	Tor	27	0	2	2	32	-3
85–86	Minn	8	0	2	2	13	+2
Totals		261	7	64	71	424	+17

Playoffs

SSN	TEAM	GP	G	A	PTS.	PIM	
77–78	Buf	8	0	2	2	0	
78–79	Buf	1	0	1	1	0	
80–81	StL	4	1	0	1	11	
Totals		13	1	3	4	11	

STIENBURG, Trevor *6–1 200 RW*
B. Kingston, Ont., May 13, 1966

SSN	TEAM	GP	G	A	PTS.	PIM	+/-
85–86	Que	2	1	0	1	0	0
86–87	Que	6	1	0	1	12	0
87–88	Que	8	0	1	1	24	-1
88–89	Que	55	6	3	9	125	-17
Totals		71	8	4	12	161	-18

Playoffs

SSN	TEAM	GP	G	A	PTS.	PIM	
85–86	Que	1	0	0	0	0	

STILES, Tony *5–11 200 D*
B. Carstairs, Alta., Aug. 12, 1959

SSN	TEAM	GP	G	A	PTS.	PIM	+/-
83–84	Calg	30	2	7	9	20	+14

STILLMAN, Cory *6–0 180 C*
B. Peterborough, Ont., Dec. 20, 1973

SSN	TEAM	GP	G	A	PTS.	PIM	+/-
94–95	Calg	10	0	2	2	2	+1
95–96	Calg	74	16	19	35	41	-5
96–97	Calg	58	6	20	26	14	-6
97–98	Van	5	0	0	0	2	-9
98–99	Van	76	27	30	57	38	+7
Totals		290	76	93	169	135	-12

Playoffs

SSN	TEAM	GP	G	A	PTS.	PIM	
95–96	Calg	2	1	1	2	0	

STOCK, P.J. *5–10 190 LW*
B. Victoriaville, Que., May 26, 1975

SSN	TEAM	GP	G	A	PTS.	PIM	+/-
97–98	NYR	38	2	3	5	114	+4
98–99	NYR	5	0	0	0	6	-1
Totals		43	2	3	5	120	+3

STODDARD, John Edward (Jack) *6–3 180 RW*
B. Stoney Creek, Ont., Sept. 26, 1926

SSN	TEAM	GP	G	A	PTS.	PIM	
51–52	NYR	20	4	2	6	2	
52–53	NYR	60	12	13	25	29	
Totals		80	16	15	31	31	

STOJANOV, Alek *6–4 220 RW*
B. Windsor, Ont., Apr. 25, 1973

SSN	TEAM	GP	G	A	PTS.	PIM	+/-
94–95	Van	4	0	0	0	13	-2
95–96	Van–Pitt	68	1	1	2	130	-13
96–97	Pitt	35	1	4	5	79	+3
Totals		107	2	5	7	222	-12

Playoffs

SSN	TEAM	GP	G	A	PTS.	PIM	
94–95	Van	5	0	0	0	2	
95–96	Pitt	9	0	0	0	19	
Totals		14	0	0	0	21	

SSN	TEAM	GP	G	A	PTS.	PIM	+/-

STOLTZ, Roland 6–1 191 RW
B. Oeverkalix, Sweden, Aug. 15, 1954

SSN	TEAM	GP	G	A	PTS.	PIM	+/-
81–82	Wash	14	2	2	4	14	-3

STONE, Stephen George 5–8 170 RW
B. Toronto, Ont., Sept. 26, 1952

| 73–74 | Van | 2 | 0 | 0 | 0 | 0 | -2 |

STORM, James David 6–2 200 LW
B. Milford, Mich., Feb. 5, 1971

93–94	Hart	68	6	10	16	27	+4
94–95	Hart	6	0	3	3	0	+2
95–96	Dal	10	1	2	3	17	-1
Totals		84	7	15	22	44	+5

STOTHERS, Michael Patrick 6–4 212 D
B. Toronto, Ont., Feb. 22, 1962

84–85	Phil	1	0	0	0	0	-1
85–86	Phil	6	0	1	1	6	+1
86–87	Phil	2	0	0	0	4	0
87–88	Phil–Tor	21	0	1	1	55	-7
Totals		30	0	2	2	65	-7

Playoffs

85–86	Phil	3	0	0	0	4	
86–87	Phil	2	0	0	0	7	
Totals		5	0	0	0	11	

STOUGHTON, Blaine 5–11 185 RW
B. Gilbert Plains, Man., Mar. 13, 1953

73–74	Pitt	34	5	6	11	8	-12
74–75	Tor	78	23	14	37	24	-7
75–76	Tor	43	6	11	17	8	-2
76–77	Cin (WHA)	81	52	52	104	39	
77–78	Cin–Ind (WHA)	77	19	26	45	64	
78–79	Ind–NE (WHA)	61	18	12	30	18	
79–80	Hart	80	56	44	100	16	+9
80–81	Hart	71	43	30	73	56	-17
81–82	Hart	80	52	39	91	57	-17
82–83	Hart	72	45	31	76	27	-23
83–84	Hart–NYR	68	28	16	44	8	-25
NHL Totals		526	258	191	449	204	-94
WHA Totals		219	89	90	179	121	

Playoffs

74–75	Tor	7	4	2	6	2	
76–77	Cin (WHA)	4	0	3	3	2	
78–79	NE (WHA)	7	4	3	7	4	
79–80	Hart	1	0	0	0	0	
NHL Totals		8	4	2	6	2	
WHA Totals		11	4	6	10	6	

STOYANOVICH, Steve 6–2 205 C
B. London, Ont., May 2, 1957

| 83–84 | Hart | 23 | 3 | 5 | 8 | 11 | -1 |

***STRAIN, Neil Gilbert** 5–9 165 LW
B. Kenora, Ont., Feb. 24, 1926

| 52–53 | NYR | 52 | 11 | 13 | 24 | 12 | |

STRAKA, Martin 5–10 178 C
B. Plzen, Czechoslovakia, Sept. 3, 1972

92–93	Pitt	42	3	13	16	29	+2
93–94	Pitt	84	30	34	64	24	+24
94–95	Pitt–Ott	37	5	13	18	16	-1
95–96	Ott–NYI–Fla	77	13	30	43	41	-19
96–97	Fla	55	7	22	29	12	+9
97–98	Pitt	75	19	23	42	28	-1
98–99	Pitt	80	35	48	83	26	+12
Totals		450	112	183	295	176	+26

Playoffs

92–93	Pitt	11	2	1	3	2	
93–94	Pitt	6	1	0	1	2	
95–96	Fla	13	2	2	4	2	
96–97	Fla	4	0	0	0	0	
97–98	Pitt	6	2	0	2	2	
98–99	Pitt	13	6	9	15	6	
Totals		53	13	12	25	14	

STRATE, Gordon Lynn 6–1 190 D
B. Edmonton, Alta., May 28, 1935

| 56–57 | Det | 5 | 0 | 0 | 0 | 4 | |

57–58	Det	45	0	0	0	24	
58–59	Det	11	0	0	0	6	
Totals		61	0	0	0	34	

STRATTON, Arthur 6–1 175 C
B. Winnipeg, Man., Oct. 8, 1935

59–60	NYR	18	2	5	7	2	
63–64	Det	5	0	3	3	2	
65–66	Chi	2	0	0	0	0	
67–68	Pitt–Phil	70	16	25	41	20	-10
Totals		95	18	33	51	24	-10

Playoffs

| 67–68 | Phil | 5 | 0 | 0 | 0 | 0 | |

STROBEL, Arthur George 5–6 160 LW
B. Regina, Sask., Nov. 28, 1922

| 43–44 | NYR | 7 | 0 | 0 | 0 | 0 | |

STRONG, Ken 5–11 185 LW
B. Toronto, Ont., May 9, 1963

82–83	Tor	2	0	0	0	0	
83–84	Tor	2	0	2	2	2	0
84–85	Tor	11	2	0	2	4	-3
Totals		15	2	2	4	6	-3

STRUCH, David 5–10 180 C
B. Flin Flon, Man., Feb. 11, 1971

| 93–94 | Calg | 4 | 0 | 0 | 0 | 4 | -2 |

STRUDWICK, Jason 6–3 210 D
B. Edmonton, Alta., July 17, 1975

95–96	NYI	1	0	0	0	7	0
97–98	NYI–Van	28	0	2	2	65	-2
98–99	Van	65	0	3	3	114	-19
Totals		94	0	5	5	186	-21

STRUEBY, Todd Kenneth 6–1 185 LW
B. Lannigan, Sask., June 15, 1963

81–82	Edm	3	0	0	0	0	
82–83	Edm	1	0	0	0	0	-2
83–84	Edm	1	0	1	1	2	+2
Totals		5	0	1	1	2	

***STUART, William (Red)** D
B. Amherst, N.S., 1899

20–21	Tor	18	2	1	3	4	
21–22	Tor	24	3	6	9	16	
22–23	Tor	23	7	3	10	16	
23–24	Tor	24	4	3	7	16	
24–25	Tor–Bos	29	5	2	7	32	
25–26	Bos	33	6	1	7	41	
26–27	Bos	42	3	1	4	20	
Totals		193	30	17	47	145	

Playoffs

20–21	Tor	2	0	0	0	0	
21–22	Tor	7	0	0	0	9	
26–27	Bos	8	0	0	0	6	
Totals		17	0	0	0	15	

STUMPEL, Jozef 6–1 208 C
B. Nitra, Czechoslovakia, June 20, 1972

91–92	Bos	4	1	0	1	0	+1
92–93	Bos	13	1	3	4	4	-3
93–94	Bos	59	8	15	23	14	+4
94–95	Bos	44	5	13	18	8	+4
95–96	Bos	76	18	36	54	14	-8
96–97	Bos	78	21	55	76	14	-22
97–98	LA	77	21	58	79	53	+17
98–99	LA	64	13	21	34	10	-18
Totals		415	88	201	289	117	-25

Playoffs

93–94	Bos	13	1	7	8	4	
94–95	Bos	5	0	0	0	0	
95–96	Bos	5	1	2	3	0	
Totals		23	2	9	11	4	

STUMPF, Robert 6–1 195 RW
B. Milo, Alta., Apr. 25, 1953

| 74–75 | StL–Pitt | 10 | 1 | 1 | 2 | 20 | -2 |

STURGEON, Peter Alexander 6–2 205 LW
B. Whitehorse, Yukon, Feb. 12, 1954

79–80	Col	2	0	0	0	0	0
80–81	Col	4	0	1	1	2	0
Totals		6	0	1	1	2	0

STURM, Marco 6–0 190 C
B. Dingolfing, Germany, Sept. 8, 1978

97–98	SJ	78	10	20	30	40	-2
98–99	SJ	78	16	22	38	52	+7
Totals		156	26	42	68	92	+5

Playoffs

97–98	SJ	2	0	0	0	0	
98–99	SJ	6	2	2	4	4	
Totals		8	2	2	4	4	

SUIKKANEN, Kai 6–2 205 D
B. Opiskelija, Finland, Sept. 29, 1960

81–82	Buf	1	0	0	0	0	-1
82–83	Buf	1	0	0	0	0	+1
Totals		2	0	0	0	0	0

SULLIMAN, Simon Douglas (Doug) 5–9 195 RW
B. Glace Bay, N.S., Aug. 29, 1959

79–80	NYR	31	4	7	11	2	0
80–81	NYR	32	4	1	5	32	-9
81–82	Hart	77	29	40	69	39	-13
82–83	Hart	77	22	19	41	14	-57
83–84	Hart	67	6	13	19	20	-11
84–85	NJ	57	22	16	38	4	-11
85–86	NJ	73	21	22	43	20	-10
86–87	NJ	78	27	26	53	14	-17
87–88	NJ	59	16	14	30	22	-8
88–89	Phil	52	6	6	12	8	-8
89–90	Phil	28	3	4	7	0	+4
Totals		631	160	168	328	175	-140

Playoffs

80–81	NYR	3	1	0	1	0	
87–88	NJ	9	0	3	3	2	
88–89	Phil	4	0	0	0	0	
Totals		16	1	3	4	2	

SULLIVAN, Barry Carter 6–0 205 RW
B. Preston, Ont., Sept. 21, 1926

| 47–48 | Det | 1 | 0 | 0 | 0 | 0 | -1 |

SULLIVAN, Brian Scott 6–4 195 RW
B. South Windsor, Conn., Apr. 23, 1969

| 92–93 | NJ | 2 | 0 | 1 | 1 | 0 | |

SULLIVAN, Frank Taylor (Sully) 5–11 178 D
B. Toronto, Ont., June 16, 1929

49–50	Tor	1	0	0	0	0	
52–53	Tor	5	0	0	0	2	
54–55	Chi	1	0	0	0	0	
55–56	Chi	1	0	0	0	0	
Totals		8	0	0	0	2	

SULLIVAN, George James (Red) 5–11 160 C
B. Peterborough, Ont., Dec. 24, 1929

49–50	Bos	3	0	1	1	0	
51–52	Bos	67	12	12	24	24	
52–53	Bos	32	3	8	11	8	
54–55	Chi	70	19	42	61	51	
55–56	Chi	63	14	26	40	58	
56–57	NYR	42	6	17	23	36	
57–58	NYR	70	11	35	46	61	
58–59	NYR	70	21	42	63	56	
59–60	NYR	70	12	25	37	81	
60–61	NYR	70	9	31	40	66	
Totals		557	107	239	346	441	

Playoffs

50–51	Bos	2	0	0	0	2	
51–52	Bos	7	0	0	0	0	
52–53	Bos	3	0	0	0	0	
56–57	NYR	5	1	2	3	4	
57–58	NYR	1	0	0	0	0	
Totals		18	1	2	3	6	

SULLIVAN, Michael *6–2 185 C*
B. Marshfield, Mass., Feb. 27, 1968

SSN	TEAM	GP	G	A	PTS.	PIM	+/-
91–92	SJ	64	8	11	19	15	-18
92–93	SJ	81	6	8	14	30	-42
93–94	SJ–Calg	45	4	5	9	10	-1
94–95	Calg	38	4	7	11	14	-2
95–96	Calg	81	9	12	21	24	-6
96–97	Calg	67	5	6	11	10	-11
97–98	Bos	77	5	13	18	34	-1
98–99	Phoe	63	2	4	6	24	-11
Totals		516	43	66	109	161	-92

Playoffs

SSN	TEAM	GP	G	A	PTS.	PIM
93–94	SJ	7	1	1	2	8
94–95	Calg	7	3	5	8	2
95–96	Calg	4	0	0	0	0
97–98	Bos	6	0	1	1	2
98–99	Phoe	5	0	0	0	2
Totals		29	4	7	11	14

SULLIVAN, Peter Gerald (Silky) *5–9 170 C*
B. Toronto, Ont., July 25, 1951

SSN	TEAM	GP	G	A	PTS.	PIM	+/-
75–76	Winn (WHA)	78	32	39	71	22	
76–77	Winn (WHA)	78	31	52	83	18	
77–78	Winn (WHA)	77	16	39	55	43	
78–79	Winn (WHA)	80	46	40	86	24	
79–80	Winn	79	24	35	59	20	-45
80–81	Winn	47	4	19	23	20	-17
NHL Totals		126	28	54	82	40	-62
WHA Totals		313	125	170	295	107	

Playoffs

SSN	TEAM	GP	G	A	PTS.	PIM
75–76	Winn (WHA)	13	6	7	13	0
76–77	Winn (WHA)	20	7	12	19	2
77–78	Winn (WHA)	9	3	4	7	4
78–79	Winn (WHA)	10	5	9	14	2
WHA Totals		52	21	32	53	8

SULLIVAN, Robert James *6–0 210 LW*
B. Noranda, Que., Nov. 29, 1957

SSN	TEAM	GP	G	A	PTS.	PIM	+/-
82–83	Hart	62	18	19	37	18	-17

SULLIVAN, Steve *5–9 155 C*
B. Timmons, Ont., July 6, 1974

SSN	TEAM	GP	G	A	PTS.	PIM	+/-
95–96	NJ	16	5	4	9	8	+2
96–97	NJ–Tor	54	13	25	38	37	+14
97–98	Tor	63	10	18	28	40	-8
98–99	Tor	63	20	20	40	28	+12
Totals		196	48	67	115	113	+20

Playoffs

SSN	TEAM	GP	G	A	PTS.	PIM
98–99	Tor	13	3	3	6	14

SUMMANEN, Raimo *5–11 191 LW*
B. Jyvaskyla, Finland, Mar. 2, 1962

SSN	TEAM	GP	G	A	PTS.	PIM	+/-
83–84	Edm	2	1	4	5	2	+4
84–85	Edm	9	0	4	4	0	-1
85–86	Edm	73	19	18	37	16	+7
86–87	Edm–Van	58	14	11	25	15	-2
87–88	Van	9	2	3	5	2	-4
Totals		151	36	40	76	35	+4

Playoffs

SSN	TEAM	GP	G	A	PTS.	PIM
83–84	Edm	5	1	4	5	0
85–86	Edm	5	1	1	2	0
Totals		10	2	5	7	0

***SUMMERHILL, William Arthur (Pee Wee)** *5–9 170 RW*
B. Toronto, Ont., July 9, 1915

SSN	TEAM	GP	G	A	PTS.	PIM
38–39	Mont	43	6	10	16	28
39–40	Mont	13	3	2	5	24
41–42	Brk	16	5	5	10	18
Totals		72	14	17	31	70

Playoffs

SSN	TEAM	GP	G	A	PTS.	PIM
38–39	Mont	3	0	0	0	2

SUNDBLAD, Niklas *6–1 200 RW*
B. Stockholm, Sweden, Jan. 3, 1973

SSN	TEAM	GP	G	A	PTS.	PIM	+/-
95–96	Calg	2	0	0	0	0	0

SUNDIN, Mats *6–2 189 C/RW*
B. Sollentuna, Sweden, Feb. 13, 1971

SSN	TEAM	GP	G	A	PTS.	PIM	+/-
90–91	Que	80	23	36	59	58	-24
91–92	Que	80	33	43	76	103	-19
92–93	Que	80	47	67	114	96	+21
93–94	Que	84	32	53	85	60	+1
94–95	Tor	47	23	24	47	14	-5
95–96	Tor	76	33	50	83	46	+8
96–97	Tor	82	41	53	94	59	+6
97–98	Tor	82	33	41	74	49	-3
98–99	Tor	82	31	52	83	58	+22
Totals		693	296	419	715	543	+7

Playoffs

SSN	TEAM	GP	G	A	PTS.	PIM
92–93	Que	6	3	1	4	6
94–95	Tor	7	5	4	9	4
95–96	Tor	6	3	1	4	4
98–99	Tor	17	8	8	16	16
Totals		36	19	14	33	30

SUNDIN, Ronnie *6–1 220 D*
B. Ludvika, Sweden, Oct. 3, 1970

SSN	TEAM	GP	G	A	PTS.	PIM	+/-
97–98	NYR	1	0	0	0	0	0

SUNDSTROM, Niklas *5–11 183 LW*
B. Ornskoldsvik, Sweden, June 6, 1975

SSN	TEAM	GP	G	A	PTS.	PIM	+/-
95–96	NYR	82	9	12	21	14	+2
96–97	NYR	82	24	28	52	20	+23
97–98	NYR	70	19	28	47	24	0
98–99	NYR	81	13	30	43	20	-2
Totals		315	65	98	163	78	+23

Playoffs

SSN	TEAM	GP	G	A	PTS.	PIM
95–96	NYR	11	4	3	7	4
96–97	NYR	9	0	5	5	2
Totals		20	4	8	12	6

SUNDSTROM, Patrik *6–1 200 C*
B. Skelleftea, Sweden, Dec. 14, 1961

SSN	TEAM	GP	G	A	PTS.	PIM	+/-
82–83	Van	74	23	23	46	30	-20
83–84	Van	78	38	53	91	37	-11
84–85	Van	71	25	43	68	46	-17
85–86	Van	79	18	48	66	28	-8
86–87	Van	72	29	42	71	40	+9
87–88	NJ	78	15	36	51	42	-16
88–89	NJ	65	28	41	69	36	+22
89–90	NJ	74	27	49	76	34	+15
90–91	NJ	71	15	31	46	48	+7
91–92	NJ	17	1	3	4	8	-5
Totals		679	219	369	588	349	-24

Playoffs

SSN	TEAM	GP	G	A	PTS.	PIM
82–83	Van	4	0	0	0	2
83–84	Van	4	0	1	1	7
85–86	Van	3	1	0	1	0
87–88	NJ	18	7	13	20	14
89–90	NJ	6	1	3	4	2
90–91	NJ	2	0	0	0	0
Totals		37	9	17	26	25

SUNDSTROM, Peter *6–0 180 LW*
B. Skelleftea, Sweden, Dec. 14, 1961

SSN	TEAM	GP	G	A	PTS.	PIM	+/-
83–84	NYR	77	22	22	44	24	+3
84–85	NYR	76	18	25	43	34	-26
85–86	NYR	53	8	15	23	12	+7
87–88	Wash	76	8	17	25	34	-2
88–89	Wash	35	4	2	6	12	-5
89–90	NJ	21	1	2	3	4	+1
Totals		338	61	83	144	120	-22

Playoffs

SSN	TEAM	GP	G	A	PTS.	PIM
83–84	NYR	5	1	3	4	0
84–85	NYR	3	0	0	0	0
85–86	NYR	1	0	0	0	2
87–88	Wash	14	2	0	2	6
Totals		23	3	3	6	8

***SUOMI, Alfred** *F*

SSN	TEAM	GP	G	A	PTS.	PIM
36–37	Chi	5	0	0	0	0

SUTER, Gary Lee *6–0 200 D*
B. Madison, Wisc., June 24, 1964

SSN	TEAM	GP	G	A	PTS.	PIM	+/-
85–86	Calg	80	18	50	68	141	+11
86–87	Calg	68	9	40	49	70	-10
87–88	Calg	75	21	70	91	124	+39
88–89	Calg	63	13	49	62	78	+26
89–90	Calg	76	16	60	76	97	+4
90–91	Calg	79	12	58	70	102	+26
91–92	Calg	70	12	43	55	128	+1
92–93	Calg	81	23	58	81	112	-1
93–94	Calg–Chi	41	6	12	18	38	-12
94–95	Chi	48	10	27	37	42	+14
95–96	Chi	82	20	47	67	80	+3
96–97	Chi	82	7	21	28	70	-4
97–98	Chi	73	14	28	42	74	+1
98–99	SJ	1	0	0	0	0	0
Totals		919	181	563	744	1156	+100

Playoffs

SSN	TEAM	GP	G	A	PTS.	PIM
85–86	Calg	10	2	8	10	8
86–87	Calg	6	0	3	3	10
87–88	Calg	9	1	9	10	6
88–89	Calg	5	0	3	3	10
89–90	Calg	6	0	1	1	14
91–92	Calg	6	2	3	5	8
93–94	Chi	6	3	2	5	6
94–95	Chi	12	2	5	7	10
95–96	Chi	10	3	3	6	8
96–97	Chi	6	1	4	5	8
Totals		83	15	47	62	100

SUTHERLAND, Ronald *5–8 180 D*
B. Eston, Sask., Feb. 8, 1913

SSN	TEAM	GP	G	A	PTS.	PIM
31–32	Bos	2	0	0	0	0

SUTHERLAND, William Fraser *5–10 176 C*
B. Regina, Sask., Nov. 10, 1934

SSN	TEAM	GP	G	A	PTS.	PIM	+/-
67–68	Phil	60	20	9	29	6	+1
68–69	Tor–Phil	56	14	8	22	18	+2
69–70	Phil	51	15	17	32	30	-2
70–71	Phil–StL	69	19	20	39	41	+13
71–72	StL–Det	14	2	4	6	4	+3
72–73	Winn (WHA)	48	6	16	22	34	
73–74	Winn (WHA)	12	4	5	9	6	
NHL Totals		250	70	58	128	99	+17
WHA Totals		60	10	21	31	40	

Playoffs

SSN	TEAM	GP	G	A	PTS.	PIM
62–63	Mont	2	0	0	0	0
67–68	Phil	7	1	3	4	0
68–69	Phil	4	1	1	2	0
70–71	StL	1	0	0	0	0
72–73	Winn (WHA)	14	5	9	14	9
73–74	Winn (WHA)	4	0	0	0	4
NHL Totals		14	2	4	6	0
WHA Totals		18	5	9	14	13

SUTTER, Brent Colin *5–11 180 C*
B. Viking, Alta., June 10, 1962

SSN	TEAM	GP	G	A	PTS.	PIM	+/-
80–81	NYI	3	2	2	4	0	+2
81–82	NYI	43	21	22	43	114	+28
82–83	NYI	80	21	19	40	128	+14
83–84	NYI	69	34	15	49	69	+4
84–85	NYI	72	42	60	102	51	+42
85–86	NYI	61	24	31	55	74	+11
86–87	NYI	69	27	36	63	73	+23
87–88	NYI	70	29	31	60	55	+13
88–89	NYI	77	29	34	63	77	-12
89–90	NYI	67	33	35	68	65	+9
90–91	NYI	75	21	32	53	49	-8
91–92	NYI–Chi	69	22	38	60	36	-10
92–93	Chi	65	20	34	54	67	+10
93–94	Chi	73	9	29	38	43	+17
94–95	Chi	47	7	8	15	51	+6
95–96	Chi	80	13	27	40	56	+14
96–97	Chi	39	7	7	14	18	+10
97–98	Chi	52	2	6	8	28	-6
Totals		1111	363	466	829	1054	+177

Playoffs

SSN	TEAM	GP	G	A	PTS.	PIM
81–82	NYI	19	2	6	8	36
82–83	NYI	20	10	11	21	26
83–84	NYI	20	4	10	14	18
84–85	NYI	3	0	1	1	2
85–86	NYI	5	1	0	1	4
86–87	NYI	6	2	1	3	18
8–90	NYI	5	2	3	5	2
91–92	Chi	18	3	5	8	22
92–93	Chi	4	1	1	2	4
93–94	Chi	6	0	0	0	2
94–95	Chi	16	1	2	3	4
95–96	Chi	10	1	1	2	6
96–97	Chi	2	0	0	0	6
Totals		144	30	44	74	164

SUTTER, Brian Louis Allen *5–11 175 LW*
B. Viking, Alta., Oct. 7, 1956

SSN	TEAM	GP	G	A	PTS.	PIM	+/-
76–77	StL	35	4	10	14	82	-8

SSN	TEAM	GP	G	A	PTS.	PIM	+/-
77–78	StL	78	9	13	22	123	-38
78–79	StL	77	41	39	80	165	-2
79–80	StL	71	23	35	58	156	+3
80–81	StL	78	35	34	69	232	+12
81–82	StL	74	39	36	75	239	+2
82–83	StL	79	46	30	76	254	0
83–84	StL	76	32	51	83	162	-6
84–85	StL	77	37	37	74	121	+11
85–86	StL	44	19	23	42	87	-12
86–87	StL	14	3	3	6	18	-5
87–88	StL	76	15	22	37	147	-18
Totals		779	303	333	636	1786	-65

Playoffs

76–77	StL	4	1	0	1	14	
79–80	StL	3	0	0	0	4	
80–81	StL	11	6	3	9	77	
81–82	StL	10	8	6	14	49	
82–83	StL	4	2	1	3	10	
83–84	StL	11	1	5	6	22	
84–85	StL	3	2	1	3	2	
85–86	StL	9	1	2	3	22	
87–88	StL	10	0	3	3	49	
Totals		65	21	21	42	249	

SUTTER, Darryl John 5–11 180 LW
B. Viking, Alta., Aug. 19, 1958

79–80	Chi	8	2	0	2	2	+1
80–81	Chi	76	40	22	62	86	-1
81–82	Chi	40	23	12	35	31	0
82–83	Chi	80	31	30	61	53	+18
83–84	Chi	59	20	20	40	44	-18
84–85	Chi	49	20	18	38	12	+8
85–86	Chi	50	17	10	27	44	-15
86–87	Chi	44	8	6	14	16	-3
Totals		406	161	118	279	288	-10

Playoffs

79–80	Chi	7	3	1	4	2	
80–81	Chi	3	3	1	4	2	
81–82	Chi	3	0	1	1	2	
82–83	Chi	13	4	6	10	8	
83–84	Chi	5	1	1	2	0	
84–85	Chi	15	12	7	19	12	
85–86	Chi	3	1	2	3	0	
86–87	Chi	2	0	0	0	0	
Totals		51	24	19	43	26	

SUTTER, Duane Calvin 6–1 185 RW
B. Viking, Alta., Mar. 16, 1960

79–80	NYI	56	15	9	24	55	+5
80–81	NYI	23	7	11	18	26	-8
81–82	NYI	77	18	35	53	100	+23
82–83	NYI	75	13	19	32	118	+8
83–84	NYI	78	17	23	40	94	+2
84–85	NYI	78	17	24	41	174	-12
85–86	NYI	80	20	33	53	157	+15
86–87	NYI	80	14	17	31	169	+1
87–88	Chi	37	7	9	16	70	+2
88–89	Chi	75	7	9	16	214	-11
89–90	Chi	72	4	14	18	156	-2
Totals		731	139	203	342	1333	+23

Playoffs

79–80	NYI	21	3	7	10	74	
80–81	NYI	12	3	1	4	10	
81–82	NYI	19	5	5	10	57	
82–83	NYI	20	9	12	21	43	
83–84	NYI	21	1	3	4	48	
84–85	NYI	10	0	2	2	47	
85–86	NYI	3	0	0	0	16	
86–87	NYI	14	1	0	1	26	
87–88	Chi	5	0	0	0	21	
88–89	Chi	16	3	1	4	15	
89–90	Chi	20	1	1	2	48	
Totals		161	36	32	58	405	

SUTTER, Richard 5–11 188 RW
B. Viking, Alta., Dec. 2, 1963

82–83	Pitt	4	0	0	0	0	-2
83–84	Pitt–Phil	75	16	12	28	93	+8
84–85	Phil	56	6	10	16	89	0
85–86	Phil	78	14	25	39	199	+28
86–87	Van	74	20	22	42	113	-17
87–88	Van	80	15	15	30	165	-4
88–89	Van	75	17	15	32	122	+3
89–90	Van–StL	74	11	9	20	155	-3
90–91	StL	77	16	11	27	122	+6
91–92	StL	77	9	16	25	107	+7
92–93	StL	84	13	14	27	100	-4
93–94	Chi	83	12	14	26	108	-8
94–95	Chi–TB–Tor	37	0	3	3	38	-6
Totals		874	149	166	315	1411	+8

Playoffs

83–84	Phil	3	0	0	0	16	
84–85	Phil	11	3	0	3	10	
85–86	Phil	5	2	0	2	19	
88–89	Van	7	2	1	3	12	
89–90	StL	12	2	1	3	39	
90–91	StL	13	4	2	6	16	
91–92	StL	6	0	0	0	8	
92–93	StL	11	0	1	1	10	
93–94	Chi	6	0	0	0	2	
94–95	Tor	4	0	0	0	2	
Totals		78	13	5	18	133	

SUTTER, Ronald 6–0 180 C
B. Viking Alta., Dec. 2, 1963

82–83	Phil	10	1	1	2	9	0
83–84	Phil	79	19	32	51	101	+4
84–85	Phil	73	16	29	45	94	+13
85–86	Phil	75	18	42	60	159	+26
86–87	Phil	39	10	17	27	69	+10
87–88	Phil	69	8	25	33	146	-9
88–89	Phil	55	26	22	48	80	+25
89–90	Phil	75	22	26	48	104	+2
90–91	Phil	80	17	28	45	92	+2
91–92	StL	68	19	27	46	91	+9
92–93	StL	59	12	15	27	99	-11
93–94	StL–Que	73	15	25	40	90	+2
94–95	NYI	27	1	4	5	21	-8
95–96	Bos	18	5	7	12	24	+10
96–97	SJ	78	5	17	12	65	-8
97–98	SJ	57	2	7	9	22	-2
98–99	SJ	59	3	6	9	40	-8
Totals		973	196	320	516	1263	+57

Playoffs

83–84	Phil	3	0	0	0	22	
84–85	Phil	19	4	8	12	28	
85–86	Phil	5	0	2	2	10	
86–87	Phil	16	1	7	8	12	
87–88	Phil	7	0	1	1	26	
88–89	Phil	19	1	9	10	51	
91–92	StL	6	1	3	4	8	
95–96	Bos	5	0	0	0	8	
97–98	SJ	6	1	0	1	14	
98–99	SJ	6	0	0	0	4	
Totals		92	8	30	38	189	

SUTTON, Andy 5–10 192 D
B. Edmonton, Alta., Oct. 24, 1977

98–99	SJ	31	0	3	3	65	-4

SUTTON, Kenneth 6–0 195 D
B. Edmonton, Alta., May 11, 1969

90–91	Buf	15	3	6	9	13	+2
91–92	Buf	64	2	18	20	71	+5
92–93	Buf	63	8	14	22	30	-3
93–94	Buf	78	4	20	24	71	-6
94–95	Buf–Edm	24	4	3	7	42	-3
95–96	Edm–StL	38	0	8	8	43	-13
97–98	NJ–SJ	21	0	0	0	21	-3
98–99	NJ	5	1	0	1	0	+1
Totals		308	22	69	91	291	-20

Playoffs

90–91	Buf	6	0	1	1	2	
91–92	Buf	7	0	2	2	4	
92–93	Buf	8	3	1	4	8	
93–94	Buf	4	0	0	0	2	
95–96	StL	1	0	0	0	0	
Totals		26	3	4	7	16	

SUZOR, Mark Joseph 6–1 212 D
B. Windsor, Ont., Nov. 5, 1956

76–77	Phil	4	0	1	1	4	+2
77–78	Col	60	4	15	19	56	-35
Totals		64	4	16	20	60	-33

SVEHLA, Robert 6–1 190 D
B. Martin, Czechoslovakia, Jan. 2, 1969

94–95	Fla	5	1	1	2	0	+3
95–96	Fla	81	8	49	57	94	-3
96–97	Fla	82	13	32	45	86	+2
97–98	Fla	79	9	34	43	113	-3
98–99	Fla	80	8	29	37	83	-13
Totals		327	39	145	184	376	-14

Playoffs

95–96	Fla	22	0	6	6	32	
96–97	Fla	5	1	4	5	4	
Totals		27	1	10	11	36	

SVEJKOVSKY, Jaroslav 5–11 185 RW
B. Plzen, Czech., Oct. 1, 1976

96–97	Wash	19	7	3	10	4	-1
97–98	Wash	17	4	1	5	10	-5
98–99	Wash	25	6	8	14	12	-2
Totals		61	17	12	29	26	-8

Playoffs

97–98	Wash	1	0	0	0	2	

SVENSSON, Leif 6–3 190 D
B. Harnosand, Sweden, July 8, 1951

78–79	Wash	74	2	29	31	28	-3
79–80	Wash	47	4	11	15	21	-10
Totals		121	6	40	46	49	-13

SVENSSON, Magnus 5–11 180 D
B. Tranas, Sweden, Mar. 1, 1963

94–95	Fla	19	2	5	7	10	+5
95–96	Fla	27	2	9	11	21	-1
Totals		46	4	14	18	31	+4

SVOBODA, Petr 6–1 174 D
B. Most, Czechoslovakia, Feb. 14, 1966

84–85	Mont	73	4	27	31	65	+16
85–86	Mont	73	1	18	19	33	+24
86–87	Mont	70	5	17	22	63	+14
87–88	Mont	69	7	22	29	149	+46
88–89	Mont	71	8	37	45	147	+28
89–90	Mont	60	5	31	36	98	+20
90–91	Mont	60	4	22	26	52	+5
91–92	Mont–Buf	71	6	22	28	146	+1
92–93	Buf	40	2	24	26	59	+3
93–94	Buf	60	2	14	16	89	+11
94–95	Buf–Phil	37	0	8	8	70	-5
95–96	Phil	73	1	28	29	105	+28
96–97	Phil	67	2	12	14	94	+10
97–98	Phil	56	3	15	18	83	+19
98–99	Phil–TB	59	5	18	23	81	+1
Totals		939	55	315	370	1394	+221

Playoffs

84–85	Mont	7	1	1	2	12	
85–86	Mont	8	0	0	0	21	
86–87	Mont	14	0	5	5	10	
87–88	Mont	10	0	5	5	12	
88–89	Mont	21	1	11	12	16	
89–90	Mont	10	0	5	5	7	
90–91	Mont	2	0	1	1	2	
91–92	Buf	7	1	4	5	6	
93–94	Buf	3	0	0	0	4	
94–95	Phil	14	0	4	4	8	
95–96	Phil	12	0	6	6	22	
96–97	Phil	16	1	2	3	16	
97–98	Phil	3	0	1	1	4	
Totals		127	4	45	49	140	

SWAIN, Garth Frederick Arthur (Garry) 5–9 164 C
B. Welland, Ont., Sept. 11, 1947

68–69	NE (WHA)	9	1	1	2	0	-1
74–75	NE (WHA)	66	7	15	22	18	
75–76	NE (WHA)	79	10	16	26	46	
76–77	NE (WHA)	26	5	2	7	6	
NHL Totals		9	1	1	2	0	-1
WHA Totals		171	22	33	55	70	
WHA Playoff Totals		25	3	5	8	56	

SWARBRICK, George Raymond 5–10 180 RW
B. Moose Jaw, Sask., Feb. 16, 1942

67–68	Oak	49	13	5	18	62	-17
68–69	Oak–Pitt	69	4	19	23	101	-17
69–70	Pitt	12	0	1	1	8	0
70–71	Phil	2	0	0	0	0	-2
Totals		132	17	25	42	171	-36

SWEENEY, Donald Clark 5–10 188 D
B. St. Stephen, N.B., Aug. 17, 1966

SSN	TEAM	GP	G	A	PTS.	PIM	+/-
88–89	Bos	36	3	5	8	20	-6
89–90	Bos	58	3	5	8	58	+11
90–91	Bos	77	8	13	21	67	+2
91–92	Bos	75	3	11	14	74	-9
92–93	Bos	84	7	27	34	68	+34
93–94	Bos	75	6	15	21	50	+29
94–95	Bos	47	3	19	22	24	+6
95–96	Bos	77	4	24	28	42	-4
96–97	Bos	82	3	23	26	39	-5
97–98	Bos	59	1	15	16	24	+12
98–99	Bos	81	2	10	12	64	+14
Totals		751	43	167	210	530	+84

Playoffs

89–90	Bos	21	1	5	6	18	
90–91	Bos	19	3	0	3	25	
91–92	Bos	15	0	0	0	10	
92–93	Bos	4	0	0	0	4	
93–94	Bos	12	2	1	3	4	
94–95	Bos	5	0	0	0	4	
95–96	Bos	5	0	2	2	6	
98–99	Bos	11	3	0	3	6	
Totals		92	9	8	17	77	

SWEENEY, Robert Emmett 6–3 200 C/RW
B. Concord, Mass., Jan. 25, 1964

86–87	Bos	14	2	4	6	21	-5
87–88	Bos	80	22	23	45	73	+11
88–89	Bos	75	14	14	28	99	-19
89–90	Bos	70	22	24	46	93	+2
90–91	Bos	80	15	33	48	115	+12
91–92	Bos	63	6	14	20	103	-9
92–93	Buf	80	21	26	47	118	+2
93–94	Buf	60	11	14	25	94	+3
94–95	Buf	45	5	4	9	18	-6
95–96	NYI–Calg	72	7	7	14	65	-20
Totals		639	125	163	288	799	-29

Playoffs

86–87	Bos	3	0	0	0	0	
87–88	Bos	23	6	8	14	66	
88–89	Bos	10	2	4	6	19	
89–90	Bos	20	0	2	2	30	
90–91	Bos	17	4	2	6	45	
91–92	Bos	14	1	0	1	25	
92–93	Buf	8	2	2	4	8	
93–94	Buf	1	0	0	0	0	
94–95	Bufkf	5	0	0	0	4	
95–96	Calg	2	0	0	0	0	
Totals		103	15	18	33	107	

SWEENEY, Timothy Paul 5–11 180 LW
B. Boston, Mass., Apr. 12, 1967

90–91	Calg	42	7	9	16	8	+1
91–92	Calg	11	1	2	3	4	+2
92–93	Bos	14	1	7	8	6	+1
93–94	Ana	78	16	27	43	49	+3
94–95	Ana	13	1	1	2	2	-3
95–96	Bos	41	8	8	16	14	+4
96–97	Bos	36	10	11	21	14	0
97–98	NYR	56	11	18	39	26	+7
Totals		291	55	83	138	123	+13

Playoffs

92–93	Bos	3	0	0	0	0	
95–96	Bos	1	0	0	0	2	
Totals		4	0	0	0	2	

*SWEENEY, William 5–10 165 C
B. Guelph, Ont., Jan. 30, 1937

| 59–60 | NYR | 4 | 1 | 0 | 1 | 0 | |

SYDOR, Darryl Marion 6–0 200 D
B. Edmonton, Alta., May 13, 1972

91–92	LA	18	1	5	6	22	-3
92–93	LA	80	6	23	29	63	-2
93–94	LA	84	8	27	35	94	-9
94–95	LA	48	4	19	23	36	-2
95–96	LA–Dal	84	3	17	20	75	-12
96–97	Dal	82	8	40	48	51	+37
97–98	Cal	79	11	35	46	51	+17
98–99	Dal	74	14	34	48	50	-1
Totals		549	55	200	255	442	+25

Playoffs

SSN	TEAM	GP	G	A	PTS.	PIM	+/-
92–93	LA	24	3	8	11	16	
96–97	Dal	7	0	2	2	0	
97–98	Dal	17	0	5	5	14	
98–99	Dal	23	3	9	12	16	
Totals		71	6	24	30	46	

SYKES, Phil 6–0 175 LW
B. Dawson Creek, B.C., Mar. 18, 1959

82–83	LA	7	2	0	2	2	+1
83–84	LA	3	0	0	0	2	-1
84–85	LA	79	17	15	32	38	+18
85–86	LA	76	20	24	44	97	-26
86–87	LA	58	6	15	21	133	+10
87–88	LA	40	9	12	21	82	+5
88–89	LA	23	0	1	1	8	-3
89–90	Winn	48	9	6	15	26	-8
90–91	Winn	70	12	10	22	59	-9
91–92	Winn	52	4	2	6	72	-12
Totals		456	79	85	164	519	-25

Playoffs

84–85	LA	3	0	1	1	0	
86–87	LA	5	0	1	1	8	
87–88	LA	4	0	0	0	0	
88–89	LA	3	0	0	0	8	
89–90	Winn	4	0	0	0	4	
91–92	Winn	7	0	1	1	9	
Totals		26	0	3	3	29	

SYKES, Robert John William 6–0 200 LW
B. Sudbury, Ont., Sept. 26, 1951

| 74–75 | Tor | 2 | 0 | 0 | 0 | 0 | -2 |

SYKORA, Michal 6–5 225 D
B. Pardubice, Czechoslovakia, July 5, 1973

93–94	SJ	22	1	4	5	14	-4
94–95	SJ	16	0	4	4	10	+6
95–96	SJ	79	4	16	20	54	-14
96–97	SJ–Chi	63	3	14	17	69	+4
97–98	Chi	28	1	3	4	12	-10
98–99	TB	10	1	2	3	0	-7
Totals		218	10	43	53	159	-25

Playoffs

| 96–97 | Chi | 1 | 0 | 0 | 0 | 0 | |

SYKORA, Petr 5–11 180 C
B. Pizen, Czech., Nov. 19, 1976

95–96	NJ	63	18	24	42	32	+7
96–97	NJ	19	1	2	3	4	-8
97–98	NJ	58	16	20	36	22	0
98–99	NJ	80	29	43	72	22	+16
Totals		220	64	89	153	80	+15

Playoffs

96–97	NJ	2	0	0	0	2	
97–98	NJ	2	0	0	0	0	
98–99	NJ	7	3	3	6	4	
Totals		11	3	3	6	6	

SYKORA, Petr 6–2 180 C
B. Pardubice, Czech., Dec. 21, 1978

| 98–99 | Nash | 2 | 0 | 0 | 0 | 0 | -1 |

SYLVESTER, Dean 6–2 185 RW
B. Hanson, Mass., Dec. 30, 1972

| 98–99 | Buf | 1 | 0 | 0 | 0 | 0 | -1 |

Playoffs

| 98–99 | Buf | 4 | 0 | 0 | 0 | 2 | |

SZURA, Joseph Boleslaw 6–2 198 C
B. Fort William, Ont., Dec. 18, 1938

67–68	Oak	20	1	3	4	10	-4
68–69	Oak	70	9	12	21	20	-5
72–73	LA (WHA)	72	13	32	45	25	
73–74	Hou (WHA)	42	8	7	15	4	
NHL Totals		90	10	15	25	30	-9
WHA Totals		114	21	39	60	29	

Playoffs

68–69	Oak	7	2	3	5	2	
73–74	Hous (WHA)	10	0	0	0	0	
NHL Totals		7	2	3	5	2	

| **WHA Totals** | | 10 | 0 | 0 | 0 | 0 | |

TAFT, John Philip 6–2 185 D
B. Minneapolis, Minn., Mar. 8, 1954

| 78–79 | Det | 15 | 0 | 2 | 2 | 4 | +2 |

TAGLIANETTI, Peter Anthony 6–2 195 D
B. Framingham, Mass., Aug. 15, 1963

84–85	Winn	1	0	0	0	0	+1
85–86	Winn	18	0	0	0	48	-1
86–87	Winn	3	0	0	0	12	-4
87–88	Winn	70	6	17	23	182	-13
88–89	Winn	66	1	14	15	226	-23
89–90	Winn	49	3	6	9	136	+20
90–91	Minn–Pitt	55	3	9	12	107	+16
91–92	Pitt	44	1	3	4	57	+7
92–93	TB–Pitt	72	2	12	14	184	+12
93–94	Pitt	60	2	12	14	142	+5
94–95	Pitt	13	0	1	1	12	+1
Totals		451	18	74	92	1106	+21

Playoffs

84–85	Winn	1	0	0	0	0	
85–86	Winn	3	0	0	0	2	
87–88	Winn	5	1	1	2	13	
89–90	Winn	5	0	0	0	6	
90–91	Pitt	19	0	3	3	49	
92–93	Pitt	11	1	2	3	16	
93–94	Pitt	5	0	2	2	16	
94–95	Pitt	4	0	0	0	10	
Totals		53	2	8	10	103	

TALAFOUS, Dean Charles 6–4 190 RW
B. Duluth, Minn., Aug. 25, 1953

74–75	Atl–Minn	61	9	21	30	19	-24
75–76	Minn	79	18	30	48	18	-12
76–77	Minn	80	22	27	49	10	-29
77–78	Minn	75	13	16	29	25	-16
78–79	NYR	68	13	16	29	29	+5
79–80	NYR	55	10	20	30	26	+1
80–81	NYR	50	13	17	30	28	+2
81–82	NYR	29	6	7	13	8	-3
Totals		497	104	154	258	163	-76

Playoffs

76–77	Minn	2	0	0	0	0	
79–80	NYR	5	1	2	3	9	
80–81	NYR	14	3	5	8	2	
Totals		21	4	7	11	11	

TALAKOSKI, Ron 6–3 220 RW
B. Thunder Bay, Ont., June 1, 1962

86–87	NYR	3	0	0	0	21	+1
87–88	NYR	6	0	1	1	12	0
Totals		9	0	1	1	33	+1

TALBOT, Jean–Guy 5–11 170 D
B. Cap–de–la–Madeleine, Que., July 11, 1932

54–55	Mont	3	0	1	1	0	
55–56	Mont	66	1	13	14	80	
56–57	Mont	59	0	13	13	70	
57–58	Mont	55	4	15	19	65	
58–59	Mont	69	4	17	21	77	
59–60	Mont	69	1	14	15	60	
60–61	Mont	70	5	26	31	143	
61–62	Mont	70	5	42	47	90	
62–63	Mont	70	3	22	25	51	
63–64	Mont	66	1	13	14	83	
64–65	Mont	67	8	14	22	64	
65–66	Mont	59	1	14	15	50	
66–67	Mont	68	3	5	8	51	
67–68	Minn–Det–StL	67	0	7	7	16	-3
68–69	StL	69	5	4	9	24	+9
69–70	StL	75	2	15	17	40	+18
70–71	StL–Buf	62	0	7	7	42	-23
Totals		1056	43	242	285	1006	+1

Playoffs

55–56	Mont	9	0	2	2	4	
56–57	Mont	10	0	2	2	10	
57–58	Mont	10	0	3	3	12	
58–59	Mont	11	0	1	1	10	
59–60	Mont	8	1	1	2	8	
60–61	Mont	6	1	1	2	10	
61–62	Mont	6	1	1	2	10	
62–63	Mont	5	0	0	0	8	
63–64	Mont	7	0	2	2	10	

SSN	TEAM	GP	G	A	PTS.	PIM	+/-
64–65	Mont	13	0	1	1	22	
65–66	Mont	10	0	2	2	8	
66–67	Mont	110	0	0	0	0	
67–68	StL	17	0	2	2	/	
68–69	StL	12	0	2	2	6	
69–70	StL	16	1	6	7	16	
Totals		150	4	26	30	142	

TALLON, Michael Dale Lee (Dale) *6–1 205 D*
B. Noranda, Que., Oct. 19, 1950

SSN	TEAM	GP	G	A	PTS.	PIM	+/-
70–71	Van	78	14	42	56	58	-25
71–72	Van	69	17	27	44	78	-24
72–73	Van	75	13	24	37	83	-30
73–74	Chi	65	15	19	34	36	+12
74–75	Chi	35	5	10	15	28	+4
75–76	Chi	80	15	47	62	101	-11
76–77	Chi	70	5	16	21	65	-21
77–78	Pitt	75	4	20	24	66	+3
78–79	Pitt	63	5	24	29	35	-15
79–80	Pitt	32	5	9	14	18	-4
Totals		642	98	238	336	568	-111

Playoffs

SSN	TEAM	GP	G	A	PTS.	PIM
73–74	Chi	11	1	3	4	29
74–75	Chi	8	1	3	4	4
75–76	Chi	4	0	1	1	8
76–77	Chi	2	0	1	1	0
77–78	Chi	4	0	2	2	0
79–80	Pitt	4	0	0	0	4
Totals		33	2	10	12	45

TAMBELLINI, Steven Anthony *6–0 184 C*
B. Trail, B.C. May 14, 1958

SSN	TEAM	GP	G	A	PTS.	PIM	+/-
78–79	NYI	1	0	0	0	0	-1
79–80	NYI	45	5	8	13	4	-1
80–81	NYI–Col	74	25	29	54	19	-13
81–82	Col	79	29	30	59	14	-33
82–83	NJ	73	25	18	43	14	-27
83–84	Calg	73	15	10	25	16	-8
84–85	Calg	47	19	10	29	4	+8
85–86	Van	48	15	15	30	12	-18
86–87	Van	72	16	20	36	14	-22
87–88	Van	41	11	10	21	8	-17
Totals		553	160	150	310	105	-132

Playoffs

SSN	TEAM	GP	G	A	PTS.	PIM
83–84	Calg	2	0	1	1	0

TAMER, Chris Thomas *6–2 185 D*
B. Dearborn, Mich., Nov. 17, 1970

SSN	TEAM	GP	G	A	PTS.	PIM	+/-
93–94	Pitt	12	0	0	0	9	+3
94–95	Pitt	36	2	0	2	82	0
95–96	Pitt	70	4	10	14	153	+20
96–97	Pitt	45	2	4	6	131	-25
97–98	Pitt	79	0	7	7	181	+4
98–99	Pitt–NYR	63	1	5	6	124	-14
Totals		305	9	26	35	680	-12

Playoffs

SSN	TEAM	GP	G	A	PTS.	PIM
93–94	Pitt	5	0	0	0	2
94–95	Pitt	4	0	0	0	18
95–96	Pitt	18	0	7	7	24
96–97	Pitt	4	0	0	0	4
97–98	Pitt	6	0	1	1	4
Totals		37	0	8	8	52

TANCILL, Christopher William *5–10 185 C*
B. Livonia, Mich., Feb. 7, 1968

SSN	TEAM	GP	G	A	PTS.	PIM	+/-
90–91	Hart	9	1	1	2	4	+2
91–92	Hart–Det	11	0	0	0	2	-6
92–93	Det	4	1	0	1	2	-2
93–94	Dal	12	1	3	4	8	-7
94–95	SJ	26	3	11	14	10	+1
95–96	SJ	45	7	16	23	20	-12
96–97	SJ	25	4	0	4	8	-5
97–98	Dal	2	0	1	1	0	-1
Totals		134	17	32	49	54	-30

Playoffs

SSN	TEAM	GP	G	A	PTS.	PIM
94–95	SJ	11	1	1	2	8

TANGUAY, Christian (Chris) *5–10 190 RW*
B. Beauport, Que., Aug. 4, 1962

SSN	TEAM	GP	G	A	PTS.	PIM	+/-
81–82	Que	2	0	0	0	0	0

TANNAHILL, Donald Andrew *5–11 175 LW*
B. Penetang, Ont., Feb. 21, 1949

SSN	TEAM	GP	G	A	PTS.	PIM	+/-
72–73	Van	78	22	21	43	21	-29
73–74	Van	33	8	12	20	4	+1
74–75	Minn (WHA)	72	23	30	53	20	
75–76	Calg (WHA)	78	25	24	49	10	
76–77	Calg (WHA)	72	10	22	32	4	
NHL Totals		111	30	33	63	25	-28
WHA Totals		222	58	76	134	34	

Playoffs

SSN	TEAM	GP	G	A	PTS.	PIM
74–75	Minn (WHA)	10	2	4	6	0
75–76	Calg (WHA)	10	2	5	7	8
WHA Totals		20	4	9	13	8

TANTI, Tony *5–9 184 RW*
B. Toronto, Ont., Sept. 7, 1963

SSN	TEAM	GP	G	A	PTS.	PIM	+/-
81–82	Chi	2	0	0	0	0	0
82–83	Chi–Van	40	9	8	17	16	-9
83–84	Van	79	45	41	86	50	-12
84–85	Van	68	39	20	59	45	-21
85–86	Van	77	39	33	72	85	-8
86–87	Van	77	41	38	79	84	+5
87–88	Van	73	40	37	77	90	-1
88–89	Van	77	24	25	49	69	-10
89–90	Van–Pitt	78	28	36	64	72	-10
90–91	Pitt–Buf	56	7	19	26	50	+3
91–92	Buf	70	15	16	31	100	-4
Totals		697	287	273	560	661	-67

Playoffs

SSN	TEAM	GP	G	A	PTS.	PIM
82–83	Van	4	0	1	1	0
83–84	Van	4	1	2	3	0
85–86	Van	3	0	1	1	11
88–89	Van	7	0	5	5	4
90–91	Buf	5	2	0	2	8
91–92	Buf	7	0	3	3	4
Totals		30	3	12	15	27

TARDIF, Marc *6–0 195 LW*
B. Granby, Que., June 12, 1949

SSN	TEAM	GP	G	A	PTS.	PIM	+/-
69–70	Mont	18	3	2	5	27	0
70–71	Mont	76	19	30	49	133	+25
71–72	Mont	75	31	22	53	81	+15
72–73	Mont	76	25	25	50	48	+18
73–74	LA (WHA)	75	40	30	70	47	
74–75	Mich–Que (WHA)	76	50	39	89	79	
75–76	Que (WHA)	81	71	77	148	79	
76–77	Que (WHA)	62	49	60	109	65	
77–78	Que (WHA)	78	65	89	154	50	
78–79	Que (WHA)	74	41	55	96	98	
79–80	Que	58	33	35	68	30	-13
80–81	Que	63	23	31	54	35	-4
81–82	Que	75	39	31	70	55	-15
82–83	Que	76	21	31	52	34	0
NHL Totals		517	194	207	401	443	+26
WHA Totals		446	316	350	666	418	

Playoffs

SSN	TEAM	GP	G	A	PTS.	PIM
70–71	Mont	20	3	1	4	40
71–72	Mont	6	2	3	5	9
72–73	Mont	14	6	6	12	6
74–75	Que (WHA)	15	10	11	21	10
75–76	Que (WHA)	2	1	0	1	2
76–77	Que (WHA)	12	4	10	14	8
77–78	Que (WHA)	11	6	9	15	11
78–79	Que (WHA)	4	2	6	8	4
80–81	Que	5	1	3	4	2
81–82	Que	13	1	2	3	16
82–83	Que	4	0	0	0	2
NHL Totals		62	13	15	28	75
WHA Totals		44	23	36	59	35

TARDIF, Patrice *6–2 202 C*
B. Thetford Mines, Que., Oct. 30, 1970

SSN	TEAM	GP	G	A	PTS.	PIM	+/-
94–95	StL	27	3	10	13	29	+4
95–96	StL–LA	38	4	1	5	49	-11
Totals		65	7	11	18	78	-7

TATARINOV, Mikhail *5–10 195 D*
B. Angarsk, Soviet Union, July 16, 1966

SSN	TEAM	GP	G	A	PTS.	PIM	+/-
90–91	Wash	65	8	15	23	82	-4
91–92	Que	66	11	27	38	72	+8
92–93	Que	28	2	6	8	28	+6
93–94	Bos	2	0	0	0	0	0
Totals		161	21	48	69	184	+10

TAYLOR, Chris *6–0 185 C*
B. Stratford, Ont., Mar. 6, 1972

SSN	TEAM	GP	G	A	PTS.	PIM	+/-
94–95	NYI	10	0	3	3	2	+1
95–96	NYI	11	0	1	1	2	+1
96–97	NYI	1	0	0	0	0	0
98–99	Bos	37	3	5	8	12	-3
Totals		59	3	9	12	16	-1

TAYLOR, David Andrew *6–0 190 RW*
B. Levack, Ont., Dec. 4, 1955

SSN	TEAM	GP	G	A	PTS.	PIM	+/-
77–78	LA	64	22	21	43	47	+14
78–79	LA	78	43	48	91	124	+27
79–80	LA	61	37	53	90	72	+39
80–81	LA	72	47	65	112	130	+47
81–82	LA	78	39	67	106	130	-4
82–83	LA	46	21	37	58	76	+4
83–84	LA	63	20	49	69	91	-3
84–85	LA	79	41	51	92	132	+13
85–86	LA	76	33	38	71	110	-16
86–87	LA	67	18	44	62	84	0
87–88	LA	68	26	41	67	129	-4
88–89	LA	70	26	37	63	80	+10
89–90	LA	58	15	26	41	96	+17
90–91	LA	73	23	30	53	148	+27
91–92	LA	77	10	19	29	63	+10
92–93	LA	48	6	9	15	49	+1
93–94	LA	33	4	3	7	28	-1
Totals		1111	431	638	1069	1589	+181

Playoffs

SSN	TEAM	GP	G	A	PTS.	PIM
77–78	LA	2	0	0	0	5
78–79	LA	2	0	0	0	2
79–80	LA	4	2	1	3	4
80–81	LA	4	2	2	4	10
81–82	LA	10	4	6	10	20
84–85	LA	3	2	1	3	4
86–87	LA	5	2	3	5	6
87–88	LA	5	3	3	6	6
88–89	LA	11	1	5	6	19
89–90	LA	6	4	4	8	2
90–91	LA	12	6	1	3	2
91–92	LA	6	1	1	2	20
92–93	LA	22	3	5	8	31
Totals		92	26	33	59	145

TAYLOR, Edward Wray (Ted) *6–0 175 LW*
B. Brandon, Man., Feb. 25, 1942

SSN	TEAM	GP	G	A	PTS.	PIM	+/-
64–65	NYR	4	0	0	0	4	
65–66	NYR	4	0	1	1	2	
66–67	Det	2	0	0	0	0	
67–68	Minn	31	3	5	8	34	-7
70–71	Van	56	11	16	27	53	-9
71–72	Van	69	9	13	22	88	-20
72–73	Hou (WHA)	72	34	42	76	103	
73–74	Hou (WHA)	75	21	23	44	143	
74–75	Hou (WHA)	73	26	27	53	130	
75–76	Hou (WHA)	68	15	26	41	80	
76–77	Hou (WHA)	78	16	35	51	90	
77–78	Hou (WHA)	54	11	11	22	46	
NHL Totals		166	23	35	58	181	-36
WHA Totals		420	123	164	287	592	

Playoffs

SSN	TEAM	GP	G	A	PTS.	PIM
72–73	Hou (WHA)	10	3	1	4	10
73–74	Hou (WHA)	14	4	8	12	60
74–75	Hou (WHA)	11	2	5	7	22
75–76	Hou (WHA)	11	2	2	4	17
76–77	Hou (WHA)	11	4	4	8	28
77–78	Hou (WHA)	6	3	1	4	10
WHA Totals		63	18	21	39	147

TAYLOR, Harry *5–8 165 C*
B. St. James, Man., Mar. 28, 1926

SSN	TEAM	GP	G	A	PTS.	PIM
46–47	Tor	9	0	2	2	0
48–49	Tor	42	4	7	11	30
51–52	Chi	15	1	1	2	0
Totals		66	5	10	15	30

Playoffs

SSN	TEAM	GP	G	A	PTS.	PIM
48–49	Tor	1	0	0	0	0

TAYLOR, Mark *5–11 185 C*
B. Vancouver, B.C., Jan. 26, 1958

SSN	TEAM	GP	G	A	PTS.	PIM	+/-
81–82	Phil	2	0	0	0	0	-1
82–83	Phil	61	8	25	33	24	+25
83–84	Phil–Pitt	60	24	31	55	24	-20
84–85	Pitt–Wash	56	8	11	19	21	-8

SSN	TEAM	GP	G	A	PTS.	PIM	+/-
85–86	Wash	30	2	1	3	4	-4
Totals		209	42	68	110	73	-8

Playoffs

SSN	TEAM	GP	G	A	PTS.	PIM
82–83	Phil	3	0	0	0	0
85–86	Wash	3	0	0	0	0
Totals		6	0	0	0	0

*TAYLOR, Ralph F. (Bouncer) *5–9 180 D*
B. Toronto, Ont., Oct. 2, 1905

SSN	TEAM	GP	G	A	PTS.	PIM
27–28	Chi	22	1	1	2	39
28–29	Chi	38	0	0	0	56
29–30	Chi–NYR	39	3	0	3	74
Totals		99	4	1	5	169

Playoffs

SSN	TEAM	GP	G	A	PTS.	PIM
29–30	NYR	4	0	0	0	10

*TAYLOR, Robert *F*
B. Newton, Mass., Aug. 12, 1904

SSN	TEAM	GP	G	A	PTS.	PIM
29–30	Bos	8	0	0	0	6

TAYLOR, Tim Robertson *6–1 185 C*
B. Stratford, Ont., Feb. 6, 1969

SSN	TEAM	GP	G	A	PTS.	PIM	+/-
93–94	Det	1	1	0	1	0	-1
94–95	Det	22	0	4	4	16	+3
95–96	Det	72	11	14	25	39	+11
96–97	Det	44	3	4	7	52	-6
97–98	Bos	79	20	11	31	57	-16
98–99	Bos	49	4	7	11	55	-10
Totals		267	39	40	79	219	-19

Playoffs

SSN	TEAM	GP	G	A	PTS.	PIM
94–95	Det	6	0	1	1	12
95–96	Det	18	0	4	4	4
96–97	Det	2	0	0	0	0
97–98	Bos	6	0	0	0	10
98–99	Bos	12	0	3	3	8
Totals		44	0	8	8	34

*TAYLOR, William Gordon *6–1 184 C*
B. Winnipeg, Man., Oct. 14, 1942

SSN	TEAM	GP	G	A	PTS.	PIM
64–65	NYR	2	0	0	0	0

*TAYLOR, William James *5–9 150 C*
B. Winnipeg, Man., May 3, 1919

SSN	TEAM	GP	G	A	PTS.	PIM
39–40	Tor	29	4	6	10	9
40–41	Tor	47	9	26	35	15
41–42	Tor	48	12	26	38	20
42–43	Tor	50	18	42	60	2
45–46	Tor	48	23	18	41	14
46–47	Det	60	17	46	63	35
47–48	Bos–NYR	41	4	16	20	25
Totals		323	87	180	267	120

Playoffs

SSN	TEAM	GP	G	A	PTS.	PIM
39–40	Tor	2	1	0	1	0
40–41	Tor	7	0	3	3	5
41–42	Tor	13	2	8	10	4
42–43	Tor	6	2	2	4	0
46–47	Det	5	1	5	6	4
Totals		33	6	18	24	13

TEAL, Allen Leslie (Skip) *C*
B. Ridgeway, Ont., July 17, 1933

SSN	TEAM	GP	G	A	PTS.	PIM
54–55	Bos	1	0	0	0	0

TEAL, Jeffrey Brad *6–3 205 RW*
B. Edina, Minn., May 30, 1960

SSN	TEAM	GP	G	A	PTS.	PIM	+/-
84–85	Mont	6	0	1	1	0	0

TEAL, Victor (Skeeter) *6–1 160 RW*
B. St. Catharines, Ont., Aug. 10, 1949

SSN	TEAM	GP	G	A	PTS.	PIM	+/-
73–74	NYI	1	0	0	0	0	+1

TEBBUTT, Gregory *6–2 215 D*
B. North Vancouver, B.C., May 11, 1957

SSN	TEAM	GP	G	A	PTS.	PIM	+/-
78–79	Birm (WHA)	38	2	5	7	83	
79–80	Que	2	0	1	1	4	-1
83–84	Pitt	24	0	2	2	31	-26
NHL Totals		26	0	3	3	35	-27
WHA Totals		38	2	5	7	83	

TEPPER, Stephen *6-4 215 RW*
B. Santa Ana, Cal., Mar. 10, 1969

SSN	TEAM	GP	G	A	PTS.	PIM	+/-
92–93	Chi	1	0	0	0	0	0

TERBENCHE, Paul Frederick *5–10 190 D*
B. Cobourg, Ont., Sept. 16, 1945

SSN	TEAM	GP	G	A	PTS.	PIM	+/-
67–68	Chi	68	3	7	10	8	-11
70–71	Buf	3	0	0	0	2	-3
71–72	Buf	9	0	0	0	2	-13
72–73	Buf	42	0	7	7	8	+7
73–74	Buf	67	2	12	14	8	+3
74–75	Van (WHA)	60	3	14	17	10	
75–76	Calg (WHA)	58	2	4	6	22	
76–77	Calg (WHA)	80	9	24	33	30	
77–78	Birm (WHA)	11	1	0	1	0	
78–79	Winn (WHA)	68	3	22	25	12	
NHL Totals		189	5	26	31	28	-17
WHA Totals		277	18	64	82	74	

Playoffs

SSN	TEAM	GP	G	A	PTS.	PIM
67–68	Chi	6	0	0	0	0
72–73	Buf	6	0	0	0	0
75–76	Calg (WHA)	10	0	6	6	6
77–78	Hou (WHA)	6	1	1	2	0
78–79	Winn (WHA)	10	1	1	2	4
NHL Totals		12	0	0	0	0
WHA Totals		26	2	8	10	10

TERRION, Greg Patrick *5–11 190 LW*
B. Marmora, Ont., May 2, 1960

SSN	TEAM	GP	G	A	PTS.	PIM	+/-
80–81	LA	73	12	25	37	99	-1
81–82	LA	61	15	22	37	23	-12
82–83	Tor	74	16	16	32	59	-3
83–84	Tor	79	15	24	39	36	-6
84–85	Tor	72	14	17	31	20	-15
85–86	Tor	76	10	22	32	31	-5
86–87	Tor	67	7	8	15	6	-5
87–88	Tor	59	4	16	20	65	-6
Totals		561	93	150	243	339	-53

Playoffs

SSN	TEAM	GP	G	A	PTS.	PIM
80–81	LA	3	1	0	1	4
82–83	Tor	4	1	2	3	2
85–86	Tor	10	0	3	3	17
86–87	Tor	13	0	2	2	14
87–88	Tor	5	0	2	2	4
Totals		35	2	9	11	41

TERRY, Bill *5–8 170 C*
B. Toronto, Ont., July 13, 1961

SSN	TEAM	GP	G	A	PTS.	PIM	+/-
87–88	Minn	5	0	0	0	0	-4

TERTYSHNY, Dimitri *6–1 176 D*
B. Chelyabinski, USSR, Dec. 26, 1976

SSN	TEAM	GP	G	A	PTS.	PIM	+/-
98–99	Phil	62	2	8	10	30	-1

Playoffs

SSN	TEAM	GP	G	A	PTS.	PIM
98–99	Phil	1	0	0	0	2

TESSIER, Orval Roy *5–8 160 C*
B. Cornwall, Ont., June 30, 1933

SSN	TEAM	GP	G	A	PTS.	PIM
54–55	Mont	4	0	0	0	0
55–56	Bos	23	2	3	5	6
60–61	Bos	32	3	4	7	0
Totals		59	5	7	12	6

TEZIKOV, Alexei *6–1 198 D*
B. Togliatti, USSR, June 22, 1978

SSN	TEAM	GP	G	A	PTS.	PIM	+/-
98–99	Van	1	0	0	0	0	-1

THATCHELL, Spencer Harold (Spence) *D*
B. Lloydminster, Sask., July 16, 1924

SSN	TEAM	GP	G	A	PTS.	PIM
42–43	NYR	1	0	0	0	0

THEBERGE, Greg Ray *5–10 185 D*
B. Peterborough, Ont., Sept. 3, 1959

SSN	TEAM	GP	G	A	PTS.	PIM	+/-
79–80	Wash	12	0	1	1	0	-3
80–81	Wash	1	1	0	1	0	-2
81–82	Wash	57	5	32	37	49	-8
82–83	Wash	70	8	28	36	20	-3
83–84	Wash	13	1	2	3	4	-4
Totals		153	15	63	78	73	-20

Playoffs

SSN	TEAM	GP	G	A	PTS.	PIM
82–83	Wash	4	0	1	1	0

THELIN, Mats *5–10 185 D*
B. Stockholm, Sweden, Mar. 30, 1961

SSN	TEAM	GP	G	A	PTS.	PIM	+/-
84–85	Bos	73	5	13	18	9	+9
85–86	Bos	31	2	3	5	29	+3
86–87	Bos	59	1	3	4	69	-8
Totals		163	8	19	27	107	+4

Playoffs

SSN	TEAM	GP	G	A	PTS.	PIM
84–85	Bos	5	0	0	0	6

THELVEN, Michael *5–11 185 D*
B. Stockholm, Sweden, Jan. 7, 1961

SSN	TEAM	GP	G	A	PTS.	PIM	+/-
85–86	Bos	60	6	20	26	48	+7
86–87	Bos	34	5	15	20	18	-2
87–88	Bos	67	6	25	31	57	+12
88–89	Bos	40	3	18	21	71	+10
89–90	Bos	6	0	2	2	23	+3
Totals		207	20	80	100	217	+30

Playoffs

SSN	TEAM	GP	G	A	PTS.	PIM
85–86	Bos	3	0	0	0	0
87–88	Bos	21	3	3	6	26
88–89	Bos	10	1	7	8	8
Totals		34	4	10	14	34

THERIEN, Chris *6–3 230 D*
B. Ottawa, Ont., Dec. 14, 1971

SSN	TEAM	GP	G	A	PTS.	PIM	+/-
94–95	Phil	48	3	10	13	38	+8
95–96	Phil	82	6	17	23	89	+16
96–97	Phil	71	2	22	24	64	+27
97–98	Phil	78	3	16	19	80	+5
98–99	Phil	74	3	15	18	48	+16
Totals		353	17	80	97	319	+72

Playoffs

SSN	TEAM	GP	G	A	PTS.	PIM
94–95	Phil	15	0	0	0	10
95–96	Phil	12	0	0	0	18
96–97	Phil	19	1	6	7	6
97–98	Phil	5	0	1	1	4
98–99	Phil	6	0	0	0	6
Totals		57	1	7	8	44

THERRIEN, Gaston *5–10 185 D*
B. Montreal, Que., May 27, 1960

SSN	TEAM	GP	G	A	PTS.	PIM	+/-
80–81	Que	3	0	1	1	2	-1
81–82	Que	14	0	7	7	6	+2
82–83	Que	5	0	0	0	4	-4
Totals		22	0	8	8	12	-3

Playoffs

SSN	TEAM	GP	G	A	PTS.	PIM
81–82	Que	9	0	1	1	4

THIBAUDEAU, Gilles *5–10 165 C*
B. Montreal, Que., Mar. 4, 1963

SSN	TEAM	GP	G	A	PTS.	PIM	+/-
86–87	Mont	9	1	3	4	0	+5
87–88	Mont	17	5	6	11	6	+6
88–89	Mont	32	6	6	12	6	+5
89–90	NYI–Tor	41	11	15	26	30	+8
90–91	Tor	20	2	7	9	4	-7
Totals		119	25	37	62	40	+17

Playoffs

SSN	TEAM	GP	G	A	PTS.	PIM
87–88	Mont	8	3	3	6	2

THIBEAULT, Laurence Lorrain *5–7 180 LW*
B. Charletone, Ont., Oct. 2, 1918

SSN	TEAM	GP	G	A	PTS.	PIM
44–45	Det	4	0	2	2	0
45–46	Mont	1	0	0	0	0
Totals		5	0	2	2	0

THIFFAULT, Leo Edmond *5–10 175 LW*
B. Drummondville, Que., Dec. 16, 1944

Playoffs

SSN	TEAM	GP	G	A	PTS.	PIM
67–68	Minn	5	0	0	0	0

THOMAS, Cyril James (Cy) *5–10 185 F*
B. Dowlais, Wales, Aug. 5, 1926

SSN	TEAM	GP	G	A	PTS.	PIM
47–48	Chi–Tor	14	2	4	6	12

THOMAS, John Scott *6–2 195 RW*
B. Buffalo, N.Y., Jan. 18, 1970

SSN	TEAM	GP	G	A	PTS.	PIM	+/-
92–93	Buf	7	1	1	2	15	+2
93–94	Buf	32	2	2	4	8	-6

Totals		39	3	3	6	23	-4

THOMAS, Reginald Kenneth 5-10 185 LW
B. Lambeth, Ont., Apr. 21, 1953

73–74	LA (WHA)	77	14	21	35	22	
74–75	Balt (WHA)	50	8	13	21	42	
75–76	Ind (WHA)	80	23	17	40	23	
76–77	Ind (WHA)	79	25	30	55	34	
77–78	Ind-Cin (WHA)	67	19	18	37	56	
78–79	Cin (WHA)	80	32	39	71	22	
79–80	Que	39	9	7	16	6	-5
NHL Totals		39	9	7	16	6	-5
WHA Totals		433	121	138	259	199	

Playoffs

75–76	Ind (WHA)	7	1	0	1	4	
76–77	Ind (WHA)	9	7	9	16	4	
78–79	Cin (WHA)	3	1	1	2	0	
WHA Totals		19	9	10	19	8	

THOMAS, Steve 5-11 185 LW
B. Stockport, England, July 15, 1963

84–85	Tor	18	1	1	2	2	-13
85–86	Tor	65	20	37	57	36	-15
86–87	Tor	78	35	27	62	114	-3
87–88	Chi	30	13	13	26	40	+1
88–89	Chi	45	21	19	40	69	-2
89–90	Chi	76	40	30	70	91	-3
90–91	Chi	69	19	35	54	129	+8
91–92	Chi-NYI	82	30	48	78	97	+8
92–93	NYI	79	37	50	87	111	+3
93–94	NYI	78	42	33	75	139	-9
94–95	NYI	47	11	15	26	60	-14
95–96	NJ	81	26	35	61	98	-2
96–97	NJ	57	15	19	34	46	+9
97–98	NJ	55	14	10	24	32	+4
98–99	Tor	78	28	45	73	33	+26
Totals		938	352	417	769	1097	-2

Playoffs

85–86	Tor	10	6	8	14	9
86–87	Tor	13	2	3	5	13
87–88	Chi	3	1	2	3	6
88–89	Chi	12	3	5	8	10
89–90	Chi	20	7	6	13	33
90–91	Chi	6	1	2	3	15
92–93	NYI	18	9	8	17	37
93–94	NYI	4	1	0	1	8
96–97	NJ	10	1	1	2	18
97–98	NJ	6	0	3	3	2
98–99	Tor	17	6	3	9	12
Totals		119	37	41	78	163

THOMLINSON, Dave 6-1 215 LW
B. Edmonton, Alta., Oct. 22, 1966

89–90	StL	19	1	2	3	12	-4
90–91	StL	3	0	0	0	0	-3
91–92	Bos	12	0	1	1	17	-2
93–94	LA	7	0	0	0	21	-6
94–95	LA	1	0	0	0	0	-1
Totals		42	1	3	4	50	-16

Playoffs

90–91	StL	9	3	1	4	4

THOMPSON, Brenton Keith 6-2 200 D
B. Calgary, Alta., Jan. 9, 1971

91–92	LA	27	0	5	5	89	-7
92–93	LA	30	0	4	4	76	-4
93–94	LA	24	1	0	1	81	-1
94–95	Winn	29	0	0	0	78	-17
95–96	Winn	10	0	1	1	21	-2
96–97	Phoe	1	0	0	0	7	-1
Totals		121	1	10	11	352	-32

Playoffs

91–92	LA	4	0	0	0	4

THOMPSON, Clifford B. 5-11 185 D
B. Winchester, Mass., Dec. 9, 1918

41–42	Bos	3	0	0	0	2
48–49	Bos	10	0	1	1	0
Totals		13	0	1	1	2

*THOMPSON, Kenneth F

17–18	Mont W	1	0	0	0	0

THOMPSON, Loran Errol (Errol) 5-8 180 LW
B. Summerside, P.E.I., May 28, 1950

70–71	Tor	1	0	0	0	0	-1
72–73	Tor	68	13	19	32	8	+4
73–74	Tor	56	7	8	15	6	+2
74–75	Tor	65	25	17	42	12	-1
75–76	Tor	75	43	37	80	26	+28
76–77	Tor	41	21	16	37	8	-10
77–78	Tor-Det	73	22	23	45	12	+13
78–79	Det	70	23	31	54	26	-28
79–80	Det	77	34	14	48	22	-10
80–81	Det-Pitt	73	20	20	40	64	-16
Totals		599	208	185	393	184	-16

Playoffs

73–74	Tor	2	0	1	1	0
74–75	Tor	6	0	0	0	9
75–76	Tor	10	3	3	6	0
76–77	Tor	9	2	0	2	0
77–78	Det	9	2	1	3	2
Totals		34	7	5	12	11

*THOMPSON, Paul Ivan 5-10 180 LW
B. Calgary, Alta., Nov. 2, 1906

26–27	NYR	43	7	3	10	12
27–28	NYR	41	4	4	8	22
28–29	NYR	44	10	7	17	38
29–30	NYR	44	7	12	19	36
30–31	NYR	44	7	7	14	36
31–32	Chi	48	8	14	22	34
32–33	Chi	48	13	20	33	27
33–34	Chi	48	20	16	36	17
34–35	Chi	48	16	23	39	20
35–36	Chi	46	17	23	40	19
36–37	Chi	47	17	18	35	28
37–38	Chi	48	22	22	44	14
38–39	Chi	37	5	10	15	33
Totals		586	153	179	332	336

Playoffs

26–27	NYR	2	0	0	0	0
27–28	NYR	8	0	0	0	30
28–29	NYR	6	0	2	2	6
29–30	NYR	4	0	0	0	2
30–31	NYR	4	3	0	3	2
31–32	Chi	2	0	0	0	2
33–34	Chi	8	4	3	7	6
35–36	Chi	2	0	3	3	0
37–38	Chi	10	4	3	7	6
Totals		48	11	11	22	54

THOMPSON, Rocky 6-2 185 D
B. Calgary, Alta., Aug. 8, 1977

97–98	Calg	12	0	0	0	61	0
98–99	Calg	3	0	0	0	25	0
Totals		15	0	0	0	86	0

*THOMS, William D. 5-9 170 C
B. Newmarket, Ont., Mar. 5, 1910

32–33	Tor	29	3	9	12	15
33–34	Tor	47	8	18	26	24
34–35	Tor	47	9	13	22	19
35–36	Tor	48	23	15	38	29
36–37	Tor	48	10	9	19	14
37–38	Tor	48	14	24	38	14
38–39	Tor-Chi	48	7	15	22	20
39–40	Chi	46	9	13	22	4
40–41	Chi	48	13	19	32	8
41–42	Chi	48	15	30	45	8
42–43	Chi	47	15	28	43	11
43–44	Chi	7	3	5	8	2
44–45	Chi-Bos	38	6	8	14	8
Totals		549	135	206	341	176

Playoffs

32–33	Tor	9	1	1	2	4
33–34	Tor	5	0	2	2	0
34–35	Tor	7	2	0	2	0
35–36	Tor	9	3	5	8	0
36–37	Tor	2	0	0	0	0
37–38	Tor	1	0	1	1	0
39–40	Chi	1	0	0	0	0
41–42	Chi	3	0	1	1	0
44–45	Bos	1	0	0	0	2
Totals		44	6	10	16	6

THOMSON, Floyd Harvey 6-0 190 LW
B. Sudbury, Ont., June 14, 1949

71–72	StL	49	4	6	10	48	-9
72–73	StL	75	14	20	34	71	-2
73–74	StL	77	11	22	33	58	-19
74–75	StL	77	9	27	36	106	+13
75–76	StL	58	8	10	18	25	-4
76–77	StL	58	7	8	15	11	+1
77–78	StL	6	1	1	2	4	-3
79–80	StL	11	2	3	5	18	-1
Totals		411	56	97	153	341	-24

Playoffs

72–73	StL	5	0	1	1	2
74–75	StL	2	0	1	1	0
76–77	StL	3	0	0	0	4
Totals		10	0	2	2	6

THOMSON, James Richard 6-0 190 D
B. Winnipeg, Man., Feb. 23, 1927

45–46	Tor	5	0	1	1	4
46–47	Tor	60	2	14	16	97
47–48	Tor	59	0	29	29	82
48–49	Tor	60	4	16	20	56
49–50	Tor	70	0	13	13	56
50–51	Tor	69	3	33	36	76
51–52	Tor	70	0	25	25	86
52–53	Tor	69	0	22	22	73
53–54	Tor	61	2	24	26	86
54–55	Tor	70	4	12	16	68
55–56	Tor	62	0	7	7	96
56–57	Tor	62	0	12	12	50
57–58	Chi	70	4	7	11	75
Totals		787	19	215	234	905

Playoffs

46–47	Tor	11	0	1	1	22
47–48	Tor	9	1	1	2	9
48–49	Tor	9	1	5	6	10
49–50	Tor	7	0	2	2	7
50–51	Tor	11	0	1	1	34
51–52	Tor	4	0	0	0	25
53–54	Tor	3	0	0	0	2
54–55	Tor	4	0	0	0	16
55–56	Tor	5	0	3	3	10
Totals		63	2	13	15	135

THOMSON, Jim 6-1 220 RW
B. Edmonton, Alta., Dec. 30, 1965

86–87	Wash	10	0	0	0	35	-2
88–89	Wash-Hart	19	2	0	2	67	-6
89–90	NJ	3	0	0	0	31	-3
90–91	LA	8	1	0	1	19	0
91–92	LA	45	1	2	3	162	-1
92–93	Ott-LA	24	0	1	1	97	-12
93–94	Ana	6	0	0	0	5	0
Totals		115	4	3	7	416	-24

Playoffs

92–93	LA	1	0	0	0	0

THOMSON, John F.. D
B. Bixbridge, England, Jan. 31, 1918

39–40	NYA	12	1	1	2	0
40–41	NYA	3	0	0	0	0
Totals		15	1	1	2	0

Playoffs

39–40	NYA	2	0	0	0	0

*THOMSON, Rhys G. D
B. Toronto, Ont., Aug. 9, 1918

39–40	Mont	7	0	0	0	16
42–43	Tor	18	0	2	2	22
Totals		25	0	2	2	38

THOMSON, William Ferguson 5-9 162 C
B. Ayshire, Scotland, Mar. 23, 1914

38–39	Det	4	0	0	0	0
43–44	Chi-Det	6	2	2	4	0
Totals		10	2	2	4	0

Playoffs

43–44	Det	2	0	0	0	0

SSN	TEAM	GP	G	A	PTS.	PIM	+/-
THORNBURY, Tom *5–11 175 D*							
B. Lindsay, Ont., Mar. 17, 1963							
83–84	Pitt	14	1	8	9	16	-19
THORNTON, Joe *6–4 198 C*							
B. London, Ont., July 7, 1979							
97–98	Bos	55	3	4	7	19	-6
98–99	Bos	81	16	25	41	69	+3
Totals		136	19	29	48	88	-3
Playoffs							
97–98	Bos	6	0	0	0	9	
98–99	Bos	11	3	6	9	4	
Totals		17	3	6	9	13	
THORNTON, Scott *6–3 210 C*							
B. London, Ont., Jan. 9, 1971							
90–91	Tor	33	1	3	4	30	-15
91–92	Edm	15	0	1	1	43	-6
92–93	Edm	9	0	1	1	0	-4
93–94	Edm	61	4	7	11	104	-15
94–95	Edm	47	10	12	22	89	-4
95–96	Edm	77	9	9	18	149	-25
96–97	Mont	73	10	10	20	128	-19
97–98	Mont	67	6	9	15	158	0
98–99	Mont	47	7	4	11	87	-2
Totals		429	47	56	103	788	-90
Playoffs							
91–92	Edm	1	0	0	0	0	
96–97	Mont	5	1	0	1	2	
97–98	Mont	9	0	2	2	10	
Totals		15	1	2	3	12	
***THORSTEINSON, Joseph** *5–9 157 RW*							
B. Winnipeg, Man., March 19, 1905							
32–33	NYA	4	0	0	0	0	
***THURIER, Alfred Michael (Fred)** *5–10 160 C*							
B. Granby, Que., Jan. 11, 1918							
40–41	NYA	3	2	1	3	0	
41–42	Brk	27	7	7	14	4	
44–45	NYR	50	16	19	35	14	
Totals		80	25	27	52	18	
THURLBY, Thomas Newman *5–10 180 D*							
B. Kingston, Ont., Nov. 9, 1938							
67–68	Oak	20	1	2	3	4	-6
THYER, Mario *5–11 170 C*							
B. Montreal, Que., Sept. 29, 1966							
89–90	Minn	5	0	0	0	0	-3
Playoffs							
89–90	Minn	1	0	0	0	2	
TICHY, Milan *6–3 198 D*							
B. Plzen, Czechoslovakia, Sept. 22, 1969							
92–93	Chi	13	0	1	1	30	+7
94–95	NYI	2	0	0	0	2	-1
95–96	NYI	8	0	4	4	8	+3
Totals		23	0	5	5	40	+9
TIDEY, Alexander *6–0 188 RW*							
B. Vancouver, B.C., Jan. 5, 1955							
75–76	SD (WHA)	74	16	11	27	46	-1
76–77	Buf	3	0	0	0	0	-1
77–78	Buf	1	0	0	0	0	-1
79–80	Edm	5	0	0	0	8	-3
NHL Totals		9	0	0	0	8	-5
WHA Totals		74	16	11	27	46	
Playoffs							
75–76	SD (WHA)	11	3	6	9	10	
76–77	Buf	2	0	0	0	0	
NHL Totals		2	0	0	0	0	
WHA Totals		11	3	6	9	10	
TIKKANEN, Esa *6–1 190 LW*							
B. Helsinki, Finland, Jan. 25, 1965							
85–86	Edm	35	7	6	13	28	+5
86–87	Edm	76	34	44	78	120	+44
87–88	Edm	80	23	51	74	153	+21
88–89	Edm	67	31	47	78	92	+10
89–90	Edm	79	30	33	63	161	+17
90–91	Edm	79	27	42	69	85	+22
91–92	Edm	40	12	16	28	44	-8
92–93	Edm–NYR	81	16	24	40	94	-24
93–94	NYR	83	22	32	54	114	+5
94–95	StL	43	12	23	35	22	+13
95–96	StL–NJ–Van	58	14	30	44	36	+1
96–97	Van–NYR	76	13	17	30	72	-9
97–98	Fla–Wash	48	3	18	21	18	-11
Totals		877	244	386	630	1077	+71
Playoffs							
84–85	Edm	3	0	0	0	2	
85–86	Edm	8	3	2	5	7	
86–87	Edm	21	7	2	9	22	
87–88	Edm	19	10	17	27	72	
88–89	Edm	7	1	3	4	12	
89–90	Edm	22	13	11	24	26	
90–91	Edm	18	12	8	20	24	
91–92	Edm	16	5	3	8	8	
94–95	StL	7	2	2	4	20	
95–96	Van	6	3	2	5	2	
96–97	NYR	15	9	3	12	26	
97–98	Wash	21	3	3	6	20	
Totals		186	72	60	132	275	
TILEY, Brad *6–1 185 D*							
B. Markdale, Ont., July 5, 1971							
97–98	Phoe	1	0	0	0	0	0
98–99	Phoe	8	0	0	0	0	-1
Totals		9	0	0	0	0	-1
Playoffs							
98–99	Phoe	1	0	0	0	0	
TILLEY, Tom *6–0 189 D*							
B. Trenton, Ont., Mar. 28, 1965							
88–89	StL	70	1	22	23	47	+1
89–90	StL	34	0	5	5	6	+17
90–91	StL	22	2	4	6	4	+5
93–94	StL	48	1	7	8	32	+3
Totals		174	4	38	42	89	+19
Playoffs							
88–89	StL	10	1	2	3	17	
93–94	StL	4	0	1	1	2	
Totals		14	1	3	4	19	
TIMANDER, Mattias *6–1 194 D*							
B. Solleftea, Sweden, April 16, 1974							
96–97	Bos	41	1	8	9	14	-9
97–98	Bos	23	1	1	2	6	-9
98–99	Bos	22	0	6	6	10	+4
Totals		86	2	15	17	30	-4
Playoffs							
98–99	Bos	4	1	1	2	2	
TIMGREN, Raymond Charles *5–9 161 LW*							
B. Windsor, Ont., Sept. 29, 1928							
48–49	Tor	36	3	12	15	9	
49–50	Tor	68	7	18	25	9	
50–51	Tor	70	1	9	10	20	
51–52	Tor	50	2	4	6	11	
52–53	Tor	12	0	0	0	4	
54–55	Chi–Tor	15	1	1	2	4	
Totals		251	14	44	58	57	
Playoffs							
48–49	Tor	9	3	3	6	2	
49–50	Tor	6	0	4	4	2	
50–51	Tor	11	0	1	1	2	
51–52	Tor	4	0	1	1	0	
Totals		30	3	9	12	6	
TIMONEN, Kimmo *5–9 180 D*							
B. Kuopio, Finland, March 18, 1975							
98–99	Nash	50	4	8	12	30	-4
TINORDI, Mark *6–4 213 D*							
B. Red Deer, Alta., May 9, 1966							
87–88	NYR	24	1	2	3	50	-5
88–89	Minn	47	2	3	5	107	-9
89–90	Minn	66	3	7	10	240	0
90–91	Minn	69	5	27	32	189	+1
91–92	Minn	63	4	24	28	179	-13
92–93	Minn	69	15	27	42	157	-1
93–94	Dal	61	6	18	24	143	+6
94–95	Wash	42	3	9	12	71	-5
95–96	Wash	71	3	10	13	113	+26
96–97	Wash	56	2	6	8	118	+3
97–98	Wash	47	8	9	17	39	+9
98–99	Wash	48	0	6	6	108	-6
Totals		663	52	148	200	1514	+6
Playoffs							
88–89	Minn	5	0	0	0	0	
89–90	Minn	7	0	1	1	16	
90–91	Minn	23	5	6	11	78	
91–92	Minn	7	1	2	3	11	
94–95	Wash	1	0	0	0	0	
95–96	Wash	6	0	0	0	16	
97–98	Wash	21	1	2	3	42	
Totals		70	7	11	18	165	
TIPPETT, Dave *5–10 180 LW*							
B. Moosomin, Sask., Aug. 25, 1961							
83–84	Hart	17	4	2	6	2	-1
84–85	Hart	80	7	12	19	12	-24
85–86	Hart	80	14	20	34	18	+9
86–87	Hart	80	9	22	31	42	0
87–88	Hart	80	16	21	37	32	-4
88–89	Hart	80	17	24	41	45	-6
89–90	Hart	66	8	19	27	32	0
90–91	Wash	61	6	9	15	24	-13
91–92	Wash	30	2	10	12	16	+2
92–93	Pitt	74	6	19	25	56	+5
93–94	Phil	73	4	11	15	38	-20
Totals		721	93	169	262	317	-52
Playoffs							
85–86	Hart	10	2	2	4	4	
86–87	Hart	6	0	2	2	4	
87–88	Hart	6	0	0	0	2	
88–89	Hart	4	0	1	1	0	
89–90	Hart	7	1	3	4	2	
90–91	Wash	10	2	3	5	8	
91–92	Wash	7	0	1	1	0	
92–93	Pitt	12	1	4	5	14	
Totals		62	6	16	22	34	
TITANIC, Morris S. *6–1 180 LW*							
B. Toronto, Ont., Jan. 7, 1953							
74–75	Buf	17	0	0	0	0	-4
75–76	Buf	2	0	0	0	0	+1
Totals		19	0	0	0	0	-3
TITOV, German *6–1 190 C*							
B. Moscow, USSR, Oct. 16, 1965							
93–94	Calg	76	27	18	45	28	+20
94–95	Calg	40	12	12	24	16	+6
95–96	Calg	82	28	39	67	24	+9
96–97	Calg	79	22	30	52	36	-12
97–98	Calg	68	18	22	40	38	-1
98–99	Pitt	72	11	45	56	34	+18
Totals		417	118	166	284	176	+40
Playoffs							
93–94	Calg	7	2	1	3	4	
94–95	Calg	7	5	3	8	10	
95–96	Calg	4	0	2	2	0	
98–99	Pitt	11	3	5	8	4	
Totals		29	10	11	21	18	
TKACHUK, Keith Matthew *6–2 210 LW*							
B. Melrose, Mass., Mar. 28, 1972							
91–92	Winn	17	3	5	8	28	0
92–93	Winn	83	28	23	51	201	-13
93–94	Winn	84	41	40	81	255	-12
94–95	Winn	48	22	29	51	152	-4
95–96	Winn	76	50	48	98	156	+11
96–97	Phoe	81	52	34	86	228	-1
97–98	Phoe	69	40	26	66	147	+9
98–99	Phoe	68	36	32	68	151	+22
Totals		526	272	237	509	1318	+12
Playoffs							
91–92	Winn	7	3	0	3	30	
92–93	Winn	6	4	0	4	14	
95–96	Winn	6	1	2	3	22	
96–97	Phoe	7	6	0	6	7	
97–98	Phoe	6	3	3	6	10	
98–	Phoe	7	1	3	4	13	

Totals	39	18	8	26	96	

TKACZUK, Walter Robert *6-0 190 C*
B. Emstedetten, West Germany, Sept. 29, 1947

SSN	TEAM	GP	G	A	PTS.	PIM	+/-
67–68	NYR	2	0	0	0	0	-1
68–69	NYR	71	12	24	36	28	-11
69–70	NYR	76	27	50	77	38	+26
70–71	NYR	77	26	47	73	48	+18
71–72	NYR	76	24	42	66	65	+34
72–73	NYR	76	27	39	66	59	+35
73–74	NYR	71	21	42	63	58	+15
74–75	NYR	62	11	25	36	34	+1
75–76	NYR	78	8	28	36	56	-10
76–77	NYR	80	12	38	50	38	+11
77–78	NYR	80	26	40	66	30	+19
78–79	NYR	77	15	27	42	38	+20
79–80	NYR	76	12	25	37	36	+19
80–81	NYR	43	6	22	28	28	+13
Totals		945	227	451	678	556	+185

Playoffs

68–69	NYR	4	0	1	1	6
69–70	NYR	6	2	1	3	17
70–71	NYR	13	1	5	6	14
71–72	NYR	16	4	6	10	35
72–73	NYR	10	7	2	9	8
73–74	NYR	13	0	5	5	22
74–75	NYR	3	1	2	3	5
77–78	NYR	3	0	2	2	0
78–79	NYR	18	4	7	11	10
79–80	NYR	7	0	1	1	2
Totals		93	19	32	51	119

TOAL, Michael James (Toaler) *6-0 175 C*
B. Red Deer, Alta., Mar. 23, 1959

79–80	Edm	3	0	0	0	0	0

TOCCHET, Rick *6-0 205 RW*
B. Scarborough, Ont., Apr. 9, 1964

84–85	Phil	75	14	25	39	181	+6
85–86	Phil	69	14	21	35	284	+12
86–87	Phil	69	21	26	47	288	+16
87–88	Phil	65	31	33	64	301	+3
88–89	Phil	66	45	36	81	183	-1
89–90	Phil	75	37	59	96	196	+4
90–91	Phil	70	40	31	71	150	+2
91–92	Phil–Pitt	61	27	32	59	151	+15
92–93	Pitt	80	48	61	109	252	+28
93–94	Pitt	51	14	26	40	134	-15
94–95	LA	36	18	17	35	70	-8
95–96	LA–Bos	71	29	31	60	181	+10
96–97	Bos–Wash	53	21	19	40	98	-3
97–98	Phoe	68	26	19	45	157	+1
98–99	Phoe	81	26	30	56	147	+5
Totals		990	411	466	877	2773	+75

Playoffs

84–85	Phil	19	3	4	7	72
85–86	Phil	5	1	2	3	26
86–87	Phil	26	11	10	21	72
87–88	Phil	5	1	4	5	55
88–89	Phil	16	6	6	12	69
91–92	Pitt	14	6	13	19	24
92–93	Pitt	12	7	6	13	24
93–94	Pitt	6	2	3	5	20
95–96	Bos	5	4	0	4	21
97–98	Phoe	6	6	2	8	25
98–99	Phoe	7	0	3	3	8
Totals		121	47	53	100	416

TODD, Kevin Lee *5-10 180 C*
B. Winnipeg, Man., May 4, 1968

88–89	NJ	1	0	0	0	0	-1
90–91	NJ	1	0	0	0	0	-1
91–92	NJ	80	21	42	63	69	+8
92–93	NJ–Edm	55	9	14	23	22	-9
93–94	Chi–LA	47	8	14	22	24	-3
94–95	LA	33	3	8	11	12	-5
95–96	LA	74	16	27	43	38	+6
96–97	Ana	65	9	21	30	44	-7
97–98	Ana	27	4	7	11	12	-5
Totals		383	70	133	203	225	-17

Playoffs

90–91	NJ	1	0	0	0	6
91–92	NJ	7	3	2	5	8
96–97	Ana	4	0	0	0	2
Totals		12	3	2	5	16

TOMALTY, Glenn *6-1 205 LW*
B. Lachute, Que., July 23, 1954

79–80	Winn	1	0	0	0	0	0

TOMLAK, Mike *6-3 205 C/LW*
B. Thunder Bay, Ont., Oct. 17, 1964

89–90	Hart	70	7	14	21	48	+5
90–91	Hart	64	8	8	16	55	-9
91–92	Hart	6	0	0	0	0	-2
93–94	Hart	1	0	0	0	0	0
Totals		141	15	22	37	103	-6

Playoffs

89–90	Hart	7	0	1	1	2
90–91	Hart	3	0	0	0	2
Totals		10	0	1	1	4

TOMLINSON, Dave *5-11 180 C*
B. North Vancouver, B.C., May 8, 1969

91–92	Tor	3	0	0	0	2	-1
92–93	Tor	3	0	0	0	2	0
93–94	Winn	31	1	3	4	24	-12
94–95	Fla	5	0	0	0	0	-2
Totals		42	1	3	4	28	-15

TOMLINSON, Kirk *5-10 175 C*
B. Toronto, Ont., May 2, 1968

87–88	Minn	1	0	0	0	0	0

TOMS, Jeff *6-3 180 LW*
B. Swift Current, Sask., June 4, 1974

95–96	TB	1	0	0	0	0	0
96–97	TB	34	2	8	10	10	+2
97–98	TB–Wash	46	4	6	10	15	-17
98–99	Wash	21	1	5	6	2	0
Totals		102	7	19	26	27	-15

Playoffs

97–98	Wash	1	0	0	0	0

TONELLI, John *6-1 200 LW*
B. Milton, Ont., Mar. 23, 1957

75–76	Hou (WHA)	79	17	14	31	66	
76–77	Hou (WHA)	80	24	31	55	109	
77–78	Hou (WHA)	65	23	41	64	103	
78–79	NYI	73	17	39	56	44	+29
79–80	NYI	77	14	30	44	49	+8
80–81	NYI	70	20	32	52	57	+8
81–82	NYI	80	35	58	93	57	+48
82–83	NYI	76	31	40	71	55	+30
83–84	NYI	73	27	40	67	66	+21
84–85	NYI	80	42	58	100	95	+50
85–86	NYI–Calg	74	23	45	68	60	+21
86–87	Calg	78	20	31	51	72	-2
87–88	Calg	74	17	41	58	84	+10
88–89	LA	77	31	33	64	110	+9
89–90	LA	73	31	37	68	62	-8
90–91	LA	71	14	16	30	49	+3
91–92	Chi–Que	52	3	11	14	51	-5
NHL Totals		1028	325	511	836	911	+222
WHA Totals		224	64	86	150	278	

Playoffs

75–76	Hou (WHA)	17	7	7	14	8
76–77	Hou (WHA)	11	3	4	7	12
77–78	Hou (WHA)	6	1	3	4	8
78–79	NYI	10	1	6	7	0
79–80	NYI	21	7	9	16	18
80–81	NYI	16	5	8	13	16
81–82	NYI	19	6	10	16	18
82–83	NYI	20	7	11	18	20
83–84	NYI	19	1	3	4	31
84–85	NYI	10	1	9	10	9
85–86	Calg	22	7	9	16	49
86–87	Calg	3	0	0	0	4
87–88	Calg	6	2	5	7	8
88–89	LA	6	0	0	0	8
89–90	LA	10	1	2	3	6
90–91	LA	12	2	4	6	12
Totals		172	40	75	115	200

TOOKEY, Timothy Raymond *5-11 185 C*
B. Edmonton, Alta., Aug. 29, 1960

80–81	Wash	29	10	13	23	18	-6
81–82	Wash	28	8	8	16	35	-9
82–83	Que	12	1	6	7	4	+2
83–84	Pitt	8	0	2	2	2	-2
86–87	Pitt	2	0	0	0	0	0
87–88	LA	20	1	6	7	8	-2
88–89	LA	7	2	1	3	4	-3
Totals		106	22	36	58	71	-20

Playoffs

86–87	Phil	10	1	3	4	2

TOOMEY, Sean *6-1 200 LW*
B. St. Paul, Minn., June 27, 1965

86–87	Minn	1	0	0	0	0	-1

TOPOROWSKI, Shayne *6-2 210 RW*
B Paddockswood, Sask., Aug. 6, 1975

96–97	Tor	3	0	0	0	7	0

TOPPAZZINI, Gerald (Jerry, Topper) *5-11 180 RW*
B. Copper Cliff, Ont., July 29, 1931

52–53	Bos	69	10	13	23	36
53–54	Bos-Chi	51	5	8	13	42
54–55	Chi	70	9	18	27	20
55–56	Det-Bos	68	8	14	22	53
56–57	Bos	55	15	23	38	26
57–58	Bos	64	25	24	49	51
58–59	Bos	70	21	23	44	61
59–60	Bos	69	12	33	45	26
60–61	Bos	67	15	35	50	35
61–62	Bos	70	19	31	50	26
62–63	Bos	65	17	18	35	6
63–64	Bos	65	7	4	11	15
Totals		783	163	244	407	397

Playoffs

52–53	Bos	11	0	3	3	9
56–57	Bos	10	0	1	1	2
57–58	Bos	12	9	3	12	2
58–59	Bos	7	4	2	6	0
Totals		40	13	9	22	13

TOPPAZZINI, Zellio Louis Peter (Topper) *5-11 180 RW*
B. Copper Cliff, Ont., Jan. 5, 1930

48–49	Bos	5	1	1	2	0
49–50	Bos	36	5	5	10	18
50–51	Bos-NYR	59	14	14	28	27
51–52	NYR	16	1	1	2	4
56–57	Chi	7	0	0	0	0
Totals		123	21	21	42	49

Playoffs

48–49	Bos	2	0	0	0	0

TORGAJEV, Pavel *6-1 187 LW*
B. Gorky, U.S.S.R., Jan. 25, 1966

95–96	Galg	41	6	10	16	14	+2

Playoffs

95–96	Calg	1	0	0	0	0

TORKKI, Jari *5-11 185 LW*
B. Rauma, Finland, Aug. 11, 1965

88–89	Chi	4	1	0	1	0	-2

TORMANNEN, Antti *6-1 198 RW*
B. Espoo, Finland, Sept. 19, 1970

95–96	Ott	50	7	8	15	28	-15

TOUHEY, William J. *5-9 155 LW*
B. Ottawa, Ont., Mar. 23, 1906

27–28	Mont M	29	2	0	2	2
28–29	Ott	44	9	3	12	28
29–30	Ott	44	10	3	13	24
30–31	Ott	44	15	15	30	8
31–32	Bos	26	5	4	9	12
32–33	Ott	47	12	7	19	12
33–34	Ott	46	12	8	20	21
Totals		280	65	40	105	107

Playoffs

29–30	Ott	2	1	0	1	0

*TOUPIN, J. Jacques *5-7 155 RW*
B. Trois Rivieres, Que., Nov. 10, 1910

43–44	Chi	8	1	2	3	0

Playoffs

SSN	TEAM	GP	G	A	PTS.	PIM	+/-
43–44	Chi	4	0	0	0	0	

*TOWNSEND, Arthur Gordon *F*

SSN	TEAM	GP	G	A	PTS.	PIM	+/-
26–27	Chi	5	0	0	0	0	

TOWNSHEND, Graeme *6–2 225 RW*
B. Kingston, Jamaica, Oct. 2, 1965

SSN	TEAM	GP	G	A	PTS.	PIM	+/-
89–90	Bos	4	0	0	0	7	-1
90–91	Bos	18	2	5	7	12	+1
91–92	NYI	7	1	2	3	0	+6
92–93	NYI	2	0	0	0	0	0
93–94	Ott	14	0	0	0	9	-7
Totals		45	3	7	10	28	-1

TRADER, Larry *6–1 180 D*
B. Barry's Bay, Ont., July 7, 1963

SSN	TEAM	GP	G	A	PTS.	PIM	+/-
82–83	Det	15	0	2	2	6	-9
84–85	Det	40	3	7	10	39	+11
86–87	StL	5	0	0	0	8	-5
87–88	StL–Mont	31	2	4	6	21	+1
Totals		91	5	13	18	74	-2

Playoffs

SSN	TEAM	GP	G	A	PTS.	PIM	+/-
84–85	Det	3	0	0	0	0	

*TRAINOR, Thomas Weston (Wes) *5–8 180 LW*
B. Charlottetown, P.E.I., Sept. 11, 1922

SSN	TEAM	GP	G	A	PTS.	PIM	+/-
48–49	NYR	17	1	2	3	6	

*TRAPP, Albert Robert (Bobby) *D*
B. 1898

SSN	TEAM	GP	G	A	PTS.	PIM	+/-
26–27	Chi	44	4	2	6	92	
27–28	Chi	38	0	2	2	37	
Totals		82	4	4	8	129	

Playoffs

SSN	TEAM	GP	G	A	PTS.	PIM	+/-
26–27	Chi	2	0	0	0	4	

TRAPP, Doug *6–0 180 LW*
B. Balcarres, Sask., Nov. 28, 1965

SSN	TEAM	GP	G	A	PTS.	PIM	+/-
86–87	Buf	2	0	0	0	0	0

*TRAUB, Percy (Puss) *D*

SSN	TEAM	GP	G	A	PTS.	PIM	+/-
26–27	Chi	42	0	2	2	93	
27–28	Det	44	3	1	4	75	
28–29	Det	44	0	0	0	46	
Totals		130	3	3	6	214	

Playoffs

SSN	TEAM	GP	G	A	PTS.	PIM	+/-
26–27	Chi	2	0	0	0	6	
28–29	Det	2	0	0	0	0	
Totals		4	0	0	0	6	

TRAVERSE, Patrick *6–3 200 D*
B. Montreal, Que., Mar. 14, 1974

SSN	TEAM	GP	G	A	PTS.	PIM	+/-
95–96	Ott	5	0	0	0	2	-1
98–99	Ott	46	1	9	10	22	+12
Totals		51	1	9	10	24	+11

TREBIL, Daniel *6–3 185 D*
B. Edina, Minn., April 10, 1974

SSN	TEAM	GP	G	A	PTS.	PIM	+/-
96–97	Ana	29	3	3	6	23	+5
97–98	Ana	21	0	1	1	2	-8
98–99	Ana	6	0	0	0	0	-2
Totals		56	34	4	7	25	-5

Playoffs

SSN	TEAM	GP	G	A	PTS.	PIM	+/-
96–97	Ana	9	0	1	1	6	
98–99	Ana	1	0	0	0	2	
Totals		10	0	1	1	8	

TREDWAY, Brock *6–0 180 RW*
B. Highland Creek, Ont., June 23, 1959

Playoffs

SSN	TEAM	GP	G	A	PTS.	PIM	+/-
81–82	LA	1	0	0	0	0	

TREMBLAY, Brent Francis *6–2 192 D*
B. North Bay, Ont., Nov. 1, 1957

SSN	TEAM	GP	G	A	PTS.	PIM	+/-
78–79	Wash	1	0	0	0	0	0
79–80	Wash	9	1	0	1	6	+1
Totals		10	1	0	1	6	+1

TREMBLAY, Jean Claude (J.C.) *5–11 190 D*
B. Bagotville, Que., Jan. 22, 1939

SSN	TEAM	GP	G	A	PTS.	PIM	+/-
59–60	Mont	11	0	1	1	0	
60–61	Mont	29	1	3	4	18	
61–62	Mont	70	3	17	20	18	
62–63	Mont	69	1	17	18	10	
63–64	Mont	70	5	16	21	24	
64–65	Mont	68	3	17	20	22	
65–66	Mont	59	6	29	35	8	
66–67	Mont	60	8	26	34	14	
67–68	Mont	73	4	26	30	18	+28
68–69	Mont	75	7	32	39	18	+29
69–70	Mont	58	2	19	21	7	+5
70–71	Mont	76	11	52	63	23	+16
71–72	Mont	76	6	51	57	24	+52
72–73	Que (WHA)	76	14	75	89	32	
73–74	Que (WHA)	68	9	44	53	10	
74–75	Que (WHA)	68	16	56	72	18	
75–76	Que (WHA)	80	12	77	89	16	
76–77	Que (WHA)	53	4	31	35	16	
77–78	Que (WHA)	54	5	37	42	26	
78–79	Que (WHA)	56	6	38	44	8	
NHL Totals		794	57	306	363	204	+130
WHA Totals		455	66	358	424	126	

Playoffs

SSN	TEAM	GP	G	A	PTS.	PIM	+/-
60–61	Mont	5	0	0	0	2	
61–62	Mont	6	0	2	2	2	
62–63	Mont	5	0	0	0	0	
63–64	Mont	7	2	1	3	9	
64–65	Mont	13	1	9	10	18	
65–66	Mont	10	2	9	11	2	
66–67	Mont	10	2	4	6	2	
67–68	Mont	13	3	6	9	2	
68–69	Mont	13	1	4	5	6	
70–71	Mont	20	3	14	17	15	
71–72	Mont	6	0	2	2	0	
74–75	Que (WHA)	11	0	10	10	2	
75–76	Que (WHA)	5	0	3	3	0	
76–77	Que (WHA)	17	2	9	11	2	
77–78	Que (WHA)	1	0	1	1	0	
NHL Totals		108	14	51	65	58	
WHA Totals		34	2	23	25	4	

*TREMBLAY, Joseph Jean–Gilles (Gilles) *5–10 175 LW*
B. Montmorency, Que., Dec. 17, 1938

SSN	TEAM	GP	G	A	PTS.	PIM	+/-
60–61	Mont	45	7	11	18	4	
61–62	Mont	70	32	22	54	28	
62–63	Mont	60	25	24	49	42	
63–64	Mont	61	22	15	37	21	
64–65	Mont	26	9	7	16	16	
65–66	Mont	70	27	21	48	24	
66–67	Mont	62	13	19	32	16	
67–68	Mont	71	23	28	51	8	+28
68–69	Mont	44	10	15	25	2	+15
Totals		509	168	162	330	161	+43

Playoffs

SSN	TEAM	GP	G	A	PTS.	PIM	+/-
60–61	Mont	6	1	3	4	0	
61–62	Mont	6	1	0	1	2	
62–63	Mont	5	2	0	2	0	
63–64	Mont	2	0	0	0	0	
65–66	Mont	10	4	5	9	0	
66–67	Mont	10	0	1	1	0	
67–68	Mont	9	1	5	6	2	
Totals		48	9	14	23	4	

TREMBLAY, Marcel *F*
B. Winnipeg, Man., July 4, 1915

SSN	TEAM	GP	G	A	PTS.	PIM	+/-
38–39	Mont	10	0	2	2	0	

TREMBLAY, Mario *6–0 190 RW*
B. Alma, Que., Sept. 2, 1956

SSN	TEAM	GP	G	A	PTS.	PIM	+/-
74–75	Mont	63	21	18	39	108	+23
75–76	Mont	71	11	16	27	88	+5
76–77	Mont	74	18	28	46	61	+25
77–78	Mont	56	10	14	24	44	+6
78–79	Mont	76	30	29	59	74	+23
79–80	Mont	77	16	26	42	105	+6
80–81	Mont	77	25	38	63	123	+16
81–82	Mont	80	33	40	73	66	+24
82–83	Mont	80	30	37	67	87	+29
83–84	Mont	67	14	25	39	112	+2
84–85	Mont	75	31	35	66	120	+21
85–86	Mont	56	19	20	39	55	+4
Totals		852	258	326	584	1043	+184

Playoffs

SSN	TEAM	GP	G	A	PTS.	PIM	+/-
74–75	Mont	11	0	1	1	7	
75–76	Mont	10	0	1	1	27	
76–77	Mont	14	3	0	3	9	
77–78	Mont	5	2	0	2	16	
78–79	Mont	13	3	4	7	13	
79–80	Mont	10	0	11	11	14	
80–81	Mont	3	0	0	0	9	
81–82	Mont	5	4	1	5	24	
82–83	Mont	3	0	1	1	7	
Totals		74	12	19	31	126	

TREMBLAY, Nelson (Nels) *5–9 170 C*
B. Quebec City, Que., July 26, 1923

SSN	TEAM	GP	G	A	PTS.	PIM	+/-
44–45	Mont	1	0	1	1	0	
45–46	Mont	2	0	0	0	0	
Totals		3	0	1	1	0	

Playoffs

SSN	TEAM	GP	G	A	PTS.	PIM	+/-
44–45	Mont	2	0	0	0	0	

TREMBLAY, Yannick *6–2 185 D*
B. Pointe–aux–Trembles, Que., Nov. 15, 1975

SSN	TEAM	GP	G	A	PTS.	PIM	+/-
96–97	Tor	5	0	0	0	0	-4
97–98	Tor	38	2	4	6	6	-6
98–99	Tor	35	2	7	9	16	0
Totals		78	4	11	15	22	-10

TREPANIER, Pascal *6–0 205 D*
B. Gaspe, Que., Apr. 9, 1973

SSN	TEAM	GP	G	A	PTS.	PIM	+/-
97–98	Col A	15	0	1	1	18	-2
98–99	Ana	45	2	4	6	48	0
Totals		61	2	5	7	66	-2

TRIMPER, Timothy Edward *5–9 185 LW*
B. Windsor, Ont., Sept. 28, 1959

SSN	TEAM	GP	G	A	PTS.	PIM	+/-
79–80	Chi	30	6	10	16	10	
80–81	Winn	56	15	14	29	28	
81–82	Winn	74	8	8	16	100	
82–83	Winn	5	0	0	0	0	
83–84	Winn	5	0	0	0	0	
84–85	Minn	20	1	4	5	15	
Totals		190	30	36	66	153	

Playoffs

SSN	TEAM	GP	G	A	PTS.	PIM	+/-
79–80	Chi	1	0	0	0	2	
81–82	Winn	1	0	0	0	0	
Totals		2	0	0	0	2	

TRNKA, Pavel *6–3 200 D*
B. Pizen, Czech., July 27, 1976

SSN	TEAM	GP	G	A	PTS.	PIM	+/-
97–98	Ana	48	3	4	7	40	-4
98–99	Ana	63	0	4	4	60	-6
Totals		111	3	8	11	100	-10

Playoffs

SSN	TEAM	GP	G	A	PTS.	PIM	+/-
98–99	Ana	4	0	1	1	2	

*TROTTIER, Bryan John *5–11 195 C*
B. Val Marie, Sask., July 17, 1956

SSN	TEAM	GP	G	A	PTS.	PIM	+/-
75–76	NYI	80	32	63	95	21	+28
76–77	NYI	76	30	42	72	34	+28
77–78	NYI	77	46	77	123	46	+52
78–79	NYI	76	47	87	134	50	+76
79–80	NYI	78	42	62	104	68	+31
80–81	NYI	73	31	72	103	74	+49
81–82	NYI	80	50	79	129	88	+70
82–83	NYI	80	34	55	89	68	+37
83–84	NYI	68	40	71	111	59	+70
84–85	NYI	68	28	31	59	47	+5
85–86	NYI	78	37	59	96	72	+29
86–87	NYI	80	23	64	87	50	+3
87–88	NYI	77	30	52	82	48	+10
88–89	NYI	73	17	28	45	44	-7
89–90	NYI	59	13	11	24	29	-11
90–91	Pitt	52	9	19	28	24	+5
91–92	Pitt	63	11	18	29	54	-11
93–94	Pitt	41	4	11	15	36	-12
Totals		1279	524	901	1425	912	+462

Playoffs

SSN	TEAM	GP	G	A	PTS.	PIM	+/-
75–76	NYI	13	1	7	8	8	
76–77	NYI	12	2	8	10	2	
77–78	NYI	7	0	3	3	4	
78–79	NYI	10	2	4	6	13	
79–80	NYI	21	12	17	29	53	

SSN	TEAM	GP	G	A	PTS.	PIM	+/-
80–81	NYI	18	11	18	29	34	
81–82	NYI	19	6	23	29	40	
82–83	NYI	17	8	12	20	18	
83–84	NYI	21	8	6	14	49	
84–85	NYI	10	4	2	6	8	
85–86	NYI	3	1	1	2	2	
86–87	NYI	14	8	5	13	12	
87–88	NYI	6	0	0	0	10	
89–90	NYI	4	1	0	1	4	
90–91	Pitt	23	3	4	7	49	
91–92	Pitt	21	4	3	7	8	
93–94	Pitt	2	0	0	0	0	
Totals		221	71	113	184	277	

***TROTTIER, David T.** *5–10 170 LW*
B. Pembroke, Ont., June 25, 1906

SSN	TEAM	GP	G	A	PTS.	PIM	+/-
28–29	Mont M	37	2	4	6	60	
29–30	Mont M	41	17	10	27	73	
30–31	Mont M	43	9	8	17	58	
31–32	Mont M	48	26	18	44	94	
32–33	Mont M	48	16	15	31	38	
33–34	Mont M	48	9	17	26	47	
34–35	Mont M	34	10	9	19	22	
35–36	Mont M	46	10	10	20	25	
36–37	Mont M	43	12	11	23	33	
37–38	Mont M	47	9	10	19	42	
38–39	Det	11	1	1	2	16	
Totals		446	121	113	234	508	

Playoffs

SSN	TEAM	GP	G	A	PTS.	PIM
29–30	Mont M	4	0	2	2	8
30–31	Mont M	2	0	0	0	6
31–32	Mont M	4	1	0	1	2
32–33	Mont M	2	0	0	0	6
33–34	Mont M	4	0	0	0	6
34–35	Mont M	7	2	1	3	4
35–36	Mont M	3	0	0	0	4
36–37	Mont M	5	1	0	1	5
Totals		31	4	3	7	41

TROTTIER, Guy *5–8 165 RW*
B. Hull, Que., Apr. 1, 1941

SSN	TEAM	GP	G	A	PTS.	PIM	+/-
68–69	NYR	2	0	0	0	0	0
70–71	Tor	61	19	5	24	21	-12
71–72	Tor	52	9	12	21	16	-12
72–73	Ott (WHA)	72	26	32	58	25	
73–74	Tor (WHA)	71	27	35	62	58	
74–75	Tor–Mich (WHA)	23	7	6	13	4	
NHL Totals		115	28	17	45	37	-24
WHA Totals		166	60	73	133	87	

Playoffs

SSN	TEAM	GP	G	A	PTS.	PIM
70–71	Tor	5	0	0	0	0
71–72	Tor	4	1	0	1	16
72–73	Ott (WHA)	5	1	2	3	0
73–74	Tor (WHA)	12	5	5	10	4
NHL Totals		9	1	0	1	16
WHA Totals		17	6	7	13	4

TROTTIER, Rocky *5–11 185 RW*
B. Climax, Sask., Apr. 11, 1964

SSN	TEAM	GP	G	A	PTS.	PIM	+/-
83–84	NJ	5	1	1	2	0	-1
84–85	NJ	33	5	3	8	2	-3
Totals		38	6	4	10	2	-4

***TRUDEL, Louis Napoleon** *5–11 167 LW*
B. Salem, Mass., July 21, 1913

SSN	TEAM	GP	G	A	PTS.	PIM	+/-
33–34	Chi	31	1	3	4	13	
34–35	Chi	47	11	11	22	28	
35–36	Chi	47	3	4	7	27	
36–37	Chi	45	6	12	18	11	
37–38	Chi	42	6	16	22	15	
38–39	Mont	31	8	13	21	2	
39–40	Mont	47	12	7	19	24	
40–41	Mont	16	2	3	5	2	
Totals		306	49	69	118	122	

Playoffs

SSN	TEAM	GP	G	A	PTS.	PIM
33–34	Chi	7	0	0	0	2
34–35	Chi	2	0	0	0	0
35–36	Chi	2	0	0	0	2
37–38	Chi	10				
38–39	Mont	3	1	0	1	0
Totals		24	1	3	4	6

***TRUDELL, Rene Joseph** *5–9 165 RW*
B. Mariapolis, Man., Jan. 31, 1919

SSN	TEAM	GP	G	A	PTS.	PIM	+/-
45–46	NYR	16	3	5	8	4	
46–47	NYR	59	8	16	24	38	
47–48	NYR	54	13	7	20	30	
Totals		129	24	28	52	72	

Playoffs

SSN	TEAM	GP	G	A	PTS.	PIM
47–48	NYR	5	0	0	0	2

TSULYGIN, Nikolai *6–4 205 D*
B. Ufa, USSR, May 29, 1975

SSN	TEAM	GP	G	A	PTS.	PIM	+/-
96–97	Ana	22	0	1	1	6	-5

TSYGUROV, Denis *6–3 198 D*
B. Chelyabinsk, USSR, Feb. 26, 1971

SSN	TEAM	GP	G	A	PTS.	PIM	+/-
93–94	Buf	8	0	0	0	8	-1
94–95	Buf–LA	25	0	0	0	15	-3
95–96	LA	18	1	5	6	22	0
Totals		51	1	5	6	45	-4

TSYPLAKOV, Vladimir *6–2 194 LW*
B. Inta, U.S.S.R., Apr. 18, 1969

SSN	TEAM	GP	G	A	PTS.	PIM	+/-
95–96	LA	23	5	5	10	4	+1
96–97	LA	67	16	23	39	12	+8
97–98	LA	73	18	34	52	18	+15
98–99	LA	69	11	12	23	32	-7
Totals		232	50	74	124	66	+17

TUCKER, Darcy *5–10 170 C*
B. Castor, Alta., Mar. 15, 1975

SSN	TEAM	GP	G	A	PTS.	PIM	+/-
95–96	Mont	3	0	0	0	0	-1
96–97	Mont	73	7	13	20	110	-5
97–98	Mont–TB	74	7	13	20	146	-14
98–99	TB	82	21	22	43	176	-34
Totals		232	35	48	83	432	-54

Playoffs

SSN	TEAM	GP	G	A	PTS.	PIM
96–97	Mont	4	0	0	0	0

TUCKER, John *6–0 200 C*
B. Windsor, Ont., Sept. 29, 1964

SSN	TEAM	GP	G	A	PTS.	PIM	+/-
83–84	Buf	21	12	4	16	4	+2
84–85	Buf	64	22	27	49	21	+6
85–86	Buf	75	31	34	65	39	0
86–87	Buf	54	17	34	51	21	-3
87–88	Buf	45	19	19	38	20	+4
88–89	Buf	60	13	31	44	31	-5
89–90	Buf–Wash	46	10	21	31	12	+8
90–91	Buf–NYI	38	4	7	11	8	-1
92–93	TB	78	17	39	56	69	-12
93–94	TB	66	17	23	40	28	+9
94–95	TB	46	12	13	25	14	-10
95–96	TB	63	3	7	10	18	-8
Totals		656	177	259	436	285	-10

Playoffs

SSN	TEAM	GP	G	A	PTS.	PIM
83–84	Buf	3	1	0	1	0
84–85	Buf	5	1	5	6	0
87–88	Buf	6	7	3	10	18
88–89	Buf	3	0	3	3	0
89–90	Wash	12	1	7	8	4
95–96	TB	2	0	0	0	2
Totals		31	10	18	28	24

***TUDIN, Cornell (Connie)** *D*

SSN	TEAM	GP	G	A	PTS.	PIM
41–42	Mont	4	0	1	1	4

TUDOR, Robert Alan *5–11 190 RW/C*
B. Cupar, Sask., June 30, 1956

SSN	TEAM	GP	G	A	PTS.	PIM	+/-
78–79	Van	24	4	4	8	19	0
79–80	Van	2	0	0	0	0	0
82–83	StL	2	0	0	0	0	0
Totals		28	4	4	8	19	0

Playoffs

SSN	TEAM	GP	G	A	PTS.	PIM
78–79	Van	2	0	0	0	0
79–80	Van	1	0	0	0	0
Totals		3	0	0	0	0

TUER, Allan *6–0 190 D*
B. North Battleford, Sask., July 19, 1963

SSN	TEAM	GP	G	A	PTS.	PIM	+/-
85–86	LA	45	0	1	1	150	-16
87–88	Minn	6	1	0	1	29	-3
88–89	Hart	4	0	0	0	23	-2
89–90	Hart	2	0	0	0	6	-1
Totals		57	1	1	2	208	-22

TUOMAINEN, Marko *6–3 203 RW*
B. Kuopio, Finland, Apr. 25, 1972

SSN	TEAM	GP	G	A	PTS.	PIM	+/-
94–95	Edm	4	0	0	0	0	0

TURCOTTE, Alfie *5–11 185 C*
B. Gary, Ind., June 5, 1965

SSN	TEAM	GP	G	A	PTS.	PIM	+/-
83–84	Mont	30	7	7	14	10	-9
84–85	Mont	53	8	16	24	35	-1
85–86	Mont	2	0	0	0	2	0
87–88	Winn	3	0	0	0	0	-4
88–89	Winn	14	1	3	4	2	-6
89–90	Wash	4	0	2	2	0	0
90–91	Wash	6	1	1	2	0	-1
Totals		112	17	29	46	49	-21

Playoffs

SSN	TEAM	GP	G	A	PTS.	PIM
84–85	Mont	5	0	0	0	4

TURCOTTE, Darren *6–0 178 C*
B. Boston, Mass., Mar. 2, 1968

SSN	TEAM	GP	G	A	PTS.	PIM	+/-
88–89	NYR	20	7	3	10	4	0
89–90	NYR	76	32	34	66	32	+3
90–91	NYR	74	26	41	67	37	-5
91–92	NYR	71	30	23	53	57	+11
92–93	NYR	71	25	28	53	40	-3
93–94	NYR–Hart	32	4	15	19	17	-13
94–95	Hart	47	17	18	35	22	+1
95–96	Winn–SJ	68	22	21	43	30	+5
96–97	SJ	65	16	21	37	16	-8
97–98	StL	62	12	6	18	26	+6
98–99	Nash	40	4	5	9	16	-11
Totals		626	195	215	410	297	-14

Playoffs

SSN	TEAM	GP	G	A	PTS.	PIM
88–89	NYR	1	0	0	0	0
89–90	NYR	10	1	6	7	4
90–91	NYR	6	1	2	3	0
91–92	NYR	8	4	0	4	6
97–98	StL	10	0	0	0	2
Totals		35	6	8	14	12

TURGEON, Pierre *6–1 195 C*
B. Rouyn, Que., Aug. 29, 1969

SSN	TEAM	GP	G	A	PTS.	PIM	+/-
87–88	Buf	76	14	28	42	34	-8
88–89	Buf	80	34	54	88	26	-2
89–90	Buf	80	40	66	106	29	+10
90–91	Buf	78	32	47	79	26	+14
91–92	Buf–NYI	77	40	55	95	20	+7
92–93	NYI	83	58	74	132	26	-1
93–94	NYI	69	38	56	94	18	+14
94–95	NYI–Mont	49	24	23	47	14	0
95–96	Mont	80	38	58	96	44	+19
96–97	Mont–StL	78	26	59	85	14	+8
97–98	StL	60	22	46	68	24	+13
98–99	StL	67	31	34	65	36	+4
Totals		877	397	600	997	311	+78

Playoffs

SSN	TEAM	GP	G	A	PTS.	PIM
87–88	Buf	6	4	3	7	4
88–89	Buf	5	3	5	8	2
89–90	Buf	6	2	4	6	2
90–91	Buf	6	3	1	4	6
92–93	NYI	11	6	7	13	0
93–94	NYI	4	0	1	1	0
95–96	Mont	6	2	4	6	2
96–97	StL	5	1	1	2	2
97–98	StL	10	4	4	8	2
98–99	StL	13	4	9	13	6
Totals		72	29	39	68	26

TURGEON, Sylvain *6–0 200 LW*
B. Noranda, Que., Jan. 17, 1965

SSN	TEAM	GP	G	A	PTS.	PIM	+/-
83–84	Hart	76	40	32	72	55	-11
84–85	Hart	64	31	31	62	67	-10
85–86	Hart	76	45	34	79	88	+1
86–87	Hart	41	23	13	36	45	-3
87–88	Hart	71	23	26	49	71	-5
88–89	Hart	42	16	14	30	40	-11
89–90	NJ	72	30	17	47	81	-8
90–91	Mont	19	5	7	12	20	-2
91–92	Mont	56	9	11	20	39	-4
92–93	Ott	72	25	18	43	104	-29
93–94	Ott	47	11	15	26	52	-25
94–95	Ott	33	11	8	19	29	-1

SSN	TEAM	GP	G	A	PTS.	PIM	+/-
Totals		669	269	226	495	691	-108
Playoffs							
85–86	Hart	9	2	3	5	4	
86–87	Hart	6	1	2	3	4	
87–88	Hart	6	0	0	0	4	
88–89	Hart	4	0	2	2	4	
89–90	NJ	1	0	0	0	0	
90–91	Mont	5	0	0	0	2	
91–92	Mont	5	1	0	1	4	
Totals		36	4	7	11	22	

TURLICK, Gordon F
B. Mickel, B.C., Sept. 17, 1939

SSN	TEAM	GP	G	A	PTS.	PIM	+/-
59–60	Bos	2	0	0	0	2	

TURNBULL, Ian Wayne 6–0 200 D
B. Montreal, Que., Dec. 22, 1953

SSN	TEAM	GP	G	A	PTS.	PIM	+/-
73–74	Tor	78	8	27	35	74	+12
74–75	Tor	22	6	7	13	44	-6
75–76	Tor	76	20	36	56	90	+24
76–77	Tor	80	22	57	79	84	+47
77–78	Tor	77	14	47	61	77	+6
78–79	Tor	80	12	51	63	80	-7
79–80	Tor	75	11	28	39	90	-23
80–81	Tor	80	19	47	66	104	-17
81–82	Tor–LA	54	11	17	28	89	-4
82–83	Pitt	6	0	0	0	4	-3
Totals		628	123	317	440	753	+29
Playoffs							
73–74	Tor	4	0	0	0	8	
74–75	Tor	7	0	2	2	4	
75–76	Tor	10	2	9	11	29	
76–77	Tor	9	4	4	8	10	
77–78	Tor	13	6	10	16	10	
78–79	Tor	6	0	4	4	27	
79–80	Tor	3	0	3	3	2	
80–81	Tor	3	1	0	1	4	
Totals		55	13	32	45	94	

TURNBULL, Perry John 6–2 200 C
B. Rimbey, Alta., Mar. 9, 1959

SSN	TEAM	GP	G	A	PTS.	PIM	+/-
79–80	StL	80	16	19	35	124	-11
80–81	StL	75	34	22	56	209	+15
81–82	StL	79	33	26	59	161	-15
82–83	StL	79	32	15	47	172	-20
83–84	StL–Mont	72	20	15	35	140	-14
84–85	Winn	66	22	21	43	130	+9
85–86	Winn	80	20	31	51	183	-18
86–87	Winn	26	1	5	6	44	-2
87–88	StL	51	10	9	19	82	+8
Totals		608	188	163	351	1245	-48
Playoffs							
79–80	StL	3	1	1	2	2	
81–82	StL	5	3	2	5	11	
82–83	StL	4	1	0	1	14	
83–84	Mont	9	1	2	3	10	
84–85	Winn	8	0	1	1	26	
85–86	Winn	3	0	1	1	11	
86–87	Winn	1	0	0	0	10	
87–88	StL	1	0	0	0	2	
Totals		34	6	7	13	86	

TURNBULL, Randy Layne 5–11 185 D
B. Bentley, Alta., Feb. 7, 1962

SSN	TEAM	GP	G	A	PTS.	PIM	+/-
81–82	Calg	1	0	0	0	2	-1

TURNER, Brad 6–2 205 D
B. Winnipeg, Man., May 25, 1968

SSN	TEAM	GP	G	A	PTS.	PIM	+/-
91–92	NYI	3	0	0	0	0	+1

TURNER, Dean Cameron 6–2 215 D
B. Dearborn, Mich., June 22, 1958

SSN	TEAM	GP	G	A	PTS.	PIM	+/-
78–79	NYR	1	0	0	0	0	-1
79–80	Col	27	1	0	1	51	0
80–81	Col	4	0	0	0	4	-4
82–83	LA	3	0	0	0	4	0
Totals		35	1	0	1	59	-59

TURNER, Robert George 6–0 178 D
B. Regina, Sask., Jan. 31, 1934

SSN	TEAM	GP	G	A	PTS.	PIM	+/-
55–56	Mont	33	1	4	5	35	
56–57	Mont	58	1	4	5	48	
57–58	Mont	66	0	3	3	30	
58–59	Mont	68	4	24	28	66	
59–60	Mont	54	0	9	9	40	
60–61	Mont	60	2	2	4	16	
61–62	Chi	69	8	2	10	52	
62–63	Chi	70	3	3	6	20	
Totals		478	19	51	70	307	
Playoffs							
55–56	Mont	10	0	1	1	10	
56–57	Mont	6	0	1	1	0	
57–58	Mont	10	0	0	0	2	
58–59	Mont	11	0	2	2	20	
59–60	Mont	8	0	0	0	0	
60–61	Mont	5	0	0	0	0	
61–62	Chi	12	1	0	1	6	
62–63	Chi	6	0	0	0	6	
Totals		68	1	4	5	44	

*TUSTIN, Norman Robert 5–11 175 LW
B. Regina, Sask., Jan. 3, 1919

SSN	TEAM	GP	G	A	PTS.	PIM	+/-
41–42	NYR	18	2	4	6	0	

TUTEN, Audley K. 5–10 180 D
B. Enterprise, Alta., Jan. 14, 1915

SSN	TEAM	GP	G	A	PTS.	PIM	+/-
41–42	Chi	5	1	1	2	10	
42–43	Chi	34	3	7	10	38	
Totals		39	4	8	12	48	

TUTT, Brian 6–1 195 D
B. Small Well, Alta., June 9, 1962

SSN	TEAM	GP	G	A	PTS.	PIM	+/-
89–90	Wash	7	1	0	1	2	-4

TUTTLE, Steve 6–1 197 RW
B. Vancouver, B.C., Jan. 5, 1966

SSN	TEAM	GP	G	A	PTS.	PIM	+/-
88–89	StL	53	13	12	25	6	+3
89–90	StL	71	12	10	22	4	-6
90–91	StL	20	3	6	9	2	+2
Totals		144	28	28	56	12	-1
Playoffs							
88–89	StL	6	1	2	3	0	
89–90	StL	5	0	1	1	2	
90–91	StL	6	0	3	3	0	
Totals		17	1	6	7	2	

TUZZOLINO, Tony 6–2 180 RW
B. Buffalo, N.Y., Oct. 9, 1975

SSN	TEAM	GP	G	A	PTS.	PIM	+/-
97–98	Ana	1	0	0	0	2	-2

TVERDOVSKY, Oleg 6–0 185 D
B. Donetsk, USSR, May 18, 1976

SSN	TEAM	GP	G	A	PTS.	PIM	+/-
94–95	Ana	36	3	9	12	14	-6
95–96	Ana–Winn	82	7	23	30	41	-7
96–97	Phoe	82	10	45	55	30	-5
97–98	Phoe	46	7	12	19	12	+1
98–99	Phoe	82	7	18	25	32	+11
Totals		228	34	107	141	129	-6
Playoffs							
95–96	Winn	6	0	1	1	0	
96–97	Phoe	7	0	1	1	0	
97–98	Phoe	6	0	7	7	0	
98–99	Phoe	6	0	2	2	6	
Totals		25	0	11	11	6	

TWIST, Anthony Rory (Tony) 6–1 220 LW/D
B. Sherwood Park, Alta., May 9, 1968

SSN	TEAM	GP	G	A	PTS.	PIM	+/-
89–90	StL	28	0	0	0	124	-2
90–91	Que	24	0	0	0	104	-4
91–92	Que	44	0	1	1	164	-3
92–93	Que	34	0	2	2	64	0
93–94	StL	49	0	4	4	101	-1
94–95	StL	28	3	0	3	89	0
95–96	StL	51	3	2	5	100	-1
96–97	StL	64	1	2	3	121	-8
97–98	StL	60	1	1	2	105	-4
98–99	StL	63	2	6	8	149	0
Totals		445	10	18	28	1121	-23
Playoffs							
94–95	StL	1	0	0	0	6	
95–96	StL	10	1	1	2	16	
96–97	StL	6	0	0	0	0	
98–99	StL	1	0	0	0	0	
Totals		18	1	1	2	22	

UBRIACO, Eugene Stephen 5–8 157 LW
B. Sault Ste. Marie, Ont., Dec. 26, 1937

SSN	TEAM	GP	G	A	PTS.	PIM	+/-
67–68	Pitt	65	18	15	33	16	-13
68–69	Pitt–Oak	75	19	18	37	28	-5
69–70	Oak–Chi	37	2	2	4	6	-2
Totals		177	39	35	74	50	-20
Playoffs							
68–69	Cal	7	2	0	2	2	
69–70	Chi	4	0	0	0	2	
Totals		11	2	0	2	4	

ULANOV, Igor 6–1 205 D
B. Perm, Soviet Union, Oct. 1, 1969

SSN	TEAM	GP	G	A	PTS.	PIM	+/-
91–92	Winn	27	2	9	11	67	+5
92–93	Winn	56	2	14	16	124	+6
93–94	Winn	74	0	17	17	165	-11
94–95	Winn–Wash	22	1	4	5	29	+1
95–96	Chi–TB	64	3	9	12	116	+11
96–97	TB	59	1	7	8	108	+2
97–98	TB–Mont	49	2	8	10	97	-7
98–99	Mont	76	3	9	12	109	-3
Totals		427	14	77	91	815	+4
Playoffs							
91–92	Winn	7	0	0	0	39	
92–93	Winn	4	0	0	0	4	
94–95	Wash	2	0	0	0	4	
95–96	TB	5	0	0	0	15	
97–98	Mont	10	1	4	5	12	
Totals		28	1	4	5	74	

ULLMAN, Norman Victor Alexander 5–10 185 C
B. Provost, Alta., Dec. 26, 1935

SSN	TEAM	GP	G	A	PTS.	PIM	+/-
55–56	Det	66	9	9	18	26	
56–57	Det	64	16	36	52	47	
57–58	Det	69	23	28	51	38	
58–59	Det	69	22	36	58	42	
59–60	Det	70	24	34	58	46	
60–61	Det	70	28	42	70	34	
61–62	Det	70	26	38	64	54	
62–63	Det	70	26	30	56	53	
63–64	Det	61	21	30	51	55	
64–65	Det	70	42	41	83	70	
65–66	Det	70	31	41	72	35	
66–67	Det	68	26	44	70	26	
67–68	Det–Tor	71	35	37	72	28	-1
68–69	Tor	75	35	42	77	41	+19
69–70	Tor	74	18	42	60	37	+20
70–71	Det–StL	73	34	51	85	24	+14
71–72	Tor	77	23	50	73	26	+8
72–73	Tor	65	20	35	55	10	-18
73–74	Tor	78	22	47	69	12	+10
74–75	Tor	80	9	26	35	8	-12
75–76	Edm (WHA)	77	31	56	87	16	
76–77	Edm (WHA)	67	16	27	43	28	
NHL Totals		1410	490	739	1229	712	+40
WHA Totals		144	47	83	130	40	
Playoffs							
55–56	Det	10	1	3	4	13	
56–57	Det	5	1	1	2	6	
57–58	Det	4	0	2	2	4	
59–60	Det	6	2	2	4	0	
60–61	Det	11	0	4	4	4	
62–63	Det	11	4	12	16	14	
63–64	Det	14	7	10	17	6	
64–65	Det	7	6	4	10	2	
65–66	Det	12	6	9	15	12	
68–69	Tor	4	1	0	1	0	
70–71	Tor	6	0	2	2	2	
71–72	Tor	5	1	3	4	2	
73–74	Tor	4	1	1	2	0	
74–75	Tor	7	0	0	0	2	
75–76	Edm (WHA)	4	1	3	4	2	
76–77	Edm (WHA)	5	0	3	3	0	
NHL Totals		106	30	53	83	67	
WHA Totals		9	1	6	7	2	

UNGER, Garry Douglas 6–0 185 C
B. Edmonton, Alta., Dec. 7, 1947

SSN	TEAM	GP	G	A	PTS.	PIM	+/-
67–68	Tor–Det	28	6	11	17	6	-1
68–69	Det	76	24	20	44	33	+6
69–70	Det	76	42	24	66	67	+24
70–71	Det–StL	79	28	28	56	104	-36
71–72	StL	78	36	34	70	104	-8

SSN	TEAM	GP	G	A	PTS.	PIM	+/-
72–73	StL	78	41	39	80	119	+7
73–74	StL	78	33	35	68	96	-17
74–75	StL	80	36	44	80	123	+5
75–76	StL	80	39	44	83	95	-12
76–77	StL	80	30	27	57	56	-35
77–78	StL	80	32	20	52	66	-44
78–79	StL	80	30	26	56	44	+2
79–80	Atl	79	17	16	33	39	-26
80–81	LA–Edm	71	10	10	20	46	+8
81–82	Edm	46	7	13	20	69	+1
82–83	Edm	16	2	0	2	8	
Totals		1105	413	391	804	1075	-131

Playoffs

69–70	Det	4	0	1	1	6	
70–71	StL	6	3	2	5	20	
71–72	StL	11	4	5	9	35	
72–73	StL	5	1	2	3	2	
74–75	StL	2	1	3	4	6	
75–76	StL	3	2	1	3	7	
76–77	StL	4	0	1	1	2	
79–80	Atl	4	0	3	3	2	
80–81	Edm	8	0	0	0	2	
81–82	Edm	4	1	0	1	23	
82–83	Edm	1	0	0	0	0	
Totals		52	12	18	30	105	

USTORF, Stefan 6–0 185 C
B. Kaufbeuren, Germany, Jan. 3, 1974

95–96	Wash	48	7	10	17	14	+8
96–97	Wash	6	0	0	0	2	-3
Totals		54	7	10	17	16	+5

Playoffs

| 95–96 | Wash | 5 | 0 | 0 | 0 | 0 | |

VACHON, Nick 5–10 185 C
B. Montreal, Que., July 20, 1972

| 96–97 | NYI | 1 | 0 | 0 | 0 | 0 | |

VADNAIS, Carol Marcel 6–1 210 D
B. Montreal, Que., Sept. 25, 1945

66–67	Mont	11	0	3	3	35	
67–68	Mont	31	1	1	2	31	-2
68–69	Oak	76	15	27	42	151	-18
69–70	Oak	76	24	20	44	212	-24
70–71	Cal	42	10	16	26	91	-3
71–72	Cal–Bos	68	18	26	44	143	-18
72–73	Bos	78	7	24	31	127	+21
73–74	Bos	78	16	43	59	123	+35
74–75	Bos	79	18	56	74	129	+10
75–76	Bos–NYR	76	22	35	57	121	-16
76–77	NYR	74	11	37	48	131	-20
77–78	NYR	80	6	40	46	115	+25
78–79	NYR	77	8	37	45	86	+14
79–80	NYR	66	3	20	23	118	-1
80–81	NYR	74	3	20	23	91	+19
81–82	NYR	50	5	6	11	45	-2
82–83	NJ	51	2	7	9	64	-34
Totals		1087	169	418	587	1813	-54

Playoffs

66–67	Mont	1	0	0	0	2	
67–68	Mont	1	0	0	0	2	
68–69	Cal	7	1	4	5	10	
69–70	Oak	4	2	1	3	15	
71–72	Bos	15	0	2	2	43	
72–73	Bos	5	0	0	0	8	
73–74	Bos	16	1	12	13	42	
74–75	Bos	3	1	5	6	0	
77–78	NYR	3	0	2	2	16	
78–79	NYR	18	2	9	11	13	
79–80	NYR	9	1	2	3	6	
80–81	NYR	16	1	3	4	26	
81–82	NYR	10	1	0	1	4	
Totals		106	10	40	50	187	

VAIC, Lubomir 5–9 178 C
B. Spisska Nova Ves, Czech., Mar. 6, 1977

| 97–98 | Van | 5 | 1 | 1 | 2 | 2 | -2 |

VAIL, Eric Douglas (Big Train) 6–2 210 LW
B. Timmins, Ont., Sept. 16, 1953

73–74	Atl	23	2	9	11	30	+2
74–75	Atl	72	39	21	60	46	+1
75–76	Atl	60	16	31	47	34	+7
76–77	Atl	78	32	39	71	22	+9
77–78	Atl	79	22	36	58	16	+3
78–79	Atl	80	35	48	83	53	+25
79–80	Atl	77	28	25	53	22	+5
80–81	Calg	64	28	36	64	23	+8
81–82	Calg–Det	58	14	15	29	35	-22
Totals		591	216	260	476	281	+38

Playoffs

73–74	Atl	1	0	0	0	2	
75–76	Atl	2	0	0	0	0	
76–77	Atl	3	1	3	4	0	
77–78	Atl	2	1	1	2	0	
78–79	Atl	2	0	1	1	2	
79–80	Atl	4	3	1	4	2	
80–81	Calg	6	0	0	0	0	
Totals		20	5	6	11	6	

*VAIL, Melville (Sparky) 6–0 185 D
B. Meaford, Ont., July 5, 1906

28–29	NYR	18	3	0	3	16	
29–30	NYR	32	1	1	2	2	
Totals		50	4	1	5	18	

Playoffs

28–29	NYR	6	0	0	0	2	
29–30	NYR	4	0	0	0	0	
Totals		10	0	0	0	2	

VAIVE, Richard Claude 6–0 200 RW
B. Ottawa, Ont., May 14, 1959

78–79	Birm (WHA)	75	26	33	59	248	
79–80	Van–Tor	69	22	15	37	188	-16
80–81	Tor	75	33	29	62	229	-16
81–82	Tor	77	54	35	89	157	+12
82–83	Tor	78	51	28	79	105	-13
83–84	Tor	76	52	41	93	114	-12
84–85	Tor	72	35	33	68	112	-26
85–86	Tor	61	33	31	64	85	-19
86–87	Tor	73	32	34	66	61	+12
87–88	Chi	76	43	26	69	108	-20
88–89	Chi–Buf	58	31	26	57	124	+2
89–90	Buf	70	29	19	48	74	+9
90–91	Buf	71	25	27	52	74	+11
91–92	Buf	20	1	3	4	14	-2
NHL Totals		876	441	347	788	1445	-78
WHA Totals		75	26	33	59	248	

Playoffs

79–80	Tor	3	1	0	1	11	
80–81	Tor	3	1	0	1	4	
82–83	Tor	4	2	5	7	6	
85–86	Tor	9	6	2	8	9	
86–87	Tor	13	4	2	6	23	
87–88	Chi	5	6	2	8	38	
88–89	Buf	5	2	1	3	8	
89–90	Buf	6	4	2	6	6	
90–91	Buf	6	1	2	3	6	
Totals		54	27	16	43	111	

VALENTINE, Christopher William 6–0 190 C
B. Belleville, Ont., Dec. 6, 1961

81–82	Wash	60	30	37	67	92	-15
82–83	Wash	23	7	10	17	14	-2
83–84	Wash	22	6	5	11	21	-8
Totals		105	43	52	95	127	-25

Playoffs

| 82–83 | Wash | 2 | 0 | 0 | 0 | 4 | |

VALICEVIC, Robert 6–2 197 RW
B. Detroit, Mich., Jan. 6, 1971

| 98–99 | Nash | 19 | 4 | 2 | 6 | 2 | +4 |

VALIQUETTE, John Joseph (Jack) 6–2 195 C
B. St. Thomas, Ont., Mar. 18, 1956

74–75	Tor	1	0	0	0	0	-4
75–76	Tor	45	10	23	33	30	-8
76–77	Tor	66	15	30	45	7	+5
77–78	Tor	60	8	13	21	15	+2
78–79	Col	76	23	34	57	12	-42
79–80	Col	77	25	25	50	8	-7
80–81	Col	25	3	9	12	7	-12
Totals		350	84	134	218	79	-66

Playoffs

75–76	Tor	10	2	3	5	2	
77–78	Tor	13	1	3	4	2	
Totals		23	3	6	9	4	

VALK, Garry 6–1 205 LW
B. Edmonton, Alta., Nov. 27, 1967

90–91	Van	59	10	11	21	67	-23
91–92	Van	65	8	17	25	56	+3
92–93	Van	48	6	7	13	77	+6
93–94	Ana	78	18	27	45	100	+8
94–95	Ana	36	3	6	9	34	-4
95–96	Ana	79	12	12	24	125	+8
96–97	Ana–Pitt	70	10	11	21	78	-8
97–98	Pitt	39	2	1	3	33	-3
98–99	Tor	77	8	21	29	53	+8
Totals		551	77	113	190	623	-5

Playoffs

90–91	Van	5	0	0	0	20	
91–92	Van	4	0	0	0	5	
92–93	Van	7	0	1	1	12	
98–99	Tor	17	3	4	7	22	
Totals		33	3	5	8	59	

VALLIS, Lindsay 6–3 207 D
B. Winnipeg, Man. Jan. 12, 1971

| 93–94 | Mont | 1 | 0 | 0 | 0 | 0 | 0 |

VAN ALLEN, Shaun Kelly 6–1 200 C
B. Shaunavon, Sask., Aug. 29, 1967

90–91	Edm	2	0	0	0	0	
92–93	Edm	21	1	4	5	6	-2
93–94	Ana	80	8	25	33	64	0
94–95	Ana	45	8	21	29	32	-4
95–96	Ana	49	8	17	25	41	+13
96–97	Ott	80	11	14	25	35	-8
97–98	Ott	80	4	15	19	48	+4
98–99	Ott	79	6	11	17	30	+3
Totals		436	46	107	153	256	+6

Playoffs

96–97	Ott	7	0	1	1	4	
97–98	Ott	11	0	1	1	10	
98–99	Ott	4	0	0	0	0	
Totals		22	0	2	2	14	

VAN BOXMEER, John Martin 6–0 190 D
B. Petrolia, Ont., Nov. 20, 1952

73–74	Mont	20	1	4	5	18	-3
74–75	Mont	9	0	2	2	0	-1
75–76	Mont	46	6	11	17	31	+17
76–77	Mont–Col	45	2	12	14	32	-19
77–78	Col	80	12	42	54	87	-12
78–79	Col	76	9	34	43	46	-26
79–80	Buf	80	11	40	51	55	+40
80–81	Buf	80	18	51	69	69	-2
81–82	Buf	69	14	54	68	62	+20
82–83	Buf	65	6	21	27	53	+7
83–84	Que	18	5	3	8	12	-1
Totals		588	84	274	358	465	+20

Playoffs

73–74	Mont	1	0	0	0	0	
77–78	Col	2	0	1	1	2	
79–80	Buf	14	3	5	8	12	
80–81	Buf	8	1	8	9	7	
81–82	Buf	4	0	1	1	6	
82–83	Buf	9	1	0	1	10	
Totals		38	5	15	20	37	

VAN DORP, Wayne 6–4 225 LW
B. Vancouver, B.C., May 19, 1961

86–87	Edm	3	0	0	0	25	-1
87–88	Pitt	25	1	3	4	75	+2
88–89	Chi	8	0	0	0	23	+1
89–90	Chi	61	7	4	11	303	-3
90–91	Que	4	1	0	1	30	+1
91–92	Que	24	3	5	8	109	+5
Totals		125	12	12	24	565	+5

Playoffs

86–87	Edm	3	0	0	0	2	
88–89	Chi	16	0	1	1	17	
89–90	Chi	8	0	0	0	23	
Totals		27	0	1	1	42	

VAN IMPE, Darren *6–0 195 D*
B. Saskatoon, Sask., May 18, 1973

SSN	TEAM	GP	G	A	PTS.	PIM	+/-
94–95	Ana	1	0	1	1	4	0
95–96	Ana	16	1	2	3	14	+8
96–97	Ana	74	4	19	23	90	+3
97–98	Ana–Bos	69	3	11	14	40	-6
98–99	Bos	60	5	15	20	66	-5
Totals		220	13	48	61	214	0

Playoffs

SSN	TEAM	GP	G	A	PTS.	PIM	+/-
96–97	Ana	9	0	2	2	16	
97–98	Bos	6	2	1	3	0	
98–99	Bos	11	1	2	3	4	
Totals		26	3	5	8	20	

VAN IMPE, Edward Charles *5–10 205 D*
B. Saskatoon, Sask., May 27, 1940

SSN	TEAM	GP	G	A	PTS.	PIM	+/-
66–67	Chi	61	8	11	19	111	
67–68	Phil	67	4	13	17	141	-5
68–69	Phil	68	7	12	19	112	-1
69–70	Phil	65	0	10	10	117	-13
70–71	Phil	77	0	11	11	80	-8
71–72	Phil	73	4	9	13	78	+22
72–73	Phil	72	1	11	12	76	+31
73–74	Phil	77	2	16	18	119	+39
74–75	Phil	78	1	17	18	109	+20
75–76	Phil–Pitt	52	0	13	13	76	-2
76–77	Pitt	10	0	3	3	6	0
Totals		700	27	126	153	1025	+70

Playoffs

SSN	TEAM	GP	G	A	PTS.	PIM	+/-
66–67	Chi	6	0	0	0	8	
67–68	Phil	7	0	4	4	11	
68–69	Phil	1	0	0	0	17	
70–71	Phil	4	0	1	1	8	
72–73	Phil	11	0	0	0	16	
73–74	Phil	17	1	2	3	41	
74–75	Phil	17	0	4	4	28	
75–76	Pitt	3	0	1	1	2	
Totals		66	1	12	13	131	

VANDENBUSSCHE, Ryan *5–11 187 RW*
B. Simcoe, Ont., Feb. 28, 1973

SSN	TEAM	GP	G	A	PTS.	PIM	+/-
96–97	NYR	11	1	0	1	30	-2
97–98	NYR–Chi	20	1	1	2	43	-2
98–99	Chi	6	0	0	0	17	0
Totals		37	2	1	3	90	-4

VARADA, Vaclav *6–0 198 LW*
B. Valasske Mezirici, Czech., Apr. 26, 1976

SSN	TEAM	GP	G	A	PTS.	PIM	+/-
95–96	Buf	1	0	0	0	0	0
96–97	Buf	5	0	0	0	2	0
97–98	Buf	27	5	6	11	15	0
98–99	Buf	72	7	24	31	61	+11
Totals		105	12	30	42	78	+11

Playoffs

SSN	TEAM	GP	G	A	PTS.	PIM	+/-
97–98	Buf	15	3	4	7	18	
98–99	Buf	21	5	4	9	14	
Totals		36	8	8	16	32	

VARIS, Petri *6–1 200 LW*
B. Varkaus, Finland, May 13, 1969

SSN	TEAM	GP	G	A	PTS.	PIM	+/-
97–98	Chi	1	0	0	0	0	0

VARLAMOV, Sergei *5–11 190 LW*
B. Kiev, USSR, July 21; 1978

SSN	TEAM	GP	G	A	PTS.	PIM	+/-
97–98	Calg	1	0	0	0	0	0

VARVIO, Jarkko *5–9 175 RW*
B. Tampere, Finland, Apr. 28, 1972

SSN	TEAM	GP	G	A	PTS.	PIM	+/-
93–94	Dal	8	2	3	5	4	+1
94–95	Dal	5	1	1	2	0	+1
Totals		13	3	4	7	4	+2

VASILEVSKI, Alexander *5–11 190 RW*
B. Kiev, U.S.S.R., Jan. 8, 1975

SSN	TEAM	GP	G	A	PTS.	PIM	+/-
95–96	StL	1	0	0	0	0	-1
96–97	StL	3	0	0	0	2	-1
Totals		4	0	0	0	2	-2

VASILJEVS, Herbert *5–11 170 C*
B. Riga, USSR, May 27, 1976

SSN	TEAM	GP	G	A	PTS.	PIM	+/-
98–99	Fla	5	0	0	0	2	-1

VASILIEV, Andrei *5–9 180 LW*
B. Voskresensk, USSR, Mar. 30, 1972

SSN	TEAM	GP	G	A	PTS.	PIM	+/-
94–95	NYI	2	0	0	0	2	0
95–96	NYI	10	2	5	7	2	+4
96–97	NYI	3	0	0	0	2	-3
98–99	Phoe	1	0	0	0	0	-2
Totals		16	2	5	7	6	-1

VASKE, Dennis James *6–2 210 D*
B. Rockford, Ill., Oct. 11, 1967

SSN	TEAM	GP	G	A	PTS.	PIM	+/-
90–91	NYI	5	0	0	0	2	+4
91–92	NYI	39	0	1	1	39	+5
92–93	NYI	27	1	5	6	32	+9
93–94	NYI	65	2	11	13	76	+21
94–95	NYI	41	1	11	12	53	+3
95–96	NYI	19	1	6	7	21	-13
96–97	NYI	17	0	4	4	12	+3
97–98	NYI	19	0	3	3	12	+2
98–99	Bos	3	0	0	0	6	-3
Totals		235	5	41	46	253	+31

Playoffs

SSN	TEAM	GP	G	A	PTS.	PIM	+/-
92–93	NYI	18	0	6	6	14	
93–94	NYI	4	0	1	1	2	
Totals		22	0	7	7	16	

VASKO, Elmer (Moose) *6–3 220 D*
B. Duparquet, Que., Dec. 11, 1935

SSN	TEAM	GP	G	A	PTS.	PIM	+/-
56–57	Chi	64	3	12	15	31	
57–58	Chi	59	6	20	26	51	
58–59	Chi	63	6	10	16	52	
59–60	Chi	69	3	27	30	110	
60–61	Chi	63	4	18	22	40	
61–62	Chi	64	2	22	24	87	
62–63	Chi	64	4	9	13	70	
63–64	Chi	70	2	18	20	65	
64–65	Chi	69	1	10	11	56	
65–66	Chi	56	1	7	8	44	
67–68	Minn	70	1	6	7	45	-36
68–69	Minn	72	1	7	8	68	-18
69–70	Minn	3	0	0	0	0	-1
Totals		786	34	166	200	719	-55

Playoffs

SSN	TEAM	GP	G	A	PTS.	PIM	+/-
58–59	Chi	6	0	1	1	4	
59–60	Chi	4	0	0	0	0	
60–61	Chi	12	1	1	2	23	
61–62	Chi	12	0	0	0	4	
62–63	Chi	6	0	1	1	8	
63–64	Chi	7	0	0	0	4	
64–65	Chi	14	1	2	3	20	
65–66	Chi	3	0	0	0	4	
67–68	Minn	14	0	2	2	6	
Totals		78	2	7	9	73	

VASKO, Richard John (Rick) *6–0 185 D*
B. St. Catharines, Ont., Jan. 12, 1957

SSN	TEAM	GP	G	A	PTS.	PIM	+/-
77–78	Det	3	0	0	0	7	-1
79–80	Det	8	0	0	0	2	-11
80–81	Det	20	3	7	10	20	-3
Totals		31	3	7	10	29	-15

VAUTOUR, Yvon *6–0 200 RW*
B. St. John, N.B., Sept. 10, 1956

SSN	TEAM	GP	G	A	PTS.	PIM	+/-
79–80	NYI	17	3	1	4	24	-6
80–81	Col	74	15	19	34	143	-20
81–82	Col	14	1	2	3	18	-6
82–83	NJ	52	4	7	11	136	-19
83–84	NJ	42	3	4	7	78	-18
84–85	Que	5	0	0	0	2	0
Totals		204	26	33	59	401	-69

VAYDIK, Gregory *6–0 185 C*
B. Yellowknife, N.W.T., Oct. 9, 1955

SSN	TEAM	GP	G	A	PTS.	PIM	+/-
76–77	Chi	5	0	0	0	0	-2

VEITCH, Darren William *5–11 195 D*
B. Saskatoon, Sask., Apr. 24, 1960

SSN	TEAM	GP	G	A	PTS.	PIM	+/-
80–81	Wash	59	4	21	25	46	-12
81–82	Wash	67	9	44	53	54	-17
82–83	Wash	10	0	8	8	0	-1
83–84	Wash	46	6	18	24	17	0
84–85	Wash	75	3	18	21	37	+31
85–86	Wash–Det	75	3	14	17	29	+12
86–87	Det	77	13	45	58	52	+14
87–88	Det	63	7	33	40	45	+11
88–89	Tor	37	3	7	10	16	-17
90–91	Tor	2	0	1	1	0	-4
Totals		511	48	209	257	296	+17

Playoffs

SSN	TEAM	GP	G	A	PTS.	PIM	+/-
83–84	Wash	5	0	1	1	15	
84–85	Wash	5	0	1	1	4	
86–87	Det	12	3	4	7	8	
87–88	Det	11	4	5	6	6	
Totals		33	4	11	15	33	

VELISCHEK, Randy *6–0 200 D*
B. Montreal, Que., Feb. 10, 1962

SSN	TEAM	GP	G	A	PTS.	PIM	+/-
82–83	Minn	3	0	0	0	2	-4
83–84	Minn	33	2	2	4	10	-6
84–85	Minn	52	4	9	13	26	+7
85–86	NJ	47	2	7	9	39	-20
86–87	NJ	64	2	16	18	52	-12
87–88	NJ	51	3	9	12	66	-13
88–89	NJ	80	4	14	18	70	-2
89–90	NJ	62	0	6	6	72	+4
90–91	Que	79	2	10	12	42	-19
91–92	Que	38	2	3	5	22	-3
Totals		509	21	76	97	401	-68

Playoffs

SSN	TEAM	GP	G	A	PTS.	PIM	+/-
82–83	Minn	9	0	0	0	0	
83–84	Minn	1	0	0	0	0	
84–85	Minn	9	2	3	5	8	
87–88	NJ	19	0	2	2	20	
89–90	NJ	6	0	0	0	4	
Totals		44	2	5	7	32	

VENASKY, Victor William *5–11 177 C*
B. Thunder Bay, Ont., June 3, 1951

SSN	TEAM	GP	G	A	PTS.	PIM	+/-
72–73	LA	77	15	19	34	10	-16
73–74	LA	32	6	5	11	12	-1
74–75	LA	17	1	2	3	0	+3
75–76	LA	80	18	26	44	12	-6
76–77	LA	80	14	26	40	18	+2
77–78	LA	71	3	10	13	6	+1
78–79	LA	73	4	13	17	8	0
Totals		430	61	101	162	66	-17

Playoffs

SSN	TEAM	GP	G	A	PTS.	PIM	+/-
75–76	LA	9	0	1	1	6	
76–77	LA	9	1	4	5	6	
77–78	LA	1	0	0	0	0	
78–79	LA	2	0	0	0	0	
Totals		21	1	5	6	12	

VENERUZZO, Gary Raymond *5–9 165 LW*
B. Fort William, Ont., June 28, 1943

SSN	TEAM	GP	G	A	PTS.	PIM	+/-
67–68	StL	5	1	1	2	0	+1
71–72	StL	2	0	0	0	0	-1
72–73	LA (WHA)	78	43	30	73	34	
73–74	LA (WHA)	78	39	29	68	68	
74–75	Balt (WHA)	77	33	27	60	57	
75–76	Cin–Phoe (WHA)	75	22	26	48	35	
76–77	SD (WHA)	40	14	11	25	18	
NHL Totals		7	1	1	2	0	0
WHA Totals		348	151	123	274	212	

Playoffs

SSN	TEAM	GP	G	A	PTS.	PIM	+/-
67–68	StL	9	0	2	2	2	
72–73	LA (WHA)	6	3	0	3	4	
75–76	Phoe (WHA)	5	2	0	2	7	
76–77	SD (WHA)	7	0	0	0	0	
NHL Totals		9	0	2	2	2	
WHA Totals		18	5	0	5	11	

VERBEEK, Patrick *5–9 190 LW/RW*
B. Sarnia, Ont., May 24, 1964

SSN	TEAM	GP	G	A	PTS.	PIM	+/-
82–83	NJ	6	3	2	5	8	-2
83–84	NJ	79	20	27	47	158	-19
84–85	NJ	78	15	18	33	162	-24
85–86	NJ	76	25	28	53	79	-24
86–87	NJ	74	35	24	59	120	-23
87–88	NJ	73	46	31	77	227	+29
88–89	NJ	77	26	21	47	189	-18
89–90	Hart	80	44	45	89	228	+1
90–91	Hart	80	43	39	82	246	0
91–92	Hart	76	22	35	57	243	-16
92–93	Hart	84	39	43	82	197	-7
93–94	Hart	84	37	38	75	177	-15
94–95	Hart–NYR	48	17	16	33	71	-2

SSN	TEAM	GP	G	A	PTS.	PIM	+/-
95–96	NYR	69	41	41	82	129	+29
96–97	Dal	81	17	36	53	128	+3
97–98	Dal	82	31	26	57	170	+15
98–99	Dal	78	17	17	34	133	+11
Totals		1225	478	487	965	2665	-62

Playoffs

SSN	TEAM	GP	G	A	PTS.	PIM
87–88	NJ	20	4	8	12	51
89–90	Hart	7	2	2	4	26
90–91	Hart	6	3	2	5	40
91–92	Hart	7	0	2	2	12
94–95	NYR	10	4	6	10	20
95–96	NYR	11	3	6	9	12
96–97	Dal	7	1	3	4	16
97–98	Dal	17	3	2	5	26
98–99	Dal	18	3	4	7	14
Totals		103	25	35	60	217

VERMETTE, Mark 6–1 203 RW
B. Cochenour, Ont., Oct. 3, 1967

SSN	TEAM	GP	G	A	PTS.	PIM	+/-
88–89	Que	12	0	4	4	7	-7
89–90	Que	11	1	5	6	8	-3
90–91	Que	34	3	4	7	10	-15
91–92	Que	10	1	0	1	8	-6
Totals		67	5	13	18	33	-31

VERRET, Claude 5–9 165 C
B. Lachine, Que., Apr. 20, 1963

SSN	TEAM	GP	G	A	PTS.	PIM	+/-
83–84	Buf	11	2	5	7	2	-3
84–85	Buf	3	0	0	0	0	-2
Totals		14	2	5	7	2	-5

VERSTRAETE, Leigh 5–11 185 RW
B. Pincher Creek, Alta., Jan. 6, 1962

SSN	TEAM	GP	G	A	PTS.	PIM	+/-
82–83	Tor	3	0	0	0	5	0
84–85	Tor	2	0	0	0	0	0
87–88	Tor	3	0	1	1	0	-2
Totals		8	0	1	1	14	-2

VERVERGAERT, Dennis Andrew 6–0 195 RW
B. Hamilton, Ont., Mar. 30, 1953

SSN	TEAM	GP	G	A	PTS.	PIM	+/-
73–74	Van	78	26	31	57	25	-20
74–75	Van	57	19	32	51	25	+6
75–76	Van	80	37	34	71	53	-1
76–77	Van	79	27	18	45	38	-35
77–78	Van	80	21	33	54	23	-24
78–79	Van–Phil	72	18	24	42	19	-1
79–80	Phil	58	14	17	31	24	+9
80–81	Wash	79	14	27	41	40	-5
Totals		583	176	216	392	247	-71

Playoffs

SSN	TEAM	GP	G	A	PTS.	PIM
74–75	Van	1	0	0	0	0
75–76	Van	2	1	0	1	4
78–79	Phil	3	0	2	2	2
79–80	Phil	2	0	0	0	0
Totals		8	1	2	3	6

VESEY, Jim 6–1 202 C/RW
B. Columbus, Mass., Oct. 29, 1965

SSN	TEAM	GP	G	A	PTS.	PIM	+/-
88–89	StL	5	1	1	2	7	-1
89–90	StL	6	0	1	1	0	-3
91–92	Bos	4	0	0	0	0	0
Totals		15	1	2	3	7	-4

VEYSEY, Sidney 5–11 175 C
B. Sherbrooke, Que., July 3, 1955

SSN	TEAM	GP	G	A	PTS.	PIM	+/-
77–78	Van	1	0	0	0	0	-1

VIAL, Dennis 6–2 215 D
B. Sault Ste. Marie, Ont., Apr. 10, 1969

SSN	TEAM	GP	G	A	PTS.	PIM	+/-
90–91	NYR–Det	30	0	0	0	77	-7
91–92	Det	27	1	0	1	72	+1
92–93	Det	9	0	1	1	20	+1
93–94	Ott	55	2	5	7	214	-9
94–95	Ott	27	0	4	4	65	0
95–96	Ott	64	1	4	5	276	-13
96–97	Ott	11	0	1	1	25	0
97–98	Ott	19	0	0	0	45	0
Totals		242	4	15	19	794	-27

VICKERS, Stephen James 6–0 185 LW
B. Toronto, Ont., Apr. 21, 1951

SSN	TEAM	GP	G	A	PTS.	PIM	+/-
72–73	NYR	61	30	23	53	37	+35
73–74	NYR	75	34	24	58	18	+6
74–75	NYR	80	41	48	89	64	+10
75–76	NYR	80	30	53	83	40	-17
76–77	NYR	75	22	31	53	26	-14
77–78	NYR	79	19	44	63	30	+10
78–79	NYR	66	13	34	47	24	-7
79–80	NYR	75	29	33	62	38	+20
80–81	NYR	73	19	39	58	40	+7
81–82	NYR	34	9	11	20	13	+4
Totals		698	246	340	586	330	+54

Playoffs

SSN	TEAM	GP	G	A	PTS.	PIM
72–73	NYR	10	5	4	9	4
73–74	NYR	13	4	4	8	17
74–75	NYR	3	2	4	6	6
77–78	NYR	3	2	1	3	0
78–79	NYR	18	5	3	8	13
79–80	NYR	9	2	2	4	4
80–81	NYR	12	4	7	11	14
Totals		68	24	25	49	58

VIGNEAULT, Alain 5–11 195 D
B. Quebec City, Que., May 14, 1961

SSN	TEAM	GP	G	A	PTS.	PIM	+/-
81–82	StL	14	1	2	3	43	-1
82–83	StL	28	1	3	4	39	-4
Totals		42	2	5	7	82	-5

Playoffs

SSN	TEAM	GP	G	A	PTS.	PIM
82–83	StL	4	0	1	1	26

VILGRAIN, Claude 6–1 205 RW
B. Port-au-Prince, Haiti, Mar. 1, 1963

SSN	TEAM	GP	G	A	PTS.	PIM	+/-
87–88	Van	6	1	1	2	0	-3
89–90	NJ	6	1	2	3	4	+7
91–92	NJ	71	19	27	46	74	+27
92–93	NJ	4	0	2	2	0	-3
93–94	Phil	2	0	0	0	0	-1
Totals		89	21	32	53	78	+19

Playoffs

SSN	TEAM	GP	G	A	PTS.	PIM
89–90	NJ	4	0	0	0	0
91–92	NJ	7	1	1	2	17
Totals		11	1	1	2	17

VINCELETTE, Daniel 6–2 202 LW
B. Verdun, Que., Aug. 1, 1967

SSN	TEAM	GP	G	A	PTS.	PIM	+/-
87–88	Chi	69	6	11	17	109	-15
88–89	Chi	66	11	4	15	119	-9
89–90	Chi–Que	13	0	1	1	29	-7
90–91	Que	16	0	1	1	38	-10
91–92	Chi	29	3	5	8	56	-6
Totals		193	20	22	42	351	-47

Playoffs

SSN	TEAM	GP	G	A	PTS.	PIM
86–87	Chi	3	0	0	0	0
87–88	Chi	4	0	0	0	0
88–89	Chi	5	0	0	0	4
Totals		12	0	0	0	4

VIPOND, Peter John 5–10 175 LW
B. Oshawa, Ont., Dec. 8, 1949

SSN	TEAM	GP	G	A	PTS.	PIM	+/-
72–73	Cal	3	0	0	0	0	0

VIRTA, Hannu 5–11 180 D
B. Turku, Finland, Mar. 22, 1963

SSN	TEAM	GP	G	A	PTS.	PIM	+/-
81–82	Buf	3	0	1	1	4	0
82–83	Buf	74	13	24	37	18	+7
83–84	Buf	70	6	30	36	12	+15
84–85	Buf	51	1	23	24	16	-2
85–86	Buf	47	5	23	28	16	+2
Totals		245	25	101	126	66	+22

Playoffs

SSN	TEAM	GP	G	A	PTS.	PIM
81–82	Buf	4	0	1	1	0
82–83	Buf	10	1	2	3	4
83–84	Buf	3	0	0	0	2
Totals		17	1	3	4	6

VIRTUE, Terry 6–0 200 D
B. Scarborough, Ont., Aug. 12, 1970

SSN	TEAM	GP	G	A	PTS.	PIM	+/-
98–99	Bos	4	0	0	0	0	+2

VISHEAU, Mark Andrew 6–4 200 D
B. Burlington, Ont., June 27, 1973

SSN	TEAM	GP	G	A	PTS.	PIM	+/-
93–94	Winn	1	0	0	0	0	0

SSN	TEAM	GP	G	A	PTS.	PIM	+/-
98–99	LA	28	1	3	4	107	-7
Totals		29	1	3	4	107	-7

VITAKOSKI, Vesa 6–3 215 LW
B. Lappeenranta, Finland, Feb. 13, 1971

SSN	TEAM	GP	G	A	PTS.	PIM	+/-
93–94	Calg	8	1	2	3	0	0
94–95	Calg	10	1	2	3	6	-1
95–96	Calg	5	0	0	0	2	-1
Totals		23	2	4	6	8	-2

VITOLINSH, Harijs 6–3 212 C
B. Riga, Latvia, Apr. 30, 1968

SSN	TEAM	GP	G	A	PTS.	PIM	+/-
93–94	Winn	8	0	0	0	4	0

VIVEIROS, Emanuel 6–0 175 D
B. St. Albert, Alta., Jan. 8, 1966

SSN	TEAM	GP	G	A	PTS.	PIM	+/-
85–86	Minn	4	0	1	1	0	+2
86–87	Minn	1	0	1	1	0	0
87–88	Minn	24	1	9	10	6	-5
Totals		29	1	11	12	6	-3

VOKES, Ed F

SSN	TEAM	GP	G	A	PTS.	PIM
30–31	Chi	5	0	0	0	0

VOLCAN, Michael Stephen (Mickey) 6–0 190 D
B. Edmonton, Alta., Mar. 3, 1962

SSN	TEAM	GP	G	A	PTS.	PIM	+/-
80–81	Hart	49	2	11	13	26	-12
81–82	Hart	26	1	5	6	29	-17
82–83	Hart	68	4	13	17	73	-30
83–84	Calg	19	1	4	5	18	-2
Totals		162	8	33	41	146	-61

VOLEK, David 6–0 185 LW/RW
B. Prague, Czechoslovakia, June 18, 1966

SSN	TEAM	GP	G	A	PTS.	PIM	+/-
88–89	NYI	77	25	34	59	24	-11
89–90	NYI	80	17	22	39	41	-2
90–91	NYI	77	22	34	56	57	-10
91–92	NYI	74	18	42	60	35	0
92–93	NYI	56	8	13	21	34	-1
93–94	NYI	32	5	9	14	10	0
Totals		396	95	154	249	201	-24

Playoffs

SSN	TEAM	GP	G	A	PTS.	PIM
89–90	NYI	5	1	4	5	0
92–93	NYI	10	4	1	5	2
Totals		15	5	5	10	2

VOLMAR, Douglas Steven 6–1 215 RW
B. Cleveland Heights, Ohio, Jan. 9, 1945

SSN	TEAM	GP	G	A	PTS.	PIM	+/-
70–71	Det	2	0	1	1	2	0
71–72	Det	39	9	5	14	8	0
72–73	LA	21	4	2	6	16	-2
74–75	SD (WHA)	10	0	1	1	4	
NHL Totals		62	13	8	21	26	-2
WHA Totals		10	0	1	1	4	

Playoffs

SSN	TEAM	GP	G	A	PTS.	PIM
69–70	Det	2	1	0	1	0

VON STEFENELLI, Phil 6–1 200 D
B. Vancouver, B.C., Apr. 10, 1969

SSN	TEAM	GP	G	A	PTS.	PIM	+/-
95–96	Bos	27	0	4	4	16	+2
96–97	Ott	6	0	1	1	7	-3
Totals		33	0	5	5	23	-1

VOPAT, Jan 6–0 198 D
B. Most, Czech., March 22, 1973

SSN	TEAM	GP	G	A	PTS.	PIM	+/-
95–96	LA	11	1	4	5	4	+3
96–97	LA	33	4	5	9	22	+3
97–98	LA	21	1	5	6	10	+8
98–99	Nash	55	5	6	11	28	0
Totals		120	11	20	31	64	+14

Playoffs

SSN	TEAM	GP	G	A	PTS.	PIM
97–98	LA	2	0	1	1	2

VOPAT, Roman 6–3 216 C
B. Litvinov, Czech., Apr. 21, 1976

SSN	TEAM	GP	G	A	PTS.	PIM	+/-
95–96	StL	25	2	3	5	48	-8
96–97	LA	29	4	5	9	60	-7
97–98	LA	25	0	3	3	55	-7
98–99	LA–Chi–Phil	54	0	3	3	90	-7
Totals		133	6	14	20	253	-29

SSN	TEAM	GP	G	A	PTS.	PIM	+/-

VOROBIEV, Vladimir *5-11 185 LW*
B. Cherepovets, USSR, Oct. 2, 1972

SSN	TEAM	GP	G	A	PTS.	PIM	+/-
96-97	NYR	16	5	5	10	6	+4
97-98	NYR	15	2	2	4	6	-10
98-99	Edm	2	2	0	2	2	+1
Totals		33	9	7	16	14	-5

Playoffs

| 98-99 | Edm | 1 | 0 | 0 | 0 | 0 | |

***VOSS, Carl Potter** 5-8 168 C*
B. Chelsea, Mass., Jan. 6, 1907

26-27	Tor	12	0	0	0	0	
28-29	Tor	2	0	0	0	0	
32-33	NYR-Det	48	8	15	23	10	
33-34	Det-Ott	48	7	18	25	12	
34-35	StL E	48	13	18	31	14	
35-36	NYA	46	3	9	12	10	
36-37	Mont M	20	0	2	2	4	
37-38	Mont M-Chi	37	3	8	11	0	
Totals		261	34	70	104	50	

Playoffs

32-33	Bos	4	1	1	2	0	
35-36	NYA	5	0	0	0	0	
36-37	Mont M	5	1	0	1	0	
37-38	Chi	10	3	2	5	0	
Totals		24	5	3	8	0	

VUJTEK, Vladimir *6-1 190 LW*
B. Ostrava Czechoslovakia, Feb. 17, 1972

91-92	Mont	2	0	0	0	0	-1
92-93	Edm	30	1	10	11	8	-1
93-94	Edm	40	4	15	19	14	-7
97-98	TB	30	2	4	6	16	-2
Totals		102	7	29	36	38	-11

VUKOTA, Mick *6-2 195 RW*
B. Saskatoon, Sask., Sept. 14, 1966

87-88	NYI	17	1	0	1	82	+1
88-89	NYI	48	2	2	4	237	-17
89-90	NYI	76	4	8	12	290	+10
90-91	NYI	60	2	4	6	238	-13
91-92	NYI	74	0	6	6	293	-6
92-93	NYI	74	2	5	7	216	+3
93-94	NYI	72	3	1	4	237	-5
94-95	NYI	40	0	2	2	109	+1
95-96	NYI	33	1	1	2	106	-3
96-97	NYI	17	1	0	1	71	-2
97-98	TB-Mont	64	1	0	1	192	-4
Totals		575	17	29	46	2071	-35

Playoffs

87-88	NYI	2	0	0	0	23	
89-90	NYI	1	0	0	0	17	
92-93	NYI	15	0	0	0	16	
93-94	NYI	4	0	0	0	17	
97-98	Mont	1	0	0	0	0	
Totals		23	0	0	0	73	

VYAZMIKIN, Igor *6-1 194 RW/LW*
B. Moscow, Soviet Union, Jan. 8, 1966

| 90-91 | Edm | 4 | 1 | 0 | 1 | 0 | 0 |

WADDELL, Donald *5-10 178 D*
B. Detroit, Mich., Aug. 19, 1958

| 80-81 | LA | 1 | 0 | 0 | 0 | 0 | -1 |

***WAITE, Frank E. (Deacon)** 5-11 150 F*
B. Qu'Appelle, Sask., Apr. 9, 1906

| 30-31 | NYR | 1 | 3 | 4 | 4 | | |

WALKER, Gord *6-0 175 RW*
B. Castiegar, B.C., Aug. 12, 1965

86-87	NYR	1	1	0	1	4	+2
87-88	NYR	18	1	4	5	17	-8
88-89	LA	11	1	0	1	2	-2
89-90	LA	1	0	0	0	0	
Totals		31	3	4	7	23	-8

WALKER, Howard *6-0 205 D*
B. Grande Prairie, Alta., Aug. 5, 1958

80-81	Wash	64	2	11	13	100	+9
81-82	Wash	16	0	2	2	26	-9
82-83	Calg	3	0	0	0	7	0

| Totals | | 83 | 2 | 13 | 15 | 133 | 0 |

***WALKER, John Phillip (Jack)** LW*
B. Silver Mountain, Ont., Nov. 28, 1888

26-27	Det	37	3	4	7	6	
27-28	Det	43	2	4	6	12	
Totals		80	5	8	13	18	

WALKER, Kurt Adrian *6-3 200 D*
B. Weymouth, Mass., June 10, 1954

75-76	Tor	5	0	0	0	49	-2
76-77	Tor	26	2	3	5	34	+5
77-78	Tor	40	2	2	4	69	-5
Totals		71	4	5	9	152	-2

Playoffs

75-76	Tor	6	0	0	0	24	
77-78	Tor	10	0	0	0	10	
Totals		16	0	0	0	34	

WALKER, Russell *6-2 185 RW*
B. Red Deer, Alta., May 24, 1953

73-74	Clev (WHA)	76	15	14	29	117	
74-75	Clev (WHA)	66	14	11	25	80	
75-76	Clev (WHA)	72	23	15	38	122	
76-77	LA	16	1	0	1	35	-2
77-78	LA	1	0	0	0	6	0
NHL Totals		17	1	0	1	41	-2
WHA Totals		214	52	40	92	319	

Playoffs

73-74	Clev (WHA)	5	1	0	1	11	
74-75	Clev (WHA)	5	1	0	1	17	
75-76	Clev (WHA)	3	0	0	0	18	
WHA Totals		13	2	0	2	46	

WALKER, Scott *5-9 180 D*
B. Montreal, Que., July 19, 1973

94-95	Van	11	0	1	1	33	0
95-96	Van	63	4	8	12	137	-7
96-97	Van	64	3	15	18	132	+2
97-98	Van	59	3	10	13	164	-8
98-99	Nash	71	15	25	40	103	0
Totals		268	25	59	84	569	-13

WALL, Robert James Albert *5-10 202 D*
B. Richmond Hill, Ont., Dec. 1, 1942

64-65	Det	1	0	0	0	0	
65-66	Det	8	1	1	2	8	
66-67	Det	31	2	2	4	26	
67-68	LA	71	5	18	23	66	-9
68-69	LA	71	13	13	26	16	-6
69-70	LA	70	5	13	18	26	-26
70-71	StL	25	2	4	6	4	-1
71-72	Det	45	2	4	6	9	-7
72-73	Alb (WHA)	78	16	29	45	20	
73-74	Edm (WHA)	74	6	31	37	46	
74-75	SD (WHA)	33	0	9	9	15	
75-76	SD (WHA)	68	1	20	21	32	
NHL Totals		322	30	55	85	155	-49
WHA Totals		253	23	89	112	113	

Playoffs

64-65	Det	1	0	0	0	0	
65-66	Det	6	0	0	0	2	
67-68	LA	7	0	1	1	0	
68-69	LA	8	0	2	2	0	
73-74	Edm (WHA)	3	0	2	2	2	
74-75	SD (WHA)	10	0	3	3	2	
75-76	SD (WHA)	11	1	3	4	4	
NHL Totals		22	0	3	3	2	
WHA Totals		26	1	8	9	8	

WALLIN, Peter *5-9 170 RW*
B. Stockholm, Sweden, Apr. 30, 1957

80-81	NYR	12	1	5	6	2	-1
81-82	NYR	40	2	9	11	12	+1
Totals		52	3	14	17	14	0

Playoffs

| 80-81 | NYR | 14 | 2 | 6 | 8 | 6 | |

WALSH, James *6-1 185 D*
B. Norfolk, Va., Oct. 26, 1956

| 81-82 | Buf | 4 | 0 | 1 | 1 | 4 | 0 |

WALSH, Mike *6-2 195 LW*
B. New York, N.Y., Apr. 3, 1962

87-88	NYI	1	0	0	0	0	0
88-89	NYI	13	2	0	2	4	-7
Totals		14	2	0	2	4	-7

WALTER, Ryan William *6-0 200 C/LW*
B. New Westminster, B.C., Apr. 23, 1958

78-79	Wash	69	28	28	56	70	-1
79-80	Wash	80	24	42	66	106	-1
80-81	Wash	80	24	44	68	150	-9
81-82	Wash	78	38	49	87	142	-3
82-83	Mont	80	29	46	75	40	+15
83-84	Mont	73	20	29	49	83	-11
84-85	Mont	72	19	19	38	59	-18
85-86	Mont	69	15	34	49	45	-9
86-87	Mont	76	23	23	46	34	-6
87-88	Mont	61	13	23	36	39	+12
88-89	Mont	78	14	17	31	48	+23
89-90	Mont	70	8	16	24	59	+4
90-91	Mont	25	0	1	1	12	-3
91-92	Van	67	6	11	17	49	+6
92-93	Van	25	3	0	3	10	-2
Totals		1003	264	382	646	946	-3

Playoffs

82-83	Mont	3	0	0	0	11	
83-84	Mont	15	2	1	3	4	
84-85	Mont	12	2	7	9	13	
85-86	Mont	5	0	1	1	2	
86-87	Mont	17	7	12	19	10	
87-88	Mont	11	2	4	6	6	
88-89	Mont	21	3	5	8	6	
89-90	Mont	11	0	2	2	0	
90-91	Mont	5	0	0	0	2	
91-92	Van	13	0	3	3	8	
Totals		113	16	35	51	62	

WALTON, Michael Robert (Shakey) *5-10 175 C*
B. Kirkland Lake, Ont., Jan. 3, 1945

65-66	Tor	6	1	3	4	0	
66-67	Tor	31	7	10	17	13	
67-68	Tor	73	30	29	59	48	+1
68-69	Tor	66	22	21	43	34	-9
69-70	Tor	58	21	34	55	68	-25
70-71	Tor-Bos	45	6	15	21	31	+11
71-72	Bos	76	28	28	56	45	+23
72-73	Bos	56	25	22	47	37	+10
73-74	Minn (WHA)	78	57	60	117	88	
74-75	Minn (WHA)	75	48	45	93	33	
75-76	Minn (WHA)	58	31	40	71	27	
75-76	Van	10	8	8	16	9	+5
76-77	Van	40	7	24	31	32	-15
77-78	Van	65	29	37	66	30	-26
78-79	StL-Bos-Chi	62	17	16	33	10	-18
NHL Totals		588	201	247	448	357	-43
WHA Totals		211	136	145	281	148	

Playoffs

66-67	Tor	12	4	3	7	2	
68-69	Tor	4	0	0	0	4	
70-71	Bos	5	2	0	2	19	
71-72	Bos	15	6	6	12	13	
72-73	Bos	5	1	1	2	2	
73-74	Minn (WHA)	11	10	8	18	16	
74-75	Minn (WHA)	12	10	7	17	10	
75-76	Van	2	0	0	0	5	
78-79	Chi	4	1	0	1	0	
NHL Totals		47	14	10	24	45	
WHA Totals		23	20	15	35	26	

WALTON, Robert Charles *5-9 165 C*
B. Ottawa, Ont., Aug. 5, 1917

| 43-44 | Mont | 4 | 0 | 0 | 0 | 0 | |

WALZ, Wes *5-10 185 C*
B. Calgary, Alta., May 15, 1970

89-90	Bos	2	1	1	2	0	-1
90-91	Bos	56	8	8	16	32	-14
91-92	Bos-Phil	17	1	3	4	12	-2
93-94	Calg	53	11	27	38	16	+20
94-95	Calg	39	6	12	18	11	+7
95-96	Det	2	0	0	0	0	0
Totals		169	27	51	78	71	+10

Playoffs

SSN	TEAM	GP	G	A	PTS.	PIM	+/-
90–91	Bos	2	0	0	0	0	
93–94	Calg	6	3	0	3	2	
94–95	Calg	1	0	0	0	0	
Totals		9	3	0	3	2	

WAPPEL, Gordon Alexander 6–2 203 D
B. Regina, Sask., July 26, 1958

79–80	Atl	2	0	0	0	0	+1
80–81	Calg	7	0	1	1	4	+1
81–82	Calg	11	1	0	1	6	-4
Totals		20	1	1	2	10	-2

Playoffs

79–80	Atl	2	0	0	0	4	

WARD, Aaron Christian 6–2 200 D
B. Windsor, Ont., Jan. 17, 1973

93–94	Det	5	1	0	1	4	+2
94–95	Det	1	0	1	1	2	-1
96–97	Det	49	2	5	7	52	-9
97–98	Det	52	5	5	10	47	+4
98–99	Det	60	3	8	11	52	-5
Totals		167	11	19	30	157	-12

Playoffs

96–97	Det	19	0	0	0	17	
98–99	Det	8	0	1	1	8	
Totals		27	0	1	1	25	

WARD, Dixon 6–0 200 RW
B. Leduc, Alta., Sept. 23, 1968

92–93	Van	70	22	30	52	82	+34
93–94	Van-LA	67	12	3	15	82	-22
94–95	Tor	22	0	3	3	31	-4
95–96	Buf	8	2	2	4	6	+1
96–97	Buf	79	13	32	45	36	+17
97–98	Buf	71	10	13	23	42	+9
98–99	Buf	78	20	24	44	44	+10
Totals		395	79	107	186	323	+45

Playoffs

92–93	Van	9	2	3	5	0	
96–97	Buf	12	2	3	5	12	
97–98	Buf	15	3	8	11	6	
98–99	Buf	21	7	5	12	32	
Totals		57	14	19	33	50	

WARD, Donald Joseph 6–2 210 D
B. Sarnia, Ont., Oct. 19, 1935

57–58	Chi	3	0	0	0	0	
59–60	Bos	31	0	1	1	160	
Totals		34	0	1	1	160	

WARD, Edward John 6–3 205 RW
B. Edmonton, Alta., Nov. 10, 1969

93–94	Que	7	1	0	1	5	0
94–95	Calg	2	1	1	2	2	-2
95–96	Calg	41	3	5	8	44	-2
96–97	Calg	40	5	8	13	49	-3
97–98	Calg	64	4	5	9	122	-1
98–99	Calg	68	3	5	8	67	-4
Totals		222	17	24	41	289	-12

*WARD, James William 5–11 167 RW
B. Fort William, Ont., Sept. 1, 1906

27–28	Mont M	44	10	2	12	44	
28–29	Mont M	44	14	8	22	46	
29–30	Mont M	43	10	7	17	54	
30–31	Mont M	42	14	8	22	52	
31–32	Mont M	48	19	19	38	39	
32–33	Mont M	48	16	17	33	52	
33–34	Mont M	48	14	9	23	46	
34–35	Mont M	42	9	6	15	24	
35–36	Mont M	48	12	19	31	30	
36–37	Mont M	41	14	14	28	34	
37–38	Mont M	48	11	15	26	34	
38–39	Mont	36	4	3	7	0	
Totals		532	147	127	274	455	

Playoffs

27–28	Mont M	9	1	1	2	6	
29–30	Mont M	4	0	1	1	4	
30–31	Mont M	2	0	0	0	2	
31–32	Mont M	4	2	1	3	0	

32–33	Mont M	2	0	0	0	0	
33–34	Mont M	4	0	0	0	0	
34–35	Mont M	2	1	1	2	0	
35–36	Mont M	3	0	0	0	6	
38–39	Mont	1	0	0	0	0	
Totals		31	4	4	8	18	

WARD, Joseph Michael 6–0 178 C
B. Sarnia, Ont., Feb. 11, 1961

80–81	Col	4	0	0	0	2	-2

WARD, Ronald Leon 5–10 180 C
B. Cornwall, Ont., Sept. 12, 1944

69–70	Tor	18	0	1	1	2	0
71–72	Van	71	2	4	6	4	-2
72–73	NY (WHA)	77	51	67	118	28	
73–74	Van-LA-Clev (WHA)	70	33	28	61	25	
74–75	Clev (WHA)	73	30	32	62	18	
75–76	Clev (WHA)	75	32	50	82	24	
76–77	Minn–Winn–Calg (WHA)	64	24	33	57	8	
NHL Totals		89	2	5	7	6	-2
WHA Totals		359	170	210	380	103	

Playoffs

73–74	Clev (WHA)	5	3	0	3	2	
74–75	Clev (WHA)	5	0	2	2	2	
75–76	Clev (WHA)	3	0	2	2	0	
WHA Totals		13	3	4	7	4	

WARE, Jeff 6–4 220 D
B. Toronto, Ont., May 19, 1977

96–97	Tor	13	0	0	0	6	+2
97–98	Tor	2	0	0	0	0	+1
98–99	Fla	6	0	1	1	6	-6
Totals		21	0	1	1	12	-3

WARE, Michael 6–5 216 RW
B. York, Ont., Mar. 22, 1967

88–89	Edm	2	0	1	1	4	+1
89–90	Edm	3	0	0	0	4	-1
Totals		5	0	1	1	15	0

WARES, Edward George 5–10 182 D
B. Calgary, Alta., Mar. 19, 1915

36–37	NYR	2	2	0	2	0	
37–38	Det	21	9	7	16	2	
38–39	Det	28	8	8	16	10	
39–40	Det	33	2	6	8	19	
40–41	Det	42	10	16	26	34	
41–42	Det	43	9	29	38	31	
42–43	Det	47	12	18	30	10	
45–46	Chi	45	4	11	15	34	
46–47	Chi	60	4	7	11	21	
Totals		321	60	102	162	161	

Playoffs

38–39	Det	6	1	0	1	8	
39–40	Det	5	0	0	0	0	
40–41	Det	9	0	0	0	0	
41–42	Det	12	1	3	4	22	
42–43	Det	10	3	3	6	4	
45–46	Chi	3	0	1	1	0	
Totals		45	5	7	12	34	

WARNER, James Francis 5–11 180 RW
B. Minneapolis, Minn., Mar. 26, 1954

78–79	NE (WHA)	41	6	9	15	20	
79–80	Hart	32	0	3	3	10	-6

Playoffs

78–79	NE (WHA)	1	0	0	0	0	

WARNER, Robert Norman 5–11 180 D
B. Grimsby, Ont., Dec. 13, 1950

76–77	Tor	10	1	1	2	4	+4

Playoffs

76–77	Tor	4	0	0	0	0	

WARRENER, Rhett 6–1 209 D
B. Shaunavon, Sask., Jan. 27, 1976

95–96	Fla	28	0	3	3	46	+4
96–97	Fla	62	4	9	13	88	+20
97–98	Fla	79	0	4	4	99	-16

98–99	Fla–Buf	61	1	7	8	84	+2
Totals		230	5	23	28	317	+10

Playoffs

95–96	Fla	21	0	1	1	0	
96–97	Fla	5	0	0	0	0	
98–99	Buf	20	1	3	4	32	
Totals		46	1	4	5	32	

WARRINER, Todd 6–1 188 LW
B. Blenheim, Ont., Jan. 3, 1974

94–95	Tor	5	0	0	0	0	-3
95–96	Tor	57	7	8	15	26	-11
96–97	Tor	75	12	21	33	41	-3
97–98	Tor	45	5	8	13	20	+5
98–99	Tor	53	9	10	19	28	-6
Totals		235	33	47	80	115	-18

Playoffs

95–96	Tor	6	1	1	2	2	
98–99	Tor	9	0	0	0	2	
Totals		15	1	1	2	4	

WARWICK, Grant David (Knobby) 5–6 165 RW
B. Regina, Sask., Oct. 11, 1921

41–42	NYR	44	16	17	33	36	
42–43	NYR	50	17	18	35	31	
43–44	NYR	18	8	9	17	14	
44–45	NYR	42	20	22	42	25	
45–46	NYR	45	19	18	37	19	
46–47	NYR	54	20	20	40	24	
47–48	NYR-Bos	58	23	17	40	38	
48–49	Bos	58	22	15	37	14	
49–50	Mont	30	2	6	8	19	
Totals		399	147	142	289	220	

Playoffs

41–42	NYR	6	0	1	1	2	
47–48	Bos	5	0	3	3	4	
48–49	Bos	5	2	0	2	0	
Totals		16	2	4	6	6	

WARWICK, William Harvey 5–6 165 LW
B. Regina, Sask., Nov. 17, 1924

42–43	NYR	1	0	1	1	4	
43–44	NYR	13	3	2	5	12	
Totals		14	3	3	6	16	

WASHBURN, Steve 6–2 191 C
B. Ottawa, Ont., April 10, 1975

95–96	Fla	1	0	1	1	0	+1
96–97	Fla	18	3	6	9	4	+2
97–98	Fla	58	11	8	19	32	-6
98–99	Fla–Van	12	0	0	0	6	-1
Totals		89	14	15	29	62	-2

Playoffs

95–96	Fla	1	0	1	1	0	

WASNIE, Nicholas 5–10 174 RW
B. Winnipeg, Man., Jan. 1, 1904

27–28	Chi	14	1	0	1	22	
29–30	Mont	44	12	11	23	64	
30–31	Mont	44	9	2	11	26	
31–32	Mont	48	10	2	12	16	
32–33	NYA	48	11	12	23	36	
33–34	Ott	37	11	6	17	10	
34–35	StL E	13	3	1	4	2	
Totals		248	57	34	91	176	

Playoffs

29–30	Mont	6	2	2	4	12	
30–31	Mont	4	4	1	5	8	
31–32	Mont	4	0	0	0	0	
Totals		14	6	3	9	20	

WATSON, Bryan Joseph (Bugsy) 5–10 175 D
B. Bancroft, Ont., Nov. 14, 1942

63–64	Mont	39	0	2	2	18	
64–65	Mont	5	0	1	1	7	
65–66	Det	70	2	7	9	133	
66–67	Det	48	0	1	1	66	
67–68	Mont	12	0	1	1	9	-3
68–69	Oak–Pitt	68	2	7	9	132	-27

SSN	TEAM	GP	G	A	PTS.	PIM	+/-
69–70	Pitt	61	1	9	10	189	-1
70–71	Pitt	43	2	6	8	119	-5
71–72	Pitt	75	3	17	20	212	+5
72–73	Pitt	69	1	17	18	179	+18
73–74	Pitt–StL—Det	70	1	9	10	255	-13
74–75	Det	70	1	13	14	238	-29
75–76	Det	79	0	18	18	322	-20
76–77	Det–Wash	70	1	15	16	130	-3
77–78	Wash	79	3	11	14	167	-12
78–79	Wash	20	0	1	1	36	-7
78–79	Cin (WHA)	21	0	2	2	56	
NHL Totals		878	17	135	152	2212	-97
WHA Totals		21	0	2	2	56	

Playoffs

63–64	Mont	6	0	0	0	2	
65–66	Det	12	2	0	2	30	
69–70	Pitt	10	0	0	0	17	
71–72	Pitt	4	0	0	0	21	
78–79	Cin (WHA)	3	0	1	1	2	
NHL Totals		32	2	0	2	70	
WHA Totals		3	0	1	1	2	

WATSON, David 6–2 190 LW
B. Kirkland Lake, Ont., May 19, 1958

79–80	Col	5	0	0	0	2	-1
80–81	Col	13	0	1	1	8	-2
Totals		18	0	1	1	10	-3

WATSON, Harry Percival (Whipper) 6–1 203 LW
B. Saskatoon, Sask., May 6, 1923

41–42	Brk	47	10	8	18	6	
42–43	Det	50	13	18	31	10	
45–46	Det	44	14	10	24	4	
46–47	Tor	44	19	15	34	10	
47–48	Tor	57	21	20	41	16	
48–49	Tor	60	26	19	45	0	
49–50	Tor	60	19	16	35	11	
50–51	Tor	68	18	19	37	18	
51–52	Tor	70	22	17	39	18	
52–53	Tor	63	16	8	24	8	
53–54	Tor	70	21	7	28	30	
54–55	Tor–Chi	51	15	17	32	4	
55–56	Chi	55	11	14	25	6	
56–57	Chi	70	11	19	30	9	
Totals		809	236	207	443	150	

Playoffs

42–43	Det	7	0	0	0	0	
45–46	Det	5	2	0	2	0	
46–47	Tor	11	3	2	5	6	
47–48	Tor	9	5	2	7	9	
48–49	Tor	9	4	2	6	2	
49–50	Tor	7	0	0	0	2	
50–51	Tor	5	1	2	3	4	
51–52	Tor	4	1	0	1	2	
53–54	Tor	5	0	1	1	2	
Totals		62	16	9	25	27	

WATSON, James Arthur (Watty) 6–2 195 D
B. Malartic, Que., June 28, 1943

63–64	Det	1	0	0	0	0	
64–65	Det	1	0	0	0	2	
65–66	Det	2	0	0	0	4	
67–68	Det	61	0	3	3	87	-20
68–69	Det	8	0	1	1	4	-3
69–70	Det	4	0	0	0	0	0
70–71	Buf	78	2	9	11	147	-28
71–72	Buf	66	2	6	8	101	-33
72–73	LA (WHA)	75	5	15	20	123	
73–74	LA–Chi (WHA)	71	0	11	11	50	
74–75	Chi (WHA)	57	3	6	9	31	
75–76	Que (WHA)	28	0	1	1	24	
NHL Totals		221	4	19	23	345	-104
WHA Totals		231	8	33	41	228	

Playoffs

72–73	LA (WHA)	4	0	1	1	2	
73–74	Chi (WHA)	18	2	3	5	18	
WHA Totals		22	2	4	6	20	

WATSON, James Charles 6–0 195 D
B. Smithers, B.C., Aug. 19, 1952

72–73	Phil	4	0	1	1	5	-1
73–74	Phil	78	2	18	20	44	+33
74–75	Phil	68	7	18	25	72	+41
75–76	Phil	79	2	34	36	66	+65
76–77	Phil	71	3	23	26	35	+34
77–78	Phil	71	5	12	17	62	+33
78–79	Phil	77	9	13	22	52	+11
79–80	Phil	71	5	18	23	51	+53
80–81	Phil	18	2	2	4	6	+14
81–82	Phil	76	3	9	12	99	+12
Totals		613	38	148	186	492	+345

Playoffs

72–73	Phil	2	0	0	0	0	
73–74	Phil	17	1	2	3	41	
74–75	Phil	17	1	8	9	10	
75–76	Phil	16	1	8	9	6	
76–77	Phil	10	1	2	3	2	
77–78	Phil	12	1	7	8	6	
78–79	Phil	8	0	2	2	2	
79–80	Phil	15	0	4	4	20	
81–82	Phil	4	0	1	1	2	
Totals		102	5	34	39	89	

WATSON, Joseph John 5–10 185 D
B. Smithers, B.C., July 6, 1943

64–65	Bos	4	0	1	1	0	
66–67	Bos	69	2	13	15	38	
67–68	Phil	73	5	14	19	56	+12
68–69	Phil	60	2	8	10	14	-21
69–70	Phil	54	3	11	14	28	0
70–71	Phil	57	3	7	10	50	+9
71–72	Phil	65	3	7	10	38	-17
72–73	Phil	63	2	24	26	46	+30
73–74	Phil	74	1	17	18	34	+28
74–75	Phil	80	6	17	23	42	+42
75–76	Phil	78	2	22	24	28	+56
76–77	Phil	77	4	26	30	39	+29
77–78	Phil	65	5	9	14	22	+23
78–79	Col	16	0	2	2	12	-13
Totals		835	38	178	216	447	+183

Playoffs

67–68	Phil	7	1	1	2	28	
68–69	Phil	4	0	0	0	0	
70–71	Phil	1	0	0	0	0	
72–73	Phil	11	0	2	2	12	
73–74	Phil	17	1	4	5	24	
74–75	Phil	17	0	4	4	6	
75–76	Phil	16	1	1	2	10	
76–77	Phil	10	0	0	0	2	
77–78	Phil	1	0	0	0	0	
Totals		84	3	12	15	82	

*WATSON, Phillipe Henri (Phil) 5–11 165 RW
B. Montreal, Que., Apr. 24, 1914

35–36	NYR	24	0	2	2	24	
36–37	NYR	48	11	17	28	22	
37–38	NYR	48	7	25	32	52	
38–39	NYR	48	15	22	37	42	
39–40	NYR	48	7	28	35	42	
40–41	NYR	40	11	25	36	49	
41–42	NYR	48	15	37	52	58	
42–43	NYR	46	14	28	42	44	
43–44	Mont	44	17	32	49	61	
44–45	NYR	45	11	8	19	24	
45–46	NYR	49	12	14	26	43	
46–47	NYR	48	6	12	18	17	
47–48	NYR	54	18	15	33	54	
Totals		590	144	265	409	532	

Playoffs

36–37	NYR	9	0	2	2	9	
37–38	NYR	3	0	2	2	0	
38–39	NYR	7	1	1	2	7	
39–40	NYR	3	3	6	9	16	
40–41	NYR	3	0	2	2	9	
41–42	NYR	6	1	4	5	8	
43–44	Mont	9	3	5	8	16	
47–48	NYR	5	2	3	5	2	
Totals		45	10	25	35	67	

WATSON, William (Bill) 6–0 185 RW
B. Pine Falls, Man., Mar. 30, 1964

85–86	Chi	52	8	16	24	2	-4
86–87	Chi	51	13	19	32	6	+19
87–88	Chi	9	2	0	2	0	-5
88–89	Chi	3	0	1	1	4	0
Totals		115	23	36	59	12	+10

Playoffs

85–86	Chi	2	0	1	1	0	
86–87	Chi	4	0	1	1	0	
Totals		6	0	2	2	0	

WATT, Mike 6–2 212 LW
B. Seaforth, Ont., Mar. 31, 1976

97–98	Edm	14	1	2	3	4	-4
98–99	NYI	75	8	17	25	12	-2
Totals		89	9	19	28	16	-6

WATTERS, Timothy John 5–11 185 D
B. Kamloops, B.C., July 25, 1959

81–82	Winn	69	2	22	24	97	+14
82–83	Winn	77	5	18	23	98	-10
83–84	Winn	74	3	20	23	169	+7
84–85	Winn	63	2	20	22	74	+20
85–86	Winn	56	6	8	14	97	-10
86–87	Winn	63	3	13	16	119	+5
87–88	Winn	36	0	0	0	106	-12
88–89	LA	76	3	18	21	168	+17
89–90	LA	62	1	10	11	92	+23
90–91	LA	45	0	4	4	92	+7
91–92	LA	37	0	7	7	92	-2
92–93	LA	22	0	2	2	18	-3
93–94	LA	60	1	9	10	67	-11
94–95	LA	1	0	0	0	0	+1
Totals		741	26	151	177	1289	+46

Playoffs

81–82	Winn	4	0	1	1	8	
82–83	Winn	3	0	0	0	2	
83–84	Winn	3	1	0	1	2	
84–85	Winn	8	0	1	1	16	
86–87	Winn	10	0	0	0	21	
87–88	Winn	4	0	0	0	4	
88–89	LA	11	0	1	1	6	
89–90	LA	4	0	0	0	6	
90–91	LA	7	0	0	0	12	
91–92	LA	6	0	0	0	8	
92–93	LA	22	0	2	2	30	
Totals		82	1	5	6	115	

WATTS, Brian Alan 6–0 180 LW
B. Hagersville, Ont., Sept. 10, 1947

75–76	Det	4	0	0	0	0	0

WEBB, Steve 6–0 195 RW
B. Peterborough, Ont., April 30, 1975

96–97	NYI	41	1	4	5	144	-10
97–98	NYI	20	0	0	0	35	-2
98–99	NYI	45	0	0	0	32	-10
Totals		106	1	4	5	211	-22

*WEBSTER, Aubrey 5–9 168 F
B. Fort William, Ont., Sept. 25, 1910

30–31	Phil Q	1	0	0	0	0	
34–35	Mont M	4	0	0	0	0	
Totals		5	0	0	0	0	

*WEBSTER, Donald 5–7 180 LW
B. Toronto, Ont., July 3, 1924

43–44	Tor	27	7	6	13	28	

Playoffs

43–44	Tor	5	0	0	0	12	

WEBSTER, John Robert (Chick) 5–10 160 C
B. Toronto, Ont., Nov. 3, 1921

49–50	NYR	14	0	0	0	4	

WEBSTER, Thomas Ronald 5–10 170 RW
B. Kirkland Lake, Ont., Oct. 4, 1948

68–69	Bos	9	0	2	2	9	-1
69–70	Bos	2	0	1	1	2	-1
70–71	Det	78	30	37	67	40	-47
71–72	Det–Cal	12	3	2	5	10	-4
72–73	NE (WHA)	77	53	50	103	89	
73–74	NE (WHA)	64	43	27	70	28	
74–75	NE (WHA)	66	40	24	64	52	
75–76	NE (WHA)	55	33	50	83	24	
76–77	NE (WHA)	70	36	49	85	43	
77–78	NE (WHA)	20	15	5	20	5	
79–80	Det	1	0	0	0	0	0
NHL Totals		102	33	42	75	61	-53
WHA Totals		352	220	205	425	241	

SSN	TEAM	GP	G	A	PTS.	PIM	+/-
Playoffs							
68–69	Bos	1	0	0	0	0	
72–73	NE (WHA)	15	12	14	26	6	
73–74	NE (WHA)	3	5	0	5	7	
74–75	NE (WHA)	3	0	2	2	0	
75–76	NE (WHA)	17	10	9	19	6	
76–77	NE (WHA)	5	1	1	2	0	
NHL Totals		1	0	0	0	0	
WHA Totals		43	28	26	54	19	

WEIGHT, Doug 5–11 191 C
B. Warren, Mich., Jan. 21, 1971

SSN	TEAM	GP	G	A	PTS.	PIM	+/-
91–92	NYR	53	8	22	30	23	-3
92–93	NYR–Edm	78	17	31	48	65	+4
93–94	Edm	84	24	50	74	47	-24
94–95	Edm	48	7	33	40	69	-17
95–96	Edm	82	25	79	104	95	-19
96–97	Edm	80	21	61	82	80	+1
97–98	Edm	79	26	44	70	69	+1
98–99	Edm	43	6	31	37	12	-8
Totals		547	134	351	485	460	-65
Playoffs							
90–91	NYR	1	0	0	0	0	
91–92	NYR	7	2	2	4	0	
96–97	Edm	12	3	8	11	8	
97–98	Edm	12	2	7	9	14	
98–99	Edm	4	1	1	2	15	
Totals		36	8	18	26	37	

*****WEILAND, Ralph C. (Cooney)** 5–7 150 C
B. Seaforth, Ont., Nov. 5, 1904

SSN	TEAM	GP	G	A	PTS.	PIM
28–29	Bos	40	11	7	18	16
29–30	Bos	44	43	30	73	27
30–31	Bos	44	25	13	38	14
31–32	Bos	47	14	12	26	20
32–33	Ott	48	16	11	27	4
33–34	Ott–Det	46	13	19	32	10
34–35	Det	48	13	25	38	10
35–36	Bos	48	14	13	27	15
36–37	Bos	48	6	9	15	6
37–38	Bos	48	11	12	23	16
38–39	Bos	47	7	9	16	9
Totals		508	173	160	333	147
Playoffs						
28–29	Bos	5	2	0	2	2
29–30	Bos	6	1	5	6	2
30–31	Bos	5	6	3	9	2
33–34	Det	9	2	2	4	4
35–36	Bos	2	1	0	1	2
36–37	Bos	3	0	0	0	0
37–38	Bos	3	0	0	0	0
38–39	Bos	12	0	0	0	0
Totals		45	12	10	22	12

WEINRICH, Eric John 6–1 210 D
B. Roanoke, Virg., Dec. 19, 1966

SSN	TEAM	GP	G	A	PTS.	PIM	+/-
88–89	NJ	2	0	0	0	0	-1
89–90	NJ	19	2	7	9	11	+1
90–91	NJ	76	4	34	38	48	+10
91–92	NJ	76	7	25	32	55	+10
92–93	Hart	79	7	29	36	76	-11
93–94	Hart–Chi	62	4	24	28	33	+1
94–95	Chi	48	3	10	13	33	+1
95–96	Chi	77	5	10	15	65	+14
96–97	Chi	81	7	25	32	62	+19
97–98	Chi	82	2	21	23	106	+10
98–99	Chi–Mont	80	7	15	22	89	-25
Totals		682	48	200	248	578	+29
Playoffs							
89–90	NJ	6	1	3	4	17	
90–91	NJ	7	1	2	3	6	
91–92	NJ	7	0	2	2	4	
93–94	Chi	6	0	2	2	6	
94–95	Chi	16	1	5	6	4	
95–96	Chi	10	1	4	5	10	
96–97	Chi	6	0	1	1	4	
Totals		58	4	19	23	51	

WEIR, Stanley Brian 6–1 180 C
B. Ponoka, Alta., Mar. 17, 1952

SSN	TEAM	GP	G	A	PTS.	PIM	+/-
72–73	Cal	78	15	24	39	16	-24
73–74	Cal	58	9	7	16	10	-33
74–75	Cal	80	18	27	45	12	-30
75–76	Tor	64	19	32	51	22	+10

SSN	TEAM	GP	G	A	PTS.	PIM	+/-
76–77	Tor	65	11	19	30	14	+2
77–78	Tor	30	12	5	17	4	0
78–79	Edm (WHA)	68	31	30	61	20	
79–80	Edm	79	33	33	66	40	+2
80–81	Edm	70	12	20	32	40	-7
81–82	Edm–Col	61	5	16	21	23	-7
82–83	Det	57	5	24	29	2	0
NHL Totals		642	139	207	346	183	-85
WHA Totals		68	31	30	61	20	
Playoffs							
75–76	Tor	9	1	3	4	0	
76–77	Tor	7	2	1	3	0	
77–78	Tor	13	3	1	4	0	
78–79	Edm (WHA)	13	2	5	7	2	
79–80	Edm	3	0	0	0	2	
80–81	Edm	5	0	0	0	0	
NHL Totals		37	6	5	11	4	
WHA Totals		13	2	5	7	2	

WEIR, Wally 6–2 205 D
B. Verdun, Que., June 3, 1954

SSN	TEAM	GP	G	A	PTS.	PIM	+/-
76–77	Que (WHA)	69	3	17	20	197	
77–78	Que (WHA)	13	0	0	0	47	
78–79	Que (WHA)	68	2	7	9	166	
79–80	Que	73	3	12	15	133	-18
80–81	Que	54	6	8	14	77	0
81–82	Que	62	3	5	8	173	-16
82–83	Que	58	5	11	16	135	+11
83–84	Que	25	2	3	5	17	+5
84–85	Hart–Pitt	48	2	6	8	90	-6
NHL Totals		320	21	45	66	625	-24
WHA Totals		150	5	24	29	410	
Playoffs							
76–77	Que (WHA)	17	1	5	6	13	
77–78	Que (WHA)	11	1	2	3	50	
78–79	Que (WHA)	4	0	1	1	4	
80–81	Que	3	0	0	0	15	
81–82	Que	15	0	0	0	45	
82–83	Que	4	0	1	1	19	
83–84	Que	1	0	0	0	17	
NHL Totals		23	0	1	1	96	
WHA Totals		32	2	8	10	67	

*****WELLINGTON, Duke** D

SSN	TEAM	GP	G	A	PTS.	PIM
19–20	Que	1	0	0	0	0

WELLS, Chris 6–6 215 C
B. Calgary, Alta., Nov. 12, 1975

SSN	TEAM	GP	G	A	PTS.	PIM	+/-
95–96	Pitt	54	2	2	4	59	-6
96–97	Fla	47	2	6	8	42	+5
97–98	Fla	61	5	10	15	47	+4
98–99	Fla	20	0	2	2	31	-4
Totals		202	9	20	29	179	-1
Playoffs							
96–97	Fla	3	0	0	0	0	

WELLS, Gordon (Jay) 6–1 210 D
B. Paris, Ont., May 18, 1959

SSN	TEAM	GP	G	A	PTS.	PIM	+/-
79–80	LA	43	0	0	0	113	-22
80–81	LA	72	5	13	18	155	+9
81–82	LA	60	1	8	9	145	+2
82–83	LA	69	3	12	15	167	+11
83–84	LA	69	3	18	21	141	-10
84–85	LA	77	2	9	11	185	+4
85–86	LA	79	11	31	42	226	+7
86–87	LA	77	7	29	36	155	-19
87–88	LA	58	2	23	25	159	-3
88–89	Phil	67	2	19	21	184	-3
89–90	Phil–Buf	60	3	17	20	129	+5
90–91	Buf	43	1	2	3	86	-18
91–92	Buf–NYR	52	2	9	11	181	-1
92–93	NYR	53	1	9	10	107	-2
93–94	NYR	79	2	7	9	110	+4
94–95	NYR	43	2	7	9	36	0
95–96	StL	76	0	3	3	67	-8
96–97	TB	21	0	0	0	13	-3
Totals		1098	47	216	263	2359	-47
Playoffs							
79–80	LA	4	0	0	0	11	
80–81	LA	4	0	0	0	27	
81–82	LA	10	1	3	4	41	
84–85	LA	3	0	1	1	0	
86–87	LA	5	1	2	3	10	
87–88	LA	18	0	2	2	51	

SSN	TEAM	GP	G	A	PTS.	PIM	+/-
89–90	Buf	6	0	0	0	12	
90–91	Buf	1	0	1	1	0	
91–92	NYR	13	0	2	2	10	
93–94	NYR	23	0	0	0	20	
94–95	NYR	10	0	0	0	8	
95–96	StL	12	0	1	1	2	
Totals		114	3	14	17	213	

WENSINK, John 6–0 200 LW
B. Cornwall, Ont., Apr. 1, 1953

SSN	TEAM	GP	G	A	PTS.	PIM	+/-
73–74	StL	3	0	0	0	0	
76–77	Bos	23	4	6	10	32	+5
77–78	Bos	80	16	20	36	181	+23
78–79	Bos	76	28	18	46	106	+20
79–80	Bos	69	9	11	20	110	+7
80–81	Col	53	6	3	9	124	-14
81–82	Col	57	5	3	8	152	-13
82–83	NJ	42	2	7	9	135	-8
Totals		403	70	68	138	840	+20
Playoffs							
76–77	Bos	13	0	3	3	8	
77–78	Bos	15	2	2	4	54	
78–79	Bos	8	0	1	1	19	
79–80	Bos	4	0	0	0	5	
80–81	Que	3	0	0	0	0	
Totals		43	2	6	8	86	

*****WENTWORTH, Marvin (Cy)** 5–9 170 D
B. Grimsby, Ont., Jan. 24, 1905

SSN	TEAM	GP	G	A	PTS.	PIM
27–28	Chi	44	5	5	10	31
28–29	Chi	44	2	1	3	44
29–30	Chi	39	3	4	7	28
30–31	Chi	43	4	4	8	12
31–32	Chi	48	3	10	13	30
32–33	Mont M	47	4	10	14	48
33–34	Mont M	48	2	5	7	31
34–35	Mont M	48	4	9	13	28
35–36	Mont M	48	4	5	9	24
36–37	Mont M	44	3	4	7	29
37–38	Mont M	48	4	5	9	32
38–39	Mont	45	0	3	3	12
39–40	Mont	32	1	3	4	6
Totals		578	39	68	107	355
Playoffs						
30–31	Chi	9	1	1	2	16
31–32	Chi	2	0	0	0	0
32–33	Mont M	2	0	1	1	0
33–34	Mont M	4	0	2	2	2
34–35	Mont M	7	3	2	5	0
35–36	Mont M	3	0	0	0	0
36–37	Mont M	5	1	0	1	0
38–39	Mont	3	0	0	0	4
Totals		35	5	6	11	22

WERENKA, Brad 6–2 210 D
B. Two Hills, Alta., Feb. 12, 1969

SSN	TEAM	GP	G	A	PTS.	PIM	+/-
92–93	Edm	27	5	3	8	24	+1
93–94	Edm–Que	26	0	11	11	22	+3
95–96	Chi	9	0	0	0	8	-2
97–98	Pitt	71	3	15	18	46	+15
98–99	Pitt	81	6	18	24	93	+17
Totals		214	14	47	61	193	+34
Playoffs							
97–98	Pitt	6	1	0	1	8	
98–99	Pitt	13	1	1	2	6	
Totals		19	2	1	3	14	

WESLEY, Glen 6–1 195 D
B. Red Deer, ALta., Oct. 2, 1968

SSN	TEAM	GP	G	A	PTS.	PIM	+/-
87–88	Bos	79	7	30	37	69	+21
88–89	Bos	77	19	35	54	61	+23
89–90	Bos	78	9	27	36	48	+6
90–91	Bos	80	11	32	43	78	0
91–92	Bos	78	9	37	46	54	+9
92–93	Bos	64	8	25	33	47	-2
93–94	Bos	81	14	44	58	64	+1
94–95	Hart	48	2	14	16	50	-6
95–96	Hart	68	8	16	24	88	-8
96–97	Hart	68	6	26	32	40	0
97–98	Car	82	6	19	25	36	+7
98–99	Car	74	7	17	24	44	+14
Totals		877	106	322	428	879	+46

Playoffs

SSN	TEAM	GP	G	A	PTS.	PIM	+/-
87–88	Bos	23	6	8	14	22	
88–89	Bos	10	0	2	2	4	
89–90	Bos	21	2	6	8	36	
90–91	Bos	19	2	9	11	19	
91–92	Bos	15	2	4	6	16	
92–93	Bos	4	0	0	0	0	
93–94	Bos	13	3	3	6	12	
98–99	Car	6	0	0	0	2	
Totals		111	15	32	47	111	

WESLEY, Trevor (Blake) 6–1 200 D
B. Red Deer, Alta., July 10, 1959

SSN	TEAM	GP	G	A	PTS.	PIM	+/-
79–80	Phil	2	0	1	1	2	-3
80–81	Phil	50	3	7	10	107	+13
81–82	Hart	78	9	18	27	123	-34
82–83	Hart-Que	74	4	9	13	130	-20
83–84	Que	46	2	8	10	75	+14
84–85	Que	21	0	2	2	28	-2
85–86	Tor	27	0	1	1	21	-4
Totals		298	18	46	64	486	-36

Playoffs

SSN	TEAM	GP	G	A	PTS.	PIM	+/-
82–83	Que	4	0	0	0	2	
83–84	Que	9	1	2	3	20	
84–85	Que	6	1	0	1	8	
Totals		19	2	2	4	30	

WESTFALL, Vernon Edwin (Ed) 6–1 197 RW
B. Belleville, Ont., Sept. 19, 1940

SSN	TEAM	GP	G	A	PTS.	PIM	+/-
61–62	Bos	63	2	9	11	53	
62–63	Bos	48	1	11	12	34	
63–64	Bos	55	1	5	6	35	
64–65	Bos	68	12	15	27	65	
65–66	Bos	59	9	21	30	42	
66–67	Bos	70	12	24	36	26	
67–68	Bos	73	14	22	36	38	+5
68–69	Bos	70	18	24	42	22	+20
69–70	Bos	72	14	22	36	28	+20
70–71	Bos	78	25	34	59	48	+58
71–72	Bos	78	18	26	44	19	+29
72–73	NYI	67	15	31	46	25	-42
73–74	NYI	68	19	23	42	28	-5
74–75	NYI	73	22	33	55	28	+19
75–76	NYI	80	25	31	56	27	+17
76–77	NYI	79	14	33	47	8	+21
77–78	NYI	71	5	19	24	14	+7
78–79	NYI	55	5	11	16	4	0
Totals		1227	231	394	625	544	+169

Playoffs

SSN	TEAM	GP	G	A	PTS.	PIM	+/-
67–68	Bos	4	2	0	2	2	
68–69	Bos	10	3	7	10	11	
69–70	Bos	14	3	5	8	4	
70–71	Bos	7	1	2	3	2	
71–72	Bos	15	4	3	7	10	
74–75	NYI	17	5	10	15	12	
75–76	NYI	8	2	3	5	0	
76–77	NYI	12	1	5	6	0	
77–78	NYI	2	0	0	0	0	
78–79	NYI	6	1	2	3	0	
Totals		95	22	37	59	41	

WHARRAM, Kenneth Malcolm 5–9 165 RW
B. Ferris, Ont., July 2, 1933

SSN	TEAM	GP	G	A	PTS.	PIM	+/-
51–52	Chi	1	0	0	0	0	
53–54	Chi	29	1	7	8	8	
55–56	Chi	3	0	0	0	0	
58–59	Chi	66	10	9	19	14	
59–60	Chi	59	14	11	25	16	
60–61	Chi	64	16	29	45	12	
61–62	Chi	62	14	23	37	29	
62–63	Chi	55	20	18	38	17	
63–64	Chi	70	39	32	71	18	
64–65	Chi	68	24	20	44	27	
65–66	Chi	69	26	17	43	28	
66–67	Chi	70	31	34	65	21	
67–68	Chi	74	27	42	69	18	-2
68–69	Chi	76	30	39	69	19	+18
Totals		766	252	281	533	227	+16

Playoffs

SSN	TEAM	GP	G	A	PTS.	PIM	+/-
58–59	Chi	6	0	2	2	2	
59–60	Chi	4	1	1	2	0	
60–61	Chi	12	3	5	8	12	
61–62	Chi	12	3	4	7	8	
62–63	Chi	6	1	5	6	0	
63–64	Chi	7	2	2	4	6	
64–65	Chi	12	2	3	5	4	
65–66	Chi	6	1	0	1	4	
66–67	Chi	6	2	2	4	2	
67–68	Chi	9	1	3	4	0	
Totals		80	16	27	43	38	

WHARTON, Leonard (Len) F
B. Winnipeg, Man., Dec. 13, 1927

SSN	TEAM	GP	G	A	PTS.	PIM	+/-
44–45	NYR	1	0	0	0	0	

WHEELDON, Simon 5–11 170 C
B. Vancouver, B.C., Aug. 30, 1966

SSN	TEAM	GP	G	A	PTS.	PIM	+/-
87–88	NYR	5	0	1	1	4	-2
88–89	NYR	6	0	1	1	2	-1
90–91	Winn	4	0	0	0	4	+2
Totals		15	0	2	2	10	-1

*WHELDON, Donald 6–2 185 D
B. Falmouth, Mass., Dec. 28, 1954

SSN	TEAM	GP	G	A	PTS.	PIM	+/-
74–75	StL	2	0	0	0	0	

WHELTON, William 6–1 180 D
B. Everett, Mass., Aug. 28, 1959

SSN	TEAM	GP	G	A	PTS.	PIM	+/-
80–81	Winn	2	0	0	0	0	

WHISTLE, Rob 6–2 195 D
B. Thunder Bay, Ont., Apr. 4, 1961

SSN	TEAM	GP	G	A	PTS.	PIM	+/-
85–86	NYR	32	4	2	6	10	
87–88	StL	19	3	3	6	6	
Totals		51	7	5	12	16	

Playoffs

SSN	TEAM	GP	G	A	PTS.	PIM	+/-
85–86	NYR	3	0	0	0	2	
87–88	StL	1	0	0	0	0	
Totals		4	0	0	0	2	

WHITE, Anthony Raymond 5–10 175 LW
B. Grand Falls, Nfld., June 16, 1954

SSN	TEAM	GP	G	A	PTS.	PIM	+/-
74–75	Wash	5	0	2	2	0	0
75–76	Wash	80	25	17	42	56	-43
76–77	Wash	72	12	9	21	44	-15
77–78	Wash	1	0	0	0	0	-4
79–80	Minn	6	0	0	0	4	-2
Totals		164	37	28	65	104	-64

Playoffs

SSN	TEAM	GP	G	A	PTS.	PIM	+/-
72–73	LA (WHA)	6	1	0	1	0	

WHITE, Brian 6–1 180 D
B. Winchester, Mass., Feb. 7, 1976

SSN	TEAM	GP	G	A	PTS.	PIM	+/-
98–99	Col A	2	0	0	0	0	0

WHITE, Leonard Arthur (Moe) 5–11 178 LW
B. Verdun, Que., July 28, 1919

SSN	TEAM	GP	G	A	PTS.	PIM	+/-
45–46	Mont	4	0	1	1	2	

WHITE, Peter Toby 5–11 200 C
B. Montreal, Que., Mar. 15, 1969

SSN	TEAM	GP	G	A	PTS.	PIM	+/-
93–94	Edm	26	3	5	8	2	+1
94–95	Edm	9	2	4	6	0	+1
95–96	Edm-Tor	27	5	3	8	0	-14
98–99	Phil	3	0	0	0	0	0
Totals		65	10	12	22	2	-12

*WHITE, Sherman Beverly 5–10 165 C
B. Amherst, N.S., May 12, 1923

SSN	TEAM	GP	G	A	PTS.	PIM	+/-
46–47	NYR	1	0	0	0	0	
49–50	NYR	3	0	2	2	0	
Totals		4	0	2	2	0	

WHITE, Todd 5–10 181 C
B. Kanata, Ont., May 21, 1975

SSN	TEAM	GP	G	A	PTS.	PIM	+/-
97–98	Chi	7	1	0	1	2	0
98–99	Chi	35	5	8	13	20	-1
Totals		42	6	8	14	22	-1

*WHITE, Wilfred Belmont (Tex) 5–11 155 F
B. 1901

SSN	TEAM	GP	G	A	PTS.	PIM	+/-
25–26	Pitt Pi	35	7	1	8	22	
26–27	Pitt Pi	43	5	4	9	21	
27–28	Pitt Pi	44	5	1	6	54	
28–29	Pitt Pi-NYA	43	5	5	10	26	
29–30	Pitt Pi	29	8	1	9	16	
30–31	Phil Q	9	3	0	3	2	
Totals		203	33	12	45	141	

Playoffs

SSN	TEAM	GP	G	A	PTS.	PIM	+/-
27–28	Pitt	2	0	0	0	4	
28–29	NYA	2	0	0	0	2	
Totals		4	0	0	0	6	

WHITE, William Earl 6–1 195 D
B. Toronto, Ont., Aug. 26, 1939

SSN	TEAM	GP	G	A	PTS.	PIM	+/-
67–68	LA	74	11	27	38	100	+17
68–69	LA	75	5	28	33	38	-20
69–70	LA-Chi	61	4	16	20	39	-12
70–71	Chi	67	4	21	25	64	+51
71–72	Chi	76	7	22	29	58	+42
72–73	Chi	72	9	38	47	80	+30
73–74	Chi	69	5	31	36	52	+51
74–75	Chi	51	4	23	27	20	+9
75–76	Chi	59	1	9	10	44	-10
Totals		604	50	215	265	495	+158

Playoffs

SSN	TEAM	GP	G	A	PTS.	PIM	+/-
67–68	LA	7	2	2	4	4	
68–69	LA	11	1	4	5	8	
69–70	LA	8	1	2	3	8	
70–71	Chi	18	1	4	5	20	
71–72	Chi	8	0	3	3	6	
72–73	Chi	16	1	6	7	10	
73–74	Chi	11	1	7	8	14	
74–75	Chi	8	0	3	3	4	
75–76	Chi	4	0	1	1	2	
Totals		91	7	32	39	76	

WHITELAW, Robert 5–11 185 D
B. Motherwell, Scotland, Oct. 5, 1916

SSN	TEAM	GP	G	A	PTS.	PIM	+/-
40–41	Det	23	0	2	2	2	
41–42	Det	9	0	0	0	0	
Totals		32	0	2	2	2	

Playoffs

SSN	TEAM	GP	G	A	PTS.	PIM	+/-
40–41	Det	8	0	0	0	0	

WHITLOCK, Robert Angus 5–10 175 C
B. Charlottetown, P.E.I., July 16, 1949

SSN	TEAM	GP	G	A	PTS.	PIM	+/-
69–70	Minn	1	0	0	0	0	+1
72–73	Chi (WHA)	75	23	30	53	53	
73–74	Chi-LA (WHA)	66	20	29	49	48	
74–75	Ind (WHA)	73	31	26	57	56	
75–76	Ind (WHA)	30	7	15	22	16	
NHL Totals		1	0	0	0	0	+1
WHA Totals		244	81	98	179	173	

WHITNEY, Ray 5–9 160 C
B. Edmonton, Alta., May 8, 1972

SSN	TEAM	GP	G	A	PTS.	PIM	+/-
91–92	SJ	2	0	3	3	0	-1
92–93	SJ	26	4	6	10	4	-14
93–94	SJ	61	14	26	40	14	+2
94–95	SJ	39	13	12	25	14	-7
95–96	SJ	60	17	24	41	16	-23
96–97	SJ	12	0	2	2	4	-6
97–98	SJ-Fla	77	33	32	65	28	+9
98–99	Fla	81	26	28	64	18	-3
Totals		358	107	143	250	98	-43

Playoffs

SSN	TEAM	GP	G	A	PTS.	PIM	+/-
93–94	SJ	14	0	4	4	8	
94–95	SJ	11	4	4	8	2	
Totals		25	4	8	12	10	

WHYTE, Sean 6–0 198 RW
B. Sudbury, Ont., May 4, 1970

SSN	TEAM	GP	G	A	PTS.	PIM	+/-
91–92	LA	3	0	0	0	0	-1
92–93	LA	18	0	2	2	12	+1
Totals		21	0	2	2	12	0

WICKENHEISER, Douglas Peter 6–1 200 C
B. Regina, SAsk., Mar. 30, 1961

SSN	TEAM	GP	G	A	PTS.	PIM	+/-
80–81	Mont	41	7	8	15	20	+5
81–82	Mont	56	12	23	35	43	+18
82–83	Mont	78	25	30	55	49	+22
83–84	Mont-StL	73	12	26	38	25	+11
84–85	StL	68	23	20	43	36	+9
85–86	Stl	36	8	11	19	16	+11
86–87	Stl	80	13	15	28	37	-22
87–88	Van	80	7	19	26	36	-15
88–89	NYR-Wash	17	3	5	8	4	+1

SSN	TEAM	GP	G	A	PTS.	PIM	+/-
89–90	Wash	27	1	8	9	20	+1
Totals		556	111	165	276	286	+41

Playoffs

SSN	TEAM	GP	G	A	PTS.	PIM	+/-
83–84	StL	11	2	2	4	2	
85–86	StL	19	2	5	7	12	
86–87	StL	6	0	0	0	2	
88–89	Wash	5	0	0	0	2	
Totals		41	4	7	11	18	

*WIDING, Juha Markku (Whitey) *6–1 190 C*
B. Uleaborg, Finland, July 4, 1947

SSN	TEAM	GP	G	A	PTS.	PIM	+/-
69–70	NYR–LA	48	7	9	16	12	+1
70–71	LA	78	25	40	65	24	-11
71–72	LA	78	27	28	55	26	-36
72–73	LA	77	16	54	70	30	-14
73–74	LA	71	27	30	57	26	-4
74–75	LA	80	26	34	60	46	+18
75–76	LA	67	7	15	22	26	-12
76–77	LA–Clev	76	9	16	25	18	-23
77–78	Edm (WHA)	71	18	24	42	8	
NHL Totals		575	144	226	370	208	-81
WHA Totals		71	18	24	42	8	

Playoffs

SSN	TEAM	GP	G	A	PTS.	PIM	+/-
73–74	LA	5	1	0	1	2	
74–75	LA	3	0	2	2	0	
77–78	Edm (WHA)	5	0	1	1	0	
NHL Totals		8	1	2	3	2	
WHA Totals		5	0	1	1	0	

WIDMER, Jason *6–0 205 D*
B. Calgary, Alta., Aug. 1, 1973

SSN	TEAM	GP	G	A	PTS.	PIM	+/-
94–95	NYI	1	0	0	0	0	-1
95–96	NYI	4	0	0	0	7	0
96–97	SJ	2	0	1	1	0	+1
Totals		7	0	1	1	7	0

*WIEBE, Arthur Walter Ronald *5–10 180 D*
B. Rosthern, Sask., Sept. 28, 1913

SSN	TEAM	GP	G	A	PTS.	PIM	+/-
32–33	Chi	3	0	0	0	0	
34–35	Chi	42	2	1	3	27	
35–36	Chi	46	1	0	1	25	
36–37	Chi	45	0	2	2	6	
37–38	Chi	44	0	3	3	24	
38–39	Chi	47	1	2	3	24	
39–40	Chi	40	3	2	5	28	
40–41	Chi	46	2	2	4	28	
41–42	Chi	44	2	4	6	20	
42–43	Chi	33	1	7	8	25	
43–44	Chi	21	2	4	6	2	
Totals		411	14	27	41	209	

Playoffs

SSN	TEAM	GP	G	A	PTS.	PIM	+/-
34–35	Chi	2	0	0	0	0	
35–36	Chi	2	0	0	0	0	
37–38	Chi	10	0	1	1	2	
39–40	Chi	2	1	0	1	2	
40–41	Chi	4	0	0	0	0	
41–42	Chi	3	0	0	0	0	
43–44	Chi	8	0	2	2	4	
Totals		31	1	3	4	8	

WIEMER, James Duncan *6–4 216 D*
B. Sudbury, Ont., Jan. 9, 1961

SSN	TEAM	GP	G	A	PTS.	PIM	+/-
83–84	Buf	64	5	15	20	48	+1
84–85	Buf–NYR	32	7	5	12	34	-15
85–86	NYR	7	3	0	3	2	0
87–88	Edm	12	1	2	3	15	+7
88–89	LA	9	2	3	5	20	+2
89–90	Bos	61	5	14	19	63	+11
90–91	Bos	61	4	19	23	62	+3
91–92	Bos	47	1	8	9	84	+10
92–93	Bos	28	1	6	7	48	+1
93–94	Bos	4	0	0	0	2	-3
Totals		325	29	72	101	378	+17

Playoffs

SSN	TEAM	GP	G	A	PTS.	PIM	+/-
82–83	Buf	1	0	0	0	0	
85–86	NYR	8	1	0	1	6	
87–88	Edm	2	0	0	0	2	
88–89	LA	10	2	1	3	19	
89–90	LA	8	0	1	1	4	
90–91	Bos	16	1	3	4	14	
91–92	Bos	15	1	3	4	14	
92–93	Bos	1	0	0	0	4	
Totals		62	5	8	13	63	

WIEMER, Jason *6–1 215 C*
B. Kimberley, B.C., Apr. 14, 1976

SSN	TEAM	GP	G	A	PTS.	PIM	+/-
94–95	TB	36	1	4	5	44	-2
95–96	TB	66	9	9	18	81	-9
96–97	TB	63	9	5	14	134	-13
97–98	TB–Calg	79	12	10	22	160	-10
98–99	Calg	78	8	13	21	177	-12
Totals		322	39	41	80	596	-46

Playoffs

SSN	TEAM	GP	G	A	PTS.	PIM	+/-
95–96	TB	6	1	0	1	28	

*WILCOX, Archibald *187 D*
B. Montreal, Que., May 9, 1903

SSN	TEAM	GP	G	A	PTS.	PIM	+/-
29–30	Mont M	40	3	5	8	38	
30–31	Mont M	40	2	2	4	42	
31–32	Mont M	48	3	3	6	37	
32–33	Mont M	47	0	3	3	37	
33–34	Mont M–Bos	26	0	1	1	4	
34–35	StL E	11	0	0	0	0	
Totals		212	8	14	22	158	

Playoffs

SSN	TEAM	GP	G	A	PTS.	PIM	+/-
29–30	Mont M	4	1	0	1	4	
30–31	Mont M	2	0	0	0	2	
31–32	Mont M	4	0	0	0	4	
32–33	Mont M	2	0	0	0	0	
Totals		12	1	0	1	10	

WILCOX, Barry Frederick *6–1 190 RW*
B. New Westminster, B.C., Apr. 23, 1948

SSN	TEAM	GP	G	A	PTS.	PIM	+/-
72–73	Van	31	3	2	5	15	-10
74–75	Van	2	0	0	0	0	0
Totals		33	3	2	5	15	-10

WILDER, Archibald *5–9 155 LW*
B. Melville, Sask., Apr. 30, 1917

SSN	TEAM	GP	G	A	PTS.	PIM	+/-
40–41	Det	18	0	2	2	2	

WILEY, James Thomas *6–2 195 C*
B. Sault Ste. Marie, Ont., Apr. 28, 1950

SSN	TEAM	GP	G	A	PTS.	PIM	+/-
72–73	Pitt	4	0	1	1	0	+1
73–74	Pitt	22	0	3	3	2	-4
74–75	Van	1	0	0	0	0	0
75–76	Van	2	0	0	0	2	-1
76–77	Van	34	4	6	10	4	-13
Totals		63	4	10	14	8	-17

WILKIE, Bob *6–2 215 D*
B. Calgary, Alta., Feb. 11, 1969

SSN	TEAM	GP	G	A	PTS.	PIM	+/-
90–91	Det	8	1	2	3	2	-2
93–94	Phil	10	1	3	4	8	-2
Totals		18	2	5	7	10	-4

WILKIE, David *6–2 210 D*
B. Ellensburgh, Wash., May 30, 1974

SSN	TEAM	GP	G	A	PTS.	PIM	+/-
94–95	Mont	1	0	0	0	0	0
95–96	Mont	24	1	5	6	10	-10
96–97	Mont	61	6	9	15	63	-8
97–98	Mont–TB	34	2	5	7	21	-22
98–99	TB	46	1	7	8	69	-19
Totals		166	10	26	36	163	-60

Playoffs

SSN	TEAM	GP	G	A	PTS.	PIM	+/-
95–96	Mont	6	1	2	3	12	
96–97	Mont	2	0	0	0	2	
Totals		8	1	2	3	14	

WILKINS, Barry James *5–11 190 D*
B. Toronto, Ont., Feb. 28, 1947

SSN	TEAM	GP	G	A	PTS.	PIM	+/-
66–67	Bos	1	0	0	0	0	
68–69	Bos	1	1	0	1	0	+1
69–70	Bos	6	0	0	0	2	-1
70–71	Van	70	5	18	23	131	-18
71–72	Van	45	2	5	7	65	-9
72–73	Van	76	11	17	28	133	-38
73–74	Van	78	3	28	31	123	-13
74–75	Van–Pitt	66	5	30	35	103	+29
75–76	Pitt	75	0	27	27	106	-1
76–77	Edm (WHA)	51	4	24	28	75	
77–78	Ind (WHA)	79	2	21	23	79	
NHL Totals		418	27	125	152	663	-50
WHA Totals		130	6	45	51	154	

Playoffs

SSN	TEAM	GP	G	A	PTS.	PIM	+/-
74–75	Pitt	3	0	0	0	0	
75–76	Pitt	3	0	1	1	4	
76–77	Edm (WHA)	4	0	1	1	2	
NHL Totals		6	0	1	1	4	
WHA Totals		4	0	1	1	2	

*WILKINSON, John H. *5–11 195 D*
B. Ottawa, Ont., July 9, 1911

SSN	TEAM	GP	G	A	PTS.	PIM	+/-
43–44	Bos	9	0	0	0	3	

WILKINSON, Neil John *6–3 190 D*
B. Selkirk, Man., Oct. 16, 1967

SSN	TEAM	GP	G	A	PTS.	PIM	+/-
89–90	Minn	36	0	5	5	100	-1
90–91	Minn	50	2	9	11	117	-5
91–92	SJ	60	4	15	19	107	-11
92–93	SJ	59	1	7	8	96	-50
93–94	Chi	72	3	9	12	115	+2
94–95	Winn	41	1	4	5	75	-26
95–96	Winn–Pitt	62	3	14	17	120	+12
96–97	Pitt	23	0	0	0	36	-12
97–98	Pitt	34	2	4	6	24	0
98–99	Pitt	24	0	0	0	22	-2
Totals		460	16	67	83	813	-93

Playoffs

SSN	TEAM	GP	G	A	PTS.	PIM	+/-
89–90	Minn	7	0	2	2	11	
90–91	Minn	22	3	3	6	12	
93–94	Chi	4	0	0	0	0	
95–96	Pitt	15	0	1	1	14	
96–97	Pitt	5	0	0	0	4	
Totals		53	3	6	9	41	

WILKS, Brian *5–11 175 C*
B. North York, Ont., Feb. 27, 1966

SSN	TEAM	GP	G	A	PTS.	PIM	+/-
84–85	LA	2	0	0	0	0	-1
85–86	LA	43	4	8	12	25	-7
86–87	LA	1	0	0	0	0	-2
88–89	LA	2	0	0	0	2	0
Totals		48	4	8	12	27	-10

WILLARD, Rod Stephen *6–0 190 LW*
B. New Liskeard, Ont., May 1, 1960

SSN	TEAM	GP	G	A	PTS.	PIM	+/-
82–83	Tor	1	0	0	0	0	-1

*WILLIAMS, Burr *5–10 183 D*
B. Okemah, Okla., Aug. 30, 1909

SSN	TEAM	GP	G	A	PTS.	PIM	+/-
33–34	Det	1	0	1	1	12	
34–35	StL E–Bos	16	0	0	0	12	
36–37	Det	2	0	0	0	4	
Totals		19	0	1	1	28	

Playoffs

SSN	TEAM	GP	G	A	PTS.	PIM	+/-
33–34	Det	2	0	0	0	8	

WILLIAMS, Darryl *5–11 185 LW*
B. Mt. Pearl, Nfld., Feb. 9, 1968

SSN	TEAM	GP	G	A	PTS.	PIM	+/-
92–93	LA	2	0	0	0	10	0

WILLIAMS, David Andrew *6–2 195 D*
B. Plainfield, N.J., Aug. 25, 1967

SSN	TEAM	GP	G	A	PTS.	PIM	+/-
91–92	SJ	56	3	25	28	40	-13
92–93	SJ	40	1	11	12	49	-27
93–94	Ana	56	5	15	20	42	+8
94–95	Ana	21	2	2	4	26	-5
Totals		173	11	53	64	157	-37

WILLIAMS, David James (Tiger) *5–11 190 LW*
B. Weyburn, Sask., Feb. 3, 1954

SSN	TEAM	GP	G	A	PTS.	PIM	+/-
74–75	Tor	42	10	19	29	187	+4
75–76	Tor	78	21	19	40	299	-1
76–77	Tor	77	18	25	43	338	+11
77–78	Tor	78	19	31	50	351	+6
78–79	Tor	77	19	20	39	298	-7
79–80	Tor–Van	78	30	23	53	278	-13
80–81	Van	77	35	27	62	343	+4
81–82	Van	77	17	21	38	341	-6
82–83	Van	68	8	13	21	265	-7
83–84	Van	67	15	16	31	294	-11
84–85	Det–LA	67	7	11	18	201	-16
85–86	LA	72	20	29	49	320	-6
86–87	LA	76	16	18	34	358	-1
87–88	LA–Hart	28	6	0	6	93	+3
Totals		962	241	272	513	3966	-40

SSN	TEAM	GP	G	A	PTS.	PIM	+/-
Playoffs							
74–75	Tor	7	1	3	4	25	
75–76	Tor	10	0	0	0	75	
76–77	Tor	9	3	6	9	29	
77–78	Tor	12	1	2	3	63	
78–79	Tor	6	0	0	0	48	
79–80	Van	3	0	0	0	20	
80–81	Van	3	0	0	0	20	
81–82	Van	17	3	7	10	116	
82–83	Van	4	0	3	3	12	
83–84	Van	4	1	0	1	13	
84–85	LA	3	0	0	0	4	
86–87	LA	5	3	2	5	30	
Totals		83	12	23	35	455	

WILLIAMS, Frederick Richard 5–11 178 C
B. Saskatoon, Sask., July 1, 1956

SSN	TEAM	GP	G	A	PTS.	PIM	+/-
76–77	Det	44	2	5	7	10	-17

WILLIAMS, Gordon James 5–11 190 RW
B. Saskatoon, Sask., Apr. 10, 1960

SSN	TEAM	GP	G	A	PTS.	PIM	+/-
81–82	Phil	1	0	0	0	2	0
82–83	Phil	1	0	0	0	0	0
Totals		2	0	0	0	2	0

WILLIAMS, Sean 6–1 182 C
B. Oshawa, Ont., Jan. 28, 1968

SSN	TEAM	GP	G	A	PTS.	PIM	+/-
91–92	Chi	2	0	0	0	4	0

*WILLIAMS, Thomas Charles 6–0 187 LW
B. Windsor, Ont., Feb. 7, 1951

SSN	TEAM	GP	G	A	PTS.	PIM	+/-
71–72	NYR	3	0	0	0	2	-1
72–73	NYR	8	0	1	1	0	+1
73–74	NYR–LA	60	12	19	31	10	+1
74–75	LA	74	24	22	46	16	+14
75–76	LA	70	19	20	39	14	0
76–77	LA	80	35	39	74	14	+14
77–78	LA	58	15	22	37	9	-14
78–79	LA	44	10	15	25	8	-7
Totals		397	115	138	253	73	+8

SSN	TEAM	GP	G	A	PTS.	PIM
Playoffs						
73–74	LA	5	3	1	4	0
74–75	LA	3	0	0	0	0
75–76	LA	9	2	2	4	2
76–77	LA	9	3	4	7	2
77–78	LA	2	0	0	0	0
78–79	LA	1	0	0	0	0
Totals		29	8	7	15	4

WILLIAMS, Thomas Mark 5–11 185 C
B. Duluth, Minn., Apr. 17, 1940

SSN	TEAM	GP	G	A	PTS.	PIM	+/-
61–62	Bos	26	6	6	12	2	
62–63	Bos	69	23	20	43	11	
63–64	Bos	37	8	15	23	8	
64–65	Bos	65	13	21	34	28	
65–66	Bos	70	16	22	38	31	
66–67	Bos	29	8	13	21	2	
67–68	Bos	68	18	32	50	14	+24
68–69	Bos	26	4	7	11	19	+6
69–70	Minn	75	15	52	67	18	-19
70–71	Minn–Cal	59	17	23	40	24	-17
71–72	Cal	32	3	9	12	2	-17
72–73	NE (WHA)	69	10	21	31	14	
73–74	NE (WHA)	70	21	37	58	6	
74–75	Wash	73	22	36	58	12	-48
75–76	Wash	34	8	13	21	6	-33
NHL Totals		663	161	269	430	177	-104
WHA Totals		139	31	58	89	20	

SSN	TEAM	GP	G	A	PTS.	PIM
Playoffs						
67–68	Bos	4	1	0	1	2
69–70	Minn	6	1	5	6	0
72–73	NE (WHA)	15	6	11	17	2
73–74	NE (WHA)	4	0	3	3	10
NHL Totals		10	2	5	7	2
WHA Totals		19	6	14	20	12

WILLIAMS, Warren Milton (Butch) 5–11 195 RW
B. Duluth, Minn., Sept. 11, 1952

SSN	TEAM	GP	G	A	PTS.	PIM	+/-
73–74	StL	31	3	10	13	6	+2
74–75	Cal	63	11	21	32	118	-16
75–76	Cal	14	0	4	4	7	-7
76–77	Edm (WHA)	29	3	10	13	16	
NHL Totals		108	14	35	49	131	-21
WHA Totals		29	3	10	13	16	

WILLIS, Shane 6–0 176 RW
B. Edmonton, Alta., June 13, 1977

SSN	TEAM	GP	G	A	PTS.	PIM	+/-
98–99	Car	7	0	0	0	0	-2

WILLSON, Donald Arthur F
B. Chatham, Ont., Jan. 1, 1914

SSN	TEAM	GP	G	A	PTS.	PIM
37–38	Mont	18	2	7	9	0
38–39	Mont	4	0	0	0	0
Totals		22	2	7	9	0

SSN	TEAM	GP	G	A	PTS.	PIM
Playoffs						
37–38	Mont	3	0	0	0	0

WILM, Clarke 6–0 202 C
B. Central Butte, Sosk., Oct. 24, 1976

SSN	TEAM	GP	G	A	PTS.	PIM	+/-
98–99	Calg	78	10	8	18	53	+11

WILSON, Behn Bevan 6–3 210 D
B. Toronto, Ont., Dec. 19, 1958

SSN	TEAM	GP	G	A	PTS.	PIM	+/-
78–79	Phil	80	13	36	49	197	+13
79–80	Phil	61	9	25	34	212	+21
80–81	Phil	77	16	47	63	237	+39
81–82	Phil	59	13	23	36	135	+6
82–83	Phil	62	8	24	32	92	+3
83–84	Chi	59	10	22	32	143	-5
84–85	Chi	76	10	23	33	185	+5
85–86	Chi	69	13	37	50	113	-11
87–88	Chi	58	6	23	29	166	-19
Totals		601	98	260	358	1480	+52

SSN	TEAM	GP	G	A	PTS.	PIM
Playoffs						
78–79	Phil	5	1	0	1	8
79–80	Phil	19	4	9	13	66
80–81	Phil	12	2	10	12	36
81–82	Phil	4	1	4	5	10
82–83	Phil	3	0	1	1	2
83–84	Chi	4	0	0	0	0
84–85	Chi	15	4	5	9	60
85–86	Chi	2	0	0	0	2
87–88	Chi	3	0	0	0	6
Totals		67	12	29	41	190

*WILSON, Bertwin Hilliard (Bert) 6–0 190 LW
B. Orangeville, Ont., Oct. 17, 1949

SSN	TEAM	GP	G	A	PTS.	PIM	+/-
73–74	NYR	5	1	1	2	2	+1
74–75	NYR	61	5	1	6	66	0
75–76	StL–LA	58	2	3	5	64	-6
76–77	LA	77	4	3	7	64	-9
77–78	LA	79	7	16	23	127	0
78–79	LA	73	9	10	19	138	-5
79–80	LA	75	4	3	7	91	-19
80–81	Calg	50	5	7	12	94	-6
Totals		478	37	44	81	646	-44

SSN	TEAM	GP	G	A	PTS.	PIM
Playoffs						
75–76	LA	9	0	0	0	24
76–77	LA	8	0	2	2	12
77–78	LA	2	0	0	0	2
79–80	LA	2	0	0	0	4
80–81	Calg	1	0	0	0	0
Totals		22	0	2	2	42

WILSON, Carey 6–2 195 C
B. Winnipeg, Man., May 19, 1962

SSN	TEAM	GP	G	A	PTS.	PIM	+/-
83–84	Calg	15	2	5	7	2	-1
84–85	Calg	74	24	48	72	27	+24
85–86	Calg	76	29	29	58	24	+1
86–87	Calg	80	20	36	56	42	-2
87–88	Calg–Hart	70	27	41	68	40	-3
88–89	Hart–NYR	75	32	45	77	59	-11
89–90	NYR	41	9	17	26	57	+4
90–91	Hart–Calg	57	11	18	29	18	-13
91–92	Calg	42	11	12	23	37	-6
92–93	Calg	22	4	7	11	8	+10
Totals		552	169	258	427	314	+3

SSN	TEAM	GP	G	A	PTS.	PIM
Playoffs						
83–84	Calg	6	3	1	4	2
84–85	Calg	4	0	0	0	0
85–86	Calg	9	0	2	2	2
86–87	Calg	6	1	1	2	6
87–88	Hart	6	2	4	6	2
88–89	NYR	4	1	2	3	2
89–90	NYR	10	2	1	3	0
90–91	Calg	7	2	2	4	0
Totals		52	11	13	24	14

*WILSON, Carol (Cully) RW
B. 1893

SSN	TEAM	GP	G	A	PTS.	PIM
19–20	Tor	23	21	5	26	79
20–21	Tor–Mont	17	8	2	10	16
21–22	Ham	23	7	9	16	21
22–23	Ham	23	16	3	19	46
26–27	Chi	39	8	4	12	40
Totals		125	60	23	83	202

SSN	TEAM	GP	G	A	PTS.	PIM
Playoffs						
26–27	Chi	2	1	0	1	6

WILSON, Douglas Jr. 6–1 187 D
B. Ottawa, Ont., July 5, 1957

SSN	TEAM	GP	G	A	PTS.	PIM	+/-
77–78	Chi	77	14	20	34	72	+11
78–79	Chi	56	5	21	26	37	+4
79–80	Chi	73	12	49	61	70	-5
80–81	Chi	76	12	39	51	80	+6
81–82	Chi	76	39	46	85	54	+1
82–83	Chi	74	18	51	69	58	+22
83–84	Chi	66	13	45	58	64	-11
84–85	Chi	78	22	54	76	44	+23
85–86	Chi	79	17	47	64	80	+24
86–87	Chi	69	16	32	48	36	+15
87–88	Chi	27	8	24	32	28	-17
88–89	Chi	66	15	47	62	69	+8
89–90	Chi	70	23	50	73	40	+13
90–91	Chi	51	11	29	40	32	+25
91–92	SJ	44	9	19	28	26	-38
92–93	SJ	42	3	17	20	40	-28
Totals		1024	237	590	827	830	+53

SSN	TEAM	GP	G	A	PTS.	PIM
Playoffs						
77–78	Chi	4	0	0	0	0
79–80	Chi	7	2	8	10	6
80–81	Chi	3	0	3	3	2
81–82	Chi	15	3	10	13	32
82–83	Chi	13	4	11	15	12
83–84	Chi	5	0	3	3	2
84–85	Chi	12	3	10	13	12
85–86	Chi	3	1	1	2	2
86–87	Chi	4	0	0	0	0
88–89	Chi	4	1	2	3	0
89–90	Chi	20	3	12	15	18
90–91	Chi	5	2	1	3	2
Totals		95	19	61	80	88

WILSON, Gordon Allan 6–1 185 LW
B. Port Arthur, Ont., Aug. 13, 1932

SSN	TEAM	GP	G	A	PTS.	PIM
Playoffs						
54–55	Bos	2	0	0	0	0

WILSON, James (Hub) 5–10 180 LW
B. Ottawa, Ont., May 13, 1909

SSN	TEAM	GP	G	A	PTS.	PIM
31–32	NYA	2	0	0	0	0

WILSON, Jerold (Jerry) 6–2 200 F
B. Edmonton, Alta., Apr. 10, 1937

SSN	TEAM	GP	G	A	PTS.	PIM
56–57	Mont	3	0	0	0	2

WILSON, John Edward (Iron Man) 5–10 175 LW
B. Kincardine, Ont., June 14, 1929

SSN	TEAM	GP	G	A	PTS.	PIM
49–50	Det	1	0	0	0	0
51–52	Det	28	4	5	9	18
52–53	Det	70	23	19	42	22
53–54	Det	70	17	17	34	22
54–55	Det	70	12	15	27	14
55–56	Det	70	24	9	33	12
56–57	Chi	70	18	30	48	24
57–58	Det	70	12	27	39	14
58–59	Det	70	11	17	28	18
59–60	Tor	70	15	16	31	8
60–61	Tor–NYR	59	14	13	27	24
61–62	NYR	40	11	3	14	14
Totals		688	161	171	332	190

SSN	TEAM	GP	G	A	PTS.	PIM
Playoffs						
49–50	Det	8	0	1	1	0
50–51	Det	1	0	0	0	0
51–52	Det	8	4	1	5	5
52–53	Det	6	2	5	7	0
53–54	Det	12	3	0	3	0
54–55	Det	11	0	1	1	0
57–58	Det	4	2	1	3	0
59–60	Tor	10	1	2	3	2
61–62	NYR	6	2	2	4	4

SSN	TEAM	GP	G	A	PTS.	PIM	+/-
Totals		66	14	13	27	11	

WILSON, Landon 6-2 202 RW
B. St. Louis, Mo., Mar. 15, 1975

SSN	TEAM	GP	G	A	PTS.	PIM	+/-
95-96	Col A	7	1	0	1	6	+3
96-97	Col A-Bos	49	8	12	20	72	-5
97-98	Bos	28	1	5	6	7	+3
98-99	Bos	22	3	3	6	17	0
Totals		106	13	20	33	102	+1

Playoffs
97-98	Bos	1	0	0	0	0	
98-99	Bos	8	1	1	2	8	
Totals		9	1	1	2	8	

*WILSON, Lawrence 5-11 170 C
B. Kincardine, Ont., Oct. 23, 1930

49-50	Det	1	0	0	0	2	
51-52	Det	5	0	0	0	4	
52-53	Det	15	0	4	4	6	
53-54	Chi	66	9	33	42	22	
54-55	Chi	63	12	11	23	39	
55-56	Chi	2	0	0	0	2	
Totals		152	21	48	69	75	

Playoffs
| 49-50 | Det | 4 | 0 | 0 | 0 | 0 | |

WILSON, Mike 6-5 180 D
B. Brampton, Ont., Feb. 26, 1975

95-96	Buf	58	4	8	12	41	+13
96-97	Buf	77	2	9	11	51	+13
97-98	Buf	66	4	4	8	48	+13
98-99	Buf-Fla	34	1	2	3	47	+12
Totals		235	11	23	34	187	+51

Playoffs
96-97	Buf	10	0	1	1	2	
97-98	Buf	15	0	1	1	13	
Totals		25	0	2	2	15	

WILSON, Mitch 5-8 199 RW
B. Kelowna, B.C., Feb. 15, 1962

84-85	NJ	9	0	2	2	21	+1
86-87	Pitt	17	2	1	3	83	-3
Totals		26	2	3	5	104	-2

WILSON, Murray Charles 6-1 185 LW
B. Ottawa, Ont., Aug. 3, 1951

72-73	Mont	52	18	9	27	16	+14
73-74	Mont	72	17	14	31	26	+4
74-75	Mont	73	24	18	42	44	+13
75-76	Mont	59	11	24	35	36	+25
76-77	Mont	60	13	14	27	26	+25
77-78	Mont	12	0	1	1	0	-1
78-79	LA	58	11	15	26	14	-7
Totals		386	94	95	189	162	+73

Playoffs
72-73	Mont	16	2	4	6	6	
73-74	Mont	5	1	0	1	2	
74-75	Mont	5	0	3	3	4	
75-76	Mont	12	1	1	2	6	
76-77	Mont	14	1	6	7	14	
78-79	LA	1	0	0	0	0	
Totals		53	5	14	19	32	

WILSON, Richard Gordon (Rick) 6-1 195 D
B. Prince Albert, Sask., Aug. 10, 1950

73-74	Mont	21	0	2	2	6	+8
74-75	StL	76	2	5	7	83	+12
75-76	StL	65	1	6	7	20	-10
76-77	Det	77	3	13	16	56	-20
Totals		239	6	26	32	165	-10

Playoffs
74-75	StL	2	0	0	0	0	
75-76	StL	1	0	0	0	0	
Totals		3	0	0	0	0	

WILSON, Richard William (Rik) 6-0 185 D
B. Long Beach, Cal., June 17, 1962

81-82	StL	48	3	18	21	24	-10
82-83	StL	56	3	11	14	50	-10
83-84	StL	48	7	11	18	53	+4
84-85	StL	51	8	16	24	39	+14
85-86	StL-Calg	34	0	4	4	48	-7
87-88	Chi	14	4	5	9	6	+4
Totals		251	25	65	90	220	-5

Playoffs
81-82	StL	9	0	3	3	14	
83-84	StL	11	0	0	0	9	
84-85	StL	2	0	1	1	0	
Totals		22	0	4	4	23	

WILSON, Robert Wayne 5-9 178 D
B. Sudbury, Ont., Feb. 18, 1934

| 53-54 | Chi | 1 | 0 | 0 | 0 | 0 | |

WILSON, Roger Sidney 6-2 210 D
B. Sudbury, Ont., Sept. 18, 1946

| 74-75 | Chi | 7 | 0 | 2 | 2 | 6 | +1 |

WILSON, Ronald Lawrence 5-10 170 D
B. Windsor, Ont., May 28, 1955

77-78	Tor	13	2	1	3	0	-5
78-79	Tor	46	5	12	17	4	-10
79-80	Tor	5	0	2	2	2	-2
84-85	Minn	13	4	8	12	2	-1
85-86	Minn	11	1	3	4	8	-2
86-87	Minn	65	12	29	41	36	-9
87-88	Minn	24	2	12	14	16	-4
Totals		177	26	67	93	68	-33

Playoffs
78-79	Tor	3	0	1	1	0	
79-80	Tor	3	1	2	3	2	
85-86	Minn	5	2	4	6	4	
Totals		11	3	7	10	6	

WILSON, Ronald Lee 5-9 180 C
B. Toronto, Ont., May 13, 1956

79-80	Winn	79	21	36	57	28	-12
80-81	Winn	77	18	33	51	55	-34
81-82	Winn	39	3	13	16	49	-3
82-83	Winn	12	6	3	9	4	+7
83-84	Winn	51	3	12	15	12	-3
84-85	Winn	75	10	9	19	31	-8
85-86	Winn	54	6	7	13	16	-2
86-87	Winn	80	3	13	16	13	+10
87-88	Winn	69	5	8	13	28	-1
89-90	StL	33	3	17	20	23	+5
90-91	StL	73	10	27	37	54	-1
91-92	StL	64	12	17	29	46	+10
92-93	StL	78	8	11	19	44	-8
93-94	Mont	48	2	10	12	12	-2
Totals		832	110	216	326	415	-42

Playoffs
82-83	Winn	3	2	2	4	2	
84-85	Winn	7	4	2	6	2	
85-86	Winn	1	0	0	0	0	
86-87	Winn	10	1	2	3	0	
87-88	Winn	1	0	0	0	2	
89-90	StL	12	3	5	8	18	
90-91	StL	7	0	0	0	28	
91-92	StL	6	0	1	1	0	
92-93	StL	11	0	0	0	12	
93-94	Mont	4	0	0	0	0	
Totals		63	10	12	22	64	

WILSON, Wallace Lloyd 5-11 165 C
B. Berwick, N.S., May 25, 1921

| 47-48 | Bos | 53 | 11 | 8 | 19 | 18 | |

Playoffs
| 47-48 | Bos | 1 | 0 | 0 | 0 | 0 | |

WING, Murray Allan 5-11 180 D
B. Thunder Bay, Ont., Oct. 14, 1950

| 73-74 | Det | 1 | 0 | 1 | 1 | 0 | -2 |

WINNES, Christopher 6-0 201 RW
B. Ridgefield, Conn., Feb. 12, 1968

91-92	Bos	24	1	3	4	6	-6
92-93	Bos	5	0	1	1	0	+1
93-94	Phil	4	0	2	2	0	+1
Totals		33	1	6	7	6	-4

Playoffs
| 90-91 | Bos | 1 | 0 | 0 | 0 | 0 | |

WISEMAN, Brian 5-8 175 C
B. Chatham, Ont., July 13, 1971

| 96-97 | Tor | 3 | 0 | 0 | 0 | 0 | 0 |

*WISEMAN, Edward Randall 5-7 160 RW
B. Newcastle, N.B., Dec. 28, 1912

32-33	Det	47	8	8	16	16	
33-34	Det	47	5	9	14	13	
34-35	Det	40	11	13	24	14	
35-36	Det-NYA	43	12	15	27	16	
36-37	NYA	43	14	19	33	12	
37-38	NYA	48	18	14	32	32	
38-39	NYA	45	12	21	33	8	
39-40	NYA-Bos	49	7	19	26	8	
40-41	Bos	47	16	24	40	10	
41-42	Bos	45	12	22	34	8	
Totals		454	115	164	279	137	

Playoffs
32-33	Det	2	0	0	0	0	
33-34	Det	9	0	1	1	4	
35-36	NYA	4	2	1	3	0	
37-38	NYA	6	0	4	4	10	
38-39	NYA	2	0	0	0	0	
39-40	Bos	6	2	1	3	2	
40-41	Bos	11	6	2	8	0	
41-42	Bos	5	0	1	1	0	
Totals		45	10	10	20	16	

WISTE, James Andrew 5-10 185 C
B. Moose Jaw, Sask., Feb. 18, 1946

68-69	Chi	3	0	0	0	0	+1
69-70	Chi	26	0	8	8	8	0
70-71	Van	23	1	2	3	0	-8
72-73	Clev (WHA)	70	28	43	71	24	
73-74	Clev (WHA)	76	23	35	58	26	
74-75	Ind (WHA)	75	13	28	41	30	
75-76	Ind (WHA)	7	0	2	2	0	
NHL Totals		52	1	10	11	8	-7
WHA Totals		228	64	108	172	80	

Playoffs
72-73	Clev (WHA)	9	3	8	11	13	
73-74	Clev (WHA)	5	0	1	1	0	
WHA Totals		14	3	9	12	13	

WITEHALL, Johan 6-1 198 LW
B. Kungsbacka, Sweden, Jan. 7, 1972

| 98-99 | NYR | 4 | 0 | 0 | 0 | 0 | 0 |

WITHERSPOON, James Douglas 6-3 205 D
B. Toronto, Ont., Oct. 3, 1951

| 75-76 | LA | 2 | 0 | 0 | 0 | 2 | -1 |

WITIUK, Stephen 5-7 165 RW
B. Winnipeg, Man., Jan. 8, 1929

| 51-52 | Chi | 33 | 3 | 8 | 11 | 14 | |

WITT, Brendan 6-1 205 D
B. Humboldt, Sask., Feb. 20, 1975

95-96	Wash	48	2	3	5	85	-4
96-97	Wash	44	3	2	5	88	-20
97-98	Wash	64	1	7	8	112	-11
98-99	Wash	54	2	5	7	87	-6
Totals		220	8	17	25	372	-41

Playoffs
| 97-98 | Wash | 16 | 1 | 0 | 1 | 14 | |

WOIT, Benedict Francis (Benny) 5-11 190 D
B. Fort William, Ont., Jan. 7, 1928

50-51	Det	2	0	0	0	0	
51-52	Det	58	3	8	11	20	
52-53	Det	70	1	5	6	40	
53-54	Det	70	0	2	2	38	
54-55	Det	62	2	3	5	22	
55-56	Chi	63	1	8	9	46	
56-57	Chi	9	0	0	0	2	
Totals		334	7	26	33	168	

Playoffs
| 50-51 | Det | 4 | 0 | 0 | 0 | 2 | |
| 51-52 | Det | 8 | 1 | 1 | 2 | 2 | |

SSN	TEAM	GP	G	A	PTS.	PIM	+/-
52–53	Det	6	1	3	4	0	
53–54	Det	12	0	1	1	8	
54–55	Det	11	0	1	1	6	
Totals		41	2	6	8	18	

WOJCIECHOWSKI, Stephen (Wochy) *5-8 160 RW*
B. Fort William, Ont., Dec. 25, 1922

SSN	TEAM	GP	G	A	PTS.	PIM	+/-
44–45	Det	49	19	20	39	17	
46–47	Det	5	0	0	0	0	
Totals		54	19	20	39	17	

Playoffs

| 44–45 | Det | 6 | 0 | 1 | 1 | 0 | |

WOLANIN, Craig *6-3 205 D*
B. Grosse Pointe, Mich., July 27, 1967

85–86	NJ	44	2	16	18	74	-7
86–87	NJ	68	4	6	10	109	-31
87–88	NJ	78	6	25	31	170	0
88–89	NJ	56	3	8	11	69	-9
89–90	NJ–Que	50	1	10	11	57	-11
90–91	Que	80	5	13	18	89	-13
91–92	Que	69	2	11	13	80	-12
92–93	Que	24	1	4	5	49	+9
93–94	Que	63	6	10	16	80	+16
94–95	Que	40	3	6	9	40	+12
95–96	Col A	75	7	20	27	50	+25
96–97	TB–Tor	38	0	4	4	21	-6
97–98	Tor	10	0	0	0	6	-9
Totals		695	40	133	173	894	-36

Playoffs

87–88	NJ	18	2	5	7	51	
92–93	Que	4	0	0	0	4	
94–95	Que	6	1	1	2	4	
95–96	Col A	7	1	0	1	8	
Totals		35	4	6	10	67	

WOLF, Bennett Martin *6-3 205 D*
B. Kitchener, Ont., Oct. 23, 1959

80–81	Pitt	24	0	1	1	94	-1
81–82	Pitt	1	0	0	0	2	0
82–83	Pitt	5	0	0	0	37	-2
Totals		30	0	1	1	133	-3

WONG, Michael Anthony *6-3 205 C*
B. Minneapolis, Minn., Jan. 14, 1955

| 75–76 | Det | 22 | 1 | 1 | 2 | 12 | |

WOOD, Dody *5-11 181 C*
B. Chetwynd, B.C., Mar. 10, 1972

92–93	SJ	13	1	1	2	71	-5
94–95	SJ	9	1	1	2	29	0
95–96	SJ	32	3	6	9	138	0
96–97	SJ	44	3	2	5	193	-3
97–98	SJ	8	0	0	0	40	-3
Totals		106	8	10	18	471	-11

WOOD, Randy *6-0 195 LW/C*
B. Princeton, N.J., Oct. 12, 1963

86–87	NYI	6	1	0	1	4	-1
87–88	NYI	75	22	16	38	80	-2
88–89	NYI	77	15	13	28	44	-18
89–90	NYI	74	24	24	48	39	-10
90–91	NYI	76	24	18	42	45	-12
91–92	NYI–Buf	78	22	18	40	86	-12
92–93	Buf	82	18	25	43	77	+6
93–94	Buf	84	22	16	38	71	+11
94–95	Tor	48	13	11	24	34	+7
95–96	Tor–Dal	76	8	13	21	62	-15
96–97	NYI	65	6	5	11	61	-7
Totals		741	175	159	334	603	-53

Playoffs

86–87	NYI	13	1	3	4	14	
87–88	NYI	5	1	0	1	6	
89–90	NYI	5	1	1	2	4	
91–92	Buf	7	2	1	3	6	
92–93	Buf	8	1	4	5	4	
93–94	Buf	6	0	0	0	0	
94–95	Tor	7	2	0	2	6	
Totals		51	8	9	17	40	

WOOD, Robert Owen *6-1 185 D*
B. Lethbridge, Alta., July 9, 1930

| 50–51 | NYR | 1 | 0 | 0 | 0 | 0 | |

WOODLEY, Dan *5-11 185 RW*
B. Oklahoma City, Okla., Dec. 29, 1967

| 87–88 | Van | 5 | 2 | 0 | 2 | 17 | +1 |

WOODS, Paul William *5-10 170 LW*
B. Hespeler, Ont., Apr. 12, 1955

77–78	Det	80	19	23	42	52	+18
78–79	Det	80	14	23	37	59	-26
79–80	Det	79	6	20	26	24	-19
80–81	Det	67	8	16	24	45	-10
81–82	Det	75	10	17	27	48	-5
82–83	Det	63	13	20	33	30	-2
83–84	Det	57	2	5	7	18	-16
Totals		501	72	124	196	276	-60

Playoffs

| 77–78 | Det | 7 | 0 | 5 | 5 | 4 | |

WOOLLEY, Jason Douglas *6-0 186 D*
B. Toronto, Ont., July 27, 1969

91–92	Wash	1	0	0	0	0	+1
92–93	Wash	26	0	2	2	10	+3
93–94	Wash	10	1	2	3	4	+2
94–95	Fla	34	4	9	13	18	-1
95–96	Fla	52	6	28	34	32	-9
96–97	Fla–Pitt	60	6	30	36	30	+4
97–98	Buf	71	9	26	35	35	+8
98–99	Buf	80	10	33	43	62	+16
Totals		334	36	130	166	191	+24

Playoffs

93–94	Wash	4	1	0	1	4	
95–96	Fla	13	2	6	8	14	
96–97	Pitt	5	0	3	3	0	
97–98	Buf	15	2	9	11	12	
98–99	Buf	21	4	11	15	10	
Totals		58	9	29	38	40	

WORRELL, Peter *6-6 225 LW*
B. Pierrefonds, Que., Aug. 18, 1977

97–98	Fla	19	0	0	0	153	-4
98–99	Fla	62	4	5	9	268	0
Totals		81	4	5	9	421	-4

WORTMAN, Kevin *6-0 200 D*
B. Sagus, Mass., Feb. 22, 1969

| 93–94 | Calg | 5 | 0 | 0 | 0 | 2 | +1 |

WOTTON, Mark *5-11 187 D*
B. Foxwarren, Man., Nov. 16, 1973

94–95	Van	1	0	0	0	0	+1
96–97	Van	36	3	6	9	19	+8
97–98	Van	5	0	0	0	6	-2
Totals		42	3	6	9	25	+7

Playoffs

| 94–95 | Van | 5 | 0 | 0 | 0 | 4 | |

*WOYTOWICH, Robert Ivan *5-11 195 D*
B. Winnipeg, Man., Aug. 18, 1941

64–65	Bos	21	2	10	12	16	
65–66	Bos	68	2	17	19	75	
66–67	Bos	64	2	7	9	43	
67–68	Minn	66	4	17	21	63	-23
68–69	Pitt	71	9	20	29	62	-26
69–70	Pitt	68	8	25	33	49	-12
70–71	Pitt	78	4	22	26	30	+8
71–72	Pitt–LA	67	1	8	9	14	-27
72–73	Winn (WHA)	62	2	4	6	47	
73–74	Winn (WHA)	72	6	28	34	43	
74–75	Winn–Ind (WHA)	66	0	12	12	36	
75–76	Ind (WHA)	42	1	7	8	14	
NHL Totals		503	32	126	158	352	-80
WHA Totals		242	9	51	60	140	

Playoffs

67–68	Minn	14	0	1	1	18	
69–70	Pitt	10	1	2	3	2	
72–73	Winn (WHA)	14	1	1	2	4	
73–74	Winn (WHA)	4	0	0	0	0	
NHL Totals		24	1	3	4	20	

| **WHA Totals** | | 18 | 1 | 1 | 2 | 4 | |

WREN, Bob *5-10 185 LW*
B. Preston, Ont., Sept. 16, 1974

| 97–98 | Ana | 3 | 0 | 0 | 0 | 0 | 0 |

WRIGHT, Jamie *6-0 172 LW*
B. Kitchener, Ont., May 13, 1976

97–98	Dal	21	4	2	6	2	+8
98–99	Dal	11	0	0	0	0	-3
Totals		32	4	2	6	2	+5

Playoffs

| 97–98 | Dal | 5 | 0 | 0 | 0 | 0 | |

WRIGHT, John Gilbert Brereton *5-11 175 C*
B. Toronto, Ont., Nov. 9, 1948

72–73	Van	71	10	27	37	32	-16
73–74	Van–StL	52	6	9	15	33	-3
74–75	KC	4	0	0	0	2	-3
Totals		127	16	36	52	67	-22

WRIGHT, Keith Edward *6-0 180 LW*
B. Newmarket, Ont., Apr. 13, 1944

| 67–68 | Phil | 1 | 0 | 0 | 0 | 0 | +1 |

WRIGHT, Larry Dale *6-1 180 C*
B. Regina, Sask., Oct. 8, 1951

71–72	Phil	27	0	1	1	2	-6
72–73	Phil	9	0	1	1	4	-3
74–75	Cal	2	0	0	0	0	-2
75–76	Phil	2	1	0	1	0	+1
77–78	Det	66	3	6	9	13	-12
Totals		106	4	8	12	19	-22

WRIGHT, Tyler *5-11 185 C*
B. Canora, Sask., Apr. 6, 1973

92–93	Edm	7	1	1	2	19	-4
93–94	Edm	5	0	0	0	4	-3
94–95	Edm	6	1	0	1	14	+1
95–96	Edm	23	1	0	1	33	-7
96–97	Pitt	45	2	2	4	70	-7
97–98	Pitt	82	3	4	7	112	-3
98–99	Pitt	61	0	0	0	90	-2
Totals		249	8	7	15	342	-25

Playoffs

97–98	Pitt	6	0	1	1	4	
98–99	Pitt	13	0	0	0	19	
Totals		19	0	1	1	23	

WYCHERLEY, Ralph H. (Bus) *6-0 185 LW*
B. Saskatoon, Sask., Feb. 26, 1920

40–41	NYA	26	4	5	9	4	
41–42	Brk	2	0	2	2	2	
Totals		28	4	7	11	6	

WYLIE, Duane Steven *5-8 170 C*
B. Spokane, Wash., Nov. 10, 1950

74–75	Chi	6	1	3	4	2	-1
76–77	Chi	8	2	0	2	0	-4
Totals		14	3	3	6	2	-5

*WYLIE, William Vance (Wiggie) *5-8 145 C*
B. Galt, Ont., July 15, 1928

| 50–51 | NYR | 1 | 0 | 0 | 0 | 0 | |

WYROZUB, William Randall (Randy) *5-11 170 C*
B. Lacombe, Alta., Apr. 8, 1950

70–71	Buf	16	2	2	4	6	-9
71–72	Buf	34	3	4	7	0	-2
72–73	Buf	45	3	3	6	4	-1
73–74	Buf	5	0	1	1	0	-1
75–76	Ind (WHA)	55	11	14	25	8	
NHL Totals		100	8	10	18	10	-13
WHA Totals		55	11	14	25	8	

YACHMENEV, Vitali *5-9 180 RW*
B. Chelyabinsk, U.S.S.R., Jan. 8, 1975

95–96	LA	80	19	34	53	16	-3
96–97	LA	65	10	22	32	10	-9
97–98	LA	4	0	1	1	4	+1
98–99	Nash	55	7	10	17	10	-10

SSN	TEAM	GP	G	A	PTS.	PIM	+/-
Totals		204	36	67	103	40	-21

*YACKEL, Kenneth James *F*
B. St. Paul, Minn., Mar. 5, 1932

SSN	TEAM	GP	G	A	PTS.	PIM	+/-
58–59	Bos	6	0	0	0	2	

Playoffs

SSN	TEAM	GP	G	A	PTS.	PIM	+/-
58–59	Bos	2	0	0	0	2	

YAKE, Terry *5–11 190 RW*
B. New Westminster, B.C., Oct. 22, 1968

SSN	TEAM	GP	G	A	PTS.	PIM	+/-
88–89	Hart	2	0	0	0	0	+1
89–90	Hart	2	0	1	1	0	-1
90–91	Hart	19	1	4	5	10	-3
91–92	Hart	15	1	1	2	4	-2
92–93	Hart	66	22	31	53	46	+3
93–94	Ana	82	21	31	52	44	+2
94–95	Tor	19	3	2	5	2	+1
97–98	StL	65	10	15	25	38	+1
98–99	StL	60	9	18	27	34	-9
Totals		330	67	103	170	178	-7

Playoffs

SSN	TEAM	GP	G	A	PTS.	PIM	+/-
90–91	Hart	6	1	1	2	16	
97–98	StL	10	2	1	3	6	
98–99	StL	13	1	2	3	14	
Totals		29	4	4	8	36	

YAREMCHUK, Gary *6–0 185 C*
B. Edmonton, Alta., Aug. 15, 1961

SSN	TEAM	GP	G	A	PTS.	PIM	+/-
81–82	Tor	18	0	3	3	10	-7
82–83	Tor	3	0	0	0	2	-1
83–84	Tor	1	0	0	0	0	-1
84–85	Tor	12	1	1	2	16	-7
Totals		34	1	4	5	28	-16

YAREMCHUK, Ken *5–11 185 C*
B. Edmonton, Alta., Jan. 1, 1964

SSN	TEAM	GP	G	A	PTS.	PIM	+/-
83–84	Chi	47	6	7	13	19	-7
84–85	Chi	63	10	16	26	16	-6
85–86	Chi	78	14	20	34	43	-17
86–87	Tor	20	3	8	11	16	0
87–88	Tor	16	2	5	7	10	-7
88–89	Tor	11	1	0	1	2	-8
Totals		235	36	56	92	106	-42

Playoffs

SSN	TEAM	GP	G	A	PTS.	PIM	+/-
83–84	Chi	1	0	0	0	0	
84–85	Chi	15	5	5	10	37	
85–86	Chi	3	1	1	2	2	
86–87	Tor	6	0	0	0	0	
87–88	Tor	6	0	2	2	10	
Totals		31	6	8	14	49	

YASHIN, Alexei *6–3 215 C*
B. Sverdlovsk, USSR, Nov. 5, 1973

SSN	TEAM	GP	G	A	PTS.	PIM	+/-
93–94	Ott	83	30	49	79	22	-49
94–95	Ott	47	21	23	44	20	-20
95–96	Ott	46	15	24	39	28	-15
96–97	Ott	82	35	40	75	44	-7
97–98	Ott	82	33	39	72	24	+6
98–99	Ott	82	44	50	94	54	+16
Totals		422	178	225	403	192	-69

Playoffs

SSN	TEAM	GP	G	A	PTS.	PIM	+/-
96–97	Ott	7	1	5	6	2	
97–98	Ott	11	5	3	8	8	
98–99	Ott	4	0	0	0	10	
Totals		22	6	8	14	20	

YATES, Richard (Ross) *6–0 180 C*
B. Montreal, Que., June 18, 1959

SSN	TEAM	GP	G	A	PTS.	PIM	+/-
83–84	Hart	7	1	1	2	4	0

YAWNEY, Trent *6–3 192 D*
B. Hudson Bay, Sask., Sept. 29, 1965

SSN	TEAM	GP	G	A	PTS.	PIM	+/-
87–88	Chi	15	2	8	10	15	-1
88–89	Chi	69	5	19	24	116	-5
89–90	Chi	70	5	15	20	82	-6
90–91	Chi	61	3	13	16	77	+6
91–92	Calg	47	4	9	13	45	-5
92–93	Calg	63	1	16	17	67	+9
93–94	Calg	58	6	15	21	60	+21
94–95	Calg	37	0	2	2	108	-4
95–96	Calg	69	0	3	3	88	-1
96–97	StL	39	0	2	2	17	+2
97–98	Chi	45	1	0	1	76	-5
98–99	Chi	20	0	0	0	32	-6
Totals		593	27	102	129	783	+5

Playoffs

SSN	TEAM	GP	G	A	PTS.	PIM	+/-
87–88	Chi	5	0	4	4	8	
88–89	Chi	15	3	6	9	20	
89–90	Chi	20	3	5	8	27	
90–91	Chi	1	0	0	0	0	
92–93	Calg	6	3	2	5	6	
93–94	Calg	7	0	0	0	16	
94–95	Calg	2	0	0	0	2	
95–96	Calg	4	0	0	0	2	
Totals		60	9	17	26	81	

YEGOROV, Alexei *5–9 174 C*
B. Leningrad, U.S.S.R., May 21, 1975

SSN	TEAM	GP	G	A	PTS.	PIM	+/-
95–96	SJ	9	3	2	5	2	-5
96–97	SJ	2	0	1	1	0	+1
Totals		11	3	3	6	2	-4

YELLE, Stephane *6–1 162 C*
B. Ottawa, Ont., May 9, 1974

SSN	TEAM	GP	G	A	PTS.	PIM	+/-
95–96	Col A	71	13	14	27	30	+15
96–97	Col A	79	9	17	26	38	+1
97–98	Col A	81	7	15	22	48	-10
98–99	Col A	72	8	7	15	40	-8
Totals		303	37	53	90	156	-2

Playoffs

SSN	TEAM	GP	G	A	PTS.	PIM	+/-
95–96	Col A	22	1	4	5	8	
96–97	Col A	12	1	6	7	2	
97–98	Col A	7	1	0	1	12	
98–99	Col A	10	0	1	1	6	
Totals		51	3	11	14	28	

YLONEN, Juha *6–0 180 C*
B. Helsinki, Finland, Feb. 13, 1972

SSN	TEAM	GP	G	A	PTS.	PIM	+/-
96–97	Phoe	2	0	0	0	0	0
97–98	Phoe	55	1	11	12	10	-3
98–99	Phoe	59	6	17	23	20	+18
Totals		116	7	28	35	30	+15

Playoffs

SSN	TEAM	GP	G	A	PTS.	PIM	+/-
98–99	Phoe	2	0	2	2	2	

YORK, Harry *6–2 215 C*
B. Panoka, Alta., April 16, 1974

SSN	TEAM	GP	G	A	PTS.	PIM	+/-
96–97	StL	74	14	18	32	24	+1
97–98	StL–NYR	60	4	6	10	31	-1
98–99	NYR–Pitt–Van	56	7	9	16	24	-3
Totals		190	25	33	58	79	-3

Playoffs

SSN	TEAM	GP	G	A	PTS.	PIM	+/-
96–97	StL	5	0	0	0	2	

YORK, Jason *6–2 195 D*
B. Ottawa, Ont., May 20, 1970

SSN	TEAM	GP	G	A	PTS.	PIM	+/-
92–93	Det	2	0	0	0	0	0
93–94	Det	7	1	2	3	2	0
94–95	Det–Ana	25	1	10	11	14	+4
95–96	Ana	79	3	21	24	88	-7
96–97	Ott	75	4	17	21	67	-8
97–98	Ott	73	3	13	16	62	+8
98–99	Ott	79	4	31	35	48	+17
Totals		340	15	94	109	281	+14

Playoffs

SSN	TEAM	GP	G	A	PTS.	PIM	+/-
96–97	Ott	7	0	0	0	4	
97–98	Ott	7	1	1	2	7	
98–99	Ott	4	1	1	2	4	
Totals		18	2	2	4	15	

YOUNG, Brian Donald *6–1 183 D*
B. Jasper, Alta., Oct. 2, 1958

SSN	TEAM	GP	G	A	PTS.	PIM	+/-
80–81	Chi	8	0	2	2	6	-4

YOUNG, C.J. *5–10 180 RW*
B. Waban, Mass., Jan. 1, 1968

SSN	TEAM	GP	G	A	PTS.	PIM	+/-
92–93	Calg–Bos	43	7	7	14	32	-6

*YOUNG, Douglas G. *5–9 190 D*
B. Medicine Hat, Alta., Oct. 1, 1908

SSN	TEAM	GP	G	A	PTS.	PIM	+/-
31–32	Det	47	10	2	12	45	
32–33	Det	48	5	6	11	59	
33–34	Det	48	4	0	4	36	
34–35	Det	48	4	6	10	37	
35–36	Det	48	5	12	17	54	
36–37	Det	10	0	0	0	6	
37–38	Det	48	3	5	8	24	
38–39	Det	44	1	5	6	16	
39–40	Mont	47	3	9	12	22	
40–41	Mont	3	0	0	0	4	
Totals		391	35	45	80	303	

Playoffs

SSN	TEAM	GP	G	A	PTS.	PIM	+/-
31–32	Det	2	0	0	0	2	
32–33	Det	4	1	1	2	0	
33–34	Det	9	0	0	0	10	
35–36	Det	7	0	2	2	0	
38–39	Det	6	0	2	2	4	
Totals		28	1	5	6	16	

YOUNG, Howard John Edward *6–0 190 D*
B. Toronto, Ont., Aug. 2, 1937

SSN	TEAM	GP	G	A	PTS.	PIM	+/-
60–61	Det	29	0	8	8	108	
61–62	Det	30	0	2	2	67	
62–63	Det	64	4	5	9	273	
63–64	Chi	39	0	7	7	99	
66–67	Det	44	3	14	17	100	
67–68	Det	62	2	17	19	112	+16
68–69	Chi	57	3	7	10	67	-13
70–71	Van	11	0	2	2	25	-7
74–75	Phoe–Winn (WHA)	72	16	22	38	86	
76–77	Phoe (WHA)	26	1	3	4	23	
NHL Totals		336	12	62	74	851	-4
WHA Totals		98	17	25	42	109	

Playoffs

SSN	TEAM	GP	G	A	PTS.	PIM	+/-
60–61	Det	11	2	2	4	30	
62–63	Det	8	0	2	2	16	
Totals		19	2	4	6	46	

YOUNG, Scott Allen *6–0 190 RW*
B. Clinton, Mass., Oct. 1, 1967

SSN	TEAM	GP	G	A	PTS.	PIM	+/-
87–88	Hart	7	0	0	0	2	-6
88–89	Hart	76	19	40	59	27	-21
89–90	Hart	80	24	40	64	47	-24
90–91	Hart–Pitt	77	15	25	42	41	-6
92–93	Que	82	30	30	60	20	+5
93–94	Que	76	26	25	51	14	-4
94–95	Que	48	18	21	39	14	+9
95–96	Col A	81	21	39	60	50	+2
96–97	Col A	72	18	19	37	14	-5
97–98	Ana	73	13	20	33	22	-13
98–99	StL	75	24	28	52	27	+8
Totals		747	210	287	497	278	-55

Playoffs

SSN	TEAM	GP	G	A	PTS.	PIM	+/-
87–88	Hart	4	1	0	1	0	
88–89	Hart	4	2	0	2	4	
89–90	Hart	7	2	0	2	2	
90–91	Pitt	17	1	6	7	2	
92–93	Que	6	4	1	5	0	
94–95	Que	6	3	3	6	2	
95–96	Col A	22	3	12	15	10	
96–97	Col A	17	4	2	6	14	
98–99	StL	13	4	7	11	10	
Totals		96	24	31	55	44	

YOUNG, Timothy Michael *6–1 190 C*
B. Scarborough, Ont., Feb. 22, 1955

SSN	TEAM	GP	G	A	PTS.	PIM	+/-
75–76	Minn	63	18	33	51	71	-10
76–77	Minn	80	29	66	95	58	-32
77–78	Minn	78	23	35	58	64	-37
78–79	Minn	73	24	32	56	46	-12
79–80	Minn	77	31	43	74	24	+14
80–81	Minn	74	25	41	66	40	+6
81–82	Minn	49	10	31	41	67	0
82–83	Minn	70	18	35	53	31	+4
83–84	Winn	44	15	19	34	25	-11
84–85	Phil	20	2	6	8	12	+2
Totals		628	195	341	536	438	-81

Playoffs

SSN	TEAM	GP	G	A	PTS.	PIM	+/-
76–77	Minn	2	1	1	2	2	
79–80	Minn	15	2	5	7	4	
80–81	Minn	12	3	14	17	9	
81–82	Minn	4	1	1	2	10	
82–83	Minn	2	0	2	2	2	
Totals		35	7	23	30	27	

SSN	TEAM	GP	G	A	PTS.	PIM	+/-
YOUNG, Warren Howard *6-3 195 C*							
B. Toronto, Ont., Jan. 11, 1956							
81–82	Minn	1	0	0	0	0	-3
82–83	Minn	4	1	1	2	0	0
83–84	Pitt	15	1	7	8	19	-2
84–85	Pitt	80	40	32	72	174	-20
85–86	Det	79	22	24	46	161	-34
86–87	Pitt	50	8	13	21	103	-5
87–88	Pitt	7	0	0	0	15	-4
Totals		236	72	77	149	472	-68

YOUNGHANS, Thomas *5-11 RW*
B. St. Paul, Minn., Jan. 22, 1953

SSN	TEAM	GP	G	A	PTS.	PIM	+/-
76–77	Minn	78	8	6	14	35	-11
77–78	Minn	72	10	8	18	100	-10
78–79	Minn	76	8	10	18	50	-23
79–80	Minn	79	10	6	16	92	-3
80–81	Minn	74	4	6	10	79	-8
81–82	Minn–NYR	50	4	5	9	17	+1
Totals		429	44	41	85	373	-54

Playoffs

76–77	Minn	2	0	0	0	0	
79–80	Minn	15	2	1	3	17	
80–81	Minn	5	0	0	0	4	
81–82	NYR	2	0	0	0	0	
Totals		24	2	1	3	21	

YSEBAERT, Paul Robert *6-1 190 C*
B. Sarnia, Ont., May 15, 1966

88–89	NJ	5	0	4	4	0	+2
89–90	NJ	5	1	2	3	0	0
90–91	NJ–Det	62	19	21	40	22	-7
91–92	Det	79	35	40	75	55	+44
92–93	Det	80	34	28	62	42	+19
93–94	Winn–Chi	71	14	21	35	26	-7
94–95	Chi–TB	44	12	16	28	18	+3
95–96	TB	55	16	15	31	16	-19
96–97	TB	39	5	12	17	4	+1
97–98	TB	82	13	27	40	32	-43
98–99	TB	10	0	1	1	2	-5
Totals		532	149	187	336	217	-12

Playoffs

90–91	Det	2	0	2	2	0	
91–92	Det	10	1	0	1	10	
92–93	Det	7	3	1	4	2	
93–94	Chi	6	0	0	0	8	
95–96	TB	5	0	0	0	0	
Totals		30	4	3	7	20	

YUSHKEVICH, Dimitri *5-11 208 D*
B. Yaroslavl, USSR, Nov. 19, 1971

92–93	Phil	82	5	27	32	71	+12
93–94	Phil	75	5	25	30	86	-8
94–95	Phil	40	5	9	14	47	-4
95–96	Tor	69	1	10	11	54	-14
96–97	Tor	74	4	10	14	56	-24
97–98	Tor	72	0	12	12	78	-13
98–99	Tor	78	6	22	28	88	+25
Totals		490	26	115	141	480	-26

Playoffs

94–95	Phil	15	1	5	6	12	
95–96	Tor	4	0	0	0	0	
98–99	Tor	17	1	5	6	22	
Totals		36	2	10	12	34	

YZERMAN, Steve *5-11 183 C*
B. Cranbrook, B.C., May 9, 1965

83–84	Det	80	39	48	87	33	-17
84–85	Det	80	30	59	89	58	-17
85–86	Det	51	14	28	42	16	-24
86–87	Det	80	31	59	90	43	-1
87–88	Det	64	50	52	102	44	+30
88–89	Det	80	65	90	155	61	+17
89–90	Det	79	62	65	127	79	-6
90–91	Det	80	51	57	108	34	-2
91–92	Det	79	45	58	103	64	+26
92–93	Det	84	58	79	137	44	+33
93–94	Det	58	24	58	82	36	+11
94–95	Det	47	12	26	38	40	+6
95–96	Det	80	36	59	95	64	+29
96–97	Det	81	22	63	85	78	+22
97–98	Det	75	24	45	69	46	+3
98–99	Det	80	29	45	74	42	+8
Totals		1178	592	891	1483	782	+118

Playoffs

83–84	Det	4	3	3	6	0	
84–85	Det	3	2	1	3	2	
86–87	Det	16	5	13	18	8	
87–88	Det	3	1	3	4	6	
88–89	Det	6	5	5	10	2	
90–91	Det	7	3	3	6	4	
91–92	Det	11	3	5	8	12	
92–93	Det	7	4	3	7	4	
93–94	Det	3	1	3	4	0	
94–95	Det	15	4	8	12	0	
95–96	Det	18	8	12	20	4	
96–97	Det	20	7	6	13	4	
97–98	Det	22	6	18	24	22	
98–99	Det	10	9	4	13	0	
Totals		145	61	87	148	68	

ZABRANSKY, Libor *6-3 196 D*
B. Brno, Czech, Nov. 25, 1973

96–97	StL	34	1	5	6	44	-1
97–98	StL	6	0	1	1	6	-3
Totals		40	1	6	7	50	-4

ZABROSKI, Martin *D*

44–45	Chi	1	0	0	0	0	

ZAHARKO, Miles *6-0 197 D*
B. Mannville, Alta., Apr. 30, 1957

77–78	Atl	71	1	19	20	26	-13
78–79	Chi	1	0	0	0	0	0
80–81	Chi	42	3	11	14	40	+22
81–82	Chi	15	1	2	3	18	-1
Totals		129	5	32	37	84	+8

Playoffs

77–78	Atl	1	0	0	0	0	
80–81	Chi	2	0	0	0	0	
Totals		3	0	0	0	0	

ZAINE, Rodney Carl (Zainer) *5-10 180 C*
B. Ottawa, Ont., May 18, 1946

70–71	Pitt	37	8	5	13	21	-8
71–72	Buf	24	2	1	3	4	-14
72–73	Chi (WHA)	74	3	14	17	25	
73–74	Chi (WHA)	78	5	13	18	17	
74–75	Chi (WHA)	68	3	6	9	16	
NHL Totals		61	10	6	16	25	-22
WHA Totals		220	11	33	44	58	

Playoffs

73–74	Chi (WHA)	18	2	1	3	2	

ZALAPSKI, Zarley *6-1 211 D*
B. Edmonton, Alta., Apr. 22, 1968

87–88	Pitt	15	3	8	11	7	+10
88–89	Pitt	58	12	33	45	57	-9
89–90	Pitt	51	6	25	31	37	-14
90–91	Pitt–Hart	77	15	39	54	65	+8
91–92	Hart	79	20	37	57	120	-7
92–93	Hart	83	14	51	65	94	-34
93–94	Hart–Calg	69	10	37	47	74	-6
94–95	Calg	48	4	24	28	46	+9
95–96	Calg	80	12	17	29	115	+11
96–97	Calg	2	0	0	0	0	-1
97–98	Calg–Mont	63	3	12	15	63	-13
Totals		625	99	283	382	676	-46

Playoffs

89–90	Pitt	11	1	8	9	13	
90–91	Hart	6	1	3	4	8	
91–92	Hart	7	2	3	5	6	
93–94	Calg	7	0	3	3	2	
94–95	Calg	7	0	4	4	4	
95–96	Calg	4	0	1	1	10	
97–98	Mont	6	0	1	1	4	
Totals		48	4	23	27	47	

ZAMUNER, Rob *6-2 202 C*
B. Oakville, Ont., Sept. 17, 1969

91–92	NYR	9	1	2	3	2	0
92–93	TB	84	15	28	43	74	-25
93–94	TB	59	6	6	12	42	-9
94–95	TB	43	9	6	15	24	-3
95–96	TB	72	15	20	35	62	+11
96–97	TB	82	17	33	50	56	+3
97–98	TB	77	14	12	26	41	-31
98–99	TB	58	8	11	19	24	-15

SSN	TEAM	GP	G	A	PTS.	PIM	+/-
Totals		484	85	118	203	325	-69

Playoffs

95–96	TB	6	2	3	5	10	

ZANUSSI, Joseph Lawrence *5-10 180 D*
B. Rossland, B.C., Sept. 25, 1947

72–73	Winn (WHA)	73	4	21	25	53	
73–74	Winn (WHA)	76	3	22	25	53	
74–75	NYR	8	0	2	2	4	+5
75–76	Bos	60	1	7	8	30	+2
76–77	Bos–StL	19	0	4	4	12	-5
NHL Totals		87	1	13	14	46	+2
WHA Totals		149	7	43	50	106	

Playoffs

72–73	Winn (WHA)	14	2	5	7	6	
73–74	Winn (WHA)	4	0	0	0	0	
75–76	Bos	4	0	1	1	2	
NHL Totals		4	0	1	1	2	
WHA Totals		18	2	5	7	6	

ZANUSSI, Ronald Kenneth *5-11 180 RW*
B. Toronto, Ont., Aug. 31, 1956

77–78	Minn	68	15	17	32	89	-20
78–79	Minn	63	14	16	30	82	+5
79–80	Minn	72	14	31	45	93	+4
80–81	Minn–Tor	53	9	11	20	95	-4
81–82	Tor	43	0	8	8	14	-4
Totals		299	52	83	135	373	-19

Playoffs

79–80	Minn	14	0	4	4	17	
80–81	Tor	3	0	0	0	0	
Totals		17	0	4	4	17	

ZAVISHA, Brad *6-2 205 LW*
B. Hines Creek, Alta., Jan. 4, 1972

93–94	Edm	2	0	0	0	0	-2

ZEDNIK, Richard *5-11 172 LW*
B. Bystrica, Czech., Jan. 6, 1976

95–96	Wash	1	0	0	0	0	0
96–97	Wash	11	2	1	3	4	-5
97–98	Wash	65	17	9	26	28	-2
98–99	Wash	49	9	8	17	50	-6
Totals		126	28	18	46	86	-13

Playoffs

97–98	Wash	17	7	3	10	16	

ZEIDEL, Lazarus (Larry) *5-11 185 D*
B. Montreal, Que., June 1, 1928

51–52	Det	19	1	0	1	14	
52–53	Det	9	0	0	0	8	
53–54	Chi	64	1	6	7	102	
67–68	Phil	57	1	10	11	68	+12
68–69	Phil	9	0	0	0	6	-3
Totals		158	3	16	19	198	+9

Playoffs

51–52	Det	5	0	0	0	0	
67–68	Phil	7	0	1	1	12	
Totals		12	0	1	1	12	

ZELEPUKIN, Valeri *5-11 190 LW*
B. Voskresensk, Soviet Union, Sept. 17, 1968

91–92	NJ	44	13	18	31	28	+11
92–93	NJ	78	23	41	64	70	+10
93–94	NJ	82	26	31	57	70	+36
94–95	NJ	4	1	2	3	6	+3
95–96	NJ	61	6	9	15	107	-10
96–97	NJ	71	14	24	38	36	-10
97–98	NJ–Edm	68	4	18	22	89	-2
98–99	Phil	74	16	9	25	48	0
Totals		482	103	152	255	454	+38

Playoffs

91–92	NJ	4	1	1	2	2	
92–93	NJ	5	0	2	2	0	
93–94	NJ	20	5	2	7	14	
94–95	NJ	18	1	2	3	12	
96–97	NJ	8	3	2	5	2	
97–98	Edm	8	1	2	3	2	
98–99	Phil	4	1	0	1	4	
Totals		67	12	11	23	46	

ZEMLAK, Richard Andrew 6–2 190 RW
B. Wynard, Sask., Mar. 3, 1963

SSN	TEAM	GP	G	A	PTS.	PIM	+/-
86–87	Que	20	0	2	2	47	0
87–88	Minn	54	1	4	5	307	-15
88–89	Minn–Pitt	34	0	0	0	148	-3
89–90	Pitt	19	1	5	6	43	-6
91–92	Calg	5	0	1	1	42	-2
Totals		**132**	**2**	**12**	**14**	**587**	**-26**

Playoffs

88–89	Pitt	1	0	0	0	10	

ZENIUK, Edward William 5–11 180 D
B. Landis, Sask., Mar. 8, 1933

SSN	TEAM	GP	G	A	PTS.	PIM	+/-
54–55	Det	2	0	0	0	0	

ZENT, Jason 5–11 180 LW
B. Buffalo, N.Y., April 15, 1971

SSN	TEAM	GP	G	A	PTS.	PIM	+/-
96–97	Ott	22	3	3	6	9	+5
97–98	Ott	3	0	0	0	4	0
98–99	Phil	2	0	0	0	0	0
Totals		**27**	**3**	**3**	**6**	**13**	**+5**

ZETTERSTROM, Lars 6–1 198 D
B. Stockholm, Sweden, Nov. 6, 1953

SSN	TEAM	GP	G	A	PTS.	PIM	+/-
78–79	Van	14	0	1	1	2	-10

ZETTLER, Rob 6–3 190 D
B. Sept Iles, Que., Mar. 8, 1968

SSN	TEAM	GP	G	A	PTS.	PIM	+/-
88–89	Minn	2	0	0	0	0	-1
89–90	Minn	31	0	8	8	45	-7
90–91	Minn	47	1	4	5	119	-10
91–92	SJ	74	1	8	9	99	-23
92–93	SJ	80	0	7	7	150	-50
93–94	SJ–Phil	75	0	7	7	134	-26
94–95	Phil	32	0	1	1	34	-3
95–96	Tor	29	0	1	1	48	-1
96–97	Tor	48	2	12	14	51	+8
97–98	Tor	59	0	7	7	108	-8
98–99	Nash	2	0	0	0	2	-2
Totals		**479**	**4**	**55**	**59**	**790**	**-123**

Playoffs

94–95	Phil	1	0	0	0	2	
95–96	Tor	2	0	0	0	0	
Totals		**3**	**0**	**0**	**0**	**2**	

ZEZEL, Peter 5–11 200 C
B. Toronto, Ont., Apr. 22, 1965

SSN	TEAM	GP	G	A	PTS.	PIM	+/-
84–85	Phil	65	15	46	61	26	+22
85–86	Phil	79	17	37	54	76	+27
86–87	Phil	71	33	39	72	71	+21
87–88	Phil	69	22	35	57	42	+7
88–89	Phil–StL	78	21	49	70	42	-14
89–90	StL	73	25	47	72	30	-9
90–91	Wash–Tor	52	21	19	40	14	-20
91–92	Tor	64	16	33	49	26	-22
92–93	Tor	70	12	23	35	24	0
93–94	Tor	41	8	8	16	19	+5
94–95	Dal	30	6	5	11	19	-6
95–96	StL	57	8	13	21	12	-2
96–97	StL–NJ	53	4	12	16	16	+10
97–98	NJ–Van	30	5	15	20	2	+15
98–99	Van	41	6	8	14	16	+5
Totals		**873**	**219**	**389**	**608**	**435**	**+39**

Playoffs

84–85	Phil	19	1	8	9	28	
85–86	Phil	5	3	1	4	4	
86–87	Phil	25	3	10	13	10	
87–88	Phil	7	3	2	5	7	
88–89	StL	10	6	6	12	4	
89–90	StL	12	1	7	8	4	
92–93	Tor	20	2	1	3	6	
93–94	Tor	18	2	4	6	8	
94–95	Dal	3	1	0	1	0	
95–96	StL	10	3	0	3	2	
96–97	NJ	2	0	0	0	10	
Totals		**131**	**25**	**39**	**64**	**83**	

ZHAMNOV, Alexei 6–1 195 C
B. Moscow, USSR, Oct. 1, 1970

SSN	TEAM	GP	G	A	PTS.	PIM	+/-
92–93	Winn	68	25	47	72	58	+7
93–94	Winn	61	26	45	71	62	-20
94–95	Winn	48	30	35	65	20	+5
95–96	Winn	58	22	37	59	65	-4
96–97	Chi	74	20	42	62	56	+18
97–98	Chi	70	21	28	49	61	+16
98–99	Chi	76	20	41	61	50	-10
Totals		**455**	**164**	**275**	**439**	**372**	**+12**

Playoffs

92–93	Winn	6	0	2	2	2	
95–96	Winn	6	2	1	3	8	
Totals		**12**	**2**	**3**	**5**	**10**	

ZHITNIK, Alexei 5–11 190 D
B. Kiev, USSR, Oct. 10, 1972

SSN	TEAM	GP	G	A	PTS.	PIM	+/-
92–93	LA	78	12	36	48	80	-3
93–94	LA	81	12	40	52	101	-11
94–95	LA–Buf	32	4	10	14	61	-6
95–96	Buf	80	6	30	36	58	-25
96–97	Buf	80	7	28	35	95	+10
97–98	Buf	78	15	30	45	102	+19
98–99	Buf	81	7	26	33	96	-6
Totals		**510**	**63**	**200**	**263**	**593**	**-22**

Playoffs

92–93	LA	24	3	9	12	26	
94–95	Buf	5	0	1	1	14	
96–97	Buf	12	1	0	1	16	
97–98	Buf	15	0	3	3	36	
98–99	Buf	21	4	11	15	52	
Totals		**77**	**8**	**24**	**32**	**120**	

ZHOLTOK, Sergei 6–0 190 C
B. Riga, Latvia, Dec. 2, 1972

SSN	TEAM	GP	G	A	PTS.	PIM	+/-
92–93	Bos	1	0	1	1	0	+1
93–94	Bos	24	2	1	3	2	-7
96–97	Ott	57	12	16	28	19	+2
97–98	Ott	78	10	13	23	16	-7
98–99	Mont	70	7	15	22	6	-12
Totals		**230**	**31**	**46**	**77**	**43**	**-23**

Playoffs

96–97	Ott	7	1	1	2	0	
97–98	Ott	11	0	2	2	0	
Totals		**18**	**1**	**3**	**4**	**0**	

ZMOLEK, Doug Allan 6–2 220 D
B. Rochester, Minn., Nov. 3, 1970

SSN	TEAM	GP	G	A	PTS.	PIM	+/-
92–93	SJ	84	5	10	15	229	-50
93–94	SJ–Dal	75	1	4	5	133	-8
94–95	Dal	42	0	5	5	67	-6
95–96	Dal–LA	58	2	5	7	87	-5
96–97	LA	57	1	0	1	116	-22
97–98	LA	46	0	8	8	111	0
98–99	Chi	62	0	14	14	102	+1
Totals		**424**	**9**	**46**	**55**	**845**	**-9**

Playoffs

93–94	Dal	7	0	1	1	14	
94–95	Dal	5	0	0	0	10	
97–98	LA	2	0	0	0	2	
Totals		**14**	**0**	**1**	**1**	**16**	

ZOMBO, Richard 6–1 202 D
B. Des Plaines, Ill., May 8, 1963

SSN	TEAM	GP	G	A	PTS.	PIM	+/-
84–85	Det	1	0	0	0	0	-3
85–86	Det	14	0	1	1	16	-10
86–87	Det	44	1	4	5	59	-6
87–88	Det	62	3	14	17	96	+24
88–89	Det	75	1	20	21	106	+22
89–90	Det	77	5	20	25	95	+13
90–91	Det	77	4	19	23	55	-2
91–92	Det–StL	67	3	15	18	61	+1
92–93	StL	71	0	15	15	78	-2
93–94	StL	74	2	8	10	85	-15
94–95	StL	23	1	4	5	24	+7
95–96	Bos	67	4	10	14	53	-7
Totals		**652**	**24**	**130**	**154**	**728**	**+22**

Playoffs

86–87	Det	7	0	1	1	9	
87–88	Det	16	0	6	6	55	
88–89	Det	6	0	1	1	16	

ZUBOV, Sergei 6–1 200 D
B. Moscow, USSR, July 22, 1970

SSN	TEAM	GP	G	A	PTS.	PIM	+/-
90–91	Det	7	1	0	1	10	
91–92	StL	6	0	2	2	12	
92–93	StL	11	0	1	1	12	
93–94	StL	4	0	0	0	11	
94–95	StL	3	0	0	0	2	
Totals		**60**	**1**	**11**	**12**	**127**	

ZUBOV, Sergei 6–1 200 D
B. Moscow, USSR, July 22, 1970

SSN	TEAM	GP	G	A	PTS.	PIM	+/-
92–93	NYR	49	8	23	31	4	-1
93–94	NYR	78	12	77	89	39	+20
94–95	NYR	38	10	26	36	18	-2
95–96	Pitt	64	11	55	66	22	+28
96–97	Dal	78	13	30	43	24	+19
97–98	Dal	73	10	47	57	16	+16
98–99	Dal	81	10	41	51	20	+9
Totals		**461**	**74**	**299**	**373**	**143**	**+89**

Playoffs

93–94	NYR	22	5	14	19	0	
94–95	NYR	10	3	8	11	2	
95–96	Pitt	18	1	14	15	26	
96–97	Dal	7	0	3	3	2	
97–98	Dal	17	4	5	9	2	
98–99	Dal	23	1	12	13	4	
Totals		**97**	**14**	**56**	**70**	**36**	

ZUBRUS, Dainius 6–3 215 RW
B. Elektrenai, USSR, June 16, 1978

SSN	TEAM	GP	G	A	PTS.	PIM	+/-
96–97	Phil	68	8	13	21	22	+3
97–98	Phil	69	8	25	33	42	+29
98–99	Phil–Mont 80	6	10	16	29	-8	
Totals		**217**	**22**	**48**	**70**	**93**	**+24**

Playoffs

96–97	Phil	19	5	4	9	12	
97–98	Phil	5	0	1	1	2	
Totals		**24**	**5**	**5**	**10**	**14**	

ZUKE, Michael 6–0 180 C
B. Sault Ste. Marie, Ont., Apr. 16, 1954

SSN	TEAM	GP	G	A	PTS.	PIM	+/-
76–77	Ind (WHA)	15	3	4	7	2	
77–78	Edm (WHA)	71	23	34	57	47	
78–79	StL	34	9	17	26	18	-8
79–80	StL	69	22	42	64	30	-2
80–81	StL	74	24	44	68	57	+15
81–82	StL	76	13	40	53	41	-18
82–83	StL	43	8	16	24	14	-3
83–84	Hart	75	6	23	29	36	-18
84–85	Hart	67	4	12	16	12	-4
85–86	Hart	17	0	2	2	12	-2
NHL Totals		**455**	**86**	**196**	**282**	**220**	**-40**
WHA Totals		**86**	**26**	**38**	**64**	**49**	

Playoffs

77–78	Edm (WHA)	5	2	3	5	0	
79–80	StL	3	0	0	0	2	
80–81	StL	11	4	5	9	4	
81–82	StL	8	1	1	2	2	
82–83	StL	4	1	0	1	4	
NHL Totals		**26**	**6**	**6**	**12**	**12**	
WHA Totals		**5**	**2**	**3**	**5**	**0**	

ZUNICH, Ralph (Ruby) D
B. Calumet, Mich., Nov. 24, 1910

SSN	TEAM	GP	G	A	PTS.	PIM	+/-
43–44	Det	2	0	0	0	2	

ZYUZIN, Andrei 6–1 195 D
B. Ufa, Russia, Jan. 21 1978

SSN	TEAM	GP	G	A	PTS.	PIM	+/-
97–98	SJ	56	6	7	13	66	+8
98–99	SJ	25	3	1	4	38	+5
Totals		**81**	**9**	**8**	**17**	**104**	**+13**

Playoffs

97–98	SJ	6	1	0	1	14	

GOALIES

SEASON TEAM	GP	MIN.	W	L	T	GA	SO.	AVG.
ABBOTT, George								
43–44 Bos	1	60	0	1	0	7	0	7.00
ADAMS, John Matthew *6–0 200*								
B. Port Arthur, Ont., July 27, 1946								
72–73 Bos	14	780	9	3	1	39	1	3.00
74–75 Wash	8	400	0	7	0	46	0	6.90
Totals	22	1180	9	10	1	85	1	4.32
AIKEN, Donald								
B. Arlington, Mass., Jan. 1, 1932								
57–58 Mont	1	34	0	1	0	6	0	10.59
AITKENHEAD, Andrew								
B. Glasgow, Scotland, Mar. 6, 1904								
32–33 NYR	48	2970	23	17	8	107	3	2.23
33–34 NYR	48	2990	21	19	8	113	7	2.35
34–35 NYR	10	610	3	7	0	37	1	3.70
Totals	106	6570	47	43	16	257	11	2.35
Playoffs								
32–33 NYR	8	488	6	1	1	13	2	1.63
33–34 NYR	2	123	0	2	0	2	1	1.00
Totals	10	608	6	3	1	15	3	1.48
ALMAS, Ralph Clayton (Red) *5–9 160*								
B. Saskatoon, Sask., Apr. 26, 1924								
46–47 Det	1	60	0	1	0	5	0	5.00
50–51 Chi	1	60	0	1	0	5	0	5.00
52–53 Det	1	60	0	0	1	3	0	3.00
Totals	3	180	0	2	1	13	0	4.33
Playoffs								
Det	5	263	1	3	0	13		02.97
ANDERSON, Lawrence Lorne *5–11 166*								
B. Renfrew, Ont., July 26, 1931								
51–52 NYR	3	180	1	2	0	18	0	6.00
ASKEY, Tom *6–2 185*								
B. Kenmore, N.Y., Oct. 4, 1972								
97–98 Ana	7	273	0	1	2	12	0	2.64
Playoffs								
98–99 Ana	1	30	0	1	0	2	0	4.00
ASTROM, Hardy *6–0 170*								
B. Skelleftea, Sweden, Mar. 29, 1951								
77–78 NYR	4	240	2	2	0	14	0	3.50
79–80 Col	49	2574	9	27	6	161	0	3.75
80–81 Col	30	1642	6	15	6	103	0	3.76
Totals	83	4456	17	44	12	278	0	3.74
AUBIN, Jean-Sebastien *5–11 179*								
B. Montreal, Que., July 19, 1977								
98–99 Pitt	17	756	4	3	6	28	2	2.22
BACH, Ryan *6–1 180*								
B. Sherwood Park, Alta., Oct. 21, 1973								
98–99 LA	3	108	0	3	0	8	0	4.44
BAILEY, Scott *5–11 185*								
B. Calgary, Alta., May 2, 1972								
95–96 Bos	11	571	5	1	2	31	0	3.26
96–97 Bos	8	394	1	5	0	24	0	3.65
Totals	19	965	6	6	2	55	0	3.42
BAKER, Steven *6–3 200*								
B. Boston, Mass., May 6, 1957								
79–80 NYR	27	1391	9	8	6	79	1	3.41
80–81 NYR	21	1260	10	6	5	73	2	3.48
81–82 NYR	6	328	1	5	0	33	0	6.04
82–83 NYR	3	102	0	1	0	5	0	2.94
Totals	57	3081	20	20	11	190	3	3.70
BALES, Michael Raymond *6–1 180*								
B. Prince Albert, Sask., Aug. 6, 1971								
92–93 Bos	1	25	0	0	0	1	0	2.40
94–95 Ott	1	3	0	0	0	0	0	0.00

SEASON TEAM	GP	MIN.	W	L	T	GA	SO.	AVG.
95–96 Tor	20	1040	2	14	1	72	0	4.15
96–97 Ott	1	52	0	1	0	4	0	4.62
Totals	23	1120	2	15	1	77	0	4.13
BANNERMAN, Murray *5–11 184*								
B. Fort Francis, Ont., Apr. 27, 1957								
77–78 Van	1	20	0	0	0	0	0	0.00
80–81 Chi	15	865	2	10	2	62	0	4.30
81–82 Chi	29	1671	11	12	4	116	1	4.17
82–83 Chi	41	2460	24	12	5	127	4	3.10
83–84 Chi	56	3335	23	29	4	188	2	3.38
84–85 Chi	60	3371	27	25	4	215	0	3.83
85–86 Chi	48	2689	20	19	6	201	1	4.48
86–87 Chi	39	2059	9	18	9	142	0	4.14
Totals	289	16470	116	125	33	1051	8	3.83
Playoffs								
81–82 Chi	10	555	5	4	0	35	0	3.78
82–83 Chi	8	480	4	4	0	32	0	4.00
83–84 Chi	5	300	2	3	0	17	0	3.40
84–85 Chi	15	906	9	6	0	72	0	4.77
85–86 Chi	2	81	0	1	0	9	0	4.85
Totals	40	2322	20	18	0	165	0	4.26
BARON, Marco Joseph *5–11 179*								
B. Montreal, Que., Apr. 8, 1959								
79–80 Bos	1	40	0	0	0	2	0	3.00
80–81 Bos	10	507	3	4	1	24	0	2.84
81–82 Bos	44	2515	22	16	4	144	1	3.44
82–83 Bos	9	516	6	3	0	33	0	3.84
83–84 LA	21	1211	3	13	4	87	0	4.31
84–85 Edm	1	33	0	1	0	2	0	3.64
Totals	86	4822	34	39	9	292	1	3.63
Playoffs								
80–81 Bos	1	20	0	1	0	3	0	9.00
BARRASSO, Thomas *6–3 207*								
B. Boston, Mass., Mar. 31, 1965								
83–84 Buf	42	2475	26	12	3	117	2	2.84
84–85 Buf	54	3248	25	18	10	144	5	2.66
85–86 Buf	60	3561	29	24	5	214	2	3.61
86–87 Buf	46	2501	17	23	2	152	2	3.65
87–88 Buf	54	3133	25	18	8	173	2	3.31
88–89 Buf–Pitt	54	2951	20	22	7	207	0	4.21
89–90 Pitt	24	1294	7	12	3	101	0	4.68
90–91 Pitt	48	2754	27	16	3	165	1	3.59
91–92 Pitt	57	3329	25	22	9	196	1	3.53
92–93 Pitt	63	3702	43	14	5	186	4	3.01
93–94 Pitt	44	2482	22	15	5	139	2	3.36
94–95 Pitt	2	125	0	1	1	8	0	3.84
95–96 Pitt	49	2799	29	16	2	160	2	3.43
96–97 Pitt	5	270	0	5	0	26	0	5.78
97–98 Pitt	63	3542	31	14	13	122	7	2.07
98–99 Pitt	43	2306	19	16	3	98	4	2.55
Totals	708	40469	345	248	79	2208	34	3.27
Playoffs								
83–84 Buf	3	139	0	2	0	8	0	3.45
84–85 Buf	5	300	2	3	0	22	0	4.40
87–88 Buf	4	224	1	3	0	16	0	4.29
88–89 Pitt	11	631	7	4	0	40	0	3.80
90–91 Pitt	20	1175	12	7	0	51	1	2.60
91–92 Pitt	21	1233	16	5	0	58	1	2.82
92–93 Pitt	12	722	7	5	0	35	2	2.91
93–94 Pitt	6	356	2	4	0	17	0	2.87
94–95 Pitt	2	80	0	1	0	8	0	6.00
95–96 Pitt	10	558	4	5	0	26	1	2.80
97–98 Pitt	6	376	2	4	0	17	0	2.71
98–99 Pitt	13	787	6	7	0	35	1	2.67
Totals	113	6581	59	50	0	333	6	3.04
BASSEN, Henry (Hank) *5–10 170*								
B. Calgary, Alta., Dec. 6, 1932								
54–55 Chi	21	1260	4	9	8	63	0	3.00
55–56 Chi	12	720	3	8	1	42	1	3.50
60–61 Det	35	2120	13	13	8	102	0	2.89
61–62 Det	27	1620	9	12	6	76	3	2.81
62–63 Det	17	980	6	5	5	53	0	3.24
63–64 Det	1	60	0	1	0	4	0	4.00
65–66 Det	11	406	3	4	0	17	0	2.51
66–67 Det	8	384	2	4	0	22	1	3.44
67–68 Pitt	25	1299	7	10	3	62	1	2.86
Totals	157	8849	47	66	31	441	6	2.99
Playoffs								
60–61 Det	4	220	1	3	0	9	0	2.45

SEASON	TEAM	GP	MIN.	W	L	T	GA	SO.	AVG.
65–66	Det	1	54	0	1	0	2	0	2.22
Totals		5	274	1	4	0	11	0	2.41

BASTIEN, Aldege (Baz) 5-7 160
B. Timmins, Ont., Aug. 29, 1920

SEASON	TEAM	GP	MIN.	W	L	T	GA	SO.	AVG.
45–46	Tor	5	300	0	4	1	20	0	4.00

BAUMAN, Gary Glenwood 5-11 175
B. Innisfail, Alta., July 21, 1940

SEASON	TEAM	GP	MIN.	W	L	T	GA	SO.	AVG.
66–67	Mont	2	120	1	1	0	5	0	2.50
67–68	Minn	26	1294	5	13	5	75	0	3.48
68–69	Minn	7	304	0	4	1	22	0	4.34
Totals		35	1718	6	18	6	102	0	3.56

BEAUPRE, Donald William 5-10 172
B. Waterloo, Ont., Sept. 19, 1961

SEASON	TEAM	GP	MIN.	W	L	T	GA	SO.	AVG.
80–81	Minn	44	2585	18	14	11	138	0	3.20
81–82	Minn	29	1634	11	8	9	101	0	3.71
82–83	Minn	36	2011	19	10	5	120	0	3.58
83–84	Minn	33	1791	16	13	2	123	0	4.12
84–85	Minn	31	1770	10	17	3	109	1	3.69
85–86	Minn	52	3073	25	20	6	182	1	3.55
86–87	Minn	47	2622	17	20	6	174	1	3.98
87–88	Minn	43	2288	10	22	3	161	0	4.22
88–89	Minn–Wash	12	637	5	5	0	31	1	2.92
89–90	Wash	48	2793	23	18	5	150	2	3.22
90–91	Wash	45	2572	20	18	3	113	5	2.64
91–92	Wash	54	3108	29	17	6	166	1	3.20
92–93	Wash	58	3282	27	23	5	181	1	3.31
93–94	Wash	53	2853	24	16	8	135	2	2.84
94–95	Ott	38	2161	8	25	3	121	1	3.36
95–96	Ott–Tor	41	2106	6	28	0	136	1	3.87
96–97	Tor	3	110	0	3	0	10	0	5.45
Totals		667	37396	268	277	75	2151	17	3.45

Playoffs

SEASON	TEAM	GP	MIN.	W	L	T	GA	SO.	AVG.
80–81	Minn	6	360	4	2	0	26	0	4.33
81–82	Minn	2	60	0	1	0	4	0	4.00
82–83	Minn	4	245	2	2	0	20	0	4.90
83–84	Minn	13	782	6	7	0	40	1	3.07
84–85	Minn	4	184	1	1	0	12	0	3.91
85–86	Minn	5	300	2	3	0	17	0	3.40
89–90	Wash	8	401	4	3	0	18	0	2.69
90–91	Wash	11	624	5	5	0	29	1	2.79
91–92	Wash	7	419	3	4	0	22	0	3.15
92–93	Wash	2	119	1	1	0	9	0	4.54
93–94	Wash	8	429	5	2	0	21	1	2.94
95–96	Tor	2	20	0	0	0	2	0	6.00
Totals		72	3943	33	31	0	220	3	3.35

BEAUREGARD, Stephane 5-11 190
B. Cowansville, Que., Jan. 10, 1968

SEASON	TEAM	GP	MIN.	W	L	T	GA	SO.	AVG.
89–90	Winn	19	1079	7	8	3	59	0	3.28
90–91	Winn	16	836	3	10	1	55	0	3.95
91–92	Winn	26	1267	6	8	6	61	2	2.89
92–93	Phil	16	802	3	9	0	59	0	4.41
93–94	Winn	13	418	0	4	1	34	0	4.88
Totals		90	4402	19	39	11	268	2	3.65

Playoffs

SEASON	TEAM	GP	MIN.	W	L	T	GA	SO.	AVG.
89–90	Winn	4	238	1	3	0	12	0	3.03

BEDARD, James Arthur 5-10 181
B. Niagara Falls, Ont., Nov. 14, 1956

SEASON	TEAM	GP	MIN.	W	L	T	GA	SO.	AVG.
77–78	Wash	43	2492	11	23	7	152	1	3.66
78–79	Wash	30	1740	6	17	6	126	0	4.34
Totals		73	4232	17	40	13	278	1	3.94

BEHREND, Marc 6-1 180
B. Madison, Wisc., Jan. 11, 1961

SEASON	TEAM	GP	MIN.	W	L	T	GA	SO.	AVG.
83–84	Winn	6	351	2	4	0	32	0	5.47
84–85	Winn	23	1173	8	10	2	87	1	4.45
85–86	Winn	9	422	2	5	0	41	0	5.83
Totals		38	1946	12	19	2	160	1	4.93

Playoffs

SEASON	TEAM	GP	MIN.	W	L	T	GA	SO.	AVG.
83–84	Winn	2	121	0	2	0	9	0	4.46
84–85	Winn	4	179	1	1	0	10	0	3.35
85–86	Winn	1	12	0	0	0	0	0	0.00
Totals		7	312	1	3	0	19	0	3.65

BELANGER, Yves 5-11 170
B. Baie Comeau, Que., Sept. 30, 1952

SEASON	TEAM	GP	MIN.	W	L	T	GA	SO.	AVG.
74–75	StL	11	640	6	3	2	29	1	2.72
75–76	StL	31	1763	11	17	1	113	0	3.85
76–77	StL	3	140	0	3	0	7	0	3.00

SEASON	TEAM	GP	MIN.	W	L	T	GA	SO.	AVG.
77–78	StL–Atl	20	1081	7	11	0	70	1	3.89
78–79	Atl	5	182	1	2	0	21	0	6.92
79–80	Bos	8	328	2	0	3	19	0	3.48
Totals		78	4134	27	36	6	259	2	3.76

BELFOUR, Ed 5-11 182
B. Carmen, Man., Apr. 21, 1965

SEASON	TEAM	GP	MIN.	W	L	T	GA	SO.	AVG.
88–89	Chi	23	1148	4	12	3	74	0	3.87
90–91	Chi	74	4127	43	19	7	170	4	2.47
91–92	Chi	52	2928	21	18	10	132	5	2.70
92–93	Chi	71	4106	41	18	11	177	7	2.59
93–94	Chi	70	3998	37	24	6	178	7	2.67
94–95	Chi	42	2450	22	15	3	93	5	2.28
95–96	Chi	50	2956	22	17	10	135	1	274
96–97	Chi–SJ	46	2723	14	24	6	131	2	2.89
97–98	Dal	61	3581	37	12	10	112	9	1.88
98–99	Dal	61	3536	35	15	9	117	5	1.99
Totals		550	31553	276	174	75	1319	45	2.51

Playoffs

SEASON	TEAM	GP	MIN.	W	L	T	GA	SO.	AVG.
89–90	Chi	9	409	4	2	0	17	0	2.49
90–91	Chi	6	295	2	4	0	20	0	4.07
91–92	Chi	18	949	12	4	0	39	1	2.47
92–93	Chi	4	249	0	4	0	13	0	3.13
93–94	Chi	6	360	2	4	0	15	0	2.50
94–95	Chi	16	1014	9	7	0	37	1	2.19
95–96	Chi	9	666	6	3	0	23	1	2.07
97–98	Dal	17	1038	10	7	0	32	1	1.79
98–99	Dal	23	1544	16	7	0	43	3	1.63
Totals		85	6524	61	42	0	239	7	2.25

BELHUMEUR, Michel 5-10 160
B. Sorel, Que., Sept. 2, 1949

SEASON	TEAM	GP	MIN.	W	L	T	GA	SO.	AVG.
72–73	Phil	23	1117	9	7	3	60	0	3.22
74–75	Wash	35	1812	0	24	3	162	0	5.36
75–76	Wash	7	377	0	5	1	32	0	5.09
Totals		65	3306	9	36	7	254	0	4.61

BELL, Gordon 5-10 164
B. Portage La Prairie, Man., Mar. 13, 1925

SEASON	TEAM	GP	MIN.	W	L	T	GA	SO.	AVG.
45–46	Tor	8	480				31	0	3.88

Playoffs

SEASON	TEAM	GP	MIN.	W	L	T	GA	SO.	AVG.
55–56	NYR	2	120	1	1	0	9	0	4.50

BENEDICT, Clinton Stephen (Benny)
B. Ottawa, Ont., 1891

SEASON	TEAM	GP	MIN.	W	L	T	GA	SO.	AVG.
17–18	Ott	22	1337	9	13	0	114	1	5.18
18–19	Ott	18	1113	12	6	0	53	2	2.94
19–20	Ott	24	1443	19	5	0	64	5	2.67
20–21	Ott	24	1457	13	11	0	75	2	3.13
21–22	Ott	24	1508	14	8	2	84	2	3.50
22–23	Ott	24	1486	14	9	1	54	4	2.25
23–24	Ott	22	1356	16	6	0	45	3	2.05
24–25	Mont M	30	1843	9	19	2	65	2	2.17
25–26	Mont M	36	2288	20	11	5	73	6	2.03
26–27	Mont M	43	2748	20	19	4	65	13	1.51
27–28	Mont M	44	2690	24	14	6	76	6	1.73
28–29	Mont M	37	2300	14	16	7	57	11	1.54
29–30	Mont M	14	752	6	6	1	38	0	2.71
Totals		362	22321	190	143	28	863	57	2.32

Playoffs

SEASON	TEAM	GP	MIN.	W	L	T	GA	SO.	AVG.
18–19	Ott	5	300	1	4	0	26	0	5.20
19–20	Ott	5	300	3	2	0	11	1	2.20
20–21	Ott	7	420	5	2	0	12	2	1.71
21–22	Ott	2	120	0	1	0	5	1	2.50
22–23	Ott	8	480	6	2	0	10	3	1.25
23–24	Ott	2	120	0	2	0	5	0	2.50
25–26	Mont M	8	480	5	1	2	8	4	1.00
26–27	Mont M	2	132	0	1	1	2	0	1.00
27–28	Mont M	9	555	5	3	1	8	4	0.89
Totals		48	2907	25	18	4	87	15	1.80

BENNETT, Harvey A. 6-0 175
B. Edington, Sask., July 23, 1925

SEASON	TEAM	GP	MIN.	W	L	T	GA	SO.	AVG.
44–45	Bos	24	1470	10	12	2	106	0	4.33

BERGERON, Jean-Claude 6-2 192
B. Hauterive, Que., Oct. 14, 1968

SEASON	TEAM	GP	MIN.	W	L	T	GA	SO.	AVG.
90–91	Mont	18	941	7	6	2	59	0	3.76
92–93	TB	21	1163	8	10	1	71	0	3.66
93–94	TB	3	134	1	1	1	7	0	3.13
94–95	TB	17	883	3	9	1	49	1	3.33
95–96	TB	12	595	2	6	2	42	0	4.24
96–97	LA	1	56	0	1	0	4	0	4.29
Totals		72	3772	21	33	7	232	1	3.69

SEASON	TEAM	GP	MIN.	W	L	T	GA	SO	AVG.

BERNHARDT, Timothy John *5–9 160*
B. Sarnia, Ont., Jan. 17, 1958

SEASON	TEAM	GP	MIN.	W	L	T	GA	SO	AVG.
82–83	Calg	6	280	0	5	0	21	0	4.50
84–85	Tor	37	2182	13	19	4	136	0	3.74
85–86	Tor	23	1266	4	12	3	107	0	5.07
86–87	Tor	1	20	0	0	0	3	0	9.00
Totals		67	3748	17	36	7	267	0	4.27

BERTHIAUME, Daniel *5–9 155*
B. Longueuil, Que., Jan. 26, 1966

SEASON	TEAM	GP	MIN.	W	L	T	GA	SO	AVG.
86–87	Winn	31	1758	18	7	3	93	1	3.17
87–88	Winn	56	3010	22	19	7	176	2	3.51
88–89	Winn	9	443	0	8	0	44	0	5.96
89–90	Winn–Minn	29	1627	11	14	3	100	1	3.69
90–91	LA	37	2119	20	11	4	117	1	3.31
91–92	LA–Bos	27	1378	8	14	3	87	0	3.79
92–93	Ott	25	1326	2	17	1	95	0	4.30
93–94	Ott	1	1	0	0	0	2	0	12.00
Totals		215	11662	81	90	21	714	5	3.67

Playoffs

SEASON	TEAM	GP	MIN.	W	L	T	GA	SO	AVG.
85–86	Winn	1	68	0	1	0	4	0	3.53
86–87	Winn	8	439	4	4	0	21	0	2.87
87–88	Winn	5	300	1	4	0	25	0	5.00
Totals		14	807	5	9	0	50	0	3.72

BESTER, Allan J. *5–7 150*
B. Hamilton, Ont., Mar. 26, 1964

SEASON	TEAM	GP	MIN.	W	L	T	GA	SO	AVG.
83–84	Tor	32	1848	11	16	4	134	0	4.35
84–85	Tor	15	767	3	9	1	54	1	4.22
85–86	Tor	1	20	0	0	0	2	0	6.00
86–87	Tor	36	1808	10	14	3	110	2	3.65
87–88	Tor	30	1607	8	12	5	102	2	3.81
88–89	Tor	43	2460	17	20	3	156	2	3.80
89–90	Tor	42	2206	20	16	0	165	0	4.49
90–91	Tor–Det	9	425	0	7	0	31	0	4.38
91–92	Det	1	31	0	0	0	2	0	3.87
95–96	Dal	10	601	4	5	1	30	0	3.00
Totals		219	11773	73	99	17	786	7	4.01

Playoffs

SEASON	TEAM	GP	MIN.	W	L	T	GA	SO	AVG.
86–87	Tor	1	39	0	0	0	1	0	1.54
87–88	Tor	5	253	2	3	0	21	0	4.98
89–90	Tor	4	196	0	3	0	14	0	4.29
90–91	Dal	1	20	0	0	0	1	0	3.00
Totals		11	508	2	6	0	37	0	4.37

BEVERIDGE, William S. *5–8 170*
B. Ottawa, Ont., July 1, 1909

SEASON	TEAM	GP	MIN.	W	L	T	GA	SO	AVG.
29–30	Det	39	2410	14	20	5	109	2	2.79
30–31	Ott	9	520	0	8	0	32	0	3.56
32–33	Ott	35	2195	7	19	8	95	5	2.71
33–34	Ott	48	3000	13	29	6	143	3	2.98
34–35	St L E	48	2990	11	31	6	144	3	3.00
35–36	Mont M	32	1970	14	13	5	71	1	2.22
36–37	Mont M	21	1290	12	6	3	47	1	2.24
37–38	Mont M	48	2980	12	30	6	149	2	3.10
42–43	NYR	17	1020	4	10	3	89	1	5.24
Totals		297	18375	87	166	42	879	18	2.87

Playoffs

SEASON	TEAM	GP	MIN.	W	L	T	GA	SO	AVG.
36–37	Mont M	5	300	2	3	0	11	0	2.20

BIBEAULT, Paul *5–9 160*
B. Montreal, Que., Apr. 13, 1919

SEASON	TEAM	GP	MIN.	W	L	T	GA	SO	AVG.
40–41	Mont	4	210	1	2	0	15	0	4.29
41–42	Mont	38	2380	17	19	1	131	1	3.45
42–43	Mont	50	3010	19	19	12	191	1	3.81
43–44	Tor	29	1740	13	14	2	87	5	3.00
44–45	Bos	26	1530	6	18	2	113	0	4.43
45–46	Bos–Mont	26	1560	12	10	4	75	2	2.88
46–47	Chi	41	2460	0	0	0	170	1	4.15
Totals		214	12890	68	82	21	782	10	3.64

Playoffs

SEASON	TEAM	GP	MIN.	W	L	T	GA	SO	AVG.
41–42	Mont	3	180	1	2	0	8	1	2.67
42–43	Mont	5	320	1	4	0	18	1	3.38
43–44	Tor	5	300	1	4	0	23	0	4.60
44–45	Bos	7	437	3	4	0	22	0	3.02
Totals		20	1237	6	14	0	71	2	3.44

BIERK, Zac *6–2 186*
B. Peterborough, Ont., Sept. 17, 1976

SEASON	TEAM	GP	MIN.	W	L	T	GA	SO	AVG.
97–98	TB	13	433	1	4	1	30	0	4.16
98–99	TB	1	59	0	1	0	2	0	2.03
Totals		14	492	1	5	1	32	0	3.90

BILLINGTON, Craig *5–10 170*
B. London, Ont., Sept. 11, 1966

SEASON	TEAM	GP	MIN.	W	L	T	GA	SO	AVG.
85–86	NJ	18	901	4	9	1	77	0	5.13
86–87	NJ	22	1114	4	13	2	89	0	4.79
88–89	NJ	3	140	1	1	0	11	0	4.71
91–92	NJ	26	1363	13	7	1	69	2	3.04
92–93	NJ	42	2389	21	6	4	146	2	3.67
93–94	Ott	63	3319	11	41	4	254	0	4.59
94–95	Ott–Bos	17	845	5	7	2	51	0	3.62
95–96	Bos	27	1380	10	13	3	79	1	3.43
96–97	Col A	23	1200	11	8	2	53	1	2.65
97–98	Col A	23	1162	8	7	4	45	1	2.32
98–99	Col A	21	1086	11	8	1	52	0	2.87
Totals		285	13899	99	130	24	926	7	3.99

Playoffs

SEASON	TEAM	GP	MIN.	W	L	T	GA	SO	AVG.
92–93	NJ	2	78	0	1	0	5	0	3.85
94–95	Bos	1	25	0	0	0	1	0	2.40
95–96	Bos	1	60	0	1	0	6	0	6.00
96–97	Col A	1	20	0	0	0	1	0	3.00
97–98	Col A	1	1	0	0	0	0	0	0.00
98–99	Col A	1	9	0	0	0	1	0	6.67
Totals		7	193	0	2	0	14	0	4.36

BINETTE, Andre *5–7 165*
B. Montreal, Que., Dec. 2, 1933

SEASON	TEAM	GP	MIN.	W	L	T	GA	SO	AVG.
54–55	Mont	1	60	1	0	0	4	0	4.00

BINKLEY, Leslie John (Les) *6–0 175*
B. Owen Sound, Ont., June 6, 1936

SEASON	TEAM	GP	MIN.	W	L	T	GA	SO	AVG.
67–68	Pitt	54	3141	20	24	10	151	6	2.88
68–69	Pitt	50	2885	10	31	8	158	0	3.29
69–70	Pitt	27	1477	10	13	1	79	3	3.21
70–71	Pitt	34	1870	11	11	10	89	2	2.86
71–72	Pitt	31	1673	7	15	5	98	0	3.51
72–73	Ott (WHA)	30	1709	10	17	1	106	0	3.72
73–74	Tor (WHA)	27	1412	14	9	1	77	1	3.27
74–75	Tor (WHA)	17	772	6	4	0	46	0	3.58
75–76	Tor (WHA)	7	335	0	6	0	32	0	5.73
NHL Totals		196	11046	58	94	34	575	11	3.12
WHA Totals		81	4228	30	36	2	261	1	3.70

Playoffs

SEASON	TEAM	GP	MIN.	W	L	T	GA	SO	AVG.
69–70	Pitt	7	428	5	2	0	15	0	2.10
72–73	Ott (WHA)	4	223	1	3	0	17	0	4.57
73–74	Tor (WHA)	5	182	2	2	0	18	0	5.93
74–75	Tor (WHA)	1	59	0	1	0	5	0	5.08
NHL Totals		7	428	5	2	0	15	0	2.10
WHA Totals		10	464	3	6	0	40	0	4.17

BIRON, Martin *6–1 154*
B. Lac St. Charles, Que., Aug. 15, 1977

SEASON	TEAM	GP	MIN.	W	L	T	GA	SO	AVG.
95–96	Buf	3	119	0	2	0	10	0	5.04
98–99	Buf	6	281	1	2	1	10	0	2.14
Totals		9	400	1	4	1	20	0	3.00

BITTNER, Richard J. *6–0 170*
B. New Haven, Conn., Jan. 12, 1922

SEASON	TEAM	GP	MIN.	W	L	T	GA	SO	AVG.
49–50	Bos	1	60	0	0	1	3	0	3.00

BLAKE, Michael W. *6–0 185*
B. Kitchener, Ont., Apr. 6, 1956

SEASON	TEAM	GP	MIN.	W	L	T	GA	SO	AVG.
81–82	LA	2	51	0	0	0	2	0	2.35
82–83	LA	9	432	4	4	0	30	0	4.17
83–84	LA	29	1634	9	11	5	118	0	4.33
Totals		40	2117	13	15	5	150	0	4.25

BLUE, John *5–10 185*
B. Huntington Beach, Cal., Feb. 19, 1966

SEASON	TEAM	GP	MIN.	W	L	T	GA	SO	AVG.
92–93	Bos	23	1322	9	8	4	64	1	2.90
93–94	Bos	18	944	5	8	3	47	0	2.99
95–96	Buf	5	255	2	2	0	15	0	3.53
Totals		46	2521	16	18	7	126	1	3.00

Playoffs

SEASON	TEAM	GP	MIN.	W	L	T	GA	SO	AVG.
92–93	Bos	2	96	0	1	0	5	0	3.13

BOISVERT, Gilles *5–8 152*
B. Trois–Rivieres, Que., Feb. 15, 1933

SEASON	TEAM	GP	MIN.	W	L	T	GA	SO	AVG.
59–60	Det	3	180	0	3	0	9	0	3.00

BOUCHARD, Daniel Hector *6–0 175*
B. Val d'Or, Que., Dec. 12, 1950

SEASON	TEAM	GP	MIN.	W	L	T	GA	SO	AVG.
72–73	Atl	34	1944	9	15	10	100	2	3.09
73–74	Atl	46	2660	18	18	8	123	5	2.77

SEASON	TEAM	GP	MIN.	W	L	T	GA	SO.	AVG.
74–75	Atl	40	2400	20	15	5	111	3	2.78
75–76	Atl	47	2671	19	17	8	113	2	2.54
76–77	Atl	42	2378	17	17	5	139	1	3.51
77–78	Atl	58	3340	25	12	19	153	2	2.75
78–79	Atl	64	3624	32	21	7	201	3	3.33
79–80	Atl	53	3076	23	19	10	163	2	3.18
80–81	Calg–Que	43	2500	23	10	8	143	2	3.43
81–82	Que	60	3572	27	22	11	230	1	3.86
82–83	Que	50	2947	20	21	8	197	1	4.01
83–84	Que	57	3373	180	1	3.20			
84–85	Que	29	1738	101	0	3.49			
85–86	Winn	32	1696	107	2	3.79			
Totals		655	37919	286	232	113	2061	27	3.26

Playoffs

73–74	Atl	1	60	0	1	0	4	0	4.00
75–76	Atl	2	120	0	2	0	3	0	1.50
76–77	Atl	1	60	0	1	0	5	0	5.00
77–78	Atl	2	120	0	2	0	7	0	3.50
78–79	Atl	2	100	0	2	0	9	0	5.40
79–80	Atl	4	241	1	3	0	14	0	3.49
80–81	Que	5	286	2	3	0	19	1	3.99
81–82	Que	11	677	4	7	0	38	0	3.37
82–83	Que	4	242	1	3	0	11	0	2.73
Totals		43	2549				147	1	3.46

BOURQUE, Claude Hennessey *5–6 140*
B. Oxford, N.S., Mar. 31, 1915

38–39	Mont	25	1560	7	13	5	69	2	2.76
39–40	Mont–Det	37	2270	9	25	3	123	3	3.25
Totals		62	3830	16	38	8	192	5	3.01

Playoffs

38–39	Mont	3	188	1	2	0	8	1	2.55

BOUTIN, Roland (Rollie) *5–9 179*
B. Westlock, Alta., Nov. 6, 1957

78–79	Wash	2	90	0	1	0	10	0	6.67
79–80	Wash	18	927	7	7	1	54	0	3.50
80–81	Wash	2	120	0	2	0	11	0	5.50
Totals		22	1137	7	10	1	75	0	3.96

BOUVRETTE, Lionel *5–9 165*
B. Hawsbury, Ont., June 10, 1914

42–43	NYR	1	60				6	0	6.00

BOWER, John William (China Wall) *5–11 189*
B. Prince Albert, Sask., Nov. 8, 1924

53–54	NYR	70	4200	29	31	10	182	5	2.60
54–55	NYR	5	300	2	2	1	13	0	2.60
56–57	NYR	2	120	0	2	0	7	0	3.50
58–59	Tor	39	2340	15	17	7	107	3	2.74
59–60	Tor	66	3960	34	24	8	180	5	2.73
60–61	Tor	58	3480	33	15	10	145	2	2.50
61–62	Tor	59	3540	32	17	10	152	2	2.58
62–63	Tor	42	2520	20	15	7	110	1	2.62
63–64	Tor	51	3009	24	16	11	106	5	2.11
64–65	Tor	34	2040	13	13	8	81	3	2.38
65–66	Tor	35	1998	18	12	5	75	3	2.25
66–67	Tor	24	1431	12	9	3	63	2	2.64
67–68	Tor	43	2239	14	18	7	84	4	2.25
68–69	Tor	20	779	5	4	3	37	2	2.85
69–70	Tor	1	60	0	1	0	5	0	5.00
Totals		549	32016	251	196	90	1347	37	2.52

Playoffs

58–59	Tor	12	746	5	7	0	39	0	3.14
59–60	Tor	10	645	4	6	0	31	0	2.88
60–61	Tor	3	180	0	3	0	9	0	3.00
61–62	Tor	10	579	5	4	0	22	0	2.28
62–63	Tor	10	600	8	2	0	16	2	1.60
63–64	Tor	14	850	8	6	0	30	20	2.12
64–65	Tor	5	321	2	3	0	13	0	2.43
65–66	Tor	2	123	0	2	0	8	0	4.00
66–67	Tor	4	155	2	0	0	5	1	1.94
68–69	Tor	4	154	0	2	0	11	0	4.29
Totals		74	4350	34	35	0	184	5	2.54

BRANNIGAN, Andrew John *5–11 190*
B. Winnipeg, Man., Apr. 11, 1922

40–41	NYA	1	7	0	0	0	0	0	0.00

BRATHWAITE, Fred *5–7 170*
B. Ottawa, Ont., Nov. 24, 1972

93–94	Edm	19	982	3	10	3	58	0	3.54
94–95	Edm	14	601	2	5	1	40	0	3.99
95–96	Edm	7	293	0	2	0	12	0	2.46

SEASON	TEAM	GP	MIN.	W	L	T	GA	SO.	AVG.
98–99	Calg	28	1663	11	9	7	68	1	2.45
Totals		68	3539	16	26	11	178	1	3.02

BRIMSEK, Francis Charles (Mr. Zero) *5–9 170*
B. Eveleth, Minn., Sept. 26, 1915

38–39	Bos	43	2610	33	9	1	68	10	1.58
39–40	Bos	48	2950	31	2	5	98	6	2.04
40–41	Bos	48	3040	27	8	13	102	6	2.13
41–42	Bos	47	2930	24	17	6	115	3	2.45
42–43	Bos	50	3000	24	17	9	176	1	3.52
45–46	Bos	34	2040	16	14	4	111	2	3.26
46–47	Bos	60	3600	26	23	11	175	3	2.92
47–48	Bos	60	3600	23	24	13	168	3	2.80
48–49	Bos	54	3240	26	20	8	147	1	2.72
49–50	Chi	70	4200	22	38	10	244	5	3.49
Totals		514	31210	252	182	80	1404	40	2.70

Playoffs

38–39	Bos	12	863	8	4	0	18	1	1.50
39–40	Bos	6	360	2	4	0	15	0	2.50
40–41	Bos	11	678	8	3	0	23	1	2.09
41–42	Bos	5	307	2	3	0	16	0	3.20
42–43	Bos	9	560	4	5	0	33	0	3.54
45–46	Bos	10	641	5	5	0	29	0	2.71
46–47	Bos	5	323	1	4	0	16	0	2.97
47–48	Bos	5	317	1	4	0	20	0	3.79
48–49	Bos	5	316	1	4	0	16	0	3.04
Totals		68	4365	32	36	0	186	2	2.56

BROCHU, Martin *5–10 200*
B. Anjou, Que., March 10, 1973

98–99	Wash	2	120	0	2	0	6	0	3.00

BRODA, Walter (Turk) *5–9 180*
B. Brandon, Man., May 15, 1914

36–37	Tor	45	2770	22	19	4	106	3	2.36
37–38	Tor	48	2980	24	15	9	127	6	2.65
38–39	Tor	48	2990	19	20	9	107	8	2.23
39–40	Tor	47	2900	25	17	5	108	4	2.30
40–41	Tor	48	2970	28	14	6	99	5	2.06
41–42	Tor	48	2960	27	18	3	136	6	2.83
42–43	Tor	50	3000	22	19	9	159	1	3.18
45–46	Tor	15	900	6	6	3	53	0	3.53
46–47	Tor	60	3600	31	19	10	172	4	2.87
47–48	Tor	60	3600	32	15	13	143	5	2.38
48–49	Tor	60	3600	22	25	13	161	5	2.68
49–50	Tor	68	4040	30	25	12	167	9	2.48
50–51	Tor	31	1827	14	11	5	68	6	2.23
51–52	Tor	1	30	0	1	0	3	0	6.00
Totals		629	38167	302	224	101	1609	62	2.53

Playoffs

36–37	Tor	2	133	0	2	0	5	0	2.50
37–38	Tor	7	452	3	4	0	13	1	1.86
38–39	Tor	10	617	4	5	0	20	2	2.00
39–40	Tor	10	657	6	4	0	19	1	1.90
40–41	Tor	7	438	3	4	0	15	0	2.14
41–42	Tor	13	780	8	5	0	31	1	2.38
42–43	Tor	6	439	2	4	0	20	0	2.73
46–47	Tor	11	680	2	3	0	27	1	2.38
47–48	Tor	9	557	8	1	0	20	1	2.15
48–49	Tor	9	574	8	1	0	15	1	1.57
49–50	Tor	7	450	3	4	0	10	3	1.33
50–51	Tor	9	509	5	3	0	9	2	1.06
51–52	Tor	2	120	0	2	0	7	0	2.50
Totals		102	6406	58	42	0	211	13	1.98

BRODERICK, Kenneth Lorne *5–10 178*
B. Toronto, Ont., Fe B. 16, 1942

69–70	Minn	7	360	2	4	0	26	0	4.33
73–74	Bos	5	300	2	2	1	16	0	3.20
74–75	Bos	15	804	7	6	0	32	1	2.39
76–77	Edm (WHA)	40	2301	18	18	1	134	4	3.49
77–78	Edm–Que (WHA)	33	1637	11	13	1	125	0	4.58
NHL Totals		27	1464	11	12	1	74	1	3.03
WHA Totals		73	3938	29	31	2	259	4	3.95

Playoffs

76–77	Edm (WHA)	3	179	1	2	0	10	0	3.35
77–78	Que (WHA)	2	48	0	1	0	2	0	2.50
Totals		5	227	1	3	0	12	0	3.17

BRODERICK, Len
B. Toronto, Ont., Oct. 11, 1930

57–58	Mont	1	60	0	0	1	2	0	2.00

BRODEUR, Martin *6–1 205*
B. Montreal, Que., May 6, 1972

SEASON	TEAM	GP	MIN.	W	L	T	GA	SO.	AVG.
91–92	NJ	4	179	2	1	0	10	0	3.35
93–94	NJ	47	2625	27	11	8	105	3	2.40
94–95	NJ	40	2184	19	11	6	89	3	2.45
95–96	NJ	77	4434	34	30	12	173	6	2.34
96–97	NJ	67	3838	37	14	13	120	10	1.88
97–98	NJ	70	4128	43	17	8	130	10	1.89
98–99	NJ	70	4239	39	21	10	162	4	2.29
Totals		375	21626	201	105	57	789	36	2.19

Playoffs

SEASON	TEAM	GP	MIN.	W	L	T	GA	SO.	AVG.
93–94	NJ	17	1171	8	9	0	38	1	1.95
94–95	NJ	20	1222	16	4	0	34	3	1.67
96–97	NJ	10	659	5	5	0	19	2	1.73
97–98	NJ	6	36	2	4	0	12	0	1.97
98–99	NJ	7	425	3	4	0	20	0	2.82
Totals		61	3799	34	27	0	126	6	1.99

BRODEUR, Richard *5–7 160*
B. Longueuil, Que., Sept. 15, 1952

SEASON	TEAM	GP	MIN.	W	L	T	GA	SO.	AVG.
72–73	Que (WHA)	24	1288	5	14	2	102	0	4.75
73–74	Que (WHA)	30	1607	15	12	1	89	1	3.32
74–75	Que (WHA)	51	2938	29	21	2	191	2	3.90
75–76	Que (WHA)	69	3967	44	21	2	244	2	3.69
76–77	Que (WHA)	53	2906	29	18	2	167	2	3.45
77–78	Que (WHA)	36	1962	18	15	2	121	0	3.70
78–79	Que (WHA)	42	2433	25	13	2	126	3	3.11
79–80	NYI	2	80	1	0	0	6	0	4.50
80–81	Van	52	3024	17	18	16	177	0	3.51
81–82	Van	52	3010	20	18	12	168	2	3.35
82–83	Van	58	3291	21	26	8	208	0	3.79
83–84	Van	36	2110	10	21	5	141	1	4.01
84–85	Van	51	2930	16	27	6	228	0	4.67
85–86	Van	64	3541	19	32	8	240	2	4.07
86–87	Van	53	2972	20	25	5	178	1	3.59
87–88	Van–Hart	17	1010	7	8	2	64	0	3.80
NHL Totals		385	21968	131	176	62	1410	6	3.85
WHA Totals		305	17101	165	114	12	1040	10	3.65

Playoffs

SEASON	TEAM	GP	MIN.	W	L	T	GA	SO.	AVG.
74–75	Que (WHA)	15	906	8	7	0	48	1	3.18
75–76	Que (WHA)	5	299	1	4	0	22	0	4.41
76–77	Que (WHA)	17	1007	12	5	0	55	1	3.28
77–78	Que (WHA)	11	622	5	5	0	38	1	3.67
78–79	Que (WHA)	3	114	0	2	0	14	0	7.37
80–81	Van	3	185	0	3	0	13	0	4.22
81–82	Van	17	1089	11	6	0	49	0	2.70
82–83	Van	3	193	0	3	0	13	0	4.04
85–86	Van	2	120	0	2	0	12	0	6.00
87–88	Hart	4	200	1	3	0	12	0	3.60
NHL Totals		33	2009	13	20	0	111	1	3.32
WHA Totals		51	2948	26	23	0	177	3	3.60

BROMLEY, Gart Bert *5–10 160*
B. Edmonton, Alta., Jan. 19, 1950

SEASON	TEAM	GP	MIN.	W	L	T	GA	SO.	AVG.
73–74	Buf	12	598	3	5	3	33	0	3.31
74–75	Buf	50	2787	26	11	11	144	4	3.10
75–76	Buf	1	60	0	1	0	7	0	7.00
76–77	Calg (WHA)	28	1237	6	9	2	79	0	3.83
77–78	Winn (WHA)	39	2252	25	12	1	124	1	3.30
78–79	Van	38	2144	11	19	6	136	2	3.81
79–80	Van	15	860	8	2	4	43	1	3.00
80–81	Van	20	978	6	6	4	62	0	3.80
NHL Totals		136	7427	54	44	28	425	7	3.43
WHA Totals		67	3489	31	21	3	203	1	3.49

Playoffs

SEASON	TEAM	GP	MIN.	W	L	T	GA	SO.	AVG.
77–78	Winn (WHA)	5	268	4	0	0	7	0	1.57
78–79	Van	3	180	1	2	0	14	0	4.67
79–80	Van	4	180	4	3	0	11	0	3.67
NHL Totals		7	360	2	5	0	25	0	4.17
WHA Totals		5	268	4	0	0	7	0	1.57

BROOKS, Arthur

SEASON	TEAM	GP	MIN.	W	L	T	GA	SO.	AVG.
17–18	Tor	4	220	2	1	0	23	0	5.75

BROOKS, Donald Ross *5–8 173*
B. Toronto, Ont., Oct. 17, 1937

SEASON	TEAM	GP	MIN.	W	L	T	GA	SO.	AVG.
72–73	Bos	16	910	11	1	3	40	1	2.64
73–74	Bos	21	1170	16	3	0	46	3	2.36
74–75	Bos	17	967	10	3	3	48	0	2.98
Totals		54	3047	37	7	6	134	4	2.64

Playoffs

SEASON	TEAM	GP	MIN.	W	L	T	GA	SO.	AVG.
72–73	Bos	1	20	0	0	0	3	0	9.00

BROPHY, Frank

SEASON	TEAM	GP	MIN.	W	L	T	GA	SO.	AVG.
19–20	Que	21	1247	3	18	0	148	0	7.05

BROWN, Andrew Conrad (Andy) *6–0 185*
B. Hamilton, Ont., Feb. 15, 1944

SEASON	TEAM	GP	MIN.	W	L	T	GA	SO.	AVG.
71–72	Det	10	560	4	5	1	37	0	3.96
72–73	Det–Pitt	16	857	5	5	4	61	0	4.27
73–74	Pitt	36	1956	13	16	4	115	1	3.53
74–75	Ind (WHA)	52	2979	15	35	0	206	2	4.15
75–76	Ind (WHA)	24	1368	9	11	2	82	1	3.60
76–77	Ind (WHA)	10	430	1	4	1	26	0	3.63
NHL Totals		62	3373	22	26	9	213	1	3.79
WHA Totals		86	4777	25	50	3	314	3	3.94

BROWN, Kenneth Murray (Ken) *5–11 175*
B. Port Arthur, Ont., Feb. 15, 1944

SEASON	TEAM	GP	MIN.	W	L	T	GA	SO.	AVG.
70–71	Chi	1	18	0	0	0	1	0	3.33
72–73	Alb (WHA)	20	1034	10	8	0	63	1	3.66
74–75	Edm (WHA)	32	1466	11	11	0	85	2	3.48
NHL Totals		1	18	0	0	0	1	0	3.33
WHA Totals		52	2500	21	19	0	148	3	3.55

BRUNETTA, Mario *6–3 180*
B. Quebec City, Que., Jan. 25, 1967

SEASON	TEAM	GP	MIN.	W	L	T	GA	SO.	AVG.
87–88	Que	29	1550	10	12	1	96	0	3.72
88–89	Que	5	226	1	3	0	19	0	5.04
89–90	Que	6	191	1	2	0	13	0	4.08
Totals		40	1967	12	17	1	128	0	3.90

BULLOCK, Bruce John *5–7 160*
B. Toronto, Ont., May 9, 1949

SEASON	TEAM	GP	MIN.	W	L	T	GA	SO.	AVG.
72–73	Van	14	840	3	8	3	67	0	4.79
74–75	Van	1	60	0	1	0	4	0	4.00
76–77	Van	1	27	0	0	0	3	0	6.67
Totals		16	927	3	9	3	74	0	4.79

BURKE, Sean *6–4 210*
B. Windsor, Ont., Jan. 29, 1967

SEASON	TEAM	GP	MIN.	W	L	T	GA	SO.	AVG.
87–88	NJ	13	689	10	1	0	35	1	3.05
88–89	NJ	62	3590	22	31	9	230	3	3.84
89–90	NJ	52	2914	22	22	6	175	0	3.60
90–91	NJ	35	1870	8	12	8	112	0	3.59
92–93	Hart	50	2656	16	27	3	184	0	4.16
93–94	Hart	47	2750	17	24	5	137	2	2.99
94–95	Hart	42	2418	17	19	4	108	0	2.68
95–96	Hart	66	3669	28	28	6	190	4	3.11
96–97	Hart	51	2985	22	22	6	134	4	2.69
97–98	Car–Van–Phil	52	2985	16	23	9	142	2	2.85
98–99	Fla	59	3402	21	24	14	151	3	2.66
Totals		529	29928	199	233	70	1598	19	3.20

Playoffs

SEASON	TEAM	GP	MIN.	W	L	T	GA	SO.	AVG.
87–88	NJ	17	1001	9	8	0	57	1	3.42
89–90	NJ	2	125	0	2	0	8	0	3.84
Totals		19	1126	9	10	0	65	1	3.46

BUZINSKI, Stephen
B. Dunblane, Sask., Oct. 15, 1917

SEASON	TEAM	GP	MIN.	W	L	T	GA	SO.	AVG.
42–43	NYR	9	560	2	6	1	55	0	5.89

CALEY, Donald Thomas *5–10 165*
B. Dauphin, Man., Oct. 9, 1945

SEASON	TEAM	GP	MIN.	W	L	T	GA	SO.	AVG.
67–68	St L	1	30	0	0	0	3	0	6.00

CAPRICE, Frank *5–9 160*
B. Hamilton, Ont., May 2, 1962

SEASON	TEAM	GP	MIN.	W	L	T	GA	SO.	AVG.
82–83	Van	1	20	0	0	0	3	0	9.00
83–84	Van	19	1098	8	8	2	62	1	3.39
84–85	Van	28	1523	8	14	3	122	0	4.81
85–86	Van	7	308	0	3	2	28	0	5.46
86–87	Van	25	1390	8	11	2	89	0	3.84
87–88	Van	22	1250	7	10	2	87	0	4.18
Totals		102	5589	31	40	11	391	1	4.20

CAREY, Jim *6–2 205*
B. Dorchester, Mass., May 31, 1974

SEASON	TEAM	GP	MIN.	W	L	T	GA	SO.	AVG.
94–95	Wash	28	1604	18	6	3	57	4	2.13
95–96	Wash	71	4069	35	24	9	153	9	2.26
96–97	Wash–Bos	59	3297	22	31	3	169	1	3.08
97–98	Bos	10	496	3	2	1	24	2	2.90
98–99	StL	4	202	1	2	0	13	0	2.86
Totals		172	9668	79	55	17	416	16	2.58

Playoffs

SEASON	TEAM	GP	MIN.	W	L	T	GA	SO.	AVG.
94–95	Wash	7	358	2	4	0	25	0	4.19

		GP	MIN.	W	L	T	GA	SO.	AVG.
95–96	Wash	3	97	0	1	0	10	0	6.19
Totals		10	455	2	5	0	35	0	4.62

CARON, Jacques Joseph *6–2 185*
B. Noranda, Que., Apr. 21, 1940

		GP	MIN.	W	L	T	GA	SO.	AVG.
67–68	LA	1	60	0	1	0	4	0	4.00
68–69	LA	3	140	0	1	0	9	0	3.86
71–72	St L	28	1619	14	8	5	68	1	2.52
72–73	St L	30	1562	8	14	5	92	1	3.53
73–74	Van	10	465	2	5	1	38	0	4.90
75–76	Clev (WHA)	2	130	1	0	1	8	1	3.69
76–77	Cin (WHA)	24	1292	13	6	3	61	3	2.83
NHL Totals		72	3846	24	29	11	211	2	3.29
WHA Totals		26	1422	14	6	3	69	4	2.91

Playoffs

		GP	MIN.	W	L	T	GA	SO.	AVG.
71–72	StL	9	499	4	5	0	26	0	3.13
72–73	StL	3	140	0	2	0	8	0	3.43
76–77	Cin (WHA)	1	14	0	1	0	3	0	12.86
NHL Totals		12	639	4	7	0	34	0	3.19
WHA Totals		1	14	0	1	0	3	0	12.86

CARTER, Lyle Dwight *6–1 185*
B. Truro, N.S., Apr. 29, 1945

		GP	MIN.	W	L	T	GA	SO.	AVG.
71–72	Cal	15	721	4	7	0	50	0	4.16

CASEY, Jon *5–10 155*
B. Grand Rapids, Minn., Aug. 29, 1962

		GP	MIN.	W	L	T	GA	SO.	AVG.
83–84	Minn	2	84	1	0	0	6	0	4.29
85–86	Minn	26	1402	11	11	1	91	0	3.89
87–88	Minn	14	663	1	7	4	41	0	3.71
88–89	Minn	55	2961	18	17	12	151	1	3.06
89–90	Minn	61	3407	31	22	4	183	3	3.22
90–91	Minn	55	3185	21	20	11	158	3	2.98
91–92	Minn	52	2911	19	23	5	165	2	3.40
92–93	Minn	60	3476	26	26	4	193	3	3.33
93–94	Bos	57	3192	30	15	9	153	4	2.88
94–95	StL	19	872	7	5	4	40	0	2.75
95–96	StL	9	395	2	3	0	25	0	3.80
96–97	StL	15	707	3	8	0	40	0	3.39
Totals		425	23255	170	157	55	1246	16	3.21

Playoffs

		GP	MIN.	W	L	T	GA	SO.	AVG.
88–89	Minn	4	211	1	3	0	16	0	4.55
89–90	Minn	7	416	3	4	0	21	1	3.04
90–91	Minn	23	1205	14	7	0	61	1	3.04
91–92	Minn	7	437	3	4	0	22	0	3.02
93–94	Bos	11	698	5	6	0	34	0	2.92
94–95	StL	2	30	0	1	0	2	0	4.00
95–96	StL	12	747	6	6	0	36	1	2.89
Totals		66	3743	32	31	0	192	3	3.08

CHABOT, Frederic *5–11 175*
B. Hebertville, Que., Feb. 12, 1968

		GP	MIN.	W	L	T	GA	SO.	AVG.
90–91	Mont	3	108	0	0	1	6	0	3.33
92–93	Mont	1	40	0	0	0	1	0	1.50
93–94	Mont–Phil	5	130	0	2	0	10	0	4.62
97–98	LA	12	554	3	3	2	29	0	3.14
98–99	Mont	11	430	1	3	0	16	0	2.23
Totals		32	1262	4	8	4	62	0	2.95

CHABOT, Lorne (Chabotsky) *6–1 185*
B. Montreal, Que., Oct. 5, 1900

		GP	MIN.	W	L	T	GA	SO.	AVG.
26–27	NYR	36	2307	22	9	5	56	10	1.56
27–28	NYR	44	2730	19	16	9	79	11	1.80
28–29	Tor	43	2458	20	18	5	67	12	1.56
29–30	Tor	42	2620	21	12	9	113	6	2.69
30–31	Tor	37	2300	21	8	8	80	6	2.16
31–32	Tor	44	2698	22	16	6	106	4	2.41
32–33	Tor	48	2948	24	18	6	111	5	2.31
33–34	Mont	47	2928	21	20	6	101	8	2.15
34–35	Chi	48	2940	26	17	5	88	8	1.83
35–36	Mont M	16	1010	8	3	5	35	2	2.19
36–37	NYA	6	370	2	3	1	25	1	4.17
Totals		411	25309	206	140	65	861	73	2.04

Playoffs

		GP	MIN.	W	L	T	GA	SO.	AVG.
26–27	NYR	2	120	0	1	1	3	1	1.50
27–28	NYR	6	321	2	2	1	8	1	1.33
28–29	Tor	4	242	2	2	0	5	0	1.25
30–31	Tor	2	139	0	1	1	4	0	2.00
31–32	Tor	7	438	5	1	1	15	0	2.14
32–33	Tor	9	686	4	5	0	18	2	2.00
33–34	Mont	2	121	0	1	1	4	0	2.00
34–35	Chi	2	124	0	1	1	1	1	0.50
35–36	Mont M	3	357	0	3	0	6	0	2.00
Totals		37	2558	13	17	6	64	5	1.50

CHADWICK, Edwin Walter *5–11 184*
B. Fergus, Ont., May 8, 1933

		GP	MIN.	W	L	T	GA	SO.	AVG.
55–56	Tor	5	300	2	0	2	3	2	0.60
56–57	Tor	70	4200	21	34	15	192	5	2.74
57–58	Tor	70	4200	21	38	11	226	4	3.23
58–59	Tor	31	1800	12	15	4	93	3	3.10
59–60	Tor	4	240	1	2	1	15	0	3.75
61–62	Bos	4	240	0	3	1	22	0	5.50
Totals		184	10980	57	92	35	551	14	3.01

CHAMPOUX, Robert Joseph *5–10 175*
B. St. Hilaire, Que., Dec. 2, 1942

		GP	MIN.	W	L	T	GA	SO.	AVG.
73–74	Cal	17	923	2	11	3	80	0	5.20

Playoffs

		GP	MIN.	W	L	T	GA	SO.	AVG.
63–64	Det	1	40	0	0	0	4	0	6.00

CHEEVERS, Gerald Michael (Cheesey) *5–11 175*
B. St. Catharines, Ont., Dec. 7, 1940

		GP	MIN.	W	L	T	GA	SO.	AVG.
61–62	Tor	2	120	1	1	0	7	0	3.50
65–66	Bos	7	340	0	4	1	34	3	6.00
66–67	Bos	22	1298	5	11	6	72	1	3.33
67–68	Bos	47	2646	23	17	5	125	3	2.83
68–69	Bos	52	3112	28	12	12	145	3	2.80
69–70	Bos	41	2384	24	8	8	108	4	2.72
70–71	Bos	40	2400	27	8	5	109	3	2.73
71–72	Bos	41	2420	27	5	8	101	2	2.50
72–73	Clev (WHA)	52	3144	32	20	0	149	5	2.84
73–74	Clev (WHA)	59	3562	30	20	6	180	4	3.03
74–75	Clev (WHA)	52	3076	26	24	2	167	4	3.26
75–76	Clev (WHA)	28	1570	11	4	1	95	1	3.63
75–76	Bos	15	900	8	2	5	41	1	2.73
76–77	Bos	45	2700	30	10	5	137	3	3.04
77–78	Bos	21	1086	10	5	2	48	1	2.65
78–79	Bos	43	2509	23	0	10	132	1	3.16
79–80	Bos	42	2479	24	11	7	116	4	2.81
NHL Totals		418	24394	230	94	74	1175	26	2.89
WHA Totals		191	11352	99	78	9	591	14	3.12

Playoffs

		GP	MIN.	W	L	T	GA	SO.	AVG.
67–68	Bos	4	240	0	4	0	15	0	3.75
68–69	Bos	9	572	0	4	4	16	3	1.68
69–70	Bos	13	781	12	1	0	29	0	2.23
70–71	Bos	6	360	3	3	0	21	0	3.50
71–72	Bos	8	483	6	2	0	21	2	2.61
72–73	Clev (WHA)	9	548	5	4	0	22	0	2.41
73–74	Clev (WHA)	5	303	1	4	0	18	0	3.56
74–75	Clev (WHA)	5	300	1	4	0	23	0	4.60
75–76	Bos	6	392	2	4	0	14	1	2.14
76–77	Bos	14	858	8	5	0	44	1	3.08
77–78	Bos	12	731	8	4	0	35	0	2.87
78–79	Bos	6	360	4	2	0	15	0	2.50
79–80	Bos	10	619	4	6	0	32	0	3.10
NHL Totals		88	5396	47	35	0	242	7	2.69
WHA Totals		19	1151	7	12	0	63	0	3.28

CHEVELDAE, Timothy *5–10 195*
B. Melville, Sask., Feb. 15, 1968

		GP	MIN.	W	L	T	GA	SO.	AVG.
88–89	Det	2	122	0	2	0	9	0	4.43
89–90	Det	28	1600	10	9	8	101	0	3.79
90–91	Det	65	3615	30	26	5	214	2	3.55
91–92	Det	72	4236	38	23	9	226	2	3.20
92–93	Det	67	3880	34	24	7	210	4	3.25
93–94	Det–Winn	44	2360	21	17	2	143	2	3.64
94–95	Winn	30	1571	8	16	3	97	0	3.70
95–96	Winn	30	1695	8	18	3	111	0	3.93
96–97	Bos	2	93	0	1	0	5	0	3.23
Totals		340	19172	149	136	37	1116	10	3.49

Playoffs

		GP	MIN.	W	L	T	GA	SO.	AVG.
90–91	Det	7	398	3	4	0	22	0	3.32
91–92	Det	11	597	3	7	0	25	2	2.51
92–93	Det	7	423	3	4	0	24	0	3.40
Totals		25	1418	9	15	0	71	2	3.00

CHEVRIER, Alain *5–8 180*
B. Cornwall, Ont., Apr. 23, 1961

		GP	MIN.	W	L	T	GA	SO.	AVG.
85–86	NJ	37	1862	11	18	2	143	0	4.61
86–87	NJ	58	3153	24	26	2	227	0	4.32
87–88	NJ	45	2354	18	19	3	148	1	3.77
88–89	Winn–Chi	49	2665	21	19	4	170	1	3.83
89–90	Chi–Pitt	42	2060	17	16	3	146	0	4.25
90–91	Det	3	108	0	2	0	11	0	6.11
Totals		234	12202	91	100	14	845	2	4.16

Playoffs

		GP	MIN.	W	L	T	GA	SO.	AVG.
88–89	Chi	16	1013	9	7	0	44	0	2.61

SEASON	TEAM	GP	MIN.	W	L	T	GA	SO.	AVG.

CLANCY, Francis Michael (King) *5–9 184*
B. Ottawa, Ont., Feb. 25, 1903

SEASON	TEAM	GP	MIN.	W	L	T	GA	SO.	AVG.
32–33	Tor	1	1	0	0	0	0	0	0.00

CLEGHORN, Ogilvie (Odie)
B. Montreal, Que.

| 25–26 | Pitt Pi | 1 | 60 | 1 | 0 | 0 | 2 | 0 | 2.00 |

CLIFFORD, Chris *5–9 167*
B. Kingston, Ont., May 26, 1966

| 88–89 | Chi | 1 | 4 | 0 | 0 | 0 | 0 | 0 | 0.00 |

CLOUTIER, Dan *6–1 182*
B. Mont-Laurier, Que., April 22, 1976

97–98	NYR	12	451	4	5	1	23	0	2.50
98–99	NYR	22	1097	6	8	3	49	0	2.68
Totals		34	1548	10	13	4	72	0	2.79

CLOUTIER, Jacques *5–7 167*
B. Noranda, Que., Jan. 3, 1960

81–82	Buf	7	311	5	1	0	13	0	2.51
82–83	Buf	25	1390	10	7	6	81	0	3.50
84–85	Buf	1	65	0	0	1	4	0	3.69
85–86	Buf	15	872	5	9	1	49	1	3.37
86–87	Buf	40	2167	11	19	5	137	0	3.79
87–88	Buf	20	851	4	8	2	67	0	4.72
88–89	Buf	36	1786	15	14	0	108	0	3.63
89–90	Chi	43	2178	18	15	2	112	2	3.09
90–91	Chi–Que	25	1232	5	11	2	85	0	4.14
91–92	Que	26	1345	6	14	3	88	0	3.93
92–93	Que	3	154	0	2	1	10	0	3.90
93–94	Que	14	475	3	2	1	24	0	3.03
Totals		255	12826	82	102	24	778	3	3.64

Playoffs

88–89	Buf	4	238	1	3	0	10	1	2.52
89–90	Chi	4	175	0	2	0	8	0	2.74
Totals		8	413	1	5	0	18	1	2.62

COLVIN, Les *5–6 150*
B. Oshawa, Ont., Feb. 8, 1921

| 48–49 | Bos | 1 | 60 | 0 | 1 | 0 | 4 | 0 | 4.00 |

CONACHER, Charles William (The Bomber) *6–1 195*
B. Toronto, Ont., Dec. 20, 1910

32–33	Tor	1	2	0	0	0	0	0	0.00
34–35	Tor	1	3	0	0	0	0	0	0.00
38–39	Det	1	4	0	0	0	0	0	0.00
Totals		3	9	0	0	0	0	0	0.00

CONNELL, Alex (The Ottawa Fireman) *5–9 150*
B. Ottawa, Ont., Feb. 8, 1902

24–25	Ott	30	1852	17	12	1	66	7	2.20
25–26	Ott	36	2231	24	8	1	42	15	1.17
26–27	Ott	44	2782	30	10	4	69	13	1.57
27–28	Ott	44	2760	20	14	10	57	15	1.30
28–29	Ott	44	2820	14	17	13	67	7	1.52
29–30	Ott	44	2780	21	15	8	118	3	2.68
30–31	Ott	36	2190	10	22	4	110	3	3.06
31–32	Det	48	3050	24	19	5	108	6	2.25
32–33	Det	15	845	4	8	2	36	1	2.57
33–34	NYA	1	40	1	0	0	2	0	3.00
34–35	Mont M	48	2970	24	19	5	92	9	1.92
36–37	Mont M	27	1710	10	11	6	63	2	2.33
Totals		417	26030	199	155	59	830	81	1.91

Playoffs

25–26	Ott	2	120	0	1	1	2	0	1.00
26–27	Ott	6	400	3	0	3	4	2	0.67
27–28	Ott	2	120	0	2	0	3	0	1.50
29–30	Ott	2	120	0	1	1	6	0	3.00
31–32	Det	2	120	0	1	1	3	0	1.50
34–35	Mont M	7	429	6	0	1	8	2	1.14
Totals		21	1309	9	5	7	26	4	1.19

CORSI, James *5–10 180*
B. Montreal, Que., June 19, 1954

77–78	Que (WHA)	23	1089	10	7	0	82	0	4.52
78–79	Que (WHA)	40	2291	16	20	1	126	3	3.30
79–80	Edm	26	1366	8	14	3	83	0	3.65
NHL Totals		26	1366	8	14	3	83	0	3.65
WHA Totals		63	3380	26	27	1	208	3	3.69

COURTEAU, Maurice Laurent *5–8 162*
B. Quebec City, Que., Feb. 18, 1920

| 43–44 | Bos | 6 | 360 | 2 | 4 | 0 | 33 | 0 | 5.50 |

COUSINEAU, Marcel *5–9 180*
B. Delson, Que., April 30, 1973

96–97	Tor	13	566	3	5	1	31	1	3.29
97–98	Tor	2	17	0	0	0	0	0	0.00
98–99	NYI	6	293	0	4	0	14	0	2.87
Totals		21	876	*3	9	1	45	1	3.08

COX, Abbie
29–30	Mont M	1	60	1	0	0	2	0	2.00
33–34	Det–NYA	3	133	0	1	1	8	0	3.61
35–36	Mont	1	70	0	0	1	1	0	0.86
Totals		5	263	1	1	2	11	0	2.51

COWLEY, Wayne *6–0 185*
B. Scarborough, Ont., Dec. 4, 1964

| 93–94 | Edm | 1 | 57 | 0 | 1 | 0 | 3 | 0 | 3.16 |

CRAIG, James *6–1 190*
B. North Easton, Me., May 31, 1957

79–80	Atl	4	206	1	2	1	13	0	3.79
80–81	Bos	23	1272	9	7	6	78	0	3.68
83–84	Minn	3	110	1	1	0	9	0	4.92
Totals		30	1588	11	10	7	100	0	3.78

CRHA, Jiri *5–11 170*
B. Pardubice, Czechoslovakia, Apr. 13, 1950

79–80	Tor	15	830	8	7	0	50	0	3.61
80–81	Tor	54	3112	20	20	11	211	0	4.07
Totals		69	3942	28	27	11	261	0	3.97

Playoffs

79–80	Tor	2	121	0	2	0	10	0	4.96
80–81	Tor	3	65	0	2	0	11	0	10.15
Totals		5	186	0	4	0	21	0	6.77

CROZIER, Roger Allan *5–8 140*
B. Bracebridge, Ont., Mar. 16, 1942

63–64	Det	15	900	5	6	4	51	2	3.40
64–65	Det	70	4167	40	23	7	168	6	2.42
65–66	Det	64	3734	28	24	12	173	7	2.78
66–67	Det	58	3256	22	30	4	182	4	3.35
67–68	Det	34	1729	9	18	2	95	1	3.30
68–69	Det	38	1820	11	16	3	101	0	3.33
69–70	Det	34	1877	16	6	9	83	0	2.65
70–71	Buf	44	2198	9	20	7	135	1	3.69
71–72	Buf	63	3654	13	34	14	214	2	3.51
72–73	Buf	49	2633	23	13	7	121	3	2.76
73–74	Buf	12	615	4	3	4	39	0	3.80
74–75	Buf	23	1260	17	2	1	55	3	2.62
75–76	Buf	11	620	8	2	0	27	1	2.61
76–77	Wash	3	103	1	0	0	2	0	1.17
Totals		518	28566	206	197	74	1446	30	3.04

Playoffs

63–64	Det	2	108	0	1	0	5	0	2.78
64–65	Det	7	420	3	4	0	23	0	3.29
65–66	Det	12	666	6	5	0	26	1	2.34
69–70	Det	1	34	0	1	0	3	0	5.29
72–73	Buf	4	249	2	2	0	11	0	2.65
74–75	Buf	5	292	3	2	0	14	0	2.88
Totals		31	1769	14	15	0	82	1	2.78

CUDE, Wilfred *5–9 146*
B. Barrie, England, July 4, 1910

30–31	Phil	29	1750	2	22	3	127	1	4.38
31–32	Bos–Chi	3	161	1	1	0	15	1	5.59
33–34	Det–Mont	30	1920	16	6	8	47	5	1.47
34–35	Mont	48	2960	19	23	6	145	1	3.02
35–36	Mont	47	2940	11	26	10	122	6	2.60
36–37	Mont	44	2730	22	17	5	99	5	2.25
37–38	Mont	47	2990	18	17	12	126	3	2.68
38–39	Mont	23	1440	8	11	4	77	2	3.35
39–40	Mont	7	415	1	5	1	24	0	3.43
40–41	Mont	3	180	2	1	0	13	0	4.33
Totals		281	17486	100	129	49	795	24	2.73

Playoffs

33–34	Det	9	653	4	5	0	21	1	2.33
34–35	Mont	2	120	0	1	1	6	0	3.00
36–37	Mont	5	352	2	3	0	13	0	2.60
37–38	Mont	3	192	1	2	0	11	0	3.67
Totals		19	1317	7	11	1	51	1	2.32

CUTTS, Donald Edward *6–3 190*
B. Edmonton, Alta., Feb. 24, 1953

79–80	Edm	6	269	1	2	1	16	0	3.57

CYR, Claude
B. Montreal, Que., Mar. 27, 1939

58–59	Mont	1	20	0	0	0	1	0	3.00

DADSWELL, Doug *5–10 180*
B. Scarborough, Ont., Feb. 7, 1964

86–87	Calg	2	125	0	1	1	10	0	4.80
87–88	Calg	25	1221	8	7	2	89	0	4.37
Totals		27	1346	8	8	3	99	0	4.41

DAFOE, Byron Jaromir *5–11 175*
B. Sussex, England, Feb. 25, 1971

92–93	Wash	1	1	0	0	0	0	0	0.00
93–94	Wash	5	230	2	2	0	13	0	3.39
94–95	Wash	4	187	1	1	1	11	0	3.53
95–96	LA	47	2666	14	24	8	172	1	3.87
96–97	LA	40	2162	13	17	5	112	0	3.11
97–98	Bos	65	3693	30	25	9	138	6	2.24
98–99	Bos	68	4001	32	23	11	133	10	1.99
Totals		230	12940	92	92	34	579	17	2.68

Playoffs

93–94	Wash	2	118	0	2	0	55	0	2.54
94–95	Wash	1	20	0	0	0	1	0	3.00
97–98	Bos	6	422	2	4	0	14	1	1.99
98–99	Bos	12	768	6	6	0	26	2	2.03
Totals		21	1328	8	12	0	46	3	2.08

D'ALESSIO, Corrie *5–11 155*
B. Cornwall, Ont., Sept. 9, 1969

92–93	Hart	1	11	0	0	0	0	0	0.00

DALEY, Thomas Joseph (Joe) *5–10 160*
B. Winnipeg, Man., Feb. 20, 1943

68–69	Pitt	29	1615	10	13	3	87	2	3.23
69–70	Pitt	9	528	1	5	3	26	0	2.95
70–71	Buf	38	2073	12	16	8	128	1	3.70
71–72	Det	29	1620	11	10	5	85	0	3.15
72–73	Winn (WHA)	29	1718	17	10	1	83	2	2.90
73–74	Winn (WHA)	41	2454	19	20	1	163	0	3.99
74–75	Winn (WHA)	51	2902	23	21	4	175	1	3.62
75–76	Winn (WHA)	62	3612	41	17	1	171	5	2.84
76–77	Winn (WHA)	65	3818	39	23	2	206	3	3.24
77–78	Winn (WHA)	37	2075	21	11	1	114	1	3.30
78–79	Winn (WHA)	23	1256	7	11	3	90	0	4.30
NHL Totals		105	5836	34	44	19	326	3	3.35
WHA Totals		308	17835	167	113	13	1002	12	3.37

Playoffs

72–73	Winn (WHA)	7	422	5	2	0	25	0	3.55
73–74	Winn (WHA)	2	119	0	2	0	8	0	4.03
75–76	Winn (WHA)	12	671	10	1	0	29	1	2.59
76–77	Winn (WHA)	20	1186	11	9	0	71	1	3.59
77–78	Winn (WHA)	5	271	4	1	0	13	0	2.88
78–79	Winn (WHA)	3	37	0	0	0	3	0	4.86
WHA Totals		49	2706	30	15	0	149	2	3.30

DAMORE, Nicholas *5–6 160*
B. Niagara Falls, Ont., July 10, 1916

41–42	Bos	1	60	0	1	0	3	0	3.00

D'AMOUR, Marc *5–9 185*
B. Sudbury, Ont., Apr. 29, 1961

85–86	Calg	16	579	2	4	2	32	0	3.32

DASKALAKIS, Cleon *5–9 175*
B. Boston, Mass., Sept. 29, 1962

84–85	Bos	8	289	1	2	1	24	0	4.98
85–86	Bos	2	120	0	2	0	10	0	5.00
86–87	Bos	2	97	2	0	0	7	0	4.33
Totals		12	506	3	4	1	41	0	4.86

DAVIDSON, John Arthur *6–3 205*
B. Ottawa, Ont., Feb. 27, 1953

73–74	St L	39	2300	13	19	7	118	0	3.08
74–75	St L	40	2360	17	15	7	144	0	3.66
75–76	NYR	56	3207	22	28	5	212	3	3.97
76–77	NYR	39	2116	14	14	6	125	1	3.54
77–78	NYR	34	1848	14	13	4	98	1	3.18
78–79	NYR	39	2232	20	.12	5	131	0	3.52
79–80	NYR	41	2306	20	15	4	122	2	3.17

80–81	NYR	10	560	1	7	1	48	0	5.14
81–82	NYR	1	60	1	0	0	1	0	1.00
82–83	NYR	2	120	1	1	0	5	0	2.50
Totals		301	17109	123	124	39	1004	7	3.52

Playoffs

74–75	StL	1	60	0	1	0	4	0	4.00
77–78	NYR	2	122	1	1	0	7	0	3.44
78–79	NYR	18	1106	11	7	0	42	1	2.28
79–80	NYR	9	541	4	5	0	21	0	2.33
81–82	NYR	1	33	0	0	0	3	0	5.45
Totals		31	1862	16	14	0	77	1	2.48

DECOURCY, Robert Phillip *5–11 160*
B. Toronto, Ont., June 12, 1927

47–48	NYR	1	29	0	1	0	6	0	12.41

DEFELICE, Norman *5–10 150*
B. Schumacher, Ont., Jan. 19, 1933

56–57	Bos	10	600	3	5	2	30	0	3.00

DeJORDY, Denis Emile *5–9 185*
B. St. Hyacinthe, Que., Nov. 12, 1938

62–63	Chi	5	290	2	1	2	12	0	2.48
63–64	Chi	6	360	2	3	1	19	0	3.17
64–65	Chi	30	1760	16	10	3	74	3	2.52
66–67	Chi	44	2536	22	12	7	104	4	2.46
67–68	Chi	50	2838	23	15	11	128	4	2.71
68–69	Chi	53	2981	22	22	7	156	2	3.14
69–70	Chi–LA	31	1704	8	16	5	87	0	3.06
70–71	LA	60	3375	18	29	11	214	1	3.80
71–72	LA–Mont	12	623	3	7	1	48	0	4.62
72–73	Det	24	1331	8	11	3	83	1	3.74
73–74	Det	1	20	0	1	0	4	0	12.00
Totals		316	17818	124	127	51	929	15	3.13

Playoffs

63–64	Chi	1	20	0	0	0	2	0	6.00
64–65	Chi	2	80	0	1	0	9	0	6.75
66–67	Chi	4	184	1	2	0	10	0	3.26
67–68	Chi	11	662	5	6	0	34	0	3.08
Totals		18	946	6	9	0	55	0	3.49

DELGUIDICE, Matthew *5–9 170*
B. West Haven, Conn., Mar. 5, 1967

90–91	Bos	1	10	0	0	0	0	0	0.00
91–92	Bos	10	424	2	5	1	28	0	3.96
Totals		11	434	2	5	1	28	0	3.87

DENIS, Marc *6–0 188*
B. Montreal, Que., Aug. 1, 1977

96–97	Col A	1	60	0	1	0	3	0	3.00
98–99	Col A	4	217	1	1	1	9	0	2.49
Totals		5	277	1	2	1	12	0	2.60

DeROUVILLE, Philippe *6–1 185*
B. Victoriaville, Que., Aug. 7, 1974

94–95	Pitt	1	60	1	0	0	3	0	3.00
96–97	Pitt	2	111	0	2	0	6	0	3.24
Totals		3	171	1	2	0	9	0	3.16

DESJARDINS, Gerard Ferdinand *5–11 190*
B. Sudbury, Ont., July 22, 1944

68–69	LA	60	3499	18	34	6	190	4	3.26
69–70	LA–Chi	47	2693	11	29	5	167	3	3.72
70–71	Chi	22	1217	12	6	3	49	0	2.42
71–72	Chi	6	360	1	2	3	21	0	3.50
72–73	NYI	44	2498	5	35	3	195	0	4.68
73–74	NYI	36	1945	9	17	6	101	0	3.12
74–75	Balt (WHA)	41	2282	9	28	1	162	0	4.26
74–75	Buf	9	540	6	2	1	25	0	2.78
75–76	Buf	55	3280	29	15	11	161	2	2.95
76–77	Buf	49	2871	31	12	6	126	3	2.63
77–78	Buf	3	111	0	1	0	7	0	3.78
NHL Totals		331	19014	122	153	44	1042	12	3.29
WHA Totals		41	2282	9	28	1	162	0	4.26

Playoffs

68–69	LA	9	431	3	4	0	28	0	3.90
71–72	Chi	1	60	1	0	0	5	0	5.00
74–75	Buf	15	760	7	5	0	43	0	3.39
75–76	Buf	9	563	4	5	0	28	0	2.98
76–77	Buf	1	60	0	1	0	4	0	4.00
Totals		35	1874	15	15	0	108	0	3.46

DICKIE, William

SEASON	TEAM	GP	MIN.	W	L	T	GA	SO.	AVG.
41–42	Chi	1	60	1	0	0	3	0	3.00

DION, Conrad 5–4 140
B. St. Remi de Tingwick, Que., Aug. 11, 1918

SEASON	TEAM	GP	MIN.	W	L	T	GA	SO.	AVG.
43–44	Det	26	1560	17	7	2	80	1	3.08
44–45	Det	12	720	6	6	2	39	0	3.25
Totals		38	2280	23	13	4	119	1	3.13

Playoffs

43–44	Det	5	300	1	4	0	17	0	3.40

DION, Michel 5–10 184
B. Granby, Que., Feb. 11, 1954

SEASON	TEAM	GP	MIN.	W	L	T	GA	SO.	AVG.
74–75	Ind (WHA)	1	59	0	1	0	4	0	4.00
75–76	Ind (WHA)	31	1860	14	15	1	85	0	2.74
76–77	Ind (WHA)	42	2286	17	19	3	128	1	3.36
77–78	Cin (WHA)	45	2356	21	17	1	140	4	3.57
78–79	Cin (WHA)	30	1681	10	14	2	93	0	3.32
79–80	Que	50	2773	15	25	6	171	2	3.70
80–81	Que–Winn	26	1445	3	14	6	122	0	5.07
81–82	Pitt	62	3580	25	24	12	226	0	3.79
82–83	Pitt	49	2791	12	30	4	198	0	4.26
83–84	Pitt	30	1553	2	19	4	138	0	5.33
84–85	Pitt	10	553	3	6	0	43	0	4.67
NHL Totals		227	12695	60	118	32	898	2	4.24
WHA Totals		149	8243	62	66	7	450	5	3.28

Playoffs

75–76	Ind (WHA)	3	126	0	2	0	5	0	2.38
76–77	Ind (WHA)	4	245	2	2	0	17	0	4.16
81–82	Pitt	5	304	2	3	0	22	0	4.34
NHL Totals		5	304	2	3	0	22	0	4.34
WHA Totals		7	371	2	4	0	22	0	3.56

DOLSON, Clarence (Dolly)

SEASON	TEAM	GP	MIN.	W	L	T	GA	SO.	AVG.
28–29	Det	44	2750	19	19	6	63	10	1.43
29–30	Det	5	320	0	4	0	24	0	4.80
30–31	Det	44	2750	16	21	7	105	6	2.39
Totals		93	5820	35	44	13	192	16	1.98

Playoffs

28–29	Det	2	120	0	2	0	7	0	3.50

DOPSON, Robert 6–0 200
B. Smiths Falls, Ont., Aug. 21, 1967

93–94	Pitt	2	45	0	0	0	3	0	4.00

DOWIE, Bruce 5–10 170
B. Oakville, Ont., Dec. 9, 1962

83–84	Tor	2	72	0	1	0	4	0	3.33

DRAPER, Thomas 5–11 180
B. Outremont, Que., Nov. 20, 1966

SEASON	TEAM	GP	MIN.	W	L	T	GA	SO.	AVG.
88–89	Winn	2	120	1	1	0	12	0	6.00
89–90	Winn	6	359	2	4	0	26	0	4.35
91–92	Buf	26	1403	10	9	5	75	1	3.21
92–93	Buf	11	664	5	6	0	41	0	3.70
93–94	NYI	7	227	1	3	0	16	0	4.23
95–96	Winn	1	34	0	0	0	3	0	5.29
Totals		53	2807	19	23	5	173	1	3.70

Playoffs

91–92	Buf	7	433	3	4	0	19	1	2.63

DRYDEN, David Murray 6–2 180
B. Hamilton, Ont., Sept. 5, 1941

SEASON	TEAM	GP	MIN.	W	L	T	GA	SO.	AVG.
61–62	NYR	1	40	0	1	0	3	0	4.50
65–66	Chi	11	453	3	4	1	23	0	3.05
67–68	Chi	27	1268	0	0	0	69	1	3.26
68–69	Chi	30	1479	0	0	0	79	3	3.20
70–71	Buf	10	409	3	3	0	23	1	3.37
71–72	Buf	20	1026	3	9	5	68	0	3.98
72–73	Buf	37	2018	14	13	7	89	3	2.65
73–74	Buf	53	2987	23	20	8	148	1	2.97
74–75	Chi (WHA)	45	2728	18	26	1	176	1	3.87
75–76	Edm (WHA)	62	3567	22	34	5	235	1	3.95
76–77	Edm (WHA)	24	1416	10	13	0	77	1	3.26
77–78	Edm (WHA)	48	2578	21	23	2	150	2	3.49
78–79	Edm (WHA)	63	3531	41	17	2	170	3	2.89
79–80	Edm	14	744	2	7	3	53	0	4.27
NHL Totals		203	10424	48	57	24	555	9	3.19
WHA Totals		242	13820	112	113	10	808	8	3.51

Playoffs

65–66	Chi	1	13	0	0	0	0	0	0.00

SEASON	TEAM	GP	MIN.	W	L	T	GA	SO.	AVG.
72–73	Buf	2	120	0	2	0	9	0	4.50
75–76	Edm (WHA)	3	180	0	3	0	15	0	5.00
77–78	Edm (WHA)	2	91	0	1	0	6	0	3.96
78–79	Edm (WHA)	13	687	6	7	0	42	0	3.67
NHL Totals		3	133	0	2	0	9	0	4.06
WHA Totals		18	958	6	11	0	63	0	3.95

DRYDEN, Kenneth Wayne 6–4 210
B. Hamilton, Ont., Aug. 8, 1947

SEASON	TEAM	GP	MIN.	W	L	T	GA	SO.	AVG.
70–71	Mont	6	327	6	0	0	9	0	1.65
71–72	Mont	64	3800	39	8	15	142	8	2.24
72–73	Mont	54	3165	33	7	13	119	6	2.26
74–75	Mont	56	3320	30	9	16	149	4	2.69
75–76	Mont	62	3580	42	10	8	121	8	2.03
76–77	Mont	56	3275	41	6	8	117	10	2.14
77–78	Mont	52	3071	37	7	7	105	5	2.05
78–79	Mont	47	2814	30	10	7	108	5	2.30
Totals		397	23352	258	57	74	870	46	2.24

Playoffs

70–71	Mont	20	1221	12	8	0	61	0	3.00
71–72	Mont	6	360	2	4	0	17	0	2.83
72–73	Mont	17	1039	12	5	0	50	1	2.89
74–75	Mont	11	688	6	5	0	29	2	2.53
75–76	Mont	13	780	12	1	0	25	1	1.92
76–77	Mont	14	849	12	2	0	22	4	1.55
77–78	Mont	15	919	12	3	0	29	2	1.89
78–79	Mont	16	990	12	4	0	41	0	2.48
Totals		112	6846	80	32	0	274	10	2.40

DUMAS, Michel 5–9 180
B. St. Antoine-de-Pontbriand, Que., July 8, 1949

SEASON	TEAM	GP	MIN.	W	L	T	GA	SO.	AVG.
74–75	Chi	3	121	2	0	0	7	0	3.47
76–77	Chi	5	241	0	1	2	17	0	4.23
Totals		8	362	2	1	2	24	0	3.98

Playoffs

74–75	Chi	1	19	0	0	0	1	0	3.16

DUNHAM, Michael 6–3 185
B. Johnson City, N.Y., June 1, 1972

SEASON	TEAM	GP	MIN.	W	L	T	GA	SO.	AVG.
96–97	NJ	26	1013	8	7	1	43	2	2.55
97–98	NJ	15	773	5	5	3	29	1	2.25
98–99	Nash	44	2472	16	23	3	127	1	3.08
Totals		115	4260	29	35	7	199	4	2.80

DUPUIS, Robert

79–80	Edm	1	60	0	1	0	4	0	4.00

* DURNAN, William 6–0 190
B. Toronto, Que., Jan. 22, 1916

SEASON	TEAM	GP	MIN.	W	L	T	GA	SO.	AVG.
43–44	Mont	50	3000	28	5	7	109	2	2.18
44–45	Mont	50	3000	28	8	4	121	1	2.42
45–46	Mont	40	2400	24	11	5	104	4	2.60
46–47	Mont	60	3600	34	16	10	138	4	2.30
47–48	Mont	59	3505	20	28	10	162	5	2.77
48–49	Mont	60	3600	28	23	9	126	10	2.10
49–50	Mont	64	3840	26	21	17	141	8	2.20
Totals		383	22945	208	112	62	901	34	2.36

Playoffs

43–44	Mont	9	549	8	1	0	14	1	1.53
44–45	Mont	6	373	2	4	0	15	0	2.41
45–46	Mont	9	581	8	1	0	20	0	2.07
46–47	Mont	11	700	6	5	0	23	1	1.97
48–49	Mont	7	468	3	4	0	17	0	2.18
49–50	Mont	3	180	0	3	0	10	0	3.33
Totals		45	2851	27	18	0	99	2	2.08

DYCK, Edwin Paul 5–11 160
B. Warman, Sask., Oct. 29, 1950

SEASON	TEAM	GP	MIN.	W	L	T	GA	SO.	AVG.
71–72	Van	12	573	1	6	2	35	0	3.66
72–73	Van	25	1297	5	17	1	98	1	4.53
73–74	Van	12	583	2	5	2	45	0	4.63
74–75	Ind (WHA)	32	1692	3	21	3	123	0	4.36
NHL Totals		49	2453	8	28	5	178	1	4.35
WHA Totals		32	1692	3	21	3	123	0	4.36

EDWARDS, Donald Laurie 5–9 160
B. Hamilton, Ont., Sept. 28, 1955

SEASON	TEAM	GP	MIN.	W	L	T	GA	SO.	AVG.
76–77	Buf	25	1480	16	7	2	62	2	2.51
77–78	Buf	72	4209	38	16	7	185	5	2.64
78–79	Buf	54	3160	26	18	9	159	2	3.02
79–80	Buf	49	2920	27	9	12	125	2	2.57
80–81	Buf	45	2700	23	10	12	133	3	2.96
81–82	Buf	62	3500	26	23	9	205	0	3.51

SEASON	TEAM	GP	MIN.	W	L	T	GA	SO.	AVG.
82–83	Calg	39	2209	16	15	6	148	1	4.02
83–84	Calg	41	2303	13	19	5	157	0	4.09
84–85	Calg	34	1691	11	15	2	115	1	4.08
85–86	Tor	38	2009	12	23	0	160	0	4.78
Totals		459	26181	208	155	74	1449	16	3.32

Playoffs

76–77	Buf	5	300	2	3	0	15	0	3.00
77–78	Buf	8	482	3	5	0	22	0	2.74
79–80	Buf	6	360	3	3	0	17	1	2.83
80–81	Buf	8	503	4	4	0	28	0	3.34
81–82	Buf	4	214	1	3	0	16	0	4.49
82–83	Calg	5	226	1	2	0	22	0	5.84
83–84	Calg	6	217	2	1	0	12	0	3.31
Totals		42	2302	16	21	0	132	1	3.44

EDWARDS, Gary William
B. Toronto, Ont., Oct. 5, 1947

68–69	St L	1	4	0	0	0	0	0	0.00
69–70	St L	1	60	0	1	0	4	0	4.00
71–72	LA	44	2503	13	23	5	150	2	3.60
72–73	LA	27	1560	9	16	1	94	1	3.62
73–74	LA	18	929	5	7	2	50	1	3.23
74–75	LA	27	1561	15	3	6	61	3	2.34
75–76	LA	29	1740	12	13	4	103	0	3.55
76–77	LA–Clev	27	1500	4	16	5	107	2	4.28
77–78	Clev	30	1700	6	18	5	128	0	4.52
78–79	Minn	25	1337	6	11	5	83	0	3.72
79–80	Minn	26	1539	9	7	10	82	0	3.20
80–81	Edm	15	729	5	3	4	44	0	3.62
81–82	St L–Pitt	16	840	4	7	2	67	1	4.79
Totals		286	16002	88	125	43	973	10	3.65

Playoffs

73–74	LA	1	60	1	0	0	1	0	1.00
75–76	LA	2	120	1	1	0	9	0	4.50
79–80	Minn	7	337	3	3	0	22	0	3.92
80–81	Edm	1	20	0	0	0	2	0	6.00
Totals		11	537	5	4	0	34	0	3.80

EDWARDS, Marvin Wayne *5–8 155*
B. St. Catharines, Ont., Aug. 15, 1935

68–69	Pitt	1	60	0	1	0	3	0	3.00
69–70	Tor	25	1420	10	9	4	77	1	3.25
72–73	Cal	21	1207	4	14	2	87	1	4.32
73–74	Cal	14	780	1	10	1	51	0	3.92
Totals		61	3467	15	34	7	218	2	3.77

EDWARDS, Roy Allen *5–8 165*
B. Seneca Township, Ont., Mar. 12, 1937

67–68	Det	41	2177	15	15	8	127	0	3.50
68–69	Det	40	2099	18	11	6	89	4	2.54
69–70	Det	47	2683	24	15	6	116	2	2.59
70–71	Det	38	2104	11	19	7	119	0	3.39
71–72	Pitt	15	847	2	8	4	36	0	2.55
72–73	Det	52	3012	22	17	7	132	6	2.63
73–74	Det	4	187	0	3	0	18	0	5.78
Totals		236	13109	92	88	38	637	12	2.92

Playoffs

69–70	Det	4	206	0	3	0	11	0	3.20

ELIOT, Darren *6–1 175*
B. Hamilton, Ont., Nov. 26, 1961

84–85	LA	33	1882	12	11	6	137	0	4.37
85–86	LA	27	1481	5	17	3	121	0	4.90
86–87	LA	24	1404	8	13	2	103	1	4.40
87–88	Det	3	97	0	0	1	9	0	5.57
88–89	Buf	2	67	0	0	0	7	0	6.27
Totals		89	4931	25	41	12	377	1	4.59

Playoffs

86–87	1	40	0	0	0	7	0	10.50	

ELLACOTT, Kenneth *5–8 160*
B. Paris, Ont., Mar. 3, 1959

82–83	Van	12	555	2	3	4	41	0	4.43

ERICKSON, Chad *5–9 175*
B. Minneapolis, Minn., Aug. 21, 1970

91–92	NJ	2	120	1	1	0	9	0	4.50

ESCHE, Robert *6–1 204*
B. Utica, N.Y., Jan. 22, 1976

98–99	Phoe	3	130	0	1	0	7	0	3.23

ESPOSITO, Anthony James (Tony O) *5–11 185*
B. Sault Ste. Marie, Ont., Apr. 23, 1943

68–69	Mont	13	746	5	3	4	34	2	2.73
69–70	Chi	63	3763	38	17	8	136	15	2.17
70–71	Chi	57	3325	35	14	6	126	6	2.27
71–72	Chi	48	2780	31	10	6	82	9	1.76
72–73	Chi	56	3340	32	17	7	140	4	2.51
73–74	Chi	70	4143	34	14	21	141	10	2.04
74–75	Chi	71	4219	34	30	7	193	6	2.74
75–76	Chi	68	4003	30	23	13	198	4	2.97
76–77	Chi	69	4067	25	36	8	234	2	3.45
77–78	Chi	64	3840	23	22	14	168	5	2.63
78–79	Chi	63	3780	24	28	11	206	4	3.27
79–80	Chi	69	4140	31	22	16	205	6	2.97
80–81	Chi	66	3935	29	23	14	246	0	3.75
81–82	Chi	52	3069	19	25	8	231	1	4.52
82–83	Chi	39	2340	23	11	5	135	1	3.46
83–84	Chi	18	1095				88	1	4.82
Totals		886	52585				2563	76	2.92

Playoffs

69–70	Chi	8	480	4	4	0	27	0	3.38
70–71	Chi	18	1151	11	7	0	42	2	2.19
71–72	Chi	5	300	2	3	0	16	0	3.20
72–73	Chi	15	895	10	5	0	46	1	3.08
73–74	Chi	10	584	6	4	0	28	2	2.88
74–75	Chi	8	472	3	5	0	34	0	4.32
75–76	Chi	4	240	0	4	0	13	0	3.25
76–77	Chi	2	120	0	2	0	6	0	3.00
77–78	Chi	4	252	0	4	0	19	0	4.52
78–79	Chi	4	243	0	4	0	14	0	3.46
79–80	Chi	6	373	3	3	0	14	0	2.25
80–81	Chi	3	215	0	3	0	15	0	4.19
81–82	Chi	7	381	3	3	0	16	1	2.52
82–83	Chi	5	311	3	2	0	18	0	3.47
Totals		99	6017	45	53	0	308	6	3.07

ESSENSA, Robert Earle *6–0 185*
B. Toronto, Ont., Jan. 14, 1965

88–89	Winn	20	1102	6	8	3	68	1	3.70
89–90	Winn	36	2035	18	9	5	107	1	3.15
90–91	Winn	55	2916	19	24	6	153	4	3.15
91–92	Winn	47	2627	21	17	6	126	5	2.88
92–93	Winn	67	3855	33	26	6	227	2	3.53
93–94	Winn–Det	69	3914	23	37	8	235	2	3.60
96–97	Edm	19	879	4	8	0	41	1	2.80
97–98	Edm	16	825	6	6	1	35	0	2.55
98–99	Edm	39	2091	12	14	6	96	0	2.75
Totals		368	20233	142	149	41	1088	16	3.23

Playoffs

89–90	Winn	4	206	2	1	0	12	0	3.50
91–92	Winn	1	33	0	0	0	3	0	5.45
92–93	Winn	6	367	2	4	0	20	0	3.27
93–94	Det	2	109	0	2	0	9	0	4.95
97–98	Edm	1	27	0	0	0	1	0	2.22
Totals		14	742	4	7	0	45	0	3.64

* EVANS, Claude *5–8 165*
B. Longueuil, Que., Apr. 28, 1933

54–55	Mont	4	220	2	2	0	12	0	3.27
57–58	Bos	1	60	0	0	1	4	0	4.00
Totals		5	280	2	2	1	16	0	3.43

EXELBY, Randy *5–9 170*
B. Toronto, Ont., Aug. 13, 1965

88–89	Mont	1	3	0	0	0	0	0	0.00
89–90	Edm	1	60	0	1	0	5	0	5.00
Totals		2	63	0	1	0	5	0	4.76

FARR, Norman Richard (Rocky) *5–11 180*
B. Toronto, Ont., Apr. 7, 1947

72–73	Buf	1	29	0	1	0	3	0	6.21
73–74	Buf	11	480	2	4	1	25	0	3.13
74–75	Buf	7	213	0	1	2	14	0	3.94
Totals		19	722	2	6	3	42	0	3.49

FAVELL, Douglas Robert *5–10 172*
B. St. Catharines, Ont., Apr. 5, 1945

67–68	Phil	37	2192	15	15	6	83	4	2.27
68–69	Phil	21	1195	3	12	5	71	1	3.56
69–70	Phil	15	820	4	5	4	43	1	3.15
70–71	Phil	44	2434	16	15	9	108	2	2.66
71–72	Phil	54	2993	18	25	9	140	5	2.81
72–73	Phil	44	2419	20	15	4	114	3	2.83
73–74	Tor	32	1752	14	7	9	79	0	2.71

SEASON	TEAM	GP	MIN.	W	L	T	GA	SO.	AVG.
74–75	Tor	39	2149	12	17	6	145	1	4.05
75–76	Tor	3	160	0	2	1	15	0	5.63
76–77	Col	30	1614	8	15	3	105	0	3.90
77–78	Col	47	2663	13	20	11	159	1	3.58
78–79	Col	7	380	0	5	2	34	0	5.37
Totals		373	20771	123	153	69	1096	18	3.17

Playoffs

SEASON	TEAM	GP	MIN.	W	L	T	GA	SO.	AVG.
67–68	Phil	2	120	0	2	0	8	0	4.00
68–69	Phil	1	60	0	1	0	5	0	5.00
70–71	Phil	2	120	0	2	0	8	0	4.00
72–73	Phil	11	669	5	6	0	29	1	2.60
73–74	Tor	3	181	0	3	0	10	0	3.31
77–78	Calg	2	120	0	2	0	6	0	3.00
Totals		21	1270	5	16	0	66	1	3.12

FERNANDEZ, Emmanuel *6–0 185*
B. Etobicoke, Ont., Aug. 27, 1974

SEASON	TEAM	GP	MIN.	W	L	T	GA	SO.	AVG.
94–95	Dal	1	59	0	1	0	3	0	3.05
95–96	Dal	5	249	0	1	1	19	0	4.58
97–98	Dal	2	69	1	0	0	2	0	1.74
98–99	Dal	1	60	0	1	0	2	0	2.00
Totals		9	437	1	3	1	26	0	3.57

FICHAUD, Eric *5–11 160*
B. Montreal, Que., Nov. 4, 1975

SEASON	TEAM	GP	MIN.	W	L	T	GA	SO.	AVG.
95–96	NYI	24	1234	7	12	2	68	1	3.31
96–97	NYI	34	1759	9	14	4	91	0	3.10
97–98	NYI	17	807	3	8	3	40	0	2.97
98–99	Nash	9	447	0	6	0	24	0	3.22
Totals		84	4247	19	40	9	223	1	3.15

FISET, Stephane *6–1 195*
B. Montreal, Que., June 17, 1970

SEASON	TEAM	GP	MIN.	W	L	T	GA	SO.	AVG.
89–90	Que	6	342	0	5	1	34	0	5.96
90–91	Que	3	186	0	2	1	12	0	3.87
91–92	Que	23	1133	7	10	2	71	1	3.76
92–93	Que	37	1939	18	9	4	110	0	3.40
93–94	Que	50	2798	20	25	4	158	2	3.39
94–95	Que	32	1879	17	10	3	87	2	2.78
95–96	Col A	37	2107	22	6	7	103	1	2.93
96–97	LA	44	2482	13	24	5	132	4	3.19
97–98	LA	60	3497	26	25	8	158	2	2.71
98–99	LA	42	2403	18	21	1	104	0	2.60
Totals		334	18766	141	137	36	969	15	3.10

Playoffs

SEASON	TEAM	GP	MIN.	W	L	T	GA	SO.	AVG.
92–93	Que	1	21	0	0	0	1	0	2.86
94–95	Que	4	209	1	2	0	16	0	4.59
95–96	Col A	1	1	0	0	0	0	0	0.00
97–98	LA	2	93	0	2	0	7	0	4.52
Totals		8	324	1	4	0	24	0	4.44

FITZPATRICK, Mark *6–2 198*
B. Toronto, Ont., Nov. 13, 1968

SEASON	TEAM	GP	MIN.	W	L	T	GA	SO.	AVG.
88–89	LA–NYI	28	1584	9	12	5	105	0	3.98
89–90	NYI	47	2653	19	19	5	150	3	3.39
90–91	NYI	2	120	1	1	0	6	0	3.00
91–92	NYI	30	1743	11	13	5	93	0	3.20
92–93	NYI	39	2253	17	15	5	130	0	3.46
93–94	Fla	28	1603	12	8	6	73	1	2.73
94–95	Fla	15	819	6	7	1	36	2	2.64
95–96	Fla	34	1786	15	11	3	88	2	2.96
96–97	Fla	30	1680	8	9	9	66	0	2.36
97–98	Fla–TB	46	2578	9	31	3	134	2	3.12
98–99	Chi	27	1403	6	8	6	64	0	2.74
Totals		326	18222	108	134	49	945	9	3.11

Playoffs

SEASON	TEAM	GP	MIN.	W	L	T	GA	SO.	AVG.
89–90	NYI	4	152	0	2	0	13	0	5.33
92–93	NYI	3	77	0	1	0	4	0	3.12
95–96	Fla	2	60	0	0	0	6	0	6.00
Totals		9	289	0	3	0	23	0	4.78

FLAHERTY, Wade *6–0 170*
B. Terrace, B.C., Jan. 11, 1968

SEASON	TEAM	GP	MIN.	W	L	T	GA	SO.	AVG.
91–92	SJ	3	178	0	3	0	13	0	4.38
92–93	SJ	1	60	0	1	0	5	0	5.00
94–95	SJ	18	852	5	6	1	44	1	3.10
95–96	SJ	24	1137	3	12	1	92	0	4.85
96–97	SJ	7	359	2	4	0	31	0	5.18
97–98	NYI	16	694	4	4	3	23	3	1.99
98–99	NYI	20	1048	5	11	2	53	0	3.03
Totals		89	4338	19	41	7	261	4	3.61

Playoffs

SEASON	TEAM	GP	MIN.	W	L	T	GA	SO.	AVG.
94–95	SJ	7	377	2	3	0	31	0	4.93

FORBES, Vernon (Jake) *5–6 140*
B. Toronto, Ont.

SEASON	TEAM	GP	MIN.	W	L	T	GA	SO.	AVG.
19–20	Tor	5	300	1	4	0	21	0	4.20
20–21	Tor	20	1221	13	7	0	78	0	3.90
22–23	Ham	24	1469	6	18	0	110	0	4.58
23–24	Ham	24	1483	9	15	0	68	1	2.83
24–25	Ham	30	1833	19	10	1	60	6	2.00
25–26	NYA	36	2241	12	19	4	86	2	2.39
26–27	NYA	44	2715	17	25	2	91	8	2.07
27–28	NYA	16	980	3	11	2	51	2	3.19
28–29	NYA	1	60	1	0	0	3	0	3.00
29–30	NYA	1	70	0	0	1	1	0	1.00
30–31	Phil Q	2	120	0	2	0	7	0	3.50
31–32	NYA	6	360	3	3	0	16	0	2.67
32–33	NYA	2	70	0	0	1	2	0	2.00
Totals		210	12922	84	114	11	594	19	2.76

Playoffs

SEASON	TEAM	GP	MIN.	W	L	T	GA	SO.	AVG.
20–21	Tor	2	120	0	2	0	7	0	3.50

FORD, Brian *5–10 170*
B. Edmonton, Alta., Sept. 22, 1961

SEASON	TEAM	GP	MIN.	W	L	T	GA	SO.	AVG.
83–84	Que	3	123	1	1	0	13	0	6.34
84–85	Pitt	8	457	2	6	0	48	0	6.30
Totals		11	580	3	7	0	61	0	6.31

FOSTER, Norm *5–9 175*
B. Vancouver, B.C., Feb. 10, 1965

SEASON	TEAM	GP	MIN.	W	L	T	GA	SO.	AVG.
90–91	Bos	3	184	2	1	0	14	0	4.57
91–92	Edm	10	439	5	3	0	20	0	2.73
Totals		13	623	7	4	0	34	0	3.27

FOUNTAIN, Mike *6–1 176*
B. North York, Ont., Jan. 26, 1972

SEASON	TEAM	GP	MIN.	W	L	T	GA	SO.	AVG.
96–97	Van	6	245	2	2	0	14	1	3.43
97–98	Car	3	163	0	3	0	10	0	3.68
Totals		9	408	2	5	0	24	1	3.53

FOWLER, Norman (Hec)

SEASON	TEAM	GP	MIN.	W	L	T	GA	SO.	AVG.
24–25	Bos	7	420	1	6	0	43	0	6.14

FRANCIS, Emile Percy (The Cat) *5–6 145*
B. North Battleford, Sask., Sept. 13, 1926

SEASON	TEAM	GP	MIN.	W	L	T	GA	SO.	AVG.
46–47	Chi	19	1140	6	12	1	104	0	5.47
47–48	Chi	54	3240	18	31	5	183	1	3.39
48–49	NYR	2	120	2	0	0	4	0	2.00
49–50	NYR	1	60	0	1	0	8	0	8.00
50–51	NYR	5	260	1	1	2	14	0	3.23
51–52	NYR	14	840	4	7	3	42	0	3.00
Totals		95	5660	31	52	11	355	1	3.76

FRANKS, James Reginald *5–11 156*
B. Melville, Sask., Nov. 8, 1914

SEASON	TEAM	GP	MIN.	W	L	T	GA	SO.	AVG.
37–38	Det	1	60	1	0	0	3	0	3.00
42–43	NYR	23	1380	5	14	4	103	0	4.48
43–44	Det–Bos	19	1140	6	9	3	79	1	4.16
Totals		43	2580	12	23	7	185	1	4.30

Playoffs

SEASON	TEAM	GP	MIN.	W	L	T	GA	SO.	AVG.
36–37	Det	1	30	0	1	0	2	0	2.00

FREDERICK, Raymond *6–0 154*
B. Fort Francis, Ont., July 31, 1929

SEASON	TEAM	GP	MIN.	W	L	T	GA	SO.	AVG.
54–55	Chi	5	300	0	4	1	22	0	4.40

FRIESEN, Karl *6–0 185*
B. Winnipeg, Man., June 30, 1958

SEASON	TEAM	GP	MIN.	W	L	T	GA	SO.	AVG.
86–87	NJ	4	130	0	2	1	16	0	7.38

FROESE, Robert Glenn *5–11 180*
B. St. Catharines, Que., June 30, 1958

SEASON	TEAM	GP	MIN.	W	L	T	GA	SO.	AVG.
82–83	Phil	25	1407	17	4	2	59	4	2.52
83–84	Phil	48	2863	28	13	7	150	2	3.14
84–85	Phil	17	923	13	2	0	37	1	2.41
85–86	Phil	51	2728	31	10	3	116	5	2.55
86–87	Phil–NYR	31	1654	17	11	0	100	0	3.63
87–88	NYR	25	1443	8	11	3	85	0	3.53
88–89	NYR	30	1621	9	14	4	102	1	3.78
89–90	NYR	15	812	5	7	1	45	0	3.33
Totals		242	13451	128	72	23	694	13	3.10

Playoffs

SEASON	TEAM	GP	MIN.	W	L	T	GA	SO.	AVG.
83–84	Phil	3	154	0	2	0	11	0	4.28
84–85	Phil	4	146	0	1	0	11	0	4.52
85–86	Phil	5	293	2	3	0	15	0	3.07
86–87	NYR	4	165	1	1	0	10	0	3.64
88–89	NYR	2	72	0	2	0	8	0	6.67
Totals		18	830	3	9	0	55	0	3.98

FUHR, Grant *5–9 190*
B. Spruce Grove, Alta., Sept. 28, 1962

SEASON	TEAM	GP	MIN.	W	L	T	GA	SO.	AVG.
81–82	Edm	48	2847	28	5	14	157	0	3.31
82–83	Edm	32	1803	13	12	5	129	0	4.29
83–84	Edm	45	2625	30	10	4	171	1	3.91
84–85	Edm	46	2559	26	8	7	165	1	3.87
85–86	Edm	40	2184	29	8	0	143	0	3.93
86–87	Edm	44	2388	22	13	3	137	0	3.44
87–88	Edm	75	4304	40	24	9	246	4	3.43
88–89	Edm	59	3341	23	26	6	213	1	3.83
89–90	Edm	21	1081	9	7	3	70	1	3.89
90–91	Edm	13	778	6	4	3	39	1	3.01
91–92	Tor	66	3774	25	33	5	230	2	3.66
92–93	Tor–Buf	58	3359	14	24	6	185	1	3.30
93–94	Buf	32	1726	13	12	3	106	2	3.68
94–95	Buf–LA	17	878	2	9	3	59	0	4.03
95–96	StL	79	4365	30	28	16	209	3	2.87
96–97	StL	73	4261	33	27	11	193	3	2.72
97–98	StL	58	3274	29	21	6	238	3	2.53
98–99	StL	39	2193	16	11	8	89	2	2.44
Totals		845	47740	398	282	112	2679	25	3.37

Playoffs

SEASON	TEAM	GP	MIN.	W	L	T	GA	SO.	AVG.
81–82	Edm	5	309	2	3	0	26	0	5.05
82–83	Edm	1	11	0	0	0	0	0	0.00
83–84	Edm	16	883	11	4	0	44	1	2.90
84–85	Edm	18	1064	15	3	0	55	0	3.10
85–86	Edm	9	541	5	4	0	28	0	3.11
86–87	Edm	19	1148	14	5	0	47	0	2.46
87–88	Edm	19	1136	16	2	0	55	0	2.90
88–89	Edm	7	417	3	4	0	24	1	3.45
90–91	Edm	17	1019	8	7	0	51	0	3.00
92–93	Buf	8	474	3	4	0	27	1	3.42
95–96	StL	2	69	1	0	0	1	0	0.87
96–97	StL	6	357	2	4	0	13	2	2.18
97–98	StL	10	616	6	4	0	28	0	2.73
98–99	StL	13	790	6	6	0	31	1	2.35
Totals		150	8834	92	50	0	430	6	2.92

GAGE, Joaquin *6–0 200*
B. Vancouver, B.C., Oct. 19, 1973

SEASON	TEAM	GP	MIN.	W	L	T	GA	SO.	AVG.
94–95	Edm	2	99	0	2	0	7	0	4.24
95–96	Edm	16	717	2	8	1	45	0	3.77
Totals		18	816	2	10	1	52	0	3.82

GAGNON, David *6–0 185*
B. Windsor, Ont., Oct. 31, 1967

SEASON	TEAM	GP	MIN.	W	L	T	GA	SO.	AVG.
90–91	Det	2	35	0	1	0	6	0	10.29

* GAMBLE, Bruce George *5–9 200*
B. Port Arthur, Ont., May 24, 1938

SEASON	TEAM	GP	MIN.	W	L	T	GA	SO.	AVG.
58–59	NYR	2	120	0	2	0	6	0	3.00
60–61	Bos	52	3120	12	23	7	195	0	3.75
61–62	Bos	28	1680	6	18	4	123	1	4.39
65–66	Tor	10	501	5	2	2	21	4	2.51
66–67	Tor	23	1185	5	10	4	67	0	3.39
67–68	Tor	41	2201	19	13	3	85	5	2.31
68–69	Tor	61	3446	28	20	11	161	3	2.80
69–70	Tor	52	3057	18	23	11	156	5	3.06
70–71	Tor–Phil	34	1946	9	20	3	120	2	3.78
71–72	Phil	24	1186	7	8	2	58	2	2.93
Totals		327	18442	109	139	47	992	22	3.23

Playoffs

SEASON	TEAM	GP	MIN.	W	L	T	GA	SO.	AVG.
68–69	Tor	2	86	0	2	0	13	0	9.07
70–71	Phil	2	120	0	2	0	12	0	6.00
Totals		4	206	0	4	0	25	0	7.28

GAMBLE, Troy *5–11 190*
B. New Glasgow, N.S., Apr. 7, 1967

SEASON	TEAM	GP	MIN.	W	L	T	GA	SO.	AVG.
86–87	Van	1	60	0	1	0	4	0	4.00
88–89	Van	5	302	2	3	0	12	0	2.38
90–91	Van	47	2433	16	16	6	140	1	3.45
91–92	Van	19	1009	4	9	3	73	0	4.34
Totals		72	3804	22	29	9	229	1	3.61

Playoffs

SEASON	TEAM	GP	MIN.	W	L	T	GA	SO.	AVG.
90–91	Van	4	249	1	3	0	16	0	3.86

* GARDINER, Charles Robert (Chuck)
B. Edinburgh, Scotland, Dec. 31, 1904

SEASON	TEAM	GP	MIN.	W	L	T	GA	SO.	AVG.
27–28	Chi	40	2420	6	32	2	114	3	2.85
28–29	Chi	44	2758	7	29	8	85	5	1.93
29–30	Chi	44	2750	21	18	5	111	3	2.52
30–31	Chi	44	2710	24	17	3	78	12	1.77
31–32	Chi	48	2989	18	19	11	92	4	1.92
32–33	Chi	48	3010	16	20	12	101	5	2.10
33–34	Chi	48	3050	20	17	11	83	10	1.73
Totals		316	19687	112	152	52	664	42	2.02

Playoffs

SEASON	TEAM	GP	MIN.	W	L	T	GA	SO.	AVG.
29–30	Chi	2	172	0	1	1	3	0	1.50
30–31	Chi	9	638	5	3	1	14	2	1.56
31–32	Chi	2	120	1	1	0	6	1	3.00
33–34	Chi	8	602	6	1	1	12	2	1.50
Totals		21	1532	12	6	3	35	5	1.37

GARDINER, Wilbert (Bert) *5–11 160*
B. Saskatoon, Sask., Mar. 25, 1913

SEASON	TEAM	GP	MIN.	W	L	T	GA	SO.	AVG.
35–36	NYR	1	60	1	0	0	1	0	1.00
40–41	Mont	42	2600	13	23	6	119	1	2.83
41–42	Mont	10	620	1	8	1	42	0	4.20
42–43	Chi	50	3020	17	18	15	180	1	3.58
43–44	Bos	41	2460	17	19	5	212	1	5.17
Totals		144	8760	49	68	27	554	3	3.79

Playoffs

SEASON	TEAM	GP	MIN.	W	L	T	GA	SO.	AVG.
38–39	NYR	6	433	3	3	0	12	0	2.00
40–41	Mont	3	214	1	2	0	8	0	2.67
Totals		9	647	4	5	0	20	0	1.85

GARDNER, George Edward (Bud) *5–10 160*
B. Lachine, Que., Oct. 8, 1942

SEASON	TEAM	GP	MIN.	W	L	T	GA	SO.	AVG.
65–66	Det	1	60	1	0	0	1	0	1.00
66–67	Det	11	560	3	6	0	36	0	3.86
67–68	Det	12	534	3	2	2	32	0	3.60
70–71	Van	18	922	6	8	1	52	0	3.38
71–72	Van	24	1237	3	14	3	86	0	4.17
72–73	LA (WHA)	49	2713	19	22	4	149	1	3.30
73–74	LA–Van (WHA)	30	1710	4	23	1	138	0	4.84
NHL Totals		66	3313	16	30	6	207	0	3.75
WHA Totals		79	4423	23	45	5	287	1	3.89

Playoffs

SEASON	TEAM	GP	MIN.	W	L	T	GA	SO.	AVG.
72–73	LA	3	116	1	2	0	11	0	5.69

GARNER, Tyrone *6–1 170*
B. Stoney Creek, Ont., July 27, 1978

SEASON	TEAM	GP	MIN.	W	L	T	GA	SO.	AVG.
98–99	Calg	3	139	0	2	0	12	0	5.18

GARRETT, John Murdock *5–8 175*
B. Trenton, Ont., June 17, 1951

SEASON	TEAM	GP	MIN.	W	L	T	GA	SO.	AVG.
73–74	Minn (WHA)	40	2290	21	18	0	137	1	3.59
74–75	Minn (WHA)	58	3294	30	23	2	180	2	3.28
75–76	Minn–Tor (WHA)	61	3730	29	28	4	210	3	3.38
76–77	Birm (WHA)	65	3803	24	34	4	224	4	3.53
77–78	Birm (WHA)	58	3306	24	31	1	210	2	3.81
78–79	NE (WHA)	41	2496	20	17	4	149	2	3.58
79–80	Hart	52	3046	16	24	11	202	0	3.98
80–81	Hart	54	3152	15	27	12	241	0	4.59
81–82	Hart–Que	28	1618	9	11	7	125	0	4.64
82–83	Que–Van	34	1887	13	14	5	112	1	3.56
83–84	Van	29	1653	14	10	2	113	0	4.10
84–85	Van	10	407	1	5	0	44	0	6.49
NHL Totals		207	11763	14	10	2	837	1	4.27
WHA Totals		323	18919	148	151	15	1110	14	3.52

Playoffs

SEASON	TEAM	GP	MIN.	W	L	T	GA	SO.	AVG.
73–74	Minn (WHA)	7	372	4	2	0	25	0	4.03
74–75	Minn (WHA)	12	726	6	6	0	41	1	3.39
77–78	Birm (WHA)	5	271	1	4	0	26	0	5.76
78–79	NE (WHA)	8	447	4	3	0	32	0	4.30
79–80	Hart	1	60	0	1	0	8	0	8.00
81–82	Que	5	323	3	2	0	21	0	3.90
82–83	Van	1	60	1	0	0	4	0	4.00
83–84	Van	2	18	0	0	0	0	0	0.00
NHL Totals		9	461	4	3	0	33	0	4.30
WHA Totals		32	1816	15	15	0	124	1	4.10

GATHERUM, David L. *5–8 170*
B. Fort William, Ont., Mar. 28, 1932

SEASON	TEAM	GP	MIN.	W	L	T	GA	SO.	AVG.
53–54	Det	3	180	2	0	1	3	1	1.00

GAUTHIER, Paul *5–5 125*
B. Winnipeg, Man., Mar. 6, 1915

SEASON	TEAM	GP	MIN.	W	L	T	GA	SO.	AVG.
37–38	Mont	1	70	0	0	1	2	0	1.71

GAUTHIER, Sean *5–11 195*
B. Sudbury, Ont., March 28, 1971

SEASON	TEAM	GP	MIN.	W	L	T	GA	SO.	AVG.
98–99	SJ	1	3	0	0	0	0	0	0.00

GELINEAU, John Edward (Jack) *6–0 180*
B. Toronto, Ont., Nov. 11, 1924

SEASON	TEAM	GP	MIN.	W	L	T	GA	SO.	AVG.
48–49	Bos	4	240	2	2	0	12	0	3.00
49–50	Bos	67	4020	22	30	15	220	3	3.28
50–51	Bos	70	4200	22	30	18	197	4	2.81
53–54	Chi	2	120	0	2	0	18	0	9.00
Totals		143	8580	46	64	33	447	7	3.13
Playoffs									
50–51	Bos	4	260	2	2	0	7	1	1.62

GIACOMIN, Edward (Fast Eddie) *5–11 180*
B. Sudbury, Ont., June 6, 1939

SEASON	TEAM	GP	MIN.	W	L	T	GA	SO.	AVG.
65–66	NYR	36	2096	8	19	7	128	0	3.66
66–67	NYR	68	3981	30	25	11	173	9	2.61
67–68	NYR	66	3940	36	20	10	160	8	2.44
68–69	NYR	70	4114	37	23	7	175	7	2.55
69–70	NYR	70	4148	35	21	14	163	6	2.36
70–71	NYR	45	2641	27	10	7	95	8	2.16
71–72	NYR	44	2551	24	10	9	115	1	2.70
72–73	NYR	43	2580	26	11	6	125	4	2.91
73–74	NYR	56	3286	30	15	10	168	5	3.07
74–75	NYR	37	2069	13	12	8	120	1	3.48
75–76	NYR–Det	33	1980	12	17	4	119	2	3.61
76–77	Det	33	1791	8	18	3	107	3	3.58
77–78	Det	9	516	3	5	1	27	0	3.14
Totals		610	35693	289	206	97	1675	54	2.82
Playoffs									
66–67	NYR	4	246	0	4	0	14	0	3.41
67–68	NYR	6	360	2	4	0	18	0	3.00
68–69	NYR	3	180	0	3	0	10	0	3.33
69–70	NYR	5	276	2	3	0	19	0	4.13
70–71	NYR	12	759	7	5	0	28	0	2.21
71–72	NYR	10	600	6	4	0	27	0	2.70
72–73	NYR	10	539	5	4	0	23	1	2.56
73–74	NYR	13	788	7	6	0	37	0	2.82
74–75	NYR	2	86	0	2	0	4	0	2.79
Totals		65	3834	29	35	0	180	1	2.82

GIGUERE, Jean–Sebastien *6–0 175*
B. Montreal, Que., May 16, 1977

SEASON	TEAM	GP	MIN.	W	L	T	GA	SO.	AVG.
96–97	Hart	8	394	1	4	0	24	0	3.65
98–99	Calg	15	860	6	7	1	46	0	3.21
Totals		23	1254	7	11	1	70	0	3.35

GILBERT, Gilles Joseph *6–1 175*
B. St. Esprit, Que., Mar. 31, 1949

SEASON	TEAM	GP	MIN.	W	L	T	GA	SO.	AVG.
69–70	Minn	1	60	0	1	0	6	0	6.00
70–71	Minn	17	931	5	9	2	59	0	3.80
71–72	Minn	4	218	1	2	1	11	0	3.03
72–73	Minn	22	1320	10	10	2	67	2	3.05
73–74	Bos	54	3210	34	12	8	158	6	2.95
74–75	Bos	53	3029	21	17	11	158	3	3.13
75–76	Bos	55	3123	33	8	10	151	3	2.90
76–77	Bos	34	2040	8	18	3	97	1	2.85
77–78	Bos	25	1326	15	6	2	56	2	2.53
78–79	Bos	23	1254	12	8	2	74	0	3.54
79–80	Bos	33	1933	20	9	3	88	1	2.73
80–81	Det	48	2618	11	24	9	175	0	4.01
81–82	Det	27	1478	6	10	6	105	0	4.26
82–83	Det	20	1137	4	14	1	85	0	4.49
Totals		416	23677	182	148	60	1290	18	3.27
Playoffs									
72–73	Minn	1	60	0	1	0	4	0	4.00
73–74	Bos	6	977	10	6	0	43	1	2.64
74–75	Bos	3	188	1	2	0	12	0	3.83
75–76	Bos	6	360	3	3	0	19	2	3.17
76–77	Bos	1	20	0	1	0	3	0	9.00
78–79	Bos	5	314	3	2	0	16	0	3.06
Totals		22	1919	17	15	0	97	3	3.03

GILL, Andre *5–7 145*
B. Sorel, Que., Sept. 19, 1941

SEASON	TEAM	GP	MIN.	W	L	T	GA	SO.	AVG.
67–68	Bos	5	270	3	2	0	13	1	2.89
72–73	Chi (WHA)	33	1709	4	24	0	118	0	4.14
73–74	Chi (WHA)	13	803	4	7	2	46	0	3.44
NHL Totals		5	270	3	2	0	13	1	2.89
WHA Totals		46	2512	8	31	2	164	0	3.92
Playoffs									
73–74	Chi (WHA)	11	614	6	5	0	38	0	3.71

*** GOODMAN, Paul** *5–9 165*
B. Selkirk, Man., Nov. 4, 1908

SEASON	TEAM	GP	MIN.	W	L	T	GA	SO.	AVG.
39–40	Chi	31	1920	16	10	5	62	4	1.94
40–41	Chi	21	1320	7	10	4	55	2	2.50
Totals		52	3240	23	20	9	117	6	2.17
Playoffs									
37–38	Chi	1	60	0	1	0	5	0	5.00
39–40	Chi	2	127	0	2	0	5	0	2.36
Totals		3	187	0	3	0	10	0	3.21

GORDON, Scott *5–10 175*
B. Brockton, Mass., Feb. 6, 1963

SEASON	TEAM	GP	MIN.	W	L	T	GA	SO.	AVG.
89–90	Que	10	597	2	8	0	53	0	5.33
90–91	Que	13	485	0	8	0	48	0	5.94
Totals		23	1082	2	16	0	101	0	5.60

GOSSELIN, Mario *5–8 165*
B. Thetford Mines, Que., June 15, 1963

SEASON	TEAM	GP	MIN.	W	L	T	GA	SO.	AVG.
83–84	Que	3	148	2	0	0	3	1	1.21
84–85	Que	35	1960	19	10	3	109	1	3.34
85–86	Que	31	1726	14	14	1	111	2	3.86
86–87	Que	30	1625	13	11	1	86	0	3.18
87–88	Que	54	3002	20	28	4	189	2	3.78
88–89	Que	39	2064	11	19	3	146	0	4.24
89–90	LA	26	1226	7	11	1	79	0	3.87
92–93	Hart	16	867	5	9	1	57	0	3.94
93–94	Hart	7	239	0	4	0	21	0	5.27
Totals		241	12857	91	106	14	801	6	3.74
Playoffs									
84–85	Que	17	1059	9	8	0	54	0	3.06
85–86	Que	1	40	0	1	0	5	0	7.50
86–87	Que	11	654	7	4	0	37	0	3.39
89–90	LA	3	63	0	2	0	3	0	2.90
Totals		32	1816	16	15	0	99	0	3.27

GOVERDE, David *6–0 210*
B. Toronto, Ont., Apr. 9, 1970

SEASON	TEAM	GP	MIN.	W	L	T	GA	SO.	AVG.
91–92	LA	2	120	1	1	0	9	0	4.50
92–93	LA	2	98	0	2	0	13	0	7.96
93–94	LA	1	60	0	1	0	7	0	7.00
Totals		5	278	1	4	0	29	0	6.26

GRAHAME, Ronald Ian *5–11 175*
B. Victoria, B.C., June 7, 1950

SEASON	TEAM	GP	MIN.	W	L	T	GA	SO.	AVG.
73–74	Hou (WHA)	4	250	3	0	1	5	1	1.20
74–75	Hou (WHA)	43	2590	33	10	0	131	4	3.03
75–76	Hou (WHA)	57	3343	39	17	0	182	3	3.27
76–77	Hou (WHA)	39	2345	27	10	2	107	4	2.74
77–78	Bos	40	2328	26	6	7	107	3	2.76
78–79	LA	34	1940	11	19	2	136	0	4.21
79–80	LA	26	1405	9	11	4	98	2	4.19
80–81	LA–Que	14	799	4	7	2	68	0	5.11
NHL Totals		114	6472	50	43	15	409	5	3.79
WHA Totals		143	8528	102	37	3	425	12	2.99
Playoffs									
74–75	Hou (WHA)	13	780	12	1	0	26	3	2.00
75–76	Hou (WHA)	14	817	6	8	0	54	1	3.97
76–77	Hou (WHA)	9	561	4	5	0	36	0	3.85
77–78	Bos	4	202	2	1	0	7	0	2.08
NHL Totals		4	202	2	1	0	7	0	2.08
WHA Totals		36	2158	22	14	0	116	4	3.23

GRANT, Benjamin Cameron *5–11 160*
B. Owen Sound, Ont., July 14, 1908

SEASON	TEAM	GP	MIN.	W	L	T	GA	SO.	AVG.
28–29	Tor	3	110	1	0	0	4	0	1.33
29–30	Tor–NYA	9	550	4	5	0	36	0	3.93
30–31	Tor	7	430	1	5	1	19	2	2.71
31–32	Tor	5	320	1	2	1	18	1	3.60
33–34	NYA	5	320	1	4	0	18	1	3.60
43–44	Tor–Bos	21	1260	9	10	2	93	0	4.43
Totals		50	2990	17	26	4	188	4	3.77

GRANT, Doug Munro *6–1 200*
B. Corner Brook, Nfld., July 27, 1948

SEASON	TEAM	GP	MIN.	W	L	T	GA	SO.	AVG.
73–74	Det	37	2018	15	16	2	140	1	4.16

SEASON	TEAM	GP	MIN.	W	L	T	GA	SO.	AVG.
74–75	Det	7	380	1	5	0	34	0	5.37
75–76	Det	2	120	1	1	0	8	0	4.00
76–77	StL	17	960	7	7	3	50	1	3.13
77–78	StL	9	500	3	3	2	24	0	2.88
78–79	StL	4	190	0	2	1	23	0	7.26
79–80	StL	1	31	0	0	0	1	0	1.94
Totals		77	4199	27	34	8	280	2	4.00

GRATTON, Gilles 5–11 160
B. La Salle, Que., July 28, 1952

72–73	Ott (WHA)	51	3021	25	22	3	187	0	3.71
73–74	Tor (WHA)	57	3200	26	24	3	188	2	3.53
74–75	Tor (WHA)	53	2881	30	20	1	185	2	3.85
75–76	StL	6	265	2	0	2	11	0	2.49
76–77	NYR	41	2034	11	18	7	143	0	4.22
NHL Totals		47	2299	13	18	9	154	0	4.02
WHA Totals		161	9102	81	66	7	560	4	3.69

Playoffs

72–73	Ott (WHA)	2	87	0	1	0	7	0	4.83
73–74	Tor (WHA)	10	539	5	3	0	25	0	2.78
74–75	Tor (WHA)	1	36	0	1	0	5	0	8.33
WHA Totals		13	662	5	5	0	37	0	3.35

GRAY, Gerald Robert (Gerry) 6–0 168
B. Brantford, Ont., Jan. 28, 1948

70–71	Det	7	380	1	4	1	30	0	4.74
72–73	NYI	1	60	0	1	0	5	0	5.00
Totals		8	440	1	5	1	35	0	4.77

GRAY, Harrison Leroy 5–11 165
B. Calgary, Alta., Sept. 5, 1941

63–64	Det	1	40	0	0	0	5	0	7.50

GREENLAY, Michael 6–3 200
B. Vitoria, Brazil, Sept, 15, 1968

89–90	Edm	2	20	0	0	0	4	0	12.00

GUENETTE, Steve 5–10 175
B. Gloucester, Ont., Nov. 13, 1965

86–87	Pitt	2	113	0	2	0	8	0	4.25
87–88	Pitt	19	1092	12	7	0	61	1	3.35
88–89	Pitt	11	574	5	6	0	41	0	4.29
89–90	Calg	2	119	1	1	0	8	0	4.03
90–91	Calg	1	60	1	0	0	4	0	4.00
Totals		35	1958	19	16	0	122	1	3.74

HACKETT, Jeff 6–1 180
B. London, Ont., June 1, 1968

88–89	NYI	13	662	4	7	0	39	0	3.53
90–91	NYI	30	1508	5	18	1	91	0	3.62
91–92	SJ	42	2314	11	27	1	148	0	3.84
92–93	SJ	36	2000	2	30	1	176	0	5.28
93–94	Chi	22	1084	2	12	3	62	0	3.43
94–95	Chi	7	328	1	3	2	13	0	2.38
95–96	Chi	35	2000	18	11	4	80	4	2.40
96–97	Chi	41	2473	19	18	4	89	2	2.16
97–98	Chi	58	3441	21	25	11	126	8	2.20
98–99	Chi-Mont	63	3615	26	26	10	150	5	2.49
Totals		347	19425	109	177	37	974	19	3.01

Playoffs

94–95	Chi	2	26	0	0	0	1	0	2.31
95–96	Chi	1	60	0	1	0	5	0	5.00
96–97	Chi	6	345	2	4	0	25	0	4.35
Totals		9	431	2	5	0	31	0	4.32

* HAINSWORTH, George 5–6 150
B. Toronto, Ont., June 26, 1895

26–27	Mont	44	2732	28	14	2	67	14	1.52
27–28	Mont	44	2730	26	11	7	48	13	1.09
28–29	Mont	44	2800	22	7	15	43	22	0.98
29–30	Mont	42	3008	21	14	9	108	4	2.57
30–31	Mont	44	2740	26	10	8	89	8	2.02
31–32	Mont	48	2998	25	16	7	110	6	2.29
32–33	Mont	48	2980	18	25	5	115	8	2.40
33–34	Tor	48	3010	26	13	9	119	3	2.48
34–35	Tor	48	2957	30	14	4	111	8	2.31
35–36	Tor	48	3000	23	19	6	106	8	2.21
36–37	Tor–Mont	7	460	2	3	2	21	0	2.74
Totals		465	29415	247	146	74	937	94	1.91

Playoffs

26–27	Mont	4	252	1	1	2	6	1	1.50
27–28	Mont	2	128	0	1	1	3	0	1.50
28–29	Mont	3	180	0	3	0	5	0	1.67

SEASON	TEAM	GP	MIN.	W	L	T	GA	SO.	AVG.
29–30	Mont	6	481	5	0	1	6	3	1.00
30–31	Mont	10	722	6	4	0	21	2	2.10
31–32	Mont	4	300	1	3	0	13	0	3.25
32–33	Mont	2	120	0	1	1	8	0	4.00
33–34	Tor	5	302	2	3	0	11	0	2.20
34–35	Tor	7	460	3	4	0	12	2	1.71
35–36	Tor	9	541	3	6	0	27	0	3.00
Totals		52	3486	21	26	5	112	8	1.93

*HALL, Glenn Henry (Mr. Goalie) 6–0 160
B. Humboldt, Sask., Oct. 3, 1931

52–53	Det	6	360	4	1	1	10	1	1.67
54–55	Det	2	120	2	0	0	2	0	1.00
55–56	Det	70	4200	30	24	16	148	12	2.11
56–57	Det	70	4200	38	20	12	157	4	2.24
57–58	Chi	70	4200	24	39	7	202	7	2.89
58–59	Chi	70	4200	28	29	13	208	1	2.97
59–60	Chi	70	4200	28	29	13	180	6	2.57
60–61	Chi	70	4200	29	24	17	180	6	2.57
61–62	Chi	70	4200	31	26	13	186	9	2.66
62–63	Chi	66	3910	30	20	16	166	5	2.55
63–64	Chi	65	3840	34	19	12	148	7	2.31
64–65	Chi	41	2440	18	18	5	99	4	2.43
65–66	Chi	64	3747	34	21	7	164	4	2.63
66–67	Chi	32	1664	19	5	5	66	2	2.38
67–68	StL	49	2858	19	21	9	118	5	2.48
68–69	StL	41	2354	19	12	8	85	8	2.17
69–70	StL	18	1010	7	8	3	49	1	2.91
70–71	StL	32	1761	13	11	8	71	2	2.42
Totals		906	53464	407	327	165	2239	84	2.51

Playoffs

55–56	Det	10	604	5	5	0	28	0	2.78
56–57	Det	5	300	1	4	0	15	0	3.00
58–59	Chi	6	360	2	4	0	21	0	3.50
59–60	Chi	4	249	0	4	0	14	0	3.37
60–61	Chi	12	772	8	4	0	27	2	2.10
61–62	Chi	12	720	6	6	0	31	2	2.58
62–63	Chi	6	360	2	4	0	25	0	4.17
63–64	Chi	7	408	3	4	0	22	0	3.24
64–65	Chi	13	760	7	6	0	28	1	2.21
65–66	Chi	6	347	2	4	0	22	0	3.80
66–67	Chi	3	176	1	2	0	8	0	2.73
67–68	StL	18	1111	8	10	0	45	1	2.43
68–69	StL	3	131	0	2	0	5	0	2.29
69–70	StL	7	421	4	3	0	21	0	2.99
70–71	StL	3	180	0	3	0	9	0	3.00
Totals		115	6899	49	65	0	321	6	2.79

HAMEL, Pierre 5–9 170
B. Montreal, Que., Sept. 16, 1952

74–75	Tor	4	195	1	2	0	18	0	5.54
78–79	Tor	1	1	0	0	0	0	0	0.00
79–80	Winn	35	1947	9	19	3	130	0	4.01
80–81	Winn	29	1623	3	20	4	128	0	4.73
Totals		69	3766	13	41	7	276	0	4.40

HANLON, Glen 6–0 185
B. Brandon, Man., Feb. 20, 1957

77–78	Van	4	200	1	2	1	9	0	2.70
78–79	Van	31	1821	12	13	5	94	3	3.10
79–80	Van	57	3341	17	29	10	193	0	3.47
80–81	Van	17	798	5	8	0	59	1	4.44
81–82	Van–StL	30	1686	8	15	5	114	1	4.06
82–83	StL–NYR	35	1844	12	18	2	117	0	3.81
83–84	NYR	50	2837	28	14	4	166	1	3.51
84–85	NYR	44	2510	14	20	7	175	0	4.18
85–86	NYR	23	1170	5	12	1	65	0	3.33
86–87	Det	36	1963	11	16	5	104	1	3.18
87–88	Det	47	2623	22	17	5	141	4	3.23
88–89	Det	39	2092	13	14	8	124	1	3.56
89–90	Det	45	2290	15	18	5	154	1	4.03
90–91	Det	19	862	4	6	3	46	0	3.20
Totals		477	26037	167	202	61	1561	13	3.60

Playoffs

79–80	Van	2	60	0	0	0	3	0	3.00
81–82	StL	3	109	0	2	0	9	0	4.95
82–83	NYR	1	60	0	1	0	5	0	5.00
83–84	NYR	5	308	2	3	0	13	1	2.53
84–85	NYR	3	168	0	3	0	14	0	5.00
85–86	NYR	3	75	0	0	0	6	0	4.80
86–87	Det	8	467	5	2	0	13	2	1.87
87–88	Det	8	431	4	3	0	22	1	3.08
88–89	Det	2	78	0	1	0	7	0	5.38
Totals		35	1756	11	12	0	92	4	3.14

HARRISON, Paul Douglas 6-1 175
B. Timmons, Ont., Feb. 11, 1955

SEASON	TEAM	GP	MIN.	W	L	T	GA	SO.	AVG.
75–76	Minn	6	307	0	0	0	28	0	5.47
76–77	Minn	2	120	0	0	0	11	0	5.50
77–78	Minn	27	1555	6	16	2	99	1	3.82
78–79	Tor	25	1403	8	12	3	82	1	3.51
79–80	Tor	30	1492	9	17	2	110	0	4.42
81–82	Pitt–Buf	19	929	5	8	1	78	0	5.04
Totals		109	5806	28	53	8	408	2	4.22

Playoffs

SEASON	TEAM	GP	MIN.	W	L	T	GA	SO.	AVG.
78–79	Tor	2	91	0	1	0	7	0	4.62
80–81	Tor	1	40	0	0	0	1	0	1.50
81–82	Buf	1	26	0	0	0	1	0	2.31
Totals		4	157	0	1	0	9	0	3.44

HASEK, Dominik 5-11 168
B. Pardubice, Czechoslovakia, Jan. 29, 1965

SEASON	TEAM	GP	MIN.	W	L	T	GA	SO.	AVG.
90–91	Chi	5	195	3	0	1	8	0	2.46
91–92	Chi	20	1014	10	4	1	44	1	2.60
92–93	Buf	28	1429	11	10	4	75	0	3.15
93–94	Buf	58	3358	30	20	6	109	7	1.95
94–95	Buf	41	2416	19	14	7	85	5	2.11
95–96	Buf	59	3417	22	30	6	161	2	2.83
96–97	Buf	67	4037	37	20	10	153	5	2.27
97–98	Buf	72	4220	33	23	13	147	13	2.09
98–99	Buf	64	3817	30	18	14	119	9	1.87
Totals		414	23903	195	139	62	901	42	2.26

Playoffs

SEASON	TEAM	GP	MIN.	W	L	T	GA	SO.	AVG.
90–91	Chi	3	69	0	0	0	3	0	2.61
91–92	Chi	3	158	0	2	0	8	0	3.04
92–93	Buf	1	45	1	0	0	1	0	1.33
93–94	Buf	7	484	3	4	0	13	2	1.61
94–95	Buf	5	309	1	4	0	18	0	3.50
96–97	Buf	3	153	1	1	0	5	0	1.96
97–98	Buf	15	948	10	5	0	32	1	2.03
98–99	Buf	19	1218	13	6	0	36	2	1.77
Totals		56	3384	29	22	0	116	5	2.07

HAYWARD, Brian 5-10 180
B. Weston, Ont., June 25, 1960

SEASON	TEAM	GP	MIN.	W	L	T	GA	SO.	AVG.
82–83	Winn	24	1440	10	12	2	89	1	3.71
83–84	Winn	28	1530	7	18	2	124	0	4.86
84–85	Winn	61	3436	33	17	7	220	0	3.84
85–86	Winn	52	2721	13	28	5	217	0	4.79
86–87	Mont	37	2178	19	13	4	102	1	2.81
87–88	Mont	39	2247	22	10	4	107	2	2.86
88–89	Mont	36	2091	20	13	3	101	1	2.90
89–90	Mont	29	1674	10	12	6	94	1	3.37
90–91	Minn	26	1473	6	15	3	77	2	3.14
91–92	SJ	7	305	1	4	0	25	0	4.92
92–93	SJ	18	930	2	14	1	86	0	5.55
Totals		357	20025	143	156	37	1242	8	3.72

Playoffs

SEASON	TEAM	GP	MIN.	W	L	T	GA	SO.	AVG.
82–83	Winn	3	160	0	3	0	14	0	5.24
84–85	Winn	6	309	2	4	0	23	0	4.47
85–86	Winn	2	68	0	1	0	6	0	5.29
86–87	Mont	13	708	6	5	0	32	0	2.71
87–88	Mont	4	230	2	2	0	9	0	2.35
88–89	Mont	2	124	1	1	0	7	0	3.39
89–90	Mont	1	33	0	0	0	2	0	3.64
90–91	Minn	6	171	0	2	0	11	0	3.86
Totals		37	1803	11	18	0	104	0	3.46

HEAD, Donald Charles
B. Mount Dennis, Ont., June 30, 1933

SEASON	TEAM	GP	MIN.	W	L	T	GA	SO.	AVG.
61–62	Bos	38	2280	9	26	3	161	2	4.24

HEALY, Glenn 5-10 185
B. Pickering, Ont., Aug. 23, 1962

SEASON	TEAM	GP	MIN.	W	L	T	GA	SO.	AVG.
85–86	LA	1	51	0	0	0	6	0	7.06
87–88	LA	34	1869	12	18	1	135	1	4.33
88–89	LA	48	2699	25	19	2	192	0	4.27
89–90	NYI	39	2197	12	19	6	128	2	3.50
90–91	NYI	53	2999	18	24	9	166	0	3.32
91–92	NYI	37	1960	14	16	4	124	1	3.80
92–93	NYI	47	2655	22	20	2	146	1	3.30
93–94	NYR	29	1368	10	12	2	69	2	3.03
94–95	NYR	17	888	8	6	1	35	1	2.36
95–96	NYR	44	2564	17	14	11	124	2	2.90
96–97	NYR	23	1357	5	12	4	59	1	2.61
97–98	Tor	21	1068	4	10	2	53	0	2.98
98–99	Tor	9	546	6	3	0	27	0	2.97
Totals		402	22221	153	173	44	1264	11	3.41

Playoffs

SEASON	TEAM	GP	MIN.	W	L	T	GA	SO.	AVG.
87–88	LA	4	240	1	3	0	20	0	5.00
88–89	LA	3	97	0	1	0	6	0	3.71
89–90	NYI	4	166	1	2	0	9	0	3.25
92–93	NYI	18	1109	9	8	0	59	0	3.19
93–94	NYR	2	68	0	0	0	1	0	0.88
94–95	NYR	5	230	2	1	0	13	0	3.39
98–99	Tor	1	20	0	0	0	0	0	0.00
Totals		37	1930	13	15	0	108	0	3.36

HEBERT, Guy Andrew 5-11 185
B. Troy, N.Y., Jan. 7, 1967

SEASON	TEAM	GP	MIN.	W	L	T	GA	SO.	AVG.
91–92	StL	13	738	5	5	1	36	0	2.93
92–93	StL	24	1210	8	8	2	74	1	3.67
93–94	Ana	52	2991	20	27	3	141	2	2.83
94–95	Ana	39	2092	13	20	4	109	2	3.13
95–96	Ana	59	3326	28	23	5	157	4	2.83
96–97	Ana	67	3863	29	22	12	172	4	2.67
97–98	Ana	46	2660	13	24	6	130	3	2.93
98–99	Ana	69	4083	31	29	9	165	6	2.42
Totals		369	20963	146	161	42	984	22	2.82

Playoffs

SEASON	TEAM	GP	MIN.	W	L	T	GA	SO.	AVG.
92–93	StL	1	2	0	0	0	0	0	0.00
96–97	Ana	9	534	4	4	0	18	1	2.02
98–99	Ana	4	208	0	3	0	15	0	4.33
Totals		14	744	4	7	0	33	1	2.66

HEBERT, Sammy
B. 1894

SEASON	TEAM	GP	MIN.	W	L	T	GA	SO.	AVG.
17–18	Tor–Ott	2	80	1	1	0	10	0	7.50
23–24	Ott	2	120	0	2	0	9	0	4.50
Totals		4	200	1	3	0	19	0	5.70

HEINZ, Richard 5-10 165
B. Essex, Ont., May 30, 1955

SEASON	TEAM	GP	MIN.	W	L	T	GA	SO.	AVG.
80–81	StL	4	220	2	1	1	8	0	2.18
81–82	StL–Van	12	613	4	6	0	44	1	4.31
82–83	StL	9	335	1	5	1	24	1	4.30
83–84	StL	22	1118	7	7	3	80	0	4.29
84–85	StL	2	70	0	0	0	3	0	2.57
Totals		49	2356	14	19	5	159	2	4.05

HENDERSON, John Duncan (Long John) 6-1 174
B. Toronto, Ont., Mar. 25, 1933

SEASON	TEAM	GP	MIN.	W	L	T	GA	SO.	AVG.
54–55	Bos	44	2628	15	14	15	109	5	2.49
55–56	Bos	1	60	0	1	0	4	0	4.00
Totals		45	2688	15	15	15	113	5	2.52

Playoffs

SEASON	TEAM	GP	MIN.	W	L	T	GA	SO.	AVG.
54–55	Bos	2	120	0	2	0	8	0	4.00

HENRY, Gordon David (Red) 6-0 185
B. Owen Sound, Ont., Aug. 17, 1926

SEASON	TEAM	GP	MIN.	W	L	T	GA	SO.	AVG.
48–49	Bos	1	60	1	0	0	0	1	0.00
49–50	Bos	2	120	0	2	0	5	0	2.50
Totals		3	180	1	2	0	5	1	1.67

Playoffs

SEASON	TEAM	GP	MIN.	W	L	T	GA	SO.	AVG.
50–51	Bos	2	120	0	2	0	10	0	5.00
52–53	Bos	3	163	0	2	0	11	0	4.05
Totals		5	283	0	4	0	21	0	4.45

HENRY, Samuel James (Sugar Jim) 5-9 165
B. Winnipeg, Man., Oct. 23, 1920

SEASON	TEAM	GP	MIN.	W	L	T	GA	SO.	AVG.
41–42	NYR	48	2960	29	17	2	143	1	2.98
45–46	NYR	11	623	1	7	2	41	1	3.95
46–47	NYR	2	120	0	2	0	9	0	4.50
47–48	NYR	48	2880	17	18	13	153	2	3.19
48–49	Chi	60	3600	21	31	8	211	0	3.52
51–52	Bos	70	4200	23	34	13	176	7	2.51
52–53	Bos	70	4200	28	29	13	172	7	2.46
53–54	Bos	70	4200	32	28	10	181	8	2.59
54–55	Bos	26	1532	8	12	6	79	1	3.09
Totals		405	24315	159	178	67	1165	27	2.87

Playoffs

SEASON	TEAM	GP	MIN.	W	L	T	GA	SO.	AVG.
41–42	NYR	6	360	2	4	0	13	1	2.17
51–52	Bos	7	448	3	4	0	18	1	2.41
52–53	Bos	9	510	5	4	0	26	0	3.06
53–54	Bos	4	240	0	4	0	16	0	4.00
54–55	Bos	3	183	1	2	0	8	0	2.62
Totals		29	1741	11	18	0	81	2	2.79

HERRON, Denis *5–11 165*
B. Chambly, Que., June 18, 1952

Season	Team	GP	MIN.	W	L	T	GA	SO.	AVG.
72–73	Pitt	18	967	6	7	2	55	2	3.41
73–74	Pitt	5	260	1	3	0	18	0	4.15
74–75	Pitt–KC	25	1388	5	14	4	91	0	3.93
75–76	KC	64	3620	11	39	11	243	0	4.03
76–77	Pitt	34	1920	15	11	5	94	1	2.94
77–78	Pitt	60	3534	20	25	15	210	0	3.57
78–79	Pitt	56	3208	22	19	12	180	0	3.37
79–80	Mont	34	1909	25	3	3	80	0	2.51
80–81	Mont	25	1147	6	9	6	67	1	3.50
81–82	Mont	27	1547	12	6	8	68	3	2.64
82–83	Pitt	31	1707	5	18	5	151	1	5.31
83–84	Pitt	38	2028	8	24	2	138	1	4.08
84–85	Pitt	42	2193	10	22	3	170	1	4.65
85–86	Pitt	3	180	0	3	0	14	0	4.67
Totals		462	25608	143	206	76	1579	10	3.70

Playoffs

Season	Team	GP	MIN.	W	L	T	GA	SO.	AVG.
76–77	Pitt	3	180	1	2	0	11	0	3.67
78–79	Pitt	7	421	2	5	0	24	0	3.42
79–80	Mont	5	300	2	3	0	15	0	3.00
Totals		15	901	5	10	0	50	0	3.33

HEXTALL, Ron *6–3 192*
B. Winnipeg, Man., May 3, 1964

Season	Team	GP	MIN.	W	L	T	GA	SO.	AVG.
86–87	Phil	66	3799	37	21	6	190	1	3.00
87–88	Phil	62	3561	30	22	7	208	0	3.50
88–89	Phil	64	3756	30	28	6	202	0	3.23
89–90	Phil	8	419	4	2	1	29	0	4.15
90–91	Phil	36	2035	13	16	5	106	0	3.13
91–92	Phil	45	2668	16	21	6	151	3	3.40
92–93	Que	54	2988	29	16	5	172	0	3.45
93–94	NYI	65	3581	27	26	6	184	5	3.08
94–95	Phil	31	1824	17	9	4	88	1	2.89
95–96	Phil	53	3102	31	13	7	112	4	2.17
96–97	Phil	55	3094	31	16	5	132	5	2.56
97–98	Phil	46	2688	21	17	7	97	4	2.17
98–99	Phil	23	1235	10	7	4	52	0	2.53
Totals		608	34750	296	214	69	1723	23	2.95

Playoffs

Season	Team	GP	MIN.	W	L	T	GA	SO.	AVG.
86–87	Phil	26	1540	15	11	0	71	2	2.77
87–88	Phil	7	379	2	4	0	30	0	4.75
88–89	Phil	15	886	8	7	0	49	0	3.32
92–93	Que	6	372	2	4	0	18	0	2.90
93–94	NYI	3	158	0	3	0	16	0	6.08
94–95	Phil	15	897	10	5	0	42	0	2.81
95–96	Phil	12	760	6	6	0	27	0	2.13
96–97	Phil	8	444	4	3	0	22	0	2.97
97–98	Phil	1	20	0	0	0	1	0	3.00
Totals		93	5456	47	43	0	276	2	3.04

HIGHTON, Hector Salisbury *6–0 175*
B. Medicine Hat, Alta., Dec. 10, 1923

Season	Team	GP	MIN.	W	L	T	GA	SO.	AVG.
43–44	Chi	24	1440	10	14	0	108	0	4.50

HIMES, Norman *5–9 145*
B. Galt, Ont., Apr. 13, 1903

Season	Team	GP	MIN.	W	L	T	GA	SO.	AVG.
27–28	NYA	1	19	0	0	0	0	0	0.00
28–29	NYA	1	60	0	0	1	3	0	3.00
Totals		2	79	0	0	1	3	0	2.28

HIRSCH, Corey *5–10 160*
B. Medicine Hat, Alta., July 1, 1972

Season	Team	GP	MIN.	W	L	T	GA	SO.	AVG.
92–93	NYR	4	224	1	2	1	14	0	3.75
95–96	Van	41	2338	17	14	6	114	1	2.93
96–97	Van	39	2127	12	20	4	116	2	3.27
97–98	Van	1	50	0	0	0	5	0	6.00
98–99	Van	20	919	3	8	3	48	1	3.13
Totals		105	5658	33	44	14	297	4	3.15

Playoffs

Season	Team	GP	MIN.	W	L	T	GA	SO.	AVG.
95–96	Van	6	338	2	3	0	21	0	3.73

HODGE, Charles Edward *5–6 150*
B. Lachine, Que., July 28, 1933

Season	Team	GP	MIN.	W	L	T	GA	SO.	AVG.
54–55	Mont	14	800	7	3	4	31	1	2.33
57–58	Mont	12	720	8	2	2	31	1	2.58
58–59	Mont	2	120	1	1	0	6	0	3.00
59–60	Mont	1	60	0	1	0	3	0	3.00
60–61	Mont	30	1800	19	8	3	76	4	2.53
63–64	Mont	62	3720	33	18	11	140	8	2.26
64–65	Mont	53	3120	26	16	10	135	3	2.60
65–66	Mont	26	1301	12	7	2	56	1	2.58
66–67	Mont	37	2055	11	15	7	88	3	2.57
67–68	Oak	58	3311	13	29	13	158	3	2.86

HODGE *(continued)*

Season	Team	GP	MIN.	W	L	T	GA	SO.	AVG.
68–69	Cal	14	781	4	6	1	48	0	3.69
69–70	Oak	14	738	3	5	2	43	0	3.50
70–71	Van	35	1967	15	13	5	112	0	3.42
Totals		358	20493	152	124	60	927	24	2.70

Playoffs

Season	Team	GP	MIN.	W	L	T	GA	SO.	AVG.
54–55	Mont	4	84	1	1	0	5	0	3.57
63–64	Mont	7	420	3	4	0	16	1	2.29
64–65	Mont	5	300	2	3	0	10	1	2.00
Totals		16	804	6	8	0	31	2	2.31

HODSON, Kevin *6–0 182*
B. Winnipeg, Man., Mar. 27, 1972

Season	Team	GP	MIN.	W	L	T	GA	SO.	AVG.
95–96	Det	4	163	2	0	0	3	1	1.10
96–97	Det	6	294	2	2	1	8	1	1.63
97–98	Det	21	988	9	3	3	44	2	2.67
98–99	Det–TB	9	413	2	3	1	20	0	2.91
Totals		40	1858	15	8	5	75	4	2.42

Playoffs

Season	Team	GP	MIN.	W	L	T	GA	SO.	AVG.
97–98	Det	1	1	0	0	0	0	0	0.00

HOFFORT, Bruce *5–10 185*
B. North Battleford, Sask., July 30, 1966

Season	Team	GP	MIN.	W	L	T	GA	SO.	AVG.
89–90	Phil	7	329	3	0	2	20	0	3.65
90–91	Phil	2	39	1	0	1	3	0	4.62
Totals		9	368	4	0	3	23	0	3.75

HOGANSON, Paul Edward *5–11 175*
B. Toronto, Ont., Nov. 12, 1949

Season	Team	GP	MIN.	W	L	T	GA	SO.	AVG.
70–71	Pitt	2	57	0	1	0	7	0	7.37
73–74	LA (WHA)	27	1308	6	16	0	102	0	4.68
74–75	Balt (WHA)	32	1776	9	19	2	121	2	4.09
75–76	NE–Cin (WHA)	49	2616	20	26	0	161	2	3.69
76–77	Cin–Ind (WHA)	28	1218	8	8	1	88	1	4.33
77–78	Cin (WHA)	7	326	1	2	1	24	0	4.42
NHL Totals		2	57	0	1	0	7	0	7.37
WHA Totals		143	7244	44	71	4	496	5	4.11

Playoffs

Season	Team	GP	MIN.	W	L	T	GA	SO.	AVG.
76–77	Ind (WHA)	5	348	3	2	0	17	1	2.93

HOGOSTA, Goran *6–1 179*
B. Appelbo, Sweden, Apr. 15, 1954

Season	Team	GP	MIN.	W	L	T	GA	SO.	AVG.
77–78	NYI	1	9	0	0	0	0	0	0.00
79–80	Que	21	1199	5	12	3	83	1	4.15
Totals		22	1208	5	12	3	83	1	4.12

HOLDEN, Mark *5–10 165*
B. Weymouth, Mass., June 12, 1957

Season	Team	GP	MIN.	W	L	T	GA	SO.	AVG.
81–82	Mont	1	20	0	0	0	0	0	0.00
82–83	Mont	2	87	0	1	1	6	0	4.14
83–84	Mont	1	52	0	1	0	4	0	4.60
84–85	Winn	4	213	2	0	0	15	0	4.23
Totals		8	372	2	2	1	25	0	4.03

HOLLAND, Kenneth Mark *5–8 160*
B. Vernon, B.C., Nov. 10, 1955

Season	Team	GP	MIN.	W	L	T	GA	SO.	AVG.
80–81	Hart	1	60	0	1	0	7	0	7.00

HOLLAND, Robert (Robbie) *6–1 182*
B. Montreal, Que., Sept, 19, 1957

Season	Team	GP	MIN.	W	L	T	GA	SO.	AVG.
79–80	Pitt	34	1974	10	17	6	126	1	3.83
80–81	Pitt	10	539	1	5	3	45	0	5.01
Totals		44	2513	11	22	9	171	1	4.08

HOLMES, Harold (Hap, Harry)
B. Aurora, Ont., Apr. 15, 1889

Season	Team	GP	MIN.	W	L	T	GA	SO.	AVG.
17–18	Tor	16	965	10	6	0	76	0	4.75
18–19	Tor	2	120	0	2	0	9	0	4.50
26–27	Det	43	2685	12	27	4	100	6	2.33
27–28	Det	44	2740	19	19	6	79	11	1.80
Totals		105	6510	41	54	10	264	17	2.43

Playoffs

Season	Team	GP	MIN.	W	L	T	GA	SO.	AVG.
17–18	Tor	7	420	4	3	0	26	0	3.71

HORNER, Reginald (Red) *6–0 190*
B. Lynden, Ont., May 28, 1909

Season	Team	GP	MIN.	W	L	T	GA	SO.	AVG.
32–33	Tor	1	1	0	0	0	1	0	60.00

SEASON	TEAM	GP	MIN.	W	L	T	GA	SO.	AVG.

HRIVNAK, Jim *6–2 195*
B. Montreal, Que., May 28, 1968

89–90	Wash	11	609	5	5	0	36	0	3.55
90–91	Wash	9	432	4	2	1	26	0	3.61
91–92	Wash	12	605	6	3	0	35	0	3.47
92–93	Wash–Winn	30	1601	15	10	2	96	0	3.60
93–94	StL	23	970	4	10	0	69	0	4.27
Totals		85	4217	34	30	3	262	0	3.73

HRUDEY, Kelly Stephen *5–10 189*
B. Edmonton, Alta., Jan. 13, 1961

83–84	NYI	12	535	7	2	0	28	0	3.14
84–85	NYI	41	2335	19	17	3	141	2	3.62
85–86	NYI	45	2563	19	15	8	137	1	3.21
86–87	NYI	46	2634	21	15	7	145	0	3.30
87–88	NYI	47	2751	22	17	5	153	3	3.34
88–89	NYI–LA	66	3774	28	28	5	230	1	3.66
89–90	LA	52	2860	22	21	6	194	2	4.07
90–91	LA	47	2730	26	13	6	132	3	2.90
91–92	LA	60	3509	26	17	13	197	1	3.39
92–93	LA	50	2718	18	21	6	175	2	3.86
93–94	LA	64	3713	22	31	7	228	1	3.68
94–95	LA	35	1894	14	13	5	99	0	3.14
95–96	LA	36	2077	7	15	10	113	0	3.26
96–97	SJ	48	2631	16	24	5	140	0	3.19
97–98	SJ	28	1360	4	16	2	62	1	2.74
Totals		677	38084	271	265	88	2174	17	3.43

Playoffs

84–85	NYI	5	281	1	3	0	8	0	1.71
85–86	NYI	2	120	0	2	0	6	0	3.00
86–87	NYI	14	842	7	7	0	38	0	2.71
87–88	NYI	6	381	2	4	0	23	0	3.62
88–89	LA	10	566	4	6	0	35	0	3.71
89–90	LA	9	539	4	4	0	39	0	4.34
90–91	LA	12	798	6	6	0	37	0	2.78
91–92	LA	6	355	2	4	0	22	0	3.72
92–93	LA	20	1261	10	10	0	74	0	3.52
97–98	SJ	1	20	0	0	0	1	0	3.00
Totals		85	5163	36	46	0	283	0	3.29

ING, Peter *6–2 170*
B. Toronto, Ont., Apr. 28, 1969

89–90	Tor	3	182	0	2	1	18	0	5.93
90–91	Tor	56	3126	16	29	8	200	1	3.84
91–92	Edm	12	463	3	4	0	33	0	4.28
93–94	Det	3	170	1	2	0	15	0	5.29
Totals		74	3941	20	37	9	266	1	4.05

INNESS, Gary George *6–0 195*
B. Toronto, Ont., May 28, 1949

73–74	Pitt	20	1032	7	10	1	56	0	3.26
74–75	Pitt	57	3122	24	18	10	161	2	3.09
75–76	Pitt–Phil	25	1332	10	9	2	85	0	3.83
76–77	Phil	6	210	1	0	2	9	0	2.57
77–78	Ind (WHA)	52	2850	14	30	1	200	0	4.21
78–79	Ind (WHA)	9	609	3	6	0	51	0	5.02
78–79	Wash	37	2107	14	14	8	130	0	3.70
79–80	Wash	14	727	2	9	2	44	0	3.63
80–81	Wash	3	180	0	1	2	9	0	3.00
NHL Totals		162	8710	58	61	27	494	2	3.40
WHA Totals		61	3459	17	36	1	251	0	4.35

Playoffs

74–75	Pitt	9	540	5	4	0	24	0	2.67

IRBE, Arturs *5–7 180*
B. Riga, Soviet Union, Feb. 2, 1967

91–92	SJ	13	645	2	6	3	48	0	4.47
92–93	SJ	36	2074	7	26	0	142	1	4.11
93–94	SJ	74	4412	30	28	16	209	3	2.84
94–95	SJ	38	2043	14	19	3	111	4	3.26
95–96	SJ	22	1112	4	12	4	85	0	4.59
96–97	Dal	35	1965	17	12	3	88	3	2.69
97–98	Van	41	1999	14	11	6	91	2	2.73
98–99	Car	62	3643	27	20	12	135	6	2.22
Totals		321	17893	115	134	47	909	19	3.05

Playoffs

93–94	SJ	14	806	7	7	0	50	0	3.72
94–95	SJ	6	316	2	4	0	27	0	5.13
96–97	Dal	1	13	0	0	0	0	0	0.00
98–99	Car	6	408	2	4	0	15	0	2.21
Totals		27	1543	11	15	0	92	0	3.58

IRELAND, Randolph *6–0 165*
B. Rosetown, Sask., Apr. 5, 1957

78–79	Buf	2	30	0	0	0	3	0	6.00

IRONS, Robert Richard (Robbie) *5–8 150*
B. Toronto, Ont., Nov. 19, 1946

68–69	StL	1	3	0	0	0	0	0	0.00

***** **IRONSTONE, Joseph**
B. 1897

25–26	NYA	1	40	0	1	0	3	0	4.50
27–28	Tor	1	70	1	0	0	0	1	0.00
Totals		2	110	1	1	0	3	1	1.64

JABLONSKI, Pat *6–0 180*
B. Toledo, Ohio, June 20, 1967

89–90	StL	4	208	0	3	0	17	0	4.90
90–91	StL	8	492	2	3	3	25	0	3.05
91–92	StL	10	468	3	6	0	38	0	4.87
92–93	TB	43	2268	8	24	4	150	1	3.97
93–94	TB	15	834	5	6	3	54	0	3.88
95–96	StL–Mont	24	1272	5	9	6	63	0	2.97
96–97	Mont–Phoe	19	813	4	7	2	52	0	3.84
97–98	Car	5	279	1	4	0	14	0	3.01
Totals		128	6634	28	62	18	413	1	3.74

Playoffs

90–91	StL	3	90	0	0	0	5	0	3.33
95–96	Mont	1	49	0	0	0	1	0	1.22
Totals		4	139	0	0	0	6	0	2.59

JACKSON, Douglas *5–10 150*
B. Winnipeg, Man., Dec. 12, 1924

47–48	Chi	6	360	2	3	1	42	0	7.00

JACKSON, Percy *5–9 165*
B. Canmore, Alta., Sept. 21, 1908

31–32	Bos	4	232	1	1	1	8	0	2.07
33–34	NYA	1	60	0	1	0	9	0	9.00
34–35	NYR	1	60	0	1	0	8	0	8.00
35–36	Bos	1	40	0	0	0	1	0	1.50
Totals		7	392	1	3	1	26	0	3.98

JAKS, Pauli *6–0 194*
B. Schaffhausen, Switzerland, Jan. 25, 1972

94–95	LA	1	40	0	0	0	2	0	3.00

JANASZAK, Steven *6–1 210*
B. St. Paul, Minn., Jan. 7, 1957

79–80	Minn	1	60	0	0	1	2	0	2.00
81–82	Col	2	100	0	1	0	13	0	7.80
Totals		3	160	0	1	1	15	0	5.63

JANECYK, Robert *6–1 180*
B. Chicago, Ill., May 18, 1957

83–84	Chi	8	412	2	3	1	28	0	4.08
84–85	LA	51	3002	22	21	8	183	2	3.66
85–86	LA	38	2083	14	16	4	162	0	4.67
86–87	LA	7	420	4	3	0	34	0	4.86
87–88	LA	5	303	1	4	0	23	0	4.55
88–89	LA	1	30	0	0	0	2	0	4.00
Totals		110	6250	43	47	13	432	2	4.15

Playoffs

84–85	LA	3	184	0	3	0	10	0	3.26

JENKINS, Joseph Roger *5–11 173*
B. Appleton, Wis., Nov. 18, 1911

38–39	NYA	1	30	0	1	0	7	0	14.00

JENSEN, Allan Raymond *5–10 180*
B. Hamilton, Ont., Nov. 27, 1958

80–81	Det	1	60	0	1	0	7	0	7.00
81–82	Wash	26	1274	8	8	4	81	0	3.81
82–83	Wash	40	2358	22	12	6	135	1	3.44
83–84	Wash	43	2414	25	13	3	117	4	2.91
84–85	Wash	14	803	10	3	1	34	1	2.54
85–86	Wash	44	2437	28	9	3	129	2	3.18
86–87	Wash–LA	11	628	2	7	1	54	0	5.16
Totals		179	9974	95	53	18	557	8	3.35

Playoffs

82–83	Wash	3	139	1	2	0	10	0	4.32
83–84	Wash	6	258	3	1	0	14	0	3.28
84–85	Wash	3	201	1	2	0	8	0	2.39
Totals		12	598	5	5	0	32	0	3.21

JENSEN, Darren Aksel 5–9 165
B. Creston, B.C., May 27, 1960

SEASON	TEAM	GP	MIN.	W	L	T	GA	SO.	AVG.
84–85	Phil	1	60	0	1	0	7	0	7.00
85–86	Phil	29	1436	15	9	1	88	2	3.68
Totals		30	1496	15	10	1	95	2	3.81

JOHNSON, Brent 6–2 190
B. Farmington, Mich., March 12, 1977

SEASON	TEAM	GP	MIN.	W	L	T	GA	SO.	AVG.
98–99	StL	6	286	3	2	0	10	0	2.10

JOHNSON, Robert Martin 6–1 185
B. Farmington, Mich., Nov. 12, 1948

SEASON	TEAM	GP	MIN.	W	L	T	GA	SO.	AVG.
72–73	StL	12	583	6	5	0	26	0	2.68
74–75	Pitt	12	476	3	4	1	40	0	5.04
75–76	Ott–Clev (WHA)	42	2377	17	22	1	144	1	3.63
NHL Totals		24	1059	9	9	1	66	0	3.74
WHA Totals		42	2377	17	22	1	144	1	3.63

Playoffs

SEASON	TEAM	GP	MIN.	W	L	T	GA	SO.	AVG.
75–76	Clev (WHA)	2	120	0	2	0	8	0	4.00

JOHNSTON, Edward Joseph 6–0 190
B. Montreal, Que., Nov. 23, 1935

SEASON	TEAM	GP	MIN.	W	L	T	GA	SO.	AVG.
62–63	Bos	50	2880	11	27	11	196	1	4.05
63–64	Bos	70	4200	18	40	12	211	6	3.01
64–65	Bos	47	2820	12	31	4	163	3	3.47
65–66	Bos	33	1743	10	19	2	108	1	3.72
66–67	Bos	34	1880	9	21	2	116	0	3.70
67–68	Bos	28	1524	11	8	5	73	0	2.87
68–69	Bos	24	1440	14	6	4	74	2	3.08
69–70	Bos	37	2176	16	9	11	108	3	2.98
70–71	Bos	38	2280	30	6	2	96	4	2.53
71–72	Bos	38	2260	27	8	3	102	2	2.71
72–73	Bos	45	2510	24	17	1	137	5	3.27
73–74	Tor	26	1516	12	9	4	78	1	3.09
74–75	StL	30	1800	12	13	5	93	2	3.10
75–76	StL	38	2152	11	7	9	130	1	3.62
76–77	StL	38	2111	13	16	5	108	1	3.07
77–78	StL–Chi	16	890	6	9	7	62	0	4.18
Totals		591	34182	236	256	87	1854	32	3.25

Playoffs

SEASON	TEAM	GP	MIN.	W	L	T	GA	SO.	AVG.
68–69	Bos	1	65	0	1	0	4	0	3.69
69–70	Bos	1	60	0	1	0	4	0	4.00
70–71	Bos	1	60	0	1	0	7	0	7.00
71–72	Bos	7	420	6	1	0	13	1	1.86
72–73	Bos	3	160	1	2	0	9	0	3.38
73–74	Tor	1	60	0	1	0	6	0	6.00
74–75	StL	1	60	0	1	0	5	0	5.00
76–77	StL	3	138	0	2	0	9	0	3.91
Totals		18	1023	7	10	0	57	1	3.34

JOSEPH, Curtis Shayne (Cujo) 5–10 182
B. Keswick, Ont., Apr. 29, 1967

SEASON	TEAM	GP	MIN.	W	L	T	GA	SO.	AVG.
89–90	StL	15	852	9	5	1	48	0	3.38
90–91	StL	30	1710	16	10	2	89	0	3.12
91–92	StL	60	3494	27	20	10	175	2	3.01
92–93	StL	68	3890	29	28	9	196	1	3.02
93–94	StL	71	4127	36	23	11	213	1	3.10
94–95	StL	36	1914	20	10	1	89	1	2.79
95–96	Edm	34	1936	15	16	2	111	0	3.44
96–97	Edm	72	4089	32	29	9	200	6	2.93
97–98	Edm	71	4132	29	31	9	181	8	2.63
98–99	Tor	67	4001	35	24	7	171	3	2.56
Totals		524	30156	248	196	61	1473	22	2.93

Playoffs

SEASON	TEAM	GP	MIN.	W	L	T	GA	SO.	AVG.
89–90	StL	6	327	4	1	0	18	0	3.30
91–92	StL	6	379	2	4	0	23	0	3.64
92–93	StL	11	715	7	4	0	27	2	2.27
93–94	StL	4	246	0	4	0	15	0	3.66
94–95	StL	7	392	3	3	0	24	0	3.67
96–97	Edm	12	767	5	7	0	36	2	2.82
97–98	Edm	12	716	5	7	0	23	3	1.93
98–99	Tor	17	1011	9	8	0	41	1	2.43
Totals		75	3955	35	38	0	207	8	3.14

JUNKIN, Joseph Brian 5–11 180
B. Lindsay, Ont., Sept. 8, 1946

SEASON	TEAM	GP	MIN.	W	L	T	GA	SO.	AVG.
68–69	Bos	1	8	0	0	0	0	0	0.00
73–74	NY–NJ (WHA)	53	3122	21	25	4	197	1	3.79
74–75	SD (WHA)	16	839	6	7	0	46	1	3.29
NHL Totals		1	8	0	0	0	0	0	0.00
WHA Totals		69	3961	27	32	4	243	2	3.68

KAARELA, Jari Pekka 5–10 165
B. Tampere, Finland, Aug. 8, 1958

SEASON	TEAM	GP	MIN.	W	L	T	GA	SO.	AVG.
80–81	Col	5	220	2	2	0	22	0	6.00

KAMPURRI, Hannu 6–0 175
B. Helsinki, Finland, June 1, 1957

SEASON	TEAM	GP	MIN.	W	L	T	GA	SO.	AVG.
84–85	NJ	13	645	1	10	1	54	0	5.02

* KARAKAS, Michael 5–11 147
B. Aurora, Minn., Dec. 12, 1911

SEASON	TEAM	GP	MIN.	W	L	T	GA	SO.	AVG.
35–36	Chi	48	2990	21	19	8	92	9	1.92
36–37	Chi	48	2978	14	27	7	131	5	2.73
37–38	Chi	48	2980	14	25	9	139	1	2.90
38–39	Chi	48	2988	12	28	8	132	5	2.75
39–40	Chi–Mont	22	1360	7	13	2	76	0	3.45
43–44	Chi	26	1560	12	9	5	79	3	3.04
44–45	Chi	48	2880	12	29	7	187	4	3.90
45–46	Chi	48	2880	22	19	7	166	1	3.46
Totals		336	20616	114	169	53	1002	28	2.92

Playoffs

SEASON	TEAM	GP	MIN.	W	L	T	GA	SO.	AVG.
35–36	Chi	2	120	1	1	0	7	0	3.50
37–38	Chi	8	525	6	2	0	15	2	1.88
43–44	Chi	9	549	4	5	0	24	1	2.62
45–46	Chi	4	240	0	4	0	26	0	6.50
Totals		23	1434	11	12	0	72	3	3.01

KEANS, Douglas Frederick 5–7 175
B. Pembroke, Ont., Jan. 7, 1958

SEASON	TEAM	GP	MIN.	W	L	T	GA	SO.	AVG.
79–80	LA	10	559	3	3	3	23	0	2.47
80–81	LA	9	454	2	3	1	37	0	4.89
81–82	LA	31	1436	8	10	7	103	0	4.30
82–83	LA	6	304	0	2	2	24	0	4.73
83–84	Bos	33	1779	19	8	3	92	2	3.10
84–85	Bos	25	1497	16	6	3	82	1	3.29
85–86	Bos	30	1757	14	13	3	107	0	3.65
86–87	Bos	36	1942	18	8	4	108	0	3.34
87–88	Bos	30	1660	16	11	0	90	1	3.25
Totals		210	11388	96	64	26	666	4	3.51

Playoffs

SEASON	TEAM	GP	MIN.	W	L	T	GA	SO.	AVG.
79–80	LA	1	40	0	1	0	7	0	10.50
81–82	LA	2	32	0	1	0	1	0	1.88
84–85	Bos	4	240	2	2	0	15	0	3.75
86–87	Bos	2	120	0	2	0	11	0	5.50
Totals		9	432	2	6	0	34	0	4.72

KEENAN, Donald
B. Bos

SEASON	TEAM	GP	MIN.	W	L	T	GA	SO.	AVG.
58–59	Bos	1	60	0	1	0	4	0	4.00

KERR, David Alexander 5–10 160
B. Toronto, Ont., Jan. 11, 1910

SEASON	TEAM	GP	MIN.	W	L	T	GA	SO.	AVG.
30–31	Mont M	28	1649	13	11	4	76	1	2.71
31–32	NYA	1	60	0	1	0	6	0	6.00
32–33	Mont M	25	1520	14	8	3	58	4	2.32
33–34	Mont M	48	3060	19	18	11	122	6	2.54
34–35	NYR	37	2290	19	12	6	94	4	2.54
35–36	NYR	47	2980	18	17	12	95	8	2.02
36–37	NYR	48	3020	19	20	9	106	4	2.21
37–38	NYR	48	2960	27	15	6	96	8	2.00
38–39	NYR	48	2970	26	16	6	105	6	2.19
39–40	NYR	48	3000	27	11	10	77	8	1.60
40–41	NYR	48	3010	21	19	8	125	2	2.60
Totals		426	26519	203	148	75	960	51	2.17

Playoffs

SEASON	TEAM	GP	MIN.	W	L	T	GA	SO.	AVG.
30–31	Mont M	2	120	0	2	0	8	0	4.00
32–33	Mont M	2	120	0	2	0	5	0	2.50
33–34	Mont M	4	240	1	2	1	7	1	1.75
34–35	NYR	4	240	1	1	2	10	0	2.50
36–37	NYR	9	553	6	3	0	10	4	1.11
37–38	NYR	3	262	1	2	0	8	0	2.67
38–39	NYR	1	119	0	1	0	2	0	2.00
39–40	NYR	12	770	8	4	0	20	3	1.67
40–41	NYR	3	192	1	2	0	6	0	2.00
Totals		40	2616	18	19	3	76	8	1.74

KHABIBULIN, Nikolai 6–1 176
B. Sverdlovsk, USSR, Jan. 13, 1973

SEASON	TEAM	GP	MIN.	W	L	T	GA	SO.	AVG.
94–95	Winn	26	1339	8	9	4	76	0	3.41
95–96	Winn	53	2914	26	20	3	152	2	3.13
96–97	Phoe	72	4091	30	33	6	193	7	2.83
97–98	Phoe	70	4026	30	28	10	184	4	2.74
98–99	Phoe	63	3657	32	23	7	130	8	2.13
Totals		284	16027	126	113	30	735	21	2.75

Playoffs

95–96	Winn	6	359	2	4	0	19	0	3.18
96–97	Phoe	7	426	3	4	0	15	1	2.11
97–98	Phoe	4	185	2	1	0	13	0	4.22
98–99	Phoe	7	449	3	4	0	18	0	2.41
Totals		24	1419	10	13	0	65	1	2.75

KIDD, Trevor *6–2 190*
B. Dugald, Man., Mar. 29, 1972

91–92	Calg	2	120	1	1	0	8	0	4.00
93–94	Calg	31	1614	13	7	6	85	0	3.16
94–95	Calg	43	2463	22	14	6	107	3	2.61
95–96	Calg	47	2570	15	21	8	119	3	2.78
96–97	Calg	55	2979	21	23	6	141	4	2.84
97–98	Car	47	2685	21	21	3	97	3	2.17
98–99	Car	25	1358	7	10	6	61	2	2.70
Totals		250	13789	100	97	35	618	15	2.69

Playoffs

94–95	Calg	7	434	3	4	0	26	1	3.59
95–96	Calg	2	83	0	1	0	9	0	6.51
Totals		9	517	3	5	0	35	1	4.06

KING, Scott *6–1 185*
B. Thunder Bay, Ont., June 25, 1967

90–91	Det	1	45	0	0	0	2	0	2.67
91–92	Det	1	16	0	0	0	1	0	3.75
Totals		2	61	0	0	0	3	0	2.95

KLEISINGER, Terry *6–0 190*
B. Regina, Sask., Oct. 10, 1960

85–86	NYR	4	191	0	2	0	14	0	4.40

KLYMKIW, Julian *5–11 180*
B. Winnipeg, Man., July 16, 1933

58–59	NYR	1	19	0	0	0	2	0	6.32

KNICKLE, Rick *5–10 175*
B. Chatham, N. B., Feb. 26, 1960

92–93	LA	10	532	6	4	0	35	0	5.95
93–94	LA	4	174	1	2	0	9	0	3.10
Totals		14	706	7	6	0	44	0	3.74

KOLZIG, Olaf *6–3 225*
B. Johannesburg, South Africa, Apr. 6, 1970

89–90	Wash	2	120	0	2	0	12	0	6.00
92–93	Wash	1	20	0	0	0	2	0	6.00
93–94	Wash	7	224	0	3	0	20	0	5.36
94–95	Wash	14	724	2	8	2	30	0	2.49
95–96	Wash	18	897	4	8	2	46	0	3.08
96–97	Wash	29	1645	8	15	4	71	2	2.59
97–98	Wash	64	3788	33	18	10	139	5	2.20
98–99	Wash	64	3586	26	31	3	154	4	2.58
Totals		199	11004	73	85	21	474	11	2.58

Playoffs

94–95	Wash	2	44	1	0	0	1	0	1.36
95–96	Wash	5	341	2	3	0	11	0	1.94
97–98	Wash	21	1351	12	9	0	44	1	1.95
Totals		28	1736	15	12	0	56	1	1.94

KUNTAR, Leslie Steven *6–2 195*
B. Elma, N.Y., July 28, 1969

93–94	Mont	6	302	2	2	0	16	0	3.18

KURT, Gary David *6–3 205*
B. Kitchener, Ont., Mar. 9, 1947

71–72	Cal	16	838	1	7	5	60	0	4.30
72–73	NY (WHA)	36	1881	10	21	0	150	0	4.78
73–74	NY–NJ (WHA)	20	1089	8	10	0	75	0	4.13
74–75	Phoe (WHA)	47	2841	25	16	4	156	2	3.29
75–76	Phoe (WHA)	40	2369	18	20	2	147	1	3.72
76–77	Phoe (WHA)	33	1752	11	9	1	162	0	5.55
NHL Totals		16	838	1	7	5	60	0	4.30
WHA Totals		176	9932	72	86	7	690	3	4.17

Playoffs

74–75	Phoe (WHA)	4	207	1	2	0	12	0	3.48

LABRECQUE, Patrick *6–0 190*
B. Laval, Que., Mar 6, 1971

95–96	Mont	2	98	0	1	0	7	0	4.29

LACHER, Blaine *6–1 205*
B. Medicine Hat, Alta., Sept. 5, 1970

94–95	Bos	35	1965	19	11	2	79	4	2.41
95–96	Bos	12	671	3	5	2	44	0	3.93
Totals		47	2636	22	16	4	123	4	2.80

Playoffs

94–95	Bos	5	283	1	4	0	12	0	2.54

LACROIX, Alphonse

25–26	Mont	5	280	1	4	0	16	0	3.20

LaFERRIERE, Richard *5–9 170*
B. Hawksbury, Ont., Jan. 3, 1961

81–82	Col	1	20	0	1	0	1	0	3.00

LaFOREST, Mark Andrew *5–11 190*
B. Welland, Ont., July 10, 1962

85–86	Det	28	1383	4	21	0	114	1	4.95
86–87	Det	5	219	2	1	0	12	0	3.29
87–88	Phil	21	972	5	9	2	60	1	3.70
88–89	Phil	17	933	5	7	2	64	0	4.12
89–90	Tor	27	1343	9	14	0	87	0	3.89
93–94	Ott	5	182	0	2	0	17	0	5.60
Totals		103	5032	25	54	4	354	2	4.22

Playoffs

87–88	Phil	2	48	1	0	0	1	0	1.25

LALIME, Patrick *6–2 170*
B. St. Bonaventure, Que., July 7, 1974

96–97	Pitt	39	2058	21	12	2	101	3	2.94

LANGKOW, Scott *5–11 190*
B. Edmonton, Alta., Apr. 21, 1975

95–96	Winn	1	6	0	0	0	0	0	0.00
97–98	Phoe	3	137	0	1	1	10	0	4.38
98–99	Phoe	1	35	0	0	0	3	0	5.17
Totals		5	178	0	1	1	13	0	4.38

LAROCQUE, Michel Raymond (Bunny) *5–10 185*
B. Hull, Que., Apr. 16, 1952

73–74	Mont	27	1431	15	8	2	69	0	2.89
74–75	Mont	25	1480	17	5	0	74	3	3.00
75–76	Mont	22	1220	16	1	3	50	2	2.46
76–77	Mont	26	1525	19	2	4	53	0	2.09
77–78	Mont	30	1729	22	3	4	77	1	2.67
78–79	Mont	34	1986	22	7	4	94	3	2.84
79–80	Mont	29	2259	17	13	8	125	3	3.32
80–81	Mont–Tor	36	2083	19	12	5	122	1	3.51
81–82	Tor	50	2647	10	24	9	207	0	4.69
82–83	Tor–Phil	18	955	3	9	4	76	0	4.77
83–84	StL	5	300	0	5	0	31	0	6.20
Totals		312	17615	160	89	45	978	17	3.33

Playoffs

73–74	Mont	6	364	2	4	0	18	0	2.97
78–79	Mont	1	20	0	0	0	0	0	0.00
79–80	Mont	5	300	4	1	0	11	1	2.20
80–81	Tor	2	75	0	1	0	8	0	6.40
Totals		14	759	6	6	0	37	1	2.92

LASKOWSKI, Gary *6–1 175*
B. Ottawa, Ont., June 6, 1959

82–83	LA	46	2227	15	20	4	173	0	4.56
83–84	LA	13	665	4	7	1	55	0	4.96
Totals		59	2942	19	27	5	228	0	4.65

LAXTON, Gordon *5–10 195*
B. Montreal, Que., Mar. 16, 1955

75–76	Pitt	8	414	3	4	0	31	0	4.49
76–77	Pitt	6	253	1	3	0	26	0	6.17
77–78	Pitt	2	73	0	1	0	9	0	7.40
78–79	Pitt	1	60	0	1	0	8	0	8.00
Totals		17	800	4	9	0	74	0	5.55

LeBLANC, Raymond *5–10 170*
B. Fitchburg, Mass., Oct. 24, 1964

91–92	Chi	1	60	1	0	0	1	0	1.00

LeDUC, Albert (Battleship) *5–9 180*
B. Valleyfield, Que., Nov. 12, 1902

31–32	Mont	1	2	0	0	0	1	0	30.00

SEASON	TEAM	GP	MIN.	W	L	T	GA	SO.	AVG.

LEGACE, Manny *5–9 162*
B. Toronto, Ont., Feb. 4, 1973

SEASON	TEAM	GP	MIN.	W	L	T	GA	SO.	AVG.
98–99	LA	17	899	2	9	2	39	0	2.60

LEGRIS, Claude *5–9 160*
B. Verdun, Que., Nov. 6, 1956

SEASON	TEAM	GP	MIN.	W	L	T	GA	SO.	AVG.
80–81	Det	3	63	0	1	0	4	0	3.81
81–82	Det	1	28	0	0	1	0	0	0.00
Totals		4	91	0	1	1	4	0	2.64

LEHMAN, Hugh
B. Pembroke, Ont., Oct. 27, 1895

SEASON	TEAM	GP	MIN.	W	L	T	GA	SO.	AVG.
26–27	Chi	44	2797	19	22	3	116	5	2.64
27–28	Chi	4	250	1	2	1	20	1	5.00
Totals		48	3047	20	24	4	136	6	2.68

Playoffs

SEASON	TEAM	GP	MIN.	W	L	T	GA	SO.	AVG.
26–27	Chi	2	120	0	1	1	10	0	5.00

LEMELIN, Rejean *5–11 170*
B. Sherbrooke, Que. Nov. 19, 1954

SEASON	TEAM	GP	MIN.	W	L	T	GA	SO.	AVG.
78–79	Atl	18	994	8	8	1	55	0	3.32
79–80	Atl	3	150	0	2	0	15	0	6.00
80–81	Calg	29	1629	14	6	7	88	2	3.24
81–82	Calg	34	1866	10	15	6	135	0	4.34
82–83	Calg	39	2211	16	12	8	133	2	3.61
83–84	Calg	51	2568	21	12	9	150	0	3.50
84–85	Calg	56	3176	30	12	10	183	1	3.46
85–86	Calg	60	3369	29	24	4	229	1	4.08
86–87	Calg	34	1735	16	9	1	94	2	3.25
87–88	Bos	49	2828	24	17	6	138	3	2.93
88–89	Bos	40	2392	19	15	6	120	0	3.01
89–90	Bos	43	2310	22	15	2	108	2	2.81
90–91	Bos	33	1829	17	10	3	111	1	3.64
91–92	Bos	8	407	5	1	0	23	0	3.39
92–93	Bos	10	542	5	4	0	31	0	3.43
Totals		507	28006	236	162	63	1613	12	3.46

Playoffs

SEASON	TEAM	GP	MIN.	W	L	T	GA	SO.	AVG.
78–79	Atl	1	20	0	0	0	0	0	0.00
80–81	Calg	6	366	3	3	0	22	0	3.61
82–83	Calg	7	327	3	3	0	27	0	4.95
83–84	Calg	8	448	4	4	0	32	0	4.29
84–85	Calg	4	248	1	3	0	15	1	3.63
85–86	Calg	3	109	0	1	0	7	0	3.85
86–87	Calg	2	101	0	1	0	6	0	3.56
87–88	Bos	17	1027	11	6	0	45	1	2.63
88–89	Bos	4	252	1	3	0	16	0	3.81
89–90	Bos	3	135	0	1	0	13	0	5.78
90–91	Bos	2	32	0	0	0	0	0	0.00
91–92	Bos	2	54	0	0	0	3	0	3.33
Totals		59	3119	23	25	0	186	2	3.58

LENARDUZZI, Mike *6–1 165*
B. London, Ont., Sept. 14, 1972

SEASON	TEAM	GP	MIN.	W	L	T	GA	SO.	AVG.
92–93	Hart	3	168	1	1	1	9	0	3.21
93–94	Hart	1	21	0	0	0	1	0	2.86
Totals		4	189	1	1	1	10	0	3.17

LESSARD, Mario *5–9 177*
B. East Broughton, Que., June 25, 1954

SEASON	TEAM	GP	MIN.	W	L	T	GA	SO.	AVG.
78–79	LA	49	2860	23	15	10	148	4	3.10
79–80	LA	50	2836	18	22	7	185	0	3.91
80–81	LA	64	3746	35	18	11	203	2	3.25
81–82	LA	52	2933	13	28	8	213	2	4.36
82–83	LA	19	888	3	10	2	68	1	4.59
83–84	LA	6	266	0	4	1	26	0	5.87
Totals		240	13529	92	97	39	843	9	3.74

Playoffs

SEASON	TEAM	GP	MIN.	W	L	T	GA	SO.	AVG.
78–79	LA	2	126	0	2	0	9	0	4.29
79–80	LA	4	207	1	2	0	14	0	4.06
80–81	LA	4	220	1	3	0	20	0	5.45
81–82	LA	10	583	4	5	0	41	0	4.22
Totals		20	1136	6	12	0	83	0	4.38

LEVASSEUR, Jean–Louis *5–10 160*
B. Noranda, Que., June 16, 1949

SEASON	TEAM	GP	MIN.	W	L	T	GA	SO.	AVG.
75–76	Minn (WHA)	4	193	2	1	0	10	0	3.11
76–77	Minn–Edm (WHA)	51	2928	21	23	5	166	2	3.40
77–78	NE (WHA)	27	1655	14	11	2	91	3	3.30
78–79	Que (WHA)	3	140	0	1	1	14	0	6.00
79–80	Minn	1	60	0	1	0	7	0	7.00
NHL Totals		1	60	0	1	0	7	0	7.00
WHA Totals		85	4916	37	36	8	281	5	3.43

Playoffs

SEASON	TEAM	GP	MIN.	W	L	T	GA	SO.	AVG.
76–77	Edm (WHA)	2	133	0	2	0	10	0	4.51
77–78	NE (WHA)	12	719	8	4	0	31	0	2.59
78–79	Que (WHA)	1	59	0	1	0	8	0	8.14
WHA Totals		15	911	8	7	0	49	0	3.23

LEVINSKY, Alexander *5–10 184*
B. Syracuse, N.Y., Feb. 2, 1910

SEASON	TEAM	GP	MIN.	W	L	T	GA	SO.	AVG.
32–33	Tor	1	1	0	0	0	1	0	60.00

* LINDBERGH, Per–Erik (Pelle) *5–9 160*
B. Stockholm, Sweden, May 24, 1959

SEASON	TEAM	GP	MIN.	W	L	T	GA	SO.	AVG.
81–82	Phil	8	480	2	4	2	35	0	4.38
82–83	Phil	40	2334	23	13	3	116	3	2.98
83–84	Phil	36	1999	16	13	3	135	1	4.05
84–85	Phil	65	3858	40	17	7	194	2	3.02
85–86	Phil	8	480	6	2	0	23	1	2.88
Totals		157	9151	87	49	15	503	7	3.30

Playoffs

SEASON	TEAM	GP	MIN.	W	L	T	GA	SO.	AVG.
82–83	Phil	3	180	0	3	0	18	0	6.00
83–84	Phil	2	26	0	1	0	3	0	6.98
84–85	Phil	18	1008	12	6	0	42	3	2.50
Totals		23	1214	12	10	0	63	3	3.11

LINDSAY, Bert A.

SEASON	TEAM	GP	MIN.	W	L	T	GA	SO.	AVG.
17–18	Mont W	4	240	1	3	0	35	0	8.75
18–19	Tor	16	979	5	11	0	83	0	5.19
Totals		20	1219	6	14	0	118	0	5.81

LITTMAN, David *6–0 183*
B. Cranston, R.I., June 13, 1967

SEASON	TEAM	GP	MIN.	W	L	T	GA	SO.	AVG.
90–91	Buf	1	36	0	0	0	3	0	5.00
91–92	Buf	1	60	0	1	0	4	0	4.00
92–93	TB	1	45	0	1	0	7	0	9.33
Totals		3	141	0	2	0	14	0	5.96

LIUT, Michael *6–2 195*
B. Weston, Ont., Jan. 7, 1956

SEASON	TEAM	GP	MIN.	W	L	T	GA	SO.	AVG.
77–78	Cin (WHA)	27	1215	8	12	0	86	0	4.25
78–79	Cin (WHA)	54	3181	23	27	4	184	3	3.47
79–80	StL	64	3661	32	23	9	194	2	3.18
80–81	StL	61	3570	33	14	13	199	1	3.34
81–82	StL	64	3691	28	28	7	250	2	4.06
82–83	StL	68	3794	21	27	13	235	1	3.72
83–84	StL	58	3425	25	29	4	197	3	3.45
84–85	StL–Hart	44	2600	16	19	7	155	2	3.58
85–86	Hart	57	3282	27	23	4	198	2	3.62
86–87	Hart	59	3476	31	22	5	187	4	3.23
87–88	Hart	60	3532	25	28	5	187	2	3.18
88–89	Hart	35	2006	13	19	1	142	1	4.25
89–90	Hart–Wash	37	2161	19	16	1	91	4	2.53
90–91	Wash	35	1834	13	16	3	114	0	3.73
91–92	Wash	21	1123	10	7	2	70	1	3.74
NHL Totals		663	38155	293	271	74	2219	25	3.49
WHA Totals		81	4396	31	39	4	270	3	3.69

Playoffs

SEASON	TEAM	GP	MIN.	W	L	T	GA	SO.	AVG.
78–79	Cin (WHA)	3	179	1	2	0	12	0	4.02
79–80	StL	3	193	0	3	0	12	0	3.73
80–81	StL	11	685	5	6	0	50	0	4.38
81–82	StL	10	494	5	3	0	27	0	3.28
82–83	StL	4	240	1	3	0	15	0	3.75
83–84	StL	11	714	6	5	0	29	1	2.44
85–86	Hart	8	441	5	2	0	14	1	1.90
86–87	Hart	6	332	2	4	0	25	0	4.52
87–88	Hart	3	160	1	1	0	11	0	4.13
89–90	Wash	9	507	4	4	0	28	0	3.31
90–91	Wash	2	48	0	1	0	4	0	5.00
NHL Totals		67	3814	29	32	0	215	2	3.38
WHA Totals		3	179	1	2	0	12	0	4.02

LOCKETT, Kenneth Richard *6–0 160*
B. Toronto, Ont., Aug. 30, 1947

SEASON	TEAM	GP	MIN.	W	L	T	GA	SO.	AVG.
74–75	Van	25	912	6	7	1	48	2	3.16
75–76	Van	30	1436	7	8	7	83	0	3.47
76–77	SD (WHA)	45	1144	18	19	1	148	1	7.76
NHL Totals		55	2348	13	15	8	131	2	3.35
WHA Totals		45	1144	18	19	1	148	1	7.76

Playoffs

SEASON	TEAM	GP	MIN.	W	L	T	GA	SO.	AVG.
74–75	Van	1	60	0	1	0	6	0	6.00
76–77	SD (WHA)	5	260	1	3	0	19	0	4.38
NHL Totals		1	60	6	0	6.00				
WHA Totals		5	260	19	0	4.38				

SEASON	TEAM	GP	MIN.	W	L	T	GA	SO.	AVG.

* LOCKHART, Howard (Holes)

SEASON	TEAM	GP	MIN.	W	L	T	GA	SO.	AVG.
19–20	Tor–Que	6	328	4	2	0	31	0	5.67
20–21	Ham	24	1454	7	17	0	132	1	5.50
21–22	Ham	24	1409	6	17	0	103	0	4.29
23–24	Tor	1	60	0	1	0	5	0	5.00
24–25	Bos	2	120	0	2	0	11	0	5.50
Totals		57	3371	17	39	0	282	1	5.02

LoPRESTI, Peter Jon *6–1 195*
B. Virginia, Minn., May 23, 1954

SEASON	TEAM	GP	MIN.	W	L	T	GA	SO.	AVG.
74–75	Minn	35	1964	9	20	3	137	1	4.19
75–76	Minn	34	1789	7	22	1	123	1	4.13
76–77	Minn	44	2590	13	20	10	156	1	3.61
77–78	Minn	53	3065	12	35	6	216	2	4.23
78–79	Minn	7	345	2	4	0	28	0	4.87
80–81	Edm	2	105	0	1	0	8	0	4.57
Totals		175	9858	43	102	20	668	5	4.07

Playoffs

SEASON	TEAM	GP	MIN.	W	L	T	GA	SO.	AVG.
76–77	Minn	2	77	0	2	0	6	0	4.68

* LoPRESTI, Samuel *5–11 200*
B. Eveleth, Minn., Jan. 30, 1917

SEASON	TEAM	GP	MIN.	W	L	T	GA	SO.	AVG.
40–41	Chi	27	1670	9	15	3	84	1	3.11
41–42	Chi	47	2860	21	23	3	152	3	3.23
Totals		74	4530	30	38	6	236	4	3.13

Playoffs

SEASON	TEAM	GP	MIN.	W	L	T	GA	SO.	AVG.
40–41	Chi	5	343	2	3	0	12	0	2.40
41–42	Chi	3	187	1	2	0	5	1	1.67
Totals		8	530	3	5	0	17	1	1.92

LORENZ, Danny *5–10 187*
B. Murrayville, B.C., Dec. 12, 1969

SEASON	TEAM	GP	MIN.	W	L	T	GA	SO.	AVG.
90–91	NYI	2	80	0	1	0	5	0	3.75
91–92	NYI	2	120	0	2	0	10	0	5.00
92–93	NYI	4	157	1	2	0	10	0	3.82
Totals		8	357	1	5	0	25	0	4.20

LOUSTEL, Ron *5–11 185*
B. Winnipeg, Man., Mar. 7, 1962

SEASON	TEAM	GP	MIN.	W	L	T	GA	SO.	AVG.
80–81	Winn	1	60	0	1	0	10	0	10.00

LOW, Ronald Albert *6–1 205*
B. Birtle, Man., June 21, 1950

SEASON	TEAM	GP	MIN.	W	L	T	GA	SO.	AVG.
72–73	Tor	42	2343	12	24	4	152	1	3.89
74–75	Wash	48	2588	8	36	2	235	1	5.45
75–76	Wash	43	2289	6	31	2	208	0	5.45
76–77	Wash	54	2918	16	27	5	188	0	3.87
77–78	Det	32	1816	9	12	9	102	1	3.37
79–80	Que–Edm	26	1478	13	9	3	88	0	3.57
80–81	Edm	24	1260	5	13	3	93	0	4.43
81–82	Edm	29	1554	17	7	1	100	0	3.86
82–83	Edm–NJ	14	712	2	8	1	51	0	4.30
83–84	NJ	44	2218	8	25	4	161	0	4.35
84–85	NJ	26	1326	6	11	4	85	1	3.85
Totals		382	20502	102	203	37	1463	4	4.28

Playoffs

SEASON	TEAM	GP	MIN.	W	L	T	GA	SO.	AVG.
77–78	Det	4	240	1	3	0	17	0	4.25
79–80	Edm	3	212	0	3	0	12	0	3.40
Totals		7	452	1	6	0	29	0	3.85

LOZINSKI, Larry Peter *5–11 175*
B. Hudson Bay, Sask., Mar. 11, 1958

SEASON	TEAM	GP	MIN.	W	L	T	GA	SO.	AVG.
80–81	Det	30	1459	105		0	4.32		

LUMLEY, Harry (Apple Cheeks) *6–0 195*
B. Owen Sound, Ont., Nov. 11, 1926

SEASON	TEAM	GP	MIN.	W	L	T	GA	SO.	AVG.
43–44	Det–NYR	3	140	0	2	0	13	0	5.57
44–45	Det	37	2220	24	10	3	119	1	3.22
45–46	Det	50	3000	20	20	10	159	2	3.18
46–47	Det	52	3120	22	20	10	159	3	3.06
47–48	Det	60	3592	30	18	12	147	7	2.46
48–49	Det	60	3600	34	19	7	145	6	2.42
49–50	Det	63	3780	33	16	14	148	7	2.35
50–51	Chi	64	3785	12	41	10	246	3	3.90
51–52	Chi	70	4180	16	44	9	241	2	3.46
52–53	Tor	70	4200	27	30	13	167	10	2.39
53–54	Tor	69	4140	32	24	13	128	13	1.86
54–55	Tor	69	4140	24	21	22	134	8	1.94
55–56	Tor	59	3520	21	28	10	159	3	2.71
57–58	Bos	25	1500	11	10	4	71	3	2.84
58–59	Bos	11	660	8	2	1	27	1	2.45
59–60	Bos	42	2520	18	19	5	147	2	3.50
Totals		804	48097	332	324	143	2210	71	2.76

Playoffs

SEASON	TEAM	GP	MIN.	W	L	T	GA	SO.	AVG.
44–45	Det	14	871	7	7	0	31	2	2.14
45–46	Det	5	310	1	4	0	16	1	3.10
47–48	Det	10	600	4	6	0	30	0	3.00
48–49	Det	11	726	4	7	0	26	0	2.15
49–50	Det	14	910	8	6	0	28	3	1.85
53–54	Tor	5	321	1	4	0	15	0	2.80
54–55	Tor	4	240	0	4	0	14	0	3.50
55–56	Tor	5	304	1	4	0	14	1	2.76
57–58	Bos	1	60	0	1	0	5	0	5.00
58–59	Bos	7	436	3	4	0	20	0	2.75
Totals		76	4778	29	47	0	199	7	2.50

MacKENZIE, Shawn *5–10 175*
B. Bedford, N.S., Aug. 22, 1962

SEASON	TEAM	GP	MIN.	W	L	T	GA	SO.	AVG.
82–83	NJ	4	130	0	1	0	15	0	6.92

MADELEY, Darrin *5–11 170*
B. Holland Landing, Ont., Feb. 25, 1968

SEASON	TEAM	GP	MIN.	W	L	T	GA	SO.	AVG.
92–93	Ott	2	90	0	2	0	10	0	6.67
93–94	Ott	32	1583	3	18	5	115	0	4.36
94–95	Ott	5	255	1	3	0	15	0	3.53
Totals		39	1928	4	23	5	140	0	4.36

MALARCHUK, Clint *6–0 187*
B. Grand Prairie, Alta., May 1, 1961

SEASON	TEAM	GP	MIN.	W	L	T	GA	SO.	AVG.
81–82	Que	2	120	0	1	0	14	0	7.00
82–83	Que	15	900	8	5	2	71	0	4.73
83–84	Que	23	1215	10	9	2	80	0	3.95
85–86	Que	46	2657	26	12	4	142	4	3.21
86–87	Que	54	3092	18	26	9	175	1	3.40
87–88	Wash	54	2926	24	20	4	154	4	3.16
88–89	Wash–Buf	49	2754	19	19	8	154	2	3.36
89–90	Buf	29	1596	14	11	2	89	0	3.35
90–91	Buf	37	2131	12	14	10	119	1	3.35
91–92	Buf	29	1639	10	13	3	102	0	3.73
Totals		338	19030	141	130	45	1100	11	3.47

Playoffs

SEASON	TEAM	GP	MIN.	W	L	T	GA	SO.	AVG.
85–86	Que	3	143	0	2	0	11	0	4.62
86–87	Que	3	140	0	2	0	8	0	3.43
87–88	Wash	4	193	0	2	0	15	0	4.66
88–89	Buf	1	59	0	1	0	5	0	5.08
90–91	Buf	4	246	2	2	0	17	0	4.15
Totals		15	781	2	9	0	56	0	4.30

MANELUK, George *5–11 185*
B. Winnipeg, Man., July 25, 1967

SEASON	TEAM	GP	MIN.	W	L	T	GA	SO.	AVG.
90–91	NYI	4	140	1	1	0	15	0	6.43

MANIAGO, Cesare *6–3 195*
B. Trail, B.C., Jan. 13, 1939

SEASON	TEAM	GP	MIN.	W	L	T	GA	SO.	AVG.
60–61	Tor	7	420	4	2	1	18	0	2.57
62–63	Mont	14	820	5	5	4	42	0	3.07
65–66	NYR	28	1613	9	16	3	94	2	3.50
66–67	NYR	6	219	0	3	1	14	0	3.84
67–68	Minn	52	2877	21	17	9	133	6	2.77
68–69	Minn	64	3599	18	33	10	198	1	3.30
69–70	Minn	50	2887	9	24	16	163	2	3.39
70–71	Minn	40	2380	19	15	6	107	5	2.70
71–72	Minn	43	2539	20	17	4	112	3	2.65
72–73	Minn	47	2736	21	18	6	132	5	2.89
73–74	Minn	40	2378	12	18	10	138	1	3.48
74–75	Minn	37	2129	11	21	4	149	1	4.20
75–76	Minn	47	2704	13	27	5	151	2	3.35
76–77	Van	47	2699	17	21	9	151	1	3.36
77–78	Van	46	2570	10	24	8	172	1	4.02
Totals		568	32570	189	261	96	1774	30	3.27

Playoffs

SEASON	TEAM	GP	MIN.	W	L	T	GA	SO.	AVG.
60–61	Tor	2	145	1	1	0	6	0	2.48
67–68	Minn	14	893	7	7	0	39	0	2.62
69–70	Minn	3	180	1	2	0	6	1	2.00
70–71	Minn	8	480	3	5	0	28	0	3.50
71–72	Minn	4	238	1	3	0	12	0	3.03
72–73	Minn	5	309	2	3	0	9	2	1.75
Totals		36	2245	15	21	0	100	3	2.67

MARACLE, Norm *5–9 175*
B. Belleville, Ont., Oct. 2, 1974

SEASON	TEAM	GP	MIN.	W	L	T	GA	SO.	AVG.
97–98	Det	4	178	2	0	1	6	0	2.02
98–99	Det	16	821	6	5	2	31	0	2.27
Totals		20	999	8	5	3	37	0	2.22

Playoffs

SEASON	TEAM	GP	MIN.	W	L	T	GA	SO.	AVG.
98–99	Det	2	58	0	0	0	3	0	3.10

MAROIS, Jean

SEASON	TEAM	GP	MIN.	W	L	T	GA	SO.	AVG.
43–44	Tor	1	60	1	0	0	4	0	4.00
53–54	Chi	2	120	0	2	0	11	0	5.50
Totals		3	180	1	2	0	15	0	5.00

MARTIN, Seth *5–11 180*
B. Rossland, B.C., May 4, 1933

67–68	StL	30	1552	8	10	7	67	1	2.59

Playoffs

67–68	StL	2	73	0	0	0	5	0	4.11

MASON, Chris *6–0 200*
B. Red Deer, Alta., Apr. 20, 1976

98–99	Nash	3	69	0	0	0	6	0	5.22

MASON, Robert *6–1 180*
B. International Falls, Minn., Apr. 22, 1961

83–84	Wash	2	120	2	0	0	3	0	1.50
84–85	Wash	12	661	8	2	1	31	1	2.81
85–86	Wash	1	16	1	0	0	0	0	0.00
86–87	Wash	45	2536	20	18	5	137	0	3.24
87–88	Chi	41	2312	13	18	8	160	0	4.15
88–89	Que	22	1168	5	14	1	92	0	4.73
89–90	Wash	16	822	4	9	1	48	0	3.50
90–91	Van	6	353	2	4	0	29	0	4.93
Totals		145	7988	55	65	16	500	1	3.76

Playoffs

86–87	Wash	4	309	2	2	0	9	1	1.75
87–88	Chi	1	60	0	1	0	3	0	3.00
Totals		5	369	2	3	0	12	1	1.95

MATTSSON, Rainer Markus *6–0 180*
B. Suoneiemi, Finland, July 30, 1957

77–78	Que–Winn (WHA)	16	777	5	8	0	60	0	4.63
78–79	Winn (WHA)	52	2990	25	21	3	181	0	3.63
79–80	Winn	21	1200	5	11	4	65	2	3.25
80–81	Winn	31	1707	3	21	4	128	1	4.50
82–83	Minn–LA	21	999	6	6	4	71	2	4.26
83–84	LA	19	1101	7	8	2	79	1	4.31
NHL Totals		92	5007	21	46	14	343	6	4.11
WHA Totals		68	3767	30	29	3	241	0	3.84

MAY, Darrell Gerald *6–0 175*
B. Edmonton, Alta., Mar. 6, 1962

85–86	StL	3	184	1	2	0	13	0	4.24
87–88	StL	3	180	0	3	0	18	0	6.00
Totals		6	364	1	5	0	31	0	5.11

MAYER, Gilles *5–6 135*
B. Ottawa, Ont., Aug. 24, 1930

49–50	Tor	1	60	0	1	0	2	0	2.00
53–54	Tor	1	60	0	0	1	3	0	3.00
54–55	Tor	1	60	0	1	0	1	0	1.00
55–56	Tor	6	360	1	5	0	19	0	3.17
Totals		9	540	1	7	1	25	0	2.78

McAULEY, Kenneth Leslie (Tubby) *5–10 190*
B. Edmonton, Alta., Jan. 9, 1921

43–44	NYR	50	2980	6	39	5	310	0	6.20
44–45	NYR	46	2760	11	25	10	227	1	4.93
Totals		96	5740	17	64	15	537	1	5.61

McCARTAN, John William (Jack) *6–1 195*
B. St. Paul, Minn., Aug. 5, 1935

59–60	NYR	4	240	2	1	1	7	0	1.75
60–61	NYR	8	440	1	6	1	36	1	4.91
72–73	Minn (WHA)	38	2160	15	19	1	129	1	3.58
73–74	Minn (WHA)	2	42	0	0	0	5	0	7.14
74–75	Minn (WHA)	2	61	1	0	0	5	0	4.92
NHL Totals		12	680	3	7	2	43	1	3.79
WHA Totals		42	2263	16	19	1	139	1	3.69

Playoffs

72–73	Minn (WHA)	4	213	1	2	0	14	0	3.94

* McCOOL, Frank *6–0 170*
B. Calgary, Alta., Oct. 27, 1918

44–45	Tor	50	3000	24	22	4	161	4	3.22
45–46	Tor	22	1320	10	9	3	81	0	3.68
Totals		72	4320	34	31	7	242	4	3.36

Playoffs

44–45	Tor	13	807	8	5	0	30	4	2.23

McDUFFE, Peter Arnold *5–9 180*
B. Milton, Ont., Feb. 16, 1948

71–72	StL	10	467	0	6	0	29	0	3.73
72–73	NYR	1	60	1	0	0	1	0	1.00
73–74	NYR	6	340	3	2	1	18	0	3.18
74–75	KC	36	2100	7	25	4	148	0	4.23
75–76	Det	4	240	0	3	1	22	0	5.50
77–78	Ind (WHA)	12	539	1	6	1	39	0	4.34
NHL Totals		57	3207	11	36	6	218	0	4.08
WHA Totals		12	539	1	6	1	39	0	4.34

Playoffs

71–72	StL	1	60	0	1	0	7	0	7.00

McGRATTON, Thomas *6–2 170*
B. Brantford, Ont., Oct. 19, 1927

47–48	Det	1	8	0	0	0	0	0	0.00

McKAY, Ross Lee *5–11 175*
B. Edmonton, Alta., Mar. 3, 1964

90–91	Hart	1	35	0	0	0	3	0	5.14

McKENZIE, William Ian *5–11 180*
B. St. Thomas, Ont., Mar. 12, 1949

73–74	Det	13	720	4	4	4	43	1	3.58
74–75	Det	13	740	1	9	2	58	0	4.70
75–76	KC	22	1120	1	16	1	97	0	5.20
76–77	Col	5	200	0	2	1	8	0	2.40
77–78	Col	12	654	3	6	2	42	0	3.85
79–80	Col	26	1342	9	12	3	78	1	3.49
Totals		91	4776	18	49	13	326	2	4.10

McKICHAN, Steve *5–11 180*
B. Strathroy, Ont., May 29, 1967

90–91	Van	1	20	0	0	0	2	0	6.00

McLACHLAN, Murray *6–0 195*
B. London, Ont., Oct. 20, 1948

70–71	Tor	2	25	0	1	0	4	0	9.60

McLEAN, Kirk *6–0 195*
B. Willowdale, Ont., June 26, 1966

85–86	NJ	2	111	1	1	0	11	0	5.95
86–87	NJ	4	160	1	1	0	10	0	3.75
87–88	Van	41	2380	11	27	3	147	1	3.71
88–89	Van	42	2477	20	17	3	127	4	3.08
89–90	Van	63	3739	21	30	10	216	0	3.47
90–91	Van	41	1969	10	22	3	131	0	3.99
91–92	Van	65	3852	38	17	9	176	5	2.74
92–93	Van	54	3261	28	21	5	184	3	3.39
93–94	Van	52	3128	23	26	3	156	3	2.99
94–95	Van	40	2374	18	12	10	109	1	2.75
95–96	Van	45	2645	15	21	9	156	2	3.54
96–97	Van	44	2581	21	18	3	138	0	3.21
97–98	Van–Car	37	1984	10	19	4	119	1	3.60
98–99	Fla	30	1597	9	10	4	73	2	2.74
Totals		560	32258	228	242	66	1753	22	3.26

Playoffs

88–89	Van	5	302	2	3	0	18	0	3.58
90–91	Van	2	123	1	1	0	7	0	3.41
91–92	Van	13	785	6	7	0	33	2	2.52
92–93	Van	12	754	6	6	0	42	0	3.34
93–94	Van	24	1544	15	9	0	59	4	2.29
94–95	Van	11	660	4	7	0	36	0	3.27
95–96	Van	1	21	0	1	0	3	0	8.57
Totals		68	4189	34	34	0	198	6	2.84

McLELLAND, David *5–9 165*
B. Penticton, B.C., Nov. 20, 1952

72–73	Van	2	120	1	1	0	10	0	5.00

McLENNAN, Jamie *6–0 190*
B. Edmonton, Alta., June 30, 1971

93–94	NYI	22	1287	8	7	6	61	0	2.84
94–95	NYI	21	1185	6	11	2	67	0	3.39
95–96	Van	13	636	3	9	1	39	0	3.68
97–98	StL	30	1658	16	8	2	60	2	2.17
98–99	StL	33	1763	13	14	4	70	3	2.38
Totals		119	6529	46	49	15	297	5	2.73

Playoffs

98–99	StL	1	37	0	1	0	0	0	0.00

McLEOD, Donald Martin 6-0 190
B. Trail, B.C., Aug. 24, 1946

SEASON	TEAM	GP	MIN.	W	L	T	GA	SO.	AVG.
70-71	Det	14	698	3	7	0	60	0	5.16
71-72	Phil	4	181	0	3	1	14	0	4.64
72-73	Hou (WHA)	41	2410	19	20	1	145	1	3.61
73-74	Hou (WHA)	49	2971	33	13	3	127	3	2.56
74-75	Van (WHA)	72	4184	33	35	2	233	1	3.34
75-76	Calg (WHA)	63	3534	30	27	3	206	1	3.50
76-77	Calg (WHA)	67	3701	25	34	5	210	3	3.40
77-78	Que-Edm (WHA)	40	2126	17	14	1	130	2	3.67
NHL Totals		18	879	3	10	1	74	0	5.05
WHA Totals		332	18926	157	143	15	1051	11	3.33

Playoffs

SEASON	TEAM	GP	MIN.	W	L	T	GA	SO.	AVG.
72-73	Hou (WHA)	3	178	0	3	0	8	0	2.70
73-74	Hou (WHA)	14	842	12	2	0	35	0	2.49
75-76	Calg (WHA)	10	559	5	5	0	37	0	3.97
77-78	Edm (WHA)	4	207	1	3	0	16	0	4.64
WHA Totals		31	1786	18	13	0	96	0	3.23

McLEOD, James Bradley 5-8 170
B. Port Arthur, Ont., Apr. 7, 1937

SEASON	TEAM	GP	MIN.	W	L	T	GA	SO.	AVG.
71-72	StL	16	880	6	6	4	44	0	3.00
72-73	Chi (WHA)	54	2996	22	25	2	166	1	3.32
73-74	NJ-LA (WHA)	27	1486	7	20	0	105	1	4.24
74-75	Balt (WHA)	16	694	3	6	1	53	0	4.58
NHL Totals		16	880	6	6	4	44	0	3.00
WHA Totals		97	5176	32	51	3	324	2	3.76

McNAMARA, Gerald 6-2 190
B. Sturgeon Falls, Ont., Sept. 22, 1934

SEASON	TEAM	GP	MIN.	W	L	T	GA	SO.	AVG.
60-61	Tor	5	300	2	2	1	13	0	2.60
69-70	Tor	2	23	0	0	0	2	0	5.22
Totals		7	323	2	2	1	15	0	2.79

McNEIL, Gerard George 5-7 155
B. Quebec City, Que., Apr. 17, 1926

SEASON	TEAM	GP	MIN.	W	L	T	GA	SO.	AVG.
47-48	Mont	2	95	0	1	1	7	0	4.42
49-50	Mont	6	360	3	1	2	9	1	1.50
50-51	Mont	70	4200	25	30	15	184	6	2.63
51-52	Mont	70	4200	34	26	10	164	5	2.34
52-53	Mont	66	3960	25	23	18	140	10	2.12
53-54	Mont	53	3180	28	19	6	114	6	2.15
56-57	Mont	9	540	4	5	0	32	0	3.56
Totals		276	16535	119	105	52	650	28	2.36

Playoffs

SEASON	TEAM	GP	MIN.	W	L	T	GA	SO.	AVG.
49-50	Mont	2	135	1	1	0	5	0	2.22
50-51	Mont	11	785	5	6	0	25	1	1.91
51-52	Mont	11	688	4	7	0	23	1	2.01
52-53	Mont	8	486	5	3	0	16	2	1.98
53-54	Mont	3	190	2	1	0	3	1	0.95
Totals		35	2284	17	18	0	72	5	1.89

McRAE, Gordon Alexander 6-0 180
B. Sherbrooke, Que., Apr. 12, 1948

SEASON	TEAM	GP	MIN.	W	L	T	GA	SO.	AVG.
72-73	Tor	11	620	7	3	0	39	0	3.77
74-75	Tor	20	1063	1	13	6	57	0	3.22
75-76	Tor	20	956	6	5	2	59	0	3.70
76-77	Tor	2	120	0	1	1	9	0	4.50
77-78	Tor	18	1040	7	10	1	57	1	3.29
Totals		71	3799	21	32	10	221	1	3.49

Playoffs

SEASON	TEAM	GP	MIN.	W	L	T	GA	SO.	AVG.
74-75	Tor	7	441	2	5	0	21	0	2.86
75-76	Tor	1	13	0	0	0	1	0	4.62
Totals		8	454	2	5	0	22	0	2.91

MELANSON, Roland Joseph (Rollie) 5-10 180
B. Moncton, N. B., June 28, 1960

SEASON	TEAM	GP	MIN.	W	L	T	GA	SO.	AVG.
80-81	NYI	11	620	8	1	1	32	0	3.10
81-82	NYI	36	2115	22	7	6	114	0	3.23
82-83	NYI	44	2460	24	12	5	109	1	2.66
83-84	NYI	37	2019	20	11	2	110	0	3.27
84-85	NYI-Minn	28	1567	8	13	3	113	0	4.33
85-86	Minn-LA	28	1571	6	17	3	111	0	4.24
86-87	LA	46	2734	18	21	6	168	1	3.69
87-88	LA	47	2676	17	20	7	195	2	4.37
88-89	LA	4	178	1	1	0	19	0	6.40
90-91	NJ	1	20	0	0	0	2	0	6.00
91-92	Mont	9	492	5	3	0	22	2	2.68
Totals		291	16452	129	103	33	995	6	3.63

Playoffs

SEASON	TEAM	GP	MIN.	W	L	T	GA	SO.	AVG.
80-81	NYI	3	92	1	0	0	6	0	3.91
81-82	NYI	3	64	0	1	0	5	0	4.69
82-83	NYI	5	238	2	2	0	10	2	2.52
83-84	NYI	6	87	0	1	0	5	0	3.45
86-87	LA	5	260	1	4	0	24	0	5.54
87-88	LA	1	60	0	1	0	9	0	9.00
Totals		23	801	4	9	0	59	0	4.42

MELOCHE, Gilles 5-10 170
B. Montreal, Que., July 12, 1950

SEASON	TEAM	GP	MIN.	W	L	T	GA	SO.	AVG.
70-71	Chi	2	120	2	0	0	6	0	3.00
71-72	Cal	56	3121	16	25	13	173	4	3.33
72-73	Cal	59	3473	12	32	14	235	1	4.06
73-74	Cal	47	2800	9	33	5	198	1	4.24
74-75	Cal	47	2771	9	27	10	186	1	4.03
75-76	Cal	41	2440	12	23	6	140	1	3.44
76-77	Clev	51	2961	19	24	6	171	2	3.47
77-78	Clev	54	3100	16	27	8	195	1	3.77
78-79	Minn	53	3118	20	25	7	173	2	3.33
79-80	Minn	54	3141	27	20	6	160	1	3.06
80-81	Minn	38	2215	17	14	6	120	2	3.25
81-82	Minn	51	3026	26	15	9	175	1	3.47
82-83	Minn	47	2689	20	13	11	160	1	3.57
83-84	Minn	52	2883	21	17	8	201	2	4.18
84-85	Minn	32	1817	10	13	8	115	0	3.80
85-86	Pitt	34	1989	13	15	5	119	0	3.59
86-87	Pitt	43	2343	13	19	7	134	0	3.43
87-88	Pitt	27	1394	8	9	5	95	0	4.09
Totals		788	45401	270	351	131	2756	20	3.64

Playoffs

SEASON	TEAM	GP	MIN.	W	L	T	GA	SO.	AVG.
79-80	Minn	11	564	5	4	0	35	1	3.62
80-81	Minn	13	802	8	5	0	47	0	3.52
81-82	Minn	4	184	1	2	0	8	0	2.61
82-83	Minn	5	319	2	3	0	18	0	3.39
83-84	Minn	4	200	1	2	0	11	0	3.30
84-85	Minn	8	395	4	3	0	25	1	3.80
Totals		45	2464	21	19	0	143	2	3.48

MICALEF, Corrado 5-8 172
B. Montreal, Que., Apr. 20, 1961

SEASON	TEAM	GP	MIN.	W	L	T	GA	SO.	AVG.
81-82	Det	18	809	4	10	1	63	0	4.67
82-83	Det	34	1756	11	13	5	106	2	3.62
83-84	Det	14	808	5	8	1	52	0	3.86
84-85	Det	36	1856	5	19	7	136	0	4.40
85-86	Det	11	565	1	9	1	52	0	5.52
Totals		113	5794	26	59	15	409	2	4.24

MIDDLEBROOK, Lindsay 5-7 160
B. Collingwood, Ont., Sept. 7, 1955

SEASON	TEAM	GP	MIN.	W	L	T	GA	SO.	AVG.
79-80	Winn	10	580	2	8	0	40	0	4.14
80-81	Winn	14	653	0	9	3	65	0	5.97
81-82	Minn	3	140	0	0	2	7	0	3.00
82-83	NJ-Edm	10	472	1	6	1	40	0	5.08
Totals		37	1845	3	23	6	152	0	4.94

* MILLAR, Al 5-11 175
B. Winnipeg, Man., Sept. 18, 1929

SEASON	TEAM	GP	MIN.	W	L	T	GA	SO.	AVG.
57-58	Bos	6	360	1	3	2	25	0	4.17

MILLEN, Greg H. 5-9 175
B. Toronto, Ont., June 25, 1957

SEASON	TEAM	GP	MIN.	W	L	T	GA	SO.	AVG.
78-79	Pitt	28	1532	14	11	1	86	2	3.37
79-80	Pitt	44	2586	18	18	7	157	2	3.64
80-81	Pitt	63	3721	25	27	10	258	0	4.16
81-82	Hart	55	3201	11	30	12	229	0	4.29
82-83	Hart	60	3520	14	38	6	282	1	4.81
83-84	Hart	60	3583	21	30	9	221	2	3.70
84-85	Hart-StL	54	3266	18	29	7	222	1	4.08
85-86	StL	36	2168	14	16	6	129	1	3.57
86-87	StL	42	2482	15	18	9	146	0	3.53
87-88	StL	48	2854	21	19	7	167	1	3.51
88-89	StL	52	3019	22	20	7	170	6	3.38
89-90	StL-Que-Chi	49	2900	19	25	5	188	1	3.89
90-91	Chi	3	58	0	1	0	4	0	4.14
91-92	Det	10	487	3	2	3	22	0	2.71
Totals		604	35347	215	284	89	2281	17	3.87

Playoffs

SEASON	TEAM	GP	MIN.	W	L	T	GA	SO.	AVG.
79-80	Pitt	5	300	2	3	0	21	0	4.20
80-81	Pitt	5	325	2	3	0	19	0	3.51
84-85	StL	1	60	0	1	0	2	0	2.00
85-86	StL	10	586	6	3	0	29	0	2.97
86-87	StL	4	250	1	3	0	10	0	2.40
87-88	StL	10	600	5	5	0	38	0	3.80

SEASON TEAM	GP	MIN.	W	L	T	GA	SO.	AVG.
88–89 StL	10	649	5	5	0	34	0	3.14
89–90 Chi	14	613	6	6	0	40	0	3.92
Totals	59	3383	27	29	0	193	0	3.42

* MILLER, Joseph *5–9 170*
B. Morrisburgh, Ont., Oct. 6, 1900

27–28 NYA	28	1721	8	16	4	77	5	2.75
28–29 Pitt Pi	44	2780	9	27	8	80	11	1.82
29–30 Pitt Pi	43	2630	5	35	3	179	0	4.16
30–31 Phil Q	15	850	2	12	1	50	0	3.33
Totals	130	7981	24	90	16	386	16	2.90

Playoffs

27–28 NYR	3	180	2	1	0	3	1	1.00

MIO, Edward *5–10 180*
B. Windsor, Ont., Jan. 31, 1954

77–78 Ind (WHA)	17	900	6	8	0	64	0	4.27
78–79 Ind–Edm (WHA)	27	1310	9	12	1	84	2	3.85
79–80 Edm	34	1711	9	13	5	120	1	4.21
80–81 Edm	43	2393	16	15	9	155	0	3.89
81–82 NYR	25	1500	13	6	5	89	0	3.56
82–83 NYR	41	2365	16	8	6	136	2	3.45
83–84 Det	24	1295	7	11	3	95	1	4.40
84–85 Det	7	376	1	3	2	27	0	4.31
85–86 Det	18	788	2	7	0	83	0	6.32
NHL Totals	192	12299	83	85	31	822	6	4.01
WHA Totals	44	2210	15	20	1	148	2	4.02

Playoffs

78–79 Edm (WHA)	3	90	0	0	0	6	0	4.00
81–82 NYR	8	443	4	3	0	28	0	3.79
82–83 NYR	8	480	5	3	0	32	0	4.00
83–84 Det	1	63	0	1	0	3	0	2.86
NHL Totals	17	986	9	7	0	63	0	3.83
WHA Totals	3	90	0	0	0	6	0	4.00

*MITCHELL, Ivan

19–20 Tor	15	872	7	7	0	65	0	4.33
20–21 Tor	4	240	2	2	0	22	0	5.50
21–22 Tor	2	120	2	0	0	6	0	3.00
Totals	21	1232	11	9	0	93	0	4.53

MOFFAT, Michael *5–10 165*
B. Galt, Ont., Feb. 4, 1962

81–82 Bos	2	120	2	0	0	6	0	3.00
82–83 Bos	13	673	4	6	1	49	0	4.37
83–84 Bos	4	186	1	1	1	15	0	4.84
Totals	19	979	7	7	2	70	0	4.29

Playoffs

81–82 Bos	11	663	6	5	0	38	0	3.44

MOOG, Donald Andrew (Andy) *5–8 170*
B. Penticton, B.C., Feb. 18, 1960

80–81 Edm	7	313	3	3	0	20	0	3.83
81–82 Edm	8	399	3	5	0	32	0	4.81
82–83 Edm	50	2833	33	8	7	167	1	3.54
83–84 Edm	38	2212	27	8	1	139	1	3.77
84–85 Edm	39	2019	22	9	3	111	1	3.30
85–86 Edm	47	2664	27	9	7	164	1	3.69
86–87 Edm	46	2461	28	11	3	144	0	3.51
87–88 Bos	6	360	4	2	0	17	1	2.83
88–89 Bos	41	2482	18	14	8	133	1	3.22
89–90 Bos	46	2536	24	10	7	122	3	2.89
90–91 Bos	51	2844	25	13	9	136	4	2.87
91–92 Bos	62	3640	28	22	9	196	1	3.23
92–93 Bos	55	3194	37	14	3	168	3	3.16
93–94 Dal	55	3121	24	20	7	170	2	3.27
94–95 Dal	31	1770	10	12	7	72	0	2.44
95–96 Dal	41	2228	13	19	7	111	1	2.99
96–97 Dal	48	2738	28	13	5	98	3	2.15
97–98 Mont	42	2337	18	17	5	97	3	2.49

Playoffs

80–81 Edm	9	526	5	4	0	32	0	3.65
82–83 Edm	16	949	11	5	0	48	0	3.03
83–84 Edm	7	263	4	0	0	12	0	2.74
84–85 Edm	2	20	0	0	0	0	0	0.00
85–86 Edm	1	60	1	0	0	1	0	1.00
86–87 Edm	2	120	2	0	0	8	0	4.00
87–88 Bos	7	354	1	4	0	25	0	4.24
89–90 Bos	6	359	4	2	0	14	0	2.34
90–91 Bos	20	1195	13	7	0	44	2	2.21
91–92 Bos	19	1133	10	9	0	60	0	3.18
92–93 Bos	15	866	8	7	0	46	1	3.19

93–94 Dal	3	161	0	3	0	14	0	5.22
94–95 Dal	4	246	1	3	0	12	0	2.93
96–97 Dal	5	277	1	4	0	16	0	3.47
97–98 Mont	9	474	4	5	0	24	1	3.04
Totals	132	7452	68	57	0	377	4	3.04

MOORE, Alfred Ernest (Alfie)
B. Toronto, Ont.

36–37 NYA	18	1110	7	11	0	64	1	3.56
38–39 NYA	2	120	0	2	0	14	0	7.00
39–40 Det	1	60	0	1	0	3	0	3.00
Totals	21	1290	7	14	0	81	1	3.77

Playoffs

37–38 Chi	1	60	1	0	0	1	0	1.00
38–39 NYA	2	120	0	2	0	6	0	3.00
Totals	3	180	1	2	0	7	0	2.33

MOORE, Robert David (Robbie) *5–5 155*
B. Sarnia, Ont., May 3, 1954

78–79 Phil	5	237	3	0	1	7	2	1.77
82–83 Wash	1	20	0	1	1	1	0	3.00
Totals	6	257	3	1	1	8	2	1.87

Playoffs

78–79 Phil	5	268	3	2	0	18	0	4.03

MORRISSETTE, Jean Guy *5–6 140*
B. Causapscal, Que., Dec. 19, 1937

63–64 Mont	1	36	0	1	0	4	0	6.67

MOSS, Tyler *6–0 184*

97–98 Calg	6	367	2	3	1	20	0	3.27
98–99 Calg	11	550	3	7	0	23	0	2.51
Totals	17	917	5	10	1	43	0	2.81

MOWERS, John Thomas *5–11 185*
B. Niagara Falls, Ont., Oct. 29, 1916

40–41 Det	48	3040	21	16	11	102	4	2.13
41–42 Det	47	2880	19	25	3	144	5	3.06
42–43 Det	50	3010	25	14	11	124	6	2.47
46–47 Det	7	420	0	0	0	29	0	4.14
Totals	152	9350	65	55	25	399	15	2.56

Playoffs

40–41 Det	9	561	4	5	0	20	0	2.22
41–42 Det	12	720	7	5	0	38	0	3.17
42–43 Det	10	679	8	2	0	22	2	1.94
46–47 Det	1	60	0	1	0	5	0	7.50
Totals	32	2000	19	13	0	85	2	2.55

MRAZEK, Jerome John *5–9 160*
B. Prince Albert, Sask., Oct. 15, 1951

75–76 Phil	1	6	0	0	0	1	0	10.00

* MUMMERY, Harry

19–20 Que	3	142	1	1	0	18	0	6.00
21–22 Ham	1	49	1	0	0	2	0	2.00
Totals	4	191	2	1	0	20	0	6.28

* MURPHY, Harold (Hal)
B. Montreal, Que., July 6, 1927

52–53 Mont	1	60	1	0	0	4	0	4.00

MURRAY, Thomas Mickey

29–30 Mont	1	60	0	1	0	4	0	4.00

MUZZATTI, Jason Mark *6–1 190*
B. Toronto, Ont., Feb. 3, 1970

93–94 Calg	1	60	0	1	0	8	0	8.00
94–95 Calg	1	10	0	0	0	0	0	0.00
95–96 Hart	22	1013	4	8	3	49	1	2.90
96–97 Hart	31	1591	9	13	5	91	0	3.43
97–98 NYR–SJ	7	340	0	3	2	19	0	3.35
Totals	62	3014	13	25	10	167	1	3.32

MYLLYS, Jarmo *5–8 150*
B. Sovanlinna, Finland, May 29, 1965

88–89 Minn	4	238	1	4	0	22	0	5.55
89–90 Minn	4	156	0	3	0	16	0	6.15
90–91 Minn	2	78	0	2	0	8	0	6.15
91–92 SJ	27	1374	3	18	1	115	0	5.02
Totals	39	1846	4	27	1	161	0	5.23

MYLNIKOV, Sergei 5-10 176
B. Chelyabinski, Soviet Union, Oct. 6, 1958

Season	Team	GP	MIN.	W	L	T	GA	SO.	AVG.
89–90	Que	10	568	1	7	2	47	0	4.96

MYRE, Louis Philippe (Phil) 6-1 185
B. Ste.–Anne–de–Bellevue, Que., Nov. 1, 1948

Season	Team	GP	MIN.	W	L	T	GA	SO.	AVG.
69–70	Mont	10	503	4	3	2	19	0	2.27
70–71	Mont	30	1677	13	11	4	87	1	3.11
71–72	Mont	9	528	4	5	0	32	0	3.64
72–73	Atl	46	2736	16	23	5	138	2	3.03
73–74	Atl	36	2020	11	16	6	112	0	3.33
74–75	Atl	40	2400	14	16	10	114	5	2.85
75–76	Atl	37	2129	16	16	4	123	1	3.47
76–77	Atl	43	2422	17	17	7	124	3	3.07
77–78	Atl–StL	53	3143	13	32	8	202	1	3.86
78–79	StL	39	2259	9	22	8	163	1	4.33
79–80	Phil	41	2367	18	7	15	141	0	3.57
80–81	Phil–Col	26	1480	9	11	5	94	0	3.81
81–82	Col	24	1256	2	17	2	112	0	5.35
82–83	Buf	5	300	3	2	0	21	0	4.20
Totals		439	25220	149	198	76	1482	14	3.53

Playoffs

Season	Team	GP	MIN.	W	L	T	GA	SO.	AVG.
73–74	Atl	3	186	0	3	0	13	0	4.19
76–77	Atl	2	120	1	1	0	5	0	2.50
79–80	Phil	6	384	5	1	0	16	1	2.50
82–83	Buf	1	57	0	0	0	7	0	7.37
Totals		12	747	6	5	0	41	1	3.29

NEWTON, Cameron Charles (Cam) 5-11 170
B. Peterborough, Ont., Feb. 25, 1950

Season	Team	GP	MIN.	W	L	T	GA	SO.	AVG.
70–71	Pitt	5	281	1	3	1	16	0	3.42
72–43	Pitt	11	533	3	4	0	35	0	3.94
73–74	Chi (WHA)	45	2732	25	18	2	143	1	3.14
74–75	Chi (WHA)	32	1905	12	20	0	126	0	3.97
75–76	Ott–Clev (WHA)	25	1469	11	13	1	83	1	3.39
NHL Totals		16	814	4	7	1	51	0	3.76
WHA Totals		102	6106	48	51	3	352	2	3.46

Playoffs

Season	Team	GP	MIN.	W	L	T	GA	SO.	AVG.
73–74	Chi (WHA)	10	486	2	5	0	34	0	4.20
75–76	Clev (WHA)	1	60	0	1	0	6	0	6.00
WHA Totals		11	546	2	6	0	40	0	4.40

NORRIS, Jack Wayne 5-10 175
B. Saskatoon, Sask., Aug. 5, 1942

Season	Team	GP	MIN.	W	L	T	GA	SO.	AVG.
64–65	Bos	23	1380	9	12	2	86	1	3.74
67–68	Chi	7	334	2	3	0	22	1	3.95
68–69	Chi	3	100	1	0	0	10	0	6.00
70–71	LA	25	1305	7	11	2	85	0	3.91
72–73	Alb (WHA)	64	3702	28	29	3	189	1	3.06
73–74	Edm (WHA)	53	2954	23	24	1	158	2	3.21
74–75	Phoe (WHA)	33	1962	14	15	4	107	1	3.27
75–76	Phoe (WHA)	41	2412	21	14	4	128	1	3.18
NHL Totals		58	3119	19	26	4	203	2	3.91
WHA Totals		191	11030	86	82	12	582	5	3.17

Playoffs

Season	Team	GP	MIN.	W	L	T	GA	SO.	AVG.
73–74	Edm (WHA)	3	111	0	2	0	9	0	4.86
74–75	Phoe (WHA)	2	100	0	2	0	10	0	6.00
75–76	Phoe (WHA)	5	298	2	3	0	17	0	3.42
WHA Totals		10	509	2	7	0	36	0	4.24

O'NEILL, Michael 5-7 160
B. LaSalle, Que., Nov. 3, 1967

Season	Team	GP	MIN.	W	L	T	GA	SO.	AVG.
91–92	Winn	1	13	0	0	0	1	0	4.62
92–93	Winn	2	73	0	0	1	6	0	4.93
93–94	Winn	17	738	0	9	1	51	0	4.15
96–97	Ana	1	31	0	0	0	3	0	5.81
Totals		21	855	0	9	2	61	0	4.28

OLESCHUK, William Stephen 6-3 194
B. Edmonton, Alta., July 20, 1955

Season	Team	GP	MIN.	W	L	T	GA	SO.	AVG.
75–76	KC	1	60	0	1	0	4	0	4.00
77–78	Col	2	100	1	2	0	9	0	5.40
78–79	Col	40	2118	6	19	8	136	1	3.85
79–80	Col	12	557	1	6	2	39	0	4.20
Totals		55	2835	7	28	10	188	1	3.98

* OLESEVICH, Daniel
B. Port Colburne, Ont., Aug. 16, 1937

Season	Team	GP	MIN.	W	L	T	GA	SO.	AVG.
61–62	NYR	1	40	0	0	1	2	0	3.00

OSGOOD, Chris 5-10 160
B. Peace River, Alta., Nov. 26, 1972

Season	Team	GP	MIN.	W	L	T	GA	SO.	AVG.
93–94	Det	41	2206	23	8	5	105	2	2.86
94–95	Det	19	1087	14	5	0	41	1	2.26
95–96	Det	50	2933	39	6	5	106	5	2.17
96–97	Det	47	2769	23	13	9	106	6	2.30
97–98	Det	64	3807	33	20	11	140	6	2.21
98–99	Det	63	3691	34	25	4	149	3	2.42
Totals		303	16493	166	77	25	647	23	2.35

Playoffs

Season	Team	GP	MIN.	W	L	T	GA	SO.	AVG.
93–94	Det	6	307	3	2	0	12	1	2.35
94–95	Det	2	68	0	0	0	2	0	1.76
95–96	Det	15	936	8	7	0	33	2	2.12
96–97	Det	2	47	0	0	0	2	0	2.55
97–98	Det	22	1361	16	6	0	48	2	2.12
98–99	Det	6	358	4	2	0	14	1	2.35
Totals		53	3077	31	17	0	111	6	2.16

OUIMET, Edward John (Ted) 6-0 175
B. Noranda, Que., July 6, 1947

Season	Team	GP	MIN.	W	L	T	GA	SO.	AVG.
68–69	StL	1	60	0	1	0	2	0	2.00
74–75	NE (WHA)	1	20	0	0	0	3	0	9.00

PAGEAU, Paul 5-9 160
B. Montreal, Que., Oct. 1, 1959

Season	Team	GP	MIN.	W	L	T	GA	SO.	AVG.
80–81	LA	1	60	0	1	0	8	0	8.00

PAILLE, Marcel 5-8 185
B. Shawinigan Falls, Que., Dec. 8, 1932

Season	Team	GP	MIN.	W	L	T	GA	SO.	AVG.
57–58	NYR	33	1980	11	15	7	102	1	3.09
58–59	NYR	1	60	0	1	4	4	0	4.00
59–60	NYR	17	1020	6	9	2	67	1	3.94
60–61	NYR	4	240	2	2	0	16	0	4.00
61–62	NYR	10	600	4	4	2	28	0	2.80
62–62	NYR	3	180	0	1	2	10	0	3.33
64–65	NYR	39	2262	10	21	7	135	0	3.58
72–73	Phil (WHA)	15	611	2	8	0	49	0	4.81
NHL Totals		107	6342	33	52	21	362	2	3.42
WHA Totals		15	611	2	8	0	49	0	4.81

Playoffs

Season	Team	GP	MIN.	W	L	T	GA	SO.	AVG.
72–73	Phi (WHA)	1	26	0	1	0	5	0	11.54

PALMATEER, Michael 5-9 170
B. Toronto, Ont., Jan. 13, 1954

Season	Team	GP	MIN.	W	L	T	GA	SO.	AVG.
76–77	Tor	50	2877	23	18	8	154	4	3.21
77–78	Tor	63	3760	34	19	9	172	5	2.74
78–79	Tor	58	3396	26	21	10	167	4	2.95
79–80	Tor	38	2039	16	14	3	125	2	3.68
80–81	Wash	49	2679	18	19	9	173	2	3.87
81–82	Wash	11	584	2	7	2	47	0	4.83
82–83	Tor	53	2965	21	23	7	197	0	3.99
83–84	Tor	34	1831	9	17	4	149	0	4.88
Totals		356	20131	149	138	52	1183	17	3.53

Playoffs

Season	Team	GP	MIN.	W	L	T	GA	SO.	AVG.
76–77	Tor	6	360	3	3	0	16	0	2.67
77–78	Tor	13	795	6	7	0	32	2	2.42
78–79	Tor	5	298	2	3	0	17	0	3.42
79–80	Tor	1	60	0	1	0	7	0	7.00
82–83	Tor	4	252	1	3	0	17	0	4.05
Totals		29	1765	12	17	0	89	2	3.03

PANG, Darren 5-5 155
B. Meaford, Ont., Feb. 17, 1964

Season	Team	GP	MIN.	W	L	T	GA	SO.	AVG.
84–85	Chi	1	60	0	1	0	4	0	4.00
87–88	Chi	45	2548	17	23	1	163	0	3.84
88–89	Chi	35	1644	10	11	6	120	0	4.38
Totals		81	4252	27	35	7	287	0	4.05

Playoffs

Season	Team	GP	MIN.	W	L	T	GA	SO.	AVG.
87–88	Chi	4	240	1	3	0	18	0	4.50
88–89	Chi	2	10	0	0	0	0	0	0.00
Totals		6	250	1	3	0	18	0	4.32

PARENT, Bernard Marcel (Bernie) 5-10 180
B. Montreal, Que., Apr. 3, 1945

Season	Team	GP	MIN.	W	L	T	GA	SO.	AVG.
65–66	Bos	39	2083	11	20	3	128	1	3.69
66–67	Bos	18	1022	3	11	2	62	0	3.64
67–68	Phil	38	2248	16	17	5	93	4	2.48
68–69	Phil	58	3365	17	23	16	151	1	2.69
69–70	Phil	62	3680	13	29	20	171	3	2.79
70–71	Phil–Tor	48	2626	16	19	9	119	3	2.72
71–72	Tor	47	2715	17	18	9	116	3	2.56
72–73	Phil (WHA)	63	3653	33	28	0	220	2	3.61

SEASON	TEAM	GP	MIN.	W	L	T	GA	SO.	AVG.
73–74	Phil	73	4314	47	13	12	136	12	1.89
74–75	Phil	68	4041	44	14	10	137	12	2.03
75–76	Phil	11	615	6	2	3	24	0	2.34
76–77	Phil	61	3525	35	13	12	159	5	2.71
77–78	Phil	49	2923	29	6	13	108	7	2.22
78–79	Phil	36	1979	16	12	7	89	4	2.70
NHL Totals		608	35136	270	197	121	1493	55	2.55
WHA Totals		63	3653	33	28	0	220	2	3.61

Playoffs

67–68	Phil	5	355	2	3	0	8	0	1.35
68–69	Phil	3	180	0	3	0	12	0	4.00
70–71	Tor	4	235	2	2	0	9	0	2.30
71–72	Tor	4	243	1	3	0	13	0	3.21
72–73	Phil (WHA)	1	70	0	1	0	3	0	2.57
73–74	Phil	17	1042	12	5	0	35	2	2.02
74–75	Phil	15	922	10	5	0	29	4	1.89
75–76	Phil	8	480	4	4	0	27	0	3.38
76–77	Phil	3	123	0	3	0	8	0	3.90
77–78	Phil	12	722	7	5	0	33	0	2.74
NHL Totals		71	4302	38	33	0	174	6	2.43
WHA Totals		1	70	0	1	0	3	0	2.57

PARENT, Rich 6–3 195

97–98	StL	1	12	0	0	0	0	0	0.00
98–99	StL	10	519	4	3	1	22	1	2.54
Totals		11	531	4	3	1	22	1	2.49

PARENT, Robert John 5–9 175
B. Windsor, Ont., Feb. 19, 1958

81–82	Tor	2	120	0	2	0	13	0	6.50
82–83	Tor	1	40	0	0	0	2	0	3.00
Totals		3	160	0	2	0	15	0	5.63

PARRO, David 5–10 155
B. Saskatoon, Sask., Apr. 30, 1957

80–81	Wash	18	811	4	7	2	49	1	3.63
81–82	Wash	52	2942	16	26	7	206	1	4.20
82–83	Wash	6	261	1	3	10	19	0	4.37
83–84	Wash	1	0	0	0	0	0	0	0.00
Totals		77	4015	21	36	10	274	2	4.09

PASSMORE, Steve 5–9 165
B. Thunder Bay, Ont., Jan. 29, 1973

98–99	Edm	6	362	1	4	1	17	0	2.82

* PATRICK, Lester 6–1 180
B. Drummondville, Que., Dec. 30, 1883

Playoffs

27–28	NYR	1	46	1	0	0	1	0	1.30

PEETERS, Peter 6–0 170
B. Edmonton, Alta., Aug. 1, 1957

78–79	Phil	6	280	1	2	1	16	0	3.43
79–80	Phil	40	2373	29	5	5	108	1	2.73
80–81	Phil	40	2333	22	12	5	115	2	2.96
81–82	Phil	44	2591	23	18	3	160	0	3.71
82–83	Bos	62	3611	40	11	9	142	8	2.36
83–84	Bos	50	2868	29	16	2	151	0	3.16
84–85	Bos	51	2975	19	26	4	172	1	3.47
85–86	Bos–Wash	42	2506	22	15	4	144	1	3.45
86–87	Wash	37	2002	17	11	4	107	0	3.21
87–88	Wash	35	1896	14	12	5	88	2	2.78
88–89	Wash	33	1854	20	7	3	88	4	2.85
89–90	Phil	24	1140	1	13	5	72	1	3.79
90–91	Phil	26	1270	9	7	1	61	1	2.88
Totals		489	27699	246	155	51	1424	21	3.08

Playoffs

79–80	Phil	13	799	8	5	0	37	1	2.78
80–81	Phil	3	180	2	1	0	12	0	4.00
81–82	Phil	4	220	1	2	0	17	0	4.64
82–83	Bos	17	1024	9	8	0	61	1	3.57
83–84	Bos	3	180	0	3	0	10	0	3.33
84–85	Bos	1	60	0	1	0	4	0	4.00
85–86	Wash	9	544	5	4	0	24	0	2.65
86–87	Wash	3	180	1	2	0	9	0	3.00
87–88	Wash	12	654	7	5	0	34	0	3.12
88–89	Wash	6	359	2	4	0	24	0	4.01
Totals		71	4200	35	35	0	232	2	3.31

PELLETIER, Jean-Marc 6–3 200
B. Atlanta, Ga., March 4, 1978

98–99	Phil	1	60	0	1	0	5	0	5.00

PELLETIER, Marcel 5–11 180
B. Drummondville, Que., Dec. 6, 1927

50–51	Chi	6	355	1	5	0	29	0	4.90
62–63	NYR	2	40	0	1	1	4	0	6.00
Totals		8	395	1	6	1	33	0	5.01

PENNEY, Steven 6–1 190
B. Ste-Foy, Que., Feb. 2, 1961

83–84	Mont	4	240	0	4	0	19	0	4.75
84–85	Mont	54	3252	26	18	8	167	1	3.08
85–86	Mont	18	990	6	8	2	72	0	4.36
86–87	Winn	7	327	1	4	1	25	0	4.59
87–88	Winn	8	385	2	4	1	30	0	4.68
Totals		91	5194	35	38	12	313	1	3.62

Playoffs

83–84	Mont	15	871	9	6	0	32	3	2.20
84–85	Mont	12	733	6	6	0	40	1	3.27
Totals		27	1604	15	12	0	72	4	2.69

* PERREAULT, Robert (Miche) 5–8 170
B. Trois-Rivieres, Que., Jan. 28, 1931

55–56	Mont	6	360	3	3	0	12	1	2.00
58–59	Det	3	180	2	1	0	9	0	3.00
62–63	Bos	22	1320	3	12	6	85	1	3.86
72–73	LA (WHA)	1	60	1	0	0	2	0	2.00
NHL Totals		31	1860	8	16	6	106	2	3.42
WHA Totals		1	60	1	0	0	2	0	2.00

PETTIE, James 6–0 195
B. Toronto, Ont., Oct. 24, 1953

76–77	Bos	1	60	1	0	0	3	0	3.00
77–78	Bos	1	60	0	1	0	6	0	6.00
78–79	Bos	19	1037	8	6	2	62	1	3.59
Totals		21	1157	9	7	2	71	1	3.68

PIETRANGELO, Frank 5–10 182
B. Niagara Falls, Ont., Dec. 17, 1964

87–88	Pitt	21	1207	9	11	0	80	1	3.98
88–89	Pitt	15	669	5	3	0	45	0	4.04
89–90	Pitt	21	1066	8	6	2	77	0	4.33
90–91	Pitt	25	1311	10	11	1	86	0	3.94
91–92	Pitt–Hart	10	531	5	2	1	32	0	3.62
92–93	Hart	30	1373	4	15	1	111	0	4.85
93–94	Hart	19	984	5	11	1	59	0	3.60
Totals		141	7141	46	59	6	490	1	4.12

Playoffs

90–91	Pitt	5	288	4	1	0	15	1	3.13
91–92	Hart	7	425	3	4	0	19	0	2.68
Totals		12	713	7	5	0	34	1	2.86

* PLANTE, Joseph Jacques (Jake the Snake) 6–0 175
B. Mont Carmel, Que., Jan. 17, 1929

52–53	Mont	3	180	2	0	1	4	0	1.33
53–54	Mont	17	1020	7	5	5	27	5	1.59
54–55	Mont	52	3080	31	13	7	110	5	2.14
55–56	Mont	64	3840	42	12	10	119	7	1.86
56–57	Mont	61	3660	31	18	12	123	9	2.02
57–58	Mont	57	3386	34	14	8	119	9	2.11
58–59	Mont	67	4000	38	16	13	144	9	2.16
59–60	Mont	69	4140	40	17	12	175	3	2.54
60–61	Mont	40	2400	22	11	7	112	2	2.80
61–62	Mont	70	4200	42	14	14	166	4	2.37
62–63	Mont	56	3320	22	14	9	138	5	2.49
63–64	NYR	65	3900	22	35	8	220	3	3.38
64–65	NYR	33	1938	10	17	5	109	2	3.37
68–69	StL	37	2139	18	12	6	70	5	1.96
69–70	StL	32	1839	18	9	5	67	5	2.19
70–71	Tor	40	2329	24	11	4	73	4	1.88
71–72	Tor	34	1965	16	13	5	86	2	2.63
72–73	Tor–Bos	40	2197	15	15	6	103	4	2.81
74–75	Edm (WHA)	31	1592	15	14	1	88	1	3.32
NHL Totals		837	49533	434	246	137	1965	82	2.38
WHA Totals		31	1592	15	14	1	88	1	3.32

Playoffs

52–53	Mont	4	240	3	1	0	7	1	1.75
53–54	Mont	8	480	5	3	0	15	2	1.88
54–55	Mont	12	639	6	4	0	31	1	2.91
55–56	Mont	10	600	8	2	0	18	2	1.80
56–57	Mont	10	616	8	2	0	18	1	1.75
57–58	Mont	10	618	8	2	0	20	1	1.94
58–59	Mont	11	670	8	3	0	28	0	2.51
59–60	Mont	8	489	8	0	0	11	3	1.35
60–61	Mont	6	412	2	4	0	16	0	2.33

SEASON	TEAM	GP	MIN.	W	L	T	GA	SO.	AVG.
61–62	Mont	6	360	2	4	0	19	0	3.17
62–63	Mont	5	300	1	4	0	14	0	2.80
68–69	StL	10	589	8	2	0	14	3	1.43
69–70	StL	6	324	4	1	0	8	1	1.48
70–71	Tor	3	134	0	2	0	7	0	3.13
71–72	Tor	1	60	0	1	0	5	0	5.00
72–73	Bos	2	120	0	2	0	10	0	5.00
Totals		112	6651	71	37	0	241	15	2.17

PLASSE, Michel Pierre *5–11 172*
B. Montreal, Que., June 1, 1948

SEASON	TEAM	GP	MIN.	W	L	T	GA	SO.	AVG.
70–71	StL	1	60	1	0	0	3	0	3.00
72–73	Mont	17	932	11	2	3	40	0	2.58
73–74	Mont	15	839	7	4	2	57	0	4.08
74–75	KC–Pitt	44	2514	13	21	7	169	0	4.03
75–76	Pitt	55	3096	24	19	10	178	2	3.45
76–77	Col	54	2986	12	29	10	190	0	3.82
77–78	Col	25	1383	3	12	8	90	0	3.90
78–79	Col	41	2302	9	29	2	152	0	3.96
79–80	Col	6	327	0	3	2	26	0	4.77
80–81	Que	33	1933	10	14	9	118	0	3.66
81–82	Que	8	388	2	3	1	35	0	5.41
Totals		299	16760	92	136	54	1058	2	3.79
Playoffs									
75–76	Pitt	3	180	1	2	0	8	1	2.67
80–81	Que	1	15	0	0	0	1	0	4.00
Totals		4	195	1	2	0	9	1	2.77

PLAXTON, Hugh John
B. Barrie, Ont., May 16, 1904

SEASON	TEAM	GP	MIN.	W	L	T	GA	SO.	AVG.
32–33	Mont M	1	59	0	1	0	5	0	5.08

POTVIN, Felix *6–0 190*
B. Anjou, Que., June 23, 1971

SEASON	TEAM	GP	MIN.	W	L	T	GA	SO.	AVG.
91–92	Tor	4	210	0	2	1	8	0	2.29
92–93	Tor	48	2781	25	15	7	116	2	2.50
93–94	Tor	66	3883	34	22	9	187	3	2.89
94–95	Tor	36	2144	15	13	7	104	0	2.91
95–96	Tor	69	4009	30	26	11	192	2	2.87
96–97	Tor	74	4271	27	36	7	224	0	3.15
97–98	Tor	67	3864	26	33	7	176	5	2.73
98–99	NYI	16	905	5	9	1	56	0	3.71
Totals		380	22067	162	156	50	1063	12	2.89
Playoffs									
92–93	Tor	21	1308	11	10	0	62	1	2.84
93–94	Tor	18	1124	9	9	0	46	3	2.46
94–95	Tor	7	424	3	4	0	20	1	2.83
95–96	Tor	6	350	2	4	0	19	0	3.26
Totals		52	3206	25	27	0	147	5	2.75

PRONOVOST, Claude
B. Shawinigan Falls, Que., July 22, 1935

SEASON	TEAM	GP	MIN.	W	L	T	GA	SO.	AVG.
55–56	Bos	1	60	1	0	0	0	1	0.00
58–59	Mont	2	60	0	1	0	7	0	7.00
Totals		3	120	1	1	0	7	1	3.50

PUPPA, Daren James *6–3 205*
B. Kirkland Lake, Ont., Mar. 23, 1963

SEASON	TEAM	GP	MIN.	W	L	T	GA	SO.	AVG.
85–86	Buf	7	401	3	4	0	21	1	3.14
86–87	Buf	3	185	0	2	1	13	0	4.22
87–88	Buf	17	874	8	6	1	61	0	4.19
88–89	Buf	37	1908	17	10	6	107	1	3.36
89–90	Buf	56	3241	31	16	6	156	1	2.89
90–91	Buf	38	2092	15	11	6	118	2	3.38
91–92	Buf	33	1757	11	14	4	114	0	3.89
92–93	Buf–Tor	32	1785	17	7	4	96	2	3.23
93–94	TB	63	3653	22	33	6	165	4	2.71
94–95	TB	36	2013	14	19	2	90	1	2.68
95–96	TB	57	3189	29	16	9	131	5	2.46
96–97	TB	6	325	1	4	1	14	0	2.58
97–98	TB	26	1456	5	14	6	66	0	2.72
98–99	TB	13	691	5	6	1	33	2	2.87
Totals		724	23570	178	159	54	1185	19	3.02
Playoffs									
87–88	Buf	3	142	1	1	0	11	0	4.65
89–90	Buf	6	370	2	4	0	15	0	2.43
90–91	Buf	2	81	0	1	0	10	0	7.41
92–93	Tor	1	20	0	0	0	1	0	3.00
95–96	TB	4	173	1	3	0	14	0	4.86
Totals		16	786	4	9	0	51	0	3.89

PUSEY, Chris *6–0 180*
B. Brantford, Ont., June 30, 1965

SEASON	TEAM	GP	MIN.	W	L	T	GA	SO.	AVG.
85–86	Det	1	40	0	0	0	3	0	4.50

RACICOT, Andre *5–11 165*
B. Rouyn, Que., June 9, 1969

SEASON	TEAM	GP	MIN.	W	L	T	GA	SO.	AVG.
89–90	Mont	1	13	0	0	0	3	0	13.85
90–91	Mont	21	975	7	9	2	52	1	3.20
91–92	Mont	9	436	0	3	3	23	0	3.17
92–93	Mont	26	1433	17	5	1	81	1	3.39
93–94	Mont	11	500	2	6	2	37	0	4.44
Totals		68	3357	26	23	8	196	2	3.50
Playoffs									
90–91	Mont	2	12	0	1	0	2	0	10.00
91–92	Mont	1	1	0	0	0	0	0	0.00
92–93	Mont	1	18	0	0	0	2	0	6.67
Totals		4	31	0	1	0	4	0	7.74

RACINE, Bruce *6–0 178*
B. Cornwall, Ont., Aug. 9, 1996

SEASON	TEAM	GP	MIN.	W	L	T	GA	SO.	AVG.
95–96	StL	11	230	0	3	0	12	0	3.13
Playoffs									
95–96	StL	1	1	0	0	0	0	0	0.00

RAM, Jamie *5–11 175*
B. Scarborough, Ont., Jan. 18, 1971

SEASON	TEAM	GP	MIN.	W	L	T	GA	SO.	AVG.
95–96	NYR	1	27	0	0	0	0	0	0.00

RANFORD, Bill *5–11 185*
B. Brandon, Man., Dec. 14, 1966

SEASON	TEAM	GP	MIN.	W	L	T	GA	SO.	AVG.
85–86	Bos	4	240	3	1	0	10	0	2.50
86–87	Bos	41	2234	16	20	2	124	3	3.33
87–88	Bos	6	325	3	0	2	16	0	2.95
88–89	Edm	29	1509	15	8	2	88	1	3.50
89–90	Edm	56	3107	24	16	9	165	1	3.19
90–91	Edm	60	3415	27	27	3	182	0	3.20
91–92	Edm	67	3822	27	26	10	228	1	3.58
92–93	Edm	67	3753	17	38	6	240	1	3.84
93–94	Edm	71	4070	22	34	11	236	1	3.48
94–95	Edm	40	2203	15	20	3	133	2	3.62
95–96	Edm–Bos	77	4322	34	30	9	237	2	3.29
96–97	Bos–Wash	55	3156	20	23	10	171	2	3.25
97–98	Wash	22	1183	7	12	2	55	0	2.79
98–99	TB–Det	36	1812	6	18	4	110	1	3.64
Totals		631	35151	236	273	73	1995	15	3.40
Playoffs									
85–86	Bos	2	120	0	2	0	7	0	3.50
86–87	Bos	2	123	0	2	0	8	0	3.90
89–90	Edm	22	1401	16	6	0	59	0	2.53
90–91	Edm	3	135	1	2	0	8	0	3.56
91–92	Edm	16	909	8	8	0	51	2	3.37
95–96	Bos	4	239	1	3	0	16	0	4.02
98–99	Det	4	183	2	2	0	10	1	3.28
Totals		53	3110	28	25	0	159	4	3.07

RAYMOND, Alain *5–10 177*
B. Rimouski, Que., June 24, 1965

SEASON	TEAM	GP	MIN.	W	L	T	GA	SO.	AVG.
87–88	Wash	1	40	0	1	0	2	0	3.00

RAYNER, Claude Earl (Chuck) *5–11 190*
B. Sutherland, Sask., Aug. 11, 1920

SEASON	TEAM	GP	MIN.	W	L	T	GA	SO.	AVG.
40–41	NYA	12	773	2	7	3	44	0	3.67
41–42	NYA	36	2230	13	21	2	129	1	3.58
45–46	NYR	41	2377	12	21	7	150	5	3.79
46–47	NYR	58	3480	22	30	6	177	5	3.05
47–48	NYR	12	691	4	7	0	42	0	3.65
48–49	NYR	58	3480	16	31	11	168	7	2.90
49–50	NYR	69	4140	28	30	11	181	6	2.62
50–51	NYR	66	3940	19	28	19	187	6	2.85
51–52	NYR	53	3180	18	25	10	159	2	3.00
52–53	NYR	20	1200	4	8	8	58	1	2.90
Totals		425	25491	138	208	77	1295	33	3.05
Playoffs									
47–48	NYR	6	360	2	4	0	17	0	2.83
49–50	NYR	12	775	7	5	0	29	1	2.25
Totals		18	1135	9	9	0	46	1	2.43

REAUGH, Daryl *6–4 200*
B. Prince George, B.C., Feb. 13, 1965

SEASON	TEAM	GP	MIN.	W	L	T	GA	SO.	AVG.
84–85	Edm	1	60	0	1	0	5	0	5.00
87–88	Edm	6	176	1	1	0	14	0	4.77
90–91	Hart	20	1010	7	7	1	53	1	3.15
Totals		27	1246	7	9	1	72	1	3.47

SEASON	TEAM	GP	MIN.	W	L	T	GA	SO.	AVG.
REDDICK, Eldon (Pokey) *5–8 170*									
B. Halifax, N.S., Oct. 6, 1964									
86–87	Winn	48	2762	21	21	4	149	0	3.24
87–88	Winn	28	1487	9	13	3	102	0	4.12
88–89	Winn	41	2109	11	17	7	144	0	4.10
89–90	Edm	11	604	5	4	2	31	0	3.08
90–91	Edm	2	120	0	2	0	9	0	4.50
93–94	Fla	2	80	0	1	0	8	0	6.00
Totals		132	7162	46	58	16	443	0	3.71
Playoffs									
86–87	Winn	3	166	0	2	0	10	0	3.61
89–90	Edm	1	2	0	0	0	0	0	0.00
Totals		4	168	0	2	0	10	0	3.57
REDQUEST, Greg *5–10 190*									
B. Toronto, Ont., July 30, 1956									
77–78	Pitt	1	13	0	0	0	3	3	13.85
REECE, David Barrett *6–1 190*									
B. Troy, N.Y., Sept. 13, 1948									
75–76	Bos	14	777	7	5	2	43	2	3.32
REESE, Jeff *5–9 175*									
B. Brantford, Ont., Mar. 24, 1966									
87–88	Tor	5	249	1	2	1	17	0	4.10
88–89	Tor	10	486	2	6	1	40	0	4.94
89–90	Tor	21	1101	9	6	3	81	0	4.41
90–91	Tor	30	1430	6	13	3	92	1	3.86
91–92	Tor–Calg	20	1000	4	7	3	57	1	3.42
92–93	Calg	26	1311	14	4	1	70	1	3.20
93–94	Calg–Hart	20	1099	5	9	3	57	1	3.11
94–95	Hart	11	477	2	5	1	26	0	3.27
95–96	Hart–TB	26	1269	9	10	1	68	1	3.22
96–97	NJ	3	139	0	2	0	13	0	5.61
98–99	Tor	2	106	1	1	0	8	0	4.53
Totals		174	8667	53	65	17	529	5	3.66
Playoffs									
89–90	Tor	2	108	1	1	0	6	0	3.33
92–93	Calg	4	209	1	3	0	17	0	4.88
95–96	TB	5	198	1	1	0	12	0	3.64
Totals		11	515	3	5	0	35	0	4.08
RESCH, Glenn Allan (Chico) *5–9 165*									
B. Moose Jaw, Sask., July 10, 1948									
73–74	NYI	2	120	1	1	0	6	0	3.00
74–75	NYI	25	1432	12	7	0	59	3	2.47
75–76	NYI	44	2546	23	11	8	88	7	2.07
76–77	NYI	46	2711	26	13	6	103	4	2.28
77–78	NYI	45	2637	28	9	7	112	3	2.55
78–79	NYI	43	2539	26	7	10	106	2	2.50
79–80	NYI	45	2606	23	14	6	132	3	3.04
80–81	NYI–Col	40	2266	20	11	7	121	3	3.20
81–82	Col	61	3424	16	31	11	230	0	4.03
82–83	NJ	65	3650	15	35	12	242	0	3.98
83–84	NJ	51	2641	9	31	3	184	1	4.18
84–85	NJ	51	2884	15	27	5	200	0	4.16
85–86	NJ–Phil	36	1956	11	22	0	136	0	4.17
86–87	Phil	17	867	6	5	2	42	0	2.91
Totals		571	32279	231	224	82	1761	26	3.27
Playoffs									
74–75	NYI	12	692	8	4	0	25	1	2.17
75–76	NYI	7	357	3	3	0	18	0	3.03
76–77	NYI	3	144	1	1	0	5	0	2.08
77–78	NYI	7	388	3	4	0	15	0	2.32
78–79	NYI	5	300	2	3	0	11	1	2.20
79–80	NYI	4	120	0	2	0	9	0	4.50
Totals		41	2044	17	17	0	85	2	2.50
RHEAUME, Herbert									
25–26	Mont	31	1889	10	19	1	92	0	2.92
RHODES, Damian *6–0 190*									
B. St. Paul, Minn., May 28, 1969									
90–91	Tor	1	60	1	0	0	1	0	1.00
93–94	Tor	22	1213	9	7	3	53	0	2.62
94–95	Tor	13	760	6	6	1	34	0	2.68
95–96	Tor–Ott	47	2747	14	27	5	127	2	2.77
96–97	Ott	50	2934	14	20	4	133	1	2.72
97–98	Ott	50	2743	19	19	7	107	5	2.34
98–99	Ott	45	2480	22	13	7	101	3	2.44
Totals		228	12937	85	92	37	556	11	2.58

SEASON	TEAM	GP	MIN.	W	L	T	GA	SO.	AVG.
Playoffs									
93–94	Tor	1	1	0	0	0	0	0	0.00
97–98	Ott	10	590	5	5	0	21	0	2.13
98–99	Ott	2	150	0	2	0	6	0	2.40
Totals		13	741	5	7	0	27	0	2.18
RICCI, Joseph Nick *5–10 160*									
B. Niagara Falls, Ont., June 3, 1959									
79–80	Pitt	4	240	2	2	0	14	0	3.50
80–81	Pitt	9	540	4	5	0	35	0	3.88
81–82	Pitt	3	160	0	3	0	14	0	5.25
82–83	Pitt	3	147	1	2	0	16	0	6.53
Totals		19	1087	7	12	0	79	0	4.36
RICHARDSON, Terrance Paul *6–1 190*									
B. Powell River, B.C., May 7, 1953									
73–74	Det	9	315	1	4	0	28	0	5.33
74–75	Det	4	202	1	2	0	23	0	6.83
75–76	Det	1	60	0	1	0	7	0	7.00
76–77	Det	5	269	1	3	0	18	0	4.01
78–79	Det	1	60	0	1	0	9	0	9.00
Totals		20	906	3	11	0	85	0	5.63
RICHTER, Michael Thomas *5–11 185*									
B. Philadelphia, Pa., Sept. 22, 1966									
89–90	NYR	23	1320	12	5	5	66	0	3.00
90–91	NYR	45	2596	21	13	7	135	0	3.12
91–92	NYR	41	2298	23	12	2	119	3	3.11
92–93	NYR	38	2105	13	19	3	134	1	3.82
93–94	NYR	68	3710	42	12	6	159	5	2.57
94–95	NYR	35	1993	14	17	2	97	2	2.92
95–96	NYR	41	2396	24	13	3	107	3	2.68
96–97	NYR	61	3598	33	22	6	161	4	2.68
97–98	NYR	72	4143	21	31	15	184	0	2.66
98–99	NYR	68	3878	27	30	8	170	4	2.63
Totals		492	28037	230	174	57	1341	22	2.87
Playoffs									
88–89	NYR	1	58	0	1	0	4	0	4.14
89–90	NYR	6	330	3	2	0	19	0	3.45
90–91	NYR	6	313	2	4	0	14	1	2.68
91–92	NYR	7	412	4	2	0	24	1	3.50
93–94	NYR	23	1417	16	7	0	49	4	2.07
94–95	NYR	7	384	2	5	0	23	0	3.59
95–96	NYR	11	661	5	6	0	36	0	3.27
96–97	NYR	15	939	9	6	0	33	3	2.11
Totals		76	4514	41	33	0	202	9	2.68
RIDLEY, Charles Curtis (Curt) *6–0 190*									
B. Minnedosa, Man., Oct. 24, 1951									
74–75	NYR	2	81	1	1	0	7	0	5.19
75–76	Van	9	500	6	0	2	19	1	2.28
76–77	Van	37	2074	8	21	4	134	0	3.88
77–78	Van	40	2010	9	17	8	136	1	4.06
79–80	Van–Tor	13	709	2	7	2	47	0	3.98
80–81	Tor	3	124	1	1	0	12	0	5.81
Totals		104	5498	27	47	16	355	1	3.87
Playoffs									
75–76	Van	2	120	0	2	0	8	0	4.00
RIENDEAU, Vincent *5–10 185*									
B. St. Hyacinthe, Que., Apr. 20, 1966									
87–88	Mont	1	36	0	0	0	5	0	8.33
88–89	StL	32	1842	11	15	5	108	0	3.52
89–90	StL	43	2551	17	19	5	149	1	3.50
90–91	StL	44	2671	29	9	6	134	3	3.01
91–92	StL–Det	5	244	3	2	0	13	0	3.20
92–93	Det	22	1193	13	4	2	64	0	3.22
93–94	Det–Bos	26	1321	9	10	1	73	1	3.32
94–95	Bos	11	565	3	6	1	27	0	2.87
Totals		184	10423	85	65	20	573	5	3.30
Playoffs									
89–90	StL	8	397	3	4	0	24	0	3.63
90–91	StL	13	687	6	7	0	35	1	3.06
91–92	Det	2	73	1	0	0	4	0	3.29
93–94	Bos	2	120	1	1	0	8	0	4.00
Totals		25	1277	11	12	0	71	1	3.34
RIGGIN, Denis Melville *5–11 156*									
B. Kincardine, Ont., Apr. 11, 1936									
59–60	Det	9	540	2	6	1	32	1	3.56
62–63	Det	9	445	3	4	1	22	0	2.97
Totals		18	985	5	10	2	54	1	3.29

SEASON	TEAM	GP	MIN.	W	L	T	GA	SO.	AVG.

RIGGIN, Patrick Michael *5-9 163*
B. Kincardine, Ont., May 26, 1959

SEASON	TEAM	GP	MIN.	W	L	T	GA	SO.	AVG.
78-79	Birm (WHA)	46	2511	16	22	5	158	1	3.78
79-80	Atl	25	1368	11	9	2	73	2	3.20
80-81	Calg	42	2411	21	16	4	154	0	3.83
81-82	Calg	52	2934	19	19	11	207	2	4.23
82-83	Wash	38	2161	17	9	9	121	0	3.36
83-84	Wash	41	2299	21	14	2	102	4	2.66
84-85	Wash	57	3388	28	20	7	168	2	2.98
85-86	Wash-Bos	46	2641	19	14	9	150	1	3.41
86-87	Bos-Pitt	27	1501	11	11	4	84	0	3.36
87-88	Pitt	22	1169	7	8	4	76	0	3.90
Totals		350	19872	153	120	52	1135	11	3.43

Playoffs

SEASON	TEAM	GP	MIN.	W	L	T	GA	SO.	AVG.
80-81	Calg	11	629	6	4	0	37	0	3.53
81-82	Calg	3	194	0	3	0	10	0	3.10
82-83	Wash	3	101	0	1	0	8	0	4.76
83-84	Wash	5	230	1	3	0	9	0	2.35
84-85	Wash	2	122	1	1	0	5	0	2.45
85-86	Bos	1	60	0	1	0	3	0	3.00
Totals		25	1336	8	13	0	72	0	3.23

RING, Robert

SEASON	TEAM	GP	MIN.	W	L	T	GA	SO.	AVG.
65-66	Bos	1	34	0	0	0	4	0	7.06

RIVARD, Fernand Joseph *5-9 160*
B. Grand Mere, Que., Jan. 18, 1946

SEASON	TEAM	GP	MIN.	W	L	T	GA	SO.	AVG.
68-69	Minn	13	657	0	0	0	48	0	4.38
69-70	Minn	14	800	3	5	5	42	1	3.15
73-74	Minn	13	701	3	6	2	50	1	4.28
74-75	Minn	15	707	3	9	0	50	0	4.24
Totals		55	2865	9	20	7	190	2	3.98

* ROACH, John Ross *5-5 130*
B. Fort Perry, Ont., June 23, 1900

SEASON	TEAM	GP	MIN.	W	L	T	GA	SO.	AVG.
21-22	Tor	22	1340	11	10	1	91	0	4.14
22-23	Tor	24	1469	13	10	1	88	1	3.67
23-24	Tor	23	1380	10	13	0	80	1	3.48
24-25	Tor	30	1800	19	11	0	84	1	2.80
25-26	Tor	36	2210	12	21	3	114	2	3.17
26-27	Tor	44	2764	15	24	5	94	4	2.14
27-28	Tor	43	2690	17	18	8	88	4	2.05
28-29	NYR	44	2760	21	13	10	65	13	1.48
29-30	NYR	44	2770	17	17	10	143	1	3.25
30-31	NYR	44	2760	19	16	9	87	7	1.98
31-32	NYR	48	3020	23	17	8	112	9	2.33
32-33	Det	48	2970	25	15	8	93	10	1.94
33-34	Det	18	1030	9	8	1	45	1	2.50
34-35	Det	23	1460	7	11	5	62	4	2.70
Totals		491	30423	218	204	69	1246	58	2.46

Playoffs

SEASON	TEAM	GP	MIN.	W	L	T	GA	SO.	AVG.
21-22	Tor	7	425	4	2	1	13	2	1.86
24-25	Tor	2	120	0	2	0	5	0	2.50
28-29	NYR	6	392	3	2	1	5	3	0.83
29-30	NYR	4	309	1	2	1	7	0	1.75
30-31	NYR	4	240	2	2	0	4	1	1.00
31-32	Det	7	480	3	4	0	27	1	3.86
32-33	Det	4	240	2	2	0	8	1	2.00
Totals		34	2206	15	16	3	69	8	1.88

* ROBERTS, Maurice (Moe) *5-9 165*
B. Waterbury, Conn., Dec. 13, 1907

SEASON	TEAM	GP	MIN.	W	L	T	GA	SO.	AVG.
25-26	Bos	2	90	0	1	0	5	0	2.50
31-32	NYA	1	60	1	0	0	1	0	1.00
33-34	NYA	6	336	1	4	0	25	0	4.17
51-52	Chi	1	20	0	0	0	0	0	0.00
Totals		10	506	2	5	0	31	0	3.68

* ROBERTSON, Earl Cooper *5-10 165*
B. Bingorgh, Sask., Nov. 24, 1910

SEASON	TEAM	GP	MIN.	W	L	T	GA	SO.	AVG.
37-38	NYA	48	3000	19	18	11	111	6	2.31
38-39	NYA	46	2850	17	18	10	136	3	2.96
39-40	NYA	48	2960	15	29	4	140	6	2.92
40-41	NYA	36	2260	6	22	8	142	1	3.94
41-42	NYA	12	750	3	8	1	46	0	3.83
Totals		190	11820	60	95	34	575	16	2.92

Playoffs

SEASON	TEAM	GP	MIN.	W	L	T	GA	SO.	AVG.
36-37	Det	6	340	3	2	0	8	2	1.33
37-38	NYA	6	475	3	3	0	12	0	2.00
39-40	NYA	3	180	0	2	0	9	0	3.00
Totals		15	995	6	7	0	29	2	1.75

ROLLINS, Elwin Ira (Al) *6-2 175*
B. Vanguard, Sask., Oct. 9, 1926

SEASON	TEAM	GP	MIN.	W	L	T	GA	SO.	AVG.
49-50	Tor	2	120	1	1	0	4	1	2.00
50-51	Tor	40	2373	27	5	8	70	5	1.77
51-52	Tor	70	4170	29	24	16	154	5	2.22
52-53	Chi	70	4200	27	28	15	175	6	2.50
53-54	Chi	66	3960	12	47	7	213	5	3.23
54-55	Chi	44	2640	9	27	8	150	0	3.41
55-56	Chi	58	3480	16	31	11	174	3	3.00
56-57	Chi	70	4200	16	39	15	225	3	3.21
59-60	NYR	8	480	1	3	4	31	0	3.88
Totals		428	25623	138	205	84	1196	28	2.80

Playoffs

SEASON	TEAM	GP	MIN.	W	L	T	GA	SO.	AVG.
50-51	Tor	4	253	3	1	0	6	0	1.42
51-52	Tor	2	120	0	2	0	6	0	3.00
52-53	Chi	7	425	3	4	0	18	0	2.54
Totals		13	798	6	7	0	30	0	2.26

ROLOSON, Dwayne *6-1 180*
B. Simcoe, Ont., Oct. 12, 1969

SEASON	TEAM	GP	MIN.	W	L	T	GA	SO.	AVG.
96-97	Calg	31	1618	9	14	3	78	1	2.89
97-98	Calg	39	2205	11	16	8	110	0	2.99
98-99	Buf	18	911	6	8	2	42	1	2.77
Totals		88	4734	26	38	13	230	2	2.92

Playoffs

SEASON	TEAM	GP	MIN.	W	L	T	GA	SO.	AVG.
98-99	Buf	4	138	1	1	1	10	0	4.32

ROMANO, Roberto *5-6 170*
B. Montreal, Que., Oct. 10, 1962

SEASON	TEAM	GP	MIN.	W	L	T	GA	SO.	AVG.
82-83	Pitt	3	155	0	3	0	18	0	6.97
83-84	Pitt	18	1020	6	11	0	78	1	4.59
84-85	Pitt	31	1629	9	17	2	120	1	4.42
85-86	Pitt	46	2684	21	20	3	159	2	3.55
86-87	Pitt-Bos	26	1498	9	12	2	93	0	3.72
93-94	Pitt	2	125	1	0	1	3	0	1.44
Totals		126	7111	46	63	8	471	4	3.97

ROSATI, Mike *5-10 170*
B. Toronto, Ont., Jan. 7, 1968

SEASON	TEAM	GP	MIN.	W	L	T	GA	SO.	AVG.
98-99	Wash	1	28	1	0	0	0	0	0.00

ROUSSEL, Dominic *6-1 191*
B. Hull, Que., Feb. 22, 1970

SEASON	TEAM	GP	MIN.	W	L	T	GA	SO.	AVG.
91-92	Phil	17	922	7	8	2	40	1	2.60
92-93	Phil	34	1769	13	11	5	111	1	3.76
93-94	Phil	60	3285	29	20	5	183	1	3.34
94-95	Phil	19	1075	11	7	0	42	1	2.34
95-96	Phil-Winn	16	741	4	5	2	38	1	3.08
98-99	Ana	18	884	4	5	4	37	1	2.51
Totals		164	8676	68	56	18	451	6	3.12

Playoffs

SEASON	TEAM	GP	MIN.	W	L	T	GA	SO.	AVG.
94-95	Phil	1	23	0	0	0	0	0	0.00

ROY, Patrick *6-0 192*
B. Quebec City, Que., Oct. 5, 1965

SEASON	TEAM	GP	MIN.	W	L	T	GA	SO.	AVG.
84-85	Mont	1	20	1	0	0	0	0	0.00
85-86	Mont	47	2651	23	18	3	148	1	3.35
86-87	Mont	46	2686	22	16	6	131	1	2.93
87-88	Mont	45	2586	23	12	9	125	3	2.90
88-89	Mont	48	2744	33	5	6	113	4	2.47
89-90	Mont	54	3173	31	16	5	134	3	2.53
90-91	Mont	48	2835	25	15	6	128	1	2.71
91-92	Mont	67	3935	36	22	8	155	5	2.36
92-93	Mont	62	3595	31	25	5	192	2	3.20
93-94	Mont	68	3867	35	17	11	161	7	2.50
94-95	Mont	43	2566	17	20	6	127	1	2.97
95-96	Mont-Col A	61	3565	34	24	2	165	2	2.78
96-97	Col A	62	3698	38	15	7	143	7	2.32
97-98	Col A	65	3835	31	19	13	153	4	2.39
98-99	Col A	61	3648	32	19	8	139	5	2.29
Totals		778	45404	412	243	95	2014	46	2.66

Playoffs

SEASON	TEAM	GP	MIN.	W	L	T	GA	SO.	AVG.
85-86	Mont	20	1218	15	5	0	39	1	1.92
86-87	Mont	6	330	4	2	0	22	0	4.00
87-88	Mont	8	430	3	4	0	24	0	3.35
88-89	Mont	19	1206	13	6	0	42	2	2.09
89-90	Mont	11	641	5	6	0	26	1	2.43
90-91	Mont	13	785	7	5	0	40	0	3.06
91-92	Mont	11	686	4	7	0	30	1	2.62
92-93	Mont	20	1293	16	4	0	46	0	2.13
93-94	Mont	6	375	3	3	0	16	0	2.56
95-96	Col A	22	1454	16	6	0	51	3	2.10
96-97	Col A	17	1034	10	7	0	38	3	2.21

SEASON	TEAM	GP	MIN.	W	L	T	GA	SO.	AVG.
97–98	Col A	7	430	3	4	0	18	0	2.51
98–99	Col A	19	1173	11	8	0	52	1	2.66
Totals		179	11055	110	67	0	444	12	2.41

RUPP, Patrick Lloyd
B. Detroit, Mich., Aug. 12, 1942

SEASON	TEAM	GP	MIN.	W	L	T	GA	SO.	AVG.
63–64	Det	1	60	0	1	0	4	0	4.00

RUTHERFORD, James Earl (Jim) *5–8 168*
B. Beeton, Ont., Feb. 17, 1949

SEASON	TEAM	GP	MIN.	W	L	T	GA	SO.	AVG.
70–71	Det	29	1498	6	15	3	94	1	3.77
71–72	Pitt	40	2160	17	15	5	116	1	3.22
72–73	Pitt	49	2660	20	22	5	129	3	2.91
73–74	Pitt–Det	51	2852	16	23	8	168	0	3.53
74–75	Det	59	3478	20	29	10	217	2	3.74
75–76	Det	44	2640	13	25	6	158	4	3.59
76–77	Det	48	2740	7	34	6	180	1	3.94
77–78	Det	43	2468	20	17	4	134	1	3.26
78–79	Det	32	1892	13	14	5	103	1	3.27
79–80	Det	23	1326	6	13	3	92	1	4.16
80–81	Det–Tor–LA	31	1741	9	16	4	135	0	4.65
81–82	LA	7	380	3	3	0	43	0	6.79
82–83	Det	1	60	0	1	0	7	0	7.00
Totals		457	25895	150	227	59	1576	14	3.65

Playoffs

SEASON	TEAM	GP	MIN.	W	L	T	GA	SO.	AVG.
71–72	Pitt	4	240	0	4	0	14	0	3.50
77–78	Det	3	180	2	1	0	12	0	4.00
80–81	LA	1	20	0	0	0	2	0	6.00
Totals		8	440	2	5	0	28	0	3.82

RUTLEDGE, Wayne Alvin *6–2 200*
B. Barrie, Ont., Jan. 5, 1942

SEASON	TEAM	GP	MIN.	W	L	T	GA	SO.	AVG.
67–68	LA	45	2444	20	18	4	117	2	2.87
68–69	LA	17	921	0	0	0	56	0	3.65
69–70	LA	20	960	2	12	1	68	0	4.25
72–73	Hou (WHA)	36	2163	20	14	2	108	0	3.00
73–74	Hou (WHA)	25	1509	12	12	1	84	0	3.34
74–75	Hou (WHA)	35	2098	20	15	0	113	2	3.23
75–76	Hou (WHA)	25	1456	14	10	0	77	1	3.17
76–77	Hou (WHA)	42	2512	23	14	4	132	3	3.15
77–78	Hou (WHA)	12	634	4	7	0	47	0	4.45
NHL Totals		82	4325	22	30	5	241	2	3.34
WHA Totals		175	10372	93	72	7	561	6	3.25

Playoffs

SEASON	TEAM	GP	MIN.	W	L	T	GA	SO.	AVG.
67–68	LA	3	149	1	1	0	8	0	3.22
68–69	LA	5	229	1	1	0	12	0	3.14
72–73	Hou (WHA)	7	423	4	3	0	20	0	2.84
75–76	Hou (WHA)	4	200	1	2	0	10	0	3.00
76–77	Hou (WHA)	2	120	2	0	0	4	0	2.00
77–8	Hou (WHA)	3	131	1	2	0	8	0	3.66
NHL Totals		8	378	2	2	0	20	0	3.17
WHA Totals		16	874	8	7	0	42	0	2.88

St. CROIX, Richard *5–10 160*
B. Kenora, Ont., Jan. 3, 1955

SEASON	TEAM	GP	MIN.	W	L	T	GA	SO.	AVG.
77–78	Phil	7	395	2	4	1	20	0	3.04
78–79	Phil	2	117	0	1	1	6	0	3.08
79–80	Phil	1	60	1	0	0	2	0	2.00
80–81	Phil	27	1567	13	7	6	65	2	2.49
81–82	Phil	29	1729	13	9	6	112	0	3.89
82–83	Phil–Tor	33	1860	13	14	4	112	0	3.61
Totals		99	5728	42	35	18	317	2	3.32

Playoffs

SEASON	TEAM	GP	MIN.	W	L	T	GA	SO.	AVG.
80–81	Phil	9	541	4	5	0	27	1	2.99
81–82	Phil	1	20	0	1	0	1	0	3.00
82–83	Tor	1	1	0	0	0	1	0	60.00
Totals		11	562	4	6	0	29	1	3.10

ST. LAURENT, Sam *5–10 190*
B. Arvida, Que., Feb. 16, 1959

SEASON	TEAM	GP	MIN.	W	L	T	GA	SO.	AVG.
85–86	NJ	4	188	2	1	0	13	1	4.15
86–87	Det	6	342	1	2	2	16	0	2.81
87–88	Det	6	294	2	2	0	16	0	3.27
88–89	Det	4	141	0	1	1	9	0	3.83
89–90	Det	14	607	2	0	1	38	0	3.76
Totals		34	1572	7	12	4	92	1	3.51

Playoffs

SEASON	TEAM	GP	MIN.	W	L	T	GA	SO.	AVG.
87–88	Det	1	10	0	0	0	1	0	6.00

SALO, Tommy *5–11 161*
B. Surahammar, Sweden, Feb. 1, 1971

SEASON	TEAM	GP	MIN.	W	L	T	GA	SO.	AVG.
94–95	NYI	6	358	1	5	0	18	0	3.02
95–96	NYI	10	523	1	7	1	35	0	4.02
96–97	NYI	58	3208	20	27	8	151	5	2.82
97–98	NYI	62	3461	23	29	5	152	4	2.64
98–99	NYI–Edm	64	3718	25	28	9	159	5	2.57
Totals		200	11268	70	96	23	515	14	2.74

Playoffs

SEASON	TEAM	GP	MIN.	W	L	T	GA	SO.	AVG.
98–99	Edm	4	296	0	4	0	11	0	2.23

SANDS, Charlie *5–9 160*
B. Fort William, Ont., Mar. 23, 1911

SEASON	TEAM	GP	MIN.	W	L	T	GA	SO.	AVG.
39–40	Mont	1	25	0	0	0	5	0	12.00

SANDS, Michael *5–9 155*
B. Mississauga, Ont., April 6, 1963

SEASON	TEAM	GP	MIN.	W	L	T	GA	SO.	AVG.
84–85	Minn	3	139	0	3	0	14	0	6.04
86–87	Minn	3	163	0	2	0	12	0	4.42
Totals		6	302	0	5	0	26	0	5.17

SARJEANT, Geoff Ian *5–9 180*
B. Newmarket, Ont., Nov. 30, 1969

SEASON	TEAM	GP	MIN.	W	L	T	GA	SO.	AVG.
94–95	StL	4	120	1	0	0	6	0	3.00
95–96	SJ	4	171	0	2	1	14	0	4.91
Totals		8	291	1	2	1	20	0	4.12

SAUVE, Robert *5–8 165*
B. Ste. Genevieve, Que., June 17, 1955

SEASON	TEAM	GP	MIN.	W	L	T	GA	SO.	AVG.
76–77	Buf	4	184	1	2	0	11	0	3.59
77–78	Buf	11	480	6	2	0	20	2	2.50
78–79	Buf	29	1610	10	10	7	100	0	3.73
79–80	Buf	32	1880	20	8	4	74	4	2.36
80–81	Buf	35	2100	16	10	9	111	2	3.17
81–82	Buf–Det	55	3125	17	26	9	200	0	3.84
82–83	Buf	54	3110	25	20	7	179	1	3.45
83–84	Buf	40	2375	22	13	4	138	0	3.49
84–85	Buf	27	1564	13	10	3	84	0	3.22
85–86	Chi	38	2099	19	13	2	138	0	3.95
86–87	Chi	46	2660	19	19	5	159	1	3.59
87–88	NJ	34	1804	10	16	3	107	0	3.56
Totals		405	22991	178	149	53	1321	8	3.45

Playoffs

SEASON	TEAM	GP	MIN.	W	L	T	GA	SO.	AVG.
78–79	Buf	3	181	1	2	0	9	0	2.98
79–80	Buf	8	501	6	2	0	17	2	2.04
82–83	Buf	10	545	6	4	0	28	2	3.08
83–84	Buf	2	41	0	1	0	5	0	7.35
85–86	Chi	2	99	0	2	0	8	0	4.85
86–87	Chi	4	245	0	4	0	15	0	3.67
87–88	NJ	5	238	2	1	0	13	0	3.28
Totals		34	1850	15	16	0	95	4	3.08

* SAWCHUK, Terrance Gordon (Terry) *6–0 195*
B. Winnipeg, Man., Dec. 28, 1929

SEASON	TEAM	GP	MIN.	W	L	T	GA	SO.	AVG.
49–50	Det	7	420	4	3	0	16	1	2.29
50–51	Det	70	4200	44	13	13	139	11	1.99
51–52	Det	70	4200	44	14	12	133	12	1.90
52–53	Det	63	3780	32	15	16	120	9	1.90
53–54	Det	67	4000	35	19	13	129	12	1.94
54–55	Det	68	4040	28	24	26	132	12	1.96
55–56	Bos	68	4080	22	33	13	181	9	2.66
56–57	Bos	34	2040	18	10	6	81	2	2.38
57–58	Det	70	4200	29	29	12	207	3	2.96
58–59	Det	67	4020	23	36	8	209	5	3.12
59–60	Det	58	3480	24	20	14	156	5	2.69
60–61	Det	37	2080	12	16	8	113	2	3.05
61–62	Det	43	2580	14	21	8	143	5	3.33
62–63	Det	48	2775	23	16	7	119	3	2.48
63–64	Det	53	3140	24	20	7	138	5	2.60
64–65	Tor	36	2160	17	13	6	92	1	2.56
65–66	Tor	27	1521	10	11	4	80	1	2.96
66–67	Tor	28	1409	15	5	4	66	2	2.81
67–68	LA	36	1936	11	14	6	99	2	3.07
68–69	Det	13	641	3	4	3	28	0	2.62
69–70	NYR	8	412	3	1	2	20	1	2.91
Totals		971	57114	435	337	188	2401	103	2.52

Playoffs

SEASON	TEAM	GP	MIN.	W	L	T	GA	SO.	AVG.
50–51	Det	6	463	2	4	0	13	1	1.68
51–52	Det	8	480	8	0	0	5	4	0.63
52–53	Det	6	372	2	4	0	21	1	3.39
53–54	Det	12	751	8	4	0	20	2	1.60
54–55	Det	11	660	8	3	0	26	1	2.36
57–58	Det	4	252	0	4	0	19	0	4.52
59–60	Det	6	405	2	4	0	20	0	2.96
60–61	Det	8	465	5	2	0	18	1	2.32
62–63	Det	11	660	5	6	0	36	0	3.27
63–64	Det	13	695	6	6	0	31	1	2.68

SEASON	TEAM	GP	MIN.	W	L	T	GA	SO.	AVG.
64–65	Tor	1	60	0	1	0	3	0	3.00
65–66	Tor	2	120	0	2	0	6	0	3.00
66–67	Tor	10	568	6	4	0	25	0	2.64
67–68	LA	5	280	2	3	0	18	1	3.86
69–70	NYR	3	80	0	1	0	6	0	4.50
Totals		106	6311	54	48	0	267	12	2.54

SCHAEFER, Joseph
B. Long Island City, N.Y., Dec. 21, 1924

SEASON	TEAM	GP	MIN.	W	L	T	GA	SO.	AVG.
59–60	NYR	1	39	0	0	0	5	0	7.69
60–61	NYR	1	47	0	1	0	3	0	3.83
Totals		2	86	0	1	0	8	0	5.58

SCHAFER, Paxton 5–9 152
B. Medicine Hat, Alta., Feb. 26, 1976

SEASON	TEAM	GP	MIN.	W	L	T	GA	SO.	AVG.
96–97	Bos	3	77	0	0	0	6	0	4.68

SCHWAB, Corey 6–0 180
B. Battleford, Sask., Nov. 4, 1970

SEASON	TEAM	GP	MIN.	W	L	T	GA	SO.	AVG.
95–96	NJ	10	331				12	0	2.18
96–97	TB	31	1462				74	2	3.04
97–98	TB	16	821	2	9	1	40	1	2.92
98–99	TB	40	2146	8	25	3	126	0	3.52
Totals		97	4760	21	49	5	252	3	3.18

SCOTT, Ron 5–8 155
B. Guelph, Ont., July 21, 1960

SEASON	TEAM	GP	MIN.	W	L	T	GA	SO.	AVG.
83–84	NYR	9	485	2	3	3	29	0	3.59
85–86	NYR	4	156	0	3	0	11	0	4.23
86–87	NYR	1	65	0	0	1	5	0	4.62
87–88	NYR	2	90	1	1	0	6	0	4.00
89–90	LA	12	654	5	6	0	40	0	3.67
Totals		28	1450	8	13	4	91	0	3.77

Playoffs

SEASON	TEAM	GP	MIN.	W	L	T	GA	SO.	AVG.
89–90	LA	1	32	0	0	0	4	0	7.50

SEVIGNY, Richard 5–8 172
B. Montreal, Que., Apr. 11, 1957

SEASON	TEAM	GP	MIN.	W	L	T	GA	SO.	AVG.
79–80	Mont	11	632	5	4	2	31	0	2.94
80–81	Mont	33	1777	20	4	3	71	2	2.40
81–82	Mont	19	1027	11	4	2	53	0	3.10
82–83	Mont	38	2130	15	11	8	122	1	3.44
83–84	Mont	40	2203	16	8	2	124	1	3.38
84–85	Que	20	1104	10	6	2	62	1	3.37
85–86	Que	11	468	3	5	1	33	0	4.23
86–87	Que	4	144	0	2	0	11	0	4.58
Totals		176	9485	90	44	20	507	5	3.21

Playoffs

SEASON	TEAM	GP	MIN.	W	L	T	GA	SO.	AVG.
80–81	Mont	3	180	0	3	0	13	0	4.33
82–83	Mont	1	28	0	0	0	0	0	0.00
Totals		4	208	0	3	0	13	0	3.75

SHARPLES, Scott 6–0 180
B. Calgary, Alta., Mar. 1, 1968

SEASON	TEAM	GP	MIN.	W	L	T	GA	SO.	AVG.
91–92	Calg	1	65	0	0	1	4	0	3.69

SHIELDS, Allen 6–0 188
B. Ottawa, Ont., May 10, 1907

SEASON	TEAM	GP	MIN.	W	L	T	GA	SO.	AVG.
31–32	NYA	2	41	0	0	0	9	0	13.17

SHIELDS, Steve 6–3 210
B. Toronto, Ont., July 19, 1972

SEASON	TEAM	GP	MIN.	W	L	T	GA	SO.	AVG.
95–96	Buf	2	75	1	0	0	4	0	3.20
96–97	Buf	13	789	3	8	2	39	0	2.97
97–98	Buf	16	785	3	6	4	37	0	2.83
98–99	SJ	37	2162	15	11	8	80	4	2.22
Totals		68	3811	22	25	16	160	4	2.52

Playoffs

SEASON	TEAM	GP	MIN.	W	L	T	GA	SO.	AVG.
97–98	Buf	10	570	4	6	0	26	1	2.74
98–99	SJ	1	60	0	1	0	6	0	6.00
Totals		11	630	4	7	0	32	1	3.05

SHTALENKOV, Mikhail 6–2 180
B. Moscow, USSR, Oct. 20, 1965

SEASON	TEAM	GP	MIN.	W	L	T	GA	SO.	AVG.
93–94	Ana	10	543	3	4	1	24	0	2.65
94–95	Ana	18	810	4	7	1	49	0	3.63
95–96	Ana	30	1637	7	16	3	85	0	3.12
96–97	Ana	24	1079	7	8	1	52	2	2.89
97–98	Ana	40	2049	13	18	5	110	1	3.22
98–99	Phoe-Edm	38	2063	13	19	4	90	3	2.62
Totals		160	8180	47	72	15	410	7	3.03

Playoffs

SEASON	TEAM	GP	MIN.	W	L	T	GA	SO.	AVG.
96–97	Ana	4	211	0	3	0	10	0	2.84

SHULMISTRA, Richard 6–2 185
B. Sudbury, Ont., Apr. 1, 1971

SEASON	TEAM	GP	MIN.	W	L	T	GA	SO.	AVG.
97–98	NJ	1	62	0	1	0	30	0	1.94

SIDORKIEWICZ, Peter 5–9 180
B. Dabrown Bialostocka, Poland, June 29, 1963

SEASON	TEAM	GP	MIN.	W	L	T	GA	SO.	AVG.
87–88	Hart	1	60	0	1	0	6	0	6.00
88–89	Hart	44	2635	22	18	4	133	4	3.03
89–90	Hart	46	2703	19	19	7	161	1	3.57
90–91	Hart	52	2953	21	22	7	164	1	3.33
91–92	Hart	35	1995	9	19	6	111	2	3.34
92–93	Ott	64	3388	8	46	3	250	0	4.43
93–94	NJ	3	130	0	3	0	6	0	2.77
97–98	NJ	1	20	0	0	0	1	0	3.00
Totals		246	13884	79	128	27	832	8	3.60

Playoffs

SEASON	TEAM	GP	MIN.	W	L	T	GA	SO.	AVG.
88–89	Hart	2	124	0	2	0	8	0	3.87
89–90	Hart	7	429	3	4	0	23	0	3.22
90–91	Hart	6	359	2	4	0	24	0	4.01
Totals		15	912	5	10	0	55	0	3.62

SIMMONS, Donald 5–10 150
B. Port Colborne, Ont., Sept. 13, 1931

SEASON	TEAM	GP	MIN.	W	L	T	GA	SO.	AVG.
56–57	Bos	26	1560	13	9	4	63	4	2.42
57–58	Bos	38	2228	15	15	7	93	5	2.50
58–59	Bos	58	3480	24	26	8	184	3	3.17
59–60	Bos	28	1680	10	15	3	94	2	3.36
60–61	Bos	18	1080	3	9	6	59	1	3.28
61–62	Tor	9	540	4	4	1	21	1	2.33
62–63	Tor	28	1680	15	8	5	70	1	2.50
63–64	Tor	21	1191	9	9	1	63	3	3.17
65–66	NYR	11	491	3	6	1	37	0	4.52
67–68	NYR	5	300	2	1	2	13	0	2.60
68–69	NYR	5	206	2	2	1	8	0	2.33
Totals		247	14436	100	104	39	705	20	2.93

Playoffs

SEASON	TEAM	GP	MIN.	W	L	T	GA	SO.	AVG.
56–57	Bos	10	600	5	5	0	29	2	2.90
57–58	Bos	11	671	6	5	0	27	1	2.41
61–62	Tor	3	165	2	1	0	8	0	2.91
Totals		24	1436	13	11	0	64	3	2.67

SIMMONS, Gary Byrne 6–2 200
B. Charlottetown, P.E.I., July 19, 1944

SEASON	TEAM	GP	MIN.	W	L	T	GA	SO.	AVG.
74–75	Cal	34	2029	10	21	3	124	2	3.67
75–76	Cal	40	2360	15	19	5	131	2	3.33
76–77	Clev-LA	19	1080	3	10	5	67	1	3.72
77–78	LA	14	693	2	7	2	44	0	3.81
Totals		107	6162	30	57	15	366	5	3.56

Playoffs

SEASON	TEAM	GP	MIN.	W	L	T	GA	SO.	AVG.
76–77	LA	1	20	0	0	0	1	0	3.00

SKIDMORE, Paul 6–0 185
B. Smithtown, N.Y., July 22, 1956

SEASON	TEAM	GP	MIN.	W	L	T	GA	SO.	AVG.
81–82	StL	2	120	1	1	0	6	0	3.00

SKORODENSKI, Warren 6–1 180
B. Winnipeg, Man., Mar. 22, 1960

SEASON	TEAM	GP	MIN.	W	L	T	GA	SO.	AVG.
81–82	Chi	1	60	0	1	0	5	0	5.00
84–85	Chi	27	1396				75	2	322
85–86	Chi	1	60				6	0	6.00
86–87	Chi	3	155				7	0	2.71
87–88	Edm	3	61				7	0	6.89
Totals		35	1732				100	2	3.46
Playoff Totals		2	33				6	0	10.91

SKUDRA, Peter 6–1 182
B. Riga, Latvia, Apr. 24, 1973

SEASON	TEAM	GP	MIN.	W	L	T	GA	SO.	AVG.
97–98	Pitt	17	851	6	4	3	26	0	1.83
98–99	Pitt	37	1914	15	11	5	89	3	2.79
Totals		54	2765	21	15	8	115	3	2.50

SMITH, Allan Robert (Al) 6–1 200
B. Toronto, Ont., Nov. 10, 1945

SEASON	TEAM	GP	MIN.	W	L	T	GA	SO.	AVG.
65–66	Tor	2	62	2	0	0	2	0	1.94
66–67	Tor	1	60	0	1	0	5	0	5.00
68–69	Tor	7	335	2	2	1	16	0	2.87
69–70	Pitt	46	2555	15	20	8	129	2	3.03
70–71	Pitt	46	2472	9	22	9	128	2	3.11
71–72	Det	43	2500	18	20	4	135	4	3.24

SEASON	TEAM	GP	MIN.	W	L	T	GA	SO.	AVG.
72–73	NE (WHA)	51	3059	31	19	1	162	3	3.18
73–74	NE (WHA)	55	3194	30	21	2	164	2	3.08
74–75	NE (WHA)	59	3494	33	21	4	202	2	3.47
75–76	Buf	14	840	9	3	2	43	0	3.07
76–77	Buf	7	265	0	3	0	19	0	4.30
77–78	NE (WHA)	55	3246	30	20	3	174	2	3.22
78–79	NE (WHA)	40	2396	17	17	5	132	1	3.31
79–80	Hart	30	1754	4	10	8	107	2	3.66
80–81	Col	37	1909	9	18	4	151	0	4.75
NHL Totals		233	12752	68	99	36	735	10	3.46
WHA Totals		260	15389	141	98	15	834	10	3.25

Playoffs

SEASON	TEAM	GP	MIN.	W	L	T	GA	SO.	AVG.
69–70	Pitt	3	180	1	2	0	10	0	3.33
72–73	NE (WHA)	15	909	12	3	0	49	0	3.23
73–74	NE (WHA)	7	399	3	4	0	21	0	3.16
74–75	NE (WHA)	6	366	2	4	0	28	0	4.59
75–76	Buf	1	17	0	0	0	1	0	3.53
77–78	NE (WHA)	3	120	0	2	0	14	0	7.00
78–79	NE (WHA)	4	153	1	2	0	12	0	4.71
79–80	Hart	2	120	0	2	0	10	0	5.00
NHL Totals		6	317	1	4	0	21	0	3.97
WHA Totals		35	1947	18	15	0	124	1	3.82

SMITH, Gary Edward (Suitcase) *6–4 215*
B. Ottawa, Ont., Feb. 4, 1944

SEASON	TEAM	GP	MIN.	W	L	T	GA	SO.	AVG.
65–66	Tor	3	118	0	2	0	7	0	3.56
66–67	Tor	2	115	0	2	0	7	0	3.65
67–68	Oak	21	1129	2	13	4	60	1	3.19
68–69	Oak	54	2993	0	0	0	148	4	2.97
69–70	Oak	65	3762	19	34	12	195	2	3.11
70–71	Cal	71	3975	19	48	4	256	2	3.86
71–72	Chi	28	1540	14	5	6	62	5	2.42
72–73	Chi	23	1340	10	10	2	79	0	3.54
73–74	Van	66	3632	20	33	8	208	3	3.44
74–75	Van	72	3823	32	24	9	197	6	3.09
75–76	Van	51	2864	20	24	6	167	2	3.50
76–77	Minn	36	2090	10	17	8	139	1	3.99
77–78	Wash–Minn	20	1160	2	14	4	77	0	3.98
78–79	Ind–Winn (WHA)	22	1290	7	13	0	92	0	4.28
79–80	Winn	20	1073	4	11	4	73	0	4.08
NHL Totals		532	29614	152	237	67	1675	26	3.39
WHA Totals		22	1290	7	13	0	92	0	4.28

Playoffs

SEASON	TEAM	GP	MIN.	W	L	T	GA	SO.	AVG.
68–69	Oak	7	420	3	4	0	23	0	3.29
69–70	Cal	4	248	0	4	0	13	0	3.15
71–72	Chi	2	120	1	1	0	3	1	1.50
72–73	Chi	2	65	0	1	0	5	0	4.62
74–75	Van	4	257	1	3	0	14	0	3.27
76–77	Minn	1	43	0	0	0	4	0	5.58
78–79	Winn (WHA)	10	563	8	2	0	35	0	3.73
NHL Totals		20	1153	5	13	0	62	1	3.23
WHA Totals		10	563	8	2	0	35	0	3.73

* SMITH, Norman *5–7 165*
B. Toronto, Ont., Mar. 18, 1908

SEASON	TEAM	GP	MIN.	W	L	T	GA	SO.	AVG.
31–32	Mont M	21	1267	5	12	4	62	0	2.95
34–35	Det	25	1550	12	11	2	52	2	2.08
35–36	Det	48	3030	24	16	8	103	6	2.15
36–37	Det	48	2980	25	14	9	102	6	2.13
37–38	Det	47	2930	11	25	11	130	3	2.77
38–39	Det	4	240	0	4	0	12	0	3.00
43–44	Det	5	240	3	1	1	11	0	2.75
44–45	Det	1	60	1	0	0	3	0	3.00
Totals		199	12297	81	83	35	475	17	2.32

Playoffs

SEASON	TEAM	GP	MIN.	W	L	T	GA	SO.	AVG.
35–36	Det	7	598	6	1	0	12	2	1.71
36–37	Det	5	282	3	1	0	6	1	1.20
Totals		12	880	9	2	0	18	3	1.23

SMITH, William John (Billy) *5–10 185*
B. Perth, Ont., Dec. 12, 1950

SEASON	TEAM	GP	MIN.	W	L	T	GA	SO.	AVG.
71–72	LA	5	300	1	3	1	23	0	4.60
72–73	NYI	37	2122	7	24	3	147	0	4.16
73–74	NYI	46	2615	9	23	12	134	0	3.07
74–75	NYI	58	3368	21	18	1	156	3	2.78
75–76	NYI	39	2254	19	10	9	98	3	2.61
76–77	NYI	36	2089	21	8	6	87	2	2.50
77–78	NYI	38	2154	20	8	8	95	2	2.65
78–79	NYI	40	2261	25	8	4	108	1	2.87
79–80	NYI	38	2114	15	14	7	104	2	2.95
80–81	NYI	41	2363	22	10	8	129	2	3.28
81–82	NYI	46	2685	32	9	4	133	0	2.97
82–83	NYI	41	2340	18	14	7	112	1	2.87
83–84	NYI	42	2279	23	13	2	130	2	3.42
84–85	NYI	37	2090	18	14	3	133	0	3.82
85–86	NYI	41	2308	20	14	4	143	1	3.72
86–87	NYI	40	2252	14	18	5	132	1	3.52
87–88	NYI	38	2107	17	14	5	113	2	3.22
88–89	NYI	17	730	3	11	0	54	0	4.44
Totals		680	38426	305	233	105	2031	22	3.17

Playoffs

SEASON	TEAM	GP	MIN.	W	L	T	GA	SO.	AVG.
74–75	NYI	6	333	1	4	0	23	0	4.14
75–76	NYI	8	437	4	3	0	21	0	2.88
76–77	NYI	10	580	7	3	0	27	0	2.79
77–78	NYI	1	47	0	0	0	1	0	1.28
78–79	NYI	5	315	4	1	0	10	1	1.90
79–80	NYI	20	1198	15	4	0	56	1	2.80
80–81	NYI	17	994	14	3	0	42	0	2.54
81–82	NYI	18	1120	15	3	0	47	1	2.52
82–83	NYI	17	962	13	3	0	43	2	2.68
83–84	NYI	21	1190	12	8	0	54	0	2.72
84–85	NYI	6	342	3	3	0	19	0	3.33
85–86	NYI	1	60	0	1	0	4	0	4.00
86–87	NYI	2	67	0	0	0	1	0	0.90
Totals		132	7645	88	36	0	348	5	2.73

SNEDDON, Robert Allan *6–2 190*
B. Montreal, Que., May 31, 1944

SEASON	TEAM	GP	MIN.	W	L	T	GA	SO.	AVG.
70–71	Cal	5	225	0	2	0	21	0	5.60

SNOW, Garth *6–3 200*
B. Wrentham, Mass., July 28, 1969

SEASON	TEAM	GP	MIN.	W	L	T	GA	SO.	AVG.
93–94	Que	5	279	3	2	0	16	0	3.44
94–95	Que	2	119	1	1	0	11	0	5.55
95–96	Phil	26	1437	12	8	4	69	0	2.88
96–97	Phil	35	1884	14	8	8	79	2	2.52
97–98	Phil–Van	41	2155	17	15	4	93	1	2.59
98–99	Van	65	3501	20	31	8	171	6	2.93
Totals		174	9375	34	65	24	439	9	2.81

Playoffs

SEASON	TEAM	GP	MIN.	W	L	T	GA	SO.	AVG.
94–95	Que	1	9	0	0	0	1	0	6.67
95–96	Phil	1	1	0	0	0	0	0	0.00
96–97	Phil	12	699	8	4	0	33	0	2.83
Totals		14	709	8	4	0	34	0	2.88

SODERSTROM, Tommy *5–9 165*
B. Stockholm, Sweden, July 17, 1969

SEASON	TEAM	GP	MIN.	W	L	T	GA	SO.	AVG.
92–93	Phil	44	2512	20	17	6	143	5	3.42
93–94	Phil	34	1736	6	18	4	116	2	4.01
94–95	NYI	26	1350	8	12	3	70	1	3.11
95–96	NYI	51	2590	11	22	6	167	2	3.87
96–97	NYI	1	0	0	0	0	0	0	0.00
Totals		156	8188	45	69	19	496	10	3.63

SOETAERT, Douglas Henry *6–0 185*
B. Edmonton, Alta., Apr. 21, 1955

SEASON	TEAM	GP	MIN.	W	L	T	GA	SO.	AVG.
75–76	NYR	8	273	2	2	0	24	0	5.27
76–77	NYR	12	570	3	4	1	28	1	2.95
77–78	NYR	6	360	2	2	2	20	0	3.33
78–79	NYR	17	900	5	7	3	57	0	3.80
79–80	NYR	8	435	5	2	0	33	0	4.55
80–81	NYR	39	2320	16	16	7	152	0	3.93
81–82	Winn	39	2157	13	14	8	155	2	4.31
82–83	Winn	44	2533	19	19	6	174	0	4.12
83–84	Winn	47	2539	18	15	7	182	0	4.30
84–85	Mont	28	1606	14	9	4	91	0	3.40
85–86	Mont	23	1215	11	6	2	56	3	2.77
86–87	NYR	13	675	2	7	2	58	0	5.16
Totals		284	15583	110	103	44	1030	6	3.97

Playoffs

SEASON	TEAM	GP	MIN.	W	L	T	GA	SO.	AVG.
81–82	Winn	2	120	1	1	0	8	0	4.00
82–83	Winn	1	20	0	0	0	0	0	0.00
83–84	Winn	1	20	0	1	0	5	0	15.00
84–85	Mont	1	20	0	0	0	1	0	3.00
Totals		5	180	1	2	0	14	0	4.67

SOUCY, Christian *5–11 160*
B. Gatineau, Que., Sept. 14, 1970

SEASON	TEAM	GP	MIN.	W	L	T	GA	SO.	AVG.
93–94	Chi	1	3	0	0	0	0	0	0.00

* SPOONER, Andy (Red)

SEASON	TEAM	GP	MIN.	W	L	T	GA	SO.	AVG.
29–30	Pitt Pi	1	60	0	1	0	6	0	6.00

STANIOWSKI, Edward *5–9 170*
B. Moose Jaw, Sask., July 7, 1955

SEASON	TEAM	GP	MIN.	W	L	T	GA	SO.	AVG.
75–76	StL	11	620	5	3	2	33	0	3.19
76–77	StL	29	1589	10	15	1	108	0	4.08

SEASON TEAM	GP	MIN.	W	L	T	GA	SO.	AVG.
77–78 StL	17	886	1	10	2	57	0	3.86
78–79 StL	39	2291	9	25	3	146	0	3.82
79–80 StL	22	1108	2	11	3	80	0	4.33
80–81 StL	19	1010	10	3	3	72	0	4.28
81–82 Winn	45	2643	20	19	6	174	1	3.95
82–83 Winn	17	827	4	8	0	65	1	4.72
83–84 Winn–Hart	19	1081	6	9	1	82	0	4.55
84–85 Hart	1	20	0	0	0	1	0	3.00
Totals	219	12075	67	104	21	818	2	4.06

Playoffs

75–76 StL	3	206	1	2	0	7	0	2.04
76–77 StL	3	102	0	2	0	9	0	5.29
81–82 Winn	2	120	0	2	0	12	0	6.00
Totals	8	428	1	6	0	28	0	3.92

STARR, Harold *5–11 176*
B. Ottawa, Ont., July 6, 1906

31–32 Mont M	1	3	0	0	0	0	0	0.00

STAUBER, Robb *5–11 180*
B. Duluth, Minn., Nov. 25, 1967

89–90 LA	2	83	0	1	0	11	0	7.95
92–93 LA	31	1735	15	8	4	111	0	3.84
93–94 LA	22	1144	4	11	5	65	1	3.41
94–95 LA–Buf	7	333	2	3	0	22	0	3.96
Totals	62	3295	21	23	9	209	1	3.81

Playoffs

92–93 LA	4	240	3	1	0	16	0	4.00

STEFAN, Gregory Steven *5–11 180*
B. Brantford, Ont., Feb. 11, 1961

81–82 Det	2	120	0	2	0	10	2	5.00
82–83 Det	35	1847	6	16	9	139	0	4.52
83–84 Det	50	2600	19	22	2	152	2	3.51
84–85 Det	46	2635	21	19	3	190	0	4.33
85–86 Det	37	2068	10	20	5	155	1	4.50
86–87 Det	43	2351	20	17	3	135	1	3.45
87–88 Det	33	1854	17	9	5	96	1	3.11
88–89 Det	46	2499	21	17	3	167	0	4.01
89–90 Det	7	359	1	5	0	24	0	4.01
Totals	299	16333	115	128	30	1068	5	3.92

Playoffs

83–84 Det	3	210	1	2	0	8	0	2.29
84–85 Det	3	138	0	3	0	17	0	7.39
86–87 Det	9	508	4	5	0	24	0	2.83
87–88 Det	10	531	5	4	0	32	1	3.62
88–89 Det	5	294	2	3	0	18	0	3.67
Totals	30	1681	12	17	0	99	1	3.53

STEIN, Phillip J.
B. Toronto, Ont., Sept. 13, 1913

39–40 Tor	1	70	0	0	1	2	0	1.71

STEPHENSON, Frederick Wayne *5–9 175*
B. Fort William, Ont., Jan. 29, 1945

71–72 StL	2	100	0	1	0	9	0	5.40
72–73 StL	45	2535	18	5	7	128	1	3.03
73–74 StL	40	2360	13	21	5	123	2	3.13
74–75 Phil	12	639	7	2	0	29	1	2.72
75–76 Phil	66	3819	40	10	11	164	1	2.58
76–77 Phil	21	1065	12	3	2	41	3	2.31
77–78 Phil	26	1482	14	10	1	68	3	2.75
78–79 Phil	40	2187	20	10	5	122	2	3.35
79–80 Wash	56	3146	18	24	10	187	0	3.57
80–81 Wash	20	1010	4	7	5	66	1	3.92
Totals	328	18343	146	93	46	937	14	3.06

Playoffs

72–73 StL	3	160	1	2	0	14	0	5.25
74–75 Phil	2	123	2	0	0	4	1	1.95
75–76 Phil	8	494	4	4	0	22	0	2.67
76–77 Phil	9	532	4	3	0	23	1	2.59
78–79 Phil	4	213	0	3	3	16	0	4.51
Totals	26	1522	11	12	0	79	2	3.11

STEVENSON, Douglas *5–8 170*
B. Regina, Sask., Apr. 6, 1924

44–45 NYR–Chi	6	360	1	5	0	27	0	4.50
45–46 Chi	2	120	1	1	0	12	0	6.00
Totals	8	480	2	6	0	39	0	4.88

STEWART, Charles (Doc)
B.

24–25 Bos	21	1266	5	16	0	65	2	3.10
25–26 Bos	35	2168	17	14	4	80	6	2.29

SEASON TEAM	GP	MIN.	W	L	T	GA	SO.	AVG.
26–27 Bos	21	1303	9	11	1	49	2	2.33
Totals	77	4737	31	41	5	194	10	2.46

STEWART, Jim

79–80 Bos	1	20	0	1	0	5	0	15.00

STORR, Jamie *6–1 192*
B. Brampton, Ont., Dec. 28, 1975

94–95 LA	5	263	1	3	1	17	0	3.88
95–96 LA	5	262	3	1	0	12	0	2.75
96–97 LA	5	265	2	1	1	11	0	2.49
97–98 LA	17	920	9	5	1	34	2	2.22
98–99 LA	28	1525	12	12	2	61	4	2.40
Totals	60	3235	27	22	5	135	6	2.50

Playoffs

97–98 LA	3	145	0	2	0	9	0	3.72

STUART, Herbert

26–27 Det	3	180	0	1	0	5	0	1.67

SYLVESTRI, Don *6–0 180*
B. Sudbury, Ont., June 2, 1961

84–85 Det	3	102	0	0	2	6	0	3.53

TABARACCI, Richard Stephen *6–1 180*
B. Toronto, Ont., Jan. 2, 1969

88–89 Pitt	1	33	0	0	0	4	0	7.27
90–91 Winn	24	1093	9	9	4	71	1	3.90
91–92 Winn	18	966	6	7	3	52	0	3.23
92–93 Winn–Wash	25	1302	8	12	0	80	2	3.69
93–94 Wash	32	1770				91	2	3.08
94–95 Wash–Calg	13	596	3	3	3	21	0	2.11
95–96 Calg	43	2391	19	16	3	117	3	2.94
96–97 Calg–TB	62	3373	22	29	6	152	5	2.70
97–98 Calg	42	2419	13	22	6	116	0	2.88
98–99 Wash	23	1193	4	12	3	50	2	2.51
Totals	283	15136	92	124	30	754	15	2.99

Playoffs

91–92 Winn	7	387	3	4	0	26	0	4.03
92–93 Wash	4	304	1	3	0	14	0	2.76
93–94 Wash	2	111	0	2	0	6	0	3.24
94–95 Calg	1	19	0	0	0	0	0	0.00
95–96 Calg	3	204	0	3	0	7	0	2.06
Totals	17	1025	4	12	0	53	0	3.10

TAKKO, Kari *6–2 185*
B. Uusikaupunki, Finland, June 23, 1963

85–86 Minn	1	60	0	1	0	3	0	3.00
86–87 Minn	38	2075	13	18	4	119	0	3.44
87–88 Minn	37	1919	8	19	6	143	1	4.47
88–89 Minn	32	1603	8	15	4	93	0	3.48
89–90 Minn	21	1012	4	12	0	68	0	4.03
90–91 Minn–Edm	13	648	4	6	0	49	0	4.54
Totals	142	7317	37	71	14	475	1	3.90

Playoffs

88–89 Minn	3	105	0	1	0	7	0	4.00
89–90 Minn	1	4	0	0	0	0	0	0.00
Totals	4	109	0	1	0	7	0	3.85

TALLAS, Robbie *6–0 178*
B. Edmonton, Alta., Mar. 20, 1973

95–96 Bos	1	60	1	0	0	3	0	3.00
96–97 Bos	28	1244	8	12	1	69	1	3.33
97–98 Bos	14	788	6	3	3	24	1	1.83
98–99 Bos	17	987	7	7	2	43	1	2.61
Totals	60	3079	22	22	6	139	3	2.71

TANNER, John *6–3 182*
B. Cambridge, Ont., Mar. 17, 1971

89–90 Que	1	60	0	1	0	3	0	3.00
90–91 Que	6	228	1	3	1	16	0	4.21
91–92 Que	14	796	1	7	4	46	1	3.47
Totals	21	1084	2	11	5	65	1	3.60

TATARYN, David Nathan *5–9 160*
B. Sudbury, Ont., July 17, 1950

75–76 Tor (WHA)	23	1261	7	12	1	100	0	4.76
76–77 NYR	2	80	1	1	0	10	0	7.50

TAYLOR, Robert Ian *6–1 180*
B. Calgary, Alta., Jan. 24, 1945

SEASON	TEAM	GP	MIN.	W	L	T	GA	SO.	AVG.
71–72	Phil	6	320	1	2	2	16	0	3.00
72–73	Phil	23	1144	8	8	4	78	0	4.09
73–74	Phil	8	366	3	3	0	26	0	4.26
74–75	Phil	3	120	0	2	0	13	0	6.50
75–76	Phil–Pitt	6	318	3	2	0	22	0	4.15
Totals		46	2268	15	17	6	155	0	4.10

TENO, Harvie
B. Windsor, Ont., Feb. 15, 1915

SEASON	TEAM	GP	MIN.	W	L	T	GA	SO.	AVG.
38–39	Det	5	300				15	0	3.00

TERRERI, Christopher Arnold *5–8 160*
B. Providence, R.I., Nov. 15, 1964

SEASON	TEAM	GP	MIN.	W	L	T	GA	SO.	AVG.
86–87	NJ	7	286	0	3	1	21	0	4.41
88–89	NJ	8	402	0	4	2	18	0	2.69
89–90	NJ	35	1931	15	12	3	110	0	3.42
90–91	NJ	53	2970	24	21	7	144	1	2.91
91–92	NJ	54	3186	22	22	10	169	1	3.18
92–93	NJ	48	2672	19	21	3	151	2	3.39
93–94	NJ	44	2340	20	11	4	106	2	2.72
94–95	NJ	15	734	3	7	2	31	0	2.53
95–96	NJ–SJ	50	2726	16	29	1	164	0	3.61
96–97	SJ–Chi	29	1629	10	11	5	74	0	2.73
97–98	Chi	21	1222	8	10	2	49	2	2.41
98–99	NJ	12	726	8	3	1	30	1	2.48
Totals		376	20824	145	154	41	1067	9	3.07

Playoffs

SEASON	TEAM	GP	MIN.	W	L	T	GA	SO.	AVG.
89–90	NJ	4	238	2	2	0	13	0	3.28
90–91	NJ	7	428	3	4	0	21	0	2.94
91–92	NJ	7	386	3	3	0	23	0	3.58
92–93	NJ	4	219	1	3	0	17	0	4.66
93–94	NJ	4	200	3	0	0	9	0	2.70
94–95	NJ	1	8	0	0	0	0	0	0.00
96–97	Chi		2	44	0	0	3	0	4.09
Totals		29	1523	12	12	0	86	0	3.39

THEODORE, Jose *5–10 180*
B. Laval, Que., Sept. 13, 1976

SEASON	TEAM	GP	MIN.	W	L	T	GA	SO.	AVG.
95–96	Mont	1	9	0	0	0	1	0	6.67
96–97	Mont	16	821	5	6	2	53	0	3.87
98–99	Mont	18	913	4	12	0	50	1	3.29
Totals		35	1743	9	18	2	104	1	3.58

Playoffs

SEASON	TEAM	GP	MIN.	W	L	T	GA	SO.	AVG.
96–97	Mont	2	168	1	1	0	7	0	2.50

THIBAULT, Jocelyn *5–11 170*
B. Montreal, Que., Jan. 12, 1975

SEASON	TEAM	GP	MIN.	W	L	T	GA	SO.	AVG.
93–94	Que	29	1504	8	13	3	83	0	3.31
94–95	Que	18	898	12	2	2	35	1	2.34
95–96	Col A–Mont	50	2892	26	17	5	138	3	2.86
96–97	Mont	61	3397	22	24	11	164	1	2.90
97–98	Mont	47	2652	19	15	8	109	2	2.47
98–99	Mont-Chi	62	3543	24	30	7	159	5	2.69
Totals		267	14886	111	101	36	688	12	2.78

Playoffs

SEASON	TEAM	GP	MIN.	W	L	T	GA	SO.	AVG.
94–95	Que	3	148	1	2	0	8	0	3.24
95–96	Mont	6	311	2	4	0	18	0	3.47
96–97	Mont	3	179	0	3	0	13	0	4.36
97–98	Mont	2	43	0	0	0	4	0	5.58
Totals		14	681	3	9	0	43	0	3.79

THOMAS, Robert Wayne *6–2 195*
B. Ottawa, Ont., Oct. 9, 1947

SEASON	TEAM	GP	MIN.	W	L	T	GA	SO.	AVG.
72–73	Mont	10	583	8	1	0	23	1	2.37
73–74	Mont	42	2410	23	12	5	111	1	2.76
75–76	Tor	64	3684	28	24	12	196	2	3.19
76–77	Tor	33	1803	10	13	6	116	1	3.86
77–78	NYR	41	2352	12	20	7	141	4	3.60
78–79	NYR	31	1668	15	10	3	101	1	3.63
79–80	NYR	12	668	4	7	0	44	0	3.95
80–81	NYR	10	600	3	6	1	34	0	3.40
Totals		243	13768	103	93	34	766	10	3.34

Playoffs

SEASON	TEAM	GP	MIN.	W	L	T	GA	SO.	AVG.
75–76	Tor	10	587	5	5	0	34	1	3.48
76–77	Tor	4	202	1	2	0	12	0	3.56
77–78	NYR	1	60	0	1	0	4	0	4.00
Totals		15	849	6	8	0	50	1	3.53

* THOMPSON, Cecil R. (Tiny) *5–10 160*
B. Sandon, B.C., May 31, 1905

SEASON	TEAM	GP	MIN.	W	L	T	GA	SO.	AVG.
28–29	Bos	44	2710	26	13	5	52	12	1.18
29–30	Bos	44	2680	38	5	1	98	3	2.23
30–31	Bos	44	2730	28	10	6	90	3	2.05
31–32	Bos	43	2698	13	19	11	103	9	2.40
32–33	Bos	48	3000	25	15	8	88	11	1.83
33–34	Bos	48	2980	18	25	5	130	5	2.71
34–35	Bos	48	2970	23	18	7	112	8	2.33
35–36	Bos	48	2930	22	20	6	82	10	1.71
36–37	Bos	48	2970	23	18	7	110	6	2.29
37–38	Bos	48	2970	30	11	7	89	7	1.85
38–39	Bos–Det	44	2706	19	18	7	109	4	2.42
39–40	Det	46	2830	16	24	6	120	3	2.61
Totals		553	34174	284	194	75	1183	81	2.08

Playoffs

SEASON	TEAM	GP	MIN.	W	L	T	GA	SO.	AVG.
29–29	Bos	5	300	5	0	0	3	3	0.60
29–30	Bos	6	432	3	3	0	12	0	2.00
30–31	Bos	5	348	2	3	0	13	0	2.60
32–33	Bos	5	429	2	3	0	9	0	1.80
34–35	Bos	4	275	1	1	0	7	1	1.75
35–36	Bos	2	120	1	1	0	8	1	4.00
36–37	Bos	3	180	1	2	0	8	1	2.67
37–38	Bos	3	212	0	3	0	6	0	2.00
38–39	Det	6	374	3	3	0	15	1	2.50
39–40	Det	5	300	2	3	0	12	0	2.40
Totals		44	2970	20	22	0	93	7	1.88

TORCHIA, Mike *5–11 215*
B. Toronto, Ont., Feb. 23, 1972

SEASON	TEAM	GP	MIN.	W	L	T	GA	SO.	AVG.
94–95	Dal	6	327	3	2	1	18	0	3.30

TREFILOV, Andrei *6–0 180*
B. Kirovo–Chepetsk, USSR, Aug. 31, 1969

SEASON	TEAM	GP	MIN.	W	L	T	GA	SO.	AVG.
92–93	Calg	1	65	0	0	1	5	0	4.62
93–94	Calg	11	623	3	4	2	26	2	2.50
94–95	Calg	6	236	0	3	0	16	0	4.07
95–96	Buf	22	1094	8	8	1	64	0	3.51
96–97	Buf	3	159	0	2	0	10	0	3.77
97–98	Chi	6	299	1	4	0	17	0	3.41
98–99	Chi-Calg	5	187	0	4	0	15		4.81
Totals		54	2663	12	25	4	153	2	3.45

Playoffs

SEASON	TEAM	GP	MIN.	W	L	T	GA	SO.	AVG.
96–97	Buf	1	5	0	0	0	0	0	0.00

TREMBLAY, Vincent *5–11 185*
B. Quebec City, Que., Oct. 21, 1959

SEASON	TEAM	GP	MIN.	W	L	T	GA	SO.	AVG.
79–80	Tor	10	329	2	1	0	28	0	5.11
80–81	Tor	3	143	0	3	0	16	0	6.71
81–82	Tor	40	2033	10	18	8	153	1	4.52
82–83	Tor	1	40				2	0	3.00
83–84	Pitt	4	240				24	0	6.00
Totals		58	2785				223	1	4.80

TUCKER, Ted *5–11 165*
B. Fort William, Ont., May 7, 1949

SEASON	TEAM	GP	MIN.	W	L	T	GA	SO.	AVG.
73–74	Cal	5	177	1	1	1	10	0	3.39

TUGNUTT, Ronald Frederick Bradley *5–11 155*
B. Scarborough, Ont., Oct. 22, 1967

SEASON	TEAM	GP	MIN.	W	L	T	GA	SO.	AVG.
87–88	Que	6	284	2	3	0	16	0	3.38
88–89	Que	26	1367	10	10	3	82	0	3.60
89–90	Que	35	1978	5	24	3	152	0	4.61
90–91	Que	56	3144	12	29	10	212	0	4.05
91–92	Que–Edm	33	1707	7	18	3	116	1	4.08
92–93	Edm	26	1338	9	12	2	93	0	4.17
93–94	Ana–Mont	36	1898	12	18	2	100	1	3.16
94–95	Mont	7	346	1	3	1	18	0	3.12
96–97	Ott	37	1991	17	15	1	93	3	2.80
97–98	Ott	42	2236	15	14	8	84	3	2.25
98–99	Ott	43	2508	22	10	8	75	3	1.79
Totals		347	18797	112	156	41	1041	11	3.32

Playoffs

SEASON	TEAM	GP	MIN.	W	L	T	GA	SO.	AVG.
91–92	Edm	2	60	0	0	0	3	0	3.00
93–94	Mont	1	59	0	1	0	5	0	5.08
96–97	Ott	7	425	3	4	0	14	1	1.98
97–98	Ott	2	74	0	1	0	6	0	4.86
98–99	Ott	2	118	0	2	0	6	0	3.05
Totals		14	736	3	8	0	34	1	2.77

TUREK, Roman *6–3 190*
B. Pisek, Czech., May 21, 1970

SEASON	TEAM	GP	MIN.	W	L	T	GA	SO.	AVG.
96–97	Dal	6	263	3	1	0	9	0	2.05

SEASON	TEAM	GP	MIN.	W	L	T	GA	SO.	AVG.
97–98	Dal	23	1324	11	10	1	49	1	2.22
98–99	Dal	26	1382	16	3	3	48	1	2.08
Totals		55	2969	30	14	4	106	2	2.14

TURNER, Joseph
41–42	Det	1	60	0	0	1	3	0	3.00

VACHON, Rogatien (Rogie) *5–7 165*
B. Palmarolle, Que., Sept. 8, 1945
66–67	Mont	19	1137	11	3	4	47	1	2.48
67–68	Mont	39	2227	23	13	2	92	4	2.48
68–69	Mont	36	2051	22	9	3	98	2	2.87
69–70	Mont	64	3697	31	18	12	162	4	2.63
70–71	Mont	47	2676	23	12	9	118	2	2.65
71–72	Mont–LA	29	1606	6	19	3	111	0	4.15
72–73	LA	53	3120	22	20	10	148	4	2.85
73–74	LA	65	3751	28	26	10	175	5	2.80
74–75	LA	54	3239	27	14	1	121	6	2.24
75–76	LA	51	3060	26	20	5	160	5	3.14
76–77	LA	68	4059	33	23	12	184	8	2.72
77–78	LA	70	4107	29	27	13	196	4	2.86
78–79	Det	50	2908	10	27	11	189	0	3.90
79–80	Det	59	3474	20	30	8	209	4	3.61
80–81	Bos	53	3021	25	19	6	168	1	3.34
81–82	Bos	38	2165	19	11	6	132	1	3.66
Totals		795	46298	355	291	115	2310	51	2.99

Playoffs
66–67	Mont	9	555	6	3	0	22	0	2.38
67–68	Mont	2	113	1	1	0	4	0	2.12
68–69	Mont	8	507	2	1	0	12	1	1.42
73–74	LA	4	140	0	4	0	7	0	1.75
74–75	LA	3	199	1	2	0	7	0	2.11
75–76	LA	7	438	4	3	0	17	1	2.33
76–77	LA	9	520	4	5	0	36	0	4.15
77–78	LA	2	120	0	2	0	11	0	5.50
80–81	Bos	3	164	0	2	0	16	0	5.85
81–82	Bos	1	20	0	0	0	1	0	3.00
Totals		48	2876	23	23	0	133	2	2.77

VANBIESBROUCK, John *5–8 175*
B. Detroit, Mich., Sept. 4, 1963
81–82	NYR	1	60	1	0	0	1	0	1.00
83–84	NYR	3	180	2	1	0	10	0	3.33
84–85	NYR	42	2358	12	24	3	166	1	4.22
85–86	NYR	61	3326	31	21	5	184	3	3.32
86–87	NYR	50	2656	18	20	5	161	0	3.64
87–88	NYR	56	3319	27	22	7	187	2	3.38
88–89	NYR	56	3207	28	21	4	197	0	3.69
89–90	NYR	47	2734	19	19	7	154	1	3.38
90–91	NYR	40	2257	15	18	6	126	3	3.35
91–92	NYR	45	2526	27	13	3	120	2	2.85
92–93	NYR	48	2757	20	18	7	152	4	3.31
93–94	Fla	57	3440	21	25	11	145	1	2.53
94–95	Fla	37	2087	14	15	4	86	4	2.47
95–96	Fla	57	3178	26	20	7	142	2	2.68
96–97	Fla	57	3347	27	19	10	128	2	2.29
97–98	Fla	60	3451	18	29	11	165	4	2.87
98–99	Phil	62	3712	27	18	15	135	6	2.18
Totals		779	44595	333	303	105	2259	85	3.04

Playoffs
83–84	NYR	1	1	0	0	0	0	0	0.00
84–85	NYR	1	20	0	0	0	0	0	0.00
85–86	NYR	16	899	8	8	0	49	1	3.27
86–87	NYR	4	195	1	3	0	11	1	3.38
88–89	NYR	2	107	0	1	0	6	0	3.36
89–90	NYR	6	298	2	3	0	15	0	3.02
90–91	NYR	1	52	0	0	0	1	0	1.15
91–92	NYR	7	368	2	5	0	23	0	3.75
95–96	Fla	22	1332	12	10	0	50	1	2.25
96–97	Fla	5	328	1	4	0	13	1	2.38
98–99	Phil	6	369	2	4	0	9	1	1.46
Totals		71	3969	28	38	0	177	5	2.68

VEISOR, Michael David *5–9 158*
B. Toronto, Ont., Aug. 25, 1952
73–74	Chi	10	537	7	0	2	20	1	2.23
74–75	Chi	9	460	1	5	1	36	0	4.70
76–77	Chi	3	180	1	2	0	13	0	4.33
77–78	Chi	12	720	3	4	5	31	2	2.58
78–79	Chi	17	1020	5	8	4	60	0	3.53
79–80	Chi	11	660	3	5	3	37	0	3.36
80–81	Hart	29	1588	6	13	6	118	1	4.46
81–82	Hart	13	701	5	5	2	53	0	4.54
82–83	Hart	23	1280	5	16	1	118	1	5.53
83–84	Hart–Winn	12	660				46	0	4.18
Totals		139	7806				532	5	4.09

Playoffs
SEASON	TEAM	GP	MIN.	W	L	T	GA	SO.	AVG.
73–74	Chi	2	80	0	1	0	5	0	3.75
79–80	Chi	1	60	0	1	0	6	0	6.00
Totals		3	140	0	2	0	11	0	4.71

VERNON, Michael *5–9 170*
B. Calgary, Alta., Feb. 24, 1963
82–83	Calg	2	100	0	2	0	11	0	6.60
83–84	Calg	1	11	0	1	0	4	0	22.22
85–86	Calg	18	921	9	3	3	52	1	3.39
86–87	Calg	54	2957	30	21	1	178	1	3.61
87–88	Calg	64	3565	39	16	7	210	1	3.53
88–89	Calg	52	2938	37	6	5	130	2	2.65
89–90	Calg	47	2795	23	14	9	146	0	3.13
90–91	Calg	54	3121	31	19	3	172	1	3.31
91–92	Calg	63	3640	24	30	9	217	0	3.58
92–93	Calg	64	3752	29	26	9	203	2	3.26
93–94	Calg	48	2798	26	17	5	131	3	2.81
94–95	Det	30	1807	19	6	4	76	1	2.52
95–96	Det	32	1855	21	7	2	70	3	2.26
96–97	Det	33	1952	13	11	8	79	0	2.43
97–98	SJ	62	3564	30	22	8	146	5	2.46
98–99	SJ	49	2831	16	22	10	107	4	2.27
Totals		673	38537	347	223	83	1932	22	3.01

Playoffs
85–86	Calg	21	1229	12	9	0	60	0	2.93
86–87	Calg	5	263	2	3	0	16	0	3.65
87–88	Calg	9	515	4	4	0	34	0	3.96
88–89	Calg	22	1381	16	5	0	52	3	2.26
89–90	Calg	6	342	2	3	0	19	0	3.33
90–91	Calg	7	427	3	4	0	21	0	2.95
92–93	Calg	4	150	1	1	0	15	0	6.00
93–94	Calg	7	466	3	4	0	23	0	2.96
94–95	Det	18	1063	12	6	0	41	1	2.31
95–96	Det	4	243	2	2	0	11	0	2.72
96–97	Det	20	1229	16	4	0	36	1	1.76
97–98	SJ	6	348	2	4	0	14	1	2.41
98–99	SJ	5	321	2	3	0	13	0	2.31
Totals		134	7977	127	80	0	355	6	2.67

* VEZINA, Georges
B. Chicoutimi, Que., Jan., 1887
17–18	Mont	22	1282	13	9	0	84	1	3.82
18–19	Mont	18	1097	10	8	0	78	1	4.33
19–20	Mont	24	1454	13	11	0	113	0	4.71
20–21	Mont	24	1436	13	11	0	99	1	4.13
21–22	Mont	24	1468	13	10	1	94	0	3.92
22–23	Mont	24	1488	13	9	2	61	2	2.54
23–24	Mont	24	1459	13	11	0	48	3	2.00
24–25	Mont	30	1860	17	11	2	56	5	1.87
25–26	Mont	1	20	0	0	0	0	0	0.00
Totals		191	11564	105	80	5	633	13	3.28

Playoffs
17–18	Mont	2	120	1	1	0	10	0	5.00
18–19	Mont	10	636	6	3	0	37	1	3.70
22–23	Mont	2	120	1	1	0	3	0	1.50
23–24	Mont	6	360	6	0	0	6	2	1.00
24–25	Mont	6	360	5	1	0	18	1	3.00
Totals		26	1596	19	6	0	74	4	2.78

VILLEMURE, Gilles *5–8 185*
B. Trois–Rivieres, Que., May 30, 1940
63–64	NYR	5	300	0	3	2	18	0	3.60
67–68	NYR	4	200	1	2	0	8	1	2.40
68–69	NYR	4	240	0	1	0	9	0	2.25
70–71	NYR	34	2039	22	8	4	78	4	2.30
71–72	NYR	37	2129	24	7	4	74	3	2.09
72–73	NYR	34	2040	20	12	2	78	3	2.29
73–74	NYR	21	1054	7	7	3	62	0	3.53
74–75	NYR	45	2470	22	14	6	130	2	3.16
75–76	Chi	15	797	2	7	5	57	0	4.29
76–77	Chi	6	312	0	4	1	28	0	5.38
Totals		205	11581	98	65	27	542	13	2.81

Playoffs
68–69	NYR	1	60	0	1	0	4	0	4.00
70–71	NYR	2	80	0	1	0	6	0	4.50
71–72	NYR	6	360	4	2	0	14	0	2.33
72–73	NYR	2	61	0	1	0	2	0	1.97
73–74	NYR	1	1	0	0	0	0	0	0.00
74–75	NYR	2	94	1	0	0	6	0	3.83
Totals		14	656	5	5	0	32	0	2.93

SEASON	TEAM	GP	MIN.	W	L	T	GA	SO.	AVG.

VUKOUN, Tomas *5–11 208*
B. Karlovy Vary, Czech., July 2, 1976

SEASON	TEAM	GP	MIN.	W	L	T	GA	SO.	AVG.
96–97	Mont	1	20	0	0	0	4	0	12.00
98–99	Nash	37	1954	12	18	4	96	1	2.95
Totals		38	1974	12	18	4	100	1	3.04

WAITE, Jimmy *6–1 180*
B. Sherbrooke, Que., Apr. 15, 1969

88–89	Chi	11	494	0	7	1	43	0	5.22
89–90	Chi	4	183	2	0	0	14	0	4.59
90–91	Chi	1	60	1	0	0	2	0	2.00
91–92	Chi	17	877	4	7	4	54	0	3.69
92–93	Chi	20	996	6	7	1	49	2	2.95
93–94	SJ	15	697	3	7	0	50	0	4.30
94–95	Chi	2	119	1	1	0	5	0	2.52
95–96	Chi	1	31	0	0	0	0	0	0.00
96–97	Chi	2	105	0	1	1	7	0	4.00
97–98	Phoe	17	793	5	6	1	28	1	2.12
98–99	Phoe	16	898	6	5	4	41	1	2.74
Totals		106	5253	28	41	12	293	4	3.35

Playoffs

93–94	SJ	2	40	0	0	0	3	0	4.50
97–98	Phoe	4	171	0	3	0	11	0	3.86
Totals		6	211	0	3	0	14	0	3.98

WAKALUK, Darcy *5–11 180*
B. Pincher Creek, Alta., Mar. 14, 1966

88–89	Buf	6	214	1	3	0	15	0	4.21
90–91	Buf	16	630	4	5	3	35	0	3.33
91–92	Minn	36	1905	13	19	1	104	1	3.28
92–93	Minn	29	1596	10	12	5	97	1	3.65
93–94	Dal	36	2000	18	9	6	88	3	2.64
94–95	Dal	15	754	4	8	0	40	2	3.18
95–96	Dal	37	1875	9	16	5	106	1	3.39
96–97	Phoe	16	782	8	3	1	39	1	2.99
Totals		191	9756	67	75	21	524	9	3.22

Playoffs

90–91	Buf	2	37	0	1	0	2	0	3.34
93–94	Dal	5	307	4	1	0	15	0	2.93
94–95	Dal	1	20	0	0	0	1	0	3.00
Totals		8	364	4	2	0	18	0	2.97

WAKELY, Ernest Alfred (Ernie) *5–11 160*
B. Flin Flon, Man., Nov. 27, 1940

62–63	Mont	1	60	1	0	0	3	0	3.00
68–69	Mont	1	60	0	1	0	4	0	4.00
69–70	StL	30	1651	12	9	4	58	4	2.11
70–71	StL	51	2859	20	14	11	133	3	2.79
71–72	StL	30	1614	8	18	2	92	1	3.42
72–73	Winn (WHA)	49	2889	26	19	3	152	2	3.16
73–74	Winn (WHA)	37	2254	15	18	4	123	3	3.27
74–75	Winn–SD (WHA)	41	2417	23	15	2	131	3	3.25
75–76	SD (WHA)	67	3824	35	27	4	208	3	3.26
76–77	SD (WHA)	46	2506	22	18	3	129	2	3.09
77–78	Cin–Hou (WHA)	57	3381	28	23	4	192	2	3.41
78–79	Birm (WHA)	37	2060	15	17	1	129	0	3.76
NHL Totals		113	6244	41	42	17	290	8	2.79
WHA Totals		334	19331	164	137	1064	153.30		

Playoffs

69–70	StL	4	216	0	4	0	17	0	4.72
70–71	StL	3	180	2	1	0	7	1	2.33
71–72	StL	3	113	0	1	0	13	0	6.90
72–73	Winn (WHA)	7	420	4	3	0	22	0	3.14
74–75	SD (WHA)	10	520	4	6	0	39	0	4.50
75–76	SD (WHA)	11	640	5	6	0	39	0	3.66
76–77	SD (WHA)	3	160	2	1	0	9	0	3.38
NHL Totals		10	509	2	6	0	37	1	4.36
WHA Totals		31	1740	15	16	0	109	0	3.76

* WALSH, James Patrick (Flat) *5–11 175*
B. Kinston, Ont., Mar. 23, 1897

26–27	Mont M	1	60	0	1	0	3	0	3.00
27–28	Mont M	1	40	0	0	0	1	0	1.00
28–29	NYA–Mont M	11	710	3	4	4	9	4	0.76
29–30	Mont M	30	1897	16	10	4	74	2	2.47
30–31	Mont M	16	781	7	7	2	30	2	1.88
31–32	Mont M	27	1670	14	10	3	77	2	2.85
32–33	Mont M	22	1303	8	11	3	56	2	2.55
Totals		108	6461	48	43	16	250	12	2.32

Playoffs

29–30	Mont M	4	312	1	3	0	11	1	2.75
30–31	Mont M	4	258	1	1	2	5	1	1.25
Totals		8	570	2	4	2	16	2	1.68

WAMSLEY, Richard *5–11 185*
B. Simcoe, Ont., May 25, 1959

80–81	Mont	5	253	3	0	1	8	1	1.90
81–82	Mont	38	2206	23	7	7	101	2	2.75
82–83	Mont	46	2583	27	12	5	151	0	3.51
83–84	Mont	42	2333	19	17	3	144	2	3.70
84–85	StL	40	2319	23	12	5	126	0	3.26
85–86	StL	42	2517	22	16	3	144	1	3.43
86–87	StL	41	2410	17	15	6	142	0	3.54
87–88	StL–Calg	33	1891	14	16	1	108	2	3.43
88–89	Calg	35	1927	17	11	4	95	2	2.96
89–90	Calg	36	1969	18	8	6	107	2	3.26
90–91	Calg	29	1670	14	7	5	85	0	3.05
91–92	Calg–Tor	17	885	7	7	0	61	0	4.14
92–93	Tor	3	160	0	3	0	15	0	5.63
Totals		407	23123	204	131	46	1287	12	3.34

Playoffs

81–82	Mont	5	300	2	3	0	11	0	2.20
82–83	Mont	3	152	0	3	0	7	0	2.77
83–84	Mont	1	32	0	0	0	0	0	0.00
84–85	StL	2	120	0	2	0	7	0	3.50
85–86	StL	10	569	4	6	0	37	0	3.90
86–87	StL	2	120	1	1	0	5	0	2.50
87–88	Calg	1	33	0	1	0	2	0	3.64
88–89	Calg	1	20	0	1	0	2	0	6.00
89–90	Calg	1	49	0	1	0	9	0	11.02
90–91	Calg	1	2	0	0	0	1	0	30.00
Totals		27	1397	7	18	0	81	0	3.48

WATT, James Magnus *5–11 180*
B. Duluth, Minn., May 11, 1950

73–74	StL	1	20	0	0	0	2	0	6.00

WEEKES, Kevin *6–0 175*
B. Toronto, Ont., Apr. 4, 1975

97–98	Fla	11	485	0	5	1	32	0	3.96
98–99	Van	11	532	0	8	1	34	0	3.83
Totals		22	1017	0	13	2	66	0	3.89

WEEKS, Stephen *5–11 170*
B. Scarborough, Ont., June 30, 1958

80–81	NYR	1	60	0	1	0	2	0	2.00
81–82	NYR	49	2852	23	16	9	179	1	3.77
82–83	NYR	18	1040	9	5	3	68	0	3.92
83–84	NYR	26	1361	10	11	2	90	0	3.97
84–85	Hart	23	1397	9	12	2	91	2	3.91
85–86	Hart	27	1544	13	13	0	99	1	3.85
86–87	Hart	25	1367	12	8	2	78	1	3.42
87–88	Hart–Van	27	1468	10	10	4	86	0	3.51
88–89	Van	35	2056	11	19	5	102	0	2.98
89–90	Van	21	1142	4	11	4	79	0	4.15
90–91	Van	1	59	0	1	0	6	0	6.10
91–92	NYI–LA	30	1284	10	7	2	79	0	3.69
92–93	Ott	7	249	0	5	0	30	0	7.23
Totals		290	15879	111	119	33	989	5	3.74

Playoffs

80–81	NYR	1	14	0	0	0	1	0	4.29
81–82	NYR	4	127	1	2	0	9	0	4.25
85–86	Hart	3	169	1	2	0	8	0	2.84
86–87	Hart	1	36	0	0	0	1	0	1.67
88–89	Van	3	140	1	1	0	8	0	3.43
Totals		12	486	3	5	0	27	0	3.33

WETNEL, Carl David *6–1 170*
B. Detroit, Mich., Dec. 12, 1938

64–65	Det	2	33	0	1	0	4	0	7.27
67–68	Minn	5	269	1	2	1	18	0	4.01
72–73	Minn (WHA)	1	60	0	1	0	3	0	3.00
NHL Totals		7	302	1	3	1	22	0	4.37
WHA Totals		1	60	0	1	0	3	0	3.00

WHITMORE, Kay *5–11 175*
B. Sudbury, Ont., Apr. 10, 1967

88–89	Hart	3	180	2	1	0	10	0	3.33
89–90	Hart	9	442	4	2	1	26	0	3.53
90–91	Hart	18	850	3	9	3	52	0	3.67
91–92	Hart	45	2567	14	21	6	155	3	3.62
92–93	Van	31	1817	18	8	4	94	1	3.10
93–94	Van	32	1921	18	14	0	113	0	3.53

SEASON	TEAM	GP	MIN.	W	L	T	GA	SO.	AVG.

SEASON	TEAM	GP	MIN.	W	L	T	GA	SO.	AVG.
94–95	Van	11	558	0	6	2	37	0	3.98
Totals		149	8335	59	61	16	487	4	3.51

Playoffs

88–89	Hart	2	135	0	2	0	10	0	4.44
91–92	Hart	1	19	0	0	0	1	0	3.16
94–95	Van	1	20	0	0	0	2	0	6.00
Totals		4	174	0	2	0	13	0	4.48

WILKINSON, Derek 6–0 160

95–96	TB	4	200	0	3	0	15	0	4.50
96–97	TB	5	169	0	2	1	12	0	4.26
97–98	TB	8	311	2	4	1	17	0	3.28
98–99	TB	5	253	1	3	1	13	0	3.08
Totals		22	933	3	12	3	57	0	3.67

WILLIS, Jordan 5–9 170
B. Kincardine, Ont., Feb. 28, 1975

95–96	Dal	1	19	0	1	0	1	0	3.16

WILSON, Duncan Shepherd (Dunc) 5–11 175
B. Toronto, Ont., Mar. 22, 1948

69–70	Phil	1	60	0	1	0	3	0	3.00
70–71	Van	35	1791	3	25	2	128	0	4.29
71–72	Van	53	2870	16	30	3	173	1	3.62
72–73	Van	43	2423	13	21	5	159	1	3.94
73–74	Tor	24	1412	9	11	3	68	1	2.89
74–75	Tor–NYR	28	1573	9	13	4	99	0	3.78
75–76	NYR	20	1080	5	9	3	76	0	4.22
76–77	Pitt	45	2627	18	19	8	129	5	2.95
77–78	Pitt	21	1180	5	11	3	95	0	4.83
78–79	Van	17	835	2	10	2	58	0	4.17
Totals		287	15851	80	150	33	988	8	3.74

WILSON, Ross Ingram (Lefty) 5–11 178
B. Toronto, Ont., Oct. 15, 1919

53–54	Det	1	20	0	0	0	0	0	0.00
55–56	Tor	1	13	0	0	0	0	0	0.00
57–58	Bos	1	52	0	0	1	1	0	1.15
Totals		3	85	0	0	1	1	0	0.71

* WINKLER, Harold Lang (Hal) 5–8 150
B. Gretna, Man., Mar. 20, 1892

26–27	NYR–Bos	31	1959	15	13	3	56	6	1.72
27–28	Bos	44	2780	20	13	11	70	15	1.59
Totals		75	4739	35	26	14	126	21	1.60

Playoffs

26–27	Bos	8	520	2	2	4	13	2	1.63
27–28	Bos	2	120	0	1	1	5	0	2.50
Totals		10	640	2	3	5	18	2	1.69

WOLFE, Bernard Ronald 5–9 165
B. Montreal, Que., Dec. 18, 1951

75–76	Wash	40	2134	5	23	7	148	0	4.16
76–77	Wash	37	1779	7	15	9	114	1	3.84
77–78	Wash	25	1328	4	14	4	94	0	4.25
78–79	Wash	18	863	4	9	1	68	0	4.73
Totals		120	6104	20	61	21	424	1	4.17

WOODS, Alec
B. Falkirk, Sask.

36–37	NYA	1	70	0	1	0	3	0	2.57

WORSLEY, Lorne John (Gump) 5–7 180
B. Montreal, Que., May 14, 1929

52–53	NYR	50	3000	13	29	8	153	2	3.06
54–55	NYR	65	3900	15	33	17	197	4	3.03
55–56	NYR	70	4200	32	28	10	203	4	2.90
56–57	NYR	68	4080	26	28	13	220	3	3.24
57–58	NYR	37	2220	21	10	6	86	4	2.32
58–59	NYR	67	4001	26	29	12	205	2	3.07
59–60	NYR	41	2301	8	25	8	137	0	3.57
60–61	NYR	58	3473	19	28	9	193	1	3.33
61–62	NYR	60	3520	22	27	9	174	2	2.97
62–63	NYR	67	3980	22	34	9	219	2	3.30
63–64	Mont	8	444	3	2	2	22	1	2.97
64–65	Mont	19	1080	10	7	1	50	1	2.78
65–66	Mont	51	2899	29	14	6	114	2	2.36
66–67	Mont	18	888	9	6	2	47	1	3.18
67–68	Mont	40	2213	19	9	8	73	6	1.98
68–69	Mont	30	1703	19	5	4	64	5	2.55
69–70	Mont–Minn	14	813	8	2	3	34	1	2.51
70–71	Minn	24	1369	4	10	8	57	0	2.50
71–72	Minn	34	1923	16	10	7	68	2	2.12
72–73	Minn	12	624	6	2	3	30	0	2.88

SEASON	TEAM	GP	MIN.	W	L	T	GA	SO.	AVG.

SEASON	TEAM	GP	MIN.	W	L	T	GA	SO.	AVG.
73–74	Minn	29	1601	8	14	5	86	0	3.22
Totals		862	50232	335	353	150	2432	43	2.90

Playoffs

55–56	NYR	3	180	0	3	0	15	0	5.00
56–57	NYR	5	316	1	4	0	22	0	4.18
57–58	NYR	6	365	2	4	0	28	0	4.60
61–62	NYR	6	384	2	4	0	22	0	3.44
64–65	Mont	8	501	6	2	0	14	2	1.68
65–66	Mont	10	600	8	2	0	20	1	2.00
66–67	Mont	2	80	0	1	0	2	0	1.50
67–68	Mont	12	669	11	0	0	21	1	1.88
68–69	Mont	7	370	5	1	0	14	0	2.27
69–70	Minn	3	180	1	2	0	14	0	4.67
70–71	Minn	4	240	3	1	0	13	0	3.25
71–72	Minn	4	194	2	1	0	7	1	2.16
Totals		70	4079	41	25	0	192	5	2.82

* WORTERS, Roy (Shrimp) 5–3 135
B. Toronto, Ont., Oct. 19, 1900

25–26	PittPi	35	2145	18	16	1	68	7	1.94
26–27	PittPi	44	2711	15	26	3	108	4	2.45
27–28	PittPi	44	2740	19	17	8	76	10	1.73
28–29	NYA	38	2390	16	13	9	46	13	1.21
29–30	NYA–Mont	37	2330	12	24	1	137	2	3.53
30–31	NYA	44	2760	18	16	0	74	8	1.68
31–32	NYA	40	2459	12	20	7	110	5	2.75
32–33	NYA	47	2970	15	22	10	116	5	2.47
33–34	NYA	36	2240	12	13	10	75	4	2.08
34–35	NYA	48	3000	12	27	9	142	3	2.96
35–36	NYA	48	3000	16	25	7	122	3	2.54
36–37	NYA	23	1430	6	14	3	69	2	3.00
Totals		484	30175	171	233	68	1143	66	2.27

Playoffs

25–26	Pitt	2	120	0	1	1	6	0	3.00
27–28	Pitt	2	120	1	1	0	6	0	3.00
28–29	NYA	2	150	0	1	1	1	1	0.50
35–36	NYA	5	300	2	3	0	11	2	2.20
Totals		11	690	3	6	2	24	3	2.09

WORTHY, Christopher John 6–0 180
B. Bristol, England, Oct. 23, 1947

68–69	Oak	14	786	4	6	3	54	0	4.12
69–70	Oak	1	60	0	1	0	5	0	5.00
70–71	Cal	11	480	1	3	1	39	0	4.88
73–74	Edm (WHA)	29	1452	11	12	1	92	0	3.80
74–75	Edm (WHA)	29	1660	11	13	3	99	1	3.58
75–76	Edm (WHA)	24	1256	5	14	0	98	1	4.68
NHL Totals		26	1326	5	10	4	98	0	4.43
WHA Totals		82	4368	27	39	4	289	2	3.97

Playoffs

73–74	Edm (WHA)	3	146	1	1	0	8	0	3.29
75–76	Edm (WHA)	1	60	0	1	0	7	0	7.00
WHA Totals		4	206	1	2	0	15	0	4.37

WREGGET, Kenneth 6–1 195
B. Brandon, Man., Mar. 25, 1964

83–84	Tor	3	165	1	1	1	14	0	5.09
84–85	Tor	23	1278	2	15	3	103	0	4.84
85–86	Tor	30	1566	9	13	4	113	0	4.33
86–87	Tor	56	3026	22	28	3	200	0	3.97
87–88	Tor	56	3000	12	35	4	222	2	4.44
88–89	Tor–Phil	35	2018	12	21	2	152	0	4.52
89–90	Phil	51	2961	22	24	3	169	0	3.42
90–91	Phil	30	1484	10	14	3	88	0	3.56
91–92	Phil–Pitt	32	1707	14	11	3	106	0	3.73
92–93	Pitt	25	1368	13	7	2	78	0	3.42
93–94	Pitt	42	2456	21	12	7	138	1	3.37
94–95	Pitt	38	2208	25	9	2	118	0	3.21
95–96	Pitt	37	2132	20	13	2	115	3	3.24
96–97	Pitt	46	2514	17	17	6	136	2	3.25
97–98	Pitt	15	611	3	6	2	28	0	2.75
Totals		519	28494	201	226	47	1780	8	3.75

Playoffs

85–86	Tor	10	607	6	4	0	32	1	3.16
86–87	Tor	13	761	7	6	0	29	1	2.29
87–88	Tor	2	108	0	1	0	11	0	6.11
88–89	Phil	5	268	2	2	0	10	0	2.24
91–92	Pitt	1	40	0	0	0	4	0	6.00
94–95	Pitt	11	661	5	6	0	33	1	3.00
95–96	Pitt	9	599	7	2	0	23	0	2.30
96–97	Pitt	5	297	1	4	0	18	0	3.64
Totals		56	3341	28	25	0	160	3	2.87

SEASON	TEAM	GP	MIN.	W	L	T	GA	SO.	AVG.
YOUNG, Douglas G. *5–9 190*									
B. Medicine Hat, Alta., Oct. 1, 1908									
33–34	Det	1	21	0	0	0	1	0	2.86
YOUNG, Wendell *5–9 185*									
B. Halifax, N.S., Aug. 1, 1963									
85–86	Van	22	1023	4	9	3	61	0	3.58
86–87	Van	8	420	1	6	1	35	0	5.00
87–88	Phil	6	320	3	2	0	20	0	3.75
88–89	Pitt	22	1150	12	9	0	92	0	4.80
89–90	Pitt	43	2318	16	20	3	161	1	4.17
90–91	Pitt	18	773	4	6	2	52	0	4.04
91–92	Pitt	18	838	7	6	0	53	0	3.79
92–93	TB	31	1591	7	19	2	97	0	3.66
93–94	TB	9	480	2	3	1	20	0	2.50
94–95	Pitt	10	497	3	6	0	27	0	3.26
Totals		187	9410	59	86	12	618	2	3.94
Playoffs									
85–86	Van	1	60	0	1	0	5	0	5.00
88–89	Pitt	1	39	0	0	0	1	0	1.54
Totals		2	99	0	1	0	6	0	3.64
ZANIER, Michael *5–11 183*									
B. Trail, B.C., Aug. 22, 1962									
84–85	Edm	3	185	1	1	1	12	0	3.89

GLOSSARY

Attacking Zone—Area from an opponent's blue line to goal line.

Back-Checking—A forward coming back into his defensive zone to check an opponent off the puck.

Backhander—Any shot or pass made with the stick turned around.

Blue Line—Two lines, one at each end of the rink, that are 60 feet from the goal line and define the attacking zone. They are also used to determine offsides. No attacking player may precede the puck over the defending team's blue line.

Boarding—To ride or drive an opponent into the dasher boards. Can result in a minor or major penalty.

Bodycheck—To use one's body to block an opponent. Legal only when the man hit has the puck or was the last player to have touched it.

Charging—Skating three strides or more and crashing into an opponent. Illegal and calls for a penalty.

Checking—Defending against or guarding an opponent. On a line, a right wing checks the other team's left wing and a left wing checks the opposing right wing. Centers check each other. Checking requires harassing an opposing skater with the aim of making him surrender the puck.

Crease—The rectangular area marked off in front of each net. Only a goalie is permitted in the crease and no player may score from there unless he is being pinned in by a defending player.

Cross-Checking—To hit an opponent with both hands on the stick and no part of the stick on the ice. Illegal and calls for a penalty.

Curved Stick—A stick with a concave rather than flat blade.

Defending Zone—The area from a team's goal line to its blue line.

Deke—To feint or shift an opponent out of position.

Delay of Game—An intentional stoppage in play (i.e., shooting the puck into the stands, pinning a

puck against the boards when unchecked, etc.). Illegal and calls for a minor penalty.

Elbowing—Hitting an opponent with the elbow. Illegal and calls for a minor penalty.

Empty-Netter—A goal scored after the opposition has pulled its goalie for an extra skater.

End-to-End Rush—A play in which a skater takes the puck deep in the defensive zone and advances it by himself deep into the attacking zone.

Faceoff—The dropping of the puck between two opposing players to start play. Faceoffs follow goals or other stoppages in action and are to hockey what the jump ball is to basketball.

Forechecking—Checking an opponent in his own zone.

Freezing the Puck—Pinning the puck against the boards with a skate or stick in order to force a stoppage in play. Can result in delay of game penalty if no opposing player is on the puck.

Goal Judge—Game official who sits in booth directly behind net and signals when a goal has been scored by turning on a red light.

Hat Trick—Three (or more) goals by a single player in a game.

Head-Manning—Always advancing the puck to a teammate up ice. Never retreating.

High-Sticking—The carrying of the stick above shoulder level. Always illegal and calls for a penalty if one player hits another in this way or a faceoff if no other infraction occurs.

Holding—To use your hands on an opponent or his equipment. Illegal and calls for a minor penalty.

Hooking—To impede an opponent with the blade of your stick. Illegal and calls for a minor penalty.

Icing the Puck—Shooting the puck from behind the center red line across an opponent's goal line.

Usually done to break up an attack and ease pressure. The puck is brought back and a faceoff takes place in the defensive zone of the team that iced the puck. No icing is called against a team that is shorthanded because of a penalty.

Interference—Body contact with a man not in possession of the puck or who was not the last man to touch the puck. Also called for knocking an opponent's fallen stick out of his reach. Illegal and calls for a minor penalty.

Kneeing—Using the knee to check an opponent. Illegal and calls for a minor penalty.

Linesman—Secondary official who makes determinations on icing and offsides calls and is empowered to call a minor penalty if a team has too many men on the ice.

Major Penalty—A five-minute penalty. (For example, for fighting or spearing.)

Match Penalty—Suspension for the balance of the game.

Minor Penalty—A two-minute penalty. Most penalties are minors.

Misconduct Penalty—A 10-minute penalty against an individual, not a team. A substitute is permitted. Called for various forms of unacceptable behavior or when a player incurs a second major penalty in a game.

Neutral Zone—The area between blue lines. The center ice area.

Offsides—Called when an attacking player precedes the puck across the opponent's blue line. Illegal and calls for a faceoff.

Offsides Pass—Called when the puck is passed to a teammate across two or more lines. Illegal and calls for a faceoff from point where the pass originated.

Penalty-Killer—A player whose job it is to use up time while a teammate is serving a penalty. The best penalty-killers are fast skaters who can break up a power play. Once in possession of the puck, the penalty-killer tries to hold onto it and

seldom tries to attack. He is content to waste time until his team is at full strength again.

Playmaker—Usually a center whose skating and puck-carrying ability enable him to set up or make a play that can lead to a goal.

Plus-Minus System—Used to determine a player's relative worth to his team. A "plus" is awarded to a player on the ice when his team scores an even-strength or shorthanded goal. A "minus" is given to a player who is on the ice when the opposition scores an even-strength or shorthanded goal. No "plus" or "minus" is given on a power-play goal.

Pokecheck—The quick thrust of the stick to take a puck away from an opposing player. Usually done best by defensemen rather than forwards. Legal.

Power Play—A manpower advantage resulting from a penalty to the opposing team.

Puck—The vulcanized rubber disc used in hockey.

Red Line—The line that divides the ice in half.

Referee—Head official in the game who has general supervision of play.

Roughing—Minor fisticuffs or shoving. Illegal and calls for a minor penalty.

Shorthanded—What a team is when it is trying to kill a penalty.

Slap Shot—When a player winds and slaps his stick at the puck. Usually a hard but erratic shot.

Slashing—To swing stick at an opponent. Illegal and calls for a minor penalty.

Slot—The area extending from in front of the net out about 30 feet. Many goals are scored from this area.

Spearing—To use the stick as one would a spear. Illegal and calls for a major penalty.

Stickhandling—The art of carrying the puck with the stick.

Sudden-Death Goal—Any goal scored in overtime of a game. Overtime is only played if a game is tied after three periods.

Sweep Check—To swing the stick along the ice to intercept the puck or hamper an opponent. It is legal.

Tip-In—A goal scored from just outside the goalie's crease.

Wash-Out—Disallowing of a goal by a referee, or disallowing of icing or offsides by a linesman.

Wrist Shot—When a player releases a shot without winding up, relying instead on the quickness of his hands.

INDEX

Duggan, Thomas J., 17
"Duke of Duluth." See Lewis, Herbert (Herbie)
Dumart, Woody, 45, 49, 54, *64*, 262, 286, 380, 441
Dunc McCallum Memorial Trophy. See McCallum (Dunc) Memorial Trophy
Duncan, Art, 35
Dunderdale, Thomas, 441
Dunham, Michael, 206, 212
Dunn, Jimmie, 460
Dunn, Richie, 367
Dupont, Andre, 121
Dupont, Arthur, 24
Durnan, Ronald (Bill), 60, 62, 64, 66, *69*, 70, 71, 88, 274, *275*, 441
Dutton, Mervyn (Red), 12, *48*, 54, 57, 59, 65, 427–28, 441
Dwyer, Bill, 43
Dye, Cecil (Babe), 9, 12, 13, 18, *322*, 323–24, 441
Dyer, Kelly, 543
Dynamite Line, 285

E

Eagles. See St. Louis Eagles
Eagleson, Robert Alan, 460
Eastern Canadian Amateur Hockey Association, 334
Eddie Powers Memorial Trophy. See Powers (Eddie) Memorial Trophy
Eddie Shore Award. See Shore (Eddie) Award
Edmonton Oilers, 139, 140, 148, 151, 156, 162, 166, 167, 172, 173, 204–5, 220, 237, 264, 299, 312, 342, 366–68, 371, 508, 517
Edmonton (Western Canada Hockey League team), 12, 13, 20
Edwards, Don, 367, 368, 399
Eisner, Michael, 188
Elliott, Chaucer, 458
Elmer Ferguson Memorial Award. See Ferguson (Elmer) Memorial Award
Emile Bouchard Trophy. See Bouchard (Emile) Trophy
Emms Family Award, 548
Emms, Hap, 36
Entry draft, 490–506, 545, 567–71
Eriksson, Anders, 285
Errey, Bob, 372
ESPN/ESPN2, game broadcasting by, 419
"Espo." See Esposito, Phil
Esposito, Patsy, 368
Esposito, Phil, 105, 110, 111, *111*, 112, 113, 114, 115, 119, 121, 122, 126, 144, 164, 222, 246–48, *247*, 259, 291, 293, 298, 319, 320, 324, *341*, 364, *365*, 366, 368, *392*, 393, 396, 441
Esposito, Tony, *111*, 112, 113, 115, 116, 122, 247, 309, 314, *319*, 319–21, 441

Eveleth, Minn., 47, 465
Evil eyes, on Billy Smith, 368
Ezinicki, Bill, 73, 230

F

F. W. "Dinty" Moore Trophy. See Moore (F. W. "Dinty") Trophy
Falcons. See Detroit Falcons
Farrell, Arthur, 441
Faulkner, Alex, 362
Faulkner, Steve, 274
Favell, Doug, 107
Fedorov, Sergei, 181, *191*, 193, 198, 202, 205, 209, 211, 264, 376
Ferguson, Elmer, 24
Ferguson (Elmer) Memorial Award, 433, 464
Ferguson, John, 390
Ferraro, Ray, 184
Fetisov, Slava, *203*, 205, 376
Fighting Saints. See Minnesota Fighting Saints
Finley, Brian, 568
Fitzgerald, Tom, 202
Fitzpatrick, Mark, 182
Flaherty, Wade, 213
Flaman, Ferdinand Charles (Fernie), 441
Flames. See Atlanta Flames
Fletcher, Cliff, 369, 371
Florida Panthers, 167, 188, 196, 198–99, 344
Fleury, Theo, 545
"The Flower." See Lafleur, Guy
Flower pot, Stanley Cup as, 337
Flu epidemic (1919), 7, 339
Flyers. See Philadelphia Flyers
Foligno, Mike, 296
Fontinato, Louie, 81, *85*, 92, 94, 225
Forbes, Dave, 124
Forsberg, Peter, 198, 202, 204, 214, 216, 567
Fort Wayne Komets, 560
Foster Hewitt Memorial Award, See Hewitt (Foster) Memorial Award
Four Broncos Memorial Trophy, 549
Fowler, Norm, 12, 18
Fox network, game broadcasting by, 419
"Fox Trax," 419
Foyston, Frank, 8, *8*, 9, 12, 21, 441
Francis, Emile (The Cat), 74, 97, 101, 359, 460
Francis, Ron, 198, 372, 375
Frank J. Selke Trophy. See Selke (Frank J.) Trophy
Fraser, Don, 560
Fred A. Huber Memorial Trophy. See Huber (Fred A.) Memorial Trophy
Fred Hunt Memorial Award. See Hunt (Fred) Memorial Award
"Freddie the Fog." See Shero, Fred
Fredrickson, Frank, 13, 18, 21, 441
Ftorek, Robbie, 513

Fuhr, Grant, 159, 164, 166, 174, 175, *312, 314*, 403

G

Gadsby, Bill, 81, 82, 86, 87, 95, 101, 246, *331*, 332, 362, 441
Gagnon, Johnny, 43
Gainey, Bob, 132, 134, 141, 143, 175, *323*, 325–27, 441
Gainor, Dutch, 285
Gallinger, Don, 68
Gallivan, Dan, 433
Gallivan, Danny, 415
Gambling scandal (1947–48), 68
Gardiner, Charles (Chuck), 34, 35, 39, *317*, 318–19, 442
Gardiner, Herbert Martin (Herb), 21, 442
Gardner, James Henry (Jimmy), 442
Garpenlov, Johan, 192, 202
Garrett (Dudley "Red") Memorial Award, 558
Garry F. Longman Memorial Trophy. See Longman (Garry F.) Memorial Trophy
Gartner, Mike, *325*, 328, 408
Gatschene (James) Memorial Trophy, 561
Gauthier, Gerard, *135*
Gee, George, 74, 359
Gelinas, Martin, 167
Gelineau, Jack, 71
Geoffrion, Bernie (Boom Boom), 74, 80, 82, 84, 86, 90, 92, 99, 101, 244, 269, 287–88, *287*, 362, 386, 442, *442*
Georges Vezina Trophy. See Vezina (Georges) Trophy
Gerard, Eddie, 11, 23–24, 339, 353, 442
Giacomin, Ed (Eddie), 101, 114, 292, 364, 442, 546
Gibson, J. L. (Jack), 460
Gilbert, Rod, 97, 101, 108, 115, 442, *443*
Gillies, Clark, 132, 134, 268
Gilmour, Doug, 164, 169, 181, 186, 371, 545
Gilmour, Hamilton Livingstone (Billy), 442
Glennie, Brian, 124
Gnida, Richard, 205
Goal lights, 64
Goalie mask, *27, 32*, 89, *434*, 540
Goaltending, positioning rule, 3
Gobuty, Michael, 517
Goheen, Frank (Moose), 442
Golden Blades. See New York Golden Blades
"Golden Jet." See Hull, Robert Marvin (Bobby)
Goldham, Bob, 68, 72, 381
Goodenow, Bob, 181
Goodfellow, Ebenezer R. (Ebbie), 34, 44, 49, 51, 443

Hull, Robert Marvin (Bobby), 57, 84, 86, *86*, 89, 90, 92, 93, 94, 95, 98, 99, *100*, 101, 103, 108, 110, 111, 113, 115, 116–17, 172, 230–33, *232*, 247, 252, 261, 271, 292, 306, 363, *363*, 364, 386, 389, 391, *392*, 393, 445, 508, 511, 519
Hume, Fred J., 461
Hunt (Fred) Memorial Award, 559
Hunter (Bill) Trophy, 550
Hunter, Dale, 165, 184, 422
Hurricanes. See Carolina Hurricanes
Hutton, John Bower (Bouse), 445
Hyland, Harry, 445

I

Ice, artificial, 9
Imlach, George (Punch), 87, 90, 93, 97, 254, 262, 289, 290, 461
Indianapolis Capitols, 555
Indianapolis Ice, 560
Indianapolis Racers, 511, 512, 517
Influenza epidemic (1919), 7, 339
Ingarfield, Earl, 268
Instigator rule, 162
International challenges, 237, 379, 398, 576
International Hockey League, 559–63
Ion, Fred J. (Mickey), 2, *422*, 423, 425, 426, 459
Irbe, Arturs, 192
Irvin, Dick, 181, 415
Irvin, James Dickenson (Dick), 12, 20, 21, 35, 38, 40, 51, 60, 65, 71–72, 76, 78, 79, 81, 148, 155, 180, 384, *444*, 445
Islanders. See New York Islanders
Ivan, Tommy, 92, 461
Izvestia Cup, 412

J

Jack Adams Award. See Adams (Jack) Award
Jackman, Barret, 569
Jackson, Art, 303
Jackson, Don, 158
Jackson, Harvey (Busher), 35, 39, 40, 43, 44, 54, 165, 273, 278, 303, *303*, 329, 326, 445
Jack A. Butterfield Trophy. See Butterfield (Jack A.) Trophy
Jacques Plante Memorial Trophy. See Plante (Jacques) Memorial Trophy
Jagr, Jaromir, 182, 198, 199, 203, *208*, 209, 212, 213, 216, 278–80, *279*, 342, 372, 567.
James, Angela, 543
James Gatschene Memorial Trophy. See Gatschene (James) Memorial Trophy
James Norris Memorial Trophy. See Norris (James) Memorial Trophy
Jarvis, Doug, 152, 161
Jean Beliveau Trophy. See Beliveau (Jean) Trophy

Jenkins, Roger, 39
Jennings, William M. (Bill), 461
Jennings (William M.) Award, *480*, 481
Jersey Knights, 510
Jerseys, numbers added to, 2
Jets. See Winnipeg Jets
Jillson, Jeff, 568
Jim Piggot Memorial Trophy. See Piggot (Jim) Memorial Trophy
Joe Louis Arena (Detroit), 151, 170, 203, 208
John B. Sollenberger Trophy. See Sollenberger (John B.) Trophy
Johnson, Bob, 179, 283, *372*, 373, 461
Johnson, Ernie (Moose), 9, 10, *11*, 445
Johnson, Ivan (Ching), 35, 37, 445
Johnson, Jim, 373
Johnson, Mark, 401
Johnson, Terry, 158
Johnson, Thomas Christian (Tom), 87, 94, 445
Jokinen, Olli, *214*
Joliat, Aurel, 13, 17, 34, 35, 36, 39, 43, *310*, 311, 445
Joseph, Curtis, 210, 408
Jubilee Rink (Montreal), 3
Juckes, Gordon, 461
Juneau, Joe, 211, 212
Junior hockey, 545–63

K

Kalamazoo Wings, 560
Kaltsov, Konstantin, 569
Kamensky, Valeri, 215
Kaminksy (Max) Trophy, 548
Kamloops Blazers, 545
Kansas City Scouts, 105, 124, 129. See also Colorado Rockies
Karakas, Mike, 42, 45, 47
Kariya, Paul, 202–03, 204, 209, 216
Kasparaitis, Darius, 184
Kasper, Steve, 145
Keane, Mike, 202
Keats, Gordon (Duke), 445
Keefe, Sheldon, 571
Keenan, Mike, 188, 192, 197, 309
Kehoe, Rick, 143
Kelley, Jack, 508
Kelly, Bob, *135*
Kelly, Leonard Patrick (Red), 72, 74, 76, 78, 80, 84, 91, 93, 103, 107, 254–56, *255*, *340*, 365, 383, 386, 445
Kelman, Scott, 568
Ken McKenzie Trophy. See McKenzie (Ken) Trophy
Kennedy, George, 10
Kennedy, Theodore (Ted), 71, 80, 223, 298, 306, *304*, 358, 382, 446
Kenney, Tom, 545
Kenora Thistles, and Stanley Cup, 338
Keon, David Michael (Dave), 90, 93, 103, 280, *313*, 313–14, 446
Kerr, Davey, 45, 49, 51, *52*

Kerr, Tim, 155, 156, 158, *159*
Khabibulin, Nikolai, 556
Kharalmov, Valery, 256
"The Kid." See Gretzky, Wayne
Kid Line, 39, 40, 43, 71, 278, 303, 329
Kilcoursie, Lord, 333
Kilpatrick, Gen. John Reed, 278, 461
Kilrea, Hec, 31, 355, 356
King Clancy Memorial Trophy. See Clancy (King) Memorial Trophy
Kings. See Los Angeles Kings
Kitchener Kids, 49. See also Kraut Line
Kitchener Rangers, 258
Klatt, Trent, 375
Klima, Petr, 173, 176
Knights. See New Jersey Knights
Knox, Seymour H., III, 461
Kocur, Joe, 212
Koharski, Don, 166
Kolzig, Olaf, 210, 211, 209, 556
Konstantinov, Vladimir, 197, *203*, 205, 209, 211, 212, 376, *377*
Kovalev, Alexei, 192, 197, 425
Kozlov, Vyacheslav (Slava), 192, 204
Kraut Line, 45, 49, 64, 71, 262, 286. See also Kitchener Kids
Kroc, Ray, 515
Krupp, Uwe, 199
Krushelnyski, Mike, 167
Kudelski, Bob, 408
Kudroc, Kristian, 569
Kuleshov, Mikhail, 569
Kurri, Jari, 150, *152*, 153, 156, 161, 163, 172, 264, 299–301, *300*, 368
Kurtenbach, Orland, *106*

L

Labine, Leo, 75
Lach, Elmer James, 60, 62, 64, 68, 69, 74, 76, 311, *312*, 312–13, 356, 446
Lacroix, Andre, 507, 511
Lacroix, Pierre, 277
Ladies Ontario Hockey Association, 540
Lady Bessborough Trophy, 541
Lady Byng Trophy, 18, 481, *481*
LaFayette, Nathan, 193, 375
Lafleur, Guy ("The Flower"), 105, 124, 126, *127*, 128, 129, 132, 133, 134, 141, 153, 167, 236–37, *236*, 256, 280, 446, *446*, 545
Lafleur (Guy) Trophy, 552
LaFontaine, Pat, 162, 294, 342, 545
Laidlaw, Tom, 371
Lajeunesse, Simon, 571
Lalonde, Edouard (Newsy), 1, 2, 4, 7, 8, 9, 11, 13, 17, *36*, 37, 271–72, *272*, 283, 290, 293, 356, 369, 446
Lamoureux (Leo P.) Memorial Trophy, 562
Langenbrunner, Jamie, 211
Langway, Rod, 149, 152
Laperriere, Jacques, 97, 98, 99, 283, *341*, 391, 446

Northcott, Baldy, 37
Northern Fusiliers (National Hockey Association team), 2
Northey, William M., 462
Nystrom, Bobby, 141, 340, *344*

O

Oakland Seals, 99, 103, 105, 107–08, 129. See also Cleveland Barons
Oates, Adam, 556
O'Brien, John Ambrose, 462
O'Connor, Herbert William (Buddy), 68, 449
Octopus (squid), 421–22
Offensive game, Hewitt, Foster, on, 416
Officials, 64, 421–30. See also Referees
Ogrodnick, John, 156
Ohlund, Mattias, 411
Oilers. See Edmonton Oilers
Oliver, Harold (Harry), 449
Oliver, Murray, 389
Olmstead, Murray Bert, 82, 87, 103, 365, 383, 385, 449
Olympia Stadium (Detroit), 95, 362
Olympic hockey, 537, 569–75, *573*
Olympic hockey, history of, 571
Olympics, NHL participating in, 569–71
Olympic Saddledome (Calgary), 151
O'Neill, Brian F., 462
Ontario Hockey Association, 1, 272
Ontario Hockey Association (OHA) Memorial Cup, 546
Ontario Hockey League, 54669
O'Reilly, Terry, 242, 422–23
Orlando, Jimmy, *58*
Orr, Bobby, *102,* 103, 105, *107,* 108, 111, 112, 113, 114, 115, 119, 122, 124, 126, 157, 219, 222–23, *222,* 241, 248, 256, 262, 267, 292–93, *392,* 449, 545
Orr, Frank, 260
Osgood, Chris, 201, 210, *210,* 211, 212, 376, 556
Ottawa Civic Centre, 183
Ottawa Generals, 1, 2, 333
Ottawa Nationals, 510. See also Toronto Toros
Ottawa Senators, 2, 5, 7, 9, 10, 12, 13, 14, 21, 34, 167, 179, 183, 205, 308, 318, 331
Ottawa Silver Seven, 333, 334, 337, 338
Otto, Joel, 170
Ouellet, Maxime, 569
Overtime, 59, 151
Owen, George, 285, 286
Ozolinsh, Sandis, 202, 204

P

Pacific Coast Hockey Association, 2, 4, 7, 10, 12, 13, 19
Pacific Coast Hockey League, Patrick brothers and, 337
Paek, Jim, 373
Page, Frederick, 462
Pappin, Jim, 103, 389
Parent, Bernard Marcel (Bernie), 107, 120, 121, 122, *123,* 124, 164, 188, 216, *308,* 309, 391, 449
Parise, J. P., 124
Park, Douglas Bradford (Brad), 113, 115, *117,* 126, 132, 155, 161, 298–99, *298,* 449
Patrick, Craig, 155, 373
Patrick, Frank, 1, 2, 7, 13, 40, 337, 462
Patrick, Lester, 1, 2, 7, 12, 21, 23–24, 29, 37, 40, 45, 290, 291, 324, 334, 337, 339, 353–55, *354,* 449, 484
Patrick (Lester) Trophy, *483,* 484
Patrick, Lynn, 45, 54, 151, 450
Patrick, Muzz, 45, 54, 81, 97
Patrick, Steve, 367
Patterson, Colin, 371
Patterson Pats (Toronto), 540
Pavelich, Mark, 465
Pavelich, Marty, 252, 382
Pavelich, Matt, *428,* 459
Payne, Steve, 151
Pearl Harbor, 54
Pearson, Lester B., 485
Pearson (Lester B.) Award, *484,* 485
Peca, Michael, 205
Peeters, Pete, 146, *148,* 149, 226, *344,* 398
Penalties, 5, 82, 94, 97, 122, 171, 175
Penalty shot, 40
Penguins. See Pittsburgh Penguins
Perreault, Gilbert, 114, 119, *131,* 158, 294–96, *295,* 397, 450
Perron, Jean, 276
Philadelphia Blazers, 508, 510. See also Vancouver Blazers
Philadelphia Flyers, 99, 103, 105, 107, 120, 122, 124, 126, 141, 156, 162, 167, 193, 202–3, 256, 302, 308, 340, 342, 344, 369, 375
Philadelphia Phantoms, 556
Philadelphia Quakers, 33
Philadelphia Ramblers, 555
Phillips, Tommy, 450
Phoenix Roadrunners, 511, 513, 515
Pickard, Allan W., 462
Pieri (Louis A. R.) Memorial Award, 559
Piggot (Jim) Memorial Trophy, 550
Pilote, Pierre, 94, 95, 97, 98, 99, 101, 307, *306,* 386, 450, 556
Pilous, Rudy, 92, 246, 462
Pinkney (Dave) Trophy, 548
Pirates. See Pittsburgh Pirates
Pitre, Didier (Pit), 271, 283, 450
Pittsburgh Penguins, 99, 103, 105, 107, 167, 172, 176, 181, 182, 225, 268, 278, 342, 364, 369, 372–71, 375
Pittsburgh Pirates, 19, 33. See also Philadelphia Quakers
Plager, Barclay, 165
Plante, Jacques, 76, 78, 80, 81, 82, *83,* 84, 86, 87, 89, 90, 93, *93,* 97, 110, 121, 239–40, *240,* 245, 306, 314, 319, 331, 360, *361,* 387, 388, 391, 450, 556
Plante (Jacques) Memorial Trophy, 552
Players, 192, 219–331, 433–58
Playfair, Larry, 294
Plett, Willi, 129
"The Pocket Rocket." See Richard, Henri
Pocklington, Peter, 167, 517
Poile (N. R. "Bud") Trophy, 563
Poile, Norman Robert (Bud), 68, 103, 462
Polis, Greg, 394
Pollock, Sam, 97, 462
Portland Buckaroos, 238
Portland (Pacific Coast Hockey Association team), 4, 17
Potvin, Denis, 122, 124, 126, 130, 132, 133, 134, 141, 143, 157–58, 161, 164, 248–50, *249,* 368, 430, 450
Potvin, Felix, 184, 192, 409, 545
Poulin, Dave, 163, *173,* 237
Power failure, Boston Garden, 166, 342
Powerplay regulation (1956), 82
Powers, Eddie, 386
Powers (Eddie) Memorial Trophy, 547
Pratt, Walter (Babe), 60, 63, 68, 329, *329,* 332, 450
Prentice, Dean, 81, 385, 392
Presidents' Trophy, 158, *484,* 485
Preston, Rich, 517
Preston Rivulettes, 540, 541
Primeau, A. Joseph (Joe), 35, 39, 43, 73, 278, 303, *327,* 329, 358
Prince of Wales Trophy, *485,* 486
Prodgers, George (Goldie), 9
Production Line, 68, 69, 70, 71, 76, 252, 325
Professional Hockey Writers' Association, 433
Pronovost, Andre, 86, 386
Pronovost, Lorne, *108*
Pronovost, Marcel, *75,* 89, 90, 388, 450, *450,* 556
Propp, Brian, 176, 285
Prospal, Vaclav, 375
Provost, Claude, 82, 98, 387
Prystai, Metro, 72
Puck, computerized, 419
Pulford, Bob, 93, 103, 386, 388, 450
Pulford, Harvey, 450
Punch Line, 60, 61, 64, 68, 71, 311, 312, 356
Puppa, Daren, 188
Pyatt, Taylor, 568

Q

Quackenbush, Bill, 68, 70, 72, 75, 450

Toros. See Toronto Toros
Torrey, Bill, 130, 188, 252, 267, 368, 463
Trades, 221, 248
Tremblay, Gilles, 95, 362
Tremblay, J. C., 114, 508
Tremblay, Mario, 199, 277
Tretiak, Vladislav, 457
Trihey, Harry, 457
Trophies, NHL, 475–86. See also specific trophy, e.g., Hart Memorial Trophy
Trottier, Bryan, 126, 130, 132, 134, 139, 141, 161, 267–69, *270*, 368, 403, 457
Trottier, Dave, 286
Tueting, Sarah, 537
Turek, Roman, 216
Turgeon, Pierre, 184, 186, 408
"Turkey Egg." See Broda, Walter (Turk)
Turner, Lloyd, 463
Turner Cup, 559, 560
Tutt, W. Thayer, 464

U

Udvari, Frank, *420*, 425, 428, 459
Ulion, Gretchen, 537, *541*
Ullman, Norm, 97, 98, 288, *325*, 328, 387, 389, 457
Unger, Garry, 161, 394, 395
United States, 419, 537, 543
United States Amateur League, 19
United States Hockey Hall of Fame, 465–66
Utah Grizzlies, 560

V

Vachon, Rogatien (Rogie), 108
Vadnais, Carol, 298
Vail, Eric, 124
Vairo, Lou, 283
Vaive, Rick, 401
van Hellemond, Andy, 197, 422, 425, 426, 427, *429*
Vanbiesbrouck, John, 159, 202
Vancouver Blazers, 510, 512. See also Calgary Cowboys
Vancouver Canucks, 105, 114, 145, 191–92, 205, 341, 342, 373–75
Vancouver Millionaires, 2, 4, 7, 9, 10, 12, 14, 16, 339
Vasko, Elmer (Moose), *89*
Verbeek, Pat, 409

Verdun Black Hawks, 241
Verdun Electric, 540
Vernon, Mike, 158, 170, 197, 201, 205, 209, 342, 376, 556
Vezina, Georges, 4, 14, 18, 19, 21, 293, *317*, 318, 457, 477
Vezina (Georges) Trophy, 21, 108, 477, *477*
Vickers, Jack, 129
Vickers, Steve, 119
Victoria (Pacific Coast Hockey Association team), 2, 7, 18
Victoria (Western Hockey League team), 20
Video replay, 181, 205
Villemure, Gilles, 114
Volek, David, 184
Voss, Carl V., 41, 464

W

Waghorne, Fred, 464
Wales Conference, in All-Star Game, 339, 395
Walker, John Phillip (Jack), 458
Walkout, players' (April 1992), 179–80
Walsh, Martin (Marty), 458
Walter, Ryan, 170, 369
Walton, Mike (Shakey), 511, *514*
Wanderers. See Montreal Wanderers
Ward, Dixon, 216
Ward, Jimmy, 355
Warwick, Grant, 54
Washington Capitals, 105, 124, 151, 161–62, 208–9, 324, 342, 344, 376
Watson, Harry, 358, 458
Watson, Harry P., 458
Watson, Jim, 121
Watson, Joe, 121
Watson, Phil, 81
Webster, Tom, 172
Weiland, Ralph (Cooney), 31, *32, 33*, 285, 458
Wensink, John, *134*
Western Canada Hockey League (Western Hockey League), 12, 20
Western Hockey League (Junior hockey), 546, 549–51
Westfall, Ed, *100*
Westmount Arena (Montreal), 3
Westwick, Harry, 458
Whalers. See Hartford Whalers; New England Whalers
Wharram, Ken, 95, 97, 103, 390
Wharton, John, 376

Whitcroft, Fred, 458
Whitney, Ray, 197
Whyte, Sandra, 537
Wickenheiser, Hayley, 543
William Hanley Trophy. See Hanley (William) Trophy
William M. Jennings Award. See Jennings (William M.) Award
Williams, Tiger, 250, 251
Wilson, Cully, 7, 8, 11
Wilson (Del) Trophy, 550
Wilson, Doug, 145
Wilson, Gordon Allan (Phat), 458
Wilson, Rik, 158
Wilson, Stacy, *542*
Windsor Godfredsons, 559
Windsor Spitfires, 559
Winnipeg Jets, 116, 139, 140, 151, 232, 508, 512, 513, 515, 517
Winter Olympics, hockey in. See Olympic hockey.
Wirtz, Arthur M., 464
Wirtz, William, 464
Wiseman, Eddie, 53
Women's hockey, 537–41
Women's Invitational Tournament, 543
Women's World Championship
Woolley, Jason, 216
World championships, 574–576
World Cup, 576
World Hockey Association, 105, 116, 139, 507–35
World War I, 2, 5, 9
World War II, 49, 53–54, 60, 63
Worsley, Lorne (Gump), 76, 93, 99, 108, *108, 341*, 362, 393, 458, 556
Worters, Roy, 26, *31*, 34, 458
Wregget, Ken, 197

Y

Yashin, Alexei, 408
Young, Howie, 94, 97, 246
Yukon Klondikes, 333–34
Yzerman, Steve, 170, 172, 201, 202, *207*, 211, 212, 264, *318*, 319, 344, *350*, 376

Z

Zalapsky, Zarley, 209
Zelepukin, Valeri, 192
Zhitnik, Alexei, 216
Ziegler, John A., Jr., 105, *130*, 133, 181, 182, 183, 371, 464
Zubov, Sergei, 190, 214

PHOTO CREDITS

Cover photo by *The Hockey News*. Back cover photo by AP/Wide World.

AP/Wide World Photos: 91, 108, 120, 135, 140, 152, 199, 200, 201, 206, 207, 208, 210, 211, 214, 215, 217, 229, 235, 238, 270, 276, 279, 284, 292, 300, 303 (right), 306 (right), 311, 321 (right), 323 (left), 326, 344, 349, 350, 359, 363, 367, 373, 377, 407, 538, 539, 540, 541, 542, 572, 573

Associated Features, Inc.: 236, 240, 304 (left), 308 (right), 309, 316 (right), 318 (right), 319, 321 (left), 323 (right), 324 (right), 325 (both), 327 (right), 328 (both), 329 (right), 331 (left)

David Bier Studios: 287

Bruce Bennett: 142, 143, 153, 154, 157, 158, 159, 160, 161, 162, 163, 164, 165, 168, 169, 172, 173, 174, 176, 178, 180, 183, 184, 185, 187, 190, 191, 194, 196, 221, 226, 247, 249, 251, 265, 303 (left), 312 (right), 314, 345, 347, 348, 370, 372, 402, 428, 429, 430, 439, 446, 451, 453, 468

Paul Bereswill: 117, 509

Cliff Boutelle: 222, 443, 452

CBC: 418

Michael DiGirolamo/B. Bennett Studios: 177

ESPN: 417

Hockey Hall of Fame: 3, 4, 5, 6, 8, 11, 12, 15, 19, 21, 22, 23, 25, 26, 27, 31, 32, 33, 34, 36, 38, 41, 44, 46, 52, 58, 59, 61, 62, 65, 67, 68, 69, 79, 80, 83, 85, 88, 242, 253, 261, 272, 273, 282, 286, 301, 302, 307, 308 (left), 310 (both), 312 (left), 315, 316 (left), 317 (both), 318 (left), 322 (both), 324 (right), 327 (left), 329 (left), 331 (right), 336, 337, 338, 339, 354, 358, 416, 422, 423, 424 (both), 427, 432, 434, 435, 437, 440, 444, 455

Nancy Hogue: 129

Rich Jaspon/B. Bennett Studios: 241

Scotty Kilpatrick: 86, 98, 228, 255, 420

Jack Mecca: 320

Brian Miller/B. Bennett Studios: 346

National Hockey League: 66, 130, 425, 475, 476, 477, 478, 479, 480, 481, 482, 483, 484, 485, 486

New York Rangers: 53, 55, 77, 304 (right), 305, 306 (left), 330

Richard Pilling: 125, 132, 147, 148, 149, 155, 258, 268, 298

Dick Raphael: 111

Ken Regan: 100, 313

Robert Shaver: 118, 123, 127, 131, 136, 146, 245, 257, 260, 295, 343, 366, 438

Barton Silverman: 96, 102, 106, 244, 266, 426

Sports Photo Sources: 263, 436, 442, 447, 448, 450, 454, 456

Toronto Maple Leafs: 289

UPI: 30, 40, 42, 48, 64, 73, 75, 89, 93, 107, 109, 114, 121, 134, 151, 189, 234, 277, 281, 290, 293, 297, 340, 341, 342, 361, 365, 392, 400, 510, 514, 515, 516, 570

HAT TRICK!

Sports fans score three times and Visible Ink Press gets the assists.

The Unauthorized NASCAR® Fan Guide 2000

From the pits to the infield to the grandstands on turn 4, this guide has the races covered. NASCAR fans will love the coverage of America's fastest growing sport. 625 pages, 225 photographs and a 16-page color insert cover race history, drivers, race results, Jeff Gordon, race etiquette, racing equipment, sponsorship, even famous crashes and the safety improvements they inspired and more.

Bill Fleischman and Al Pearce • February 2000 • Paperback • 625 pp.
ISBN 1-57859-102-3

Unauthorized NASCAR "... is what everybody has been asking for ... I'll just say, 'Get it.' It's everything you need to know about our favorite sport."
— Stooges NASCAR Page (Geocities.com)

Bud Collins' Tennis Encyclopedia

The book Tennis Magazine says is "a must have" for every tennis fan. You'll love learning about the game from its inception to modern day. You'll feel like a champion at Wimbledon when you learn all about the tournaments, players, equipment, rules, innovations and more that are served up by experts on the game.

Bud Collins • 1997 • Paperback • 700 pp.
ISBN 1-57859-000-0

"Collins is deadly serious when it comes to the sports history ... there are hundreds of entertaining anecdotes." — Inside Tennis

The Handy Sports Answer Book™

The next time someone pitches you a trivia question, hit a home run with help from a *Handy* source. Commonly asked sports questions cover a variety of sports, rules, notable figures, statistics, highlights, lowlights — even halftime shows and a whole lot more. A friendly, informative Q and A format, complete with 140 photos, covers 1,100 sports questions — making it the perfect sports guide for the fan in all of us.

Roger Matuz, Laurie Hillstrom, Kevin Hillstrom • 1999 • Paperback • 550 pp.
ISBN 1-57859-075-2

VISIBLE INK PRESS